Occupational Outlook Handbook 2008-2009

Compiled by
The United States Department of Labor

Mc Graw Hill

New York   Chicago   San Francisco   Lisbon   London   Madrid   Mexico City
Milan   New Delhi   San Juan   Seoul   Singapore   Sydney   Toronto

This McGraw-Hill edition is an unabridged publication of the *Occupational Outlook Handbook, 2008–09 Edition*, compiled by the United States Department of Labor, Bureau of Labor Statistics.

1 2 3 4 5 6 7 8 9 10 11 12 13 14 15 16 17 18 19 20 21 22   WCK/WCK   0 9 8

ISBN 978-0-07-149214-0
MHID   0-07-149214-3
ISSN   0082-9072

McGraw-Hill books are available at special quantity discounts to use as premiums and sales promotions or for use in corporate training programs. To contact a representative, please visit the Contact Us pages at www.mhprofessional.com.

This book is printed on acid-free paper.

Contents

Tomorrow's Jobs

Making informed career decisions requires reliable information about opportunities in the future. Opportunities result from the relationships between the population, labor force, and the demand for goods and services.

Population ultimately limits the size of the labor force—individuals working or looking for work—which limits the goods and services that can be produced. Demand for various goods and services is largely responsible for employment in the industries providing them. Employment opportunities, in turn, result from demand for skills needed within specific industries. Opportunities for medical assistants and other healthcare occupations, for example, have surged in response to rapid growth in demand for health services.

Examining the past and present, and projecting changes in these relationships is the foundation of the Occupational Outlook Program. This chapter presents highlights of Bureau of Labor Statistics' projections of the labor force and occupational and industry employment that can help guide your career plans. Sources of additional information about the projections appear on the preceding page.

Population

Population trends affect employment opportunities in a number of ways. Changes in population influence the demand for goods and services. For example, a growing and aging population has increased the demand for health services. Equally important, population changes produce corresponding changes in the size and demographic composition of the labor force.

The U.S. civilian noninstitutional population is expected to increase by 21.8 million over the 2006-2016 period (chart 1). The 2006-2016 rate of growth is slower than the growth rate over the 1986-1996 and 1996-2006 periods—9 percent, 11 percent, and 13 percent, respectively. Continued growth, however, will mean more consumers of goods and services, spurring demand for workers in a wide range of occupations and industries. The effects of population growth on various occupations will differ. The differences are partially accounted for by the age distribution of the future population.

As the baby boomers continue to age, the 55 to 64 age group will increase by 30.3 percent or 9.5 million persons, more than any other group. The 35 to 44 age group will decrease by 5.5 percent, reflecting a slowed birth rate following the baby boom generation, while the youth population, aged 16 to 24, will decline 1.1 percent over the 2006-2016 period.

Minorities and immigrants will constitute a larger share of the U.S. population in 2016. The number of Asians and people of Hispanic origin are projected to continue to grow much faster than other racial and ethnic groups.

Labor force

Population is the single most important factor in determining the size and composition of the labor force—people either working or looking for work. The civilian labor force is projected to increase by 12.8 million, or 8.5 percent, to 164.2 million over the 2006-2016 period.

The U.S. workforce will become more diverse by 2016. White, non-Hispanic persons will continue to make up a decreasing share of the labor force, falling from 69.1 percent in 2006 to 64.6 percent in 2016 (chart 2). However, despite rela-

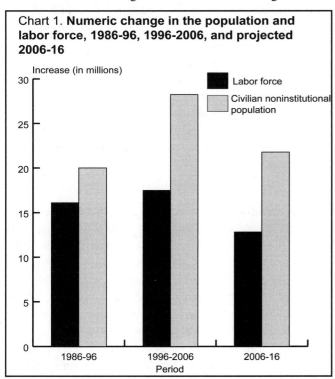

Chart 1. **Numeric change in the population and labor force, 1986-96, 1996-2006, and projected 2006-16**

Increase (in millions)

Labor force

Civilian noninstitutional population

Period

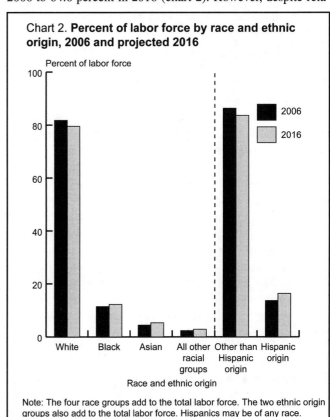

Chart 2. **Percent of labor force by race and ethnic origin, 2006 and projected 2016**

Percent of labor force

2006

2016

White   Black   Asian   All other racial groups   Other than Hispanic origin   Hispanic origin

Race and ethnic origin

Note: The four race groups add to the total labor force. The two ethnic origin groups also add to the total labor force. Hispanics may be of any race.

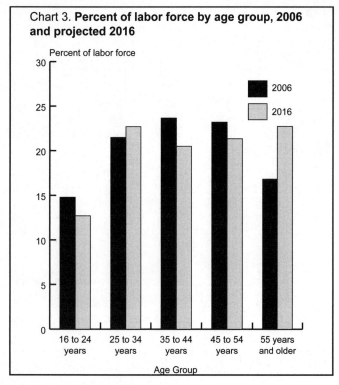

Chart 3. **Percent of labor force by age group, 2006 and projected 2016**

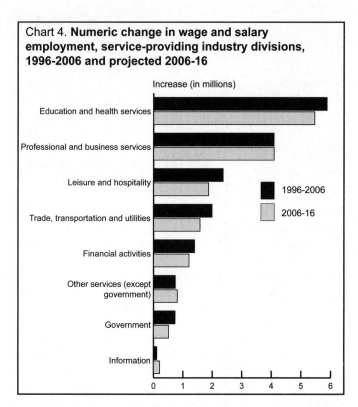

Chart 4. **Numeric change in wage and salary employment, service-providing industry divisions, 1996-2006 and projected 2006-16**

tively slow growth, white non-Hispanics will remain the overwhelming majority of the labor force. Hispanics are projected be the fastest growing ethnic group, growing by 29.9 percent. By 2016, Hispanics will continue to constitute an increasing proportion of the labor force, growing from 13.7 percent to 16.4 percent. Asians are projected to account for an increasing share of the labor force by 2016, growing from 4.4 to 5.3 percent. Blacks will also increase their share of the labor force, growing from 11.4 percent to 12.3 percent.

The numbers of men and women in the labor force will grow, but the number of women will grow at a slightly faster rate than the number of men. The male labor force is projected to grow by 8.0 percent from 2006 to 2016, compared with 8.9 percent for women, down from 12.7 and 13.4 percent, respectively, from 1996 to 2006. As a result, men's share of the labor force is expected to decrease from 53.7 to 53.4 percent, while women's share is expected to increase from 46.3 to 46.6 percent.

The youth labor force, aged 16 to 24, is expected to decrease its share of the labor force to 12.7 percent by 2016. The primary working age group, between 25 and 54 years old, is projected to decline from 68.4 percent of the labor force in 2006 to 64.6 percent by 2016. Workers 55 and older, on the other hand, are projected to leap from 16.8 percent to 22.7 percent of the labor force between 2006 and 2016 (chart 3). The aging of the baby boom generation will cause not only an increase in the percentage of workers in the oldest age category, but a decrease in the percentage of younger workers.

Employment

Total employment is expected to increase from 150.6 million in 2006 to 166.2 million in 2016, or by 10 percent. The 15.6 million jobs that will be added by 2016 will not be evenly distributed across major industrial and occupational groups. Changes in consumer demand, technology, and many other factors will

contribute to the continually changing employment structure in the U.S. economy.

The following two sections examine projected employment change from industrial and occupational perspectives. The industrial profile is discussed in terms of primary wage and salary employment. Primary employment excludes secondary jobs for those who hold multiple jobs. The exception is employment in agriculture, which includes self-employed and unpaid family workers in addition to wage and salary workers.

The occupational profile is viewed in terms of total employment—including primary and secondary jobs for wage and salary, self-employed, and unpaid family workers. Of the roughly 150 million jobs in the U.S. economy in 2006, wage and salary workers accounted for 138.3 million, self-employed workers accounted for 12.2 million, and unpaid family workers accounted for about 130,000. Secondary employment accounted for 1.8 million jobs. Self-employed workers held nearly 9 out of 10 secondary jobs and wage and salary workers held most of the remainder.

Industry

Service-providing industries. The long-term shift from goods-producing to service-providing employment is expected to continue. Service-providing industries are expected to account for approximately 15.7 million new wage and salary jobs generated over the 2006-2016 period (chart 4), while goods-producing industries will see overall job loss.

Education and health services. This industry supersector is projected to grow by 18.8 percent, and add more jobs, nearly 5.5 million, than any other industry supersector. More than 3 out of every 10 new jobs created in the U.S. economy will be in either the healthcare and social assistance or public and private educational services sectors.

Healthcare and social assistance—including public and private hospitals, nursing and residential care facilities, and individual and family services—will grow by 25.4 percent and add 4 million new jobs. Employment growth will be driven by increasing demand for healthcare and social assistance because of an aging population and longer life expectancies. Also, as more women enter the labor force, demand for childcare services is expected to grow.

Public and private educational services will grow by 10.7 percent and add 1.4 million new jobs through 2016. Rising student enrollments at all levels of education will create demand for educational services.

Professional and business services. This industry supersector, which includes some of the fastest growing industries in the U.S. economy, will grow by 23.3 percent and add 4.1 million new jobs.

Employment in administrative and support and waste management and remediation services will grow by 20.3 percent and add 1.7 million new jobs to the economy by 2016. The largest industry growth in this sector will be enjoyed by employment services, which will be responsible for 692,000 new jobs, or over 40 percent of all new jobs in administrative and support and waste management and remediation services. Employment services ranks second among industries with the most new employment opportunities in the Nation and is expected to have a growth rate that is faster than the average for all industries. This will be due to the need for seasonal and temporary workers and for highly specialized human resources services.

Employment in professional, scientific, and technical services will grow by 28.8 percent and add 2.1 million new jobs by 2016. Employment in computer systems design and related services will grow by 38.3 percent and add nearly one-fourth of all new jobs in professional, scientific, and technical services. Employment growth will be driven by the increasing reliance of businesses on information technology and the continuing importance of maintaining system and network security. Management, scientific, and technical consulting services also will grow at a staggering 78 percent and account for another third of growth in this supersector. Demand for these services will be spurred by the increased use of new technology and computer software and the growing complexity of business.

Management of companies and enterprises will grow by 14.9 percent and add 270,000 new jobs.

Information. Employment in the information supersector is expected to increase by 6.9 percent, adding 212,000 jobs by 2016. Information contains some of the fast-growing computer-related industries such as software publishing, Internet publishing and broadcasting, and wireless telecommunication carriers. Employment in these industries is expected to grow by 32 percent, 44.1 percent, and 40.9 percent, respectively. The information supersector also includes motion picture production; broadcasting; and newspaper, periodical, book, and directory publishing. Increased demand for telecommunications services, cable service, high-speed Internet connections, and software will fuel job growth among these industries.

Leisure and hospitality. Overall employment will grow by 14.3 percent. Arts, entertainment, and recreation will grow by 30.9 percent and add 595,000 new jobs by 2016. Most of these new job openings, 79 percent, will be in the amusement, gambling, and recreation sector. Job growth will stem from public participation in arts, entertainment, and recreation activities—reflecting increasing incomes, leisure time, and awareness of the health benefits of physical fitness.

Accommodation and food services is expected to grow by 11.4 percent and add 1.3 million new jobs through 2016. Job growth will be concentrated in food services and drinking places, reflecting increases in population, dual-income families, and the convenience of many new food establishments.

Trade, transportation, and utilities. Overall employment in this industry supersector will grow by 6 percent between 2006 and 2016. Transportation and warehousing is expected to increase by 496,000 jobs, or by 11.1 percent through 2016. Truck transportation will grow by 11 percent, adding 158,000 new jobs, while rail transportation is projected to decline. The warehousing and storage sector is projected to grow rapidly at 23.5 percent, adding 150,000 jobs. Demand for truck transportation and warehousing services will expand as many manufacturers concentrate on their core competencies and contract out their product transportation and storage functions.

Employment in retail trade is expected to increase by 4.5 percent. Despite slower than average growth, this industry will add almost 700,000 new jobs over the 2006-2016 period, growing from 15.3 million employees to 16 million. While consumers will continue to demand more goods, consolidation among grocery stores and department stores will temper growth. Wholesale trade is expected to increase by 7.3 percent, growing from 5.9 million to 6.3 million jobs.

Employment in utilities is projected to decrease by 5.7 percent through 2016. Despite increased output, employment in electric power generation, transmission, and distribution and natural gas distribution is expected to decline through 2016 due to improved technology that increases worker productivity. However, employment in water, sewage, and other systems is expected to increase 18.7 percent by 2016. Jobs are not easily eliminated by technological gains in this industry because water treatment and waste disposal are very labor-intensive activities.

Financial activities. Employment is projected to grow 14.4 percent over the 2006-2016 period. Real estate and rental and leasing is expected to grow by 18 percent and add 392,000 jobs by 2016. Growth will be due, in part, to increased demand for housing as the population grows. The fastest growing industry in the real estate and rental and leasing services sector will be activities related to real estate, such as property management and real estate appraisal, which will grow by 29 percent—remnants of the housing boom that pervaded much of the first half of the decade.

Finance and insurance are expected to add 815,000 jobs, an increase of 13.2 percent, by 2016. Employment in securities, commodity contracts, and other financial investments and related activities is expected to grow 46 percent by 2016, reflecting the increased number of baby boomers in their peak savings years, the growth of tax-favorable retirement plans, and the globalization of the securities markets. Employment in credit intermediation and related services, including banks, will grow by 8.2 percent and add almost one-third of all new jobs within

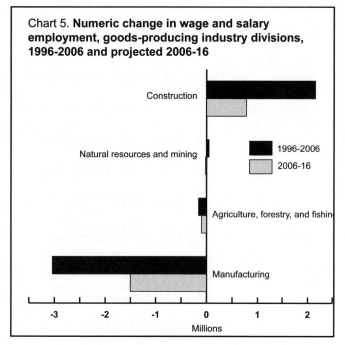

Chart 5. **Numeric change in wage and salary employment, goods-producing industry divisions, 1996-2006 and projected 2006-16**

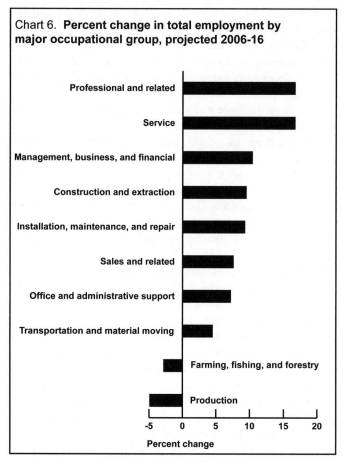

Chart 6. **Percent change in total employment by major occupational group, projected 2006-16**

finance and insurance. Insurance carriers and related activities are expected to grow by 7.4 percent and add 172,000 new jobs by 2016. The number of jobs within agencies, brokerages, and other insurance related activities is expected to grow about 15.4 percent. Growth will stem from the needs of an increasing population and new insurance products on the market.

Government. Between 2006 and 2016, government employment, not including employment in public education and hospitals, is expected to increase by 4.8 percent, from 10.8 million to 11.3 million jobs. Growth in government employment will be fueled by an increased demand for pubic safety, but dampened by budgetary constraints and outsourcing of government jobs to the private sector. State and local governments, excluding education and hospitals, are expected to grow by 7.7 percent as a result of the continued shift of responsibilities from the Federal Government to State and local governments. Federal Government employment, including the Postal Service, is expected to decrease by 3.8 percent.

Other services (except government and private households). Employment will grow by 14.9 percent. About 2 out of every 5 new jobs in this supersector will be in religious organizations, which are expected to grow by 18.9 percent. Other automotive repair and maintenance will be the fastest growing industry at 40.7 percent, reflecting demand for quick maintenance services for the increasing number of automobiles on the Nation's roads. Also included among other services are business, professional, labor, political, and similar organizations, which are expected to increase by 13.6 percent and add 68,000 new jobs. This industry includes homeowner, tenant, and property owner associations.

Goods-producing industries. Employment in the goods-producing industries has been relatively stagnant since the early 1980s. Overall, this sector is expected to decline 3.3 percent over the 2006-2016 period. Although employment is expected to decline overall, projected growth among goods-producing industries varies considerably (chart 5).

Construction. Employment in construction is expected to increase by 10.2 percent, from 7.7 million to 8.5 million. Demand for commercial construction and an increase in road, bridge, and tunnel construction will account for the bulk of job growth in this supersector.

Manufacturing. While overall employment in this supersector will decline by 10.6 percent or 1.5 million jobs, employment in a few detailed manufacturing industries will increase. For example, employment in pharmaceutical and medicine manufacturing is expected to grow by 23.8 percent and add 69,000 new jobs by 2016. However, productivity gains, job automation, and international competition will adversely affect employment in most manufacturing industries. Employment in household appliance manufacturing is expected to decline by 25.8 percent and lose 21,000 jobs over the decade. Similarly, employment in machinery manufacturing, apparel manufacturing, and computer and electronic product manufacturing will decline by 146,000, 129,000, and 157,000 jobs, respectively.

Agriculture, forestry, fishing, and hunting. Overall employment in agriculture, forestry, fishing, and hunting is expected to decrease by 2.8 percent. Employment is expected to continue to decline due to rising costs of production, increasing consolidation, and more imports of food and lumber. The only industry within this supersector expected to grow is support activities for agriculture and forestry, which includes farm labor contractors and farm management services. This industry is expected to grow by 10.5 percent and add 12,000 new jobs. Crop production will see the largest job loss, with 98,000 fewer jobs in 2016 than in 2006.

Mining. Employment in mining is expected to decrease 1.6 percent, or by some 10,000 jobs, by 2016. Employment in support activities for mining will be responsible for most of the employment decline in this industry, seeing a loss of 17,000 jobs. Other mining industries, such as coal mining and metal ore mining, are expected to see little or no change or a small increase in employment. Employment stagnation in these industries is attributable mainly to technology gains that boost worker productivity and strict environmental regulations.

Occupation

Expansion of service-providing industries is expected to continue, creating demand for many occupations. However, projected job growth varies among major occupational groups (chart 6).

Professional and related occupations. These occupations include a wide variety of skilled professions. Professional and related occupations will be one of the two fastest growing major occupational groups, and will add the most new jobs. Over the 2006-2016 period, a 16.7-percent increase in the number of professional and related jobs is projected, which translates into nearly 5 million new jobs. Professional and related workers perform a wide variety of duties, and are employed throughout private industry and government. Almost three-quarters of the job growth will come from three groups of professional occupations—computer and mathematical occupations, healthcare practitioners and technical occupations, and education, training, and library occupations—which together will add 3.5 million jobs.

Service occupations. Duties of service workers range from fighting fires to cooking meals. Employment in service occupations is projected to increase by 4.8 million, or 16.7 percent, the second largest numerical gain and tied with professional and related occupations for the fastest rate of growth among the major occupational groups. Food preparation and serving related occupations are expected to add the most jobs among the service occupations, 1.4 million, by 2016. However, healthcare support occupations and personal care and service occupations are expected to grow the fastest, at 26.8 percent and 22 percent, respectively. Combined, these two occupational groups will account for 2.1 million new jobs.

Management, business, and financial occupations. Workers in management, business, and financial occupations plan and direct the activities of business, government, and other organizations. Their employment is expected to increase by 1.6 million, or 10.4 percent, by 2016. Among management occupations, the numbers of social and community service mangers and gaming managers will grow the fastest, by 24.7 percent and 24.4 percent, respectively. Construction managers will add the most new jobs—77,000—by 2016. Farmers and ranchers are the only workers whose numbers are expected to see a large decline, losing 90,000 jobs. Among business and financial occupations, accountants and auditors and all other business operation specialists will add the most jobs, 444,000 combined. Financial analysts and personal financial advisors will be the fastest growing occupations in this group, with growth rates of 33.8 percent and 41 percent, respectively.

Construction and extraction occupations. Construction and extraction workers build new residential and commercial build-

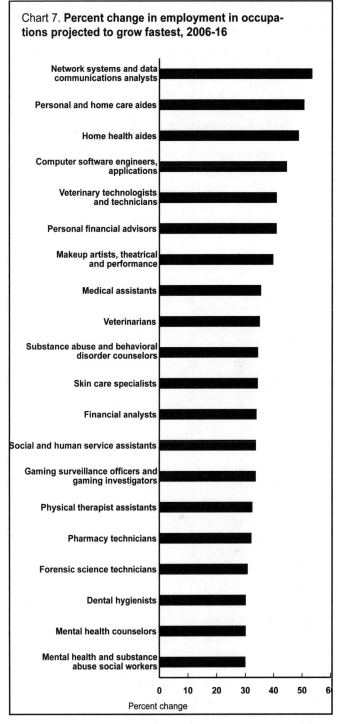

Chart 7. Percent change in employment in occupations projected to grow fastest, 2006-16

- Network systems and data communications analysts
- Personal and home care aides
- Home health aides
- Computer software engineers, applications
- Veterinary technologists and technicians
- Personal financial advisors
- Makeup artists, theatrical and performance
- Medical assistants
- Veterinarians
- Substance abuse and behavioral disorder counselors
- Skin care specialists
- Financial analysts
- Social and human service assistants
- Gaming surveillance officers and gaming investigators
- Physical therapist assistants
- Pharmacy technicians
- Forensic science technicians
- Dental hygienists
- Mental health counselors
- Mental health and substance abuse social workers

Percent change
0   10   20   30   40   50   60

ings, and also work in mines, quarries, and oil and gas fields. Employment of these workers is expected to grow 9.5 percent, adding 785,000 new jobs. Construction trades and related workers will account for nearly 4 out of 5 of these new jobs, or 622,000, by 2016. Minor declines in extraction occupations will reflect overall employment stagnation in the mining and oil and gas extraction industries.

Installation, maintenance, and repair occupations. Workers in installation, maintenance, and repair occupations install new equipment and maintain and repair older equipment. These occupations will add 550,000 jobs by 2016, growing by 9.3 percent. Automotive service technicians and mechanics and general maintenance and repair workers will account for close to

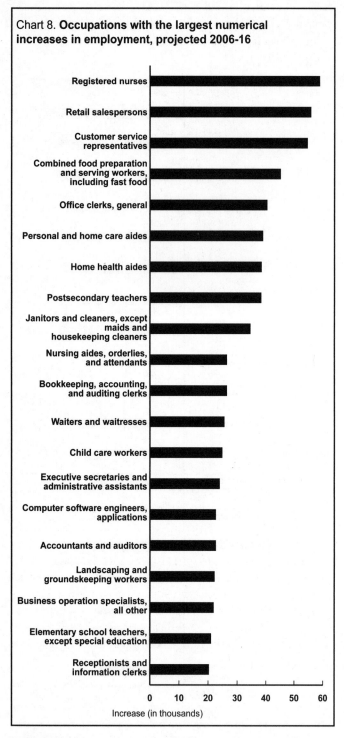

Chart 8. **Occupations with the largest numerical increases in employment, projected 2006-16**

Registered nurses

Retail salespersons

Customer service representatives

Combined food preparation and serving workers, including fast food

Office clerks, general

Personal and home care aides

Home health aides

Postsecondary teachers

Janitors and cleaners, except maids and housekeeping cleaners

Nursing aides, orderlies, and attendants

Bookkeeping, accounting, and auditing clerks

Waiters and waitresses

Child care workers

Executive secretaries and administrative assistants

Computer software engineers, applications

Accountants and auditors

Landscaping and groundskeeping workers

Business operation specialists, all other

Elementary school teachers, except special education

Receptionists and information clerks

0   10   20   30   40   50   60

Increase (in thousands)

half of all new installation, maintenance, and repair jobs. The fastest growth rate will be among locksmiths and safe repairers, an occupation that is expected to grow 22.1 percent over the 2006-2016 period.

Transportation and material moving occupations. Transportation and material moving workers transport people and materials by land, sea, or air. Employment of these workers should increase by 4.5 percent, accounting for 462,000 new jobs by 2016. Among transportation occupations, motor vehicle operators will add the most jobs, 368,000. Material moving occupations will decline slightly, 0.5 percent, losing 25,000 jobs.

Sales and related occupations. Sales and related workers solicit goods and services to businesses and consumers. Sales and related occupations are expected to add 1.2 million new jobs by 2016, growing by 7.6 percent. Retail salespersons will contribute the most to this grow by adding 557,000 new jobs.

Office and administrative support occupations. Office and administrative support workers perform the day-to-day activities of the office, such as preparing and filing documents, dealing with the public, and distributing information. Employment in these occupations is expected to grow by 7.2 percent, adding 1.7 million new jobs by 2016. Customer service representatives will add the most new jobs, 545,000, while stock clerks and order fillers is expected to see the largest employment decline among all occupations, losing 131,000 jobs.

Farming, fishing, and forestry occupations. Farming, fishing, and forestry workers cultivate plants, breed and raise livestock, and catch animals. These occupations will decline 2.8 percent and lose 29,000 jobs by 2016. Agricultural workers, including farmworkers and laborers, will account for nearly 3 out of 4 lost jobs in this group. The number of fishing and hunting workers is expected to decline by 16.2 percent, while the number of forest, conservation, and logging workers is expected to decline by 1.4 percent.

Production occupations. Production workers are employed mainly in manufacturing, where they assemble goods and operate plants. Production occupations are expected to decline by 4.9 percent, losing 528,000 jobs by 2016. Some jobs will be created in production occupations, mostly in food processing and woodworking. Metal workers and plastic workers; assemblers and fabricators; textile, apparel, and furnishings occupations; and other production workers will account for most of the job loss among production occupations.

Among all occupations in the economy, healthcare occupations are expected to make up 7 of the 20 fastest growing occupations, the largest proportion of any occupational group (chart 7). These 7 healthcare occupations, in addition to exhibiting high growth rates, will add nearly 750,000 new jobs between 2006 and 2016. Other occupational groups that have more than one occupation in the 20 fastest growing occupations are computer occupations, personal care and service occupations, community and social services occupations, and business and financial operations occupations. High growth rates among occupations in the top 20 fastest growing occupations reflect projected rapid growth in the health care and social assistance industries and the professional, scientific, and technical services industries.

The 20 occupations listed in chart 8 will account for more than one-third of all new jobs, 6.6 million combined, over the 2006-2016 period. The occupations with the largest numerical increases cover a wider range of occupational categories than do those occupations with the fastest growth rates. Health occupations will account for some of these increases in employment, as will occupations in education, sales, and food service. Occupations in office and administrative services will grow by 1.7 million jobs, one-fourth of the job growth among the 20 occupations with the largest job growth. Many of the occupations listed below are very large, and will create more new jobs than will those with high growth rates. Only 3 out of the 20 fastest growing occupations—home health aides, personal and home care aides, and computer software application engineers—also

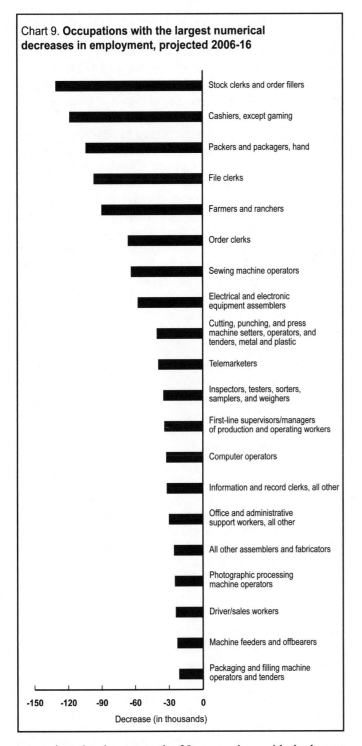

Chart 9. Occupations with the largest numerical decreases in employment, projected 2006-16

Stock clerks and order fillers

Cashiers, except gaming

Packers and packagers, hand

File clerks

Farmers and ranchers

Order clerks

Sewing machine operators

Electrical and electronic equipment assemblers

Cutting, punching, and press machine setters, operators, and tenders, metal and plastic

Telemarketers

Inspectors, testers, sorters, samplers, and weighers

First-line supervisors/managers of production and operating workers

Computer operators

Information and record clerks, all other

Office and administrative support workers, all other

All other assemblers and fabricators

Photographic processing machine operators

Driver/sales workers

Machine feeders and offbearers

Packaging and filling machine operators and tenders

Decrease (in thousands): -150 -120 -90 -60 -30 0

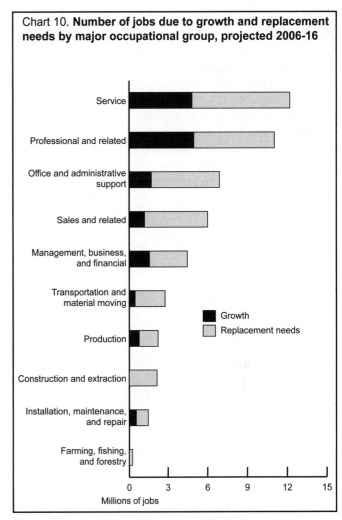

Chart 10. Number of jobs due to growth and replacement needs by major occupational group, projected 2006-16

Service

Professional and related

Office and administrative support

Sales and related

Management, business, and financial

Transportation and material moving

Production

Construction and extraction

Installation, maintenance, and repair

Farming, fishing, and forestry

■ Growth
▨ Replacement needs

Millions of jobs: 0 3 6 9 12 15

are projected to be among the 20 occupations with the largest numerical increases in employment.

Declining occupational employment stems from declining industry employment, technological advances, changes in business practices, and other factors. For example, installation of self-checkouts and other forms of automation will increase productivity and are expected to contribute to a decline of 118,000 cashiers over the 2006-2016 period (chart 9). Fourteen of the 20 occupations with the largest numerical decreases are either production occupations or office and administrative support occupations, which are affected by increasing plant and factory automation and the implementation of office technology that reduces the need for these workers. The difference between the office and administrative occupations that are expected to experience the largest declines and those that are expected to see the largest increases is the extent to which job functions can be easily automated or performed by other workers. For instance, the duties of executive secretaries and administrative assistants involve a great deal of personal interaction that cannot be automated, while the duties of file clerks—adding, locating, and removing business records—can be automated or performed by other workers.

Education and training

For 12 of the 20 fastest growing occupations, an associate degree or higher is the most significant level of postsecondary education or training. On-the-job training is the most significant level of postsecondary education or training for another 6 of the 20 fastest growing occupations. In contrast, on-the-job training is the most significant level of postsecondary education or training for 12 of the 20 occupations with the largest numerical increases, while 6 of these 20 occupations have an associate degree or higher as the most significant level of postsecondary education or training. On-the-job training is the most significant level of postsecondary education or training for 19 of the 20 occupations with the largest numerical decreases. Table 1 lists the fastest growing occupations and occupations projected to have the largest numerical increases in employment between 2006 and 2016, by level of postsecondary education or training.

Total job openings

Job openings stem from both employment growth and replacement needs (chart 10). Replacement needs arise as workers leave occupations. Some transfer to other occupations while others retire, return to school, or quit to assume household responsibilities. Replacement needs are projected to account for 68 percent of the approximately 50 million job openings between 2006 and 2016. Thus, even occupations projected to experience slower than average growth or to decline in employment still may offer many job openings.

Service occupations are projected to have the largest number of total job openings, 12.2 million, and 60 percent of those will be due to replacement needs. A large number of replacements will be necessary as young workers leave food preparation and service occupations. Replacement needs generally are greatest in the largest occupations and in those with relatively low pay or limited training requirements.

Professional and related occupations are projected to be one of the two fastest growing major occupational groups, and are expected to add more jobs than any other major occupational group, about 5 million, by 2016. However, the majority of job openings are expected to come from more than 6 million replacements.

Office automation will significantly affect many individual office and administrative support occupations. While these occupations are projected to grow about as fast as average, some are projected to decline rapidly. Office and administrative support occupations are projected to create 6.9 million total job openings over the 2006-2016 period, ranking third behind service occupations and professional and related occupations.

Farming, fishing, and forestry occupations and production occupations should offer job opportunities despite overall declines in employment. These occupations will lose 29,000 and 528,000 jobs, respectively, but are expected to provide more than 2.4 million total job openings. Job openings among these groups will be solely due to the replacement needs of a workforce that is exhibiting high levels of retirement and job turnover.

Table 1. Fastest growing occupations and occupations projected to have the largest numerical increases in employment between 2006 and 2016, by level of postsecondary education or training

Fastest growing occupations	*Occupations having the largest numerical job growth*
First-professional degree	
Veterinarians	Physicians and surgeons
Pharmacists	Lawyers
Chiropractors	Pharmacists
Physicians and surgeons	Veterinarians
Optometrists	Dentists
Doctoral degree	
Postsecondary teachers	Postsecondary teachers
Computer and information scientists, research	Clinical, counseling, and school psychologists
Medical scientists, except epidemiologists	Medical scientists, except epidemiologists
Biochemists and biophysicists	Computer and information scientists, research
Clinical, counseling, and school psychologists	Biochemists and biophysicists
Master's degree	
Mental health counselors	Clergy
Mental health and substance abuse social workers	Physical therapists
Marriage and family counselors	Mental health and substance abuse social workers
Physical therapists	Educational, vocational, and school counselors
Physician assistants	Rehabilitation counselors
Bachelor's or higher degree, plus work experience	
Actuaries	Management analysts
Education administrators, preschool and child care center/program	Financial managers
Management analysts	Computer and information systems managers
Training and development specialists	Medical and health services managers
Public relations managers	Training and development specialists
Bachelor's degree	
Network systems and data communications analysts	Computer software engineers, applications
Computer software engineers, applications	Accountants and auditors
Personal financial advisors	Business operations specialists, all other
Substance abuse and behavioral disorder counselors	Elementary schoolteachers, except special education
Financial analysts	Computer systems analysts
Associate degree	
Veterinary technologists and technicians	Registered nurses
Physical therapist assistant	Computer support specialists
Dental hygienists	Paralegals and legal assistants
Environmental science and protection technicians, including health	Dental hygienists
Cardiovascular technologists and technicians	Legal secretaries
Postsecondary vocational award	
Makeup artists, theatrical and performance	Nursing aides, orderlies, and attendants
Skin care specialists	Preschool teachers, except special education
Manicurists and pedicurists	Automotive service technicians and mechanics
Fitness trainers and aerobics instructors	Licensed practical and licensed vocational nurses
Preschool teachers, except special education	Hairdressers, hairstylists, and cosmetologists
Work experience in a related occupation	
Sales representatives, services, all other	Executive secretaries and administrative assistants
Gaming managers	Sales representatives, services, all other
Gaming supervisors	Sales representatives, wholesale and manufacturing, except technical and scientific products
Aircraft cargo handling supervisors	First-line supervisors/managers of food preparation and serving workers
Self-enrichment education teachers	First-line supervisors/managers of office and administrative support workers
Long-term on-the-job training	
Audio and video equipment technicians	Carpenters
Interpreters and translators	Cooks, restaurant
Athletes and sports competitors	Police and sheriff's patrol officers
Motorboat mechanics	Plumbers, pipefitters, and steamfitters
Automotive glass installers and repairers	Electricians
Moderate-term on-the-job training	
Medical assistants	Customer service representatives
Social and human service assistants	Bookkeeping, accounting, and auditing clerks
Gaming surveillance officers and gaming investigators	Truck drivers, heavy and tractor-trailer
Pharmacy technicians	Medical assistants
Dental assistants	Maintenance and repair workers, general
Short-term on-the-job training	
Personal and home care aides	Retail salespersons
Home health aides	Combined food preparation and serving workers, including fast food
Gaming and sports book writers and runners	Office clerks, general
Physical therapist aides	Personal and home care aides
Amusement and recreation attendants	Home health aides

Sources of Career Information

This section identifies some major sources of information on careers. These sources are meant to be used in addition to those listed at the end of each *Handbook* statement, and may provide additional information.

How to best use this information. The sources mentioned in this section offer different types of information. For example, people you know may provide very specific information because they have knowledge of you, your abilities and interests, and your qualifications. Other sources, such as those found in State Sources below, provide information on occupations in each State. Gathering information from a wide range of sources is the best way to determine what occupations may be appropriate for you, and in what geographic regions these occupations are found. The sources of information discussed in this section are not exhaustive, and other sources could prove equally valuable in your career search.

Career information

Like any major decision, selecting a career involves a lot of fact finding. Fortunately, some of the best informational resources are easily accessible. You should assess career guidance materials carefully. Information that seems out of date or glamorizes an occupation—overstates its earnings or exaggerates the demand for workers, for example—should be evaluated with skepticism. Gathering as much information as possible will help you make a more informed decision.

People you know. One of the best resources can be those you know, such as friends and family. They may answer some questions about a particular occupation or put you in touch with someone who has some experience in the field. This personal networking can be invaluable in evaluating an occupation or an employer. These people will be able to tell you about their specific duties and training, as well as what they did or did not like about a job. People who have worked in an occupation locally also may be able to recommend and get you in touch with specific employers.

Employers. This is the primary source of information on specific jobs. Employers may post lists of job openings and application requirements, including the exact training and experience required, starting wages and benefits, and advancement opportunities and career paths.

Informational interviews. People already working in a particular field often are willing to speak with people interested in joining their field. An informational interview will allow you to get good information from experts in a specific career without the pressure of a job interview. These interviews allow you to determine how a certain career may appeal to you while helping you build a network of personal contacts.

Professional societies, trade groups, and labor unions. These groups have information on an occupation or various related occupations with which they are associated or which they actively represent. This information may cover training requirements, earnings, and listings of local employers. These groups may train members or potential members themselves, or may be able to put you in contact with organizations or individuals who perform such training.

Each occupational statement in the *Handbook* concludes with a section on sources of additional information, which lists organizations that may be contacted for more information. Another valuable source for finding organizations associated with occupations is *The Encyclopedia of Associations*, an annual publication that lists trade associations, professional societies, labor unions, and other organizations.

Guidance and career counselors. Counselors can help you make choices about which careers might suit you best. They can help you determine what occupations suit your skills by testing your aptitude for various types of work, and determining your strengths and interests. Counselors can help you evaluate your options and search for a job in your field or help you select a new field altogether. They can also help you determine which educational or training institutions best fit your goals, and find ways to finance them. Some counselors offer other services such as interview coaching, résumé building, and help in filling out various forms. Counselors in secondary schools and post-secondary institutions may arrange guest speakers, field trips, or job fairs.

Common places where guidance and career counselors are employed include:

* High school guidance offices
* College career planning and placement offices
* Placement offices in private vocational or technical schools and institutions
* Vocational rehabilitation agencies
* Counseling services offered by community organizations
* Private counseling agencies and private practices
* State employment service offices

When using a private counselor, check to see that the counselor is experienced. One way to do so is to ask people who have used their services in the past. The National Board of Certified Counselors and Affiliates is an institution which accredits career counselors. To verify the credentials of a career counselor and to find a career counselor in your area, contact:

➤ National Board for Certified Counselor and Affiliates, 3 Terrace Way, Suite D, Greensboro, NC 27403-3660. Internet: **http://www.nbcc.org/cfind**

Postsecondary institutions. Colleges, universities, and other postsecondary institutions may put a lot of effort into helping place their graduates in good jobs, because the success of their graduates may indicate the quality of their institution and may affect the institution's ability to attract new students. Postsecondary institutions typically have career centers with libraries of information on different careers, listings of related jobs, and alumni contacts in various professions. Career centers frequently employ career counselors who generally provide their services only to their students and alumni. Career centers can help you build your résumé, find internships and co-ops—which can lead to full-time positions—and tailor your course selection or program to make you a more attractive job applicant.

Local libraries. Libraries can be an invaluable source of information. Since most areas have libraries, they can be a convenient place to look for information. Also, many libraries provide access to the Internet and e-mail.

Libraries may have information on job openings, locally and nationally; potential contacts within occupations or industries; colleges and financial aid; vocational training; individual businesses or careers; and writing résumés. Libraries frequently have subscriptions to various trade magazines that can provide information on occupations and industries. Your local library also may have video materials. These sources often have references to organizations which can provide additional information about training and employment opportunities.

If you need help getting started or finding a resource, ask your librarian for assistance.

Internet resources. With the growing popularity of the Internet, a wide verity of career information has become easily accessible. Many online resources include job listings, résumé posting services, and information on job fairs, training, and local wages. Many of the resources listed elsewhere in this section have Internet sites that include valuable information on potential careers. Since no single source contains all information on an occupation, field, or employer, you will likely need to use a variety of sources.

When using Internet resources, be sure that the organization is a credible, established source of information on the particular occupation. Individual companies may include job listings on their Web sites, and may include information about required credentials, wages and benefits, and the job's location. Contact information, such as whom to call or where to send a résumé, is usually included.

Some sources exist primarily as a Web service. These services often have information on specific jobs, and can greatly aid in the job hunting process. Some commercial sites offer these services, as do Federal, State, and some local governments. *Career OneStop*, a joint program by the Department of Labor and the States as well as local agencies, provides these services free of charge.

Online Sources from the Department of Labor. A major portion of the U.S. Department of Labor's Labor Market Information System is the Career OneStop site. This site includes:

- *State Job Banks* allow you to search over a million job openings listed with State employment agencies.
- *America's Career InfoNet* provides data on employment growth and wages by occupation; the knowledge, skills, and abilities required by an occupation; and links to employers.
- *America's Service Locator* is a comprehensive database of career centers and information on unemployment benefits, job training, youth programs, seminars, educational opportunities, and disabled or older worker programs.

Career OneStop, along with the National Toll free Helpline (877-USA-JOBS) and the local One-Stop Career Centers in each State, combine to provide a wide range of workforce assistance and resources:

➤ Career OneStop. Internet: **http://www.careeronestop.org**

Use the O*NET numbers at the start of each *Handbook* statement to find more information on specific occupations:

➤ O*NET Online. Internet: **http://www.onetcenter.org**

Provided in collaboration with the U.S. Department of Education, *Career Voyages* has information on certain high-demand occupations:

➤ Career Voyages. Internet: **http://www.careervoyages.gov**

The Department of Labor's Bureau of Labor Statistics publishes a wide range of labor market information, from regional wages for specific occupations to statistics on National, State, and area employment.

➤ Bureau of Labor Statistics. Internet: **http://www.bls.gov**

While the *Handbook* discusses careers from an occupational perspective, a companion publication—*Career Guide to Industries*—discusses careers from an industry perspective. The *Career Guide* is also available at your local career center and library:

➤ *Career Guide to Industries.*
Internet: **http://www.bls.gov/oco/cg/home.htm**

For information on occupational wages:

➤ Wage Data. Internet: **http://www.bls.gov/bls/blswage.htm**

For information on training, workers' rights, and job listings:

➤ Education and Training Administration.
Internet: **http://www.doleta.gov/jobseekers**

Organizations for specific groups. Some organizations provide information designed to help specific groups of people. Consult directories in your library's reference center or a career guidance office for information on additional organizations associated with specific groups.

Disabled workers:
State counseling, training, and placement services for those with disabilities are available from:

➤ State Vocational Rehabilitation Agency. Internet: **http://wdcrobcolp01.ed.gov/Programs/EROD**

Information on employment opportunities, transportation, and other considerations for people with all types of disabilities is available from:

➤ National Organization on Disability, 910 Sixteenth St. NW., Suite 600, Washington, DC 20006. Telephone: (202) 293-5960. TTY: (202) 293-5968. Internet: **http://www.nod.org/economic**

For information on making accommodations in the work place for people with disabilities:

➤ Job Accommodation Network (JAN), P.O. Box 6080, Morgantown, WV 26506. Internet: **http://www.jan.wvu.edu**

A comprehensive Federal Web site of disability-related resources is accessible at:

Blind workers:

Information on the free national reference and referral service for the blind can be obtained by contacting:

➤ National Federation of the Blind, Job Opportunities for the Blind (JOB), 1800 Johnson St., Baltimore, MD 21230. Telephone: (410) 659-9314. Internet: **http://www.nfb.org**

Older workers:

➤ National Council on the Aging, 1901 2nd St. NW., 4th Floor., Washington, DC 20036. Telephone: (202) 479-1200. Internet: **http://www.ncoa.org**

➤ National Caucus and Center on Black Aged, Inc., Senior Employment Programs, 1220 L St. NW., Suite 800, Washington, DC 20005. Telephone: (202) 637-8400. Fax: (202) 347-0895. Internet: **http://www.ncba-aged.org**

Veterans:

Contact the nearest regional office of the U.S. Department of Labor's Veterans Employment and Training Service or:

➤ Credentialing Opportunities Online (COOL), which explains how military personnel can meet civilian certification and license requirements related to their Military Occupational Specialty (MOS). Internet: **http://www.cool.army.mil/index.htm**

Women:

➤ Department of Labor, Women's Bureau, 200 Constitution Ave. NW., Washington, DC 20210. Telephone: (800) 827-5335. Internet: **http://www.dol.gov/wb**

Federal laws, executive orders, and selected Federal grant programs bar discrimination in employment based on race, color, religion, sex, national origin, age, and handicap. Information on how to file a charge of discrimination is available from U.S. Equal Employment Opportunity Commission offices around the country. Their addresses and telephone numbers are listed in telephone directories under U.S. Government, EEOC. Telephone: (800) 669-4000. TTY: (800) 669-6820). Internet: **http://www.eeoc.gov**

Office of Personnel Management. Information on obtaining civilian positions within the Federal Government is available

from the U.S. Office of Personnel Management through USA-Jobs, the Federal Government's official employment information system. This resource for locating and applying for job opportunities can be accessed through the Internet or through an interactive voice response telephone system at (703) 724-1850 or TDD (978) 461-8404. These numbers are not toll free, and charges may result.

➤ USA Jobs: **http://www.usajobs.opm.gov**

Military. The military employs and has information on hundreds of occupations. Information is available on the Montgomery G.I. Bill, which provides money for school and educational debt repayments. Information on military service can be provided by your local recruiting office. Also see the *Handbook* statement on Job Opportunities in the Armed Forces. You will find more information on careers in the military at:

➤ Today's Military. Internet: **http://www.todaysmilitary.com**

State Sources. Most States have career information delivery systems (CIDS), which may be found in secondary and post-secondary institutions, as well as libraries, job training sites, vocational-technical schools, and employment offices. A wide range of information is provided, from employment opportunities to unemployment insurance claims.

Whereas the *Handbook* provides information for occupations on a national level, each State has detailed information on occupations and labor markets within their respective jurisdictions. State occupational projections are available at: **http://www.projectionscentral.com**

Alabama
Labor Market Information Division, Alabama Department of Industrial Relations, 649 Monroe St., Room 422, Montgomery, AL 36131. Telephone: (334) 242-8859. Internet: **http://dir.alabama.gov**

Alaska
Research and Analysis Section, Department of Labor and Workforce Development, P.O. Box 25501, Juneau, AK 99802-5501. Telephone: (907) 465-4500. Internet: **http://www.jobs.state.ak.us**

Arizona
Arizona Department of Economic Security, P.O. Box 6123 SC 733A, Phoenix, AZ 85005-6123. Telephone: (602) 542-5984. Internet: **http://www.workforce.az.gov**

Arkansas
Labor Market Information, Department of Workforce Services, #2 Capital Mall, Little Rock, AR 72201. Telephone: (501) 682-3198. Internet: **http://www.arkansas.gov/esd**

California
State of California Employment Development Department, Labor Market Information Division, P.O. Box 826880, Sacramento, CA 94280-0001. Telephone: (916) 262-2162. Internet: **http://www.labormarketinfo.edd.ca.gov**

Colorado

Labor Market Information, Colorado Department of Labor and Employment, 633 17th St., Suite 201, Denver, CO 80202-3660. Telephone: (303) 318-8000. Internet: **http://www.coworkforce.com/lmi**

Connecticut

Office of Research, Connecticut Department of Labor, 200 Folly Brook Blvd., Wethersfield, CT 06109-1114. Telephone: (860) 263-6275. Internet: **http://www.ctdol.state.ct.us/lmi**

Delaware

Office of Occupational and Labor Market Information, Department of Labor, 19 West Lea Blvd., Wilmington, DE 19802-. Telephone: (302) 761-8069.
Internet: **http://www.delawareworks.com/oolmi/welcome.shtml**

District of Columbia

DC Department of Employment Services, 609 H St. NE., Washington, D.C. 20002. Telephone: (202) 724-7000.
Internet: **http://www.does.dc.gov/does**

Florida

Labor Market Statistics, Agency for Workforce Innovation, MSC G-020, 107 E. Madison St., Tallahassee, FL 32399-4111. Telephone: (850) 245-7205. Internet: **http://www.labormarketinfo.com**

Georgia

Workforce Information and Analysis, Room 300, Department of Labor, 223 Courtland St., CWC Building, Atlanta, GA 30303. Telephone: (404) 232-3875. Internet:
http://www.dol.state.ga.us/em/get_labor_market_information.htm

Guam

Guam Department of Labor, 504 D St., Tiyan, Guam 96910. Telephone: (671) 475-0101.

Hawaii

Research and Statistics Office, Department of Labor and Industrial Relations, 830 Punchbowl St., Room 304, Honolulu, HI 96813. Telephone: (808) 586-8999. Internet: **http://www.hiwi.org**

Idaho

Research and Analysis Bureau, Department of Commerce and Labor, 317 West Main St., Boise, ID 83735-0670. Telephone: (208) 332-3570. Internet: **http://lmi.idaho.gov**

Illinois

Illinois Department of Employment Security, Economic Information and Analysis Division, 33 S. State St., 9th Floor , Chicago, IL 60603. Telephone: (312) 793-2316. Internet: **http://lmi.ides.state.il.us**

Indiana

Research and Analysis—Indiana Workforce Development, Indiana Government Center South, 10 North Senate Ave., Indianapolis, IN 46204. Telephone: (800) 891-6499. Internet: **http://www.in.gov/dwd**

Iowa

Policy and Information Division, Iowa Workforce Development, 1000 East Grand Ave., Des Moines, IA 50319-0209. Telephone: (515) 281-5116. Internet: **http://www.iowaworkforce.org/lmi**

Kansas

Kansas Department of Labor, Labor Market Information Services, 401 SW Topeka Blvd., Topeka, KS 66603-3182. Telephone: (785) 296-5000. Internet: **http://laborstats.dol.ks.gov**

Kentucky

Research and Statistics Branch, Office of Employment and Training, 275 East Main St., Frankfort, KY 40621. Telephone: (502) 564-7976. Internet: **http://www.workforcekentucky.ky.gov**

Louisiana

Research and Statistics Division, Department of Labor, 1001 North 23rd St., Baton Rouge, LA 70802-3338. Telephone: (225) 342-3111. Internet: **http://www.laworks.net**

Maine

Labor Market Information Services Division, Maine Department of Labor, State House Station 54, P.O. Box 259 45 Commerce Dr., Augusta, ME 04330. Telephone: (207) 621-5182.
Internet: **http://www.state.me.us/labor/lmis/index.html**

Maryland

Maryland Department of Labor Licensing and Regulation, Office of Labor Market Analysis and Information, Room 316, 1100 N. Eutaw, Baltimore, MD 21201. Telephone: (410) 767-2250. Internet: **http://www.dllr.state.md.us/lmi/index.htm**

Massachusetts

Executive Office of Labor and Workforce Development, Division of Career Services, 19 Staniford St., Boston, MA 02114. Telephone: (617) 626-5300. Internet: **http://www.detma.org/LMIdataprog.htm**

Michigan

Bureau of Labor Market Information and Strategic Initiatives, Department of Labor and Economic Growth, 3032 West Grand Blvd., Suite 9-100, Detroit, MI 48202. Telephone: (313) 456-3090. Internet: **http://www.milmi.org**

Minnesota

Department of Employment and Economic Development, Labor Market Information Office, 1st National Bank Building, 332 Minnesota St., Suite E200, St. Paul, MN 55101-1351. Telephone: (888) 234-1114. Internet: **http://www.deed.state.mn.us/lmi**

Mississippi

Labor Market Information Division, Mississippi Department of Employment Security , 1235 Echelon Pkwy., P.O. Box 1699, Jackson, MS 39215. Telephone: (601) 321-6000. Internet: **http://mdes.ms.gov**

Missouri
Missouri Economic Research and Information Center, P.O. Box 3150, Jefferson City, MO 65102-3150. Telephone: (866) 225-8113. Internet: **http://www.missourieconomy.org**

Montana
Research and Analysis Bureau, P.O. Box 1728, Helena, MT 59624. Telephone: (800) 541-3904. Internet: **http://www.ourfactsyourfuture.org**

Nebraska
Nebraska Workforce Development—Labor Market Information, Nebraska Department of Labor, 550 South 16tth St., P.O. Box 94600, Lincoln, NE 68509. Telephone: (402) 471-2600. Internet: **http://www.dol.state.ne.us/nelmi.htm**

Nevada
Research and Analysis, Department of Employment Training and Rehabilitation, 500 East Third St., Carson City, NV 89713. Telephone: (775) 684-0450. Internet: **http://www.nevadaworkforce.com**

New Hampshire
Economic and Labor Market Information Bureau, New Hampshire Employment Security, 32 South Main St., Concord, NH 03301-4857. Telephone: (603) 228-4124. Internet: **http://www.nhes.state.nh.us/elmi**

New Jersey
Division of Labor Market and Demographic Research, Department of Labor and Workforce Development, P.O. Box 388, Trenton, NJ 08625-0388. Telephone: (609) 984-2593. Internet: **http://www.wnjpin.net**

New Mexico
New Mexico Department of Labor , Economic Research and Analysis, 401 Broadway NE., Albuquerque, NM 87102. Telephone: (505) 222-4683. Internet: **http://www.dws.state.nm.us/dws-lmi.html**

New York
Research and Statistics, New York State Department of Labor, State Office Campus, Room 490, Albany, NY 12240. Telephone: (518) 457-2919.
Internet: **http://www.labor.state.ny.us/workforceindustrydata/index.asp**

North Carolina
Labor Market Information Division, Employment Security Commission, 700 Wade Ave., Raleigh, NC 27605. Telephone: (919) 733-4329. Internet: **http://www.ncesc.com**

North Dakota
Labor Market Information Manager, Job Service North Dakota, 1000 East Divide Ave., Bismarck, ND 58506. Telephone: (800) 732-9787. Internet: **http://www.ndworkforceintelligence.com**

Ohio
Bureau of Labor Market Information, Office of Workforce Development, Ohio Department of Job and Family Services, P.O. Box 1618, Columbus, OH 43216-1618.Telephone: (614) 752-9494. Internet: **http://www.ohioworkforceinformer.org**

Oklahoma
Labor Market Information, Oklahoma Employment Security Commission, 2401 N. Lincoln Blvd., Oklahoma City, OK 73105. Telephone: (405) 557-7100. Internet: **http://www.oesc.state.ok.us/lmi/default.htm**

Oregon
Oregon Employment Department, Research Division, 875 Union St. NE., Salem, OR 97311.Telephone: (503) 947-1200. Internet: **http://www.qualityinfo.org/olmisj/OlmisZine**

Pennsylvania
Center for Workforce Information & Analysis, Pennsylvania Department of Labor and Industry, 220 Labor and Industry Building, Seventh and Forster Sts., Harrisburg, PA 17121. Telephone: (877) 493-3282. Internet: **http://www.paworkstats.state.pa.us**

Puerto Rico
Labor Market Information Office, P.O. Box 195540, San Juan, Puerto Rico 00919-5540.Telephone: (787) 281-5760. Internet: **http://www.dtrh.gobierno.pr/oficina_procurador_del_trabajo.asp**

Rhode Island
Labor Market Information, Rhode Island Department of Labor and Training, 1511 Pontiac Ave., Cranston, RI 02920. Telephone: (401) 462-8740. Internet: **http://www.dlt.ri.gov/lmi**

South Carolina
Labor Market Information Department, South Carolina Employment Security Commission, 631 Hampton St., Columbia, SC 29202. Telephone: (803) 737-2660. Internet: **http://www.sces.org/lmi/index.asp**

South Dakota
Labor Market Information Center, Department of Labor, P.O. Box 4730, Aberdeen, SD 57402-4730. Telephone: (605) 626-2314. Internet: **http://www.state.sd.us/dol/lmic/index.htm**

Tennessee
Research and Statistics Division, Department of Labor and Workforce Development, 710 James Robertson Pkwy., Nashville, TN 37243. Telephone: (615) 741-6642. Internet: **http://www.state.tn.us/labor-wfd/lmi.htm**

Texas
Labor Market Information, Texas Workforce Commission, 9001 North IH-35, Suite 103A, Austin, TX 75753. Telephone: (866) 938-4444. Internet: **http://www.tracer2.com**

Utah
Director of Workforce Information, Utah Department of Workforce Services, P.O. Box 45249, Salt Lake City, UT 84145-0249. Telephone: (801) 526-9675. Internet: **http://jobs.utah.gov/opencms/wi**

Vermont
Research and Analysis, Vermont Department of Labor, P.O. Box 488, Montpelier, VT 05601-0488. Telephone: (802) 828-4000. Internet: **http://www.labor.vermont.gov**

Virgin Islands
Bureau of Labor Statistics, Department of Labor, P.O. Box 302608, St Thomas, VI 00803-2608.Telephone: (340) 776-3700. Internet: **http://www.vidol.gov**

Virginia
Economic Information Services, Virginia Employment Commission, P.O. Box 1358, Richmond, VA 23218-1358. Telephone: (804) 786-8223. Internet: **http://velma.virtuallmi.com**

Washington
Labor Market and Economic Analysis, Washington Employment Security Department, PO Box 9046, Olympia, WA 98507-9046. Telephone: (800) 215-1617. Internet: **http://www.workforceexplorer.com**

West Virginia
WORKFORCE West Virginia, Research, Information and Analysis Division, 112 California Ave., Charleston, WV 25303-0112. Telephone: (304) 558-2660. Internet: **http://www.wvbep.org/bep/lmi**

Wisconsin
Bureau of Workforce Information, Department of Workforce Development, P.O.Box 7944, Madison, WI 53707-7944. Telephone: (608) 266-8212. Internet: **http://worknet.wisconsin.gov/worknet**

Wyoming
Research and Planning, Wyoming Department of Employment, 246 S. Center St., Casper, WY 82602. Telephone: (307) 473-3807. Internet: **http://doe.state.wy.us/lmi**

Sources of Education, Training, and Financial Aid

Education can present opportunities for those looking to start a new career or change specialty within their current occupation. This section outlines some major sources of education and training required to enter many occupations, as well as some ways to finance that education or training.

For information on the specific training and educational requirements for a particular occupation, and what training is typically provided by an employer, consult the Training, Other Qualifications, and Advancement section of the appropriate *Handbook* statement.

Sources of Education and Training

Four-year colleges and universities. These institutions provide detailed information on theory and practice for a wide variety of subjects. Colleges and universities can provide students with the knowledge and background necessary to be successful in many fields. They also can help to place students in cooperative education programs—often called "co-ops"—or internships. Co-ops and internships are short-term jobs with firms related to a student's field of study that lead to college credit. In co-ops and internships, students learn the specifics of a job while making valuable contacts that can lead to a permanent position.

For more information on colleges and universities, go to your local library, consult your high school guidance counselor, or contact individual colleges. Also check with your State's higher education agency. A list of these agencies is available on the Internet: **http://wdcrobcolp01.ed.gov/Programs/EROD**.

Junior and community colleges. Junior and community colleges offer a mixture of programs that lead to associate degrees and training certificates. Community colleges tend to be less expensive than 4-year colleges and universities. They usually are more willing to accommodate part-time students than colleges and universities, and their programs are more tailored to the needs of local employers. Many community colleges have an open admissions policy, and they often offer weekend and night classes.

Community colleges often form partnerships with local businesses that allow students to gain job-specific training. For students who may not be able to enroll in a college or university because of their academic record, limited finances, or distance from such an institution, junior or community colleges are often used as a place to earn credits that can be applied toward a degree at a 4-year college. Junior and community colleges also are noted for their extensive role in continuing and adult education.

For more information on junior and community colleges, go to your local library, consult your high school guidance counselor, or contact individual schools. Also check with your State's higher education agency. A list of these agencies is available on the Internet: **http://wdcrobcolp01.ed.gov/Programs/EROD**.

Online colleges and universities. Online colleges and universities offer classes over the Internet that cover most of the same material as their traditional classroom counterparts. Offering classes on the Internet provides a great deal of flexibility to students, allowing many who work, travel frequently, or lack the ability or means to attend a traditional university to earn a degree from an accredited institution.

A prospective student should talk to a guidance counselor or advisor before deciding to enroll in an online college or university. Additionally, the prospective student should check the college or university's accreditation with the U.S. Department of Education. This can be done online at: **http://www.ope.ed.gov/accreditation/Search.asp**.

Vocational and trade schools. These institutions train people in specific trades. They offer courses designed to provide hands-on experience. Vocational and trade schools tend to concentrate on trades, services, and other types of skilled work.

Vocational and trade schools frequently engage students in real-world projects, allowing them to apply field methods while learning theory in classrooms. Graduates of vocational and trade schools have an advantage over informally trained or self-trained job seekers because graduates have an independent organization certifying that they have the knowledge, skills, and abilities necessary to perform the duties of a particular occupation. These schools also help students to acquire any license or other credentials needed to enter the job market.

For more information on vocational and trade schools, go to your local library, consult your high school guidance counselor, or contact individual schools. Also check with your State's director of vocational-technical education. A list of State directors of vocational-technical education is available on the Internet: **http://wdcrobcolp01.ed.gov/Programs/EROD**.

Apprenticeships. An apprenticeship provides work experience as well as education and training for people entering certain occupations. Apprenticeships are offered by sponsors, who employ and train the apprentice. The apprentice follows a training course under close supervision and receives some formal education to learn the theory related to the job.

Apprenticeships are a way for inexperienced people to become skilled workers that generally last between 1 and 4 years. Some apprenticeships allow the apprentice to earn an associate degree. An *Apprenticeship Completion Certificate* is granted to those completing programs. This certificate is administered by federally approved State agencies.

Information on apprenticeships is available from the Office of Apprenticeship Training, Employer, and Labor Services on the Internet: **http://www.doleta.gov/atels_bat**. For assistance finding an apprenticeship program, go to: **http://www.doleta.gov/atels_bat/fndprgm.cfm**.

Professional societies, trade associations, and labor unions. These groups are made up of people with common interests, usually in related occupations or industries. The groups frequently are able to provide training, access to training through their affiliates, or information on acceptable sources of training for their field. If licensing or certification is required, they also may be able to assist you in meeting those requirements.

For a listing of professional societies, trade associations, and labor unions related to an occupation, check the Sources of Additional Information section at the end of that occupational statement in the *Handbook*.

Employers. Many employers provide on-the-job training, which can range from spending a few minutes watching another employee demonstrate a task to participating in formal training programs that may last for several months. In some jobs, employees may continually undergo training to stay up to date with new developments and technologies, or to add new skills.

Military. The United States Armed Forces trains and employs people in more than 4,100 different occupations. For more information, see the *Handbook* statement on "Job Opportunities in The Armed Forces." For detailed answers to specific questions, contact your local recruiting office. Valuable resources also are available on the Internet: **http://www.todaysmilitary.com.**

Sources of Financial Aid

Many people fund their education or training through financial aid or tuition assistance programs. Federal student aid comes in three forms: grants, work-study programs, and loans. All Federal student aid applicants must first fill out a Free Application for Federal Student Aid (FAFSA), which provides a Student Aid Report (SAR) and eligibility rating. Forms must be submitted to desired institutions of study, which determine the amount of aid you will receive.For information on applying for Federal financial aid, visit the FAFSA Internet site: **http://www.fafsa.ed.gov.**A U.S. Department of Education publication describing Federal financial aid programs, called *The Student Guide,* is available at: **http://www.studentaid.ed.gov/students/publications/student_guide/index.html.** Information on Federal programs is available from: **http://www.studentaid.ed.gov** and **www.students.gov.** Information on State programs is available from your State's higher education agency. A list of these agencies is available at: **http://wdcrobcolp01.ed.gov/Programs/EROD.**

Grants. A grant is money which is given to students or the institution they are attending in order to pay for their education or training and any associated expenses. Grants are usually given on the basis of financial need. Grants are considered gifts and are not paid back. Federal grants are almost exclusively for undergraduate students. They include Pell Grants, which can be worth up to $4,310 annually. Pell Grants of up to $4,800 will be available beginning in July 2008, with further increases to $5,000 and $5,400 available in July 2010 and July 2012, respectively. Federal Supplemental Educational Opportunity Grants (FSEOG) can be worth up to $4,000 annually. Priority for FSEOG awards is given to those who have also received the Pell Grant and have exceptional financial need.

Additional information on grants is available on the Internet: **http://www.studentaid.ed.gov.** Information also is available from your State Higher Education agency. A list of these agencies is available at: **http://wdcrobcolp01.ed.gov/Programs/EROD.**

Federal Work-Study program. The Federal Work-Study program is offered at most institutions and consists of Federal sponsorship of a student who works part time at the institution he or she is attending. The money a student earns through this program goes directly toward the cost of attending the institution. There are no set minimum or maximum amounts for this type of aid, although, on average, a student can expect to earn about $2,000 per school year.

For additional information on work-study opportunities offered, check with individual institutions. General information on the Federal Work-Study program is available at: **http://www.studentaid.ed.gov/students/publications/student_guide/2005-2006/english/types-fed-workstudy.htm.**

Scholarships. A scholarship is a sum of money donated to a student to help pay for his or her education or training and any associated costs. Scholarships can range from small amounts up to the full cost of schooling. They are based on financial need, academic merit, athletic ability, or a wide variety of other criteria set by the organizations that provide the scholarships. Frequently, students must meet minimum academic requirements to be considered for a scholarship. Other qualifying requirements—such as intended major field of study, heritage, or group membership—may be added by the organization providing the scholarship.

Scholarships are provided by a wide variety of institutions, including educational institutions, State and local governments, private associations, social groups, and individuals. There are no federally awarded scholarships based on academic merit. Most large scholarships are awarded to students by the institution they plan to attend. Students who have received State scholarships and plan to attend a school in another State should check with their State to see if the scholarship can be transferred.

Information on scholarships is typically available from high school guidance counselors and local libraries. Additional scholarship information is available from State higher education agencies. A list of these agencies is available at: **http://wdcrobcolp01.ed.gov/Programs/EROD.** The College Board has information on available scholarships at: **http://www.collegeboard.com/pay.**

Student loans. Many institutions, both public and private, provide low-interest loans to students and their parents or guardians. The Federal Government also provides several types of student loans based on the applicant's level of financial need. The amount of money a student can receive in loans varies by the distributing institution and depends on whether the student is claimed by a parent or guardian as a dependent. Since the process of applying for a loan may take several months, it is a good idea to start applying for Federal student loans well in advance.

The available Federal loan programs can accommodate prospective undergraduate, graduate, vocational, and disabled students. Federal loans can be distributed through the school that the student is attending, from the Federal Government directly, or from a third-party private lender or bank. Perkins loans are distributed through the school the student is attending. Loans coming from the Federal Government directly from the William D. Ford Federal Direct Loan Program are dispersed by the Department of Education. Third-party loans through a private lender or bank are from the Federal Family Education Loan (FFEL) program. For all federally funded loans, payments are made to the institution that originally dispersed the funds.

For those with financial need, Federal Perkins loans and both Direct and FFEL-subsidized Stafford loans are available. Perkins loans have no minimum amount; they are capped at $4,000 per year for undergraduates, but will be increasing to $6,000 a year by 2012. Students should visit the Department of Education's Web site (**http://www.studentaid.ed.gov/PORTALSWebApp/ students/english/fafsa.jsp**) to learn about the current level of aid available because it will vary by year and a student's status (married, single, dependent, or independent). Subsidized Stafford loans vary in size and can increase as a student completes more years of undergraduate, graduate, or professional education. Interest rates for both loans will be gradually decreasing until 2012. Information on specific interest rates is available through the school's financial aid officer or the Department of Education's Web site. Those with Perkins loans are not responsible for starting to repay the loan until they have been out of school for 9 months. Those with subsidized Stafford loans must begin payments within 6 to 9 months of leaving school but are not charged monthly interest while in school.

For those who do not demonstrate financial need, Direct and FFEL-unsubsidized Stafford Loans and Federal Parent Loans for Students (PLUS) are available. Unsubsidized Stafford loans vary in value and are capped at the cost of attendance. With Federal unsubsidized Stafford Loans, interest payments start almost immediately and can be paid monthly or accrued until the completion of studies. The latter option results in a larger total loan cost but may be more convenient for some students. With PLUS loans, the parent must pay interest and principal payments while the student is enrolled in school and must continue payments after completion. Check with your lender for available repayment schedules. Students usually have 10 years to repay Perkins loans and from 10 to 30 years for unsubsidized Stafford loans.

Subsidized and unsubsidized Stafford loans are only available to students who are enrolled in an academic program at least half time. As with any loan, be sure to investigate different lenders, and understand what your loan contract requires of you before agreeing to any loan. Check with established financial institutions to compare the terms of available private student loans. Comparisons of the various types of loans are available on the Internet: **http://www.studentaid.ed.gov/students/publications/ student_guide/index.html**. The College Board has information on available loans at: **http://www.collegeboard.com/pay**.

Employer tuition support programs. Some employers offer tuition assistance programs as part of their employee benefits package. The terms of these programs depend on the firm and can vary by the type and amount of training subsidized, as well as by eligibility requirements. Consult your human resources department for information on tuition support programs offered by your employer.

Military tuition support programs. The United States Armed Forces offer various tuition assistance and loan repayment programs for military personnel. See the *Handbook* statement on "Job Opportunities in the Armed Forces" for more information. Also go to: **http://www.todaysmilitary.com/app/tm/get/col- legehelp/support**.

Finding and Applying for Jobs and Evaluating Offers

Finding—and getting—a job you want can be a challenging process, but knowing more about job search methods and application techniques can increase your chances of success. And knowing how to judge the job offers you receive makes it more likely that you will end up with the best possible job.

Where to learn about job openings

Personal contacts
School career planning and placement offices
Employers
Classified ads
    —National and local newspapers
    —Professional journals
    —Trade magazines
Internet resources
Professional associations
Labor unions
State employment service offices
Federal Government
Community agencies
Private employment agencies and career consultants
Internships

Job search methods

Finding a job can take months of time and effort. But you can speed the process by using many methods to find job openings. Data from the Bureau of Labor Statistics suggest that people who use many job search methods find jobs faster than people who use only one or two.

In the box above, some sources of job openings are listed. Those sources are described more fully below.

Personal contacts. Many jobs are never advertised. People get them by talking to friends, family, neighbors, acquaintances, teachers, former coworkers, and others who know of an opening. Be sure to tell people that you are looking for a job because the people you know may be some of the most effective resources for your search. To develop new contacts, join student, community, or professional organizations.

School career planning and placement offices. High school and college placement offices help their students and alumni find jobs. Some invite recruiters to use their facilities for interviews or career fairs. They also may have lists of open jobs. Most also offer career counseling, career testing, and job search advice. Some have career resource libraries; host workshops on job search strategy, resume writing, letter writing, and effective interviewing; critique drafts of resumes; conduct mock interviews; and sponsor job fairs.

Employers. Directly contacting employers is one of the most successful means of job hunting. Through library and Internet research, develop a list of potential employers in your desired career field. Then call these employers and check their Web sites for job openings. Web sites and business directories can tell you how to apply for a position or whom to contact. Even if no open positions are posted, do not hesitate to contact the employer: You never know when a job might become available. Consider asking for an informational interview with people working in the career you want to learn more. Ask them how they got started, what they like and dislike about the work, what type of qualifications are necessary for the job, and what type of personality succeeds in that position. In addition to giving you career information, they may be able to put you in contact with other people who might hire you, and they can keep you in mind if a position opens up.

Classified ads. The "Help Wanted" ads in newspapers and the Internet list numerous jobs, and many people find work by responding to these ads. But when using classified ads, keep the following in mind:

- Follow all leads to find a job; do not rely solely on the classifieds.
- Answer ads promptly, because openings may be filled quickly, even before the ad stops appearing in the paper.
- Read the ads every day, particularly the Sunday edition, which usually includes the most listings.
- Keep a record of all ads to which you have responded, including the specific skills, educational background, and personal qualifications required for the position.

Internet resources. The Internet includes many job hunting Web sites with job listings. Some job boards provide National listings of all kinds; others are local. Some relate to a specific type of work; others are general. To find good prospects, begin with an Internet search using keywords related to the job you want. Also look for the sites of related professional associations.

Also consider checking Internet forums, also called message boards. These are online discussion groups where anyone may post and read messages. Use forums specific to your profession or to career-related topics to post questions or messages and to read about the job searches or career experiences of other people.

In online job databases, remember that job listings may be posted by field or discipline, so begin your search using keywords. Many Web sites allow job seekers to post their resumes online for free.

Professional associations. Many professions have associations that offer employment information, including career planning, educational programs, job listings, and job placement. To use these services, associations usually require that you be a member; information can be obtained directly from an association through the Internet, by telephone, or by mail.

Labor unions. Labor unions provide various employment services to members and potential members, including apprenticeship programs that teach a specific trade or skill. Contact the appropriate labor union or State apprenticeship council for more information.

State employment service offices. The State employment service, sometimes called the Job Service, operates in coordination with the U.S. Department of Labor's Employment and Training Administration. Local offices, found nationwide, help job seekers to find jobs and help employers to find qualified workers at no cost to either. To find the office nearest you, look in the State government telephone listings under "Job Service" or "Employment."

Job matching and referral. At the State employment service office, an interviewer will determine if you are "job ready" or if you need help from counseling and testing services to assess your occupational aptitudes and interests and to help you choose and prepare for a career. After you are job ready, you may examine available job listings and select openings that interest you. A staff member can then describe the job openings in detail and arrange for interviews with prospective employers.

Services for special groups. By law, veterans are entitled to priority job placement at State employment service centers. If you are a veteran, a veterans' employment representative can inform you of available assistance and help you to deal with problems.

State employment service offices also refer people to opportunities available under the Workforce Investment Act (WIA) of 1998. Educational and career services and referrals are provided to employers and job seekers, including adults, dislocated workers, and youth. These programs help to prepare people to participate in the State's workforce, increase their employment and earnings potential, improve their educational and occupational skills, and reduce their dependency on welfare.

Federal Government. Information on obtaining a position with the Federal Government is available from the U.S. Office of Personnel Management (OPM) through USAJOBS, the Federal Government's official employment information system. This resource for locating and applying for job opportunities can be accessed through the Internet at **http://www.usajobs.opm.gov** or through an interactive voice response telephone system at (703) 724-1850 or TDD (978) 461-8404. These numbers are not toll free, and charges may result.

Community agencies. Many nonprofit organizations, including religious institutions and vocational rehabilitation agencies, offer counseling, career development, and job placement services, generally targeted to a particular group, such as women, youths, minorities, ex-offenders, or older workers.

Private employment agencies and career consultants. Private agencies can save you time and they will contact employers who otherwise might be difficult to locate. But these agencies may charge for their services. Most operate on a commission basis, charging a percentage of the first-year salary paid to a successful applicant. You or the hiring company will pay the fee. Find out the exact cost and who is responsible for paying associated fees before using the service. When determining if the service is worth the cost, consider any guarantees that the agency offers.

Internships. Many people find jobs with business and organizations with whom they have interned or volunteered. Look for internships and volunteer opportunities on job boards, career centers, and company and association Web sites, but also check community service organizations and volunteer opportunity databases. Some internships and long-term volunteer positions come with stipends and all provide experience and the chance to meet employers and other good networking contacts.

Applying for a job

After you have found some jobs that interest you, the next step is to apply for them. You will almost always need to complete resumes or application forms and cover letters. Later, you will probably need to go on interviews to meet with employers face to face.

Resumes and application forms. Resumes and application forms give employers written evidence of your qualifications and skills. The goal of these documents is to prove—as clearly and directly as possible—how your qualifications match the job's requirements. Do this by highlighting the experience, accomplishments, education, and skills that most closely fit the job you want.

Gathering information. Resumes and application forms both include the same information. As a first step, gather the following facts:

- Contact information, including your name, mailing address, e-mail address (if you have one you check often), and telephone number.

- Type of work or specific job you are seeking or a qualifications summary, which describes your best skills and experience in just a few lines.

- Education, including school name and its city and State, months and years of attendance, highest grade completed or diploma or degree awarded, and major subject or subjects studied. Also consider listing courses and awards that might be relevant to the position. Include a grade point average if you think it would help in getting the job.

- Experience, paid and volunteer. For each job, include the job title, name and location of employer, and dates of employment. Briefly describe your job duties and major accomplishments. In a resume, use phrases instead of sentences to describe your work; write, for example, "Supervised 10 children" instead of writing "I supervised 10 children."

- Special skills. You might list computer skills, proficiency in foreign languages, achievements, or and membership in organizations in a separate section.

• References. Be ready to provide references if requested. Good references could be former employers, coworkers, or teachers or anyone else who can describe your abilities and job-related traits. You will be asked to provide contact information for the people you choose.

Throughout the application or resume, focus on accomplishments that relate most closely to the job you want. You can even use the job announcement as a guide, using some of the same words and phrases to describe your work and education.

Look for concrete examples that show your skills. When describing your work experience, for instance, you might say that you increased sales by 10 percent, finished a task in half the usual time, or received three letters of appreciation from customers.

Choosing a format. After gathering the information you want to present, the next step is to put it in the proper format. In an application form, the format is set. Just fill in the blanks. But make sure you fill it out completely and follow all instructions. Do not omit any requested information. Consider making a copy of the form before filling it out, in case you make a mistake and have to start over. If possible, have someone else look over the form before submitting it.

In a resume, there are many ways of organizing the information you want to include, but the most important information should usually come first. Most applicants list their past jobs in reverse chronological order, describing their most recent employment first and working backward. But some applicants use a functional format, organizing their work experience under headings that describe their major skills. They then include a brief work history section that lists only job titles, employers, and dates of employment. Still other applicants choose a format that combines these two approaches in some way. Choose the style that best showcases your skills and experience.

Whatever format you choose, keep your resume short. Many experts recommend that new workers use a one-page resume. Avoid long blocks of text and italicized material. Consider using bullets to highlight duties or key accomplishments.

Before submitting your resume, make sure that it is easy to read. Are the headings clear and consistently formatted with bold or some other style of type? Is the type face large enough? Then, ask at least two people to proofread the resume for spelling and other errors and make sure you use your computer's spell checker.

Keep in mind that many employers scan resumes into databases, which they then search for specific keywords or phrases. The keywords are usually nouns referring to experience, education, personal characteristics, or industry buzz words. Identify keywords by reading the job description and qualifications in the job ad; use these same words in your resume. For example, if the job description includes customer service tasks, use the words "customer service" on your resume. Scanners sometimes misread paper resumes, which could mean some of your keywords don't get into the database. So, if you know that your resume will be scanned, and you have the option, e-mail an electronic version. If you must submit a paper resume, make it scannable by using a simple font and avoiding underlines, italics, and graphics. It is also a good idea to send a tradition-

ally formatted resume along with your scannable resume, with a note on each marking its purpose.

Cover letters. When sending a resume, most people include a cover letter to introduce themselves to the prospective employer. Most cover letters are no more than three short paragraphs. Your cover letter should capture the employer's attention, follow a business letter format, and usually should include the following information:

• Name and address of the specific person to whom the letter is addressed.
• Reason for your interest in the company or position.
• Your main qualifications for the position.
• Request for an interview.
• Your home and work telephone numbers.

If you send a scannable resume, you should also include a scannable cover letter, which avoids graphics, fancy fonts, italics, and underlines.

As with your resume, it may be helpful to look for examples on the Internet or in books at your local library or bookstore, but be sure not to copy letters directly from other sources.

Interviewing. An interview gives you the opportunity to showcase your qualifications to an employer, so it pays to be well prepared. The accompanying box provides some helpful hints.

Evaluating a job offer

Once you receive a job offer, you must decide if you want the job. Fortunately, most organizations will give you a few days to accept or reject an offer.

There are many issues to consider when assessing a job offer. Will the organization be a good place to work? Will the job be interesting? Are there opportunities for advancement? Is the salary fair? Does the employer offer good benefits? Now is the time to ask the potential employer about these issues—and to do some checking on your own.

The organization. Background information on an organization can help you to decide whether it is a good place for you to work. Factors to consider include the organization's business or activity, financial condition, age, size, and location.

You generally can get background information on an organization, particularly a large organization, on its Internet site or by telephoning its public relations office. A public company's annual report to the stockholders tells about its corporate philosophy, history, products or services, goals, and financial status. Most government agencies can furnish reports that describe their programs and missions. Press releases, company newsletters or magazines, and recruitment brochures also can be useful. Ask the organization for any other items that might interest a prospective employee. If possible, speak to current or former employees of the organization.

Background information on the organization may be available at your public or school library. If you cannot get an annual report, check the library for reference directories that may provide basic facts about the company, such as earnings, products and services, and number of employees. Some directories

Job interview tips

Preparation:
Learn about the organization.
Have a specific job or jobs in mind.
Review your qualifications for the job.
Be ready to briefly describe your experience, showing how it relates it the job.
Be ready to answer broad questions, such as "Why should I hire you?" "Why do you want this job?" "What are your strengths and weaknesses?"
Practice an interview with a friend or relative.

Personal appearance:
Be well groomed.
Dress appropriately.
Do not chew gum or smoke.

The interview:
Be early.
Learn the name of your interviewer and greet him or her with a firm handshake.
Use good manners with everyone you meet.
Relax and answer each question concisely.
Use proper English—avoid slang.
Be cooperative and enthusiastic.
Use body language to show interest—use eye contact and don't slouch.
Ask questions about the position and the organization, but avoid questions whose answers can easily be found on the company Web site.
Also avoid asking questions about salary and benefits unless a job offer is made.
Thank the interviewer when you leave and shake hands.
Send a short thank you note.

Information to bring to an interview:
Social Security card.
Government-issued identification (driver's license).
Resume or application. Although not all employers require a resume, you should be able to furnish the interviewer information about your education, training, and previous employment.
References. Employers typically require three references. Get permission before using anyone as a reference. Make sure that they will give you a good reference. Try to avoid using relatives as references.
Transcripts. Employers may require an official copy of transcripts to verify grades, coursework, dates of attendance, and highest grade completed or degree awarded.

widely available in libraries either in print or as online databases include:

- *Dun & Bradstreet's Million Dollar Directory*
- *Standard and Poor's Register of Corporations*
- *Mergent's Industry Review (formerly Moody's Industrial Manual)*
- *Thomas Register of American Manufacturers*
- *Ward's Business Directory*

Stories about an organization in magazines and newspapers can tell a great deal about its successes, failures, and plans for the future. You can identify articles on a company by looking under its name in periodical or computerized indexes in libraries, or by using one of the Internet's search engines. However, it probably will not be useful to look back more than 2 or 3 years.

The library also may have government publications that present projections of growth for the industry in which the organization is classified. Long-term projections of employment and output for detailed industries, covering the entire U.S. economy, are developed by the Bureau of Labor Statistics and revised every 2 years. (See the *Career Guide to Industries*, online at **http://www.bls.gov/oco/cg**.) Trade magazines also may include articles on the trends for specific industries.

Career centers at colleges and universities often have information on employers that is not available in libraries. Ask a career center representative how to find out about a particular organization.

During your research consider the following questions:

Does the organization's business or activity match your own interests and beliefs?
It is easier to apply yourself to the work if you are enthusiastic about what the organization does.

How will the size of the organization affect you?
Large firms generally offer a greater variety of training programs and career paths, more managerial levels for advancement, and better employee benefits than do small firms. Large employers also may have more advanced technologies. However, many jobs in large firms tend to be highly specialized.

Jobs in small firms may offer broader authority and responsibility, a closer working relationship with top management, and a chance to clearly see your contribution to the success of the organization.

Should you work for a relatively new organization or one that is well established?
New businesses have a high failure rate, but for many people, the excitement of helping to create a company and the potential for sharing in its success more than offset the risk of job loss. However, it may be just as exciting and rewarding to work for a young firm that already has a foothold on success.

The job. Even if everything else about the job is attractive, you will be unhappy if you dislike the day-to-day work. Determining in advance whether you will like the work may be difficult. However, the more you find out about the job before accepting or rejecting the offer, the more likely you are to make the right choice. Consider the following questions:

Where is the job located?
If the job is in another section of the country, you need to consider the cost of living, the availability of housing and transportation, and the quality of educational and recreational facilities in that section of the country. Even if the job location is in your area, you should consider the time and expense of commuting.

Does the work match your interests and make good use of your skills?

The duties and responsibilities of the job should be explained in enough detail to answer this question.

How important is the job to the company or organization?

An explanation of where you fit in the organization and how you are supposed to contribute to its overall goals should give you an idea of the job's importance.

What will the hours be?

Most jobs involve regular hours—for example, 40 hours a week, during the day, Monday through Friday. Other jobs require night, weekend, or holiday work. In addition, some jobs routinely require overtime to meet deadlines or sales or production goals, or to better serve customers. Consider the effect that the work hours will have on your personal life.

How long do most people who enter this job stay with the company?

High turnover can mean dissatisfaction with the nature of the work or something else about the job.

Opportunities offered by employers. A good job offers you opportunities to learn new skills, increase your earnings, and rise to positions of greater authority, responsibility, and prestige. A lack of opportunities can dampen interest in the work and result in frustration and boredom.

The company should have a training plan for you. What valuable new skills does the company plan to teach you?

The employer should give you some idea of promotion possibilities within the organization. What is the next step on the career ladder? If you have to wait for a job to become vacant before you can be promoted, how long does this usually take? When opportunities for advancement do arise, will you compete with applicants from outside the company? Can you apply for jobs for which you qualify elsewhere within the organization, or is mobility within the firm limited?

Salaries and benefits. When an employer makes a job offer, information about earnings and benefits are usually included. You will want to research to determine if the offer is fair. If you choose to negotiate for higher pay and better benefits, objective research will help you strengthen your case.

You may have to go to several sources for information. One of the best places to start is the information from the Bureau of Labor Statistics. Data on earnings by detailed occupation from the Occupational Employment Statistics (OES) Survey are available from:

➤ Bureau of Labor Statistics, Office of Occupational Statistics and Employment Projections, 2 Massachusetts Ave. NE., Room 2135, Washington, DC 20212-0001. Telephone: (202) 691-6569. Internet: **http://www.bls.gov/oes**.

Data from the Bureau's National Compensation Survey are available from:

➤ Bureau of Labor Statistics, Office of Compensation Levels and Trends, 2 Massachusetts Ave. NE., Room 4175, Washington, DC 20212-0001. Telephone: (202) 691-6199. Internet: **http://www.bls.gov/ncs**.

You should also look for additional information, specifically tailored to your job offer and circumstances. Try to find family, friends, or acquaintances who recently were hired in similar jobs. Ask your teachers and the staff in placement offices about starting pay for graduates with your qualifications. Help-wanted ads in newspapers sometimes give salary ranges for similar positions. Check the library or your school's career center for salary surveys such as those conducted by the National Association of Colleges and Employers or various professional associations.

If you are considering the salary and benefits for a job in another geographic area, make allowances for differences in the cost of living, which may be significantly higher in a large metropolitan area than in a smaller city, town, or rural area.

You also should learn the organization's policy regarding overtime. Depending on the job, you may or may not be exempt from laws requiring the employer to compensate you for overtime. Find out how many hours you will be expected to work each week and whether you receive overtime pay or compensatory time off for working more than the specified number of hours in a week.

Also take into account that the starting salary is just that—the start. Your salary should be reviewed on a regular basis; many organizations do it every year. How much can you expect to earn after 1, 2, or 3 or more years? An employer cannot be specific about the amount of pay if it includes commissions and bonuses.

Benefits also can add a lot to your base pay, but they vary widely. Find out exactly what the benefit package includes and how much of the cost you must bear.

For more information

To learn more about finding and applying for jobs, visit your local library and career center. You can find career centers that are part of the U.S. Department of Labor One-Stop Career system by calling toll free (877) 348-0502.

The *Occupational Outlook Quarterly*, a career magazine published by the Bureau of Labor Statistics, is one of the resources available at many libraries and career centers. The magazine includes many articles about finding, applying for, and choosing jobs. See, for example:

➤ "Employment interviewing: Seizing the opportunity and the job," online at **http://www.bls.gov/opub/ooq/2000/summer/art02.pdf**.

➤ "Getting back to work: Returning to the labor force after an absence," online at **http://www.bls.gov/opub/ooq/2004/winter/art03.pdf**.

➤ "How to get a job in the Federal Government," online at **http://www.bls.gov/opub/ooq/2004/summer/art01.pdf**.

➤ "Internships: Previewing a profession," online at **http://www.bls.gov/opub/ooq/2006/summer/art02.pdf**.

➤ "Resumes, applications, and cover letters," online at **http://www.bls.gov/opub/ooq/1999/summer/art01.pdf**.

Occupational Information Included in the Handbook

The *Occupational Outlook Handbook* is a career guidance resource that provides information on hundreds of occupations that comprise 9 out of 10 jobs in the United States. Each occupation is presented in its own chapter, or "statement," that discusses the type of work that is performed, the work environment, the education and training requirements, the possibilities for advancement, and the typical earnings. Each statement is presented in a standard format, making it easy to compare occupations.

Because the *Handbook* covers so many occupations, it is best used as a reference, and is not meant to be read from cover to cover. Readers should begin by looking at the table of contents, in which similar occupations are grouped in clusters, or by looking at the index, in which occupations are listed alphabetically.

About those numbers at the beginning of each statement

The numbers in parentheses that appear just below the title of every detailed occupational statement are from the Occupational Information Network (O*NET)—a system used by State employment service offices to classify applicants and job openings, and by some career information centers and libraries to file occupational information.

You can use O*NET to search for occupations that match your skills, or you may search by keyword or O*NET code. For each occupation, O*NET reports information about different aspects of the job, including tasks performed, knowledge, skills, abilities, and work activities. It also lists interests, work styles, such as independence, and work values, such as achievement, that are well suited to the occupation. O*NET ranks and scores the descriptors in each category by their importance to the occupation.

Occupational Information Network Coverage, a section beginning on page 859, cross-references O*NET codes to occupations covered in the *Handbook*. O*NET codes are based on the 2000 Standard Occupational Classification (SOC) system. You can access O*NET on the Internet at **http://www.online.onetcenter.org**.

Sections of Occupational Statements

Significant Points
This section highlights key occupational characteristics discussed in the statement.

Nature of the Work
What workers do on the job, what tools and equipment they use, and how closely they are supervised is discussed in this section. The statement on fire fighting occupations, for example, gives a detailed account of the responsibilities of a firefighter, which include operating the fire hose, providing emergency medical care, and cleaning and maintaining equipment. Some statements mention common alternative job titles or occupational specialties. The statement on accountants and auditors, for example, discusses several specialties, including public accountants, management accountants, and internal auditors.

The *Handbook* is revised every 2 years. This section may be revised for several reasons. One is the emergence of occupational specialties. For instance, webmasters—who are responsible for the technical aspects of operating a Web site—constitute a specialty within computer scientists and database administrators. Another reason for revision is a change in technology that affects the way in which a job is performed. The Internet, for example, allows purchasers to acquire supplies with a click of the mouse, saving time and money. Furthermore, job duties may be affected by modifications to business practices, such as organizational restructuring or changes in response to new government regulations. An example is paralegals and legal assistants, who are increasingly being used by law firms in order to lower costs and increase the efficiency of legal services.

Work environment. This subsection discusses the workplace, physical activities, and typical hours of workers in the occupation. It also describes opportunities for part-time work, the extent of travel required, any special equipment that is used, and the risk of injury that workers may face.

In many occupations, people work regular business hours—40 hours a week, Monday through Friday—but many do not. Waiters and waitresses, for example, often work evenings and weekends. The work setting can range from a hospital, to a mall, to an offshore oil rig. Truck drivers might be susceptible to injury, while paramedics have high job-related stress. Semiconductor processors may wear protective clothing or equipment, some construction laborers do physically demanding work, and top executives may travel frequently.

Information on various worker characteristics, such as the average number of hours worked per week, is obtained from the Current Population Survey (CPS)—a survey of households conducted by the U.S. Census Bureau for the Bureau of Labor Statistics (BLS).

Economists in BLS consult many sources before making changes to the nature of the work section, or any other section, of a *Handbook* statement. Usual sources include articles from newspapers, magazines, and professional journals, as well as the Web sites of professional associations, unions, and trade groups. Information found on the Internet or in periodicals is verified through interviews with individuals employed in the occupation, professional associations, unions, and others with occupational knowledge, such as university professors and career counselors.

Training, Other qualifications, and Advancement

After gathering your initial impressions of what a job is all about, it is important to understand how to prepare for it. The training, other qualifications, and advancement section explains all of the steps necessary to enter and advance in an occupation.

Education and training. This subsection describes the most significant sources of education and training, the type education or training preferred by employers, and the typical length of training. Some common forms of training include a high school diploma, informal on-the-job training, previous work experience, and a college degree. Other types of training include, but are not limited to, formal training (including internships), the U.S. Armed Forces, and graduate or professional degrees. The type of education or training required for each occupation in the *Handbook* varies, and two similar occupations can have very different requirements. For example, sales experience is particularly important for many sales jobs, but other sales jobs require formal postsecondary education, such as a bachelor's degree.

Licensure. The kinds of mandatory licenses or certifications associated with an occupation are described in this subsection. To be certified or licensed, a worker usually is required to complete one or more training courses and pass one or more examinations. Most occupations do not have mandatory licensure or certification requirements, but those that do, for example, include lawyers, pharmacists, and social workers. Some occupations have numerous professional credentials granted by different organizations, in which case the most widely recognized organizations are listed in the *Handbook.*

Other qualifications. Any additional qualifications that are not included in the previous subsections, such as the desirable skills, aptitudes, and personal characteristics that employers look for would be discussed in this section. For example, meeting and convention planners must have excellent interpersonal and organizational skills, the ability to work under pressure, and must pay attention to detail. For some entry-level jobs, personal characteristics are more important than formal training. Employers generally seek people who read, write, and speak well; compute accurately; think logically; learn quickly; get along with others; and demonstrate dependability. This subsection also includes information about voluntary, entry-level certifications.

Advancement. This subsection details possible advancement opportunities after gaining experience in an occupation. Advancement can come in several forms, including advancement within the occupation, such as promotion to a management position; advancement into other occupations, such as leaving a job as a lawyer to become a judge; and advancement to self-employment, such as an automotive technician opening his or her own repair shop.

Certain types of certification can also serve as a form of advancement. Voluntary certification often demonstrates a level of competency to employers, and can result in more responsibility, higher pay, or a new job. Accountants, for example, generally begin their careers without the Certified Public Accountant (CPA) designation. Many choose to pursue a CPA, however, because it increases their chances for advancement.

Information in the training, other qualifications, and advancement section comes from personal interviews with individuals employed in the occupation, Web sites, published training materials, and interviews with the organizations that grant degrees, certifications, or licenses, or are otherwise associated with the occupation.

Employment

This section reports the number of jobs that the occupation provided in 2006, the key industries in which those jobs were found, and, if significant, the number or proportion of self-employed workers in the occupation.

The source of estimated employment in a particular occupation in the *Handbook* is the Bureau's National Employment Matrix, which presents current and projected employment for 311 detailed industries and 754 detailed occupations over the 2006-2016 period. Data in the matrix come primarily from the establishment-based Occupational Employment Statistics (OES) Survey, which reports employment of wage and salary workers only for each occupation in every industry except agriculture and private households. Matrix data also come from the household-based Current Population Survey (CPS), which provides estimates of the number of self-employed and unpaid family workers in each occupation. The matrix also incorporates CPS data on total employment—wage and salary, self-employed, and unpaid family workers—in the agriculture and private household industries.

The estimate of total employment in each *Handbook* occupation combines data from several different sources. Furthermore, some *Handbook* occupations combine several matrix occupations. For these reasons, employment numbers cited in the *Handbook* often differ from employment data provided by the OES, CPS, and other employment surveys.

When significant, the geographic distribution of jobs is mentioned, reflecting CPS data. On the basis of OES survey data, some *Handbook* statements, such as textile, apparel, and furnishings occupations, list States that employ substantial numbers of workers in the occupation.

Job Outlook

In planning for the future, it is important to consider potential job growth and job opportunities. This section describes the factors that affect employment growth or decline, and in some instances, describes the relationship between the number of job seekers and the number of job openings.

Employment change. This subsection reflects the occupational projections in the National Employment Matrix. Each occupation is assigned a descriptive phrase based on its projected percent change in employment over the 2006-2016 period. This phrase describes the occupation's projected employment change relative to the projected average employment change for all occupations combined. (These phrases are listed at the end of *Occupational Information Included in the Handbook.*)

Many factors are examined in projecting the employment change for each occupation. One such factor is changes in technology. New technology can either create new job opportunities or eliminate jobs by making workers obsolete. The Internet has increased the demand for workers in the computer and information technology fields, such as computer support specialists and systems administrators. However, the Internet also has adversely affected travel agents, because many people now book tickets, hotels, and rental cars online.

Another factor that influences employment trends is demographic change. By affecting the services demanded, demographic change can influence occupational growth or decline. For example, an aging population will demand more health care services, leading to occupational growth in health care occupations.

Another factor affecting job growth or decline is changes in business practices, such as restructuring businesses or outsourcing (contracting out) work. Corporate restructuring has made many organizations "flatter," resulting in fewer middle management positions. Also, in the past few years, insurance carriers have been outsourcing sales and claims adjuster jobs to large, 24-hour call centers in order to reduce costs. Jobs in some occupations, such as computer programmers and customer service representatives, have been "offshored"—moved to low-wage foreign countries.

The substitution of one product or service for another can also affect employment projections. For example, consumption of plastic products has grown as they have been substituted for metal goods in consumer and manufactured products in recent years. The process is likely to continue and should result in stronger demand for machine operators in plastics than in metal.

Competition from foreign trade usually has a negative affect on employment. Often, foreign manufacturers can produce goods more cheaply than they can be produced in the United States, and the cost savings can be passed on in the form of lower prices with which U.S. manufacturers cannot compete. Increased international competition is a major reason for the decline in employment among textile, apparel, and furnishings workers.

Another factor is job growth or decline in key industries. If an occupation is concentrated in an industry that is growing rapidly, it is likely that that occupation will grow rapidly as well. For example, the growing need for business expertise is fueling demand for consulting services. This is expected to cause rapid growth in the management, scientific, and technical consulting services industry, which, in turn, will lead to rapid growth in the employment of management analysts.

Job prospects. In some cases, the *Handbook* mentions that an occupation is likely to provide numerous job openings or, in others, that an occupation likely will have relatively few openings. This information reflects the projected change in employment, as well as replacement needs. Large occupations in which workers frequently enter and leave, such as food and beverage serving occupations, generally provide the most job openings—reflecting the need to replace workers who transfer to other occupations or who stop working.

Some *Handbook* statements discuss the relationship between the number of job seekers and the number of job openings. (The phrases used to describe that relationship appear at the end of *Occupational Information Included in the Handbook*.) Job opportunities are affected by several factors, including the creation of new jobs, the number of people who apply for jobs, and the number of people who leave the occupation. In some oc-

cupations, there is a rough balance between job seekers and job openings, resulting in *good* opportunities. In other occupations, employers may report difficulty finding qualified applicants, resulting in *excellent* job opportunities. Still other occupations are characterized by a surplus of applicants, leading to *keen* competition for jobs. Variation in job opportunities by industry, educational attainment, size of firm, or geographic location also may be discussed. Even in crowded occupations, job openings do exist. Good students or highly qualified individuals should not be deterred from undertaking training for, or seeking entry into, those occupations.

Employment projections table. The employment projections table lists employment statistics from the National Employment Matrix. It includes 2006 employment, projected 2016 employment, and the 2006-2016 change in employment in both numerical and percent forms. Numbers below ten thousand are rounded to the nearest hundred, numbers above ten thousand are rounded to the nearest thousand, and percents are rounded to the nearest whole number. Numerical and percent changes are calculated using non-rounded 2006 and 2016 employment figures, and then are rounded for presentation in the employment projections table.

Earnings

This section discusses typical earnings and how workers are compensated—by means of annual salaries, hourly wages, commissions, piece rates, tips, or bonuses. Within every occupation, earnings vary by experience, responsibility, performance, tenure, and geographic area. Almost every statement in the *Handbook* contains 2006 OES-survey earnings data for wage and salary workers. Information on earnings in the major industries in which the occupation is employed, also supplied by the OES survey, may be given as well.

In addition to presenting earnings data from the OES survey, some statements contain additional earnings data from non-BLS sources. Starting and average salaries of Federal workers are based on 2007 data from the U.S. Office of Personnel Management. The National Association of Colleges and Employers supplies information on average salary offers in 2007 for students graduating with a bachelor's, master's, or Ph.D. degree in certain fields. A few statements contain additional earnings information from other sources, such as unions, professional associations, and private companies. These data sources are cited in the text.

Benefits account for a significant portion of total compensation costs to employers. Benefits such as paid vacation, health insurance, and sick leave may not be mentioned, because they are widespread. In some occupational statements, the absence of these traditional benefits is pointed out. Although not as common as traditional benefits, flexible hours and profit-sharing plans may be offered to attract and retain highly qualified workers. Less common benefits also include childcare, tuition for dependents, housing assistance, summers off, and free or discounted merchandise or services. For certain occupations, the percentage of workers affiliated with a union is listed. These data come from the CPS survey.

Unless otherwise noted, the source of employment and earnings data presented in the *Handbook* is the Bureau of

Labor Statistics. Nearly all *Handbook* statements cite employment and wage data from the OES survey, and some include data from outside sources. OES data may be used to compare wages among occupations; outside data, however, may not be used in this manner, because characteristics of these data vary widely.

Related occupations

Occupations involving similar duties, skills, interests, education, and training are listed.

Sources of additional information

No single publication can describe all aspects of an occupation. Thus, the *Handbook* lists the mailing addresses of associations, government agencies, unions, and other organizations that can provide occupational information. In some cases, toll free telephone numbers and Internet addresses also are listed. Free or relatively inexpensive publications offering more information may be mentioned; some of these publications also may be available in libraries, in school career centers, in guidance offices, or on the Internet. Most of the organizations listed in this section were sources of information on the nature of the work, training, and job outlook discussed in the *Handbook*.

For additional sources of information, also read the earlier chapters, "Sources of Career Information" and "Sources of Education, Training, and Financial Aid."

Key phrases in the *Handbook*

This box explains how to interpret the key phrases used to describe projected changes in employment. It also explains the terms used to describe the relationship between the number of job openings and the number of job seekers. The description of this relationship in a particular occupation reflects the knowledge and judgment of economists in the BLS Office of Occupational Statistics and Employment Projections.

Changing employment between 2006 and 2016

If the statement reads:	Employment is projected to:
Grow much faster than average	increase 21 percent or more
Grow faster than average	increase 14 to 20 percent
Grow about as fast as average	increase 7 to 13 percent
Grow more slowly than average	increase 3 to 6 percent
Little or no change	decrease 2 percent to increase 2 percent
Decline slowly or moderately	decrease 3 to 9 percent
Decline rapidly	decrease 10 percent or more

Opportunities and competition for jobs

If the statement reads:	Job openings compared with job seekers may be:
Very good to excellent opportunities	More numerous
Good or favorable opportunities	In rough balance
May face, or can expect, keen competition	Fewer

Management, Business, and Financial Occupations

Management Occupations

Administrative Services Managers

(O*NET 11-3011.00)

Significant Points

- Applicants will face keen competition for the limited number of top-level management jobs, but competition should be less severe for lower-level management jobs; demand should be strong for facility managers.

- Administrative services managers work throughout private industry and government and have a wide range of responsibilities, experience, earnings, and education.

- Like other managers, administrative services managers should be analytical, detail-oriented, flexible, decisive, and have good leadership and communication skills.

Nature of the Work

Administrative services managers coordinate and direct the many support services that allow organizations to operate efficiently. They perform a broad range of duties. They might, for example, oversee secretarial and reception services, administration, payroll, conference planning and travel, information and data processing, mail, materials scheduling and distribution, printing and reproduction, records management, telecommunications management, security, parking, energy consumption, and personal property procurement, supply, recycling, and disposal. They manage support services for organizations as diverse as insurance companies, computer manufacturers, and government offices.

Specific duties for these managers vary by degree of responsibility and authority. First-line administrative services managers directly supervise a staff that performs various support services. Mid-level managers, on the other hand, develop departmental plans, set goals and deadlines, implement procedures to improve productivity and customer service, and define the responsibilities of supervisory-level managers. Some mid-level administrative services managers oversee first-line supervisors from various departments, including the clerical staff. Mid-level managers also may be involved in the hiring and dismissal of employees, but they generally have no role in the formulation of personnel policy. Some of these managers advance to upper level positions, such as vice president of administrative

services, which are discussed in the *Handbook* statement on top executives.

In small organizations, a single administrative services manager may oversee all support services. In larger ones, however, first-line administrative services managers often report to mid-level managers who, in turn, report to owners or top-level managers, sometimes called director of administration, or vice president of administration.

The nature of managerial jobs varies as significantly as the range of administrative services required by organizations. For example, *administrative services managers* who work as contract administrators oversee the preparation, analysis, negotiation, and review of contracts related to the purchase or sale of equipment, materials, supplies, products, or services. In addition, some administrative services managers acquire, distribute,

Administrative services managers coordinate and direct support services that allow organizations to operate efficiently.

and store supplies, while others dispose of surplus property or oversee the disposal of unclaimed property.

Administrative services managers who work as *facility managers* plan, design, and manage buildings, grounds, equipment, and supplies, in addition to people. This task requires integrating the principles of business administration, information technology, architecture, engineering, and behavioral science. Although the specific tasks assigned to facility managers vary substantially depending on the organization, the duties fall into several categories, relating to operations and maintenance, real estate, project planning and management, leadership and communication, finance, quality assessment, facility function, technology integration, and management of human and environmental factors. Tasks within these broad categories may include space and workplace planning, budgeting, purchase and sale of real estate, lease management, renovations, or architectural planning and design. Facility managers may suggest and oversee renovation projects for a variety of reasons, ranging from improving efficiency to ensuring that facilities meet government regulations and environmental, health, and security standards. For example, they may influence a building renovation project toward a greater use of "green" energy–electricity generated from alternative and cost efficient energy sources, such as solar panels or fuel cells. Additionally, facility managers continually monitor the facility to ensure that it remains safe, secure, and well-maintained. Often, the facility manager is responsible for directing staff, including maintenance, grounds, and custodial workers.

Work environment. Administrative services managers generally work in comfortable offices. Managers involved in contract administration and personal property procurement, use, and disposal may travel between their home office, branch offices, vendors' offices, and property sales sites. Also, facility managers who are responsible for the design of workspaces may spend time at construction sites and may travel between different facilities while monitoring the work of maintenance and custodial staffs. However, new technology has increased the number of managers who telecommute from home or other offices, and teleconferencing has reduced the need for travel. Facility managers also may spend time outdoors, supervising and handling a variety of issues related to groundskeeping, landscaping, construction, security, and parking.

Most administrative services managers work a standard 40-hour week. However, uncompensated overtime frequently is required to resolve problems and meet deadlines. Facility managers often are "on call" to address a variety of problems that can arise in a facility during nonwork hours.

Training, Other Qualifications, and Advancement

Education and experience requirements for these managers vary widely, depending on the size and complexity of the organization. In small organizations, experience may be the only requirement needed to enter a position as an office manager. When an opening in administrative services management occurs, the office manager may be promoted to the position based on past performance. In large organizations, however, administrative services managers normally are hired from outside and each position has formal education and experience require-

ments. Some administrative services managers have advanced degrees.

Education and training. Specific requirements vary by job responsibility. For first-line administrative services managers of secretarial, mailroom, and related support activities, many employers prefer to hire people who have an associate degree in business or management, although a high school diploma may suffice when combined with appropriate experience.

For managers of audiovisual, graphics, and other technical activities, postsecondary technical school training is preferred. Managers of highly complex services, such as contract administration, generally need at least a bachelor's degree in business, human resources, or finance. Regardless of major, the curriculum should include courses in office technology, accounting, business mathematics, computer applications, human resources, and business law.

Most facility managers have an undergraduate or graduate degree in engineering, architecture, construction management, business administration, or facility management. Many have a background in real estate, construction, or interior design, in addition to managerial experience.

Whatever the manager's educational background, it must be accompanied by related work experience reflecting their ability. For this reason, many administrative services managers have advanced through the ranks of their organization, acquiring work experience in various administrative positions before assuming first-line supervisory duties. All managers who oversee departmental supervisors should be familiar with office procedures and equipment. Managers of personal property acquisition and disposal need experience in purchasing and sales, and knowledge of a variety of supplies, machinery, and equipment. Managers concerned with supply, inventory, and distribution should be experienced in receiving, warehousing, packaging, shipping, transportation, and related operations. Contract administrators may have worked as contract specialists, cost analysts, or procurement specialists. Managers of unclaimed property often have experience in insurance claims analysis and records management.

Other qualifications. Persons interested in becoming administrative services managers should have good leadership and communication skills and be able to establish effective working relationships with many different people, ranging from managers, supervisors, and professionals, to clerks and blue-collar workers. They should be analytical, detail-oriented, flexible, and decisive. They must be able to coordinate several activities at once, quickly analyze and resolve specific problems, and cope with deadlines.

Certification and advancement. Most administrative services managers in small organizations advance by moving to other management positions or to a larger organization. Advancement is easier in large firms that employ several levels of administrative services managers. Attainment of the Certified Manager (CM) designation offered by the Institute of Certified Professional Managers (ICPM), through education, work experience, and successful completion of examinations, can enhance a manager's advancement potential. In addition, a master's degree in business administration or a related field enhances a first-level manager's opportunities to advance to a mid-level management position, such as director of administrative services, and eventually to a top-level management position, such as executive vice president for administrative services. Those with enough money and experience can establish their own management consulting firm.

Advancement of facility managers is based on the practices and size of individual companies. Some facility managers transfer from other departments within the organization or work their way up from technical positions. Others advance through a progression of facility management positions that offer additional responsibilities. Completion of the competency-based professional certification program offered by the International Facility Management Association can give prospective candidates an advantage. In order to qualify for this Certified Facility Manager (CFM) designation, applicants must meet certain educational and experience requirements. People entering the profession also may obtain the Facility Management Professional (FMP) credential, a stepping stone to the CFM.

Employment

Administrative services managers held about 247,000 jobs in 2006. About 65 percent worked in service-providing industries, including Federal, State, and local government; health care; finance and insurance; professional, scientific, and technical services; administrative and support services; and educational services, public and private. Most of the remaining managers worked in wholesale and retail trade, in management of companies and enterprises, or in manufacturing.

Job Outlook

The number of jobs is projected to grow as fast as average for all occupations. Applicants will face keen competition for the limited number of top-level management jobs through 2016. Better opportunities are expected for lower-level management jobs. Demand should be strong for facility managers.

Employment change. Employment of administrative services managers is projected to grow 12 percent over the 2006-16 decade, about as fast as the average for all occupations. Demand should be strong for facility managers because businesses increasingly realize the importance of maintaining, securing, and efficiently operating their facilities, which are very large investments for most organizations. Cost-cutting measures to improve profitability, streamline operations, and compete globally will continue to be addressed by many public and private organizations, resulting in more firms outsourcing facility management services or hiring qualified facility managers who are capable achieving these goals in-house.

Administrative services managers employed in management services and management consulting should be in demand. The proliferation of facility management outsourcing should result in employment growth in facilities management firms as companies increasingly look to outside specialists to handle the myriad of tasks that have become increasingly complex and expensive. Some of the services outsourced include food service, space planning and design, janitorial, power plant, grounds, office, safety, property, video surveillance, maintenance and repairs, and parking management.

Job prospects. Applicants will face keen competition for the limited number of top-level management jobs; competition should be less severe for lower-level management jobs.

Despite average job growth, continuing corporate restructuring and increasing use of office technology may result in a more streamlined organizational structure with fewer levels of management, reducing the need for some middle management positions. This should adversely affect administrative services managers who oversee first-line managers. However, the effects of these changes on employment should be less severe for facility managers and other administrative services managers who have a wide range of responsibilities, than for other middle managers who specialize in certain functions. In addition to new administrative services management jobs created over the 2006-16 projection period, many job openings will stem from the need to replace workers who transfer to other jobs, retire, or leave the occupation for other reasons.

Job opportunities may vary from year to year because the strength of the economy affects demand for administrative services managers. Industries least likely to be affected by economic fluctuations tend to be the most stable places for employment.

Earnings

Earnings of administrative services managers vary greatly depending on the employer, the specialty, and the geographic area. In general, however, median annual earnings of wage and salary administrative services managers in May 2006 were $67,690. The middle 50 percent earned between $48,200 and $90,350. The lowest 10 percent earned less than $34,970, and the highest 10 percent earned more than $117,610. Median annual earnings in the industries employing the largest numbers of these managers were:

Management of companies and enterprises $77,040
General medical and surgical hospitals................................72,210
State government...68,410
Local government 67,050
Colleges, universities, and professional schools..................64,810

In the Federal Government, industrial specialists averaged $74,042 a year in 2007. Corresponding averages were $73,455 for facility operations services managers, $72,730 for industrial property managers, $65,351 for property disposal specialists,

Projections data from the National Employment Matrix

Occupational Title	SOC Code	Employment, 2006	Projected employment, 2016	Change, 2006-16	
				Number	Percent
Administrative services managers	11-3011	247,000	276,000	29,000	12

NOTE: Data in this table are rounded. See the discussion of the employment projections table in the *Handbook* introductory chapter on *Occupational Information Included in the Handbook.*

$71,948 for administrative officers, and $63,756 for support services administrators.

Related Occupations

Administrative services managers direct and coordinate support services and oversee the purchase, use, and disposal of personal property. Occupations with similar functions include office and administrative support worker supervisors and managers; cost estimators; property, real estate, and community association managers; purchasing managers, buyers, and purchasing agents; and top executives.

Sources of Additional Information

For information about careers and education and degree programs in facility management, as well as the Certified Facility Manager designation, contact:

➤ International Facility Management Association, 1 East Greenway Plaza, Suite 1100, Houston, TX 77046-0194. Internet: **http://www.ifma.org**

For information about the Certified Manager (CM) designation, contact:

➤ Institute of Certified Professional Managers, James Madison University, MSC 5504, Harrisonburg, VA 22807.

For information on training and classes for professional office management personnel, contact:

➤ Association of Professional Office Managers, 1 Research Court, Suite #450, Rockville, MD 20850. Internet: **http://www.apomonline.org**

Advertising, Marketing, Promotions, Public Relations, and Sales Managers

(O*NET 11-2011.00, 11-2021.00, 11-2022.00, 11-2031.00)

Significant Points

- Keen competition is expected for these highly coveted jobs.

- College graduates with related experience, a high level of creativity, strong communication skills, and computer skills should have the best job opportunities.

- High earnings, substantial travel, and long hours, including evenings and weekends, are common.

- Because of the importance and high visibility of their jobs, these managers often are prime candidates for advancement to the highest ranks.

Nature of the Work

Advertising, marketing, promotions, public relations, and sales managers coordinate their companies' market research, marketing strategy, sales, advertising, promotion, pricing, product development, and public relations activities. In small firms, the owner or chief executive officer might assume all advertising, promotions, marketing, sales, and public relations responsibilities. In large firms, which may offer numerous products and

These managers have a wide range of educational backgrounds.

services nationally or even worldwide, an executive vice president directs overall advertising, marketing, promotions, sales, and public relations policies. (Executive vice presidents are included in the *Handbook* statement on top executives.)

Advertising managers. Advertising managers oversee advertising and promotion staffs, which usually are small, except in the largest firms. In a small firm, managers may serve as liaisons between the firm and the advertising or promotion agency to which many advertising or promotional functions are contracted out. In larger firms, advertising managers oversee in-house account, creative, and media services departments. The *account executive manages* the account services department, assesses the need for advertising and, in advertising agencies, maintains the accounts of clients. The creative services department develops the subject matter and presentation of advertising. The *creative director* oversees the copy chief, art director, and associated staff. The *media director* oversees planning groups that select the communication media—for example, radio, television, newspapers, magazines, the Internet, or outdoor signs—to disseminate the advertising.

Marketing managers. Marketing managers develop the firm's marketing strategy in detail. With the help of subordinates, including *product development managers* and *market research managers*, they estimate the demand for products and services offered by the firm and its competitors. In addition, they identify potential markets—for example, business firms, wholesalers, retailers, government, or the general public. Marketing managers develop pricing strategy to help firms maximize profits and market share while ensuring that the firm's customers are satisfied. In collaboration with sales, product development, and other managers, they monitor trends that indicate the need for new products and services, and they oversee product development. Marketing managers work with advertising and promotion managers to promote the firm's products and services and to attract potential users.

Promotions managers. Promotions managers supervise staffs of promotions specialists. These managers direct promotions programs that combine advertising with purchase incentives to increase sales. In an effort to establish closer contact with purchasers—dealers, distributors, or consumers—promotions programs may use direct mail, telemarketing, television or radio advertising, catalogs, exhibits, inserts in newspapers, Internet advertisements or Web sites, in-store displays or product endorsements, and special events. Purchasing incentives may include discounts, samples, gifts, rebates, coupons, sweepstakes, and contests.

Public relations managers. Public relations managers supervise public relations specialists. (See the *Handbook* statement on public relations specialists.) These managers direct publicity programs to a targeted audience. They often specialize in a specific area, such as crisis management, or in a specific industry, such as health care. They use every available communication medium to maintain the support of the specific group upon whom their organization's success depends, such as consumers, stockholders, or the general public. For example, public relations managers may clarify or justify the firm's point of view on health or environmental issues to community or special-interest groups.

Public relations managers also evaluate advertising and promotions programs for compatibility with public relations efforts and serve as the eyes and ears of top management. They observe social, economic, and political trends that might ultimately affect the firm, and they make recommendations to enhance the firm's image on the basis of those trends.

Public relations managers may confer with labor relations managers to produce internal company communications—such as newsletters about employee-management relations—and with financial managers to produce company reports. They assist company executives in drafting speeches, arranging interviews, and maintaining other forms of public contact; oversee company archives; and respond to requests for information. In addition, some of these managers handle special events, such as the sponsorship of races, parties introducing new products, or other activities that the firm supports in order to gain public attention through the press without advertising directly.

Sales managers. Sales managers direct the firm's sales program. They assign sales territories, set goals, and establish training programs for the sales representatives. (See the *Handbook* statement on sales representatives, wholesale and manufacturing). Sales managers advise the sales representatives on ways to improve their sales performance. In large, multi-product firms, they oversee regional and local sales managers and their staffs. Sales managers maintain contact with dealers and distributors. They analyze sales statistics gathered by their staffs to determine sales potential and inventory requirements and to monitor customers' preferences. Such information is vital in the development of products and the maximization of profits.

Work environment. Advertising, marketing, promotions, public relations, and sales managers work in offices close to those of top managers. Working under pressure is unavoidable when schedules change and problems arise, but deadlines and goals must still be met.

Substantial travel may be involved. For example, attendance at meetings sponsored by associations or industries often is mandatory. Sales managers travel to national, regional, and local offices and to the offices of various dealers and distributors. Advertising and promotions managers may travel to meet with

clients or representatives of communications media. At times, public relations managers travel to meet with special-interest groups or government officials. Job transfers between headquarters and regional offices are common, particularly among sales managers.

Long hours, including evenings and weekends are common. In 2006, about two-thirds of advertising, marketing, and public relations managers worked more than 40 hours a week.

Training, Other Qualifications, and Advancement

A wide range of educational backgrounds is suitable for entry into advertising, marketing, promotions, public relations, and sales managerial jobs, but many employers prefer those with experience in related occupations.

Education and training. For marketing, sales, and promotions management positions, some employers prefer a bachelor's or master's degree in business administration with an emphasis on marketing. Courses in business law, management, economics, accounting, finance, mathematics, and statistics are advantageous. Additionally, the completion of an internship while the candidate is in school is highly recommended. In highly technical industries, such as computer and electronics manufacturing, a bachelor's degree in engineering or science, combined with a master's degree in business administration, is preferred.

For advertising management positions, some employers prefer a bachelor's degree in advertising or journalism. A course of study should include, for example, marketing, consumer behavior, market research, sales, communication methods and technology, and visual arts, and art history and photography.

For public relations management positions, some employers prefer a bachelor's or master's degree in public relations or journalism. The applicant's curriculum should include courses in advertising, business administration, public affairs, public speaking, political science, and creative and technical writing.

Most advertising, marketing, promotions, public relations, and sales management positions are filled by promoting experienced staff or related professional personnel. For example, many managers are former sales representatives, purchasing agents, buyers, or product, advertising, promotions, or public relations specialists. In small firms, where the number of positions is limited, advancement to a management position usually comes slowly. In large firms, promotion may occur more quickly.

Other qualifications. Familiarity with word-processing and database applications is important for most positions. Computer skills are vital because marketing, product promotion, and advertising on the Internet are increasingly common. Also, the ability to communicate in a foreign language may open up employment opportunities in many rapidly growing areas around the country, especially cities with large Spanish-speaking populations.

Persons interested in becoming advertising, marketing, promotions, public relations, and sales managers should be mature, creative, highly motivated, resistant to stress, flexible, and decisive. The ability to communicate persuasively, both orally and in writing, with other managers, staff, and the public is vital. These managers also need tact, good judgment, and exceptional ability to establish and maintain effective personal relationships with supervisory and professional staff members and client firms.

Certification and advancement. Some associations offer certification programs for these managers. Certification—an indication of competence and achievement—is particularly important in a competitive job market. While relatively few advertising, marketing, promotions, public relations, and sales managers currently are certified, the number of managers who seek certification is expected to grow. Today, there are numerous management certification programs based on education and job performance. In addition, The Public Relations Society of America offers a certification program for public relations practitioners based on years of experience and performance on an examination.

Although experience, ability, and leadership are emphasized for promotion, advancement can be accelerated by participation in management training programs conducted by larger firms. Many firms also provide their employees with continuing education opportunities—either in-house or at local colleges and universities—and encourage employee participation in seminars and conferences, often held by professional societies. In collaboration with colleges and universities, numerous marketing and related associations sponsor national or local management training programs. Course subjects include brand and product management, international marketing, sales management evaluation, telemarketing and direct sales, interactive marketing, promotion, marketing communication, market research, organizational communication, and data-processing systems procedures and management. Many firms pay all or part of the cost for employees who successfully complete courses.

Because of the importance and high visibility of their jobs, advertising, marketing, promotions, public relations, and sales managers often are prime candidates for advancement to the highest ranks. Well-trained, experienced, and successful managers may be promoted to higher positions in their own or another firm; some become top executives. Managers with extensive experience and sufficient capital may open their own businesses.

Employment

Advertising, marketing, promotions, public relations, and sales managers held about 583,000 jobs in 2006. The following tabulation shows the distribution of jobs by occupational specialty:

Sales managers...318,000
Marketing managers..167,000
Public relations managers 50,000
Advertising and promotions managers 47,000

These managers were found in virtually every industry. Sales managers held more than half of the jobs; most were employed in wholesale trade, retail trade, manufacturing, and finance and insurance industries. Marketing managers held more than a fourth of the jobs; the professional, scientific, and technical services, and the finance and insurance industries employed almost one-third of marketing managers. About one-fourth of advertising and promotions managers worked in the professional, scientific, and technical services industries and the wholesale trade. Most public relations managers were employed in service-providing industries, such as professional, scientific, and technical services; educational services, public and private; finance and insurance; and health care and social assistance.

Job Outlook

Average job growth is projected, but keen competition is expected for these highly coveted jobs.

Employment change. Employment of advertising, marketing, promotions, public relations, and sales managers is expected to increase by 12 percent through 2016—about as fast as the average for all occupations. Job growth will be spurred by intense domestic and global competition in products and services offered to consumers and increasing activity in television, radio, and outdoor advertising.

Projected employment growth varies by industry. For example, employment is projected to grow much faster than average in scientific, professional, and related services—such as computer systems design and related services, and advertising and related services—as businesses increasingly hire contractors for these services instead of additional full-time staff. By contrast, a decline in employment is expected in many manufacturing industries.

Job prospects. Advertising, marketing, promotions, public relations, and sales manager jobs are highly coveted and will be sought by other managers or highly experienced professionals, resulting in keen competition. College graduates with related experience, a high level of creativity, and strong communication skills should have the best job opportunities. In particular, employers will seek those who have the computer skills to con-

Projections data from the National Employment Matrix

Occupational Title	SOC Code	Employment, 2006	Projected employment, 2016	Change, 2006-16	
				Number	Percent
Advertising, marketing, promotions, public relations, and sales managers	11-2000	583,000	651,000	68,000	12
Advertising and promotions managers	11-2011	47,000	50,000	3,000	6
Marketing and sales managers	11-2020	486,000	542,000	57,000	12
Marketing managers	11-2021	167,000	192,000	24,000	14
Sales managers	11-2022	318,000	351,000	33,000	10
Public relations managers	11-2031	50,000	58,000	8,400	17

NOTE: Data in this table are rounded. See the discussion of the employment projections table in the *Handbook* introductory chapter on *Occupational Information Included in the Handbook.*

duct advertising, marketing, promotions, public relations, and sales activities on the Internet.

Earnings

Median annual earnings in May 2006 were $73,060 for advertising and promotions managers, $98,720 for marketing managers, $91,560 for sales managers, and $82,180 for public relations managers.

Median annual earnings of wage and salary advertising and promotions managers in May 2006 in the advertising and related services industry were $97,540.

Median annual earnings in the industries employing the largest numbers of marketing managers were:

Computer systems design and related services $119,540
Management of companies and enterprises 103,070
Management, scientific, and technical consulting
  services...100,200
Architectural, engineering, and related services 92,480
Depository credit intermediation 91,420

Median annual earnings in the industries employing the largest numbers of sales managers were:

Professional and commercial equipment and supplies
  merchant wholesalers...$112,810
Wholesale electronic markets and agents and brokers........107,420
Automobile dealers 101,110
Management of companies and enterprises 98,240
Machinery, equipment, and supplies
  merchant wholesalers...93,450

Salary levels vary substantially, depending upon the level of managerial responsibility, length of service, education, size of firm, location, and industry. For example, manufacturing firms usually pay these managers higher salaries than nonmanufacturing firms. For sales managers, the size of their sales territory is another important determinant of salary. Many managers earn bonuses equal to 10 percent or more of their salaries.

According to a survey by the National Association of Colleges and Employers, starting salaries for marketing majors graduating in 2007 averaged $40,161 and those for advertising majors averaged $33,831.

Related Occupations

Advertising, marketing, promotions, public relations, and sales managers direct the sale of products and services offered by their firms and the communication of information about their firms' activities. Other workers involved with advertising, marketing, promotions, public relations, and sales include actors, producers, and directors; advertising sales agents; artists and related workers; demonstrators, product promoters, and models; market and survey researchers; public relations specialists; sales representatives, wholesale and manufacturing; and writers and editors.

Sources of Additional Information

For information about careers in advertising management, contact:

➤ American Association of Advertising Agencies, 405 Lexington Ave., New York, NY 10174-1801.
Internet: **http://www.aaaa.org**

Information about careers and professional certification in public relations management is available from:
➤ Public Relations Society of America, 33 Maiden LaNE., New York, NY 10038-5150. Internet: **http://www.prsa.org**

Computer and Information Systems Managers

(O*NET 11-3021.00)

Significant Points

- Employment of computer and information systems managers is expected to grow faster than the average for all occupations through the year 2016.

- Many managers possess advanced technical knowledge gained from working in a computer occupation.

- Job opportunities will be best for applicants with a strong understanding of business and good communication skills.

Nature of the Work

In the modern workplace, it is imperative that technology works both effectively and reliably. Computer and information systems managers play a vital role in the implementation of technology within their organizations. They do everything from helping to construct a business plan to overseeing network security to directing Internet operations.

Computer and information systems managers plan, coordinate, and direct research and facilitate the computer-related activities of firms. They help determine both technical and business goals in consultation with top management and make detailed plans for the accomplishment of these goals. This requires a strong understanding of both technology and business practices.

Computer and information systems managers direct the work of systems analysts, computer programmers, support specialists, and other computer-related workers. They plan and coordinate activities such as installation and upgrading of hardware and software, programming and systems design, development of computer networks, and implementation of Internet and intranet sites. They are increasingly involved with the upkeep, maintenance, and security of networks. They analyze the computer and information needs of their organizations from an operational and strategic perspective and determine immediate and long-range personnel and equipment requirements. They assign and review the work of their subordinates and stay abreast of the latest technology to ensure the organization does not lag behind competitors.

The duties of computer and information systems managers vary greatly. *Chief technology officers (CTOs)*, for example, evaluate the newest and most innovative technologies and determine how these can help their organizations. The chief technology officer often reports to the organization's chief information officer, manages and plans technical standards, and tends to the daily information technology issues of the firm. (Chief information officers are covered in a separate *Handbook* statement on top executives.) Because of the rapid pace of technological change, chief technology officers must constantly be on the lookout for developments that could benefit their organizations. Once a useful tool has been identified, the CTO must determine an implementation strategy and sell that strategy to management.

Management information systems (MIS) directors or *information technology (IT) directors* manage computing resources for their organizations. They often work under the chief information officer and plan and direct the work of subordinate information technology employees. These managers ensure the availability, continuity, and security of data and information technology services in their organizations. In this capacity, they oversee a variety of user services such as an organization's help desk, which employees can call with questions or problems. MIS directors also may make hardware and software upgrade recommendations based on their experience with an organization's technology.

Project managers develop requirements, budgets, and schedules for their firms' information technology projects. They coordinate such projects from development through implementation, working with internal and external clients, vendors, consultants, and computer specialists. These managers are increasingly involved in projects that upgrade the information security of an organization.

Work environment. Computer and information systems managers spend most of their time in offices. Most work at least 40 hours a week and some may have to work evenings and weekends to meet deadlines or solve unexpected problems. Some computer and information systems managers may experience considerable pressure in meeting technical goals with short deadlines or tight budgets. As networks continue to expand and more work is done remotely, computer and information systems managers have to communicate with and oversee offsite employees using modems, laptops, e-mail, and the Internet.

Computer and information systems managers supervise other information technology employees.

Like other workers who spend most of their time using computers, computer and information systems managers are susceptible to eyestrain, back discomfort, and hand and wrist problems such as carpal tunnel syndrome.

Training, Other Qualifications, and Advancement
Computer and information systems managers are generally experienced workers who have both technical expertise and an understanding of business and management principles. A strong educational background and experience in a variety of technical fields is needed.

Education and training. A bachelor's degree usually is required for management positions, although employers often prefer a graduate degree, especially an MBA with technology as a core component. This degree differs from a traditional MBA in that there is a heavy emphasis on information technology in addition to the standard business curriculum. This preparation is becoming important because more computer and information systems managers are making important technology decisions as well as business decisions for their organizations.

Some universities offer degrees in management information systems. These degrees blend technical subjects with business, accounting, and communications courses. A few computer and information systems managers attain their positions with only an associate or trade school degree, but they must have sufficient experience and must have acquired additional skills on the job. To aid their professional advancement, many managers with an associate degree eventually earn a bachelor's or master's degree while working.

Certification and other qualifications. Computer and information systems managers need a broad range of skills. Employers look for managers who have experience with the specific software or technology used on the job, as well as a background in either consulting or business management. The expansion of electronic commerce has elevated the importance of business insight and, consequently, many computer and information systems managers are called on to make important business decisions. Managers need a keen understanding of people, management processes, and customers' needs.

Advanced technical knowledge is essential for computer and information systems managers, who must understand and guide the work of their subordinates yet also explain the work in nontechnical terms to senior managers and potential customers. Therefore, many computer and information systems managers have worked as a systems analyst, for example, or as a computer support specialist, programmer, or other information technology professional.

Although certification is not necessarily required for most computer and information systems manager positions, there is a wide variety of certifications available that may be helpful in getting a job. These certifications are often product-specific, and are generally administered by software or hardware companies rather than independent organizations.

As computer systems become more closely connected with day-to-day operations of businesses, computer and information systems managers are also expected to be aware of business practices. They must possess strong interpersonal, communication, and leadership skills because they are required to interact not only with staff members, but also with other people inside and outside their organizations. They must possess team skills to work on group projects and other collaborative efforts. They also must have an understanding of how a business functions, how it earns revenue, and how technology relates to the core competencies of the business. As a result, many firms now prefer to give these positions to people who have spent time outside purely technical fields.

Advancement. Computer and information systems managers may advance to progressively higher leadership positions in the information technology department. A project manager might, for instance, move up to the chief technology officer position and then to chief information officer. On occasion, some may become managers in non-technical areas such as marketing, human resources, or sales because in high technology firms an understanding of technical issues is helpful in those areas.

Employment

Computer and information systems managers held about 264,000 jobs in 2006. About 1 in 4 computer managers worked in service-providing industries, mainly in computer systems design and related services. This industry provides services related to the commercial use of computers on a contract basis, including custom computer programming services; computer systems integration design services; computer facilities management services, including computer systems or data-processing facilities support services; and other computer-related services, such as disaster recovery services and software installation. Other large employers include insurance and financial firms, government agencies, and manufacturers.

Job Outlook

The increasing use of technology in the workplace is projected to lead to faster than average growth in this occupation. Due to employment increases and because of the high demand for technical workers, prospects should be excellent for qualified job candidates.

Employment change. Employment of computer and information systems managers is expected to grow 16 percent over the 2006-16 decade, which is faster than the average for all occupations. New applications of technology in the workplace will continue to drive demand for workers, fueling the need for more managers.

Despite the downturn in the technology sector in the early part of the decade, the outlook for computer and information systems managers remains strong. To remain competitive, firms will continue to install sophisticated computer networks and set up more complex intranets and websites. Keeping a computer network running smoothly is essential to almost every organization.

Because so much business is carried out over computer networks, security will continue to be an important issue for businesses and other organizations. Although software developers continue to improve their products to remove vulnerabilities, attackers are becoming ever more complex in their methods. Organizations need to understand how their systems are vulnerable and how to protect their infrastructure and Internet sites from hackers, viruses, and other attacks. The emergence of security as a key concern for businesses should lead to strong growth for computer managers. Firms will increasingly hire security experts to fill key leadership roles in their information technology departments because the integrity of their computing environments is of utmost importance. As a result, there will be a high demand for managers proficient in computer security issues.

With the explosive growth of electronic commerce and the capacity of the Internet to create new relationships with customers, the role of computer and information systems managers will continue to evolve. Workers who have experience in web applications and Internet technologies will become increasingly vital to their companies.

Opportunities for those who wish to become computer and information systems managers should be closely related to the growth of the occupations they supervise and the industries in which they are found. (See the statements on computer programmers, computer software engineers, computer support specialists and systems administrators, computer systems analysts, and computer scientists and database administrators elsewhere in the *Handbook*.)

Job prospects. Prospects for qualified computer and information systems managers should be excellent. Fast-paced occupational growth and the limited supply of technical workers will lead to a wealth of opportunities for qualified individuals. While technical workers remain relatively scarce in the United States, the demand for them continues to rise. This situation was exacerbated by the economic downturn in the early 2000s, when many technical professionals lost their jobs. Since then, many workers have chosen to avoid this work since it is perceived to have poor prospects.

Workers with specialized technical knowledge and strong communications skills will have the best prospects. People with management skills and an understanding of business practices and principles will have excellent opportunities, as companies are increasingly looking to technology to drive their revenue.

Earnings

Earnings for computer and information systems managers vary by specialty and level of responsibility. Median annual earnings of these managers in May 2006 were $101,580. The middle 50 percent earned between $79,240 and $129,250. Median

Projections data from the National Employment Matrix

Occupational Title	SOC Code	Employment, 2006	Projected employment, 2016	Change, 2006-16	
				Number	Percent
Computer and information systems managers...................................	11-3021	264,000	307,000	43,000	16

NOTE: Data in this table are rounded. See the discussion of the employment projections table in the *Handbook* introductory chapter on *Occupational Information Included in the Handbook.*

annual earnings in the industries employing the largest numbers of computer and information systems managers in May 2006 were as follows:

Computer systems design and related services.................$109,130
Management of companies and enterprises........................105,980
Data processing, hosting, and related services...................105,200
Insurance carriers..102,180
Colleges, universities, and professional schools..................83,280

The Robert Half Technology 2007 Salary Guide lists the following annual salary ranges for various computer and information systems manager positions: Chief Technology Officer (CTO), $101,000-$157,750; Chief Security Officer, $97,500-$141,000; Vice President of Information Technology, $107,500-$157,750; Information Technology Manager, Technical Services Manager, $62,500-$88,250.

In addition, computer and information systems managers, especially those at higher levels, often receive employment-related benefits, such as expense accounts, stock option plans, and bonuses.

Related Occupations

The work of computer and information systems managers is closely related to that of computer programmers, computer software engineers, computer systems analysts, computer scientists and database administrators, and computer support specialists and systems administrators. Computer and information systems managers also have some high-level responsibilities similar to those of top executives.

Sources of Additional Information

For information about a career as a computer and information systems manager, contact:

➤ Association of Information Technology Professionals, 401 North Michigan Ave., Suite 2400, Chicago, IL 60611. Internet: **http://www.aitp.org**

Construction Managers

(O*NET 11-9021.00)

Significant Points

- Construction managers must be available—often 24 hours a day—to deal with delays, bad weather, or emergencies at the jobsite.

- Employers prefer jobseekers who combine construction industry work experience with a bachelor's degree in construction science, construction management, or civil engineering.

- Although certification is not required, there is a growing movement toward certification of construction managers.

- Excellent job opportunities are expected.

Nature of the Work

Construction managers plan, direct, and coordinate a wide variety of construction projects, including the building of all types of residential, commercial, and industrial structures, roads, bridges, wastewater treatment plants, and schools and hospitals. Construction managers may oversee an entire project or just part of one. They schedule and coordinate all design and construction processes, including the selection, hiring, and oversight of specialty trade contractors, but they usually do not do any actual construction of the structure.

Construction managers are salaried or self-employed managers who oversee construction supervisors and workers. They are often called project managers, constructors, construction superintendents, project engineers, program managers, construction supervisors, or general contractors. Construction managers may be owners or salaried employees of a construction management or contracting firm, or may work under contract or as a salaried employee of the property owner, developer, or contracting firm overseeing the construction project.

These managers coordinate and supervise the construction process from the conceptual development stage through final construction, making sure that the project gets done on time and within budget. They often work with owners, engineers, architects, and others who are involved in the construction process. Given the designs for buildings, roads, bridges, or other projects, construction managers oversee the planning, scheduling, and implementation of those designs.

Large construction projects, such as an office building or industrial complex, are often too complicated for one person to manage. These projects are divided into many segments: site preparation, including land clearing and earth moving; sewage systems; landscaping and road construction; building construction, including excavation and laying of foundations and erection of the structural framework, floors, walls, and roofs; and building systems, including fire-protection, electrical, plumbing, air-conditioning, and heating. Construction managers may be in charge of one or more of these activities.

Construction managers determine the best way to get materials to the building site and the most cost-effective plan and schedule for completing the project. They divide all required construc-

Construction managers must be available—often 24 hours a day— to deal with delays, bad weather, or emergencies at the job site.

tion site activities into logical steps, budgeting the time required to meet established deadlines. This may require sophisticated estimating and scheduling techniques and use of computers with specialized software. (See the section on cost estimators elsewhere in the *Handbook*.)

They also oversee the selection of general contractors and trade contractors to complete specific pieces of the project—which could include everything from structural metalworking and plumbing to painting and carpet installation. Construction managers determine the labor requirements and, in some cases, supervise or monitor the hiring and dismissal of workers. They oversee the performance of all trade contractors and are responsible for ensuring that all work is completed on schedule.

Construction managers direct and monitor the progress of construction activities, sometimes through construction supervisors or other construction managers. They oversee the delivery and use of materials, tools, and equipment; worker productivity and safety; and the quality of construction. They are responsible for obtaining all necessary permits and licenses and, depending upon the contractual arrangements, direct or monitor compliance with building and safety codes, other regulations, and requirements set by the project's insurers.

Work environment. Working out of a main office or out of a field office at the construction site, construction managers monitor the overall construction project. Decisions regarding daily construction activities generally are made at the jobsite. Managers may travel extensively when the construction site is not close to their main office or when they are responsible for activities at two or more sites. Management of overseas construction projects usually entails temporary residence in another country.

Often "on call" 24 hours a day, construction managers deal with delays, the effects of bad weather, or emergencies at the site. Most work more than a standard 40-hour week because construction may proceed around-the-clock. They may need to work this type of schedule for days or weeks to meet special project deadlines, especially if there are delays.

Although the work usually is not considered inherently dangerous, construction managers must be careful while performing onsite services.

Training, Other Qualifications, and Advancement

Employers increasingly prefer to hire construction managers with a bachelor's degree in construction science, construction management, building science, or civil engineering, although it is also possible for experienced construction workers to move up to become construction managers. In addition to having education and experience, construction mangers must understand contracts, plans, specifications, and regulations.

Education and training. For construction manager jobs, employers increasingly prefer to hire individuals who have a bachelor's degree in construction science, construction management, building science, or civil engineering, plus work experience. Practical construction experience is very important, whether gained through an internship, a cooperative education program, a job in the construction trades, or another job in the industry. Traditionally, people advanced to construction management positions after having substantial experience as construction craftworkers—carpenters, masons, plumbers, or electricians, for example—or after

having worked as construction supervisors or as owners of independent specialty contracting firms. However, as construction processes become increasingly complex, employers are placing more importance on specialized education after high school.

About 105 colleges and universities offer bachelor's degree programs in construction science, building science, and construction engineering. These programs include courses in project control and development, site planning, design, construction methods, construction materials, value analysis, cost estimating, scheduling, contract administration, accounting, business and financial management, safety, building codes and standards, inspection procedures, engineering and architectural sciences, mathematics, statistics, and information technology. Graduates from 4-year degree programs usually are hired as assistants to project managers, field engineers, schedulers, or cost estimators. An increasing number of graduates in related fields—engineering or architecture, for example—also enter construction management, often after acquiring substantial experience on construction projects.

About 60 colleges and universities offer a master's degree program in construction management or construction science. Master's degree recipients, especially those with work experience in construction, typically become construction managers in very large construction or construction management companies. Often, individuals who hold a bachelor's degree in an unrelated field seek a master's degree in construction management or construction science to work in the construction industry. Some construction managers obtain a master's degree in business administration or finance to further their career prospects. Doctoral degree recipients usually become college professors or conduct research.

A number of 2-year colleges throughout the country offer construction management or construction technology programs. Many individuals also attend training and educational programs sponsored by industry associations, often in collaboration with postsecondary institutions.

Other qualifications. Construction managers should be flexible and work effectively in a fast-paced environment. They should be decisive and work well under pressure, particularly when faced with unexpected occurrences or delays. The ability to coordinate several major activities at once, while analyzing and resolving specific problems, is essential, as is an understanding of engineering, architectural, and other construction drawings. Familiarity with computers and software programs for job costing, online collaboration, scheduling, and estimating also is important.

Good oral and written communication skills also are important, as are leadership skills. Managers must be able to establish a good working relationship with many different people, including owners, other managers, designers, supervisors, and craftworkers. The ability to converse fluently in Spanish is increasingly an asset because Spanish is the first language of many workers in the construction industry.

Certification and advancement. There is a growing movement toward certification of construction managers. Although certification is not required to work in the construction industry, it can be valuable because it provides evidence of competence and experience. Both the American Institute of Constructors and the Construction Management Association of America have es-

Projections data from the National Employment Matrix

Occupational Title	SOC Code	Employment, 2006	Projected employment, 2016	Change, 2006-16	
				Number	Percent
Construction managers..	11-9021	487,000	564,000	77,000	16

NOTE: Data in this table are rounded. See the discussion of the employment projections table in the *Handbook* introductory chapter on *Occupational Information Included in the Handbook.*

tablished voluntary certification programs for construction managers. Requirements combine written examinations with verification of education and professional experience. The American Institute of Constructors awards the Associate Constructor (AC) and Certified Professional Constructor (CPC) designations to candidates who meet its requirements and pass the appropriate construction examinations. The Construction Management Association of America awards the Certified Construction Manager (CCM) designation to workers who have the required experience and who pass a technical examination. Applicants for this designation also must complete a self-study course that covers the professional role of a construction manager, legal issues, allocation of risk, and other topics related to construction management.

Advancement opportunities for construction managers vary depending upon an individual's performance and the size and type of company for which they work. Within large firms, managers may eventually become top-level managers or executives. Highly experienced individuals may become independent consultants; some serve as expert witnesses in court or as arbitrators in disputes. Those with the required capital may establish their own construction management services, specialty contracting, or general contracting firm.

Employment

Construction managers held 487,000 jobs in 2006. About 57 percent were self-employed, many as owners of general or specialty trade construction firms. Most salaried construction managers were employed in the construction industry, 13 percent by specialty trade contractor businesses—for example, plumbing, heating, air-conditioning, and electrical contractors—9 percent in residential building construction; and 9 percent in nonresidential building construction. Others were employed by architectural, engineering, and related services firms and by local governments.

Job Outlook

Faster than average employment growth is expected. Additionally, excellent job opportunities will exist as the number of job openings exceeds the number of qualified applicants.

Employment change. Employment of construction managers is projected to increase by 16 percent during the 2006-16 decade, faster than the average for all occupations. More construction managers will be needed as the level of construction activity continues to grow. Population and business growth will result in more construction of residential homes, office buildings, shopping malls, hospitals, schools, restaurants, and other structures that require construction managers.

The increasing complexity of construction projects will also boost demand for specialized management-level personnel within the construction industry. Sophisticated technology and the proliferation of laws setting standards for buildings and construc-

tion materials, worker safety, energy efficiency, environmental protection, and the potential for adverse litigation have further complicated the construction process. Advances in building materials and construction methods; the need to replace portions of the Nation's infrastructure; and the growing number of multipurpose buildings and energy-efficient structures will further add to the demand for more construction managers.

Job prospects. Excellent employment opportunities for construction managers are expected through 2016 because the number of job openings will exceed the number of qualified individuals seeking to enter the occupation. This situation is expected to continue even as college construction management programs expand to meet the current high demand for graduates. The construction industry often does not attract sufficient numbers of qualified job seekers because working conditions are considered poor.

In addition to job openings arising from employment growth, many additional openings should result annually from the need to replace workers who transfer to other occupations or leave the labor force for other reasons. A substantial number of seasoned managers are also expected to retire over the next decade, likely resulting in a large number of openings.

Prospects for individuals seeking construction manager jobs in construction management, architectural and engineering services, and construction contracting firms should be best for people who have a bachelor's or higher degree in construction science, construction management, or civil engineering plus practical experience working in construction. Employers will increasingly prefer applicants with college degrees, internships, and a strong background in building technology. Construction managers will also have many opportunities to start their own firms.

Employment of construction managers, like that of many other construction workers, is sensitive to the fluctuations of the economy. Workers in these trades may experience periods of unemployment when the overall level of construction falls. On the other hand, shortages of these workers may occur in some areas during peak periods of building activity.

Earnings

Earnings of salaried construction managers and self-employed independent construction contractors vary depending upon the size and nature of the construction project, its geographic location, and economic conditions. In addition to typical benefits, many salaried construction managers receive bonuses and use of company motor vehicles.

Median annual earnings of wage and salary construction managers in May 2006 were $73,700. The middle 50 percent earned between $56,090 and $98,350. The lowest paid 10 percent earned less than $43,210, and the highest paid 10 percent earned more than $135,780. Median annual earnings in the industries employing the largest numbers of construction managers were as follows:

Building equipment contractors $75,200

Electrical contractors 74,380

Nonresidential building construction 74,080

Foundation, structure, and building exterior contractors 71,640

Residential building construction..69,400

The earnings of self-employed workers are not included in these numbers.

According to a July 2007 salary survey by the National Association of Colleges and Employers, people with a bachelor's degree in construction science/management received job offers averaging $46,930 a year.

Related Occupations

Construction managers participate in the conceptual development of a construction project and oversee its organization, scheduling, and implementation. Other workers who perform similar functions include architects, except landscape and naval; civil engineers; cost estimators; landscape architects; and engineering and natural sciences managers.

Sources of Additional Information

For information about constructor certification, contact:

➤ American Institute of Constructors, 717 Princess St., Alexandria, VA 22314. Internet: **http://www.aicnet.org**

For information about construction management and construction manager certification, contact:

➤ Construction Management Association of America, 7918 Jones Branch Dr., Suite 540, McLean, VA 22102.

Internet: **http://www.cmaanet.org**

Information on accredited construction science and management educational programs and accreditation requirements is available from:

➤ American Council for Construction Education, 1717 North Loop 1604 E, Suite 320, San Antonio, TX 78232.

Internet: **http://www.acce-hq.org**

➤ National Center for Construction Education and Research, P.O. Box 141104, Gainesville, FL 32614.

Internet: **http://www.nccer.org**

Education Administrators

(O*NET 11-9031.00, 11-9032.00, 11-9033.00, 11-9039.99)

Significant Points

- Many jobs require a master's or doctoral degree and experience in a related occupation, such as teaching or admissions counseling.

- Strong interpersonal and communication skills are essential because much of an administrator's job involves working and collaborating with others.

- Excellent opportunities are expected since a large proportion of education administrators is expected to retire over the next 10 years.

Nature of the Work

Successful operation of an educational institution requires competent administrators. Education administrators provide instructional leadership and manage the day-to-day activities in schools, preschools, day care centers, and colleges and universities. They also direct the educational programs of businesses, correctional institutions, museums, and job training and community service organizations. (College presidents and school superintendents are covered in the *Handbook* statement on general managers and top executives.)

Education administrators set educational standards and goals and establish the policies and procedures to achieve them. They also supervise managers, support staff, teachers, counselors, librarians, coaches, and other employees. They develop academic programs, monitor students' educational progress, train and motivate teachers and other staff, manage career counseling and other student services, administer recordkeeping, prepare budgets, and perform many other duties. They also handle relations with parents, prospective and current students, employers, and the community. In an organization such as a small day care center, one administrator may handle all these functions. In universities or large school systems, responsibilities are divided among many administrators, each with a specific function.

Educational administrators who manage elementary, middle, and secondary schools are called *principals*. They set the academic tone and actively work with teachers to develop and maintain high curriculum standards, develop mission statements, and set performance goals and objectives. Principals confer with staff to advise, explain, or answer procedural questions. They hire, evaluate, and help improve the skills of teachers and other staff. They visit classrooms, observe teaching methods, review instructional objectives, and examine learning materials. Principals must use clear, objective guidelines for teacher appraisals, because pay often is based on performance ratings.

Principals also meet and interact with other administrators, students, parents, and representatives of community organizations. Decision-making authority has increasingly shifted from school district central offices to individual schools. School principals have greater flexibility in setting school policies and goals, but when making administrative decisions they must pay attention to the concerns of parents, teachers, and other members of the community.

Preparing budgets and reports on various subjects, including finances and attendance, and overseeing the requisition and allocation of supplies also is an important responsibility of principals. As school budgets become tighter, many principals have become more involved in public relations and fundraising to secure financial support for their schools from local businesses and the community.

Principals must take an active role to ensure that students meet national, State, and local academic standards. Many principals develop partnerships with local businesses and school-to-work transition programs for students. Increasingly, principals must be sensitive to the needs of the rising number of non-English speaking and culturally diverse student body. In some areas, growing enrollments also are a cause for concern because they lead to overcrowding at many schools. When addressing problems of inadequate resources, administrators serve as advocates for the building of new schools or the repair of existing ones. During summer months, principals are responsible for planning for the upcoming year, overseeing summer school, participating in workshops for teachers and administrators, supervising building repairs and improvements, and working to make sure the school has adequate staff for the school year.

Schools continue to be involved with students' emotional welfare as well as their academic achievement. As a result, principals face responsibilities outside the academic realm. For example, many schools have growing numbers of students from dual-income and single-parent families or students who are themselves teenage parents. To support these students and their families, some schools have established before- and after-school childcare programs or family resource centers, which also may offer parenting classes and social service referrals. With the help of community organizations, some principals have established programs to combat increases in crime, drug and alcohol abuse, and sexually transmitted diseases among students.

Assistant principals aid the principal in the overall administration of the school. Some assistant principals hold this position for several years, during which time they prepare for advancement to principal; others are assistant principals throughout their careers. They are primarily responsible for scheduling student classes, ordering textbooks and supplies, and coordinating transportation, custodial, cafeteria, and other support services. They usually handle student discipline and attendance problems, social and recreational programs, and health and safety matters. They also may counsel students on personal, educational, or vocational matters. With the advent of site-based management, assistant principals are playing a greater role in ensuring the academic success of students by helping to develop new curriculums, evaluating teachers, and dealing with school-community relations—responsibilities previously assumed solely by the principal. The number of assis-

Most education administrators begin their careers as teachers.

tant principals that a school employs may vary, depending on the number of students.

Administrators in school district central offices oversee public schools under their jurisdiction. This group includes those who direct subject-area programs such as English, music, vocational education, special education, and mathematics. They supervise instructional coordinators and curriculum specialists, and work with them to evaluate curriculums and teaching techniques and improve them. (Instructional coordinators are covered elsewhere in the *Handbook*.) Administrators also may oversee career counseling programs and testing that measures students' abilities and helps to place them in appropriate classes. Others may also direct programs such as school psychology, athletics, curriculum and instruction, and professional development. With site-based management, administrators have transferred primary responsibility for many of these programs to the principals, assistant principals, teachers, instructional coordinators, and other staff in the schools.

In preschools and childcare centers, which are usually much smaller than other educational institutions, the director or supervisor of the school or center often serves as the sole administrator. Their job is similar to that of other school administrators in that they oversee daily activities and operation of the schools, hire and develop staff, and make sure that the school meets required regulations and educational standards.

In colleges and universities, *provosts*, also known as *chief academic officers*, assist presidents, make faculty appointments and tenure decisions, develop budgets, and establish academic policies and programs. With the assistance of *academic deans* and *deans of faculty*, they also direct and coordinate the activities of deans of individual colleges and chairpersons of academic departments. Fundraising is the chief responsibility of the *director of development* and also is becoming an essential part of the job for all administrators.

College or university department heads or *chairpersons* are in charge of departments that specialize in particular fields of study, such as English, biological science, or mathematics. In addition to teaching, they coordinate schedules of classes and teaching assignments; propose budgets; recruit, interview, and hire applicants for teaching positions; evaluate faculty members; encourage faculty development; serve on committees; and perform other administrative duties. In overseeing their departments, chairpersons must consider and balance the concerns of faculty, administrators, and students.

Higher education administrators also direct and coordinate the provision of student services. *Vice presidents of student affairs or student life, deans of students*, and *directors of student services* may direct and coordinate admissions, foreign student services, health and counseling services, career services, financial aid, and housing and residential life, as well as social, recreational, and related programs. In small colleges, they may counsel students. In larger colleges and universities, separate administrators may handle each of these services. *Registrars* are custodians of students' records. They register students, record grades, prepare student transcripts, evaluate academic records, assess and collect tuition and fees, plan and implement commencement, oversee the preparation of college catalogs and schedules of classes, and analyze enrollment and demographic statistics. *Directors of admissions* manage the process of recruiting, evaluating, and admitting students, and work closely with *financial aid directors*, who oversee scholarship, fellowship, and loan programs. Registrars and admissions officers at most institutions need computer skills because they use electronic student information systems. For example, for those whose institutions present college catalogs, schedules, and other information on the Internet, knowledge of online resources, imaging, and other computer skills is important. *Athletic directors* plan and direct intramural and intercollegiate athletic activities, seeing to publicity for athletic events, preparation of budgets, and supervision of coaches. Other increasingly important administrators direct public relations, distance learning, and technology.

Work environment. Education administrators hold leadership positions with significant responsibility. Most find working with students extremely rewarding, but as the responsibilities of administrators have increased in recent years, so has the stress. Coordinating and interacting with faculty, parents, students, community members, business leaders, and State and local policymakers can be fast-paced and stimulating, but also stressful and demanding. Principals and assistant principals, whose varied duties include discipline, may find working with difficult students to be challenging. They are also increasingly being held accountable for ensuring that their schools meet recently imposed State and Federal guidelines for student performance and teacher qualifications.

About 1 in 3 education administrators work more than 40 hours a week and often supervise school activities at night and on weekends. Most administrators work year round, although some work only during the academic year.

Training, Other Qualifications, and Advancement

Most education administrators begin their careers as teachers and prepare for advancement into education administration by completing a master's or doctoral degree. Because of the diversity of duties and levels of responsibility, educational backgrounds and experience vary considerably among these workers.

Education and training. Principals, assistant principals, central office administrators, academic deans, and preschool directors usually have held teaching positions before moving into administration. Some teachers move directly into principal positions; others first become assistant principals, or gain experience in other administrative jobs at either the school or district level in positions such as department head, curriculum specialist, or subject matter advisor. In some cases, administrators move up from related staff jobs such as recruiter, school counselor, librarian, residence hall director, or financial aid or admissions counselor.

In most public schools, principals, assistant principals, and school district administrators need a master's degree in education administration or educational leadership. Some principals and central office administrators have a doctorate or specialized degree in education administration. In private schools, some principals and assistant principals hold only a bachelor's degree, but the majority have a master's or doctoral degree.

Educational requirements for administrators of preschools and childcare centers vary depending on the setting of the program and the State of employment. Administrators who oversee preschool programs in public schools are often required to have at least a bachelor's degree. Child care directors who supervise private programs are usually not required to have a degree; however, most States require a preschool education credential, which often includes some postsecondary coursework.

College and university academic deans and chairpersons usually advance from professorships in their departments, for which they need a master's or doctoral degree; further education is not typically necessary. Admissions, student affairs, and financial aid directors and registrars sometimes start in related staff jobs with bachelor's degrees—any field usually is acceptable—and obtain advanced degrees in college student affairs, counseling, or higher education administration. A Ph.D. or Ed.D. usually is necessary for top student affairs positions. Computer literacy and a background in accounting or statistics may be assets in admissions, records, and financial work.

Advanced degrees in higher education administration, educational leadership, and college student affairs are offered in many colleges and universities. Education administration degree programs include courses in school leadership, school law, school finance and budgeting, curriculum development and evaluation, research design and data analysis, community relations, politics in education, and counseling. The National Council for Accreditation of Teacher Education (NCATE) and the Educational Leadership Constituent Council (ELCC) accredit programs designed for elementary and secondary school administrators. Although completion of an accredited program is not required, it may assist in fulfilling licensure requirements.

Licensure and certification. Most States require principals to be licensed as school administrators. License requirements vary by State, but nearly all States require either a master's degree or some other graduate-level training. Some States also require candidates for licensure to pass a test. On-the-job training, often with a mentor, is increasingly required or recommended for new school leaders. Some States require administrators to take continuing education courses to keep their license, thus ensuring that administrators have the most up-to-date skills. The number and types of courses required to maintain licensure vary by State. Principals in private schools are not subject to State licensure requirements.

Nearly all States require child care and preschool center directors to be licensed. Licensing usually requires a number of years of experience or hours of coursework or both. Sometimes, it requires a college degree. Often, directors are also required to earn a general preschool education credential, such as the Child Development Associate credential (CDA) sponsored by the Council for Professional Recognition, or some other credential designed specifically for directors.

One credential specifically for directors is the National Administration Credential, offered by the National Child Care Association. The credential requires experience and training in child care center management.

There are usually no licensing requirements for administrators at postsecondary institutions.

Other qualifications. To be considered for education administrator positions, workers must first prove themselves in their current jobs. In evaluating candidates, supervisors look for leadership, determination, confidence, innovativeness, and motivation. The ability to make sound decisions and to organize and coordinate work efficiently is essential. Because much of an administrator's job involves interacting with others—such as students, parents, teachers, and the community—a person in such a position must have strong interpersonal skills and be an effective communicator and motivator. Knowledge of leadership principles and practices, gained through work experience and formal education, is important. A familiarity with computer technology is a necessity for principals, who are required to gather information and coordinate technical resources for their students, teachers, and classrooms.

Advancement. Education administrators advance through promotion to higher level administrative positions or by transferring to comparable positions at larger schools or systems. They also may become superintendents of school systems or presidents of educational institutions.

Employment

Education administrators held about 443,000 jobs in 2006. Of these, 56,000 were preschool or child care administrators, 226,000 were elementary or secondary school administrators, and 131,000 were postsecondary administrators. The great majority—over 80 percent—worked in public or private educational institutions. Most of the remainder worked in child daycare centers, religious organizations, job training centers, and businesses and other organizations that provided training for their employees.

Job Outlook

Employment of education administrators is projected to grow about as fast as average, as education and training take on greater importance in everyone's lives. Job opportunities for many of these positions should be excellent because a large proportion of education administrators are expected to retire over the next 10 years.

Employment change. Employment of education administrators is expected to grow by 12 percent between 2006 and 2016, about as fast as the average for all occupations, primarily due to growth in enrollments of school-age children. Enrollment of students in elementary and secondary schools is expected to grow slowly over the next decade, which will limit the growth of principals and other administrators in these schools. However,

the number of administrative positions will continue to increase as more administrative responsibilities are placed on individual schools, particularly related to monitoring student achievement. Preschool and childcare center administrators are expected to experience substantial growth due to increasing enrollments in formal child care programs as fewer young children are cared for in private homes. Additionally, as more States implement or expand public preschool programs, more preschool directors will be needed.

The number of students at the postsecondary level is projected to grow more rapidly than other student populations, creating significant demand for administrators at that level. A significant portion of the growth will occur in the private and for-profit segments of higher education. Many of these schools cater to working adults who might not ordinarily participate in postsecondary education. These schools allow students to earn a degree, receive job-specific training, or update their skills in a convenient manner, such as through part-time programs or distance learning. As the number of these schools continues to grow, more administrators will be needed to oversee them.

Job prospects. Principals and assistant principals should have very favorable job prospects. A sharp increase in responsibilities in recent years has made the job more stressful and has discouraged some teachers from taking positions in administration. Principals are now being held more accountable for the performance of students and teachers, while at the same time they are required to adhere to a growing number of government regulations. In addition, overcrowded classrooms, safety issues, budgetary concerns, and teacher shortages in some areas all are creating additional stress for administrators. Many teachers feel that the increase in pay for becoming an administrator is not high enough to compensate for the greater responsibilities.

Opportunities may vary by region of the country. Enrollments are expected to increase the fastest in the West and South, where the population is growing faster, and to decline or remain stable in the Northeast and the Midwest. School administrators also are in greater demand in rural and urban areas, where pay is generally lower than in the suburbs.

Although competition among faculty for prestigious positions as academic deans and department heads is likely to remain keen, fewer applicants are expected for nonacademic administrative jobs, such as director of admissions or student affairs. Furthermore, many people are discouraged from seeking administrator jobs by the requirement that they have a master's or doctoral degree in education administration—as well as by the opportunity to earn higher salaries in other occupations.

Projections data from the National Employment Matrix

Occupational Title	SOC Code	Employment, 2006	Projected employment, 2016	Change, 2006-16	
				Number	Percent
Education administrators	11-9030	443,000	496,000	53,000	12
Education administrators, preschool and child care center/ program	11-9031	56,000	69,000	13,000	24
Education administrators, elementary and secondary school	11-9032	226,000	243,000	17,000	8
Education administrators, postsecondary....................................	11-9033	131,000	150,000	19,000	14
Education administrators, all other...	11-9039	30,000	33,000	3,700	13

NOTE: Data in this table are rounded. See the discussion of the employment projections table in the *Handbook* introductory chapter on *Occupational Information Included in the Handbook.*

Earnings

In May 2006, elementary and secondary school administrators had median annual earnings of $77,740; postsecondary school administrators had median annual earnings of $73,990, while administrators in preschool and childcare centers earned a median of $37,740 per year. Salaries of education administrators depend on several factors, including the location and enrollment level in the school or school district.

According to a survey of public schools, conducted by the Educational Research Service, average salaries for principals and assistant principals in the 2006-07 school year were as follows:

Principals:
Senior high school...$92,965
Jr. high/middle school 87,866
Elementary school..82,414

Assistant principals:
Senior high school...$75,121
Jr. high/middle school 73,020
Elementary school..67,735

According to the College and University Professional Association for Human Resources, median annual salaries for selected administrators in higher education in 2006-07 were as follows:

Chief academic officer...$140,595
Academic deans:
Business $135,080
Arts and sciences..121,942
Graduate programs..120,120
Education 117,450
Nursing...112,497
Health-related professions 110,346
Continuing education...99,595
Occupational studies/vocational education.........................83,108

Other administrators:
Chief development officer..$125,000
Dean of students..80,012
Director, student financial aid 68,000
Registrar...66,008
Director, student activities 50,000

Benefits for education administrators are generally very good. Many get 4 or 5 weeks of vacation every year and have generous health and pension packages. Many colleges and universities offer free tuition to employees and their families.

Related Occupations

Education administrators apply organizational and leadership skills to provide services to individuals. Workers in related occupations include administrative services managers; office and administrative support worker supervisors and managers; and human resource, training, and labor relations managers and specialists. Education administrators also work with students and have backgrounds similar to those of counselors; librarians; instructional coordinators; teachers—preschool, kindergarten, elementary, middle, and secondary; and teachers—postsecondary.

Sources of Additional Information

For information on principals, contact:
➤ The National Association of Elementary School Principals, 1615 Duke St., Alexandria, VA 22314-3483.
Internet: **http://www.naesp.org**
➤ The National Association of Secondary School Principals, 1904 Association Drive, Reston, VA 20191-1537.
Internet: **http://www.nassp.org**

For a list of nationally recognized programs in elementary and secondary educational administration, contact:
➤ The Educational Leadership Constituent Council, 1904 Association Drive, Reston, VA 20191.
Internet: **http://www.npbea.org/ELCC/index.html**

For information on collegiate registrars and admissions officers, contact:
➤ American Association of Collegiate Registrars and Admissions Officers, One Dupont Circle NW., Suite 520, Washington, DC 20036-1171. Internet: **http://www.aacrao.org**

For information on professional development and graduate programs for college student affairs administrators, contact:
➤ NASPA, Student Affairs Administrators in Higher Education, 1875 Connecticut Ave. NW., Suite 418, Washington, DC 20009.
Internet: **http://www.naspa.org**

For information on the National Administrator Credential for child care directors, contact:
➤ National Child Care Association, 2025 M St NW., Suite 800, Washington, DC 20036. Internet: **http://www.nccanet.org**

For information on the Child Development Associate Credential, contact:
➤ Council for Professional Recognition, 2460 16th St., NW., Washington, DC 20009. Internet: **http://www.cdacouncil.org**

Engineering and Natural Sciences Managers

(O*NET 11-9041.00, 11-9121.00)

Significant Points

- Most engineering and natural sciences managers have formal education and work experience as engineers, scientists, or mathematicians.

- Projected employment growth for engineering and natural sciences managers is closely related to growth in employment of the engineers and scientists they supervise and the industries in which they work.

- Opportunities will be best for workers with strong communication and business management skills.

Nature of the Work

Engineering and natural sciences managers plan, coordinate, and direct research, design, and production activities. They may supervise engineers, scientists, and technicians, along with support personnel. These managers use their knowledge of engineering and natural sciences to oversee a variety of activities. They determine scientific and technical goals within broad outlines provided by top executives, who are discussed elsewhere in the *Handbook*. These goals may include improving manufacturing processes, advancing scientific research, or developing new products. Managers make detailed plans to accomplish these goals. For example, they may develop the overall concepts of a new product or identify technical problems preventing the completion of a project.

To perform effectively, these managers also must apply knowledge of administrative procedures, such as budgeting, hiring, and supervision. They propose budgets for projects and programs and determine staff, training, and equipment needs. They hire and assign scientists, engineers, and support personnel to carry out specific parts of each project. They also supervise the work of these employees, check the technical accuracy of their work and the soundness of their methods, review their output, and establish administrative procedures and policies—including environmental standards, for example.

In addition, these managers use communication skills extensively. They spend a great deal of time coordinating the activities of their unit with those of other units or organizations. They confer with higher levels of management; with financial, production, marketing, and other managers; and with contractors and equipment and materials suppliers.

Engineering managers may supervise people who design and develop machinery, products, systems, and processes. They might also direct and coordinate production, operations, quality assurance, testing, or maintenance in industrial plants. Many are plant engineers, who direct and coordinate the design, installation, operation, and maintenance of equipment and machinery in industrial plants. Others manage research and development teams that produce new products and processes or improve existing ones.

Natural sciences managers oversee the work of life and physical scientists, including agricultural scientists, chemists, biologists, geologists, medical scientists, and physicists. These managers direct research and development projects and coordinate

Engineering and science managers must have well-developed business and communication skills.

activities such as testing, quality control, and production. They may work on basic research projects or on commercial activities. Science managers sometimes conduct their own research in addition to managing the work of others.

Work environment. Engineering and natural sciences managers spend most of their time in an office. Some managers, however, also may work in laboratories, where they may be exposed to the same conditions as research scientists, or in industrial plants, where they may be exposed to the same conditions as production workers. Most managers work at least 40 hours a week and may work much longer on occasion to meet project deadlines. Some may experience considerable pressure to meet technical or scientific goals on a short deadline or within a tight budget.

Training, Other Qualifications, and Advancement

Strong technical knowledge is essential for engineering and natural sciences managers, who must understand and guide the work of their subordinates and explain the work in nontechnical terms to senior management and potential customers. Therefore, most managers have formal education and work experience as an engineer, scientist, or mathematician.

Education and training. These managers usually have education similar to that of the workers they supervise. Most engineering managers, for example, begin their careers as engineers, after completing a bachelor's degree in the field. Many engineers gain business management skills by completing a master's degree in engineering management (MEM) or business administration (MBA). Employers often pay for such training. In large firms, some courses required in these degree programs may be offered onsite. Typically, engineers who prefer to manage in technical areas pursue an MEM, and those interested in less technical management earn an MBA.

Similarly, many science managers begin their careers as scientists, such as chemists, biologists, geologists, or mathematicians. Most scientists and mathematicians engaged in basic research have a Ph.D. degree; some who work in applied research and other activities may have a bachelor's or master's degree. Graduate programs allow scientists to augment their undergraduate training with instruction in other fields, such as management or computer technology. Natural science managers interested in more technical management may earn traditional master's or Ph.D. degrees in natural sciences or master's degrees in science that incorporate business management skills. Those interested in more general management may pursue an MBA. Given the rapid pace of scientific developments, science managers must continuously upgrade their knowledge.

Other qualifications. Engineering and natural sciences managers must be specialists in the work they supervise. To advance to these positions, engineers and scientists generally must gain experience and assume management responsibility. To fill management positions, employers seek engineers and scientists who possess administrative and communication skills in addition to technical knowledge in their specialty. In fact, because engineering and natural sciences managers must effectively lead groups and coordinate projects, they usually need excellent communication and administrative skills.

Advancement. Engineering and natural sciences managers may advance to progressively higher leadership positions within their disciplines. Some may become managers in nontechnical areas such as marketing, human resources, or sales. In high technology firms, managers in nontechnical areas often must possess the same specialized knowledge as do managers in technical areas. For example, employers in an engineering firm may prefer to hire experienced engineers as sales workers because the complex services offered by the firm can be marketed only by someone with specialized engineering knowledge. Such sales workers could eventually advance to jobs as sales managers.

Employment

Engineering and natural sciences managers held about 228,000 jobs in 2006. Manufacturing industries employed 38 percent of engineering and natural sciences managers. Manufacturing industries with the largest employment are those which produce computer and electronic equipment and those which produce transportation equipment, including aerospace products and parts. Another 31 percent worked in professional, scientific, and technical services industries, primarily for firms providing architectural, engineering, and related services and firms providing scientific research and development services. Other large employers include Federal, State, and local government agencies.

Job Outlook

Employment of engineering and natural sciences managers is projected to grow about as fast as the average for all occupations, similar to the growth rate of engineers and life and physical scientists. Opportunities will be best for workers with strong communication and business management skills.

Employment change. Employment of engineering and natural sciences managers is expected to grow 8 percent over the 2006-16 decade, about as fast as the average for all occupations. Projected employment growth for engineering and natural sciences managers should be in line with growth of the engineers and scientists they supervise and the industries in which they work. Because many employers find it more efficient to contract engineering and science work to specialty firms, there should be strong demand for engineering managers in the scientific research and development services industry and for both engineering and natural science managers in the architectural, engineering, and related services industry.

Job prospects. Opportunities for engineering managers should be better in rapidly growing areas of engineering—such as environmental and biomedical engineering—than in more slowly growing areas—such as electronics and materials engi-neering. Opportunities for natural sciences managers should likewise be best in the rapidly growing medical and environmental sciences. (See the statements on engineers and life and physical scientists elsewhere in the *Handbook.*) Engineers and scientists with advanced technical knowledge and strong communication skills will be in the best position to become managers. Because engineering and natural sciences managers are involved in the financial, production, and marketing activities of their firm, business management skills are also advantageous for those seeking management positions. In addition to those openings resulting from employment growth, job openings will result from the need to replace managers who retire or move into other occupations.

Earnings

Earnings for engineering and natural sciences managers vary by specialty and by level of responsibility. Median annual earnings of wage and salary engineering managers were $105,430 in May 2006. The middle 50 percent earned between $84,090 and $130,170. Median annual earnings in the industries employing the largest numbers of engineering managers were:

Semiconductor and other electronic component manufacturing	$120,740
Federal executive branch	116,140
Navigational, measuring, electromedical, and control instruments manufacturing	115,150
Aerospace product and parts manufacturing	111,020
Engineering services	103,570

Median annual earnings of wage and salary natural sciences managers were $100,080 in May 2006. The middle 50 percent earned between $77,320 and $130,900. Median annual earnings in the industries employing the largest numbers of natural sciences managers were:

Research and development in the physical, engineering, and life sciences	$120,780
Pharmaceutical and medicine manufacturing	111,070
Federal executive branch	96,100
Architectural, engineering, and related services	88,990
State government	65,570

In addition, engineering and natural sciences managers, especially those at higher levels, often receive more benefits—such as expense accounts, stock option plans, and bonuses—than do nonmanagerial workers in their organizations.

Projections data from the National Employment Matrix

Occupational Title	SOC Code	Employment, 2006	Projected employment, 2016	Change, 2006-16	
				Number	Percent
Engineering and natural sciences managers	—	228,000	246,000	18,000	8
Engineering managers	11-9041	187,000	201,000	14,000	7
Natural sciences managers	11-9121	41,000	45,000	4,600	11

NOTE: Data in this table are rounded. See the discussion of the employment projections table in the *Handbook* introductory chapter on *Occupational Information Included in the Handbook.*

Related Occupations

The work of engineering and natural sciences managers is closely related to that of engineers; mathematicians; and physical and life scientists, including agricultural and food scientists, atmospheric scientists, biological scientists, conservation scientists and foresters, chemists and materials scientists, environmental scientists and hydrologists, geoscientists, medical scientists, and physicists and astronomers. It also is related to the work of other managers, especially top executives.

Sources of Additional Information

For information about a career as an engineering and natural sciences manager, contact the sources of additional information for engineers, life scientists, and physical scientists that are listed at the end of statements on these occupations elsewhere in the *Handbook*.

Additional information on science and engineering master's degrees is available from:

➤ Commission on Professionals in Science and Technology, 1200 New York Ave. NW., Suite 113, Washington, DC 20005. Internet: **http://www.sciencemasters.org**

To learn more about managing scientists and engineers in research and development, see the *Occupational Outlook Quarterly* article, "Careers for scientists—and others—in scientific research and development," in print at many libraries and career centers. and online at:
http://www.bls.gov/opub/ooq/2005/summer/art04.htm

Farmers, Ranchers, and Agricultural Managers

(O*NET 11-9011.00 11–9011.01, 11–9011.02, 11–9011.03, 11–9012.00)

Significant Points

- Modern farming requires knowledge of new developments in agriculture, as well as work experience often gained through growing up on a farm or through postsecondary education.

- Overall employment is projected to decline because of increasing productivity and consolidation of farms.

- Horticulture and organic farming will provide better employment opportunities.

- Small-scale farming is a major growth area and offers the best opportunity for entering the occupation.

Nature of the Work

American farmers, ranchers, and agricultural managers direct the activities of one of the world's largest and most productive agricultural sectors. They produce enough food and fiber to meet the needs of the United States and for export. *Farmers and ranchers* own and operate mainly family-owned farms. They also may lease land from a landowner and operate it as a working farm. *Agricultural managers* manage the day-to-day activities of one or more farms, ranches, nurseries, timber tracts, greenhouses, or other agricultural establishments for farmers, absentee landowners, or corporations. Their duties and responsibilities vary widely but focus on the business aspects of running a farm. On small farms, they may oversee the entire operation; on larger farms, they may oversee a single activity, such as marketing.

Farmers, ranchers, and agricultural managers make many managerial decisions. Farm output and income are strongly influenced by the weather, disease, fluctuations in prices of domestic and foreign farm products, and Federal farm programs. In crop-production operations, farmers and managers usually determine the best time to plant seed, apply fertilizer and chemicals, and harvest and market the crops. Many carefully plan the combination of crops they grow, so that if the price of one crop drops, they will have sufficient income from another crop to make up the loss. Farmers, ranchers, and managers monitor the constantly changing prices for their products. They use different strategies to protect themselves from unpredictable changes in the markets for agricultural products. If they plan ahead, they may be able to store their crops or keep their livestock to take advantage of higher prices later in the year. Those who participate in the risky futures market buy contracts on future production of agricultural goods. These contracts can minimize the risk of sudden price changes by guaranteeing a certain price for farmers' and ranchers' agricultural goods when they are ready to sell.

Farmers need in-depth knowledge of many kinds of crops.

While most farm output is sold directly to food-processing companies, some farmers—particularly operators of smaller farms—may choose to sell their goods directly to consumers through farmers' markets. Some use cooperatives to reduce their financial risk and to gain a larger share of the prices consumers pay. For example, in community-supported agriculture, cooperatives sell shares of a harvest to consumers prior to the planting season, thus freeing the farmer from having to bear all the financial risks and ensuring the farmer a market for the produce of the coming season. Farmers, ranchers, and agricultural managers also negotiate with banks and other credit lenders to get the best financing deals for their equipment, livestock, and seed.

Like other businesses, farming operations have become more complex in recent years, so many farmers use computers to keep financial and inventory records. They also use computer databases and spreadsheets to manage breeding, dairy, and other farm operations.

The type of farm farmers, ranchers, and agricultural managers operate determines their specific tasks. On crop farms—farms growing grain, cotton, other fibers, fruit, and vegetables—farmers are responsible for preparing, tilling, planting, fertilizing, cultivating, spraying, and harvesting. After the harvest, they make sure that the crops are properly packaged, stored, and marketed. Livestock, dairy, and poultry farmers and ranchers feed and care for animals and keep barns, pens, coops, and other farm buildings clean and in good condition. They also plan and oversee breeding and marketing activities. Both farmers and ranchers operate machinery and maintain equipment and facilities, and both track technological improvements in animal breeding and seeds, and choose new or existing products.

The size of the farm or ranch often determines which of these tasks farmers and ranchers handle themselves. Operators of small farms usually perform all tasks, physical and administrative. They keep records for management and tax purposes, service machinery, maintain buildings, and grow vegetables and raise animals. Operators of large farms, by contrast, have employees who help with the physical work that small-farm operators do themselves. Although employment on most farms is limited to the farmer and 1 or 2 family workers or hired employees, some large farms have 100 or more full-time and seasonal workers. Some of these employees are in nonfarm occupations, working as truck drivers, sales representatives, bookkeepers, and computer specialists.

Agricultural managers usually do not plant, harvest, or perform other production activities; instead, they hire and supervise farm and livestock workers, who perform most daily production tasks. Managers may establish output goals; determine financial constraints; monitor production and marketing; hire, assign, and supervise workers; determine crop transportation and storage requirements; and oversee maintenance of the property and equipment.

Two types of farmers that are growing in importance are horticultural specialty farmers and aquaculture farmers. *Horticultural specialty farmers* oversee the production of fruits, vegetables, flowers, and ornamental plants used in landscaping, including turf. They also grow nuts, berries, and grapes for wine. *Aquaculture farmers* raise fish and shellfish in marine, brackish, or fresh water, usually in ponds, floating net pens, raceways, or recirculating systems. They stock, feed, protect, and otherwise manage aquatic life sold for consumption or used for recreational fishing.

Work environment. The work of full-time farmers, ranchers, and agricultural managers is often strenuous; work hours are frequently long; and these workers rarely have days off during the planting, growing, and harvesting seasons. Nevertheless, for those who enter farming or ranching, the hard work is counterbalanced by their enjoyment of living in a rural area, working outdoors, being self-employed, and making a living off the land.

Farmers and farm managers on crop farms usually work from sunrise to sunset during the planting and harvesting seasons. The rest of the year, they plan next season's crops, market their output, and repair machinery.

On livestock-producing farms and ranches, work goes on throughout the year. Animals, unless they are grazing, must be fed and watered every day, and dairy cows must be milked two or three times a day. Many livestock and dairy farmers monitor and attend to the health of their herds, which may include assisting in the birthing of animals. Such farmers and farm managers rarely get the chance to get away, unless they hire an assistant or arrange for a temporary substitute.

Farmers and farm managers who grow produce and perishables have different demands on their time depending on the crop grown and the season. They may work very long hours during planting and harvesting season, but shorter hours at other times. Some farmers maintain cover crops during the cold months, which keep them busy beyond the typical growing season.

On very large farms, farmers and farm managers spend substantial time meeting farm supervisors in charge of various activities. Professional farm managers overseeing several farms may divide their time between traveling to meet farmers or landowners and planning the farm operations in their offices. As farming practices and agricultural technology become more sophisticated, farmers and farm managers are spending more time in offices and at computers, where they electronically manage many aspects of their businesses. Some farmers also attend conferences exchanging information, particularly during the winter months.

Farm work can be hazardous. Tractors and other farm machinery can cause serious injury, and workers must be constantly alert on the job. The proper operation of equipment and handling of chemicals are necessary to avoid accidents, safeguard health, and protect the environment.

Training, Other Qualifications, and Advancement

Experience gained from growing up on or working on a family farm is the most common way farmers learn their trade. However, modern farming requires increasingly complex scientific, business, and financial decisions, so postsecondary education in agriculture is important even for people who were raised on farms.

Education and training. Most farmers receive their training on the job, often by being raised on a farm. However, the completion of a 2-year associate degree or a 4-year bachelor's degree at a college of agriculture is becoming increasingly important for farm managers and for farmers and ranchers who expect to make a living at farming. A degree in farm management or in business with a concentration in agriculture is important.

Students should select the college most appropriate to their interests and location. All State university systems have at least one land-grant college or university with a school of agriculture. Common programs of study include agronomy, dairy science, agricultural economics and business, horticulture, crop and fruit science, and animal science. For students interested in aquaculture, formal programs are available and include coursework in fisheries biology, fish culture, hatchery management and maintenance, and hydrology.

Agricultural colleges teach technical knowledge of crops, growing conditions, and plant diseases. They also teach prospective ranchers and dairy farmers the basics of veterinary science and animal husbandry. Students also study how the environment is affected by farm operations, for example, how the various pesticides affect local animals.

New farmers, ranchers, and agricultural managers often spend time working under an experienced farmer to learn how to apply the skills learned through academic training. Those without academic training often take many years to learn how weather, fertilizers, seed, feeding or breeding affect the growth of crops or the raising of animals in addition to other aspects of farming. A small number of farms offer formal apprenticeships to help young people learn the practical skills of farming and ranching.

Other qualifications. Farmers, ranchers, and agricultural managers need managerial skills to organize and operate a business. A basic knowledge of accounting and bookkeeping is essential in keeping financial records, and knowledge of credit sources is vital for buying seed, fertilizer, and other needed inputs. Workers must also be familiar with complex safety regulations and requirements of governmental agricultural support programs. Computer skills are becoming increasingly important, especially on large farms, where computers are widely used for recordkeeping and business analysis. In addition, skills in personnel management, communication, and conflict resolution are important in the operation of a farm or ranch business.

Mechanical aptitude and the ability to work with tools of all kinds also are valuable skills for a small-farm operator, who often maintains and repairs machinery or farm structures.

Certification and advancement. Because of rapid changes in the industry, farmers, ranchers, and agricultural managers need to stay informed about continuing advances in agricul-

tural methods, both in the United States and abroad. They need to monitor changes in governmental regulations that may affect production methods or markets for particular crops. Besides print journals that inform the agricultural community, farmers and managers use the Internet for quick access to the latest developments in areas such as agricultural marketing, legal arrangements, and growing crops, vegetables, and livestock.

Agricultural managers can enhance their professional status through voluntary certification as an Accredited Farm Manager (AFM) by the American Society of Farm Managers and Rural Appraisers. Accreditation requires several years of farm management experience, the appropriate academic background—a bachelor's degree or, preferably, a master's degree in a field of agricultural science—and the passing of courses and examinations related to the business, financial, and legal aspects of farm and ranch management.

Employment

Farmers, ranchers, and agricultural managers held nearly 1.3 million jobs in 2006. About 80 percent are self-employed farmers and ranchers, and the remainder is agricultural managers. Most farmers, ranchers, and agricultural managers oversee crop-production activities, while others manage livestock and dairy production. Most farmers and ranchers operate small farms on a part-time basis.

The soil, topography of the land, and climate often determine the type of farming and ranching done in a particular area. California, Texas, Iowa, Nebraska, and Kansas are the leading agricultural States in terms of agricultural output measured in dollars. Texas, Missouri, Iowa, Kentucky, and Tennessee are the leading agricultural States in terms of numbers of farms.

Job Outlook

The long-term trend toward the consolidation of farms into fewer and larger ones is expected to continue over the 2006–16 decade and to result in a continued, moderate decline in employment of self-employed farmers and ranchers and little or no change in employment of salaried agricultural managers. Nevertheless, a number of jobs will be available due to the need to replace the large number of farmers expected to retire or leave the profession over the next decade.

Employment change. Employment of self-employed farmers is expected to decline moderately by 8 percent over the 2006–2016 decade. The continuing ability of the agriculture sector to produce more with fewer workers will cause some farmers to go out of business as market pressures leave little room for the marginally successful farmer. As land, machin-

Projections data from the National Employment Matrix

Occupational Title	SOC Code	Employment, 2006	Projected employment, 2016	Change, 2006-16	
				Number	Percent
Agricultural managers	11-9010	1,317,000	1,230,000	-87,000	-7
Farm, ranch, and other agricultural managers	11-9011	258,000	261,000	2,900	1
Farmers and ranchers	11-9012	1,058,000	969,000	-90,000	-8

NOTE: Data in this table are rounded. See the discussion of the employment projections table in the *Handbook* introductory chapter on *Occupational Information Included in the Handbook.*

ery, seed, and chemicals become more expensive, only well-capitalized farmers and corporations will be able to buy many of the farms that become available. These larger, more productive farms are better able to withstand the adverse effects of climate and price fluctuations on farm output and income. Larger farms also have advantages in obtaining government subsidies and payments because these payments are usually based on acreage owned and per-unit production.

In contrast, agricultural managers are projected to gain jobs, growing by 1 percent—effectively little or no change in the occupation. Owners of large tracts of land, who often do not live on the property they own, increasingly will seek the expertise of agricultural managers to run their farms and ranches in a business-like manner.

Despite the expected continued consolidation of farmland and the projected decline in overall employment of this occupation, an increasing number of small-scale farmers have developed successful market niches that involve personalized, direct contact with their customers. Many are finding opportunities in organic food production, which is the fastest growing segment in agriculture. Others use farmers' markets that cater directly to urban and suburban consumers, allowing the farmers to capture a greater share of consumers' food dollars. Some small-scale farmers belong to collectively owned marketing cooperatives that process and sell their product. Other farmers participate in community-supported agriculture cooperatives that allow consumers to directly buy a share of the farmer's harvest.

Aquaculture may continue to provide some new employment opportunities over the 2006–16 decade. Concerns about overfishing and the depletion of the stock of some wild fish species will likely lead to more restrictions on deep-sea fishing, even as public demand for the consumption of seafood continues to grow. This has spurred the growth of aquaculture farms that raise selected aquatic species—such as shrimp, salmon, trout, and catfish—in pens or ponds. Aquaculture has increased even in landlocked States, as farmers attempt to diversify.

Job prospects. Job prospects are expected to be favorable for those who want to go into farming. With fewer people wanting to become farmers and a large number of farmers expected to retire or give up their farms in the next decade, there will be some opportunities to own or lease a farm. The market for agricultural products is projected to be good for most products over the next decade, and thus many farmers who retire will need to be replaced. Farmers who produce corn used to produce ethanol will be in particular demand as ethanol plays a greater role in energy production as fuel for automobiles. Farmers who grow crops used in landscaping, such as trees, shrubs, turf, and other ornamentals, also will have better job prospects, as people put more money into landscaping their homes and businesses.

Earnings

Incomes of farmers and ranchers vary greatly from year to year, because prices of farm products fluctuate with weather conditions and the other factors that influence the quantity and quality of farm output and the demand for those products. A farm that shows a large profit one year may show a loss the

following year. According to the U.S. Department of Agriculture, the average net cash farm business income for farm operator households in 2005 was $15,603. This figure, however, does not reflect that farmers often receive government subsidies or other payments that supplement their incomes and reduce some of the risk of farming. Additionally, most farmers—primarily operators of small farms—have income from off-farm business activities or careers, often greater than that of their farm income.

Full-time, salaried farm managers had median weekly earnings of $1,001 in May 2006. The middle half earned between $766 and $1,382. The highest paid 10 percent earned more than $1,924, and the lowest paid 10 percent earned less than $572.

Self-employed farmers must procure their own health and life insurance. As members of farm organizations, they may receive group discounts on health and life insurance premiums.

Related Occupations

Farmers, ranchers, and agricultural managers strive to improve the quality of agricultural products and the efficiency of farms. Others whose work relates to agriculture include agricultural engineers, agricultural and food scientists, agricultural workers, and purchasing agents and buyers of farm products.

Sources of Additional Information

For general information about farming and agricultural occupations, contact either of the following organizations:
➤ Center for Rural Affairs, P.O. Box 406, Walthill, NE 68067. Internet: **http://www.cfra.org**
➤ National FFA Organization, The National FFA Center, Attention Career Information Requests, P.O. Box 68690, Indianapolis, IN 46268. Internet: **http://www.ffa.org**

For information about certification as an accredited farm manager, contact:
➤ American Society of Farm Managers and Rural Appraisers, 950 Cherry St., Suite 508, Denver, CO 80222. Internet: **http://www.asfmra.org**

For information on the USDA's program to help small farmers get started, contact:
➤ Small Farm Program, U.S. Department of Agriculture, Cooperative State, Research, Education, and Extension Service, Stop 2220, Washington, DC 20250.
Internet: **http://www.csrees.usda.gov/smallfarms.cfm**

For information about organic farming, horticulture, and internships, contact:
➤ Alternative Farming System Information Center, NAL, 10301 Baltimore Ave., Room 132, Beltsville, MD 20705. Internet: **http://www.nal.usda.gov**
➤ ATTRA, National Sustainable Agriculture Information Service, P.O. Box 3657, Fayetteville, AR 72702.
Internet: **http://www.attra.ncat.org**

To learn more about how technological and other changes are affecting agricultural careers, see the *Occupational Outlook Quarterly* article "Farming in the 21st century: A modern business in the modern world," in print at many libraries and career centers and online at:
http://www.bls.gov/opub/ooq/2005/spring/art02.pdf

Financial Managers

(O*NET 11-3031.00, 11-3031.01, 11-3031.02)

Significant Points

- Jobseekers are likely to face competition.

- About 3 out of 10 work in finance and insurance industries.

- A bachelor's degree in finance, accounting, or a related field is the minimum academic preparation, but employers increasingly seek graduates with a master's degree in business administration, economics, finance, or risk management.

- Experience may be more important than formal education for some financial manager positions—most notably, branch managers in banks.

Nature of the Work

Almost every firm, government agency, and other type of organization has one or more financial managers. Financial managers oversee the preparation of financial reports, direct investment activities, and implement cash management strategies. Managers also develop strategies and implement the long-term goals of their organization.

The duties of financial managers vary with their specific titles, which include controller, treasurer or finance officer, credit manager, cash manager, risk and insurance manager, and manager of international banking. *Controllers* direct the preparation of financial reports, such as income statements, balance sheets, and analyses of future earnings or expenses, that summarize and forecast the organization's financial position. Controllers also are in charge of preparing special reports required by regulatory authorities. Often, controllers oversee the accounting, audit, and budget departments. *Treasurers* and *finance officers* direct the organization's budgets to meet its financial goals. They oversee the investment of funds, manage associated risks, supervise cash management activities, execute capital-raising strategies to support a firm's expansion, and deal with mergers

Financial managers develop strategies for achieving the long-term goals of their organization.

and acquisitions. *Credit managers* oversee the firm's issuance of credit, establishing credit-rating criteria, determining credit ceilings, and monitoring the collections of past-due accounts.

Cash managers monitor and control the flow of cash receipts and disbursements to meet the business and investment needs of the firm. For example, cash flow projections are needed to determine whether loans must be obtained to meet cash requirements or whether surplus cash should be invested in interest-bearing instruments. *Risk* and *insurance managers* oversee programs to minimize risks and losses that might arise from financial transactions and business operations. They also manage the organization's insurance budget. Managers specializing in international finance develop financial and accounting systems for the banking transactions of multinational organizations. (Chief financial officers and other executives are included with top executives elsewhere in the *Handbook*.)

Financial institutions—such as commercial banks, savings and loan associations, credit unions, and mortgage and finance companies—employ additional financial managers who oversee various functions, such as lending, trusts, mortgages, and investments, or programs, including sales, operations, or electronic financial services. These managers may solicit business, authorize loans, and direct the investment of funds, always adhering to Federal and State laws and regulations.

Branch managers of financial institutions administer and manage all of the functions of a branch office. Job duties may include hiring personnel, approving loans and lines of credit, establishing a rapport with the community to attract business, and assisting customers with account problems. Branch mangers also are becoming more oriented toward sales and marketing. As a result, it is important that they have substantial knowledge about all types of products that the bank sells. Financial managers who work for financial institutions must keep abreast of the rapidly growing array of financial services and products.

In addition to the preceding duties, all financial managers perform tasks unique to their organization or industry. For example, government financial managers must be experts on the government appropriations and budgeting processes, whereas health care financial managers must be knowledgeable about issues surrounding health care financing. Moreover, financial managers must be aware of special tax laws and regulations that affect their industry.

Financial managers play an increasingly important role in mergers and consolidations and in global expansion and related financing. These areas require extensive, specialized knowledge to reduce risks and maximize profit. Financial managers increasingly are hired on a temporary basis to advise senior managers on these and other matters. In fact, some small firms contract out all their accounting and financial functions to companies that provide such services.

The role of the financial manager, particularly in business, is changing in response to technological advances that have significantly reduced the amount of time it takes to produce financial reports. Financial managers now perform more data analysis and use it to offer senior managers ideas on how to maximize profits. They often work on teams, acting as business advisors to top management. Financial managers need to keep abreast of the latest computer technology to increase the efficiency of their firm's financial operations.

Work environment. Working in comfortable offices, often close to top managers and to departments that develop the financial data those managers need, financial managers typically have direct access to state-of-the-art computer systems and information services. They commonly work long hours, often up to 50 or 60 per week. Financial managers generally are required to attend meetings of financial and economic associations and may travel to visit subsidiary firms or to meet customers.

Training, Other Qualifications, and Advancement

Most financial managers need a bachelor's degree, and many have a master's degree or professional certification. Bank managers often have experience as loan officers. Financial managers also need strong interpersonal and business skills.

Education and training. A bachelor's degree in finance, accounting, economics, or business administration is the minimum academic preparation for financial managers. However, many employers now seek graduates with a master's degree, preferably in business administration, economics, finance, or risk management. These academic programs develop analytical skills and teach the latest financial analysis methods and technology.

Experience may be more important than formal education for some financial manager positions—most notably, branch managers in banks. Banks typically fill branch manager positions by promoting experienced loan officers and other professionals who excel at their jobs. Other financial managers may enter the profession through formal management training programs offered by the company. The American Institute of Banking, which is affiliated with the American Bankers Association, sponsors educational and training programs for bank officers at banking schools and educational conferences.

Other qualifications. Candidates for financial management positions need many different skills. Interpersonal skills are important because these jobs involve managing people and working as part of a team to solve problems. Financial managers must have excellent communication skills to explain complex financial data. Because financial managers work extensively with various departments in their firm, a broad understanding of business is essential.

Financial managers should be creative thinkers and problem-solvers, applying their analytical skills to business. They must be comfortable with the latest computer technology. Financial managers must have knowledge of international finance because financial operations are increasingly being affected by the global economy. Proficiency in a foreign language also may be important. In addition, a good knowledge of compliance procedures is essential because of the many recent regulatory changes.

Certification and advancement. Financial managers may broaden their skills and exhibit their competency by attaining professional certification. Many associations offer professional certification programs. For example, the CFA Institute confers the Chartered Financial Analyst designation on investment professionals who have a bachelor's degree, pass three sequential examinations, and meet work experience requirements. The Association for Financial Professionals confers the Certified Treasury Professional credentials to those who pass a computer-based exam and have a minimum of 2 years of relevant experience. Continuing education is required to maintain these credentials. Also, financial managers who specialize in accounting sometimes earn the Certified Public Accountant (CPA) or the Certified Management Accountant (CMA) designation. The CMA is offered by the Institute of Management Accountants to its members who have a bachelor's degree and at least 2 years of work experience and who pass the institute's four-part examination and fulfill continuing education requirements. (See accountants and auditors elsewhere in the *Handbook* for additional information on CPA and CMA designations.)

Continuing education is vital to financial managers, who must cope with the growing complexity of global trade, changes in Federal and State laws and regulations, and the proliferation of new and complex financial instruments. Firms often provide opportunities for workers to broaden their knowledge and skills by encouraging them to take graduate courses at colleges and universities or attend conferences related to their specialty. Financial management, banking, and credit union associations, often in cooperation with colleges and universities, sponsor numerous national and local training programs. Trainees prepare extensively at home and then attend sessions on subjects such as accounting management, budget management, corporate cash management, financial analysis, international banking, and information systems. Many firms pay all or part of the costs for employees who successfully complete the courses. Although experience, ability, and leadership are emphasized for promotion, advancement may be accelerated by this type of special study.

Because financial management is so important to efficient business operations, well-trained, experienced financial managers who display a strong grasp of the operations of various departments within their organization are prime candidates for promotion to top management positions. Some financial managers transfer to closely related positions in other industries. Those with extensive experience and access to sufficient capital may start their own consulting firms.

Employment

Financial managers held about 506,000 jobs in 2006. Although they can be found in every industry, approximately 3 out of 10 were employed by finance and insurance establishments, such

Projections data from the National Employment Matrix

Occupational Title	SOC Code	Employment, 2006	Projected employment, 2016	Change, 2006-16	
				Number	Percent
Financial managers	11-3031	506,000	570,000	64,000	13

NOTE: Data in this table are rounded. See the discussion of the employment projections table in the *Handbook* introductory chapter on *Occupational Information Included in the Handbook.*

as banks, savings institutions, finance companies, credit unions, insurance carriers, and securities dealers. About 8 percent worked for Federal, State, or local government.

Job Outlook

Employment growth for financial managers is expected is to be about as fast as the average for all occupations. However, applicants will likely face strong competition for jobs. Those with a masters' degree and a certification will have the best opportunities.

Employment change. Employment of financial managers over the 2006-16 decade is expected to grow by 13 percent, which is about as fast as the average for all occupations. Regulatory reforms and the expansion and globalization of the economy will increase the need for financial expertise and drive job growth. As the economy expands, both the growth of established companies and the creation of new businesses will spur demand for financial managers. Employment of bank branch managers is expected to increase because banks are refocusing on the importance of their existing branches and are creating new branches to service a growing population. However, mergers, acquisitions, and corporate downsizing are likely to restrict the employment growth of financial managers to some extent.

The long-run prospects for financial managers in the securities and commodities industry should be favorable, because more people will be needed to handle increasingly complex financial transactions and manage a growing amount of investments. Financial managers also will be needed to handle mergers and acquisitions, raise capital, and assess global financial transactions. Risk managers, who assess risks for insurance and investment purposes, also will be in demand.

Some companies may hire financial managers on a temporary basis, to see the organization through a short-term crisis or to offer suggestions for boosting profits. Other companies may contract out all accounting and financial operations. Even in these cases, however, financial managers may be needed to oversee the contracts.

Job prospects. As with other managerial occupations, job-seekers are likely to face competition because the number of job openings is expected to be less than the number of applicants. Candidates with expertise in accounting and finance—particularly those with a master's degree and or certification—should enjoy the best job prospects. Strong computer skills and knowledge of international finance are important; as are excellent communication skills because financial management involves working on strategic planning teams.

As banks expand the range of products and services they offer to include insurance and investment products, branch managers with knowledge in these areas will be needed. As a result, candidates who are licensed to sell insurance or securities will have the most favorable prospects. (See the *Handbook* statements on insurance sales agents; and securities, commodities, and financial services sales agents.)

Earnings

Median annual earnings of wage and salary financial managers were $90,970 in May 2006. The middle 50 percent earned between $66,690 and $125,180. The lowest 10 percent earned less than $50,290 while the top 10 percent earned more than $145,600. Median annual earnings in the industries employing the largest numbers of financial managers were:

Securities and commodity contracts intermediation	$131,730
Management of companies and enterprises	105,410
Nondepository credit intermediation	86,340
Local government	72,790
Depository credit intermediation	72,580

According to a survey by Robert Half International, a staffing services firm specializing in accounting and finance professionals, directors of finance earned between $79,000 and $184,000 in 2007, and corporate controllers earned between $61,250 and $149,250.

Large organizations often pay more than small ones, and salary levels also can depend on the type of industry and location. Many financial managers in both public and private industry receive additional compensation in the form of bonuses, which, like salaries, vary substantially by size of firm. Deferred compensation in the form of stock options is becoming more common, especially for senior-level executives.

Related Occupations

Financial managers combine formal education with experience in one or more areas of finance, such as asset management, lending, credit operations, securities investment, or insurance risk and loss control. Workers in other occupations requiring similar training and skills include accountants and auditors; budget analysts; financial analysts and personal financial advisors; insurance sales agents; insurance underwriters; loan officers; securities, commodities, and financial services sales agents; and real estate brokers and sales agents.

Sources of Additional Information

For information about careers and certification in financial management, contact:

➤ Financial Management Association International, College of Business Administration, University of South Florida, Tampa, FL 33620. Internet: **http://www.fma.org**

For information about careers in financial and treasury management and the Certified Treasury Professional program, contact:

➤ Association for Financial Professionals, 7315 Wisconsin Ave., Suite 600 West, Bethesda, MD 20814.
Internet: **http://www.afponline.org**

For information about the Chartered Financial Analyst program, contact:

➤ CFA Institute, P.O. Box 3668, 560 Ray Hunt Dr., Charlottesville, VA 22903. Internet: **http://www.cfainstitute.org**

For information on The American Institute of Banking and its programs, contact:

➤ American Bankers Association, 1120 Connecticut Ave. NW., Washington, DC 20036.

For information about the Certified in Management Accounting designation, contact:

➤ Institute of Management Accountants, 10 Paragon Dr., Montvale, NJ, 07645. Internet: **http://www.imanet.org**

Food Service Managers

(O*NET 11-9051.00)

Significant Points

- Experience in food and beverage preparation and serving jobs is necessary for most food service manager positions.

- Food service managers coordinate a wide range of activities, but their most difficult task may be dealing with irate customers and uncooperative employees.

- Job opportunities for food service managers should be good as the number of outlets of restaurant chains increases to meet customer demand for convenience and value.

Nature of the Work

Food service managers are responsible for the daily operations of restaurants and other establishments that prepare and serve meals and beverages to customers. Besides coordinating activities among various departments, such as kitchen, dining room, and banquet operations, food service managers ensure that customers are satisfied with their dining experience. In addition, they oversee the inventory and ordering of food, equipment, and supplies and arrange for the routine maintenance and upkeep of the restaurant's equipment and facilities. Managers generally are responsible for all of the administrative and human-resource functions of running the business, including recruiting new employees and monitoring employee performance and training.

Managers interview, hire, train, and when necessary, fire employees. Retaining good employees is a major challenge facing food service managers. Managers recruit employees at career fairs, contact schools that offer academic programs in hospitality or culinary arts, and arrange for newspaper advertising to attract additional applicants. Managers oversee the training of new employees and explain the establishment's policies and practices. They schedule work hours, making sure that enough workers are present to cover each shift. If employees are unable to work, managers may have to call in alternates to cover for them or fill in themselves when needed. Some managers may help with cooking, clearing tables, or other tasks when the restaurant becomes extremely busy.

Food service managers ensure that diners are served properly and in a timely manner. They investigate and resolve customers' complaints about food quality or service. They monitor orders in the kitchen to determine where backups may occur, and they work with the chef to remedy any delays in service. Managers direct the cleaning of the dining areas and the washing of tableware, kitchen utensils, and equipment to comply with company and government sanitation standards. Managers also monitor the actions of their employees and patrons on a continual basis to ensure the personal safety of everyone. They make sure that health and safety standards and local liquor regulations are obeyed.

In addition to their regular duties, food service managers perform a variety of administrative assignments, such as keeping employee work records, preparing the payroll, and completing paperwork to comply with licensing laws and tax, wage and hour, unemployment compensation, and Social Security laws. Some of this work may be delegated to an assistant manager or bookkeeper, or it may be contracted out, but most general managers retain responsibility for the accuracy of business records. Managers also maintain records of supply and equipment purchases and ensure that accounts with suppliers are paid.

Managers tally the cash and charge receipts received and balance them against the record of sales. They are responsible for depositing the day's receipts at the bank or securing them in a safe place. Finally, managers are responsible for locking up the establishment, checking that ovens, grills, and lights are off, and switching on alarm systems.

Technology influences the jobs of food service managers in many ways, enhancing efficiency and productivity. Many restaurants use computers to track orders, inventory, and the seating of patrons. Point-of-service (POS) systems allow servers to key in a customer's order, either at the table using a hand-held device, or from a computer terminal in the dining room, and send the order to the kitchen instantaneously so preparation can begin. The same system totals and prints checks, functions like a cash register, connects to credit card authorizers, and tracks sales. To minimize food costs and spoilage, many managers

Food service managers keep an inventory of food and supplies and perform other bookkeeping functions.

use inventory-tracking software to compare sales records with a record of the current inventory. Some establishments enter an inventory of standard ingredients and suppliers into their POS system. When supplies of particular ingredients run low, they can be ordered directly from the supplier using preprogrammed information. Computers also allow restaurant and food service managers to keep track of employee schedules and paychecks more efficiently.

Food service managers use the Internet to track industry news, find recipes, conduct market research, purchase supplies or equipment, recruit employees, and train staff. Internet access also makes service to customers more efficient. Many restaurants maintain Web sites that include menus and online promotions, provide information about the restaurant's location, and offer patrons the option of making a reservation.

In most full-service restaurants and institutional food service facilities, the management team consists of a *general manager*, one or more *assistant managers*, and an *executive chef*. The executive chef is responsible for all food preparation activities, including running kitchen operations, planning menus, and maintaining quality standards for food service. In limited-service eating places, such as sandwich shops, coffee bars, or fast-food establishments, managers, not executive chefs, are responsible for supervising routine food preparation operations. Assistant managers in full-service facilities generally oversee service in the dining rooms and banquet areas. In larger restaurants and fast-food or other food service facilities that serve meals daily and maintain longer business hours, individual assistant managers may supervise different shifts of workers. In smaller restaurants, formal titles may be less important, and one person may undertake the work of one or more food service positions. For example, the executive chef also may be the general manager or even sometimes an owner. (For additional information on these other workers, see material on top executives and chefs, cooks, and food preparation workers elsewhere in the *Handbook*.)

In restaurants where there are both food service managers and executive chefs, the managers often help the chefs select successful menu items. This task varies by establishment depending on the seasonality of menu items, the frequency with which restaurants change their menus, and the introduction of daily, weekly, or seasonal specials. Many restaurants rarely change their menus while others make frequent alterations. Managers or executive chefs select menu items, taking into account the likely number of customers and the past popularity of dishes. Other issues considered when planning a menu include whether there was any food left over from prior meals that should not be wasted, the need for variety, and the seasonal availability of foods. Managers or executive chefs analyze the recipes of the dishes to determine food, labor, and overhead costs, work out the portion size and nutritional content of each plate, and assign prices to various menu items. Menus must be developed far enough in advance that supplies can be ordered and received in time.

Managers or executive chefs estimate food needs, place orders with distributors, and schedule the delivery of fresh food and supplies. They plan for routine services or deliveries, such as linen services or the heavy cleaning of dining rooms or kitchen equipment, to occur during slow times or when the dining room is closed. Managers also arrange for equipment maintenance and repairs, and coordinate a variety of services such as waste removal and pest control. Managers or executive chefs receive deliveries and check the contents against order records. They inspect the quality of fresh meats, poultry, fish, fruits, vegetables, and baked goods to ensure that expectations are met. They meet with representatives from restaurant supply companies and place orders to replenish stocks of tableware, linens, paper products, cleaning supplies, cooking utensils, and furniture and fixtures.

Work environment. Food service managers are among the first to arrive in the morning and the last to leave at night. Long hours—12 to 15 per day, 50 or more per week, and sometimes 7 days a week—are common. Managers of institutional food service facilities, such as school, factory, or office cafeterias, work more regular hours because the operating hours of these establishments usually conform to the operating hours of the business or facility they serve. However, hours for many managers are unpredictable.

Managers should be calm, flexible, and able to work through emergencies, such as a fire or flood, to ensure everyone's safety. They also should be able to fill in for absent workers on short notice. Managers often experience the pressures of simultaneously coordinating a wide range of activities. When problems occur, it is the manager's responsibility to resolve them with minimal disruption to customers. The job can be hectic, and dealing with irate customers or uncooperative employees can be stressful.

Managers also may experience the typical minor injuries of other restaurant workers, such as muscle aches, cuts, or burns. They might endure physical discomfort from moving tables or chairs to accommodate large parties, receiving and storing daily supplies from vendors, or making minor repairs to furniture or equipment.

Training, Other Qualifications, and Advancement

Experience in the food services industry, whether as a cook, waiter or waitress, or counter attendant, is the most common training for food service managers. Many restaurant and food service manager positions, particularly self-service and fast-food, are filled by promoting experienced food and beverage preparation and service workers.

Education and training. Experience as a waiter or waitress, cook, or counter help is the most common way to enter the occupation. Executive chefs, in particular, need extensive experience working as chefs. Many food service management companies and national or regional restaurant chains recruit management trainees from 2- and 4-year college hospitality management programs, which require internships and real-life experience to graduate. Some restaurant chains prefer to hire people with degrees in restaurant and institutional food service management, but they often hire graduates with degrees in other fields who have demonstrated experience, interest, and aptitude.

Postsecondary education is preferred for many food service manager positions, but it is not a significant qualification for many others: More than 40 percent of food service managers have a high school diploma or less; less than one-quarter have a bachelor's or graduate degree. However, a postsecondary degree is preferred by higher end full-service restaurants and for many corporate positions, such as managing a regional or national restaurant chain or franchise or overseeing contract food service operations at sports and entertainment complexes, school campuses, and institutional facilities. A college degree also is beneficial for those who want to own or manage their own restaurant.

Almost 1,000 colleges and universities offer 4-year programs in restaurant and hospitality management or institutional food service management; a growing number of university programs offer graduate degrees in hospitality management or similar fields. For those not interested in pursuing a 4-year degree, community and junior colleges, technical institutes, and other institutions offer programs in the field leading to an associate degree or other formal certification.

Both 2- and 4-year programs provide instruction in subjects such as nutrition, sanitation, and food planning and preparation, as well as accounting, business law and management, and computer science. Some programs combine classroom and laboratory study with internships providing on-the-job experience. In addition, many educational institutions offer culinary programs in food preparation. Such training can lead to careers as cooks or chefs and provide a foundation for advancement to executive chef positions.

Many larger food service operations will provide, or offer to pay for, technical training, such as computer or business courses, so that employees can acquire the business skills necessary to read spreadsheets or understand the concepts and practices of running a business. Generally, this requires a long-term commitment on the employee's part to both the employer and to the profession.

Most restaurant chains and food service management companies have rigorous training programs for management positions. Through a combination of classroom and on-the-job training, trainees receive instruction and gain work experience in all aspects of the operation of a restaurant or institutional food service facility. Areas include food preparation, nutrition, sanitation, security, company policies and procedures, personnel management, recordkeeping, and preparation of reports. Training on use of the restaurant's computer system is increasingly important as well. Usually, after 6 months or a year, trainees receive their first permanent assignment as an assistant manager.

Other qualifications. Most employers emphasize personal qualities when hiring managers. Workers who are reliable, show initiative, and have leadership qualities are highly sought after for promotion. Other qualities that managers look for are good problem-solving skills and the ability to concentrate on details. A neat and clean appearance is important, because food service managers must convey self-confidence and show respect in dealing with the public. Because food service management can be physically demanding, good health and stamina are important.

Managers must be good communicators as they deal with customers, employees, and suppliers for most of the day. They must be able to motivate employees to work as a team, to ensure that food and service meet appropriate standards. Additionally, the ability to speak multiple languages is helpful to communicate with staff and patrons.

Certification and advancement. The certified Foodservice Management Professional (FMP) designation is a measure of professional achievement for food service managers, and although not a requirement for employment or necessary for advancement, voluntary certification can provide recognition of professional competence, particularly for managers who acquired their skills largely on the job. The National Restaurant Association Educational Foundation awards the FMP designation to managers who achieve a qualifying score on a written examination, complete a series of courses that cover a range of food service management topics, and meet standards of work experience in the field.

Willingness to relocate often is essential for advancement to positions with greater responsibility. Managers typically advance to larger or more prominent establishments or regional management positions within restaurant chains. Some may open their own food service establishments or franchise operation.

Employment

Food service managers held about 350,000 jobs in 2006. The majority of managers are salaried, but 45 percent are self-employed as owners of independent restaurants or other small food service establishments. Thirty-eight percent of all salaried jobs for food service managers are in full-service restaurants or limited-service eating places, such as fast-food restaurants and cafeterias. Other salaried jobs are in special food services—an industry that includes food service contractors who supply food services at institutional, governmental, commercial, or industrial locations, and educational services, primarily in elementary and secondary schools. A smaller number of salaried jobs are in hotels; amusement, gambling, and recreation industries; nursing care facilities; and hospitals. Jobs are located throughout the country, with large cities and resort areas providing more opportunities for full-service dining positions.

Job Outlook

Food service manager jobs are expected to grow 5 percent, or more slowly than the average for all occupations through 2016. However, job opportunities should be good because, in addition

Projections data from the National Employment Matrix

Occupational Title	SOC Code	Employment, 2006	Projected employment, 2016	Change, 2006-16	
				Number	Percent
Food service managers...	11-9051	350,000	368,000	18,000	5

NOTE: Data in this table are rounded. See the discussion of the employment projections table in the *Handbook* introductory chapter on *Occupational Information Included in the Handbook.*

to job growth, many more openings will arise from the need to replace managers who leave the occupation.

Employment change. Employment of food service managers is expected to grow 5 percent, or more slowly than the average for all occupations, during the 2006-16 decade. New eating and drinking places will open to meet the growing demand for convenience and value from a growing population, generating new employment opportunities for food service managers. Employment growth is projected to vary by industry. Most new jobs will be in full-service restaurants, but they are expected to decline among limited service restaurants. Manager jobs will also increase in special food services, an industry that includes food service contractors that provide food for schools, health care facilities, and other commercial businesses and in nursing and residential care for the elderly. Self-employment of these workers will generate nearly 30 percent of new jobs.

Job prospects. In addition to job openings from employment growth, the need to replace managers who transfer to other occupations or stop working will create good job opportunities. Although practical experience is an integral part of finding a food service management position, applicants with a degree in restaurant, hospitality or institutional food service management will have an edge when competing for jobs at upscale restaurants and for advancement in a restaurant chain or into corporate management.

Earnings

Median annual earnings of salaried food service managers were $43,020 in May 2006. The middle 50 percent earned between $34,210 and $55,100. The lowest 10 percent earned less than $27,400, and the highest 10 percent earned more than $70,810. Median annual earnings in the industries employing the largest numbers of food service managers were as follows:

Traveler accommodation	$48,890
Special food services	48,710
Full-service restaurants	45,650
Elementary and secondary schools	39,650
Limited-service eating places	39,070

In addition to receiving typical benefits, most salaried food service managers are provided free meals and the opportunity for additional training, depending on their length of service. Some food service managers, especially those in full-service restaurants, may earn bonuses depending on sales volume or revenue.

Related Occupations

Food service managers direct the activities of a hospitality-industry business and provide a service to customers. Other managers and supervisors in hospitality-oriented businesses include gaming managers, lodging managers, sales worker supervisors, and first-line supervisors or managers of food preparation and serving workers.

Sources of Additional Information

Information about a career as a food service manager, 2- and 4-year college programs in restaurant and food service manage-

ment, and certification as a Foodservice Management Professional is available from:

➤ National Restaurant Association Educational Foundation, 175 West Jackson Blvd., Suite 1500, Chicago, IL 60604-2702. Internet: **http://www.nraef.org**

Career information about food service managers, as well as a directory of 2- and 4-year colleges that offer courses or programs that prepare persons for food service careers is available from:

➤ National Restaurant Association, 1200 17th St.NW., Washington, DC 20036-3097. Internet: **http://www.restaurant.org**

General information on hospitality careers may be obtained from:

➤ The International Council on Hotel, Restaurant, and Institutional Education, 2810 North Parham Rd., Suite 230, Richmond, VA 23294. Internet: **http://www.chrie.org**

Additional information about job opportunities in food service management may be obtained from local employers and from local offices of State employment services agencies.

Funeral Directors

(O*NET 11-9061.00)

Significant Points

- Job opportunities should be good, particularly for those who also embalm.

- Some mortuary science graduates relocate to get a job.

- Funeral directors are licensed by the State in which they practice.

- Funeral directors need the ability to communicate easily and compassionately and to comfort people in a time of sorrow.

Nature of the Work

Funeral practices and rites vary greatly among cultures and religions. However, funeral practices usually share some common elements—removing the deceased to a mortuary, preparing the remains, performing a ceremony that honors the deceased and addresses the spiritual needs of the family, and carrying out final disposition of the deceased. Funeral directors arrange and direct these tasks for grieving families.

Funeral directors also are called morticians or undertakers. This career may not appeal to everyone, but those who work as funeral directors take great pride in their ability to provide comforting and appropriate services.

Funeral directors arrange the details and handle the logistics of funerals. They interview the family to learn their wishes about the funeral, the clergy or other people who will officiate, and the final disposition of the remains. Sometimes, the deceased leaves detailed instructions for his or her own funeral. Together with the family, funeral directors establish the location, dates, and times of wakes, memorial services, and burials.

They arrange for a hearse to carry the body to the funeral home or mortuary. They also comfort the family and friends of the deceased.

Funeral directors prepare obituary notices and have them placed in newspapers, arrange for pallbearers and clergy, schedule the opening and closing of a grave with a representative of the cemetery, decorate and prepare the sites of all services, and provide transportation for the deceased, mourners, and flowers between sites. They also direct preparation and shipment of the body for out-of-State burial.

Most funeral directors also are trained, licensed, and practicing embalmers. Embalming is a sanitary, cosmetic, and preservative process through which the body is prepared for interment. If more than 24 hours elapse between death and interment, State laws usually require that the remains be refrigerated or embalmed.

When embalming a body, funeral directors wash the body with germicidal soap and replace the blood with embalming fluid to preserve the tissues. They may reshape and reconstruct bodies using materials such as clay, cotton, plaster of Paris, and wax. They also may apply cosmetics to provide a natural appearance, dress the body, and place it in a casket. Funeral directors maintain records such as embalming reports and itemized lists of clothing or valuables delivered with the body. In large funeral homes, an embalming staff of two or more, plus several apprentices may be employed.

Funeral services may take place in a home, house of worship, funeral home, or at the gravesite or crematory. Some services are not religious, but many are, reflecting the religion of the family. Funeral directors must be familiar with the funeral and burial customs of many faiths, ethnic groups, and fraternal organizations. For example, members of some religions seldom have the deceased embalmed or cremated.

Burial in a casket is the most common method of disposing of remains in this country, although entombment also occurs. Cremation, which is the burning of the body in a special furnace, is increasingly selected because it can be less expensive and is becoming more appealing, in part because memorial services can be held anywhere, and at any time, sometimes months later when all relatives and friends can come together. A funeral service followed by cremation need not be any different from a funeral service followed by a burial. Usually, cremated remains are placed in some type of permanent receptacle, or urn, before being committed to a final resting place. The urn may be buried, placed in an indoor or outdoor mausoleum or columbarium, or interred in a special urn garden that many cemeteries provide for cremated remains.

Funeral directors handle the paperwork involved with the person's death, including submitting papers to State authorities so that a formal death certificate may be issued and copies distributed to the heirs. They may help family members apply for veterans' burial benefits, and they notify the Social Security Administration of the death. Also, funeral directors may apply for the transfer of any pensions, insurance policies, or annuities on behalf of survivors.

Funeral directors also work with those who want to plan their own funerals in advance. This provides peace of mind by en-

Funeral directors explain various details of burial options and arrange funerals.

suring that the client's wishes will be taken care of in a way that is satisfying to the client and to the client's survivors.

Most funeral homes are small, family-run businesses, and many funeral directors are owner-operators or employees with managerial responsibilities. Funeral directors, therefore, are responsible for the success and the profitability of their businesses. Directors keep records of expenses, purchases, and services rendered; prepare and send invoices for services; prepare and submit reports for unemployment insurance; prepare Federal, State, and local tax forms; and prepare itemized bills for customers. Funeral directors increasingly use computers for billing, bookkeeping, and marketing. Some are beginning to use the Internet to communicate with clients who are planning their funerals in advance or to assist them by developing electronic obituaries and guest books. Directors strive to foster a cooperative spirit and friendly attitude among employees and a compassionate demeanor toward the families. Increasingly, funeral directors also are helping individuals adapt to changes in their lives following a death through aftercare services and support groups.

Most funeral homes have a chapel, one or more viewing rooms, a casket-selection room, and a preparation room. Many also have a crematory on the premises. Equipment may include a hearse, a flower car, limousines, and sometimes an ambulance. Funeral homes usually stock a selection of caskets and urns for families to purchase or rent.

Work environment. Funeral directors occasionally come into contact with bodies that had contagious diseases, but the possibility of infection is remote if health regulations are followed.

Funeral directors often work long, irregular hours, and the occupation can be highly stressful. Many are on call at all hours because they may be needed to remove remains in the middle of the night. Shift work sometimes is necessary because funeral home hours include evenings and weekends. In smaller funeral homes, working hours vary, but in larger establishments, employees usually work 8 hours a day, 5 or 6 days a week.

Training, Other Qualifications, and Advancement

Funeral directors are licensed in all States. State licensing laws vary, but most require applicants to be 21 years old, have 2 years of formal education, serve a 1-year apprenticeship, and pass an examination.

Education and training. College programs in mortuary science usually last from 2 to 4 years. The American Board of Funeral Service Education accredits about 50 mortuary science programs. A few community and junior colleges offer 2-year programs, and a few colleges and universities offer both 2-year and 4-year programs. Mortuary science programs include courses in anatomy, physiology, pathology, embalming techniques, restorative art, business management, accounting and use of computers in funeral home management, and client services. They also include courses in the social sciences and in legal, ethical, and regulatory subjects such as psychology, grief counseling, oral and written communication, funeral service law, business law, and ethics.

Many State and national associations offer continuing education programs designed for licensed funeral directors. These programs address issues in communications, counseling, and management. More than 30 States have requirements that funeral directors receive continuing education credits to maintain their licenses.

Apprenticeships must be completed under the direction of an experienced and licensed funeral director. Some States require apprenticeships. Depending on State regulations, apprenticeships last from 1 to 3 years and may be served before, during, or after mortuary school. Apprenticeships provide practical experience in all facets of the funeral service, from embalming to transporting remains.

High school students can start preparing for a career as a funeral director by taking courses in biology and chemistry and participating in public speaking or debate clubs. Part-time or summer jobs in funeral homes also provide good experience. These jobs consist mostly of maintenance and cleanup tasks, such as washing and polishing limousines and hearses, but they can help students become familiar with the operation of funeral homes.

Licensure. All States require funeral directors to be licensed. Licensing laws vary by State, but most require applicants to be 21 years old, have 2 years of formal education that includes studies in mortuary science, serve a 1-year apprenticeship, and pass a qualifying examination. After becoming licensed, new funeral directors may join the staff of a funeral home.

Some States require all funeral directors to be licensed in embalming. Others have separate licenses for directors and embalmers, but in those States funeral directors who embalm need to be licensed in embalming, and most workers obtain both licenses.

State board licensing examinations vary, but they usually consist of written and oral parts and include a demonstration of practical skills. People who want to work in another State may have to pass the examination for that State; however, some States have reciprocity arrangements and will grant licenses to funeral directors from another State without further examination. People interested in a career as a funeral director should contact their State licensing board for specific requirements.

Other qualifications. Funeral directors need composure, tact, and the ability to communicate easily and compassionately with the public. Funeral directors also should have the desire and ability to comfort people in a time of sorrow.

To show proper respect and consideration for the families and the dead, funeral directors must dress appropriately. The professions usually require short, neat haircuts and trim beards, if any, for men. Suits and ties for men and dresses for women are customary.

Advancement. Advancement opportunities generally are best in larger funeral homes. Funeral directors may earn promotions to higher paying positions such as branch manager or general manager. Some directors eventually acquire enough money and experience to establish their own funeral home businesses.

Employment

Funeral directors held about 29,000 jobs in 2006. About 20 percent were self-employed. Nearly all worked in the death care services industry.

Job Outlook

Job opportunities are expected to be good, particularly for those who also embalm. Some mortuary science graduates relocate to get a job.

Employment change. Employment of funeral directors is expected to increase by 12 percent during the 2006-16 decade, about as fast as the average for all occupations. Projected job growth reflects growth in the death care services industry, where funeral directors are employed.

Job prospects. In addition to employment growth, the need to replace funeral directors who retire or leave the occupation for other reasons will provide a number of job opportunities. Funeral directors are older, on average, than workers in most other occupations and are expected to retire in greater numbers over the coming decade. In addition, some funeral directors leave the profession because of the long and irregular hours. Some mortuary science graduates relocate to get a job.

Earnings

Median annual earnings for wage and salary funeral directors were $49,620 in May 2006. The middle 50 percent earned between $37,200 and $65,260. The lowest 10 percent earned less than $28,410 and the top 10 percent earned more than $91,800.

Salaries of funeral directors depend on the number of years of experience in funeral service, the number of services performed, the number of facilities operated, the area of the coun-

Projections data from the National Employment Matrix

Occupational Title	SOC Code	Employment, 2006	Projected employment, 2016	Change, 2006-16	
				Number	Percent
Funeral directors	11-9061	29,000	32,000	3,600	12

NOTE: Data in this table are rounded. See the discussion of the employment projections table in the *Handbook* introductory chapter on *Occupational Information Included in the Handbook.*

try, and the director's level of formal education. Funeral directors in large cities usually earn more than their counterparts in small towns and rural areas.

Related Occupations

The job of a funeral director requires tact, discretion, and compassion when dealing with grieving people. Others who need these qualities include social workers, psychologists, physicians and surgeons, and other health practitioners involved in diagnosis and treatment.

Sources of Additional Information

For a list of accredited mortuary science programs and information on the funeral service profession, write to:

➤ The National Funeral Directors Association, 13625 Bishop's Dr., Brookfield, WI 53005. Internet: **http://www.nfda.org**

For information about college programs in mortuary science, scholarships, and funeral service as a career, contact:

➤ The American Board of Funeral Service Education, 3432 Ashland Ave., Suite U, St.Joseph, MO 64506.

Internet: **http://www.abfse.org**

For information on specific State licensing requirements, contact the State's licensing board.

For more information about funeral directors and their work, see the *Occupational Outlook Quarterly* article, "Jobs in weddings and funerals: Working with the betrothed and the bereaved," available in many libraries and career centers and online at:

http://www.bls.gov/opub/ooq/2006/winter/art03.pdf

Human Resources, Training, and Labor Relations Managers and Specialists

(O*NET 11-3041.00, 11-3042.00, 11-3049.99, 13-1071.00, 13-1071.01, 13-1071.02, 13-1072.00, 13-1073.00, 13-1079.99)

Significant Points

- The educational backgrounds of these workers vary considerably, reflecting the diversity of duties and levels of responsibility.

- Certification and previous experience are assets for most specialties, and are essential for more advanced positions, including managers, arbitrators, and mediators.

- College graduates who have earned certification should have the best job opportunities.

Nature of the Work

Every organization wants to attract the most qualified employees and match them to jobs for which they are best suited. However, many enterprises are too large to permit close contact between top management and employees. Human resources, training, and labor relations managers and specialists provide this connection. In the past, these workers performed the administrative function of an organization, such as handling employee benefits questions or recruiting, interviewing, and hiring new staff in accordance with policies established by top management. Today's human resources workers manage these tasks, but, increasingly, they also consult with top executives regarding strategic planning. They have moved from behind-the-scenes staff work to leading the company in suggesting and changing policies.

In an effort to enhance morale and productivity, limit job turnover, and help organizations increase performance and improve business results, these workers also help their firms effectively use employee skills, provide training and development opportunities to improve those skills, and increase employees' satisfaction with their jobs and working conditions. Although some jobs in the human resources field require only limited contact with people outside the human resources office, dealing with people is an important part of the job.

There are many types of human resources, training, and labor relations managers and specialists. In a small organization, a *human resources generalist* may handle all aspects of human resources work, and thus require an extensive range of knowledge. The responsibilities of human resources generalists can vary widely, depending on their employer's needs.

In a large corporation, the *director of human resources* may supervise several departments, each headed by an experienced manager who most likely specializes in one human resources activity, such as employment and placement; compensation, and benefits; training and development; or labor relations. The director may report to a top human resources executive. (Executives are included in the *Handbook* statement on top executives.)

Employment and placement. Employment and placement managers supervise the hiring and separation of employees. They also supervise employment, recruitment, and placement specialists, including recruitment specialists and employment interviewers. Employment, recruitment, and placement specialists recruit and place workers.

Recruiters maintain contacts within the community and may travel considerably, often to college campuses, to search for promising job applicants. Recruiters screen, interview, and occasionally test applicants. They also may check references and extend job offers. These workers must be thoroughly familiar with the organization and its human resources policies in order to discuss wages, working conditions, and promotional opportunities with prospective employees. They also must stay informed about equal employment opportunity (EEO) and affirmative action guidelines and laws, such as the Americans with Disabilities Act.

Employment interviewers—whose many job titles include *human resources consultants*, *human resources development specialists*, and *human resources coordinators*—help to match employers with qualified jobseekers. Similarly, employer relations representatives, who usually work in government agencies, maintain working relationships with local employers and promote the use of public employment programs and services.

Compensation, benefits, and job analysis. Compensation, benefits, and job analysis specialists conduct compensation

College graduates with certification should have the best opportunities for jobs as human resources, training, and labor relations managers and specialists.

programs for employers and may specialize in specific areas such as pensions or position classifications. For example, *job analysts*, occasionally called *position classifiers*, collect and examine detailed information about job duties in order to prepare job descriptions. These descriptions explain the duties, training, and skills that each job requires. Whenever a large organization introduces a new job or reviews existing jobs, it calls upon the expert knowledge of the job analyst.

Occupational analysts conduct research, usually in large firms. They are concerned with occupational classification systems and study the effects of industry and occupational trends on worker relationships. They may serve as technical liaison between the firm and other firms, government, and labor unions.

Establishing and maintaining a firm's pay system is the principal job of the *compensation manager*. Assisted by staff specialists, compensation managers devise ways to ensure fair and equitable pay rates. They may conduct surveys to see how their firm's rates compare with others, and they ensure that the firm's pay scale complies with changing laws and regulations. In addition, compensation managers often manage their firm's performance evaluation system, and they may design reward systems such as pay-for-performance plans.

Employee benefits managers and specialists manage the company's employee benefits program, notably its health insurance and pension plans. Expertise in designing and administering benefits programs continues to take on importance as employer-provided benefits account for a growing proportion of overall compensation costs, and as benefit plans increase in number and complexity. For example, pension benefits might include a 401K or thrift savings, profit-sharing, and stock ownership plans; health benefits might include long-term catastrophic illness insurance and dental insurance. Familiarity with health benefits is a top priority for employee benefits managers and specialists, as more firms struggle to cope with the rising cost of health care for employees and retirees. In addition to health insurance and pension coverage, some firms offer employees life and accidental death and dismemberment insurance, disability insurance, and relatively new benefits designed to meet the needs of a changing workforce, such as pa-

rental leave, child and elder care, long-term nursing home care insurance, employee assistance and wellness programs, and flexible benefits plans. Benefits managers must keep abreast of changing Federal and State regulations and legislation that may affect employee benefits.

Employee assistance plan managers, also called *employee welfare managers*, are responsible for a wide array of programs. These include occupational safety and health standards and practices; health promotion and physical fitness, medical examinations, and minor health treatment, such as first aid; plant security; publications; food service and recreation activities; carpooling and transportation programs, such as transit subsidies; employee suggestion systems; child care and elder care; and counseling services. Child care and elder care are increasingly significant because of growth in the number of dual-income households and the elderly population. Counseling may help employees deal with emotional disorders, alcoholism, or marital, family, consumer, legal, and financial problems. Some employers offer career counseling as well. In large firms, certain programs, such as those dealing with security and safety, may be in separate departments headed by other managers.

Training and development. *Training and development managers and specialists* conduct and supervise training and development programs for employees. Increasingly, management recognizes that training offers a way of developing skills, enhancing productivity and quality of work, and building worker loyalty to the firm, and most importantly, increasing individual and organizational performance to achieve business results. Training is widely accepted as an employee benefit and a method of improving employee morale, and enhancing employee skills has become a business imperative. Increasingly, managers and leaders realize that the key to business growth and success is through developing the skills and knowledge of its workforce.

Other factors involved in determining whether training is needed include the complexity of the work environment, the rapid pace of organizational and technological change, and the growing number of jobs in fields that constantly generate new knowledge, and thus, require new skills. In addition, advances in learning theory have provided insights into how adults learn, and how training can be organized most effectively for them.

Training managers provide worker training either in the classroom or onsite. This includes setting up teaching materials prior to the class, involving the class, and issuing completion certificates at the end of the class. They have the responsibility for the entire learning process, and its environment, to ensure that the course meets its objectives and is measured and evaluated to understand how learning impacts business results.

Training specialists plan, organize, and direct a wide range of training activities. Trainers respond to corporate and worker service requests. They consult with onsite supervisors regarding available performance improvement services and conduct orientation sessions and arrange on-the-job training for new employees. They help all employees maintain and improve their job skills, and possibly prepare for jobs requiring greater skill. They help supervisors improve their interpersonal skills in order to deal effectively with employees. They may set up individualized training plans to strengthen an employee's existing skills or teach new ones. Training specialists in some companies set up leadership or executive development programs among employees in lower level positions. These programs are designed to develop leaders, or "groom" them, to replace those leaving the organization and as part of a succession plan. Trainers also lead programs to assist employees with job transitions as a result of mergers and acquisitions, as well as technological changes. In government-supported training programs, training specialists function as case managers. They first assess the training needs of clients and then guide them through the most appropriate training method. After training, clients may either be referred to employer relations representatives or receive job placement assistance.

Planning and program development is an essential part of the training specialist's job. In order to identify and assess training needs within the firm, trainers may confer with managers and supervisors or conduct surveys. They also evaluate training effectiveness to ensure that the training employees receive helps the organization meet its strategic business goals and achieve results.

Depending on the size, goals, and nature of the organization, trainers may differ considerably in their responsibilities and in the methods they use. Training methods include on-the-job training; operating schools that duplicate shop conditions for trainees prior to putting them on the shop floor; apprenticeship training; classroom training; and electronic learning, which may involve interactive Internet-based training, multimedia programs, distance learning, satellite training, other computer-aided instructional technologies, videos, simulators, conferences, and workshops.

Employee relations. An organization's *director of industrial relations* forms labor policy, oversees industrial labor relations, negotiates collective bargaining agreements, and coordinates grievance procedures to handle complaints resulting from management disputes with unionized employees. The director of industrial relations also advises and collaborates with the director of human resources, other managers, and members of their staff, because all aspects of human resources policy—such as wages, benefits, pensions, and work practices—may be involved in drawing up a new or revised union contract.

Labor relations managers and their staffs implement industrial labor relations programs. Labor relations specialists prepare information for management to use during collective bargaining agreement negotiations, a process that requires the specialist to be familiar with economic and wage data and to have extensive knowledge of labor law and collective bargaining trends. The labor relations staff interprets and administers the contract with respect to grievances, wages and salaries, employee welfare, health care, pensions, union and management practices, and other contractual stipulations. As union membership continues to decline in most industries, industrial relations personnel are working more often with employees who are not members of a labor union.

Dispute resolution—attaining tacit or contractual agreements—has become increasingly significant as parties to a dispute attempt to avoid costly litigation, strikes, or other disruptions. Dispute resolution also has become more complex, involving employees, management, unions, other firms, and government agencies. Specialists involved in dispute resolution must be highly knowledgeable and experienced, and often report to the director of industrial relations. *Conciliators*, or *mediators*, advise and counsel labor and management to prevent and, when necessary, resolve disputes over labor agreements or other labor relations issues. *Arbitrators*, occasionally called umpires or referees, decide disputes that bind both labor and management to specific terms and conditions of labor contracts. Labor relations specialists who work for unions perform many of the same functions on behalf of the union and its members.

EEO officers, representatives, or *affirmative action coordinators* handle EEO matters in large organizations. They investigate and resolve EEO grievances, examine corporate practices for possible violations, and compile and submit EEO statistical reports.

Other emerging specialties in human resources include *international human resources managers*, who handle human resources issues related to a company's foreign operations; and *human resources information system specialists*, who develop and apply computer programs to process human resources information, match job seekers with job openings, and handle other human resources matters.

Work environment. Human resources work usually takes place in clean, pleasant, and comfortable office settings. Arbitrators and mediators may work out of their homes.

Although most human resources, training, and labor relations managers and specialists work in the office, some travel extensively. For example, recruiters regularly attend professional meetings and visit college campuses to interview prospective employees; arbitrators and mediators often must travel to the site chosen for negotiations.

Many human resources, training, and labor relations managers and specialists work a standard 35- to 40-hour week. However, longer hours might be necessary for some workers—for example, labor relations managers and specialists, arbitrators, and mediators—when contract agreements are being prepared and negotiated.

Training, Other Qualifications, and Advancement

The educational backgrounds of human resources, training, and labor relations managers and specialists vary considerably, reflecting the diversity of duties and levels of responsibility. In filling entry-level jobs, many employers seek college graduates who have majored in human resources, human resources administration, or industrial and labor relations. Other employers look for college graduates with a technical or business background or a well-rounded liberal arts education.

Education and training. Many colleges and universities have programs leading to a degree in personnel, human resources, or labor relations. Some offer degree programs in human resources administration or human resources management, training and development, or compensation and benefits. Depending on the school, courses leading to a career in human resources management may be found in departments of business administration, education, instructional technology, organizational development, human services, communication, or public administration, or within a separate human resources institution or department.

Because an interdisciplinary background is appropriate in this field, a combination of courses in the social sciences, business, and behavioral sciences is useful. Some jobs may require a more technical or specialized background in engineering, science, finance, or law, for example. Most prospective human resources specialists should take courses in compensation, recruitment, training and development, and performance appraisal, as well as courses in principles of management, organizational structure, and industrial psychology. Other relevant courses include business administration, public administration, psychology, sociology, political science, economics, and statistics. Courses in labor law, collective bargaining, labor economics, labor history, and industrial psychology also provide a valuable background for the prospective labor relations specialist. As in many other fields, knowledge of computers and information systems also is useful.

An advanced degree is increasingly important for some jobs. Many labor relations jobs require graduate study in industrial or labor relations. A strong background in industrial relations and law is highly desirable for contract negotiators, mediators, and arbitrators; in fact, many people in these specialties are lawyers. A background in law also is desirable for employee benefits managers and others who must interpret the growing number of laws and regulations. A master's degree in human resources, labor relations, or in business administration with a concentration in human resources management is highly recommended for those seeking general and top management positions.

The duties given to entry-level workers will vary, depending on whether the new workers have a degree in human resource management, have completed an internship, or have some other type of human resources-related experience. Entry-level employees commonly learn the profession by performing administrative duties—helping to enter data into computer systems, compiling employee handbooks, researching information for a supervisor, or answering the phone and handling routine questions. Entry-level workers often enter formal or on-the-job training programs in which they learn how to classify jobs, interview applicants, or administer employee benefits. They then are assigned to specific areas in the human resources department to gain experience. Later, they may advance to a managerial position, supervising a major element of the human resources program—compensation or training, for example.

Other qualifications. Previous experience is an asset for many specialties in the human resources field, and is essential for more advanced positions, including managers, arbitrators, and mediators. Many employers prefer entry-level workers who have gained some experience through an internship or work-study program while in school. Human resources administration and human resources development require the ability to work with individuals as well as a commitment to

organizational goals. This field also demands other skills that people may develop elsewhere—using computers, selling, teaching, supervising, and volunteering, among others. The field offers clerical workers opportunities for advancement to professional positions. Responsible positions occasionally are filled by experienced individuals from other fields, including business, government, education, social services administration, and the military.

The human resources field demands a range of personal qualities and skills. Human resources, training, and labor relations managers and specialists must speak and write effectively. The growing diversity of the workforce requires that they work with or supervise people with various cultural backgrounds, levels of education, and experience. They must be able to cope with conflicting points of view, function under pressure, and demonstrate discretion, integrity, fair-mindedness, and a persuasive, congenial personality.

Certification and advancement. Most organizations specializing in human resources offer classes intended to enhance the skills of their members. Some organizations offer certification programs, which are signs of competence and credibility and can enhance one's advancement opportunities. For example, the International Foundation of Employee Benefit Plans confers a designation in three distinct areas of specialization—group benefit, retirement, and compensation—to persons who complete a series of college-level courses and pass exams. Candidates can earn a designation in each of the specialty tracks and, simultaneously, receive credit toward becoming a Certified Employee Benefits Specialist (CEBP). The American Society for Training and Development (ASTD) Certification Institute offers professional certification in the learning and performance field. Addressing nine areas of expertise, it requires passing a knowledge-based exam and successful work experience. In addition, ASTD offers 16 short-term certificate and workshop programs covering a broad range of professional training and development topics. The Society for Human Resource Management offers two levels of certification, including the Professional in Human Resources (PHR) and the Senior Professional in Human Resources (SPHR). Additionally, the organization offers the Global Professional in Human Resources for those with international and cross-border responsibilities and the California Certification in Human Resources for those who plan to work in the State and are unfamiliar with California's labor and human resource laws. All designations require experience and a passing score on a comprehensive exam. World at Work Society of Certified Professionals offers four levels of designations in the areas of compensation, benefits, work life, and total rewards management practices. Through the Society, candidates can obtain the designation of Certified Compensation Professional (CCP), Certified Benefits Professional (CBP), Global Remuneration Professional (GRP), and Work-Life Certified Professional (WLCP).

Exceptional human resources workers may be promoted to director of human resources or industrial relations, which can eventually lead to a top managerial or executive position. Others may join a consulting or outsourcing firm or open their own business. A Ph.D. is an asset for teaching, writing, or consulting work.

Employment

Human resources, training, and labor relations managers and specialists held about 868,000 jobs in 2006. The following tabulation shows the distribution of jobs by occupational specialty:

Training and development specialists 210,000
Employment, recruitment, and placement specialists 197,000
Human resources managers 136,000
Compensation, benefits, and job analysis specialists 110,000
Human resources, training, and labor
   relations specialists, all other..214,000

Human resources, training, and labor relations managers and specialists were employed in virtually every industry. About 17,000 managers and specialists were self-employed, working as consultants to public and private employers.

The private sector accounted for nearly 9 out of 10 salaried jobs, including 13 percent in administrative and support services; 10 percent in professional, scientific, and technical services; 9 percent in health care and social assistance; 9 percent in finance and insurance firms; and 7 percent in manufacturing.

Government employed 13 percent of human resources managers and specialists. They handled the recruitment, interviewing, job classification, training, salary administration, benefits, employee relations, and other matters related to the Nation's public employees.

Job Outlook

Employment of human resources, training, and labor relations managers and specialists is expected to grow faster than the average for all occupations. College graduates who have earned certification should have the best job opportunities.

Employment change. Overall employment is projected to grow by 17 percent between 2006 and 2016, faster than the average for all occupations. Legislation and court rulings setting standards in various areas—occupational safety and health, equal employment opportunity, wages, health care, pensions, and family leave, among others—will increase demand for human resources, training, and labor relations experts. Rising health care costs should continue to spur demand for specialists to develop creative compensation and benefits packages that firms can offer prospective employees.

Employment of labor relations staff, including arbitrators and mediators, should grow as firms become more involved in labor relations and attempt to resolve potentially costly labor-management disputes out of court. Additional job growth may stem from increasing demand for specialists in international human resources management and human resources information systems.

Job growth could be limited by the widespread use of computerized human resources information systems that make workers more productive. Like other workers, employment of human resources, training, and labor relations managers and specialists, particularly in larger firms, may be adversely affected by corporate downsizing, restructuring, and mergers and acquisitions.

Demand may be particularly strong for certain specialists. For example, employers are expected to devote greater resources to job-specific training programs in response to the increasing complexity of many jobs and technological advances that can leave employees with obsolete skills. Additionally, as highly trained and skilled baby boomers retire, there should be strong demand for training and development specialists to impart needed skills to their replacements. In addition, increasing efforts throughout industry to recruit and retain quality employees should create many jobs for employment, recruitment, and placement specialists.

Among industries, firms involved in management, consulting, and employment services should offer many job opportunities, as businesses increasingly contract out human resources functions or hire human resources specialists on a temporary basis in order to deal with the increasing cost and complexity of training and development programs. Demand for specialists also should increase in outsourcing firms that develop and administer complex employee benefits and compensation packages for other organizations.

Job prospects. College graduates who have earned certification should have the best job opportunities. Graduates with a bachelor's degree in human resources, human resources administration, or industrial and labor relations should be in demand; those with a technical or business background or a well-rounded liberal arts education also should find opportunities. Demand for human resources, training, and labor relations managers and specialists is governed by the staffing needs of the firms for which

Projections data from the National Employment Matrix

Occupational Title	SOC Code	Employment, 2006	Projected employment, 2016	Change, 2006-16	
				Number	Percent
Human resources, training, and labor relations managers and specialists	—	868,000	1,015,000	147,000	17
Compensation and benefits managers..	11-3041	49,000	55,000	5,900	12
Training and development managers	11-3042	29,000	33,000	4,500	16
Human resources managers, all other...	11-3049	58,000	65,000	6,600	11
Employment, recruitment, and placement specialists..................	13-1071	197,000	233,000	36,000	18
Compensation, benefits, and job analysis specialists...................	13-1072	110,000	130,000	20,000	18
Training and development specialists	13-1073	210,000	249,000	38,000	18
Human resources, training, and labor relations specialists, all other...	13-1079	214,000	250,000	35,000	16

NOTE: Data in this table are rounded. See the discussion of the employment projections table in the *Handbook* introductory chapter on *Occupational Information Included in the Handbook.*

they work. A rapidly expanding business is likely to hire additional human resources workers—either as permanent employees or consultants—while a business that has experienced a merger or a reduction in its workforce will require fewer of these workers. Also, as human resources management becomes increasingly important to the success of an organization, some small and medium-size businesses that do not have a human resources department may assign employees various human resources duties together with other unrelated responsibilities.

In addition to human resources management and specialist jobs created over the 2006-2016 projection period, many job openings will arise from the need to replace workers who transfer to other occupations, retire, or leave the labor force for other reasons.

Earnings

Annual salary rates for human resources workers vary according to occupation, level of experience, training, location, and firm size.

Median annual earnings of compensation and benefits managers were $74,750 in May 2006. The middle 50 percent earned between $55,370 and $99,690. The lowest 10 percent earned less than $42,750, and the highest 10 percent earned more than $132,820. In 2006, median annual earnings were $85,330 in the management of companies and enterprises industry.

Median annual earnings of training and development managers were $80,250 in May 2006. The middle 50 percent earned between $58,770 and $107,450. The lowest 10 percent earned less than $43,530, and the highest 10 percent earned more than $141,140.

Median annual earnings of human resources managers, all other were $88,510 in May 2006. The middle 50 percent earned between $67,710 and $114,860. The lowest 10 percent earned less than $51,810, and the highest 10 percent earned more than $145,600. In May 2006, median annual earnings were $98,400 in the management of companies and enterprises industry.

Median annual earnings of employment, recruitment, and placement specialists were $42,420 in May 2006. The middle 50 percent earned between $32,770 and $58,320. The lowest 10 percent earned less than $26,590, and the highest 10 percent earned more than $81,680. Median annual earnings in the industries employing the largest numbers of employment, recruitment, and placement specialists were:

Management, scientific, and technical consulting services	$53,060
Management of companies and enterprises	48,360
Local government	40,660
Employment services	39,720
State government	36,320

Median annual earnings of compensation, benefits, and job analysis specialists were $50,230 in May 2006. The middle 50 percent earned between $39,400 and $63,800. The lowest 10 percent earned less than $32,180, and the highest 10 percent earned more than $80,150. Median annual earnings in the industries employing the largest numbers of compensation, benefits, and job analysis specialists were:

Local government	$53,440
Management of companies and enterprises	52,960
Insurance carriers	50,510
Agencies, brokerages, and other insurance related activities	49,100
State government	46,100

Median annual earnings of training and development specialists were $47,830 in May 2006. The middle 50 percent earned between $35,980 and $63,200. The lowest 10 percent earned less than $27,450, and the highest 10 percent earned more than $80,630. Median annual earnings in the industries employing the largest numbers of training and development specialists were:

Computer systems design and related services	$60,430
Management of companies and enterprises	50,850
Insurance carriers	50,060
State government	49,040
Local government	47,990

The average salary for human resources managers employed by the Federal Government was $76,503 in 2007; for labor-management relations examiners, $94,927; and for manpower development specialists, $86,071. Salaries were slightly higher in areas where the prevailing local pay level was higher. There are no formal entry-level requirements for managerial positions. Applicants must possess a suitable combination of educational attainment, experience, and record of accomplishment.

According to a July 2007 salary survey conducted by the National Association of Colleges and Employers, bachelor's degree candidates majoring in human resources, including labor and industrial relations, received starting offers averaging $41,680 a year.

Related Occupations

All human resources occupations are closely related. Other workers with skills and expertise in interpersonal relations include counselors, education administrators, public relations specialists, lawyers, psychologists, social and human service assistants, and social workers.

Sources of Additional Information

For information about human resource management careers and certification, contact:
➤ Society for Human Resource Management, 1800 Duke St., Alexandria, VA 22314. Internet: **http://www.shrm.org**

For information about careers in employee training and development and certification, contact:
➤ American Society for Training and Development, 1640 King St., Box 1443, Alexandria, VA 22313-2043.
Internet: **http://www.astd.org**

For information about careers and certification in employee compensation and benefits, contact:
➤ International Foundation of Employee Benefit Plans, 18700 W. Bluemound Rd., P.O. Box 69, Brookfield, WI 53008-0069.
Internet: **http://www.ifebp.org**
➤ World at Work, 14040 N. Northsight Blvd., Scottsdale, AZ 85260. Internet: **http://www.worldatwork.org**

Industrial Production Managers

(O*NET 11-3051.00)

Significant Points

- Industrial production managers coordinate all the people and equipment involved in the manufacturing process.

- Most employers prefer to hire workers with a college degree; experience in some part of production operations is also usually required.

- Employment is expected to decline as overall employment in manufacturing declines.

Nature of the Work

Industrial production managers plan, direct, and coordinate the production activities required to produce the vast array of goods manufactured every year in the United States. They make sure that production meets output and quality goals while remaining within budget. Depending on the size of the manufacturing plant, industrial production managers may oversee the entire plant or just one area.

Industrial production managers devise methods to use the plant's personnel and capital resources to best meet production goals. They may determine which machines will be used, whether new machines need to be purchased, whether overtime or extra shifts are necessary, and what the sequence of production will be. They monitor the production run to make sure that it stays on schedule and correct any problems that may arise.

Part of an industrial production manager's job is to come up with ways to make the production process more efficient. Traditional factory methods, such as mass assembly lines, have given way to "lean" production techniques, which give managers more flexibility. While in a traditional assembly line, each worker was responsible for only a small portion of the assembly, repeating that task on every product, lean production employs teams to build and assemble products in stations or cells, so rather than specializing in a specific task, workers are capable of performing all jobs within a team. Without the constraints of the traditional assembly line, industrial production managers can more easily change production levels and staffing on different product lines to minimize inventory levels and more quickly react to changing customer demands.

Industrial production managers also monitor product standards and implement quality control programs. They make sure the finished product meets a certain level of quality, and if not, they try to find out what the problem is and find a solution. While traditional quality control programs reacted only to problems that reached a certain significant level, newer management techniques and programs, such as ISO 9000, Total Quality Management (TQM), or Six Sigma, emphasize continuous quality improvement. If the problem relates to the quality of work performed in the plant, the manager may implement better training programs or reorganize the manufacturing process, often based upon the suggestions of employee teams. If the

Industrial production managers monitor the quantity and quality of goods produced.

cause is substandard materials or parts from outside suppliers, the industrial production manager may work with the supplier to improve their quality.

Industrial production managers work closely with the other managers of the firm to implement the company's policies and goals. They also must work with the financial departments in order to come up with a budget and spending plan. They work the closest with the heads of sales, procurement, and logistics. Sales managers relay the client's needs and the price the client is willing to pay to the production department, which must then fulfill the order. The logistics or distribution department handles the delivery of the goods, which often needs to be coordinated with the production department. The procurement department orders the supplies that the production department needs to make its products. It is also responsible for making sure that the inventories of supplies are maintained at proper levels so production proceeds without interruption. A breakdown in communications between the production manager and the procurement department can cause slowdowns and a failure to meet production schedules. Just-in-time production techniques have reduced inventory levels, making constant communication among managers, suppliers, and procurement departments even more important.

Work environment. Most industrial production managers divide their time between production areas and their offices. While in the production area, they must follow established health and safety practices and wear the required protective clothing and equipment. The time in the office, which often is located near production areas, usually is spent meeting with subordinates or other department managers, analyzing production data, and writing and reviewing reports.

Many industrial production managers work extended hours, especially when production deadlines must be met. In 2006, about a third of all workers worked more than 50 hours a week, on average. In facilities that operate around-the-clock, managers often work late shifts and may be called at any hour to deal with emergencies. This could mean going to the plant to resolve the problem, regardless of the hour, and staying until the situation is under control. Dealing with production workers as well as superiors when working under the pressure of production deadlines or emergency situations can be stressful.

Corporate restructuring has eliminated levels of management and support staff, thus shifting more responsibilities to production managers and compounding this stress.

Training, Other Qualifications, and Advancement

Because of the diversity of manufacturing operations and job requirements, there is no standard preparation for this occupation. Most employers prefer to hire workers with a college degree. Experience in some part of production operations is also usually required, although some college graduates are hired directly into management positions.

Education and training. Many industrial production managers have a college degree in business administration, management, industrial technology, or industrial engineering. However, although employers may prefer candidates with a business or engineering background, some companies will hire well-rounded liberal arts graduates who are willing to spend time in a production-related job.

Some industrial production managers enter the occupation after working their way up through the ranks, starting as production workers and then advancing to supervisory positions before being selected for management. These workers already have an intimate knowledge of the production process and the firm's organization. To be selected for promotion, workers can expand their skills by obtaining a college degree, demonstrating leadership qualities, or by taking company-sponsored courses to learn the additional skills needed for management.

As production operations become more sophisticated, an increasing number of employers look for candidates with graduate degrees in industrial management or business administration, particularly for positions at larger plants where managers have more oversight responsibilities. Combined with an undergraduate degree in engineering, either of these graduate degrees is considered particularly good preparation. Managers who do not have graduate degrees often take courses in decision sciences, which provide them with techniques and statistical formulas that can be used to maximize efficiency and improve quality. Those who enter the field directly from college or graduate school often are unfamiliar with the firm's production process. As a result, they may spend their first few months in the company's training program. These programs familiarize trainees with the production process, company policies, and the requirements of the job. In larger companies, they also may include assignments to other departments, such as purchasing and accounting. A number of companies hire college graduates as first-line supervisors and later promote them to management positions.

Other qualifications. Companies are placing greater importance on a candidate's interpersonal skills. Because the job requires the ability to compromise, persuade, and negotiate, successful production managers must be well-rounded and have excellent communication skills. Strong computer skills are also essential.

Industrial production managers must continually keep informed of new production technologies and management practices. Many belong to professional organizations and attend trade shows or industry conferences where new equipment is displayed and new production methods and technologies discussed.

Certification and advancement. Some industrial production managers earn certifications that show their competency in various quality and management systems. Although certification is not required for industrial production manager jobs, it may improve job prospects.

One credential, Certified in Production and Inventory Management (CPIM), is offered by the Association for Operations Management and requires passing a series of exams that cover supply chain management, resource planning, scheduling, production operations, and strategic planning. Certification holders must complete a set number of professional development activities every 3 years to maintain their certification.

The American Society for Quality offers the Certified Manager of Quality/Organizational Excellence (CMQ/OE) credential. This certification is open to managers who pass an exam and who have at least 10 years of experience or education, 5 of which must be in a decision-making position. It is intended for managers who lead process improvement initiatives. To maintain certification, workers must complete a set number of professional development units every 3 years.

Industrial production managers with a proven record of superior performance may advance to plant manager or vice president for manufacturing. Others transfer to jobs with more responsibilities at larger firms. Opportunities also exist for managers to become consultants. (For more information, see the statement on management analysts elsewhere in the *Handbook*.)

Employment

Industrial production managers held about 157,000 jobs in 2006. About 4 out of 5 are employed in manufacturing industries, including the fabricated metal product, transportation equipment, and computer and electronic product manufacturing sectors. Production managers work in all parts of the country, but jobs are most plentiful in areas where manufacturing is concentrated.

Job Outlook

Employment of industrial production managers is expected to decline. Applicants with experience in production occupations along with a college degree in industrial engineering, management, or a related field will enjoy the best job prospects.

Employment change. Employment of industrial production managers is expected to decline moderately by 6 percent over

Projections data from the National Employment Matrix

Occupational Title	SOC Code	Employment, 2006	Projected employment, 2016	Change, 2006-16	
				Number	Percent
Industrial production managers..	11-3051	157,000	148,000	-9,200	-6

NOTE: Data in this table are rounded. See the discussion of the employment projections table in the *Handbook* introductory chapter on *Occupational Information Included in the Handbook.*

the 2006-2016 decade, mirroring the overall decline in manufacturing employment. Some declines will result from manufacturing plants moving abroad, but domestic production in manufacturing is expected to continue to increase. However, as plants produce more goods with fewer people, there will be less need for industrial production managers.

Efforts to increase efficiency at the management level have led companies to ask production managers to assume more responsibilities, particularly as computers allow managers to more easily coordinate scheduling, planning, and communication among departments. In addition, more emphasis on quality in the production process has redistributed some of the production manager's oversight responsibilities to supervisors and workers on the production line. However, most of the decision making work of production managers cannot be automated, which will limit the declines in employment.

Job prospects. Despite employment declines, a number of jobs are expected to open due to the need to replace workers who retire or transfer to other occupations. Applicants with experience in production occupations along with a college degree in industrial engineering, management, or business administration, and particularly those with an undergraduate engineering degree and a master's degree in business administration or industrial management, will enjoy the best job prospects. Employers also are likely to seek candidates who have excellent communication skills, related work experience, and who are personable, flexible, and eager to enhance their knowledge and skills through ongoing training.

Earnings
Median annual earnings for industrial production managers were $77,670 in May 2006. The middle 50 percent earned between $59,650 and $100,810. The lowest 10 percent earned less than $47,230, and the highest 10 percent earned more than $130,680. Median annual earnings in the manufacturing industries employing the largest numbers of industrial production managers were:

Management of companies and enterprises	$88,820
Aerospace product and parts manufacturing	87,750
Motor vehicle parts manufacturing	79,360
Printing and related support activities	73,350
Plastics product manufacturing	70,180

Related Occupations
Industrial production managers oversee production staff and equipment, ensure that production goals and quality standards are being met, and implement company policies. Other managerial occupations with similar responsibilities are general and operations managers, construction managers, and sales managers. Occupations requiring comparable training and problem-solving skills are engineers, management analysts, and operations research analysts.

Sources of Additional Information
General information on careers in industrial production management is available from local manufacturers and schools with programs in industrial management.

For more information on careers in production management and information on the CPIM certification, contact:
➤ APICS, the Association for Operations Management, 5301 Shawnee Road, Alexandria, VA 22312.
Internet: **http://www.apics.org**

For more information on quality management and the CMQ/OE certification, contact:
➤ American Society for Quality, 600 North Plankinton Ave., Milwaukee, WI 53203. Internet: **http://www.asq.org**

Lodging Managers

(O*NET 11-9081.00)

Significant Points

- Long hours, including night and weekend work, are common.

- Employment is projected to grow about as fast as the average for all occupations.

- College graduates with degrees in hotel or hospitality management should have better opportunities for jobs at full-service hotels and for advancement than those without a degree.

Nature of the Work
A comfortable room, good food, and a helpful staff can make being away from home an enjoyable experience for both vacationing families and business travelers. Lodging managers make sure that these conveniences are provided, while also ensuring that the establishments are run efficiently and profitably. Most lodging managers work in traditional hotels and motels, but some work in other lodging establishments, such as recreational camps and RV parks, inns, boardinghouses, and youth hostels.

Lodging establishments can vary significantly in size and in the number of services they provide, which can range from supplying a simple in-room television and continental breakfast to operating a casino and accommodating a convention. These factors affect the number and type of lodging managers employed at each property. However, the one person who oversees all lodging operations at a property is usually called a *general manager*. At larger hotels with several departments and multiple layers of management, one general manager and multiple assistant managers coordinate the activities of separate departments. (See related sections elsewhere in the *Handbook* on supervisors and managers of housekeeping and janitorial workers, human resources, training, and labor relations managers and specialists, financial managers, advertising, marketing, promotions, public relations and sales managers, and food service managers.) In smaller limited-service hotels—mainly those without food and beverage service—one lodging manager may direct all the activities of the property.

Lodging managers have overall responsibility for the operation and profitability of the hotel. Depending on the hotel and the size of its staff, lodging managers may either perform or direct housekeeping, personnel, office administration, marketing and sales, purchasing, security, maintenance, oversight of recreation facilities, and other activities. They may hire and train staff, set schedules, and lend a hand when needed.

Within guidelines established by the owners of the hotel or executives of the hotel chain, lodging managers set room rates, allocate funds to departments, approve expenditures, and ensure that standards for guest service, decor, housekeeping, food quality, and banquet operations are met. Increasingly, lodging managers are also responsible for ensuring that the information technology that is common in today's hotels is operational. Some lodging managers work in financial management, monitoring room sales and reservations, overseeing accounting and cash-flow matters at the hotel, projecting occupancy levels, and deciding which rooms to discount and when to offer rate specials.

Front office managers, a category of lodging manager, coordinate reservations and room assignments and train and direct the hotel's front desk staff. They ensure that guests are treated courteously, complaints and problems are resolved, and requests for special services are carried out. Any adjustments to bills often are referred to front office managers for resolution.

Some lodging managers, called *convention services managers*, coordinate the activities of various departments to accommodate meetings, conventions, and special events. They meet with representatives of groups or organizations to plan the number of conference rooms to reserve, the configuration of the meeting space, and determine what other services the group will need, such as catering or banquets and audio, visual, or other electronic requirements. During the meeting or event, they resolve unexpected problems and monitor activities to ensure that hotel operations conform to the group's expectations.

Lodging managers may work with hotel sales and marketing directors and public relations directors to manage and coordinate the advertising and promotion of the hotel. They help develop lodging and dining specials and coordinate special events, such as holiday or seasonal specials. They may direct their staff to purchase advertising and to market their property to organizations or groups seeking a venue for conferences, conventions, business meetings, trade shows, and special events.

Lodging managers who oversee the personnel functions of a hotel or serve as human resource directors ensure that all accounting, payroll, and employee relations matters are handled in compliance with hotel policy and applicable laws. They also oversee hiring practices and standards and ensure that training and promotion programs reflect appropriate employee development guidelines.

Computers are used extensively by lodging managers and their assistants to keep track of guests' bills, reservations, room assignments, meetings, and special events. In addition, computers are used to order food, beverages, and supplies, as well as to prepare reports for hotel owners and top-level managers. Many hotels also provide extensive information technology services for their guests. Managers work with computer specialists and other information technology specialists to ensure that

Lodging managers ensure that standards for guest service are met.

the hotel's computer systems, Internet, and communications networks function properly.

Work environment. Because hotels are open around the clock, night and weekend work is common. Many lodging managers work more than 40 hours per week and are often on-call, which means they may be called back to work at any time. In some hotels and resort properties where work is seasonal, managers may have other duties less related to guest services during the off season or they may find work in other hotels or occupations.

The pressures of coordinating a wide range of activities, turning a profit for investors, and dealing with guests who are sometimes angry can be stressful. Managing conferences and working at the front desk during check-in and check-out times can be particularly hectic.

Training, Other Qualifications, and Advancement

Management trainees for larger upscale hotel chains almost always need a bachelor's or master's degree, preferably in hospitality or hotel management. If not coming directly from college, experience working at a hotel is generally required to get a position as a lodging manager.

Education and training. Most large, full-service hotel chains usually hire people who have a bachelor's degree in business, hotel, or hospitality management for management trainee positions; however, a liberal arts degree coupled with experience in the hospitality field may be sufficient. At other hotels, especially those with fewer services, employers look for applicants with an associate degree or certificate in hotel, restaurant, or hospitality management along with experience. Formal internships or part-time or summer work in a hotel are an asset. Most degree programs include work-study opportunities.

Community colleges, junior colleges, and many universities offer certificate or degree programs in hotel, restaurant, or hospitality management leading to an associate, bachelor's, or graduate degree. Technical institutes, vocational and trade schools, and other academic institutions also offer courses leading to formal recognition in hospitality management. More than 800 educational facilities across the United States provide academic training for would-be lodging managers.

Projections data from the National Employment Matrix

Occupational Title	SOC Code	Employment, 2006	Projected employment, 2016	Change, 2006-16	
				Number	Percent
Lodging managers..	11-9081	71,000	80,000	8,700	12

NOTE: Data in this table are rounded. See the discussion of the employment projections table in the *Handbook* introductory chapter on *Occupational Information Included in the Handbook*.

Hotel management programs include instruction in hotel administration, accounting, economics, marketing, housekeeping, food service management and catering, and hotel maintenance and engineering. Computer training also is an integral part of hotel management training due to the widespread use of computers in reservations, billing, and housekeeping management. Lodging managers also need to know how to generate and read profit-and-loss reports and other business and economic data.

More than 450 high schools in 45 States offer the Lodging Management Program created by the Educational Institute of the American Hotel and Lodging Association. This 2-year program offered to high school juniors and seniors teaches management principles and leads to a professional certification called the "Certified Rooms Division Specialist." Many colleges and universities grant participants in this program credit towards a postsecondary degree in hotel management.

Hotel employees who do not have hospitality training or a college degree but who do demonstrate leadership potential and possess sufficient experience may be invited to participate in a management training program sponsored by the hotel or a hotel chain's corporate parent. Those who already possess the people skills and service orientation needed to succeed in hotel management can usually train for technical expertise in areas such as computer use and accounting principles while on the job. Trainees usually begin as assistant managers and may rotate assignments among the hotel's departments to gain a wide range of experiences. Relocation to another property may be required to help round out the experience and to help a trainee grow into a more responsible management position in a larger or busier hotel.

Other qualifications. Lodging managers must be able to get along with many different types of people, even in stressful situations. They must be able to solve problems quickly and concentrate on details. Initiative, self-discipline, effective communication skills, and the ability to organize and direct the work of others are essential for lodging managers. Managers must have a good knowledge of hotel operations, including safety and security measures, repair and maintenance, and personnel practices. Knowledge of hotel financing is essential to operate a hotel profitably.

Certification and advancement. Large hotel chains may offer better opportunities for advancement than small, independently owned establishments, but relocation every several years often is necessary for advancement. Large chains have more extensive career ladder programs and offer managers the opportunity to transfer to another hotel in the chain or to a regional or central office. Career advancement can be accelerated by the completion of certification programs offered by various hotel and lodging associations. Certification usually requires a combination of course work, examinations, and experience.

Employment

Most lodging managers work in the traveler accommodation industry, including hotels and motels, although they can work for any business that provides room or shelter for people. Companies that manage hotels under contract also employ managers. Lodging managers held about 71,000 jobs in 2006. The majority of lodging managers—54 percent—were self-employed, primarily as owners of small hotels and bed-and-breakfast inns.

Job Outlook

Steady growth in travel will provide average job growth and very good job opportunities for lodging managers. However, those seeking jobs at hotels with the highest level of guest services will face strong competition.

Employment change. Employment of lodging managers is expected to grow 12 percent from 2006 to 2016, which is about as fast as the average for all occupations. Steady business travel and increased domestic and foreign tourism will drive job growth. The many new hotels being planned or built will need lodging managers to run them. In 2007 alone, over 600 new hotels will open. Many of these will be located in suburbs where population and business activity are growing fastest. Most of these new hotels, however, will offer limited services and will not have large staffs or need many managers, somewhat moderating job growth. Some lodging places also do not require a manager to be available 24 hours a day; instead front desk clerks assume some managerial duties at night. Still, there are expected to be a significant number of full-service hotels built, including resort, casino, and luxury hotels, which should generate many additional job openings for experienced managers and management trainees.

Job prospects. In addition to job openings from employment growth, additional job openings are expected to occur as experienced managers leave the labor force or transfer to other occupations, in part because of the long hours and stressful working conditions. Job opportunities are expected to be good for people with good customer service skills and experience in the food service or hospitality industries. People with a college degree in hotel or hospitality management are expected to have the best opportunities at upscale and luxury hotels.

Earnings

Median annual earnings of lodging managers were $42,320 in May 2006. The middle 50 percent earned between $31,870 and $58,380. The lowest 10 percent earned less than $25,120 and the highest 10 percent earned more than $82,510. Median annual earnings for lodging managers in traveler accommodations were $41,880.

Salaries of lodging managers vary greatly according to their responsibilities, location, and the segment of the hotel industry in which they work. Managers may earn bonuses of up to 25 percent of their basic salary in some hotels and also may be furnished with meals, parking, laundry, and other services. In addition to providing typical benefits, some hotels offer profit-sharing plans and educational assistance to their employees.

Related Occupations

Other workers who organize and direct a business focused on customer service include food service managers, gaming managers, sales worker supervisors, and property, real estate, and community association managers.

Sources of Additional Information

For information on careers and scholarships in hotel management, contact:

➤ American Hotel and Lodging Association, 1201 New York Ave. NW., Suite 600, Washington, DC 20005. Internet: **http://www.ahla.com**

Information on careers in the lodging industry and professional development and training programs may be obtained from:

➤ Educational Institute of the American Hotel and Lodging Association, 800 N. Magnolia Ave., Suite 1800, Orlando, FL 32853. Internet: **http://www.ei-ahla.org**

For information on educational programs in hotel and restaurant management, including correspondence courses, write to:

➤ International Council on Hotel, Restaurant, and Institutional Education, 2810 North Parham Rd., Suite 230, Richmond, VA 23294. Internet: **http://www.chrie.org**

Medical and Health Services Managers

(O*NET 11-9111.00)

Significant Points

- Job opportunities will be good, especially for applicants with work experience in health care and strong business and management skills.

- A master's degree is the standard credential, although a bachelor's degree is adequate for some entry-level positions.

- Medical and health services managers typically work long hours and may be called at all hours to deal with problems.

Nature of the Work

Health care is a business and, like every business, it needs good management to keep it running smoothly. Medical and health services managers, also referred to as *health care executives* or *health care administrators*, plan, direct, coordinate, and supervise the delivery of health care. These workers are either specialists in charge of a specific clinical department or generalists who manage an entire facility or system.

The structure and financing of health care are changing rapidly. Future medical and health services managers must be pre-pared to deal with the integration of health care delivery systems, technological innovations, an increasingly complex regulatory environment, restructuring of work, and an increased focus on preventive care. They will be called on to improve efficiency in health care facilities and the quality of the care provided.

Large facilities usually have several assistant administrators who aid the top administrator and handle daily decisions. Assistant administrators direct activities in clinical areas such as nursing, surgery, therapy, medical records, or health information.

In smaller facilities, top administrators handle more of the details of daily operations. For example, many nursing home administrators manage personnel, finances, facility operations, and admissions while also providing resident care.

Clinical managers have training or experience in a specific clinical area and, accordingly, have more specific responsibilities than do generalists. For example, directors of physical therapy are experienced physical therapists, and most health information and medical record administrators have a bachelor's degree in health information or medical record administration. Clinical managers establish and implement policies, objectives, and procedures for their departments; evaluate personnel and work quality; develop reports and budgets; and coordinate activities with other managers.

Health information managers are responsible for the maintenance and security of all patient records. Recent regulations enacted by the Federal Government require that all health care providers maintain electronic patient records and that these records be secure. As a result, health information managers must keep up with current computer and software technology and with legislative requirements. In addition, as patient data become more frequently used for quality management and in medical research, health information managers ensure that databases are complete, accurate, and available only to authorized personnel.

In group medical practices, managers work closely with physicians. Whereas an office manager might handle business affairs in small medical groups, leaving policy decisions to the physicians themselves, larger groups usually employ a full-time administrator to help formulate business strategies and coordinate day-to-day business.

A small group of 10 to 15 physicians might employ 1 administrator to oversee personnel matters, billing and collection, budgeting, planning, equipment outlays, and patient flow. A large practice of 40 to 50 physicians might have a chief administrator and several assistants, each responsible for different areas.

Medical and health services managers in managed care settings perform functions similar to those of their counterparts in large group practices, except that they could have larger staffs to manage. In addition, they might do more community outreach and preventive care than do managers of a group practice.

Some medical and health services managers oversee the activities of a number of facilities in health systems. Such systems might contain both inpatient and outpatient facilities and offer a wide range of patient services.

Work environment. Some managers work in comfortable, private offices; others share space with other staff. Most medi-

Medical and health services managers may deal with personnel, billing and collection, budget, and procurement issues.

cal and health services managers work long hours. Nursing care facilities and hospitals operate around the clock; administrators and managers be called at all hours to deal with problems. They also travel to attend meetings or inspect satellite facilities.

Training, Other Qualifications, and Advancement

A master's degree in one of a number of fields is the standard credential for most generalist positions as a medical or health care manager. A bachelor's degree is sometimes adequate for entry-level positions in smaller facilities and departments. In physicians' offices and some other facilities, on-the-job experience may substitute for formal education.

Education and training. Medical and health services managers must be familiar with management principles and practices. A master's degree in health services administration, long-term care administration, health sciences, public health, public administration, or business administration is the standard credential for most generalist positions in this field. However, a bachelor's degree is adequate for some entry-level positions in smaller facilities, at the departmental level within health care organizations, and in health information management. Physicians' offices and some other facilities hire those with on-the-job experience instead of formal education.

Bachelor's, master's, and doctoral degree programs in health administration are offered by colleges; universities; and schools of public health, medicine, allied health, public administration, and business administration. In 2007, 72 schools had accredited programs leading to the master's degree in health services administration, according to the Commission on Accreditation of Healthcare Management Education.

For people seeking to become heads of clinical departments, a degree in the appropriate field and work experience may be sufficient early in their career. However, a master's degree in health services administration or a related field might be required to advance. For example, nursing service administrators usually are chosen from among supervisory registered nurses with administrative abilities and graduate degrees in nursing or health services administration.

Health information managers require a bachelor's degree from an accredited program. In 2007, there were 42 accredited bachelor's degree programs and 3 master's degree programs in

health information management according to the Commission on Accreditation for Health Informatics and Information Management Education.

Some graduate programs seek students with undergraduate degrees in business or health administration; however, many graduate programs prefer students with a liberal arts or health profession background. Candidates with previous work experience in health care also may have an advantage. Competition for entry into these programs is keen, and applicants need above-average grades to gain admission. Graduate programs usually last between 2 and 3 years. They may include up to 1 year of supervised administrative experience and coursework in areas such as hospital organization and management, marketing, accounting and budgeting, human resources administration, strategic planning, law and ethics, biostatistics or epidemiology, health economics, and health information systems. Some programs allow students to specialize in one type of facility—hospitals, nursing care facilities, mental health facilities, or medical groups. Other programs encourage a generalist approach to health administration education.

Licensure. All States and the District of Columbia require nursing care facility administrators to have a bachelor's degree, pass a licensing examination, complete a State-approved training program, and pursue continuing education. Some States also require licenses for administrators in assisted living facilities. A license is not required in other areas of medical and health services management.

Certification and other qualifications. Medical and health services managers often are responsible for facilities and equipment worth millions of dollars, and for hundreds of employees. To make effective decisions, they need to be open to different opinions and good at analyzing contradictory information. They must understand finance and information systems and be able to interpret data. Motivating others to implement their decisions requires strong leadership abilities. Tact, diplomacy, flexibility, and communication skills are essential because medical and health services managers spend most of their time interacting with others.

Health information managers who have a bachelor's degree or postbaccalaureate from an approved program and who pass an exam can earn certification as a Registered Health Information Administrator from the American Health Information Management Association.

Advancement. Medical and health services managers advance by moving into more responsible and higher paying positions, such as assistant or associate administrator, department head, or chief executive officer, or by moving to larger facilities. Some experienced managers also may become consultants or professors of health care management.

New graduates with master's degrees in health services administration may start as department managers or as supervisory staff. The level of the starting position varies with the experience of the applicant and the size of the organization. Hospitals and other health facilities offer postgraduate residencies and fellowships, which usually are staff positions. Graduates from master's degree programs also take jobs in large medical group practices, clinics, mental health facilities, nursing care corporations, and consulting firms.

Projections data from the National Employment Matrix

Occupational Title	SOC Code	Employment, 2006	Projected employment, 2016	Change, 2006-16	
				Number	Percent
Medical and health services managers..	11-9111	262,000	305,000	43,000	16

NOTE: Data in this table are rounded. See the discussion of the employment projections table in the *Handbook* introductory chapter on *Occupational Information Included in the Handbook.*

Graduates with bachelor's degrees in health administration usually begin as administrative assistants or assistant department heads in larger hospitals. They also may begin as department heads or assistant administrators in small hospitals or nursing care facilities.

Employment

Medical and health services managers held about 262,000 jobs in 2006. About 37 percent worked in hospitals, and another 22 percent worked in offices of physicians or in nursing and residential care facilities. Most of the remainder worked in home health care services, Federal Government health care facilities, outpatient care centers, insurance carriers, and community care facilities for the elderly.

Job Outlook

Employment of medical and health services managers is expected to grow faster than average. Job opportunities should be good, especially for applicants with work experience in the health care field and strong business management skills.

Employment change. Employment of medical and health services managers is expected to grow 16 percent from 2006 to 2016, faster than the average for all occupations. The health care industry will continue to expand and diversify, requiring managers to help ensure smooth business operations.

Managers in all settings will be needed to improve quality and efficiency of health care while controlling costs, as insurance companies and Medicare demand higher levels of accountability. Managers also will be needed to oversee the computerization of patient records and to ensure their security as required by law. Additional demand for managers will stem from the need to recruit workers and increase employee retention, to comply with changing regulations, to implement new technology, and to help improve the health of their communities by emphasizing preventive care.

Hospitals will continue to employ the most medical and health services managers over the 2006-16 decade. However, the number of new jobs created is expected to increase at a slower rate in hospitals than in many other industries because of the growing use of clinics and other outpatient care sites. Despite relatively slow employment growth, a large number of new jobs will be created because of the industry's large size.

Employment will grow fastest in practitioners' offices and in home health care agencies. Many services previously provided in hospitals will continue to shift to these settings, especially as medical technologies improve. Demand in medical group practice management will grow as medical group practices become larger and more complex.

Medical and health services managers also will be employed by health care management companies that provide management services to hospitals and other organizations and to spe-

cific departments such as emergency, information management systems, managed care contract negotiations, and physician recruiting.

Job prospects. Job opportunities will be good, especially for applicants with work experience in the health care field and strong business management skills should have the best opportunities. Medical and health services managers with experience in large hospital facilities will enjoy an advantage in the job market, as hospitals become larger and more complex. Competition for jobs at the highest management levels will be keen because of the high pay and prestige.

Earnings

Median annual earnings of wage and salary medical and health services managers were $73,340 in May 2006. The middle 50 percent earned between $57,240 and $94,780. The lowest 10 percent earned less than $45,050, and the highest 10 percent earned more than $127,830. Median annual earnings in the industries employing the largest numbers of medical and health services managers in May 2006 were:

General medical and surgical hospitals..............................$78,660
Outpatient care centers..67,920
Offices of physicians..67,540
Nursing care facilities 66,730
Home health care services 66,720

Earnings of medical and health services managers vary by type and size of the facility and by level of responsibility. For example, the Medical Group Management Association reported that, in 2006, median salaries for administrators were $72,875 in practices with 6 or fewer physicians, $95,766 in practices with 7 to 25 physicians, and $132,955 in practices with 26 or more physicians.

According to a survey by the Professional Association of Health Care Office Management, 2006 average total compensation for office managers in specialty physicians' practices was $70,474 in gastroenterology, $70,599 in dermatology, $76,392 in cardiology, $67,317 in ophthalmology, $67,222 in obstetrics and gynecology, $77,621 in orthopedics, $62,125 in pediatrics, $66,853 in internal medicine, and $60,040 in family practice.

Related Occupations

Medical and health services managers have training or experience in both health and management. Other occupations requiring knowledge of both fields are insurance underwriters and social and community service managers.

Sources of Additional Information

Information about undergraduate and graduate academic programs in this field is available from:

➤ Association of University Programs in Health Administration, 2000 North 14th St., Suite 780, Arlington, VA 22201.
Internet: **http://www.aupha.org**

For a list of accredited graduate programs in medical and health services administration, contact:
➤ Commission on Accreditation of Healthcare Management Education, 2000 North 14th St., Suite 780, Arlington, VA 2220.
Internet: **http://www.cahme.org**

For information about career opportunities in health care management, contact:
➤ American College of Healthcare Executives, One N. Franklin St., Suite 1700, Chicago, IL 60606.
Internet: **http://www.healthmanagementcareers.org**

For information about career opportunities in long-term care administration, contact:
➤ American College of Health Care Administrators, 300 N. Lee St., Suite 301, Alexandria, VA 22314.
Internet: **http://www.achca.org**

For information about career opportunities in medical group practices and ambulatory care management, contact:
➤ Medical Group Management Association, 104 Inverness Terrace East, Englewood, CO 80112.
Internet: **http://www.mgma.org**

For information about medical and health care office managers, contact:
➤ Professional Association of Health Care Office Management, 461 East Ten Mile Rd., Pensacola, FL 32534.

For information about career opportunities in health information management, contact:
➤ American Health Information Management Association, 233 N. Michigan Ave., Suite 2150, Chicago, IL 60601.
Internet: **http://www.ahima.org**

Property, Real Estate, and Community Association Managers

(O*NET 11–9141.00)

Significant Points

- Opportunities should be best for those with college degrees in business administration, real estate, or related fields, and with professional designations.

- Particularly good opportunities are expected for those with experience managing housing for older people or with experience running a health unit.

- More than half of property, real estate, and community association managers are self-employed.

Nature of the Work

To businesses and investors, properly managed real estate is a source of income and profits; to homeowners, well-managed property is a way to preserve and enhance resale values and increase comfort. Property, real estate, and community association managers maintain and increase the value of real estate investments by handling the logistics of running a property. *Property*

and real estate managers oversee the performance of income-producing commercial or residential properties and ensure that real estate investments achieve their expected revenues. *Community association managers* manage the common property and services of condominiums, cooperatives, and planned communities through their homeowner or community associations.

When owners of apartments, office buildings, or retail or industrial properties lack the time or expertise needed for the day-to-day management of their real estate investments or homeowner associations, they often hire a property or real estate manager or a community association manager. The manager is employed either directly by the owner or indirectly through a contract with a property management firm.

Generally, property and real estate managers handle the financial operations of the property, ensuring that rent is collected and that mortgages, taxes, insurance premiums, payroll, and maintenance bills are paid on time. In community associations, homeowners pay no rent and pay their own real estate taxes and mortgages, but community association managers collect association dues. Some property managers, usually senior-level property managers, supervise the preparation of financial statements and periodically report to the owners on the status of the property, occupancy rates, expiration dates of leases, and other matters.

Often, property managers negotiate contracts for janitorial, security, groundskeeping, trash removal, and other services. When contracts are awarded competitively, managers solicit bids from several contractors and advise the owners on which bid to accept. They monitor the performance of contractors, and investigate and resolve complaints from residents and tenants when services are not properly provided. Managers also purchase supplies and equipment for the property, and make arrangements with specialists for repairs that cannot be handled by regular property maintenance staff.

In addition to fulfilling these duties, property managers must understand and comply with relevant legislation, such as the Americans with Disabilities Act, the Federal Fair Housing Amendment Act, and local fair housing laws. They must ensure that their renting and advertising practices are not discriminatory, and that the property itself complies with all of the local, State, and Federal regulations and building codes.

Onsite property managers are responsible for the day-to-day operations of a single property, such as an office building, a shopping center, a community association, or an apartment complex. To ensure that the property is safe and properly maintained, onsite managers routinely inspect the grounds, facilities, and equipment to determine whether repairs or maintenance are needed. In handling requests for repairs or trying to resolve complaints, they meet not only with current residents, but also with prospective residents or tenants to show vacant apartments or office space. Onsite managers also are responsible for enforcing the terms of rental or lease agreements, such as rent collection, parking and pet restrictions, and termination-of-lease procedures. Other important duties of onsite managers include keeping accurate, up-to-date records of income and expenditures from property operations and submitting regular expense reports to the senior-level property manager or owners.

Property managers who do not work onsite act as a liaison between the onsite manager and the owner. They also market vacant space to prospective tenants by hiring a leasing agent, advertising, or other means, and they establish rental rates in accordance with prevailing local economic conditions.

Some property and real estate managers, often called *real estate asset managers*, act as the property owners' agent and adviser for the property. They plan and direct the purchase, development, and disposition of real estate on behalf of the business and investors. These managers focus on long-term strategic financial planning, rather than on day-to-day operations of the property.

In deciding to acquire property, real estate asset managers consider several factors, such as property values, taxes, zoning, population growth, transportation, and traffic volume and patterns. Once a site is selected, they negotiate contracts for the purchase or lease of the property, securing the most beneficial terms. Real estate asset managers review their company's real estate holdings periodically and identify properties that are no longer financially profitable. They then negotiate the sale of, or terminate the lease on, such properties.

Community association managers, on the other hand, do work that more closely parallels that of onsite property managers. They collect monthly assessments, prepare financial statements and budgets, negotiate with contractors, and help to resolve complaints. In other respects, however, the work of association managers differs from that of other residential property and real estate managers because they interact with homeowners and other residents on a daily basis. Usually hired by a volunteer board of directors of the association, they administer the daily affairs, and oversee the maintenance, of property and facilities that the homeowners own and use jointly through the association. They also assist the board and owners in complying with association and government rules and regulations.

Some associations encompass thousands of homes and employ their own onsite staff and managers. In addition to administering the associations' financial records and budget, managers may be responsible for the operation of community pools, golf courses, and community centers, and for the maintenance of landscaping and parking areas. Community association managers also may meet with the elected boards of directors to discuss and resolve legal issues or disputes that may affect the owners, as well as to review any proposed changes or improvements by homeowners

Property, real estate, and community association managers handle the logistics of running a property.

to their properties, to make sure that they comply with community guidelines.

Work environment. The offices of most property, real estate, and community association managers are clean, modern, and well lighted. However, many managers spend a major portion of their time away from their desks. Onsite managers, in particular, may spend a large portion of their workday away from their offices, visiting the building engineer, showing apartments, checking on the janitorial and maintenance staff, or investigating problems reported by tenants. Property and real estate managers frequently visit the properties they oversee, sometimes daily when contractors are doing major repair or renovation work. Real estate asset managers may spend time away from home while traveling to company real estate holdings or searching for properties to acquire.

Property, real estate, and community association managers often must attend evening meetings with residents, property owners, community association boards of directors, or civic groups. Not surprisingly, many managers put in long workweeks, especially before financial and tax reports are due and before board and annual meetings. Some apartment managers are required to live in the apartment complexes where they work, so that they are available to handle emergencies, even when they are off duty. They usually receive compensatory time off for working nights or weekends. Many apartment managers receive time off during the week so that they are available on weekends to show apartments to prospective residents.

Training, Other Qualifications, and Advancement

Employers increasingly are hiring college graduates with a bachelor's or master's degree in business administration, accounting, finance, or real estate, even if they don't have much practical experience.

Education and training. Most employers prefer to hire college graduates for property management positions. In fact, employers increasingly are hiring inexperienced college graduates with a bachelor's or master's degree in business administration, accounting, finance, real estate, or public administration for these positions. Those with degrees in the liberal arts also may qualify, especially if they have relevant coursework. Many people entering jobs such as assistant property manager have onsite management experience.

Licensure. Managers of public housing subsidized by the Federal Government are required to be certified, but many property, real estate, and community association managers who work with all types of property choose to earn a professional designation voluntarily, because it represents formal recognition of their achievements and affords status in the occupation. Real estate managers who buy or sell property are required to be licensed by the State in which they practice. In a few States, property association managers must be licensed.

Other qualifications. Previous employment as a real estate sales agent may be an asset to onsite managers, because it provides experience that is useful in showing apartments or office space. In the past, those with backgrounds in building maintenance have advanced to onsite manager positions on the strength of their knowledge of building mechanical systems, but this path is becoming less common as employers place greater emphasis on administrative, financial, and communication abilities for managerial jobs.

People most commonly enter real estate asset manager jobs by transferring from positions as property managers or real estate brokers. Real estate asset managers must be good negotiators, adept at persuading and working with people, and good at analyzing data in order to assess the fair-market value of property or its development potential. Resourcefulness and creativity in arranging financing are essential for managers who specialize in land development.

Good speaking, writing, computer, and financial skills, as well as an ability to deal tactfully with people, are essential in all areas of property management.

Certification and advancement. Many people begin property management careers as assistants. Assistants work closely with a property manager and learn how to prepare budgets, analyze insurance coverage and risk options, market property to prospective tenants, and collect overdue rent payments. In time, many assistants advance to property manager positions.

Some people start as onsite managers of apartment buildings, office complexes, or community associations. As they acquire experience, often working under the direction of a more experienced property manager, they may advance to positions of greater responsibility. Those who excel as onsite managers often transfer to assistant offsite property manager positions, in which they can acquire experience handling a broad range of property management responsibilities.

The responsibilities and compensation of property, real estate, and community association managers increase as these workers manage more and larger properties. Most property managers, often called portfolio managers, are responsible for several properties at a time. As their careers advance, they gradually are entrusted with larger properties that are more complex to manage. Many specialize in the management of one type of property, such as apartments, office buildings, condominiums, cooperatives, homeowners' associations, or retail properties. Managers who excel at marketing properties to tenants might specialize in managing new properties, while those who are particularly knowledgeable about buildings and their mechanical systems might specialize in the management of older properties requiring renovation or more frequent repairs. Some experienced managers open their own property management firms.

Many employers encourage attendance at short-term formal training programs conducted by various professional and trade associations that are active in the real estate field. Employers send managers to these programs to improve their management skills and expand their knowledge of specialized subjects, such as the operation and maintenance of building mechanical systems, the enhancement of property values, insurance and risk management, personnel management, business and real estate law, community association risks and liabilities, tenant relations,

communications, accounting and financial concepts, and reserve funding. Managers also participate in these programs to prepare themselves for positions of greater responsibility in property management. The completion of these programs, plus related job experience and a satisfactory score on a written examination can lead to certification, or the formal award of a professional designation, by the sponsoring association. (Some organizations offering certifications are listed as sources of additional information at the end of this statement.) Some associations also require their members to adhere to a specific code of ethics.

Employment

Property, real estate, and community association managers held about 329,000 jobs in 2006. About 36 percent worked for real estate agents and brokers, lessors of real estate, or activities related to real estate. Others worked for real estate development companies, government agencies that manage public buildings, and corporations with extensive holdings of commercial properties. More than half of property, real estate, and community association managers are self-employed.

Job Outlook

Faster than average employment growth is expected. Opportunities should be best for jobseekers with a college degree in business administration, real estate, or a related field, and for those who attain a professional designation. Particularly good opportunities are expected for those with experience managing housing for older people or with experience running a health unit.

Employment change. Employment of property, real estate, and community association managers is projected to increase by 15 percent during the 2006–16 decade, faster than the average for all occupations. Job growth among onsite property managers in commercial real estate is expected to accompany the projected expansion of the real estate and rental and leasing industry. An increase in the Nation's stock of apartments, houses, and offices also should require more property managers. Developments of new homes are increasingly being organized with community or homeowner associations that provide community services and oversee jointly owned common areas requiring professional management. To help properties become more profitable or to enhance the resale values of homes, more commercial and residential property owners are expected to place their investments in the hands of professional managers. Moreover, the number of older people will grow during the 2006–16 projection period, increasing the need for specialized housing, such as assisted-living facilities and retirement communities that require management.

Job prospects. In addition to openings from job growth, a number of openings are expected as managers transfer to other occupations or leave the labor force. Opportunities should be best for jobseekers with a college degree in business administration, real estate, or a related field, and for those who attain a professional

Projections data from the National Employment Matrix

Occupational Title	SOC Code	Employment, 2006	Projected employment, 2016	Change, 2006-16	
				Number	Percent
Property, real estate, and community association managers.............	11-9141	329,000	379,000	50,000	15

NOTE: Data in this table are rounded. See the discussion of the employment projections table in the *Handbook* introductory chapter on *Occupational Information Included in the Handbook.*

designation. Because of the expected increase in assisted-living and retirement communities, particularly good opportunities are expected for those with experience managing housing for older people or with experience running a health unit.

Earnings

Median annual earnings of salaried property, real estate, and community association managers were $43,070 in May 2006. The middle 50 percent earned between $28,700 and $64,200 a year. The lowest 10 percent earned less than $20,140, and the highest 10 percent earned more than $95,170 a year. Median annual earnings of salaried property, real estate, and community association managers in the largest industries that employed them in May 2006 were:

Land subdivision	$78,040
Local government	55,210
Activities related to real estate	40,590
Offices of real estate agents and brokers	40,500
Lessors of real estate	37,480

Many resident apartment managers and onsite association managers receive the use of an apartment as part of their compensation package. Managers often are reimbursed for the use of their personal vehicles, and managers employed in land development often receive a small percentage of ownership in the projects that they develop.

Related Occupations

Property, real estate, and community association managers plan, organize, staff, and manage the real estate operations of businesses. Workers who perform similar functions in other fields include administrative services managers, education administrators, food service managers, lodging managers, medical and health services managers, real estate brokers and sales agents, and urban and regional planners.

Sources of Additional Information

For information about education and careers in property management, as well as information about professional designation and certification programs in both residential and commercial property management, contact:

➤ Institute of Real Estate Management, 430 N. Michigan Ave., Chicago, IL 60611. Internet: **http://www.irem.org**

For information on careers and certification programs in commercial property management, contact:

➤ Building Owners and Managers Institute, 1521 Ritchie Hwy., Arnold, MD 21012. Internet: **http://www.bomi.org**

For information on careers and professional designation and certification programs in residential property management and community association management, contact:

➤ Community Associations Institute, 225 Reinekers Ln., Suite 300, Alexandria, VA 22314.
Internet: **http://www.caionline.org**

➤ National Board of Certification for Community Association Managers, 225 Reinekers Ln., Suite 310, Alexandria, VA 22314.
Internet: **http://www.nbccam.org**

Purchasing Managers, Buyers, and Purchasing Agents

(O*NET 11-3061.00, 13-1021.00, 13-1022.00, 13-1023.00)

Significant Points

- About 43 percent are employed in wholesale trade or manufacturing establishments.

- Some firms prefer to promote existing employees to these positions, while others recruit and train college graduates.

- Employment is projected to have little or no job growth.

- Opportunities should be best for those with a college degree.

Nature of the Work

Purchasing managers, buyers, and purchasing agents shop for a living. They buy the goods and services the company or institution needs to either resell to customers or for the establishment's own use. *Wholesale and retail buyers* purchase goods, such as clothing or electronics, for resale. *Purchasing agents* buy goods and services for use by their own company or organization; they might buy raw materials for manufacturing or office supplies, for example. *Purchasing agents and buyers of farm products* purchase goods such as grain, Christmas trees, and tobacco for further processing or resale.

Purchasing professionals consider price, quality, availability, reliability, and technical support when choosing suppliers and merchandise. They try to get the best deal for their company, meaning the highest quality goods and services at the lowest possible cost to their companies. In order to accomplish this successfully, purchasing managers, buyers, and purchasing agents study sales records and inventory levels of current stock, identify foreign and domestic suppliers, and keep abreast of changes affecting both the supply of, and demand for, needed products and materials. To be effective, purchasing specialists must have a working technical knowledge of the goods or services to be purchased.

In large industrial organizations, a distinction often is drawn between the work of a buyer or purchasing agent and that of a *purchasing manager*. Purchasing agents commonly focus on routine purchasing tasks, often specializing in a commodity or group of related commodities, such as steel, lumber, cotton, grains, fabricated metal products, or petroleum products. Purchasing agents usually track market conditions, price trends, and futures markets. Purchasing managers usually handle the more complex or critical purchases and may supervise a group of purchasing agents handling other goods and services. Whether a person is titled purchasing manager, buyer, or purchasing agent depends somewhat on specific industry and employer practices. But purchasing managers often have a much larger range of duties than purchasing agents. They may actively seek new technologies and suppliers. They may create and oversee systems that allow individuals within their organizations to buy their own supplies, lowering the cost of each transaction.

Purchasing specialists employed by government agencies or manufacturing firms usually are called purchasing directors, managers, or agents; or contract specialists. These workers acquire materials, parts, machines, supplies, services, and other inputs to the production of a final product. Purchasing agents and managers obtain items ranging from raw materials, fabricated parts, machinery, and office supplies to construction services and airline tickets. Some purchasing managers specialize in negotiating and supervising supply contracts and are called contract or supply managers.

Often, purchasing specialists in government place solicitations for services and accept bids and offers through the Internet. Government purchasing agents and managers must follow strict laws and regulations in their work, in order to avoid any appearance of impropriety.

Purchasing specialists who buy finished goods for resale are employed by wholesale and retail establishments, where they commonly are known as buyers or merchandise managers. Wholesale and retail buyers are an integral part of a complex system of distribution and merchandising that caters to the vast array of consumer needs and desires. Wholesale buyers purchase goods directly from manufacturers or from other wholesale firms for resale to retail firms, commercial establishments, institutions, and other organizations. In retail firms, buyers purchase goods from wholesale firms or directly from manufacturers for resale to the public.

Buyers largely determine which products their establishment will sell. Therefore, it is essential that they have the ability to predict what will appeal to consumers. They must constantly stay informed of the latest trends, because failure to do so could jeopardize profits and the reputation of their company. They keep track of inventories and sales levels through computer software that is linked to the store's cash registers. Buyers also follow ads in newspapers and other media to check competitors' sales activities, and they watch general economic conditions to anticipate consumer buying patterns. Buyers working for large and medium-sized firms usually specialize in acquiring one or two lines of merchandise, whereas buyers working for small stores may purchase the establishment's complete inventory.

The use of private-label merchandise and the consolidation of buying departments have increased the responsibilities of retail buyers. Private-label merchandise, produced for a particular retailer, requires buyers to work closely with vendors to develop and obtain the desired product. The downsizing and consolidation of buying departments increases the demands placed on buyers because, although the amount of work remains unchanged, there are fewer people to accomplish it. The result is an increase in the workloads and levels of responsibility for all.

Many merchandise managers assist in the planning and implementation of sales promotion programs. Working with merchandise executives, they determine the nature of the sale and purchase items accordingly. Merchandise managers may work with advertising personnel to create an ad campaign. For example, they may determine in which media the advertisement will be placed—newspapers, direct mail, television, or some combination of all three. In addition, merchandise managers often visit

the selling floor to ensure that goods are properly displayed. Buyers stay in constant contact with store and department managers to find out what products are selling well and which items the customers are demanding to be added to the product line. Often, assistant buyers are responsible for placing orders and checking shipments.

Evaluating suppliers is one of the most critical functions of a purchasing manager, buyer, or purchasing agent. Many firms now run on a lean manufacturing schedule and use just-in-time inventories so any delays in the supply chain can shut down production and cost the firm its customers and reputation. Purchasing professionals use many resources to find out all they can about potential suppliers. The Internet has become an effective tool in searching catalogs, trade journals, and industry and company publications, and directories. Purchasing professionals will attend meetings, trade shows, and conferences to learn of new industry trends and make contacts with suppliers. Purchasing managers, agents, and buyers will usually interview prospective suppliers and visit their plants and distribution centers to asses their capabilities. It is important to make certain that the supplier is capable of delivering the desired goods or services on time, in the correct quantities without sacrificing quality. Once all of the necessary information on suppliers is gathered, orders are placed and contracts are awarded to those suppliers who meet the purchaser's needs. Most of the transaction process is now automated using electronic purchasing systems that link the supplier and firms together through the Internet.

Purchasing professionals can gain instant access to specifications for thousands of commodities, inventory records, and their customers' purchase records to avoid overpaying for goods and to avoid shortages of popular goods or surpluses of goods that do not sell as well. These systems permit faster selection, customization, and ordering of products, and they allow buyers to concentrate on the qualitative and analytical aspects of the job. Long-term contracts are an important strategy of purchasing professionals because it allows purchasers to consolidate their supply bases around fewer suppliers. In today's global economy, purchasing managers, buyers, and purchasing agents should expect to deal with foreign suppliers which may require travel to other countries and to be familiar with other cultures and languages.

Changing business practices have altered the traditional roles of purchasing or supply management specialists in many industries. For example, manufacturing companies increasingly involve workers in this occupation at most stages of product development because of their ability to forecast a part's or material's cost, availability, and suitability for its intended purpose. Furthermore, potential problems with the supply of materials may be avoided by consulting the purchasing department in the early stages of product design.

Purchasing specialists often work closely with other employees in their own organization when deciding on purchases, an arrangement sometimes called "team buying." For example, before submitting an order, they may discuss the design of custom-made products with company design engineers, talk about problems involving the quality of purchased goods with quality assurance engineers and production supervisors, or mention shipment problems to managers in the receiving department.

Purchasing managers, buyers, and purchasing agents work to get the best merchandise at the lowest cost.

Work environment. Most purchasing managers, buyers, and purchasing agents work in comfortable offices. They frequently work more than the standard 40-hour week, because of special sales, conferences, or production deadlines. Evening and weekend work also is common before holiday and back-to-school seasons for those working in retail trade. Consequently, many retail firms discourage the use of vacation time during peak periods.

Buyers and merchandise managers often work under great pressure. Because wholesale and retail stores are so competitive, buyers need physical stamina to keep up with the fast-paced nature of their work.

Many purchasing managers, buyers, and purchasing agents travel at least several days a month. Purchasers for worldwide manufacturing companies and large retailers, as well as buyers of high fashion, may travel outside the United States.

Training, Other Qualifications, and Advancement

Qualified people may begin as trainees, purchasing clerks, expediters, junior buyers, or assistant buyers. They often need continuing education, certification, or a bachelor's degree to advance. Retail and wholesale firms prefer to hire applicants who have a college degree and who are familiar with the merchandise they sell and with wholesaling and retailing practices. Some retail firms promote qualified employees to assistant buyer positions; others recruit and train college graduates as assistant buyers. Most employers use a combination of methods.

Education and training. Educational requirements tend to vary with the size of the organization. Large stores and distributors prefer applicants who have completed a bachelor's degree program with a business emphasis. Many manufacturing firms put an even greater emphasis on formal training, preferring applicants with a bachelor's or master's degree in engineering, business, economics, or one of the applied sciences. A master's degree is essential for advancement to many top-level purchasing manager jobs.

Regardless of academic preparation, new employees must learn the specifics of their employer's business. Training periods vary in length, with most lasting 1 to 5 years. In wholesale and retail establishments, most trainees begin by selling merchandise, supervising sales workers, checking invoices on material received,

and keeping track of stock. As they progress, trainees are given increased buying-related responsibilities.

In manufacturing, new purchasing employees often are enrolled in company training programs and spend a considerable amount of time learning about their firm's operations and purchasing practices. They work with experienced purchasers to learn about commodities, prices, suppliers, and markets. In addition, they may be assigned to the production planning department to learn about the material requirements system and the inventory system the company uses to keep production and replenishment functions working smoothly.

Other qualifications. Purchasing managers, buyers, and purchasing agents must know how to use word processing and spreadsheet software and the Internet. Other important qualities include the ability to analyze technical data in suppliers' proposals; good communication, negotiation, and mathematical skills; knowledge of supply-chain management; and the ability to perform financial analyses.

People who wish to become wholesale or retail buyers should be good at planning and decisionmaking and have an interest in merchandising. Anticipating consumer preferences and ensuring that goods are in stock when they are needed requires resourcefulness, good judgment, and self-confidence. Buyers must be able to make decisions quickly and to take risks. Marketing skills and the ability to identify products that will sell also are very important. Employers often look for leadership ability, too, because buyers spend a large portion of their time supervising assistant buyers and dealing with manufacturers' representatives and store executives.

Experienced buyers may advance by moving to a department that manages a larger volume or by becoming a merchandise manager. Others may go to work in sales for a manufacturer or wholesaler.

Certification and advancement. An experienced purchasing agent or buyer may become an assistant purchasing manager in charge of a group of purchasing professionals before advancing to purchasing manager, supply manager, or director of materials management. At the top levels, duties may overlap with other management functions, such as production, planning, logistics, and marketing.

Regardless of industry, continuing education is essential for advancement. Many purchasing managers, buyers, and purchasing agents participate in seminars offered by professional societies and take college courses in supply management. Professional certification is becoming increasingly important, especially for those just entering the occupation.

There are several recognized credentials for purchasing agents and purchasing managers. The Certified Purchasing Manager (C.P.M.) designation is conferred by the Institute for Supply Management. In 2008, this certification will be replaced by the Certified Professional in Supply Management (CPSM) credential, covering the wider scope of duties now performed by purchasing professionals. The Certified Purchasing Professional (CPP) and Certified Professional Purchasing Manager (CPPM) designations are conferred by the American Purchasing Society. The Certified Supply Chain Professional credential is conferred by APICS, the Association for Operations Management. For workers in Federal, State, and local government, the National Institute of Governmental Purchasing offers the designations of Certified Professional Public Buyer (CPPB) and Certified Public Purchasing Officer (CPPO). Most of these certifications are awarded only after work-related experience and education requirements are met and written or oral exams are successfully completed.

Employment

Purchasing managers, buyers, and purchasing agents held about 529,000 jobs in 2006. About 43 percent worked in the wholesale trade and manufacturing industries and another 11 percent worked in retail trade. The remainder worked mostly in service establishments, such as management of companies and enterprises, or different levels of government. A small number were self-employed.

The following tabulation shows the distribution of employment by occupational specialty:

Purchasing agents, except wholesale,
   retail, and farm products..287,000
Wholesale and retail buyers, except farm products 157,000
Purchasing managers...70,000
Purchasing agents and buyers, farm products..........................16,000

Job Outlook

Employment of purchasing managers, buyers, and purchasing agents is expected to have little or no job growth through the year 2016. Generally, opportunities will be best for individuals with a bachelor's degree. In government and in large companies, opportunities will be best for those with a master's degree.

Employment change. No change in overall employment of purchasing managers, buyers, and purchasing agents is expected during the 2006-16 decade.

Demand for purchasing workers will be limited by improving software, which has eliminated much of the paperwork involved in ordering and procuring supplies, and also by the growing number of purchases being made electronically through the Internet and electronic data interchange (EDI). Demand will also be limited by offshoring of routine purchasing actions to other countries and by consolidation of purchasing departments, which makes purchasing agents more efficient.

Demand for purchasing workers in the manufacturing sector will be less than demand in the services sector, as the overall service sector grows more rapidly than the manufacturing sector. Also, many purchasing agents are now charged with procuring services that traditionally had been done in-house, such as

computer and IT (information technology) support in addition to traditionally contracted services such as advertising.

Employment of purchasing managers is expected to grow more slowly than average. The use of the Internet to conduct electronic commerce has made information easier to obtain, thus increasing the productivity of purchasing managers. The Internet also allows both large and small companies to bid on contracts. Exclusive supply contracts and long-term contracting have allowed companies to negotiate with fewer suppliers less frequently.

Employment of wholesale and retail buyers, except farm products, is expected to have little or no change in employment. In the retail industry, mergers and acquisitions have caused buying departments to consolidate. In addition, larger retail stores are eliminating local buying departments and centralizing them at their headquarters.

Employment of purchasing agents, except wholesale, retail, and farm products, is expected to have little or no change in employment, primarily because of the increased globalization of the U.S. economy. As more materials and supplies come from abroad, firms have begun to outsource more of their purchasing duties to foreign purchasing agents who are located closer to the foreign suppliers of goods and materials they will need. This trend is expected to continue, but it will likely be limited to routine transactions with complex and critical purchases still being handled in-house.

Finally, employment of purchasing agents and buyers, farm products, is projected to decline 9 percent, as overall growth in agricultural industries and retailers in the grocery-related industries consolidate.

Job prospects. Persons who have a bachelor's degree in business should have the best chance of obtaining a buyer position in wholesale or retail trade or within government. A bachelor's degree, combined with industry experience and knowledge of a technical field, will be an advantage for those interested in working for a manufacturing or industrial company. Government agencies and larger companies usually require a master's degree in business or public administration for top-level purchasing positions.

Earnings

Median annual earnings of purchasing managers were $81,570 in May 2006. The middle 50 percent earned between $60,890 and $105,780 a year. The lowest 10 percent earned less than $46,540, and the highest 10 percent earned more than $132,040 a year.

Median annual earnings for purchasing agents and buyers of farm products were $46,770 in May 2006. The middle 50 percent earned between $34,770 and $64,100 a year. The lowest

Projections data from the National Employment Matrix

Occupational Title	SOC Code	Employment, 2006	Projected employment, 2016	Change, 2006-16	
				Number	Percent
Purchasing managers, buyers, and purchasing agents	—	529,000	531,000	1,200	0
Purchasing managers	11-3061	70,000	72,000	2,400	3
Purchasing agents and buyers, farm products.............................	13-1021	16,000	15,000	-1,400	-9
Wholesale and retail buyers, except farm products	13-1022	157,000	156,000	-200	0
Purchasing agents, except wholesale, retail, and farm products...	13-1023	287,000	288,000	400	0

NOTE: Data in this table are rounded. See the discussion of the employment projections table in the *Handbook* introductory chapter on *Occupational Information Included in the Handbook.*

10 percent earned less than $26,520, and the highest 10 percent earned more than $88,650 a year.

Median annual earnings for wholesale and retail buyers, except farm products, were $44,640 in May 2006. The middle 50 percent earned between $33,640 and $60,590 a year. The lowest 10 percent earned less than $26,270, and the highest 10 percent earned more than $83,080 a year. Median annual earnings in the industries employing the largest numbers of wholesale and retail buyers, except farm products, were:

Management of companies and enterprises............................$54,390
Grocery and related product wholesalers.................................46,080
Wholesale electronic markets and agents and brokers............45,020
Building material and supplies dealers.....................................40,380
Grocery stores..34,210

Median annual earnings for purchasing agents, except wholesale, retail, and farm products, were $50,730 in May 2006. The middle 50 percent earned between $39,000 and $66,730 a year. The lowest 10 percent earned less than $31,350, and the highest 10 percent earned more than $83,900 a year. Median annual earnings in the industries employing the largest numbers of purchasing agents, except wholesale, retail, and farm products, were:

Federal executive branch...$68,500
Aerospace product and parts manufacturing............................59,390
Navigational, measuring, electromedical,
   and control instruments manufacturing................................55,620
Management of companies and enterprises..............................54,820
Local government..48,170

Purchasing managers, buyers, and purchasing agents receive the same benefits package as other workers, including vacations, sick leave, life and health insurance, and pension plans. In addition to receiving standard benefits, retail buyers often earn cash bonuses based on their performance and may receive discounts on merchandise bought from their employer.

Related Occupations

Like purchasing managers, buyers, and purchasing agents, procurement clerks work to obtain materials and goods for businesses. Workers in other occupations who need a knowledge of marketing and the ability to assess consumer demand include those in advertising, marketing, promotions, public relations, and sales managers; food service managers: insurance sales agents; lodging managers; sales engineers; and sales representatives, wholesale and manufacturing.

Sources of Additional Information

Further information about education, training, employment, and certification for purchasing careers is available from:

➤ American Purchasing Society, North Island Center, Suite 203, 8 East Galena Blvd., Aurora, IL 60506.

➤ Association for Operations Management, APICS, 5301 Shawnee Rd., Alexandria, VA 22312-2317. Internet: **http://www.apics.org**

➤ Institute for Supply Management, P.O. Box 22160, Tempe, AZ 85285-2160. Internet: **http://www.ism.ws**

➤ National Institute of Governmental Purchasing, Inc., 151 Spring St., Suite 300, Herndon, VA 20170-5223. Internet: **http://www.nigp.org**

Top Executives

(O*NET 11-1011.00, 11-1021.00)

Significant Points

- Keen competition is expected because the prestige and high pay of these jobs attract a large number of applicants.

- Top executives are among the highest paid workers; however, long hours, considerable travel, and intense pressure to succeed are common.

- The formal education and experience of top executives vary as widely as the nature of their responsibilities.

Nature of the Work

All organizations have specific goals and objectives that they strive to meet. Top executives devise strategies and formulate policies to ensure that these objectives are met. Although they have a wide range of titles—such as chief executive officer, chief operating officer, board chair, president, vice president, school superintendent, county administrator, or tax commissioner—all formulate policies and direct the operations of businesses and corporations, public sector organizations, nonprofit institutions, and other organizations.

A corporation's goals and policies are established by the *chief executive officer* in collaboration with other top executives, who are overseen by a board of directors. In a large corporation, the chief executive officer meets frequently with subordinate executives to ensure that operations are conducted in accordance with these policies. The chief executive officer of a corporation retains overall accountability; however, a *chief operating officer* may be delegated several responsibilities, including the authority to oversee executives who direct the activities of various departments and implement the organization's policies on a day-to-day basis. In publicly held and nonprofit corporations, the board of directors ultimately is accountable for the success or failure of the enterprise, and the chief executive officer reports to the board.

In addition to being responsible for the operational success of a company, top executives also are increasingly being held accountable for the accuracy of their financial reporting, particularly among publicly traded companies. For example, recently enacted legislation contains provisions for corporate governance, internal control, and financial reporting.

The nature of the responsibilities of other high-level executives depends on the size of the organization. In small organizations, such as independent retail stores or small manufacturers, a partner, owner, or general manager often is responsible for purchasing, hiring, training, quality control, and day-to-day supervisory duties. In large organizations, the duties of executives

While top executives are among the highest paid workers, long hours and intense pressure to succeed are common.

are highly specialized. Some managers, for instance, are responsible for the overall performance of one aspect of the organization, such as manufacturing, marketing, sales, purchasing, finance, personnel, training, administrative services, computer and information systems, property management, transportation, or legal services. (Some of these and other management occupations are discussed elsewhere in this section of the *Handbook*.)

Chief financial officers direct the organization's financial goals, objectives, and budgets. They oversee the investment of funds and manage associated risks, supervise cash management activities, execute capital-raising strategies to support a firm's expansion, and deal with mergers and acquisitions.

Chief information officers are responsible for the overall technological direction of their organizations. They are increasingly involved in the strategic business plan of a firm as part of the executive team. To perform effectively, they also need knowledge of administrative procedures, such as budgeting, hiring, and supervision. These managers propose budgets for projects and programs and make decisions on staff training and equipment purchases. They hire and assign computer specialists, information technology workers, and support personnel to carry out specific parts of the projects. They supervise the work of these employees, review their output, and establish administrative procedures and policies. Chief information officers also provide organizations with the vision to master information technology as a competitive tool.

Chief executives have overall responsibility for the operation of their organizations. Working with executive staff, they set goals and arrange programs to attain these goals. Executives also appoint department heads, who manage the employees who carry out programs. Chief executives also oversee budgets and ensure that resources are used properly and that programs are carried out as planned.

Chief executive officers carry out a number of other important functions, such as meeting with staff and board members to determine the level of support for proposed programs. Chief executive officers in government often nominate citizens to boards and commissions, encourage business investment, and promote economic development in their communities. To do

all of these varied tasks effectively, chief executives rely on a staff of highly skilled personnel. Executives who control small companies, however, often do this work by themselves.

General and operations managers plan, direct, or coordinate the operations of companies or public and private sector organizations. Their duties include formulating policies, managing daily operations, and planning the use of materials and human resources, but are too diverse and general in nature to be classified in any one area of management or administration, such as personnel, purchasing, or administrative services. In some organizations, the duties of general and operations managers may overlap the duties of chief executive officers.

Work environment. Top executives typically have spacious offices and numerous support staff. General managers in large firms or nonprofit organizations usually have comfortable offices close to those of the top executives to whom they report. Long hours, including evenings and weekends, are standard for most top executives and general managers, although their schedules may be flexible.

Substantial travel between international, national, regional, and local offices to monitor operations and meet with customers, staff, and other executives often is required of managers and executives. Many managers and executives also attend meetings and conferences sponsored by various associations. The conferences provide an opportunity to meet with prospective donors, customers, contractors, or government officials and allow managers and executives to keep abreast of technological and managerial innovations.

In large organizations, job transfers between local offices or subsidiaries are common for persons on the executive career track. Top executives are under intense pressure to succeed; depending on the organization, this may mean earning higher profits, providing better service, or attaining fundraising and charitable goals. Executives in charge of poorly performing organizations or departments usually find their jobs in jeopardy.

Training, Other Qualifications, and Advancement

The formal education and experience required by top executives vary as widely as their responsibilities do, but many of these workers have at least a bachelor's degree and considerable experience.

Education and training. Many top executives have a bachelor's or graduate degree in business administration, liberal arts, or a more specialized discipline. The specific degree required often depends on the type of organization for which they work. College presidents, for example, typically have a doctorate in the field in which they originally taught, and school superintendents often have a master's degree in education administration. (For information on lower-level managers in educational services, see the *Handbook* statement on education administrators.) A brokerage office manager needs a strong background in securities and finance, and department store executives generally have extensive experience in retail trade.

Some top executives in the public sector have a background in public administration or liberal arts. Others might have a more specific background related to their jobs. For example, a health commissioner might have a graduate degree in health services administration or business administration. (For information on lower-level managers in health services, see the *Handbook* statement on medical and health services managers.)

Many top executive positions are filled from within the organization by promoting experienced, lower-level managers when an opening occurs. In industries such as retail trade or transportation, for instance, it is possible for individuals without a college degree to work their way up within the company and become managers. However, many companies prefer that their top executives have extensive managerial experience and, therefore, hire individuals who have been managers in other organizations.

Other qualifications. Top executives must have highly developed personal skills. An analytical mind able to quickly assess large amounts of information and data is very important, as is the ability to consider and evaluate the relationships between numerous factors. Top executives also must be able to communicate clearly and persuasively. For managers to succeed they need other important qualities as well, including leadership, self-confidence, motivation, decisiveness, flexibility, sound business judgment, and determination.

Certification and advancement. Advancement may be accelerated by participation in company training programs that impart a broader knowledge of company policy and operations. Managers also can help their careers by becoming familiar with the latest developments in management techniques at national or local training programs sponsored by various industry and trade associations. To facilitate their promotion to an even higher level, managers who have experience in a particular field, such as accounting or engineering, may attend executive development programs geared towards their background.

Participation in conferences and seminars can expand knowledge of national and international issues influencing the organization and can help the participants develop a network of useful contacts. For example, the Institute of Certified Professional Managers offers the Certified Manager (CM) credential, which is earned by completing training and passing an exam. The certification is held by individuals at all experience levels, from those seeking to enter management to those who are already senior executives. Certification is not necessary for advancement but may be helpful in developing and demonstrating valuable management skills.

General managers may advance to a top executive position, such as executive vice president, in their own firm or they may take a corresponding position in another firm. They may even advance to peak corporate positions such as chief operating officer or chief executive officer. Chief executive officers often become members of the board of directors of one or more firms, typically as a director of their own firm and often as chair of its board of directors. Some top executives establish their own firms or become independent consultants.

Employment

Top executives held about 2.2 million jobs in 2006. Employment by detailed occupation was distributed as follows:

General and operations managers 1,720,000
Chief executives 402,000

Top executives are found in every industry, but service-providing industries, including government, employed over 3 out of 4 top executives.

Job Outlook

Employment of top executives is projected to have little or no change. Keen competition for jobs is expected because of the prestige and high pay of these positions.

Employment change. Employment of top executives—including chief executives, general and operations managers, and legislators—is expected to grow 2 percent from 2006 to 2016. Because top managers are essential to the success of any organization, their jobs are unlikely to be automated or offshored to other countries. Some top executive jobs may be eliminated through industry consolidation, as upper management is streamlined after mergers and acquisitions. Employment of top executives is not as sensitive to growth in business as employment in many other occupations. As a business grows, the number of top executives changes little relative to the total number of employees. Therefore, top executives are not expected to experience as much employment growth as workers in the occupations they oversee.

Projected employment growth of top executives varies by industry. For example, employment growth is expected to grow faster than average in professional, scientific, and technical services and about as fast as the average in administrative and support services. However, employment is projected to decline in some manufacturing industries.

Job prospects. Keen competition is expected for top executive positions because the prestige and high pay attract a large number of qualified applicants. Because this is a large occupation, numerous openings will occur each year as executives transfer to other positions, start their own businesses, or retire. However, many executives who leave their jobs transfer to other executive positions, a pattern that tends to limit the number of job openings for new entrants to the occupation.

Experienced managers whose accomplishments reflect strong leadership qualities and the ability to improve the efficiency or competitive position of an organization will have the best opportunities. In an increasingly global economy, experience in international economics, marketing, information systems, and knowledge of several languages also may be beneficial.

Projections data from the National Employment Matrix

Occupational Title	SOC Code	Employment, 2006	Projected employment, 2016	Change, 2006-16	
				Number	Percent
Top executives..	—	2,123,000	2,157,000	34,000	2
Chief executives	11-1011	402,000	410,000	8,200	2
General and operations managers...........................	11-1021	1,720,000	1,746,000	26,000	2

NOTE: Data in this table are rounded. See the discussion of the employment projections table in the *Handbook* introductory chapter on *Occupational Information Included in the Handbook.*

Earnings

Top executives are among the highest paid workers in the U.S. economy. However, salary levels vary substantially depending on the level of managerial responsibility; length of service; and type, size, and location of the firm. For example, a top manager in a very large corporation can earn significantly more than a counterpart in a small firm.

Median annual earnings of wage and salary general and operations managers in May 2006 were $85,230. The middle 50 percent earned between $58,230 and $128,580. Because the specific responsibilities of general and operations managers vary significantly within industries, earnings also tend to vary considerably. Median annual earnings in the industries employing the largest numbers of general and operations managers were:

Architectural, engineering, and related services $113,280
Management of companies and enterprises 105,130
Building equipment contractors 85,270
Depository credit intermediation 85,050
Local government 74,950

Median annual earnings of wage and salary chief executives in May 2006 were greater than $145,600; some chief executives of large companies earn hundreds of thousands to over a million dollars annually, although salaries vary substantially by type and level of responsibilities and by industry.

In addition to salaries, total compensation often includes stock options and other performance bonuses. The use of executive dining rooms and company aircraft and cars, expense allowances, and company-paid insurance premiums and physical examinations also are among benefits commonly enjoyed by top executives in private industry. A number of chief executive officers also are provided with company-paid club memberships and other amenities.

Related Occupations

Top executives plan, organize, direct, control, and coordinate the operations of an organization and its major departments or programs. The members of the board of directors and lower-level managers also are involved in these activities. Many other management occupations have similar responsibilities; however, they are concentrated in specific industries or are responsible for a specific department within an organization. A few examples are administrative services managers; education administrators; financial managers; food service managers; and advertising, marketing, promotions, public relations, and sales managers. Legislators oversee their staffs and help set public policies in Federal, State, and local governments.

Sources of Additional Information

For more information on top executives, including educational programs and job listings, contact:
➤ American Management Association, 1601 Broadway, 6th Floor, New York, NY 10019.
Internet: **http://www.amanet.org**
➤ National Management Association, 2210 Arbor Blvd., Dayton, OH 45439. Internet: **http://www.nma1.org**

For more information on executive financial management careers, contact:
➤ Financial Executives International, 200 Campus Dr., P.O. Box 674, Florham Park, NJ 07932.
Internet: **http://www.financialexecutives.org**
➤ Financial Management Association International, College of Business Administration, University of South Florida, 4202 East Fowler Ave., BSN 3331, Tampa, FL 33620.
Internet: **http://www.fma.org**

For information about management skills development, including the Certified Manager (CM) credential, contact:
➤ Institute for Certified Professional Managers, 1598 S. Main St., Harrisonburg, VA 22801. Internet: **http://www.icpm.biz**

Business and Financial Operations Occupations

Accountants and Auditors

(O*NET 13-2011.00, 13-2011.01, 13-2011.02)

Significant Points

- Most jobs require at least a bachelor's degree in accounting or a related field.

- Opportunities will be best for jobseekers who have a master's degree, obtain certification or licensure or who are proficient in the use of accounting and auditing computer software.

- Faster-than-average growth of accountant and auditor jobs will result from an increase in the number of businesses, changing financial laws and regulations, and greater scrutiny of company finances.

Nature of the Work

Accountants and auditors help to ensure that the Nation's firms are run efficiently, its public records kept accurately, and its taxes paid properly and on time. They analyze and communicate financial information for various entities such as companies, individual clients, and government. Beyond carrying out the fundamental tasks of the occupation—preparing, analyzing, and verifying financial documents in order to provide information to clients—many accountants also offer budget analysis, financial and investment planning, information technology consulting, and limited legal services.

Specific job duties vary widely among the four major fields of accounting and auditing: *public, management, government accounting*, and *internal auditing*.

Public accountants perform a broad range of accounting, auditing, tax, and consulting activities for their clients, which may be corporations, governments, nonprofit organizations, or individuals. For example, some public accountants concentrate

Many accountants produce extensive financial reports for a company's recordkeeping.

on tax matters, such as advising companies about the tax advantages and disadvantages of certain business decisions and preparing individual income tax returns. Others offer advice in areas such as compensation or employee health care benefits, the design of accounting and data-processing systems, and the selection of controls to safeguard assets. Still others audit clients' financial statements and inform investors and authorities that the statements have been correctly prepared and reported. These accountants are also referred to as *external auditors*. Public accountants, many of whom are Certified Public Accountants (CPAs), generally have their own businesses or work for public accounting firms.

Some public accountants specialize in forensic accounting—investigating and interpreting white-collar crimes such as securities fraud and embezzlement, bankruptcies and contract disputes, and other complex and possibly criminal financial transactions, including money laundering by organized criminals. Forensic accountants combine their knowledge of accounting and finance with law and investigative techniques to determine whether an activity is illegal. Many forensic accountants work closely with law enforcement personnel and lawyers during investigations and often appear as expert witnesses during trials.

In response to recent accounting scandals, new Federal legislation restricts the nonauditing services that public accountants can provide to clients. If an accounting firm audits a client's financial statements, that same firm cannot provide advice on human resources, technology, investment banking, or legal matters, although accountants may still advise on tax issues. Accountants may also advise other clients in these areas and may provide advice within their own firm.

Management accountants—also called cost, managerial, industrial, corporate, or private accountants—record and analyze the financial information of the companies for which they work. Among their other responsibilities are budgeting, performance evaluation, cost management, and asset management. Usually, management accountants are part of executive teams involved in strategic planning or the development of new products. They analyze and interpret the financial information that corporate executives need in order to make sound business decisions.

They also prepare financial reports for other groups, including stockholders, creditors, regulatory agencies, and tax authorities. Within accounting departments, management accountants may work in various areas, including financial analysis, planning and budgeting, and cost accounting.

Government accountants and auditors work in the public sector, maintaining and examining the records of government agencies and auditing private businesses and individuals whose activities are subject to government regulations or taxation. Accountants employed by Federal, State, and local governments ensure that revenues are received and expenditures are made in accordance with laws and regulations. Those employed by the Federal Government may work as Internal Revenue Service agents or in financial management, financial institution examination, or budget analysis and administration.

Internal auditors verify the effectiveness of their organization's internal controls and check for mismanagement, waste, or fraud. They examine and evaluate their firms' financial and information systems, management procedures, and internal controls to ensure that records are accurate and controls are adequate. They also review company operations, evaluating their efficiency, effectiveness, and compliance with corporate policies and government regulations. Because computer systems commonly automate transactions and make information readily available, internal auditors may also help management evaluate the effectiveness of their controls based on real-time data, rather than personal observation. They may recommend and review controls for their organization's computer systems, to ensure their reliability and integrity of the data.

Internal auditors may also have specialty titles, such as information technology auditors, environmental auditors, and compliance auditors.

Technology is rapidly changing the nature of the work of most accountants and auditors. With the aid of special software packages, accountants summarize transactions in the standard formats of financial records and organize data in special formats employed in financial analysis. These accounting packages greatly reduce the tedious work associated with data management and recordkeeping. Computers enable accountants and auditors to be more mobile and to use their clients' computer systems to extract information from databases and the Internet. As a result, a growing number of accountants and auditors with extensive computer skills specialize in correcting problems with software or in developing software to meet unique data management and analytical needs. Accountants also are beginning to perform more technical duties, such as implementing, controlling, and auditing computer systems and networks and developing a business's technology plans.

Accountants also act as personal advisors. They not only provide clients with accounting and tax help, but also help them develop personal budgets, manage assets and investments, plan for retirement, and recognize and reduce their exposure to risks. This role is in response to clients' demands for a single trustworthy individual or firm to meet all of their financial needs. However, accountants are restricted from providing these services to clients whose financial statements they also prepare. (See financial analysts and personal financial advisors elsewhere in the *Handbook*.)

Work environment. Most accountants and auditors work in a typical office setting. Some may be able to do part of their work at home. Accountants and auditors employed by public accounting firms, government agencies, and organizations with multiple locations may travel frequently to perform audits at branches, clients' places of business, or government facilities.

Most accountants and auditors usually work a standard 40-hour week, but many work longer hours, particularly if they are self-employed and have numerous clients. Tax specialists often work long hours during the tax season.

Training, Other Qualifications, and Advancement

Most accountants and auditors need at least a bachelor's degree in business, accounting, or a related field. Many accountants and auditors choose to obtain certification to help advance their careers, such as becoming a Certified Public Accountant (CPA).

Education and training. Most accountant and auditor positions require at least a bachelor's degree in accounting or a related field. Beginning accounting and auditing positions in the Federal Government, for example, usually require 4 years of college (including 24 semester hours in accounting or auditing) or an equivalent combination of education and experience. Some employers prefer applicants with a master's degree in accounting, or with a master's degree in business administration with a concentration in accounting. Some universities and colleges are now offering programs to prepare students to work in growing specialty professions such as internal auditing,. Many professional associations offer continuing professional education courses, conferences, and seminars.

Some graduates of junior colleges or business or correspondence schools, as well as bookkeepers and accounting clerks who meet the education and experience requirements set by their employers, can obtain junior accounting positions and advance to accountant positions by demonstrating their accounting skills on the job.

Most beginning accountants and auditors may work under supervision or closely with an experienced accountant or auditor before gaining more independence and responsibility.

Licensure and certification. Any accountant filing a report with the Securities and Exchange Commission (SEC) is required by law to be a Certified Public Accountant (CPA). This may include senior level accountants working for or on behalf of public companies that are registered with the SEC. CPAs are licensed by their State Board of Accountancy. Any accountant who passes a national exam and meets the other requirements of the State where they practice can become a CPA. The vast majority of States require CPA candidates to be college graduates, but a few States will substitute a number of years of public accounting experience for a college degree.

As of 2007, 42 States and the District of Columbia required CPA candidates to complete 150 semester hours of college coursework—an additional 30 hours beyond the usual 4-year bachelor's degree. Several other States have adopted similar legislation that will become effective before 2009. Colorado, Delaware, New Hampshire, and Vermont are the only States that do not have any immediate plans to require the 150 semester hours. In response to this trend, many schools have altered their curricula accordingly, with most programs offering master's degrees as part of the 150 hours. Prospective accounting majors should carefully research accounting curricula and the requirements of any States in which they hope to become licensed.

All States use the four-part Uniform CPA Examination prepared by the American Institute of Certified Public Accountants (AICPA). The CPA examination is rigorous, and less than one-half of those who take it each year pass every part they attempt on the first try. Candidates are not required to pass all four parts at once, but most States require candidates to pass all four sections within 18 months of passing their first section. The CPA exam is now computerized and is offered 2 months out of every quarter at various testing centers throughout the United States. Most States also require applicants for a CPA certificate to have some accounting experience; however requirements vary by State or jurisdiction.

Nearly all States require CPAs and other public accountants to complete a certain number of hours of continuing professional education before their licenses can be renewed. The professional associations representing accountants sponsor numerous courses, seminars, group study programs, and other forms of continuing education.

Other qualifications. Previous experience in accounting or auditing can help an applicant get a job. Many colleges offer students the opportunity to gain experience through summer or part-time internship programs conducted by public accounting or business firms. In addition, as many business processes are now automated, practical knowledge of computers and their applications is a great asset for jobseekers in the accounting and auditing fields.

People planning a career in accounting and auditing should have an aptitude for mathematics and be able to analyze, compare, and interpret facts and figures quickly. They must be able to clearly communicate the results of their work to clients and managers both verbally and in writing. Accountants and auditors must be good at working with people, business systems, and computers. At a minimum, accountants and auditors should be familiar with basic accounting and computer software packages. Because financial decisions are made on the basis of their statements and services, accountants and auditors should have high standards of integrity.

Certification and advancement. Professional recognition through certification, or a designation other than the CPA, provides a distinct advantage in the job market. Certification can attest to professional competence in a specialized field of accounting and auditing. Accountants and auditors can seek credentials from a wide variety of professional societies.

The Institute of Management Accountants confers the Certified Management Accountant (CMA) designation upon applicants who complete a bachelor's degree or who attain a minimum score or higher on specified graduate school entrance exams. Applicants must have worked at least 2 years in management accounting, pass a four-part examination, agree to meet continuing education requirements, and comply with standards of professional conduct. The exam covers areas such as financial statement analysis, working-capital policy, capital structure, valuation issues, and risk management.

The Institute of Internal Auditors offers the Certified Internal Auditor (CIA) designation to graduates from accredited colleges and universities who have worked for 2 years as internal auditors and have passed a four-part examination. The IIA also offers the designations of Certified in Control Self-Assessment (CCSA), Certified Government Auditing Professional (CGAP), and Certified Financial Services Auditor (CFSA) to those who pass the exams and meet educational and experience requirements.

The ISACA, formerly known as the Information Systems Audit and Control Association, confers the Certified Information Systems Auditor (CISA) designation upon candidates who pass an examination and have 5 years of experience auditing information systems. Information systems experience, financial or operational auditing experience, or related college credit hours can be substituted for up to 2 years information systems auditing, control or security experience.

The Accreditation Council for Accountancy and Taxation, a satellite organization of the National Society of Accountants, confers four designations: Accredited Business Accountant (ABA), Accredited Tax Advisor (ATA), Accredited Tax Preparer (ATP), and Elder Care Specialist (ECS)—on accountants specializing in tax preparation for small and medium-sized businesses. Candidates for the ABA must pass an exam; candidates for the other designations must complete the required coursework and in some cases pass an exam.

The Association of Certified Fraud Examiners offers the Certified Fraud Examiner (CFE) designation for forensic or public accountants involved in fraud prevention, detection, deterrence, and investigation. To obtain the designation, individuals must have a bachelor's degree, 2 years of relevant experience, pass a four-part examination, and abide by a code of professional ethics. Related work experience may be substituted for the educational requirement.

The Association of Government Accountants grants the Certified Government Financial Manager (CGFM) designation for accountants, auditors, and other government financial workers at the Federal, State, and local levels. Candidates must have a minimum of a bachelor's degree, 24 hours of study in financial management, 2 years of experience in government, and passing scores on a series of three exams. The exams cover topics in governmental environment; governmental accounting, financial reporting, and budgeting; and financial management and control.

For those accountants with their CPA, the AICPA offers the option to receive any or all of the Accredited in Business Valuation (ABV), Certified Information Technology Professional (CITP), or Personal Financial Specialist (PFS) designations. CPA's with these designations demonstrate a level of expertise in these areas in which accountants practice ever more frequently. The business valuation designation requires a written exam and the completion of a minimum of 10 business valuation projects that demonstrate a candidate's experience and competence. The technology designation requires the achievement of a set number of points awarded for business technology experience and educa-

tion. Candidates for the personal financial specialist designation also must achieve a certain level of points based on experience and education, pass a written exam, and submit references.

Many senior corporation executives have a background in accounting, internal auditing, or finance. Beginning public accountants often advance to positions with more responsibility in 1 or 2 years and to senior positions within another few years. Those who excel may become supervisors, managers, or partners; open their own public accounting firm; or transfer to executive positions in management accounting or internal auditing in private firms.

Management accountants often start as cost accountants, junior internal auditors, or trainees for other accounting positions. As they rise through the organization, they may advance to accounting manager, chief cost accountant, budget director, or manager of internal auditing. Some become controllers, treasurers, financial vice presidents, chief financial officers, or corporation presidents.

Public accountants, management accountants, and internal auditors usually have much occupational mobility. Practitioners often shift into management accounting or internal auditing from public accounting, or between internal auditing and management accounting. It is less common for accountants and auditors to move from either management accounting or internal auditing into public accounting. Additionally, because they learn about and review the internal controls of various business units within a company, internal auditors often gain the experience needed to become upper-level managers.

Employment

Accountants and auditors held about 1.3 million jobs in 2006. They worked throughout private industry and government, but 21 percent of wage and salary accountants worked for accounting, tax preparation, bookkeeping, and payroll services firms. Approximately 10 percent of accountants or auditors was self-employed.

Many management accountants, internal auditors, or government accountants and auditors are not CPAs; however, a large number are licensed CPAs. Most accountants and auditors work in urban areas, where public accounting firms and central or regional offices of businesses are concentrated.

Some individuals with backgrounds in accounting and auditing are full-time college and university faculty; others teach part time while working as self-employed accountants or as accountants for private industry or government. (See teachers—postsecondary elsewhere in the *Handbook.*)

Job Outlook

Strong growth of accountants and auditor jobs over the 2006-16 decade is expected to result from stricter accounting and auditing regulations, along with an expanding economy. The best job

Projections data from the National Employment Matrix

Occupational Title	SOC Code	Employment, 2006	Projected employment, 2016	Change, 2006-16	
				Number	Percent
Accountants and auditors..	13-2011	1,274,000	1,500,000	226,000	18

NOTE: Data in this table are rounded. See the discussion of the employment projections table in the *Handbook* introductory chapter on *Occupational Information Included in the Handbook.*

prospects will be for accountants and auditors who have a college degree or any certification, but especially a CPA.

Employment change. Employment of accountants and auditors is expected to grow by 18 percent between 2006 and 2016, which is faster than the average for all occupations. This occupation will have a very large number of new jobs arise, almost 226,000 over the projections decade. An increase in the number of businesses, changing financial laws, and corporate governance regulations, and increased accountability for protecting an organization's stakeholders will drive growth.

As the economy grows, the number of business establishments will increase, requiring more accountants and auditors to set up books, prepare taxes, and provide management advice. As these businesses grow, the volume and complexity of information reviewed by accountants and auditors regarding costs, expenditures, taxes, and internal controls will expand as well. The globalization of business also has led to more demand for accounting expertise and services related to international trade and accounting rules and international mergers and acquisitions.

An increased need for accountants and auditors also will arise from changes in legislation related to taxes, financial reporting standards, business investments, mergers, and other financial events. As a result of accounting scandals at several large corporations, Congress passed the Sarbanes-Oxley Act of 2002 in an effort to curb corporate accounting fraud. This legislation requires public companies to maintain well-functioning internal controls to ensure the accuracy and reliability of their financial reporting. It also holds the company's chief executive personally responsible for falsely reporting financial information.

These changes are expected to lead to increased scrutiny of company finances and accounting procedures and should create opportunities for accountants and auditors, particularly CPAs, to audit financial records more thoroughly. Management accountants and internal auditors increasingly will also be needed to discover and eliminate fraud before audits, and ensure that important processes and procedures are documented accurately and thoroughly. Also, efforts to make government agencies more efficient and accountable will increase demand for government accountants.

Increased focus on and numbers of financial crimes such as embezzlement, bribery, and securities fraud will increase the demand for forensic accountants to detect illegal financial activity by individuals, companies, and organized crime rings. Computer technology has made these crimes easier to commit, and they are on the rise. At the same time, the development of new computer software and electronic surveillance technology has made tracking down financial criminals easier, thus increasing the ease, and likelihood of, discovery. As success rates of investigations grow, demand for forensic accountants will increase.

The changing role of accountants and auditors also will spur job growth, although this will be slower than in the past because of changes in the law. Federal legislation now prohibits accountants from providing many types of management and consulting services to clients whose books they audit. However, accountants will still be able to advise clients that are not publicly traded companies and those they do not audit.

Also, the increasing popularity of tax preparation firms and computer software will shift accountants away from tax prepara-

tion. As computer programs continue to simplify some accounting-related tasks, clerical staff will increasingly handle many routine calculations.

Job prospects. Overall, job opportunities for accountants and auditors should be favorable. Those who earn a CPA should have excellent job prospects. After most States instituted the 150-hour rule for CPAs, enrollment in accounting programs declined. However, enrollment is again growing as more students have become attracted to the profession by the attention from the accounting scandals.

In the aftermath of the accounting scandals, professional certification is even more important to ensure that accountants' credentials and knowledge of ethics are sound. Regardless of specialty, accountants and auditors who have earned professional recognition through certification or licensure should have the best job prospects. Applicants with a master's degree in accounting or a master's degree in business administration with a concentration in accounting also will have an advantage.

Individuals who are proficient in accounting and auditing computer software or have expertise in specialized areas—such as international business, specific industries, or current legislation—may have an advantage in getting some accounting and auditing jobs. In addition, employers increasingly seek applicants with strong interpersonal and communication skills. Many accountants work on teams with others who have different backgrounds, so they must be able to communicate accounting and financial information clearly and concisely. Regardless of qualifications, however, competition will remain keen for the most prestigious jobs in major accounting and business firms.

In addition to openings from job growth, the need to replace accountants and auditors who retire or transfer to other occupations will produce numerous job openings in this large occupation.

Earnings

Median annual earnings of wage and salary accountants and auditors were $54,630 in May 2006. The middle half of the occupation earned between $42,520 and $71,960. The top 10 percent earned more than $94,050, and the bottom 10 percent earned less than $34,470. Median annual earnings in the industries employing the largest numbers of accountants and auditors were as follows:

Accounting, tax preparation, bookkeeping, and payroll services	$57,020
Management of companies and enterprises	55,560
Local government	50,120
Depository credit intermediation	49,380
State government	47,200

According to a salary survey conducted by the National Association of Colleges and Employers, bachelor's degree candidates in accounting received starting offers averaging $46,718 a year in 2006; master's degree candidates in accounting were offered $49,277 initially.

According to a 2007 salary survey conducted by Robert Half International, a staffing services firm specializing in accounting and finance, general accountants and internal auditors with up to 1 year of experience earned between $31,500 and $48,250 a year. Those with 1 to 3 years of experience earned between

$36,000 and $60,000. Senior accountants and auditors earned between $43,250 and $79,250, managers between $51,250 and $101,500, and directors of accounting and internal auditing between $68,000 and $208,000. The variation in salaries reflects differences in size of firm, location, level of education, and professional credentials.

In the Federal Government, the starting annual salary for junior accountants and auditors was $28,862 in 2007. Candidates who had a superior academic record might start at $35,752, while applicants with a master's degree or 2 years of professional experience usually began at $43,731. Beginning salaries were slightly higher in selected geographic areas where the prevailing local pay level was higher. Accountants employed by the Federal Government in nonsupervisory, supervisory, and managerial positions averaged $78,665 a year in 2007; auditors averaged $83,322.

Wage and salary accountants and auditors usually receive standard benefits, including health and medical insurance, life insurance, a 401(k) plan, and paid annual leave. High-level senior accountants may receive additional benefits, such as the use of a company car and an expense account.

Related Occupations

Accountants and auditors design internal control systems and analyze financial data. Others for whom training in accounting is valuable include budget analysts; cost estimators; loan officers; financial analysts and personal financial advisors; tax examiners, collectors, and revenue agents; bill and account collectors; and bookkeeping, accounting, and auditing clerks. Recently, some accountants have assumed the role of management analysts and are involved in the design, implementation, and maintenance of accounting software systems. Others who perform similar work include computer programmers, computer software engineers, and computer support specialists and systems administrators.

Sources of Additional Information

Information on accredited accounting programs can be obtained from:
➤ AACSB International—Association to Advance Collegiate Schools of Business, 777 South Harbour Island Blvd., Suite 750, Tampa FL 33602-5730.
Internet:
http://www.aacsb.edu/accreditation/AccreditedMembers.asp

Information about careers in certified public accounting and CPA standards and examinations may be obtained from:
➤ American Institute of Certified Public Accountants, 1211 Avenue of the Americas, New York, NY 10036.
Internet: **http://www.aicpa.org**
➤ The Uniform CPA Examination, 1211 Avenue of the Americas, New York, NY 10036. Internet: **http://www.cpa-exam.org**

Information on CPA licensure requirements by State may be obtained from:
➤ National Association of State Boards of Accountancy, 150 Fourth Ave. North, Suite 700, Nashville, TN 37219-2417.
Internet: **http://www.nasba.org**

Information on careers in management accounting and the CMA designation may be obtained from:
➤ Institute of Management Accountants, 10 Paragon Dr., Montvale, NJ 07645-1718. Internet: **http://www.imanet.org**

Information on the Accredited in Accountancy, Accredited Business Accountant, Accredited Tax Advisor, or Accredited Tax Preparer designation may be obtained from:
➤ Accreditation Council for Accountancy and Taxation, 1010 North Fairfax St., Alexandria, VA 22314.-1574.
Internet: **http://www.acatcredentials.org**

Information on the Certified Fraud Examiner designation may be obtained from:
➤ Association of Certified Fraud Examiners, 716 West Ave, Austin, TX 78701-2727.

Information on careers in internal auditing and the CIA designation may be obtained from:
➤ The Institute of Internal Auditors, 247 Maitland Ave., Altamonte Springs, FL 32701-4201.
Internet: **http://www.theiia.org**

Information on careers in information systems auditing and the CISA designation may be obtained from:
➤ ISACA, 3701 Algonquin Rd., Suite 1010, Rolling Meadows, IL 60008. Internet: **http://www.isaca.org**

Information on careers in government accounting and the CGFM designation may be obtained from:
➤ Association of Government Accountants, 2208 Mount Vernon Ave., Alexandria, VA 22301.
Internet: **http://www.agacgfm.org**

Information on obtaining positions as an accountant or auditor with the Federal Government is available from the Office of Personnel Management through USAJOBS, the Federal Government's official employment information system. This resource for locating and applying for job opportunities can be accessed through the Internet at **http://www.usajobs.opm.gov** or through an interactive voice response telephone system at (703) 724-1850 or TDD (978) 461-8404. These numbers are not toll free, and charges may result. For advice on how to find and apply for Federal jobs, see the *Occupational Outlook Quarterly* article "How to get a job in the Federal Government," online at:
http://www.bls.gov/opub/ooq/2004/summer/art01.pdf

Appraisers and Assessors of Real Estate

(O*NET 13-2021.00, 13-2021.01, 13-2021.02)

Significant Points

- Appraisers and assessors must meet licensing and/or certification requirements which vary by State, but generally include specific training requirements, a period of work as a trainee, and passing one or more examinations.

- More than 3 out of 10 were self-employed; salaried assessors worked primarily in local government, while salaried appraisers worked mainly for real estate firms.

- Employment is expected to grow faster than average.

Nature of the Work

Appraisers and assessors of real estate estimate the value of property for a variety of purposes, such as to assess property tax, to confirm adequate collateral for mortgages, to confirm or help set a good sales price, to settle an estate, or to aid in a divorce settlement. They often specialize in appraising or assessing a certain type of real estate such as residential buildings or commercial properties. However, they may be called on to estimate the value of any type of real estate, ranging from farmland to a major shopping center. Assessors estimate the value of all properties in a locality for property tax purposes whereas appraisers appraise properties one at a time.

Valuations of all types of real property are conducted using similar methods, regardless of the type of property or who employs the appraiser or assessor. Appraisers and assessors work in localities they are familiar with so they have knowledge of any environmental or other concerns that may affect the value of a property. They note any unique characteristics of the property and of the surrounding area, such as a specific architectural style of a building or a major highway located next to the parcel. They also take into account additional aspects of a property like the condition of the foundation and roof of a building or any renovations that may have been done. Additionally, they may take pictures to document a certain room or feature, in addition to taking pictures of the exterior of the building. After visiting the property, the appraiser or assessor will estimate the fair value of the property by taking into consideration such things as comparable home sales, lease records, location, view, previous appraisals, and income potential.

Appraisers and assessors write detailed reports on their research and observations, stating the value of the parcel as well as the precise reasoning and methodology of how they arrived at the estimate. Writing reports has become faster and easier through the use of laptop computers, allowing them to access data and write at least some of the report on-site. Another computer technology that has affected this occupation is the electronic map of a given jurisdiction and its respective property distribution. Appraisers and assessors use these maps to obtain an accurate perspective on the property and buildings surrounding a property. Digital photos also are commonly used to document the physical appearance of a building or land at the time of appraisal.

Appraisers have independent clients and focus solely on valuing one property at a time. They primarily work on a client-to-client basis, and make appraisals for a variety of reasons. Real property appraisers often specialize by the type of real estate they appraise, such as residential properties, golf courses, or strip malls. In general, commercial appraisers have the ability to appraise any real property but may specialize only in property used for commercial purposes, such as stores or hotels. Residential appraisers focus on appraising homes or other residences and only value those that house 1 to 4 families. Other appraisers have a general practice and value any type of real property.

Assessors predominately work for local governments and are responsible for valuing properties for property tax assessment purposes. Most senior assessors are appointed or elected to their position. Unlike appraisers, assessors often value entire

Appraisers and assessors of real estate may use photographs to help analyze a property.

neighborhoods using mass appraisal techniques to value all the homes in a local neighborhood at one time. Although they do not usually focus on a single property they may assess a single property if the property owner challenges the assessment. They may use a computer-programmed automated valuation model specifically developed for their assigned jurisdictions. In most jurisdictions the entire community must be revalued annually or every few years. Depending on the size of the jurisdiction and the number of staff in an assessor's office, an appraisal firm, often called a revaluation firm, may do much of the work of valuing the properties in the jurisdiction. These results are then officially certified by the assessor.

When properties are reassessed, assessors issue notices of assessments and taxes that each property owner must pay. Assessors must be current on tax assessment procedures and must be able to defend the accuracy of their property assessments, either to the owner directly or at a public hearing, since assessors also are responsible for dealing with tax payers who want to contest their assigned property taxes. Assessors also keep a database of every parcel in their jurisdiction labeling the property owner, issued tax assessment, and size of the property, as well as property maps of the jurisdiction that detail the property distribution of the jurisdiction.

Work environment. Appraisers and assessors spend much of their time researching and writing reports. However, with the advancement of computers and other technologies, such as wireless Internet, time spent in the office has decreased as research can now be done in less time or on-site or at home. Records that once required a visit to a courthouse or city hall often can be found online. This has especially affected self-employed appraisers, often called independent fee appraisers, who make their own office hours, allowing them to spend much more time on-site doing research and less time in their office. Time spent on-site versus in the office also depends on the specialty. For example, residential appraisers tend to spend less time on office work than commercial appraisers, who could spend up to several weeks at one site analyzing documents and writing reports. Appraisers who work for private institutions generally spend most of their time inside the office, making on-site visits when necessary. Appraisers and assessors usually conduct on-site appraisal work alone.

Independent fee appraisers tend to work more than a standard 40 hour work week, in addition to working evenings and weekends writing reports. On-site visits usually occur during daylight hours, and according to the client's schedule. Assessors and privately employed appraisers, on the other hand, usually work a standard 40-hour work week. Occasionally they work an evening or Saturday, to speak with a concerned tax payer, for example. More than 10 percent of appraisers and assessors worked part time in 2006.

Most independent fee appraisers' offices are relatively small, consisting of either just themselves or a small staff. However, private institutions such as banks and mortgage broker offices may employ several appraisers in one office. The size of the office employing assessors depends on the size of the local government; in some States assessments are by counties whereas in other States assessments are made by municipalities or other local governments. Therefore a county assessor's office probably would employ more assessors than a small town, which may only employ a single assessor.

Training, Other Qualifications, and Advancement

The requirements to become a fully qualified appraiser or assessor are complex and vary by State and, sometimes, by the value or type of property. In general, both appraisers and assessors must be licensed or certified requirements. Prospective appraisers and assessors should check with their State to determine the specific requirements.

Education and training. Currently, no formal degree requirements exist to become an appraiser or assessor. However, starting in 2008 all appraisers and assessors who need a license will be required to have a bachelor's degree or the equivalent in credit hours. Most practicing appraisers and assessors have at least a bachelor's degree, sometimes in a related field such as economics, finance, or real estate. The specific training courses necessary, however, are not commonly available as part of most bachelor's programs and must be taken separately, usually at community colleges or through appraisal- or assessor-related organizations.

Obtaining on-the-job training is also an essential part of becoming a fully qualified assessor or appraiser and is required for obtaining a license or certification. In the past, many appraisers obtained experience working in financial institutions or real estate offices. However, the current trend is for candidates to get their initial experience in the office of an independent fee appraiser.

Assessors tend to start out in an assessor's office that is willing to provide on-the-job training; smaller municipalities are often unable to provide this experience. An alternate source of experience for aspiring assessors is through a revaluation firm.

Licensure. Federal law requires that any appraiser involved in a Federally-related transaction with a loan amount of $250,000 or more must have a State-issued license or certification. Licensing requirements vary by State, but they typically include specific training requirements, a period of work as a trainee, and passing one or more examinations.

All States also are required to conform, at a minimum, to the licensing and certification requirements established by the Appraisal Qualifications Board (AQB) of The Appraisal Foundation, a Congressionally-authorized organization dedicated to this purpose. The AQB requires that appraisers pass a Foundation-approved State examination as well as meet education and experience requirements. The education requirements include a course and examination on the Uniform Standards of Professional Appraisal Practice (USPAP) set forth by the Appraisal Standards Board (ASB) of The Appraisal Foundation.

Although Federal standards do not require an appraisal license for appraisers valuing real property with loan amounts of less than $250,000, many States require any practicing appraiser to obtain a license or certification, regardless of transaction value. In addition, many States have different, more stringent requirements for licensure than those set forth by the AQB.

One State-issued appraiser license is the State Certified General Real Property Appraiser license, which allows an appraiser to value any type of real property regardless of value. Another State-issued license is the State Certified Residential Real Property Appraiser license, which allows an appraiser to value any residential unit of 1 to 4 families regardless of value, and any other type of property with a value of up to $250,000. An additional license, which is recommended or used by many States, is the State Licensed Residential Appraiser license, which permits its holder to appraise commercial property up to $250,000 and 1 to 4 family residential units worth up to $1 million.

Starting in 2008, several new educational requirements enacted by the AQB for State Licensure will take effect. For the State Licensed Residential Appraiser license, which is available or required in a majority of States, the candidate must obtain 150 qualifying education hours, 15 of which must be on the National USPAP Course, and at least 2,000 hours of on-the-job training. For the State Certified Residential Appraiser and the State Certified General Appraiser licenses, the required education hours are much more rigorous, at 200 hours and 300 hours, respectively. In addition, all candidates must pass an examination. Also starting in 2008, individuals wishing to become State certified appraisers will need to either possess a college degree or complete a specified number of hours in certain college-level courses. Requirements vary by State so candidates should contact their appropriate State agency to see what specific criteria are mandated.

In many States, those working on their appraiser requirements for licensure are classified as a "trainee." Some of these States have their own training programs while others use the AQB's recommended program. The program varies by State but usually requires at least 75 hours of specified appraisal education, 15 of which must be on the National USPAP Course, before applying for a trainee position. The number of additional courses a trainee must take depends on the State requirements for the license they wish to obtain.

The qualifications necessary to become an assessor also vary by State, but often are similar to the requirements for becoming an appraiser. In most States, the State assessor board sets education and experience requirements that must be met to obtain a certificate to practice as an assessor. A few States have no State-wide requirements; rather, standards are set by each locality.

States mandating assessor certification have requirements similar to those for appraisers. Some States also have more than one level of certification. All candidates must attend State-approved schools and facilities and take basic appraisal courses. Although appraisers value one property at a time while an assessor typically values many, the methods and techniques used are the same. As a result, the main courses assessors take are the same as those for appraisers. In addition, there usually is a set number of on-the-job hours that must be completed and all assessor candidates in these States must pass an examination. In some States, assessors must abide by the USPAP standards and are strongly encouraged to follow these standards in most other States. For those States not requiring certificates, the hiring assessor's office usually will require the candidate to take basic appraisal courses, complete on-the-job training, and accrue a sufficient number of work hours to meet the requirements for appraisal licenses or certificates. Many assessors also possess a State appraisal license.

For both appraisers and assessors, continuing education is necessary to maintain a license or certification. The minimum continuing education requirement for appraisers, as set by the AQB, is 14 hours per year. Appraisers must also complete a 7 hour National USPAP Update Course every 2 years. Some States have further requirements. Continuing education can be obtained in any State-approved school or facility, as well as recognized seminars and conferences held by associations or related organizations. Assessors also must fulfill a continuing education requirement in most States, but the amount varies by State.

Other qualifications. Appraisers and assessors must possess good analytical skills, mathematical skills, and the ability to pay attention to detail. They also must work well with people and alone. Since they will work with the public, politeness is a must, along with the ability to listen and thoroughly answer any questions about their work.

Certification and advancement. Many appraisers and assessors choose to become a designated member of a regional or nationally recognized appraiser or assessor association. Designations are particularly useful in States or types of practices where a license is not mandatory or a certificate has not been established. Designations are another way for appraisers or assessors to establish themselves in the profession, and are recognizable credentials to show employers and potential clients a higher level of education and experience. Obtaining a designation usually requires 5 to 10 years of training and experience, often more than the minimum licensing requirements of the AQB. Many appraisers and assessors start with getting their license or certificate and work their way up to a designation. Many appraisal associations have a membership category specifically for trainees, who then can receive full membership after licensure. Since States differ greatly on the requirements to become an assessor, licensure is not necessarily required for

membership or designations; however, the imposed designation qualifications tend to be very stringent.

Advancement within the occupation comes with experience. The higher the level of appraiser licensure, for example, the higher the fees an independent fee appraiser may charge. Staying in one particular region or focusing on one type of appraising specialty also will help to establish one's business, reputation, and expertise. Assessors often have a career progression within their office, starting as a trainee and eventually ending up appointed or elected as a senior appraiser or supervisor.

Employment

In 2006, appraisers and assessors of real estate held about 101,000 jobs. Most appraisers and assessors work full-time. More than 3 out of 10 were self-employed; virtually all were appraisers. Employment was concentrated in areas with high levels of real estate activity, such as major metropolitan areas. Assessors are more uniformly spread throughout the country than appraisers because every locality has at least one assessor.

About 25 percent worked in local government; almost all were assessors. Another 30 percent, mainly appraisers, worked for real estate firms, while a relatively small number worked for financial institutions, such as banks and credit unions.

Job Outlook

Employment of appraisers and assessors of real estate is expected to grow faster than average for all occupations. Job opportunities should be favorable for those who meet licensing qualifications and have several years of experience.

Employment change. Employment of appraisers and assessors of real estate is expected to grow by 17 percent, which is faster than the average for all occupations, over the 2006-16 decade. Employment of appraisers will grow with increases in the level of real estate activity. Additionally, more appraisers will be hired to help with litigation claims, probate cases, foreclosures, business valuations, and divorce settlements. Employment of assessors will grow with the increase in the amount of real property to be assessed. However, employment will be held down to a certain extent by productivity increases brought about by the increased use of computers and other technologies, which make for faster valuations and allow appraisers to take on more customers and each assessor to assess more properties.

Independent fee appraisers will see the strongest growth because banks and other financial institutions increasingly are contracting work out to them to make loan appraisals on a case-by-case basis. The increased use of automated valuation models to conduct appraisals for loan and mortgage purposes also will shift work out of the financial sector. Additionally, more work is being done in service sectors of the economy, such as in the legal and accounting sectors.

Projections data from the National Employment Matrix

Occupational Title	SOC Code	Employment, 2006	Projected employment, 2016	Change, 2006-16	
				Number	Percent
Appraisers and assessors of real estate	13-2021	101,000	118,000	17,000	17

NOTE: Data in this table are rounded. See the discussion of the employment projections table in the *Handbook* introductory chapter on *Occupational Information Included in the Handbook.*

Job prospects. Employment opportunities should be best in areas with active real estate markets, such as the East and West coasts and major cities and suburbs. Although opportunities for established appraisers and assessors are expected to be good in these areas, those wishing to enter the occupation may have difficulty locating a trainee position because traditional sources of training positions increasingly are prefer not to take on new trainees.

The cyclical nature of the real estate market also will have a direct effect on the job prospects of appraisers, especially those who appraise residential properties. In times of recession, fewer people buy or sell real estate, causing a decrease in the demand for appraisers. As a result, opportunities will be best for appraisers who are able to switch specialties and appraise different types of properties.

Because assessors are needed in every local or State jurisdiction to make assessments for property tax purposes regardless of the state of the local economy, assessors are less affected by economic and real estate market fluctuations than are appraisers. In addition to growth openings, there should be numerous openings because of the need to replace the many appraisers and assessors who are expected to retire or decrease their working hours over the projection period.

Earnings

Median annual earnings of wage and salary appraisers and assessors of real estate were $44,460 in May 2006. The middle 50 percent earned between $32,080 and $64,460. The lowest 10 percent earned less than $24,000 and the highest 10 percent earned more than $86,140. Median annual earnings of those working for local governments were $40,650. Median annual earnings of those working for real estate firms were $44,120. Generally, those working in urban and coastal regions earned more than those working in rural locations.

Related Occupations

Other occupations that involve the inspection of real estate include construction and building inspectors, real estate brokers and sales agents, and urban and regional planners. Appraisers and assessors must also place a monetary value on properties. Occupations also involved in valuing items include claims adjusters, appraisers, examiners and investigators, as well as cost estimators.

Sources of Additional Information

For more information on licensure requirements, contact:
➤ The Appraisal Foundation, 1155 15th Street NW., Suite 1111, Washington, DC 20005.
Internet: **http://www.appraisalfoundation.org**

For more information on individual State licensure requirements, contact:
➤ Appraisal Subcommittee (ASC), 2000 K Street, NW., Suite 310; Washington, D.C. 20006. Internet: **http://www.asc.gov**

For more information on appraisers of real estate, contact:
➤ American Society of Appraisers, 555 Herndon Pkwy., Suite 125, Herndon, VA 20170. Internet: **http://www.appraisers.org**
➤ Appraisal Institute, 550 W. Van Buren St., Suite 1000, Chicago, IL 60607. Internet: **http://www.appraisalinstitute.org**

➤ National Association of Independent Fee Appraisers, 401 N. Michigan Ave. Suite 2200, Chicago, IL 60611.
➤ National Association of Real Estate Appraisers, 1224 North Nokomis NE., Alexandria, MN 56308.

For more information on assessors of real estate, contact:
➤ International Association of Assessing Officers, 314 W 10th St., Kansas City, MO 64105. Internet: **http://www.iaao.org**

Budget Analysts

(O*NET 13-2031.00)

Significant Points

- Good job opportunities are expected.

- A bachelor's degree generally is the minimum educational requirement, but many employers prefer or require a master's degree.

- About 44 percent of all budget analysts work in Federal, State, and local governments.

Nature of the Work

Efficiently distributing limited financial resources is an important challenge in all organizations. In most large and complex organizations, this task would be nearly impossible without budget analysts. These workers develop, analyze, and execute budgets, which are used to allocate current resources and estimate future financial needs.

Budget analysts work in private industry, nonprofit organizations, and the public sector. In private sector firms, a budget analyst's main responsibility is to examine the budget and seek new ways to improve efficiency and increase profits. In nonprofit and governmental organizations, which usually are not concerned with profits, analysts try to find the most efficient way to distribute funds and other resources among various departments and programs.

In recent years, as limited funding has led to downsizing and restructuring throughout private industry and government, budget analysts have seen their role broadened. In addition to managing an organization's budget, they are often involved in program performance evaluation, policy analysis, and the drafting of budget-related legislation. At times, they also conduct training sessions for company or government agency personnel regarding new budget procedures.

At the beginning of each budget cycle, managers and department heads submit proposed operational and financial plans to budget analysts for review. These plans outline the organization's programs, estimate the financial needs of these programs, and propose funding initiatives to meet those needs.

Analysts examine budget estimates and proposals for completeness; accuracy; and conformance with established procedures, regulations, and organizational objectives. Sometimes they employ cost-benefit analyses to review financial requests, assess program tradeoffs, and explore alternative funding methods. They also examine past budgets and research economic and financial developments that affect the organization's spending.

This process enables analysts to evaluate proposals in terms of the organization's priorities and financial resources.

After the initial review process, budget analysts consolidate individual departmental budgets into operating and capital budget summaries. These summaries contain statements that argue for or against funding requests. Budget summaries are then submitted to senior management, or, as is often the case in State and local governments, to appointed or elected officials. Budget analysts then help the chief operating officer, agency head, or other top managers analyze the proposed plan and devise possible alternatives if the projected results are unsatisfactory. The final decision to approve the budget usually is made by the organization head in a private firm, or, in government, by elected officials such as State legislators.

Throughout the year, analysts periodically monitor the budget by reviewing reports and accounting records to determine if allocated funds have been spent as specified. If deviations appear between the approved budget and actual performance, budget analysts may write a report explaining the variations and recommending revised procedures. To avoid or alleviate deficits, budget analysts may recommend program cuts or a reallocation of excess funds. They also inform program managers and others within the organization of the status and availability of funds in different accounts. Before new programs begin or existing programs are changed, a budget analyst must assess the program's efficiency and effectiveness. Analysts also may be involved in long-range financial planning.

Financial software has greatly increased the amount of data and information that budget analysts can consider. The analysts also make extensive use of spreadsheet, database, and word-processing software.

Work environment. Budget analysts usually work in a comfortable office setting. They spend the majority of their time working independently, compiling and analyzing data and preparing budget proposals. Some budget analysts travel to obtain budget details first-hand or to personally verify funding allocation.

The schedules of budget analysts vary throughout the budget cycle, and many are required to work additional hours during the initial development, midyear reviews, and final reviews of budgets. In 2006, about 65 percent of budget analysts worked between 35 and 44 hours per week, while about 17 percent worked more than 44 hours per week, and about 10 percent worked fewer than 35 hours per week. The pressures of deadlines and tight work schedules can be stressful.

Training, Other Qualifications, and Advancement
A bachelor's degree usually is the minimum educational requirement for budget analyst jobs, but some organizations prefer or require a master's degree. Entry-level budget analysts usually begin with limited responsibilities but can be promoted to intermediate-level positions within 1 to 2 years, and to senior positions with additional experience.

Education and training. Private firms and government agencies generally require budget analysts to have at least a bachelor's degree, but many prefer or require a master's degree. Within the Federal Government, a bachelor's degree in any field is sufficient for an entry-level budget analyst position, but mas-

ter's degrees are preferred. State and local governments have varying requirements, but a bachelor's degree in one of many areas, including accounting, finance, business, public administration, economics, statistics, political science, or sociology, is a common requirement. Many States, especially larger, more urban States, require a master's degree. Many government employers prefer candidates with strong analytic and policy analysis backgrounds that may be obtained through such majors as political science, economics, public administration, or public finance.

Some firms prefer candidates with a degree in business because business courses emphasize both quantitative and analytical skills, which are equally important in budget analysis. Sometimes a degree in a field closely related to that of the employing industry or organization, such as engineering, may be preferred. Because developing a budget requires strong numerical and analytical skills, courses in statistics or accounting are helpful, regardless of the prospective budget analyst's major field of study. Occasionally, budget-related or finance-related work experience can be substituted for formal education.

Entry-level budget analysts in the Federal Government receive extensive on-the-job and classroom training. In most other organizations, however, budget analysts usually learn the job by working through one complete budget cycle. During the cycle, which typically lasts 1 year, analysts become familiar with the various steps involved in the budgeting process. Many budget analysts also take professional development classes throughout their careers.

Other qualifications. Budget analysts must abide by strict ethical standards. Integrity, objectivity, and confidentiality are all essential when dealing with financial information, and budget analysts must avoid any personal conflicts of interest. Most budget analysts also need mathematical skills and should be able to use software packages, including spreadsheet, database,

Almost half of all budget analysts work in Federal, State, and local governments.

Projections data from the National Employment Matrix

Occupational Title	SOC Code	Employment, 2006	Projected employment, 2016	Change, 2006-16	
				Number	Percent
Budget analysts	13-2031	62,000	66,000	4,400	7

NOTE: Data in this table are rounded. See the discussion of the employment projections table in the *Handbook* introductory chapter on *Occupational Information Included in the Handbook.*

data-mining, financial analysis, and graphics programs. Strong oral and written communication skills also are essential, because budget analysts must prepare, present, and defend budget proposals to decision makers. In addition, budget analysts must be able to work under strict time constraints.

Certification and advancement. Entry-level budget analysts usually begin with limited responsibilities, working under close supervision. Capable entry-level analysts can be promoted to intermediate-level positions within 1 to 2 years, and to senior positions with additional experience. Because of the importance and high visibility of their jobs, senior budget analysts are prime candidates for promotion to management positions in various parts of their organizations, or with other organizations with which they have worked.

Some government budget analysts employed at the Federal, State, or local level may earn the Certified Government Financial Manager designation granted by the Association of Government Accountants. Other government financial officers also may earn this designation. To do so, candidates must have a minimum of a bachelor's degree, 24 credit hours of study in financial management, and 2 years of government work experience in financial management. They also must pass a series of three exams that cover topics on the government; governmental accounting, financial reporting, and budgeting; and financial management and control. To maintain the designation, individuals must complete 80 hours of continuing professional education every 2 years.

Employment

Budget analysts held 62,000 jobs throughout private industry and government in 2006. Federal, State, and local governments are major employers, accounting for 44 percent of budget analyst jobs. Many other budget analysts worked in manufacturing; financial services; management services; professional, scientific, and technical services; and schools.

Job Outlook

Budget analyst jobs are expected to increase about as fast as the average, and job prospects should generally be good, especially for applicants with a master's degree.

Employment change. Employment of budget analysts is expected to increase by 7 percent between 2006 and 2016, which is about as fast as the average for all occupations. Employment growth will be driven by the continuing demand for sound financial analysis in both the public and the private sectors.

As businesses and other organizations become more complex and specialized, budget planning and financial control will demand greater attention. In recent years, computer applications used in budget analysis have become increasingly sophisticated, allowing more data to be processed in a shorter time. As a result, budget analysts have seen their workload broadened, and they are expected to produce more than they have in the past.

Budget analysts will also continue to acquire new responsibilities in other areas, such as policy analysis and performance evaluation, which make them more important to their organizations.

Job prospects. Good job prospects are expected for budget analysts over the 2006-16 decade. Job openings should result from employment growth and from the need to replace workers who retire or leave the occupation for other reasons. Candidates with a master's degree are expected to have the best opportunities. Familiarity with spreadsheet, database, data-mining, financial-analysis, and graphics software packages also should enhance a jobseeker's prospects.

Because of the importance of financial analysis, and because financial and budget reports must be completed during all phases of the business cycle, budget analysts usually are less vulnerable to layoffs than many other types of workers.

Earnings

Salaries of budget analysts vary widely by experience, education, and employer. Median annual earnings of wage-and-salary budget analysts in May 2006 were $61,430. The middle 50 percent earned between $49,070 and $77,000. The lowest 10 percent earned less than $40,070, and the highest 10 percent earned more than $93,080. Median annual earnings in the industries employing the largest numbers of budget analysts were:

Management of companies and enterprises $65,280
Federal Government..65,240
State government...55,990
Local government 55,120
Colleges, universities, and professional schools..................51,270

In the Federal Government, budget analysts usually start as trainees, earning $28,862 or $35,752 per year in 2007. Candidates with a master's degree began at $43,731. Beginning salaries were slightly higher in areas where the prevailing local pay level was higher. The average annual salary in 2007 for budget analysts employed by the Federal Government was $71,267.

According to a 2007 survey conducted by Robert Half International—a staffing services firm specializing in accounting and finance—starting salaries of financial, budget, treasury, and cost analysts in small companies ranged from $32,750 to $39,250. In large companies, starting salaries ranged from $36,500 to $43,750.

Related Occupations

Budget analysts analyze and interpret financial data, make recommendations for the future, and assist in the implementation of new ideas and financial strategies. Other workers who have similar duties include accountants and auditors, cost estimators, economists, financial analysts and personal financial advisors, financial managers, loan officers, and management analysts.

Sources of Additional Information

Information about career opportunities as a budget analyst may be available from your State or local employment service.

Information on careers and certification in government financial management may be obtained from:

➤ Association of Government Accountants, 2208 Mount Vernon Ave., Alexandria, VA 22301.
Internet: **http://www.agacgfm.org**

Information on careers in budget analysis at the State government level may be obtained from:

➤ National Association of State Budget Officers, Hall of the States Building, Suite 642, 444 North Capitol St.NW., Washington, DC 20001. Internet: **http://www.nasbo.org**

Information on obtaining budget analyst positions with the Federal Government is available from the Office of Personnel Management through USAJOBS, the Federal Government's official employment information system. This resource for locating and applying for job opportunities can be accessed through the Internet at **http://www.usajobs.opm.gov** or through an interactive voice response telephone system at (703) 724-1850. This number is not toll free, and charges may result. For advice on how to find and apply for Federal jobs, see the *Occupational Outlook Quarterly* article "How to get a job in the Federal Government," online at:

http://www.bls.gov/opub/ooq/2004/summer/art01.pdf

Claims Adjusters, Appraisers, Examiners, and Investigators

(O*NET 13-1031.00, 13-1031.01, 13-1031.02, 13-1032.00)

Significant Points

- Employment is expected to increase moderately, but many job openings will arise from the need to replace workers who retire or leave for other reasons.

- Licensing and continuing education requirements vary by State.

- College graduates have the best opportunities; competition will be keen for jobs as investigators because this occupation attracts many qualified people.

Nature of the Work

Individuals and businesses purchase insurance policies to protect against monetary losses. In the event of a loss, policyholders submit claims, or requests for payment, seeking compensation for their loss. Adjusters, appraisers, examiners, and investigators deal with those claims. They work primarily for property and casualty insurance companies, for whom they handle a wide variety of claims alleging property damage, liability, or bodily injury. Their main role is to investigate the claims, negotiate settlements, and authorize payments to claimants, all the while mindful not to violate the claimant's rights under Federal and State privacy laws. They must determine whether the customer's insurance policy covers the loss and how much of the loss should be paid to the claimant. Although many adjusters, appraisers, examiners, and investigators have overlapping functions and may even perform the same tasks, the insurance industry generally assigns specific roles to each of these claims workers.

Adjusters plan and schedule the work required to process a claim. They might, for example, handle the claim filed after an automobile accident or after a storm damages a customer's home. Adjusters investigate claims by interviewing the claimant and witnesses, consulting police and hospital records, and inspecting property damage to determine the extent of the company's liability. Adjusters may consult with other professionals, such as accountants, architects, construction workers, engineers, lawyers, and physicians, who can offer a more expert evaluation of a claim. The information gathered—including photographs and statements, either written, audio, or on video tape—is set down in a report that is then used to evaluate the associated claim. When the policyholder's claim is legitimate, the claims adjuster negotiates with the claimant and settles the claim. When claims are contested, adjusters will work with attorneys and expert witnesses to defend the insurer's position.

Many companies centralize claims adjustment in a claims center, where the cost of repair is estimated and a check is issued immediately. More complex cases, usually involving bodily injury, are referred to senior adjusters. Some adjusters work with multiple types of insurance, but most specialize in homeowner claims, business losses, automotive damage, or workers' compensation.

Claimants can opt not to rely on the services of their insurance company's adjuster and may instead choose to hire a public adjuster. These workers assist clients in preparing and presenting claims to insurance companies and in trying to negotiate a fair settlement. They perform the same services as adjusters who work directly for companies, but they work in the best interests of the client, rather than the insurance company. Independent adjusters are also self-employed and are typically hired by an insurance carrier on a freelance or contractual basis. Insurance companies may choose to hire independent adjusters in lieu of hiring them as regular employees.

Claims examiners within property and casualty insurance firms may have duties similar to those of an adjuster, but often their primary job is to review the claims submitted in order to ensure that proper guidelines have been followed. They may assist adjusters with complex and complicated claims or when a disaster suddenly greatly increases the volume of claims.

Most claims examiners work for life or health insurance companies. In health insurance companies, examiners review health-related claims to see whether costs are reasonable given the diagnosis. Examiners use guides with information on the average period of disability, the expected treatments, and the average hospital stay for the various ailments. Examiners check claim applications for completeness and accuracy, interview medical specialists, and consult policy files to verify the information reported in a claim. Examiners will then either authorize the appropriate payment or refer the claim to an investigator for a more thorough review. Claims examiners usually specialize in group or individual insurance plans and in hospital, dental, or prescription drug claims.

In life insurance, claims examiners review the causes of death, particularly in the case of an accident, because most life insurance policies pay additional benefits if a death is accidental. Claims examiners also may review new applications for life insurance to make sure that the applicants have no serious illnesses that would make them a high risk to insure and thus disqualify them from obtaining insurance.

Another occupation that plays an important role in the accurate settlement of claims is that of the *appraiser*, whose role is to estimate the cost or value of an insured item. The majority of appraisers employed by insurance companies and independent adjusting firms are *auto damage appraisers*. These appraisers inspect damaged vehicles after an accident and estimate the cost of repairs. This information is then relayed to the adjuster, who incorporates the appraisal into the settlement. Auto damage appraisers are valued by insurance companies because they can provide an unbiased judgment of repair costs. Otherwise, the companies would have to rely on auto mechanics' estimates, which might be unreasonably high.

Many claims adjusters and auto damage appraisers are equipped with laptop computers from which they can download the necessary forms and files from insurance company databases. They also may use digital cameras, which allow photographs of the damage to be sent to the company via the Internet. Many also input information about the damage directly into their computers, where software programs produce estimates of damage on standard forms. These new technologies allow for faster and more efficient processing of claims.

When adjusters or examiners suspect fraud, they refer the claim to an investigator. *Insurance investigators* in an insurance company's special investigative unit handle claims in which the company suspects fraudulent or criminal activity, such as arson, falsified workers' disability claims, staged accidents, or unnecessary medical treatments. The severity of insurance fraud cases can vary greatly, from claimants simply overstating the damage to a vehicle to complicated fraud rings responsible for many claimants and supported by dishonest doctors, lawyers, and even insurance personnel.

Investigators usually start with a database search to obtain background information on claimants and witnesses. Investigators can access certain personal information and identify Social Security numbers, aliases, driver's license numbers, addresses, phone numbers, criminal records, and past claims histories to establish whether a claimant has ever attempted insurance fraud. Then, investigators may visit claimants and witnesses to obtain a recorded statement, take photographs, and inspect facilities, such as doctors' offices, to determine whether the doctors have a proper license. Investigators often consult with legal counsel and can be expert witnesses in court cases.

Often, investigators also perform surveillance work. For example, in a case involving fraudulent workers' compensation claims, an investigator may covertly observe the claimant for several days or even weeks. If the investigator observes the subject performing an activity that is ruled out by injuries stated in a workers' compensation claim, the investigator will take video or still photographs to document the activity and report it to the insurance company.

Work environment. Working environments of claims adjusters, appraisers, examiners, and investigators vary greatly. Many claims adjusters and auto damage appraisers, often work outside the office, inspecting damaged buildings and automobiles. Adjusters who inspect damaged buildings must be wary of potential hazards such as collapsed roofs and floors, as well as weakened structures.

Adjusters report to the office every morning to get their assignments, while others simply call in from home and spend their days traveling to claim sites. New technology, such as laptop computers and cellular telephones, is making telecommuting easier for claims adjusters and auto damage appraisers. Many adjusters work inside their office only a few hours a week, while others conduct their business entirely out of their home and automobile. Occasionally, experienced adjusters must be away from home for days—for example, when they travel to the scene of a disaster such as a tornado, hurricane, or flood—to work with local adjusters and government officials.

Most claims examiners employed by life and health insurance companies work a standard 5-day, 40-hour week in a typical office environment. In contrast, adjusters often must arrange their work schedules to accommodate evening and weekend appointments with clients. This sometimes results in adjusters working irregular schedules or more than 40 hours a week, especially when they have a lot of claims to investigate. Adjusters often are called to work in the event of emergencies and may have to work 50 or 60 hours a week until all claims are resolved.

Appraisers spend much of their time offsite at automotive body shops estimating vehicle damage costs. The remaining time may be spent working in the office. Many independent appraisers work from home, which has been made easier through new computer software valuation programs. Auto damage appraisers typically work regular hours, and rarely work on the weekends. Self employed appraisers also have the flexibility to make their own hours, as many appraisals are done by appointment.

Some days, investigators will spend all day in the office, searching databases, making telephone calls, and writing re-

Auto damage appraisers may document the state of the automobile in their loss estimation reports.

ports. Other times, they may be away, performing surveillance activities or interviewing witnesses. Some of the work can involve confrontation with claimants and others involved in a case, so the job can be stressful and dangerous. Insurance investigators often work irregular hours because of the need to conduct surveillance and contact people who are not available during normal working hours. Early morning, evening, and weekend work is common.

Training, Other Qualifications, and Advancement

Training and entry requirements vary widely for claims adjusters, appraisers, examiners, and investigators. Although many in these occupations do not have a college degree, most companies prefer to hire college graduates.

Education and training. There are no formal education requirements for any of these occupations, and a high school degree is typically the minimal requirement needed to obtain employment. However, most employers prefer to hire college graduates or people who have some postsecondary training.

No specific college major is recommended, but a variety of degrees can be an asset. For example, a claims adjuster who has a business or an accounting background might be suited to specialize in claims of financial loss due to strikes, breakdowns of equipment, or damage to merchandise. College training in architecture or engineering is helpful in adjusting industrial claims, such as those involving damage from fires or other accidents. A legal background can be beneficial to someone handling workers' compensation and product liability cases. A medical background is useful for those examiners working on medical and life insurance claims.

The following tabulation presents the 2006 percent distribution of all claims adjusters, appraisers, examiners, and investigators by their highest level of educational attainment:

	Percent
High school graduate or less	22
Some college, no degree	17
Associate's degree	12
Bachelor's degree	45
Graduate degree	5

For auto damage appraiser jobs, firms typically prefer to hire people who also have experience as an estimator or as a manager of an auto body repair shop. Also, an appraiser must know how to repair vehicles in order to identify and estimate damage. Technical skills are essential. While auto damage appraisers do not require a college education, most companies prefer to hire persons with formal training. Many vocational colleges offer 2-year programs in auto body repair and teach students how to estimate the costs to repair damaged vehicles.

For investigator jobs, most insurance companies prefer to hire people trained as law enforcement officers, private investigators, claims adjusters, or examiners because these workers have good interviewing and interrogation skills.

Beginning claims adjusters, appraisers, examiners, and investigators work on small claims under the supervision of an experienced workers. As they learn more about claims investigation and settlement, they are assigned larger, more complex claims. Trainees take on more responsibility as they demonstrate competence in handling assignments and progress in their coursework. Auto damage appraisers may also receive some on-the-job training, which may last several months. They may work under close supervision while estimating damage costs until their employer decides they are ready to perform estimates on their own.

Continuing education is very important for claims adjusters, appraisers, examiners, and investigators because Federal and State laws and court decisions affect how claims are handled or who is covered by insurance policies. Also, examiners working on life and health claims must be familiar with new medical procedures and prescription drugs. Examiners working on auto claims must be familiar with new car models and repair techniques.

Many companies offer training sessions to inform their employees of industry changes, and a number of schools and associations give courses and seminars on various topics having to with claims. Correspondence courses via the Internet are also making long-distance learning possible.

Licensure. Licensing requirements for claims adjusters, appraisers, examiners, and investigators vary by State. Some States have few requirements, while others require either the completion of prelicensing education, a satisfactory score on a licensing exam, or both. Earning a voluntary professional designation can sometimes substitute for completing an exam. In some States, claims adjusters employed by insurance companies can work under the company license and need not become licensed themselves. Public adjusters may need to meet separate or additional requirements. For example, some States require public adjusters to file a surety bond.

Some States that require licensing also require a certain number of continuing education credits per year in order to renew the license. Workers can fulfill their continuing education requirements by attending classes or workshops, by writing articles for claims publications, or by giving lectures and presentations.

Other qualifications. Claims adjusters, appraisers, and examiners often work closely with claimants, witnesses, and other insurance professionals, so they must be able to communicate effectively with others. Knowledge of computer applications also is very helpful. In addition, a valid driver's license and a good driving record are required for workers who must travel on the job. Some companies require applicants to pass a series of written aptitude tests designed to measure their communication, analytical, and general mathematical skills.

When hiring investigators, employers look for individuals who have ingenuity and who are persistent and assertive. Investigators should not be afraid of confrontation, should communicate well, and should be able to think on their feet. Good interviewing and interrogation skills also are important and usually are acquired in earlier careers in law enforcement.

Certification and advancement. Employees who demonstrate competence in claims work or administrative skills may be promoted to more responsible managerial or administrative jobs. Similarly, claims investigators may rise to become supervisor or manager of the investigations department. Once they achieve expertise, many choose to start their own independent adjusting or auto damage appraising firms.

Projections data from the National Employment Matrix

Occupational Title	SOC Code	Employment, 2006	Projected employment, 2016	Change, 2006-16	
				Number	Percent
Claims adjusters, appraisers, examiners, and investigators	13-1030	319,000	347,000	29,000	9
Claims adjusters, examiners, and investigators............................	13-1031	305,000	332,000	27,000	9
Insurance appraisers, auto damage	13-1032	13,000	15,000	1,700	13

NOTE: Data in this table are rounded. See the discussion of the employment projections table in the *Handbook* introductory chapter on *Occupational Information Included in the Handbook*.

Numerous examiners and adjusters also earn professional certifications and designations to demonstrate their professional expertise. Although requirements for these designations vary, many entail at least 5 to 10 years of experience in the claims field and the successful completion of an examination; in addition, a certain number of continuing education credits must be earned each year to retain the designation.

Employment

Adjusters, appraisers, examiners, and investigators held about 319,000 jobs in 2006. Insurance carriers, agencies, brokerages, and related industries, such as private claims adjusting companies, employed more than 7 out of 10 claims adjusters, appraisers, examiners, and investigators. Less than 5 percent of these jobs were held by auto damage insurance appraisers. Relatively few adjusters, appraisers, examiners, and investigators were self-employed.

Job Outlook

Despite average job growth, keen competition for claims adjuster, appraiser, examiner, and investigator jobs is expected, especially in smaller, privately owned companies. For claims adjusters, opportunities will be best for those who have a license and related experience. For appraiser jobs, opportunities will be best for those who have some vocational training and previous auto body repair experience.

Employment change. Employment of claims adjusters, appraisers, examiners, and investigators is expected to grow by 9 percent over the 2006-16 decade, which is about as fast as the average for all occupations. Many insurance carriers are downsizing their claims staff in an effort to contain costs. Larger companies are relying more on customer service representatives in call centers, for example, to handle the recording of the necessary details of the claim, allowing adjusters to spend more of their time investigating claims. New technology is reducing the amount of time it takes for an adjuster to complete a claim, thereby increasing the number of claims that one adjuster can handle. The demand for these jobs will increase regardless of new technology, however, because they cannot be easily automated. Additionally, a growing need for adjusters, appraisers, examiners, and investigators will stem from more insurance policies being sold to accommodate a growing population. Further, as the elderly population increases, there will be a greater need for health care, resulting in more health insurance claims.

Employment of insurance investigators is not expected to grow significantly, despite the expected increase in the number of claims in litigation and the number and complexity of insurance fraud cases. Technology, such as the Internet, reduces the amount of time it takes investigators to perform background checks, allowing them to handle more cases. However, adjusters are still needed to contact policyholders, inspect damaged property, and consult with experts.

As with claims adjusters, examiners, and investigators, employment of auto damage appraisers should grow by 13 percent, which is also about as fast as the average for all occupations. Insurance companies and agents continue to sell growing numbers of auto insurance policies, leading to more claims being filed that require the attention of an auto damage appraiser. The work of auto damage appraisers is also not easily automated because most appraisals require an onsite inspection, but new technology is making them somewhat more efficient. In addition, some insurance companies are opening their own repair facilities, which may reduce the need for auto damage appraisers.

Job prospects. Numerous job openings also will result from job growth and the need to replace workers who transfer to other occupations or leave the labor force. Overall, college graduates and those with previous related experience will have the best opportunities for jobs as claims adjusters, examiners, and investigators. Auto damage appraisers with related vocational training and auto body shop experience will also have good prospects. People entering these occupations with no previous experience or formal training may find more opportunities working directly for an insurance carrier.

Competition for investigator jobs will remain keen because the occupation attracts many qualified people, including retirees from law enforcement, the military, and experienced claims adjusters and examiners who choose to get an investigator license. Heightened media and public awareness of insurance fraud also may attract qualified candidates to this occupation.

Earnings

Earnings of claims adjusters, appraisers, examiners, and investigators vary significantly. Median annual earnings were $50,660 in May 2006 for wage and salary workers. The middle 50 percent earned between $38,520 and $65,210. The lowest 10 percent earned less than $30,890, and the highest 10 percent earned more than $79,170.

Median annual earnings of wage and salary auto damage insurance appraisers were $49,180 in May 2006. The middle 50 percent earned between $40,870 and $57,830. The lowest 10 percent earned less than $34,220, and the highest 10 percent earned more than $68,420.

Many claims adjusters, especially those who work for insurance companies, receive additional bonuses or benefits as part of their job. Adjusters often are furnished a laptop computer, a cellular telephone, and a company car, or are reimbursed for the use of their own vehicle for business purposes.

Related Occupations

Property-casualty insurance adjusters and life and health insurance examiners must determine the validity of a claim and negotiate a settlement. They also are responsible for determining how much to reimburse the client. Occupations similar to those of claims adjusters, appraisers, examiners, and investigators include cost estimators; bill and account collectors; medical records and health information technicians; billing and posting clerks; credit authorizers, checkers, and clerks; and bookkeeping, accounting, and auditing clerks.

In determining the validity of a claim, insurance adjusters must inspect the damage in order to assess the magnitude of the loss. Workers who perform similar duties include fire inspectors and investigators and construction and building inspectors.

To ensure that company practices and procedures are followed, property and casualty examiners review insurance claims to which a claims adjuster has already proposed a settlement. Others in occupations that review documents for accuracy and compliance with a given set of rules and regulations are tax examiners, collectors, and revenue agents, as well as accountants and auditors.

Like automotive body and related repairers and automotive service technicians and mechanics, auto damage appraisers must be familiar with the structure and functions of various automobiles and their parts. They must also be familiar with techniques to estimate value, which is a requirement similar to appraisers and assessors of real estate.

Insurance investigators detect and investigate fraudulent claims and criminal activity. Their work is similar to that of private detectives and investigators.

Sources of Additional Information

General information about a career as a claims adjuster, appraiser, examiner, or investigator is available from the home offices of many insurance companies.

Information about licensing requirements for claims adjusters may be obtained from the department of insurance in each State.

Information about the property-casualty insurance field can be obtained by contacting:

➤ Insurance Information Institute, 110 William St., New York, NY 10038. Internet: **http://www.iii.org**

Information about the health insurance field can be obtained by contacting:

➤ National Association of Health Underwriters, 2000 North 14th Street, Suite 450, Arlington, VA 22201.
Internet: **http://www.nahu.org**

For information about professional designation and training programs, contact any of the following organizations:

➤ American College, 270 South Bryn Mawr Ave., Bryn Mawr, PA 19010–2196.
Internet: **http://www.theamericancollege.edu**

➤ American Institute for Chartered Property Casualty Underwriters and the Insurance Institute of America, 720 Providence Rd., P.O. Box 3016, Malvern, PA 19355–0716.
Internet: **http://www.aicpcu.org**

➤ International Claim Association, 1255 23rd St. NW., Washington, DC 20037. Internet: **http://www.claim.org**

➤ LOMA, 2300 Windy Ridge Parkway, Suite 600, Atlanta, GA 30339-8443. Internet: **http://www.loma.org**

Information on careers in auto damage appraising can be obtained from:

➤ Independent Automotive Damage Appraisers Association, P.O. Box 12291 Columbus, GA 31917–2291.
Internet: **http://www.iada.org**

Cost Estimators

(O*NET 13-1051.00)

Significant Points

- About 62 percent of cost estimators work in the construction industry, and another 15 percent are employed in manufacturing industries.

- Voluntary certification can be valuable to cost estimators; some individual employers may require professional certification for employment.

- Very good employment opportunities are expected.

- In construction and manufacturing, job prospects should be best for those with industry work experience and a bachelor's degree in a related field.

Nature of the Work

Accurately forecasting the scope, cost, and duration of future projects is vital to the survival of any business. Cost estimators develop the cost information that business owners or managers need to make a bid for a contract or to decide on the profitability of a proposed new product or project. They also determine which endeavors are making a profit.

Regardless of the industry in which they work, estimators compile and analyze data on all of the factors that can influence costs, such as materials, labor, location, duration of the project, and special machinery requirements, including computer hardware and software. Job duties vary widely depending on the type and size of the project.

The methods for estimating costs can differ greatly by industry. On a construction project, for example, the estimating process begins with the decision to submit a bid. After reviewing various preliminary drawings and specifications, the estimator visits the site of the proposed project. The estimator needs to gather information on access to the site; the availability of electricity, water, and other services; and surface topography and drainage. The estimator usually records this information in a signed report that is included in the final project estimate.

After the site visit, the estimator determines the quantity of materials and labor the firm will need to furnish. This process, called the quantity survey or "takeoff," involves completing standard estimating forms, filling in dimensions, numbers of units, and other information. A cost estimator working for a general contractor, for example, estimates the costs of all of the items that the contractor must provide. Although subcontractors estimate their costs as part of their own bidding process, the general contractor's cost estimator often analyzes bids made by subcontractors. Also during the takeoff process, the estimator must make decisions concerning equipment needs, the sequence of operations, the size of the crew required, and physical constraints at the site. Allowances for wasted materials, inclement weather, shipping delays, and other factors that may increase costs also must be incorporated in the estimate.

After completing the quantity surveys, the estimator prepares a cost summary for the entire project, including the costs of labor, equipment, materials, subcontracts, overhead, taxes, insurance, markup, and any other costs that may affect the project. The chief estimator then prepares the bid proposal for submission to the owner.

Construction cost estimators also may be employed by the project's architect or owner to estimate costs or to track actual costs relative to bid specifications as the project develops. Estimators often specialize in large construction companies employing more than one estimator. For example, one may estimate only electrical work and another may concentrate on excavation, concrete, and forms.

In manufacturing and other firms, cost estimators usually are assigned to the engineering, cost, or pricing department. The estimator's goal is to accurately estimate the costs associated with making products. The job may begin when management requests an estimate of the costs associated with a major redesign of an existing product or the development of a new product or production process. When estimating the cost of developing a new product, for example, the estimator works with engineers, first reviewing blueprints or conceptual drawings to determine the machining operations, tools, gauges, and materials that would be required. The estimator then prepares a parts list and determines whether it is more efficient to produce or to purchase the parts. To do this, the estimator asks for price information from potential suppliers. The next step is to determine the cost of manufacturing each component of the product. Some high-technology products require a considerable amount of computer programming during the design phase. The cost of software development is one of the fastest growing and most difficult activities to estimate. As a result, some cost estimators now specialize in estimating only computer software development and related costs.

The cost estimator then prepares time-phase charts and learning curves. Time-phase charts indicate the time required for tool design and fabrication, tool "debugging"—finding and correcting all problems—manufacturing of parts, assembly, and testing. Learning curves graphically represent the rate at which the performance of workers producing parts for the new product improves with practice. These curves are commonly called "cost reduction" curves, because many problems—such as engineering changes, rework, shortages of parts, and lack of operator skills—diminish as the number of units produced increases, resulting in lower unit costs.

Using all of this information, the estimator then calculates the standard labor hours necessary to produce a specified number of units. Standard labor hours are then converted to dollar values, to which are added factors for waste, overhead, and profit to yield the unit cost in dollars. The estimator then compares the cost of purchasing parts with the firm's estimated cost of manufacturing them to determine which is cheaper.

Cost estimators analyze data on factors that influence costs to determine whether a contract is viable.

Computers play an integral role in cost estimation because estimating often involves complex mathematical calculations and requires advanced mathematical techniques. For example, to undertake a parametric analysis (a process used to estimate costs per unit based on square footage or other specific requirements of a project), cost estimators use a computer database containing information on the costs and conditions of many other similar projects. Although computers cannot be used for the entire estimating process, they can relieve estimators of much of the drudgery associated with routine, repetitive, and time-consuming calculations. New and improved cost estimating software has lead to more efficient computations, leaving estimators greater time to visit and analyze projects.

Operations research, production control, cost, and price analysts who work for government agencies may do significant amounts of cost estimating in the course of their regular duties. In addition, the duties of construction managers may include estimating costs. (For more information, see the statements on operations research analysts and construction managers elsewhere in the *Handbook*.)

Work environment. Although estimators spend most of their time in a comfortable office, construction estimators also visit worksites that can be dusty, dirty, and occasionally hazardous. Likewise, estimators in manufacturing spend time on the factory floor, where it also can be noisy and dirty. In some industries, frequent travel between a firm's headquarters and its subsidiaries or subcontractors may be required.

Estimators normally work a 40-hour week, but overtime is common. Cost estimators often work under pressure and stress, especially when facing bid deadlines. Inaccurate estimating can cause a firm to lose a bid or to lose money on a job that was not accurately estimated.

Training, Other Qualifications, and Advancement

Job entry requirements for cost estimators vary by industry. In the construction industry, employers increasingly prefer to hire cost estimators with a bachelor's degree in construction science, construction management, or building science, although it is also possible for experienced construction workers to become cost estimators. Employers in manufacturing usually prefer someone with a bachelor's degree in mathematics, statistics, or engineering.

Education and training. In the construction industry, employers increasingly prefer individuals with a degree in building science, construction management, or construction science, all of which usually include several courses in cost estimating. Most construction estimators also have considerable construction experience, gained through work in the industry, internships, or cooperative education programs. Applicants with a thorough knowledge of construction materials, costs, and procedures in areas ranging from heavy construction to electrical work, plumbing systems, or masonry work have a competitive edge.

In manufacturing industries, employers prefer to hire individuals with a degree in engineering, physical science, operations research, mathematics, or statistics or in accounting, finance, business, economics, or a related subject. In most industries, experience in quantitative techniques is important.

Many colleges and universities include cost estimating as part of bachelor's and associate degree curriculums in civil engineering, industrial engineering, and construction management or construction engineering technology. In addition, cost estimating is often part of master's degree programs in construction science or construction management. Organizations representing cost estimators, such as the Association for the Advancement of Cost Engineering (AACE International) and the Society of Cost Estimating and Analysis (SCEA), also sponsor educational and professional development programs. These programs help students, estimators-in-training, and experienced estimators learn about changes affecting the profession. Specialized courses and programs in cost-estimating techniques and procedures also are offered by many technical schools, community colleges, and universities.

Estimators also receive much training on the job because every company has its own way of handling estimates. Work-

ing with an experienced estimator, newcomers become familiar with each step in the process. Those with no experience reading construction specifications or blueprints first learn that aspect of the work. Then they may accompany an experienced estimator to the construction site or shop floor, where they observe the work being done, take measurements, or perform other routine tasks. As they become more knowledgeable, estimators learn how to tabulate quantities and dimensions from drawings and how to select the appropriate prices for materials.

Other qualifications. Cost estimators should have an aptitude for mathematics; be able to quickly analyze, compare, and interpret detailed but sometimes poorly defined information; and be able to make sound and accurate judgments based on this information. The ability to focus on details, while analyzing and overcoming larger obstacles, is essential. Assertiveness and self-confidence in presenting and supporting conclusions are also important, as are strong communications and interpersonal skills, because estimators may work as part of a team alongside managers, owners, engineers, and design professionals. Cost estimators also need knowledge of computers, including word-processing and spreadsheet packages. In some instances, familiarity with special estimation software or programming skills also may be required.

Certification and advancement. Voluntary certification can be valuable to cost estimators because it provides professional recognition of the estimator's competence and experience. In some instances, individual employers may even require professional certification for employment. Both AACE International and SCEA administer certification programs. To become certified, estimators usually must have between 2 and 8 years of estimating experience and must pass an examination. In addition, certification requirements may include the publication of at least one article or paper in the field.

For most estimators, advancement takes the form of higher pay and prestige. Some move into management positions, such as project manager for a construction firm or manager of the industrial engineering department for a manufacturer. Others may go into business for themselves as consultants, providing estimating services for a fee to government or to construction or manufacturing firms.

Employment

Cost estimators held about 221,000 jobs in 2006. About 62 percent of estimators were in the construction industry, and another 15 percent were employed in manufacturing. The remainder worked in a wide range of other industries.

Cost estimators work throughout the country, usually in or near major industrial, commercial, and government centers and in cities and suburban areas undergoing rapid change or development.

Projections data from the National Employment Matrix

Occupational Title	SOC Code	Employment, 2006	Projected employment, 2016	Change, 2006-16	
				Number	Percent
Cost estimators..	13-1051	221,000	262,000	41,000	19

NOTE: Data in this table are rounded. See the discussion of the employment projections table in the *Handbook* introductory chapter on *Occupational Information Included in the Handbook.*

Job Outlook

Employment of cost estimators is expected to grow faster than average. Very good employment opportunities are expected.

Employment change. Employment is expected to grow by 19 percent between 2006 and 2016, which is faster than the average for all occupations. Employment growth in the construction industry, in which most cost estimators are employed, will account for the majority of new jobs in this occupation. Construction and repair of highways, streets, bridges, subway systems, airports, water and sewage systems, and electric power plants and transmission lines will stimulate demand for many more cost estimators. Similarly, increasing population and business growth will result in more construction of residential homes, office buildings, shopping malls, hospitals, schools, restaurants, and other structures that require cost estimators. As the population ages, the demand for nursing and extended-care facilities will also increase. The growing complexity of construction projects will also boost demand for cost estimators as a larger number of workers specialize in a particular area of construction.

Job prospects. Because there are no formal bachelor's degree programs in cost estimating, some employers have difficulty recruiting qualified cost estimators, resulting in very good employment opportunities. Job prospects in construction should be best for those who have a degree in construction science, construction management, or building science plus practical experience in the various phases of construction or in a specialty craft area. For cost estimating jobs in manufacturing, those with degrees in mathematics, statistics, engineering, accounting, business administration, or economics should have the best job prospects.

In addition to job openings arising from employment growth, many additional openings should result annually from the need to replace workers who transfer to other occupations due to the sometimes stressful nature of the work, or who retire or leave the occupation for other reasons.

Employment of cost estimators, like that of many other construction workers, is sensitive to the fluctuations of the economy. Workers in these trades may experience periods of unemployment when the overall level of construction falls. On the other hand, shortages of these workers may occur in some areas during peak periods of building activity.

Earnings

Salaries of cost estimators vary widely by experience, education, size of firm, and industry. Median annual earnings of wage and salary cost estimators in May 2006 were $52,940. The middle 50 percent earned between $40,320 and $69,460. The lowest 10 percent earned less than $31,600, and the highest 10 percent earned more than $88,310. Median annual earnings in the industries employing the largest numbers of cost estimators were:

Nonresidential building construction	$60,870
Building equipment contractors	56,170
Foundation, structure, and building exterior contractors	52,520
Residential building construction	52,460
Building finishing contractors	51,610

According to a July 2007 salary survey by the National Association of Colleges and Employers, those with bachelor's degrees in construction science/management received job offers averaging $46,930 a year.

Related Occupations

Other workers who quantitatively analyze information include accountants and auditors; budget analysts; claims adjusters, appraisers, examiners, and investigators; economists; financial analysts and personal financial advisors; insurance underwriters; loan officers; market and survey researchers; and operations research analysts. In addition, the duties of industrial production managers and construction managers also may involve analyzing costs.

Sources of Additional Information

Information about career opportunities, certification, educational programs, and cost-estimating techniques may be obtained from the following organizations:

➤ Association for the Advancement of Cost Engineering (AACE International), 209 Prairie Ave., Suite 100, Morgantown, WV 26501. Internet: **http://www.aacei.org**

➤ Society of Cost Estimating and Analysis, 527 Maple Ave. East, Suite 301, Vienna, VA 22180.
Internet: **http://www.sceaonline.net**

Financial Analysts and Personal Financial Advisors

(O*NET 13-2051.00, 13-2052.00)

Significant Points

- Good interpersonal skills and an aptitude for working with numbers are among the most important qualifications for financial analysts and personal financial advisors.

- Keen competition is anticipated for these highly paid positions, despite rapid job growth; those who have earned a professional designation or an MBA are expected to have the best opportunities.

- Almost one third of personal financial advisors are self-employed.

Nature of the Work

Financial analysts and personal financial advisors provide analysis and guidance to businesses and individuals in making investment decisions. Both types of specialists gather financial information, analyze it, and make recommendations. However, their job duties differ because of the type of investment information they provide and their relationships with investors.

Financial analysts assess the economic performance of companies and industries for firms and institutions with money to invest. Also called *securities analysts* and *investment analysts*, they work for investment banks, insurance companies, mutual and pension funds, securities firms, the business media, and other businesses, helping them make investment decisions or recommendations. Financial analysts read company financial statements and analyze commodity prices, sales, costs, expenses, and tax rates in order to determine a company's value and to project its future earnings. They often meet with company officials to gain a better insight into the firm's prospects and to determine its managerial effectiveness.

Financial analysts can usually be divided into two basic types: those who work on the *buy side* and those who work on the *sell side*. Analysts on the buy side work for companies that have a great deal of money to invest. These companies, called institutional investors, include mutual funds, hedge funds, insurance companies, independent money managers, and charitable organizations, such as universities and hospitals, with large endowments. Buy side financial analysts work to devise investment strategies for a company's portfolio. Conversely, analysts on the sell side help securities dealers to sell their products. These companies include investment banks and securities firms. The business media also hire financial advisors that are supposed to be impartial, and as such occupy a role somewhere in the middle.

Financial analysts generally focus on a specific industry, region, or type of product. For example, an analyst may focus on the utilities industry, Latin America, or the options market. Firms with larger research departments may divide the work even further so their analysts can maintain sharp focus. Within their areas of specialty, analysts assess current trends in business practices, products, and competition. They must keep abreast of new regulations or policies that may affect the investments they are watching and monitor the economy to determine its effect on earnings. Some experienced analysts called *portfolio managers* supervise a team of analysts and help guide a company in selecting the right mix of products, industries, and regions for their investment portfolio. Others who manage mutual funds or hedge funds perform a similar role and are generally called *fund managers*. Other analysts, called *risk managers*, analyze portfolio decisions and determine how to maximize profits through diversification and hedging.

Some financial analysts, called *ratings analysts*, evaluate the ability of companies or governments that issue bonds to repay their debts. On the basis of their evaluation, a management team assigns a rating to a company's or government's bonds, which helps them to decide whether to include them in a portfolio. Other financial analysts perform budget, cost, and credit analysis as part of their responsibilities.

Financial analysts use spreadsheet and statistical software packages to analyze financial data, spot trends, and develop forecasts. Analysts also use the data they find to measure the financial risks associated with making a particular investment decision. On the basis of their results, they write reports and make presentations, usually with recommendations to buy or sell particular investments.

Personal financial advisors assess the financial needs of individuals. Advisors use their knowledge of investments, tax laws, and insurance to recommend financial options to individuals. They help them to identify and plan to meet short- and long-term goals. Planners help clients with retirement and estate planning, funding the college education of children, and gen-

Personal financial advisors often meet with their clients to help them make investment decisions.

eral investment choices. Many also provide tax advice or sell life insurance. Although most planners offer advice on a wide range of topics, some specialize in areas such as retirement and estate planning or risk management.

Personal financial advisors usually work with many clients, and they often must find their own customers. Many personal financial advisors spend a great deal of their time making sales calls and marketing their services. Many advisors also meet potential clients by giving seminars or lectures or through business and social contacts. Finding clients and building a customer base is one of the most important aspects of becoming successful as a financial advisor.

Financial advisors begin work with a client by setting up a consultation. This is usually an in-person meeting where the advisor obtains as much information as possible about the client's finances and goals. The advisor then develops a comprehensive financial plan that identifies problem areas, makes recommendations for improvement, and selects appropriate investments compatible with the client's goals, attitude toward risk, and expectation or need for a return on the investment. Sometimes this plan is written, but more often it is in the form of verbal advice. Advisors sometimes meet with accountants or legal professionals for help.

Financial advisors usually meet with established clients at least once a year to update them on potential investments and adjust their financial plan to any life changes—such as marriage, disability, or retirement. Financial advisors also answer clients' questions regarding changes in benefit plans or the consequences of a change in their jobs or careers. Financial planners must educate their clients about risks and various possible scenarios so that the clients don't harbor unrealistic expectations.

Most personal financial advisors buy and sell financial products, such as securities and life insurance. Fees and commissions from the purchase and sale of securities and life insurance plans are one of the major sources of income for most personal financial advisors.

Private bankers or *wealth managers* are personal financial advisors who work for people who have a lot of money to invest. While most investors are simply saving for retirement or their children's college education, these individuals have large amounts of capital and often use the returns on their investments as a major source of income. Because they have so much capital, these clients resemble institutional investors and approach investing differently from the general public. Private bankers manage portfolios for these individuals using the resources of the bank, including teams of financial analysts, accountants, lawyers, and other professionals. Private bankers sell these services to wealthy individuals, generally spending most of their time working with a small number of clients. Unlike most personal financial advisors, private bankers meet with their clients regularly to keep them abreast of financial matters; they often have the responsibility of directly managing customers' finances.

Work environment. Financial analysts and personal financial advisors usually work in offices or their own homes. Financial analysts may work long hours, travel frequently to visit companies or potential investors, and face the pressure of deadlines. Much of their research must be done after office hours because their days are filled with telephone calls and meetings.

Personal financial advisors usually work standard business hours, but they also schedule meetings with clients in the evenings or on weekends. Many also teach evening classes or hold seminars in order to bring in more clients. Some personal financial advisors spend a fair amount of their time traveling, usually to attend conferences and training sessions, but also occasionally to visit clients.

Private bankers also generally work during standard business hours, but because they work so closely with their clients, they may have to be available outside normal hours upon request.

Training, Other Qualifications, and Advancement

Financial analysts and most personal financial advisors must have a bachelor's degree. Many also earn a master's degree in finance or business administration or get professional designations. Because the field is so specialized, workers frequently attend training and seminars to learn the latest developments.

Education and training. A bachelor's or graduate degree is required for financial analysts and is strongly preferred for personal financial advisors. Most companies require financial analysts to have at least a bachelor's degree in finance, business administration, accounting, statistics, or economics. Coursework in statistics, economics, and business is required, and knowledge of accounting policies and procedures, corporate budgeting, and financial analysis methods is recommended. A master's degree in finance or business administration also is desirable. Also useful are advanced courses in options pricing or bond valuation and knowledge of risk management.

Employers usually do not require a specific field of study for personal financial advisors, but a bachelor's degree in accounting, finance, economics, business, mathematics, or law provides good preparation for the occupation. Courses in investments, taxes, estate planning, and risk management are also helpful.

Programs in financial planning are becoming more widely available in colleges and universities.

Licensure. The Financial Industry Regulatory Authority (FINRA) is the main licensing organization for the securities industry. Depending on an individual's work, many different licenses may be required, although buy side analysts are less likely to need licenses. The majority of these licenses require sponsorship by an employer, so companies do not expect individuals to have these licenses before starting a job. Experienced workers who change jobs will need to have their licenses renewed with the new company.

Almost all personal financial advisors need the Series 7 and Series 63 or 66 licenses. These licenses give their holders the right to act as a registered representative of a securities firm and to give financial advice. Because the Series 7 license requires sponsorship, self-employed personal financial advisors must maintain a relationship with a large securities firm. This relationship allows them to act as representatives of that firm in the buying and selling of securities.

If personal financial advisors choose to sell insurance, they need additional licenses issued by State licensing boards.

Other qualifications. Strong math, analytical, and problem-solving skills are essential qualifications for financial analysts. Good communication skills also are necessary, because these workers must present complex financial concepts and strategies. Self-confidence, maturity, and the ability to work independently are important as well. Financial analysts must be detail-oriented, motivated to seek out obscure information, and familiar with the workings of the economy, tax laws, and money markets. Financial analysts should also be very comfortable with computers, as they are frequently used in doing work. Although much of the software they use is proprietary, they must be comfortable working with spreadsheets and statistical packages.

Personal financial advisors need many of the same skills, but they must emphasize customer service. They need strong sales ability, including the ability to make customers feel comfortable. It is important for them to be able to present financial concepts to clients in easy-to-understand language. Personal financial advisors must also be able to interact casually with people from many different backgrounds. Some advisors have experience in a related occupation, such as accountant, auditor, insurance sales agent, or broker.

Private bankers work directly with wealthy individuals, so they must be polished and refined. They should be able to interact comfortably with people who may be well-known in the community.

Certification and advancement. Although not required, certifications can enhance professional standing and is recommended by many employers.

Financial analysts can earn the Chartered Financial Analyst (CFA) designation, sponsored by the CFA Institute. To qualify for this designation, applicants need a bachelor's degree and four years of work experience in a related field and must pass three examinations. The first exam is administered twice per year, while the second and third are administered annually. These exams cover subjects such as accounting, economics, securities analysis, financial markets and instruments, corporate finance, asset valuation, and portfolio management. Increasingly, personal financial advisors, sometimes called wealth managers, working with wealthy individuals have the CFA designation.

Personal financial advisors may obtain the Certified Financial Planner credential, often referred to as CFP. This certification, issued by the Certified Financial Planner Board of Standards, requires 3 years of relevant experience; the completion of education requirements, including a bachelor's degree; passing a comprehensive examination, and adherence to a code of ethics. The exams test the candidate's knowledge of the financial planning process, insurance and risk management, employee benefits planning, taxes and retirement planning, and investment and estate planning. Candidates are also required to have a working knowledge of debt management, planning liability, emergency fund reserves, and statistical modeling.

Financial analysts advance by moving into positions where they are responsible for larger or more important products. They may also supervise teams of financial analysts. Eventually, they may become portfolio managers or fund managers, directing the investment portfolios of their companies or funds.

Personal financial advisors have several different paths to advancement. Many accumulate clients and manage more assets. Those who work in firms may move into managerial positions. Others may choose to open their own branch offices for large securities firms and serve as independent registered representatives for those firms. In most cases, employees of established firms are barred from keeping their clients after they leave a firm, so an advisor who leaves a firm to establish a new business must find new customers. Many newly independent personal financial advisors sell their services to family and friends, hoping to win business through referrals.

Employment

Financial analysts and personal financial advisors held 397,000 jobs in 2006, of which financial analysts held 221,000. Many financial analysts work at the headquarters of large financial institutions, most of which are based in New York City or other major financial centers. More than 2 out of 5 financial analysts worked in the finance and insurance industries, including securities and commodity brokers, banks and credit institutions, and insurance carriers. Others worked throughout private industry and government.

Personal financial advisors held 176,000 jobs in 2006. Jobs were spread throughout the country. Much like financial analysts, more than half worked in finance and insurance industries, including securities and commodity brokers, banks, insurance carriers, and financial investment firms. However, about 30 percent of personal financial advisors were self-employed, operating small investment advisory firms, usually in urban areas.

Job Outlook

Employment of financial analysts and personal financial advisors is expected to grow much faster than the average for all occupations. Growth will be especially strong for personal financial advisors, which are projected to be among the 10 fastest growing occupations. Despite strong job growth, keen competition will continue for these well paid jobs, especially for new entrants.

Employment change. As the level of investment increases, overall employment of financial analysts and personal financial advisors is expected to increase by 37 percent during the 2006-16 decade, which is much faster than the average for all occupations.

Personal financial advisors are projected to grow by 41 percent, which is much faster than the average for all occupations, over the projections decade. Growing numbers of advisors will be needed to assist the millions of workers expected to retire in the next 10 years. As more members of the large baby boom generation reach their peak years of retirement savings, personal investments are expected to increase and more people will seek the help of experts. Many companies also have replaced traditional pension plans with retirement savings programs, so more individuals are managing their own retirements than in the past, creating jobs for advisors. In addition, people are living longer and must plan to finance longer retirements.

Deregulation of the financial services industry also is expected to continue to spur demand for personal financial advisors in the banking industry. In recent years, banks and insurance companies have been allowed to expand into the securities industry. Many firms are adding investment advice to their services and are expected to increase their hiring of personal financial advisors.

Employment of financial analysts is expected to grow by 34 percent between 2006 and 2016, which is also much faster than the average for all occupations. Primary factors for this growth are increasing complexity of investments and growth in the industry. As the number and type of mutual funds and the amount of assets invested in these funds increase, mutual fund companies will need more financial analysts to research and recommend investments.

Job prospects. Despite overall employment growth, competition for jobs is expected to be keen in these high-paying occupations. Growth in the industry will create many new positions, but there are still far more people who would like to enter the occupation. For those aspiring to financial analyst jobs, a strong academic background is absolutely essential. Good grades in

Projections data from the National Employment Matrix

Occupational Title	SOC Code	Employment, 2006	Projected employment, 2016	Change, 2006-16	
				Number	Percent
Financial analysts and personal financial advisors	—	397,000	544,000	147,000	37
Financial analysts..	13-2051	221,000	295,000	75,000	34
Personal financial advisors...	13-2052	176,000	248,000	72,000	41

NOTE: Data in this table are rounded. See the discussion of the employment projections table in the *Handbook* introductory chapter on *Occupational Information Included in the Handbook.*

courses such as finance, accounting, and economics are very important to employers. An MBA or certification is helpful in maintaining employment.

Personal financial advisors will also face competition, as many other services compete for customers. Many individuals enter the field by working for a bank or full-service brokerage. Most independent advisories fail within the first year of business, making self-employment challenging. Because the occupation requires sales, people who have strong selling skills will ultimately be most successful. A college degree and certification can lend credibility.

Earnings. Median annual earnings, including bonuses, of wage and salary financial analysts were $66,590 in May 2006. The middle 50 percent earned between $50,700 and $90,690. The lowest 10 percent earned less than $40,340, and the highest 10 percent earned more than $130,130. The bonuses that many financial analysts receive in addition to their salary can be a significant part of their total earnings. Usually, the bonus is based on how well their predictions compare to the actual performance of a benchmark investment.

Median annual earnings of wage and salary personal financial advisors were $66,120 in May 2006. The middle 50 percent earned between $44,130 and $114,260. The lowest 10 percent earned less than $32,340 and the highest 10 percent earned more than $145,600. Personal financial advisors who work for financial services firms are generally paid a salary plus bonus. Advisors who work for financial investment or planning firms or who are self-employed either charge hourly fees for their services or opt to earn their money through fees on stock and insurance purchases. Advisors generally receive commissions for financial products they sell, in addition to charging a fee. Those who manage a client's assets may charge a percentage of those assets. Earnings of self-employed workers are not included in the medians given here.

Related Occupations

Other jobs requiring expertise in finance and investment or in the sale of financial products include accountants and auditors, financial managers, insurance sales agents real estate brokers and sales agents, budget analysts, insurance underwriters, actuaries, and securities, commodities, and financial services sales agents.

Sources of Additional Information

For general information on securities industry employment, contact:

➤ Financial Industry Regulatory Authority (FINRA), 1735 K St.NW., Washington, DC 20006.
Internet: **http://www.finra.org**
➤ Securities Industry and Financial Markets Association, 120 Broadway, 35th Floor, New York, NY 10271.
Internet: **http://www.sifma.org**

For information on financial analyst careers, contact:

➤ American Academy of Financial Management, 2 Canal St., Suite 2317, New Orleans, LA 70130.
Internet: **http://www.aafm.org**
➤ CFA Institute, P.O. Box 3668, 560 Ray C. Hunt Dr., Charlottesville, VA 22903.
Internet: **http://www.cfainstitute.org**

For information on personal financial advisor careers, contact:

➤ Certified Financial Planner Board of Standards, Inc., 1670 Broadway, Suite 600, Denver, CO 80202.
Internet: **http://www.cfp.net**
➤ Financial Planning Association, 4100 E. Mississippi Ave., Suite 400, Denver, CO 80246-3053.
Internet: **http://www.fpanet.org**
➤ Investment Management Consultants Association, 5619 DTC Parkway, Suite 500, Greenwood Village, CO 80111.
Internet: **http://www.imca.org**

For additional career information, see the *Occupational Outlook Quarterly* article "Financial analysts and personal financial advisors" in print at many libraries and career centers. and online:

http://www.bls.gov/opub/ooq/2000/summer/art03.pdf

Insurance Underwriters

(O*NET 13-2053.00)

Significant Points

- Most large insurance companies prefer to hire people who have a college degree in business administration or finance with courses in accounting.

- Continuing education is necessary for advancement.

- Employment is expected to grow more slowly than average as the spread of underwriting software increases worker productivity.

- Job opportunities should be best for those with a background in finance and strong computer and communication skills.

Nature of the Work

Insurance companies protect individuals and organizations from financial loss by assuming billions of dollars in risk each year—risks of car accident, property damage, illness, and other occurrences. Underwriters decide if insurance is provided and under what terms. They are needed to identify and calculate the risk of loss from policyholders, establish who receives a policy, determine the appropriate premium, and write policies that cover this risk. An insurance company may lose business to competitors if the underwriter appraises risks too conservatively, or it may have to pay excessive claims if the underwriting actions are too liberal.

With the aid of computers, underwriters analyze information in insurance applications to determine whether a risk is acceptable and will not result in a loss. Insurance applications often are supplemented with reports from loss-control representatives, medical reports, reports from data vendors, and actuarial studies. Underwriters then must decide whether to issue the policy and, if so, determine the appropriate premium to charge. In making this determination, underwriters consider a wide variety of factors about the applicant. For example, an underwriter working in health insurance may consider age, family history,

Underwriters consider many factors when determining eligibility for an insurance policy.

and current health whereas an underwriter working for a property-casualty insurance company is concerned with the causes of loss to which property is exposed and the safeguards taken by the applicant. Therefore, underwriters serve as the main link between the insurance carrier and the insurance agent. On occasion, they accompany sales agents to make presentations to prospective clients.

Technology plays an important role in an underwriter's job. Underwriters use computer applications called "smart systems" to manage risks more efficiently and accurately. These systems analyze and rate insurance applications, recommend acceptance or denial of the risk, and adjust the premium rate in accordance with the risk. With these systems, underwriters are better equipped to make sound decisions and avoid excessive losses.

The Internet also has affected the work of underwriters. Many insurance carriers' computer systems are now linked to various databases on the Internet that allow immediate access to information—such as driving records—necessary in determining a potential client's risk. This kind of access reduces the amount of time and paperwork necessary for an underwriter to complete a risk assessment.

Although there are many possible lines of insurance to work in, most underwriters specialize in one of four broad categories: life, health, mortgage, and property and casualty. Life and health insurance underwriters may further specialize in group or individual policies.

An increasing proportion of insurance sales, particularly in life and health insurance, are being made through group contracts. A standard group policy insures everyone in a specified group through a single contract at a standard premium rate. The group underwriter analyzes the overall composition of the group to ensure that the total risk is not excessive. Another type of group policy provides members of a group—senior citizens, for example—with individual policies reflecting their needs. These usually are casualty policies, such as those covering automobiles. The casualty underwriter analyzes the application of each group member and makes individual appraisals. Some group underwriters meet with union or employer representatives to discuss the types of policies available to their group.

Property and casualty underwriters usually specialize in either commercial or personal insurance and then by type of risk insured, as in fire, homeowners', automobile, marine, or liability insurance, as well as workers' compensation. In cases where property-casualty companies provide insurance through a single "package" policy covering various types of risks, the underwriter must be familiar with different lines of insurance. For business insurance, the underwriter often must be able to evaluate the firm's entire operation in appraising its application for insurance.

Work environment. Underwriters have desk jobs that require no unusual physical activity. Their offices usually are comfortable and pleasant. Most underwriters are based in a company headquarters or regional branch office, but they occasionally attend meetings away from home for several days. Construction and marine underwriters frequently travel to inspect worksites and assess risks.

Although underwriters typically work a standard 40-hour week, more are working longer hours due to the downsizing of many insurance companies. For some underwriters, evening and weekend hours are not uncommon.

Training, Other Qualifications, and Advancement
Although there are no formal education requirements for becoming an underwriter, many employers prefer candidates with a bachelor's degree or professional designation, some insurance-related experience, and strong computer skills. Much of what an underwriter does may be learned through on-the-job training, so the majority of underwriters start their careers as trainees.

Education and training. For entry-level underwriting jobs, most large insurance companies prefer college graduates who have a degree in business administration or finance with courses or experience in accounting. However, a bachelor's degree in almost any field—plus courses in business law and accounting—provides a good general background and may be sufficient to qualify an individual. Because computers are an integral part of most underwriters' jobs, some coursework with computers is also beneficial. Many employers prefer to hire candidates with several years of related experience in underwriting or insurance.

New employees usually start as underwriter trainees or assistant underwriters. They may help collect information on applicants and evaluate routine applications under the supervision of an experienced risk analyst. Property and casualty trainees study claims files to become familiar with factors associated with certain types of losses. Many larger insurers offer work-study training programs, lasting from a few months to a year. As trainees gain experience, they are assigned policy applications that are more complex and cover greater risks.

The computer programs many underwriters use to assess risk are always being improved upon and updated, so on-the-job computer training may continue throughout an underwriter's career.

Other qualifications. Underwriting can be a satisfying career for people who enjoy analyzing information and paying attention to detail. In addition, underwriters must possess good judgment in order to make sound decisions. Excellent communication and interpersonal skills also are essential, as much of

Projections data from the National Employment Matrix

Occupational Title	SOC Code	Employment, 2006	Projected employment, 2016	Change, 2006-16	
				Number	Percent
Insurance underwriters..	13-2053	104,000	111,000	6,600	6

NOTE: Data in this table are rounded. See the discussion of the employment projections table in the *Handbook* introductory chapter on *Occupational Information Included in the Handbook.*

the underwriter's work involves dealing with agents and other insurance professionals.

Certification and advancement. Continuing education is necessary for advancement. Independent-study programs for experienced underwriters are available. The Insurance Institute of America offers a training program for beginning underwriters. It also offers the designation of Associate in Commercial Underwriting (ACU) for those starting a career in underwriting business insurance policies. People interested in underwriting personal insurance policies may earn the Associate in Personal Insurance (API) designation. To earn either the ACU or API designation, underwriters complete a series of courses and examinations that generally lasts 1 to 2 years.

The American Institute for Chartered Property Casualty Underwriters awards the Chartered Property and Casualty Underwriter (CPCU) designation to experienced underwriters. Earning the CPCU designation requires passing 8 exams, having at least 3 years of insurance experience, and abiding by the Institute's and CPCU Society's code of professional ethics.

The American College offers the equivalent Chartered Life Underwriter (CLU) designation and the Registered Health Underwriter (RHU) designation for life and health insurance professionals.

Experienced underwriters who complete courses of study may advance to senior underwriter or underwriting manager positions. Some underwriting managers are promoted to senior managerial jobs. Some employers require a master's degree to achieve this level. Other underwriters are attracted to the earnings potential of sales and, therefore, obtain State licenses to sell insurance and related financial products as agents or brokers.

Employment

Insurance underwriters held about 104,000 jobs in 2006. Insurance carriers employed 65 percent of all underwriters. Most of the remaining underwriters work in insurance agencies or for organizations that offer insurance services to insurance companies and policyholders. A small number of underwriters work in agencies owned and operated by banks, mortgage companies, and real estate firms.

Most underwriters are based in the insurance company's home office, but some, mainly in the property and casualty area, work out of regional branch offices of the insurance company. These underwriters usually have the authority to underwrite most risks and determine an appropriate rating without consulting the home office.

Job Outlook

Although growth is expected to be more slowly than the average for all occupations, job prospects will remain good because of the continuous turnover experienced in this occupation.

Employment change. Employment of underwriters is expected to grow by 6 percent during the 2006-16 decade, which is slower than the average for all occupations. Underwriting software will continue to make workers more productive, but it does not do away with the need for human skills. As a result, employment of underwriters will increase as a growing economy and population expands the insurance needs of businesses and individuals.

Demand for underwriters also is expected to improve as insurance carriers try to restore profitability to make up for an unusually large number of underwriting losses in recent years. As the carriers' returns on their investments have declined, insurers are placing more emphasis on underwriting to generate revenues. This renewed interest in underwriting should result in some long-term growth for underwriters.

Job prospects. Job opportunities should be best for those with experience in related insurance jobs, a background in finance, and strong computer and communication skills. In addition to openings arising from job growth, openings also will be created by the need to replace underwriters who retire or transfer to another occupation.

New and emerging fields of insurance will be the source of the most job opportunities for underwriters. Insurance carriers are always assessing new risks and offering new types of policies to meet changing circumstances. Underwriters are needed particularly in the area of product development, where they assess risks and set the premiums for new lines of insurance. One new line of insurance being offered by life insurance carriers is long-term care insurance and it may provide job opportunities for underwriters.

Earnings

Median annual earnings of wage and salary insurance underwriters were $52,350 in May 2006. The middle 50 percent earned between $40,000 and $71,070 a year. The lowest 10 percent earned less than $32,270, while the highest 10 percent earned more than $92,240. Median annual earnings of underwriters working with insurance carriers were $52,900, while underwriters' median annual earnings in agencies, brokerages, and other insurance related activities were $51,820.

Insurance companies usually provide better-than-average benefits, including retirement plans and employer-financed group life and health insurance. Insurance companies usually pay tuition for underwriting courses that their trainees complete, and some also offer salary incentives.

Related Occupations

Underwriters make decisions on the basis of financial and statistical data. Other workers with the same type of responsibility include accountants and auditors, actuaries, budget analysts, cost estimators, financial managers, loan officers, and credit analysts. Other related jobs in the insurance industry include insurance sales agents and claims adjusters, appraisers, examiners, and investigators.

Sources of Additional Information

Information about a career as an insurance underwriter is available from the home offices of many insurance companies.

Information about the property-casualty insurance field can be obtained by contacting:

➤ Insurance Information Institute, 110 William St., New York, NY 10038. Internet: **http://www.iii.org**

Information about the health insurance field can be obtained by contacting:

➤ National Association of Health Underwriters, 2000 North 14th Street, Suite 450, Arlington, VA 22201.
Internet: **http://www.nahu.org**

Information on the underwriting function and the CPCU and AU designations can be obtained from:

➤ American Institute for Chartered Property and Casualty Underwriters and Insurance Institute of America, 720 Providence Rd., P.O. Box 3016, Malvern, PA 19355.
Internet: **http://www.aicpcu.org**

➤ CPCU Society, 720 Providence Road, Malvern, PA 19355.
Internet: **http://www.cpcusociety.org**

Information on the CLU and RHU designations can be obtained from:

➤ American College, 270 South Bryn Mawr Ave., Bryn Mawr, PA 19010. Internet: **http://www.theamericancollege.edu**

Loan Officers

(O*NET 13-2072.00)

Significant Points

- About 9 out of 10 loan officers work for commercial banks, savings institutions, credit unions, and related financial institutions.

- Loan officers usually need a bachelor's degree in finance, economics, or a related field; training or experience in banking, lending, or sales is advantageous.

- Earnings often fluctuate with the number of loans generated, rising substantially when the economy is good and interest rates are low.

Nature of the Work

For many individuals, taking out a loan is the only way to buy a house, car, or college education. For businesses, loans likewise are essential to start many companies, purchase inventory, or invest in capital equipment. *Loan officers* facilitate this lending by finding potential clients and helping them to apply for loans. Loan officers also gather personal information about clients and businesses to ensure an informed decision regarding their creditworthiness and the probability of repayment. Loan officers may also provide guidance to prospective borrowers who have problems qualifying for traditional loans. For example, loan

Loan officers determine the creditworthiness of prospective clients.

officers might determine the most appropriate type of loan for a particular customer and explain specific requirements and restrictions associated with the loan.

Loan officers guide clients through the process of applying for a loan. The process begins with a meeting or telephone call with a prospective client, during which the loan officer obtains basic information about the purpose of the loan and explains the different types of loans and credit terms available to the applicant. Loan officers answer questions about the process and sometimes assist clients in filling out the application.

After a client completes the application, the loan officer begins the process of analyzing and verifying the information on the application to determine the client's creditworthiness. Often, loan officers can quickly access the client's credit history by computer and obtain a credit "score," representing a software program's assessment of the client's creditworthiness. When a credit history is not available or when unusual financial circumstances are present, the loan officer may request additional financial information from the client or, in the case of commercial loans, copies of the company's financial statements. Loan officers include such information and their written comments in a loan file, which is used to analyze whether the prospective loan meets the lending institution's requirements. Loan officers then decide, in consultation with their managers, whether to grant the loan. If the loan is approved, a repayment schedule is arranged with the client.

Loan officers usually specialize in commercial, consumer, or mortgage loans. Commercial or business loans help companies pay for new equipment or expand operations; consumer loans include home equity, automobile, and personal loans; mortgage loans are made to purchase real estate or to refinance an existing mortgage. As banks and other financial institutions begin to offer new types of loans and a growing variety of financial services, loan officers will have to learn about these new product lines.

In many instances, loan officers act as salespeople. Commercial loan officers, for example, contact firms to determine their needs for loans. If a firm is seeking new funds, the loan officer will try to persuade the company to obtain the loan from his or her institution. Similarly, mortgage loan officers develop relationships with commercial and residential real estate agencies so that, when an individual or firm buys a property, the real estate agent might recommend contacting a specific loan officer for financing.

Some loan officers, called loan underwriters, specialize in evaluating a client's creditworthiness and may conduct a financial analysis or other risk assessment.

Other loan officers, referred to as *loan collection officers*, contact borrowers with delinquent loan accounts to help them find a method of repayment to avoid their defaulting on the loan. If a repayment plan cannot be developed, the loan collection officer initiates collateral liquidation, in which the lender seizes the collateral used to secure the loan—a home or car, for example—and sells it to repay the loan.

Work environment. Working as a loan officer usually involves considerable travel. For example, commercial and mortgage loan officers frequently work away from their offices and rely on laptop computers, cellular telephones, and pagers to keep in contact with their employers and clients. Mortgage loan officers often work out of their home or car, visiting offices or homes of clients to complete loan applications. Commercial loan officers sometimes travel to other cities to prepare complex loan agreements. Consumer loan officers, however, are likely to spend most of their time in an office.

Most loan officers work a standard 40-hour week, but many work longer, depending on the number of clients and the demand for loans. Mortgage loan officers can work especially long hours because they are free to take on as many customers as they choose. Loan officers are especially busy when interest rates are low, causing a surge in loan applications.

Training, Other Qualifications, and Advancement

Loan officers usually need a bachelor's degree in finance, economics, or a related field. Previous banking, lending, or sales experience is also highly valued by employers.

Education and training. Loan officer positions generally require a bachelor's degree in finance, economics, or a related field. Loan officers without a college degree often advance to their positions after gaining several years of work experience in various other related occupations, such as teller or customer service representative.

Licensure. There are currently no specific licensing requirements for loan officers working in banks or credit unions. Training and licensing requirements for loan officers who work in mortgage banks or brokerages vary by State and may include continuing education requirements. As the types of mortgages offered to prospective homebuyers increases, licensing requirements may become more stringent as regulators and lawmakers become more leery of possible predatory lending.

Other qualifications. People planning a career as a loan officer should be good at working with others, confident in their abilities, and highly motivated. Loan officers must be willing to attend community events as representatives of their employer. Sales ability, good interpersonal and communication skills, and a strong desire to succeed also are important qualities for loan officers. Most employers also prefer applicants who are familiar with computers and their applications in banking.

Certification and advancement. Capable loan officers may advance to larger branches of their firms or to managerial positions. Some loan officers advance to supervise other loan officers and clerical staff.

Various banking associations and private schools offer courses and programs for students interested in lending and for experienced loan officers who want to keep their skills current. For example, the Bank Administration Institute, an affiliate of the American Banker's Association, offers the Loan Review Certificate Program for people who review and approve loans. This program enhances the quality of reviews and improves the early detection of deteriorating loans, thereby contributing to the safety and soundness of the loan portfolio.

The Mortgage Bankers Association offers the Certified Mortgage Banker (CMB) designation to loan officers in real estate finance. The association offers three CMB designations: residential, commerce, and masters to candidates who have 3 years of experience, earn educational credits, and pass an exam. Completion of these courses and programs generally enhances employment and advancement opportunities.

Employment

Loan officers held about 373,000 jobs in 2006. About 9 out of 10 loan officers were employed by commercial banks, savings institutions, credit unions, and related financial institutions. Loan officers are employed throughout the Nation, but most work in urban and suburban areas. At some banks, particularly in rural areas, the branch or assistant manager often handles the loan application process.

Job Outlook

Loan officers can expect average employment growth. Job opportunities will be best for people with a college education and related experience.

Employment change. Employment of loan officers is projected to increase 11 percent between 2006 and 2016, which is about as fast as the the average for all occupations. Employment growth stemming from economic expansion and population increases—factors that generate demand for loans—will be partially offset by increased automation that speeds the lending process and by the growing use of the Internet to apply for and obtain loans.

The use of credit scoring has made the loan evaluation process much simpler than in the past and even unnecessary in some cases. Credit scoring allows loan officers—particularly

Projections data from the National Employment Matrix

Occupational Title	SOC Code	Employment, 2006	Projected employment, 2016	Change, 2006-16	
				Number	Percent
Loan officers	13-2072	373,000	415,000	43,000	11

NOTE: Data in this table are rounded. See the discussion of the employment projections table in the *Handbook* introductory chapter on *Occupational Information Included in the Handbook.*

loan underwriters—to evaluate many more loans in less time than previously. In addition, the mortgage application process has become highly automated and standardized, a simplification that has enabled mortgage loan vendors to offer their services over the Internet. Online vendors accept loan applications from customers over the Internet and determine which lenders have the best interest rates for particular loans. With this knowledge, customers can go directly to the lending institution, thereby bypassing mortgage loan brokers. Shopping for loans on the Internet, especially for mortgages, is expected to become more common in the future and to slow job growth for loan officers.

Job prospects. Besides openings arising from growth, additional job openings will result from the need to replace workers who retire or otherwise leave the occupation permanently.

College graduates and those with banking, lending, or sales experience should have the best job prospects.

Job opportunities for loan officers are influenced by the volume of applications, which is determined largely by interest rates and by the overall level of economic activity. Although loans remain a major source of revenue for banks, demand for new loans fluctuates and affects the income and employment opportunities of loan officers. An upswing in the economy or a decline in interest rates often results in a surge in real estate buying and mortgage refinancing, requiring loan officers to work long hours processing applications and inducing lenders to hire additional loan officers. Loan officers often are paid by commission on the value of the loans they place, and when the real estate market slows, they often suffer a decline in earnings and may even be subject to layoffs. The same applies to commercial loan officers, whose workloads increase during good economic times as companies seek to invest more in their businesses. In difficult economic conditions, an increase in the number of delinquent loans results in more demand for loan collection officers.

Earnings

Median annual earnings of wage and salary loan officers were $51,760 in May 2006. The middle 50 percent earned between $37,590 and $73,630. The lowest 10 percent earned less than $29,590 while the top 10 percent earned more than $107,040. Median annual earnings in the industries employing the largest numbers of loan officers were as follows:

The form of compensation for loan officers varies. Most are paid a commission based on the number of loans they originate. Some institutions pay only salaries, while others pay their loan officers a salary plus a commission or bonus based on the number of loans originated. Loan officers who are paid on commission usually earn more than those who earn only a salary, and those who work for smaller banks generally earn less than those employed by larger institutions.

According to a salary survey conducted by Robert Half International, a staffing services firm specializing in accounting and finance, consumer loan officers, referred to as personal bankers, with 1 to 3 years of experience earned between $30,750 and $36,250 in 2007, and commercial loan officers with 1 to 3 years of experience made between $45,750 and $70,250. Commercial loan officers with more than 3 years of experience made between $61,750 and $100,750, and consumer loan officers earned between $36,250 and $51,250. Earnings of loan officers with graduate degrees or professional certifications are higher.

Banks and other lenders sometimes may offer their loan officers free checking privileges and somewhat lower interest rates on personal loans.

Related Occupations

Loan officers help people manage financial assets and secure loans. Occupations that involve similar functions include those of securities, commodities, and financial services sales agents; financial analysts and personal financial advisors; real estate brokers and sales agents; insurance underwriters; insurance sales agents; and loan counselors.

Sources of Additional Information

Information about a career as a mortgage loan officer can be obtained from:

➤ Mortgage Bankers Association, 1919 Pennsylvania Ave. NW., Washington, DC 20006.
Internet: **http://www.mortgagebankers.org**

State bankers' associations can furnish specific information about job opportunities in their State. Also, individual banks can supply information about job openings and the activities, responsibilities, and preferred qualifications of their loan officers.

Management Analysts

(O*NET 13-1111.00)

Significant Points

- Despite much faster than average employment growth, keen competition is expected for jobs; opportunities should be best for those with a graduate degree, specialized expertise, and a talent for salesmanship and public relations.

- About 27 percent, over three times the average for all occupations, are self-employed.

- A bachelor's degree is sufficient for many entry-level government jobs; many positions in private industry require a master's degree, specialized expertise, or both.

Nature of the Work

As business becomes more complex, firms are continually faced with new challenges. They increasingly rely on management analysts to help them remain competitive amidst these changes. Management analysts, often referred to as *management consultants* in private industry, analyze and propose ways to improve an organization's structure, efficiency, or profits.

For example, a small but rapidly growing company might employ a consultant who is an expert in just-in-time inventory management to help improve its inventory-control system. In another case, a large company that has recently acquired a new division may hire management analysts to help reorganize the corporate structure and eliminate duplicate or nonessential jobs. In recent years, information technology and electronic commerce have provided new opportunities for management analysts. Companies hire consultants to develop strategies for entering and remaining competitive in the new electronic marketplace. (For information on computer specialists working in consulting, see the following statements elsewhere in the *Handbook*: computer software engineers; systems analysts, computer scientists, and database administrators; and computer programmers.)

Management analysts might be single practitioners or part of large international organizations employing thousands of other consultants. Some analysts and consultants specialize in a specific industry, such as health care or telecommunications, while others specialize by type of business function, such as human resources, marketing, logistics, or information systems. In government, management analysts tend to specialize by type of agency. The work of management analysts and consultants varies with each client or employer, and from project to project. Some projects require a team of consultants, each specializing in one area. In other projects, consultants work independently with the organization's managers. In all cases, analysts and consultants collect, review, and analyze information in order to make recommendations to managers.

Both public and private organizations use consultants for a variety of reasons. Some lack the internal resources needed to handle a project, while others need a consultant's expertise to determine what resources will be required and what problems may be encountered if they pursue a particular opportunity. To retain a consultant, a company first solicits proposals from a number of consulting firms specializing in the area in which it needs assistance. These proposals include the estimated cost and scope of the project, staffing requirements, references from a number of previous clients, and a completion deadline. The company then selects the proposal that best suits its needs. Some firms, however, employ internal management consulting groups rather than hiring outside consultants.

After obtaining an assignment or contract, management analysts first define the nature and extent of the problem that they have been asked to solve. During this phase, they analyze relevant data—which may include annual revenues, employment, or expenditures—and interview managers and employees while observing their operations. The analysts or consultants then develop solutions to the problem. While preparing their rec-

Many management analysts are self-employed.

ommendations, they take into account the nature of the organization, the relationship it has with others in the industry, and its internal organization and culture. Insight into the problem often is gained by building and solving mathematical models, such as one that shows how inventory levels affect costs and product delivery times.

Once they have decided on a course of action, consultants report their findings and recommendations to the client. Their suggestions usually are submitted in writing, but oral presentations regarding findings also are common. For some projects, management analysts are retained to help implement the suggestions they have made.

Like their private-sector colleagues, management analysts in government agencies try to increase efficiency and worker productivity and to control costs. For example, if an agency is planning to purchase personal computers, it must first determine which type to buy, given its budget and data-processing needs. In this case, management analysts would assess the prices and characteristics of various machines and determine which ones best meet the agency's goals. Analysts may manage contracts for a wide range of goods and services to ensure quality performance and to prevent cost overruns.

Work environment. Management analysts usually divide their time between their offices and the client's site. In either situation, much of an analyst's time is spent indoors in clean, well-lit offices. Because they must spend a significant portion of their time with clients, analysts travel frequently.

Analysts and consultants generally work at least 40 hours a week. Uncompensated overtime is common, especially when project deadlines are approaching. Analysts may experience a great deal of stress when trying to meet a client's demands, often on a tight schedule.

Self-employed consultants can set their workload and hours and work at home. On the other hand, their livelihood depends on their ability to maintain and expand their client base. Salaried consultants also must impress potential clients to get and keep clients for their company.

Training, Other Qualifications, and Advancement

Entry requirements for management analysts vary. For some entry-level positions, a bachelor's degree is sufficient. For others, a master's degree, specialized expertise, or both is required.

Education and training. Educational requirements for entry-level jobs in this field vary between private industry and government. Many employers in private industry generally seek individuals with a master's degree in business administration or a related discipline. Some employers also require additional years of experience in the field or industry in which the worker plans to consult. Other firms hire workers with a bachelor's degree as research analysts or associates and promote them to consultants after several years. Some government agencies require experience, graduate education, or both, but many also hire people with a bachelor's degree and little work experience for entry-level management analyst positions.

Few universities or colleges offer formal programs in management consulting; however, many fields of study provide a suitable educational background for this occupation because of the wide range of areas addressed by management analysts. Common fields of study include business, management, accounting, marketing, economics, statistics, computer and information science, or engineering. Most analysts also have years of experience in management, human resources, information technology, or other specialties. Analysts also routinely attend conferences to keep abreast of current developments in their field.

Other qualifications. Management analysts often work with minimal supervision, so they need to be self-motivated and disciplined. Analytical skills, the ability to get along with a wide range of people, strong oral and written communication skills, good judgment, time-management skills, and creativity are other desirable qualities. The ability to work in teams also is an important attribute as consulting teams become more common.

Certification and advancement. As consultants gain experience, they often become solely responsible for specific projects, taking on more responsibility and managing their own hours. At the senior level, consultants may supervise teams working on more complex projects and become more involved in seeking out new business. Those with exceptional skills may eventually become partners in the firm, focusing on attracting new clients and bringing in revenue. Senior consultants who leave their consulting firms often move to senior management positions at non-consulting firms. Others with entrepreneurial ambition may open their own firms.

A high percentage of management consultants are self-employed, partly because business startup and overhead costs are low. Since many small consulting firms fail each year because of lack of managerial expertise and clients, persons interested in opening their own firm must have good organizational and marketing skills. Several years of consulting experience are also helpful.

The Institute of Management Consultants USA, Inc. offers the Certified Management Consultant (CMC) designation to those who meet minimum levels of education and experience, submit client reviews, and pass an interview and exam covering the IMC USA's Code of Ethics. Management consultants with a CMC designation must be recertified every 3 years. Certification is not mandatory for management consultants, but it may give a jobseeker a competitive advantage.

Employment

Management analysts held about 678,000 jobs in 2006. About 27 percent of these workers, over three times the average for all occupations, were self-employed. Management analysts are found throughout the country, but employment is concentrated in large metropolitan areas. Management analysts work in a range of industries, including management, scientific, and technical consulting firms; computer systems design and related services firms; and Federal, State, and local governments.

Job Outlook

Employment of management analysts is expected to grow much faster than average. Despite projected rapid employment growth, keen competition is expected for jobs as management analysts because of the independent and challenging nature of the work and the high earnings potential that make this occupation attractive to many.

Employment change. Employment of management analysts is expected to grow 22 percent over the 2006-16 decade, much faster than the average for all occupations, as industry and government increasingly rely on outside expertise to improve the performance of their organizations. Job growth is projected in very large consulting firms with international expertise and in smaller consulting firms that specialize in specific areas, such as biotechnology, health care, information technology, human resources, engineering, and marketing. Growth in the number of individual practitioners may be hindered by increasing use of consulting teams that are often more versatile.

Job growth for management analysts has been driven by a number of changes in the business environment that have forced firms to take a closer look at their operations. These changes include regulatory changes, developments in information technology, and the growth of electronic commerce. Firms hire consultants to help them adapt to new business regulations, such as the Sarbanes-Oxley Act, which tightened financial reporting rules. Traditional companies hire analysts to help design intranets or company Web sites or to establish online businesses. New Internet startup companies hire analysts not only to design Web sites but also to advise them in traditional business practices, such as pricing strategies, marketing, and inventory and human resource management.

To offer clients better quality and a wider variety of services, consulting firms are partnering with traditional computer software and technology firms. Also, many computer firms are developing consulting practices of their own to take advantage of this expanding market. Although information technology consulting should remain one of the fastest growing consulting areas, employment in the computer services industry can be volatile so the most successful management analysts may also consult in other business areas.

The growth of international business also has contributed to an increase in demand for management analysts. As U.S. firms expand their business abroad, many will hire management analysts to help them form the right strategy for entering the market; to advise them on legal matters pertaining to specific countries; or to help them with organizational, administrative, and other issues, especially if the U.S. company is involved in a partnership or merger with a local firm. These trends provide management analysts with more opportunities to travel or work abroad but also require them to have a more comprehensive knowledge of international business and foreign cultures and

Projections data from the National Employment Matrix

Occupational Title	SOC Code	Employment, 2006	Projected employment, 2016	Change, 2006-16	
				Number	Percent
Management analysts...	13-1111	678,000	827,000	149,000	22

NOTE: Data in this table are rounded. See the discussion of the employment projections table in the *Handbook* introductory chapter on *Occupational Information Included in the Handbook.*

languages. Just as globalization creates new opportunities for management analysts, it also allows U.S. firms to hire management analysts in other countries; however, because international work is expected to increase the total amount of work, this development is not expected to adversely affect employment in this occupation.

Furthermore, as international and domestic markets have become more competitive, firms have needed to use resources more efficiently. Management analysts increasingly are sought to help reduce costs, streamline operations, and develop marketing strategies. As this process continues and businesses downsize, even more opportunities will be created for analysts to perform duties that previously were handled internally. Finally, more management analysts also will be needed in the public sector, as Federal, State, and local government agencies seek ways to become more efficient.

Job prospects. Despite rapid employment growth, keen competition is expected. The pool of applicants from which employers can draw is quite large since analysts can have very diverse educational backgrounds and work experience. Furthermore, the independent and challenging nature of the work, combined with high earnings potential, makes this occupation attractive to many. Job opportunities are expected to be best for those with a graduate degree, specialized expertise, and a talent for salesmanship and public relations.

Economic downturns also can have adverse effects on employment for some management consultants. In these times, businesses look to cut costs, and consultants may be considered an excess expense. On the other hand, some consultants might experience an increase in work during recessions because they advise businesses on how to cut costs and remain profitable.

Earnings

Salaries for management analysts vary widely by years of experience and education, geographic location, specific expertise, and size of employer. Generally, management analysts employed in large firms or in metropolitan areas have the highest salaries. Median annual earnings of wage and salary management analysts in May 2006 were $68,050. The middle 50 percent earned between $50,860 and $92,390. The lowest 10 percent earned less than $39,840, and the highest 10 percent earned more than $128,330. Median annual earnings in the industries employing the largest numbers of management analysts were:

Management, scientific, and technical consulting services	$76,600
Computer systems design and related services	76,130
Federal executive branch	73,800
Management of companies and enterprises	68,660
State government	50,270

Salaried management analysts usually receive common benefits, such as health and life insurance, a retirement plan, vacation, and sick leave, as well as less common benefits, such as profit sharing and bonuses for outstanding work. In addition, all travel expenses usually are reimbursed by the employer.

Self-employed consultants have to maintain their own office and provide their own benefits.

Related Occupations

Management analysts collect, review, and analyze data; make recommendations; and implement their ideas. Occupations with similar duties include accountants and auditors; budget analysts; cost estimators; financial analysts and personal financial advisors; operations research analysts; economists; and market and survey researchers. Some management analysts specialize in information technology and work with computers, as do computer systems analysts and computer scientists and database administrators. Most management analysts also have managerial experience similar to that of administrative services managers; advertising, marketing, promotions, public relations, and sales managers; financial managers; human resources, training, and labor relations managers and specialists; industrial production managers; or top executives.

Sources of Additional Information

Information about career opportunities in management consulting is available from:

➤ Association of Management Consulting Firms, 380 Lexington Ave., Suite 1700, New York, NY 10168. Internet: **http://www.amcf.org**

Information about the Certified Management Consultant designation can be obtained from:

➤ Institute of Management Consultants USA, Inc., 2025 M St.NW., Suite 800, Washington, DC 20036. Internet: **http://www.imcusa.org**

Information on obtaining a management analyst position with the Federal Government is available from the Office of Personnel Management (OPM) through USAJOBS, the Federal Government's official employment information system. This resource for locating and applying for job opportunities can be accessed through the Internet at **http://www.usajobs.opm.gov** or through an interactive voice response telephone system at (703) 724-1850 or TDD (978) 461-8404. These numbers are not toll free, and charges may result. For advice on how to find and apply for Federal jobs, see the *Occupational Outlook Quarterly* article "How to get a job in the Federal Government," online at:

http://www.bls.gov/opub/ooq/2004/summer/art01.pdf

Meeting and Convention Planners

(O*NET 13-1121.00)

Significant Points

- Planners often work long hours in the period prior to and during a meeting or convention, and extensive travel may be required.

- Employment is expected to grow faster than average.

- Opportunities will be best for individuals with a bachelor's degree and some experience as a meeting planner.

Nature of the Work

Meetings and conventions bring people together for a common purpose, and meeting and convention planners work to ensure that this purpose is achieved seamlessly. Meeting planners coordinate every detail of meetings and conventions, from the speakers and meeting location to arranging for printed materials and audio-visual equipment.

The first step in planning a meeting or convention is determining the purpose, message, or impression that the sponsoring organization wants to communicate. Planners increasingly focus on how meetings affect the goals of their organizations; for example, they may survey prospective attendees to find out what motivates them and how they learn best. Planners then choose speakers, entertainment, and content, and arrange the program to present the organization's information in the most effective way.

Meeting and convention planners search for prospective meeting sites, which may be hotels, convention centers, or conference centers. They issue requests for proposals to all the sites in which they are interested. These requests state the meeting dates and outline the planners' needs for the meeting or convention, including meeting and exhibit space, lodging, food and beverages, telecommunications, audio-visual requirements, transportation, and any other necessities. The establishments respond with proposals describing what space and services they can supply, and at what prices. Meeting and convention planners review these proposals and either make recommendations to top management or choose the site themselves.

Once the location is selected, meeting and convention planners arrange support services, coordinate with the facility, prepare the site staff for the meeting, and set up all forms of electronic communication needed for the meeting or convention, such as e-mail, voice mail, video, and online communication.

Meeting logistics, the management of the details of meetings and conventions, such as labor and materials, is another major component of the job. Planners register attendees and issue name badges, coordinate lodging reservations, and arrange transportation. They make sure that all necessary supplies are ordered and transported to the meeting site on time, that meeting rooms are equipped with sufficient seating and audio-visual equipment, that all exhibits and booths are set up properly, and that all materials are printed. They also make sure that the meeting adheres to fire and labor regulations and oversee food and beverage distribution.

There also is a financial management component of the work. Planners negotiate contracts with facilities and suppliers. These contracts, which have become increasingly complex, are often drawn up more than a year in advance of the meeting or convention. Contracts may include clauses requiring the planner to book a certain number of rooms for meeting attendees and imposing penalties if the rooms are not filled. Therefore, it is important that the planner closely estimate how many people will attend the meeting based on previous meeting attendance and current circumstances. Planners must also oversee the finances of meetings and conventions. They are given overall budgets by their organizations and must create a detailed budget, forecasting what each aspect of the event will cost. Additionally, some planners oversee meetings that contribute significantly to their

Meeting and convention planners often work long hours before and during a meeting or convention.

organization's operating budget and must ensure that the event meets income goals.

An increasingly important part of the work is measuring how well the meeting's purpose was achieved, and planners begin this measurement as they outline the meeting's goals. Planners set their own specific goals after learning an organization's goals for a meeting or convention. They choose objectives for which success is measurable and define what will constitute achievement of each goal. The most obvious way to gauge their success is to have attendees fill out surveys about their experiences at the event. Planners can ask specific questions about what the attendees learned, how well organized the meeting or convention appeared, and how they felt about the overall experience. If the purpose of a meeting or convention is publicity, a good measure of success would be how much press coverage the event received. A more precise measurement of meeting success, and one that is gaining importance, is return on investment. Planners compare the costs and benefits of an event and show whether it was worthwhile to the organization. For example, if a company holds a meeting to motivate its employees and improve company morale, the planner might track employee turnover before and after the meeting.

An important part of all these different functions of meeting professionals is establishing and maintaining relationships. Meeting and convention planners interact with a variety of people and must communicate effectively. They must understand their organization's goals for the meeting or convention, be able to communicate their needs clearly to meeting site staff and other suppliers, maintain contact with many different people, and inform people about changes as they occur.

Some aspects of the work vary by the type of organization for which planners work. Those who work for associations must market their meetings to association members, convincing members that attending the meeting is worth their time and expense. Marketing is usually less important for corporate meeting planners because employees are generally required to attend company meetings. Corporate planners usually have shorter time frames in which to prepare their meetings. Planners who work in Federal, State, and local governments must learn how to operate within established government procedures, such as procedures and rules for procuring materials and booking lodging for government employees.

Convention service managers, meeting professionals who work in hotels, convention centers, and similar establishments, act as liaisons between the meeting facility and planners who work for associations, businesses, or governments. They present food service options to outside planners, coordinate special requests, suggest hotel services based on the planners' budgets, and otherwise help outside planners present effective meetings and conventions in their facilities.

Meeting planners in small organizations perform a wider range of duties, with perhaps one person coordinating an entire meeting. These planners usually need to multi-task even more than planners in larger organizations.

In large organizations or those that sponsor large meetings or conventions, meeting professionals are more likely to specialize in a particular aspect of meeting planning. Some specialties are conference coordinators, who handle most of the meeting logistics; registrars, who handle advance registration and payment, name badges, and the set-up of on-site registration; and education planners, who coordinate the meeting content, including speakers and topics. In organizations that hold very large or complex meetings, there may be several senior positions, such as manager of registration, education seminar coordinator, or conference services director, with the entire meeting planning department headed by a department director.

Work environment. The work of meeting and convention planners may be considered either stressful or energizing, but there is no question that it is fast-paced and demanding. Planners oversee multiple operations at one time, face numerous deadlines, and orchestrate the activities of several different groups of people. Meeting and convention planners spend the majority of their time in offices; but during meetings, they work on-site at the hotel, convention center, or other meeting location. They travel regularly to attend meetings and to visit prospective meeting sites. The extent of travel depends upon the type of organization for which the planner works. Local and regional organizations require mostly regional travel, while national and international organizations require travel to more distant locales, including travel abroad.

Work hours can be long and irregular, with planners working more than 40 hours per week in the time leading up to a meeting and fewer hours after finishing a meeting. During meetings or conventions, planners may work very long days, possibly starting as early as 5:00 a.m. and working until midnight. They are sometimes required to work on weekends.

Some physical activity is required, including long hours of standing and walking and some lifting and carrying of boxes of materials, exhibits, or supplies. Planners work with the public and with workers from diverse backgrounds. They may get to travel to beautiful hotels and interesting places and meet speakers and meeting attendees from around the world, and they usually enjoy a high level of autonomy.

Training, Other Qualifications, and Advancement

People with a variety of educational or work backgrounds may seek meeting and convention planning positions. Many migrate into the occupation after gaining planning experience.

For example, an administrative assistant may begin planning small meetings and gradually move into a full-time position as a meeting and convention planner. Although there are some certification programs and college courses in meeting and convention planning available, most needed skills are learned through experience.

Education and training. Many employers prefer applicants who have a bachelor's degree, but this is not always required. The proportion of planners with a bachelor's degree is increasing because the work and responsibilities are becoming more complex.

Planners have backgrounds in a variety of disciplines, but some useful undergraduate majors are marketing, public relations, communications, business, and hotel or hospitality management. Individuals who have studied hospitality management may start out with greater responsibilities than those with other academic backgrounds.

Several universities offer bachelors or masters degrees with majors in meetings management. Additionally, meeting and convention planning continuing education programs are offered by a few universities and colleges. These programs are designed for career development of meeting professionals as well as for people wishing to enter the occupation. Some programs may require 40 to more than 100 classroom hours and may last anywhere from 1 semester to 2 years.

Most of the training is done informally on the job. Entry-level planners, depending upon their education, generally begin by performing small tasks under the supervision of senior meeting professionals. For example, they may issue requests for proposals and discuss the resulting proposals with higher level planners. They also may assist in registration, review of contracts, or the creation of meeting timelines, schedules, or objectives. They may start by planning small meetings, such as committee meetings. Those who start at small organizations have the opportunity to learn more quickly since they will be required to take on a larger number of tasks.

Other qualifications. Meeting and convention planners must have excellent written and verbal communications skills and interpersonal skills. They must be detail-oriented with excellent organizational skills, and they must be able to multi-task, meet tight deadlines, and maintain composure under pressure in a fast-paced environment. Quantitative and analytic skills are needed to formulate and follow budgets and to understand and negotiate contracts. The ability to speak multiple languages is a plus, since some planners must communicate with meeting attendees and speakers from around the world. Planners also need computer skills, such as the ability to use financial and registration software and the Internet. In the course of their careers, planners may work in a number of different, unrelated industries, and they must be able to learn independently about each new industry so they can coordinate programs that address the industry's important issues.

Some meeting and convention planners enter the occupation after working in hotel sales or as marketing or catering coordinators. These are effective ways to learn about meeting and convention planning because these hotel personnel work with numerous meeting planners, participate in negotiations for hotel services, and witness many different meetings. Workers who enter the occupation in these ways often start at a higher level than those with bachelor's degrees and no experience.

Certification and advancement. To advance in this occupation, planners must volunteer to take on more responsibility and find new and better ways of doing things in their organizations. The most important factors are demonstrated skill on the job, determination, and gaining the respect of others within the organization. Because formal education is increasingly important, those who enter the occupation may enhance their professional standing by enrolling in meeting planning courses offered by professional meeting and convention planning organizations, colleges, or universities. Education may improve work performance, and therefore may be an important factor in career development. However, advancement based solely on education is uncommon.

As meeting and convention planners prove themselves, they are given greater responsibilities. This may mean taking on a wider range of duties or moving to another planning specialty to gain experience in that area before moving to a higher level. For example, a planner may be promoted from conference coordinator, with responsibility for meeting logistics, to program coordinator, with responsibility for booking speakers and formatting the meeting's program. The next step up may be meeting manager, who supervises all parts of the meeting, and then director of meetings, and then possibly department director of meetings and education. Another path for promotion is to move from a small organization to a larger one, taking on responsibility for larger meetings and conventions.

The Convention Industry Council offers the Certified Meeting Professional (CMP) credential, a voluntary certification for meeting and convention planners. Although the CMP is not required, it is widely recognized in the industry and may help in career advancement. To qualify, candidates must have a minimum of 3 years of meeting management experience, full-time employment in a meeting management capacity, and proof of accountability for successfully completed meetings. Those who qualify must then pass an examination that covers topics such as adult learning, financial management, facilities and services, logistics, and meeting programs.

The Society of Government Meeting Professionals (SGMP) offers the Certified Government Meeting Professional credential. This certification is not required to work as a government meeting planner. It may, however, be helpful to those who want to demonstrate knowledge of issues specific to planning government meetings, such as regulations and policies governing procurement and travel. To qualify for certification, candidates must have at least 1 year of membership in SGMP. Membership requires employment as a meeting planner within Federal, State, or local government or for firm that works on government contracts. To become certified, members must take a 3-day course and pass an exam.

With significant experience, meeting planners may become independent meeting consultants, advance to vice president or executive director of an association, or start their own meeting planning firms.

Employment

Meeting and convention planners held about 51,000 jobs in 2006. About 27 percent worked for religious, grantmaking, civic, professional, and similar organizations; 17 percent worked in accommodation, including hotels and motels; 8 percent worked for educational services, public and private; 3 percent worked for governments; and 6 percent were self-employed. The rest were employed by convention and trade show organizing firms and in other industries as corporate meeting and convention planners.

Job Outlook

Employment of meeting and convention planners is expected to grow faster than the average for all occupations over the 2006-16 decade. Some additional job openings will arise from the need to replace workers who leave the workforce or transfer to other occupations. Opportunities will be best for individuals with a bachelors degree and some meeting planning experience.

Employment change. Employment of meeting and convention planners is expected to grow 20 percent over the 2006-16 decade, faster than the average for all occupations.

As businesses and organizations become increasingly international, meetings and conventions become even more important. In organizations that span the country or the globe, the periodic meeting is increasingly the only time the organization can bring all of its members together. Despite the proliferation of alternative forms of communication, such as e-mail, videoconferencing, and the Web, face-to-face interaction is still a necessity. In fact, new forms of communication foster interaction and connect individuals and groups that previously would not have collaborated. By increasing the number of human connections, electronic forms of communication actually increase the demand for meetings, which may offer the only opportunity for these people to interact in person.

Industries that are experiencing high growth tend to experience corresponding growth in meetings and conferences. For example, the medical and pharmaceutical sectors will experience large increases in meeting activity because of their high growth and their knowledge-intensive natures. These increases will spur employment growth of meeting professionals in medical and pharmaceutical associations. Professional associations hold conferences and conventions that offer the continuing education, training, and opportunities to exchange ideas that are vital to medical and pharmaceutical professionals.

Projections data from the National Employment Matrix

Occupational Title	SOC Code	Employment, 2006	Projected employment, 2016	Change, 2006-16	
				Number	Percent
Meeting and convention planners	13-1121	51,000	61,000	10,000	20

NOTE: Data in this table are rounded. See the discussion of the employment projections table in the *Handbook* introductory chapter on *Occupational Information Included in the Handbook.*

Job prospects. In addition to openings from employment growth, there will also be some job openings that arise due to the need to replace workers who leave the workforce or transfer to other occupations. Opportunities will be best for individuals with a bachelor's degree and some meeting planning experience.

Unlike workers in some occupations, meeting and convention planners often can change industries relatively easily, so they often are able to move to different industries in response to the growth or declines in particular sectors of the economy.

Demand for corporate meeting planners is highly susceptible to business cycle fluctuations because meetings are usually among the first expenses cut when budgets are tight. For associations, fluctuations are less pronounced because meetings are generally a source of revenue rather than an expense. However, since fewer people are able to attend association meetings during recessions, associations often reduce their meeting staff as well. Associations for industries such as health care, in which meeting attendance is required for professionals to maintain their licensure, are the least likely to experience cutbacks during downturns in the economy.

Earnings

Median annual earnings of wage and salary meeting and convention planners in May 2006 were $42,180. The middle 50 percent earned between $32,840 and $55,040. The lowest 10 percent earned less than $25,880, and the highest 10 percent earned more than $70,950. In 2006, median annual earnings in the industries employing the largest numbers of meeting and convention planners were as follows:

Business, professional, labor, political, and similar organizations	$45,850
Other support services	44,770
Local government	41,110
Colleges, universities, and professional schools	39,400
Traveler accommodation	38,270

Related Occupations

Meeting and convention planners work to communicate a particular message or impression about an organization, as do public relations specialists. They coordinate the activities of several operations to create a service for large numbers of people, using organizational, logistical, communication, budgeting, and interpersonal skills. Food service managers use the same skills for similar purposes. Like meeting and convention planners, producers and directors coordinate a range of activities to produce a television show or movie, negotiate contracts, and communicate with a wide variety of people. Travel agents also use similar skills, such as interacting with many people and coordinating travel arrangements, including hotel accommodations, transportation, and advice on destinations.

Sources of Additional Information

For information about meeting planner certification, contact:
➤ Convention Industry Council, 8201 Greensboro Dr., Suite 300, McLean, VA 22102.
Internet: **http://www.conventionindustry.org**

For information about the Certified Government Meeting Professional designation, contact:
➤ Society of Government Meeting Professionals, 908 King St., Lower Level, Alexandria, VA 22314.
Internet: **http://www.sgmp.org**

For information about internships and on-campus student meeting planning organizations, contact:
➤ Professional Convention Management Association, 2301 S. Lake Shore Dr., Suite 1001, Chicago, IL 60616-1419.
Internet: **http://www.pcma.org**

For information about meeting planning education, entering the profession, and career paths, contact:
➤ Meeting Professionals International, 3030 LBJ Fwy., Suite 1700, Dallas, TX 75244-5903.
Internet: **http://www.mpiweb.org**

For general career information about meeting and convention planners, see the *Occupational Outlook Quarterly* article "Meeting and convention planners," online at:
http://www.bls.gov/opub/ooq/2005/fall/art03.pdf

Tax Examiners, Collectors, and Revenue Agents

(O*NET 13-2081.00)

Significant Points

- Tax examiners, collectors, and revenue agents work for Federal, State, and local governments.

- Employment is expected to have little or no change, but the large number of retirements over the next 10 years should create many job openings.

- Competition will be greatest for positions with the Internal Revenue Service.

Nature of the Work

Taxes are one of the certainties of life, and as long as governments collect taxes, there will be jobs for tax examiners, collectors, and revenue agents. By reviewing tax returns, conducting audits, identifying taxes payable, and collecting overdue tax dollars, these workers ensure that governments obtain revenues from businesses and citizens.

Tax examiners do similar work whether they are employed at the Federal, State, or local government level. They review filed tax returns for accuracy and determine whether tax credits and deductions are allowed by law. Because many States assess individual income taxes based on the taxpayer's reported Federal adjusted gross income, tax examiners working for the Federal Government report any adjustments or corrections they make to the States. State tax examiners then determine whether the adjustments affect the taxpayer's State tax liability. At the local level, tax examiners often have additional duties, but an integral part of the work still includes the need to determine the factual basis for claims for refunds.

Tax examiners usually deal with the simplest tax returns—those filed by individual taxpayers with few deductions or those filed by small businesses. At the entry level, many tax examiners perform clerical duties, such as reviewing tax returns and entering them into a computer system for processing. If there is a problem, tax examiners may contact the taxpayer to resolve it.

Tax examiners also review returns for accuracy, checking taxpayers' math and making sure that the amounts that they report match those reported from other sources, such as employers and banks. In addition, examiners verify that Social Security numbers match names and that taxpayers have correctly interpreted the instructions on tax forms.

Much of a tax examiner's job involves making sure that tax credits and deductions claimed by taxpayers are legitimate. Tax examiners contact taxpayers by mail or telephone to address discrepancies and request supporting documentation. They may notify taxpayers of any overpayment or underpayment and either issue a refund or request further payment. If a taxpayer owes additional taxes, tax examiners adjust the total amount by assessing fees, interest, and penalties and notify the taxpayer of the total liability. Although most tax examiners deal with uncomplicated returns, some may work in more complex tax areas, such as pensions or business net operating losses.

Revenue agents specialize in tax-related accounting work for the U.S. Internal Revenue Service (IRS) and for equivalent agencies in State and local governments. Like tax examiners, they audit returns for accuracy. However, revenue agents handle complicated income, sales, and excise tax returns of businesses and large corporations. As a result, their work differs in a number of ways from that of tax examiners.

Entry-level Federal revenue agents usually audit tax returns of small businesses whose market specializations are similar. As they develop expertise in an industry, such as construction, retail sales, or finance, insurance, and real estate, revenue agents work with tax returns of larger corporations.

Many experienced revenue agents specialize; for example, they may focus exclusively on multinational businesses. But all revenue agents working for the Federal Government must keep abreast of the lengthy, complex, and frequently changing tax code. Computer technology has simplified the research process, allowing revenue agents Internet access to relevant legal bulletins, IRS notices, and tax-related court decisions. Revenue agents are increasingly using computers to analyze data and identify trends that help pinpoint tax offenders.

At the State level, revenue agents have duties similar to those of their counterparts in the Federal Government. State revenue agents use revenue adjustment reports forwarded by the IRS to determine whether adjustments made by Federal revenue agents affect a taxpayer's taxable income in the eyes of the States. In addition, State agents consider the sales and income taxes for their own States.

At the local level, revenue agents have varying titles and duties, but they still perform field audits or office audits of financial records for business firms. In some cases, local revenue agents also examine financial records of individuals. These local agents, like their State counterparts, rely on the information contained in Federal tax returns. However, local agents also must be knowledgeable enough to apply local tax laws regarding income, utility fees, or school taxes.

Collectors, also called *revenue officers* in the IRS, deal with delinquent accounts. The process of collecting a delinquent account starts with the revenue agent or tax examiner sending a report to the taxpayer. If the taxpayer makes no effort to resolve the delinquent account, the case is assigned to a collector. When a collector takes a case, he or she first sends the taxpayer a notice. The collector then works with the taxpayer on how to settle the debt.

In cases in which taxpayers fail to file a tax return, Federal collectors may request that the IRS prepare the return on a taxpayer's behalf. In other instances, collectors are responsible for verifying claims that delinquent taxpayers cannot pay their taxes. They investigate these claims by researching court information on the status of liens, mortgages, or financial statements; locating assets through third parties, such as neighbors or local departments of motor vehicles; and requesting legal summonses for other records. Ultimately, collectors must decide whether the IRS should take a lien—a claim on an asset such as a bank account, real estate, or an automobile—to settle a debt. Collectors also have the discretion to garnish wages—that is, take a portion of earned wages—to collect taxes owed.

A big part of a collector's job at the Federal level is imposing and following up on delinquent taxpayers' payment deadlines.

Little or no change in employment is projected, but expected retirements should create many job openings.

For each case file, collectors must maintain records, including contacts, telephone numbers, and actions taken.

Like tax examiners and revenue agents, collectors use computers to maintain files. Computer technology also gives collectors access to data to help them identify high-risk debtors—those who are unlikely to pay or are likely to flee. Collectors at the IRS usually work independently. However, they call on experts when tax examiners or revenue agents find fraudulent returns, or when the seizure of a property will involve complex legal steps.

At the State level, collectors decide whether to take action on the basis of their own States' tax returns. Collection work may be handled over the telephone or turned over to a collector who specializes in obtaining settlements. These collectors contact people directly and have the authority to issue subpoenas and request seizures of property. At the local levels, collectors have less power than their State and Federal counterparts. Although they can start the processes leading to the seizure of property and garnishment of wages, they must go through the local court system.

Work environment. Tax examiners, collectors, and revenue agents work in clean, pleasant, and comfortable office settings. Sometimes travel is necessary. Revenue agents at both the Federal and State levels spend a significant portion of their time in the offices of private firms, accessing tax-related records. Some agents may be permanently stationed in the offices of large corporations with complicated tax structures. Agents at the local level usually work in city halls or municipal buildings. Collectors travel to local courthouses, county and municipal seats of government, businesses, and taxpayers' homes to look up records, search for assets, and settle delinquent accounts.

Stress can result from the need to work under a deadline in checking returns and evaluating taxpayer claims. Collectors also must face the unpleasant task of confronting delinquent taxpayers.

Tax examiners, collectors, and revenue agents generally work a 40-hour week, although some overtime might be needed during the tax season. State and local tax examiners, who may review sales, gasoline, and cigarette taxes instead of handling tax returns, may have a steadier workload year-round.

Training, Other Qualifications, and Advancement

Many tax examiners, collectors, and revenue agents have a bachelor's degree. But relevant experience, or a combination of postsecondary education and experience, is sufficient qualification for many jobs. Specialized experience is sufficient to qualify for many jobs in State and local government.

Education and training. As shown in the table below, a bachelor's degree was the most common level of educational attainment among tax examiners, collectors, and revenue agents in 2006.

	Percent
High school graduate or less	25
Some college, no degree	19
Associate degree	10
Bachelor's degree	39
Graduate degree	6

In the Federal Government, workers must have a bachelor's degree or a combination of some college education and related experience. But in State and local governments, workers often have an associate degree, some college-level business classes and specialized experience, or a high school diploma and specialized experience.

For more advanced entry-level positions, applicants often must have a bachelor's degree. Candidates may sometimes qualify without a bachelor's degree, however, if they can demonstrate experience working with tax records, tax laws and regulations, documents, financial accounts, or similar records.

Specific education and training requirements vary by occupational specialty.

Tax examiners usually must have a bachelor's degree in accounting or a related discipline or a combination of education and full-time accounting, auditing, or tax compliance work. Tax examiner candidates at the IRS must have a bachelor's degree or 1 year of full-time specialized experience, which could include full-time work in accounting, bookkeeping, or tax analysis. After they are hired, tax examiners receive some formal training. In addition, annual employer-provided updates keep tax examiners current with changes in procedures and regulations.

Collectors usually must have some combination of college education and experience in collections, management, customer service, or tax compliance, or as a loan officer or credit manager. A bachelor's degree is required for employment as a collector with the IRS. No additional experience is required, and experience may not be substituted for the degree. Degrees in business, finance, accounting, and criminal justice are good backgrounds.

Entry-level collectors receive formal and on-the-job training under an instructor's guidance before working independently. Collectors usually complete initial training by the end of their second year of service, but may receive advanced technical instruction as they gain seniority and take on more difficult cases. Also, collectors are encouraged to continue their professional education by attending meetings to exchange information about how changes in tax laws affect collection methods.

Revenue agents usually must have a bachelor's degree in accounting, business administration, economics, or a related discipline or a combination of education and full-time business administration, accounting, or auditing work. Revenue agents with the IRS must have either a bachelor's degree or 30 semester hours of accounting coursework along with specialized experience. Specialized experience includes full-time work in accounting, bookkeeping, or tax analysis.

Other qualifications. Tax examiners, collectors, and revenue agents work with confidential financial and personal information; therefore, trustworthiness is crucial for maintaining the confidentiality of individuals and businesses. Applicants for Federal Government jobs must submit to a background investigation.

Collectors need good interpersonal and communication skills because they deal directly with the public and because their reports are scrutinized when the tax agency must legally justify attempts to seize assets. They must be able to negotiate well

Projections data from the National Employment Matrix

Occupational Title	SOC Code	Employment, 2006	Projected employment, 2016	Change, 2006-16	
				Number	Percent
Tax examiners, collectors, and revenue agents	13-2081	81,000	82,000	1,700	2

NOTE: Data in this table are rounded. See the discussion of the employment projections table in the *Handbook* introductory chapter on *Occupational Information Included in the Handbook*.

and deal effectively with others in potentially confrontational situations.

Revenue agents need strong analytical, organizational, and time management skills. They also must be able to work independently, because they spend so much time away from their home office, and they must keep current with changes in the tax code and laws.

Advancement. Advancement potential within Federal, State, and local agencies varies for tax examiners, revenue agents, and collectors. For related jobs outside government, experienced workers can take a licensing exam administered by the Federal Government to become enrolled agents—nongovernment tax professionals authorized to represent taxpayers before the IRS.

Collectors who demonstrate leadership skills and a thorough knowledge of collection activities may advance to supervisory or managerial collector positions, in which they oversee the activities of other collectors. It is only these higher level supervisors and managers who may authorize the more serious actions against individuals and businesses. The more complex collection attempts which usually are directed at larger businesses are reserved for collectors at these higher levels.

Newly hired revenue agents expand their accounting knowledge and remain up to date by consulting auditing manuals and other sources for detailed information about individual industries. Employers also continually offer training in new auditing techniques and tax-related issues and court decisions. As revenue agents gain experience, they may specialize in an industry, work with larger corporations, and cover increasingly complex tax returns. Some revenue agents also specialize in assisting in criminal investigations, auditing the books of known or suspected criminals such as drug dealers or money launderers. Some agents work with grand juries to help secure indictments. Others become international agents, assessing taxes on companies with subsidiaries abroad.

Employment

In 2006, tax examiners, revenue agents, and collectors held about 81,000 jobs at all levels of government.

About 44 percent worked for the Federal Government, 37 percent for State governments, and the remainder for local governments. In the IRS, tax examiners and revenue agents predominate because of the need to examine or audit tax returns. Collectors make up a smaller proportion, because most disputed tax liabilities do not require enforced collection.

Job Outlook

Little or no change in employment is expected, but the large number of retirements expected over the next 10 years should create many job openings at all levels of government.

Employment change. Employment of tax examiners, collectors, and revenue agents is projected to grow 2 percent during the 2006-16 decade, which is considered little or no change. Demand for tax examiners, revenue agents, and tax collectors will stem from changes in government policy toward tax enforcement and from growth in the number of businesses.

The Federal Government is expected to increase its tax enforcement efforts. Also, new technology and information sharing among tax agencies make it easier for agencies to pinpoint potential offenders, increasing the number of cases for audit and collection. These two factors should increase the demand for revenue agents and tax collectors.

The work of tax examiners is especially well suited to automation, adversely affecting demand for these workers in particular. In addition, more than 40 States and many local tax agencies contract out their tax collection functions to private-sector collection agencies in order to reduce costs, and this trend is likely to continue. The IRS has begun outsourcing some tax collection, but it is unclear whether the agency will continue or expand this practice. If IRS outsourcing continues, it will dampen growth in employment of revenue officers but is not expected to affect employment of revenue agents.

Job prospects. The large number of retirements expected over the next 10 years is expected to create many job openings at all levels of government. Both State and Federal tax agencies are turning their enforcement focus to higher income taxpayers and businesses, which file more complicated tax returns. Because of this, workers with knowledge of tax laws and experience working with complex tax issues will have the best opportunities.

Competition will be greatest for positions with the IRS. Opportunities at the Federal level will reflect the tightening or relaxation of budget constraints imposed on the IRS, the primary employer of these workers.

Employment at the State and local levels may fluctuate with the overall state of the economy. When the economy is contracting, State and local governments are likely to freeze hiring and lay off workers in response to budgetary constraints.

Earnings

In May 2006, median annual earnings for all tax examiners, collectors, and revenue agents were $45,620. The middle 50 percent earned between $34,840 and $62,530. The bottom 10 percent earned less than $27,290, and the top 10 percent earned more than $81,890. However, median earnings vary considerably, depending on the level of government. At the Federal level, May 2006 median annual earnings for tax examiners were $52,630; at the State level, they were $44,110; and at the local level, they were $33,120.

Earnings also vary by occupational specialty. For example, in the Federal Government in 2006, tax examiners earned an average of $38,290, revenue agents earned $82,204, and tax specialists earned $55,100.

IRS employees receive family, vacation, and sick leave. Full-time permanent IRS employees are offered tax deferred retirement savings and investment plans with employer matching contributions, health insurance, and life insurance.

Related Occupations

Tax examiners, collectors, and revenue agents analyze and interpret financial data. Occupations with similar responsibilities include accountants and auditors, budget analysts, cost estimators, financial analysts and personal financial advisors, financial managers, and loan officers.

Sources of Additional Information

Information on obtaining positions as tax examiners, collectors, or revenue agents with the Federal Government is available from the Office of Personnel Management through USAJOBS, the Federal Government's official employment information system. This resource for locating and applying for job opportunities can be accessed through the Internet at **http://www.usajobs.opm.gov** or through an interactive voice response telephone system at (703) 724-1850 or TDD (978) 461-8404. These numbers are not tollfree, and charges may result.

State or local government personnel offices can provide information about tax examiner, collector, or revenue agent jobs at those levels of government.

For information about careers at the Internal Revenue Service, contact:

➤ Internal Revenue Service, 1111 Constitution Ave. NW., Washington, D.C. 20224. Internet: **http://www.jobs.irs.gov**

Professional and Related Occupations

Computer and Mathematical Occupations

Actuaries

(O*NET 15-2011.00)

Significant Points

- A strong background in mathematics is essential; actuaries must pass a series of examinations to gain full professional status.

- About 6 out of 10 actuaries are employed in the insurance industry.

- Employment opportunities should remain good for those who qualify, because the stringent qualifying examination system restricts the number of candidates.

Nature of the Work

Through their knowledge of statistics, finance, and business, actuaries assess the risk of events occurring and help create policies that minimize risk and its financial impact on companies and clients. One of the main functions of actuaries is to help businesses assess the risk of certain events occurring and formulate policies that minimize the cost of that risk. For this reason, actuaries are essential to the insurance industry.

Actuaries assemble and analyze data to estimate the probability and likely cost of an event such as death, sickness, injury, disability, or loss of property. Actuaries also address financial questions, including those involving the level of pension contributions required to produce a certain retirement income level and the way in which a company should invest resources to maximize return on investments in light of potential risk. Using their broad knowledge of statistics, finance, and business, actuaries help design insurance policies, pension plans, and other financial strategies in a manner which will help ensure that the plans are maintained on a sound financial basis.

Most actuaries are employed in the insurance industry, specializing in either life and health insurance or property and casualty insurance. They produce probability tables or use more sophisticated dynamic modeling techniques that determine the likelihood that a potential event will generate a claim. From these tables, they estimate the amount a company can expect to pay in claims. For example, property and casualty actuaries calculate the expected number of claims resulting from automobile accidents, which varies depending on the insured person's age, sex, driving history, type of car, and other factors. Actuaries ensure that the price, or premium, charged for such insurance will enable the company to cover claims and other expenses. This premium must be profitable, yet competitive with other insurance companies. Within the life and health in-surance fields, actuaries help to develop long-term-care insurance and annuity policies, the latter a growing investment tool for many individuals.

Actuaries in other financial service industries manage credit and help price corporate security offerings. They also devise new investment tools to help their firms compete with other financial service companies. Pension actuaries work under the provisions of the Employee Retirement Income Security Act (ERISA) of 1974 to evaluate pension plans covered by that Act and report on the plans' financial soundness to participants, sponsors, and Federal regulators. Actuaries working for the government help manage social programs such as Social Security and Medicare.

Actuaries may help determine company policy and may need to explain complex technical matters to company executives, government officials, shareholders, policyholders, or the public in general. They may testify before public agencies on proposed legislation that affects their businesses or explain changes in contract provisions to customers. They also may help companies develop plans to enter new lines of business or new geographic markets by forecasting demand in competitive settings.

Consulting actuaries provide advice to clients on a contract basis. The duties of most consulting actuaries are similar to those of other actuaries. For example, some may evaluate company pension plans by calculating the future value of employee and employer contributions and determining whether the amounts are sufficient to meet the future needs of retirees. Others help companies reduce their insurance costs by lowering the level of risk the companies take on. For example, they may provide advice on how to lessen the risk of injury on the job. Consulting actuaries sometimes testify in court regarding the value of potential lifetime earnings of a person who is disabled or killed in an accident, the current value of future pen-

Actuaries need a strong background in mathematics and statistics.

sion benefits (in divorce cases), or other values arrived at by complex calculations. Some actuaries work in reinsurance, a field in which one insurance company arranges to share a large prospective liability policy with another insurance company in exchange for a percentage of the premium.

Work environment. Actuaries have desk jobs, and their offices usually are comfortable and pleasant. They often work at least 40 hours a week. Some actuaries—particularly consulting actuaries—may travel to meet with clients. Consulting actuaries also may experience more erratic employment and be expected to work more than 40 hours per week.

Training, Other Qualifications, and Advancement

Actuaries need a strong foundation in mathematics, statistics, and general business. They generally have a bachelor's degree and are required to pass a series of exams in order to become certified.

Education and training. Actuaries need a strong background in mathematics and general business. Usually, actuaries earn an undergraduate degree in mathematics, statistics or actuarial science, or a business-related field such as finance, economics or business. While in college, students should complete coursework in economics, applied statistics and corporate finance, which is a requirement for professional certification. Furthermore, many students obtain internships to gain experience in the profession prior to graduation. About 100 colleges and universities offer an actuarial science program, and most offer a degree in mathematics, statistics, economics, or finance.

Some companies hire applicants without specifying a major, provided that the applicant has a working knowledge of mathematics—including calculus, probability, and statistics—and has demonstrated this knowledge by passing one or two actuarial exams required for professional designation. Companies increasingly prefer well-rounded individuals who, in addition to having acquired a strong technical background, have some training in business and liberal arts and possess strong communication skills.

Beginning actuaries often rotate among different jobs in an organization, such as marketing, underwriting, financial reporting and product development, to learn various actuarial operations and phases of insurance work. At first, they prepare data for actuarial projects or perform other simple tasks. As they gain experience, actuaries may supervise clerks, prepare correspondence, draft reports, and conduct research. They may move from one company to another early in their careers as they advance to higher positions.

Licensure. Two professional societies sponsor programs leading to full professional status in their specialty: the Society of Actuaries (SOA) and the Casualty Actuarial Society (CAS). The SOA certifies actuaries in the fields of life insurance, health benefits systems, retirement systems, and finance and investment. The CAS gives a series of examinations in the property and casualty field, which includes car, homeowners, medical malpractice, workers compensation, and personal injury liability.

Three of the first four exams in the SOA and CAS examination series are jointly sponsored by the two societies and cover the same material. For this reason, students do not need to commit themselves to a specialty until they have taken the initial examinations, which test an individual's competence in probability, statistics, and other branches of mathematics and finance. The first few examinations help students evaluate their potential as actuaries. Many prospective actuaries begin taking the exams in college with the help of self-study guides and courses. Those who pass one or more examinations have better opportunities for employment at higher starting salaries than those who do not.

Many candidates find work as an actuary immediately after graduation and work through the certification process while gaining some experience in the field. In fact, many employers pay the examination fees and provide their employees time to study. As actuaries pass exams, they are often rewarded with a pay increase. Despite the fact that employers are supportive during the exam process, home study is necessary and many actuaries study for months to prepare for each exam.

The process for gaining certification in the Casualty Actuarial Society is predominantly exam based. To reach the first level of certification, the Associate or ACAS level, a candidate must complete seven exams, attend one course on professionalism and complete the coursework in applied statistics, corporate finance, and economics required by both the SOA and CAS. This process generally takes from 4 to 6 years. The next level, the Fellowship or FCAS level, requires passing two additional exams in advanced topics, including investment and assets and dynamic financial analysis and the valuation of insurance. Most actuaries reach the fellowship level 2 to 3 years after attaining Associate status.

The certification process of the Society of Actuaries blends exams with computer learning modules and coursework. After taking the initial exams, candidates must choose a specialty: group and health benefits, individual life and annuities, retirement benefits, pensions, investments or finance/enterprise risk management. To reach the Associate or ASA level, a candidate must complete the initial four exams, the coursework in applied statistics, corporate finance and economics required by the SOA and CAS, eight computer modules with two corresponding assessments and a course in professionalism. This process generally takes from 4 to 6 years. To attain the Fellowship or FSA level, a candidate must pass two additional exams within a chosen specialty and must complete three computer modules and a professionalism course. Attaining Fellowship status usually takes an additional 2 to 3 years after becoming an Associate.

Specific requirements apply to pension actuaries, who verify the financial status of defined benefit pension plans for the Federal Government. These actuaries must be enrolled by the Joint Board of the U.S. Treasury Department and the U.S. Department of Labor for the Enrollment of Actuaries. To qualify for enrollment, applicants must meet certain experience and examination requirements, as stipulated by the Board.

Other qualifications. In addition to knowledge of mathematics, computer skills are becoming increasingly important. Actuaries should be able to develop and use spreadsheets and databases, as well as standard statistical analysis software. Knowledge of computer programming languages, such as Visual Basic for Applications, SAS, or SQL, is also useful.

To perform their duties effectively, actuaries must keep up with current economic and social trends and legislation, as well as with developments in health, business, and finance that could affect insurance or investment practices. Good communication and interpersonal skills also are important, particularly for prospective consulting actuaries.

Advancement. Advancement depends largely on job performance and the number of actuarial examinations passed. Actuaries with a broad knowledge of the insurance, pension, investment, or employee benefits fields can rise to administrative and executive positions in their companies. Actuaries with supervisory ability may advance to management positions in other areas, such as underwriting, accounting, data processing, marketing, and advertising. Increasingly, actuaries with knowledge of business are beginning to rise to high-level positions within their companies, such as Chief Risk Officer, Chief Financial Officer, or other executive level positions. These generally require that actuaries use their abilities for assessing risk and apply it to the entire company as a whole. Furthermore, some experienced actuaries move into consulting, often by opening their own consulting firm. Some actuaries transfer to college and university faculty positions. (See the section on teachers—postsecondary elsewhere in the *Handbook*.)

Employment

Actuaries held about 18,000 jobs in 2006. Over half of all actuaries were employed by insurance carriers. Approximately 21 percent work for professional, scientific and technical consulting services. Others worked for insurance agents and brokers and in the management of companies and enterprises industry. A relatively small number of actuaries are employed by government agencies.

Job Outlook

Employment of actuaries is expected to grow rapidly through 2016. Job opportunities should remain good for those who qualify, because the stringent qualifying examination system restricts the number of candidates.

Employment change. Employment of actuaries is expected to increase by about 24 percent over the 2006-16 period, which is much faster than the average for all other occupations. Employment growth in the insurance industry—the largest employer of actuaries—is expected to continue at a stable pace, while more significant job growth is likely in other industries, such as health care and consulting firms.

Steady demand by the insurance industry should ensure that actuarial jobs in this key industry will remain stable during the projection period. Although relatively few new jobs will be created, actuaries will continue to be needed to develop, price, and evaluate a variety of insurance products and calculate the costs of new risks. The demand for actuaries in life insurance

has been growing rapidly as a result of the rise in popularity of annuities, a financial product offered primarily by life insurance companies. In addition, the risk of terrorism and natural disasters has created a large demand for actuaries in property insurance.

Some new employment opportunities for actuaries should also become available in the health-care field as health-care issues and Medicare reform continue to receive attention. Increased regulation of managed health-care companies and the desire to contain health-care costs will continue to provide job opportunities for actuaries, who will also be needed to evaluate the risks associated with new medical issues, such as genetic testing and the impact of new diseases. Others in this field are involved in drafting health-care legislation.

A significant proportion of new actuaries will find employment with consulting firms. Companies that may not find it cost effective to employ their own actuaries are increasingly hiring consulting actuaries to analyze various risks. Other areas with notable growth prospects are information services and accounting services. Also, because actuarial skills are increasingly seen as useful to other industries that deal with risk, such as the airline and the banking industries, additional job openings may be created in these industries.

Despite the increase in employment overall, there has been some decline in the demand for pension actuaries. This is due in large part to the decline of defined benefit plans, which required review by an actuary, in favor of investment based retirement funds, such as 401ks.

Job prospects. Opportunities for actuaries should be good, particularly for those who have passed at least one or two of the initial exams. In addition, a small number of jobs will open up each year to replace actuaries who leave the occupation to retire or transfer new jobs. Candidates with additional knowledge or experience, such as computer programming skills, will be particularly attractive to employers. Most jobs in this occupation are located in urban areas, but opportunities vary by geographic location.

Earnings

Median annual earnings of actuaries were $82,800 in May 2006. The middle 50 percent earned between $58,710 and $114,570. The lowest 10 percent had earnings of less than $46,470 while the top 10 percent earned more than $145,600.

According to the National Association of Colleges and Employers, annual starting salaries for graduates with a bachelor's degree in actuarial science averaged $53,754 in 2007.

Insurance companies and consulting firms give merit increases to actuaries as they gain experience and pass examinations. Some companies also offer cash bonuses for each professional designation achieved. A 2007 survey by Life Office Management Association, Inc. of the largest U.S. insurance and finan-

Projections data from the National Employment Matrix

Occupational Title	SOC Code	Employment, 2006	Projected employment, 2016	Change, 2006-2016	
				Number	Percent
Actuaries	15-2011	18,000	22,000	4,300	24

NOTE: Data in this table are rounded. See the discussion of the employment projections table in the *Handbook* introductory chapter on *Occupational Information Included in the Handbook*.

cial services companies indicated that the average base salary for an entry-level actuary was $53,111. Associate actuaries, who direct and provide leadership in the design, pricing, and implementation of insurance products, received an average salary of $109,167. Actuaries at the highest technical level without managerial responsibilities reportedly were paid an average of $125,946.

Related Occupations

Actuaries need a strong background in mathematics, statistics, and related fields. Other workers whose jobs involve such skills include accountants and auditors, budget analysts, economists, market and survey researchers, financial analysts and personal financial advisors, insurance underwriters, mathematicians, and statisticians.

Sources of Additional Information

Career information on actuaries specializing in pensions is available from:

➤ American Society of Pension Actuaries, 4245 N. Fairfax Dr., Suite 750, Arlington, VA 22203.
Internet: **http://www.aspa.org**

For information about actuarial careers in life and health insurance, employee benefits and pensions, and finance and investments, contact:

➤ Society of Actuaries (SOA), 475 N. Martingale Rd., Suite 600, Schaumburg, IL 60173-2226.
Internet: **http://www.soa.org**

For information about actuarial careers in property and casualty insurance, contact:

➤ Casualty Actuarial Society (CAS), 4350 N. Fairfaix Dr., Suite 250 Arlington, VA 22203.
Internet: **http://www.casact.org**

The SOA and CAS jointly sponsor a Web site for those interested in pursuing an actuarial career.
Internet: **http://www.BeAnActuary.org**

For general information on a career as an actuary, contact:

➤ American Academy of Actuaries, 1100 17th St.NW., 7th Floor, Washington, DC 20036.
Internet: **http://www.actuary.org**

Computer Programmers

(O*NET 15-1021.00)

Significant Points

- Almost 8 out of 10 computer programmers held an associate's degree or higher in 2006; nearly half held a bachelor's degree, and 2 out of 10 held a graduate degree.

- Employment of computer programmers is expected to decline by four percent through 2016.

- Job prospects will be best for applicants with a bachelor's degree and experience with a variety of programming languages and tools.

Nature of the Work

Computer programmers write, test, and maintain the detailed instructions, called programs, that computers follow to perform their functions. Programmers also conceive, design, and test logical structures for solving problems by computer. With the help of other computer specialists, they figure out which instructions to use to make computers do specific tasks. Many technical innovations in programming—advanced computing technologies and sophisticated new languages and programming tools, for example—have redefined the role of a programmer and elevated much of the programming work done today.

Job titles and descriptions may vary, depending on the organization, but computer programmers are individuals whose main job function is programming. Programmers usually write programs according to the specifications given by computer software engineers and systems analysts. (Sections on computer software engineers and on computer systems analysts appear elsewhere in the *Handbook*.) After engineers and analysts design software—describing how it will work—the programmer converts that design into a logical series of instructions that the computer can follow. The programmer codes these instructions in a conventional programming language such as COBOL; an artificial intelligence language such as Prolog; or one of the more advanced object-oriented languages, such as Java, C++, or ACTOR.

Different programming languages are used depending on the purpose of the program. Programmers generally know more than one programming language, and because many languages are similar, they often can learn new languages relatively easily. In practice, programmers often are referred to by the language they know, such as Java programmers, or by the type of function they perform or environment in which they work—for example, database programmers, mainframe programmers, or Web programmers.

Programmers also update, repair, modify, and expand existing programs. Some, especially those working on large projects that involve many programmers, use computer-assisted software engineering (CASE) tools to automate much of the coding process. These tools enable a programmer to concentrate on writing the unique parts of a program. Programmers working on smaller projects often use "programmer environments," applications that increase productivity by combining compiling, code walk through, code generation, test data generation, and debugging functions. Programmers also use libraries of basic code that can be modified or customized for a specific application. This approach yields more reliable and consistent programs and increases programmers' productivity by eliminating some routine steps.

Programs vary widely depending on the type of information they will access or generate. For example, the instructions involved in updating financial records are very different from those required to simulate flight for pilot training. Simple programs can be written in a few hours, but some programs draw data from many existing systems or use complex mathematical formulas. These programs may take more than a year to create. In most cases, several programmers work together as a team under a senior programmer's supervision.

Programmers test a program by running it to ensure that the instructions are correct and that the program produces the desired outcome. If errors do occur, the programmer must make the appropriate change and recheck the program until it produces the correct results. This process is called testing and debugging. Programmers may continue to fix problems for as long as a program is used.

Programmers working on a mainframe, a large centralized computer, may prepare instructions for a computer operator who will run the program. (A section on computer operators appears elsewhere in the *Handbook*.) Programmers also may contribute to the instruction manual for a program.

Programmers in software development companies may work directly with experts from various fields to create specialized software—either programs designed for specific clients or packaged software for general use—ranging from games and educational software to programs for desktop publishing and financial planning. Programming of packaged software constitutes one of the most rapidly growing segments of the computer services industry.

Increasingly, advanced software platforms are bridging the gap between computer programmers and computer users. New platforms, such as spreadsheet, accounting, and enterprise resource planning applications, have created demand for computer specialists who have first-hand knowledge of a user-base. These workers use such platforms to develop programs that meet the specific needs of this base. Computer programmers often are responsible for creating the software platform, and then fine-tuning the final program after it has been made.

Computer programmers often are grouped into two broad types—applications programmers and systems programmers. *Applications programmers* write programs to handle a specific job, such as a program to track inventory within an organization. They also may revise existing packaged software or customize generic applications purchased from vendors. *Systems programmers*, in contrast, write programs to maintain and control computer systems software for operating systems, networked systems, and database systems. These workers make changes in the instructions that determine how the network, workstations, and central processing unit of a system handle the various jobs they have been given, and how they communicate with peripheral equipment such as terminals, printers, and disk drives. Because of their knowledge of the entire computer system, systems programmers often help applications programmers determine the source of problems that may occur with their programs.

In some organizations, workers known as *programmer-analysts* are responsible for both the systems analysis and programming. (A more detailed description of the work of programmer-analysts is presented in the section on computer systems analysts elsewhere in the *Handbook*.)

Work environment. Programmers spend the majority of their time in front of a computer terminal, and work in clean, comfortable offices. Telecommuting is becoming more common, however, as technological advances allow more work to be done from remote locations.

Most computer programmers work about 40 hours per week. Long hours or weekend work may be required, however, to

Computer programmers write, test, and maintain the detailed instructions that computers follow.

meet deadlines or fix unexpected technical problems. About four percent work part-time, compared with about 15 percent for all occupations.

Like other workers who spend long periods in front of a computer terminal typing at a keyboard, programmers are susceptible to eyestrain, back discomfort, and hand and wrist problems such as carpal tunnel syndrome.

Training, Other Qualifications, and Advancement

A bachelor's degree commonly is required for computer programming jobs, although a two-year degree or certificate may be adequate for some positions. Employers favor applicants who already have relevant programming skills and experience. Skilled workers who keep up to date with the latest technology usually have good opportunities for advancement.

Education and training. Most programmers have a bachelor's degree, but a two-year degree or certificate may be adequate for some jobs. Some computer programmers hold a college degree in computer science, mathematics, or information systems, whereas others have taken special courses in computer programming to supplement their degree in a field such as accounting, finance, or another area of business. In 2006, more than 68 percent of computer programmers had a bachelor's degree or higher, but as the level of education and training required by employers continues to rise, this proportion is expected to increase.

Employers who use computers for scientific or engineering applications usually prefer college graduates who have a degree in computer or information science, mathematics, engineering, or the physical sciences. Employers who use computers for business applications prefer to hire people who have had college courses in management information systems and business, and who possess strong programming skills. A graduate degree in a related field is required for some jobs.

Most systems programmers hold a four-year degree in computer science. Extensive knowledge of a variety of operating systems is essential for such workers. This includes being able to configure an operating system to work with different types of hardware and being able to adapt the operating system to best meet the needs of a particular organization. Systems programmers also must be able to work with database systems, such as DB2, Oracle, or Sybase.

In addition to educational attainment, employers highly value relevant programming skills, as well as experience. Although knowledge of traditional programming languages still is important, employers are placing an emphasis on newer, object-oriented languages and tools such as C++ and Java. Additionally, employers seek people familiar with fourth- and fifth-generation languages that involve graphic user interface and systems programming. College graduates who are interested in changing careers or developing an area of expertise may return to a two-year community college or technical school for specialized training. In the absence of a degree, substantial specialized experience or expertise may be needed.

Entry-level or junior programmers may work alone on simple assignments after some initial instruction, or they may be assigned to work on a team with more experienced programmers. Either way, beginning programmers generally must work under close supervision.

Because technology changes so rapidly, programmers must continuously update their knowledge and skills by taking courses sponsored by their employer or by software vendors, or offered through local community colleges and universities.

Certification and other qualifications. When hiring programmers, employers look for people with the necessary programming skills who can think logically and pay close attention to detail. Programming calls for patience, persistence, and the ability to perform exacting analytical work, especially under pressure. Ingenuity and creativity are particularly important when programmers design solutions and test their work for potential failures. The ability to work with abstract concepts and to do technical analysis is especially important for systems programmers because they work with the software that controls the computer's operation.

Because programmers are expected to work in teams and interact directly with users, employers want programmers who are able to communicate with non-technical personnel. Business skills are also important, especially for those wishing to advance to managerial positions.

Certification is a way to demonstrate a level of competence and may provide a jobseeker with a competitive advantage. In addition to language-specific certificates, product vendors or software firms also offer certification and may require professionals who work with their products to be certified. Voluntary certification also is available through various other organizations.

Advancement. For skilled workers who keep up to date with the latest technology, prospects for advancement are good. In large organizations, programmers may be promoted to lead programmer and be given supervisory responsibilities. Some applications programmers may move into systems programming

after they gain experience and take courses in systems software. With general business experience, programmers may become programmer-analysts or systems analysts, or may be promoted to managerial positions. Programmers with specialized knowledge and experience with a language or operating system may work in research and development and may even become computer software engineers. As employers increasingly contract with outside firms to do programming jobs, more opportunities should arise for experienced programmers with expertise in a specific area to work as consultants.

Employment

Computer programmers held about 435,000 jobs in 2006. Programmers are employed in almost every industry, but the largest concentration is in computer systems design and related services. Large numbers of programmers also work for software publishers, financial institutions, insurance carriers, educational institutions, government agencies, and management of companies and enterprises. Many computer programmers work independently as consultants on a temporary or contract basis, some of whom are self-employed. About 17,000 computer programmers were self-employed in 2006.

Job Outlook

Employment of computer programmers is expected to decline slowly. Job prospects should be best for those with a bachelor's degree and experience with a variety of programming languages and tools.

Employment change. Employment of computer programmers is expected to decline slowly, decreasing by 4 percent from 2006 to 2016. The consolidation and centralization of systems and applications, developments in packaged software, advances in programming languages and tools, and the growing ability of users to design, write, and implement more of their own programs mean that more programming functions can be performed by other types of information workers, such as computer software engineers.

Another factor contributing to employment decline will be the offshore outsourcing of programming jobs. Because they can transmit their programs digitally, computer programmers can perform their job function from anywhere in the world, allowing companies to employ workers in countries that have lower prevailing wages. Computer programmers are at a much higher risk of having their jobs outsourced abroad than are workers involved in more complex and sophisticated information technology functions, such as software engineering. Much of the work of computer programmers requires little localized or specialized knowledge and can be made routine once knowledge of a particular programming language is mastered—and computer programming languages have become known internationally.

Projections data from the National Employment Matrix

Occupational Title	SOC Code	Employment, 2006	Projected employment, 2016	Change, 2006-2016	
				Number	Percent
Computer programmers	15-1021	435,000	417,000	-18,000	-4

NOTE: Data in this table are rounded. See the discussion of the employment projections table in the *Handbook* introductory chapter on *Occupational Information Included in the Handbook.*

Nevertheless, employers will continue to need some local programmers, especially those who have strong technical skills and who understand an employer's business and its programming requirements. This means that programmers will have to keep abreast of changing programming languages and techniques. Given the importance of networking and the expansion of client/server, Web-based, and wireless environments, organizations will look for programmers who can support data communications and help implement business and intranet strategies. Demand for programmers with strong object-oriented programming capabilities and technical specialization in areas such as client/server programming, wireless applications, multimedia technology, and graphic user interface likely will stem from the expansion of intranets, extranets, and Internet applications. Programmers also will be needed to create and maintain expert systems and embed these technologies in more products. Finally, a growing emphasis on cybersecurity will lead to increased demand for programmers who are familiar with digital security issues, and are skilled in using appropriate security technology.

Job prospects. Although employment is projected to decline, numerous job openings will result from the need to replace programmers who leave the labor force or transfer to other occupations. Prospects for these openings should be best for applicants with a bachelor's degree and experience with a variety of programming languages and tools. The languages that are in demand today include C++, Java, and other object-oriented languages, as well as newer, domain-specific languages that apply to computer networking, database management, and Internet application development. As technology evolves, however, and newer, more sophisticated tools emerge, programmers will need to update their skills in order to remain competitive. Obtaining vendor-specific or language-specific certification also can provide a competitive edge.

Jobs for both systems and applications programmers should be most plentiful in computer consulting businesses. These establishments are part of the computer systems design and related services industry, which is projected to be among the fastest growing industries in the economy over the 2006 to 2016 period.

Earnings

Median annual earnings of wage-and-salary computer programmers were $65,510 in May 2006. The middle 50 percent earned between $49,580 and $85,080 a year. The lowest 10 percent earned less than $38,460, and the highest 10 percent earned more than $106,610. Median annual earnings in the industries employing the largest numbers of computer programmers in May 2006 are shown below:

Software publishers	$79,270
Computer systems design and related services	67,880
Management of companies and enterprises	67,170
Insurance carriers	65,650

According to the National Association of Colleges and Employers, starting salary offers for computer programmers averaged $49,928 per year in 2007.

According to Robert Half Technology, a firm providing specialized staffing services, average annual starting salaries in 2007 ranged from $55,250 to $90,250 for applications development programmers/analysts, and from $60,250 to $94,750 for software developers. Average starting salaries for mainframe systems programmers ranged from $52,250 to $70,750.

Related Occupations

Other professional workers who deal extensively with data include computer software engineers, computer scientists and database administrators, computer systems analysts, statisticians, mathematicians, engineers, commercial and industrial designers, and operations research analysts.

Sources of Additional Information

State employment service offices can provide information about job openings for computer programmers. Municipal chambers of commerce are an additional source of information on an area's largest employers.

Further information about computer careers is available from:

➤ Association for Computing Machinery, 2 Penn Plaza, Suite 701, New York, NY 10121-0701.
Internet: **http://www.acm.org**
➤ Institute of Electrical and Electronics Engineers Computer Society, Headquarters Office, 1730 Massachusetts Ave. NW., Washington, DC 20036-1992.
Internet: **http://www.computer.org**
➤ National Workforce Center for Emerging Technologies, 3000 Landerholm Circle SE., Bellevue, WA 98007.
Internet: **http://www.nwcet.org**
➤ University of Washington Computer Science and Engineering Department, AC101 Paul G. Allen Center, Box 352350, 185 Stevens Way, Seattle, WA 98195-2350.
Internet: **http://www.cs.washington.edu/WhyCSE**

Computer Scientists and Database Administrators

(O*NET 15-1011.00, 15-1061.00, 15-1081.00, 15-1099.99)

Significant Points

- Education requirements range from an associate degree to a doctoral degree.

- Employment is expected to increase much faster than the average as organizations continue to expand their use of technology.

- Workers must be able to learn new technologies quickly for these constantly evolving occupations.

Nature of the Work

The rapid and widespread use of computers and information technology has generated a need for highly trained workers proficient in various job functions. These computer specialists include computer scientists, database administrators, and network systems and data communication analysts. Job tasks and occupational titles used to describe these workers evolve rapidly and continually, reflecting new areas of specialization or changes in technology, as well as the preferences and practices of employers.

Computer scientists work as theorists, researchers, or inventors. Their jobs are distinguished by the higher level of theoretical expertise and innovation they apply to complex problems and the creation or application of new technology. The areas of computer science research range from complex theory to hardware design to programming-language design. Some researchers work on multidisciplinary projects, such as developing and advancing uses of virtual reality, extending human-computer interaction, or designing robots. They may work on design teams with electrical engineers and other specialists.

Computer science researchers employed by academic institutions (covered in the statement on teachers—postsecondary, elsewhere in the *Handbook*) have job functions that are similar in many ways to those employed by other organizations. In general, researchers in academic settings have more flexibility to focus on pure theory, while those working in other organizations usually focus on projects that have the possibility of producing patents and profits. However, some researchers in non-academic settings have considerable latitude in determining the direction of their research.

With the Internet and electronic business generating large volumes of data, there is a growing need to be able to store, manage, and extract data effectively. *Database administrators* work with database management systems software and determine ways to organize and store data. They identify user needs and set up new computer databases. In many cases, database administrators must integrate data from outdated systems into a new system. They also test and coordinate modifications to the system when needed, and troubleshoot problems when they occur. An organization's database administrator ensures the performance of the system, understands the platform on which the database runs, and adds new users to the system. Because many databases are connected to the Internet, database administrators also must plan and coordinate security measures with network administrators. With the growing volume of sensitive data and the increasing interconnectedness of computer networks, data integrity, backup systems, and database security have become increasingly important aspects of the job of database administrators.

Network systems and data communications analysts, also referred to as *network architects*, design, test, and evaluate systems such as local area networks (LANs), wide area networks (WANs), the Internet, intranets, and other data communications systems. Systems are configured in many ways and can range from a connection between two offices in the same building to globally distributed networks, voice mail, and e-mail systems of a multinational organization. Network systems and data communications analysts perform network modeling, analysis, and planning, often requiring both hardware and software solutions. For example, a network may involve the installation of several pieces of hardware, such as routers and hubs, wireless adaptors, and cables, while also requiring the installation and configuration of software, such as network drivers. Analysts also may research related products and make necessary hardware and software recommendations.

Telecommunications specialists focus on the interaction between computer and communications equipment. These workers design voice and data communication systems, supervise the installation of the systems, and provide maintenance and other services to clients after the systems are installed.

The growth of the Internet and the expansion of the World Wide Web (the graphical portion of the Internet) have generated a variety of occupations related to the design, development, and maintenance of Web sites and their servers. For example, *webmasters* are responsible for all technical aspects of a Web site, including performance issues such as speed of access, and for approving the content of the site. *Internet developers* or *Web developers*, also called *Web designers*, are responsible for day-to-day site creation and design.

Work environment. Computer scientists and database administrators normally work in offices or laboratories in comfortable surroundings. They typically work about 40 hours a week, the same as many other professional or office workers. However, evening or weekend work may be necessary to meet deadlines or to solve specific problems. Telecommuting is increasingly common for many computer professionals as networks expand, allowing more work to be done from remote locations through modems, laptops, electronic mail, and the Internet. However,

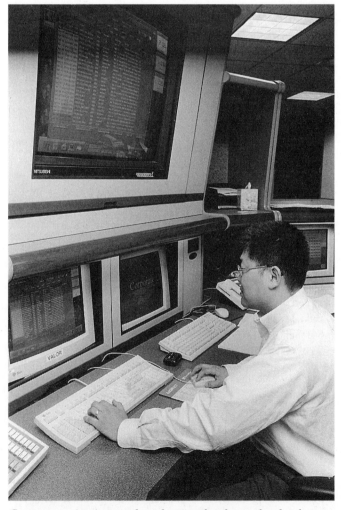

Computer scientists work at the very forefront of technology.

some work still must be done in the office for security or other reasons.

Like other workers who spend long periods in front of a computer terminal typing on a keyboard, computer scientists and database administrators are susceptible to eyestrain, back discomfort, and hand and wrist problems such as carpal tunnel syndrome or cumulative trauma disorder.

Training, Other Qualifications, and Advancement

Rapidly changing technology requires an increasing level of skill and education on the part of workers in these occupations. Employers look for professionals with an ever-broader background and range of skills, including technical knowledge and also communication and other interpersonal skills.

Education and training. While there is no universally accepted way to prepare for a job as a network systems analyst, computer scientist, or database administrator, most employers place a premium on some formal college education. A bachelor's degree is a prerequisite for many jobs; however, some jobs may require only a 2-year degree. Relevant work experience also is very important. For more technically complex jobs, persons with graduate degrees are preferred. Most computer scientist positions require a Ph.D. degree, as their main job function is research. Computer scientists having only a bachelor's or master's degree are generally limited in their ability to advance.

For database administrator and network systems and data communication analyst positions, most employers seek applicants who have bachelor's degrees in computer science, information science, or management information systems (MIS). MIS programs usually are part of the business school or college and differ considerably from computer science programs, emphasizing business and management-oriented coursework and business computing courses. Employers increasingly prefer applicants with a master's degree in business administration (MBA) with a concentration in information systems, as more firms move their business to the Internet. For some network systems and data communication analysts, such as webmasters, an associate degree or certificate is sufficient, although more advanced positions might require a computer-related bachelor's degree.

Most community colleges and many independent technical institutes and proprietary schools offer an associate's degree in computer science or a related information technology field. Many of these programs may be geared more toward meeting the needs of local businesses and are more occupation specific than are 4-year degree programs. Some jobs may be better suited to the level of training that such programs offer. Employers usually look for people who have broad knowledge and experience related to computer systems and technologies, strong problem-solving and analytical skills, and good interpersonal skills. Courses in computer science or systems design offer good preparation for a job in these computer occupations. For jobs in a business environment, employers usually want systems analysts to have business management or closely related skills, while a background in the physical sciences, applied mathematics, or engineering is preferred for work in scientifically oriented organizations. Art or graphic design skills may be desirable for webmasters or Web developers.

Despite employers' preference for those with technical degrees, individuals with post-secondary degrees in a variety of other subjects may find employment in these occupations. Given the rapid pace of technological change, a degree generally has more value as a demonstration of an individual's ability to learn, rather than as a certification of a certain skill set. Generally speaking, coursework in computer science and an undergraduate degree are sufficient qualifications, especially if the applicant has a reasonable amount of experience.

Certification and other qualifications. Computer scientists and database administrators must be able to think logically and have good communication skills. Because they often deal with a number of tasks simultaneously, the ability to concentrate and pay close attention to detail also is important. Although computer specialists sometimes work independently, they frequently work in teams on large projects. As a result, they must be able to communicate effectively with computer personnel, such as programmers and managers, as well as with users or other staff who may have no technical computer background.

Jobseekers can enhance their employment opportunities by earning certifications, most of which are offered through private companies, with many related to specific products. Many employers regard these certifications as the industry standard. For example, one method of acquiring enough knowledge to get a job as a database administrator is to become certified in database management with a certain software package. Voluntary certification also is available through various organizations associated with computer specialists. Professional certification may afford a jobseeker a competitive advantage.

Because technology is so closely connected to the functioning of businesses, many workers in these occupations come from elsewhere in the business or industry to become computer specialists. This background can be very useful, in that it helps them to better understand how their networking and database tools are being used within the organization.

Advancement. Computer scientists may advance into managerial or project leadership positions. Many having advanced degrees choose to leave private industry for academic positions. Database administrators may advance into managerial positions, such as chief technology officer, on the basis of their experience managing data and enforcing security. Computer specialists with work experience and considerable expertise in a particular subject or a certain application may find lucrative opportunities as independent consultants or may choose to start their own computer consulting firms.

Technological advances come so rapidly in the computer field that continuous study is necessary to keep one's skills up to date. Employers, hardware and software vendors, colleges and universities, and private training institutions offer continuing education. Additional training may come from professional development seminars offered by professional computing societies.

Employment

Computer scientists and database administrators held about 542,000 jobs in May 2006, including about 58,000 who were self-employed. Employment was distributed among the detailed occupations as follows:

Network systems and data communication analysts...........262,000
Computer specialists, all other...136,000
Database administrators...119,000
Computer and information scientists, research....................25,000

Although they are increasingly employed in every sector of the economy, the greatest concentration of these workers is in the computer systems design and related services industry. Firms in this industry provide services related to the commercial use of computers on a contract basis, including custom computer programming services; computer systems integration design services; computer facilities management services, including computer systems or data processing facilities support services for clients; and other computer-related services, such as disaster recovery services and software installation. Many computer scientists and database administrators are employed by Internet service providers; Web search portals; and data processing, hosting, and related services firms. Others work for government, manufacturers of computer and electronic products, insurance companies, financial institutions, and universities.

A growing number of computer specialists, such as network and data communications analysts, are employed on a temporary or contract basis; many of these individuals are self-employed, working independently as contractors or consultants. For example, a company installing a new computer system may need the services of several network systems and data communication analysts just to get the system running. Because not all of the analysts would be needed once the system is functioning, the company might contract for such employees with a temporary help agency or consulting firm, or with the network systems analysts themselves. Such jobs may last from several months to 2 years or more. This growing practice enables companies to bring in people with the exact skills they need to complete a particular project, rather than having to spend time or money training or retraining existing workers. Often, experienced consultants then train a company's in-house staff as a project develops.

Job Outlook
Computer scientists and database administrators are projected to be one of the fastest growing occupations over the next decade. Strong employment growth combined with a limited supply of qualified workers will result in excellent employment prospects for this occupation and a high demand for their skills.

Employment change. The computer scientists and database administrators occupation is expected to grow 37 percent from 2006 to 2016, much faster than average for all occupations. Employment of these computer specialists is expected to grow as organizations continue to adopt and integrate increasingly sophisticated technologies. Job increases will be driven by very rapid growth in computer systems design and related services, which is projected to be one of the fastest growing industries in the U.S. economy.

The demand for networking to facilitate the sharing of information, the expansion of client-server environments, and the need for computer specialists to use their knowledge and skills in a problem-solving capacity will be major factors in the rising demand for computer scientists and database administrators. Firms will continue to seek out computer specialists who are able to implement the latest technologies and are able to apply them to meet the needs of businesses as they struggle to maintain a competitive advantage.

As computers continue to become more central to business functions, more sophisticated and complex technology is being implemented across all organizations, fueling demand for computer scientists and database administrators. There is growing demand for network systems and data communication analysts to help firms maximize their efficiency with available technology. Expansion of electronic commerce—doing business on the Internet—and the continuing need to build and maintain databases that store critical information on customers, inventory, and projects are fueling demand for database administrators familiar with the latest technology. Because of the increasing reliance on the Internet among businesses, information security is an increasing concern.

The development of new technologies leads to demand for various kinds of workers. The expanding integration of Internet technologies into businesses, for example, has resulted in a growing need for specialists who can develop and support Internet and intranet applications. The growth of electronic commerce means that more establishments use the Internet to conduct their business online. It also means more security specialists are needed to protect their systems. The spread of such new technologies translates into a need for information technology professionals who can help organizations use technology to communicate with employees, clients, and consumers. Explosive growth in these areas also is expected to fuel demand for specialists who are knowledgeable about network, data, and communications security.

Projections data from the National Employment Matrix

Occupational Title	SOC Code	Employment, 2006	Projected employment, 2016	Change, 2006-2016	
				Number	Percent
Computer scientists and database administrators	—	542,000	742,000	200,000	37
Computer and information scientists, research............................	15-1011	25,000	31,000	5,400	22
Database administrators..	15-1061	119,000	154,000	34,000	29
Network systems and data communications analysts..................	15-1081	262,000	402,000	140,000	53
Computer specialists, all other..	15-1099	136,000	157,000	21,000	15

NOTE: Data in this table are rounded. See the discussion of the employment projections table in the *Handbook* introductory chapter on *Occupational Information Included in the Handbook.*

Job prospects. Computer scientists and database administrators should continue to enjoy excellent job prospects. As technology becomes more sophisticated and complex, however, these positions will demand a higher level of skill and expertise from their employees. Individuals with an advanced degree in computer science or computer engineering or with an MBA with a concentration in information systems should enjoy favorable employment prospects. College graduates with a bachelor's degree in computer science, computer engineering, information science, or MIS also should enjoy favorable prospects, particularly if they have supplemented their formal education with practical experience. Because employers continue to seek computer specialists who can combine strong technical skills with good business skills, individuals with a combination of experience inside and outside the IT arena will have the best job prospects.

In addition to growth, many job openings will arise from the need to replace workers who move into managerial positions or other occupations or who leave the labor force.

Earnings

Median annual earnings of computer and information scientists, research, were $93,950 in May 2006. The middle 50 percent earned between $71,930 and $118,100. The lowest 10 percent earned less than $53,590, and the highest 10 percent earned more than $144,880. Median annual earnings of computer and information scientists employed in computer systems design and related services in May 2006 were $95,340.

Median annual earnings of database administrators were $64,670 in May 2006. The middle 50 percent earned between $48,560 and $84,830. The lowest 10 percent earned less than $37,350, and the highest 10 percent earned more than $103,010. In May 2006, median annual earnings of database administrators employed in computer systems design and related services were $72,510, and for those in management of companies and enterprises, earnings were $67,680.

Median annual earnings of network systems and data communication analysts were $64,600 in May 2006. The middle 50 percent earned between $49,510 and $82,630. The lowest 10 percent earned less than $38,410, and the highest 10 percent earned more than $101,740. Median annual earnings in the industries employing the largest numbers of network systems and data communications analysts in May 2006 are shown below:

Wired telecommunications carriers	$72,480
Management of companies and enterprises	68,490
Management, scientific, and technical consulting services	67,830
Computer systems design and related services	67,080
State government	52,020

Median annual earnings of all other computer specialists were $68,570 in May 2006. Median annual earnings of all other computer specialists employed in computer systems design and related services were $67,370, and, for those in management of companies and enterprises, earnings were $63,610 in May 2006.

Robert Half International, a firm providing specialized staffing services, noted the following salary ranges for computer-related occupations in their 2007 Salary Guide:

Database manager	$84,750 - $116,000
Network architect	78,000 - 112,250
Database developer	73,500 - 103,000
Senior web developer	71,000 - 102,000
Database administratort	70,250 - 102,000
Network manager	68,750 - 93,000
Web developer	54,750 - 81,500
LAN/WAN administrator	51,000 - 71,500
Web administrator	49,750 - 74,750
Web designer	47,000 - 71,500
Telecommunications specialist	47,500 - 69,500

Related Occupations

Others who work with large amounts of data are computer programmers, computer software engineers, computer and information systems managers, engineers, mathematicians, statisticians, and actuaries.

Sources of Additional Information

Further information about computer careers is available from:
➤ Association for Computing Machinery (ACM), 1515 Broadway, New York, NY 10036.
Internet: **http://www.acm.org**
➤ Institute of Electrical and Electronics Engineers Computer Society, Headquarters Office, 1730 Massachusetts Ave. NW., Washington, DC 20036-1992.
Internet: **http://www.computer.org**
➤ Software & Information Industry Association, 1090 Vermont Ave. NW., 6th floor, Washington, DC 20005.
Internet: **http://www.siia.net**

Computer Software Engineers

(O*NET 15-1031.00, 15-1032.00)

Significant Points

- Computer software engineers are one of the occupations projected to grow the fastest and add the most new jobs over the 2006-16 decade.

- Excellent job prospects are expected for applicants with at least bachelor's degree in computer engineering or computer science and with practical work experience.

- Computer software engineers must continually strive to acquire new skills in conjunction with the rapid changes that occur in computer technology.

Nature of the Work

Computer software engineers apply the principles of computer science and mathematical analysis to the design, development, testing, and evaluation of the software and systems that make computers work. The tasks performed by these workers evolve quickly, reflecting new areas of specialization or changes in technology, as well as the preferences and practices of employers. (A separate section on computer hardware engineers appears in the engineers section of the *Handbook*.)

Software engineers can be involved in the design and development of many types of software, including computer games, word processing and business applications, operating systems and network distribution, and compilers, which convert programs to machine language for execution on a computer.

Computer software engineers begin by analyzing users' needs, and then design, test, and develop software to meet those needs. During this process they create the detailed sets of instructions, called algorithms, that tell the computer what to do. They also may be responsible for converting these instructions into a computer language, a process called programming or coding, but this usually is the responsibility of *computer programmers*. (A separate section on computer programmers appears elsewhere in the *Handbook*.) Computer software engineers must be experts in operating systems and middleware to ensure that the underlying systems will work properly.

Computer applications software engineers analyze users' needs and design, construct, and maintain general computer applications software or specialized utility programs. These workers use different programming languages, depending on the purpose of the program. The programming languages most often used are C, C++, and Java, with Fortran and COBOL used less commonly. Some software engineers develop both packaged systems and systems software or create customized applications.

Computer systems software engineers coordinate the construction, maintenance, and expansion of an organization's computer systems. Working with the organization, they coordinate each department's computer needs—ordering, inventory, billing, and payroll recordkeeping, for example—and make suggestions about its technical direction. They also might set up the organization's intranets—networks that link computers within the organization and ease communication among various departments.

Computer software engineers design, create, and modify computer applications and systems.

Systems software engineers also work for companies that configure, implement, and install the computer systems of other organizations. These workers may be members of the marketing or sales staff, serving as the primary technical resource for sales workers. They also may help with sales and provide customers with technical support. Since the selling of complex computer systems often requires substantial customization to meet the needs of the purchaser, software engineers help to identify and explain needed changes. In addition, systems software engineers are responsible for ensuring security across the systems they are configuring.

Computer software engineers often work as part of a team that designs new hardware, software, and systems. A core team may comprise engineering, marketing, manufacturing, and design people, who work together to release a product.

Work environment. Computer software engineers normally work in clean, comfortable offices or in laboratories in which computer equipment is located. Software engineers who work for software vendors and consulting firms frequently travel overnight to meet with customers. Telecommuting is also becoming more common, allowing workers to do their jobs from remote locations.

Most software engineers work at least 40 hours a week, but about 17 percent work more than 50 hours a week. Software engineers also may have to work evenings or weekends to meet deadlines or solve unexpected technical problems.

Like other workers who spend long hours typing at a computer, software engineers are susceptible to eyestrain, back discomfort, and hand and wrist problems such as carpal tunnel syndrome.

Training, Other Qualifications, and Advancement

Most employers prefer applicants who have at least a bachelor's degree and experience with a variety of computer systems and technologies. In order to remain competitive, computer software engineers must continually strive to acquire the latest technical skills. Advancement opportunities are good for those with relevant experience.

Education and training. Most employers prefer applicants who have at least a bachelor's degree and broad knowledge of, and experience with, a variety of computer systems and technologies. The usual college major for applications software engineers is computer science or software engineering. Systems software engineers often study computer science or computer information systems. Graduate degrees are preferred for some of the more complex jobs. In 2006, about 80 percent of workers had a bachelor's degree or higher.

Academic programs in software engineering may offer the program as a degree option or in conjunction with computer science degrees. Because of increasing emphasis on computer security, software engineers with advanced degrees in areas such as mathematics and systems design will be sought after by software developers, government agencies, and consulting firms.

Students seeking software engineering jobs enhance their employment opportunities by participating in internships or co-ops. These experiences provide students with broad knowledge and experience, making them more attractive to employers. Inexperienced college graduates may be hired by large computer and consulting firms that train new employees in intensive, company-based programs.

Certification and other qualifications. Systems software vendors offer certification and training programs, but most training authorities say that program certification alone is not sufficient for the majority of software engineering jobs.

People interested in jobs as computer software engineers must have strong problem-solving and analytical skills. They also must be able to communicate effectively with team members, other staff, and the customers they meet. Because they often deal with a number of tasks simultaneously, they must be able to concentrate and pay close attention to detail.

As technology advances, employers will need workers with the latest skills. Computer software engineers must continually strive to acquire new skills if they wish to remain in this dynamic field. To help keep up with changing technology, workers may take continuing education and professional development seminars offered by employers, software vendors, colleges and universities, private training institutions, and professional computing societies. Computer software engineers also need skills related to the industry in which they work. Engineers working for a bank, for example, should have some expertise in finance so that they understand banks' computer needs.

Advancement. As with most occupations, advancement opportunities for computer software engineers increase with experience. Entry-level computer software engineers are likely to test designs. As they become more experienced, engineers may begin helping to design and develop software. Eventually, they may advance to become a project manager, manager of information systems, or chief information officer, especially if they have business skills and training. Some computer software engineers with several years of experience or expertise find lucrative opportunities working as systems designers or independent consultants.

Employment

Computer software engineers held about 857,000 jobs in 2006. Approximately 507,000 were computer applications software engineers, and about 350,000 were computer systems software engineers. Although they are employed in most industries, the largest concentration of computer software engineers—more than 29 percent—is in computer systems design and related services. Many computer software engineers also work for establishments in other industries, such as software publishers, government agencies, manufacturers of computers and related electronic equipment, financial institutions, insurance providers, and management of companies and enterprises.

An increasing number of computer software engineers work as independent consultants on a temporary or contract basis, many of whom are self-employed. About 17,000 computer software engineers were self-employed in 2006.

Job Outlook

Job prospects should be excellent, as computer software engineers are expected to be among the fastest-growing occupations through the year 2016.

Employment change. Employment of computer software engineers is projected to increase by 38 percent over the 2006 to 2016 period, which is much faster than the average for all occupations. This occupation will generate about 324,000 new jobs, over the projections decade, one of the largest employment increases of any occupation.

Employment growth will result as businesses and other organizations adopt and integrate new technologies and seek to maximize the efficiency of their computer systems. Competition among businesses will continue to create incentive for sophisticated technological innovations, and organizations will need more computer software engineers to implement these changes.

Demand for computer software engineers will also increase as computer networking continues to grow. For example, expanding Internet technologies have spurred demand for computer software engineers who can develop Internet, intranet, and World Wide Web applications. Likewise, electronic data-processing systems in business, telecommunications, government, and other settings continue to become more sophisticated and complex. Implementing, safeguarding, and updating computer systems and resolving problems will fuel the demand for growing numbers of systems software engineers.

New growth areas will also continue to arise from rapidly evolving technologies. The increasing uses of the Internet, the proliferation of Web sites, and mobile technology such as wireless Internet have created a demand for a wide variety of new products. As individuals and businesses rely more on handheld computers and wireless networks, it will be necessary to integrate current computer systems with this new, more mobile technology.

In addition, information security concerns have given rise to new software needs. Concerns over "cyber security" should result in businesses and government continuing to invest heavily in software that protects their networks and vital electronic infrastructure from attack. The expansion of this technology in the next 10 years will lead to an increased need for computer engineers to design and develop the software and systems to run these new applications and integrate them into older systems.

Projections data from the National Employment Matrix

Occupational Title	SOC Code	Employment, 2006	Projected employment, 2016	Change, 2006-2016	
				Number	Percent
Computer software engineers	15-1030	857,000	1,181,000	324,000	38
Computer software engineers, applications	15-1031	507,000	733,000	226,000	45
Computer software engineers, systems software	15-1032	350,000	449,000	99,000	28

NOTE: Data in this table are rounded. See the discussion of the employment projections table in the *Handbook* introductory chapter on *Occupational Information Included in the Handbook.*

As with other information technology jobs, outsourcing of software development to other countries may temper somewhat employment growth of computer software engineers. Firms may look to cut costs by shifting operations to foreign countries with lower prevailing wages and highly educated workers. Jobs in software engineering are less prone to being offshored than are jobs in other computer specialties, however, because software engineering requires innovation and intense research and development.

Job prospects. As a result of rapid employment growth over the 2006 to 2016 decade, job prospects for computer software engineers should be excellent. Those with practical experience and at least a bachelor's degree in computer engineering or computer science should have the best opportunities. Employers will continue to seek computer professionals with strong programming, systems analysis, interpersonal, and business skills. In addition to jobs created through employment growth, many job openings will result from the need to replace workers who move into managerial positions, transfer to other occupations, or leave the labor force. Consulting opportunities for computer software engineers also should continue to grow as businesses seek help to manage, upgrade, and customize their increasingly complicated computer systems.

Earnings

In May 2006, median annual earnings of wage-and-salary computer applications software engineers were $79,780. The middle 50 percent earned between $62,830 and $98,470. The lowest 10 percent earned less than $49,350, and the highest 10 percent earned more than $119,770. Median annual earnings in the industries employing the largest numbers of computer applications software engineers in May 2006 were as follows:

Software publishers	$84,560
Computer systems design and related services	78,850
Management, scientific, and technical consulting services	78,850
Management of companies and enterprises	78,580
Insurance carriers	74,230

In May 2006, median annual earnings of wage-and-salary computer systems software engineers were $85,370. The middle 50 percent earned between $67,620 and $105,330. The lowest 10 percent earned less than $53,580, and the highest 10 percent earned more than $125,750. Median annual earnings in the industries employing the largest numbers of computer systems software engineers in May 2006 are as follows:

Research and development in the physical, engineering, and life sciences	$97,220
Scientific research and development services	97,180
Computer and peripheral equipment manufacturing	93,240
Software publishers	87,450
Computer systems design and related services	84,660
Data processing, hosting, and related services	78,270

According to the National Association of Colleges and Employers, starting salary offers for graduates with a bachelor's degree in computer engineering averaged $56,201 in 2007.

Starting salary offers for graduates with a bachelor's degree in computer science averaged $53,396.

According to Robert Half Technology, starting salaries for software engineers in software development ranged from $66,500 to $99,750 in 2007. For network engineers, starting salaries ranged from $65,750 to $90,250.

Related Occupations

Other workers who use mathematics and logic extensively include computer systems analysts, computer scientists and database administrators, computer programmers, computer hardware engineers, computer support specialists and systems administrators, engineers, commercial and industrial designers, statisticians, mathematicians, and actuaries.

Sources of Additional Information

Additional information on a career in computer software engineering is available from the following organizations:

➤ Association for Computing Machinery (ACM), 2 Penn Plaza, Suite 701, NY 10121-0701.
Internet: **http://www.acm.org**
➤ Institute of Electronics and Electrical Engineers Computer Society, Headquarters Office, 1730 Massachusetts Ave. N.W., Washington, DC 20036-1992.
Internet: **http://www.computer.org**
➤ National Workforce Center for Emerging Technologies, 3000 Landerholm Circle S.E., Bellevue, WA 98007.
Internet: **http://www.nwcet.org**
➤ University of Washington Computer Science and Engineering Department, AC101 Paul G. Allen Center, Box 352350, 185 Stevens Way, Seattle, WA 98195-2350.
Internet: **http://www.cs.washington.edu/WhyCSE**

Computer Support Specialists and Systems Administrators

(O*NET 15-1041.00, 15-1071.00, 15-1071.01)

Significant Points

- Growth in computer support specialist jobs will be about as fast as the average, while growth in network and computer system administrator jobs will be much faster than average

- There are many paths of entry to these occupations.

- Job prospects should be best for college graduates with relevant skills and experience; certifications and practical experience are essential for people without degrees.

Nature of the Work

In the last decade, computers have become an integral part of everyday life at home, work, school, and nearly everywhere else. Of course, almost every computer user encounters a problem occasionally, whether it is the annoyance of a forgotten password or the disaster of a crashing hard drive. The explosive use of computers has created demand for specialists who provide advice to users, as well as for the day-to-day administration, maintenance, and support of computer systems and networks.

Computer support specialists provide technical assistance, support, and advice to customers and other users. This occupational group includes *technical support specialists* and *help-desk technicians*. These troubleshooters interpret problems and provide technical support for hardware, software, and systems. They answer telephone calls, analyze problems by using automated diagnostic programs, and resolve recurring difficulties. Support specialists work either within a company that uses computer systems or directly for a computer hardware or software vendor. Increasingly, these specialists work for help-desk or support services firms, for which they provide computer support to clients on a contract basis.

Technical support specialists respond to inquiries from their organizations' computer users and may run automatic diagnostics programs to resolve problems. They also install, modify, clean, and repair computer hardware and software. In addition, they may write training manuals and train computer users in how to use new computer hardware and software. These workers also oversee the daily performance of their company's computer systems and evaluate how useful software programs are.

Help-desk technicians respond to telephone calls and e-mail messages from customers looking for help with computer problems. In responding to these inquiries, help-desk technicians must listen carefully to the customer, ask questions to diagnose the nature of the problem, and then patiently walk the customer through the problem-solving steps.

Help-desk technicians deal directly with customer issues and companies value them as a source of feedback on their products. They are consulted for information about what gives customers the most trouble, as well as other customer concerns. Most computer support specialists start out at the help desk.

Network and *computer systems administrators* design, install, and support an organization's computer systems. They are responsible for local-area networks (LAN), wide-area networks (WAN), network segments, and Internet and intranet systems. They work in a variety of environments, including professional offices, small businesses, government organizations, and large corporations. They maintain network hardware and software, analyze problems, and monitor networks to ensure their availability to system users. These workers gather data to identify customer needs and then use the information to identify, interpret, and evaluate system and network requirements. Administrators also may plan, coordinate, and implement network security measures.

Systems administrators are responsible for maintaining network efficiency. They ensure that the design of an organization's computer system allows all of the components, including computers, the network, and software, to work properly together. Furthermore, they monitor and adjust the performance of existing networks and continually survey the current computer site to determine future network needs. Administrators also troubleshoot problems reported by users and by automated network monitoring systems and make recommendations for future system upgrades.

Computer support specialists provide technical assistance, support, and advice to computer users.

In some organizations, *computer security specialists* may plan, coordinate, and implement the organization's information security. These workers educate users about computer security, install security software, monitor networks for security breaches, respond to cyber attacks, and, in some cases, gather data and evidence to be used in prosecuting cyber crime. The responsibilities of computer security specialists have increased in recent years as cyber attacks have become more common. This and other growing specialty occupations reflect an increasing emphasis on client-server applications, the expansion of Internet and intranet applications, and the demand for more end-user support.

Work environment. Computer support specialists and systems administrators normally work in well-lighted, comfortable offices or computer laboratories. They usually work about 40 hours a week, but if their employer requires computer support over extended hours, they may be "on call" for rotating evening or weekend work. Overtime may be necessary when unexpected technical problems arise. Like other workers who type on a keyboard for long periods, computer support specialists and systems administrators are susceptible to eyestrain, back discomfort, and hand and wrist problems such as carpal tunnel syndrome.

Computer support specialists and systems administrators constantly interact with customers and fellow employees as they answer questions and give advice. Those who work as consultants are away from their offices much of the time, sometimes spending months working in a client's office.

As computer networks expand, more computer support specialists and systems administrators may be able to provide technical support from remote locations. This capability would reduce or eliminate travel to the customer's workplace. Systems administrators also can administer and configure networks and servers remotely, although this practice is not as common as it is among computer support specialists.

Training, Other Qualifications, and Advancement

A college degree is required for some computer support specialist positions, but certification and relevant experience may be sufficient for others. A bachelor's degree is required for many network and computer systems administrator positions.

For both occupations, strong analytical and communication skills are essential.

Education and training. Due to the wide range of skills required, there are many paths of entry to a job as a computer support specialist or systems administrator. Training requirements for computer support specialist positions vary, but many employers prefer to hire applicants with some formal college education. A bachelor's degree in computer science or information systems is a prerequisite for some jobs; other jobs, however, may require only a computer-related associate degree. And for some jobs, relevant computer experience and certifications may substitute for formal education. For systems administrator jobs, many employers seek applicants with bachelor's degrees, although not necessarily in a computer-related field.

A number of companies are becoming more flexible about requiring a college degree for support positions. In the absence of a degree, however, certification and practical experience are essential. Certification training programs, offered by a variety of vendors and product makers, may help some people to qualify for entry-level positions.

Other qualifications. People interested in becoming a computer support specialist or systems administrator must have strong problem-solving, analytical, and communication skills because troubleshooting and helping others are vital parts of the job. The constant interaction with other computer personnel, customers, and employees requires computer support specialists and systems administrators to communicate effectively on paper, via e-mail, over the phone, or in person. Strong writing skills are useful in preparing manuals for employees and customers.

Advancement. Beginning computer support specialists usually work for organizations that deal directly with customers or in-house users. Support specialists may advance into positions in which they use what they have learned from customers to improve the design and efficiency of future products. Job promotions usually depend more on performance than on formal education. Eventually, some computer support specialists become software engineers, designing products rather than assisting users. Computer support specialists in hardware and software companies often enjoy great upward mobility; advancement sometimes comes within months of becoming employed.

Entry-level network and computer systems administrators are involved in routine maintenance and monitoring of computer systems, typically working behind the scenes in an organization. After gaining experience and expertise, they often are able to advance to more senior-level positions. For example, senior network and computer systems administrators may make presentations to executives and managers on the security of the company computer network. They also may translate the needs of an organization into a set of technical requirements based on the available technology. As with support specialists, administrators may become software engineers involved in system and network design.

As technology continues to improve, computer support specialists and systems administrators must strive to acquire new skills. Many continuing education programs are provided by employers, hardware and software vendors, colleges and universities, and private training institutions. Professional development seminars offered by computing services firms also can enhance skills and advancement opportunities.

Employment

Computer support specialists and systems administrators held about 862,000 jobs in 2006. Of these, approximately 552,000 were computer support specialists and about 309,000 were network and computer systems administrators. Although they worked in a wide range of industries, about 23 percent of all computer support specialists and systems administrators were employed in professional, scientific, and technical services industries, principally computer systems design and related services. Substantial numbers of these workers were also employed in administrative and support services companies, financial institutions, insurance companies, government agencies, educational institutions, software publishers, telecommunications organizations, health care organizations, and management of companies and enterprises.

Employers of computer support specialists and systems administrators range from startup companies to established industry leaders. As computer networks become an integral part of business, industries not typically associated with computers—such as construction—increasingly need computer support workers.

Job Outlook

Employment of computer support specialists and systems administrators is expected to increase faster than the average. Job prospects should be best for those with a college degree and relevant experience.

Employment change. Employment of computer support specialists and systems administrators is expected to increase by 18 percent from 2006 to 2016, which is much faster than the average for all occupations. In addition, this occupation is expected to add 155,000 jobs over the projection decade.

Employment of computer support specialists is expected to increase by 13 percent from 2006 to 2016, which is about as fast as the average for all occupations. Demand for these workers

Projections data from the National Employment Matrix

Occupational Title	SOC Code	Employment, 2006	Projected employment, 2016	Change, 2006-2016	
				Number	Percent
Computer support specialists and systems administrators................	—	862,000	1,016,000	155,000	18
Computer support specialists.......................................	15-1041	552,000	624,000	71,000	13
Network and computer systems administrators...........................	15-1071	309,000	393,000	83,000	27

NOTE: Data in this table are rounded. See the discussion of the employment projections table in the *Handbook* introductory chapter on *Occupational Information Included in the Handbook.*

will result as organizations and individuals continue to adopt increasingly sophisticated technology. Job growth will continue to be driven by the ongoing expansion of the computer system design and related services industry, which is projected to remain one of the fastest-growing industries in the U.S. economy. Growth will not be as explosive as during the previous decade, however, because the information technology industry is maturing and because some of these jobs are expected to be outsourced offshore where prevailing wages are lower. Physical location is not as important for computer support specialists as it is for other occupations because these workers can provide assistance remotely and support services are provided around the clock across time zones.

Job growth among computer support specialists reflects the rapid evolution of technology. As computers and software become more complex, support specialists will be needed to provide technical assistance to customers and other users. The adoption of new mobile technologies, such as the wireless Internet, will continue to create a need for these workers to familiarize and educate computer users. Consulting jobs for computer support specialists also should continue to increase as businesses seek help managing, upgrading, and customizing ever more complex computer systems.

Employment of network and computer systems administrators is expected to increase by 27 percent from 2006 to 2016, which is much faster than the average for all occupations. Computer networks have become an integral part of business, and demand for these workers will increase as firms continue to invest in new technologies. The wide use of electronic commerce and the increasing adoption of mobile technologies mean that more establishments will use the Internet to conduct business online. This growth translates into a need for systems administrators who can help organizations use technology to communicate with employees, clients, and consumers.

Demand for computer security specialists will grow as businesses and government continue to invest heavily in "cyber security," protecting vital computer networks and electronic infrastructures from attack. The information security field is expected to generate many new system administrator jobs over the next decade as firms across all industries place a high priority on safeguarding their data and systems.

Employment of network and computer systems administrators, however, may be tempered somewhat by offshore outsourcing, as firms transfer work to countries with lower-prevailing wages and highly skilled work forces. Systems administrators may increasingly be able to manage computer systems from remote locations as technology advances.

Job prospects. Job prospects should be best for college graduates who possess the latest technological skills, particularly graduates who have supplemented their formal education with relevant work experience. Employers will continue to seek computer specialists who possess strong fundamental computer skills combined with good interpersonal and communication skills. Due to the demand for computer support specialists and systems administrators over the next decade, those who have strong computer skills but do not have a college degree should continue to qualify for some entry-level positions.

Earnings

Median annual earnings of wage-and-salary computer support specialists were $41,470 in May 2006. The middle 50 percent earned between $32,110 and $53,640. The lowest 10 percent earned less than $25,290, and the highest 10 percent earned more than $68,540. Median annual earnings in the industries employing the largest numbers of computer support specialists in May 2006 were as follows:

Software publishers	$46,270
Management of companies and enterprises	42,770
Computer systems design and related services	42,510
Colleges, universities, and professional schools	40,130
Elementary and secondary schools	37,880

Median annual earnings of wage-and-salary network and computer systems administrators were $62,130 in May 2006. The middle 50 percent earned between $48,520 and $79,160. The lowest 10 percent earned less than $38,610, and the highest 10 percent earned more than $97,080. Median annual earnings in the industries employing the largest numbers of network and computer systems administrators in May 2006 were as follows:

Wired telecommunications carriers	$70,790
Computer systems design and related services	66,680
Management of companies and enterprises	66,020
Colleges, universities, and professional schools	54,590
Elementary and secondary schools	53,750

According to Robert Half Technology, starting salaries in 2007 ranged from $27,500 to $37,000 for help-desk workers. Starting salaries for desktop support analysts ranged from $46,500 to $65,250. For systems administrators, starting salaries ranged from $50,000 to $75,750.

Related Occupations

Other computer specialists include computer programmers, computer software engineers, computer systems analysts, and computer scientists and database administrators. Other workers who respond to customer inquiries are customer service representatives.

Sources of Additional Information

For additional information about a career as a computer support specialist, contact:
➤ Association of Support Professionals, 122 Barnard Ave., Watertown, MA 02472.

For additional information about a career as a systems administrator, contact:
➤ The League of Professional System Administrators, 15000 Commerce Parkway, Suite C, Mount Laurel, NJ 08054.
Internet: **http://lopsa.org/**
➤ National Workforce Center for Emerging Technologies, 3000 Landerholm Circle SE., Bellevue, WA 98007.
Internet: **http://www.nwcet.org**

Computer Systems Analysts

(O*NET 15-1051.00)

Significant Points

- Employers generally prefer applicants who have at least a bachelor's degree in computer science, information science, or management information systems (MIS).

- Employment is expected to increase much faster than the average and more new jobs are expected to arise than in all but a few other occupations.

- Very good job prospects are expected as organizations continue to adopt increasingly sophisticated technologies.

Nature of the Work

All organizations rely on computer and information technology to conduct business and operate efficiently. Computer systems analysts help organizations to use technology effectively and to incorporate rapidly changing technologies into their existing systems. The work of computer systems analysts evolves rapidly, reflecting new areas of specialization and changes in technology.

Computer systems analysts solve computer problems and use computer technology to meet the needs of an organization. They may design and develop new computer systems by choosing and configuring hardware and software. They may also devise ways to apply existing systems' resources to additional tasks. Most systems analysts work with specific types of computer systems—for example, business, accounting, or financial systems or scientific and engineering systems—that vary with the kind of organization. Analysts who specialize in helping an organization select the proper system software and infrastructure are often called *system architects*. Analysts who specialize in developing and fine-tuning systems often are known as *systems designers*.

To begin an assignment, systems analysts consult managers and users to define the goals of the system. Analysts then design a system to meet those goals. They specify the inputs that the system will access, decide how the inputs will be processed, and format the output to meet users' needs. Analysts use techniques such as structured analysis, data modeling, information engineering, mathematical model building, sampling, and cost accounting to make sure their plans are efficient and complete. They also may prepare cost-benefit and return-on-investment analyses to help management decide whether implementing the proposed technology would be financially feasible.

When a system is approved, systems analysts determine what computer hardware and software will be needed to set it up. They coordinate tests and observe the initial use of the system to ensure that it performs as planned. They prepare specifications, flow charts, and process diagrams for computer programmers to follow; then they work with programmers to "debug," or eliminate errors, from the system. Systems analysts who do

Computer systems analysts use information technology to help meet the needs of an organization.

more in-depth testing may be called *software quality assurance analysts*. In addition to running tests, these workers diagnose problems, recommend solutions, and determine whether program requirements have been met.

In some organizations, *programmer-analysts* design and update the software that runs a computer. They also create custom applications tailored to their organization's tasks. Because they are responsible for both programming and systems analysis, these workers must be proficient in both areas. (A separate section on computer programmers appears elsewhere in the *Handbook*.) As this dual proficiency becomes more common, analysts are increasingly working with databases, object-oriented programming languages, client–server applications, and multimedia and Internet technology.

One challenge created by expanding computer use is the need for different computer systems to communicate with each other. Systems analysts work to make the computer systems within an organization, or across organizations, compatible so that information can be shared. Many systems analysts are involved with these "networking" tasks, connecting all the computers internally, in an individual office, department, or establishment, or externally, as when setting up e-commerce networks to facilitate business among companies.

Work environment. Computer systems analysts work in offices or laboratories in comfortable surroundings. They usually work about 40 hours a week—about the same as many other professional or office workers. Evening or weekend work may be necessary, however, to meet deadlines or solve specific problems. Many analysts telecommute, using computers to work from remote locations.

Like other workers who spend long periods typing on a computer, computer systems analysts are susceptible to eyestrain, back discomfort, and hand and wrist problems such as carpal tunnel syndrome or cumulative trauma disorder.

Training, Other Qualifications, and Advancement

Training requirements for computer systems analysts vary depending on the job, but many employers prefer applicants who have a bachelor's degree. Relevant work experience also is very important. Advancement opportunities are good for those with the necessary skills and experience.

Education and training. When hiring computer systems analysts, employers usually prefer applicants who have at least a bachelor's degree. For more technically complex jobs, people with graduate degrees are preferred.

The level and type of education that employers require reflects changes in technology. Employers often scramble to find workers capable of implementing the newest technologies. Workers with formal education or experience in information security, for example, are currently in demand because of the growing use of computer networks, which must be protected from threats.

For jobs in a technical or scientific environment, employers often seek applicants who have at least a bachelor's degree in a technical field, such as computer science, information science, applied mathematics, engineering, or the physical sciences. For jobs in a business environment, employers often seek applicants with at least a bachelor's degree in a business-related field such as management information systems (MIS). Increasingly, employers are seeking individuals who have a master's degree in business administration (MBA) with a concentration in information systems.

Despite the preference for technical degrees, however, people who have degrees in other majors may find employment as systems analysts if they also have technical skills. Courses in computer science or related subjects combined with practical experience can qualify people for some jobs in the occupation.

Employers generally look for people with expertise relevant to the job. For example, systems analysts who wish to work for a bank should have some expertise in finance, and systems analysts who wish to work for a hospital should have some knowledge of health management.

Technological advances come so rapidly in the computer field that continuous study is necessary to remain competitive. Employers, hardware and software vendors, colleges and universities, and private training institutions offer continuing education to help workers attain the latest skills. Additional training may come from professional development seminars offered by professional computing societies.

Other qualifications. Employers usually look for people who have broad knowledge and experience related to computer systems and technologies, strong problemsolving and analytical skills, and the ability to think logically. In addition, because they often deal with a number of tasks simultaneously, the ability to concentrate and pay close attention to detail is important. Although these workers sometimes work independently, they frequently work in teams on large projects. Therefore, they must have good interpersonal skills and be able to communicate effectively with computer personnel, users, and other staff who may have no technical background.

Advancement. With experience, systems analysts may be promoted to senior or lead systems analyst. Those who possess leadership ability and good business skills also can become computer and information systems managers or can advance into other management positions such as manager of information systems or chief information officer. Those with work experience and considerable expertise in a particular subject or application may find lucrative opportunities as independent consultants, or may choose to start their own computer consulting firms.

Employment

Computer systems analysts held about 504,000 jobs in 2006. Although they are increasingly employed in every sector of the economy, the greatest concentration of these workers is in the computer systems design and related services industry. Computer systems analysts are also employed by governments; insurance companies; financial institutions; hospitals; management, scientific, and technical consulting services firms; data processing services firms; professional and commercial equipment wholesalers; universities; and management of companies and enterprises.

A growing number of systems analysts are employed on a temporary or contract basis; many of these individuals are self-employed, working independently as contractors or consultants. About 29,000 computer systems analysts were self-employed in 2006.

Job Outlook

Employment is expected to grow much faster than the average for all occupations. As a result of this rapid growth, job prospects should be very good.

Employment change. Employment of computer systems analysts is expected to grow by 29 percent from 2006 to 2016, which is much faster than the average for all occupations. In addition, the 146,000 new jobs that are expected to arise over the projections decade will be substantial. Demand for these workers will increase as organizations continue to adopt and integrate increasingly sophisticated technologies. Job growth will not be as rapid as during the preceding decade, however, as the information technology sector matures and as routine work is increasingly outsourced offshore to foreign countries with lower prevailing wages.

The growth of electronic commerce and the integration of Internet technologies into business have resulted in a growing need for specialists who can develop and support Internet and intranet applications. Moreover, falling prices of computer hardware and software should continue to induce more businesses to expand their computerized operations and incorporate new technologies.

The demand for computer networking within organizations will also drive demand for computer systems analysts. The introduction of the wireless Internet, known as WiFi, and of personal mobile computers has created a need for new systems

Projections data from the National Employment Matrix

Occupational Title	SOC Code	Employment, 2006	Projected employment, 2016	Change, 2006-2016	
				Number	Percent
Computer systems analysts..	15-1051	504,000	650,000	146,000	29

NOTE: Data in this table are rounded. See the discussion of the employment projections table in the *Handbook* introductory chapter on *Occupational Information Included in the Handbook.*

that can integrate these technologies into existing networks. Explosive growth in these areas is expected to fuel demand for analysts who are knowledgeable about systems integration and network, data, and communications security.

As more sophisticated and complex technology is implemented across all organizations, demand for systems analysts will remain strong. These workers will be called upon to solve problems and to integrate new technologies with existing ones. Also, the increasing importance being placed on "cyber-security"—the protection of electronic information—will result in a need for workers skilled in information security.

As with other information technology jobs, employment growth may be tempered somewhat as some computer systems analyst jobs are outsourced offshore. Firms may look to cut costs by shifting operations to foreign countries with lower prevailing wages and highly educated workers who have strong technical skills.

Job prospects. Job prospects should be very good. Job openings will occur as a result of strong job growth and from the need to replace workers who move into managerial positions or other occupations, or who leave the labor force. As technology becomes more sophisticated and complex, employers demand a higher level of skill and expertise from their employees. Individuals with an advanced degree in computer science or computer engineering or with an MBA with a concentration in information systems should have the best prospects. College graduates with a bachelor's degree in computer science, computer engineering, information science, or management information systems also should enjoy very good prospects, particularly if they have supplemented their formal education with practical experience. Because employers continue to seek computer specialists who can combine strong technical skills with good interpersonal and business skills, graduates with non-computer-science degrees who have had courses in computer programming, systems analysis, and other information technology subjects also should continue to find jobs in computer fields.

Earnings

Median annual earnings of wage-and-salary computer systems analysts were $69,760 in May 2006. The middle 50 percent earned between $54,320 and $87,600 a year. The lowest 10 percent earned less than $42,780, and the highest 10 percent earned more than $106,820. Median annual earnings in the industries employing the largest numbers of computer systems analysts in May 2006 were:

Professional and commercial equipment and supplies merchant wholesalers	$81,080
Computer systems design and related services	71,680
Management of companies and enterprises	71,090
Insurance carriers	69,990
State government	61,340

According to the National Association of Colleges and Employers, starting offers for graduates with a bachelor's degree in computer science averaged $53,396. Starting offers for graduates with a bachelor's degree in information sciences and systems averaged $50,852. For those with a degree in manage-

ment information systems/business data processing, starting offers averaged $47,648.

According to Robert Half Technology, starting salaries for systems analysts ranged from $64,000 to $87,000 in 2007. Starting salaries for business systems analysts ranged from $61,250 to $86,500. Starting salaries for developer/programmer analysts ranged from $55,250 to $90,250.

Related Occupations

Other workers who use computers extensively and who use logic and creativity to solve business and technical problems include computer programmers, computer software engineers, computer and information systems managers, engineers, mathematicians, statisticians, operations research analysts, management analysts, and actuaries.

Sources of Additional Information

Further information about computer careers is available from:
➤ Association for Computing Machinery (ACM), 2 Penn Plaza, Suite 701, New York, NY 10121-0701.
Internet: **http://www.acm.org**
➤ Institute of Electrical and Electronics Engineers Computer Society, Headquarters Office, 1730 Massachusetts Ave. NW., Washington, DC 20036-1992.
Internet: **http://www.computer.org**
➤ National Workforce Center for Emerging Technologies, 3000 Landerholm Circle SE., Bellevue, WA 98007.
Internet: **http://www.nwcet.org**
➤ University of Washington Computer Science and Engineering Department, AC101 Paul G. Allen Center, Box 352350, 185 Stevens Way, Seattle, WA 98195-2350.
Internet: **http://www.cs.washington.edu/WhyCSE**

Mathematicians

(O*NET 15–2021.00)

Significant Points

- A Ph.D. in mathematics usually is the minimum educational requirement, except in the Federal Government.

- Master's degree and Ph.D. holders with a strong background in mathematics and a related field, such as computer science or engineering, should have better employment opportunities in related occupations.

- Average employment growth is expected for mathematicians.

Nature of the Work

Mathematics is one of the oldest and most fundamental sciences. Mathematicians use mathematical theory, computational techniques, algorithms, and the latest computer technology to solve economic, scientific, engineering, physics, and business problems. The work of mathematicians falls into two broad classes—theoretical (pure) mathematics and applied mathematics. These classes, however, are not sharply defined and often overlap.

Theoretical mathematicians advance mathematical knowledge by developing new principles and recognizing previously unknown relationships between existing principles of mathematics. Although these workers seek to increase basic knowledge without necessarily considering its practical use, such pure and abstract knowledge has been instrumental in producing or furthering many scientific and engineering achievements. Many theoretical mathematicians are employed as university faculty, dividing their time between teaching and conducting research. (See the statement on teachers—postsecondary elsewhere in the *Handbook*.)

Applied mathematicians, on the other hand, use theories and techniques, such as mathematical modeling and computational methods, to formulate and solve practical problems in business, government, engineering, and the physical, life, and social sciences. For example, they may analyze the most efficient way to schedule airline routes between cities, the effects and safety of new drugs, the aerodynamic characteristics of an experimental automobile, or the cost-effectiveness of alternative manufacturing processes.

Applied mathematicians working in industrial research and development may develop or enhance mathematical methods when solving a difficult problem. Some mathematicians, called cryptanalysts, analyze and decipher encryption systems—codes—designed to transmit military, political, financial, or law enforcement-related information.

Applied mathematicians start with a practical problem, envision its separate elements, and then reduce the elements to mathematical variables. They often use computers to analyze relationships among the variables and solve complex problems by developing models with alternative solutions.

Individuals with titles other than mathematician do much of the work in applied mathematics. In fact, because mathematics is the foundation on which so many other academic disciplines are built, the number of workers using mathematical techniques is much greater than the number formally called mathematicians. For example, engineers, computer scientists, physicists, and economists are among those who use mathematics exten-

Applied mathematicians start with a practical problem, envision its separate elements, and then reduce the elements to mathematical variables.

sively. Some professionals, including statisticians, actuaries, and operations research analysts, are actually specialists in a particular branch of mathematics. (For more information, see the statements on actuaries, operations research analysts, and statisticians elsewhere in the *Handbook*.) Applied mathematicians are frequently required to collaborate with other workers in their organizations to find common solutions to problems.

Work environment. Mathematicians usually work in comfortable offices. They often are part of interdisciplinary teams that may include economists, engineers, computer scientists, physicists, technicians, and others. Deadlines, overtime work, special requests for information or analysis, and prolonged travel to attend seminars or conferences may be part of their jobs.

Mathematicians who work in academia usually have a mix of teaching and research responsibilities. These mathematicians may conduct research alone or in close collaboration with other mathematicians. Collaborators may work together at the same institution or from different locations, using technology such as e-mail to communicate. Mathematicians in academia also may be aided by graduate students.

Training, Other Qualifications, and Advancement

A Ph.D. degree in mathematics usually is the minimum educational requirement for prospective mathematicians, except in the Federal Government.

Education and training. In the Federal Government, entry-level job candidates usually must have at least a bachelor's degree with a major in mathematics or 24 semester hours of mathematics courses. Outside the Federal Government, bachelor's degree holders in mathematics usually are not qualified for most jobs, and many seek advanced degrees in mathematics or a related discipline.

Most colleges and universities offer a bachelor's degree in mathematics. Courses usually required for this degree include calculus, differential equations, and linear and abstract algebra. Additional courses might include probability theory and statistics, mathematical analysis, numerical analysis, topology, discrete mathematics, and mathematical logic. Many colleges and universities advise or require students majoring in mathematics to take courses in a closely related field, such as computer science, engineering, life science, physical science, or economics. A double major in mathematics and another related discipline is particularly desirable to many employers. High school students who are prospective college mathematics majors should take as many mathematics courses as possible while in high school.

In private industry, candidates for mathematician jobs typically need a Ph.D., although there may be opportunities for those with a master's degree. Most of the positions designated for mathematicians are in research and development laboratories, as part of technical teams.

In 2007, there were more than 300 graduate programs, offering both master's and doctoral degrees, in pure or applied mathematics around the country. In graduate school, students conduct research and take advanced courses, usually specializing in a subfield of mathematics.

Other qualifications. For jobs in applied mathematics, training in the field in which mathematics will be used is very important. Mathematics is used extensively in physics, actuarial science, statistics, engineering, and operations research. Computer science, business and industrial management, economics, finance, chemistry, geology, life sciences, and behavioral sciences are likewise dependent on applied mathematics. Mathematicians also should have substantial knowledge of computer programming, because most complex mathematical computation and much mathematical modeling are done on a computer.

Mathematicians need to have good reasoning to identify, analyze, and apply basic principles to technical problems. Communication skills also are important, as mathematicians must be able to interact and discuss proposed solutions with people who may not have extensive knowledge of mathematics.

Advancement. Bachelor's degree holders who meet State certification requirements may become primary or secondary school mathematics teachers. (For additional information, see the statement on teachers—preschool, kindergarten, elementary, middle, and secondary elsewhere in the *Handbook*.)

The majority of those with a master's degree in mathematics who work in private industry do so not as mathematicians but in related fields such as computer science, where they have titles such as computer programmer, systems analyst, or systems engineer.

Employment

Mathematicians held about 3,000 jobs in 2006. Many people with mathematical backgrounds also worked in other occupations. For example, there were about 54,000 jobs as postsecondary mathematical science teachers in 2006.

Many mathematicians work for Federal or State governments. The U.S. Department of Defense is the primary Federal employer, accounting for about 37 percent of the mathematicians employed by the Federal Government. Many of the other mathematicians employed by the Federal Government work for the National Aeronautics and Space Administration (NASA).

In the private sector, major employers include scientific research and development services and management, scientific, and technical consulting services. Some mathematicians also work for software publishers, insurance companies, and in aerospace or pharmaceutical manufacturing.

Job Outlook

Employment of mathematicians is expected to grow as fast as the average. However, keen competition for jobs is expected.

Employment change. Employment of mathematicians is expected to increase by 10 percent during the 2006–16 decade, as fast as the average for all occupations. Advancements in technology usually lead to expanding applications of mathematics, and more workers with knowledge of mathematics will be required in the future. However, jobs in industry and government often require advanced knowledge of related scientific disciplines in addition to mathematics. The most common fields in which mathematicians study and find work are computer

science and software development, physics, engineering, and operations research. More mathematicians also are becoming involved in financial analysis.

Job prospects. Job competition will remain keen because employment in this occupation is relatively small and few new jobs are expected. Master's degree and Ph.D. holders with a strong background in mathematics and a related discipline, such as engineering or computer science, and who apply mathematical theory to real-world problems will have the best job prospects in related occupations.

Holders of a master's degree in mathematics will face very strong competition for jobs in theoretical research. Because the number of Ph.D. degres awarded in mathematics continues to exceed the number of available university positions—especially those that are tenure tracked—many graduates will need to find employment in industry and government.

Additionally, employment in theoretical mathematical research is sensitive to general economic fluctuations and to changes in government spending. Job prospects will be greatly influenced by changes in public and private funding for research and development.

Earnings

Median annual earnings of mathematicians were $86,930 in May 2006. The middle 50 percent earned between $62,970 and $106,250. The lowest 10 percent had earnings of less than $43,500, while the highest 10 percent earned more than $132,190.

In early 2007, the average annual salary for mathematicians employed by the Federal Government in supervisory, nonsupervisory, and managerial positions was $93,539; for mathematical statisticians, $96,121; and for cryptanalysts, the average was $90,435.

Related Occupations

Other occupations that require extensive knowledge of mathematics or, in some cases, a degree in mathematics include actuaries, statisticians, computer programmers, computer systems analysts, computer scientists and database administrators, computer software engineers, and operations research analysts. A strong background in mathematics also facilitates employment as teachers—postsecondary; teachers—preschool, kindergarten, elementary, middle, and secondary; engineers; economists; market and survey researchers; financial analysts and personal financial advisors; and physicists and astronomers.

Sources of Additional Information

For more information about careers and training in mathematics, especially for doctoral-level employment, contact:
➤ American Mathematical Society, 201 Charles St., Providence, RI 02904-2294. Internet: **http://www.ams.org**

Projections data from the National Employment Matrix

Occupational Title	SOC Code	Employment, 2006	Projected employment, 2016	Change, 2006-2016	
				Number	Percent
Mathematicians..	15-2021	3,000	3,300	300	10

NOTE: Data in this table are rounded. See the discussion of the employment projections table in the *Handbook* introductory chapter on *Occupational Information Included in the Handbook*.

For specific information on careers in applied mathematics, contact:

➤ Society for Industrial and Applied Mathematics, 3600 University City Science Center, Philadelphia, PA 19104-2688. Internet: **http://www.siam.org**

Information on obtaining positions as mathematicians with the Federal Government is available from the Office of Personnel Management through USAJOBS, the Federal Government's official employment information system. This resource for locating and applying for job opportunities can be accessed through the Internet at **http://www.usajobs.gov** or through an interactive voice response telephone system at (703) 724-1850 or TDD (978) 461-8404. These numbers are not tollfree, and charges may result. For advice on how to find and apply for Federal jobs, see the *Occupational Outlook Quarterly* article "How to get a job in the Federal Government," online at: **http://www.bls.gov/opub/ooq/2004/summer/art01.pdf**

Operations Research Analysts

(O*NET 15-2031.00)

Significant Points

- While a bachelor's degree is the minimum requirement, employers generally prefer applicants with at least a master's degree in operations research or a closely related field.

- Computer programming skills and keeping up to date with technological advances and improvements in analytical methods are essential.

- Employment growth is projected to be as fast as the average for all occupations.

- Individuals with a master's or Ph.D. degree in operations research or a closely related subject should find opportunities in a number of occupations that use their computer, mathematical, and problem-solving skills.

Nature of the Work

"Operations research" and "management science" are terms that are used interchangeably to describe the discipline of using advanced analytical techniques to make better decisions and to solve problems. The procedures of operations research were first formalized by the military. They have been used in wartime to effectively deploy radar, search for enemy submarines, and get supplies to where they are most needed. In peacetime and in private enterprises, operations research is used in planning business ventures and analyzing options by using statistical analysis, data and computer modeling, linear programming, and other mathematical techniques.

Large organizations are very complex. They must effectively manage money, materials, equipment, and people. Operations research analysts find better ways to coordinate these elements by applying analytical methods from mathematics, science, and engineering. Analysts often find many possible solutions for

meeting the goals of a project. These potential solutions are presented to managers, who choose the course of action that they think best.

Operations research analysts are often involved in top-level strategizing, planning, and forecasting. They help to allocate resources, measure performance, schedule, design production facilities and systems, manage the supply chain, set prices, coordinate transportation and distribution, or analyze large databases.

The duties of the operations research analyst vary according to the structure and management of the organization they are assisting. Some firms centralize operations research in one department; others use operations research in each division. Operations research analysts also may work closely with senior managers to identify and solve a variety of problems. Analysts often have one area of specialization, such as working in the transportation or the financial services industry.

Operations research analysts start a project by listening to managers describe a problem. Then, analysts ask questions and formally define the problem. For example, an operations research analyst for an auto manufacturer may be asked to determine the best inventory level for each of the parts needed on a production line and to ascertain the optimal number of windshields to be kept in stock. Too many windshields would be wasteful and expensive, whereas too few could halt production.

Analysts would study the problem, breaking it into its components. Then they would gather information from a variety of sources. To determine the optimal inventory, operations research analysts might talk with engineers about production levels, discuss purchasing arrangements with buyers, and examine storage-cost data provided by the accounting department.

Relevant information in hand, the analysts determine the most appropriate analytical technique. Techniques used may include a Monte Carlo simulation, linear and nonlinear programming, dynamic programming, queuing and other stochastic-process models, Markov decision processes, econometric methods, data envelopment analysis, neural networks, expert systems, decision analysis, and the analytic hierarchy process. Nearly all of these techniques involve the construction of a mathemati-

Operations research analysts need strong computer, mathematical, and problem-solving skills.

cal model that attempts to describe the system being studied. So, the problem of the windshields, for example, would be described as a set of equations that try to model real-world conditions.

The use of models enables the analyst to explicitly describe the different components and clarify the relationships among them. The descriptions can be altered to examine what may happen to the system under different circumstances. In most cases, a computer program is developed to numerically evaluate the model.

Usually the model chosen is modified and run repeatedly to obtain different solutions. A model for airline flight scheduling, for example, might stipulate such things as connecting cities, the amount of fuel required to fly the routes, projected levels of passenger demand, varying ticket and fuel prices, pilot scheduling, and maintenance costs. By assessing different possible schedules, the analyst is able to determine the best flight schedule consistent with particular assumptions.

Based on the results of the analysis, the operations research analyst presents recommendations to managers. The analyst may need to modify and rerun the computer program to consider different assumptions before presenting the final recommendation. Once managers reach a decision, the analyst usually works with others in the organization to ensure the plan's successful implementation.

Work environment. Operations research analysts generally work regular hours in an office environment. However, because they work on projects that are of immediate interest to top managers, operations research analysts often are under pressure to meet deadlines and may work more than 40 hours a week.

Training, Other Qualifications, and Advancement
A college degree in operations research generally is required. Computer programming skills are essential.

Education and training. Employers generally prefer applicants with at least a master's degree in operations research or a closely related field—such as computer science, engineering, business, mathematics, information systems, or management science—coupled with a bachelor's degree in computer science or a quantitative discipline such as economics, mathematics, or statistics. Dual graduate degrees in operations research and computer science are especially attractive to employers. There are more than 130 programs in operations research and related studies in colleges and universities across the United States.

Continuing education is important for operations research analysts. Keeping up to date with technological advances and improvements in analytical methods is vital for maintaining their problem-solving skills.

Other qualifications. Computers are the most important tools used by operations research analysts, so analysts must have training and experience in programming. Analysts typically also need to be proficient in database collection and management, and the development and use of sophisticated software packages.

Operations research analysts must be able to think logically, work well with people, and write and speak well.

Advancement. Beginning analysts usually perform routine work under the supervision of more experienced analysts. As novices gain knowledge and experience, they are assigned more complex tasks and are given greater autonomy to design models and solve problems.

Operations research analysts can advance by becoming technical specialists or supervisors on more complicated projects. Analysts also gain valuable insights into the industry where they work and may assume higher level managerial or administrative positions. Operations research analysts with significant experience or expertise may become consultants, and some open their own consulting practices.

Employment
Operations research analysts held about 58,000 jobs in 2006. Major employers include computer systems design firms; insurance carriers and other financial institutions; telecommunications companies; management, scientific, and technical consulting services firms; and Federal, State, and local governments. Most operations research analysts in the Federal Government work for the Department of Defense, and many in private industry work directly or indirectly on national defense.

Job Outlook
Employment of operations research analysts is projected to grow as fast as the average for all occupations. Individuals with a master's or Ph.D. degree in operations research or a closely related subject should find job opportunities in a number of occupations that use their computer, mathematical, and problem-solving skills.

Employment change. Employment of operations research analysts is expected to grow 11 percent, as fast as the average for all occupations between 2006 and 2016. Demand for operations research analysis should continue to grow. Organizations increasingly will be faced with the pressure of growing domestic and international competition and must work to make their operations as effective as possible. As a result, businesses increasingly will rely on operations research analysts to optimize profits by improving productivity and reducing costs. As new technology is introduced into the marketplace, operations research analysts will be needed to determine how to use the technology in the best way.

Additionally, technological advancements have extended the availability of data access and storage, making information more readily available. Advancements in computing capabilities and analytical software have made it cheaper and faster

Projections data from the National Employment Matrix

Occupational Title	SOC Code	Employment, 2006	Projected employment, 2016	Change, 2006-2016	
				Number	Percent
Operations research analysts...	15-2031	58,000	65,000	6,200	11

NOTE: Data in this table are rounded. See the discussion of the employment projections table in the *Handbook* introductory chapter on *Occupational Information Included in the Handbook.*

for analysts to solve problems. As problem solving becomes cheaper and faster with technological advances, more firms will have the ability to employ or consult with analysts.

Job prospects. Graduates with degrees in operations research or closely related fields should find opportunities in a number of occupations where their computer, mathematical, and problem-solving skills are needed—operations research analyst, systems analyst, computer scientist, or management analyst, for example. In addition to job growth, some openings will result from the need to replace analysts retiring or leaving the occupation permanently for other reasons. Analysts who keep up with the latest technological advancements and software will have the best opportunities.

Jobs for operations research analysts exist in almost every industry because of the diversity of applications for their work. As businesses and government agencies continue to contract out jobs to cut costs, opportunities for operations research analysts will be best in management, scientific, and technical consulting firms. Opportunities in the military exist as well, but will depend on the size of future military budgets. Military leaders rely on operations research analysts to test and evaluate the accuracy and effectiveness of new weapons systems and strategies. (See the *Handbook* statement on job opportunities in the Armed Forces.)

Earnings

Median annual earnings of operations research analysts were $64,650 in May 2006. The middle 50 percent earned between $48,820 and $85,760. The lowest 10 percent had earnings of less than $38,760, while the highest 10 percent earned more than $108,290. Median annual earnings of operations research analysts working in management, scientific, and technical consulting services were $69,870.

The average annual salary for operations research analysts in the Federal Government in nonsupervisory, supervisory, and managerial positions was $91,207 in 2007.

Employer-sponsored training is often another part of an analyst's compensation. Some analysts attend advanced university classes on these subjects at their employer's expense.

Related Occupations

Operations research analysts apply advanced analytical methods to large, complicated problems. Economists, computer systems analysts, mathematicians, and engineers also use advanced analysis and often apply the principles of operations research. Workers in other occupations that also stress advanced analysis include computer scientists and database administrators, computer programmers, statisticians, and market and survey researchers. Because its goal is improved organizational effectiveness, operations research also is closely allied to managerial occupations such as computer and information systems managers, and management analysts.

Sources of Additional Information

For information on career opportunities and a list of degree programs for operations research analysts, contact:

➤ Institute for Operations Research and the Management Sciences, 7240 Parkway Dr., Suite 310, Hanover, MD 21076. Internet: **http://www.informs.org**

For information on operations research careers and degree programs in the Armed Forces, contact:
➤ Military Operations Research Society, 1703 N. Beauregard St., Suite 450, Alexandria, VA 22311.
Internet: **http://www.mors.org**

Information on obtaining positions as operations research analysts with the Federal Government is available from the Office of Personnel Management through USAJOBS, the Federal Government's official employment information system. This resource for locating and applying for job opportunities can be accessed through the Internet at **http://www.usajobs.opm.gov** or through an interactive voice response telephone system at (703) 724-1850 or TDD (978) 461-8404. These numbers are not toll free, and charges may result. For advice on how to find and apply for Federal jobs, see the *Occupational Outlook Quarterly* article "How to get a job in the Federal Government," online at:
http://www.bls.gov/opub/ooq/2004/summer/art01.pdf.

Statisticians

(O*NET 15-2041.00)

Significant Points

- About 30 percent of statisticians work for Federal, State, and local governments; other employers include scientific research and development services and finance and insurance firms.

- A master's degree in statistics or mathematics is the minimum educational requirement for most jobs as a statistician.

- Employment of statisticians is projected to grow about as fast as average.

- Individuals with a degree in statistics should have opportunities in a variety of fields.

Nature of the Work

Statistics is the scientific application of mathematical principles to the collection, analysis, and presentation of numerical data. Statisticians apply their mathematical and statistical knowledge to the design of surveys and experiments; the collection, processing, and analysis of data; and the interpretation of the experiment and survey results. Opinion polls, statements of accuracy on scales and other measuring devises, and information about average earnings in an occupation are all usually the work of statisticians.

Statisticians may apply their knowledge of statistical methods to a variety of subject areas, such as biology, economics, engineering, medicine, public health, psychology, marketing, education, and sports. Many economic, social, political, and military decisions cannot be made without statistical techniques, such as the design of experiments to gain Federal approval of a newly manufactured drug. Statistics might be needed to show whether the seemingly good results of a drug were likely be-

Individuals with a degree in statistics should have opportunities in a variety of fields.

cause of the drug rather than just the effect of random variation in patient outcomes.

One technique that is especially useful to statisticians is sampling—obtaining information about a population of people or group of things by surveying a small portion of the total. For example, to determine the size of the audience for particular programs, television-rating services survey only a few thousand families, rather than all viewers. Statisticians decide where and how to gather the data, determine the type and size of the sample group, and develop the survey questionnaire or reporting form. They also prepare instructions for workers who will collect and tabulate the data. Finally, statisticians analyze, interpret, and summarize the data using computer software.

In business and industry, statisticians play an important role in quality control and in product development and improvement. In an automobile company, for example, statisticians might design experiments to determine the failure time of engines exposed to extreme weather conditions by running individual engines until failure and breakdown. Working for a pharmaceutical company, statisticians might develop and evaluate the results of clinical trials to determine the safety and effectiveness of new medications. At a computer software firm, statisticians might help construct new statistical software packages to analyze data more accurately and efficiently. In addition to product development and testing, some statisticians also are involved in deciding what products to manufacture, how much to charge for them, and to whom the products should be marketed. Statisticians also may manage assets and liabilities, determining the risks and returns of certain investments.

Statisticians also are employed by nearly every government agency. Some government statisticians develop surveys that measure population growth, consumer prices, or unemployment. Other statisticians work for scientific, environmental, and agricultural agencies and may help figure out the average level of pesticides in drinking water, the number of endangered species living in a particular area, or the number of people afflicted with a particular disease. Statisticians also are employed in national defense agencies, determining the accuracy of new weapons and the likely effectiveness of defense strategies.

Because statistical specialists are employed in so many work areas, specialists who use statistics often have different profes-

sional designations. For example, a person using statistical methods to analyze economic data may have the title econometrician, while statisticians in public health and medicine may hold titles such as biostatistician or biometrician.

Work environment. Statisticians generally work regular hours in an office environment. Sometimes, they may work more hours to meet deadlines.

Some statisticians travel to provide advice on research projects, supervise and set up surveys, or gather statistical data. While advanced communications devices such as e-mail and teleconferencing are making it easier for statisticians to work with clients in different areas, there still are situations that require the statistician to be present, such as during meetings or while gathering data.

Training, Other Qualifications, and Advancement

A master's degree in statistics or mathematics is the minimum educational requirement, but research and academic jobs generally require a Ph.D., Federal Government jobs require at least a bachelor's degree.

Education and training. A master's degree in statistics or mathematics usually is the minimum educational requirement for most statistician jobs. Research and academic positions usually require a Ph.D. in statistics. Beginning positions in industrial research often require a master's degree combined with several years of experience.

Jobs with the Federal Government require at least a bachelor's degree. The training required for employment as an entry-level statistician in the Federal Government is a bachelor's degree, including at least 15 semester hours of statistics or a combination of 15 hours of mathematics and statistics, if at least 6 semester hours are in statistics. Qualifying as a mathematical statistician in the Federal Government requires 24 semester hours of mathematics and statistics, with a minimum of 6 semester hours in statistics and 12 semester hours in an area of advanced mathematics, such as calculus, differential equations, or vector analysis.

In 2007, more than 200 universities offered a degree program in statistics, biostatistics, or mathematics. Many other schools also offered graduate-level courses in applied statistics for students majoring in biology, business, economics, education, engineering, psychology, and other fields. Acceptance into graduate statistics programs does not require an undergraduate degree in statistics, although good training in mathematics is essential.

Many schools also offered degrees in mathematics, operations research, and other fields that include a sufficient number of courses in statistics to qualify graduates for some entry-level positions with the Federal Government. Required subjects for statistics majors include differential and integral calculus, statistical methods, mathematical modeling, and probability theory. Additional recommended courses for undergraduates include linear algebra, design and analysis of experiments, applied multivariate analysis, and mathematical statistics.

Because computers are used extensively for statistical applications, a strong background in computer science is highly recommended. For positions involving quality and productivity improvement, training in engineering or physical science is useful. A background in biological, chemical, or health science is important for positions involving the preparation and testing of pharmaceutical or agricultural products. Courses in economics and business administration are helpful for many jobs in market research, business analysis, and forecasting.

Advancements in technology have made a great impact on statistics. Statistical modeling continues to become quicker and easier because of increased computational power and new analytical methods or software. Continuing education is important for statisticians; they need to stay abreast emerging technologies to perform well.

Other qualifications. Good communications skills are important for prospective statisticians in industry, who often need to explain technical matters to persons without statistical expertise. An understanding of business and the economy also is valuable for those who plan to work in private industry.

Advancement. Beginning statisticians generally are supervised by an experienced statistician. With experience, they may advance to positions with more technical responsibility and, in some cases, supervisory duties. Opportunities for promotion are greater for people with advanced degrees. Master's and Ph.D. degree holders usually enjoy independence in their work and may engage in research; develop statistical methods; or, after a number of years of experience in a particular area, become statistical consultants.

Employment

Statisticians held about 22,000 jobs in 2006. About 20 percent of these jobs were in the Federal Government, where statisticians were concentrated in the Departments of Commerce, Agriculture, and Health and Human Services. Another 10 percent were found in State and local governments, including State colleges and universities. Most of the remaining jobs were in private industry, especially in scientific research and development services, insurance carriers, and pharmaceutical and medicine manufacturing.

Job Outlook

Average employment growth is projected. Individuals with a degree in statistics should have opportunities in a variety of fields.

Employment change. Employment of statisticians is projected to grow 9 percent from 2006 to 2016, about as fast as the average for all occupations. The demand for individuals with a background is statistics is expected to grow, although some jobs will be in occupations with titles other than "statistician."

The use of statistics is widespread and growing. Statistical models aid in decision making in both private industry and government. There will always be a demand for the skills statistical modeling provides. Technological advances are expected to

spur demand for statisticians. Ever faster computer processing allows statisticians to analyze greater amounts of data much more quickly, and to gather and sort through large amounts of data that would not have been analyzed in the past. As these processes continue to become more efficient and less expensive, an increasing number of employers will want to employ statisticians to take advantage of the new information available.

Biostatisticians should experience employment growth, primarily because of the booming pharmaceuticals business. As pharmaceutical companies develop new treatments and medical technologies, biostatisticians will be needed to do research and clinical trials.

Job prospects. Individuals with a degree in statistics should have opportunities in a variety of fields. For example, many jobs involve the analysis and interpretation of data from economics, biological science, psychology, computer software engineering, education, and other disciplines. Additional job openings will become available as statisticians transfer to other occupations, retire, or leave the workforce for other reasons.

Among graduates with a master's degree in statistics, those with a strong background in an allied field, such as finance, biology, engineering, or computer science, should have the best prospects of finding jobs related to their field of study.

Those who meet State certification requirements may become high school statistics teachers, for example. (For additional information, see the statement on teachers—preschool, kindergarten, elementary, middle, and secondary elsewhere in the *Handbook.*)

Earnings

Median annual wage-and-salary earnings of statisticians were $65,720 in May 2006. The middle 50 percent earned between $48,480 and $87,850. The lowest 10 percent earned less than $37,010, while the highest 10 percent earned more than $108,630.

The average annual salary for statisticians in the Federal Government was $85,690 in 2007, while mathematical statisticians averaged $96,121.

Some employers offer tuition reimbursement.

Related Occupations

People in diverse occupations work with statistics. Among these are actuaries; mathematicians; operations research analysts; computer scientists and database administrators; computer systems analysts; computer programmers; computer software engineers; engineers; economists, market and survey researchers, and other social scientists; and financial analysts and personal financial advisors. Some statisticians also work as secondary school teachers or postsecondary teachers.

Projections data from the National Employment Matrix

Occupational Title	SOC Code	Employment, 2006	Projected employment, 2016	Change, 2006-2016	
				Number	Percent
Statisticians	15-2041	22,000	24,000	1,900	9

NOTE: Data in this table are rounded. See the discussion of the employment projections table in the *Handbook* introductory chapter on *Occupational Information Included in the Handbook.*

Sources of Additional Information

For information about career opportunities in statistics, contact:

➤ American Statistical Association, 1429 Duke St., Alexandria, VA 22314. Internet: **http://www.amstat.org**

For more information on doctoral-level careers and training in mathematics, a field closely related to statistics, contact:

➤ American Mathematical Society, 201 Charles St., Providence, RI 02904. Internet: **http://www.ams.org**

Information on obtaining positions as statisticians with the Federal Government is available from the Office of Personnel Management through USAJOBS, the Federal Government's official employment information system. This resource for locating and applying for job opportunities can be accessed through the Internet at **http://www.usajobs.opm.gov** or through an interactive voice response telephone system at (703) 724-1850 or TDD (978) 461-8404. These numbers are not toll free, and charges may result. For advice on how to find and apply for Federal jobs, see the *Occupational Outlook Quarterly* article "How to get a job in the Federal Government," online at: **http://www.bls.gov/opub/ooq/2004/summer/art01.pdf**.

Architects, Surveyors, and Cartographers

Architects, Except Landscape and Naval

(O*NET 17-1011.00)

Significant Points

- About 1 in 5 architects are self-employed—more than 2 times the proportion for all occupations.

- Licensing requirements include a professional degree in architecture, at least 3 years of practical work training, and passing all divisions of the Architect Registration Examination.

- Architecture graduates may face competition, especially for jobs in the most prestigious firms.

Nature of the Work

People need places in which to live, work, play, learn, worship, meet, govern, shop, and eat. These places may be private or public; indoors or out; rooms, buildings, or complexes, and architects design them. Architects are licensed professionals trained in the art and science of building design who develop the concepts for structures and turn those concepts into images and plans.

Architects create the overall aesthetic and look of buildings and other structures, but the design of a building involves far more than its appearance. Buildings also must be functional, safe, and economical and must suit the needs of the people who use them. Architects consider all these factors when they design buildings and other structures.

Architects may be involved in all phases of a construction project, from the initial discussion with the client through the entire construction process. Their duties require specific skills—designing, engineering, managing, supervising, and communicating with clients and builders. Architects spend a great deal of time explaining their ideas to clients, construction contractors, and others. Successful architects must be able to communicate their unique vision persuasively.

The architect and client discuss the objectives, requirements, and budget of a project. In some cases, architects provide various predesign services: conducting feasibility and environmental impact studies, selecting a site, preparing cost analysis and land-use studies, or specifying the requirements the design must meet. For example, they may determine space requirements by researching the numbers and types of potential users of a building. The architect then prepares drawings and a report presenting ideas for the client to review.

After discussing and agreeing on the initial proposal, architects develop final construction plans that show the building's appearance and details for its construction. Accompanying these plans are drawings of the structural system; air-conditioning, heating, and ventilating systems; electrical systems; communications systems; plumbing; and, possibly, site and landscape plans. The plans also specify the building materials and, in some cases, the interior furnishings. In developing designs, architects follow building codes, zoning laws, fire regulations, and other ordinances, such as those requiring easy access by people who are disabled. Computer-aided design and drafting (CADD) and Building Information Modeling (BIM) technology has replaced traditional paper and pencil as the most common method for creating design and construction drawings. Continual revision of plans on the basis of client needs and budget constraints is often necessary.

Architects may also assist clients in obtaining construction bids, selecting contractors, and negotiating construction contracts. As construction proceeds, they may visit building sites to make sure that contractors follow the design, adhere to the schedule, use the specified materials, and meet work quality standards. The job is not complete until all construction is finished, required tests are conducted, and construction costs are paid. Sometimes, architects also provide postconstruction services, such as facilities management. They advise on energy efficiency measures, evaluate how well the building design adapts to the needs of occupants, and make necessary improvements.

Often working with engineers, urban planners, interior designers, landscape architects, and other professionals, architects in fact spend a great deal of their time coordinating information from, and the work of, other professionals engaged in the same project.

They design a wide variety of buildings, such as office and apartment buildings, schools, churches, factories, hospitals, houses, and airport terminals. They also design complexes such

Architects design buidings.

as urban centers, college campuses, industrial parks, and entire communities.

Architects sometimes specialize in one phase of work. Some specialize in the design of one type of building—for example, hospitals, schools, or housing. Others focus on planning and predesign services or construction management and do minimal design work.

Work environment. Usually working in a comfortable environment, architects.spend most of their time in offices consulting with clients, developing reports and drawings, and working with other architects and engineers. However, they often visit construction sites to review the progress of projects. Although most architects work approximately 40 hours per week, they often have to work nights and weekends to meet deadlines.

Training, Other Qualifications, and Advancement

There are three main steps in becoming an architect. First is the attainment of a professional degree in architecture. Second is work experience through an internship, and third is licensure through the passing of the Architect Registration Exam.

Education and training. In most States, the professional degree in architecture must be from one of the 114 schools of architecture that have degree programs accredited by the National Architectural Accrediting Board. However, State architectural registration boards set their own standards, so graduation from a non-accredited program may meet the educational requirement for licensing in a few States.

Three types of professional degrees in architecture are available: a 5-year bachelor's degree, which is most common and is intended for students with no previous architectural training; a 2-year master's degree for students with an undergraduate degree in architecture or a related area; and a 3- or 4-year master's degree for students with a degree in another discipline.

The choice of degree depends on preference and educational background. Prospective architecture students should consider the options before committing to a program. For example,

although the 5-year bachelor of architecture offers the fastest route to the professional degree, courses are specialized, and if the student does not complete the program, transferring to a program in another discipline may be difficult. A typical program includes courses in architectural history and theory, building design with an emphasis on CADD, structures, technology, construction methods, professional practice, math, physical sciences, and liberal arts. Central to most architectural programs is the design studio, where students apply the skills and concepts learned in the classroom, creating drawings and three-dimensional models of their designs.

Many schools of architecture also offer postprofessional degrees for those who already have a bachelor's or master's degree in architecture or other areas. Although graduate education beyond the professional degree is not required for practicing architects, it may be required for research, teaching, and certain specialties.

All State architectural registration boards require architecture graduates to complete a training period—usually at least 3 years—before they may sit for the licensing exam. Every State, with the exception of Arizona, has adopted the training standards established by the Intern Development Program, a branch of the American Institute of Architects and the National Council of Architectural Registration Boards (NCARB). These standards stipulate broad training under the supervision of a licensed architect. Most new graduates complete their training period by working as interns at architectural firms. Some States allow a portion of the training to occur in the offices of related professionals, such as engineers or general contractors. Architecture students who complete internships while still in school can count some of that time toward the 3-year training period.

Interns in architectural firms may assist in the design of one part of a project, help prepare architectural documents or drawings, build models, or prepare construction drawings on CADD. Interns also may research building codes and materials or write specifications for building materials, installation criteria, the quality of finishes, and other, related details.

Licensure. All States and the District of Columbia require individuals to be licensed (registered) before they may call themselves architects and contract to provide architectural services. During the time between graduation and becoming licensed, architecture school graduates generally work in the field under the supervision of a licensed architect who takes legal responsibility for all work. Licensing requirements include a professional degree in architecture, a period of practical training or internship, and a passing score on all divisions of the Architect Registration Examination. The examination is broken into nine divisions consisting of either multiple choice or graphical questions. The eligibility period for completion of all divisions of the exam varies by State.

Most States also require some form of continuing education to maintain a license, and many others are expected to adopt mandatory continuing education. Requirements vary by State but usually involve the completion of a certain number of credits annually or biennially through workshops, formal university classes, conferences, self-study courses, or other sources.

Other qualifications. Architects must be able to communicate their ideas visually to their clients. Artistic and drawing ability is helpful, but not essential, to such communication.

More important are a visual orientation and the ability to understand spatial relationships. Other important qualities for anyone interested in becoming an architect are creativity and the ability to work independently and as part of a team. Computer skills are also required for writing specifications, for 2- and 3-dimensional drafting using CADD programs, and for financial management.

Certification and advancement. A growing number of architects voluntarily seek certification by the National Council of Architectural Registration Boards. Certification is awarded after independent verification of the candidate's educational transcripts, employment record, and professional references. Certification can make it easier to become licensed across States. In fact, it is the primary requirement for reciprocity of licensing among State Boards that are NCARB members. In 2007, approximately one-third of all licensed architects had this certification.

After becoming licensed and gaining experience, architects take on increasingly responsible duties, eventually managing entire projects. In large firms, architects may advance to supervisory or managerial positions. Some architects become partners in established firms, while others set up their own practices. Some graduates with degrees in architecture also enter related fields, such as graphic, interior, or industrial design; urban planning; real estate development; civil engineering; and construction management.

Employment

Architects held about 132,000 jobs in 2006. Approximately 7 out of 10 jobs were in the architectural, engineering, and related services industry—mostly in architectural firms with fewer than five workers. A small number worked for residential and nonresidential building construction firms and for government agencies responsible for housing, community planning, or construction of government buildings, such as the U.S. Departments of Defense and Interior, and the General Services Administration. About 1 in 5 architects are self-employed.

Job Outlook

Employment of architects is expected to grow faster than the average for all occupations through 2016. Keen competition is expected for positions at the most prestigious firms, and opportunities will be best for those architects who are able to distinguish themselves with their creativity.

Employment change. Employment of architects is expected to grow by 18 percent between 2006 and 2016, which is faster than the average for all occupations. Employment of architects is strongly tied to the activity of the construction industry. Strong growth is expected to come from nonresidential construction as demand for commercial space increases. Residential construction, buoyed by low interest rates, is also expected to grow as more people become homeowners. If interest rates

rise significantly, home building may fall off, but residential construction makes up only a small part of architects' work.

Current demographic trends also support an increase in demand for architects. As the population of Sunbelt States continues to grow, the people living there will need new places to live and work. As the population continues to live longer and babyboomers begin to retire, there will be a need for more healthcare facilities, nursing homes, and retirement communities. In education, buildings at all levels are getting older and class sizes are getting larger. This will require many school districts and universities to build new facilities and renovate existing ones.

In recent years, some architecture firms have outsourced the drafting of construction documents and basic design for large-scale commercial and residential projects to architecture firms overseas. This trend is expected to continue and may have a negative impact on employment growth for lower level architects and interns who would normally gain experience by producing these drawings.

Job prospects. Besides employment growth, additional job openings will arise from the need to replace the many architects who are nearing retirement, and others who transfer to other occupations or stop working for other reasons. Internship opportunities for new architectural students are expected to be good over the next decade, but more students are graduating with architectural degrees and some competition for entry-level jobs can be anticipated. Competition will be especially keen for jobs at the most prestigious architectural firms as prospective architects try to build their reputation. Prospective architects who have had internships while in school will have an advantage in obtaining intern positions after graduation. Opportunities will be best for those architects that are able to distinguish themselves from others with their creativity.

Prospects will also be favorable for architects with knowledge of "green" design. Green design, also known as sustainable design, emphasizes energy efficiency, renewable resources such as energy and water, waste reduction, and environmentally friendly design, specifications, and materials. Rising energy costs and increased concern about the environment has led to many new buildings being built green.

Some types of construction are sensitive to cyclical changes in the economy. Architects seeking design projects for office and retail construction will face especially strong competition for jobs or clients during recessions, and layoffs may ensue in less successful firms. Those involved in the design of institutional buildings, such as schools, hospitals, nursing homes, and correctional facilities, will be less affected by fluctuations in the economy. Residential construction makes up a small portion of work for architects, so major changes in the housing market would not be as significant as fluctuations in the nonresidential market.

Despite good overall job opportunities some architects may not fare as well as others. The profession is geographically

Projections data from the National Employment Matrix

Occupational Title	SOC Code	Employment, 2006	Projected employment, 2016	Change, 2006-2016	
				Number	Percent
Architects, except landscape and naval...	17-1011	132,000	155,000	23,000	18

NOTE: Data in this table are rounded. See the discussion of the employment projections table in the *Handbook* introductory chapter on *Occupational Information Included in the Handbook.*

sensitive, and some parts of the Nation may have fewer new building projects. Also, many firms specialize in specific buildings, such as hospitals or office towers, and demand for these buildings may vary by region. Architects may find it increasingly necessary to gain reciprocity in order to compete for the best jobs and projects in other States.

Earnings

Median annual earnings of wage-and-salary architects were $64,150 in May 2006. The middle 50 percent earned between $49,780 and $83,450. The lowest 10 percent earned less than $39,420, and the highest 10 percent earned more than $104,970. Those just starting their internships can expect to earn considerably less.

Earnings of partners in established architectural firms may fluctuate because of changing business conditions. Some architects may have difficulty establishing their own practices and may go through a period when their expenses are greater than their income, requiring substantial financial resources.

Many firms pay tuition and fees toward continuing education requirements for their employees.

Related Occupations

Architects design buildings and related structures. Construction managers, like architects, also plan and coordinate activities concerned with the construction and maintenance of buildings and facilities. Others who engage in similar work are landscape architects, civil engineers, urban and regional planners, and designers, including interior designers, commercial and industrial designers, and graphic designers.

Sources of Additional Information

Information about education and careers in architecture can be obtained from:

➤ The American Institute of Architects, 1735 New York Ave. NW., Washington, DC 20006. Internet: **http://www.aia.org**

➤ Intern Development Program, National Council of Architectural Registration Boards, Suite 1100K, 1801 K St. NW., Washington, D.C. 20006.
Internet: **http://www.ncarb.org**

Landscape Architects

(O*NET 17-1012.00)

Significant Points

- Almost 19 percent of all landscape architects are self-employed—more than 2 times the proportion for all occupations.

- 49 States require landscape architects to be licensed.

- New graduates can expect to face competition for jobs in the largest and most prestigious landscape architecture firms, but there should be good job opportunities overall as demand for landscape architecture services increases.

Nature of the Work

Everyone enjoys attractively designed residential areas, public parks and playgrounds, college campuses, shopping centers, golf courses, and parkways. Landscape architects design these areas so that they are not only functional, but also beautiful, and compatible with the natural environment. They plan the location of buildings, roads, and walkways, and the arrangement of flowers, shrubs, and trees. They also design and plan the restoration of natural places disturbed by humans such as wetlands, stream corridors, mined areas and forested land.

Landscape architects work for many types of organizations—from real estate development firms starting new projects to municipalities constructing airports or parks—and they often are involved with the development of a site from its conception. Working with architects, surveyors, and engineers, landscape architects help determine the best arrangement of roads and buildings. They also collaborate with environmental scientists, foresters, and other professionals to find the best way to conserve or restore natural resources. Once these decisions are made, landscape architects create detailed plans indicating new topography, vegetation, walkways, and other landscaping details, such as fountains and decorative features.

In planning a site, landscape architects first study the project holistically. They also consider the purpose of the project and the funds available. They analyze the natural elements of the site, such as the climate, soil, slope of the land, drainage, and vegetation; observe where sunlight falls on the site at different times of the day; and assess the effect of existing buildings, roads, walkways, and utilities.

After studying and analyzing the site, landscape architects prepare a preliminary design. To address the needs of the client as well as the conditions at the site, they frequently make changes before a final design is approved. They also take into account any local, State, or Federal regulations, such as those protecting wetlands or historic resources. In preparing designs, computer-aided design (CAD) has become an essential tool for most landscape architects. Many landscape architects also use video simulation to help clients envision the proposed ideas and plans. For larger scale site planning, landscape architects also use geographic information systems (GIS) technology, a computer mapping system.

Throughout all phases of planning and design, landscape architects consult with other professionals, such as civil engineers, hydrologists, or architects, involved in the project. Once the design is complete, they prepare a proposal for the client. They produce detailed plans of the site, including written reports, sketches, models, photographs, land-use studies, and cost estimates, and submit them for approval by the client and by regulatory agencies. When the plans are approved, landscape architects prepare working drawings showing all existing and proposed features. They also outline in detail the methods of construction and draw up a list of necessary materials. Landscape architects then monitor the implementation of their design, while general contractors or landscape contractors usually direct the actual construction of the site and installation of plantings.

Some landscape architects work on a variety of projects. Others specialize in a particular area, such as street and highway beautification, waterfront improvement projects, parks and playgrounds, or shopping centers. Still others work in regional planning and resource management; feasibility, environmental impact, and cost studies; or site construction. Increasingly, landscape architects work in environmental remediation, such as preservation and restoration of wetlands or abatement of stormwater run-off in new developments. Historic landscape preservation and restoration is another area where landscape architects increasingly play a role.

Landscape architects who work for government agencies do site and landscape design for government buildings, parks, and other public lands, as well as park and recreation planning in national parks and forests. In addition, they prepare environmental impact statements and studies on environmental issues such as public land-use planning. Some restore degraded land, such as mines or landfills. Others use their skills in traffic-calming, the "art" of slowing traffic through the use of traffic design, enhancement of the physical environment, and greater attention to aesthetics.

Work environment. Landscape architects spend most of their time in offices creating plans and designs, preparing models and cost estimates, doing research, or attending meetings with clients and other professionals involved in a design or planning project. The remainder of their time is spent at the site. During the design and planning stage, landscape architects visit and analyze the site to verify that the design can be incorporated into the landscape. After the plans and specifications are completed, they may spend additional time at the site observing or supervising the construction. Those who work in large national or regional firms may spend considerably more time out of the office, traveling to sites.

Salaried employees in both government and landscape architectural firms usually work regular hours. However, they may occasionally work overtime to meet a project deadline. Hours of self-employed landscape architects vary depending on the demands of their projects.

Landscape architects consult with clients and other professionals throughout the plannining and design of a project.

Training, Other Qualifications, and Advancement

Almost every state requires landscape architects to be licensed. While requirements vary among the states, they usually include a degree in landscape architecture from an accredited school, work experience, and the passage of the Landscape Architect Registration Exam.

Education and training. A bachelor's or master's degree in landscape architecture usually is necessary for entry into the profession. There are two undergraduate professional degrees: a Bachelor of Landscape Architecture (BLA) and a Bachelor of Science in Landscape Architecture (BSLA). These usually require four or five years of study in design, construction techniques, art, history, natural and social sciences. There are generally two types of graduate degree programs. For those who hold an undergraduate degree in a field other than landscape architecture and intend to become landscape architecture practitioners, the Master of Landscape Architecture (MLA) typically takes three years of full-time study. Those who hold undergraduate degrees in landscape architecture can earn their MLA in two years.

In 2007, 61 colleges and universities offered 79 undergraduate and graduate programs in landscape architecture that were accredited by the Landscape Architecture Accreditation Board of the American Society of Landscape Architects. Courses required in these programs usually include subjects such as surveying, landscape design and construction, landscape ecology, site design, and urban and regional planning. Other courses include history of landscape architecture, plant and soil science, geology, professional practice, and general management. The design studio is another important aspect of many curriculums. Whenever possible, students are assigned real projects, providing them with valuable hands-on experience. While working on these projects, students become proficient in the use of computer-aided design, geographic information systems, and video simulation.

Licensure and certification. As of January 2008, 49 states required landscape architects to be licensed. Licensing is based on the Landscape Architect Registration Examination (L.A.R.E.), sponsored by the Council of Landscape Architectural Registration Boards and administered in two portions, graphic and multiple choice. Admission to the exam usually requires a degree from an accredited school plus 1 to 4 years of work experience under the supervision of a licensed landscape architect, although standards vary from State to State. For those without an accredited landscape architecture degree, most states provide alternative paths to qualify to take the L.A.R.E., usually requiring more work experience. Currently, 15 States require that a State examination be passed in addition to the L.A.R.E. to satisfy registration requirements. State examinations focus on laws, environmental regulations, plants, soils, climate, and any other characteristics unique to the State.

Because requirements for licensure are not uniform, landscape architects may find it difficult to transfer their registration from one State to another. However, those who meet the national standards of graduating from an accredited program, serving 3 years of internship under the supervision of a registered landscape architect, and passing the L.A.R.E. can satisfy requirements in most States. By meeting national requirements, a landscape architect can also obtain certification from the Council of Landscape Architectural Registration Boards which can be useful in obtaining reciprocal licensure in other states.

In States where licensure is required, new hires may be called "apprentices" or "intern landscape architects" until they become licensed. Their duties vary depending on the type and size of the employing firm. They may do project research or prepare working drawings, construction documents, or base maps of the area to be designed. Some are allowed to participate in the actual design of a project. However, interns must perform all work under the supervision of a licensed landscape architect. Additionally, all drawings and specifications must be signed and sealed by the licensed landscape architect, who takes legal responsibility for the work. After gaining experience and becoming licensed, landscape architects usually can carry a design through all stages of development.

Many States require some form of continuing education to maintain a license. Requirements usually involve the completion of workshops, seminars, formal university classes, conferences, self-study courses, or other classes.

The Federal Government does not require its landscape architects to be licensed. Candidates for entry positions with the Federal Government should have a bachelor's or master's degree in landscape architecture.

Other qualifications. People planning a career in landscape architecture should appreciate nature, enjoy working with their hands, and possess strong analytical skills. Creative vision and artistic talent also are desirable qualities. Good oral communication skills are essential. Landscape architects must be able to convey their ideas to other professionals and clients and to make presentations before large groups. Strong writing skills also are valuable, as is knowledge of computer applications of all kinds, including word processing, desktop publishing, and spreadsheets. Landscape architects use these tools to develop presentations, proposals, reports, and land impact studies for clients, colleagues, and superiors. Landscape architects must also be able to draft and design using CAD software. Many employers recommend that prospective landscape architects complete at least one summer internship with a landscape architecture firm to hone their technical skills and to gain an understanding of the day-to-day operations of the business, including how to win clients, generate fees, and work within a budget.

Advancement. After several years, landscape architects may become project managers, taking on the responsibility for meeting schedules and budgets, in addition to overseeing the project design. Later, they may become associates or partners of a firm, with a proprietary interest in the business.

Many landscape architects are self-employed. Self-discipline, business acumen, and good marketing skills are important qualities for those who choose to open their own business.

Even with these qualities, however, some may struggle while building a client base.

Those with landscape architecture training also qualify for jobs closely related to landscape architecture, and may, after gaining some experience, become construction supervisors, land or environmental planners, or landscape consultants.

Employment

Landscape architects held about 28,000 jobs in 2006. More than 1 out of 2 landscape architects were employed in architectural, engineering, and related services. State and local governments employed approximately 6 percent of all landscape architects. About 2 out of 10 landscape architects were self-employed.

Employment of landscape architects is concentrated in urban and suburban areas throughout the country; some landscape architects work in rural areas, particularly those employed by the Federal Government to plan and design parks and recreation areas.

Job Outlook

Employment of landscape architects is expected to grow faster than the average for all occupations through the year 2016. There should be good job prospects for landscape architects overall, but opportunities may depend on geographic location and local real estate and construction markets.

Employment change. Employment of landscape architects is expected to increase by 16 percent during the 2006-16 decade, which is faster than the average for all occupations. Employment will grow because the expertise of landscape architects will be sought after in the planning and development of new construction to meet the needs of a growing population. With land costs rising and the public desiring more beautiful spaces, the importance of good site planning and landscape design is growing.

New construction will spur demand for landscape architects to help plan sites that meet with environmental regulations and zoning laws and integrate new structures with the natural environment in the least disruptive way. For example, landscape architects will be needed to manage stormwater run-off to avoid pollution of waterways and conserve water resources. Landscape architects also will be increasingly involved in preserving and restoring wetlands and other environmentally sensitive sites.

Continuation of the Safe, Accountable, Flexible, Efficient, Transportation, Equity Act: A Legacy for Users also is expected to spur employment for landscape architects, particularly in State and local governments. This Act, known as SAFE-TEA-LU, provides funds for surface transportation and transit programs, such as interstate highway construction and maintenance, pedestrian and bicycle trails, and safe routes to schools.

Projections data from the National Employment Matrix

Occupational Title	SOC Code	Employment, 2006	Projected employment, 2016	Change, 2006-2016	
				Number	Percent
Landscape architects	17-1012	28,000	32,000	4,600	16

NOTE: Data in this table are rounded. See the discussion of the employment projections table in the *Handbook* introductory chapter on *Occupational Information Included in the Handbook.*

In addition to the work related to new development and construction, landscape architects are expected to be involved in historic preservation, land reclamation, and refurbishment of existing sites. Additionally, landscape architects will be needed to create security perimeters that are better integrated with their surroundings for many of the Nation's landmarks, monuments, and buildings.

Job prospects. In addition to growth, the need to replace landscape architects who retire or leave the labor force will produce some additional job openings.

Opportunities will vary by year and geographic region, depending on local economic conditions. During a recession, when real estate sales and construction slow down, landscape architects may face greater competition for jobs and sometimes layoffs. But because landscape architects can work on many different types of projects, they may have steadier work than other design professionals when traditional construction slows.

New graduates can expect to face competition for jobs in the largest and most prestigious landscape architecture firms, but there should be good job opportunities overall as demand for landscape architecture services increases. Many employers prefer to hire entry-level landscape architects who have internship experience, which significantly reduces the amount of on-the-job training required. Opportunities will be best for landscape architects who develop strong technical skills—such as computer design—communication skills, and knowledge of environmental codes and regulations. Those with additional training or experience in urban planning increase their opportunities for employment in landscape architecture firms that specialize in site planning as well as landscape design.

Earnings

In May 2006, median annual earnings for landscape architects were $55,140. The middle 50 percent earned between $42,720 and $73,240. The lowest 10 percent earned less than $34,230 and the highest 10 percent earned over $95,420. Architectural, engineering, and related services employed more landscape architects than any other group of industries, and there the median annual earnings were $56,060 in May 2006.

Related Occupations

Landscape architects use their knowledge of design, construction, land-use planning, and environmental issues to develop a landscape project. Others whose work requires similar skills are architects, except landscape and naval; surveyors, cartographers, photogrammetrists, and surveying technicians; civil engineers; and urban and regional planners. Landscape architects also must know how to grow and use plants in the landscape. Some conservation scientists and foresters and biological scientists also study plants and do related work. Environmental scientists and hydrologists, and geoscientists, like many landscape architects, work in the area of environmental remediation.

Sources of Additional Information

Additional information, including a list of colleges and universities offering accredited programs in landscape architecture, is available from:

➤ American Society of Landscape Architects, Career Information, 636 Eye St.NW., Washington, DC 20001-3736. Internet: **http://www.asla.org**

General information on registration or licensing requirements is available from:

➤ Council of Landscape Architectural Registration Boards, 3949 Pender Dr., Suite 120, Vienna, VA 22030. Internet: **http://www.clarb.org**

Surveyors, Cartographers, Photogrammetrists, and Surveying and Mapping Technicians

(O*NET 17-1021.00, 17-1022.00, 17-3031.00, 17-3031.01, 17-3031.02)

Significant Points

- About 7 out of 10 jobs were in architectural, engineering, and related services.

- Opportunities will be best for surveyors, cartographers, and photogrammetrists who have a bachelor's degree and strong technical skills.

- Overall employment of surveyors, cartographers, photogrammetrists, and surveying technicians is expected to grow much faster than the average for all occupations through the year 2016.

Nature of the Work

Surveyors, cartographers, and photogrammetrists are responsible for measuring and mapping the Earth's surface. *Surveyors* establish official land, airspace, and water boundaries. They write descriptions of land for deeds, leases, and other legal documents; define airspace for airports; and take measurements of construction and mineral sites. Other surveyors provide data about the shape, contour, location, elevation, or dimension of land or land features. *Cartographers and photogrammetrists* collect, analyze, interpret, and map geographic information from surveys and from data and photographs collected using airplanes and satellites. *Surveying and mapping technicians* assist these professionals by collecting data in the field, making calculations, and helping with computer-aided drafting. Collectively, these occupations play key roles in the field of geospatial information.

Surveyors measure distances, directions, and angles between points and elevations of points, lines, and contours on, above, and below the Earth's surface. In the field, they select known survey reference points and determine the precise location of important features in the survey area using specialized equipment. Surveyors also research legal records, look for evidence of previous boundaries, and analyze data to determine the location of boundary lines. They are sometimes called to provide expert testimony in court about their work. Surveyors also record their results, verify the accuracy of data, and prepare plots, maps, and reports.

Some surveyors perform specialized functions closer to those of cartographers and photogrammetrists than to those of traditional surveyors. For example, *geodetic surveyors* use high-accuracy techniques, including satellite observations, to measure large areas of the earth's surface. *Geophysical prospecting surveyors* mark sites for subsurface exploration, usually to look for petroleum. *Marine or hydrographic surveyors* survey harbors, rivers, and other bodies of water to determine shorelines, the topography of the bottom, water depth, and other features.

Surveyors use the Global Positioning System (GPS) to locate reference points with a high degree of precision. To use this system, a surveyor places a satellite signal receiver—a small instrument mounted on a tripod—on a desired point, and another receiver on a point for which the geographic position is known. The receiver simultaneously collects information from several satellites to establish a precise position. The receiver also can be placed in a vehicle for tracing out road systems. Because receivers now come in different sizes and shapes, and because the cost of receivers has fallen, much more surveying work can be done with GPS. Surveyors then interpret and check the results produced by the new technology.

Field measurements are often taken by a survey party that gathers the information needed by the surveyor. A typical survey party consists of a party chief and one or more surveying technicians and helpers. The party chief, who may be either a surveyor or a senior surveying technician, leads day-to-day work activities. Surveying technicians assist the party chief by adjusting and operating surveying instruments, such as the total station, which measures and records angles and distances simultaneously. Surveying technicians or assistants position and hold the vertical rods, or targets, that the operator sights on to measure angles, distances, or elevations. They may hold measuring tapes if electronic distance-measuring equipment is not used. Surveying technicians compile notes, make sketches, and enter the data obtained from surveying instruments into computers either in the field or at the office. Survey parties also may include laborers or helpers who perform less-skilled duties, such as clearing brush from sight lines, driving stakes, or carrying equipment.

Photogrammetrists and cartographers measure, map, and chart the Earth's surface. Their work involves everything from performing geographical research and compiling data to producing maps. They collect, analyze, and interpret both spatial data—such as latitude, longitude, elevation, and distance—and nonspatial data—for example, population density, land-use patterns, annual precipitation levels, and demographic characteristics. Their maps may give both physical and social characteristics of the land. They prepare maps in either digital or graphic form, using information provided by geodetic surveys and remote sensing systems including aerial cameras, satellites, and LIDAR.

LIDAR—light-imaging detection and ranging—uses lasers attached to planes and other equipment to digitally map the topography of the Earth. It is often more accurate than traditional surveying methods and also can be used to collect other forms of data, such as the location and density of forests. Data developed by LIDAR can be used by surveyors, cartographers, and photogrammetrists to provide spatial information to specialists in geology, seismology, forestry, and construction, and other fields.

Geographic Information Systems (GIS) have become an integral tool for surveyors, cartographers and photogrammetrists, and surveying and mapping technicians. Workers use GIS to assemble, integrate, analyze, and display data about location in a digital format. They also use GIS to compile information from a variety of sources. GIS typically are used to make maps which combine information useful for environmental studies, geology, engineering, planning, business marketing, and other disciplines. As more of these systems are developed, many mapping specialists are being called *geographic information specialists*.

Work environment. Surveyors and surveying technicians usually work an 8-hour day, 5 days a week and may spend a lot of time outdoors. Sometimes, they work longer hours during the summer, when weather and light conditions are most suitable for fieldwork. Construction-related work may be limited during times of inclement weather.

Surveyors and technicians engage in active, sometimes strenuous, work. They often stand for long periods, walk considerable distances, and climb hills with heavy packs of instruments and other equipment. They also can be exposed to all types of weather. Traveling is sometimes part of the job, and land surveyors and technicians may commute long distances, stay away from home overnight, or temporarily relocate near a survey site. Surveyors also work indoors while planning surveys, searching court records for deed information, analyzing data, and preparing reports and maps.

Cartographers and photogrammetrists spend most of their time in offices using computers. However, certain jobs may require extensive field work to verify results and acquire data.

Surveyors use sophisticated equipment to take measurements.

Training, Other Qualifications, and Advancement

Most surveyors, cartographers, and photogrammetrists have a bachelor's degree in surveying or a related field. Every State requires that surveyors be licensed.

Education and training. In the past, many people with little formal training started as members of survey crews and worked their way up to become licensed surveyors, but this has become increasingly difficult to do. Now, most surveyors need a bachelor's degree. A number of universities offer bachelor's degree programs in surveying, and many community colleges, technical institutes, and vocational schools offer 1-, 2-, and 3-year programs in surveying or surveying technology.

Cartographers and photogrammetrists usually have a bachelor's degree in cartography, geography, surveying, engineering, forestry, computer science, or a physical science, although a few enter these positions after working as technicians. With the development of GIS, cartographers and photogrammetrists need more education and stronger technical skills—including more experience with computers—than in the past.

Most cartographic and photogrammetric technicians also have specialized postsecondary education. High school students interested in surveying and cartography should take courses in algebra, geometry, trigonometry, drafting, mechanical drawing, and computer science.

Licensure. All 50 States and all U.S. territories license surveyors. For licensure, most State licensing boards require that individuals pass a written examination given by the National Council of Examiners for Engineering and Surveying (NCEES). Most States also require surveyors to pass a written examination prepared by the State licensing board.

Licensing happens in stages. After passing a first exam, the Fundamentals of Surveying, most candidates work under the supervision of an experienced surveyor for 4 years and then for licensure take a second exam, the Principles and Practice of Surveyors.

Specific requirements for training and education vary among the States. An increasing number of States require a bachelor's degree in surveying or in a closely related field, such as civil engineering or forestry, regardless of the number of years of experience. Some States require the degree to be from a school accredited by the Accreditation Board for Engineering and Technology. Many States also have a continuing education requirement.

Additionally a number of States require cartographers and photogrammetrists to be licensed as surveyors, and some States have specific licenses for photogrammetrists.

Other qualifications. Surveyors, cartographers, and photogrammetrists should be able to visualize objects, distances, sizes, and abstract forms. They must work with precision and accuracy because mistakes can be costly.

Members of a survey party must be in good physical condition because they work outdoors and often carry equipment over difficult terrain. They need good eyesight, coordination, and hearing to communicate verbally and using hand signals. Surveying is a cooperative operation, so good interpersonal skills and the ability to work as part of a team is important. Good office skills also are essential because surveyors must be able to research old deeds and other legal papers and prepare reports that document their work.

Certification and advancement. High school graduates with no formal training in surveying usually start as apprentices. Beginners with postsecondary school training in surveying usually can start as technicians or assistants. With on-the-job experience and formal training in surveying—either in an institutional program or from a correspondence school—workers may advance to senior survey technician, then to party chief. Depending on State licensing requirements, in some cases they may advance to licensed surveyor.

The National Society of Professional Surveyors, a member organization of the American Congress on Surveying and Mapping, has a voluntary certification program for surveying technicians. Technicians are certified at four levels requiring progressive amounts of experience and the passing of written examinations. Although not required for State licensure, many employers require certification for promotion to positions with greater responsibilities.

The American Society for Photogrammetry and Remote Sensing has voluntary certification programs for technicians and professionals in photogrammetry, remote sensing, and GIS. To qualify for these professional distinctions, individuals must meet work experience and training standards and pass a written examination. The professional recognition these certifications can help workers gain promotions.

Employment

Surveyors, cartographers, photogrammetrists, and surveying technicians held about 148,000 jobs in 2006. Employment was distributed by occupational specialty as follows:

Surveying and mapping technicians	76,000
Surveyors	60,000
Cartographers and photogrammetrists	12,000

The architectural, engineering, and related services industry—including firms that provided surveying and mapping services to other industries on a contract basis—provided 7 out of 10 jobs for these workers. Federal, State, and local governmental agencies provided about 14 percent of these jobs. Major Federal Government employers are the U.S. Geological Survey (USGS), the Bureau of Land Management (BLM), the National Geodetic Survey, the National Geospatial Intelligence Agency, and the Army Corps of Engineers. Most surveyors in State and local government work for highway departments or urban planning and redevelopment agencies. Construction, mining and utility companies also employ surveyors, cartographers, photogrammetrists, and surveying technicians.

Job Outlook

Surveyors, cartographers, photogrammetrists, and surveying and mapping technicians should have favorable job prospects. These occupations should experience much faster than average employment growth.

Employment change. Overall employment of surveyors, cartographers, photogrammetrists, and surveying and mapping technicians is expected to increase by 21 percent from 2006 to 2016, which is much faster than the average for all occupations. Increasing demand for fast, accurate, and complete geographic information will be the main source of growth for these occupations.

Projections data from the National Employment Matrix

Occupational Title	SOC Code	Employment, 2006	Projected employment, 2016	Change, 2006-2016	
				Number	Percent
Surveyors, cartographers, photogrammetrists, and surveying technicians..	—	148,000	179,000	31,000	21
Cartographers and photogrammetrists	17-1021	12,000	15,000	2,500	20
Surveyors	17-1022	60,000	74,000	14,000	24
Surveying and mapping technicians	17-3031	76,000	90,000	15,000	19

NOTE: Data in this table are rounded. See the discussion of the employment projections table in the *Handbook* introductory chapter on *Occupational Information Included in the Handbook.*

An increasing number of firms are interested in geographic information and its applications. For example, GIS can be used to create maps and information used in emergency planning, security, marketing, urban planning, natural resource exploration, construction, and other applications. Also, the increased popularity of online mapping systems has created a higher demand for and awareness of geographic information among consumers.

Job prospects. In addition to openings from growth, job openings will continue to arise from the need to replace workers who transfer to other occupations or who leave the labor force altogether. Many of the workers in these occupations are approaching retirement age.

Opportunities for surveyors, cartographers, and photogrammetrists should remain concentrated in engineering, surveying, mapping, building inspection, and drafting services firms. However, employment may fluctuate from year to year with construction activity or with mapping needs for land and resource management.

Opportunities should be stronger for professional surveyors than for surveying and mapping technicians. Advancements in technology, such as total stations and GPS, have made surveying parties smaller than they once were. Additionally, cartographers, photogrammetrists, and technicians who produce more basic GIS data may face competition for jobs from offshore firms and contractors.

As technologies become more complex, opportunities will be best for surveyors, cartographers, and photogrammetrists who have a bachelor's degree and strong technical skills. Increasing demand for geographic data, as opposed to traditional surveying services, will mean better opportunities for cartographers and photogrammetrists who are involved in the development and use of geographic and land information systems.

Earnings

Median annual earnings of cartographers and photogrammetrists were $48,240 in May 2006. The middle 50 percent earned between $37,480 and $65,240. The lowest 10 percent earned less than $30,910 and the highest 10 percent earned more than $80,520.

Median annual earnings of surveyors were $48,290 in May 2006. The middle 50 percent earned between $35,720 and $63,990. The lowest 10 percent earned less than $26,690 and the highest 10 percent earned more than $79,910. Median annual earnings of surveyors employed in architectural, engineering, and related services were $47,570 in May 2006.

Median annual earnings of surveying and mapping technicians were $32,340 in May 2006. The middle 50 percent earned

between $25,070 and $42,230. The lowest 10 percent earned less than $20,020, and the highest 10 percent earned more than $53,310. Median annual earnings of surveying and mapping technicians employed in architectural, engineering, and related services were $30,670 in May 2006, while those employed by local governments had median annual earnings of $37,550.

Related Occupations

Surveying is related to the work of civil engineers, architects, and landscape architects because an accurate survey is the first step in land development and construction projects. Cartographic and geodetic surveying are related to the work of environmental scientists and geoscientists, who study the earth's internal composition, surface, and atmosphere. Cartography also is related to the work of geographers and urban and regional planners, who study and decide how the earth's surface is being and may be used.

Sources of Additional Information

For career information on surveyors, cartographers, photogrammetrists, and surveying technicians, contact:
➤ American Congress on Surveying and Mapping, Suite 403, 6 Montgomery Village Ave., Gaithersburg, MD 20879. Internet: **http://www.acsm.net**

Information about career opportunities, licensure requirements, and the surveying technician certification program is available from:
➤ National Society of Professional Surveyors, Suite 403, 6 Montgomery Village Ave., Gaithersburg, MD 20879.

For information on a career as a geodetic surveyor, contact:
➤ American Association of Geodetic Surveying (AAGS), Suite 403, 6 Montgomery Village Ave., Gaithersburg, MD 20879.

For career information on photogrammetrists, photogrammetric technicians, remote sensing scientists and image-based cartographers or geographic information system specialists, contact:
➤ ASPRS: Imaging and Geospatial Information Society, 5410 Grosvenor Lane., Suite 210, Bethesda, MD 20814-2160. Internet: **http://www.asprs.org**

General information on careers in photogrammetry, mapping, and surveying is available from:
➤ MAPPS: Management Association for Private Photogrammetric Surveyors, 1760 Reston Parkway, Suite 515, Reston, VA 20190. Internet: **http://www.mapps.org**

Information on about careers in remote sensing, photogrammetry, surveying, GIS, and other geography-related disciplines also is available from the Spring 2005 Occupational Outlook Quarterly article, "Geography Jobs", available online at:
http://www.bls.gov/opub/ooq/2005/spring/art01.pdf

Engineers

(O*NET 17-2011.00, 17-2021.00, 17-2031.00, 17-2041.00, 17-2051.00, 17-2061.00, 17-2071.00, 17-2072.00, 17-2081.00, 17-2111.00, 17-2111.01, 17-2111.02, 17-2111.03, 17-2112.00, 17-2121.00, 17-2121.01, 17-2121.02, 17-2131.00, 17-2141.00, 17-2151.00, 17-2161.00, 17-2171.00, 17-2199.99)

Significant Points

- Overall job opportunities in engineering are expected to be good, but will vary by specialty.

- A bachelor's degree in engineering is required for most entry-level jobs.

- Starting salaries are among the highest of all college graduates.

- Continuing education is critical for engineers as technology evolves.

Nature of the Work

Engineers apply the principles of science and mathematics to develop economical solutions to technical problems. Their work is the link between scientific discoveries and the commercial applications that meet societal and consumer needs.

Many engineers develop new products. During this process, they consider several factors. For example, in developing an industrial robot, engineers precisely specify the functional requirements; design and test the robot's components; integrate the components to produce the final design; and evaluate the design's overall effectiveness, cost, reliability, and safety. This process applies to the development of many different products, such as chemicals, computers, power plants, helicopters, and toys.

In addition to design and development, many engineers work in testing, production, or maintenance. These engineers supervise production in factories, determine the causes of component failure, and test manufactured products to maintain quality. They also estimate the time and cost to complete projects. Supervisory engineers are responsible for major components or entire projects. (See the statement on engineering and natural sciences managers elsewhere in the *Handbook*.)

Engineers use computers extensively to produce and analyze designs; to simulate and test how a machine, structure, or system operates; to generate specifications for parts; and to monitor product quality and control process efficiency. Nanotechnology, which involves the creation of high-performance materials and components by integrating atoms and molecules, also is introducing entirely new principles to the design process.

Most engineers specialize. Following are details on the 17 engineering specialties covered in the Federal Government's Standard Occupational Classification (SOC) system. Numerous other specialties are recognized by professional societies, and each of the major branches of engineering has numerous subdivisions. Civil engineering, for example, includes structural and transportation engineering, and materials engineering includes ceramic, metallurgical, and polymer engineering. Engineers also may specialize in one industry, such as motor vehicles, or in one type of technology, such as turbines or semiconductor materials.

- Aerospace engineers design, develop, and test aircraft, spacecraft, and missiles and supervise the manufacture of these products. Those who work with aircraft are called *aeronautical engineers*, and those working specifically with spacecraft are *astronautical engineers*. Aerospace engineers develop new technologies for use in aviation, defense systems, and space exploration, often specializing in areas such as structural design, guidance, navigation and control, instrumentation and communication, or production methods. They also may specialize in a particular type of aerospace product, such as commercial aircraft, military fighter jets, helicopters, spacecraft, or missiles and rockets, and may become experts in aerodynamics, thermodynamics, celestial mechanics, propulsion, acoustics, or guidance and control systems.

- Agricultural engineers apply knowledge of engineering technology and science to agriculture and the efficient use of biological resources. Because of this, they are also referred to as *biological and agricultural engineers*. They design agricultural machinery, equipment, sensors, processes, and structures, such as those used for crop storage. Some engineers specialize in areas such as power systems and machinery design; structures and environment engineering; and food and bioprocess engineering. They develop ways to conserve soil and water and to improve the processing of agricultural products. Agricultural engineers often work in research and development, production, sales, or management.

- Biomedical engineers develop devices and procedures that solve medical and health-related problems by combining their knowledge of biology and medicine with engineering principles and practices. Many do research, along with life scientists, chemists, and medical scientists, to develop and evaluate systems and products such as artificial organs, prostheses (artificial devices that replace missing body parts), instrumentation, medical information systems, and health management and care delivery systems. Biomedical engineers may also design devices used in various medical procedures, imaging systems such as magnetic resonance imaging (MRI), and devices for automating insulin injections or controlling body functions. Most engineers in this specialty need a sound background in another engineering specialty, such as mechanical or electronics engineering, in addition to specialized biomedical training. Some specialties within biomedical engineering include biomaterials, biomechanics, medical imaging, rehabilitation engineering, and orthopedic engineering.

- Chemical engineers apply the principles of chemistry to solve problems involving the production or use of chemicals and biochemicals. They design equipment and processes for large-scale chemical manufacturing, plan and test methods of manufacturing products and treating byproducts, and supervise production. Chemical engineers also work in a variety of manufacturing industries other than chemical manufacturing, such as those producing energy, electronics, food, clothing, and paper. They also work in health care, biotechnology, and business services. Chemical engineers apply principles of physics, mathematics, and mechanical and electrical engineering, as well as chemistry. Some may specialize in a particular chemical process, such as oxidation or polymerization. Others specialize in a particular field, such as nanomaterials, or in the development of specific products. They must be aware of all aspects of chemicals manufacturing and how the manufacturing process affects the environment and the safety of workers and consumers.

- Civil engineers design and supervise the construction of roads, buildings, airports, tunnels, dams, bridges, and water supply and sewage systems. They must consider many factors in the design process, from the construction costs and expected lifetime of a project to government regulations and potential environmental hazards such as earthquakes and hurricanes. Civil engineering, considered one of the oldest engineering disciplines, encompasses many specialties. The major ones are structural, water resources, construction, environmental, transportation, and geotechnical engineering. Many civil engineers hold supervisory or administrative positions, from supervisor of a construction site to city engineer. Others may work in design, construction, research, and teaching.

- Computer hardware engineers research, design, develop, test, and oversee the manufacture and installation of computer hardware. Hardware includes computer chips, circuit boards, computer systems, and related equipment such as keyboards, modems, and printers. (Computer software engineers—often simply called computer engineers—design and develop the software systems that control computers. These workers are covered elsewhere in the *Handbook*.) The work of computer hardware engineers is very similar to that of electronics engineers in that they may design and test circuits and other electronic components, but computer hardware engineers do that work only as it relates to computers and computer-related equipment. The rapid advances in computer technology are largely a result of the research, development, and design efforts of these engineers.

- Electrical engineers design, develop, test, and supervise the manufacture of electrical equipment. Some of this equipment includes electric motors; machinery controls, lighting, and wiring in buildings; automobiles; aircraft; radar and navigation systems; and power generation, control, and transmission devices used by electric utilities. Although the terms "electrical" and "electronics" engineering often are used interchangeably in academia and industry, electrical engineers have traditionally focused on the generation and supply of power, whereas electronics engineers have worked on applications of electricity to control systems or signal processing. Electrical engineers specialize in areas such as power systems engineering or electrical equipment manufacturing.

- Electronics engineers, except computer are responsible for a wide range of technologies, from portable music players to the global positioning system (GPS), which can continuously

Engineers sometimes perform tests in laboratories.

provide the location, for example, of a vehicle. Electronics engineers design, develop, test, and supervise the manufacture of electronic equipment such as broadcast and communications systems. Many electronics engineers also work in areas closely related to computers. However, engineers whose work is related exclusively to computer hardware are considered computer hardware engineers. Electronics engineers specialize in areas such as communications, signal processing, and control systems or have a specialty within one of these areas—control systems or aviation electronics, for example.

- Environmental engineers develop solutions to environmental problems using the principles of biology and chemistry. They are involved in water and air pollution control, recycling, waste disposal, and public health issues. Environmental engineers conduct hazardous-waste management studies in which they evaluate the significance of the hazard, advise on treatment and containment, and develop regulations to prevent mishaps. They design municipal water supply and industrial wastewater treatment systems. They conduct research on the environmental impact of proposed construction projects, analyze scientific data, and perform quality-control checks. Environmental engineers are concerned with local and worldwide environmental issues. They study and attempt to minimize the effects of acid rain, global warming, automobile emissions, and ozone depletion. They may also be involved in the protection of wildlife. Many environmental engineers work as consultants, helping their clients to comply with regulations, to prevent environmental damage, and to clean up hazardous sites.

- Health and safety engineers, except mining safety engineers and inspectors prevent harm to people and property by applying knowledge of systems engineering and mechanical, chemical, and human performance principles. Using this specialized knowledge, they identify and measure potential hazards, such as the risk of fires or the dangers involved in handling of toxic chemicals. They recommend appropriate loss prevention measures according to the probability of harm and potential damage. Health and safety engineers develop procedures and designs to reduce the risk of illness, injury, or damage. Some work in manufacturing industries to ensure the designs of new products do not create unnecessary hazards. They must be able to anticipate, recognize, and evaluate hazardous conditions, as well as develop hazard control methods.

• Industrial engineers determine the most effective ways to use the basic factors of production—people, machines, materials, information, and energy—to make a product or provide a service. They are primarily concerned with increasing productivity through the management of people, methods of business organization, and technology. To maximize efficiency, industrial engineers carefully study the product requirements and design manufacturing and information systems to meet those requirements with the help of mathematical methods and models. They develop management control systems to aid in financial planning and cost analysis, and design production planning and control systems to coordinate activities and ensure product quality. They also design or improve systems for the physical distribution of goods and services and determine the most efficient plant locations. Industrial engineers develop wage and salary administration systems and job evaluation programs. Many industrial engineers move into management positions because the work is closely related to the work of managers.

• Marine engineers and naval architects are involved in the design, construction, and maintenance of ships, boats, and related equipment. They design and supervise the construction of everything from aircraft carriers to submarines, and from sailboats to tankers. Naval architects work on the basic design of ships, including hull form and stability. Marine engineers work on the propulsion, steering, and other systems of ships. Marine engineers and naval architects apply knowledge from a range of fields to the entire design and production process of all water vehicles. Other workers who operate or supervise the operation of marine machinery on ships and other vessels sometimes may be called marine engineers or, more frequently, ship engineers, but they do different work and are covered under water transportation occupations elsewhere in the *Handbook*.

• Materials engineers are involved in the development, processing, and testing of the materials used to create a range of products, from computer chips and aircraft wings to golf clubs and snow skis. They work with metals, ceramics, plastics, semiconductors, and composites to create new materials that meet certain mechanical, electrical, and chemical requirements.

Some engineers, such as these mining engineers, work part of their time outdoors.

They also are involved in selecting materials for new applications. Materials engineers have developed the ability to create and then study materials at an atomic level, using advanced processes to replicate the characteristics of materials and their components with computers. Most materials engineers specialize in a particular material. For example, metallurgical engineers specialize in metals such as steel, and ceramic engineers develop ceramic materials and the processes for making them into useful products such as glassware or fiber optic communication lines.

• Mechanical engineers research, design, develop, manufacture, and test tools, engines, machines, and other mechanical devices. Mechanical engineering is one of the broadest engineering disciplines. Engineers in this discipline work on power-producing machines such as electric generators, internal combustion engines, and steam and gas turbines. They also work on power-using machines such as refrigeration and air-conditioning equipment, machine tools, material handling systems, elevators and escalators, industrial production equipment, and robots used in manufacturing. Mechanical engineers also design tools that other engineers need for their work. In addition, mechanical engineers work in manufacturing or agriculture production, maintenance, or technical sales; many become administrators or managers.

• Mining and geological engineers, including mining safety engineers find, extract, and prepare coal, metals, and minerals for use by manufacturing industries and utilities. They design open-pit and underground mines, supervise the construction of mine shafts and tunnels in underground operations, and devise methods for transporting minerals to processing plants. Mining engineers are responsible for the safe, economical, and environmentally sound operation of mines. Some mining engineers work with geologists and metallurgical engineers to locate and appraise new ore deposits. Others develop new mining equipment or direct mineral-processing operations that separate minerals from the dirt, rock, and other materials with which they are mixed. Mining engineers frequently specialize in the mining of one mineral or metal, such as coal or gold. With increased emphasis on protecting the environment, many mining engineers work to solve problems related to land reclamation and water and air pollution. Mining safety engineers use their knowledge of mine design and practices to ensure the safety of workers and to comply with State and Federal safety regulations. They inspect walls and roof surfaces, monitor air quality, and examine mining equipment for compliance with safety practices.

• Nuclear engineers research and develop the processes, instruments, and systems used to derive benefits from nuclear energy and radiation. They design, develop, monitor, and operate nuclear plants to generate power. They may work on the nuclear fuel cycle—the production, handling, and use of nuclear fuel and the safe disposal of waste produced by the generation of nuclear energy—or on the development of fusion energy. Some specialize in the development of nuclear power sources for naval vessels or spacecraft; others find industrial and medical uses for radioactive materials, as in equipment used to diagnose and treat medical problems.

• Petroleum engineers search the world for reservoirs containing oil or natural gas. Once these resources are discovered, petroleum engineers work with geologists and other specialists to understand the geologic formation and properties of the rock containing the reservoir, determine the drilling methods to be used, and monitor drilling and production operations. They design equipment and processes to achieve the maximum profitable recovery of oil and gas. Because only a small proportion of oil and gas in a reservoir flows out under natural forces, petroleum engineers develop and use various enhanced recovery methods. These include injecting water, chemicals, gases, or steam into an oil reservoir to force out more of the oil and doing computer-controlled drilling or fracturing to connect a larger area of a reservoir to a single well. Because even the best techniques in use today recover only a portion of the oil and gas in a reservoir, petroleum engineers research and develop technology and methods to increase recovery and lower the cost of drilling and production operations.

Work environment. Most engineers work in office buildings, laboratories, or industrial plants. Others may spend time outdoors at construction sites and oil and gas exploration and production sites, where they monitor or direct operations or solve onsite problems. Some engineers travel extensively to plants or worksites here and abroad.

Many engineers work a standard 40-hour week. At times, deadlines or design standards may bring extra pressure to a job, requiring engineers to work longer hours.

Training, Other Qualifications, and Advancement

Engineers typically enter the occupation with a bachelor's degree in an engineering specialty, but some basic research positions may require a graduate degree. Engineers offering their services directly to the public must be licensed. Continuing education to keep current with rapidly changing technology is important for engineers.

Education and training. A bachelor's degree in engineering is required for almost all entry-level engineering jobs. College graduates with a degree in a natural science or mathematics occasionally may qualify for some engineering jobs, especially in specialties in high demand. Most engineering degrees are granted in electrical, electronics, mechanical, or civil engineering. However, engineers trained in one branch may work in related branches. For example, many aerospace engineers have training in mechanical engineering. This flexibility allows employers to meet staffing needs in new technologies and specialties in which engineers may be in short supply. It also allows engineers to shift to fields with better employment prospects or to those that more closely match their interests.

Most engineering programs involve a concentration of study in an engineering specialty, along with courses in both mathematics and the physical and life sciences. Many programs also include courses in general engineering. A design course, sometimes accompanied by a computer or laboratory class or both, is part of the curriculum of most programs. General courses not directly related to engineering, such as those in the social sciences or humanities, are also often required.

In addition to the standard engineering degree, many colleges offer 2-year or 4-year degree programs in engineering technology. These programs, which usually include various hands-on laboratory classes that focus on current issues in the applica-

A bachelor's degree in engineering is required for most entry-level jobs.

tion of engineering principles, prepare students for practical design and production work, rather than for jobs that require more theoretical and scientific knowledge. Graduates of 4-year technology programs may get jobs similar to those obtained by graduates with a bachelor's degree in engineering. Engineering technology graduates, however, are not qualified to register as professional engineers under the same terms as graduates with degrees in engineering. Some employers regard technology program graduates as having skills between those of a technician and an engineer.

Graduate training is essential for engineering faculty positions and many research and development programs, but is not required for the majority of entry-level engineering jobs. Many experienced engineers obtain graduate degrees in engineering or business administration to learn new technology and broaden their education. Many high-level executives in government and industry began their careers as engineers.

About 1,830 programs at colleges and universities offer bachelor's degrees in engineering that are accredited by the Accreditation Board for Engineering and Technology (ABET), Inc., and there are another 710 accredited programs in engineering technology. ABET accreditation is based on a program's faculty, curriculum, and facilities; the achievement of a program's students; program improvements; and institutional commitment to specific principles of quality and ethics. Although most institutions offer programs in the major branches of engineering, only a few offer programs in the smaller specialties. Also, programs of the same title may vary in content. For example, some programs emphasize industrial practices, preparing students for a job in industry, whereas others are more theoretical and are designed to prepare students for graduate work. Therefore, students should investigate curriculums and check accreditations carefully before selecting a college.

Admissions requirements for undergraduate engineering schools include a solid background in mathematics (algebra, geometry, trigonometry, and calculus) and science (biology, chemistry, and physics), with courses in English, social studies, and humanities. Bachelor's degree programs in engineering typically are designed to last 4 years, but many students find that it takes between 4 and 5 years to complete their studies. In a typical 4-year college curriculum, the first 2 years are spent studying mathematics, basic sciences, introductory engineering, humanities, and social sciences. In the last 2 years, most courses are in engineering, usually with a concentration in one specialty. Some programs offer a general engineering curriculum; students then specialize on the job or in graduate school.

Some engineering schools have agreements with 2-year colleges whereby the college provides the initial engineering education, and the engineering school automatically admits students for their last 2 years. In addition, a few engineering schools have arrangements that allow students who spend 3 years in a liberal arts college studying pre-engineering subjects and 2 years in an engineering school studying core subjects to receive a bachelor's degree from each school. Some colleges and universities offer 5-year master's degree programs. Some 5-year or even 6-year cooperative plans combine classroom study and practical work, permitting students to gain valuable experience and to finance part of their education.

Licensure. All 50 States and the District of Columbia require licensure for engineers who offer their services directly to the public. Engineers who are licensed are called professional engineers (PE). This licensure generally requires a degree from an ABET-accredited engineering program, 4 years of relevant work experience, and successful completion of a State examination. Recent graduates can start the licensing process by taking the examination in two stages. The initial Fundamentals of Engineering (FE) examination can be taken upon graduation. Engineers who pass this examination commonly are called engineers in training (EIT) or engineer interns (EI). After acquiring suitable work experience, EITs can take the second examination, the Principles and Practice of Engineering exam. Several States have imposed mandatory continuing education requirements for relicensure. Most States recognize licensure from other States, provided that the manner in which the initial license was obtained meets or exceeds their own licensure requirements. Many civil, electrical, mechanical, and chemical engineers are licensed PEs. Independent of licensure, various certification programs are offered by professional organizations to demonstrate competency in specific fields of engineering.

Other qualifications. Engineers should be creative, inquisitive, analytical, and detail oriented. They should be able to work as part of a team and to communicate well, both orally and in writing. Communication abilities are becoming increasingly important as engineers frequently interact with specialists in a wide range of fields outside engineering.

Certification and advancement. Beginning engineering graduates usually work under the supervision of experienced engineers and, in large companies, also may receive formal classroom or seminar-type training. As new engineers gain knowledge and experience, they are assigned more difficult projects with greater independence to develop designs, solve problems, and make decisions. Engineers may advance to become technical specialists or to supervise a staff or team of engineers and technicians. Some may eventually become engineering managers or enter other managerial or sales jobs. In sales, an engineering background enables them to discuss a product's technical aspects and assist in product planning, installation, and use. (See the statements under management and business

and financial operations occupations, and the statement on sales engineers elsewhere in the *Handbook.*)

Numerous professional certifications for engineers exist and may be beneficial for advancement to senior technical or managerial positions. Many certification programs are offered by the professional societies listed as sources of additional information for engineering specialties at the end of this statement.

Employment

In 2006, engineers held about 1.5 million jobs. The distribution of employment by engineering specialty follows:

Civil engineers	256,000
Mechanical engineers	227,000
Industrial engineers	201,000
Electrical engineers	153,000
Electronics engineers, except computer	138,000
Aerospace engineers	90,000
Computer hardware engineers	79,000
Environmental engineers	54,000
Chemical engineers	30,000
Health and safety engineers, except mining safety engineers and inspectors	25,000
Materials engineers	22,000
Petroleum engineers	17,000
Nuclear engineers	15,000
Biomedical engineers	14,000
Marine engineers and naval architects	9,200
Mining and geological engineers, including mining safety engineers	7,100
Agricultural engineers	3,100
All other engineers	170,000

About 37 percent of engineering jobs were found in manufacturing industries and another 28 percent were in the professional, scientific, and technical services sector, primarily in architectural, engineering, and related services. Many engineers also worked in the construction, telecommunications, and wholesale trade industries.

Federal, State, and local governments employed about 12 percent of engineers in 2006. About half of these were in the Federal Government, mainly in the U.S. Departments of Defense, Transportation, Agriculture, Interior, and Energy, and in the National Aeronautics and Space Administration. Most engineers in State and local government agencies worked in highway and public works departments. In 2006, about 3 percent of engineers were self-employed, many as consultants.

Engineers are employed in every State, in small and large cities and in rural areas. Some branches of engineering are concentrated in particular industries and geographic areas—for example, petroleum engineering jobs tend to be located in areas with sizable petroleum deposits, such as Texas, Louisiana, Oklahoma, Alaska, and California. Others, such as civil engineering, are widely dispersed, and engineers in these fields often move from place to place to work on different projects.

Engineers are employed in every major industry. The industries employing the most engineers in each specialty are given in table 1, along with the percent of occupational employment in the industry.

Table 1. Percent concentration of engineering specialty employment in key industries, 2006

Specialty	Industry	Percent
Aerospace engineers	Aerospace product and parts manufacturing	49
Agricultural engineers	Food manufacturing	25
	Architectural, engineering, and related services	15
Biomedical engineers	Medical equipment and supplies manufacturing	20
	Scientific research and development services	20
Chemical engineers	Chemical manufacturing	29
	Architectural, engineering, and related services	15
Civil engineers	Architectural, engineering, and related services	49
Computer hardware engineers	Computer and electronic product manufacturing	41
	Computer systems design and related services	19
Electrical engineers	Architectural, engineering, and related services	21
Electronics engineers, except computer	Computer and electronic product manufacturing	26
	Telecommunications	15
Environmental engineers	Architectural, engineering, and related services	29
	State and local government	21
Health and safety engineers, except mining safety engineers and inspectors	State and local government	10
Industrial engineers	Transportation equipment manufacturing	18
	Machinery manufacturing	8
Marine engineers and naval architects	Architectural, engineering, and related services	29
Materials engineers	Primary metal manufacturing	11
	Semiconductor and other electronic component manufacturing	9
Mechanical engineers	Architectural, engineering, and related services	22
	Transportation equipment manufacturing	14
Mining and geological engineers, including mining safety engineers	Mining	58
Nuclear engineers	Research and development in the physical, engineering, and life sciences	30
	Electric power generation, transmission and distribution	27
Petroleum engineers	Oil and gas extraction	43

Job Outlook

Employment of engineers is expected to grow about as fast as the average for all occupations over the next decade, but growth will vary by specialty. Environmental engineers should experience the fastest growth, while civil engineers should see the largest employment increase. Overall job opportunities in engineering are expected to be good.

Overall employment change. Overall engineering employment is expected to grow by 11 percent over the 2006-16 decade, about as fast as the average for all occupations. Engineers have traditionally been concentrated in slower growing or declining manufacturing industries, in which they will continue to be needed to design, build, test, and improve manufactured products. However, increasing employment of engineers in faster growing service industries should generate most of the employment growth. Job outlook varies by engineering specialty, as discussed later.

Competitive pressures and advancing technology will force companies to improve and update product designs and to optimize their manufacturing processes. Employers will rely on engineers to increase productivity and expand output of goods and services. New technologies continue to improve the design process, enabling engineers to produce and analyze various product designs much more rapidly than in the past. Unlike in some other occupations, however, technological advances are not expected to substantially limit employment opportunities in engineering because engineers will continue to develop new products and processes that increase productivity.

Offshoring of engineering work will likely dampen domestic employment growth to some degree. There are many well-trained, often English-speaking engineers available around the world willing to work at much lower salaries than U.S. engineers. The rise of the Internet has made it relatively easy for part of the engineering work previously done by engineers in this country to be done by engineers in other countries, a factor that will tend to hold down employment growth. Even so, there will always be a need for onsite engineers to interact with other employees and clients.

Overall job outlook. Overall job opportunities in engineering are expected to be good because the number of engineering graduates should be in rough balance with the number of job openings between 2006 and 2016. In addition to openings from job growth, many openings will be created by the need to replace current engineers who retire; transfer to management, sales, or other occupations; or leave engineering for other reasons.

Many engineers work on long-term research and development projects or in other activities that continue even during economic slowdowns. In industries such as electronics and aerospace, however, large cutbacks in defense expenditures and in government funding for research and development have resulted in significant layoffs of engineers in the past. The trend toward contracting for engineering work with engineering services firms, both domestic and foreign, has also made engineers more vulnerable to layoffs during periods of lower demand.

It is important for engineers, as it is for workers in other technical and scientific occupations, to continue their education throughout their careers because much of their value to their employer depends on their knowledge of the latest technology. Engineers in high-technology areas, such as biotechnology or information technology, may find that technical knowledge becomes outdated rapidly. By keeping current in their field, engineers are able to deliver the best solutions and greatest value to their employers. Engineers who have not kept current in their field may find themselves at a disadvantage when seeking promotions or during layoffs.

Employment change and job outlook by engineering specialty.

• Aerospace engineers are expected to have 10 percent growth in employment over the projections decade, about as fast as the average for all occupations. Increases in the number and scope of military aerospace projects likely will generate new jobs. In addition, new technologies expected to be used on commercial aircraft produced during the next decade should spur demand for aerospace engineers. The employment outlook for aerospace engineers appears favorable. The number of degrees granted in aerospace engineering has declined for many years because of a perceived lack of opportunities in this field. Although this trend has reversed, new graduates continue to be needed to replace aerospace engineers who retire or leave the occupation for other reasons.

• Agricultural engineers are expected to have employment growth of 9 percent over the projections decade, about as fast as the average for all occupations. More engineers will be needed to meet the increasing demand for using biosensors to determine the optimal treatment of crops. Employment growth should also result from the need to increase crop yields to feed an expanding population and produce crops used as renewable energy sources. Moreover, engineers will be needed to develop more efficient agricultural production and conserve resources.

• Biomedical engineers are expected to have 21 percent employment growth over the projections decade, much faster than the average for all occupations. The aging of the population and the focus on health issues will drive demand for better medical devices and equipment designed by biomedical engineers. Along with the demand for more sophisticated medical equipment and procedures, an increased concern for cost-effectiveness will boost demand for biomedical engineers, particularly in pharmaceutical manufacturing and related industries. However, because of the growing interest in this field, the number of degrees granted in biomedical engineering has increased greatly. Biomedical engineers, particularly those with only a bachelor's degree, may face competition for jobs. Unlike many other engineering specialties, a graduate degree is recommended or required for many entry-level jobs.

• Chemical engineers are expected to have employment growth of 8 percent over the projections decade, about as fast as the average for all occupations. Although overall employment in the chemical manufacturing industry is expected to decline, chemical companies will continue to research and develop new chemicals and more efficient processes to increase output of existing chemicals. Among manufacturing industries, pharmaceuticals may provide the best opportunities for jobseekers. However, most employment growth for chemical engineers will be in service-providing industries such as professional, scien-

Projections data from the National Employment Matrix

Occupational Title	SOC Code	Employment, 2006	Projected employment, 2016	Change, 2006-2016	
				Number	Percent
Engineers..	17-2000	1,512,000	1,671,000	160,000	11
Aerospace engineers	17-2011	90,000	99,000	9,200	10
Agricultural engineers....................................	17-2021	3,100	3,400	300	9
Biomedical engineers.....................................	17-2031	14,000	17,000	3,000	21
Chemical engineers..	17-2041	30,000	33,000	2,400	8
Civil engineers	17-2051	256,000	302,000	46,000	18
Computer hardware engineers	17-2061	79,000	82,000	3,600	5
Electrical and electronics engineers...............	17-2070	291,000	306,000	15,000	5
Electrical engineers.......................................	17-2071	153,000	163,000	9,600	6
Electronics engineers, except computer..........	17-2072	138,000	143,000	5,100	4
Environmental engineers................................	17-2081	54,000	68,000	14,000	25
Industrial engineers, including health and safety........................	17-2110	227,000	270,000	43,000	19
Health and safety engineers, except mining safety engineers and inspectors	17-2111	25,000	28,000	2,400	10
Industrial engineers.......................................	17-2112	201,000	242,000	41,000	20
Marine engineers and naval architects	17-2121	9,200	10,000	1,000	11
Materials engineers	17-2131	22,000	22,000	900	4
Mechanical engineers.....................................	17-2141	226,000	235,000	9,400	4
Mining and geological engineers, including mining safety engineers	17-2151	7,100	7,800	700	10
Nuclear engineers..	17-2161	15,000	16,000	1,100	7
Petroleum engineers.......................................	17-2171	17,000	18,000	900	5
Engineers, all other	17-2199	170,000	180,000	9,400	6

NOTE: Data in this table are rounded. See the discussion of the employment projections table in the *Handbook* introductory chapter on *Occupational Information Included in the Handbook.*

tific, and technical services, particularly for research in energy and the developing fields of biotechnology and nanotechnology.

• Civil engineers are expected to experience 18 percent employment growth during the projections decade, faster than the average for all occupations. Spurred by general population growth and the related need to improve the Nation's infrastructure, more civil engineers will be needed to design and construct or expand transportation, water supply, and pollution control systems and buildings and building complexes. They also will be needed to repair or replace existing roads, bridges, and other public structures. Because construction industries and architectural, engineering and related services employ many civil engineers, employment opportunities will vary by geographic area and may decrease during economic slowdowns, when construction is often curtailed.

• Computer hardware engineers are expected to have 5 percent employment growth over the projections decade, slower than the average for all occupations. Although the use of information technology continues to expand rapidly, the manufacture of computer hardware is expected to be adversely affected by intense foreign competition. As computer and semiconductor manufacturers contract out more of their engineering needs to both domestic and foreign design firms, much of the growth in employment of hardware engineers is expected in the computer systems design and related services industry.

• Electrical engineers are expected to have employment growth of 6 percent over the projections decade, slower than the average for all occupations. Although strong demand for electrical devices—including electric power generators, wireless phone transmitters, high-density batteries, and navigation systems—should spur job growth, international competition and the use of engineering services performed in other countries will limit employment growth. Electrical engineers working in firms providing engineering expertise and design services to manufacturers should have better job prospects.

• Electronics engineers, except computer are expected to have employment growth of 4 percent during the projections decade, slower than the average for all occupations. Although rising demand for electronic goods—including communications equipment, defense-related equipment, medical electronics, and consumer products—should continue to increase demand for electronics engineers, foreign competition in electronic products development and the use of engineering services performed in other countries will limit employment growth. Growth is expected to be fastest in service-providing industries—particularly in firms that provide engineering and design services.

• Environmental engineers should have employment growth of 25 percent during the projections decade, much faster than the average for all occupations. More environmental engineers will be needed to comply with environmental regulations and to develop methods of cleaning up existing hazards. A shift in emphasis toward preventing problems rather than controlling those that already exist, as well as increasing public health concerns resulting from population growth, also are expected to spur demand for environmental engineers. Because of this employment growth, job opportunities should be good even as more students earn degrees. Even though employment of

Overall job opportunities in engineering are expected to be good.

environmental engineers should be less affected by economic conditions than most other types of engineers, a significant economic downturn could reduce the emphasis on environmental protection, reducing job opportunities.

• Health and safety engineers, except mining safety engineers and inspectors are projected to experience 10 percent employment growth over the projections decade, about as fast as the average for all occupations. Because health and safety engineers make production processes and products as safe as possible, their services should be in demand as concern increases for health and safety within work environments. As new technologies for production or processing are developed, health and safety engineers will be needed to ensure that they are safe.

• Industrial engineers are expected to have employment growth of 20 percent over the projections decade, faster than the average for all occupations. As firms look for new ways to reduce costs and raise productivity, they increasingly will turn to industrial engineers to develop more efficient processes and reduce costs, delays, and waste. This should lead to job growth for these engineers, even in manufacturing industries with slowly growing or declining employment overall. Because their work is similar to that done in management occupations, many industrial engineers leave the occupation to become managers. Many openings will be created by the need to replace industrial engineers who transfer to other occupations or leave the labor force.

• Marine engineers and naval architects are expected to experience employment growth of 11 percent over the projections decade, about as fast as the average for all occupations. Strong demand for naval vessels and recreational small craft should more than offset the long-term decline in the domestic design and construction of large oceangoing vessels. Good prospects are expected for marine engineers and naval architects because of growth in employment, the need to replace workers who retire or take other jobs, and the limited number of students pursuing careers in this occupation.

• Materials engineers are expected to have employment growth of 4 percent over the projections decade, slower than the average for all occupations. Although employment is expected to decline in many of the manufacturing industries in which materials engineers are concentrated, growth should be strong for materials engineers working on nanomaterials and biomaterials. As manufacturing firms contract for their materials engineering needs, employment growth is expected in professional, scientific, and technical services industries also.

• Mechanical engineers are projected to have 4 percent employment growth over the projections decade, slower than the average for all occupations. This is because total employment in manufacturing industries—in which employment of mechanical engineers is concentrated—is expected to decline. Some new job opportunities will be created due to emerging technologies in biotechnology, materials science, and nanotechnology. Additional opportunities outside of mechanical engineering will exist because the skills acquired through earning a degree in mechanical engineering often can be applied in other engineering specialties.

• Mining and geological engineers, including mining safety engineers are expected to have 10 percent employment growth over the projections decade, about as fast as the average for all occupations. Following a lengthy period of decline, strong growth in demand for minerals and increased use of mining engineers in the oil and gas extraction industry is expected to create some employment growth over the 2006-16 period. Moreover, many mining engineers currently employed are approaching retirement age, a factor that should create additional job openings. Furthermore, relatively few schools offer mining engineering programs, resulting in good job opportunities for graduates. The best opportunities may require frequent travel or even living overseas for extended periods of time as mining operations around the world recruit graduates of U.S. mining engineering programs.

• Nuclear engineers are expected to have employment growth of 7 percent over the projections decade, about as fast as the average for all occupations. Most job growth will be in research and development and engineering services. Although no commercial nuclear power plants have been built in the United States for many years, nuclear engineers will be needed to operate existing plants and design new ones, including researching future nuclear power sources. They also will be needed to work in defense-related areas, to develop nuclear medical technology, and to improve and enforce waste management and safety standards. Nuclear engineers are expected to have good employment opportunities because the small number of nuclear engineering graduates is likely to be in rough balance with the number of job openings.

• Petroleum engineers are expected to have 5 percent employment growth over the projections decade, more slowly than the average for all occupations. Even though most of the potential petroleum-producing areas in the United States already have been explored, petroleum engineers will increasingly be needed to develop new methods of extracting more resources from existing sources. Favorable opportunities are expected for petroleum engineers because the number of job openings is likely to exceed the relatively small number of graduates. Petroleum engineers work around the world and, in fact, the best employment opportunities may include some work in other countries.

Table 2: Earnings distribution by engineering specialty, May 2006

Specialty	Lowest 10%	Lowest 25%	Median	Highest 25%	Highest 10%
Aerospace engineers	59,610	71,360	87,610	106,450	124,550
Agricultural engineers	42,390	53,040	66,030	80,370	96,270
Biomedical engineers	44,930	56,420	73,930	93,420	116,330
Chemical engineers	50,060	62,410	78,860	98,100	118,670
Civil engineers	44,810	54,520	68,600	86,260	104,420
Computer hardware engineers	53,910	69,500	88,470	111,030	135,260
Electrical engineers	49,120	60,640	75,930	94,050	115,240
Electronics engineers, except computer	52,050	64,440	81,050	99,630	119,900
Environmental engineers	43,180	54,150	69,940	88,480	106,230
Health and safety engineers, except mining safety engineers and inspectors	41,050	51,630	66,290	83,240	100,160
Industrial engineers	44,790	55,060	68,620	84,850	100,980
Marine engineers and naval architects	45,200	56,280	72,990	90,790	113,320
Materials engineers	46,120	57,850	73,990	92,210	112,140
Mechanical engineers	45,170	55,420	69,850	87,550	104,900
Mining and geological engineers, including mining safety engineers	42,040	54,390	72,160	94,110	128,410
Nuclear engineers	65,220	77,920	90,220	105,710	124,510
Petroleum engineers	57,960	75,880	98,380	123,130	145,600+
All other engineers	46,080	62,710	81,660	100,320	120,610

Table 3: Average starting salary by engineering specialty and degree , 2007

Curriculum	Bachelor's	Master's	Ph.D.
Aerospace/aeronautical/astronautical	$53,408	$62,459	$73,814
Agricultural	49,764	—	—
Architectual	48,664	—	—
Bioengineering and biomedical	51,356	59,240	—
Chemical	59,361	68,561	73,667
Civil	48,509	48,280	62,275
Computer	56,201	60,000	92,500
Electrical/electronics and communications	55,292	66,309	75,982
Environmental/environmental health	47,960	—	—
Industrial/manufacturing	55,067	64,759	77,364
Materials	56,233	—	—
Mechanical	54,128	62,798	72,763
Mining and mineral	54,381	—	—
Nuclear	56,587	59,167	—
Petroleum	60,718	57,000	—

Source: National Association of Colleges and Employers

Earnings

Earnings for engineers vary significantly by specialty, industry, and education. Variation in median earnings and in the earnings distributions for engineers in various specialties is especially significant. Table 2 shows wage-and-salary earnings distributions in May 2006 for engineers in specialties covered in this statement.

In the Federal Government, mean annual salaries for engineers ranged from $75,144 in agricultural engineering to $107,546 in ceramic engineering in 2007.

As a group, engineers earn some of the highest average starting salaries among those holding bachelor's degrees. Table 3 shows average starting salary offers for engineers, according to a 2007 survey by the National Association of Colleges and Employers.

Related Occupations

Engineers apply the principles of physical science and mathematics in their work. Other workers who use scientific and mathematical principles include architects, except landscape and naval; engineering and natural sciences managers; computer and information systems managers; computer programmers; computer software engineers; mathematicians; drafters; engineering technicians; sales engineers; science technicians; and physical and life scientists, including agricultural and food scientists, biological scientists, conservation scientists and foresters, atmospheric scientists, chemists and materials scientists, environmental scientists and hydrologists, geoscientists, and physicists and astronomers.

Sources of Additional Information

Information about careers in engineering is available from:
➤ JETS, 1420 King St., Suite 405, Alexandria, VA 22314. Internet: **http://www.jets.org**

Information on ABET-accredited engineering programs is available from:
➤ ABET, Inc., 111 Market Place, Suite 1050, Baltimore, MD 21202. Internet: **http://www.abet.org**

Those interested in information on the Professional Engineer licensure should contact:
➤ National Council of Examiners for Engineering and Surveying, P.O. Box 1686, Clemson, SC 29633. Internet: **http://www.ncees.org**
➤ National Society of Professional Engineers, 1420 King St., Alexandria, VA 22314. Internet: **http://www.nspe.org**

Information on general engineering education and career resources is available from:
➤ American Society for Engineering Education, 1818 N St.NW., Suite 600, Washington, DC 20036. Internet: **http://www.asee.org**

Information on obtaining engineering positions with the Federal Government is available from the Office of Personnel Management through USAJOBS, the Federal Government's official employment information system. This resource for locating and applying for job opportunities can be accessed through the Internet at **http://www.usajobs.opm.gov** or through an interactive voice response telephone system at (703) 724-1850 or TDD (978) 461-8404. These numbers are not toll free, and charges may result. For advice on how to find and apply for Federal jobs, see the Occupational Outlook Quarterly article "How to get a job in the Federal Government," online at: **http://www.bls.gov/opub/ooq/2004/summer/art01.pdf**.

For more detailed information on an engineering specialty, contact societies representing the individual branches of engineering. Each can provide information about careers in the particular branch.

Aerospace engineers
➤ Aerospace Industries Association, 1000 Wilson Blvd., Suite 1700, Arlington, VA 22209. Internet: **http://www.aia-aerospace.org**
➤ American Institute of Aeronautics and Astronautics, Inc., 1801 Alexander Bell Dr., Suite 500, Reston, VA 20191. Internet: **http://www.aiaa.org**

Agricultural engineers
➤ American Society of Agricultural and Biological Engineers, 2950 Niles Rd., St.Joseph, MI 49085. Internet: **http://www.asabe.org**

Biomedical engineers
➤ Biomedical Engineering Society, 8401 Corporate Dr., Suite 140, Landover, MD 20785. Internet: **http://www.bmes.org**

Chemical engineers
➤ American Chemical Society, Department of Career Services, 1155 16th St.NW., Washington, DC 20036. Internet: **http://www.chemistry.org**
➤ American Institute of Chemical Engineers, 3 Park Ave., New York, NY 10016. Internet: **http://www.aiche.org**

Civil engineers
➤ American Society of Civil Engineers, 1801 Alexander Bell Dr., Reston, VA 20191. Internet: **http://www.asce.org**

Computer hardware engineers
➤ IEEE Computer Society, 1730 Massachusetts Ave. NW., Washington, DC 20036. Internet: **http://www.computer.org**

Electrical and electronics engineers
➤ Institute of Electrical and Electronics Engineers–USA, 1828 L St.NW., Suite 1202, Washington, DC 20036. Internet: **http://www.ieeeusa.org**

Environmental engineers
➤ American Academy of Environmental Engineers, 130 Holiday Court, Suite 100, Annapolis, MD 21401. Internet: **http://www.aaee.net**

Health and safety engineers
➤ American Society of Safety Engineers, 1800 E Oakton St., Des Plaines, IL 60018. Internet: **http://www.asse.org**
➤ Board of Certified Safety Professionals, 208 Burwash Ave., Savoy, IL 61874. Internet: **http://www.bcsp.org**

Industrial engineers
➤ Institute of Industrial Engineers, 3577 Parkway LaNE., Suite 200, Norcross, GA 30092. Internet: **http://www.iienet.org**

Marine engineers and naval architects
➤ Society of Naval Architects and Marine Engineers, 601 Pavonia Ave., Jersey City, NJ 07306. Internet: **http://www.sname.org**

Materials engineers
➤ ASM International, 9639 Kinsman Rd., Materials Park, OH 44073. Internet: **http://www.asminternational.org**

➤ Minerals, Metals, and Materials Society, 184 Thorn Hill Rd., Warrendale, PA 15086. Internet: **http://www.tms.org**

Mechanical engineers
➤ American Society of Heating, Refrigerating, and Air-Conditioning Engineers, Inc., 1791 Tullie Circle NE., Atlanta, GA 30329. Internet: **http://www.ashrae.org**
➤ American Society of Mechanical Engineers, 3 Park Ave., New York, NY 10016. Internet: **http://www.asme.org**
➤ SAE International, 400 Commonwealth Dr., Warrendale, PA 15096. Internet: **http://www.sae.org**

Mining and geological engineers, including mining safety engineers
➤ Society for Mining, Metallurgy, and Exploration, Inc., 8307 Shaffer Parkway, Littleton, CO 80127. Internet: **http://www.smenet.org**

Nuclear engineers
➤ American Nuclear Society, 555 North Kensington Ave., La Grange Park, IL 60526. Internet: **http://www.ans.org**

Petroleum engineers
➤ Society of Petroleum Engineers, P.O. Box 833836, Richardson, TX 75083. Internet: **http://www.spe.org**

Drafters and Engineering Technicians

Drafters

(O*NET 17-3011.00, 17-3011.01, 17-3011.02, 17-3012.00, 17-3012.01, 17-3012.02, 17-3013.00, 17-3019.99)

Significant Points

- The type and quality of training programs vary considerably so prospective students should be careful in selecting a program.

- Opportunities should be best for individuals with at least 2 years of postsecondary training in drafting and considerable skill and experience using computer-aided design and drafting systems.

- Employment is projected to grow more slowly than average.

- Demand for drafters varies by specialty and depends on the needs of local industry.

Nature of the Work

Drafters prepare technical drawings and plans, which are used to build everything from manufactured products such as toys, toasters, industrial machinery, and spacecraft to structures such as houses, office buildings, and oil and gas pipelines.

In the past, drafters sat at drawing boards and used pencils, pens, compasses, protractors, triangles, and other drafting devices to prepare a drawing by hand. Now, most drafters use Computer Aided Design and Drafting (CADD) systems to prepare drawings. Consequently, some drafters may be referred to as *CADD operators.*

With CADD systems, drafters can create and store drawings electronically so that they can be viewed, printed, or programmed directly into automated manufacturing systems. CADD systems also permit drafters to quickly prepare variations of a design. Although drafters use CADD extensively, it is only a tool. Drafters still need knowledge of traditional drafting techniques, in addition to CADD skills. Despite the nearly universal use of CADD systems, manual drafting and sketching are used in certain applications.

Drafters' drawings provide visual guidelines and show how to construct a product or structure. Drawings include technical details and specify dimensions, materials, and procedures. Drafters fill in technical details using drawings, rough sketches, specifications, and calculations made by engineers, surveyors, architects, or scientists. For example, drafters use their knowledge of standardized building techniques to draw in the details of a structure. Some use their understanding of engineering and manufacturing theory and standards to draw the parts of a machine; they determine design elements, such as the numbers and kinds of fasteners needed to assemble the machine. Drafters use technical handbooks, tables, calculators, and computers to complete their work.

Drafting work has many specialties:

Aeronautical drafters prepare engineering drawings detailing plans and specifications used in the manufacture of aircraft, missiles, and related parts.

Architectural drafters draw architectural and structural features of buildings and other structures. These workers may specialize in a type of structure, such as residential or commercial, or in a kind of material used, such as reinforced concrete, masonry, steel, or timber.

Civil drafters prepare drawings and topographical and relief maps used in major construction or civil engineering projects, such as highways, bridges, pipelines, flood control projects, and water and sewage systems.

Electrical drafters prepare wiring and layout diagrams used by workers who erect, install, and repair electrical equipment and wiring in communication centers, power plants, electrical distribution systems, and buildings.

Electronics drafters draw wiring diagrams, circuit board assembly diagrams, schematics, and layout drawings used in the manufacture, installation, and repair of electronic devices and components.

Mechanical drafters prepare drawings showing the detail and assembly of a wide variety of machinery and mechanical devices, indicating dimensions, fastening methods, and other requirements.

Process piping or pipeline drafters prepare drawings used in the layout, construction, and operation of oil and gas fields, refineries, chemical plants, and process piping systems.

Work environment. Drafters usually work in comfortable offices. They may sit at adjustable drawing boards or drafting tables when doing manual drawings, although most drafters work at computer terminals much of the time. Because they spend long periods in front of computers doing detailed work, drafters may be susceptible to eyestrain, back discomfort, and hand and wrist problems. Most drafters work a standard 40-hour week; only a small number work part time.

Drafters pay careful attention to detail in their technical drawings.

Training, Other Qualifications, and Advancement

Employers prefer applicants who have completed postsecondary school training in drafting, which is offered by technical institutes, community colleges, and some 4-year colleges and universities. Employers are most interested in applicants with well-developed drafting and mechanical drawing skills; knowledge of drafting standards, mathematics, science, and engineering technology; and a solid background in CADD techniques.

Education and training. High school courses in mathematics, science, computer technology, design, computer graphics, and, where available, drafting are useful for people considering a drafting career. Employers prefer applicants who have also completed training after high school at a technical institute, community college, or 4-year college or university.

The kind and quality of drafting training programs vary considerably so prospective students should be careful in selecting a program. They should contact prospective employers to ask which schools they prefer and contact schools to ask for information about the kinds of jobs their graduates have, the type and condition of instructional facilities and equipment, and teacher qualifications.

Technical institutes offer intensive technical training, but they provide a less general education than do community colleges. Either certificates or diplomas may be awarded. Many technical institutes offer 2-year associate degree programs, which are similar to, or part of, the programs offered by community colleges or State university systems. Their programs vary considerably in length and in the type of courses offered. Some public vocational-technical schools serve local students and emphasize the type of training preferred by local employers. Most require a high school diploma or its equivalent for admission. Other technical institutes are run by private, often for-profit, organizations sometimes called proprietary schools.

Community colleges offer courses similar to those in technical institutes but include more classes in theory and liberal arts. Often, there is little or no difference between technical institute and community college programs. However, courses taken at community colleges are more likely to be accepted for credit at 4-year colleges. After completing a 2-year associate degree program, graduates may obtain jobs as drafters or continue their education in a related field at a 4-year college. Most 4-year colleges do not offer training in drafting, but they do offer classes in engineering, architecture, and mathematics that are useful for obtaining a job as a drafter.

Technical training obtained in the Armed Forces also can be applied in civilian drafting jobs. Some additional training may be necessary, depending on the technical area or military specialty.

Training differs somewhat within the drafting specialties, although the basics, such as mathematics, are similar. In an electronics drafting program, for example, students learn how to depict electronic components and circuits in drawings. In architectural drafting, they learn the technical specifications of buildings.

Certification and other qualifications. Mechanical ability and visual aptitude are important for drafters. Prospective drafters should be able to draw well and perform detailed work accurately and neatly. Artistic ability is helpful in some specialized fields, as is knowledge of manufacturing and construction methods. In addition, prospective drafters should have good interpersonal skills because they work closely with engineers, surveyors, architects, and other professionals and, sometimes, with customers.

The American Design Drafting Association (ADDA) has established a certification program for drafters. Although employers usually do not require drafters to be certified, certification demonstrates knowledge and an understanding of nationally recognized practices. Individuals who wish to become certified must pass the Drafter Certification Test, administered periodically at ADDA-authorized sites. Applicants are tested on basic drafting concepts, such as geometric construction, working drawings, and architectural terms and standards.

Advancement. Entry-level or junior drafters usually do routine work under close supervision. After gaining experience, they may become intermediate drafters and progress to more difficult work with less supervision. At the intermediate level, they may need to exercise more judgment and perform calculations when preparing and modifying drawings. Drafters may eventually advance to senior drafter, designer, or supervisor. Many employers pay for continuing education, and, with appropriate college degrees, drafters may go on to become engineering technicians, engineers, or architects.

Employment

Drafters held about 253,000 jobs in 2006. Architectural and civil drafters held 46 percent of all jobs for drafters, mechanical drafters held about 31 percent, and electrical and electronics drafters held about 14 percent.

About 49 percent of all jobs for drafters were in architectural, engineering, and related services firms that design construction projects or do other engineering work on a contract basis for other industries. Another 25 percent of jobs were in manufacturing industries such as machinery manufacturing, including metalworking and other general machinery; fabricated metal products manufacturing, including architectural and structural metals; computer and electronic products manufacturing, including navigational, measuring, electromedical, and control instruments; and transportation equipment manufacturing, including aerospace products and parts manufacturing, as well as ship and boat building. Most of the rest were employed in construction, government, wholesale trade, utilities, and employment services. Approximately 5 percent were self-employed in 2006.

Job Outlook

Drafters can expect slower than average employment growth through 2016, with the best opportunities expected for those with 2 years of professional training.

Employment change. Employment of drafters is expected to grow by 6 percent between 2006 and 2016, which is slower than the average for all occupations. Industrial growth and increasingly complex design problems associated with new products and manufacturing processes will increase the demand for drafting services. Furthermore, drafters are beginning to break out of the traditional drafting role and do work traditionally performed by engineers and architects, also increasing demand. However, drafters tend to be concentrated in slow-growing or declining manufacturing industries. In addition, CADD systems that are more powerful and easier to use are also expected to limit demand for lesser skilled drafters because simple tasks will be made easier or able to be done by other technical professionals. Employment growth also should be slowed by the offshore outsourcing to other countries of some drafting work because some drafting can be done by sending CADD files over the Internet.

Although growth is expected to be greatest for mechanical, architectural, and civil drafters, demand for particular drafting specialties varies throughout the country because employment usually is contingent on the needs of local industry.

Job prospects. Most job openings are expected to arise from the need to replace drafters who transfer to other occupations, leave the labor force, or retire.

Opportunities should be best for individuals with at least 2 years of postsecondary training in a drafting program that provides strong technical skills and considerable experience with CADD systems. CADD has increased the complexity of drafting applications while enhancing the productivity of drafters. It also has enhanced the nature of drafting by creating more possibilities for design and drafting. As technology continues to advance, employers will look for drafters with a strong background in fundamental drafting principles, a high level of technical sophistication, and the ability to apply their knowledge to a broader range of responsibilities.

Employment of drafters remains highly concentrated in industries that are sensitive to cyclical changes in the economy, primarily manufacturing industries. During recessions, drafters may be laid off. However, a growing number of drafters should continue to find employment on a temporary or contract basis as more companies turn to the employment services industry to meet their changing needs.

Earnings

Drafters' earnings vary by specialty, location, and level of responsibility. Median annual earnings of architectural and civil drafters were $41,960 in May 2006. The middle 50 percent earned between $33,550 and $52,220. The lowest 10 percent

Projections data from the National Employment Matrix

Occupational Title	SOC Code	Employment, 2006	Projected employment, 2016	Change, 2006-2016	
				Number	Percent
Drafters	17-3010	253,000	268,000	15,000	6
Architectural and civil drafters	17-3011	116,000	123,000	7,000	6
Electrical and electronics drafters	17-3012	35,000	36,000	1,400	4
Mechanical drafters	17-3013	78,000	82,000	4,100	5
Drafters, all other	17-3019	25,000	27,000	2,700	11

NOTE: Data in this table are rounded. See the discussion of the employment projections table in the *Handbook* introductory chapter on *Occupational Information Included in the Handbook.*

earned less than $27,010, and the highest 10 percent earned more than $63,310.

Median annual earnings of mechanical drafters were $43,700 in May 2006. The middle 50 percent earned between $34,680 and $55,130. The lowest 10 percent earned less than $28,230, and the highest 10 percent earned more than $67,860. Median annual earnings for mechanical drafters in architectural, engineering, and related services were $44,120.

Median annual earnings of electrical and electronics drafters were $46,830 in May 2006. The middle 50 percent earned between $36,660 and $60,160. The lowest 10 percent earned less than $29,290, and the highest 10 percent earned more than $74,490. In architectural, engineering, and related services, median annual earnings for electrical and electronics drafters were $44,140.

Related Occupations

Other workers who prepare or analyze detailed drawings and make precise calculations and measurements include architects, except landscape and naval; landscape architects; commercial and industrial designers; engineers; engineering technicians; science technicians; and surveyors, cartographers, photogrammetrists, and surveying technicians.

Sources of Additional Information

Information on schools offering programs in drafting and related fields is available from:

➤ Accrediting Commission of Career Schools and Colleges of Technology, 2101 Wilson Blvd., Suite 302, Arlington, VA 22201. Internet: **http://www.accsct.org**

Information about certification is available from:

➤ American Design Drafting Association, 105 E. Main St., Newbern, TN 38059. Internet: **http://www.adda.org**

Engineering Technicians

(O*NET 17-3021.00, 17-3022.00, 17-3023.00, 17-3023.01, 17-3023.03, 17-3024.00, 17-3025.00, 17-3026.00, 17-3027.00, 17-3029.99)

Significant Points

- Because the type and quality of training programs vary considerably, prospective students should carefully investigate training programs before enrolling.

- Electrical and electronic engineering technicians make up 33 percent of all engineering technicians.

- Employment of engineering technicians often is influenced by the same economic conditions that affect engineers; as a result, job outlook varies by specialty.

- Opportunities will be best for individuals with an associate degree or extensive job training in engineering technology.

Nature of the Work

Engineering technicians use the principles and theories of science, engineering, and mathematics to solve technical problems in research and development, manufacturing, sales, construction, inspection, and maintenance. Their work is more narrowly focused and application-oriented than that of scientists and engineers. Many engineering technicians assist engineers and scientists, especially in research and development. Others work in quality control, inspecting products and processes, conducting tests, or collecting data. In manufacturing, they may assist in product design, development, or production. Although many workers who repair or maintain various types of electrical, electronic, or mechanical equipment are called technicians, these workers are covered in the *Handbook* section on installation, maintenance, and repair occupations.

Engineering technicians who work in research and development build or set up equipment; prepare and conduct experiments; collect data; calculate or record results; and help engineers or scientists in other ways, such as making prototype versions of newly designed equipment. They also assist in design work, often using computer-aided design and drafting (CADD) equipment.

Most engineering technicians specialize, learning skills and working in the same disciplines as engineers. Occupational titles, therefore, tend to reflect this similarity. The *Handbook* does not cover in detail some branches of engineering technology, such as chemical engineering technology (the development of new chemical products and processes) and bioengineering technology (the development and implementation of biomedical equipment), for which there are accredited programs of study.

Aerospace engineering and operations technicians construct, test, and maintain aircraft and space vehicles. They may calibrate test equipment and determine causes of equipment malfunctions. Using computer and communications systems, aerospace engineering and operations technicians often record and interpret test data.

Civil engineering technicians help civil engineers plan and oversee the building of highways, buildings, bridges, dams, wastewater treatment systems, and other structures and do related research. Some estimate construction costs and specify materials to be used, and some may even prepare drawings or perform land-surveying duties. Others may set up and monitor instruments used to study traffic conditions. (Cost estimators; construction and building inspectors; drafters; and surveyors, cartographers, photogrammetrists, and surveying technicians are covered elsewhere in the *Handbook*.)

Electrical and electronics engineering technicians help design, develop, test, and manufacture electrical and electronic equipment such as communication equipment; radar, industrial, and medical monitoring or control devices; navigational equipment; and computers. They may work in product evaluation and testing, using measuring and diagnostic devices to adjust, test, and repair equipment. (Workers whose jobs primarily involve repairing electrical and electronic equipment are often referred to as electronics technicians, but they are included with electrical and electronics installers and repairers discussed elsewhere in the *Handbook*.)

Electromechanical engineering technicians combine knowledge of mechanical engineering technology with knowledge of electrical and electronic circuits to design, develop, test, and manufacture electronic and computer-controlled mechanical systems. Their work often overlaps that of both electrical and

Some engineering technicians assist engineers and scientists in data analysis.

electronics engineering technicians and mechanical engineering technicians.

Environmental engineering technicians work closely with environmental engineers and scientists in developing methods and devices used in the prevention, control, or correction of environmental hazards. They inspect and maintain equipment related to air pollution and recycling. Some inspect water and wastewater treatment systems to ensure that pollution control requirements are met.

Industrial engineering technicians study the efficient use of personnel, materials, and machines in factories, stores, repair shops, and offices. They prepare layouts of machinery and equipment, plan the flow of work, conduct statistical studies of production time or quality, and analyze production costs.

Mechanical engineering technicians help engineers design, develop, test, and manufacture industrial machinery, consumer products, and other equipment. They may assist in product tests by, for example, setting up instrumentation for auto crash tests. They may make sketches and rough layouts, record and analyze data, make calculations and estimates, and report on their findings. When planning production, mechanical engineering technicians prepare layouts and drawings of the assembly process and of parts to be manufactured. They estimate labor costs, equipment life, and plant space. Some test and inspect machines and equipment or work with engineers to eliminate production problems.

Work environment. Most engineering technicians work 40 hours a week in laboratories, offices, manufacturing or industrial plants, or on construction sites. Some may be exposed to hazards from equipment, chemicals, or toxic materials.

Training, Other Qualifications, and Advancement

Most engineering technicians enter the occupation with an associate degree in engineering technology. Training is available at technical institutes, community colleges, extension divisions of colleges and universities, public and private vocational-technical schools, and in the Armed Forces. Because the type and quality of training programs vary considerably, prospective students should carefully investigate training programs before enrolling.

Education and training. Although it may be possible to qualify for certain engineering technician jobs without formal training, most employers prefer to hire someone with at least a 2-year associate degree in engineering technology. People with college courses in science, engineering, and mathematics may qualify for some positions but may need additional specialized training and experience. Prospective engineering technicians should take as many high school science and math courses as possible to prepare for programs in engineering technology after high school.

Most 2-year associate degree programs accredited by the Technology Accreditation Commission of the Accreditation Board for Engineering and Technology (ABET) include at least college algebra and trigonometry and one or two basic science courses. Depending on the specialty, more math or science may be required. About 710 ABET-accredited programs are offered in engineering technology specialties.

The type of technical courses required depends on the specialty. For example, prospective mechanical engineering technicians may take courses in fluid mechanics, thermodynamics, and mechanical design; electrical engineering technicians may need classes in electrical circuits, microprocessors, and digital electronics; and those preparing to work in environmental engineering technology need courses in environmental regulations and safe handling of hazardous materials.

Many publicly and privately operated schools provide technical training, but the type and quality of training vary considerably. Therefore, prospective students should carefully select a program in line with their goals. They should ascertain prospective employers' preferences and ask schools to provide information about the kinds of jobs obtained by program graduates, about instructional facilities and equipment, and about faculty qualifications. Graduates of ABET-accredited programs usually are recognized as having achieved an acceptable level of competence in the mathematics, science, and technical courses required for this occupation.

Technical institutes offer intensive technical training through application and practice, but they provide less theory and general education than do community colleges. Many technical institutes offer 2-year associate degree programs and are similar to or part of a community college or State university system. Other technical institutes are run by private organizations, with programs that vary considerably in length and types of courses offered.

Community colleges offer curriculums that are similar to those in technical institutes but include more theory and liberal arts. There may be little or no difference between programs at technical institutes and community colleges, as both offer associate degrees. After completing the 2-year program, some graduates get jobs as engineering technicians, whereas others continue their education at 4-year colleges. However, an associate degree in pre-engineering is different from one in engineering technology. Students who enroll in a 2-year pre-engineering program may find it very difficult to find work as an engineering technician if they decide not to enter a 4-year engineering program because pre-engineering programs usually focus less on hands-on applications and more on academic preparatory work. Conversely, graduates of 2-year engineering technology programs may not receive credit for some of the courses they have taken if they choose to transfer to a 4-year engineering program. Colleges having 4-year programs usually do not offer engineering technician training, but college courses in science, engineering, and mathematics are useful for obtaining a job as an engineering technician. Many 4-year colleges offer bachelor's degrees in engineering technology, but graduates of these programs often are hired to work as technologists or applied engineers, not technicians.

Area vocational-technical schools, another source of technical training, include postsecondary public institutions that serve local students and emphasize training needed by local employers. Most require a high school diploma or its equivalent for admission.

Other training in technical areas may be obtained in the Armed Forces. Many military technical training programs are highly regarded by employers. However, skills acquired in military programs are often narrowly focused and may be of limited applicability in civilian industry, which often requires broader training. Therefore, some additional training may be needed, depending on the acquired skills and the kind of job.

Other qualifications. Because many engineering technicians assist in design work, creativity is desirable. Good communication skills and the ability to work well with others also are important as engineering technicians are typically part of a team of engineers and other technicians.

Certification and advancement. Although employers usually do not require engineering technicians to be certified, such certification may provide jobseekers a competitive advantage. The National Institute for Certification in Engineering Technologies has established voluntary certification programs for several engineering technology specialties. Certification is available at various levels, each level combining a written examination in a specialty with a certain amount of job-related experience, a supervisory evaluation, and a recommendation.

Engineering technicians usually begin by performing routine duties under the close supervision of an experienced technician, technologist, engineer, or scientist. As they gain experience, they are given more difficult assignments with only general supervision. Some engineering technicians eventually become supervisors.

Employment

Engineering technicians held 511,000 jobs in 2006. Approximately 33 percent were electrical and electronics engineering technicians, as indicated by the following tabulation.

Electrical and electronic engineering technicians...............170,000
Civil engineering technicians...91,000
Industrial engineering technicians 75,000
Mechanical engineering technicians.....................................48,000
Environmental engineering technicians...............................21,000
Electro-mechanical technicians 16,000
Aerospace engineering and operations technicians 8,500
Engineering technicians, except drafters, all other 82,000

About 35 percent of all engineering technicians worked in manufacturing, mainly in the computer and electronic equipment, transportation equipment, and machinery manufacturing industries. Another 25 percent worked in professional, scientific, and technical service industries, mostly in engineering or business services companies that do engineering work on contract for government, manufacturing firms, or other organizations.

In 2006, the Federal Government employed 37,000 engineering technicians. State governments employed 29,000, and local governments employed 25,000.

Job Outlook

Overall employment of engineering technicians is expected to grow about as fast as the average for all occupations, but projected growth and job prospects vary by specialty. Opportunities will be best for individuals with an associate degree or extensive job training in engineering technology.

Employment change. Overall employment of engineering technicians is expected to grow 7 percent between 2006 and 2016, about as fast as the average for all occupations. Competitive pressures will force companies to improve and update manufacturing facilities and product designs, resulting in more jobs for engineering technicians.

Growth of engineering technician employment in some design functions may be dampened by increasing globalization of the development process. To reduce costs and speed project completion, some companies may relocate part of their development operations to facilities overseas, impacting both engi-

Projections data from the National Employment Matrix

Occupational Title	SOC Code	Employment, 2006	Projected employment, 2016	Change, 2006-2016	
				Number	Percent
Engineering technicians, except drafters	17-3020	511,000	545,000	34,000	7
Aerospace engineering and operations technicians	17-3021	8,500	9,400	900	10
Civil engineering technicians..	17-3022	91,000	100,000	9,200	10
Electrical and electronic engineering technicians.........................	17-3023	170,000	177,000	6,100	4
Electro-mechanical technicians	17-3024	16,000	16,000	400	3
Environmental engineering technicians	17-3025	21,000	26,000	5,200	25
Industrial engineering technicians	17-3026	75,000	82,000	7,500	10
Mechanical engineering technicians..	17-3027	48,000	51,000	3,100	6
Engineering technicians, except drafters, all other	17-3029	82,000	83,000	1,600	2

NOTE: Data in this table are rounded. See the discussion of the employment projections table in the *Handbook* introductory chapter on *Occupational Information Included in the Handbook.*

neers and engineering technicians—particularly in electronics and computer-related specialties. However, much of the work of engineering technicians requires on-site presence, so demand for engineering technicians within the U.S. should continue to grow—particularly in the environmental, civil, and industrial specialties.

Because engineering technicians work closely with engineers, employment of engineering technicians is often influenced by the same local and national economic conditions that affect engineers. As a result, the employment outlook varies with industry and specialization.

Aerospace engineering and operations technicians are expected to have 10 percent employment growth between 2006 and 2016, about as fast as the average for all occupations. Increases in the number and scope of military aerospace projects likely will generate new jobs. New technologies to be used on commercial aircraft produced during the next decade should also spur demand for these workers.

Civil engineering technicians are expected to have 10 percent employment growth between 2006 and 2016, about as fast as the average for all occupations. Spurred by population growth and the related need to improve the Nation's infrastructure, more civil engineering technicians will be needed to expand transportation, water supply, and pollution control systems, as well as large buildings and building complexes. They also will be needed to repair or replace existing roads, bridges, and other public structures.

Electrical and electronic engineering technicians are expected to have 4 percent employment growth between 2006 and 2016, more slowly than the average for all occupations. Although rising demand for electronic goods—including communications equipment, defense-related equipment, medical electronics, and consumer products—should continue to drive demand, foreign competition in design and manufacturing will limit employment growth.

Electro-mechanical technicians are expected to have 3 percent employment growth between 2006 and 2016, more slowly than the average for all occupations. As with the closely-related electrical and electronic engineering technicians and mechanical engineering technicians, job growth should be driven by increasing demand for electro-mechanical products such as unmanned aircraft and robotic equipment. However, growth will be tempered by advances in productivity and strong foreign competition.

Environmental engineering technicians are expected to have 25 percent employment growth between 2006 and 2016, much faster than the average for all occupations. More environmental engineering technicians will be needed to comply with environmental regulations and to develop methods of cleaning up existing hazards. A shift in emphasis toward preventing problems rather than controlling those that already exist, as well as increasing public health concerns resulting from population growth, also will spur demand.

Industrial engineering technicians are expected to have 10 percent employment growth between 2006 and 2016, about as fast as the average for all occupations. As firms continue to seek new means of reducing costs and increasing productivity, demand for industrial engineering technicians to analyze and improve production processes should increase. This should lead to some job growth even in manufacturing industries with slowly growing or declining employment.

Mechanical engineering technicians are expected to have 6 percent employment growth between 2006 and 2016, more slowly than the average for all occupations. As mechanical products and components become increasingly complex, demand for improvements in these products should drive employment growth of mechanical engineering technicians. However, growth is expected to be limited by foreign competition in both design services and manufacturing.

Job prospects. Job prospects will vary by specialty and location, depending on the health and composition of local industry. In general, opportunities will be best for individuals with an associate degree or extensive job training in engineering technology. As technology becomes more sophisticated, employers will continue to look for technicians who are skilled in new technology and require little additional training. An increase in the number of jobs related to public health and safety should create job opportunities for engineering technicians with the appropriate training and certification. In addition to openings from job growth, many job openings will stem from the need to replace technicians who retire or leave the labor force.

Earnings

Median annual earnings in May 2006 of engineering technicians by specialty are shown in the following tabulation.

Aerospace engineering and operations technicians $53,300
Electrical and electronic engineering technicians.................50,660
Industrial engineering technicians 46,810
Mechanical engineering technicians.....................................45,850
Electro-mechanical technicians 44,720
Civil engineering technicians...40,560
Environmental engineering technicians 40,560

Median annual earnings of wage-and-salary electrical and electronics engineering technicians were $50,660 in May 2006. The middle 50 percent earned between $39,270 and $60,470. The lowest 10 percent earned less than $30,120, and the highest 10 percent earned more than $73,200. Median annual earnings in the industries employing the largest numbers of electrical and electronics engineering technicians are:

Wired telecommunications carriers $54,780
Engineering services 48,330
Semiconductor and other
    electronic component manufacturing................................45,720
Navigational, measuring, electromedical,
    and control instruments manufacturing 45,140
Employment services...38,910

Median annual earnings of wage-and-salary civil engineering technicians were $40,560 in May 2006. The middle 50 percent earned between $31,310 and $51,230. The lowest 10 percent earned less than $25,250, and the highest 10 percent earned more than $62,920. Median annual earnings in the industries employing the largest numbers of civil engineering technicians are:

Local government $45,800
Architectural services..42,310
Engineering services 41,180
State government...35,870
Testing laboratories..31,800

In May 2006, the median annual salary for aerospace engineering and operations technicians in the aerospace products and parts manufacturing industry was $52,060, and the median annual salary for environmental engineering technicians in the architectural, engineering, and related services industry was $38,060. The median annual salary for industrial engineering technicians in the aerospace product and parts manufacturing industry was $57,330. In the architectural, engineering, and related services industry, the median annual salary for mechanical engineering technicians was $43,920. Electro-mechanical technicians earned a median salary of $41,550 in the navigational, measuring, electromedical, and control instruments manufacturing industry.

Related Occupations

Engineering technicians apply scientific and engineering skills usually gained in postsecondary programs below the bachelor's degree level. Similar occupations include science technicians; drafters; surveyors, cartographers, photogrammetrists, and surveying technicians; and broadcast and sound engineering technicians and radio operators.

Sources of Additional Information

For information about careers in engineering technology, contact:

➤ JETS (Junior Engineering Technical Society) Guidance, 1420 King St., Suite 405, Alexandria, VA 22314.
Internet: **http://www.jets.org**

Information on engineering technology programs accredited by the Accreditation Board for Engineering and Technology is available from:

➤ ABET, Inc., 111 Market Place, Suite 1050, Baltimore, MD 21202. Internet: **http://www.abet.org**

Information on certification, as well as job and career information, is available from:

➤ National Institute for Certification in Engineering Technologies, 1420 King St., Alexandria, VA 22314.
Internet: **http://www.nicet.org**

Life Scientists

Agricultural and Food Scientists

(O*NET 19–1011.00, 19–1012.00, 19–1013.00)

Significant Points

- About 14 percent of agricultural and food scientists work for Federal, State, or local governments.

- A bachelor's degree in agricultural science is sufficient for some jobs in product development; a master's or Ph.D. degree is required for research or teaching.

- Opportunities for agricultural and food scientists are expected to be good over the next decade, particularly for those holding a master's or Ph.D. degree.

Nature of the Work

The work of agricultural and food scientists plays an important part in maintaining the Nation's food supply by ensuring agricultural productivity and food safety. Agricultural scientists study farm crops and animals and develop ways of improving their quantity and quality. They look for ways to improve crop yield with less labor, control pests and weeds more safely and effectively, and conserve soil and water. They research methods of converting raw agricultural commodities into attractive and healthy food products for consumers. Some agricultural scientists look for ways to use agricultural products for fuels.

In the past two decades, rapid advances in the study of genetics have spurred the growth of biotechnology. Some agricultural and food scientists use biotechnology to manipulate the genetic material of plants and crops, attempting to make these organisms more productive or resistant to disease. Advances in biotechnology have opened up research opportunities in many areas of agricultural and food science, including commercial applications in agriculture, environmental remediation, and the food industry. Interest in the production of biofuels, or fuels manufactured from agricultural derivatives, has also increased. Some agricultural scientists work with biologists and chemists to develop processes for turning crops into energy sources, such as ethanol produced from corn.

Another emerging technology expected to affect agriculture is nanotechnology—a molecular manufacturing technology which promises to revolutionize methods of testing agricultural and food products for contamination or spoilage. Some food scientists are using nanotechnology to develop sensors that can quickly and accurately detect contaminant molecules in food.

Many agricultural scientists work in basic or applied research and development. Basic research seeks to understand the biological and chemical processes by which crops and livestock grow, such as determining the role of a particular gene in plant growth. Applied research uses this knowledge to discover mechanisms to improve the quality, quantity, or safety of agricultural products. Other agricultural scientists manage or administer research and development programs, or manage marketing or production operations in companies that produce food products or agricultural chemicals, supplies, and machinery. Some agricultural scientists are consultants to business firms, private clients, or government.

Depending on the agricultural or food scientist's area of specialization, the nature of the work performed varies.

Food scientists and technologists usually work in the food processing industry, universities, or the Federal Government to create and improve food products. They use their knowledge of chemistry, physics, engineering, microbiology, biotechnology, and other sciences to develop new or better ways of preserving, processing, packaging, storing, and delivering foods. Some food scientists engage in basic research, discovering new food sources; analyzing food content to determine levels of vitamins, fat, sugar, or protein; or searching for substitutes for harmful or undesirable additives, such as nitrites. Others engage in applied research, finding ways to improve the content of food or to remove harmful additives. They also develop ways to process, preserve, package, or store food according to industry and government regulations. Traditional food processing research into baking, blanching, canning, drying, evaporation, and pasteurization also continues. Other food scientists enforce government regulations, inspecting food processing areas and ensuring that sanitation, safety, quality, and waste management standards are met.

Food technologists generally work in product development, applying the findings from food science research to improve the selection, preservation, processing, packaging, and distribution of food.

Plant scientists study plants, helping producers of food, feed, and fiber crops to feed a growing population and conserve natural resources. *Agronomists* and *crop scientists* not only help increase productivity, but also study ways to improve the nutritional value of crops and the quality of seed, often through biotechnology. Some crop scientists study the breeding, physiology, and management of crops and use genetic engineering to develop crops resistant to pests and drought. Some plant scientists develop new technologies to control or eliminate pests and prevent their spread in ways appropriate to the specific environment. They also conduct research or oversee activities to halt the spread of insect-borne disease.

Soil scientists study the chemical, physical, biological, and mineralogical composition of soils as it relates to plant growth. They also study the responses of various soil types to fertilizers, tillage practices, and crop rotation. Many soil scientists who work for the Federal Government conduct soil surveys, classifying and mapping soils. They provide information and recommendations to farmers and other landowners regarding the best use of land and plants to avoid or correct problems, such as erosion. They may also consult with engineers and other technical personnel working on construction projects about the effects of, and solutions to, soil problems. Because soil science is closely related to environmental science, persons trained in soil science also work to ensure environmental quality and effective land use.

Animal scientists work to develop better, more efficient ways of producing and processing meat, poultry, eggs, and milk. Dairy scientists, poultry scientists, animal breeders, and other scientists in related fields study the genetics, nutrition, repro-

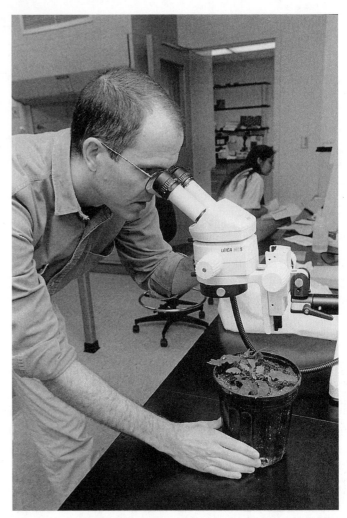

Agicultural and food scientists often work in offices or labratories.

duction, and growth of domestic farm animals. Some animal scientists inspect and grade livestock food products, purchase livestock, or work in technical sales or marketing. As extension agents or consultants, animal scientists advise agricultural producers on how to upgrade animal housing facilities properly, lower mortality rates, handle waste matter, or increase production of animal products, such as milk or eggs.

Work environment. Agricultural scientists involved in management or basic research tend to work regular hours in offices and laboratories. The work environment for those engaged in applied research or product development varies, depending on specialty and on type of employer. For example, food scientists in private industry may work in test kitchens while investigating new processing techniques. Animal scientists working for Federal, State, or university research stations may spend part of their time at dairies, farrowing houses, feedlots, farm animal facilities, or outdoors conducting research. Soil and crop scientists also spend time outdoors conducting research on farms and agricultural research stations.

Training, Other Qualifications, and Advancement

Most agricultural and food scientists need at least a master's degree to work in basic or applied research, whereas a bachelor's degree is sufficient for some jobs in applied research or product development, or jobs in other occupations related to agricultural science.

Education and training. Training requirements for agricultural scientists depend on the type of work they perform. A bachelor's degree in agricultural science is sufficient for some jobs in product development or assisting in applied research, but a master's or doctoral degree is generally required for basic research or for jobs directing applied research. A Ph.D. in agricultural science usually is needed for college teaching and for advancement to senior research positions. Degrees in related sciences such as biology, chemistry, or physics or in related engineering specialties also may qualify people for many agricultural science jobs.

All States have a land-grant college that offers agricultural science degrees. Many other colleges and universities also offer agricultural science degrees or agricultural science courses. However, not every school offers all specialties. A typical undergraduate agricultural science curriculum includes communications, mathematics, economics, business, and physical and life sciences courses, in addition to a wide variety of technical agricultural science courses. For prospective animal scientists, these technical agricultural science courses might include animal breeding, reproductive physiology, nutrition, and meats and muscle biology. Graduate students usually specialize in a subfield of agricultural science, such as animal breeding and genetics, crop science, or horticulture science, depending on their interests. For example, those interested in doing genetic and biotechnological research in the food industry need a strong background in life and physical sciences, such as cell and molecular biology, microbiology, and inorganic and organic chemistry. Undergraduate students, however, need not specialize. In fact, undergraduates who are broadly trained often have greater career flexibility.

Students preparing to be food scientists take courses such as food chemistry, food analysis, food microbiology, food engineering, and food processing operations. Those preparing as soil and plant scientists take courses in plant pathology, soil chemistry, entomology, plant physiology, and biochemistry, among others. Advanced degree programs include classroom and fieldwork, laboratory research, and a thesis or dissertation based on independent research.

Other qualifications. Agricultural and food scientists should be able to work independently or as part of a team and be able to communicate clearly and concisely, both orally and in writing. Most of these scientists also need an understanding of basic business principles, the ability to apply statistical techniques, and the ability to use computers to analyze data and to control biological and chemical processing.

Certification and advancement. Agricultural scientists who have advanced degrees usually begin in research or teaching. With experience, they may advance to jobs as supervisors of research programs or managers of other agriculture-related activities.

The American Society of Agronomy certifies agronomists and crop advisors, and the Soil Science Society of America certifies soil scientists and soil classifiers. To become certified in soil science or soil classification, applicants must have a bachelor's degree in soil science and 5 years of experience or a graduate degree and 3 years experience. Certification in agronomy requires a bachelor's degree in agronomy or a related field and 5 years experience or a graduate degree and 3 years. Crop advising certification requires either 4 years of experience or a bachelor's degree in agriculture and 2 years of experience. To receive any of these certifications, applicants must also pass designated examinations and agree to adhere to a code of ethics. Each certification is maintained through continuing education.

Employment

Agricultural and food scientists held about 33,000 jobs in 2006. In addition, many people trained in these sciences held faculty positions in colleges and universities. (See the statement on postsecondary teachers elsewhere in the *Handbook*.)

About 14 percent of agricultural and food scientists work for Federal, State, or local governments. State and local governments employed about 5 percent, while the Federal Government employed another 9 percent in 2006, mostly in the U.S. Department of Agriculture. Educational services accounted for another 18 percent of jobs. Other agricultural and food scientists worked for agricultural service companies, commercial research and development laboratories, seed companies, wholesale distributors, and food products companies. About 5,500 agricultural scientists were self-employed in 2006, mainly as consultants.

Job Outlook

Job growth among agricultural and food scientists should be about as fast as the average for all occupations. Opportunities are expected to be good over the next decade, particularly for those holding a master's or Ph.D. degree.

Employment change. Employment of agricultural and food scientists is expected to grow 9 percent between 2006 and 2016, about as fast as the average for all occupations. Past agricultural research has created higher yielding crops, crops with bet-

Projections data from the National Employment Matrix

Occupational Title	SOC Code	Employment, 2006	Projected employment, 2016	Change, 2006-2016	
				Number	Percent
Agricultural and food scientists	19-1010	33,000	36,000	3,100	9
Animal scientists..	19-1011	5,400	5,900	500	10
Food scientists and technologists...............................	19-1012	12,000	13,000	1,200	10
Soil and plant Scientists..	19-1013	16,000	17,000	1,300	8

NOTE: Data in this table are rounded. See the discussion of the employment projections table in the *Handbook* introductory chapter on *Occupational Information Included in the Handbook*.

ter resistance to pests and plant pathogens, and more effective fertilizers and pesticides. Research is still necessary, however, particularly as insects and diseases continue to adapt to pesticides and as soil fertility and water quality continue to need improvement. This creates more jobs for agricultural scientists.

Emerging biotechnologies will play an ever larger role in agricultural research. Scientists will be needed to apply these technologies to the creation of new food products and other advances. Moreover, increasing demand is expected for biofuels and other agricultural products used in industrial processes. Agricultural scientists will be needed to find ways to increase the output of crops used in these products.

Agricultural scientists will also be needed to balance increased agricultural output with protection and preservation of soil, water, and ecosystems. They increasingly encourage the practice of sustainable agriculture by developing and implementing plans to manage pests, crops, soil fertility and erosion, and animal waste in ways that reduce the use of harmful chemicals and do little damage to farms and the natural environment.

Job growth for food scientists and technologists will be driven by the demand for new food products and food safety measures. Food research is expected to increase because of heightened public awareness of diet, health, food safety, and biosecurity—preventing the introduction of infectious agents into herds of animals. Advances in biotechnology and nanotechnology should also spur demand, as food scientists and technologists apply these technologies to testing and monitoring food safety.

Fewer new jobs for agricultural and food scientists are expected in the Federal Government, mostly because of budgetary constraints at the U.S. Department of Agriculture.

Job prospects. Opportunities should be good for agricultural and food scientists with a master's degree, particularly those seeking applied research positions in a laboratory. Master's degree candidates also can seek to become certified crop advisors, helping farmers better manage their crops. Those with a Ph.D. in agricultural and food science will experience the best opportunities, especially in basic research and teaching positions at colleges and universities.

Graduates with a bachelor's degree in agricultural or food science can sometimes work in applied research and product development positions under the guidance of a Ph.D. scientist, but usually only in certain subfields, such as food science and technology. The Federal Government also hires bachelor's degree holders to work as soil scientists.

Most people with bachelor's degrees find work in positions related to agricultural or food science rather than in jobs as agricultural or food scientists. A bachelor's degree in agricultural science is useful for managerial jobs in farm-related or ranch-related businesses, such as farm credit institutions or companies that manufacture or sell feed, fertilizer, seed, and farm equipment. In some cases, people with a bachelor's degree can provide consulting services or work in sales and marketing—promoting high-demand products such as organic foods. Bachelor's degrees also may help people become farmers, ranchers, and agricultural managers; agricultural inspectors; or purchasing agents for agricultural commodity or farm supply companies.

Employment of agricultural and food scientists is relatively stable during periods of economic recession. Layoffs are less likely among agricultural and food scientists than in some other occupations because food is a staple item and its demand fluctuates very little with economic activity.

Earnings

Median annual earnings of food scientists and technologists were $53,810 in May 2006. The middle 50 percent earned between $37,740 and $76,960. The lowest 10 percent earned less than $29,620, and the highest 10 percent earned more than $97,350. Median annual earnings of soil and plant scientists were $56,080 in May 2006. The middle 50 percent earned between $42,410 and $72,020. The lowest 10 percent earned less than $33,650, and the highest 10 percent earned more than $93,460. In May 2006, median annual earnings of animal scientists were $47,800.

The average Federal salary in 2007 was $91,491 in animal science and $79,051 in agronomy.

According to the National Association of Colleges and Employers, beginning salary offers in 2007 for graduates with a bachelor's degree in animal sciences averaged $35,035 a year; plant sciences, $31,291 a year; and in other agricultural sciences, $37,908 a year.

Related Occupations

The work of agricultural scientists is closely related to that of other scientists, including biological scientists, chemists, and conservation scientists and foresters. It also is related to the work of managers of agricultural production, such as farmers, ranchers, and agricultural managers. Certain specialties of agricultural science also are related to other occupations. For example, the work of animal scientists is related to the work of veterinarians.

Sources of Additional Information

Information on careers in agricultural science is available from:

➤ American Society of Agronomy, Crop Science Society of America, Soil Science Society of America, 677 S. Segoe Rd., Madison, WI 53711-1086.
Internet: **http://www.agronomy.org**

➤ Living Science, Purdue University, 1140 Agricultural Administration Bldg., West Lafayette, IN 47907-1140.
Internet: **http://www.agriculture.purdue.edu/USDA/careers**

Information on careers in food science and technology is available from:

➤ Institute of Food Technologists, 525 W. Van Buren, Suite 1000, Chicago, IL 60607. Internet: **http://www.ift.org**

Information on getting a job as an agricultural scientist with the Federal Government is available from the Office of Personnel Management through USAJOBS, the Federal Government's official employment information system. This resource for locating and applying for job opportunities can be accessed through the Internet at **http://www.usajobs.opm.gov** or through an interactive voice response telephone system at (703) 724-1850 or TDD (978) 461-8404. These numbers are not tollfree, and charges may result.

Biological Scientists

(O*NET 19-1021.00, 19-1022.00, 19-1023.00, 19-1029.99)

Significant Points

- Biotechnological research and development should continue to drive employment growth.

- A Ph.D. degree usually is required for independent research, but a master's degree is sufficient for some jobs in applied research or product development; temporary postdoctoral research positions are common.

- Competition for jobs is expected.

Nature of the Work

Biological scientists study living organisms and their relationship to the environment. They perform research to gain a better understanding of fundamental life processes or apply that understanding to developing new products or processes. Most specialize in one area of biology, such as zoology (the study of animals) or microbiology (the study of microscopic organisms). (Medical scientists, whose work is closely related to that of biological scientists, are discussed elsewhere in the *Handbook*.)

Many biological scientists work in research and development. Some conduct basic research to advance our knowledge of living organisms, including bacteria and other infectious agents. Basic biological research enhances our understanding so that we can develop solutions to human health problems and improve the natural environment. These biological scientists mostly work in government, university, or private industry laboratories, often exploring new areas of research. Many expand on specialized research they started in graduate school.

Many research scientists must submit grant proposals to obtain funding for their projects. Colleges and universities, private industry, and Federal Government agencies such as the National Institutes of Health and the National Science Foundation contribute to the support of scientists whose research proposals are determined to be financially feasible and to have the potential to advance new ideas or processes.

Biological scientists who work in applied research or product development use knowledge gained by basic research to develop new drugs, treatments, and medical diagnostic tests; increase crop yields; and develop new biofuels. They usually have less freedom than basic researchers do to choose the emphasis of their research, and they spend more time working on marketable treatments to meet the business goals of their employers. Biological scientists doing applied research and product development in private industry may be required to describe their research plans or results to nonscientists who are in a position to veto or approve their ideas. These scientists must consider the business effects of their work. Scientists often work in teams, interacting with engineers, scientists of other disciplines, business managers, and technicians. Some biological scientists also work with customers or suppliers and manage budgets.

Scientists usually conduct research in laboratories using a wide variety of other equipment. Some conduct experiments involving animals or plants. This is particularly true of botanists, physiologists, and zoologists. Some biological research also takes place outside the laboratory. For example, a botanist might do field research in tropical rain forests to see which plants grow there, or an ecologist might study how a forest area recovers after a fire. Some marine biologists also work outdoors, often on research vessels from which they study fish, plankton, or other marine organisms.

Swift advances in knowledge of genetics and organic molecules spurred growth in the field of biotechnology, transforming the industries in which biological scientists work. Biological scientists can now manipulate the genetic material of animals and plants, attempting to make organisms more productive or resistant to disease. Basic and applied research on biotechnological processes, such as recombining DNA, has led to the production of important substances, including human insulin and growth hormone. Many other substances not previously available in large quantities are now produced by biotechnological means. Some of these substances are useful in treating diseases.

Today, many biological scientists are involved in biotechnology. Those working on various genome (chromosomes with their associated genes) projects isolate genes and determine their function. This work continues to lead to the discovery of genes associated with specific diseases and inherited health risks, such as sickle cell anemia. Advances in biotechnology have created research opportunities in almost all areas of biology, with commercial applications in areas such as medicine, agriculture, and environmental remediation.

Most biological scientists specialize in the study of a certain type of organism or in a specific activity, although recent advances have blurred some traditional classifications.

Aquatic biologists study micro-organisms, plants, and animals living in water. *Marine biologists* study salt water organisms, and *limnologists* study fresh water organisms. Much of the work of marine biology centers on molecular biology, the study of the biochemical processes that take place inside living cells. Marine biologists sometimes are mistakenly called oceanographers, but oceanography is the study of the physical characteristics of oceans and the ocean floor. (See the *Handbook* statements on environmental scientists and hydrologists and on geoscientists.)

Biochemists study the chemical composition of living things. They analyze the complex chemical combinations and reactions involved in metabolism, reproduction, and growth. Biochemists do most of their work in biotechnology, which involves understanding the complex chemistry of life.

Botanists study plants and their environments. Some study all aspects of plant life, including algae, fungi, lichens, mosses, ferns, conifers, and flowering plants; others specialize in areas such as identification and classification of plants, the structure and function of plant parts, the biochemistry of plant processes, the causes and cures of plant diseases, the interaction of plants with other organisms and the environment, and the geological record of plants.

Microbiologists investigate the growth and characteristics of microscopic organisms such as bacteria, algae, or fungi. Most microbiologists specialize in environmental, food, agricultural, or industrial microbiology; virology (the study of viruses); immunology (the study of mechanisms that fight infections); or bioinformatics (the use of computers to handle or characterize biological information, usually at the molecular level). Many microbiologists use biotechnology to advance knowledge of cell reproduction and human disease.

Physiologists study life functions of plants and animals, both in the whole organism and at the cellular or molecular level, under normal and abnormal conditions. Physiologists often specialize in functions such as growth, reproduction, photosynthesis, respiration, or movement, or in the physiology of a certain area or system of the organism.

Biophysicists study how physics, such as electrical and mechanical energy and related phenomena, relates to living cells and organisms. They perform research in fields such as neuroscience or bioinformatics.

Zoologists and wildlife biologists study animals and wildlife—their origin, behavior, diseases, and life processes. Some experiment with live animals in controlled or natural surroundings, while others dissect dead animals to study their structure. Zoologists and wildlife biologists also may collect and analyze biological data to determine the environmental effects of current and potential uses of land and water areas. Zoologists usually are identified by the animal group they study—ornithologists study birds, for example, mammalogists study mammals, herpetologists study reptiles, and ichthyologists study fish.

Ecologists investigate the relationships among organisms and between organisms and their environments, examining the effects of population size, pollutants, rainfall, temperature, and altitude. Using knowledge of various scientific disciplines, ecologists may collect, study, and report data on the quality of air, food, soil, and water.

(Agricultural and food scientists, sometimes referred to as biological scientists, are discussed elsewhere in the *Handbook*, as are medical scientists, whose work is closely related to that of biological scientists.)

Work environment. Biological scientists usually are not exposed to unsafe or unhealthy conditions. Those who work with dangerous organisms or toxic substances in the laboratory must follow strict safety procedures to avoid contamination. Many biological scientists, such as botanists, ecologists, and zoologists, do field studies that involve strenuous physical activity and primitive living conditions. Biological scientists in the field may work in warm or cold climates, in all kinds of weather.

Marine biologists encounter a variety of working conditions. Some work in laboratories; others work on research ships, and those who work underwater must practice safe diving while working around sharp coral reefs and hazardous marine life. Although some marine biologists obtain their specimens from the sea, many still spend a good deal of their time in laboratories and offices, conducting tests, running experiments, recording results, and compiling data.

Many biological scientists depend on grant money to support their research. They may be under pressure to meet deadlines and to conform to rigid grant-writing specifications when preparing proposals to seek new or extended funding.

Biological scientists typically work regular hours. While the 40-hour workweek is common, longer hours are not uncommon.

A Ph.D. usually is required for independent research.

Researchers may be required to work odd hours in laboratories or other locations (especially while in the field), depending on the nature of their research.

Training, Other Qualifications, and Advancement
Most biological scientists need a Ph.D. degree in biology or one of its subfields to work in research or development positions. A period of postdoctoral work in the laboratory of a senior researcher has become common for biological scientists who intend to conduct research or teach at the university level.

Education and training. A Ph.D. degree usually is necessary for independent research, industrial research, and college teaching, as well as for advancement to administrative positions. A master's degree is sufficient for some jobs in applied research, product development, management, or inspection; it also may qualify one to work as a research technician or a teacher. The bachelor's degree is adequate for some nonresearch jobs. For example, graduates with a bachelor's degree may start as biological scientists in testing and inspection or may work in jobs related to biological science, such as technical sales or service representatives. Some work as research assistants, laboratory technicians, or high school biology teachers. (See the statements elsewhere in the *Handbook* on clinical laboratory technologists and technicians; science technicians; and teachers—preschool, kindergarten, elementary, middle, and secondary.) Many with a bachelor's degree in biology enter medical, dental, veterinary, or other health profession schools.

In addition to required courses in chemistry and biology, undergraduate biological science majors usually study allied disciplines such as mathematics, physics, engineering, and computer science. Computer courses are beneficial for modeling and simulating biological processes, operating some laboratory equipment, and performing research in the emerging field of bioinformatics. Those interested in studying the environment also should take courses in environmental studies and become familiar with applicable legislation and regulations. Prospective biological scientists who hope to work as marine biologists should have at least a bachelor's degree in a biological or marine science. However, students should not overspecialize in undergraduate study, as knowledge of marine biology often is acquired in graduate study.

Most colleges and universities offer bachelor's degrees in biological science, and many offer advanced degrees. Advanced degree programs often emphasize a subfield such as microbiology or botany, but not all universities offer curricula in all subfields. Larger universities frequently have separate departments specializing in different areas of biological science. For example, a program in botany might cover agronomy, horticulture, or plant pathology. Advanced degree programs typically include classroom and fieldwork, laboratory research, and a thesis or dissertation.

Biological scientists with a Ph.D. often take temporary postdoctoral research positions that provide specialized research experience. Postdoctoral positions may offer the opportunity to publish research findings. A solid record of published research is essential in obtaining a permanent position involving basic research, especially for those seeking a permanent college or university faculty position.

Other qualifications. Biological scientists should be able to work independently or as part of a team and be able to communicate clearly and concisely, both orally and in writing. Those in private industry, especially those who aspire to management or administrative positions, should possess strong business and communication skills and be familiar with regulatory issues and marketing and management techniques. Those doing field research in remote areas must have physical stamina. Biological scientists also must have patience and self-discipline to conduct long and detailed research projects.

Advancement. As they gain experience, biological scientists typically gain greater control over their research and may advance to become lead researchers directing a team of scientists and technicians. Some work as consultants to businesses or to government agencies. However, those dependent on research grants are still constrained by funding agencies, and they may spend much of their time writing grant proposals. Others choose to move into managerial positions and become natural science managers (see engineering and natural science managers elsewhere in the *Handbook*). They may plan and administer programs for testing foods and drugs, for example, or direct activities at zoos or botanical gardens. Those who pursue management careers spend much of their time preparing budgets and schedules. Some leave biology for nontechnical managerial, administrative, or sales jobs.

Employment

Biological scientists held about 87,000 jobs in 2006. In addition, many biological scientists held biology faculty positions in colleges and universities but are not included in these numbers. Those whose primary work involves teaching and research are considered postsecondary teachers. (See the statement on teachers—postsecondary elsewhere in the *Handbook*.)

About 39 percent of all biological scientists were employed by Federal, State, and local governments. Federal biological scientists worked mainly for the U.S. Departments of Agriculture, Interior, and Defense and for the National Institutes of Health. Most of the rest worked in scientific research and testing laboratories, the pharmaceutical and medicine manufacturing industry, or colleges and universities.

Job Outlook

Biological scientists can expect to face competition for jobs. After a recent period of rapid expansion in research funding, moderate growth in research grants should drive average employment growth over the next decade.

Employment change. Employment of biological scientists is projected to grow 9 percent over the 2006-16 decade, about as fast as the average for all occupations, as biotechnological research and development continues to drive job growth. The Federal Government funds much basic research and development, including many areas of medical research that relate to biological science. Recent budget increases at the National Institutes of Health have led to large increases in Federal basic research and development expenditures, with research grants growing both in number and dollar amount. Nevertheless, the increase in expenditures has slowed substantially and is not expected to match its past growth over the 2006-16 projection period. This may result in a highly competitive environment for winning and renewing research grants.

Biological scientists enjoyed very rapid employment gains since the 1980s—reflecting, in part, the growth of biotechnology companies. Employment growth should slow somewhat,

Projections data from the National Employment Matrix

Occupational Title	SOC Code	Employment, 2006	Projected employment, 2016	Change, 2006-2016	
				Number	Percent
Biological scientists	19-1020	87,000	95,000	8,000	9
Biochemists and biophysicists....................................	19-1021	20,000	23,000	3,200	16
Microbiologists	19-1022	17,000	19,000	1,900	11
Zoologists and wildlife biologists..............................	19-1023	20,000	22,000	1,700	9
Biological scientists, all other....................................	19-1029	29,000	30,000	1,100	4

NOTE: Data in this table are rounded. See the discussion of the employment projections table in the *Handbook* introductory chapter on *Occupational Information Included in the Handbook.*

as fewer new biotechnology firms are founded and existing firms merge or are absorbed by larger biotechnology or pharmaceutical firms. Some companies may conduct a portion of their research and development in other lower-wage countries, further limiting employment growth. However, much of the basic biological research done in recent years has resulted in new knowledge, including the isolation and identification of genes. Biological scientists will be needed to take this knowledge to the next stage, which is the understanding how certain genes function within an entire organism, so that medical treatments can be developed to treat various diseases. Even pharmaceutical and other firms not solely engaged in biotechnology use biotechnology techniques extensively, spurring employment increases for biological scientists. For example, biological scientists are continuing to help farmers increase crop yields by pinpointing genes that can help crops such as wheat grow worldwide in areas that currently are hostile to the crop. Continued work on chronic diseases should also lead to growing demand for biological scientists.

In addition, efforts to discover new and improved ways to clean up and preserve the environment will continue to add to job growth. More biological scientists will be needed to determine the environmental impact of industry and government actions and to prevent or correct environmental problems such as the negative effects of pesticide use. Some biological scientists will find opportunities in environmental regulatory agencies, while others will use their expertise to advise lawmakers on legislation to save environmentally sensitive areas. New industrial applications of biotechnology, such as new methods for making ethanol for transportation fuel, also will spur demand for biological scientists.

There will continue to be demand for biological scientists specializing in botany, zoology, and marine biology, but opportunities will be limited because of the small size of these fields. Marine biology, despite its attractiveness as a career, is a very small specialty within biological science.

Job prospects. Doctoral degree holders are expected to face competition for basic research positions. Furthermore, should the number of advanced degrees awarded continue to grow, applicants for research grants are likely to face even more competition. Currently, about 1 in 4 grant proposals are approved for long-term research projects. In addition, applied research positions in private industry may become more difficult to obtain if increasing numbers of scientists seek jobs in private industry because of the competitive job market for independent research positions in universities and for college and university faculty.

Prospective marine biology students should be aware that those who would like to enter this specialty far outnumber the very few openings that occur each year for the type of glamorous research jobs that many would like to obtain. Almost all marine biologists who do basic research have a Ph.D.

People with bachelor's and master's degrees are expected to have more opportunities in nonscientist jobs related to biology. The number of science-related jobs in sales, marketing, and research management is expected to exceed the number of independent research positions. Non-Ph.D.s also may fill positions as science or engineering technicians or as medical health technologists and technicians. Some become high school biology teachers.

Biological scientists are less likely to lose their jobs during recessions than are those in many other occupations because many are employed on long-term research projects. However, an economic downturn could influence the amount of money allocated to new research and development efforts, particularly in areas of risky or innovative research. An economic downturn also could limit the possibility of extension or renewal of existing projects.

Earnings

Median annual earnings of biochemists and biophysicists were $76,320 in 2006. The middle 50 percent earned between $53,390 and $100,060. The lowest 10 percent earned less than $40,820, and the highest 10 percent earned more than $129,510. Median annual earnings of biochemists and biophysicists employed in scientific research and development services were $79,990 in 2006.

Median annual earnings of microbiologists were 57,980 in 2006. The middle 50 percent earned between $43,850 and $80,550. The lowest 10 percent earned less than $35,460, and the highest 10 percent earned more than $108,270.

Median annual earnings of zoologists and wildlife biologists were $53,300 in 2006. The middle 50 percent earned between $41,400 and $67,200. The lowest 10 percent earned less than $32,800, and the highest 10 percent earned more than $84,580.

According to the National Association of Colleges and Employers, beginning salary offers in 2007 averaged $34,953 a year for bachelor's degree recipients in biological and life sciences.

In the Federal Government in 2007, general biological scientists earned an average salary of $72,146; microbiologists, $87,206; ecologists, $76,511; physiologists, $100,745; geneticists, $91,470; zoologists, $110,456; and botanists, $67,218.

Related Occupations

Many other occupations deal with living organisms and require a level of training similar to that of biological scientists. These include medical scientists, agricultural and food scientists, conservation scientists and foresters, and engineering and natural sciences managers, as well as health occupations such as physicians and surgeons, dentists, and veterinarians.

Sources of Additional Information

For information on careers in the biological sciences, contact:
➤ American Institute of Biological Sciences, 1444 I St.NW., Suite 200, Washington, DC 20005.
Internet: **http://www.aibs.org**

For information on careers in biochemistry or biological sciences, contact:
➤ Federation of American Societies for Experimental Biology, 9650 Rockville Pike, Bethesda, MD 20814.
Internet: **http://www.faseb.org**

For information on careers in botany, contact:
➤ The Botanical Society of America, 4475 Castleman Ave., P.O. Box 299, St.Louis, MO 63166.
Internet: **http://www.botany.org**

For information on careers in physiology, contact:

➤ American Physiology Society, 9650 Rockville Pike, Bethesda, MD 20814. Internet: **http://www.the-aps.org**

Information on obtaining a biological scientist position with the Federal Government is available from the Office of Personnel Management through USAJOBS, the Federal Government's official employment information system. This resource for locating and applying for job opportunities can be accessed through the Internet at **http://www.usajobs.opm.gov** or through an interactive voice response telephone system at (703) 724-1850 or TDD (978) 461-8404. These numbers are not tollfree, and charges may result.

Conservation Scientists and Foresters

(O*NET 19-1031.00, 19-1031.01, 19-1031.02, 19-1031.03, 19-1032.00)

Significant Points

- About 2 of 3 conservation scientists and foresters work for Federal, State, or local governments.

- Workers in this occupation need, at a minimum, a bachelor's degree in forestry, environmental science, range management, or a related discipline.

- Slower than average job growth is projected; most new jobs will be in governments and in private sector forestry and conservation consulting.

Nature of the Work

Forests and rangelands supply wood products, livestock forage, minerals, and water. They serve as sites for recreational activities and provide habitats for wildlife. Conservation scientists and foresters manage the use and development of these lands and help to protect them. Some advise landowners on the use and management of their land. Conservation scientists and foresters often specialize in one area, such as wildlife management, soil conservation, urban forestry, pest management, native species, or forest economics. But most work falls into one of three categories: forestry, conservation science focusing on range lands, and conservation science focusing on farming and soil.

Foresters oversee our Nation's forests and direct activities on them for economic, recreational, conservational, and environmental purposes. Individual landowners, the public, and industry own most of the forested land in this country, and they require the expertise of foresters to keep the forests healthy and sustainable. Often this means coming up with a plan to keep the forests free from disease, harmful insects, and damaging wildfires, for example, planning when and where to plant trees and vegetation and when to cut timber. It may also mean coming up with ways to make the land profitable but still protected for future generations.

Foresters have a wide range of duties, often depending on who they are working for. Some primary duties of foresters include drawing up plans to regenerate forested lands, monitoring their progress, and supervising harvests. Land management foresters choose and direct the preparation of sites on which trees will be planted. They oversee controlled burning and the use of bulldozers or herbicides to clear weeds, brush, and logging debris. They advise on the type, number, and placement of trees to be planted. Foresters then monitor the seedlings to ensure healthy growth and to determine the best time for harvesting. If they detect signs of disease or harmful insects, they consult with specialists in forest pest management to decide on the best course of treatment. When the trees reach a certain size, foresters decide which trees and how many should be harvested and sold to sawmills.

Procurement foresters make up a large share of foresters. Their job is to buy timber, typically for a sawmill or wood products manufacturer, by contacting local forest owners and negotiating a sale contract. This typically involves taking inventory of the type, amount, and location of all standing timber on the property, a process known as timber cruising. They then appraise the timber's worth, negotiate its purchase, and draw up a contract for purchase. The forester next subcontracts with loggers or pulpwood cutters for tree removal and to aid in laying out roads to access the timber. Throughout the process, foresters maintain close contact with the subcontractor and the landowner to ensure that the work meets the landowner's requirements and Federal, State, and local environmental regulations.

Throughout the forest management and procurement processes, foresters are often responsible for conserving wildlife habitats and creek beds within forests, maintaining water quality and soil stability, and complying with environmental regulations. Foresters must balance the desire to conserve forested ecosystems with the need to use forest resources for recreational or economic purposes. For example, foresters are increasingly working with landowners to find ways to generate money from forested lands, such as for hunting or other recreational activity, without cutting down trees. An increasing concern of foresters is the prevention of devastating wildfires. Using a variety of techniques, including the thinning of forests or using controlled burns to clear brush, foresters work with governments and private landowners to minimize the impact of fire on the forest. During fires, they work with or supervise fire fighters and plan ways to attack the fire.

Some foresters, mostly in the Federal Government, perform research on issues facing forests and related natural resources. They may study tree improvement and harvesting techniques; global change; protection of forests from pests, diseases, and fire; improving wildlife habitats; forest recreation; and other topics. State foresters may perform some research but more often work with private landowners in developing forest management plans. Both Federal and State foresters enforce relevant environmental laws, including laws on water quality and fire suppression.

Relatively new fields in forestry are urban forestry and conservation education. Urban foresters live and work in larger cities and manage urban forests. They are concerned with quality of life issues, such as air quality, shade, beautification, storm water runoff, and property values. Conservation education foresters train teachers and students about sound forest stewardship.

Foresters use a number of tools to perform their jobs. Clinometers measure the height of trees; diameter tapes measure tree diameter; and increment borers and bark gauges measure the growth of trees so that timber volumes can be computed and growth rates estimated. Remote sensing (aerial photographs and other imagery taken from airplanes and satellites) and Geographic Information Systems (GIS) data often are used for mapping large forest areas and for detecting widespread trends of forest and land use. Once a map is generated, data are digitized to create a computerized inventory of information required to manage the forest land and its resources. Moreover, hand-held computers, Global Positioning Systems (GPS), and Internet-based applications are used extensively.

Conservation scientists manage, improve, and protect the country's natural resources. They work with landowners and Federal, State, and local governments to devise ways to use and improve the land while safeguarding the environment. Conservation scientists mainly advise farmers, farm managers, and ranchers on how they can improve their land for agricultural purposes and to control erosion. A growing number of conservation scientists are also advising landowners and governments on recreational uses for the land.

Two of the more common conservation scientists are range managers and soil conservationists. Range managers, also called range conservationists, range ecologists, or range scientists, study, manage, improve, and protect rangelands to maximize their use without damaging the environment. Rangelands cover hundreds of millions of acres of the United States, mostly in Western States and Alaska. They contain many natural resources, including grass and shrubs for animal grazing, wildlife habitats, water from vast watersheds, recreation facilities, and valuable mineral and energy resources. Range managers may inventory soils, plants, and animals; develop resource management plans; help to restore degraded ecosystems; or assist in managing a ranch. For example, they may help ranchers attain optimum livestock production by determining the number and kind of animals to graze, the grazing system to use, and the best season for grazing. At the same time, however, range managers maintain soil stability and vegetation for other uses such as wildlife habitats and outdoor recreation. They also plan and implement revegetation of disturbed sites.

Soil and water conservationists provide technical assistance to farmers, ranchers, forest managers, State and local agencies, and others concerned with the conservation of soil, water, and related natural resources. They develop programs for private landowners designed to make the most productive use of land without damaging it. Soil conservationists also assist landowners by visiting areas with erosion problems, finding the source of the problem, and helping landowners and managers develop management practices to combat it. Water conservationists also assist private landowners and Federal, State, and local governments by advising on water quality, preserving water supplies, groundwater contamination, and management and conservation of water resources.

Work environment. Working conditions vary considerably. Some foresters and conservation scientists work regular hours in offices or labs, but others may split their time between fieldwork and office work. Independent consultants and new, less

Conservation scientsts and foresters keep careful data on plant growth to protect natural resources.

experienced workers spend the majority of their time outdoors overseeing or participating in hands-on work. Fieldwork can involve long hours alone.

The work can be physically demanding. Some conservation scientists and foresters work outdoors in all types of weather, sometimes in isolated areas, and consequently may need to walk long distances through densely wooded land to carry out their work. Natural disasters may also cause foresters and conservation scientists to work long hours during emergencies. For example, foresters often have to work long hours during fire season, and conservation scientists often are called to prevent erosion after a forest fire and to provide emergency help after floods, mudslides, and tropical storms.

Foresters employed by the Federal Government and the States usually work 40 hours a week, but not always on a standard schedule. In field positions, foresters often work for long blocks of time, working 10 days straight, followed by 4 days off, for example. Overtime may be necessary when working in fire fighting, law enforcement, or natural disaster response.

Training, Other Qualifications, and Advancement

Most forester and conservation scientist jobs require a bachelor's degree. Research and teaching positions usually need a graduate degree.

Education and training. A bachelor's degree in forestry, biology, natural resource management, environmental sciences, or a related discipline is the minimum educational requirement for careers in forestry. In the Federal Government, a combination of experience and appropriate education occasionally may substitute for a bachelor's degree, but competition for jobs makes this difficult. Foresters who wish to do research or to teach usually need an advanced degree, preferably a Ph.D.

Conservation scientists generally have at least a bachelor's degree in fields such as ecology, natural resource management, agriculture, biology, or environmental science. A master's degree or Ph.D. is usually required for teaching and research positions.

Most land-grant colleges and universities offer degrees in forestry. The Society of American Foresters accredits about 50 degree programs throughout the country. Curricula focus on four areas: forest ecology and biology, measurement of forest resources, management of forest resources, and public policy. Students should balance general science courses such as ecology, biology, tree physiology, taxonomy, and soil formation with technical forestry courses, such as forest inventory, wildlife habitat assessment, remote sensing, land surveying, GPS technology, integrated forest resource management, forest protection, and silviculture, which is the care and cultivation of forest trees. In addition, mathematics, statistics, and computer science courses are recommended. Courses in resource policy and administration, specifically forest economics and business administration, are also helpful. Forestry curricula increasingly include courses on wetlands analysis and sustainability and regulatory issues because prospective foresters need a strong grasp of Federal, State, and local policy issues and an understanding of complex environmental regulations.

Many colleges require students to complete a field session either in a camp operated by the college or in a cooperative work-study program with a Federal or State agency or with private industry. All schools encourage students to take summer jobs that provide experience in forestry or conservation work.

Range managers usually have a degree in range management or range science. Nine colleges and universities offer degrees in range management that are accredited by the Society of Range Management. More than 40 other schools offer coursework in range science or in a closely related discipline. Range management courses combine plant, animal, and soil sciences with principles of ecology and resource management. Desirable electives include statistics, forestry, hydrology, agronomy, wildlife, animal husbandry, computer science, and recreation. Selection of a minor in range management, such as wildlife ecology, watershed management, animal science, or agricultural economics, can often enhance qualifications for certain types of employment.

Very few colleges and universities offer degrees in soil conservation. Most soil conservationists have degrees in environmental studies, agronomy, general agriculture, hydrology, or crop or soil science; a few have degrees in related fields such as wildlife biology, forestry, and range management. Programs of study usually include 30 semester hours in natural resources or agriculture, including at least 3 hours in soil science.

Licensure. Sixteen States sponsor some type of credentialing process for foresters. Alabama, California, Connecticut, Maine, Maryland, Massachusetts, and New Hampshire have licensing statutes. Arkansas, Georgia, Mississippi, North Carolina, and South Carolina have mandatory registration statutes, and Michigan, New Jersey, Oklahoma, and West Virginia have voluntary registration statutes. Both licensing and registration requirements usually entail completing a 4-year degree in forestry and several years of forestry work experience. Candidates pursuing licensing also may be required to pass a comprehensive written exam.

Other qualifications. Foresters and conservation scientists usually enjoy working outdoors, are able to tolerate extensive walking and other types of physical exertion, and are willing to relocate to find work. They also must work well with people and have good communication skills.

Certification and advancement. One option to advance in these occupations is to become certified. The Society of American Foresters certifies foresters who have at least a bachelor's degree from one of the 50 forestry programs accredited by the Society or from a forestry program that, though not accredited by the Society, is substantially equivalent. In addition, the candidate must have 5 years of qualifying professional experience and pass an examination.

The Society for Range Management offers two types of certification: one as a certified professional in rangeland management and another as a certified range management consultant. Candidates seeking certification must have at least a bachelor's degree in range science or a closely related field, a minimum of 6 years of full-time work experience, and a passing score on an exam.

Additionally, a graduate with the proper coursework in college can seek certification as a wetland scientist through the Society of Wetland Scientists.

Recent forestry and conservation scientist graduates usually work under the supervision of experienced foresters or scientists. After gaining experience, they may advance to more responsible positions. In the Federal Government, most entry-level foresters work in forest resource management. An experienced Federal forester may supervise a ranger district and may advance to forest supervisor, regional forester, or a top administrative position in the national headquarters.

In private industry, foresters start by learning the practical and administrative aspects of the business and by acquiring comprehensive technical training. They are then introduced to contract writing, timber harvesting, and decision making. Some foresters work their way up to top managerial positions. Foresters in management usually leave fieldwork behind, spending more of their time in an office, working with teams to develop management plans and supervising others. After gaining several years of experience, some foresters may become consultants, working alone or with one or several partners. They contract with State or local governments, private landowners, private industry, or other forestry consulting groups.

Soil conservationists usually begin working within one county or conservation district and, with experience, may advance to the area, State, regional, or national level. Also, soil conservationists can transfer to related occupations, such as farm or ranch management advisor or land appraiser.

Employment

Conservation scientists and foresters held about 33,000 jobs in 2006. Conservation scientist jobs are heavily concentrated in government where nearly 3 in 4 are employed. Soil conservationists are employed primarily in the U.S. Department of Agriculture's (USDA) Natural Resource Conservation Service. Most range managers work in the USDA's Forest Service, the U.S. Department of the Interior's Bureau of Land Management, and the Natural Resource Conservation Service. A small number are self-employed and others work for nonprofit organizations or in consulting firms.

More than half of all foresters work for Federal, State and local governments. Federal Government foresters are concentrated in the USDA's Forest Service. A few foresters are self-employed, generally working as consultants or procurement foresters. Others work for sawmills, wood products manufacturers, logging companies, and the forestry industry.

Although conservation scientists and foresters work in every State, employment of foresters is concentrated in the Western and Southeastern States, where many national and private forests and parks—and most of the lumber and pulpwood-producing forests—are located. Range managers work almost entirely in the Western States, where most of the rangeland is located. Soil conservationists, on the other hand, are employed in almost every county in the country. Besides the jobs described above, some foresters and conservation scientists held faculty positions in colleges and universities. (See the section on teachers—postsecondary elsewhere in the *Handbook*.)

Job Outlook

Employment of conservation scientists and foresters is expected to grow more slowly than the average for all occupations through 2016. In addition to job openings from growth, many openings are expected as today's scientists and foresters retire.

Employment change. Employment of conservation scientists and foresters is expected to grow by 5 percent during the 2006-16 decade, more slowly than the average for all occupations. Recent large-scale sales of forestlands by industry has resulted in a loss of jobs within the traditional forest industry while creating limited opportunities with Timber Investment Management Organizations and Real Estate Investment Trusts.

Fire prevention and suppression will become a main activity for some conservation scientists and foresters, especially within the Federal Government, as the human population spreads into previously uninhabited lands. The Federal Government employs more conservation scientists and foresters than any other industry. Overall employment of conservation scientists and foresters in the Federal government is expected to grow more slowly than the average for all occupations, mostly because of budgetary constraints and the trend toward contracting these functions out to private consulting firms. Also, Federal land management agencies, such as the United States Forest Service, have de-emphasized their timber programs and increasingly focused on wildfire suppression and law enforcement, which may require hiring people with other skills.

State governments are the second largest employer of conservation and forest workers, and they are expected to have little or no growth in their employment of conservation scientists and foresters due to budgetary restrictions. A few States are now working to provide market-based incentives to private landowners to encourage them to use forest land for the public benefit by cleaning watersheds, keeping trees, or doing other environmentally focused activities. More State foresters are being asked to design and help implement such eco-management plans.

The management of storm water and coastlines has created demand for people knowledgeable about runoff and erosion on farms and in cities and suburbs. The opening of Federal lands to leasing by oil and gas companies is creating healthy demand for range scientists and range managers, who are finding work with consulting companies to help write environmental impact statements. Additionally, soil and water quality experts will still be needed as States design initiatives to improve water resources by preventing pollution by agricultural producers and industrial plants. A small number of new jobs will result from the need for range and soil conservationists to provide technical assistance to owners of grazing land through the Natural Resource Conservation Service. Salaried foresters working for private industry—such as paper companies, sawmills, and pulpwood mills—will be needed, though in smaller numbers than in the past, to provide technical assistance and management plans to landowners.

Establishments in management, scientific, and technical consulting services have increased their hiring of conservation scientists and foresters in recent years in response to demand for professionals to prepare environmental impact statements and erosion and sediment control plans, monitor water quality near logging sites, and advise on tree harvesting practices required by Federal, State, or local regulations. Hiring by these firms should continue during the 2006-16 decade.

Job prospects. The Federal Government and some State governments expect a large number of workers to retire over the next decade. This is likely to create a large number of job openings for foresters and conservation scientists in government despite the projection for slower than average growth of this occupation in all State, local, and Federal governments combined. However, the best opportunities for foresters and conservation scientists will be in consulting. Government and businesses are increasingly contracting out forestry and conservation services to companies that specialize in providing them.

Foresters involved with timber harvesting will find better opportunities in the Southeast, where much forested land is privately owned. However, the recent opening of public lands, especially in the West, to commercial activity will also help the outlook for foresters.

Earnings

Median annual earnings of conservation scientists in May 2006 were $54,970. The middle 50 percent earned between $40,950 and $68,460. The lowest 10 percent earned less than $29,860, and the highest 10 percent earned more than $80,260.

Median annual earnings of foresters in 2006 were $51,190. The middle 50 percent earned between $40,870 and $62,290.

Projections data from the National Employment Matrix

Occupational Title	SOC Code	Employment, 2006	Projected employment, 2016	Change, 2006-2016	
				Number	Percent
Conservation scientists and foresters	19-1030	33,000	35,000	1,700	5
Conservation scientists...	19-1031	20,000	21,000	1,100	5
Foresters..	19-1032	13,000	14,000	700	5

NOTE: Data in this table are rounded. See the discussion of the employment projections table in the *Handbook* introductory chapter on *Occupational Information Included in the Handbook*.

The lowest 10 percent earned less than $33,490, and the highest 10 percent earned more than $74,570.

In 2006, most bachelor's degree graduates entering the Federal Government as foresters, range managers, or soil conservationists started at $28,862 or $35,752, depending on academic achievement. Those with a master's degree could start at $43,731 or $52,912. Holders of doctorates could start at $63,417. Beginning salaries were slightly higher in selected areas where the prevailing local pay level was higher. In 2007, the average Federal salary for foresters was $65,964; for soil conservationists, $64,284; and for rangeland managers, $60,828.

According to the National Association of Colleges and Employers, graduates with a bachelor's degree in conservation and renewable natural resources received an average starting salary offer of $34,678 in July 2007.

In private industry, starting salaries for students with a bachelor's degree were comparable with starting salaries in the Federal Government, but starting salaries in State and local governments were usually lower.

Conservation scientists and foresters who work for Federal, State, and local governments and large private firms generally receive more generous benefits than do those working for smaller firms. Governments usually have good pension, health, and leave plans.

Related Occupations

Conservation scientists and foresters manage, develop, and protect natural resources. Other workers with similar responsibilities include environmental engineers, agricultural and food scientists, biological scientists, environmental scientists and hydrologists, geoscientists, and farmers, ranchers, and agricultural managers.

Sources of Additional Information

For information about forestry careers and schools offering education in forestry, send a self-addressed, stamped business envelope to:

➤ Society of American Foresters, 5400 Grosvenor Ln., Bethesda, MD 20814-2198. Internet: **http://www.safnet.org**

Information about a career as a range manager, and a list of schools offering training, is available from:

➤ Society for Range Management, 10030 West 27th Ave., Wheat Ridge, CO 80215-6601.
Internet: **http://www.rangelands.org/srm.shtml**

Information on getting a job as a conservation scientist or forester with the Federal Government is available from the Office of Personnel Management (OPM) through USAJOBS, the Federal Government's official employment information system. This resource for locating and applying for job opportunities can be accessed through the Internet at **http://www.usajobs.opm.gov** or through an interactive voice response telephone system at (703) 724-1850 or TDD (978) 461-8404. These numbers are not toll free, and charges may result. For advice on how to find and apply for jobs, see the Occupational Outlook Quarterly article "How to get a job in the Federal Government," online at: **http://www.bls.gov/opub/ooq/2004/summer/art01.pdf**.

Medical Scientists

(O*NET 19-1041.00, 19-1042.00)

Significant Points

- Most medical scientists need a Ph.D. in a biological science; some hold a medical degree.

- Epidemiologists typically need a master's degree in public health or, in some cases, a Ph.D. or medical degree.

- Competition is expected for most positions; however, those with both a Ph.D. and M.D. are likely to have very good opportunities.

Nature of the Work

Medical scientists research human diseases to improve human health. Most medical scientists conduct biomedical research and development to advance knowledge of life processes and living organisms, including viruses, bacteria, and other infectious agents. Past research has resulted in advances in diagnosis, treatment, and prevention of many diseases. Basic medical research continues to build the foundation for new vaccines, drugs, and treatment procedures. Medical scientists engage in laboratory research, clinical investigation, technical writing, drug application review, and related activities.

Medical scientists study biological systems to understand the causes of disease and other health problems. They develop treatments and design research tools and techniques that have medical applications. Some try to identify changes in cells or in chromosomes that signal the development of medical problems. For example, medical scientists involved in cancer research may formulate a combination of drugs that will lessen the effects of the disease. Medical scientists who are also physicians can administer these drugs to patients in clinical trials, monitor their reactions, and observe the results. They may draw blood, excise tissue, or perform other invasive procedures. Those who are not physicians normally collaborate with physicians who deal directly with patients. Medical scientists examine the results of clinical trials and adjust the dosage levels to reduce negative side effects or to induce better results. In addition to developing treatments for medical conditions, medical scientists attempt to discover ways to prevent health problems. For example, they may study the link between smoking and lung cancer or between alcoholism and liver disease.

Medical scientists who work in applied research or product development use knowledge discovered through basic research to develop new drugs and medical treatments. They usually have less autonomy than basic medical researchers do to choose the emphasis of their research. They spend more time working on marketable treatments to meet the business goals of their employers. Medical scientists doing applied research and product development in private industry may also be required to explain their research plans or results to nonscientists who are in a position to reject or approve their ideas. These scientists must consider the business effects of their work. Scientists increasingly work as part of teams, interacting with engineers, scientists of other disciplines, business managers, and technicians.

Swift advances in basic medical knowledge related to genetics and organic molecules have spurred growth in the field of biotechnology. Discovery of important drugs, including human insulin and growth hormone, is the result of research using biotechnology techniques, such as recombining DNA. Many other substances not previously available in large quantities are now produced by biotechnological means; some may one day be useful in treating diseases such as Parkinson's or Alzheimer's. Today, many medical scientists are involved in the science of genetic engineering—isolating, identifying, and sequencing human genes to determine their functions. This work continues to lead to the discovery of genes associated with specific diseases and inherited health risks, such as sickle cell anemia. These advances in biotechnology have opened up research opportunities in almost all areas of medical science.

Some medical scientists specialize in epidemiology. This branch of medical science investigates and describes the causes and spread of disease and develops the means for prevention or control. Epidemiologists may study many different illnesses, often focusing on major infectious diseases such as influenza or cholera. Epidemiologists can be separated into two groups—research and clinical.

Research epidemiologists conduct research in an effort to eradicate or control infectious diseases. Many work on illnesses that affect the entire body, such as AIDS or typhus, while others focus on localized infections such as those of the brain, lungs, or digestive tract. Research epidemiologists work at colleges and universities, schools of public health, medical schools, and independent research firms. For example, Federal Government agencies, such as the U.S. Department of Defense, may contract with a research firm to evaluate the incidence of malaria in certain parts of the world. Other research epidemiologists may work as college and university faculty and are counted as postsecondary teachers.

Clinical epidemiologists work primarily in consulting roles at hospitals, informing the medical staff of infectious outbreaks and providing containment solutions. These epidemiologists sometimes are referred to as infection control professionals, and some of them are also physicians. Clinical epidemiologists who are not also physicians often collaborate with physicians to find ways to contain outbreaks of diseases. In addition to traditional duties of studying and controlling diseases, clinical epidemiologists also may be required to develop standards and guidelines for the treatment and control of communicable diseases. Some clinical epidemiologists may work in outpatient settings.

Work environment. Many medical scientists work independently in private industry, university, or government laboratories, exploring new areas of research or expanding on specialized research that they began in graduate school. Medical scientists working in colleges and universities, hospitals, and nonprofit medical research organizations typically submit grant proposals to obtain funding for their projects. Colleges and universities, private industry, and Federal Government agencies—particularly the National Institutes of Health and the National Science Foundation—provide the primary support for

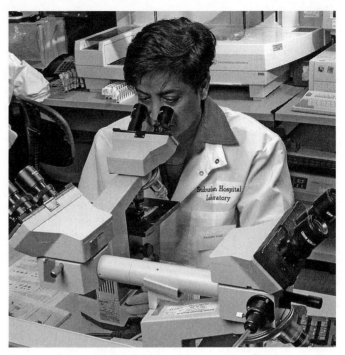

Opportunities will be best for medical scientists with both a Ph.D. and M.D.

researchers whose proposals are determined to be financially feasible and to have the potential to advance new ideas or processes. Medical scientists who rely on grant money may be under pressure to meet deadlines and to conform to rigid grant-writing specifications when preparing proposals to seek new or extended funding.

Medical scientists who conduct research usually work in laboratories and use a wide variety of equipment. Some may work directly with individual patients or larger groups as they administer drugs and monitor patients during clinical trials. Often, these medical scientists also spend time working in clinics and hospitals.

Medical scientists usually are not exposed to unsafe or unhealthy conditions; however, those scientists who work with dangerous organisms or toxic substances must follow strict safety procedures to avoid contamination.

Medical scientists typically work regular hours in offices or laboratories, but longer hours are not uncommon. Researchers may be required to work odd hours in laboratories or other locations, depending on the nature of their research. On occasion, epidemiologists may be required to travel to meetings and hearings for medical investigations.

Training, Other Qualifications, and Advancement

A Ph.D. in a biological science is the minimum education required for most prospective medical scientists, except epidemiologists. However, some medical scientists pursue medical degrees to perform clinical work. Epidemiologists typically need at least a master's degree in public health, but some work requires a Ph.D. or medical degree. A period of postdoctoral work in the laboratory of a senior researcher is becoming increasingly common for medical scientists.

Education and training. A Ph.D. typically qualifies people to research basic life processes or particular medical problems and to analyze the results of experiments. Some medical scientists obtain a medical degree instead of a Ph.D., but some do not become licensed physicians because they prefer research to clinical practice. It is particularly helpful for medical scientists to earn both a Ph.D. and a medical degree.

Students planning careers as medical scientists should have a bachelor's degree in a biological science. In addition to required courses in chemistry and biology, undergraduates should study allied disciplines, such as mathematics, engineering, physics, and computer science, or courses in their field of interest. Once they have completed undergraduate studies, they can then select a specialty for their advanced degree, such as cytology, bioinformatics, genomics, or pathology.

The minimum educational requirement for epidemiologists is a master's degree from a school of public health. Some jobs may require a Ph.D. or medical degree, depending on the work performed. Epidemiologists who work in hospitals and health care centers often must have a medical degree with specific training in infectious diseases. Some employees in research epidemiology positions are required to be licensed physicians because they must administer drugs in clinical trials.

Few students select epidemiology for undergraduate study. Undergraduates, nonetheless, should study biological sciences and should have a solid background in chemistry, mathematics, and computer science. Once a student is prepared for graduate studies, he or she can choose a specialty within epidemiology. For example, those interested in studying environmental epidemiology should focus on environmental coursework, such as water pollution, air pollution, pesticide use, toxicology, and molecular biology. Other specialties include occupational epidemiology, infection processes, infection control precautions, surveillance methodology, and outbreak investigation. Some epidemiologists begin their careers in other health care occupations, such as registered nurse or medical technologist.

In addition to formal education, medical scientists usually spend some time in a postdoctoral position before they apply for permanent jobs. Postdoctoral work provides valuable laboratory experience, including experience in specific processes and techniques such as gene splicing, which is transferable to other research projects. In some institutions, the postdoctoral position can lead to a permanent job.

Licensure. Medical scientists who administer drug or gene therapy to human patients, or who otherwise interact medically with patients—drawing blood, excising tissue, or performing other invasive procedures—must be licensed physicians. To be licensed, physicians must graduate from an accredited medical school, pass a licensing examination, and complete 1 to 7 years of graduate medical education. (See the statement on physicians and surgeons elsewhere in the *Handbook*.)

Epidemiologists who perform laboratory tests often require the knowledge and expertise of a licensed physician to administer drugs to patients in clinical trials. Epidemiologists who are not physicians frequently work closely with one.

Other qualifications. Medical scientists should be able to work independently or as part of a team and be able to communicate clearly and concisely, both orally and in writing. Those in private industry, especially those who aspire to consulting and administrative positions, should possess strong communication skills so that they can provide instruction and advice to physicians and other health care professionals.

Certification and advancement. The Association for Professionals in Infection Control and Epidemiology offers continuing education courses and certification programs in infection prevention and control and applied epidemiology. To become certified as an infection control professional, applicants must pass an examination. Certification can be an advantage for those seeking advancement in this rapidly evolving field.

Advancement among medical scientists usually takes the form of greater independence in their work, larger budgets, or tenure in university positions. Others choose to move into managerial positions and become natural science managers (see engineering and natural science managers elsewhere in the *Handbook*). Those who pursue management careers spend more time preparing budgets and schedules.

Employment

Medical scientists held about 92,000 jobs in 2006. Epidemiologists accounted for only 5 percent of that total. In addition, many medical scientists held faculty positions in colleges and universities, but they are classified as college or university faculty. (See teachers—postsecondary, elsewhere in the *Handbook*.)

About 34 percent of medical scientists, except epidemiologists, were employed in colleges and universities. About 28 percent were employed in scientific research and development services firms; 12 percent were employed in pharmaceutical and medicine manufacturing; 9 percent were employed in hospitals; and most of the remainder were employed in private educational services and ambulatory health care services.

Among epidemiologists, 57 percent were employed in government; 12 percent were employed in hospitals; 11 percent were employed in colleges and universities; and 9 percent were employed in scientific research and development services.

Job Outlook

Medical scientists can expect to face competition for most jobs, in part because of the attractiveness of the career. However,

Projections data from the National Employment Matrix

Occupational Title	SOC Code	Employment, 2006	Projected employment, 2016	Change, 2006-2016	
				Number	Percent
Medical scientists..	19-1040	92,000	110,000	18,000	20
Epidemiologists..	19-1041	4,500	5,100	600	14
Medical scientists, except epidemiologists..................................	19-1042	87,000	105,000	18,000	20

NOTE: Data in this table are rounded. See the discussion of the employment projections table in the *Handbook* introductory chapter on *Occupational Information Included in the Handbook*.

those with both a Ph.D. and M.D. are likely to experience very good opportunities.

Employment change. Employment of medical scientists is expected to increase 20 percent over the 2006-16 decade, faster than the average for all occupations. The Federal Government funds much basic research and development, including many areas of medical research. Although previous budget increases at the National Institutes of Health have led to large increases in the number of grants awarded to researchers, the increase in expenditures has slowed significantly, causing expected future employment growth to be more modest than in the past despite the faster than average projected growth.

Medical scientists enjoyed rapid gains in employment since the 1980s—reflecting, in part, the growth of biotechnology companies. Job growth should be dampened somewhat as fewer new biotechnology firms are founded and as existing firms merge or are absorbed by larger biotechnology or pharmaceutical firms. Some companies may conduct a portion of their research and development in other lower-wage countries, further limiting employment growth. However, much of the basic medical research done in recent years has resulted in new knowledge, including the isolation and identification of new genes. Medical scientists will be needed to take this knowledge to the next stage—understanding how certain genes function within an entire organism—so that medical treatments can be developed for various diseases. Even pharmaceutical and other firms not solely engaged in biotechnology have largely adopted biotechnology techniques, thus creating employment for medical scientists.

Employment growth should also occur as a result of the expected expansion in research related to illnesses such as AIDS, cancer, and avian influenza, along with growing treatment problems such as antibiotic resistance. Moreover, environmental conditions such as overcrowding and the increasing frequency of international travel will tend to spread existing diseases and give rise to new ones. Medical scientists will continue to be needed because they greatly contribute to the development of treatments and medicines that improve human health.

An increasing focus on monitoring patients at hospitals and health care centers to ensure positive patient outcomes will contribute to job growth for epidemiologists. In addition, a heightened awareness of bioterrorism and rare, but infectious diseases such as West Nile Virus or severe acute respiratory syndrome (SARS) should spur demand for these workers. As hospitals enhance their infection control programs, many will seek to boost the quality and quantity of their staff.

Job prospects. Besides job openings due to employment growth, openings will arise as workers leave the labor force or transfer to other occupations. However, doctoral degree holders can expect to face considerable competition for basic research positions and for research grants. If the number of advanced degrees awarded continues to grow, applicants are likely to face even more competition.

Although medical scientists can expect competition for jobs, those with both doctoral and medical degrees are likely to experience very good opportunities. As funding for research becomes more difficult to obtain, those with both a biological and professional medical background will have a distinct ad-

vantage. Opportunities in epidemiology also should be highly competitive, as the number of available positions will continue to be limited.

Medical scientists and epidemiologists are less likely to lose their jobs during recessions than are those in many other occupations because they are employed on long-term research projects. However, a recession could influence the amount of money allocated to new research and development, particularly in areas of risky or innovative medical research. A recession also could limit extensions or renewals of existing projects.

Earnings

Median annual earnings of wage and salary medical scientists, except epidemiologists, were $61,680 in May 2006. The middle 50 percent of these workers earned between $44,830 and $88,130. The lowest 10 percent earned less than $35,490, and the highest 10 percent earned more than $117,520. Median annual earnings in the industries employing the largest numbers of medical scientists were:

Pharmaceutical and medicine manufacturing	$82,640
Research and development in the physical, engineering, and life sciences	71,490
Offices of physicians	70,000
General medical and surgical hospitals	64,700
Colleges, universities, and professional schools	44,600

Median annual earnings of wage and salary epidemiologists were $56,670 in May 2006. The middle 50 percent earned between $45,220 and $71,080. The lowest 10 percent earned less than $36,920, and the highest 10 percent earned more than $87,300.

Related Occupations

Many other occupations deal with living organisms and require a level of training similar to that of medical scientists. These occupations include biological scientists, agricultural and food scientists, pharmacists, engineering and natural sciences managers, and health occupations such as physicians and surgeons, dentists, and veterinarians.

Sources of Additional Information

For information on pharmaceutical scientists, contact:

➤ American Association of Pharmaceutical Scientists (AAPS), 2107 Wilson Blvd., Suite 700, Arlington, VA 22201. Internet: **http://www.aapspharmaceutica.org**

For information on careers in microbiology, contact:

➤ American Society for Microbiology, Career Information— Education Department, 1752 N St.NW., Washington, DC 20036. Internet: **http://www.asm.org**

For information on infectious diseases training programs, contact:

➤ Infectious Diseases Society of America, Guide to Training Programs, 66 Canal Center Plaza, Suite 600, Alexandria, VA 22314. Internet: **http://www.idsociety.org**

Information on obtaining a medical scientist position with the Federal Government is available from the Office of Personnel Management through USAJOBS, the Federal Government's official employment information system. This resource for locating and applying for job opportunities can be accessed through the Internet at **http://www.usajobs.opm.gov** or through an interactive voice response telephone system at (703) 724-1850 or TDD (978) 461-8404. These numbers are not toll free, and

charges may result. For advice on how to find and apply for Federal jobs, see the Occupational Outlook Quarterly article "How to get a job in the Federal Government," online at: **http://www.bls.gov/opub/ooq/2004/summer/art01.pdf**.

Physical Scientists

Atmospheric Scientists

(O*NET 19-2021.00)

Significant Points

- About 37 percent of atmospheric scientists are employed by the Federal Government; most of these work in the National Weather Service.

- A bachelor's degree in meteorology, or in a closely related field with courses in meteorology, is the minimum educational requirement; a master's degree is necessary for some positions, and a Ph.D. degree is required for most basic research positions.

- Atmospheric scientists should have favorable job prospects, but opportunities as weather broadcasters are rare and highly competitive.

Nature of the Work

Atmospheric science is the study of the atmosphere—the blanket of air covering the Earth. Atmospheric scientists, commonly called *meteorologists*, study the atmosphere's physical characteristics, motions, and processes, and the way in which these factors affect the rest of our environment. The best known application of this knowledge is forecasting the weather. In addition to predicting the weather, atmospheric scientists attempt to identify and interpret climate trends, understand past weather, and analyze today's weather. Weather information and meteorological research are also applied in air-pollution control, agriculture, forestry, air and sea transportation, defense, and the study of possible trends in the Earth's climate, such as global warming, droughts, and ozone depletion.

Atmospheric scientists who forecast the weather are known as *operational meteorologists*; they are the largest group of specialists. These scientists study the Earth's air pressure, temperature, humidity, and wind velocity, and they apply physical and mathematical relationships to make short-range and long-range weather forecasts. Their data come from weather satellites, radars, sensors, and stations in many parts of the world. Meteorologists use sophisticated computer models of the world's atmosphere to make long-term, short-term, and local-area forecasts. More accurate instruments for measuring and observing weather conditions, as well as high-speed computers to process and analyze weather data, have revolutionized weather forecasting. Using satellite data, climate theory, and sophisticated computer models of the world's atmosphere, meteorologists can more effectively interpret the results of these models to make

local-area weather predictions. These forecasts inform not only the general public, but also those who need accurate weather information for both economic and safety reasons, such as the shipping, air transportation, agriculture, fishing, forestry, and utilities industries.

The use of weather balloons, launched a few times a day to measure wind, temperature, and humidity in the upper atmosphere, is currently supplemented by sophisticated atmospheric satellite monitoring equipment that transmits data as frequently as every few minutes. Doppler radar, for example, can detect airflow patterns in violent storm systems, allowing forecasters to better predict thunderstorms, flash floods, tornadoes, and other hazardous winds, and to monitor the direction and intensity of storms.

Some atmospheric scientists work in research. *Physical meteorologists*, for example, study the atmosphere's chemical and physical properties; the transmission of light, sound, and radio waves; and the transfer of energy in the atmosphere. They also study factors affecting the formation of clouds, rain, and snow; the dispersal of air pollutants over urban areas; and other weather phenomena, such as the mechanics of severe storms. *Synoptic meteorologists* develop new tools for weather forecasting using computers and sophisticated mathematical models of atmospheric activity. *Climatologists* study climactic variations spanning hundreds or even millions of years. They also may collect, analyze, and interpret past records of wind, rainfall, sunshine, and temperature in specific areas or regions. Their studies are used to design buildings, plan heating and cooling systems, and aid in effective land use and agricultural production. Environmental problems, such as pollution and shortages of fresh water, have widened the scope of the meteorological profession. *Environmental meteorologists* study these problems and may evaluate and report on air quality for environmental impact statements. Other research meteorologists examine the most effective ways to control or diminish air pollution.

Work environment. Weather stations are found everywhere—at airports, in or near cities, and in isolated and remote areas. Some atmospheric scientists also spend time observing weather conditions and collecting data from aircraft. Weather forecasters who work for radio or television stations broadcast their reports from station studios, and may work evenings and weekends. Meteorologists in smaller weather offices often work alone; in larger ones, they work as part of a team. Those who work for private consulting firms or for companies analyzing and monitoring emissions to improve air quality usually work with other scientists or engineers; fieldwork and travel may be common for these workers.

Most weather stations operate around the clock, 7 days a week. Jobs in such facilities usually involve night, weekend,

Atmospheric scientists in smaller weather offices often work alone.

and holiday work, often with rotating shifts. During weather emergencies, such as hurricanes, meteorologists may work overtime. Operational meteorologists also are often under pressure to meet forecast deadlines. Meteorologists who are not involved in forecasting tasks work regular hours, usually in offices.

Training, Other Qualifications, and Advancement

A bachelor's degree in meteorology or atmospheric science, or in a closely related field with courses in meteorology, usually is the minimum educational requirement for an entry-level position as an atmospheric scientist. A master's degree is necessary for some positions, and a Ph.D. degree is required for most basic research positions.

Education and training. The preferred educational requirement for entry-level meteorologists in the Federal Government is a bachelor's degree—not necessarily in meteorology—with at least 24 semester hours of meteorology/atmospheric science courses, including 6 hours in the analysis and prediction of weather systems, 6 hours of atmospheric dynamics and thermodynamics, 3 hours of physical meteorology, and 2 hours of remote sensing of the atmosphere or instrumentation. Other required courses include 3 semester hours of ordinary differential equations, 6 hours of college physics, and at least 9 hours of courses appropriate for a physical science major—such as statistics, chemistry, physical oceanography, physical climatology, physical hydrology, radiative transfer, aeronomy (the study of the upper atmosphere), advanced thermodynamics, advanced electricity and magnetism, light and optics, and computer science. Sometimes, a combination of education and appropriate experience may be substituted for a degree.

Although positions in operational meteorology are available for those with only a bachelor's degree, obtaining a second bachelor's degree or a master's degree enhances employment opportunities, pay, and advancement potential. A master's degree usually is necessary for conducting applied research and development, and a Ph.D. is required for most basic research positions. Students planning on a career in research and development do not necessarily need to major in atmospheric science or meteorology as an undergraduate. In fact, a bachelor's degree in mathematics, physics, or engineering provides excellent preparation for graduate study in atmospheric science.

Because atmospheric science is a small field, relatively few colleges and universities offer degrees in meteorology or atmospheric science, although many departments of physics, earth science, geography, and geophysics offer atmospheric science and related courses. In 2007, the American Meteorological Society listed approximately 100 undergraduate and graduate atmospheric science programs. Many of these programs combine the study of meteorology with another field, such as agriculture, hydrology, oceanography, engineering, or physics. For example, hydrometeorology is the blending of hydrology (the science of Earth's water) and meteorology, and is the field concerned with the effect of precipitation on the hydrologic cycle and the environment.

Prospective students should make certain that courses required by the National Weather Service and other employers are offered at the college they are considering. Computer science courses, additional meteorology courses, a strong background in mathematics and physics, and good communication skills are important to prospective employers.

Students should also take courses in subjects that are most relevant to their desired area of specialization. For example, those who wish to become broadcast meteorologists for radio or television stations should develop excellent communication skills through courses in speech, journalism, and related fields. Students interested in air quality work should take courses in chemistry and supplement their technical training with coursework in policy or government affairs. Prospective meteorologists seeking opportunities at weather consulting firms should possess knowledge of business, statistics, and economics, as an increasing emphasis is being placed on long-range seasonal forecasting to assist businesses.

Beginning atmospheric scientists often do routine data collection, computation, or analysis, and some basic forecasting. Entry-level operational meteorologists in the Federal Government usually are placed in intern positions for training and experience. During this period, they learn about the Weather Service's forecasting equipment and procedures, and rotate to different offices to learn about various weather systems. After completing the training period, they are assigned to a permanent duty station.

Certification and advancement. The American Meteorological Society (AMS) offers professional certification for consulting meteorologists, administered by a Board of Certified Consulting Meteorologists. Applicants must meet formal education requirements, pass an examination to demonstrate thorough meteorological knowledge, have a minimum of 5 years of experience or a combination of experience plus an advanced degree, and provide character references from fellow professionals. In addition, AMS also offers professional certification for broadcast meteorologists.

Experienced meteorologists may advance to supervisory or administrative jobs, or may handle more complex forecasting jobs. After several years of experience, some meteorologists establish their own weather consulting services.

Employment

Atmospheric scientists held about 8,800 jobs in 2006. Although several hundred people teach atmospheric science and related courses in college and university departments of meteorology or atmospheric science, physics, earth science, or geophysics, these individuals are classified as college or university faculty, rather than atmospheric scientists. (See the statement on post-secondary teachers elsewhere in the *Handbook*.)

The Federal Government was the largest single employer of civilian meteorologists, accounting for about 37 percent. The National Oceanic and Atmospheric Administration (NOAA) employed most Federal meteorologists in National Weather Service stations throughout the Nation; the remainder of NOAA's meteorologists worked mainly in research and development or management. The U.S. Department of Defense employed several hundred civilian meteorologists. In addition to civilian meteorologists, hundreds of Armed Forces members are involved in forecasting and other meteorological work. (See the statement on job opportunities in the Armed Forces elsewhere in the *Handbook*.) Others worked for professional, scientific, and technical services firms, including private weather consulting services; radio and television broadcasting; air carriers; and State government.

Job Outlook

Employment is expected to increase about as fast as the average. Atmospheric scientists should have favorable job prospects, but opportunities in broadcasting are rare and highly competitive.

Employment change. Employment of atmospheric scientists is projected to grow 11 percent over the 2006-16 decade, about as fast as the average for all occupations. The National Weather Service has completed an extensive modernization of its weather forecasting equipment and finished all hiring of meteorologists needed to staff the upgraded stations. The Service has no plans to increase the number of weather stations or the number of meteorologists in existing stations. Employment of meteorologists in other Federal agencies is expected to decline.

In private industry, on the other hand, job opportunities for atmospheric scientists are expected to be better than in the Federal Government. As research leads to continuing improvements in weather forecasting, demand should grow for private weather consulting firms to provide more detailed information than has formerly been available, especially to climate-sensitive industries. Farmers, commodity investors, radio and television stations, and utilities, transportation, and construction firms can greatly benefit from additional weather information more closely targeted to their needs than the general information provided by the National Weather Service. Additionally, research on seasonal and other long-range forecasting is yielding positive results, which should spur demand for more atmospheric scientists to interpret these forecasts and advise climate-sensitive industries. However, because many customers for private weather services are in industries sensitive to fluctuations in the economy, the sales and growth of private weather services depend on the health of the economy.

There will continue to be demand for atmospheric scientists to analyze and monitor the dispersion of pollutants into the air to ensure compliance with Federal environmental regulations, but related employment increases are expected to be small. Efforts toward making and improving global weather observations also could have a positive impact on employment.

Job prospects. Atmospheric scientists should have favorable job prospects, as the number of graduates is expected to be in rough balance with the number of openings. Opportunities in broadcasting are rare and there will be very few job openings in this industry. Openings for academic and government positions should result primarily from replacement needs as older workers retire or leave the occupation for other reasons.

Earnings

Median annual earnings of atmospheric scientists in May 2006 were $77,150. The middle 50 percent earned between $55,530 and $96,490. The lowest 10 percent earned less than $39,090, and the highest 10 percent earned more than $119,700.

The average salary for meteorologists employed by the Federal Government was $84,882 in 2007. Many meteorologists in the Federal Government with a bachelor's degree received a starting salary of $35,752, or slightly higher in areas of the country where the prevailing local pay level is higher.

Related Occupations

Workers in other occupations concerned with the physical environment include environmental scientists and hydrologists, geoscientists, physicists and astronomers, mathematicians, and engineers.

Sources of Additional Information

Information about careers in meteorology and a listing of colleges and universities offering meteorology programs is provided by the American Meteorological Society on the Internet at: **http://www.ametsoc.org**

General information about meteorology and careers in atmospheric science can also be obtained from the National Oceanic and Atmospheric Administration on the Internet at: **http://www.noaa.gov**

Information on obtaining a position as a meteorologist with the Federal Government is available from the Office of Personnel Management through USAJOBS, the Federal Government's official employment information system. This resource for locating and applying for job opportunities can be accessed through the Internet at **http://www.usajobs.opm.gov** or through an interactive voice response telephone system at (703) 724-1850 or TDD (978) 461-8404. These numbers are not toll free, and charges may result.

Projections data from the National Employment Matrix

Occupational Title	SOC Code	Employment, 2006	Projected employment, 2016	Change, 2006-2016	
				Number	Percent
Atmospheric and space scientists..	19-2021	8,800	9,700	900	11

NOTE: Data in this table are rounded. See the discussion of the employment projections table in the *Handbook* introductory chapter on *Occupational Information Included in the Handbook.*

Chemists and Materials Scientists

(O*NET 19-2031.00, 19-2032.00)

Significant Points

- A bachelor's degree in chemistry or a related discipline is the minimum educational requirement; however, many research jobs require a master's degree or, more often, a Ph.D.

- Job growth will occur in professional, scientific, and technical services firms as manufacturing companies continue to outsource their research and development and testing operations to these smaller, specialized firms.

- New chemists at all levels may experience competition for jobs, particularly in declining chemical manufacturing industries; graduates with a master's degree, and particularly those with a Ph.D., will enjoy better opportunities at larger pharmaceutical and biotechnology firms.

Nature of the Work

Everything in the environment, whether naturally occurring or of human design, is composed of chemicals. Chemists and materials scientists search for and use new knowledge about chemicals. Chemical research has led to the discovery and development of new and improved synthetic fibers, paints, adhesives, drugs, cosmetics, electronic components, lubricants, and thousands of other products. Chemists and materials scientists also develop processes such as improved oil refining and petrochemical processing that save energy and reduce pollution. Applications of materials science include studies of superconducting materials, graphite materials, integrated-circuit chips, and fuel cells. Research on the chemistry of living things spurs advances in medicine, agriculture, food processing, and other fields.

Many chemists and materials scientists work in research and development (R&D). In basic research, they investigate the properties, composition, and structure of matter and the laws that govern the combination of elements and reactions of substances to each other. In applied R&D, these scientists create new products and processes or improve existing ones, often using knowledge gained from basic research. For example, synthetic rubber and plastics resulted from research on small molecules uniting to form large ones, a process called polymerization. R&D chemists and materials scientists use computers and a wide variety of sophisticated laboratory instrumentation for modeling, simulation, and experimental analysis.

The use of computers to analyze complex data has allowed chemists and materials scientists to practice combinatorial chemistry. This technique makes and tests large quantities of chemical compounds simultaneously to find those with certain desired properties. Combinatorial chemistry has allowed chemists to produce thousands of compounds more quickly and inexpensively than was formerly possible and assisted in the sequencing of human genes. Specialty chemists, such as medicinal and organic chemists, work with life scientists to translate this knowledge into new drugs.

Developments in the field of chemistry that involve life sciences will expand, resulting in more interaction among biologists, engineers, computer specialists, and chemists. (*Biochemists*, whose work encompasses both biology and chemistry, are discussed in the *Handbook* statement on biological scientists.)

Chemists also work in production and quality control in chemical manufacturing plants. They prepare instructions for plant workers that specify ingredients, mixing times, and temperatures for each stage in the process. They also monitor automated processes to ensure proper product yield and test samples of raw materials or finished products to ensure that they meet industry and government standards, including regulations governing pollution. Chemists report and document test results and analyze those results in hopes of improving existing theories or developing new test methods.

Chemists often specialize. *Analytical chemists* determine the structure, composition, and nature of substances by examining and identifying their various elements or compounds. These chemists are absolutely crucial to the pharmaceutical industry because pharmaceutical companies need to know the identity of compounds that they hope to turn into drugs. Furthermore, analytical chemists develop analytical techniques and study the relationships and interactions among the parts of compounds. They also identify the presence and concentration of chemical pollutants in air, water, and soil.

Organic chemists study the chemistry of the vast number of carbon compounds that make up all living things. Organic chemists who synthesize elements or simple compounds to create new compounds or substances that have different properties and applications have developed many commercial products, such as drugs, plastics, and elastomers (elastic substances similar to rubber). *Inorganic chemists* study compounds consisting mainly of elements other than carbon, such as those in electronic components.

Physical and *theoretical chemists* study the physical characteristics of atoms and molecules and the theoretical properties of matter; and they investigate how chemical reactions work. Their research may result in new and better energy sources. *Macromolecular chemists* study the behavior of atoms and molecules. *Medicinal chemists* study the structural properties of compounds intended for applications to human medicine.

Materials chemists study and develop new materials to improve existing products or make new ones. In fact, virtually all chemists are involved in this quest in one way or another.

The work of materials chemists is similar to, but separate from, the work of materials scientists. Materials scientists apply physics as well as chemistry to study all aspects of materials. Chemistry, however, plays an increasingly dominant role in materials science because it provides information about the structure and composition of materials.

Materials scientists study the structures and chemical properties of various materials to develop new products or enhance existing ones. They also determine ways to strengthen or combine materials or develop new materials for use in a variety of products. Materials science encompasses the natural and synthetic materials used in a wide range of products and structures, from airplanes, cars, and bridges to clothing and household goods. Materials scientists often specialize in specific areas such as ceramics or metals.

Work environment. Chemists and materials scientists usually work regular hours in offices and laboratories. R&D chemists and materials scientists spend much time in laboratories but also work in offices when they do theoretical research or plan, record, and report on their lab research. Although some laboratories are small, others are large enough to incorporate prototype chemical manufacturing facilities as well as advanced testing equipment. In addition to working in a laboratory, materials scientists also work with engineers and processing specialists in industrial manufacturing facilities. Chemists do some of their work in a chemical plant or outdoors—gathering water samples to test for pollutants, for example. Some chemists are exposed to health or safety hazards when handling certain chemicals, but there is little risk if proper procedures are followed.

Chemists and materials scientists typically work regular hours. A 40-hour workweek is usual, but longer hours are not uncommon. Researchers may be required to work odd hours in laboratories or other locations, depending on the nature of their research.

Opportunities will be best for chemists and material scientists at large biotechnology and pharmaceutical firms.

Training, Other Qualifications, and Advancement

A bachelor's degree in chemistry or a related discipline is the minimum educational requirement; however, many research jobs require a master's degree or, more often, a Ph.D.

Education and training. A bachelor's degree in chemistry or a related discipline usually is the minimum educational requirement for entry-level chemist jobs. While some materials scientists hold a degree in materials science, degrees in chemistry, physics, or electrical engineering are also common. Most research jobs in chemistry and materials science require a master's degree or, more frequently, a Ph.D.

Many colleges and universities offer degree programs in chemistry. In 2007, the American Chemical Society (ACS) had approved approximately 640 bachelors, 310 masters, and 200 doctoral degree programs. In addition to these programs, other advanced degree programs in chemistry were offered at several hundred colleges and universities. The number of colleges that offer a degree program in materials science is small but gradually increasing.

Students planning careers as chemists and materials scientists should take courses in science and mathematics, should like working with their hands building scientific apparatus and performing laboratory experiments, and should like computer modeling.

In addition to taking required courses in analytical, inorganic, organic, and physical chemistry, undergraduate chemistry majors usually study biological sciences; mathematics; physics; and increasingly, computer science. Computer courses are essential because employers prefer job applicants who are able to apply computer skills to modeling and simulation tasks and operate computerized laboratory equipment. This is increasingly important as combinatorial chemistry and advanced screening techniques are more widely applied. Courses in statistics are useful because both chemists and materials scientists need the ability to apply basic statistical techniques.

People interested in environmental specialties also should take courses in environmental studies and become familiar with current legislation and regulations. Specific courses should include atmospheric, water, and soil chemistry, and energy.

Graduate students studying chemistry commonly specialize in a subfield, such as analytical chemistry or polymer chemistry, depending on their interests and the kind of work they wish to do. For example, those interested in doing drug research in the pharmaceutical industry usually develop a strong background in medicinal or synthetic organic chemistry. However, students normally need not specialize at the undergraduate level. In fact, undergraduates who are broadly trained have more flexibility when searching for jobs than if they have narrowly defined their interests. Most employers provide new graduates additional training or education.

In government or industry, beginning chemists with a bachelor's degree work in quality control, perform analytical testing, or assist senior chemists in R&D laboratories. Many employers prefer chemists and materials scientists with a Ph.D., or at least a master's degree, to lead basic and applied research. Within materials science, a broad background in various sciences is preferred. This broad base may be obtained through degrees in physics, engineering, or chemistry. Although many companies prefer hiring Ph.D.s, some may employ materials scientists with bachelor's and master's degrees.

Other qualifications. Because R&D chemists and materials scientists are increasingly expected to work on interdisciplinary teams, some understanding of other disciplines, including business and marketing or economics, is desirable, along with leadership ability and good oral and written communication skills. Interaction among specialists in this field is increasing, especially for specialty chemists in drug development. One type of chemist often relies on the findings of another type of chemist. For example, an organic chemist must understand findings on the identity of compounds prepared by an analytical chemist.

Experience, either in academic laboratories or through internships, fellowships, or work-study programs in industry, also is useful. Some employers of research chemists, particularly in the pharmaceutical industry, prefer to hire individuals with several years of postdoctoral experience.

Perseverance, curiosity, and the ability to concentrate on detail and to work independently are essential.

Advancement. Advancement among chemists and materials scientists usually takes the form of greater independence in their work or larger budgets. Others choose to move into managerial positions and become natural science managers (listed elsewhere in the *Handbook*). Those who pursue management careers spend more time preparing budgets and schedules and setting research strategy. Chemists or materials scientists who develop new products or processes sometimes form their own companies or join new firms to develop these ideas.

Employment

Chemists and materials scientists held about 93,000 jobs in 2006. Chemists accounted for about 84,000 of these, while materials scientists accounted for about 9,700 jobs. In addition, many chemists and materials scientists held faculty positions in colleges and universities but are not included in these numbers. (See the statement on teachers—postsecondary, elsewhere in the *Handbook*.)

About 41 percent of all chemists and material scientists are employed in manufacturing firms—mostly in the chemical manufacturing industry; firms in this industry produce plastics and synthetic materials, drugs, soaps and cleaners, pesticides and fertilizers, paint, industrial organic chemicals, and other chemical products. About 18 percent of chemists and material scientists work in scientific research and development services; 12 percent work in architectural, engineering, and related services. Companies whose products are made of metals, ceramics, and rubber employ most materials scientists. In addition, thousands of people with a background in chemistry and materials science hold teaching positions in high schools and in colleges and universities. (See the statements on teachers—post-

secondary, and teachers—preschool, kindergarten, elementary, middle, and secondary, elsewhere in the *Handbook*.)

Chemists and materials scientists are employed in all parts of the country, but they are mainly concentrated in large industrial areas.

Job Outlook

Average job growth is expected. New chemists at all levels may experience competition for jobs, particularly in declining chemical manufacturing industries. Graduates with a master's degree or a Ph.D., will enjoy better opportunities, especially at larger pharmaceutical and biotechnology firms.

Employment change. Employment of chemists and materials scientists is expected to grow 9 percent over the 2006-16 decade, about as fast as the average for all occupations. Job growth will occur in professional, scientific, and technical services firms as manufacturing companies continue to outsource their R&D and testing operations to these smaller, specialized firms.

Chemists should experience employment growth in pharmaceutical and biotechnology research, as recent advances in genetics open new avenues of treatment for diseases. Employment of chemists in the nonpharmaceutical chemical manufacturing industries is expected to decline over the projection period, along with overall declining employment in these industries.

Employment of materials scientists should continue to grow as manufacturers of diverse products seek to improve their quality by using new materials and manufacturing processes.

Within the chemical manufacturing industries, job growth for chemists is expected to be strongest in pharmaceutical and biotechnology firms. Biotechnological research, including studies of human genes, continues to offer possibilities for the development of new drugs and products to combat illnesses and diseases that have previously been unresponsive to treatments derived by traditional chemical processes. Stronger competition among drug companies and an aging population are contributing to the need for new drugs.

The remaining chemical manufacturing industries are expected to employ fewer chemists as companies divest their R&D operations. To control costs, most chemical companies, including many large pharmaceutical and biotechnology companies, will increasingly turn to scientific R&D services firms to perform specialized research and other work formerly done by in-house chemists. As a result, these firms will experience healthy growth. Also, some companies are expected to conduct an increasing amount of manufacturing and research in lower-wage countries, further limiting domestic employment growth. Quality control will continue to be an important issue in chemical manufacturing and other industries that use chemicals in their manufacturing processes.

Projections data from the National Employment Matrix

Occupational Title	SOC Code	Employment, 2006	Projected employment, 2016	Change, 2006-2016	
				Number	Percent
Chemists and materials scientists..	19-2030	93,000	102,000	8,500	9
Chemists...	19-2031	84,000	91,000	7,600	9
Materials scientists..	19-2032	9,700	11,000	800	9

NOTE: Data in this table are rounded. See the discussion of the employment projections table in the *Handbook* introductory chapter on *Occupational Information Included in the Handbook.*

Chemists also will be employed to develop and improve the technologies and processes used to produce chemicals for all purposes, and to monitor and measure air and water pollutants to ensure compliance with local, State, and Federal environmental regulations. Environmental research will offer many new opportunities for chemists and materials scientists. To satisfy public concerns and to comply with government regulations, chemical manufacturing industries will continue to invest billions of dollars each year in technology that reduces pollution and cleans up existing waste sites. Research into traditional and alternative energy sources should also lead to employment growth among chemists.

Job prospects. New chemists at all levels may experience competition for jobs, particularly in declining chemical manufacturing industries. Graduates with a bachelor's degree in chemistry may find science-related jobs in sales, marketing, and middle management. Some become chemical technicians or technologists or high school chemistry teachers. In addition, bachelor's degree holders are increasingly finding assistant research positions at smaller research organizations.

Graduates with an advanced degree, and particularly those with a Ph.D., will enjoy better opportunities. Larger pharmaceutical and biotechnology firms will offer more openings for these workers. Furthermore, chemists with an advanced degree will continue to fill most senior research and upper management positions; however, similar to other occupations, applicants face strong competition for the limited number of upper management jobs.

In addition to jobs openings resulting from employment growth, some job openings will result from the need to replace chemists and materials scientists who retire or otherwise leave the labor force, although not all positions will be filled.

During periods of economic recession, layoffs of chemists may occur—especially in the industrial chemicals industry. Layoffs are less likely in the pharmaceutical industry, where long development cycles generally overshadow short-term economic conditions. The traditional chemical industries, however, provide many raw materials to the automotive manufacturing and construction industries, both of which are vulnerable to temporary slowdowns during recessions.

Earnings

Median annual earnings of chemists in 2006 were $59,870. The middle 50 percent earned between $44,780 and $82,610. The lowest 10 percent earned less than $35,480, and the highest 10 percent earned more than $106,310. Median annual earnings of materials scientists in 2006 were $74,610. The middle 50 percent earned between $55,170 and $96,800. The lowest 10 percent earned less than $41,810, and the highest 10 percent earned more than $118,670. Median annual earnings in the industries employing the largest numbers of chemists in 2006 are shown below:

Federal executive branch	$88,930
Scientific research and development services	68,760
Basic chemical manufacturing	62,340
Pharmaceutical and medicine manufacturing	57,210
Testing laboratories	45,730

According to the National Association of Colleges and Employers, beginning salary offers in July 2007 for graduates with bachelor's degrees in chemistry averaged $41,506 a year.

In 2007, annual earnings of chemists in nonsupervisory, supervisory, and managerial positions in the Federal Government averaged $89,954.

Related Occupations

The research and analysis conducted by chemists and materials scientists is closely related to work done by agricultural and food scientists, biological scientists, medical scientists, engineering and natural sciences managers, chemical engineers, materials engineers, physicists and astronomers, and science technicians.

Sources of Additional Information

General information on career opportunities and earnings for chemists is available from:

➤ American Chemical Society, Education Division, 1155 16th St.NW., Washington, DC 20036. Internet: **http://www.acs.org**

Information on obtaining a position as a chemist with the Federal Government is available from the Office of Personnel Management through USAJOBS, the Federal Government's official employment information system. This resource for locating and applying for job opportunities can be accessed through the Internet at **http://www.usajobs.opm.gov** or through an interactive voice response telephone system at (703) 724-1850 or TDD (978) 461-8404. These numbers are not toll free, and charges may result.

Environmental Scientists and Hydrologists

(O*NET 19-2041.00, 19-2043.00)

Significant Points

- Environmental scientists and hydrologists often work in offices, laboratories, and field sites.

- Federal, State, and local governments employ 43 percent of all environmental scientists and hydrologists.

- Although a bachelor's degree in an earth science is adequate for a few entry-level jobs, employers prefer a master's degree; a Ph.D. degree generally is required for research or college teaching positions.

- Job prospects are expected to be favorable, particularly for hydrologists.

Nature of the Work

Environmental scientists and hydrologists use their knowledge of the physical makeup and history of the Earth to protect the environment, study the properties of underground and surface waters, locate water and energy resources, predict water-related geologic hazards, and provide environmental site assessments and advice on indoor air quality and hazardous-waste-site remediation.

Environmental scientists conduct research to identify, abate, and eliminate hazards that affect people, wildlife, and their environments. These workers analyze measurements or observations of air, food, water, and soil to determine the way to clean and preserve the environment. Understanding the issues involved in protecting the environment—degradation, conservation, recycling, and replenishment—is central to the work of environmental scientists. They often use this understanding to design and monitor waste disposal sites, preserve water supplies, and reclaim contaminated land and water to comply with Federal environmental regulations. They also write risk assessments, describing the likely affect of construction and other environmental changes; write technical proposals; and give presentations to managers and regulators.

Hydrologists study the quantity, distribution, circulation, and physical properties of bodies of water. Often, they specialize in either underground water or surface water. They examine the form and intensity of precipitation, its rate of infiltration into the soil, its movement through the Earth, and its return to the ocean and atmosphere. Hydrologists use sophisticated techniques and instruments. For example, they may use remote sensing technology, data assimilation, and numerical modeling to monitor the change in regional and global water cycles. Some surface-water hydrologists use sensitive stream-measuring devices to assess flow rates and water quality.

Many environmental scientists and hydrologists work at consulting firms, helping businesses and government agencies comply with environmental policy, particularly with regard to ground-water decontamination and flood control. They are usually hired to solve problems. Most consulting firms fall into two categories: large multidisciplinary engineering companies, the largest of which may employ thousands of workers, and small niche firms that may employ only a few workers. When looking for jobs, environmental scientists and hydrologists should consider the type of firm and the scope of the projects it undertakes. In larger firms, environmental scientists are more likely to engage in large, long-term projects in which they will work with people in other scientific disciplines. In smaller specialty firms, however, they work more often with business professionals and clients in government and the private sector.

Environmental scientists who work on policy formation may help identify ways that human behavior can be modified in the future to avoid such problems as ground-water contamination and depletion of the ozone layer. Some environmental scientists work in managerial positions, usually after spending some time performing research or learning about environmental laws and regulations.

Many environmental scientists do work and have training that is similar to other physical or life scientists, but they focus on environmental issues. Many specialize in subfields such as environmental ecology and conservation, environmental chemistry, environmental biology, or fisheries science. Specialties affect the specific activities that environmental scientists perform, although recent understandings of the interconnectedness of life processes have blurred some traditional classifications. For example, *environmental ecologists* study the relationships between organisms and their environments and the effects of factors such as population size, pollutants, rainfall, tempera-

Environmental scientists and hydrologists work in labratories, offices, and in the field.

ture, and altitude, on both. They may collect, study, and report data on air, soil, and water using their knowledge of various scientific disciplines. *Ecological modelers* study ecosystems, pollution control, and resource management using mathematical modeling, systems analysis, thermodynamics, and computer techniques. *Environmental chemists* study the toxicity of various chemicals, that is, how those chemicals affect plants, animals, and people. (Information on geoscientists, who also study the Earth, is located elsewhere in the *Handbook.*)

Environmental scientists and hydrologists in research positions with the Federal Government or in colleges and universities often have to find funding for their work by writing grant proposals. Consultants face similar pressures to market their skills and write proposals so that they will have steady work.

Work environment. Most entry-level environmental scientists and hydrologists spend the majority of their time in the field, while more experienced workers generally devote more time to office or laboratory work. Many beginning hydrologists and some environmental scientists, such as environmental ecologists and environmental chemists, often take field trips that involve physical activity. Environmental scientists and hydrologists in the field may work in warm or cold climates, in all kinds of weather. In their research, they may dig or chip with a hammer, scoop with a net, come in contact with water, and carry equipment. Travel often is required to meet with prospective clients or investors.

Researchers and consultants might face stress when looking for funding. Occasionally, those who write technical reports to business clients and regulators may be under pressure to meet deadlines and thus have to work long hours.

Training, Other Qualifications, and Advancement

Most environmental scientists and hydrologists need a master's degree. A Ph.D. is usually necessary for jobs in college teaching or research.

Education and training. A bachelor's degree in an earth science is adequate for a few entry-level positions, but environmental scientists increasingly need a master's degree in environmental science, hydrology, or a related natural science. A master's degree also is the minimum educational requirement for most entry-level applied research positions in private industry, in State and Federal agencies, and at State geological surveys. A doctoral degree generally is necessary for college teaching and most research positions.

Some environmental scientists have a degree in environmental science. Many, however, earn degrees in life science, chemistry, geology, geophysics, atmospheric science, or physics and then apply their education to the environment. They often need research or work experience related to environmental science.

A bachelor's degree in environmental science offers an interdisciplinary approach to the natural sciences, with an emphasis on biology, chemistry, and geology. Undergraduate environmental science majors typically focus on data analysis and physical geography, which are particularly useful in studying pollution abatement, water resources, or ecosystem protection, restoration, and management. Understanding the geochemistry of inorganic compounds is becoming increasingly important in developing remediation goals. Students interested in working in the environmental or regulatory fields, either in environmental consulting firms or for Federal or State governments, should take courses in hydrology, hazardous-waste management, environmental legislation, chemistry, fluid mechanics, and geologic logging, which is the gathering of geologic data. An understanding of environmental regulations and government permit issues also is valuable for those planning to work in mining and oil and gas extraction.

Students interested in hydrology should take courses in the physical sciences, geophysics, chemistry, engineering science, soil science, mathematics, aquatic biology, atmospheric science, geology, oceanography, hydrogeology, and the management or conservation of water resources. In some cases, a bachelor's degree in a hydrologic science is sufficient for positions consulting about water quality or wastewater treatment.

For environmental scientists and hydrologists who consult, courses in business, finance, marketing, or economics may be useful. In addition, combining environmental science training with other disciplines such as engineering or business, qualifies these scientists for the widest range of jobs.

Other qualifications. Computer skills are essential for prospective environmental scientists and hydrologists. Students who have some experience with computer modeling, data analysis and integration, digital mapping, remote sensing, and Geographic Information Systems (GIS) will be the most prepared to enter the job market. Familiarity with the Global Positioning System (GPS)—a locator system that uses satellites—is vital.

Environmental scientists and hydrologists must have good interpersonal skills, because they usually work as part of a team with other scientists, engineers, and technicians. Strong oral and written communication skills also are essential because writing technical reports and research proposals and communicating results to company managers, regulators, and the public are important aspects of the work. Because international work is becoming increasingly pervasive, knowledge of a second language can be an advantage. Those involved in fieldwork must have physical stamina.

Certification and advancement. Environmental scientists and hydrologists often begin their careers in field exploration or, occasionally, as research assistants or technicians in laboratories or offices. They are given more difficult assignments as they gain experience. Eventually, they may be promoted to project leader, program manager, or some other management and research position. (Information on engineering and natural science managers is located elsewhere in the *Handbook.*)

The American Institute of Hydrology offers certification programs in professional hydrology. Certification may be beneficial for those seeking advancement.

Employment

Environmental scientists and hydrologists held about 92,000 jobs in 2006. Jobs for hydrologists accounted for only 9 percent of the total. Many more individuals held environmental science faculty positions in colleges and universities, but they are classified as postsecondary teachers. (See the statement on teachers—postsecondary elsewhere in the *Handbook.*)

About 35 percent of environmental scientists were employed in State and local governments; 21 percent in management, scientific, and technical consulting services; 15 percent in architectural, engineering and related services; and 8 percent in the Federal Government. About 2 percent were self-employed.

Among hydrologists, 26 percent were employed in architectural, engineering, and related services, and 18 percent worked for management, scientific, and technical consulting services. In 2006, the Federal Government employed about 28 percent of hydrologists, mostly within the U.S. Department of the Interior for the U.S. Geological Survey (USGS) and within the U.S. Department of Defense. Another 21 percent worked for State agencies, such as State geological surveys and State departments of conservation. About 2 percent of hydrologists were self-employed, most as consultants to industry or government.

Job Outlook

Employment of environmental scientists and hydrologists is expected to grow much faster than the average for all occupations. Job prospects are expected to be favorable, particularly for hydrologists.

Employment change. Employment of environmental scientists is expected to increase by 25 percent between 2006 and 2016, much faster than the average for all occupations. Over the same period, employment of hydrologists should increase by 24 percent, also much faster than the average. Job growth for environmental scientists and hydrologists should be strongest in private-sector consulting firms. Growth in employment of environmental scientists and hydrologists will be spurred largely by the increasing demands placed on the environment and water resources by population growth. Further demand should result from the need to comply with complex environmental laws and regulations, particularly those regarding ground-water decontamination, clean air, and flood control.

Much job growth will result from a continued need to monitor the quality of the environment, to interpret the impact of human actions on terrestrial and aquatic ecosystems, and to develop strategies for restoring ecosystems. In addition, environmental

Projections data from the National Employment Matrix

Occupational Title	SOC Code	Employment, 2006	Projected employment, 2016	Change, 2006-2016	
				Number	Percent
Environmental scientists and hydrologists...	—	92,000	114,000	23,000	25
Environmental scientists and specialists, including health	19-2041	83,000	104,000	21,000	25
Hydrologists...	19-2043	8,300	10,000	2,000	24

NOTE: Data in this table are rounded. See the discussion of the employment projections table in the *Handbook* introductory chapter on *Occupational Information Included in the Handbook*.

scientists will be needed to help planners develop and construct buildings, transportation corridors, and utilities that protect water resources and reflect efficient and beneficial land use.

Demand for hydrologists should also be strong as the population increases and moves to more environmentally sensitive locations. As people increasingly migrate toward coastal regions, for example, hydrologists will be needed to assess building sites for potential geologic hazards and to mitigate the effects of natural hazards such as floods, landslides, and hurricanes. Hydrologists also will be needed to study hazardous-waste sites and determine the effect of pollutants on soil and ground water so that engineers can design remediation systems. Increased government regulations, such as those regarding the management of storm water, and issues related to water conservation, deteriorating coastal environments, and rising sea levels also will stimulate employment growth for these workers.

Many environmental scientists and hydrologists work in consulting. Consulting firms have hired these scientists to help businesses and government address issues related to underground tanks, land disposal areas, and other hazardous-waste-management facilities. Currently, environmental consulting is evolving from investigations to creating remediation and engineering solutions. At the same time, the regulatory climate is moving from a rigid structure to a more flexible risk-based approach. These factors, coupled with new Federal and State initiatives that integrate environmental activities into the business process itself, will result in a greater focus on waste minimization, resource recovery, pollution prevention, and the consideration of environmental effects during product development. This shift in focus to preventive management will provide many new opportunities for environmental scientists and hydrologists in consulting roles.

Job prospects. In addition to job openings due to growth, there will be additional demand for new environmental scientists and hydrologists to replace those who retire, advance to management positions, or change careers. Job prospects for hydrologists should be favorable, particularly for those with field experience. Demand for hydrologists who understand both the scientific and engineering aspects of waste remediation should be strong. Few colleges and universities offer programs in hydrology, so the number of qualified workers may be limited.

Job prospects for environmental scientists also will be good, but less favorable than for hydrologists because of the larger number of workers seeking to enter the field.

Funding for Federal and State geological surveys depend largely on the political climate and the current budget. Thus, job security for environmental scientists and hydrologists may vary. During periods of economic recession, layoffs of envi-

ronmental scientists and hydrologists may occur in consulting firms; layoffs are much less likely in government.

Earnings

Median annual earnings of environmental scientists were $56,100 in May 2006. The middle 50 percent earned between $42,840 and $74,480. The lowest 10 percent earned less than $34,590, and the highest 10 percent earned more than $94,670.

Median annual earnings of hydrologists were $66,260 in 2006, with the middle 50 percent earning between $51,370 and $82,140, the lowest 10 percent earning less than $42,080, and the highest 10 percent earning more than $98,320.

Median annual earnings in the industries employing the largest number of environmental scientists in 2006 were as follows:

Federal executive branch	$82,490
Management, scientific, and technical consulting services	57,280
Engineering services	56,080
Local government	52,100
State government	50,590

According to the National Association of Colleges and Employers, beginning salary offers in July 2007 for graduates with bachelor's degrees in an environmental science averaged $38,336 a year.

In 2007, the Federal Government's average salary for hydrologists was $82,217.

Related Occupations

Environmental scientists and hydrologists perform investigations for the purpose of abating or eliminating pollutants or hazards that affect the environment or plants, animals, and humans. Many other occupations deal with preserving or researching the natural environment, including conservation scientists and foresters, atmospheric scientists, and some biological scientists, science technicians, and engineering technicians. Environmental scientists and hydrologists have extensive training in physical sciences, and many apply their knowledge of chemistry, physics, biology, and mathematics to the study of the Earth, work closely related to that of geoscientists.

Using problem-solving skills, physicists; chemists; engineers; mathematicians; surveyors, cartographers, photogrammetrists, and surveying technicians; computer systems analysts; and computer scientists and database administrators may also perform similar work related to the environment.

Sources of Additional Information

Information on training and career opportunities for environmental scientists is available from:

➤ American Geological Institute, 4220 King St., Alexandria, VA 22302. Internet: **http://www.agiweb.org**

For information on careers in hydrology, contact:

➤ American Institute of Hydrology, 300 Village Green Circle, Suite #201, Smyrna, GA 30080.
Internet: **http://www.aihydro.org**

Information on obtaining a position as a hydrologist or an environmental protection specialist with the Federal Government is available from the Office of Personnel Management through USAJOBS, the Federal Government's official employment information system. This resource for locating and applying for job opportunities can be accessed through the Internet at **http://www.usajobs.opm.gov** or through an interactive voice response telephone system at (703) 724-1850 or TDD (978) 461-8404. These numbers are not toll free, and charges may result.

Geoscientists

(O*NET 19-2042)

Significant Points

- Work at remote field sites is common.

- Federal, State, and local governments employ 18 percent of all geoscientists.

- Employers prefer applicants with a master's degree for most positions; a Ph.D. degree is required for most high-level research and college teaching positions.

- Excellent job opportunities are expected for graduates with a master's degree.

Nature of the Work

Geoscientists study the composition, structure, and other physical aspects of the Earth. They study the Earth's geologic past and present by using sophisticated instruments to analyze the composition of earth, rock, and water. Many geoscientists help to search for natural resources such as groundwater, metals, and petroleum. Others work closely with environmental and other scientists to preserve and clean up the environment.

Geoscientists usually study and work in one of several closely related fields of geoscience. *Geologists* study the composition, processes, and history of the Earth. They try to find out how rocks were formed and what has happened to them since their formation. They also study the evolution of life by analyzing plant and animal fossils. *Geophysicists* use the principles of physics, mathematics, and chemistry to study not only the Earth's surface, but also its internal composition, ground and surface waters, atmosphere, oceans, and magnetic, electrical, and gravitational forces.

Within these two major disciplines of geology and geophysics are numerous subspecialties. For example, *petroleum geologists* map the subsurface of the ocean or land as they explore the terrain for oil and gas deposits. They use sophisticated instrumentation and computers to interpret geological information. *Engineering*

geologists apply geologic principles to the fields of civil and environmental engineering, offering advice on major construction projects and assisting in environmental remediation and natural hazard-reduction projects. *Mineralogists* analyze and classify minerals and precious stones according to their composition and structure. They study the environment surrounding rocks in order to find new mineral resources. *Sedimentologists* study the nature, origin, distribution, and alteration of sediments, such as sand, silt, and mud. These sediments may contain oil, gas, coal, and many other mineral deposits. *Paleontologists* study fossils found in geological formations to trace the evolution of plant and animal life and the geologic history of the Earth. *Stratigraphers* examine the formation and layering of rocks to understand the environment which formed them. *Volcanologists* investigate volcanoes and volcanic phenomena to try to predict the potential for future eruptions and hazards to human health and welfare. *Glacial geologists* study the physical properties and movement of glaciers and ice sheets. *Geochemists* study the nature and distribution of chemical elements in groundwater and earth materials.

Geophysicists specialize in areas such as geodesy, seismology, and magnetic geophysics. *Geodesists* study the Earth's size, shape, gravitational field, tides, polar motion, and rotation. *Seismologists* interpret data from seismographs and other geophysical instruments to detect earthquakes and locate earthquake-related faults. *Geomagnetists* measure the Earth's magnetic field and use measurements taken over the past few centuries to devise theoretical models that explain the Earth's origin. *Paleomagnetists* interpret fossil magnetization in rocks and sediments from the continents and oceans to record the spreading of the sea floor, the wandering of the continents, and the many reversals of polarity that the Earth's magnetic field has undergone through time. Other geophysicists study atmospheric sciences and space physics. (See the statement on atmospheric scientists, and physicists and astronomers, elsewhere in the *Handbook*.)

Oceanographers use their knowledge of geology and geophysics, in addition to biology and chemistry, to study the world's oceans and coastal waters. They study the motion and circulation of the ocean waters; the physical and chemical properties of the oceans; and how these properties affect coastal areas, climate, and weather. Oceanographers are further broken down according to their areas of expertise. For example, *physical oceanographers* study the tides, waves, currents, temperatures, density, and salinity of the ocean. They examine the interaction of various forms of energy, such as light, radar, sound, heat, and wind, with the sea, in addition to investigating the relationship between the sea, weather, and climate. *Chemical oceanographers* study the distribution of chemical compounds and chemical interactions that occur in the ocean and on the sea floor. They may investigate how pollution affects the chemistry of the ocean. *Geological and geophysical oceanographers* study the topographic features and the physical makeup of the ocean floor. Their knowledge can help companies find oil and gas off coastal waters. (*Biological oceanographers*, often called marine biologists, study the distribution and migration patterns of the many diverse forms of sea life in the ocean; the statement on biological scientists discusses this occupation elsewhere in the *Handbook*.)

Geoscientists in research positions with the Federal Government or in colleges and universities frequently are required to design programs and write grant proposals in order to fund their research. Geoscientists in consulting jobs face similar pressures to market their skills and write proposals so that they will have steady work.

Work environment. Geoscientists can spend a large part of their time in the field, identifying and examining rocks, studying information collected by remote sensing instruments in satellites, conducting geological surveys, constructing field maps, and using instruments to measure the Earth's gravity and magnetic field. They often perform seismic studies, for example, which involve bouncing energy waves off buried layers of rock, to search for oil and gas or to understand the structure of the subsurface layers. Similarly, they use seismic signals generated by an earthquake to determine the earthquake's location and intensity. In laboratories, geologists and geophysicists examine the chemical and physical properties of specimens. They study fossil remains of animal and plant life or experiment with the flow of water and oil through rocks.

Some geoscientists spend the majority of their time in an office, but many others divide their time between fieldwork and office or laboratory work. Work at remote field sites is common. Many geoscientists, such as volcanologists, often take field trips that involve physical activity. Geoscientists in the field may work in warm or cold climates and in all kinds of weather. In their research, they may dig or chip with a hammer, scoop with a net, and carry equipment in a backpack. Oceanographers may spend

Excellent employment opportunities are expected for geoscientists with a master's degree.

considerable time at sea on academic research ships. Geologists frequently travel to remote field sites by helicopter or 4-wheel-drive vehicles and cover large areas on foot. Many exploration geologists and geophysicists work in foreign countries, sometimes in remote areas and under difficult conditions. Travel often is required to meet with prospective clients or investors. Fieldwork often requires working long hours.

Training, Other Qualifications, and Advancement

A master's degree is the primary educational requirement for most entry-level positions. A Ph.D. is necessary for most high-level research and college teaching positions, but a master's degree is preferred for most other geoscience jobs.

Education and training. A bachelor's degree is adequate for a few entry-level positions, but most geoscientists need a master's degree in geology or earth science. A master's degree is the preferred educational requirement for most entry-level research positions in private industry, Federal agencies, and State geological surveys. A Ph.D. is necessary for most high-level research and college teaching positions, but it may not be preferred for other jobs.

Many colleges and universities offer a bachelor's or higher degree in a geoscience. Traditional geoscience courses emphasizing classical geologic methods and topics (such as mineralogy, petrology, paleontology, stratigraphy, and structural geology) are important for all geoscientists. People who study physics, chemistry, biology, mathematics, engineering, or computer science may also qualify for some geoscience positions if their course work includes geology.

Licensure. A number of States require geoscientists who offer their services directly to the public, particularly geologists, to obtain a license from a State licensing board. Licensing requirements vary but often include education, experience, and a passing score on an examination.

Other qualifications. Computer skills are essential for prospective geoscientists; students who have experience with computer modeling, data analysis and integration, digital mapping, remote sensing, and Geographic Information Systems (GIS) will be the most prepared entering the job market. Knowledge of the Global Positioning System (GPS)—a locator system that uses satellites—has also become essential. Some employers seek applicants with field experience, so a summer internship is often helpful.

Geoscientists must have good interpersonal skills because they usually work as part of a team with other geoscientists and with environmental scientists, engineers, and technicians. Strong oral and written communication skills also are important because writing technical reports and research proposals and explaining research results in person are important aspects of the work. Because many jobs require foreign travel, knowledge of a second language is becoming increasingly beneficial.

Geoscientists must be inquisitive, able to think logically, and capable of complex analytical thinking, including spatial visualization and the ability to infer conclusions from sparse data. Those involved in fieldwork must have physical stamina.

Advancement. Geoscientists often begin their careers in field exploration or as research assistants or technicians in laboratories or offices. As they gain experience, they get more assignments that are difficult. Eventually, some are promoted to project leader, program manager, or to a senior research position. Those who choose to work in management will spend more time scheduling, budgeting, and reporting to top executives or clients. (See the statement on engineering and natural sciences managers elsewhere in the *Handbook*.)

Employment

Geoscientists held about 31,000 jobs in 2006. Many more individuals held geoscience faculty positions in colleges and universities, but they are classified as college and university faculty. (See the statement on teachers—postsecondary elsewhere in the *Handbook*.)

About 24 percent of geoscientists were employed in architectural, engineering, and related services, and 18 percent worked for oil and gas extraction companies. In 2006, State agencies such as State geological surveys and State departments of conservation employed about 2,900 geoscientists. Another 2,600 worked for the Federal Government, including geologists, geophysicists, and oceanographers, mostly within the U.S. Department of the Interior for the U.S. Geological Survey (USGS) and within the U.S. Department of Defense. About 2 percent of geoscientists were self-employed, most as consultants to industry or government.

Job Outlook

Although employment growth will vary by industry, overall employment of geoscientists is expected to grow much faster than the average for all occupations. Graduates with a master's degree can expect excellent job opportunities; very few geoscientist jobs are available to bachelor's degree holders. Ph.D.s should face competition for basic research and college teaching jobs.

Employment change. Employment growth of 22 percent for geoscientists is expected between 2006 and 2016, much faster than the average for all occupations. The need for energy, environmental protection, and responsible land and water management will spur employment demand. Employment in management, scientific, and technical consulting services should continue to grow as more geoscientists work as consultants. These services have increased their hiring of geoscientists in recent years because of increased government contracting, and private corporations' need for technical assistance and environmental management plans. Moreover, many geoscientists monitor the quality of the environment, including aquatic ecosystems, deteriorating coastal environments, and rising sea levels—all of which will create employment growth for them. An expected increase in highway building and other infrastructure projects will also be a source of jobs for engineering geologists.

Employment is also expected to increase in the oil and gas extraction industry. Many geoscientists work in the exploration and production of oil and gas. Historically, employment of petroleum geologists, geophysicists, and some other geoscientists has been cyclical and affected considerably by the price of oil and gas. When prices are low, oil and gas producers curtail explora-

tion activities and lay off geologists. When prices were higher, companies had the funds and incentive to renew exploration efforts and to hire geoscientists in larger numbers. In recent years, however, a growing worldwide demand for oil and gas and for new exploration and recovery techniques—particularly in deep water and previously inaccessible sites in Alaska and the Gulf of Mexico—has created some stability to the petroleum industry. Geoscientists who speak a foreign language and who are willing to work abroad should enjoy the best opportunities, as the need for energy, construction materials, and a broad range of geoscience expertise grows in developing nations.

Job prospects. Graduates with a master's degree should have excellent opportunities, especially in the management, scientific and technical consulting industry and in the engineering services industries. In addition to demand resulting from job growth, replacing those who leave the occupation for retirement, managerial positions, or other careers will generate a number of jobs. With relatively few students earning master's degrees in the geosciences, job openings may exceed the number of qualified job seekers over the 2006-16 projection decade. However, geoscientists with doctoral degrees, who primarily work as college and university faculty or do basic research, may face competition. There are few openings for new graduates with only a bachelor's degree in geoscience, but these graduates may have favorable opportunities in related occupations, such as high school science teacher or science technician.

There will be fewer opportunities for geoscientists in Federal and State government, mostly because of budget constraints at key agencies, such as the USGS, and the trend among governments toward contracting out to consulting firms instead of hiring new government employees. However, departures of geoscientists who retire or leave the government for other reasons will result in some job openings over the next decade.

Geoscientists may face layoffs during periods of economic recession. Especially vulnerable are those in consulting and, to a lesser extent, workers in Government. Employment for those working in the production of oil and gas, however, will largely be dictated by the cyclical nature of the energy sector and changes in government policy, although less so than in the past.

Earnings

Median annual earnings of geoscientists were $72,660 in May 2006. The middle 50 percent earned between $51,860 and $100,650; the lowest 10 percent earned less than $39,740, the highest 10 percent more than $135,950.

The petroleum, mineral, and mining industries offer higher salaries, but less job security, than other industries because economic downturns sometimes cause layoffs.

According to the National Association of Colleges and Employers, beginning salary offers in July 2007 for graduates with bachelor's degrees in geology and related sciences averaged $40,786 a year.

Projections data from the National Employment Matrix

Occupational Title	SOC Code	Employment, 2006	Projected employment, 2016	Change, 2006-2016	
				Number	Percent
Geoscientists, except hydrologists and geographers.........................	19-2042	31,000	38,000	6,800	22

NOTE: Data in this table are rounded. See the discussion of the employment projections table in the *Handbook* introductory chapter on *Occupational Information Included in the Handbook*.

In 2007, the Federal Government's average salary was $87,392 for geologists, $100,585 for geophysicists, and 93,461 for oceanographers.

Related Occupations

Many geoscientists work in the petroleum and natural gas industry, an industry that also employs numerous other workers whose jobs deal with the scientific and technical aspects of the exploration and extraction of petroleum and natural gas. Among these other workers are engineering technicians; science technicians; petroleum engineers; and surveyors, cartographers, photogrammetrists, and surveying technicians. Also, some physicists and astronomers, chemists and materials scientists, atmospheric scientists, biological scientists, and environmental scientists and hydrologists perform related work both in the exploration and extraction of petroleum and natural gas and in activities having to do with the environment.

Sources of Additional Information

Information on training and career opportunities for geologists is available from either of the following organizations:

➤ American Association of Petroleum Geologists, P.O. Box 979, Tulsa, OK 74101. Internet: **http://www.aapg.org**

➤ American Geological Institute, 4220 King St., Alexandria, VA 22302-1502. Internet: **http://www.agiweb.org**

Information on obtaining a position as a geologist, geophysicist, or oceanographer with the Federal Government is available from the Office of Personnel Management through USAJOBS, the Federal Government's official employment information system. This resource for locating and applying for job opportunities can be accessed through the Internet at **http://www.usajobs.opm.gov** or through an interactive voice response telephone system at (703) 724-1850 or TDD (978) 461-8404. These numbers are not toll free, and charges may result.

Physicists and Astronomers

(O*NET 19-2011.00, 19-2012.00)

Significant Points

- Scientific research and development services firms and the Federal Government employ over half of all physicists and astronomers.

- Most jobs are in basic research, usually requiring a doctoral degree; master's degree holders qualify for some jobs in applied research and development; bachelor's degree holders often qualify as research assistants or for other physics-related occupations, such as technicians.

- Applicants may face competition for basic research positions due to limited funding; however, those with a background in physics or astronomy may have good opportunities in related occupations.

Nature of the Work

Physicists and astronomers conduct research to understand the nature of the universe and everything in it. These researchers observe, measure, interpret, and develop theories to explain celestial and physical phenomena using mathematics. From the vastness of space to the infinitesimal scale of subatomic particles, they study the fundamental properties of the natural world and apply the knowledge gained to design new technologies.

Physicists explore and identify basic principles and laws governing the motion, energy, structure, and interactions of matter. Some physicists study theoretical areas, such as the nature of time and the origin of the universe; others apply their knowledge of physics to practical areas, such as the development of advanced materials, electronic and optical devices, and medical equipment.

Physicists design and perform experiments with lasers, particle accelerators, electron microscopes, mass spectrometers, and other equipment. On the basis of their observations and analysis, they attempt to discover and explain laws describing the forces of nature, such as gravity, electromagnetism, and nuclear interactions. Experiments also help physicists find ways to apply physical laws and theories to problems in nuclear energy, electronics, optics, materials, communications, aerospace technology, and medical instrumentation.

Astronomers use the principles of physics and mathematics to learn about the fundamental nature of the universe, including the sun, moon, planets, stars, and galaxies. As such, astronomy is sometimes considered a subfield of physics. They also apply their knowledge to solve problems in navigation, space flight, and satellite communications and to develop the instrumentation and techniques used to observe and collect astronomical data.

Most physicists work in research and development. Some do basic research to increase scientific knowledge. Others conduct applied research to build upon the discoveries made through basic research and work to develop new devices, products, and processes. For example, basic research in solid-state physics led to the development of transistors and, then, integrated circuits used in computers.

Physicists also design research equipment, which often has additional unanticipated uses. For example, lasers are used in surgery, microwave devices function in ovens, and measuring instruments can analyze blood or the chemical content of foods.

A small number of physicists work in inspection, testing, quality control, and other production-related jobs in industry.

Much physics research is done in small or medium-sized laboratories. However, experiments in plasma, nuclear, and high-energy physics, as well as in some other areas of physics, require extremely large, expensive equipment, such as particle accelerators. Physicists in these subfields often work in large teams. Although physics research may require extensive experimentation in laboratories, research physicists still spend much time in offices planning, recording, analyzing, and reporting on research.

Physicists generally specialize in one of many subfields: elementary particle physics, nuclear physics, atomic and molecular physics, condensed matter physics (solid-state physics), optics, acoustics, space physics, plasma physics, or the physics of fluids. Some specialize in a subdivision of one of these subfields. For example, within condensed-matter physics, specialties include superconductivity, crystallography, and semiconductors. However, all physics involves the same fundamental principles, so specialties may overlap, and physicists may switch from one subfield to another. Also, growing numbers of physicists work in interdisciplinary fields, such as biophysics, chemical physics, and geophysics.

Almost all astronomers do research. Some are theoreticians, working on the laws governing the structure and evolution of astronomical objects. Others analyze large quantities of data gathered by observatories and satellites and write scientific papers or reports on their findings. Some astronomers actually operate large space-based or ground-based telescopes, usually as part of a team. However, astronomers may spend only a few weeks each year making observations with optical telescopes, radio telescopes, and other instruments.

For many years, satellites and other space-based instruments, such as the Hubble space telescope, have provided prodigious amounts of astronomical data. New technology has lead to improvements in analytical techniques and instruments, such as

Most jobs for physicists and astronomers are in research and usually require a doctoral degree.

computers and optical telescopes and mounts, and is creating a resurgence in ground-based research.

A small number of astronomers work in museums housing planetariums. These astronomers develop and revise programs presented to the public and may direct planetarium operations.

Work environment. Most physicists and astronomers do not encounter unusual hazards in their work. Some physicists temporarily work away from home at national or international facilities with unique equipment, such as particle accelerators. Astronomers who make observations with ground-based telescopes may spend many hours working in observatories; this work usually involves travel to remote locations and may require working at night. Physicists and astronomers whose work depends on grant money often are under pressure to write grant proposals to keep their work funded.

Physicists often work regular hours in laboratories and offices. At times, however, those who are deeply involved in research may work long or irregular hours. Astronomers may need to work at odd hours to observe celestial phenomena, particularly those working with ground-based telescopes.

Training, Other Qualifications, and Advancement

Because most jobs are in basic research and development, a doctoral degree is the usual educational requirement for physicists and astronomers. Master's degree holders qualify for some jobs in applied research and development, whereas bachelor's degree holders often qualify as research assistants or for other occupations related to physics.

Education and training. A Ph.D. degree in physics or closely related fiends is typically required for basic research positions, independent research in industry, faculty positions, and advancement to managerial positions. This prepares students for a career in research through rigorous training in theory, methodology, and mathematics. Most physicists specialize in a subfield during graduate school and continue working in that area afterwards.

Additional experience and training in a postdoctoral research appointment, although not required, is important for physicists and astronomers aspiring to permanent positions in basic research in universities and government laboratories. Many physics and astronomy Ph.D. holders ultimately teach at the college or university level.

Master's degree holders usually do not qualify for basic research positions, but may qualify for many kinds of jobs requiring a physics background, including positions in manufacturing and applied research and development. Increasingly, many master's degree programs are specifically preparing students for physics-related research and development that does not require a Ph.D. degree. These programs teach students specific research skills that can be used in private-industry jobs. In addition, a master's degree coupled with State certification usually qualifies one for teaching jobs in high schools or at 2-year colleges.

Those with bachelor's degrees in physics are rarely qualified to fill positions in research or in teaching at the college level. They are, however, usually qualified to work as technicians or research assistants in engineering-related areas, in software development and other scientific fields, or in setting up computer networks and sophisticated laboratory equipment. Increasingly, some may qualify for applied research jobs in private industry or take on nontraditional physics roles, often in computer science, such as systems analysts or database administrators. Some become science teachers in secondary schools.

Holders of a bachelor's or master's degree in astronomy often enter an unrelated field. However, they are also qualified to work in planetariums running science shows, to assist astronomers doing research, and to operate space-based and ground-based telescopes and other astronomical instrumentation. (See the statements on engineers, geoscientists, computer programmers, computer scientists and database administrators, computer software engineers, and computer systems analysts elsewhere in the *Handbook*.)

About 760 colleges and universities offer a bachelor's degree in physics. Undergraduate programs provide a broad background in the natural sciences and mathematics. Typical physics courses include electromagnetism, optics, thermodynamics, atomic physics, and quantum mechanics.

Approximately 185 colleges and universities have departments offering Ph.D. degrees in physics; about 70 additional colleges offer a master's as their highest degree in physics. Graduate students usually concentrate in a subfield of physics, such as elementary particles or condensed matter. Many begin studying for their doctorate immediately after receiving their bachelor's degree.

About 80 universities grant degrees in astronomy, either through an astronomy, physics, or combined physics-astronomy department. Currently, about 40 astronomy departments are combined with physics departments, and the same number are administered separately. With about 40 doctoral programs in astronomy, applicants face considerable competition for available slots. Those planning a career in the subject should have a strong physics background. In fact, an undergraduate degree in either physics or astronomy is excellent preparation, followed by a Ph.D. in astronomy.

Many physics and astronomy Ph.D. holders begin their careers in a postdoctoral research position, in which they may work with experienced physicists as they continue to learn about their specialties or develop a broader understanding of related areas of research. Initial work may be under the close supervision of senior scientists. As they gain experience, physicists perform increasingly complex tasks and achieve greater independence in their work. Experience, either in academic laboratories or through internships, fellowships, or work-study programs in industry, also is useful. Some employers of research physicists, particularly in the information technology industry, prefer to hire individuals with several years of postdoctoral experience.

Other qualifications. Mathematical ability, problem-solving and analytical skills, an inquisitive mind, imagination, and initiative are important traits for anyone planning a career in physics or astronomy. Prospective physicists who hope to work in industrial laboratories applying physics knowledge to practical problems should broaden their educational background to include courses outside of physics, such as econom-

ics, information technology, and business management. Good oral and written communication skills also are important because many physicists work as part of a team, write research papers or proposals, or have contact with clients or customers with nonphysics backgrounds.

Advancement. Advancement among physicists and astronomers usually takes the form of greater independence in their work, larger budgets, or tenure in university positions. Others choose to move into managerial positions and become natural science managers (listed elsewhere in the *Handbook*). Those who pursue management careers spend more time preparing budgets and schedules. Those who develop new products or processes sometimes form their own companies or join new firms to develop these ideas.

Employment

Physicists and astronomers held about 18,000 jobs in 2006. Physicists accounted for about 17,000 of these, while astronomers accounted for only about 1,700 jobs. Many physicists and astronomers held faculty positions in colleges and universities. Those classified as postsecondary teachers are not included in these employment numbers. (See the statement on teachers—postsecondary elsewhere in the *Handbook*.)

About 38 percent of physicists and astronomers worked for scientific research and development services firms. The Federal Government employed 21 percent, mostly in the U.S. Department of Defense, but also in the National Aeronautics and Space Administration (NASA) and in the U.S. Departments of Commerce, Health and Human Services, and Energy. Other physicists and astronomers worked in colleges and universities in nonfaculty, usually research, positions, or for State governments, information technology companies, pharmaceutical and medicine manufacturing companies, or electronic equipment manufacturers.

Although physicists and astronomers are employed in all parts of the country, most work in areas in which universities, large research laboratories, or observatories are located.

Job Outlook

Physicists and astronomers should experience average job growth but may face competition for basic research positions due to limited funding. However, those with a background in physics or astronomy may have good opportunities in related occupations.

Employment change. Employment of physicists and astronomers is expected to grow at 7 percent, about as fast as the average for all occupations during the 2006-16 decade. The need to replace physicists and astronomers who retire or otherwise leave the occupation permanently will account for many additional expected job openings.

Federal research expenditures are the major source of physics- and astronomy-related research funds, especially for basic research. Although these expenditures are expected to increase over the 2006-16 projection period, resulting in some growth in employment and opportunities, the limited science research funds available still will result in competition for basic research jobs among Ph.D. holders. However, research relating to biotechnology and nanotechnology should continue to see strong growth.

Although research and development expenditures in private industry will continue to grow, many research laboratories in private industry are expected to continue to reduce basic research, which includes much physics research, in favor of applied or manufacturing research and product and software development. Nevertheless, people with a physics background continue to be in demand in information technology, semiconductor technology, and other applied sciences. This trend is expected to continue; however, many of the new workers will have job titles such as computer software engineer, computer programmer, or systems analyst or developer, rather than physicist.

Job prospects. In recent years the number of doctorates granted in physics has been somewhat greater than the number of job openings for traditional physics research positions in colleges and universities and in research centers. Recent increases in undergraduate physics enrollments may also lead to growth in enrollments in graduate physics programs, so that there may be an increase in the number of doctoral degrees granted that could intensify the competition for basic research positions. However, demand has grown in other related occupations for those with advanced training in physics. Prospects should be favorable for physicists in applied research, development, and related technical fields.

Opportunities should also be numerous for those with a master's degree, particularly graduates from programs preparing students for related work in applied research and development, product design, and manufacturing positions in private industry. Many of these positions, however, will have titles other than physicist, such as engineer or computer scientist.

People with only a bachelor's degree in physics or astronomy are usually not qualified for physics or astronomy research jobs, but they may qualify for a wide range of positions related to engineering, mathematics, computer science, environmental science, and some nonscience fields, such as finance. Those who meet State certification requirements can become high school physics teachers, an occupation in strong demand in many school districts. Some States require new teachers to obtain a master's degree in education within a certain time. (See the statement on teachers—preschool, kindergarten, elementary, middle, and secondary elsewhere in the *Handbook.*) Despite competition for traditional physics and astronomy research jobs, graduates with a physics or astronomy degree at any level will find their knowledge of science and mathematics useful for entry into many other occupations.

Despite their small numbers, astronomers can expect good job prospects in government and academia over the projection period. Since astronomers are particularly dependent upon government funding, Federal budgetary decisions will have a sizable influence on job prospects for astronomers.

Earnings

Median annual earnings of physicists were 94,240 in May 2006. The middle 50 percent earned between $72,910 and $117,080. The lowest 10 percent earned less than $52,070, and the highest 10 percent earned 143,570.

Median annual earnings of astronomers were $95,740 in 2006. The middle 50 percent earned between $62,050 and $125,420, the lowest 10 percent less than $44,590, and the highest 10 percent more than $145,600.

According to a 2007 National Association of Colleges and Employers survey, the average annual starting salary offer to physics doctoral degree candidates was $52,469.

The American Institute of Physics reported a median annual salary of $80,000 in 2006 for its members with Ph.D.'s (excluding those in postdoctoral positions) who were employed by a university on a 9-10 month salary; the median was $112,700 for those who held a Ph.D. and worked at a federally funded research and development center; and $110,000 for self-employed physicists who hold a Ph.D. Those working in temporary postdoctoral positions earned significantly less.

The average annual salary for physicists employed by the Federal Government was $111,769 in 2007; for astronomy and space scientists, it was $117,570.

Related Occupations

The work of physicists and astronomers relates closely to that of engineers, chemists and materials scientists, atmospheric scientists, environmental scientists and hydrologists, geoscientists, computer systems analysts, computer scientists and database administrators, computer programmers, mathematicians, and engineering and natural sciences managers.

Sources of Additional Information

Further information on career opportunities in physics is available from the following organizations:

➤ American Institute of Physics, Career Services Division and Education and Employment Division, One Physics EllipSE., College Park, MD 20740-3843. Internet: **http://www.aip.org**

➤ American Physical Society, One Physics EllipSE., College Park, MD 20740-3844. Internet: **http://www.aps.org**

Projections data from the National Employment Matrix

Occupational Title	SOC Code	Employment, 2006	Projected employment, 2016	Change, 2006-2016	
				Number	Percent
Astronomers and physicists	19-2010	18,000	19,000	1,200	7
Astronomers..	19-2011	1,700	1,700	100	6
Physicists..	19-2012	17,000	18,000	1,100	7

NOTE: Data in this table are rounded. See the discussion of the employment projections table in the *Handbook* introductory chapter on *Occupational Information Included in the Handbook.*

Social Scientists and Related Occupations

Economists

(O*NET 19-3011.00)

Significant Points

- Slower than average job growth is expected as firms increasingly employ workers with titles that reflect specialized duties rather than the general title of economist.

- Job seekers with a background in economics should have opportunities in various occupations.

- Candidates who hold a master's or Ph.D. degree in economics will have the best employment prospects and advancement opportunities.

- Quantitative skills are important in all economics specialties.

Nature of the Work

Economists study how society distributes resources, such as land, labor, raw materials, and machinery, to produce goods and services. They may conduct research, collect and analyze data, monitor economic trends, or develop forecasts. Economists research a wide variety of issues including energy costs, inflation, interest rates, exchange rates, business cycles, taxes, and employment levels, among others.

Economists develop methods for obtaining the data they need. For example, sampling techniques may be used to conduct a survey and various mathematical modeling techniques may be used to develop forecasts. Preparing reports, including tables and charts, on research results also is an important part of an economist's job. Presenting economic and statistical concepts in a clear and meaningful way is particularly important for economists whose research is intended for managers and others who do not have a background in economics. Some economists also perform economic analysis for the media.

Many economists specialize in a particular area of economics, although general knowledge of basic economic principles is essential. *Microeconomists* study the supply and demand decisions of individuals and firms, such as how profits can be maximized and the quantity of a good or service that consumers will demand at a certain price. *Industrial economists* or *organizational economists* study the market structure of particular industries in terms of the number of competitors within those industries and examine the market decisions of competitive firms and monopolies. These economists also may be concerned with antitrust policy and its impact on market structure. *Macroeconomists* study historical trends in the whole economy and forecast future trends in areas such as unemployment, inflation, economic growth, productivity, and investment. Doing similar work as macroeconomists are *monetary economists* or *financial economists*, who study the money and banking system and the effects of changing interest rates. *International economists* study international financial markets, exchange rates, and the effects of various trade policies such as tariffs. *Labor economists* or *demographic economists* study the supply and demand for labor and the determination of wages. These economists also try to explain the reasons for unemployment and the effects of changing demographic trends, such as an aging population and increasing immigration, on labor markets. *Public finance economists* are involved primarily in studying the role of the government in the economy and the effects of tax cuts, budget deficits, and welfare policies. *Econometricians* investigate all areas of economics and apply mathematical techniques such as calculus, game theory, and regression analysis to their research. With these techniques, they formulate economic models that help explain economic relationships and that can be used to develop forecasts about business cycles, the effects of a specific rate of inflation on the economy, the effects of tax legislation on unemployment levels, and other economic phenomena.

Many economists apply these areas of economics to health, education, agriculture, urban and regional economics, law, history, energy, the environment, or other issues. Most economists are concerned with practical applications of economic policy. Economists working for corporations are involved primarily in microeconomic issues, such as forecasting consumer demand and sales of the firm's products. Some analyze their competitors' growth and market share and advise their company on how to handle the competition. Others monitor legislation passed by Congress, such as environmental and worker safety regulations, and assess how the new laws will affect the corporation. Corporations with many international branches or subsidiaries might employ economists to monitor the economic situations in countries where they do business or to provide a risk assessment of a country into which the company is considering expanding.

Economists working in economic consulting or research firms sometimes perform the same tasks as economists working for corporations. However, economists in consulting firms also perform much of the macroeconomic analysis and forecasting conducted in the United States. These economists collect data on various economic indicators, maintain databases, analyze historical trends, and develop models to forecast growth, inflation, unemployment, or interest rates. Their analyses and forecasts are frequently published in newspapers and journal articles.

Another large employer of economists is the government. Economists in the Federal Government administer most of the surveys and collect the majority of the economic data about the United States. For example, economists in the U.S. Department of Commerce collect and analyze data on the production, distribution, and consumption of commodities produced in the United States and overseas, and economists employed by the U.S. Department of Labor collect and analyze data on the domestic economy, including data on prices, wages, employment, productivity, and safety and health.

Economists spend much of their time conducting research and writing reports.

Economists who work for government agencies also assess economic conditions in the United States or abroad to estimate the effects of specific changes in legislation or public policy. Government economists advise policy makers in areas such as the deregulation of industries, the effects of changes to Social Security, the effects of tax cuts on the budget deficit, and the effectiveness of imposing tariffs on imported goods. An economist working in State or local government might analyze data on the growth of school-age or prison populations and on employment and unemployment rates in order to project future spending needs.

Work environment. Economists have structured work schedules. They often work alone, writing reports, preparing statistical charts, and using computers, but they also may be an integral part of a research team. Most work under pressure of deadlines and tight schedules, which may require overtime. Their routine may be interrupted by special requests for data and by the need to attend meetings or conferences. Frequent travel may be necessary.

Training, Other Qualifications, and Advancement

Some entry-level positions for economists are available to those with a bachelor's degree, but higher degrees are required for many positions. Prospective economists need good quantitative skills.

Education and training. A master's or Ph.D. degree in economics is required for many private sector economist jobs and for advancement to more responsible positions. In the Federal Government, candidates for entry-level economist positions must have a bachelor's degree with a minimum of 21 semester hours of economics and 3 hours of statistics, accounting, or calculus.

Economics includes numerous specialties at the graduate level, such as econometrics, international economics, and labor economics. Students should select graduate schools that are strong in the specialties that interest them. Some schools help graduate students find internships or part-time employment in government agencies, economic consulting or research firms, or financial institutions before graduation.

Undergraduate economics majors can choose from a variety of courses, ranging from microeconomics, macroeconomics,

and econometrics to more philosophical courses, such as the history of economic thought. Because of the importance of quantitative skills to economists, courses in mathematics, statistics, econometrics, sampling theory and survey design, and computer science are extremely helpful.

Whether working in government, industry, research organizations, or consulting firms, economists with a bachelor's degree usually qualify for entry-level positions as a research assistant, for administrative or management trainee positions, or for various sales jobs. A master's degree usually is required to qualify for more responsible research and administrative positions. A Ph.D. is necessary for top economist positions in many organizations. Also, many corporation and government executives have a strong background in economics.

Aspiring economists should gain experience gathering and analyzing data, conducting interviews or surveys, and writing reports on their findings while in college. This experience can prove invaluable later in obtaining a full-time position in the field because much of the economist's work, especially in the beginning, may center on these duties. With experience, economists eventually are assigned their own research projects. Related job experience, such as work as a stock or bond trader, might be advantageous.

Other qualifications. Those considering careers as economists should be able to pay attention to details because much time is spent on precise data analysis. Candidates also should have strong computer and quantitative skills and be able to perform complex research. Patience and persistence are necessary qualities, given that economists must spend long hours on independent study and problem solving. Good communication skills also are useful, as economists must be able to present their findings, both orally and in writing, in a clear, concise manner.

Advancement. With experience or an advanced degree, economists may advance into positions of greater responsibility, including administration and independent research.

Many people with an economics background become teachers. (See the statement on teachers—postsecondary elsewhere in the *Handbook.*) A master's degree usually is the minimum requirement for a job as an instructor in a junior or community college. In most colleges and universities, however, a Ph.D. is necessary for appointment as an instructor. A Ph.D. and extensive publications in academic journals are required for a professorship, tenure, and promotion.

Employment

Economists held about 15,000 jobs in 2006. Government employed 52 percent of economists, in a wide range of agencies, with 32 percent in Federal Government and 20 percent in State and local government. The remaining jobs were spread throughout private industry, particularly in scientific research and development services and management, scientific, and technical consulting services. A number of economists combine a full-time job in government, academia, or business with part-time or consulting work in another setting.

Employment of economists is concentrated in large cities. Some work abroad for companies with major international operations, for U.S. Government agencies, and for international organizations, such as the World Bank, International Monetary Fund, and United Nations.

In addition to the previously mentioned jobs, economists hold faculty positions in colleges and universities. Economics faculties have flexible work schedules and may divide their time among teaching, research, consulting, and administration. These workers are counted as postsecondary teachers, not economists.

Job Outlook

Employment of economists is expected to grow about as fast as the average for all occupations. The demand for workers who have knowledge and skill in economics is projected to grow faster, but these workers are often in occupations other than economist. Job prospects will be best for those with graduate degrees in economics.

Employment change. Employment of economists is expected to grow seven percent from 2006 to 2016, about as fast as the average for all occupations. Demand for economic analysis should grow, but the increase in the number of economist jobs will be tempered as firms hire workers for more specialized jobs with specialized titles. Many workers with economic backgrounds will work in related occupations with more specific job titles, such as financial analyst, market analyst, public policy consultant, researcher or research assistant, and purchasing manager. Overall employment growth also will be slowed because of the relatively high number of economists employed in slow growing or declining government sectors. Employment in Federal government agencies is expected to decrease, and employment in State and local government is expected to grow more slowly than employment in the private sector.

Employment growth should be fastest in private industry, especially in management, scientific, and technical consulting services. Rising demand for economic analysis in virtually every industry should stem from the growing complexity of the global economy, the effects of competition on businesses, and increased reliance on quantitative methods for analyzing and forecasting business, sales, and other economic trends. Some corporations choose to hire economic consultants to fill these needs, rather than keeping an economist on staff. This practice should result in more economists being employed in consulting services.

Job prospects. In addition to job openings from growth, the need to replace experienced workers who transfer to other occupations or who retire or leave the labor force for other reasons will create openings for economists.

Individuals with a background in economics should have opportunities in various occupations. As indicated earlier, some examples of job titles often held by those with an economics background are financial analyst, market analyst, public policy consultant, researcher or research assistant, and purchasing manager.

People who have a master's or Ph.D. degree in economics, who are skilled in quantitative techniques and their application to economic modeling and forecasting, and who also have good communications skills, should have the best job opportunities. Like those in many other disciplines, some economists leave the occupation to become professors, but competition for tenured teaching positions is expected to be keen.

Bachelor's degree holders may face competition for the limited number of economist positions for which they qualify. However, they will qualify for a number of other positions that can use their economic knowledge. Many graduates with bachelor's degrees will find jobs in industry and business as management or sales trainees. Bachelor's degree holders with good quantitative skills and a strong background in mathematics, statistics, survey design, and computer science also may be hired as researchers. Some will find jobs in government.

Candidates who meet State certification requirements may become high school economics teachers. The demand for secondary school economics teachers is expected to grow, as economics becomes an increasingly important and popular course. (See the statement on teachers—preschool, kindergarten, elementary, middle, and secondary elsewhere in the *Handbook*.)

Earnings

Median annual wage and salary earnings of economists were $77,010 in May 2006. The middle 50 percent earned between $55,740 and $103,500. The lowest 10 percent earned less than $42,280, and the highest 10 percent earned more than $136,550.

In the Federal Government, the starting salary for economists having a bachelor's degree was $35,752 in 2007. Those having a master's degree could qualify for positions with an annual salary of $43,731. Those with a Ph.D. could begin at $52,912, and some individuals with experience and an advanced degree could start at $63,417. Starting salaries were higher in selected geographical areas where the prevailing local pay was higher. The average annual salary for economists employed by the Federal Government was $94,098 a year in 2007.

Related Occupations

Economists are concerned with understanding and interpreting financial matters, among other subjects. Other occupations in this area include accountants and auditors; actuaries; budget analysts; cost estimators; financial analysts and personal financial advisors; financial managers; insurance underwriters; loan officers; and purchasing managers, buyers, and purchasing agents. Economists also rely heavily on quantitative analysis, as do mathematicians, statisticians, and operations research analysts. Other occupations involved in market research and

Projections data from the National Employment Matrix

Occupational Title	SOC Code	Employment, 2006	Projected employment, 2016	Change, 2006-2016	
				Number	Percent
Economists..	19-3011	15,000	16,000	1,100	7

NOTE: Data in this table are rounded. See the discussion of the employment projections table in the *Handbook* introductory chapter on *Occupational Information Included in the Handbook.*

data collection are management analysts and market and survey researchers. Economists also study consumer behavior, similar to the work of sociologists.

Sources of Additional Information

For information on careers in business economics, contact:
➤ National Association for Business Economics, 1233 20th St.NW., Suite 505, Washington, DC 20036.

Information on obtaining positions as economists with the Federal Government is available from the Office of Personnel Management through USAJOBS, the Federal Government's official employment information system. This resource for locating and applying for job opportunities can be accessed through the Internet at **http://www.usajobs.opm.gov** or through an interactive voice response telephone system at (703) 724-1850 or TDD (978) 461-8404. These numbers are not toll free, and charges may result. For advice on how to find and apply for Federal jobs, see the Occupational Outlook Quarterly article "How to get a job in the Federal Government," online at: **http://www.bls.gov/opub/ooq/2004/summer/art01.pdf**

Market and Survey Researchers

(O*NET 19-3021.00, 19-3022.00)

Significant Points

- Market and survey researchers need at least a bachelor's degree.

- Continuing education and keeping current with the latest methods of developing, conducting, and analyzing surveys and other data is important for advancement.

- Employment is expected to grow faster than average.

- Job opportunities should be best for those with a master's or Ph.D. degree in marketing or a related field and with strong quantitative skills.

Nature of the Work

Market and survey researchers gather information about what people think. *Market*, or *marketing*, *research analysts* help companies understand what types of products people want and at what price. They also help companies market their products to the people most likely to buy them. Gathering statistical data on competitors and examining prices, sales, and methods of marketing and distribution, they analyze data on past sales to predict future sales.

Market research analysts devise methods and procedures for obtaining the data they need. Often, they design surveys to assess consumer preferences through Internet, telephone, or mail responses. They conduct some surveys as personal interviews, going door-to-door, leading focus group discussions, or setting up booths in public places such as shopping malls. Trained interviewers usually conduct the surveys under the market research analyst's direction.

After compiling and evaluating the data, market research analysts make recommendations to their client or employer. They provide a company's management with information needed to make decisions on the promotion, distribution, design, and pricing of products or services. The information also may be used to determine the advisability of adding new lines of merchandise, opening branches of the company in a new location, or otherwise diversifying the company's operations. Market research analysts also might develop advertising brochures and commercials, sales plans, and product promotions such as rebates and giveaways.

Survey researchers also gather information about people and their opinions, but these workers focus exclusively on designing and conducting surveys. They work for a variety of clients, such as corporations, government agencies, political candidates, and providers of various services. The surveys collect information that is used in performing research, making fiscal or policy decisions, measuring the effectiveness of those decisions, or improving customer satisfaction. Analysts may conduct opinion research to determine public attitudes on various issues; the research results may help political or business leaders to measure public support for their electoral prospects or social policies. Like market research analysts, survey researchers may use a variety of mediums to conduct surveys, such as the Internet, personal or telephone interviews, or questionnaires sent through the mail. They also may supervise interviewers who conduct surveys in person or over the telephone.

Survey researchers design surveys in many different formats, depending upon the scope of their research and the method of collection. Interview surveys, for example, are common because they can increase participation rates. Survey researchers may consult with economists, statisticians, market research analysts, or other data users in order to design surveys. They also may present survey results to clients.

Work environment. Market and survey researchers generally have structured work schedules. They often work alone, writing reports, preparing statistical charts, and using computers, but they also may be an integral part of a research team. Market researchers who conduct personal interviews have frequent contact with the public. Most work under pressure of deadlines

Market and survey researchers conduct research and design surveys.

and tight schedules, which may require overtime. Travel may be necessary.

Training, Other Qualifications, and Advancement

A bachelor's degree is usually sufficient for entry-level market and survey research positions. Higher degrees may be required for some positions, however. Continuing education and keeping current with the latest methods of developing, conducting, and analyzing surveys and other data also is important for advancement.

Education and training. A bachelor's degree is the minimum educational requirement for many market and survey research jobs. However, a master's degree may be required, especially for technical positions.

In addition to completing courses in business, marketing, and consumer behavior, prospective market and survey researchers should take other liberal arts and social science courses, including economics, psychology, English, and sociology. Because of the importance of quantitative skills to market and survey researchers, courses in mathematics, statistics, sampling theory and survey design, and computer science are extremely helpful. Market and survey researchers often earn advanced degrees in business administration, marketing, statistics, communications, or other closely related disciplines.

While in college, aspiring market and survey researchers should gain experience gathering and analyzing data, conducting interviews or surveys, and writing reports on their findings. This experience can prove invaluable later in obtaining a full-time position in the field, because much of the initial work may center on these duties. Some schools help graduate students find internships or part-time employment in government agencies, consulting firms, financial institutions, or marketing research firms prior to graduation.

Other qualifications. Market and survey researchers spend a lot of time performing precise data analysis, so those considering careers in the occupation should be able to pay attention to detail. Patience and persistence are also necessary qualities because these workers must spend long hours on independent study and problem solving. At the same time, they must work well with others; often, market and survey researchers oversee the interviewing of a wide variety of individuals. Communication skills are important, too, because researchers must be able to present their findings well both orally and in writing.

Certification and advancement. The Marketing Research Association (MRA) offers a certification program for professional researchers who wish to demonstrate their expertise. Certification is based on education and experience and requires ongoing continuing education.

Researchers and analysts often begin by assisting others. With experience, market and survey analysts are eventually are assigned their own research projects. Continuing education and advanced degrees will be helpful to those looking to advance to more responsible positions in this occupation. It also is important to keep current with the latest methods of developing, conducting, and analyzing surveys and other data.

Some people with expertise in marketing or survey research choose to teach others these skills. (See the statement on teachers—postsecondary elsewhere in the *Handbook*.) A master's degree usually is the minimum educational requirement for a job as a marketing or survey research instructor in junior and community colleges. In most colleges and universities, however, a Ph.D. is necessary for appointment as an instructor. A Ph.D. and extensive publications in academic journals are required for professorship, tenure, and promotion. Others advance to supervisory or managerial positions. Many corporation and government executives have a strong background in marketing.

Employment

Market and survey researchers held about 261,000 jobs in 2006, most of which—234,000—were held by market research analysts. Because of the applicability of market research to many industries, market research analysts are employed throughout the economy. The industries that employ the largest number of market research analysts were management of companies and enterprises; management, scientific, and technical consulting services; insurance carriers; computer systems design and related services; and other professional, scientific, and technical services—which includes marketing research and public opinion polling.

Survey researchers held about 27,000 jobs in 2006. Survey researchers were employed primarily by firms in other professional, scientific, and technical services—which include market research and public opinion polling; scientific research and development services; and management, scientific, and technical consulting services. Colleges, universities, and professional schools also provided many jobs for survey researchers.

A number of market and survey researchers combine a full-time job in government, academia, or business with part-time consulting work in another setting. About seven percent of market and survey researchers are self-employed.

Besides holding the previously mentioned jobs, many people who do market and survey research work held faculty positions in colleges and universities. These workers are counted as postsecondary teachers rather than market and survey researchers.

Job Outlook

Employment growth of market and survey researchers is projected to be faster than average. Bachelor's degree holders may face competition for employment in these occupations. Job opportunities should be best for jobseekers with a master's or Ph.D. degree in marketing or a related field and with strong quantitative skills.

Employment change. Employment of market and survey researchers is projected to grow 20 percent from 2006 to 2016, faster than the average for all occupations. As companies seek to expand their market and as consumers become better informed, the need for marketing professionals will increase. In addition, globalization of the marketplace creates a need for more market and survey researchers to analyze foreign markets and competition.

Marketing research provides organizations valuable feedback from purchasers, allowing companies to evaluate consumer satisfaction and plan more effectively for the future. Survey researchers also will be needed to meet the growing demand for market and opinion research as an increasingly competitive economy requires businesses to allocate advertising funds more effectively and efficiently.

Projections data from the National Employment Matrix

Occupational Title	SOC Code	Employment, 2006	Projected employment, 2016	Change, 2006-2016	
				Number	Percent
Market and survey researchers...	19-3020	261,000	313,000	51,000	20
Market research analysts...	19-3021	234,000	281,000	47,000	20
Survey researchers	19-3022	27,000	31,000	4,300	16

NOTE: Data in this table are rounded. See the discussion of the employment projections table in the *Handbook* introductory chapter on *Occupational Information Included in the Handbook*.

Job prospects. Bachelor's degree holders may face competition for jobs, as many positions, especially the more technical ones, require a master's or doctorate degree. Among bachelor's degree holders, those with good quantitative skills, including a strong background in mathematics, statistics, survey design, and computer science, will have the best opportunities. Job opportunities should be best for jobseekers with a master's or Ph.D. degree in marketing or a related field and with strong quantitative skills. Ph.D. holders in marketing and related fields should have a range of opportunities in many industries, especially in consulting firms. Like those in many other disciplines, however, Ph.D. holders probably will face keen competition for tenured teaching positions in colleges and universities.

Market research analysts should have the best opportunities in consulting firms and marketing research firms as companies find it more profitable to contract for market research services rather than support their own marketing department. However, other organizations, including computer systems design companies, software publishers, financial services organizations, health care institutions, advertising firms, and insurance companies, may also offer job opportunities for market research analysts. Increasingly, market research analysts not only collect and analyze information, but also help clients implement analysts' ideas and recommendations.

There will be fewer job opportunities for survey researchers since it is a relatively smaller occupation. The best prospects will come from growth in the market research and public opinion polling industry, which employs many survey researchers.

Earnings

Median annual earnings of market research analysts in May 2006 were $58,820. The middle 50 percent earned between $42,190 and $84,070. The lowest 10 percent earned less than $32,250, and the highest 10 percent earned more than $112,510. Median annual earnings in the industries employing the largest numbers of market research analysts in May 2006 were:

Computer systems design and related services	$76,220
Management of companies and enterprises	62,680
Other professional, scientific, and technical services	57,520
Management, scientific, and technical consulting services	54,040
Insurance carriers	53,430

Median annual earnings of survey researchers in May 2006 were $33,360. The middle 50 percent earned between $22,150 and $50,960. The lowest 10 percent earned less than $16,720, and the highest 10 percent earned more than $73,630. Median

annual earnings of survey researchers in other professional, scientific, and technical services were $27,440.

Related Occupations

Market and survey researchers perform research to find out how well the market will receive products, services, and ideas. Such research may include planning, implementing, and analyzing surveys to determine the needs and preferences of people. Other jobs using these skills include economists, psychologists, sociologists, statisticians, operations research analysts, management analysts, and urban and regional planners. Market and survey researchers often work closely with advertising, marketing, promotions, public relations, and sales managers. When analyzing data, market and survey researchers must use quantitative skills similar to those of mathematicians, cost estimators, and actuaries. Also, market and survey researchers often are concerned with public opinion, as are public relations specialists.

Sources of Additional Information

For information about careers and certification in market research, contact:

➤ Marketing Research Association, 110 National Dr., Glastonbury, CT 06033. Internet: **http://www.mra-net.org**

For information about careers in survey research, contact:

➤ Council of American Survey Research Organizations, 170 North Country Rd., Suite 4, Port Jefferson, NY 11777. Internet: **http://www.casro.org**

Psychologists

(O*NET 19-3031.00, 19-3031.01, 19-3031.02, 19-3031.03, 19-3032.00, 19-3039.99)

Significant Points

- About 34 percent of psychologists are self-employed, compared with only 8 percent of all workers.

- Competition for admission to graduate psychology programs is keen.

- Overall employment of psychologists is expected to grow faster than average.

- Job prospects should be the best for people who have a doctoral degree in an applied specialty, such as counseling or health, and those with a specialist or doctoral degree in school psychology.

Nature of the Work

Psychologists study the human mind and human behavior. Research psychologists investigate the physical, cognitive, emotional, or social aspects of human behavior. Psychologists in health service fields provide mental health care in hospitals, clinics, schools, or private settings. Psychologists employed in applied settings, such as business, industry, government, or nonprofit organizations, provide training, conduct research, design organizational systems, and act as advocates for psychology.

Like other social scientists, psychologists formulate hypotheses and collect data to test their validity. Research methods vary with the topic under study. Psychologists sometimes gather information through controlled laboratory experiments or by administering personality, performance, aptitude, or intelligence tests. Other methods include observation, interviews, questionnaires, clinical studies, and surveys.

Psychologists apply their knowledge to a wide range of endeavors, including health and human services, management, education, law, and sports. They usually specialize in one of a number of different areas.

Clinical psychologists—who constitute the largest specialty—work most often in counseling centers, independent or group practices, hospitals, or clinics. They help mentally and emotionally distressed clients adjust to life and may assist medical and surgical patients in dealing with illnesses or injuries. Some clinical psychologists work in physical rehabilitation settings, treating patients with spinal cord injuries, chronic pain or illness, stroke, arthritis, or neurological conditions. Others help people deal with personal crisis, such as divorce or the death of a loved one.

Clinical psychologists often interview patients and give diagnostic tests. They may provide individual, family, or group psychotherapy and may design and implement behavior modification programs. Some clinical psychologists collaborate with physicians and other specialists to develop and implement treatment and intervention programs that patients can understand and comply with. Other clinical psychologists work in universities and medical schools, where they train graduate students in the delivery of mental health and behavioral medicine services. Some administer community mental health programs.

Areas of specialization within clinical psychology include health psychology, neuropsychology, and geropsychology. *Health psychologists* study how biological, psychological, and social factors affect health and illness. They promote healthy living and disease prevention through counseling, and they focus on how patients adjust to illnesses and treatments and view their quality of life. *Neuropsychologists* study the relation between the brain and behavior. They often work in stroke and head injury programs. *Geropsychologists* deal with the special problems faced by the elderly. The emergence and growth of these specialties reflects the increasing participation of psychologists in direct services to special patient populations.

Often, clinical psychologists consult with other medical personnel regarding the best treatment for patients, especially treatment that includes medication. Clinical psychologists generally are not permitted to prescribe medication to treat patients; only psychiatrists and other medical doctors may prescribe most medications. (See the statement on physicians and surgeons elsewhere in the *Handbook*.) However, two States—Louisiana and New Mexico—currently allow appropriately trained clinical psychologists to prescribe medication with some limitations.

Counseling psychologists use various techniques, including interviewing and testing, to advise people on how to deal with problems of everyday living, including career or work problems and problems faced in different stages of life. They work in settings such as university counseling centers, hospitals, and individual or group practices. (See also the statements on counselors and social workers elsewhere in the *Handbook*.)

School psychologists work with students in early childhood and elementary and secondary schools. They collaborate with teachers, parents, and school personnel to create safe, healthy, and supportive learning environments for all students. School psychologists address students' learning and behavioral problems, suggest improvements to classroom management strategies or parenting techniques, and evaluate students with disabilities and gifted and talented students to help determine the best way to educate them.

They improve teaching, learning, and socialization strategies based on their understanding of the psychology of learning environments. They also may evaluate the effectiveness of academic programs, prevention programs, behavior management procedures, and other services provided in the school setting.

Industrial-organizational psychologists apply psychological principles and research methods to the workplace in the interest of improving productivity and the quality of worklife. They also are involved in research on management and marketing problems. They screen, train, and counsel applicants for jobs, as well as perform organizational development and analysis. An industrial psychologist might work with management to reorganize the work setting in order to improve productivity or quality of life in the workplace. Industrial psychologists frequently act as consultants, brought in by management to solve a particular problem.

Developmental psychologists study the physiological, cognitive, and social development that takes place throughout life. Some specialize in behavior during infancy, childhood, and adolescence, or changes that occur during maturity or old age. Developmental psychologists also may study developmental disabilities and their effects. Increasingly, research is developing ways to help elderly people remain independent as long as possible.

Social psychologists examine people's interactions with others and with the social environment. They work in organizational consultation, marketing research, systems design, or other applied psychology fields. Prominent areas of study include group behavior, leadership, attitudes, and perception.

Experimental or *research psychologists* work in university and private research centers and in business, nonprofit, and governmental organizations. They study the behavior of both human beings and animals, such as rats, monkeys, and pigeons. Prominent areas of study in experimental research include motivation, thought, attention, learning and memory, sensory and perceptual processes, effects of substance abuse, and genetic and neurological factors affecting behavior.

Psychologists interact with people daily, and need good communication and personal skills.

Work environment. Psychologists' work environments vary by subfield and place of employment. For example, clinical, school, and counseling psychologists in private practice frequently have their own offices and set their own hours. However, they usually offer evening and weekend hours to accommodate their clients. Those employed in hospitals, nursing homes, and other health care facilities may work shifts that include evenings and weekends, and those who work in schools and clinics generally work regular daytime hours. Most psychologists in government and industry have structured schedules.

Psychologists employed as faculty by colleges and universities divide their time between teaching and research and also may have administrative responsibilities; many have part-time consulting practices.

Increasingly, many psychologists work as part of a team, consulting with other psychologists and professionals. Many experience pressures because of deadlines, tight schedules, and overtime. Their routine may be interrupted frequently. Travel may be required in order to attend conferences or conduct research.

Training, Other Qualifications, and Advancement

A master's or doctoral degree, and a license, are required for most psychologists.

Education and training. A doctoral degree usually is required for independent practice as a psychologist. Psychologists with a Ph.D. or Doctor of Psychology (Psy.D.) qualify for a wide range of teaching, research, clinical, and counseling positions in universities, health care services, elementary and secondary schools, private industry, and government. Psychologists with a doctoral degree often work in clinical positions or in private practices, but they also sometimes teach, conduct research, or carry out administrative responsibilities.

A doctoral degree generally requires 5 to 7 years of graduate study, culminating in a dissertation based on original research.

Courses in quantitative research methods, which include the use of computer-based analysis, are an integral part of graduate study and are necessary to complete the dissertation. The Psy. D. degree may be based on practical work and examinations rather than a dissertation. In clinical, counseling, and school psychology, the requirements for the doctoral degree include at least a 1-year internship.

A specialist degree or its equivalent is required in most States for an individual to work as a school psychologist, although a few States still credential school psychologists with master's degrees. A specialist (Ed.S.) degree in school psychology requires a minimum of 3 years of full-time graduate study (at least 60 graduate semester hours) and a 1-year full-time internship. Because their professional practice addresses educational and mental health components of students' development, school psychologists' training includes coursework in both education and psychology.

People with a master's degree in psychology may work as industrial-organizational psychologists. They also may work as psychological assistants under the supervision of doctoral-level psychologists and may conduct research or psychological evaluations. A master's degree in psychology requires at least 2 years of full-time graduate study. Requirements usually include practical experience in an applied setting and a master's thesis based on an original research project.

Competition for admission to graduate psychology programs is keen. Some universities require applicants to have an undergraduate major in psychology. Others prefer only coursework in basic psychology with additional courses in the biological, physical, and social sciences and in statistics and mathematics.

A bachelor's degree in psychology qualifies a person to assist psychologists and other professionals in community mental health centers, vocational rehabilitation offices, and correctional programs. Bachelor's degree holders may also work as research or administrative assistants for psychologists. Some work as technicians in related fields, such as marketing research. Many find employment in other areas, such as sales, service, or business management.

In the Federal Government, candidates having at least 24 semester hours in psychology and one course in statistics qualify for entry-level positions. However, competition for these jobs is keen because this is one of the few ways in which one can work as a psychologist without an advanced degree.

The American Psychological Association (APA) presently accredits doctoral training programs in clinical, counseling, and school psychology, as well as institutions that provide internships for doctoral students in school, clinical, and counseling psychology. The National Association of School Psychologists, with the assistance of the National Council for Accreditation of Teacher Education, helps to approve advanced degree programs in school psychology.

Licensure. Psychologists in independent practice or those who offer any type of patient care—including clinical, counseling, and school psychologists—must meet certification or licensing requirements in all States and the District of Columbia. Licensing laws vary by State and by type of position and require licensed or certified psychologists to limit their practice to areas in which they have developed professional competence through training and experience. Clinical and counseling psychologists usually need a doctorate in psychology, an approved internship, and 1 to 2 years of professional experience. In addition, all States require that applicants pass an examination. Most State licensing boards administer a standardized test, and many supplement that with additional oral or essay questions. Some States require continuing education for renewal of the license.

The National Association of School Psychologists (NASP) awards the Nationally Certified School Psychologist (NCSP) designation, which recognizes professional competency in school psychology at a national, rather than State, level. Currently, 29 States recognize the NCSP and allow those with the certification to transfer credentials from one State to another without taking a new certification exam. In States that recognize the NCSP, the requirements for certification or licensure and those for the NCSP often are the same or similar. Requirements for the NCSP include the completion of 60 graduate semester hours in school psychology; a 1,200-hour internship, 600 hours of which must be completed in a school setting; and a passing score on the National School Psychology Examination.

Other qualifications. Aspiring psychologists who are interested in direct patient care must be emotionally stable, mature, and able to deal effectively with people. Sensitivity, compassion, good communication skills, and the ability to lead and inspire others are particularly important qualities for people wishing to do clinical work and counseling. Research psychologists should be able to do detailed work both independently and as part of a team. Patience and perseverance are vital qualities, because achieving results in the psychological treatment of patients or in research may take a long time.

Certification and advancement. The American Board of Professional Psychology (ABPP) recognizes professional achievement by awarding specialty certification in 13 different areas. Candidates for ABPP certification need a doctorate in psychology, postdoctoral training in their specialty, several years of experience, professional endorsements, and are required to pass the specialty board examination.

Psychologists can improve their advancement opportunities by earning an advanced degree and by participation in continuing education. Many psychologists opt to start their own practice after gaining experience working in the field.

Employment

Psychologists held about 166,000 jobs in 2006. Educational institutions employed about 29 percent of psychologists in positions other than teaching, such as counseling, testing, research, and administration. About 21 percent were employed in health care, primarily in offices of mental health practitioners, hospitals, physicians' offices, and outpatient mental health and substance abuse centers. Government agencies at the State and local levels employed psychologists in correctional facilities, law enforcement, and other settings.

After several years of experience, some psychologists—usually those with doctoral degrees—enter private practice or set up private research or consulting firms. About 34 percent of psychologists were self-employed in 2006, compared with only 8 percent of all professional workers.

In addition to the previously mentioned jobs, many psychologists held faculty positions at colleges and universities and as high school psychology teachers. (See the statements on teachers—postsecondary and teachers—preschool, kindergarten, elementary, middle, and secondary elsewhere in the *Handbook*.)

Job Outlook

Faster-than-average employment growth is expected for psychologists. Job prospects should be the best for people who have a doctoral degree from a leading university in an applied specialty, such as counseling or health, and those with a specialist or doctoral degree in school psychology. Master's degree holders in fields other than industrial-organizational psychology will face keen competition. Opportunities will be limited for bachelor's degree holders.

Employment change. Employment of psychologists is expected to grow 15 percent from 2006 to 2016, faster than the average for all occupations. Employment will grow because of increased demand for psychological services in schools, hospitals, social service agencies, mental health centers, substance abuse treatment clinics, consulting firms, and private companies.

Employment growth will vary by specialty. Growing awareness of how students' mental health and behavioral problems, such as bullying, affect learning will increase demand for school psychologists to offer student counseling and mental health services.

The rise in health care costs associated with unhealthy lifestyles, such as smoking, alcoholism, and obesity, has made prevention and treatment more critical. An increase in the number of employee assistance programs, which help workers deal with personal problems, also should lead to employment growth for clinical and counseling specialties. Clinical and counseling psychologists also will be needed to help people deal with depression and other mental disorders, marriage and family problems, job stress, and addiction. The growing number of elderly will increase the demand for psychologists trained in geropsychology to help people deal with the mental and physi-

Projections data from the National Employment Matrix

Occupational Title	SOC Code	Employment, 2006	Projected employment, 2016	Change, 2006-2016	
				Number	Percent
Psychologists...	19-3030	166,000	191,000	25,000	15
Clinical, counseling, and school psychologists...........................	19-3031	152,000	176,000	24,000	16
Industrial-organizational psychologists	19-3032	1,900	2,400	400	21
Psychologists, all other	19-3039	12,000	13,000	900	8

NOTE: Data in this table are rounded. See the discussion of the employment projections table in the *Handbook* introductory chapter on *Occupational Information Included in the Handbook.*

cal changes that occur as individuals grow older. There also will be increased need for psychologists to work with returning veterans.

Industrial-organizational psychologists also will be in demand to help to boost worker productivity and retention rates in a wide range of businesses. Industrial-organizational psychologists will help companies deal with issues such as workplace diversity and antidiscrimination policies. Companies also will use psychologists' expertise in survey design, analysis, and research to develop tools for marketing evaluation and statistical analysis.

Job prospects. Job prospects should be the best for people who have a doctoral degree from a leading university in an applied specialty, such as counseling or health, and those with a specialist or doctoral degree in school psychology. Psychologists with extensive training in quantitative research methods and computer science may have a competitive edge over applicants without such background.

Master's degree holders in fields other than industrial-organizational psychology will face keen competition for jobs because of the limited number of positions that require only a master's degree. Master's degree holders may find jobs as psychological assistants or counselors, providing mental health services under the direct supervision of a licensed psychologist. Still others may find jobs involving research and data collection and analysis in universities, government, or private companies.

Opportunities directly related to psychology will be limited for bachelor's degree holders. Some may find jobs as assistants in rehabilitation centers or in other jobs involving data collection and analysis. Those who meet State certification requirements may become high school psychology teachers.

Earnings

Median annual earnings of wage and salary clinical, counseling, and school psychologists in May 2006 were $59,440. The middle 50 percent earned between $45,300 and $77,750. The lowest 10 percent earned less than $35,280, and the highest 10 percent earned more than $102,730. Median annual earnings in the industries employing the largest numbers of clinical, counseling, and school psychologists were:

Offices of mental health practitioners $69,510
Elementary and secondary schools 61,290
Local government 58,770
Individual and family services 50,780
Outpatient care centers 50,310

Median annual earnings of wage and salary industrial-organizational psychologists in May 2006 were $86,420. The middle 50 percent earned between $66,310 and $115,000. The lowest 10 percent earned less than $48,380, and the highest 10 percent earned more than $139,620.

Related Occupations

Psychologists work with people, developing relationships and comforting them. Other occupations with similar duties include counselors, social workers, clergy, sociologists, special education teachers, funeral directors, market and survey researchers, recreation workers, and human resources, training, and labor

relations managers and specialists. Psychologists also sometimes diagnose and treat problems and help patients recover. These duties are similar to those for physicians and surgeons, radiation therapists, audiologists, dentists, optometrists, and speech-language pathologists.

Sources of Additional Information

For information on careers, educational requirements, financial assistance, and licensing in all fields of psychology, contact:
➤ American Psychological Association, Center for Psychology Workforce Analysis and Research and Education Directorate, 750 1st St.NE., Washington, DC 20002.
Internet: **http://www.apa.org/students**

For information on careers, educational requirements, certification, and licensing of school psychologists, contact:
➤ National Association of School Psychologists, 4340 East West Hwy., Suite 402, Bethesda, MD 20814.
Internet: **http://www.nasponline.org**

Information about State licensing requirements is available from:
➤ Association of State and Provincial Psychology Boards, P.O. Box 241245, Montgomery, AL 36124.
Internet: **http://www.asppb.org**

Information about psychology specialty certifications is available from:
➤ American Board of Professional Psychology, Inc., 300 Drayton St., 3rd Floor, Savannah, GA 31401.
Internet: **http://www.abpp.org**

Urban and Regional Planners

(O*NET 19-3051.00)

Significant Points

- Local governments employ about 68 percent of urban and regional planners.

- Most new jobs will be in affluent, rapidly growing communities.

- Job prospects will be best for those with a master's degree and strong computer skills; bachelor's degree holders may find positions, but advancement opportunities are limited.

Nature of the Work

Urban and regional planners develop long- and short-term plans for the use of land and the growth and revitalization of urban, suburban, and rural communities and the region in which they are located. They help local officials alleviate social, economic, and environmental problems by recommending locations for roads, schools, and other infrastructure and suggesting zoning regulations for private property. This work includes forecasting the future needs of the population. Because local governments employ the majority of urban and regional planners, they often are referred to as community or city planners.

Planners promote the best use of a community's land and resources for residential, commercial, institutional, and recreational purposes. They address environmental, economic, and social health issues of a community as it grows and changes. They may formulate plans relating to the construction of new school buildings, public housing, or other kinds of infrastructure. Planners also may help to make decisions about developing resources and protecting ecologically sensitive regions. Some planners are involved in environmental issues including pollution control, wetland preservation, forest conservation, and the location of new landfills. Planners also may help to draft legislation on environmental, social, and economic issues, such as planning a new park, sheltering the homeless, or making the region more attractive to businesses.

Before preparing plans for community development, planners study and report on the current use of land for residential, business, and community purposes. Their reports include information on the location and capacity of streets, highways, airports, water and sewer lines, schools, libraries, and cultural and recreational sites. They also provide data on the types of industries in the community, the characteristics of the population, and employment and economic trends. Using this information, along with input from citizens, planners try to optimize land use for buildings and other public facilities. Planners prepare reports showing how their programs can be carried out and what they will cost.

Planners examine proposed community facilities, such as schools, to be sure that these facilities will meet the needs of a growing or changing population. They keep abreast of economic and legal issues involved in zoning codes, building codes, and environmental regulations and ensure that builders and developers follow these codes and regulations. Planners also deal with land-use issues created by population movements. For example, as suburban growth and economic development create more jobs outside cities, the need for public transportation that gets workers to those jobs increases. In response, planners develop and model possible transportation systems and explain them to planning boards and the general public.

Planners use computers to record and analyze information and to prepare reports and recommendations for government executives and others. Computer databases, spreadsheets, and analytical techniques are used to project program costs and forecast future trends in employment, housing, transportation, or population. Computerized geographic information systems (GIS) enable planners to map land areas, to overlay maps with geographic variables such as population density, and to combine or manipulate geographic information to produce alternative plans for land use or development.

Urban and regional planners often confer with land developers, civic leaders, and public officials and may function as mediators in community disputes, presenting alternatives that are acceptable to opposing parties. Planners may prepare material for community relations programs, speak at civic meetings, and appear before legislative committees and elected officials to explain and defend their proposals.

Most urban and regional planners focus on one or more areas of specialization. Among the most common are community development and redevelopment and land-use or code enforce-

Urban and regional planners develop plans for communities to best use land and other resources.

ment. While planners may specialize in areas such as transportation planning or urban design, they are also required to keep the bigger picture in mind, and do what's best for the community as a whole.

Work environment. Urban and regional planners often travel to inspect the features of land under consideration for development or regulation. Some local government planners involved in site development inspections spend most of their time in the field. Although most planners have a scheduled 40-hour workweek, they frequently attend evening or weekend meetings or public hearings with citizens' groups. Planners may experience the pressure of deadlines and tight work schedules, as well as political pressure generated by interest groups affected by proposals related to urban development and land use.

Training, Other Qualifications, and Advancement
A master's degree from an accredited planning program provides the best training for a wide range of planning positions. Experience and acquiring and maintaining certification lead to the best opportunities for advancement.

Education and training. Most entry-level jobs in Federal, State, and local governments require a master's degree from an accredited program in urban or regional planning or a related field, such as urban design or geography. Students are admitted to master's degree programs in planning with a wide range of undergraduate backgrounds; a bachelor's degree in economics, geography, political science, or environmental design is especially good preparation. A few schools offer a bachelor's degree in urban planning, and graduates from these programs qualify for some entry-level positions, but their advancement opportunities are often limited unless they acquire an advanced degree.

In 2007, 66 colleges and universities offered an accredited master's degree program, and 15 offered an accredited bachelor's degree program, in planning. Accreditation for these programs is from the Planning Accreditation Board, which consists of representatives of the American Institute of Certified Planners, the American Planning Association, and the Association of Collegiate Schools of Planning. Most graduate programs in planning require at least 2 years of study.

Most college and university planning departments offer specialization in areas such as community development and redevelopment, land-use or code enforcement, transportation planning, environmental and natural resources planning, urban design, and economic planning and development.

Highly recommended also are courses in related disciplines, such as architecture, law, earth sciences, demography, economics, finance, health administration, and management, in addition to courses in planning. Because familiarity with computer models and statistical techniques is important, courses in statistics, computer science, and geographic information systems also are recommended or required.

Graduate students spend considerable time in studios, workshops, and laboratory courses, learning to analyze and solve planning problems. They often are required to work in a planning office part time or during the summer. Local government planning offices frequently offer students internships, providing experience that proves invaluable in obtaining a full-time planning position after graduation.

Licensure. As of 2007, New Jersey was the only State that required planners to be licensed, although Michigan required registration to use the title "community planner." Licensure in New Jersey is based on two examinations—one testing generalized knowledge of planning and another testing knowledge of New Jersey planning laws. Registration as a community planner in Michigan is based on professional experience and national and State examinations.

Other qualifications. Planners must be able to think in terms of spatial relationships and visualize the effects of their plans and designs. They should be flexible and be able to reconcile different viewpoints and make constructive policy recommendations. The ability to communicate effectively, both orally and in writing, is necessary for anyone interested in this field.

Certification and advancement. The American Institute of Certified Planners, a professional institute within the American Planning Association, grants certification to individuals who have the appropriate combination of education and professional experience and pass an examination. Professional development activities are required to maintain certification. Certification may be helpful for promotion.

After a few years of experience, planners may advance to assignments requiring a high degree of independent judgment, such as designing the physical layout of a large development or recommending policy and budget options. Some public sector planners are promoted to community planning director and spend a great deal of time meeting with officials, speaking to civic groups, and supervising a staff. Further advancement occurs through a transfer to a larger jurisdiction with more complex problems and greater responsibilities or into related occupations, such as director of community or economic development.

Employment

Urban and regional planners held about 34,000 jobs in 2006. About 68 percent were employed by local governments. Companies involved with architectural, engineering, and related services, as well as management, scientific, and technical consulting services, employ an increasing proportion of planners in the private sector. Others are employed in State government agencies dealing with housing, transportation, or environmental protection, and a small number work for the Federal Government.

Job Outlook

Faster than average employment growth is projected for urban and regional planners. Most new jobs will be in affluent, rapidly expanding communities. Job prospects will be best for those with a master's degree and strong computer skills.

Employment change. Employment of urban and regional planners is expected to grow 15 percent from 2006 to 2016, faster than the average for all occupations. Employment growth will be driven by the need for State and local governments to provide public services such as regulation of commercial development, the environment, transportation, housing, and land use and development for an expanding population. Nongovernmental initiatives dealing with historic preservation and redevelopment will also create employment growth.

Most new jobs for urban and regional planners will be in local government, as planners will be needed to address an array of problems associated with population growth, especially in affluent, rapidly expanding communities. For example, new housing developments require roads, sewer systems, fire stations, schools, libraries, and recreation facilities that must be planned for within budgetary constraints.

The fastest job growth for urban and regional planners will occur in the private sector, primarily in the professional, scientific, and technical services industries. For example, planners may be employed by firms to help design security measures for a building that are effective but also subtle and able to blend in with the surrounding area. However, because the private sector employs only 21 percent of urban and regional planners, not as many new jobs will be created in the private sector as in government.

Job prospects. In addition to those from employment growth, job openings will arise from the need to replace experienced planners who transfer to other occupations, retire, or leave the labor force for other reasons. Graduates with a master's degree from an accredited program should have better job opportunities than those with only a bachelor's degree. Also, computers and software—especially GIS software—are increasingly being used in planning, and those with strong computer skills and GIS experience will have an advantage in the job market.

Projections data from the National Employment Matrix

Occupational Title	SOC Code	Employment, 2006	Projected employment, 2016	Change, 2006-2016	
				Number	Percent
Urban and regional planners	19-3051	34,000	39,000	4,900	15

NOTE: Data in this table are rounded. See the discussion of the employment projections table in the *Handbook* introductory chapter on *Occupational Information Included in the Handbook.*

Earnings

Median annual wage-and-salary earnings of urban and regional planners were $56,630 in May 2006. The middle 50 percent earned between $44,480 and $71,390. The lowest 10 percent earned less than $35,610, and the highest 10 percent earned more than $86,880. Median annual earnings in the industries employing the largest numbers of urban and regional planners in May 2006 were:

Engineering services	$63,840
Architectural, engineering, and related services	62,890
Architectural services	61,700
State government	57,490
Local government	54,550

Related Occupations

Urban and regional planners develop plans for the growth of urban, suburban, and rural communities. Others whose work is similar include architects; civil engineers; environmental engineers; landscape architects: geographers; property, real estate, and community association managers; surveyors, cartographers, photogrammetrists, and surveying technicians; and market and survey researchers.

Sources of Additional Information

Information on careers, salaries, and certification in urban and regional planning is available from:

➤ American Planning Association, 1776 Massachusetts Ave. N.W., Washington, DC 20036.
Internet: **http://www.planning.org**

Information on accredited urban and regional planning programs is available from:

➤ Association of Collegiate Schools of Planning, 6311 Mallard Trace, Tallahassee, FL 32312. Internet: **http://www.acsp.org**

For addition information on urban and regional planning and on related occupations, see "Geography jobs" in the Spring 2005 Occupational Outlook Quarterly. The article is online at: **http://www.bls.gov/opub/ooq/2005/spring/art01.pdf**

Social Scientists, Other

(O*NET 19-3041.00, 19-3091.01, 19-3091.02, 19-3092.00, 19-3093.00, 19-3094.00)

Significant Points

- About 41 percent of these workers are employed by governments, mostly by the Federal Government.

- The educational attainment of social scientists is among the highest of all occupations, with most positions requiring a master's or Ph.D. degree.

- Overall employment is projected to grow about as fast as the average for all occupations, but varies by specialty.

- Job seekers may face competition, and those with higher educational attainment will have the best prospects.

Nature of the Work

The major social science occupations covered in this statement are anthropologists, archaeologists, geographers, historians, political scientists, and sociologists. (Economists, market and survey researchers, psychologists, and urban and regional planners are covered elsewhere in the *Handbook*.)

Social scientists study all aspects of society—from past events and achievements to human behavior and relationships among groups. Their research provides insights into the different ways individuals, groups, and institutions make decisions, exercise power, and respond to change. Through their studies and analyses, social scientists suggest solutions to social, business, personal, governmental, and environmental problems. In fact, many work as policy analysts for government or private organizations.

Research is a major activity of many social scientists, who use a variety of methods to assemble facts and construct theories. Applied research usually is designed to produce information that will enable people to make better decisions or manage their affairs more effectively. Social scientists often begin by collecting existing information. Collecting information takes many forms, including conducting interviews and questionnaires to gather demographic and opinion data, living and working among the population being studied, performing other field investigations, and experimenting with human or animal subjects in a laboratory. Social scientists also look at data in detail, such as studying the data they've collected, reanalyzing already existing data, analyzing historical records and documents, and interpreting maps and the effect of location on culture and other aspects of society. Following are several major types of social scientists. Specialists in one field may find that their research overlaps work being conducted in another discipline.

Anthropologists study the origin and the physical, social, and cultural development and behavior of humans. They may examine the way of life, archaeological remains, language, or physical characteristics of people in various parts of the world. Some compare the customs, values, and social patterns of different cultures. Anthropologists usually concentrate in sociocultural anthropology, linguistics, biophysical, or physical anthropology. Sociocultural anthropologists study the customs, cultures, and social lives of groups in settings that range from unindustrialized societies to modern urban centers. Linguistic anthropologists investigate the role of, and changes to, language over time in various cultures. Biophysical anthropologists research the evolution of the human body, look for the earliest evidences of human life, and analyze how culture and biology influence one another. Physical anthropologists examine human remains found at archaeological sites in order to understand population demographics and factors, such as nutrition and disease, which affected these populations. *Archaeologists* examine and recover material evidence including the ruins of buildings, tools, pottery, and other objects remaining from past human cultures in order to determine the history, customs, and living habits of earlier civilizations. With continued technological advances making it increasingly possible to detect the presence of underground anomalies without digging, archaeologists will be able to better target excavation sites. Another technological advancement is the use of geographic information systems (GIS) for tasks such as analyzing how environmental factors near a site may have affected the development of a society. Most anthropologists and archaeologists specialize in a particular region of the world.

Political scientists study the origin, development, and operation of political systems and public policy. They conduct research on a wide range of subjects, such as relations between the United States and other countries, the institutions and political life of nations, the politics of small towns or major metropolises, and the decisions of the U.S. Supreme Court. Studying topics such as public opinion, political decision making, ideology, and public policy, they analyze the structure and operation of governments, as well as various political entities. Depending on the topic, a political scientist might conduct a public-opinion survey, analyze election results or public documents, or interview public officials.

Sociologists study society and social behavior by examining the groups, cultures, organizations, and social institutions people form. They also study the activities in which people participate, including social, religious, political, economic, and business organizations. They study the behavior of, and interaction among, groups, organizations, institutions, and nations and how they react to phenomena such as the spread of technology, health epidemics, crime, and social movements. They also trace the origin and growth of these groups and interactions. Sociologists analyze how social influences affect different individuals. They also are concerned with the ways organizations and institutions affect the daily lives of individuals and groups. To analyze social patterns, sociologists design research projects that use a variety of methods, including historical analysis, comparative analysis, and quantitative and qualitative techniques. The results of sociological research aid educators, lawmakers, administrators, and others who are interested in resolving social problems and formulating public policy. Most sociologists work in one or more specialties, such as social organization, stratification, and mobility; racial and ethnic relations; education; the family; social psychology; urban, rural, political, and comparative sociology; gender relations; demography; gerontology; criminology; and sociological practice.

Geographers analyze distributions of physical and cultural phenomena on local, regional, continental, and global scales. Economic geographers study the distribution of resources and economic activities. Political geographers are concerned with the relationship of geography to political phenomena, and cultural geographers study the geography of cultural phenomena. Physical geographers examine variations in climate, vegetation, soil, and landforms and their implications for human activity. Urban and transportation geographers study cities and metropolitan areas. Regional geographers study the physical, economic, political, and cultural characteristics of regions ranging in size from a congressional district to entire continents. Medical geographers investigate health care delivery systems, epidemiology (the study of the causes and control of epidemics), and the effect of the environment on health. Most geographers use GIS technology to assist with their work. For example, they may use GIS to create computerized maps that can track information such as population growth, traffic patterns, environmental hazards, natural resources, and weather patterns, after which they use the information to advise governments on the develop-

ment of houses, roads, or landfills. Many of the people who study geography and work with GIS technology are classified in other occupations, such as surveyors, cartographers, photogrammetrists, and survey technicians (who develop maps and other location-based information), urban and regional planners (who help to decide on and evaluate the locations of building and roads and other aspects of physical society), and geoscientists (who study earthquakes and other physical aspects of the Earth). (These occupations are described elsewhere in the *Handbook*.)

Historians research, analyze, and interpret the past. They use many sources of information in their research, including government and institutional records, newspapers and other periodicals, photographs, interviews, films, and unpublished manuscripts such as personal diaries and letters. Historians usually specialize in a country or region, a particular period, or a particular field, such as social, intellectual, cultural, political, or diplomatic history. Other historians help study and preserve archival materials, artifacts, and historic buildings and sites.

Work environment. Most social scientists have regular hours. Generally working behind a desk, either alone or in collaboration with other social scientists, they read and write research articles or reports. Many experience the pressures of writing and publishing, as well as those associated with deadlines and tight schedules. Sometimes they must work overtime, for which they usually are not compensated. Social scientists often work as an integral part of a research team. Travel may be necessary to collect information or attend meetings. Social scientists on foreign assignment must adjust to unfamiliar cultures, climates, and languages.

Some social scientists do fieldwork. For example, anthropologists, archaeologists, and geographers may travel to remote areas, live among the people they study, learn their languages, and stay for long periods at the site of their investigations. They may work under rugged conditions, and their work may involve strenuous physical exertion.

Social scientists employed by colleges and universities usually have flexible work schedules, often dividing their time among teaching, research, writing, consulting, and administra-

Social scientists need strong research, analytical, and writing skills.

tive responsibilities. Those who teach in these settings are classified as postsecondary teachers.

Training, Other Qualifications, and Advancement

The educational attainment of social scientists is among the highest of all occupations, with most positions requiring a master's or Ph.D. degree.

Education and training. Graduates with master's degrees in applied specialties usually are qualified for positions outside of colleges and universities, although requirements vary by field. A Ph.D. degree may be required for higher-level positions. Bachelor's degree holders have limited opportunities and do not qualify for most of the occupations discussed above. A bachelor's degree does, however, provide a suitable background for many different kinds of entry-level jobs in related occupations, such as research assistant, writer, management trainee, or market analyst.

Training in statistics and mathematics is essential for many social scientists Geographers, political scientists, and those in other fields increasingly use mathematical and quantitative research methods. The ability to use computers for research purposes is mandatory in most disciplines. Social scientists also must keep up-to date on the latest technological advances that affect their discipline and research. For example, most geographers use GIS technology extensively, and GIS is also becoming more commonly used by archaeologists, sociologists, and other workers.

Many social science students also benefit from internships or field experience. Numerous local museums, historical societies, government agencies, non-profit and other organizations offer internships or volunteer research opportunities. Archaeological field schools instruct future anthropologists, archaeologists, and historians in how to excavate, record, and interpret historical sites.

Other qualifications. Social scientists need excellent written and oral communication skills to report research findings and to collaborate on research. Successful social scientists also need intellectual curiosity and creativity because they constantly seek new information about people, things, and ideas. The ability to think logically and methodically is also essential to analyze complicated issues, such as the relative merits of various forms of government. Objectivity, an open mind, and systematic work habits are important in all kinds of social science research. Perseverance, too, is often necessary, as when an anthropologist spends years studying artifacts from an ancient civilization before making a final analysis and interpretation.

Advancement. Some social scientists advance to top-level research and administrative positions. Advancement often depends on the number and quality of reports that social scientists publish or their ability to design studies.

Many social scientists choose to teach in their field, often while pursuing their own research. These workers are usually classified as postsecondary teachers. The minimum requirement for most positions in colleges and universities is a Ph.D. degree. Graduates with a master's degree in a social science may qualify for teaching positions in community colleges. Social science graduates with sufficient education courses can qualify for teaching positions in secondary and elementary schools.

Employment

Social scientists held about 18,000 jobs in 2006. Many worked as researchers, administrators, and counselors for a wide range of employers. About 41 percent worked for Federal, State, and local governments, mostly for the Federal Government. Other employers included scientific research and development services; management, scientific, and technical consulting services; business, professional, labor, political, and similar organizations; and architectural, engineering, and related firms.

Many individuals with training in a social science discipline teach in colleges and universities and in secondary and elementary schools. (For more information, see teachers—postsecondary and teachers—preschool, kindergarten, elementary, middle, and secondary elsewhere in the *Handbook.*) The proportion of social scientists who teach varies by specialty. For example, graduates in history are more likely to teach than are graduates in most other social science fields.

The following tabulation shows employment, by social science specialty.

Anthropologists and archeologists...5,500
Political scientists...4,700
Sociologists 3,700
Historians 3,400
Geographers 1,100

Job Outlook

Overall employment is projected to grow about as fast as average, but varies by detailed occupation. Job seekers may face competition, and those with higher educational attainment will have the best prospects.

Projections data from the National Employment Matrix

Occupational Title	SOC Code	Employment, 2006	Projected employment, 2016	Change, 2006-2016	
				Number	Percent
Social scientists, other..	—	18,000	20,000	1,800	10
Sociologists...	19-3041	3,700	4,100	400	10
Anthropologists and archeologists..............................	19-3091	5,500	6,400	800	15
Geographers	19-3092	1,100	1,200	100	6
Historians	19-3093	3,400	3,700	300	8
Political scientists..	19-3094	4,700	4,900	300	5

NOTE: Data in this table are rounded. See the discussion of the employment projections table in the *Handbook* introductory chapter on *Occupational Information Included in the Handbook.*

Employment change. Overall employment of social scientists is expected to grow 10 percent from 2006 to 2016, about as fast as the average for all occupations. However, projected growth rates vary by specialty. Anthropologists and archaeologists, sociologists, and historians are projected to grow about as fast as average. Employment of geographers and political scientists is projected to grow more slowly than average, reflecting the relatively few opportunities outside of the Federal Government. Employment is projected to decline slowly in the Federal Government, a key employer of social scientists.

The following tabulation shows projected percent change in employment, by social science specialty.

	Percent
Anthropologists and archeologists	15
Sociologists	10
Historians	8
Geographers	6
Political scientists	5

Anthropologists and archaeologists will experience the majority of their job growth in the management, scientific, and technical consulting services industry. Anthropologists who work as consultants apply anthropological knowledge and methods to problems ranging from economic development issues to forensics. As construction projects increase, more archaeologists also will be needed to monitor the work, ensuring that historical sites and artifacts are preserved.

Political scientists, sociologists, and historians will mainly find jobs in policy or research. Demand for political science research is growing because of increasing interest about politics and foreign affairs, including social and environmental policy issues and immigration. Political scientists will use their knowledge of political institutions to further the interests of nonprofit, political lobbying, and social organizations. Likewise, the incorporation of sociology into research in other fields will continue to increase the need for sociologists. They may find work conducting policy research for consulting firms and nonprofit organizations, and their knowledge of society and social behavior may be used by a variety of companies in product development, marketing, and advertising. Historians may find opportunities with historic preservation societies or working as a consultant as public interest in preserving and restoring historical sites increases.

Geographers will work advising government, real estate developers, utilities, and telecommunications firms on where to build new roads, buildings, power plants, and cable lines. Geographers also will advise on environmental matters, such as where to build a landfill or preserve wetland habitats. Geographers with a background in GIS will find numerous job opportunities applying GIS technology in nontraditional areas, such as emergency assistance, where GIS can track locations of ambulances, police, and fire rescue units and their proximity to the emergency. Workers in these jobs may not necessarily be called "geographers," but instead may be referred to by a different title, such as "GIS analyst" or "GIS specialist."

Job prospects. In addition to opportunities from employment growth, some job openings for social scientists will come from the need to replace those who retire, enter teaching or other occupations, or leave their social science occupation for other reasons.

People seeking social science positions may face competition for jobs, and those with higher educational attainment will have the best prospects. Many jobs in policy, research, or marketing for which social scientists qualify are not advertised exclusively as social scientist positions. Because of the wide range of skills and knowledge possessed by these social scientists, many compete for jobs with other workers, such as market and survey researchers, psychologists, engineers, urban and regional planners, and statisticians.

Some people with social science degrees will find opportunities as university faculty rather than as applied social scientists. Although there will be keen competition for tenured positions, the number of faculty expected to retire over the decade and the increasing number of part-time or short-term faculty positions will lead to better opportunities in colleges and universities than in the past. The growing importance and popularity of social science subjects in secondary schools also is strengthening the demand for social science teachers at that level.

Earnings

In May 2006, anthropologists and archaeologists had median annual wage-and-salary earnings of $49,930; geographers, $62,990; historians, $48,520; political scientists, $90,140; and sociologists, $60,290.

In the Federal Government, social scientists with a bachelor's degree and no experience often started at a yearly salary of $28,862 or $35,572 in 2007, depending on their college records. Those with a master's degree could start at $43,731, and those with a Ph.D. degree could begin at $52,912, while some individuals with experience and an advanced degree could start at $63,417. Beginning salaries were higher in selected areas of the country where the prevailing local pay level was higher.

Related Occupations

The duties and training of these social scientists are similar to other social scientists, including economists, market and survey researchers, psychologists, and urban and regional planners. Many social scientists conduct surveys, study social problems, teach, and work in museums, performing tasks similar to those of statisticians; counselors; social workers; teachers—postsecondary; teachers—preschool, kindergarten, elementary, middle, and secondary; and archivists, curators, and museum technicians.

Political scientists often research the function of government, including the legal system, as do lawyers; paralegals and legal assistants; and judges, magistrates, and other judicial workers. Many political scientists analyze and report on current events, as do news analysts, reporters, and correspondents.

Geographers often study the Earth's environment and natural resources, as do conservation scientists and foresters, atmospheric scientists, and environmental scientists and hydrologists. Geographers also use GIS computer technology to make maps. Other occupations with similar duties include surveyors, cartographers, photogrammetrists, and surveying technicians; computer systems analysts; and computer scientists and database administrators.

Sources of Additional Information

For information about careers in anthropology, contact:

➤ American Anthropological Association, 2200 Wilson Blvd., Suite 600, Arlington, VA 22201.
Internet: **http://www.aaanet.org**

For information about careers in archaeology, contact:

➤ Archaeological Institute of America, 656 Beacon St., 6th Floor, Boston, MA 02215. Internet: **http://www.archaeological.org**

➤ Society for American Archaeology, 900 2nd St.NE., Suite 12, Washington, DC 20002. Internet: **http://www.saa.org**

For information about careers in geography, contact:

➤ Association of American Geographers, 1710 16th St.NW., Washington, DC 20009. Internet: **http://www.aag.org**

Also see "Geography jobs," in the spring 2005 issue of the Occupational Outlook Quarterly and online at:
http://www.bls.gov/opub/ooq/2005/spring/art01.pdf

Information on careers for historians is available from:

➤ American Historical Association, 400 A St.SE., Washington, DC 20003. Internet: **http://www.historians.org**

For information about careers in political science, contact:

➤ American Political Science Association, 1527 New Hampshire Ave. NW., Washington, DC 20036.
Internet: **http://www.apsanet.org**

➤ National Association of Schools of Public Affairs and Administration, 1029 Vermont Ave. NW., Suite 1100, Washington, DC 20005. Internet: **http://www.naspaa.org**

Information about careers in sociology is available from:

➤ American Sociological Association, 1307 New York Ave. NW., Suite 700, Washington, DC 20005.
Internet: **http://www.asanet.org**

For information about careers in policy analysis, an important task for some social scientists, see "Policy analysts: Shaping society through research and problem-solving," online at **http://www.bls.gov/opub/ooq/2007/spring/art03.pdf** and in the spring 2007 issue of the Occupational Outlook Quarterly.

Science Technicians

(O*NET 19-4011.00, 19-4011.01, 19-4011.02, 19-4021.00, 19-4031.00, 19-4041.00, 19-4041.01, 19-4041.02, 19-4051.00, 19-4051.01, 19-4051.02, 19-4091.00, 19-4092.00, 19-4093.00, 19-4099.99)

Significant Points

- Science technicians in production jobs can be employed on day, evening, or night shifts; other technicians work outdoors, sometimes in remote locations.

- Most science technicians need an associate degree or a certificate in applied science or science-related technology; biological and forensic science technicians usually need a bachelor's degree.

- Projected job growth varies among occupational specialties; for example, forensic science technicians will grow much faster than average, while chemical technicians will grow more slowly than average.

- Job opportunities are expected to be best for graduates of applied science technology programs who are well trained on equipment used in laboratories or production facilities.

Nature of the Work

Science technicians use the principles and theories of science and mathematics to solve problems in research and development and to help invent and improve products and processes. However, their jobs are more practically oriented than those of scientists. Technicians set up, operate, and maintain laboratory instruments, monitor experiments, make observations, calculate and record results, and often develop conclusions. They must keep detailed logs of all of their work. Those who perform production work monitor manufacturing processes and may ensure quality by testing products for proper proportions of ingredients, for purity, or for strength and durability.

As laboratory instrumentation and procedures have become more complex, the role of science technicians in research and development has expanded. In addition to performing routine tasks, many technicians, under the direction of scientists, now develop and adapt laboratory procedures to achieve the best results, interpret data, and devise solutions to problems. Technicians must develop expert knowledge of laboratory equipment so that they can adjust settings when necessary and recognize when equipment is malfunctioning.

Most science technicians specialize, learning their skills and working in the same disciplines in which scientists work. Occupational titles, therefore, tend to follow the same structure as those for scientists.

Agricultural and food science technicians work with related scientists to conduct research, development, and testing on food and other agricultural products. Agricultural technicians are involved in food, fiber, and animal research, production, and processing. Some conduct tests and experiments to improve the yield and quality of crops or to increase the resistance of plants and animals to disease, insects, or other hazards. Other agricultural technicians breed animals for the purpose of investigating nutrition. Food science technicians assist food scientists and technologists in research and development, production technology, and quality control. For example, food science technicians may conduct tests on food additives and preservatives to ensure compliance with Food and Drug Administration regulations regarding color, texture, and nutrients. These technicians analyze, record, and compile test results; order supplies to maintain laboratory inventory; and clean and sterilize laboratory equipment.

Biological technicians work with biologists studying living organisms. Many assist scientists who conduct medical research—helping to find a cure for cancer or AIDS, for example. Those who work in pharmaceutical companies help develop and manufacture medicine. Those working in the field of microbiology generally work as laboratory assistants, studying living organisms and infectious agents. Biological technicians also analyze organic substances, such as blood, food, and drugs. Biological technicians working in biotechnology apply knowledge and techniques gained from basic research, including gene splicing and recombinant DNA, and apply them to product development.

Chemical technicians work with chemists and chemical engineers, developing and using chemicals and related products and equipment. Generally, there are two types of chemical technicians: research technicians who work in experimental laboratories and process control technicians who work in manufacturing or other industrial plants. Many chemical technicians working in research and development conduct a variety of laboratory procedures, from routine process control to complex research projects. For example, they may collect and analyze samples of air and water to monitor pollution levels, or they may produce compounds through complex organic synthesis. Most *process technicians* work in manufacturing, testing packaging for design, integrity of materials, and environmental acceptability. Often, process technicians who work in plants focus on quality assurance, monitoring product quality or production processes and developing new production techniques. A few work in shipping to provide technical support and expertise.

Environmental science and protection technicians perform laboratory and field tests to monitor environmental resources and determine the contaminants and sources of pollution in the environment. They may collect samples for testing or be involved in abating and controlling sources of environmental pollution. Some are responsible for waste management operations, control and management of hazardous materials inventory, or general activities involving regulatory compliance. Many environmental science technicians employed at private consulting firms work directly under the supervision of an environmental scientist.

Forensic science technicians investigate crimes by collecting and analyzing physical evidence. Often, they specialize in areas such as DNA analysis or firearm examination, performing tests on weapons or on substances such as fiber, glass, hair, tissue, and body fluids to determine their significance to the investigation. Proper collection and storage methods are important to protect the evidence. Forensic science technicians also prepare reports to document their findings and the laboratory techniques used, and they may provide information and expert opinions to investigators. When criminal cases come to trial, forensic science technicians often give testimony as expert witnesses on laboratory findings by identifying and classifying substances, materials, and other evidence collected at the scene of a crime. Some forensic science technicians work closely with other experts or technicians. For example, a forensic science technician may consult either a medical expert about the exact time and cause of a death or another technician who specializes in DNA typing in hopes of matching a DNA type to a suspect.

Forest and conservation technicians compile data on the size, content, and condition of forest land. These workers usually work in a forest under the supervision of a forester, doing specific tasks such as measuring timber, supervising harvesting operations, assisting in road building operations, and locating property lines and features. They also may gather basic information, such as data on populations of trees, disease and insect damage, tree seedling mortality, and conditions that may pose a fire hazard. In addition, forest and conservation technicians train and lead forest and conservation workers in seasonal activities, such as planting tree seedlings, and maintaining recreational facilities. Increasing numbers of forest and conservation technicians work in urban forestry—the study of individual trees in cities—and other nontraditional specialties, rather than in forests or rural areas.

Geological and petroleum technicians measure and record physical and geologic conditions in oil or gas wells, using advanced instruments lowered into the wells or analyzing the mud from the wells. In oil and gas exploration, technicians collect and examine geological data or test geological samples to determine their petroleum content and their mineral and element composition. Some petroleum technicians, called scouts, collect information about oil well and gas well drilling operations, geological and geophysical prospecting, and land or lease contracts.

Nuclear technicians operate nuclear test and research equipment, monitor radiation, and assist nuclear engineers and physicists in research. Some also operate remote controlled equipment to manipulate radioactive materials or materials exposed to radioactivity. Workers who control nuclear reactors are classified as *nuclear power reactor operators*, and are not included in this statement. (See the statement on power plant operators, distributors, and dispatchers elsewhere in the *Handbook*.)

Other science technicians perform a wide range of activities. Some collect weather information or assist oceanographers; others work as laser technicians or radiographers.

Work environment. Science technicians work under a wide variety of conditions. Most work indoors, usually in laboratories, and have regular hours. Some occasionally work irregular hours to monitor experiments that cannot be completed during regular working hours. Production technicians often work in 8-hour shifts around the clock. Others, such as agricultural, forest and conservation, geological and petroleum, and environmental science and protection technicians, perform much of their work outdoors, sometimes in remote locations.

Advances in automation and information technology require technicians to operate more sophisticated laboratory equipment. Science technicians make extensive use of computers, electronic measuring equipment, and traditional experimental apparatus.

Some science technicians may be exposed to hazards from equipment, chemicals, or toxic materials. Chemical technicians sometimes work with toxic chemicals or radioactive isotopes; nuclear technicians may be exposed to radiation, and biological technicians sometimes work with disease-causing

Job opportunities will be best for graduates who are trained on equipment used in labratories or production facilities.

organisms or radioactive agents. Forensic science technicians often are exposed to human body fluids and firearms. However, these working conditions pose little risk if proper safety procedures are followed. For forensic science technicians, collecting evidence from crime scenes can be distressing and unpleasant.

Training, Other Qualifications, and Advancement

Most science technicians need an associate degree or a certificate in applied science or science-related technology. Biological and forensic science technicians usually need a bachelor's degree. Science technicians with a high school diploma and no college degree typically begin work as trainees under the direct supervision of a more experienced technician, and eventually earn a 2-year degree in science technology.

Education and training. There are several ways to qualify for a job as a science technician. Many employers prefer applicants who have at least 2 years of specialized training or an associate degree in applied science or science-related technology. Because employers' preferences vary, however, some science technicians have a bachelor's degree in chemistry, biology, or forensic science or have completed several science and math courses at a 4-year college.

Most biological technician jobs, for example, require a bachelor's degree in biology or a closely related field. Forensic science positions also typically require a bachelor's degree to work in the field. Knowledge and understanding of legal procedures also can be helpful. Chemical technician positions in research and development also often have a bachelor's degree, but most chemical process technicians have a 2-year degree instead, usually an associate degree in process technology. In some cases, a high school diploma is sufficient. These workers usually receive additional on-the-job training. Entry-level workers whose college training encompasses extensive hands-on experience with a variety of diagnostic laboratory equipment generally require less on-the-job training.

Whatever their degree, science technicians usually need hands-on training either in school or on the job. Most can get good career preparation through 2-year formal training programs that combine the teaching of scientific principles and theory with practical hands-on application in a laboratory setting with up-to-date equipment. Graduates of bachelor's degree programs in science who have considerable experience in laboratory-based courses, have completed internships, or have held summer jobs in laboratories also are well qualified for science technician positions and are preferred by some employers.

Job candidates, who have extensive hands-on experience with a variety of laboratory equipment, including computers and related equipment, usually require a short period of on-the-job training. Those with a high school diploma and no college degree typically begin work as trainees under the direct supervision of a more experienced technician. Many with a high school diploma eventually earn a 2-year degree in science technology, often paid for by their employer.

Many technical and community colleges offer associate degrees in a specific technology or more general education in science and mathematics. A number of associate degree programs are designed to provide easy transfer to bachelor's degree programs at colleges or universities. Technical institutes usually offer technician training, but they provide less theory and general education than do community colleges. The length of programs at technical institutes varies, although 1-year certificate programs and 2-year associate degree programs are common. Prospective forestry and conservation technicians can choose from more than 20 associate degree programs in forest technology accredited by the Society of American Foresters.

Approximately 30 colleges and universities offer a bachelor's degree program in forensic science; about another 25 schools offer a bachelor's degree in a natural science with an emphasis on forensic science or criminology; a few additional schools offer a bachelor's degree with an emphasis in a specialty area, such as criminology, pathology, jurisprudence, investigation, odontology, toxicology, or forensic accounting.

Some schools offer cooperative-education or internship programs, allowing students the opportunity to work at a local company or some other workplace while attending classes during alternate terms. Participation in such programs can significantly enhance a student's employment prospects.

People interested in careers as science technicians should take as many high school science and math courses as possible. Science courses taken beyond high school, in an associate or bachelor's degree program, should be laboratory oriented, with an emphasis on bench skills. A solid background in applied chemistry, physics, and math is vital.

Other qualifications. Communication skills are important because technicians are often required to report their findings both orally and in writing. In addition, technicians should be able to work well with others. Because computers often are used in research and development laboratories, technicians should also have strong computer skills, especially in computer modeling. Organizational ability, an eye for detail, and skill in interpreting scientific results are important as well, as are a high mechanical aptitude, attention to detail, and analytical thinking.

Advancement. Technicians usually begin work as trainees in routine positions under the direct supervision of a scientist or a more experienced technician. As they gain experience, technicians take on more responsibility and carry out assignments under only general supervision, and some eventually become supervisors. However, technicians employed at universities often have job prospects tied to those of particular professors; when those professors retire or leave, these technicians face uncertain employment prospects.

Employment

Science technicians held about 267,000 jobs in 2006. As indicated by the following tabulation, chemical and biological technicians accounted for 52 percent of all jobs:

Biological technicians 79,000
Chemical technicians 61,000
Environmental science and
    protection technicians, including health............................37,000
Forest and conservation technicians....................................34,000
Agricultural and food science technicians............................26,000
Forensic science technicians 13,000
Geological and petroleum technicians 12,000
Nuclear technicians 6,500

About 30 percent of biological technicians worked in professional, scientific, or technical services firms; most other biological technicians worked in educational services, Federal, State, and local governments, or pharmaceutical and medicine manufacturing. Chemical technicians held jobs in a wide range of manufacturing and service-providing industries. About 39 percent worked in chemical manufacturing and another 30 percent worked in professional, scientific, or technical services firms. Most environmental science and protection technicians worked for State and local governments and professional, scientific, and technical services firms. About 76 percent of forest and conservation technicians held jobs in the Federal Government, mostly in the Forest Service; another 17 percent worked for State governments. Around 32 percent of agricultural and food science technicians worked in educational services and 20 percent worked for food processing companies; most of the rest were employed in agriculture. Forensic science technicians worked primarily for State and local governments. Approximately 37 percent of all geological and petroleum tech-

nicians worked for oil and gas extraction companies and 49 percent of nuclear technicians worked for utilities.

Job Outlook

Employment of science technicians is projected to grow about as fast as the average, although employment change will vary by specialty. Job opportunities are expected to be best for graduates of applied science technology programs who are well trained on equipment used in laboratories or production facilities.

Employment change. Overall employment of science technicians is expected to grow 12 percent during the 2006-16 decade, about as fast as the average for all occupations. The continued growth of scientific and medical research—particularly research related to biotechnology—will be the primary driver of employment growth, but the development and production of technical products should also stimulate demand for science technicians in many industries.

Employment of biological technicians should increase faster than the average, as the growing number of agricultural and medicinal products developed with the use of biotechnology techniques boosts demand for these workers. Also, an aging population and stronger competition among pharmaceutical companies are expected to contribute to the need for innovative and improved drugs, further spurring demand. Most growth in employment will be in professional, scientific, and technical services and in educational services.

Job growth for chemical technicians is projected to grow more slowly than the average. The chemical manufacturing industry, except pharmaceutical and medicine manufacturing, is anticipated to experience a decline in overall employment as companies downsize and turn to outside contractors to provide specialized services. Some of these contractors will be in other countries with lower average wages, further limiting employment growth. An increasing focus on quality assurance will require a greater number of process technicians, however, stimulating demand for these workers.

Employment of environmental science and protection technicians is expected to grow much faster than the average; these workers will be needed to help regulate waste products; to collect air, water, and soil samples for measuring levels of pollutants; to monitor compliance with environmental regulations;

Projections data from the National Employment Matrix

Occupational Title	SOC Code	Employment, 2006	Projected employment, 2016	Change, 2006-2016	
				Number	Percent
Science technicians	—	267,000	300,000	33,000	12
Agricultural and food science technicians...................................	19-4011	26,000	28,000	1,700	7
Biological technicians...	19-4021	79,000	91,000	13,000	16
Chemical technicians	19-4031	61,000	65,000	3,600	6
Geological and petroleum technicians.......................................	19-4041	12,000	13,000	1,000	9
Nuclear technicians...	19-4051	6,500	6,900	400	7
Environmental science and protection technicians, including health..	19-4091	37,000	47,000	10,000	28
Forensic science technicians	19-4092	13,000	17,000	4,000	31
Forest and conservation technicians	19-4093	34,000	33,000	-700	-2

NOTE: Data in this table are rounded. See the discussion of the employment projections table in the *Handbook* introductory chapter on *Occupational Information Included in the Handbook.*

and to clean up contaminated sites. Over 80 percent of this growth is expected to be in professional, scientific, and technical services as environmental monitoring, management, and regulatory compliance increase.

An expected decline in employment of forest and conservation technicians within the Federal Government will lead to little or no change in employment in this specialty, due to budgetary constraints and continued reductions in demand for timber management on Federal lands. However, opportunities at State and local governments within specialties such as urban forestry may provide some new jobs. In addition, an increased emphasis on specific conservation issues, such as environmental protection, preservation of water resources, and control of exotic and invasive pests, may provide some employment opportunities.

Employment of agricultural and food science technicians is projected to grow about as fast as the average. Research in biotechnology and other areas of agricultural science will increase as it becomes more important to balance greater agricultural output with protection and preservation of soil, water, and the ecosystem. In particular, research will be needed to combat insects and diseases as they adapt to pesticides and as soil fertility and water quality continue to need improvement.

Jobs for forensic science technicians are expected to increase much faster than the average. Employment growth in State and local government should be driven by the increasing application of forensic science to examine, solve, and prevent crime. Crime scene technicians who work for State and county crime labs should experience favorable employment prospects resulting from strong job growth.

Average employment growth is expected for geological and petroleum technicians. Job growth should be strongest in professional, scientific, and technical services firms because geological and petroleum technicians will be needed to assist environmental scientists and geoscientists as they provide consultation services for companies regarding environmental policy and Federal Government mandates, such as those requiring lower sulfur emissions.

Nuclear technicians should grow about as fast as the average as more are needed to monitor the Nation's aging fleet of nuclear reactors and research future advances in nuclear power. Although no new nuclear powerplants have been built for decades in the United States, energy demand has recently renewed interest in this form of electricity generation and may lead to future construction. Technicians also will be needed to work in defense-related areas, to develop nuclear medical technology, and to improve and enforce waste management and safety standards.

Job prospects. In addition to job openings created by growth, many openings should arise from the need to replace technicians who retire or leave the labor force for other reasons. Job opportunities are expected to be best for graduates of applied science technology programs who are well trained on equipment used in laboratories or production facilities. As the instrumentation and techniques used in industrial research, development, and production become increasingly more complex, employers will seek individuals with highly developed

technical skills. Good communication skills are also increasingly sought by employers.

Job opportunities vary by specialty. The best opportunities for agricultural and food science technicians will be in agricultural biotechnology, specifically in research and development on biofuels. Geological and petroleum technicians should experience little competition for positions because of the relatively small number of new entrants. Forensic science technicians with a bachelor's degree in a forensic science will enjoy much better opportunities than those with an associate degree. During periods of economic recession, science technicians may be laid off.

Earnings
Median hourly earnings of science technicians in May 2006 were as follows:

Nuclear technicians $31.49
Geological and petroleum technicians 22.19
Forensic science technicians 21.79
Chemical technicians 18.87
Environmental science and
    protection technicians, including health 18.31
Biological technicians 17.17
Agricultural and food science technicians............................15.26
Forest and conservation technicians 14.84

In 2007, the average annual salary in the Federal Government was $40,629 for biological science technicians; $53,026 for physical science technicians; $40,534 for forestry technicians; $54,081 for geodetic technicians; $50,337 for hydrologic technicians; and $63,396 for meteorological technicians.

Related Occupations
Other technicians who apply scientific principles and who usually have a 2-year associate degree include engineering technicians, broadcast and sound engineering technicians and radio operators, drafters, and health technologists and technicians— especially clinical laboratory technologists and technicians, diagnostic medical sonographers, and radiologic technologists and technicians.

Sources of Additional Information
For information about a career as a chemical technician, contact:
➤ American Chemical Society, Education Division, Career Publications, 1155 16th St.NW., Washington, DC 20036. Internet: **http://www.acs.org**

For career information and a list of undergraduate, graduate, and doctoral programs in forensic sciences, contact:
➤ American Academy of Forensic Sciences, P.O. Box 669, Colorado Springs, CO, 80901. Internet: **http://www.aafs.org**

For general information on forestry technicians and a list of schools offering education in forestry, send a self-addressed, stamped business envelope to:
➤ Society of American Foresters, 5400 Grosvenor Ln., Bethesda, MD 20814. Internet: **http://www.safnet.org**

Community and Social Services Occupations

Counselors

(O*NET 21-1011.00, 21-1012.00, 21-1013.00, 21-1014.00, 21-1015.00, 21-1019.99)

Significant Points

- A master's degree generally is required to become a licensed counselor.

- Job opportunities for counselors should be very good because job openings are expected to exceed the number of graduates from counseling programs.

- The health care and social assistance industry employs about 47 percent of counselors, and state and local government employ about 11 percent.

Nature of the Work

Counselors assist people with personal, family, educational, mental health, and career problems. Their duties vary greatly depending on their occupational specialty, which is determined by the setting in which they work and the population they serve.

Educational, vocational, and school counselors provide individuals and groups with career and educational counseling. School counselors assist students of all levels, from elementary school to postsecondary education. They advocate for students and work with other individuals and organizations to promote the academic, career, personal, and social development of children and youth. School counselors help students evaluate their abilities, interests, talents, and personalities to develop realistic academic and career goals. Counselors use interviews, counseling sessions, interest and aptitude assessment tests, and other methods to evaluate and advise students. They also operate career information centers and career education programs. Often, counselors work with students who have academic and social development problems or other special needs.

Elementary school counselors observe children during classroom and play activities and confer with their teachers and parents to evaluate the children's strengths, problems, or special needs. In conjunction with teachers and administrators, they make sure that the curriculum addresses both the academic and the developmental needs of students. Elementary school counselors do less vocational and academic counseling than high school counselors.

High school counselors advise students regarding college majors, admission requirements, entrance exams, financial aid, trade or technical schools, and apprenticeship programs. They help students develop job search skills, such as resume writing and interviewing techniques. College career planning and placement counselors assist alumni or students with career development and job-hunting techniques.

School counselors at all levels help students to understand and deal with social, behavioral, and personal problems. These counselors emphasize preventive and developmental counseling to provide students with the life skills needed to deal with problems before they worsen and to enhance students' personal, social, and academic growth. Counselors provide special services, including alcohol and drug prevention programs and conflict resolution classes. They also try to identify cases of domestic abuse and other family problems that can affect a student's development.

Counselors interact with students individually, in small groups, or as an entire class. They consult and collaborate with parents, teachers, school administrators, school psychologists, medical professionals, and social workers to develop and implement strategies to help students succeed.

Vocational counselors, also called *employment* or *career counselors*, provide mainly career counseling outside the school setting. Their chief focus is helping individuals with career decisions. Vocational counselors explore and evaluate the client's education, training, work history, interests, skills, and personality traits. They may arrange for aptitude and achievement tests to help the client make career decisions. They also work with individuals to develop their job-search skills and assist clients in locating and applying for jobs. In addition, career counselors provide support to people experiencing job loss, job stress, or other career transition issues.

Rehabilitation counselors help people deal with the personal, social, and vocational effects of disabilities. They counsel people with disabilities resulting from birth defects, illness or disease, accidents, or other causes. They evaluate the strengths and limitations of individuals, provide personal and vocational counseling, and arrange for medical care, vocational training, and job placement. Rehabilitation counselors interview both individuals with disabilities and their families, evaluate school and medical reports, and confer with physicians, psychologists, occupational therapists, and employers to determine the capabilities and skills of the individual. They develop rehabilitation programs by conferring with clients; these programs often include training to help clients develop job skills. Rehabilitation counselors also work toward increasing the client's capacity to live independently.

Mental health counselors work with individuals, families, and groups to address and treat mental and emotional disorders and to promote mental health. They are trained in a variety of therapeutic techniques used to address issues, including depression, addiction and substance abuse, suicidal impulses, stress, problems with self-esteem, and grief. They also help with job and career concerns, educational decisions, issues related to mental and emotional health, and family, parenting, marital, or other relationship problems. Mental health counselors often work closely with other mental health specialists, such as psychiatrists, psychologists, clinical social workers, psychiatric nurses, and school counselors. (Information on psychologists, registered nurses, social workers and physicians and surgeons, which includes psychiatrists, appears elsewhere in the *Handbook*.)

Substance abuse and behavioral disorder counselors help people who have problems with alcohol, drugs, gambling, and eating disorders. They counsel individuals who are addicted to drugs, helping them to identify behaviors and problems related to their addiction. Counseling can be done on an individual basis, but is frequently done in a group setting. These counselors will often also work with family members who are affected by the addictions of their loved ones. Counselors also conduct programs aimed at preventing addictions.

Marriage and family therapists apply family systems theory, principals and techniques to individuals, families, and couples to resolve emotional conflicts. In doing so, they modify people's perceptions and behaviors, enhance communication and understanding among family members, and help to prevent family and individual crises. Marriage and family therapists also may engage in psychotherapy of a non-medical nature, make appropriate referrals to psychiatric resources, perform research, and teach courses about human development and interpersonal relationships.

Other counseling specialties include gerontological, multicultural, and genetic counseling. A gerontological counselor provides services to elderly people and their families as they face changing lifestyles. Genetic counselors provide information and support to families who have members with birth defects or genetic disorders and to families who may be at risk for a variety of inherited conditions. These counselors identify families at risk, interpret information about the disorder, analyze inheritance patterns and risks of recurrence, and review available options with the family.

Work environment. Work environment can vary greatly depending on occupational specialty. School counselors work predominantly in schools, where they usually have an office but also may work in classrooms. Other counselors may work in a private practice, community health organization, or hospital. Many counselors work in an office where they see clients throughout the day. Because privacy is essential for confidential and frank discussions with clients, counselors usually have private offices.

Counselors often work with clients one-on-one to assist with personal, family, educational, and career problems and decisions.

The work schedules of counselors depend on occupational specialty and work setting. Some school counselors work the traditional 9- to 10-month school year with a 2- to 3-month vacation, but increasing numbers, are employed on 11-month or full-year contracts, particularly those working in middle and high schools. They usually work the same hours as teachers, but they may travel more frequently to attend conferences and conventions. College career planning and placement counselors work long and irregular hours during student recruiting periods.

Rehabilitation counselors usually work a standard 40-hour week. Self-employed counselors and those working in mental health and community agencies, such as substance abuse and behavioral disorder counselors, frequently work evenings to counsel clients who work during the day. Both mental health counselors and marriage and family therapists also often work flexible hours to accommodate families in crisis or working couples who must have evening or weekend appointments.

Training, Other Qualifications, and Advancement

Education and training requirements for counselors are often very detailed and vary by State and specialty. Prospective counselors should check with State and local governments, employers, and national voluntary certification organizations to determine which requirements apply.

Education and training. Education requirements vary based on occupational specialty and State licensure and certification requirements. A master's degree is usually required to be licensed as a counselor. Some States require counselors in public employment to have a master's degree; others accept a bachelor's degree with appropriate counseling courses. Counselor education programs in colleges and universities are often found in departments of education or psychology. Fields of study include college student affairs, elementary or secondary school counseling, education, gerontological counseling, marriage and family therapy, substance abuse counseling, rehabilitation counseling, agency or community counseling, clinical mental health counseling, career counseling, and related fields. Courses are often grouped into eight core areas: human growth and development, social and cultural diversity, relationships, group work, career development, assessment, research and program evaluation, and professional identity. In an accredited master's degree program, 48 to 60 semester hours of graduate study, including a period of supervised clinical experience in counseling, are required.

Some employers provide training for newly hired counselors. Others may offer time off or tuition assistance to complete a graduate degree. Often counselors must participate in graduate studies, workshops, and personal studies to maintain their certificates and licenses.

Licensure. Licensure requirements differ greatly by State, occupational specialty, and work setting. Many States require school counselors to hold a State school counseling certification and to have completed at least some graduate course work; most require the completion of a master's degree. Some States require school counselors to be licensed, which generally requires continuing education credits. Some States require public school counselors to have both counseling and teaching certificates and to have had some teaching experience.

For counselors based outside of schools, 49 States and the District of Columbia have some form of counselor licensure that governs the practice of counseling. Requirements typically include the completion of a master's degree in counseling, the accumulation of 2 years or 3,000 hours of supervised clinical experience beyond the master's degree level, the passage of a State-recognized exam, adherence to ethical codes and standards, and the completion of annual continuing education requirements. However, counselors working in certain settings or in a particular specialty may face different licensure requirements. For example, a career counselor working in private practice may need a license, but a counselor working for a college career center may not. In addition, substance abuse and behavior disorder counselors are generally governed by a different State agency or board than other counselors. The criteria for their licensure vary greatly and in some cases, these counselors may only need a high school diploma and certification. Those interested in entering the field must research State and specialty requirements to determine what qualifications they must have.

Other qualifications. People interested in counseling should have a strong desire to help others and should be able to inspire respect, trust, and confidence. They should be able to work independently or as part of a team. Counselors must follow the code of ethics associated with their respective certifications and licenses.

Counselors must possess high physical and emotional energy to handle the array of problems that they address. Dealing daily with these problems can cause stress.

Certification and advancement. Some counselors elect to be certified by the National Board for Certified Counselors, Inc., which grants a general practice credential of National Certified Counselor. To be certified, a counselor must hold a master's degree with a concentration in counseling from a regionally accredited college or university; have at least 2 years of supervised field experience in a counseling setting (graduates from counselor education programs accredited by the Council for Accreditation of Counseling and Related Educational Programs are exempted); provide two professional endorsements, one of which must be from a recent supervisor; and must have a passing score on the board's examination. This national certification is voluntary and is distinct from State licensing. However, in some States, those who pass the national exam are exempted from taking a State certification exam. The board also offers specialty certifications in school, clinical mental health, and addiction counseling. These specialty certifications require passage of a supplemental exam. To maintain their certifications, counselors retake and pass the exam or complete 100 credit hours of acceptable continuing education every 5 years.

The Commission on Rehabilitation Counselor Certification offers voluntary national certification for rehabilitation counselors. Many State and local governments and other employers require rehabilitation counselors to have this certification. To become certified, rehabilitation counselors usually must graduate from an accredited educational program, complete an internship, and pass a written examination. Certification requirements vary, however, according to an applicant's educational history. Employment experience, for example, is required for those with a counseling degree in a specialty other than reha-

bilitation. To maintain their certification, counselors must successfully retake the certification exam or complete 100 credit hours of acceptable continuing education every 5 years.

Other counseling organizations also offer certification in particular counseling specialties. Usually, becoming certified is voluntary, but having certification may enhance job prospects.

Prospects for advancement vary by counseling field. School counselors can become directors or supervisors of counseling, guidance, or pupil personnel services; or, usually with further graduate education, become counselor educators, counseling psychologists, or school administrators. (Psychologists and education administrators are covered elsewhere in the *Handbook*.) Some counselors choose to work for a State's department of education.

Some marriage and family therapists, especially those with doctorates in family therapy, become supervisors, teachers, researchers, or advanced clinicians in the discipline. Counselors may also become supervisors or administrators in their agencies. Some counselors move into research, consulting, or college teaching or go into private or group practice. Some may choose to pursue a doctoral degree to improve their chances for advancement.

Employment

Counselors held about 635,000 jobs in 2006. Employment was distributed among the counseling specialties as follows:

Educational, vocational, and school counselors..................260,000
Rehabilitation counselors.....................................141,000
Mental health counselors 100,000
Substance abuse and behavioral disorder counselors 83,000
Marriage and family therapists 25,000
Counselors, all other 27,000

Educational, vocational, and school counselors work primarily in elementary and secondary schools and colleges and universities. Other types of counselors work in a wide variety of public and private establishments, including healthcare facilities; job training, career development, and vocational rehabilitation centers; social agencies; correctional institutions; and residential care facilities, such as halfway houses for criminal offenders and group homes for children, the elderly, and the disabled. Some substance abuse and behavioral disorder counselors work in therapeutic communities where people with addictions live while undergoing treatment. Counselors also work in organizations engaged in community improvement and social change, drug and alcohol rehabilitation programs, and State and local government agencies.

A growing number of counselors are self-employed and work in group practices or private practice, due in part to new laws allowing counselors to be paid for their services by insurance companies and to the growing recognition that counselors are well-trained, effective professionals.

Job Outlook

Employment for counselors is expected to grow much faster than the average for all occupations through 2016. However, job growth will vary by location and occupational specialty.

Projections data from the National Employment Matrix

Occupational Title	SOC Code	Employment, 2006	Projected employment, 2016	Change, 2006-2016	
				Number	Percent
Counselors...	21-1010	635,000	771,000	136,000	21
Substance abuse and behavioral disorder counselors..................	21-1011	83,000	112,000	29,000	34
Educational, vocational, and school counselors...........................	21-1012	260,000	292,000	33,000	13
Marriage and family therapists	21-1013	25,000	32,000	7,400	30
Mental health counselors	21-1014	100,000	130,000	30,000	30
Rehabilitation counselors...	21-1015	141,000	173,000	32,000	23
Counselors, all other..	21-1019	27,000	32,000	4,500	17

NOTE: Data in this table are rounded. See the discussion of the employment projections table in the *Handbook* introductory chapter on *Occupational Information Included in the Handbook*.

Job prospects should be good due to growth and the need to replace people leaving the field.

Employment change. Overall employment of counselors is expected to increase by 21 percent between 2006 and 2016, which is much faster than the average for all occupations. However, growth is expected to vary by specialty.

Employment of substance abuse and behavioral disorder counselors is expected to grow 34 percent, which is much faster than the average for all occupations. As society becomes more knowledgeable about addiction, it is increasingly common for people to seek treatment. Furthermore, drug offenders are increasingly being sent to treatment programs rather than jail.

Employment for educational, vocational and school counselors is expected to grow 13 percent, which is about as fast as the average for all occupations. Demand for vocational or career counselors should grow as multiple job and career changes become common and as workers become increasingly aware of counseling services. In addition, State and local governments will employ growing numbers of counselors to assist beneficiaries of welfare programs who exhaust their eligibility and must find jobs. Other opportunities for employment of counselors will arise in private job-training centers that provide training and other services to laid-off workers and others seeking to acquire new skills or careers. Demand for school counselors may increase due in large part to increases in student enrollments at postsecondary schools and colleges and as more States require elementary schools to employ counselors. Expansion of the responsibilities of school counselors should also lead to increases in their employment. For example, counselors are becoming more involved in crisis and preventive counseling, helping students deal with issues ranging from drug and alcohol abuse to death and suicide. Although schools and governments realize the value of counselors in helping their students to achieve academic success, budget constraints at every school level will dampen job growth of school counselors. Federal grants and subsidies may help to offset tight budgets and allow the reduction in student-to-counselor ratios to continue.

Employment of mental health counselors is expected to grow by 30 percent, which is much faster than the average for all occupations. Mental health counselors will be needed to staff statewide networks that are being established to improve services for children and adolescents with serious emotional disturbances and for their families. Under managed care systems, insurance companies are increasingly providing for reimbursement of counselors as a less costly alternative to psychiatrists and psychologists.

Jobs for rehabilitation counselors are expected to grow by 23 percent, which is much faster than the average for all occupations. The number of people who will need rehabilitation counseling is expected to grow as advances in medical technology allow more people to survive injury or illness and live independently again. In addition, legislation requiring equal employment rights for people with disabilities will spur demand for counselors, who not only help these people make a transition to the workforce but also help companies to comply with the law.

Marriage and family therapists will experience growth of 30 percent, which is much faster than the average for all occupations. This is due in part to an increased recognition of the field. It is more common for people to seek help for their marital and family problems than it was in the past.

Job prospects. Job prospects vary greatly based on the occupational specialty. Prospects for rehabilitation counselors are excellent because many people are leaving the field or retiring. Furthermore, opportunities are very good in substance abuse and behavioral disorder counseling because relatively low wages and long hours make recruiting new entrants difficult. For school counselors, job prospects should be good because many people are leaving the occupation to retire; however, opportunities may be more favorable in rural and urban areas, rather than the suburbs, because it is often difficult to recruit people to these areas.

Earnings

Median annual earnings of wage and salary educational, vocational, and school counselors in May 2006 were $47,530. The middle 50 percent earned between $36,120 and $60,990. The lowest 10 percent earned less than $27,240, and the highest 10 percent earned more than $75,920. School counselors can earn additional income working summers in the school system or in other jobs. Median annual earnings in the industries employing the largest numbers of educational, vocational, and school counselors were as follows:

Elementary and secondary schools $53,750
Junior colleges 48,240
Colleges, universities, and professional schools...................41,780
Individual and family services 32,370
Vocational rehabilitation services 31,340

Median annual earnings of wage and salary substance abuse and behavioral disorder counselors in May 2006 were $34,040. The middle 50 percent earned between $27,330 and $42,650. The lowest 10 percent earned less than $22,600, and the highest 10 percent earned more than $52,340.

Median annual earnings of wage and salary mental health counselors in May 2006 were $34,380. The middle 50 percent earned between $26,780 and $45,610. The lowest 10 percent earned less than $21,890, and the highest 10 percent earned more than $59,700.

Median annual earnings of wage and salary rehabilitation counselors in May 2006 were $29,200. The middle 50 percent earned between $22,980 and $39,000. The lowest 10 percent earned less than $19,260, and the highest 10 percent earned more than $53,170.

For substance abuse, mental health, and rehabilitation counselors, government employers generally pay the highest wages, followed by hospitals and social service agencies. Residential care facilities often pay the lowest wages.

Median annual earnings of wage and salary marriage and family therapists in May 2006 were $43,210. The middle 50 percent earned between $32,950 and $54,150. The lowest 10 percent earned less than $25,280, and the highest 10 percent earned more than $69,050. Median annual earnings were $36,020 in individual and family social services, the industry employing the largest number of marriage and family therapists.

Self-employed counselors who have well-established practices, as well as counselors employed in group practices, usually have the highest earnings.

Related Occupations

Counselors help people evaluate their interests, abilities, and disabilities and deal with personal, social, academic, and career problems. Others who help people in similar ways include teachers, social and human service assistants, social workers, psychologists, physicians and surgeons, registered nurses, occupational therapists, and human resources, training, and labor relations managers and specialists.

Sources of Additional Information

For general information about counseling, as well as information on specialties such as college, mental health, rehabilitation, multicultural, career, marriage and family, and gerontological counseling, contact:

➤ American Counseling Association, 5999 Stevenson Ave., Alexandria, VA 22304. Internet: **http://www.counseling.org**

For information on school counselors, contact:

➤ American School Counselors Association, 1101 King St., Suite 625, Alexandria, VA 22314.
Internet: **http://www.schoolcounselor.org**

For information on mental health counselors, contact:

➤ American Mental Health Counselors Association, 801 N. Fairfax Street, Suite 304, Alexandria, VA 22314.
Internet: **http://www.amhca.org**

For information on marriage and family therapists, contact:

➤ American Association for Marriage and Family Therapy, 112 South Alfred Street, Alexandria, VA 22314
Internet: **http://www.aamft.org**

For information on accredited counseling and related training programs, contact:

➤ Council for Accreditation of Counseling and Related Educational Programs, American Counseling Association, 5999 Stevenson Ave., 4th floor, Alexandria, VA 22304.
Internet: **http://www.cacrep.org**

For information on national certification requirements for counselors, contact:

➤ National Board for Certified Counselors, Inc, 3 Terrace Way, Suite D, Greensboro, NC 27403.
Internet: **http://www.nbcc.org**

State departments of education can supply information on colleges and universities offering guidance and counseling training that meets State certification and licensure requirements.

State employment service offices have information about job opportunities and entrance requirements for counselors.

Health Educators

(O*NET 21-1091.00)

Significant Points

- 5 out of 10 health educators work in health care and social assistance and an additional 2 out of 10 work in State and local government.

- A bachelor's degree is the minimum requirement for entry level jobs, but many employers prefer to hire workers with a master's degree.

- Rapid job growth is expected, but the relatively small number of jobs in this occupation will limit the number of job openings.

Nature of the Work

Health educators work to encourage healthy lifestyles and wellness through educating individuals and communities about behaviors that promote healthy living and prevent diseases and other health problems.

They attempt to prevent illnesses by informing and educating individuals and communities about health-related topics, such as proper nutrition, the importance of exercise, how to avoid sexually transmitted diseases, and the habits and behaviors necessary to avoid illness. They begin by assessing the needs of their audience, which includes determining which topics to cover and how to best present the information. For example, they may hold programs on self-examinations for breast cancer to women who are at higher risk or may teach classes on the effects of binge drinking to college students. Health educators must take the cultural norms of their audience into account. For example, programs targeted at the elderly need to be drastically different from those aimed at a college-aged population.

After assessing their audiences' needs, health educators must decide how to meet those needs. Health educators have a lot of options in putting together programs to that end. They may organize a lecture, class, demonstration or health screening, or create a video, pamphlet or brochure. Often, planning a program requires working with other people in a team or on a committee within the organization that employs them. Also, health educators must plan programs that are consistent with the goals and objectives of their employers. For example, many nonprofit organizations educate the public about just one disease or health issue and, therefore, limit their programs to cover topics related to that disease or issue.

Next, health educators need to implement their proposed plan. This may require finding funding by applying for grants, writing curriculums for classes, or creating written materials that would be made available to the public. Also, programs may require dealing with basic logistics problems, such as finding speakers or locations for the event.

Generally, after a program is presented, health educators evaluate its success. This could include tracking the absentee rate of employees from work and students from school, surveying participants on their opinions about the program, or other methods of collecting evidence that suggests whether the programs were effective. Through evaluation, they can improve plans for the future by learning from mistakes and capitalizing on strengths.

Although programming is a large part of their job, health educators also serve as a resource on health topics. This may include locating services, reference material and other resources that may be useful to the community they serve and referring individuals or groups to organizations or medical professionals.

The basic goals and duties of health educators are the same but their jobs vary greatly depending on the type of organization in which they work. Most health educators work in medical care settings, colleges and universities, schools, public health departments, nonprofit organizations, and private business.

Within medical care facilities, health educators tend to work one-on-one with patients and their families. Their goal in this setting is to educate individual patients on their diagnosis and how that may change or affect their lifestyle. Often, this includes explaining the necessary procedures or surgeries as well as how patients will need to change their lifestyles in order to manage their illness or return to full health. This may include directing patients to outside resources that may be useful in their transition, such as support groups, home health agencies or social services. Often, health educators work closely with physicians, nurses, and other staff to create educational programs or materials, such as brochures, Web sites, and classes, for other departments. In some cases, health educators train hospital staff about how to better interact with patients.

Health educators in colleges and universities work primarily with the student population. Generally, they create programs on topics that affect young adults, like sexual activity, smoking, and nutrition. They may need to alter their teaching methods to attract audiences to their events. For example, they might show a popular movies followed by a discussion or hold programs in dormitories or cafeterias. They may teach courses for credit or give lectures on health-related topics. Often they train students as peer educators, who then lead their own programs.

Health educators in schools are typically found in secondary schools, where they generally teach health class. They develop lesson plans that are relevant and age appropriate to their stu-

Health educators teach individuals and groups about topics related to a healthy lifestyle.

dents. They may need to cover sensitive topics, like sexually transmitted diseases, alcohol and drugs. They may be required to be able to also teach another subject such as science or physical education. Sometimes they may develop the health education curriculum for the school or the entire school district. (For more information see the statement on secondary school teachers elsewhere in the *Handbook*.)

Heath educators in public health are employed primarily by State and local departments of public health and, therefore, administer State-mandated programs. They often serve as members of statewide councils or national committees on topics like aging. As part of this work, they inform other professionals in changes to health policy. They work closely with nonprofit organizations to help them get the resources they need, such as grants, to continue serving the community.

Health educators in nonprofits strive to get information out to the public on various health problems and make people aware of the resources their programs have to help people to the community. While some organizations target a particular audience, others educate the community regarding one disease or health issue. Therefore, in this setting, health educators may be limited in the topics they cover or the population they serve. Work in this setting may include creating print-based material for distribution to the community, often in conjunction with organizing lectures, health screenings, and activities related to increasing awareness.

In private industry, health educators create programs to inform the employees of an entire firm or organization. They organize programs that fit into workers' schedules by arranging lunchtime speakers or daylong health screenings so that workers may come when it is most convenient. Educators in this setting must align their work with the overall goals of their employers. For example, a health educator working for a medical supply company may hold a program related to the company's newest product.

Work environment. Health educators work in various environments based on the industry in which they work. In public health, nonprofit organizations, business work sites, colleges and universities, and medical care settings they work primarily in offices. However, they may spend a lot of time away from the office implementing and attending programs, meeting with community organizers, speaking with patients, or teaching classes. Health educators in schools spend the majority of their day in classrooms.

Health educators generally work 40 hour weeks. However, when programs, events, or meetings are scheduled they may need to work evening or weekends.

Training, Other Qualifications, and Advancement

A bachelor's degree is generally required for entry level health educator positions, but some employers prefer a bachelor's degree and some related experience gained through an internship or volunteer work. A master's degree may be required for some positions and is usually required for advancement. In addition, some employers may require candidates to be Certified Health Education Specialists.

Education and training. Entry level health educator positions generally require a bachelor's degree in health education. Over 250 colleges and universities offer bachelor's programs in health education or a similarly titled major. These programs teach students the theories of health education and develop the skills necessary to implement health education programs. Courses in psychology, human development, and a foreign language are helpful, and experience gained through an internship or other volunteer opportunities can make graduates more appealing to employers.

Graduate health education programs are often offered under titles such as community health education, school health education, or health promotion and lead to a Master of Arts, Master of Science, Master of Education, or a Master of Public Health degree. Many students pursue their master's in health education after majoring or working in another related field, such as nursing or psychology. A master's degree is required for most health educator positions in public health.

Once hired, on-the-job training for health educators varies greatly depending on the type and size of employer. State and local public health departments and other larger offices may have a formal training program, while smaller health education offices and departments may train new employees through less formal means, such as mentoring or working with more experienced staff. Some employers may require and pay for educators to take continuing education courses to keep their skills up-to-date.

Other qualifications. Health educators spend much of their time working with people and must be comfortable working with both individuals and large groups. They need to be good communicators and comfortable speaking in public as they may need to teach classes or give presentations. Health educators often work with a very diverse population so they must be sensitive to cultural differences and open to working with people of varied backgrounds. Health educators often create new pro-

grams or materials so they should be creative and skilled writers.

Certification and advancement. Health educators may choose to become a Certified Health Education Specialist, a credential offered by the National Commission of Health Education Credentialing, Inc. The certification is awarded after passing an examination on the basic areas of responsibility for a health educator. The exam is aimed at entry level educators who have already completed a degree in health education or are within 3 months of completion. In addition, to maintain certification, health educators must complete 75 hours of approved continuing education courses or seminars over a 5-year period. Some employers prefer to hire applicants who are certified and some States require health educators certification to work in a public health department.

A graduate degree is usually required to advance past an entry level position to jobs such as executive director, supervisor, or senior health educator. These positions may spend more time on planning and evaluating programs than on their implementation, but may require supervising other health educators who implement the programs. Health educators at this level may also work with other administrators of related programs. Some health educators pursue a doctoral degree in health education and may transfer to research positions or become professors of health education (see the statement on postsecondary teachers elsewhere in the *Handbook*)

Employment

Health educators held about 62,000 jobs in 2006. They work primarily in two industries with 20 percent working in State and local government and 53 percent working in health care and social assistance. In addition, a small percent of health educators work in grant-making services and social advocacy organizations.

Job Outlook

Employment of health educators is expected to grow much faster than the average for all occupations and job prospects are expected to be favorable.

Employment change. Employment of health educators is expected to grow by 26 percent, which is much faster than the average for all occupations. Growth will result from the rising cost of health care and the increased recognition of the need for qualified health educators.

The rising cost of healthcare has increased the need for health educators. As health care costs continue to rise, insurance companies, employers and governments are attempting to find ways to curb the cost. One of the more cost effective ways is to employ health educators to teach people how to live healthy lives and avoid costly treatments for illnesses. Awareness of the number of illnesses, such as lung cancer, HIV, heart disease

Projections data from the National Employment Matrix

Occupational Title	SOC Code	Employment, 2006	Projected employment, 2016	Change, 2006-2016	
				Number	Percent
Health educators..	21-1091	62,000	78,000	16,000	26

NOTE: Data in this table are rounded. See the discussion of the employment projections table in the *Handbook* introductory chapter on *Occupational Information Included in the Handbook*.

and skin cancer, that may be avoided with lifestyle changes has increased. These diseases may be avoidable if the public better understands the effects of their behavior on their health. In addition, many illnesses, such as breast and testicular cancer are best treated with early detection so it is important for people to understand how to detect possible problems on their own. The need to provide the public with this information will result in State and local governments, hospitals, and businesses employing a growing number of health educators.

The emphasis on health education has been coupled with a growing demand for qualified health educators. In the past, it was thought that anyone could do the job of a health educator and the duties were often given to nurses or other healthcare professionals. However, in recent years, employers have recognized that those trained specifically in health education are better qualified to perform those duties. Therefore, demand for health professionals with a background specifically in health education has increased.

Demand for health educators will increase in most industries, but their employment may decrease in secondary schools. Many schools, facing budget cuts, ask teachers trained in other fields, like science or physical education, to teach the subject of health education.

Job prospects. Job prospects for health educators with bachelor's degrees will be favorable, but better for those who have acquired experience through internships or volunteer jobs. A graduate degree is preferred by many employers.

Earnings

Median annual earnings of health educators was $41,330 in May 2006; the middle 50 percent earned between $31,300 and $56,580. The lowest 10 percent earned less than $24,750, and the highest 10 percent earned more than $72,500.

Median annual earnings in the industries employing the largest numbers of health educators in May 2006 were as follows:

General medical and surgical hospitals...............................$40,890
State government...33,100
Local government 32,420
Outpatient care centers..27,530
Individual and family services 25,760

Related Occupations

Health educators work closely with people to alter their behavior. Other professions with similar skills include counselors, social workers, psychologists, teachers, social and human service assistances, and nurses.

Sources of Additional Information

For further information about health educators, contact:
➤ American Association for Health Education, 1900 Association Drive, Reston, VA 20191
Internet: **http://www.aahperd.org/aahe/**

For information on voluntary credentialing and job opportunities, contact:
➤ The National Commission for Health Education Credentialing, Inc. 1541 Alta Drive, Suite 303, Whitehall, PA 18052-5642 Internet: **http://www.nchec.org**

Probation Officers and Correctional Treatment Specialists

(O*NET 21-1092.00)

Significant Points

- State and local governments employ most of these workers.

- A bachelor's degree in social work, criminal justice, or a related field usually is required.

- Employment growth, which is projected to be as fast as the average, depends on government funding.

- Job opportunities are expected to be excellent.

Nature of the Work

Many people who are convicted of crimes are placed on probation instead of being sent to prison. People who have served time in prison are often released on parole. During probation and parole, offenders must stay out of trouble and meet various other requirements. Probation officers, parole officers, and correctional treatment specialists work with and monitor offenders to prevent them from committing new crimes.

Probation officers, who are called community supervision officers in some States, supervise people who have been placed on probation. *Correctional treatment specialists*, who may also be known as case managers, counsel offenders and create rehabilitation plans for them to follow when they are no longer in prison or on parole. *Parole officers* perform many of the same duties that probation officers perform. The difference is that parole officers supervise offenders who have been released from prison, whereas probation officers work with those who are sentenced to probation instead of prison. *Pretrial services officers* conduct pretrial investigations, the findings of which help determine whether suspects should be released before their trial.

Probation and parole officers supervise offenders on probation or parole through personal contact with the offenders and their families. Instead of requiring offenders to meet officers in their offices, many officers meet offenders in their homes and at their places of employment or therapy. Probation and parole agencies also seek the assistance of community organizations, such as religious institutions, neighborhood groups, and local residents, to monitor the behavior of many offenders. Some offenders are required to wear an electronic device so that probation officers can monitor their location and movements. Probation and parole officers may arrange for offenders to get substance abuse rehabilitation or job training. Probation officers usually work with either adults or juveniles exclusively. Only in small, usually rural, jurisdictions do probation officers counsel both adults and juveniles. In some States, the jobs of parole and probation officers are combined.

Probation officers also spend much of their time working for the courts. They investigate the backgrounds of the accused, write presentence reports, and recommend sentences. They review sentencing recommendations with offenders and their families before submitting them to the court. Probation officers may be required to testify in court as to their findings and recommendations. They also attend hearings to update the court on offenders' efforts at rehabilitation and compliance with the terms of their sentences.

Correctional treatment specialists work in jails, prisons, or parole or probation agencies. In jails and prisons, they evaluate the progress of inmates. They may evaluate inmates using questionnaires and psychological tests. They also work with inmates, probation officers, and other agencies to develop parole and release plans. Their case reports, which discuss the inmate's history and likelihood of committing another crime, are provided to the appropriate parole board when their clients are eligible for release. In addition, they plan education and training programs to improve offenders' job skills and provide them with coping, anger management, and drug and sexual abuse counseling either individually or in groups. They usually write treatment plans and summaries for each client. Correctional treatment specialists working in parole and probation agencies perform many of the same duties as their counterparts who work in correctional institutions.

The number of cases a probation officer or correctional treatment specialist handles at one time depends on the needs of offenders and the risks they pose. Higher risk offenders and those who need more counseling usually command more of the officer's time and resources. Caseload size also varies by agency jurisdiction. Consequently, officers may handle from 20 to more than 100 active cases at a time.

Computers, telephones, and fax machines enable the officers to handle the caseload. Probation officers may telecommute from their homes. Other technological advancements, such as electronic monitoring devices and drug screening, also have assisted probation officers and correctional treatment specialists in supervising and counseling offenders.

Pretrial services officers conduct pretrial investigations, the findings of which help determine whether suspects should be released before their trial. When suspects are released before their trial, pretrial services officers supervise them to make sure they adhere to the terms of their release and that they show up for trial. In the Federal courts system, probation officers perform the functions of pretrial services officers.

Work environment. Probation officers and correctional treatment specialists work with criminal offenders, some of whom may be dangerous. In the course of supervising offenders, they usually interact with many other individuals, such as family members and friends of their clients, who may be angry, upset, or difficult to work with. Workers may be assigned to fieldwork in high-crime areas or in institutions where there is a risk of violence or communicable disease.

Probation officers and correctional treatment specialists are required to meet many court-imposed deadlines, which contribute to heavy workloads. In addition, extensive travel and fieldwork may be required to meet with offenders who are on probation or parole. Workers may be required to carry a firearm or other weapon for protection. They also may be required to collect and transport urine samples of offenders for drug testing. All of these factors make for a stressful work environment. Although the high stress levels can make these jobs very difficult

Most probation officers and correctional treatment specialists work in State or local government.

at times, this work also can be very rewarding. Many workers obtain personal satisfaction from counseling members of their community and helping them become productive citizens.

Probation officers and correctional treatment specialists generally work a 40-hour week, but some may work longer. They may be on call 24 hours a day to supervise and assist offenders at any time.

Training, Other Qualifications, and Advancement

Qualifications vary by agency, but a bachelor's degree is usually required. Most employers require candidates to pass oral, written, and psychological examinations.

Education and training. A bachelor's degree in social work, criminal justice, psychology, or a related field is usually required. Some employers require a master's degree in criminal justice, social work, psychology, or a related field for candidates who do not have previous related experience. Different employers have different requirements for what counts as related experience. It may include work in probation, pretrial services, parole, corrections, criminal investigations, substance abuse treatment, social work, or counseling.

Most probation officers and some correctional treatment specialists are required to complete a training program sponsored by their State government or the Federal Government, after which a certification test may be required. Most probation officers and correctional treatment specialists work as trainees or on a probationary period for up to a year before being offered a permanent position.

Other qualifications. Applicants usually take written, oral, psychological, and physical examinations. Prospective probation officers or correctional treatment specialists should be in good physical and emotional condition. Most agencies require applicants to be at least 21 years old and, for Federal employment, not older than 37. Those convicted of felonies may not be eligible for employment in this occupation.

Familiarity with the use of computers often is required due to the increasing use of computer technology in probation and parole work. Candidates also should be knowledgeable about laws and regulations pertaining to corrections. Probation officers and correctional treatment specialists should have strong writing skills because they are required to prepare many reports.

Projections data from the National Employment Matrix

Occupational Title	SOC Code	Employment, 2006	Projected employment, 2016	Change, 2006-2016	
				Number	Percent
Probation officers and correctional treatment specialists.................	21-1092	94,000	105,000	10,000	11

NOTE: Data in this table are rounded. See the discussion of the employment projections table in the *Handbook* introductory chapter on *Occupational Information Included in the Handbook*.

They should also have excellent listening and interpersonal skills to work effectively with offenders.

Advancement. A typical agency has several levels of probation and parole officers and correctional treatment specialists, as well as supervisors. Advancement is primarily based on length of experience and performance. A graduate degree, such as a master's degree in criminal justice, social work, or psychology, may be helpful for advancement.

Employment

Probation officers and correctional treatment specialists held about 94,000 jobs in 2006. Most jobs are in State or local governments. In some States, the State government employs all probation officers and correctional treatment specialists; in other States, local governments are the only employers. In still other States, both levels of government employ these workers. Jobs are more plentiful in urban areas. In the Federal Government, probation officers are employed by the U.S. courts, and correctional treatment specialists are employed by the U.S. Department of Justice's Bureau of Prisons.

Job Outlook

Employment of probation officers and correctional treatment specialists is projected to grow as fast as the average for all occupations through 2016. Job opportunities are expected to be excellent.

Employment change. Employment of probation officers and correctional treatment specialists is projected to grow 11 percent between 2006 and 2016, as fast as the average for all occupations. Mandatory sentencing guidelines calling for longer sentences and reduced parole for inmates have resulted in a large increase in the prison population. However, mandatory sentencing guidelines are being reconsidered in many States because of budgetary constraints, court decisions, and doubts about the guidelines' effectiveness. Instead, there may be more emphasis in many States on rehabilitation and alternate forms of punishment, such as probation, spurring demand for probation and parole officers and correctional treatment specialists. Additionally, there will be a need for parole officers to supervise the large numbers of people who are currently incarcerated and will be released from prison.

However, the job outlook depends primarily on the amount of government funding that is allocated to corrections, and especially to probation systems. Although community supervision is far less expensive than keeping offenders in prison, a change in political trends toward more imprisonment and away from community supervision could result in reduced employment opportunities.

Job prospects. In addition to openings due to growth, many openings will be created by replacement needs, especially openings due to the large number of these workers who are expected to retire. This occupation is not attractive to some potential entrants due to relatively low earnings, heavy workloads, and high stress. For these reasons, job opportunities are expected to be excellent.

Earnings

Median annual earnings of probation officers and correctional treatment specialists in May 2006 were $42,500. The middle 50 percent earned between $33,880 and $56,280. The lowest 10 percent earned less than $28,000, and the highest 10 percent earned more than $71,160. In May 2006, median annual earnings for probation officers and correctional treatment specialists employed in State government were $42,970; those employed in local government earned $43,100. Higher wages tend to be found in urban areas.

Related Occupations

Probation officers and correctional treatment specialists counsel criminal offenders while they are in prison or on parole. Other occupations that involve similar responsibilities include social workers, social and human service assistants, and counselors.

Probation officers and correctional treatment specialists also play a major role in maintaining public safety. Other occupations related to corrections and law enforcement include police and detectives, correctional officers, and firefighting occupations.

Sources of Additional Information

For information about criminal justice job opportunities in your area, contact your State's department of corrections, criminal justice, or probation.

Further information about probation officers and correctional treatment specialists is available from:

➤ American Probation and Parole Association, P.O. Box 11910, Lexington, KY 40578. Internet: **http://www.appa-net.org**

Social and Human Service Assistants

(O*NET 21-1093.00)

Significant Points

- A bachelor's degree usually is not required for these jobs, but employers increasingly seek individuals with relevant work experience or education beyond high school.

- Employment is projected to grow much faster than average for all occupations.

- Job opportunities should be excellent, particularly for applicants with appropriate postsecondary education, but wages remain low.

Nature of the Work

Social and human service assistants help social workers, health care workers, and other professionals to provide services to people. Social and human service assistant is a generic term for workers with a wide array of job titles, including human service worker, case management aide, social work assistant, community support worker, mental health aide, community outreach worker, life skills counselor, or gerontology aide. They usually work under the direction of workers from a variety of fields, such as nursing, psychiatry, psychology, rehabilitative or physical therapy, or social work. The amount of responsibility and supervision they are given varies a great deal. Some have little direct supervision—they may run a group home, for example. Others work under close direction.

Social and human service assistants provide services to clients to help them improve their quality of life. They assess clients' needs, investigate their eligibility for benefits and services such as food stamps, Medicaid, or welfare, and help to obtain them. They also arrange for transportation and escorts, if necessary, and provide emotional support. Social and human service assistants monitor and keep case records on clients and report progress to supervisors and case managers.

Social and human service assistants play a variety of roles in a community. They may organize and lead group activities, assist clients in need of counseling or crisis intervention, or administer food banks or emergency fuel programs, for example. In halfway houses, group homes, and government-supported housing programs, they assist adults who need supervision with personal hygiene and daily living skills. They review clients' records, ensure that they take their medication, talk with family members, and confer with medical personnel and other caregivers to provide insight into clients' needs. Social and human service assistants also give emotional support and help clients become involved in community recreation programs and other activities.

In psychiatric hospitals, rehabilitation programs, and outpatient clinics, social and human service assistants work with psychiatrists, psychologists, social workers, and others to help clients master everyday living skills, communicate more effectively, and live well with others. They support the client's participation in a treatment plan, such as individual or group counseling or occupational therapy.

The work, while satisfying, can be emotionally draining. Understaffing and relatively low pay may add to the pressure.

Work environment. Working conditions of social and human service assistants vary. Some work in offices, clinics, and hospitals, while others work in group homes, shelters, sheltered workshops, and day programs. Traveling to see clients is also required for some jobs. Sometimes working with clients can be dangerous even though most agencies do everything they can to ensure their workers' safety. Most assistants work 40 hours a week; some work in the evening and on weekends.

Training, Other Qualifications, and Advancement

A bachelor's degree is not required for most jobs in this occupation, but employers increasingly seek individuals with relevant work experience or education beyond high school.

Education and training. Many employers prefer to hire people with some education beyond high school. Certificates or associate degrees in subjects such as human services, gerontology or one of the social or behavioral sciences meet many employers' requirements. Some jobs may require a bachelor's or master's degree in human services or a related field, such as counseling, rehabilitation, or social work.

Human services degree programs have a core curriculum that trains students to observe patients and record information, conduct patient interviews, implement treatment plans, employ problem-solving techniques, handle crisis intervention matters, and use proper case management and referral procedures. Many programs utilize field work to give students hands-on experience. General education courses in liberal arts, sciences, and the humanities also are part of most curriculums. Most programs also offer specialized courses related to addictions, gerontology, child protection, and other areas. Many degree programs require completion of a supervised internship.

The level of education workers have often influenced the kind of work they are assigned and the degree of responsibility that is given to them. For example, workers with no more than a high school education are likely to receive extensive on-the-job training to work in direct-care services, helping clients to fill out paperwork, for example. Workers with a college degree, however, might do supportive counseling, coordinate program activities, or manage a group home. Social and human service assistants with proven leadership ability, especially from paid or volunteer experience in social services, often have greater autonomy in their work. Regardless of the academic or work background of employees, most employers provide some form of in-service training to their employees such as seminars and workshops.

Other qualifications. These workers should have a strong desire to help others, effective communication skills, a sense of responsibility, and the ability to manage time effectively. Many human services jobs involve direct contact with people who are vulnerable to exploitation or mistreatment; so patience and understanding are also highly valued characteristics.

Social and human service assistants help clients apply for benefits and services, like food stamps or welfare.

Projections data from the National Employment Matrix

Occupational Title	SOC Code	Employment, 2006	Projected employment, 2016	Change, 2006-2016	
				Number	Percent
Social and human service assistants	21-1093	339,000	453,000	114,000	34

NOTE: Data in this table are rounded. See the discussion of the employment projections table in the *Handbook* introductory chapter on *Occupational Information Included in the Handbook.*

It is becoming more common for employers to require a criminal background check, and in some settings, workers may be required to have a valid driver's license.

Advancement. Formal education is almost always necessary for advancement. In general, advancement to case management, rehabilitation, or social work jobs requires a bachelor's or master's degree in human services, counseling, rehabilitation, social work, or a related field.

Employment

Social and human service assistants held about 339,000 jobs in 2006. Over 60 percent were employed in the health care and social assistance industries. Nearly 3 in 10 were employed by State and local governments, primarily in public welfare agencies and facilities for mentally disabled and developmentally challenged individuals.

Job Outlook

Employment of social and human service assistants is expected to grow by nearly 34 percent through 2016. Job prospects are expected to be excellent, particularly for applicants with appropriate postsecondary education.

Employment change. The number of social and human service assistants is projected to grow by nearly 34 percent between 2006 and 2016, which is much faster than the average for all occupations. This occupation will have a very large number of new jobs arise, about 114,000 over the projections decade. Faced with rapid growth in the demand for social and human services, many employers increasingly rely on social and human service assistants.

Demand for social services will expand with the growing elderly population, who are more likely to need adult day care, meal delivery programs, support during medical crises, and other services. In addition, more social and human service assistants will be needed to provide services to pregnant teenagers, people who are homeless, people who are mentally disabled or developmentally challenged, and people who are substance abusers.

Job training programs are also expected to require additional social and human service assistants. As social welfare policies shift focus from benefit-based programs to work-based initiatives, there will be more demand for people to teach job skills to the people who are new to, or returning to, the workforce.

Residential care establishments should face increased pressures to respond to the needs of the mentally and physically disabled. The number of people who are disabled is increasing, and many need help to care for themselves. More community-based programs and supportive independent-living sites are expected to be established to house and assist the homeless and the mentally and physically disabled. Furthermore,

as substance abusers are increasingly being sent to treatment programs instead of prison, employment of social and human service assistants in substance abuse treatment programs also will grow.

Opportunities are expected to be good in private social service agencies. Employment in private agencies will grow as State and local governments continue to contract out services to the private sector in an effort to cut costs. Also, some private agencies have been employing more social and human service assistants in place of social workers, who are more educated and more highly paid.

The number of jobs for social and human service assistants in local governments will grow but not as fast as employment for social and human service assistants in other industries. Employment in the public sector may fluctuate with the level of funding provided by State and local governments and with the number of services contracted out to private organizations.

Job prospects. Job prospects for social and human service assistants are expected to be excellent, particularly for individuals with appropriate education after high school. Job openings will come from job growth, but also from the need to replace workers who advance into new positions, retire, or leave the workforce for other reasons. There will be more competition for jobs in urban areas than in rural ones, but qualified applicants should have little difficulty finding employment.

Earnings

Median annual earnings of social and human service assistants were $25,580 in May 2006. The middle 50 percent earned between $20,350 and $32,440. The top 10 percent earned more than $40,780, while the lowest 10 percent earned less than $16,180.

Median annual earnings in the industries employing the largest numbers of social and human service assistants in May 2006 were:

Local government	$30,510
State government	29,810
Individual and family services	24,490
Vocational rehabilitation services	22,530
Residential mental retardation, mental health and substance abuse facilities	22,380

Related Occupations

Workers in other occupations that require skills similar to those of social and human service assistants include social workers, clergy, counselors, child care workers; occupational therapist assistants and aides, physical therapist assistants and aides, and nursing, psychiatric, and home health aides.

Sources of Additional Information

For information on programs and careers in human services, contact:

➤ Council for Standards in Human Services Education, PMB 703, 1050 Larrabee Avenue, Suite 104, Bellingham, WA 98225-7367. Internet: **http://www.cshse.org**

➤ National Organization for Human Services, 90 Madison Street, Suite 206, Denver, CO 80206. Internet: **http://www.nationalhumanservices.org**

Information on job openings may be available from State employment service offices or directly from city, county, or State departments of health, mental health and mental retardation, and human resources.

Social Workers

(O*NET 21-1021.00, 21-1022.00, 21-1023.00, 21-1029.99)

Significant Points

- Employment is projected to grow much faster than average.

- About 5 out of 10 jobs were in health care and social assistance industries and 3 in 10 work for State and local government agencies.

- While a bachelor's degree is the minimum requirement, a master's degree in social work or a related field has become the standard for many positions.

- Competition for jobs is expected in cities, but opportunities should be good in rural areas.

Nature of the Work

Social work is a profession for those with a strong desire to help improve people's lives. Social workers assist people by helping them cope with issues in their everyday lives, deal with their relationships, and solve personal and family problems. Some social workers help clients who face a disability or a life-threatening disease or a social problem, such as inadequate housing, unemployment, or substance abuse. Social workers also assist families that have serious domestic conflicts, sometimes involving child or spousal abuse. Some social workers conduct research, advocate for improved services, engage in systems design or are involved in planning or policy development. Many social workers specialize in serving a particular population or working in a specific setting.

Child, family, and school social workers provide social services and assistance to improve the social and psychological functioning of children and their families and to maximize the well-being of families and the academic functioning of children. They may assist single parents, arrange adoptions, or help find foster homes for neglected, abandoned, or abused children. Some specialize in services for senior citizens. These social workers may run support groups for the children of aging parents; advise elderly people or family members about housing, transportation, long-term care, and other services; and coordinate and monitore

these services. Through employee assistance programs, social workers may help people cope with job-related pressures or with personal problems that affect the quality of their work.

In schools, social workers often serve as the link between students' families and the school, working with parents, guardians, teachers, and other school officials to ensure students reach their academic and personal potential. In addition, they address problems such as misbehavior, truancy, and teenage pregnancy and advise teachers on how to cope with difficult students. Increasingly, school social workers teach workshops to entire classes.

Child, family, and school social workers may also be known as child welfare social workers, family services social workers, child protective services social workers, occupational social workers, or gerontology social workers. They often work for individual and family services agencies, schools, or State or local governments.

Medical and public health social workers provide psychosocial support to people, families, or vulnerable populations so they can cope with chronic, acute, or terminal illnesses, such as Alzheimer's disease, cancer, or AIDS. They also advise family caregivers, counsel patients, and help plan for patients' needs after discharge from hospitals. They may arrange for at-home services, such as meals-on-wheels or home care. Some work on interdisciplinary teams that evaluate certain kinds of patients—geriatric or organ transplant patients, for example. Medical and public health social workers may work for hospitals, nursing and personal care facilities, individual and family services agencies, or local governments.

Mental health and substance abuse social workers assess and treat individuals with mental illness or substance abuse problems, including abuse of alcohol, tobacco, or other drugs. Such services include individual and group therapy, outreach, crisis intervention, social rehabilitation, and teaching skills needed for everyday living. They also may help plan for supportive services to ease clients' return to the community. Mental health and substance abuse social workers are likely to work in hospitals, substance abuse treatment centers, individual and family services agencies, or local governments. These social workers may be known as clinical social workers. (Counselors and psychologists, who may provide similar services, are discussed elsewhere in the *Handbook*.)

Other types of social workers include social work administrators, planners and policymakers, who develop and implement programs to address issues such as child abuse, homelessness, substance abuse, poverty, and violence. These workers research and analyze policies, programs, and regulations. They identify social problems and suggest legislative and other solutions. They may help raise funds or write grants to support these programs.

Work environment. Social workers usually spend most of their time in an office or residential facility, but they also may travel locally to visit clients, meet with service providers, or attend meetings. Some may meet with clients in one of several offices within a local area. Social work, while satisfying, can be challenging. Understaffing and large caseloads add to the pressure in some agencies. To tend to patient care or client needs, many hospitals and long-term care facilities employ social workers on teams with a broad mix of occupations, including clinical specialists, registered nurses, and health aides. Full-time social

Social workers help clients with problems such as unemployment, life-threatening illnesses, or substance abuse.

workers usually work a standard 40-hour week, but some occasionally work evenings and weekends to meet with clients, attend community meetings, and handle emergencies. Some work part time, particularly in voluntary nonprofit agencies.

Training, Other Qualifications, and Advancement

A bachelor's degree is the minimum requirement for entry into the occupation, but many positions require an advanced degree. All States and the District of Columbia have some licensure, certification, or registration requirement, but the regulations vary.

Education and training. A bachelor's degree in social work (BSW) is the most common minimum requirement to qualify for a job as a social worker; however, majors in psychology, sociology, and related fields may qualify for some entry-level jobs, especially in small community agencies. Although a bachelor's degree is sufficient for entry into the field, an advanced degree has become the standard for many positions. A master's degree in social work (MSW) is typically required for positions in health settings and is required for clinical work as well. Some jobs in public and private agencies also may require an advanced degree, such as a master's degree in social services policy or administration. Supervisory, administrative, and staff training positions usually require an advanced degree. College and university teaching positions and most research appointments normally require a doctorate in social work (DSW or Ph.D.).

As of 2006, the Council on Social Work Education accredited 458 bachelor's programs and 181 master's programs. The Group for the Advancement of Doctoral Education listed 74 doctoral programs in social work (DSW or Ph.D.) in the United States. Bachelor's degree programs prepare graduates for direct service positions, such as caseworker, and include courses in social work values and ethics, dealing with a culturally diverse clientele and at-risk populations, promotion of social and economic justice, human behavior and the social environment, social welfare policy and services, social work practice, social research methods, and field education. Accredited programs require a minimum of 400 hours of supervised field experience.

Master's degree programs prepare graduates for work in their chosen field of concentration and continue to develop the skills required to perform clinical assessments, manage large caseloads, take on supervisory roles, and explore new ways of draw-

ing upon social services to meet the needs of clients. Master's programs last 2 years and include a minimum of 900 hours of supervised field instruction or internship. A part-time program may take 4 years. Entry into a master's program does not require a bachelor's degree in social work, but courses in psychology, biology, sociology, economics, political science, and social work are recommended. In addition, a second language can be very helpful. Most master's programs offer advanced standing for those with a bachelor's degree from an accredited social work program.

Licensure. All States and the District of Columbia have licensing, certification, or registration requirements regarding social work practice and the use of professional titles. Although standards for licensing vary by State, a growing number of States are placing greater emphasis on communications skills, professional ethics, and sensitivity to cultural diversity issues. Most States require 2 years (3,000 hours) of supervised clinical experience for licensure of clinical social workers.

Other qualifications. Social workers should be emotionally mature, objective, and sensitive to people and their problems. They must be able to handle responsibility, work independently, and maintain good working relationships with clients and coworkers. Volunteer or paid jobs as a social work aide can help people test their interest in this field.

Certification and advancement. The National Association of Social Workers offers voluntary credentials. Social workers with a master's degree in social work may be eligible for the Academy of Certified Social Workers (ACSW), the Qualified Clinical Social Worker (QCSW), or the Diplomate in Clinical Social Work (DCSW) credential, based on their professional experience. Credentials are particularly important for those in private practice; some health insurance providers require social workers to have them in order to be reimbursed for services.

Advancement to supervisor, program manager, assistant director, or executive director of a social service agency or department usually requires an advanced degree and related work experience. Other career options for social workers include teaching, research, and consulting. Some of these workers also help formulate government policies by analyzing and advocating policy positions in government agencies, in research institutions, and on legislators' staffs.

Some social workers go into private practice. Most private practitioners are clinical social workers who provide psychotherapy, usually paid for through health insurance or by the client themselves. Private practitioners must have at least a master's degree and a period of supervised work experience. A network of contacts for referrals also is essential. Many private practitioners split their time between working for an agency or hospital and working in their private practice. They may continue to hold a position at a hospital or agency in order to receive health and life insurance.

Employment

Social workers held about 595,000 jobs in 2006. About 5 out of 10 jobs were in health care and social assistance industries and 3 out of 10 are employed by State and local government agencies. Although most social workers are employed in cities or suburbs, some work in rural areas. Employment by type of social worker in 2006, follows:

Child, family, and school social workers..............................282,000
Medical and public health social workers............................124,000
Mental health and substance abuse social workers..............122,000
Social workers, all other..66,000

Job Outlook

Employment for social workers is expected grow much faster than the average for all occupations through 2016. Job prospects are expected to be favorable, particularly for social workers who specialize in the aging population or work in rural areas.

Employment change. Employment of social workers is expected to increase by 22 percent during the 2006-16 decade, which is much faster than the average for all occupations. The growing elderly population and the aging baby boom generation will create greater demand for health and social services, resulting in rapid job growth among gerontology social workers. Employment of social workers in private social service agencies also will increase. However, agencies increasingly will restructure services and hire more social and human service assistants, who are paid less, instead of social workers. Employment in State and local government agencies may grow somewhat in response to growing needs for public welfare, family services, and child protective services, but many of these services will be contracted out to private agencies. Employment levels in public and private social services agencies may fluctuate, depending on need and government funding levels.

Opportunities for social workers in private practice will expand, but growth may be somewhat hindered by restrictions that managed care organizations put on mental health services. The growing popularity of employee assistance programs is expected to spur demand for private practitioners, some of whom provide social work services to corporations on a contractual basis. However, the popularity of employee assistance programs will fluctuate with the business cycle because businesses are not likely to offer these services during recessions.

Employment of child, family and school social workers is expected to grow by 19 percent, which is faster than the average for all occupations. One of the major contributing factors is the rise in the elderly population. Social workers, particularly family social workers, will be needed to assist in finding the best care for the aging and to support their families. Furthermore, demand for school social workers will increase and lead to more jobs as efforts are expanded to respond to rising student enrollments as well as the continued emphasis on integrating disabled children into the general school population. There could be competition for school social work jobs in some areas because of the limited number of openings. The availability of Federal, State, and local funding will be a major factor in determining the actual job growth in schools. The demand for child and family social workers may also be tied to the availability of government funding.

Mental health and substance abuse social workers will grow by 29 percent, which is much faster than the average, over the 2006-16 decade. In particular, social workers specializing in substance abuse will experience strong demand. Substance abusers are increasingly being placed into treatment programs instead of being sentenced to prison. Also, growing numbers of the substance abusers sentenced to prison or probation are, increasingly being required by correctional systems to have substance abuse treatment added as a condition to their sentence or probation. As this trend grows, demand will strengthen for treatment programs and social workers to assist abusers on the road to recovery.

Growth of medical and public health social workers is expected to be 24 percent, which is much faster than the average for all occupations. Hospitals continue to limit the length of patient stays, so the demand for social workers in hospitals will grow more slowly than in other areas. But hospitals are releasing patients earlier than in the past, so social worker employment in home health care services is growing. However, the expanding senior population is an even larger factor. Employment opportunities for social workers with backgrounds in gerontology should be good in the growing numbers of assisted-living and senior-living communities. The expanding senior population also will spur demand for social workers in nursing homes, long-term care facilities, and hospices. However, in these settings other types of workers are often being given tasks that were previously done by social workers.

Job prospects. Job prospects are generally expected to be favorable. Many job openings will stem from growth and the need to replace social workers who leave the occupation. However, competition for social worker jobs is expected in cities, where training programs for social workers are prevalent. Opportunities should be good in rural areas, which often find it difficult to attract and retain qualified staff. By specialty, job prospects may be best for those social workers with a background in gerontology and substance abuse treatment.

Earnings

Median annual earnings of child, family, and school social workers were $37,480 in May 2006. The middle 50 percent earned between $29,590 and $49,060. The lowest 10 percent earned

Projections data from the National Employment Matrix

Occupational Title	SOC Code	Employment, 2006	Projected employment, 2016	Change, 2006-2016	
				Number	Percent
Social workers..	21-1020	595,000	727,000	132,000	22
Child, family, and school social workers	21-1021	282,000	336,000	54,000	19
Medical and public health social workers....................................	21-1022	124,000	154,000	30,000	24
Mental health and substance abuse social workers.......................	21-1023	122,000	159,000	37,000	30
Social workers, all other...	21-1029	66,000	78,000	12,000	18

NOTE: Data in this table are rounded. See the discussion of the employment projections table in the *Handbook* introductory chapter on *Occupational Information Included in the Handbook.*

less than $24,480, and the top 10 percent earned more than $62,530. Median annual earnings in the industries employing the largest numbers of child, family, and school social workers in May 2006 were:

Elementary and secondary schools	$48,360
Local government	43,500
State government	39,000
Individual and family services	32,680
Other residential care facilities	32,590

Median annual earnings of medical and public health social workers were $43,040 in May 2006. The middle 50 percent earned between $34,110 and $53,740. The lowest 10 percent earned less than $27,280, and the top 10 percent earned more than $64,070. Median annual earnings in the industries employing the largest numbers of medical and public health social workers in May 2006 were:

General medical and surgical hospitals	$48,420
Home health care services	44,470
Local government	41,590
Nursing care facilities	38,550
Individual and family services	35,510

Median annual earnings of mental health and substance abuse social workers were $35,410 in May 2006. The middle 50 percent earned between $27,940 and $45,720. The lowest 10 percent earned less than $22,490, and the top 10 percent earned more than $57,630. Median annual earnings in the industries employing the largest numbers of mental health and substance abuse social workers in May 2006 were:

Local government	$39,550
Psychiatric and substance abuse hospitals	39,240
Individual and family services	34,920
Residential mental retardation, mental health and substance abuse facilities	30,590
Outpatient mental health and substance abuse centers	34,290

Median annual earnings of social workers, all other were $43,580 in May 2006. The middle 50 percent earned between $32,530 and $56,420. The lowest 10 percent earned less than $25,540, and the top 10 percent earned more than $68,500. Median annual earnings in the industries employing the largest numbers of social workers, all other in May 2006 were:

Local government	$46,330
State government	45,070
Individual and family services	35,150

About 20 percent of social workers are members of a union. Many belong to the union that represents workers in other occupations at their place of employment.

Related Occupations

Through direct counseling or referral to other services, social workers help people solve a range of personal problems. Workers in occupations with similar duties include the clergy, counselors, probation officers and correctional treatment specialists, psychologists, and social and human services assistants.

Sources of Additional Information

For information about career opportunities in social work and voluntary credentials for social workers, contact:

➤ National Association of Social Workers, 750 First St.N.E., Suite 700, Washington, DC 20002-4241.
Internet: **http://www.socialworkers.org**

For a listing of accredited social work programs, contact:

➤ Council on Social Work Education, 1725 Duke St., Suite 500, Alexandria, VA 22314-3457. Internet: **http://www.cswe.org**

Information on licensing requirements and testing procedures for each State may be obtained from State licensing authorities, or from:

➤ Association of Social Work Boards, 400 South Ridge Pkwy., Suite B, Culpeper, VA 22701. Internet: **http://www.aswb.org**

Legal Occupations

Court Reporters

(O*NET 23-2091.00)

Significant Points

- Job prospects are expected to be excellent, especially for those with certification.

- Demand for real-time broadcast captioning and translating will spur employment growth.

- The amount of training required to become a court reporter varies by specialization; licensure requirements vary by State.

Nature of the Work

Court reporters usually create verbatim transcripts of speeches, conversations, legal proceedings, meetings, and other events. Sometimes written accounts of spoken words are necessary for correspondence, records, or legal proof, and court reporters provide those accounts. They play a critical role not only in judicial proceedings, but also at every meeting where the spoken word must be preserved as a written transcript. They are responsible for ensuring a complete, accurate, and secure legal record. In addition to preparing and protecting the legal record, many court reporters assist judges and trial attorneys in a variety of ways, such as organizing and searching for information in the official record or making suggestions to judges and attorneys regarding courtroom administration and procedure. Increasingly, court reporters provide closed-captioning and real-time translating services to the deaf and hard-of-hearing community.

There are several methods of court reporting. The most common method is called stenographic. Using a stenotype machine, stenotypists document all statements made in official proceedings. The machine allows them to press multiple keys at once to record combinations of letters representing sounds, words, or phrases. These symbols are electronically recorded and then translated and displayed as text in a process called computer-aided transcription (CAT). In real-time court reporting, the stenotype machine is linked to computers for real-time captioning, often of television programs. As the reporter keys in the symbols, the spoken word instantly appear as text on the screen.

Another method of court reporting is electronic reporting. This method uses audio equipment to record court proceedings. The court reporter monitors the process, takes notes to identify speakers, and listens to the recording to ensure clarity and quality. The equipment used may include analog tape recorders or digital equipment. Electronic reporters and transcribers often are responsible for producing a written transcript of the recorded proceeding.

Yet another method of court reporting is voice writing. Using the voice-writing method, a court reporter speaks directly into a voice silencer—a hand-held mask containing a microphone. As the reporter repeats the testimony into the recorder, the mask prevents the reporter from being heard during testimony. Voice writers record everything that is said by judges, witnesses, attorneys, and other parties to a proceeding, including gestures and emotional reactions, and prepare transcripts afterwards.

Court reporters are responsible for a number of duties both before and after transcribing events. Stenographic or voice writing reporters must create and maintain the computer dictionary that they use to translate their keystroke codes or voice files into written text. They may customize the dictionary with parts of words, entire words, or terminology specific to the proceeding, program, or event—such as a religious service—they plan to transcribe. After documenting proceedings, stenographic reporters must edit the computer-generated translation for correct grammar. All reporters are responsible for accurate identification of proper names and places. Electronic reporters ensure that the record or testimony is discernible. Reporters usually prepare written transcripts, make copies, and provide information from the transcript to courts, counsels, parties, and the public on request. Court reporters also develop procedures for easy storage and retrieval of all stenographic notes, voice files, commonly referred to as "stenograms", or audio recordings in paper or digital format.

Although many court reporters record official proceedings in the courtroom, others work outside the courts. For example, court reporters—called webcasters—capture sales meetings, press conferences, product introductions, and technical training seminars and instantly transmit them to all parties involved via computers. As participants speak into telephones or microphones, the words appear on all of the participants' computer monitors simultaneously. Still others capture the proceedings taking place in government agencies at all levels, from the U.S. Congress to State and local governing bodies. Court report-

ers who specialize in captioning live television programming for people with hearing loss are commonly known as broadcast captioners. They work for television networks or cable stations, captioning news, emergency broadcasts, sporting events, and other programming.

A version of the captioning process that allows reporters to provide more personalized services for deaf and hard-of-hearing people is Communication Access Real-time Translation (CART). CART reporters often work with hard-of-hearing students and people who are learning English as a second language, captioning high school and college classes and providing transcripts at the end of the sessions. CART reporters also accompany deaf clients to events, including conventions, doctor appointments, or wherever communication access is needed. CART providers increasingly furnish this service remotely, as an Internet or phone connection allows for immediate communication access regardless of location. With CART and broadcast captioning, the level of understanding gained by a person with hearing loss depends entirely on the skill of the court reporter. In an emergency, such as a tornado or a hurricane, people's safety may depend on the accuracy of information provided in the form of captioning.

Some voice writers produce a transcript in real time, using computer speech recognition technology. Other voice writers prefer to translate their voice files after the proceeding is over, or they transcribe the files manually, without using speech recognition at all. In any event, speech recognition-enabled voice writers pursue not only court reporting careers, but also careers as closed captioners, CART reporters for hearing-impaired individuals, and Internet streaming text providers or caption providers.

Stenographic or voice writing reporters create and maintain the computer dictionary that they use to translate their keystroke codes or voice files into written text.

Work environment. The majority of court reporters work in comfortable settings, such as offices of attorneys, courtrooms, legislatures, and conventions. An increasing number of court reporters work from home-based offices as independent contractors, or freelancers.

Work in this occupation presents few hazards, although sitting in the same position for long periods can be tiring, and workers can suffer wrist, back, neck, or eye strain. Workers also risk repetitive stress injuries such as carpal tunnel syndrome. In addition, the pressure to be accurate and fast can be stressful.

Many official court reporters work a standard 40-hour week, and they often work additional hours at home preparing transcripts. Self-employed court reporters, or freelancers, usually work flexible hours, including part time, evenings, and weekends, or they may be on call.

Training, Other Qualifications, and Advancement

The amount of training required to become a court reporter varies by specialization. Licensure requirements vary by State.

Education and training. The amount of training required to become a court reporter varies with the type of reporting chosen. It usually takes less than a year to become a novice voice writer, although it takes at least two years to become proficient at realtime voice writing. Electronic reporters and transcribers learn their skills on the job. The average length of time it takes to become a realtime stenotypist is 33 months. Training is offered by about 130 postsecondary vocational and technical schools and colleges. The National Court Reporters Association (NCRA) has certified about 70 programs, all of which offer courses in stenotype computer-aided transcription and real-time reporting. NCRA-certified programs require students to capture a minimum of 225 words per minute, a requirement for Federal Government employment as well.

Electronic court reporters use audio-capture technology and, therefore, usually learn their skills on the job. Students read manuals, review them with their trainers, and observe skilled electronic transcribers perform procedures. Court electronic transcribers generally obtain initial technical training from a vendor when it is placed in service, with further court-specific training provided on the job. If working for a private company or organization, hands-on training occurs under direct supervision of an established practitioner or firm.

Licensure. Some States require voice writers to pass a test and to earn State licensure. As a substitute for State licensure, the National Verbatim Reporters Association offers three national certifications to voice writers: Certified Verbatim Reporter (CVR), Certificate of Merit (CM), and Real-Time Verbatim Reporter (RVR). Earning these certifications is sufficient to be licensed in States where the voice method of court reporting is permitted. Candidates for the first certification—the CVR—must pass a written test of spelling, punctuation, vocabulary, legal and medical terminology and three 5-minute dictation and transcription examinations that test for speed, accuracy, and silence. The second certification, the CM, requires additional levels of speed, knowledge, and accuracy. The RVR certification measures the candidate's skill at real-time transcription, judicial reporting, CART provision, and captioning, including Webcasting. To retain these certifications, the voice writer must

obtain continuing education credits. Credits are given for voice writer education courses, continuing legal education courses, and college courses.

Some States require court reporters to be notary publics. Others require the Certified Court Reporter (CCR) designation, for which a reporter must pass a State test administered by a board of examiners.

Other qualifications. In addition to possessing speed and accuracy, court reporters must have excellent listening skills and hearing, good English grammar and vocabulary, and punctuation skills. They must be aware of business practices and current events as well as the correct spelling of names of people, places, and events that may be mentioned in a broadcast or in court proceedings. For those who work in courtrooms, an expert knowledge of legal terminology and criminal and appellate procedure is essential. Because capturing proceedings requires the use of computerized stenography or speech recognition equipment, court reporters must be knowledgeable about computer hardware and software applications. Voice writers must learn to listen and speak simultaneously and very quickly and quietly, while also identifying speakers and describing peripheral activities in the courtroom or deposition room.

Certification and advancement. Certifications can help court reporters get jobs and advance in their careers. Several associations offer certifications for different types of reporters.

The National Court Reporters Association confers the entry-level designation Registered Professional Reporter (RPR) upon those who pass a four-part examination and participate in mandatory continuing education programs. Although voluntary, the designation is recognized as a mark of distinction in the field.

A court reporter may obtain additional certifications that demonstrate higher levels of experience and competency, such as Registered Merit Reporter (RMR) or Registered Diplomate Reporter (RDR). The NCRA also offers the designations Certified Realtime Reporter (CRR), Certified Broadcast Captioner (CBC), and Certified CART Provider (CCP), designed primarily for those who caption media programs or assist people who are deaf.

With experience and education, court reporters can also receive certification in administrative and management, consulting, or teaching positions.

The United States Court Reporters Association offers another voluntary certification designation, the Federal Certified Real-time Reporter (FCRR), for court reporters working in Federal courts. The exam is designed to test the basic real-time skills of Federal court reporters and is recognized by the Administrative Office for the United States District Courts for purposes of real-time certification.

The American Association of Electronic Reporters and Transcribers (AAERT) certifies electronic court reporters. Certification is voluntary and includes a written and a practical examination. To be eligible to take the exams, candidates must have at least 2 years of court reporting or transcribing experience, must be eligible for notary public commissions in their States, and must have completed high school. AAERT offers three types of certificates—Certified Electronic Court Reporter (CER), Certified Electronic Court Transcriber (CET), and Certified Electronic Court Reporter and Transcriber (CERT). Some employers may require electronic court reporters and transcribers to obtain certificates once they are eligible.

Employment

Court reporters held about 19,000 jobs in 2006. More than half worked for State and local governments, a reflection of the large number of court reporters working in courts, legislatures, and various agencies. Most of the remaining wage and salary workers were employed by court reporting agencies. Around 8 percent of court reporters were self-employed.

Job Outlook

Employment is projected to grow much faster than the average, reflecting the demand for real-time broadcast captioning and translating. Job opportunities should be excellent, especially for those with certification.

Employment change. Employment of court reporters is projected to grow 25 percent, much faster than the average for all occupations between 2006 and 2016. Demand for court reporter services will be spurred by the continuing need for accurate transcription of proceedings in courts and in pretrial depositions, by the growing need to create captions for live television, and by the need to provide other real-time broadcast captioning and translating services for the deaf and hard-of-hearing.

Increasing numbers of civil and criminal cases are expected to create new jobs for court reporters, but budget constraints are expected to limit the ability of Federal, State, and local courts to expand, and thereby also limit the demand for traditional court reporting services in courtrooms and other legal venues. Further, because of the difficulty in attracting court reporters and in efforts to control costs, many courtrooms have installed tape recorders that are maintained by electronic court reporters and transcribers to record court proceedings. However, because courts use electronic reporters and transcribers only in a limited capacity traditional stenographic court reporters will continue to be used in felony trials and other proceedings. Despite the use of audiotape and videotape technology, court reporters can quickly turn spoken words into readable, searchable, permanent text, and they will continue to be needed to produce written legal transcripts and proceedings for publication.

Voice writers have become more widely accepted as the accuracy of speech recognition technology improves. Still, many courts allow only stenotypists to perform court reporting duties.

In addition, more court reporters will be needed to caption outside of legal proceedings. Not only is there Federal legislation mandating that all new television programming be captioned for the deaf and hard-of-hearing, all new Spanish-language programming likewise must be captioned by 2010. In addition, the Americans with Disabilities Act gives deaf and hard-of-hearing students in colleges and universities the right to request access to real-time translation in their classes. These factors are expected to continue to increase the demand for court reporters who provide CART services. Although these services forgo transcripts and differ from traditional court reporting, they require the same skills that court reporters learn in their training.

Job prospects. Job opportunities for court reporters are expected to be excellent as job openings continue to outnumber jobseekers in some areas. Court reporters with certification and those who choose to specialize in providing CART, broadcast captioning, and or webcasting services should have the best job opportunities. The favorable job market reflects the fact that fewer people are entering this profession, particularly as stenographic typists.

Earnings

Wage and salary court reporters had median annual earnings of $45,610 in May 2006. The middle 50 percent earned between $33,160 and $61,530. The lowest paid 10 percent earned less than $23,430, and the highest paid 10 percent earned more than $77,770. Median annual earnings in May 2006 were $45,080 for court reporters working in local government and $41,720 for those working in business support services.

Compensation and compensation methods for court reporters vary with the type of reporting job, the experience of the individual reporter, the level of certification achieved, and the region of the country. Official court reporters earn a salary and a per-page fee for transcripts. Many salaried court reporters supplement their income by doing freelance work. Freelance court reporters are paid per job and receive a per-page fee for transcripts. CART providers are paid by the hour. Captioners receive a salary and benefits if they work as employees of a captioning company; Captioners working as independent contractors are paid by the hour.

Related Occupations

Workers in several other occupations also type, record information, and process paperwork. Among these are secretaries and administrative assistants; medical transcriptionists; data entry and information processing workers; receptionists and information clerks; and human resources assistants, except payroll and timekeeping. Other workers who provide legal support include paralegals and legal assistants.

Sources of Additional Information

State employment service offices can provide information about job openings for court reporters. For information about careers, training, and certification in court reporting contact:

➤ American Association of Electronic Reporters and Transcribers, 23812 Rock Circle, Bothell, WA 98021. Internet: **http://www.aaert.org**

Projections data from the National Employment Matrix

Occupational Title	SOC Code	Employment, 2006	Projected employment, 2016	Change, 2006-2016	
				Number	Percent
Court reporters	23-2091	19,000	24,000	4,700	25

NOTE: Data in this table are rounded. See the discussion of the employment projections table in the *Handbook* introductory chapter on *Occupational Information Included in the Handbook.*

➤ National Court Reporters Association, 8224 Old Courthouse Rd., Vienna, VA 22182.
Internet: **http://www.ncraonline.org**
➤ National Verbatim Reporters Association, 207 Third Ave., Hattiesburg, MS 39401. Internet: **http://www.nvra.org**
➤ United States Court Reporters Association, 4731 N. Western Ave., Chicago, IL 60625-2012.
Internet: **http://www.uscra.org**

Judges, Magistrates, and Other Judicial Workers

(O*NET 23-1021.00, 23-1022.00, 23-1023.00)

Significant Points

- A bachelor's degree and work experience are the minimum requirements for a judgeship or magistrate position, but most workers have law degrees, and some are elected.

- Overall employment is projected to grow more slowly than average, but varies by occupational specialty.

- Judges and magistrates are expected encounter competition for jobs because of the prestige associated with serving on the bench.

Nature of the Work

Judges, magistrates, and other judicial workers apply the law and oversee the legal process in courts. They preside over cases concerning every aspect of society, from traffic offenses to disputes over the management of professional sports to issues concerning the rights of huge corporations. All judicial workers must ensure that trials and hearings are conducted fairly and that the court safeguards the legal rights of all parties involved.

The most visible responsibility of judges is presiding over trials or hearings and listening as attorneys represent their clients. Judges rule on the admissibility of evidence and the methods of conducting testimony, and they may be called on to settle disputes between opposing attorneys. Also, they ensure that rules and procedures are followed, and if unusual circumstances arise for which standard procedures have not been established, judges interpret the law to determine how the trial will proceed.

Judges often hold pretrial hearings for cases. They listen to allegations and determine whether the evidence presented merits a trial. In criminal cases, judges may decide that people charged with crimes should be held in jail pending trial, or they may set conditions for their release. In civil cases, judges and magistrates occasionally impose restrictions on the parties until a trial is held.

In many trials, juries are selected to decide guilt or innocence in criminal cases or liability and compensation in civil cases. Judges instruct juries on applicable laws, direct them to deduce the facts from the evidence presented, and hear their verdict. When the law does not require a jury trial or when the parties waive their right to a jury, judges decide cases. In such instances, the judge determines guilt in criminal cases and imposes sentences on the guilty; in civil cases, the judge awards relief—such as compensation for damages—to the winning parties to the lawsuit.

Judges also work outside the courtroom in their chambers or private offices. There, judges read documents on pleadings and motions, research legal issues, write opinions, and oversee the court's operations. In some jurisdictions, judges also manage the courts' administrative and clerical staff.

Judges' duties vary according to the extent of their jurisdictions and powers. *General trial court judges* of the Federal and State court systems have jurisdiction over any case in their system. They usually try civil cases transcending the jurisdiction of lower courts and all cases involving felony offenses. Federal and State *appellate court judges*, although few in number, have the power to overrule decisions made by trial court or *administrative law judges*. Appellate court judges overrule decisions if they determine that legal errors were made in a case or if legal precedent does not support the judgment of the lower court. Appellate court judges rule on a small number of cases and rarely have direct contact with litigants—the people who bring the case or who are on trial. Instead, they usually base their decisions on the lower court's records and on lawyers' written and oral arguments.

Many State court judges only hear certain types of cases. A variety of titles are assigned to these judges; among the most common are *municipal court judge, county court judge, magistrate*, and *justice of the peace*. Traffic violations, misdemeanors, small-claims cases, and pretrial hearings constitute the bulk of the work of these judges, but some States allow them to handle cases involving domestic relations, probate, contracts, and other selected areas of the law.

Administrative law judges, sometimes called *hearing officers or adjudicators*, are employed by government agencies to make determinations for administrative agencies. These judges make decisions, for example, on a person's eligibility for various Social Security or workers' compensation benefits, on protection of the environment, on the enforcement of health and safety regulations, on employment discrimination, and on compliance with economic regulatory requirements.

Some people work as arbitrators, mediators, or conciliators instead of as judges or magistrates. They assist with alternative dispute resolution—processes used to settle disputes outside of court. All hearings are private and confidential, and the processes are less formal than a court trial. If no settlement is reached, no statements made during the proceedings are admissible as evidence in any subsequent litigation.

There are two types of arbitration—compulsory and voluntary. During compulsory arbitration, opposing parties submit their dispute to one or more impartial persons, called arbitrators, for a final and nonbinding decision. Either party may reject the ruling and request a trial in court. Voluntary arbitration is a process in which opposing parties choose one or more arbitrators to hear their dispute and submit a final, binding decision.

Arbitrators usually are attorneys or business people with expertise in a particular field. The parties identify, in advance, the issues to be resolved by arbitration, the scope of the relief to be awarded, and many of the procedural aspects of the process.

Mediators are neutral parties who help people to resolve their disputes outside of court. People often use mediators when they wish to preserve their relationship. A mediator may offer suggestions, but resolution of the dispute rests with the parties themselves. Mediation proceedings also are confidential and private. If the parties are unable to reach a settlement, they are free to pursue other options. The parties usually decide in advance how they will share the cost of mediation. However, many mediators volunteer their services, or they may be court staff. Courts ask that mediators provide their services at the lowest possible rate and that parties split the cost.

Conciliation, or facilitation, is similar to mediation. The conciliator's role is to guide the parties to a settlement. The parties must decide in advance whether they will be bound by the conciliator's recommendations.

Work environment. Judges, magistrates, and other judicial workers do most of their work in offices, law libraries, and courtrooms. Work in these occupations presents few hazards, although sitting in the same position in the courtroom for long periods can be tiring. Most judges wear robes when they are in

Judges preside over cases concerning every aspect of society, from traffic offenses to disputes over the management of professional sports.

a courtroom. Judges typically work a standard 40-hour week, but many work more than 50 hours per week. Some judges with limited jurisdiction are employed part time and divide their time between their judicial responsibilities and other careers.

Arbitrators, mediators, and conciliators usually work in private offices or meeting rooms; no public record is made of the proceedings. Arbitrators, mediators, and conciliators often travel to a site chosen for negotiations, but some work from their home. Arbitrators, mediators, and conciliators usually work a standard 35- to 40-hour week. However, longer hours might be necessary when contract agreements are being prepared and negotiated.

Training, Other Qualifications, and Advancement
A bachelor's degree and work experience usually constitute the minimum requirements for judges and magistrates, but most workers have law degrees, and some are elected. Training requirements for arbitrators, mediators, and conciliators vary.

Education and training. Most judges have first been lawyers. In fact, Federal and State judges usually are required to be lawyers, which means that they have attended law school and passed an examination. About 40 States allow nonlawyers to hold limited-jurisdiction judgeships, but opportunities are better for those with law experience.

Federal administrative law judges must be lawyers and pass a competitive examination administered by the U.S. Office of Personnel Management. Some State administrative law judges and other hearing officials are not required to be lawyers.

All States have some type of orientation for newly elected or appointed judges. The Federal Judicial Center, American Bar Association, National Judicial College, and National Center for State Courts provide judicial education and training for judges and other judicial-branch personnel. General and continuing education courses usually last from a few days to 3 weeks. More than half of all States, as well as Puerto Rico, require judges to take continuing education courses while serving on the bench.

Training for arbitrators, mediators, and conciliators is available through independent mediation programs, national and local mediation membership organizations, and postsecondary schools. To practice in State-funded or court-funded mediation programs, mediators usually must meet specific training or experience standards, which vary by State and court. Most mediators complete a 40-hour basic course and a 20-hour advanced training course. Some people receive training by volunteering at a community mediation center or co-mediating cases with an experienced mediator. Others go on to complete an advanced degree or certificate program in conflict resolution at a college or university. Degrees in public policy, law, and related fields also provide good background for prospective arbitrators, mediators, and conciliators.

Licensure. There are no national credentials or licensure requirements for arbitrators, mediators, and conciliators. In fact, State regulatory requirements vary widely. Some States require arbitrators to be experienced lawyers. Some States "license" mediators while other States "register" or "certify." Currently, only four States—Florida, New Hampshire, Texas, and Virginia—have certification programs. Increasingly, credentialing programs are being offered through professional organizations. For example, the American Arbitration Association requires mediators listed on its mediation panel to complete their training course, receive recommendations from the trainers, and complete an apprenticeship.

Other qualifications. Judges and magistrates must be appointed or elected. That often takes political support. Federal administrative law judges are appointed by various Federal agencies, with virtually lifetime tenure. Federal magistrate judges are appointed by district judges—the life-tenured Federal judges of district courts—to serve in a U.S. district court for 8 years. A part-time Federal magistrate judge's term of office is 4 years. Some State judges are appointed, but the remainder are elected in partisan or nonpartisan State elections. Many State and local judges serve fixed renewable terms ranging from 4 or 6 years for some trial court judgeships to as long as 14 years or even life for other trial or appellate court judgeships. Judicial nominating commissions, composed of members of the bar and the public, are used to screen candidates for judgeships in many States and for some Federal judgeships.

Advancement. Some judicial workers move to higher courts or courts with broader jurisdiction. Advancement for alternative dispute workers includes taking on more complex cases or starting a business.

Employment

Judges, magistrates, and other judicial workers held 51,000 jobs in 2006. Judges, magistrates, and magistrate judges held 27,000 jobs, all in State and local governments. Administrative law judges, adjudicators, and hearing officers held 15,000 jobs, with 59 percent in State governments, 22 percent in the Federal Government, and 19 percent in local governments. Arbitrators, mediators, and conciliators held another 8,500 jobs. Approximately 29 percent worked for State and local governments. The remainder worked for labor organizations, law offices, insurance carriers, and other private companies and for organizations that specialize in providing dispute resolution services.

Job Outlook

Overall employment is projected to grow more slowly than average, but varies by specialty. Judges and magistrates are expected encounter competition for jobs because of the prestige associated with serving on the bench.

Employment change. Overall employment of judges, magistrates, and other judicial workers is expected to grow 4 percent over the 2006-16 projection decade, slower than the aver-

age for all occupations. Budgetary pressures at all levels of government are expected to hold down the hiring of judges, despite rising caseloads, particularly in Federal courts. However, the continued need to cope with crime and settle disputes, as well as the public's willingness to go to court to settle disputes, should spur demand for judges. Also, economic growth is expected to lead to more business contracts and transactions and, thus, more legal disputes.

Demographic shifts in the population will also spur demand for judges. For instance, the number of immigrants migrating to the U.S. will continue to rise, thereby increasing the demand for judges to handle the complex issues of immigrant legal status. Demand for judges will also increase because as the American population ages, the courts are expected to reform guardianship policies and practices and develop new strategies to address elder abuse. Both the quantity and the complexity of judges' work have increased because of developments in information technology, medical science, electronic commerce, and globalization.

Employment of arbitrators, mediators, and conciliators is expected to grow about as fast as the average for all occupations through 2016. Many individuals and businesses try to avoid litigation, which can involve lengthy delays, high costs, unwanted publicity, and ill will. Arbitration and other alternatives to litigation usually are faster, less expensive, and more conclusive, spurring demand for the services of arbitrators, mediators, and conciliators. Demand also will continue to increase for arbitrators, mediators, and conciliators as all jurisdictions now have some type of alternative dispute resolution program. Some jurisdictions have programs requiring disputants to meet with a mediator, in certain circumstances, such as when attempting to resolve child custody issues.

Job prospects. The prestige associated with serving on the bench will ensure continued competition for judge and magistrate positions. However, a growing number of candidates choose to forgo the bench and work in the private sector, where pay may be significantly higher. This movement may lessen the competition somewhat. Most job openings will arise as judges retire. However, additional openings will occur when new judgeships are authorized by law or when judges are elevated to higher judicial offices.

Earnings

Judges, magistrate judges, and magistrates had median annual earnings of $101,690 in May 2006. The middle 50 percent earned between $53,920 and $135,010. The top 10 percent earned more than $145,600, while the bottom 10 percent

Projections data from the National Employment Matrix

Occupational Title	SOC Code	Employment, 2006	Projected employment, 2016	Change, 2006-2016	
				Number	Percent
Judges, magistrates, and other judicial workers................................	23-1020	51,000	53,000	2,300	4
Administrative law judges, adjudicators, and hearing officers	23-1021	15,000	15,000	0	0
Arbitrators, mediators, and conciliators......................................	23-1022	8,500	9,400	900	11
Judges, magistrate judges, and magistrates.................................	23-1023	27,000	29,000	1,400	5

NOTE: Data in this table are rounded. See the discussion of the employment projections table in the *Handbook* introductory chapter on *Occupational Information Included in the Handbook.*

earned less than $29,540. Median annual earnings in the industries employing the largest numbers of judges, magistrate judges, and magistrates in May 2006 were $117,760 in State government and $74,630 in local government. Administrative law judges, adjudicators, and hearing officers earned a median of $72,600, and arbitrators, mediators, and conciliators earned a median of $49,490.

In the Federal court system, the Chief Justice of the U.S. Supreme Court earned $212,100 in 2006, and the Associate Justices earned $203,000. Federal court of appeals judges earned $175,100 a year, while district court judges had salaries of $165,200, as did judges in the Court of Federal Claims and the Court of International Trade. Federal judges with limited jurisdiction, such as magistrates and bankruptcy judges, had salaries of $151,984.

According to a 2006 survey by the National Center for State Courts, salaries of chief justices of State high courts averaged $142,264 and ranged from $102,466 to $200,613. Annual salaries of associate justices of the State highest courts averaged $136,810 and ranged from $100,884 to $184,300. Salaries of State intermediate appellate court judges averaged $132,102 and ranged from $101,612 to $172,452. Salaries of State judges of general jurisdiction trial courts averaged $122,559 and ranged from $94,093 to $168,100.

Most salaried judges are provided health, life, and dental insurance; pension plans; judicial immunity protection; expense accounts; vacation, holiday, and sick leave; and contributions to retirement plans made on their behalf. In many States, judicial compensation committees, which make recommendations on the amount of salary increases, determine judicial salaries. States without commissions have statutes that regulate judicial salaries, link judicial salaries to the increases in pay for Federal judges, or adjust annual pay according to the change in the Consumer Price Index, calculated by the U.S. Bureau of Labor Statistics.

Related Occupations

Legal training and mediation skills are useful to those in many other occupations, including counselors; lawyers; paralegals and legal assistants; title examiners, abstractors, and searchers; law clerks; and detectives and criminal investigators.

Sources of Additional Information

Information on judges, magistrates, and other judicial workers may be obtained from:
➤ National Center for State Courts, 300 Newport Ave., Williamsburg, VA 23185-4147.
Internet: **http://www.ncsconline.org**

Information on arbitrators, mediators, and conciliators may be obtained from:
➤ American Arbitration Association, 1633 Broadway, Floor 10, New York, NY 10019. Internet: **http://www.adr.org**

Information on Federal judges can be found at:
➤ Administrative Office of the United States Courts, One Columbus Circle, NE., Washington, DC 20544.
Internet: **http://www.uscourts.gov**

Lawyers

(O*NET 23-1011.00)

Significant Points

- About 27 percent of lawyers are self-employed, either as partners in law firms or in solo practices.

- Formal requirements to become a lawyer usually include a 4-year college degree, 3 years of law school, and passing a written bar examination; however, some requirements may vary by State.

- Competition for admission to most law schools is intense.

- Competition for job openings should be keen because of the large number of students graduating from law school each year.

Nature of the Work

The legal system affects nearly every aspect of our society, from buying a home to crossing the street. Lawyers form the backbone of this system, linking it to society in numerous ways. They hold positions of great responsibility and are obligated to adhere to a strict code of ethics.

Lawyers, also called *attorneys*, act as both advocates and advisors in our society. As advocates, they represent one of the parties in criminal and civil trials by presenting evidence and arguing in court to support their client. As advisors, lawyers counsel their clients about their legal rights and obligations and suggest particular courses of action in business and personal matters. Whether acting as an advocate or an advisor, all attorneys research the intent of laws and judicial decisions and apply the law to the specific circumstances faced by their clients.

The more detailed aspects of a lawyer's job depend upon his or her field of specialization and position. Although all lawyers are licensed to represent parties in court, some appear in court more frequently than others. Trial lawyers, who specialize in trial work, must be able to think quickly and speak with ease and authority. In addition, familiarity with courtroom rules and strategy is particularly important in trial work. Still, trial lawyers spend the majority of their time outside the courtroom, conducting research, interviewing clients and witnesses, and handling other details in preparation for a trial.

Lawyers may specialize in a number of areas, such as bankruptcy, probate, international, elder, or environmental law. Those specializing in environmental law, for example, may represent interest groups, waste disposal companies, or construction firms in their dealings with the U.S. Environmental Protection Agency and other Federal and State agencies. These lawyers help clients prepare and file for licenses and applications for approval before certain activities may occur. Some lawyers specialize in the growing field of intellectual property, helping to protect clients' claims to copyrights, artwork under contract, product designs, and computer programs. Other lawyers advise insurance companies about the legality of insurance transactions, guiding the company in writing insurance policies to conform to the law and to protect the companies from unwarranted claims. When claims are filed against insurance companies, these attorneys review the claims and represent the companies in court.

Most lawyers are in private practice, concentrating on criminal or civil law. In criminal law, lawyers represent individuals who have been charged with crimes and argue their cases in courts of law. Attorneys dealing with civil law assist clients with litigation, wills, trusts, contracts, mortgages, titles, and leases. Other lawyers handle only public-interest cases—civil or criminal—concentrating on particular causes and choosing cases that might have an impact on the way law is applied. Lawyers are sometimes employed full time by a single client. If the client is a corporation, the lawyer is known as "house counsel" and usually advises the company concerning legal issues related to its business activities. These issues might involve patents, government regulations, contracts with other companies, property interests, or collective bargaining agreements with unions.

A significant number of attorneys are employed at the various levels of government. Some work for State attorneys general, prosecutors, and public defenders in criminal courts. At the Federal level, attorneys investigate cases for the U.S. Department of Justice and other agencies. Government lawyers also help develop programs, draft and interpret laws and legislation, establish enforcement procedures, and argue civil and criminal cases on behalf of the government.

Other lawyers work for legal aid societies—private, nonprofit organizations established to serve disadvantaged people. These lawyers generally handle civil, rather than criminal, cases.

Lawyers increasingly use various forms of technology to perform more efficiently. Although all lawyers continue to use law libraries to prepare cases, most supplement conventional printed sources with computer sources, such as the Internet and legal databases. Software is used to search this legal literature automatically and to identify legal texts relevant to a specific case. In litigation involving many supporting documents, lawyers may use computers to organize and index material. Lawyers must be geographically mobile and able to reach their clients in a timely matter, so they might use electronic filing, web and videoconferencing, and voice-recognition technology to share information more effectively.

Lawyers use law libraries and other sources, such as the Internet and legal databases, to prepare cases.

Work environment. Lawyers do most of their work in offices, law libraries, and courtrooms. They sometimes meet in clients' homes or places of business and, when necessary, in hospitals or prisons. They may travel to attend meetings, gather evidence, and appear before courts, legislative bodies, and other authorities. They may also face particularly heavy pressure when a case is being tried. Preparation for court includes understanding the latest laws and judicial decisions.

Salaried lawyers usually have structured work schedules. Lawyers who are in private practice may work irregular hours while conducting research, conferring with clients, or preparing briefs during nonoffice hours. Lawyers often work long hours; of those who work full time, about 37 percent work 50 hours or more per week.

Training, Other Qualifications, and Advancement

Formal requirements to become a lawyer usually include a 4-year college degree, 3 years of law school, and passing a written bar examination; however, some requirements may vary by State. Competition for admission to most law schools is intense. Federal courts and agencies set their own qualifications for those practicing before or in them.

Education and training. Becoming a lawyer usually takes 7 years of full-time study after high school—4 years of undergraduate study, followed by 3 years of law school. Law school applicants must have a bachelor's degree to qualify for admission. To meet the needs of students who can attend only part time, a number of law schools have night or part-time divisions.

Although there is no recommended "prelaw" undergraduate major, prospective lawyers should develop proficiency in writing and speaking, reading, researching, analyzing, and thinking logically—skills needed to succeed both in law school and in the law. Regardless of major, a multidisciplinary background is recommended. Courses in English, foreign languages, public speaking, government, philosophy, history, economics, mathematics, and computer science, among others, are useful. Students interested in a particular aspect of law may find related courses helpful. For example, prospective patent lawyers need a strong background in engineering or science, and future tax lawyers must have extensive knowledge of accounting.

Acceptance by most law schools depends on the applicant's ability to demonstrate an aptitude for the study of law, usually through undergraduate grades, the Law School Admission Test (LSAT), the quality of the applicant's undergraduate school, any prior work experience, and sometimes, a personal interview. However, law schools vary in the weight they place on each of these and other factors.

All law schools approved by the American Bar Association require applicants to take the LSAT. As of 2006, there were 195 ABA-accredited law schools; others were approved by State authorities only. Nearly all law schools require applicants to have certified transcripts sent to the Law School Data Assembly Service, which then submits the applicants' LSAT scores and their standardized records of college grades to the law schools of their choice. The Law School Admission Council administers both this service and the LSAT. Competition for admission to many law schools—especially the most prestigious ones—is usually intense, with the number of applicants greatly exceeding the number that can be admitted.

During the first year or year and a half of law school, students usually study core courses, such as constitutional law, contracts, property law, torts, civil procedure, and legal writing. In the remaining time, they may choose specialized courses in fields such as tax, labor, or corporate law. Law students often gain practical experience by participating in school-sponsored legal clinics; in the school's moot court competitions, in which students conduct appellate arguments; in practice trials under the supervision of experienced lawyers and judges; and through research and writing on legal issues for the school's law journals.

A number of law schools have clinical programs in which students gain legal experience through practice trials and projects under the supervision of lawyers and law school faculty. Law school clinical programs might include work in legal aid offices, for example, or on legislative committees. Part-time or summer clerkships in law firms, government agencies, and corporate legal departments also provide valuable experience. Such training can lead directly to a job after graduation and can help students decide what kind of practice best suits them. Law school graduates receive the degree of *juris doctor* (J.D.), a first professional degree.

Advanced law degrees may be desirable for those planning to specialize, research, or teach. Some law students pursue joint degree programs, which usually require an additional semester or year of study. Joint degree programs are offered in a number of areas, including business administration or public administration.

After graduation, lawyers must keep informed about legal and nonlegal developments that affect their practices. In 2006, 43 States and jurisdictions required lawyers to participate in mandatory continuing legal education. Many law schools and State and local bar associations provide continuing education courses that help lawyers stay abreast of recent developments. Some States allow continuing education credits to be obtained through participation in seminars on the Internet.

Licensure. To practice law in the courts of any State or other jurisdiction, a person must be licensed, or admitted to its bar, under rules established by the jurisdiction's highest court. All States require that applicants for admission to the bar pass a written bar examination; most States also require applicants to pass a separate written ethics examination. Lawyers who have been admitted to the bar in one State occasionally may be admitted to the bar in another without taking another examination if they meet the latter jurisdiction's standards of good moral character and a specified period of legal experience. In most cases, however, lawyers must pass the bar examination in each State in which they plan to practice. Federal courts and agencies set their own qualifications for those practicing before or in them.

To qualify for the bar examination in most States, an applicant must earn a college degree and graduate from a law school accredited by the American Bar Association (ABA) or the proper State authorities. ABA accreditation signifies that the law school, particularly its library and faculty, meets certain standards. With certain exceptions, graduates of schools not approved by the ABA are restricted to taking the bar examination and practicing

in the State or other jurisdiction in which the school is located; most of these schools are in California.

Although there is no nationwide bar examination, 48 States, the District of Columbia, Guam, the Northern Mariana Islands, Puerto Rico, and the Virgin Islands require the 6-hour Multistate Bar Examination (MBE) as part of their overall bar examination; the MBE is not required in Louisiana or Washington. The MBE covers a broad range of issues, and sometimes a locally prepared State bar examination is given in addition to it. The 3-hour Multistate Essay Examination (MEE) is used as part of the bar examination in several States. States vary in their use of MBE and MEE scores.

Many States also require Multistate Performance Testing to test the practical skills of beginning lawyers. Requirements vary by State, although the test usually is taken at the same time as the bar exam and is a one-time requirement.

In 2007, law school graduates in 52 jurisdictions were required to pass the Multistate Professional Responsibility Examination (MPRE), which tests their knowledge of the ABA codes on professional responsibility and judicial conduct. In some States, the MPRE may be taken during law school, usually after completing a course on legal ethics.

Other qualifications. The practice of law involves a great deal of responsibility. Individuals planning careers in law should like to work with people and be able to win the respect and confidence of their clients, associates, and the public. Perseverance, creativity, and reasoning ability also are essential to lawyers, who often analyze complex cases and handle new and unique legal problems.

Advancement. Most beginning lawyers start in salaried positions. Newly hired attorneys usually start as associates and work with more experienced lawyers or judges. After several years, some lawyers are admitted to partnership in their firm, which means they are partial owners of the firm, or go into practice for themselves. Some experienced lawyers are nominated or elected to judgeships. (See the section on judges, magistrates, and other judicial workers elsewhere in the *Handbook*.) Others become full-time law school faculty or administrators; a growing number of these lawyers have advanced degrees in other fields as well.

Some attorneys use their legal training in administrative or managerial positions in various departments of large corporations. A transfer from a corporation's legal department to another department often is viewed as a way to gain administrative experience and rise in the ranks of management.

Employment

Lawyers held about 761,000 jobs in 2006. Approximately 27 percent of lawyers were self-employed, practicing either as partners in law firms or in solo practices. Most salaried lawyers held positions in government, in law firms or other corporations, or in nonprofit organizations. Most government-employed lawyers worked at the local level. In the Federal Government, lawyers worked for many different agencies but were concentrated in the Departments of Justice, Treasury, and Defense. Many salaried lawyers working outside of government were employed as house counsel by public utilities, banks, insurance companies, real estate agencies, manufacturing firms, and other business firms and nonprofit organizations. Some also had part-time independent practices, while others worked part time as lawyers and full time in another occupation.

A relatively small number of trained attorneys work in law schools, and are not included in the employment estimate for lawyers. Most are faculty members who specialize in one or more subjects; however, some serve as administrators. Others work full time in nonacademic settings and teach part time. (For additional information, see the *Handbook* section on teachers—postsecondary.)

Job Outlook

Average employment growth is projected, but job competition is expected to be keen.

Employment change. Employment of lawyers is expected to grow 11 percent during the 2006-16 decade, about as fast as the average for all occupations. The growth in the population and in the level of business activity is expected create more legal transactions, civil disputes, and criminal cases. Job growth among lawyers also will result from increasing demand for legal services in such areas as health care, intellectual property, venture capital, energy, elder, antitrust, and environmental law. In addition, the wider availability and affordability of legal clinics should result in increased use of legal services by middle-income people. However, growth in demand for lawyers will be constrained as businesses increasingly use large accounting firms and paralegals to perform some of the same functions that lawyers do. For example, accounting firms may provide employee-benefit counseling, process documents, or handle various other services previously performed by a law firm. Also, mediation and dispute resolution increasingly are being used as alternatives to litigation.

Job growth for lawyers will continue to be concentrated in salaried jobs, as businesses and all levels of government employ a growing number of staff attorneys. Most salaried positions are in urban areas where government agencies, law firms, and big corporations are concentrated. The number of self-employed lawyers is expected to grow slowly, reflecting the difficulty of establishing a profitable new practice in the face of competition from larger, established law firms. Moreover, the growing complexity of law, which encourages specialization, along with the cost of maintaining up-to-date legal research materials, favors larger firms.

Job prospects. Competition for job openings should continue to be keen because of the large number of students graduating from law school each year. Graduates with superior academic records from highly regarded law schools will have the best job opportunities. Perhaps as a result of competition for attorney positions, lawyers are increasingly finding work in less traditional areas for which legal training is an asset, but not normally a requirement—for example, administrative, managerial, and

business positions in banks, insurance firms, real estate companies, government agencies, and other organizations. Employment opportunities are expected to continue to arise in these organizations at a growing rate.

As in the past, some graduates may have to accept positions outside of their field of interest or for which they feel overqualified. Some recent law school graduates who have been unable to find permanent positions are turning to the growing number of temporary staffing firms that place attorneys in short-term jobs. This service allows companies to hire lawyers on an "as-needed" basis and permits beginning lawyers to develop practical skills.

Because of the keen competition for jobs, a law graduate's geographic mobility and work experience assume greater importance. The willingness to relocate may be an advantage in getting a job, but to be licensed in another State, a lawyer may have to take an additional State bar examination. In addition, employers increasingly seek graduates who have advanced law degrees and experience in a specialty, such as tax, patent, or admiralty law.

Job opportunities often are adversely affected by cyclical swings in the economy. During recessions, demand declines for some discretionary legal services, such as planning estates, drafting wills, and handling real estate transactions. Also, corporations are less likely to litigate cases when declining sales and profits restrict their budgets. Some corporations and law firms will not hire new attorneys until business improves, and these establishments may even cut staff to contain costs. Several factors, however, mitigate the overall impact of recessions on lawyers; during recessions, for example, individuals and corporations face other legal problems, such as bankruptcies, foreclosures, and divorces requiring legal action.

For lawyers who wish to work independently, establishing a new practice will probably be easiest in small towns and expanding suburban areas. In such communities, competition from larger, established law firms is likely to be less than in big cities, and new lawyers may find it easier to establish a reputation among potential clients.

Earnings

In May 2006, the median annual earnings of all wage-and-salaried lawyers were $102,470. The middle half of the occupation earned between $69,910 and $145,600. Median annual earnings in the industries employing the largest numbers of lawyers in May 2006 were:

Management of companies and enterprises.........................$128,610
Federal Government 119,240
Legal services 108,100
Local government 78,810
State government 75,840

Projections data from the National Employment Matrix

Occupational Title	SOC Code	Employment, 2006	Projected employment, 2016	Change, 2006-2016	
				Number	Percent
Lawyers..	23-1011	761,000	844,000	84,000	11

NOTE: Data in this table are rounded. See the discussion of the employment projections table in the *Handbook* introductory chapter on *Occupational Information Included in the Handbook.*

Table 1. Median salaries of lawyers 9 months after graduation, 2005

All graduates	$60,000
Type of work	
Private practice	$85,000
Business	60,000
Government	46,158
Academic/judicial clerkships	45,000
Source: National Association of Law Placement	

Salaries of experienced attorneys vary widely according to the type, size, and location of their employer. Lawyers who own their own practices usually earn less than those who are partners in law firms. Lawyers starting their own practice may need to work part time in other occupations to supplement their income until their practice is well established.

Median salaries of lawyers 9 months after graduation from law school in 2005 varied by type of work, as indicated in table 1.

Most salaried lawyers are provided health and life insurance, and contributions are made to retirement plans on their behalf. Lawyers who practice independently are covered only if they arrange and pay for such benefits themselves.

Related Occupations

Legal training is necessary in many other occupations, including paralegals and legal assistants; law clerks; title examiners, abstractors, and searchers; and judges, magistrates, and other judicial workers.

Sources of Additional Information

Information on law schools and a career in law may be obtained from the following organizations:

➤ American Bar Association, 321 North Clark St., Chicago, IL 60610. Internet: **http://www.abanet.org**

➤ National Association for Law Placement, 1025 Connecticut Ave. NW., Suite 1110, Washington, DC 20036.
Internet: **http://www.nalp.org**

Information on the LSAT, the Law School Data Assembly Service, the law school application process, and financial aid available to law students may be obtained from:

➤ Law School Admission Council, P.O. Box 40, Newtown, PA 18940. Internet: **http://www.lsac.org**

Information on obtaining positions as lawyers with the Federal Government is available from the Office of Personnel Management through USAJOBS, the Federal Government's official employment information system. This resource for locating and applying for job opportunities can be accessed through the Internet at **http://www.usajobs.opm.gov** or through an interactive voice response telephone system at (703) 724-1850 or TDD (978) 461-8404. These numbers are not toll free, and charges may result. For advice on how to find and apply for Federal jobs, see the Occupational Outlook Quarterly article "How to get a job in the Federal Government," online at:
http://www.bls.gov/opub/ooq/2004/summer/art01.pdf.

The requirements for admission to the bar in a particular State or other jurisdiction may be obtained at the State capital, from the clerk of the Supreme Court, or from the administrator of the State Board of Bar Examiners.

Paralegals and Legal Assistants

(O*NET 23-2011.00)

Significant Points

- Most entrants have an associate degree in paralegal studies, or a bachelor's degree coupled with a certificate in paralegal studies.

- About 7 out of 10 work for law firms; others work for corporate legal departments and government agencies.

- Employment is projected to grow much faster than average, as employers try to reduce costs by hiring paralegals to perform tasks once done by lawyers.

- Competition for jobs should continue; experienced, formally trained paralegals should have the best employment opportunities.

Nature of the Work

While lawyers assume ultimate responsibility for legal work, they often delegate many of their tasks to paralegals. In fact, paralegals—also called legal assistants—are continuing to assume a growing range of tasks in legal offices and perform many of the same tasks as lawyers. Nevertheless, they are explicitly prohibited from carrying out duties considered to be the practice of law, such as setting legal fees, giving legal advice, and presenting cases in court.

One of a paralegal's most important tasks is helping lawyers prepare for closings, hearings, trials, and corporate meetings. Paralegals might investigate the facts of cases and ensure that all relevant information is considered. They also identify appropriate laws, judicial decisions, legal articles, and other materials that are relevant to assigned cases. After they analyze and organize the information, paralegals may prepare written reports that attorneys use in determining how cases should be handled. If attorneys decide to file lawsuits on behalf of clients, paralegals may help prepare the legal arguments, draft pleadings and motions to be filed with the court, obtain affidavits, and assist attorneys during trials. Paralegals also organize and track files of all important case documents and make them available and easily accessible to attorneys.

In addition to this preparatory work, paralegals perform a number of other functions. For example, they help draft contracts, mortgages, and separation agreements. They also may assist in preparing tax returns, establishing trust funds, and planning estates. Some paralegals coordinate the activities of other law office employees and maintain financial office records.

Computer software packages and the Internet are used to search legal literature stored in computer databases and on CD-ROM. In litigation involving many supporting documents, paralegals usually use computer databases to retrieve, organize, and index various materials. Imaging software allows paralegals to scan documents directly into a database, while billing programs help them to track hours billed to clients. Computer software packages also are used to perform tax computations and explore the consequences of various tax strategies for clients.

Paralegals are found in all types of organizations, but most are employed by law firms, corporate legal departments, and various government offices. In these organizations, they can work in many different areas of the law, including litigation, personal injury, corporate law, criminal law, employee benefits, intellectual property, labor law, bankruptcy, immigration, family law, and real estate. As the law becomes more complex, paralegals become more specialized. Within specialties, functions are often broken down further. For example, paralegals specializing in labor law may concentrate exclusively on employee benefits. In small and medium-size law firms, duties are often more general.

The tasks of paralegals differ widely according to the type of organization for which they work. A corporate paralegal often assists attorneys with employee contracts, shareholder agreements, stock-option plans, and employee benefit plans. They also may help prepare and file annual financial reports, maintain corporate minutes' record resolutions, and prepare forms to secure loans for the corporation. Corporate paralegals often monitor and review government regulations to ensure that the corporation is aware of new requirements and is operating within the law. Increasingly, experienced corporate paralegals or paralegal managers are assuming additional supervisory responsibilities such as overseeing team projects.

The duties of paralegals who work in the public sector usually vary by agency. In general, litigation paralegals analyze legal material for internal use, maintain reference files, conduct research for attorneys, and collect and analyze evidence for agency hearings. They may prepare informative or explanatory material on laws, agency regulations, and agency policy for general use by the agency and the public. Paralegals employed in community legal-service projects help the poor, the aged, and others who are in need of legal assistance. They file forms, conduct research, prepare documents, and,

In addition to investigating the facts of cases, paralegals identify relevant laws, judicial decisions, legal articles, and other materials.

when authorized by law, may represent clients at administrative hearings.

Work environment. Paralegals handle many routine assignments, particularly when they are inexperienced. As they gain experience, paralegals usually assume more varied tasks with additional responsibility. Paralegals do most of their work in offices and law libraries. Occasionally, they travel to gather information and perform other duties.

Paralegals employed by corporations and government usually work a standard 40-hour week. Although most paralegals work year round, some are temporarily employed during busy times of the year and then released. Paralegals who work for law firms sometimes work very long hours when under pressure to meet deadlines.

Training, Other Qualifications, and Advancement

Most entrants have an associate degree in paralegal studies, or a bachelor's degree coupled with a certificate in paralegal studies. Some employers train paralegals on the job.

Education and training. There are several ways to become a paralegal. The most common is through a community college paralegal program that leads to an associate degree. Another common method of entry, mainly for those who already have a college degree, is earning a certificate in paralegal studies. A small number of schools offer a bachelor's and master's degree in paralegal studies. Finally, some employers train paralegals on the job.

Associate and bachelor's degree programs usually combine paralegal training with courses in other academic subjects. Certificate programs vary significantly, with some only taking a few months to complete. Most certificate programs provide intensive paralegal training for individuals who already hold college degrees.

About 1,000 colleges and universities, law schools, and proprietary schools offer formal paralegal training programs. Approximately 260 paralegal programs are approved by the American Bar Association (ABA). Although many employers do not require such approval, graduation from an ABA-approved program can enhance employment opportunities. Admission requirements vary. Some require certain college courses or a bachelor's degree, while others accept high school graduates or those with legal experience. A few schools require standardized tests and personal interviews.

The quality of paralegal training programs varies; some programs may include job placement services. If possible, prospective students should examine the experiences of recent graduates before enrolling in a paralegal program. Any training program usually includes courses in legal research and the legal applications of computers. Many paralegal training programs also offer an internship in which students gain practical experience by working for several months in a private law firm, the office of a public defender or attorney general, a corporate legal department, a legal aid organization, a bank, or a government agency. Internship experience is an asset when one is seeking a job after graduation.

Some employers train paralegals on the job, hiring college graduates with no legal experience or promoting experienced legal secretaries. Other entrants have experience in a technical field that is useful to law firms, such as a background in tax preparation or criminal justice. Nursing or health administration experience is valuable in personal injury law practices.

Certification and other qualifications. Although most employers do not require certification, earning a voluntary certification from a professional society may offer advantages in the labor market. The National Association of Legal Assistants (NALA), for example, has established standards for certification requiring various combinations of education and experience. Paralegals who meet these standards are eligible to take a 2-day examination. Those who pass the exam may use the Certified Legal Assistant (CLA) or Certified Paralegal (CP) credential. The NALA also offers the Advanced Paralegal Certification for experienced paralegals who want to specialize. The Advanced Paralegal Certification program is a curriculum based program offered on the Internet.

The American Alliance of Paralegals, Inc. offers the American Alliance Certified Paralegal (AACP) credential, a voluntary certification program. Paralegals seeking the AACP certification must possess at least five years of paralegal experience and meet one of the three educational criteria. Certification must be renewed every two years, including the completion 18 hours of continuing education.

In addition, the National Federation of Paralegal Association offers the Registered Paralegal (RP) designation to paralegals with a bachelor's degree and at least 2 years of experience who pass an exam. To maintain the credential, workers must complete 12 hours of continuing education every 2 years. The National Association for Legal Professionals offers the Professional Paralegal (PP) certification to those who pass a four-part exam. Recertification requires 75 hours of continuing education.

Paralegals must be able to document and present their findings and opinions to their supervising attorney. They need to understand legal terminology and have good research and investigative skills. Familiarity with the operation and applications of computers in legal research and litigation support also is important. Paralegals should stay informed of new developments in the laws that affect their area of practice. Participation in continuing legal education seminars allows paralegals to maintain and expand their knowledge of the law. In fact, all paralegals in California must complete 4 hours of mandatory continuing education in either general law or in a specialized area of law.

Because paralegals frequently deal with the public, they should be courteous and uphold the ethical standards of the legal profession. The National Association of Legal Assistants, the National Federation of Paralegal Associations, and a few States have established ethical guidelines for paralegals to follow.

Advancement. Paralegals usually are given more responsibilities and require less supervision as they gain work experience. Experienced paralegals who work in large law firms, corporate legal departments, or government agencies may supervise and delegate assignments to other paralegals and clerical staff. Advancement opportunities also include promotion to managerial and other law-related positions within the firm or corporate legal department. However, some paralegals find it easier to move to another law firm when seeking increased responsibility or advancement.

Employment

Paralegals and legal assistants held about 238,000 jobs in 2006. Private law firms employed 7 out of 10 paralegals and legal assistants; most of the remainder worked for corporate legal departments and various levels of government. Within the Federal Government, the U.S. Department of Justice is the largest employer, followed by the Social Security Administration and the U.S. Department of the Treasury. A small number of paralegals own their own businesses and work as freelance legal assistants, contracting their services to attorneys or corporate legal departments.

Job Outlook

Despite projected rapid employment growth, competition for jobs is expected to continue as many people seek to go into this profession; experienced, formally trained paralegals should have the best employment opportunities.

Employment change. Employment of paralegals and legal assistants is projected to grow 22 percent between 2006 and 2016, much faster than the average for all occupations. Employers are trying to reduce costs and increase the availability and efficiency of legal services by hiring paralegals to perform tasks once done by lawyers. Paralegals are performing a wider variety of duties, making them more useful to businesses.

Demand for paralegals also is expected to grow as an expanding population increasingly requires legal services, especially in areas such as intellectual property, health care, international law, elder issues, criminal law, and environmental law. The growth of prepaid legal plans also should contribute to the demand for legal services.

Private law firms will continue to be the largest employers of paralegals, but a growing array of other organizations, such as corporate legal departments, insurance companies, real estate and title insurance firms, and banks also hire paralegals. Corporations in particular are expected to increase their in-house legal departments to cut costs. In part because of the

Projections data from the National Employment Matrix

Occupational Title	SOC Code	Employment, 2006	Projected employment, 2016	Change, 2006-2016	
				Number	Percent
Paralegals and legal assistants..	23-2011	238,000	291,000	53,000	22

NOTE: Data in this table are rounded. See the discussion of the employment projections table in the *Handbook* introductory chapter on *Occupational Information Included in the Handbook.*

range of tasks they can perform, paralegals are also increasingly employed in small and medium-size establishments of all types.

Job prospects. In addition to new jobs created by employment growth, more job openings will arise as people leave the occupation. There will be demand for paralegals who specialize in areas such as real estate, bankruptcy, medical malpractice, and product liability. Community legal service programs, which provide assistance to the poor, elderly, minorities, and middle-income families, will employ additional paralegals to minimize expenses and serve the most people. Job opportunities also are expected in Federal, State, and local government agencies, consumer organizations, and the courts. However, this occupation attracts many applicants, creating competition for jobs. Experienced, formally trained paralegals should have the best job prospects.

To a limited extent, paralegal jobs are affected by the business cycle. During recessions, demand declines for some discretionary legal services, such as planning estates, drafting wills, and handling real estate transactions. Corporations are less inclined to initiate certain types of litigation when falling sales and profits lead to fiscal belt tightening. As a result, full-time paralegals employed in offices adversely affected by a recession may be laid off or have their work hours reduced. However, during recessions, corporations and individuals are more likely to face problems that require legal assistance, such as bankruptcies, foreclosures, and divorces. Paralegals, who provide many of the same legal services as lawyers at a lower cost, tend to fare relatively better in difficult economic conditions.

Earnings

Earnings of paralegals and legal assistants vary greatly. Salaries depend on education, training, experience, the type and size of employer, and the geographic location of the job. In general, paralegals who work for large law firms or in large metropolitan areas earn more than those who work for smaller firms or in less populated regions. In May 2006, full-time wage-and-salary paralegals and legal assistants had median annual earnings, including bonuses, of $43,040. The middle 50 percent earned between $33,920 and $54,690. The top 10 percent earned more than $67,540, and the bottom 10 percent earned less than $27,450. Median annual earnings in the industries employing the largest numbers of paralegals were:

Federal Government	$56,080
Management of companies and enterprises	52,220
Local government	42,170
Legal services	41,460
State government	38,020

In addition to earning a salary, many paralegals receive bonuses, in part, to compensate them for sometimes having to work long hours. Paralegals also receive vacation, paid sick leave, a 401 savings plan, life insurance, personal paid time off, dental insurance, and reimbursement for continuing legal education.

Related Occupations

Among the other occupations that call for a specialized understanding of the law but do not require the extensive training of a lawyer, are law clerks; title examiners, abstractors, and searchers; claims adjusters, appraisers, examiners, and investigators; and occupational health and safety specialists and technicians.

Sources of Additional Information

General information on a career as a paralegal can be obtained from:

➤ Standing Committee on Paralegals, American Bar Association, 321 North Clark St., Chicago, IL 60610. Internet: **http://www.abanet.org/legalservices/paralegals**

For information on the Certified Legal Assistant exam, schools that offer training programs in a specific State, and standards and guidelines for paralegals, contact:

➤ National Association of Legal Assistants, Inc., 1516 South Boston St., Suite 200, Tulsa, OK 74119. Internet: **http://www.nala.org**

Information on the Paralegal Advanced Competency Exam, paralegal careers, paralegal training programs, job postings, and local associations is available from:

➤ National Federation of Paralegal Associations, PO Box 2016, Edmonds, WA 98020. Internet: **http://www.paralegals.org**

Information on paralegal training programs, including the pamphlet *How to Choose a Paralegal Education Program*, may be obtained from:

➤ American Association for Paralegal Education, 19 Mantua Rd., Mt. Royal, NJ 08061. Internet: **http://www.aafpe.org**

Information on paralegal careers, certification, and job postings is available from:

➤ American Alliance of Paralegals, Inc., 16815 East Shea Boulevard, Suite 110, No. 101, Fountain Hills, Arizona, 85268. Internet: **http://www.aapipara.org**

For information on the Professional Paralegal exam, schools that offer training programs in a specific State, and standards and guidelines for paralegals, contact:

➤ NALS, 314 E. 3rd St., Suite 210, Tulsa, OK 74120. Internet: **http://www.nals.org**

Information on obtaining positions as a paralegal or legal assistant with the Federal Government is available from the Office of Personnel Management through USAJOBS, the Federal Government's official employment information system. This resource for locating and applying for job opportunities can be accessed through the Internet at **http://www.usajobs.opm.gov** or through an interactive voice response telephone system at (703) 724-1850 or TDD (978) 461-8404. These numbers are not toll free, and charges may result. For advice on how to find and apply for Federal jobs, see the Occupational Outlook Quarterly article "How to get a job in the Federal Government," online at:

http://www.bls.gov/opub/ooq/2004/summer/art01.pdf.

Education, Training, Library, and Museum Occupations

Archivists, Curators, and Museum Technicians

(O*NET 25-4011.00, 25-4012.00, 25-4013.00)

Significant Points

- Most worked in museums, historical sites, and similar venues; in educational institutions; or in Federal, State, or local government.

- A graduate degree and related work experience are required for most positions; museum technicians may enter with a bachelor's degree.

- Keen competition is expected for most jobs because qualified applicants generally outnumber job openings.

Nature of the Work

Archivists, curators, and museum technicians work for museums, governments, zoos, colleges and universities, corporations, and other institutions that require experts to preserve important records and artifacts. These workers preserve important objects and documents, including works of art, transcripts of meetings, photographs, coins and stamps, living and preserved plants and animals, and historic objects, including, for example, turn-of-the-century immigration records, buildings, and sites.

Archivists and curators plan and oversee the arrangement, cataloguing, and exhibition of collections and, along with technicians and conservators, maintain collections. They acquire and preserve important documents and other valuable items for permanent storage or display. They also describe, catalogue, and analyze, valuable objects for the benefit of researchers and the public.

Archivists and curators may coordinate educational and public outreach programs, such as tours, workshops, lectures, and classes, and may work with the boards of institutions to administer plans and policies. They also may research topics or items relevant to their collections.

Although some duties of archivists and curators are similar, the types of items they deal with differ: curators usually handle objects with cultural, biological, or historical significance, such as sculptures, textiles, and paintings, while archivists handle mainly records and documents that are retained because of their importance and potential value in the future.

Archivists collect, organize, and maintain control over a wide range of information deemed important enough for permanent safekeeping. This information takes many forms: photographs, films, video and sound recordings, and electronic data files in a wide variety of formats, as well as more traditional paper records, letters, and documents.

Archivists maintain records in accordance with accepted standards and practices that ensure the long-term preservation and easy retrieval of the documents. Records may be saved on any medium, including paper, film, videotape, audiotape, computer disk, or DVD. They also may be copied onto some other format to protect the original and to make the records more accessible to researchers who use them. As various storage media evolve, archivists must keep abreast of technological advances in electronic information storage.

Archivists often specialize in an area of history so they can more accurately determine which records in that area qualify for retention and should become part of the archives. Archivists also may work with specialized forms of records, such as manuscripts, electronic records, photographs, cartographic records, motion pictures, and sound recordings.

Computers are increasingly being used to generate and maintain archival records. Professional standards for the use of computers in handling archival records are still evolving. Expanding computer capabilities that allow more records to be stored and exhibited electronically have transformed, and are expected to continue to transform, many aspects of archival collections.

Curators administer museums, zoos, aquariums, botanical gardens, nature centers, and historic sites. The head curator of the museum is usually called the *museum director*. Curators direct the acquisition, storage, and exhibition of collections, including negotiating and authorizing the purchase, sale, exchange, or loan of collections. They are also responsible for authenticating, evaluating, and categorizing the specimens in a collection. Curators oversee and help conduct the institution's research projects and related educational programs. Today, an increasing part of a curator's duties involves fundraising and promotion, which may include the writing and reviewing of grant proposals, journal articles, and publicity materials, as well as attendance at meetings, conventions, and civic events.

Most curators specialize in a particular field, such as botany, art, paleontology, or history. Those working in large institutions may be highly specialized. A large natural history museum, for example, would employ separate curators for its collections of birds, fishes, insects, and mammals. Some curators maintain their collections, others do research, and others perform administrative tasks. In small institutions with only one or a few curators, one curator may be responsible for a number of tasks, from maintaining collections to directing the affairs of the museum.

Conservators manage, care for, preserve, treat, and document works of art, artifacts, and specimens—work that may require substantial historical, scientific, and archaeological research. They use x-rays, chemical testing, microscopes, special lights, and other laboratory equipment and techniques to examine objects and determine their condition and the appropriate method for preserving them. Conservators document their findings and treat items to minimize their deterioration or to restore them to their original state. Conservators usually specialize in a particular material or group of objects, such as documents and books, paintings, decorative arts, textiles, metals, or architectural material. In addition to their conservation work, conservators par-

Keen competition is expected for most jobs because qualified applicants generally outnumber job openings.

ticipate in outreach programs, research topics in their area of specialty, and write articles for scholarly journals.

Museum technicians assist curators by performing various preparatory and maintenance tasks on museum items. They also answer public inquiries and assist curators and outside scholars in using collections. Archives technicians help archivists organize, maintain, and provide access to historical documentary materials.

Work environment. The working conditions of archivists and curators vary. Some spend most of their time working with the public, providing reference assistance and educational services. Others perform research or process records, which often means working alone or in offices with only a few people. Those who restore and install exhibits or work with bulky, heavy record containers may lift objects, climb, or stretch. Those in zoos, botanical gardens, and other outdoor museums and historic sites frequently walk great distances. Conservators work in conservation laboratories. The size of the objects in the collection they are working with determines the amount of effort involved in lifting, reaching, and moving objects.

Curators who work in large institutions may travel extensively to evaluate potential additions to the collection, organize exhibitions, and conduct research in their area of expertise. However, travel is rare for curators employed in small institutions.

Training, Other Qualifications, and Advancement

Employment as an archivist, conservator, or curator usually requires graduate education and related work experience. Museum technicians often start work with a bachelor's degree. While completing their formal education, many archivists and curators work in archives or museums to gain "hands-on" experience.

Education and training. Although archivists earn a variety of undergraduate degrees, a graduate degree in history or library science with courses in archival science is preferred by most employers. Many colleges and universities offer courses or practical training in archival techniques as part of their history, library science, or other curriculum. A few institutions now offer master's degrees in archival studies. Some positions may require knowledge of the discipline related to the collection, such as business or medicine.

For employment as a curator, most museums require a master's degree in an appropriate discipline of the museum's specialty—art, history, or archaeology—or in museum studies. Many employers prefer a doctoral degree, particularly for curators in natural history or science museums. Earning two graduate degrees—in museum studies (museology) and a specialized subject—gives a candidate a distinct advantage in this competitive job market. In small museums, curatorial positions may be available to individuals with a bachelor's degree. Because curators, particularly those in small museums, may have administrative and managerial responsibilities, courses in business administration, public relations, marketing, and fundraising also are recommended. For some positions, an internship of full-time museum work supplemented by courses in museum practices is needed.

When hiring conservators, employers look for a master's degree in conservation or in a closely related field, together with substantial experience. There are only a few graduate programs in museum conservation techniques in the United States. Competition for entry to these programs is keen; to qualify, a student must have a background in chemistry, archaeology or studio art, and art history, as well as work experience. For some programs, knowledge of a foreign language also is helpful. Conservation apprenticeships or internships as an undergraduate can enhance one's admission prospects. Graduate programs last 2 to 4 years, the latter years of which include internship training. A few individuals enter conservation through apprenticeships with museums, nonprofit organizations, and conservators in private practice. Apprenticeships should be supplemented with courses in chemistry, studio art, and history. Apprenticeship training, although accepted, is a more difficult route into the conservation profession.

Museum technicians usually need a bachelor's degree in an appropriate discipline of the museum's specialty, training in museum studies, or previous experience working in museums, particularly in the design of exhibits. Similarly, archives technicians usually need a bachelor's degree in library science or history, or relevant work experience. Relatively few schools grant a bachelor's degree in museum studies. More common are undergraduate minors or tracks of study that are part of an undergraduate degree in a related field, such as art history, history, or archaeology. Students interested in further study may obtain a master's degree in museum studies, offered in colleges and universities throughout the country. However, many employers feel that, while museum studies are helpful, a thorough knowledge of the museum's specialty and museum work experience are more important.

Certification and other qualifications. The Academy of Certified Archivists offers voluntary certification for archivists. The designation "Certified Archivist" can be obtained by those with at least a master's degree and a year of appropriate archival experience. The certification process requires candidates to pass a written examination, and they must renew their certification periodically.

Archivists need research skills and analytical ability to understand the content of documents and the context in which they were created and to decipher deteriorated or poor-quality printed matter, handwritten manuscripts, photographs, or films. A background in preservation management is often required of archivists because they are responsible for taking proper care of their records. Archivists also must be able to organize large amounts of information and write clear instructions for its retrieval and use. In addition, computer skills and the ability to work with electronic records and databases are very important. Because electronic records are becoming the prevalent form of record-keeping, and archivists must create searchable databases, knowledge of Web technology is increasingly being required.

Curatorial positions often require knowledge in a number of fields. For historic and artistic conservation, courses in chemistry, physics, and art are desirable. Like archivists, curators need computer skills and the ability to work with electronic databases. Many curators are responsible for posting information on the Internet, so they also need to be familiar with digital imaging, scanning technology, and copyright law.

Curators must be flexible because of their wide variety of duties, among which are the design and presentation of exhibits. In small museums, curators need manual dexterity to build exhibits or restore objects. Leadership ability and business skills are important for museum directors, while marketing skills are valuable in increasing museum attendance and fundraising.

Advancement. Continuing education is available through meetings, conferences, and workshops sponsored by archival, historical, and museum associations. Some larger organizations, such as the National Archives in Washington, D.C., offer such training in-house.

Many archives, including one-person shops, are very small and have limited opportunities for promotion. Archivists typically advance by transferring to a larger unit that has supervisory positions. A doctorate in history, library science, or a related field may be needed for some advanced positions, such as director of a State archive.

In large museums, curators may advance through several levels of responsibility, eventually becoming the museum director. Curators in smaller museums often advance to larger ones. Individual research and publications are important for advancement in larger institutions.

Technician positions often serve as a steppingstone for individuals interested in archival and curatorial work. Except in small museums, a master's degree is needed for advancement.

Employment

Archivists, curators, and museum technicians held about 27,000 jobs in 2006. About 38 percent were employed in museums, historical sites, and similar institutions, and 18 percent worked for State and private educational institutions, mainly college and university libraries. Nearly 31 percent worked in Federal, State, and local government, excluding educational institutions. Most

Federal archivists work for the National Archives and Records Administration; others manage military archives in the U.S. Department of Defense. Most Federal Government curators work at the Smithsonian Institution, in the military museums of the Department of Defense, and in archaeological and other museums and historic sites managed by the U.S. Department of the Interior. All State governments have archival or historical record sections employing archivists. State and local governments also have numerous historical museums, parks, libraries, and zoos employing curators.

Some large corporations that have archives or record centers employ archivists to manage the growing volume of records created or maintained as required by law or necessary to the firms' operations. Religious and fraternal organizations, professional associations, conservation organizations, major private collectors, and research firms also employ archivists and curators.

Conservators may work under contract to treat particular items, rather than as regular employees of a museum or other institution. These conservators may work on their own as private contractors, or they may work as an employee of a conservation laboratory or regional conservation center that contracts their services to museums.

Job Outlook

Faster than average employment growth is expected through 2016. Keen competition is expected for most jobs as archivists, curators, and museum technicians because qualified applicants generally outnumber job openings.

Employment change. Employment of archivists, curators, and museum technicians is expected to increase 18 percent over the 2006-16 decade, faster than the average for all occupations. Jobs for archivists are expected to increase as public and private organizations require organization of and access to increasing volumes of records and information. Public interest in science, art, history, and technology will continue, creating opportunities for curators, conservators, and museum technicians. Museum attendance has held steady in recent years, many museums are financially healthy, and many have pursued building and renovation projects.

There has been an increase in self-employment among conservators, as many museums move toward hiring these workers on contract rather than keeping them permanently on staff. This trend is expected to continue.

Demand for archivists who specialize in electronic records and records management will grow more rapidly than the demand for archivists who specialize in older media formats.

Job prospects. Keen competition is expected for most jobs as archivists, curators, and museum technicians because quali-

Projections data from the National Employment Matrix

Occupational Title	SOC Code	Employment, 2006	Projected employment, 2016	Change, 2006-2016	
				Number	Percent
Archivists, curators, and museum technicians	25-4010	27,000	33,000	5,000	18
Archivists	25-4011	6,400	7,400	900	14
Curators	25-4012	10,000	13,000	2,400	23
Museum Technicians and Conservators	25-4013	11,000	12,000	1,700	16

NOTE: Data in this table are rounded. See the discussion of the employment projections table in the *Handbook* introductory chapter on *Occupational Information Included in the Handbook.*

fied applicants generally outnumber job openings. Graduates with highly specialized training, such as master's degrees in both library science and history, with a concentration in archives or records management and extensive computer skills, should have the best opportunities for jobs as archivists. Opportunities for those who manage electronic records are expected to be better than for those who specialize in older media formats.

Curator jobs, in particular, are attractive to many people, and many applicants have the necessary training and knowledge of the subject. But because there are relatively few openings, candidates may have to work part time, as an intern, or even as a volunteer assistant curator or research associate after completing their formal education. Substantial work experience in collection management, research, exhibit design, or restoration, as well as database management skills, will be necessary for permanent status.

Conservators also can expect competition for jobs. Competition is stiff for the limited number of openings in conservation graduate programs, and applicants need a technical background. Conservation program graduates with knowledge of a foreign language and a willingness to relocate will have an advantage over less qualified candidates.

Museums and other cultural institutions can be subject to cuts in funding during recessions or periods of budget tightening, reducing demand for these workers. Although the number of archivists and curators who move to other occupations is relatively low, the need to replace workers who retire will create some additional job openings.

Earnings

Median annual earnings of archivists in May 2006 were $40,730. The middle 50 percent earned between $30,610 and $53,990. The lowest 10 percent earned less than $23,890, and the highest 10 percent earned more than $73,060. Median annual earnings of curators in May 2006 were $46,300. The middle 50 percent earned between $34,410 and $61,740. The lowest 10 percent earned less than $26,320, and the highest 10 percent earned more than $80,030. Median annual earnings of museum technicians and conservators in May 2006 were $34,340. The middle 50 percent earned between $26,360 and $46,120. The lowest 10 percent earned less than $20,600, and the highest 10 percent earned more than $61,270.

In 2007, the average annual salary for archivists in the Federal Government was $79,199; for museum curators, $80,780; for museum specialists and technicians, $58,855; and for archives technicians, $44,547.

Related Occupations

The skills that archivists, curators, and museum technicians use in preserving, organizing, and displaying objects or information of historical interest are shared by artists and related workers; librarians; and anthropologists and archeologists, historians, and other social scientists.

Sources of Additional Information

For information on archivists and on schools offering courses in archival studies, contact:

➤ Society of American Archivists, 527 South Wells St., 5th floor, Chicago, IL 60607-3922. Internet: **http://www.archivists.org**

For general information about careers as a curator and schools offering courses in museum studies, contact:

➤ American Association of Museums, 1575 Eye St.NW., Suite 400, Washington, DC 20005. Internet: **http://www.aam-us.org**

For information about careers and education programs in conservation and preservation, contact:

➤ American Institute for Conservation of Historic and Artistic Works, 1717 K St.NW., Suite 200, Washington, DC 20006. Internet: **http://aic-faic.org**

For information about archivists and archivist certification, contact:

➤ Academy of Certified Archivists, 90 State St., Suite 1009, Albany, NY 12207. Internet: **http://www.certifiedarchivists.org**

For information about government archivists, contact:

➤ National Association of Government Archivists and Records Administrators, 90 State St., Suite 1009, Albany, NY 12207. Internet: **http://www.nagara.org**

Information on obtaining positions as archivists, curators, and museum technicians with the Federal Government is available from the Office of Personnel Management through USAJOBS, the Federal Government's official employment information system. This resource for locating and applying for job opportunities can be accessed through the Internet at **http://www.usajobs.opm.gov** or through an interactive voice response telephone system at (703) 724-1850 or TDD (978) 461-8404. These numbers are not toll free, and charges may result.

Instructional Coordinators

(O*NET 25-9031.00)

Significant Points

- Many instructional coordinators have experience as teachers or education administrators.

- A master's degree is required for positions in public schools and preferred for jobs in other settings.

- Employment is projected to grow much faster than average, reflecting the need to meet new educational standards, train teachers, and develop new materials.

- Favorable job prospects are expected.

Nature of the Work

Instructional coordinators—also known as curriculum specialists, personnel development specialists, instructional coaches, or directors of instructional material—play a large role in improving the quality of education in the classroom. They develop curricula, select textbooks and other materials, train teachers, and assess educational programs for quality and adherence to regulations and standards. They also assist in implementing new technology in the classroom.

At the primary and secondary school level, instructional coordinators often specialize in specific subjects, such as reading, language arts, mathematics, or science. At the postsecondary level, coordinators may work with employers to develop training programs that produce qualified workers.

Instructional coordinators evaluate how well a school or training program's curriculum, or plan of study, meets students' needs. Based on their research and observations of instructional practice, they recommend improvements. They research teaching methods and techniques and develop procedures to ensure that instructors are implementing the curriculum successfully and meeting program goals. To aid in their evaluation, they may meet with members of educational committees and advisory groups to learn about subjects—for example, English, history, or mathematics—and explore how curriculum materials meet students' needs and relate to occupations. Coordinators also may develop questionnaires and interview school staff about the curriculum.

Some instructional coordinators also review textbooks, software, and other educational materials and make recommendations on purchases. They monitor the ways in which teachers use materials in the classroom, and they supervise workers who catalogue, distribute, and maintain a school's educational materials and equipment.

Some instructional coordinators find ways to use technology to enhance student learning. They monitor the introduction of new technology, including the Internet, into a school's curriculum. In addition, instructional coordinators might recommend installing educational software, such as interactive books and exercises designed to enhance student literacy and develop math skills. Instructional coordinators may invite experts—such as computer hardware, software, and library or media specialists—to help integrate technological materials into the curriculum.

In addition to developing curriculum and instructional materials, many instructional coordinators also plan and provide onsite education for teachers and administrators. Instructional coordinators mentor new teachers and train experienced ones in the latest instructional methods. This role becomes especially important when a school district introduces new content, program innovations, or a different organizational structure. For example, when a State or school district introduces standards or tests that students must pass, instructional coordinators often advise teachers on the content of these standards and provide instruction on how to implement them in the classroom.

Instructional coordinators train teachers on new curriculum standards.

Work environment. Many instructional coordinators work long hours. They often work year round. Some spend much of their time traveling between schools meeting with teachers and administrators. The opportunity to shape and improve instructional curricula and work in an academic environment can be satisfying. However, some instructional coordinators find the work stressful because they are continually accountable to school administrators.

Training, Other Qualifications, and Advancement
The minimum educational requirement for most instructional coordinator positions in public schools is a master's or higher degree—usually in education—plus a State teacher or administrator license. A master's degree also is preferred for positions in other settings.

Education and training. Instructional coordinators should have training in curriculum development and instruction or in the specific field for which they are responsible, such as mathematics or history. Courses in research design teach how to create and implement research studies to determine the effectiveness of a given method of instruction or curriculum and how to measure and improve student performance.

Instructional coordinators usually are also required to take continuing education courses to keep their skills current. Topics may include teacher evaluation techniques, curriculum training, new teacher induction, consulting and teacher support, and observation and analysis of teaching.

Licensure. Instructional coordinators must be licensed to work in public schools. Some States require a teaching license, whereas others require an education administrator license.

Other qualifications. Instructional coordinators must have a good understanding of how to teach specific groups of students and expertise in developing educational materials. As a result, many people become instructional coordinators after working for several years as teachers. Also beneficial is work experience in an education administrator position, such as a principal or assistant principal, or in another advisory role, such as a master teacher.

Instructional coordinators must be able to make sound decisions about curriculum options and to organize and coordinate work efficiently. They should have strong interpersonal and communication skills. Familiarity with computer technology also is important for instructional coordinators, who are increasingly involved in gathering technical information for students and teachers.

Advancement. Depending on experience and educational attainment, instructional coordinators may advance to higher administrative positions in a school system or to management or executive positions in private industry.

Employment
Instructional coordinators held about 129,000 jobs in 2006. Almost 40 percent worked in public or private elementary and secondary schools, while more than 20 percent worked in public or private junior colleges, colleges and universities, and professional schools. Other employing industries included State and local government; individual and family services; child day care services; scientific research and development services; and management, scientific, and technical consulting services.

Projections data from the National Employment Matrix

Occupational Title	SOC Code	Employment, 2006	Projected employment, 2016	Change, 2006-2016	
				Number	Percent
Instructional coordinators	25-9031	129,000	159,000	29,000	22

NOTE: Data in this table are rounded. See the discussion of the employment projections table in the *Handbook* introductory chapter on *Occupational Information Included in the Handbook.*

Job Outlook

Much faster-than-average job growth is projected. Job opportunities generally should be favorable, particularly for those with experience in math and reading curriculum development.

Employment change. The number of instructional coordinators is expected to grow by 22 percent over the 2006-16 decade, much faster than the average for all occupations, as they will be instrumental in developing new curricula to meet the demands of a changing society and in training teachers. Although budget constraints may limit employment growth to some extent, a continuing emphasis on improving the quality of education should result in an increasing demand for these workers. The emphasis on accountability also should increase at all levels of government and cause more schools to focus on improving standards of educational quality and student performance. Growing numbers of coordinators will be needed to incorporate the new standards into existing curricula and make sure teachers and administrators are informed of changes.

Additional job growth for instructional coordinators will stem from the increasing emphasis on lifelong learning and on programs for students with special needs, including those for whom English is a second language. These students often require more educational resources and consolidated planning and management within the educational system.

Job prospects. Favorable job prospects are expected. Opportunities should be best for those who specialize in subjects targeted for improvement by the No Child Left Behind Act—namely, reading, math, and science. There also will be a need for more instructional coordinators to show teachers how to use technology in the classroom.

Earnings

Median annual earnings of instructional coordinators in May 2006 were $52,790. The middle 50 percent earned between $38,800 and $70,320. The lowest 10 percent earned less than $29,040, and the highest 10 percent earned more than $87,510.

Related Occupations

Instructional coordinators are professionals involved in education, training, and development. Occupations with similar characteristics include preschool, kindergarten, elementary, middle, and secondary school teachers; postsecondary teachers; education administrators; counselors; and human resources, training, and labor relations managers and specialists.

Sources of Additional Information

Information on requirements and job opportunities for instructional coordinators is available from local school systems and State departments of education.

Librarians

(O*NET 25-4021.00)

Significant Points

- Librarians use the latest information technology to perform research, classify materials, and help students and library patrons seek information.

- A master's degree in library science is the main qualification for most librarian positions, although school librarians often need experience as teachers to meet State licensing requirements.

- Despite slower-than-average projected employment growth, job opportunities are still expected to be favorable because a large number of librarians are expected to retire in the coming decade.

Nature of the Work

The traditional concept of a library is being redefined from a place to access paper records or books to one that also houses the most advanced electronic resources, including the Internet, digital libraries, and remote access to a wide range of information sources. Consequently, librarians, often called information professionals, increasingly combine traditional duties with tasks involving quickly changing technology. Librarians help people find information and use it effectively for personal and professional purposes. They must have knowledge of a wide variety of scholarly and public information sources and must follow trends related to publishing, computers, and the media in order to oversee the selection and organization of library materials. Librarians manage staff and develop and direct information programs and systems for the public and ensure that information is organized in a manner that meets users' needs.

Most librarian positions focus on one of three aspects of library work: user services, technical services, and administrative services. Still, even librarians specializing in one of these areas have other responsibilities, too. Librarians in user services, such as reference and children's librarians, work with patrons to help them find the information they need. The job involves analyzing users' needs to determine what information is appropriate and searching for, acquiring, and providing the information. The job also includes an instructional role, such as showing users how to find information. For example, librarians commonly help users navigate the Internet so they can search for and evaluate information efficiently. Librarians in technical services, such as acquisitions and cataloguing, acquire, prepare, and classify materials so that patrons can find it easily. Some write abstracts and summaries. Often, these librarians do not deal directly with the public. Librarians in administrative services oversee the management and planning of libraries: they negotiate contracts for services, materials, and equipment; supervise library employees; perform public-relations and fundraising duties; prepare budgets; and direct activities to ensure that everything functions properly.

In small libraries or information centers, librarians usually handle all aspects of library operations. They read book reviews, publishers' announcements, and catalogues to keep up with current literature and other available resources, and they select and purchase materials from publishers, wholesalers, and distributors. Librarians prepare new materials, classifying them by subject matter and describing books and other library materials to make them easy to find. Librarians supervise assistants, who enter classification information and descriptions of materials into electronic catalogs. In large libraries, librarians often specialize in a single area, such as acquisitions, cataloguing, bibliography, reference, special collections, or administration. Teamwork is increasingly important.

Librarians also recommend materials. Many compile lists of books, periodicals, articles, audiovisual materials, and electronic resources on particular subjects and analyze collections. They collect and organize books, pamphlets, manuscripts, and other materials in a specific field, such as rare books, genealogy, or music. In addition, they coordinate programs such as storytelling for children and literacy skills and book talks for adults. Some conduct classes, publicize services, write grants, and oversee other administrative matters.

Many libraries have access to remote databases and maintain their own computerized databases. The widespread use of electronic resources makes database-searching skills important for librarians. Librarians develop and index databases and help train users to develop searching skills. Some libraries are forming consortiums with other libraries to allow patrons to access a wider range of databases and to submit information requests to several libraries simultaneously. The Internet also has greatly expanded the amount of available reference information. Librarians must know how to use these resources and inform the public about the wealth of information available in them.

Librarians are classified according to the type of library in which they work: a public library; school library media center; college, university, or other academic library; or special library. Librarians in special libraries work in information centers or libraries maintained by government agencies or corporations, law firms, advertising agencies, museums, professional associations, unions, medical centers, hospitals, religious organizations, and research laboratories. They acquire and arrange an organization's information resources, which usually are limited to subjects of special interest to the organization. They can provide vital information services by preparing abstracts and indexes of current periodicals, organizing bibliographies, or analyzing background information and preparing reports on areas of particular interest. For example, a special librarian working for a corporation could provide the sales department with information on competitors or new developments affecting the field. A medical librarian may provide information about new medical treatments, clinical trials, and standard procedures to health professionals, patients, consumers, and corporations. Government document librarians, who work for government agencies and depository libraries in each of the States, preserve government publications, records, and other documents that make up a historical record of government actions.

Some librarians work with specific groups, such as children, young adults, adults, or the disadvantaged. In school library media centers, librarians—often called school media specialists—help teachers develop curricula and acquire materials for classroom instruction. They also conduct classes for students on how to use library resources for research projects.

Librarians with computer and information systems skills can work as automated-systems librarians, planning and operating computer systems, and as information architects, designing information storage and retrieval systems and developing procedures for collecting, organizing, interpreting, and classifying information. These librarians analyze and plan for future information needs. (See the section on computer scientists and database administrators elsewhere in the *Handbook*.) Automated information systems enable librarians to focus on administrative and budgeting responsibilities, grant writing, and specialized research requests, while delegating more routine services responsibilities to technicians. (See the section on library technicians elsewhere in the *Handbook*.)

More and more, librarians apply their information management and research skills to arenas outside of libraries—for example, database development, reference tool development, information systems, publishing, Internet coordination, marketing, Web content management and design, and training of database users. Entrepreneurial librarians sometimes start their own consulting practices, acting as freelance librarians or information brokers and providing services to other libraries, businesses, or government agencies.

Work environment. Librarians spend a significant portion of time at their desks or in front of computer terminals; extended work at video display terminals can cause eyestrain and headaches. Assisting users in obtaining information or books for their jobs, homework, or recreational reading can be chal-

Librarians assist patrons with their research and resource needs.

lenging and satisfying, but working with users under deadlines can be demanding and stressful. Some librarians lift and carry books, and some climb ladders to reach high stacks, although most modern libraries have readily accessible stacks. Librarians in small settings without support staff sometimes shelve books themselves.

More than 20 percent of librarians work part time. Public and college librarians often work weekends, evenings, and some holidays. School librarians usually have the same workday and vacation schedules as classroom teachers. Special librarians usually work normal business hours, but in fast-paced industries—such as advertising or legal services—they can work longer hours when needed.

Training, Other Qualifications, and Advancement
A master's degree in library science (MLS) is necessary for librarian positions in most public, academic, and special libraries. Librarians in the Federal Government need an MLS or the equivalent in education and experience. School librarians do not typically need an MLS but must meet State licensing requirements.

Education and training. Entry into a library science graduate program requires a bachelor's degree, but any undergraduate major is acceptable. Many colleges and universities offer library science programs, but employers often prefer graduates of the 56 schools accredited by the American Library Association. Most programs take 1 year to complete; some take 2. A typical graduate program includes courses in the foundations of library and information science, such as the history of books and printing, intellectual freedom and censorship, and the role of libraries and information in society. Other basic courses cover the selection and processing of materials, the organization of information, research methods and strategies, and user services. Prospective librarians also study online reference systems, Internet search methods, and automated circulation systems. Elective course options include resources for children or young adults; classification, cataloguing, indexing, and abstracting; and library administration. Computer-related course work is an increasingly important part of an MLS degree. Some programs offer interdisciplinary degrees combining technical courses in information science with traditional training in library science.

The MLS degree provides general preparation for library work, but some individuals specialize in a particular area, such as reference, technical services, or children's services. A Ph.D. in library and information science is advantageous for a college teaching position or a top administrative job in a college or university library or large public library system.

Licensure. States generally have certification requirements for librarians in public schools and local libraries, though there are wide variations among States. School librarians in 14 States need a master's degree, either an MLS or a master's in education with a specialization in library media. In addition, about half of all States require that school librarians hold teacher certifications, although not all require teaching experience. Some States may also require librarians to pass a comprehensive assessment. Most States also have developed certification standards for local public libraries, although in some States these guidelines are only voluntary.

Other qualifications. In addition to an MLS degree, librarians in a special library, such as a law or corporate library, usually supplement their education with knowledge of the field in which they are specializing, sometimes earning a master's, doctoral, or professional degree in the subject. Areas of specialization include medicine, law, business, engineering, and the natural and social sciences. For example, a librarian working for a law firm may hold both library science and law degrees, while medical librarians should have a strong background in the sciences. In some jobs, knowledge of a foreign language is needed.

Librarians participate in continuing education and training to stay up to date with new information systems and technology.

Advancement. Experienced librarians can advance to administrative positions, such as department head, library director, or chief information officer.

Employment
Librarians held about 158,000 jobs in 2006. Most worked in school and academic libraries, but more than one-fourth worked in public libraries. The remainder worked in special libraries or as information professionals for companies and other organizations.

Job Outlook
Despite slower-than-average projected employment growth, job opportunities are still expected to be favorable because a large number of librarians are expected to retire in the coming decade.

Employment change. Employment of librarians is expected to grow by 4 percent between 2006 and 2016, slower than the average for all occupations. Growth in the number of librarians will be limited by government budget constraints and the increasing use of electronic resources. Both will result in the hiring of fewer librarians and the replacement of librarians with less costly library technicians and assistants. As electronic resources become more common and patrons and support staff become more familiar with their use, fewer librarians are needed to maintain and assist users with these resources. In addition, many libraries are equipped for users to access library resources directly from their homes or offices through library Web sites. Some users bypass librarians altogether and conduct research on their own. However, librarians will still

Projections data from the National Employment Matrix

Occupational Title	SOC Code	Employment, 2006	Projected employment, 2016	Change, 2006-2016	
				Number	Percent
Librarians..	25-4021	158,000	164,000	5,800	4

NOTE: Data in this table are rounded. See the discussion of the employment projections table in the *Handbook* introductory chapter on *Occupational Information Included in the Handbook.*

be needed to manage staff, help users develop database-searching techniques, address complicated reference requests, choose materials, and help users to define their needs.

Jobs for librarians outside traditional settings will grow the fastest over the decade. Nontraditional librarian jobs include working as information brokers and working for private corporations, nonprofit organizations, and consulting firms. Many companies are turning to librarians because of their research and organizational skills and their knowledge of computer databases and library automation systems. Librarians can review vast amounts of information and analyze, evaluate, and organize it according to a company's specific needs. Librarians also are hired by organizations to set up information on the Internet. Librarians working in these settings may be classified as systems analysts, database specialists and trainers, webmasters or web developers, or local area network (LAN) coordinators.

Job prospects. More than 2 out of 3 librarians are aged 45 or older, which will result in many job openings over the next decade as many librarians retire. However, recent increases in enrollments in MLS programs will prepare a sufficient number of new librarians to fill these positions. Opportunities for public school librarians, who are usually drawn from the ranks of teachers, should be particularly favorable.

Earnings

Salaries of librarians vary according to the individual's qualifications and the type, size, and location of the library. Librarians with primarily administrative duties often have greater earnings. Median annual earnings of librarians in May 2006 were $49,060. The middle 50 percent earned between $39,250 and $60,800. The lowest 10 percent earned less than $30,930, and the highest 10 percent earned more than $74,670. Median annual earnings in the industries employing the largest numbers of librarians in 2006 were as follows:

Junior colleges	$52,030
Colleges, universities, and professional schools	51,160
Elementary and secondary schools	50,710
Local government	44,960
Other information services	44,170

The average annual salary for all librarians in the Federal Government in nonsupervisory, supervisory, and managerial positions was $80,873 in 2007.

About 1 in 4 librarians are a member of a union or are covered under a union contract.

Related Occupations

Librarians play an important role in the transfer of knowledge and ideas by providing people with information. Jobs requiring similar analytical, organizational, and communication skills include archivists, curators, and museum technicians and computer and information scientists, research. School librarians have many duties similar to those of school teachers. Librarians increasingly store, catalogue, and access information with computers. Other jobs that use computer skills include computer systems analysts, and computer scientists and database administrators.

Sources of Additional Information

For information on a career as a librarian and information on accredited library education programs and scholarships, contact:

➤ American Library Association, Office for Human Resource Development and Recruitment, 50 East Huron St., Chicago, IL 60611. Internet: **http://www.ala.org/ala/education/educationcareers.htm**

For information on a career as a special librarian, contact:

➤ Special Libraries Association, 331 South Patrick St., Alexandria, VA 22314. Internet: **http://www.sla.org**

For information on a career as a law librarian, scholarship information, and a list of ALA-accredited schools offering programs in law librarianship, contact:

➤ American Association of Law Libraries, 53 West Jackson Blvd., Suite 940, Chicago, IL 60604.
Internet: **http://www.aallnet.org**

For information on employment opportunities for health sciences librarians and for scholarship information, credentialing information, and a list of MLA-accredited schools offering programs in health sciences librarianship, contact:

➤ Medical Library Association, 65 East Wacker Place, Suite 1900, Chicago, IL 60601. Internet: **http://www.mlanet.org**

Information concerning requirements and application procedures for positions in the Library of Congress can be obtained directly from:

➤ Human Resources Office, Library of Congress, 101 Independence Ave. SE., Washington, DC 20540-2231.
Internet: **http://www.loc.gov/hr**

State library agencies can furnish information on scholarships available through their offices, requirements for certification, and general information about career prospects in the particular State of interest. Several of these agencies maintain job hot lines reporting openings for librarians.

State departments of education can furnish information on certification requirements and job opportunities for school librarians.

Library Technicians

(O*NET 25-4031.00)

Significant Points

- Increasing use of electronic resources enables library technicians to perform tasks once done by librarians.

- Training requirements range from a high school diploma to an associate degree, but computer skills are necessary for all workers.

- Employment should grow more rapidly in special libraries because increasing numbers of professionals and other workers use those libraries.

- Opportunities will be best for those with specialized postsecondary library training.

Nature of the Work

Library technicians help librarians acquire, prepare, and organize materials and help users to find those materials. Library technicians usually work under the supervision of a librarian, although they sometimes work independently. Technicians in small libraries handle a range of duties; those in large libraries usually specialize. The duties of technicians are expanding and evolving as libraries increasingly use the Internet and other technologies to share information. Depending on where they work, library technicians can have other titles, such as *library technical assistant* or *media aide*.

Library technicians direct library users to standard references, organize and maintain periodicals, prepare volumes for binding, handle interlibrary loan requests, prepare invoices, perform routine cataloguing and coding of library materials, retrieve information from computer databases, and supervise support staff.

Technicians also market library services. They participate in and help plan reader advisory programs, used-book sales, and outreach programs. They may also design posters, bulletin boards, or displays to inform patrons of library events and services.

As libraries increasingly use the Internet, virtual libraries, and other electronic resources, the duties of library technicians are changing. In fact, new technologies allow some technicians to assume responsibilities which were previously performed only by librarians. Technicians now catalog new acquisitions and oversee the circulation of all library materials. They often maintain, update, and help customize electronic databases. Technicians also may help to maintain the library's Web site and instruct patrons in how to use the library's computers.

The automation of recordkeeping has reduced the amount of clerical work performed by library technicians. Many libraries now offer self-service registration and circulation areas, where patrons can register for library cards and check out materials themselves. These technologies decrease the time library technicians spend recording and inputting records.

Some library technicians operate and maintain audiovisual equipment, such as projectors, tape and CD players, and DVD and videocassette players. They also assist users with microfilm or microfiche readers.

Library technicians in school libraries encourage and teach students to use the library and media center. They also help teachers obtain instructional materials, and they assist students with assignments.

Some technicians work in special libraries maintained by government agencies, corporations, law firms, advertising agencies, museums, professional societies, medical centers, or research laboratories. These technicians conduct literature searches, compile bibliographies, and prepare abstracts, usually on subjects of particular interest to the organization.

To extend library services to more patrons, many libraries operate bookmobiles, which are often run by library technicians. The technicians take bookmobiles—trucks stocked with books—to shopping centers, apartment complexes, schools, nursing homes, and other places. Technicians may operate a bookmobile alone or with other library employees.

Library technicians may process materials for circulation.

Library technicians who drive bookmobiles are responsible for answering patrons' questions, receiving and checking out books, collecting fines, maintaining the book collection, shelving materials, and occasionally operating audiovisual equipment to show slides or movies. Technicians who drive the bookmobile keep track of mileage and sometimes are responsible for maintenance of the vehicle and any equipment, such as photocopiers, in it. Many bookmobiles are equipped with personal computers linked to the main library Internet system, allowing patrons access to electronic resources as well as books.

Work environment. Library technicians who prepare library materials sit at desks or computer terminals for long periods and can develop headaches or eyestrain. They may lift and carry books, climb ladders to reach high stacks, and bend low to shelve books on bottom shelves. Technicians who work in bookmobiles may assist handicapped or elderly patrons to the bookmobile or shovel snow to ensure their safety. They may enter hospitals or nursing homes to deliver books.

Library technicians in school libraries work regular school hours. Those in public libraries and college and university libraries may work weekends, evenings, and some holidays. Library technicians in corporate libraries usually work normal business hours, although they often work overtime as well. The schedules of technicians who drive bookmobiles often depend on the size of the area being served.

Training, Other Qualifications, and Advancement

Training requirements for library technicians vary widely, ranging from a high school diploma to specialized postsecondary training. Some employers only hire individuals who have library work experience or college training related to libraries; others train inexperienced workers on the job.

Education and training. Most libraries prefer to hire technicians who have earned a certificate or associate degree, but some smaller libraries may hire individuals with only a high school diploma.

Many library technicians in public schools must meet the same requirements as teacher assistants. Those in Title 1 schools—schools that receive special funding because of the high percentage of poor students enrolled—must hold an associate or higher degree, have a minimum of 2 years of college, or pass a rigorous State or local exam.

Associate degree and certificate programs for library technicians include courses in liberal arts and subjects related to libraries. Students learn about library organization and operation and how to order, process, catalogue, locate, and circulate library materials and media. They often learn to use library automation systems. Libraries and associations offer continuing education courses to inform technicians of new developments in the field.

Other qualifications. Given the rapid spread of automation in libraries, computer skills are a necessity. Knowledge of databases, library automation systems, online library systems, online public access systems, and circulation systems is particularly valuable. Many bookmobile drivers must have a commercial driver's license.

Advancement. Library technicians usually advance by assuming added responsibilities. For example, technicians often start at the circulation desk, checking books in and out. After gaining experience, they may become responsible for storing and verifying information. As they advance, they may become involved in budget and personnel matters. Some library technicians advance to supervisory positions and are in charge of the day-to-day operation of their departments or, sometimes, a small library. Those who earn a graduate degree in library sciences can become librarians.

Employment

Library technicians held about 121,000 jobs in 2006; about half worked in local public libraries. Most of the rest worked in school or academic libraries, but some worked in special libraries in health care and legal settings. The Federal Government employs library technicians primarily at the U.S. Department of Defense and the U.S. Library of Congress.

Job Outlook

Employment of library technicians is expected to grow about as fast as average. Opportunities will be best for those with specialized postsecondary library training.

Employment change. The number of library technicians is expected to grow by 8 percent between 2006 and 2016, about as fast as the average for all occupations, as the increasing use of library automation creates more opportunities for these workers. Electronic information systems have simplified some tasks, enabling them to be performed by technicians rather than librarians, and spurring demand for technicians. However, job growth in educational institutions will be limited by slowing enrollment growth. In addition, public libraries often face budget pressures, which hold down overall growth in library services. However, this may result in the hiring of more library technicians because they are paid less than librarians and, thus, represent a lower-cost way to offer some library services. Employment should grow more rapidly in special libraries be-cause increasing numbers of professionals and other workers use those libraries.

Job prospects. In addition to job openings from employment growth, some openings will result from the need to replace library technicians who transfer to other occupations or leave the labor force. Opportunities will be best for library technicians with specialized postsecondary library training. Increased use of special libraries in businesses, hospitals, and other places should result in good job opportunities for library technicians in those settings.

Earnings

Median annual earnings of library technicians in May 2006 were $26,560. The middle 50 percent earned between $20,220 and $34,280. The lowest 10 percent earned less than $15,820, and the highest 10 percent earned more than $42,850. Median annual earnings in the industries employing the largest numbers of library technicians in 2006 were as follows:

Colleges, universities, and professional schools	$29,950
Junior colleges	29,470
Local government	25,610
Elementary and secondary schools	24,760
Other information services	23,420

Salaries of library technicians in the Federal Government averaged $43,238 in 2007.

Related Occupations

Library technicians perform organizational and administrative duties. Workers in other occupations with similar duties include library assistants, clerical; information and record clerks; and medical records and health information technicians. Technicians also support and assist librarians in much the same way as teacher assistants support teachers.

Sources of Additional Information

For general career information on library technicians, including information on training programs, contact:

➤ American Library Association, Office for Human Resource Development and Recruitment, 50 East Huron St., Chicago, IL 60611. Internet:

http://www.ala.org/ala/education/educationcareers.htm

➤ Council on Library/Media Technology, P.O. Box 42048, Mesa, AZ 85274-2048. Internet: **http://colt.ucr.edu**

Information concerning requirements and application procedures for positions in the Library of Congress can be obtained directly from:

➤ Human Resources Office, Library of Congress, 101 Independence Ave. SE., Washington, DC 20540-2231. Internet: **http://www.loc.gov/hr**

Projections data from the National Employment Matrix

Occupational Title	SOC Code	Employment, 2006	Projected employment, 2016	Change, 2006-2016	
				Number	Percent
Library technicians	25-4031	121,000	132,000	10,000	8

NOTE: Data in this table are rounded. See the discussion of the employment projections table in the *Handbook* introductory chapter on *Occupational Information Included in the Handbook*.

State library agencies can furnish information on requirements for technicians and general information about career prospects in the State. Several of these agencies maintain job hot lines that report openings for library technicians.

State departments of education can furnish information on requirements and job opportunities for school library technicians.

Teacher Assistants

(O*NET 25-9041.00)

Significant Points

- Almost 4 in 10 teacher assistants work part time.

- Educational requirements range from a high school diploma to some college training.

- Favorable job prospects are expected.

- Opportunities should be best for those with at least 2 years of formal postsecondary education, those with experience in helping special education students, or those who can speak a foreign language.

Nature of the Work

Teacher assistants provide instructional and clerical support for classroom teachers, allowing teachers more time for lesson planning and teaching. They support and assist children in learning class material using the teacher's lesson plans, providing students with individualized attention. Teacher assistants also supervise students in the cafeteria, schoolyard, and hallways, or on field trips; they record grades, set up equipment, and help prepare materials for instruction. Teacher assistants also are called teacher aides or instructional aides. Some assistants refer to themselves as paraeducators or paraprofessionals.

Some teacher assistants perform exclusively noninstructional or clerical tasks, such as monitoring nonacademic settings. Playground and lunchroom attendants are examples of such assistants. Most teacher assistants, however, perform a combination of instructional and clerical duties. They generally provide instructional reinforcement to children, under the direction and guidance of teachers. They work with students individually or in small groups—listening while students read, reviewing or reinforcing class lessons, or helping them find information for reports. At the secondary school level, teacher assistants often specialize in a certain subject, such as math or science. Teacher assistants often take charge of special projects and prepare equipment or exhibits, such as for a science demonstration. Some assistants work in computer laboratories, helping students to use computers and educational software programs.

In addition to instructing, assisting, and supervising students, teacher assistants may grade tests and papers, check homework, keep health and attendance records, do typing and filing, and duplicate materials. They also stock supplies, operate audiovisual equipment, and keep classroom equipment in order.

Many teacher assistants work extensively with special education students. As schools become more inclusive and integrate special education students into general education classrooms, teacher assistants in both general education and special education classrooms increasingly assist students with disabilities. They attend to the physical needs of students with disabilities, including feeding, teaching good grooming habits, or assisting students riding the schoolbus. They also provide personal attention to students with other special needs, such as those who speak English as a second language or those who need remedial education. Some work with young adults to help them obtain a job or to apply for community services to support them after schooling. Teacher assistants help assess a student's progress by observing performance and recording relevant data.

While the majority of teacher assistants work in primary and secondary educational settings, others work in preschools and other child care centers. Often one or two assistants will work with a lead teacher in order to better provide the individual attention that young children require. In addition to assisting in educational instruction, they also supervise the children at play and assist in feeding and other basic care activities.

Teacher assistants also work with infants and toddlers who have developmental delays or other disabilities. Under the guidance of a teacher or therapist, teacher assistants perform exercises or play games to help the child develop physically and behaviorally.

Teacher assistants work with small groups of students during reading lessons.

Work environment. Teacher assistants work in a variety of settings—including preschools, child care centers, and religious and community centers, where they work with young adults—but most work in classrooms in elementary, middle, and secondary schools. They also work outdoors supervising recess when weather allows, and they spend much of their time standing, walking, or kneeling.

Approximately 4 in 10 teacher assistants work part time. However, even among full-time workers, about 17 percent work less than 40 hours per week. Most assistants who provide educational instruction work the traditional 9-month to 10-month school year.

Seeing students develop and gain appreciation of the joy of learning can be very rewarding. However, working closely with students can be both physically and emotionally tiring. Teacher assistants who work with special education students often perform more strenuous tasks, including lifting, as they help students with their daily routine. Those who perform clerical work may tire of administrative duties, such as copying materials or entering data.

Training, Other Qualifications, and Advancement

Training requirements for teacher assistants vary by State or school district and range from a high school diploma to some college training. Increasingly, employers prefer applicants with some related college coursework.

Education and training. Many teacher assistants need only a high school diploma and on-the-job training. A college degree or related coursework in child development improves job opportunities, however. In fact, teacher assistants who work in Title 1 schools—those with a large proportion of students from low-income households—must have college training or proven academic skills. They face new Federal requirements as of 2006: assistants must hold a 2-year or higher degree, have a minimum of 2 years of college, or pass a rigorous State or local assessment.

A number of colleges offer associate degrees or certificate programs that either prepare graduates to work as teacher assistants or provide additional training for current teacher assistants.

All teacher assistants receive some on-the-job training. Teacher assistants need to become familiar with the school system and with the operation and rules of the school. Those who tutor and review lessons with students, must learn and understand the class materials and instructional methods used by the teacher. Teacher assistants also must know how to operate audiovisual equipment, keep records, and prepare instructional materials, as well as have adequate computer skills.

Other qualifications. Many schools require previous experience in working with children and a valid driver's license. Some schools may require the applicant to pass a background check. Teacher assistants should enjoy working with children from a wide range of cultural backgrounds and be able to handle classroom situations with fairness and patience. Teacher assistants also must demonstrate initiative and a willingness to follow a teacher's directions. They must have good writing skills and be able to communicate effectively with students and teachers. Teacher assistants who speak a second language, especially Spanish, are in great demand for communicating with growing numbers of students and parents whose primary language is not English.

Advancement. Advancement for teacher assistants—usually in the form of higher earnings or increased responsibility—comes primarily with experience or additional education. Some school districts provide time away from the job or tuition reimbursement so that teacher assistants can earn their bachelor's degrees and pursue licensed teaching positions. In return for tuition reimbursement, assistants are often required to teach for a certain length of time in the school district.

Employment

Teacher assistants held 1.3 million jobs in 2006. About 3 out of 4 worked for public and private elementary and secondary schools. Child care centers and religious organizations employed most of the rest.

Job Outlook

Many job openings are expected for teacher assistants due to turnover and average employment growth in this large occupation, resulting in favorable job prospects.

Employment change. Employment of teacher assistants is expected to grow by 10 percent between 2006 and 2016, about as fast as the average for all occupations. A large number of new jobs, 137,000, will arise over the 2006-16 period because of the size of the occupation. School enrollments are projected to increase slowly over the next decade, but faster growth is expected among special education students and students for whom English is a second language, and they will increase as a share of the total school-age population. These students are the ones who most need teacher assistants.

Legislation requires students with disabilities and non-native English speakers to receive an education equal to that of other students, so it will continue to generate jobs for teacher assistants, who help to accommodate these students' special needs. Children with special needs require much personal attention, and teachers rely heavily on teacher assistants to provide much of that attention. An increasing number of after-school programs and summer programs also will create new opportunities for teacher assistants.

The greater focus on school quality and accountability in recent years also is likely to lead to an increased demand for teacher assistants. Growing numbers of teacher assistants may be needed to help teachers prepare students for standardized testing and to provide extra assistance to students who perform

Projections data from the National Employment Matrix

Occupational Title	SOC Code	Employment, 2006	Projected employment, 2016	Change, 2006-2016	
				Number	Percent
Teacher assistants..	25-9041	1,312,000	1,449,000	137,000	10

NOTE: Data in this table are rounded. See the discussion of the employment projections table in the *Handbook* introductory chapter on *Occupational Information Included in the Handbook.*

poorly on these tests. Job growth of assistants may be moderated, however, if schools are encouraged to hire more full-fledged teachers for instructional purposes.

Job prospects. Favorable job prospects are expected. Opportunities for teacher assistant jobs should be best for those with at least 2 years of formal postsecondary education, those with experience in helping special education students, or those who can speak a foreign language. Demand is expected to vary by region of the country. Regions in which the population and school enrollments are expected to grow faster, such as many communities in the South and West, should have rapid growth in the demand for teacher assistants.

In addition to job openings stemming from employment growth, numerous openings will arise as assistants leave their jobs and must be replaced. Many assistant jobs require limited formal education and offer relatively low pay so many workers transfer to other occupations or leave the labor force to assume family responsibilities, to return to school, or for other reasons.

Earnings

Median annual earnings of teacher assistants in May 2006 were $20,740. The middle 50 percent earned between $16,430 and $26,160. The lowest 10 percent earned less than $13,910, and the highest 10 percent earned more than $31,610.

Full-time workers usually receive health coverage and other benefits. Teacher assistants who work part time ordinarily do not receive benefits. In 2006, about 3 out of 10 teacher assistants belonged to unions—mainly the American Federation of Teachers and the National Education Association—which bargain with school systems over wages, hours, and the terms and conditions of employment.

Related Occupations

Teacher assistants who instruct children have duties similar to those of preschool, kindergarten, elementary, middle, and secondary school teachers, as well as special education teachers. However, teacher assistants do not have the same level of responsibility or training. The support activities of teacher assistants and their educational backgrounds are similar to those of childcare workers, library technicians, and library assistants. Teacher assistants who work with children with disabilities perform many of the same functions as occupational therapist assistants and aides.

Sources of Additional Information

For information on teacher assistants, including training and certification, contact:

➤ American Federation of Teachers, Paraprofessional and School Related Personnel Division, 555 New Jersey Ave. NW., Washington, DC 20001.
Internet: **http://www.aft.org/psrp/index.html**
➤ National Education Association, Educational Support Personnel Division, 1201 16th Street, NW., Washington, DC 20036. Internet: **http://www.nea.org/esphome**
➤ National Resource Center for Paraprofessionals, 6526 Old Main Hill, Utah State University, Logan, UT 84322.
Internet: **http://www.nrcpara.org**

Human resource departments of school systems, school administrators, and State departments of education also can provide details about employment opportunities and required qualifications for teacher assistant jobs.

Teachers—Adult Literacy and Remedial Education

(O*NET 25-3011.00)

Significant Points

- Many adult literacy and remedial education teachers work part time and receive no benefits; unpaid volunteers also teach these subjects.

- Most programs require teachers to have at least a bachelor's degree; a public school teaching license is required for publicly run programs in some States.

- Job opportunities are expected to be favorable, particularly for teachers of English to speakers of other languages.

Nature of the Work

Adult literacy and remedial education teachers instruct adults and out-of-school youths in reading, writing, speaking English, and performing elementary mathematical calculations—basic skills that equip them to solve problems well enough to become active participants in our society, to hold a job, and to further their education. The instruction provided by these teachers can be divided into three principle categories: *remedial* or *adult basic education (ABE)* is geared toward adults whose skills are either at or below an eighth-grade level; *adult secondary education (ASE)* is geared towards students who wish to obtain their General Educational Development (GED) certificate or other high school equivalency credential; and *English literacy* instruction for adults with limited proficiency in English. For the most part, students in these adult education classes traditionally have been those who did not graduate from high school or who passed through school without acquiring the knowledge needed to meet their education goals or to participate fully in today's high-skill society. Increasingly, however, students in these classes are immigrants or other people whose native language is not English. Educators who work with adult English-language learners are usually called *teachers of English as a second language (ESL)* or *teachers of English to speakers of other languages (ESOL)*.

Remedial education teachers, more commonly called adult basic education teachers, teach basic academic courses in mathematics, languages, history, reading, writing, science, and other areas, using instructional methods geared toward adult learning. They teach these subjects to students 16 years of age and older who demonstrate the need to increase their skills in one or more of the subject areas mentioned. Classes are taught to appeal to a variety of learning styles and usually include large-group, small-group, and one-on-one instruction. Because the students often are at different proficiency levels for different subjects, adult basic education teachers must make individual assessments of each student's abilities beforehand. In many programs, the assessment is used to develop an individualized education plan for each student. Teachers are required to evaluate students periodically to determine their progress and potential for advancement to the next level.

Teachers in remedial or adult basic education may have to assist students in acquiring effective study skills and the self-confidence they need to reenter an academic environment. Teachers also may encounter students with learning or physical disabilities that require additional expertise. Teachers should possess an understanding of how to help these students achieve their goals, but they also may need to have the knowledge to detect challenges their students may have and provide them with access to a broader system of additional services that are required to address their challenges.

For students who wish to get a GED credential in order to get a job or qualify for postsecondary education, adult secondary education, or GED, teachers provide help in acquiring the necessary knowledge and skills to pass the test. Earning a GED requires passing a series of five tests in reading, writing, mathematics, science, and social studies; most teachers instruct students in all subject areas. To help students pass the tests and succeed later in life, teachers not only provide subject matter instruction but also focus on improving the communication, information-processing, problem-solving, and critical-thinking skills necessary for further education and successful careers.

ESOL teachers help adults to speak, listen, read, and write in English, often in the context of real-life situations to promote learning. More advanced students may concentrate on writing and conversational skills or focus on learning more academic or job-related communication skills. ESOL teachers work with adults from a wide range of backgrounds. They must be prepared to work with students of all ages and from many different language backgrounds. Some students may have extensive educational experiences in their native language, while others may have very little. As a result, some students may progress faster than others, so teachers must be able to tailor their instruction to the needs and abilities of their students. Because the teacher and students often do not share a common language, creativity is an important part of fostering communication in the classroom and achieving learning goals.

All adult literacy and remedial teachers must prepare lessons beforehand, do any related paperwork, and stay current in their fields. Attendance for students is mostly voluntary and course work is rarely graded. Because computers are increasingly being used to supplement instruction in basic skills and in teaching ESOL, many teachers also must learn the latest applications for computers in the classroom.

Work environment. Because many adult literacy and remedial education teachers work with adult students, they do not encounter some of the behavioral or social problems sometimes found with younger students. Adults attend by choice, are highly motivated, and bring years of experience to the classroom—attributes that can make teaching these students rewarding and satisfying. However, many adult education programs are located in cramped facilities that lack modern amenities, which can be frustrating for teachers.

A large number of these teachers work part time. Some have several part-time teaching assignments or work full time in addition to their part-time teaching job. Classes for adults are held

Adult literacy teachers help students learn by using examples from everyday life.

on days and at times that best accommodate students who may have a job or family responsibilities, so evening and weekend work is common.

Training, Other Qualifications, and Advancement

Nearly all programs require teachers to have at least a bachelor's degree, but some require a master's degree in adult education or ESOL instruction. Some States require teachers to have a public school teacher license or a license specifically for adult education teachers.

Education and training. Adult education teachers need at least a bachelor's degree, although some programs prefer or require a master's degree. Programs may also prefer to hire those with teaching experience, especially with adults. Many colleges and universities offer master's degrees or graduate certificates in adult education, although some adult education programs offer classes or workshops themselves on topics relevant for their teachers. These include classes on teaching adults, using technology to teach, working with learners from a variety of cultures, and teaching adults with learning disabilities. ESOL teachers also should have courses or training in second-language acquisition theory and linguistics. In addition, knowledge of the citizenship and naturalization process may be useful. Knowledge of a second language is not necessary to teach ESOL students, but can be helpful in understanding the students' perspectives. GED teachers should know what is required to pass the GED and be able to instruct students in the subject matter.

Professional development among adult education and literacy teachers varies widely. Both part-time and full-time teachers are expected to participate in ongoing professional development activities in order to keep current on new developments in the field and to enhance skills already acquired. Each State's professional development system reflects the unique needs and organizational structure of that State. Attendance by teachers at professional development workshops and other activities is often outlined in State or local policy. Some teachers are able to access professional development activities through alternative delivery systems such as the Internet or distance learning.

Licensure. Most States require teachers in these programs to have some form of license if they are employed in a State or local government-run program. Some States have specific licenses for adult education teachers, while others require a public school teacher license. Requirements for a license typically consist of a bachelor's degree and completion of an approved teacher training program.

Other qualifications. Adult education and literacy teachers must have the ability to work with students who come from a variety of cultural, educational, and economic backgrounds. They must be understanding and respectful of their students' circumstances and be familiar with their concerns. All teachers, both paid and volunteer, should be able to communicate well and motivate their students.

Advancement. Opportunities for advancement for adult education and literacy teachers again vary from State to State and program to program. Some part-time teachers are able to move into full-time teaching positions or program administrator positions, such as coordinator or director, when such vacancies occur. Others may decide to use their classroom experience to move into policy work at a nonprofit organization or with the local, State, or Federal Government or to perform research.

Employment

Teachers of adult literacy and remedial education held about 76,000 jobs in 2006. Many additional teachers worked as unpaid volunteers. Many of the jobs are federally funded, with additional funds coming from State and local governments. The overwhelming majority of these teachers are employed by the educational services industry, primarily in local school districts, adult learning centers, and community colleges.

Job Outlook

Employment is expected to grow faster than the average for all occupations, and a large number of job openings is expected due to the need to replace people who leave the occupation or retire. Job opportunities are expected to be favorable, particularly for teachers of English to speakers of other languages.

Employment change. Employment of adult literacy and remedial education teachers is expected to grow by 14 percent through 2016, faster than the average for all occupations. As employers increasingly require a more literate workforce, workers' demand for adult literacy, basic education, and secondary education classes is expected to grow. Significant employment growth is anticipated especially for ESOL teachers, who will be needed by the increasing number of immigrants and other residents living in this country who need to learn or improve their English skills. In addition, greater proportions of these groups are expected to take ESOL classes.

The demand for adult literacy and basic and secondary education often fluctuates with the economy. When the economy is good and workers are hard to find, employers may relax their standards and hire workers without a degree or GED or good proficiency in English. As the economy softens, employers can be more selective, and more students may find that they need additional education to get a job. In addition, adult education classes often are subject to changes in funding levels, which can cause the number of teaching jobs to fluctuate from year to year. In particular, budget pressures may limit Federal funding of adult education, which may cause programs to rely more on volunteers if other organizations and governments do not make up the difference. Other factors such as immigration policies and the relative prosperity of the United States compared with other countries also may have an impact on the number of immigrants entering this country and, consequently, on the demand for ESOL teachers.

Job prospects. Job prospects should be favorable as high turnover of part time jobs in this occupation creates many openings. Opportunities will be best for ESOL teachers, particularly in States that have large populations of residents who have limited English skills—such as California, Florida, Texas, and New York. However, many other parts of the Nation have begun to attract large numbers of immigrants, making good opportunities in this field widely available.

Earnings

Median hourly earnings of adult literacy and remedial education teachers were $43,910 in May 2006. The middle 50 percent earned between $32,660 and $57,310. The lowest 10 percent earned less than $24,610, and the highest 10 percent earned more than $75,680. Part-time adult literacy and remedial education instructors are usually paid by the hour or for each class that they teach, and receive few or no benefits. Full-time teachers are generally paid a salary and receive health insurance and other benefits if they work for a school system or government.

Projections data from the National Employment Matrix

Occupational Title	SOC Code	Employment, 2006	Projected employment, 2016	Change, 2006-2016	
				Number	Percent
Adult literacy, remedial education, and GED teachers and instructors..	25-3011	76,000	87,000	11,000	14

NOTE: Data in this table are rounded. See the discussion of the employment projections table in the *Handbook* introductory chapter on *Occupational Information Included in the Handbook*.

Related Occupations

The work of adult literacy and remedial education teachers is closely related to that of other types of teachers, especially preschool, kindergarten, elementary school, middle school, and secondary school teachers. In addition, adult literacy and basic and secondary education teachers require a wide variety of skills and aptitudes. Not only must they be able to teach and motivate students (including, at times, those with learning disabilities), but they also must often take on roles as advisers and mentors. Workers in other occupations that require these aptitudes include special-education teachers, counselors, and social workers. Other occupations that involve working with speakers of languages other than English include interpreters and translators.

Sources of Additional Information

Information on adult literacy, basic and secondary education programs, and teacher certification requirements is available from State departments of education, local school districts, and literacy resource centers. Information also may be obtained through local religious and charitable organizations.

For information on adult education and family literacy programs, contact:

➤ The U.S. Department of Education, Office of Vocational and Adult Education, Potomac Center Plaza, 400 Maryland Ave. SW., Washington, DC 20202.
Internet:

http://www.ed.gov/about/offices/list/ovae/index.html

For information on teaching English as a second language, contact:

➤ The Center for Adult English Language Acquisition, 4646 40th St.NW., Washington, DC 20016.
Internet: **http://www.cal.org/caela**

Teachers—Postsecondary

(O*NET 25-1011.00, 25-1021.00, 25-1022.00, 25-1031.00, 25-1032.00, 25-1041.00, 25-1042.00, 25-1043.00, 25-1051.00, 25-1052.00, 25-1053.00, 25-1054.00, 25-1061.00, 25-1062.00, 25-1063.00, 25-1064.00, 25-1065.00, 25-1066.00, 25-1067.00, 25-1069.99, 25-1071.00, 25-1072.00, 25-1081.00, 25-1082.00, 25-1111.00, 25-1112.00, 25-1113.00, 25-1121.00, 25-1122.00, 25-1123.00, 25-1124.00, 25-1125.00, 25-1126.00, 25-1191.00, 25-1192.00, 25-1193.00, 25-1194.00, 25-1199.99)

Significant Points

- Educational qualifications range from expertise in a particular field to a Ph.D., depending on the subject taught and the type of educational institution.

- Job opportunities are expected to be very good, but many new openings will be for part-time or non-tenure-track positions.

- Prospects will be better and earnings higher in rapidly growing fields that offer many nonacademic career options.

Nature of the Work

Postsecondary teachers instruct students in a wide variety of academic and vocational subjects beyond the high school level. Most of theses students are working toward a degree, but many others are studying for a certificate or certification to improve their knowledge or career skills. Postsecondary teachers include college and university faculty, postsecondary career and technical education teachers, and graduate teaching assistants. Teaching in any venue involves forming a lesson plan, presenting material to students, responding to students learning needs, and evaluating student progress. In addition to instruction, postsecondary teachers, particularly those at 4-year colleges and universities, also perform a significant amount of research in the subject they teach. They must also keep up with new developments in their field and may consult with government, business, nonprofit, and community organizations.

College and university faculty make up the majority of postsecondary teachers. Faculty usually are organized into departments or divisions, based on academic subject or field. They typically teach several different related courses in their subject—algebra, calculus, and statistics, for example. They may instruct undergraduate or graduate students, or both. College and university faculty may give lectures to several hundred students in large halls, lead small seminars, or supervise students in laboratories. They prepare lectures, exercises, and laboratory experiments; grade exams and papers; and advise and work with students individually. In universities, they also supervise graduate students' teaching and research. College faculty work with an increasingly varied student population made up of growing shares of part-time, older, and culturally and racially diverse students.

Faculty keep up with developments in their field by reading current literature, talking with colleagues, and participating in professional conferences. They also are encouraged to do their own research to expand knowledge in their field by performing experiments; collecting and analyzing data; or examining original documents, literature, and other source material. They publish their findings in scholarly journals, books, and electronic media.

Most postsecondary teachers extensively use computer technology, including the Internet, e-mail, and software programs. They may use computers in the classroom as teaching aids and may post course content, class notes, class schedules, and other information on the Internet. The use of e-mail, chat rooms, and other techniques has greatly improved communications between students and teachers and among students.

Some instructors use the Internet to teach courses to students at remote sites. These so-called "distance learning" courses are an increasingly popular option for students who work while attending school. Faculty who teach these courses must be able to adapt existing courses to make them successful online or design a new course that takes advantage of the format.

Most full-time faculty members serve on academic or administrative committees that deal with the policies of their institution, departmental matters, academic issues, curricula, budgets, equipment purchases, and hiring. Some work with student and community organizations. Department chairpersons are faculty members who usually teach some courses but have heavier administrative responsibilities.

The proportion of time spent on research, teaching, administrative, and other duties varies by individual circumstance and type of institution. Faculty members at universities normally spend a significant part of their time doing research; those in 4-year colleges, somewhat less; and those in 2-year colleges, relatively little. The teaching load, however, often is heavier in 2-year colleges and somewhat lighter at 4-year institutions. At all types of institutions, full professors—those that have reached the highest level in their field—usually spend a larger portion of their time conducting research than do assistant professors, instructors, and lecturers.

In addition to traditional 2- and 4-year institutions, an increasing number of postsecondary educators work in alternative schools or in programs aimed at providing career-related education for working adults. Courses are usually offered online or on nights and weekends. Instructors at these programs generally work part time and are only responsible for teaching, with little to no administrative and research responsibilities.

Postsecondary vocational education teachers, also known as *postsecondary career and technical education teachers*, provide instruction for occupations that require specialized training but not usually a 4-year degree. They may teach classes in welding, dental hygienics, x-ray technician techniques, auto mechanics, or cosmetology, for example. Classes often are taught in an industrial or laboratory setting where students are provided hands-on experience. For example, welding instructors show students various welding techniques and essential safety practices, watch them use tools and equipment, and have them repeat procedures until they meet the specific standards required by the trade. Increasingly, career and technical education teachers are integrating academic and vocational curriculums so that students obtain a variety of skills that can be applied on the job. In addition, career and technical education teachers at community colleges and career and technical schools also often play a key role in students' transition from school to work by helping to establish internship programs for students and by facilitating contact between students and prospective employers.

Graduate teaching assistants, often referred to as *graduate TAs*, assist faculty, department chairs, or other professional staff at colleges and universities by performing teaching or teaching-related duties. In addition to their work responsibilities, assistants have their own school commitments, as they are also students who are working towards earning a graduate degree, such as a Ph.D. Some teaching assistants have full responsibility for teaching a course—usually one that is introductory—which can include preparation of lectures and exams, and assigning final grades to students. Others help faculty members, which may include doing a variety of tasks such as grading papers, monitoring exams, holding office hours or help-sessions for students, conducting laboratory sessions, or administering quizzes to the class. Teaching assistants generally meet initially with the faculty member whom they are going to assist to determine exactly what is expected of them, as each faculty member may have his or her own needs. For example, some faculty members prefer assistants to sit in on classes, but others assign them other tasks

to do during class time. Graduate teaching assistants may work one-on-one with a faculty member or, for large classes, they may be one of several assistants.

Work environment. Many postsecondary teachers find the environment intellectually stimulating and rewarding because they are surrounded by others who enjoy their subject. The ability to share their expertise with others is also appealing to many.

Most postsecondary teachers have flexible schedules. They must be present for classes, usually 12 to 16 hours per week, and for faculty and committee meetings. Most establish regular office hours for student consultations, usually 3 to 6 hours per week. Otherwise, teachers are free to decide when and where they will work, and how much time to devote to course preparation, grading, study, research, graduate student supervision, and other activities.

Classes are typically scheduled during weekdays, although some occur at night or during the weekend. This is particularly true for teachers at 2-year community colleges or institutions with large enrollments of older students who have full-time jobs or family responsibilities. Most colleges and universities require teachers to work 9 months of the year, which allows them time during the summer and school holidays to teach ad-

Postsecondary teachers conduct research and publish articles and papers, in addition to instructing students.

ditional courses, do research, travel, or pursue nonacademic interests.

About 30 percent of college and university faculty worked part time in 2006. Some part-timers, known as "adjunct faculty," have primary jobs outside of academia—in government, private industry, or nonprofit research—and teach "on the side." Others may have multiple part-time teaching positions at different institutions. Most graduate teaching assistants work part time while working on their graduate studies. The number of hours that they work may vary, depending on their assignments.

University faculty may experience a conflict between their responsibilities to teach students and the pressure to do research and publish their findings. This may be a particular problem for young faculty seeking advancement in 4-year research universities. Also, recent cutbacks in support workers and the hiring of more part-time faculty have put a greater administrative burden on full-time faculty. Requirements to teach online classes also have added greatly to the workloads of postsecondary teachers. Many find that developing the courses to put online is very time-consuming, especially when learning how to operate the technology and answering large amounts of e-mail.

Graduate TAs usually have flexibility in their work schedules like college and university faculty, but they also must spend a considerable amount of time pursuing their own academic coursework and studies. Work may be stressful, particularly when assistants are given full responsibility for teaching a class. However, these types of positions allow graduate students the opportunity to gain valuable teaching experience, which is especially helpful for those who seek to become college faculty members after completing their degree.

Training, Other Qualifications, and Advancement

The education and training required of postsecondary teachers varies widely, depending on the subject taught and educational institution employing them. Educational requirements for teachers are generally highest at research universities, where a Ph.D. is the most commonly held degree; at career and technical institutes, experience and expertise in a related occupation is the principal qualification.

Education and training. Four-year colleges and universities usually require candidates for full-time, tenure-track positions, to hold a doctoral degree. However, they may hire master's degree holders or doctoral candidates for certain disciplines, such as the arts, or for part-time and temporary jobs.

Doctoral programs take an average of 6 years of full-time study beyond the bachelor's degree; this includes time spent completing a master's degree and a dissertation. Some programs, such as those in the humanities, may take longer to complete; others, such as those in engineering, usually are shorter. Candidates specialize in a subfield of a discipline, for example, organic chemistry, counseling psychology, or European history, and also take courses covering the entire discipline. Programs typically include 20 or more increasingly specialized courses and seminars plus comprehensive examinations on all major areas of the field. Candidates also must complete a dissertation—a written report on original research in the candidate's major field of study. The dissertation sets forth an original hypothesis or proposes a model and tests it. Students in the natural sciences and engineering usually do laboratory work; in the humanities, they study original documents and other published material. The dissertation is done under the guidance of one or more faculty advisors and usually takes 1 or 2 years of full-time work.

In 2-year colleges, master's degree holders fill most full-time teaching positions. However, in certain fields where there may be more applicants than available jobs, institutions can be more selective in their hiring practices. In these fields, master's degree holders may be passed over in favor of candidates holding Ph.Ds. Many 2-year institutions increasingly prefer job applicants to have some teaching experience or experience with distance learning. Preference also may be given to those holding dual master's degrees, especially at smaller institutions, because they can teach more subjects.

Training requirements for postsecondary career and technical education teachers vary by State and subject. In general, career and technical education teachers need a bachelor's or graduate degree, plus at least 3 years of work experience in their field. In some fields, a license or certificate that demonstrates one's qualifications may be all that is required. These teachers may need to update their skills through continuing education to maintain certification. They must also maintain ongoing dialogue with businesses to determine the skills most needed in the current workplace.

Other qualifications. Postsecondary teachers should communicate and relate well with students, enjoy working with them, and be able to motivate them. They should have inquiring and analytical minds, and a strong desire to pursue and disseminate knowledge. Additionally, they must be self-motivated and able to work in an environment in which they receive little direct supervision.

Obtaining a position as a graduate teaching assistant is a good way to gain college teaching experience. To qualify, candidates must be enrolled in a graduate school program. In addition, some colleges and universities require teaching assistants to attend classes or take some training prior to being given responsibility for a course.

Although graduate teaching assistants usually work at the institution and in the department where they are earning their degree, teaching or internship positions for graduate students at institutions that do not grant a graduate degree have become more common in recent years. For example, a program called Preparing Future Faculty, administered by the Association of American Colleges and Universities and the Council of Graduate Schools, has led to the creation of many programs that are now independent. These programs offer graduate students at research universities the opportunity to work as teaching assistants at other types of institutions, such as liberal arts or community colleges. Working with a mentor, the graduate students teach classes and learn how to improve their teaching techniques. They may attend faculty and committee meetings, develop a curriculum, and learn how to balance the teaching, research, and administrative roles that faculty play. These programs provide valuable learning opportunities for graduate students interested in teaching at the postsecondary level, and also help to make these students aware of the differences among the various types of institutions at which they may someday work.

Some degree holders, particularly those who studied in the natural sciences, spend additional years after earning their graduate degree on postdoctoral research and study before taking a faculty position. Some Ph.D.s are able to extend postdoctoral appointments, or take new ones, if they are unable to find a faculty job. Most of these appointments offer a nominal salary.

Advancement. For faculty, a major goal in the traditional academic career is attaining tenure. The process of attaining tenure can take approximately 7 years with faculty moving up the ranks in tenure-track positions as they meet specific criteria. The ranks are instructor, assistant professor, associate professor, and professor. Colleges and universities usually hire new tenure-track faculty as instructors or assistant professors under term contracts. At the end of the period, their record of teaching, research, and overall contribution to the institution is reviewed and tenure may be granted if the review is favorable. Those denied tenure usually must leave the institution. Tenured professors cannot be fired without just cause and due process. Tenure protects the faculty's academic freedom—the ability to teach and conduct research without fear of being fired for advocating controversial or unpopular ideas. It also gives both faculty and institutions the stability needed for effective research and teaching, and provides financial security for faculty. Some institutions have adopted post-tenure review policies to encourage ongoing evaluation of tenured faculty.

The number of tenure-track positions is declining as institutions seek flexibility in dealing with financial matters and changing student interests. Institutions rely more heavily on limited term contracts and part-time, or adjunct, faculty, thus shrinking the total pool of tenured faculty. Limited-term contracts—typically 2- to 5 years, may be terminated or extended when they expire but generally do not lead to the granting of tenure. In addition, some institutions have limited the percentage of faculty who can be tenured.

For tenured postsecondary teachers, further advancement involves a move into administrative and managerial positions, such as departmental chairperson, dean, and president. At 4-year institutions, such advancement requires a doctoral degree. At 2-year colleges, a doctorate is helpful but not usually required, except for advancement to some top administrative positions. (Deans and departmental chairpersons are covered in the *Handbook* statement on education administrators, while college presidents are included in the *Handbook* statement on top executives.)

Employment

Postsecondary teachers held nearly 1.7 million jobs in 2006. Most were employed in 4-year colleges and universities and in 2-year community colleges. Other postsecondary teachers are employed by schools and institutes that specialize in training people in a specific field, such as technology centers or culinary schools, or work for businesses that provide professional development courses to employees of companies. Some career and technical education teachers work for State and local governments and job training facilities. The following tabulation shows postsecondary teaching jobs in specialties having 20,000 or more jobs in 2006:

Health specialties teachers 145,000
Graduate teaching assistants 144,000
Vocational education teachers 119,000
Art, drama, and music teachers 88,000
Business teachers 82,000
English language and literature teachers 72,000
Education teachers 67,000
Biological science teachers 65,000
Mathematical science teachers 54,000
Nursing instructors and teachers 46,000
Computer science teachers 44,000
Engineering teachers 40,000
Psychology teachers 37,000
Foreign language and literature teachers 30,000
Communications teachers 29,000
History teachers 26,000
Philosophy and religion teachers 25,000
Chemistry teachers 24,000
Recreation and fitness studies teachers 20,000

Job Outlook

Employment of postsecondary teachers is expected to grow much faster than average as student enrollments continue to increase. However, a significant proportion of these new jobs will be part-time and non-tenure-track positions. Retirements of current postsecondary teachers should create numerous openings for all types of postsecondary teachers, so job opportunities are generally expected to be very good, although they will vary by the subject taught and the type of educational institution.

Employment change. Postsecondary teachers are expected to grow by 23 percent between 2006 and 2016, much faster than the average for all occupations. Because of the size of this occupation and its much faster than average growth rate, postsecondary teachers will account for 382,000 new jobs, which is among the largest number of new jobs for an occupation. Projected growth in the occupation will be primarily due to increases in college and university enrollment over the next decade. This enrollment growth stems mainly from the expected increase in the population of 18- to 24-year-olds, who constitute the majority of students at postsecondary institutions, and from

Projections data from the National Employment Matrix

Occupational Title	SOC Code	Employment, 2006	Projected employment, 2016	Change, 2006-2016	
				Number	Percent
Postsecondary teachers	25-1000	1,672,000	2,054,000	382,000	23

NOTE: Data in this table are rounded. See the discussion of the employment projections table in the *Handbook* introductory chapter on *Occupational Information Included in the Handbook.*

the increasing number of high school graduates who choose to attend these institutions. Adults returning to college to enhance their career prospects or to update their skills also will continue to create new opportunities for postsecondary teachers, particularly at community colleges and for-profit institutions that cater to working adults. However, many postsecondary educational institutions receive a significant portion of their funding from State and local governments, so expansion of public higher education will be limited by State and local budgets.

Job prospects. A significant number of openings in this occupation will be created by growth in enrollments and the need to replace the large numbers of postsecondary teachers who are likely to retire over the next decade. Many postsecondary teachers were hired in the late 1960s and the 1970s to teach members of the baby boom generation, and they are expected to retire in growing numbers in the years ahead. As a result, Ph.D. recipients seeking jobs as postsecondary teachers will experience favorable job prospects over the next decade.

Although competition will remain tight for tenure-track positions at 4-year colleges and universities, there will be available a considerable number of part-time or renewable, term appointments at these institutions and at community colleges. Opportunities for master's degree holders are also expected to be favorable because there will be considerable growth at community colleges, career education programs, and other institutions that employ them.

Opportunities for graduate teaching assistants are expected to be very good, reflecting expectations of higher undergraduate enrollments coupled with more modest increases in graduate student enrollment. Constituting almost 9 percent of all postsecondary teachers, graduate teaching assistants play an integral role in the postsecondary education system, and they are expected to continue to do so in the future.

Opportunities will also be excellent for postsecondary vocational teachers due to an increased emphasis on career and technical education at the postsecondary level. Job growth, combined with a large number of expected retirements, will result in many job openings for these workers. Prospects will be best for instructors in specialties that pay well outside of the teaching field, such as the construction trades and manufacturing technology.

One of the main reasons why students attend postsecondary institutions is to prepare themselves for careers, so the best job prospects for postsecondary teachers are likely to be in rapidly growing fields that offer many nonacademic career options. These will include fields such as business, nursing and other health specialties, and biological sciences. Community colleges and other institutions offering career and technical education have been among the most rapidly growing, and these institutions are expected to offer some of the best opportunities for postsecondary teachers.

Earnings

Median annual earnings of all postsecondary teachers in 2006 were $56,120. The middle 50 percent earned between $39,610 and $80,390. The lowest 10 percent earned less than $27,590, and the highest 10 percent earned more than $113,450.

Earnings for college faculty vary according to rank and type of institution, geographic area, and field. According to a 2006-07 survey by the American Association of University Professors, salaries for full-time faculty averaged $73,207. By rank, the average was $98,974 for professors, $69,911 for associate professors, $58,662 for assistant professors, $42,609 for instructors, and $48,289 for lecturers. Faculty in 4-year institutions earn higher salaries, on average, than do those in 2-year schools. In 2006-07, faculty salaries averaged $84,249 in private independent institutions, $71,362 in public institutions, and $66,118 in religiously affiliated private colleges and universities. In fields with high-paying nonacademic alternatives—medicine, law, engineering, and business, among others—earnings exceed these averages. In others fields, such as the humanities and education, earnings are lower. Earnings for postsecondary career and technical education teachers vary widely by subject, academic credentials, experience, and region of the country.

Many faculty members have significant earnings in addition to their base salary from consulting, teaching additional courses, research, writing for publication, or other employment. In addition, many college and university faculty enjoy unique benefits, including access to campus facilities, tuition waivers for dependents, housing and travel allowances, and paid leave for sabbaticals. Part-time faculty and instructors usually have fewer benefits than full-time faculty.

Related Occupations

Postsecondary teaching requires the ability to communicate ideas well, motivate students, and be creative. Workers in other occupations that require these skills are preschool, kindergarten, elementary, middle, and secondary school teachers; education administrators; librarians; counselors; writers and editors; public relations specialists; and management analysts. Faculty research activities often are similar to those of life, physical, and social scientists, as well as to those of managers and administrators in industry, government, and nonprofit research organizations.

Sources of Additional Information

Professional societies related to a field of study often provide information on academic and nonacademic employment opportunities. Names and addresses of many of these societies appear in statements elsewhere in the *Handbook*.

Special publications on higher education, such as The Chronicle of Higher Education, list specific employment opportunities for faculty. These publications are available in libraries.

For information on the Preparing Future Faculty program, contact:

➤ Council of Graduate Schools, One Dupont Circle, NW., Suite 430, Washington, DC 20036-1173. Internet: **http://www.preparing-faculty.org**

For information on postsecondary career and technical education teaching positions, contact State departments of career and technical education. General information on adult and career and technical education is available from:

➤ Association for Career and Technical Education, 1410 King St., Alexandria, VA 22314. Internet: **http://www.acteonline.org**

Teachers—Preschool, Kindergarten, Elementary, Middle, and Secondary

(O*NET 25-2011.00, 25-2012.00, 25-2021.00, 25-2022.00, 25-2023.00, 25-2031.00, 25-2032.00)

Significant Points

- Public school teachers must be licensed, which typically requires a bachelor's degree and completion of an approved teacher education program.

- Many States offer alternative licensing programs to attract people into teaching, especially for hard-to-fill positions.

- Job prospects should be favorable; opportunities will vary by geographic area and subject taught.

Nature of the Work

Teachers play an important role in fostering the intellectual and social development of children during their formative years. The education that teachers impart plays a key role in determining the future prospects of their students. Whether in preschools or high schools or in private or public schools, teachers provide the tools and the environment for their students to develop into responsible adults.

Teachers act as facilitators or coaches, using classroom presentations or individual instruction to help students learn and apply concepts in subjects such as science, mathematics, or English. They plan, evaluate, and assign lessons; prepare, administer, and grade tests; listen to oral presentations; and maintain classroom discipline. Teachers observe and evaluate a student's performance and potential and increasingly are asked to use new assessment methods. For example, teachers may examine a portfolio of a student's artwork or writing in order to judge the student's overall progress. They then can provide additional assistance in areas in which a student needs help. Teachers also grade papers, prepare report cards, and meet with parents and school staff to discuss a student's academic progress or personal problems.

Many teachers use a "hands-on" approach that uses "props" or "manipulatives" to help children understand abstract concepts, solve problems, and develop critical thought processes. For example, they teach the concepts of numbers or of addition and subtraction by playing board games. As the children get older, teachers use more sophisticated materials, such as science apparatus, cameras, or computers. They also encourage collaboration in solving problems by having students work in groups to discuss and solve problems together. To be prepared for success later in life, students must be able to interact with others, adapt to new technology, and think through problems logically.

Preschool, kindergarten, and elementary school teachers play a vital role in the development of children. What children learn and experience during their early years can shape their views of themselves and the world and can affect their later success or failure in school, work, and their personal lives. Pre-

school, kindergarten, and elementary school teachers introduce children to mathematics, language, science, and social studies. They use games, music, artwork, films, books, computers, and other tools to teach basic skills.

Preschool children learn mainly through play and interactive activities. *Preschool teachers* capitalize on children's play to further language and vocabulary development (using storytelling, rhyming games, and acting games), improve social skills (having the children work together to build a neighborhood in a sandbox), and introduce scientific and mathematical concepts (showing the children how to balance and count blocks when building a bridge or how to mix colors when painting). Thus, a less structured approach, including small-group lessons, one-on-one instruction, and learning through creative activities such as art, dance, and music, is adopted to teach preschool children. Play and hands-on teaching also are used by *kindergarten teachers*, but academics begin to take priority in kindergarten classrooms. Letter recognition, phonics, numbers, and awareness of nature and science, introduced at the preschool level, are taught primarily in kindergarten.

Most *elementary school teachers* instruct one class of children in several subjects. In some schools, two or more teachers work as a team and are jointly responsible for a group of students in at least one subject. In other schools, a teacher may teach one special subject—usually music, art, reading, science, arithmetic, or physical education—to a number of classes. A small but growing number of teachers instruct multilevel classrooms, with students at several different learning levels.

Middle school teachers and *secondary school teachers* help students delve more deeply into subjects introduced in elementary school and expose them to more information about the world. Middle and secondary school teachers specialize in a specific subject, such as English, Spanish, mathematics, history, or biology. They also may teach subjects that are career oriented. *Vocational education teachers*, also referred to as career and technical or career-technology teachers, instruct and train students to work in a wide variety of fields, such as healthcare, business, auto repair, communications, and, increasingly, technology. They often teach courses that are in high demand by area employers, who may provide input into the curriculum and offer internships to students. Many vocational teachers play an active role in building and overseeing these partnerships. Additional responsibilities of middle and secondary school teachers may include career guidance and job placement, as well as follow-ups with students after graduation. (*Special education teachers*—who instruct elementary and secondary school students who have a variety of disabilities—are discussed separately in this section of the *Handbook*.)

In addition to conducting classroom activities, teachers oversee study halls and homerooms, supervise extracurricular activities, and accompany students on field trips. They may identify students with physical or mental problems and refer the students to the proper authorities. Secondary school teachers occasionally assist students in choosing courses, colleges, and careers. Teachers also participate in education conferences and workshops.

Computers play an integral role in the education teachers provide. Resources such as educational software and the Internet expose students to a vast range of experiences and promote interactive learning. Through the Internet, students can communicate with other students anywhere in the world, allowing them to share experiences and differing viewpoints. Students also use the Internet for individual research projects and to gather information. Computers are used in other classroom activities as well, from solving math problems to learning English as a second language. Teachers also may use computers to record grades and perform other administrative and clerical duties. They must continually update their skills so that they can instruct and use the latest technology in the classroom.

Teachers often work with students from varied ethnic, racial, and religious backgrounds. With growing minority populations in most parts of the country, it is important for teachers to work effectively with a diverse student population. Accordingly, some schools offer training to help teachers enhance their awareness and understanding of different cultures. Teachers may also include multicultural programming in their lesson plans, to address the needs of all students, regardless of their cultural background.

In recent years, site-based management, which allows teachers and parents to participate actively in management decisions regarding school operations, has gained popularity. In many schools, teachers are increasingly involved in making decisions regarding the budget, personnel, textbooks, curriculum design, and teaching methods.

Work environment. Seeing students develop new skills and gain an appreciation of knowledge and learning can be very rewarding. However, teaching may be frustrating when one is dealing with unmotivated or disrespectful students. Occasionally, teachers must cope with unruly behavior and violence in the schools. Teachers may experience stress in dealing with large classes, heavy workloads, or old schools that are run down and lack many modern amenities. Accountability standards also may increase stress levels, with teachers expected to produce students who are able to exhibit satisfactory performance on standardized tests in core subjects. Many teachers, particularly in public schools, are also frustrated by the lack of control they have over what they are required to teach.

Teachers in private schools generally enjoy smaller class sizes and more control over establishing the curriculum and setting standards for performance and discipline. Their students also tend to be more motivated, since private schools can be selective in their admissions processes.

Teachers are sometimes isolated from their colleagues because they work alone in a classroom of students. However, some schools allow teachers to work in teams and with mentors to enhance their professional development.

Including school duties performed outside the classroom, many teachers work more than 40 hours a week. Part-time schedules are more common among preschool and kindergarten teachers. Although most school districts have gone to all-day kindergartens, some kindergarten teachers still teach two kindergarten classes a day. Most teachers work the traditional 10-month school year with a 2-month vacation during the summer. During the vacation break, those on the 10-month schedule may teach in summer sessions, take other jobs, travel, or pursue personal interests. Many enroll in college courses or workshops

Teachers instruct students in both academic and personal enrichment subjects.

to continue their education. Teachers in districts with a year-round schedule typically work 8 weeks, are on vacation for 1 week, and have a 5-week midwinter break. Preschool teachers working in day care settings often work year round.

Most States have tenure laws that prevent public school teachers from being fired without just cause and due process. Teachers may obtain tenure after they have satisfactorily completed a probationary period of teaching, normally 3 years. Tenure does not absolutely guarantee a job, but it does provide some security.

Training, Other Qualifications, and Advancement

The traditional route to becoming a public school teacher involves completing a bachelor's degree from a teacher education program and then obtaining a license. However, most States now offer alternative routes to licensure for those who have a college degree in other fields. Private school teachers do not have to be licensed but still need a bachelor's degree. A bachelor's degree may not be needed by preschool teachers and vocational education teachers, who need experience in their field rather than a specific degree.

Education and training. Traditional education programs for kindergarten and elementary school teachers include courses designed specifically for those preparing to teach. These courses include mathematics, physical science, social science, music, art, and literature, as well as prescribed professional education courses, such as philosophy of education, psychology of learning, and teaching methods. Aspiring secondary school teachers most often major in the subject they plan to teach while also taking a program of study in teacher preparation. Many 4-year colleges require students to wait until their sophomore year before applying for admission to teacher education programs. To maintain their accreditation, teacher education programs are now required to include classes in the use of computers and other technologies. Most programs require students to perform a student-teaching internship. Teacher education programs are accredited by the National Council for Accreditation of Teacher Education and the Teacher Education Accreditation Council. Graduation from an accredited program is not necessary to become a teacher, but it may make fulfilling licensure requirements easier.

Many States now offer professional development schools, which are partnerships between universities and elementary or secondary schools. Professional development schools merge theory with practice and allow the student to experience a year of teaching firsthand, under professional guidance. Students enter these 1-year programs after completion of their bachelor's degree.

Licensure and certification. All 50 States and the District of Columbia require public school teachers to be licensed. Licensure is not required for teachers in most private schools. Usually licensure is granted by the State Board of Education or a licensure advisory committee. Teachers may be licensed to teach the early childhood grades (usually preschool through grade 3); the elementary grades (grades 1 through 6 or 8); the middle grades (grades 5 through 8); a secondary-education subject area (usually grades 7 through 12); or a special subject, such as reading or music (usually grades kindergarten through 12).

Requirements for regular licenses to teach kindergarten through grade 12 vary by State. However, all States require general education teachers to have a bachelor's degree and to have completed an approved teacher training program with a prescribed number of subject and education credits, as well as supervised practice teaching. Some States also require technology training and the attainment of a minimum grade point average. A number of States require that teachers obtain a master's degree in education within a specified period after they begin teaching.

Almost all States require applicants for a teacher's license to be tested for competency in basic skills, such as reading and writing, and in teaching. Almost all also require teachers to exhibit proficiency in their subject. Many school systems are presently moving toward implementing performance-based systems for licensure, which usually require teachers to demonstrate satisfactory teaching performance over an extended period in order to obtain a provisional license, in addition to passing an examination in their subject. Most States require teachers to complete a minimum number of hours of continuing education to renew their license. Many States have reciprocity agreements that make it easier for teachers licensed in one State to become licensed in another.

Licensing requirements for preschool teachers also vary by State. Requirements for public preschool teachers are generally more stringent than those for private preschool teachers. Some States require a bachelor's degree in early childhood education, while others require an associate's degree, and still others require certification by a nationally recognized authority. The Child Development Associate (CDA) credential, the most common type of certification, requires a mix of classroom training and experience working with children, along with an independent assessment of the teacher's competence.

Nearly all States now also offer alternative licensure programs for teachers who have a bachelor's degree in the subject they will teach, but who lack the necessary education courses required for a regular license. Many of these alternative licensure programs are designed to ease shortages of teachers of certain subjects, such as mathematics and science. Other programs provide teachers for urban and rural schools that have difficulty filling positions with teachers from traditional licensure programs. Alternative licensure programs are intended to attract people into teaching who do not fulfill traditional licensing standards, including recent college graduates who did not complete education programs and those changing from another career to teaching. In some programs, individuals begin teaching quickly under provisional licensure under the close supervision of experienced educators while taking education courses outside school hours. If they progress satisfactorily, they receive regular licensure after working for 1 or 2 years. In other programs, college graduates who do not meet licensure requirements take only those courses that they lack and then become licensed. This approach may take 1 or 2 semesters of full-time study. The coursework for alternative certification programs often leads to a master's degree. In extreme circumstances, when schools cannot attract enough qualified teachers to fill positions, States may issue emergency licenses to individuals who do not meet the requirements for a regular license that let them begin teaching immediately.

In many States, vocational teachers have many of the same licensure requirements as other teachers. However, knowledge and experience in a particular field are important, so some States will license vocational education teachers without a bachelor's degree, provided they can demonstrate expertise in their field. A minimum number of hours in education courses may also be required.

Private schools are generally exempt from meeting State licensing standards. For secondary school teacher jobs, they prefer candidates who have a bachelor's degree in the subject they intend to teach, or in childhood education for elementary school teachers. They seek candidates among recent college graduates as well as from those who have established careers in other fields.

Other qualifications. In addition to being knowledgeable about the subjects they teach, teachers must have the ability to communicate, inspire trust and confidence, and motivate students, as well as understand the students' educational and emotional needs. Teachers must be able to recognize and respond to individual and cultural differences in students and employ different teaching methods that will result in higher student achievement. They should be organized, dependable, patient, and creative. Teachers also must be able to work cooperatively and communicate effectively with other teachers, support staff, parents, and members of the community. Private schools associated with religious institutions also desire candidates who share the values that are important to the institution.

Additional certifications and advancement. In some cases, teachers of kindergarten through high school may attain professional certification in order to demonstrate competency beyond that required for a license. The National Board for Professional Teaching Standards offers a voluntary national certification. To become nationally certified, experienced teachers must prove their aptitude by compiling a portfolio showing their work in the classroom and by passing a written assessment and evaluation of their teaching knowledge. Currently, teachers may become certified in a variety of areas, on the basis of the age of the students and, in some cases, the subject taught. For example, teachers may obtain a certificate for teaching English language arts to early adolescents (aged 11 to 15), or they may become certified as early childhood generalists. All States recognize national certification, and many States and school districts provide special benefits to teachers who earn certification. Benefits typically include higher salaries and reimbursement for continuing education and certification fees. In addition, many States allow nationally certified teachers to carry a license from one State to another.

With additional preparation, teachers may move into such positions as school librarians, reading specialists, instructional coordinators, or guidance counselors. Teachers may become administrators or supervisors, although the number of these positions is limited and competition for them can be intense. In some systems, highly qualified, experienced teachers can become senior or mentor teachers, with higher pay and additional responsibilities. They guide and assist less experienced teachers while keeping most of their own teaching responsibilities. Preschool teachers usually work their way up from assistant teacher, to teacher, to lead teacher—who may be responsible for the instruction of several classes—and, finally, to director of the center. Preschool teachers with a bachelor's degree frequently are qualified to teach kindergarten through grade 3 as well. Teaching at these higher grades often results in higher pay.

Employment

Preschool, kindergarten, elementary school, middle school, and secondary school teachers, except special education, held about 4.0 million jobs in 2006. Of the teachers in those jobs, about 1.5 million are elementary school teachers, 1.1 million are secondary school teachers, 673,000 are middle school teachers, 437,000 are preschool teachers, and 170,000 are kindergarten teachers. The vast majority work in elementary and secondary schools. Preschool teachers, except special education, are most often employed in child daycare services (59 percent), public and private educational services (16 percent), and religious organizations (15 percent). Employment of teachers is geographically distributed much the same as the population.

Job Outlook

Employment of preschool, kindergarten, elementary, middle, and secondary school teachers is projected to grow about as fast as average. Job prospects are expected to be favorable, with particularly good prospects for teachers in high-demand fields like math, science, and bilingual education, or in less desirable urban or rural school districts.

Employment change. Employment of school teachers is expected to grow by 12 percent between 2006 and 2016, about as fast as the average for all occupations. However, because of the size of the occupations in this group, this growth will create 479,000 additional teacher positions, more than all but a few occupations.

Through 2016, overall student enrollments in elementary, middle, and secondary schools—a key factor in the demand for teachers—are expected to rise more slowly than in the past as children of the baby boom generation leave the school system. This will cause employment of teachers from kindergarten through the secondary grades to grow as fast as the average. Projected enrollments will vary by region. Fast-growing States in the South and West—led by Nevada, Arizona, Texas, and Georgia—will experience the largest enrollment increases. Enrollments in the Midwest are expected to hold relatively steady, while those in the Northeast are expected to decline. Teachers who are geographically mobile and who obtain licensure in more than one subject should have a distinct advantage in finding a job.

The number of teachers employed is dependent on State and local expenditures for education and on the enactment of legislation to increase the quality and scope of public education. At the Federal level, there has been a large increase in funding for education, particularly for the hiring of qualified teachers in lower income areas. Also, some States are instituting programs to improve early childhood education, such as offering full day kindergarten and universal preschool. These programs, along with projected higher enrollment growth for preschool age children, will create many new jobs for preschool teachers, which are expected to grow much faster than the average for all occupations.

Projections data from the National Employment Matrix

Occupational Title	SOC Code	Employment, 2006	Projected employment, 2016	Change, 2006-2016	
				Number	Percent
Teachers—preschool, kindergarten, elementary, middle, and secondary	—	3,954,000	4,433,000	479,000	12
Preschool and kindergarten teachers	25-2010	607,000	750,000	143,000	23
Preschool teachers, except special education	25-2011	437,000	552,000	115,000	26
Kindergarten teachers, except special education	25-2012	170,000	198,000	28,000	16
Elementary and middle school teachers	25-2020	2,214,000	2,496,000	282,000	13
Elementary school teachers, except special education	25-2021	1,540,000	1,749,000	209,000	14
Middle school teachers, except special and vocational education	25-2022	658,000	732,000	74,000	11
Vocational education teachers, middle school	25-2023	16,000	15,000	-800	-5
Secondary school teachers	25-2030	1,133,000	1,187,000	54,000	5
Secondary school teachers, except special and vocational education	25-2031	1,038,000	1,096,000	59,000	6
Vocational education teachers, secondary school	25-2032	96,000	91,000	-4,400	-5

NOTE: Data in this table are rounded. See the discussion of the employment projections table in the *Handbook* introductory chapter on *Occupational Information Included in the Handbook.*

Job prospects. Job opportunities for teachers over the next 10 years will vary from good to excellent, depending on the locality, grade level, and subject taught. Most job openings will result from the need to replace the large number of teachers who are expected to retire over the 2006-16 period. Also, many beginning teachers decide to leave teaching for other careers after a year or two—especially those employed in poor, urban schools—creating additional job openings for teachers.

The job market for teachers also continues to vary by school location and by subject taught. Job prospects should be better in inner cities and rural areas than in suburban districts. Many inner cities—often characterized by overcrowded, ill-equipped schools and higher-than-average poverty rates—and rural areas—characterized by their remote location and relatively low salaries—have difficulty attracting and retaining enough teachers. Currently, many school districts have difficulty hiring qualified teachers in some subject areas—most often mathematics, science (especially chemistry and physics), bilingual education, and foreign languages. Increasing enrollments of minorities, coupled with a shortage of minority teachers, should cause efforts to recruit minority teachers to intensify. Also, the number of non-English-speaking students will continue to grow, creating demand for bilingual teachers and for those who teach English as a second language. Qualified vocational teachers also are currently in demand in a variety of fields at both the middle school and secondary school levels. Specialties that have an adequate number of qualified teachers include general elementary education, physical education, and social studies.

The supply of teachers is expected to increase in response to reports of improved job prospects, better pay, more teacher involvement in school policy, and greater public interest in education. In addition, more teachers may be drawn from a reserve pool of career changers, substitute teachers, and teachers completing alternative certification programs. In recent years, the total number of bachelor's and master's degrees granted in education has been increasing slowly. But many States have implemented policies that will encourage even more students to become teachers because of a shortage of teachers in certain locations and in anticipation of the loss of a number of teachers to retirement.

Earnings

Median annual earnings of kindergarten, elementary, middle, and secondary school teachers ranged from $43,580 to $48,690 in May 2006; the lowest 10 percent earned $28,590 to $33,070; the top 10 percent earned $67,490 to $76,100. Median earnings for preschool teachers were $22,680.

According to the American Federation of Teachers, beginning teachers with a bachelor's degree earned an average of $31,753 in the 2004–05 school year. The estimated average salary of all public elementary and secondary school teachers in the 2004–05 school year was $47,602.

In 2006, more than half of all elementary, middle, and secondary school teachers belonged to unions—mainly the American Federation of Teachers and the National Education Association—that bargain with school systems over salaries, hours, and other terms and conditions of employment. Fewer preschool

and kindergarten teachers were union members—about 17 percent in 2006.

Teachers can boost their earnings in a number of ways. In some schools, teachers receive extra pay for coaching sports and working with students in extracurricular activities. Getting a master's degree or national certification often results in a raise in pay, as does acting as a mentor. Some teachers earn extra income during the summer by teaching summer school or performing other jobs in the school system. Although private school teachers generally earn less than public school teachers, they may be given other benefits, such as free or subsidized housing.

Related Occupations

Preschool, kindergarten, elementary school, middle school, and secondary school teaching requires a variety of skills and aptitudes, including a talent for working with children; organizational, administrative, and recordkeeping abilities; research and communication skills; the power to influence, motivate, and train others; patience; and creativity. Workers in other occupations requiring some of these aptitudes include teachers—postsecondary; counselors; teacher assistants; education administrators; librarians; child care workers; public relations specialists; social workers; and athletes, coaches, umpires, and related workers.

Sources of Additional Information

Information on licensure or certification requirements and approved teacher training institutions is available from local school systems and State departments of education.

Information on teachers' unions and education-related issues may be obtained from the following sources:

➤ American Federation of Teachers, 555 New Jersey Ave. NW., Washington, DC 20001. Internet: **http://www.aft.org**

➤ National Education Association, 1201 16th St.NW., Washington, DC 20036. Internet: **http://www.nea.org**

A list of institutions with accredited teacher education programs can be obtained from:

➤ National Council for Accreditation of Teacher Education, 2010 Massachusetts Ave. NW., Suite 500, Washington, DC 20036-1023. Internet: **http://www.ncate.org**

➤ Teacher Education Accreditation Council, Suite 300, One Dupont Circle, Washington, DC 20036.
Internet: **http://www.teac.org**

Information on alternative certification programs can be obtained from:

➤ National Center for Alternative Certification, 1901 Pennsylvania Ave NW., Suite 201, Washington, DC 20006.
Internet: **http://www.teach-now.org**

Information on National Board Certification can be obtained from:

➤ National Board for Professional Teaching Standards, 1525 Wilson Blvd., Suite 500, Arlington, VA 22209.
Internet: **http://www.nbpts.org**

For information on vocational education and vocational education teachers, contact:

➤ Association for Career and Technical Education, 1410 King St., Alexandria, VA 22314. Internet: **http://www.acteonline.org**

For information on careers in educating children and issues affecting preschool teachers, contact either of the following organizations:

➤ National Association for the Education of Young Children, 1509 16th St.NW., Washington, DC 20036.
Internet: **http://www.naeyc.org**

➤ Council for Professional Recognition, 2460 16th St.NW., Washington, DC 20009-3575.
Internet: **http://www.cdacouncil.org**

Teachers—Self-Enrichment Education

(O*NET 25-3021.00)

Significant Points

- Many self-enrichment teachers are self-employed or work part time.

- Teachers should have knowledge and enthusiasm for their subject, but little formal training is required.

- Employment is projected to grow much faster than average, and job prospects should be favorable; opportunities may vary by subject taught.

Nature of the Work

Self-enrichment teachers provide instruction in a wide variety of subjects that students take for fun or self-improvement. Some teach a series of classes that provide students with useful life skills, such as cooking, personal finance, and time management. Others provide group instruction intended solely for recreation, such as photography, pottery, and painting. Many others provide one-on-one instruction in a variety of subjects, including dance, singing, or playing a musical instrument. Some teachers conduct courses on academic subjects, such as literature, foreign language, and history, in a non-academic setting. The classes self-enrichment teachers give seldom lead to a degree and attendance is voluntary, but dedicated, talented students sometimes go on to careers in the arts.

Self-enrichment teachers may have styles and methods of instruction that differ greatly. Most self-enrichment classes are relatively informal. Some classes, such as pottery or sewing, may be largely hands-on, with the instructor demonstrating methods or techniques for the class, observing students as they attempt to do it themselves, and pointing out mistakes to students and offering suggestions to improve techniques. Other classes, such as those involving financial planning or religion and spirituality, may center on lectures or might rely more heavily on group discussions. Self-enrichment teachers may also teach classes offered through religious institutions, such as marriage preparation or classes in religion for children.

Many of the classes that self-enrichment educators teach are shorter in duration than classes taken for academic credit; some finish in 1 or 2 days or several weeks. These brief classes tend to be introductory in nature and generally focus on only one topic—for example, a cooking class that teaches students how to make bread. Some self-enrichment classes introduce chil-

dren and youth to activities, such as piano or drama, and may be designed to last anywhere from 1 week to several months.

Many self-enrichment teachers provide one-on-one lessons to students. The instructor may only work with the student for an hour or two a week, but tells the student what to practice in the interim until the next lesson. Many instructors work with the same students on a weekly basis for years and derive satisfaction from observing them mature and gain expertise. The most talented students may go on to paid careers as craft artists, painters, sculptors, dancers, singers, or musicians.

All self-enrichment teachers must prepare lessons beforehand and stay current in their fields. Many self-enrichment teachers are self employed and provide instruction as a business. As such, they must collect any fees or tuition and keep records of students whose accounts are prepaid or in arrears. Although not a requirement for most types of classes, teachers may use computers and other modern technologies in their instruction or to maintain business records.

Work environment. Few self-enrichment education teachers are full-time salaried workers. Most either work part time or are self-employed. Some have several part-time teaching assignments, but it is most common for teachers to have a full-time job in another occupation, often related to the subject that they teach, in addition to their part-time teaching job. Although jobs in this occupation are primarily part time and pay is low, most teachers enjoy their work because it gives them the opportunity to share a subject they enjoy with others.

Many classes for adults are held in the evenings and on weekends to accommodate students who have a job or family responsibilities. Similarly, self-enrichment classes for children are usually held after school, on weekends, or during school vacations.

Students in self-enrichment programs attend by choice so they tend to be highly motivated and eager to learn. Students

Self-enrichment teachers cover a wide range of subjects, including gardening, photography, and personal finance.

also often bring their own unique experiences to class, which can make teaching them rewarding and satisfying. Self-enrichment teachers must have a great deal of patience, however, particularly when working with young children.

Training, Other Qualifications, and Advancement
The main qualification for self-enrichment teachers is expertise in their subject area, but requirements vary greatly with the type of class taught and the place of employment.

Education and training. In general, there are few educational or training requirements for a job as a self-enrichment teacher beyond being an expert in the subject taught. To demonstrate expertise, however, self enrichment teachers may be required to have formal training in disciplines, such as art or music, where specific teacher training programs are available. Prospective dance teachers, for example, may complete programs that prepare them to teach many types of dance—from ballroom to ballet. Other employers may require a portfolio of a teacher's work. For example, to secure a job teaching a photography course, an applicant often needs to show examples of previous work. Some self-enrichment teachers are trained educators or other professionals who teach enrichment classes in their spare time. In many self-enrichment fields, however, instructors are simply experienced in the field, and want to share that experience with others.

Other qualifications. In addition to knowledge of their subject, self-enrichment teachers should have good speaking skills and a talent for making the subject interesting. Patience and the ability to explain and instruct students at a basic level are important as well, particularly for teachers who work with children.

Advancement. Opportunities for advancement in this profession are limited. Some part-time teachers are able to move into full-time teaching positions or program administrator positions, such as coordinator or director. Experienced teachers may mentor new instructors.

Employment
Teachers of self-enrichment education held about 261,000 jobs in 2006. The largest numbers of teachers were employed by public and private educational institutions, religious organizations, and providers of social assistance and amusement and recreation services. More than 20 percent of workers were self employed.

Job Outlook
Employment of self-enrichment education teachers is expected to grow much faster than average, and job prospects should be favorable. A large number of job openings are expected due to job growth, the retirement of existing teachers, and because of those who leave their jobs for other reasons. New opportunities

arise constantly because many jobs are short term and are often held as a second job.

Employment change. Employment of self-enrichment education teachers is expected to increase by 23 percent between 2006 and 2016, much faster than the average for all occupations. The need for self-enrichment teachers is expected to grow as more people embrace lifelong learning and as course offerings expand. Demand for self-enrichment education will also increase as a result of demographic changes. Retirees are one of the larger groups of participants in self-enrichment education because they have more time for classes. As members of the baby boom generation begin to retire, demand for self-enrichment education should grow. At the same time, the children of the baby boomers will be entering the age range of another large group of participants, young adults—who often are single and participate in self-enrichment classes for the social, as well as the educational, experience.

Job prospects. Job prospects should be favorable as increasing demand and high turnover creates many opportunities, but opportunities may vary as some fields have more prospective teachers than others. Opportunities should be best for teachers of subjects that are not easily researched on the Internet and those that benefit from hands-on experiences, such as cooking, crafts, and the arts. Classes on self-improvement, personal finance, and computer and Internet-related subjects are also expected to be popular.

Earnings
Median hourly earnings of wage-and-salary self-enrichment teachers were $16.08 in May 2006. The middle 50 percent earned between $11.29 and $23.08. The lowest 10 percent earned less than $8.53, and the highest 10 percent earned more than $32.02. Self-enrichment teachers are generally paid by the hour or for each class that they teach. Earnings may also be tied to the number of students enrolled in the class.

Part-time instructors are usually paid for each class that they teach, and receive few benefits. Full-time teachers are generally paid a salary and may receive health insurance and other benefits.

Related Occupations
The work of self-enrichment teachers is closely related to that of other types of teachers, especially preschool, kindergarten, elementary school, middle school, and secondary school teachers. Self-enrichment teachers also teach a wide variety of subjects that may be related to the work done by those in many other occupations, such as dancers and choreographers; artists and related workers; musicians, singers, and related workers; recreation workers; and athletes, coaches, umpires, and related workers.

Projections data from the National Employment Matrix

Occupational Title	SOC Code	Employment, 2006	Projected employment, 2016	Change, 2006-2016	
				Number	Percent
Self-enrichment education teachers	25-3021	261,000	322,000	60,000	23

NOTE: Data in this table are rounded. See the discussion of the employment projections table in the *Handbook* introductory chapter on *Occupational Information Included in the Handbook.*

Sources of Additional Information

For information on employment of self-enrichment teachers, contact local schools, colleges, or companies that offer self-enrichment programs.

Teachers—Special Education

(O*NET 25-2041.00, 25-2042.00, 25-2043.00)

Significant Points

- All States require teachers to be licensed; traditional licensing requires the completion of a special education teacher training program and at least a bachelor's degree, though many States require a master's degree.

- Many States offer alternative licensure programs to attract college graduates who do not have training in education.

- Excellent job prospects are expected due to rising enrollments of special education students and reported shortages of qualified teachers.

Nature of the Work

Special education teachers work with children and youths who have a variety of disabilities. A small number of special education teachers work with students with severe cases of mental retardation or autism, primarily teaching them life skills and basic literacy. However, the majority of special education teachers work with children with mild to moderate disabilities, using or modifying the general education curriculum to meet the child's individual needs. Most special education teachers instruct students at the elementary, middle, and secondary school level, although some work with infants and toddlers.

The various types of disabilities that may qualify individuals for special education programs include specific learning disabilities, speech or language impairments, mental retardation, emotional disturbance, multiple disabilities, hearing impairments, orthopedic impairments, visual impairments, autism, combined deafness and blindness, traumatic brain injury, and other health impairments. Students are classified under one of the categories, and special education teachers are prepared to work with specific groups. Early identification of a child with special needs is an important part of a special education teacher's job, because early intervention is essential in educating children with disabilities.

Special education teachers use various techniques to promote learning. Depending on the disability, teaching methods can include individualized instruction, problem-solving assignments, and small-group work. When students need special accommodations to take a test, special education teachers see that appropriate ones are provided, such as having the questions read orally or lengthening the time allowed to take the test.

Special education teachers help to develop an Individualized Education Program (IEP) for each student. The IEP sets personalized goals for the student and is tailored to that student's individual needs and ability. When appropriate, the program includes a transition plan outlining specific steps to prepare students with disabilities for middle school or high school or, in the case of older students, a job or postsecondary study. Teachers review the IEP with the student's parents, school administrators, and the student's general education teachers. Teachers work closely with parents to inform them of their child's progress and suggest techniques to promote learning at home.

Special education teachers design and teach appropriate curricula, assign work geared toward each student's needs and abilities, and grade papers and homework assignments. They are involved in the students' behavioral, social, and academic development, helping them develop emotionally, feel comfortable in social situations, and be aware of socially acceptable behavior. Preparing special education students for daily life after graduation also is an important aspect of the job. Teachers provide students with career counseling or help them learn routine skills, such as balancing a checkbook.

As schools become more inclusive, special education teachers and general education teachers increasingly work together in general education classrooms. Special education teachers help general educators adapt curriculum materials and teaching techniques to meet the needs of students with disabilities. They coordinate the work of teachers, teacher assistants, and related personnel, such as therapists and social workers, to meet the individualized needs of the student within inclusive special education programs. A large part of a special education teacher's job involves communicating and coordinating with others involved in the child's well being, including parents, social workers, school psychologists, occupational and physical therapists, school administrators, and other teachers.

Special education teachers work in a variety of settings. Some have their own classrooms and teach only special education students; others work as special education resource teachers and offer individualized help to students in general education classrooms; still others teach together with general education teachers in classes including both general and special education students. Some teachers work with special education students for several hours a day in a resource room, separate from their general education classroom. Considerably fewer special education teachers work in residential facilities or tutor students in homebound or hospital environments.

Some special education teachers work with infants and usually travel to the child's home to work with the parents. Many of these infants have medical problems that slow or preclude normal development. Special education teachers show parents techniques and activities designed to stimulate the infant and encourage the growth and development of the child's skills. Toddlers usually receive their services at a preschool where special education teachers help them develop social, self-help, motor, language, and cognitive skills, often through the use of play.

Technology is becoming increasingly important in special education. Teachers use specialized equipment such as computers with synthesized speech, interactive educational software programs, and audiotapes to assist children.

Work environment. Special education teachers enjoy the challenge of working with students with disabilities and the

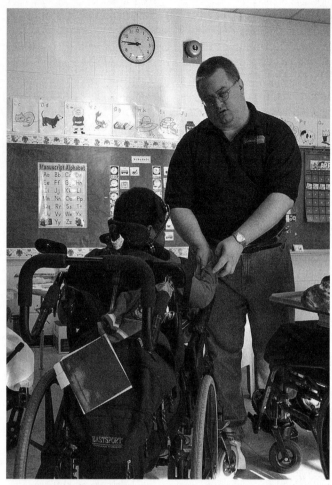

Special education teachers adapt learning plans to the individual needs of their students.

opportunity to establish meaningful relationships with them. Although helping these students can be highly rewarding, the work also can be emotionally and physically draining. Many special education teachers are under considerable stress due to heavy workloads and administrative tasks. They must produce a substantial amount of paperwork documenting each student's progress and work under the threat of litigation against the school or district by parents if correct procedures are not followed or if they feel that their child is not receiving an adequate education. Recently passed legislation, however, is intended to reduce the burden of paperwork and the threat of litigation. The physical and emotional demands of the job cause some special education teachers to leave the occupation.

Some schools offer year-round education for special education students, but most special education teachers work only the traditional 10-month school year.

Training, Other Qualifications, and Advancement
All States require special education teachers to be licensed, which typically requires at least a bachelor's degree and completion of an approved training program in special education teaching. Many States require a master's degree. Most States have alternative methods for entry for bachelor's degree holders who do not have training in education.

Education and training. Many colleges and universities across the United States offer programs in special education

at the undergraduate, master's, and doctoral degree levels. Special education teachers usually undergo longer periods of training than do general education teachers. Most bachelor's degree programs last years and include general and specialized courses in special education. However, an increasing number of institutions require a 5th year or other graduate-level preparation. Among the courses offered are educational psychology, legal issues of special education, child growth and development, and strategies for teaching students with disabilities. Some programs require specialization, while others offer generalized special education degrees or a course of study in several specialized areas. The last year of the program usually is spent student teaching in a classroom supervised by a certified teacher.

Licensure. All 50 States and the District of Columbia require special education teachers to be licensed. The State board of education or a licensure advisory committee usually grants licenses, and licensure varies by State. In some States, special education teachers receive a general education credential to teach kindergarten through grade 12. These teachers then train in a specialty, such as learning disabilities or behavioral disorders. Many States offer general special education licenses across a variety of disability categories, while others license several different specialties within special education.

For traditional licensing, all States require a bachelor's degree and the completion of an approved teacher preparation program with a prescribed number of subject and education credits and supervised practice teaching. However, many States also require a master's degree in special education, involving at least 1 year of additional course work, including a specialization, beyond the bachelor's degree. Often a prospective teacher must pass a professional assessment test as well. Some States have reciprocity agreements allowing special education teachers to transfer their licenses from one State to another, but many others still require that experienced teachers reapply and pass licensing requirements to work in the State.

Most States also offer alternative routes to licensing which are intended to attract people into teaching who do not fulfill traditional licensing standards. Most alternative licensure programs are open to anyone with a bachelor's degree, although some are designed for recent college graduates or professionals in other education occupations. Programs typically require the successful completion of a period of supervised preparation and instruction and passing an assessment test. Individuals can then begin teaching under a provisional license and can obtain a regular license after teaching under the supervision of licensed teachers for a period of 1 to 2 years and completing required education courses through a local college or other provider.

Other qualifications. Special education teachers must be patient, able to motivate students, understanding of their students' special needs, and accepting of differences in others. Teachers must be creative and apply different types of teaching methods to reach students who are having difficulty learning. Communication and cooperation are essential skills because special education teachers spend a great deal of time interacting with others, including students, parents, and school faculty and administrators.

Advancement. Special education teachers can advance to become supervisors or administrators. They may also earn advanced degrees and become instructors in colleges that prepare others to teach special education. In some school systems, highly experienced teachers can become mentors to less experienced ones, providing guidance to those teachers while maintaining a light teaching load.

Employment

Special education teachers held a total of about 459,000 jobs in 2006. Nearly all work in public and private educational institutions. A few worked for individual and social assistance agencies or residential facilities, or in homebound or hospital environments.

Job Outlook

Employment of special education teachers is expected to increase faster than average. Job prospects should be excellent as many districts report problems finding adequate numbers of certified special education teachers.

Employment change. The number of special education teachers is expected to increase by 15 percent from 2006 to 2016, faster than the average for all occupations. Although student enrollments in general are expected to grow slowly, continued increases in the number of special education students needing services will generate a greater need for special education teachers.

The number of students requiring special education services has grown steadily in recent years due to improvements that have allowed learning disabilities to be diagnosed at earlier ages and medical advances that have resulted in more children surviving serious accidents or illnesses, but with impairments that require special accommodations. In addition, legislation emphasizing training and employment for individuals with disabilities and educational reforms requiring higher standards for graduation has increased demand for special education services. The percentage of foreign-born special education students also is expected to grow, as teachers become more adept in recognizing disabilities in that population. Finally, more parents are expected to seek special services for their children who have difficulty meeting the new, higher standards required of students.

Job prospects. In addition to job openings resulting from growth, a large number of openings will result from the need to replace special education teachers who switch to teaching general education, change careers altogether, or retire. At the same time, many school districts report difficulty finding sufficient

numbers of qualified teachers. As a result, special education teachers should have excellent job prospects.

The job outlook does vary by geographic area and specialty. Although most areas of the country report difficulty finding qualified applicants, positions in inner cities and rural areas usually are more plentiful than job openings in suburban or wealthy urban areas. Student populations also are expected to increase more rapidly in certain parts of the country, such as the South and West, resulting in increased demand for special education teachers in those regions. In addition, job opportunities may be better in certain specialties—such as teachers who work with children with multiple disabilities or severe disabilities like autism—because of large increases in the enrollment of special education students classified under those categories. Legislation encouraging early intervention and special education for infants, toddlers, and preschoolers has created a need for early childhood special education teachers. Bilingual special education teachers and those with multicultural experience also are needed to work with an increasingly diverse student population.

Earnings

Median annual earnings in May 2006 of wage-and-salary special education teachers who worked primarily in preschools, kindergartens, and elementary schools were $46,360. The middle 50 percent earned between $37,500 and $59,320. The lowest 10 percent earned less than $31,320, and the highest 10 percent earned more than $73,620.

Median annual earnings of wage-and-salary middle school special education teachers were $47,650. The middle 50 percent earned between $38,460 and $61,530. The lowest 10 percent earned less than $32,420, and the highest 10 percent earned more than $80,170.

Median annual earnings of wage-and-salary special education teachers who worked primarily in secondary schools were $48,330. The middle 50 percent earned between $38,910 and $62,640. The lowest 10 percent earned less than $32,760, and the highest 10 percent earned more than $78,020.

In 2006, about 58 percent of special education teachers belonged to unions—mainly the American Federation of Teachers and the National Education Association—that bargain with school systems over wages, hours, and the terms and conditions of employment.

In most schools, teachers receive extra pay for coaching sports and working with students in extracurricular activities. Some teachers earn extra income during the summer, working in the school system or in other jobs.

Projections data from the National Employment Matrix

Occupational Title	SOC Code	Employment, 2006	Projected employment, 2016	Change, 2006-2016	
				Number	Percent
Special education teachers	25-2040	459,000	530,000	71,000	15
Special education teachers, preschool, kindergarten, and elementary school	25-2041	219,000	262,000	43,000	20
Special education teachers, middle school.................................	25-2042	102,000	118,000	16,000	16
Special education teachers, secondary school	25-2043	138,000	150,000	12,000	9

NOTE: Data in this table are rounded. See the discussion of the employment projections table in the *Handbook* introductory chapter on *Occupational Information Included in the Handbook.*

Related Occupations

Special education teachers work with students who have disabilities and special needs. Other occupations involved with the identification, evaluation, and development of students with disabilities include psychologists, social workers, speech-language pathologists, audiologists, counselors, teacher assistants, occupational therapists, recreational therapists, and teachers—preschool, kindergarten, elementary, middle, and secondary.

Sources of Additional Information

For information on professions related to early intervention and education for children with disabilities, listings of schools with special education training programs, information on teacher certification, and general information on related personnel issues, contact:

➤ The Council for Exceptional Children, 1110 N. Glebe Rd., Suite 300, Arlington, VA 22201.
Internet: **http://www.cec.sped.org**

➤ National Center for Special Education Personnel & Related Service Providers, National Association of State Directors of Special Education, 1800 Diagonal Rd., Suite 320, Alexandria, VA 22314. Internet: **http://www.personnelcenter.org**

To learn more about the special education teacher certification and licensing requirements in individual States, contact the State's department of education.

Art and Design Occupations

Artists and Related Workers

(O*NET 27-1011.00, 27-1012.00, 27-1013.00, 27-1014.00, 27-1019.99)

Significant Points

- About 62 percent of artists and related workers are self-employed.

- Keen competition is expected for both salaried jobs and freelance work because the arts attract many talented people with creative ability.

- Artists usually develop their skills through a bachelor's degree program or other postsecondary training in art or design.

- Earnings for self-employed artists vary widely; some well-established artists earn more than salaried artists, while others find it difficult to rely solely on income earned from selling art.

Nature of the Work

Artists create art to communicate ideas, thoughts, or feelings. They use a variety of methods—painting, sculpting, or illustration—and an assortment of materials, including oils, watercolors, acrylics, pastels, pencils, pen and ink, plaster, clay, and computers. Artists' works may be realistic, stylized, or abstract and may depict objects, people, nature, or events.

Artists generally fall into one of four categories. Art directors formulate design concepts and presentation approaches for visual communications. Craft artists create or reproduce handmade objects for sale or exhibition. Fine artists, including painters, sculptors, and illustrators, create original artwork, using a variety of media and techniques. Multi-media artists and animators create special effects, animation, or other visual images on film, on video, or with computers or other electronic media. (Designers, including graphic designers, are discussed elsewhere in the *Handbook*.)

Art directors develop design concepts and review material that is to appear in periodicals, newspapers, and other printed or digital media. They decide how best to present information visually, so that it is eye catching, appealing, and organized. Art directors decide which photographs or artwork to use and oversee the design, layout, and production of material to be published. They may direct workers engaged in artwork, design, layout, and copywriting.

Craft artists make a wide variety of objects, mostly by hand, that are sold either in their own studios, in retail outlets, or at arts-and-crafts shows. Some craft artists display their works in galleries and museums. Craft artists work with many different materials, including ceramics, glass, textiles, wood, metal, and paper, to create unique pieces of art, such as pottery, stained glass, quilts, tapestries, lace, candles, and clothing. Many craft artists also use fine-art techniques—for example, painting, sketching, and printing—to add finishing touches to their art.

Fine artists typically display their work in museums, commercial art galleries, corporate collections, and private homes. Some of their artwork may be commissioned (done on request from clients), but most is sold by the artist or through private art galleries or dealers. The gallery and the artist predetermine how much each will earn from the sale. Only the most successful fine artists are able to support themselves solely through the sale of their works. Most fine artists have at least one other job to support their art careers. Some work in museums or art galleries as fine-arts directors or as curators, planning and setting up art exhibits. A few artists work as art critics for newspapers or magazines or as consultants to foundations or institutional collectors. Other artists teach art classes or conduct workshops in schools or in their own studios. Some artists also hold full-time or part-time jobs unrelated to art and pursue fine art as a hobby or second career.

Usually, fine artists specialize in one or two art forms, such as painting, illustrating, sketching, sculpting, printmaking, and restoring. Painters, illustrators, cartoonists, and sketch artists work with two-dimensional art forms, using shading, perspective, and color to produce realistic scenes or abstractions.

Illustrators usually create pictures for books, magazines, and other publications and for commercial products such as textiles, wrapping paper, stationery, greeting cards, and calendars. Increasingly, illustrators are working in digital format, preparing work directly on a computer. This has created new opportunities for illustrators to work with animators and in broadcast media.

Medical and *scientific illustrators* combine drawing skills with knowledge of biology or other sciences. Medical illustrators work digitally or traditionally to create images of human anatomy and surgical procedures as well as 3-dimensional models and animations. Scientific illustrators draw animal and plant life, atomic and molecular structures, and geologic and planetary formations. These illustrations are used in medical and scientific publications and in audiovisual presentations for teaching purposes. Illustrators also work for lawyers, producing exhibits for court cases.

Cartoonists draw political, advertising, social, and sports cartoons. Some cartoonists work with others who create the idea or story and write captions. Some cartoonists write captions themselves. Most cartoonists have comic, critical, or dramatic talents in addition to drawing skills.

Sketch artists create likenesses of subjects with pencil, charcoal, or pastels. Sketches are used by law enforcement agencies to assist in identifying suspects, by the news media to depict courtroom scenes, and by individual patrons for their own enjoyment.

Sculptors design three-dimensional artworks, either by molding and joining materials such as clay, glass, wire, plastic, fabric, or metal or by cutting and carving forms from a block of plaster, wood, or stone. Some sculptors combine various materials to create mixed-media installations. Some incorporate light, sound, and motion into their works.

Printmakers create printed images from designs cut or etched into wood, stone, or metal. After creating the design, the artist inks the surface of the woodblock, stone, or plate and uses a printing press to roll the image onto paper or fabric. Some make prints by pressing the inked surface onto paper by hand or by graphically encoding and processing data, using a computer. The digitized images are then printed on paper with the use of a computer printer.

Painting restorers preserve and restore damaged and faded paintings. They apply solvents and cleaning agents to clean the surfaces of the paintings, they reconstruct or retouch damaged areas, and they apply preservatives to protect the paintings. Restoration is highly detailed work and usually is reserved for experts in the field.

Multi-media artists and animators work primarily in motion picture and video industries, advertising, and computer systems design services. They draw by hand and use computers to create the series of pictures that form the animated images or special effects seen in movies, television programs, and computer games. Some draw storyboards for television commercials, movies, and animated features. Storyboards present television commercials in a series of scenes similar to a comic strip and allow an advertising agency to evaluate commercials proposed by advertising companies. Storyboards also serve as guides to placing actors and cameras on the television or mo-

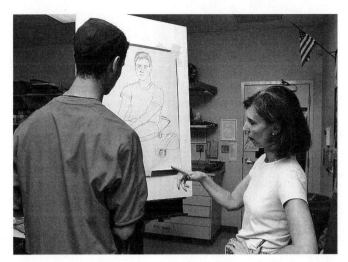
Many artists develop their skills through formal training in art and design.

tion picture set and to other production details. Many multimedia artists model objects in three dimensions by computer and work with programmers to make those images move.

Work environment. Many artists work in fine art or commercial art studios located in office buildings, warehouses, or lofts. Others work in private studios in their homes. Some fine artists share studio space, where they also may exhibit their work. Studio surroundings usually are well lighted and ventilated; however, fine artists may be exposed to fumes from glue, paint, ink, and other materials and to dust or other residue from filings, splattered paint, or spilled cleaners and other fluids. Artists who sit at drafting tables or who use computers for extended periods may experience back pain, eyestrain, or fatigue.

Artists employed by publishing companies, advertising agencies, and design firms generally work a standard workweek. During busy periods, they may work overtime to meet deadlines. Self-employed artists can set their own hours. They may spend much time and effort selling their artwork to potential customers or clients and building a reputation.

Training, Other Qualifications, and Advancement

Artists usually develop their skills through a bachelor's degree program or other postsecondary training in art or design. Although formal schooling is not strictly required for craft and fine artists, it is very difficult to become skilled enough to make a living without some training. Art directors usually have years of work experience and generally need at least a bachelor's degree. Due to the level of technical expertise demanded, multimedia artists and animators generally also need a bachelor's degree.

Education and training. Many colleges and universities offer programs leading to a bachelor's or master's degree in fine arts. Courses usually include core subjects such as English, social science, and natural science, in addition to art history and studio art. Independent schools of art and design also offer postsecondary studio training in the craft, fine, and multi-media arts leading to certificates in the specialties or to an associate or bachelor's degree in fine arts. Typically, these programs focus more intensively on studio work than do the academic programs in a university setting. In 2007 the

National Association of Schools of Art and Design accredited 282 postsecondary institutions with programs in art and design; most of these schools award a degree in art.

Many educational programs in art also provide training in computer techniques. Computers are used widely in the visual arts, and knowledge and training in computer graphics and other visual display software are critical elements of many jobs in these fields.

Medical illustrators must have both a demonstrated artistic ability and a detailed knowledge of living organisms, surgical and medical procedures, and human and animal anatomy. A bachelor's degree combining art and premedical courses usually is required. However, most medical illustrators also choose to pursue a master's degree in medical illustration. This degree is offered in four accredited schools in the United States.

Art directors usually begin as entry-level artists in advertising, publishing, design, and motion picture production firms. Artists are promoted to art director after demonstrating artistic and leadership abilities. Some art schools offer coursework in art direction as part of their curricula. Depending on the scope of their responsibilities, some art directors also may pursue a degree in art administration, which teaches non-artistic skills such as project management and finance.

Those who want to teach fine arts at public elementary or secondary schools usually must have a teaching certificate in addition to a bachelor's degree. An advanced degree in fine arts or arts administration is usually necessary for management or administrative positions in government or in foundations or for teaching in colleges and universities. (See the statements for teachers—postsecondary; and teachers—preschool, kindergarten, elementary, middle, and secondary school elsewhere in the *Handbook*.)

Other qualifications. Evidence of appropriate talent and skill, displayed in an artist's portfolio, is an important factor used by art directors, clients, and others in deciding whether to hire an individual or contract for their work. A portfolio is a collection of handmade, computer-generated, photographic, or printed samples of the artist's best work. Assembling a successful portfolio requires skills usually developed through postsecondary training in art or visual communications. Internships also provide excellent opportunities for artists to develop and enhance their portfolios.

Advancement. Artists hired by firms often start with relatively routine work. While doing this work, however, they may observe other artists and practice their own skills.

Craft and fine artists advance professionally as their work circulates and as they establish a reputation for a particular style. Many of the most successful artists continually develop new ideas, and their work often evolves over time.

Many artists freelance part-time while continuing to hold a full-time job until they are established. Others freelance part time while still in school, to develop experience and to build a portfolio of published work.

Freelance artists try to develop a set of clients who regularly contract for work. Some freelance artists are widely recognized for their skill in specialties such as cartooning or children's book illustration. These artists may earn high incomes and can choose the type of work they do.

Employment

Artists held about 218,000 jobs in 2006. About 62 percent were self-employed. Employment was distributed as follows:

Multimedia artists and animators......................................87,000
Art directors 78,000
Fine artists, including painters,
    sculpters and illustrators...30,000
Craft artists..8,800
Artists and related workers, all other...............................14,000

Of the artists who were not self-employed, many worked for advertising and related services; newspaper, periodical, book, and software publishers; motion picture and video industries; specialized design services; and computer systems design and related services. Some self-employed artists offered their services to advertising agencies, design firms, publishing houses, and other businesses.

Job Outlook

Employment of artists is projected to grow faster than average. Competition for jobs is expected to be keen for both salaried and freelance jobs in all specialties because the number of people with creative ability and an interest in this career is expected to continue to exceed the number of available openings. Despite the competition, employers and individual clients are always on the lookout for talented and creative artists.

Employment change. Employment of artists and related workers is expected to grow 16 percent through 2016, faster than the average for all occupations.

Projections data from the National Employment Matrix

Occupational Title	SOC Code	Employment, 2006	Projected employment, 2016	Change, 2006-2016	
				Number	Percent
Artists and related workers	27-1010	218,000	253,000	34,000	16
Art directors	27-1011	78,000	85,000	7,000	9
Craft artists...	27-1012	8,800	9,500	700	8
Fine artists, including painters, sculptors, and illustrators...........	27-1013	30,000	33,000	3,000	10
Multi-media artists and animators	27-1014	87,000	110,000	23,000	26
Artists and related workers, all other..................................	27-1019	14,000	15,000	1,200	8

NOTE: Data in this table are rounded. See the discussion of the employment projections table in the *Handbook* introductory chapter on *Occupational Information Included in the Handbook.*

Demand for illustrators who work on a computer will increase as Web sites use more detailed images and backgrounds in their designs. Many cartoonists, in particular, opt to post their work on political Web sites and online publications. Cartoonists often create animated or interactive images to satisfy readers' demands for more sophisticated images. The small number of medical illustrators will also be in greater demand as medical research continues to grow.

Demand for multimedia artists and animators will increase as consumers continue to demand more realistic video games, movie and television special effects, and 3D animated movies. Additional job openings will arise from an increasing demand for Web site development and for computer graphics adaptation from the growing number of mobile technologies. Animators are also increasingly finding work in alternative areas such as scientific research or design services.

Job prospects. Competition for jobs as artists and related workers will be keen because there are more qualified candidates than available jobs. Employers in all industries should be able to choose from among the most qualified candidates.

Despite the competition, studios, galleries, and individual clients are always on the lookout for artists who display outstanding talent, creativity, and style. Among craft and fine artists, talented individuals who have developed a mastery of artistic techniques and skills will have the best job prospects. Multi-media artists and animators should have better job opportunities than other artists, but still will experience competition. Job opportunities for animators of lower-technology cartoons could be hampered as these jobs continue to be outsourced overseas.

Despite an expanding number of opportunities, art directors should experience keen competition for the available openings. Craft and fine artists work mostly on a freelance or commission basis and may find it difficult to earn a living solely by selling their artwork. Only the most successful craft and fine artists receive major commissions for their work. Competition among artists for the privilege of being shown in galleries is expected to remain acute, as will competition for grants from sponsors such as private foundations, State and local arts councils, and the National Endowment for the Arts.

The growth in computer graphics packages and stock art Web sites is making it easier for writers, publishers, and art directors to create their own illustrations. As the use of this technology grows, there will be fewer opportunities for illustrators. However, it also has opened up new opportunities for illustrators who prefer to work digitally. Salaried cartoonists will have fewer job opportunities because many newspapers and magazines increasingly rely on freelance work.

Earnings

Median annual earnings of salaried art directors were $68,100 in May 2006. The middle 50 percent earned between $49,480 and $94,920. The lowest 10 percent earned less than $37,920, and the highest 10 percent earned more than $135,090. Median annual earnings were $70,630 in advertising and related services.

Median annual earnings of salaried craft artists were $24,090. The middle 50 percent earned between $18,860 and $35,840. The lowest 10 percent earned less than $14,130, and the highest 10 percent earned more than $46,700. Earnings data for the many self-employed craft artists were not available.

Median annual earnings of salaried fine artists, including painters, sculptors, and illustrators were $41,970. The middle 50 percent earned between $28,500 and $58,550. The lowest 10 percent earned less than $18,350, and the highest 10 percent earned more than $79,390. Earnings data for the many self-employed fine artists were not available.

Median annual earnings of salaried multi-media artists and animators were $51,350, not including the earnings of the self-employed. The middle 50 percent earned between $38,980 and $70,050. The lowest 10 percent earned less than $30,390, and the highest 10 percent earned more than $92,720. Median annual earnings were $57,310 in motion picture and video industries and $48,860 in advertising and related services.

Earnings for self-employed artists vary widely. Some charge only a nominal fee while they gain experience and build a reputation for their work. Others, such as well-established freelance fine artists and illustrators, can earn more than salaried artists. Many, however, find it difficult to rely solely on income earned from selling paintings or other works of art. Like other self-employed workers, freelance artists must provide their own benefits.

Related Occupations

Other workers who apply artistic skills include architects, except landscape and naval; archivists, curators, and museum technicians; commercial and industrial designers; fashion designers; floral designers; graphic designers; interior designers; jewelers and precious stone and metal workers; landscape architects; photographers; and woodworkers. Some workers who use computers extensively, including computer software engineers and desktop publishers, may require art skills.

Sources of Additional Information

For general information about art and design and a list of accredited college-level programs, contact:
➤ National Association of Schools of Art and Design, 11250 Roger Bacon Dr., Suite 21, Reston, VA 20190. Internet: **http://nasad.arts-accredit.org**

For information on careers in the craft arts and for a list of schools and workshops, contact:
➤ American Craft Council Library, 72 Spring St., 6th Floor, New York, NY 10012. Internet: **http://www.craftcouncil.org**

For information on careers in illustration, contact:
➤ Society of Illustrators, 128 E. 63rd St., New York, NY 10021. Internet: **http://www.societyillustrators.org**

For information on careers in medical illustration, contact:
➤ Association of Medical Illustrators, 245 First St., Suite 1800, Cambridge, MA 02142. Internet: **http://www.ami.org**

For information on workshops, scholarships, internships, and competitions for art students interested in advertising careers, contact:
➤ Art Directors Club, 106 W. 29th St., New York, NY 10001. Internet: **http://www.adcglobal.org**

Commercial and Industrial Designers

(O*NET 27-1021.00)

Significant Points

- Commercial and industrial designers usually work closely with a range of specialists including engineers, materials scientists, marketing and corporate strategy staff, cost estimators, and accountants.

- About 30 percent are self-employed; many designers work for services firms.

- A bachelor's degree is usually required to start; many designers pursue a master's degree.

- Keen competition for jobs is expected; those with strong backgrounds in engineering and computer-aided design and extensive business expertise will have the best prospects.

Nature of the Work

Commercial and industrial designers combine the fields of art, business, and engineering to design the products people use every day. In fact, these designers are responsible for the style, function, quality, and safety of almost every manufactured good. Usually designers specialize in one particular product category, such as automobiles and other transportation vehicles, appliances, technology goods, medical equipment, furniture, toys, tools and construction equipment, or housewares.

The first steps in developing a new design, or altering an existing one, are to determine the requirements of the client, the purpose of the product, and to the tastes of customers or users. When creating a new design, designers often begin by researching the product user or the context in which the product will be used. They ascertain desired product characteristics, such as size, shape, weight, color, materials used, cost, ease of use, fit, and safety. To gather this information, designers meet with clients, conduct market research, read design and consumer publications, attend trade shows, and visit potential users, suppliers and manufacturers.

Next, designers prepare conceptual sketches or diagrams—by hand or with the aid of a computer—to illustrate their vision of the product. After conducting research and consulting with a creative director or other members of the product development team, designers then create detailed sketches or renderings. Many designers use computer-aided design (CAD) tools to create these renderings. Computer models make it easier to adjust designs and to experiment with a greater number of alternatives, speeding and improving the design process. Industrial designers who work for manufacturing firms also use computer-aided industrial design (CAID) tools to create designs and machine-readable instructions that can direct automated production tools to build the designed product to exact specifications. Often, designers will also create physical models out of clay, wood, and other materials to give clients a better idea of what the finished product will look like.

Designers present the designs and prototypes to their client or managers and incorporate any changes and suggestions. Designers often work with engineers, accountants, and cost estimators to determine if a product can be made safer, easier to assemble or use, or cheaper to manufacture. Before a product is completed and manufactured, designers may participate in usability and safety tests, watching consumers use prototypes and then making adjustments based on those observations.

Increasingly, designers are working with corporate strategy staff to ensure that their designs fit into the company's business plan and strategic vision. They work with marketing staff to develop plans to best market new product designs to consumers. They work to design products that accurately reflect the company's image and values. And although designers have always tried to identify and design products that fit consumers' needs, more designers are now focused on creating that product before a competitor does. More of today's designers must also focus on creating innovative products as well as considering the style and technical aspects of the product.

Work environment. Designers employed by manufacturing establishments, large corporations, or design firms generally work regular hours in well-lighted and comfortable settings. Designers in smaller design consulting firms, or those who freelance, may work under a contract to do specific tasks or designs. They frequently adjust their workday to suit their clients' schedules and deadlines, meeting with the clients evenings

Most commercial and industrial designers use computer-aided software to prepare conceptual diagrams.

or weekends when necessary. Consultants and self-employed designers tend to work longer hours and in smaller, more congested, environments. Additional hours may be required to meet deadlines.

Designers may work in their own offices or studios or in clients' homes or offices. They also may travel to other locations, such as testing facilities, design centers, clients' exhibit sites, users' homes or workplaces, and manufacturing facilities. With the increased speed and sophistication of computers and advanced communications networks, designers may form international design teams and serve a more geographically dispersed clientele.

Training, Other Qualifications, and Advancement
A bachelor's degree is required for most entry-level commercial and industrial design positions. Many designers also pursue a master's degree to increase their employment opportunities.

Education and training. A bachelor's degree in industrial design, architecture, or engineering is required for most entry-level commercial and industrial design jobs. Coursework includes principles of design, sketching, computer-aided design, industrial materials and processes, manufacturing methods, and some classes in engineering, physical science, mathematics, psychology, and anthropology. Many programs also include internships at design or manufacturing firms.

Many aspiring commercial and industrial designers earn a master's degree in industrial design. Some already have a bachelor's degree in the field, but an increasing number have degrees and experience in other areas, such as marketing, information technology, or engineering, and are hoping to transfer into a design occupation.

Also, because of the growing emphasis on strategic design and how products fit into a firm's overall business plan, an increasing number of designers are pursing a master's degree in business administration to gain business skills.

The National Association of Schools of Art and Design accredits approximately 250 postsecondary colleges, universities, and private institutes with programs in art and design. About 45 of these schools award a degree in industrial design; some offer a bachelor's of art, some a bachelor's of science. Many schools require the successful completion of 1 year of basic art and design courses before entry into a bachelor's degree program. Applicants also may be required to submit sketches and other examples of their artistic ability.

Other qualifications. Creativity and technical knowledge are crucial in this occupation. People in this field must have a strong sense of the esthetic—an eye for color and detail and a sense of balance and proportion. Despite the advancement of computer-aided design, sketching ability remains an important advantage. Designers must also understand the technical aspects of how products function. Most employers also expect new designers to know computer-aided design software. The deciding factor in getting a job often is a good portfolio—examples of a person's best work.

Designers must also be imaginative and persistent and must be able to communicate their ideas visually, verbally, and in writing. Because tastes and styles can change quickly, designers need to be well read, open to new ideas and influences, and quick to react to changing trends. Problem-solving skills and the ability to work independently and under pressure also are important traits. People in this field need self-discipline to start projects on their own, to budget their time, and to meet deadlines and production schedules.

As strategic design becomes more important, employers will seek designers with project management skills and knowledge of accounting, marketing, quality assurance, purchasing, and strategic planning. Good business sense and sales ability are important, especially for those who freelance or run their own business.

Advancement. Beginning commercial and industrial designers usually receive on-the-job training and normally need 1 to 3 years of training before they can advance to higher level positions. Experienced designers in large firms may advance to chief designer, design department head, or other supervisory positions. Some designers leave the occupation to become teachers in design schools or in colleges and universities. Many faculty members continue to consult privately or operate small design studios to complement their classroom activities. Some experienced designers open their own design firms.

Employment
Commercial and industrial designers held about 48,000 jobs in 2006. About 30 percent were self-employed. Another 15 percent of designers were employed in either engineering or specialized design services firms. Manufacturing firms and service providing companies employed most of the rest of commercial and industrial designers.

Job Outlook
Employment is expected to grow about as fast as average. Keen competition for jobs is expected; those with strong backgrounds in engineering and computer-aided design and extensive business expertise will have the best prospects.

Employment change. Employment of commercial and industrial designers is expected to grow 7 percent between 2006 and 2016, about as fast as the average for all occupations. Employment growth will arise from an expanding economy and from an increase in consumer and business demand for new or upgraded products.

Increasing demand for commercial and industrial designers will also stem from the continued emphasis on the quality and safety of products, the increasing demand for new products

Projections data from the National Employment Matrix

Occupational Title	SOC Code	Employment, 2006	Projected employment, 2016	Change, 2006-2016	
				Number	Percent
Commercial and industrial designers..	27-1021	48,000	51,000	3,400	7

NOTE: Data in this table are rounded. See the discussion of the employment projections table in the *Handbook* introductory chapter on *Occupational Information Included in the Handbook.*

that are easy and comfortable to use, and the development of high-technology products in consumer electronics, medicine, transportation, and other fields. But increasingly, manufacturers have been outsourcing design work to design services firms to cut costs and to find the most qualified design talent, increasing employment in these firms and reducing it in others, such as manufacturing. Additionally, some companies use design firms overseas, especially for the design of high-technology products. These overseas design firms are located closer to their suppliers, which reduces the time it takes to design and sell a product—an important consideration when technology is changing quickly. This offshoring of design work could continue to slow employment growth of U.S. commercial and industrial designers.

Despite the increase in design work performed overseas, most design jobs, particularly jobs not related to high-technology product design, will still remain in the U.S. Design is essential to a firm's success, and firms will want to retain control over the design process.

Job prospects. Competition for jobs will be keen because many talented individuals are attracted to the design field. The best job opportunities will be in specialized design firms which are used by manufacturers to design products or parts of products. Designers with strong backgrounds in engineering and computer-aided design and extensive business expertise will have the best prospects.

As the demand for design work becomes more consumer-driven, designers who can closely monitor, and react to, changing customer demands—and who can work with marking and strategic planning staffs to come up with new products—will also improve their job prospects.

Employment of designers can be affected by fluctuations in the economy. For example, during periods of economic downturns, companies may cut research and development spending, including new product development.

Earnings

Median annual wage-and-salary earnings for commercial and industrial designers were $54,560 in May 2006. The middle 50 percent earned between $41,270 and $72,610. The lowest 10 percent earned less than $31,510, and the highest 10 percent earned more than $92,970. Earnings information for the self-employed are not available. Median annual earnings of salaried commercial and industrial designers in the largest industries that employed them in May 2006 were:

Management of companies and enterprises $64,700
Architectural, engineering, and related services 61,890
Engineering services 60,440
Specialized design services..52,500

Related Occupations

Workers in other art and design occupations include artists and related workers; fashion designers; floral designers; graphic designers; and interior designers. Some other occupations that require computer-aided design skills are architects, except landscape and naval; computer software engineers; desktop publishers; drafters; and engineers.

Sources of Additional Information

For general career information on commercial and industrial design, contact:

➤ Industrial Designers Society of America, 45195 Business Court, Suite 250, Dulles, VA 20166.
Internet: **http://www.idsa.org**

For general information about art and design and a list of accredited college-level programs, contact:

➤ National Association of Schools of Art and Design, 11250 Roger Bacon Dr., Suite 21, Reston, VA 20190.
Internet: **http://nasad.arts-accredit.org**

Fashion Designers

(O*NET 27-1022.00)

Significant Points

- Almost one-forth are self-employed.

- In 2006, the highest concentrations of fashion designers were employed in New York and California.

- Employers usually seek designers with a 2- or 4-year degree who are knowledgeable about textiles fabrics, ornamentation, and fashion trends.

- Slower-than-average job growth is projected, and competition for jobs is expected to be keen.

Nature of the Work

Fashion designers help create the billions of dresses, suits, shoes, and other clothing and accessories purchased every year by consumers. Designers study fashion trends, sketch designs of clothing and accessories, select colors and fabrics, and oversee the final production of their designs. *Clothing designers* create and help produce men's, women's, and children's apparel, including casual wear, suits, sportswear, formalwear, outerwear, maternity, and intimate apparel. *Footwear designers* help create and produce different styles of shoes and boots. *Accessory designers* help create and produce items such as handbags, belts, scarves, hats, hosiery, and eyewear, which add the finishing touches to an outfit. (The work of jewelers and precious stone and metal workers is described elsewhere in the *Handbook.*) Some fashion designers specialize in clothing, footwear, or accessory design, but others create designs in all three fashion categories.

The design process from initial design concept to final production takes between 18 and 24 months. The first step in creating a design is researching current fashion and making predictions of future trends. Some designers conduct their own research, while others rely on trend reports published by fashion industry trade groups. Trend reports indicate what styles, colors, and fabrics will be popular for a particular season in the future. Textile manufacturers use these trend reports to begin designing fabrics and patterns while fashion designers begin to sketch preliminary designs. Designers then visit manufacturers or trade shows to procure samples of fabrics and decide which fabrics to use with which designs.

Once designs and fabrics are chosen, a prototype of the article using cheaper materials is created and then tried on a model to see what adjustments to the design need to be made. This also helps designers to narrow their choices of designs to offer for sale. After the final adjustments and selections have been made, samples of the article using the actual materials are sewn and then marketed to clothing retailers. Many designs are shown at fashion and trade shows a few times a year. Retailers at the shows place orders for certain items, which are then manufactured and distributed to stores.

Computer-aided design (CAD) is increasingly being used in the fashion design industry. Although most designers initially sketch designs by hand, a growing number also translate these hand sketches to the computer. CAD allows designers to view designs of clothing on virtual models and in various colors and shapes, thus saving time by requiring fewer adjustments of prototypes and samples later.

Depending on the size of their design firm and their experience, fashion designers may have varying levels of involvement in different aspects of design and production. In large design firms, fashion designers often are the lead designers who are responsible for creating the designs, choosing the colors and fabrics, and overseeing technical designers who turn the designs into a final product. They are responsible for creating the prototypes and patterns and work with the manufacturers and suppliers during the production stages. Large design houses also employ their own patternmakers, tailors, and sewers who create the master patterns for the design and sew the prototypes and samples. Designers working in small firms, or those new to the job, usually perform most of the technical, patternmaking, and sewing tasks, in addition to designing the clothing. (The work of pattern makers, hand sewers, and tailors is covered in the statement on textile, apparel, and furnishings occupations elsewhere in the *Handbook*.)

Fashion designers working for apparel wholesalers or manufacturers create designs for the mass market. These designs are manufactured in various sizes and colors. A small number of high-fashion (haute couture) designers are self-employed and create custom designs for individual clients, usually at very high prices. Other high-fashion designers sell their designs in their own retail stores or cater to specialty stores or high-fashion department stores. These designers create a mixture of original garments and those that follow established fashion trends.

Some fashion designers specialize in costume design for performing arts, motion picture, and television productions. The work of costume designers is similar to other fashion designers. Costume designers, however, perform extensive research on the styles worn during the period in which the performance takes place, or they work with directors to select and create appropriate attire. They make sketches of designs, select fabric and other materials, and oversee the production of the costumes. They also must stay within the costume budget for the particular production item.

Work environment. Fashion designers employed by manufacturing establishments, wholesalers, or design firms generally work regular hours in well-lighted and comfortable settings. Designers who freelance generally work on a contract, or by the job. They frequently adjust their workday to suit their

Designers visit manufacturers or trade shows to procure samples of fabrics.

clients' schedules and deadlines, meeting with the clients during evenings or weekends when necessary. Freelance designers tend to work longer hours and in smaller, more congested, environments, and are under pressure to please clients and to find new ones in order to maintain a steady income. Regardless of their work setting, all fashion designers occasionally work long hours to meet production deadlines or prepare for fashion shows.

The global nature of the fashion business requires constant communication with suppliers, manufacturers, and customers all over the United States and the world. Most fashion designers travel several times a year to trade and fashion shows to learn about the latest fashion trends. Designers also may travel frequently to meet with fabric and materials suppliers and with manufacturers who produce the final apparel products.

Training, Other Qualifications, and Advancement
In fashion design, employers usually seek individuals with a 2- or 4-year degree who are knowledgeable about textiles, fabrics, ornamentation, and fashion trends.

Education and training. Bachelor's of fine arts and associate degree programs in fashion design are offered at many colleges, universities, and private art and design schools. Some fashion designers also combine a fashion design degree with a business, marketing, or fashion merchandising degree, especially those who want to run their own business or retail store. Basic coursework includes color, textiles, sewing and tailoring, pattern making, fashion history, computer-aided design (CAD), and design of different types of clothing such as menswear or footwear. Coursework in human anatomy, mathematics, and psychology also is useful.

The National Association of Schools of Art and Design accredits approximately 250 postsecondary institutions with programs in art and design. Most of these schools award degrees in fashion design. Many schools do not allow formal entry into a program until a student has successfully completed basic art and design courses. Applicants usually have to submit sketches and other examples of their artistic ability.

Aspiring fashion designers can learn these necessary skills through internships with design or manufacturing firms. Some designers also gain valuable experience working in retail stores, as personal stylists, or as custom tailors. Such experience can help designers gain sales and marketing skills while learning what styles and fabrics look good on different people.

Designers also can gain exposure to potential employers by entering their designs in student or amateur contests. Because of the global nature of the fashion industry, experience in one of the international fashion centers, such as Milan or Paris, can be useful.

Other qualifications. Designers must have a strong sense of the esthetic—an eye for color and detail, a sense of balance and proportion, and an appreciation for beauty. Fashion designers also need excellent communication and problem-solving skills. Despite the advancement of computer-aided design, sketching ability remains an important advantage in fashion design. A good portfolio—a collection of a person's best work—often is the deciding factor in getting a job.

In addition to creativity, fashion designers also need to have sewing and patternmaking skills, even if they do not perform these tasks themselves. Designers need to be able to understand these skills so they can give proper instruction in how the garment should be constructed. Fashion designers also need strong sales and presentation skills to persuade clients to purchase their designs. Good teamwork and communication skills also are necessary because increasingly the business requires constant contact with suppliers, manufacturers, and buyers around the world.

Advancement. Beginning fashion designers usually start out as pattern makers or sketching assistants for more experienced designers before advancing to higher level positions. Experienced designers may advance to chief designer, design department head, or another supervisory position. Some designers may start their own design company, or sell their designs in their own retail stores. A few of the most successful designers can work for high-fashion design houses that offer personalized design services to wealthy clients.

Employment

Fashion designers held about 20,000 jobs in 2006. About 28 percent of fashion designers worked for apparel, piece goods, and notions merchant wholesalers; and the remainder worked for corporate offices involved in the management of companies and enterprises, clothing stores, performing arts companies, and specialized design services firms. Another 24 percent were self-employed.

Employment of fashion designers tends to be concentrated in regional fashion centers. In 2006, the highest concentrations of fashion designers were employed in New York and California.

Job Outlook

Slower-than-average job growth is projected. Competition for jobs is expected to be keen as many designers are attracted to the creativity and glamour associated with the occupation.

Employment change. Employment of fashion designers is projected to grow 5 percent between 2006 and 2016, more slowly than the average for all occupations. Job growth will stem from a growing population demanding more clothing, footwear, and accessories. Demand is increasing for stylish clothing that is affordable, especially among middle income consumers. However, employment declines in cut and sew apparel manufacturing are projected to offset job increases among apparel wholesalers.

Job opportunities in cut and sew manufacturing will continue to decline as apparel is increasingly manufactured overseas. However, employment of fashion designers in this industry will not decline as fast as other occupations because firms are more likely to keep design work in-house.

Job prospects. Job competition is expected be keen as many designers are attracted to the creativity and glamour associated with the occupation. Relatively few job openings arise because of low job turnover and the small number of new openings created every year.

The best job opportunities will be in design firms that design mass market clothing sold in department stores and retail chain stores, such as apparel wholesale firms. Few employment opportunities are expected in design firms that cater to high-end department stores and specialty boutiques as demand for expensive, high-fashion design declines relative to other luxury goods and services.

Earnings

Median annual earnings for salaried fashion designers were $62,610 in May 2006. The middle 50 percent earned between $42,140 and $87,510. The lowest 10 percent earned less than $30,000, and the highest 10 percent earned more than $117,120. Median annual earnings of salaried fashion designers in the largest industries that employed them in May 2006 were:

Management of companies and enterprises $70,570
Cut and sew apparel manufacturing......................................69,810
Apparel, piece goods, and
 notions merchant wholesalers...62,910

Earnings in fashion design can vary widely based on the employer and years of experience. Starting salaries in fashion design tend to be very low until designers are established in the industry. Salaried fashion designers usually earn higher and more stable incomes than self-employed or freelance designers. However, a few of the most successful self-employed fashion designers may earn many times the salary of the highest paid salaried designers. Self-employed fashion designers must provide their own benefits and retirement.

Projections data from the National Employment Matrix

Occupational Title	SOC Code	Employment, 2006	Projected employment, 2016	Change, 2006-2016	
				Number	Percent
Fashion designers..	27-1022	20,000	21,000	1,000	5

NOTE: Data in this table are rounded. See the discussion of the employment projections table in the *Handbook* introductory chapter on *Occupational Information Included in the Handbook.*

Related Occupations

Workers in other art and design occupations include artists and related workers, commercial and industrial designers, floral designers, graphic designers, and interior designers. Jewelers and precious stone and metal workers also design wearable accessories. Other common occupations in the fashion industry include demonstrators, product promoters, and models; photographers; purchasing managers, buyers, and purchasing agents; retail salespersons; and textile, apparel, and furnishings occupations.

Sources of Additional Information

For general information about art and design and a list of accredited college-level programs, contact:

➤ National Association of Schools of Art and Design, 11250 Roger Bacon Dr., Suite 21, Reston, VA 20190. Internet: **http://nasad.arts-accredit.org**

For general information about careers in fashion design, contact:

➤ Fashion Group International, 8 West 40th St., 7th Floor, New York, NY 10018. Internet: **http://www.fgi.org**

Floral Designers

(O*NET 27-1023.00)

Significant Points

- Despite the projected decline in employment, job opportunities should be good because of relatively high replacement needs.

- Floral design is the only design specialty that does not require formal postsecondary training.

- Many floral designers work long hours on weekends and holidays, filling orders and setting up decorations for weddings and other events.

- About one-third are self-employed.

Nature of the Work

Floral designers, or florists, cut live, dried, or silk flowers and other greenery and arrange them into displays of various sizes and shapes. These workers design these displays by selecting flowers, containers, and ribbons and arranging them into bouquets, corsages, centerpieces of tables, wreaths, and the like for weddings, funerals, holidays, and other special occasions. Some floral designers also use accessories such as balloons, candles, toys, candy, and gift baskets as part of their displays.

Job duties often vary by employment setting. Most floral designers work in small independent floral shops that specialize in custom orders and also handle large orders for weddings, caterers, or interior designers. Floral designers may meet with customers to discuss the arrangement or work from a written order. They note the occasion, the customer's preferences, the price of the order, the time the floral display or plant is to be ready, and the place to which it is to be delivered. For special occasions, floral designers usually will help set up floral decorations. Floral designers also will prearrange a few displays to have available for walk-in customers or last-minute orders. Some floral designers also assist interior designers in creating live or silk displays for hotels, restaurants, and private residences.

A number of floral designers, also known as florists, work in the floral departments of grocery stores or for Internet florists, which specialize in creating prearranged floral decorations and bouquets. These floral retailers also may fill small custom orders for special occasions and funerals, but some grocery store florists do not deliver to clients or handle large custom orders.

Florists who work for wholesale flower distributors assist in the selection of different types of flowers and greenery to purchase and sell to retail florists. Wholesale floral designers also select flowers for displays that they use as examples for retail florists.

Self-employed floral designers must handle the various aspects of running their own businesses, such as selecting and purchasing flowers, hiring and supervising staff, and maintaining financial records. Self-employed designers also may run gift shops or wedding consultation businesses in addition to providing floral design services. Some conduct design work-

Floral designers cut live, dried, or silk flowers and other greenery and arrange them into displays of various sizes and shapes.

shops for amateur gardeners or others with an interest in floral design.

Work environment. Most floral designers work in comfortable and well-lit spaces in retail outlets or at home, although working outdoors sometimes is required. Designers also may frequently make short trips delivering flowers, setting up arrangements for special events, and procuring flowers and other supplies.

Floral designers have frequent contact with customers and must work to satisfy their demands, including last-minute holiday and funeral orders. Because many flowers are perishable, most orders cannot be completed too far in advance. Consequently, some designers work long hours before and during holidays. Some also work nights and weekends to complete large orders for weddings and other special events.

Floral designers may suffer muscle strain from long periods of standing and from repeated finger and arm movements required to make floral arrangements. They are susceptible to back strain from lifting and carrying heavy flower arrangements. Designers also may suffer allergic reactions to certain types of pollen when working with flowers. In addition, they frequently use sharp objects—scissors, knives, and metal wire—that can cause injuries if handled improperly.

Training, Other Qualifications, and Advancement

Floral design is the only design occupation that does not require formal postsecondary training; most floral designers learn their skills on the job. Employers generally look for high school graduates who have creativity, a flair for arranging flowers, and a desire to learn.

Education and training. Floral design is the only design occupation that does not require formal postsecondary training; most floral designers learn their skills on the job. Private floral schools, vocational schools, and community colleges award certificates in floral design. These programs generally require a high school diploma for admission and last from several weeks to 1 year. Floral design courses teach the basics of arranging flowers, including the different types of flowers, their color and texture, cutting and taping techniques, tying bows and ribbons, proper handling and care of flowers, floral trends, and pricing.

Some floral designers also may earn an associate or bachelor's degree at a community college or university. Some programs offer formal degrees in floral design, while others offer degrees in floriculture, horticulture, or ornamental horticulture. In addition to floral design courses, these programs teach courses in botany, chemistry, hydrology, microbiology, pesticides, and soil management.

Since many floral designers manage their own business, additional courses in business, accounting, marketing, and computer technology can be helpful.

Certification and other qualifications. The American Institute of Floral Designers offers an accreditation examination as an indication of professional achievement in floral design. The exam consists of a written part covering floral terminology and an onsite floral-arranging part in which candidates have 4 hours to complete five floral designs: funeral tributes, table arrangements, wedding arrangements, wearable flowers, and a category of the candidate's choosing.

Floral designers must be creative, service oriented, and able to communicate their ideas visually and verbally. Because trends in floral design change quickly, designers must be open to new ideas and react quickly to changing trends. Problem-solving skills and the ability to work independently and under pressure also are important traits. Individuals in this field need self-discipline to budget their time and meet deadlines.

Advancement. Many florists gain their initial experience working as cashiers or delivery people in retail floral stores. The completion of formal design training, however, is an asset for floral designers, particularly those interested in advancing to chief floral designer or in opening their own businesses.

Advancement in the floral field is limited. After a few years of on-the-job training, designers can either advance to a supervisory position or open their own floral shop.

Employment

Floral designers held about 87,000 jobs in 2006. Approximately 33 percent were self-employed. About 45 percent of all floral designers worked in florist shops. Another 10 percent worked in the floral departments of grocery stores. Others were employed by miscellaneous nondurable goods merchant wholesalers, other general merchandise stores, and in lawn and garden equipment and supply stores.

Job Outlook

Despite the projected decline in employment, job opportunities are expected to be good because of the need to replace workers who leave the occupation.

Employment change. Employment of floral designers is expected to decline moderately, 9 percent, between 2006 and 2016. The demand for floral decorations will continue to grow as flower sales increase with the population and the lavishness of weddings and other special events that require floral decorations. As disposable incomes rise, more people also will demand fresh flowers in their homes and offices. Increased spending on interior design also is expected to create more demand for stylish artificial arrangements for homes and businesses.

Despite growing demand for floral decorations, few job opportunities are expected in floral wholesalers, primarily because an increasing number of shops are purchasing flowers

Projections data from the National Employment Matrix

Occupational Title	SOC Code	Employment, 2006	Projected employment, 2016	Change, 2006-2016	
				Number	Percent
Floral designers..	27-1023	87,000	79,000	-7,700	-9

NOTE: Data in this table are rounded. See the discussion of the employment projections table in the *Handbook* introductory chapter on *Occupational Information Included in the Handbook.*

and supplies directly from growers in order to cut costs. In addition, the growth of electronic commerce in the floral industry will make it easier for retail florists to locate their own suppliers. Discretionary spending on flowers and floral products is highly sensitive to the state of the economy, and during economic downturns employment may fall off as floral expenditures decline.

Job prospects. Job opportunities should be good because of the relatively high replacement needs in retail florists. Many people leave the occupation after a time because of its comparatively low starting pay and limited opportunities for advancement. Opportunities should be good in grocery store and Internet floral shops as sales of floral arrangements from these outlets grow. The prearranged displays and gifts available in these stores appeal to consumers because of the convenience and because of prices that are lower than can be found in independent floral shops.

As mass marketers capture more of the small flower orders, independent floral shops are increasingly finding themselves under pressure to remain profitable. Many independent shops have added online ordering systems in order to compete with Internet florists. Others are trying to distinguish their services by specializing in certain areas of floral design or by combining floral design with event planning and interior design services. Some florists also are adding holiday decorating services in which they will set up decorations for businesses and residences.

Earnings
Median annual earnings for wage and salary floral designers were $21,700 in May 2006. The middle 50 percent earned between $17,690 and $27,330. The lowest 10 percent earned less than $15,040, and the highest 10 percent earned more than $33,650. Median annual earnings were $23,990 in grocery stores and $21,210 in florists.

Related Occupations
Other art and design occupations include artists and related workers, commercial and industrial designers, fashion designers, graphic designers, and interior designers. Landscape architects also create designs involving plants and flowers. Other occupations involved directly with plants and flowers include soil and plant scientists; and farm workers and laborers, crop, nursery, and greenhouse.

Sources of Additional Information
For information about careers in floral design, contact:
➤ American Institute of Floral Designers, 720 Light St., Baltimore, MD 21230. Internet: **http://www.aifd.org**
➤ Society of American Florists, 1601 Duke St., Alexandria, VA 22314. Internet: **http://www.safnow.org**

To learn more about designing flowers for weddings and funerals, see "Jobs in weddings and funerals: Working with the betrothed and the bereaved," in the winter 2006 Occupational Outlook Quarterly and online at:
http://www.bls.gov/opub/ooq/2006/winter/art03.pdf.

Graphic Designers
(O*NET 27-1024.00)

Significant Points

- About 25 percent are self-employed; many do freelance work in addition to holding a salaried job in design or in another occupation.

- A bachelor's degree is required for most entry-level positions; however, an associate degree may be sufficient for some technical positions.

- Job seekers are expected to face keen competition; individuals with a bachelor's degree and knowledge of computer design software, particularly those with Web site design and animation experience will have the best opportunities.

Nature of the Work
Graphic designers—or graphic artists—plan, analyze, and create visual solutions to communications problems. They find the most effective way to get messages across in print, electronic, and film media using a variety of methods such as color, type, illustration, photography, animation, and various print and layout techniques. Graphic designers develop the overall layout and production design of magazines, newspapers, journals, corporate reports, and other publications. They also produce promotional displays, packaging, and marketing brochures for products and services, design distinctive logos for products and businesses, and develop signs and signage systems—called environmental graphics—for business and government. An increasing number of graphic designers also develop material for Internet Web pages, interactive media, and multimedia projects. Graphic designers also may produce the credits that appear before and after television programs and movies.

The first step in developing a new design is to determine the needs of the client, the message the design should portray, and its appeal to customers or users. Graphic designers consider cognitive, cultural, physical, and social factors in planning and executing designs for the target audience. Designers gather relevant information by meeting with clients, creative or art directors, and by performing their own research. Identifying the needs of consumers is becoming increasingly important for graphic designers as they continue to develop corporate communication strategies in addition to creating designs and layouts.

Graphic designers prepare sketches or layouts—by hand or with the aid of a computer—to illustrate their vision for the design. They select colors, sound, artwork, photography, animation, style of type, and other visual elements for the design. Designers also select the size and arrangement of the different elements on the page or screen. They may create graphs and charts from data for use in publications, and they often consult with copywriters on any text that accompanies the design. Designers then present the completed design to their clients or

Graphic designers use specialized software packages to create layouts and graphics.

art or creative director for approval. In printing and publishing firms, graphic designers also may assist the printers by selecting the type of paper and ink for the publication and reviewing the mock-up design for errors before final publication.

Graphic designers use specialized computer software packages to help them create layouts and design elements and to program animated graphics.

Graphic designers sometimes supervise assistants who follow instructions to complete parts of the design process. Designers who run their own businesses also may devote a considerable time to developing new business contacts, choosing equipment, and performing administrative tasks, such as reviewing catalogues and ordering samples. The need for up-to-date computer and communications equipment is an ongoing consideration for graphic designers.

Work environment. Working conditions and places of employment vary. Graphic designers employed by large advertising, publishing, or design firms generally work regular hours in well-lighted and comfortable settings. Designers in smaller design consulting firms and those who freelance generally work on a contract, or job, basis. They frequently adjust their workday to suit their clients' schedules and deadlines. Consultants and self-employed designers tend to work longer hours and in smaller, more congested, environments.

Designers may work in their own offices or studios or in clients' offices. Designers who are paid by the assignment are under pressure to please existing clients and to find new ones to maintain a steady income. All designers sometimes face frustration when their designs are rejected or when their work is not as creative as they wish. Graphic designers may work evenings or weekends to meet production schedules, especially in the printing and publishing industries where deadlines are shorter and more frequent.

Training, Other Qualifications, and Advancement

A bachelor's or an associate degree in graphic design is usually required for a job as a graphic designer. Creativity, communication, and problem solving skills and familiarity with computer graphics and design software also are important.

Education and training. A bachelor's degree is required for most entry-level and advanced graphic design positions; al-

though some entry-level technical positions may only require an associate degree. Bachelor's degree programs in fine arts or graphic design are offered at many colleges, universities, and private design schools. Most curriculums include studio art, principles of design, computerized design, commercial graphics production, printing techniques, and Web site design. In addition to design courses, a liberal arts education that includes courses in art history, writing, psychology, sociology, foreign languages and cultural studies, marketing, and business are useful in helping designers work effectively.

Associate degrees and certificates in graphic design also are available from 2-year and 3-year professional schools. These programs usually focus on the technical aspects of graphic design and include few liberal arts courses. Graduates of 2-year programs normally qualify as assistants to graphic designers or for positions requiring technical skills only. Individuals who wish to pursue a career in graphic design—and who already possess a bachelor's degree in another field—can complete a 2-year or 3-year program in graphic design to learn the technical requirements.

The National Association of Schools of Art and Design accredits about 250 postsecondary institutions with programs in art and design. Most of these schools award a degree in graphic design. Many schools do not allow formal entry into a bachelor's degree program until a student has successfully finished a year of basic art and design courses. Applicants may be required to submit sketches and other examples of their artistic ability.

Increasingly, employers expect new graphic designers to be familiar with computer graphics and design software. Graphic designers must keep up with new and updated software, on their own or through software training programs.

Other qualifications. In addition to postsecondary training in graphic design, creativity, communication, and problem-solving skills are crucial. Graphic designers must be creative and able to communicate their ideas visually, verbally, and in writing. They also must have an eye for details. Designers show employers these traits by putting together a portfolio—a collection of examples of a person's best work. A good portfolio often is the deciding factor in getting a job.

Because consumer tastes can change quickly, designers also need to be well read, open to new ideas and influences, and quick to react to changing trends. The ability to work independently and under pressure are equally important traits. People in this field need self-discipline to start projects on their own, to budget their time, and to meet deadlines and production schedules. Good business sense and sales ability also are important, especially for those who freelance or run their own firms.

Advancement. Beginning graphic designers usually receive on-the-job training and normally need 1 to 3 years of training before they can advance to higher positions. Experienced graphic designers in large firms may advance to chief designer, art or creative director, or other supervisory positions. Some designers leave the occupation to become teachers in design schools or in colleges and universities. Many faculty members continue to consult privately or operate small design studios to complement their classroom activities. Some experienced designers open their own firms or choose to specialize in one area of graphic design.

Employment

Graphic designers held about 261,000 jobs in 2006. Most graphic designers worked in specialized design services; advertising and related services; printing and related support activities; or newspaper, periodical, book, and directory publishers. Other designers produced computer graphics for computer systems design firms or motion picture production firms. A small number of designers also worked in engineering services or for management, scientific, and technical consulting firms.

About 25 percent of designers were self-employed. Many did freelance work—full time or part time—in addition to holding a salaried job in design or in another occupation.

Job Outlook

Employment of graphic designers is expected grow about as fast as average. Keen competition for jobs is expected; individuals with a bachelor's degree and knowledge of computer design software, particularly those with Web site design and animation experience will have the best opportunities.

Employment change. Employment of graphic designers is expected to grow 10 percent, about as fast as the average for all occupations from 2006 to 2016, as demand for graphic design continues to increase from advertisers, publishers, and computer design firms. Some of this increase is expected to stem from the expansion of the video entertainment market, including television, movies, video, and made-for-Internet outlets.

Moreover, graphic designers with Web site design and animation experience will especially be needed as demand increases for design projects for interactive media—Web sites, video games, cellular telephones, personal digital assistants, and other technology. Demand for graphic designers also will increase as advertising firms create print and Web marketing and promotional materials for a growing number of products and services.

In recent years, some computer, printing, and publishing firms have outsourced basic layout and design work to design firms overseas. This trend is expected to continue and may have a negative impact on employment growth for low-level, technical graphic design workers. However, most high-level graphic design jobs will remain in the U.S. Strategic design, the work of developing communication strategies for clients and firms to help them to gain competitive advantages in the market, requires close proximity to the consumer in order to identify and target their needs and interests.

Job prospects. Graphic designers are expected to face keen competition for available positions. Many talented individuals are attracted to careers as graphic designers. Individuals with a bachelor's degree and knowledge of computer design software, particularly those with Web site design and animation experience will have the best opportunities.

Graphic designers with a broad liberal arts education and experience in marketing and business management will be best suited for positions developing communication strategies.

Earnings

Median annual earnings for wage and salary graphic designers were $39,900 in May 2006. The middle 50 percent earned between $30,600 and $53,310. The lowest 10 percent earned less than $24,120, and the highest 10 percent earned more than $69,730. May 2006 median annual earnings in the industries employing the largest numbers of graphic designers were:

```
Specialized design services..................................................$43,410
Advertising and related services ..........................................41,600
Newspaper, periodical, book, and directory publishers ........34,290
Printing and related support activities..................................33,930
Newspaper publishers .........................................................31,540
```

According to the American Institute of Graphic Arts, median annual total cash compensation for entry-level designers was $35,000 in 2007. Staff-level graphic designers earned a median of $45,000. Senior designers, who may supervise junior staff or have some decision-making authority that reflects their knowledge of graphic design, earned a median of $62,000. Solo designers who freelanced or worked under contract to another company reported median earnings of $60,000. Design directors, the creative heads of design firms or in-house corporate design departments, earned $98,600. Graphic designers with ownership or partnership interests in a firm or who were principals of the firm in some other capacity earned $113,000.

Related Occupations

Workers in other occupations in the art and design field include artists and related workers; commercial and industrial designers; fashion designers; floral designers; and interior designers. Other occupations that require computer-aided design skills include computer software engineers, drafters, and desktop publishers. Other occupations involved in the design, layout, and copy of publications include advertising, marketing, promotions, public relations, and sales managers; photographers; writers and editors; and prepress technicians and workers.

Sources of Additional Information

For general information about art and design and a list of accredited college-level programs, contact:
➤ National Association of Schools of Art and Design, 11250 Roger Bacon Dr., Suite 21, Reston, VA 20190-5248.
Internet: **http://nasad.arts-accredit.org**

Projections data from the National Employment Matrix

Occupational Title	SOC Code	Employment, 2006	Projected employment, 2016	Change, 2006-2016	
				Number	Percent
Graphic designers...	27-1024	261,000	286,000	26,000	10

NOTE: Data in this table are rounded. See the discussion of the employment projections table in the *Handbook* introductory chapter on *Occupational Information Included in the Handbook*.

For information about graphic, communication, or interaction design careers, contact:

➤ American Institute of Graphic Arts, 164 Fifth Ave., New York, NY 10010. Internet: **http://www.aiga.org**

For information on workshops, scholarships, internships, and competitions for graphic design students interested in advertising careers, contact:

➤ Art Directors Club, 106 West 29th St., New York, NY 10001. Internet: **http://www.adcglobal.org**

Interior Designers

(O*NET 27-1025.00)

Significant Points

- Keen competition is expected for jobs because many talented individuals are attracted to this occupation.

- About 26 percent are self-employed.

- Postsecondary education—especially a bachelor's degree—is recommended for entry-level positions; some States license interior designers.

Nature of the Work

Interior designers draw upon many disciplines to enhance the function, safety, and aesthetics of interior spaces. Their main concerns are with how different colors, textures, furniture, lighting, and space work together to meet the needs of a building's occupants. Designers plan interior spaces of almost every type of building, including offices, airport terminals, theaters, shopping malls, restaurants, hotels, schools, hospitals, and private residences. Good design can boost office productivity, increase sales, attract a more affluent clientele, provide a more relaxing hospital stay, or increase a building's market value.

Traditionally, most interior designers focused on decorating—choosing a style and color palette and then selecting appropriate furniture, floor and window coverings, artwork, and lighting. However, an increasing number of designers are becoming involved in architectural detailing, such as crown molding and built-in bookshelves, and in planning layouts of buildings undergoing renovation, including helping to determine the location of windows, stairways, escalators, and walkways.

Interior designers must be able to read blueprints, understand building and fire codes, and know how to make space accessible to people who are disabled. Designers frequently collaborate with architects, electricians, and building contractors to ensure that designs are safe and meet construction requirements.

Whatever space they are working on, almost all designers follow the same process. The first step, known as programming, is to determine the client's needs and wishes. The designer usually meets face-to-face with the client to find out how the space will be used and to get an idea of the client's preferences and budget. For example, the designer might inquire about a family's cooking habits if the family is remodeling a kitchen or ask about a store or restaurant's target customer in order to pick an appropriate motif. The designer also will visit the space to take inventory of existing furniture and equipment and identify positive attributes of the space and potential problems.

Then, the designer formulates a design plan and estimates costs. Today, designs often are created with the use of computer-aided design (CAD), which provides more detail and easier corrections than sketches made by hand. Once the designer completes the proposed design, he or she will present it to the client and make revisions based on the client's input.

When the design concept is decided upon, the designer will begin specifying the materials, finishes, and furnishings required, such as furniture, lighting, flooring, wall covering, and artwork. Depending on the complexity of the project, the designer also might submit drawings for approval by a construction inspector to ensure that the design meets building codes. If a project requires structural work, the designer works with an architect or engineer for that part of the project. Most designs also require the hiring of contractors to do technical work, such as lighting, plumbing, or electrical wiring. Often designers choose contractors and write work contracts.

Finally, the designer develops a timeline for the project, coordinates contractor work schedules, and makes sure work is completed on time. The designer oversees the installation of the design elements, and after the project is complete, the designer, together with the client, pay follow-up visits to the building site to ensure that the client is satisfied. If the client is not satisfied, the designer makes corrections.

Designers who work for furniture or home and garden stores sell merchandise in addition to offering design services. In-store designers provide services, such as selecting a style and color scheme that fits the client's needs or finding suitable accessories and lighting, similar to those offered by other interior designers. However, in-store designers rarely visit clients' spaces and use only a particular store's products or catalogs.

Interior designers sometimes supervise assistants who carry out their plans and perform administrative tasks, such as reviewing catalogues and ordering samples. Designers who run their own businesses also may devote considerable time to developing new business contacts, examining equipment and space needs, and attending to business matters.

Although most interior designers do many kinds of projects, some specialize in one area of interior design. Some specialize in the type of building space—usually residential or commercial—while others specialize in a certain design element or type of client, such as health care facilities. The most common specialties of this kind are lighting, kitchen and bath, and closet designs. However, designers can specialize in almost any area of design, including acoustics and noise abatement, security, electronics and home theaters, home spas, and indoor gardens.

Three areas of design that are becoming increasingly popular are ergonomic design, elder design, and environmental—or green—design. Ergonomic design involves designing work spaces and furniture that emphasize good posture and minimize muscle strain on the body. Elder design involves planning interior space to aid in the movement of people who are elderly and disabled. Green design involves selecting furniture and carpets that are free of chemicals and hypoallergenic and selecting construction materials that are energy efficient or are made from renewable resources

Work environment. Working conditions and places of employment vary. Interior designers employed by large corporations or design firms generally work regular hours in well-lighted and comfortable settings. Designers in smaller design consulting firms or those who freelance generally work on a contract, or job, basis. They frequently adjust their workday to suit their clients' schedules and deadlines, meeting with clients during evening or weekend hours when necessary. Consultants and self-employed designers tend to work longer hours and in smaller, more congested environments.

Interior designers may work under stress to meet deadlines, stay on budget, and please clients. Self-employed designers also are under pressure to find new clients to maintain a steady income.

Designers may work in their own offices or studios or in clients' homes or offices. They also may travel to other locations, such as showrooms, design centers, clients' exhibit sites, and manufacturing facilities. With the increased speed and sophistication of computers and advanced communications networks, designers may form international design teams, serve a more geographically dispersed clientele, research design alternatives by using information on the Internet, and purchase supplies electronically.

Interior designers often review a large number of samples in order to choose an appropriate design for interior spaces.

Training, Other Qualifications, and Advancement

Postsecondary education, especially a bachelor's degree, is recommended for entry-level positions in interior design. Two-year and 3-year programs also are available. Some States license interior designers.

Education and training. Postsecondary education, especially a bachelor's degree, is recommended for entry-level positions in interior design. Training programs are available from professional design schools or from colleges and universities and usually take 2 to 4 years to complete. Graduates of 2-year or 3-year programs are awarded certificates or associate degrees in interior design and normally qualify as assistants to interior designers upon graduation. Graduates with a bachelor's degree usually qualify for a formal design apprenticeship program.

The National Association of Schools of Art and Design accredits approximately 250 postsecondary institutions with programs in art and design. Most of these schools award a degree in interior design. Applicants may be required to submit sketches and other examples of their artistic ability. Basic coursework includes computer-aided design (CAD), drawing, perspective, spatial planning, color and fabrics, furniture design, architecture, ergonomics, ethics, and psychology.

The National Council for Interior Design Accreditation also accredits interior design programs that lead to a bachelor's degree. In 2007, there were 145 accredited bachelor's degree programs in interior design in the United States; most are part of schools or departments of art, architecture, and home economics.

After the completion of formal training, interior designers will enter a 1-year to 3-year apprenticeship to gain experience before taking a licensing exam. Most apprentices work in design or architecture firms under the supervision of an experienced designer. Apprentices also may choose to gain experience working as an in-store designer in furniture stores. The National Council of Interior Design offers the Interior Design Experience Program, which helps entry-level interior designers gain valuable work experience by supervising work experience and offering mentoring services and workshops to new designers.

Licensure. Twenty-three States, the District of Columbia, and Puerto Rico register or license interior designers. The National Council administers the licensing exam for Interior Design Qualification. To be eligible to take the exam, applicants must have at least 6 years of combined education and experience in interior design, of which at least 2 years must be postsecondary education in design.

Once candidates have passed the qualifying exam, they are granted the title of Certified, Registered, or Licensed Interior Designer, depending on the State. Continuing education is required to maintain licensure.

Other qualifications. Membership in a professional association is one indication of an interior designer's qualifications and professional standing. The American Society of Interior Designers is the largest professional association for interior designers in the United States. Interior designers can qualify for membership with at least a 2-year degree and work experience.

Employers increasingly prefer interior designers who are familiar with computer-aided design software and the basics of architecture and engineering to ensure that their designs meet building safety codes.

In addition to possessing technical knowledge, interior designers must be creative, imaginative, and persistent and must be able to communicate their ideas visually, verbally, and in writing. Because tastes in style can change quickly, designers need to be well read, open to new ideas and influences, and quick to react to changing trends. Problem-solving skills and the ability to work independently and under pressure are additional important traits. People in this field need self-discipline to start projects on their own, to budget their time, and to meet deadlines and production schedules. Good business sense and sales ability also are important, especially for those who freelance or run their own business.

Certification and advancement. Optional certifications in kitchen and bath design are available from the National Kitchen and Bath Association. The association offers three different levels of certification for kitchen and bath designers, each achieved through training seminars and certification exams.

Beginning interior designers receive on-the-job training and normally need 1 to 3 years of training before they can advance to higher level positions. Experienced designers in large firms may advance to chief designer, design department head, or some other supervisory position. Some experienced designers open their own firms or decide to specialize in one aspect of interior design. Other designers leave the occupation to become teachers in schools of design or in colleges and universities. Many faculty members continue to consult privately or operate small design studios to complement their classroom activities.

Employment

Interior designers held about 72,000 jobs in 2006. Approximately 26 percent were self-employed. About 26 percent of interior designers worked in specialized design services. The rest of the interior designers provided design services in architectural and landscape architectural services, furniture and home-furnishing stores, building material and supplies dealers, and residential building construction companies. Many interior designers also performed freelance work in addition to holding a salaried job in interior design or another occupation.

Job Outlook

Employment of interior designers is expected to be faster than average; however, keen competition for jobs is expected.

Employment change. Employment of interior designers is expected to grow 19 percent from 2006 to 2016, faster than the average for all occupations. Economic expansion, growing homeowner wealth, and an increasing interest in interior design will increase demand for designers.

Recent increases in homeowner wealth and the growing popularity of home improvement television programs have increased demand for residential design services. Homeowners have been using the equity in their homes to finance new additions, remodel aging kitchens and bathrooms, and update the general décor of the home. Many homeowners also have requested design help in creating year-round outdoor living spaces.

However, this same growth in home improvement television programs and discount furniture stores has spurred a trend in do-it-yourself design, which could hamper employment growth of designers. Nevertheless, some clients will still hire designers for initial consultations.

Demand from businesses in the hospitality industry—hotels, resorts, and restaurants—is expected to be high because of an expected increase in tourism. Demand for interior design services from the health care industry also is expected to be high because of an anticipated increase in demand for facilities that will accommodate the aging population. Designers will be needed to make these facilities as comfortable and homelike as possible for patients.

Some interior designers choose to specialize in one design element to create a niche for themselves in an increasingly competitive market. The demand for kitchen and bath design is growing in response to the growing demand for home remodeling. Designs using the latest technology in, for example, home theaters, state-of-the-art conference facilities, and security systems are expected to be especially popular. In addition, demand for home spas, indoor gardens, and outdoor living space should continue to increase.

Extensive knowledge of ergonomics and green design are expected to be in demand. Ergonomic design has gained in popularity with the growth in the elderly population and workplace safety requirements. The public's growing awareness of environmental quality and the growing number of individuals with allergies and asthma are expected to increase the demand for green design.

Job prospects. Interior designers are expected to face keen competition for available positions because many talented individuals are attracted to this profession. Individuals with little or no formal training in interior design, as well as those lacking creativity and perseverance, will find it very difficult to establish and maintain a career in this occupation.

As the economy grows, more private businesses and consumers will request the services of interior designers. However, design services are considered a luxury expense and may be subject to fluctuations in the economy. For example, decreases in consumer and business income and spending caused by a slow economy can have a detrimental effect on employment of interior designers.

Earnings

Median annual earnings for wage and salary interior designers were $42,260 in May 2006. The middle 50 percent earned

Projections data from the National Employment Matrix

Occupational Title	SOC Code	Employment, 2006	Projected employment, 2016	Change, 2006-2016	
				Number	Percent
Interior designers	27-1025	72,000	86,000	14,000	19

NOTE: Data in this table are rounded. See the discussion of the employment projections table in the *Handbook* introductory chapter on *Occupational Information Included in the Handbook.*

between $31,830 and $57,230. The lowest 10 percent earned less than $24,270, and the highest 10 percent earned more than $78,760. Median annual earnings in the industries employing the largest numbers of interior designers in May 2006 were:

Architectural, engineering, and related services	$46,750
Architectural services	46,750
Specialized design services	43,250
Furniture stores	38,980
Building material and supplies dealers	36,650

Interior design salaries vary widely with the specialty, type of employer, number of years of experience, and reputation of the individuals. Among salaried interior designers, those in large specialized design and architectural firms tend to earn higher and more stable salaries. Interior designers working in retail stores usually earn a commission, which can be irregular.

For residential design projects, self-employed interior designers and those working in smaller firms usually earn a per-hour consulting fee, plus a percentage of the total cost of furniture, lighting, artwork, and other design elements. For commercial projects, they might charge a per-hour consulting fee, charge by the square footage, or charge a flat fee for the whole project. Also, designers who use specialty contractors usually earn a percentage of the contractor's earnings on the project in return for hiring the contractor. Self-employed designers must provide their own benefits.

Related Occupations

Workers in other occupations who design or arrange objects to enhance their appearance and function include architects, except landscape and naval; artists and related workers; commercial and industrial designers; fashion designers; floral designers; graphic designers; and landscape architects.

Sources of Additional Information

For information on degrees, continuing education, and licensure programs in interior design and interior design research, contact:

➤ American Society of Interior Designers, 608 Massachusetts Ave. NE., Washington, DC 20002.
Internet: **http://www.asid.org**

For a list of schools with accredited bachelor's degree programs in interior design, contact:

➤ Foundation for Interior Design Education Research, 146 Monroe Center NW., Suite 1318, Grand Rapids, MI 49503.
Internet: **http://www.fider.org**

For general information about art and design and a list of accredited college-level programs, contact:

➤ National Association of Schools of Art and Design, 11250 Roger Bacon Dr., Suite 21, Reston, VA 20190.
Internet: **http://nasad.arts-accredit.org**

For information on State licensing requirements and exams, and the Interior Design Experience Program, contact:

➤ National Council for Interior Design Qualification, 1200 18th St.NW., Suite 1001, Washington, DC 20036-2506.
Internet: **http://www.ncidq.org**

For information on careers, continuing education, and certification programs in the interior design specialty of residential kitchen and bath design, contact:

➤ National Kitchen and Bath Association, 687 Willow Grove St., Hackettstown, NJ 07840.
Internet: **http://www.nkba.org/student**

Entertainers and Performers, Sports and Related Occupations

Actors, Producers, and Directors

(O*NET 27-2011.00, 27-2012.00, 27-2012.01, 27-2012.02, 27-2012.03, 27-2012.04, 27-2012.05)

Significant Points

- Actors endure long periods of unemployment, intense competition for roles, and frequent rejections in auditions.

- Formal training through a university or acting conservatory is typical; however, many actors, producers, and directors find work on the basis of their experience and talent alone.

- Because earnings may be erratic, many supplement their incomes by holding jobs in other fields; however, the most successful actors, producers, and directors may have extraordinarily high earnings.

Nature of the Work

Actors, producers, and directors express ideas and create images in theater, film, radio, television, and other performing arts media. They interpret a writer's script to entertain, inform, or instruct an audience. Although many actors, producers, and directors work in New York or Los Angeles, far more work in other places. They perform, direct, and produce in local or regional television studios, theaters, or film production companies, often creating advertising or training films or small-scale independent movies.

Actors perform in stage, radio, television, video, or motion picture productions. They also work in cabarets, nightclubs, and theme parks. Actors portray characters, and, for more complex roles, they research their character's traits and circumstances so that they can better understand a script.

Most actors struggle to find steady work and only a few achieve recognition as stars. Some well-known, experienced performers may be cast in supporting roles or make brief, cameo appearances, speaking only one or two lines. Others work as "extras," with no lines to deliver. Some actors do voiceover and narration work for advertisements, animated features, books on tape, and other electronic media. They also teach in high school or university drama departments, acting conservatories, or public programs.

Producers are entrepreneurs who make the business and financial decisions involving a motion picture, made-for-television feature, or stage production. They select scripts, approve the development of ideas, arrange financing, and determine the size and cost of the endeavor. Producers hire or approve directors, principal cast members, and key production staff members. They also negotiate contracts with artistic and design personnel in accordance with collective bargaining agreements. They guarantee payment of salaries, rent, and other expenses.

Television and radio producers determine which programs, episodes, or news segments get aired. They may research material, write scripts, and oversee the production of individual pieces. Producers in any medium coordinate the activities of writers, directors, managers, and agents to ensure that each project stays on schedule and within budget.

Directors are responsible for the creative decisions of a production. They interpret scripts, audition and select cast members, conduct rehearsals, and direct the work of cast and crew. They approve the design elements of a production, including the sets, costumes, choreography, and music. Assistant directors cue the performers and technicians, telling them when to make entrances or light, sound, or set changes.

Work environment. Actors, producers, and directors work under constant pressure. Many face stress from the continual need to find their next job. To succeed, actors, producers, and directors need patience and commitment to their craft. Actors strive to deliver flawless performances, often while working under undesirable and unpleasant conditions. Producers and directors organize rehearsals and meet with writers, designers, financial backers, and production technicians. They experience stress not only from these activities, but also from the need to adhere to budgets, union work rules, and production schedules.

Acting assignments typically are short term—ranging from 1 day to a few months—which means that actors frequently experience long periods of unemployment between jobs. The uncertain nature of the work results in unpredictable earnings and intense competition for jobs. Often, actors, producers, and directors must hold other jobs in order to sustain a living.

When performing, actors typically work long, irregular hours. For example, stage actors may perform one show at night while rehearsing another during the day. They also might travel with a show when it tours the country. Movie actors may work on location, sometimes under adverse weather conditions, and may spend considerable time waiting to perform their scenes. Actors who perform in a television series often appear on camera with little preparation time, because scripts tend to be revised frequently or even written moments before taping. Those who appear live or before a studio audience must be able to handle impromptu situations and calmly ad lib, or substitute, lines when necessary.

Evening and weekend work is a regular part of a stage actor's life. On weekends, more than one performance may be held per day. Actors and directors working on movies or television programs, especially those who shoot on location, may work in

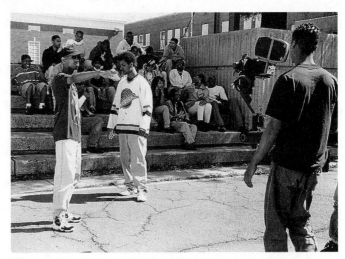

Actors, producers, and directors work in various locations.

the early morning or late evening hours to film night scenes or tape scenes inside public facilities outside of normal business hours.

Actors should be in good physical condition and have the necessary stamina and coordination to move about theater stages and large movie and television studio lots. They also need to maneuver about complex technical sets while staying in character and projecting their voices audibly. Actors must be fit to endure heat from stage or studio lights and the weight of heavy costumes. Producers and directors ensure the safety of actors by conducting extra rehearsals on the set so that the actors can learn the layout of set pieces and props, by allowing time for warmups and stretching exercises to guard against physical and vocal injuries, and by providing an adequate number of breaks to prevent heat exhaustion and dehydration.

Training, Other Qualifications, and Advancement

People who become actors, producers, and directors follow many paths to employment. The most important qualities employers look for are creative instincts, innate talent, and the intellectual capacity to perform. The best way to prepare for a career as an actor, especially in the theater, is through formal dramatic training, preferably obtained as part of a bachelor's degree program. Producers and especially directors need experience in the field, either as actors or in other related jobs.

Education and training. Formal dramatic training, either through an acting conservatory or a university program, generally is necessary for these jobs, but some people successfully enter the field without it. Most people studying for a bachelor's degree take courses in radio and television broadcasting, communications, film, theater, drama, or dramatic literature. Many stage actors continue their academic training and receive a Master of Fine Arts (MFA) degree. Advanced curricula may include courses in stage speech and movement, directing, playwriting, and design, as well as intensive acting workshops. The National Association of Schools of Theatre accredits 150 programs in theater arts.

Most aspiring actors participate in high school and college plays, work in college radio or television stations, or perform with local community theater groups. Local and regional theater experience and work in summer stock, on cruise lines, or in theme parks helps many young actors hone their skills. Membership in one of the actors' unions and work experience in smaller communities may lead to work in larger cities, notably New York, Chicago, or Los Angeles. In television and film, actors and directors typically start in smaller television markets or with independent movie production companies and then work their way up to larger media markets and major studio productions. A few people go into acting after successful careers in other fields, such as broadcasting or announcing.

Actors, regardless of experience level, may pursue workshop training through acting conservatories or mentoring by a drama coach. Sometimes actors learn a foreign language or train with a dialect coach to develop an accent to make their characters more realistic.

There are no specific training requirements for producers. They come from many different backgrounds. Actors, writers, film editors, and business managers commonly enter the field. Producers often start in a theatrical management office, working for a press agent, managing director, or business manager. Some start in a performing arts union or service organization. Others work behind the scenes with successful directors, serve on the boards of art companies, or promote their own projects. Although there are no formal training programs for producers, a number of colleges and universities offer degree programs in arts management and in managing nonprofit organizations.

Directors often start out as actors. Many also have formal training in directing. The Directors Guild of America and the Alliance of Motion Picture and Television Producers jointly sponsor the Assistant Directors Training Program. To be accepted to this highly competitive program, an individual must have either a bachelor's or associate degree or 2 years of experience and must complete a written exam and other assessments. Program graduates are eligible to become a member of the Directors Guild and typically find employment as a second assistant director.

Other qualifications. Actors need talent and creativity that will enable them to portray different characters. Because competition for parts is fierce, versatility and a wide range of related performance skills, such as singing, dancing, skating, juggling, acrobatics, or miming are especially useful. Experience in horseback riding, fencing, linguistics, or stage combat also can lift some actors above the average and get them noticed by producers and directors. Actors must have poise, stage presence, the ability to affect an audience, and the ability to follow direction. Modeling experience also may be helpful. Physical appearance, such as having certain features and being the specified size and weight, often is a deciding factor in who gets a particular role.

Many professional actors rely on agents or managers to find work, negotiate contracts, and plan their careers. Agents generally earn a percentage of the pay specified in an actor's contract. Other actors rely solely on attending open auditions for parts. Trade publications list the times, dates, and locations of these auditions.

Some actors begin as movie extras. To become an extra, one usually must be listed by casting agencies that supply extras to the major movie studios in Hollywood. Applicants are accepted only when the numbers of people of a particular type on the list, for example, athletic young women, old men, or small children,

falls below what is needed. In recent years, only a very small proportion of applicants have succeeded in being listed.

Like actors, directors and producers need talent and creativity. They also need business acumen.

Advancement. As the reputations and box-office draw of actors, producers, and directors grow, they might work on bigger budget productions, on network or syndicated broadcasts, or in more prestigious theaters. Actors may advance to lead roles and receive star billing. A few actors move into acting-related jobs, such as drama coaches or directors of stage, television, radio, or motion picture productions. Some teach drama privately or in colleges and universities.

Employment

In May 2006, actors, producers, and directors held about 163,000 jobs, primarily in motion picture and video, performing arts, and broadcast industries. Because many others were between jobs, the total number of actors, producers, and directors available for work was higher. Employment in the theater, and other performing arts companies, is cyclical—higher in the fall and spring seasons—and concentrated in New York and other major cities with large commercial houses for musicals and touring productions. Also, many cities support established professional regional theaters that operate on a seasonal or year-round basis. About 28 percent of actors, producers, and directors were self-employed.

Actors, producers, and directors may find work in summer festivals, on cruise lines, and in theme parks. Many smaller, nonprofit professional companies, such as repertory companies, dinner theaters, and theaters affiliated with drama schools, acting conservatories, and universities, provide employment opportunities for local amateur talent and professional entertainers. Auditions typically are held in New York for many productions across the country and for shows that go on the road.

Employment in motion pictures and in films for television is centered in New York and Los Angeles. However, small studios exist throughout the country. Many films are shot on location and may employ local professional and nonprofessional actors. In television, opportunities are concentrated in the network centers of New York and Los Angeles, but cable television services and local television stations around the country also employ many actors, producers, and directors.

Job Outlook

Employment of actors, producers, and directors is expected to grow about as fast as the average for all occupations. Competition for jobs will be keen. Although a growing number of people aspire to enter these professions, many will leave the field early because the work—when it is available—is hard, the hours are long, and the pay may be low.

Employment change. Employment in these occupations is expected to grow 11 percent during the 2006-16 decade, about as fast as the average for all occupations. Expanding cable and satellite television operations, increasing production and distribution of major studio and independent films, and rising demand for films in other countries should create more employment opportunities for actors, producers, and directors. Also fueling job growth is the continued development of interactive media, direct-for-Web movies, and mobile content, produced

Projections data from the National Employment Matrix

Occupational Title	SOC Code	Employment, 2006	Projected employment, 2016	Change, 2006-2016	
				Number	Percent
Actors, producers, and directors	27-2010	163,000	182,000	18,000	11
Actors...	27-2011	70,000	78,000	8,100	12
Producers and directors...	27-2012	93,000	103,000	10,000	11

NOTE: Data in this table are rounded. See the discussion of the employment projections table in the *Handbook* introductory chapter on *Occupational Information Included in the Handbook*.

for cell phones or other portable electronic devices. However, greater emphasis on national, rather than local, entertainment productions may restrict employment opportunities in the broadcasting industry.

Job prospects. Competition for jobs will be stiff. The large number of highly trained and talented actors auditioning for roles generally exceeds the number of parts that become available. Only performers with the most stamina and talent will find regular employment.

Venues for live entertainment, such as Broadway and Off-Broadway theaters, touring productions, and repertory theaters in many major metropolitan areas, as well as theme parks and resorts, are expected to offer many job opportunities. However, prospects in these venues are variable because they fluctuate with economic conditions.

Earnings

The most successful actors, producers, and directors may have extraordinarily high earnings but for others, because earnings may be erratic, many supplement their income by holding jobs in other fields.

Median hourly earnings of actors were $11.61 in May 2006. The middle 50 percent earned between $8.47 and $22.51. The lowest 10 percent earned less than $7.31, and the highest 10 percent earned more than $51.02. Median hourly earnings were $16.82 in performing arts companies and $10.69 in the motion picture and video industry. Annual earnings data for actors were not available because of the wide variation in the number of hours worked by actors and the short-term nature of many jobs, which may last for 1 day or 1 week; it is extremely rare for actors to have guaranteed employment that exceeded 3 to 6 months.

Median annual earnings of salaried producers and directors were $56,310 in 2006. The middle 50 percent earned between $37,980 and $88,700. Median annual earnings were $70,750 in the motion picture and video industry and $47,530 in radio and television broadcasting.

Minimum salaries, hours of work, and other conditions of employment are often covered in collective bargaining agreements between the producers and the unions representing workers. The Actors' Equity Association (AEA) represents stage actors; the Screen Actors Guild (SAG) covers actors in motion pictures, including television, commercials, and film; and the American Federation of Television and Radio Artists (AFTRA) represents television and radio studio performers. Some actors who regularly work in several media find it advantageous to join multiple unions, while SAG and AFTRA may share jurisdiction for work in additional areas, such as the production of training or educational films not slated for broadcast, television

commercial work, and interactive media. While these unions generally determine minimum salaries, any actor or director may negotiate for a salary higher than the minimum.

Under terms of a joint SAG and AFTRA contract covering all unionized workers, motion picture and television actors with speaking parts earned a minimum daily rate of $759 or $2,634 for a 5-day week as of July 1, 2007. Actors also receive contributions to their health and pension plans and additional compensation for reruns and foreign telecasts of the productions in which they appear.

According to AEA, the minimum weekly salary for actors in Broadway productions as of June 2007 was $1,509. Actors in Off-Broadway theaters received minimums ranging from $516 to $976 a week as of October 29, 2007, depending on the seating capacity of the theater. Regional theaters that operate under an Equity agreement pay actors $544 to $840 per week. For touring productions, actors receive an additional $113 per day for living expenses ($119 per day in higher cost cities). New terms were negotiated under an "experimental touring program" provision for lower budget musicals that tour to smaller cities or that perform for fewer performances at each stop. In an effort to increase the number of paid workweeks while on tour, actors may be paid less than the full production rate for touring shows in exchange for higher per diems and profit participation.

Some well-known actors—stars—earn well above the minimum; their salaries are many times the figures cited, creating the false impression that all actors are highly paid. For example, of the nearly 100,000 SAG members, only about 50 might be considered stars. The average income that SAG members earn from acting, less than $5,000 a year, is low because employment is sporadic. Therefore, most actors must supplement their incomes by holding jobs in other occupations.

Many actors who work more than a qualifying number of days, or weeks per year or earn over a set minimum pay, are covered by a union health, welfare, and pension fund, which includes hospitalization insurance to which employers contribute. Under some employment conditions, Equity and AFTRA members receive paid vacations and sick leave.

Many stage directors belong to the Society of Stage Directors and Choreographers (SSDC), and film and television directors belong to the Directors Guild of America. Earnings of stage directors vary greatly. The SSDC usually negotiates salary contracts which include royalties (additional income based on the number of performances) with smaller theaters. Directing a production at a dinner theater generally will pay less than directing one at a summer theater, but has more potential for generating income from royalties. Regional theaters may hire directors for longer periods, increasing compensation accordingly. The highest-paid directors work on Broadway and commonly earn over $50,000 per show. However, they also receive payment in the form of royalties—a negotiated percentage of gross box office receipts—that can exceed their contract fee for long-running box office successes.

Stage producers seldom get a set fee; instead, they get a percentage of a show's earnings or ticket sales.

Related Occupations

People who work in performing arts occupations that may require acting skills include announcers; dancers and choreographers; and musicians, singers, and related workers. Others working in occupations related to film and theater include makeup artists, theatrical and performance; fashion designers; and set and exhibit designers. Producers share many responsibilities with those who work as top executives.

Sources of Additional Information

For general information about theater arts and a list of accredited college-level programs, contact:

➤ National Association of Schools of Theater, 11250 Roger Bacon Dr., Suite 21, Reston, VA 20190.
Internet: **http://nast.arts-accredit.org**

For general information on actors, producers, and directors, contact any of the following organizations:

➤ Actors Equity Association, 165 West 46th St., New York, NY 10036. Internet: **http://www.actorsequity.org**

➤ Screen Actors Guild, 5757 Wilshire Blvd., Los Angeles, CA 90036-3600. Internet: **http://www.sag.org**

➤ American Federation of Television and Radio Artists—Screen Actors Guild, 4340 East-West Hwy., Suite 204, Bethesda, MD 20814-4411.
Internet: **http://www.aftra.org or http://www.sag.org**

Athletes, Coaches, Umpires, and Related Workers

(O*NET 27-2021.00, 27-2022.00, 27-2023.00)

Significant Points

- Work hours are often irregular and extensive travel may be required.

- Career-ending injuries are always a risk for athletes.

- Job opportunities will be best for part-time coaches, sports instructors, umpires, referees, and sports officials in high schools, sports clubs, and other settings.

- Competition to become a professional athlete will continue to be extremely intense; athletes who seek to compete professionally must have extraordinary talent, desire, and dedication to training.

Nature of the Work

We are a Nation of sports fans and sports players. Some of those who participate in amateur sports dream of becoming paid professional athletes, coaches, or sports officials, but very

few beat the long and daunting odds of making a full-time living from professional athletics. Those athletes who make it to the professional level find that careers are short and jobs are insecure. Even though the chances of employment as a professional athlete are slim, there are many opportunities for at least a part-time job as a coach, instructor, referee, or umpire in amateur athletics or in high school, college, or university sports.

Athletes and *sports competitors* compete in organized, officiated sports events to entertain spectators. When playing a game, athletes are required to understand the strategies of their game while obeying the rules and regulations of the sport. The events in which they compete include both team sports, such as baseball, basketball, football, hockey, and soccer, and individual sports, such as golf, tennis, and bowling. The level of play varies from unpaid high school athletics to professional sports, in which the best from around the world compete in events broadcast on international television.

Being an athlete involves more than competing in athletic events. Athletes spend many hours each day practicing skills and improving teamwork under the guidance of a coach or a sports instructor. They view videotapes to critique their own performances and techniques and to learn their opponents' tendencies and weaknesses to gain a competitive advantage. Some athletes work regularly with strength trainers to gain muscle and stamina and to prevent injury. Many athletes push their bodies to the limit during both practice and play, so career-ending injury always is a risk; even minor injuries may put a player at risk of replacement. Because competition at all levels is extremely intense and job security is always precarious, many athletes train year round to maintain excellent form and technique and peak physical condition. Very little downtime from the sport exists at the professional level. Athletes also must conform to regimented diets during their sports season to supplement any physical training program.

Coaches organize amateur and professional athletes and teach them the fundamentals of individual and team sports. (In individual sports, *instructors* sometimes may fill this role.) Coaches train athletes for competition by holding practice sessions to perform drills that improve the athletes' form, technique, skills, and stamina. Along with refining athletes' individual skills, coaches are responsible for instilling good sportsmanship, a competitive spirit, and teamwork and for managing their teams during both practice sessions and competitions. Before competition, coaches evaluate or scout the opposing team to determine game strategies and practice specific plays. During competition, coaches may call specific plays intended to surprise or overpower the opponent, and they may substitute players for optimum team chemistry and success. Coaches' additional tasks may include selecting, storing, issuing, and taking inventory of equipment, materials, and supplies.

Many coaches in high schools are primarily teachers of academic subjects who supplement their income by coaching part time. (For more information on high school teachers, see the statement on teachers—preschool, kindergarten, elementary, middle, and secondary, elsewhere in the *Handbook*.) College coaches consider coaching a full-time discipline and may be away from home frequently as they travel to scout and recruit prospective players.

Sports instructors teach professional and nonprofessional athletes individually. They organize, instruct, train, and lead athletes in indoor and outdoor sports such as bowling, tennis, golf, and swimming. Because activities are as diverse as weight lifting, gymnastics, scuba diving, and karate, instructors tend to specialize in one or a few activities. Like coaches, sports instructors also may hold daily practice sessions and be responsible for any needed equipment and supplies. Using their knowledge of their sport and of physiology, they determine the type and level of difficulty of exercises, prescribe specific drills, and correct athletes' techniques. Some instructors also teach and demonstrate the use of training apparatus, such as trampolines or weights, for correcting athletes' weaknesses and enhancing their conditioning. Like coaches, sports instructors evaluate the athlete and the athlete's opponents to devise a competitive game strategy.

Coaches and sports instructors sometimes differ in their approaches to athletes because of the focus of their work. For example, while coaches manage the team during a game to optimize its chance for victory, sports instructors—such as those who work for professional tennis players—often are not permitted to instruct their athletes during competition. Sports instructors spend more of their time with athletes working one-on-one, which permits them to design customized training programs for each individual. Motivating athletes to play hard challenges most coaches and sports instructors but is vital for the athlete's success. Many coaches and instructors derive great satisfaction working with children or young adults, helping them to learn new physical and social skills, improve their physical condition, and achieve success in their sport.

Umpires, referees, and other sports officials officiate at competitive athletic and sporting events. They observe the play, detect infractions of rules, and impose penalties established by the rules and regulations of the various sports. Umpires, referees, and sports officials anticipate play and position themselves to best see the action, assess the situation, and determine any violations. Some sports officials, such as boxing referees, may work independently, while others such as umpires work in groups. Regardless of the sport, the job is highly stressful because officials are often required to make a decision in a split second, sometimes resulting in strong disagreement among competitors, coaches, and spectators.

Professional *scouts* evaluate the skills of both amateur and professional athletes to determine talent and potential. As a sports intelligence agent, the scout's primary duty is to seek out top athletic candidates for the team he or she represents. At the professional level, scouts typically work for scouting organizations or as freelance scouts. In locating new talent, scouts perform their work in secrecy so as not to "tip off" their opponents about their interest in certain players. At the college level, the head scout often is an assistant coach, although freelance scouts may aid colleges by reporting to coaches about exceptional players. Scouts at this level seek talented high school athletes by reading newspapers, contacting high school coaches and alumni, attending high school games, and study-

Coaches need good communication and leadership skills.

ing videotapes of prospects' performances. They also evaluate potential players' background and personal characteristics, such as motivation and discipline, by talking to the players' coaches, parents, and teachers.

Work environment. Irregular work hours are the trademark of the athlete. They also are common for coaches, umpires, referees, and other sports officials. Athletes and others in sports related occupations often work Saturdays, Sundays, evenings, and holidays. Athletes and full-time coaches usually work more than 40 hours a week for several months during the sports season, if not most of the year. Some coaches in educational institutions may coach more than one sport, particularly in high schools.

Athletes, coaches, and sports officials who participate in competitions that are held outdoors may be exposed to all weather conditions of the season. Those involved in events that are held indoors tend to work in climate-controlled comfort, often in arenas, enclosed stadiums, or gymnasiums. Athletes, coaches, and some sports officials frequently travel to sporting events by bus or airplane. Scouts also travel extensively in locating talent, often by automobile.

Umpires, referees, and other sports officials regularly encounter verbal abuse by fans, coaches, and athletes. The officials also face possible physical assault and, increasingly, lawsuits from injured athletes based on their officiating decisions.

Training, Other Qualifications, and Advancement

Education and training requirements for athletes, coaches, umpires, and related workers vary greatly by the level and type of sport. Regardless of the sport or occupation, these jobs require immense overall knowledge of the game, usually acquired through years of experience at lower levels.

Education and training. Becoming a professional athlete is the culmination of years of effort. Athletes usually begin competing in their sports while in elementary or middle school, and continue through high school and sometimes college. They play in amateur tournaments and on high school and college teams, where the best attract the attention of professional scouts. Most schools require that participating athletes maintain specific academic standards to remain eligible to play. Athletes who seek to compete professionally must have extraordinary talent, desire, and dedication to training.

Head coaches at public secondary schools and sports instructors at all levels usually must have a bachelor's degree. For high school coaching and sports instructor jobs, schools usually prefer to hire teachers willing to take on the jobs part time. (For information on teachers, including those specializing in physical education, see the section on teachers—preschool, kindergarten, elementary, middle, and secondary elsewhere in the *Handbook*.) If no suitable teacher is found, schools hire someone from outside. Some entry-level positions for coaches or instructors require only experience derived as a participant in the sport or activity. Those who are not teachers must meet State requirements for certification to become a head coach. Certification, however, may not be required for coaching and sports instructor jobs in private schools. Degree programs specifically related to coaching include exercise and sports science, physiology, kinesiology, nutrition and fitness, physical education, and sports medicine.

Each sport has specific requirements for umpires, referees, and other sports officials. Umpires, referees, and other sports officials often begin their careers by volunteering for intramural, community, and recreational league competitions.

Scouting jobs require experience playing a sport at the college or professional level that makes it possible to spot young players who possess extraordinary athletic ability and skills. Most beginning scouting jobs are as part-time talent spotters in a particular area or region. Hard work and a record of success often lead to full-time jobs responsible for bigger territories. Some scouts advance to scouting director jobs or various administrative positions in sports.

Certification and other qualifications. Athletes, coaches, umpires, and related workers must relate well to others and possess good communication and leadership skills. Coaches also must be resourceful and flexible to successfully instruct and motivate individuals and groups of athletes.

To officiate at high school athletic events, officials must register with the State agency that oversees high school athletics and pass an exam on the rules of the particular game. For college refereeing, candidates must be certified by an officiating school and be evaluated during a probationary period. Some larger college sports conferences require officials to have certification and other qualifications, such as residence in or near the conference boundaries, along with several years of experience officiating at high school, community college, or other college conference games.

For those interested in becoming a tennis, golf, karate, or other kind of instructor, certification is highly desirable. Often, one must be at least 18 years old and certified in cardiopulmonary resuscitation (CPR). There are many certifying organizations specific to the various sports, and their training requirements vary. Participation in a clinic, camp, or school usually is required for certification. Part-time workers and those in smaller facilities are less likely to need formal education or training.

Standards for officials become more stringent as the level of competition advances. Whereas umpires for high school baseball need a high school diploma or its equivalent, 20/20 vision, and quick reflexes, those seeking to officiate at minor or major league games must attend professional umpire training school. Top graduates are selected for further evaluation while officiating in a rookie minor league. Umpires then usually need 7 to 10 years of experience in various minor leagues before being considered for major league jobs. Becoming an official for professional football also is competitive, as candidates must have at least 10 years of officiating experience, with 5 of them at a collegiate varsity or minor professional level. For the National Football League (NFL), prospective trainees are interviewed by clinical psychologists to determine levels of intelligence and ability to handle extremely stressful situations. In addition, the NFL's security department conducts thorough background checks. Potential candidates are likely to be interviewed by a panel from the NFL officiating department and are given a comprehensive examination on the rules of the sport.

Advancement. Many coaches begin their careers as assistant coaches to gain the knowledge and experience needed to become a head coach. Head coaches at large schools that strive to compete at the highest levels of a sport require substantial experience as a head coach at another school or as an assistant coach. To reach the ranks of professional coaching, a person usually needs years of coaching experience and a winning record in the lower ranks.

Employment

Athletes, coaches, umpires, and related workers held about 253,000 jobs in 2006. Coaches and scouts held 217,000 jobs; athletes, 18,000; and umpires, referees, and other sports officials, 19,000. Nearly 42 percent of athletes, coaches, umpires, and related workers worked part time, while 15 percent maintained variable schedules. Many sports officials and coaches receive such small and irregular payments for their services—occasional officiating at club games, for example—that they may not consider themselves employed in these occupations, even part time.

Among those employed in wage and salary jobs, 47 percent held jobs in public and private educational services. About 13 percent worked in amusement, gambling, and recreation industries, including golf and tennis clubs, gymnasiums, health clubs, judo and karate schools, riding stables, swim clubs, and other sports and recreation facilities. Another 6 percent worked in the spectator sports industry.

About 1 out of 5 workers in this occupation was self-employed, earning prize money or fees for lessons, scouting, or officiating assignments. Many other coaches and sports officials, although technically not self-employed, have such irregular or tenuous working arrangements that their working conditions resemble those of self-employment.

Job Outlook

Employment of athletes, coaches, umpires, and related workers is expected to grow faster than the average for all occupations through 2016. Very keen competition is expected for jobs at the highest levels of sports.

Employment change. Employment of athletes, coaches, umpires, and related workers is expected to increase by 15 per-

Projections data from the National Employment Matrix

Occupational Title	SOC Code	Employment, 2006	Projected employment, 2016	Change, 2006-2016	
				Number	Percent
Athletes, coaches, umpires, and related workers	27-2020	253,000	291,000	38,000	15
Athletes and sports competitors..	27-2021	18,000	21,000	3,400	19
Coaches and scouts	27-2022	217,000	249,000	32,000	15
Umpires, referees, and other sports officials...............................	27-2023	19,000	22,000	3,000	16

NOTE: Data in this table are rounded. See the discussion of the employment projections table in the *Handbook* introductory chapter on *Occupational Information Included in the Handbook.*

cent from 2006 to 2016, which is faster than the average for all occupations. Employment will grow as the general public continues to participate in organized sports for entertainment, recreation, and physical conditioning. Increasing participation in organized sports by girls and women will boost demand for coaches, umpires, and related workers. Job growth also will be driven by the increasing number of baby boomers approaching retirement, during which they are expected to participate more in leisure activities such as golf and tennis which require instruction.

Employment of coaches and instructors also will increase with expansion of school and college athletic programs and growing demand for private sports instruction. Sports-related job growth within education also will be driven by the decisions of local school boards. Population growth dictates the construction of additional schools, particularly in the expanding suburbs, but funding for athletic programs often is cut first when budgets become tight. Still, the popularity of team sports often enables shortfalls to be offset somewhat by assistance from fundraisers, booster clubs, and parents.

Job prospects. Persons who are State-certified to teach academic subjects in addition to physical education are likely to have the best prospects for obtaining coaching and instructor jobs. The need to replace the many high school coaches who change occupations or leave the labor force entirely also will provide some coaching opportunities.

Competition for professional athlete jobs will continue to be extremely intense. Opportunities to make a living as a professional in individual sports such as golf or tennis may grow as new tournaments are established and as prize money distributed to participants increases. Because most professional athletes' careers last only a few years due to debilitating injuries and age, annual replacement needs for these jobs is high, creating some job opportunities. However, the talented young men and women who dream of becoming sports superstars greatly outnumber the number of openings.

Opportunities should be best for persons seeking part-time umpire, referee, and other sports official jobs at the high school level. Competition is expected for higher paying jobs at the college level and will be even greater for jobs in professional sports. Competition should be keen for jobs as scouts, particularly for professional teams, because the number of available positions is limited.

Earnings

Median annual wage and salary earnings of athletes were $41,060 in May 2006. However, the highest paid professional athletes earn much more.

Median annual wage and salary earnings of umpires and related workers were $22,880 in May 2006. The middle 50 percent earned between $17,090 and $33,840. The lowest paid 10 percent earned less than $14,120, and the highest paid 10 percent earned more than $45,430.

In May 2006, median annual wage and salary earnings of coaches and scouts were $26,950. The middle 50 percent earned between $17,510 and $40,850. The lowest paid 10 percent earned less than $13,990, and the highest paid 10 percent earned more than $58,890. However, the highest paid professional coaches earn much more. Median annual earnings in the industries employing the largest numbers of coaches and scouts in May 2006 are shown below:

Colleges, universities, and professional schools................$37,530
Other amusement and recreation industries 27,180
Fitness and recreational sports centers...............................26,150
Other schools and instruction..23,840
Elementary and secondary schools......................................21,960

Earnings vary by level of education, certification, and geographic region. Some instructors and coaches are paid a salary, while others may be paid by the hour, per session, or based on the number of participants.

Related Occupations

Athletes and coaches use their extensive knowledge of physiology and sports to instruct, inform, and encourage sports participants. Other workers with similar duties include dietitians and nutritionists; physical therapists; recreation workers; fitness workers; recreational therapists; and teachers—preschool, kindergarten, elementary, middle, and secondary.

Sources of Additional Information

For information about sports officiating for team and individual sports, contact:

➤ National Association of Sports Officials, 2017 Lathrop Ave., RaciNE., WI 53405. Internet: **http://www.naso.org**

For more information about certification of tennis instructors and coaches, contact:

➤ Professional Tennis Registry, P.O. Box 4739, Hilton Head Island, SC 29938. Internet: **http://www.ptrtennis.org**

➤ U.S. Professional Tennis Association, 3535 Briarpark Dr., Suite ONE., Houston, TX 77042.
Internet: **http://www.uspta.org**

Dancers and Choreographers

(O*NET 27-2031.00, 27-2032.00)

Significant Points

- Many dancers stop performing by their late thirties, but some remain in the field as choreographers, dance teachers, or artistic directors.

- Most dancers begin formal training at an early age—between 5 and 15—and many have their first professional audition by age 17 or 18.

- Dancers and choreographers face intense competition; only the most talented find regular work.

Nature of the Work

From ancient times to the present, dancers have expressed ideas, stories, and rhythm with their bodies. They use a variety of dance forms that allow free movement and self-expression, including classical ballet, modern dance, and culturally specific dance styles. Many dancers combine performance work with teaching or choreography.

Dancers perform in a variety of settings, including opera, musical theater, and other musical productions, and may present folk, ethnic, tap, jazz, and other popular kinds of dance. They also perform in television, movies, music videos, and commercials, in which they also may sing and act. Dancers most often perform as part of a group, although a few top artists perform solo.

Dancers work with choreographers, who create original dances and develop new interpretations of existing dances. Because few dance routines are written down, choreographers instruct performers at rehearsals to achieve the desired effect. In addition, choreographers usually are involved in auditioning performers.

Work environment. Dance is strenuous. Many dancers stop performing by their late thirties because of the physical demands on the body. However, some continue to work in the

Most dancers need long-term on-the-job training to be successful.

field as choreographers, dance teachers and coaches, or artistic directors. Others move into administrative positions, such as company managers. A few celebrated dancers, however, continue performing most of their lives.

Daily rehearsals require very long hours. Many dance companies tour for part of the year to supplement a limited performance schedule at home. Dancers who perform in musical productions and other family entertainment spend much of their time on the road; others work in nightclubs or on cruise ships. Most dance performances are in the evening, whereas rehearsals and practice take place during the day. As a result, dancers often work very long and late hours. Generally, dancers and choreographers work in modern and temperature-controlled facilities; however, some studios may be older and less comfortable.

Training, Other Qualifications, and Advancement

Most dancers need long-term on-the-job training to be successful. Some earn a bachelor's degree or attend dance school, although neither is required. Becoming a choreographer usually requires years of dancing experience.

Education and training. Training varies with the type of dance and is a continuous part of all dancers' careers. Many dancers and dance instructors believe that dancers should start with a good foundation in classical technique before selecting a particular dance style. Ballet training for girls usually begins at 5 to 8 years of age with a private teacher or through an independent ballet school. Serious training traditionally begins between the ages of 10 and 12. Boys often begin their ballet training between the ages of 10 and 15. Students who demonstrate potential in their early teens may seek out more intensive and advanced professional training. At about this time, students should begin to focus their training on a particular style and decide whether to pursue additional training through a dance company's school or a college dance program. Leading dance school companies often have summer training programs from which they select candidates for admission to their regular full-time training programs. Formal training for modern and culturally specific dancers often begins later than training in ballet; however, many folk dance forms are taught to very young children. Many dancers have their first professional auditions by age 17 or 18.

Training is an important component of professional dancers' careers. Dancers normally spend 8 hours a day in class and rehearsal, keeping their bodies in shape and preparing for performances. Their daily training period includes time to warm up and cool down before and after classes and rehearsals.

Because of the strenuous and time-consuming training required, some dancers view formal education as secondary. However, a broad, general education including music, literature, history, and the visual arts is helpful in the interpretation of dramatic episodes, ideas, and feelings. Dancers sometimes conduct research to learn more about the part they are playing.

Many colleges and universities award bachelor's or master's degrees in dance, typically through departments of dance, theater, or fine arts. The National Association of Schools of Dance accredits 65 programs in dance. Many programs concentrate on modern dance, but some also offer courses in jazz, culturally specific dance, ballet, or classical techniques. Courses in dance composition, history and criticism, and movement analysis are also available.

A college education is not essential for employment as a professional dancer; however, many dancers obtain degrees in unrelated fields to prepare themselves for careers after dance. The completion of a college program in dance and education is usually essential to qualify to teach dance in college, high school, or elementary school. Colleges and conservatories sometimes require graduate degrees but may accept performance experience. A college background is not necessary, however, for teaching dance or choreography in local recreational programs. Studio schools prefer teachers to have experience as performers.

Other qualifications. Because of the rigorous practice schedules of most dancers, self-discipline, patience, perseverance, and a devotion to dance are essential for success in the field. Dancers also must possess good problem-solving skills and an ability to work with people. Good health and physical stamina also are necessary attributes. Above all, dancers must have flexibility, agility, coordination, and grace, a sense of rhythm, a feeling for music, and a creative ability to express themselves through movement.

Because dancers typically perform as members of an ensemble made up of other dancers, musicians, and directors or choreographers, they must be able to function as part of a team. They also should be highly motivated and prepared to face the anxiety of intermittent employment and rejections when auditioning for work.

Advancement. For dancers, advancement takes the form of a growing reputation, more frequent work, bigger and better roles, and higher pay. Some dancers may take on added responsibilities, such as by becoming a dance captain in musical theater or ballet master/ballet mistress in concert dance companies, by leading rehearsals, or by working with less experienced dancers in the absence of the choreographer.

Choreographers typically are experienced dancers with years of practice working in the theater. Through their performance as dancers, they develop reputations that often lead to opportunities to choreograph productions.

Employment

Professional dancers and choreographers held about 40,000 jobs in 2006. Many others were between engagements, so that the total number of people available for work as dancers over the course of the year was greater. Dancers and choreographers worked in a variety of industries, such as private educational services, which includes dance studios and schools, as well as colleges and universities; food services and drinking establishments; performing arts companies, which include dance, theater, and opera companies; and amusement and recreation venues, such as casinos and theme parks. About 17 percent of dancers and choreographers were self-employed.

Most major cities serve as home to major dance companies; however, many smaller communities across the Nation also support home-grown, full-time professional dance companies.

Job Outlook

Employment of dancers and choreographers is expected to grow more slowly than the average for all occupations. Dancers and choreographers face intense competition for jobs. Only the most talented find regular employment.

Employment change. Employment of dancers and choreographers is expected to grow 6 percent during the 2006-16 decade, more slowly than the average for all occupations. The public's continued interest in dance will sustain large and midsize dance companies, but funding from public and private organizations is not expected to keep pace with rising production costs. For many small organizations, the result will be fewer performances and more limited employment opportunities.

Job prospects. Because many people enjoy dance and would like to make their careers in dance, dancers and choreographers face intense competition for jobs. Only the most talented find regular employment. However, there are always some jobs available.

Although job openings will arise each year because dancers and choreographers retire or leave the occupation for other reasons, the number of applicants will continue to vastly exceed the number of job openings.

National dance companies likely will continue to provide jobs in this field. Opera companies and dance groups affiliated with television and motion pictures also will offer some opportunities. Moreover, the growing popularity of dance for recreational and fitness purposes has resulted in increased opportunities to teach dance, especially for older dancers who may be transitioning to another field. Finally, music video channels will provide opportunities for both dancers and choreographers.

Earnings

Median hourly earnings of dancers were $9.55 in May 2006. The middle 50 percent earned between $7.31 and $17.50. The lowest 10 percent earned less than $6.62, and the highest 10 percent earned more than $25.75. Annual earnings data for dancers were not available, because of the wide variation in the number of hours worked by dancers and the short-term nature of many jobs—which may last for 1 day or 1 week—make it rare for dancers to have guaranteed employment that exceeds a

Projections data from the National Employment Matrix

Occupational Title	SOC Code	Employment, 2006	Projected employment, 2016	Change, 2006-2016	
				Number	Percent
Dancers and choreographers	27-2030	40,000	43,000	2,400	6
Dancers	27-2031	20,000	22,000	1,900	9
Choreographers	27-2032	20,000	21,000	500	2

NOTE: Data in this table are rounded. See the discussion of the employment projections table in the *Handbook* introductory chapter on *Occupational Information Included in the Handbook.*

few months. Median hourly earnings in the industries employing the largest number of dancers were as follows:

Theater companies and dinner theaters...............................$15.28
Other schools and instruction..11.71
Other amusement and recreation industries............................8.58
Drinking places (alcoholic beverages).....................................7.76
Full-service restaurants 7.13

Median annual earnings of salaried choreographers were $34,660 in May 2006. The middle 50 percent earned between $21,910 and $49,810. The lowest 10 percent earned less than $15,710, and the highest 10 percent earned more than $64,010. Median annual earnings were $34,460 in "other schools and instruction," a North American Industry Classification System category that includes dance studios and schools.

Dancers who were on tour usually received an additional allowance for room and board, as well as extra compensation for overtime. Earnings from dancing are usually low because employment is irregular. Dancers often supplement their income by working as guest artists with other dance companies, teaching dance, or taking jobs unrelated to the field.

Earnings of dancers at many of the largest companies and in commercial settings are governed by union contracts. Dancers in the major opera ballet, classical ballet, and modern dance corps belong to the American Guild of Musical Artists, Inc. of the AFL-CIO; those who appear on live or videotaped television programs belong to the American Federation of Television and Radio Artists; those who perform in films and on television belong to the Screen Actors Guild; and those in musical theater are members of the Actors' Equity Association. The unions and producers sign basic agreements specifying minimum salary rates, hours of work, benefits, and other conditions of employment. However, the contract each dancer signs with the producer of the show may be more favorable than the basic agreement.

Most salaried dancers and choreographers covered by union contracts receive some paid sick leave and various health and pension benefits, including extended sick pay and family-leave benefits provided by their unions. Employers contribute toward these benefits. Dancers and choreographers not covered by union contracts usually do not enjoy such benefits.

Related Occupations

People who work in other performing arts occupations include actors, producers, and directors; and musicians, singers, and related workers. Those directly involved in the production of dance programs include set and exhibit designers; fashion designers; and barbers, cosmetologists, and other personal appearance workers. Like dancers, athletes, coaches, umpires, and related workers need strength, flexibility, and agility.

Sources of Additional Information

For general information about dance and a list of accredited college-level programs, contact:
➤ National Association of Schools of Dance, 11250 Roger Bacon Dr., Suite 21, Reston, VA 20190.
Internet: **http://nasd.arts-accredit.org**

For information about dance and dance companies, contact:
➤ Dance/USA, 1156 15th St.NW., Suite 820, Washington, DC 20005. Internet: **http://www.danceusa.org**

Musicians, Singers, and Related Workers

(O*NET 27-2041.00, 27-2041.01, 27-2041.04, 27-2042.00, 27-2042.01, 27-2042.02)

Significant Points

- Part-time schedules—typically at night and on weekends—intermittent unemployment, and rejection when auditioning for work are common; many musicians and singers supplement their income with earnings from other sources.

- Aspiring musicians and singers begin studying an instrument or training their voices at an early age.

- Competition for jobs is keen; talented individuals who can play several instruments and perform a wide range of musical styles should enjoy the best job prospects.

Nature of the Work

Musicians, singers, and related workers play musical instruments, sing, compose or arrange music, or conduct groups in instrumental or vocal performances. They may perform solo or as part of a group. Musicians, singers, and related workers entertain live audiences in nightclubs, concert halls, and theaters; others perform in recording or production studios. Regardless of the setting, musicians, singers, and related workers spend considerable time practicing, alone and with their bands, orchestras, or other musical ensembles.

Musicians play one or more musical instruments. Many musicians learn to play several related instruments and can perform equally well in several musical styles. Instrumental musicians, for example, may play in a symphony orchestra, rock group, or jazz combo one night, appear in another ensemble the next, and work in a studio band the following day. Some play a variety of string, brass, woodwind, or percussion instruments or electronic synthesizers.

Singers interpret music and text, using their knowledge of voice production, melody, and harmony. They sing character parts or perform in their own individual style. Singers are often classified according to their voice range—soprano, contralto, tenor, baritone, or bass, for example—or by the type of music they sing, such as rock, pop, folk, opera, rap, or country.

Music directors and *conductors* conduct, direct, plan, and lead instrumental or vocal performances by musical groups, such as orchestras, choirs, and glee clubs. These leaders audition and select musicians, choose the music most appropriate for their talents and abilities, and direct rehearsals and performances. *Choral directors* lead choirs and glee clubs, sometimes working with a band or an orchestra conductor. Directors audition and select singers and lead them at rehearsals and performances to achieve harmony, rhythm, tempo, shading, and other desired musical effects.

Composers create original music such as symphonies, operas, sonatas, radio and television jingles, film scores, and popular songs. They transcribe ideas into musical notation, using

Keen competition is expected for jobs as musicians and singers.

harmony, rhythm, melody, and tonal structure. Although most composers and songwriters practice their craft on instruments and transcribe the notes with pen and paper, some use computer software to compose and edit their music.

Arrangers transcribe and adapt musical compositions to a particular style for orchestras, bands, choral groups, or individuals. Components of music—including tempo, volume, and the mix of instruments needed—are arranged to express the composer's message. While some arrangers write directly into a musical composition, others use computer software to make changes.

Work environment. Musicians typically perform at night and on weekends. They spend much additional time practicing or in rehearsal. Full-time musicians with long-term employment contracts, such as those with symphony orchestras or television and film production companies, enjoy steady work and less travel. Nightclub, solo, or recital musicians frequently travel to perform in a variety of local settings and may tour nationally or internationally. Because many musicians find only part-time or intermittent work, experiencing unemployment between engagements, they often supplement their income with other types of jobs. The stress of constantly looking for work leads many musicians to accept permanent, full-time jobs in other occupations, while working part time as musicians.

Most instrumental musicians work closely with a variety of other people, including their colleagues, agents, employers, sponsors, and audiences. Although they usually work indoors, some perform outdoors for parades, concerts, and festivals. In some nightclubs and restaurants, smoke and odors may be present and lighting and ventilation may be poor.

Training, Other Qualifications, and Advancement

Long-term on-the-job training is the most common way people learn to become musicians or singers. Aspiring musicians begin studying an instrument at an early age. They may gain valuable experience playing in a school or community band or an orchestra or with a group of friends. Singers usually start training when their voices mature. Participation in school musicals or choirs often provides good early training and experience. Composers and music directors usually require a bachelor's degree in a related field.

Education and training. Musicians need extensive and prolonged training and practice to acquire the necessary skills and knowledge to interpret music at a professional level. Like other artists, musicians and singers continually strive to improve their abilities. Formal training may be obtained through private study with an accomplished musician, in a college or university music program, or in a music conservatory. An audition generally is necessary to qualify for university or conservatory study. The National Association of Schools of Music accredits more than 600 college-level programs in music. Courses typically include music theory, music interpretation, composition, conducting, and performance in a particular instrument or in voice. Music directors, composers, conductors, and arrangers need considerable related work experience or advanced training in these subjects.

A master's or doctoral degree usually is required to teach advanced music courses in colleges and universities; a bachelor's degree may be sufficient to teach basic courses. A degree in music education qualifies graduates for a State certificate to teach music in public elementary or secondary schools. Musicians who do not meet public school music education requirements may teach in private schools and recreation associations or instruct individual students in private sessions.

Other qualifications. Musicians must be knowledgeable about a broad range of musical styles as well as the type of music that interests them most. Having a broader range of interest, knowledge, and training can help expand employment opportunities and musical abilities. Voice training and private instrumental lessons, especially when taken at a young age, also help develop technique and enhance one's performance.

Young persons considering careers in music should have musical talent, versatility, creativity, poise, and a good stage presence. Self-discipline is vital because producing a quality performance on a consistent basis requires constant study and practice. Musicians who play in concerts or in nightclubs and those who tour must have physical stamina to endure frequent travel and an irregular performance schedule. Musicians and singers also must be prepared to face the anxiety of intermittent employment and of rejection when auditioning for work.

Advancement. Advancement for musicians usually means becoming better known, finding work more easily, and performing for higher earnings. Successful musicians often rely on agents or managers to find them performing engagements, negotiate contracts, and develop their careers.

Employment

Musicians, singers, and related workers held about 264,000 jobs in 2006. Around 35 percent worked part time; 48 percent were self-employed. Many found jobs in cities in which entertainment and recording activities are concentrated, such as New York, Los Angeles, Las Vegas, Chicago, and Nashville.

Musicians, singers, and related workers are employed in a variety of settings. Of those who earn a wage or salary, 35 percent were employed by religious organizations and 11 percent by performing arts companies such as professional orchestras, small chamber music groups, opera companies, musical theater companies, and ballet troupes. Musicians and singers also perform in nightclubs and restaurants and for weddings and other events. Well-known musicians and groups may perform in concerts, appear on radio and television broadcasts, and make recordings and music videos. The U.S. Armed Forces also offer careers in their bands and smaller musical groups.

Job Outlook

Employment is expected to grow about as fast as the average for all occupations. Keen competition for jobs, especially full-time jobs, is expected to continue. Talented individuals who are skilled in multiple instruments or musical styles will have the best job prospects.

Employment change. Overall employment of musicians, singers, and related workers is expected to grow 11 percent during the 2006-16 decade, about as fast as the average for all occupations. Most new wage-and-salary jobs for musicians will arise in religious organizations. Five percent growth is expected for self-employed musicians, who generally perform in nightclubs, concert tours, and other venues. The Internet and other new forms of media may provide independent musicians and singers alternative methods to distribute music.

Job prospects. Growth in demand for musicians will generate a number of job opportunities, and many openings also will arise from the need to replace those who leave the field each year because they are unable to make a living solely as musicians or singers, or for other reasons.

Competition for jobs as musicians, singers, and related workers is expected to be keen, especially for full-time jobs. The vast number of people with the desire to perform will continue to greatly exceed the number of openings. New musicians or singers will have their best chance of landing a job with smaller, community-based performing arts groups or as freelance artists. Talented individuals who are skilled in multiple instruments or musical styles will have the best job prospects. However, talent alone is no guarantee of success: many people start out to become musicians or singers but leave the profession because they find the work difficult, the discipline demanding, and the long periods of intermittent unemployment a hardship.

Earnings

Median hourly earnings of wage-and-salary musicians and singers were $19.73 in May 2006. The middle 50 percent earned between $10.81 and $36.55. The lowest 10 percent earned less than $7.08, and the highest 10 percent earned more than $57.37. Median hourly earnings were $23.37 in performing arts companies and $13.57 in religious organizations. Annual earnings data for musicians and singers were not available because of the wide variation in the number of hours worked by musicians and singers and the short-term nature of many jobs. It is rare for musicians and singers to have guaranteed employment that exceeds 3 to 6 months.

Median annual earnings of salaried music directors and composers were $39,750 in May 2006. The middle 50 percent earned between $23,660 and $60,350. The lowest 10 percent earned less than $15,210, and the highest 10 percent earned more than $110,850.

For self-employed musicians and singers, earnings typically reflect the number of jobs a freelance musician or singer played or the number of hours and weeks of contract work, in addition to a performer's professional reputation and setting. Performers who can fill large concert halls, arenas, or outdoor stadiums generally command higher pay than those who perform in local clubs. Soloists or headliners usually receive higher earnings than band members or opening acts. The most successful musicians earn performance or recording fees that far exceed the median earnings.

The American Federation of Musicians negotiates minimum contracts for major orchestras during the performing season. Each orchestra works out a separate contract with its local union, but individual musicians may negotiate higher salaries. In regional orchestras, minimum salaries are often less because fewer performances are scheduled. Regional orchestra musicians often are paid for their services, without any guarantee of future employment. Community orchestras often have more limited funding and offer salaries that are much lower for seasons of shorter duration.

Although musicians employed by some symphony orchestras work under master wage agreements, which guarantee a season's work up to 52 weeks, many other musicians face relatively long periods of unemployment between jobs. Even when employed, many musicians and singers work part time in unrelated occupations. Thus, their earnings for music usually are lower than earnings in many other occupations. Moreover, because they may not work steadily for one employer, some performers cannot qualify for unemployment compensation, and few have typical benefits such as sick leave or paid vacations. For these reasons, many musicians give private lessons or take jobs unrelated to music to supplement their earnings as performers.

Many musicians belong to a local of the American Federation of Musicians. Professional singers who perform live often belong to a branch of the American Guild of Musical Artists; those who record for the broadcast industries may belong to the American Federation of Television and Radio Artists.

Related Occupations

Musical instrument repairers and tuners (part of the precision instrument and equipment repairers occupation) require tech-

Projections data from the National Employment Matrix

Occupational Title	SOC Code	Employment, 2006	Projected employment, 2016	Change, 2006-2016	
				Number	Percent
Musicians, singers, and related workers	27-2040	264,000	293,000	29,000	11
Music directors and composers..	27-2041	68,000	77,000	8,800	13
Musicians and singers...	27-2042	196,000	216,000	20,000	10

NOTE: Data in this table are rounded. See the discussion of the employment projections table in the *Handbook* introductory chapter on *Occupational Information Included in the Handbook.*

nical knowledge of musical instruments. Others whose work involves the performing arts include actors, producers, and directors; announcers; and dancers and choreographers. School teachers and self-enrichment education teachers who teach music often use some of the same knowledge and skills as musicians and singers.

Sources of Additional Information

For general information about music and music teacher education and a list of accredited college-level programs, contact:

➤ National Association of Schools of Music, 11250 Roger Bacon Dr., Suite 21, Reston, VA 20190.
Internet: **http://nasm.arts-accredit.org**

Media and Communication-Related Occupations

Announcers

(O*NET 27-3011.00, 27-3012.00)

Significant Points

- Competition for announcer jobs will continue to be keen.

- Jobs at small stations usually have low pay, but offer the best opportunities for inexperienced announcers.

- Applicants who have completed internships or have related work experience, and those with computer skills, may have an advantage in the job market.

- Employment is projected to decline.

Nature of the Work

Radio and television announcers perform a variety of tasks on and off the air. They announce station program information, such as program schedules and station breaks for commercials, or public service information, and they introduce and close programs. Announcers read prepared scripts or make ad lib commentary on the air, as they present news, sports, the weather, time, and commercials. If a written script is required, they may do the research and writing. Announcers also interview guests and moderate panels or discussions. Some provide commentary for the audience during sporting events, at parades, and on other occasions. Announcers often are well known to radio and television audiences and may make promotional appearances and do remote broadcasts for their stations.

Announcers at smaller stations may cover all of these areas and tend to have more off-air duties as well. They may operate the control board, monitor the transmitter, sell commercial time to advertisers, keep a log of the station's daily programming, and produce advertisements and other recorded material. Advances in technology make it possible for announcers to do some work previously performed by editors and broadcast technicians. At many music stations, the announcer is simultaneously responsible both for announcing and for operating the control board, which is used to broadcast programming, commercials, and public-service announcements according to the station's schedule. Much of the recorded material that used to be on records or tape is now in the form of digital files on computers. (See the statement on broadcast and sound engineering technicians and radio operators elsewhere in the *Handbook*.)

Public radio and television announcers are involved in station fundraising efforts.

Changes in technology have led to more remote operation of stations. Several stations in different locations of the same region may be operated from one office. Some stations operate overnight without any staff, playing programming from a satellite feed or using programming that was recorded earlier, including segments from announcers.

Announcers frequently participate in community activities. Sports announcers, for example, may serve as masters of ceremonies at sports club banquets or may greet customers at openings of sporting goods stores.

Radio announcers who broadcast music often are called *disc jockeys (DJs)*. Some DJs specialize in one kind of music, announcing selections as they air them. Most DJs do not select much of the music they play (although they often did so in the past); instead, they follow schedules of commercials, talk, and music provided to them by management. While on the air, DJs comment on the music, weather, and traffic. They may take requests from listeners, interview guests, and manage listener contests.

Some DJs announce and play music at clubs, dances, restaurants, and weddings. They often have their own equipment with which to play the music. Many are self-employed and rent their services out on a job-by-job basis.

Show hosts may specialize in a certain area of interest, such as politics, personal finance, sports, or health. They contribute to the preparation of the program's content, interview guests, and discuss issues with viewers, listeners, or the studio audience.

Public address system announcers provide information to the audience at sporting, performing arts, and other events.

Work environment. Announcers usually work in well-lighted, air-conditioned, soundproof studios. Announcers often work within tight schedules, which can be physically and mentally stressful. For many announcers, the intangible rewards—creative work, many personal contacts, and the satisfaction of becoming widely known—far outweigh the disadvantages of irregular and often unpredictable hours, work pressures, and disrupted personal lives.

The broadcast day is long for radio and TV stations—many are on the air 24 hours a day—so announcers can expect to work unusual hours. Many present early-morning shows, when most people are getting ready for work or commuting, while others do late-night programs. The shifts, however, may not be as varied as in the past because new technology is allowing stations to eliminate some of the overnight hours.

Announcers may read prepared scripts or make ad-lib commentary on the air.

Training, Other Qualifications, and Advancement

Entry into this occupation is highly competitive, and postsecondary education or long-term on-the-job training is common. Trainees usually must have several years of experience in the industry before receiving an opportunity to work on the air. An applicant's delivery and—in television—appearance and style is important.

Education and training. Formal training in broadcasting from a college, a technical school, or a private broadcasting school is valuable. These programs prepare students to work with emerging technologies, a skill that is becoming increasingly important. Many announcers have a bachelor's degree in a subject such as communications, broadcasting, or journalism. High school and college courses in English, public speaking, drama, foreign languages, and computer science are valuable, and hobbies such as sports and music are additional assets.

Individuals considering enrolling in a broadcasting school should contact personnel managers of radio and television stations, as well as broadcasting trade organizations, to determine the school's reputation for producing suitably trained candidates.

Announcers are often required to complete long-term on-the-job training. This can be accomplished at campus radio or TV facilities and at commercial stations while students serve as interns. Paid or unpaid internships provide students with hands-on training and the chance to establish contacts in the industry. Unpaid interns often receive college credit and are allowed to observe and assist station employees. Although the Fair Labor Standards Act limits the amount of work that unpaid interns may perform in a station, unpaid internships are more common than paid internships. Unpaid internships sometimes lead to paid internships, however, which are valuable because interns do work ordinarily performed by regular employees and may even go on the air.

Once hired by a television station, an employee usually starts out as a production assistant, researcher, or reporter and is given a chance to move into announcing if they show an aptitude for "on-air" work. A beginner's chance of landing an on-air job is remote. The best chances for an on-air job for inexperienced announcers may be as a substitute for a familiar announcer at a small radio station or on the late-night shift at a larger station. In radio, newcomers usually start out taping interviews and operating equipment.

Other qualifications. Announcers must have a pleasant and well-controlled voice, good timing, excellent pronunciation, and correct grammar. College broadcasting programs offer courses, such as voice and diction, to help students improve their vocal qualities. Television announcers need a neat, pleasing appearance as well. Knowledge of theater, sports, music, business, politics, and other subjects likely to be covered in broadcasts improves one's chances for success. Announcers, especially those seeking radio careers, should have good information technology skills and be capable of using computers, editing equipment, and other broadcast-related devices because new advances in technology have made these abilities increasingly important. Announcers also need strong writing skills, because they normally write their own material. In addition, they should be able to ad lib all or part of a show and to work under tight deadlines. The most successful announcers attract a large audience by combining a pleasing personality and voice with an appealing style.

Advancement. Announcers usually begin at a station in a small community and, if they are qualified, may move to a better paying job in a large city. They also may advance by hosting a regular program as a disc jockey, sportscaster, or other specialist. Competition for employment by networks is particularly intense, and employers look for college graduates with at least several years of successful announcing experience.

Employment

Announcers held about 71,000 jobs in 2006. About 42 percent of all announcers worked part time. About 54 percent were employed in radio and television broadcasting. Another 30 percent were self-employed freelance announcers who sold their services for individual assignments to networks and stations, to advertising agencies, other independent producers, or to sponsors of local events.

Job Outlook

Competition for jobs as announcers will be keen because the broadcasting field attracts many more jobseekers than there are jobs. Furthermore, employment of announcers is projected to decline. In some cases, announcers leave the field because they cannot advance to better paying jobs. Changes in station ownership, format, and ratings frequently cause periods of unemployment for many announcers.

Employment change. Employment of announcers is expected to decline moderately by 7 percent from 2006 to 2016. Increasing consolidation of radio and television stations, the advent of new technology, and growth of alternative media sources, such as satellite radio, will contribute to the expected decline. Consolidation among broadcasting companies may lead to an increased use of syndicated programming and pro-

Projections data from the National Employment Matrix

Occupational Title	SOC Code	Employment, 2006	Projected employment, 2016	Change, 2006-2016	
				Number	Percent
Announcers	27-3010	71,000	66,000	-4,900	-7
Radio and television announcers.................................	27-3011	59,000	54,000	-4,900	-8
Public address system and other announcers	27-3012	12,000	12,000	0	0

NOTE: Data in this table are rounded. See the discussion of the employment projections table in the *Handbook* introductory chapter on *Occupational Information Included in the Handbook.*

grams originating outside a station's viewing or listening area. Digital technology is increasing the productivity of announcers, reducing the time required to edit material or perform other off-air technical and production work.

Job prospects. Some job openings will arise from the need to replace those who transfer to other kinds of work or leave the labor force. Nevertheless, competition for jobs as announcers will be keen because the broadcasting field attracts many more jobseekers than there are jobs. Small radio stations are more inclined to hire beginners, but the pay is low. Applicants who have completed internships and those with related work experience usually receive preference for available positions. Job seekers with good computer and technical skills also will have an advantage because announcers are now doing more of the computer work that was previously carried out by technicians. In radio, announcers are increasingly using computers to edit their programs. Because competition for ratings is so intense in major metropolitan areas, large stations will continue to seek announcers who have proven that they can attract and retain a sizable audience. Announcers who are knowledgeable about business, consumer, and health news also may have an advantage over others. While subject-matter specialization is more common at large stations and the networks, many small stations also encourage it. There will be some opportunities for self-employed DJ's who provide music at clubs and special events but most of these jobs will be part time.

Earnings

Salaries in broadcasting vary widely, but generally are relatively low, except for announcers who work for large stations in major markets or for networks. Earnings are higher in television than in radio and higher in commercial broadcasting than in public broadcasting.

Median hourly earnings of wage and salary radio and television announcers in May 2006 were $11.69. The middle 50 percent earned between $8.10 and $18.62. The lowest 10 percent earned less than $6.55, and the highest 10 percent earned more than $32.98. Median hourly earnings of announcers in the radio and television broadcasting industry were $11.52.

Median hourly earnings of wage and salary public address and other system announcers in May 2006 were $12.02. The middle 50 percent earned between $8.41 and $19.38. The lowest 10 percent earned less than $6.73 and the highest 10 percent earned more than $29.69.

Related Occupations

The success of announcers depends upon how well they communicate. Others who must be skilled at oral communication include news analysts, reporters, and correspondents; interpreters

and translators; salespersons and those in related occupations; and public relations specialists. Many announcers also must entertain their audience, so their work is similar to other entertainment-related occupations, such as actors, producers, and directors; and musicians, singers, and related workers. Some announcers write their own material, as do writers and editors. Announcers perform a variety of duties, including some technical operations similar to those performed by broadcast and sound engineering technicians and radio operators.

Sources of Additional Information

General information on the broadcasting industry, where many announcers are employed, is available from:

➤ National Association of Broadcasters, 1771 N St.NW., Washington, DC 20036. Internet: **http://www.nab.org**

Broadcast and Sound Engineering Technicians and Radio Operators

(O*NET 27-4011.00, 27-4012.00, 27-4013.00, 27-4014.00)

Significant Points

- Job applicants will face keen competition for jobs in major metropolitan areas, where pay generally is higher; prospects are expected to be better in small cities and towns.

- Technical school, community college, or college training in broadcast technology, electronics, or computer networking provides the best preparation.

- About 30 percent of these workers are in broadcasting, mainly in radio and television stations, and 17 percent work in the motion picture, video, and sound recording industries.

- Evening, weekend, and holiday work is common.

Nature of the Work

Broadcast and sound engineering technicians and radio operators set up, operate, and maintain a wide variety of electrical and electronic equipment used in almost any radio or television broadcast, concert, play, musical recording, television show, or movie. With such a range of work, there are many specialized occupations within the field.

Audio and video equipment technicians set up and operate audio and video equipment, including microphones, sound speakers, video screens, projectors, video monitors, and recording equipment. They also connect wires and cables and set up and operate sound and mixing boards and related electronic equipment for concerts, sports events, meetings and conventions, presentations, and news conferences. They may set up and operate associated spotlights and other custom lighting systems.

Broadcast technicians set up, operate, and maintain equipment that regulates the signal strength, clarity, and the range of sounds and colors of radio or television broadcasts. These technicians also operate control panels to select the source of the material. Technicians may switch from one camera or studio to another, from film to live programming, or from network to local programming.

Sound engineering technicians operate machines and equipment to record, synchronize, mix, or reproduce music, voices, or sound effects in recording studios, sporting arenas, theater productions, or movie and video productions.

Radio operators mainly receive and transmit communications using a variety of tools. These workers also repair equipment, using such devices as electronic testing equipment, handtools, and power tools. One of their major duties is to help to maintain communication systems in good condition.

The transition to digital recording, editing, and broadcasting has greatly changed the work of broadcast and sound engineering technicians and radio operators. Software on desktop computers has replaced specialized electronic equipment in many recording and editing functions. Most radio and television stations have replaced videotapes and audiotapes with computer hard drives and other computer data storage systems. Computer networks linked to specialized equipment dominate modern broadcasting. This transition has forced technicians to learn computer networking and software skills. (See the statement on computer support specialists and systems administrators elsewhere in the *Handbook*.)

Broadcast and sound engineering technicians and radio operators perform a variety of duties in small stations. In large stations and at the networks, technicians are more specialized, although job assignments may change from day to day. The terms "operator," "engineer," and "technician" often are used interchangeably to describe these jobs. Workers in these positions may monitor and log outgoing signals and operate transmitters; set up, adjust, service, and repair electronic broadcasting equipment; and regulate fidelity, brightness, contrast, volume, and sound quality of television broadcasts.

Technicians also work in program production. *Recording engineers* operate and maintain video and sound recording equipment. They may operate equipment designed to produce special effects, such as the illusions of a bolt of lightning or a police siren. *Sound mixers* or *re-recording mixers* produce soundtracks for movies or television programs. After filming or recording is complete, these workers may use a process called "dubbing" to insert sounds. *Field technicians* set up and operate portable transmission equipment outside the studio. Because television news coverage requires so much electronic equipment and the technology is changing so rapidly, many stations assign technicians exclusively to news.

Chief engineers, *transmission engineers*, and *broadcast field supervisors* oversee other technicians and maintain broadcasting equipment.

Evening, weekend, and holiday work is common for some broadcast and sound engineering technicians and radio operators.

Work environment. Broadcast and sound engineering technicians and radio operators generally work indoors in pleasant surroundings. However, those who broadcast news and other programs from locations outside the studio may work outdoors in all types of weather or in other dangerous conditions. Technicians doing maintenance may climb poles or antenna towers, while those setting up equipment do heavy lifting.

Technicians at large stations and the networks usually work a 40-hour week under great pressure to meet broadcast deadlines, and may occasionally work overtime. Technicians at small stations routinely work more than 40 hours a week. Evening, weekend, and holiday work is usual because most stations are on the air 18 to 24 hours a day, 7 days a week. Even though a technician may not be on duty when the station is broadcasting, some technicians may be on call during nonwork hours; these workers must handle any problems that occur when they are on call.

Technicians who work on motion pictures may be on a tight schedule and may work long hours to meet contractual deadlines.

Training, Other Qualifications, and Advancement

Both broadcast and sound engineering technicians usually receive some kind of formal training prior to beginning work. Audio and video technicians usually learn the skills they need through a year or more of on-the-job training, but some have formal education after high school. Radio operators usually train for several months on the job

Education and training. The best way to prepare for a broadcast and sound engineering technician job is to obtain technical school, community college, or college training in broadcast technology, electronics, or computer networking. For broadcast technicians, an associate degree is recommended. Sound engineering technicians usually complete vocational programs, which usually takes about a year, although there are shorter programs. Prospective technicians should take high school courses in math, physics, and electronics.

When starting out, broadcast and sound engineering technicians learn skills on the job from experienced technicians and supervisors. These beginners often start their careers in small stations and, once experienced, transfer to larger ones. Large stations usually hire only technicians with experience. Many employers pay tuition and expenses for courses or seminars to help technicians keep abreast of developments in the field.

Audio and video equipment technicians generally need a high school diploma. Many recent entrants have a community college degree or other forms of postsecondary degrees, although they are not always required. These technicians may substitute on-the-job training for formal education requirements. Many audio and video technicians learn through long-term on-the-job training, lasting from 1 to several years, depending on the specifics of their job. Working in a studio as an assistant is a good way of gaining experience and knowledge.

Radio operators usually are not required to complete any formal training. This is an entry-level position that generally requires on-the-job training.

In the motion picture industry, people are hired as apprentice editorial assistants and work their way up to more skilled jobs. Employers in the motion picture industry usually hire experienced freelance technicians on a picture-by-picture basis. Reputation and determination are important in getting jobs.

Continuing education to become familiar with emerging technologies is recommended for all broadcast and sound engineering technicians and radio operators.

Other qualifications. Building electronic equipment from hobby kits and operating a "ham," or amateur, radio are good ways to prepare for these careers, as is working in college radio and television stations. Information technology skills also are valuable because digital recording, editing, and broadcasting are now the norm. Broadcast and sound engineering technicians and radio operators must have manual dexterity and an aptitude for working with electrical, electronic, and mechanical systems and equipment.

Certification and advancement. Licensing is not required for broadcast technicians. However, certification by the Society of Broadcast Engineers is a mark of competence and experience. The certificate is issued to experienced technicians who pass an examination.

Experienced technicians can become supervisory technicians or chief engineers. A college degree in engineering is needed to become chief engineer at a large television station.

Employment

Broadcast and sound engineering technicians and radio operators held about 105,000 jobs in 2006. Their employment was distributed among the following detailed occupations:

Audio and video equipment technicians 50,000
Broadcast technicians...38,000
Sound engineering technicians 16,000
Radio operators 1,500

About 30 percent worked in broadcasting (except Internet) and 17 percent worked in the motion picture, video, and sound recording industries. About 13 percent were self-employed. Television stations employ, on average, many more technicians than radio stations. Some technicians are employed in other industries, producing employee communications, sales, and training programs. Technician jobs in television and radio are located in virtually all cities; jobs in radio also are found in many small towns. The highest paying and most specialized jobs are concentrated in New York City, Los Angeles, Chicago, and Washington, DC—the originating centers for most network or news programs. Motion picture production jobs are concentrated in Los Angeles and New York City.

Job Outlook

Employment is expected to grow faster than average through 2016. But people seeking entry-level jobs as technicians in broadcasting are expected to face keen competition in major metropolitan areas. Prospects are expected to be better in small cities and towns.

Employment change. Overall employment of broadcast and sound engineering technicians and radio operators is expected to grow 17 percent over the 2006-16 decade, which is faster than the average for all occupations. Job growth in radio and television broadcasting will be limited by consolidation of ownership of radio and television stations and by labor-saving technical advances, such as computer-controlled programming and remotely controlled transmitters. Stations often are consolidated and operated from a single location, reducing employment because one or a few technicians can provide support to multiple stations. Offsetting these trends, however, is a move toward digital broadcasting that will increase employment opportunities. As of February 2009, television stations will only be allowed to broadcast digital signals and, by law, will be forced to turn off their analog signals. Technicians who can install and operate digital transmitters will be in demand as stations attempt to meet this deadline. Radio stations are beginning to

Projections data from the National Employment Matrix

Occupational Title	SOC Code	Employment, 2006	Projected employment, 2016	Change, 2006-2016	
				Number	Percent
Broadcast and sound engineering technicians and radio operators ..	27-4010	105,000	123,000	18,000	17
Audio and video equipment technicians	27-4011	50,000	62,000	12,000	24
Broadcast technicians..	27-4012	38,000	42,000	4,600	12
Radio operators	27-4013	1,500	1,300	-300	-16
Sound engineering technicians	27-4014	16,000	18,000	1,500	9

NOTE: Data in this table are rounded. See the discussion of the employment projections table in the *Handbook* introductory chapter on *Occupational Information Included in the Handbook.*

broadcast digital signals as well, but there is no law that will require them to do so.

Projected job growth varies among detailed occupations in this field. Employment of audio and video equipment technicians is expected to grow 24 percent through 2016, which is much faster than the average for all occupations. Not only will these workers have to set up audio and video equipment, but they will have to maintain and repair it as well. Employment of broadcast technicians and sound engineering technicians is expected to grow 12 percent and 9 percent respectively, through 2016, about as fast as the average for all occupations. Advancements in technology will enhance the capabilities of technicians to produce higher quality radio and television programming. Employment of radio operators, on the other hand, is projected to decline rapidly by 16 percent through 2016 as more stations control programming and operate transmitters remotely.

Employment of broadcast and sound engineering technicians in the cable and pay television portion of the broadcasting industry is expected to grow as the range of products and services expands, including cable Internet access and video-on-demand. Employment of these workers in the motion picture industry is expected to grow rapidly. However, this job market is expected to remain competitive because of the large number of people who are attracted by the glamour of working in motion pictures.

Job prospects. People seeking entry-level jobs as technicians in broadcasting are expected to face keen competition in major metropolitan areas, where pay generally is higher and the number of qualified jobseekers typically exceeds the number of openings. Prospects for entry-level positions are expected to be better in small cities and towns for beginners with appropriate training.

In addition to employment growth, job openings will result from the need to replace experienced technicians who leave this field. Some of these workers leave for other jobs that require knowledge of electronics, such as computer repairer or industrial machinery repairer.

Earnings

Television stations usually pay higher salaries than radio stations; commercial broadcasting usually pays more than public broadcasting; and stations in large markets pay more than those in small markets.

Median annual earnings of audio and video equipment technicians in May 2006 were $34,840. The middle 50 percent earned between $26,090 and $46,320. The lowest 10 percent earned less than $19,980, and the highest 10 percent earned more than $62,550. Median annual earnings in motion picture and video industries, which employed the largest number of audio and video equipment technicians, were $34,530.

Median annual earnings of broadcast technicians in May 2006 were $30,690. The middle 50 percent earned between $20,880 and $45,310. The lowest 10 percent earned less than $15,680, and the highest 10 percent earned more than $64,860. Median annual earnings in radio and television broadcasting, which employed the largest number of broadcast technicians, were $27,380.

Median annual earnings of sound engineering technicians in May 2006 were $43,010. The middle 50 percent earned between $29,270 and $65,590. The lowest 10 percent earned less than $21,050, and the highest 10 percent earned more than $90,770.

Median annual earnings of radio operators in May 2006 were $37,890. The middle 50 percent earned between $28,860 and $48,280. The lowest 10 percent earned less than $20,790, and the highest 10 percent earned more than $57,920.

Related Occupations

Broadcast and sound engineering technicians and radio operators need the electronics training necessary to operate technical equipment, and they generally complete specialized postsecondary programs. Occupations with similar characteristics include engineering technicians, science technicians, and electrical and electronics installers and repairers. Broadcast and sound engineering technicians also may operate computer networks, as do computer support specialists and systems administrators. Broadcast technicians on some live radio and television programs screen incoming calls; these workers have responsibilities similar to those of communications equipment operators.

Sources of Additional Information

For career information and links to employment resources, contact:

➤ National Association of Broadcasters, 1771 N St.NW., Washington, DC 20036. Internet: **http://www.nab.org**

For information on certification, contact:

➤ Society of Broadcast Engineers, 9182 North Meridian St., Suite 150, Indianapolis, IN 46260. Internet: **http://www.sbe.org**

For information on audio and video equipment technicians, contact:

➤ InfoComm International, 11242 Waples Mill Rd., Suite 200, Fairfax, VA 22030. Internet: **http://www.infocomm.org**

Interpreters and Translators

(O*NET 27-3091.00)

Significant Points

- About 22 percent of interpreters and translators are self-employed.

- Work is often sporadic, and many of these workers are part time.

- In addition to needing fluency in at least two languages, many interpreters and translators need a bachelor's degree. Many also complete job-specific training programs.

- Job outlook varies by specialty.

Nature of the Work

Interpreters and translators enable the cross-cultural communication necessary in today's society by converting one language into another. However, these language specialists do more than simply translate words—they relay concepts and ideas between languages. They must thoroughly understand the subject matter in which they work in order to accurately convert information from one language, known as the source language, into another, the target language. In addition, they must be sensitive to the cultures associated with their languages of expertise.

Interpreters and translators are often discussed together because they share some common traits. For example, both must be fluent in at least two languages—a native, or active, language and a secondary, or passive, language; a small number of interpreters and translators are fluent in two or more passive languages. Their active language is the one that they know best and into which they interpret or translate, and their passive language is one for which they have nearly perfect knowledge.

Although some people do both, interpretation and translation are different professions. Interpreters deal with spoken words, translators with written words. Each task requires a distinct set of skills and aptitudes, and most people are better suited for one or the other. While interpreters often work into and from both languages, translators generally work only into their active language.

Interpreters convert one spoken language into another—or, in the case of sign-language interpreters, between spoken communication and sign language. This requires interpreters to pay attention carefully, understand what is communicated in both languages, and express thoughts and ideas clearly. Strong research and analytical skills, mental dexterity, and an exceptional memory also are important.

The first part of an interpreter's work begins before arriving at the jobsite. The interpreter must become familiar with the subject matter that the speakers will discuss, a task that may involve research to create a list of common words and phrases associated with the topic. Next, the interpreter usually travels to the location where his or her services are needed. Physical presence may not be required for some work, such as telephone interpretation. But it is usually important that the interpreter see the communicators in order to hear and observe the person speaking and to relay the message to the other party.

There are two types of interpretation: simultaneous and consecutive. Simultaneous interpretation requires interpreters to listen and speak (or sign) at the same time. In simultaneous interpretation, the interpreter begins to convey a sentence being spoken while the speaker is still talking. Ideally, simultaneous interpreters should be so familiar with a subject that they are able to anticipate the end of the speaker's sentence. Because they need a high degree of concentration, simultaneous interpreters work in pairs, with each interpreting for 20- to 30-minute periods. This type of interpretation is required at international conferences and is sometimes used in the courts.

In contrast to simultaneous interpretation's immediacy, consecutive interpretation begins only after the speaker has verbalized a group of words or sentences. Consecutive interpreters often take notes while listening to the speakers, so they must develop some type of note-taking or shorthand system. This form of interpretation is used most often for person-to-person communication, during which the interpreter is positioned near both parties.

Translators convert written materials from one language into another. They must have excellent writing and analytical ability. And because the documents that they translate must be as flawless as possible, they also need good editing skills.

Assignments may vary in length, writing style, and subject matter. When translators first receive text to convert into another language, they usually read it in its entirety to get an idea of the subject. Next, they identify and look up any unfamiliar words. Multiple additional readings are usually needed before translators begin to actually write and finalize the translation. Translators also might do additional research on the subject matter if they are unclear about anything in the text. They consult with the text's originator or issuing agency to clarify unclear or unfamiliar ideas, words, or acronyms.

Translating involves more than replacing a word with its equivalent in another language; sentences and ideas must be manipulated to flow with the same coherence as those in the source document so that the translation reads as though it originated in the target language. Translators also must bear in mind any cultural references that may need to be explained to the intended audience, such as colloquialisms, slang, and other expressions that do not translate literally. Some subjects may be more difficult than others to translate because words or passages may have multiple meanings that make several translations possible. Not surprisingly, translated work often goes through multiple revisions before final text is submitted.

The way in which translators do their jobs has changed with advances in technology. Today, nearly all translation work is done on a computer, and most assignments are received and submitted electronically. This enables translators to work from almost anywhere, and a large percentage of them work from home. The Internet provides advanced research capabilities and valuable language resources, such as specialized dictionaries and glossaries. In some cases, use of machine-assisted translation—including memory tools that provide comparisons of previous translations with current work—helps save time and reduce repetition.

The services of interpreters and translators are needed in a number of subject areas. While these workers may not completely specialize in a particular field or industry, many do focus on one area of expertise. Some of the most common areas are described below; however, interpreters and translators also may work in a variety of other areas, including business, social services, or entertainment.

Conference interpreters work at conferences that have non-English-speaking attendees. This work includes international business and diplomacy, although conference interpreters interpret for any organization that works with foreign language speakers. Employers prefer high-level interpreters who have the ability to translate from at least two passive languages into one active (native) language—for example, the ability to interpret from Spanish and French into English. For some positions, such as those with the United Nations, this qualification is mandatory.

Much of the interpreting performed at conferences is simultaneous; however, at some meetings with a small number of attendees, consecutive interpreting also may be used. Usually, interpreters sit in soundproof booths, listening to the speakers through headphones and interpreting into a microphone what is said. The interpreted speech is then relayed to the listener through headsets. When interpreting is needed for only one or two people, the interpreter generally sits behind or next to the attendee and whispers a translation of the proceedings.

Guide or escort interpreters accompany either U.S. visitors abroad or foreign visitors in the United States to ensure that they are able to communicate during their stay. These specialists interpret on a variety of subjects, both on an informal basis and on a professional level. Most of their interpretation is consecutive, and work is generally shared by two interpreters when the assignment requires more than an 8-hour day. Frequent travel, often for days or weeks at a time, is common, an aspect of the job that some find particularly appealing.

Judiciary interpreters and translators help people appearing in court who are unable or unwilling to communicate in English. These workers must remain detached from the content of their work and not alter or modify the meaning or tone of what is said. Legal translators must be thoroughly familiar with the language and functions of the U.S. judicial system, as well as other countries' legal systems. Court interpreters work in a variety of legal settings, such as attorney-client meetings, preliminary hearings, depositions, trials, and arraignments. Success as a court interpreter requires an understanding of both legal terminology and colloquial language. In addition to interpreting what is said, court interpreters also may be required to translate written documents and read them aloud, also known as sight translation.

Literary translators adapt written literature from one language into another. They may translate any number of documents, including journal articles, books, poetry, and short stories. Literary translation is related to creative writing; literary translators must create a new text in the target language that reproduces the content and style of the original. Whenever possible, literary translators work closely with authors to best capture their intended meanings and literary characteristics.

This type of work often is done as a sideline by university professors; however, opportunities exist for well-established literary translators. As with writers, finding a publisher and maintaining a network of contacts in the publishing industry is a critical part of the job. Most aspiring literary translators begin by submitting a short sample of their work, in the hope that it will be printed and give them recognition. For example, after receiving permission from the author, they might submit to a publishing house a previously unpublished short work, such as a poem or essay.

Localization translators constitute a relatively recent and rapidly expanding specialty. Localization involves the complete adaptation of a product for use in a different language and culture. At its earlier stages, this work dealt primarily with software localization, but the specialty has expanded to include the adaptation of Internet sites and products in manufacturing and other business sectors. The goal of these specialists is to make the product to appear as if it were originally manufactured in the country where it will be sold and supported.

Medical interpreters and translators provide language services to health care patients with limited English proficiency. Medical interpreters help patients to communicate with doctors, nurses, and other medical staff. Translators working in this specialty primarily convert patient materials and informational brochures issued by hospitals and medical facilities into the desired language. Medical interpreters need a strong grasp of medical and colloquial terminology in both languages, along with cultural sensitivity regarding how the patient receives the information. They must remain detached but aware of the patient's feelings and pain.

Sign language interpreters facilitate communication between people who are deaf or hard of hearing and people who can hear. Sign language interpreters must be fluent in English and in American Sign Language (ASL), which combines signing, finger spelling, and specific body language. ASL has its own grammatical rules, sentence structure, idioms, historical contexts, and cultural nuances. Sign language interpreting, like foreign language interpreting, involves more than simply replacing a word of spoken English with a sign representing that word.

Most sign language interpreters either interpret, aiding communication between English and ASL, or transliterate, facilitating communication between English and contact signing—a form of signing that uses a more English language-based word order. Some interpreters specialize in oral interpreting for deaf or hard of hearing people who lip-read instead of sign. Other specialties include tactile signing, which is interpreting for people who are blind as well as deaf by making manual signs into a person's hands; cued speech; and signing exact English.

Self-employed and freelance interpreters and translators need general business skills to successfully manage their finances and careers. They must set prices for their work, bill customers, keep financial records, and market their services to attract new business and build their client base.

Work environment. Interpreters work in a variety of settings, such as hospitals, courtrooms, and conference centers. They are required to travel to the site—whether it is in a neighboring town or on the other side of the world—where their services are needed. Interpreters who work over the telephone generally work in call centers in urban areas, and keep to a standard 5-day, 40-hour workweek. Interpreters for deaf students in schools usually work in a school setting for 9 months out of the year. Translators usually work alone, and they must frequently perform under pressure of deadlines and tight schedules. Many translators choose to work at home; however, technology allows translators to work from almost anywhere.

Because many interpreters and translators freelance, their schedules are often erratic, with extensive periods of no work interspersed with periods requiring long, irregular hours. For those who freelance, a significant amount of time must be dedicated to looking for jobs. In addition, freelancers must manage their own finances, and payment for their services may not always be prompt. Freelancing, however, offers variety and flexibility, and allows many workers to choose which jobs to accept or decline.

The work can be stressful and exhausting, and translation can be lonesome. However, interpreters and translators may use their irregular schedules to pursue other interests, such as traveling, dabbling in a hobby, or working a second job. Many interpreters and translators enjoy what they do and value the ability to control their schedules and workloads.

Interpreters and translators need fluency in at least two languages and, in many cases, a bachelor's degree.

Training, Other Qualifications, and Advancement

Interpreters and translators must be fluent in at least two languages. Their educational backgrounds may vary widely, but most have a bachelor's degree. Many also complete job-specific training programs.

Education and training. The educational backgrounds of interpreters and translators vary. Knowing at least two languages is essential. Although it is not necessary to have been raised bilingual to succeed, many interpreters and translators grew up speaking two languages.

In high school, students can prepare for these careers by taking a broad range of courses that include English writing and comprehension, foreign languages, and basic computer proficiency. Other helpful pursuits include spending time abroad, engaging in direct contact with foreign cultures, and reading extensively on a variety of subjects in English and at least one other language.

Beyond high school, there are many educational options. Although a bachelor's degree is often required, interpreters and translators note that it is acceptable to major in something other than a language. An educational background in a particular field of study provides a natural area of subject matter expertise. However, specialized training in how to do the work is generally required. Formal programs in interpreting and translation are available at colleges nationwide and through nonuniversity training programs, conferences, and courses. Many people who work as conference interpreters or in more technical areas—such as localization, engineering, or finance—have master's degrees, while those working in the community as court or medical interpreters or translators are more likely to complete job-specific training programs.

Other qualifications. Experience is an essential part of a successful career in either interpreting or translation. In fact, many agencies or companies use only the services of people who have worked in the field for 3 to 5 years or who have a degree in translation studies or both.

A good way for translators to learn firsthand about the profession is to start out working in-house for a translation company; however, such jobs are not very numerous. People seeking to enter interpreter or translator jobs should begin by getting experience whatever way they can—even if it means doing informal or unpaid work.

Volunteer opportunities are available through community organizations, hospitals, and sporting events, such as marathons, that involve international competitors. The American Translators Association works with the Red Cross to provide volunteer interpreters in crisis situations. All translation can be used as examples for potential clients, even translation done as practice.

Paid or unpaid internships and apprenticeships are other ways for interpreters and translators to get started. Escort interpreting may offer an opportunity for inexperienced candidates to work alongside a more seasoned interpreter. Interpreters might also find it easier to break into areas with particularly high demand for language services, such as court or medical interpretation.

Whatever path of entry they pursue, new interpreters and translators should establish mentoring relationships to build their skills, confidence, and a professional network. Mentoring may be formal, such as through a professional association, or informal with a coworker or an acquaintance who has experience as an interpreter or translator. Both the American Translators Association and the Registry of Interpreters for the Deaf offer formal mentoring programs.

Translators working in localization need a solid grasp of the languages to be translated, a thorough understanding of technical concepts and vocabulary, and a high degree of knowledge about the intended target audience or users of the product. Because software often is involved, it is not uncommon for people who work in this area of translation to have a strong background in computer science or to have computer-related work experience.

Certification and advancement. There is currently no universal form of certification required of interpreters and translators in the United States, but there are a variety of different tests that workers can take to demonstrate proficiency. The American Translators Association provides certification in more than 24 language combinations for its members; other options include a certification program offered by The Translators and Interpreters Guild. Many interpreters are not certified.

Federal courts have certification for Spanish, Navajo, and Haitian Creole interpreters, and many State and municipal courts offer their own forms of certification. The National Association of Judiciary Interpreters and Translators also offers certification for court interpreting.

The U.S. Department of State has a three-test series for interpreters, including simple consecutive interpreting (for escort work), simultaneous interpreting (for court or seminar work), and conference-level interpreting (for international conferences). These tests are not referred to directly as certification, but successful completion often indicates that a person has an adequate level of skill to work in the field.

The National Association of the Deaf and the Registry of Interpreters for the Deaf (RID) jointly offer certification for general sign interpreters. In addition, the registry offers specialty tests in legal interpreting, speech reading, and deaf-to-deaf interpreting—which includes interpreting between deaf speakers with different native languages and from ASL to tactile signing.

Once interpreters and translators have gained sufficient experience, they may then move up to more difficult or prestigious assignments, may seek certification, may be given editorial responsibility, or may eventually manage or start a translation agency.

Many self-employed interpreters and translators start businesses by submitting resumes and samples to many different employment agencies and then wait to be contacted when an agency matches their skills with a job. After establishing a few regular clients, interpreters and translators may receive enough work from a few clients to stay busy, and they often hear of subsequent jobs by word of mouth or through referrals from existing clients.

Employment

Interpreters and translators held about 41,000 jobs in 2006. However, the actual number of interpreters and translators is probably significantly higher because many work in the occupation only sporadically. Interpreters and translators are employed in a variety of industries, reflecting the diversity of employment options in the field. About 33 worked in public and private educational institutions, such as schools, colleges, and universities. About 12 worked in health care and social assistance, many of whom worked for hospitals. Another 10 worked in other areas of government, such as Federal, State and local courts. Other employers of interpreters and translators include publishing companies, telephone companies, airlines, and interpreting and translating agencies.

About 22 percent of interpreters and translators are self-employed. Many who freelance in the occupation work only part time, relying on other sources of income to supplement earnings from interpreting or translation.

Job Outlook

Interpreters and translators can expect much faster than average employment growth over the next decade. Job prospects vary by specialty.

Employment change. Employment of interpreters and translators is projected to increase 24 percent over the 2006-16 decade, much faster than the average for all occupations. This growth will be driven partly by strong demand in health care settings and work related to homeland security. Additionally, higher demand for interpreters and translators results directly from the broadening of international ties and the increase in the number of foreign language speakers in the United States. Both of these trends are expected to continue, contributing to relatively rapid growth in the number of jobs for interpreters and translators.

Current events and changing political environments, often difficult to foresee, will increase the need for people who can work with other languages. For example, homeland security

needs are expected to drive increasing demand for interpreters and translators of Middle Eastern and North African languages, primarily in Federal Government agencies.

Demand will remain strong for translators of the languages referred to as "PFIGS"—Portuguese, French, Italian, German, and Spanish; Arabic and other Middle Eastern languages; and the principal Asian languages—Chinese, Japanese, and Korean. Demand for American Sign Language interpreters will grow rapidly, driven by the increasing use of video relay services, which allow individuals to conduct video calls using a sign language interpreter over an Internet connection.

Technology has made the work of interpreters and translators easier. However, technology is not likely to have a negative impact on employment of interpreters and translators because such innovations are incapable of producing work comparable with work produced by these professionals.

Job prospects. Urban areas, especially Washington D.C., New York, and cities in California, provide the largest numbers of employment possibilities, especially for interpreters; however, as the immigrant population spreads into more rural areas, jobs in smaller communities will become more widely available.

Job prospects for interpreters and translators vary by specialty. There should be demand for specialists in localization, driven by imports and exports and the expansion of the Internet; however, demand may be dampened somewhat by outsourcing of localization work to other countries. Demand is expected to be strong in other technical areas, such as medicine and law. Given the shortage of interpreters and translators meeting the desired skill level of employers, interpreters for the deaf will continue to have favorable employment prospects. On the other hand, job opportunities are expected to be limited for both conference interpreters and literary translators.

Earnings

Salaried interpreters and translators had median hourly earnings of $17.10 in May 2006. The middle 50 percent earned between $12.94 and $22.60. The lowest 10 percent earned less than $9.88, and the highest 10 percent earned more than $30.91.

Earnings depend on language, subject matter, skill, experience, education, certification, and type of employer, and salaries of interpreters and translators can vary widely. Interpreters and translators who know languages for which there is a greater demand, or which relatively few people can translate, often have higher earnings as do those with specialized expertise, such as those working in software localization. Individuals classified as language specialists for the Federal Government earned an average of $76,287 annually in 2007. Limited information suggests that some highly skilled interpreters and translators—for example, high-level conference interpreters—working full time can earn more than $100,000 annually.

Projections data from the National Employment Matrix

Occupational Title	SOC Code	Employment, 2006	Projected employment, 2016	Change, 2006-2016	
				Number	Percent
Interpreters and translators...	27-3091	41,000	51,000	9,700	24

NOTE: Data in this table are rounded. See the discussion of the employment projections table in the *Handbook* introductory chapter on *Occupational Information Included in the Handbook.*

For those who are not salaried, earnings may fluctuate, depending on the availability of work. Freelance interpreters usually earn an hourly rate, whereas translators who freelance typically earn a rate per word or per hour.

Related Occupations

Interpreters and translators use their multilingual skills, as do teachers of languages. These include preschool, kindergarten, elementary, middle, and secondary school teachers; postsecondary school teachers; special education teachers; adult literacy and remedial education teachers; and self-enrichment education teachers. The work of interpreters, particularly guide or escort interpreters, is similar to that of tour guides and escorts, in that they accompany individuals or groups on tours or to places of interest.

The work of translators is similar to that of writers and editors, in that they communicate information and ideas in writing and prepare texts for publication or dissemination. Furthermore, interpreters or translators working in a legal or health care environment are required to have a knowledge of terms and concepts that is similar to that of professionals working in these fields, such as court reporters or medical transcriptionists.

Sources of Additional Information

Organizations dedicated to these professions can provide valuable advice and guidance to people interested in learning more about interpretation and translation. The language services division of local hospitals or courthouses also may have information about available opportunities.

For general career information, contact the organizations listed below:

➤ American Translators Association, 225 Reinekers Ln., Suite 590, Alexandria, VA 22314. Internet: **http://www.atanet.org**

For more detailed information by specialty, contact the association affiliated with that subject area:

➤ American Literary Translators Association, The University of Texas at Dallas, Box 830688 Mail Station JO51, Richardson, TX 75083-0688. Internet: **http://www.literarytranslators.org**

➤ Localization Industry Standards Association, Domaine en Prael, CH-1323 Romainmôtier, Switzerland. Internet: **http://www.lisa.org**

➤ National Association of Judiciary Interpreters and Translators, 603 Stewart St., Suite 610, Seattle, WA 98101. Internet: **http://www.najit.org**

➤ National Council on Interpreting in Health Care, 270 West Lawrence St., Albany, NY 12208. Internet: **http://www.ncihc.org**

➤ Registry of Interpreters for the Deaf, 333 Commerce St., Alexandria, VA 22314. Internet: **http://www.rid.org**

For information about testing to become a contract interpreter or translator with the U.S. State Department, contact:

➤ U.S. Department of State, Office of Language Services, 2401 E St.NW., SA-1, Room H1400, Washington, DC 20520-2204.

Information on obtaining positions as interpreters and translators with the Federal Government is available from the Office of Personnel Management through USAJOBS, the Federal Government's official employment information system. This resource for locating and applying for job opportunities can be accessed through the Internet at **http://www.usajobs.opm.gov**

or through an interactive voice response telephone system at (703) 724-1850 or TDD (978) 461-8404. These numbers are not toll free, and charges may result. For advice on how to find and apply for Federal jobs, see the Occupational Outlook Quarterly article "How to get a job in the Federal Government," online at:
http://www.bls.gov/opub/ooq/2004/summer/art01.pdf.

News Analysts, Reporters, and Correspondents

(O*NET 27-3021.00, 27-3022.00)

Significant Points

● Competition will be keen for jobs at large metropolitan and national newspapers, broadcast stations, and magazines; small publications and broadcast stations and online newspapers and magazines should provide the best opportunities.

● Most employers prefer individuals with a bachelor's degree in journalism or mass communications and experience gained at school newspapers or broadcasting stations or through internships with news organizations.

● Jobs often involve long, irregular hours and pressure to meet deadlines.

Nature of the Work

News analysts, reporters, and correspondents gather information, prepare stories, and make broadcasts that inform us about local, State, national, and international events; present points of view on current issues; and report on the actions of public officials, corporate executives, interest groups, and others who exercise power.

News analysts—also called *newscasters* or *news anchors*—examine, interpret, and broadcast news received from various sources. News anchors present news stories and introduce videotaped news or live transmissions from on-the-scene reporters. *News correspondents* report on news occurring in the large U.S. and foreign cities where they are stationed.

In covering a story, *reporters* investigate leads and news tips, look at documents, observe events at the scene, and interview people. Reporters take notes and also may take photographs or shoot videos. At their office, they organize the material, determine the focus or emphasis, write their stories, and edit accompanying video material. Many reporters enter information or write stories using laptop computers and electronically submit the material to their offices from remote locations. In some cases, *newswriters* write a story from information collected and submitted by reporters. Radio and television reporters often compose stories and report "live" from the scene. At times, they later tape an introduction to or commentary on their story in the studio. Some journalists also interpret the news or offer opinions to readers, viewers, or listeners. In this role, they are called commentators or columnists.

Newscasters at large stations and networks usually specialize in a particular type of news, such as sports or weather. *Weathercasters*, also called weather reporters, report current and forecasted weather conditions. They gather information from national satellite weather services, wire services, and local and regional weather bureaus. Some weathercasters are trained meteorologists and can develop their own weather forecasts. (See the statement on atmospheric scientists elsewhere in the *Handbook*.) *Sportscasters* select, write, and deliver sports news. This may include interviews with sports personalities and coverage of games and other sporting events.

General-assignment reporters write about newsworthy occurrences—such as accidents, political rallies, visits of celebrities, or business closings—as assigned. Large newspapers and radio and television stations assign reporters to gather news about specific topics, such as crime or education. Some reporters specialize in fields such as health, politics, foreign affairs, sports, theater, consumer affairs, social events, science, business, or religion. Investigative reporters cover stories that may take many days or weeks of information gathering.

Some publications use teams of reporters instead of assigning each reporter one specific topic, allowing reporters to cover a greater variety of stories. News teams may include reporters, editors, graphic artists, and photographers working together to complete a story.

Reporters on small publications cover all aspects of the news. They take photographs, write headlines, lay out pages, edit wire-service stories, and write editorials. Some also solicit advertisements, sell subscriptions, and perform general office work.

Work environment. The work of news analysts, reporters, and correspondents is usually hectic. They are under great pressure to meet deadlines. Broadcasts sometimes are aired with

Large newspapers and radio and television stations assign reporters to cover specific topics.

little or no time for preparation. Some news analysts, reporters, and correspondents work in comfortable, private offices; others work in large rooms filled with the sound of keyboards and computer printers, as well as the voices of other reporters. Curious onlookers, police, or other emergency workers can distract those reporting from the scene for radio and television. Covering wars, political uprisings, fires, floods, and similar events is often dangerous.

Working hours vary. Reporters on morning papers often work from late afternoon until midnight. Radio and television reporters usually are assigned to a day or evening shift. Magazine reporters usually work during the day.

Reporters sometimes have to change their work hours to meet a deadline or to follow late-breaking developments. Their work demands long hours, irregular schedules, and some travel. Because many stations and networks are on the air 24 hours a day, newscasters can expect to work unusual hours.

Training, Other Qualifications, and Advancement

Most employers prefer individuals with a bachelor's degree in journalism or mass communications, but some hire graduates with other majors. They look for experience at school newspapers or broadcasting stations, and internships with news organizations. Large-city newspapers and stations also may prefer candidates with a degree in a subject-matter specialty such as economics, political science, or business. Some large newspapers and broadcasters may hire only experienced reporters.

Education and training. More than 1,500 institutions offer programs in communications, journalism, and related programs. In 2007, 109 of these were accredited by the Accrediting Council on Education in Journalism and Mass Communications. Most of the courses in a typical curriculum are in liberal arts; the remaining courses are in journalism. Examples of journalism courses are introductory mass media, basic reporting and copy editing, history of journalism, and press law and ethics. Students planning a career in broadcasting take courses in radio and television news and production. Those planning newspaper or magazine careers usually specialize in news-editorial journalism. To create stories for online media, they need to learn to use computer software to combine online story text with audio and video elements and graphics.

Some schools also offer a master's or Ph.D. degree in journalism. Some graduate programs are intended primarily as preparation for news careers, while others prepare journalism teachers, researchers and theorists, and advertising and public relations workers. A graduate degree may help those looking to advance more quickly.

High school courses in English, journalism, and social studies provide a good foundation for college programs. Useful college liberal arts courses include English with an emphasis on writing, sociology, political science, economics, history, and psychology. Courses in computer science, business, and speech are useful as well. Fluency in a foreign language is necessary in some jobs.

Employers report that practical experience is the most important part of education and training. Upon graduation many students already have gained much practical experience through part-time or summer jobs or through internships with news organizations. Most newspapers, magazines, and broadcast news organizations offer reporting and editing internships. Work on high school and college newspapers, at broadcasting stations, or on community papers or U.S. Armed Forces publications also provides practical training. In addition, journalism scholarships, fellowships, and assistantships awarded to college journalism students by universities, newspapers, foundations, and professional organizations are helpful. Experience as a stringer or freelancer—a part-time reporter who is paid only for stories printed—is advantageous.

Other qualifications. Reporters typically need more than good word-processing skills. Computer graphics and desktop-publishing skills also are useful. Computer-assisted reporting involves the use of computers to analyze data in search of a story. This technique and the interpretation of the results require computer skills and familiarity with databases. Knowledge of news photography also is valuable for entry-level positions, which sometimes combine the responsibilities of a reporter with those of a camera operator or photographer.

Reporters should be dedicated to providing accurate and impartial news. Accuracy is important, both to serve the public and because untrue or libelous statements can lead to lawsuits. A nose for news, persistence, initiative, poise, resourcefulness, a good memory, and physical stamina are important, as is the emotional stability to deal with pressing deadlines, irregular hours, and dangerous assignments. Broadcast reporters and news analysts must be comfortable on camera. All reporters must be at ease in unfamiliar places and with a variety of people. Positions involving on-air work require a pleasant voice and appearance.

Advancement. Most reporters start at small publications or broadcast stations as general assignment reporters or copy editors. They are usually assigned to cover court proceedings and civic and club meetings, summarize speeches, and write obituaries. With experience, they report more difficult assignments or specialize in a particular field. Large publications and stations hire few recent graduates; as a rule, they require new reporters to have several years of experience.

Some news analysts and reporters can advance by moving to larger newspapers or stations. A few experienced reporters become columnists, correspondents, writers, announcers, or public relations specialists. Others become editors in print journalism or program managers in broadcast journalism, who supervise reporters. Some eventually become broadcasting or publishing industry managers.

Employment

News analysts, reporters, and correspondents held about 67,000 jobs in 2006. About 59 percent worked for newspaper, periodi-

cal, book, and directory publishers. Another 23 percent worked in radio and television broadcasting. About 11 percent of news analysts, reporters, and correspondents were self-employed (free lancers or stringers).

Job Outlook

There is expected to be little or no change in employment through 2016. Competition will continue to be keen for jobs on large metropolitan and national newspapers, broadcast stations and networks, and magazines. Small broadcast stations and publications and online newspapers and magazines should provide the best opportunities. Talented writers who can handle highly specialized scientific or technical subjects will have an advantage.

Employment change. Employment of news analysts, reporters, and correspondents is expected to grow 2 percent between 2006 and 2016, which is considered to be little or no change in employment. Many factors will contribute to the limited job growth in this occupation. Consolidation and convergence should continue in the publishing and broadcasting industries. As a result, companies will be better able to allocate their news analysts, reporters, and correspondents to cover news stories. Constantly improving technology also is allowing workers to do their jobs more efficiently, another factor that will limit the number of workers needed to cover a story or certain type of news. However, the continued demand for news will create some job opportunities. Job openings also will result from the need to replace workers who leave their occupations permanently; some news analysts, reporters, and correspondents find the work too stressful and hectic or do not like the lifestyle, and transfer to other occupations.

Job prospects. Competition will continue to be keen for jobs on large metropolitan and national newspapers, broadcast stations and networks, and magazines. Job opportunities will be best for applicants in the expanding world of new media, such as online newspapers or magazines. Small, local papers and news stations also will provide greater job prospects for potential reporters and news analysts. For beginning newspaper reporters, freelancing will supply more opportunities for employment as well. Students with a background in journalism as well as another specific subject matter, such as politics, economics, or biology, will have an advantage over those without additional background knowledge.

Journalism graduates have the background for work in closely related fields such as advertising and public relations, and many take jobs in these fields. Other graduates accept sales, managerial, or other nonmedia positions.

The number of job openings in the newspaper and broadcasting industries—in which news analysts, reporters, and corre-

Projections data from the National Employment Matrix

Occupational Title	SOC Code	Employment, 2006	Projected employment, 2016	Change, 2006-2016	
				Number	Percent
News analysts, reporters and correspondents	27-3020	67,000	68,000	1,200	2
Broadcast news analysts..	27-3021	7,700	8,200	500	6
Reporters and correspondents	27-3022	59,000	60,000	700	1

NOTE: Data in this table are rounded. See the discussion of the employment projections table in the *Handbook* introductory chapter on *Occupational Information Included in the Handbook.*

spondents are employed—is sensitive to economic upswings and downturns because these industries depend on advertising revenue.

Earnings

Salaries for news analysts, reporters, and correspondents vary widely. Median annual earnings of reporters and correspondents were $33,470 in May 2006. The middle 50 percent earned between $24,370 and $51,700. The lowest 10 percent earned less than $19,180, and the highest 10 percent earned more than $73,880. Median annual earnings of reporters and correspondents were $31,690 in newspaper, periodical, book, and directory publishing, and $38,050 in radio and television broadcasting.

Median annual earnings of broadcast news analysts were $46,710 in May 2006. The middle 50 percent earned between $30,080 and $83,370. The lowest 10 percent earned less than $22,430, and the highest 10 percent earned more than $145,600. Median annual earnings of broadcast news analysts were $48,790 in radio and television broadcasting.

Related Occupations

News analysts, reporters, and correspondents must write clearly and effectively to succeed in their profession. Others for whom good writing ability is essential include writers and editors and public relations specialists. Many news analysts, reporters, and correspondents also must communicate information orally. Others for whom oral communication skills are important are announcers, interpreters and translators, those in sales and related occupations, and teachers.

Sources of Additional Information

For information on broadcasting education and scholarship resources, contact:

➤ National Association of Broadcasters, 1771 N St.NW., Washington, DC 20036. Internet: **http://www.nab.org**

Information on careers in journalism, colleges and universities offering degree programs in journalism or communications, and journalism scholarships and internships may be obtained from:

➤ Dow Jones Newspaper Fund, Inc., P.O. Box 300, Princeton, NJ 08543-0300.

Information on union wage rates for newspaper and magazine reporters is available from:

➤ Newspaper Guild, Research and Information Department, 501 Third St.NW., Suite 250, Washington, DC 20001.

For a list of schools with accredited programs in journalism and mass communications, send a stamped, self-addressed envelope to:

➤ Accrediting Council on Education in Journalism and Mass Communications, University of Kansas School of Journalism and Mass Communications, Stauffer-Flint Hall, 1435 Jayhawk Blvd., Lawrence, KS 66045. Internet: **http://www.ku.edu/~ acejmc/STUDENT/STUDENT.SHTML**

Names and locations of newspapers and a list of schools and departments of journalism are published in the Editor and Publisher International Year Book, available in most public libraries and newspaper offices.

Photographers

(O*NET 27-4021.00)

Significant Points

- Competition for jobs is expected to be keen because the work is attractive to many people.

- Technical expertise, a "good eye," imagination, and creativity are essential.

- More than half of all photographers are self-employed, a much higher proportion than for most occupations.

Nature of the Work

Photographers produce and preserve images that paint a picture, tell a story, or record an event. To create commercial-quality photographs, photographers need technical expertise, creativity, and the appropriate professional equipment. Producing a successful picture requires choosing and presenting a subject to achieve a particular effect, and selecting the right cameras and other photographic enhancing tools. For example, photographers may enhance the subject's appearance with natural or artificial light, shoot the subject from an interesting angle, draw attention to a particular aspect of the subject by blurring the background, or use various lenses to produce desired levels of detail at various distances from the subject.

Today, most photographers use digital cameras instead of traditional silver-halide film cameras, although some photographers use both types, depending on their own preference and the nature of the assignment. Regardless of the camera they use, photographers also employ an array of other equipment—from lenses, filters, and tripods to flash attachments and specially constructed lighting equipment—to improve the quality of their work.

Digital cameras capture images electronically, allowing them to be edited on a computer. Images can be stored on portable memory devices such as compact disks or on smaller storage devices such as memory cards used in digital cameras and flash drives. Once the raw image has been transferred to a computer, photographers can use processing software to crop or modify the image and enhance it through color correction and other specialized effects. As soon as a photographer has finished editing the image, it can be sent anywhere in the world over the Internet.

Photographers also can create electronic portfolios of their work and display them on their own webpage, allowing them to reach prospective customers directly. Digital technology also allows the production of larger, more colorful, and more accurate prints or images for use in advertising, photographic art, and scientific research. Photographers who process their own digital images need to be proficient in the use of computers, high-quality printers, and editing software.

Photographers who use cameras with silver-halide film often send their film to laboratories for processing. Color film requires expensive equipment and exacting conditions for correct processing and printing. (See the statement on photographic process workers and processing machine operators elsewhere in the *Handbook*.) Other photographers develop and print their own photographs using their own fully equipped darkrooms, especially if they use black and white film or seek to achieve special effects. Photographers who do their own film developing must invest in additional developing and printing equipment and acquire the technical skills to operate it.

Some photographers specialize in areas such as portrait, commercial and industrial, scientific, news, or fine arts photography. *Portrait photographers* take pictures of individuals or groups of people and often work in their own studios. Some specialize in weddings, religious ceremonies, or school photographs and may work on location. Portrait photographers who own and operate their own business have many responsibilities in addition to taking pictures. They must arrange for advertising, schedule appointments, set and adjust equipment, purchase supplies, keep records, bill customers, pay bills, and—if they have employees—hire, train, and direct their workers. Many also process their own images, design albums, and mount and frame the finished photographs.

Commercial and industrial photographers take pictures of various subjects, such as buildings, models, merchandise, artifacts, and landscapes. These photographs are used in a variety of media, including books, reports, advertisements, and catalogs. Industrial photographers often take pictures of equipment, machinery, products, workers, and company officials. The pictures are used for various purposes—for example, analysis of engineering projects, publicity, or records of equipment development or deployment, such as placement of an offshore oil rig. This photography frequently is done on location.

Scientific photographers take images of a variety of subjects to illustrate or record scientific or medical data or phenomena, using knowledge of scientific procedures. They typically possess additional knowledge in areas such as engineering, medicine, biology, or chemistry.

News photographers, also called *photojournalists*, photograph newsworthy people, places, and sporting, political, and community events for newspapers, journals, magazines, or television.

Fine arts photographers sell their photographs as fine artwork. In addition to technical proficiency, fine arts photographers need artistic talent and creativity.

Self-employed, or freelance, photographers usually specialize in one of the above fields. In addition to carrying out assignments under direct contract with clients, they may license the use of their photographs through stock-photo agencies or market their work directly to the public. Stock-photo agencies sell magazines and other customers the right to use photographs, and pay the photographer a commission. These agencies require an application from the photographer and a sizable portfolio of pictures. Once accepted, photographers usually are required to submit a large number of new photographs each year. Self-employed photographers must also have a thorough understanding of copyright laws in order to protect their work.

Most photographers spend only a small portion of their work schedule actually taking photographs. Their most common activities are editing images on a computer—if they use a digital camera—and looking for new business—if they are self-employed.

Work environment. Working conditions for photographers vary considerably. Photographers employed in government and

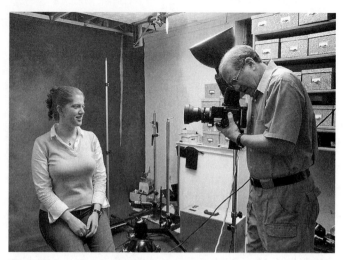

Technical expertise, imagination and creativity, and a "good eye" are important for photographers.

advertising studios usually work a 5-day, 40-hour week. On the other hand, news photographers often work long, irregular hours and must be available to work on short notice. Many photographers work part time or on variable schedules.

Portrait photographers usually work in their own studios but also may travel to take photographs at the client's location, such as a school, a company office, or a private home. News and commercial photographers frequently travel locally, stay overnight on assignments, or travel to distant places for long periods.

Some photographers work in uncomfortable or even dangerous surroundings, especially news photographers covering accidents, natural disasters, civil unrest, or military conflicts. Many photographers must wait long hours in all kinds of weather for an event to take place and stand or walk for long periods while carrying heavy equipment. News photographers often work under strict deadlines.

Self-employment allows for greater autonomy, freedom of expression, and flexible scheduling. However, income can be uncertain and the continuous, time consuming search for new clients can be stressful. Some self-employed photographers hire assistants who help seek out new business.

Training, Other Qualifications, and Advancement

Employers usually seek applicants with a "good eye," imagination, and creativity, as well as a good technical understanding of photography. Photojournalists or industrial or scientific photographers generally need a college degree. Freelance and portrait photographers need technical proficiency, gained through a degree, training program, or experience.

Education and training. Entry-level positions in photojournalism or in industrial or scientific photography generally require a college degree in photography or in a field related to the industry in which the photographer seeks employment. Entry-level freelance or portrait photographers need technical proficiency. Some complete a college degree or vocational training programs.

Photography courses are offered by many universities, community and junior colleges, vocational-technical institutes, and private trade and technical schools. Basic courses in photography cover equipment, processes, and techniques. Learning good business skills is important and some bachelor's degree programs offer courses focusing on them. Art schools offer useful training in photographic design and composition.

Photographers may start out as assistants to experienced photographers. Assistants acquire the technical knowledge needed to be a successful photographer and also learn other skills necessary to run a portrait or commercial photography business.

Some photographers enter the field by submitting unsolicited a portfolio of photographs to magazines and to art directors at advertising agencies; for freelance photographers, a good portfolio is essential.

Individuals interested in a career in photography should try to develop contacts in the field by subscribing to photographic newsletters and magazines, joining camera clubs, and seeking summer or part-time employment in camera stores, newspapers, or photo studios.

Other qualifications. Photographers need good eyesight, artistic ability, and good hand-eye coordination. They should be patient, accurate, and detail-oriented and should be able to work well with others, as they frequently deal with clients, graphic designers, and advertising and publishing specialists. Photographers need to know how to use computer software programs and applications that allow them to prepare and edit images, and those who market directly to clients should know how to use the Internet to display their work.

Portrait photographers need the ability to help people relax in front of the camera. Commercial and fine arts photographers must be imaginative and original. News photographers must not only be good with a camera, but also understand the story behind an event so that their pictures match the story. They must be decisive in recognizing a potentially good photograph and act quickly to capture it.

Photographers who operate their own business, or freelance, need business skills as well as talent. These individuals must know how to prepare a business plan; submit bids; write contracts; keep financial records; market their work; hire models, if needed; get permission to shoot on locations that normally are not open to the public; obtain releases to use photographs of people; license and price photographs; and secure copyright protection for their work. To protect their rights and their work, self-employed photographers require basic knowledge of licensing and copyright laws, as well as knowledge of contracts and negotiation procedures.

Freelance photographers also should develop an individual style of photography to differentiate themselves from the competition.

Advancement. After several years of experience, magazine and news photographers may advance to photography or picture editor positions. Some photographers teach at technical schools, film schools, or universities.

Employment

Photographers held about 122,000 jobs in 2006. More than half were self-employed, a much higher proportion than for most occupations. Some self-employed photographers have contracts with advertising agencies, magazine publishers, or other businesses to do individual projects for a set fee, while others operate portrait studios or provide photographs to stock-photo agencies.

Most salaried photographers work in portrait or commercial photography studios; most of the others work for newspapers, magazines, and advertising agencies. Photographers work in all areas of the country, but most are employed in metropolitan areas.

Job Outlook

Employment of photographers is expected to grow about as fast as the average for all occupations through 2016. Photographers can expect keen competition for job openings because the work is attractive to many people.

Employment change. Demand for portrait photographers should increase as the population grows. Moreover, growth of Internet versions of magazines, journals, and newspapers will require increasing numbers of commercial photographers to provide digital images. The Internet and improved data management programs also should make it easier for freelancers to market directly to their customers, increasing opportunities for self-employment and decreasing reliance on stock photo agencies. As a result, employment of photographers is expected to grow 10 percent over the 2006-16 projection period, about as fast as the average for all occupations.

Job growth, however, will be constrained somewhat by the widespread use of digital photography and the falling price of digital equipment. Improvements in digital technology reduce barriers of entry into this profession and allow more individual consumers and businesses to produce, store, and access photographic images on their own. Photojournalists may be adversely affected by the increase in "citizen journalism"—when newspapers buy images taken by non-professionals who happen to be at the scene of an event. Declines in the newspaper industry also will reduce demand for photographers to provide still images for print.

Job prospects. Photographers can expect keen competition for job openings because the work is attractive to many people. The number of individuals interested in positions as commercial and news photographers usually is much greater than the number of openings. Salaried jobs in particular may be difficult to find as more companies contract with freelancers rather than hire their own photographers. Those who succeed in landing a salaried job or attracting enough work to earn a living by freelancing are likely to be adept at operating a business and to be among the most creative. They will be able to find and exploit the new opportunities available from rapidly changing technologies. Relat-

Projections data from the National Employment Matrix

Occupational Title	SOC Code	Employment, 2006	Projected employment, 2016	Change, 2006-2016	
				Number	Percent
Photographers	27-4021	122,000	135,000	13,000	10

NOTE: Data in this table are rounded. See the discussion of the employment projections table in the *Handbook* introductory chapter on *Occupational Information Included in the Handbook.*

ed work experience, job-related training, or some unique skill or talent—such as a background in computers or electronics—also improve a photographer's job prospects.

Earnings

Median annual earnings of salaried photographers were $26,170 in May 2006. The middle 50 percent earned between $18,680 and $38,730. The lowest 10 percent earned less than $15,540, and the highest 10 percent earned more than $56,640. Median annual earnings in the industry employing the largest numbers of salaried photographers were $22,860 in the photographic services industry.

Salaried photographers—more of whom work full time—tend to earn more than those who are self-employed. Because most freelance and portrait photographers purchase their own equipment, they incur considerable expense acquiring and maintaining cameras and accessories. Unlike news and commercial photographers, few fine arts photographers are successful enough to support themselves solely through their art.

Related Occupations

Other occupations requiring artistic talent and creativity include architects, except landscape and naval; artists and related workers; commercial and industrial designers, fashion designers, and graphic designers; and television, video, and motion picture camera operators and editors. Photojournalists are often required to cover news stories much the same as news analysts, reporters, and correspondents. The processing work that photographers do on computers is similar to the work of prepress technicians and workers and desktop publishers.

Sources of Additional Information

Career information on photography is available from:

➤ Professional Photographers of America, Inc., 229 Peachtree St.NE., Suite 2200, Atlanta, GA 30303.
Internet: **http://www.ppa.com**

➤ National Press Photographers Association, Inc., 3200 Croasdaile Dr., Suite 306, Durham, NC 27705.
Internet: **http://www.nppa.org**

➤ American Society of Media Photographers, Inc., 150 North Second St., Philadelphia, PA 19106.
Internet: **http://www.asmp.org**

Public Relations Specialists

(O*NET 27-3031.00)

Significant Points

- Although employment is projected to grow faster than average, keen competition is expected for entry-level jobs.

- Opportunities should be best for college graduates who combine a degree in public relations, journalism, or another communications-related field with a public relations internship or other related work experience.

- The ability to communicate effectively is essential.

Nature of the Work

An organization's reputation, profitability, and even its continued existence can depend on the degree to which its targeted "publics" support its goals and policies. Public relations specialists—also referred to as communications specialists and media specialists, among other titles—serve as advocates for businesses, nonprofit associations, universities, hospitals, and other organizations, and build and maintain positive relationships with the public. As managers recognize the importance of good public relations to the success of their organizations, they increasingly rely on public relations specialists for advice on the strategy and policy of such programs.

Public relations specialists handle organizational functions such as media, community, consumer, industry, and governmental relations; political campaigns; interest-group representation; conflict mediation; and employee and investor relations. They do more than "tell the organization's story." They must understand the attitudes and concerns of community, consumer, employee, and public interest groups and establish and maintain cooperative relationships with them and with representatives from print and broadcast journalism.

Public relations specialists draft press releases and contact people in the media who might print or broadcast their material. Many radio or television special reports, newspaper stories, and magazine articles start at the desks of public relations specialists. Sometimes the subject is an organization and its policies toward its employees or its role in the community. Often the subject is a public issue, such as health, energy, or the environment, and what an organization does to advance that issue.

Public relations specialists also arrange and conduct programs to keep up contact between organization representatives and the public. For example, they set up speaking engagements and often prepare speeches for company officials. These media specialists represent employers at community projects; make film, slide, or other visual presentations at meetings and school assemblies; and plan conventions. In addition, they are responsible for preparing annual reports and writing proposals for various projects.

In government, public relations specialists—who may be called press secretaries, information officers, public affairs specialists, or communication specialists—keep the public informed about the activities of agencies and officials. For example, public affairs specialists in the U.S. Department of State keep the public informed of travel advisories and of U.S. positions on foreign issues. A press secretary for a member of Congress keeps constituents aware of the representative's accomplishments.

In large organizations, the key public relations executive, who often is a vice president, may develop overall plans and policies with other executives. In addition, public relations departments employ public relations specialists to write, research, prepare materials, maintain contacts, and respond to inquiries.

People who handle publicity for an individual or who direct public relations for a small organization may deal with all aspects of the job. They contact people, plan and research, and prepare materials for distribution. They also may handle advertising or sales promotion work to support marketing efforts.

Public relations specialists draft press releases and contact people in the media who print or broadcast their material.

Work environment. Public relations specialists work in busy offices. The pressures of deadlines and tight work schedules can be stressful.

Some public relations specialists work a standard 35- to 40-hour week, but unpaid overtime is common and work schedules can be irregular and frequently interrupted. Occasionally, they must be at the job or on call around the clock, especially if there is an emergency or crisis. Schedules often have to be rearranged so that workers can meet deadlines, deliver speeches, attend meetings and community activities, and travel.

Training, Other Qualifications, and Advancement

There are no defined standards for entry into a public relations career. A college degree in a communications-related field combined with public relations experience is excellent preparation for public relations work.

Education and training. Many entry-level public relations specialists have a college degree in public relations, journalism, advertising, or communication. Some firms seek college graduates who have worked in electronic or print journalism. Other employers seek applicants with demonstrated communication skills and training or experience in a field related to the firm's business—information technology, health care, science, engineering, sales, or finance, for example.

Many colleges and universities offer bachelor's and postsecondary degrees in public relations, usually in a journalism or communications department. In addition, many other colleges offer at least one course in this field. A common public relations sequence includes courses in public relations principles and techniques; public relations management and administration, including organizational development; writing, emphasizing news releases, proposals, annual reports, scripts, speeches, and related items; visual communications, including desktop publishing and computer graphics; and research, emphasizing social science research and survey design and implementation.

Courses in advertising, journalism, business administration, finance, political science, psychology, sociology, and creative writing also are helpful. Specialties are offered in public relations for business, government, and nonprofit organizations.

Many colleges help students gain part-time internships in public relations that provide valuable experience and training. Membership in local chapters of the Public Relations Student Society of America (affiliated with the Public Relations Society of America) or in student chapters of the International Association of Business Communicators provides an opportunity for students to exchange views with public relations specialists and to make professional contacts that may help them find a job in the field. A portfolio of published articles, television or radio programs, slide presentations, and other work is an asset in finding a job. Writing for a school publication or television or radio station provides valuable experience and material for one's portfolio.

Some organizations, particularly those with large public relations staffs, have formal training programs for new employees. In smaller organizations, new employees work under the guidance of experienced staff members. Beginners often maintain files of material about company activities, scan newspapers and magazines for appropriate articles to clip, and assemble information for speeches and pamphlets. They also may answer calls from the press and the public, work on invitation lists and details for press conferences, or escort visitors and clients. After gaining experience, they write news releases, speeches, and articles for publication or plan and carry out public relations programs. Public relations specialists in smaller firms usually get all-around experience, whereas those in larger firms tend to be more specialized.

Other qualifications. Public relations specialists must show creativity, initiative, and good judgment and have the ability to communicate thoughts clearly and simply. Decision-making, problem-solving, and research skills also are important. People who choose public relations as a career need an outgoing personality, self-confidence, an understanding of human psychology, and an enthusiasm for motivating people. They should be competitive, yet able to function as part of a team and be open to new ideas.

Certification and advancement. The Universal Accreditation Board accredits public relations specialists who are members of the Public Relations Society of America and who participate in the Examination for Accreditation in Public Relations process. This process includes both a readiness review and an examination, which are designed for candidates who have at least 5 years of full-time work or teaching experience in public relations and who have earned a bachelor's degree in a communications-related field. The readiness review includes a written submission by each candidate, a portfolio review, and dialogue between the candidate and a three-member panel. Candidates who successfully advance through readiness review and pass the computer-based examination earn the Accredited in Public Relations (APR) designation.

The International Association of Business Communicators (IABC) also has an accreditation program for professionals in the communications field, including public relations specialists. Those who meet all the requirements of the program earn the

Accredited Business Communicator (ABC) designation. Candidates must have at least 5 years of experience and a bachelor's degree in a communications field and must pass written and oral examinations. They also must submit a portfolio of work samples demonstrating involvement in a range of communications projects and a thorough understanding of communications planning.

Employers may consider professional recognition through accreditation as a sign of competence in this field, which could be especially helpful in a competitive job market.

Promotion to supervisory jobs may come to public relations specialists who show that they can handle more demanding assignments. In public relations firms, a beginner might be hired as a research assistant or account coordinator and be promoted to account executive, senior account executive, account manager, and eventually vice president. A similar career path is followed in corporate public relations, although the titles may differ.

Some experienced public relations specialists start their own consulting firms. (For more information on public relations managers, see the *Handbook* statement on advertising, marketing, promotions, public relations, and sales managers.)

Employment

Public relations specialists held about 243,000 jobs in 2006. They are concentrated in service-providing industries such as advertising and related services; health care and social assistance; educational services; and government. Others work for communications firms, financial institutions, and government agencies.

Public relations specialists are concentrated in large cities, where press services and other communications facilities are readily available and many businesses and trade associations have their headquarters. Many public relations consulting firms, for example, are in New York, Los Angeles, San Francisco, Chicago, and Washington, DC. There is a trend, however, for public relations jobs to be dispersed throughout the Nation, closer to clients.

Job Outlook

Employment is projected to grow faster than average; however, keen competition is expected for entry-level jobs.

Employment change. Employment of public relations specialists is expected to grow by 18 percent from 2006 to 2016, faster than average for all occupations. The need for good public relations in an increasingly competitive business environment should spur demand for these workers in organizations of all types and sizes. Those with additional language capabilities also are in great demand.

Employment in public relations firms should grow as firms hire contractors to provide public relations services rather than support full-time staff.

Among detailed industries, the largest job growth will continue to be in advertising and related services.

Job prospects. Keen competition likely will continue for entry-level public relations jobs, as the number of qualified applicants is expected to exceed the number of job openings. Many people are attracted to this profession because of the high profile nature of the work. Opportunities should be best for college graduates who combine a degree in journalism, public relations, advertising, or another communications-related field with a public relations internship or other related work experience. Applicants without the appropriate educational background or work experience will face the toughest obstacles.

Additional job opportunities should result from the need to replace public relations specialists who retire or leave the occupation for other reasons.

Earnings

Median annual earnings for salaried public relations specialists were $47,350 in May 2006. The middle 50 percent earned between $35,600 and $65,310; the lowest 10 percent earned less than $28,080, and the top 10 percent earned more than $89,220. Median annual earnings in the industries employing the largest numbers of public relations specialists in May 2006 were:

Management of companies and enterprises	$52,940
Business, professional, labor, political, and similar organizations	51,400
Advertising and related services	49,980
Local government	47,550
Colleges, universities, and professional schools	43,330

Related Occupations

Public relations specialists create favorable attitudes among various organizations, interest groups, and the public through effective communication. Other workers with similar jobs include advertising, marketing, promotions, public relations, and sales managers; demonstrators, product promoters, and models; news analysts, reporters, and correspondents; lawyers; market and survey researchers; sales representatives, wholesale and manufacturing; and police and detectives involved in community relations.

Sources of Additional Information

A comprehensive directory of schools offering degree programs, a sequence of study in public relations, a brochure on careers in public relations, and an online brochure entitled *Where Shall*

Projections data from the National Employment Matrix

Occupational Title	SOC Code	Employment, 2006	Projected employment, 2016	Change, 2006-2016	
				Number	Percent
Public relations specialists	27-3031	243,000	286,000	43,000	18

NOTE: Data in this table are rounded. See the discussion of the employment projections table in the *Handbook* introductory chapter on *Occupational Information Included in the Handbook.*

I Go to Study Advertising and Public Relations?, are available from:

➤ Public Relations Society of America, Inc., 33 Maiden LaNE., New York, NY 10038-5150. Internet: **http://www.prsa.org**

For information on accreditation for public relations professionals and the IABC Student Web site, contact:

➤ International Association of Business Communicators, One Hallidie Plaza, Suite 600, San Francisco, CA 94102.

Television, Video, and Motion Picture Camera Operators and Editors

(O*NET 27-4031.00, 27-4032.00)

Significant Points

- Workers acquire their skills through on-the-job or formal postsecondary training.

- Keen competition for jobs is expected due to the large number of people who wish to enter the broadcasting and motion picture industries, where many camera operators and editors are employed.

- Those with the most experience and the most advanced computer skills will have the best job opportunities.

Nature of the Work

Television, video, and motion picture camera operators produce images that tell a story, inform or entertain an audience, or record an event. *Film and video editors* edit soundtracks, film, and video for the motion picture, cable, and broadcast television industries. Some camera operators do their own editing.

Camera operators use television, video, or motion picture cameras to shoot a wide range of material, including television series, studio programs, news and sporting events, music videos, motion pictures, documentaries, and training sessions. This material is constructed from many different shots by film and video editors. With the increase in digital technology, much of the editing work is now done on a computer. Many camera operators and editors are employed by independent television stations; local affiliate stations of television networks; large cable and television networks; or smaller, independent production companies.

Making commercial-quality movies and video programs requires technical expertise and creativity. Producing successful images requires choosing and presenting interesting material, selecting appropriate equipment, and applying a good eye and a steady hand to ensure smooth, natural movement of the camera.

Some camera operators film or videotape private ceremonies and special events, such as weddings and conference program sessions. Those who record these images on videotape are often called *videographers*. *Studio camera operators* work in a broadcast studio and usually videotape their subjects from a fixed position. *News camera operators*, also called *electronic news gathering (ENG) operators*, work as part of a reporting team, following newsworthy events as they unfold. To capture live events, they must anticipate the action and act quickly. ENG operators sometimes edit raw footage on the spot for relay to a television affiliate for broadcast.

Camera operators employed in the entertainment field use motion picture cameras to film movies, television programs, and commercials. Those who film motion pictures also are known as *cinematographers*. Some specialize in filming cartoons or special effects. Cinematographers may be an integral part of the action, using cameras in any of several different mounts. For example, the camera can be stationary and shoot whatever passes in front of the lens, or it can be mounted on a track, with the camera operator responsible for shooting the scene from different angles or directions. Wider use of digital cameras has enhanced the number of angles and the clarity that a camera operator can provide. Other camera operators sit on cranes and follow the action while crane operators move them into position. *Steadicam operators* mount a harness and carry the camera on their shoulders to provide a clear picture while they move about the action. Camera operators who work in the entertainment field often meet with directors, actors, editors, and camera assistants to discuss ways of filming, editing, and improving scenes.

Work environment. ENG operators and those who cover major events, such as conventions or sporting events, frequently travel locally and stay overnight or travel to distant places for longer periods. Camera operators filming television programs or motion pictures may travel to film on location.

Some camera operators—especially ENG operators covering accidents, natural disasters, civil unrest, or military conflicts—work in uncomfortable or even dangerous surroundings. Many camera operators must wait long hours in all kinds of weather for an event to take place and must stand or walk for long periods while carrying heavy equipment. ENG operators often work under strict deadlines.

Hours of work and working schedules for camera operators and editors vary considerably. Those employed by television and cable networks and advertising agencies usually work a 5-day, 40-hour week; however, they may work longer hours to meet production schedules. ENG operators often work long, irregular hours and must be available to work on short notice.

Film and video editors use computers to create a finished product.

Camera operators and editors working in motion picture production also may work long, irregular hours.

Training, Other Qualifications, and Advancement

Television, video, and motion picture camera operators and editors usually acquire their skills through formal postsecondary training at vocational schools, colleges, universities, or photographic institutes. A bachelor's degree may be required for some positions, particularly those for film and video editors. Employers usually seek applicants with a good eye, imagination, and creativity, as well as a good technical understanding of how the camera operates.

Education and training. Many universities, community and junior colleges, vocational-technical institutes, and private trade and technical schools offer courses in camera operation and videography. Basic courses cover equipment, processes, and techniques. It is increasingly important for camera operators to have a good understanding of computer technology. Bachelor's degree programs, especially those including business courses, provide a well-rounded education. Film schools also may provide training on the artistic or aesthetic aspects of filmmaking.

Individuals interested in camera operations should subscribe to videographic newsletters and magazines, join audio-video clubs, and seek summer or part-time employment in cable and television networks, motion picture studios, or camera and video stores.

To enter the occupation, many camera operators first become production assistants to learn how film and video production works. In entry-level jobs they learn to set up lights, cameras, and other equipment. They also may receive routine assignments requiring adjustments to their cameras or decisions on what subject matter to capture. Camera operators in the film and television industries usually are hired for a project on the basis of recommendations from individuals such as producers, directors of photography, and camera assistants from previous projects or through interviews with the producer. ENG and studio camera operators who work for television affiliates usually start in small markets to gain experience.

Other qualifications. Camera operators need good eyesight, artistic ability, and hand-eye coordination. They should be patient, accurate, and detail oriented. Camera operators also should have good communication skills and, if needed, the ability to hold a camera by hand for extended periods.

Camera operators, who run their own businesses or do freelance work, need business skills as well as talent. These individuals must know how to submit bids, write contracts, get permission to shoot on locations that normally are not open to the public, obtain releases to use film or tape of people, price

their services, secure copyright protection for their work, and keep financial records.

Advancement. With experience, operators may advance to more demanding assignments or to positions with larger or network television stations. Advancement for ENG operators may mean moving to larger media markets. Other camera operators and editors may become directors of photography for movie studios, advertising agencies, or television programs. Some teach at technical schools, film schools, or universities.

Employment

Television, video, and motion picture camera operators and editors held about 47,000 jobs in 2006. About 27,000 were camera operators and film and video editors held about 21,000 jobs.

Many are employed by independent television stations, local affiliate stations of television networks or broadcast groups, large cable and television networks, or smaller independent production companies. About 17 percent of camera operators and film editors were self-employed. Some self-employed camera operators contracted with television networks, documentary or independent filmmakers, advertising agencies, or trade show or convention sponsors to work on individual projects for a set fee, often at a daily rate.

Most of the salaried camera operators and editors were employed by television broadcasting stations or motion picture studios. More than half of the salaried film and video editors worked for motion picture studios. Most camera operators and editors worked in large metropolitan areas.

Job Outlook

Keen competition for jobs is expected due to the large number of people who wish to enter the broadcasting and motion picture industries, where many camera operators and editors are employed. Those with the most experience and the most advanced computer skills will have the best job opportunities. Employment is expected to grow about as fast as the average.

Employment change. Employment of camera operators and editors is expected to grow 12 percent over the 2006-16 decade, which is about as fast as the average for all occupations through 2016. Rapid expansion of the entertainment market, especially motion picture production and distribution, will spur growth of camera operators. In addition, computer and Internet services will provide new outlets for interactive productions. Camera operators will be needed to film made-for-Internet broadcasts, such as live music videos, digital movies, sports features, and general information or entertainment programming. These images can be delivered directly into the home either on compact discs or as streaming video over the Internet. Growth will be tempered, however, by the increased offshore production of

Projections data from the National Employment Matrix

Occupational Title	SOC Code	Employment, 2006	Projected employment, 2016	Change, 2006-2016	
				Number	Percent
Television, video, and motion picture camera operators and editors	27-4030	47,000	53,000	5,700	12
Camera operators, television, video, and motion picture..............	27-4031	27,000	30,000	3,100	12
Film and video editors	27-4032	21,000	23,000	2,600	13

NOTE: Data in this table are rounded. See the discussion of the employment projections table in the *Handbook* introductory chapter on *Occupational Information Included in the Handbook.*

motion pictures. Job growth in television broadcasting will be tempered by the use of automated cameras under the control of a single person working either on the studio floor or in a director's booth.

Job prospects. Television, video, and motion picture camera operators and editors can expect keen competition for job openings because of the large number of people who wish to enter the broadcasting and motion picture industries, where many of these workers are employed. The number of individuals interested in positions as videographers and movie camera operators usually is much greater than the number of openings. Those who succeed in landing a salaried job or attracting enough work to earn a living by freelancing are likely to be the most creative and highly motivated people, able to adapt to rapidly changing technologies and adept at operating a business. The change to digital cameras has increased the importance of strong computer skills. Those with the most experience and the most advanced computer skills will have the best job opportunities.

Earnings

Median annual earnings for television, video, and motion picture camera operators were $40,060 in May 2006. The middle 50 percent earned between $26,930 and $59,440. The lowest 10 percent earned less than $18,810, and the highest 10 percent earned more than $84,500. Median annual earnings were $44,010 in the motion picture and video industries and $32,200 in radio and television broadcasting.

Median annual earnings for film and video editors were $46,670 in May 2006. The middle 50 percent earned between $30,610 and $74,650. The lowest 10 percent earned less than $22,710, and the highest 10 percent earned more than $110,720. Median annual earnings were $53,580 in the motion picture and video industries, which employed the largest numbers of film and video editors.

Many camera operators who work in film or video are freelancers, whose earnings tend to fluctuate each year. Because most freelance camera operators purchase their own equipment, they incur considerable expense acquiring and maintaining cameras and accessories. Some camera operators belong to unions, including the International Alliance of Theatrical Stage Employees, and the National Association of Broadcast Employees and Technicians.

Related Occupations

Related arts and media occupations include artists and related workers, broadcast and sound engineering technicians and radio operators, graphic designers, and photographers.

Sources of Additional Information

For information about careers as a camera operator, contact:
➤ International Cinematographer's Guild, 80 Eighth Ave., 14th Floor, New York, NY 10011.
➤ National Association of Broadcast Employees and Technicians, 501 Third St.NW., 6th floor, Washington, DC 20001. Internet: **http://www.nabetcwa.org**

Information about career and employment opportunities for camera operators and film and video editors also is available from local offices of State employment service agencies, local offices of the relevant trade unions, and local television and film production companies that employ these workers.

Writers and Editors

(O*NET 23-2091.00, 27-3041.00, 27-3042.00, 27-3043.00, 27-3043.04, 27-3043.05)

Significant Points

- Most jobs in this occupation require a college degree preferably in communications, journalism, or English, but a degree in a technical subject may be useful for technical writing positions.

- The outlook for most writing and editing jobs is expected to be competitive because many people are attracted to the occupation.

- Online publications and services are growing in number and sophistication, spurring the demand for writers and editors with Web or multimedia experience.

Nature of the Work

Writers and editors produce a wide variety of written materials delivered to an audience in an increasing number of ways. They develop content using any number of multimedia formats for readers, listeners, or viewers. Although many people write as part of their primary job, or on on-line chats or blogs, only writers and editors who are paid for their work are included in this occupation. (News analysts, reporters and correspondents, who gather information and prepare stories about newsworthy events, are described elsewhere in the *Handbook.*)

Writers fall into two main categories—writers and authors and technical writers. *Writers and authors* develop original written materials for books, magazines, trade journals, online publications, company newsletters, radio and television broadcasts, motion pictures, and advertisements. Their works are classified broadly as either fiction or nonfiction and writers often are identified by the type of writing they do—for example, novelists, playwrights, biographers, screenwriters, and textbook writers. Some freelance writers may be commissioned by a sponsor to write a script; others may be contracted to write a book on the basis of a proposal in the form of a draft or an outline. Writers may produce materials for publication or performance, such as songwriters or scriptwriters.

Writers work with editors and publishers throughout the writing process to review edits, topics, and production schedules. Editors and publishers may assign topics to staff writers or review proposals from freelance writers. All writers conduct research on their topics, which they gather through personal observation, library and Internet research, and interviews. Writers, especially of nonfiction, are expected to establish their credibility with editors and readers through strong research and the use of appropriate sources and citations. Writers and authors then select the material they want to use, organize it, and use the written word to express story lines, ideas, or to convey information. With help from editors, they may revise or rewrite sections, searching for the best organization or the right phrasing.

Copy writers are a very specialized type of writer. They prepare advertising copy for use in publications or for broadcasting and they write other materials to promote the sale of a good or service. They often must work with the client to produce advertising themes or slogans and may be involved in the marketing of the product or service.

Technical writers put technical information into easily understandable language. They prepare product documentation, such as operating and maintenance manuals, catalogs, assembly instructions, and project proposals. Technical writers primarily are found in the information technology industry, writing operating instructions for online Help and documentation for computer programs. Many technical writers work with engineers on technical subject matters to prepare written interpretations of engineering and design specifications and other information for a general readership. Technical writers also may serve as part of a team conducting usability studies to help improve the design of a product that still is in the prototype stage. They plan and edit technical materials and oversee the preparation of illustrations, photographs, diagrams, and charts.

Most writers and editors have at least a basic familiarity with technology, regularly using personal computers, desktop or electronic publishing systems, scanners, and other electronic communications equipment. Many writers prepare material directly for the Internet. For example, they may write for electronic editions of newspapers or magazines, create short fiction or poetry, or produce technical documentation that is available only online. These writers also may prepare text for Web sites. As a result, they should be knowledgeable about graphic design, page layout, and multimedia software. In addition, they should be familiar with interactive technologies of the Web so that they can blend text, graphics, and sound together. Bloggers who are paid to write may be considered writers.

Many writers are considered *freelance writers*. They are self-employed and sell their work to publishers, publication enterprises, manufacturing firms, public relations departments, or advertising agencies. Sometimes, they contract with publishers first to write a book or an article. Others may be hired to complete specific short-term or recurring assignments, such as writing about a new product or contributing to an organization's quarterly newsletter.

Editors review, rewrite, and edit the work of writers. They also may do original writing. An editor's responsibilities vary with the employer and type and level of editorial position held. Editorial duties may include planning the content of books, technical journals, trade magazines, and other general-interest publications. Editors also review story ideas proposed by staff and freelance writers then decide what material will appeal to readers. They review and edit drafts of books and articles, offer comments to improve the work, and suggest possible titles. In addition, they may oversee the production of publications. In the book-publishing industry, an editor's primary responsibility is to review proposals for books and decide whether to buy the publication rights from the author.

Major newspapers and newsmagazines usually employ several types of editors. The *executive editor* oversees *assistant editors*, and generally has the final say about what stories are published and how they are covered. Assistant editors have responsibility for particular subjects, such as local news, international news, feature stories, or sports. The *managing editor* usually is responsible for the daily operation of the news department. *Assignment editors* determine which reporters will cover a given story. *Copy editors* mostly review and edit a reporter's copy for accuracy, content, grammar, and style.

In smaller organizations—such as small daily or weekly newspapers—a single editor may do everything or share responsibility with only a few other people. Executive and managing editors typically hire writers, reporters, and other employees. They also plan budgets and negotiate contracts with freelance writers, sometimes called "stringers" in the news industry.

Editors often have assistants, many of whom hold entry-level jobs. These assistants, frequently called copy editors, review copy for errors in grammar, punctuation, and spelling and check the copy for readability, style, and agreement with editorial policy. They suggest revisions, such as changing words and rearranging sentences and paragraphs, to improve clarity or accuracy. They also carry out research for writers and verify facts, dates, and statistics. In addition, they may arrange page layouts of articles, photographs, and advertising; compose headlines; and prepare copy for printing. *Publication assistants* who work for publishing houses may read and evaluate manuscripts submitted by freelance writers, proofread printers' galleys, and answer letters about published material. Assistants on small newspapers or in radio stations compile articles available from wire services or the Internet, answer phones, and make photocopies.

Work environment. While some writers and editors work in comfortable, private offices, others work in noisy rooms filled with the sounds of keyboards and the voices of other writers tracking down information or interviewing sources. The search for information sometimes requires that writers travel to diverse workplaces, such as factories, offices, or laboratories, but many find their material through telephone interviews, the library, and the Internet.

Advances in electronic communications have changed the work environment for many writers. Laptop computers and wireless communications technologies allow growing numbers of writers to work from home and on the road. The ability to e-mail, transmit and download stories, research, or review materials using the Internet allows writers and editors greater flexibility in where and how they complete assignments.

Some writers keep regular office hours, either to maintain contact with sources and editors or to establish a writing routine, but most writers set their own hours. Many writers—especially freelance writers—are paid per assignment; therefore, they work any number of hours necessary to meet a deadline. As a result, writers must be willing to work evenings, nights, or weekends to produce a piece acceptable to an editor or client by the publication deadline. Those who prepare morning or weekend publications and broadcasts also may regularly work nights, early mornings, and weekends.

While many freelance writers enjoy running their own businesses and the advantages of working flexible hours, most routinely face the pressures of juggling multiple projects with competing demands and the continual need to find new work. Deadline pressures and long, erratic work hours—often part of the daily routine in these jobs—may cause stress, fatigue, or burnout. In addition, the use of computers for extended periods

Writers and editors use reference books and other resources to research or verify information.

may cause some individuals to experience back pain, eyestrain, or fatigue.

Training, Other Qualifications, and Advancement

A college degree generally is required for a position as a writer or editor. Good facility with computers and communications equipment is necessary in order to stay in touch with sources, editors, and other writers while working on assignments, whether from home, an office, or while traveling.

Education and training. Some employers look for a broad liberal arts background, while others prefer to hire people with degrees in communications, journalism, or English. For those who specialize in a particular area, such as fashion, business, or law, additional background in the chosen field is expected. Increasingly, technical writing requires a degree in, or some knowledge about, a specialized field—for example, engineering, business, or one of the sciences. Knowledge of a second language is helpful for some positions. A background in web design, computer graphics, or other technology field is increasingly practical, because of the growing use of graphics and representational design in developing technical documentation. In many cases, people with good writing skills may transfer from jobs as technicians, scientists, or engineers into jobs as writers or editors. Others begin as research assistants or as trainees in a technical information department, develop technical communication skills, and then assume writing duties.

Other qualifications. Writers and editors must be able to express ideas clearly and logically and should enjoy writing. Creativity, curiosity, a broad range of knowledge, self-motivation, and perseverance also are valuable. Writers and editors must demonstrate good judgment and a strong sense of ethics in deciding what material to publish. In addition, the ability to concentrate amid confusion and to work under pressure often is essential. Editors also need tact and the ability to guide and encourage others in their work.

Familiarity with electronic publishing, graphics, and video production increasingly is needed. Use of electronic and wireless communications equipment to send e-mail, transmit work, and review copy often is necessary. Online newspapers and magazines require knowledge of computer software used to combine online text with graphics, audio, video, and animation.

High school and college newspapers, literary magazines, community newspapers, and radio and television stations all provide valuable—but sometimes unpaid—practical writing experience. Many magazines, newspapers, and broadcast stations have internships for students. Interns write short pieces, conduct research and interviews, and learn about the publishing or broadcasting business.

Advancement. In small firms, beginning writers and editors hired as assistants may actually begin writing or editing material right away. Opportunities for advancement and also full-time work can be limited, however. Many small or not-for-profit organizations either do not have enough regular work or cannot afford to employ writers on a full-time basis. However, they routinely contract out work to freelance writers.

In larger businesses, jobs usually are more formally structured. Beginners generally do research, fact check articles, or copy edit drafts. Advancement to full-scale writing or editing assignments may occur more slowly for newer writers and editors in larger organizations than for employees of smaller companies. Advancement often is more predictable, though, coming with the assignment of more important articles.

Advancement for writers, especially freelancers, often means working on larger, more complex projects for better known publications or for more money. Building a reputation and establishing a track record for meeting deadlines also makes it easier to get future assignments. Experience, credibility, and reliability often lead to long-term freelance relationships with the same publications and to contacts with editors who will seek you out for particular assignments.

The growing popularity of blogging could allow some writers to get their work read. For example, a few well-written blogs may garner some recognition for the author and may lead to a few paid pieces in other print or electronic publications. Some established staff writers contribute to blogs on the on-line versions of publications in conjunction with their routine work. However, most bloggers do not earn a considerable amount of money writing their blogs.

Employment

Writers and editors held about 306,000 jobs in 2006. More than one-third were self-employed Writers and authors held about 135,000 jobs; editors, about 122,000 jobs; and technical writers, about 49,000 jobs. About one-third of the salaried jobs for writers and editors were in the information sector, which includes newspaper, periodical, book, and directory publishers; radio and television broadcasting; software publishers; motion picture and sound-recording industries; Internet service providers, Web search portals and data-processing services; and Internet publishing and broadcasting. Substantial numbers also worked in professional, scientific, and technical services. Other salaried writers and editors work in computer systems design and related services, public and private educational services, and religious organizations.

Jobs with major book publishers, magazines, broadcasting companies, advertising agencies, and public relations firms are concentrated in New York, Chicago, Los Angeles, Boston, Philadelphia, and San Francisco. However, many writers work outside these cities and travel regularly to meet with personnel at the headquarters. Jobs with newspapers, business and professional journals, and technical and trade magazines are more widely dispersed throughout the country. Technology permits writers and editors to work from distant and remote locations and still communicate with editors and publishers. As a result, geographic concentration is less of a requirement for many writing or editing positions than it once was.

Thousands of other individuals work primarily as freelance writers, earning income from their articles, books, and less commonly, television and movie scripts. Many support themselves with income derived from other sources.

Job Outlook

Employment of writers and editors is expected to grow about as fast as the average for all occupations. Competition is expected for writing and editing jobs because many people with the appropriate training and talent are attracted to the occupation.

Employment change. Employment of writers and editors is expected to grow 10 percent, or about as fast as the average for all occupations, from 2006 to 2016. Employment of salaried writers and editors is expected to increase as demand grows for web-based publications. Technical writing, blogging, and other writing for interactive media that provide readers with nearly real-time information will provide opportunities for writers. Print magazines and other periodicals increasingly are developing market niches, appealing to readers with special interests, and making Internet-only content available on their websites. Businesses and organizations are developing newsletters and websites, and more companies are publishing materials directly for the Internet. Online publications and services are growing in number and sophistication, spurring the demand for writers and editors, especially those with Web experience. Professional, scientific, and technical services firms, including advertising and public relations agencies, also are growing and should be another source of new jobs.

Job prospects. Opportunities should be best for technical writers and those with training in a specialized field. Demand for technical writers and writers with expertise in areas such as law, medicine, or economics is expected to increase because of the continuing expansion of scientific and technical information and the need to communicate it to others. Legal, scientific, and

technological developments and discoveries generate demand for people to interpret technical information for a more general audience. Rapid growth and change in the high-technology and electronics industries result in a greater need for people to write users' guides, instruction manuals, and training materials. This work requires people who not only are technically skilled as writers, but also are familiar with the subject area.

In addition to job openings created by employment growth, some openings will arise as experienced workers retire, transfer to other occupations, or leave the labor force. Replacement needs are relatively high in this occupation because many freelancers leave because they cannot earn enough money.

Earnings

Median annual earnings for salaried writers and authors were $48,640 in May 2006. The middle 50 percent earned between $34,850 and $67,820. The lowest 10 percent earned less than $25,430, and the highest 10 percent earned more than $97,700. Median annual earnings were $50,650 in advertising and related services and $40,880 in newspaper, periodical, book, and directory publishers.

Median annual earnings for salaried editors were $46,990 in May 2006. The middle 50 percent earned between $35,250 and $64,140. The lowest 10 percent earned less than $27,340, and the highest 10 percent earned more than $87,400. Median annual earnings of those working for newspaper, periodical, book, and directory publishers were $45,970.

Median annual earnings for salaried technical writers were $58,050 in May 2006. The middle 50 percent earned between $45,130 and $73,750. The lowest 10 percent earned less than $35,520, and the highest 10 percent earned more than $91,720. Median annual earnings in computer systems design and related services were $59,830.

According to the Society for Technical Communication, the median annual salary for entry level technical writers was $40,400 in 2005. The median annual salary for midlevel non-supervisory technical writers was $52,140, and for senior non-supervisory technical writers, $69,000.

Related Occupations

Writers and editors communicate ideas and information. Other communications occupations include announcers; interpreters and translators; news analysts, reporters, and correspondents; and public relations specialists.

Sources of Additional Information

For information on careers in technical writing, contact:
➤ Society for Technical Communication, Inc., 901 N. Stuart St., Suite 904, Arlington, VA 22203. Internet: **http://www.stc.org**

Projections data from the National Employment Matrix

Occupational Title	SOC Code	Employment, 2006	Projected employment, 2016	Change, 2006-2016	
				Number	Percent
Writers and editors..	27-3040	306,000	336,000	30,000	10
Editors..	27-3041	122,000	124,000	2,800	2
Technical writers..	27-3042	49,000	59,000	9,600	20
Writers and authors...	27-3043	135,000	153,000	17,000	13

NOTE: Data in this table are rounded. See the discussion of the employment projections table in the *Handbook* introductory chapter on *Occupational Information Included in the Handbook.*

Health Diagnosing and Treating Practitioners

Audiologists

(O*NET 29-1121.00)

Significant Points

- More than half worked in health care facilities; many others were employed by educational services.

- A master's degree in audiology (hearing) is the standard level of education required; however, a doctoral degree is becoming more common for new entrants.

- Few openings are expected because of the small size of the occupation.

- Job prospects will be favorable for those possessing the doctoral (Au.D.) degree.

Nature of the Work

Audiologists work with people who have hearing, balance, and related ear problems. They examine individuals of all ages and identify those with the symptoms of hearing loss and other auditory, balance, and related sensory and neural problems. They then assess the nature and extent of the problems and help the individuals manage them. Using audiometers, computers, and other testing devices, they measure the loudness at which a person begins to hear sounds, the ability to distinguish between sounds, and the impact of hearing loss on an individual's daily life. In addition, audiologists use computer equipment to evaluate and diagnose balance disorders. Audiologists interpret these results and may coordinate them with medical, educational, and psychological information to make a diagnosis and determine a course of treatment.

Hearing disorders can result from a variety of causes including trauma at birth, viral infections, genetic disorders, exposure to loud noise, certain medications, or aging. Treatment may include examining and cleaning the ear canal, fitting and

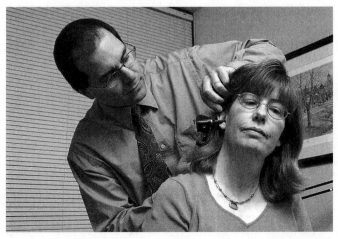

Audiologists usually work at a desk or table in clean, comfortable surroundings.

dispensing hearing aids, and fitting and programming cochlear implants. Audiologic treatment also includes counseling on adjusting to hearing loss, training on the use of hearing instruments, and teaching communication strategies for use in a variety of environments. For example, they may provide instruction in listening strategies. Audiologists also may recommend, fit, and dispense personal or large area amplification systems and alerting devices.

In audiology clinics, audiologists may independently develop and carry out treatment programs. They keep records on the initial evaluation, progress, and discharge of patients. In other settings, audiologists may work with other health and education providers as part of a team in planning and implementing services for children and adults. Audiologists who diagnose and treat balance disorders often work in collaboration with physicians, and physical and occupational therapists.

Some audiologists specialize in work with the elderly, children, or hearing-impaired individuals who need special treatment programs. Others develop and implement ways to protect workers' hearing from on-the-job injuries. They measure noise levels in workplaces and conduct hearing protection programs in factories and in schools and communities.

Audiologists who work in private practice also manage the business aspects of running an office, such as developing a patient base, hiring employees, keeping records, and ordering equipment and supplies.

A few audiologists conduct research on types of, and treatment for, hearing, balance, and related disorders. Others design and develop equipment or techniques for diagnosing and treating these disorders.

Work environment. Audiologists usually work at a desk or table in clean, comfortable surroundings. The job is not physically demanding but does require attention to detail and intense concentration. The emotional needs of patients and their families may be demanding. Most full-time audiologists work about 40 hours per week, which may include weekends and evenings to meet the needs of patients. Some work part time. Those who work on a contract basis may spend a substantial amount of time traveling between facilities.

Training, Other Qualifications, and Advancement

All States require audiologists to be licensed or registered. Licensure or registration requires at least a master's degree in audiology; however, a first professional, or doctoral, degree is becoming increasingly necessary.

Education and training. Individuals must have at least a master's degree in audiology to qualify for a job. However, a first professional or doctoral degree is becoming more common. As of early 2007, eight States required a doctoral degree or its equivalent. The professional doctorate in audiology (Au. D.) requires approximately 8 years of university training and supervised professional experience.

In early 2007, the Accreditation Commission of Audiology Education accredited more than 50 Au.D. programs and the

Council on Academic Accreditation in Audiology and Speech-Language Pathology (CAA) accredited over 70 graduate programs in audiology. Graduation from an accredited program may be required to obtain a license in some States. Requirements for admission to programs in audiology include courses in English, mathematics, physics, chemistry, biology, psychology, and communication. Graduate coursework in audiology includes anatomy; physiology; physics; genetics; normal and abnormal communication development; auditory, balance, and neural systems assessment and treatment; diagnosis and treatment; pharmacology; and ethics.

Licensure and certification. Audiologists are regulated by licensure or registration in all 50 States. Forty-one States have continuing education requirements for licensure renewal, the number of hours required varies by State. Twenty States and the District of Columbia also require audiologists to have a Hearing Aid Dispenser license to dispense hearing aids; for the remaining 30 States, an audiologist license is all that is needed to dispense hearing aids. Third-party payers generally require practitioners to be licensed to qualify for reimbursement. States set requirements for education, mandating a master's or doctoral degree, as well as other requirements. For information on the specific requirements of your State, contact that State's licensing board.

In some States, specific certifications from professional associations satisfy some or all of the requirements for State licensure. Certification can be obtained from two certifying bodies. Audiologists can earn the Certificate of Clinical Competence in Audiology (CCC-A) offered by the American Speech-Language-Hearing Association; they may also be certified through the American Board of Audiology.

Other qualifications. Audiologists should be able to effectively communicate diagnostic test results, diagnoses, and proposed treatments in a manner easily understood by their patients. They must be able to approach problems objectively and provide support to patients and their families. Because a patient's progress may be slow, patience, compassion, and good listening skills are necessary.

It is important for audiologists to be aware of new diagnostic and treatment technologies. Most audiologists participate in continuing education courses to learn new methods and technologies.

Advancement. With experience, audiologists can advance to open their own private practice. Audiologist working in hospitals and clinics can advance to management or supervisory positions.

Employment

Audiologists held about 12,000 jobs in 2006. More than half of all jobs were in health care facilities—offices of physicians or other health practitioners, including audiologists; hospitals; and outpatient care centers. About 13 percent of jobs were in educational services, including elementary and secondary schools. Other jobs for audiologists were in health and personal care stores, including hearing aid stores; scientific research and development services; and State and local governments.

A small number of audiologists were self-employed in private practice. They provided hearing health care services in their own offices or worked under contract for schools, health care facilities, or other establishments.

Job Outlook

Average employment growth is projected. However, because of the small size of the occupation, few job openings are expected. Job prospects will be favorable for those possessing the Au.D. degree.

Employment change. Employment of audiologists is expected to grow 10 percent from 2006 to 2016, about as fast as the average for all occupations. Hearing loss is strongly associated with aging, so rapid growth in older population groups will cause the number of people with hearing and balance impairments to increase markedly. Medical advances also are improving the survival rate of premature infants and trauma victims, who then need assessment and sometimes treatment. Greater awareness of the importance of early identification and diagnosis of hearing disorders in infants also will increase employment. A number of States require that newborns be screened for hearing loss and receive appropriate early intervention services.

Employment in educational services will increase along with growth in elementary and secondary school enrollments, including enrollment of special education students.

Growth in employment of audiologists will be moderated by limitations on reimbursements made by third-party payers for the tests and services they provide.

Job prospects. Job prospects will be favorable for those possessing the Au.D. degree. Only a few job openings for audiologists will arise from the need to replace those who leave the occupation, because the occupation is relatively small and workers tend to stay in this occupation until they retire.

Earnings

Median annual earnings of wage-and-salary audiologists were $57,120 in May 2006. The middle 50 percent earned between $47,220 and $70,940. The lowest 10 percent earned less than $38,370, and the highest 10 percent earned more than $89,160. Some employers may pay for continuing education courses.

Related Occupations

Audiologists specialize in the prevention, diagnosis, and treatment of hearing problems. Workers in related occupations include occupational therapists, optometrists, physical therapists,

Projections data from the National Employment Matrix

Occupational Title	SOC Code	Employment, 2006	Projected employment, 2016	Change, 2006-2016	
				Number	Percent
Audiologists	29-1121	12,000	13,000	1,200	10

NOTE: Data in this table are rounded. See the discussion of the employment projections table in the *Handbook* introductory chapter on *Occupational Information Included in the Handbook.*

psychologists, recreational therapists, rehabilitation counselors, and speech-language pathologists.

Sources of Additional Information

State licensing boards can provide information on licensure requirements. State departments of education can supply information on certification requirements for those who wish to work in public schools.

For information on the specific requirements of your State, contact that State's licensing board. Career information, a description of the CCC-A credential, and information on State licensure is available from:

➤ American Speech-Language-Hearing Association, 10801 Rockville Pike, Rockville, MD 20852.
Internet: **http://www.asha.org**

Information on American Board of Audiology certification is available from:

➤ American Board of Audiology, 11730 Plaza America Dr., Suite 300, Reston, VA 20190.
Internet: **http://www.americanboardofaudiology.org**

For information on the Au.D. degree, contact:

➤ Audiology Foundation of America, 8 N. 3rd St., Suite 406, Lafayette, IN 47901. Internet: **http://www.audfound.org**

Chiropractors

(O*NET 29-1011.00)

Significant Points

- Job prospects should be good; employment is expected to grow faster than average because of increasing consumer demand for alternative health care.

- Chiropractors must be licensed, requiring 2 to 4 years of undergraduate education, the completion of a 4-year chiropractic college course, and passing scores on national and State examinations.

- About 52 percent of chiropractors were self employed.

- Earnings are relatively low in the beginning but increase as the practice grows.

Nature of the Work

Chiropractors, also known as *doctors of chiropractic* or *chiropractic physicians*, diagnose and treat patients with health problems of the musculoskeletal system and treat the effects of those problems on the nervous system and on general health. Many chiropractic treatments deal specifically with the spine and the manipulation of the spine. Chiropractic medicine is based on the principle that spinal joint misalignments interfere with the nervous system and can result in lower resistance to disease and many different conditions of diminished health.

The chiropractic approach to health care stresses the patient's overall health. Chiropractors provide natural, drugless, nonsurgical health treatments, relying on the body's inherent recuperative abilities. They also recognize that many factors affect health, including exercise, diet, rest, environment, and heredity. Chiropractors recommend changes in lifestyle that affect those factors. In some situations, chiropractors refer patients to or consult with other health practitioners.

Like other health practitioners, chiropractors follow a standard routine to get information needed to diagnose and treat patients. They take the patient's medical history; conduct physical, neurological, and orthopedic examinations; and may order laboratory tests. X-rays and other diagnostic images are important tools because of the chiropractor's emphasis on the spine and its proper function. Chiropractors also analyze the patient's posture and spine using a specialized technique. For patients whose health problems can be traced to the musculoskeletal system, chiropractors manually adjust the spinal column.

Some chiropractors use other alternative medicines in their practices, including therapies using water, light, massage, ultrasound, electric, acupuncture, and heat. They also may apply supports such as straps, tapes, and braces to manually adjust the spine. Chiropractors counsel patients about health concepts such as nutrition, exercise, changes in lifestyle, and stress management, but chiropractors do not prescribe drugs or perform surgery.

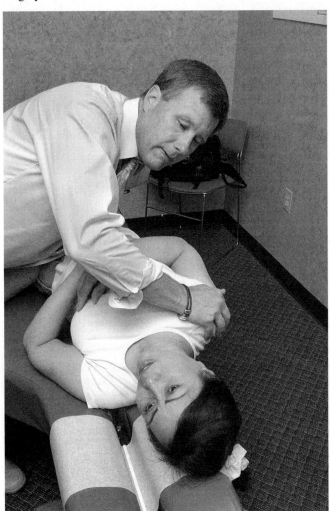

Chiropractors provide natural, drugless, nonsurgical health treatments to patients, including spinal adjustments.

In addition to general chiropractic practice, some chiropractors specialize in sports injuries, neurology, orthopedics, pediatrics, nutrition, internal disorders, or diagnostic imaging.

Many chiropractors are solo or group practitioners who also have the administrative responsibilities of running a practice. In larger offices, chiropractors delegate these tasks to office managers and chiropractic assistants. Chiropractors in private practice are responsible for developing a patient base, hiring employees, and keeping records.

Work environment. Chiropractors work in clean, comfortable offices. Like other health practitioners, chiropractors are sometimes on their feet for long periods. Chiropractors who take x-rays must employ appropriate precautions against the dangers of repeated exposure to radiation.

Chiropractors work, on average, about 40 hours per week, although longer hours are not uncommon. Solo practitioners set their own hours but may work evenings or weekends to accommodate patients. Like other health care practitioners, chiropractors in a group practice will sometimes be on call or treat patients of other chiropractors in the group.

Training, Other Qualifications, and Advancement

Chiropractors must be licensed, which requires 2 to 4 years of undergraduate education, the completion of a 4-year chiropractic college course, and passing scores on national and State examinations.

Education and training. In 2007, 16 chiropractic programs and 2 chiropractic institutions in the United States were accredited by the Council on Chiropractic Education. Applicants must have at least 90 semester hours of undergraduate study leading toward a bachelor's degree, including courses in English, the social sciences or humanities, organic and inorganic chemistry, biology, physics, and psychology. Many applicants have a bachelor's degree, which may eventually become the minimum entry requirement. Several chiropractic colleges offer prechiropractic study, as well as a bachelor's degree program. Recognition of prechiropractic education offered by chiropractic colleges varies among the States.

Chiropractic programs require a minimum of 4,200 hours of combined classroom, laboratory, and clinical experience. During the first 2 years, most chiropractic programs emphasize classroom and laboratory work in sciences such as anatomy, physiology, public health, microbiology, pathology, and biochemistry. The last 2 years focus on courses in manipulation and spinal adjustment and provide clinical experience in physical and laboratory diagnosis, neurology, orthopedics, geriatrics, physiotherapy, and nutrition. Chiropractic programs and institutions grant the degree of Doctor of Chiropractic.

Chiropractic colleges also offer postdoctoral training in orthopedics, neurology, sports injuries, nutrition, rehabilitation, radiology, industrial consulting, family practice, pediatrics, and applied chiropractic sciences. Once such training is complete, chiropractors may take specialty exams leading to "diplomate" status in a given specialty. Exams are administered by specialty chiropractic associations.

Licensure. All States and the District of Columbia regulate the practice of chiropractic and grant licenses to chiropractors who meet the educational and examination requirements established by the State. Chiropractors can practice only in States where they are licensed. Some States have agreements permitting chiropractors licensed in one State to obtain a license in another without further examination, provided that their educational, examination, and practice credentials meet State specifications.

Most State licensing boards require at least 2 years of undergraduate education, but an increasing number are requiring a 4-year bachelor's degree. All boards require the completion of a 4-year program at an accredited chiropractic college leading to the Doctor of Chiropractic degree.

For licensure, most State boards recognize either all or part of the four-part test administered by the National Board of Chiropractic Examiners. State examinations may supplement the National Board tests, depending on State requirements. All States except New Jersey require the completion of a specified number of hours of continuing education each year in order to maintain licensure. Chiropractic associations and accredited chiropractic programs and institutions offer continuing education programs.

Other qualifications. Chiropractic requires keen observation to detect physical abnormalities. It also takes considerable manual dexterity, but not unusual strength or endurance, to perform adjustments. Chiropractors should be able to work independently and handle responsibility. As in other health-related occupations, empathy, understanding, and the desire to help others are good qualities for dealing effectively with patients.

Advancement. Newly licensed chiropractors can set up a new practice, purchase an established one, or enter into partnership with an established practitioner. They also may take a salaried position with an established chiropractor, a group practice, or a health care facility

Employment

Chiropractors held about 53,000 jobs in 2006. Most chiropractors work in a solo practice, although some are in group practice or work for other chiropractors. A small number teach, conduct research at chiropractic institutions, or work in hospitals and clinics. Approximately 52 percent of chiropractors were self employed.

Many chiropractors are located in small communities. However, the distribution of chiropractors is not geographically uniform. This occurs primarily because new chiropractors frequently establish their practices in close proximity to one of the few chiropractic educational institutions.

Job Outlook

Employment is expected to grow faster than average because of increasing consumer demand for alternative health care. Job prospects should be good.

Employment change. Employment of chiropractors is expected to increase 14 percent between 2006 and 2016, faster than the average for all occupations. Projected job growth stems from increasing consumer demand for alternative health care. Because chiropractors emphasize the importance of healthy lifestyles and do not prescribe drugs or perform surgery, chiropractic care is appealing to many health-conscious Americans. Chiropractic treatment of the back, neck, extremities, and joints has become more accepted as a result of re-

Projections data from the National Employment Matrix

Occupational Title	SOC Code	Employment, 2006	Projected employment, 2016	Change, 2006-2016 Number	Change, 2006-2016 Percent
Chiropractors...	29-1011	53,000	60,000	7,600	14

NOTE: Data in this table are rounded. See the discussion of the employment projections table in the *Handbook* introductory chapter on *Occupational Information Included in the Handbook.*

search and changing attitudes about alternative, noninvasive health care practices. The rapidly expanding older population, with its increased likelihood of mechanical and structural problems, also will increase demand for chiropractors.

Demand for chiropractic treatment, however, is related to the ability of patients to pay, either directly or through health insurance. Although more insurance plans now cover chiropractic services, the extent of such coverage varies among plans. Chiropractors must educate communities about the benefits of chiropractic care in order to establish a successful practice.

Job prospects. Job prospects for new chiropractors are expected to be good. In this occupation, replacement needs arise almost entirely from retirements. Chiropractors usually remain in the occupation until they retire; few transfer to other occupations. Establishing a new practice will be easiest in areas with a low concentration of chiropractors.

Earnings
Median annual earnings of salaried chiropractors were $65,220 in 2006. The middle 50 percent earned between $45,710 and $96,500 a year.

In 2005, the mean salary for chiropractors was $104,363 according to a survey conducted by Chiropractic Economics magazine.

In chiropractic, as in other types of independent practice, earnings are relatively low in the beginning and increase as the practice grows. Geographic location and the characteristics and qualifications of the practitioner also may influence earnings.

Salaried chiropractors typically receive heath insurance and retirement benefits from their employers, whereas self-employed chiropractors must provide for their own health insurance and retirement.

Related Occupations
Chiropractors treat patients and work to prevent bodily disorders and injuries. So do athletic trainers, massage therapists, occupational therapists, physical therapists, physicians and surgeons, podiatrists, and veterinarians.

Sources of Additional Information
General information on a career as a chiropractor is available from the following organizations:

➤ American Chiropractic Association, 1701 Clarendon Blvd., Arlington, VA 22209. Internet: **http://www.acatoday.org**

➤ International Chiropractors Association, 1110 North Glebe Rd., Suite 650, Arlington, VA 22201.
Internet: **http://www.chiropractic.org**

➤ World Chiropractic Alliance, 2950 N. Dobson Rd., Suite 3, Chandler, AZ 85224.

For a list of chiropractic programs and institutions, as well as general information on chiropractic education, contact:

➤ Council on Chiropractic Education, 8049 North 85th Way, Scottsdale, AZ 85258-4321. Internet: **http://www.cce-usa.org**

For information on State education and licensure requirements, contact:

➤ Federation of Chiropractic Licensing Boards, 5401 W. 10th St., Suite 101, Greeley, CO 80634-4400.
Internet: **http://www.fclb.org**

For more information on the national chiropractic licensing exam, contact:

➤ National Board of Chiropractic Examiners, 901 54th Ave., Greeley, CO 80634-4400. Internet: **http://www.nbce.org**

For information on admission requirements to a specific chiropractic college, as well as scholarship and loan information, contact the college's admissions office.

Dentists

(O*NET 29-1021.00, 29-1022.00, 29-1023.00, 29-1024.00, 29-1029.99)

Significant Points

- Most dentists are solo practitioners.

- Dentists usually complete at least 8 years of education beyond high school.

- Average employment growth will generate some job openings, but most openings will result from the need to replace the large number of dentists expected to retire.

- Job prospects should be good.

Nature of the Work
Dentists diagnose and treat problems with teeth and tissues in the mouth, along with giving advice and administering care to help prevent future problems. They provide instruction on diet, brushing, flossing, the use of fluorides, and other aspects of dental care. They remove tooth decay, fill cavities, examine x-rays, place protective plastic sealants on children's teeth, straighten teeth, and repair fractured teeth. They also perform corrective surgery on gums and supporting bones to treat gum diseases. Dentists extract teeth and make models and measurements for dentures to replace missing teeth. They also administer anesthetics and write prescriptions for antibiotics and other medications.

Dentists use a variety of equipment, including x-ray machines, drills, mouth mirrors, probes, forceps, brushes, and scalpels. They wear masks, gloves, and safety glasses to protect themselves and their patients from infectious diseases.

Dentists in private practice oversee a variety of administrative tasks, including bookkeeping and the buying of equipment and supplies. They may employ and supervise dental hygienists, dental assistants, dental laboratory technicians, and receptionists. (These occupations are described elsewhere in the *Handbook.*)

Most dentists are general practitioners, handling a variety of dental needs. Other dentists practice in any of nine specialty areas. *Orthodontists*, the largest group of specialists, straighten teeth by applying pressure to the teeth with braces or retainers. The next largest group, *oral and maxillofacial surgeons*, operates on the mouth and jaws. The remainder may specialize as *pediatric dentists* (focusing on dentistry for children); *periodontists* (treating gums and bone supporting the teeth); *prosthodontists* (replacing missing teeth with permanent fixtures, such as crowns and bridges, or with removable fixtures such as dentures); *endodontists* (performing root canal therapy); *public health dentists* (promoting good dental health and preventing dental diseases within the community); *oral pathologists* (studying oral diseases); or *oral and maxillofacial radiologists*

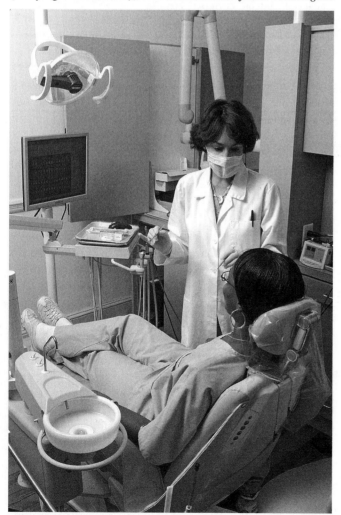

Dentists use various equipment to diagnose and treat problems with teeth and tissues in the mouth.

(diagnosing diseases in the head and neck through the use of imaging technologies).

Work environment. Most dentists are solo practitioners, meaning that they own their own businesses and work alone or with a small staff. Some dentists have partners, and a few work for other dentists as associate dentists.

Most dentists work 4 or 5 days a week. Some work evenings and weekends to meet their patients' needs. The number of hours worked varies greatly among dentists. Most full-time dentists work between 35 and 40 hours a week. However, others, especially those who are trying to establish a new practice, work more. Also, experienced dentists often work fewer hours. It is common for dentists to continue in part-time practice well beyond the usual retirement age.

Training, Other Qualifications, and Advancement

All 50 States and the District of Columbia require dentists to be licensed. To qualify for a license in most States, candidates must graduate from an accredited dental school and pass written and practical examinations.

Education and training. In 2006, there were 56 dental schools accredited by the American Dental Association's (ADA's) Commission on Dental Accreditation. Dental schools require a minimum of 2 years of college-level predental education prior to admittance. Most dental students have at least a bachelor's degree before entering dental school, although a few applicants are accepted to dental school after 2 or 3 years of college and complete their bachelor's degree while attending dental school.

High school and college students who want to become dentists should take courses in biology, chemistry, physics, health, and mathematics. College undergraduates planning on applying to dental school are required to take many science courses. Because of this, some choose a major in a science, such as biology or chemistry, while others take the required science coursework while pursuing a major in another subject.

All dental schools require applicants to take the Dental Admissions Test (DAT). When selecting students, schools consider scores earned on the DAT, applicants' grade point averages, and information gathered through recommendations and interviews. Competition for admission to dental school is keen.

Dental school usually lasts 4 academic years. Studies begin with classroom instruction and laboratory work in science, including anatomy, microbiology, biochemistry, and physiology. Beginning courses in clinical sciences, including laboratory techniques, are also completed. During the last 2 years, students treat patients, usually in dental clinics, under the supervision of licensed dentists. Most dental schools award the degree of Doctor of Dental Surgery (DDS). Others award an equivalent degree, Doctor of Dental Medicine (DMD).

Some dental school graduates work for established dentists as associates for 1 to 2 years to gain experience and save money to equip an office of their own. Most dental school graduates, however, purchase an established practice or open a new one immediately after graduation.

Licensure. Licensing is required to practice as a dentist. In most States, licensure requires passing written and practical examinations in addition to having a degree from an accredited dental school. Candidates may fulfill the written part of the State licensing requirements by passing the National Board Dental Examinations. Individual States or regional testing agencies administer the written or practical examinations.

In 2006, 17 States licensed or certified dentists who intended to practice in a specialty area. Requirements include 2 to 4 years of postgraduate education and, in some cases, the completion of a special State examination. Most State licenses permit dentists to engage in both general and specialized practice.

Other qualifications. Dentistry requires diagnostic ability and manual skills. Dentists should have good visual memory, excellent judgment regarding space, shape, and color, a high degree of manual dexterity, and scientific ability. Good business sense, self-discipline, and good communication skills are helpful for success in private practice.

Advancement. Dentists who want to teach or conduct research usually spend an additional 2 to 5 years in advanced dental training, in programs operated by dental schools or hospitals. A recent survey by the American Dental Education Association showed that 11 percent of new graduates enrolled in postgraduate training programs to prepare for a dental specialty.

Employment

Dentists held about 161,000 jobs in 2006. Employment was distributed among general practitioners and specialists as follows:

Dentists, general	136,000
Orthodontists	9,200
Oral and maxillofacial surgeons	7,700
Prosthodontists	1,000
Dentists, all other specialists	6,900

About one third of dentists were self-employed and not incorporated. Almost all dentists work in private practice. According to the ADA, about 3 out of 4 dentists in private practice are sole proprietors, and 1 in 7 belongs to a partnership. A few salaried dentists work in hospitals and offices of physicians.

Job Outlook

Average employment growth will generate some job openings, but most openings will result from the need to replace the large number of dentists expected to retire. Job prospects should be good as new dentists take over established practices or start their own.

Employment change. Employment of dentists is projected to grow nine percent through 2016, about as fast as the average for all occupations. The demand for dental services is expected to continue to increase. The overall population is growing, particularly the number of older people, which will increase the demand for dental care. As members of the baby-boom generation advance into middle age, a large number will need complicated dental work, such as bridges. In addition, elderly people are more likely to retain their teeth than were their predecessors, so they will require much more care than in the past. The younger generation will continue to need preventive checkups despite an overall increase in the dental health of the public over the last few decades. Recently, some private insurance providers have increased their dental coverage. If this trend continues, those with new or expanded dental insurance will be more likely to visit a dentist than in the past. Also, while they are currently a small proportion of dental expenditures, cosmetic dental services, such as fitting braces for adults as well as children and providing teeth-whitening treatments, have become increasingly popular.

However, employment of dentists is not expected to keep pace with the increased demand for dental services. Productivity increases from new technology, as well as having dental hygienists and assistants perform some tasks, will allow dentists to perform more work than they have in the past. As their practices expand, dentists are likely to hire more hygienists and dental assistants to handle routine services.

Dentists will increasingly provide care and instruction aimed at preventing the loss of teeth, rather than simply providing treatments such as fillings. Improvements in dental technology also will allow dentists to offer more effective and less painful treatment to their patients.

Job prospects. As an increasing number of dentists from the baby-boom generation reach retirement age, many of them will retire or work fewer hours. However, the number of applicants to, and graduates from, dental schools has increased in recent years. Therefore, younger dentists will be able to take over the work from older dentists who retire or cut back on hours, as well as provide dental services to accommodate the growing demand.

Demand for dental services tends to follow the business cycle, primarily because these services usually are paid for either by the patient or by private insurance companies. As a result, during slow times in the economy, demand for dental services can decrease; dentists may have difficulty finding employment,

Projections data from the National Employment Matrix

Occupational Title	SOC Code	Employment, 2006	Projected employment, 2016	Change, 2006-2016	
				Number	Percent
Dentists	29-1020	161,000	176,000	15,000	9
Dentists, general	29-1021	136,000	149,000	13,000	9
Oral and maxillofacial surgeons	29-1022	7,700	8,400	700	9
Orthodontists	29-1023	9,200	10,000	800	9
Prosthodontists	29-1024	1,000	1,100	100	11
Dentists, all other specialists	29-1029	6,900	7,400	500	7

NOTE: Data in this table are rounded. See the discussion of the employment projections table in the *Handbook* introductory chapter on *Occupational Information Included in the Handbook.*

or if already in an established practice, they may work fewer hours because of reduced demand.

Earnings

Median annual earnings of salaried dentists were $136,960 in May 2006. Earnings vary according to number of years in practice, location, hours worked, and specialty. Self-employed dentists in private practice tend to earn more than do salaried dentists.

Dentists who are salaried often receive benefits paid by their employer, with health insurance and malpractice insurance being among the most common. However, like other business owners, self-employed dentists must provide their own health insurance, life insurance, retirement plans, and other benefits.

Related Occupations

Dentists examine, diagnose, prevent, and treat diseases and abnormalities. Chiropractors, optometrists, physicians and surgeons, podiatrists, psychologists, and veterinarians do similar work.

Sources of Additional Information

For information on dentistry as a career, a list of accredited dental schools, and a list of State boards of dental examiners, contact:
➤ American Dental Association, Commission on Dental Accreditation, 211 E. Chicago Ave., Chicago, IL 60611. Internet: **http://www.ada.org**

For information on admission to dental schools, contact:
➤ American Dental Education Association, 1400 K St. NW., Suite 1100, Washington, DC 20005. Internet: **http://www.adea.org**

Persons interested in practicing dentistry should obtain the requirements for licensure from the board of dental examiners of the State in which they plan to work.

To obtain information on scholarships, grants, and loans, including Federal financial aid, prospective dental students should contact the office of student financial aid at the schools to which they apply.

Dietitians and Nutritionists

(O*NET 29-1031.00)

Significant Points

- Most jobs are in hospitals, nursing care facilities, outpatient care centers, and offices of physicians or other health practitioners.

- Dietitians and nutritionists need at least a bachelor's degree in dietetics, foods and nutrition, food service systems management, or a related area; licensure, certification, or registration requirements vary by State.

- Employment is projected to grow about as fast as the average for all occupations; however, growth may be constrained if employers substitute other workers for dietitians and if limitations are placed on insurance reimbursement for dietetic services.

- Good job opportunities are expected.

Nature of the Work

Dietitians and nutritionists plan food and nutrition programs, supervise meal preparation, and oversee the serving of meals. They prevent and treat illnesses by promoting healthy eating habits and recommending dietary modifications. For example, dietitians might teach a patient with high blood pressure how to use less salt when preparing meals, or create a diet reduced in fat and sugar for an overweight patient.

Dietitians manage food service systems for institutions such as hospitals and schools, promote sound eating habits through education, and conduct research. Many dietitians specialize, becoming a clinical dietitian, community dietitian, management dietitian, or consultant.

Clinical dietitians provide nutritional services to patients in hospitals, nursing care facilities, and other institutions. They assess patients' nutritional needs, develop and implement nutrition programs, and evaluate and report the results. They also confer with doctors and other health care professionals to coordinate medical and nutritional needs. Some clinical dietitians specialize in managing the weight of overweight patients or in the care of renal (kidney), diabetic, or critically ill patients. In addition, clinical dietitians in nursing care facilities, small hospitals, or correctional facilities may manage the food service department.

Community dietitians counsel individuals and groups on nutritional practices designed to prevent disease and promote health. Working in places such as public health clinics, home health agencies, and health maintenance organizations, community dietitians evaluate individual needs, develop nutritional care plans, and instruct individuals and their families. Dietitians working in home health agencies provide instruction on grocery shopping and food preparation to the elderly, children, and individuals with special needs.

Increased public interest in nutrition has led to job opportunities in food manufacturing, advertising, and marketing. In these areas, dietitians analyze foods, prepare literature for distribution, or report on issues such as dietary fiber, vitamin supplements, or the nutritional content of recipes.

Management dietitians oversee large-scale meal planning and preparation in health care facilities, company cafeterias, prisons, and schools. They hire, train, and direct other dietitians and food service workers; budget for and purchase food, equipment, and supplies; enforce sanitary and safety regulations; and prepare records and reports.

Consultant dietitians work under contract with health care facilities or in their own private practice. They perform nutrition screenings for their clients and offer advice on diet-related concerns such as weight loss and cholesterol reduction. Some work for wellness programs, sports teams, supermarkets, and other nutrition-related businesses. They may consult with food service managers, providing expertise in sanitation, safety procedures, menu development, budgeting, and planning.

Work environment. Dietitians and nutritionists usually work in clean, well-lighted, and well-ventilated areas. However, some work in hot, congested kitchens. Many dietitians and nutritionists are on their feet for much of the workday.

Dietitians and nutritionists plan food and nutrition programs to reach the client's health goals.

Most full-time dietitians and nutritionists work a regular 40-hour week, although some work weekends. About 1 in 3 worked part time in 2006.

Training, Other Qualifications, and Advancement

Dietitians and nutritionists need at least a bachelor's degree. Licensure, certification, or registration requirements vary by State.

Education and training. Becoming a dietitian or nutritionist usually requires at least a bachelor's degree in dietetics, foods and nutrition, food service systems management, or a related area. Graduate degrees also are available. College students in these majors take courses in foods, nutrition, institution management, chemistry, biochemistry, biology, microbiology, and physiology. Other suggested courses include business, mathematics, statistics, computer science, psychology, sociology, and economics. High school students interested in becoming a dietitian or nutritionist should take courses in biology, chemistry, mathematics, health, and communications.

As of 2007, there were 281 bachelor's degree programs and 22 master's degree programs approved by the American Dietetic Association's Commission on Accreditation for Dietetics Education.

Licensure. Of the 48 States and jurisdictions with laws governing dietetics, 35 require licensure, 12 require statutory certification, and 1 requires registration. Requirements vary by State. As a result, interested candidates should determine the requirements of the State in which they want to work before sitting for any exam.

In States that require licensure, only people who are licensed can work as dietitians and nutritionists. States that require statutory certification limit the use of occupational titles to people who meet certain requirements; individuals without certification can still practice as a dietitian or nutritionist but

without using certain titles. Registration is the least restrictive form of State regulation of dietitians and nutritionists. Unregistered people are permitted to practice as a dietitian or nutritionist.

Certification and other qualifications. Although not required, the Commission on Dietetic Registration of the American Dietetic Association awards the Registered Dietitian credential to those who pass an exam after completing academic coursework and a supervised internship. This certification is different from the statutory certification regulated by some States and discussed in the previous section. To maintain a Registered Dietitian status, workers must complete at least 75 credit hours in approved continuing education classes every 5 years.

A supervised internship, required for certification, can be completed in one of two ways. The first requires the completion of a program accredited by the Commission on Dietetic Registration. As of 2007, there were 53 accredited programs that combined academic and supervised practice experience and generally lasted 4 to 5 years. The second option requires the completion of 900 hours of supervised practice experience in any of the 265 accredited internships. These internships may be full-time programs lasting 6 to 12 months or part-time programs lasting 2 years.

Advancement. Experienced dietitians may advance to management positions, such as assistant director, associate director, or director of a dietetic department, or may become self-employed. Some dietitians specialize in areas such as renal, diabetic, cardiovascular, or pediatric dietetics. Others leave the occupation to become sales representatives for equipment, pharmaceutical, or food manufacturers. A master's degree can help some workers to advance their careers, particularly in career paths related to research, advanced clinical positions, or public health.

Employment

Dietitians and nutritionists held about 57,000 jobs in 2006. More than half of all jobs were in hospitals, nursing care facilities, outpatient care centers, or offices of physicians and other health practitioners. State and local government agencies provided additional jobs—mostly in correctional facilities, health departments, and other public-health-related areas. Some dietitians and nutritionists were employed in special food services, an industry made up of firms providing food services on contract to facilities such as colleges and universities, airlines, correctional facilities, and company cafeterias.

Other jobs were in public and private educational services, community care facilities for the elderly (which includes assisted-living facilities), individual and family services, home health care services, and the Federal Government—mostly in the U.S. Department of Veterans Affairs. Some dietitians were self-employed, working as consultants to facilities such as hospitals and nursing care facilities or providing dietary counseling to individuals.

Job Outlook

Average employment growth is projected. Good job opportunities are expected, especially for dietitians with specialized

Projections data from the National Employment Matrix

Occupational Title	SOC Code	Employment, 2006	Projected employment, 2016	Change, 2006-2016	
				Number	Percent
Dietitians and nutritionists	29-1031	57,000	62,000	4,900	9

NOTE: Data in this table are rounded. See the discussion of the employment projections table in the *Handbook* introductory chapter on *Occupational Information Included in the Handbook.*

training, an advanced degree, or certifications beyond the particular State's minimum requirement.

Employment change. Employment of dietitians and nutritionists is expected to increase 9 percent during the 2006-16 projection decade, about as fast as the average for all occupations. Job growth will result from an increasing emphasis on disease prevention through improved dietary habits. A growing and aging population will boost demand for nutritional counseling and treatment in hospitals, residential care facilities, schools, prisons, community health programs, and home health care agencies. Public interest in nutrition and increased emphasis on health education and prudent lifestyles also will spur demand, especially in food service management.

Employment growth, however, may be constrained if some employers substitute other workers, such as health educators, food service managers, and dietetic technicians, to do work related to nutrition. Also, demand for nutritional therapy services is related to the ability of patients to pay, either out-of-pocket or through health insurance, and although more insurance plans now cover nutritional therapy services, the extent of such coverage varies among plans. Growth may be curbed by limitations on insurance reimbursement for dietetic services.

Hospitals will continue to employ a large number of dietitians and nutritionists to provide medical nutritional therapy and plan meals. But hospitals also will continue to contract with outside agencies for food service and move medical nutritional therapy to outpatient care facilities, slowing job growth in hospitals relative to food service, outpatient facilities, and other employers.

The number of dietitian positions in nursing care facilities is expected to decline, as these establishments continue to contract with outside agencies for food services. However, employment is expected to grow rapidly in contract providers of food services, in outpatient care centers, and in offices of physicians and other health practitioners.

Finally, with increased public awareness of obesity and diabetes, Medicare coverage may be expanded to include medical nutrition therapy for renal and diabetic patients, creating job growth for dietitians and nutritionists specializing in those diseases.

Job prospects. In addition to employment growth, job openings will result from the need to replace experienced workers who retire or leave the occupation for other reasons. Overall, job opportunities will be good for dietitians and nutritionists, particularly for licensed and registered dietitians. Job opportunities should be particularly good in outpatient care facilities, offices of physicians, and food service management. Dietitians and nutritionists without a bachelor's degree will face keen competition for jobs.

Dietitians with specialized training, an advanced degree, or certifications beyond the particular State's minimum requirement will experience the best job opportunities. Those specializing in renal and diabetic nutrition or gerontological nutrition will benefit from the growing number of diabetics and the aging of the population.

Earnings

Median annual earnings of dietitians and nutritionists were $46,980 in May 2006. The middle 50 percent earned between $38,430 and $57,090. The lowest 10 percent earned less than $29,860, and the highest 10 percent earned more than $68,330. Median annual earnings in the industries employing the largest numbers of dietitians and nutritionists in May 2006 were:

Outpatient care centers	$49,950
General medical and surgical hospitals.............................	47,320
State government	46,690
Nursing care facilities...	46,660
Local government..	43,250

According to the American Dietetic Association, median annualized wages for registered dietitians in 2005 varied by practice area as follows: $53,800 in consultation and business; $60,000 in food and nutrition management; $60,200 in education and research; $48,800 in clinical nutrition/ambulatory care; $50,000 in clinical nutrition/long-term care; $44,800 in community nutrition; and $45,000 in clinical nutrition/acute care. Salaries also vary by years in practice, education level, and geographic region.

Related Occupations

Workers in other occupations who may apply the principles of dietetics include food service managers, health educators, dietetic technicians, and registered nurses.

Sources of Additional Information

For a list of academic programs, scholarships, and other information about dietetics, contact:

➤ The American Dietetic Association, 120 South Riverside Plaza, Suite 2000, Chicago, IL 60606-6995.
Internet: **http://www.eatright.org**

For information on the Registered Dietitian exam and other specialty credentials, contact:

➤ The Commission on Dietetic Registration, 120 South Riverside Plaza, Suite 2000, Chicago, IL 60606-6995.
Internet: **http://www.cdrnet.org**

Occupational Therapists

(O*NET 29-1122.00)

Significant Points

- Employment is expected to grow much faster than average and job opportunities should be good, especially for therapists treating the elderly.

- Occupational therapists must be licensed, requiring a master's degree in occupational therapy, 6 months of supervised fieldwork, and passing scores on national and State examinations.

- Occupational therapists are increasingly taking on supervisory roles, allowing assistants and aides to work more closely with clients under the guidance of a therapist.

- More than a quarter of occupational therapists work part time.

Nature of the Work

Occupational therapists help patients improve their ability to perform tasks in living and working environments. They work with individuals who suffer from a mentally, physically, developmentally, or emotionally disabling condition. Occupational therapists use treatments to develop, recover, or maintain the daily living and work skills of their patients. The therapist helps clients not only to improve their basic motor functions and reasoning abilities, but also to compensate for permanent loss of function. The goal is to help clients have independent, productive, and satisfying lives.

Occupational therapists help clients to perform all types of activities, from using a computer to caring for daily needs such as dressing, cooking, and eating. Physical exercises may be used to increase strength and dexterity, while other activities may be chosen to improve visual acuity or the ability to discern patterns. For example, a client with short-term memory loss might be encouraged to make lists to aid recall, and a person with coordination problems might be assigned exercises to improve hand-eye coordination. Occupational therapists also use computer programs to help clients improve decision-making, abstract-reasoning, problem-solving, and perceptual skills, as well as memory, sequencing, and coordination—all of which are important for independent living.

Patients with permanent disabilities, such as spinal cord injuries, cerebral palsy, or muscular dystrophy, often need special instruction to master certain daily tasks. For these individuals, therapists demonstrate the use of adaptive equipment, including wheelchairs, orthoses, eating aids, and dressing aids. They also design or build special equipment needed at home or at work, including computer-aided adaptive equipment. They teach clients how to use the equipment to improve communication and control various situations in their environment.

Some occupational therapists treat individuals whose ability to function in a work environment has been impaired. These practitioners might arrange employment, evaluate the work space, plan work activities, and assess the client's progress. Therapists also may collaborate with the client and the employer to modify the work environment so that the client can successfully complete the work.

Assessing and recording a client's activities and progress is an important part of an occupational therapist's job. Accurate records are essential for evaluating clients, for billing, and for reporting to physicians and other health care providers.

Occupational therapists may work exclusively with individuals in a particular age group or with a particular disability. In schools, for example, they evaluate children's capabilities, recommend and provide therapy, modify classroom equipment, and help children participate in school activities. A therapist may work with children individually, lead small groups in the classroom, consult with a teacher, or serve on an administrative committee. Some therapists provide early intervention therapy to infants and toddlers who have, or are at risk of having, developmental delays. Therapies may include facilitating the use of the hands and promoting skills for listening, following directions, social play, dressing, or grooming.

Other occupational therapists work with elderly patients. These therapists help the elderly lead more productive, active, and independent lives through a variety of methods. Therapists with specialized training in driver rehabilitation assess an individual's ability to drive using both clinical and on-the-road tests. The evaluations allow the therapist to make recommendations for adaptive equipment, training to prolong driving independence, and alternative transportation options. Occupational therapists also work with clients to assess their homes for hazards and to identify environmental factors that contribute to falls.

Occupational therapists in mental health settings treat individuals who are mentally ill, developmentally challenged, or emotionally disturbed. To treat these problems, therapists

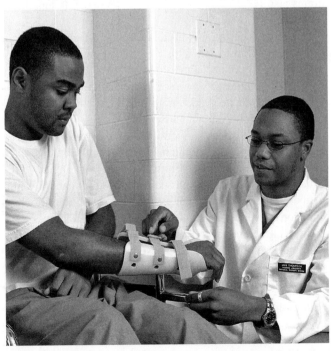

Occupational therapists help people improve their ability to perform tasks in their daily living and working environments.

choose activities that help people learn to engage in and cope with daily life. Activities might include time management skills, budgeting, shopping, homemaking, and the use of public transportation. Occupational therapists also work with individuals who are dealing with alcoholism, drug abuse, depression, eating disorders, or stress-related disorders.

Work environment. In large rehabilitation centers, therapists may work in spacious rooms equipped with machines, tools, and other devices generating noise. The work can be tiring because therapists are on their feet much of the time. Those providing home health care services may spend time driving from appointment to appointment. Therapists also face hazards such as back strain from lifting and moving clients and equipment.

Occupational therapists in hospitals and other health care and community settings usually work a 40-hour week. Those in schools may participate in meetings and other activities during and after the school day. In 2006, more than a quarter of occupational therapists worked part time.

Training, Other Qualifications, and Advancement

Occupational therapists must be licensed, requiring a master's degree in occupational therapy, 6 months of supervised fieldwork, and passing scores on national and State examinations.

Education and training. A master's degree or higher in occupational therapy is the minimum requirement for entry into the field. In 2007, 124 master's degree programs offered entry-level education, 66 programs offered a combined bachelor's and master's degree, and 5 offered an entry-level doctoral degree. Most schools have full-time programs, although a growing number are offering weekend or part-time programs as well. Coursework in occupational therapy programs include the physical, biological, and behavioral sciences as well as the application of occupational therapy theory and skills. Programs also require the completion of 6 months of supervised fieldwork.

People considering this profession should take high school courses in biology, chemistry, physics, health, art, and the social sciences. College admissions offices also look favorably on paid or volunteer experience in the health care field. Relevant undergraduate majors include biology, psychology, sociology, anthropology, liberal arts, and anatomy.

Licensure. All States, Puerto Rico, Guam, and the District of Columbia regulate the practice of occupational therapy. To obtain a license, applicants must graduate from an accredited educational program and pass a national certification examination. Those who pass the exam are awarded the title "Occupational Therapist Registered (OTR)." Some States have additional requirements for therapists who work in schools or early intervention programs. These requirements may include education-related classes, an education practice certificate, or early intervention certification.

Other qualifications. Occupational therapists need patience and strong interpersonal skills to inspire trust and respect in their clients. Patience is necessary because many clients may not show rapid improvement. Ingenuity and imagination in adapting activities to individual needs are assets. Those working in home health care services also must be able to adapt to a variety of settings.

Advancement. Occupational therapists are expected to continue their professional development by participating in continuing education courses and workshops. In fact, a number of States require continuing education as a condition of maintaining licensure.

Therapists are increasingly taking on supervisory roles. Because of rising health care costs, third-party payers are beginning to encourage occupational therapist assistants and aides to take more hands-on responsibility for clients. Occupational therapists can choose to advance their careers by taking on administrative duties and supervising assistants and aides.

Occupational therapists also can advance by specializing in a clinical area and gaining expertise in treating a certain type of patient or ailment. Therapists have specialized in gerontology, mental health, pediatrics, and physical rehabilitation. In addition, some occupational therapists choose to teach classes in accredited occupational therapy educational programs.

Employment

Occupational therapists held about 99,000 jobs in 2006. About 1 in 10 occupational therapists held more than one job. The largest number of jobs was in hospitals. Other major employers were offices of other health practitioners (including offices of occupational therapists), public and private educational services, and nursing care facilities. Some occupational therapists were employed by home health care services, outpatient care centers, offices of physicians, individual and family services, community care facilities for the elderly, and government agencies.

A small number of occupational therapists were self-employed in private practice. These practitioners treated clients referred by other health professionals. They also provided contract or consulting services to nursing care facilities, schools, adult day care programs, and home health care agencies.

Job Outlook

Employment of occupational therapists is expected to grow much faster than the average for all occupations. Job opportunities should be good, especially for occupational therapists treating the elderly.

Employment change. Employment of occupational therapists is expected to increase 23 percent between 2006 and

Projections data from the National Employment Matrix

Occupational Title	SOC Code	Employment, 2006	Projected employment, 2016	Change, 2006-2016	
				Number	Percent
Occupational therapists..	29-1122	99,000	122,000	23,000	23

NOTE: Data in this table are rounded. See the discussion of the employment projections table in the *Handbook* introductory chapter on *Occupational Information Included in the Handbook.*

2016, much faster than the average for all occupations. The increasing elderly population will drive growth in the demand for occupational therapy services. In the short run, the impact of proposed Federal legislation imposing limits on reimbursement for therapy services may adversely affect the job market for occupational therapists. However, over the long run, the demand for occupational therapists should continue to rise as a result of the increasing number of individuals with disabilities or limited function who require therapy services. The baby-boom generation's movement into middle age, a period when the incidence of heart attack and stroke increases, will spur demand for therapeutic services. Growth in the population 75 years and older—an age group that suffers from high incidences of disabling conditions—also will increase demand for therapeutic services. In addition, medical advances now enable more patients with critical problems to survive—patients who ultimately may need extensive therapy.

Hospitals will continue to employ a large number of occupational therapists to provide therapy services to acutely ill inpatients. Hospitals also will need occupational therapists to staff their outpatient rehabilitation programs.

Employment growth in schools will result from the expansion of the school-age population, the extension of services for disabled students, and an increasing prevalence of sensory disorders in children. Therapists will be needed to help children with disabilities prepare to enter special education programs.

Job prospects. Job opportunities should be good for licensed occupational therapists in all settings, particularly in acute hospital, rehabilitation, and orthopedic settings because the elderly receive most of their treatment in these settings. Occupational therapists with specialized knowledge in a treatment area also will have increased job prospects. Driver rehabilitation and fall-prevention training for the elderly are emerging practice areas for occupational therapy.

Earnings

Median annual earnings of occupational therapists were $60,470 in May 2006. The middle 50 percent earned between $50,450 and $73,710. The lowest 10 percent earned less than $40,840, and the highest 10 percent earned more than $89,450. Median annual earnings in the industries employing the largest numbers of occupational therapists in May 2006 were:

Home health care services	$67,600
Nursing care facilities	64,750
Offices of physical, occupational and speech therapists, and audiologists	62,290
General medical and surgical hospitals	61,610
Elementary and secondary schools	54,260

Related Occupations

Occupational therapists use specialized knowledge to help individuals perform daily living skills and achieve maximum independence. Other workers performing similar duties include athletic trainers, audiologists, chiropractors, physical therapists, recreational therapists, rehabilitation counselors, respiratory therapists, and speech-language pathologists.

Sources of Additional Information

For more information on occupational therapy as a career, contact:

➤ American Occupational Therapy Association, 4720 Montgomery LaNE., Bethesda, MD 20824-1220. Internet: **http://www.aota.org**

For information regarding the requirements to practice as an occupational therapist in schools, contact the appropriate occupational therapy regulatory agency for your State.

Optometrists

(O*NET 29-1041.00)

Significant Points

- Admission to optometry school is competitive.

- To be licensed, optometrists must earn a Doctor of Optometry degree from an accredited optometry school and pass the appropriate exams administered by the National Board of Examiners in Optometry.

- Employment is expected to grow as fast as average in response to the vision care needs of a growing and aging population.

Nature of the Work

Optometrists, also known as *doctors of optometry*, or *ODs*, are the main providers of vision care. They examine people's eyes to diagnose vision problems, such as nearsightedness and farsightedness, and they test patients' depth and color perception and ability to focus and coordinate the eyes. Optometrists may prescribe eyeglasses or contact lenses, or they may prescribe or provide other treatments, such as vision therapy or low-vision rehabilitation.

Optometrists also test for glaucoma and other eye diseases and diagnose conditions caused by systemic diseases such as diabetes and high blood pressure, referring patients to other health practitioners as needed. They administer drugs to patients to aid in the diagnosis of vision problems and to treat eye diseases. Optometrists often provide preoperative and postoperative care to cataract patients, as well as to patients who have had laser vision correction or other eye surgery.

Most optometrists are in general practice. Some specialize in work with the elderly, children, or partially sighted persons who need specialized visual devices. Others develop and implement ways to protect workers' eyes from on-the-job strain or injury. Some specialize in contact lenses, sports vision, or vision therapy. A few teach optometry, perform research, or consult.

Most optometrists are private practitioners who also handle the business aspects of running an office, such as developing a patient base, hiring employees, keeping paper and electronic records, and ordering equipment and supplies. Optometrists who operate franchise optical stores also may have some of these duties.

Optometrists should not be confused with ophthalmologists or dispensing opticians. *Ophthalmologists* are physicians who

Optometrists use specialized equipment to test vision and detect diseases of the eye.

perform eye surgery, as well as diagnose and treat eye diseases and injuries. Like optometrists, they also examine eyes and prescribe eyeglasses and contact lenses. *Dispensing opticians* fit and adjust eyeglasses and, in some States, may fit contact lenses according to prescriptions written by ophthalmologists or optometrists. (See the sections on physicians and surgeons; and opticians, dispensing, elsewhere in the *Handbook.*)

Work environment. Optometrists work in places—usually their own offices—that are clean, well lighted, and comfortable. Most full-time optometrists work about 40 hours a week. Many work weekends and evenings to suit the needs of patients. Emergency calls, once uncommon, have increased with the passage of therapeutic-drug laws expanding optometrists' ability to prescribe medications.

Optometrists who work in solo practice or with a partner tend to work longer hours because they must tend to administrative duties in addition to their medical ones. According to the American Optometric Association surveys, optometrists worked about 49 hours per week, on average, in 2004, and were available to see patients about 38 hours per week.

Training, Other Qualifications, and Advancement
The Doctor of Optometry degree requires the completion of a 4-year program at an accredited optometry school, preceded by at least 3 years of preoptometric study at an accredited college or university. All States require optometrists to be licensed.

Education and training. Optometrists need a Doctor of Optometry degree, which requires the completion of a 4-year program at an accredited optometry school. In 2006, there were 16 colleges of optometry in the U.S. and 1 in Puerto Rico that offered programs accredited by the Accreditation Council on Optometric Education of the American Optometric Association. Requirements for admission to optometry schools include college courses in English, mathematics, physics, chemistry, and biology. Because a strong background in science is important, many applicants to optometry school major in a science, such as biology or chemistry as undergraduates. Others major in another subject and take many science courses offering laboratory experience.

Admission to optometry school is competitive. Applicants must take the Optometry Admissions Test, which measures academic ability and scientific comprehension. As a result, most applicants take the test after their sophomore or junior year in college, allowing them an opportunity to take the test again and raise their score. A few applicants are accepted to optometry school after 3 years of college and complete their bachelor's degree while attending optometry school. However, most students accepted by a school or college of optometry have completed an undergraduate degree. Each institution has its own undergraduate prerequisites, so applicants should contact the school or college of their choice for specific requirements.

Optometry programs include classroom and laboratory study of health and visual sciences and clinical training in the diagnosis and treatment of eye disorders. Courses in pharmacology, optics, vision science, biochemistry, and systemic diseases are included.

One-year postgraduate clinical residency programs are available for optometrists who wish to obtain advanced clinical competence. Specialty areas for residency programs include family practice optometry, pediatric optometry, geriatric optometry, vision therapy and rehabilitation, low-vision rehabilitation, cornea and contact lenses, refractive and ocular surgery, primary eye care optometry, and ocular disease.

Licensure. All States and the District of Columbia require that optometrists be licensed. Applicants for a license must have a Doctor of Optometry degree from an accredited optometry school and must pass both a written National Board examination and a National, regional, or State clinical examination. The written and clinical examinations of the National Board of Examiners in Optometry usually are taken during the student's academic career. Many States also require applicants to pass an examination on relevant State laws. Licenses must be renewed every 1 to 3 years and, in all States, continuing education credits are needed for renewal.

Other qualifications. Business ability, self-discipline, and the ability to deal tactfully with patients are important for success. The work of optometrists also requires attention to detail and manual dexterity.

Advancement. Optometrists wishing to teach or conduct research may study for a master's degree or Ph.D. in visual science, physiological optics, neurophysiology, public health, health administration, health information and communication, or health education.

Employment
Optometrists held about 33,000 jobs in 2006. Salaried jobs for optometrists were primarily in offices of optometrists; offices of physicians, including ophthalmologists; and health and personal care stores, including optical goods stores. A few salaried jobs for optometrists were in hospitals, the Federal Government, or outpatient care centers including health maintenance organizations. Nearly 25 percent of optometrists are self-employed. According to a 2005 survey by the American Optometric Association most self-employed optometrists worked in private practice or in partnership with other health care professionals. A small number worked for optical chains or franchises or as independent contractors.

Job Outlook
Employment of optometrists is expected to grow as fast as average for all occupations through 2016, in response to the vision

Projections data from the National Employment Matrix

Occupational Title	SOC Code	Employment, 2006	Projected employment, 2016	Change, 2006-2016	
				Number	Percent
Optometrists..	29-1041	33,000	36,000	3,700	11

NOTE: Data in this table are rounded. See the discussion of the employment projections table in the *Handbook* introductory chapter on *Occupational Information Included in the Handbook.*

care needs of a growing and aging population. Greater recognition of the importance of vision care, along with growth in employee vision care plans, will also spur job growth.

Employment change. Employment of optometrists is projected to grow 11 percent between 2006 and 2016. A growing population that recognizes the importance of good eye care will increase demand for optometrists. Also, an increasing number of health insurance plans that include vision care, should generate more job growth.

As the population ages, there will likely be more visits to optometrists and ophthalmologists because of the onset of vision problems that occur at older ages, such as cataracts and glaucoma. In addition, increased incidences of diabetes and hypertension in the general population as well as in the elderly will generate greater demand for optometric services as these diseases often affect eyesight.

Employment of optometrists would grow more rapidly if not for productivity gains expected to allow each optometrist to see more patients. These expected gains stem from greater use of optometric assistants and other support personnel, who can reduce the amount of time optometrists need with each patient.

The increasing popularity of laser surgery to correct some vision problems may reduce some of the demand for optometrists as patients often do not require eyeglasses afterward. But optometrists still will be needed to provide preoperative and postoperative care for laser surgery patients.

Job prospects. Job opportunities for optometrists should be very good over the next decade. Demand is expected to be much higher, and because there are only 16 schools of optometry, the number of students who can get a degree in optometry is limited. In addition to growth, the need to replace optometrists who retire or leave the occupation for other reasons will create more employment opportunities.

Earnings

Median annual earnings of salaried optometrists were $91,040 in May 2006. The middle 50 percent earned between $66,530 and $118,490. Median annual earnings of salaried optometrists in offices of optometrists were $86,760. Salaried optometrists tend to earn more initially than do optometrists who set up their own practices. In the long run, however, those in private practice usually earn more.

According to the American Optometric Association, median net annual income for all optometrists, including the self-employed, was $105,000 in 2006. The middle 50 percent earned between $84,000 and $150,000.

Self-employed optometrists, including those working in partnerships, must provide their own benefits. Optometrists employed by others typically enjoy paid vacation, sick leave, and pension contributions.

Related Occupations

Other workers who apply scientific knowledge to prevent, diagnose, and treat disorders and injuries are chiropractors, dentists, physicians and surgeons, psychologists, podiatrists, and veterinarians.

Sources of Additional Information

For information on optometry as a career and a list of accredited optometric institutions of education, contact:

➤ Association of Schools and Colleges of Optometry, 6110 Executive Blvd., Suite 510, Rockville, MD 20852.
Internet: **http://www.opted.org**

Additional career information is available from:

➤ American Optometric Association, Educational Services, 243 North Lindbergh Blvd., St.Louis, MO 63141.
Internet: **http://www.aoa.org**

The board of optometry in each State can supply information on licensing requirements.

For information on specific admission requirements and sources of financial aid, contact the admissions officers of individual optometry schools.

Pharmacists

(O*NET 29-1051.00)

Significant Points

- Excellent job opportunities are expected.

- Earnings are high, but some pharmacists are required to work nights, weekends, and holidays.

- Pharmacists are becoming more involved in counseling patients and planning drug therapy programs.

- A license is required; the prospective pharmacist must graduate from an accredited college of pharmacy and pass a series of examinations.

Nature of the Work

Pharmacists distribute prescription drugs to individuals. They also advise their patients, as well as physicians and other health practitioners, on the selection, dosages, interactions, and side effects of medications. Pharmacists monitor the health and progress of patients to ensure the safe and effective use of medication. Compounding—the actual mixing of ingredients to form medications—is a small part of a pharmacist's practice, because most medicines are produced by pharmaceutical companies in a standard dosage and drug delivery form. Most pharmacists work in a community setting, such as a retail drugstore, or in a health care facility, such as a hospital, nursing home, mental health institution, or neighborhood health clinic.

Pharmacists in community pharmacies dispense medications, counsel patients on the use of prescription and over-the-counter medications, and advise physicians about patients' medication therapy. They also advise patients about general health topics such as diet, exercise, and stress management, and provide information on products such as durable medical equipment or home health care supplies. In addition, they may complete third-party insurance forms and other paperwork. Those who own or manage community pharmacies may sell non-health-related merchandise, hire and supervise personnel, and oversee the general operation of the pharmacy. Some community pharmacists provide specialized services to help patients with conditions such as diabetes, asthma, smoking cessation, or high blood pressure; others also are trained to administer vaccinations.

Pharmacists in health care facilities dispense medications and advise the medical staff on the selection and effects of drugs. They may make sterile solutions to be administered intravenously. They also plan, monitor and evaluate drug programs or regimens. They may counsel hospitalized patients on the use of drugs before the patients are discharged.

Pharmacists who work in home health care monitor drug therapy and prepare infusions—solutions that are injected into patients—and other medications for use in the home.

Some pharmacists specialize in specific drug therapy areas, such as intravenous nutrition support, oncology (cancer), nuclear pharmacy (used for chemotherapy), geriatric pharmacy, and psychiatric pharmacy (the use of drugs to treat mental disorders).

Most pharmacists keep confidential computerized records of patients' drug therapies to prevent harmful drug interactions. Pharmacists are responsible for the accuracy of every prescription that is filled, but they often rely upon pharmacy technicians and pharmacy aides to assist them in the dispensing process. Thus, the pharmacist may delegate prescription-filling and administrative tasks and supervise their completion. Pharmacists also frequently oversee pharmacy students serving as interns.

Increasingly, pharmacists are pursuing nontraditional pharmacy work. Some are involved in research for pharmaceutical manufacturers, developing new drugs and testing their effects. Others work in marketing or sales, providing clients with expertise on the use, effectiveness, and possible side effects of drugs. Some pharmacists work for health insurance companies, developing pharmacy benefit packages and carrying out cost-benefit analyses on certain drugs. Other pharmacists work for the government, managed care organizations, public health care services, the armed services, or pharmacy associations. Finally, some pharmacists are employed full time or part time as college faculty, teaching classes and performing research in a wide range of areas.

Work environment. Pharmacists work in clean, well-lighted, and well-ventilated areas. Many pharmacists spend most of their workday on their feet. When working with sterile or dangerous pharmaceutical products, pharmacists wear gloves, masks, and other protective equipment.

Pharmacists counsel patients and answer questions about medications.

Most full-time salaried pharmacists work approximately 40 hours a week, and about 10 percent work more than 50 hours. Many community and hospital pharmacies are open for extended hours or around the clock, so pharmacists may be required to work nights, weekends, and holidays. Consultant pharmacists may travel to nursing homes or other facilities to monitor patients' drug therapy. About 16 percent of pharmacists worked part time in 2006.

Training, Other Qualifications, and Advancement

A license is required in all States, the District of Columbia, and all U.S. territories. In order to obtain a license, pharmacists must earn a Doctor of Pharmacy (Pharm.D.) degree from a college of pharmacy and pass several examinations.

Education and training. Pharmacists must earn a Pharm.D. degree from an accredited college or school of pharmacy. The Pharm.D. degree has replaced the Bachelor of Pharmacy degree, which is no longer being awarded. To be admitted to a Pharm.D. program, an applicant must have completed at least 2 years of postsecondary study, although most applicants have completed 3 or more years. Other entry requirements usually include courses in mathematics and natural sciences, such as chemistry, biology, and physics, as well as courses in the humanities and social sciences. In 2007, 92 colleges and schools of pharmacy were accredited to confer degrees by the Accreditation Council for Pharmacy Education (ACPE). About 70 percent of Pharm.D. programs require applicants to take the Pharmacy College Admissions Test (PCAT).

Courses offered at colleges of pharmacy are designed to teach students about all aspects of drug therapy. In addition, students learn how to communicate with patients and other health care providers about drug information and patient care. Students also learn professional ethics, concepts of public health, and medication distribution systems management. In addition to receiving classroom instruction, students in Pharm.D. programs spend about one-forth of their time in a variety of pharmacy practice settings under the supervision of licensed pharmacists.

In the 2006–07 academic year, 70 colleges of pharmacy also awarded the master-of-science degree or the Ph.D. degree. Both degrees are awarded after the completion of a Pharm.D. degree and are designed for those who want additional clinical, laboratory, and research experience. Areas of graduate study include pharmaceutics and pharmaceutical chemistry (physical and chemical properties of drugs and dosage forms), pharmacology (effects of drugs on the body), and pharmacy administration. Many master's and Ph.D. degree holders go on to do research for a drug company or teach at a university.

Other options for pharmacy graduates who are interested in further training include 1-year or 2-year residency programs or fellowships. Pharmacy residencies are postgraduate training programs in pharmacy practice and usually require the completion of a research project. These programs are often mandatory for pharmacists who wish to work in hospitals. Pharmacy fellowships are highly individualized programs that are designed to prepare participants to work in a specialized area of pharmacy, such clinical practice or research laboratories. Some pharmacists who own their own pharmacy obtain a master's degree in business administration (MBA). Others may obtain a degree in public administration or public health.

Licensure. A license to practice pharmacy is required in all States, the District of Columbia, and all U.S. territories. To obtain a license, a prospective pharmacist must graduate from a college of pharmacy that is accredited by the ACPE and pass a series of examinations. All States, U.S. territories, and the District of Columbia require the North American Pharmacist Licensure Exam (NAPLEX), which tests pharmacy skills and knowledge. Forty-four States and the District of Columbia also require the Multistate Pharmacy Jurisprudence Exam (MPJE), which tests pharmacy law. Both exams are administered by the National Association of Boards of Pharmacy (NABP). Each of the eight States and territories that do not require the MJPE has its own pharmacy law exam. In addition to the NAPLEX and MPJE, some States and territories require additional exams that are unique to their jurisdiction.

All jurisdictions except California currently grant license transfers to qualified pharmacists who already are licensed by another jurisdiction. Many pharmacists are licensed to practice in more than one jurisdiction. Most jurisdictions require continuing education for license renewal. Persons interested in a career as a pharmacist should check with individual jurisdiction boards of pharmacy for details on license renewal requirements and license transfer procedures.

Graduates of foreign pharmacy schools may also qualify for licensure in some U.S. States and territories. These individuals must apply for certification from the Foreign Pharmacy Graduate Examination Committee (FPGEC). Once certified, they must pass the Foreign Pharmacy Graduate Equivalency Examination (FPGEE), Test of English as a Foreign Language (TOEFL) exam, and Test of Spoken English (TSE) exam. They then must pass all of the exams required by the licensing jurisdiction, such as the NAPLEX and MJPE. Applicants who graduated from programs accredited by the Canadian Council for Accreditation of Pharmacy Programs (CCAPP) between 1993 and 2004 are exempt from FPGEC certification and examination requirements.

Other qualifications. Prospective pharmacists should have scientific aptitude, good interpersonal skills, and a desire to help others. They also must be conscientious and pay close attention to detail, because the decisions they make affect human lives.

Advancement. In community pharmacies, pharmacists usually begin at the staff level. Pharmacists in chain drugstores may be promoted to pharmacy supervisor or manager at the store level, then to manager at the district or regional level, and later to an executive position within the chain's headquarters. Hospital pharmacists may advance to supervisory or administrative positions. After they gain experience and secure the necessary capital, some pharmacists become owners or part owners of independent pharmacies. Pharmacists in the pharmaceutical industry may advance in marketing, sales, research, quality control, production, or other areas.

Employment

Pharmacists held about 243,000 jobs in 2006. About 62 percent worked in community pharmacies that were either independently owned or part of a drugstore chain, grocery store, department store, or mass merchandiser. Most community pharmacists were salaried employees, but some were self-employed owners. About 23 percent of pharmacists worked in hospitals. A small proportion worked in mail-order and Internet pharmacies, pharmaceutical wholesalers, offices of physicians, and the Federal Government.

Job Outlook

Employment is expected to increase much faster than the average through 2016. As a result of rapid growth and the need to replace workers who leave the occupation, job prospects should be excellent.

Employment change. Employment of pharmacists is expected to grow by 22 percent between 2006 and 2016, which is much faster than the average for all occupations. The increasing numbers of middle-aged and elderly people—who use more prescription drugs than younger people—will continue to spur demand for pharmacists throughout the projection period. Other factors likely to increase the demand for pharmacists include scientific advances that will make more drug products available and the coverage of prescription drugs by a greater number of health insurance plans and Medicare.

As the use of prescription drugs increases, demand for pharmacists will grow in most practice settings, such as community pharmacies, hospital pharmacies, and mail-order pharmacies. As the population ages, assisted living facilities and home care organizations should see particularly rapid growth. Demand will also increase as cost conscious insurers, in an attempt to

Projections data from the National Employment Matrix

Occupational Title	SOC Code	Employment, 2006	Projected employment, 2016	Change, 2006-2016	
				Number	Percent
Pharmacists	29-1051	243,000	296,000	53,000	22

NOTE: Data in this table are rounded. See the discussion of the employment projections table in the *Handbook* introductory chapter on *Occupational Information Included in the Handbook.*

improve preventative care, use pharmacists in areas such as patient education and vaccination administration.

Demand is also increasing in managed care organizations where pharmacists analyze trends and patterns in medication use, and in pharmacoeconomics—the cost and benefit analysis of different drug therapies. New jobs also are being created in disease management—the development of new methods for curing and controlling diseases—and in sales and marketing. Rapid growth is also expected in pharmacy informatics—the use of information technology to improve patient care.

Job prospects. Excellent opportunities are expected for pharmacists over the 2006 to 2016 period. Job openings will result from rapid employment growth, and from the need to replace workers who retire or leave the occupation for other reasons.

Earnings

Median annual of wage-and-salary pharmacists in May 2006 were $94,520. The middle 50 percent earned between $83,180 and $108,140 a year. The lowest 10 percent earned less than $67,860, and the highest 10 percent earned more than $119,480 a year. Median annual earnings in the industries employing the largest numbers of pharmacists in May 2006 were:

Department stores	$99,050
Grocery stores	95,600
Pharmacies and drug stores	94,640
General medical and surgical hospitals	93,640

According to a 2006 survey by *Drug Topics Magazine*, pharmacists in retail settings earned an average of $92,291 per year, while pharmacists in institutional settings earned an average of $97,545. Full-time pharmacists earned an average of $102,336, while part-time pharmacists earned an average of $55,589.

Related Occupations

Pharmacy technicians and pharmacy aides also work in pharmacies. Persons in other professions who may work with pharmaceutical compounds include biological scientists, medical scientists, and chemists and materials scientists. Increasingly, pharmacists are involved in patient care and therapy, work that they have in common with physicians and surgeons.

Sources of Additional Information

For information on pharmacy as a career, preprofessional and professional requirements, programs offered by colleges of pharmacy, and student financial aid, contact:

➤ American Association of Colleges of Pharmacy, 1426 Prince St., Alexandria, VA 22314. Internet: **http://www.aacp.org**

General information on careers in pharmacy is available from:

➤ American Society of Health-System Pharmacists, 7272 Wisconsin Ave., Bethesda, MD 20814.

Internet: **http://www.ashp.org**

➤ National Association of Chain Drug Stores, 413 N. Lee St., P.O. Box 1417-D49, Alexandria, VA 22313-1480.

Internet: **http://www.nacds.org**

➤ Academy of Managed Care Pharmacy, 100 North Pitt St., Suite 400, Alexandria, VA 22314. Internet: **http://www.amcp.org**

➤ American Pharmacists Association, 1100 15th Street, NW. Suite 400., Washington, DC 20005.

Internet: **http://www.aphanet.org**

Information on the North American Pharmacist Licensure Exam (NAPLEX) and the Multistate Pharmacy Jurisprudence Exam (MPJE) is available from:

➤ National Association of Boards of Pharmacy, 1600 Feehanville Dr., Mount Prospect, IL 60056.

Internet: **http://www.nabp.net**

State licensure requirements are available from each State's board of pharmacy. Information on specific college entrance requirements, curriculums, and financial aid is available from any college of pharmacy.

Physical Therapists

(O*NET 29-1123.00)

Significant Points

- Employment is expected to increase much faster than average.

- Job opportunities should be good, particularly in acute hospital, rehabilitation, and orthopedic settings.

- Physical therapists need a master's degree from an accredited physical therapy program and a State license, requiring passing scores on national and State examinations.

- About 6 out of 10 physical therapists work in hospitals or in offices of physical therapists.

Nature of the Work

Physical therapists provide services that help restore function, improve mobility, relieve pain, and prevent or limit permanent physical disabilities of patients suffering from injuries or disease. They restore, maintain, and promote overall fitness and health. Their patients include accident victims and individuals with disabling conditions such as low-back pain, arthritis, heart disease, fractures, head injuries, and cerebral palsy.

Therapists examine patients' medical histories and then test and measure the patients' strength, range of motion, balance and coordination, posture, muscle performance, respiration, and motor function. Next, physical therapists develop plans describing a treatment strategy and its anticipated outcome.

Treatment often includes exercise, especially for patients who have been immobilized or who lack flexibility, strength, or endurance. Physical therapists encourage patients to use their muscles to increase their flexibility and range of motion. More advanced exercises focus on improving strength, balance, coordination, and endurance. The goal is to improve how an individual functions at work and at home.

Physical therapists also use electrical stimulation, hot packs or cold compresses, and ultrasound to relieve pain and reduce swelling. They may use traction or deep-tissue massage to relieve pain and improve circulation and flexibility. Therapists also teach patients to use assistive and adaptive devices, such as

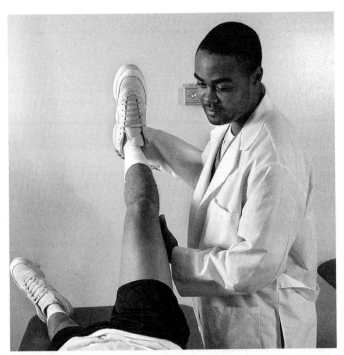

Physical therapists use traction or deep-tissue massage to relieve pain.

crutches, prostheses, and wheelchairs. They also may show patients how to do exercises at home to expedite their recovery.

As treatment continues, physical therapists document the patient's progress, conduct periodic examinations, and modify treatments when necessary.

Physical therapists often consult and practice with a variety of other professionals, such as physicians, dentists, nurses, educators, social workers, occupational therapists, speech-language pathologists, and audiologists.

Some physical therapists treat a wide range of ailments; others specialize in areas such as pediatrics, geriatrics, orthopedics, sports medicine, neurology, and cardiopulmonary physical therapy.

Work environment. Physical therapists practice in hospitals, clinics, and private offices that have specially equipped facilities. They also treat patients in hospital rooms, homes, or schools. These jobs can be physically demanding because therapists often have to stoop, kneel, crouch, lift, and stand for long periods. In addition, physical therapists move heavy equipment and lift patients or help them turn, stand, or walk.

In 2006, most full-time physical therapists worked a 40-hour week; some worked evenings and weekends to fit their patients' schedules. About 1 in 5 physical therapists worked part time.

Training, Other Qualifications, and Advancement

Physical therapists need a master's degree from an accredited physical therapy program and a State license, requiring passing scores on national and State examinations.

Education and training. According to the American Physical Therapy Association, there were 209 accredited physical therapist education programs in 2007. Of the accredited programs, 43 offered master's degrees and 166 offered doctoral degrees. Only master's degree and doctoral degree programs are accredited, in accordance with the Commission on Accreditation in Physical Therapy Education. In the future, a doctoral degree might be the required entry-level degree. Master's degree programs typically last 2 years, and doctoral degree programs last 3 years.

Physical therapist education programs start with basic science courses such as biology, chemistry, and physics and then introduce specialized courses, including biomechanics, neuroanatomy, human growth and development, manifestations of disease, examination techniques, and therapeutic procedures. Besides getting classroom and laboratory instruction, students receive supervised clinical experience.

Among the undergraduate courses that are useful when one applies to a physical therapist education program are anatomy, biology, chemistry, social science, mathematics, and physics. Before granting admission, many programs require volunteer experience in the physical therapy department of a hospital or clinic. For high school students, volunteering with the school athletic trainer is a good way to gain experience.

Licensure. All States require physical therapists to pass national and State licensure exams before they can practice. They must also graduate from an accredited physical therapist education program.

Other qualifications. Physical therapists should have strong interpersonal skills so that they can educate patients about their physical therapy treatments and communicate with patients' families. Physical therapists also should be compassionate and possess a desire to help patients.

Advancement. Physical therapists are expected to continue their professional development by participating in continuing education courses and workshops. In fact, a number of States require continuing education as a condition of maintaining licensure.

Employment

Physical therapists held about 173,000 jobs in 2006. The number of jobs is greater than the number of practicing physical therapists because some physical therapists hold two or more jobs. For example, some may work in a private practice, but also work part time in another health care facility.

About 6 out of 10 physical therapists worked in hospitals or in offices of physical therapists. Other jobs were in the home health care services industry, nursing care facilities, outpatient care centers, and offices of physicians. Some physical therapists were self-employed in private practices, seeing individual patients and contracting to provide services in hospitals, rehabilitation centers, nursing care facilities, home health care agencies, adult day care programs, and schools. Physical therapists also teach in academic institutions and conduct research.

Job Outlook

Employment of physical therapists is expected to grow much faster than average. Job opportunities will be good, especially in acute hospital, rehabilitation, and orthopedic settings.

Employment change. Employment of physical therapists is expected to grow 27 percent from 2006 to 2016, much faster than the average for all occupations. The impact of proposed Federal legislation imposing limits on reimbursement for therapy services may adversely affect the short-term job outlook for physical therapists. However, the long-run demand for physical therapists should continue to rise as new treatments

Projections data from the National Employment Matrix

Occupational Title	SOC Code	Employment, 2006	Projected employment, 2016	Change, 2006-2016	
				Number	Percent
Physical therapists..	29-1123	173,000	220,000	47,000	27

NOTE: Data in this table are rounded. See the discussion of the employment projections table in the *Handbook* introductory chapter on *Occupational Information Included in the Handbook.*

and techniques expand the scope of physical therapy practices. Moreover, demand will be spurred by the increasing numbers of individuals with disabilities or limited function.

The increasing elderly population will drive growth in the demand for physical therapy services. The elderly population is particularly vulnerable to chronic and debilitating conditions that require therapeutic services. Also, the baby-boom generation is entering the prime age for heart attacks and strokes, increasing the demand for cardiac and physical rehabilitation. And increasing numbers of children will need physical therapy as technological advances save the lives of a larger proportion of newborns with severe birth defects.

Future medical developments also should permit a higher percentage of trauma victims to survive, creating additional demand for rehabilitative care. In addition, growth may result from advances in medical technology that could permit the treatment of an increasing number of disabling conditions that were untreatable in the past.

Widespread interest in health promotion also should increase demand for physical therapy services. A growing number of employers are using physical therapists to evaluate worksites, develop exercise programs, and teach safe work habits to employees.

Job prospects. Job opportunities will be good for licensed physical therapists in all settings. Job opportunities should be particularly good in acute hospital, rehabilitation, and orthopedic settings, where the elderly are most often treated. Physical therapists with specialized knowledge of particular types of treatment also will have excellent job prospects.

Earnings

Median annual earnings of physical therapists were $66,200 in May 2006. The middle 50 percent earned between $55,030 and $78,080. The lowest 10 percent earned less than $46,510, and the highest 10 percent earned more than $94,810. Median annual earnings in the industries employing the largest numbers of physical therapists in May 2006 were:

Home health care services	$70,920
Nursing care facilities	68,650
General medical and surgical hospitals................................	66,630
Offices of physicians..	65,900
Offices of physical, occupational and speech therapists, and audiologists	65,150

Related Occupations

Physical therapists rehabilitate people with physical disabilities. Others who work in the rehabilitation field include audiologists, chiropractors, occupational therapists, recreational therapists, rehabilitation counselors, respiratory therapists, and speech-language pathologists.

Sources of Additional Information

Additional career information and a list of accredited educational programs in physical therapy are available from:

➤ American Physical Therapy Association, 1111 North Fairfax St, Alexandria, VA 22314-1488.
Internet: **http://www.apta.org**

Physician Assistants

(O*NET 29-1071.00)

Significant Points

- Physician assistant programs usually last at least 2 years; admission requirements vary by program, but many require at least 2 years of college and some health care experience.

- All States require physician assistants to complete an accredited education program and to pass a national exam in order to obtain a license.

- Employment is projected to grow much faster than average as health care establishments increasingly use physician assistants to contain costs.

- Job opportunities should be good, particularly in rural and inner-city clinics.

Nature of the Work

Physician assistants (PAs) practice medicine under the supervision of physicians and surgeons. They should not be confused with medical assistants, who perform routine clinical and clerical tasks. (Medical assistants are discussed elsewhere in the *Handbook.*) PAs are formally trained to provide diagnostic, therapeutic, and preventive health care services, as delegated by a physician. Working as members of the health care team, they take medical histories, examine and treat patients, order and interpret laboratory tests and x-rays, and make diagnoses. They also treat minor injuries, by suturing, splinting, and casting. PAs record progress notes, instruct and counsel patients, and order or carry out therapy. In 48 States and the District of Columbia, physician assistants may prescribe some medications. In some establishments, a PA is responsible for managerial duties, such as ordering medical supplies or equipment and supervising technicians and assistants.

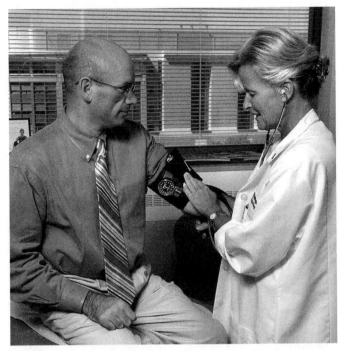

Physician assistants may be the principal care providers in rural or inner city clinics, where a physician is present for only one or two days each week.

Physician assistants work under the supervision of a physician. However, PAs may be the principal care providers in rural or inner city clinics where a physician is present for only one or two days each week. In such cases, the PA confers with the supervising physician and other medical professionals as needed and as required by law. PAs also may make house calls or go to hospitals and nursing care facilities to check on patients, after which they report back to the physician.

The duties of physician assistants are determined by the supervising physician and by State law. Aspiring PAs should investigate the laws and regulations in the States in which they wish to practice.

Many PAs work in primary care specialties, such as general internal medicine, pediatrics, and family medicine. Other specialty areas include general and thoracic surgery, emergency medicine, orthopedics, and geriatrics. PAs specializing in surgery provide preoperative and postoperative care and may work as first or second assistants during major surgery.

Work environment. Although PAs usually work in a comfortable, well-lighted environment, those in surgery often stand for long periods. At times, the job requires a considerable amount of walking. Schedules vary according to the practice setting, and often depend on the hours of the supervising physician. The workweek of hospital-based PAs may include weekends, nights, or early morning hospital rounds to visit patients. These workers also may be on call. PAs in clinics usually work a 40-hour week.

Training, Other Qualifications, and Advancement

Physician assistant programs usually last at least 2 years. Admission requirements vary by program, but many require at least 2 years of college and some health care experience. All States require that PAs complete an accredited, formal education program and pass a National exam to obtain a license.

Education and training. Physician assistant education programs usually last at least 2 years and are full time. Most programs are in schools of allied health, academic health centers, medical schools, or 4-year colleges; a few are in community colleges, the military, or hospitals. Many accredited PA programs have clinical teaching affiliations with medical schools.

In 2007, 136 education programs for physician assistants were accredited or provisionally accredited by the American Academy of Physician Assistants. More than 90 of these programs offered the option of a master's degree, and the rest offered either a bachelor's degree or an associate degree. Most applicants to PA educational programs already have a bachelor's degree.

Admission requirements vary, but many programs require 2 years of college and some work experience in the health care field. Students should take courses in biology, English, chemistry, mathematics, psychology, and the social sciences. Many PAs have prior experience as registered nurses, and others come from varied backgrounds, including military corpsman or medics and allied health occupations such as respiratory therapists, physical therapists, and emergency medical technicians and paramedics.

PA education includes classroom instruction in biochemistry, pathology, human anatomy, physiology, microbiology, clinical pharmacology, clinical medicine, geriatric and home health care, disease prevention, and medical ethics. Students obtain supervised clinical training in several areas, including family medicine, internal medicine, surgery, prenatal care and gynecology, geriatrics, emergency medicine, psychiatry, and pediatrics. Sometimes, PA students serve one or more of these rotations under the supervision of a physician who is seeking to hire a PA. The rotations often lead to permanent employment.

Licensure. All States and the District of Columbia have legislation governing the qualifications or practice of physician assistants. All jurisdictions require physician assistants to pass the Physician Assistant National Certifying Examination, administered by the National Commission on Certification of Physician Assistants (NCCPA) and open only to graduates of accredited PA education programs. Only those successfully completing the examination may use the credential "Physician Assistant-Certified." To remain certified, PAs must complete 100 hours of continuing medical education every 2 years. Every 6 years, they must pass a recertification examination or complete an alternative program combining learning experiences and a take-home examination.

Other qualifications. Physician assistants must have a desire to serve patients and be self-motivated. PAs also must have a good bedside manner, emotional stability, and the ability to make decisions in emergencies. Physician assistants must be willing to study throughout their career to keep up with medical advances.

Certification and advancement. Some PAs pursue additional education in a specialty such as surgery, neonatology, or emergency medicine. PA postgraduate educational programs are available in areas such as internal medicine, rural primary care, emergency medicine, surgery, pediatrics, neonatology, and occupational medicine. Candidates must be graduates of an accredited program and be certified by the NCCPA.

As they attain greater clinical knowledge and experience, PAs can advance to added responsibilities and higher earnings. However, by the very nature of the profession, clinically practicing PAs always are supervised by physicians.

Employment

Physician assistants held about 66,000 jobs in 2006. The number of jobs is greater than the number of practicing PAs because some hold two or more jobs. For example, some PAs work with a supervising physician, but also work in another practice, clinic, or hospital. According to the American Academy of Physician Assistants, about 15 percent of actively practicing PAs worked in more than one clinical job concurrently in 2006.

More than half of jobs for PAs were in the offices of physicians. About a quarter were in hospitals, public or private. The rest were mostly in outpatient care centers, including health maintenance organizations; the Federal Government; and public or private colleges, universities, and professional schools. A few were self-employed.

Job Outlook

Employment is expected to grow much faster than the average as health care establishments increasingly use physician assistants to contain costs. Job opportunities for PAs should be good, particularly in rural and inner city clinics, as these settings typically have difficulty attracting physicians.

Employment change. Employment of physician assistants is expected to grow 27 percent from 2006 to 2016, much faster than the average for all occupations. Projected rapid job growth reflects the expansion of health care industries and an emphasis on cost containment, which results in increasing use of PAs by health care establishments.

Physicians and institutions are expected to employ more PAs to provide primary care and to assist with medical and surgical procedures because PAs are cost-effective and productive members of the health care team. Physician assistants can relieve physicians of routine duties and procedures. Telemedicine—using technology to facilitate interactive consultations between physicians and physician assistants—also will expand the use of physician assistants.

Besides working in traditional office-based settings, PAs should find a growing number of jobs in institutional settings such as hospitals, academic medical centers, public clinics, and prisons. PAs also may be needed to augment medical staffing in inpatient teaching hospital settings as the number of hours physician residents are permitted to work is reduced, encouraging hospitals to use PAs to supply some physician resident services.

Job prospects. Job opportunities for PAs should be good, particularly in rural and inner-city clinics because those settings have difficulty attracting physicians. In addition to job openings from employment growth, openings will result from the need to replace physician assistants who retire or leave the occupation permanently during the 2006-16 decade. Opportunities will be best in States that allow PAs a wider scope of practice, such as allowing PAs to prescribe medications.

Earnings

Median annual earnings of wage-and-salary physician assistants were $74,980 in May 2006. The middle 50 percent earned between $62,430 and $89,220. The lowest 10 percent earned less than $43,100, and the highest 10 percent earned more than $102,230. Median annual earnings in the industries employing the largest numbers of physician assistants in May 2006 were:

Outpatient care centers $80,960
General medical and surgical hospitals 76,710
Offices of physicians 74,160

According to the American Academy of Physician Assistants, median income for physician assistants in full-time clinical practice was $80,356 in 2006; median income for first-year graduates was $69,517. Income varies by specialty, practice setting, geographical location, and years of experience. Employers often pay for their employees' liability insurance, registration fees with the Drug Enforcement Administration, State licensing fees, and credentialing fees.

Related Occupations

Other health care workers who provide direct patient care that requires a similar level of skill and training include audiologists, occupational therapists, physical therapists, registered nurses, and speech-language pathologists.

Sources of Additional Information

For information on a career as a physician assistant, including a list of accredited programs, contact:

➤ American Academy of Physician Assistants Information Center, 950 North Washington St., Alexandria, VA 22314. Internet: **http://www.aapa.org**

For eligibility requirements and a description of the Physician Assistant National Certifying Examination, contact:

➤ National Commission on Certification of Physician Assistants, Inc., 12000 Findley Rd., Suite 200, Duluth, GA 30097. Internet: **http://www.nccpa.net**

Projections data from the National Employment Matrix

Occupational Title	SOC Code	Employment, 2006	Projected employment, 2016	Change, 2006-2016	
				Number	Percent
Physician assistants	29-1071	66,000	83,000	18,000	27

NOTE: Data in this table are rounded. See the discussion of the employment projections table in the *Handbook* introductory chapter on *Occupational Information Included in the Handbook.*

Physicians and Surgeons

(O*NET 29-1061.00, 29-1062.00, 29-1063.00, 29-1064.00, 29-1065.00, 29-1066.00, 29-1067.00, 29-1069.99)

Significant Points

- Many physicians and surgeons work long, irregular hours; more than one-third of full-time physicians worked 60 hours or more a week in 2006.

- Acceptance to medical school is highly competitive.

- Formal education and training requirements are among the most demanding of any occupation, but earnings are among the highest.

- Job opportunities should be very good, particularly in rural and low-income areas.

Nature of the Work

Physicians and surgeons diagnose illnesses and prescribe and administer treatment for people suffering from injury or disease. Physicians examine patients, obtain medical histories, and order, perform, and interpret diagnostic tests. They counsel patients on diet, hygiene, and preventive health care.

There are two types of physicians: M.D.—Doctor of Medicine—and D.O.—Doctor of Osteopathic Medicine. M.D.s also are known as allopathic physicians. While both M.D.s and D.O.s may use all accepted methods of treatment, including drugs and surgery, D.O.s place special emphasis on the body's musculoskeletal system, preventive medicine, and holistic patient care. D.O.s are most likely to be primary care specialists although they can be found in all specialties. About half of D.O.s practice general or family medicine, general internal medicine, or general pediatrics.

Physicians work in one or more of several specialties, including, but not limited to, anesthesiology, family and general medicine, general internal medicine, general pediatrics, obstetrics and gynecology, psychiatry, and surgery.

Anesthesiologists focus on the care of surgical patients and pain relief. Like other physicians, they evaluate and treat patients and direct the efforts of their staffs. Through continual monitoring and assessment, these critical care specialists are responsible for maintenance of the patient's vital life functions—heart rate, body temperature, blood pressure, breathing—during surgery. They also work outside of the operating room, providing pain relief in the intensive care unit, during labor and delivery, and for those who suffer from chronic pain. Anesthesiologists confer with other physicians and surgeons about appropriate treatments and procedures before, during, and after operations.

Family and general practitioners often provide the first point of contact for people seeking health care, by acting as the traditional family doctor. They assess and treat a wide range of conditions, from sinus and respiratory infections to broken bones. Family and general practitioners typically have a base of regular, long-term patients. These doctors refer patients with more serious conditions to specialists or other health care facilities for more intensive care.

General internists diagnose and provide nonsurgical treatment for a wide range of problems that affect internal organ systems, such as the stomach, kidneys, liver, and digestive tract. Internists use a variety of diagnostic techniques to treat patients through medication or hospitalization. Like general practitioners, general internists commonly act as primary care specialists. They treat patients referred from other specialists, and, in turn they refer patients to other specialists when more complex care is required.

General pediatricians care for the health of infants, children, teenagers, and young adults. They specialize in the diagnosis and treatment of a variety of ailments specific to young people and track patients' growth to adulthood. Like most physicians, pediatricians work with different health care workers, such as nurses and other physicians, to assess and treat children with various ailments. Most of the work of pediatricians involves treating day-to-day illnesses—minor injuries, infectious diseases, and immunizations—that are common to children, much as a general practitioner treats adults. Some pediatricians specialize in pediatric surgery or serious medical conditions, such as autoimmune disorders or serious chronic ailments.

Obstetricians and gynecologists (OB/GYNs) specialize in women's health. They are responsible for women's general medical care, and they also provide care related to pregnancy and the reproductive system. Like general practitioners, OB/GYNs attempt to prevent, diagnose, and treat general health problems, but they focus on ailments specific to the female anatomy, such as cancers of the breast or cervix, urinary tract and pelvic disorders, and hormonal disorders. OB/GYNs also specialize in childbirth, treating and counseling women throughout their pregnancy, from giving prenatal diagnoses to assisting with delivery and providing postpartum care.

Psychiatrists are the primary caregivers in the area of mental health. They assess and treat mental illnesses through a combination of psychotherapy, psychoanalysis, hospitalization, and medication. Psychotherapy involves regular discussions with patients about their problems; the psychiatrist helps them find solutions through changes in their behavioral patterns, the exploration of their past experiences, or group and family therapy sessions. Psychoanalysis involves long-term psychotherapy and counseling for patients. In many cases, medications are administered to correct chemical imbalances that cause emotional problems. Psychiatrists also may administer electroconvulsive therapy to those of their patients who do not respond to, or who cannot take, medications.

Surgeons specialize in the treatment of injury, disease, and deformity through operations. Using a variety of instruments, and with patients under anesthesia, a surgeon corrects physical deformities, repairs bone and tissue after injuries, or performs preventive surgeries on patients with debilitating diseases or disorders. Although a large number perform general surgery, many surgeons choose to specialize in a specific area. One of the most prevalent specialties is orthopedic surgery: the treatment of the musculoskeletal system. Others include neurological surgery (treatment of the brain and nervous system), cardiovascular surgery, otolaryngology (treatment of the ear, nose,

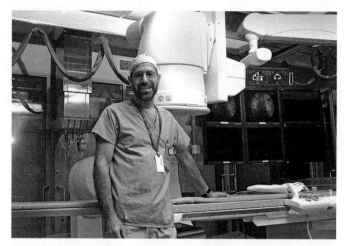

Physicians increasingly practice in groups or health care organizations that provide backup coverage and allow for more time off.

and throat), and plastic or reconstructive surgery. Like other physicians, surgeons also examine patients, perform and interpret diagnostic tests, and counsel patients on preventive health care.

Other physicians and surgeons work in a number of other medical and surgical specialists, including allergists, cardiologists, dermatologists, emergency physicians, gastroenterologists, ophthalmologists, pathologists, and radiologists.

Work environment. Many physicians—primarily general and family practitioners, general internists, pediatricians, OB/GYNs, and psychiatrists—work in small private offices or clinics, often assisted by a small staff of nurses and other administrative personnel. Increasingly, physicians are practicing in groups or health care organizations that provide backup coverage and allow for more time off. Physicians in a group practice or health care organization often work as part of a team that coordinates care for a number of patients; they are less independent than the solo practitioners of the past. Surgeons and anesthesiologists usually work in well-lighted, sterile environments while performing surgery and often stand for long periods. Most work in hospitals or in surgical outpatient centers.

Many physicians and surgeons work long, irregular hours. Over one-third of full-time physicians and surgeons worked 60 hours or more a week in 2006. Only 8 percent of all physicians and surgeons worked part-time, compared with 15 percent for all occupations. Physicians and surgeons must travel frequently between office and hospital to care for their patients. While on call, a physician will deal with many patients' concerns over the phone and make emergency visits to hospitals or nursing homes.

Training, Other Qualifications, and Advancement
The common path to practicing as a physician requires 8 years of education beyond high school and 3 to 8 additional years of internship and residency. All States, the District of Columbia, and U.S. territories license physicians.

Education and training. Formal education and training requirements for physicians are among the most demanding of any occupation—4 years of undergraduate school, 4 years of medical school, and 3 to 8 years of internship and residency,

depending on the specialty selected. A few medical schools offer combined undergraduate and medical school programs that last 6 years rather than the customary 8 years.

Premedical students must complete undergraduate work in physics, biology, mathematics, English, and inorganic and organic chemistry. Students also take courses in the humanities and the social sciences. Some students volunteer at local hospitals or clinics to gain practical experience in the health professions.

The minimum educational requirement for entry into medical school is 3 years of college; most applicants, however, have at least a bachelor's degree, and many have advanced degrees. There are 146 medical schools in the United States—126 teach allopathic medicine and award a Doctor of Medicine (M.D.) degree; 20 teach osteopathic medicine and award the Doctor of Osteopathic Medicine (D.O.) degree.

Acceptance to medical school is highly competitive. Applicants must submit transcripts, scores from the Medical College Admission Test, and letters of recommendation. Schools also consider an applicant's character, personality, leadership qualities, and participation in extracurricular activities. Most schools require an interview with members of the admissions committee.

Students spend most of the first 2 years of medical school in laboratories and classrooms, taking courses such as anatomy, biochemistry, physiology, pharmacology, psychology, microbiology, pathology, medical ethics, and laws governing medicine. They also learn to take medical histories, examine patients, and diagnose illnesses. During their last 2 years, students work with patients under the supervision of experienced physicians in hospitals and clinics, learning acute, chronic, preventive, and rehabilitative care. Through rotations in internal medicine, family practice, obstetrics and gynecology, pediatrics, psychiatry, and surgery, they gain experience in the diagnosis and treatment of illness.

Following medical school, almost all M.D.s enter a residency—graduate medical education in a specialty that takes the form of paid on-the-job training, usually in a hospital. Most D.O.s serve a 12-month rotating internship after graduation and before entering a residency, which may last 2 to 6 years.

A physician's training is costly. According to the Association of American Medical Colleges, in 2004 more than 80 percent of medical school graduates were in debt for educational expenses.

Licensure and certification. All States, the District of Columbia, and U.S. territories license physicians. To be licensed, physicians must graduate from an accredited medical school, pass a licensing examination, and complete 1 to 7 years of graduate medical education. Although physicians licensed in one State usually can get a license to practice in another without further examination, some States limit reciprocity. Graduates of foreign medical schools generally can qualify for licensure after passing an examination and completing a U.S. residency.

M.D.s and D.O.s seeking board certification in a specialty may spend up to 7 years in residency training, depending on the specialty. A final examination immediately after residency or after 1 or 2 years of practice also is necessary for certification by a member board of the American Board of Medical Special-

Table 1. Percent distribution of active physicians in patient care by specialty, 2005

	Percent
Total	100.0
Primary care	40.4
Family medicine and general practice	12.3
Internal medicine	15.0
Obstetrics & gynecology	5.5
Pediatrics	7.5
Specialties	59.6
Anesthesiology	5.2
Psychiatry	5.1
Surgical specialties, selected	10.8
All other specialties	38.5

SOURCE: American Medical Association, Physician Characteristics and Distribution in the US, 2007.

ists (ABMS) or the American Osteopathic Association (AOA). The ABMS represents 24 boards related to medical specialties ranging from allergy and immunology to urology. The AOA has approved 18 specialty boards, ranging from anesthesiology to surgery. For certification in a subspecialty, physicians usually need another 1 to 2 years of residency.

Other qualifications. People who wish to become physicians must have a desire to serve patients, be self-motivated, and be able to survive the pressures and long hours of medical education and practice. Physicians also must have a good bedside manner, emotional stability, and the ability to make decisions in emergencies. Prospective physicians must be willing to study throughout their career to keep up with medical advances.

Advancement. Some physicians and surgeons advance by gaining expertise in specialties and subspecialties and by developing a reputation for excellence among their peers and patients. Many physicians and surgeons start their own practice or join a group practice. Others teach residents and other new doctors, and some advance to supervisory and managerial roles in hospitals, clinics, and other settings.

Employment

Physicians and surgeons held about 633,000 jobs in 2006; approximately 15 percent were self-employed. About half of wage-and-salary physicians and surgeons worked in offices of physicians, and 18 percent were employed by hospitals. Others practiced in Federal, State, and local governments, including colleges, universities, and professional schools; private colleges, universities, and professional schools; and outpatient care centers.

According to 2005 data from the American Medical Association (AMA), about two in five physicians in patient care were in primary care, but not in a subspecialty of primary care. (See table 1.)

A growing number of physicians are partners or wage-and-salary employees of group practices. Organized as clinics or as associations of physicians, medical groups can more easily afford expensive medical equipment, can share support staff, and benefit from other business advantages.

According to the AMA, the New England and Middle Atlantic States have the highest ratio of physicians to population; the South Central and Mountain States have the lowest. D.O.s are more likely than M.D.s to practice in small cities and towns and in rural areas. M.D.s tend to locate in urban areas, close to hospitals and education centers.

Job Outlook

Employment of physicians and surgeons is expected to grow faster than the average for all occupations. Job opportunities should be very good, especially for physicians and surgeons willing to practice in specialties—including family practice, internal medicine, and OB/GYN—or in rural and low-income areas where there is a perceived shortage of medical practitioners.

Employment change. Employment of physicians and surgeons is projected to grow 14 percent from 2006 to 2016, faster than the average for all occupations. Job growth will occur because of continued expansion of health care related industries. The growing and aging population will drive overall growth in the demand for physician services, as consumers continue to demand high levels of care using the latest technologies, diagnostic tests, and therapies.

Demand for physicians' services is highly sensitive to changes in consumer preferences, health care reimbursement policies, and legislation. For example, if changes to health coverage result in consumers facing higher out-of-pocket costs, they may demand fewer physician services. Patients relying more on other health care providers—such as physician assistants, nurse practitioners, optometrists, and nurse anesthetists—also may temper demand for physician services. In addition, new technologies will increase physician productivity. These technologies include electronic medical records, test and prescription orders, billing, and scheduling.

Job prospects. Opportunities for individuals interested in becoming physicians and surgeons are expected to be very good. In addition to job openings from employment growth, numerous openings will result from the need to replace physicians and surgeons who retire over the 2006-16 decade.

Unlike their predecessors, newly trained physicians face radically different choices of where and how to practice. New physicians are much less likely to enter solo practice and more likely to take salaried jobs in group medical practices, clinics, and health networks.

Reports of shortages in some specialties, such as general or family practice, internal medicine, and OB/GYN, or in rural

Projections data from the National Employment Matrix

Occupational Title	SOC Code	Employment, 2006	Projected employment, 2016	Change, 2006-2016 Number	Change, 2006-2016 Percent
Physicians and surgeons	29-1060	633,000	723,000	90,000	14

NOTE: Data in this table are rounded. See the discussion of the employment projections table in the *Handbook* introductory chapter on *Occupational Information Included in the Handbook.*

Table 2. Median compensation for physicians, 2005

Specialty	Less than two years in specialty	Over one year in specialty
Anesthesiology....................................	$259,948	$321,686
Surgery: General	228,839	282,504
Obstetrics/gynecology: General..........	203,270	247,348
Psychiatry: General............................	173,922	180,000
Internal medicine: General..................	141,912	166,420
Pediatrics: General.............................	132,953	161,331
Family practice (without obstetrics) ...	137,119	156,010

SOURCE: Medical Group Management Association, Physician Compensation and Production Report, 2005.

or low-income areas should attract new entrants, encouraging schools to expand programs and hospitals to increase available residency slots. However, because physician training is so lengthy, employment change happens gradually. In the short term, to meet increased demand, experienced physicians may work longer hours, delay retirement, or take measures to increase productivity, such as using more support staff to provide services. Opportunities should be particularly good in rural and low-income areas, as some physicians find these areas unattractive because of less control over work hours, isolation from medical colleagues, or other reasons.

Earnings

Earnings of physicians and surgeons are among the highest of any occupation. The Medical Group Management Association's Physician Compensation and Production Survey, reports that median total compensation for physicians in 2005 varied by specialty, as shown in table 2. Total compensation for physicians reflects the amount reported as direct compensation for tax purposes, plus all voluntary salary reductions. Salary, bonus and incentive payments, research stipends, honoraria, and distribution of profits were included in total compensation.

Self-employed physicians—those who own or are part owners of their medical practice—generally have higher median incomes than salaried physicians. Earnings vary according to number of years in practice, geographic region, hours worked, skill, personality, and professional reputation. Self-employed physicians and surgeons must provide for their own health insurance and retirement.

Related Occupations

Physicians work to prevent, diagnose, and treat diseases, disorders, and injuries. Other health care practitioners who need similar skills and who exercise critical judgment include chiropractors, dentists, optometrists, physician assistants, podiatrists, registered nurses, and veterinarians.

Sources of Additional Information

For a list of medical schools and residency programs, as well as general information on premedical education, financial aid, and medicine as a career, contact:

➤ American Association of Colleges of Osteopathic MediciNE., 5550 Friendship Blvd., Suite 310, Chevy ChaSE., MD 20815. Internet: **http://www.aacom.org**

➤ Association of American Medical Colleges, Section for Student Services, 2450 N St.NW., Washington, DC 20037. Internet: **http://www.aamc.org/students**

For general information on physicians, contact:

➤ American Medical Association, 515 N. State St., Chicago, IL 60610. Internet: **http://www.ama-assn.org**

➤ American Osteopathic Association, Department of Communications, 142 East Ontario St., Chicago, IL 60611. Internet: **http://www.osteopathic.org**

For information about various medical specialties, contact:

➤ American Academy of Family Physicians, Resident Student Activities Department, 11400 Tomahawk Creek Pkwy., Leawood, KS 66211. Internet: **http://fmignet.aafp.org**

➤ American Academy of Pediatrics, 141 Northwest Point Blvd., Elk Grove Village, IL 60007. Internet: **http://www.aap.org**

➤ American Board of Medical Specialties, 1007 Church St., Suite 404, Evanston, IL 60201. Internet: **http://www.abms.org**

➤ American College of Obstetricians and Gynecologists, 409 12th St.SW., P.O. Box 96920, Washington, DC 20090. Internet: **http://www.acog.org**

➤ American College of Physicians, 190 North Independence Mall West, Philadelphia, PA 19106. Internet: **http://www.acponline.org**

➤ American College of Surgeons, Division of Education, 633 North Saint Clair St., Chicago, IL 60611. Internet: **http://www.facs.org**

➤ American Psychiatric Association, 1000 Wilson Blvd., Suite 1825, Arlington, VA 22209. Internet: **http://www.psych.org**

➤ American Society of Anesthesiologists, 520 N. Northwest Hwy., Park Ridge, IL 60068. Internet: **http://www.asahq.org/career/homepage.htm**

Information on Federal scholarships and loans is available from the directors of student financial aid at schools of medicine. Information on licensing is available from State boards of examiners.

Podiatrists

(O*NET 29-1081.00)

Significant Points

- Podiatrists must be licensed, requiring 3 to 4 years of undergraduate education, the completion of a 4-year podiatric college program, and passing scores on national and State examinations.

- While the occupation is small, job opportunities should be good for entry-level graduates of accredited podiatric medicine programs.

- Opportunities for newly trained podiatrists will be better in group medical practices, clinics, and health networks than in traditional, solo practices.

- Podiatrists enjoy very high earnings.

Nature of the Work

Americans spend a great deal of time on their feet. As the Nation becomes more active across all age groups, the need for foot care will become increasingly important.

The human foot is a complex structure. It contains 26 bones—plus muscles, nerves, ligaments, and blood vessels—and is designed for balance and mobility. The 52 bones in the feet make up about one-fourth of all the bones in the human body. Podiatrists, also known as *doctors of podiatric medicine* (DPMs), diagnose and treat disorders, diseases, and injuries of the foot and lower leg.

Podiatrists treat corns, calluses, ingrown toenails, bunions, heel spurs, and arch problems; ankle and foot injuries, deformities, and infections; and foot complaints associated with diabetes and other diseases. To treat these problems, podiatrists prescribe drugs and physical therapy, set fractures, and perform surgery. They also fit corrective shoe inserts called orthotics, design plaster casts and strappings to correct deformities, and design custom-made shoes. Podiatrists may use a force plate or scanner to help design the orthotics: patients walk across a plate connected to a computer that "reads" their feet, picking up pressure points and weight distribution. From the computer readout, podiatrists order the correct design or recommend another kind of treatment.

To diagnose a foot problem, podiatrists also order x-rays and laboratory tests. The foot may be the first area to show signs of serious conditions such as arthritis, diabetes, and heart disease. For example, patients with diabetes are prone to foot ulcers and infections because of poor circulation. Podiatrists consult with and refer patients to other health practitioners when they detect symptoms of these disorders.

Most podiatrists have a solo practice, although more are forming group practices with other podiatrists or health practitioners. Some specialize in surgery, orthopedics, primary care, or public health. Besides these board-certified specialties, podiatrists may practice other specialties, such as sports medicine, pediatrics, dermatology, radiology, geriatrics, or diabetic foot care.

Podiatrists who are in private practice are responsible for running a small business. They may hire employees, order supplies, and keep records, among other tasks. In addition, some educate the community on the benefits of foot care through speaking engagements and advertising.

Work environment. Podiatrists usually work in small private offices or clinics, sometimes supported by a small staff of assistants and other administrative personnel. They also may spend time visiting patients in nursing homes or performing surgery at hospitals or ambulatory surgical centers. Podiatrists with private practices set their own hours but may work evenings and weekends to accommodate their patients. Podiatrists usually treat fewer emergencies than other doctors.

Training, Other Qualifications, and Advancement

Podiatrists must be licensed, requiring 3 to 4 years of undergraduate education, the completion of a 4-year podiatric college program, and passing scores on national and State examinations.

Education and training. Prerequisites for admission to a college of podiatric medicine include the completion of at least 90 semester hours of undergraduate study, an acceptable grade point average, and suitable scores on the Medical College Admission Test. (Some colleges also may accept the Dental Admission Test or the Graduate Record Exam.)

Admission to podiatric colleges usually requires at least 8 semester hours each of biology, inorganic chemistry, organic chemistry, and physics and at least 6 hours of English. The science courses should be those designed for premedical students. Extracurricular and community activities, personal interviews, and letters of recommendation are also important. About 95 percent of podiatric students have at least a bachelor's degree.

In 2007, there were seven colleges of podiatric medicine fully accredited by the Council on Podiatric Medical Education. Colleges of podiatric medicine offer a 4-year program whose core curriculum is similar to that in other schools of medicine. During the first 2 years, students receive classroom instruction in basic sciences, including anatomy, chemistry, pathology, and pharmacology. Third-year and fourth-year students have clinical rotations in private practices, hospitals, and clinics. During these rotations, they learn how to take general and podiatric histories, perform routine physical examinations, interpret tests and findings, make diagnoses, and perform therapeutic procedures. Graduates receive the degree of Doctor of Podiatric Medicine (DPM).

Most graduates complete a hospital-based residency program after receiving a DPM. Residency programs last from 2 to 4 years. Residents receive advanced training in podiatric medicine and surgery and serve clinical rotations in anesthesiology,

Podiatrists diagnose and treat disorders of the feet and ankles.

internal medicine, pathology, radiology, emergency medicine, and orthopedic and general surgery. Residencies lasting more than 1 year provide more extensive training in specialty areas.

Licensure. All States and the District of Columbia require a license for the practice of podiatric medicine. Each State defines its own licensing requirements, although many States grant reciprocity to podiatrists who are licensed in another State. Applicants for licensure must be graduates of an accredited college of podiatric medicine and must pass written and oral examinations. Some States permit applicants to substitute the examination of the National Board of Podiatric Medical Examiners, given in the second and fourth years of podiatric medical college, for part or all of the written State examination. In general, States require a minimum of 2 years of postgraduate residency training in an approved health care institution. For licensure renewal, most States require continuing education.

Other qualifications. People planning a career in podiatry should have scientific aptitude, manual dexterity, interpersonal skills, and a friendly bedside manner. In private practice, podiatrists also should have good business sense.

Certification and advancement. There are a number of certifying boards for the podiatric specialties of orthopedics, primary medicine, and surgery. Certification has requirements beyond licensure. Each board requires advanced training, the completion of written and oral examinations, and experience as a practicing podiatrist. Most managed-care organizations prefer board-certified podiatrists.

Podiatrists may advance to become professors at colleges of podiatric medicine, department chiefs in hospitals, or general health administrators.

Employment

Podiatrists held about 12,000 jobs in 2006. About 24 percent of podiatrists were self-employed. Most podiatrists were solo practitioners, although more are entering group practices with other podiatrists or other health practitioners. Solo practitioners primarily were unincorporated self-employed workers, although some also were incorporated wage and salary workers in offices of other health practitioners. Other podiatrists were employed by hospitals, long-term care facilities, the Federal Government, and municipal health departments.

Job Outlook

Employment is expected to increase about as fast as average because of increasing consumer demand for podiatric medicine services. Job prospects should be good.

Employment change. Employment of podiatrists is expected to increase 9 percent from 2006 to 2016, about as fast as the average for all occupations. More people will turn to podiatrists for foot care because of the rising number of injuries sustained by a more active and increasingly older population.

Medicare and most private health insurance programs cover acute medical and surgical foot services, as well as diagnostic x-rays and leg braces. Details of such coverage vary among plans. However, routine foot care, including the removal of corns and calluses, is not usually covered unless the patient has a systemic condition that has resulted in severe circulatory problems or areas of desensitization in the legs or feet. Like dental services, podiatric care is often discretionary and, therefore, more dependent on disposable income than some other medical services.

Employment of podiatrists would grow even faster were it not for continued emphasis on controlling the costs of specialty health care. Insurers will balance the cost of sending patients to podiatrists against the cost and availability of substitute practitioners, such as physicians and physical therapists.

Job prospects. Although the occupation is small and most podiatrists continue to practice until retirement, job opportunities should be good for entry-level graduates of accredited podiatric medicine programs. Job growth and replacement needs should create enough job openings for the supply of new podiatric medicine graduates. Opportunities will be better for board-certified podiatrists because many managed-care organizations require board certification. Newly trained podiatrists will find more opportunities in group medical practices, clinics, and health networks than in traditional solo practices. Establishing a practice will be most difficult in the areas surrounding colleges of podiatric medicine, where podiatrists concentrate.

Earnings

Podiatrists enjoy very high earnings. Median annual earnings of salaried podiatrists were $108,220 in 2006. Additionally, a survey by *Podiatry Management Magazine* reported median net income of $114,000 in 2006. Podiatrists in partnerships tended to earn higher net incomes than those in solo practice. A salaried podiatrist typically receives heath insurance and retirement benefits from their employer, whereas self-employed chiropractors must provide for their own health insurance and retirement. Also, solo practitioners must absorb the costs of running their own offices.

Related Occupations

Other workers, who apply medical knowledge to prevent, diagnose, and treat muscle and bone disorders and injuries include athletic trainers, chiropractors, massage therapists, occupational therapists, physical therapists, and physicians and surgeons. Workers who specialize in developing orthopedic shoe inserts, braces, and prosthetic limbs are orthotists and prosthetists.

Sources of Additional Information

For information on a career in podiatric medicine, contact:
➤ American Podiatric Medical Association, 9312 Old Georgetown Rd., Bethesda, MD 20814-1621.
Internet: **http://www.apma.org**

Projections data from the National Employment Matrix

Occupational Title	SOC Code	Employment, 2006	Projected employment, 2016	Change, 2006-2016	
				Number	Percent
Podiatrists..	29-1081	12,000	13,000	1,100	9

NOTE: Data in this table are rounded. See the discussion of the employment projections table in the *Handbook* introductory chapter on *Occupational Information Included in the Handbook.*

Information on colleges of podiatric medicine and their entrance requirements, curricula, and student financial aid is available from:

➤ American Association of Colleges of Podiatric MediciNE., 15850 Crabbs Branch Way, Suite 320, Rockville, MD 20855-2622. Internet: **http://www.aacpm.org**

Radiation Therapists

(O*NET 29-1124.00)

Significant Points

- A bachelor's degree, associate degree, or certificate in radiation therapy is generally required.

- Good job opportunities are expected.

- Employment is projected to grow much faster than the average for all occupations.

Nature of the Work

Treating cancer in the human body is the principal use of radiation therapy. As part of a medical radiation oncology team, radiation therapists use machines—called linear accelerators—to administer radiation treatment to patients. Linear accelerators, used in a procedure called external beam therapy, project high-energy x-rays at targeted cancer cells. As the x-rays collide with human tissue, they produce highly energized ions that can shrink and eliminate cancerous tumors. Radiation therapy is sometimes used as the sole treatment for cancer, but is usually used in conjunction with chemotherapy or surgery.

The first step in the radiation therapy process is simulation. During simulation, the radiation therapist uses an x-ray imaging machine or computer tomography (CT) scan to pinpoint the location of the tumor. The therapist then positions the patient and adjusts the linear accelerator so that, when treatment begins, radiation exposure is concentrated on the tumor cells. The radiation therapist then develops a treatment plan in conjunction with a radiation oncologist (a physician who specializes in therapeutic radiology), and a dosimetrist (a technician who calculates the dose of radiation that will be used for treatment). The therapist later explains the treatment plan to the patient and answers any questions that the patient may have.

The next step in the process is treatment. To begin, the radiation therapist positions the patient and adjusts the linear accelerator according to the guidelines established in simulation. Then, from a separate room that is protected from the x-ray radiation, the therapist operates the linear accelerator and monitors the patient's condition through a TV monitor and an intercom system. Treatment can take anywhere from 10 to 30 minutes and is usually administered once a day, 5 days a week, for 2 to 9 weeks.

During the treatment phase, the radiation therapist monitors the patient's physical condition to determine if any adverse side effects are taking place. The therapist must also be aware of the patient's emotional wellbeing. Because many patients are under stress and are emotionally fragile, it is important for the therapist to maintain a positive attitude and provide emotional support.

Radiation therapists keep detailed records of their patients' treatments. These records include information such as the dose of radiation used for each treatment, the total amount of radiation used to date, the area treated, and the patient's reactions. Radiation oncologists and dosimetrists review these records to ensure that the treatment plan is working, to monitor the amount of radiation exposure that the patient has received, and to keep side effects to a minimum.

Radiation therapists also assist medical radiation physicists, workers who monitor and adjust the linear accelerator. Because radiation therapists often work alone during the treatment phase, they need to be able to check the linear accelerator for problems and make any adjustments that are needed. Therapists also may assist dosimetrists with routine aspects of dosimetry, the process used to calculate radiation dosages.

Work environment. Radiation therapists work in hospitals or in cancer treatment centers. These places are clean, well lighted, and well ventilated. Therapists do a considerable amount of lifting and must be able to help disabled patients get on and off treatment tables. They spend most of their time on their feet

Radiation therapists generally work 40 hours a week, and unlike those in other health care occupations, they normally work only during the day. However, because radiation therapy emer-

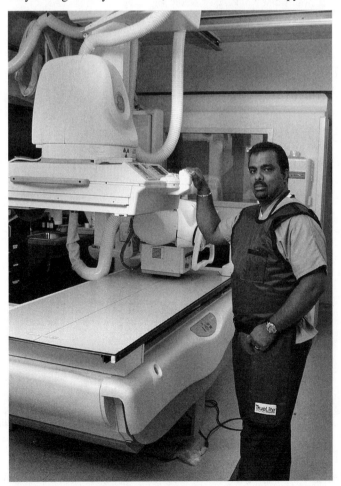

Radiation therapists work in hospitals and cancer treatment centers.

gencies do occur, some therapists are required to be on call and may have to work outside of their normal hours.

Working with cancer patients can be stressful, but many radiation therapists also find it rewarding. Because they work around radioactive materials, radiation therapists take great care to ensure that they are not exposed to dangerous levels of radiation. Following standard safety procedures can prevent overexposure.

Training, Other Qualifications, and Advancement
A bachelor's degree, associate degree, or certificate in radiation therapy generally is required. Many States also require radiation therapists to be licensed. With experience, therapists can advance to managerial positions.

Education and training. Employers usually require applicants to complete an associate or a bachelor's degree program in radiation therapy. Individuals also may become qualified by completing an associate or a bachelor's degree program in radiography, which is the study of radiological imaging, and then completing a 12-month certificate program in radiation therapy. Radiation therapy programs include core courses on radiation therapy procedures and the scientific theories behind them. In addition, such programs often include courses on human anatomy and physiology, physics, algebra, precalculus, writing, public speaking, computer science, and research methodology. In 2007 there were 123 radiation therapy programs accredited by the American Registry of Radiologic Technologists (ARRT).

Licensure. In 2007, 32 States required radiation therapists to be licensed by a State accrediting board. Licensing requirements vary by State, but many States require applicants to pass the ARRT certification examination. Further information is available from individual State licensing offices.

Certification and other qualifications. Some States, as well as many employers, require that radiation therapists be certified by ARRT. To become ARRT-certified, an applicant must complete an accredited radiation therapy program, adhere to ARRT ethical standards, and pass the ARRT certification examination. The examination and accredited academic programs cover radiation protection and quality assurance, clinical concepts in radiation oncology, treatment planning, treatment delivery, and patient care and education. Candidates also must demonstrate competency in several clinical practices including patient care activities; simulation procedures; dosimetry calculations; fabrication of beam modification devices; low-volume, high-risk procedures, and the application of radiation.

ARRT certification is valid for 1 year, after which therapists must renew their certification. Requirements for renewal include abiding by the ARRT ethical standards, paying annual dues, and satisfying continuing education requirements. Continuing education requirements must be met every 2 years and include either the completion of 24 credits of radiation thera-

py-related courses or the attainment of ARRT certification in a discipline other than radiation therapy. Certification renewal, however, may not be required by all States or employers that require initial certification.

All radiation therapists need good communication skills because their work involves a great deal of patient interaction. Individuals interested in becoming radiation therapists should be psychologically capable of working with cancer patients. They should be caring and empathetic because they work with patients who are ill and under stress. They should be able to keep accurate, detailed records. They also should be physically fit because they work on their feet for long periods and lift and move disabled patients.

Advancement. Experienced radiation therapists may advance to manage radiation therapy programs in treatment centers or other health care facilities. Managers generally continue to treat patients while taking on management responsibilities. Other advancement opportunities include teaching, technical sales, and research. With additional training and certification, therapists also can become dosimetrists, who use complex mathematical formulas to calculate proper radiation doses.

Employment
Radiation therapists held about 15,000 jobs in 2006. About 73 percent worked in hospitals, and about 17 percent worked in the offices of physicians. A small proportion worked in outpatient care centers.

Job Outlook
Employment is expected to increase much faster than the average from 2006 to 2016, and job prospects should be good.

Employment change. Employment of radiation therapists is projected to grow by 25 percent between 2006 and 2016, which is much faster than the average for all occupations. As the U.S. population grows and an increasing share of it is in the older age groups, the number of people needing treatment is expected to increase and to spur demand for radiation therapists. In addition, as radiation technology advances and is able to treat more types of cancer, radiation therapy will be prescribed more often.

Job prospects. Job prospects are expected to be good. Job openings will result from employment growth and from the need to replace workers who retire or leave the occupation for other reasons. Applicants who are certified should have the best opportunities.

Earnings
Median annual earnings of wage-and-salary radiation therapists were $66,170 in May 2006. The middle 50 percent earned between $54,170 and $78,550. The lowest 10 percent earned less than $44,840, and the highest 10 percent earned more than

Projections data from the National Employment Matrix

Occupational Title	SOC Code	Employment, 2006	Projected employment, 2016	Change, 2006-2016	
				Number	Percent
Radiation therapists...	29-1124	15,000	18,000	3,600	25

NOTE: Data in this table are rounded. See the discussion of the employment projections table in the *Handbook* introductory chapter on *Occupational Information Included in the Handbook.*

$92,110. Median annual earnings in the industries that employed the largest numbers of radiation therapists in May 2006 are as follows:

Outpatient care centers..$73,810
Offices of physicians..70,050
General medical and surgical hospitals..................63,580

Some employers also reimburse their employees for the cost of continuing education.

Related Occupations

Radiation therapists use advanced machinery to administer medical treatment to patients. Other occupations that perform similar duties include radiologic technologists and technicians, diagnostic medical sonographers, nuclear medicine technologists, cardiovascular technologists and technicians, dental hygienists, respiratory therapists, physical therapist assistants and aides, registered nurses, and physicians and surgeons.

Other occupations that build relationships with patients and provide them with emotional support include nursing, psychiatric, and home health aides; counselors; psychologists; social workers; and social and human service assistants.

Sources of Additional Information

Information on certification by the American Registry of Radiologic Technologists and on accredited radiation therapy programs may be obtained from:
➤ American Registry of Radiologic Technologists, 1255 Northland Dr., St.Paul, MN 55120.
Internet: **http://www.arrt.org**

Information on careers in radiation therapy may be obtained from:
➤ American Society of Radiologic Technologists, 15000 Central Ave., SE., Albuquerque, NM 87123.
Internet: **http://www.asrt.org**

Recreational Therapists

(O*NET 29-1125.00)

Significant Points

- Recreational therapists will experience competition for jobs.

- A bachelor's degree in therapeutic recreation is the usual requirement for entry-level positions.

- Recreational therapists should be comfortable working with persons who are ill or who have disabilities.

Nature of the Work

Recreational therapists, also referred to as *therapeutic recreation specialists*, provide treatment services and recreation activities for individuals with disabilities or illnesses. Using a variety of techniques, including arts and crafts, animals, sports, games, dance and movement, drama, music, and community outings, therapists improve and maintain the physical, mental, and emotional well-being of their clients. Therapists help individuals reduce depression, stress, and anxiety; recover basic motor functioning and reasoning abilities; build confidence; and socialize effectively so that they can enjoy greater independence and reduce or eliminate the effects of their illness or disability. In addition, therapists help people with disabilities integrate into the community by teaching them how to use community resources and recreational activities. Recreational therapists are different from recreation workers, who organize recreational activities primarily for enjoyment. (Recreation workers are discussed elsewhere in the *Handbook*.)

In acute health care settings, such as hospitals and rehabilitation centers, recreational therapists treat and rehabilitate individuals with specific health conditions, usually in conjunction or collaboration with physicians, nurses, psychologists, social workers, and physical and occupational therapists. In long-term and residential care facilities, recreational therapists use leisure activities—especially structured group programs—to improve and maintain their clients' general health and well-being. They also may provide interventions to prevent the client from suffering further medical problems and complications.

Recreational therapists assess clients using information from observations, medical records, standardized assessments, the medical staff, the clients' families, and the clients themselves. They then develop and carry out therapeutic interventions consistent with the clients' needs and interests. For example, they may encourage clients who are isolated from others or who have limited social skills to play games with others, and they may teach right-handed people with right-side paralysis how to use their unaffected left side to throw a ball or swing a racket. Recreational therapists may instruct patients in relaxation techniques to reduce stress and tension, stretching and

Recreational therapists use various techniques, including cognitive tests, to treat clients and maintain their well-being.

limbering exercises, proper body mechanics for participation in recreational activities, pacing and energy conservation techniques, and team activities. As they work, therapists observe and document a patient's participation, reactions, and progress.

Community-based recreational therapists may work in park and recreation departments, special-education programs for school districts, or assisted-living, adult day care, and substance abuse rehabilitation centers. In these programs, therapists use interventions to develop specific skills, while providing opportunities for exercise, mental stimulation, creativity, and fun. Those few who work in schools help counselors, teachers, and parents address the special needs of students, including easing disabled students' transition into adult life.

Work environment. Recreational therapists provide services in special activity rooms but also plan activities and prepare documentation in offices. When working with clients during community integration programs, they may travel locally to teach clients how to use public transportation and other public areas, such as parks, playgrounds, swimming pools, restaurants, and theaters. Therapists often lift and carry equipment. Recreational therapists generally work a 40-hour week that may include some evenings, weekends, and holidays.

Training, Other Qualifications, and Advancement

A bachelor's degree with a major or concentration in therapeutic recreation is the usual requirement for entry-level positions. Some States regulate recreational therapists, but requirements vary.

Education and training. Most entry-level recreational therapists need a bachelor's degree in therapeutic recreation, or in recreation with a concentration in therapeutic recreation. People may qualify for paraprofessional positions with an associate degree in therapeutic recreation or another subject related to health care. An associate degree in recreational therapy; training in art, drama, or music therapy; or qualifying work experience may be sufficient for activity director positions in nursing homes.

Approximately 130 academic programs prepare students to become recreational therapists. Most offer bachelor's degrees, although some also offer associate, master's, or doctoral degrees. Therapeutic recreation programs include courses in assessment, treatment and program planning, intervention design, and evaluation. Students also study human anatomy, physiology, abnormal psychology, medical and psychiatric terminology, characteristics of illnesses and disabilities, professional ethics, and the use of assistive devices and technology.

Licensure. Some States regulate recreational therapists through licensure, registration, or regulation of titles. Requirements vary by State. In 2006, North Carolina, Utah, and

New Hampshire required licensure to practice as a recreational therapist.

Certification and other qualifications. Although certification is usually voluntary, most employers prefer to hire candidates who are certified therapeutic recreation specialists. In 2006, about 3 out of 4 recreational therapists worked in a clinical setting, which often requires certification by the National Council for Therapeutic Recreation Certification. The council offers the Certified Therapeutic Recreation Specialist credential to candidates who have a bachelor's or graduate degree from an accredited educational institution, pass a written certification examination, and complete a supervised internship of at least 480 hours. Therapists must meet additional requirements to maintain certification.

Therapists can also earn certifications in specific areas, such as art therapy and aquatic therapy.

Recreational therapists must be comfortable working with people who are ill or disabled. Therapists must be patient, tactful, and persuasive when working with people who have a variety of special needs. Ingenuity, a sense of humor, and imagination are needed to adapt activities to individual needs, and good physical coordination is necessary to demonstrate or participate in recreational activities.

Advancement. Therapists may advance to supervisory or administrative positions. Some teach, conduct research, or consult for health or social services agencies.

Employment

Recreational therapists held about 25,000 jobs in 2006. About 70 percent were in nursing and residential care facilities and hospitals. Others worked in State and local government agencies and in community care facilities for the elderly, including assisted-living facilities. The rest worked primarily in residential mental retardation, mental health, and substance abuse facilities; individual and family services; Federal Government agencies; educational services; and outpatient care centers. Only a small number of therapists were self-employed, generally contracting with long-term care facilities or community agencies to develop and oversee programs.

Job Outlook

Overall employment of recreational therapists is expected to grow more slowly than the average for all occupations. Competition for jobs is expected.

Employment change. Employment of recreational therapists is expected to increase 4 percent from 2006 to 2016, slower than the average for all occupations. Employment of recreational therapists will grow to meet the therapy needs of the increasing number of older adults. In nursing care facilities—the largest industry employing recreational therapists—employment will grow slightly faster than the occupation as a

Projections data from the National Employment Matrix

Occupational Title	SOC Code	Employment, 2006	Projected employment, 2016	Change, 2006-2016	
				Number	Percent
Recreational therapists...	29-1125	25,000	26,000	900	4

NOTE: Data in this table are rounded. See the discussion of the employment projections table in the *Handbook* introductory chapter on *Occupational Information Included in the Handbook.*

whole as the number of older adults continues to grow. Fast employment growth is expected in the residential and outpatient settings that serve people who are physically disabled, cognitively disabled, or elderly or who have mental illness or substance abuse problems Employment is expected to decline in hospitals, however, as services shift to outpatient settings and employers emphasize cost containment.

Health care facilities will support a growing number of jobs in adult day care and outpatient programs offering short-term mental health and alcohol or drug abuse services. Rehabilitation, home health care, and transitional programs will provide additional jobs.

Job prospects. Recreational therapists will experience competition for jobs. Job opportunities should be best for people with a bachelor's degree in therapeutic recreation or in recreation with courses in therapeutic recreation. Opportunities also should be good for therapists who hold specialized certifications such as aquatic therapy, meditation, or crisis intervention. Recreational therapists might experience more competition for jobs in certain regions of the country.

Earnings

Median annual earnings of recreational therapists were $34,990 in May 2006. The middle 50 percent earned between $26,780 and $44,850. The lowest 10 percent earned less than $20,880, and the highest 10 percent earned more than $55,530. Median annual earnings in the industries employing the largest numbers of recreational therapists in May 2006 were:

General medical and surgical hospitals	$39,320
State government	38,260
Psychiatric and substance abuse hospitals	37,560
Nursing care facilities	30,440
Community care facilities for the elderly	28,980

Related Occupations

Recreational therapists primarily design activities to help people with disabilities lead more fulfilling and independent lives. Other workers who have similar jobs are occupational therapists, physical therapists, recreation workers, rehabilitation counselors, and teachers—special education.

Sources of Additional Information

For information and materials on careers and academic programs in recreational therapy, contact:

➤ American Therapeutic Recreation Association, 1414 Prince St., Suite 204, Alexandria, VA 22314-2853.
Internet: **http://www.atra-tr.org**

➤ National Therapeutic Recreation Society, 22377 Belmont Ridge Rd., Ashburn, VA 20148-4501. Internet:
http://www.nrpa.org/content/default.aspx?documentid=530

Information on certification may be obtained from:

➤ National Council for Therapeutic Recreation Certification, 7 Elmwood Dr., New City, NY 10956.
Internet: **http://www.nctrc.org**

For information on licensure requirements, contact the appropriate recreational therapy regulatory agency for your State.

Registered Nurses

(O*NET 29-1111.00)

Significant Points

- Registered nurses constitute the largest health care occupation, with 2.5 million jobs.

- About 59 percent of jobs are in hospitals.

- The three major educational paths to registered nursing are a bachelor's degree, an associate degree, and a diploma from an approved nursing program.

- Registered nurses are projected to generate about 587,000 new jobs over the 2006-16 period, one of the largest numbers among all occupations; overall job opportunities are expected to be excellent, but may vary by employment setting.

Nature of the Work

Registered nurses (RNs), regardless of specialty or work setting, treat patients, educate patients and the public about various medical conditions, and provide advice and emotional support to patients' family members. RNs record patients' medical histories and symptoms, help perform diagnostic tests and analyze results, operate medical machinery, administer treatment and medications, and help with patient follow-up and rehabilitation.

RNs teach patients and their families how to manage their illness or injury, explaining post-treatment home care needs; diet, nutrition, and exercise programs; and self-administration of medication and physical therapy. Some RNs work to promote general health by educating the public on warning signs and symptoms of disease. RNs also might run general health screening or immunization clinics, blood drives, and public seminars on various conditions.

When caring for patients, RNs establish a plan of care or contribute to an existing plan. Plans may include numerous activities, such as administering medication, including careful checking of dosages and avoiding interactions; starting, maintaining, and discontinuing intravenous (IV) lines for fluid, medication, blood, and blood products; administering therapies and treatments; observing the patient and recording those observations; and consulting with physicians and other health care clinicians. Some RNs provide direction to licensed practical nurses and nursing aids regarding patient care. RNs with advanced educational preparation and training may perform diagnostic and therapeutic procedures and may have prescriptive authority.

RNs can specialize in one or more areas of patient care. There generally are four ways to specialize. RNs can choose a particular work setting or type of treatment, such as perioperative nurses, who work in operating rooms and assist surgeons. RNs also may choose to specialize in specific health conditions, as do diabetes management nurses, who assist patients to manage diabetes. Other RNs specialize in working with one or more organs or body system types, such as dermatology nurses, who work with patients who have skin disorders. RNs also can choose to work with a well-defined population, such as geriatric nurses, who work with the elderly. Some RNs may combine specialties. For example, pediatric oncology nurses deal with children and adolescents who have cancer.

There are many options for RNs who specialize in a work setting or type of treatment. *Ambulatory care nurses* provide preventive care and treat patients with a variety of illnesses and injuries in physicians' offices or in clinics. Some ambulatory care nurses are involved in telehealth, providing care and advice through electronic communications media such as videoconferencing, the Internet, or by telephone. *Critical care nurses* provide care to patients with serious, complex, and acute illnesses or injuries that require very close monitoring and extensive medication protocols and therapies. Critical care nurses often work in critical or intensive care hospital units. *Emergency*, or *trauma*, *nurses* work in hospital or stand-alone emergency departments, providing initial assessments and care for patients with life-threatening conditions. Some emergency nurses may become qualified to serve as transport nurses, who provide medical care to patients who are transported by helicopter or airplane to the nearest medical facility. *Holistic nurses* provide care such as acupuncture, massage and aroma therapy, and biofeedback, which are meant to treat patients' mental and spiritual health in addition to their physical health. *Home health care nurses* provide at-home nursing care for patients, often as follow-up care after discharge from a hospital or from a rehabilitation, long-term care, or skilled nursing facility. *Hospice and palliative care nurses* provide care, most often in home or hospice settings, focused on maintaining quality of life for terminally ill patients. *Infusion nurses* administer medications, fluids, and blood to patients through injections into patients' veins. *Long- term care nurses* provide health care services on a recurring basis to patients with chronic physical or mental disorders, often in long-term care or skilled nursing facilities. *Medical-surgical nurses* provide health promotion and basic medical care to patients with various medical and surgical diagnoses. *Occupational health nurses* seek to prevent job-related injuries and illnesses, provide monitoring and emergency care services, and help employers implement health and safety standards. *Perianesthesia nurses* provide preoperative and postoperative care to patients undergoing anesthesia during surgery or other procedure. *Perioperative nurses* assist surgeons by selecting and handling instruments, controlling bleeding, and suturing incisions. Some of these nurses also can specialize in plastic and reconstructive surgery. *Psychiatric-mental health nurses* treat patients with personality and mood disorders. *Radiology nurses* provide care to patients undergoing diagnostic radiation procedures such as ultrasounds, magnetic resonance imaging, and radiation therapy for oncology diagnoses. *Rehabilitation nurses* care for patients with temporary and permanent disabilities. *Transplant nurses* care for both transplant recipients and living donors and monitor signs of organ rejection.

RNs specializing in a particular disease, ailment, or health care condition are employed in virtually all work settings, including physicians' offices, outpatient treatment facilities, home health care agencies, and hospitals. *Addictions nurses* care for patients seeking help with alcohol, drug, tobacco, and other addictions. *Intellectual and developmental disabilities nurses*

provide care for patients with physical, mental, or behavioral disabilities; care may include help with feeding, controlling bodily functions, sitting or standing independently, and speaking or other communication. *Diabetes management nurses* help diabetics to manage their disease by teaching them proper nutrition and showing them how to test blood sugar levels and administer insulin injections. *Genetics nurses* provide early detection screenings, counseling, and treatment of patients with genetic disorders, including cystic fibrosis and Huntington's disease. *HIV/AIDS nurses* care for patients diagnosed with HIV and AIDS. *Oncology nurses* care for patients with various types of cancer and may assist in the administration of radiation and chemotherapies and follow-up monitoring. *Wound, ostomy, and continence nurses* treat patients with wounds caused by traumatic injury, ulcers, or arterial disease; provide postoperative care for patients with openings that allow for alternative methods of bodily waste elimination; and treat patients with urinary and fecal incontinence.

RNs specializing in treatment of a particular organ or body system usually are employed in hospital specialty or critical care units, specialty clinics, and outpatient care facilities. *Cardiovascular nurses* treat patients with coronary heart disease and those who have had heart surgery, providing services such as postoperative rehabilitation. *Dermatology nurses* treat patients with disorders of the skin, such as skin cancer and psoriasis. *Gastroenterology nurses* treat patients with digestive and intestinal disorders, including ulcers, acid reflux disease, and abdominal bleeding. Some nurses in this field also assist in specialized procedures such as endoscopies, which look inside the gastrointestinal tract using a tube equipped with a light and a camera that can capture images of diseased tissue. *Gynecology nurses* provide care to women with disorders of the reproductive system, including endometriosis, cancer, and sexually transmitted diseases. *Nephrology nurses* care for patients with kidney disease caused by diabetes, hypertension, or substance abuse. *Neuroscience nurses* care for patients with dysfunctions of the nervous system, including brain and spinal cord injuries and seizures. *Ophthalmic nurses* provide care to patients with disorders of the eyes, including blindness and glaucoma, and to patients undergoing eye surgery. *Orthopedic nurses* care for patients with muscular and skeletal problems, including arthritis, bone fractures, and muscular dystrophy. *Otorhinolaryngology nurses* care for patients with ear, nose, and throat disorders, such as cleft palates, allergies, and sinus disorders. *Respiratory nurses* provide care to patients with respiratory disorders such as asthma, tuberculosis, and cystic fibrosis. *Urology nurses* care for patients with disorders of the kidneys, urinary tract, and male reproductive organs, including infections, kidney and bladder stones, and cancers.

RNs who specialize by population provide preventive and acute care in all health care settings to the segment of the population in which they specialize, including newborns (neonatology), children and adolescents (pediatrics), adults, and the elderly (gerontology or geriatrics). RNs also may provide basic health care to patients outside of health care settings in such venues as including correctional facilities, schools, summer camps, and the military. Some RNs travel around the United

States and abroad providing care to patients in areas with shortages of health care workers.

Most RNs work as staff nurses as members of a team providing critical health care . However, some RNs choose to become advanced practice nurses, who work independently or in collaboration with physicians, and may focus on the provision of primary care services. *Clinical nurse specialists* provide direct patient care and expert consultations in one of many nursing specialties, such as psychiatric-mental health. *Nurse anesthetists* provide anesthesia and related care before and after surgical, therapeutic, diagnostic and obstetrical procedures. They also provide pain management and emergency services, such as airway management. *Nurse-midwives* provide primary care to women, including gynecological exams, family planning advice, prenatal care, assistance in labor and delivery, and neonatal care. *Nurse practitioners* serve as primary and specialty care providers, providing a blend of nursing and health care services to patients and families. The most common specialty areas for nurse practitioners are family practice, adult practice, women's health, pediatrics, acute care, and geriatrics. However, there are a variety of other specialties that nurse practitioners can choose, including neonatology and mental health. Advanced practice nurses can prescribe medications in all States and in the District of Columbia.

Some nurses have jobs that require little or no direct patient care, but still require an active RN license. *Case managers* ensure that all of the medical needs of patients with severe injuries and severe or chronic illnesses are met. *Forensics nurses* participate in the scientific investigation and treatment of abuse victims, violence, criminal activity, and traumatic accident. *Infection control nurses* identify, track, and control infectious outbreaks in health care facilities and develop programs for outbreak prevention and response to biological terrorism. *Legal nurse consultants* assist lawyers in medical cases by interviewing patients and witnesses, organizing medical records, determining damages and costs, locating evidence, and educating lawyers about medical issues. *Nurse administrators* supervise nursing staff, establish work schedules and budgets, maintain medical supply inventories, and manage resources to ensure high-quality care. *Nurse educators* plan, develop, implement, and evaluate educational programs and curricula for the professional development of student nurses and RNs. *Nurse informaticists* manage and communicate nursing data and information to improve decision making by consumers, patients, nurses, and other health care providers. RNs also may work as health care consultants, public policy advisors, pharmaceutical and medical supply researchers and salespersons, and medical writers and editors.

Work environment. Most RNs work in well-lighted, comfortable health care facilities. Home health and public health nurses travel to patients' homes, schools, community centers, and other sites. RNs may spend considerable time walking, bending, stretching, and standing. Patients in hospitals and nursing care facilities require 24-hour care; consequently, nurses in these institutions may work nights, weekends, and holidays. RNs also may be on call—available to work on short notice. Nurses who work in offices, schools, and other settings that do not provide 24-hour care are more likely to work regular

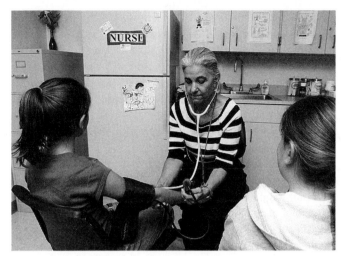

Registered nurses who work in schools provide general health care to students.

business hours. About 21 percent of RNs worked part time in 2006, and 7 percent held more than one job.

Nursing has its hazards, especially in hospitals, nursing care facilities, and clinics, where nurses may be in close contact with individuals who have infectious diseases and with toxic, harmful, or potentially hazardous compounds, solutions, and medications. RNs must observe rigid, standardized guidelines to guard against disease and other dangers, such as those posed by radiation, accidental needle sticks, chemicals used to sterilize instruments, and anesthetics. In addition, they are vulnerable to back injury when moving patients, shocks from electrical equipment, and hazards posed by compressed gases. RNs also may suffer emotional strain from caring for patients suffering unrelieved intense pain, close personal contact with patients' families, the need to make critical decisions, and ethical dilemmas and concerns.

Training, Other Qualifications, and Advancement
The three major educational paths to registered nursing are a bachelor's degree, an associate degree, and a diploma from an approved nursing program. Nurses most commonly enter the occupation by completing an associate degree or bachelor's degree program. Individuals then must complete a national licensing examination in order to obtain a nursing license. Further training or education can qualify nurses to work in specialty areas, and may help improve advancement opportunities.

Education and training. There are three major educational paths to registered nursing—a bachelor's of science degree in nursing (BSN), an associate degree in nursing (ADN), and a diploma. BSN programs, offered by colleges and universities, take about 4 years to complete. In 2006, 709 nursing programs offered degrees at the bachelor's level. ADN programs, offered by community and junior colleges, take about 2 to 3 years to complete. About 850 RN programs granted associate degrees. Diploma programs, administered in hospitals, last about 3 years. Only about 70 programs offered diplomas. Generally, licensed graduates of any of the three types of educational programs qualify for entry-level positions.

Many RNs with an ADN or diploma later enter bachelor's programs to prepare for a broader scope of nursing practice. Often, they can find an entry-level position and then take advantage of tuition reimbursement benefits to work toward a BSN by completing an RN-to-BSN program. In 2006, there were 629 RN-to-BSN programs in the United States. Accelerated master's degree in nursing (MSN) programs also are available by combining 1 year of an accelerated BSN program with 2 years of graduate study. In 2006, there were 149 RN-to-MSN programs.

Accelerated BSN programs also are available for individuals who have a bachelor's or higher degree in another field and who are interested in moving into nursing. In 2006, 197 of these programs were available. Accelerated BSN programs last 12 to 18 months and provide the fastest route to a BSN for individuals who already hold a degree. MSN programs also are available for individuals who hold a bachelor's or higher degree in another field.

Individuals considering nursing should carefully weigh the advantages and disadvantages of enrolling in a BSN or MSN program because, if they do, their advancement opportunities usually are broader. In fact, some career paths are open only to nurses with a bachelor's or master's degree. A bachelor's degree often is necessary for administrative positions and is a prerequisite for admission to graduate nursing programs in research, consulting, and teaching, and all four advanced practice nursing specialties—clinical nurse specialists, nurse anesthetists, nurse-midwives, and nurse practitioners. Individuals who complete a bachelor's receive more training in areas such as communication, leadership, and critical thinking, all of which are becoming more important as nursing care becomes more complex. Additionally, bachelor's degree programs offer more clinical experience in nonhospital settings. Education beyond a bachelor's degree can also help students looking to enter certain fields or increase advancement opportunities. In 2006, 448 nursing schools offered master's degrees, 108 offered doctoral degrees, and 58 offered accelerated BSN-to-doctoral programs.

All four advanced practice nursing specialties require at least a master's degree. Most programs include about 2 years of full-time study and require a BSN degree for entry; some programs require at least 1 to 2 years of clinical experience as an RN for admission. In 2006, there were 342 master's and post-master's programs offered for nurse practitioners, 230 master's and post-master's programs for clinical nurse specialists, 106 programs for nurse anesthetists, and 39 programs for nurse-midwives.

All nursing education programs include classroom instruction and supervised clinical experience in hospitals and other health care facilities. Students take courses in anatomy, physiology, microbiology, chemistry, nutrition, psychology and other behavioral sciences, and nursing. Coursework also includes the liberal arts for ADN and BSN students.

Supervised clinical experience is provided in hospital departments such as pediatrics, psychiatry, maternity, and surgery. A growing number of programs include clinical experience in nursing care facilities, public health departments, home health agencies, and ambulatory clinics.

Licensure and certification. In all States, the District of Columbia, and U.S. territories, students must graduate from an approved nursing program and pass a national licensing examination, known as the NCLEX-RN, in order to obtain a nursing license. Nurses may be licensed in more than one State, either

by examination or by the endorsement of a license issued by another State. The Nurse Licensure Compact Agreement allows a nurse who is licensed and permanently resides in one of the member States to practice in the other member States without obtaining additional licensure. In 2006, 20 states were members of the Compact, while 2 more were pending membership. All States require periodic renewal of licenses, which may require continuing education.

Certification is common, and sometimes required, for the four advanced practice nursing specialties—clinical nurse specialists, nurse anesthetists, nurse-midwives, and nurse practitioners. Upon completion of their educational programs, most advanced practice nurses become nationally certified in their area of specialty. Certification also is available in specialty areas for all nurses. In some States, certification in a specialty is required in order to practice that specialty.

Foreign-educated and foreign-born nurses wishing to work in the United States must obtain a work visa. To obtain the visa, nurses must undergo a federal screening program to ensure that their education and licensure are comparable to that of a U.S. educated nurse, that they have proficiency in written and spoken English, and that they have passed either the Commission on Graduates of Foreign Nursing Schools (CGFNS) Qualifying Examination or the NCLEX-RN. CGFNS administers the VisaScreen Program. (The Commission is an immigration-neutral, nonprofit organization that is recognized internationally as an authority on credentials evaluation in the health care field.) Nurses educated in Australia, Canada (except Quebec), Ireland, New Zealand, and the United Kingdom, or foreign-born nurses who were educated in the United States, are exempt from the language proficiency testing. In addition to these national requirements, foreign-born nurses must obtain state licensure in order to practice in the United States. Each State has its own requirements for licensure.

Other qualifications. Nurses should be caring, sympathetic, responsible, and detail oriented. They must be able to direct or supervise others, correctly assess patients' conditions, and determine when consultation is required. They need emotional stability to cope with human suffering, emergencies, and other stresses.

Advancement. Some RNs start their careers as licensed practical nurses or nursing aides, and then go back to school to receive their RN degree. Most RNs begin as staff nurses in hospitals, and with experience and good performance often move to other settings or are promoted to more responsible positions. In management, nurses can advance from assistant unit manger or head nurse to more senior-level administrative roles of assistant director, director, vice president, or chief nurse. Increasingly, management-level nursing positions require a graduate or an advanced degree in nursing or health services administration. Administrative positions require leadership, communication and negotiation skills, and good judgment.

Some nurses move into the business side of health care. Their nursing expertise and experience on a health care team equip them to manage ambulatory, acute, home-based, and chronic care. Employers—including hospitals, insurance companies, pharmaceutical manufacturers, and managed care organizations, among others—need RNs for health planning and development, marketing, consulting, policy development, and quality assurance. Other nurses work as college and university faculty or conduct research.

Employment

As the largest health care occupation, registered nurses held about 2.5 million jobs in 2006. Hospitals employed the majority of RNs, with 59 percent of jobs. Other industries also employed large shares of workers. About 8 percent of jobs were in offices of physicians, 5 percent in home health care services, 5 percent in nursing care facilities, 4 percent in employment services, and 3 percent in outpatient care centers. The remainder worked mostly in government agencies, social assistance agencies, and educational services. About 21 percent of RNs worked part time.

Job Outlook

Overall job opportunities for registered nurses are expected to be excellent, but may vary by employment and geographic setting. Employment of RNs is expected to grow much faster than the average for all occupations through 2016 and, because the occupation is very large, many new jobs will result. In fact, registered nurses are projected to generate 587,000 new jobs, among the largest number of new jobs for any occupation. Additionally, hundreds of thousands of job openings will result from the need to replace experienced nurses who leave the occupation.

Employment change. Employment of registered nurses is expected to grow 23 percent from 2006 to 2016, much faster than the average for all occupations. Growth will be driven by technological advances in patient care, which permit a greater number of health problems to be treated, and by an increasing emphasis on preventive care. In addition, the number of older people, who are much more likely than younger people to need nursing care, is projected to grow rapidly.

However, employment of RNs will not grow at the same rate in every industry. The projected growth rates for RNs in the industries with the highest employment of these workers are:

	Percent
Offices of physicians	39
Home health care services	39
Outpatient care centers, except mental health and substance abuse	34
Employment services	27
General medical and surgical hospitals, public and private	22
Nursing care facilities	20

Employment is expected to grow more slowly in hospitals— health care's largest industry—than in most other health care industries. While the intensity of nursing care is likely to increase, requiring more nurses per patient, the number of inpatients (those who remain in the hospital for more than 24 hours) is not likely to grow by much. Patients are being discharged earlier, and more procedures are being done on an outpatient basis, both inside and outside hospitals. Rapid growth is expected in hospital outpatient facilities, such as those providing same-day surgery, rehabilitation, and chemotherapy.

More and more sophisticated procedures, once performed only in hospitals, are being performed in physicians' offices and in outpatient care centers, such as freestanding ambulatory surgical and emergency centers. Accordingly, employment is expected to grow very fast in these places as health care in general expands.

Employment in nursing care facilities is expected to grow because of increases in the number of elderly, many of whom require long-term care. However, this growth will be relatively slower than in other health care industries because of the desire of patients to be treated at home or in residential care facilities, and the increasing availability of that type of care. The financial pressure on hospitals to discharge patients as soon as possible should produce more admissions to nursing and residential care facilities and to home health care. Job growth also is expected in units that provide specialized long-term rehabilitation for stroke and head injury patients, as well as units that treat Alzheimer's victims.

Employment in home health care is expected to increase rapidly in response to the growing number of older persons with functional disabilities, consumer preference for care in the home, and technological advances that make it possible to bring increasingly complex treatments into the home. The type of care demanded will require nurses who are able to perform complex procedures.

Rapid employment growth in employment services industry is expected as hospitals, physician's offices, and other health care establishments utilize temporary workers to fill short-term staffing needs. And as the demand for nurses grows, temporary nurses will be needed more often, further contributing to employment growth in this industry.

Job prospects. Overall job opportunities are expected to be excellent for registered nurses. Employers in some parts of the country and in certain employment settings report difficulty in attracting and retaining an adequate number of RNs, primarily because of an aging RN workforce and a lack of younger workers to fill positions. Enrollments in nursing programs at all levels have increased more rapidly in the past few years as students seek jobs with stable employment. However, many qualified applicants are being turned away because of a shortage of nursing faculty. The need for nursing faculty will only increase as many instructors near retirement. Many employers also are relying on foreign-educated nurses to fill vacant positions.

Projections data from the National Employment Matrix

Occupational Title	SOC Code	Employment, 2006	Projected employment, 2016	Change, 2006-2016	
				Number	Percent
Registered nurses	29-1111	2,505,000	3,092,000	587,000	23

NOTE: Data in this table are rounded. See the discussion of the employment projections table in the *Handbook* introductory chapter on *Occupational Information Included in the Handbook.*

Even though overall employment opportunities for all nursing specialties are expected to be excellent, they can vary by employment setting. Despite the slower employment growth in hospitals, job opportunities should still be excellent because of the relatively high turnover of hospital nurses. RNs working in hospitals frequently work overtime and night and weekend shifts and also treat seriously ill and injured patients, all of which can contribute to stress and burnout. Hospital departments in which these working conditions occur most frequently—critical care units, emergency departments, and operating rooms—generally will have more job openings than other departments. To attract and retain qualified nurses, hospitals may offer signing bonuses, family-friendly work schedules, or subsidized training. A growing number of hospitals also are experimenting with online bidding to fill open shifts, in which nurses can volunteer to fill open shifts at premium wages. This can decrease the amount of mandatory overtime that nurses are required to work.

Although faster employment growth is projected in physicians' offices and outpatient care centers, RNs may face greater competition for these positions because they generally offer regular working hours and more comfortable working environments. There also may be some competition for jobs in employment services, despite a high rate of employment growth, because a large number of workers are attracted by the industry's relatively high wages and the flexibility of the work in this industry.

Generally, RNs with at least a bachelor's degree will have better job prospects than those without a bachelor's. In addition, all four advanced practice specialties—clinical nurse specialists, nurse practitioners, nurse-midwives, and nurse anesthetists—will be in high demand, particularly in medically underserved areas such as inner cities and rural areas. Relative to physicians, these RNs increasingly serve as lower-cost primary care providers.

Earnings

Median annual earnings of registered nurses were $57,280 in May 2006. The middle 50 percent earned between $47,710 and $69,850. The lowest 10 percent earned less than $40,250, and the highest 10 percent earned more than $83,440. Median annual earnings in the industries employing the largest numbers of registered nurses in May 2006 were:

Employment services	$64,260
General medical and surgical hospitals	58,550
Home health care services	54,190
Offices of physicians	53,800
Nursing care facilities	52,490

Many employers offer flexible work schedules, child care, educational benefits, and bonuses.

Related Occupations

Because of the number of specialties for registered nurses, and the variety of responsibilities and duties, many other health care occupations are similar in some aspect of the job. Other occupations that deal directly with patients when providing care include licensed practical and licensed vocational nurses, physicians and surgeons, athletic trainers, respiratory therapists, massage therapists, dietitians and nutritionists, occupational therapists, physical therapists, and emergency medical technicians and paramedics. Other occupations that use advanced medical equipment to treat patients include cardiovascular technologists and technicians, diagnostic medical sonographers, radiologic technologists and technicians, radiation therapists, and surgical technologists. Workers who also assist other health care professionals in providing care include nursing, psychiatric, and home health aides; physician assistants; and dental hygienists. Some nurses take on a management role, similar to medical and health services managers.

Sources of Additional Information

For information on a career as a registered nurse and nursing education, contact:

➤ National League for Nursing, 61 Broadway, New York, NY 10006. Internet: **http://www.nln.org**

For information on baccalaureate and graduate nursing education, nursing career options, and financial aid, contact:

➤ American Association of Colleges of Nursing, 1 Dupont Circle NW., Suite 530, Washington, DC 20036. Internet: **http://www.aacn.nche.edu**

For additional information on registered nurses, including credentialing, contact:

➤ American Nurses Association, 8515 Georgia Ave., Suite 400, Silver Spring, MD 20910. Internet: **http://nursingworld.org**

For information on the NCLEX-RN exam and a list of individual State boards of nursing, contact:

➤ National Council of State Boards of Nursing, 111 E. Wacker Dr., Suite 2900, Chicago, IL 60611. Internet: **http://www.ncsbn.org**

For information on the nursing population, including workforce shortage facts, contact:

➤ Bureau of Health Professions, 5600 Fishers LaNE., Room 8-05, Rockville, MD 20857. Internet: **http://bhpr.hrsa.gov**

For information on obtaining U.S. certification and work visas for foreign-educated nurses, contact:

➤ Commission on Graduates of Foreign Nursing Schools, 3600 Market St., Suite 400, Philadelphia, PA 19104. Internet: **http://www.cgfns.org**

For a list of accredited clinical nurse specialist programs, contact:

➤ National Association of Clinical Nurse Specialists, 2090 Linglestown Rd., Suite 107, Harrisburg, PA 17110. Internet: **http://www.nacns.org**

For information on nurse anesthetists, including a list of accredited programs, contact:

➤ American Association of Nurse Anesthetists, 222 Prospect Ave., Park Ridge, IL 60068.

For information on nurse-midwives, including a list of accredited programs, contact:

➤ American College of Nurse-Midwives, 8403 Colesville Rd., Suite 1550, Silver Spring, MD 20910. Internet: **http://www.midwife.org**

For information on nurse practitioners, including a list of accredited programs, contact:

➤ American Academy of Nurse Practitioners, P.O. Box 12846, Austin, TX 78711. Internet: **http://www.aanp.org**

For information on nurse practitioners education, contact:

➤ National Organization of Nurse Practitioner Faculties, 1522 K St. NW., Suite 702, Washington, DC 20005. Internet: **http://www.nonpf.org**

For information on critical care nurses, contact:

➤ American Association of Critical-Care Nurses, 101 Columbia, Aliso Viejo, CA 92656. Internet: **http://www.aacn.org**

For additional information on registered nurses in all fields and specialties, contact:

➤ American Society of Registered Nurses, 1001 Bridgeway, Suite 411, Sausalito, CA 94965. Internet: **http://www.asrn.org**

Respiratory Therapists

(O*NET 29-1126.00, 29-2054.00)

Significant Points

- Job opportunities should be very good.

- An associate degree is the minimum educational requirement, but a bachelor's or master's degree may be important for advancement.

- All States, except Alaska and Hawaii, require respiratory therapists to be licensed.

- Hospitals will account for the vast majority of job openings, but a growing number of openings will arise in other settings.

Nature of the Work

Respiratory therapists and *respiratory therapy technicians*—also known as respiratory care practitioners—evaluate, treat, and care for patients with breathing or other cardiopulmonary disorders. Practicing under the direction of a physician, respiratory therapists assume primary responsibility for all respiratory care therapeutic treatments and diagnostic procedures, including the supervision of respiratory therapy technicians. Respiratory therapy technicians follow specific, well-defined respiratory care procedures under the direction of respiratory therapists and physicians.

In clinical practice, many of the daily duties of therapists and technicians overlap. However, therapists generally have greater responsibility than technicians. For example, respiratory therapists consult with physicians and other health care staff to help develop and modify patient care plans. Respiratory therapists also are more likely to provide complex therapy requiring considerable independent judgment, such as caring for patients on life support in intensive-care units of hospitals. In this *Handbook* statement, the term *respiratory therapist* includes both respiratory therapists and respiratory therapy technicians.

Respiratory therapists evaluate and treat all types of patients, ranging from premature infants whose lungs are not fully developed to elderly people whose lungs are diseased. Respiratory therapists provide temporary relief to patients with chronic asthma or emphysema, and they give emergency care to patients who are victims of a heart attack, stroke, drowning, or shock.

To evaluate patients, respiratory therapists interview them, perform limited physical examinations, and conduct diagnostic tests. For example, respiratory therapists test a patient's breathing capacity and determine the concentration of oxygen and other gases in a patient's blood. They also measure a patient's pH, which indicates the acidity or alkalinity of the blood. To evaluate a patient's lung capacity, respiratory therapists have the patient breathe into an instrument that measures the volume and flow of oxygen during inhalation and exhalation. By comparing the reading with the norm for the patient's age, height, weight, and sex, respiratory therapists can provide information that helps determine whether the patient has any lung deficiencies. To analyze oxygen, carbon dioxide, and blood pH levels, therapists draw an arterial blood sample, place it in a blood gas analyzer, and relay the results to a physician, who then makes treatment decisions.

To treat patients, respiratory therapists use oxygen or oxygen mixtures, chest physiotherapy, and aerosol medications—liquid medications suspended in a gas that forms a mist which is inhaled. They teach patients how to inhale the aerosol properly to ensure its effectiveness. When a patient has difficulty getting enough oxygen into his or her blood, therapists increase the patient's concentration of oxygen by placing an oxygen mask or nasal cannula on the patient and setting the oxygen flow at the level prescribed by a physician. Therapists also connect patients who cannot breathe on their own to ventilators that deliver pressurized oxygen into the lungs. The therapists insert a tube into the patient's trachea, or windpipe; connect the tube to the ventilator; and set the rate, volume, and oxygen concentration of the oxygen mixture entering the patient's lungs.

Therapists perform regular assessments of patients and equipment. If a patient appears to be having difficulty breathing or if the oxygen, carbon dioxide, or pH level of the blood is abnormal, therapists change the ventilator setting according to the doctor's orders or check the equipment for mechanical problems.

Respiratory therapists perform chest physiotherapy on patients to remove mucus from their lungs and make it easier for them to breathe. Therapists place patients in positions that help drain mucus, and then vibrate the patients' rib cages, often by tapping on the chest, and tell the patients to cough. Chest physiotherapy may be needed after surgery, for example, because anesthesia depresses respiration. As a result, physiotherapy may be prescribed to help get the patient's lungs back to normal and to prevent congestion. Chest physiotherapy also helps patients suffering from lung diseases, such as cystic fibrosis, that cause mucus to collect in the lungs.

Therapists who work in home care teach patients and their families to use ventilators and other life-support systems. In addition, these therapists visit patients in their homes to inspect and clean equipment, evaluate the home environment, and ensure that patients have sufficient knowledge of their diseases and the proper use of their medications and equipment. Therapists also make emergency visits if equipment problems arise.

In some hospitals, therapists perform tasks that fall outside their traditional role. Therapists are becoming involved in areas such as pulmonary rehabilitation, smoking cessation counseling, disease prevention, case management, and polysomnogra-

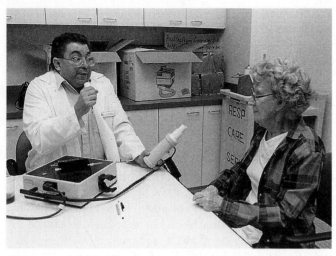

Respiratory therapists sometimes conduct diagnostic tests to evaluate patients.

phy—the diagnosis of breathing disorders during sleep, such as apnea. Respiratory therapists also increasingly treat critical care patients, either as part of surface and air transport teams or as part of rapid-response teams in hospitals.

Work environment. Respiratory therapists generally work between 35 and 40 hours a week. Because hospitals operate around the clock, therapists may work evenings, nights, or weekends. They spend long periods standing and walking between patients' rooms. In an emergency, therapists work under the stress of the situation. Respiratory therapists employed in home health care must travel frequently to patients' homes.

Respiratory therapists are trained to work with gases stored under pressure. Adherence to safety precautions and regular maintenance and testing of equipment minimize the risk of injury. As in many other health occupations, respiratory therapists are exposed to infectious diseases, but by carefully following proper procedures they can minimize the risks.

Training, Other Qualifications, and Advancement
An associate degree is the minimum educational requirement, but a bachelor's or master's degree may be important for advancement. All States, except Alaska and Hawaii, require respiratory therapists to be licensed.

Education and training. An associate degree is required to become a respiratory therapist. Training is offered at the postsecondary level by colleges and universities, medical schools, vocational-technical institutes, and the Armed Forces. Most programs award associate or bachelor's degree and prepare graduates for jobs as advanced respiratory therapists. A limited number of associate degree programs lead to jobs as entry-level respiratory therapists. According to the Commission on Accreditation of Allied Health Education Programs (CAAHEP), 45 entry-level and 334 advanced respiratory therapy programs were accredited in the United States in 2006.

Among the areas of study in respiratory therapy programs are human anatomy and physiology, pathophysiology, chemistry, physics, microbiology, pharmacology, and mathematics. Other courses deal with therapeutic and diagnostic procedures and tests, equipment, patient assessment, cardiopulmonary resuscitation, the application of clinical practice guidelines, patient care outside of hospitals, cardiac and pulmonary rehabilitation,

respiratory health promotion and disease prevention, and medical recordkeeping and reimbursement.

High school students interested in applying to respiratory therapy programs should take courses in health, biology, mathematics, chemistry, and physics. Respiratory care involves basic mathematical problem solving and an understanding of chemical and physical principles. For example, respiratory care workers must be able to compute dosages of medication and calculate gas concentrations.

Licensure and certification. A license is required to practice as a respiratory therapist, except in Alaska and Hawaii. Also, most employers require respiratory therapists to maintain a cardiopulmonary resuscitation (CPR) certification.

Licensure is usually based, in large part, on meeting the requirements for certification from the National Board for Respiratory Care (NBRC). The board offers the Certified Respiratory Therapist (CRT) credential to those who graduate from entry-level or advanced programs accredited by CAAHEP or the Committee on Accreditation for Respiratory Care (CoARC) and who also pass an exam.

The board also awards the Registered Respiratory Therapist (RRT) to CRTs who have graduated from advanced programs and pass two separate examinations. Supervisory positions and intensive-care specialties usually require the RRT.

Other qualifications. Therapists should be sensitive to a patient's physical and psychological needs. Respiratory care practitioners must pay attention to detail, follow instructions, and work as part of a team. In addition, operating advanced equipment requires proficiency with computers.

Advancement. Respiratory therapists advance in clinical practice by moving from general care to the care of critically ill patients who have significant problems in other organ systems, such as the heart or kidneys. Respiratory therapists, especially those with a bachelor's or master's degree, also may advance to supervisory or managerial positions in a respiratory therapy department. Respiratory therapists in home health care and equipment rental firms may become branch managers. Some respiratory therapists advance by moving into teaching positions. Some others use the knowledge gained as a respiratory therapist to work in another industry, such as developing, marketing, or selling pharmaceuticals and medical devices.

Employment
Respiratory therapists held about 122,000 jobs in 2006. About 79 percent of jobs were in hospitals, mainly in departments of respiratory care, anesthesiology, or pulmonary medicine. Most of the remaining jobs were in offices of physicians or other health practitioners, consumer-goods rental firms that supply respiratory equipment for home use, nursing care facilities, and home health care services. Holding a second job is relatively common for respiratory therapists. About 12 percent held another job, compared with 5 percent of workers in all occupations.

Job Outlook
Faster-than-average employment growth is projected for respiratory therapists. Job opportunities should be very good, especially for respiratory therapists with cardiopulmonary care skills or experience working with infants.

Projections data from the National Employment Matrix

Occupational Title	SOC Code	Employment, 2006	Projected employment, 2016	Change, 2006-2016	
				Number	Percent
Respiratory therapists..	—	122,000	145,000	23,000	19
Respiratory therapists..	29-1126	102,000	126,000	23,000	23
Respiratory therapy technicians.................................	29-2054	19,000	19,000	200	1

NOTE: Data in this table are rounded. See the discussion of the employment projections table in the *Handbook* introductory chapter on *Occupational Information Included in the Handbook*.

Employment change. Employment of respiratory therapists is expected to grow 19 percent from 2006 to 2016, faster than the average for all occupations. The increasing demand will come from substantial growth in the middle-aged and elderly population—a development that will heighten the incidence of cardiopulmonary disease. Growth in demand also will result from the expanding role of respiratory therapists in case management, disease prevention, emergency care, and the early detection of pulmonary disorders.

Older Americans suffer most from respiratory ailments and cardiopulmonary diseases such as pneumonia, chronic bronchitis, emphysema, and heart disease. As their numbers increase, the need for respiratory therapists is expected to increase as well. In addition, advances in inhalable medications and in the treatment of lung transplant patients, heart attack and accident victims, and premature infants (many of whom are dependent on a ventilator during part of their treatment) will increase the demand for the services of respiratory care practitioners.

Job prospects. Job opportunities are expected to be very good. The vast majority of job openings will continue to be in hospitals. However, a growing number of openings are expected to be outside of hospitals, especially in home health care services, offices of physicians or other health practitioners, consumer-goods rental firms, or in the employment services industry as a temporary worker in various settings.

Earnings

Median annual earnings of wage-and-salary respiratory therapists were $47,420 in May 2006. The middle 50 percent earned between $40,840 and $56,150. The lowest 10 percent earned less than $35,200, and the highest 10 percent earned more than $64,190.

Median annual earnings of wage-and-salary respiratory therapy technicians were $39,120 in May 2006. The middle 50 percent earned between $32,050 and $46,930. The lowest 10 percent earned less than $25,940, and the highest 10 percent earned more than $56,220.

Related Occupations

Under the supervision of a physician, respiratory therapists administer respiratory care and life support to patients with heart and lung difficulties. Other workers who care for, treat, or train people to improve their physical condition include registered nurses, occupational therapists, physical therapists, radiation therapists, and athletic trainers. Respiratory care practitioners work with advanced medical technology, as do other health care technicians including cardiovascular technologists and technicians, nuclear medicine technologists, radiologic technologists and technicians, and diagnostic medical sonographers.

Sources of Additional Information

Information concerning a career in respiratory care is available from:

➤ American Association for Respiratory Care, 9425 N. MacArthur Blvd., Suite 100, Irving, TX 75063. Internet: **http://www.aarc.org**

For a list of accredited educational programs for respiratory care practitioners, contact either of the following organizations:

➤ Commission on Accreditation for Allied Health Education Programs, 1361 Park St., Clearwater, FL 33756. Internet: **http://www.caahep.org**

➤ Committee on Accreditation for Respiratory Care, 1248 Harwood Rd., Bedford, TX 76021.

Information on gaining credentials in respiratory care and a list of State licensing agencies can be obtained from:

➤ National Board for Respiratory Care, Inc., 18000 W. 105th St., Olathe, KS 66061. Internet: **http://www.nbrc.org**

Speech-Language Pathologists

(O*NET 29-1127.00)

Significant Points

- About half worked in educational services; most others were employed by health care and social assistance facilities.

- A master's degree in speech-language pathology is the standard credential required for licensing in most States.

- Excellent job opportunities are expected.

Nature of the Work

Speech-language pathologists, sometimes called *speech therapists*, assess, diagnose, treat, and help to prevent disorders related to speech, language, cognitive-communication, voice, swallowing, and fluency.

Speech-language pathologists work with people who cannot produce speech sounds or cannot produce them clearly; those with speech rhythm and fluency problems, such as stuttering; people with voice disorders, such as inappropriate pitch or harsh voice; those with problems understanding and producing language; those who wish to improve their communication skills by modifying an accent; and those with cognitive communication impairments, such as attention, memory, and problem solving disorders. They also work with people who have swallowing difficulties.

Speech, language, and swallowing difficulties can result from a variety of causes including stroke, brain injury or deterioration, developmental delays or disorders, learning disabilities, cerebral palsy, cleft palate, voice pathology, mental retardation, hearing loss, or emotional problems. Problems can be congenital, developmental, or acquired. Speech-language pathologists use special instruments and qualitative and quantitative assessment methods, including standardized tests, to analyze and diagnose the nature and extent of impairments.

Speech-language pathologists develop an individualized plan of care, tailored to each patient's needs. For individuals with little or no speech capability, speech-language pathologists may select augmentative or alternative communication methods, including automated devices and sign language, and teach their use. They teach patients how to make sounds, improve their voices, or increase their oral or written language skills to communicate more effectively. They also teach individuals how to strengthen muscles or use compensatory strategies to swallow without choking or inhaling food or liquid. Speech-language pathologists help patients develop, or recover, reliable communication and swallowing skills so patients can fulfill their educational, vocational, and social roles.

Speech-language pathologists keep records on the initial evaluation, progress, and discharge of clients. This helps pinpoint problems, tracks client progress, and justifies the cost of treatment when applying for reimbursement. They counsel individuals and their families concerning communication disorders and how to cope with the stress and misunderstanding that often accompany them. They also work with family members to recognize and change behavior patterns that impede communication and treatment and show them communication-enhancing techniques to use at home.

Most speech-language pathologists provide direct clinical services to individuals with communication or swallowing disorders. In medical facilities, they may perform their job in conjunction with physicians, social workers, psychologists, and other therapists. Speech-language pathologists in schools collaborate with teachers, special educators, interpreters, other school personnel, and parents to develop and implement individual or group programs, provide counseling, and support classroom activities.

Some speech-language pathologists conduct research on how people communicate. Others design and develop equipment or techniques for diagnosing and treating speech problems.

Work environment. Speech-language pathologists usually work at a desk or table in clean comfortable surroundings. In medical settings, they may work at the patient's bedside and assist in positioning the patient. In schools, they may work with students in an office or classroom. Some work in the client's home.

Although the work is not physically demanding, it requires attention to detail and intense concentration. The emotional needs of clients and their families may be demanding. Most full-time speech-language pathologists work 40 hours per week. Those who work on a contract basis may spend a substantial amount of time traveling between facilities.

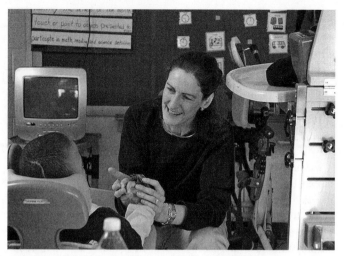

Speech-language pathologists tailor a plan of care for each patient.

Training, Other Qualifications, and Advancement
A master's degree is the most common level of education among speech-language pathologists. Licensure or certification requirements also exist, but vary by State.

Education and training. Most speech-language pathologist jobs require a master's degree. In 2007, more than 230 colleges and universities offered graduate programs in speech-language pathology accredited by the Council on Academic Accreditation in Audiology and Speech-Language Pathology. While graduation from an accredited program is not always required to become a speech-language pathologist, it may be helpful in obtaining a license or may be required to obtain a license in some States.

Speech-language pathology courses cover anatomy, physiology, and the development of the areas of the body involved in speech, language, and swallowing; the nature of disorders; principles of acoustics; and psychological aspects of communication. Graduate students also learn to evaluate and treat speech, language, and swallowing disorders and receive supervised clinical training in communication disorders.

Licensure and certification. In 2007, 47 States regulated speech-language pathologists through licensure or registration. A passing score on the national examination on speech-language pathology, offered through the Praxis Series of the Educational Testing Service, is required. Other usual requirements include 300 to 375 hours of supervised clinical experience and 9 months of postgraduate professional clinical experience. Forty-one States have continuing education requirements for licensure renewal. Medicaid, Medicare, and private health insurers generally require a practitioner to be licensed to qualify for reimbursement.

Only 12 States require this same license to practice in the public schools. The other States issue a teaching license or certificate that typically requires a master's degree from an approved college or university. Some States will grant a provisional teaching license or certificate to applicants with a bachelor's degree, but a master's degree must be earned within 3 to 5 years. A few States grant a full teacher's certificate or license to bachelor's degree applicants.

In some States, the Certificate of Clinical Competence in Speech-Language Pathology (CCC-SLP) offered by the American Speech-Language-Hearing Association meets some or all of the requirements for licensure. To earn a CCC, a person must have a graduate degree from an accredited university, 400 hours of supervised clinical experience, complete a 36-week postgraduate clinical fellowship, and pass the Praxis Series examination in speech-language pathology administered by the Educational Testing Service. Contact your State's Licensing Board for details on your State's requirements.

Other qualifications. Speech-language pathologists should be able to effectively communicate diagnostic test results, diagnoses, and proposed treatment in a manner easily understood by their patients and their families. They must be able to approach problems objectively and be supportive. Because a patient's progress may be slow, patience, compassion, and good listening skills are necessary.

Advancement. As speech-language pathologists gain clinical experience and engage in continuing professional education, many develop expertise with certain populations, such as preschoolers and adolescents, or disorders, such as aphasia and learning disabilities. Some may obtain board recognition in a specialty area, such as child language, fluency, or feeding and swallowing. Experienced clinicians may become mentors or supervisors of other therapists or be promoted to administrative positions.

Employment

Speech-language pathologists held about 110,000 jobs in 2006. About half were employed in educational services, primarily in preschools and elementary and secondary schools. Others were employed in hospitals; offices of other health practitioners, including speech-language pathologists; nursing care facilities; home health care services; individual and family services; outpatient care centers; and child day care centers.

A few speech-language pathologists are self-employed in private practice. They contract to provide services in schools, offices of physicians, hospitals, or nursing care facilities, or work as consultants to industry.

Job Outlook

Average employment growth is projected. Job opportunities are expected to be excellent.

Employment change. Employment of speech-language pathologists is expected to grow 11 percent from 2006 to 2016, about as fast as the average for all occupations. As the members of the baby boom generation continue to age, the possibility of neurological disorders and associated speech, language, and swallowing impairments increases. Medical advances also are improving the survival rate of premature infants and trauma and stroke victims, who then need assessment and sometimes treatment.

Employment in educational services will increase with the growth in elementary and secondary school enrollments, including enrollment of special education students. Federal law guarantees special education and related services to all eligible children with disabilities. Greater awareness of the importance of early identification and diagnosis of speech and language disorders in young children will also increase employment.

In health care facilities, restrictions on reimbursement for therapy services may limit the growth of speech-language pathologist jobs in the near term. However, the long-run demand for therapists should continue to rise as growth in the number of individuals with disabilities or limited function spurs demand for therapy services.

The number of speech-language pathologists in private practice will rise because of the increasing use of contract services by hospitals, schools, and nursing care facilities.

Job prospects. The combination of growth in the occupation and an expected increase in retirements over the coming years should create excellent job opportunities for speech-language pathologists. Opportunities should be particularly favorable for those with the ability to speak a second language, such as Spanish. Job prospects also are expected to be especially favorable for those who are willing to relocate, particularly to areas experiencing difficulty in attracting and hiring speech-language pathologists.

Earnings

Median annual earnings of wage-and-salary speech-language pathologists were $57,710 in May 2006. The middle 50 percent earned between $46,360 and $72,410. The lowest 10 percent earned less than $37,970, and the highest 10 percent earned more than $90,400. Median annual earnings in the industries employing the largest numbers of speech-language pathologists were:

Nursing care facilities $70,180
Offices of other health practitioners.....................................63,240
General medical and surgical hospitals................................61,970
Elementary and secondary schools 53,110

Some employers may reimburse speech-language pathologists for their required continuing education credits.

Related Occupations

Speech-language pathologists specialize in the prevention, diagnosis, and treatment of speech and language problems. Workers in related occupations include audiologists, occupational therapists, optometrists, physical therapists, psychologists, and recreational therapists. Speech-language pathologists in school

Projections data from the National Employment Matrix

Occupational Title	SOC Code	Employment, 2006	Projected employment, 2016	Change, 2006-2016	
				Number	Percent
Speech-language pathologists...	29-1127	110,000	121,000	12,000	11

NOTE: Data in this table are rounded. See the discussion of the employment projections table in the *Handbook* introductory chapter on *Occupational Information Included in the Handbook.*

systems often work closely with special education teachers in assisting students with disabilities.

Sources of Additional Information

State licensing boards can provide information on licensure requirements. State departments of education can supply information on certification requirements for those who wish to work in public schools.

For information on careers in speech-language pathology, a description of the CCC-SLP credential, and a listing of accredited graduate programs in speech-language pathology, contact:

➤ American Speech-Language-Hearing Association, 10801 Rockville Pike, Rockville, MD 20852.
Internet: **http://www.asha.org**

Veterinarians

(O*NET 29-1131.00)

Significant Points

- Veterinarians should have an affinity for animals and the ability to get along with their owners.

- Graduation from an accredited college of veterinary medicine and a State license are required.

- Competition for admission to veterinary school is keen; however, graduates should have excellent job opportunities.

- About 3 out of 4 veterinarians work in private practice.

Nature of the Work

Veterinarians care for the health of pets, livestock, and animals in zoos, racetracks, and laboratories. Some veterinarians use their skills to protect humans against diseases carried by animals and conduct clinical research on human and animal health problems. Others work in basic research, broadening our knowledge of animals and medical science, and in applied research, developing new ways to use knowledge.

Most veterinarians diagnose animal health problems; vaccinate against diseases, such as distemper and rabies; medicate animals suffering from infections or illnesses; treat and dress wounds; set fractures; perform surgery; and advise owners about animal feeding, behavior, and breeding.

According to the American Medical Veterinary Association, more than 70 percent of veterinarians who work in private medical practices predominately, or exclusively, treat small animals. Small-animal practitioners usually care for companion animals, such as dogs and cats, but also treat birds, reptiles, rabbits, ferrets, and other animals that can be kept as pets. About one-fourth of all veterinarians work in mixed animal practices, where they see pigs, goats, cattle, sheep, and some wild animals in addition to companion animals.

A small number of private-practice veterinarians work exclusively with large animals, mostly horses or cattle; some also care for various kinds of food animals. These veterinarians usually drive to farms or ranches to provide veterinary services for herds or individual animals. Much of this work involves preventive care to maintain the health of the animals. These veterinarians test for and vaccinate against diseases and consult with farm or ranch owners and managers regarding animal production, feeding, and housing issues. They also treat and dress wounds, set fractures, and perform surgery, including cesarean sections on birthing animals. Other veterinarians care for zoo, aquarium, or laboratory animals. Veterinarians of all types euthanize animals when necessary.

Veterinarians who treat animals use medical equipment such as stethoscopes, surgical instruments, and diagnostic equipment, including radiographic and ultrasound equipment. Veterinarians working in research use a full range of sophisticated laboratory equipment.

Veterinarians contribute to human as well as animal health. A number of veterinarians work with physicians and scientists as they research ways to prevent and treat various human health problems. For example, veterinarians contributed greatly in conquering malaria and yellow fever, solved the mystery of botulism, produced an anticoagulant used to treat some people with heart disease, and defined and developed surgical techniques for humans, such as hip and knee joint replacements and limb and organ transplants. Today, some determine the effects of drug therapies, antibiotics, or new surgical techniques by testing them on animals.

Some veterinarians are involved in food safety and inspection. Veterinarians who are livestock inspectors, for example, check animals for transmissible diseases, such as E. coli, advise owners on the treatment of their animals, and may quarantine animals. Veterinarians who are meat, poultry, or egg product inspectors examine slaughtering and processing plants, check live animals and carcasses for disease, and enforce government regulations regarding food purity and sanitation. More veterinarians are finding opportunities in food security as they ensure that the Nation has abundant and safe food supplies. Veterinarians involved in food security often work along the Nation's borders as animal and plant health inspectors, where they examine imports and exports of animal products to prevent disease here and in foreign countries. Many of these workers are employed by the Department of Homeland Security or the Department of Agriculture's Animal and Plant Health Inspection Service division.

Work environment. Veterinarians in private or clinical practice often work long hours in a noisy indoor environment. Sometimes they have to deal with emotional or demanding pet owners. When working with animals that are frightened or in pain, veterinarians risk being bitten, kicked, or scratched.

Veterinarians in large-animal practice spend time driving between their office and farms or ranches. They work outdoors in all kinds of weather and may have to treat animals or perform surgery, under unsanitary conditions.

Veterinarians working in nonclinical areas, such as public health and research, have working conditions similar to those of other professionals in those lines of work. These veterinarians enjoy clean, well-lit offices or laboratories and spend much of their time dealing with people rather than animals.

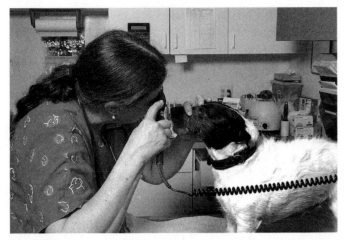

Most veterinarians perform clinical work in private practices on small animals.

Veterinarians often work long hours. Those in group practices may take turns being on call for evening, night, or weekend work; solo practitioners may work extended and weekend hours, responding to emergencies or squeezing in unexpected appointments.

Training, Other Qualifications, and Advancement
Veterinarians must obtain a Doctor of Veterinary Medicine degree and a State license. There is keen competition for admission to veterinary school.

Education and training. Prospective veterinarians must graduate with a Doctor of Veterinary Medicine (D.V.M. or V.M.D.) degree from a 4-year program at an accredited college of veterinary medicine. There are 28 colleges in 26 States that meet accreditation standards set by the Council on Education of the American Veterinary Medical Association (AVMA).

The prerequisites for admission to veterinary programs vary. Many programs do not require a bachelor's degree for entrance, but all require a significant number of credit hours—ranging from 45 to 90 semester hours—at the undergraduate level. However, most of the students admitted have completed an undergraduate program and earned a bachelor's degree. Applicants without a degree face a difficult task gaining admittance.

Preveterinary courses should emphasize the sciences. Veterinary medical colleges typically require applicants to have taken classes in organic and inorganic chemistry, physics, biochemistry, general biology, animal biology, animal nutrition, genetics, vertebrate embryology, cellular biology, microbiology, zoology, and systemic physiology. Some programs require calculus; some require only statistics, college algebra and trigonometry, or pre-calculus. Most veterinary medical colleges also require some courses in English or literature, other humanities, and the social sciences. Increasingly, courses in general business management and career development have become a standard part of the curriculum to teach new graduates how to effectively run a practice.

In addition to satisfying preveterinary course requirements, applicants must submit test scores from the Graduate Record Examination (GRE), the Veterinary College Admission Test (VCAT), or the Medical College Admission Test (MCAT), depending on the preference of the college to which they are applying. Currently, 22 schools require the GRE, 4 require the VCAT, and 2 accept the MCAT.

There is keen competition for admission to veterinary school. The number of accredited veterinary colleges has remained largely the same since 1983, but the number of applicants has risen significantly. Only about 1 in 3 applicants was accepted in 2005.

New graduates with a Doctor of Veterinary Medicine degree may begin to practice veterinary medicine once they receive their license, but many new graduates choose to enter a 1-year internship. Interns receive a small salary but often find that their internship experience leads to better paying opportunities later, relative to those of other veterinarians. Veterinarians who then seek board certification also must complete a 3- to 4-year residency program that provides intensive training in one of the 20 AVMA-recognized veterinary specialties including internal medicine, oncology, pathology, dentistry, nutrition, radiology, surgery, dermatology, anesthesiology, neurology, cardiology, ophthalmology, preventive medicine, and exotic small-animal medicine.

Licensure. All States and the District of Columbia require that veterinarians be licensed before they can practice. The only exemptions are for veterinarians working for some Federal agencies and some State governments. Licensing is controlled by the States and is not strictly uniform, although all States require the successful completion of the D.V.M. degree—or equivalent education—and a passing grade on a national board examination, the North American Veterinary Licensing Exam. This 8-hour examination consists of 360 multiple-choice questions covering all aspects of veterinary medicine as well as visual materials designed to test diagnostic skills.

The Educational Commission for Foreign Veterinary Graduates grants certification to individuals trained outside the United States who demonstrate that they meet specified requirements for English language and clinical proficiency. This certification fulfills the educational requirement for licensure in all States.

Most States also require candidates to pass a State jurisprudence examination covering State laws and regulations. Some States do additional testing on clinical competency as well. There are few reciprocal agreements between States, veterinarians who wish to practice in a different State usually must first pass that State's examinations.

Other qualifications. When deciding whom to admit, some veterinary medical colleges place heavy consideration on a candidate's veterinary and animal experience. Formal experience, such as work with veterinarians or scientists in clinics, agribusiness, research, or some area of health science, is particularly advantageous. Less formal experience, such as working with animals on a farm or ranch or at a stable or animal shelter, also can be helpful. Students must demonstrate ambition and an eagerness to work with animals.

Prospective veterinarians must have good manual dexterity. They should have an affinity for animals and the ability to get along with their owners, especially pet owners, who usually have strong bonds with their pets. Veterinarians who intend to go into private practice should possess excellent communication and business skills, because they will need to manage their practice and employees successfully and to promote, market, and sell their services.

Advancement. Most veterinarians begin as employees in established group practices. Despite the substantial financial investment in equipment, office space, and staff, many veterinarians with experience eventually set up their own practice or purchase an established one.

Newly trained veterinarians can become U.S. Government meat and poultry inspectors, disease-control workers, animal welfare and safety workers, epidemiologists, research assistants, or commissioned officers in the U.S. Public Health Service or various branches of the U.S. Armed Forces. A State license may be required.

Nearly all States have continuing education requirements for licensed veterinarians. Requirements differ by State and may involve attending a class or otherwise demonstrating knowledge of recent medical and veterinary advances.

Employment

Veterinarians held about 62,000 jobs in 2006. According to the American Veterinary Medical Association, about 3 out of 4 veterinarians were employed in a solo or group practice. Most others were salaried employees of another veterinary practice. Data from the U.S. Bureau of Labor Statistics show that the Federal Government employed about 1,400 civilian veterinarians, chiefly in the U.S. Departments of Agriculture, Health and Human Services, and, increasingly, Homeland Security. Other employers of veterinarians are State and local governments, colleges of veterinary medicine, medical schools, research laboratories, animal food companies, and pharmaceutical companies. A few veterinarians work for zoos, but most veterinarians caring for zoo animals are private practitioners who contract with the zoos to provide services, usually on a part-time basis.

In addition, many veterinarians hold veterinary faculty positions in colleges and universities and are classified as teachers. (See the statement on teachers—postsecondary elsewhere in the *Handbook*.)

Job Outlook

Employment is expected to increase much faster than average. Excellent job opportunities are expected.

Employment change. Employment of veterinarians is expected to increase 35 percent over the 2006-16 decade, much faster than the average for all occupations. Veterinarians usually practice in animal hospitals or clinics and care primarily for companion animals. Recent trends indicate particularly strong interest in cats as pets. Faster growth of the cat population is expected to increase the demand for feline medicine and veterinary services, while demand for veterinary care for dogs should continue to grow at a more modest pace.

Many pet owners are relatively affluent and consider their pets a member of the family. These owners are becoming more aware of the availability of advanced care and are more willing to pay for intensive veterinary care than owners in the past. Furthermore, the number of pet owners purchasing pet insurance is rising, increasing the likelihood that considerable money will be spent on veterinary care.

More pet owners also will take advantage of nontraditional veterinary services, such as cancer treatment and preventive dental care. Modern veterinary services have caught up to human medicine; certain procedures, such as hip replacement, kidney transplants, and blood transfusions, which were once only available for humans, are now available for animals.

Continued support for public health and food and animal safety, national disease control programs, and biomedical research on human health problems will contribute to the demand for veterinarians, although the number of positions in these areas is limited. Homeland security also may provide opportunities for veterinarians involved in efforts to maintain abundant food supplies and minimize animal diseases in the U.S. and in foreign countries.

Job prospects. Excellent job opportunities are expected because there are only 28 accredited schools of veterinary medicine in the United States, resulting in a limited number of graduates—about 2,700—each year. However, applicants face keen competition for admission to veterinary school.

New graduates continue to be attracted to companion-animal medicine because they prefer to deal with pets and to live and work near heavily populated areas, where most pet owners live. Employment opportunities are good in cities and suburbs, but even better in rural areas because fewer veterinarians compete to work there.

Beginning veterinarians may take positions requiring evening or weekend work to accommodate the extended hours of operation that many practices are offering. Some veterinarians take salaried positions in retail stores offering veterinary services. Self-employed veterinarians usually have to work hard and long to build a sufficient client base.

The number of jobs for large-animal veterinarians is likely to grow more slowly than jobs for companion-animal veterinarians. Nevertheless, job prospects should be better for veterinarians who specialize in farm animals because of lower earnings in the farm-animal specialty and because many veterinarians do not want to work in rural or isolated areas.

Veterinarians with training in food safety and security, animal health and welfare, and public health and epidemiology should have the best opportunities for a career in the Federal Government.

Earnings

Median annual earnings of veterinarians were $71,990 in May 2006. The middle 50 percent earned between $56,450 and $94,880. The lowest 10 percent earned less than $43,530, and the highest 10 percent earned more than $133,150.

Projections data from the National Employment Matrix

Occupational Title	SOC Code	Employment, 2006	Projected employment, 2016	Change, 2006-2016	
				Number	Percent
Veterinarians	29-1131	62,000	84,000	22,000	35

NOTE: Data in this table are rounded. See the discussion of the employment projections table in the *Handbook* introductory chapter on *Occupational Information Included in the Handbook.*

The average annual salary for veterinarians in the Federal Government was $84,335 in 2007.

According to a survey by the American Veterinary Medical Association, average starting salaries of veterinary medical college graduates in 2006 varied by type of practice as follows:

Large animals, exclusively	$61,029
Small animals, predominantly	57,117
Small animals, exclusively	56,241
Private clinical practice	55,031
Large animals, predominantly	53,397
Mixed animals	52,254
Equine (horses)	40,130

Related Occupations

Veterinarians prevent, diagnose, and treat diseases, disorders, and injuries in animals. Those who do similar work for humans include chiropractors, dentists, optometrists, physicians and surgeons, and podiatrists. Veterinarians have extensive training in physical and life sciences, and some do scientific and medical research, as do biological scientists and medical scientists.

Animal care and service workers and veterinary technologists and technicians also work extensively with animals. Like veterinarians, they must have patience and feel comfortable with animals. However, the level of training required for these occupations is substantially less than that needed by veterinarians.

Sources of Additional Information

For additional information on careers in veterinary medicine, a list of U.S. schools and colleges of veterinary medicine, and ac-creditation policies, send a letter-size, self-addressed, stamped envelope to:

➤ American Veterinary Medical Association, 1931 N. Meacham Rd., Suite 100, Schaumburg, IL 60173.
Internet: **http://www.avma.org**

For information on veterinary education, contact:
➤ Association of American Veterinary Medical Colleges, 1101 Vermont Ave. NW., Suite 301, Washington, DC 20005.
Internet: **http://www.aavmc.org**

For information on scholarships, grants, and loans, contact the financial aid officer at the veterinary schools to which you wish to apply.

For information on veterinarians working in zoos, see the Occupational Outlook Quarterly article "Wild jobs with wildlife," online at:
http://www.bls.gov/opub/ooq/2001/spring/art01.pdf.

Information on obtaining a veterinary position with the Federal Government is available from the Office of Personnel Management through USAJOBS, the Federal Government's official employment information system. This resource for locating and applying for job opportunities can be accessed through the Internet at **http://www.usajobs.opm.gov** or through an interactive voice response telephone system at (703) 724-1850 or TDD (978) 461-8404. These numbers are not toll free, and charges may result. For advice on how to find and apply for Federal jobs, see the Occupational Outlook Quarterly article "How to get a job in the Federal Government," online at:
http://www.bls.gov/opub/ooq/2004/summer/art01.pdf

Health Technologists and Technicians

Athletic Trainers

(O*NET 29-9091.00)

Significant Points

- Long hours, sometimes including nights and weekends, are common.

- A bachelor's degree is usually the minimum requirement, but many athletic trainers hold a master's or doctoral degree.

- Employment is projected to grow much faster than average.

- Job prospects should be good in the health care industry, but competition is expected for positions with sports teams.

Nature of the Work

Athletic trainers help prevent and treat injuries for people of all ages. Their clients include everyone from professional athletes to industrial workers. Recognized by the American Medical Association as allied health professionals, athletic trainers specialize in the prevention, assessment, treatment, and rehabilitation of musculoskeletal injuries. Athletic trainers often are one of the first heath care providers on the scene when injuries occur, and therefore they must be able to recognize, evaluate, and assess injuries and provide immediate care when needed. They also are heavily involved in the rehabilitation and reconditioning of injuries. Athletic trainers should not be confused with fitness trainers or personal trainers, who are not health care workers, but rather train people to become physically fit. (Fitness workers are discussed elsewhere in the *Handbook*.)

Athletic trainers often help prevent injuries by advising on the proper use of equipment and applying protective or injury-preventive devices such as tape, bandages, and braces. Injury prevention also often includes educating people on what they should do to avoid putting themselves at risk for injuries.

Athletic trainers work under the supervision of a licensed physician, and in cooperation with other health care providers. The level of medical supervision varies, depending upon the setting. Some athletic trainers meet with the team physician or consulting physician once or twice a week; others interact with a physician every day. The extent of the supervision ranges from discussing specific injuries and treatment options with a physician to performing evaluations and treatments as directed by a physician.

Athletic trainers often have administrative responsibilities. These may include regular meetings with an athletic director or other administrative officer to deal with budgets, purchasing, policy implementation, and other business-related issues.

Work environment. The work of athletic trainers requires frequent interaction with others. This includes consulting with physicians as well as frequent contact with athletes and patients to discuss and administer treatments, rehabilitation programs, injury-preventive practices, and other health-related issues. Many athletic trainers work indoors most of the time; others, especially those in some sports-related jobs, spend much of their time working outdoors. The job also might require standing for long periods, working with medical equipment or machinery, and being able to walk, run, kneel, crouch, stoop, or crawl. Travel may be required.

Schedules vary by work setting. Athletic trainers in nonsports settings generally have an established schedule—usually about 40 to 50 hours per week—with nights and weekends off. Athletic trainers working in hospitals and clinics may spend part of their time working at other locations doing outreach. Most commonly, these outreach programs include conducting athletic training services and speaking at high schools, colleges, and commercial businesses.

Athletic trainers in sports settings have schedules that are longer and more variable. These athletic trainers must be present for team practices and games, which often are on evenings and weekends, and their schedules can change on short notice when games and practices have to be rescheduled. As a result, athletic trainers in sports settings may regularly work 6 or 7 days per week, including late hours.

In high schools, athletic trainers who also teach may work 60 to 70 hours a week, or more. In National Collegiate Athletic Association Division I colleges and universities, athletic trainers generally work with one team; when that team's sport is in season, working at least 50 to 60 hours a week is common. Athletic trainers in smaller colleges and universities often work with several teams and have teaching responsibilities. During

the off-season, a 40-hour to 50-hour work week may be normal in most settings. Athletic trainers for professional sports teams generally work the most hours per week. During training camps, practices, and competitions, they may be required to work up to 12 hours a day.

There is some stress involved with being an athletic trainer, as there is with most health-related occupations. Athletic trainers are responsible for their clients' health, and sometimes have to make quick decisions that could affect the health or career of their clients. Athletics trainers also can be affected by the pressure to win that is typical of competitive sports teams.

Training, Other Qualifications, and Advancement

A bachelor's degree is usually the minimum requirement to work as an athletic trainer, but many athletic trainers hold a master's or doctoral degree. In 2006, 46 States required athletic trainers to be licensed or hold some form of registration.

Education and training. A bachelor's degree from an accredited college or university is required for almost all jobs as an athletic trainer. In 2006, there were more than 350 accredited programs nationwide. Students in these programs are educated both in the classroom and in clinical settings. Formal education includes many science and health-related courses, such as human anatomy, physiology, nutrition, and biomechanics.

According to the National Athletic Trainers Association, 68 percent of athletic trainers have a master's or doctoral degree. Athletic trainers may need a master's or higher degree to be eligible for some positions, especially those in colleges and universities, and to increase their advancement opportunities. Because some positions in high schools involve teaching along with athletic trainer responsibilities, a teaching certificate or license could be required.

Licensure and certification. In 2006, 46 States required athletic trainers to be licensed or registered; this requires certification from the Board of Certification, Inc. (BOC). For certification, athletic trainers need a bachelor's degree from an accredited athletic training program. In addition, a successful candidate for BOC certification must pass a rigorous examination. To retain certification, credential holders must continue taking medical-related courses and adhere to the BOC standards of practice. In States where licensure is not required, certification is voluntary but may be helpful for those seeking jobs and advancement.

Other qualifications. Because all athletic trainers deal directly with a variety of people, they need good social and communication skills. They should be able to manage difficult situations and the stress associated with them, such as when disagreements arise with coaches, clients, or parents regarding suggested treatment. Athletic trainers also should be organized, be able to manage time wisely, be inquisitive, and have a strong desire to help people.

Advancement. There are a number ways for athletic trainers to advance or move into related positions. Assistant athletic trainers may become head athletic trainers and, eventually, athletic directors. Athletic trainers also might enter a physician group practice and assume a management role. Some athletic trainers move into sales and marketing positions, using their

Athletic trainers apply protective devices such as tape, bandages, and braces to help prevent injuries.

athletic trainer expertise to sell medical and athletic equipment.

Employment

Athletic trainers held about 17,000 jobs in 2006 and are found in every part of the country. Most athletic trainer jobs are related to sports, although an increasing number also work in nonsports settings. About 34 percent of athletic trainers worked in health care, including jobs in hospitals, offices of physicians, and offices of other health practitioners. Another 34 percent were found in public and private educational services, primarily in colleges, universities, and high schools. About 20 percent worked in fitness and recreational sports centers.

Job Outlook

Employment is projected to grow much faster than average. Job prospects should be good in the health care industry, but competition is expected for positions with sports teams.

Employment change. Employment of athletic trainers is expected to grow 24 percent from 2006 to 2016, much faster than the average for all occupations. Job growth will be concentrated in the health care industry, including hospitals and offices of health practitioners. Fitness and recreation sports centers also will provide many new jobs, as these establishments become more common and continue to need athletic trainers to care for their clients. Growth in positions with sports teams will be somewhat slower, however, as most professional sports clubs and colleges and universities already have complete athletic training staffs.

The demand for health care should grow dramatically as the result of advances in technology, increasing emphasis on preventive care, and an increasing number of older people who are more likely to need medical care. Athletic trainers will benefit from this expansion because they provide a cost-effective way to increase the number of health professionals in an office or other setting.

Also, employers increasingly emphasize sports medicine, in which an immediate responder, such as an athletic trainer, is on site to help prevent injuries and provide immediate treatment for any injuries that do occur. Increased licensure requirements and regulation has led to a greater acceptance of athletic trainers as qualified health care providers. As a result, third-party reimbursement is expected to continue to grow for athletic training services.

As athletic trainers continue to expand their services, more employers are expected to use these workers to realize the cost savings of providing health care in-house. There should be strong demand for athletic trainers in settings outside the sports world, especially those that focus on health care. Continuing efforts to have an athletic trainer in every high school reflect concern for the health of student-athletes as well as efforts to provide more funding for schools, and may lead to growth in the number of athletic trainers employed in high schools.

Job prospects. Job prospects should be good for athletic trainers in the health care industry. Those looking for a position with a sports team, however, may face competition. Turnover among athletic trainers is limited. When working with sports teams, many athletic trainers prefer to continue to work with the same coaches, administrators, and players when a good working relationship already exists.

Because of relatively low turnover, the settings with the best job prospects will be the ones that are expected to have the most job growth, primarily positions in the heath care industry and fitness and recreational sports centers. Additional job opportunities are expected in elementary and secondary schools as more positions are created. Some of these positions also will require teaching responsibilities. There will be more competition for positions within colleges and universities as well as professional sports clubs.

The occupation is expected to continue to change over the next decade, including more administrative responsibilities, adapting to new technology, and working with larger populations, and job seekers must be able to adapt to these changes.

Earnings

Most athletic trainers work in full-time positions, and typically receive benefits. The salary of an athletic trainer depends on experience and job responsibilities, and varies by job setting. Median annual earnings of wage-and-salary athletic trainers were $36,560 in May 2006. The middle 50 percent earned between $28,920 and $45,690. The lowest 10 percent earned less than $21,940, while the top 10 percent earned more than $57,580.

Many employers pay for some of the continuing education required for athletic trainers to remain certified, although the amount covered varies from employer to employer.

Related Occupations

The American Medical Association recognizes athletic trainers as allied health professionals. They work under the direction of physicians and provide immediate and ongoing care for injuries. Also, they provide education and advice on the prevention of injuries and work closely with injured patients to rehabilitate and recondition injuries, often through therapy. Other occupations that may require similar responsibilities include emergency medical technicians and paramedics, physical therapists, physician assistants, registered nurses, licensed practical and licensed vocational nurses, recreational therapists, occupational therapists, respiratory therapists, chiropractors, podiatrists, and massage therapists.

There also are opportunities for athletic trainers to join the military, although they would not be classified as an athletic trainer. Enlisted soldiers and officers who are athletic trainers

Projections data from the National Employment Matrix

Occupational Title	SOC Code	Employment, 2006	Projected employment, 2016	Change, 2006-2016	
				Number	Percent
Athletic trainers..	29-9091	17,000	21,000	4,200	24

NOTE: Data in this table are rounded. See the discussion of the employment projections table in the *Handbook* introductory chapter on *Occupational Information Included in the Handbook.*

are usually placed in another program, such as health educator or training specialist, in which their skills are useful. (For information on military careers, see the *Handbook* statement on job opportunities in the Armed Forces.)

Sources of Additional Information

For further information on careers in athletic training, contact:
➤ National Athletic Trainers Association, 2952 Stemmons Freeway, Dallas, TX 75247. Internet: **http://www.nata.org**

For further information on certification, contact:
➤ Board of Certification, Inc., 4223 South 143rd Circle, Omaha, NE 68137. Internet: **http://www.bocatc.org**

Cardiovascular Technologists and Technicians

(O*NET 29-2031.00)

Significant Points

- Employment is expected to grow much faster than average; technologists and technicians trained to perform certain procedures will be in particular demand.

- About 3 out of 4 jobs are in hospitals.

- The vast majority of workers complete a 2-year junior or community college program.

Nature of the Work

Cardiovascular technologists and technicians assist physicians in diagnosing and treating cardiac (heart) and peripheral vascular (blood vessel) ailments.

Cardiovascular technologists and technicians schedule appointments perform ultrasound or cardiovascular procedures, review doctors' interpretations and patient files, and monitor patients' heart rates. They also operate and care for testing equipment, explain test procedures, and compare findings to a standard to identify problems. Other day-to-day activities vary significantly between specialties.

Cardiovascular technologists may specialize in any of three areas of practice: invasive cardiology, echocardiography, or vascular technology.

Invasive cardiology. Cardiovascular technologists specializing in invasive procedures are called *cardiology technologists*. They assist physicians with cardiac catheterization procedures in which a small tube, or catheter, is threaded through a patient's artery from a spot on the patient's groin to the heart. The procedure can determine whether a blockage exists in the blood vessels that supply the heart muscle. The procedure also can help to diagnose other problems. Part of the procedure may involve balloon angioplasty, which can be used to treat blockages of blood vessels or heart valves without the need for heart surgery. Cardiology technologists assist physicians as they insert a catheter with a balloon on the end to the point of the obstruction. Another procedure using the catheter is electrophysiology test, which help locate the specific areas of heart tissue that give rise to the abnormal electrical impulses that cause arrhythmias.

Technologists prepare patients for cardiac catheterization by first positioning them on an examining table and then shaving, cleaning, and administering anesthesia to the top of their leg near the groin. During the procedures, they monitor patients' blood pressure and heart rate with EKG equipment and notify the physician if something appears to be wrong. Technologists also may prepare and monitor patients during open-heart surgery and during the insertion of pacemakers and stents that open up blockages in arteries to the heart and major blood vessels.

Noninvasive technology. Technologists who specialize in vascular technology or echocardiography perform noninvasive tests using. Tests are called "noninvasive" if they do not require the insertion of probes or other instruments into the patient's body. For example, procedures such as Doppler ultrasound transmit high-frequency sound waves into areas of the patient's body and then processes reflected echoes of the sound waves to form an image. Technologists view the ultrasound image on a screen and may record the image on videotape or photograph it for interpretation and diagnosis by a physician. As the technologist uses the instrument to perform scans and record images, technologists check the image on the screen for subtle differences between healthy and diseased areas, decide which images to include in the report to the physician, and judge whether the images are satisfactory for diagnostic purposes. They also explain the procedure to patients, record any additional medical history the patient relates, select appropriate equipment settings, and change the patient's position as necessary. (See the statement on diagnostic medical sonographers elsewhere in the *Handbook* to learn more about other sonographers.)

Vascular technology. Technicians who assist physicians in the diagnosis of disorders affecting the circulation are known as *vascular technologists* or *vascular sonographers*. Vascular technologists complete patients' medical history, evaluate pulses and assess blood flow in arteries and veins by listening to the vascular flow sounds for abnormalities, and assure the appropriate vascular test has been ordered. Then they perform a noninvasive procedure using ultrasound instruments to record vascular information such as vascular blood flow, blood pressure, oxygen saturation, cerebral circulation, peripheral circulation, and abdominal circulation. Many of these tests are performed during or immediately after surgery. Vascular technologists then provide a summary of findings to the physician to aid in patient diagnosis and management.

Echocardiography. This area of practice includes giving electrocardiograms (EKGs) and sonograms of the heart. Cardiovascular technicians who specialize in EKGs, stress testing, and those who perform Holter monitor procedures are known as cardiographic or *electrocardiograph* (or *EKG*) *technicians*.

To take a basic EKG, which traces electrical impulses transmitted by the heart, technicians attach electrodes to the patient's chest, arms, and legs, and then manipulate switches on an EKG machine to obtain a reading. An EKG is printed out for interpretation by the physician. This test is done before most kinds of surgery or as part of a routine physical examination, especially on persons who have reached middle age or who have a history of cardiovascular problems.

EKG technicians with advanced training perform Holter monitor and stress testing. For Holter monitoring, technicians place electrodes on the patient's chest and attach a portable EKG monitor to the patient's belt. Following 24 or more hours of normal activity by the patient, the technician removes a tape from the monitor and places it in a scanner. After checking the quality of the recorded impulses on an electronic screen, the technician usually prints the information from the tape for analysis by a physician. Physicians use the output from the scanner to diagnose heart ailments, such as heart rhythm abnormalities or problems with pacemakers.

For a treadmill stress test, EKG technicians document the patient's medical history, explain the procedure, connect the patient to an EKG monitor, and obtain a baseline reading and resting blood pressure. Next, they monitor the heart's performance while the patient is walking on a treadmill, gradually increasing the treadmill's speed to observe the effect of increased exertion. Like vascular technologists and cardiac sonographers, cardiographic technicians who perform EKG, Holter monitor, and stress tests are known as "noninvasive" technicians.

Technologists who use ultrasound to examine the heart chambers, valves, and vessels are referred to as *cardiac sonographers*, or *echocardiographers*. They use ultrasound instrumentation to create images called echocardiograms. An echocardiogram may be performed while the patient is either resting or physically active. Technologists may administer medication to physically active patients to assess their heart function. Cardiac sonographers also may assist physicians who perform transesophageal echocardiography, which involves placing a tube in the patient's esophagus to obtain ultrasound images.

Work environment. Cardiovascular technologists and technicians spend a lot of time walking and standing. Heavy lifting may be involved to move equipment or transfer patients. These workers wear heavy protective aprons while conducting some procedures. Those who work in catheterization laboratories may face stressful working conditions because they are in close

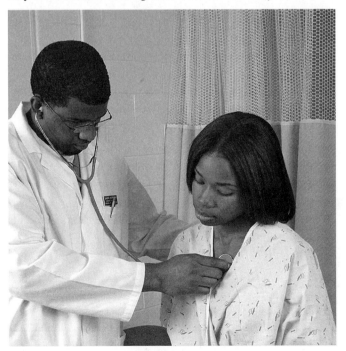

About 3 out of 4 cardiovascular technologists and technicians work in hospitals.

contact with patients with serious heart ailments. For example, some patients may encounter complications that have life-or-death implications.

Some cardiovascular technologists and technicians may have the potential for radiation exposure, which is kept to a minimum by strict adherence to radiation safety guidelines. In addition, those who use sonography can be at an increased risk for musculoskeletal disorders such as carpel tunnel syndrome, neck and back strain, and eye strain. However, greater use of ergonomic equipment and an increasing awareness will continue to minimize such risks.

Technologists and technicians generally work a 5-day, 40-hour week that may include weekends. Those in catheterization laboratories tend to work longer hours and may work evenings. They also may be on call during the night and on weekends.

Training, Other Qualifications, and Advancement

The most common level of education completed by cardiovascular technologists and technicians is an associate degree. Certification, although not required in all cases, is available.

Education and training. Although a few cardiovascular technologists, vascular technologists, and cardiac sonographers are currently trained on the job, most receive training in 2- to 4-year programs. The majority of technologists complete a 2-year junior or community college program, but 4-year programs are increasingly available. The first year is dedicated to core courses and is followed by a year of specialized instruction in either invasive, noninvasive cardiovascular, or noninvasive vascular technology. Those who are qualified in an allied health profession need to complete only the year of specialized instruction.

The Joint Review Committee on Education in Cardiovascular Technology reviews education programs seeking accreditation. The Commission on Accreditation of Allied Health Professionals (CAAHEP) accredits these education programs; as of 2006, there were 31 programs accredited in cardiovascular technology in the United States. Similarly, those who want to study echocardiography or vascular sonography may also attend CAAHEP accredited programs in diagnostic medical sonography. In 2006, there were 147 diagnostic medical sonography programs accredited by CAAHEP. Those who attend these accredited programs are eligible to obtain professional certification.

Unlike most other cardiovascular technologists and technicians, most EKG technicians are trained on the job by an EKG supervisor or a cardiologist. On-the-job training usually lasts about 8 to 16 weeks. Most employers prefer to train people already in the health care field—nursing aides, for example. Some EKG technicians are students enrolled in 2-year programs to become technologists, working part time to gain experience and make contact with employers. One-year certification programs exist for basic EKGs, Holter monitoring, and stress testing.

Licensure and certification. Some States require workers in this occupation to be licensed. For information on a particular State, contact that State's medical board. Certification is available from two organizations: Cardiovascular Credentialing International (CCI) and the American Registry of Diagnostic Medical Sonographers (ARDMS). The CCI offers four certifications—Certified Cardiographic Technician (CCT), Registered Cardiac Sonographer (RCS), Registered Vascular Specialist (RVS), and Registered Cardiovascular Invasive Specialist (RCIS). The ARDMS offers Registered Diagnostic Cardiac Sonographer (RDCS) and Registered Vascular Technologist (RVT) credentials. Some States require certification as part of licensure. In other States, certification is not required but many employers prefer it.

Other qualifications. Cardiovascular technologists and technicians must be reliable, have mechanical aptitude, and be able to follow detailed instructions. A pleasant, relaxed manner for putting patients at ease is an asset. They must be articulate as they must communicate technically with physicians and also explain procedures simply to patients.

Advancement. Technologists and technicians can advance to higher levels of the profession as many institutions structure the occupation with multiple levels, each having an increasing amount of responsibility. Technologists and technicians also can advance into supervisory or management positions. Other common possibilities include working in an educational setting or conducting laboratory work.

Employment

Cardiovascular technologists and technicians held about 45,000 jobs in 2006. About 3 out of 4 jobs were in hospitals (public and private), primarily in cardiology departments. The remaining jobs were mostly in offices of physicians, including cardiologists, or in medical and diagnostic laboratories, including diagnostic imaging centers.

Job Outlook

Employment is expected to grow much faster than average; technologists and technicians trained to perform certain procedures will be in particular demand.

Employment change. Employment of cardiovascular technologists and technicians is expected to increase by 26 percent through the year 2016, much faster than the average for all occupations. Growth will occur as the population ages, because older people have a higher incidence of heart disease and other complications of the heart and vascular system. Procedures such as ultrasound are being performed more often as a replacement for more expensive and more invasive procedures. Due to advances in medicine and greater public awareness, signs of vascular disease can be detected earlier, creating demand for cardiovascular technologists and technicians to perform various procedures.

Employment of vascular technologists and echocardiographers will grow as advances in vascular technology and sonography reduce the need for more costly and invasive procedures. Electrophysiology is also becoming a rapidly growing specialty. However, fewer EKG technicians will be needed, as hospitals train nursing aides and others to perform basic EKG

procedures. Individuals trained in Holter monitoring and stress testing are expected to have more favorable job prospects than those who can perform only a basic EKG.

Medicaid has relaxed some of the rules governing reimbursement for vascular exams, which is resulting in vascular studies becoming a more routine practice. As a result of increased use of these procedures, individuals with training in vascular studies should have more favorable employment opportunities.

Job prospects. Some additional job openings for cardiovascular technologists and technicians will arise from replacement needs as individuals transfer to other jobs or leave the labor force. Although growing awareness of musculoskeletal disorders has made prevention easier, some cardiovascular technologists and technicians have been forced to leave the occupation early because of this disorder.

It is not uncommon for cardiovascular technologists and technicians to move between the specialties within the occupation by obtaining certification in more than one specialty.

Earnings

Median annual earnings of cardiovascular technologists and technicians were $42,300 in May 2006. The middle 50 percent earned between $29,900 and $55,670. The lowest 10 percent earned less than $23,670, and the highest 10 percent earned more than $67,410. Median annual earnings of cardiovascular technologists and technicians in 2006 were $41,960 in offices of physicians and $41,950 in general medical and surgical hospitals.

Related Occupations

Cardiovascular technologists and technicians operate sophisticated equipment that helps physicians and other health practitioners to diagnose and treat patients. So do diagnostic medical sonographers, nuclear medicine technologists, radiation therapists, radiologic technologists and technicians, and respiratory therapists.

Sources of Additional Information

For general information about a career in cardiovascular technology, contact:

➤ Alliance of Cardiovascular Professionals, Thalia Landing Offices, Bldg. 2, 4356 Bonney Rd., Suite 103, Virginia Beach, VA 23452-1200. Internet: **http://www.acp-online.org**

For a list of accredited programs in cardiovascular technology, contact:

➤ Committee on Accreditation for Allied Health Education Programs, 1361 Park St, Clearwater, FL 33756.
Internet: **http://www.caahep.org**

➤ Society for Vascular Ultrasound, 4601 Presidents Dr., Suite 260, Lanham, MD 20706-4381.
Internet: **http://www.svunet.org**

Projections data from the National Employment Matrix

Occupational Title	SOC Code	Employment, 2006	Projected employment, 2016	Change, 2006-2016	
				Number	Percent
Cardiovascular technologists and technicians....................................	29-2031	45,000	57,000	12,000	26

NOTE: Data in this table are rounded. See the discussion of the employment projections table in the *Handbook* introductory chapter on *Occupational Information Included in the Handbook.*

For information on echocardiography, contact:

➤ American Society of Echocardiography, 1500 Sunday Dr., Suite 102, Raleigh, NC 27607.
Internet: **http://www.asecho.org**

For information regarding registration and certification, contact:

➤ Cardiovascular Credentialing International, 1500 Sunday Dr., Suite 102, Raleigh, NC 27607.
Internet: **http://www.cci-online.org**

➤ American Registry of Diagnostic Medical Sonographers, 51 Monroe St., Plaza East ONE., Rockville, MD 20850-2400.
Internet: **http://www.ardms.org**

Clinical Laboratory Technologists and Technicians

(O*NET 29-2011.00, 29-2012.00)

Significant Points

- Faster than average employment growth and excellent job opportunities are expected.

- Clinical laboratory technologists usually have a bachelor's degree with a major in medical technology or in one of the life sciences; clinical laboratory technicians generally need either an associate degree or a certificate.

- Most jobs will continue to be in hospitals, but employment will grow faster in other settings.

Nature of the Work

Clinical laboratory testing plays a crucial role in the detection, diagnosis, and treatment of disease. Clinical laboratory technologists—also referred to as clinical laboratory scientists or medical technologists—and clinical laboratory technicians, also known as medical technicians or medical laboratory technicians, perform most of these tests.

Clinical laboratory personnel examine and analyze body fluids, and cells. They look for bacteria, parasites, and other microorganisms; analyze the chemical content of fluids; match blood for transfusions; and test for drug levels in the blood that show how a patient is responding to treatment. Technologists also prepare specimens for examination, count cells, and look for abnormal cells in blood and body fluids. They use microscopes, cell counters, and other sophisticated laboratory equipment. They also use automated equipment and computerized instruments capable of performing a number of tests simultaneously. After testing and examining a specimen, they analyze the results and relay them to physicians.

With increasing automation and the use of computer technology, the work of technologists and technicians has become less hands-on and more analytical. The complexity of tests performed, the level of judgment needed, and the amount of responsibility workers assume depend largely on the amount of education and experience they have. Clinical laboratory tech-nologists usually do more complex tasks than clinical laboratory technicians do.

Clinical laboratory technologists perform complex chemical, biological, hematological, immunologic, microscopic, and bacteriological tests. Technologists microscopically examine blood and other body fluids. They make cultures of body fluid and tissue samples, to determine the presence of bacteria, fungi, parasites, or other microorganisms. Technologists analyze samples for chemical content or a chemical reaction and determine concentrations of compounds such as blood glucose and cholesterol levels. They also type and cross match blood samples for transfusions.

Clinical laboratory technologists evaluate test results, develop and modify procedures, and establish and monitor programs, to ensure the accuracy of tests. Some technologists supervise clinical laboratory technicians.

Technologists in small laboratories perform many types of tests, whereas those in large laboratories generally specialize. Clinical chemistry technologists, for example, prepare specimens and analyze the chemical and hormonal contents of body fluids. Microbiology technologists examine and identify bacteria and other microorganisms. Blood bank technologists, or immunohematology technologists, collect, type, and prepare blood and its components for transfusions. Immunology technologists examine elements of the human immune system and its response to foreign bodies. Cytotechnologists prepare slides of body cells and examine these cells microscopically for abnormalities that may signal the beginning of a cancerous growth. Molecular biology technologists perform complex protein and nucleic acid testing on cell samples.

Clinical laboratory technicians perform less complex tests and laboratory procedures than technologists do. Technicians may prepare specimens and operate automated analyzers, for example, or they may perform manual tests in accordance with detailed instructions. They usually work under the supervision of medical and clinical laboratory technologists or laboratory managers. Like technologists, clinical laboratory technicians may work in several areas of the clinical laboratory or specialize in just one. Phlebotomists collect blood samples, for example, and histotechnicians cut and stain tissue specimens for microscopic examination by pathologists.

Work environment. Clinical laboratory personnel are trained to work with infectious specimens. When proper methods of infection control and sterilization are followed, few hazards exist. Protective masks, gloves, and goggles often are necessary to ensure the safety of laboratory personnel.

Working conditions vary with the size and type of employment setting. Laboratories usually are well lighted and clean; however, specimens, solutions, and reagents used in the laboratory sometimes produce fumes. Laboratory workers may spend a great deal of time on their feet.

Hours of clinical laboratory technologists and technicians vary with the size and type of employment setting. In large hospitals or in independent laboratories that operate continuously, personnel usually work the day, evening, or night shift and may work weekends and holidays. Laboratory personnel in small facilities may work on rotating shifts, rather than on a regular

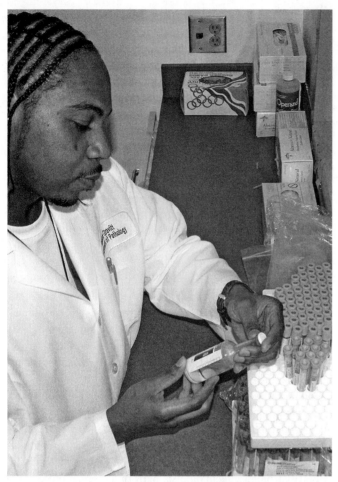

Clinical laboratory personnel look for bacteria, parasites, and other microorganisms; analyze the chemical content of fluids; match blood for transfusions; and test for drug levels in the blood that show how a patient is responding to treatment.

shift. In some facilities, laboratory personnel are on call several nights a week or on weekends, in case of an emergency.

Training, Other Qualifications, and Advancement

Clinical laboratory technologist generally require a bachelor's degree in medical technology or in one of the life sciences; clinical laboratory technicians usually need an associate degree or a certificate.

Education and training. The usual requirement for an entry-level position as a clinical laboratory technologist is a bachelor's degree with a major in medical technology or one of the life sciences; however, it is possible to qualify for some jobs with a combination of education and on-the-job and specialized training. Universities and hospitals offer medical technology programs.

Bachelor's degree programs in medical technology include courses in chemistry, biological sciences, microbiology, mathematics, and statistics, as well as specialized courses devoted to knowledge and skills used in the clinical laboratory. Many programs also offer or require courses in management, business, and computer applications. The Clinical Laboratory Improvement Act requires technologists who perform highly complex tests to have at least an associate degree.

Medical and clinical laboratory technicians generally have either an associate degree from a community or junior college or a certificate from a hospital, a vocational or technical school, or the Armed Forces. A few technicians learn their skills on the job.

The National Accrediting Agency for Clinical Laboratory Sciences (NAACLS) fully accredits about 470 programs for medical and clinical laboratory technologists, medical and clinical laboratory technicians, histotechnologists and histotechnicians, cytogenetic technologists, and diagnostic molecular scientists. NAACLS also approves about 60 programs in phlebotomy and clinical assisting. Other nationally recognized agencies that accredit specific areas for clinical laboratory workers include the Commission on Accreditation of Allied Health Education Programs and the Accrediting Bureau of Health Education Schools.

Licensure. Some States require laboratory personnel to be licensed or registered. Licensure of technologists often requires a bachelor's degree and the passing of an exam, but requirements vary by State and specialty. Information on licensure is available from State departments of health or boards of occupational licensing.

Certification and other qualifications. Many employers prefer applicants who are certified by a recognized professional association. Associations offering certification include the Board of Registry of the American Society for Clinical Pathology, the American Medical Technologists, the National Credentialing Agency for Laboratory Personnel, and the Board of Registry of the American Association of Bioanalysts. These agencies have different requirements for certification and different organizational sponsors.

In addition to certification, employers seek clinical laboratory personnel with good analytical judgment and the ability to work under pressure. Technologists in particular are expected to be good at problem solving. Close attention to detail is also essential for laboratory personnel because small differences or changes in test substances or numerical readouts can be crucial to a diagnosis. Manual dexterity and normal color vision are highly desirable, and with the widespread use of automated laboratory equipment, computer skills are important.

Advancement. Technicians can advance and become technologists through additional education and experience. Technologists may advance to supervisory positions in laboratory work or may become chief medical or clinical laboratory technologists or laboratory managers in hospitals. Manufacturers of home diagnostic testing kits and laboratory equipment and supplies also seek experienced technologists to work in product development, marketing, and sales.

Professional certification and a graduate degree in medical technology, one of the biological sciences, chemistry, management, or education usually speeds advancement. A doctorate usually is needed to become a laboratory director. Federal regulation requires directors of moderately complex laboratories to have either a master's degree or a bachelor's degree, combined with the appropriate amount of training and experience.

Employment

Clinical laboratory technologists and technicians held about 319,000 jobs in 2006. More than half of jobs were in hospitals.

Most of the remaining jobs were in offices of physicians and in medical and diagnostic laboratories. A small proportion was in educational services and in all other ambulatory health care services.

Job Outlook

Rapid job growth and excellent job opportunities are expected. Most jobs will continue to be in hospitals, but employment will grow faster in other settings.

Employment change. Employment of clinical laboratory workers is expected to grow 14 percent between 2006 and 2016, faster than the average for all occupations. The volume of laboratory tests continues to increase with both population growth and the development of new types of tests.

Technological advances will continue to have opposing effects on employment. On the one hand, new, increasingly powerful diagnostic tests will encourage additional testing and spur employment. On the other, research and development efforts targeted at simplifying routine testing procedures may enhance the ability of nonlaboratory personnel—physicians and patients in particular—to perform tests now conducted in laboratories.

Although hospitals are expected to continue to be the major employer of clinical laboratory workers, employment is expected to grow faster in medical and diagnostic laboratories, offices of physicians, and all other ambulatory health care services.

Job prospects. Job opportunities are expected to be excellent because the number of job openings is expected to continue to exceed the number of job seekers. Although significant, job growth will not be the only source of opportunities. As in most occupations, many additional openings will result from the need to replace workers who transfer to other occupations, retire, or stop working for some other reason.

Earnings

Median annual wage-and-salary earnings of medical and clinical laboratory technologists were $49,700 in May 2006. The middle 50 percent earned between $41,680 and $58,560. The lowest 10 percent earned less than $34,660, and the highest 10 percent earned more than $69,260. Median annual earnings in the industries employing the largest numbers of medical and clinical laboratory technologists were:

Federal Government...$57,360
Medical and diagnostic laboratories 50,740
General medical and surgical hospitals.................................49,930
Offices of physicians...45,420
Colleges, universities, and professional schools..................45,080

Median annual wage-and-salary earnings of medical and clinical laboratory technicians were $32,840 in May 2006. The middle 50 percent earned between $26,430 and $41,020. The lowest 10 percent earned less than $21,830, and the highest 10 percent earned more than $50,250. Median annual earnings in the industries employing the largest numbers of medical and clinical laboratory technicians were:

General medical and surgical hospitals..............................$34,200
Colleges, universities, and professional schools..................33,440
Offices of physicians...31,330
Medical and diagnostic laboratories 30,240
Other ambulatory health care services................................29,560

According to the American Society for Clinical Pathology, median hourly wages of staff clinical laboratory technologists and technicians in 2005 in various specialties and laboratory types were:

Specialty	Hospital	Private clinic	Physician office laboratory
Cytotechnoligist	$26.39	$31.64	$25.69
Histotechnologist	21.50	21.63	23.29
Medical technologist.................	21.77	20.00	20.00
Histotechnician	18.50	20.86	18.27
Medical laboratory technician	17.41	16.94	16.63
Phlebotomist	11.70	12.15	11.25

Related Occupations

Clinical laboratory technologists and technicians analyze body fluids, tissue, and other substances, using a variety of tests. Similar or related procedures are performed by chemists and materials scientists, science technicians, and veterinary technologists and technicians.

Sources of Additional Information

For a list of accredited and approved educational programs for clinical laboratory personnel, contact:
➤ National Accrediting Agency for Clinical Laboratory Sciences, 8410 W. Bryn Mawr Ave., Suite 670, Chicago, IL 60631. Internet: **http://www.naacls.org**

Information on certification is available from:
➤ American Association of Bioanalysts, Board of Registry, 906 Olive St., Suite 1200, St.Louis, MO 63101.
Internet: **http://www.aab.org**
➤ American Medical Technologists, 10700 Higgins Rd., Suite 150, Rosemont, IL 60018. Internet: **http://www.amt1.com**
➤ American Society for Clinical Pathology, 33 West Monroe Street, Suite 1600, Chicago, IL 60603.
Internet: **http://www.ascp.org**

Projections data from the National Employment Matrix

Occupational Title	SOC Code	Employment, 2006	Projected employment, 2016	Change, 2006-2016	
				Number	Percent
Clinical laboratory technologists and technicians............................	29-2010	319,000	362,000	43,000	14
Medical and clinical laboratory technologists	29-2011	167,000	188,000	21,000	12
Medical and clinical laboratory technicians	29-2012	151,000	174,000	23,000	15

NOTE: Data in this table are rounded. See the discussion of the employment projections table in the *Handbook* introductory chapter on *Occupational Information Included in the Handbook.*

➤ National Credentialing Agency for Laboratory Personnel, P.O. Box 15945, Lenexa, KS 66285.
Internet: **http://www.nca-info.org**

Additional career information is available from:

➤ American Association of Blood Banks, 8101 Glenbrook Rd., Bethesda, MD 20814. Internet: **http://www.aabb.org**

➤ American Society for Clinical Laboratory Science, 6701 Democracy Blvd., Suite 300, Bethesda, MD 20817.
Internet: **http://www.ascls.org**

➤ American Society for Cytopathology, 400 West 9th St., Suite 201, Wilmington, DE 19801.
Internet: **http://www.cytopathology.org**

➤ Clinical Laboratory Management Association, 989 Old Eagle School Rd., Suite 815, WayNE., PA 19087.
Internet: **http://www.clma.org**

Dental Hygienists

(O*NET 29-2021.00)

Significant Points

- A degree from an accredited dental hygiene school and a State license are required for this job.

- Dental hygienists rank among the fastest growing occupations.

- Job prospects are expected to remain excellent.

- More than half work part time, and flexible scheduling is a distinctive feature of this job.

Nature of the Work

Dental hygienists remove soft and hard deposits from teeth, teach patients how to practice good oral hygiene, and provide other preventive dental care. They examine patients' teeth and gums, recording the presence of diseases or abnormalities.

Dental hygienists use an assortment of different tools to complete their tasks. Hand and rotary instruments and ultrasonic devices are used to clean and polish teeth, including removing calculus, stains, and plaque. Hygienists use x-ray machines to take dental pictures, and sometimes develop the film. They may use models of teeth to explain oral hygiene, perform root planning as a periodontal therapy, or apply cavity-preventative agents such as fluorides and pit and fissure sealants. In some States, hygienists are allowed to administer anesthetics, while in others they administer local anesthetics using syringes. Some States also allow hygienists to place and carve filling materials, temporary fillings, and periodontal dressings; remove sutures; and smooth and polish metal restorations.

Dental hygienists also help patients develop and maintain good oral health. For example, they may explain the relationship between diet and oral health or inform patients how to select toothbrushes and show them how to brush and floss their teeth.

Hygienists sometimes make a diagnosis and other times may prepare clinical and laboratory diagnostic tests for the dentist to interpret. Hygienists sometimes work chair side with the dentist during treatment.

Work environment. Dental hygienists work in clean, well-lighted offices. Important health safeguards include strict adherence to proper radiological procedures and the use of appropriate protective devices when administering anesthetic gas. Dental hygienists also wear safety glasses, surgical masks, and gloves to protect themselves and patients from infectious diseases.

Flexible scheduling is a distinctive feature of this job. Full-time, part-time, evening, and weekend schedules are widely available. Dentists frequently hire hygienists to work only 2 or 3 days a week, so hygienists may hold jobs in more than one dental office. More than half of all dental hygienists worked part time—less than 35 hours a week.

Training, Other Qualifications, and Advancement

Prospective dental hygienists must become licensed in the State in which they wish to practice. A degree from an accredited dental hygiene school is usually required along with licensure examinations.

Education and training. A high school diploma and college entrance test scores are usually required for admission to a dental hygiene program. High school students interested in becoming a dental hygienist should take courses in biology, chemistry, and mathematics. Also, some dental hygiene programs require applicants to have completed at least 1 year of college. Specific entrance requirements vary from one school to another.

In 2006, there were 286 dental hygiene programs accredited by the Commission on Dental Accreditation. Most dental hygiene programs grant an associate degree, although some also offer a certificate, a bachelor's degree, or a master's degree. A

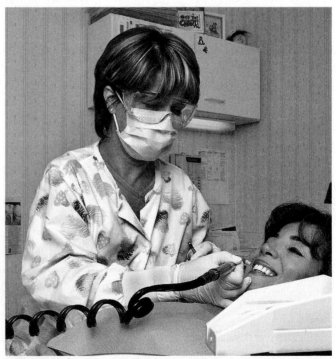

Dental hygienists use hand and rotary instruments to clean and polish teeth.

minimum of an associate degree or certificate in dental hygiene is generally required for practice in a private dental office. A bachelor's or master's degree usually is required for research, teaching, or clinical practice in public or school health programs.

Schools offer laboratory, clinical, and classroom instruction in subjects such as anatomy, physiology, chemistry, microbiology, pharmacology, nutrition, radiography, histology (the study of tissue structure), periodontology (the study of gum diseases), pathology, dental materials, clinical dental hygiene, and social and behavioral sciences.

Licensure. Dental hygienists must be licensed by the State in which they practice. Nearly all States require candidates to graduate from an accredited dental hygiene school and pass both a written and clinical examination. The American Dental Association's Joint Commission on National Dental Examinations administers the written examination, which is accepted by all States and the District of Columbia. State or regional testing agencies administer the clinical examination. In addition, most States require an examination on the legal aspects of dental hygiene practice. Alabama is the only State that allows candidates to take its examinations if they have been trained through a State-regulated on-the-job program in a dentist's office.

Other qualifications. Dental hygienists should work well with others because they work closely with dentists and dental assistants as well as dealing directly with patients. Hygienists also need good manual dexterity, because they use dental instruments within a patient's mouth, with little room for error.

Employment

Dental hygienists held about 167,000 jobs in 2006. Because multiple job holding is common in this field, the number of jobs exceeds the number of hygienists. Almost all jobs for dental hygienists were in offices of dentists. A very small number worked for employment services, offices of physicians, or other industries.

Job Outlook

Dental hygienists rank among the fastest growing occupations, and job prospects are expected to remain excellent.

Employment change. Employment of dental hygienists is expected to grow 30 percent through 2016, much faster than the average for all occupations. This projected growth ranks dental hygienists among the fastest growing occupations, in response to increasing demand for dental care and the greater use of hygienists.

The demand for dental services will grow because of population growth, older people increasingly retaining more teeth, and a growing focus on preventative dental care. To meet this demand, facilities that provide dental care, particularly dentists' offices, will increasingly employ dental hygienists, and more hygienists per office, to perform services that have been performed by dentists in the past.

Job prospects. Job prospects are expected to remain excellent. Older dentists, who have been less likely to employ dental hygienists, are leaving the occupation and will be replaced by recent graduates, who are more likely to employ one or more hygienists. In addition, as dentists' workloads increase, they are expected to hire more hygienists to perform preventive dental care, such as cleaning, so that they may devote their own time to more complex procedures.

Earnings

Median hourly earnings of dental hygienists were $30.19 in May 2006. The middle 50 percent earned between $24.63 and $35.67 an hour. The lowest 10 percent earned less than $19.45, and the highest 10 percent earned more than $41.60 an hour.

Earnings vary by geographic location, employment setting, and years of experience. Dental hygienists may be paid on an hourly, daily, salary, or commission basis.

Benefits vary substantially by practice setting and may be contingent upon full-time employment. According to the American Dental Association, 86 percent of hygienists receive hospital and medical benefits.

Related Occupations

Other workers supporting health practitioners in an office setting include dental assistants, medical assistants, occupational therapist assistants and aides, physical therapist assistants and aides, physician assistants, and registered nurses. Dental hygienists sometimes work with radiation technology, as do radiation therapists.

Sources of Additional Information

For information on a career in dental hygiene, including educational requirements, contact:

➤ Division of Education, American Dental Hygienists Association, 444 N. Michigan Ave., Suite 3400, Chicago, IL 60611. Internet: **http://www.adha.org**

For information about accredited programs and educational requirements, contact:

➤ Commission on Dental Accreditation, American Dental Association, 211 E. Chicago Ave., Suite 1814, Chicago, IL 60611. Internet: **http://www.ada.org**

The State Board of Dental Examiners in each State can supply information on licensing requirements.

Projections data from the National Employment Matrix

Occupational Title	SOC Code	Employment, 2006	Projected employment, 2016	Change, 2006-2016	
				Number	Percent
Dental hygienists..	29-2021	167,000	217,000	50,000	30

NOTE: Data in this table are rounded. See the discussion of the employment projections table in the *Handbook* introductory chapter on *Occupational Information Included in the Handbook.*

Diagnostic Medical Sonographers

(O*NET 29-2032.00)

Significant Points

- Job opportunities should be favorable.

- Employment growth is expected to be faster than average as sonography becomes an increasingly attractive alternative to radiologic procedures.

- More than half of all sonographers were employed by hospitals, and most of the rest were employed by offices of physicians, medical and diagnostic laboratories, and mobile imaging services.

- Sonographers may train in hospitals, vocational-technical institutions, colleges and universities, and the Armed Forces; employers prefer those who trained in accredited programs and who are registered.

Nature of the Work

Diagnostic imaging embraces several procedures that aid in diagnosing ailments. The most familiar procedures are the x-ray and the magnetic resonance imaging; however, not all imaging technologies use ionizing radiation or radio waves. Sonography, or ultrasonography, is the use of sound waves to generate an image for the assessment and diagnosis of various medical conditions. Sonography commonly is associated with obstetrics and the use of ultrasound imaging during pregnancy, but this technology has many other applications in the diagnosis and treatment of medical conditions throughout the body.

Diagnostic medical sonographers use special equipment to direct nonionizing, high frequency sound waves into areas of the patient's body. Sonographers operate the equipment, which collects reflected echoes and forms an image that may be videotaped, transmitted, or photographed for interpretation and diagnosis by a physician.

Sonographers begin by explaining the procedure to the patient and recording any medical history that may be relevant to the condition being viewed. They then select appropriate equipment settings and direct the patient to move into positions that will provide the best view. To perform the exam, sonographers use a transducer, which transmits sound waves in a cone- or rectangle-shaped beam. Although techniques vary with the area being examined, sonographers usually spread a special gel on the skin to aid the transmission of sound waves.

Viewing the screen during the scan, sonographers look for subtle visual cues that contrast healthy areas with unhealthy ones. They decide whether the images are satisfactory for diagnostic purposes and select which ones to store and show to the physician. Sonographers take measurements, calculate values, and analyze the results in preliminary findings for the physicians.

In addition to working directly with patients, diagnostic medical sonographers keep patient records and adjust and maintain equipment. They also may prepare work schedules, evaluate equipment purchases, or manage a sonography or diagnostic imaging department.

Diagnostic medical sonographers may specialize in obstetric and gynecologic sonography (the female reproductive system), abdominal sonography (the liver, kidneys, gallbladder, spleen, and pancreas), neurosonography (the brain), or breast sonography. In addition, sonographers may specialize in vascular sonography or cardiac sonography. (Vascular sonographers and cardiac sonographers are covered in the *Handbook* statement on cardiovascular technologists and technicians.)

Obstetric and gynecologic sonographers specialize in the imaging of the female reproductive system. Included in the discipline is one of the more well-known uses of sonography: examining the fetus of a pregnant woman to track the baby's growth and health.

Abdominal sonographers inspect a patient's abdominal cavity to help diagnose and treat conditions primarily involving the gallbladder, bile ducts, kidneys, liver, pancreas, spleen, and male reproductive system. Abdominal sonographers also are able to scan parts of the chest, although studies of the heart using sonography usually are done by echocardiographers.

Neurosonographers focus on the nervous system, including the brain. In neonatal care, neurosonographers study and diagnose neurological and nervous system disorders in premature infants. They also may scan blood vessels to check for abnormalities indicating a stroke in infants diagnosed with sickle-cell anemia. Like other sonographers, neurosonographers operate transducers to perform the sonogram, but use frequencies and beam shapes different from those used by obstetric and abdominal sonographers.

Breast sonographers use sonography to study diseases of the breasts. Sonography aids mammography in the detection of breast cancer. Breast sonography can also track tumors, blood

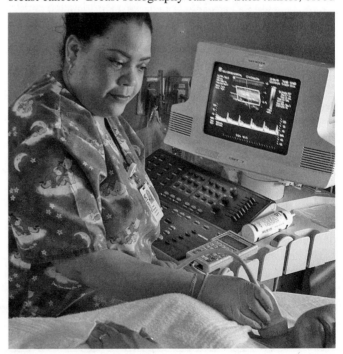

Diagnostic medical sonographers use special equipment to direct nonionizing, high frequency sound waves into areas of the patient's body.

supply conditions, and assist in the accurate biopsy of breast tissue. Breast sonographers use high-frequency transducers, made exclusively to study breast tissue.

Work environment. Sonographers typically work in health care facilities that are clean. They usually work at diagnostic imaging machines in darkened rooms, but also may perform procedures at patients' bedsides. Sonographers may be on their feet for long periods of time and may have to lift or turn disabled patients. In addition, the nature of their work can put sonographers at an increased risk for musculoskeletal disorders such as carpel tunnel syndrome, neck and back strain, and eye strain: however, greater use of ergonomic equipment and an increasing awareness will continue to minimize such risks

Some sonographers work as contract employees and may travel to several health care facilities in an area. Similarly, some sonographers work with mobile imaging service providers and travel to patients and use mobile diagnostic imaging equipment to provide service in areas that otherwise do not have the access to such services.

Most full-time sonographers work about 40 hours a week. Hospital-based sonographers may have evening and weekend hours and times when they are on call and must be ready to report to work on short notice.

Training, Other Qualifications, and Advancement

Diagnostic medical sonography is an occupation where there is no preferred level of education and several avenues of education are widely accepted by employers. Although no level of education is preferred, employers do prefer sonographers who trained in accredited programs and who are registered.

Education and training. There are several avenues for entry into the field of diagnostic medical sonography. Sonographers may train in hospitals, vocational-technical institutions, colleges and universities, and the Armed Forces. Some training programs prefer applicants with a background in science or experience in other health care professions. Some also may consider high school graduates with courses in mathematics and science, as well as applicants with liberal arts backgrounds, but this practice is infrequent.

Colleges and universities offer formal training in both 2- and 4-year programs, culminating in an associate or a bachelor's degree. Two-year programs are most prevalent. Course work includes classes in anatomy, physiology, instrumentation, basic physics, patient care, and medical ethics.

A few 1-year programs that may result in a certificate also are accepted as proper education by employers. These programs typically are satisfactory education for workers already in health care who seek to increase their marketability by training in sonography. These programs are not accredited.

The Commission on Accreditation for Allied Health Education Programs (CAAHEP) accredited 147 training programs in 2006. These programs typically are the formal training programs offered by colleges and universities. Some hospital programs are accredited as well.

Certification and other qualifications. Although no State requires licensure in diagnostic medical sonography, organizations such as the American Registry for Diagnostic Medical Sonography (ARDMS) certify the skills and knowledge of sonographers through credentialing, including registration. Because registration provides an independent, objective measure of an individual's professional standing, many employers prefer to hire registered sonographers. Sonographers registered by the ARDMS are Registered Diagnostic Medical Sonographers (RDMS). Registration with ARDMS requires passing a general physical principles and instrumentation examination, in addition to passing an exam in a specialty such as obstetric and gynecologic sonography, abdominal sonography, or neurosonography. Sonographers must complete a required number of continuing education hours to maintain registration with the ARDMS and to stay abreast of technological advancements related to the occupation.

Sonographers need good communication and interpersonal skills because they must be able to explain technical procedures and results to their patients, some of whom may be nervous about the exam or the problems it may reveal. Good hand-eye coordination is particularly important to obtaining quality images. It is also important that sonographers enjoy learning because continuing education is the key to sonographers staying abreast of the ever-changing field of diagnostic medicine. A background in mathematics and science is helpful for sonographers as well.

Advancement. Sonographers specializing in one particular discipline often seek competency in others. For example, obstetric sonographers might seek training in abdominal sonography to broaden their opportunities and increase their marketability.

Sonographers may also have advancement opportunities in education, administration, research, sales, or technical advising.

Employment

Diagnostic medical sonographers held about 46,000 jobs in 2006. More than half of all sonographer jobs were in public and private hospitals. The rest were typically in offices of physicians, medical and diagnostic laboratories, and mobile imaging services.

Job Outlook

Faster-than-average employment growth is expected. Job opportunities should be favorable.

Employment change. Employment of diagnostic medical sonographers is expected to increase by about 19 percent through

Projections data from the National Employment Matrix

Occupational Title	SOC Code	Employment, 2006	Projected employment, 2016	Change, 2006-2016	
				Number	Percent
Diagnostic medical sonographers	29-2032	46,000	54,000	8,700	19

NOTE: Data in this table are rounded. See the discussion of the employment projections table in the *Handbook* introductory chapter on *Occupational Information Included in the Handbook.*

2016—faster than the average for all occupations—as the population ages, increasing the demand for diagnostic imaging and therapeutic technology.

Additional job growth is expected as sonography becomes an increasingly attractive alternative to radiologic procedures, as patients seek safer treatment methods. Unlike most diagnostic imaging methods, sonography does not involve radiation, so harmful side effects and complications from repeated use are less likely for both the patient and the sonographer. Sonographic technology is expected to evolve rapidly and to spawn many new sonography procedures, such as 3D- and 4D-sonography for use in obstetric and ophthalmologic diagnosis. However, high costs and approval by the Federal Government may limit the rate at which some promising new technologies are adopted. Ultrasound currently is only approved for cardiovascular imaging but is awaiting Federal Government approval for other applications.

Hospitals will remain the principal employer of diagnostic medical sonographers. However, employment is expected to grow more rapidly in offices of physicians and in medical and diagnostic laboratories, including diagnostic imaging centers. Healthcare facilities such as these are expected to grow very rapidly through 2016 because of the strong shift toward outpatient care, encouraged by third-party payers and made possible by technological advances that permit more procedures to be performed outside the hospital.

Job prospects. Job opportunities should be favorable. In addition to job openings from growth, some openings will arise from the need to replace sonographers who retire or leave the occupation permanently for some other reason. Pain caused by musculoskeletal disorders has made it difficult for sonographers to perform well. Some are forced to leave the occupation early because of this disorder.

Earnings

Median annual earnings of diagnostic medical sonographers were $57,160 in May 2006. The middle 50 percent earned between $48,890 and $67,670 a year. The lowest 10 percent earned less than $40,960, and the highest 10 percent earned more than $77,520. Median annual earnings of diagnostic medical sonographers in May 2006 were $56,970 in offices of physicians and $56,850 in general medical and surgical hospitals.

Related Occupations

Diagnostic medical sonographers operate sophisticated equipment to help physicians and other health practitioners diagnose and treat patients. Workers in related occupations include cardiovascular technologists and technicians, clinical laboratory technologists and technicians, nuclear medicine technologists, radiologic technologists and technicians, and respiratory therapists.

Sources of Additional Information

For information on a career as a diagnostic medical sonographer, contact:

➤ Society of Diagnostic Medical Sonography, 2745 Dallas Pkwy., Suite 350, Plano, TX 75093-8730.
Internet: **http://www.sdms.org**

For information on becoming a registered diagnostic medical sonographer, contact:
➤ American Registry for Diagnostic Medical Sonography, 51 Monroe St., Plaza East 1, Rockville, MD 20850-2400.
Internet: **http://www.ardms.org**

For more information on ultrasound in medicine, contact:
➤ American Institute of Ultrasound in MediciNE., 14750 Sweitzer LaNE., Suite 100, Laurel, MD 20707-5906.
Internet: **http://www.aium.org**

For a current list of accredited education programs in diagnostic medical sonography, contact:
➤ Joint Review Committee on Education in Diagnostic Medical Sonography, 2025 Woodlane Dr., St.Paul, MN 55125-2998.
Internet: **http://www.jrcdms.org**
➤ Commission on Accreditation for Allied Health Education Programs, 35 East Wacker Dr., Suite1970, Chicago, IL 60601.
Internet: **http://www.caahep.org**

Emergency Medical Technicians and Paramedics

(O*NET 29-2041.00)

Significant Points

- Employment is projected to grow faster than the average as paid positions replace unpaid volunteers.

- Emergency medical technicians and paramedics need formal training and certification, but requirements vary by State.

- Emergency services function 24 hours a day so emergency medical technicians and paramedics have irregular working hours.

- Opportunities will be best for those who have earned advanced certifications.

Nature of the Work

People's lives often depend on the quick reaction and competent care of emergency medical technicians (EMTs) and paramedics. Incidents as varied as automobile accidents, heart attacks, slips and falls, childbirth, and gunshot wounds all require immediate medical attention. EMTs and paramedics provide this vital service as they care for and transport the sick or injured to a medical facility.

In an emergency, EMTs and paramedics are typically dispatched by a 911 operator to the scene, where they often work with police and fire fighters. (Police and detectives and firefighting occupations are discussed elsewhere in the *Handbook*.) Once they arrive, EMTs and paramedics assess the nature of the patient's condition while trying to determine whether the patient has any pre-existing medical conditions. Following medical protocols and guidelines, they provide appropriate emergency care and, when necessary, transport the patient. Some paramedics are trained to treat patients with minor injuries on the scene of an accident or they may treat them at their home without transporting them to a medical facility. Emergency treatment is carried out under the medical direction of physicians.

EMTs and paramedics may use special equipment, such as backboards, to immobilize patients before placing them on stretchers and securing them in the ambulance for transport to a medical facility. These workers generally work in teams. During the transport of a patient, one EMT or paramedic drives while the other monitors the patient's vital signs and gives additional care as needed. Some paramedics work as part of a helicopter's flight crew to transport critically ill or injured patients to hospital trauma centers.

At the medical facility, EMTs and paramedics help transfer patients to the emergency department, report their observations and actions to emergency department staff, and may provide additional emergency treatment. After each run, EMTs and paramedics replace used supplies and check equipment. If a transported patient had a contagious disease, EMTs and paramedics decontaminate the interior of the ambulance and report cases to the proper authorities.

EMTs and paramedics also provide transportation for patients from one medical facility to another, particularly if they work for private ambulance services. Patients often need to be transferred to a hospital that specializes in their injury or illness or to a nursing home.

Beyond these general duties, the specific responsibilities of EMTs and paramedics depend on their level of qualification and training. The National Registry of Emergency Medical Technicians (NREMT) certifies emergency medical service providers at five levels: First Responder; EMT-Basic; EMT-Intermediate, which has two levels called 1985 and 1999; and Paramedic. Some States, however, have their own certification programs and use distinct names and titles.

The EMT-Basic represents the first component of the emergency medical technician system. An EMT trained at this level is prepared to care for patients at the scene of an accident and while transporting patients by ambulance to the hospital under medical direction. The EMT-Basic has the emergency skills to assess a patient's condition and manage respiratory, cardiac, and trauma emergencies.

The EMT-Intermediate has more advanced training. However, the specific tasks that those certified at this level are allowed to perform varies greatly from by State.

EMT-Paramedics provide the most extensive pre-hospital care. In addition to carrying out the procedures of the other levels, paramedics may administer drugs orally and intravenously, interpret electrocardiograms (EKGs), perform endotracheal intubations, and use monitors and other complex equipment. However, like EMT-Immediate, what Paramedics are permitted to do varies from State to State.

Work environment. EMTs and paramedics work both indoors and out, in all types of weather. They are required to do considerable kneeling, bending, and heavy lifting. These workers risk noise-induced hearing loss from sirens and back injuries from lifting patients. In addition, EMTs and paramedics may be exposed to diseases such as hepatitis-B and AIDS, as well as violence from mentally unstable patients. The work is not only physically strenuous but can be stressful, sometimes involving life-or-death situations and suffering patients. None-

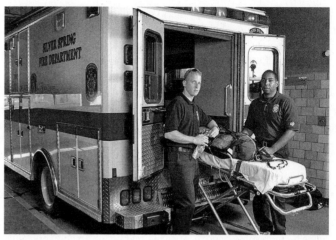

Emergency medical technicians and paramedics often work in pairs, where one person drives the ambulance and the other monitors the patient.

theless, many people find the work exciting and challenging and enjoy the opportunity to help others.

EMTs and paramedics employed by fire departments work about 50 hours a week. Those employed by hospitals frequently work between 45 and 60 hours a week, and those in private ambulance services, between 45 and 50 hours. Some of these workers, especially those in police and fire departments, are on call for extended periods. Because emergency services function 24 hours a day, EMTs and paramedics have irregular working hours.

Training, Other Qualifications, and Advancement
Generally, a high school diploma is required to enter a training program to become an EMT or paramedic. Workers must complete a formal training and certification process.

Education and training. A high school diploma is usually required to enter a formal emergency medical technician training program. Training is offered at progressive levels: EMT-Basic, EMT-Intermediate, and EMT-Paramedic.

At the EMT-Basic level, coursework emphasizes emergency skills, such as managing respiratory, trauma, and cardiac emergencies, and patient assessment. Formal courses are often combined with time in an emergency room or ambulance. The program provides instruction and practice in dealing with bleeding, fractures, airway obstruction, cardiac arrest, and emergency childbirth. Students learn how to use and maintain common emergency equipment, such as backboards, suction devices, splints, oxygen delivery systems, and stretchers. Graduates of approved EMT-Basic training programs must pass a written and practical examination administered by the State certifying agency or the NREMT.

At the EMT-Intermediate level, training requirements vary by State. The nationally defined levels (EMT-Intermediate 1985 and EMT-Intermediate 1999) typically require 30 to 350 hours of training based on scope of practice. Students learn advanced skills such the use of advanced airway devices, intravenous fluids, and some medications.

The most advanced level of training for this occupation is EMT-Paramedic. At this level, the caregiver receives training in anatomy and physiology as well as advanced medical skills.

Most commonly, the training is conducted in community colleges and technical schools over 1 to 2 years and may result in an associate's degree. Such education prepares the graduate to take the NREMT examination and become certified as a Paramedic. Extensive related coursework and clinical and field experience is required. Refresher courses and continuing education are available for EMTs and paramedics at all levels.

Licensure. All 50 States require certification for each of the EMT levels. In most States and the District of Columbia registration with the NREMT is required at some or all levels of certification. Other States administer their own certification examination or provide the option of taking either the NREMT or State examination. To maintain certification, EMTs and paramedics must recertify, usually every 2 years. Generally, they must be working as an EMT or paramedic and meet a continuing education requirement.

Other qualifications. EMTs and paramedics should be emotionally stable, have good dexterity, agility, and physical coordination, and be able to lift and carry heavy loads. They also need good eyesight (corrective lenses may be used) with accurate color vision.

Advancement. Paramedics can become supervisors, operations managers, administrative directors, or executive directors of emergency services. Some EMTs and paramedics become instructors, dispatchers, or physician assistants; others move into sales or marketing of emergency medical equipment. A number of people become EMTs and paramedics to test their interest in health care before training as registered nurses, physicians, or other health workers.

Employment

EMTs and paramedics held about 201,000 jobs in 2006. Most career EMTs and paramedics work in metropolitan areas. Volunteer EMTs and paramedics are more common in small cities, towns, and rural areas. These individuals volunteer for fire departments, emergency medical services, or hospitals and may respond to only a few calls per month. About 30 percent of EMTs or paramedics belong to a union.

Paid EMTs and paramedics were employed in a number of industries. About 4 out of 10 worked as employees of private ambulance services. About 3 out of 10 worked in local government for fire departments, public ambulance services, and emergency medical services. Another 2 out of 10 worked full time in hospitals within the medical facility or responded to calls in ambulances or helicopters to transport critically ill or injured patients. The remainder worked in various industries providing emergency services.

Job Outlook

Employment for EMTs and paramedics is expected to grow faster than the average for all occupations through 2016. Job prospects should be good, particularly in cities and private ambulance services.

Employment change. Employment of emergency medical technicians and paramedics is expected to grow by 19 percent between 2006 and 2016, which is faster than the average for all occupations. Full-time paid EMTs and paramedics will be needed to replace unpaid volunteers. It is becoming increasing difficult for emergency medical services to recruit and retain unpaid volunteers because of the amount of training and the large time commitment these positions require. As a result, more paid EMTs and paramedics are needed. Furthermore, as a large segment of the population—aging members of the baby boom generation—becomes more likely to have medical emergencies, demand will increase for EMTs and paramedics. There also will still be demand for part-time, volunteer EMTs and paramedics in rural areas and smaller metropolitan areas.

Job prospects. Job prospects should be favorable. Many job openings will arise from growth and from the need to replace workers who leave the occupation because of the limited potential for advancement, as well as the modest pay and benefits in private-sector jobs.

Job opportunities should be best in private ambulance services. Competition will be greater for jobs in local government, including fire, police, and independent third-service rescue squad departments which tend to have better salaries and benefits. EMTs and paramedics who have advanced education and certifications, such as Paramedic level certification, should enjoy the most favorable job prospects as clients and patients demand higher levels of care before arriving at the hospital.

Earnings

Earnings of EMTs and paramedics depend on the employment setting and geographic location of their jobs, as well as their training and experience. Median annual earnings of EMTs and paramedics were $27,070 in May 2006. The middle 50 percent earned between $21,290 and $35,210. The lowest 10 percent earned less than $17,300, and the highest 10 percent earned more than $45,280. Median annual earnings in the industries employing the largest numbers of EMTs and paramedics in May 2006 were $23,250 in general medical and surgical hospitals and $20,350 in ambulance services.

Those in emergency medical services who are part of fire or police departments typically receive the same benefits as firefighters or police officers. For example, many are covered by pension plans that provide retirement at half pay after 20 or 25 years of service or if the worker is disabled in the line of duty.

Related Occupations

Other workers in occupations that require quick and level-headed reactions to life-or-death situations are air traffic controllers,

Projections data from the National Employment Matrix

Occupational Title	SOC Code	Employment, 2006	Projected employment, 2016	Change, 2006-2016	
				Number	Percent
Emergency medical technicians and paramedics............................	29-2041	201,000	240,000	39,000	19

NOTE: Data in this table are rounded. See the discussion of the employment projections table in the *Handbook* introductory chapter on *Occupational Information Included in the Handbook.*

firefighting occupations, physician assistants, police and detectives, and registered nurses.

Sources of Additional Information
General information about emergency medical technicians and paramedics is available from:

➤ National Association of Emergency Medical Technicians, P.O. Box 1400, Clinton, MS 39060-1400.
Internet: **http://www.naemt.org**

➤ National Highway Traffic Safety Administration, EMS Division, 400 7th St.SW., NTS-14, Washington, DC 20590.
Internet: **http://www.ems.gov**

➤ National Registry of Emergency Medical Technicians, Rocco V. Morando Bldg., 6610 Busch Blvd., P.O. Box 29233, Columbus, OH 43229. Internet: **http://www.nremt.org**

Licensed Practical and Licensed Vocational Nurses

(O*NET 29-2061.00)

Significant Points

- Most training programs, lasting about 1 year, are offered by vocational or technical schools or community or junior colleges.

- Overall job prospects are expected to be very good, but job outlook varies by industry.

- Replacement needs will be a major source of job openings, as many workers leave the occupation permanently.

Nature of the Work
Licensed practical nurses (LPNs), or licensed vocational nurses (LVNs), care for people who are sick, injured, convalescent, or disabled under the direction of physicians and registered nurses. (The work of physicians and surgeons and of registered nurses is described elsewhere in the *Handbook*.) The nature of the direction and supervision required varies by State and job setting.

LPNs care for patients in many ways. Often, they provide basic bedside care. Many LPNs measure and record patients' vital signs such as height, weight, temperature, blood pressure, pulse, and respiration. They also prepare and give injections and enemas, monitor catheters, dress wounds, and give alcohol rubs and massages. To help keep patients comfortable, they assist with bathing, dressing, and personal hygiene, moving in bed, standing, and walking. They might also feed patients who need help eating. Experienced LPNs may supervise nursing assistants and aides.

As part of their work, LPNs collect samples for testing, perform routine laboratory tests, and record food and fluid intake and output. They clean and monitor medical equipment. Sometimes, they help physicians and registered nurses perform tests and procedures. Some LPNs help to deliver, care for, and feed infants.

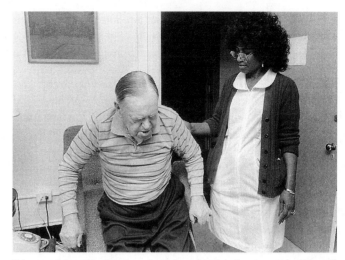

Licensed practical nurses care for people who are sick, injured, convalescent, and disabled.

LPNs also monitor their patients and report adverse reactions to medications or treatments. LPNs gather information from patients, including their health history and how they are currently feeling. They may use this information to complete insurance forms, pre-authorizations, and referrals, and they share information with registered nurses and doctors to help determine the best course of care for a patient.

LPNs often teach family members how to care for a relative or teach patients about good health habits.

Most LPNs are generalists and work in all areas of health care. However, some work in a specialized setting, such as a nursing home, a doctor's office, or in home health care. LPNs in nursing care facilities help to evaluate residents' needs, develop care plans, and supervise the care provided by nursing aides. In doctors' offices and clinics, they may be responsible for making appointments, keeping records, and performing other clerical duties. LPNs who work in home health care may prepare meals and teach family members simple nursing tasks.

In some States, LPNs are permitted to administer prescribed medicines, start intravenous fluids, and provide care to ventilator-dependent patients.

Work environment. Most licensed practical nurses in hospitals and nursing care facilities work a 40-hour week, but because patients need round-the-clock care, some work nights, weekends, and holidays. They often stand for long periods and help patients move in bed, stand, or walk.

LPNs may face hazards from caustic chemicals, radiation, and infectious diseases. They are subject to back injuries when moving patients. They often must deal with the stress of heavy workloads. In addition, the patients they care for may be confused, agitated, or uncooperative.

Training, Other Qualifications, and Advancement
Most training programs, lasting about 1 year, are offered by vocational or technical schools or community or junior colleges. LPNs must be licensed to practice. Successful completion of a practical nurse program and passing an examination are required to become licensed.

Education and training. All States and the District of Columbia require LPNs to pass a licensing examination, known as the NCLEX-PN, after completing a State-approved practical nursing program. A high school diploma or its equivalent usually is required for entry, although some programs accept candidates without a diploma, and some programs are part of a high school curriculum.

In 2006, there were more than 1,500 State-approved training programs in practical nursing. Most training programs are available from technical and vocational schools or community and junior colleges. Other programs are available through high schools, hospitals, and colleges and universities.

Most year-long practical nursing programs include both classroom study and supervised clinical practice (patient care). Classroom study covers basic nursing concepts and subjects related to patient care, including anatomy, physiology, medical-surgical nursing, pediatrics, obstetrics, psychiatric nursing, the administration of drugs, nutrition, and first aid. Clinical practice usually is in a hospital but sometimes includes other settings.

Licensure. The NCLEX-PN licensing exam is required in order to obtain licensure as an LPN. The exam is developed and administered by the National Council of State Boards of Nursing. The NCLEX-PN is a computer-based exam and varies in length. The exam covers four major categories: safe and effective care environment, health promotion and maintenance, psychosocial integrity, and physiological integrity.

Other qualifications. LPNs should have a caring, sympathetic nature. They should be emotionally stable because working with the sick and injured can be stressful. They also need to be observant, and to have good decision-making and communication skills. As part of a health-care team, they must be able to follow orders and work under close supervision.

Advancement. In some employment settings, such as nursing homes, LPNs can advance to become charge nurses who oversee the work of other LPNs and of nursing aides. Some LPNs also choose to become registered nurses through numerous LPN-to-RN training programs.

Employment

Licensed practical nurses held about 749,000 jobs in 2006. About 26 percent of LPNs worked in hospitals, 26 percent in nursing care facilities, and another 12 percent in offices of physicians. Others worked for home health care services; employment services; residential care facilities; community care facilities for the elderly; outpatient care centers; and Federal, State, and local government agencies. About 19 percent worked part time.

Job Outlook

Employment of LPNs is projected to grow faster than average. Overall job prospects are expected to be very good, but job outlook varies by industry. The best job opportunities will occur in nursing care facilities and home health care services, while applicants for jobs in hospitals may face competition.

Employment change. Employment of LPNs is expected to grow 14 percent between 2006 and 2016, faster than the average for all occupations, in response to the long-term care needs of an increasing elderly population and the general increase in demand for health care services.

Many procedures once performed only in hospitals are being performed in physicians' offices and in outpatient care centers such as ambulatory surgical and emergency medical centers, largely because of advances in technology. LPNs care for patients who undergo these and other procedures, so employment of LPNs is projected to decline in traditional hospitals, but is projected to grow faster than average in most settings outside of hospitals. However, some hospitals are assigning a larger share of nursing duties to LPNs, which will temper the employment decline in the industry.

Employment of LPNs is expected to grow much faster than average in home health care services. Home health care agencies will offer a large number of new jobs for LPNs because of an increasing number of older people with functional disabilities, consumer preference for care in the home, and technological advances that make it possible to bring increasingly complex treatments into the home.

Employment of LPNs in nursing care facilities is expected to grow faster than average, and provide the most new jobs for LPNs, because of the growing number of people who are aged and disabled and in need of long-term care. In addition, LPNs in nursing care facilities will be needed to care for the increasing number of patients who have been discharged from the hospital but who have not recovered enough to return home.

Job prospects. Replacement needs will be a major source of job openings, as many workers leave the occupation permanently. Very good job opportunities are expected. Rapid employment growth is projected in most health care industries, with the best job opportunities occurring in nursing care facilities and in home health care services. However, applicants for jobs in hospitals may face competition as the number of hospital jobs for LPNs declines.

Earnings

Median annual earnings of licensed practical nurses were $36,550 in May 2006. The middle 50 percent earned between $31,080 and $43,640. The lowest 10 percent earned less than $26,380, and the highest 10 percent earned more than $50,480. Median annual earnings in the industries employing the largest numbers of licensed practical nurses in May 2006 were:

Employment services $42,110
Nursing care facilities 38,320
Home health care services 37,880
General medical and surgical hospitals...............................35,000
Offices of physicians..32,710

Projections data from the National Employment Matrix

Occupational Title	SOC Code	Employment, 2006	Projected employment, 2016	Change, 2006-2016	
				Number	Percent
Licensed practical and licensed vocational nurses..........................	29-2061	749,000	854,000	105,000	14

NOTE: Data in this table are rounded. See the discussion of the employment projections table in the *Handbook* introductory chapter on *Occupational Information Included in the Handbook.*

Related Occupations

LPNs work closely with people while helping them. So do emergency medical technicians and paramedics; medical assistants; nursing, psychiatric, and home health aides; registered nurses; athletic trainers; social and human service assistants; pharmacy technicians; pharmacy aides; and surgical technologists.

Sources of Additional Information

For information about practical nursing, contact the following organizations:

➤ National Association for Practical Nurse Education and Service, Inc., P.O. Box 25647, Alexandria, VA 22313. Internet: **http://www.napnes.org**

➤ National Federation of Licensed Practical Nurses, Inc., 605 Poole Dr., Garner, NC 27529. Internet: **http://www.nflpn.org**

➤ National League for Nursing, 61 Broadway, New York, NY 10006. Internet: **http://www.nln.org**

Information on the NCLEX-PN licensing exam is available from:

➤ National Council of State Boards of Nursing, 111 East Wacker Dr., Suite 2900, Chicago, IL 60611. Internet: **http://www.ncsbn.org**

A list of State-approved LPN programs is available from individual State boards of nursing.

Medical Records and Health Information Technicians

(O*NET 29-2071.00)

Significant Points

- Employment is expected to grow faster than average.

- Job prospects should be very good; technicians with a strong background in medical coding will be in particularly high demand.

- Entrants usually have an associate degree.

- This is one of the few health occupations in which there is little or no direct contact with patients.

Nature of the Work

Every time a patient receives health care, a record is maintained of the observations, medical or surgical interventions, and treatment outcomes. This record includes information that the patient provides concerning his or her symptoms and medical history, the results of examinations, reports of x-rays and laboratory tests, diagnoses, and treatment plans. Medical records and health information technicians organize and evaluate these records for completeness and accuracy.

Technicians assemble patients' health information, making sure that patients' initial medical charts are complete, that all forms are completed and properly identified and authenticated, and that all necessary information is in the computer. They regularly communicate with physicians and other health care professionals to clarify diagnoses or to obtain additional in-

formation. Technicians regularly use computer programs to tabulate and analyze data to improve patient care, better control cost, provide documentation for use in legal actions, or use in research studies.

Medical records and health information technicians' duties vary with the size of the facility where they work. In large to medium-size facilities, technicians might specialize in one aspect of health information or might supervise health information clerks and transcriptionists while a medical records and health information administrator manages the department. (See the statement on medical and health services managers elsewhere in the *Handbook*.) In small facilities, a credentialed medical records and health information technician may have the opportunity to manage the department.

Some medical records and health information technicians specialize in coding patients' medical information for insurance purposes. Technicians who specialize in coding are called *health information coders*, *medical record coders*, *coder/abstractors*, or *coding specialists*. These technicians assign a code to each diagnosis and procedure, relying on their knowledge of disease processes. Technicians then use classification systems software to assign the patient to one of several hundred "diagnosis-related groups," or DRGs. The DRG determines the amount for which the hospital will be reimbursed if the patient is covered by Medicare or other insurance programs using the DRG system. In addition to the DRG system, coders use other coding systems, such as those required for ambulatory settings, physician offices, or long-term care.

Medical records and health information technicians also may specialize in cancer registry. *Cancer* (or tumor) *registrars* maintain facility, regional, and national databases of cancer patients. Registrars review patient records and pathology reports, and assign codes for the diagnosis and treatment of different

Medical records and health information technicians comprise one of the few health occupations that involve little or no direct contact with patients.

cancers and selected benign tumors. Registrars conduct annual followups on all patients in the registry to track their treatment, survival, and recovery. Physicians and public health organizations then use this information to calculate survivor rates and success rates of various types of treatment, locate geographic areas with high incidences of certain cancers, and identify potential participants for clinical drug trials. Public health officials also use cancer registry data to target areas for the allocation of resources to provide intervention and screening.

Work environment. Medical records and health information technicians work in pleasant and comfortable offices. This is one of the few health-related occupations in which there is little or no direct contact with patients. Because accuracy is essential in their jobs, technicians must pay close attention to detail. Technicians who work at computer monitors for prolonged periods must guard against eyestrain and muscle pain.

Medical records and health information technicians usually work a 40-hour week. Some overtime may be required. In hospitals—where health information departments often are open 24 hours a day, 7 days a week—technicians may work day, evening, and night shifts.

Training, Other Qualifications, and Advancement

Medical records and health information technicians entering the field usually have an associate degree from a community or junior college. Many employers favor technicians who have become Registered Health Information Technicians (RHIT). Advancement opportunities for medical record and health information technicans are typically achieved by specialization or promotion to a management position.

Education and training. Medical records and health information technicians generally obtain an associate degree from a community or junior college. Typically, community and junior colleges offer flexible course scheduling or online distance learning courses. (See the Sources of Education, Training, and Financial Aid section of the *Handbook* for more information regarding community and junior colleges.) In addition to general education, coursework includes medical terminology, anatomy and physiology, legal aspects of health information, health data standards, coding and abstraction of data, statistics, database management, quality improvement methods, and computer science. Applicants can improve their chances of admission into a program by taking biology, math, chemistry, health, and computer science courses in high school.

Certification and other qualifications. Most employers prefer to hire Registered Health Information Technicians (RHIT), who must pass a written examination offered by the American Health Information Management Association (AHIMA). To take the examination, a person must graduate from a 2-year associate degree program accredited by the Commission on Accreditation for Health Informatics and Information Management Education (CAHIIM). Technicians trained in non-CAHIIM-accredited programs or trained on the job are not eligible to take the examination. In 2007, there were about 245 CAHIIM accredited programs in Health Informantics and Information Management Education.

Some employers prefer candidates with experience in a health care setting. Experience is valuable in demonstrating certain skills or desirable qualities. It is beneficial for health information technicians to possess good communication skills, as they often serve as a liaison between health care facilities, insurance companies, and other establishments. Accuracy is also essential to technicians because they must pay close attention to detail. A candidate who exhibits proficiency with computers will become more valuable as health care facilities continue to adopt electronic medical records.

Certification and advancement. Experienced medical records and health information technicians usually advance in one of two ways—by specializing or by moving into a management position. Many senior technicians specialize in coding, in cancer registry, or in privacy and security. Most coding and registry skills are learned on the job. A number of schools offer certificate programs in coding or include coding as part of the associate degree program for health information technicians, although there are no formal degree programs in coding. For cancer registry, there are a few formal 2-year certificate programs approved by the National Cancer Registrars Association (NCRA). Some schools and employers offer intensive 1- to 2-week training programs in either coding or cancer registry.

Certification in coding is available from several organizations. Coding certification within specific medical specialty areas is available from the Board of Medical Specialty Coding and the Professional Association of Healthcare Coding Specialist (PAHCS). The American Academy of Professional Coders (AAPC) offers three distinct certification programs in coding. The AHIMA also offers certification for Certified Healthcare Privacy and Security because of growing concerns for the security of electronic medical records. Certification in cancer registry is available from the NCRA. Continuing education units are typically required to renew credentials.

In large medical records and health information departments, experienced technicians may advance to section supervisor, overseeing the work of the coding, correspondence, or discharge sections, for example. Senior technicians with RHIT credentials may become director or assistant director of a medical records and health information department in a small facility. However, in larger institutions, the director usually is an administrator with a bachelor's degree in medical records and health information administration.

Hospitals sometimes advance promising health information clerks to jobs as medical records and health information technicians, although this practice may be less common in the future. Advancement usually requires 2 to 4 years of job experience and completion of a hospital's in-house training program.

Employment

Medical records and health information technicians held about 170,000 jobs in 2006. About 2 out of 5 jobs were in hospitals. The rest were mostly in offices of physicians, nursing care facilities, outpatient care centers, and home health care services. Insurance firms that deal in health matters employ a small number of health information technicians to tabulate and analyze health information. Public health departments also employ technicians to supervise data collection from health care institutions and to assist in research.

Projections data from the National Employment Matrix

Occupational Title	SOC Code	Employment, 2006	Projected employment, 2016	Change, 2006-2016	
				Number	Percent
Medical records and health information technicians	29-2071	170,000	200,000	30,000	18

NOTE: Data in this table are rounded. See the discussion of the employment projections table in the *Handbook* introductory chapter on *Occupational Information Included in the Handbook*.

Job Outlook

Employment is expected to grow faster than average. Job prospects should be very good; technicians with a strong background in medical coding will be in particularly high demand.

Employment change. Employment of medical records and health information technicians is expected to increase by 18 percent through 2016—faster than the average for all occupations—because of rapid growth in the number of medical tests, treatments, and procedures that will be increasingly scrutinized by health insurance companies, regulators, courts, and consumers. Also, technicians will be needed to enter patient information into computer databases to comply with Federal legislation mandating the use of electronic medical records.

New jobs are expected in offices of physicians as a result of increasing demand for detailed records, especially in large group practices. New jobs also are expected in home health care services, outpatient care centers, and nursing and residential care facilities. Although employment growth in hospitals will not keep pace with growth in other health care industries, many new jobs will, nevertheless, be created.

Cancer registrars should experience job growth. As the population continues to age, the incidence of cancer may increase.

Job prospects. Job prospects should be very good. In addition to job growth, openings will result from the need to replace technicians who retire or leave the occupation permanently.

Technicians with a strong background in medical coding will be in particularly high demand. Changing government regulations and the growth of managed care have increased the amount of paperwork involved in filing insurance claims. Additionally, health care facilities are having some difficulty attracting qualified workers, primarily because employers prefer trained and experienced technicians prepared to work in an increasingly electronic environment with the integration of electronic health records. Job opportunities may be especially good for coders employed through temporary help agencies or by professional services firms.

Earnings

Median annual earnings of medical records and health information technicians were $28,030 in May 2006. The middle 50 percent earned between $22,420 and $35,990. The lowest 10 percent earned less than $19,060, and the highest 10 percent earned more than $45,260. Median annual earnings in the industries employing the largest numbers of medical records and health information technicians in May 2006 were:

General medical and surgical hospitals	$29,400
Nursing care facilities	28,410
Outpatient care centers	26,680
Offices of physicians	24,170

Related Occupations

Medical records and health information technicians need a strong clinical background to analyze the contents of medical records. Medical secretaries and medical transcriptionists also must be knowledgeable about medical terminology, anatomy, and physiology even though they have little or no direct contact with patients.

Sources of Additional Information

Information on careers in medical records and health information technology, and a list of accredited training programs is available from:

➤ American Health Information Management Association, 233 N. Michigan Ave., Suite 2150, Chicago, IL 60601-5800. Internet: **http://www.ahima.org**

Information on training and certification for medical coders is available from:

➤ American Academy of Professional Coders, 2480 South 3850 West, Suite B, Salt Lake City, UT 84120. Internet: **http://www.aapc.com**

Information on cancer registrars is available from:

➤ National Cancer Registrars Association, 1340 Braddock Place Suite 203, Alexandria, VA 22314. Internet: **http://www.ncra-usa.org**

Nuclear Medicine Technologists

(O*NET 29-2033.00)

Significant Points

- Two-thirds of nuclear medicine technologists worked in hospitals.

- Nuclear medicine technology programs range in length from 1 to 4 years and lead to a certificate, an associate degree, or a bachelor's degree.

- Faster-than-average job growth will arise from an increase in the number of middle-aged and elderly persons, who are the primary users of diagnostic and treatment procedures.

- The number of job openings each year will be relatively low because the occupation is small; technologists who also are trained in other diagnostic methods, such as radiologic technology or diagnostic medical sonography, will have the best prospects.

Nature of the Work

Diagnostic imaging embraces several procedures that aid in diagnosing ailments, the most familiar being the x-ray. In nuclear medicine, radionuclides—unstable atoms that emit radiation spontaneously—are used to diagnose and treat disease. Radionuclides are purified and compounded to form radiopharmaceuticals. Nuclear medicine technologists administer radiopharmaceuticals to patients and then monitor the characteristics and functions of tissues or organs in which the drugs localize. Abnormal areas show higher-than-expected or lower-than-expected concentrations of radioactivity. Nuclear medicine differs from other diagnostic imaging technologies because it determines the presence of disease on the basis of metabolic changes rather than changes in organ structure.

Nuclear medicine technologists operate cameras that detect and map the radioactive drug in a patient's body to create diagnostic images. After explaining test procedures to patients, technologists prepare a dosage of the radiopharmaceutical and administer it by mouth, injection, inhalation, or other means. They position patients and start a gamma scintillation camera, or "scanner," which creates images of the distribution of a radiopharmaceutical as it localizes in, and emits signals from, the patient's body. The images are produced on a computer screen or on film for a physician to interpret.

When preparing radiopharmaceuticals, technologists adhere to safety standards that keep the radiation exposure as low as possible to workers and patients. Technologists keep patient records and document the amount and type of radionuclides that they receive, use, and discard.

Work environment. Physical stamina is important because nuclear medicine technologists are on their feet much of the day and may have to lift or turn disabled patients. In addition, technologists must operate complicated equipment that requires mechanical ability and manual dexterity.

Although the potential for radiation exposure exists in this field, it is minimized by the use of shielded syringes, gloves, and other protective devices and by adherence to strict radiation safety guidelines. The amount of radiation in a nuclear medicine procedure is comparable to that received during a diagnostic x-ray procedure. Technologists also wear badges that measure radiation levels. Because of safety programs, badge measurements rarely exceed established safety levels.

Nuclear medicine technologists generally work a 40-hour week, perhaps including evening or weekend hours, in departments that operate on an extended schedule. Opportunities for part-time and shift work also are available. In addition, technologists in hospitals may have on-call duty on a rotational basis, and those employed by mobile imaging services may be required to travel to several locations.

Training, Other Qualifications, and Advancement

Nuclear medicine technology programs range in length from 1 to 4 years and lead to a certificate, an associate degree, or a bachelor's degree. Many employers and an increasing number of States require certification or licensure. Aspiring nuclear medicine technologists should check the requirements of the State in which they plan to work.

Education and training. Completion of a nuclear medicine technology program takes 1 to 4 years and leads to a certificate, an associate degree, or a bachelor's degree. Generally, certificate programs are offered in hospitals, associate degree programs in community colleges, and bachelor's degree programs in 4-year colleges and universities. Courses cover the physical sciences, biological effects of radiation exposure, radiation protection and procedures, the use of radiopharmaceuticals, imaging techniques, and computer applications.

One-year certificate programs are for health professionals who already possess an associate degree—especially radiologic technologists and diagnostic medical sonographers—but who wish to specialize in nuclear medicine. The programs also attract medical technologists, registered nurses, and others who wish to change fields or specialize.

The Joint Review Committee on Education Programs in Nuclear Medicine Technology accredits most formal training programs in nuclear medicine technology. In 2006, there were about 100 accredited programs in the continental United States and Puerto Rico.

Licensure and certification. Educational requirements for nuclear medicine technologists vary from State to State, so it is important that aspiring technologists check the requirements of the State in which they plan to work. More than half of all States require certification or licensing of nuclear medicine technicians. Certification is available from the American Registry of Radiologic Technologists (ARRT) and from the Nuclear Medicine Technology Certification Board (NMTCB). Although not required, some workers receive certification from both agencies. Nuclear medicine technologists must meet the minimum Federal standards on the administration of radioactive drugs and the operation of radiation detection equipment.

The most common way to become eligible for certification by ARRT or NMTCB is to complete a training program recognized by those organizations. Other ways to become eligible are completing a bachelor's or associate degree in biological science or related health field, such as registered nursing, or acquiring, under supervision, a certain number of hours of experience in nuclear medicine technology. ARRT and NMTCB have different requirements, but in all cases, one must pass a comprehensive exam to become certified.

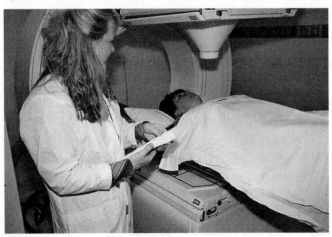

Nuclear medicine technologists operate cameras that detect and map the radioactive drugs in a patient's body to create diagnostic images.

In addition to the general certification requirements, certified technicians also must complete a certain number of continuing education hours. Continuing education is required primarily because of the frequent technological and innovative changes in the field of nuclear medicine. Typically, technologists must register annually with both the ARRT and the NMTCB.

Other qualifications. Nuclear medicine technologists should have excellent communication skills, be detail-oriented, and have a desire to continue learning. Technologists must effectively interact with patients and their families and should be sensitive to patients' physical and psychological needs. Nuclear medicine technologists must be able to work independently as they usually have little direct supervision. Technologists also must be detailed-oriented and meticulous when performing procedures to assure that all regulations are being followed.

Advancement. Technologists may advance to supervisor, then to chief technologist, and to department administrator or director. Some technologists specialize in a clinical area such as nuclear cardiology or computer analysis or leave patient care to take positions in research laboratories. Some become instructors in, or directors of, nuclear medicine technology programs, a step that usually requires a bachelor's or master's degree in the subject. Others leave the occupation to work as sales or training representatives for medical equipment and radiopharmaceutical manufacturing firms or as radiation safety officers in regulatory agencies or hospitals.

Employment

Nuclear medicine technologists held about 20,000 jobs in 2006. About 67 percent of all nuclear medicine technologists jobs were in hospitals—private and government. Most of the rest were in offices of physicians or in medical and diagnostic laboratories, including diagnostic imaging centers.

Job Outlook

Faster-than-average job growth will arise from an increase in the number of middle-aged and elderly persons, who are the primary users of diagnostic and treatment procedures. However, the number of job openings each year will be relatively low because the occupation is small.

Employment change. Employment of nuclear medicine technologists is expected to increase by 15 percent from 2006 to 2016, faster than the average for all occupations. Growth will arise from technological advancement, the development of new nuclear medicine treatments, and an increase in the number of middle-aged and older persons, who are the primary users of diagnostic procedures, including nuclear medicine tests.

Technological innovations may increase the diagnostic uses of nuclear medicine. New nuclear medical imaging technologies, including positron emission tomography (PET) and single photon emission computed tomography (SPECT), are expected to be used increasingly and to contribute further to employment growth. The wider use of nuclear medical imaging to observe metabolic and biochemical changes during neurology, cardiology, and oncology procedures also will spur demand for nuclear medicine technologists.

Nonetheless, cost considerations will affect the speed with which new applications of nuclear medicine grow. Some promising nuclear medicine procedures, such as positron emission tomography, are extremely costly, and hospitals contemplating these procedures will have to consider equipment costs, reimbursement policies, and the number of potential users.

Job prospects. In spite of fast growth in nuclear medicine, the number of openings into the occupation each year will be relatively low because of the small size of the occupation. Technologists who have additional training in other diagnostic methods, such as radiologic technology or diagnostic medical sonography, will have the best prospects.

Earnings

Median annual earnings of nuclear medicine technologists were $62,300 in May 2006. The middle 50 percent earned between $53,530 and $72,410. The lowest 10 percent earned less than $46,490, and the highest 10 percent earned more than $82,310. Median annual earnings of nuclear medicine technologists in 2006 were $61,230 in general medical and surgical hospitals.

Related Occupations

Nuclear medical technologists operate sophisticated equipment to help physicians and other health practitioners diagnose and treat patients. Cardiovascular technologists and technicians, clinical laboratory technologists and technicians, diagnostic medical sonographers, radiation therapists, radiologic technologists and technicians, and respiratory therapists perform similar functions.

Sources of Additional Information

Additional information on a career as a nuclear medicine technologist is available from:

➤ American Society of Radiologic Technologists, 15000 Central Ave. S.E., Albuquerque, NM 87123-3917. Internet: **http://www.asrt.org**

➤ American Registry of Radiologic Technologists, 1255 Northland Dr., St.Paul, MN 55120-1155. Internet: **http://www.arrt.org**

➤ Society of Nuclear Medicine Technologists, 1850 Samuel Morse Dr., Reston, VA 20190-5316. Internet: **http://www.snm.org**

For a list of accredited programs in nuclear medicine technology, contact:

➤ Joint Review Committee on Educational Programs in Nuclear Medicine Technology, 716 Black Point Rd., Polson, MT 59860. Internet: **http://www.jrcnmt.org**

Projections data from the National Employment Matrix

Occupational Title	SOC Code	Employment, 2006	Projected employment, 2016	Change, 2006-2016	
				Number	Percent
Nuclear medicine technologists..	29-2033	20,000	23,000	2,900	15

NOTE: Data in this table are rounded. See the discussion of the employment projections table in the *Handbook* introductory chapter on *Occupational Information Included in the Handbook.*

Information on certification is available from:

> Nuclear Medicine Technology Certification Board, 2970 Clairmont Rd., Suite 935, Atlanta, GA 30329-4421. Internet: **http://www.nmtcb.org**

Occupational Health and Safety Specialists and Technicians

(O*NET 29-9011.00, 29-9012.00)

Significant Points

- About 2 out of 5 specialists and technicians worked in Federal, State, and local government agencies that enforce rules on safety, health, and the environment.

- Some specialist jobs require a bachelor's degree in occupational health, safety, or a related field.

- Projected average employment growth reflects a balance of continuing public demand for a safe and healthy work environment against the desire for smaller government and fewer regulations.

Nature of the Work

Occupational health and safety specialists and technicians, also known as *safety and health professionals* or *occupational health and safety inspectors*, help prevent harm to workers, property, the environment, and the general public. For example, they might design safe work spaces, inspect machines, or test air quality. In addition to making workers safer, specialists and technicians aim to increase worker productivity by reducing absenteeism and equipment downtime—and to save money by lowering insurance premiums and workers' compensation payments, and preventing government fines. Some specialists and technicians work for governments, conducting safety inspections and imposing fines.

Occupational health and safety specialists analyze work environments and design programs to control, eliminate, and prevent disease or injury. They look for chemical, physical, radiological, and biological hazards, and they work to make more equipment ergonomic—designed to promote proper body positioning, increase worker comfort, and decrease fatigue. Specialists may conduct inspections and inform an organization's management of areas not in compliance with State and Federal laws or employer policies. They also advise management on the cost and effectiveness of safety and health programs. Some provide training on new regulations and policies or on how to recognize hazards.

Sometimes, specialists develop methods to predict hazards from historical data and other information sources. They use these methods and their own knowledge and experience to evaluate current equipment, products, facilities, or processes and those planned for use in the future. For example, they might uncover patterns in injury data that show that many injuries are caused by a specific type of system failure, human error, or weakness in procedures. They evaluate the probability and severity of accidents and identify where controls need to be implemented to reduce or eliminate risk. If a new program or practice is required, they propose it to management and monitor results if it is implemented. Specialists also might conduct safety training for management, supervisors, and workers. Training sessions might show how to recognize hazards, for example, or explain new regulations and production processes.

Some specialists, often called *loss prevention specialists*, work for insurance companies, inspecting the facilities that they insure and suggesting and helping to implement improvements.

Occupational health and safety technicians often focus on testing air, water, machines, and other elements of the work environment. They collect data that occupational health and safety specialists then analyze. Usually working under the supervision of specialists, they also help to implement and evaluate safety programs.

To measure hazards, such as noise or radiation, occupational health and safety technicians prepare and calibrate scientific equipment. They must properly collect and handle samples of dust, gases, vapors, and other potentially toxic materials to ensure personal safety and accurate test results. Occupational health and safety specialists also may perform this work, especially if it is complex.

To ensure that machinery and equipment complies with appropriate safety regulations, occupational health and safety specialists and technicians both may examine and test machinery and equipment, such as lifting devices, machine guards, or scaffolding. They may check that personal protective equipment, such as masks, respirators, protective eyewear, or hardhats, is being used according to regulations. They also check that hazardous materials are stored correctly. They test and identify work areas for potential accident and health hazards, such as toxic vapors, mold, mildew, and explosive gas-air mixtures and help implement appropriate control measures, such as adjustments to ventilation systems. Their inspection of the workplace might involve talking with workers and observing their work, as well as inspecting elements in their work environment, such as lighting, tools, and equipment.

If an injury or illness occurs, occupational health and safety specialists and technicians help investigate, studying its causes and recommending remedial action. Some occupational health and safety specialists and technicians help workers to return to work after accidents and injuries.

Occupational health and safety specialists and technicians frequently communicate with management about the status of health and safety programs. They also might consult with engineers or physicians.

Specialists and technicians write reports, including accident reports, and enter information on Occupational Safety and Health Administration recordkeeping forms. They may prepare documents used in legal proceedings and give testimony in court. Those who develop expertise in specific areas may develop occupational health and safety systems, including policies, procedures, and manuals.

The responsibilities of occupational health and safety specialists and technicians vary by industry, workplace, and types of hazards affecting employees. Mine examiners, for example, are technicians who inspect mines for proper air flow and health hazards such as the buildup of methane or other noxious gases. Environmental protection officers evaluate and coordinate the storage and handling of hazardous waste, the cleanup of contaminated soil or water, or other activities that affect the environment. Ergonomists consider the design of industrial, office, and other equipment to maximize worker comfort, safety, and productivity. Health physicists work in places that use radiation and radioactive material, helping to protect people and the environment from hazardous radiation exposure. And industrial hygienists examine the workplace for health hazards, such as exposure to lead, asbestos, pesticides, or communicable diseases.

Work environment. Occupational health and safety specialists and technicians work in a variety of settings from offices and factories to mines. Their jobs often involve considerable fieldwork, and some require frequent travel.

Occupational health and safety specialists and technicians may be exposed to many of the same strenuous, dangerous, or stressful conditions faced by industrial employees. They may find themselves in an adversarial role if an organization disagrees with their recommendations. Many occupational health and safety specialists and technicians work long, and often irregular, hours.

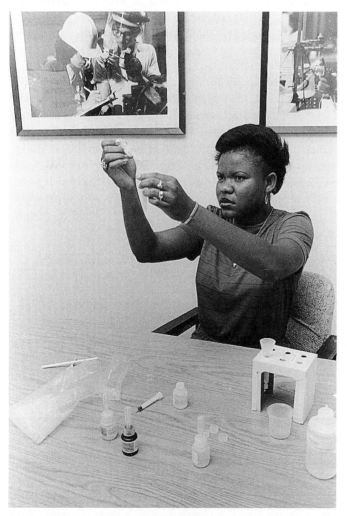

Occupational health and safety technicians use scientific equipment to measure hazards, such as noise or radiation.

Training, Other Qualifications, and Advancement

All occupational health and safety specialists and technicians are trained in the applicable laws or inspection procedures through some combination of classroom and on-the-job training.

Education and training. Some employers require occupational health and safety specialists to have a bachelor's degree in occupational health, safety, or a related field, such as engineering, biology, or chemistry. For some positions, a master's degree in industrial hygiene or a related subject is required. There also are associate degree and 1-year certificate programs, which primarily are intended for technicians.

As of February 2007, the Accreditation Board for Engineering and Technology accredited 45 programs in health physics, industrial hygiene, and safety.

Certification and other qualifications. Although voluntary, many employers encourage certification. Certification is available through several organizations. The Board of Certified Safety Professionals offers the Certified Safety Professional (CSP) credential. The American Board of Industrial Hygiene offers the Certified Industrial Hygienist (CIH) credential. Also, the Council on Certification of Health, Environmental, and Safety Technologists certifies people as Occupational Health and Safety Technologists (OHST), who may be called Certified Loss Control Specialists (CLCS), Construction Health and Safety Technicians (CHST), and Safety Trained Supervisors (STS). The Indoor Air Quality Association awards the Certified Indoor Environmentalist (CIE) credential. The Board of Certification in Professional Ergonomics offers the Certified Professional Ergonomist (CPE) and the Certified Ergonomics Associate (CEA) credentials. The American Board of Health Physicists awards the Certified Health Physicist (CHP) credential.

Requirements for these credentials differ. Usually, they include specific education and experience, passing an examination, and completing periodic continuing education for recertification.

In general, people who want to enter this occupation should be responsible and like detailed work. Occupational health and safety specialists and technicians also should be able to communicate well. Recommended high school courses include English, mathematics, chemistry, biology, and physics. Experience as an occupational health and safety professional is also a prerequisite for many positions.

Advancement. Occupational health and safety specialists and technicians who work for the Federal Government advance through their career ladder to a specified full-performance level if their work is satisfactory. For positions above this level, usually supervisory positions, advancement is competitive and based on agency needs and individual merit. Advancement opportunities in State and local governments and the private sector are often similar to those in the Federal Government.

Specialists and technicians with broad education and experience and those who are well versed in numerous business functions usually have the best advancement opportunities. One way to keep up with current professional developments is to join a professional society, such as those that offer the certifications mentioned earlier. These organizations offer journals, continuing education courses, and conferences, which offer learning and networking opportunities and can help workers and students to advance.

With an advanced degree, professionals can become professors or do research. Promotion to senior specialist positions is likely to require an advanced degree and substantial experience in several areas of practice.

Employment

Occupational health and safety specialists and technicians held about 56,000 jobs in 2006. While the majority of jobs were spread throughout the private sector; about 2 out of 5 specialists worked for government agencies. Local governments employed 15 percent, the Federal Government employed 13 percent, and State governments employed 12 percent.

Within the Federal Government, most jobs are as Occupational Safety and Health Administration inspectors, who enforce U.S. Department of Labor regulations and impose fines. Within the U.S. Department of Health and Human Services, the National Institute of Occupational Safety and Health hires occupational health and safety specialists to offer companies help in evaluating safety without the risk of fines. Most large government agencies also employ occupational health and safety specialists and technicians who work to protect agency employees.

Most private companies either employ their own occupational health and safety workers or contract with them. Most contract work is done through consulting companies, but some specialists and technicians are self-employed.

In addition to working for governments, occupational health and safety specialists and technicians were employed in manufacturing firms; private general medical and surgical hospitals; private colleges, universities, and professional schools; scientific and technical consulting services; research and development in the physical, engineering, and life sciences; and electric power generation, transmission, and distribution. Insurance companies and technical consulting services also often employed specialists, whereas employment services and testing laboratories often employed technicians.

Job Outlook

Average employment growth is expected; additional opportunities will arise from the need to replace workers who leave the occupation.

Employment change. Employment of occupational health and safety specialists and technicians is expected to increase 9 percent during the 2006-16 decade, about as fast as the average for all occupations, reflecting a balance of continuing public demand for a safe and healthy work environment against the desire for smaller government and fewer regulations. Emergency preparedness will continue to increase in importance, creating demand for these workers. More specialists will be needed to cope with technological advances in safety equipment and threats, changing regulations, and increasing public expectations. In private industry, employment growth will reflect overall business growth and continuing self-enforcement of government and company regulations and policies.

Over the past two decades, insurance and worker's compensation costs have risen and have become a financial concern for many employers and insurance companies. As a result, job growth should be good for those specializing in loss prevention, especially in construction safety and in ergonomics.

Job prospects. In addition to job openings from growth, job openings will arise from the need to replace workers who transfer to other occupations, retire, or leave for other reasons. An aging population paired with a decline in the number of postsecondary students studying the sciences, especially health physics, will create opportunities for those with technical skill.

Employment of occupational health and safety specialists and technicians in the private sector is somewhat affected by general economic fluctuations. Federal, State, and local governments, which employ about 2 out of 5 of all specialists and technicians, provide considerable job security; workers are less likely to be affected by changes in the economy.

Earnings

Median annual earnings of occupational health and safety specialists and technicians were $54,920 in May 2006. The middle 50 percent earned between $41,800 and $70,230. The lowest 10 percent earned less than $32,230, and the highest 10 percent earned more than $83,720. Median annual earnings in the industries employing the largest numbers of occupational health and safety specialists and technicians in May 2006 were:

Federal Government $68,890
Management, scientific, and
   technical consulting services 63,130
General medical and surgical hospitals 59,200
Local government 52,110
State government 49,690

Most occupational health and safety specialists and technicians work in large private firms or for Federal, State, and local governments, most of which generally offer benefits more generous than those offered by smaller firms.

Projections data from the National Employment Matrix

Occupational Title	SOC Code	Employment, 2006	Projected employment, 2016	Change, 2006-2016	
				Number	Percent
Occupational health and safety specialists and technicians..............	29-9010	56,000	61,000	5,200	9
Occupational health and safety specialists..................................	29-9011	45,000	49,000	3,700	8
Occupational health and safety technicians	29-9012	10,000	12,000	1,500	15

NOTE: Data in this table are rounded. See the discussion of the employment projections table in the *Handbook* introductory chapter on *Occupational Information Included in the Handbook.*

Related Occupations

Occupational health and safety specialists and technicians help to ensure that laws and regulations are obeyed. Others who enforce laws and regulations include agricultural inspectors, construction and building inspectors, correctional officers, financial examiners, fire inspectors, police and detectives, and transportation inspectors. Occupational health and safety specialists also analyze work environments and processes, topics that industrial engineers also study.

Sources of Additional Information

Information about jobs in Federal, State, and local governments and in private industry is available from State employment service offices.

For information on a career as an industrial hygienist, including a list of colleges and universities offering industrial hygiene and related degrees, contact:

➤ American Industrial Hygiene Association, 2700 Prosperity Ave., Suite 250, Fairfax, VA 22031. Internet: **http://www.aiha.org**

For information on the Certified Industrial Hygienist or Certified Associate Industrial Hygienist credential, contact:

➤ American Board of Industrial HygieNE., 6015 West St.Joseph Hwy., Suite 102, Lansing, MI 48917. Internet: **http://www.abih.org**

For more information on professions in safety, a list of safety and related academic programs, and the Certified Safety Professional credential, contact:

➤ Board of Certified Safety Professionals, 208 Burwash Ave., Savoy, IL 61874. Internet: **http://www.bcsp.org**

For information on the Occupational Health and Safety Technologist, Construction Health and Safety Technician credentials, and Safety Trained Supervisors, contact:

➤ Council on Certification of Health, Environmental, and Safety Technologists, 208 Burwash Ave., Savoy, IL 61874. Internet: **http://www.cchest.org**

For information on a career as a health physicist, contact:

➤ Health Physics Society, 1313 Dolley Madison Blvd., Suite 402, McLean, VA 22101. Internet: **http://www.hps.org**

For additional career information, contact:

➤ U.S. Department of Health and Human Services, Center for Disease Control and Prevention, National Institute of Occupational Safety and Health, Hubert H. Humphrey Bldg., 200 Independence Ave. SW., Room 715H, Washington, DC 20201. Internet: **http://www.cdc.gov/niosh**

➤ U.S. Department of Labor, Occupational Safety and Health Administration, Office of Communication, 200 Constitution Ave. NW., Washington, DC 20210. Internet: **http://www.osha.gov**

Information on obtaining positions as occupational health and safety specialists and technicians with the Federal Government is available from the Office of Personnel Management through USAJOBS, the Federal Government's official employment information system. This resource for locating and applying for job opportunities can be accessed through the Internet at **http://www.usajobs.opm.gov** or through an interactive voice response telephone system at (703) 724-1850 or TDD (978) 461-8404. These numbers are not toll free, and charges may result.

Opticians, Dispensing

(O*NET 29-2081.00)

Significant Points

- Most dispensing opticians receive training on the job or through apprenticeships lasting 2 or more years, but some employers seek graduates of postsecondary training programs in opticianry.

- A license to practice is required by 22 States.

- Employment growth is projected to be average and reflect the steady demand for corrective lenses and fashionable eyeglass frames.

Nature of the Work

Helping people see better and look good at the same time is the job of a dispensing optician. Dispensing opticians help select and then fit eyeglasses and contact lenses for people with eye problems, following prescriptions written by ophthalmologists or optometrists. (The work of optometrists is described elsewhere in the *Handbook*. See the section on physicians and surgeons for information about ophthalmologists.) Dispensing opticians recommend eyeglass frames, lenses, and lens coatings after considering the prescription and the customer's occupation, habits, and facial features. They measure clients' eyes, including the distance between the centers of the pupils and the distance between the ocular surface and the lens. For customers without prescriptions, dispensing opticians may use a focimeter to record eyeglass measurements in order to duplicate their existing eyeglasses. They also may obtain a customer's previous record to re-make eyeglasses or contact lenses, or they may verify a prescription with the examining optometrist or ophthalmologist.

Dispensing opticians prepare work orders that give ophthalmic laboratory technicians the information they need to grind and insert lenses into a frame. (See the section on ophthalmic laboratory technicians elsewhere in the *Handbook*.) The work order includes prescriptions for lenses and information on their size, material, color, and style. Some dispensing opticians grind and insert lenses themselves. They may also apply tint to glasses. After the glasses are made, dispensing opticians verify that the lenses have been ground to specifications. Then they may reshape or bend the frame by hand or using pliers so that the eyeglasses fit the customer properly and comfortably.

Many opticians also spend time fixing, adjusting, and refitting broken frames. They instruct clients about adapting to, wearing, or caring for eyeglasses. Additionally, administrative duties have become a major part of their work, including keeping records on customers' prescriptions, work orders, and payments, and tracking inventory and sales.

Some dispensing opticians, after additional education and training, specialize in fitting contacts, artificial eyes, or cosmetic shells to cover blemished eyes. To fit contact lenses, dispensing opticians measure the shape and size of the eye, select the type of contact lens material, and prepare work orders

Opticians take measurements to ensure that eyeglasses fit properly.

specifying the prescription and lens size. Fitting contact lenses requires considerable skill, care, and patience. Dispensing opticians observe customers' eyes, corneas, lids, and contact lenses with specialized instruments and microscopes. During several follow-up visits, opticians teach proper insertion, removal, and care of contact lenses.

Work environment. Dispensing opticians work indoors mainly in medical offices, optical stores, or in large department or club stores. Opticians spend a fair amount of time on their feet. If they prepare lenses, they need to take precautions against the hazards of glass cutting, chemicals, and machinery. Most dispensing opticians work about 40 hours a week, although a few work longer hours. Those in retail stores may work evenings and weekends. Some work part time.

Training, Other Qualifications, and Advancement

Most workers entering this occupation receive their training on the job, mainly through apprenticeship programs that may last 2 years or longer. Some employers, though, prefer to hire people who have graduated from an opticianry program.

Education and training. A high school diploma is all that is required to get into this occupation, but most workers have completed at least some college courses or a degree. Classes in physics, basic anatomy, algebra, and trigonometry as well as experience with computers are particularly valuable. These prepare dispensing opticians to learn job skills, including optical mathematics, optical physics, and the use of precision measuring instruments and other machinery and tools.

Most applicants for optician positions do not have any background in the field and learn mainly on the job. Large employers usually offer structured apprenticeship programs; small employers provide more informal, on-the-job training. Apprentices receive technical training and also learn office management and sales. Under the supervision of an experienced optician, optometrist, or ophthalmologist, apprentices work directly with patients, fitting eyeglasses and contact lenses.

Formal training in the field is offered in community colleges and in a few 4-year colleges and universities. As of 2007, the Commission on Opticianry Accreditation accredited 21 associate degree programs. Graduation from an accredited program in opticianry provides a nationally recognized credential. There also are shorter programs of 1 year or less.

Licensure. Twenty-one States require dispensing opticians to be licensed. States may require individuals to pass one or more of the following for licensure: a State practical examination, a State written examination, and certification examinations offered by the American Board of Opticianry (ABO) and the National Contact Lens Examiners (NCLE). To qualify for the examinations, States often require applicants to complete postsecondary training or work as apprentices for 2 to 4 years.

Some States that license dispensing opticians allow graduates of opticianry programs to take the licensure exam immediately upon graduation; others require a few months to a year of experience. Continuing education is commonly required for licensure renewal. Information about specific licensing requirements is available from the State board of occupational licensing.

Certification and other qualifications. Any optician can apply to the ABO and the NCLE for certification of their skills, whether or not their State requires it. Certification signifies to customers and employers that an optician has a certain level of expertise. All applicants age 18 or older who have a high school diploma or equivalent are eligible for the exam, but some State licensing boards have additional eligibility requirements. Certification must be renewed every 3 years through continuing education. The State of Texas offers voluntary registration for the occupation.

Dispensing opticians deal directly with the public, so they should be tactful, pleasant, and communicate well. Manual dexterity and the ability to do precision work are essential.

Advancement. Many experienced dispensing opticians open their own optical stores. Others become managers of optical stores or sales representatives for wholesalers or manufacturers of eyeglasses or lenses.

Employment

Dispensing opticians held about 66,000 jobs in 2006. About one-third of dispensing opticians worked in offices of optometrists. Nearly one-third worked in health and personal care stores, including optical goods stores. Many of these stores offer one-stop shopping. Customers may have their eyes examined, choose frames, and have glasses made on the spot. Some opticians work in optical departments of department stores or other general merchandise stores, such as warehouse clubs and superstores. Eleven percent worked in offices of physicians, primarily ophthalmologists, who sell glasses directly to patients. Two percent were self-employed and ran their own unincorporated businesses.

Job Outlook

Employment of dispensing opticians is expected to grow about as fast as average for all occupations through 2016, as the population ages and demand for corrective lenses increases. Good job prospects are expected, but the occupation will remain relatively small.

Employment change. Employment in this occupation is expected to rise 9 percent over the 2006-16 decade. Middle age is a time when many individuals use corrective lenses for the first time, and elderly persons generally require more vision care than others. As the share of the population in these older age groups increases, more opticians will be needed to provide service to them. In addition, awareness is increasing of the importance of regular eye exams across all age groups. A small,

Projections data from the National Employment Matrix

Occupational Title	SOC Code	Employment, 2006	Projected employment, 2016	Change, 2006-2016	
				Number	Percent
Opticians, dispensing	29-2081	66,000	72,000	5,700	9

NOTE: Data in this table are rounded. See the discussion of the employment projections table in the *Handbook* introductory chapter on *Occupational Information Included in the Handbook.*

but growing number of States require children as young as 5 to get eye exams, which is expected to increase the need for eye care services in those States. Fashion also influences demand. Frames come in a growing variety of styles, colors, and sizes, encouraging people to buy more than one pair.

Moderating the need for optician services is the increasing use of laser surgery to correct vision problems. Although the surgery remains relatively more expensive than eyewear, patients who successfully undergo this surgery may not require glasses or contact lenses for several years. Also, new technology is allowing people with minimal training to make the measurements needed to fit glasses and may allow dispensing opticians to work faster, limiting the need for more workers. There also is proposed legislation that, if passed, may require contact lens manufacturers to make lenses available to nonoptical retail outlets, which may allow them to be sold over the Internet, reducing the need for opticians to provide contact lens services.

Job prospects. Job prospects for entering the profession should be good as there is a regular need to replace those who leave the occupation or retire. Nevertheless, the number of job openings will be limited because the occupation is small. Also, dispensing opticians are vulnerable to changes in the business cycle because eyewear purchases often can be deferred for a time. Job prospects will be best for those who have taken formal opticianry classes and those who master new technology, including new refraction systems, framing materials, and edging techniques.

Earnings

Median annual earnings of dispensing opticians were $30,300 in May 2006. The middle 50 percent earned between $23,560 and $38,950. The lowest 10 percent earned less than $19,290, and the highest 10 percent earned more than $47,630. Median annual earnings in the industries employing the largest numbers of dispensing opticians in May 2006 were:

Offices of physicians	$32,770
Health and personal care stores	31,850
Offices of health practitioner	29,200
Offices of optometrists	29,190

Benefits for opticians are generally determined by the industries in which they are employed. In general, those who work part-time or in small retail shops generally have fewer benefits than those who may work for large optical chains or department stores. Self-employed opticians must provide their own benefits.

Related Occupations

Other workers who deal with customers and perform delicate work include jewelers and precious stone and metal workers,

orthotists and prosthetists, and precision instrument and equipment repairers. Ophthalmic laboratory technicians also perform many of the tasks that opticians perform. And because many opticians work in the retail industry, retail salesworkers also perform some of the same duties.

Sources of Additional Information

To learn about voluntary certification for opticians who fit eyeglasses, as well as a list of State licensing boards for opticians, contact:

➤ American Board of Opticianry, 6506 Loisdale Rd., Suite 209, Springfield, VA 22150. Internet: **http://www.abo.org**

For information on voluntary certification for dispensing opticians who fit contact lenses, contact:

➤ National Contact Lens Examiners, 6506 Loisdale Rd., Suite 209, Springfield, VA 22150.
Internet: **http://www.abo-ncle.org**

Pharmacy Technicians

(O*NET 29-2052.00)

Significant Points

- Job opportunities are expected to be good, especially for those with certification or previous work experience.

- Many technicians work evenings, weekends, and holidays.

- About 71 percent of jobs were in retail pharmacies, grocery stores, department stores, or mass retailers.

Nature of the Work

Pharmacy technicians help licensed pharmacists provide medication and other health care products to patients. Technicians usually perform routine tasks to help prepare prescribed medication, such as counting tablets and labeling bottles. They also perform administrative duties, such as answering phones, stocking shelves, and operating cash registers. Technicians refer any questions regarding prescriptions, drug information, or health matters to a *pharmacist.* (See the statement on pharmacists elsewhere in the *Handbook.*)

Pharmacy technicians who work in retail or mail-order pharmacies have varying responsibilities, depending on State rules and regulations. Technicians receive written prescriptions or requests for prescription refills from patients. They also may receive prescriptions sent electronically from the doctor's office. They must verify that information on the prescription is complete and accurate. To prepare the prescription, technicians must retrieve, count, pour, weigh, measure, and sometimes mix the medication. Then, they prepare the prescription labels, select the type of prescription container, and affix the prescription and auxiliary labels to the container. Once the prescription is filled, technicians price and file the prescription, which must be checked by a pharmacist before it is given to the patient. Technicians may establish and maintain patient profiles, prepare insurance claim forms, and stock and take inventory of prescription and over-the-counter medications.

In hospitals, nursing homes, and assisted-living facilities, technicians have added responsibilities, including reading patients' charts and preparing the appropriate medication. After the pharmacist checks the prescription for accuracy, the pharmacy technician may deliver it to the patient. The technician then copies the information about the prescribed medication onto the patient's profile. Technicians also may assemble a 24-hour supply of medicine for every patient. They package and label each dose separately. The packages are then placed in the medicine cabinets of patients until the supervising pharmacist checks them for accuracy, and only then is the medication given to the patients.

Pharmacy aides work closely with pharmacy technicians. They often are clerks or cashiers who primarily answer telephones, handle money, stock shelves, and perform other clerical duties. (See the statement on pharmacy aides elsewhere in the *Handbook.*) Pharmacy technicians usually perform more complex tasks than pharmacy aides, although in some States their duties and job titles may overlap.

Work environment. Pharmacy technicians work in clean, organized, well-lighted, and well-ventilated areas. Most of their workday is spent on their feet. They may be required to lift heavy boxes or to use stepladders to retrieve supplies from high shelves.

Technicians work the same hours that pharmacists work. These may include evenings, nights, weekends, and holidays, particularly in facilities that are open 24 hours a day such as hospitals and some retail pharmacies. As their seniority increases, technicians often acquire increased control over the hours they work. There are many opportunities for part-time work in both retail and hospital settings.

Pharmacy technicians prepare prescription medications for patients.

Training, Other Qualifications, and Advancement

Most pharmacy technicians are trained on-the-job, but employers favor applicants who have formal training, certification, or previous experience. Strong customer service skills also are important. Pharmacy technicians may become supervisors, may move into specialty positions or into sales, or may become pharmacists.

Education and training. Although most pharmacy technicians receive informal on-the-job training, employers favor those who have completed formal training and certification. However, there are currently few State and no Federal requirements for formal training or certification of pharmacy technicians. Employers who have insufficient resources to give on-the-job training often seek formally educated pharmacy technicians. Formal education programs and certification emphasize the technician's interest in and dedication to the work. In addition to the military, some hospitals, proprietary schools, vocational or technical colleges, and community colleges offer formal education programs.

Formal pharmacy technician education programs require classroom and laboratory work in a variety of areas, including medical and pharmaceutical terminology, pharmaceutical calculations, pharmacy recordkeeping, pharmaceutical techniques, and pharmacy law and ethics. Technicians also are required to learn medication names, actions, uses, and doses. Many training programs include internships, in which students gain hands-on experience in actual pharmacies. After completion, students receive a diploma, a certificate, or an associate's degree, depending on the program.

Prospective pharmacy technicians with experience working as an aide in a community pharmacy or volunteering in a hospital may have an advantage. Employers also prefer applicants with experience managing inventories, counting tablets, measuring dosages, and using computers. In addition, a background in chemistry, English, and health education may be beneficial.

Certification and other qualifications. Two organizations, the Pharmacy Technician Certification Board and the Institute for the Certification of Pharmacy Technicians, administer national certification examinations. Certification is voluntary in most States, but is required by some States and employers. Some technicians are hired without formal training, but under the condition that they obtain certification within a specified period of time. To be eligible for either exam, candidates must have a high school diploma or GED, no felony convictions of any kind within 5 years of applying, and no drug or pharmacy related felony convictions at any point. Employers, often pharmacists, know that individuals who pass the exam have a standardized body of knowledge and skills. Many employers also will reimburse the costs of the exam.

Under both programs, technicians must be recertified every 2 years. Recertification requires 20 hours of continuing education within the 2-year certification period. At least 1 hour must be in pharmacy law. Continuing education hours can be earned from several different sources, including colleges, pharmacy associations, and pharmacy technician training programs. Up to 10 hours of continuing education can be earned on the job under the direct supervision and instruction of a pharmacist.

Strong customer service and teamwork skills are needed because pharmacy technicians interact with patients, coworkers, and health care professionals. Mathematics, spelling, and reading skills also are important. Successful pharmacy technicians are alert, observant, organized, dedicated, and responsible. They should be willing and able to take directions, but be able to work independently without constant instruction. They must be precise; details are sometimes a matter of life and death. Candidates interested in becoming pharmacy technicians cannot have prior records of drug or substance abuse.

Advancement. In large pharmacies and health-systems, pharmacy technicians with significant training, experience and certification can be promoted to supervisory positions, mentoring and training pharmacy technicians with less experience. Some may advance into specialty positions such as chemo therapy technician and nuclear pharmacy technician. Others move into sales. With a substantial amount of formal training, some pharmacy technicians go on to become pharmacists.

Employment

Pharmacy technicians held about 285,000 jobs in 2006. About 71 percent of jobs were in retail pharmacies, either independently owned or part of a drugstore chain, grocery store, department store, or mass retailer. About 18 percent of jobs were in hospitals and a small proportion was in mail-order and Internet pharmacies, offices of physicians, pharmaceutical wholesalers, and the Federal Government.

Job Outlook

Employment is expected to increase much faster than the average through 2016, and job opportunities are expected to be good.

Employment change. Employment of pharmacy technicians is expected to increase by 32 percent from 2006 to 2016, which is much faster than the average for all occupations. The increased number of middle-aged and elderly people—who use more prescription drugs than younger people—will spur demand for technicians throughout the projection period. In addition, as scientific advances bring treatments for an increasing number of conditions, more pharmacy technicians will be needed to fill a growing number of prescriptions.

As cost-conscious insurers begin to use pharmacies as patient-care centers, pharmacy technicians will assume responsibility for some of the more routine tasks previously performed by pharmacists. In addition, they will adopt some of the administrative duties that were previously performed by pharmacy aides, such as answering phones and stocking shelves.

Reducing the need for pharmacy technicians to some degree, however, will be the growing use of drug dispensing machines. These machines increase productivity by completing some of the pharmacy technician's duties, namely counting pills and placing them into prescription containers. These machines are only used for the most common medications, however, and their effect on employment should be minimal.

Almost all States have legislated the maximum number of technicians who can safely work under a pharmacist at one time. Changes in these laws could directly affect employment.

Job prospects. Good job opportunities are expected for full-time and part-time work, especially for technicians with formal training or previous experience. Job openings for pharmacy technicians will result from employment growth, and from the need to replace workers who transfer to other occupations or leave the labor force.

Earnings

Median hourly earnings of wage-and-salary pharmacy technicians in May 2006 were $12.32. The middle 50 percent earned between $10.10 and $14.92. The lowest 10 percent earned less than $8.56, and the highest 10 percent earned more than $17.65. Median hourly earnings in the industries employing the largest numbers of pharmacy technicians in May 2006 were:

General medical and surgical hospitals................................$13.86
Grocery stores 12.78
Pharmacies and drug stores..11.50

Certified technicians may earn more. Shift differentials for working evenings or weekends also can increase earnings. Some technicians belong to unions representing hospital or grocery store workers.

Related Occupations

This occupation is most closely related to pharmacists and pharmacy aides. Workers in other medical support occupations include dental assistants, medical transcriptionists, medical records and health information technicians, occupational therapist assistants and aides, and physical therapist assistants and aides.

Sources of Additional Information

For information on pharmacy technician certification programs, contact:
➤ Pharmacy Technician Certification Board, 2215 Constitution Ave. NW., Washington DC 20037-2985.
Internet: **http://www.ptcb.org**
➤ Institute for the Certification of Pharmacy Technicians, 2536 S. Old Hwy 94, Suite 214, St.Charles, MO 63303.
Internet: **http://www.nationaltechexam.org**
For a list of accredited pharmacy technician training programs, contact:
➤ American Society of Health-System Pharmacists, 7272 Wisconsin Ave., Bethesda, MD 20814.
Internet: **http://www.ashp.org**

Projections data from the National Employment Matrix

Occupational Title	SOC Code	Employment, 2006	Projected employment, 2016	Change, 2006-2016	
				Number	Percent
Pharmacy technicians...	29-2052	285,000	376,000	91,000	32

NOTE: Data in this table are rounded. See the discussion of the employment projections table in the *Handbook* introductory chapter on *Occupational Information Included in the Handbook.*

For pharmacy technician career information, contact:
➤ National Pharmacy Technician Association, P.O. Box 683148, Houston, TX 77268.
Internet: **http://www.pharmacytechnician.org**

Radiologic Technologists and Technicians

(O*NET 29-2034.00, 29-2034.01, 29-2034.02)

Significant Points

- Employment is projected to grow faster than average, and job opportunities are expected to be favorable.

- Formal training programs in radiography are offered in hospitals, colleges and universities, and less frequently at vocational-technical institutes; range in length from 1 to 4 years; and lead to a certificate, an associate degree, or a bachelor's degree.

- Although hospitals will remain the primary employer, a number of new jobs will be found in physicians' offices and diagnostic imaging centers.

Nature of the Work

Radiologic technologists take x-rays and administer nonradioactive materials into patients' bloodstreams for diagnostic purposes.

Radiologic technologists also referred to as *radiographers*, produce x-ray films (radiographs) of parts of the human body for use in diagnosing medical problems. They prepare patients for radiologic examinations by explaining the procedure, removing jewelry and other articles through which x-rays cannot pass, and positioning patients so that the parts of the body can be appropriately radiographed. To prevent unnecessary exposure to radiation, these workers surround the exposed area with radiation protection devices, such as lead shields, or limit the size of the x-ray beam. Radiographers position radiographic equipment at the correct angle and height over the appropriate area of a patient's body. Using instruments similar to a measuring tape, they may measure the thickness of the section to be radiographed and set controls on the x-ray machine to produce radiographs of the appropriate density, detail, and contrast. They place the x-ray film under the part of the patient's body to be examined and make the exposure. They then remove the film and develop it.

Radiologic technologists must follow physicians' orders precisely and conform to regulations concerning the use of radiation to protect themselves, their patients, and their co-workers from unnecessary exposure.

In addition to preparing patients and operating equipment, radiologic technologists keep patient records and adjust and maintain equipment. They also may prepare work schedules, evaluate purchases of equipment, or manage a radiology department.

Experienced radiographers may perform more complex imaging procedures. When performing fluoroscopies, for example, radiographers prepare a solution of contrast medium for the patient to drink, allowing the radiologist (a physician who interprets radiographs) to see soft tissues in the body.

Some radiographers specialize in computed tomography (CT), and are sometimes referred to as *CT technologists*. CT scans produce a substantial amount of cross-sectional x-rays of an area of the body. From those cross-sectional x-rays a three-dimensional image is made. The CT uses ionizing radiation; therefore, it requires the same precautionary measures that radiographers use with other x-rays.

Radiographers also can specialize in Magnetic Resonance Imaging as an *MR technologist*. MR, like CT, produces multiple cross-sectional images to create a 3-dimensional image. Unlike CT, MR uses non-ionizing radio frequency to generate image contrast.

Another common specialty for radiographers specialize in is mammography. Mammographers use low dose x-ray systems to produce images of the breast.

In addition to radiologic technologists, others who conduct diagnostic imaging procedures include cardiovascular technologists and technicians, diagnostic medical sonographers, and nuclear medicine technologists. (Each is discussed elsewhere in the *Handbook*.)

Work environment. Physical stamina is important in this occupation because technologists are on their feet for long periods and may lift or turn disabled patients. Technologists work at diagnostic machines but also may perform some procedures at patients' bedsides. Some travel to patients in large vans equipped with sophisticated diagnostic equipment.

Although radiation hazards exist in this occupation, they are minimized by the use of lead aprons, gloves, and other shielding devices, as well as by instruments monitoring exposure

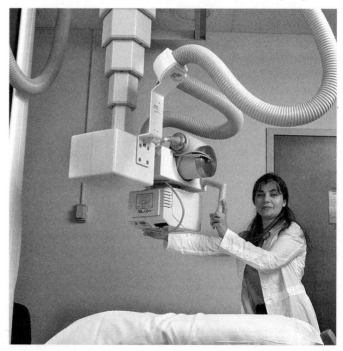

Radiographers position equipment at the correct angle and height over the appropriate area of a patient's body.

to radiation. Technologists wear badges measuring radiation levels in the radiation area, and detailed records are kept on their cumulative lifetime dose.

Most full-time radiologic technologists work about 40 hours a week. They may, however, have evening, weekend, or on-call hours. Opportunities for part-time and shift work also are available.

Training, Other Qualifications, and Advancement

Preparation for this profession is offered in hospitals, colleges and universities, and less frequently at vocational-technical institutes. Hospitals employ most radiologic technologists. Employers prefer to hire technologists with formal training.

Education and training. Formal training programs in radiography range in length from 1 to 4 years and lead to a certificate, an associate degree, or a bachelor's degree. Two-year associate degree programs are most prevalent.

Some 1-year certificate programs are available for experienced radiographers or individuals from other health occupations, such as medical technologists and registered nurses, who want to change fields. A bachelor's or master's degree in one of the radiologic technologies is desirable for supervisory, administrative, or teaching positions.

The Joint Review Committee on Education in Radiologic Technology accredits most formal training programs for the field. The committee accredited more than 600 radiography programs in 2007. Admission to radiography programs require, at a minimum, a high school diploma or the equivalent. High school courses in mathematics, physics, chemistry, and biology are helpful. The programs provide both classroom and clinical instruction in anatomy and physiology, patient care procedures, radiation physics, radiation protection, principles of imaging, medical terminology, positioning of patients, medical ethics, radiobiology, and pathology.

Licensure. Federal legislation protects the public from the hazards of unnecessary exposure to medical and dental radiation by ensuring that operators of radiologic equipment are properly trained. Under this legislation, the Federal Government sets voluntary standards that the States may use for accrediting training programs and licensing individuals who engage in medical or dental radiography. In 2007, 40 states required licensure for practicing radiologic technologists and technicians.

Certification and other qualifications. The American Registry of Radiologic Technologists (ARRT) offers voluntary certification for radiologic technologists. In addition, 35 States use ARRT-administered exams for State licensing purposes. To be eligible for certification, technologists generally must graduate from an accredited program and pass an examination. Many employers prefer to hire certified radiographers.

To be recertified, radiographers must complete 24 hours of continuing education every 2 years.

Radiologic technologists should be sensitive to patients' physical and psychological needs. They must pay attention to detail, follow instructions, and work as part of a team. In addition, operating complicated equipment requires mechanical ability and manual dexterity.

Advancement. With experience and additional training, staff technologists may become specialists, performing CT scanning, MR, and angiography, a procedure during which blood vessels are x-rayed to find clots. Technologists also may advance, with additional education and certification, to become a radiologist assistant.

Experienced technologists also may be promoted to supervisor, chief radiologic technologist, and, ultimately, department administrator or director. Depending on the institution, courses or a master's degree in business or health administration may be necessary for the director's position.

Some technologists progress by specializing in the occupation to become instructors or directors in radiologic technology programs; others take jobs as sales representatives or instructors with equipment manufacturers.

Employment

Radiologic technologists held about 196,000 jobs in 2006. More than 60 percent of all jobs were in hospitals. Most other jobs were in offices of physicians; medical and diagnostic laboratories, including diagnostic imaging centers; and outpatient care centers.

Job Outlook

Employment is projected to grow faster than average, and job opportunities are expected to be favorable.

Employment change. Employment of radiologic technologists is expected to increase by about 15 percent from 2006 to 2016, faster than the average for all occupations. As the population grows and ages, there will be an increasing demand for diagnostic imaging. Although health care providers are enthusiastic about the clinical benefits of new technologies, the extent to which they are adopted depends largely on cost and reimbursement considerations. As technology advances many imaging modalities are becoming less expensive and their adoption is becoming more widespread. For example, digital imaging technology can improve the quality of the images and the efficiency of the procedure, but it remains slightly more expensive than analog imaging, a procedure during which the image is put directly on film. Despite this, digital imaging is becoming more widespread in many imaging facilities because of the advantages it provides over analog.

Although hospitals will remain the principal employer of radiologic technologists, a number of new jobs will be found

Projections data from the National Employment Matrix

Occupational Title	SOC Code	Employment, 2006	Projected employment, 2016	Change, 2006-2016	
				Number	Percent
Radiologic technologists and technicians	29-2034	196,000	226,000	30,000	15

NOTE: Data in this table are rounded. See the discussion of the employment projections table in the *Handbook* introductory chapter on *Occupational Information Included in the Handbook.*

in offices of physicians and diagnostic imaging centers. Health facilities such as these are expected to grow through 2016, because of the shift toward outpatient care, encouraged by third-party payers and made possible by technological advances that permit more procedures to be performed outside the hospital.

Job prospects. In addition to job growth, job openings also will arise from the need to replace technologists who leave the occupation. Radiologic technologists are willing to relocate and who also are experienced in more than one diagnostic imaging procedure—such as CT, MR, and mammography—will have the best employment opportunities as employers seek to control costs by using multi-credentialed employees.

CT is becoming a frontline diagnosis tool. Instead of taking x-rays to decide whether a CT is needed, as was the practice before, it is often the first choice for imaging because of its accuracy. MR also is increasing in frequency of use. Technologists with credentialing in either of these specialties will be very marketable to employers.

Earnings

Median annual earnings of radiologic technologists were $48,170 in May 2006. The middle 50 percent earned between $39,840 and $57,940. The lowest 10 percent earned less than $32,750, and the highest 10 percent earned more than $68,920. Median annual earnings in the industries employing the largest numbers of radiologic technologists in 2006 were:

Medical and diagnostis laboratories $51,280
General medical and surgical hospitals............................48,830
Offices of physicians 45,500

Related Occupations

Radiologic technologists operate sophisticated equipment to help physicians, dentists, and other health practitioners diagnose and treat patients. Workers in related occupations include cardiovascular technologists and technicians, clinical laboratory technologists and technicians, diagnostic medical sonographers, nuclear medicine technologists, radiation therapists, and respiratory therapists.

Sources of Additional Information

For information on careers in radiologic technology, contact:
➤ American Society of Radiologic Technologists, 15000 Central Ave. SE., Albuquerque, NM 87123-3917.
Internet: **http://www.asrt.org**

For the current list of accredited education programs in radiography, write to:
➤ Joint Review Committee on Education in Radiologic Technology, 20 N. Wacker Dr., Suite 2850, Chicago, IL 60606-3182. Internet: **http://www.jrcert.org**

For certification information, contact:
➤ American Registry of Radiologic Technologists, 1255 Northland Dr., St.Paul, MN 55120-1155.
Internet: **http://www.arrt.org**

Surgical Technologists

(O*NET 29-2055.00)

Significant Points

- Employment is expected to grow much faster than average.

- Job opportunities will be best for technologists who are certified.

- Training programs last 9 to 24 months and lead to a certificate, diploma, or associate degree.

- Hospitals will continue to be the primary employer, although much faster employment growth is expected in other health care industries.

Nature of the Work

Surgical technologists, also called scrubs and surgical or operating room technicians, assist in surgical operations under the supervision of surgeons, registered nurses, or other surgical personnel. Surgical technologists are members of operating room teams, which most commonly include surgeons, anesthesiologists, and circulating nurses.

Before an operation, surgical technologists help prepare the operating room by setting up surgical instruments and equipment, sterile drapes, and sterile solutions. They assemble both sterile and nonsterile equipment, as well as check and adjust it to ensure it is working properly. Technologists also get patients ready for surgery by washing, shaving, and disinfecting incision sites. They transport patients to the operating room, help position them on the operating table, and cover them with sterile surgical drapes. Technologists also observe patients' vital signs, check charts, and help the surgical team put on sterile gowns and gloves.

During surgery, technologists pass instruments and other sterile supplies to surgeons and surgeon assistants. They may hold retractors, cut sutures, and help count sponges, needles, supplies, and instruments. Surgical technologists help prepare, care for, and dispose of specimens taken for laboratory analysis and help apply dressings. Some operate sterilizers, lights, or suction machines, and help operate diagnostic equipment.

After an operation, surgical technologists may help transfer patients to the recovery room and clean and restock the operating room.

Certified surgical technologists with additional specialized education or training also may act in the role of the surgical first assistant or circulator. The surgical first assistant, as defined by the American College of Surgeons (ACS,) provides aid in exposure, hemostasis (controlling blood flow and stopping or preventing hemorrhage), and other technical functions under the surgeon's direction that help the surgeon carry out a safe operation. A circulating technologist is the "unsterile" member of the surgical team who interviews the patient before surgery; prepares the patient; helps with anesthesia; obtains

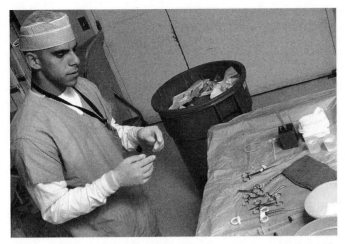

Surgical technologists assemble, check, and adjust both sterile and nonsterile equipment.

and opens packages for the "sterile" people to remove the sterile contents during the procedure; keeps a written account of the surgical procedure; and answers the surgeon's questions about the patient during the surgery.

Work environment. Surgical technologists work in clean, well-lighted, cool environments. They must stand for long periods and remain alert during operations. At times, they may be exposed to communicable diseases and unpleasant sights, odors, and materials.

Most surgical technologists work a regular 40-hour week, although they may be on call or work nights, weekends, and holidays on a rotating basis.

Training, Other Qualifications, and Advancement

Training programs last 9 to 24 months and lead to a certificate, diploma, or associate degree. Professional certification can help in getting jobs and promotions.

Education and training. Surgical technologists receive their training in formal programs offered by community and junior colleges, vocational schools, universities, hospitals, and the military. In 2006, the Commission on Accreditation of Allied Health Education Programs (CAAHEP) recognized more than 400 accredited training programs. Programs last from 9 to 24 months and lead to a certificate, diploma, or associate degree. High school graduation normally is required for admission. Recommended high school courses include health, biology, chemistry, and mathematics.

Programs provide classroom education and supervised clinical experience. Students take courses in anatomy, physiology, microbiology, pharmacology, professional ethics, and medical terminology. Other topics covered include the care and safety of patients during surgery, sterile techniques, and surgical procedures. Students also learn to sterilize instruments; prevent and control infection; and handle special drugs, solutions, supplies, and equipment.

Certification and other qualifications. Most employers prefer to hire certified technologists. Technologists may obtain voluntary professional certification from the Liaison Council on Certification for the Surgical Technologist by graduating from a CAAHEP-accredited program and passing a national certification examination. They may then use the Certified Surgical Technologist (CST) designation. Continuing education or reexamination is required to maintain certification, which must be renewed every 4 years.

Certification also may be obtained from the National Center for Competency Testing (NCCT). To qualify to take the exam, candidates follow one of three paths: complete an accredited training program; undergo a 2-year hospital on-the-job training program; or acquire 7 years of experience working in the field. After passing the exam, individuals may use the designation Tech in Surgery-Certified, TS-C (NCCT). This certification must be renewed every 5 years through either continuing education or reexamination.

Surgical technologists need manual dexterity to handle instruments quickly. They also must be conscientious, orderly, and emotionally stable to handle the demands of the operating room environment. Technologists must respond quickly and must be familiar with operating procedures in order to have instruments ready for surgeons without having to be told. They are expected to keep abreast of new developments in the field.

Advancement. Technologists advance by specializing in a particular area of surgery, such as neurosurgery or open heart surgery. They also may work as circulating technologists. With additional training, some technologists advance to first assistant. Some surgical technologists manage central supply departments in hospitals, or take positions with insurance companies, sterile supply services, and operating equipment firms.

Employment

Surgical technologists held about 86,000 jobs in 2006. About 70 percent of jobs for surgical technologists were in hospitals, mainly in operating and delivery rooms. Other jobs were in offices of physicians or dentists who perform outpatient surgery and in outpatient care centers, including ambulatory surgical centers. A few technologists, known as private scrubs, are employed directly by surgeons who have special surgical teams, like those for liver transplants.

Job Outlook

Employment of surgical technologists is expected to grow much faster than the average for all occupations. Job opportunities will be best for technologists who are certified.

Projections data from the National Employment Matrix

Occupational Title	SOC Code	Employment, 2006	Projected employment, 2016	Change, 2006-2016	
				Number	Percent
Surgical technologists	29-2055	86,000	107,000	21,000	24

NOTE: Data in this table are rounded. See the discussion of the employment projections table in the *Handbook* introductory chapter on *Occupational Information Included in the Handbook.*

Employment change. Employment of surgical technologists is expected to grow 24 percent between 2006 and 2016, much faster than the average for all occupations, as the volume of surgeries increases. The number of surgical procedures is expected to rise as the population grows and ages. Older people, including the baby boom generation, who generally require more surgical procedures, will account for a larger portion of the general population. In addition, technological advances, such as fiber optics and laser technology, will permit an increasing number of new surgical procedures to be performed and also will allow surgical technologists to assist with a greater number of procedures.

Hospitals will continue to be the primary employer of surgical technologists, although much faster employment growth is expected in offices of physicians and in outpatient care centers, including ambulatory surgical centers.

Job prospects. Job opportunities will be best for technologists who are certified.

Earnings

Median annual earnings of wage-and-salary surgical technologists were $36,080 in May 2006. The middle 50 percent earned between $30,300 and $43,560. The lowest 10 percent earned less than $25,490, and the highest 10 percent earned more than $51,140. Median annual earnings in the industries employing the largest numbers of surgical technologists were:

Offices of physicians	$37,300
Outpatient care centers	37,280
General medical and surgical hospitals	35,840
Offices of dentists	34,160

Benefits provided by most employers include paid vacation and sick leave, health, medical, vision, dental insurance and life insurance, and retirement program. A few employers also provide tuition reimbursement and child care benefits.

Related Occupations

Other health occupations requiring approximately 1 year of training after high school include dental assistants, licensed practical and licensed vocational nurses, clinical laboratory technologists and technicians, and medical assistants.

Sources of Additional Information

For additional information on a career as a surgical technologist and a list of CAAHEP-accredited programs, contact:

➤ Association of Surgical Technologists, 6 West Dry Creek Circle, Suite 200, Littleton, CO 80120.
Internet: **http://www.ast.org**

For information on becoming a Certified Surgical Technologist, contact:

➤ Liaison Council on Certification for the Surgical Technologist, 6 West Dry Creek Circle, Suite 100, Littleton, CO 80120. Internet: **http://www.lcc-st.org**

For information on becoming a Tech in Surgery-Certified, contact:

➤ National Center for Competency Testing, 7007 College Blvd., Suite 705, Overland Park, KS 66211.

Veterinary Technologists and Technicians

(O*NET 29-2056.00)

Significant Points

- Animal lovers get satisfaction from this occupation, but aspects of the work can be unpleasant, physically and emotionally demanding, and sometimes dangerous.

- Entrants generally complete a 2-year or 4-year veterinary technology program and must pass a State examination.

- Employment is expected to grow much faster than average.

- Overall job opportunities should be excellent; however, keen competition is expected for jobs in zoos and aquariums.

Nature of the Work

Owners of pets and other animals today expect state-of-the-art veterinary care. To provide this service, veterinarians use the skills of veterinary technologists and technicians, who perform many of the same duties for a veterinarian that a nurse would for a physician, including routine laboratory and clinical procedures. Although specific job duties vary by employer, there often is little difference between the tasks carried out by technicians and by technologists, despite some differences in formal education and training. As a result, most workers in this occupation are called technicians.

Veterinary technologists and technicians typically conduct clinical work in a private practice under the supervision of a licensed veterinarian. They often perform various medical tests and treat and diagnose medical conditions and diseases in animals. For example, they may perform laboratory tests such as urinalysis and blood counts, assist with dental prophylaxis, prepare tissue samples, take blood samples, or assist veterinarians in a variety of tests and analyses in which they often use various items of medical equipment, such as test tubes and diagnostic equipment. While most of these duties are performed in a laboratory setting, many are not. For example, some veterinary technicians obtain and record patients' case histories, expose and develop x-rays and radiographs, and provide specialized nursing care. In addition, experienced veterinary technicians may discuss a pet's condition with its owners and train new clinic personnel. Veterinary technologists and technicians assisting small-animal practitioners usually care for companion animals, such as cats and dogs, but can perform a variety of duties with mice, rats, sheep, pigs, cattle, monkeys, birds, fish, and frogs. Very few veterinary technologists work in mixed animal practices where they care for both small companion animals and larger, nondomestic animals.

Besides working in private clinics and animal hospitals, veterinary technologists and technicians may work in research facilities, where they administer medications orally or topically, prepare samples for laboratory examinations, and record infor-

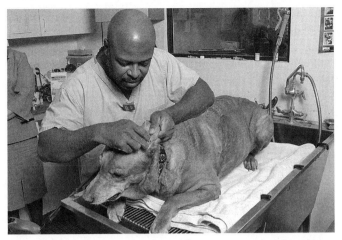

Many veterinary technologists and technicians assist veterinarians in routine laboratory and clinical procedures.

mation on an animal's genealogy, diet, weight, medications, food intake, and clinical signs of pain and distress. Some may sterilize laboratory and surgical equipment and provide routine post-operative care. At research facilities, veterinary technologists typically work under the guidance of veterinarians or physicians. Some veterinary technologists vaccinate newly admitted animals and occasionally may have to euthanize seriously ill, severely injured, or unwanted animals.

While the goal of most veterinary technologists and technicians is to promote animal health, some contribute to human health as well. Veterinary technologists occasionally assist veterinarians in implementing research projects as they work with other scientists in medical-related fields such as gene therapy and cloning. Some find opportunities in biomedical research, wildlife medicine, the military, livestock management, or pharmaceutical sales.

Work environment. People who love animals get satisfaction from working with and helping them. However, some of the work may be unpleasant, physically and emotionally demanding, and sometimes dangerous. At times, veterinary technicians must clean cages and lift, hold, or restrain animals, risking exposure to bites or scratches. These workers must take precautions when treating animals with germicides or insecticides. The work setting can be noisy.

Veterinary technologists and technicians who witness abused animals or who euthanize unwanted, aged, or hopelessly injured animals may experience emotional stress. Those working for humane societies and animal shelters often deal with the public, some of whom might react with hostility to any implication that the owners are neglecting or abusing their pets. Such workers must maintain a calm and professional demeanor while they enforce the laws regarding animal care.

In some animal hospitals, research facilities, and animal shelters, a veterinary technician is on duty 24 hours a day, which means that some may work night shifts. Most full-time veterinary technologists and technicians work about 40 hours a week, although some work 50 or more hours a week.

Training, Other Qualifications, and Advancement

There are primarily two levels of education and training for entry to this occupation: a 2-year program for veterinary technicians and a 4-year program for veterinary technologists.

Education and training. Most entry-level veterinary technicians have a 2-year associate degree from an American Veterinary Medical Association (AVMA)-accredited community college program in veterinary technology in which courses are taught in clinical and laboratory settings using live animals. About 16 colleges offer veterinary technology programs that are longer and that culminate in a 4-year bachelor's degree in veterinary technology. These 4-year colleges, in addition to some vocational schools, also offer 2-year programs in laboratory animal science. Several schools offer distance learning.

In 2006, 131 veterinary technology programs in 44 States were accredited by the American Veterinary Medical Association (AVMA). Graduation from an AVMA-accredited veterinary technology program allows students to take the credentialing exam in any State in the country.

Persons interested in careers as veterinary technologists and technicians should take as many high school science, biology, and math courses as possible. Science courses taken beyond high school, in an associate or bachelor's degree program, should emphasize practical skills in a clinical or laboratory setting.

Technologists and technicians usually begin work as trainees in routine positions under the direct supervision of a veterinarian. Entry-level workers whose training or educational background encompasses extensive hands-on experience with a variety of laboratory equipment, including diagnostic and medical equipment, usually require a shorter period of on-the-job training.

Licensure and certification. Each State regulates veterinary technicians and technologists differently; however, all States require them to pass a credentialing exam following coursework. Passing the State exam assures the public that the technician or technologist has sufficient knowledge to work in a veterinary clinic or hospital. Candidates are tested for competency through an examination that includes oral, written, and practical portions and that is regulated by the State Board of Veterinary Examiners or the appropriate State agency. Depending on the State, candidates may become registered, licensed, or certified. Most States, however, use the National Veterinary Technician (NVT) exam. Prospects usually can have their passing scores transferred from one State to another, so long as both States use the same exam.

Employers recommend American Association for Laboratory Animal Science (AALAS) certification for those seeking employment in a research facility. AALAS offers certification for three levels of technician competence, with a focus on three principal areas—animal husbandry, facility management, and animal health and welfare. Those who wish to become certified must satisfy a combination of education and experience requirements prior to taking the AALAS examination. Work experience must be directly related to the maintenance, health, and well-being of laboratory animals and must be gained in a laboratory animal facility as defined by AALAS. Candidates who meet the necessary criteria can begin pursuing the desired certification on the basis of their qualifications. The lowest level of certification is Assistant Laboratory Animal Technician (ALAT), the second level is Laboratory Animal Technician (LAT), and the highest level of certification is Laboratory Animal Technologist (LATG). The AALAS examination consists of multiple-choice questions and is longer and more difficult for higher levels of certification, ranging from 2 hours and 120 multiple choice questions for the ALAT to 3 hours and 180 multiple choice questions for the LATG.

Other qualifications. As veterinary technologists and technicians often deal with pet owners, communication skills are very important. In addition, technologists and technicians should be able to work well with others, because teamwork with veterinarians is common. Organizational ability and the ability to pay attention to detail also are important.

Advancement. As they gain experience, technologists and technicians take on more responsibility and carry out more assignments under only general veterinary supervision. Some eventually may become supervisors.

Employment

Veterinary technologists and technicians held about 71,000 jobs in 2006. About 91 percent worked in veterinary services. The remainder worked in boarding kennels, animal shelters, stables, grooming salons, zoos, State and private educational institutions, and local, State, and Federal agencies.

Job Outlook

Excellent job opportunities will stem from the need to replace veterinary technologists and technicians who leave the occupation and from the limited output of qualified veterinary technicians from 2-year programs, which are not expected to meet the demand over the 2006-16 period. Employment is expected to grow much faster than average.

Employment change. Employment of veterinary technologists and technicians is expected to grow 41 percent over the 2006-16 projection period, which is much faster than the average for all occupations. Pet owners are becoming more affluent and more willing to pay for advanced veterinary care because many of them consider their pet to be part of the family. This growing affluence and view of pets will continue to increase the demand for veterinary care. The vast majority of veterinary technicians work at private clinical practice under veterinarians. As the number of veterinarians grows to meet the demand for veterinary care, so will the number of veterinary technicians needed to assist them.

The number of pet owners who take advantage of veterinary services for their pets—currently about 6 in 10—is expected to grow over the projection period, increasing employment opportunities. The availability of advanced veterinary services, such as preventive dental care and surgical procedures, also will provide opportunities for workers specializing in those areas as they will be needed to assist licensed veterinarians. The rapidly growing number of cats kept as companion pets is expected to boost the demand for feline medicine and services. Further demand for these workers will stem from the desire to replace veterinary assistants with more highly skilled technicians and technologists in animal clinics and hospitals, shelters, boarding kennels, and humane societies.

Biomedical facilities, diagnostic laboratories, wildlife facilities, humane societies, animal control facilities, drug or food manufacturing companies, and food safety inspection facilities will provide additional jobs for veterinary technologists and technicians. However, keen competition is expected for veterinary technologist and technician jobs in zoos and aquariums, due to expected slow growth in facility capacity, low turnover among workers, the limited number of positions, and the fact that the work in zoos and aquariums attracts many candidates.

Job prospects. Excellent job opportunities are expected because of the relatively few veterinary technology graduates each year. The number of 2-year programs has recently grown to 131, but due to small class sizes, fewer than 3,000 graduates are anticipated each year, which is not expected to meet demand. Additionally, many veterinary technicians remain in the field for only 7-8 years, so the need to replace workers who leave the occupation each year also will produce many job opportunities.

Employment of veterinary technicians and technologists is relatively stable during periods of economic recession. Layoffs are less likely to occur among veterinary technologists and technicians than in some other occupations because animals will continue to require medical care.

Earnings

Median hourly earnings of veterinary technologists and technicians were $12.88 in May 2006. The middle 50 percent earned between $10.44 and $15.77. The bottom 10 percent earned less than $8.79, and the top 10 percent earned more than $18.68.

Related Occupations

Others who work extensively with animals include animal care and service workers, and veterinary assistants and laboratory animal caretakers. Like veterinary technologists and technicians, they must have patience and feel comfortable with animals. However, the level of training required for these occupations is less than that needed by veterinary technologists and technicians. Veterinarians, who need much more formal education, also work extensively with animals, preventing, diagnosing, and treating their diseases, disorders, and injuries.

Sources of Additional Information

For information on certification as a laboratory animal technician or technologist, contact:

➤ American Association for Laboratory Animal Science, 9190 Crestwyn Hills Dr., Memphis, TN 38125.
Internet: **http://www.aalas.org**

For information on careers in veterinary medicine and a listing of AVMA-accredited veterinary technology programs, contact:
➤ American Veterinary Medical Association, 1931 N. Meacham Rd., Suite 100, Schaumburg, IL 60173-4360.
Internet: **http://www.avma.org**

Projections data from the National Employment Matrix

Occupational Title	SOC Code	Employment, 2006	Projected employment, 2016	Change, 2006-2016	
				Number	Percent
Veterinary technologists and technicians	29-2056	71,000	100,000	29,000	41

NOTE: Data in this table are rounded. See the discussion of the employment projections table in the *Handbook* introductory chapter on *Occupational Information Included in the Handbook.*

Service Occupations

Healthcare Support Occupations

Dental Assistants

(O*NET 31-9091.00)

Significant Points

- Job prospects should be excellent.

- Dentists are expected to hire more assistants to perform routine tasks so that they may devote their own time to more complex procedures.

- Many assistants learn their skills on the job, although an increasing number are trained in dental-assisting programs; most programs take 1 year or less to complete.

Nature of the Work

Dental assistants work closely with, and under the supervision of, dentists. (See the statement on dentists elsewhere in the *Handbook*.) Assistants perform a variety of patient care, office, and laboratory duties.

Dental assistants should not be confused with dental hygienists, who are licensed to perform different clinical tasks. (See the statement on dental hygienists elsewhere in the *Handbook*.)

Dental assistants sterilize and disinfect instruments and equipment, prepare and lay out the instruments and materials required to treat each patient, and obtain patients' dental records. Assistants make patients as comfortable as possible in the dental chair and prepare them for treatment. During dental procedures, assistants work alongside the dentist to provide assistance. They hand instruments and materials to dentists and keep patients' mouths dry and clear by using suction or other devices. They also instruct patients on postoperative and general oral health care.

Dental assistants may prepare materials for impressions and restorations, take dental x-rays, and process x-ray film as directed by a dentist. They also may remove sutures, apply topical anesthetics to gums or cavity-preventive agents to teeth, remove excess cement used in the filling process, and place rubber dams on the teeth to isolate them for individual treatment. Some States are expanding dental assistants' duties to include tasks such as coronal polishing and restorative dentistry functions for those assistants that meet specific training and experience requirements.

Dental assistants with laboratory duties make casts of the teeth and mouth from impressions, clean and polish removable appliances, and make temporary crowns. Those with office duties schedule and confirm appointments, receive patients, keep treatment records, send bills, receive payments, and order dental supplies and materials.

Work environment. Dental assistants work in a well-lighted, clean environment. Their work area usually is near the dental chair so that they can arrange instruments, materials, and medication and hand them to the dentist when needed. Dental assistants must wear gloves, masks, eyewear, and protective clothing to protect themselves and their patients from infectious diseases. Assistants also follow safety procedures to minimize the risks associated with the use of x-ray machines.

About half of dental assistants have a 35- to 40-hour workweek. Most of the rest work part-time or have variable schedules. Depending on the hours of the dental office where they work, assistants may have to work on Saturdays or evenings. Some dental assistants hold multiple jobs by working at dental offices that are open on different days or scheduling their work at a second office around the hours they work at their primary office.

Training, Other Qualifications, and Advancement

Many assistants learn their skills on the job, although an increasing number are trained in dental-assisting programs offered by community and junior colleges, trade schools, technical institutes, or the Armed Forces.

Education and training. High school students interested in a career as a dental assistant should take courses in biology, chemistry, health, and office practices. For those wishing to pursue further education, the Commission on Dental Accreditation within the American Dental Association (ADA) approved 269 dental-assisting training programs in 2006. Programs include classroom, laboratory, and preclinical instruction in dental-assisting skills and related theory. In addition, students gain practical experience in dental schools, clinics, or dental offices. Most programs take 1 year or less to complete and lead to a certificate or diploma. Two-year programs offered in community

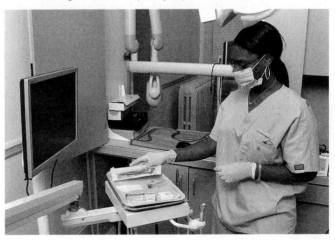

Dental assistants prepare and lay out the instruments and materials required to treat each patient.

and junior colleges lead to an associate degree. All programs require a high school diploma or its equivalent, and some require science or computer-related courses for admission. A number of private vocational schools offer 4- to 6-month courses in dental assisting, but the Commission on Dental Accreditation does not accredit these programs.

A large number of dental assistants learn through on-the-job training. In these situations, the employing dentist or other dental assistants in the dental office teach the new assistant dental terminology, the names of the instruments, how to perform daily duties, how to interact with patients, and other things necessary to help keep the dental office running smoothly. While some things can be picked up easily, it may be a few months before new dental assistants are completely knowledgeable about their duties and comfortable doing all of their tasks without assistance.

A period of on-the-job training is often required even for those that have completed a dental-assisting program or have some previous experience. Different dentists may have their own styles of doing things that need to be learned before an assistant can be comfortable working with them. Office-specific information, such as where files are kept, will need to be learned at each new job. Also, as dental technology changes, dental assistants need to stay familiar with the tools and procedures that they will be using or helping dentists to use. On-the-job training is often sufficient to keep assistants up-to-date on these matters.

Licensure. Most States regulate the duties that dental assistants are allowed to perform. Some States require licensure or registration, which may include passing a written or practical examination. There are a variety of schools offering courses—approximately 10 to 12 months in length—that meet their State's requirements. Other States require dental assistants to complete State-approved education courses of 4 to 12 hours in length. Some States offer registration of other dental assisting credentials with little or no education required. Some States require continuing education to maintain licensure or registration. A few States allow dental assistants to perform any function delegated to them by the dentist.

Individual States have adopted different standards for dental assistants who perform certain advanced duties. In some States, for example, dental assistants who perform radiological procedures must complete additional training. Completion of the Radiation Health and Safety examination offered by Dental Assisting National Board (DANB) meets the standards in more than 30 States. Some States require completion of a State-approved course in radiology as well.

Certification and other qualifications. Certification is available through the Dental Assisting National Board (DANB) and is recognized or required in more than 30 States. Certification is an acknowledgment of an assistant's qualifications and pro-

fessional competence and may be an asset when one is seeking employment. Candidates may qualify to take the DANB certification examination by graduating from an ADA-accredited dental assisting education program or by having 2 years of full-time, or 4 years of part-time, experience as a dental assistant. In addition, applicants must have current certification in cardiopulmonary resuscitation. For annual recertification, individuals must earn continuing education credits. Other organizations offer registration, most often at the State level.

Dental assistants must be a second pair of hands for a dentist; therefore, dentists look for people who are reliable, work well with others, and have good manual dexterity.

Advancement. Without further education, advancement opportunities are limited. Some dental assistants become office managers, dental-assisting instructors, dental product sales representatives, or insurance claims processors for dental insurance companies. Others go back to school to become dental hygienists. For many, this entry-level occupation provides basic training and experience and serves as a steppingstone to more highly skilled and higher paying jobs.

Employment

Dental assistants held about 280,000 jobs in 2006. Almost all jobs for dental assistants were in offices of dentists. A small number of jobs were in the Federal, State, and local governments or in offices of physicians. About 35 percent of dental assistants worked part time, sometimes in more than one dental office.

Job Outlook

Employment is expected to increase much faster than average; job prospects are expected to be excellent.

Employment change. Employment is expected to grow 29 percent from 2006 to 2016, which is much faster than the average for all occupations. In fact, dental assistants are expected to be among the fastest growing occupations over the 2006-16 projection period.

Population growth, greater retention of natural teeth by middle-aged and older people, and an increased focus on preventative dental care for younger generations will fuel demand for dental services. Older dentists, who have been less likely to employ assistants or have employed fewer, are leaving the occupation and will be replaced by recent graduates, who are more likely to use one or more assistants. In addition, as dentists' workloads increase, they are expected to hire more assistants to perform routine tasks, so that they may devote their own time to more complex procedures.

Job prospects. Job prospects for dental assistants should be excellent. In addition to job openings due to employment growth, numerous job openings will arise out of the need to replace assistants who transfer to other occupations, retire, or

Projections data from the National Employment Matrix

Occupational Title	SOC Code	Employment, 2006	Projected employment, 2016	Change, 2006-16	
				Number	Percent
Dental assistants..	31-9091	280,000	362,000	82,000	29

NOTE: Data in this table are rounded. See the discussion of the employment projections table in the *Handbook* introductory chapter on *Occupational Information Included in the Handbook.*

leave for other reasons. Many opportunities for entry-level positions offer on-the-job training, but some dentists prefer to hire experienced assistants or those who have completed a dental-assisting program.

Earnings

Median hourly earnings of dental assistants were $14.53 in May 2006. The middle 50 percent earned between $11.94 and $17.44 an hour. The lowest 10 percent earned less than $9.87, and the highest 10 percent earned more than $20.69 an hour.

Benefits vary substantially by practice setting and may be contingent upon full-time employment. According to the American Dental Association, 87 percent of dentists offer reimbursement for continuing education courses taken by their assistants.

Related Occupations

Other workers supporting health practitioners include dental hygienists, medical assistants, surgical technologists, pharmacy aides, pharmacy technicians, occupational therapist assistants and aides, and physical therapist assistants and aides.

Sources of Additional Information

Information about career opportunities and accredited dental assistant programs is available from:

➤ Commission on Dental Accreditation, American Dental Association, 211 East Chicago Ave., Suite 1814, Chicago, IL 60611. Internet: **http://www.ada.org**

For information on becoming a Certified Dental Assistant and a list of State boards of dentistry, contact:

➤ Dental Assisting National Board, Inc., 676 North Saint Clair St., Suite 1880, Chicago, IL 60611.
Internet: **http://www.danb.org**

For more information on a career as a dental assistant and general information about continuing education, contact:

➤ American Dental Assistants Association, 35 East Wacker Dr., Suite 1730, Chicago, IL 60601.
Internet: **http://www.dentalassistant.org**

For more information about continuing education courses, contact:

➤ National Association of Dental Assistants, 900 South Washington St., Suite G-13, Falls Church, VA 22046.

Massage Therapists

(O*NET 31-9011.00)

Significant Points

- Employment is expected to grow faster than average over the 2006-16 period as more people learn about the benefits of massage therapy.

- Many States require formal training and national certification in order to practice massage therapy.

- This occupation includes a large percentage of part-time and self-employed workers.

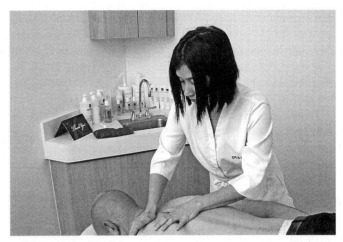

Massage therapists improve circulation by rubbing or applying pressure to muscles.

Nature of the Work

The medical benefits of "friction" were first documented in Western culture by the Greek physician Hippocrates around 400 BC. Today, massage therapy is being used as a means of treating painful ailments, decompressing tired and overworked muscles, reducing stress, rehabilitating sports injuries, and promoting general health. This is done by manipulating the soft tissue muscles of the body in order to improve circulation and remove waste products from the muscles.

Clients may seek massage for medical benefit or for relaxation purposes, and there is a wide range of massage treatment available to meet these distinct needs. Massage therapy that aims to improve physical health typically differs in duration and technique from massage that is intended to simply relax or rejuvenate clients. The training background of those who perform the two types of massage therapy differs as well.

Massage therapists can specialize in over 80 different types of massage, called modalities. Swedish massage, deep tissue massage, reflexology, acupressure, sports massage, and neuromuscular massage are just a few of the many approaches to massage therapy. Most massage therapists specialize in several modalities, which require different techniques. Some use exaggerated strokes ranging the length of a body part, while others use quick, percussion-like strokes with a cupped or closed hand. A massage can be as long as 2 hours or as short as 5 or 10 minutes. Usually, the type of massage given depends on the client's needs and the client's physical condition. For example, therapists may use special techniques for elderly clients that they would not use for athletes, and they would use approaches for clients with injuries that would not be appropriate for clients seeking relaxation. There are also some forms of massage that are given solely to one type of client, for example prenatal massage and infant massage.

Massage therapists work by appointment. Before beginning a massage therapy session, therapists conduct an informal interview with the client to find out about the person's medical history and desired results from the massage. This gives therapists a chance to discuss which techniques could be beneficial to the client and which could be harmful. Because massage therapists tend to specialize in only a few areas of massage, customers will often be referred to or seek a therapist with a certain type of massage in mind. Based on the person's goals, ailments, medical history, and stress- or pain-related problem areas, a massage therapist will conclude whether a massage would be harmful, and if not, move forward with the session. While giving the massage, therapists alter their approach or concentrate on any areas of particular discomfort as necessary.

Many modalities of massage therapy use massage oils, lotions, or creams to massage and rub the client's muscles. Most massage therapists, particularly those who are self-employed, supply their own table or chair, sheets, pillows, and body lotions or oils. Most modalities of massage require clients to be covered in a sheet or blanket, and require clients to be undressed or to wear loose-fitting clothing. The therapist only exposes the body part being massaged. Some types of massage are done without oils or lotions and are performed with the client fully-clothed.

Massage therapists must develop a rapport with their clients if repeat customers are to be secured. Because those who seek a therapist tend to make regular visits, developing a loyal clientele is an important part of becoming successful.

Work environment. Massage therapists work in an array of settings both private and public: private offices, studios, hospitals, nursing homes, fitness centers, sports medicine facilities, airports, and shopping malls, for example. Some massage therapists also travel to clients' homes or offices to provide a massage. It is not uncommon for full-time massage therapists to divide their time among several different settings, depending on the clients and locations scheduled.

Most massage therapists give massages in dimly lit settings. Using candles and/or incense is not uncommon. Ambient or other calm, soothing music is often played. The dim lighting, smells, and background noise are meant to put clients at ease. On the other hand, when visiting a client's office, a massage therapist may not have those amenities. The working conditions depend heavily on a therapist's location and what the client wants.

Because massage is physically demanding, massage therapists can succumb to injury if the proper technique is not used. Repetitive motion problems and fatigue from standing for extended periods of time are most common. This risk can be limited by use of good technique, proper spacing between sessions, exercise, and in many cases by the therapists themselves receiving a massage on a regular basis.

Because of the physical nature of the work and time needed in between sessions, massage therapists typically give massages less than 40 hours per week. Most therapists who work 15 to 30 hours per week consider themselves to be full-time workers, because when time for travel, equipment set-up, and business functions, such as billing, are added, a massage therapist's hours per week may very well be more than 40 hours. About 42 percent of all massage therapists worked part time and 20 percent had variable schedules in 2006.

Training, Other Qualifications, and Advancement
In 2007, 38 States and the District of Columbia had laws regulating massage therapy in some way. Most of the boards governing massage therapy in these States require practicing massage therapists to complete a formal education program and pass a national certification examination or a State exam. It is best to check information on licensing, certification, and accreditation on a State-by-State basis.

Education and training. Training standards and requirements for massage therapists vary greatly by State and locality. There are roughly 1,500 massage therapy postsecondary schools, college programs, and training programs throughout the country. Massage therapy programs generally cover subjects such as anatomy; physiology, the study of organs and tissues; kinesiology, the study of motion and body mechanics; business; ethics; as well as hands-on practice of massage techniques. Training programs may concentrate on certain modalities of massage. Several programs also provide alumni services such as postgraduate job placement and continuing educational services. Both full- and part-time programs are available.

These programs vary in accreditation. Massage therapy training programs are generally approved by a State board, and may also be accredited by an independent accrediting agency. In States that regulate massage therapy, graduation from an approved school or training program is usually required in order to practice. Some State regulations require that therapists keep up on their knowledge and technique through continuing education.

Licensure. After completion of a training program, many massage therapists opt to take the National Certification Examination for Therapeutic Massage and Bodywork (NCETMB.) Many States require that therapists pass this test in order to practice massage therapy. The exam is administered by the National Certification Board for Therapeutic Massage and Bodywork (NCBTMB), which has several eligibility requirements. In States that require massage therapy program approval, a candidate must graduate from a State-approved training institute or submit a portfolio of training experience for NCBTMB review to qualify for the test. In locations that do not require accredited training programs, this is unnecessary.

When a therapist passes the NCETMB, he or she can use the recognized national credential: Nationally Certified in Therapeutic Massage and Bodywork (NCTMB). The credential must be renewed every 4 years. In order to remain certified, a therapist must perform at least 200 hours of therapeutic massage and complete continuing education requirements during this time. In 2005, the NCBTMB introduced a new national certification test and corresponding professional credential. The new test covers the same topics as the traditional national certification exam, but covers fewer modalities of massage therapy. Recognition of this new national certification varies by State.

Recently, a second multi-State examination program has begun to take shape. The Federation of State Massage Therapy Boards offers a licensure program that is also accepted by many States.

Massage therapy licensure boards decide which certifications and tests to accept on a State-by-State basis. Therefore, those wishing to practice massage therapy should look into legal requirements for the State and locality in which they intend to practice.

Other qualifications. Both strong communication skills and a friendly, empathetic personality are extremely helpful qualities for fostering a trusting relationship with clients and in turn, expanding one's client base. Massage can be a delicate issue for some clients and because of this, making clients feel comfortable is one of the most important abilities for massage therapists.

Advancement. Membership in a professional massage therapy association may help therapists network and in turn, find new clients. Some of these associations require that members graduate from a nationally credentialed training program, have a State license, or be nationally certified by the NCBTMB.

Because of the nature of massage therapy, opportunities for advancement are limited. However, with increased experience and an expanding client base, there are opportunities for therapists to increase client fees and, therefore, income. In addition, those who are well organized and have an entrepreneurial spirit may go into business for themselves. Self-employed massage therapists with a large client base have the highest earnings.

Employment

Massage therapists held about 118,000 jobs in 2006. About 64 percent were self-employed. There are many more people who practice massage therapy as a secondary source of income. As a result, some industry sources estimate that more than 200,000 people practice massage therapy in some capacity.

Of those self-employed, most owned their own business, and the rest worked as independent contractors. Others found employment in salons and spas; the offices of physicians and chiropractors; fitness and recreational sports centers; and hotels. While massage therapists can find jobs throughout the country, employment is concentrated in metropolitan areas, as well as resort and destination locales.

Job Outlook

Employment growth for massage therapists is expected to be faster than average for all occupations with very good job prospects, particularly for those seeking part-time work.

Employment change. Employment for massage therapists is expected to increase 20 percent from 2006 to 2016, faster than average for all occupations. Employment will grow as more people learn about the benefits of massage therapy.

Increased interest in alternative medicine and holistic healing will translate into new openings for those skilled in massage therapy. Healthcare providers and medical insurance companies are beginning to recognize massage therapy as a legitimate treatment and preventative measure for several types of injuries and illnesses. The health care industry is using massage therapy more often as a supplement to conventional medical techniques for ailments such as muscle problems, some sicknesses and diseases, and stress-related health problems. Massage therapy's growing acceptance as a medical tool, particularly by the medical provider and insurance industries, will have the greatest impact on new job growth for massage therapists.

Massage is an increasingly popular technique for relaxation and reduction of stress. As workplaces try to distinguish themselves as employee-friendly, providing professional in-office, seated massages for employees is becoming a popular on-the-job benefit.

Older citizens in nursing homes or assisted living facilities are also finding benefits from massage, such as increased energy levels and reduced health problems. Demand for massage therapy should grow among older age groups because they increasingly enjoy longer, more active lives and persons age 55 and older are projected to be the most rapidly growing segment of the U.S. population over the next decade. However, demand for massage therapy is presently greatest among young adults, and they are likely to continue to enjoy the benefits of massage therapy as they age.

Job prospects. In States that regulate massage therapy, those who complete formal training programs and pass the national certification exam are likely to have very good opportunities. However, new massage therapists should expect to work only part-time in spas, hotels, hospitals, physical therapy centers, and other businesses until they can build a client base of their own. Because referrals are a very important source of work for massage therapists, networking will increase the number of job opportunities. Joining a State or local chapter of a professional association can also help build strong contacts and further increase the likelihood of steady work.

Female massage therapists will continue to enjoy slightly better job prospects, as some clients—both male and female—are uncomfortable with male physical contact. In 2006, 84 percent of all massage therapists were female.

Earnings

Median wage and salary hourly earnings of massage therapists, including gratuities, were $16.06 in May 2006. The middle 50 percent earned between $10.98 and $24.22. The lowest 10 percent earned less than $7.48, and the highest 10 percent earned more than $33.83. Generally, massage therapists earn 15 to 20 percent of their income as gratuities. For those who work in a hospital or other clinical setting, however, tipping is not common.

As is typical for most workers who are self-employed and work part-time, few benefits are provided.

Related Occupations

Other workers associated with the healthcare industry who provide therapy to clients include athletic trainers, physical therapists, physical therapist assistants and aides, chiropractors, and workers in other occupations that use touch to aid healing or relieve stress.

Sources of Additional Information

General information on becoming a massage therapist is available from State regulatory boards.

Projections data from the National Employment Matrix

Occupational Title	SOC Code	Employment, 2006	Projected employment, 2016	Change, 2006-16	
				Number	Percent
Massage therapists	31-9011	118,000	142,000	24,000	20

NOTE: Data in this table are rounded. See the discussion of the employment projections table in the *Handbook* introductory chapter on *Occupational Information Included in the Handbook.*

For more information on becoming a massage therapist, contact:

➤ Associated Bodywork & Massage Professionals, 1271 Sugarbush Dr., Evergreen, CO 80439.
Internet: **http://www.massagetherapy.com/careers/index.php**
➤ American Massage Therapy Association, 500 Davis St., Suite 900, Evanston, IL 60201.
Internet: **http://www.amtamassage.org**

For a directory of schools providing accredited massage therapy training programs, contact:

➤ Commission on Massage Therapy Accreditation, 1007 Church St., Suite 302, Evanston, IL 60201.
Internet: **http://www.comta.org**
➤ Accrediting Commission of Career Schools and Colleges of Technology, 2101 Wilson Blvd., Suite 302, Arlington, VA 22201. Internet: **http://www.accsct.org**

Information on national testing and national certification is available from:

➤ National Certification Board for Therapeutic Massage and Bodywork, 1901 S. Meyers Rd., Suite 240, Oakbrook Terrace, IL 60181. Internet: **http://www.ncbtmb.com**
➤ Federation of State Massage Therapy Boards, 7111 W 151st Street, Suite 356, Overland Park, Kansas 66223.
Internet: **http://www.fsmtb.org**

Medical Assistants

(O*NET 31-9092.00)

Significant Points

- About 62 percent of medical assistants work in offices of physicians.

- Some medical assistants are trained on the job, but many complete 1-year or 2-year programs.

- Employment is projected to grow much faster than average, ranking medical assistants among the fastest growing occupations over the 2006-16 decade.

- Job prospects should be excellent.

Nature of the Work

Medical assistants perform administrative and clinical tasks to keep the offices of physicians, podiatrists, chiropractors, and other health practitioners running smoothly. They should not be confused with physician assistants, who examine, diagnose, and treat patients under the direct supervision of a physician. (Physician assistants are discussed elsewhere in the *Handbook*.)

The duties of medical assistants vary from office to office, depending on the location and size of the practice and the practitioner's specialty. In small practices, medical assistants usually do many different kinds of tasks, handling both administrative and clinical duties and reporting directly to an office manager, physician, or other health practitioner. Those in large practices tend to specialize in a particular area, under the supervision of department administrators.

Medical assistants who perform administrative tasks have many duties. They update and file patients' medical records, fill out insurance forms, and arrange for hospital admissions and laboratory services. They also perform tasks less specific to medical settings, such as answering telephones, greeting patients, handling correspondence, scheduling appointments, and handling billing and bookkeeping.

For clinical medical assistants, duties vary according to what is allowed by State law. Some common tasks include taking medical histories and recording vital signs, explaining treatment procedures to patients, preparing patients for examinations, and assisting physicians during examinations. Medical assistants collect and prepare laboratory specimens and sometimes perform basic laboratory tests on the premises, dispose of contaminated supplies, and sterilize medical instruments. They might instruct patients about medications and special diets, prepare and administer medications as directed by a physician, authorize drug refills as directed, telephone prescriptions to a pharmacy, draw blood, prepare patients for x-rays, take electrocardiograms, remove sutures, and change dressings.

Medical assistants also may arrange examining room instruments and equipment, purchase and maintain supplies and equipment, and keep waiting and examining rooms neat and clean.

Ophthalmic medical assistants, optometric assistants, and *podiatric medical assistants* are examples of specialized assistants who have additional duties. Ophthalmic medical assistants help ophthalmologists provide eye care. They conduct diagnostic tests, measure and record vision, and test eye muscle function. They also show patients how to insert, remove, and care for contact lenses, and they apply eye dressings. Under the direction of the physician, ophthalmic medical assistants may administer eye medications. They also maintain optical and surgical instruments and may assist the ophthalmologist in surgery. Optometric assistants also help provide eye care, working with optometrists. They provide chair-side assistance, instruct patients about contact lens use and care, conduct preliminary tests on patients, and otherwise provide assistance while working directly with an optometrist. Podiatric medical assistants make castings of feet, expose and develop x-rays, and assist podiatrists in surgery.

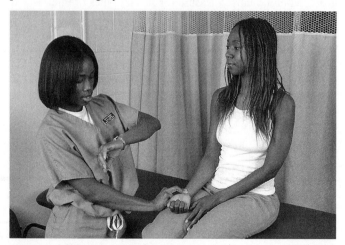

Medical assistants who perform clinical tasks often record vital signs of patients.

Work environment. Medical assistants work in well-lighted, clean environments. They constantly interact with other people and may have to handle several responsibilities at once. Most full-time medical assistants work a regular 40-hour week. However, many medical assistants work part time, evenings, or weekends.

Training, Other Qualifications, and Advancement

Some medical assistants are trained on the job, but many complete 1-year or 2-year programs.

Education and training. Postsecondary medical assisting programs are offered in vocational-technical high schools, postsecondary vocational schools, and community and junior colleges. Programs usually last either 1 year and result in a certificate or diploma, or 2 years and result in an associate degree. Courses cover anatomy, physiology, and medical terminology, as well as typing, transcription, recordkeeping, accounting, and insurance processing. Students learn laboratory techniques, clinical and diagnostic procedures, pharmaceutical principles, the administration of medications, and first aid. They study office practices, patient relations, medical law, and ethics. There are various organizations that accredit medical assisting programs. Accredited programs often include an internship that provides practical experience in physicians' offices, hospitals, or other health care facilities.

Formal training in medical assisting, while generally preferred, is not always required. Some medical assistants are trained on the job, although this practice is less common than in the past. Applicants usually need a high school diploma or the equivalent. Recommended high school courses include mathematics, health, biology, typing, bookkeeping, computers, and office skills. Volunteer experience in the health care field also is helpful. Medical assistants who are trained on the job usually spend their first few months attending training sessions and working closely with more experienced workers.

Some States allow medical assistants to perform more advanced procedures, such as giving injections, after passing a test or taking a course.

Certification and other qualifications. Employers prefer to hire experienced workers or those who are certified. Although not required, certification indicates that a medical assistant meets certain standards of competence. There are various associations—some listed in the sources of information below—that award certification credentials to medical assistants, and the certification process varies. It also is possible to become certified in a specialty, such as podiatry, optometry, or ophthalmology.

Medical assistants deal with the public; therefore, they must be neat and well groomed and have a courteous, pleasant manner and they must be able to put patients at ease and explain physicians' instructions. They must respect the confidential nature of medical information. Clinical duties require a reasonable level of manual dexterity and visual acuity.

Advancement. Medical assistants may advance to other occupations through experience or additional training. For example, some may go on to teach medical assisting, and others pursue additional education to become nurses or other health care workers. Administrative medical assistants may advance to office manager, or qualify for a variety of administrative support occupations.

Employment

Medical assistants held about 417,000 jobs in 2006. About 62 percent worked in offices of physicians; 12 percent worked in public and private hospitals, including inpatient and outpatient facilities; and 11 percent worked in offices of other health practitioners, such as chiropractors, optometrists, and podiatrists. Most of the remainder worked in other health care industries such as outpatient care centers and nursing and residential care facilities.

Job Outlook

Employment is projected to grow much faster than average, ranking medical assistants among the fastest growing occupations over the 2006-16 decade. Job opportunities should be excellent, particularly for those with formal training or experience, and certification.

Employment change. Employment of medical assistants is expected to grow 35 percent from 2006 to 2016, much faster than the average for all occupations. As the health care industry expands because of technological advances in medicine and the growth and aging of the population, there will be an increased need for all health care workers. Increasing use of medical assistants in the rapidly growing health care industry will further stimulate job growth.

Helping to drive job growth is the increasing number of group practices, clinics, and other health care facilities that need a high proportion of support personnel, particularly medical assistants who can handle both administrative and clinical duties. In addition, medical assistants work primarily in outpatient settings, a rapidly growing sector of the health care industry.

Job prospects. Job seekers who want to work as a medical assistant should find excellent job prospects. Medical assistants are projected to account for a very large number of new jobs, and many other opportunities will come from the need to replace workers leaving the occupation. Those with formal training or experience—particularly those with certification—should have the best job opportunities.

Earnings

The earnings of medical assistants vary, depending on their experience, skill level, and location. Median annual earnings of

Projections data from the National Employment Matrix

Occupational Title	SOC Code	Employment, 2006	Projected employment, 2016	Change, 2006-16	
				Number	Percent
Medical assistants	31-9092	417,000	565,000	148,000	35

NOTE: Data in this table are rounded. See the discussion of the employment projections table in the *Handbook* introductory chapter on *Occupational Information Included in the Handbook.*

wage-and-salary medical assistants were $26,290 in May 2006. The middle 50 percent earned between $21,970 and $31,210. The lowest 10 percent earned less than $18,860, and the highest 10 percent earned more than $36,840. Median annual earnings in the industries employing the largest numbers of medical assistants in May 2006 were:

General medical and surgical hospitals..............................$27,340
Outpatient care centers..26,840
Offices of physicians...26,620
Offices of chiropractors...22,940
Offices of optometrists..22,850

Related Occupations

Medical assistants perform work similar to the tasks completed by other workers in medical support occupations. Administrative medical assistants do work similar to that of medical secretaries, medical transcriptionists, and medical records and health information technicians. Clinical medical assistants perform duties similar to those of dental assistants; dental hygienists; occupational therapist assistants and aides; pharmacy aides; licensed practical and licensed vocational nurses; surgical technologists; physical therapist assistants and aides; and nursing, psychiatric, and home health aides.

Sources of Additional Information

Information about career opportunities and certification for medical assistants is available from:

➤ American Association of Medical Assistants, 20 North Wacker Dr., Suite 1575, Chicago, IL 60606.
Internet: **http://www.aama-ntl.org**
➤ American Medical Technologists, 10700 West Higgins Rd., Suite 150, Rosemont, IL 60018.
Internet: **http://www.amt1.com**
➤ National Healthcareer Association, 7 Ridgedale Ave., Suite 203, Cedar Knolls, NJ 07927.

Information about career opportunities, training programs, and certification for ophthalmic medical personnel is available from:
➤ Joint Commission on Allied Health Personnel in Ophthalmology, 2025 Woodlane Dr., St.Paul, MN 55125.
Internet: **http://www.jcahpo.org/newsite/index.htm**

Information about career opportunities, training programs and certification for optometric assistants is available from:
➤ American Optometric Association, 243 N. Lindbergh Blvd., St.Louis, MO 63141. Internet: **http://www.aoa.org**

Information about certification for podiatric assistants is available from:
➤ American Society of Podiatric Medical Assistants, 2124 South Austin Blvd., Cicero, IL 60804.
Internet: **http://www.aspma.org**

For lists of accredited educational programs in medical assisting, contact:
➤ Accrediting Bureau of Health Education Schools, 7777 Leesburg Pike, Suite 314 N, Falls Church, VA 22043.
Internet: **http://www.abhes.org**
➤ Commission on Accreditation of Allied Health Education Programs, 1361 Park St., Clearwater, FL 33756.
Internet: **http://www.caahep.org**

Medical Transcriptionists

(O*NET 31-9094.00)

Significant Points

- Job opportunities will be good.

- Employers prefer medical transcriptionists who have completed a postsecondary training program.

- Many medical transcriptionists telecommute from home-based offices.

- About 41 percent worked in hospitals, and another 29 percent worked in offices of physicians.

Nature of the Work

Medical transcriptionists listen to dictated recordings made by physicians and other health care professionals and transcribe them into medical reports, correspondence, and other administrative material. They generally listen to recordings on a headset, using a foot pedal to pause the recording when necessary, and key the text into a personal computer or word processor, editing as necessary for grammar and clarity. The documents they produce include discharge summaries, medical history and physical examination reports, operative reports, consultation reports, autopsy reports, diagnostic imaging studies, progress notes, and referral letters. Medical transcriptionists return transcribed documents to the physicians or other health care professionals who dictated them for review and signature or correction. These documents eventually become part of patients' permanent files.

To understand and accurately transcribe dictated reports, medical transcriptionists must understand medical terminology, anatomy and physiology, diagnostic procedures, pharmacology, and treatment assessments. They also must be able to translate medical jargon and abbreviations into their expanded forms. To help identify terms appropriately, transcriptionists refer to standard medical reference materials—both printed and electronic; some of these are available over the Internet. Medical transcriptionists must comply with specific standards that apply to the style of medical records and to the legal and ethical requirements for keeping patient information confidential.

Experienced transcriptionists spot mistakes or inconsistencies in a medical report and check to correct the information. Their ability to understand and correctly transcribe patient assessments and treatments reduces the chance of patients receiving ineffective or even harmful treatments and ensures high-quality patient care.

Currently, most health care providers transmit dictation to medical transcriptionists using either digital or analog dictating equipment. The Internet has grown to be a popular mode for transmitting documentation. Many transcriptionists receive dictation over the Internet and are able to quickly return transcribed documents to clients for approval. Another increasingly popular method uses speech recognition technology, which electronically translates sound into text and creates drafts of reports. Transcriptionists then format the reports; edit them for mistakes in translation, punctuation, or grammar; and check for consistency and any wording that doesn't make sense medically. Transcriptionists working in specialties, such as radiology or pathology, with standardized terminology are more likely to use speech recognition technology. However, speech recognition technology will become more widespread in all specialties as the technology becomes more sophisticated, that is, better able to recognize and more accurately transcribe diverse modes of speech.

Medical transcriptionists who work in physicians' offices may have other office duties, such as receiving patients, scheduling appointments, answering the telephone, and handling incoming and outgoing mail. Medical secretaries, discussed in the statement on secretaries and administrative assistants elsewhere in the *Handbook*, also may transcribe as part of their jobs.

Work environment. The majority of these workers are employed in comfortable settings, such as hospitals, physicians' offices, transcription service offices, clinics, laboratories, medical libraries, government medical facilities, or their own homes. Many medical transcriptionists telecommute from home-based offices.

Workers usually sit in the same position for long periods. They can suffer wrist, back, neck, or eye problems due to strain and risk repetitive motion injuries such as carpal tunnel syn-

Medical transcriptionists listen to recordings on a headset, key the text into a personal computer or word processor, and edit for grammar and clarity.

drome. The constant pressure to be accurate and productive also can be stressful.

Many medical transcriptionists work a standard 40-hour week. Self-employed medical transcriptionists are more likely to work irregular hours—including part time, evenings, weekends, or on call at any time.

Training, Other Qualifications, and Advancement
Postsecondary training in medical transcription is preferred by employers; writing and computer skills also are important.

Education and training. Employers prefer to hire transcriptionists who have completed postsecondary training in medical transcription offered by many vocational schools, community colleges, and distance-learning programs.

Completion of a 2-year associate degree or 1-year certificate program—including coursework in anatomy, medical terminology, legal issues relating to health care documentation, and English grammar and punctuation—is highly recommended, but not always required. Many of these programs include supervised on-the-job experience. Some transcriptionists, especially those already familiar with medical terminology from previous experience as a nurse or medical secretary, become proficient through refresher courses and training.

Formal accreditation is not required for medical transcription programs. However, the Approval Committee for Certificate Programs (AACP)—established by the Association for Healthcare Documentation Integrity (AHDI) and the American Health Information Management Association—offers voluntary accreditation for medical transcription programs. Although voluntary, completion of an ACCP approved program may be required for transcriptionists seeking certification.

Certification and other qualifications. The AHDI awards two voluntary designations, the Registered Medical Transcriptionist (RMT) and the Certified Medical Transcriptionist (CMT). Medical transcriptionists who are recent graduates of medical transcription educational programs, or have fewer than 2 years experience in acute care, may become a registered RMT. The RMT credential is awarded upon successfully passing the AHDI level 1 registered medical transcription exam. The CMT designation requires at least 2 years of acute care experience working in multiple specialty surgery areas using different format, report, and dictation types. Candidates also must earn a passing score on a certification examination. Because medicine is constantly evolving, medical transcriptionists are encouraged to update their skills regularly. RMTs and CMTs must earn continuing education credits every 3 years to be recertified. As in many other fields, certification is recognized as a sign of competence.

Graduates of an ACCP approved program who earn the RMT credential are eligible to participate in the Registered Apprenticeship Program sponsored by the Medical Transcription Industry Association through the U.S. Department of Labor. The Registered Apprenticeship program offers structured on-the-job learning and related technical instruction for qualified medical transcriptionists entering the profession.

In addition to understanding medical terminology, transcriptionists must have good English grammar and punctuation skills and proficiency with personal computers and word processing

Projections data from the National Employment Matrix

Occupational Title	SOC Code	Employment, 2006	Projected employment, 2016	Change, 2006-16	
				Number	Percent
Medical transcriptionists..	31-9094	98,000	112,000	13,000	14

NOTE: Data in this table are rounded. See the discussion of the employment projections table in the *Handbook* introductory chapter on *Occupational Information Included in the Handbook*.

software. Normal hearing acuity and good listening skills also are necessary. Employers usually require applicants to take pre-employment tests.

Advancement. With experience, medical transcriptionists can advance to supervisory positions, home-based work, editing, consulting, or teaching. Some become owners of medical transcription businesses. With additional education or training, some become medical records and health information technicians, medical coders, or medical records and health information administrators.

Employment

Medical transcriptionists held about 98,000 jobs in 20006. About 41 percent worked in hospitals and another 29 percent worked in offices of physicians. Others worked for business support services; medical and diagnostic laboratories; outpatient care centers; and offices of physical, occupational, and speech therapists, and audiologists.

Job Outlook

Employment of medical transcriptionists is projected to grow faster than the average; job opportunities should be good, especially for those who are certified.

Employment change. Employment of medical transcriptionists is projected to grow 14 percent from 2006 to 2016, faster than the average for all occupations. Demand for medical transcription services will be spurred by a growing and aging population. Older age groups receive proportionately greater numbers of medical tests, treatments, and procedures that require documentation. A high level of demand for transcription services also will be sustained by the continued need for electronic documentation that can be shared easily among providers, third-party payers, regulators, consumers, and health information systems. Growing numbers of medical transcriptionists will be needed to amend patients' records, edit documents from speech recognition systems, and identify discrepancies in medical reports.

Contracting out transcription work overseas and advancements in speech recognition technology are not expected to significantly reduce the need for well-trained medical transcriptionists. Outsourcing transcription work abroad—to countries such as India, Pakistan, Philippines, and the Caribbean—has grown more popular as transmitting confidential health information over the Internet has become more secure; however, the demand for overseas transcription services is expected only to supplement the demand for well-trained domestic medical transcriptionists. In addition, reports transcribed by overseas medical transcription services usually require editing for accuracy by domestic medical transcriptionists before they meet U.S. quality standards.

Speech-recognition technology allows physicians and other health professionals to dictate medical reports to a computer that immediately creates an electronic document. In spite of the advances in this technology, the software has been slow to grasp and analyze the human voice and the English language, and the medical vernacular with all its diversity. As a result, there will continue to be a need for skilled medical transcriptionists to identify and appropriately edit the inevitable errors created by speech recognition systems, and to create a final document.

Job prospects. Job opportunities will be good, especially for those who are certified. Hospitals will continue to employ a large percentage of medical transcriptionists, but job growth there will not be as fast as in other industries. An increasing demand for standardized records should result in rapid employment growth in physicians' offices, especially in large group practices.

Earnings

Wage-and-salary medical transcriptionists had median hourly earnings of $14.40 in May 2006. The middle 50 percent earned between $12.17 and $17.06. The lowest 10 percent earned less than $10.22, and the highest 10 percent earned more than $20.15. Median hourly earnings in the industries employing the largest numbers of medical transcriptionists were:

Medical and diagnostic laboratories $15.68
General medical and surgical hospitals...................................14.62
Business support services 14.34
Outpatient care centers...14.31
Offices of physicians...14.00

Compensation methods for medical transcriptionists vary. Some are paid based on the number of hours they work or on the number of lines they transcribe. Others receive a base pay per hour with incentives for extra production. Employees of transcription services and independent contractors almost always receive production-based pay. Independent contractors earn more than do transcriptionists who work for others, but independent contractors have higher expenses than their corporate counterparts, receive no benefits, and may face higher risk of termination than do wage-and-salary transcriptionists.

Related Occupations

Workers in other occupations also type, record information, and process paperwork. Among these are court reporters; human resources assistants, except payroll and timekeeping; receptionists and information clerks; and secretaries and administrative assistants. Other workers who provide medical support include medical assistants and medical records and health information technicians.

Sources of Additional Information

For information on a career as a medical transcriptionist, contact:

➤ Association for Healthcare Documentation Integrity, 4230 Kiernan Ave., Suite 130, Modesto, CA 95356. Internet: **http://www.ahdionline.org**

State employment service offices can provide information about job openings for medical transcriptionists.

Nursing, Psychiatric, and Home Health Aides

(O*NET 31-1011.00, 31-1012.00, 31-1013.00)

Significant Points

- Numerous job openings and excellent job opportunities are expected.

- Most jobs are in nursing and residential care facilities, hospitals, and home health care services.

- This occupation is characterized by modest entry requirements, low pay, high physical and emotional demands, and limited advancement opportunities.

Nature of the Work

Nursing and psychiatric aides help care for physically or mentally ill, injured, disabled, or infirm individuals in hospitals, nursing care facilities, and mental health settings. Home health aides have duties that are similar, but they work in patients' homes or residential care facilities. Nursing aides and home health aides are among the occupations commonly referred to as direct care workers, due to their role in working with patients who need long-term care. The specific care they give depends on their specialty.

Nursing aides—also known as nurse aides, nursing assistants, certified nursing assistants, geriatric aides, unlicensed assistive personnel, orderlies, or hospital attendants—provide hands-on care and perform routine tasks under the supervision of nursing and medical staff. Specific tasks vary, with aides handling many aspects of a patient's care. They often help patients to eat, dress, and bathe. They also answer calls for help, deliver messages, serve meals, make beds, and tidy up rooms. Aides sometimes are responsible for taking a patient's temperature, pulse rate, respiration rate, or blood pressure. They also may help provide care to patients by helping them get into and out of bed and walk, escorting them to operating and examining rooms, or providing skin care. Some aides help other medical staff by setting up equipment, storing and moving supplies, and assisting with some procedures. Aides also observe patients' physical, mental, and emotional conditions and report any change to the nursing or medical staff.

Nurse aides employed in nursing care facilities often are the principal caregivers, having far more contact with residents than do other members of the staff. Because some residents may stay in a nursing care facility for months or even years, aides develop ongoing relationships with them and interact with them in a positive, caring way.

Home health aides help elderly, convalescent, or disabled persons live in their own homes instead of health care facilities. Under the direction of nursing or medical staff, they provide health-related services, such as administering oral medications. (Personal and home care aides, who provide mainly housekeeping and routine personal care services, are discussed elsewhere in the *Handbook*.) Like nursing aides, home health aides may check patients' pulse rate, temperature, and respiration rate; help with simple prescribed exercises; and help patients to get in and out of bed, bathe, dress, and groom. Occasionally, they change nonsterile dressings, give massages and provide skin care, or assist with braces and artificial limbs. Experienced home health aides, with training, also may assist with medical equipment such as ventilators, which help patients breathe.

Most home health aides work with elderly or disabled persons who need more extensive care than family or friends can provide. Some help discharged hospital patients who have relatively short-term needs.

In home health agencies, a registered nurse, physical therapist, or social worker usually assigns specific duties to and supervises home health aides, who keep records of the services they perform and record each patient's condition and progress. The aides report changes in a patient's condition to the supervisor or case manager.

Psychiatric aides, also known as mental health assistants or psychiatric nursing assistants, care for mentally impaired or emotionally disturbed individuals. They work under a team that may include psychiatrists, psychologists, psychiatric nurses, social workers, and therapists. In addition to helping patients to dress, bathe, groom themselves, and eat, psychiatric aides socialize with them and lead them in educational and recreational activities. Psychiatric aides may play card games or other games with patients, watch television with them, or participate in group activities, such as playing sports or going on field trips. They observe patients and report any physical or behavioral signs that might be important for the professional staff to know. They accompany patients to and from therapy and treatment. Because they have such close contact with patients, psychiatric aides can have a great deal of influence on their outlook and treatment.

Work environment. Work as an aide can be physically demanding. Aides spend many hours standing and walking, and they often face heavy workloads. Aides must guard against back injury because they may have to move patients into and out of bed or help them to stand or walk. It is important for aides to be trained in and to follow the proper procedures for lifting and moving patients. Aides also may face hazards from minor infections and major diseases, such as hepatitis, but can avoid infections by following proper procedures.

Aides also perform tasks that some may consider unpleasant, such as emptying bedpans and changing soiled bed linens. The patients they care for may be disoriented, irritable, or uncooperative. Psychiatric aides must be prepared to care for patients whose illness may cause violent behavior. Although their work can be emotionally demanding, many aides gain satisfaction from assisting those in need.

Home health aides may go to the same patient's home for months or even years. However, most aides work with a number of different patients, each job lasting a few hours, days, or weeks. Home health aides often visit multiple patients on the same day.

Home health aides generally work alone, with periodic visits from their supervisor. They receive detailed instructions explaining when to visit patients and what services to perform. Aides are individually responsible for getting to patients' homes, and they may spend a good portion of the working day traveling from one patient to another. Because mechanical lifting devices available in institutional settings are not as frequently available in patients' homes, home health aides must take extra care to avoid injuries resulting from overexertion when they assist patients.

Most full-time aides work about 40 hours per week, but because patients need care 24 hours a day, some aides work evenings, nights, weekends, and holidays. In 2006, 23 percent of aides worked part time compared with 15 percent of all workers.

Training, Other Qualifications, and Advancement

In many cases, a high school diploma or equivalent is necessary for a job as a nursing or psychiatric aide. However, a high school diploma generally is not required for jobs as home health aides. Specific qualifications vary by occupation, State laws, and work setting. Advancement opportunities are limited.

Education and training. Nursing and psychiatric aide training is offered in high schools, vocational-technical centers, some nursing care facilities, and some community colleges. Courses cover body mechanics, nutrition, anatomy and physiology, infection control, communication skills, and resident rights. Personal care skills, such as how to help patients to bathe, eat, and groom themselves, also are taught. Hospitals may require previous experience as a nursing aide or home health aide. Some States also require psychiatric aides to complete a formal training program. However, most psychiatric aides learn their skills on the job from experienced workers.

Home health aides are generally not required to have a high school diploma. They usually are trained on the job by registered nurses, licensed practical nurses, or experienced aides. Also, clients may prefer that tasks are done a certain way, and make those suggestions to the home health aide. A competency evaluation may be required to ensure the aide can perform the required tasks.

Some employers provide classroom instruction for newly hired aides, while others rely exclusively on informal on-the-job instruction by a licensed nurse or an experienced aide. Such training may last from several days to a few months. Aides also may attend lectures, workshops, and in-service training.

Licensure and certification. The Federal Government has guidelines for home health aides whose employers receive reimbursement from Medicare. Federal law requires home health aides to pass a competency test covering a wide range of areas. A home health aide may receive training before taking the competency test. In addition, the National Association for Home Care and Hospice offers voluntary certification for home health aides. Some States also require aides to be licensed.

Similar Federal requirements exist for nurse aides who work in nursing care facilities. These aides must complete a minimum of 75 hours of state-approved training and pass a competency evaluation. Aides who complete the program are known as certified nurse assistants (CNAs) and are placed on the State registry of nurse aides.

Other qualifications. Aides must be in good health. A physical examination, including State-regulated tests such as those for tuberculosis, may be required. A criminal background check also is usually required for employment.

Applicants should be tactful, patient, understanding, emotionally stable, and dependable and should have a desire to help people. They also should be able to work as part of a team, have good communication skills, and be willing to perform repetitive, routine tasks. Home health aides should be honest and discreet because they work in private homes. They also will need access to a car or public transportation to reach patients' homes.

Advancement. Opportunities for advancement within these occupations are limited. Aides generally need additional formal training or education to enter other health occupations. The most common health care occupations for former aides are licensed practical nurse, registered nurse, and medical assistant.

For some individuals, these occupations serve as entry-level jobs. For example, some high school and college students gain experience working in these occupations while attending school. In addition, experience as an aide can help individuals decide whether to pursue a career in health care.

Employment

Nursing, psychiatric, and home health aides held about 2.3 million jobs in 2006. Nursing aides held the most jobs—approximately 1.4 million. Home health aides held roughly 787,000 jobs, and psychiatric aides held about 62,000 jobs. About 52 percent of nursing aides worked in nursing and residential care facilities and another 29 percent worked in hospitals. Home health aides were mainly employed by home health care services, nursing and residential care facilities and social assistance agencies. About 47 percent of all psychiatric aides worked in

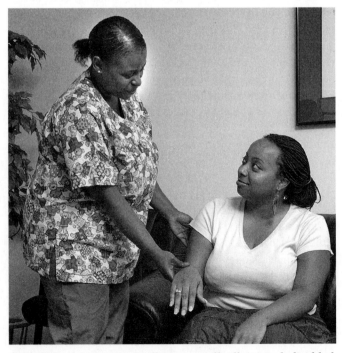

Aides help care for physically or mentally ill, injured, disabled, or infirm individuals in a variety of settings.

Projections data from the National Employment Matrix

Occupational Title	SOC Code	Employment, 2006	Projected employment, 2016	Change, 2006-16	
				Number	Percent
Nursing, psychiatric, and home health aides	31-1000	2,296,000	2,944,000	647,000	28
Home health aides...	31-1011	787,000	1,171,000	384,000	49
Nursing aides, orderlies, and attendants	31-1012	1,447,000	1,711,000	264,000	18
Psychiatric aides...	31-1013	62,000	62,000	0	0

NOTE: Data in this table are rounded. See the discussion of the employment projections table in the *Handbook* introductory chapter on *Occupational Information Included in the Handbook.*

hospitals, primarily in psychiatric and substance abuse hospitals, although some also worked in the psychiatric units of general medical and surgical hospitals. Others were employed in State government agencies; residential mental retardation, mental health, and substance abuse facilities; and nursing and residential care facilities.

Job Outlook

Excellent job opportunities for nursing, psychiatric, and home health aides will arise from a combination of rapid employment growth and the need to replace the many workers who leave the occupation each year.

Employment change. Overall employment of nursing, psychiatric, and home health aides is projected to grow 28 percent between 2006 and 2016, much faster than the average for all occupations. However, growth will vary for the individual occupations. Home health aides are expected to gain jobs faster than other aides as a result of growing demand for home services from an aging population and efforts to contain costs by moving patients out of hospitals and nursing care facilities as quickly as possible. Consumer preference for care in the home and improvements in medical technologies for in-home treatment also will contribute to much-faster-than-average employment growth for home health aides.

Nursing aide employment will not grow as fast as home health aide employment, largely because nursing aides are concentrated in relatively slower-growing industries. Employment of nursing aides is expected to grow faster than the average for all occupations through 2016, in response to the long-term care needs of an increasing elderly population. Financial pressures on hospitals to discharge patients as soon as possible should boost admissions to nursing care facilities. As a result, job openings will be more numerous in nursing and residential care facilities than in hospitals. Modern medical technology also will drive demand for nursing aides because as the technology saves and extends more lives, it increases the need for long-term care provided by aides.

Little or no change is expected in employment of psychiatric aides—the smallest of the three occupations. Most psychiatric aides currently work in hospitals, but the industries most likely to see growth will be residential facilities for people with developmental disabilities, mental illness, and substance abuse problems. There is a long-term trend toward treating psychiatric patients outside of hospitals because it is more cost effective and allows patients to live more independent lives. Demand for psychiatric aides in residential facilities will rise in response to the increase in the number of older persons, many of whom will require mental health services. Growing demand for these workers also rests on an increasing number of mentally disabled

adults who were formerly cared for by their elderly parents and who will continue to need care. Job growth also could be affected by changes in government funding of programs for the mentally ill.

Job prospects. High replacement needs for nursing, psychiatric, and home health aides reflect modest entry requirements, low pay, high physical and emotional demands, and limited opportunities for advancement within the occupation. For these same reasons, the number of people looking to enter the occupation will be limited. Many aides leave the occupation to attend training programs for other health care occupations. Therefore, people who are interested in, and suited for, this work should have excellent job opportunities.

Earnings

Median hourly earnings of nursing aides, orderlies, and attendants were $10.67 in May 2006. The middle 50 percent earned between $9.09 and $12.80 an hour. The lowest 10 percent earned less than $7.78, and the highest 10 percent earned more than $14.99 an hour. Median hourly earnings in the industries employing the largest numbers of nursing aides, orderlies, and attendants in May 2006 were:

Local government	$12.15
Employment services	11.47
General medical and surgical hospitals.................................	11.06
Nursing care facilities	10.37
Community care facilities for the elderly	10.07

Nursing and psychiatric aides in hospitals generally receive at least 1 week of paid vacation after 1 year of service. Paid holidays and sick leave, hospital and medical benefits, extra pay for late-shift work, and pension plans also are available to many hospital employees and to some nursing care facility employees.

Median hourly earnings of home health aides were $9.34 in May 2006. The middle 50 percent earned between $7.99 and $10.90 an hour. The lowest 10 percent earned less than $7.06, and the highest 10 percent earned more than $13.00 an hour. Median hourly earnings in the industries employing the largest numbers of home health aides in May 2006 were:

Nursing care facilities	$9.76
Residential mental retardation facilities................................	9.34
Services for the elderly and persons with disabilities..	9.26
Home health care services	9.14
Community care facilities for the elderly	8.87

Home health aides receive slight pay increases with experience and added responsibility. Usually, they are paid only for the time worked in the home, not for travel time between jobs, and must pay for their travel costs from their earnings. Most employers hire only on-call hourly workers and provide no benefits.

Median hourly earnings of psychiatric aides were $11.49 in May 2006. The middle 50 percent earned between $9.20 and $14.46 an hour. The lowest 10 percent earned less than $7.75, and the highest 10 percent earned more than $17.32 an hour. Median hourly earnings in the industries employing the largest numbers of psychiatric aides in May 2006 were:

State government	$13.27
General medical and surgical hospitals	12.31
Psychiatric and substance abuse hospitals	11.76
Residential mental health and substance abuse facilities	9.65
Residential mental retardation facilities	8.80

Related Occupations

Nursing, psychiatric, and home health aides help people who need routine care or treatment. So do child care workers, licensed practical and licensed vocational nurses, medical assistants, occupational therapist assistants and aides, personal and home care aides, physical therapist assistants and aides, radiation therapists, and registered nurses. Social and human service assistants, who sometimes work with mental health patients, do work similar to that of psychiatric aides.

Sources of Additional Information

Information about employment opportunities may be obtained from local hospitals, nursing care facilities, home health care agencies, psychiatric facilities, State boards of nursing, and local offices of the State employment service.

Information on licensing requirements for nursing and home health aides, and lists of State-approved nursing aide programs are available from State departments of public health, departments of occupational licensing, boards of nursing, and home care associations.

For more information on training and requirements for home health aides, contact:

➤ National Association for Home Care and Hospice, 228 7th St.SE., Washington, DC 20003.
Internet: **http://www.nahc.org**

For more information on the home health care industry, contact:

➤ Visiting Nurse Associations of America, 8403 Colesville Rd., Suite 1550, Silver Spring, MD 20910-6374.
Internet: **http://www.vnaa.org**

For more information on the health care workforce, contact:

➤ The Center for the Health Professions, 3333 California St., San Francisco, CA 94118.
Internet: **http://www.futurehealth.ucsf.edu**

Occupational Therapist Assistants and Aides

(O*NET 31-2011.00, 31-2012.00)

Significant Points

- Occupational therapist assistants generally must complete an associate degree or a certificate program; in contrast, occupational therapist aides usually receive most of their training on the job.

- Employment is projected to grow much faster than the average as demand for occupational therapy services rises and as occupational therapists increasingly use assistants and aides.

- Job prospects should be very good for occupational therapist assistants; job seekers holding only a high school diploma might face keen competition for occupational therapist aide jobs.

Nature of the Work

Occupational therapist assistants and aides work under the direction of occupational therapists to provide rehabilitative services to persons with mental, physical, emotional, or developmental impairments. The ultimate goal is to improve clients' quality of life and ability to perform daily activities. For example, occupational therapist assistants help injured workers re-enter the labor force by teaching them how to compensate for lost motor skills or help individuals with learning disabilities increase their independence.

Occupational therapist assistants, commonly known as *occupational therapy assistants*, help clients with rehabilitative activities and exercises outlined in a treatment plan developed in collaboration with an occupational therapist. Activities range from teaching the proper method of moving from a bed into a wheelchair to the best way to stretch and limber the muscles of the hand. Assistants monitor an individual's activities to make sure that they are performed correctly and to provide encouragement. They also record their client's progress for the occupational therapist. If the treatment is not having the intended effect, or the client is not improving as expected, the therapist may alter the treatment program in hopes of obtaining better results. In addition, occupational therapist assistants document the billing of the client's health insurance provider.

Occupational therapist aides typically prepare materials and assemble equipment used during treatment. They are responsible for a range of clerical tasks, including scheduling appointments, answering the telephone, restocking or ordering depleted supplies, and filling out insurance forms or other paperwork. Aides are not licensed, so the law does not allow them to perform as wide a range of tasks as occupational therapist assistants.

Work environment. Occupational therapist assistants and aides need to have a moderate degree of strength because of

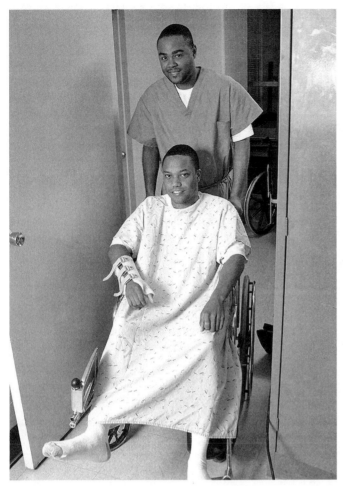

Occupational therapist assistants and aides provide rehabilitative services to persons with mental, physical, emotional, or developmental impairments.

the physical exertion required to assist patients. For example, assistants and aides may need to lift patients. Constant kneeling, stooping, and standing for long periods also are part of the job.

The hours and days that occupational therapist assistants and aides work vary by facility and with whether they are full- or part time. For example, many outpatient therapy offices and clinics have evening and weekend hours to coincide with patients' schedules.

Training, Other Qualifications, and Advancement

An associate degree or a certificate from an accredited community college or technical school is generally required to qualify for occupational therapist assistant jobs. In contrast, occupational therapist aides usually receive most of their training on the job.

Education and training. There were 126 accredited occupational therapist assistant programs in 2007. The first year of study typically involves an introduction to health care, basic medical terminology, anatomy, and physiology. In the second year, courses are more rigorous and usually include occupational therapist courses in areas such as mental health, adult physical disabilities, gerontology, and pediatrics. Students also must complete 16 weeks of supervised fieldwork in a clinic or community setting.

Applicants to occupational therapist assistant programs can improve their chances of admission by taking high school courses in biology and health and by performing volunteer work in nursing care facilities, occupational or physical therapists' offices, or other health care settings.

Occupational therapist aides usually receive most of their training on the job. Qualified applicants must have a high school diploma, strong interpersonal skills, and a desire to help people in need. Applicants may increase their chances of getting a job by volunteering their services, thus displaying initiative and aptitude to the employer.

Licensure. In most States, occupational therapist assistants are regulated and must pass a national certification examination after they graduate. Those who pass the test are awarded the title "Certified Occupational Therapy Assistant."

Other qualifications. Assistants and aides must be responsible, patient, and willing to take directions and work as part of a team. Furthermore, they should be caring and want to help people who are not able to help themselves.

Advancement. Occupational therapist assistants may advance into administration positions. They might organize all the assistants in a large occupational therapy department or act as the director for a specific department such as sports medicine. Some assistants go on to teach classes in accredited occupational therapist assistant academic programs or lead health risk reduction classes for the elderly.

Employment

Occupational therapist assistants and aides held about 33,000 jobs in 2006. Occupational therapist assistants held about 25,000 jobs, and occupational therapist aides held approximately 8,000. About 29 percent of jobs for assistants and aides were in hospitals, 23 percent were in offices of occupational therapists, and 21 percent were in nursing and residential care facilities. The rest were primarily in community care facilities for the elderly, home health care services, individual and family services, and State government agencies.

Job Outlook

Employment is expected to grow much faster than average as demand for occupational therapy services rises and as occupational therapists increasingly use assistants and aides. Job prospects should be very good for occupational therapist assistants. Job seekers holding only a high school diploma might face keen competition for occupational therapist aide jobs.

Employment change. Employment of occupational therapist assistants and aides is expected to grow 25 percent from 2006 to 2016, much faster than the average for all occupations. In the short run, the impact of proposed Federal legislation imposing limits on reimbursement for therapy services may adversely affect the job market for occupational therapist assistants and aides. Over the long run, however, demand for occupational therapist assistants and aides will continue to rise because of the increasing number of individuals with disabilities or limited function.

The growing elderly population is particularly vulnerable to chronic and debilitating conditions that require therapeutic services. These patients often need additional assistance in their treatment, making the roles of assistants and aides vital. Also,

Projections data from the National Employment Matrix

Occupational Title	SOC Code	Employment, 2006	Projected employment, 2016	Change, 2006-16	
				Number	Percent
Occupational therapist assistants and aides	31-2010	33,000	41,000	8,200	25
Occupational therapist assistants	31-2011	25,000	31,000	6,400	25
Occupational therapist aides	31-2012	8,200	10,000	1,800	22

NOTE: Data in this table are rounded. See the discussion of the employment projections table in the *Handbook* introductory chapter on *Occupational Information Included in the Handbook.*

the large baby-boom generation is entering the prime age for heart attacks and strokes, further increasing the demand for cardiac and physical rehabilitation. In addition, future medical developments should permit an increased percentage of trauma victims to survive, creating added demand for therapy services. An increase of sensory disorders in children will also spur demand for occupational therapy services.

Occupational therapists are expected to increasingly utilize assistants and aides to reduce the cost of occupational therapy services. Once a patient is evaluated and a treatment plan is designed by the therapist, the occupational therapist assistant can provide many aspects of treatment, as prescribed by the therapist.

Job prospects. Opportunities for individuals interested in becoming occupational therapist assistants are expected to be very good. In addition to employment growth, job openings will result from the need to replace occupational therapist assistants and aides who leave the occupation permanently over the 2006-16 period. Occupational therapist assistants and aides with prior experience working in an occupational therapy office or other health care setting will have the best job opportunities. However, individuals with only a high school diploma may face keen competition for occupational therapist aide jobs.

Earnings

Median annual earnings of occupational therapist assistants were $42,060 in May 2006. The middle 50 percent earned between $34,130 and $50,230. The lowest 10 percent earned less than $26,050, and the highest 10 percent earned more than $58,270. Median annual earnings in the industries employing the largest numbers of occupational therapist assistants in May 2006 were:

Offices of physical, occupational and speech therapists,
and audiologists $45,130
Nursing care facilities 43,280
General medical and surgical hospitals................................40,060

Median annual earnings of occupational therapist aides were $25,020 in May 2006. The middle 50 percent earned between $20,460 and $32,160. The lowest 10 percent earned less than $17,060, and the highest 10 percent earned more than $44,130. Median annual earnings in the industries employing the largest numbers of occupational therapist aides in May 2006 were:

Offices of physical, occupational and speech therapists,
and audiologists $26,960
General medical and surgical hospitals................................26,360
Nursing care facilities 25,520

Related Occupations

Occupational therapist assistants and aides work under the supervision and direction of occupational therapists. Other workers in the health care field who work under similar supervision include dental assistants; medical assistants; nursing, psychiatric, and home health aides; personal and home care aides; pharmacy aides; pharmacy technicians; and physical therapist assistants and aides.

Sources of Additional Information

For information on a career as an occupational therapist assistant or aide, and a list of accredited programs, contact:
➤ American Occupational Therapy Association, 4720 Montgomery Lane, Bethesda, MD 20824-1220.
Internet: **http://www.aota.org**

Pharmacy Aides

(O*NET 31-9095.00)

Significant Points

- Job opportunities are expected to be good for full-time and part-time work, especially for those with related work experience.

- Many pharmacy aides work evenings, weekends, and holidays.

- About 82 percent work in retail pharmacies, grocery stores, department stores, or mass retailers.

Nature of the Work

Pharmacy aides perform administrative duties in pharmacies. Aides often are clerks or cashiers who primarily answer telephones, handle money, stock shelves, and perform other clerical duties. They work closely with pharmacy technicians. Pharmacy technicians usually perform more complex tasks than do aides, although in some States the duties and titles of the jobs overlap. (See the statement on pharmacy technicians elsewhere in the *Handbook.*) Aides refer any questions regarding prescriptions, drug information, or health matters to a pharmacist. (See the statement on pharmacists elsewhere in the *Handbook.*)

Pharmacy aides may establish and maintain patient profiles, prepare insurance claim forms, and stock and take inventory of prescription and over-the-counter medications. Accurate recordkeeping is necessary to help avert dangerous drug interactions. In addition, because many people have medical insurance to help pay for prescriptions, it is essential that pharmacy aides correspond efficiently and correctly with third-party insurance providers to obtain payment. Pharmacy aides also maintain inventory and inform the supervisor of stock needs so that the pharmacy does not run out of vital medications that customers need. Some aides also help with the maintenance of equipment and supplies.

Work environment. Pharmacy aides work in clean, organized, well-lighted, and well-ventilated areas. Most of their workday is spent on their feet. They may be required to lift heavy boxes or to use stepladders to retrieve supplies from high shelves.

Aides work the same hours that pharmacists do. These include evenings, nights, weekends, and some holidays, particularly in facilities that are open 24 hours a day such as hospitals and some retail pharmacies.

Training, Other Qualifications, and Advancement

Most pharmacy aides are trained on the job. Employers prefer applicants with previous experience and strong customer service skills. Many pharmacy aides go on to become pharmacy technicians.

Education and training. Most pharmacy aides receive informal on-the-job training, but employers favor those with at least a high school diploma. Prospective pharmacy aides with experience working as cashiers may have an advantage when applying for jobs. Employers also prefer applicants with experience managing inventories and using computers.

Pharmacy aides begin their training by observing a more experienced worker. After they become familiar with the store's equipment, policies, and procedures, they begin to work on their own. Once they become experienced, aides are not likely to receive additional training, except when new equipment is introduced or when policies or procedures change.

Other qualifications. Strong customer service and communication skills are essential, as pharmacy aides frequently interact with patients, fellow employees, and other health-care professionals. Aides entering the field also need strong spelling, reading, and mathematics skills. Successful pharmacy aides are organized, dedicated, friendly, and responsible. They should be willing and able to take directions. Candidates interested in becoming pharmacy aides cannot have prior records of drug or substance abuse.

Advancement. With experience or certification, many pharmacy aides go on to become pharmacy technicians. Some become pharmacists after completing a substantial amount of formal training.

Employment

Pharmacy aides held about 50,000 jobs in 2006. About 82 percent worked in retail pharmacies, most of which were in drug stores but some of which were in grocery stores, department

Pharmacy aides perform administrative duties in pharmacies, such as answering phones and stocking shelves.

stores, or mass retailers. About 7 percent of aides worked in hospitals.

Job Outlook

Employment of pharmacy aides is expected to decline rapidly from 2006 to 2016. Job prospects, however, should be good.

Employment change. Employment of pharmacy aides is expected to decline rapidly, decreasing by 11 percent over the 2006 to 2016 period. Demand for pharmacy aides will fall as pharmacy technicians become increasingly responsible for answering phones, stocking shelves, operating cash registers, and performing other administrative tasks. In addition, with increased training, many pharmacy aides will become pharmacy technicians, which will result in further declines in pharmacy aide jobs.

Job prospects. Despite declining employment, job opportunities for full-time and part-time work are expected to be good. The frequent need to replace workers who leave the occupation will create opportunities for interested applicants. Aides with related work experience in pharmacies, or as cashiers or stock clerks in other retail settings, should have the best opportunities.

Earnings

Median hourly earnings of wage-and-salary pharmacy aides were $9.35 in May 2006. The middle 50 percent earned between $7.89 and $11.58; the lowest 10 percent earned less than $6.92, and the highest 10 percent earned more than $14.64. Median hourly earnings in the industries employing the largest numbers of pharmacy aides in May 2006 were:

General medical and surgical hospitals...............................$11.53
Grocery stores 9.87
Pharmacies and drug stores..8.97

Projections data from the National Employment Matrix

Occupational Title	SOC Code	Employment, 2006	Projected employment, 2016	Change, 2006-16	
				Number	Percent
Pharmacy aides	31-9095	50,000	45,000	-5,600	-11

NOTE: Data in this table are rounded. See the discussion of the employment projections table in the *Handbook* introductory chapter on *Occupational Information Included in the Handbook.*

Related Occupations

The work of pharmacy aides is closely related to that of pharmacy technicians, cashiers, and stock clerks and order fillers.

Sources of Additional Information

For information on employment opportunities, contact local employers or local offices of the State employment service.

Physical Therapist Assistants and Aides

(O*NET 31-2021.00, 31-2022.00)

Significant Points

- Employment is projected to increase much faster than average.

- Assistants should have very good job prospects; on the other hand, aides may face keen competition from the large pool of qualified applicants.

- Aides usually learn skills on the job, while assistants generally have an associate degree; some States require licensing for assistants.

- About 71 percent of jobs were in offices of physical therapists or in hospitals.

Nature of the Work

Physical therapist assistants and aides help physical therapists to provide treatment that improves patient mobility, relieves pain, and prevents or lessens physical disabilities of patients. A physical therapist might ask an assistant to help patients exercise or learn to use crutches, for example, or an aide to gather and prepare therapy equipment. Patients include accident victims and individuals with disabling conditions such as lower-back pain, arthritis, heart disease, fractures, head injuries, and cerebral palsy.

Physical therapist assistants perform a variety of tasks. Under the direction and supervision of physical therapists, they provide part of a patient's treatment. This might involve exercises, massages, electrical stimulation, paraffin baths, hot and cold packs, traction, and ultrasound. Physical therapist assistants record the patient's responses to treatment and report the outcome of each treatment to the physical therapist.

Physical therapist aides help make therapy sessions productive, under the direct supervision of a physical therapist or physical therapist assistant. They usually are responsible for keeping the treatment area clean and organized and for preparing for each patient's therapy. When patients need assistance moving to or from a treatment area, aides push them in a wheelchair or provide them with a shoulder to lean on. Because they are not licensed, aides do not perform the clinical tasks of a physical therapist assistant in States where licensure is required.

The duties of aides include some clerical tasks, such as ordering depleted supplies, answering the phone, and filling out insurance forms and other paperwork. The extent to which an aide or an assistant performs clerical tasks depends on the size and location of the facility.

Work environment. Physical therapist assistants and aides need a moderate degree of strength because of the physical exertion required in assisting patients with their treatment. In some cases, assistants and aides need to lift patients. Frequent kneeling, stooping, and standing for long periods also are part of the job.

The hours and days that physical therapist assistants and aides work vary with the facility. About 23 percent of all physical therapist assistants and aides work part time. Many outpatient physical therapy offices and clinics have evening and weekend hours, to coincide with patients' personal schedules.

Training, Other Qualifications, and Advancement

Most physical therapist aides are trained on the job, but most physical therapist assistants earn an associate degree from an accredited physical therapist assistant program. Some States require licensing for physical therapist assistants.

Education and training. Employers typically require physical therapist aides to have a high school diploma. They are trained on the job, and most employers provide clinical on-the-job training.

In many States, physical therapist assistants are required by law to hold at least an associate degree. According to the American Physical Therapy Association, there were 233 accredited physical therapist assistant programs in the United States as of 2006. Accredited programs usually last 2 years, or 4 semesters, and culminate in an associate degree.

Programs are divided into academic study and hands-on clinical experience. Academic course work includes algebra, anatomy and physiology, biology, chemistry, and psychology. Clinical work includes certifications in CPR and other first aid and field experience in treatment centers. Both educators and prospective employers view clinical experience as essential to ensuring that students understand the responsibilities of a physical therapist assistant.

Licensure. Licensing is not required to practice as a physical therapist aide. However, some States require licensure or registration in order to work as a physical therapist assistant.

Physical therapist assistants have very good job prospects, but physical therapist aides should experience keen competition for jobs.

Projections data from the National Employment Matrix

Occupational Title	SOC Code	Employment, 2006	Projected employment, 2016	Change, 2006-16	
				Number	Percent
Physical therapist assistants and aides	31-2020	107,000	137,000	31,000	29
Physical therapist assistants	31-2021	60,000	80,000	20,000	32
Physical therapist aides	31-2022	46,000	58,000	11,000	24

NOTE: Data in this table are rounded. See the discussion of the employment projections table in the *Handbook* introductory chapter on *Occupational Information Included in the Handbook.*

States that require licensure stipulate specific educational and examination criteria. Additional requirements may include certification in cardiopulmonary resuscitation (CPR) and other first aid and a minimum number of hours of clinical experience. Complete information on regulations can be obtained from State licensing boards.

Other qualifications. Physical therapist assistants and aides should be well-organized, detail oriented, and caring. They usually have strong interpersonal skills and a desire to help people in need.

Advancement. Some physical therapist aides advance to become therapist assistants after gaining experience and, often, additional education. Sometimes, this education is required by law.

Some physical therapist assistants advance by specializing in a clinical area. They gain expertise in treating a certain type of patient, such as geriatric or pediatric, or a type of ailment, such as sports injuries. Many physical therapist assistants advance to administration positions. These positions might include organizing all the assistants in a large physical therapy organization or acting as the director for a specific department such as sports medicine. Other assistants go on to teach in an accredited physical therapist assistant academic program, lead health risk reduction classes for the elderly, or organize community activities related to fitness and risk reduction.

Employment

Physical therapist assistants and aides held about 107,000 jobs in 2006. Physical therapist assistants held about 60,000 jobs; physical therapist aides, approximately 46,000. Both work with physical therapists in a variety of settings. About 71 percent of jobs were in offices of physical therapists or in hospitals. Others worked primarily in nursing care facilities, offices of physicians, home health care services, and outpatient care centers.

Job Outlook

Employment is expected to grow much faster than average because of increasing consumer demand for physical therapy services. Job prospects for physical therapist assistants are expected to be very good. Aides should experience keen competition for jobs.

Employment change. Employment of physical therapist assistants and aides is expected to grow by 29 percent over the 2006-16 decade, much faster than the average for all occupations. The impact of Federal limits on Medicare and Medicaid reimbursement for therapy services may adversely affect the short-term job outlook for physical therapist assistants and aides. However, long-term demand for physical therapist assis-

tants and aides will continue to rise, as the number of individuals with disabilities or limited function grows.

The increasing number of people who need therapy reflects, in part, the increasing elderly population. The elderly population is particularly vulnerable to chronic and debilitating conditions that require therapeutic services. These patients often need additional assistance in their treatment, making the roles of assistants and aides vital. In addition, the large baby-boom generation is entering the prime age for heart attacks and strokes, further increasing the demand for cardiac and physical rehabilitation. Moreover, future medical developments should permit an increased percentage of trauma victims to survive, creating added demand for therapy services.

Physical therapists are expected to increasingly use assistants to reduce the cost of physical therapy services. Once a patient is evaluated and a treatment plan is designed by the physical therapist, the physical therapist assistant can provide many parts of the treatment, as approved by the therapist.

Job prospects. Opportunities for individuals interested in becoming physical therapist assistants are expected to be very good. Physical therapist aides may face keen competition from the large pool of qualified individuals. In addition to employment growth, job openings will result from the need to replace workers who leave the occupation permanently. Physical therapist assistants and aides with prior experience working in a physical therapy office or other health care setting will have the best job opportunities.

Earnings

Median annual earnings of physical therapist assistants were $41,360 in May 2006. The middle 50 percent earned between $33,840 and $49,010. The lowest 10 percent earned less than $26,190, and the highest 10 percent earned more than $57,220. Median annual earnings in the industries employing the largest numbers of physical therapist assistants in May 2006 were:

Home health care services	$46,390
Nursing care facilities	44,460
Offices of physical, occupational and speech therapists, and audiologists	40,780
General medical and surgical hospitals................................	40,670
Offices of physicians	39,290

Median annual earnings of physical therapist aides were $22,060 in May 2006. The middle 50 percent earned between $18,550 and $26,860. The lowest 10 percent earned less than $15,850, and the highest 10 percent earned more than $32,600. Median annual earnings in the industries employing the largest numbers of physical therapist aides in May 2006 were:

Nursing care facilities $24,170
Offices of physicians...22,680
General medical and surgical hospitals..................................22,680
Offices of physical, occupational and speech
   therapists, and audiologists 21,230

Related Occupations

Physical therapist assistants and aides work under the supervision of physical therapists. Other workers in the health care field who work under similar supervision include dental assistants; medical assistants; occupational therapist assistants and aides; pharmacy aides; pharmacy technicians; nursing, psychiatric, and home health aides; personal and home care aides; and social and human service assistants.

Sources of Additional Information

Career information on physical therapist assistants and a list of schools offering accredited programs can be obtained from:
➤ The American Physical Therapy Association, 1111 North Fairfax St., Alexandria, VA 22314-1488.
Internet: **http://www.apta.org**

Protective Service Occupations

Correctional Officers

(O*NET 33-1011.00, 33-3011.00, 33-3012.00)

Significant Points

- The work can be stressful and hazardous.

- Most correctional officers are employed in State and local government prisons and jails.

- Job opportunities are expected to be excellent.

Nature of the Work

Correctional officers, also known as *detention officers*, are responsible for overseeing individuals who have been arrested and are awaiting trial or who have been convicted of a crime and sentenced to serve time in a jail, reformatory, or penitentiary.

The jail population changes constantly as some are released, some are convicted and transferred to prison, and new offenders are arrested and enter the system. Correctional officers in local jails admit and process about 12 million people a year, with about 700,000 offenders in jail at any given time. Correctional officers in State and Federal prisons watch over the approximately 1.5 million offenders who are incarcerated there at any given time.

Correctional officers maintain security and inmate accountability to prevent disturbances, assaults, and escapes. Officers have no law enforcement responsibilities outside the institution where they work. (For more information on related occupations, see the statements on police and detectives and on probation officers and correctional treatment specialists, elsewhere in the *Handbook*.)

Regardless of the setting, correctional officers maintain order within the institution and enforce rules and regulations. To help ensure that inmates are orderly and obey rules, correctional officers monitor the activities and supervise the work assignments of inmates. Sometimes, officers must search inmates and their living quarters for contraband like weapons or drugs, settle disputes between inmates, and enforce discipline. Correctional officers periodically inspect the facilities, checking cells and other areas of the institution for unsanitary conditions, contraband, fire hazards, and any evidence of infractions of rules. In addition, they routinely inspect locks, window bars, grilles, doors, and gates for signs of tampering. Finally, officers inspect mail and visitors for prohibited items.

Correctional officers report orally and in writing on inmate conduct and on the quality and quantity of work done by inmates. Officers also report security breaches, disturbances, violations of rules, and any unusual occurrences. They usually keep a daily log or record of their activities. Correctional officers cannot show favoritism and must report any inmate who violates the rules. If a crime is committed within their institution or an inmate escapes, they help the responsible law enforcement authorities investigate or search for the escapee. In jail and prison facilities with direct supervision of cellblocks, officers work unarmed. They are equipped with communications devices so that they can summon help if necessary. These officers often work in a cellblock alone, or with another officer, among the 50 to 100 inmates who reside there. The officers enforce regulations primarily through their interpersonal communication skills and through the use of progressive sanctions, such as the removal of some privileges.

In the highest security facilities, where the most dangerous inmates are housed, correctional officers often monitor the activities of prisoners from a centralized control center with closed-circuit television cameras and a computer tracking system. In such an environment, the inmates may not see anyone but officers for days or weeks at a time and may leave their cells only for showers, solitary exercise time, or visitors. Depending on the offenders' security classification within the institution, correctional officers may have to restrain inmates in handcuffs and leg irons to safely escort them to and from cells and other areas and to see authorized visitors. Officers also escort prisoners between the institution and courtrooms, medical facilities, and other destinations outside the institution.

Bailiffs, also known as *marshals* or *court officers*, are law enforcement officers who maintain safety and order in courtrooms. Their duties, which vary by location, include enforcing courtroom rules, assisting judges, guarding juries from outside contact, delivering court documents, and providing general security for courthouses.

Work environment. Working in a correctional institution can be stressful and hazardous. Every year, correctional officers are injured in confrontations with inmates. Correctional officers may work indoors or outdoors. Some correctional institutions are well lighted, temperature controlled, and ventilated, but others are old, overcrowded, hot, and noisy. Although both jails and prisons can be dangerous places to work, prison populations are more stable than jail populations, and correctional officers in prisons know the security and custodial requirements of the prisoners with whom they are dealing.

Correctional officers usually work an 8-hour day, 5 days a week, on rotating shifts. Because prison and jail security must be provided around the clock, officers work all hours of the day and night, weekends, and holidays. In addition, officers may be required to work paid overtime.

Training, Other Qualifications, and Advancement

Correctional officers learn most of what they need to know for their work through on-the-job training. Qualifications vary by agency, but all agencies require a high school diploma or equivalent, and some also require some college education or full-time work experience.

Education and training. A high school diploma or graduation equivalency degree is required by all employers. The Federal Bureau of Prisons requires entry-level correctional officers to have at least a bachelor's degree; 3 years of full-time experience in a field providing counseling, assistance, or supervision to individuals; or a combination of the two. Some State and local corrections agencies require some college credits, but law enforcement or military experience may be substituted to fulfill this requirement.

Federal, State, and some local departments of corrections provide training for correctional officers based on guidelines established by the American Correctional Association and the American Jail Association. Some States have regional training academies that are available to local agencies. At the conclu-

Job opportunities for correctional officers should be excellent.

sion of formal instruction, all State and local correctional agencies provide on-the-job training, including training on legal restrictions and interpersonal relations. Many systems require firearms proficiency and self-defense skills. Officer trainees typically receive several weeks or months of training in an actual job setting under the supervision of an experienced officer. However, on-the-job training varies widely from agency to agency.

Academy trainees generally receive instruction in a number of subjects, including institutional policies, regulations, and operations, as well as custody and security procedures. New Federal correctional officers must undergo 200 hours of formal training within the first year of employment. They also must complete 120 hours of specialized training at the U.S. Federal Bureau of Prisons residential training center at Glynco, GA, within 60 days of their appointment. Experienced officers receive annual in-service training to keep abreast of new developments and procedures.

Some correctional officers are members of prison tactical response teams, which are trained to respond to disturbances, riots, hostage situations, forced cell moves, and other potentially dangerous confrontations. Team members practice disarming prisoners wielding weapons, protecting themselves and inmates against the effects of chemical agents, and other tactics.

Other qualifications. All institutions require correctional officers to be at least 18 to 21 years of age, be a U.S. citizen or permanent resident, and have no felony convictions. Some require previous experience in law enforcement or the military, but college credits can be substituted to fulfill this requirement. Others require demonstration of job stability, usually by accumulating 2 years of work experience, which need not be related to corrections or law enforcement.

Correctional officers must be in good health. Candidates for employment generally are required to meet formal standards of physical fitness, eyesight, and hearing. In addition, many jurisdictions use standard tests to determine applicant suitability to work in a correctional environment. Good judgment and the ability to think and act quickly are indispensable. Applicants are typically screened for drug abuse, subject to background checks, and required to pass a written examination.

Advancement. Qualified officers may advance to the position of correctional sergeant. Correctional sergeants supervise correctional officers and usually are responsible for maintaining security and directing the activities of other officers during an assigned shift or in an assigned area. Ambitious and qualified correctional officers can be promoted to supervisory or administrative positions all the way up to warden. Promotion prospects may be enhanced by attending college. Officers sometimes transfer to related jobs, such as probation officer, parole officer, and correctional treatment specialist.

Employment

Correctional officers held about 500,000 jobs in 2006. About 3 of every 5 jobs were in State correctional institutions such as prisons, prison camps, and youth correctional facilities. About 18,000 jobs for correctional officers were in Federal correctional institutions, and about 16,000 jobs were in privately owned and managed prisons.

Projections data from the National Employment Matrix

Occupational Title	SOC Code	Employment, 2006	Projected employment, 2016	Change, 2006-16	
				Number	Percent
Correctional officers..	—	500,000	582,000	82,000	16
First-line supervisors/managers of correctional officers..............	33-1011	40,000	45,000	5,000	13
Bailiffs, correctional officers, and jailers.....................................	33-3010	460,000	537,000	77,000	17
Bailiffs..	33-3011	19,000	21,000	2,100	11
Correctional officers and jailers..	33-3012	442,000	516,000	75,000	17

NOTE: Data in this table are rounded. See the discussion of the employment projections table in the *Handbook* introductory chapter on *Occupational Information Included in the Handbook*.

Most of the remaining jobs were in city and county jails or in other institutions run by local governments. Some 300 of these jails, all of them in urban areas, are large, housing over 1,000 inmates. Most correctional officers employed in jails, however, work in institutions located in rural areas with smaller inmate populations.

Other correctional officers oversee individuals being held by the U.S. Immigration and Naturalization Service pending release or deportation or work for correctional institutions that are run by private, for-profit organizations.

Job Outlook

Employment growth is expected to be faster than the average for all occupations, and job opportunities are expected to be excellent.

Employment change. Employment of correctional officers is expected to grow 16 percent between 2006 and 2016, faster than the average for all occupations. Increasing demand for correctional officers will stem from population growth and rising rates of incarceration. Mandatory sentencing guidelines calling for longer sentences and reduced parole for inmates are a primary reason for historically increasing incarceration rates. Some States are reconsidering mandatory sentencing guidelines because of budgetary constraints, court decisions, and doubts about their effectiveness. Additionally, the Supreme Court recently ruled to make Federal sentencing guidelines voluntary, rather than mandatory, for judges. It is unclear how many States will change their sentencing policies and how long it will be before any changes affect the prison population. Nevertheless, these developments could moderate future increases in the prison population and cause employment of correctional officers to grow more slowly than they have in the past.

Some employment opportunities also will arise in the private sector, as public authorities contract with private companies to provide and staff corrections facilities. Both State and Federal corrections agencies are increasingly using private prisons.

Job prospects. Job opportunities for correctional officers are expected to be excellent. The need to replace correctional officers who transfer to other occupations, retire, or leave the labor force, coupled with rising employment demand, will generate thousands of job openings each year. In the past, some local and State corrections agencies have experienced difficulty in attracting and keeping qualified applicants, largely because of low salaries, shift work, and the concentration of jobs in rural locations. This situation is expected to continue.

Layoffs of correctional officers are rare because of increasing offender populations.

Earnings

Median annual earnings of correctional officers and jailers were $35,760 in May 2006. The middle 50 percent earned between $28,320 and $46,500. The lowest 10 percent earned less than $23,600, and the highest 10 percent earned more than $58,580. Median annual earnings in the public sector were $47,750 in the Federal Government, $36,140 in State government, and $34,820 in local government. In the facilities support services industry, where the relatively small number of officers employed by privately operated prisons is classified, median annual earnings were $25,050.

Median annual earnings of first-line supervisors/managers of correctional officers were $52,580 in May 2006. The middle 50 percent earned between $38,920 and $67,820. The lowest 10 percent earned less than $33,270, and the highest 10 percent earned more than $81,230. Median annual earnings were $51,500 in State government and $52,940 in local government.

Median annual earnings of bailiffs were $34,210 in May 2006. The middle 50 percent earned between $25,130 and $48,010. The lowest 10 percent earned less than $18,390, and the highest 10 percent earned more than $58,270. Median annual earnings were $30,510 in local government.

According to the Federal Bureau of Prisons, the starting salary for Federal correctional officers was $28,862 a year in 2007. Starting Federal salaries were slightly higher in areas where prevailing local pay levels were higher.

In addition to typical benefits, correctional officers employed in the public sector usually are provided with uniforms or a clothing allowance to purchase their own uniforms. Civil service systems or merit boards cover officers employed by the Federal Government and most State governments. Their retirement coverage entitles correctional officers to retire at age 50 after 20 years of service or at any age with 25 years of service.

Related Occupations

A number of options are available to those interested in careers in protective services and security. Security guards and gaming surveillance officers protect people and property against theft, vandalism, illegal entry, and fire. Police and detectives maintain law and order, prevent crime, and arrest offenders. Probation officers and correctional treatment specialists monitor and counsel offenders and evaluate their progress in becoming productive members of society.

Sources of Additional Information

Further information about correctional officers is available from:

➤ American Correctional Association, 206 N. Washington St., Suite 200, Alexandria, VA 22314.
Internet: **http://www.aca.org**
➤ American Jail Association, 1135 Professional Ct., Hagerstown, MD 21740.
Internet: **http://www.corrections.com/a**ja

Information on entrance requirements, training, and career opportunities for correctional officers at the Federal level may be obtained from the Federal Bureau of Prisons.
Internet: **http://www.bop.gov**

Information on obtaining a position as a correctional officer with the Federal Government is available from the Office of Personnel Management through USAJOBS, the Federal Government's official employment information system. This resource for locating and applying for job opportunities can be accessed through the Internet at **http://www.usajobs.opm.go**v or through an interactive voice response telephone system at (703) 724-1850 or TDD (978) 461-8404. These numbers are not tollfree, and charges may result.

Fire Fighting Occupations

(O*NET 33-1021.00, 33-1021.01, 33-1021.02, 33-2011.00, 33-2011.01, 33-2011.02, 33-2021.00, 33-2021.01,33-2021.02, 33-2022.00)

Significant Points

- Fire fighting involves hazardous conditions and long, irregular hours.

- About 9 out of 10 fire fighting workers were employed by local governments.

- Applicants for city fire fighting jobs generally must pass written, physical, and medical examinations.

- Although employment is expected to grow faster than the average, keen competition for jobs is expected because this occupation attracts many qualified candidates.

Nature of the Work

Every year, fires and other emergencies take thousands of lives and destroy property worth billions of dollars. Fire fighters help protect the public against these dangers by responding to fires and a variety of other emergencies. In addition to putting out fires, they are frequently the first emergency personnel at the scene of a traffic accident or medical emergency and may be called upon to treat injuries or perform other vital functions.

During duty hours, fire fighters must be prepared to respond immediately to a fire or others emergency. Fighting fires is dangerous and complex, therefore requires organization and teamwork. At every emergency scene, fire fighters perform specific duties assigned by a superior officer. At fires, they connect hose lines to hydrants and operate a pump to send water to high-pressure hoses. Some carry hoses, climb ladders, and enter burning buildings—using systematic and careful procedures—to put out fires. At times, they may need to use tools, like an ax, to make their way through doors, walls, and debris sometimes with the aid of information about a building's floor plan. Some find and rescue occupants who are unable to safely leave the building without assistance. They also provide emergency medical attention, ventilate smoke-filled areas, and attempt to salvage the contents of buildings. Fire fighters' duties may change several times while the company is in action. Sometimes they remain at the site of a disaster for days at a time, rescuing trapped survivors, and assisting with medical treatment.

Fire fighters work in a variety of settings, including metropolitan areas, rural areas with grasslands and forests, airports, chemical plants and other industrial sites. They have also assumed a range of responsibilities, including emergency medical services. In fact, most calls to which fire fighters respond involve medical emergencies. In addition, some fire fighters work in hazardous materials units that are specially trained for the control, prevention, and cleanup of hazardous materials, such as oil spills or accidents involving the transport of chemicals. (For more information, see the *Handbook* section on hazardous material removal workers.)

Workers specializing forest fires utilize different methods and equipment than other fire fighters. In national forests and parks, *forest fire inspectors and prevention specialists* spot fires from watchtowers and report the fires to headquarters by telephone or radio. Forest rangers also patrol to ensure that travelers and campers comply with fire regulations. When fires break out, crews of fire fighters are brought in to suppress the blaze with heavy equipment and water hoses. Fighting forest fires, like fighting urban fires, is rigorous work. One of the most effective means of fighting a forest fire is creating fire lines—cutting down trees and digging out grass and all other combustible vegetation in the path of the fire—to deprive it of fuel. Elite fire fighters called smoke jumpers parachute from airplanes to reach otherwise inaccessible areas. This tactic, however, can be extremely hazardous.When they aren't responding to fires and other emergencies, fire fighters clean and maintain equipment, study fire science and fire fighting techniques, conduct practice drills and fire inspections, and participate in physical fitness activities. They also prepare written reports on fire incidents and review fire science literature to stay informed about technological developments and changing administrative practices and policies.

Most fire departments have a fire prevention division, usually headed by a fire marshal and staffed by *fire inspectors*. Workers in this division conduct inspections of structures to prevent fires by ensuring compliance with fire codes. These inspectors also work with developers and planners to check and approve plans for new buildings and inspect buildings under construction.

Some fire fighters become *fire investigators*, who determine the causes of fires. They collect evidence, interview witnesses, and prepare reports on fires in cases where the cause may be arson or criminal negligence. They often are asked to testify in court. In some cities, these investigators work in police departments, and some are employed by insurance companies.

Work environment. Fire fighters spend much of their time at fire stations, which are usually similar to dormitories. When an alarm sounds, fire fighters respond, regardless of the weather or hour. Fire fighting involves the risk of death or injury from floors caving in, walls toppling, traffic accidents, and exposure to flames and smoke. Fire fighters also may come into contact with poisonous, flammable, or explosive gases and chemicals and radioactive materials, which may have immediate or long-term effects on their health. For these reasons, they must wear protective gear that can be very heavy and hot.

Work hours of fire fighters are longer and more varied than the hours of most other workers. Many fire fighters work more than 50 hours a week, and sometimes they may work longer. In some agencies, fire fighters are on duty for 24 hours, then off for 48 hours, and receive an extra day off at intervals. In others, they work a day shift of 10 hours for 3 or 4 days, a night shift of 14 hours for 3 or 4 nights, have 3 or 4 days off, and then repeat the cycle. In addition, fire fighters often work extra hours at fires and other emergencies and are regularly assigned to work on holidays. Fire lieutenants and fire captains often work the same hours as the fire fighters they supervise.

Training, Other Qualifications, and Advancement

Applicants for fire fighting jobs are usually required to have at least a high school diploma, but candidates with some education after high school are increasingly preferred. Most municipal jobs require passing written and physical tests. All fire fighters receive extensive training after being hired.

Education and training. Most fire fighters have a high school diploma, however, the completion of community college courses, or in some cases, an associate degree, in fire science may improve an applicant's chances for a job. A number of colleges and universities offer courses leading to 2- or 4-year degrees in fire engineering or fire science. In recent years, an increasing proportion of new fire fighters have had some education after high school.

As a rule, entry-level workers in large fire departments are trained for several weeks at the department's training center or academy. Through classroom instruction and practical training, the recruits study fire fighting techniques, fire prevention, hazardous materials control, local building codes, and emergency medical procedures, including first aid and cardiopulmonary resuscitation (CPR). They also learn how to use axes, chain saws, fire extinguishers, ladders, and other fire fighting and rescue equipment. After successfully completing this training, the recruits are assigned to a fire company, where they undergo a period of probation.

Many fire departments have accredited apprenticeship programs lasting up to 4 years. These programs combine formal instruction with on-the-job training under the supervision of experienced fire fighters.

Almost all departments require fire fighters to be certified as emergency medical technicians. (For more information, see the section of the *Handbook* on emergency medical technicians and paramedics.) Although most fire departments require the lowest level of certification, Emergency Medical Technician-Basic (EMT-Basic), larger departments in major metropolitan areas increasingly require paramedic certification. Some departments include this training in the fire academy, whereas others prefer that recruits earn EMT certification on their own but will give them up to 1 year to do it.

Fire fighters respond to emergencies, such as car accidents and fires.

In addition to participating in training programs conducted by local fire departments, some fire fighters attend training sessions sponsored by the U.S. National Fire Academy. These training sessions cover topics such as executive development, anti-arson techniques, disaster preparedness, hazardous materials control, and public fire safety and education. Some States also have either voluntary or mandatory fire fighter training and certification programs. Many fire departments offer fire fighters incentives such as tuition reimbursement or higher pay for completing advanced training.

Other qualifications. Applicants for municipal fire fighting jobs usually must pass a written exam; tests of strength, physical stamina, coordination, and agility; and a medical examination that includes a drug screening. Workers may be monitored on a random basis for drug use after accepting employment. Examinations are generally open to people who are at least 18 years of age and have a high school education or its equivalent. Those who receive the highest scores in all phases of testing have the best chances of being hired.

Among the personal qualities fire fighters need are mental alertness, self-discipline, courage, mechanical aptitude, endurance, strength, and a sense of public service. Initiative and good judgment also are extremely important because fire fighters make quick decisions in emergencies. Members of a crew live and work closely together under conditions of stress and danger for extended periods, so they must be dependable and able to get along well with others. Leadership qualities are necessary for officers, who must establish and maintain discipline and efficiency, as well as direct the activities of the fire fighters in their companies.

Advancement. Most experienced fire fighters continue studying to improve their job performance and prepare for promotion examinations. To progress to higher level positions, they acquire expertise in advanced fire fighting equipment and techniques, building construction, emergency medical technology, writing, public speaking, management and budgeting procedures, and public relations.

Opportunities for promotion depend upon the results of written examinations, as well as job performance, interviews, and

Projections data from the National Employment Matrix

Occupational Title	SOC Code	Employment, 2006	Projected employment, 2016	Change, 2006-16	
				Number	Percent
Fire fighting occupations..	—	361,000	404,000	43,000	12
First-line supervisors/managers of fire fighting and prevention workers..	33-1021	52,000	58,000	6,000	11
Fire fighting and prevention workers	33-2000	308,000	345,000	37,000	12
Fire fighters	33-2011	293,000	328,000	35,000	12
Fire inspectors..	33-2020	16,000	17,000	1,600	10
Fire inspectors and investigators...	33-2021	14,000	15,000	1,500	11
Forest fire inspectors and prevention specialists..................	33-2022	1,800	1,900	0	2

NOTE: Data in this table are rounded. See the discussion of the employment projections table in the *Handbook* introductory chapter on *Occupational Information Included in the Handbook*.

seniority. Hands-on tests that simulate real-world job situations are also used by some fire departments.

Usually, fire fighters are first promoted to engineer, then lieutenant, captain, battalion chief, assistant chief, deputy chief, and, finally, chief. For promotion to positions higher than battalion chief, many fire departments now require a bachelor's degree, preferably in fire science, public administration, or a related field. An associate degree is required for executive fire officer certification from the National Fire Academy.

Employment

In 2006, total paid employment in firefighting occupations was about 361,000. Fire fighters held about 293,000 jobs, first-line supervisors/managers of fire fighting and prevention workers held about 52,000, and fire inspectors and investigators held about 14,000 jobs. These employment figures include only paid career fire fighters—they do not cover volunteer fire fighters, who perform the same duties and may constitute the majority of fire fighters in a residential area. According to the U.S. Fire Administration, about 71 percent of fire companies were staffed entirely by volunteer fire fighters in 2005.

About 9 out of 10 fire fighting workers were employed by local government. Some large cities have thousands of career fire fighters, while many small towns have only a few. Most of the remainder worked in fire departments on Federal and State installations, including airports. Private fire fighting companies employ a small number of fire fighters.

In response to the expanding role of fire fighters, some municipalities have combined fire prevention, public fire education, safety, and emergency medical services into a single organization commonly referred to as a public safety organization. Some local and regional fire departments are being consolidated into countywide establishments to reduce administrative staffs, cut costs, and establish consistent training standards and work procedures.

Job Outlook

Although employment is expected to grow as fast as the average for all jobs, candidates for these positions are expected to face keen competition as these positions are highly attractive and sought after.

Employment change. Employment of workers in fire fighting occupations is expected to grow by 12 percent over the 2006-2016 decade, which is as fast as the average for all occupations. Most job growth will stem from volunteer fire fighting positions being converted to paid positions. In recent years, it has become more difficult for volunteer fire departments to recruit and retain volunteers. This may be the result of the considerable amount of training and time commitment required. Furthermore, a trend towards more people living in and around cities has increased the demand for fire fighters. When areas develop and become more densely populated, emergencies and fires affect more buildings and more people and therefore require more fire fighters.

Job prospects. Prospective fire fighters are expected to face keen competition for available job openings. Many people are attracted to fire fighting because, it is challenging and provides the opportunity to perform an essential public service; a high school education is usually sufficient for entry; and a pension is usually guaranteed after 25 years work. Consequently, the number of qualified applicants in most areas far exceeds the number of job openings, even though the written examination and physical requirements eliminate many applicants. This situation is expected to persist in coming years. Applicants with the best chances are those who are physically fit and score the highest on physical conditioning and mechanical aptitude exams. Those who have completed some fire fighter education at a community college and have EMT or paramedic certification will have an additional advantage.

Earnings

Median annual earnings of fire fighters were $41,190 in May 2006. The middle 50 percent earned between $29,550 and $54,120. The lowest 10 percent earned less than $20,660, and the highest 10 percent earned more than $66,140. Median annual earnings were $41,600 in local government, $41,070 in the Federal Government, and $37,000 in State governments.

Median annual earnings of first-line supervisors/managers of fire fighting and prevention workers were $62,900 in May 2006. The middle 50 percent earned between $50,180 and $79,060. The lowest 10 percent earned less than $36,820, and the highest 10 percent earned more than $97,820. First-line supervisors/managers of fire fighting and prevention workers employed in local government earned a median of about $64,070 a year.

Median annual earnings of fire inspectors and investigators were $48,050 in May 2006. The middle 50 percent earned between $36,960 and $61,160 a year. The lowest 10 percent earned less than $29,840, and the highest 10 percent earned more than $74,930. Fire inspectors and investigators employed in local government earned a median of about $49,690 a year.

According to the International City-County Management Association, average salaries in 2006 for sworn full-time positions were as follows:

Rank	Minimum annual base salary	Maximum annual base salary
Fire chief	$73,435	$95,271
Deputy chief	66,420	84,284
Battalion chief	62,199	78,611
Assistant fire chief	61,887	78,914
Fire captain	51,808	62,785
Fire lieutenant	47,469	56,511
Fire prevention/code inspector	45,951	58,349
Engineer	43,232	56,045

Fire fighters who average more than a certain number of work hours per week are required to be paid overtime. The hours threshold is determined by the department. Fire fighters often earn overtime for working extra shifts to maintain minimum staffing levels or during special emergencies.

Fire fighters receive benefits that usually include medical and liability insurance, vacation and sick leave, and some paid holidays. Almost all fire departments provide protective clothing (helmets, boots, and coats) and breathing apparatus, and many also provide dress uniforms. Fire fighters generally are covered by pension plans, often providing retirement at half pay after 25 years of service or if the individual is disabled in the line of duty.

Related Occupations

Like fire fighters, emergency medical technicians and paramedics and police and detectives respond to emergencies and save lives.

Sources of Additional Information

Information about a career as a fire fighter may be obtained from local fire departments and from either of the following organizations:

➤ International Association of Fire Fighters, 1750 New York Ave. NW., Washington, DC 20006.
Internet: **http://www.iaff.org**
➤ U.S. Fire Administration, 16825 South Seton Ave., Emmitsburg, MD 21727.
Internet: **http://www.usfa.dhs.gov**

Information about professional qualifications and a list of colleges and universities offering 2- or 4-year degree programs in fire science or fire prevention may be obtained from:
➤ National Fire Academy, 16825 South Seton Ave., Emmitsburg, MD 21727.
Internet: **http://www.usfa.dhs.gov/nfa/index.htm**

Police and Detectives

(O*NET 33-1012.00, 33-3021.00, 33-3021.01, 33-3021.02, 33-3021.03, 33-3021.05, 33-3031.00, 33-3051.00, 33-3051.01, 33-3051.03, 33-3052.00)

Significant Points

- Police work can be dangerous and stressful.

- Education requirements range from a high school diploma to a college degree or higher.

- Job opportunities in most local police departments will be excellent for qualified individuals, while competition is expected for jobs in State and Federal agencies.

- Applicants with college training in police science or military police experience will have the best opportunities.

Nature of the Work

People depend on police officers and detectives to protect their lives and property. Law enforcement officers, some of whom are State or Federal special agents or inspectors, perform these duties in a variety of ways depending on the size and type of their organization. In most jurisdictions, they are expected to exercise authority when necessary, whether on or off duty.

Police and detectives pursue and apprehend individuals who break the law and then issue citations or give warnings. A large proportion of their time is spent writing reports and maintaining records of incidents they encounter. Most police officers patrol their jurisdictions and investigate any suspicious activity they notice. Detectives, who are often called agents or special agents, perform investigative duties such as gathering facts and collecting evidence.

The daily activities of police and detectives differ depending on their occupational specialty—such as police officer, game warden, or detective—and whether they are working for a local, State, or Federal agency. Duties also differ substantially among various Federal agencies, which enforce different aspects of the law. Regardless of job duties or location, police officers and detectives at all levels must write reports and maintain meticulous records that will be needed if they testify in court.

Uniformed police officers have general law enforcement duties, including maintaining regular patrols and responding to calls for service. Much of their time is spent responding to calls and doing paperwork. They may direct traffic at the scene of an accident, investigate a burglary, or give first aid to an accident victim. In large police departments, officers usually are assigned to a specific type of duty. Many urban police agencies are involved in community policing—a practice in which an officer builds relationships with the citizens of local neighborhoods and mobilizes the public to help fight crime.

Police agencies are usually organized into geographic districts, with uniformed officers assigned to patrol a specific area such as part of the business district or outlying residential neighborhoods. Officers may work alone, but in large agencies, they often patrol with a partner. While on patrol, officers attempt to become thoroughly familiar with their patrol area and remain alert for anything unusual. Suspicious circumstances and hazards to public safety are investigated or noted, and officers are dispatched to individual calls for assistance within their district. During their shift, they may identify, pursue, and arrest suspected criminals; resolve problems within the community; and enforce traffic laws.

Some agencies have special geographic jurisdictions and enforcement responsibilities. Public college and university police forces, public school district police, and agencies serving transportation systems and facilities are examples. Most law enforcement workers in special agencies are uniformed officers; a smaller number are investigators.

Some police officers specialize in a particular field, such as chemical and microscopic analysis, training and firearms instruction, or handwriting and fingerprint identification. Others work with special units, such as horseback, bicycle, motorcycle, or harbor patrol; canine corps; special weapons and tactics (SWAT); or emergency response teams. A few local and special law enforcement officers primarily perform jail-related duties or work in courts. (For information on other officers who work in jails and prisons, see correctional officers elsewhere in the *Handbook*.)

Sheriffs and *deputy sheriffs* enforce the law on the county level. Sheriffs are usually elected to their posts and perform duties similar to those of a local or county police chief. Sheriffs' departments tend to be relatively small, most having fewer than 50 sworn officers. Deputy sheriffs have law enforcement duties similar to those of officers in urban police departments. Police and sheriffs' deputies who provide security in city and county courts are sometimes called bailiffs

State police officers, sometimes called *State troopers* or *highway patrol officers*, arrest criminals Statewide and patrol highways to enforce motor vehicle laws and regulations. State police officers often issue traffic citations to motorists. At the scene of accidents, they may direct traffic, give first aid, and call for emergency equipment. They also write reports used to determine the cause of the accident. State police officers are frequently called upon to render assistance to other law enforcement agencies, especially those in rural areas or small towns.

State law enforcement agencies operate in every State except Hawaii. Most full-time sworn personnel are uniformed officers who regularly patrol and respond to calls for service. Others work as investigators, perform court-related duties, or carry out administrative or other assignments.

Detectives are plainclothes investigators who gather facts and collect evidence for criminal cases. Some are assigned to interagency task forces to combat specific types of crime. They conduct interviews, examine records, observe the activities of suspects, and participate in raids or arrests. Detectives and State and Federal agents and inspectors usually specialize in investigating one type of violation, such as homicide or fraud. They are assigned cases on a rotating basis and work on them until an arrest and conviction is made or until the case is dropped.

Fish and game wardens enforce fishing, hunting, and boating laws. They patrol hunting and fishing areas, conduct search and rescue operations, investigate complaints and accidents, and aid in prosecuting court cases.

The Federal Government works in many areas of law enforcement. *Federal Bureau of Investigation (FBI) agents* are the Government's principal investigators, responsible for investigating violations of more than 200 categories of Federal law and conducting sensitive national security investigations. Agents may conduct surveillance, monitor court-authorized wiretaps, examine business records, investigate white-collar crime, or participate in sensitive undercover assignments. The FBI investigates a wide range of criminal activity, including organized crime, public corruption, financial crime, bank robbery, kidnapping, terrorism, espionage, drug trafficking, and cyber crime.

There are many other Federal agencies that enforce particular types of laws. *U.S. Drug Enforcement Administration (DEA) agents* enforce laws and regulations relating to illegal drugs. *U.S. marshals and deputy marshals* protect the Federal courts and ensure the effective operation of the judicial system. *Bureau of Alcohol, Tobacco, Firearms, and Explosives agents* enforce and investigate violations of Federal firearms and explosives laws, as well as Federal alcohol and tobacco tax regulations. The *U.S. Department of State Bureau of Diplomatic Security special agents* are engaged in the battle against terrorism.

The Department of Homeland Security also employs numerous law enforcement officers within several different agencies, including Customs and Border Protection, Immigration and Customs Enforcement, and the U.S. Secret Service. *U.S. Border Patrol agents* protect more than 8,000 miles of international land and water boundaries. *Immigration inspectors* interview and examine people seeking entrance to the United States and its territories. *Customs inspectors* enforce laws governing imports and exports by inspecting cargo, baggage, and articles worn or carried by people, vessels, vehicles, trains, and aircraft entering or leaving the United States. *Federal Air Marshals* provide air security by guarding against attacks targeting U.S. aircraft, passengers, and crews. *U.S. Secret Service special agents* and *U.S.*

Job opportunities in most local police departments will be excellent, while competition is expected for jobs in State and Federal agencies.

Secret Service uniformed officers protect the President, Vice President, their immediate families, and other public officials. Secret Service special agents also investigate counterfeiting, forgery of Government checks or bonds, and fraudulent use of credit cards.

Other Federal agencies employ police and special agents with sworn arrest powers and the authority to carry firearms. These agencies include the Postal Service, the Bureau of Indian Affairs Office of Law Enforcement, the Forest Service, and the National Park Service.

Work environment. Police and detective work can be very dangerous and stressful. In addition to the obvious dangers of confrontations with criminals, police officers and detectives need to be constantly alert and ready to deal appropriately with a number of other threatening situations. Many law enforcement officers witness death and suffering resulting from accidents and criminal behavior. A career in law enforcement may take a toll on their private lives.

The jobs of some Federal agents such as U.S. Secret Service and DEA special agents require extensive travel, often on very short notice. They may relocate a number of times over the course of their careers. Some special agents in agencies such as the U.S. Border Patrol work outdoors in rugged terrain for long periods and in all kinds of weather.

Uniformed officers, detectives, agents, and inspectors are usually scheduled to work 40-hour weeks, but paid overtime is common. Shift work is necessary because protection must be provided around the clock. Junior officers frequently work weekends, holidays, and nights. Police officers and detectives are required to work whenever they are needed and may work long hours during investigations. Officers in most jurisdictions, whether on or off duty, are expected to be armed and to exercise their authority when necessary.

Training, Other Qualifications, and Advancement

Most police and detectives learn much of what they need to know on the job, often in their agency's police academy. Civil service regulations govern the appointment of police and detectives in most States, large municipalities, and special police agencies, as well as in many smaller jurisdictions. Candidates must be U.S. citizens, usually at least 20 years old, and must meet rigorous physical and personal qualifications.

Education and training. Applicants usually must have at least a high school education, and some departments require 1 or 2 years of college coursework or, in some cases, a college degree.

Law enforcement agencies encourage applicants to take courses or training related to law enforcement subjects after high school. Many entry-level applicants for police jobs have completed some formal postsecondary education, and a significant number are college graduates. Many junior colleges, colleges, and universities offer programs in law enforcement or administration of justice.

Physical education classes and participating in sports are also helpful in developing the competitiveness, stamina, and agility needed for many law enforcement positions. Knowledge of a foreign language is an asset in many Federal agencies and urban departments.

Many agencies pay all or part of the tuition for officers to work toward degrees in criminal justice, police science, administration of justice, or public administration and pay higher salaries to those who earn such a degree.

Before their first assignments, officers usually go through a period of training. In State and large local police departments, recruits get training in their agency's police academy, often for 12 to 14 weeks. In small agencies, recruits often attend a regional or State academy. Training includes classroom instruction in constitutional law and civil rights, State laws and local ordinances, and accident investigation. Recruits also receive training and supervised experience in patrol, traffic control, the use of firearms, self-defense, first aid, and emergency response. Police departments in some large cities hire high school graduates who are still in their teens as police cadets or trainees. They do clerical work and attend classes, usually for 1 to 2 years, until they reach the minimum age requirement and can be appointed to the regular force.

To be considered for appointment as an FBI agent, an applicant must be a college graduate and have at least 3 years of professional work experience, or have an advanced degree plus 2 years of professional work experience. An applicant who meets these criteria must also have one of the following: a college major in accounting, electrical engineering, information technology, or computer science; fluency in a foreign language; a degree from an accredited law school; or 3 years of related full-time work experience. All new FBI agents undergo 18 weeks of training at the FBI Academy on the U.S. Marine Corps base in Quantico, Virginia.

Most other Federal law enforcement agencies require either a bachelor's degree or related work experience or a combination of the two. Federal law enforcement agents undergo extensive training, usually at the U.S. Marine Corps base in Quantico, Virginia, or the Federal Law Enforcement Training Center in Glynco, Georgia. The educational requirements, qualifications, and training information for a particular Federal agency can be found on the agency's Web site, most of which are listed in the last section of this statement.

Fish and game wardens also must meet specific requirements. Most States require at least 2 years of college study. Once hired, fish and game wardens attend a training academy lasting from 3 to 12 months, sometimes followed by further training in the field.

Other qualifications. Civil service regulations govern the appointment of police and detectives in most States, large municipalities, and special police agencies, as well as in many smaller jurisdictions. Candidates must be U.S. citizens, usually at least 20 years old, and must meet rigorous physical and personal qualifications. Physical examinations for entrance into law enforcement often include tests of vision, hearing, strength, and agility. Eligibility for appointment usually depends on performance in competitive written examinations and previous education and experience.

Candidates should enjoy working with people and meeting the public. Because personal characteristics such as honesty, sound judgment, integrity, and a sense of responsibility are especially important in law enforcement, candidates are interviewed by senior officers, and their character traits and backgrounds are

Projections data from the National Employment Matrix

Occupational Title	SOC Code	Employment, 2006	Projected employment, 2016	Change, 2006-16	
				Number	Percent
Police and detectives..	—	861,000	959,000	97,000	11
First-line supervisors/managers of police and detectives	33-1012	93,000	102,000	8,500	9
Detectives and criminal investigators..	33-3021	106,000	125,000	18,000	17
Fish and game wardens..	33-3031	8,000	8,000	0	0
Police officers..	33-3050	654,000	724,000	70,000	11
Police and sheriff's patrol officers	33-3051	648,000	719,000	70,000	11
Transit and railroad police	33-3052	5,600	5,900	400	6

NOTE: Data in this table are rounded. See the discussion of the employment projections table in the *Handbook* introductory chapter on *Occupational Information Included in the Handbook*.

investigated. In some agencies, candidates are interviewed by a psychiatrist or a psychologist or given a personality test. Most applicants are subjected to lie detector examinations or drug testing. Some agencies subject sworn personnel to random drug testing as a condition of continuing employment.

Advancement. Police officers usually become eligible for promotion after a probationary period ranging from 6 months to 3 years. In large departments, promotion may enable an officer to become a detective or to specialize in one type of police work, such as working with juveniles. Promotions to corporal, sergeant, lieutenant, and captain usually are made according to a candidate's position on a promotion list, as determined by scores on a written examination and on-the-job performance.

Continuing training helps police officers, detectives, and special agents improve their job performance. Through police department academies, regional centers for public safety employees established by the States, and Federal agency training centers, instructors provide annual training in self-defense tactics, firearms, use-of-force policies, sensitivity and communications skills, crowd-control techniques, relevant legal developments, and advances in law enforcement equipment.

Employment

Police and detectives held about 861,000 jobs in 2006. Seventy-nine percent were employed by local governments. State police agencies employed about 11 percent, and various Federal agencies employed about 7 percent. A small proportion worked for educational services, rail transportation, and contract investigation and security services.

According to the U.S. Bureau of Justice Statistics, police and detectives employed by local governments primarily worked in cities with more than 25,000 inhabitants. Some cities have very large police forces, while thousands of small communities employ fewer than 25 officers each.

Job Outlook

Job opportunities in most local police departments will be excellent for qualified individuals, while competition is expected for jobs in State and Federal agencies. Average employment growth is expected.

Employment change. Employment of police and detectives is expected to grow 11 percent over the 2006-16 decade, about as fast as the average for all occupations. A more security-conscious society and population growth will contribute to the increasing demand for police services.

Job prospects. Overall opportunities in local police departments will be excellent for individuals who meet the psychological, personal, and physical qualifications. In addition to openings from employment growth, many openings will be created by the need to replace workers who retire and those who leave local agencies for Federal jobs and private sector security jobs. There will be more competition for jobs in Federal and State law enforcement agencies than for jobs in local agencies. Less competition for jobs will occur in departments that offer relatively low salaries or those in urban communities where the crime rate is relatively high. Applicants with military experience or college training in police science will have the best opportunities in local and State departments. Applicants with a bachelor's degree and several years of law enforcement or military experience, especially investigative experience, will have the best opportunities in Federal agencies.

The level of government spending determines the level of employment for police and detectives. The number of job opportunities, therefore, can vary from year to year and from place to place. Layoffs, on the other hand, are rare because retirements enable most staffing cuts to be handled through attrition. Trained law enforcement officers who lose their jobs because of budget cuts usually have little difficulty finding jobs with other agencies.

Earnings

Police and sheriff's patrol officers had median annual earnings of $47,460 in May 2006. The middle 50 percent earned between $35,600 and $59,880. The lowest 10 percent earned less than $27,310, and the highest 10 percent earned more than $72,450. Median annual earnings were $43,510 in Federal Government, $52,540 in State government, and $47,190 in local government.

In May 2006, median annual earnings of police and detective supervisors were $69,310. The middle 50 percent earned between $53,900 and $83,940. The lowest 10 percent earned less than $41,260, and the highest 10 percent earned more than $104,410. Median annual earnings were $85,170 in Federal Government, $68,990 in State government, and $68,670 in local government.

In May 2006, median annual earnings of detectives and criminal investigators were $58,260. The middle 50 percent earned between $43,920 and $76,350. The lowest 10 percent earned less than $34,480, and the highest 10 percent earned more than $92,590. Median annual earnings were $69,510 in Federal

Government, $49,370 in State government, and $52,520 in local government.

Federal law provides special salary rates to Federal employees who serve in law enforcement. Additionally, Federal special agents and inspectors receive law enforcement availability pay (LEAP)—equal to 25 percent of the agent's grade and step—awarded because of the large amount of overtime that these agents are expected to work. For example, in 2007, FBI agents entered Federal service as GS-10 employees on the pay scale at a base salary of $48,159, yet they earned about $60,199 a year with availability pay. They could advance to the GS-13 grade level in field nonsupervisory assignments at a base salary of $75,414, which was worth $94,268 with availability pay. FBI supervisory, management, and executive positions in grades GS-14 and GS-15 paid a base salary of about $89,115 and $104,826 a year, respectively, which amounted to $111,394 or $131,033 per year including availability pay. Salaries were slightly higher in selected areas where the prevailing local pay level was higher. Because Federal agents may be eligible for a special law enforcement benefits package, applicants should ask their recruiter for more information.

Total earnings for local, State, and special police and detectives frequently exceed the stated salary because of payments for overtime, which can be significant.

According to the International City-County Management Association's annual Police and Fire Personnel, Salaries, and Expenditures Survey, average salaries for sworn full-time positions in 2006 were:

Rank	Minimum annual base salary	Maximum annual base salary
Police chief	$78,547	$99,698
Deputy chief	68,797	87,564
Police captain	65,408	81,466
Police lieutenant	59,940	72,454
Police sergeant	53,734	63,564
Police corporal	44,160	55,183

In addition to the common benefits—paid vacation, sick leave, and medical and life insurance—most police and sheriffs' departments provide officers with special allowances for uniforms. Because police officers usually are covered by liberal pension plans, many retire at half-pay after 25 or 30 years of service.

Related Occupations

Police and detectives maintain law and order, collect evidence and information, and conduct investigations and surveillance. Workers in related occupations include correctional officers, private detectives and investigators, probation officers and correctional treatment specialists, and security guards and gaming surveillance officers. Like police and detectives, firefighters and emergency medical technicians and paramedics provide public safety services and respond to emergencies.

Sources of Additional Information

Information about entrance requirements may be obtained from Federal, State, and local law enforcement agencies.

For general information about sheriffs and to learn more about the National Sheriffs' Association scholarship, contact:
➤ National Sheriffs' Association, 1450 Duke St., Alexandria, VA 22314. Internet: **http://www.sheriffs.org**

Information about qualifications for employment as a FBI Special Agent is available from the nearest State FBI office. The address and phone number are listed in the local telephone directory. Internet: **http://www.fbi.gov**

Information on career opportunities, qualifications, and training for U.S. Secret Service Special Agents and Uniformed Officers is available from the Secret Service Personnel Division at (202) 406-5800, (888) 813-877, or (888) 813-USSS.
Internet: **http://www.secretservice.gov/join**

Information about qualifications for employment as a DEA Special Agent is available from the nearest DEA office, or call (800) DEA-4288. Internet: **http://www.usdoj.gov/dea**

Information about career opportunities, qualifications, and training to become a deputy marshal is available from:
➤ U.S. Marshals Service, Human Resources Division—Law Enforcement Recruiting, Washington, DC 20530-1000. Internet: **http://www.usmarshals.gov**

For information on operations and career opportunities in the U.S. Bureau of Alcohol, Tobacco, Firearms, and Explosives, contact:
➤ U.S. Bureau of Alcohol, Tobacco, Firearms, and Explosives, Office of Governmental and Public Affairs, 650 Massachusetts Ave., NW., Room 8290, Washington D.C., 20226.
Internet: **http://www.atf.gov**

Information about careers in U.S. Customs and Border Protection is available from:
➤ U.S. Customs and Border Protection, 1300 Pennsylvania Ave. NW., Washington, DC 20229. Internet: **http://www.cbp.gov**

Information about law enforcement agencies within the Department of Homeland Security is available from:
➤ U.S. Department of Homeland Security, Washington, DC 20528. Internet: **http://www.dhs.gov**

To find Federal, State, and local law enforcement job fairs and other recruiting events across the country, contact:
➤ National Law Enforcement Recruiters Association, 2045 15th St.North, Suite 210, Arlington, VA 22201.
Internet: **http://www.nlera.org**

Private Detectives and Investigators

(O*NET 33-9021.00)

Significant Points

- Work hours are often irregular, and the work can be dangerous.

- About 30 percent are self-employed.

- Applicants typically have related experience in areas such as law enforcement, insurance, the military, or government investigative or intelligence jobs.

- Keen competition is expected for most jobs despite faster-than-average employment growth.

Nature of the Work

Private detectives and investigators assist individuals, businesses, and attorneys by finding and analyzing information. They connect small clues to solve mysteries or to uncover facts about legal, financial, or personal matters. Private detectives and investigators offer many services, including executive, corporate, and celebrity protection; pre-employment verification; and individual background profiles. Some investigate computer crimes, such as identity theft, harassing e-mails, and illegal downloading of copyrighted material. They also provide assistance in criminal and civil liability cases, insurance claims and fraud, child custody and protection cases, missing persons cases, and premarital screening. They are sometimes hired to investigate individuals to prove or disprove infidelity.

Private detectives and investigators have many methods to choose from when determining the facts in a case. Much of their work is done using a computer, recovering deleted e-mails and documents, for example. They may also perform computer database searches or work with someone who does. Computers allow investigators to quickly obtain huge amounts of information such as a subject's prior arrests, convictions, and civil legal judgments; telephone numbers; motor vehicle registrations; association and club memberships; and even photographs.

Detectives and investigators also perform various other types of surveillance or searches. To verify facts, such as an individual's income or place of employment, they may make phone calls or visit a subject's workplace. In other cases, especially those involving missing persons and background checks, investigators interview people to gather as much information as possible about an individual. Sometimes investigators go undercover, pretending to be someone else to get information or to observe a subject inconspicuously.

Most detectives and investigators are trained to perform physical surveillance, which may be high-tech or low-tech. They may observe a site, such as the home of a subject, from an inconspicuous location or a vehicle. Using photographic and video cameras, binoculars, and cell phones, detectives often use surveillance to gather information on an individual; this can be quite time consuming.

The duties of private detectives and investigators depend on the needs of their clients. In cases that involve fraudulent workers' compensation claims, for example, investigators may carry out long-term covert observation of a person suspected of fraud. If an investigator observes him or her performing an activity that contradicts injuries stated in a worker's compensation claim, the investigator would take video or still photographs to document the activity and report it to the client.

Detectives and investigators must be mindful of the law when conducting investigations. They keep up with Federal, State, and local legislation, such as privacy laws and other legal issues affecting their work. The legality of certain methods may be unclear, and investigators and detectives must make judgment calls when deciding how to pursue a case. They must also know how to collect evidence properly so that they do not compromise its admissibility in court.

Private detectives and investigators often specialize. Those who focus on intellectual property theft, for example, investigate and document acts of piracy, help clients stop illegal activity, and provide intelligence for prosecution and civil action. Other investigators specialize in developing financial profiles and asset searches. Their reports reflect information gathered through interviews, investigation and surveillance, and research, including review of public documents.

Computer forensic investigators specialize in recovering, analyzing, and presenting data from computers for use in investigations or as evidence. They determine the details of intrusions into computer systems, recover data from encrypted or erased files, and recover e-mails and deleted passwords.

Legal investigators assist in preparing criminal defenses, locating witnesses, serving legal documents, interviewing police and prospective witnesses, and gathering and reviewing evidence. Legal investigators also may collect information on the parties to the litigation, take photographs, testify in court, and assemble evidence and reports for trials. They often work for law firms or lawyers.

Corporate investigators conduct internal and external investigations for corporations. In internal investigations, they may investigate drug use in the workplace, ensure that expense accounts are not abused, or determine whether employees are stealing merchandise or information. External investigations attempt to thwart criminal schemes from outside the corporation, such as fraudulent billing by a supplier.

Financial investigators may be hired to develop confidential financial profiles of individuals or companies that are prospective parties to large financial transactions. These investigators often are certified public accountants (CPAs) who work closely with investment bankers and other accountants. They might also search for assets in order to recover damages awarded by a court in fraud or theft cases.

Detectives who work for retail stores or hotels are responsible for controlling losses and protecting assets. *Store detectives*, also known as *loss prevention agents*, safeguard the assets of retail stores by apprehending anyone attempting to steal merchandise or destroy store property. They prevent theft by shoplifters, vendor representatives, delivery personnel and even store employees. Store detectives also conduct periodic inspections of stock areas, dressing rooms, and restrooms, and sometimes assist in opening and closing the store. They may prepare loss prevention and security reports for management and testify in court against people they apprehend. *Hotel detectives* protect guests of the establishment from theft of their belongings and preserve order in hotel restaurants and bars. They also may keep undesirable individuals, such as known thieves, off the premises.

Work environment. Many detectives and investigators spend time away from their offices conducting interviews or doing surveillance, but some work in their office most of the day conducting computer searches and making phone calls. When the investigator is working on a case, the environment might range from plush boardrooms to seedy bars. Store and hotel detectives work in the businesses that they protect.

Investigators generally work alone, but they sometimes work with others during surveillance or when following a subject in order to avoid detection by the subject. Some of the work involves confrontation, so the job can be stressful and dangerous. Some situations call for the investigator to be armed, such as

Despite rapid employment growth, keen competition is expected for private detective jobs.

certain bodyguard assignments for corporate or celebrity clients. In most cases, however, a weapon is not necessary because the purpose of the work is gathering information and not law enforcement or criminal apprehension. Owners of investigative agencies have the added stress of having to deal with demanding and sometimes distraught clients.

Private detectives and investigators often work irregular hours because of the need to conduct surveillance and contact people who are not available during normal working hours. Early morning, evening, weekend, and holiday work is common.

Training, Other Qualifications, and Advancement

Most private detectives and investigators have some college education and previous experience in investigative work. In most States, they are required to be licensed.

Education and training. There are no formal education requirements for most private detective and investigator jobs, although many have college degrees. Courses in criminal justice and police science are helpful to aspiring private detectives and investigators. Although related experience is usually required, some people enter the occupation directly after graduation from college, generally with an associate or bachelor's degree in criminal justice or police science. The 2006 educational attainment for private detectives and investigators, in percent, was as follows:

	Percent
High school graduate or equivalent	18
Some college, no degree	26
Associate's degree	8
Bachelor's degree	34
Master's degree	13
Professional degree or PhD	3

Most corporate investigators must have a bachelor's degree, preferably in a business-related field. Some corporate investigators have a master's degree in business administration or a law degree; others are CPAs.

For computer forensics work, a computer science or accounting degree is more helpful than a criminal justice degree. An accounting degree provides good background knowledge for investigating fraud through computer forensics. Either of these two degrees provides a good starting point after which investigative techniques can be learned on the job. Alternatively, many colleges and universities now offer certificate programs, requiring from 15 to 21 credits, in computer forensics. These programs are most beneficial to law enforcement officers, paralegals, or others who are already involved in investigative work. A few colleges and universities now offer bachelor's or master's degrees in computer forensics, and others are planning to begin offering such degrees.

Most of the work of private detectives and investigators is learned on the job. New investigators will usually start by learning how to use databases to gather information. The training they receive depends on the type of firm. At an insurance company, a new investigator will learn to recognize insurance fraud. At a firm that specializes in domestic cases, a new worker might observe a senior investigator performing surveillance. Learning by doing, in which new investigators are put on cases and gain skills as they go, is a common approach. Corporate investigators hired by large companies, however, may receive formal training in business practices, management structure, and various finance-related topics.

Because they work with changing technologies, computer forensic investigators never stop training. They learn the latest methods of fraud detection and new software programs and operating systems by attending conferences and courses offered by software vendors and professional associations.

Licensure. The majority of States and the District of Columbia require private detectives and investigators to be licensed. Licensing requirements vary, however. Seven States—Alabama, Alaska, Colorado, Idaho, Mississippi, Missouri, and South Dakota—have no Statewide licensing requirements, some States have few requirements, and many others have stringent regulations. For example, the Bureau of Security and Investigative Services of the California Department of Consumer Affairs requires private investigators to be 18 years of age or older; have a combination of education in police science, criminal law, or justice and experience equaling 3 years (6,000 hours); pass a criminal history background check by the California Department of Justice and the FBI (in most States, convicted felons cannot be issued a license); and receive a qualifying score on a 2-hour written examination covering laws and regulations. Detectives and investigators in all States who carry handguns must meet additional requirements for a firearms permit.

There are no licenses specifically for computer forensic investigators, but some States require them to be licensed private investigators. Even where licensure is not required, a private investigator license is useful to some because it allows them to perform follow-up or complementary tasks.

Other qualifications. Private detectives and investigators typically have previous experience in other occupations. Some have worked in other occupations for insurance or collections companies, in the private security industry, or as paralegals. Many investigators enter the field after serving in law enforcement, the military, government auditing and investigative positions, or Federal intelligence jobs. Former law enforcement officers, military investigators, and government agents, who are frequently able to retire after 25 years of service, often become private detectives or investigators in a second career.

Others enter from jobs in finance, accounting, commercial credit, investigative reporting, insurance, and law. These individuals often can apply their prior work experience in a related investigative specialty.

Most computer forensic investigators learn their trade while working for a law enforcement agency, either as a sworn officer or a civilian computer forensic analyst. They are trained at their agency's computer forensics training program. Many people enter law enforcement specifically to get this training and establish a reputation before moving to the private sector.

For private detective and investigator jobs, most employers look for individuals with ingenuity, persistence, and assertiveness. A candidate must not be afraid of confrontation, should communicate well, and should be able to think on his or her feet. Good interviewing and interrogation skills also are important and usually are acquired in earlier careers in law enforcement or other fields. Because the courts often are the judge of a properly conducted investigation, the investigator must be able to present the facts in a manner that a jury will believe. The screening process for potential employees typically includes a background check for a criminal history.

Certification and advancement. Some investigators receive certification from a professional organization to demonstrate competency in a field. For example, the National Association of Legal Investigators confers the Certified Legal Investigator designation to licensed investigators who devote a majority of their practice to negligence or criminal defense investigations. To receive the designation, applicants must satisfy experience, educational, and continuing-training requirements and must pass written and oral exams.

ASIS, a trade organization for the security industry, offers the Professional Certified Investigator certification. To qualify, applicants must have a high school diploma or equivalent; have 5 years of investigations experience, including 2 years managing investigations; and must pass an exam.

Most private-detective agencies are small, with little room for advancement. Usually, there are no defined ranks or steps, so advancement takes the form of increases in salary and assignment status. Many detectives and investigators start their own firms after gaining a few years of experience. Corporate and legal investigators may rise to supervisor or manager of the security or investigations department.

Employment

Private detectives and investigators held about 52,000 jobs in 2006. About 30 percent were self-employed, including many for whom investigative work was a second job. Around 34 percent of detective and investigator jobs were in investigation and security services, including private detective agencies, while another 9 percent were in department or other general merchandise stores. The rest worked mostly in State and local government, legal services firms, employment services companies, insurance agencies, and credit mediation establishments, including banks and other depository institutions.

Job Outlook

Keen competition is expected for most jobs despite faster-than-average employment growth.

Employment change. Employment of private detectives and investigators is expected to grow 18 percent over the 2006-16 decade, faster than the average for all occupations. Increased demand for private detectives and investigators will result from heightened security concerns, increased litigation, and the need to protect confidential information and property of all kinds. The proliferation of criminal activity on the Internet, such as identity theft, spamming, e-mail harassment, and illegal downloading of copyrighted materials, will also increase the demand for private investigators. Employee background checks, conducted by private investigators, will become standard for an increasing number of jobs. Growing financial activity worldwide will increase the demand for investigators to control internal and external financial losses, to monitor competitors, and to prevent industrial spying.

Job prospects. Keen competition is expected for most jobs because private detective and investigator careers attract many qualified people, including relatively young retirees from law enforcement and military careers. The best opportunities for new jobseekers will be in entry-level jobs in detective agencies or stores, particularly large chain and discount stores that hire detectives on a part-time basis. Opportunities are expected to be excellent for qualified computer forensic investigators.

Earnings

Median annual earnings of salaried private detectives and investigators were $33,750 in May 2006. The middle 50 percent earned between $24,180 and $47,740. The lowest 10 percent earned less than $19,720, and the highest 10 percent earned more than $64,380. Earnings of private detectives and investigators vary greatly by employer, specialty, and geographic area.

Related Occupations

Private detectives and investigators often collect information and protect the property and other assets of companies and individuals. Others with related duties include bill and account collectors; claims adjusters, appraisers, examiners, and investigators; police and detectives; and security guards and gaming surveillance officers. Investigators who specialize in conducting financial profiles and asset searches perform work closely

Projections data from the National Employment Matrix

Occupational Title	SOC Code	Employment, 2006	Projected employment, 2016	Change, 2006-16	
				Number	Percent
Private detectives and investigators..	33-9021	52,000	61,000	9,400	18

NOTE: Data in this table are rounded. See the discussion of the employment projections table in the *Handbook* introductory chapter on *Occupational Information Included in the Handbook.*

related to that of accountants and auditors, as well as financial analysts and personal financial advisors.

Sources of Additional Information

For information on local licensing requirements, contact your State Department of Public Safety, State Division of Licensing, or local or State police headquarters.

For information on a career as a legal investigator and about the Certified Legal Investigator credential, contact:

➤ National Association of Legal Investigators, 908 21st St., Sacramento, CA 95814-3118.
Internet: **http://www.nalionline.org**

For more information about investigative and other security careers, about the Professional Certified Investigator credential, and for a list of colleges and universities offering security-related courses and majors, contact:

➤ ASIS, 1625 Prince St., Alexandria, VA 22314-2818.
Internet: **http://www.asisonline.org**

Security Guards and Gaming Surveillance Officers

(O*NET 33-9031.00, 33-9032.00)

Significant Points

- Jobs should be plentiful, but competition is expected for higher paying positions at facilities requiring longer periods of training and a high level of security, such as nuclear power plants and weapons installations.

- Because of limited formal training requirements and flexible hours, this occupation attracts many individuals seeking a second or part-time job.

- Some positions, such as those of armored car guards, are hazardous.

Nature of the Work

Security guards, also called *security officers*, patrol and inspect property to protect against fire, theft, vandalism, terrorism, and illegal activity. These workers protect their employer's investment, enforce laws on the property, and deter criminal activity and other problems. They use radio and telephone communications to call for assistance from police, fire, or emergency medical services as the situation dictates. Security guards write comprehensive reports outlining their observations and activities during their assigned shift. They also may interview witnesses or victims, prepare case reports, and testify in court.

Although all security guards perform many of the same duties, their specific tasks depend on whether they work in a "static" security position or on a mobile patrol. Guards assigned to static security positions usually stay at one location for a specified length of time. These guards must become closely acquainted with the property and people associated with their station and must often monitor alarms and closed-circuit TV cameras. In contrast, guards assigned to mobile patrol drive or walk from one location to another and conduct security checks within an assigned geographical zone. They may detain or arrest criminal violators, answer service calls concerning criminal activity or problems, and issue traffic violation warnings.

The security guard's job responsibilities also vary with the size, type, and location of the employer. In department stores, guards protect people, records, merchandise, money, and equipment. They often work with undercover store detectives to prevent theft by customers or employees, and help apprehend shoplifting suspects prior to the arrival of the police. Some shopping centers and theaters have officers who patrol their parking lots to deter car thefts and robberies. In office buildings, banks, and hospitals, guards maintain order and protect the institution's customers, staff and property. At air, sea, and rail terminals and other transportation facilities, guards protect people, freight, property, and equipment. Using metal detectors and high-tech equipment, they may screen passengers and visitors for weapons and explosives, ensure that nothing is stolen while a vehicle is being loaded or unloaded, and watch for fires and criminals.

Guards who work in public buildings such as museums or art galleries protect paintings and exhibits by inspecting people and packages entering and leaving the building. In factories, laboratories, government buildings, data processing centers, and military bases, security officers protect information, products, computer codes, and defense secrets and check the credentials of people and vehicles entering and leaving the premises. Guards working at universities, parks, and sports stadiums perform crowd control, supervise parking and seating, and direct traffic. Security guards stationed at the entrance to bars and nightclubs, prevent access by minors, collect cover charges at the door, maintain order among customers, and protect patrons and property.

Armored car guards protect money and valuables during transit. In addition, they protect individuals responsible for making commercial bank deposits from theft or injury. They pick up money or other valuables from businesses to transport to another location. Carrying money between the truck and the business can be extremely hazardous. As a result, armored car guards usually wear bulletproof vests.

Gaming surveillance officers, also known as surveillance agents, and gaming investigators act as security agents for casino managers and patrons. Using primarily audio and video equipment in an observation room, they observe casino operations for irregular activities, such as cheating or theft, and monitor compliance to rules, regulations and laws. They maintain and organize recordings from security cameras as they are sometimes used as evidence in police investigations. Some casinos use a catwalk over one-way mirrors located above the casino floor to augment electronic surveillance equipment. Surveillance agents occasionally leave the surveillance room and walk the casino floor.

All security officers must show good judgment and common sense, follow directions, testify accurately in court, and follow company policy and guidelines. In an emergency, they must be able to take charge and direct others to safety. In larger organizations, a security manager might oversee a group of security officers. In smaller organizations, however, a single worker may be solely responsible for all security.

Work environment. Most security guards and gaming surveillance officers spend considerable time on their feet, either assigned to a specific post or patrolling buildings and grounds. Guards may be stationed at a guard desk inside a building to monitor electronic security and surveillance devices or to check the credentials of people entering or leaving the premises. They also may be stationed at a guardhouse outside the entrance to a gated facility or community and may use a portable radio or cellular telephone to be in constant contact with a central station. The work usually is routine, but guards must be constantly alert for threats to themselves and the property they are protecting. Guards who work during the day may have a great deal of contact with other employees and the public. Gaming surveillance officers often work behind a bank of monitors controlling numerous cameras in a casino and thus can develop eyestrain.

Guards usually work shifts of 8 hours or longer for 40 hours per week and are often on call in case of an emergency. Some employers offer three shifts, and guards rotate to divide daytime, weekend, and holiday work equally. Guards usually eat on the job instead of taking a regular break away from the site. In 2006, about 15 percent of guards worked part time, and some held a second job as a guard to supplement their primary earnings.

Training, Other Qualifications, and Advancement

Generally, there are no specific education requirements for security guards, but employers usually prefer to fill armed guard positions with people who have at least a high school diploma. Gaming surveillance officers often need some education beyond high school. In most States, guards must be licensed.

Education and training. Many employers of unarmed guards do not have any specific educational requirements. For armed guards, employers usually prefer individuals who are high school graduates or who hold an equivalent certification.

Many employers give newly hired guards instruction before they start the job and provide on-the-job training. The amount of training guards receive varies. Training is more rigorous for armed guards because their employers are legally responsible for any use of force. Armed guards receive formal training in areas such as weapons retention and laws covering the use of force. They may be periodically tested in the use of firearms.

An increasing number of States are making ongoing training a legal requirement for retention of licensure. Guards may receive training in protection, public relations, report writing, crisis deterrence, first aid, and specialized training relevant to their particular assignment.

The American Society for Industrial Security International has written voluntary training guidelines that are intended to provide regulating bodies consistent minimum standards for the quality of security services. These guidelines recommend that security guards receive at least 48 hours of training within the first 100 days of employment. The guidelines also suggest that security guards be required to pass a written or performance examination covering topics such as sharing information with law enforcement, crime prevention, handling evidence, the

Security guards patrol property and buildings to deter crime.

use of force, court testimony, report writing, interpersonal and communication skills, and emergency response procedures. In addition, they recommend annual retraining and additional firearms training for armed officers.

Guards who are employed at establishments that place a heavy emphasis on security usually receive extensive formal training. For example, guards at nuclear power plants undergo several months of training before going on duty—and even then, they perform their tasks under close supervision for a significant period of time. They are taught to use firearms, administer first aid, operate alarm systems and electronic security equipment, and spot and deal with security problems.

Gaming surveillance officers and investigators usually need some training beyond high school but not usually a bachelor's degree. Several educational institutes offer certification programs. Classroom training usually is conducted in a casino-like atmosphere and includes the use of surveillance camera equipment. Previous security experience is a plus. Employers prefer either individuals with casino experience and significant knowledge of casino operations or those with law enforcement and investigation experience.

Licensure. Most States require that guards be licensed. To be licensed as a guard, individuals must usually be at least 18 years old, pass a background check, and complete classroom training in such subjects as property rights, emergency procedures, and detention of suspected criminals. Drug testing often is required and may be random and ongoing.

Guards who carry weapons must be licensed by the appropriate government authority, and some receive further certification as special police officers, allowing them to make limited types of arrests while on duty. Armed guard positions have more stringent background checks and entry requirements than those of unarmed guards.

Other qualifications. Most jobs require a driver's license. For positions as armed guards, employers often seek people who have had responsible experience in other occupations.

Rigorous hiring and screening programs consisting of background, criminal record, and fingerprint checks are becoming the norm in the occupation. Applicants are expected to have good character references, no serious police record, and good health. They should be mentally alert, emotionally stable, and physically fit to cope with emergencies. Guards who have frequent contact with the public should communicate well.

Like security guards, gaming surveillance officers and gaming investigators must have keen observation skills and excellent verbal and writing abilities to document violations or suspicious behavior. They also need to be physically fit and have quick reflexes because they sometimes must detain individuals until local law enforcement officials arrive.

Advancement. Compared with unarmed security guards, armed guards and special police usually enjoy higher earnings and benefits, greater job security, and more potential for advancement. Because many people do not stay long in this occupation, opportunities for advancement are good for those who make a career in security. Most large organizations use a military type of ranking that offers the possibility of advancement in both position and salary. Some guards may advance to supervisor or security manager positions. Guards with management skills may open their own contract security guard agencies. Guards can also move to an organization with more stringent security and higher pay.

Employment

Security guards and gaming surveillance officers held over 1 million jobs in 2006. More than half of all jobs for security guards were in investigation and security services, including guard and armored car services. These organizations provide security on a contract basis, assigning their guards to buildings and other sites as needed. Most other security officers were employed directly by educational services, hospitals, food services and drinking places, traveler accommodation (hotels), department stores, manufacturing firms, lessors of real estate (residential and nonresidential buildings), and governments. Guard jobs are found throughout the country, most commonly in metropolitan areas.

Gaming surveillance officers work primarily in gambling industries; traveler accommodation, which includes casino hotels; and local government. They are employed only in those States and on those Indian reservations where gambling is legal.

A significant number of law enforcement officers work as security guards when they are off duty, in order to supplement their incomes. Often working in uniform and with the official cars assigned to them, they add a high-profile security presence to the establishment with which they have contracted. At construction sites and apartment complexes, for example, their presence often deters crime. (Police and detectives are discussed elsewhere in the *Handbook*.)

Job Outlook

Opportunities for security guards and gaming surveillance officers should be favorable. Numerous job openings will stem from employment growth, driven by the demand for increased security, and from the need to replace those who leave this large occupation each year.

Employment change. Employment of security guards is expected to grow by 17 percent between 2006 and 2016, which is faster than the average for all occupations. This occupation will have a very large number of new jobs arise, about 175,000 over the projections decade. Concern about crime, vandalism, and terrorism continues to increase the need for security. Demand for guards also will grow as private security firms increasingly perform duties—such as providing security at public events and in residential neighborhoods—that were formerly handled by police officers.

Employment of gaming surveillance officers is expected to grow by 34 percent between 2006 and 2016, which is much faster than the average for all occupations. Casinos will continue to hire more surveillance officers as more States legalize gambling and as the number of casinos increases in States where gambling is already legal. In addition, casino security forces will employ more technically trained personnel as technology becomes increasingly important in thwarting casino cheating and theft.

Job prospects. Job prospects for security guards should be excellent because of growing demand for these workers and the need to replace experienced workers who leave the occupation. In addition to full-time job opportunities, the limited training requirements and flexible hours attract many people seeking part-time or second jobs. However, competition is expected for higher paying positions that require longer periods of training; these positions usually are found at facilities that require a high level of security, such as nuclear power plants or weapons installations. Job prospects for gaming surveillance officers should be good, but they will be better for those with experience in the gaming industry.

Earnings

Median annual wage-and-salary earnings of security guards were $21,530 in May 2006. The middle 50 percent earned

Projections data from the National Employment Matrix

Occupational Title	SOC Code	Employment, 2006	Projected employment, 2016	Change, 2006-16	
				Number	Percent
Security guards and gaming surveillance officers.............................	33-9030	1,049,000	1,227,000	178,000	17
Gaming surveillance officers and gaming investigators	33-9031	8,700	12,000	2,900	34
Security guards...	33-9032	1,040,000	1,216,000	175,000	17

NOTE: Data in this table are rounded. See the discussion of the employment projections table in the *Handbook* introductory chapter on *Occupational Information Included in the Handbook*.

between $17,620 and $27,430. The lowest 10 percent earned less than $15,030, and the highest 10 percent earned more than $35,840. Median annual earnings in the industries employing the largest numbers of security guards were:

General medical and surgical hospitals...............................$26,610
Elementary and secondary schools 26,290
Local government 24,950
Investigation, guard and armored car services.....................20,280

Gaming surveillance officers and gaming investigators had median annual wage-and-salary earnings of $27,130 in May 2006. The middle 50 percent earned between $21,600 and $35,970. The lowest 10 percent earned less than $18,720, and the highest 10 percent earned more than $45,940.

Related Occupations

Guards protect property, maintain security, and enforce regulations and standards of conduct in the establishments at which they work. Related security and protective service occupations include correctional officers, police and detectives, private detectives and investigators, and gaming services occupations.

Sources of Additional Information

Further information about work opportunities for guards is available from local security and guard firms and State employment service offices. Information about licensing requirements for guards may be obtained from the State licensing commission or the State police department. In States where local jurisdictions establish licensing requirements, contact a local government authority such as the sheriff, county executive, or city manager.

Food Preparation and Serving Related Occupations

Chefs, Cooks, and Food Preparation Workers

(O*NET 35-1011.00, 35-2011.00, 35-2012.00, 35-2013.00, 35-2014.00, 35-2015.00, 35-2019.99, 35-2021.00)

Significant Points

- Many cooks and food preparation workers are young—37 percent are below the age of 24.

- One-third of these workers are employed part time.

- Job openings are expected to be plentiful because many of these workers will leave the occupation for full-time employment or better wages.

Nature of the Work

Chefs, cooks, and food preparation workers prepare, season, and cook a wide range of foods—from soups, snacks, and salads to entrees, side dishes, and desserts. They work in a variety of restaurants and other food services establishments. Chefs and cooks create recipes and prepare meals, while food preparation workers peel and cut vegetables, trim meat, prepare poultry, and perform other duties, such as keeping work areas clean and monitoring temperatures of ovens and stovetops.

Specifically, *chefs* and cooks measure, mix, and cook ingredients according to recipes, using a variety of equipment, including pots, pans, cutlery, ovens, broilers, grills, slicers, grinders, and blenders. Chefs and head cooks also are responsible for directing the work of other kitchen workers, estimating food requirements, and ordering food supplies.

Food preparation workers perform routine, repetitive tasks under the direction of chefs and cooks. These workers ready the ingredients for complex dishes by slicing and dicing vegetables, and composing salads and cold items. They weigh and measure ingredients, go after pots and pans, and stir and strain soups and sauces. Food preparation workers may cut and grind meats, poultry, and seafood in preparation for cooking. They also clean work areas, equipment, utensils, dishes, and silverware.

Larger restaurants and food services establishments tend to have varied menus and larger kitchen staffs. Staffs often include several chefs and cooks, sometimes called assistant or line cooks. Each chef or cook works an assigned station that is equipped with the types of stoves, grills, pans, and ingredients needed for the foods prepared at that station. Job titles often reflect the principal ingredient prepared or the type of cooking performed—vegetable cook, fry cook, or grill cook, for example. These cooks also may direct or work with other food preparation workers.

Executive chefs and *head cooks* coordinate the work of the kitchen staff and direct the preparation of meals. They determine serving sizes, plan menus, order food supplies, and oversee kitchen operations to ensure uniform quality and presentation of meals. An executive chef, for example, is in charge of all food service operations and also may supervise the many kitchens of a hotel, restaurant group, or corporate dining operation. A *chef de cuisine* reports to an executive chef and is responsible for the daily operations of a single kitchen. A *sous chef*, or sub chef, is the second-in-command and runs the kitchen in the absence of the chef. Many chefs earn fame both for themselves and for their kitchens because of the quality and distinctive nature of the food they serve.

Responsibilities depend on where cooks work. *Institution* and *cafeteria cooks*, for example, work in the kitchens of schools, cafeterias, businesses, hospitals, and other institutions. For each meal, they prepare a large quantity of a limited number of entrees, vegetables, and desserts according to preset menus. Meals generally are prepared in advance so diners seldom get the opportunity to special order a meal. Restaurant cooks usually prepare a wider selection of dishes, cooking most orders individually. *Short-order cooks* prepare foods in restaurants and coffee shops that emphasize fast service and quick food preparation. They grill and garnish hamburgers, prepare sandwiches, fry eggs, and cook French fries, often working on several orders at the same time. *Fast-food cooks* prepare a limited selection of menu items in fast-food restaurants. They cook and package batches of food, such as hamburgers and fried chicken, to be kept warm until served. (*Combined food preparation and service workers*, who both prepare and serve items in fast-food restaurants, are included with the material on food and beverage serving and related workers elsewhere in the *Handbook*.)

The number and types of workers employed in kitchens also depends on the type of establishment. Small, full-service restaurants offering casual dining often feature a limited number of easy-to-prepare items supplemented by short-order specialties and ready-made desserts. Typically, one cook prepares all the food with the help of a short-order cook and one or two other kitchen workers.

Grocery and specialty food stores employ chefs, cooks, and food preparation workers to develop recipes and prepare meals for customers to carry out. Typically, entrees, side dishes, salads, or other items are prepared in large quantities and stored at an appropriate temperature. Counter assistants portion and package items according to customer orders for serving at home.

Some cooks, called *research chefs*, combine culinary skills with knowledge of food science to develop recipes for chain restaurants and food processors and manufacturers. They test new formulas and flavors for prepared foods and determine the most efficient and safest way to prepare new foods.

Some cooks work for individuals rather than for restaurants, cafeterias, or food manufacturers. These *private household cooks* plan and prepare meals in private homes according to the client's tastes or dietary needs. They order groceries and supplies, clean the kitchen, and wash dishes and utensils. They also may serve meals. Private chefs are employed directly by a single individual or family or sometimes by corporations or institutions, such as universities and embassies, to perform cooking and entertaining tasks. These chefs usually live in and may travel with their employer. Because of the sensitive nature of their employment, they are usually required to sign confidentiality agreements. As part of the job, private chefs often perform additional services, such as paying bills, coordinating schedules, and planning events.

Another type of private household cooks, called personal chefs, usually prepare a week's worth of meals in the client's home for the client to heat and serve according to directions throughout the week. Personal chefs are self-employed or employed by a company that provides this service.

Work environment. Many restaurant and institutional kitchens have modern equipment, convenient work areas, and air conditioning, but kitchens in older and smaller eating places are often not as well designed. Kitchen staffs invariably work in small quarters against hot stoves and ovens. They are under constant pressure to prepare meals quickly, while ensuring quality is maintained and safety and sanitation guidelines are observed. Because the pace can be hectic during peak dining times, workers must be able to communicate clearly so that food orders are completed correctly.

Chefs, cooks, and food preparation workers often prepare ingredients ahead of time so that they can be cooked quickly when ordered.

Working conditions vary with the type and quantity of food prepared and the local laws governing food service operations. Workers usually must stand for hours at a time, lifting heavy pots and kettles, and working near hot ovens and grills. Job hazards include slips and falls, cuts, and burns, but injuries are seldom serious.

Work hours in restaurants may include early mornings, late evenings, holidays, and weekends. Work schedules of chefs, cooks and other kitchen workers in factory and school cafeterias may be more regular. In 2006, about 29 percent of cooks and 44 percent of food preparation workers had part-time schedules, compared to 15 percent of workers throughout the economy. Work schedules in fine-dining restaurants, however, tend to be longer because of the time required to prepare ingredients in advance. Many executive chefs regularly work 12-hour days because they oversee the delivery of foodstuffs early in the day, plan the menu, and prepare those menu items that take the most skill.

The wide range in dining hours and the need for fully-staffed kitchens during all open hours creates work opportunities for students, youth, and other individuals seeking supplemental income, flexible work hours, or variable schedules. Eighteen percent of cooks and food preparation workers were 16 to 19 years old in 2006; nineteen percent were age 20 to 24. Ten percent had variable schedules. Kitchen workers employed by schools may work during the school year only, usually for 9 or 10 months. Similarly, resort establishments usually only offer seasonal employment.

Training, Other Qualifications, and Advancement
On-the-job training is most common for fast-food cooks, short-order cooks, and food preparation workers. Chefs and others with more advanced cooking duties often attend cooking school. Vocational training programs are available to many high school students, but advanced positions usually require training after high school. Experience, an ability to develop and enhance cooking skills, and a strong desire to cook are the most common requirements for advancement.

Education and training. A high school diploma is not required for beginning jobs, but it is recommended for those planning a career as a cook or chef. Most fast-food or short-order cooks and food preparation workers require little education or training to start because most skills are learned on the job. Training generally starts with basic sanitation and workplace safety and continues with instruction on food handling, preparation, and cooking procedures. Training in food handling, sanitation, and health and safety procedures are mandatory in most jurisdictions for all workers. Those who become proficient and who show an interest in learning complicated cooking techniques may advance to more demanding cooking positions or into supervisory positions.

Some high school or vocational school programs offer courses in basic food safety and handling procedures, cooking, and general business and computer classes that can be helpful for those who might someday want to be a chef or to open their own restaurant. Many school districts, in cooperation with State departments of education, provide on-the-job training and summer workshops for cafeteria kitchen workers who aspire to become cooks. Food service management companies or hotel and restaurant chains, also offer paid internships and summer jobs to those starting out in the field. Internships provide valuable experience and can lead to placement in more formal chef training programs.

When hiring chefs and others in advanced cooking positions, however, employers usually prefer applicants who have training after high school. These training programs range from a few months to 2 years or more. Vocational or trade-school programs typically offer basic training in food handling and sanitation procedures, nutrition, slicing and dicing methods for various kinds of meats and vegetables, and basic cooking methods, such as baking, broiling, and grilling. Longer programs leading to a certificate or a 2- or 4-year degree train chefs for fine-dining or upscale restaurants. They offer a wider array of training specialties, such as advanced cooking techniques; cooking for banquets, buffets, or parties; and cuisines and cooking styles from around the world.

A growing number of chefs participate in these longer training programs through independent cooking schools, professional culinary institutes, 2- or 4-year college degree programs in hospitality or culinary arts, or in the armed forces. Some large hotels and restaurants also operate their own training and job-placement programs for chefs and cooks. Executive chefs and head cooks who work in fine-dining restaurants require many years of training and experience and an intense desire to cook.

Although curricula may vary, students in culinary training programs spend most of their time in kitchens learning to prepare meals by practicing cooking skills. They learn good knife techniques and proper use and care of kitchen equipment. Training programs also include courses in nutrition, menu planning, portion control, purchasing and inventory methods, proper food storage procedures, and use of leftover food to minimize waste. Students also learn sanitation and public health rules for handling food. Training in food service management, computer accounting and inventory software, and banquet service are featured in some training programs. Most formal training programs also require students to get experience in a commercial kitchen through an internship, apprenticeship, or out-placement program.

Many chefs are trained on the job, receiving real work experience and training from chef-mentors in the restaurants where they work. Professional culinary institutes, industry associations, and trade unions sponsor formal apprenticeship programs in coordination with the U.S. Department of Labor.

The American Culinary Federation accredits more than 200 formal academic training programs and sponsors apprenticeship programs around the country. Typical apprenticeships last 2 years and combine classroom training and work experience. Accreditation is an indication that a culinary program meets recognized standards regarding course content, facilities, and quality of instruction.

Other qualifications. Chefs, cooks, and food preparation workers must be efficient, quick, and work well as part of a team. Manual dexterity is helpful for cutting, chopping, and plating. These workers also need creativity and a keen sense of taste and smell. Personal cleanliness is essential because most States require health certificates indicating that workers are free from communicable diseases. Knowledge of a foreign language can be an asset because it may improve communication with other restaurant staff, vendors, and the restaurant's clientele.

Certification and advancement. The American Culinary Federation certifies pastry professionals, personal chefs, and culinary educators in addition to various levels of chefs. Certification standards are based primarily on experience and formal training. Although certification is not required, it can help to prove accomplishment and lead to advancement and higher-paying positions.

Advancement opportunities for chefs, cooks, and food preparation workers depend on their training, work experience, and ability to perform more responsible and sophisticated tasks. Many food preparation workers, for example, may move into assistant or line cook positions. Chefs and cooks who demonstrate an eagerness to learn new cooking skills and to accept greater responsibility may also move up and be asked to train or supervise lesser skilled kitchen staff. Others may move to larger or more prestigious kitchens and restaurants.

Some chefs and cooks go into business as caterers or personal chefs or open their own restaurant. Others become instruc-

Projections data from the National Employment Matrix

Occupational Title	SOC Code	Employment, 2006	Projected employment, 2016	Change, 2006-16	
				Number	Percent
Chefs, cooks, and food preparation workers.................................	—	3,113,000	3,464,000	351,000	11
Chefs and head cooks..	35-1011	115,000	124,000	8,700	8
Cooks and food preparation workers	35-2000	2,998,000	3,340,000	342,000	11
Cooks	35-2010	2,097,000	2,301,000	204,000	10
Cooks, fast food	35-2011	629,000	681,000	52,000	8
Cooks, institution and cafeteria..	35-2012	401,000	445,000	43,000	11
Cooks, private household..	35-2013	4,900	5,400	400	9
Cooks, restaurant...	35-2014	850,000	948,000	98,000	12
Cooks, short order..	35-2015	195,000	205,000	9,500	5
Cooks, all other	35-2019	16,000	16,000	500	3
Food preparation workers	35-2021	902,000	1,040,000	138,000	15

NOTE: Data in this table are rounded. See the discussion of the employment projections table in the *Handbook* introductory chapter on *Occupational Information Included in the Handbook.*

tors in culinary training programs. A number of cooks and chefs advance to executive chef positions or food service management positions, particularly in hotels, clubs, or larger, more elegant restaurants. (See the section on food service managers elsewhere in the *Handbook*.)

Employment
Chefs, cooks, and food preparation workers held 3.1 million jobs in 2006. The distribution of jobs among the various types of chefs, cooks, and food preparation workers was as follows:

Food preparation workers	902,000
Cooks, restaurant	850,000
Cooks, fast food	629,000
Cooks, institution and cafeteria	401,000
Cooks, short order	195,000
Chefs and head cooks	115,000
Cooks, private household	4,900
Cooks, all other	16,000

Two-thirds of all chefs, cooks, and food preparation workers were employed in restaurants and other food services and drinking places. About 15 percent worked in institutions such as schools, universities, hospitals, and nursing care facilities. Grocery stores, hotels, and gasoline stations with convenience stores employed most of the remainder.

Job Outlook
Job opportunities for chefs, cooks, and food preparation workers are expected to be plentiful because of the continued growth and expansion of food services outlets, resulting in average employment growth, and because of the large numbers of workers who leave these occupations and need to be replaced. However, those seeking the highest-paying positions will face keen competition.

Employment change. Employment of chefs, cooks, and food preparation workers is expected to increase by 11 percent over the 2006-16 decade, which is about as fast as the average for all occupations. This occupation will have among the largest numbers of new jobs arise, about 351,000 over the period. Growth will be spurred by increases in population, household

income, and demand for convenience that will lead to more people dining out and taking vacations that include hotel stays and restaurant visits. In addition, employment of chefs, cooks, and food preparation workers who prepare meals-to-go, such as those who work in the prepared foods sections of grocery or specialty food stores, should grow faster than average as these stores compete with restaurants for people's food dollars. Also, there is a growing consumer desire for convenient, healthier, made-from-scratch meals.

Projected employment growth varies by detailed occupation. The number of higher-skilled chefs and cooks working in full-service restaurants—those that offer table service and more varied menus—is expected to increase about as fast as the average for all occupations. Much of this increase will come from job growth in more casual dining settings, rather than in up-scale full-service restaurants. Dining trends suggest that an increasing number of meals are eaten away from home, which creates growth in family dining restaurants, but greater limits on expense-account meals is expected to generate slower growth for up-scale restaurants.

Employment of food preparation workers is expected to grow faster than the average for all occupations, reflecting diners' desires for convenience as they shop for carryout meals in a greater variety of places, including full-service restaurants, limited-service eating places, and grocery stores.

Employment of fast-food cooks is expected to grow about as fast as the average for all occupations. Duties of cooks in fast-food restaurants are limited; most workers are likely to be combined food preparation and serving workers, rather than fast-food cooks. Employment of short-order cooks is expected to increase more slowly than average.

Employment of institution and cafeteria chefs and cooks will show growth about as fast as the average. Their employment will not keep pace with the rapid growth in the educational and health services industries—where their employment is concentrated. Offices, schools, and hospitals increasingly contract out their food services in an effort to make "institutional food" more attractive to office workers, students, staff, visitors, and patients. Much of the growth of these workers will be in contract food service establishments that provide catering services or food management and staff for employee dining rooms, sports complexes, convention centers, and educational or health care facilities.

Employment of private household cooks is projected to grow by 9 percent, about as fast as the average. While the employment of personal chefs is expected to increase—reflecting the growing popularity and convenience of eating restaurant-quality meals at home—the number of private chefs will not grow as fast, reflecting slower growth in private household service employment.

Job prospects. Job openings for chefs, cooks, and food preparation workers are expected to be plentiful through 2016; however, competition should be keen for jobs in the top kitchens of higher end restaurants. Although job growth will create many new positions, the overwhelming majority of job openings will stem from the need to replace workers who leave this large occupational group. Many chef, cook, and food preparation worker jobs are attractive to people seeking first-time or short-term employment, additional income, or a flexible schedule. Employers typically hire a large number of part-time workers, but many of these workers soon transfer to other occupations or stop working, creating numerous openings for those entering the field. At higher end restaurants, the fast pace, long hours, and high energy levels required to succeed also cause some top chefs and cooks to leave for other jobs, creating job openings.

Earnings

Earnings of chefs, cooks, and food preparation workers vary greatly by region and the type of employer. Earnings usually are highest in elegant restaurants and hotels, where many executive chefs are employed, and in major metropolitan and resort areas.

Median annual wage-and-salary earnings of chefs and head cooks were $34,370 in May 2006. The middle 50 percent earned between $25,910 and $46,040. The lowest 10 percent earned less than $20,160, and the highest 10 percent earned more than $60,730. Median annual earnings in the industries employing the largest number of chefs and head cooks were:

Other amusement and recreations industries $46,460
Traveler accommodation..40,020
Special food services 36,450
Full-service restaurants 32,360
Limited-service eating places 27,560

Median annual wage-and-salary earnings of cooks, private household were $22,870 in May 2006. The middle 50 percent earned between $17,960 and $31,050. The lowest 10 percent earned less than $14,690, and the highest 10 percent earned more than $55,040.

Median annual wage-and-and salary earnings of institution and cafeteria cooks were $20,410 in May 2006. The middle 50 percent earned between $16,280 and $25,280. The lowest 10 percent earned less than $13,450, and the highest 10 percent earned more than $30,770. Median annual earnings in the industries employing the largest numbers of institution and cafeteria cooks were:

General medical and surgical hospitals............................$22,980
Special food services...21,650
Community care facilities for the elderly 20,910
Nursing care facilities 20,470
Elementary and secondary schools 18,770

Median annual wage-and-salary earnings of restaurant cooks were $20,340 in May 2006. The middle 50 percent earned between $16,860 and $24,260. The lowest 10 percent earned less than $14,370, and the highest 10 percent earned more than $28,850. Median annual earnings in the industries employing the largest numbers of restaurant cooks were:

Traveler accommodations $23,400
Full-service restaurants 20,100
Limited-service eating places 18,200

Median annual wage-and-salary earnings of short-order cooks were $17,880 in May 2006. The middle 50 percent earned between $14,960 and $21,820. The lowest 10 percent earned less than $12,930, and the highest 10 percent earned more than $26,110. Median annual earnings in full-service restaurants were $18,340.

Median annual wage-and-salary earnings of food preparation workers were $17,410 in May 2006. The middle 50 percent earned between $14,920 and $21,230. The lowest 10 percent earned less than $13,190, and the highest 10 percent earned more than $25,940. Median annual earnings in the industries employing the largest number of food preparation workers were:

Grocery stores $18,920
Full-service restaurants 17,390
Limited-service eating places 15,550

Median annual wage-and-salary earnings of fast-food cooks were $15,410 in May 2006. The middle 50 percent earned between $13,730 and $17,700. The lowest 10 percent earned less than $12,170, and the highest 10 percent earned more than $20,770. Median annual earnings were $15,360 in full-service restaurants and $15,350 in limited-service eating places.

Some employers provide employees with uniforms and free meals, but Federal law permits employers to deduct from their employees' wages the cost or fair value of any meals or lodging provided, and some employers do so. Chefs, cooks, and food preparation workers who work full time often receive typical benefits, but part-time and hourly workers usually do not.

In some large hotels and restaurants, kitchen workers belong to unions. The principal unions are the Hotel Employees and Restaurant Employees International Union and the Service Employees International Union.

Related Occupations

People who perform tasks similar to those of chefs, cooks, and food preparation workers include those in food processing occupations, such as butchers and meat cutters, and bakers. Others who work closely with these workers include food service managers and food and beverage serving and related workers.

Sources of Additional Information

Information about job opportunities may be obtained from local employers and local offices of the State employment service.

Career information about chefs, cooks, and other kitchen workers, including a directory of 2- and 4-year colleges that offer courses or training programs is available from:

➤ National Restaurant Association, 1200 17th St.NW., Washington, DC 20036.
Internet: **http://www.restaurant.org**

Information on the American Culinary Federation's apprenticeship and certification programs for cooks and a list of accredited culinary programs is available from:

➤ American Culinary Federation, 180 Center Place Way, St.Augustine, FL 32095.
Internet: **http://www.acfchefs.org**

For information about becoming a personal or private chef, contact:

➤ American Personal & Private Chef Association, 4572 Delaware St., San Diego, CA 92116.
Internet: **http://www.personalchef.com**

For information about culinary apprenticeship programs registered with the U.S. Department of Labor, contact the local office of your State employment service agency, check the department's apprenticeship Web site: **http://www.doleta.gov/atels_bat** or call the toll free helpline: (877) 872-5627.

Food and Beverage Serving and Related Workers

(O*NET 35-3011.00, 35-3021.00, 35-3022.00, 35-3031.00, 35-3041.00, 35-9011.00, 35-9021.00, 35-9031.00, 35-9099.99)

Significant Points

- Most jobs are part time and have few educational requirements, attracting many young people to the occupation—more than one-fifth of these workers were 16 to 19 years old, about five times the proportion for all workers.

- Job openings are expected to be abundant through 2016, which will create excellent opportunities for jobseekers.

- Tips comprise a major portion of earnings, so keen competition is expected for jobs in fine dining and more popular restaurants where potential tips are greatest.

Nature of the Work

Food and beverage serving and related workers are the front line of customer service in restaurants, coffee shops, and other food service establishments. These workers greet customers, escort them to seats and hand them menus, take food and drink orders, and serve food and beverages. They also answer questions, explain menu items and specials, and keep tables and din-

ing areas clean and set for new diners. Most work as part of a team, helping coworkers to improve workflow and customer service.

Waiters and *waitresses*, the largest group of these workers, take customers' orders, serve food and beverages, prepare itemized checks, and sometimes accept payment. Their specific duties vary considerably, depending on the establishment. In coffee shops serving routine, straightforward fare, such as salads, soups, and sandwiches, servers are expected to provide fast, efficient, and courteous service. In fine dining restaurants, where more complicated meals are prepared and often served over several courses, waiters and waitresses provide more formal service emphasizing personal, attentive treatment and a more leisurely pace. They may recommend certain dishes and identify ingredients or explain how various items on the menu are prepared. Some prepare salads, desserts, or other menu items tableside. Additionally, servers may meet with managers and chefs, before each shift to discuss the menu and any new items or specials, review ingredients for any potential food allergies, or talk about any food safety concerns, coordination between the kitchen and the dining room, and any customer service issues from the previous day or shift. Servers usually also check the identification of patrons to ensure they meet the minimum age requirement for the purchase of alcohol and tobacco products wherever those items are sold.

Waiters and waitresses sometimes perform the duties of other food and beverage service workers. These tasks may include escorting guests to tables, serving customers seated at counters, clearing and setting up tables, or operating a cash register. However, full-service restaurants frequently hire other staff, such as hosts and hostesses, cashiers, or dining room attendants, to perform these duties.

Bartenders fill drink orders either taken directly from patrons at the bar or through waiters and waitresses who place drink

Food and beverage serving and related workers need good interpersonal skills to deal with customers.

orders for dining room customers. Bartenders check the identification of customers seated at the bar to ensure they meet the minimum age requirement for the purchase of alcohol and tobacco products. They prepare mixed drinks, serve bottled or draught beer, and pour wine or other beverages. Bartenders must know a wide range of drink recipes and be able to mix drinks accurately, quickly, and without waste. Besides mixing and serving drinks, bartenders stock and prepare garnishes for drinks; maintain an adequate supply of ice, glasses, and other bar supplies; and keep the bar area clean for customers. They also may collect payment, operate the cash register, wash glassware and utensils, and serve food to customers who dine at the bar. Bartenders usually are responsible for ordering and maintaining an inventory of liquor, mixes, and other bar supplies.

Most bartenders directly serve and interact with patrons. Bartenders should be friendly and at ease talking with customers. Bartenders at service bars, on the other hand, have less contact with customers. They work in small bars often located off the kitchen in restaurants, hotels, and clubs where only waiters and waitresses place drink orders. Some establishments, especially larger, higher volume ones, use equipment that automatically measures, pours, and mixes drinks at the push of a button. Bartenders who use this equipment, however, still must work quickly to handle a large volume of drink orders and be familiar with the ingredients for special drink requests. Much of a bartender's work still must be done by hand.

Hosts and *hostesses* welcome guests and maintain reservation or waiting lists. They may direct patrons to coatrooms, restrooms, or to a place to wait until their table is ready. Hosts and hostesses assign guests to tables suitable for the size of their group, escort patrons to their seats, and provide menus. They also schedule dining reservations, arrange parties, and organize any special services that are required. In some restaurants, they act as cashiers.

Dining room and cafeteria attendants and bartender helpers assist waiters, waitresses, and bartenders by cleaning tables, removing dirty dishes, and keeping serving areas stocked with supplies. Sometimes called backwaiters or runners, they bring meals out of the kitchen and assist waiters and waitresses by distributing dishes to individual diners. They also replenish the supply of clean linens, dishes, silverware, and glasses in the dining room and keep the bar stocked with glasses, liquor, ice, and drink garnishes. Dining room attendants set tables with clean tablecloths, napkins, silverware, glasses, and dishes and serve ice water, rolls, and butter. At the conclusion of meals, they remove dirty dishes and soiled linens from tables. Cafeteria attendants stock serving tables with food, trays, dishes, and silverware and may carry trays to dining tables for patrons. Bartender helpers keep bar equipment clean and glasses washed. *Dishwashers* clean dishes, cutlery, and kitchen utensils and equipment.

Counter attendants take orders and serve food in cafeterias, coffee shops, and carryout eateries. In cafeterias, they serve food displayed on steam tables, carve meat, dish out vegetables, ladle sauces and soups, and fill beverage glasses. In lunchrooms and coffee shops, counter attendants take orders from customers seated at the counter, transmit orders to the kitchen, and pick up and serve food. They also fill cups with coffee, soda, and other beverages and prepare fountain specialties, such as milkshakes and ice cream sundaes. Counter attendants also take carryout orders from diners and wrap or place items in containers. They clean counters, write itemized bills, and sometimes accept payment. Some counter attendants may prepare short-order items, such as sandwiches and salads.

Some food and beverage serving workers take orders from customers at counters or drive-through windows at fast-food restaurants. They assemble orders, hand them to customers, and accept payment. Many of these are *combined food preparation and serving workers* who also cook and package food, make coffee, and fill beverage cups using drink-dispensing machines.

Other workers serve food to patrons outside of a restaurant environment. They might deliver room service meals in hotels or meals to hospital rooms or act as carhops, bringing orders to parked cars.

Work environment. Food and beverage service workers are on their feet most of the time and often carry heavy trays of food, dishes, and glassware. During busy dining periods, they are under pressure to serve customers quickly and efficiently. The work is relatively safe, but care must be taken to avoid slips, falls, and burns.

Part-time work is more common among food and beverage serving and related workers than among workers in almost any other occupation. In 2006, those on part-time schedules included half of all waiters and waitresses and 39 percent of all bartenders.

Food service and drinking establishments typically maintain long dining hours and offer flexible and varied work opportunities. Many food and beverage serving and related workers work evenings, weekends, and holidays. Many students and teenagers seek part time or seasonal work as food and beverage serving and related workers as a first job to gain work experience or to earn spending money. More than one-fifth of all food and beverage serving and related workers were 16 to 19 years old—about five times the proportion for all workers.

Training, Other Qualifications, and Advancement

Most food and beverage service jobs require little or no previous experience and provide training on the job.

Education and training. There are no specific educational requirements for most food and beverage service jobs. Many employers prefer to hire high school graduates for waiter and waitress, bartender, and host and hostess positions, but completion of high school usually is not required for fast-food workers, counter attendants, dishwashers, and dining room attendants and bartender helpers. For many people, a job as a food and beverage service worker serves as a source of immediate income, rather than a career. Many entrants to these jobs are in their late teens or early twenties and have a high school education or less. Usually, they have little or no work experience. Many are full-time students or homemakers. Food and beverage service jobs are a major source of part-time employment for high school and college students.

All new employees receive some training from their employer. They learn safe food handling procedures and sanitation practices, for example. Some employers, particularly those in fast-food restaurants, teach new workers using self-study programs, on-line programs, audiovisual presentations, and instructional booklets that explain food preparation and service skills. But most food and beverage serving and related workers pick up their skills by observing and working with more experienced workers. Some full-service restaurants also provide new dining room employees with some form of classroom training that alternates with periods of on-the-job work experience. These training programs communicate the operating philosophy of the restaurant, help establish a personal rapport with other staff, teach formal serving techniques, and instill a desire to work as a team. They also provide an opportunity to discuss customer service situations and the proper ways of handling unpleasant circumstances or unruly patrons.

Some food serving workers can acquire more skills by attending relevant classes offered by public or private vocational schools, restaurant associations, or large restaurant chains. Some bartenders also acquire their skills by attending a bartending or vocational and technical school. These programs often include instruction on State and local laws and regulations, cocktail recipes, proper attire and conduct, and stocking a bar. Some of these schools help their graduates find jobs. Although few employers require any minimum level of educational attainment, some specialized training is usually needed in food handling and legal issues surrounding serving alcoholic beverages. Employers are more likely to hire and promote based on people skills and personal qualities rather than education.

Other qualifications. Restaurants rely on good food and quality customer service to retain loyal customers and succeed in a competitive industry. Food and beverage serving and related workers who exhibit excellent personal qualities—such as a neat clean appearance, a well-spoken manner, an ability to work as a part of a team, and a pleasant way with patrons—will be highly sought after. All workers who serve alcoholic beverages must be at least 21 years of age in most jurisdictions and should be familiar with State and local laws concerning the sale of alcoholic beverages. For bartender jobs, many employers prefer to hire people who are 25 or older.

Waiters and waitresses need a good memory to avoid confusing customers' orders and to recall faces, names, and preferences of frequent patrons. These workers also should be comfortable using computers to place orders and generate customers' bills. Some may need to be quick at arithmetic so they can total bills manually. Knowledge of a foreign language is helpful to communicate with a diverse clientele and staff. Prior experience waiting on tables is preferred by restaurants and hotels that have rigid table service standards. Jobs at these establishments often offer higher wages and have greater income potential from tips, but they may also have stiffer employment requirements, such as prior table service experience or higher education than other establishments.

Advancement. Due to the relatively small size of most food-serving establishments, opportunities for promotion are limited. After gaining experience, some dining room and cafeteria attendants and bartender helpers advance to waiter, waitress, or bartender jobs. For waiters, waitresses, and bartenders, advancement usually is limited to finding a job in a busier or more expensive restaurant or bar where prospects for tip earnings are better. Some bartenders, hosts and hostesses, and waiters and waitresses advance to supervisory jobs, such as dining room supervisor, maitre d'hotel, assistant manager, or restaurant general manager. A few bartenders open their own businesses. In larger restaurant chains, food and beverage service workers who excel often are invited to enter the company's formal management training program. (For more information, see the section on food service managers elsewhere in the *Handbook*.)

Employment

Food and beverage serving and related workers held 7.4 million jobs in 2006. The distribution of jobs among the various food and beverage serving occupations was as follows:

Combined food preparation and serving workers,
  including fast food 2,503,000
Waiters and waitresses 2,361,000
Counter attendants, cafeteria, food concession, and
  coffee shop 533,000
Dishwashers 517,000
Bartenders 495,000
Dining room and cafeteria attendants and
  bartender helpers 416,000
Hosts and hostesses, restaurant, lounge, and coffee shop   351,000
Food servers, non restaurant 189,000
All other food preparation and serving related workers 56,000

The overwhelming majority of jobs for food and beverage serving and related workers were found in food services and drinking places, such as restaurants, sandwich shops, and catering or contract food service operators. Other jobs were in hotels, motels, and other traveler accommodation establishments; amusement, gambling, and recreation establishments; educational services; grocery stores; nursing care facilities; civic and social organizations; and hospitals.

Jobs are located throughout the country but are typically plentiful in large cities and tourist areas. Vacation resorts offer seasonal employment, and some workers alternate between summer and winter resorts.

Job Outlook

Average employment growth is expected, and job opportunities should be excellent for food and beverage serving and related workers, but job competition is often keen at upscale restaurants.

Employment change. Overall employment of these workers is expected to increase by 13 percent over the 2006-16 decade, which is about as fast as the average for all occupations. Food and beverage serving and related workers are projected to have one of the largest numbers of new jobs arise, about 993,000, over this period. The popularity of eating out is expected to increase as the population expands and as customers seek the convenience of restaurants and other dining options. Projected employment growth varies somewhat by job type. Employment of combined food preparation and serving workers, which includes fast-food workers, is expected to increase faster than the average in response to the continuing fast-paced lifestyle of many Americans and the addition of healthier foods at many fast-food restaurants. Average employment growth is expected

Projections data from the National Employment Matrix

Occupational Title	SOC Code	Employment, 2006	Projected employment, 2016	Change, 2006-16	
				Number	Percent
Food and beverage serving and related workers	—	7,422,000	8,415,000	993,000	13
Food and beverage serving workers...	35-3000	6,081,000	6,927,000	846,000	14
Bartenders	35-3011	495,000	551,000	56,000	11
Fast food and counter workers......................................	35-3020	3,036,000	3,542,000	506,000	17
Combined food preparation and serving workers, including fast food	35-3021	2,503,000	2,955,000	452,000	18
Counter attendants, cafeteria, food concession, and coffee shop..	35-3022	533,000	587,000	54,000	10
Waiters and waitresses	35-3031	2,361,000	2,615,000	255,000	11
Food servers, nonrestaurant	35-3041	189,000	219,000	30,000	16
Other food preparation and serving related workers....................	35-9000	1,341,000	1,488,000	147,000	11
Dining room and cafeteria attendants and bartender helpers....	35-9011	416,000	466,000	49,000	12
Dishwashers..	35-9021	517,000	571,000	54,000	10
Hosts and hostesses, restaurant, lounge, and coffee shop.........	35-9031	351,000	388,000	37,000	10
Food preparation and serving related workers, all other...........	35-9099	56,000	64,000	7,300	13

NOTE: Data in this table are rounded. See the discussion of the employment projections table in the *Handbook* introductory chapter on *Occupational Information Included in the Handbook*.

for waiters and waitresses, hosts and hostesses, and bartenders. Restaurants that offer table service, more varied menus, and an active bar scene are growing in number in response to consumer demands for convenience and to increases in disposable income, especially among families who frequent casual family-oriented restaurants; affluent young professionals, who patronize trendier, more upscale establishments; and retirees and others who dine out as a way to socialize. Employment of dishwashers, dining room and cafeteria attendants, and bartender helpers also will grow about as fast as average.

Job prospects. Job opportunities at most eating and drinking places will be excellent because many people in service sector occupations change jobs frequently and the number of food service outlets needing food service workers will continue to grow. Many of these workers, such as teens, those seeking part-time employment, or multiple jobholders, do so to satisfy short-term income needs before moving on to jobs in other occupations or leaving the workforce. Keen competition is expected, however, for jobs in popular restaurants and fine dining establishments, where potential earnings from tips are greatest.

Earnings

Food and beverage serving and related workers derive their earnings from a combination of hourly wages and customer tips. Earnings vary greatly, depending on the type of job and establishment. For example, fast-food workers and hosts and hostesses usually do not receive tips, so their wage rates may be higher than those of waiters and waitresses and bartenders in full-service restaurants but their overall earnings might be lower. In many full-service restaurants, tips are higher than wages. In some restaurants, workers contribute all or a portion of their tips to a tip pool, which is distributed among qualifying workers. Tip pools allow workers who don't usually receive tips directly from customers, such as dining room attendants, to feel a part of a team and to share in the rewards of good service.

In May 2006, median hourly wage-and-salary earnings (including tips) of waiters and waitresses were $7.14. The middle 50 percent earned between $6.42 and $9.14. The lowest 10 per-

cent earned less than $5.78, and the highest 10 percent earned more than $12.46 an hour. For most waiters and waitresses, higher earnings are primarily the result of receiving more in tips rather than higher hourly wages. Tips usually average between 10 and 20 percent of guests' checks; waiters and waitresses working in busy, expensive restaurants earn the most.

Bartenders had median hourly wage-and-salary earnings (including tips) of $7.86. The middle 50 percent earned between $6.77 and $10.10. The lowest 10 percent earned less than $6.00, and the highest 10 percent earned more than $13.56 an hour. Like waiters and waitresses, bartenders employed in public bars may receive more than half of their earnings as tips. Service bartenders often are paid higher hourly wages to offset their lower tip earnings.

Median hourly wage-and-salary earnings (including tips) of dining room and cafeteria attendants and bartender helpers were $7.36. The middle 50 percent earned between $6.62 and $8.59. The lowest 10 percent earned less than $5.91, and the highest 10 percent earned more than $10.60 an hour. Most received over half of their earnings as wages; the rest of their income was a share of the proceeds from tip pools.

Median hourly wage-and-salary earnings of hosts and hostesses were $7.78. The middle 50 percent earned between $6.79 and $8.97. The lowest 10 percent earned less than $5.99, and the highest 10 percent earned more than $10.80 an hour. Wages comprised the majority of their earnings. In some cases, wages were supplemented by proceeds from tip pools.

Median hourly wage-and-salary earnings of combined food preparation and serving workers, including fast food, were $7.24. The middle 50 percent earned between $6.47 and $8.46. The lowest 10 percent earned less than $5.79, and the highest 10 percent earned more than $10.16 an hour. Although some combined food preparation and serving workers receive a part of their earnings as tips, fast-food workers usually do not.

Median hourly wage-and-salary earnings of counter attendants in cafeterias, food concessions, and coffee shops (including tips) were $7.76. The middle 50 percent earned between $6.85 and $9.00 an hour. The lowest 10 percent earned less than $6.11, and the highest 10 percent earned more than $10.86 an hour.

Median hourly wage-and-salary earnings of dishwashers were $7.57. The middle 50 percent earned between $6.78 and $8.62. The lowest 10 percent earned less than $6.01, and the highest 10 percent earned more than $10.00 an hour.

Median hourly wage-and-salary earnings of food servers outside of restaurants were $8.70. The middle 50 percent earned between $7.27 and $10.87. The lowest 10 percent earned less than $6.36, and the highest 10 percent earned more than $13.81 an hour.

Many beginning or inexperienced workers earn the Federal minimum wage of $5.85 an hour. However, a few States set minimum wages higher than the Federal minimum. Under Federal law, this wage will increase to $6.55 in the summer of 2008 and to $7.25 in the summer of 2009. Also, various minimum wage exceptions apply under specific circumstances to disabled workers, full-time students, youth under age 20 in their first 90 days of employment, tipped employees, and student-learners. Tipped employees are those who customarily and regularly receive more than $30 a month in tips. The employer may consider tips as part of wages, but the employer must pay at least $2.13 an hour in direct wages.

Many employers provide free meals and furnish uniforms, but some may deduct from wages the cost, or fair value, of any meals or lodging provided. Food and beverage service workers who work full time often receive typical benefits, but part-time workers usually do not. In some large restaurants and hotels, food and beverage serving and related workers belong to unions—principally the Unite HERE and the Service Employees International Union.

Related Occupations

Other workers who prepare food for diners include chefs, cooks, and food preparation workers. Those whose job involves serving customers and handling money include cashiers, flight attendants, gaming services workers, and retail salespersons.

Sources of Additional Information

Information about job opportunities may be obtained from local employers and local offices of State employment services agencies.

A guide to careers in restaurants plus a list of 2- and 4-year colleges offering food service programs and related scholarship information is available from:

➤ National Restaurant Association, 1200 17th St.NW., Washington, DC20036. Internet: **http://www.restaurant.org**

For general information on hospitality careers, contact:

➤ International Council on Hotel, Restaurant, and Institutional Education, 2810 North Parham Rd., Suite 230, Richmond, VA 23294. Internet:**http://www.chrie.org**

Building and Grounds Cleaning and Maintenance Occupations

Building Cleaning Workers

(O*NET 37-1011.00, 37-2011.00, 37-2012.00, 37-2019.99)

Significant Points

- This very large occupation requires few skills to enter and each year has one of the largest numbers of job openings of any occupation.

- Most job openings result from the need to replace the many workers who leave these jobs because they provide low pay and few benefits, limited opportunities for training or advancement, and often only part-time or temporary work.

- Most new jobs will occur in businesses providing janitorial and cleaning services on a contract basis.

Nature of the Work

Building cleaning workers—including janitors, maids, housekeeping cleaners, window washers, and rug shampooers—keep office buildings, hospitals, stores, apartment houses, hotels, and residences clean, sanitary, and in good condition. Some do only cleaning, while others have a wide range of duties.

Janitors and *cleaners* perform a variety of heavy cleaning duties, such as cleaning floors, shampooing rugs, washing walls and glass, and removing rubbish. They may fix leaky faucets, empty trash cans, do painting and carpentry, replenish bathroom supplies, mow lawns, and see that heating and air-conditioning equipment works properly. On a typical day, janitors may wet- or dry-mop floors, clean bathrooms, vacuum carpets, dust furniture, make minor repairs, and exterminate insects and rodents. They may also clean snow or debris from sidewalks in front of buildings and notify management of the need for major repairs. While janitors typically perform most of the duties mentioned, cleaners tend to work for companies that specialize in one type of cleaning activity, such as washing windows.

Maids and *housekeeping cleaners* perform any combination of light cleaning duties to keep private households or commercial establishments, such as hotels, restaurants, hospitals, and nursing homes, clean and orderly. In hotels, aside from cleaning and maintaining the premises, maids and housekeeping cleaners may deliver ironing boards, cribs, and rollaway beds to guests' rooms. In hospitals, they also may wash bed frames, make beds, and disinfect and sanitize equipment and supplies with germicides. Janitors, maids, and cleaners use many kinds of equipment, tools, and cleaning materials. For one job they may need standard cleaning implements; another may require an electric floor polishing machine and a special cleaning solution. Improved building materials, chemical cleaners, and power equipment have made many tasks easier and less time consuming, but cleaning workers must learn the proper use of equipment and cleaners to avoid harming floors, fixtures, building occupants, and themselves.

Cleaning supervisors coordinate, schedule, and supervise the activities of janitors and cleaners. They assign tasks and inspect building areas to see that work has been done properly; they also issue supplies and equipment and inventory stocks to ensure that supplies on hand are adequate. They may be expected to screen and hire job applicants; train new and experienced employees; and recommend promotions, transfers, or dismissals. Supervisors may prepare reports concerning the occupancy of rooms, hours worked, and department expenses. Some also perform cleaning duties.

Cleaners and *servants in private households* dust and polish furniture; sweep, mop, and wax floors; vacuum; and clean ovens, refrigerators, and bathrooms. They also may wash dishes, polish silver, and change and make beds. Some wash, fold, and iron clothes; a few wash windows. General houseworkers also may take clothes and laundry to the cleaners, buy groceries, and perform many other errands.

Building cleaning workers in large office and residential buildings, and more recently in large hotels, often work in teams consisting of workers who specialize in vacuuming, picking up trash, and cleaning restrooms, among other things. Supervisors conduct inspections to ensure that the building is cleaned properly and the team is functioning efficiently. In hotels, one member of the team is responsible for reporting electronically to the supervisor when rooms are cleaned.

Work environment. Because most office buildings are cleaned while they are empty, many cleaning workers work evening hours. Some, however, such as school and hospital custodians, work in the daytime. When there is a need for 24-hour maintenance, janitors may be assigned to shifts. Most full-time building cleaners work about 40 hours a week. Part-time cleaners usually work in the evenings and on weekends.

Most building cleaning workers work indoors, but some work outdoors part of the time, sweeping walkways, mowing lawns, or shoveling snow. Working with machines can be

Building cleaning workers often work indoors and use specialized equipment.

noisy, and some tasks, such as cleaning bathrooms and trash rooms, can be dirty and unpleasant. Janitors may suffer cuts, bruises, and burns from machines, handtools, and chemicals. They spend most of their time on their feet, sometimes lifting or pushing heavy furniture or equipment. Many tasks, such as dusting or sweeping, require constant bending, stooping, and stretching. Lifting the increasingly heavier mattresses at nicer hotels in order to change the linens can cause back injuries and sprains.

Training, Other Qualifications, and Advancement
Most building cleaning workers, except supervisors, have a high school degree or less and mainly learn their skills on the job or in informal training sessions sponsored by their employers. Supervisors, though, generally have at least a high school diploma and often some college.

Education and training. No special education is required for most entry-level janitorial or cleaning jobs, but workers should be able to perform simple arithmetic and follow instructions. High school shop courses are helpful for jobs involving repair work. Most building cleaners learn their skills on the job. Beginners usually work with an experienced cleaner, doing routine cleaning. As they gain more experience, they are assigned more complicated tasks. In some cities, programs run by unions, government agencies, or employers teach janitorial skills. Students learn how to clean buildings thoroughly and efficiently; how to select and safely use various cleansing agents; and how to operate and maintain machines, such as wet and dry vacuums, buffers, and polishers. Students learn to plan their work, to follow safety and health regulations, to interact positively with people in the buildings they clean, and to work without supervision. Instruction in minor electrical, plumbing, and other repairs also may be given.

Supervisors of building cleaning workers usually need at least a high school diploma, but many have some college or more, especially those who work at places where clean rooms and well-functioning buildings are a necessity, such as in hospitals and hotels.

Other qualifications. Those who come in contact with the public should have good communication skills. Employers usually look for dependable, hard-working individuals who are in good health, follow directions well, and get along with other people.

Certification and advancement. A small number of cleaning supervisors and managers are members of the International Executive Housekeepers Association, which offers two kinds of certification programs for cleaning supervisors and managers: Certified Executive Housekeeper (CEH) and Registered Executive Housekeeper (REH). The CEH designation is offered to those with a high school education, while the REH designation is offered to those who have a 4-year college degree. Both designations are earned by attending courses and passing exams and both must be renewed every 3 years to ensure that workers keep abreast of new cleaning methods. Those with the REH designation usually oversee the cleaning services of hotels, hospitals, casinos, and other

Projections data from the National Employment Matrix

Occupational Title	SOC Code	Employment, 2006	Projected employment, 2016	Change, 2006-16	
				Number	Percent
Building cleaning workers	—	4,154,000	4,723,000	569,000	14
First-line supervisors/managers of housekeeping and janitorial workers...	37-1011	282,000	318,000	36,000	13
Building cleaning workers	37-2010	3,872,000	4,405,000	533,000	14
Janitors and cleaners, except maids and housekeeping cleaners	37-2011	2,387,000	2,732,000	345,000	14
Maids and housekeeping cleaners..	37-2012	1,470,000	1,656,000	186,000	13
Building cleaning workers, all other..	37-2019	16,000	18,000	2,400	15

NOTE: Data in this table are rounded. See the discussion of the employment projections table in the *Handbook* introductory chapter on *Occupational Information Included in the Handbook*.

large institutions that rely on well-trained experts for their cleaning needs.

Advancement opportunities for workers usually are limited in organizations where they are the only maintenance worker. Where there is a large maintenance staff, however, cleaning workers can be promoted to supervisor or to area supervisor or manager. In many establishments, they are required to take some in-service training to improve their housekeeping techniques and procedures and to enhance their supervisory skills. A high school diploma improves the chances for advancement. Some janitors set up their own maintenance or cleaning businesses.

Employment

Building cleaning workers held about 4.2 million jobs in 2006. More than 7 percent were self-employed.

Janitors and cleaners worked in nearly every type of establishment and held about 2.4 million jobs. They accounted for more than 57 percent of all building cleaning workers. More than 31 percent worked for firms supplying building maintenance services on a contract basis, about 20 percent were employed in public or private educational services, and 2 percent worked in hotels or motels. Other employers included hospitals; restaurants; religious institutions; manufacturing firms; government agencies; and operators of apartment buildings, office buildings, and other types of real estate.

First-line supervisors of housekeeping and janitorial workers held more than 282,000 jobs. Approximately 20 percent worked in firms supplying building maintenance services on a contract basis, while approximately 11 percent were employed in hotels or motels. About 4 percent worked for State and local governments, primarily at schools and colleges. Others worked for hospitals, nursing homes and other residential care facilities.

Maids and housekeepers held about 1.5 million jobs. Private households employed the most maids and housekeepers—almost 29 percent—while hotels, motels, and other traveler accommodations employed about the same percentage, almost 29 percent. Hospitals, nursing homes, and other residential care facilities employed large numbers, also. Although cleaning jobs can be found in all cities and towns, most are located in highly populated areas where there are many office build-

ings, schools, apartment houses, nursing homes, and hospitals.

Job Outlook

Overall employment of building cleaning workers is expected to grow faster than average for all occupations through 2016, as more office complexes, apartment houses, schools, factories, hospitals, and other buildings requiring cleaning are built to accommodate a growing population and economy.

Employment change. The number of building cleaning workers is expected to grow 14 percent between 2006 and 2016, which is faster than the average for all occupations. This occupation will have, in fact, one of the largest numbers of new jobs arise, about 570,000 over the 2006-16 period.

Much of the growth in these occupations will come from cleaning residential properties. As families become more pressed for time, they increasingly hire cleaning and handyman services to perform a variety of tasks in their homes. Also, as the population ages, older people will need to hire cleaners to help maintain their houses. In addition, housekeeping cleaners will be needed to clean the growing number of residential care facilities for the elderly. These facilities, including assisted-living residences, generally provide housekeeping services as part of the rent. Although there have been some improvements in productivity in the way buildings are cleaned and maintained—using teams of cleaners, for example, and better cleaning supplies—cleaning still is very much a labor-intensive job.

As many firms reduce costs by contracting out the cleaning and maintenance of buildings, businesses providing janitorial and cleaning services on a contract basis are expected to have the greatest number of new jobs in this field.

Job prospects. In addition to job openings arising due to growth, numerous openings should result from the need to replace those who leave this very large occupation each year. Limited promotion potential, low pay, and the fact that many jobs are part-time and temporary, induce many to leave the occupation, thereby contributing to the number of job openings and the need to replace these workers.

Building cleaners usually find work by answering newspaper advertisements, applying directly to organizations where they would like to work, contacting local labor unions, or contacting State employment service offices.

Earnings

Median annual earnings of janitors and cleaners, except maids and housekeeping cleaners, were $19,930 in May 2006. The middle 50 percent earned between $16,220 and $25,640. The lowest 10 percent earned less than $14,010 and the highest 10 percent earned more than $33,060. Median annual earnings in 2006 in the industries employing the largest numbers of janitors and cleaners, except maids and housekeeping cleaners, were as follows:

Elementary and secondary schools	$24,010
Local government	23,930
Colleges, universities, and professional schools	23,170
General medical and surgical hospitals	21,670
Services to buildings and dwellings	17,870

Median annual earnings of maids and housekeepers were $17,580 in May 2006. The middle 50 percent earned between $15,060 and $21,440. The lowest 10 percent earned less than $13,140, and the highest 10 percent earned more than $26,390. Median annual earnings in 2006 in the industries employing the largest numbers of maids and housekeepers were as follows:

General medical and surgical hospitals	$20,080
Community care facilities for the elderly	17,900
Nursing care facilities	17,690
Services to buildings and dwellings	17,540
Traveler accommodation	16,790

Median annual earnings of first-line supervisors and managers of housekeeping and janitorial workers were $31,290 in May 2006. The middle 50 percent earned between $24,230 and $40,670. The lowest 10 percent earned less than $19,620, and the highest 10 percent earned more than $51,490. Median annual earnings in May 2006 in the industries employing the largest numbers of first-line supervisors and managers of housekeeping and janitorial workers were as follows:

Local government	$38,170
Elementary and secondary schools	35,660
Nursing care facilities	30,570
Services to buildings and dwellings	29,730
Traveler accommodation	26,730

Related Occupations

Workers who specialize in one of the many job functions of janitors and cleaners include pest control workers; general maintenance and repair workers; and grounds maintenance workers.

Sources of Additional Information

Information about janitorial jobs may be obtained from State employment service offices.

For information on certification in executive housekeeping, contact:

➤ International Executive Housekeepers Association, Inc., 1001 Eastwind Dr., Suite 301, Westerville, OH 43081-3361. Internet: **http://www.ieha.org**

Grounds Maintenance Workers

(O*NET 37-1012.00, 37-3011.00, 37-3012.00, 37-3013.00, 37-3019.99)

Significant Points

- Opportunities should be very good, especially for workers willing to work seasonal or variable schedules, because of significant job turnover and increased demand for landscaping.

- Many beginning jobs have low earnings and are physically demanding.

- Most workers learn through short-term on-the-job training.

Nature of the Work

Attractively designed, healthy, and well-maintained lawns, gardens, and grounds create a positive impression, establish a peaceful mood, and increase property values. Grounds maintenance workers perform the variety of tasks necessary to achieve a pleasant and functional outdoor environment. They also care for indoor gardens and plantings in commercial and public facilities, such as malls, hotels, and botanical gardens.

These workers use handtools such as shovels, rakes, pruning and handsaws, hedge and brush trimmers, and axes, as well as power lawnmowers, chain saws, snowblowers, and electric clippers. Some use equipment such as tractors and twin-axle vehicles. Landscaping and groundskeeping workers at parks, schools, cemeteries, and golf courses may lay sod after preparing the ground. Workers at sod farms use sod cutters to harvest sod that will be replanted elsewhere.

Grounds maintenance workers can be divided into landscaping workers and groundskeeping workers, depending on whether they mainly install new landscape elements or maintain existing ones, but their duties often overlap. Other grounds maintenance workers are pesticide handlers and tree trimmers.

Landscaping workers install plants and other elements into landscaped areas and often maintain them. They might mow, edge, trim, fertilize, dethatch, water, and mulch lawns and grounds many times during the growing season. They grade property by creating or smoothing hills and inclines, install lighting or sprinkler systems, and build walkways, terraces, patios, decks, and fountains. They also transport and plant new vegetation, and transplant, mulch, fertilize, and water existing plants, trees, and shrubs. A growing number of residential and commercial clients, such as managers of office buildings, shopping malls, multiunit residential buildings, and hotels and motels, favor full-service landscape maintenance.

Groundskeeping workers, also called *groundskeepers*, usually focus on maintaining existing grounds. They might work on athletic fields, golf courses, cemeteries, university campuses, and parks. In addition to caring for sod, plants, and trees, they rake and mulch leaves, clear snow from walkways and parking lots, and use irrigation methods to adjust the amount of water consumption and prevent waste. They see to the proper upkeep and repair of sidewalks, parking lots, groundskeeping equipment, pools, fountains, fences, planters, and benches.

Groundskeeping workers who care for athletic fields keep natural and artificial turf in top condition, mark out boundaries, and paint turf with team logos and names before events. They must make sure that the underlying soil on fields with natural turf has the required composition to allow proper drainage and to support the grasses used on the field. Groundskeeping workers mow, water, fertilize, and aerate the fields regularly. In sports venues, they vacuum and disinfect synthetic turf after its use to prevent the growth of harmful bacteria, and they remove the turf and replace the cushioning pad periodically.

Groundskeepers in parks and recreation facilities care for lawns, trees, and shrubs; maintain playgrounds; clean buildings; and keep parking lots, picnic areas, and other public spaces free of litter. They also may erect and dismantle snow fences, and maintain swimming pools. These workers inspect buildings and equipment, make needed repairs, and keep everything freshly painted.

Workers who maintain golf courses are called greenskeepers. Greenskeepers do many of the same things as other groundskeepers, but they also periodically relocate the holes on putting greens to prevent uneven wear of the turf and to add interest and challenge to the game. Greenskeepers also keep canopies, benches, ball washers, and tee markers repaired and freshly painted.

Some groundskeepers specialize in caring for cemeteries and memorial gardens. They dig graves to specified depths, generally using a backhoe. They mow grass regularly, apply fertilizers and other chemicals, prune shrubs and trees, plant flowers, and remove debris from graves.

Pesticide handlers, sprayers, and applicators, vegetation mix herbicides, fungicides, or insecticides and apply them through sprays, dusts, or vapors into the soil or onto plants. Those working for chemical lawn service firms are more specialized, inspecting lawns for problems and applying fertilizers, pesticides, and other chemicals to stimulate growth and prevent or control weeds, diseases, or insect infestation. Many practice integrated pest-management techniques.

Tree trimmers and *pruners* cut away dead or excess branches from trees or shrubs to clear roads, sidewalks, or utilities' equipment or to improve the appearance, health, and value of trees. Some of these workers also specialize in pruning, trimming and shaping ornamental trees and shrubs for private residences, golf courses, or other institutional grounds. Tree trimmers and pruners use handsaws, pole saws, shears, and clippers. When trimming near power lines, they usually work on truck-mounted lifts and use power pruners.

Supervisors of landscaping and groundskeeping workers oversee grounds maintenance work. They prepare cost estimates, schedule work for crews on the basis of weather conditions or the availability of equipment, perform spot checks to ensure the quality of the service, and suggest changes in work procedures. In addition, supervisors train workers in their tasks; keep employees' time records and record work performed; and even assist workers when deadlines are near. Supervisors who own their own business are also known as *landscape contractors*. They also often call themselves *landscape designers* if

Grounds maintenance workers often use power equipment.

they create landscape design plans. Landscape designers also design exterior floral displays by planting annual or perennial flowers. Some work with landscape architects. (Landscape architects, discussed elsewhere in the *Handbook*, create more technical architectural plans and usually work on larger projects.) Supervisors of workers on golf courses are known as superintendents.

Supervisors of tree trimmers and pruners are called *arborists*. Arborists specialize in the care of individual trees, diagnosing and treating tree diseases and recommending preventative health measures. Some arborists plant trees. Most can recommend types of trees that are appropriate for a specific location, as the wrong tree in the wrong location could lead to future problems with crowding, insects, diseases, or poor growth.

Arborists are employed by cities to improve urban green space, utilities to maintain power distribution networks, companies to care for residential and commercial properties, as well as many other settings.

Work environment. Many grounds maintenance jobs are seasonal, available mainly in the spring, summer, and fall, when most planting, mowing, trimming, and cleanup are necessary. Most of the work is performed outdoors in all kinds of weather. It can be physically demanding and repetitive, involving much bending, lifting, and shoveling. Workers in landscaping and groundskeeping may be under pressure to get the job completed, especially when they are preparing for scheduled events such as athletic competitions.

Those who work with pesticides, fertilizers, and other chemicals, as well as dangerous equipment and tools such as power lawnmowers, chain saws, and power clippers, must exercise safety precautions. Workers who use motorized equipment must take care to protect their hearing.

Training, Other Qualifications, and Advancement
Most grounds maintenance workers learn on-the-job. However, some occupations may require formal training in areas such as landscape design, horticulture, or business management.

Education and training. There usually are no minimum educational requirements for entry-level positions in grounds maintenance. In 2006, most workers had a high school education or less. Short-term on-the-job training generally is sufficient to teach new hires how to operate and repair equipment such as mowers, trimmers, leaf blowers, and small tractors and to follow correct safety procedures. They must also learn proper planting and maintenance procedures for their localities. Large institutional employers such as golf courses or municipalities may supplement on-the-job training with coursework in subjects like horticulture or small engine repair for those employees showing ability and willingness to learn.

Landscaping supervisors or contractors who own their own business, arborists, and landscape designers usually need formal training in landscape design, horticulture, arboriculture, or business. A bachelor's degree may be needed for those who want to become specialists or own their own business.

Licensure. Most States require licensure or certification for workers who apply pesticides. Requirements vary but usually include passing a test on the proper use and disposal of insecticides, herbicides, and fungicides. Some States require that landscape contractors be licensed.

Other qualifications. Employers look for responsible, self-motivated individuals because grounds maintenance workers often work with little supervision. Employers want people who can learn quickly and follow instructions accurately so that time is not wasted and plants are not damaged. Workers who deal directly with customers must get along well with people.

Driving a vehicle is often needed for these jobs. If driving is required, preference is given to applicants with a driver's license, a good driving record, and experience driving a truck.

Certification and advancement. The Professional Grounds Management Society offers voluntary certification to grounds managers who have a bachelor's degree in a relevant major with at least 4 years of experience, including 2 years as a supervisor; an associate degree in a relevant major with 6 years of experience, including 3 years as a supervisor; or 8 years of experience including 4 years as a supervisor, and no degree. Additionally, candidates for certification must pass an examination covering subjects such as equipment management, personnel management, environmental issues, turf care, ornamentals, and circulatory systems. Certification as a grounds technician is also offered by this organization.

The Professional Landcare Network offers six certifications to those who seek to demonstrate specific knowledge in an area of landscaping and grounds maintenance. Obtaining certification may be an asset for career advancement. The Tree Care Industry Association offers four levels of credentials. Currently available credentials include Tree Care Apprentice, Ground Operations Specialist, Tree Climber Specialist, and Tree Care Specialist, as well as a certification program in safety.

Laborers who demonstrate a willingness to work hard and quickly, have good communication skills, and take an interest in the business may advance to crew leader or other supervisory positions. Becoming a grounds manager or landscape contractor usually requires some formal education beyond high school and several years of progressively more responsible experience. Some workers with groundskeeping backgrounds may start their own businesses after several years of experience.

Employment

Grounds maintenance workers held about 1.5 million jobs in 2006. Employment was distributed as follows:

Landscaping and groundskeeping workers	1,220,000
First-line supervisors/managers of landscaping, lawn service, and groundskeeping workers	202,000
Tree trimmers and pruners	41,000
Pesticide handlers, sprayers, and applicators, vegetation	31,000
Grounds maintenance workers, all other	28,000

More than one-third of the workers in grounds maintenance were employed in companies providing landscaping services to buildings and dwellings. Others worked for amusement and recreation facilities, such as golf courses and racetracks; educational institutions, both public, and private; and property management and real-estate development firms. Some were employed by local governments, installing and maintaining landscaping for parks, hospitals, and other public facilities. Almost 24 percent of grounds maintenance workers were self-employed, providing landscape maintenance directly to customers on a contract basis.

About 14 percent of grounds maintenance workers worked part time; about 9 percent were younger than age twenty.

Job Outlook

Those interested in grounds maintenance occupations should find very good job opportunities in the future. Employment of grounds maintenance workers is expected to grow faster than average for all occupations through the year 2016.

Projections data from the National Employment Matrix

Occupational Title	SOC Code	Employment, 2006	Projected employment, 2016	Change, 2006-16	
				Number	Percent
Grounds maintenance workers and related first-line supervisors/managers	—	1,521,000	1,791,000	270,000	18
First-line supervisors/managers of landscaping, lawn service, and groundskeeping workers	37-1012	202,000	237,000	36,000	18
Grounds maintenance workers	37-3000	1,319,000	1,554,000	235,000	18
Landscaping and groundskeeping workers	37-3011	1,220,000	1,441,000	221,000	18
Pesticide handlers, sprayers, and applicators, vegetation	37-3012	31,000	35,000	4,300	14
Tree trimmers and pruners	37-3013	41,000	45,000	4,500	11
Grounds maintenance workers, all other	37-3019	28,000	33,000	4,600	17

NOTE: Data in this table are rounded. See the discussion of the employment projections table in the *Handbook* introductory chapter on *Occupational Information Included in the Handbook.*

Employment change. Employment of grounds maintenance workers is expected to grow about 18 percent during the 2006-16 decade. Grounds maintenance workers will have among the largest numbers of new jobs arise, around 270,000 over the 2006-16 period.

More workers will be needed to keep up with increasing demand by lawn care and landscaping companies. Increased construction of office buildings, shopping malls, and residential housing and of highways and parks is expected to increase demand for grounds maintenance workers. In addition, the upkeep and renovation of existing landscaping and grounds are continuing sources of demand for grounds maintenance workers. Major institutions, such as universities and corporate headquarters, recognize the importance of good landscape design in attracting personnel and clients and are expected to use grounds maintenance services more extensively to maintain and upgrade their properties. Grounds maintenance workers working for State and local governments, however, may face budget cuts, which may affect hiring.

Homeowners are a growing source of demand for grounds maintenance workers. Many two-income households lack the time to take care of their lawns so they increasingly hire people to maintain them. Also, as the population ages, more elderly homeowners will require lawn care services to help maintain their yards. In addition, there is a growing interest by homeowners in their backyards and a desire to make yards more attractive for outdoor entertaining. With many newer homes having more and bigger windows overlooking the property, it is becoming more important to maintain and beautify the grounds.

Job opportunities for tree trimmers and pruners should also increase as utility companies step up pruning of trees around electric lines to prevent power outages. Additionally, tree trimmers and pruners will be needed to help combat infestations caused by new species of insects from other countries. For example, ash trees from Chicago to Washington, D.C. are under threat by a pest from China, and preventative eradication may be employed to control the pest.

Job prospects. Jobs for grounds maintenance workers are increasing, and because wages for beginners are low and the work is physically demanding, many employers have difficulty attracting enough workers to fill all openings, creating very good job opportunities.

Job opportunities for nonseasonal work are more numerous in regions with temperate climates, where landscaping and lawn services are required all year. Opportunities may vary with local economic conditions.

Earnings

Median hourly earnings in May 2006 of grounds maintenance workers were as follows:

First-line supervisors/managers of landscaping,
lawn service, and groundskeeping workers $17.93
Tree trimmers and pruners 13.58
Pesticide handlers, sprayers, and applicators, vegetation 12.84
Landscaping and groundskeeping workers............................10.22
Grounds maintenance workers, all others 9.82

Median hourly earnings in the industries employing the largest numbers of landscaping and groundskeeping workers were as follows:

Local government $11.64
Services to buildings and dwellings......................................10.17
Landscaping services 10.17
Other amusement and recreation industries.............................9.47
Employment services...9.09

Related Occupations

Grounds maintenance workers perform most of their work outdoors and have some knowledge of plants and soils. Others whose jobs may require that they work outdoors are agricultural workers; farmers, ranchers, and agricultural managers; forest, conservation, and logging workers; landscape architects; and biological scientists.

Sources of Additional Information

For career and certification information on tree trimmers and pruners, contact:
➤ Tree Care Industry Association, 3 Perimeter Rd., Unit I, Manchester, NH 03103-3341.
Internet: **http://www.treecareindustry.org**
➤ International Society of Arboriculture, P.O. Box 3129, Champaign, IL 61826-3129.
Internet:
   http://www.isa-arbor.com/careersInArboriculture/careers.aspx
For information on work as a landscaping and groundskeeping worker, contact the following organizations:
➤ Professional Grounds Management Society, 720 Light St., Baltimore, MD 21230-3816. Internet: **http://www.pgms.org**
➤ Professional Landcare Network, 950 Herndon Parkway, Suite 450, Herndon, VA 20170-5528.
Internet: **http://www.landcarenetwork.org/**
For information on becoming a licensed pesticide applicator, contact your State's Department of Agriculture or Department of Environmental Protection or Conservation.

Pest Control Workers

(O*NET 37-2021.00)

Significant Points

- A high school diploma is the minimum educational requirement; however, about 4 in 10 workers
- have either attended college or earned a degree.
- Laws require pest control workers to be certified through training and examination.
- Job prospects should be favorable, especially in warmer climates.

Nature of the Work

Unwanted creatures that infest households, buildings, or surrounding areas are pests that can pose serious risks to health and safety. The most common pests are roaches, rats, mice, spiders, termites, fleas, ants, and bees. It is a pest control worker's job to remove them.

Pest control workers locate, identify, destroy, control, and repel pests. They use their knowledge of pests' biology and habits, along with an arsenal of pest management techniques such as applying chemicals, setting traps, operating equipment, and even modifying structures to alleviate pest problems. The final choice of which type of pest management is used often is decided by the consumer.

After a pest management plan is agreed upon, action needs to be taken. Some pests need to be eliminated and require pesticide application. Pest control workers use two different types of pesticides—general use and restricted use. General use pesticides are the most widely used and are readily available. They are available to the public in diluted concentrations. Restricted use pesticides are available only to certified professionals for controlling the most severe infestations. Their registration, labeling, and application are regulated by Federal law and interpreted by the U.S. Environmental Protection Agency (EPA), because of their potential harm to pest control workers, customers, and the environment.

Pesticides are not pest control workers' only tool. Pest control workers increasingly use a combination of pest management techniques, known as integrated pest management. One method involves using proper sanitation and creating physical barriers. Pests cannot survive without food and will not infest a building if they cannot enter it. Another method involves using baits, some of which destroy the pests and others that prevent them from reproducing. Yet another method involves using mechanical devices, such as traps, that remove pests from the immediate environment.

Integrated pest management is popular for several reasons. Pesticides can pose environmental and health risks and some States heavily restrict the application of pesticides. Some pests are becoming more resistant to pesticides in certain situations. Finally, an integrated pest management plan is more effective in the long term than use of a pesticide alone.

New technology has been introduced that allows pest control workers to conduct home inspections, mainly of termites, in much less time. The technology works by implanting microchips in baiting stations, which emit signals that can tell pest control workers if there is termite activity at one of the baiting stations. Workers pick up the signals using a device similar to a metal detector and it allows them to more quickly assess the presence of termites.

Most pest control workers are employed as pest control technicians, applicators, or supervisors. Position titles vary by State, but the hierarchy—based on the training and responsibility required—remains consistent.

Pest control technicians identify potential pest problems, conduct inspections, and design control strategies. They work directly with the customer. Some technicians require a higher level of training depending on their task. If certain products

Laws require pest control workers to be certified through training and examination.

are used, the technician may be required to become a certified applicator.

Applicators that specialize in controlling termites are called termite control technicians. They use chemicals and modify structures to eliminate termites and prevent future infestation. To treat infested areas, termite control technicians drill holes and cut openings into buildings to access infestations and install physical barriers or bait systems around the structure. Some termite control technicians even repair structural damage caused by termites.

Fumigators are applicators who control pests using poisonous gases called fumigants. Fumigators pretreat infested buildings by examining, measuring, and sealing the buildings. Then, using cylinders, hoses, and valves, they fill structures with the proper amount and concentration of fumigant. They also monitor the premises during treatment for leaking gas. To prevent accidental fumigant exposure, fumigators padlock doors and post warning signs.

Pest control supervisors, also known as *operators*, direct service technicians and certified applicators. Supervisors are licensed to apply pesticides, but they usually are more involved in running the business. Supervisors are responsible for ensuring that employees obey rules regarding pesticide use, and they must resolve any problems that arise with regulatory officials or customers. Most States require each pest control establishment to have a supervisor. Self-employed business owners usually are supervisors.

Work environment. Pest control workers travel to visit clients. Pest control workers must kneel, bend, reach, and crawl to inspect, modify, and treat structures. They work both indoors and out, in all weather conditions. During warm weather, applicators may be uncomfortable wearing the heavy protective gear; such as respirators, gloves, and goggles that are required for working with pesticides.

There are health risks associated with pesticide use. Various pest control chemicals are toxic and could be harmful if not used properly. Health risks are minimized, however, by the extensive training required for certification and the use of recommended protective equipment, resulting in fewer reported cases of lost work.

About 47 percent of all pest control workers work a 40-hour week, but 26 percent work more hours. Pest control workers often work evenings and weekends, but many work consistent shifts.

Training, Other Qualifications, and Advancement

Both Federal and State laws require pest control workers to be certified. Although a high school diploma is generally the minimum educational requirement, about 4 in 10 pest control workers have either attended college or earned a degree. Most pest control workers begin their careers as apprentice technicians.

Education and training. A high school diploma or equivalent is the minimum qualification for most pest control jobs. Pest control workers must have the basic knowledge needed to pass certification tests. In many States, training usually involves spending 10 hours in the classroom and 60 hours on the job for each category of work that the pest control worker would like to perform. Categories may include general pest control, rodent control, termite control, fumigation, and ornamental and turf control. In addition, technicians must attend general training in pesticide safety and use. After completing the required training, workers can provide supervised pest control services.

Pest control workers usually begin their careers as apprentice technicians. They receive both formal classroom and on-the-job training provided by the employer, but they also must study on their own. Because pest control methods change, workers must attend continuing education classes to maintain their certification, often provided by product manufacturers

Licensure and certification. Both Federal and State laws regulate pest control workers. These laws require them to be certified through training and examination. Most pest control firms provide training and help their employees prepare for the examination. Requirements for pest control workers vary by State. To be eligible to become applicators, technicians must have a combination of experience and education and pass a test. This requirement is sometimes waived for individuals who

have either a college degree in biological sciences or extensive related work experience. To become certified as applicators, technicians must pass an additional set of category exams. Depending on the State, applicators must attend additional classes every 1 to 6 years to be recertified. The amount of time allowed to pass the basic certification depends on the State.

Other qualifications. Because of the extensive interaction that pest control workers have with their customers, employers prefer to hire people who have good communication and interpersonal skills. In addition, most pest control companies require their employees to have a good driving record. Some states require a background check for workers prior to certification. Pest control workers must be in good health because of the physical demands of the job, and they also must be able to withstand extreme conditions—such as the heat of climbing into an attic in the summertime or the chill of sliding into a crawlspace during winter.

Advancement. Applicators with several years of experience often become supervisors. To qualify as a pest control supervisor, applicators may have to pass State-administered exams and have relevant experience, usually a minimum of 2 years. Others may choose to take the knowledge and experience that they have gained, and start their own pest management company.

Employment

Pest control workers held about 70,000 jobs in 2006; about 85 percent of workers were employed in the services to buildings and dwellings industry, which includes pest control firms. About 9 percent of workers were self employed. Jobs are concentrated in States with warmer climates and larger cities, due to the greater number of pests in these areas that thrive year round.

Job Outlook

With faster-than-average growth and a limited supply of workers, job prospects should be favorable, especially in warmer climates.

Employment change. Employment of pest control workers is expected to grow 15 percent between 2006 and 2016, which is faster than the average for all occupations. One factor limiting job growth, however, is the lack of sufficient numbers of workers willing to go into this field. Demand for pest control workers is projected to increase for a number of reasons. Growth in the population will generate new residential and commercial buildings that will require inspections by pest control workers. Also, more people are expected to use pest control services as environmental and health concerns, greater numbers of dual-income households, and improvements in the standard of living convince more people to hire professionals rather than attempt pest control work themselves. In addition, tougher regulations

Projections data from the National Employment Matrix

Occupational Title	SOC Code	Employment, 2006	Projected employment, 2016	Change, 2006-16	
				Number	Percent
Pest control workers..	37-2021	70,000	81,000	11,000	15

NOTE: Data in this table are rounded. See the discussion of the employment projections table in the *Handbook* introductory chapter on *Occupational Information Included in the Handbook.*

limiting pesticide use will demand more complex integrated pest management strategies.

Concerns about the effects of pesticide use in schools have increasingly prompted more school districts to investigate alternative means of pest control, such as integrated pest management. Furthermore, use of some newer materials for insulation around foundations has made many homes more susceptible to pest infestation. Finally, continuing population shifts to the more pest-prone Sunbelt States should increase the number of households in need of pest control.

Job prospects. Job prospects should be favorable for qualified applicants because of relatively fast job growth and because the nature of pest control work is not appealing to many people. In addition to job openings arising from employment growth, opportunities will result from the need to replace workers who leave the occupation.

Earnings

Median hourly earnings of full-time wage and salary pest control workers were $13.41 in May 2006. The middle 50 percent earned between $10.79 and $16.76. The lowest 10 percent earned less than $8.88, and the top 10 percent earned over $20.85. Pest control supervisors usually earn the most and technicians the least, with earnings of certified applicators falling somewhere in between. Some pest control workers earn commissions based on the number of contracts for pest control

services they sell. Others may earn bonuses for exceeding performance goals.

Related Occupations

Pest control workers visit homes and places of business to provide building services. Other workers who provide services to buildings include building cleaning workers; grounds maintenance workers; various construction trades workers, such as carpenters and hazardous materials removal workers; and heating, air-conditioning, and refrigeration mechanics and installers. Similar to pest control workers, pesticide handlers, sprayers, and applicators, vegetation also apply pesticides in a safe manner to lawns, trees, and other plants.

Sources of Additional Information

Private employment agencies and State employment services offices have information about available job opportunities for pest control workers.

For information about the training and certification required in your State, contact your local office of the U.S. Department of Agriculture or your State's Environmental Protection (or Conservation) Agency.

For more information about pest control careers and training, contact:

➤ National Pest Management Association, Suite 301, 9300 Lee Hgwy., Fairfax, VA 22031.
Internet: **http://www.npmapestworld.org/PTPP/**

Personal Care and Service Occupations

Animal Care and Service Workers

(O*NET 39-2011.00, 39-2021.00)

Significant Points

- Animal lovers get satisfaction in this occupation, but the work can be unpleasant, physically and emotionally demanding, and sometimes dangerous.

- Most workers are trained on the job, but employers generally prefer to hire people who have experience with animals; some jobs require a bachelor's degree in biology, animal science, or a related field.

- Most positions will present good employment opportunities; however, keen competition is expected for jobs as zookeepers and marine mammal trainers.

- Earnings are relatively low.

Nature of the Work

Many people like animals. But, as pet owners can attest, taking care of them is hard work. Animal care and service workers—who include animal caretakers and animal trainers—train, feed, water, groom, bathe, and exercise animals and clean, disinfect, and repair their cages. They also play with the animals, provide

companionship, and observe behavioral changes that could indicate illness or injury. Boarding kennels, pet stores, animal shelters, veterinary hospitals and clinics, stables, laboratories, aquariums and natural aquatic habitats, and zoological parks all house animals and employ animal care and service workers. Job titles and duties vary by employment setting.

Kennel attendants care for pets while their owners are working or traveling out of town. Beginning attendants perform basic tasks, such as cleaning cages and dog runs, filling food and water dishes, and exercising animals. Experienced attendants may provide basic animal healthcare, as well as bathe animals, trim nails, and attend to other grooming needs. Attendants who work in kennels also may sell pet food and supplies, assist in obedience training, help with breeding, or prepare animals for shipping.

Groomers are animal caretakers who specialize in grooming or maintaining a pet's appearance. Most groom dogs and a few groom cats. Some groomers work in kennels, veterinary clinics, animal shelters, or pet-supply stores. Others operate their own grooming business, typically at a salon, or increasingly, by making house calls. Such mobile services are growing rapidly as they offer convenience for pet owners, flexibility of schedules for groomers, and minimal trauma for pets resulting from their being in unfamiliar surroundings. Groomers clean and sanitize equipment to prevent the spread of disease, maintain grooming equipment, and maintain a clean and safe environment for the animals. Groomers also schedule appointments, discuss pets' grooming needs with clients, and collect information on the pet's disposition and its veterinarian. Groomers often are the first to notice a medical problem, such as an ear or skin infection that requires veterinary care.

Grooming the pet involves several steps: an initial brush-out is followed by a first clipping of hair or fur using electric clippers, combs, and grooming shears; the groomer then cuts the nails, cleans the ears, bathes, and blow-dries the animal, and ends with a final clipping and styling.

Animal caretakers in animal shelters perform a variety of duties and work with a wide variety of animals. In addition to attending to the basic needs of the animals, caretakers at shelters also must keep records of the animals received and discharged and any tests or treatments done. Some vaccinate newly admitted animals under the direction of a veterinarian or veterinary technician, and euthanize (painlessly put to death) seriously ill, severely injured, or unwanted animals. Animal caretakers in animal shelters also interact with the public, answering telephone inquiries, screening applicants for animal adoption, or educating visitors on neutering and other animal health issues.

Grooms, or caretakers, care for horses in stables. They saddle and unsaddle horses, give them rubdowns, and walk them to cool them off after a ride. They also feed, groom, and exercise the horses; clean out stalls and replenish bedding; polish saddles; clean and organize the tack (harness, saddle, and bridle) room; and store supplies and feed. Experienced grooms may help train horses.

In zoos, animal care and service workers, called *keepers*, prepare the diets and clean the enclosures of animals, and sometimes assist in raising them when they are very young. They watch for any signs of illness or injury, monitor eating patterns or any changes in behavior, and record their observations. Keepers also may answer questions and ensure that the visiting public behaves responsibly toward the exhibited animals. Depending on the zoo, keepers may be assigned to work with a broad group of animals such as mammals, birds, or reptiles, or they may work with a limited collection of animals such as primates, large cats, or small mammals.

Animal trainers train animals for riding, security, performance, obedience, or assisting people with disabilities. Animal trainers do this by accustoming the animal to human voice and contact and conditioning the animal to respond to commands. The three most commonly trained animals are dogs, horses, and marine mammals, including dolphins. Trainers use several techniques to help them train animals. One technique, known as a bridge, is a stimulus that a trainer uses to communicate the precise moment an animal does something correctly. When the animal responds correctly, the trainer gives positive reinforcement in a variety of ways: food, toys, play, rubdowns, or speaking the word "good." Animal training takes place in small steps and often takes months and even years of repetition. During the conditioning process, trainers provide animals with mental stimulation, physical exercise, and husbandry care. A relatively new form of training teaches animals to cooperate with workers giving medical care. Ani-

Most pet groomers work in kennels, veterinary clinics, or pet supply stores, but an increasing number operate their own salon or make house calls.

mals learn "veterinary" behaviors, such as allowing and even cooperating with the collection of blood samples; physical, x-ray, ultrasonic, and dental exams; physical therapy; and the administration of medicines and replacement fluids.

Training also can be a good tool for facilitating the relocation of animals from one habitat to another, easing, for example, the process of loading horses on trailers. Trainers often work in competitions or shows, such as circuses or marine parks, aquariums, animal shelters, dog kennels and salons, or horse farms. Trainers in shows work to display the talent and ability of an animal, such as a dolphin, through interactive programs to educate and entertain the public.

In addition to their hands-on work with the animals, trainers often oversee other aspects of animals' care, such as preparing their diet and providing a safe and clean environment and habitat.

Work environment. People who love animals get satisfaction from working with and helping them. However, some of the work may be unpleasant, physically and emotionally demanding, and sometimes dangerous. Most animal caretakers and service workers have to clean animal cages and lift, hold, or restrain animals, risking exposure to bites or scratches. Their work often involves kneeling, crawling, repeated bending, and lifting heavy supplies like bales of hay or bags of feed. Animal caretakers must take precautions when treating animals with germicides or insecticides. They may work outdoors in all kinds of weather, and the work setting can be noisy. Caretakers of show and sports animals travel to competitions.

Animal caretaker and service workers who witness abused animals or who assist in euthanizing unwanted, aged, or hopelessly injured animals may experience emotional distress. Those working for private humane societies and municipal animal shelters often deal with the public, some of whom might react with hostility to the implication that they are neglecting or abusing their pets. Such workers must maintain a calm and professional demeanor while helping to enforce the laws regarding animal care.

Animal care and service workers often work irregular hours. Most animals are fed every day, so caretakers often work weekend and holiday shifts. Some zoo animals skip one meal a week to mimic their lives in the wild. In some animal hospitals, research facilities, and animal shelters, an attendant is on duty 24 hours a day, which means night shifts.

Training, Other Qualifications, and Advancement

On-the-job training is the most common way animal caretakers and service workers learn their work; however, employers generally prefer to hire people who have experience with animals. Some preparatory programs are available for specific types of caretakers, such as groomers.

Education and training. Animal trainers often need a high school diploma or GED equivalent. Some animal training jobs may require a bachelor's degree and additional skills. For example, marine mammal trainers usually need a bachelor's degree in biology, marine biology, animal science, psychology, or a related field. An animal health technician degree also may qualify trainers for some jobs.

Most equine trainers learn their trade by working as a groom at a stable. Some study at an accredited private training school. Because large animals are involved, most horse-training jobs have minimum weight requirements for candidates.

Many dog trainers attend workshops and courses at community colleges and vocational schools. Topics include basic study of canines, learning theory of animals, teaching obedience cues, problem solving methods, and safety. Many also offer business training.

Many zoos require their caretakers to have a bachelor's degree in biology, animal science, or a related field. Most require experience with animals, preferably as a volunteer or paid keeper in a zoo.

Most pet groomers learn their trade by completing an informal apprenticeship, usually lasting 6 to 10 weeks, under the guidance of an experienced groomer. Prospective groomers also may attend one of the 52 State-licensed grooming schools throughout the country, with programs varying in length from 2 to 18 weeks. Beginning groomers often start by taking on one duty, such as bathing and drying the pet. They eventually assume responsibility for the entire grooming process, from the initial brush-out to the final clipping.

Animal caretakers in animal shelters are not required to have any specialized training, but training programs and workshops are available through the Humane Society of the United States, the American Humane Association, and the National Animal Control Association. Workshop topics include cruelty investigations, appropriate methods of euthanasia for shelter animals, proper guidelines for capturing animals, techniques for preventing problems with wildlife, and dealing with the public.

Beginning animal caretakers in kennels learn on the job and usually start by cleaning cages and feeding and watering animals.

Certification and other qualifications. Certifications are available in many animal service occupations. For dog trainers, certification by a professional association or one of the hundreds of private vocational or State-approved trade schools can be advantageous. The National Dog Groomers Association of America offers certification for master status as a groomer. The American Boarding Kennels Association offers a three-stage, home-study program for individuals interested in pet care. Those who complete the third stage and pass oral and written examinations become Certified Kennel Operators (CKO).

All animal caretakers and service workers need patience, sensitivity, and problem solving ability. They also need tact and communication skills. This is particularly true for those in shelters, who often deal with individuals who abandon their pets. The ability to handle emotional people is vital for workers at shelters.

Animal trainers especially need problem-solving skills and experience in animal obedience. Successful marine mammal trainers should also have good public speaking skills as seminars and presentations are a large part of the job. Usually 4 to 5 trainers work with a group of animals at one time, therefore, each trainer should be able to work as part of a team. Marine mammal trainers must also be good swimmers; certification in SCUBA is a plus.

Advancement. With experience and additional training, caretakers in animal shelters may become adoption coordinators, animal control officers, emergency rescue drivers, assistant shelter managers, or shelter directors. Pet groomers who work in large retail establishments or kennels may, with experience, move into supervisory or managerial positions. Experienced groomers often choose to open their own salons. Advancement for kennel caretakers takes the form of promotion to kennel supervisor, assistant manager, and manager; those with enough capital and experience may open up their own

Projections data from the National Employment Matrix

Occupational Title	SOC Code	Employment, 2006	Projected employment, 2016	Change, 2006-16	
				Number	Percent
Animal care and service workers	39-2000	200,000	238,000	39,000	19
Animal trainers..	39-2011	43,000	53,000	9,800	23
Nonfarm animal caretakers	39-2021	157,000	185,000	29,000	18

NOTE: Data in this table are rounded. See the discussion of the employment projections table in the *Handbook* introductory chapter on *Occupational Information Included in the Handbook.*

kennels. Zookeepers may advance to senior keeper, assistant head keeper, head keeper, and assistant curator, but very few openings occur, especially for the higher-level positions.

Employment

Animal caretakers and service workers held 200,000 jobs in 2006. Over 3 out of 4 worked as nonfarm animal caretakers; the remainder worked as animal trainers. Nonfarm animal caretakers often worked in boarding kennels, animal shelters, stables, grooming shops, pet stores, animal hospitals, and veterinary offices. A significant number of caretakers worked for animal humane societies, racing stables, dog and horse racetrack operators, zoos, theme parks, circuses, and other amusement and recreations services.

Employment of animal trainers is concentrated in animal services that specialize in training and in commercial sports, where they train racehorses and dogs. About 57 percent of animal trainers were self-employed.

Job Outlook

Because many workers leave this occupation each year, there will be good job opportunities for most positions. Faster-than-average employment growth also will add to job openings, in addition to replacement needs.

Employment change. Employment of animal care and service workers is expected to grow 19 percent over the 2006-16 decade, faster than the average for all occupations. The companion pet population, which drives employment of animal caretakers in kennels, grooming shops, animal shelters, and veterinary clinics and hospitals, is expected to increase. Pet owners—including a large number of baby boomers, whose disposable income is expected to increase as they age—are expected to increasingly purchase grooming services, daily and overnight boarding services, training services, and veterinary services, resulting in more jobs for animal care and service workers. As more pet owners consider their pets part of the family, demand for luxury animal services and the willingness to spend greater amounts of money on pets should continue to grow. Demand for marine mammal trainers, on the other hand, should grow slowly.

Demand for animal care and service workers in animal shelters is expected to grow as communities increasingly recognize the connection between animal abuse and abuse toward humans, and continue to commit private funds to animal shelters, many of which are working hand-in-hand with social service agencies and law enforcement teams.

Job prospects. Due to employment growth and the need to replace workers who leave the occupation, job opportunities for most positions should be good. The need to replace workers leaving the field will create the overwhelming majority of job openings. Many animal caretaker jobs require little or no training and have flexible work schedules, making them suitable for people seeking a first job or for temporary or part-time work. The outlook for caretakers in zoos and aquariums, however, is not favorable due to slow job growth and keen competition for the few positions.

Prospective mammal trainers will face keen competition as the number of applicants greatly exceeds the number of available positions. Prospective horse trainers should anticipate an equally challenging labor market as the number of entry-level positions is limited. Dog trainers, however, should experience conditions that are more favorable. Opportunities for dog trainers should be best in large metropolitan areas.

Job opportunities for animal care and service workers may vary from year to year because the strength of the economy affects demand for these workers. Pet owners tend to spend more on animal services when the economy is strong.

Earnings

Earnings are relatively low. Median hourly earnings of nonfarm animal caretakers were $8.72 in May 2006. The middle 50 percent earned between $7.50 and $10.95. The bottom 10 percent earned less than $6.56, and the top 10 percent earned more than $14.64. Median hourly earnings in the industries employing the largest numbers of nonfarm animal caretakers in May 2006 were:

Spectator sports	$9.38
Other personal services	8.78
Social advocacy organizations	8.31
Other professional, scientific, and technical services	8.23
Veterinary services	8.23
Other miscellaneous store retailers	8.22

Median hourly earnings of animal trainers were $12.65 in May 2006. The middle 50 percent earned between $9.11 and $17.39. The lowest 10 percent earned less than $7.66, and the top 10 percent earned more than $22.42.

Related Occupations

Others who work extensively with animals include farmers, ranchers, and agricultural managers; agricultural workers; veterinarians; veterinary technologists and technicians; veterinary assistants; and biological scientists.

Sources of Additional Information

For career information and information on training, certification, and earnings of the related occupation of animal control officers, contact:

➤ National Animal Control Association, P.O. Box 1480851, Kansas City, MO 64148-0851.
Internet: **http://www.nacanet.org**

For information on becoming an advanced pet care technician at a kennel, contact:

➤ American Boarding Kennels Association, 1702 East Pikes Peak Ave., Colorado Springs, CO 80909.
Internet: **http://www.abka.com/abka**

For general information on pet grooming careers, including certification information, contact:

➤ National Dog Groomers Association of America, P.O. Box 101, Clark, PA 16113.
Internet: **http://www.nationaldoggroomers.com**

Barbers, Cosmetologists, and Other Personal Appearance Workers

(O*NET 39-5011.00, 39-5012.00, 39-5091.00, 39-5092.00, 39-5093.00,39-5094.00)

Significant Points

- A State license is required for barbers, cosmetologists, and most other personal appearance workers, although qualifications vary by State.

- About 46 percent of workers are self employed; many also work flexible schedules.

Nature of the Work

Barbers and cosmetologists focus on providing hair care services to enhance the appearance of consumers. Other personal appearance workers, such as manicurists and pedicurists, shampooers, theatrical and performance makeup artists, and skin care specialists provide specialized beauty services that help clients look and feel their best.

Barbers cut, trim, shampoo, and style hair mostly for male clients. They also may fit hairpieces and offer scalp treatments and facial shaving. In many States, barbers are licensed to color, bleach, or highlight hair and to offer permanent-wave services. Barbers also may provide skin care and nail treatments.

Hairdressers, hairstylists, and *cosmetologists* offer a wide range of beauty services, such as shampooing, cutting, coloring, and styling of hair. They may advise clients on how to care for their hair at home. In addition, cosmetologists may be trained to give manicures, pedicures, and scalp and facial treatments; provide makeup analysis; and clean and style wigs and hairpieces.

A number of workers offer specialized services. *Manicurists* and *pedicurists*, called *nail technicians* in some States, work exclusively on nails and provide manicures, pedicures, polishing, and nail extensions to clients. Another group of specialists is *skin care specialists*, or *estheticians*, who cleanse and

Manicurists and pedicurists rank among the fastest growing occupations.

beautify the skin by giving facials, full-body treatments, and head and neck massages as well as apply makeup. They also may remove hair through waxing or, if properly trained, laser treatments. *Theatrical and performance makeup artists*, apply makeup to enhance performing artists' appearance for movie, television, or stage performances. Finally, in larger salons, *shampooers* specialize in shampooing and conditioning hair.

In addition to working with clients, personal appearance workers may keep records of hair color or skin care regimens used by their regular clients. A growing number actively sell hair, skin, and nail care products. Barbers, cosmetologists, and other personal appearance workers who operate their own salons have managerial duties that may include hiring, supervising, and firing workers, as well as keeping business and inventory records, ordering supplies, and arranging for advertising.

Work environment. Most full-time barbers, cosmetologists, and other personal appearance workers put in a 40-hour week, but longer hours are common, especially among self-employed workers. Work schedules may include evenings and weekends, the times when beauty salons and barbershops are busiest. In 2006, about 31 percent of cosmetologists and 19 percent of barbers worked part time, and 16 percent of cosmetologists and 11 percent of barbers had variable schedules.

Barbers, cosmetologists, and other personal appearance workers usually work in clean, pleasant surroundings with good lighting and ventilation. Good health and stamina are important, because these workers are on their feet for most of their shift. Prolonged exposure to some hair and nail chemicals may cause irritation, so protective clothing, such as plastic gloves or aprons, may be worn.

Training, Other Qualifications, and Advancement

All States require barbers, cosmetologists, and other personal appearance workers to be licensed, with the exceptions of shampooers and makeup artists. To qualify for a license, most job seekers are required to graduate from a State-licensed barber or cosmetology school.

Education and training. A high school diploma or GED is required for some personal appearance workers in some States. In addition, most States require that barbers and cosmetologists complete a program in a State-licensed barber or cosmetology school. Programs in hairstyling, skin care, and other personal appearance services can be found in both high schools and in public or private postsecondary vocational schools.

Full-time programs in barbering and cosmetology usually last 9 months and may lead to an associate degree, but training for manicurists and pedicurists and skin care specialists requires significantly less time. Makeup artists can attend schools that specialize in this subject, but it is not required. Shampooers generally do not need formal training. Most professionals take advanced courses in hairstyling or other personal appearance services to keep up with the latest trends. They also may take courses in sales and marketing.

During their first weeks on the job, new workers may be given relatively simple tasks. Once they have demonstrated their skills, they are gradually permitted to perform more complicated procedures, such as coloring hair. As they continue to work in the field, more training usually is required to help workers

Projections data from the National Employment Matrix

Occupational Title	SOC Code	Employment, 2006	Projected employment, 2016	Change, 2006-16	
				Number	Percent
Personal appearance workers..	39-5000	825,000	942,000	117,000	14
Barbers and cosmetologists...	39-5010	677,000	755,000	77,000	11
Barbers...	39-5011	60,000	61,000	600	1
Hairdressers, hairstylists, and cosmetologists..........................	39-5012	617,000	694,000	77,000	12
Miscellaneous personal appearance workers	39-5090	148,000	187,000	39,000	27
Makeup artists, theatrical and performance	39-5091	2,100	3,000	900	40
Manicurists and pedicurists..	39-5092	78,000	100,000	22,000	28
Shampooers...	39-5093	29,000	33,000	3,900	13
Skin care specialists	39-5094	38,000	51,000	13,000	34

NOTE: Data in this table are rounded. See the discussion of the employment projections table in the *Handbook* introductory chapter on *Occupational Information Included in the Handbook*.

learn the techniques particular to each salon and to build on the basics learned in cosmetology school. Personal appearance workers attend training at salons, cosmetology schools, or industry trade shows throughout their careers.

Licensure. All States require barbers, cosmetologists, and other personal appearance workers to be licensed, with the exceptions of shampooers and makeup artists. Qualifications for a license vary by State, but generally a person must have a high school diploma or GED, be at least 16 years old, and have graduated from a State-licensed barber or cosmetology school. After graduating from a State approved training program, students take a State licensing examination. The exam consists of a written test and, in some cases, a practical test of styling skills or an oral examination. In many States, cosmetology training may be credited toward a barbering license, and vice versa, and a few States combine the two licenses. Most States require separate licensing examinations for manicurists, pedicurists, and skin care specialists.

Some States have reciprocity agreements that allow licensed barbers and cosmetologists to obtain a license in a different State without additional formal training, but such agreements are uncommon. Consequently, persons who wish to work in a particular State should review the laws of that State before entering a training program.

Other qualifications. Successful personal appearance workers should have an understanding of fashion, art, and technical design. They also must keep a neat personal appearance and a clean work area. Interpersonal skills, image, and attitude play an important role in career success. As client retention and retail sales become an increasingly important part of salons' revenue, the ability to be an effective salesperson becomes ever more vital for salon workers. Some cosmetology schools consider "people skills" to be such an integral part of the job that they require coursework in that area. Business skills are important for those who plan to operate their own salons.

Advancement. Advancement usually takes the form of higher earnings as barbers and cosmetologists gain experience and build a steady clientele. Some barbers and cosmetologists manage salons, lease booth space in salons, or open their own salons after several years of experience. Others teach in barber or cosmetology schools or provide training through vocational schools. Still others advance to become sales representatives,

image or fashion consultants, or examiners for State licensing boards.

Employment

Barbers, cosmetologists, and other personal appearance workers held about 825,000 jobs in 2006. Of these, barbers and cosmetologists held 677,000 jobs, manicurists and pedicurists 78,000, skin care specialists 38,000, and shampooers 29,000. Theatrical and performance makeup artists held 2,100 jobs.

Most of these workers are employed in beauty salons or barber shops, but they also are found in nail salons, day and resort spas, and nursing and other residential care homes. Nearly every town has a barbershop or beauty salon, but employment in this occupation is concentrated in the most populous cities and States. Theatrical and performance makeup artists work for movie and television studios, performing arts companies, and event promoters. Some apply makeup in retail stores.

About 46 percent of all barbers, cosmetologists, and other personal appearance workers are self-employed. Many of these workers own their own salon, but a growing number of the self-employed lease booth space or a chair from the salon's owner.

Job Outlook

Overall employment of barbers, cosmetologists, and other personal appearance workers is projected to grow slightly faster than the average for all occupations. Opportunities for entry level workers should be favorable, while job candidates at high-end establishments will face keen competition.

Employment change. Personal appearance workers will grow by 14 percent from 2006 to 2016, which is faster than the average for all occupations. This growth primarily will be a result of an increasing population and from the growing demand for personal appearance services, particularly skin care services.

Employment trends are expected to vary among the different occupational specialties. Employment of hairdressers, hairstylists, and cosmetologists should increase by 12 percent because many now cut and style both men's and women's hair and because the demand for hair treatment by teens and aging baby boomers is expected to remain steady or even grow. As a result, fewer people are expected to go to barber shops and employment of barbers is expected to see relatively little change in employment.

Continued growth in the number of nail salons and full-service day spas will generate numerous job openings for manicurists, pedicurists, and skin care specialists. Employment of manicurists and pedicurists will grow by 28 percent, while employment of shampooers will increase by 13 percent. Estheticians and other skin care specialists will see large gains in employment, and are expected to grow 34 percent as more facial procedures to improve one's complexion become available and become more popular in spas and some medical settings. Makeup artists are expected to grow by 40 percent, but because of its relatively small size, the occupation will only add a few hundred jobs over the decade.

Job prospects. Job opportunities generally should be good. However, competition is expected for jobs and clients at higher paying salons as applicants compete with a large pool of licensed and experienced cosmetologists for these positions. More numerous than those arising from job growth, an abundance of job openings will come about from the need to replace workers who transfer to other occupations, retire, or leave the labor force for other reasons. Opportunities will be best for those with previous experience and for those licensed to provide a broad range of services.

Earnings

Median hourly earnings in May 2006 for salaried hairdressers, hairstylists, and cosmetologists, including tips and commission, were $10.25. The middle 50 percent earned between $7.92 and $13.75. The lowest 10 percent earned less than $6.68, and the highest 10 percent earned more than $18.78.

Median hourly earnings in May 2006 for salaried barbers, including tips, were $11.13. The middle 50 percent earned between $8.71 and $14.25. The lowest 10 percent earned less than $7.12, and the highest 10 percent earned more than $20.56.

Among skin care specialists, median hourly earnings, including tips, were $12.58, for manicurists and pedicurists $9.23, and for shampooers $7.78.

While earnings for entry-level workers usually are low, earnings can be considerably higher for those with experience. A number of factors, such as the size and location of the salon, determine the total income of personal appearance workers. They may receive commissions based on the price of the service, or a salary based on the number of hours worked, and many receive commissions on the products they sell. In addition, some salons pay bonuses to employees who bring in new business. For many personal appearance workers the ability to attract and hold regular clients are key factors in determining earnings.

Although some salons offer paid vacations and medical benefits, many self-employed and part-time workers in this occupation do not enjoy such benefits. Some personal appearance workers receive free trail products from manufacturers in the hope that they will recommend the products to clients.

Related Occupations

Other workers who provide a personal service to clients and are usually professionally licensed or certified include massage therapists and fitness workers.

Sources of Additional Information

For details on State licensing requirements and approved barber or cosmetology schools, contact your State boards of barber or cosmetology examiners.

State licensing board requirements and a list of licensed training schools for cosmetologists may be obtained from:
➤ National Accrediting Commission of Cosmetology Arts and Sciences, 4401 Ford Ave., Suite 1300, Alexandria, VA 22302. Internet: **http://www.naccas.org**

Information about a career in cosmetology is available from:
➤ National Cosmetology Association, 401 N. Michigan Ave., 22nd floor, Chicago, IL 60611.
Internet: **http://www.ncacares.org**

For information on a career as a barber, contact:
➤ National Association of Barber Boards of America, 2703 Pine Street, Arkadelphia, AR 71923.
Internet: **http://www.nationalbarberboards.com**

An additional list of private schools for several different types of personal appearance workers is available from:
➤ Beauty Schools Directory.
Internet: **http://www.beautyschoolsdirectory.com**

Child Care Workers

(O*NET 39-9011.00)

Significant Points

- About 35 percent of child care workers are self-employed, most of whom provided child care in their homes.

- Training requirements range from a high school diploma to a college degree, although a high school diploma and a little experience are adequate for many jobs.

- Many workers leave these jobs every year, creating good job opportunities.

Nature of the Work

Child care workers nurture and care for children who have not yet entered formal schooling. They also supervise older children before and after school. These workers play an important role in children's development by caring for them when parents are at work or away for other reasons. In addition to attending to children's basic needs, child care workers organize activities and implement curricula that stimulate children's physical, emotional, intellectual, and social growth. They help children explore individual interests, develop talents and independence, build self-esteem, and learn how to get along with others.

Child care workers generally are classified into three different groups based on where they work: private household workers, who care for children at the children's home; family child care providers, who care for children in the provider's own home; and child care workers who work at separate child care centers.

Private household workers who are employed on an hourly basis usually are called *babysitters*. These child care workers bathe, dress, and feed children; supervise their play; wash their clothes; and clean their rooms. Babysitters also may put children to bed and wake them, read to them, involve them in educational games, take them for doctors' visits, and discipline them. Those who are in charge of infants, sometimes called *infant nurses*, also prepare bottles and change diapers. *Nannies* work for a single family. They generally take care of children from birth to age 12, tending to the child's early education, nutrition, health, and other needs. They also may perform the duties of a housekeeper, including cleaning and laundry.

Family child care providers often work alone with a small group of children, though some work in larger settings with multiple adults. Child care centers generally have more than one adult per group of children; in groups of older children, a child care worker may assist a more experienced preschool teacher.

Most child care workers perform a combination of basic care and teaching duties, but the majority of their time is spent on care giving activities. Workers whose primary responsibility is teaching are classified as preschool teachers. (Teachers—preschool, kindergarten, elementary, middle, and secondary are covered elsewhere in the *Handbook*.) However, many basic care activities also are opportunities for children to learn. For example, a worker who shows a child how to tie a shoelace teaches the child while also providing for that child's basic needs.

Child care workers spend most of their day working with children. However, they do maintain contact with parents or guardians through informal meetings or scheduled conferences to discuss each child's progress and needs. Many child care workers keep records of each child's progress and suggest ways in which parents can stimulate their child's learning and development at home. Some child care centers and before- and after-school programs actively recruit parent volunteers to work with the children and participate in administrative decisions and program planning.

Young children learn mainly through play. Child care workers recognize this and capitalize on children's play to further language development (storytelling and acting games), improve social skills (working together to build a neighborhood in a sandbox), and introduce scientific and mathematical concepts (balancing and counting blocks when building a bridge or mixing colors when painting). Often a less structured approach is used

Child care workers nurture and care for young children.

to teach young children, including small-group lessons; one-on-one instruction; and creative activities such as art, dance, and music. Child care workers play a vital role in preparing children to build the skills they will need in school.

Child care workers in child care centers or family child care homes greet young children as they arrive, help them with their jackets, and select an activity of interest. When caring for infants, they feed and change them. To ensure a well-balanced program, child care workers prepare daily and long-term schedules of activities. Each day's activities balance individual and group play, as well as quiet and active time. Children are given some freedom to participate in activities in which they are interested. As children age, child care workers may provide more guided learning opportunities, particularly in the areas of math and reading.

Concern over school-aged children being home alone before and after school has spurred many parents to seek alternative ways for their children to constructively spend their time. The purpose of before- and after-school programs is to watch over school-aged children during the gap between school hours and the end of their parents' daily work hours. These programs also may operate during the summer and on weekends. Workers in before- and after-school programs may help students with their homework or engage them in other extracurricular activities. These activities may include field trips, sports, or learning about computers, painting, photography, or other fun subjects. Some child care workers are responsible for taking children to school in the morning and picking them up from school in the afternoon. Before- and after-school programs may be operated by public school systems, local community centers, or other private organizations.

Helping to keep children healthy is another important part of the job. Child care workers serve nutritious meals and snacks and teach good eating habits and personal hygiene. They ensure that children have proper rest periods. They identify children who may not feel well and, in some cases, may help parents locate programs that will provide basic health services. Child care workers also watch for children who show signs of emotional or developmental problems and discuss these matters with their supervisor and the child's parents. Early identification of children with special needs—such as those with behavioral, emotional, physical, or learning disabilities—is important to improve their future learning ability. Special education teachers often work with preschool children to provide the individual attention they need. (Special education teachers are discussed elsewhere in the *Handbook*.)

Work environment. Helping children grow, learn, and gain new skills can be very rewarding. The work is sometimes routine but new activities and challenges mark each day. Child care can be physically and emotionally taxing, as workers constantly stand, walk, bend, stoop, and lift to attend to each child's interests and problems.

States regulate child care facilities, the number of children per child care worker, staff qualifications, and the health and safety of the children. State regulations in all of these areas vary. To ensure that children in child care centers receive proper supervision, State or local regulations may require a certain ratio of workers to children. The ratio varies with the age of the children. Child development experts generally recommend that a single caregiver be responsible for no more than 3 or 4 infants (less than 1 year old) and toddler's (1 to 2 years old) or 6 or 7 preschool-aged children (between 2 and 5 years old). In before- and after-school programs, workers may be responsible for many school-aged children at a time.

Family child care providers work out of their own homes. While this arrangement provides convenience, it also requires that their homes be accommodating to young children. Private household workers usually work in the homes or apartments of their employers. Most live in their own homes and travel to work, though some live in the home of their employer and generally are provided with their own room and bath. They often come to feel like part of their employer's family.

The work hours of child care workers vary widely. Child care centers usually are open year round, with long hours so that parents can drop off and pick up their children before and after work. Some centers employ full-time and part-time staff with staggered shifts to cover the entire day. Some workers are unable to take regular breaks during the day due to limited staffing. Public and many private preschool programs operate during the typical 9- or 10-month school year, employing both full-time and part-time workers. Family child care providers have flexible hours and daily routines, but they may work long or unusual hours to fit parents' work schedules. Live-in nannies usually work longer hours than do those who have their own homes. However, although nannies may work evenings or weekends, they usually get other time off.

Training, Other Qualifications, and Advancement

Licensure and training requirements vary greatly by State, but many jobs require little more than a high school diploma.

Education and training. The training and qualifications required of child care workers vary widely. Each State has its own licensing requirements that regulate caregiver training. These requirements range from a high school diploma, a national Child Development Associate (CDA) credential to community college courses or a college degree in child development or early childhood education. State requirements are generally higher for workers at child care centers than for family child care providers. Child care workers in private settings who care for only a few children often are not regulated by States at all. Child care workers generally can obtain some form of employment with a high school diploma and little or no experience, but certain private firms and publicly funded programs have more demanding training and education requirements. Some employers may prefer workers who have taken secondary or postsecondary courses in child development and early childhood education or who have work experience in a child care setting. Other employers require their own specialized training. An increasing number of employers require an associate degree in early childhood education.

Licensure. Many States require child care centers, including those in private homes, to be licensed if they care for more than a few children. In order to obtain their license, child care centers may require child care workers to pass a background check and get immunizations. Furthermore, child care workers may need to be trained in first aid and CPR and receive continuous training on topics of health and safety.

Other qualifications. Child care workers must anticipate and prevent problems, deal with disruptive children, provide fair but firm discipline, and be enthusiastic and constantly alert. They must communicate effectively with the children and their parents, as well as with teachers and other child care workers. Workers should be mature, patient, understanding, and articulate and have energy and physical stamina. Skills in music, art, drama, and storytelling also are important. Self-employed child care workers must have business sense and management abilities.

Certification and advancement. Some employers prefer to hire child care workers who have earned a nationally recognized Child Development Associate (CDA) credential or the Certified Childcare Professional (CCP) designation from the Council for Professional Recognition and the National Child Care Association, respectively. Requirements include child care experience and coursework, such as college courses or employer-provided seminars.

Opportunities for advancement are limited. However, as child care workers gain experience, some may advance to supervisory or administrative positions in large child care centers or preschools. Often, these positions require additional training, such as a bachelor's or master's degree. Other workers move on to work in resource and referral agencies, consulting with parents on available child services. A few workers become involved in policy or advocacy work related to child care and early childhood education. With a bachelor's degree, workers may become preschool teachers or become certified to teach in public or private schools. Some workers set up their own child care businesses.

Employment

Child care workers held about 1.4 million jobs in 2006. Many worked part time. About 35 percent of child care workers were self-employed; most of these were family child care providers.

Child day care services employed about 18 percent of all child care workers and about 20 percent work for private households. The remainder worked primarily in educational services; nursing and residential care facilities; religious organizations; amusement and recreation industries; civic and social organizations; individual and family services; and local government, excluding education and hospitals. Some child care programs are for-profit centers, which may be affiliated with a local or national company. Religious institutions, community agencies,

Projections data from the National Employment Matrix

Occupational Title	SOC Code	Employment, 2006	Projected employment, 2016	Change, 2006-16	
				Number	Percent
Child care workers	39-9011	1,388,000	1,636,000	248,000	18

NOTE: Data in this table are rounded. See the discussion of the employment projections table in the *Handbook* introductory chapter on *Occupational Information Included in the Handbook.*

school systems, and State and local governments operate non-profit programs. A very small percentage of private industry establishments operate onsite child care centers for the children of their employees.

Job Outlook

Child care workers are expected to experience job growth that is faster than the average for all occupations. Job prospects will be excellent because of the many workers who leave and need to be replaced.

Employment change. Employment of child care workers is projected to increase by 18 percent between 2006 and 2016, which is faster than the average for all occupations. Child care workers will have a very large number of new jobs arise, almost 248,000 over the projections decade. The proportion of children being cared for exclusively by parents or other relatives is likely to continue to decline, spurring demand for additional child care workers. Concern about the safety and supervision of school-aged children during nonschool hours also should increase demand for before- and after-school programs and the child care workers who staff them.

The growth in demand for child care workers will be moderated, however, by an increasing emphasis on early childhood education programs, which hire mostly preschool workers instead of child care workers. While only a few States currently provide targeted or universal preschool programs, many more are considering or starting such programs. A rise in enrollment in private preschools is likely as the value of formal education before kindergarten becomes more widely accepted. Since the majority of workers in these programs are classified as preschool teachers, this growth in preschool enrollment will mean less growth among child care workers.

Job prospects. High replacement needs should create good job opportunities for child care workers. Qualified persons who are interested in this work should have little trouble finding and keeping a job. Many child care workers must be replaced each year as they leave the occupation to fulfill family responsibilities, to study, or for other reasons. Others leave because they are interested in pursuing other occupations or because of low wages.

Earnings

Pay depends on the educational attainment of the worker and the type of establishment. Although the pay generally is very low, more education usually means higher earnings. Median annual earnings of wage-and-salary child care workers were $17,630 in May 2006. The middle 50 percent earned between $14,790 and $21,930. The lowest 10 percent earned less than $12,910, and the highest 10 percent earned more than $27,050. Median annual earnings in the industries employing the largest numbers of child care workers in 2006 were as follows:

Other residential care facilities $20,770
Elementary and secondary schools 20,220
Civic and social organizations 16,460
Child day care services 16,320
Other amusement and recreation industries........................16,300

Earnings of self-employed child care workers vary depending on the number of hours worked, the number and ages of the children, and the location.

Benefits vary but are minimal for most child care workers. Many employers offer free or discounted child care to employees. Some offer a full benefits package, including health insurance and paid vacations, but others offer no benefits at all. Some employers offer seminars and workshops to help workers learn new skills. A few are willing to cover the cost of courses taken at community colleges or technical schools. Live-in nannies receive free room and board.

Related Occupations

Child care work requires patience; creativity; an ability to nurture, motivate, teach, and influence children; and leadership, organizational, and administrative skills. Others who work with children and need these qualities and skills include teacher assistants; teachers—preschool, kindergarten, elementary, middle, and secondary; and teachers—special education.

Sources of Additional Information

For an electronic question-and-answer service on child care, information on becoming a child care provider, and other resources, contact:
➤ National Child Care Information Center, 243 Church St.NW., 2nd floor, Vienna, VA 22180.
Internet: **http://www.nccic.org**

For eligibility requirements and a description of the Child Development Associate credential, contact:
➤ Council for Professional Recognition, 2460 16th St., NW., Washington, DC 20009-3575.
Internet: **http://www.cdacouncil.org**

For eligibility requirements and a description of the Certified Childcare Professional designation, contact:
➤ National Child Care Association, 2025 M St., NW., Suite 800, Washington, DC 20036. Internet: **http://www.nccanet.org**

For information about a career as a nanny, contact:
➤ International Nanny Association, 191 Clarksville Rd., Princeton Junction, NJ 08550-3111. Telephone (tollfree): 888-878-1477. Internet: **http://www.nanny.org**

State departments of human services or social services can supply State regulations and training requirements for child care workers.

Fitness Workers

(O*NET 39-9031.00)

Significant Points

- Many fitness and personal training jobs are part time, but many workers increase their hours by working at several different facilities or at clients' homes.

- Night and weekend hours are common.

- Most fitness workers need to be certified.

- Job prospects are expected to be good.

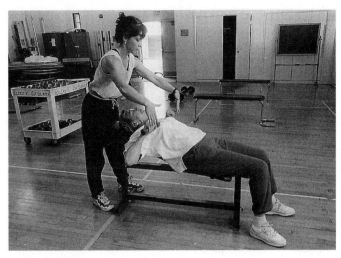

Personal trainers usually must have certification to begin working with clients.

Nature of the Work

Fitness workers lead, instruct, and motivate individuals or groups in exercise activities, including cardiovascular exercise, strength training, and stretching. They work in health clubs, country clubs, hospitals, universities, yoga and Pilates studios, resorts, and clients' homes. Increasingly, fitness workers also are found in workplaces, where they organize and direct health and fitness programs for employees of all ages. Although gyms and health clubs offer a variety of exercise activities such as weightlifting, yoga, cardiovascular training, and karate, fitness workers typically specialize in only a few areas.

Personal trainers work one-on-one with clients either in a gym or in the client's home. They help clients assess their level of physical fitness and set and reach fitness goals. Trainers also demonstrate various exercises and help clients improve their exercise techniques. They may keep records of their clients' exercise sessions to monitor clients' progress toward physical fitness. They may also advise their clients on how to modify their lifestyle outside of the gym to improve their fitness.

Group exercise instructors conduct group exercise sessions that usually include aerobic exercise, stretching, and muscle conditioning. Cardiovascular conditioning classes are often set to music. Instructors choose and mix the music and choreograph a corresponding exercise sequence. Two increasingly popular conditioning methods taught in exercise classes are Pilates and yoga. In these classes, instructors demonstrate the different moves and positions of the particular method; they also observe students and correct those who are doing the exercises improperly. Group exercise instructors are responsible for ensuring that their classes are motivating, safe, and challenging, yet not too difficult for the participants.

Fitness directors oversee the fitness-related aspects of a health club or fitness center. They create and oversee programs that meet the needs of the club's members, including new member orientations, fitness assessments, and workout incentive programs. They also select fitness equipment; coordinate personal training and group exercise programs; hire, train, and supervise fitness staff; and carry out administrative duties.

Fitness workers in smaller facilities with few employees may perform a variety of functions in addition to their fitness duties, such as tending the front desk, signing up new members, giving tours of the fitness center, writing newsletter articles, creating posters and flyers, and supervising the weight training and cardiovascular equipment areas. In larger commercial facilities, personal trainers are often required to sell their services to members and to make a specified number of sales. Some fitness workers may combine the duties of group exercise instructors and personal trainers, and in smaller facilities, the fitness director may teach classes and do personal training.

Work environment. Most fitness workers spend their time indoors at fitness centers and health clubs. Fitness directors and supervisors, however, typically spend most of their time in an office. Those in smaller fitness centers may split their time among office work, personal training, and teaching classes. Directors and supervisors generally engage in less physical activity than do lower-level fitness workers. Nevertheless, workers at all levels risk suffering injuries during physical activities.

Since most fitness centers are open long hours, fitness workers often work nights and weekends and even occasional holidays. Some may travel from place to place throughout the day, to different gyms or to clients' homes, to maintain a full work schedule.

Fitness workers generally enjoy a lot of autonomy. Group exercise instructors choreograph or plan their own classes, and personal trainers have the freedom to design and implement their clients' workout routines.

Training, Other Qualifications, and Advancement

For most fitness workers, certification is critical. Personal trainers usually must have certification to begin working with clients or with members of a fitness facility. Group fitness instructors may begin without a certification, but they are often encouraged or required by their employers to become certified.

Education and training. Fitness workers usually do not receive much on-the-job training; they are expected to know how to do their jobs when they are hired. Workers may receive some organizational training to learn about the operations of their new employer. They occasionally receive specialized training if they are expected to teach or lead a specific method of exercise or focus on a particular age or ability group. Because the requirements vary from employer to employer, it may be helpful to contact your local fitness centers or other potential employers to find out what background they prefer before pursuing training.

The education and training required depends on the specific type of fitness work: personal training, group fitness, or a specialization such as Pilates or yoga each need different preparation. Personal trainers often start out by taking classes to become certified. They then may begin by working alongside an experienced trainer before being allowed to train clients alone. Group fitness instructors often get started by participating in exercise classes until they are ready to successfully audition as instructors and begin teaching class. They also may improve their skills by taking training courses or attending fitness conventions. Most employers require instructors to work toward becoming certified.

Training for Pilates and yoga instructors is changing. Because interest in these forms of exercise has exploded in recent years, the demand for teachers has grown faster than the ability to train them properly. However, because inexperienced teachers have contributed to student injuries, there has been a push toward more standardized, rigorous requirements for teacher training.

Pilates and yoga teachers need specialized training in their particular method of exercise. For Pilates, training options range from weekend-long workshops to year-long programs, but the trend is toward requiring more training. The Pilates Method Alliance has established training standards that recommend at least 200 hours of training; the group also has standards for training schools and maintains a list of training schools that meet the requirements. However, some Pilates teachers are certified group exercise instructors who attend short Pilates workshops; currently, many fitness centers hire people with minimal Pilates training if the applicants have a fitness certification and group fitness experience.

Training requirements for yoga teachers are similar to those for Pilates teachers. Training programs range from a few days to more than 2 years. Many people get their start by taking yoga; eventually, their teachers may consider them ready to assist or to substitute teach. Some students may begin teaching their own classes when their yoga teachers think they are ready; the teachers may even provide letters of recommendation. Those who wish to pursue teaching more seriously usually pursue formal teacher training.

Currently, there are many training programs through the yoga community as well as programs through the fitness industry. The Yoga Alliance has established training standards requiring at least 200 training hours, with a specified number of hours in areas including techniques, teaching methodology, anatomy, physiology, and philosophy. The Yoga Alliance also registers schools that train students to its standards. Because some schools may meet the standards but not be registered, prospective students should check the requirements and decide if particular schools meet them.

An increasing number of employers require fitness workers to have a bachelor's degree in a field related to health or fitness, such as exercise science or physical education. Some employers allow workers to substitute a college degree for certification, but most employers who require a bachelor's degree also require certification.

Certification and other qualifications. Most personal trainers must obtain certification in the fitness field to gain employment. Group fitness instructors do not necessarily need certification to begin working. The most important characteristic that an employer looks for in a new fitness instructor is the ability to plan and lead a class that is motivating and safe. However, most organizations encourage their group instructors to become certified over time, and many require it.

In the fitness field, there are many organizations—some of which are listed in the last section of this statement—that offer certification. Becoming certified by one of the top certification organizations is increasingly important, especially for personal trainers. One way to ensure that a certifying organization is reputable is to see that it is accredited by the National Commission for Certifying Agencies.

Most certifying organizations require candidates to have a high school diploma, be certified in cardiopulmonary resuscitation (CPR), and pass an exam. All certification exams have a written component, and some also have a practical component. The exams measure knowledge of human physiology, proper exercise techniques, assessment of client fitness levels, and development of appropriate exercise programs. There is no particular training program required for certifications; candidates may prepare however they prefer. Certifying organizations do offer study materials, including books, CD-ROMs, other audio and visual materials, and exam preparation workshops and seminars, but exam candidates are not required to purchase materials to take exams.

Certification generally is good for 2 years, after which workers must become recertified by attending continuing education classes or conferences, writing articles, or giving presentations. Some organizations offer more advanced certification, requiring an associate or bachelor's degree in an exercise-related subject for individuals interested in training athletes, working with people who are injured or ill, or advising clients on general health.

Pilates and yoga instructors usually do not need group exercise certifications to maintain employment. It is more important that they have specialized training in their particular method of exercise. However, the Pilates Method Alliance does offer certification.

People planning fitness careers should be outgoing, excellent communicators, good at motivating people, and sensitive to the needs of others. Excellent health and physical fitness are important due to the physical nature of the job. Those who wish to be personal trainers in a large commercial fitness center should have strong sales skills. All personal trainers should have the personality and motivation to attract and retain clients.

Advancement. A bachelor's degree in exercise science, physical education, kinesiology (the study of muscles, especially the mechanics of human motion), or a related area, along with experience, usually is required to advance to management positions in a health club or fitness center. Some organizations require a master's degree. As in other occupations, managerial skills are also needed to advance to supervisory or managerial positions. College courses in management, business administration, accounting, and personnel management may be helpful, but many fitness companies have corporate universities in which they train employees for management positions.

Personal trainers may advance to head trainer, with responsibility for hiring and overseeing the personal training staff and for bringing in new personal training clients. Group fitness instructors may be promoted to group exercise director, responsible for hiring instructors and coordinating exercise classes. Later, a worker might become the fitness director, who manages the fitness budget and staff. Workers might also become the general manager, whose main focus is the financial aspects of an organization, particularly setting and achieving sales goals; in a small fitness center, however, the general manager is usually involved with all aspects of running the facility. Some

Projections data from the National Employment Matrix

Occupational Title	SOC Code	Employment, 2006	Projected employment, 2016	Change, 2006-16	
				Number	Percent
Fitness trainers and aerobics instructors	39-9031	235,000	298,000	63,000	27

NOTE: Data in this table are rounded. See the discussion of the employment projections table in the *Handbook* introductory chapter on *Occupational Information Included in the Handbook.*

workers go into business for themselves and open their own fitness centers.

Employment

Fitness workers held about 235,000 jobs in 2006. Almost all personal trainers and group exercise instructors worked in physical fitness facilities, health clubs, and fitness centers, mainly in the amusement and recreation industry or in civic and social organizations. About 8 percent of fitness workers were self-employed; many of these were personal trainers, while others were group fitness instructors working on a contract basis with fitness centers. Many fitness jobs are part time, and many workers hold multiple jobs, teaching or doing personal training at several different fitness centers and at clients' homes.

Job Outlook

Jobs for fitness workers are expected to increase much faster than the average for all occupations. Fitness workers should have good opportunities due to rapid job growth in health clubs, fitness facilities, and other settings where fitness workers are concentrated.

Employment change. Employment of fitness workers is expected to increase 27 percent over the 2006-2016 decade, much faster than the average for all occupations. These workers are expected to gain jobs because an increasing number of people are spending time and money on fitness, and more businesses are recognizing the benefits of health and fitness programs for their employees.

Aging baby boomers are concerned with staying healthy, physically fit, and independent. Moreover, the reduction of physical education programs in schools, combined with parents' growing concern about childhood obesity, has resulted in rapid increases in children's health club membership. Increasingly, parents are also hiring personal trainers for their children, and the number of weight-training gyms for children is expected to continue to grow. Health club membership among young adults also has grown steadily, driven by concern with physical fitness and by rising incomes.

As health clubs strive to provide more personalized service to keep their members motivated, they will continue to offer personal training and a wide variety of group exercise classes. Participation in yoga and Pilates is expected to continue to increase, driven partly by the aging population that demands low-impact forms of exercise and seeks relief from arthritis and other ailments.

Job prospects. Opportunities are expected to be good for fitness workers because of rapid job growth in health clubs, fitness facilities, and other settings where fitness workers are concentrated. In addition, many job openings will stem from the need to replace the large numbers of workers who leave these occupations each year. Part-time jobs will be easier to find than full-time jobs.

Earnings

Median annual earnings of fitness trainers and aerobics instructors in May 2006 were $25,910. The middle 50 percent earned between $18,010 and $41,040. The bottom 10 percent earned less than $14,880, while the top 10 percent earned $56,750 or more. These figures do not include the earnings of the self-employed. Earnings of successful self-employed personal trainers can be much higher. Median annual earnings in the industries employing the largest numbers of fitness workers in 2006 were as follows:

General medical and surgical hospitals	$29,640
Local government	27,720
Fitness and recreational sports centers	27,200
Other schools and instruction	22,770
Civic and social organizations	22,630

Because many fitness workers work part time, they often do not receive benefits such as health insurance or retirement plans from their employers. They are able to use fitness facilities at no cost, however.

Related Occupations

Other occupations that focus on physical fitness include athletes, coaches, umpires, and related workers. Physical therapists also do related work when they create exercise plans to improve their patients' flexibility, strength, and endurance. Dietitians and nutritionists advise individuals on improving and maintaining their health, like fitness workers do. Also like fitness workers, many recreation workers lead groups in physical activities.

Sources of Additional Information

For more information about fitness careers and universities and other institutions offering programs in health and fitness, contact:

➤ IDEA Health and Fitness Association, 10455 Pacific Center Court., San Diego, CA 92121-4339.

➤ National Strength and Conditioning Association, 1885 Bob Johnson Drive, Colorado Springs, CO 80906.
Internet: **http://www.nsca-lift.org**

For information about personal trainer and group fitness instructor certifications, contact:

➤ American College of Sports Medicine, P.O. Box 1440, Indianapolis, IN 46206-1440. Internet: **http://www.acsm.org**

➤ American Council on Exercise, 4851 Paramount Dr., San Diego, CA 92123. Internet: **http://www.acefitness.org**

➤ National Academy of Sports Medicine, 26632 Agoura Rd., Calabasas, CA 91302. Internet: **http://www.nasm.org**

➤ NSCA Certification Commission, 3333 Landmark Circle, Lincoln, NE 68504. Internet: **http://www.nsca-cc.org**

For information about Pilates certification and training programs, contact:

➤ Pilates Method Alliance, P.O. Box 370906, Miami, FL 33137-0906.

Internet: **http://www.pilatesmethodalliance.org**

For information on yoga teacher training programs, contact:

➤ Yoga Alliance, 7801 Old Branch Ave., Suite 400, Clinton, MD 20735. Internet: **http://www.yogaalliance.org**

To find accredited fitness certification programs, contact:

➤ National Commission for Certifying Agencies, 2025 M St., NW., Suite 800, Washington, DC 20036.

Internet: **http://www.noca.org/ncca/accredorg.htm**

For information about health clubs and sports clubs, contact:

➤ International Health, Racquet, and Sportsclub Association, 263 Summer St., Boston, MA 02210.

Internet: **http://www.ihrsa.org**

Flight Attendants

(O*NET 39-6031.00)

Significant Points

- Competition for positions is expected to remain keen because the opportunity for travel attracts more applicants than there are jobs.

- Job duties are learned through formal on-the-job training at a flight training center.

- A high school diploma is the minimum educational requirement; however, applicants with a college degree and with experience in dealing with the public are likely to have the best job opportunities.

Nature of the Work

Major airlines are required by law to provide flight attendants for the safety and security of the traveling public. Although the primary job of the flight attendants is to ensure that security and safety regulations are followed, attendants also try to make flights comfortable and enjoyable for passengers.

At least 1 hour before each flight, attendants are briefed by the captain—the pilot in command—on such things as emergency evacuation procedures, coordination of the crew, the length of the flight, expected weather conditions, and special issues having to do with passengers. Flight attendants make sure that first-aid kits and other emergency equipment are aboard and in working order and that the passenger cabin is in order, with adequate supplies of food, beverages, and any other provided amenities. As passengers board the plane, flight attendants greet them, check their tickets, and tell them where to store carry-on items.

Before the plane takes off, flight attendants instruct all passengers in the use of emergency equipment and check to see that seatbelts are fastened, seat backs are in upright positions, and all carry-on items are properly stowed. In the air, helping passengers in the event of an emergency is the most important responsibility of a flight attendant. Safety-related actions may range from reassuring passengers during rough weather to directing passengers who must evacuate a plane following an emergency landing. Flight attendants also answer questions about the flight; distribute reading material, pillows, and blankets; and help small children, elderly or disabled persons, and any others needing assistance. They may administer first aid to passengers who become ill. Flight attendants generally serve beverages and other refreshments and, on many flights, especially international, heat and distribute precooked meals or snacks. Prior to landing, flight attendants take inventory of headsets, alcoholic beverages, and moneys collected. They also report any medical problems passengers may have had, the condition of cabin equipment, and lost and found articles.

Lead, or first, flight attendants, sometimes known as pursers, oversee the work of the other attendants aboard the aircraft, while performing most of the same duties.

Work environment. Because airlines operate around the clock and year round, flight attendants may work nights, holidays, and weekends. In most cases, agreements between the airline and the employees' union determine the total daily and monthly working time. Scheduled on-duty time usually is limited to 12 hours per day although some contracts provide daily actual maximums of 14 hours, with somewhat greater maximums for international flying.

Attendants usually fly 65 to 90 hours a month and generally spend another 50 hours a month on the ground preparing planes for flights, writing reports following completed flights, and waiting for planes to arrive. Most airlines guarantee a minimum of 65 to 85 flight hours per month, with the option to work additional hours. Flight attendants receive extra compensation for increased hours.

Flight attendants may be away from their home base at least one-third of the time. During this period, the airlines provide hotel accommodations and an allowance for meal expenses.

Flight attendants must be flexible and willing to relocate. However, many flight attendants elect to live in one place and commute to their assigned home base. Home bases and routes worked are bid for on a seniority basis. The longer the flight attendant has been employed, the more likely he or she is to work on chosen flights. Almost all flight attendants start out working on reserve status or on call. On small corporate airlines, flight attendants often work on an as-needed basis and must adapt to varying environments and passengers.

The combination of free time and discount airfares provides flight attendants the opportunity to travel and see new places. However, the work can be strenuous and trying. Flight attendants stand during much of the flight and must remain pleasant and efficient, regardless of how tired they are or how demanding passengers may be. Occasionally, flight attendants must deal with disruptive passengers. Also, turbulent flights can add to possible difficulties regarding service, including potential injuries to passengers.

Working in a moving aircraft leaves flight attendants susceptible to injuries. For example, back injuries and mishaps can

In addition to flying, flight attendants also work on the ground preparing planes for flights, writing reports following completed flights, and waiting for planes to arrive.

occur when opening overhead compartments or while pushing heavy service carts. In addition, medical problems can arise from irregular sleeping and eating patterns, dealing with stressful passengers, working in a pressurized environment, and breathing recycled air.

Training, Other Qualifications, and Advancement

Flight attendants must be certified by the Federal Aviation Administration (FAA). A high school diploma is the minimum educational requirement, but airlines increasingly prefer applicants who have a college degree. Experience in dealing with the public is important because flight attendants must be able to interact comfortably with strangers and remain calm under duress.

Education and training. A high school diploma is the minimum educational requirement. However, airlines increasingly prefer applicants with a college degree and with experience in dealing with the public. Applicants who attend schools and colleges that offer flight attendant training may have an advantage over other applicants. Highly desirable areas of concentration include people-oriented disciplines such as psychology, communications, sociology, nursing, anthropology, police or fire science, travel and tourism, hospitality and education. Flight attendants for international airlines generally must speak a foreign language fluently. For their international flights, some of the major airlines prefer candidates who can speak two major foreign languages.

Once hired, all candidates must undergo a period of formal training. The length of training, ranging from 3 to 8 weeks, depends on the size and type of carrier and takes place at the airline's flight training center. Airlines that do not operate training centers generally send new employees to the center of another airline. Some airlines may provide transportation to the training centers and an allowance for room, board, and school supplies, while other airlines charge individuals for training. New trainees are not considered employees of the airline until they successfully complete the training program. Trainees learn emergency procedures such as evacuating an airplane, operating emergency systems and equipment, administering first aid, and surviving in the water. In addition, trainees are taught how to deal with disruptive passengers and with hijacking and terrorist situations. New hires learn flight regulations and duties, gain knowledge of company operations and policies, and receive instruction on personal grooming and weight control. Trainees for the international routes get additional instruction in passport and customs regulations. Trainees must perform many drills and duties unaided, in front of the training staff. Throughout training, they also take tests designed to eliminate unsuccessful trainees. Toward the end of their training, students go on practice flights. Upon successful completion of training, flight attendants receive the FAA's Certificate of Demonstrated Proficiency. Flight attendants also are required to go through periodic retraining and pass an FAA safety examination to continue flying.

Licensure and certification. All flight attendants must be certified by the FAA. In order to be certified, flight attendants are required to successfully complete training requirements, such as evacuation, fire fighting, medical emergency, and security procedures established by the FAA and the Transportation Security Administration. They also must perform the assigned duties of a cabin crew member and complete an approved proficiency check. Flight attendants are certified for specific types of aircraft, regardless of the carrier. Therefore, only 1-day or 2-day recurrent training, with the new carrier, is needed for those flight attendants who change airlines, as long as the type of aircraft remains the same.

Other qualifications. Airlines prefer to hire poised, tactful, and resourceful people who can interact comfortably with strangers and remain calm under duress. Flight attendants must be in excellent health, and have the ability to speak clearly. Airlines usually have age, physical, and appearance requirements. Applicants usually must be at least 18 to 21 years old, although some carriers may have higher minimum-age requirements. Applicants must meet height requirements for reaching overhead bins, which often contain emergency equipment, and most airlines want candidates with weight proportionate to height. Vision is required to be correctable to 20/30 or better with glasses or contact lenses (uncorrected no worse than 20/200). Men must have their hair cut above the collar and be clean shaven. Airlines prefer applicants with no visible tattoos, body piercing, or unusual hairstyles or makeup.

In addition to education and training, airlines conduct a thorough background check as required by the FAA, which goes back as many as 10 years. Everything about an applicant is investigated, including date of birth, employment history, criminal record, school records, and gaps in employment. Employment is contingent on a successful background check. An applicant will not be offered a job or will be immediately dismissed if his or her background check shows any discrepancies. All U.S. airlines require that applicants be citizens of the United States

Projections data from the National Employment Matrix

Occupational Title	SOC Code	Employment, 2006	Projected employment, 2016	Change, 2006-16	
				Number	Percent
Flight attendants..	39-6031	97,000	107,000	10,000	11

NOTE: Data in this table are rounded. See the discussion of the employment projections table in the *Handbook* introductory chapter on *Occupational Information Included in the Handbook.*

or registered aliens with legal rights to obtain employment in the United States.

Advancement. After completing initial training, flight attendants are assigned to one of their airline's bases. New flight attendants are placed on reserve status and are called either to staff extra flights or to fill in for crewmembers who are sick, on vacation, or rerouted. When they are not on duty, reserve flight attendants must be available to report for flights on short notice. They usually remain on reserve for at least 1 year but, in some cities, it may take 5 to 10 years or longer to advance from reserve status. Flight attendants who no longer are on reserve bid monthly for regular assignments. Because assignments are based on seniority, usually only the most experienced attendants get their choice of assignments. Advancement takes longer today than in the past because experienced flight attendants are remaining in this career longer than in the past.

Some flight attendants become supervisors, moving from senior or lead flight attendant, to check flight attendant, to flight attendant supervisor, then on to base manager, and finally to manager or vice president of in-flight operations. They may take on additional duties such as recruiting, instructing, or developing in-flight products. Their experience also may qualify them for numerous airline-related jobs involving contact with the public, such as reservation ticket agent or public relations specialist. Flight attendants who do not want to travel often for various reasons may move to a position as an administrative assistant. With additional education, some flight attendants may decide to transfer to other areas of the airline for which they work, such as risk management or human resources.

Employment

Flight attendants held about 97,000 jobs in 2006. Commercial airlines employed the vast majority of flight attendants, most of whom lived in their employer's home-base city. A small number of flight attendants worked for large companies that operated aircraft for business purposes.

Job Outlook

Competition for jobs is expected to remain keen because the opportunity for travel attracts more applicants than there are jobs.

Employment change. Employment of flight attendants is expected to grow 11 percent, about as fast as the average for all occupations over the 2006-16 projection period. Population growth and an improving economy are expected to boost the number of airline passengers. As airlines expand their capacity to meet rising demand by increasing the number and size of planes in operation, more flight attendants will be needed.

Job prospects. Despite growing demand for flight attendants, competition is expected to be keen because this job usually attracts more applicants than there are jobs, with only the most qualified eventually being hired. College graduates who have

experience dealing with the public should have the best chance of being hired. Job opportunities may be better with the faster growing regional and commuter, low-cost, and charter airlines. There also are job opportunities for professionally trained flight attendants to work for companies operating private aircraft for their executives.

The majority of job opportunities through the year 2016 will arise from the need to replace flight attendants who leave the labor force or transfer to other occupations, often for higher earnings or a more stable lifestyle. With the job now viewed increasingly as a profession, however, fewer flight attendants leave their jobs, and job turnover is not as high as in the past. The average job tenure of attendants is currently more than 14 years and is increasing.

In the long run, opportunities for persons seeking flight attendant jobs should improve as the airline industry expands. Over the next decade, however, demand for flight attendants will fluctuate with the demand for air travel, which is highly sensitive to swings in the economy. During downturns, as air traffic declines, the hiring of flight attendants declines, and some experienced attendants may be laid off until traffic recovers.

Earnings

Median annual earnings of flight attendants were $53,780 in May 2006. The middle 50 percent earned between $33,320 and $77,410. The lowest 10 percent earned less than $24,250, and the highest 10 percent earned more than $99,300.

According to data from the Association of Flight Attendants, beginning attendants had median earnings of $15,849 a year in 2006. Beginning pay scales for flight attendants vary by carrier, however. New hires usually begin at the same pay scale regardless of experience, and all flight attendants receive the same future pay increases based on an established pay scale.

Some airlines offer incentive pay for working holidays, night and international flights, or taking positions that require additional responsibility or paperwork.

Flight attendants and their immediate families are entitled to free or discounted fares on their own airline and reduced fares on most other airlines. Some airlines require that the flight attendant be with an airline for 3 to 6 months before taking advantage of this benefit. Other benefits may include medical, dental, and life insurance; 401K or other retirement plan; sick leave; paid holidays; stock options; paid vacations; and tuition reimbursement. Flight attendants also receive a "per diem" allowance for meal expenses while on duty away from home. Flight attendants are required to purchase uniforms and wear them while on duty. The airlines usually pay for uniform replacement items, and may provide a small allowance to cover cleaning and upkeep of the uniforms.

The majority of flight attendants hold union membership, primarily with the Association of Flight Attendants. Other unions that represent flight attendants include the Transport Workers Union of America and the International Brotherhood of Teamsters.

Related Occupations

Other jobs that involve helping people as a safety professional, while requiring the ability to be calm even under trying circumstances, include emergency medical technicians and paramedics as well as firefighting occupations.

Sources of Additional Information

Information about job opportunities and qualifications required for work at a particular airline may be obtained by writing to the airline's human resources office.

For further information on flight attendants, contact:
➤ Association of Flight Attendants, 501 Third St. NW., Washington, DC 20001. Internet: **http://www.afanet.org**

Gaming Services Occupations

(O*NET 11-9071.00, 39-1011.00, 39-1012.00, 39-3011.00, 39-3012.00)

Significant Points

- Job opportunities are available nationwide and are no longer limited to Nevada and New Jersey.

- Workers need a license issued by a regulatory agency, such as a State casino control board or commission.

- Employment is projected to grow much faster than average.

- Job prospects will be best for those with a degree or certification in gaming or a hospitality-related field, previous training or experience in casino gaming, and strong interpersonal and customer service skills.

Nature of the Work

Legalized gambling in the United States today includes casino gaming, State lotteries, pari-mutuel wagering on contests such as horse or dog racing, and charitable gaming. Gaming, the playing of games of chance, is a multibillion-dollar industry that is responsible for the creation of a number of unique service occupations.

The majority of all gaming services workers are employed in casinos. Their duties and titles may vary from one establishment to another. Some positions are associated with oversight and direction—supervision, surveillance, and investigation—while others involve working with the games or patrons themselves by tending slot machines, dealing cards or running games, handling money, writing and running tickets, and other activities. In nearly any gaming job, workers interact directly with patrons, and part of their responsibility is to make those interactions enjoyable.

Like nearly every business establishment, casinos have workers who direct and oversee day-to-day operations.

Gaming service workers are required to have a license.

Gaming supervisors and *gaming managers* oversee the gaming operations and personnel in an assigned area. They circulate among the tables and observe the operations to ensure that all of the stations and games are covered for each shift and workers and gamblers adhere to the rules of the games. Gaming supervisors and gaming managers often explain and interpret the operating rules of the house to patrons who may have difficulty understanding the rules. They also may plan and organize activities to create a friendly atmosphere for the guests staying in casino hotels. Periodically, they address complaints about service.

Gaming managers also have additional responsibilities beyond those of supervisors. For example, gaming managers prepare work schedules and station assignments for their subordinates. They are responsible for interviewing, hiring, training, and evaluating new workers.

Managers supervise a variety of other workers. Some of these workers need specialized skills—dealing blackjack, for example—that are unique to casino work. Others require skills common to most business workers, such as the ability to conduct financial transactions.

Slot key persons coordinate and supervise the slot machine department and its workers. Their duties include verifying and handling payoff winnings to patrons, resetting slot machines after completing the payoff, and refilling machines with money. Slot key persons must be familiar with a variety of slot machines and be able to make minor repairs and adjustments to the machines as needed. If major repairs are required, slot key persons determine whether the slot machine should be removed from the floor. Working the floor as frontline personnel, they enforce safety rules and report hazards.

Gaming and sportsbook writers and runners assist in the operations of games such as bingo and keno, in addition to taking bets on sporting events. They scan tickets presented by patrons and calculate and distribute winnings. Some writers and runners operate the equipment that randomly selects the numbers. Others may announce numbers selected, pick up tickets from patrons, collect bets, or receive, verify, and record patrons' cash wagers.

Gaming dealers operate table games such as craps, black-jack, and roulette. Standing or sitting behind the table, dealers provide dice, dispense cards to players, or run the equipment. Some dealers also monitor the patrons for infractions of casino rules. Gaming dealers must be skilled in customer service and in executing their game. Dealers determine winners, calculate and pay winning bets, and collect losing bets. Because of the fast-paced work environment, most gaming dealers are competent in at least two games, usually black-jack and craps.

Work environment. Most casinos are open 24 hours a day, 7 days a week and offer 3 staggered shifts. Employees can be expected to work weekends and holidays. The atmosphere in casinos is generally filled with fun and often considered glamorous. However, casino work can also be physically demanding. Most occupations require that workers stand for long periods; some require the lifting of heavy items. The atmosphere in casinos exposes workers to certain hazards, such as cigarette, cigar, and pipe smoke. Noise from slot machines, gaming tables, and talking workers and patrons may be distracting to some, although workers wear protective headgear in areas where loud machinery is used to count money.

Training, Other Qualifications, and Advancement
Each casino establishes its own education, training, and experience requirements, but all gaming service workers must obtain a license from a regulatory agency, such as a State casino control board or commission.

Education and training. There usually are no minimum educational requirements for entry-level gaming jobs, although most employers prefer workers with at least a high school diploma or GED.

Each casino establishes its own requirements for education, training, and experience. Some of the major casinos and slot manufacturers run their own training schools, and almost all provide some form of in-house training in addition to requiring certification. The type and quantity of classes needed may vary. Many institutions of higher learning give training toward certificates in gaming, as well as offering an associate, bachelor's, or master's degree in a hospitality-related field such as hospitality management, hospitality administration, or hotel management. Some schools offer training in games, gaming supervision, slot attendant and slot repair

technician work, slot department management, and surveillance and security.

Slot key persons do not need to meet formal educational requirements to enter the occupation, but completion of slot attendant or slot technician training is helpful. As with most other gaming workers, slot key persons receive on-the-job training during the first several weeks of employment.

Gaming and sports book writers and runners must have at least a high school diploma or GED. Most of these workers receive on-the-job training. Because gaming and sportsbook writers and runners work closely with patrons, they need excellent customer service skills.

Most gaming dealers acquire their skills by attending a dealer school or vocational and technical school. They teach the rules and procedures of the games as well as State and local laws and regulations. Graduation from one of these schools does not guarantee a job at a casino, however, as most casinos also require prospective dealers to audition for open positions. During the audition, personal qualities are assessed along with knowledge of the games.

For most gaming supervisor and gaming manager positions, an associate or bachelor's degree is beneficial, but it is not required. Most employees in these occupations have experience in other gaming occupations, typically as dealers, and have a broad knowledge of casino rules, regulations, procedures, and games.

Licensure. Gaming services workers are required to be licensed by a regulatory agency, such as a State casino control board or commission. Applicants for a license must provide photo identification and pay a fee. Some States may require gaming service workers to be residents of that State. Age requirements vary by State. The licensing application process also includes a background investigation and drug test.

Other qualifications. In addition to possessing a license, gaming services workers need superior customer service skills. Casino gaming workers provide entertainment and hospitality to patrons, and the quality of their service contributes to an establishment's success or failure. Therefore, gaming workers need good communication skills, an outgoing personality, and the ability to maintain their composure even when dealing with angry or demanding patrons. Personal integrity also is important because workers handle large amounts of money.

Gaming services workers who manage money should have some experience handling cash or using calculators or com-

Projections data from the National Employment Matrix

Occupational Title	SOC Code	Employment, 2006	Projected employment, 2016	Change, 2006-16	
				Number	Percent
Gaming services occupations...	—	174,000	214,000	40,000	23
Gaming managers	11-9071	4,000	5,000	1,000	24
First-line supervisors/managers of gaming workers.....................	39-1010	54,000	64,000	10,000	19
Gaming supervisors	39-1011	34,000	42,000	7,900	23
Slot key persons	39-1012	20,000	22,000	2,200	11
Gaming dealers	39-3011	84,000	104,000	20,000	24
Gaming and sports book writers and runners	39-3012	18,000	24,000	5,200	28

NOTE: Data in this table are rounded. See the discussion of the employment projections table in the *Handbook* introductory chapter on *Occupational Information Included in the Handbook.*

puters. For such positions, most casinos administer a math test to assess an applicant's level of competency.

Gaming supervisors and gaming managers must have strong leadership, organizational, and communication skills. Excellent customer service and employee relations skills also are necessary.

Advancement. Advancement opportunities in casino gaming depend less on workers' previous casino duties and titles than on their ability and eagerness to learn new jobs. For example, an entry-level gaming worker eventually might advance to become a dealer or card room manager or to assume some other supervisory position.

Employment

Gaming services occupations provided 174,000 jobs in 2006. Gaming services workers are found mainly in the traveler accommodation and gaming industries. Most are employed in commercial casinos, including riverboat casinos, casino hotels, and pari-mutuel racetracks—known as "racinos"—that in 20 States offer casino games. The largest number work in casinos in Nevada. Mississippi, which boasts the greatest number of riverboat casinos in operation, employs the most workers in that venue. In addition, there are 28 States with Indian casinos. Legal lotteries are held in 41 States and the District of Columbia, and pari-mutuel wagering is legal in 43 States. Forty-seven States and the District of Columbia also allow charitable gaming. Other States are considering legislation to permit gambling, but no casinos have been opened as of yet.

For most workers, gaming licensure requires proof of residency in the State in which gaming workers are employed. But some gaming services workers do not limit themselves to one State or even one country, finding jobs on the small number of casinos located on luxury cruise liners that travel the world. These individuals live and work aboard the vessel.

Job Outlook

Employment of gaming service workers is expected to grow much faster than the average for all occupations., Opportunities will be best for those with previous casino gaming experience, a degree or technical or vocational training in gaming or a hospitality-related field, and strong customer service skills.

Employment change. With demand for gaming showing no sign of waning, employment in gaming services occupations is projected to grow by 23 percent between 2006 and 2016, which is much faster than the average for all occupations. The increasing popularity and prevalence of Indian casinos and racinos will provide substantial new job openings. With many States benefiting from casino gambling in the form of tax revenue or agreements with Indian tribes, additional States are reconsidering their opposition to legalized gambling and will likely approve the construction of more casinos and other gaming establishments during the next decade. Additional job growth will occur in established gaming areas in Nevada and Atlantic City, New Jersey, as they solidify their positions as tourist destinations.

The increase in gaming reflects growth in the population and in its disposable income, both of which are expected to continue. Higher expectations for customer service among gaming patrons also should result in more jobs for gaming services workers. Because of increasing demand in gaming establishments for additional table games, particularly poker, the largest growth is expected among gaming dealers. Conversely, advancements in slot machine technology, such as coinless slot machines—known as "Ticket-in, Ticket-Out machines"—will limit job growth for slot key persons relative to other gaming service occupations. Ticket-in, Ticket-out technology reduces the need for slot key persons to pay-out jackpots, fill hoppers, and reset machines. Additionally, slot machines linked to a network allow adjustments to be made from a central computer server rather than from the floor by a slot key person. However, there will still be some new jobs for slot key persons because of the casino industry's focus on customer service and the rising popularity of racinos and slot machines in States that have recently legalized gambling or are expected to do so in the future.

Job prospects. Job prospects in gaming services occupations will be best for those with previous casino gaming experience, a degree or technical or vocational training in gaming or a hospitality-related field, and strong interpersonal and customer service skills.

In addition to job openings arising from employment growth, opportunities will result from the need to replace workers transferring to other occupations or leaving the labor force. Despite this, keen competition for jobs as gaming dealers is expected. There are generally more applicants than jobs. Experienced dealers who are able to attract new or return business will have the best job prospects.

Earnings

Wage earnings for gaming services workers vary according to occupation, level of experience, training, location, and size of the gaming establishment. The following were median earnings for various gaming services occupations in May 2006:

Gaming managers $62,820
Gaming supervisors 41,160
Slot key persons...22,720
Gaming and sports book writers and runners 18,800
Gaming dealers...14,730

Gaming dealers generally receive a large portion of their earnings from tokes, which are tips in the form of tokens received from players. Earnings from tokes vary depending on the table games the dealer operates, the personal traits of the dealer, and the pooling policies of the casino.

Related Occupations

Many other occupations provide hospitality and customer service. Some examples of related occupations are security guards and gaming surveillance officers, sales worker supervisors, cashiers, gaming change persons and booth cashiers, retail salespersons, gaming cage workers, and tellers.

Sources of Additional Information

For additional information on careers in gaming, visit your public library and your State gaming regulatory agency or casino control commission.

Information on careers in gaming also is available from:
➤ American Gaming Association, 1299 Pennsylvania Ave. NW., Suite 1175, Washington, DC 20004.
Internet: **http://www.americangaming.org**

Personal and Home Care Aides

(O*NET 39-9021.00)

Significant Points

- Job opportunities are expected to be excellent because of rapid growth in home health care and high replacement needs.

- Skill requirements are low, as is the pay.

- About 1 out of 3 personal and home care aides work part time; most aides work with a number of different clients, each job lasting a few hours, days, or weeks.

Nature of the Work

Personal and home care aides help people who are elderly, disabled, ill, and/or mentally disabled to live in their own homes or in residential care facilities instead of in health facilities or institutions. Most personal and home care aides work with elderly or physically or mentally disabled clients who need more extensive personal and home care than family or friends can provide. Some aides work with families in which a parent is incapacitated and small children need care. Others help discharged hospital patients who have relatively short-term needs. (*Home health aides*—who provide health-related services are discussed in the section on nursing, psychiatric, and home health aides, elsewhere in the *Handbook*.)

Personal and home care aides—also called *homemakers, caregivers, companions*, and *personal attendants*—provide housekeeping and routine personal care services. They clean clients' houses, do laundry, and change bed linens. Aides may plan meals (including special diets), shop for food, and cook. Aides also may help clients get out of bed, bathe, dress, and groom. Some accompany clients to doctors' appointments or on other errands.

Personal and home care aides provide instruction and psychological support to their patients. They may advise families and patients on nutrition, cleanliness, and household tasks. Aides also may assist in toilet training a severely mentally handicapped child, or they may just listen to clients talk.

In home health care agencies, a registered nurse, physical therapist, or social worker assigns specific duties and supervises personal and home care aides. Aides keep records of services performed and of clients' condition and progress. They report changes in the client's condition to the supervisor or case manager. In carrying out their work, aides cooperate with health care professionals, including registered nurses, therapists, and other medical staff.

The personal and home care aide's daily routine may vary. Aides may go to the same home every day for months or even years. Aides often visit four or five clients on the same day. However, some aides may work solely with one client who is in need of more care and attention. In some situations, this may involve working with other aides in shifts so the client has an aide throughout the day and night.

Personal and home care aides generally work on their own, with periodic visits by their supervisor. They receive detailed instructions explaining when to visit clients and what services to perform for them.

Aides are individually responsible for getting to the client's home. They may spend a good portion of the work day traveling from one client to another. Aides must be careful to avoid over-exertion or injury when they assist clients.

Work environment. Surroundings differ from case to case. Some homes are neat and pleasant, whereas others are untidy and depressing. Some clients are pleasant and cooperative; others are angry, abusive, depressed, or otherwise difficult. Aides may spend a large portion of each day traveling between clients' homes.

About 33 percent of aides work part time, and some work weekends or evenings to suit the needs of their clients.

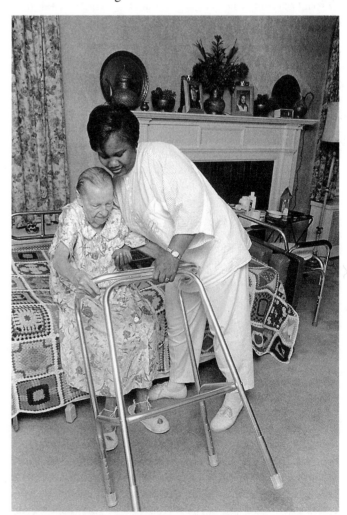

Personal and home care aides assist elderly and disabled clients with daily tasks, like housekeeping and personal hygiene.

Projections data from the National Employment Matrix

Occupational Title	SOC Code	Employment, 2006	Projected employment, 2016	Change, 2006-16	
				Number	Percent
Personal and home care aides	39-9021	767,000	1,156,000	389,000	51

NOTE: Data in this table are rounded. See the discussion of the employment projections table in the *Handbook* introductory chapter on *Occupational Information Included in the Handbook.*

Training, Other Qualifications, and Advancement

In some States, the only requirement for employment is on-the-job training, which generally is provided by employers. Other States may require formal training, which is available from community colleges, vocational schools, elder care programs, and home health care agencies.

Education and training. Most personal and home care aides receive short term on-the-job training in a range of job functions. Aides are instructed on how to properly cook for a client, which includes iinformation on nutrition and special diets. Furthermore, they may be trained on basic housekeeping tasks, such as making a bed and keeping the home sanitary and safe for the client. Generally, they are taught how to respond to an emergency situation, learning basic safety techniques. Employers may also train aides to conduct themselves in a professional and courteous manner while in a clients' home.

Other qualifications. Personal and home care aides should have a desire to help people and not mind hard work. They should be responsible, compassionate, patient, emotionally stable, and cheerful. In addition, aides should be tactful, honest, and discreet because they work in private homes. Aides also must be in good health. A physical examination, including State-mandated tests for tuberculosis and other diseases, may be required. A criminal background check, credit check, and good driving record may also be required for employment. Additionally, personal and home care aides are responsible for their own transportation to reach patients' homes.

Certification and advancement. The National Association for Home Care and Hospice (NAHC) offers national certification for personal and home care aides. Certification is a voluntary demonstration that the individual has met industry standards. Certification requires the completion of a 75-hour course, observation and documentation of 17 skills for competency assessed by a registered nurse and passing a written exam developed by NAHC.

Advancement for personal and home care aides is limited. In some agencies, workers start out performing homemaker duties, such as cleaning. With experience and training, they may take on more personal care duties. Some aides choose to receive additional training to become nursing and home health aides, licensed practical nurses, or registered nurses. Some experienced personal and home care aides may start their own home care agency or work as a self-employed aide. Self-employed aides have no agency affiliation or supervision and accept clients, set fees, and arrange work schedules on their own.

Employment

Personal and home care aides held about 767,000 jobs in 2006. The majority of jobs were in home health care services; individual and family services; residential care facilities; and private households. In 2006, about 8 percent of personal and home care aides were self-employed.

Job Outlook

Excellent job opportunities are expected for this occupation because rapid employment growth and high replacement needs are projected to produce a large number of job openings.

Employment change. Employment of personal and home care aides is projected to grow by 51 percent between 2006 and 2016, which is much faster than the average for all occupations. This occupation will be amongst the occupations adding the most new jobs, growing by about 389,000 jobs. The expected growth is due, in large part, to the projected rise in the number of elderly people, an age group that often has mounting health problems and that needs some assistance with daily activities. The elderly and other patients, such as the mentally disabled, increasingly rely on home care.

This trend reflects several developments. Inpatient care in hospitals and nursing homes can be extremely expensive, so more patients return to their homes from these facilities as quickly as possible to contain costs. Patients who need assistance with everyday tasks and household chores rather than medical care can reduce medical expenses by returning to their homes. Furthermore, most patients—particularly the elderly—increasingly prefer care in their homes rather than in nursing homes or other in-patient facilities. This trend is aided by the realization that treatment can be more effective in familiar surroundings. Finally, home care has become easier and more feasible with the development of better medical technologies for in-home treatment.

Job prospects. In addition to job openings created by the increased demand for these workers, replacement needs are expected to lead to many openings. The relatively low skill requirements, low pay, and high emotional demands of the work result in high replacement needs. For these same reasons, many people are reluctant to seek jobs in the occupation. Therefore, persons who are interested in and suited for this work—particularly those with experience or training as personal care, home health, or nursing aides—should have excellent job prospects.

Earnings

Median hourly earnings of wage-and-salary personal and home care aides were $8.54 in May 2006. The middle 50 percent earned between $7.09 and $10.19 an hour. The lowest 10 percent earned less than $6.05, and the highest 10 percent earned more than $11.60 an hour. Median hourly earnings in the industries employing the largest numbers of personal and home care aides were as follows:

Residential mental retardation facilities..................................$9.54
Services for the elderly and persons with disabilities...............9.18
Home health care services 7.19

Most employers give slight pay increases with experience and added responsibility. Aides usually are paid only for the time they work in the home, not for travel time between jobs. Employers often hire on-call hourly workers and provide no benefits.

Related Occupations

Personal and home care aides combine the duties of caregivers and social service workers. Workers in related occupations that involve personal contact to help others include childcare workers; nursing, psychiatric, and home health aides; occupational therapist assistants and aides; physical therapist assistants and aides; and social and human service assistants.

Sources of Additional Information

Information about employment opportunities may be obtained from local hospitals, nursing care facilities, home health care agencies, psychiatric facilities, residential mental health facilities, social assistance agencies, and local offices of the State employment service.

For information about voluntary credentials for personal and home care aides, contact:

➤ National Association for Homecare and Hospice, 228 Seventh St., SE., Washington, DC 20003. Internet: **http://www.nahc.org**

Recreation Workers

(O*NET 39-9032.00)

Significant Points

- The recreation field offers an unusually large number of part-time and seasonal job opportunities.

- Educational requirements range from a high school diploma to a graduate degree.

- Opportunities for part-time, seasonal, and temporary recreation jobs will be good, but competition will remain keen for full-time career positions.

Nature of the Work

People spend much of their leisure time participating in a wide variety of organized recreational activities, such as arts and crafts, the performing arts, camping, and sports. Recreation workers plan, organize, and direct these activities in local playgrounds and recreation areas, parks, community centers, religious organizations, camps, theme parks, and tourist attractions. Increasingly, recreation workers also are found in businesses where they organize and direct leisure activities for employees.

Recreation workers hold a variety of positions at different levels of responsibility. Workers who provide instruction and coaching in art, music, drama, swimming, tennis, or other activities may be called *activity specialists*.

Camp counselors lead and instruct children and teenagers in outdoor recreation, such as swimming, hiking, horseback rid-

Many recreation workers are only seasonally employed.

ing, and camping. In addition, counselors teach campers special subjects such as archery, boating, music, drama, gymnastics, tennis, and computers. In residential camps, counselors also provide guidance and supervise daily living and socialization. *Camp directors* typically supervise camp counselors, plan camp activities or programs, and perform the various administrative functions of a camp.

Recreation leaders, who are responsible for a recreation program's daily operation, primarily organize and direct participants. They may lead and give instruction in dance, drama, crafts, games, and sports; schedule the use of facilities; keep records of equipment use; and ensure that recreation facilities and equipment are used properly.

Recreation supervisors oversee recreation leaders and plan, organize, and manage recreational activities to meet the needs of a variety of populations. These workers often serve as liaisons between the director of the park or recreation center and the recreation leaders. Recreation supervisors with more specialized responsibilities also may direct special activities or events or oversee a major activity, such as aquatics, gymnastics, or performing arts.

Directors of recreation and parks develop and manage comprehensive recreation programs in parks, playgrounds, and other settings. Directors usually serve as technical advisors to State and local recreation and park commissions and may be responsible for recreation and park budgets. (Workers in a related occupation, *recreational therapists*, help individuals to recover from or adjust to illness, disability, or specific social problems; this occupation is described elsewhere in the *Handbook*.)

Work environment. Recreation workers may work in a variety of settings—for example, a cruise ship, a woodland recreational park, a summer camp, or a playground in the center of a large urban community. Regardless of the setting, most recreation workers spend much of their time outdoors and may work in a variety of weather conditions. Recreation directors and supervisors, however, typically spend most of their time in an office, planning programs and special events. Directors and supervisors generally engage in less physical activity than do lower level recreation workers. Nevertheless, recreation workers at all levels risk suffering injuries during physical activities.

Some recreation workers work about 40 hours a week. However, many people entering this field, such as camp counselors, may have some night and weekend work, irregular hours, and seasonal employment.

Training, Other Qualifications, and Advancement

The educational and training requirements for recreation workers vary widely depending on the type of job. Full-time career positions usually require a college degree. Many jobs, however, can be learned with only a short period of on-the-job training.

Education and training. Educational requirements for recreation workers range from a high school diploma—or sometimes less for those seeking summer jobs—to graduate degrees for some administrative positions in large public recreation systems. Full-time career professional positions usually require a college degree with a major in parks and recreation or leisure studies, but a bachelor's degree in any liberal arts field may be sufficient for some jobs in the private sector. In industrial recreation, or "employee services" as it is more commonly called, companies prefer to hire those with a bachelor's degree in recreation or leisure studies and a background in business administration. Some college students work part time as recreation workers while earning degrees.

Employers seeking candidates for some administrative positions favor those with at least a master's degree in parks and recreation, business administration, or public administration. Most required at least an associate degree in recreation studies or a related field.

An associate or bachelor's degree in a recreation-related discipline and experience are preferred for most recreation supervisor jobs and are required for most higher level administrative jobs. Graduates of associate degree programs in parks and recreation, social work, and other human services disciplines also enter some career recreation positions. High school graduates occasionally enter career positions, but this is not common.

Programs leading to an associate or bachelor's degree in parks and recreation, leisure studies, or related fields are offered at several hundred colleges and universities. Many also offer master's or doctoral degrees in the field. In 2006, about 100 bachelor's degree programs in parks and recreation were accredited by the National Recreation and Park Association (NRPA). Accredited programs provide broad exposure to the history, theory, and practice of park and recreation management. Courses offered include community organization; supervision and administration; recreational needs of special popula-

tions, such as the elderly or disabled; and supervised fieldwork. Students may specialize in areas such as therapeutic recreation, park management, outdoor recreation, industrial or commercial recreation, or camp management.

Specialized training or experience in a particular field, such as art, music, drama, or athletics, is an asset for many jobs. Some jobs also require certification. For example, a lifesaving certificate is a prerequisite for teaching or coaching water-related activities.

The large number of seasonal and part-time workers learn through on-the-job training.

Licensure and certification. The NRPA certifies individuals for professional and technical jobs. Certified Park and Recreation Professionals must pass an exam; earn a bachelor's degree with a major in recreation, park resources, or leisure services from a program accredited by the NRPA or earn a bachelor's degree and have at least 5 years of relevant full-time work experience. Continuing education is necessary to remain certified.

Many areas require lifeguards to be certified. Training and certification details vary from State to State and county to county. Information on lifeguards is available from your local Parks and Recreation Department.

Other qualifications. People planning recreation careers should be outgoing, good at motivating people, and sensitive to the needs of others. Excellent health and physical fitness are often required, due to the physical nature of some jobs. Volunteer experience, part-time work during school, or a summer job can lead to a full-time career as a recreation worker.

Advancement. Recreation workers with experience and managerial skills may advance to supervisory or managerial positions.

Employment

Recreation workers held about 320,000 jobs in 2006, and many additional workers held summer jobs in the occupation. About 32 percent of recreation workers worked for local governments, primarily in park and recreation departments. About 16 percent of recreation workers were employed by nursing and residential care facilities and another 10 percent were employed in civic and social organizations, such as the Boy Scouts or Girl Scouts or the Red Cross.

Job Outlook

Jobs opportunities for part-time, seasonal, and temporary recreation workers will be good, but competition will remain keen for career positions as recreation workers. Average growth is expected.

Employment change. Overall employment of recreation workers is projected to increase by 13 percent between 2006 and 2016, which is about as fast as the average for all occupations. Although people will spend more time and money on

Projections data from the National Employment Matrix

Occupational Title	SOC Code	Employment, 2006	Projected employment, 2016	Change, 2006-16	
				Number	Percent
Recreation workers	39-9032	320,000	360,000	41,000	13

NOTE: Data in this table are rounded. See the discussion of the employment projections table in the *Handbook* introductory chapter on *Occupational Information Included in the Handbook.*

recreation, budget restrictions in State and local government will moderate the number of jobs added. Many of the new jobs will be in social assistance organizations and in nursing and residential care facilities.

Growth will be driven by retiring baby boomers who, with more leisure time, high disposable income, and concern for health and fitness, are expected to increase the demand for recreation services.

Job prospects. Applicants for part-time, seasonal, and temporary recreation jobs should have good opportunities, but competition will remain keen for career positions because the recreation field attracts many applicants and because the number of career positions is limited compared with the number of lower-level seasonal jobs. Opportunities for staff positions should be best for people with formal training and experience in part-time or seasonal recreation jobs. Those with graduate degrees should have the best opportunities for supervisory or administrative positions. Job openings will stem from growth and the need to replace the large numbers of workers who leave the occupation each year.

Earnings

In May 2006, median annual earnings of recreation workers who worked full time were $20,470. The middle 50 percent earned between $16,360 and $27,050. The lowest paid 10 percent earned less than $14,150, while the highest paid 10 percent earned $35,780 or more. However, earnings of recreation directors and others in supervisory or managerial positions can be substantially higher. Most public and private recreation agencies provide full-time recreation workers with typical benefits; part-time workers receive few, if any, benefits. In May 2006, median annual earnings in the industries employing the largest numbers of recreation workers were as follows:

Nursing care facilities	$21,510
Individual and family services	20,410
Local government	20,100
Other amusement and recreation industries	18,810
Civic and social organizations	17,920

The large numbers of temporary, seasonal jobs in the recreation field typically are filled by high school or college students, generally do not have formal education requirements, and are open to anyone with the desired personal qualities. Employers compete for a share of the vacationing student labor force, and although salaries in recreation often are lower than those in other fields, the nature of the work and the opportunity to work outdoors are attractive to many.

Part-time, seasonal, and volunteer jobs in recreation include summer camp counselors, craft specialists, and after-school and weekend recreation program leaders. In addition, many teachers and college students accept jobs as recreation workers when school is not in session. The vast majority of volunteers serve as activity leaders at local day camp programs, or in youth organizations, camps, nursing homes, hospitals, senior centers, and other settings.

Related Occupations

Recreation workers must exhibit leadership and sensitivity when dealing with people. Other occupations that require similar personal qualities include counselors; probation officers and correctional treatment specialists; psychologists; recreational therapists; teachers—self enrichment education; athletes, coaches, umpires, and related workers; and social workers.

Sources of Additional Information

For information on jobs in recreation, contact employers such as local government departments of parks and recreation, nursing and personal care facilities, the Boy Scouts or Girl Scouts, or local social or religious organizations.

For career, certification, and academic program information in parks and recreation, contact:
➤ National Recreation and Park Association, 22377 Belmont Ridge Rd., Ashburn, VA 20148-4501.
Internet: **http://www.nrpa.org**

For career information about camp counselors, contact:
➤ American Camping Association, 5000 State Road 67 North, Martinsville, IN 46151-7902.
Internet: **http://www.acacamps.org**

Sales and Related Occupations

Advertising Sales Agents

(O*NET 41-3011.00)

Significant Points

- Overall earnings are higher than average but vary considerably because they usually are based on a salary plus performance-based commissions and bonuses.

- Pressure to meet monthly sales quotas can be stressful.

Nature of the Work

Advertising sales agents—often referred to as *account executives* or *advertising sales representatives*—sell or solicit advertising primarily for newspapers and periodicals, television and radio, websites, telephone directories, and direct mail and outdoor advertisers. Because such a large share of revenue for many of these media outlets is generated from advertising, advertising sales agents play an important role in their success.

More than half of all advertising sales agents work in the information sector, mostly for media firms including television and radio broadcasters, print and Internet publishers, and cable program distributors. Firms that are regionally based often need the help of two types of advertising sales agents, one to handle local clients and one to solicit advertising from national advertisers. Print publications and radio and television stations employ local sales agents who are responsible for sales in an immediate territory, while separate companies known as media representative firms sell advertising space or time for media owners at the national level with their own teams of advertising sales agents. Sales agents employed in media representation work exclusively through executives at advertising agencies, called media buyers, who purchase advertising space for their clients that want to initiate national advertising campaigns. When a local television broadcaster, radio station, print, or online publisher is working with a media representative firm, the media company normally employs a national sales manager to coordinate efforts with the media representative.

Local sales agents are often referred to as *outside sales agents* or *inside sales agents*. Outside sales agents call on clients and prospects at their places of business. They may have an appointment, or they may practice cold calling—arriving without an appointment. For these sales agents, obtaining new accounts is an important part of the job, and they may spend much of their time traveling to and visiting prospective advertisers and current clients. Inside sales agents work on their employer's premises and handle sales for customers who walk in or telephone the firm to inquire about advertising. Some may also make telephone sales calls—calling prospects, attempting to sell the media firm's advertising space or time, and arranging follow-up appointments between interested prospects and outside sales agents.

A critical part of building a relationship with a client is to find out as much as possible about the client. Before the first meeting with a client, sales agents gather background information on the client's products, current customers, prospective customers, and the geographic area of the target market. They then meet with the clients to explain how specific types of advertising will help promote the client's products or services most effectively. If a client wishes to proceed, the advertising sales agent prepares an advertising proposal to present to the client. This entails determining the advertising medium to be used, preparing sample advertisements, and providing clients with cost estimates for the proposal. Because consolidation among media industries has brought the sales of different types of advertising under one roof, advertising sales are increasingly in the form of integrated packages. This means that advertising sales agents may sell packages that include print and online ad space and time slots with a broadcast subsidiary.

After a contract has been established, advertising sales agents serve as the main contact between the advertiser or ad agency and the media firm. They handle communication between the parties and assist in developing sample artwork or radio and television spots, if needed. For radio and television advertisements, they may also arrange for commercial taping sessions and accompany clients to these sessions.

In addition to maintaining sales and overseeing clients' accounts, advertising sales agents' other duties include analyzing sales statistics and audience demographics, preparing reports on client's accounts, and scheduling and keeping their appointments and work hours. They read about new and existing products and monitor the sales, prices, and products of their competitors. In many firms, the advertising sales agent handles the drafting of contracts specifying the advertising work to be performed and its cost, and may undertake customer service responsibilities such as answering questions or addressing any problems the client may have with the proposal. Sales agents are also responsible for developing sales tools, promotional plans, and media kits, which they use to help make the sale.

Work environment. Selling can be stressful work because income and job security depend directly on the agent's ability to maintain and expand clientele. Companies generally set monthly sales quotas and place considerable pressure on advertising sales agents to meet those quotas. The added stress of rejection places more pressure on the agent.

Although agents work long and often irregular hours, most have the freedom to determine their own schedule. The Internet and other electronic tools allow agents to do more work from home or while on the road, enabling them to send messages and documents to clients and coworkers, keep up with industry news, and access databases that help them target potential customers. Advertising sales agents use e-mail to conduct much of the business with their clients.

Many advertising sales agents work more than 40 hours per week. This frequently involves irregular hours and may also include working on weekends and holidays. However, most advertising sales agents are able to set their own schedule. Eleven percent of advertising sales agents were employed part time in 2006.

Training, Other Qualifications, and Advancement

For sales positions that require meeting with clients, large employers prefer applicants with a college degree. Smaller companies generally are more willing to hire individuals with a high school degree. Successful sales experience and the ability to communicate effectively become more important than educational attainment once hired. Most training for advertising sales agents takes place informally on the job.

Education and training. Some employers, large companies in particular, prefer applicants with a college degree, particularly for sales positions that require meeting with clients. Courses in marketing, leadership, communication, business, and advertising are helpful. For those who sell over the telephone or who have a proven record of successfully selling other products, a high school degree may be sufficient. In 2006, the highest level of educational attainment for advertising sales agents was as follows.

	Percent
High school graduate or less	20
Some college, no degree	19
Associate's degree	10
Bachelor's degree or higher	52

Most training, however, takes place on the job, and can be formal or informal in nature. In most cases, an experienced sales manager instructs a newly hired advertising sales agent who lacks sales experience. In this one-on-one environment, supervisors typically coach new hires and observe as they make sales calls and contact clients. Supervisors then advise new hires on ways to improve their interaction with clients. Employers may bring in consultants to lead formal training sessions when agents sell to a specialized market segment. This practice is common when advertising sales agents sell space to automotive dealers and real estate professionals.

Other qualifications. Employers look for applicants who are honest and possess a pleasant personality and neat professional appearance. After gaining entry into the occupation, successful sales experience and the ability to communicate effectively become more important than educational attainment. In fact, when selling or soliciting ad space, personality traits are equally, if not more, important than academic background. In general, smaller companies are more willing to hire unproven individuals.

Because they represent their employers to the executives of client organizations, advertising sales agents must have excellent interpersonal and written communication skills. Being multi-lingual, particularly in English and Spanish, is another trait that will benefit prospective advertising agents as media increasingly seek to market to Hispanics and other foreign-born persons. Self-motivation, organization, persistence, independence, and the ability to multitask are required because advertising sales agents set their own schedules and perform their duties without much supervision.

Many advertising sales agents work long and irregular hours to meet sales goals.

Advancement. Advancement in the occupation means taking on bigger, more important clients. Agents with proven leadership ability and a strong sales record may advance to supervisory and managerial positions such as sales supervisor, sales manager, or vice president of sales. Frequent contact with managers of other departments and people in other firms provides sales agents with leads about job openings, enhancing advancement opportunities. In small firms, where the number of supervisory and management positions is limited, advancement may come slowly. Promotion may occur more quickly in larger media firms and in media representative firms.

Employment

Advertising sales agents held over 170,000 jobs in 2006. Workers were concentrated in three industries: More than 3 in 10 jobs were in newspaper, periodical, book, and directory publishers; 3 in 10 in advertising and related services; and nearly 2 in 10 in radio and television broadcasting. Media representative firms are in the advertising and related services industry. A relatively small number of jobs were found in specialized design services, including industrial and graphic designers; printing and related support activities; computer systems design and related services; business support services; and cable and other program distribution.

Employment is spread around the country, but jobs in radio and television stations and large, well-known publications are concentrated in big metropolitan areas. Media representative firms are also concentrated in large cities with many advertising agencies, such as New York City.

Job Outlook

Employment growth of advertising sales agents is expected to grow faster than average for all occupations for the 2006-2016 period. Because of growth in new media outlets, such as the

Projections data from the National Employment Matrix

Occupational Title	SOC Code	Employment, 2006	Projected employment, 2016	Change, 2006-16	
				Number	Percent
Advertising sales agents..	41-3011	170,000	205,000	35,000	20

NOTE: Data in this table are rounded. See the discussion of the employment projections table in the *Handbook* introductory chapter on *Occupational Information Included in the Handbook.*

Internet, advertising agents with an ability to sell, should see good job opportunities.

Employment change. Employment of advertising sales agents is expected to increase by 20 percent from 2006 to 2016, which is faster than the average for all occupations. Fast growth in the number of cable channels, online advertisers, and other advertising mediums will create many new opportunities for advertisers. These opportunities, along with increased efforts by media outlets to market to the growing Hispanic population, will lead to the growth of advertising sales agents.

The industries employing advertising sales agents, particularly the newspaper, periodical, radio, and television industries, have experienced considerable consolidation in recent years, which created efficiencies in the sale of advertising and reduced the need for more sales agents. While this trend is expected to continue over the next decade, it should do so at a slower pace and not affect employment of advertising sales agents significantly.

While advances in technology have made advertising sales agents more productive, allowing agents to take on additional duties and improve the quality of the services they provide, technological advances have not substantially decreased overall demand for these workers. Productivity gains have had the largest effect on miscellaneous services that workers provide, such as accounting, proposal creation, and customer service responsibilities, allowing them to provide faster, improved services to their clients. For example, the use of e-mail has considerably shortened the time it takes to negotiate a sale and place an ad. Sales agents may accomplish more in less time, but many work more hours than in the past, spending additional time on follow-up and service calls. Thus, while productivity gains will temper the growth of advertising sales agents, who can now manage more accounts, the increasing growth in advertising across all industries will ensure that new advertising sales agents will continue to be needed in the future.

Job prospects. Those interested in ad sales positions can expect good job opportunities. This is particularly true for sales people with experience and those with a college degree. For those with a proven sales record in advertising sales, opportunities should be excellent. In addition to the job openings generated by employment growth, openings will occur each year because of the need to replace sales representatives who transfer to other occupations or leave the labor force. Each year, many advertising sales agents discover they are unable to earn enough money and leave the occupation.

Advertising revenues are sensitive to economic downturns, which cause the industries and companies that advertise to reduce both the frequency of campaigns and the overall level of spending on advertising. Advertising sales agents must work hard to get the most out of every dollar spent on advertising under these conditions. Therefore, the number of opportunities

for advertising sales agents fluctuates with the business cycle. So while advertising sales candidates can expect good opportunities, applicants can expect keen competition for job openings during downturns in advertising spending.

Earnings

Including commissions, median annual earnings for all advertising sales agents were $42,750 in May 2006. The middle 50 percent earned between $29,450 and $63,120 a year. The lowest 10 percent earned less than $21,460, and the highest 10 percent earned more than $91,280 a year. Median annual earnings for sales agents in the industries in which they were concentrated were:

Motion picture and video industries	$55,340
Cable and other subscription programming	50,260
Advertising and related services	47,640
Radio and television broadcasting	41,110
Newspaper, periodical, book, and directory publishers	36,880

Performance-based pay, including bonuses and commissions, can make up a large portion of advertising sales agents' earnings. Most employers pay some combination of salaries, commissions, and bonuses. Commissions are usually based on individual sales numbers, whereas bonuses may depend on individual performance, on the performance of all sales workers in a group or district, or on the performance of the entire company. For agents covering multiple areas or regions, commissions also may be based on the difficulty in making a sale in that particular area. Sales revenue is affected by the economic conditions and business expectations facing the industries that tend to advertise. Earnings from commissions are likely to be high when these industries are doing well and low when companies decide not to advertise as frequently.

In addition to their earnings, advertising sales agents are usually reimbursed for entertaining clients and for other business expenses such as transportation costs, meals, and hotel stays. They often receive benefits such as health and life insurance, pension plans, vacation and sick leave, personal use of a company car, and frequent flier mileage. Some companies offer incentives such as free vacation trips or gifts for outstanding sales workers.

Related Occupations

Advertising sales agents must have sales ability and knowledge of their clients' business and personal needs. Workers in other occupations requiring these skills include telemarketers; advertising, marketing, promotions, public relations, and sales managers; insurance sales agents; purchasing managers, buyers, and purchasing agents; real estate brokers and sales agents; sales engineers; sales representatives, wholesale and manufacturing; and securities, commodities, and financial services sales agents.

Sources of Additional Information

To learn about opportunities for employment as an advertising sales agent, contact local broadcasters, radio stations, and publishers for advertising sales representative positions, or look for media representative firms in your area.

For information about advertising sales careers in newspaper publishing, contact:

➤ The Newspaper Association of America, 1921 Gallows Rd., Suite 600, Vienna, VA 22182. Internet: **http://www.naa.org**

Cashiers

(O*NET 41-2011.00, 41-2012.00)

Significant Points

- Cashiers need little or no work experience, and are trained on the job.

- Overall employment is projected to decline; however, job growth will be strong for gaming cashiers.

- Opportunities for full-time and part-time jobs are expected to be good because of the need to replace the large number of workers who leave cashier jobs.

- Many cashiers start at minimum wage.

Nature of the Work

Supermarkets, department stores, gasoline service stations, movie theaters, restaurants, and many other businesses employ cashiers to register the sale of their merchandise. Almost all cashiers total bills on a cash register, receive money, make change, fill out charge forms, and give receipts. A few still use pencil and paper or an adding machine.

Although specific job duties vary by employer, cashiers usually are assigned to a register at the beginning of their shifts and are given a drawer containing a specific amount of money with which to start—their "till." They must count their till to ensure that it contains the correct amount of money and adequate supplies of change. Cashiers also handle returns and exchanges. They must ensure that returned merchandise is in good condition, and determine where and when it was purchased and what type of payment was used.

After entering charges for all items and subtracting the value of any coupons or special discounts, cashiers total the customer's bill and take payment. Forms of payment include cash, personal checks, credit cards, and debit cards. Cashiers must know the store's policies and procedures for each type of payment the store accepts. For checks and credit and debit card charges, they may request additional identification from the customer or call in for an authorization. They must verify the age of customers purchasing alcohol or tobacco. When the sale is complete, cashiers issue a receipt to the customer and return the appropriate change. They may also wrap or bag the purchase.

Cashiers total bills on a cash register, handle money, and interact with customers.

At the end of their shifts, cashiers once again count the drawers' contents and compare the totals with sales data. An occasional shortage of small amounts may be overlooked but, in many establishments, repeated shortages are grounds for dismissal. In addition to counting the contents of their drawers at the end of their shifts, cashiers usually separate and total charge forms, return slips, coupons, and any other noncash items.

Most cashiers use scanners and computers, but some establishments still require price and product information to be entered manually. In a store with scanners, a cashier passes a product's Universal Product Code over the scanning device, which transmits the code number to a computer. The computer identifies the item and its price. In other establishments, cashiers manually enter codes into computers and then descriptions of the items and their prices appear on the screen.

Depending on the type of establishment, cashiers may have other duties as well. In many supermarkets, for example, cashiers weigh produce and bulk food, as well as return unwanted items to the shelves. In convenience stores, cashiers may be required to know how to use a variety of machines other than cash registers, and how to furnish money orders and sell lottery tickets. Operating ticket-dispensing machines and answering customers' questions are common duties for cashiers who work at movie theaters and ticket agencies. In casinos, *gaming change persons* and *booth cashiers* exchange coins and tokens and may issue payoffs. They also may operate a booth in the slot-machine area and furnish change to people or count and audit money in drawers.

Work environment. Most cashiers work indoors, usually standing in booths or behind counters. Often, they are not allowed to leave their workstations without supervisory approval because they are responsible for large sums of money. The work of cashiers can be very repetitious, but improvements in workstation design in many stores are alleviating problems caused by repetitive motion. In addition, the work can sometimes be dangerous; the risk from robberies and homicides is much higher for cashiers than for other workers, although more safety precautions are being taken to help deter robbers.

Gaming change persons and booth cashiers can expect a safer work environment than cashiers in other industries. However, casinos are not without their hazards such as exposure to fumes from cigarettes, cigars, and pipes and noise from slot machines.

About 46 percent of all cashiers work part time. Hours of work often vary depending on the needs of the employer. Generally, cashiers are expected to work weekends, evenings, and holidays to accommodate customers' needs. However, many employers offer flexible schedules. Because the holiday season is the busiest time for most retailers, many employers restrict the use of vacation time from Thanksgiving through the beginning of January.

Training, Other Qualifications, and Advancement
Cashier jobs usually are entry-level positions requiring little or no previous work experience. They require good customer service skills.

Education and training. Although there are no specific educational requirements, employers filling full-time jobs often prefer applicants with high school diplomas.

Nearly all cashiers are trained on the job. In small businesses, an experienced worker often trains beginners. The trainee spends the first day observing the operation and becoming familiar with the store's equipment, policies, and procedures. After this, trainees are assigned to a register—frequently under the supervision of an experienced worker. In larger businesses, trainees spend several days in classes before being placed at cash registers. Topics typically covered in class include a description of the industry and the company, store policies and procedures, equipment operation, and security.

Training for experienced workers is not common, except when new equipment is introduced or when procedures change. In these cases, the employer or a representative of the equipment manufacturer trains workers on the job.

Licensure. Gaming change persons and booth cashiers are required to obtain a license and background check from their State's gaming board and must meet an age requirement, usually set at 21 years old.

Other qualifications. People who want to become cashiers should be able to do repetitious work accurately. They also need basic mathematics skills and good manual dexterity. Because cashiers deal constantly with the public, they should be neat in appearance and able to deal tactfully and pleasantly with customers. In addition, some businesses prefer to hire workers who can operate specialized equipment or who have business experience, such as typing, selling, or handling money.

Advancement. Advancement opportunities for cashiers vary. For those working part time, promotion may be to a full-time position. Others advance to head cashier or cash-office clerk. In addition, this job offers a good opportunity to learn about an employer's business and can serve as a steppingstone to a more responsible position.

Employment
Cashiers held about 3.5 million jobs in 2006. Of these, 27,000 were employed as gaming change persons and booth cashiers. Although cashiers are employed in almost every industry, 26 percent of all jobs were in food and beverage stores. Gasoline stations, department stores, other retail establishments, and restaurants also employed large numbers of these workers. Outside of retail establishments, many cashiers worked in amusement, gambling, and recreation industries, local government, and personal and laundry services.

Job Outlook
Overall cashier employment is expected to decline, but job growth will be strong for gaming cashiers. Opportunities for full-time and part-time jobs are expected to be good because of the need to replace the large number of workers who leave this occupation.

Employment change. Employment of cashiers is expected to decline 3 percent between 2006 and 2016. The rising popularity of purchasing goods online will negatively affect the employment growth of cashiers, although many customers still prefer the traditional method of purchasing goods at stores. Also, the growing use of self-service check-out systems in retail trade, especially at grocery stores, should have an adverse effect on employment of cashiers. These self-checkout systems may outnumber checkouts with cashiers in the future in many establishments. The impact on job growth for cashiers will largely depend on the public's acceptance of this self-service technology.

Job growth will be strong for gaming cashiers as more States legalize casinos and gaming becomes more popular. An increasing number of gaming venues will generate new jobs. However, many casinos are finding ways to use less cash in their operations, particularly the slot machines, which now generate tickets that can be accepted by other slot machines.

Job prospects. Opportunities for full-time and part-time cashier jobs should continue to be good because of the need to replace the large number of workers who transfer to other occupations or leave the labor force. There is substantial movement into and out of the occupation because education and training requirements are minimal and the predominance of part-time jobs is attractive to people seeking a short-term source of income rather than a full-time career. Historically, workers under the age of 25 have filled many of the openings in this occupation. In 2006, almost half of all cashiers were 24 years of age or younger.

Projections data from the National Employment Matrix

Occupational Title	SOC Code	Employment, 2006	Projected employment, 2016	Change, 2006-16	
				Number	Percent
Cashiers..	41-2010	3,527,000	3,411,000	-116,000	-3
Cashiers, except gaming	41-2011	3,500,000	3,382,000	-118,000	-3
Gaming change persons and booth cashiers	41-2012	27,000	29,000	1,800	7

NOTE: Data in this table are rounded. See the discussion of the employment projections table in the *Handbook* introductory chapter on *Occupational Information Included in the Handbook.*

Because cashiers are needed in businesses and organizations of all types and sizes, job opportunities are found throughout the country. But job opportunities may vary from year to year because the strength of the economy affects demand for cashiers. Companies tend to hire more cashiers when the economy is strong. Seasonal demand for cashiers also causes fluctuations in employment.

Earnings

Many cashiers start at the Federal minimum wage, which was $5.85 an hour in 2007. Some State laws set the minimum wage higher, and establishments must pay at least that amount. Wages tend to be higher in areas where there is intense competition for workers.

Median hourly earnings of cashiers, except gaming in May 2006 were $8.08. The middle 50 percent earned between $6.99 and $9.44 an hour. The lowest 10 percent earned less than $6.18, and the highest 10 percent earned more than $11.64 an hour. Median hourly earnings in the industries employing the largest numbers of cashiers in May 2006 were:

Grocery stores	$8.20
Health and personal care stores	8.15
Department stores	8.10
Other general merchandise stores	8.09
Gasoline stations	7.82

Median hourly earnings for gaming cashiers in May 2006 were $9.94. The middle 50 percent earned between $8.16 and $12.22 an hour. The lowest 10 percent earned less than $6.98, and the highest 10 percent earned more than $14.50 an hour. Median hourly earnings in the industries employing the largest numbers of gaming cashiers in May 2006 were:

Casino hotels	$11.64
Traveler accommodation	11.61
Local government	9.50
Gambling industries	9.45

Benefits for full-time cashiers tend to be better than those for cashiers working part time. In addition to typical benefits, those working in retail establishments often receive discounts on purchases, and cashiers in restaurants may receive free or low-cost meals. Some employers also offer employee stock option plans and education reimbursement plans.

Related Occupations

Cashiers accept payment for the purchase of goods and services. Other workers with similar duties include tellers, counter and rental clerks, food and beverage serving and related workers, gaming cage workers, Postal Service workers, and retail salespersons.

Sources of Additional Information

General information on careers in grocery stores is available from:

➤ Food Marketing Institute, 2345 Crystal Dr., Arlington, VA 22202. Internet: **http://www.fmi.org**

For information about employment opportunities as a cashier, contact:

➤ National Association of Convenience Stores, 1600 Duke St., Alexandria, VA 22314.

➤ United Food and Commercial Workers International Union, Education Office, 1775 K St.NW., Washington, DC 20006. Internet: **http://www.ufcw.org**

Counter and Rental Clerks

(O*NET 41-2021.00)

Significant Points

- Jobs usually require little or no experience or formal education.

- Employment is projected to grow much faster than average as businesses strive to improve customer service.

- Many full-time and part-time job opportunities should be available, primarily because of the need to replace workers who leave this occupation.

Nature of the Work

Counter and rental clerks take orders for rentals and services. Many rent cars or home improvement equipment, for example. Regardless of where they work, counter and rental clerks must be knowledgeable about the company's goods and services, policies, and procedures. Depending on the type of establishment, counter and rental clerks use their knowledge to give advice on a wide variety of products and services, ranging from hydraulic tools to shoe repair. For example, in the car rental industry, these workers tell customers about the features of different types of automobiles and about daily and weekly rental costs. They also ensure that customers meet age and other requirements for renting cars, and they indicate when and in what condition the cars must be returned. Those in the equipment rental industry have similar duties but also must know how to operate and care for the machinery rented. In drycleaning establishments, counter clerks inform customers when items will be ready and about the effects, if any, of the chemicals used on certain garments. In video rental stores, counter clerks advise customers about the use of video and game players and the length of the rental period. They scan returned movies and games, restock shelves, handle money, and log daily reports.

When taking orders, counter and rental clerks use various types of equipment. In some establishments, they write out tickets and order forms, although most use computers or barcode scanners. Most of these computer systems are user friendly, require very little data entry, and are customized for each firm. Scanners read the product code and display a description of the item on a computer screen. However, clerks must ensure that the information on the screen matches the product.

Work environment. Firms employing counter and rental clerks usually operate nights and weekends for the convenience of their customers. As a result, many employers offer flexible

In video rental stores, counter clerks advise customers about the use of video and game players and the length of a rental, restock shelves, and handle money.

schedules. Some counter and rental clerks work 40-hour weeks, but many are on part-time schedules—usually during rush periods, such as weekends, evenings, and holidays.

Working conditions usually are pleasant; most stores and service establishments are clean, well lighted, and temperature controlled. However, clerks are on their feet much of the time and may be confined behind a small counter area. Some may need to move, lift, or carry heavy machinery or other equipment. The job requires constant interaction with the public and can be stressful, especially during busy periods.

Training, Other Qualifications, and Advancement

Most counter and rental clerk jobs are entry-level positions that require little or no experience and minimal formal education.

Education and training. Many employers prefer workers with at least a high school diploma. In most companies, counter and rental clerks are trained on the job, sometimes through the use of videos, brochures, and pamphlets.

Clerks usually learn the firm's policies and procedures and how to operate a firm's equipment from more experienced workers. However, some employers have formal classroom training programs lasting between a few hours and a few weeks. Topics covered in this training include the nature of the industry, the company and its policies and procedures, operation of equipment, sales techniques, and customer service. Counter and rental clerks also must become familiar with the different products and services rented or provided by their company to give customers the best possible service.

Other qualifications. Counter and rental clerks should enjoy working with people and should be tactful and polite, even with difficult customers. They also should be able to handle several tasks at once, while continuing to provide friendly service. In addition, good oral and written communication skills are essential.

Advancement. Advancement opportunities depend on the size and type of company. Many establishments that employ counter or rental clerks tend to be small businesses, making advancement difficult. In larger establishments, however, jobs such as counter and rental clerks offer good opportunities for workers to learn about their company's products and business practices. That can lead to more responsible positions. Some counter and rental clerks are promoted to event planner, assistant manager, or salesperson. Some pursue related positions. A clerk that fixes rented equipment might become a mechanic, for example.

In certain industries, such as equipment repair, counter and rental jobs may be an additional or alternative source of income for workers with multiple jobs or for those who are semiretired. For example, retired mechanics could prove invaluable at tool rental centers because of their knowledge of, and familiarity with, tools.

Employment

Counter and rental clerks held about 477,000 jobs in 2006. About 22 percent of clerks worked in consumer goods rental, which includes video rental stores. Other large employers included drycleaning and laundry services; automotive equipment rental and leasing services; automobile dealers; amusement, gambling, and recreation industries; and grocery stores.

Counter and rental clerks are employed throughout the country but are concentrated in metropolitan areas, where personal services and renting and leasing services are in greater demand.

Job Outlook

Much faster than average employment growth coupled with the need to replace workers who leave this occupation should result in many full-time and part-time job opportunities.

Projections data from the National Employment Matrix

Occupational Title	SOC Code	Employment, 2006	Projected employment, 2016	Change, 2006-16	
				Number	Percent
Counter and rental clerks	41-2021	477,000	586,000	109,000	23

NOTE: Data in this table are rounded. See the discussion of the employment projections table in the *Handbook* introductory chapter on *Occupational Information Included in the Handbook.*

Employment change. Employment of counter and rental clerks is expected to increase by 23 percent during the 2006-16 decade, much faster than the average for all occupations. Because all types of businesses strive to improve customer service by hiring more clerks, fast employment growth is expected in most industries; growth in amusement and recreation industries is expected to be especially fast.

Job prospects. Many full-time and part-time job opportunities should be available, primarily because of the need to replace experienced workers who transfer to other occupations or leave the labor force.

Earnings

Counter and rental clerks typically start at the minimum wage, which, in establishments covered by Federal law, was $5.85 an hour in 2007. In some States, the law sets the minimum wage higher, and establishments must pay at least that amount. Wages also tend to be higher in areas where there is intense competition for workers. In addition to wages, some counter and rental clerks receive commissions based on the number of contracts they complete or services they sell.

Median hourly earnings of counter and rental clerks in May 2006 were $9.41. The middle 50 percent earned between $7.58 and $13.05 an hour. The lowest 10 percent earned less than $6.56 an hour, and the highest 10 percent earned more than $18.17 an hour. Median hourly earnings in the industries employing the largest number of counter and rental clerks in May 2006 were:

Automobile dealers	$19.15
Automotive equipment rental and leasing	10.79
Lessors of real estate	10.31
Consumer goods rental	8.07
Drycleaning and laundry services	7.95

Full-time workers typically receive health and life insurance, paid vacation, and sick leave. Benefits for counter and rental clerks who work part time or work for independent stores tend to be significantly less than for those who work full time. Many companies offer discounts to full-time and part-time employees on the goods or services they provide.

Related Occupations

Counter and rental clerks take orders and receive payment for services rendered. Other workers with similar duties include tellers, cashiers, food and beverage serving and related workers, gaming cage workers, Postal Service workers, and retail salespersons.

Sources of Additional Information

For general information on employment in the equipment rental industry, contact:

➤ American Rental Association, 1900 19th St., Moline, IL 61265. Internet: **http://www.ararental.org**

For more information about the work of counter clerks in drycleaning and laundry establishments, contact:

➤ International Fabricare Institute, 14700 Sweitzer Ln., Laurel, MD 20707. Internet: **http://www.ifi.org**

Demonstrators, Product Promoters, and Models

(O*NET 41-9011.00, 41-9012.00)

Significant Points

- Job openings should be plentiful for demonstrators and product promoters, but keen competition is expected for modeling jobs.

- Most jobs are part time or have variable work schedules, and many jobs require frequent travel.

- Formal training is limited and education beyond high school usually is not required.

Nature of the Work

Demonstrators, product promoters, and models create public interest in buying products such as clothing, cosmetics, food, and housewares. The information they provide helps consumers make choices among the wide variety of products and services they can buy.

Demonstrators and *product promoters* encourage people and stores to buy a product by demonstrating it to prospective customers and answering their questions. They may sell the demonstrated merchandise or gather names of prospects to contact later or pass on to sales staff. Demonstrators promote sales of a product to consumers, while product promoters encourage sales to retail stores and help them market products effectively.

Demonstrators and product promoters generate sales of both sophisticated and simple products, ranging from computer software to mops. They attract an audience by offering samples, administering contests, distributing prizes and coupons, and using direct-mail advertising. They must greet and catch the attention of possible customers and quickly identify those who are interested and able to buy. They inform and educate customers about the features of products and demonstrate their use with apparent ease to inspire confidence in the product and its manufacturer. They also distribute information, such as brochures and order forms. Some demonstrations are intended to generate immediate sales through impulse buying, whereas others increase the likelihood of future sales by increasing brand awareness.

Demonstrations and product promotions are conducted in retail and grocery stores, shopping malls, trade shows, and outdoor fairs. Locations are selected based on the nature of the product and the type of audience. Demonstrations at large events may require teams of demonstrators to efficiently handle large crowds. Some demonstrators promote products on videotape or on television programs, such as "infomercials" or home shopping programs.

Demonstrators and product promoters may prepare the content of a presentation and alter it to target a specific audience or to keep it current. They may participate in the design of an exhibit or customize it for particular audiences. Results obtained by demonstrators and product promoters are analyzed, and presentations are adjusted to make them more effective.

Demonstrators and product promoters also may be involved in transporting, assembling, and disassembling materials used in demonstrations.

A demonstrator's presentation may include visuals, models, case studies, testimonials, test results, and surveys. The equipment used for a demonstration varies with the product being demonstrated. A food product demonstration might require the use of cooking utensils, while a software demonstration could require the use of a multimedia computer. Demonstrators must be familiar with the product to be able to relate detailed information to customers and to answer any questions that arise before, during, or after a demonstration. Therefore, they may research the product presented, the products of competitors, and the interests and concerns of the target audience before conducting a demonstration. Demonstrations of complex products often need practice.

Models pose for photos, paintings, or sculptures. They display clothing, such as dresses, coats, underclothing, swimwear, and suits, for a variety of audiences and in various types of media. They model accessories, such as handbags, shoes, and jewelry, and promote beauty products, including fragrances and cosmetics. The most successful models, called supermodels, hold celebrity status and often use their image to sell books, calendars, fitness videos, and other products. In addition to modeling, they may appear in movies and television shows.

Models appear in printed publications, live modeling events, and television to advertise and promote products and services. Most modeling jobs are for printed publications, and models usually do a combination of editorial, commercial, and catalog work. Editorial print modeling uses still photographs of models for fashion magazine covers and to accompany feature articles. Commercial print modeling includes work for advertisements in magazines, newspapers, and billboards. Catalog models appear in department store and mail order catalogs.

During a photo shoot, a model poses to demonstrate the features of clothing and products. Models make small changes in posture and facial expression to capture the look desired by the client. As they shoot film, photographers instruct models to pose in certain positions and to interact with their physical surroundings. Models work closely with photographers, hair and clothing stylists, makeup artists, and clients to produce the desired look and to finish the photo shoot on schedule. Stylists and makeup artists prepare the model for the photo shoot, provide touchups, and change the look of models throughout the day. If stylists are not provided, models must apply their own makeup and bring their own clothing. Because the client spends time and money planning for and preparing an advertising campaign, the client usually is present to ensure that the work is satisfactory.

Editorial printwork generally pays less than other types of modeling but provides exposure for a model and can lead to commercial modeling opportunities. Often, beginning fashion models work in foreign countries where fashion magazines are more plentiful.

Live modeling is done in a variety of locations. Live models stand, turn, and walk to demonstrate clothing to a variety of audiences. At fashion shows and in showrooms, garment buyers are the primary audience. Runway models display clothes that either are intended for direct sale to consumers or are the artistic expressions of the designer. High fashion, or haute couture, runway models walk a runway before an audience of photographers, journalists, designers, and garment buyers. Live modeling also is done in apparel marts, department stores, and fitting rooms of clothing designers. In retail establishments, models display clothing directly for shoppers and may be required to describe the features and price of the clothing. Other models pose for sketch artists, painters, and sculptors.

Models may compete with actors and actresses for work in television and may even receive speaking parts. Television work includes commercials, cable television programs, and even game shows. However, competition for television work is intense because of the potential for high earnings and extensive exposure.

Because advertisers need to target very specific segments of the population, models may specialize in a certain area. Petite and plus-size fashions are modeled by women whose dress size is smaller or larger than that worn by the typical model. Models who are disabled may be used to model fashions or products for disabled consumers. "Parts" models have a body part, such as a hand or foot, which is particularly well-suited to model products such as fingernail polish or shoes.

Almost all models work through agents. Agents provide a link between models and clients. Clients pay models, while the agency receives a portion of the model's earnings for its services. Agents scout for new faces, advise and train new models, and promote them to clients. A typical modeling job lasts only 1 day, so modeling agencies differ from other employment agencies in that they maintain an ongoing relationship with the model. Agents find and nurture relationships with clients, arrange auditions called "go-sees," and book shoots if a model is hired. They also provide bookkeeping and billing services to models and may offer them financial planning services. Relatively short careers and variable incomes make financial planning an important issue for many models.

With the help of agents, models spend a considerable amount of time promoting and developing themselves. Models assemble and maintain portfolios, print composite cards, and travel to go-sees. A portfolio is a collection of a model's previous work that is carried to all go-sees and bookings. A composite card, contains the best photographs from a model's portfolio, along with his or her measurements. Increasingly, composite cards are being sent electronically to clients and printed portfolios are being replaced with digital portfolios.

Models must gather information before a job. From an agent, they learn the pay, date, time, and length of the shoot. Also, models need to ask if hair, makeup, and clothing stylists will be provided. It is helpful to know what product is being promoted and what image they should project. Some models research the client and the product being modeled to prepare for a shoot. Models use a document called a voucher to record the rate of pay and the actual duration of the job. The voucher is used for billing purposes after both the client and model sign it. Once a job is completed, models must check in with their agency and plan for the next appointment.

Work environment. More than half of all demonstrators, product promoters, and models work part time and about 1 in

4 have variable work schedules. Many positions last 6 months or less.

Demonstrators and product promoters may work long hours while standing or walking, with little opportunity to rest. Some of them travel frequently, and night and weekend work often is required. The atmosphere of a crowded trade show or State fair is often hectic, and demonstrators and product promoters may feel pressure to influence the greatest number of consumers possible in a very limited amount of time. However, many enjoy the opportunity to interact with a variety of people.

Models work under a variety of conditions, which can often be both difficult and glamorous. The coming season's fashions may be modeled in a comfortable, climate-controlled studio or in a cold, damp outdoor location. Schedules can be demanding, and models must keep in constant touch with an agent so that they do not miss an opportunity for work. Being away from friends and family, and needing to focus on the photographer's instructions despite constant interruption for touchups, clothing, and set changes can be stressful. Yet, successful models interact with a variety of people and enjoy frequent travel. They may meet potential clients at several go-sees in one day and often travel to work in distant cities, foreign countries, and exotic locations.

Training, Other Qualifications, and Advancement
Postsecondary education, while helpful, usually is not required for demonstrators, product promoters, and models.

Education and training. Demonstrators and product promoters usually receive on-the-job training. Training is primarily product oriented because a demonstrator must be familiar with the product to demonstrate it properly. The length of training varies with the complexity of the product. Experience with the product or familiarity with similar products may be required for demonstration of complex products, such as computers. During the training process, demonstrators may be introduced to the manufacturer's corporate philosophy and preferred methods for dealing with customers.

Some aspiring models opt to attend modeling schools. Modeling schools provide training in posing, walking, makeup application, and other basic tasks, but attending such schools does not necessarily lead to job opportunities. In fact, many agents prefer beginning models with little or no previous experience and discourage models from attending modeling schools and purchasing professional photographs. Agents continually scout for new faces, and many of the top models are discovered in this way. Most agencies review snapshots or have "open calls", during which models are seen in person; this service usually is provided free of charge. Some agencies sponsor modeling contests and searches. Very few people who send in snapshots or attend open calls are offered contracts.

Agencies advise models on how to dress, wear makeup, and conduct themselves properly during go-sees and bookings. Because models' advancement depends on their previous work, development of a good portfolio is key to getting assignments. . The higher the quality and currency of the photos in the portfolio, the more likely it is that the model will find work.

Other qualifications. Employers look for demonstrators and product promoters with good communication skills and a

Demonstrators and product promoters often provide customers with free samples to encourage them to buy a product.

pleasant appearance and personality. Demonstrators and product promoters must be comfortable with public speaking. They should be able to entertain an audience and use humor, spontaneity, and personal interest in the product as promotional tools. Foreign language skills are helpful.

Models should be photogenic and have a basic knowledge of hair styling, makeup, and clothing. Some local governments require models under the age of 18 to hold a work permit. An attractive physical appearance is necessary to become a successful model. A model should have flawless skin, healthy hair, and attractive facial features. Specific requirements depend on the client, but most models must be within certain ranges for height, weight, and clothing size in order to meet the practical needs of fashion designers, photographers, and advertisers. Requirements may change slightly from time to time as our society's perceptions of physical beauty change. However, most fashion designers feel that their clothing looks best on tall, thin models. Although physical requirements may be relaxed for some types of modeling jobs, opportunities are limited for those who do not meet these basic requirements.

A model's career depends on preservation of his or her physical characteristics, so models must control their diet, exercise regularly, and get enough sleep in order to stay healthy. Haircuts, pedicures, and manicures are necessary work-related expenses for models.

In addition to being attractive, models must be photogenic. The ability to relate to the camera in order to capture the desired look on film is essential and agents test prospective models using snapshots or professional photographs. For photographic and runway work, models must be able to move gracefully and confidently. Training in acting, voice, and dance is useful and allows a model to be considered for television work. Foreign language skills are useful because successful models travel frequently to foreign countries.

Models must interact with a large number of people and personality plays an important role in success. They must be professional, polite, and prompt as every contact could lead to future employment. Organizational skills are necessary to manage personal lives, financial matters, and work and travel

Projections data from the National Employment Matrix

Occupational Title	SOC Code	Employment, 2006	Projected employment, 2016	Change, 2006-16	
				Number	Percent
Models, demonstrators, and product promoters.............................	41-9010	107,000	126,000	19,000	18
Demonstrators and product promoters...	41-9011	105,000	124,000	19,000	18
Models...	41-9012	2,000	2,200	200	10

NOTE: Data in this table are rounded. See the discussion of the employment projections table in the *Handbook* introductory chapter on *Occupational Information Included in the Handbook*.

schedules. Competition for jobs is keen and clients' needs are very specific so patience and persistence are essential.

Advancement. Demonstrators and product promoters who perform well and show leadership abilities may advance to other marketing and sales occupations or open their own business.

Models advance by working more regularly and being selected for assignments that have higher pay. They may begin to appear in magazine, print campaigns, commercials, or runway shows with a higher profile. They may begin to work with clients who will provide them with more national exposure. A model's selection of an agency is an important factor for advancement in the occupation. The better the reputation and skill of the agency, the more assignments a model is likely to get. Prospective clients prefer to work with agents, making it very difficult for a model to pursue a freelance career. Modeling careers are relatively short and most models eventually transfer to other occupations.

Employment

Demonstrators, product promoters, and models held about 107,000 jobs in 2006. Of these, models held only about 2,000 jobs in 2006. About 22 percent of all salaried jobs for demonstrators, product promoters, and models were in retail trade, especially general merchandise stores, and 14 percent were in administrative and support services—which includes employment services. Other jobs were found in advertising and related services.

Job Outlook

Employment of demonstrators, product promoters, and models is expected to grow faster than the average for all occupations through 2016. Job openings for demonstrators and product promoters should be plentiful over the next decade but models should face keen competition for the small number of openings.

Employment change. Demonstrators and product promoters are expected to experience 18 percent growth between 2006 and 2016, which is faster than the average for all occupations. Job growth should be driven by increases in the number and size of trade shows and greater use of these workers in department stores and various retail shops for in-store promotions. Product demonstration is considered a very effective marketing tool. New jobs should arise as firms devote a greater percentage of marketing budgets to product demonstration. However, it is also an expensive method of marketing, which will somewhat limit growth.

Employment of models is expected to grow by 10 percent between 2006 and 2016, which is as fast as the average for all oc-

cupations. Growth in the employment of models will be driven by their continued use in advertising products. Advertisers will continue to use models in fashion shows, catalogs, and print campaigns as a method to increase awareness of their product.

Job prospects. Job openings should be plentiful for demonstrators and product promoters. Employers may have difficulty finding qualified demonstrators who are willing to fill part-time, short-term positions. On the other hand, modeling is considered a glamorous occupation, with limited formal entry requirements. Consequently, those who wish to pursue a modeling career can expect keen competition for jobs. The modeling profession typically attracts many more jobseekers than there are job openings available. Only models who closely meet the unique requirements of the occupation will achieve regular employment. The increasing diversification of the general population should boost demand for models more representative of diverse racial and ethnic groups. Work for male models also should increase as society becomes more receptive to the marketing of men's fashions. Because fashions change frequently, demand for a model's look may fluctuate. Most models experience periods of unemployment.

Employment of demonstrators, product promoters, and models is affected by downturns in the business cycle. Many firms tend to reduce advertising budgets during recessions

Earnings

Demonstrators and product promoters had median hourly earnings of $10.65 in May 2006. The middle 50 percent earned between $8.77 and $13.91. The lowest 10 percent earned less than $7.70, and the highest 10 percent earned more than $19.27. Employers of demonstrators, product promoters, and models generally pay for job-related travel expenses.

Median hourly earnings of models were $11.22 in May 2006. The middle 50 percent earned between $9.52 and $14.42. The lowest 10 percent earned less than $7.67, and the highest 10 percent earned more than $18.68. Earnings vary for different types of modeling, and depend on the experience and reputation of the model. Female models typically earn more than male models for similar work. Hourly earnings can be relatively high, particularly for supermodels and others in high demand, but models may not have work every day, and jobs may last only a few hours. Models occasionally receive clothing or clothing discounts instead of, or in addition to, regular earnings. Almost all models work with agents, and pay 15 to 20 percent of their earnings in return for an agent's services. Models who do not find immediate work may receive payments, called advances, from agents to cover promotional and living expenses. Models must provide their own health and retirement benefits.

Related Occupations

Demonstrators, product promoters, and models create public interest in buying clothing, products, and services. Others who create interest in a product or service include actors, producers, and directors; insurance sales agents; real estate brokers; retail salespersons; sales representatives, wholesale and manufacturing; and reservation and transportation ticket agents and travel clerks.

Sources of Additional Information

For information about modeling schools and agencies in your area, contact a local consumer affairs organization such as the Better Business Bureau.

Insurance Sales Agents

(O*NET 41-3021.00)

Significant Points

- In addition to offering insurance policies, agents increasingly sell mutual funds, annuities, and securities and offer comprehensive financial planning services, including retirement and estate planning.

- Agents must obtain a license in the States where they sell.

- Job opportunities should be good for college graduates who have sales ability, excellent interpersonal skills, and expertise in a wide range of insurance and financial services.

Nature of the Work

Most people have their first contact with an insurance company through an insurance sales agent. These workers help individuals, families, and businesses select insurance policies that provide the best protection for their lives, health, and property.

Insurance sales agents, commonly referred to as "producers" in the insurance industry, sell one or more types of insurance, such as property and casualty, life, health, disability, and long-term care. Property and casualty insurance agents sell policies that protect individuals and businesses from financial loss resulting from automobile accidents, fire, theft, storms, and other events that can damage property. For businesses, property and casualty insurance can also cover injured workers' compensation, product liability claims, or medical malpractice claims.

Life insurance agents specialize in selling policies that pay beneficiaries when a policyholder dies. Depending on the policyholder's circumstances, a cash-value policy can be designed to provide retirement income, funds for the education of children, or other benefits as well. Life insurance agents also sell annuities that promise a retirement income. Health insurance agents sell health insurance policies that cover the costs of medical care and loss of income due to illness or injury. They also may sell dental insurance and short-term and long-term-disability insurance policies. Agents may specialize in any one

of these product areas, or function as generalists, providing multiple products to a single customer.

An increasing number of insurance sales agents are offering comprehensive financial planning services to their clients. These services include retirement planning, estate planning, and assistance in setting up pension plans for businesses. As a result, many insurance agents are involved in "cross-selling" or "total account development". Besides offering insurance, these agents may become licensed to sell mutual funds, variable annuities, and other securities. This practice is most common with life insurance agents who already sell annuities, but many property and casualty agents also sell financial products. (See the statement on securities, commodities, and financial services sales agents elsewhere in the *Handbook*.)

Insurance sales agents also prepare reports, maintain records, and seek out new clients. In the event that policy holders experience a loss, agents help them settle their insurance claims. Increasingly, some agents are also offering their clients financial analysis or advice on how to minimize risk.

Insurance sales agents working exclusively for one insurance company are referred to as captive agents. Independent insurance agents, or brokers, represent several companies and match insurance policies for their clients with the company that offers the best rate and coverage.

Technology has greatly affected the insurance business, making it much more efficient and giving the agent the ability to take on more clients. Agents' computers are now linked directly to insurance carriers via the Internet, making the tasks of obtaining price quotes and processing applications and service requests faster and easier. Computers also allow agents to be better informed about new products that the insurance carriers may be offering.

The growing use of the Internet in the insurance industry has altered the relationship between agent and client. Agents formerly used to devote much of their time to marketing and selling products to new clients. Now, clients are increasingly obtaining insurance quotes from a company's Web site and then contacting the company directly to purchase policies. This interaction gives the client a more active role in selecting their policy, while reducing the amount of time agents spend actively seeking new clients. Insurance sales agents also obtain many new accounts through referrals, so it is important that they maintain regular contact with their clients to ensure that the clients' financial needs are being met. Developing a satisfied clientele that will recommend an agent's services to other potential customers is a key to success for agents.

Increasing competition in the insurance industry has spurred carriers and agents to find new ways to keep their clients satisfied. One solution is to increase the use of call centers, which usually are accessible to clients 24 hours a day, 7 days a week. Insurance carriers and sales agents also are hiring customer service representatives to handle routine tasks such as answering questions, making changes in policies, processing claims, and selling more products to clients. The opportunity to cross-sell new products to clients will help agents' businesses grow. The use of call centers also allows agents to concentrate their efforts on seeking out new clients and maintaining relationships with old ones. (See elsewhere in the *Handbook* the statements on

Insurance sales agents carefully review the terms of a new policy with their clients.

customer service representatives and claims adjusters, appraisers, examiners, and investigators.)

Work environment. Insurance sales agents working as captive agents are usually based in small offices, from which they contact clients and provide information on the policies they sell. Independent insurance agents, or brokers, may work in offices of varying sizes, depending on the size of the agency. However, much of their time may be spent outside their offices, traveling locally to meet with clients, close sales, or investigate claims. Agents usually determine their own hours of work and often schedule evening and weekend appointments for the convenience of clients. Some sales agents may meet with clients during business hours and then spend evenings doing paperwork and preparing presentations to prospective clients. Although most agents work a 40-hour week, some work 60 hours a week or longer.

Training, Other Qualifications, and Advancement

Every sales agent involved in the solicitation, selling, or negotiation of insurance must have a State issued license. Licensure requirements vary by State but typically require some insurance-related coursework and the passing of several exams. Although some agents are hired right out of college, many are hired by insurance companies as customer service representatives and are later promoted to sales agent.

Education and training. For insurance sales agent jobs, many companies and independent agencies prefer to hire college graduates—especially those who have majored in business or economics. High school graduates may be hired if they have proven sales ability or have been successful in other types of work.

College training can help agents grasp the technical aspects of insurance policies as well as the industry fundamentals and operational procedures of selling insurance. Many colleges and universities offer courses in insurance, and a few schools offer a bachelor's degree in the field. College courses in finance, mathematics, accounting, economics, business law, marketing, and business administration enable insurance sales agents to understand how social and economic conditions relate to the insurance industry. Courses in psychology, sociology, and public speaking can prove useful in improving sales techniques. In addition, familiarity with computers and popular software packages has become very important because computers provide instantaneous information on a wide variety of financial products and greatly improve agents' efficiency.

Agents learn many of their job duties on the job from other agents. Many employers have their new agents shadow an experienced agent for a period of time. This allows the agent to learn how to conduct their business, how the agency interacts with clients, and how to write policies.

Employers also are placing greater emphasis on continuing professional education as the diversity of financial products sold by insurance agents increases. It is important for insurance agents to keep up to date on issues concerning clients. Changes in tax laws, government benefits programs, and other State and Federal regulations can affect the insurance needs of clients and the way in which agents conduct business. Agents can enhance their selling skills and broaden their knowledge of insurance and other financial services by taking courses at colleges and universities and by attending institutes, conferences, and seminars sponsored by insurance organizations.

Licensure. Insurance sales agents must obtain a license in the States where they plan to work. Separate licenses are required for agents to sell life and health insurance and property and casualty insurance. In most States, licenses are issued only to applicants who complete specified prelicensing courses and who pass State examinations covering insurance fundamentals and State insurance laws. The insurance industry is increasingly moving toward uniform State licensing standards and reciprocal licensing, allowing agents who earn a license in one State to become licensed in other States more easily. Most State licensing authorities also have mandatory continuing education requirements focusing on insurance laws, consumer protection, ethics, and the technical details of various insurance policies.

As the demand for financial products and financial planning increases, many insurance agents, especially those involved in life insurance, are choosing to gain the proper licensing and certification to sell securities and other financial products. Doing so, however, requires substantial study and passing an additional examination—either the Series 6 or Series 7 licensing exam, both of which are administered by the National Association of Securities Dealers (NASD). The Series 6 exam is for individuals who wish to sell only mutual funds and variable annuities, whereas the Series 7 exam is the main NASD series license that qualifies agents as general securities sales representatives.

Other qualifications. Previous experience in sales or insurance jobs can be very useful in becoming an insurance sales agent. In fact, many entrants to insurance sales agent jobs transfer from other sales related occupations, such as customer service representative positions. In selling commercial insurance, technical experience in a particular field can help sell policies to those in the same profession. As a result, new agents tend to be older than entrants in many other occupations.

Insurance sales agents should be flexible, enthusiastic, confident, disciplined, hard working, and willing to solve problems. They should communicate effectively and inspire customer confidence. Because they usually work without supervision, sales agents must be able to plan their time well and have the initiative to locate new clients.

Certification and advancement. A number of organizations offer professional designation programs that certify agents' expertise in specialties such as life, health, and property and casualty insurance, as well as financial consulting. For example, The National Alliance for Education and Research offers a wide variety of courses in health, life and property, and casualty insurance for independent insurance agents. Although voluntary, such programs assure clients and employers that an agent has a thorough understanding of the relevant specialty. Agents are usually required to complete a specified number of hours of continuing education to retain their designation.

In the area of financial planning, many agents find it worthwhile to demonstrate competency by earning the certified financial planner or chartered financial consultant designation. The Certified Financial Planner credential, issued by the Certified Financial Planner Board of Standards, requires relevant experience, completion of education requirements, passing a comprehensive examination, and adherence to an enforceable code of ethics. The exam tests the candidate's knowledge of the financial planning process, insurance and risk management, employee benefits planning, taxes and retirement planning, and investment and estate planning.

The Chartered Financial Consultant (ChFC) and the Chartered Life Underwriter (CLU) designations, issued by the American College in Bryn Mawr, Pennsylvania, typically require professional experience and the completion of an eight-course program of study. Many property and casualty insurance agents obtain the Chartered Property Casualty Underwriter (CPCU) designation, offered by the American Institute for Chartered Property Casualty Underwriter. The majority of professional designations in insurance have continuing education requirements.

An insurance sales agent who shows ability and leadership may become a sales manager in a local office. A few advance to agency managerial or executive positions. However, many who have built up a good clientele prefer to remain in sales work. Some—particularly in the property and casualty field—establish their own independent agencies or brokerage firms.

Employment

Insurance sales agents held about 436,000 jobs in 2006. Almost 50 percent of insurance sales agents work for insurance agencies and brokerages. About 23 percent work directly for insurance carriers. Although most insurance agents specialize in life and health insurance or property and casualty insurance, a growing number of "multiline" agents sell all lines of insurance. A small number of agents work for banks and securities brokerages as a result of the increasing integration of the finance and insurance industries. Approximately 26 percent of insurance sales agents are self employed.

Insurance sales agents are employed throughout the country, but most work in or near large urban centers. Some are employed in the headquarters of insurance companies, but the majority work out of local offices or independent agencies.

Job Outlook

Employment of insurance sales agents is expected to grow about average for all occupations through 2016, and opportunities will be favorable for persons who are college graduates and who have sales ability, excellent interpersonal skills, and expertise in a wide range of insurance and financial services.

Employment change. Employment of insurance sales agents is expected to increase by 13 percent over the 2006-16 period, which is about as fast as average for all occupations. Future demand for insurance sales agents depends largely on the volume of sales of insurance and other financial products. Sales of health insurance and long-term-care insurance are expected to rise sharply as the population ages. In addition, a growing population will increase demand for insurance for automobiles, homes, and high-priced valuables and equipment. As new businesses emerge and existing firms expand their insurance coverage, sales of commercial insurance also should increase, including coverage such as product liability, workers' compensation, employee benefits, and pollution liability insurance.

Employment of agents will not keep up with the rising level of insurance sales, however. Many insurance carriers are trying to contain costs and are shedding their captive agents—those agents working directly for insurance carriers. Instead carriers are relying more on independent agents or direct marketing through the mail, by phone, or on the Internet.

In many ways, the Internet should not greatly threaten agents' jobs as was widely thought. The automation of policy and claims processing is allowing insurance agents to take on more clients. Most clients value their relationship with their agent and still prefer discussing their policies directly with their agents, rather than through a computer.

Insurance and investments are becoming more complex, and many people and businesses lack the time and expertise to buy insurance without the advice of an agent.

Job prospects. Multilingual agents should have good job prospects because they can serve a wider range of customers. Additionally, insurance language tends to be quite technical, so agents who have a firm understanding of relevant technical and legal terms will also be desirable to employers. Many beginning agents fail to earn enough from commissions to meet their

Projections data from the National Employment Matrix

Occupational Title	SOC Code	Employment, 2006	Projected employment, 2016	Change, 2006-16	
				Number	Percent
Insurance sales agents	41-3021	436,000	492,000	56,000	13

NOTE: Data in this table are rounded. See the discussion of the employment projections table in the *Handbook* introductory chapter on *Occupational Information Included in the Handbook.*

income goals and eventually transfer to other careers. Many job openings are likely to result from the need to replace agents who leave the occupation or retire, as a large number of agents are expected to retire over the next decade.

Agents may face increased competition from traditional securities brokers and bankers as they begin to sell insurance policies. Insurance sales agents will need to expand the products and services they offer as consolidation increases among insurance companies, banks, and brokerage firms and as demands increase from clients for more comprehensive financial planning.

Independent agents who incorporate new technology into their existing businesses will remain competitive. Agents who use the Internet to market their products will reach a broader client base and expand their business. Agents who offer better customer service also will remain competitive. Carriers and agencies are increasingly using call centers in an effort to offer better service to customers because they provide greater access to clients' policies and more prompt services.

Most individuals and businesses consider insurance a necessity, regardless of economic conditions, so agents are not likely to face unemployment because of a recession.

Earnings

The median annual earnings of wage and salary insurance sales agents were $43,870 in May 2006. The middle 50 percent earned between $31,640 and $69,180. The lowest 10 percent had earnings of $24,600 or less, while the highest 10 percent earned more than $115,090. Median annual earnings in May 2006 in the two industries employing the largest number of insurance sales agents were $46,210 for insurance carriers, and $42,950 for agencies, brokerages, and other insurance related activities.

Many independent agents are paid by commission only, whereas sales workers who are employees of an agency or an insurance carrier may be paid in one of three ways: salary only, salary plus commission, or salary plus bonus. In general, commissions are the most common form of compensation, especially for experienced agents. The amount of the commission depends on the type and amount of insurance sold and on whether the transaction is a new policy or a renewal. Bonuses usually are awarded when agents meet their sales goals or when an agency meets its profit goals. Some agents involved with financial planning receive a fee for their services, rather than a commission.

Company-paid benefits to insurance sales agents usually include continuing education, training to qualify for licensing, group insurance plans, office space, and clerical support services. Some companies also may pay for automobile and transportation expenses, attendance at conventions and meetings, promotion and marketing expenses, and retirement plans. Independent agents working for insurance agencies receive fewer benefits, but their commissions may be higher to help them pay for marketing and other expenses.

Related Occupations

Other workers who provide or sell financial products or services include real estate brokers and sales agents; securities, commodities, and financial services sales agents; financial analysts and personal financial advisors; and financial managers. Occupations with similar sales duties include sales representatives, wholesale and manufacturing; customer service representatives, and advertising sales agents. Other occupations in the insurance industry include insurance underwriters and claims adjusters, examiners, and investigators.

Sources of Additional Information

Occupational information about insurance sales agents is available from the home office of many insurance companies. Information on State licensing requirements may be obtained from the department of insurance at any State capital.

For information about insurance sales careers and training, contact:

➤ Independent Insurance Agents and Brokers of America, 127 S. Peyton St., Alexandria, VA 22314.
Internet: **http://www.iiaba.org**
➤ Insurance Vocational Education Student Training (InVEST), 127 S. Peyton St., Alexandria, VA 22314.
Internet: **http://www.investprogram.org**
➤ National Association of Professional Insurance Agents, 400 N. Washington Street, Alexandria, VA 22314.
Internet: **http://www.pianet.org**

For information about health insurance sales careers, contact:
➤ National Association of Health Underwriters, 2000 N. 14th St., Suite 450, Arlington, VA 22201.
Internet: **http://www.nahu.org**

For general information on the property and casualty field, contact:
➤ Insurance Information Institute, 110 William St., New York, NY 10038. Internet: **http://www.iii.org**

For information about professional designation programs, contact:
➤ The American Institute for Chartered Property and Casualty Underwriters/Insurance Institute of America, 720 Providence Rd., P.O. Box 3016, Malvern, PA 19355-0716.
Internet: **http://www.aicpcu.org**
➤ The American College, 270 Bryn Mawr Ave., Bryn Mawr, PA 19010-2195. Internet: **http://www.theamericancollege.edu**

Real Estate Brokers and Sales Agents

(O*NET 41-9021.00, 41-9022.00)

Significant Points

- Real estate brokers and sales agents often work evenings and weekends and usually are on call to suit the needs of clients.

- A license is required in every State and the District of Columbia.

- Although gaining a job may be relatively easy, beginning workers face competition from well-established, more experienced agents and brokers.

- Employment is sensitive to swings in the economy, especially interest rates; during periods of declining economic activity and rising interest rates, the volume of sales and the resulting demand for sales workers fall.

Nature of the Work

One of the most complex and significant financial events in peoples' lives is the purchase or sale of a home or investment property. Because of this complexity and significance, people typically seek the help of real estate brokers and sales agents when buying or selling real estate.

Real estate brokers and sales agents have a thorough knowledge of the real estate market in their communities. They know which neighborhoods will best fit clients' needs and budgets. They are familiar with local zoning and tax laws and know where to obtain financing. Agents and brokers also act as intermediaries in price negotiations between buyers and sellers.

When selling property, brokers and agents arrange for title searches to verify ownership and for meetings between buyers and sellers during which they agree to the details of the transactions and in a final meeting, the new owners take possession of the property. They also may help to arrange favorable financing from a lender for the prospective buyer; often, this makes the difference between success and failure in closing a sale. In some cases, brokers and agents assume primary responsibility for closing sales; in others, lawyers or lenders do.

Agents and brokers spend a significant amount of time looking for properties to sell. They obtain listings—agreements by owners to place properties for sale with the firm. When listing a property for sale, agents and brokers compare the listed property with similar properties that recently sold, in order to determine a competitive market price for the property. Following the sale of the property, both the agent who sold it and the agent who obtained the listing receive a portion of the commission. Thus, agents who sell a property that they themselves have listed can increase their commission.

Before showing residential properties to potential buyers, agents meet with them to get an idea of the type of home the buyers would like. In this prequalifying phase, the agent determines how much the buyers can afford to spend. In addition, the agent and the buyer usually sign a loyalty contract, which states that the agent will be the only one to show houses to the buyer. An agent or broker then generates lists of properties for sale, their location and description, and available sources of financing. In some cases, agents and brokers use computers to give buyers a virtual tour of properties that interest them.

Agents may meet several times with prospective buyers to discuss and visit available properties. Agents identify and emphasize the most pertinent selling points. To a young family looking for a house, for example, they may emphasize the convenient floor plan, the area's low crime rate, and the proximity to schools and shopping. To a potential investor, they may point out the tax advantages of owning a rental property and the ease of finding a renter. If bargaining over price becomes necessary, agents must follow their client's instructions carefully and may have to present counteroffers to get the best possible price.

Once the buyer and seller have signed a contract, the real estate broker or agent must make sure that all special terms of the contract are met before the closing date. The agent must make sure that any legally mandated or agreed-upon inspections, such as termite and radon inspections, take place. In addition, if the seller agrees to any repairs, the broker or agent ensures they are made. Increasingly, brokers and agents are handling environmental problems as well, by making sure that the properties they sell meet environmental regulations. For example, they may be responsible for dealing with lead paint on the walls. Loan officers, attorneys, or other people handle many details, but the agent must ensure that they are carried out.

Most real estate brokers and sales agents sell residential property. A small number—usually employed in large or specialized firms—sell commercial, industrial, agricultural, or other types of real estate. Every specialty requires knowledge of that particular type of property and clientele. Selling or leasing business property requires an understanding of leasing practices, business trends, and the location of the property. Agents who sell or lease industrial properties must know about the region's transportation, utilities, and labor supply. Whatever the type of property, the agent or broker must know how to meet the client's particular requirements.

Brokers and agents do the same type of work, but brokers are licensed to manage their own real estate businesses. Agents must work with a broker. They usually provide their services to a licensed real estate broker on a contract basis. In return, the broker pays the agent a portion of the commission earned from the agent's sale of the property. Brokers, as independent businesspeople, often sell real estate owned by others; they also may rent or manage properties for a fee.

Work environment. Advances in telecommunications and the ability to retrieve data about properties over the Internet allow many real estate brokers and sales agents to work out of their homes instead of real estate offices. Even with this convenience, workers spend much of their time away from their desks—showing properties to customers, analyzing properties for sale, meeting with prospective clients, or researching the real estate market.

Agents and brokers often work more than a standard 40-hour week. They usually work evenings and weekends and are usually on call to respond to the needs of clients. Although the hours are long and frequently irregular, most agents and brokers have the freedom to determine their own schedule. They can arrange their work so that they have time off when they want it. Business usually is slower during the winter season.

Training, Other Qualifications, and Advancement

In every State and the District of Columbia, real estate brokers and sales agents must be licensed. Prospective agents must be high school graduates, be at least 18 years old, and pass a written test.

Education and training. Agents and brokers must be high school graduates. In fact, as real estate transactions have become more legally complex, many firms have turned to college graduates to fill positions. A large number of agents and brokers have some college training. College courses in real estate, finance, business administration, statistics, economics, law, and English are helpful. For those who intend to start their own company, business courses such as marketing and accounting are as important as courses in real estate or finance.

More than 1,000 universities, colleges, and community colleges offer courses in real estate. Most offer an associate or bachelor's degree in real estate; some offer graduate degrees. Many local real estate associations that are members of the National Association of Realtors sponsor courses covering the fundamentals and legal aspects of the field. Advanced courses in mortgage financing, property development and management, and other subjects also are available.

Many firms offer formal training programs for both beginners and experienced agents. Larger firms usually offer more extensive programs than smaller firms do.

Licensure. In every State and the District of Columbia, real estate brokers and sales agents must be licensed. Prospective brokers and agents must pass a written examination. The examination—more comprehensive for brokers than for agents—includes questions on basic real estate transactions and laws affecting the sale of property. Most States require candidates for the general sales license to complete between 30 and 90 hours of classroom instruction. To get a broker's license an individual needs between 60 and 90 hours of formal training and a specific amount of experience selling real estate, usually 1 to 3 years. Some States waive the experience requirements for the broker's license for applicants who have a bachelor's degree in real estate.

State licenses typically must be renewed every 1 or 2 years; usually, no examination is needed. However, many States require continuing education for license renewals. Prospective agents and brokers should contact the real estate licensing commission of the State in which they wish to work to verify the exact licensing requirements.

Other qualifications. Personality traits are as important as academic background. Brokers look for agents who have a pleasant personality, honesty, and a neat appearance. Maturity, good judgment, trustworthiness, and enthusiasm for the job are required to attract prospective customers in this highly competitive field. Agents should be well organized, be detail oriented, and have a good memory for names, faces, and business particulars. They must be at least 18 years old.

Those interested in jobs as real estate agents often begin in their own communities. Their knowledge of local neighborhoods is a clear advantage. Under the direction of an experienced agent, beginners learn the practical aspects of the job, including the use of computers to locate or list available properties and identify sources of financing.

Advancement. As agents gain knowledge and expertise, they become more efficient in closing a greater number of transactions and increase their earnings. In many large firms, experienced agents can advance to sales manager or general man-

Real estate brokers and sales agents have knowledge of the real estate market and are on call to suit the needs of clients.

ager. People who earn their broker's license may open their own offices. Others with experience and training in estimating property value may become real estate appraisers, and people familiar with operating and maintaining rental properties may become property managers. (See the *Handbook* statements on property, real estate, and community association managers; and appraisers and assessors of real estate.) Experienced agents and brokers with a thorough knowledge of business conditions and property values in their localities may enter mortgage financing or real estate investment counseling.

Employment

In 2006, real estate brokers and sales agents held about 564,000 jobs; real estate sales agents held approximately 77 percent of these jobs.

Many real estate brokers and sales agents worked part time, combining their real estate activities with other careers. About 61 percent real estate brokers and sales agents were self-employed. Real estate is sold in all areas, but employment is concentrated in large urban areas and in rapidly growing communities.

Most real estate firms are relatively small; indeed, some are one-person businesses. By contrast, some large real estate firms have several hundred agents operating out of numerous branch offices. Many brokers have franchise agreements with national or regional real estate organizations. Under this type of arrangement, the broker pays a fee in exchange for the privilege of using the more widely known name of the parent organization. Although franchised brokers often receive help in training sales staff and running their offices, they bear the ultimate responsibility for the success or failure of their firms.

Job Outlook

Average employment growth is expected because of the increasing housing needs of a growing population, as well as the perception that real estate is a good investment. Beginning agents and brokers face competition from their well-established, more experienced counterparts.

Employment change. Employment of real estate brokers and sales agents is expected to grow 11 percent during the 2006-16 projection decade—about as fast as the average for all occupations. Relatively low interest rates and the perception that real estate usually is a good investment may continue to stimulate sales of real estate, resulting in the need for more agents and brokers. However, job growth will be somewhat limited by the increasing use of technology, which is improving the productivity of agents and brokers. For example, prospective customers often can perform their own searches for properties that meet their criteria by accessing real estate information on the Internet. The increasing use of technology is likely to be more detrimental to part-time or temporary real estate agents than to full-time agents because part-time agents generally are not able to compete with full-time agents who have invested in new technology. Changing legal requirements, such as disclosure laws, also may dissuade some who are not serious about practicing full time from continuing to work part time.

Job prospects. In addition to job growth, a large number of job openings will arise from the need to replace workers who transfer to other occupations or leave the labor force. Real estate

Projections data from the National Employment Matrix

Occupational Title	SOC Code	Employment, 2006	Projected employment, 2016	Change, 2006-16	
				Number	Percent
Real estate brokers and sales agents	41-9020	564,000	624,000	60,000	11
Real estate brokers	41-9021	131,000	146,000	15,000	11
Real estate sales agents	41-9022	432,000	478,000	46,000	11

NOTE: Data in this table are rounded. See the discussion of the employment projections table in the *Handbook* introductory chapter on *Occupational Information Included in the Handbook*.

brokers and sales agents are older, on average, than are most other workers. Historically, many homemakers and retired people were attracted to real estate sales by the flexible and part-time work schedules characteristic of the field. These individuals could enter, leave, and later return to the occupation, depending on the strength of the real estate market, their family responsibilities, or other personal circumstances. Recently, however, the attractiveness of part-time real estate work has declined, as increasingly complex legal and technological requirements are raising startup costs associated with becoming an agent.

Employment of real estate brokers and sales agents often is sensitive to swings in the economy, especially interest rates. During periods of declining economic activity and rising interest rates, the volume of sales and the resulting demand for sales workers falls. As a result, the earnings of agents and brokers decline, and many work fewer hours or leave the occupation altogether.

This occupation is relatively easy to enter and is attractive because of its flexible working conditions; the high interest in, and familiarity with, local real estate markets that entrants often have; and the potential for high earnings. Therefore, although gaining a job as a real estate agent or broker may be relatively easy, beginning agents and brokers face competition from their well-established, more experienced counterparts in obtaining listings and in closing an adequate number of sales.

Well-trained, ambitious people who enjoy selling—particularly those with extensive social and business connections in their communities—should have the best chance for success.

Earnings

The median annual earnings, including commissions, of salaried real estate sales agents were $39,760 in May 2006. The middle 50 percent earned between $26,790 and $65,270 a year. The lowest 10 percent earned less than $20,170, and the highest 10 percent earned more than $111,500. Median annual earnings in the industries employing the largest number of real estate sales agents in May 2006 were:

Residential building construction..	$53,390
Land subdivision	49,230
Offices of real estate agents and brokers...............................	39,930
Activities related to real estate	36,510
Lessors of real estate	32,580

Median annual earnings, including commissions, of salaried real estate brokers were $60,790 in May 2006. The middle 50 percent earned between $37,800 and $102,180 a year. Median annual earnings in the industries employing the largest number of real estate brokers in May 2006 were:

Offices of real estate agents and brokers.............................	$64,350
Lessors of real estate	61,030
Activities related to real estate	48,250

Commissions on sales are the main source of earnings of real estate agents and brokers. The rate of commission varies according to whatever the agent and broker agree on, the type of property, and its value. The percentage paid on the sale of farm and commercial properties or unimproved land is typically higher than the percentage paid for selling a home.

Commissions may be divided among several agents and brokers. The broker or agent who obtains a listing usually shares the commission with the broker or agent who sells the property and with the firms that employ each of them. Although an agent's share varies greatly from one firm to another, often it is about half of the total amount received by the firm. Agents who both list and sell a property maximize their commission.

Income usually increases as an agent gains experience, but individual motivation, economic conditions, and the type and location of the property affect earnings, too. Sales workers who are active in community organizations and in local real estate associations can broaden their contacts and increase their earnings. A beginner's earnings often are irregular because a few weeks or even months may go by without a sale. Although some brokers allow an agent to draw against future earnings from a special account, the practice is not common with new employees. The beginner, therefore, should have enough money to live for about 6 months or until commissions increase.

Related Occupations

Selling expensive items such as homes requires maturity, tact, and a sense of responsibility. Other sales workers who find these character traits important in their work include insurance sales agents; retail salespersons; sales representatives, wholesale and manufacturing; and securities, commodities, and financial services sales agents. Although not involving sales, others who need an understanding of real estate include property, real estate, and community association managers, as well as appraisers and assessors of real estate.

Sources of Additional Information

Information on licensing requirements for real estate brokers and sales agents is available from most local real estate organizations or from the State real estate commission or board.

More information about opportunities in real estate is available on the Internet site of the following organization:

➤ National Association of Realtors.
Internet: **http://www.realtor.org**

Retail Salespersons

(O*NET 41-2031.00)

Significant Points

- Good employment opportunities are expected because of the need to replace the large number of workers who leave the occupation each year.

- Most salespersons work evenings and weekends, particularly during sales and other peak retail periods.

- Employers look for people who enjoy working with others and who have tact, patience, an interest in sales work, a neat appearance, and the ability to communicate clearly.

Nature of the Work

Consumers spend millions of dollars every day on merchandise and often rely on a store's sales force for help. Whether selling shoes, computer equipment, or automobiles, retail salespersons assist customers in finding what they are looking for and try to interest them in buying the merchandise. Most are able to describe a product's features, demonstrate its use, or show various models and colors.

In addition to selling, most retail salespersons—especially those who work in department and apparel stores—make out sales checks; receive cash, checks, debit, and charge payments; bag or package purchases; and give change and receipts. Depending on the hours they work, retail salespersons may have to open or close cash registers. This work may include counting the money in the register; separating charge slips, coupons, and exchange vouchers; and making deposits at the cash office. Salespersons often are held responsible for the contents of their registers, and repeated shortages are cause for dismissal in many organizations. (Cashiers, who have similar duties, are discussed elsewhere in the *Handbook.*)

Retailers stress the importance of providing courteous and efficient service to remain competitive. For example, when a customer wants an item that is not on the sales floor, the salesperson may check the stockroom, place a special order, or call another store to locate the item.

For some sales jobs, particularly those involving expensive and complex items, retail salespersons need special knowledge or skills. For example, salespersons who sell automobiles must be able to explain the features of various models, the manufacturers' specifications, the types of options and financing available, and the warranty.

Salespersons also may handle returns and exchanges of merchandise, wrap gifts, and keep their work areas neat. In addition, they may help stock shelves or racks, arrange for mailing or delivery of purchases, mark price tags, take inventory, and prepare displays.

Frequently, salespersons must be aware of special sales and promotions. They also must recognize security risks and thefts and know how to handle or prevent such situations.

Work environment. Most salespersons in retail trade work in clean, comfortable, well-lit stores. However, they often stand for long periods and may need supervisory approval to leave the sales floor. They also may work outdoors if they sell items such as cars, plants, or lumber yard materials.

The Monday-through-Friday, 9-to-5 workweek is the exception rather than the rule in retail trade. Most salespersons work evenings and weekends, particularly during sales and other peak retail periods. The end-of-year holiday season is the busiest time for most retailers. As a result, many employers limit the use of vacation time between Thanksgiving and the beginning of January.

This occupation offers many opportunities for part-time work and is especially appealing to students, retirees, and others seeking to supplement their income. More than 32 percent of retail salespersons worked part-time in 2006. However, most of those selling big-ticket items work full time and have substantial experience.

Training, Other Qualifications, and Advancement

Retail salespeople typically learn their skills through on-the-job training. Although advancement opportunities are limited, having a college degree or a great deal of experience may help retail salespersons move into management positions.

Education and training. There usually are no formal education requirements for this type of work, although a high school diploma or the equivalent is often preferred. A college degree may be required for management trainee positions, especially in larger retail establishments.

In most small stores, an experienced employee or the store owner instructs newly hired sales personnel in making out sales checks and operating cash registers. In large stores, training programs are more formal and are usually conducted over several days. Topics discussed often include customer service, security, the store's policies and procedures, and how to work a cash register. Depending on the type of product they are selling, employees may be given additional specialized training by sales representatives. For example, those working in cosmetics receive instruction on the types of products the store offers and for whom the cosmetics would be most beneficial. Likewise, salespersons employed by motor vehicle dealers may be in-

Retail salespersons must know about the products they are selling, and answer questions from customers.

Projections data from the National Employment Matrix

Occupational Title	SOC Code	Employment, 2006	Projected employment, 2016	Change, 2006-16	
				Number	Percent
Retail salespersons	41-2031	4,477,000	5,034,000	557,000	12

NOTE: Data in this table are rounded. See the discussion of the employment projections table in the *Handbook* introductory chapter on *Occupational Information Included in the Handbook.*

structed on the technical details of standard and optional equipment available on new vehicle models. Since providing the best possible service to customers is a high priority for many employers, employees often are given periodic training to update and refine their skills.

Other qualifications. Employers look for people who enjoy working with others and who have the tact and patience to deal with difficult customers. Among other desirable characteristics are an interest in sales work, a neat appearance, and the ability to communicate clearly and effectively. The ability to speak more than one language may be helpful for employment in communities where people from various cultures live and shop. Before hiring a salesperson, some employers may conduct a background check, especially for a job selling high-priced items.

Advancement. Opportunities for advancement vary. In some small establishments, advancement is limited because one person—often the owner—does most of the managerial work. In others, some salespersons are promoted to assistant manager. Large retail businesses usually prefer to hire college graduates as management trainees, making a college education increasingly important. However, motivated and capable employees without college degrees still may advance to administrative or supervisory positions in large establishments.

As salespersons gain experience and seniority, they usually move to positions of greater responsibility and may be given their choice of departments in which to work. This often means moving to areas with higher potential earnings and commissions. The highest earnings potential usually lies in selling "big-ticket" items—such as cars, jewelry, furniture, and electronic equipment—although doing so often requires extensive knowledge of the product and an extraordinary talent for persuasion.

Retail selling experience may be an asset when applying for sales positions with larger retailers or in nonretail industries, such as financial services, wholesale trade, or manufacturing.

Employment

Retail salespersons held about 4.5 million jobs in 2006. They worked in stores ranging from small specialty shops employing a few workers to giant department stores with hundreds of salespersons. In addition, some were self-employed representatives of direct-sales companies and mail-order houses. The largest employers of retail salespersons are department stores, clothing and clothing accessories stores, building material and garden equipment and supplies dealers, other general merchandise stores, and motor vehicle and parts dealers.

Because retail stores are found in every city and town, employment is distributed geographically in much the same way as the population.

Job Outlook

Due to the high level of turnover in this occupation, opportunities are expected to be good. The average projected employment growth in this occupation reflects the expansion of the economy and consumer spending.

Employment change. Employment is expected to grow by 12 percent over the 2006-16 decade, which is about as fast as the average for all occupations. In fact, due to the size of this occupation, retail salespersons will have one of the largest numbers of new jobs arise, about 557,000 over the projections decade. This growth reflects rising retail sales stemming from a growing population. Many retail establishments will continue to expand in size and number, leading to new retail sales positions. Since retail salespeople must be available to assist customers in person, this is not an occupation that will suffer negative effects from advancements in technology. To the contrary, software that integrates purchase transactions, inventory management, and purchasing has greatly changed retailing, but retail salespersons continue to be essential in dealing with customers. There will also be an increased demand for retail salespersons in warehouse clubs and supercenters, which sell a wide assortment of goods at low prices, since they continue to grow as many consumers prefer these stores.

Despite the growing popularity of electronic commerce, the impact of electronic commerce on employment of retail salespersons is expected to be minimal. Internet sales have not decreased the need for retail salespersons. Retail stores commonly use an online presence to complement their in-store sales; there are a limited number of Internet-only apparel and specialty stores. Retail salespersons will remain important in assuring customers, providing specialized service, and increasing customer satisfaction. Most shoppers continue to prefer to make their purchases in stores, and growth of retail sales will continue to generate employment growth in various retail establishments.

Job prospects. As in the past, employment opportunities for retail salespersons are expected to be good because of the need to replace the large number of workers who transfer to other occupations or leave the labor force each year. Warehouse clubs and supercenters are expected to have excellent job prospects as they continue to grow in popularity with consumers. In addition, many new jobs will be created for retail salespersons as businesses seek to expand operations and enhance customer service.

Opportunities for part-time work should be abundant, and demand will be strong for temporary workers during peak selling periods, such as the end-of-year holiday season. The availability of part-time and temporary work attracts many people seeking to supplement their income.

During economic downturns, sales volumes and the resulting demand for sales workers usually decline. Purchases of costly items, such as cars, appliances, and furniture, tend to be postponed during difficult economic times. In areas of high unemployment, sales of many types of goods decline. However, because many retail salespersons constantly transfer to other occupations in search of better pay or career opportunities, employers often can adjust employment levels simply by not replacing all those who leave.

Earnings

Median hourly earnings of retail salespersons, including commissions, were $9.50 in May 2006. The middle 50 percent earned between $7.81 and $12.83 an hour. The lowest 10 percent earned less than $6.79, and the highest 10 percent earned more than $18.48 an hour. Median hourly earnings in the industries employing the largest numbers of retail salespersons in May 2006 were as follows:

Automobile dealers	$18.70
Building material and supplies dealers	11.37
Other general merchandise stores	8.79
Department stores	8.70
Clothing stores	8.53

Many beginning or inexperienced workers earn the Federal minimum wage of $5.85 an hour, but many States set minimum wages higher than the Federal minimum. Under Federal law, this wage will increase to $6.55 in the summer of 2008 and to $7.25 in the summer of 2009. In areas where employers have difficulty attracting and retaining workers, wages tend to be higher than the legislated minimum.

Compensation systems can vary by type of establishment and merchandise sold. Salespersons receive hourly wages, commissions, or a combination thereof. Under a commission system, salespersons receive a percentage of the sales they make. This system offers sales workers the opportunity to increase their earnings considerably, but they may find that their earnings strongly depend on their ability to sell their product and on the ups and downs of the economy.

Benefits may be limited in smaller stores, but benefits in large establishments usually are comparable to those offered by other employers. In addition, nearly all salespersons are able to buy their store's merchandise at a discount, with the savings depending on the type of merchandise. Also, to bolster revenue, employers may use incentive programs such as awards, banquets, bonuses, and profit-sharing plans to promote teamwork among the sales staff.

Related Occupations

Salespersons use sales techniques, coupled with their knowledge of merchandise, to assist customers and encourage purchases. Workers in other occupations who use these same skills include sales representatives, wholesale and manufacturing; securities, commodities, and financial services sales agents; counter and rental clerks; real estate brokers and sales agents; purchasing managers, buyers, and purchasing agents; insurance sales agents; sales engineers; and cashiers.

Sources of Additional Information

Information on careers in retail sales may be obtained from the personnel offices of local stores or from State merchants' associations.

General information about retailing is available from:

➤ National Retail Federation, 325 7th St.NW., Suite 1100, Washington, DC 20004.

Information about training for a career in automobile sales is available from:

➤ National Automobile Dealers Association, Public Relations Department, 8400 Westpark Dr., McLean, VA 22102-3591. Internet: **http://www.nada.org**

Sales Engineers

(O*NET 41-9031.00)

Significant Points

- A bachelor's degree in engineering usually is required; many sales engineers have previous work experience in an engineering specialty.

- Projected employment growth will stem from the increasing numbers of technical products and services for sale.

- More job opportunities are expected in independent sales agencies.

- Earnings are typically based on a combination of salary and commission.

Nature of the Work

Many products and services, especially those purchased by large companies and institutions, are highly complex. Sales engineers—who also may be called *manufacturers' agents, sales representatives,* or *technical sales support workers*—work with the production, engineering, or research and development departments of their companies, or with independent sales firms, to determine how products and services could be designed or modified to suit customers' needs. They also may advise customers on how best to use the products or services provided.

Sales engineers sell and consult on technologically and scientifically advanced products. They should possess extensive knowledge of these products, including their components and processes. Sales engineers then use their technical skills to demonstrate to potential customers how and why the products or services they are selling would suit the customer better than competitors' products. Often, there may not be a directly competitive product. In these cases, the job of the sales engineer is to demonstrate to the customer the usefulness of the product or service—for example, how much money new production machinery would save.

Engineers apply the theories and principles of science and mathematics to technical problems. Their work is the link between scientific discoveries and commercial applications. Many sales engineers specialize in products that are related to their engineering specialty. For example, sales engineers selling chemical products may have chemical engineering backgrounds, while those selling business software or information systems may have degrees in computer engineering. (Information on engineers, including 17 engineering specialties, appears elsewhere in the *Handbook*.)

Many of the duties of sales engineers are similar to those of other salespersons. They must interest the client in purchasing their products, many of which are durable manufactured products such as turbines. Sales engineers often are teamed with other salespersons who concentrate on the marketing and sales, enabling the sales engineer to concentrate on the technical aspects of the job. By working on a sales team, each member is able to focus on his or her strengths and expertise. (Information on other sales occupations, including sales representatives, wholesale and manufacturing, appears elsewhere in the *Handbook*.)

Sales engineers tend to employ selling techniques that are different from those used by most other sales workers. They generally use a "consultative" style; that is, they focus on the client's problem and show how it could be solved or mitigated with their product or service. This selling style differs from the "benefits and features" method, whereby the salesperson describes the product and leaves the customer to decide how it would be useful.

In addition to maintaining current clients and attracting new ones, sales engineers help clients solve any problems that arise when the product is installed. Afterward, they may continue to serve as a liaison between the client and their company. Increasingly, sales engineers are asked to undertake tasks related to sales, such as market research, because of their familiarity with clients' purchasing needs. Drawing on this same familiarity, sales engineers may help identify and develop new products.

Work environment. Sales engineers may work directly for manufacturers or service providers, or they may work in small independent sales firms. In an independent firm, they may sell complementary products from several different suppliers.

Workers in this occupation can encounter pressure and stress because their income and job security often depend directly on their success in sales and customer service. Many sales engineers work more than 40 hours per week to meet sales goals and client needs. Although the hours may be long and often irregular, many sales engineers have the freedom to determine their own schedules. Consequently, they often can arrange their appointments so that they can have time off when they want it.

Some sales engineers have large territories and travel extensively. Because sales regions may cover several States, sales engineers may be away from home for several days or even weeks at a time. Others work near their home base and travel mostly by car. International travel to secure contracts with foreign clients is becoming more common.

Training, Other Qualifications, and Advancement

Most sales engineers have a bachelor's degree in engineering, and many have previous work experience in an engineering specialty. New sales engineers may need some on-the-job training in sales or may work closely with a sales mentor familiar with

Most sales engineers have a bachelor's degree in engineering.

company policies and practices before they can work on their own.

Education and training. A bachelor's degree in engineering usually is required to become a sales engineer. However, some workers with previous experience in sales combined with technical experience or training sometimes hold the title of sales engineer. Also, workers who have a degree in a science, such as chemistry, or even a degree in business with little or no previous sales experience, may be termed sales engineers.

Admissions requirements for undergraduate engineering schools include a solid background in mathematics (algebra, geometry, trigonometry, and calculus) and the physical sciences (biology, chemistry, and physics), as well as basic courses in English, social studies, humanities, and computer science. University programs vary in content, though all require the development of computer skills. Once a university has been selected, a student must choose an area of engineering in which to specialize. Some programs offer a general engineering curriculum; students then specialize on the job or in graduate school. Most engineering degrees are granted in electrical, mechanical, or civil engineering. However, engineers trained in one branch may work in related branches.

New graduates with engineering degrees may need sales experience and training before they can work independently as sales engineers. Training may involve teaming with a sales mentor who is familiar with the employer's business practices, customers, procedures, and company culture. After the training period has been completed, sales engineers may continue to partner with someone who lacks technical skills, yet excels in the art of sales.

It is important for sales engineers to continue their engineering and sales education throughout their careers. Much of their value to their employers depends on their knowledge of and ability to sell the latest technologies. Sales engineers in high-technology fields, such as information technology or advanced electronics, may find that technical knowledge rapidly becomes obsolete.

Other qualifications. Many sales engineers first work as engineers. For some, engineering experience is necessary to obtain the technical background needed to sell their employers' products or services effectively. Others move into the occupation because it offers better earnings and advancement potential than engineering or because they are looking for a new challenge.

Advancement. Promotion may include a higher commission rate, larger sales territory, or elevation to the position of supervisor or marketing manager. Alternatively, sales engineers may leave their companies and form independent firms. Independent firms tend to be small, and relatively few sales engineers are self-employed.

Employment

Sales engineers held about 76,000 jobs in 2006. About 37 percent were employed in wholesale trade and another 26 percent were employed in the manufacturing industries. Smaller numbers of sales engineers worked in information industries, such as software publishing and telecommunications; professional, scientific, and technical services, such as computer systems design and related services; architectural, engineering, and related services; and other industries. Unlike workers in many other sales occupations, very few sales engineers are self-employed.

Job Outlook

Job growth for sales engineers is projected to be about average through 2016, and opportunities will be good in independent sales agencies because of the increase in outsourcing of sales departments by manufacturers.

Employment change. Employment of sales engineers is expected to grow by 9 percent between 2006 and 2016, which is about as fast as the average for all occupations. Projected employment growth stems from the increasing variety and technical nature of goods and services to be sold. Competitive pressures and advancing technology will force companies to improve and update product designs more frequently and to optimize their manufacturing and sales processes, and thus require the services of a sales engineer.

In wholesale trade, both outsourcing to independent sales agencies and the use of information technology are expected to create some job growth for sales engineers. Although outsourcing should lead to more jobs in independent agencies, employment growth for sales engineers in wholesale trade likely will be dampened by the increasing ability of businesses to find, order, and track shipments directly from wholesalers through the Internet, without assistance from sales engineers. However, since direct purchases from wholesalers are more likely to be non-scientific or non-technical products, their impact on sales engineers should remain somewhat limited.

Job prospects. Manufacturers, especially foreign manufacturers that sell their products in the United States, are expected to continue outsourcing more of their sales functions to independent sales agencies in an attempt to control costs. Additionally, since independent agencies can carry multiple lines of products, a single sales engineer can handle more products than the single product line they would have handled under a manufacturer. This should result in more job opportunities for sales engineers in independent agencies.

Employment opportunities may fluctuate from year to year because sales are affected by changing economic conditions, legislative issues, and consumer preferences. Prospects will be best for those with the appropriate knowledge or technical expertise, as well as the personal traits necessary for successful sales work. In addition to new positions created as companies expand their sales forces, some openings will arise each year from the need to replace sales engineers who transfer to other occupations or leave the labor force.

Earnings

Median annual earnings, including commissions, of wage and salary sales engineers were $77,720 in May 2006. The middle 50 percent earned between $59,490 and $100,280 a year. The lowest 10 percent earned less than $47,010, and the highest 10 percent earned more than $127,680 a year. Median annual earnings of those employed by firms in the computer systems design and related services industry were $90,950.

Compensation varies significantly by the type of firm and the product sold. Most employers offer a combination of salary and commission payments or a salary plus a bonus. Those working in independent sales companies may solely earn commissions. Commissions usually are based on the amount of sales, whereas bonuses may depend on individual performance, on the performance of all workers in the group or district, or on the company's performance. Earnings from commissions and bonuses may vary greatly from year to year, depending on sales ability, the demand for the company's products or services, and the overall economy.

In addition to their earnings, sales engineers who work for manufacturers usually are reimbursed for expenses such as transportation, meals, hotels, and customer entertainment. In addition to typical benefits, sales engineers may get personal use of a company car and frequent-flyer mileage. Some companies offer incentives such as free vacation trips or gifts for outstanding performance. Sales engineers who work in independent firms may have higher but less stable earnings and, often, relatively few benefits. Most independent sales engineers do not earn any income while on vacation.

Related Occupations

Sales engineers must have sales ability and knowledge of the products and services they sell, as well as technical and analytical skills. Other occupations that require similar skills include advertising, marketing, promotions, public relations, and sales managers; engineers; insurance sales agents; purchasing man-

Projections data from the National Employment Matrix

Occupational Title	SOC Code	Employment, 2006	Projected employment, 2016	Change, 2006-16	
				Number	Percent
Sales engineers..	41-9031	76,000	82,000	6,500	9

NOTE: Data in this table are rounded. See the discussion of the employment projections table in the *Handbook* introductory chapter on *Occupational Information Included in the Handbook.*

agers, buyers and purchasing agents; real estate brokers and sales agents; sales representatives, wholesale and manufacturing; and securities, commodities, and financial services sales agents.

Sources of Additional Information

Information on careers for manufacturers' representatives and agents is available from:

➤ Manufacturers' Agents National Association, P.O. Box 3467, Laguna Hills, CA 92654.
Internet: **http://www.manaonline.org**
➤ Manufacturers' Representatives Educational Research Foundation, 8329 Cole St., Arvada, CO 80005.
Internet: **http://www.mrerf.org**

Sales Representatives, Wholesale and Manufacturing

(O*NET 41-4011.00, 41-4012.00)

Significant Points

- Competition for jobs is expected, but opportunities will be best for those with a college degree, the appropriate technical expertise, and the personal traits necessary for successful selling.

- Job prospects for sales representatives will be better for those working with essential goods, since the demand for these products do not fluctuate with the economy.

- Earnings of sales representatives are relatively high and usually are based on a combination of salary and commission.

Nature of the Work

Sales representatives are an important part of manufacturers' and wholesalers' success. Regardless of the type of product they sell, sales representatives' primary duties are to make wholesale and retail buyers and purchasing agents interested in their merchandise and to address any of their clients' questions and concerns. Sales representatives demonstrate their products and explain how using those products can reduce costs and increase sales.

Sales representatives may represent one or several manufacturers or wholesale distributors by selling one product or a complementary line of products. The clients of sales representatives span almost every industry and include other manufacturers, wholesale and retail establishments, construction contractors, and government agencies. (Retail salespersons, who sell directly to consumers, and sales engineers, who specialize in sales of technical products and services, are discussed elsewhere in the *Handbook*.)

The process of promoting and selling products can take up to several months. Sales representatives present their products to a customer and negotiate the sale. Whether in person or over the phone, they can make a persuasive sales pitch and often

will immediately answer technical and non-technical questions about the products. They may also record any interactions with clients and their respective sales to better match their future needs and sales potential.

There are two major categories of products that sales representatives work with: technical and scientific products and all products except technical and scientific products. Technical and scientific products may include anything from agricultural and mechanical equipment to electrical and pharmaceutical goods. Products included in the later category are more everyday items, including goods such as food, office supplies, and apparel.

Sales representatives stay abreast of new products and the changing needs of their customers in a variety of ways. They attend trade shows at which new products and technologies are showcased. They also attend conferences and conventions to meet other sales representatives and clients and discuss new product developments. In addition, the entire sales force may participate in company-sponsored meetings to review sales performance, product development, sales goals, and profitability.

Frequently, sales representatives who lack the necessary expertise about a given product may team with a technical expert. In this arrangement, the technical expert—sometimes a sales engineer—attends the sales presentation to explain the product and answer questions or concerns. The sales representative makes the preliminary contact with customers, introduces the company's product, and closes the sale. The representative is then able to spend more time maintaining and soliciting accounts and less time acquiring technical knowledge. After the sale, representatives may make follow-up visits to ensure that the equipment is functioning properly and may even help train customers' employees to operate and maintain new equipment. Those selling technical goods may also help set up the installation. Those selling consumer goods often suggest how and where merchandise should be displayed. When working with retailers, they may help arrange promotional programs, store displays, and advertising.

Obtaining new accounts is an important part of the job for all sales representatives. Sales representatives follow leads from other clients, track advertisements in trade journals, participate in trade shows and conferences, and may visit potential clients unannounced. In addition, they may spend time meeting with and entertaining prospective clients during evenings and weekends.

Sales representatives have several duties beyond selling products. They analyze sales statistics; prepare reports; and handle administrative duties, such as filing expense accounts, scheduling appointments, and making travel plans. They also read about new and existing products and monitor the sales, prices, and products of their competitors.

Sales representatives, regardless of where they are employed, may work in either inside sales or outside "field" sales. *Inside sales representatives* may spend a lot of their time on the phone, taking orders and resolving any problems or complaints about the merchandise. These sales representatives typically do not leave the office. *Outside sales representatives* spend much of their time traveling to and visiting with current clients and prospective buyers. During a sales call, they discuss the client's needs and suggest how their merchandise or services can meet

Sales representatives may travel to meet with prospective clients to discuss products and their uses.

those needs. They may show samples or catalogs that describe items their company stocks and inform customers about prices, availability, and ways in which their products can save money and boost productivity. Given that a number of manufacturers and wholesalers sell similar products, sales representatives must emphasize any unique qualities of their products and services. Since many sales representatives sell several complementary products made by different manufacturers, they may take a broad approach to their customers' business. For example, sales representatives may help install new equipment and train employees in its use.

Sales representatives working at an independent sales agency usually sell several products from multiple manufacturers. Additionally, these firms may only cover a certain territory, ranging from local areas to several States. These independent firms are called "manufacturers' representative companies" because their selling is on behalf of the manufacturers.

Depending on where they work, sales representatives may have different job titles. *Manufacturers' agents* or *manufacturers' representatives,* for example, are self-employed sales workers who own independent firms which contract their services to all types of manufacturing companies.

Work environment. Some sales representatives have large territories and travel considerably. Because a sales region may cover several States, representatives may be away from home for several days or weeks at a time. Others work near their home base and travel mostly by car. Sales representatives often are on their feet for long periods and may carry heavy sample products, necessitating some physical stamina.

Sales representatives may work more than 40 hours per week because of the nature of the work and the amount of travel. Since sales calls take place during regular working hours, most of the planning and paperwork involved with sales must be completed during the evening and on the weekends. Although the

hours are long and often irregular, many sales representatives working for independent sales companies have the freedom to determine their own schedules.

Dealing with different types of people can be stimulating but demanding. Sales representatives often face competition from representatives of other companies. Companies usually set goals or quotas that representatives are expected to meet. Because their earnings depend on commissions, manufacturers' representatives are also under the added pressure to maintain and expand their clientele.

Training, Other Qualifications, and Advancement

Many employers hire individuals with previous sales experience who lack a college degree, but hiring candidates with a college degree is becoming increasingly common. Regardless of educational background, factors such as personality, the ability to sell, and familiarity with brands are essential to being a successful sales representative.

Education and training. Since there is no formal educational requirement for sales representative, their levels of education varies. Having a bachelor's degree can be highly desirable, especially for sales representatives who work with technical and scientific products. This is because technological advances result in new and more complex products. Additionally, manufacturers' representatives who start their own independent sales company might have an MBA. As shown in the tabulation below, in 2006 many sales representatives had a bachelor's degree, and many others had some college classes. Some, however, had no degree or formal training, but these workers often had sales experience or potential.

	Percent
High school graduate or less	27
Some college, no degree	19
Associate's degree	9
Bachelor's degree	38
Graduate degree	6

Many sales representatives attend seminars in sales techniques or take courses in marketing, economics, communication, or even a foreign language to provide the extra edge needed to make sales. Often, companies have formal training programs for beginning sales representatives lasting up to 2 years. However, most businesses accelerate these programs to reduce costs and expedite the returns from training. In some programs, trainees rotate among jobs in plants and offices to learn all phases of production, installation, and distribution of the product. In others, trainees take formal classroom instruction at the plant, followed by on-the-job training under the supervision of a field sales manager.

Regardless of where they work, new employees may get training by accompanying experienced workers on their sales calls. As they gain familiarity with the firm's products and clients, the new workers are given increasing responsibility until they are eventually assigned their own territory. As businesses experience greater competition, representatives face more pressure to produce sales.

Other qualifications. For sales representative jobs, companies seek the best and brightest individuals who have the per-

Projections data from the National Employment Matrix

Occupational Title	SOC Code	Employment, 2006	Projected employment, 2016	Change, 2006-16	
				Number	Percent
Sales representatives, wholesale and manufacturing	41-4000	1,973,000	2,155,000	182,000	9
Sales representatives, wholesale and manufacturing, technical and scientific products	41-4011	411,000	462,000	51,000	12
Sales representatives, wholesale and manufacturing, except technical and scientific products	41-4012	1,562,000	1,693,000	131,000	8

NOTE: Data in this table are rounded. See the discussion of the employment projections table in the *Handbook* introductory chapter on *Occupational Information Included in the Handbook*.

sonality and desire to sell. Those who want to become sales representatives should be goal oriented, persuasive, and able to work well both independently and as part of a team. A pleasant personality and appearance, the ability to communicate well with people, and problem-solving skills are highly valued. Patience and perseverance are also keys to completing a sale, which can take up to several months. Sales representatives also need to be able to work with computers since computers are increasingly used to place and track orders and to monitor inventory levels.

Manufacturers' representatives who operate a sales agency must also manage their business. This requires organizational and general business skills, as well as knowledge of accounting, marketing, and administration. Usually, however, sales representatives gain experience and recognition with a manufacturer or wholesaler before becoming self-employed.

Certification and advancement. Certifications are available that provide formal recognition of the skills of sales representatives, wholesale and manufacturing. Many obtaining certification in this profession have either the Certified Professional Manufacturers' Representative (CPMR) or the Certified Sales Professional (CSP), offered by the Manufacturers' Representatives Education Research Foundation. Certification typically involves completion of formal training and passing an examination.

Frequently, promotion takes the form of an assignment to a larger account or territory where commissions are likely to be greater. Those who have good sales records and leadership ability may advance to higher level positions such as sales supervisor, district manager, or vice president of sales. Others find opportunities in purchasing, advertising, or marketing research.

Advancement opportunities typically depend on whether the sales representatives are working directly for a manufacturer or wholesaler or if they are working with an independent sales agency. Experienced sales representatives working directly for a manufacturer or wholesaler may move into jobs as sales trainers and instruct new employees on selling techniques and company policies and procedures. Some leave the manufacturer or wholesaler and start their own independent sales company. Those working for an independent sales company can also advance by going into business for themselves or by receiving higher pay.

Employment

Manufacturers' and wholesale sales representatives held about 2 million jobs in 2006. About 21 percent worked with technical and scientific products. Almost 60 percent of all representatives worked in wholesale trade. Others were employed in manufacturing, retail trade, information, and construction. Because of the diversity of products and services sold, employment opportunities are available throughout the country in a wide range of industries. In addition to those working directly for a firm, some sales representatives are self-employed manufacturers' agents. They often form small sales firms that may start with just themselves and gradually grow to employ a small staff.

Job Outlook

Job growth of sales representatives, wholesale and manufacturing, is expected to be average, but keen competition is expected for these highly paid sales jobs.

Employment change. Employment of sales representatives, wholesale and manufacturing, is expected to grow by 9 percent between 2006 and 2016, which is about as fast as the average for all occupations. Given the size of this occupation, a large number of new jobs, about 182,000 will arise over the projections decade. This is primarily because of continued growth in the variety and number of goods sold throughout the economy. Technological progress will also have an impact on job growth. Sales representatives can help ensure that retailers offer the latest technology available to their customers or that businesses acquire the right technical products that will increase their efficiency in operations. Advances in technology will therefore lead to more products being demanded and sold, and thus growth in the sales representative profession.

At the same time, however, computers and other information technology are also making sales representatives more effective and productive, allowing sales representatives to handle more clients, and thus hindering job growth somewhat.

Employment growth will be greatest in independent sales companies as manufacturers and wholesalers continue to outsource sales activities to independent agents rather than using in-house or direct sales workers. Independent agent companies are paid only if they sell, a practice that reduces the overhead cost to their clients. Also, by using agents who usually contract their services to more than one company, companies can share costs of the agents with each other. As the customers of independent agents continue to merge with other companies, independent agent companies and other wholesale trade firms will also merge with each other in response to better serve their clients.

Job prospects. Earnings of sales representatives, wholesale and manufacturing are relatively high, especially for those selling technical and scientific products, so keen competition is likely for jobs. Prospects will be best for those with a solid technical background and the personal traits necessary for successful selling. Opportunities will be better for sales representatives working for an independent sales company as opposed to working directly for a manufacturer because manufacturers are expected to continue contracting out field sales duties.

Opportunities for sales representatives in manufacturing are likely to be best for those selling products for which there is strong demand. Jobs will be most plentiful in small wholesale and manufacturing firms because a growing number of these companies will rely on agents to market their products as a way to control their costs and expand their customer base.

Employment opportunities and earnings may fluctuate from year to year because sales are affected by changing economic conditions, legislative issues, and consumer preferences. Also, many job openings will result from the need to replace workers who transfer to other occupations or leave the labor force.

Earnings
Median annual earnings of wage and salary sales representatives, wholesale and manufacturing, technical and scientific products, were $64,440, including commissions, in May 2006. The middle 50 percent earned between $45,630 and $91,090 a year. The lowest 10 percent earned less than $33,410, and the highest 10 percent earned more than $121,850 a year. Median annual earnings in the industries employing the largest numbers of sales representatives, technical and scientific products, were as follows:

Computer systems design and related services	$75,240
Wholesale electronic markets and agents and brokers	69,510
Professional and commercial equipment and supplies merchant wholesalers	67,700
Drugs and druggists' sundries merchant wholesalers	66,210
Electrical and electronic goods merchant wholesalers	61,000

Median annual earnings of wage and salary sales representatives, wholesale and manufacturing, except technical and scientific products, were $49,610, including commission, in May 2006. The middle 50 percent earned between $35,460 and $71,650 a year. The lowest 10 percent earned less than $26,030, and the highest 10 percent earned more than $101,030 a year. Median annual earnings in the industries employing the largest numbers of sales representatives, except technical and scientific products, were as follows:

Wholesale electronic markets and agents and brokers	$54,900
Professional and commercial equipment and supplies merchant wholesalers	49,730
Machinery, equipment, and supplies merchant wholesalers	48,620
Grocery and related product wholesalers	46,150
Miscellaneous nondurable goods merchant wholesalers	42,530

Compensation methods for those representatives working for an independent sales company vary significantly by the type of firm and the product sold. Most employers use a combination of salary and commissions or salary plus bonus. Commissions usually are based on the amount of sales, whereas bonuses may depend on individual performance, on the performance of all sales workers in the group or district, or on the company's performance. Unlike those working directly for a manufacturer or wholesaler, sales representatives working for an independent sales company usually are not reimbursed for expenses. Depending on the type of product or products they are selling, their experience in the field, and the number of clients they have, they can earn significantly more or less than those working in direct sales for a manufacturer or wholesaler.

In addition to their earnings, sales representatives working directly for a manufacturer or wholesaler usually are reimbursed for expenses such as transportation costs, meals, hotels, and entertaining customers. They often receive benefits such as health and life insurance, pension plans, vacation and sick leave, personal use of a company car, and frequent flyer mileage. Some companies offer incentives such as free vacation trips or gifts for outstanding sales workers.

Related Occupations
Sales representatives, wholesale and manufacturing, must have sales ability and knowledge of the products they sell. Other occupations that require similar skills include advertising, marketing, promotions, public relations, and sales managers; insurance sales agents; purchasing managers, buyers, and purchasing agents; real estate brokers and sales agents; retail salespersons; sales engineers; and securities, commodities, and financial services sales agents.

Sources of Additional Information
Information on careers for manufacturers' representatives and sales agents is available from:
➤ Manufacturers' Agents National Association, One Spectrum Pointe, Suite 150, Lake Forest, CA 92630.
Internet: **http://www.manaonline.org**
➤ Manufacturers' Representatives Educational Research Foundation, 8329 Cole St., Arvada, CO 80005.
Internet: **http://www.mrerf.org**

Sales Worker Supervisors

(O*NET 41-1011.00, 41-1012.00)

Significant Points

- Overall employment is projected to grow more slowly than average.

- Applicants with retail experience should have the best job opportunities.

- Long, irregular hours, including evenings and weekends, are common.

Nature of the Work
Sales worker supervisors oversee the work of sales and related workers, such as retail salespersons, cashiers, customer service representatives, stock clerks and order fillers, sales engineers, and wholesale sales representatives. Sales worker supervisors are responsible for interviewing, hiring, and training employ-

Sales worker supervisors monitor their staff to ensure high quality service to customers.

ees. They also may prepare work schedules and assign workers to specific duties. Many of these supervisors hold job titles such as *sales manager* or *department manager*. Under the occupational classification system used in the *Handbook*, however, workers who mainly supervise workers and who do not focus on broader managerial issues of planning and strategy are classified as supervisors.

In retail establishments, sales worker supervisors ensure that customers receive satisfactory service and quality goods. They also answer customers' inquiries, deal with complaints, and sometimes handle purchasing, budgeting, and accounting.

Responsibilities vary with the size and type of establishment. As the size of retail stores and the types of goods and services increase, supervisors tend to specialize in one department or one aspect of merchandising. Sales worker supervisors in large retail establishments are often referred to as department supervisors or managers. They provide day-to-day oversight of individual departments, such as shoes, cosmetics, or housewares in department stores; produce or meat in grocery stores; and car sales in automotive dealerships. Department supervisors establish and implement policies, goals, and procedures for their specific departments; coordinate activities with other department heads; and strive for smooth operations within their departments. They supervise employees who price and ticket goods and place them on display; clean and organize shelves, displays, and inventories in stockrooms; and inspect

merchandise to ensure that nothing is outdated. Sales worker supervisors also review inventory and sales records, develop merchandising techniques, and coordinate sales promotions. In addition, they may greet and assist customers and promote sales and good public relations.

Sales worker supervisors in non-retail establishments oversee and coordinate the activities of sales workers who sell industrial products, insurance policies, or services such as advertising, financial, or Internet services. They may prepare budgets, make personnel decisions, devise sales-incentive programs, and approve sales contracts.

In small or independent companies and retail stores, sales worker supervisors not only directly supervise sales associates, but they also are responsible for the operation of the entire company or store. Some are self-employed business or store owners.

Work environment. Most sales worker supervisors have offices. In retail trade, their offices are within the stores, usually close to the areas they oversee. Although they spend some time in the office completing merchandise orders or arranging work schedules, a large portion of their workday is spent on the sales floor, supervising employees or selling.

Work hours of supervisors vary greatly among establishments because work schedules usually depend on customers' needs. Supervisors generally work at least 40 hours a week. Long, irregular hours are common, particularly during sales, holidays, and busy shopping seasons and at times when inventory is taken. Supervisors are expected to work some evenings and weekends but usually are given a day off during the week. Hours can change weekly, and supervisors sometimes must report to work on short notice, especially when employees are absent. Independent owners often can set their own schedules, but hours must be convenient to customers.

Training, Other Qualifications, and Advancement
Sales worker supervisors usually gain knowledge of management principles and practices through work experience. Many supervisors begin their careers on the sales floor as salespersons, cashiers, or customer service representatives. These workers should be patient, decisive, and sales-oriented.

Education and training. The educational backgrounds of sales worker supervisors vary widely. Supervisors who have postsecondary education often hold associate or bachelor's degrees in liberal arts, social sciences, business, or management. Recommended high school or college courses include those related to business, such as accounting, marketing, management, and sales, and those related to social science, such as psychology, sociology, and communication. Supervisors also must know how to use computers because almost all cash registers, inventory control systems, and sales quotes and contracts are computerized. To gain experience, many college students participate in internship programs that usually are developed jointly by schools and businesses.

Having previous sales experience is usually a requirement for becoming a sales worker supervisor. Most sales worker supervisors have retail sales experience or experience as a customer service representative. In these positions, they learn merchandising, customer service, and the basic policies and procedures of the company.

The type and amount of training available to supervisors varies by company. Many national retail chains and companies have formal training programs for management trainees that include both classroom and on-site training. Training time may be as brief as 1 week or may last more than 1 year, giving trainees experience during all sales seasons.

Ordinarily, classroom training includes topics such as interviewing, customer service skills, inventory management, employee relations, and scheduling. Management trainees may work in one specific department while training on the job, or they may rotate through several departments to gain a well-rounded knowledge of the company's operation. Training programs for retail franchises are generally extensive, covering all functions of the company's operation, including budgeting, marketing, management, finance, purchasing, product preparation, human resource management, and compensation. College graduates usually can enter management training programs directly, without much experience.

Other qualifications. Sales worker supervisors must get along with all types of people. They need initiative, self-discipline, good judgment, and decisiveness. Patience and a conciliatory temperament are necessary when dealing with demanding customers. Supervisors also must be able to motivate, organize, and direct the work of subordinates and communicate clearly and persuasively with customers and other supervisors.

Advancement. Supervisors who display leadership and team-building skills, self-confidence, motivation, and decisiveness become candidates for promotion to assistant manager or manager. A postsecondary degree may speed their advancement into management because employers view it as a sign of motivation and maturity—qualities deemed important for promotion to more responsible positions. In many retail establishments, managers are promoted from within the company. In small retail establishments, where the number of positions is limited, advancement to a higher management position may come slowly. Large establishments often have extensive career ladder programs and may offer supervisors the opportunity to transfer to another store in the chain or to the central office. Although promotions may occur more quickly in large establishments, some managers may need to relocate every several years in order to advance.

Supervisors also can become advertising, marketing, promotions, public relations, and sales managers—workers who coordinate marketing plans, monitor sales, and propose advertisements and promotions—or purchasing managers, buyers, or purchasing agents—workers who purchase goods and supplies for their organization or for resale. (These occupations are covered elsewhere in the *Handbook.*)

Some supervisors who have worked in their industry for a long time open their own stores or sales firms. However, retail trade and sales occupations are highly competitive, and although many independent owners succeed, some fail to cover expenses and eventually go out of business. To prosper, owners usually need good business sense and strong customer service and public relations skills.

Employment

Sales worker supervisors held about 2.2 million jobs in 2006. Approximately 37 percent were self-employed, most of whom were store owners. About 44 percent of sales worker supervisors were wage-and-salary workers employed in the retail sector; some of the largest employers were grocery stores, department stores, motor vehicle and parts dealers, and clothing and clothing accessory stores. The remaining sales worker supervisors worked in non-retail establishments.

Job Outlook

Despite slower than average growth, retail sales worker supervisors with previous experience in sales are expected to have good job prospects because of the large size of the occupation and the need to replace workers who leave their positions.

Employment change. Employment of sales worker supervisors is expected to grow by 4 percent between 2006 and 2016, which is more slowly than the average for all occupations. Growth in the occupation will be limited as retail companies increase the responsibilities of retail salespersons and existing sales worker supervisors.

The Internet and electronic commerce are creating new opportunities to reach and communicate with potential customers. Some firms are hiring Internet sales supervisors, who are in charge of maintaining an Internet site and answering inquiries relating to the product, to prices, and to the terms of delivery. However, Internet sales and electronic commerce may reduce the number of additional sales workers needed in stores, thus reducing the total number of additional supervisors required. Overall, the impact of electronic commerce on employment of sales worker supervisors should be minimal.

Projected employment growth of sales worker supervisors will mirror, in part, the patterns of employment growth in the industries in which they work. For example, faster-than-average employment growth is expected in many of the rapidly growing service-providing industries. In contrast, the number of self-employed sales worker supervisors is expected to grow slowly as independent retailers face increasing competition from national chains.

Projections data from the National Employment Matrix

Occupational Title	SOC Code	Employment, 2006	Projected employment, 2016	Change, 2006-16	
				Number	Percent
Supervisors, sales workers	41-1000	2,206,000	2,296,000	91,000	4
First-line supervisors/managers of retail sales workers	41-1011	1,676,000	1,747,000	71,000	4
First-line supervisors/managers of non-retail sales workers	41-1012	530,000	549,000	19,000	4

NOTE: Data in this table are rounded. See the discussion of the employment projections table in the *Handbook* introductory chapter on *Occupational Information Included in the Handbook.*

Unlike mid-level and top-level managers, retail store managers generally will not be affected by the restructuring and consolidation taking place at the corporate headquarters of many retail chains.

Job prospects. Candidates who have retail experience—as a salesperson, cashier, or customer service representative, for example—will have the best opportunities for jobs as supervisors, especially in retail establishments. Stronger competition for supervisory jobs is expected in non-retail establishments, particularly those with the most attractive earnings and work environment.

Some of the job openings over the next decade will occur as experienced supervisors move into higher levels of management, transfer to other occupations, or leave the labor force. However, these job openings will not be great in number since, as with other supervisory and managerial occupations, the separation rate is low. This is the case especially for non-retail sales worker supervisors.

Earnings

Salaries of sales worker supervisors vary substantially, depending on a worker's level of responsibility and length of service and the type, size, and location of the firm.

Salaried supervisors of retail sales workers had median annual earnings of $33,960, including commissions, in May 2006. The middle 50 percent earned between $26,490 and $44,570 a year. The lowest 10 percent earned less than $21,420, and the highest 10 percent earned more than $59,710 a year. Median annual earnings in the industries employing the largest numbers of salaried supervisors of retail sales workers were as follows:

Building material and supplies dealers	$35,820
Grocery stores	33,390
Clothing stores	33,140
Gasoline stations	29,270
Other general merchandise stores	28,870

Salaried supervisors of nonretail sales workers had median annual earnings of, $65,510, including commissions, in May 2006. The middle 50 percent earned between $48,900 and $94,670 a year. The lowest 10 percent earned less than $34,840, and the highest 10 percent earned more than $135,270 a year. Median annual earnings in the industries employing the largest numbers of salaried supervisors of nonretail sales workers were as follows:

Professional and commercial equipment and supplies merchant wholesalers	$80,650
Wholesale electronic markets and agents and brokers	78,260
Machinery, equipment, and supplies merchant wholesalers	65,660
Postal service	58,640
Business support services	45,490

Compensation systems vary by type of establishment and by merchandise sold. Many supervisors receive a commission or a combination of salary and commission. Under a commission system, supervisors receive a percentage of department or store sales. Thus, these supervisors' earnings depend on their ability to sell their product and the condition of the economy. Those who sell large amounts of merchandise or exceed sales goals often receive bonuses or other awards.

Related Occupations

Sales worker supervisors serve customers, supervise workers, and direct and coordinate the operations of an establishment. Workers with similar responsibilities include financial managers, food service managers, lodging managers, office and administrative support worker supervisors and managers, and medical and health services managers.

Sources of Additional Information

Information on employment opportunities for sales worker supervisors may be obtained from the employment offices of various retail establishments or from State employment service offices.

General information on management careers in retail establishments is available from:

➤ National Retail Federation, 325 7th St.NW., Suite 1100, Washington, DC 20004.

Information about management careers and training programs in the motor vehicle dealers industry is available from:

➤ National Automobile Dealers Association, Public Relations Dept., 8400 Westpark Dr., McLean, VA 22102-3591.
Internet: **http://www.nada.org**

Information about management careers in convenience stores is available from:

➤ National Association of Convenience Stores, 1600 Duke St., Alexandria, VA 22314-3436.

Securities, Commodities, and Financial Services Sales Agents

(O*NET 41-3031.00, 41-3031.01, 41-3031.02)

Significant Points

- A college degree, sales ability, good interpersonal and communication skills, and a strong desire to succeed are important qualifications.

- Competition for entry-level jobs usually is keen, especially in investment banks; opportunities should be better in smaller firms.

- Many people leave the occupation because of underperformance, but those who are successful have a very strong attachment to their occupation because of high earnings and considerable investment in training.

Nature of the Work

Each day, hundreds of billions of dollars change hands on the major United States securities exchanges. This money is used to purchase stocks, bonds, mutual funds, and other financial instruments, called securities. Securities are bought and sold by large institutional investors, wealthy individuals, mutual funds and pension plans, and the general public. In fact, about half of

American households own stock. Most securities trades are arranged through securities, commodities, and financial services sales agents, whether they are between individuals with a few hundred dollars to invest or between large institutions having millions of dollars. The duties of sales agents vary greatly depending on occupational specialty.

The most common type of securities sales agent is called a *broker* or *stock broker*. These are the people who sell securities to everyday people, also known as retail investors. Although only about 2 out of every 10 equities are held by small investors, most investors fall into this category. Because there are so many retail investors, they must work through a broker rather than trading directly on an exchange. First, the investor speaks with the broker, discussing the terms of the trade. Then, the broker relays this information to a trader at the company's headquarters. Because most securities companies are very large, they can often find other company clients who are willing to buy or sell the same security. Otherwise, the stock trader places an order with a floor broker at an exchange, or trades the stock on an electronic network. The broker charges a fee for this service, and may also make money by finding a lower price for the security than was arranged with the investor.

The most important part of a broker's job is finding clients and building a customer base. Thus, beginning securities and commodities sales agents spend much of their time searching for customers, often relying heavily on telephone solicitation. They also may meet clients through business and social contacts. Agents also join civic organizations and other social groups to expand their networks of possible clients. Many find it useful to contact potential clients by teaching adult education investment courses or by giving lectures at libraries or social clubs. Brokerage firms may give sales agents lists of people with whom the firm has done business in the past. Some agents inherit the clients of agents who have retired. After an agent is established, referrals from satisfied clients are an important source of new business.

Investment bankers are sales agents who connect businesses that need money to finance their operations or expansion plans with investors who are interested in providing that funding in exchange for debt (in the form of bonds) or equity (in the form of stock). This process is called underwriting, and it is the main function of the investment bank. Investment bankers have to sell twice: first, they sell their advisory services to help companies set up issuing new stock or bonds, and second, they then sell the securities they issue to investors.

Perhaps the most important advisory service provided by investment banks is to help companies new to the public investment arena issue stock for the first time. This process, known as an initial public offering, or IPO, can take a great deal of effort because private companies must meet stringent requirements to become public or be allowed to issue stocks and bonds. Corporate finance departments also help private companies sell stock to institutional investors or wealthy individuals. They also advise companies that are interested in funding their operations by taking on debt. This debt can be issued in the form of bonds. Unlike a stock, which entitles its holder to partial ownership of a company, a bond entitles its holder to be repaid with a predetermined rate of interest.

Another important advisory service is provided by the mergers and acquisitions department. Bankers in this area advise companies that are interested in merging with or purchasing other companies. They also help companies that would like to be acquired. Once a potential seller or buyer is found, bankers advise their client on how to execute the agreement. Generally both buyers and sellers have investment banks working for them to make sure that the transaction goes smoothly.

Investment banking sales agents and traders sell stocks and bonds to investors. Instead of selling their services to companies for fees, salespeople and traders sell securities to customers for commissions. These sales agents generally work by telephone, calling customers and their agents to discuss new stock and bond issues. When an investor decides to make a purchase, the order goes to the trading floor. Traders execute buy and sell orders from clients and make trades on behalf of the bank itself. Because markets fluctuate so much, trading is a split-second decision making process. If a trader cannot secure the promised price on an exchange, millions of dollars could potentially be lost. On the other hand, if a trader finds a better deal, the bank could make millions more.

A small but powerful group of sales agents work directly on the floor of a stock or commodities exchange. When a firm or investor wishes to buy or sell a security or commodity, sales agents relay the order through their firm's computers to the floor of the exchange. There, *floor brokers* negotiate the price with other floor brokers, make the sale, and forward the purchase price to the sales agents. In addition to floor brokers, who work for individual securities dealers, there are also independent brokers. These are similar to floor brokers, except that they are not buyers for specific firms. Instead, they can buy and sell stocks for their own accounts, or corporate accounts that they manage,, or they can sell their services to floor brokers who are too busy to execute all of the trades they are responsible for making. Specialists or market makers also work directly on the exchange floor, and there is generally one for each security or commodity being traded. They facilitate the trading process by quoting prices and by buying or selling shares when there are too many or too few available.

Financial services sales agents sell a wide variety of banking, accounting, securities, insurance, tax preparation, and other related services. They contact potential customers to explain their services and to ascertain customers' banking and other financial needs. They also may solicit businesses to participate in consumer credit card programs.

Work environment. Most securities and commodities sales agents work in offices under fairly stressful conditions. The pace of work is very fast, and managers tend to be very demanding of their workers since both commissions and advancement are tied to sales.

Stock brokers and investment advisors generally work somewhat more than 40 hours a week, but they may not work at traditional times. Evening and weekend work is often necessary, as many of their clients work during the day. A growing number of securities sales agents, employed mostly by discount or online brokerage firms, work in call-center environments. In these centers, hundreds of agents spend much of the day on the telephone taking orders from clients or offering advice and in-

Securities, commodities, and financial services sales agents spend much of their time on the telephone with clients.

formation on different securities. Often, such call centers operate 24 hours a day, requiring agents to work in shifts.

Investment bankers in corporate finance or mergers and acquisitions typically work long hours and endure extreme stress, especially at the junior levels. Evening and weekend work is common. Because banks work with companies all over the world, extensive travel is often part of the job. With some experience, the workload becomes more manageable, but since higher-level workers generally have more contact with clients, they also tend to travel more.

Sales and trading departments typically work somewhat more than 40 hours a week, but not nearly as much as their counterparts in investment banking. They also travel less, and many only travel a few times a year for conferences or training. On the other hand, their jobs are incredibly stressful. For sales agents, every minute of the day that is wasted means they might have made another sale. Since both commissions and advancement are tied to sales, this can be very stressful. Traders have perhaps the most stressful jobs of all, as split second decisions can lead to millions of dollars being won or lost. Trading floors are very busy and often very loud. Exchange workers, much like traders, have highly stressful jobs because the bulk of their work takes place on the floor of the exchanges. However, exchange traders and workers typically work shorter hours than

many other agents since most of their work is done while the market is open.

Exchange workers, much like traders, have highly stressful jobs, but the bulk of their work takes place on the floor of the exchanges, so hours are not very long. Trading floors of exchanges are even busier and louder than those inside of investment banks. Stress is very high, as millions of dollars are on the line for almost every trade, but workers who have made it to this level are generally up to the task.

Financial services sales agents normally work 40 hours a week in a comfortable, less stressful office environment. They may spend considerable time outside the office, meeting with current and prospective clients, attending civic functions, and participating in trade association meetings. Some financial services sales agents work exclusively inside banks, providing service to walk-in customers.

Training, Other Qualifications, and Advancement

Most positions require a bachelor's degree, although few require a specific major. An MBA or professional certification can also be very helpful. Advancement is often very difficult, but those who are successful can have extremely lucrative careers.

Education and training. A college education is important for securities and commodities sales agents, especially in larger firms, because they must be knowledgeable about economic conditions and trends. Most workers have a bachelor's degree in business, finance, accounting, or economics, although this is not necessarily a requirement. Many firms hire summer interns before their last year of college and those who are most successful are offered full-time jobs after they graduate.

After working for a few years, many agents get Master's degrees in Business Administration (MBA). This degree is a requirement for many of the high-level positions in the securities industry. Because the MBA is a professional degree designed to expose students to real-world business practices, it is considered to be a major asset for jobseekers. Employers often reward MBA-holders with higher-level positions, better compensation, and even large signing bonuses.

Most employers provide intensive on-the-job training, especially for entry-level employees. While college coursework is helpful, most firms have a specialized business model which employees must learn. New employees must also come to know the large number of products and services offered by most firms. Trainees in large firms may receive classroom instruction in securities analysis, effective speaking, and the finer points of selling. Firms often rotate their trainees among various departments, to give them a broad perspective of the securities business. In small firms, sales agents often receive training in outside institutions and on the job.

Securities and commodities sales agents must keep up with new products and services and other developments. Because of this, brokers regularly attend conferences and training seminars.

Licensure. Brokers and investment advisors must register as representatives of their firm with the Financial Industry Regulatory Authority (FINRA). Before beginners can qualify as registered representatives, they must be an employee of a registered firm for at least 4 months and pass the General Securities

Registered Representative Examination—known as the Series 7 Exam—administered by FINRA. The exam takes 6 hours and contains 250 multiple-choice questions; a passing score is above 70 percent.

Most States require a second examination—the Uniform Securities Agents State Law Examination (Series 63 or 66). This test measures the prospective representative's knowledge of the securities business in general, customer protection requirements, and recordkeeping procedures. Most firms offer training to help their employees pass these exams.

There are many other licenses available, each of which gives the holder the right to sell different products and services. Most experienced representatives have several. Traders and some other workers also need licenses, although these vary greatly by firm and specialization. Financial services sales agents may also need to be licensed, especially if they sell securities or insurance.

Registered representatives must attend periodic continuing education classes to maintain their licenses. Courses consist of computer-based training in regulatory matters and company training on new products and services.

Other qualifications. Many employers consider personal qualities and skills more important than academic training. Employers seek applicants who have excellent interpersonal and communication skills, a strong work ethic, the ability to work in a team, and a desire to succeed. The ability to understand and analyze numbers is also especially important. Because securities, commodities, and financial services sales agents are entrusted with large sums of money and personal information, employers also make sure that applicants have a good credit history and a clean record. Self-confidence and an ability to handle frequent rejection are important ingredients for success.

Maturity and the ability to work independently are important so many employers prefer to hire those who have achieved success in other jobs. Most firms prefer candidates with sales experience, particularly those who have worked on commission in areas such as real estate or insurance. Other firms prefer to hire workers right out of college, with the intention of molding them to their corporate image.

Advancement. The principal form of advancement for brokers, investment advisors, and financial services sales agents is an increase in the number and size of the accounts they handle. Although beginners usually service the accounts of individual investors, they may eventually handle very large institutional accounts, such as those of banks and pension funds. After taking a series of tests, some brokers become portfolio managers and have greater authority to make investment decisions regarding an account. Some experienced sales agents become branch office managers and supervise other sales agents while continuing to provide services for their own customers. A few agents advance to top management positions or become partners in their firms.

Investment bankers who enter the occupation directly after college generally start as analysts. At this level, employees have some contact with clients but spend most of their time producing "pitchbooks," information booklets used to sell products. They also receive intensive training. After 2 to 3 years, top analysts may be promoted to an associate position or asked to leave. Recent graduates from MBA programs can start as associates, which is similar to the analyst position, but with more responsibilities. Associate may lead a group of analysts and tend to have more contact with clients. After 2 to 3 years, associates are promoted or terminated. Successful associates can become vice presidents, who manage the work of analysts and associates and have a great deal of contact with clients. Vice presidents may advance to become directors, sometimes called executive directors.

Employment

Securities, commodities, and financial services sales agents held about 320,000 jobs in 2006. More than half of jobs were in the securities, commodity contracts, and other financial investments and related activities industry. One in 5 worked in the depository and nondepository credit intermediation industries, which include commercial banks, savings institutions, and credit unions. About 1 out of 6 securities, commodities, and financial services sales agents were self-employed.

Although securities and commodities sales agents are employed by firms in all parts of the country, about 1 in 10 jobs were located in New York City, including the majority of those in investment banking. Because of their close relationship to stock exchanges and large banking operations, most of the major investment banks in the United States are based in New York City. Smaller investment banks can be found in many major American cities and some major investment banks have operations in other cities, although most of their business remains in New York.

Job Outlook

Securities, commodities, and financial services sales agent jobs are projected to grow rapidly over the next decade, especially in the banking industry. However, the number of applicants will continue to far exceed the number of job openings in this high-paying occupation.

Employment change. Employment of securities, commodities, and financial services sales agents is expected to grow 25 percent during the 2006-16 decade, which is much faster than the average for all occupations. The replacement of traditional pension plans with self-directed retirement accounts has led more Americans to hold stock in recent years. This change

Projections data from the National Employment Matrix

Occupational Title	SOC Code	Employment, 2006	Projected employment, 2016	Change, 2006-16	
				Number	Percent
Securities, commodities, and financial services sales agents............	41-3031	320,000	399,000	79,000	25

NOTE: Data in this table are rounded. See the discussion of the employment projections table in the *Handbook* introductory chapter on *Occupational Information Included in the Handbook.*

means that where companies were making investments to secure their employees' retirements in the past, individuals now save money for their own retirements. About half of American households now own stock, and the number of new investors grows daily. While these individual investors are still only a small part of the total, the nationwide interest in owning securities will greatly increase the number of brokers and investment advisors.

Members of the baby boomer generation, in their peak savings years, will fuel much of this increase in investment. As they begin to retire, the number of transactions they make will go up, fueling the need for more investment advisors and brokers. The growing demand for brokers will also stem from the increasing number and complexity of investment products, as well as the effects of globalization. As the public and businesses become more sophisticated about investing, they are venturing into the options and futures markets. Also, markets for investment are expanding with the increase in global trading of stocks and bonds.

The deregulation of financial markets has broken down the barriers between investment activities and banking. The result is that banks now compete with securities companies on all levels. Many of the major investment banks are now owned by large banks and most major banks also have brokerages, which allow their customers to quickly and easily transfer money between their personal banking and investment accounts. This will lead to increased employment of financial services sales agents in banks as they expand their product offerings in order to compete directly with other investment firms.

Job prospects. Despite job growth, competition for jobs in this occupation usually is keen with more applicants than jobs, especially in larger companies. Jobs in brokerages are competitive but are accessible to graduates who have first-rate résumés, strong interpersonal skills, and good grades. Opportunities for beginning sales agents should be better in smaller firms. Investment banking is especially known for its competitive hiring process. Having a degree from a prestigious undergraduate institution is very helpful, as are excellent grades in finance, economics, accounting, and business courses. Competition is even greater for positions working in exchanges.

Employment in the securities industry is closely connected with market conditions and the state of the overall economy and is highly volatile during recessionary periods. Turnover is high for newcomers, who face difficult prospects no matter when they join the industry. Once established, however, securities and commodities sales agents have a very strong attachment to their profession because of their high earnings and considerable investment in training.

Earnings

The median annual wage-and-salary earnings of securities, commodities, and financial services sales agents were $68,500 in May 2006. The middle half earned between $42,630 and $126,290. The lowest 10 percent earned less than $31,170, and the highest 10 percent made more than $145,600.

Median annual earnings in the industries employing the largest numbers of securities, commodities, and financial services sales agents were:

Other financial investment activities	$103,640
Security and commodity contracts intermediation and brokerage	81,050
Activities related to credit intermediation	67,080
Other nondepository credit intermediation	53,750
Nondepository credit intermediation	52,100

Because this is a sales occupation, many workers are paid a commission based on the amount of stocks, bonds, mutual funds, insurance, and other products they sell. Earnings from commissions are likely to be high when there is much buying and selling, and low when there is a slump in market activity. Most firms provide sales agents with a steady income by paying a "draw against commission"—a minimum salary based on commissions they can be expected to earn. Trainee brokers usually are paid a salary until they develop a client base. The salary gradually decreases in favor of commissions as the broker gains clients.

Investment bankers in corporate finance and mergers and acquisitions are generally paid a base salary with the opportunity to earn a substantial bonus. At the higher levels, bonuses far exceed base salary. This arrangement works similarly to commissions but gives banks greater flexibility to reward members of the team who were more effective. Since investment bankers in sales and trading departments generally work alone, they generally work on commissions.

Brokers who work for discount brokerage firms that promote the use of telephone and online trading services usually are paid a salary, sometimes boosted by bonuses that reflect the profitability of the office. Financial services sales agents usually are paid a salary also, although bonuses or commissions from sales are starting to account for a larger share of their income.

Benefits in the securities industry are generally very good. They normally include health care, retirement, and life insurance. Securities firms may also give discounts to employees on financial services that they sell to customers. Other benefits may include paid lunches with clients, paid dinners for employees who work late, and often extensive travel opportunities

Related Occupations

Other jobs requiring knowledge of finance and an ability to sell include insurance sales agents, real estate brokers and sales agents, financial analysts and personal financial advisors, and loan officers.

Sources of Additional Information

For information on securities industry employment, contact:

➤ American Academy of Financial Management, 245 Glendale Dr., Metairie, LA 70001. Internet: **http://www.aafm.org**

➤ Securities Industry and Financial Markets Association, 120 Broadway, 35th Floor, New York, NY 10271. Internet: **http://www.sifma.org**

For information on licensing, contact:

➤ Financial Industry Regulatory Authority (FINRA). 1735 K St., NW., Washington, DC 20006. Internet: **http://www.finra.org**

Travel Agents

(O*NET 41-3041.00)

Significant Points

- Travel benefits, such as reduced rates for transportation and lodging, attract people to this occupation.

- Training at a postsecondary vocational school, college, or university is increasingly important.

- Travel agents increasingly specialize in specific destinations or by type of travel or traveler.

Nature of the Work

Travel agents help travelers sort through vast amounts of information to help them make the best possible travel arrangements. They offer advice on destinations and make arrangements for transportation, hotel accommodations, car rentals, and tours for their clients. They are also the primary source of bookings for most of the major cruise lines. In addition, resorts and specialty travel groups use travel agents to promote travel packages to their clients.

Travel agents are also increasingly expected to know about and be able to advise travelers about their destinations, such as the weather conditions, local ordinances and customs, attractions, and exhibitions. For those traveling internationally, agents also provide information on customs regulations, required papers (passports, visas, and certificates of vaccination), travel advisories, and currency exchange rates. In the event of changes in itinerary in the middle of a trip, travel agents intercede on the traveler's behalf to make alternate booking arrangements.

Travel agents use a variety of published and computer-based sources for information on departure and arrival times, fares, quality of hotel accommodations, and group discounts. They may also visit hotels, resorts, and restaurants themselves to evaluate the comfort, cleanliness, and the quality of specific hotels and restaurants so that they can base recommendations on their own experiences or those of colleagues or clients.

Travel agents who primarily work for tour operators and other travel arrangers may help develop, arrange, and sell the company's own package tours and travel services. They may promote these services, using telemarketing, direct mail, and the Internet. They make presentations to social and special-interest groups, arrange advertising displays, and suggest company-sponsored trips to business managers.

Agents face increasing competition from travel and airline websites for low-cost fares, but travelers still prefer using travel agents who can provide customized service and planning for complex itineraries to remote or multiple destinations. To attract these travelers, many travel agents specialize in specific interest destinations, travel to certain regions, or in selling to particular demographic groups.

Work environment. Travel agents spend most of their time behind a desk conferring with clients, completing paperwork, contacting airlines and hotels to make travel arrangements, and

Travel agents collect information from clients concerning travel dates and destinations before researching fares and routes on computers.

promoting tours. Most of their time is spent either on the telephone or on the computer researching travel itineraries or updating reservations and travel documents. Agents may be under a great deal of pressure during travel emergencies or when they need to reschedule missed reservations. Peak vacation times, such as summer and holiday travel periods, also tend to be hectic.

Many agents, especially those who are self-employed, frequently work long hours. Advanced computer systems and telecommunications networks make it possible for a growing number of travel agents to work at home; however, some agents feel a need to have an office presence to attract walk-in business.

Training, Other Qualifications, and Advancement

A love of travel and knowledge and enthusiasm for advising people about travel destinations and itineraries are important traits for a travel agent to have. Superb communication and computer skills are essential for talking with clients and making travel reservations.

Education and training. The minimum requirement for those interested in becoming a travel agent is a high school diploma or equivalent; although many travel agencies prefer applicants who have a college degree and business or travel experience. Much of the training is provided on the job, a significant part of which consists of instruction on how to use reservation systems.

Training specific to becoming a travel agent is available at the many vocational schools that offer full-time travel agent programs leading to a postsecondary vocational award. Travel agent courses also are offered in public adult education programs, online, and in community colleges. These programs teach students about cruise lines and sales techniques and how to use the reservations systems. They also provide general information about travel destinations. A few colleges offer bachelor's or master's degrees in travel and tourism. Some employers prefer agents who have backgrounds in computer science, geography, communication, foreign languages, or world history, because these backgrounds suggest an existing interest in travel and culture and help agents develop a rapport with clients. Courses in accounting and business management also are important, especially for those who expect to manage or start their own travel agencies. Continuing education is critical because the abundance of travel information readily available through the Internet and other sources has resulted in a more informed consumer who wants to deal with an expert when choosing a travel agent.

Other qualifications. Travel agents must be well-organized, accurate, and detail-oriented in order to compile information from various sources and to plan and organize their clients' travel itineraries. Agents also must be professional and courteous when dealing with travel representatives and clients. Other desirable qualifications include good writing and interpersonal skills and sales abilities.

Personal travel experience is an asset because knowledge about a city or foreign country often helps influence a client's travel plans. Business experience or training increasingly is important because agents need to know how to run a business profitably. As the Internet has become an important tool for making travel arrangements, more travel agencies use websites to provide their services to clients. This trend has increased the importance of computer skills in this occupation.

Certification and advancement. Some employees start as reservation clerks or receptionists in travel agencies. With experience and some formal training, they can take on greater responsibilities and eventually assume travel agent duties. In agencies with many offices, travel agents may advance to busier offices or to office manager or other managerial position.

Those who start their own agencies generally have experience in an established agency. These agents must gain formal approval from suppliers or corporations, such as airlines, ship lines, or rail lines to extend credit on reservations and ensure payment. The Airlines Reporting Corporation and the International Airlines Travel Agency Network, for example, are the approving bodies for airlines. To gain approval, an agency must be financially sound and employ at least one experienced manager or travel agent.

The National Business Travel Association offers three types of designations for corporate travel professionals—Corporate Travel Expert, Certified Corporate Travel Executive, and Global Leadership Professional.

Experienced travel agents can take advanced self-study or group-study courses from the Travel Institute, leading to the Certified Travel Counselor designation. The Travel Institute also offers marketing and sales skills development programs and destination specialist programs, which provide detailed knowledge of regions such as North America, Western Europe, the Caribbean, and the Pacific Rim. With the trend toward more specialization, these and other destination specialist courses are increasingly important.

Employment

Travel agents held about 101,000 jobs in May 2006 and are found in every part of the country. Nearly two-thirds worked for travel agencies. Another 13 percent were self-employed. The remainder worked for tour operators, visitor's bureaus, reservation offices, and other travel arrangers.

Job Outlook

Employment of travel agents is expected to change little through 2016. Travel agents who specialize in a travel destination, type of traveler, or mode of transportation will have the best chances for success.

Employment change. Employment of travel agents is expected to increase by 1 percent, which is considered little or no growth. As spending on travel and tourism rebound from recent recessionary periods and as more travelers begin taking more exotic and customized trips, the demands for the specialized services offered by travel agents will offset the service lost to Internet bookings for simpler itineraries. The ease of Internet use and the ready availability of travel and airline websites that allow people to research and plan their own trips, make their own reservations, and purchase their own tickets will result in less demand for travel agents for routine travel arrangements. There will be, however, many consumers who still prefer to use a professional travel agent to plan a complete trip; to deal with more complex transactions; to ensure reliability; to suggest excursions or destinations that might otherwise be missed; to save time; or, in some cases, to save money. In addition, higher projected levels of travel, especially from businesses and retiring baby boomers will offset the loss of routine transactions. Furthermore, luxury and specialty travel is expected to increase among the growing number of Americans who are seeking out exotic and unique vacations and a growing part of travel agents' business is organizing and selling tours for the growing number of international visitors.

Projections data from the National Employment Matrix

Occupational Title	SOC Code	Employment, 2006	Projected employment, 2016	Change, 2006-16	
				Number	Percent
Travel agents	41-3041	101,000	102,000	1,000	1

NOTE: Data in this table are rounded. See the discussion of the employment projections table in the *Handbook* introductory chapter on *Occupational Information Included in the Handbook.*

Job prospects. Applicants for travel agent jobs should face fair to good job opportunities, depending on one's qualifications and experience. Opportunities should be better for agents who specialize in specific destinations, luxury travel, or particular types of travelers such as ethnic groups or groups with a special interest or hobby.

The demand for travel is sensitive to economic downturns and international political crises, when travel plans are likely to be deferred. Thus job opportunities for travel agents will fluctuate with changing economic and political times. Many openings, though, are expected to occur as agents leave for other occupations or retire.

Earnings

Experience, sales ability, and the size and location of the agency determine the salary of a travel agent. Median annual earnings of travel agents were $29,210 in May 2006. The middle 50 percent earned between $23,020 and $36,920. The lowest 10 percent earned less than $18,100, while the top 10 percent earned more than $46,270. Median earnings in May 2006 for travel agents employed in the travel arrangement and reservation services industry were $29,160.

Salaried agents usually enjoy standard employer-paid benefits that self-employed agents must provide for themselves. When traveling for personal reasons, agents usually get reduced rates for transportation and accommodations. In addition, agents sometimes take "familiarization" trips, at lower cost or no cost to themselves, to learn about various vacation sites. These benefits often attract people to this occupation.

Earnings of travel agents who own their agencies depend mainly on commissions from travel-related bookings and service fees they charge clients. Often it takes time to acquire a sufficient number of clients to have adequate earnings, so it is not unusual for new self-employed agents to have low earnings. Established agents may have lower earnings during economic downturns.

Related Occupations

Travel agents organize and schedule business, educational, or recreational travel or activities. Other workers with similar responsibilities include tour guides and escorts, travel guides, reservation and transportation ticket agents and travel clerks, retail salespersons, and hotel, motel, and resort desk clerks.

Sources of Additional Information

For further information on training opportunities, contact:
➤ American Society of Travel Agents, Education Department, 1101 King St., Alexandria, VA 22314.
Internet: **http://www.asta.org**

For information on training and certification qualifications for business travel management, contact:
➤ National Business Travel Association, 110 North Royal Street, 4th Floor, Alexandria, VA 22314. Internet: **www.nbta.org**

Office and Administrative Support Occupations

Financial Clerks

Bill and Account Collectors

(O*NET 43-3011.00)

Significant Points

- Almost 1 in 4 collectors works for a collection agency; others work in banks, retail stores, government, physicians' offices, hospitals, and other institutions that lend money and extend credit.

- Most jobs in this occupation require only a high school diploma, though many employers prefer workers with some postsecondary training.

- Much faster than average employment growth is expected as companies focus more efforts on collecting unpaid debts.

Nature of the Work

Bill and account collectors, often called simply *collectors,* keep track of accounts that are overdue and attempt to collect payment on them. Some are employed by third-party collection agencies, while others—known as "in-house collectors"—work directly for the original creditors, such as department stores, hospitals, or banks.

The duties of bill and account collectors are similar across the many different organizations in which they work. First, collectors are called upon to locate and notify customers of delinquent accounts, usually over the telephone, but sometimes by letter. When customers move without leaving a forwarding address, collectors may check with the post office, telephone companies, credit bureaus, or former neighbors to obtain the new address. The attempt to find the new address is called "skip tracing." New computer systems assist in tracing by automatically tracking when customers change their address or contact information on any of their open accounts.

Once collectors find the debtor, they inform him or her of the overdue account and solicit payment. If necessary, they review the terms of the sale, service, or credit contract with the customer. Collectors also may attempt to learn the cause of the delay in payment. Where feasible, they offer the customer advice on how to pay off the debts, such as taking out a bill consolidation loan. However, the collector's prime objective is always to ensure that the customer pays the debt in question.

If a customer agrees to pay, collectors record this commitment and check later to verify that the payment was made. Collectors may have authority to grant an extension of time if

Bill and account collectors call customers to ask for payment on late or delinquent bills.

customers ask for one. If a customer fails to pay, collectors prepare a statement indicating the customer's action for the credit department of the establishment. In more extreme cases, collectors may initiate repossession proceedings, disconnect the customer's service, or hand the account over to an attorney for legal action. Most collectors handle other administrative functions for the accounts assigned to them, including recording changes of address and purging the records of the deceased.

Collectors use computers and a variety of automated systems to keep track of overdue accounts. In sophisticated predictive dialer systems, a computer dials the telephone automatically, and the collector speaks only when a connection has been made. Such systems eliminate time spent calling busy or non-answering numbers. Many collectors use regular telephones, but others wear headsets like those used by telephone operators.

Work environment. In-house bill and account collectors typically are employed in an office environment, and those who work for third-party collection agencies may work in a call-center environment. Workers spend most of their time on the phone tracking down and contacting people with debts. The work can be stressful as some customers are confrontational when pressed about their debts. Still, some appreciate assistance in resolving their outstanding debt. Collectors may also feel pressured to meet targets for debt recovered in a certain period.

Bill and account collectors often have to work evenings and weekends, when it is easier to reach people. Many collectors work part time or on flexible work schedules, though the majority work 40 hours per week.

Projections data from the National Employment Matrix

Occupational Title	SOC Code	Employment, 2006	Projected employment, 2016	Change, 2006-16	
				Number	Percent
Bill and account collectors..	43-3011	434,000	534,000	99,000	23

NOTE: Data in this table are rounded. See the discussion of the employment projections table in the *Handbook* introductory chapter on *Occupational Information Included in the Handbook*.

Training, Other Qualifications, and Advancement

Most employers require collectors to have at a least a high school diploma and prefer some customer service experience. Employers usually provide on-the-job training to new employees.

Education and training. Most bill and account collectors are required to have at least a high school diploma. However, employers prefer workers who have completed some college or who have experience in other occupations that involve contact with the public.

Once hired, workers usually receive on-the-job training. Under the guidance of a supervisor or some other senior worker, new employees learn company procedures. Some formal classroom training also may be necessary, such as training in specific computer software. Additional training topics usually include telephone techniques and negotiation skills. Workers are also instructed in the laws governing the collection of debt as mandated by the Fair Debt Collection Practices Act, which applies to all third party and some in-house collectors.

Other qualifications. Workers should have good communication and people skills because they need to speak to customers daily, some of whom may be in stressful financial situations. In addition, collectors should be computer literate, and experience with advanced telecommunications equipment is also useful.

Advancement. Collectors most often advance by taking on more complex cases. Some might become team leaders or supervisors. Workers who acquire additional skills, experience, and training improve their advancement opportunities.

Employment

Bill and account collectors held about 434,000 jobs in 2006. About 24 percent of collectors work in the business support services industries, which includes collection agencies. Many others work in banks, retail stores, government, physician's offices, hospitals, and other institutions that lend money and extend credit.

Job Outlook

Employment of bill and account collectors is expected to grow much faster than the average for all occupations through 2016. Job prospects are expected to be favorable because growth in the occupation and the many people who leave the occupation are expected to create plentiful openings.

Employment change. Over the 2006-16 decade, employment of bill and account collectors is expected to grow by 23 percent, which is much faster than the average for all occupations. Cash flow is becoming increasingly important to companies, which are now placing greater emphasis on collecting unpaid debts sooner. Thus, the workload for collectors is expected to continue to increase as they seek to collect not only debts that are relatively old, but also ones that are more recent. In addition,

as more companies in a wide range of industries get involved in lending money and issuing credit cards, they will need to hire collectors because debt levels will likely continue to rise.

Hospitals and physicians' offices are two of the fastest growing industries requiring collectors. With insurance reimbursements not keeping up with cost increases, the health care industry is seeking to recover more money from patients. Government agencies also are making more use of collectors to collect on everything from parking tickets to child-support payments and past-due taxes. In addition, the Internal Revenue Service (IRS) has begun outsourcing the collection of overdue Federal taxes to third-party collection agencies, adding to the need for workers in this occupation.

Despite the increasing demand for bill collectors, employment growth may be somewhat constrained by the increased use of third-party debt collectors, who are generally more efficient than in-house collectors. Also, some firms are beginning to use offshore collection agencies, whose lower cost structures allow them to collect debts that are too small for domestic collection agencies.

Job prospects. Job openings will not be created from employment growth alone. A significant number of openings will result from the many people who leave the occupation and must be replaced. As a result, job opportunities should be favorable.

Contrary to the pattern in most occupations, employment of bill and account collectors tends to rise during recessions, reflecting the difficulty that many people have in meeting their financial obligations. However, collectors usually have more success at getting people to repay their debts when the economy is good.

Earnings

Median hourly earnings of bill and account collectors were $13.97 in May 2006. The middle 50 percent earned between $11.49 and $17.14. The lowest 10 percent earned less than $9.61, and the highest 10 percent earned more than $21.12. Many bill and account collectors earn commissions based on the amount of debt they recover.

Related Occupations

Bill and account collectors review and collect information on accounts. Other occupations with similar responsibilities include credit authorizers, checkers, and clerks; loan officers; and interviewers.

Sources of Additional Information

Career information on bill and account collectors is available from:

➤ ACA International, The Association of Credit and Collection Professionals, P.O. Box 390106, Minneapolis, MN 55439. Internet: **http://www.acainternational.org**

Billing and Posting Clerks and Machine Operators

(O*NET 43-3021.00, 43-3021.01, 43-3021.02, 43-3021.03)

Significant Points

- About 35 percent of these workers are employed in the health care industry.

- Most jobs in this occupation require only a high school diploma; however, many employers prefer to hire workers who have completed some college courses or a degree.

- Slower than average employment growth is expected as increased automation of billing services reduces the need for billing clerks.

Nature of the Work

Billing and posting clerks and machine operators, commonly called billing clerks, calculate charges, develop bills, and prepare them to be mailed to customers. By reviewing purchasing records and making or verifying calculations, they ensure that even the most complicated bills are accurate.

Billing clerks review hospital records, purchase orders, sales tickets, or charge slips to calculate the total amount due from a customer. They must take into account any discounts, special rates, or credit terms. A billing clerk for a trucking company, for example, often needs to consult a rate book to determine shipping costs. A hospital's billing clerk may need to contact an insurance company to determine what items will be reimbursed. In accounting, law, consulting, and similar firms, billing clerks calculate client fees based on the time required to perform the service being purchased. They keep track of the accumulated hours spent on a job, the fees to charge, the type of job performed for a customer, and the percentage of work completed.

After billing clerks review all necessary information, they compute the charges, using calculators or computers. They then prepare itemized statements, bills, or invoices used for billing and recordkeeping purposes. In some organizations, the clerk might prepare a bill containing the amount due and the date and type of service; in others, the clerk might produce a more detailed invoice with codes for all goods and services provided. They might also list the items sold, the terms of credit, the date of shipment or of service, and a salesperson's or doctor's identification.

Computers and specialized billing software allow many clerks to calculate charges and prepare bills in one step. Computer packages prompt clerks to enter data from handwritten forms and to manipulate the necessary information on quantities, labor, and rates to be charged. Billing clerks verify the entry of information and check for errors before the computer prints the bill. After the bills are printed, billing clerks review them again for accuracy. Computer software also allows bills to be sent electronically if both the biller and the customer pre-

fer not to use paper copies; this, coupled with the prevalence of electronic payment options, allows a completely paperless billing process. In offices that are not automated, *billing machine operators* produce the bill on a billing machine to send to the customer.

In addition to producing invoices, billing clerks may be asked to handle follow-up questions from customers and resolve any discrepancies or errors. Finally, all changes must be entered in the accounting records.

Work environment. Billing clerks typically are employed in an office environment, although a growing number—particularly medical billers—work at home. Most billing clerks work 40 hours per week during regular business hours, though about 16 percent work part time. Billing clerks use computers on a daily basis, so workers may have to sit for extended periods and also may experience eye and muscle strain, backaches, headaches, and repetitive motion injuries.

Training, Other Qualifications, and Advancement

Billing clerks generally need at least a high school diploma, but many employers prefer workers who have completed some college courses.

Education and training. Most billing clerks need at least a high school diploma. However, many employers prefer to hire

Billing and posting clerks prepare statements to be sent to customers.

Projections data from the National Employment Matrix

Occupational Title	SOC Code	Employment, 2006	Projected employment, 2016	Change, 2006-16	
				Number	Percent
Billing and posting clerks and machine operators	43-3021	542,000	566,000	24,000	4

NOTE: Data in this table are rounded. See the discussion of the employment projections table in the *Handbook* introductory chapter on *Occupational Information Included in the Handbook*.

workers who have completed some college courses or a degree. Workers with an associate or bachelor's degree are likely to start at higher salaries and advance more easily than those without degrees. Employers also seek workers who are comfortable using computers, especially billing software programs.

Billing clerks usually receive on-the-job training from their supervisor or some other senior worker. Some formal classroom training also may be necessary, such as training in the specific computer software used by the company. A number of community and career colleges offer certificate programs in medical billing. Courses typically cover basic biology, anatomy, and physiology in addition to training on coding and computer billing software.

Other qualifications. Workers must be careful, orderly, and detail oriented. They must be good at working with numbers to avoid making errors and to recognize errors made by others. Workers also should be discreet and trustworthy because they frequently come in contact with confidential material. Medical billers in particular need to understand and follow the regulations of the Health Insurance Portability and Accountability Act (HIPAA), which were enacted to maintain the confidentiality of patient medical records.

Advancement. Billing clerks usually advance by taking on more duties for higher pay or by transferring to a closely related occupation. Some become supervisors because most companies fill supervisory and managerial positions by promoting individuals from within the organization. Workers who acquire additional skills, experience, and training improve their advancement opportunities. With appropriate experience and education, some billing clerks may become accountants, human resource specialists, or buyers.

Employment

In 2006, billing and posting clerks and machine operators held about 542,000 jobs. Although all industries employ billing clerks, the health care industry employs the most, with over a third of all billing clerks. The wholesale and retail trade industries also employ a large number. Third-party billing companies—companies that provide billing services for other companies—are employing a growing number. Industries that provide this service are the accounting, tax preparation, bookkeeping, and payroll services industry and administrative and support services industry. These industries currently employ around 11 percent of this occupation, although a portion of these clerks do billing for their employers rather than for an outside client. Another 2 percent—mostly medical billers—were self-employed.

Job Outlook

Employment of billing and posting clerks and machine operators is expected to grow more slowly than the average for all

occupations through 2016. Despite slow growth, job prospects should be good as workers leave the occupation creating many job openings.

Employment change. Employment of billing and posting clerks and machine operators is expected to grow by about 4 percent from 2006 to 2016, which is slower than the average for all occupations. Automated and electronic billing processes have greatly simplified billing and allow companies to send bills out faster without hiring additional workers. In addition, as the billing process becomes simplified, other workers, particularly accounting and bookkeeping clerks, are taking on the billing function. More billing clerks will be needed in medical billing, however, because medical bills are complicated and health care services are growing.

Employment growth for billing clerks will occur in most health care related industries, but growth will be limited as more hospitals and physicians' offices use contract billing companies. Contract billing companies generally have much more sophisticated technology and software, enabling each clerk to produce more bills, limiting the need for more clerks. In all industries, including health care, the billing function is becoming increasingly automated and invoices and statements are automatically generated upon delivery of the service or shipment of goods. Bills also are increasingly delivered electronically over the Internet, eliminating the production and mailing of paper bills.

Job prospects. Although growth will be limited, many job openings will occur as workers transfer to other occupations or leave the labor force. A relatively large number of workers leave jobs in this occupation and must be replaced, as is common among entry-level occupations that usually require only a high school diploma.

Earnings

Median hourly earnings of billing and posting clerks and machine operators were $28,850 in May 2006. The middle 50 percent earned between $24,080 and $34,970. The lowest 10 percent earned less than $20,140, and the highest 10 percent earned more than $41,750.

Related Occupations

Billing clerks create and process financial records; other occupations with similar responsibilities include payroll and timekeeping clerks; bookkeeping, auditing, and accounting clerks; tellers; and order clerks.

Sources of Additional Information

Information on employment opportunities for billing clerks is available from local offices of the State employment service.

Bookkeeping, Accounting, and Auditing Clerks

(O*NET 43-3031.00)

Significant Points

- Bookkeeping, accounting, and auditing clerks held more than 2.1 million jobs in 2006 and are employed in every industry.

- Employment is projected to grow as fast as the average due to a growing economy.

- The large size of this occupation ensures plentiful job openings, including many opportunities for temporary and part-time work.

Nature of the Work

Bookkeeping, accounting, and auditing clerks are financial recordkeepers. They update and maintain accounting records, including those which calculate expenditures, receipts, accounts payable and receivable, and profit and loss. These workers have a wide range of skills from full-charge bookkeepers who can maintain an entire company's books to accounting clerks who handle specific tasks. All of these clerks make numerous computations each day and increasingly must be comfortable using computers to calculate and record data.

In small businesses, *bookkeepers* and *bookkeeping clerks* often have responsibility for some or all of the accounts, known as the general ledger. They record all transactions and post debits (costs) and credits (income). They also produce financial statements and prepare reports and summaries for supervisors and managers. Bookkeepers also prepare bank deposits by compiling data from cashiers, verifying and balancing receipts, and sending cash, checks, or other forms of payment to the bank. They also may handle payroll, make purchases, prepare invoices, and keep track of overdue accounts.

In large-companies' accounting departments, *accounting clerks* have more specialized tasks. Their titles, such as accounts payable clerk or accounts receivable clerk, often reflect the type of accounting they do. In addition, their responsibilities vary by level of experience. Entry-level accounting clerks post details of transactions, total accounts, and compute interest charges. They also may monitor loans and accounts to ensure that payments are up to date. More advanced accounting clerks may total, balance, and reconcile billing vouchers; ensure the completeness and accuracy of data on accounts; and code documents according to company procedures.

Accounting clerks post transactions in journals and on computer files and update the files when needed. Senior clerks also review computer printouts against regularly maintained journals and make necessary corrections. They may review invoices and statements to ensure that all the information appearing on them is accurate and complete, and they may reconcile computer reports with operating reports.

Auditing clerks verify records of transactions posted by other workers. They check figures, postings, and documents to en-

sure that they are correct, mathematically accurate, and properly coded. They also correct or note errors for accountants or other workers to fix.

As organizations continue to computerize their financial records, many bookkeeping, accounting, and auditing clerks use specialized accounting software, spreadsheets, and databases. Most clerks now enter information from receipts or bills into computers, and the information is then stored either electronically or as computer printouts, or both. The widespread use of computers also has enabled bookkeeping, accounting, and auditing clerks to take on additional responsibilities, such as payroll, procurement, and billing. Many of these functions require these clerks to write letters and make phone calls to customers or clients.

Work environment. Bookkeeping, accounting, and auditing clerks work in an office environment. They may experience eye and muscle strain, backaches, headaches, and repetitive motion injuries from using computers on a daily basis. Clerks may have to sit for extended periods while reviewing detailed data.

Many bookkeeping, accounting, and auditing clerks work regular business hours and a standard 40-hour week, although some may work occasional evenings and weekends. About 24 percent of these clerks worked part time in 2006.

Bookkeeping, accounting, and auditing clerks may work longer hours to meet deadlines at the end of the fiscal year, during tax time, or when monthly or yearly accounting audits are performed. Additionally, those who work in hotels, restaurants, and stores may put in overtime during peak holiday and vacation seasons.

Training, Other Qualifications, and Advancement

Employers usually prefer bookkeeping, accounting, and auditing clerks to have at least a high school diploma and some accounting coursework or relevant work experience. Clerks should also have good communication skills, be detail-oriented, and trustworthy.

Education and training. Most bookkeeping, accounting, and auditing clerks are required to have a high school degree at a minimum. However, having some college is increasingly important and an associate degree in business or accounting is required for some positions. Although a bachelor's degree is

Bookkeeping, accounting, and auditing clerks keep records of business and financial documents.

Projections data from the National Employment Matrix

Occupational Title	SOC Code	Employment, 2006	Projected employment, 2016	Change, 2006-16	
				Number	Percent
Bookkeeping, accounting, and auditing clerks	43-3031	2,114,000	2,377,000	264,000	12

NOTE: Data in this table are rounded. See the discussion of the employment projections table in the *Handbook* introductory chapter on *Occupational Information Included in the Handbook*.

rarely required, graduates may accept bookkeeping, accounting, and auditing clerk positions to get into a particular company or to enter the accounting or finance field with the hope of eventually being promoted.

Once hired, bookkeeping, accounting, and auditing clerks usually receive on-the-job training. Under the guidance of a supervisor or another more experienced employee, new clerks learn company procedures. Some formal classroom training also may be necessary, such as training in specialized computer software.

Other qualifications. Experience in a related job and working in an office environment also is recommended. Employers prefer workers who can use computers; knowledge of word processing and spreadsheet software is especially valuable.

Bookkeeping, accounting, and auditing clerks must be careful, orderly, and detail-oriented in order to avoid making errors and to recognize errors made by others. These workers also should be discreet and trustworthy because they frequently come in contact with confidential material. They should also have good communication skills because they increasingly work with customers. In addition, all bookkeeping, accounting, and auditing clerks should have a strong aptitude for numbers.

Certification and advancement. Bookkeeping, accounting, and auditing clerks, particularly those who handle all the recordkeeping for a company, may find it beneficial to become certified. The Certified Bookkeeper (CB) designation, awarded by the American Institute of Professional Bookkeepers, demonstrates that individuals have the skills and knowledge needed to carry out all bookkeeping functions, including overseeing payroll and balancing accounts according to accepted accounting procedures. For certification, candidates must have at least 2 years of bookkeeping experience, pass a four-part examination, and adhere to a code of ethics. Several colleges and universities offer a preparatory course for certification; some offer courses online.

Bookkeeping, accounting, and auditing clerks usually advance by taking on more duties for higher pay or by transferring to a closely related occupation. Most companies fill office and administrative support supervisory and managerial positions by promoting individuals from within their organizations, so clerks who acquire additional skills, experience, and training improve their advancement opportunities. With appropriate experience and education, some bookkeeping, accounting, and auditing clerks may become accountants or auditors.

Employment

Bookkeeping, accounting, and auditing clerks held more than 2.1 million jobs in 2006. They work in all industries and at all levels of government. Local government and the accounting, tax preparation, bookkeeping, and payroll services industry are among the individual industries employing the largest numbers of these clerks.

Job Outlook

Job growth is projected to be average through 2016, and job prospects should be good as a large number of bookkeeping, accounting, and auditing clerks are expected to retire or transfer to other occupations.

Employment change. Employment of bookkeeping, accounting, and auditing clerks is projected to grow by 12 percent during the 2006-16 decade, which is as fast as the average for all occupations. Due its size, this occupation will have among the largest numbers of new jobs arise, about 264,000 over the projections decade.

A growing economy will result in more financial transactions and other activities that require recordkeeping by these workers. Additionally, the Sarbanes-Oxley Act of 2002 calls for more accuracy and transparency in the reporting of financial data for public companies, which will increase the demand for these workers. Moreover, companies will continue to outsource their bookkeeping and accounting departments to independent accounting, tax preparation, bookkeeping, and payroll services firms. However, at the same time, the increasing use of tax preparation software in place of the services of tax professionals will hinder growth somewhat.

Clerks who can carry out a wider range of bookkeeping and accounting activities will be in greater demand than specialized clerks. Demand for full-charge bookkeepers is expected to increase, for example, because they do much of the work of accountants and perform a wider variety of financial transactions, from payroll to billing. Technological advances will continue to change the way these workers perform their daily tasks, such as using computer software programs to maintain records, but will not decrease the demand for these workers, especially in smaller establishments.

Job prospects. Some job openings are expected to result from job growth, but even more openings will stem from the need to replace existing workers who leave. Each year, numerous jobs will become available as clerks transfer to other occupations or leave the labor force. The large size of this occupation ensures plentiful job openings, including many opportunities for temporary and part-time work. Certified Bookkeepers (CBs) and those with several years of accounting or bookkeeping experience will have the best job prospects.

Earnings

In May 2006, the median wage and salary earnings of bookkeeping, accounting, and auditing clerks were $30,560. The middle half of the occupation earned between $24,540 and $37,780. The top 10 percent of bookkeeping, accounting, and auditing clerks more than $46,020, and the bottom 10 percent earned less than $19,760.

Benefits offered by employers may vary by the type and size of establishment, but health insurance and paid leave are common.

Related Occupations

Bookkeeping, accounting, and auditing clerks work with financial records. Other workers who perform similar duties include accountants and auditors; bill and account collectors; billing and posting clerks and machine operators; brokerage clerks; credit authorizers, checkers, and clerks; payroll and timekeeping clerks; procurement clerks; and tellers.

Sources of Additional Information

For information on the Certified Bookkeeper designation, contact:

➤ American Institute of Professional Bookkeepers, 6001 Montrose Rd., Suite 500, Rockville, MD 20852. Internet: **http://www.aipb.org**

Gaming Cage Workers

(O*NET 43-3041.00)

Significant Points

- Job opportunities are available nationwide and are no longer limited to Nevada and New Jersey.

- Most employers prefer applicants who have at least a high school diploma as well as experience in handling money or previous casino employment.

- Workers need a license issued by a regulatory agency, such as a State casino control board or commission; licensure requires a background investigation.

Nature of the Work

Gaming cage workers, more commonly called *cage cashiers*, work in casinos and other gaming establishments. The "cage" where these workers can be found is the central depository for money, gaming chips, and paperwork necessary to support casino play.

Cage workers carry out a wide range of financial transactions and handle any paperwork that may be required. They perform credit checks and verify credit references for people who want to open a house credit account. They cash checks according to rules established by the casino. Cage workers sell gambling chips, tokens, or tickets to patrons or to other workers for resale to patrons and exchange chips and tokens for cash. They may use cash registers, adding machines, or computers to calculate and record transactions. At the end of their shift, cage cashiers must balance the books.

Because gaming establishments are closely scrutinized, cage workers must follow a number of rules and regulations related to their handling of money. For example, they monitor large cash transactions and report these transactions to the Internal Revenue Service to help enforce tax regulations and prevent money

laundering. Also, in determining when to extend credit or cash a check, cage workers must follow detailed procedures.

Work environment. The atmosphere in casinos is often considered glamorous. However, casino work can also be physically demanding. This occupation requires workers to stand for long periods with constant reaching and grabbing. Sometimes cage workers may be expected to lift and carry relatively heavy items. The casino atmosphere exposes workers to certain hazards, such as cigarette, cigar, and pipe smoke. Noise from slot machines, gaming tables, and talking workers and patrons may be distracting to some, although workers wear protective headgear in areas where loud machinery is used to count money.

Most casinos are open 24 hours a day, 7 days a week and offer 3 staggered shifts. Casinos typically require cage workers to work on nights, weekends, and holidays.

Training, Other Qualifications, and Advancement

While there are no mandatory education requirements, gaming cage workers typically receive on-the-job training and are licensed by a regulatory agency, such as a State casino control board or commission.

Education and training. There usually are no minimum educational requirements, although most employers prefer at least a high school diploma or the equivalent.

Once hired, gaming cage workers usually receive on-the-job training. Under the guidance of a supervisor or other senior worker, new employees learn company procedures. Some formal classroom training also may be necessary, such as training in specific gaming regulations and procedures.

Licensure. All gaming workers are required to have a license issued by a regulatory agency, such as a State casino control board or commission. Applicants for a license must provide photo identification and pay a fee. Some States may require gaming cage workers to be residents of that State. Age require-

Gaming cage workers must be careful, orderly, and detail-oriented to avoid making errors.

Projections data from the National Employment Matrix

Occupational Title	SOC Code	Employment, 2006	Projected employment, 2016	Change, 2006-16	
				Number	Percent
Gaming cage workers..	43-3041	18,000	20,000	2,000	11

NOTE: Data in this table are rounded. See the discussion of the employment projections table in the *Handbook* introductory chapter on *Occupational Information Included in the Handbook.*

ments vary by State. The licensing application process also includes a background investigation and drug test.

Other qualifications. Experience in handling money or previous casino employment is preferred. Prospective gaming cage workers are sometimes required to pass a basic math test, and they must be careful, orderly, and detail-oriented to avoid making errors and to recognize errors made by others. These workers also should be discreet and trustworthy because they frequently come in contact with confidential material. Good customer service skills and computer proficiency are also necessary for this occupation. Each casino establishes its own requirements for education, training, and experience.

Advancement. Advancement opportunities in casino gaming depend less on workers' previous casino duties and titles than on their ability and eagerness to learn new jobs. For example, in addition to advancement opportunities available in the cage, such as head cage cashier or supervisor, cage workers may advance onto the floor and become dealers or supervisors.

Employment

Gaming cage workers held about 18,000 jobs in 2006. All of these individuals work in establishments that offer gaming; employment is concentrated in Nevada, Louisiana, Mississippi, and Atlantic City, New Jersey. However, a growing number of States and Indian reservations have legalized gambling, and gaming establishments can now be found in many parts of the country.

Job Outlook

Employment of gaming cage workers is expected to grow about as fast as the average for all occupations through 2016. Job seekers should have favorable prospects due primarily to the spread of legalized gambling.

Employment change. Employment of gaming cage workers is expected to increase by 11 percent between 2006 and 2016, which is about as fast as the average for all occupations. The outlook for gaming cage workers depends on the demand for gaming, which is expected to remain strong. No longer confined to Nevada and New Jersey, gaming is becoming legalized in more States that consider gaming an effective way to increase revenues. A substantial portion of this growth will come from the construction of new Indian casinos and of "racinos," which are pari-mutuel racetracks that offer casino games.

Gaming cage workers, however, will experience slower growth than others in gaming establishments, as casinos find ways to reduce the amount of cash handled by employees. For example, self-serve cash-out and change machines are common along with automated teller machines. In addition, slot machines are now able to make payouts in tickets, instead of coins. Tickets can be read by other slot machines and the amount on the ticket transferred to the new machine. Known as Ticket-in,

Ticket-Out game play, these technologies reduce the number of cash transactions needed to play and speed up the exchange process, which means fewer workers are needed to handle the cage than in the past.

Job prospects. In addition to job openings arising from employment growth, a fair number of openings will result from high turnover in this occupation caused by the high level of scrutiny workers receive and the need to be accurate. People with good mathematics abilities, previous casino experience, some background in accounting or bookkeeping, and good customer service skills should have the best opportunities.

Earnings

Earnings for gaming cage workers vary according to level of experience, training, location, and size of the gaming establishment. Median hourly earnings of gaming cage workers were $11.13 in May 2006. The middle 50 percent earned between $9.49 and $13.52 an hour. The lowest 10 percent earned less than $8.19, and the highest 10 percent earned more than $15.92 an hour.

Related Occupations

Many other occupations provide hospitality and customer service. Some examples of related occupations are credit authorizers, checkers, and clerks; gaming services occupations; sales worker supervisors; cashiers; retail salespersons; and tellers.

Sources of Additional Information

Information on employment opportunities for gaming cage workers is available from local offices of the State employment service.

Information on careers in gaming also is available from:
➤ American Gaming Association, 1299 Pennsylvania Ave. NW., Suite 1010 East, Washington, DC 20004. Internet: **http://www.americangaming.org**

Payroll and Timekeeping Clerks

(O*NET 43-3051.00)

Significant Points

- Payroll and timekeeping clerks are found in every industry.

- Workers train on the job; employers prefer high school graduates who have computer skills.

- Those who have completed a certification program will have an advantage in the job market.

Nature of the Work

Payroll and timekeeping clerks perform a vital function: ensuring that employees are paid on time and that their paychecks are accurate. If inaccuracies occur, such as monetary errors or incorrect amounts of vacation time, these clerks research and correct the records. In addition, they may perform other clerical tasks. Automated timekeeping systems that allow employees to enter the number of hours they have worked directly into a computer have eliminated much of the data entry and review by timekeepers and have elevated the job of payroll clerks, allowing them to perform more complex tasks. In offices that have not automated this function, however, payroll and timekeeping clerks still perform many of the traditional job functions.

The fundamental task of *timekeeping clerks* is distributing and collecting timecards each pay period. These workers review employee work charts, timesheets, and timecards to ensure that information is properly recorded and that records have the signatures of authorizing officials. In companies that bill clients for the time worked by staff—law or accounting firms, for example—timekeeping clerks make sure that the hours recorded are charged to the correct job so that clients can be properly billed. These clerks also review computer reports listing timecards that cannot be processed because of errors, and they contact the employee or the employee's supervisor to resolve the problem. In addition, timekeeping clerks are responsible for informing managers and other employees about procedural changes in payroll policies.

Payroll clerks, also called payroll technicians, screen timecards for calculating, coding, or other errors. They compute pay by subtracting allotments, including Federal and State taxes and contributions to retirement, insurance, and savings plans, from gross earnings. Increasingly, computers perform these calculations and alert payroll clerks to problems or errors in the data. In small organizations or for new employees whose records are not yet entered into a computer system, clerks may perform the necessary calculations manually. In some small offices, clerks or other employees in the accounting department process payrolls.

Payroll and timekeeping clerks review work charts and timesheets to ensure that employees are paid on time.

Payroll clerks record changes in employees' addresses; close out files when workers retire, resign, or transfer; and advise employees on income tax withholding and other mandatory deductions. These workers also issue and record adjustments to workers' pay because of previous errors or retroactive increases. Periodically, they prepare and mail earnings and tax-withholding statements for employees' use in preparing income tax returns. Payroll clerks need to be aware of changes in tax and deduction laws, so that they can implement them.

In small offices, payroll and timekeeping duties are likely to be included in the duties of a general office clerk, a secretary, or an accounting clerk. However, large organizations employ specialized payroll and timekeeping clerks to perform these functions. In offices that have automated timekeeping systems, payroll clerks perform more analysis of the data, examining trends and working with computer systems. They also spend more time answering employees' questions and processing unique data.

Work environment. Payroll and timekeeping clerks usually work in clean, pleasant, and comfortable office settings, but they also may face pressure to meet deadlines. Clerks usually work a standard 35- to 40-hour week; however, longer hours might be necessary during busy periods.

Training, Other Qualifications, and Advancement

Payroll and timekeeping clerks train on the job. Employers prefer high school graduates who have computer skills.

Education and training. Most employers prefer applicants with a high school diploma or GED. Payroll and timekeeping clerks train on the job, gaining skills by watching and learning from other workers. New workers receive training in payroll, timekeeping, personnel issues, workplace practices, and company policies. Some also complete training programs in high schools, business schools, or community colleges.

Other qualifications. Computer skills are very desirable. In addition, payroll and timekeeping clerks must be able to interact and communicate with individuals at all levels of the organization. Clerks need poise, tactfulness, and diplomacy, and the interpersonal skills to handle sensitive and confidential situations.

Certification and advancement. Many professional organizations for payroll and timekeeping offer classes to enhance the skills of their members. Some organizations offer certification programs; completion of a certification program can show competence and can enhance advancement opportunities. For example, the American Payroll Association offers two levels of certification, the Fundamental Payroll Certification and the Certified Payroll Professional. The first is open to all individuals who wish to demonstrate basic payroll competency. The second and more advanced credential is available to those who have been employed in the practice of payroll for at least 3 years, among other requirements. Both certifications require experience and a passing score on an exam.

Employment

Payroll and timekeeping clerks held about 214,000 jobs in 2006. They can be found in every industry, but a growing

Projections data from the National Employment Matrix

Occupational Title	SOC Code	Employment, 2006	Projected employment, 2016	Change, 2006-16	
				Number	Percent
Payroll and timekeeping clerks..	43-3051	214,000	220,000	6,600	3

NOTE: Data in this table are rounded. See the discussion of the employment projections table in the *Handbook* introductory chapter on *Occupational Information Included in the Handbook*.

number work for employment services companies as temporary employees. Many also work for accounting, tax preparation, bookkeeping, and payroll services firms, which increasingly perform the payroll function as a service to other companies. Approximately 16 percent of all payroll and timekeeping clerks worked part time in 2006.

Job Outlook

Slower-than-average job growth is expected. Those who have completed a certification program will have an advantage in the job market.

Employment change. Employment of payroll and timekeeping clerks is expected to grow 3 percent during the 2006-16 decade, slower than the average for all occupations. The increasing use of computers will limit employment growth of payroll and timekeeping clerks. For example, automated time clocks, which calculate employee hours, allow large organizations to centralize their timekeeping duties in one location. At individual sites, employee hours increasingly are tracked by computer and verified by managers. This information is compiled and sent to a central office to be processed by payroll clerks. In addition, the growing use of direct deposit will reduce the need to draft paychecks because pay is transferred automatically each pay period. Also, more organizations are allowing employees to update their payroll records electronically. In smaller organizations, payroll and timekeeping duties are being assigned to secretaries, general office clerks, or accounting clerks.

As entering and recording payroll and timekeeping information becomes more simplified, the job itself is becoming more varied and complex. For example, companies now offer a greater variety of pension, 401(k), and other investment plans to their employees. Also, the growing use of wage garnishment for child support is adding to the complexity. These developments will contribute to job growth for payroll and timekeeping clerks, who will be needed to record and monitor such information.

As firms increasingly outsource the payroll function, most job growth is expected to be in companies that specialize in payroll—including companies in the employment services industry and the accounting, tax preparation, bookkeeping, and payroll services industry. Many of these companies are data processing facilities, but accounting firms also are taking on the payroll function to supplement their accounting work.

Job prospects. In addition to job growth, numerous job openings will arise each year as payroll and timekeeping clerks leave the labor force or transfer to other occupations. Those who have completed a certification program, indicating

that they can handle more complex payroll issues, will have an advantage in the job market.

Earnings

Salaries of payroll and timekeeping clerks may vary considerably. The region of the country, size of city, and type and size of establishment all influence salary levels. Also, the level of expertise required and the complexity and uniqueness of a clerk's responsibilities may affect earnings.

Median annual earnings of payroll and timekeeping clerks in May 2006 were $32,400. The middle 50 percent earned between $26,190 and $39,420. The lowest 10 percent earned less than $21,150, and the highest 10 percent earned more than $46,500. Median annual earnings in the industries employing the largest numbers of payroll and timekeeping clerks in May 2006 were:

Management of companies and enterprises	$33,880
Accounting, tax preparation, bookkeeping, and payroll services	33,700
Elementary and secondary schools	33,600
Local government	33,490
Employment services	30,290

Some employers offer educational assistance to payroll and timekeeping clerks.

Related Occupations

Payroll and timekeeping clerks perform a vital financial function—ensuring that employees are paid on time and that their paychecks are accurate. In addition, they may perform various other office and administrative support duties. Other financial clerks include bill and account collectors; billing and posting clerks and machine operators; bookkeeping, accounting, and auditing clerks; gaming cage workers; procurement clerks; and tellers.

Sources of Additional Information

For general information about payroll and timekeeping clerks, contact:

➤ American Payroll Association, 660 North Main Ave., Suite 100, Suite 660, San Antonio, TX 78205-1217. Internet: **http://www.americanpayroll.org**

➤ WorldatWork, 14040 N. Northsight Blvd., Scottsdale, AZ 85260. Internet: **http://www.worldatwork.org**

Information on employment opportunities for payroll and timekeeping clerks is available from local offices of the State employment service.

Procurement Clerks

(O*NET 43-3061.00)

Significant Points

- About 23 percent of procurement clerks work for Federal, State, and local governments.

- Overall employment is expected to experience little or no change as a result of increasing automation, offshoring, and restructuring of business.

- High school graduates with good communication and computer skills should have the best job opportunities.

Nature of the Work

Procurement clerks compile requests for materials, prepare purchase orders, keep track of purchases and supplies, and handle inquiries about orders. Usually called purchasing clerks or *purchasing technicians*, they perform a variety of tasks related to ordering goods and supplies for an organization. They make sure that what was purchased arrives on schedule and meets the purchaser's specifications.

Automation is having a profound effect on this occupation. Orders for goods now can be placed electronically when supplies are low. However, automation is still years away for many firms, and the role of the procurement clerk is unchanged in many organizations.

Procurement clerks perform a wide range of tasks. Some clerks perform strictly clerical functions, but others, particularly at small or medium-sized companies, do more complex tasks. In general, procurement clerks process requests for purchases. They first determine whether there is any of the requested product left in inventory and may go through catalogs or to the Internet to find suppliers. They may prepare invitation-to-bid forms and mail them to suppliers or distribute them for public posting. Procurement clerks may interview potential suppliers by telephone or face-to-face to check on prices and specifications and then put together spreadsheets with price comparisons and other facts about each supplier. Upon the organization's approval, clerks prepare and mail purchase orders and enter them into computers.

Procurement clerks keep track of orders and determine the causes of any delays. If the supplier has questions, clerks try to answer them and resolve any problems. When the shipment arrives, procurement clerks may reconcile the purchase order with the shipment, making sure that they match; notify the vendors when invoices are not received; and verify that the bills match the purchase orders.

Some purchasing departments, particularly in small companies, are responsible for overseeing the organization's inventory control system. At these organizations, procurement clerks monitor in-house inventory movement and complete inventory transfer forms for bookkeeping purposes. They may keep inventory spreadsheets and place orders when materials on hand are insufficient.

Work environment. Procurement clerks usually work a standard 40-hour week. Most procurement clerks work in areas that are clean, well lit, and relatively quiet. These workers sit for long periods of time in front of computer terminals, which many cause eyestrain and headaches. Workers in this occupation may sometimes work overtime or on varied shifts.

Training, Other Qualifications, and Advancement

Most employers prefer applicants with a high school diploma or its equivalent. To advance to purchasing agent jobs, a bachelor's degree is usually required and certification is helpful.

Education and training. Most employers prefer applicants who have a high school diploma or its equivalent or a mix of education and related experience. Most procurement clerks are trained on the job under close supervision of more experienced employees. Training usually lasts less than a few months.

Other qualifications. Employers prefer workers who are computer-literate and have a working knowledge of word processing and spreadsheet software. Proficiency with computer software is important because most tasks, such as preparing purchase orders, are performed electronically.

Certification and advancement. Some procurement clerks who obtain a bachelor's degree and show a greater understanding of contracts and purchasing may be promoted to the position of purchasing agent or buyer. Useful fields of study include business, supply management, engineering, and economics.

Getting a certification may help procurement clerks demonstrate that they have the knowledge and skills necessary to take on more advanced purchasing tasks. There are several recognized credentials for purchasing agents and purchasing managers. The Certified Purchasing Manager (CPM) designation is conferred by the Institute for Supply Management. In 2008, this certification will be replaced by the Certified Professional in Supply Management (CPSM) credential, covering the wider scope of duties now performed by purchasing professionals. The Certified Purchasing Professional (CPP) and Certified Professional Purchasing Manager (CPPM) designations are conferred by the American Purchasing Society. The Certified Supply Chain Professional (CSCP) and Certified in Production and Inventory Management (CPIM) credentials are conferred by APICS, also known as the Association for Operations Management. In Federal, State, and

Procurement clerks prepare purchase orders and make sure that the shipment and the bills agree with the order.

Projections data from the National Employment Matrix

Occupational Title	SOC Code	Employment, 2006	Projected employment, 2016	Change, 2006-16	
				Number	Percent
Procurement clerks..	43-3061	78,000	76,000	-1,600	-2

NOTE: Data in this table are rounded. See the discussion of the employment projections table in the *Handbook* introductory chapter on *Occupational Information Included in the Handbook*.

local government, the indications of professional competence are Certified Professional Public Buyer (CPPB) and Certified Public Purchasing Officer (CPPO), conferred by the National Institute of Governmental Purchasing. Most of these certifications are awarded only after experience and education requirements are met and written or oral exams are successfully completed.

Employment

In 2006, procurement clerks held about 78,000 jobs in every industry, including manufacturing, retail and wholesale trade, health care, and government. About 23 percent of procurement clerks work for Federal, State, and local governments; most of these work for the Federal Government.

Job Outlook

Employment in the occupation is expected to experience little or no change. High school graduates with good communication and computer skills should have the best job opportunities.

Employment change. Employment of procurement clerks is expected to decline by 2 percent during the 2006-16 decade, which is considered little or no change, as a result of increasing automation, offshoring, and business restructuring. The need for procurement clerks will be reduced as the use of computers to place orders directly with suppliers—called electronic data interchange—and as ordering over the Internet—known as "e-procurement"—become more commonplace. In addition, procurement authority for some purchases is now being given to employees in the departments originating the purchase. These departments may be issued procurement cards, which are similar to credit cards that enable a department to charge purchases up to a specified amount.

Job prospects. Despite the expected little or no change in employment, job openings will arise out of the need to replace workers who transfer to other occupations or leave the labor force. High school graduates with good communication and computer skills should have the best job opportunities.

Earnings

Median hourly earnings of procurement clerks in May 2006 were $15.91. The middle 50 percent earned between $12.65 and $19.41. The lowest 10 percent earned less than $10.16 and the highest 10 percent earned more than $22.68. Procurement clerks working for the Federal Government had an average annual income of $41,716 in 2007.

Related Occupations

Procurement clerks compile information and records to draw up purchase orders for materials and services. Other workers who perform similar duties are purchasing agents and buyers, stock clerks and order fillers, and order clerks. Procurement clerks provide office support services for businesses and other organizations. Other workers who perform similar duties are file clerks; secretaries and administrative assistants; receptionists and information clerks; bookkeeping, accounting, and auditing clerks; and payroll and timekeeping clerks.

Sources of Additional Information

Information on obtaining positions as procurement clerks or procurement technicians with the Federal Government is available from the Office of Personnel Management through USAJOBS, the Federal Government's official employment information system. This resource for locating and applying for job opportunities can be accessed through the Internet at **http://www.usajobs.opm.gov** or through an interactive voice response telephone system at (703) 724-1850 or TDD (978) 461-8404. These numbers are not toll free, and charges may result.

State or local government personnel offices and their Web sites can provide information about procurement clerk jobs at those levels of government.

Information on employment opportunities for procurement clerks in the public or private sector is available from local offices of the State employment service.

Further information about education, training, employment, and certification for purchasing careers is available from:

➤ APICS, The Association for Operations Management, 5301 Shawnee Rd., Alexandria, VA 22312-2317. Internet: **http://www.apics.org**
➤ American Purchasing Society, North Island Center, Suite 203, 8 East Galena Blvd., Aurora, IL 60506.
➤ Institute for Supply Management, P.O. Box 22160, Tempe, AZ 85285-2160. Internet: **http://www.ism.ws**
➤ National Institute of Governmental Purchasing, Inc., 151 Spring St., Suite 300, Herndon, VA 20170-5223. Internet: **http://www.nigp.org**

Tellers

(O*NET 43-3071.00)

Significant Points

- Tellers should enjoy working with the public, feel comfortable handling large amounts of money, and be discreet and trustworthy.

- About 1 out of 4 tellers work part time.

- Many job openings will arise from replacement needs because many tellers eventually leave for jobs in other occupations that offer higher pay or more responsibility.

- Employment of tellers is projected to grow as fast as the average; good job prospects are expected.

Nature of the Work

The teller is the worker most people associate with their bank. Among the responsibilities of tellers are cashing checks, accepting deposits and loan payments, and processing withdrawals. Tellers make up approximately one-fourth of bank employees and conduct most of a bank's routine transactions.

Prior to starting their shifts, tellers receive and count an amount of working cash for their drawers. A supervisor—usually the head teller—verifies this amount. Tellers disburse this cash during the day and are responsible for its safe and accurate handling. Before leaving, tellers count their cash on hand, list the currency received on a balance sheet making sure that the accounts balance, and sort checks and deposit slips. Over the course of a workday, tellers also may process numerous mail transactions. They also may sell savings bonds, accept payment for customers' utility bills and charge cards, process necessary paperwork for certificates of deposit, and sell travelers' checks. Some tellers specialize in handling foreign currencies or commercial or business accounts. Other tellers corroborate deposits and payments to automated teller machines (ATMs).

Being a teller requires a great deal of attention to detail. Before cashing a check, a teller must verify the date, the name of the bank, the identity of the person who is to receive payment, and the legality of the document. A teller also must make sure that the written and numerical amounts agree and that the account has sufficient funds to cover the check. The teller then must carefully count cash to avoid errors. Sometimes a customer withdraws money in the form of a cashier's check, which the teller prepares and verifies. When accepting a deposit, tellers must check the accuracy of the deposit slip before processing the transaction.

As banks begin to offer more and increasingly complex financial services, tellers are being trained to identify customers who might want to buy these services. This task requires them to learn about the various financial products and services the bank offers so that they can explain them to customers and refer interested customers to appropriate specialized sales personnel. In addition, tellers in many banks are being cross-trained to perform some of the functions of customer service representatives. (Customer service representatives are discussed separately in the *Handbook*.)

Technology continues to play a large role in the job duties of all tellers. In most banks, for example, tellers use computer terminals to record deposits and withdrawals. These terminals often give them quick access to detailed information on customer accounts. Tellers can use this information to tailor the bank's services to fit a customer's needs or to recommend an appropriate bank product or service.

In most banks, head tellers manage teller operations. They set work schedules, ensure that the proper procedures are adhered to, and act as mentors to less experienced tellers. In addition, head tellers may perform the typical duties of a front-line teller, as needed, and may deal with the more difficult customer problems. They may access the vault, ensure that the correct cash balance is in the vault, and oversee large cash transactions.

Work environment. Tellers work in an office environment. They may experience eye and muscle strain, backaches, headaches, and repetitive motion injuries as a result of using computers every day. Tellers may have to sit for extended periods while reviewing detailed data.

Many tellers work regular business hours and a standard 40-hour week. Sometimes, they work evenings and weekends to accommodate extended bank hours. About 1 in 4 tellers worked part time.

Training, Other Qualifications, and Advancement

Most teller jobs require a high school diploma or higher degree. Tellers are usually trained on the job.

Education and training. Most tellers are required to have at least a high school diploma, but some have completed some college training or even a bachelor's degree in business, accounting, or liberal arts. Although a college degree is rarely required, graduates sometimes accept teller positions to get started in banking or in a particular company with the hope of eventually being promoted to managerial or other positions.

Once hired, tellers usually receive on-the-job training. Under the guidance of a supervisor or other senior worker, new employees learn company procedures. Some formal class-

Tellers must have good customer service skills.

Projections data from the National Employment Matrix

Occupational Title	SOC Code	Employment, 2006	Projected employment, 2016	Change, 2006-16	
				Number	Percent
Tellers...	43-3071	608,000	689,000	82,000	13

NOTE: Data in this table are rounded. See the discussion of the employment projections table in the *Handbook* introductory chapter on *Occupational Information Included in the Handbook*.

room training also may be necessary, such as training in specific computer software.

Other qualifications. Experience working in an office environment or in customer service, and particularly in cash-handling can be important for tellers. Regardless of experience, employers prefer workers who have good communication and customer service skills. Knowledge of word processing and spreadsheet software is also valuable.

Tellers should enjoy contact with the public. They must have a strong aptitude for numbers and feel comfortable handling large amounts of money. They should be discreet and trustworthy because they frequently come in contact with confidential material. Tellers also must be careful, orderly, and detail-oriented to avoid making errors and to recognize errors made by others.

Advancement. Tellers usually advance by taking on more duties and being promoted to head teller or to another supervisory job. Many banks and other employers fill supervisory and managerial positions by promoting individuals from within their organizations, so outstanding tellers who acquire additional skills, experience, and training improve their advancement opportunities. Tellers can prepare for jobs with better pay or more responsibility by taking courses offered by banking and financial institutes, colleges and universities, and private training institutions.

Employment

Tellers held about 608,000 jobs in 2006. The overwhelming majority of tellers worked in commercial banks, savings institutions, or credit unions. The remainder worked in a variety of other finance and other industries.

Job Outlook

Employment of tellers is expected to grow about as fast as the average for all occupations. Overall job prospects should be favorable due to the need to replace workers who retire or otherwise leave the occupation.

Employment change. Employment is projected to grow by 13 percent between 2006 and 2016, which is about as fast as the average for all occupations. To attract customers, banks are opening new branch offices in a variety of locations, such as grocery stores and shopping malls. Banks are also keeping their branches open longer during the day and on weekends. Both of these trends are expected to increase job opportunities for tellers, particularly those who work part time.

Despite the improved outlook, automation and technology will continue to reduce the need for tellers who perform only routine transactions. For example, increased use of ATMs, debit cards, credit cards, and the direct deposit of pay and benefit checks have reduced the need for bank customers to interact with tellers for routine transactions. Electronic banking—conducted over the telephone or the Internet—also is spreading rapidly throughout the banking industry and will reduce the need for tellers in the long run.

Employment of tellers also is being affected by the increasing use of 24-hour telephone centers by many large banks. These centers allow a customer to interact with a bank representative at a distant location, either by telephone or by video terminal. Such centers usually are staffed by customer service representatives.

Job prospects. Job prospects for tellers are expected to be favorable. In addition to job openings expected from growth, most openings will arise from the need to replace the many tellers who transfer to other occupations—which is common for large occupations that normally require little formal education and offer relatively low pay. Prospects will be best for tellers with excellent customer service skills, knowledge about a variety of financial services, and the ability to sell those services.

Earnings

Salaries of tellers vary with experience, region of the country, size of city, and type and size of establishment. Median annual earnings of tellers were $22,140 in May 2006. The middle 50 percent earned between $19,300 and $25,880 a year. The lowest 10 percent earned less than $16,770, and the highest 10 percent earned more than $30,020 a year in May 2006.

Related Occupations

Tellers enter data into a computer, handle cash, and keep track of financial transactions. Other clerks who perform similar duties include bill and account collectors; billing and posting clerks and machine operators; bookkeeping, accounting, and auditing clerks; gaming cage workers; brokerage clerks; and credit authorizers, checkers, and clerks.

Sources of Additional Information

Information on employment opportunities for tellers is available from banks and other employers, local offices of the State employment service, and from:

➤ Bank Administration Institute, 1 North Franklin St., Suite 1000 Chicago, IL 60606. Internet: **http://www.bai.org**

Information and Record Clerks

Brokerage Clerks

(O*NET 43-4011.00)

Significant Points

- More than 9 out of 10 brokerage clerks worked for securities and commodities firms, banks, and other establishments in the financial services industry.

- High school graduates qualify for many of these positions, but many workers now hold associate or bachelor's degrees.

- Good prospects are expected for qualified jobseekers as employment grows and as existing brokerage clerks advance to other occupations.

Nature of the Work

For a typical investor, buying and selling stock is a simple process. Often, it is as easy as calling a broker on the phone or entering the trade into a computer. Behind the scenes, however, buying and selling stock is more complicated, involving trade execution and a fair amount of paperwork. While brokers do some of this work themselves, much of it is delegated to brokerage clerks.

Brokerage clerks perform a number of different tasks with a wide range of responsibilities. Most involve computing and recording data pertaining to securities transactions. Brokerage clerks may also contact customers, take orders, and inform clients of changes to their accounts. Brokerage clerks work in the operations departments of securities firms, on trading floors, and in branch offices. Technology has had a major impact on these positions over the last several years. A significant and growing number of brokerage clerks use custom-designed software programs to process transactions more quickly. Only a few customized accounts are still handled manually.

A broker's assistant, also called a sales assistant, is the most common type of brokerage clerk. These clerks typically assist a small number of brokers, for whom they take client calls, write up order tickets, process the paperwork for opening and closing accounts, record a client's purchases and sales, and inform clients of changes to their accounts. All broker's assistants must be knowledgeable about investment products so that they can communicate clearly with clients. Those who are licensed by the Financial Industry Regulatory Authority (FINRA) can make recommendations to clients at the instruction of the broker. (Securities, commodities, and financial services sales agents are discussed elsewhere in the *Handbook*.)

Brokerage clerks in the operations areas of securities firms perform many duties to help the sale and purchase of stocks, bonds, commodities, and other kinds of investments. They also produce the necessary records of all transactions that occur in their area of the business. Purchase-and-sale clerks match orders to buy with orders to sell. They balance and verify trades of stock by comparing the records of the selling firm with those of the buying firm. Dividend clerks ensure timely payments of stock or cash dividends to clients of a particular brokerage firm. Transfer clerks execute customer requests for changes to security registration and examine stock certificates to make sure that they adhere to banking regulations. Receive-and-deliver clerks handle the receipt and delivery of securities among firms and institutions. Margin clerks record and monitor activity in customers' accounts to ensure that clients make payments and stay within legal boundaries concerning their purchases of stock.

Work environment. Brokerage clerks work in offices and on trading floors, areas that are clean and well lit but which may be noisy at times. The workload is generally manageable but can become very heavy when the market fluctuates rapidly. Brokerage clerks generally work a standard 40-hour week, but they may work overtime during particularly busy periods.

Training, Other Qualifications, and Advancement

Most brokerage clerks learn their jobs through a few months of on-the-job training and experience. Once they have worked in the firm for a few years, many clerks advance to sales representative or broker positions.

Education and training. Some brokerage clerk positions require only a high school diploma, but graduates from 2- and 4-year college degree programs are increasingly preferred. Positions dealing with the public, such as broker's or sales assistant, and those dealing with more complicated financial records are especially likely to require a college degree.

Most new employees are trained on the job, working under the close supervision of more experienced employees. Some firms offer formal training that may include courses in telephone etiquette, computer use, and customer service skills. They may also offer training programs to help clerks study for the broker licensing exams.

Brokerage clerks assist with tasks such as executing trades and filing paperwork.

Projections data from the National Employment Matrix

Occupational Title	SOC Code	Employment, 2006	Projected employment, 2016	Change, 2006-16	
				Number	Percent
Brokerage clerks	43-4011	73,000	88,000	15,000	20

NOTE: Data in this table are rounded. See the discussion of the employment projections table in the *Handbook* introductory chapter on *Occupational Information Included in the Handbook.*

Licensure. Licenses are not strictly required for most brokerage clerk positions, but a Series 7 brokerage license can make a clerk more valuable to the broker. This license gives the holder the ability to act as a registered representative of the firm. A registered representative has the right to answer more of a client's questions and to pass along securities recommendations from the broker. In order to receive this license, a clerk must pass the General Securities Registered Representative Examination (Series 7 exam), administered by FINRA, and be an employee of a registered firm for at least 4 months.

Other qualifications. Brokerage clerk jobs require good organizational and communication skills, as well as attention to detail. Computer skills are extremely important, as most of the work is done by computer. An aptitude for working with numbers is also very helpful, as is a basic knowledge of accounting.

Advancement. Clerks may be promoted to sales representative positions or other professional positions within the securities industry. Employment as a brokerage clerk may also be a stepping-stone into a position as a broker.

Employment

Brokerage clerks held about 73,000 jobs in 2006. More than 9 out of 10 worked for securities and commodities, banking, and other financial industries.

Job Outlook

The job outlook for prospective brokerage clerks is good. As the securities industry grows, the number of clerks will increase. Opportunities will be abundant relative to other securities industry occupations, due to advancement of other clerks and job growth.

Employment change. Employment of brokerage clerks is expected to grow by 20 percent during the 2006-16 decade, which is faster than the average for all occupations. With more people investing in securities, brokerage clerks will be required to process larger volumes of transactions. Moreover, regulatory changes have resulted in more legal documentation and record-keeping requirements. Demand will be tempered, however, by continually improving technologies that allow increased automation of many tasks. Further, clerks are often seen as reducing profits, since they do not bring in customers, making them particularly prone to layoffs. Because of intense competition, especially among discount brokerages, companies must continually focus on cutting costs, meaning that many responsibilities formerly handled by clerks are now handled by the brokers themselves.

Job prospects. Because brokerage clerks are often entry-level workers, many opportunities will result from the advancement of other clerks. Prospects will be good for qualified workers. New entrants who have strong sales skills and an aptitude for

understanding numbers will have the best opportunities. While not required, a 4-year degree can also be very helpful.

Earnings

Median annual earnings of brokerage clerks were $36,390 in May 2006. The middle 50 percent earned between $29,480 and $46,030. The lowest 10 percent earned less than $24,590 and the highest 10 percent earned more than $57,600.

Related Occupations

Brokerage clerks compute and record data. Other workers who perform calculations and record data include bill and account collectors; billing and posting clerks and machine operators; bookkeeping, accounting, and auditing clerks; and tellers.

Sources of Additional Information

For more information on employment in the securities industry, contact:

➤ Securities Industry and Financial Markets Association, 120 Broadway, 35th Floor, New York, NY 10271.
Internet: **http://www.sifma.org**

For information on licensing, contact:

➤ Financial Industry Regulatory Authority (FINRA), 1735 K St. NW. Washington, DC 20006. Internet: **http://www.finra.org**

Credit Authorizers, Checkers, and Clerks

(O*NET 43-4041.00, 43-4041.01, 43-4041.02)

Significant Points

- Most jobs require only a high school diploma.

- Employment is expected to decline.

Nature of the Work

Credit authorizers, checkers, and clerks review credit history and obtain the information needed to determine the creditworthiness of individuals or businesses applying for credit. They spend much of their day on the telephone or on the Internet obtaining information from credit bureaus, employers, banks, credit institutions, and other sources to determine applicants' credit history and ability to repay what they borrow or charge.

Credit authorizers, checkers, and clerks process and authorize applications for credit, including applications for credit cards. Although the distinctions among the three job titles are disappearing, some general differences remain. *Credit clerks* typically handle the processing of credit applications by verify-

Credit authorizers review a customer's credit history.

ing the information on the application, calling applicants if additional data are needed, contacting credit bureaus for a credit rating, and obtaining any other information necessary to determine applicants' creditworthiness. If clerks work in a department store or other establishment that offers instant credit, they enter the applicant's information into a computer at the point of sale. A credit rating is then transmitted from a central office within seconds to indicate whether the application should be rejected or approved.

Credit checkers investigate the credit history and current credit standing of a person or business prior to the issuance of a loan or line of credit. Credit checkers also may contact credit departments of businesses and service companies to obtain information about an applicant's credit standing. Credit reporting agencies and bureaus hire checkers to secure, update, and verify information for credit reports. These workers often are called credit investigators or credit reporters.

Credit authorizers approve charges against customers' existing accounts. Most charges are approved automatically by computer. However, when accounts are past due, overextended, or invalid, or when they show a change of address, salespersons refer the associated transactions to credit authorizers located in a central office. These authorizers evaluate the customers' computerized credit records and payment histories and quickly decide whether to approve new charges.

Work environment. Credit authorizers, checkers, and clerks usually work a standard 40-hour week. However, they may work overtime during particularly busy periods, such as holiday shopping seasons and store sales. Most credit authorizers, checkers, and clerks work in areas that are clean, well lit, and relatively quiet. These workers sit for long periods of time in front of computer screens, which may cause eyestrain and headaches. Part-time work is available, and temporary workers are often hired during peak workloads.

Training, Other Qualifications, and Advancement
Employers generally prefer workers with a least a high school diploma or its equivalent and usually provide on-the-job training.

Education and training. A high school diploma or its equivalent is usually the minimum requirement for these workers. Most new employees are trained on the job, working under close supervision of more experienced employees. Some firms offer formal training that may include courses in telephone etiquette, computer use, and customer service skills. Some credit authorizers, checkers, and clerks also take courses in credit offered by banking and credit associations, public and private vocational schools, and colleges and universities.

Experience and other qualifications. Other requirements of the job include good telephone and organizational skills and the ability to pay close attention to details and meet tight deadlines. Computer skills also are important in order to enter and retrieve data quickly.

Advancement. These workers typically can advance to supervisory positions. They may become loan or credit department supervisor or team leader of a small group of clerks.

Employment
Credit authorizers, checkers, and clerks held about 69,000 jobs in 2006. Nearly half of these workers were employed by finance and insurance industries, mainly firms in credit intermediation and related activities, such as commercial and savings banks; credit unions; and mortgage, finance, and loan companies. Credit bureaus, collection agencies, and wholesale and retail trade establishments also employ these clerks.

Job Outlook
Employment for this occupation is expected to decline moderately through the year 2016. However, job openings will still arise from the need to replace workers leaving the occupation.

Projections data from the National Employment Matrix

Occupational Title	SOC Code	Employment, 2006	Projected employment, 2016	Change, 2006-16	
				Number	Percent
Credit authorizers, checkers, and clerks	43-4041	69,000	63,000	-5,800	-8

NOTE: Data in this table are rounded. See the discussion of the employment projections table in the *Handbook* introductory chapter on *Occupational Information Included in the Handbook.*

Employment change. Employment of credit authorizers, checkers, and clerks is expected to decline moderately by about 8 percent between 2006 and 2016. Despite a projected increase in the number of credit applications, technology will allow these applications to be processed, checked, and authorized by fewer workers than were required in the past.

Credit scoring is a major development that has improved the productivity of credit authorizers, checkers, and clerks, thus limiting employment growth in the occupation. Companies and credit bureaus now can purchase software that quickly analyzes an applicant's creditworthiness and summarizes it with a "score." Credit issuers then can easily decide whether to accept or reject an application on the basis of its score, speeding up the authorization of loans or credit. Obtaining credit ratings also has become much easier for credit checkers and authorizers because businesses now have computer systems directly linked to credit bureaus that provide immediate access to a person's credit history.

Job prospects. Despite an expected decline in employment, job prospects for credit authorizers, checkers, and clerks will remain good. Openings will arise from the need to replace workers who leave the occupation for various reasons. However, the job outlook is sensitive to overall economic activity. A downturn in the economy or a rise in interest rates usually leads to a decline in demand for credit.

Earnings

Median hourly earnings of credit authorizers, checkers, and clerks in May 2006 were $14.41. The middle 50 percent earned between $11.25 and $18.10. The lowest 10 percent earned less than $8.72, and the highest 10 percent earned more than $22.30. Median hourly earnings in nondepository credit intermediation were $15.21 in 2006, while median earnings in depository credit intermediation were $15.01.

Related Occupations

Credit authorizers, checkers, and clerks obtain and analyze credit histories. Other workers who review account information include bill and account collectors, loan officers, and insurance underwriters.

Sources of Additional Information

State employment service offices and agencies can provide information about job openings for credit authorizers, checkers, and clerks.

Customer Service Representatives

(O*NET 43-4051.00)

Significant Points

- Job prospects are expected to be excellent.

- Most jobs require only a high school diploma but educational requirements are rising.

- Strong verbal communication and listening skills are important.

Nature of the Work

Customer service representatives are employed by many different types of companies to serve as a direct point of contact for customers. They are responsible for ensuring that their company's customers receive an adequate level of service or help with their questions and concerns. These customers may be individual consumers or other companies, and their service needs can vary considerably.

All customer service representatives interact with customers to provide information in response to inquiries about products or services and to handle and resolve complaints. They communicate with customers through a variety of means—by telephone; by e-mail, fax, regular mail; or in person. Some customer service representatives handle general questions and complaints, whereas others specialize in a particular area.

Many customer inquiries involve routine questions and requests. For example, customer service representatives may be asked to provide a customer with their credit card balance, or to check on the status of an order. However, other questions are more involved, and may require additional research or further explanation on the part of the customer service representative. In handling customers' complaints, they must attempt to resolve the problem according to guidelines established by the company. These procedures may involve asking questions to determine the validity of a complaint; offering possible solutions; or providing customers with refunds, exchanges, or other offers, like discounts or coupons. In some cases, customer service representatives are required to follow up with an individual customer until a question is answered or an issue is resolved.

Some customer service representatives help people decide what types of products or services would best suit their needs. They may even aid customers in completing purchases or transactions. Although the primary function of customer service representatives is not sales, some may spend time encouraging customers to purchase additional products or services. (For information on workers whose primary function is sales, see the statements on sales and related occupations elsewhere in the *Handbook.*) Customer service representatives also may make changes or updates to a customer's profile or account information. They may keep records of transactions and update and maintain databases of information.

Most customer service representatives use computers and telephones extensively in their work. Customer service representatives frequently enter information into a computer as they are speaking to customers. Often, companies have large amounts of data, such as account information, that is pulled up on a computer screen while the representative is talking to a customer so he or she can answer specific questions. Customer service representatives also usually have answers to the most common customer questions, or guidelines for dealing with complaints. In the event that they encounter a question or situation to which they do not know how to respond, workers consult with a supervisor to determine the best course of action. They generally use multiline telephone systems, which may route calls directly to the most appropriate representative. However, at times, they must transfer calls to someone who may be better able to respond to the customer's needs.

In some organizations, customer service representatives spend their entire day on the telephone. In others, they may spend part of their day answering e-mails and the remainder of the day taking calls. For some, most of their contact with the customer is face to face. Customer service representatives need to remain aware of the amount of time spent with each customer so that they can fairly distribute their time among the people who require their assistance. This is particularly important for those whose primary activities are answering telephone calls and whose conversations are required to be kept within a set time limit. For those working in call centers, there is usually very little time between telephone calls. When working in call centers, customer service representatives are likely to be under close supervision. Telephone calls may be taped and reviewed by supervisors to ensure that company policies and procedures are being followed.

Job responsibilities also can differ, depending on the industry in which a customer service representative is employed. For example, those working in the branch office of a bank may assume the responsibilities of other workers, such as teller or new account clerk, as needed. In insurance agencies, a customer service representative interacts with agents, insurance companies, and policyholders. These workers handle much of the paperwork related to insurance policies, such as policy appli-

Customer service representatives answer questions and assist customers over the phone.

cations and changes and renewals to existing policies. They answer questions regarding policy coverage, help with reporting claims, and do anything else that may need to be done. Although they must have similar credentials and knowledge of insurance products as insurance agents, the duties of a customer service representative differ from those of an agent as they are not responsible for seeking potential customers. Customer service representatives employed by utilities and communications companies assist individuals interested in opening accounts for various utilities such as electricity and gas, or for communication services such as cable television and telephone. They explain various options and receive orders for services to be installed, turned on, turned off, or changed. They also may look into and resolve complaints about billing and other service.

Work environment. Although customer service representatives work in a variety of settings, most work in areas that are clean and well lit. Many work in call or customer contact centers where workers generally have their own workstation or cubicle space equipped with a telephone, headset, and computer. Because many call centers are open extended hours, beyond the traditional work day, or are staffed around the clock, these positions may require workers to take on early morning, evening, or late night shifts. Weekend or holiday work also may be necessary. As a result, the occupation is well suited to flexible work schedules. About 17 percent of customer service representatives work part time. The occupation also offers the opportunity for seasonal work in certain industries, often through temporary help agencies.

Call centers may be crowded and noisy, and work may be repetitious and stressful, with little time between calls. Workers usually must attempt to minimize the length of each call, while still providing excellent service. To ensure that these procedures are followed, conversations may be monitored by supervisors, which be stressful. Also, long periods spent sitting, typing, or looking at a computer screen may cause eye and muscle strain, backaches, headaches, and repetitive motion injuries.

Customer service representatives working outside of a call center environment may interact with customers through several different means. For example, workers employed by an insurance agency or in a grocery store may have customers approach them in person or contact them by telephone, computer, mail, or fax. Many of these customer service representatives work a standard 40-hour week; however, their hours generally depend on their employer's hours of operation. Work environments outside of a call center also vary accordingly. Most customer service representatives work either in an office or at a service or help desk.

Customer service representatives may have to deal with difficult or irate customers, which can be challenging. However, the ability to resolve customers' problems has the potential to be very rewarding.

Training, Other Qualifications, and Advancement

Most jobs require at least a high school diploma. However, employers are increasingly seeking candidates with some college education. Most employers provide training to workers before they begin serving customers.

Projections data from the National Employment Matrix

Occupational Title	SOC Code	Employment, 2006	Projected employment, 2016	Change, 2006-16	
				Number	Percent
Customer service representatives..	43-4051	2,202,000	2,747,000	545,000	25

NOTE: Data in this table are rounded. See the discussion of the employment projections table in the *Handbook* introductory chapter on *Occupational Information Included in the Handbook*.

Education and training. Most customer service representative jobs require only a high school diploma. However, because employers are demanding a higher skilled workforce, many customer service jobs now require an associate or bachelor's degree. High school and college level courses in computers, English, or business are helpful in preparing for a job in customer service.

Training requirements vary by industry. Almost all customer service representatives are provided with some training prior to beginning work. This training generally includes customer service and phone skills; information on products and services; information about common customer problems; the use of the telephone and computer systems; and company policies and regulations. Length of training varies, but usually lasts at least several weeks. Because of a constant need to update skills and knowledge, most customer service representatives continue to receive training throughout their career. This is particularly true of workers in industries such as banking, in which regulations and products are continually changing.

Other qualifications. Because customer service representatives constantly interact with the public, good communication and problem-solving skills are a must. Verbal communication and listening skills are especially important. For workers who communicate through e-mail, good typing, spelling, and writing skills are necessary. Basic to intermediate computer knowledge and good interpersonal skills also are important qualities for people who wish to be successful in the field.

Customer service representatives play a critical role in providing an interface between customers and companies. As a result, employers seek out people who are friendly and possess a professional manner. The ability to deal patiently with problems and complaints and to remain courteous when faced with difficult or angry people is very important. Also, a customer service representative needs to be able to work independently within specified time constraints. Workers should have a clear and pleasant speaking voice and be fluent in English. However, the ability to speak a foreign language is becoming increasingly necessary.

Although some positions may require previous industry, office, or customer service experience, many customer service jobs are entry level. However, within insurance agencies and brokerages, these jobs usually are not entry-level positions. Workers must have previous experience in insurance and often are required by State regulations to be licensed like insurance sales agents. A variety of designations are available to demonstrate that a candidate has sufficient knowledge and skill, and continuing education courses and training often are offered through the employer.

Advancement. Customer service jobs are often good introductory positions into a company or an industry. In some cases, experienced workers can move up within the company into supervisory or managerial positions or they may move into areas such as product development, in which they can use their knowledge to improve products and services. As they gain more knowledge of industry products and services, customer service representatives in insurance may advance to other, higher level positions, such as insurance sales agent.

Employment

Customer service representatives held about 2.2 million jobs in 2006. Although they were found in a variety of industries, about 23 percent of customer service representatives worked in finance and insurance. The largest numbers were employed by insurance carriers, insurance agencies and brokerages, and banks and credit unions.

About 14 percent of customer service representatives were employed in administrative and support services. These workers were concentrated in the business support services industry (which includes telephone call centers) and employment services (which includes temporary help services and employment placement agencies). Another 11 percent of customer service representatives were employed in retail trade establishments such as general merchandise stores and food and beverage stores. Other industries that employ significant numbers of customer service representatives include information, particularly the telecommunications industry; manufacturing, such as printing and related support activities; and wholesale trade.

Job Outlook

Customer service representatives are expected to experience growth that is much faster than the average for all occupations through the projection period. Furthermore, job prospects should excellent as workers who leave the occupation will need to be replaced.

Employment change. Employment of customer service representatives is expected to increase 25 percent from 2006 to 2016, which is much faster than the average for all occupations. This occupation will have one of the largest numbers of new jobs arise, about 545,000 over the 2006-16 projection period. Beyond growth stemming from expansion of the industries in which customer service representatives are employed, a need for additional customer service representatives is likely to result from heightened reliance on these workers. Customer service is very important to the success of any organization that deals with customers, and strong customer service can build sales, visibility, and loyalty as companies try to distinguish themselves from competitors. In many industries, gaining a competitive edge and retaining customers will be increasingly important over the next decade. This is particularly true in industries such as financial services, communications, and utilities, which already employ numerous customer service representatives. As the trend towards consolidation in industries continues, centralized call centers will provide an effective method for delivering a high level of customer service. As a result, employment of customer service representatives may grow at a faster rate in call centers than in other areas. However, this growth may be tempered by a variety of factors such as technological improvements that make it increasingly feasible and cost-effective for call centers to be built or relocated outside of the United States.

Technology is affecting the occupation in many ways. The Internet and automated teller machines have provided customers with means of obtaining information and conducting transactions that do not entail interacting with another person. Technology also allows for greater streamlining of processes, while at the same time increasing the productivity of workers. The use of computer software to filter e-mails, generating automatic responses or directing messages to the appropriate representative, and the use of similar systems to answer or route telephone inquiries are likely to become more prevalent in the future. Also, with rapidly improving telecommunications, some organizations have begun to position their call centers overseas.

Despite such developments, the need for customer service representatives is expected to remain strong. In many ways, technology has heightened consumers' expectations for information and services, and the availability of information online seems to have generated more need for customer service representatives, particularly to respond to e-mail. Also, technology cannot replace human skills. As more sophisticated technologies are able to resolve many customers' questions and concerns, the nature of the inquiries handled by customer service representatives is likely to become increasingly complex.

Furthermore, the job responsibilities of customer service representatives are expanding. As companies downsize or take other measures to increase profitability, workers are being trained to perform additional duties such as opening bank accounts or cross-selling products. As a result, employers increasingly may prefer customer service representatives who have education beyond high school, such as some college or even a college degree.

While jobs in some industries—such as retail trade—may be affected by economic downturns, the customer service occupation generally is resistant to major fluctuations in employment.

Job prospects. Prospects for obtaining a job in this field are expected to be excellent, with more job openings than jobseekers. Bilingual jobseekers, in particular, may enjoy favorable job prospects. In addition, numerous job openings will result from the need to replace experienced customer service representatives who transfer to other occupations or leave the labor force. Replacement needs are expected to be significant in this large occupation because many young people work as customer service representatives before switching to other jobs.

This occupation is well suited to flexible work schedules, and many opportunities for part-time work will continue to be available, particularly as organizations attempt to cut labor costs by hiring more temporary workers.

Earnings

In May 2006, median hourly earnings for wage and salary customer service representatives were $13.62. The middle 50 percent earned between $10.73 and $17.40. The lowest 10 percent earned less than $8.71 and the highest 10 percent earned more than $22.11.

Earnings for customer service representatives vary according to level of skill required, experience, training, location, and size of firm. Median hourly earnings in the industries employing the largest numbers of these workers in May 2006 were:

Insurance carriers	$15.00
Agencies, brokerages, and other insurance related activities	14.51
Depository Credit Intermediation	13.68
Employment services	11.74
Telephone call centers	10.29

In addition to receiving an hourly wage, full-time customer service representatives who work evenings, nights, weekends, or holidays may receive shift differential pay. Also, because call centers are often open during extended hours, or even 24 hours a day, some customer service representatives have the benefit of being able to work a schedule that does not conform to the traditional workweek. Other benefits can include life and health insurance, pensions, bonuses, employer-provided training, and discounts on the products and services the company offers.

Related Occupations

Customer service representatives interact with customers to provide information in response to inquiries about products and services and to handle and resolve complaints. Other occupations in which workers have similar dealings with customers and the public are information and record clerks; financial clerks, such as tellers and new account clerks; insurance sales agents; securities, commodities, and financial services sales agents; retail salespersons; computer support specialists; and gaming services workers.

Sources of Additional Information

State employment service offices can provide information about employment opportunities for customer service representatives.

File Clerks

(O*NET 43-4071.00)

Significant Points

- About 1 out of 4 file clerks work part time.
- A high school diploma or its equivalent is the most common educational requirement.
- Employment is expected to decline through the year 2016.

Nature of the Work

The amount of information generated by organizations continues to grow rapidly. File clerks classify, store, retrieve, and update this information. In many small offices, they often have

File clerks are responsible for sorting, storing, and retrieving an organization's records.

additional responsibilities, such as entering data, performing word processing, sorting mail, and operating copying or fax machines.

File clerks, also called record, information, or record center clerks, examine incoming material and code it numerically, alphabetically, or by subject matter. Paper forms, letters, receipts, or reports are stored in files while necessary information may be entered, often electronically, into other storage devices. Some clerks operate mechanized files that rotate to bring the needed records to them; others convert documents to film that is then stored on microfilm or microfiche. A growing number of file clerks use imaging systems that scan paper files or film and store the material on computers.

In order for records to be useful, they must be up to date and accurate and readily available. File clerks ensure that new information is added to files in a timely manner and discard outdated materials or transfer them to inactive storage. Clerks also check files at regular intervals to make sure that all items are correctly sequenced and placed. When records cannot be found, file clerks attempt to locate them. As an organization's needs for information change, file clerks implement changes to the filing system.

When records are requested, file clerks locate them and give them to the person requesting them. A record may be a sheet of paper stored in a file cabinet or an image on microform. In the former case, the clerk retrieves the document manually. In the latter case, the clerk retrieves the microform and displays it on a microform reader. If necessary, file clerks make copies of records and distribute them. In addition, they keep track of materials removed from the files to ensure that borrowed files are returned.

Increasingly, file clerks use computerized filing and retrieval systems that have a variety of storage devices, such as a mainframe computer, CD-ROM, or DVD-ROM. To retrieve a docu- ment in these systems, the clerk enters the document's identification code, obtains the location of the document, and gets the document. Accessing files in a computer database is much quicker than locating and physically retrieving paper files. Still, even when files are stored electronically, backup paper or electronic copies usually are also kept.

Work environment. File clerks usually work in areas that are clean, well lit, and relatively quiet. The work is not overly strenuous but may involve a lot of standing, walking, reaching, pulling, and bending, depending on the method used to retrieve files. Prolonged exposure to computer screens may lead to eyestrain for the many file clerks who work with computers.

Training, Other Qualifications, and Advancement

File clerks must be alert, accurate, and able to work with others. Most train on the job.

Education and training. Most employers prefer applicants with a high school diploma or a GED or a mix of education and related experience. Most new employees are trained on the job under close supervision of more experienced employees.

Other qualifications. File clerks must be able to work with others since part of the job is helping fellow workers. Clerks must be alert, accurate, and attentive while performing repetitive tasks. Willingness to do routine and detailed work is also important. Proficiency with desktop computer software is becoming increasingly important as more files are being stored electronically.

Advancement. File clerks can advance to more senior clerical office positions such as receptionist or bookkeeping clerk.

Employment

File clerks held about 234,000 jobs in 2006. Although file clerk jobs are found in nearly every sector of the economy, more than 90 percent of these workers are employed in service-providing industries, including government. Health care establishments employed around 3 out of every 10 file clerks. About 1 out of every 4 file clerks worked part time in 2006.

Job Outlook

Rapid declines in employment are expected through 2016. Job prospects should be best for jobseekers who have general office skills and who are familiar with personal computers and other office machines.

Employment change. Employment of file clerks is expected to decline rapidly by 41 percent between 2006 and 2016, largely due to productivity gains from office automation and the consolidation of clerical jobs. Most files are stored digitally and can be retrieved electronically, reducing the demand for file clerks.

Job prospects. There will be job openings for file clerks because a large number of workers will be needed to replace the

Projections data from the National Employment Matrix

Occupational Title	SOC Code	Employment, 2006	Projected employment, 2016	Change, 2006-16	
				Number	Percent
File clerks...	43-4071	234,000	137,000	-97,000	-41

NOTE: Data in this table are rounded. See the discussion of the employment projections table in the *Handbook* introductory chapter on *Occupational Information Included in the Handbook.*

workers who leave the occupation each year. The high number of separations from file clerk jobs reflects the lack of formal training requirements, limited advancement potential, and relatively low pay. Organizations across the economy will continue to need to hire file clerks to record and retrieve information. File clerks should find opportunities for temporary or part-time work, especially during peak business periods.

Jobseekers who have typing and other secretarial skills and who are familiar with a wide range of office machines, especially personal computers, should have the best job opportunities.

Earnings

Median hourly earnings of file clerks were $10.62 in May 2006. The middle 50 percent earned between $8.64 and $13.31. The lowest 10 percent earned less than $7.27, and the highest 10 percent earned more than $16.71. Median hourly earnings in the industries employing the largest number of file clerks in May 2006 are shown below:

Local government	$12.18
Legal services	11.08
General medical and surgical hospitals	11.02
Employment services	10.19
Offices of physicians	9.50

Related Occupations

File clerks classify and retrieve files. Other workers who perform similar duties include receptionists and information clerks and stock clerks and order fillers.

Sources of Additional Information

State employment service offices and agencies can provide information about job openings for file clerks.

Hotel, Motel, and Resort Desk Clerks

(O*NET 43-4081.00)

Significant Points

- Job opportunities should be good, because of industry growth and substantial replacement needs.

- Evening, weekend, and part-time work hours create the potential for flexible schedules.

- Professional appearance and personality are more important than formal academic training in getting a job.

Nature of the Work

Hotel, motel, and resort desk clerks are always in the public eye and are usually the first line of customer service for a lodging property. Their attitude and behavior greatly influence the public's impressions of the establishment.

Front-desk clerks perform a variety of services for guests of hotels, motels, and other lodging establishments. Regardless of the type of accommodation, most desk clerks have similar responsibilities. They register arriving guests, assign rooms, and check out guests at the end of their stay. They also keep records of room assignments and other registration-related information on computers. When guests check out, desk clerks prepare and explain the charges and process payments.

Desk clerks answer questions about services, checkout times, the local community, or other matters of public interest. They report problems with guest rooms or public facilities to members of the housekeeping or maintenance staff. In larger hotels or in larger cities, desk clerks may refer queries about area attractions to a concierge and may direct more complicated questions to the appropriate manager.

In some smaller hotels and motels where smaller staffs are employed, clerks may take on a variety of additional responsibilities, such as bringing fresh linens to rooms, and they are often responsible for all front-office operations, information, and services. For example, they may perform the work of a bookkeeper, advance reservation agent, cashier, laundry attendant, and telephone switchboard operator.

Work environment. Hotels are open around the clock, creating the need for night and weekend work. About half of all desk clerks work a 40-hour week. Nearly one in five work part-time. Others work full-time, but with varying schedules. Most clerks work in areas that are clean, well lit, and relatively quiet, although lobbies can become crowded and noisy when busy. Many hotels have stringent dress guidelines for desk clerks.

Desk clerks may experience particularly hectic times during check-in and check-out times or when convention guests or large groups arrive at once. Moreover, dealing with irate guests can be stressful. Computer failures can further complicate an already busy time and add to stress levels. Hotel desk clerks may be on their feet most of the time and may occasionally be asked to lift heavy guest luggage.

Hotel, motel, and resort desk clerks regularly use computers to store and retrieve guest reservation information.

Projections data from the National Employment Matrix

Occupational Title	SOC Code	Employment, 2006	Projected employment, 2016	Change, 2006-16	
				Number	Percent
Hotel, motel, and resort desk clerks..	43-4081	219,000	257,000	38,000	17

NOTE: Data in this table are rounded. See the discussion of the employment projections table in the *Handbook* introductory chapter on *Occupational Information Included in the Handbook.*

Training, Other Qualifications, and Advancement

Employers look for clerks who are friendly and customer-service oriented, well groomed, and display maturity, self confidence, and good judgment.

Education and training. Most hotel, motel, and resort desk clerks receive orientation and training on the job. Orientation may include an explanation of the job duties and information about the establishment, such as the arrangement of guest rooms, availability of additional services, such as a business or fitness center, and location of guest services, such as ice and vending machines, restaurants, and nearby retail stores and attractions. New employees learn job tasks under the guidance of a supervisor or an experienced desk clerk. They often receive additional training on interpersonal or customer service skills and on how to use the computerized reservation, room assignment, and billing systems and equipment. Desk clerks often learn new procedures and company policies after their initial training ends. While postsecondary education is not usually required for this job, formal training in a hospitality management degree or certificate program may be an advantage for getting positions in larger or more upscale properties.

Other qualifications. Desk clerks, especially in high-volume and higher-end properties, should be quick-thinking, energetic, and able to work as a member of a team. Hotel managers typically look for these personal characteristics when hiring desk clerks, because personality traits are difficult to teach. A clear speaking voice and fluency in English are essential when talking with guests and using the telephone or public-address systems. Good spelling and computer literacy are also needed because most of the work involves a computer. In addition, speaking a foreign language fluently is increasingly helpful because of the growing international clientele of many properties.

Advancement. Large hotel and motel chains may offer better opportunities for advancement than small, independently owned establishments. Large chains have more extensive career ladder programs and may offer desk clerks an opportunity to participate in management training programs. Also, the Educational Institute of the American Hotel and Lodging Association offers home-study or group-study courses in lodging management, which may help some desk clerks obtain promotions more rapidly.

Employment

Hotel, motel, and resort desk clerks held about 219,000 jobs in 2006. Almost all were in hotels, motels, and other establishments in the accommodation industry.

Job Outlook

Hotel, motel, and resort desk clerks will experience faster-than-average job growth through the 2006-16 decade because additional hotel properties continue to be built and more people are expected to travel for business and leisure. Good job opportunities are expected.

Employment change. Employment of hotel, motel, and resort desk clerks is expected to grow 17 percent between 2006 and 2016, which is faster than the average for all occupations. As more lodging establishments open and as people and companies have more money and travel more, occupancy rates will increase and create demand for desk clerks.

Employment of hotel and motel desk clerks should benefit from steady or increasing business and leisure travel. Shifts in preferences away from long vacations and toward long weekends and other, more frequent, shorter trips also should boost demand for these workers. While many lower budget and extended-stay establishments are being built to cater to families and the leisure traveler, many new luxury and resort accommodations also are opening to serve the upscale client. With the increased number of units requiring staff, employment opportunities for desk clerks should be good.

Growth of hotel, motel, and resort desk clerk jobs will be moderated somewhat by technology. Automated check-in and check-out procedures and on-line reservations networks free up staff time for other tasks and reduce the amount of time spent with each guest.

Job prospects. In addition to job growth, job opportunities for hotel and motel desk clerks are expected to be good because of the need to replace the many clerks who either transfer to other occupations that offer better pay and advancement opportunities or who leave the workforce altogether. Opportunities for those willing to work a variable schedule should continue to be plentiful.

Employment of desk clerks is sensitive to cyclical swings in the economy. During recessions, vacation and business travel declines, and hotels and motels need fewer desk clerks. Similarly, employment is affected by special events, convention business, and seasonal fluctuations.

Earnings

Median annual earnings of hotel, motel and resort desk clerks were $18,460 in May 2006. The middle 50 percent earned between $15,930 and $22,220. The lowest 10 percent earned less than $13,690, and the highest 10 percent earned more than $27,030.

Earnings of hotel, motel, and resort desk clerks vary by worker characteristics, season, and geographic factors, such as whether the establishment is in a major metropolitan area or a resort community. Earnings also vary according to the size of the hotel and the level of service offered. For example, luxury hotels that offer guests more personal attention and a greater number of services typically have stricter and more demanding requirements for their desk staff and often provide higher earnings.

Related Occupations

Lodging managers, particularly at smaller hotels and lodging establishments, may perform some of the same duties as desk clerks. Other occupations that require workers to assist the public include counter and rental clerks, customer service representatives, receptionists and information clerks, and retail salespersons.

Sources of Additional Information

Information about the hotel and lodging industry and links to State lodging associations may be obtained from:
➤ American Hotel & Lodging Association, 1201 New York Ave., NW., #600 Washington, DC 20005.
Internet: **http://www.ahla.com**

Information on careers in the lodging industry, as well as information about professional development and training programs, may be obtained from:
➤ Educational Institute of the American Hotel and Lodging Association, 800 N. Magnolia Ave., Suite 1800, Orlando, FL 32803. Internet: **http://www.ei-ahla.org**

Human Resources Assistants, Except Payroll and Timekeeping

(O*NET 43-4161.00)

Significant Points

- About 17 percent work for Federal, State, and local governments.

- Employment will grow as human resources assistants assume more responsibilities.

- Job opportunities should be best for those with excellent communication and computer skills and a broad based knowledge of general office functions, as assistants assume more responsibilities.

Nature of the Work

Human resources assistants maintain the human resource records of an organization's employees. These records include information such as name, address, job title, and earnings; benefits such as health and life insurance; and tax withholding. They also undertake a variety of other personnel and general office related tasks.

On a daily basis, these assistants record information and answer questions about and for employees. They might look up information about absences or job performance, for instance. When an employee receives a promotion or switches health insurance plans, the human resources assistant updates the appropriate form. Human resources assistants also may prepare reports for managers. For example, they might compile a list of employees eligible for an award.

In small organizations, some human resources assistants perform a variety of other clerical duties, including answering telephone calls or letters, sending out announcements of job openings or job examinations, signing for packages, ordering office supplies, and issuing application forms. When credit bureaus and finance companies request confirmation of a person's employment, the human resources assistant provides authorized information from the employee's personnel records. Assistants also may contact payroll departments and insurance companies to verify changes to records.

Some human resources assistants are involved in hiring. They screen job applicants to obtain information such as their education and work experience; administer aptitude, personality, and interest tests; explain the organization's employment policies and refer qualified applicants to the employing official; and request references from present or past employers. Also, human resources assistants inform job applicants, by telephone, letter, or e-mail, of their acceptance for or denial of employment.

In some job settings, human resources assistants have more specific job titles. For example, *assignment clerks* notify a firm's existing employees of upcoming vacancies, identify applicants who qualify for the vacancies, and assign those who are qualified to various positions. They also keep track of vacancies that arise throughout the organization, and they complete and distribute forms advertising vacancies. When completed applications are returned, these clerks review and verify the information in them, using personnel records. After a selection for a position is made, they notify all of the applicants of their acceptance or rejection.

As another example, *identification clerks* are responsible for security matters at defense installations. They compile and record personal data about vendors, contractors, and civilian and military personnel and their dependents. The identification clerk's job duties include interviewing applicants; corresponding with law enforcement authorities; and preparing badges, passes, and identification cards.

Work environment. Human resources assistants usually work in clean, pleasant, and comfortable office settings, but prolonged exposure to video display terminals may lead to eyestrain for assistants who work with computers. They usually work a standard 35- to 40-hour week.

Human resources assistants explain the organization's employment policies, screen job applicants, and request references.

Projections data from the National Employment Matrix

Occupational Title	SOC Code	Employment, 2006	Projected employment, 2016	Change, 2006-16	
				Number	Percent
Human resources assistants, except payroll and timekeeping	43-4161	168,000	187,000	19,000	11

NOTE: Data in this table are rounded. See the discussion of the employment projections table in the *Handbook* introductory chapter on *Occupational Information Included in the Handbook*.

Training, Other Qualifications, and Advancement

Employers prefer to hire people who have a high school diploma. Computer, communication, and interpersonal skills are important.

Education and training. A high school diploma or GED usually is preferred for these jobs. Generally, training beyond high school is not required. However, training in computers, in filing and maintaining filing systems, in organizing, and in human resources practices is helpful. Proficiency using Microsoft Word, Excel, and other computer applications also is very desirable. Many of these skills can be learned in a vocational high school program aimed at office careers, and the remainder can be learned on the job.

Formal training is also available at a small number of colleges, most of which offer diploma programs in office automation. Many proprietary schools also offer such programs.

Other qualifications. Human resources assistants must be able to interact and communicate with individuals at all levels of the organization. In addition, assistants should demonstrate poise, tactfulness, diplomacy, and good interpersonal skills in order to handle sensitive and confidential situations.

Employment

Human resources assistants held about 168,000 jobs in 2006. About 17 percent work for Federal, State, and local governments. Other jobs for human resources assistants were in various industries such as health care and social assistance; educational services, public and private; management of companies and enterprises; administrative and support services; and finance and insurance.

Job Outlook

Employment of human resources assistants is expected to grow as fast as the average for all occupations. Job opportunities should be best for those with excellent communication and computer skills and a broad based knowledge of general office functions, as assistants assume more responsibilities.

Employment change. The number of jobs for human resources assistants is expected to grow by 11 percent between 2006 and 2016, as fast as the average for all occupations. In a favorable job market, more emphasis is placed on human resources departments, thus increasing the demand for assistants. However, even in economic downturns there is demand for assistants, as human resources departments in all industries try to make their organizations more efficient by determining what type of employees to fire or hire, and strategically filling job openings. Human resources assistants may play an instrumental role in their organization's human resources policies. For example, they may talk to staffing firms and consulting firms, conduct other research, and then offer their ideas on issues

such as whether to hire temporary contract workers or full-time staff.

As with other office and administrative support occupations, the growing use of computers in human resources departments means that much of the data entry that is done by human resources assistants can be eliminated, as employees themselves enter the data and send the electronic file to the human resources office. Such an arrangement, which is most feasible in large organizations with multiple human resources offices, could limit job growth among human resources assistants.

Job prospects. Job opportunities should be best for those with excellent communication and computer skills and a broad based knowledge of general office functions, as assistants assume more responsibilities. For example, workers conduct Internet research to locate resumes, they must be able to scan resumes of job candidates quickly and efficiently, and they must be increasingly sensitive to confidential information such as salaries and Social Security numbers.

In addition to positions arising from job growth, replacement needs will account for many job openings for human resources assistants as they advance within the human resources department, take jobs unrelated to human resources administration, or leave the labor force.

Earnings

Median annual earnings of human resources assistants in May 2006 were $33,750. The middle 50 percent earned between $27,430 and $41,080. The lowest 10 percent earned less than $22,700 and the highest 10 percent earned more than $48,670. Median annual earnings in the industries employing the largest number of human resources assistants in 2006 were:

Federal executive branch...	$37,000
Local government	35,440
Management of companies and enterprises	34,260
Colleges, universities, and professional schools..................	33,870
Employment services	29,330

In 2007, the Federal Government typically paid salaries ranging from $33,336 to $42,236 a year. Beginning human resources assistants with a high school diploma or 6 months of experience were paid an average annual salary of $26,685. The average salary for all human resources assistants employed by the Federal Government was $37,835 in 2007.

Some employers offer educational assistance to human resources assistants.

Related Occupations

Human resources assistants maintain the personnel records of an organization's employees. On a daily basis, these assistants record information and answer questions about employee absences and supervisory reports on employees' job performance. Other workers with similar skills and expertise in interpersonal relations include bookkeeping, accounting, and auditing clerks; communications equipment operators; customer service representatives; data entry and information processing workers; order clerks; receptionists and information clerks; secretaries and administrative assistants; stock clerks and order fillers; and tellers.

Sources of Additional Information

For information about human resources careers, contact:
➤ Society for Human Resource Management, 1800 Duke St., Alexandria, VA 22314. Internet: **http://www.shrm.org**

Interviewers

(O*NET 43-4061.00, 43-4111.00, 43-4131.00)

Significant Points

- A high school diploma or its equivalent is the most common educational requirement.

- Familiarity with computers and strong interpersonal skills are very important

Nature of the Work

Interviewers obtain information from individuals and business representatives who are opening bank accounts, trying to obtain loans, seeking admission to medical facilities, participating in consumer surveys, applying to receive aid from government programs, or providing data for various other purposes. By mail, by telephone, or in person, these workers solicit and verify information, create files, and perform a number of other related tasks.

The specific duties and job titles of *interviewers* depend upon the type of employer. In doctors' offices and other health care facilities, for example, interviewing clerks also are known as *admitting interviewers* or *patient representatives.* These workers obtain all preliminary information required for a patient's record or for his or her admission to a hospital, such as the patient's name, address, age, medical history, present medications, previous hospitalizations, religion, people to notify in case of emergency, attending physician, and party responsible for payment. In some cases, interviewing clerks may be required to verify that an individual is eligible for health benefits or to work out financing options for those who might need them.

Other duties of interviewers in health care include assigning patients to rooms and summoning escorts to take patients to their rooms; sometimes, interviewers may escort patients themselves. Using the facility's computer system, interviewers schedule laboratory work, x-rays, and surgeries; prepare admission and discharge records; and route these medical records to appropriate departments. They also may bill patients, receive payments, and answer the telephone. In an outpatient or office setting, interviewers schedule appointments, keep track of cancellations, and provide general information about care. In addition, the role of the admissions staff, particularly in hospitals,

is expanding to include a wide range of patient services, from assisting patients with financial and medical questions to helping family members find hotel rooms.

Interviewing clerks who conduct market research surveys and polls for research firms have somewhat different responsibilities. These interviewers ask a series of prepared questions, record the responses, and forward the results to management. They may ask individuals questions about their occupation and earnings, political preferences, buying habits, satisfaction with certain goods or services sold to them, or other aspects of their lives. Although most interviews are conducted over the telephone, some are conducted in focus groups or by randomly polling people in a public place. More recently, the Internet is being used to elicit people's opinions. Almost all interviewers use computers or similar devices to enter the responses to questions.

Eligibility interviewers, government programs, determine the eligibility of individuals applying to receive government assistance, such as welfare, unemployment benefits, Social Security benefits, and public housing. These interviewers gather the relevant personal and financial information about an applicant and, on the basis of the rules and regulations of the particular government program, grant, modify, deny, or terminate an individual's eligibility for the program. They also help to detect fraud committed by people who try to obtain benefits that they are not eligible to receive.

Loan interviewers and clerks review individuals' credit history and obtain the information needed to determine the creditworthiness of applicants for loans and credit cards. These workers spend much of their day on the telephone, obtaining information from credit bureaus, employers, banks, credit institutions, and other sources to determine an applicant's credit history and ability to pay back a loan or charge.

Loan interviewers interview potential borrowers; help them fill out applications for loans; investigate the applicant's background and references; verify the information on the application; and forward any findings, reports, or documents to the company's appraisal department. Finally, interviewers inform the applicant as to whether the loan has been accepted or denied.

Interviewers may ask questions over the phone or face-to-face.

Projections data from the National Employment Matrix

Occupational Title	SOC Code	Employment, 2006	Projected employment, 2016	Change, 2006-16	
				Number	Percent
Interviewers..	—	589,000	612,000	22,000	4
Eligibility interviewers, government programs...........................	43-4061	112,000	116,000	3,500	3
Interviewers, except eligibility and loan......................................	43-4111	221,000	242,000	21,000	10
Loan interviewers and clerks..	43-4131	256,000	254,000	-2,300	-1

NOTE: Data in this table are rounded. See the discussion of the employment projections table in the *Handbook* introductory chapter on *Occupational Information Included in the Handbook*.

Loan clerks, also called *loan processing clerks, loan closers, or loan service clerks,* assemble documents pertaining to a loan, process the paperwork associated with the loan, and ensure that all information is complete and verified. Mortgage loans are the primary type of loan handled by loan clerks, who also may have to order appraisals of the property, set up escrow accounts, and secure any additional information required to transfer the property.

The specific duties of loan clerks vary by specialty. Loan closers, for example, complete the loan process by gathering the proper documents for signature at the closing, including deeds of trust, property insurance papers, and title commitments. They set the time and place for the closing, make sure that all parties are present, and ensure that all conditions for settlement have been met. After the settlement, the loan closer records all of the documents involved and submits the final package to the owner of the loan. Loan service clerks maintain the payment records on a loan once it is issued. These clerical workers process the paperwork for payment of fees to insurance companies and tax authorities, and also may record changes in clients' addresses and ownership of a loan. When necessary, they answer calls from customers with routine inquiries.

Work environment. Working conditions vary for different types of interviewers, but most of these workers work in areas that are clean, well lit, and relatively quiet. Most of these workers work a standard 35 to 40 hour week, but evening and weekend work may be required in some establishments. Some interviewers may conduct surveys on the street or in shopping malls, or they may go door to door.

Training, Other Qualifications, and Advancement

There are minimal formal educational requirements for interviewers, and most new employees receive on-the-job training. Employers seek applicants with strong interpersonal skills, including a pleasant personality, clear voice, and the ability to communicate with others.

Education and training. Most employers prefer applicants with a high school diploma or its equivalent or a mix of education and related experience.

New employees generally train on the job, working under the close supervision of more experienced employees, although some firms offer formal training. Some loan interviewers also take courses about credit that are offered by banking and credit associations, public and private vocational schools, and colleges and universities.

Other qualifications. Because interviewers deal with the public, they must have a pleasant personality, clear speaking voice, and professional appearance. Familiarity with comput-

ers and strong interpersonal skills are very important. Fluency in a foreign language also can be beneficial.

Advancement. Experienced interviewers may advance to positions with added responsibilities or supervisory duties. Many organizations fill open supervisory positions by promoting qualified individuals from within the company. Interviewers who obtain additional skills or training will have the best opportunities. For some managerial positions, a college degree may be required.

Employment

Interviewers held about 589,000 jobs in 2006. Approximately 221,000 were interviewers, except eligibility and loan; 256,000 were loan interviewers and clerks; and 112,000 were eligibility interviewers, government programs. About half of all interviewers, except eligibility and loan, worked in health care and social assistance industries, and about 23 percent of these interviewers worked part time. Most loan interviewers and clerks worked in financial institutions. About 7 out of every 10 eligibility interviewers for government programs, worked in State and local government.

Job Outlook

Slower than average growth is expected for interviewers during the projection period, but levels of employment change vary significantly with occupational specialty. Prospects will be best for applicants with a broad range of job skills, including good customer service, math, and telephone skills.

Employment change. Employment of interviewers is expected to grow by 4 percent from 2006 to 2016, which is slower than the average for all occupations. However, the projected change in employment varies by specialty.

The number of interviewers, except eligibility and loan, is projected to grow about as fast as average, with the most growth in the health care and social assistance sector. This sector will hire more admissions interviewers as health care facilities consolidate staff and expand the role of the admissions staff and as an aging and growing population requires more visits to health care practitioners. However increases in the use of online surveys and questionnaires, which are often cheaper than other data collection methods, should reduce the demand for interviewers who conduct market research interviews over the phone relative to other jobs involved in marketing.

Employment of eligibility interviewers for government programs is projected to grow slower than the average for all occupations. The increase in the number of retiring baby boomers becoming eligible for Social Security and other government entitlement programs will be the main cause of growth in this occupation. Automation should have an effect on some eligibility interviewers because, as with credit and loan ratings, eligibility for government aid programs can be determined instantaneously by entering information into a computer.

Little or no change in employment is projected for loan interviewers and clerks due to advances in technology that are making these workers more productive. Despite a projected increase in the number of applications for loans, automation will increase productivity so that fewer workers will be required to process, check, and authorize applications than in the past. The effects of automation on employment will be moderated, however, by the many interpersonal aspects of the job. Mortgage loans, for example, require loan processors to personally verify financial data on the application, and loan closers are needed to assemble documents and prepare them for settlement.

Moreover, employment will be adversely affected by changes in the financial services industry. For example, significant consolidation has occurred among mortgage loan servicing companies. As a result, fewer mortgage banking companies are involved in servicing loans, making the function more efficient and reducing the need for loan service clerks.

Job prospects. Some job openings will come from employment growth, but most job openings should arise from the need to replace the numerous interviewers who leave the occupation each year. Prospects for filling these openings will be best for applicants with a broad range of job skills, including good customer service, math, and telephone skills. In addition to openings for full-time jobs, opportunities also should be available for part-time and temporary jobs.

The job outlook for loan interviewers and clerks is sensitive to overall economic activity. A downturn in the economy or a rise in interest rates usually leads to a decline in the demand for loans, particularly mortgage loans and can result in layoffs. Even in slow economic times, however, job openings will arise from the need to replace workers who leave the occupation for various reasons.

The job outlook for eligibility interviewers also is sensitive to overall economic activity; a severe slowdown in the economy will cause more people to apply for government aid programs, increasing demand for eligibility interviewers.

Earnings

Median hourly wage and salary earnings of eligibility interviewers, government programs, in May 2006 were $18.05. The middle 50 percent earned between $14.40 and $21.92. The lowest 10 percent earned less than $12.18, and the highest 10 percent earned more than $24.30. Median hourly earnings in the industries employing the largest number eligibility interviewers, government programs were:

Federal Government	$21.20
Local government	17.52
State government	16.35

Median hourly wage and salary earnings of loan interviewers and clerks in May 2006 were $14.89. The middle 50 percent earned between $12.07 and $18.69. The lowest 10 percent earned less than $9.88, and the highest 10 percent earned more

than $22.66. Median hourly earnings of loan interviewers and clerks in depository credit intermediation was $15.22, while median hourly earnings in nondepository credit intermediation was $14.35.

Median hourly wage and salary earnings of interviewers, except eligibility and loan, in May 2006 were $12.64. The middle 50 percent earned between $10.12 and $15.31. The lowest 10 percent earned less than $8.35, and the highest 10 percent earned more than $18.57. Median hourly earnings in the industries employing the largest number of interviewers, except eligibility and loan, were:

State government	$15.27
Colleges, universities, and professional schools	15.05
General medical and surgical hospitals	12.69
Offices of physicians	12.55
Other professional, scientific, and technical services	10.10

Related Occupations

Interviewers obtain information from individuals. Other workers who perform similar duties include procurement clerks, customer service representatives, and bill and account collectors.

Sources of Additional Information

State employment service offices can provide information about employment opportunities for interviewers.

For specific information on a career as a loan processor or loan closer, contact:

➤ Mortgage Bankers Association, 1919 Pennsylvania Ave. NW., Washington, DC 20006.
Internet: **http://www.mortgagebankers.org**

Library Assistants, Clerical

(O*NET 43-4121.00)

Significant Points

- Flexible schedules and ample opportunities for part-time work characterize this occupation.

- Library assistants train on the job; most libraries use electronic cataloging systems so computers skills are essential.

- Job prospects should be good.

Nature of the Work

Library assistants, clerical—sometimes referred to as library media assistants, library aides, or circulation assistants—help librarians and library technicians organize library resources and make them available to users. (Librarians and library technicians are discussed elsewhere in the *Handbook*.)

At the circulation desk, library assistants lend and collect books, periodicals, videotapes, and other materials. When an item is borrowed, assistants scan it and the patron's library card to record the transaction in the library database; they then stamp the due date on the item or print a receipt with the due date.

Library assistants reshelve books after they are returned.

When an item is returned, assistants inspect it for damage and scan it to record its return. Electronic circulation systems automatically generate notices reminding patrons that their materials are overdue, but library assistants may review the record for accuracy before sending out the notice. Library assistants also register new patrons and issue them library cards. They answer patrons' questions or refer them to a librarian.

Throughout the library, assistants sort returned books, periodicals, and other items and put them on their designated shelves, in the appropriate files, or in storage areas. Before reshelving returned materials, they look for any damage and try to make repairs. For example, they may use tape or paste to repair torn pages or book covers and use other specialized processes to repair more valuable materials.

Assistants also locate materials being lent to a patron or another library. Because nearly all library catalogs are computerized, library assistants must be familiar with computers. They sometimes help patrons with computer searches.

Some library assistants specialize in helping patrons who have vision problems. Sometimes referred to as *braille-and-talking-books clerks*, these assistants review the borrower's list of desired reading materials, and locate those materials or close substitutes from the library collection of large-type or braille volumes and books on tape. Then, they give or mail the materials to the borrower.

Work environment. Library assistants who prepare library materials may sit at desks or computer terminals for long periods and can develop headaches or eyestrain. Some duties can be repetitive and boring, such as shelving new or returned materials. Others can be rewarding, such as assisting patrons who are performing computer searches with the use of local and regional library networks. Library assistants may lift and carry books, climb ladders to reach high stacks, and bend low to shelve books on bottom shelves.

Library assistants in school libraries work regular school hours. Those in public libraries and college and university libraries also work weekends, evenings, and some holidays. About 60 percent of library assistants work part time, making the job appealing to retirees, students, and others interested in flexible schedules.

Training, Other Qualifications, and Advancement

Library assistants receive most of their training on the job. No formal education is required, although familiarity with computers is helpful.

Education and training. Training requirements for library assistants are generally minimal; most libraries prefer to hire workers with a high school diploma or GED, although libraries also hire high school students for these positions. No formal postsecondary training is expected. Some employers hire individuals with experience in other clerical jobs; others train inexperienced workers on the job.

Other qualifications. Given the extensive use of electronic resources in libraries, computer skills are needed for most jobs; knowledge of databases and other library automation systems is especially useful. Library assistants should be able to pay close attention to detail, as the proper shelving or storage of materials is essential.

Advancement. Library assistants usually advance by assuming added responsibilities. Many begin by performing simple jobs such as shelving books or adding new books and periodicals to the database when they arrive. After gaining experience, they may move into positions that allow them to interact with patrons, such as staffing the circulation desk. Experienced assistants may be able to advance to library technician positions, which involve more responsibility. Eventually they may advance to supervise a public service or technical service area. Advancement opportunities are greater in large libraries.

Employment

Library assistants held about 116,000 jobs in 2006. More than half of these workers were employed by local governments in public libraries; most of the remaining employees worked in school, college, and university libraries. Many of these jobs are part time.

Job Outlook

Employment of library assistants is expected to grow about as fast as average. Prospects should be good because many workers leave these jobs and need to be replaced.

Employment change. The number of library assistants is expected to increase by 8 percent between 2006 and 2016, about as fast as the average for all occupations. Efforts to contain costs in local governments and academic institutions of all types will slow overall growth in library services, but may result

Projections data from the National Employment Matrix

Occupational Title	SOC Code	Employment, 2006	Projected employment, 2016	Change, 2006-16	
				Number	Percent
Library assistants, clerical..	43-4121	116,000	125,000	9,100	8

NOTE: Data in this table are rounded. See the discussion of the employment projections table in the *Handbook* introductory chapter on *Occupational Information Included in the Handbook.*

in the hiring of more library support staff, who are paid less than librarians and who take on more responsibility. Because library assistants work for public institutions, they are not directly affected by the ups and downs of the business cycle, but they may be affected by changes in the level of government funding for libraries.

Job prospects. Each year, many people leave this relatively low-paying occupation for other occupations that offer higher pay or full-time work. This creates good job opportunities for those who want to become library assistants.

Earnings

Median hourly earnings of library assistants were $10.40 in May 2006. The middle 50 percent earned between $8.07 and $13.45. The lowest 10 percent earned less than $6.77, and the highest 10 percent earned more than $16.73.

Related Occupations

Library assistants, store materials and help customers retrieve it. File clerks have similar duties. Library assistants also work closely with library technicians in providing library services to patrons.

Sources of Additional Information

Information about a career as a library assistant can be obtained from either of the following organizations:

➤ Council on Library/Media Technology, P.O. Box 42048, Mesa, AZ 85274-2048. Internet: **http://colt.ucr.edu**

➤ American Library Association, 50 East Huron St., Chicago, IL 60611.
Internet:
http://www.ala.org/ala/education/educationcareers.htm

Public libraries and libraries in academic institutions also can provide information about job openings for library assistants.

Order Clerks

(O*NET 43-4151.00)

Significant Points

- Employment is expected to decline through 2016 due to growth in online retailing and in business-to-business electronic commerce, and because of the increasing use of automated systems that make placing orders easy and convenient.

- A high school diploma or GED is the most common educational requirement.

Nature of the Work

Order clerks receive and process orders for a variety of goods or services, such as spare parts, consumer appliances, gas and electric power connections, film rentals, and articles of clothing. They sometimes are called order-entry clerks, order processors, or order takers.

Orders for materials, merchandise, or services can come from inside or from outside of an organization. Inside order clerks re-

ceive orders from other workers employed by the same company or from salespersons in the field. In large companies with many worksites, such as automobile manufacturers, clerks order parts and equipment from the company's warehouses.

Many other order clerks, called outside order clerks, receive orders from outside companies or directly from consumers. Order clerks in wholesale businesses, for instance, receive orders from retail establishments for merchandise that the retailer, in turn, sells to the public. An increasing number of order clerks work for catalog companies and online retailers, receiving orders from individual customers by telephone, fax, regular mail, or e-mail.

Computers provide order clerks with ready access to information such as stock numbers, prices, and inventory. The successful filling of an order frequently depends on having the right products in stock and being able to determine which products are most appropriate for the customer's needs. Some order clerks—especially those in industrial settings—must be able to give price estimates for entire jobs, not just single parts. Others must be able to take special orders, give expected arrival dates, prepare contracts, and handle complaints.

Many order clerks receive orders directly by telephone, recording the required information as the customer places the order. However, a rapidly increasing number of orders now are received through computer systems, the Internet, faxes, and e-mail. In some cases, these orders are sent directly from the customer's terminal to the order clerk's terminal. Orders received by regular mail are sometimes scanned into a database that is instantly accessible to clerks.

Clerks review orders for completeness and clarity. They may fill in missing information or contact the customer for the information. Clerks also contact customers if the customers need additional information, such as prices or shipping dates, or if delays in filling the order are anticipated. For orders received by regular mail, clerks remove checks or money orders, sort them, and send them for processing.

After an order has been verified and entered, the customer's final cost is calculated. The clerk then routes the order to the proper department—such as the warehouse—which actually sends out or delivers the item in question.

In organizations with sophisticated computer systems, inventory records are adjusted automatically, as sales are made. In

Order clerks work in areas that are clean, well lit, and relatively quiet.

Projections data from the National Employment Matrix

Occupational Title	SOC Code	Employment, 2006	Projected employment, 2016	Change, 2006-16	
				Number	Percent
Order clerks..	43-4151	271,000	205,000	-66,000	-24

NOTE: Data in this table are rounded. See the discussion of the employment projections table in the *Handbook* introductory chapter on *Occupational Information Included in the Handbook*.

less automated organizations, order clerks may adjust or verify inventory records. Clerks also may notify other departments when inventories are low or when filling certain orders would deplete supplies.

Some order clerks must establish priorities in filling orders. For example, an order clerk in a blood bank may receive a request from a hospital for a certain type of blood. The clerk must first find out whether the request is routine or an emergency and then take appropriate action.

Work environment. Most order clerks work in areas that are clean, well lit, and relatively quiet. These workers sit for long periods of time in front of computer terminals, which may cause eyestrain and headaches.

Order clerks usually work a standard 40-hour workweek. Clerks in retail establishments typically work overtime during peak holiday seasons, when sales volume is high. Some firms may have shifts round-the-clock to accommodate customers' time zones.

Training, Other Qualifications, and Advancement
Most order clerks are trained on the job. Employers prefer workers who are computer literate and proficient in word-processing and spreadsheet software.

Education and training. Employers prefer applicants with a high school diploma or GED or a mix of education and related experience. Most order clerks are trained on the job under the close supervision of more experienced employees.

Other qualifications. It is helpful for clerks to be comfortable using computers and to have a working knowledge of word-processing and spreadsheet software. Proficiency with computer software is increasingly important because most orders are being filled and filed electronically.

Advancement. By taking on more duties, ambitious order clerks can receive higher pay or become eligible for advancement opportunities. Some use their experience as an order clerk to move into sales positions.

Employment
Order clerks held about 271,000 jobs in 2006. Over half of all order clerks were employed in wholesale and retail trade establishments, and another 15 percent were employed in manufacturing firms. Approximately 1 out every 10 order clerks worked in the electronic shopping and mail order houses sector of retail trade. Other order clerk jobs were in industries such as information, warehousing and storage, couriers, and business support services.

Job Outlook
Overall employment of order clerks is expected to decline rapidly through the year 2016 due to improvements in technology and office automation. However, numerous job openings are

expected because some of the clerks who leave the occupation will need to be replaced.

Employment change. Employment of order clerks is expected to decline rapidly by 24 percent from 2006 to 2016 as improvements in technology and office automation continue to increase worker productivity.

Growth in electronic commerce, and the use of automated systems that make placing orders easy and convenient, will decrease demand for order clerks. The spread of electronic data interchange, which enables computers to communicate directly with each other, allows orders within establishments to be placed with little human interaction. In addition, internal systems allowing a firm's employees to place orders directly are becoming increasingly common. Outside orders placed over the Internet often are entered directly into the computer by the customer; the order clerk is not involved in placing the order. Some companies also use automated phone menus to receive orders. Others use answering machines. Developments in voice recognition technology may further reduce the demand for order clerks.

Furthermore, increased automation will allow current order clerks to be more productive, with each clerk able to handle an increasingly higher volume of orders. Sophisticated inventory control and automatic billing systems permit companies to track inventory and accounts with much less help from order clerks than in the past.

Job prospects. While overall employment of order clerks is expected to decline through the year 2016, numerous openings will occur each year to replace order clerks who transfer to other occupations or leave the labor force. Many of these openings will be for seasonal work, especially in catalog companies or online retailers catering to holiday gift buyers.

Earnings
Median hourly earnings of order clerks in May 2006 were $12.66. The middle 50 percent earned between $9.91 and $16.22. The lowest 10 percent earned less than $8.18, and the highest 10 percent earned more than $20.69. Median hourly earnings in electronic shopping and mail-order houses were $10.50.

Related Occupations
Order clerks receive and process orders. Other workers who perform similar duties include stock clerks and order fillers and hotel, motel, and resort desk clerks.

Sources of Additional Information
State employment service offices and agencies can provide information about job openings for order clerks.

Receptionists and Information Clerks

(O*NET 43-4171.00)

Significant Points

- Good interpersonal skills are critical.

- A high school diploma or its equivalent is the most common educational requirement.

- Employment is expected to grow faster than average for all occupations.

Nature of the Work

Receptionists and information clerks are charged with a responsibility that may affect the success of an organization: making a good first impression. Receptionists and information clerks answer telephones, route and screen calls, greet visitors, respond to inquiries from the public, and provide information about the organization. Some are responsible for the coordination of all mail into and out of the office. In addition, they contribute to the security of an organization by helping to monitor the access of visitors—a function that has become increasingly important.

Whereas some tasks are common to most receptionists and information clerks, their specific responsibilities vary with the type of establishment in which they work. For example, receptionists and information clerks in hospitals and in doctors' offices may gather patients' personal and insurance information and direct them to the proper waiting rooms. In corporate headquarters, they may greet visitors and manage the scheduling of the board room or common conference area. In beauty or hair salons, they arrange appointments, direct customers to the hairstylist, and may serve as cashiers. In factories, large corporations, and government offices, receptionists and information clerks may provide identification cards and arrange for escorts to take visitors to the proper office. Those working for bus and train companies respond to inquiries about departures, arrivals, stops, and other related matters.

Increasingly, receptionists and information clerks use multi-line telephone systems, personal computers, and fax machines. Despite the widespread use of automated answering systems or voice mail, many receptionists and clerks still take messages and inform other employees of visitors' arrivals or cancellation of an appointment. When they are not busy with callers, most workers are expected to perform a variety of office duties, including opening and sorting mail, collecting and distributing parcels, and transmitting and delivering facsimiles. Other duties include updating appointment calendars, preparing travel vouchers, and performing basic bookkeeping, word processing, and filing.

Work environment. Receptionists and information clerks who greet customers and visitors usually work in areas that are highly visible and designed and furnished to make a good impression. Most work stations are clean, well lighted, and relatively quiet. The work performed by some receptionists and information clerks may be tiring, repetitive, and stressful

Receptionists and information clerks must be courteous, professional, and helpful when greeting people.

as they may spend all day answering continuously ringing telephones and sometimes encounter difficult or irate callers. The work environment, however, may be very friendly and motivating for individuals who enjoy greeting customers face to face and making them feel comfortable.

Training, Other Qualifications, and Advancement

A high school diploma or its equivalent is the most common educational requirement, although hiring requirements for receptionists and information clerks vary by industry. Good interpersonal skills and being technologically proficient also are important to employers.

Education and training. Receptionists and information clerks generally need a high school diploma or equivalent as most of their training is received on the job. However, employers often look for applicants who already possess certain skills, such as prior computer experience or answering telephones. Some employers also may prefer some formal office education or training. On the job, they learn how to operate the telephone system and computers. They also learn the proper procedures for greeting visitors and for distributing mail, fax messages, and parcels. While many of these skills can be learned quickly, those who are charged with relaying information to visitors or customers may need several months to learn details about the organization.

Other qualifications. Good interpersonal and customer service skills—being courteous, professional, and helpful—are critical for this job. Being an active listener often is a key quality needed by receptionists and information clerks that requires the ability to listen patiently to the points being made, to wait to speak until others have finished, and to ask appropriate questions when necessary. In addition, the ability to relay information accurately to others is important.

The ability to operate a wide range of office technology also is helpful, as receptionists and information clerks are often asked to work on other assignments during the day.

Advancement. Advancement for receptionists generally comes about either by transferring to an occupation with more responsibility or by being promoted to a supervisory position. Receptionists with especially strong computer skills may ad-

Projections data from the National Employment Matrix

Occupational Title	SOC Code	Employment, 2006	Projected employment, 2016	Change, 2006-16	
				Number	Percent
Receptionists and information clerks..	43-4171	1,173,000	1,375,000	202,000	17

NOTE: Data in this table are rounded. See the discussion of the employment projections table in the *Handbook* introductory chapter on *Occupational Information Included in the Handbook.*

vance to a better paying job as a secretary or an administrative assistant.

Employment

Receptionists and information clerks held about 1.2 million jobs in 2006. The health care and social assistance industries—including offices of physicians, hospitals, nursing homes, and outpatient care facilities—employed about 33 percent of all receptionists and information clerks. Manufacturing, wholesale and retail trade, government, and real estate industries also employed large numbers of receptionists and information clerks. More than 3 of every 10 receptionists and information clerks work part time.

Job Outlook

Employment of receptionists and information clerks is expected to grow faster than average for all occupations. Receptionists and information clerks will have a very large number of new jobs arise, more than 200,000 over the 2006-16 period. Additional job opportunities will result from the need to replace workers who transfer to other occupations or leave the labor force.

Employment change. Receptionists and information clerks are expected to increase by 17 percent from 2006 to 2016, which is faster than the average for all occupations. Employment growth will result from rapid growth in the following industries: offices of physicians, legal services, employment services, and management and technical consulting.

Technology will have conflicting effects on employment growth for receptionists and information clerks. The increasing use of voice mail and other telephone automation reduces the need for receptionists by allowing one receptionist to perform work that formerly required several. At the same time, however, the increasing use of other technology has caused a consolidation of clerical responsibilities and growing demand for workers with diverse clerical and technical skills. Because receptionists and information clerks may perform a wide variety of clerical tasks, they should continue to be in demand. Further, they perform many tasks that are interpersonal in nature and are not easily automated, ensuring continued demand for their services in a variety of establishments.

Job prospects. In addition to job growth, numerous job opportunities will be created as receptionists and information clerks transfer to other occupations or leave the labor force altogether. Opportunities should be best for persons with a wide range of clerical and technical skills, particularly those with related work experience.

Earnings

Median hourly earnings of receptionists and information clerks in May 2006 were $11.01. The middle 50 percent earned between $9.06 and $13.51. The lowest 10 percent earned less than $7.54, and the highest 10 percent earned more than $16.23. Median hourly earnings in the industries employing the largest number of receptionists and information clerks in May 2006 were:

Offices of dentists	$12.89
General medical and surgical hospitals..................................	11.74
Offices of physicians...	11.44
Employment services...	10.72
Personal care services	8.57

Related Occupations

Receptionists deal with the public and often direct people to others who can assist them. Other workers who perform similar duties include dispatchers, secretaries and administrative assistants, and customer service representatives.

Sources of Additional Information

State employment offices can provide information on job openings for receptionists.

Reservation and Transportation Ticket Agents and Travel Clerks

(O*NET 43-4181.00)

Significant Points

- Most jobs are found in large metropolitan airports, reservation call centers, and train or bus stations.

- A high school diploma or its equivalent is the most common educational requirement.

- Employment is expected to show little or no growth because of the significant impact of technology on worker productivity.

Nature of the Work

Each year, millions of people travel by plane, train, ship, bus, and automobile. Many of these travelers rely on the services of reservation and transportation ticket agents and travel clerks. Agents and clerks perform functions as varied as selling tickets, confirming reservations, checking baggage, and providing useful travel information.

Most *reservation agents* work for airlines or large hotel chains, helping people plan trips and make reservations. They usually work in reservation call centers, answering telephone or e-mail inquiries and offering travel arrangement suggestions and information such as routes, schedules, fares, and types of accommodations. They also change or confirm transportation and lodging reservations. Most agents use their own company's reservation system to obtain information needed to make, change, or cancel traveler reservations.

Transportation ticket agents are sometimes known as passenger service agents, passenger booking clerks, reservation clerks, airport service agents, ticket clerks, or ticket sellers. They work in airports, train stations, and bus stations, selling tickets, assigning seats to passengers, and checking baggage. In addition, they may answer inquiries and give directions, examine passports and visas, or check in pets. They may be required to assist customers who have trouble operating self-service ticketing machines or kiosks. Other ticket agents, more commonly known as *gate or station agents*, work in airport terminals, assisting passengers boarding airplanes. These workers direct passengers to the correct boarding area, check tickets and seat assignments, make boarding announcements, and provide special assistance to young, elderly, or disabled passengers.

Travel clerks provide travelers information on points of interest, restaurants, overnight accommodations, and availability of emergency services. In some cases, they make rental car, hotel, and restaurant reservations. Clerks also may provide assistance in filling out travel documents and answer other travel-related questions.

Work environment. Most reservation and transportation ticket agents and travel clerks work in airports, call centers, and train and bus terminals that generally are clean and safe. Reservation and ticket agents who work in large, centralized reservation centers spend much of their day talking with customers on the telephone and using a computer to plan itineraries and to make reservations. The call center environment is often hectic and noisy. Ticket agents, who work at transportation sites may stand on their feet for long periods of time, and may have to lift heavy baggage.

Although most reservation and transportation ticket agents and travel clerks work a standard 40-hour week, about 14 percent work part time. Some agents work evenings, late nights, weekends, and holidays. In general, employees with the most seniority tend to be assigned the more desirable shifts.

The work performed by reservation and transportation ticket agents and travel clerks may be repetitive and stressful. They often work under stringent time constraints. Agents and clerks must work quickly and accurately to avoid mistakes and angering customers. Difficult or angry customers also can create stressful situations as agents usually bear the brunt of customers' dissatisfaction. In addition, prolonged computer use, which is common in this occupation, may lead to eyestrain.

Training, Other Qualifications, and Advancement

Most reservation and transportation ticket agents spend several weeks in company-sponsored training programs learning the reservation system and other travel-related information.

Good customer service skills and the ability to work quickly are important.

Education and training. A high school diploma or its equivalent is the most common educational requirement for reservation and transportation ticket agents and travel clerks. Most airline reservation and ticket agents learn their skills through formal company training programs that can last several weeks. They learn company and industry policies as well as ticketing procedures. Trainees also learn to use the airline's computer system to obtain information on schedules, fares, and the availability of seats; to make reservations for passengers; and to prepare passenger itineraries. In addition, they must become familiar with train, airport, and airline code designations, security regulations, and safety procedures. After completing classroom instruction, new agents work under the direct guidance of a supervisor or experienced agent. During this time the supervisors may monitor telephone conversations to improve the quality of customer service so that agents learn to provide customer service in a courteous manner, while limiting the time spent on each call.

In contrast to those who work for airlines, reservation and transportation ticket agents and travel clerks who work for bus lines and railroads are trained on the job through short in-house classes that last several days.

Other qualifications. Applicants usually must be 18 years of age and older and a valid driver's license may be required. Also, experience with computers and good typing skills usually are required. Agents who handle passenger luggage must be able to lift heavy objects.

Many reservation and transportation ticket agents and travel clerks deal directly with the public, so a professional appearance and a pleasant personality are important. A clear speaking voice and fluency in English also are essential, because these employees frequently use the telephone or public-address systems. In addition, fluency in a foreign language is becoming increasingly helpful for those who deal with the public, because of the growing number of international and non-English speaking travelers.

Advancement. Reservation and transportation ticket agents and travel clerks may advance by being transferred to a po-

Reservation and transportation ticket agents and travel clerks verify schedules before printing tickets.

Projections data from the National Employment Matrix

Occupational Title	SOC Code	Employment, 2006	Projected employment, 2016	Change, 2006-16	
				Number	Percent
Reservation and transportation ticket agents and travel clerks	43-4181	165,000	167,000	1,800	1

NOTE: Data in this table are rounded. See the discussion of the employment projections table in the *Handbook* introductory chapter on *Occupational Information Included in the Handbook.*

sition with more responsibilities or by being promoted to a supervisory position. Many travel companies fill supervisory and managerial positions by promoting individuals within their organization, so those who acquire additional skills, experience, and training improve their opportunities for advancement. Some companies require that candidates for supervisory positions have an associate degree in a business-related field, such as management, business administration, or marketing. Within the airline industry, a ticket agent may advance to lead worker on the shift.

Employment

Reservation and transportation ticket agents and travel clerks held about 165,000 jobs in 2006. About six out of ten agents and clerks are employed by airlines. Others work for tour operators and reservation services, hotels and other lodging places, and other companies that provide transportation services.

Although agents and clerks are found throughout the country, most work in large metropolitan airports, reservation call centers, and train or bus stations. The remainder work in small, regional airports, or in small communities served only by intercity bus or railroad lines.

Job Outlook

Employment of reservation and transportation ticket agents and travel clerks is expected to show little or no growth during the projection period. Additionally, applicants for these jobs are likely to encounter keen competition.

Employment change. Employment of reservation and transportation ticket agents is expected grow only 1 percent from 2006 to 2016, reflecting little or no change to employment. Despite a growing and more mobile population who will likely travel more frequently, newer automated reservations and ticketing operations will speed transaction time and reduce the need for more workers to handle the expected higher volume of business. Most train stations and airports now have self-service ticket printing machines, or kiosks, which enable passengers to make reservations, purchase tickets, and check-in for train rides and flights themselves. Many passengers also are able to check travel times and fares, make reservations, purchase tickets, and check-in for most domestic flights on the Internet. Nevertheless, not all travel-related passenger services can be fully automated, primarily for safety and security reasons, and not all passengers use these automated services. As a result, job openings will continue to become available as increasing numbers of people travel more frequently. Additional growth will result to meet the travel needs of the growing retirement population, particularly in less traditional transportation centers, such as with boat or cruise operators or with companies who rent recreational vehicles.

Job prospects. Job applicants often face competition for these jobs, because entry requirements are relatively low and benefits for those who like to travel, particularly on the airlines, are high. Applicants who have previous experience in the travel industry, in sales, or in customer service should have the best job prospects. Those who possess a pleasant personality and strong customer service skills also should have good job opportunities. Additional job opportunities will result from the need to replace workers who transfer to other occupations, retire, or leave the labor force altogether.

Employment in these occupations may fluctuate with the economy. During recessions, discretionary passenger travel often declines, and transportation service companies are less likely to hire new workers and may institute layoffs.

Earnings

Median annual earnings of reservation and transportation ticket agents and travel clerks in May 2006 were $28,540. The middle 50 percent earned between $21,640 and $38,540. The lowest 10 percent earned less than $17,670, and the highest 10 percent earned more than $45,400. Many employers offer discounts on travel services to their employees. In May 2006, median annual earnings in the industries employing the largest number of agents were:

Scheduled air transportation $32,850
Traveler accommodation..23,630
Travel arrangement and reservation services 22,630

Related Occupations

Other occupations that provide travel-related services include hotel, motel, and resort desk clerks; travel agents; and flight attendants. Other occupations that make sales and provide information to customers include counter and rental clerks, order clerks, customer service representatives, and receptionists and information clerks.

Sources of Additional Information

For information about job opportunities as reservation and transportation ticket agents and travel clerks, write to the personnel manager of individual transportation companies. Addresses of airlines are available from:

➤ Air Transport Association of America, 1301 Pennsylvania Ave. NW., Suite 1100, Washington, DC 20004.
Internet: **http://www.airlines.org**

Material Recording, Scheduling, Dispatching, and Distributing Occupations

Cargo and Freight Agents

(O*NET 43-5011.00)

Significant Points

- Cargo and freight agents need no more than a high school diploma and learn their duties informally on the job.

- Faster than average employment growth is expected.

Nature of the Work

Cargo and freight agents arrange for and track incoming and outgoing shipments in airline, train, or trucking terminals or on shipping docks. They expedite shipments by determining the route that shipments will take and by preparing all necessary documents. Agents take orders from customers and arrange for the pickup of freight or cargo and its delivery to loading platforms. Cargo and freight agents may keep records of the cargo, including its amount, type, weight, dimensions, destination, and time of shipment. They keep a tally of missing items and record the condition of damaged items.

Cargo and freight agents arrange cargo according to its destination. They also determine any shipping rates and other charges that usually apply to freight. For imported or exported freight, they verify that the proper customs paperwork is in order. Cargo and freight agents often track shipments electronically, using bar codes, and answer customers' questions about the status of their shipments.

Work environment. Cargo and freight agents work in a wide variety of businesses, institutions, and industries. Some work in warehouses, stockrooms, or shipping and receiving rooms that may not be temperature controlled. Others may spend time in cold storage rooms or outside on loading platforms, where they are exposed to the weather.

Most jobs for cargo and freight agents involve frequent standing, bending, walking, and stretching. Some lifting and carrying of small items may be involved. Although automated devices have lessened the physical demands of this occupation, not every employer has these devices. The work still can be strenuous, even though mechanical material-handling equipment is used to move heavy items.

The typical workweek is Monday through Friday. However, evening and weekend hours are common in jobs involving large shipments.

Training, Other Qualifications, and Advancement

Cargo and freight agents need no more than a high school diploma and learn their duties informally on the job.

Education and training. Many jobs are entry level and require only a high school diploma. Cargo and freight agents undergo informal on-the-job training. They start out by checking items to be shipped, attaching labels to them, and making sure that addresses are correct. As this occupation becomes more automated, workers may need longer periods of training to master the use of equipment.

Other qualifications. Employers prefer to hire people who can use computers. Typing, filing, recordkeeping, and other clerical skills also are important.

Advancement. Advancement opportunities for cargo and freight agents are usually limited, but some agents may become team leaders or use their hands-on experience to switch to other clerical occupations in the businesses where they work.

Employment

Cargo and freight agents held about 86,000 jobs in 2006. Most agents were employed in transportation. Approximately 44 percent worked for firms engaged in support activities for the transportation industry, 23 percent were in the air transportation industry, 9 percent worked for courier businesses, and 7 percent were in the truck transportation industry.

Job Outlook

Employment is expected to grow faster than average.

Employment change. Employment of cargo and freight agents is expected to increase by 16 percent during the 2006-16 decade, faster than the average for all occupations. A growing number of agents will be needed to handle the increasing number of shipments resulting from increases in cargo traffic.

Cargo and freight agents determine the route that shipments will take and prepare all necessary documents.

Projections data from the National Employment Matrix

Occupational Title	SOC Code	Employment, 2006	Projected employment, 2016	Change, 2006-16	
				Number	Percent
Cargo and freight agents	43-5011	86,000	100,000	14,000	16

NOTE: Data in this table are rounded. See the discussion of the employment projections table in the *Handbook* introductory chapter on *Occupational Information Included in the Handbook.*

Additional demand will stem from the growing popularity of online shopping and same-day delivery.

Job prospects. In addition to new job growth, openings will be created by the need to replace cargo and freight agents who leave the occupation.

Earnings

Median annual earnings of cargo and freight agents in May 2006 were $37,110. The middle 50 percent earned between $27,750 and $46,440. The lowest 10 percent earned less than $22,470, and the highest 10 percent earned more than $57,440. Median annual earnings in the industries employing the largest numbers of cargo and freight agents in May 2006 were:

Scheduled air transportation	$38,340
Freight transportation arrangement	37,130
Couriers	36,750
General freight trucking	34,010
Support activities for air transportation	23,770

These workers usually receive the same benefits as most other workers. If uniforms are required, employers generally provide them or offer an allowance to purchase them.

Related Occupations

Cargo and freight agents plan and coordinate shipments of cargo by airlines, trains, and trucks. They also arrange freight pickup with customers. Others who do similar work are couriers and messengers; shipping, receiving, and traffic clerks; weighers, measurers, checkers, and samplers, recordkeeping; truck drivers and driver/sales workers; and Postal Service workers.

Sources of Additional Information

Information about job opportunities may be obtained from local employers and local offices of the State employment service.

Couriers and Messengers

(O*NET 43-5021.00)

Significant Points

- Most jobs do not require more than a high school diploma.

- Employment is expected to have little to no change, reflecting the more widespread use of electronic information-handling technologies such as e-mail and fax.

Nature of the Work

Couriers and messengers move and distribute information, documents, and small packages for businesses, institutions, and government agencies. They pick up and deliver letters, important business documents, or packages that need to be sent or received quickly within a local area. Couriers and messengers use trucks and vans for larger deliveries, such as legal caseloads and conference materials. By sending an item by courier or messenger, the sender ensures that it reaches its destination the same day or even within the hour. Couriers and messengers also deliver items that the sender is unwilling to entrust to other means of delivery, such as important legal or financial documents, passports, airline tickets, or medical samples to be tested.

Couriers and messengers receive their instructions either in person—by reporting to their office—or by telephone, two-way radio, or wireless data service. Then they pick up the item and carry it to its destination. After each pickup or delivery, they check in with their dispatcher to receive instructions. Sometimes the dispatcher will contact them while they are between stops and reroute them to pick up a new delivery. Consequently, most couriers and messengers spend much of their time outdoors or in their vehicle. They usually maintain records of deliveries and often obtain signatures from the people receiving the items.

Most couriers and messengers deliver items within a limited geographic area, such as a city or metropolitan area. Mail or overnight delivery service is the preferred delivery method for items that need to go longer distances. Some couriers and messengers carry items only for their employer, often a law firm, bank, medical laboratory, or financial institution. Others may act as part of an organization's internal mail system and carry items mainly within the organization's buildings or entirely within one building. Many couriers and messengers work for messenger or courier services; for a fee, they pick up items from anyone and deliver them to specified destinations within a local area. Most are paid on a commission basis.

Couriers and messengers reach their destination by several methods. Many drive vans or cars or ride motorcycles. A few travel by foot, especially in urban areas or when making deliveries nearby. In congested urban areas, messengers often use bicycles to make deliveries. Messenger or courier services usually employ the bicycle messengers.

Work environment. Couriers and messengers spend most of their time alone, making deliveries, and usually are not closely supervised. Those who deliver by bicycle must be physically fit and must cope with all weather conditions and the hazards of heavy traffic. Car, van, and truck couriers must sometimes carry heavy loads, either manually or with the aid of a hand truck. They also have to deal with difficult parking situations, traffic jams, and road construction. The pressure of making as many

Couriers and messengers spend most of their time making deliveries, and usually are not closely supervised.

deliveries as possible to increase one's earnings can be stressful and may lead to unsafe driving or bicycling practices. The typical workweek is Monday through Friday; however, evening and weekend hours are common.

Training, Other Qualifications, and Advancement

Most couriers and messengers train on the job. Communication skills, a good driving record, and good sense of direction are helpful.

Education and training. Most courier and messenger jobs do not require workers to have more than a high school diploma. Couriers and messengers usually learn as they work, training with an experienced worker for a short time.

Other qualifications. Couriers and messengers need a good knowledge of the area in which they travel and a good sense of direction. Employers also prefer to hire people who are familiar with computers and other electronic office and business equipment. In addition, good oral and written communication skills are important because communicating with customers and dispatchers is an integral part of some courier and messenger jobs.

Those who work as independent contractors for a messenger or delivery service may be required to have a valid driver's license, a registered and inspected vehicle, a good driving record, and insurance coverage. Many couriers and messengers, who are employees rather than independent contractors, also are required to provide and maintain their own vehicle. Although

some companies have spare bicycles or mopeds that their riders may rent for a short period, almost all two-wheeled couriers own their own bicycle, moped, or motorcycle.

Advancement. Couriers and messengers have limited advancement opportunities. However, one avenue for advancement is to learn dispatching or to take service requests by phone.

Some independent contractors become master contractors. Master contractors organize routes for multiple independent contractors through courier agencies.

Employment

Couriers and messengers together held about 134,000 jobs in 2006. About 25 percent were employed in the couriers and messengers industry; 15 percent worked in health care; and 9 percent worked in legal services. About 19 percent were self-employed independent contractors; they provide their own vehicles and, to a certain extent, set their own schedules. However, they are like employees in some respects, because they often contract with one company.

Job Outlook

Employment of couriers and messengers should have little to no change through 2016, despite an increasing volume of parcels, business documents, and other materials to be delivered. The need to replace workers who leave the occupation will create some job openings.

Employment change. Employment in this occupation is expected to remain unchanged during the 2006-16 decade. Employment will be unchanged because of the more widespread use of electronic information-handling technologies such as e-mail and fax. Electronic transmission of many documents, forms, and other materials is replacing items that had been hand delivered. Many legal and financial documents, which formerly were delivered by hand because they required a handwritten signature, can now be delivered electronically with online signatures. However, for items that are unable to be sent electronically—such as blueprints and other oversized materials, securities, and passports—couriers and messengers will still be needed. They still will also be required by medical and dental laboratories to pick up and deliver medical samples, specimens, and other materials.

Job prospects. Despite the lack of job growth, some job opportunities will arise out of the need to replace couriers and messengers who leave the occupation. Demand for couriers and messengers may be particularly strong in certain activities, like transporting donor organs for hospitals.

Earnings

Median annual earnings of couriers and messengers in May 2006 were $21,540. The middle 50 percent earned between

Projections data from the National Employment Matrix

Occupational Title	SOC Code	Employment, 2006	Projected employment, 2016	Change, 2006-16	
				Number	Percent
Couriers and messengers....................................	43-5021	134,000	134,000	-200	0

NOTE: Data in this table are rounded. See the discussion of the employment projections table in the *Handbook* introductory chapter on *Occupational Information Included in the Handbook.*

$17,430 and $27,080. The lowest 10 percent earned less than $14,870, and the highest 10 percent earned more than $34,510. Median annual earnings in the industries employing the largest numbers of couriers and messengers in May 2006 were:

Medical and diagnostic laboratories $23,020
Depository credit intermediation 20,680
Couriers...20,650
Legal services..20,610
Local messengers and local delivery 19,560

Couriers employed by a courier service usually receive the same benefits as most other workers. If uniforms are required, employers generally provide them or offer an allowance to purchase them. Most independent contractors do not receive benefits, but usually have higher earnings.

Related Occupations

Messengers and couriers deliver letters, parcels, and other items. They also keep accurate records of their work. Others who do similar work are Postal Service workers; truck drivers and driver/sales workers; shipping, receiving, and traffic clerks; and cargo and freight agents.

Sources of Additional Information

Local employers and local offices of the State employment service can provide additional information about job opportunities. People interested in courier and messenger jobs also may contact messenger and courier services, mail-order firms, banks, printing and publishing firms, utility companies, retail stores, or other large companies.

Information on careers as couriers and messengers is available from:

➤ Messengers and Couriers Association of the Americas, 1156 15th St. NW., Suite 900, Washington, DC 20005.

Dispatchers

(O*NET 43-5031.00, 43-5032.00)

Significant Points

- Alternative work schedules are necessary to accommodate evening, weekend, and holiday work and 24-hour-per-day, 7-day-per-week operations.

- Dispatchers generally are entry-level workers who are trained on the job and need no more than a high school diploma.

- Many States require specific types of training or certification.

Nature of the Work

Dispatchers schedule and dispatch workers, equipment, or service vehicles to carry materials or passengers. Some dispatchers take calls for taxi companies, for example, or for police or ambulance assistance. They keep records, logs, and schedules of the calls that they receive and of the transportation vehicles

Many dispatchers use computer-aided systems.

that they monitor and control. In fact, they usually prepare a detailed report on all activities occurring during their shifts. Many dispatchers employ computer-aided dispatch systems to accomplish these tasks.

All dispatchers are assigned a specific territory and have responsibility for all communications within that area. Many work in teams, especially dispatchers in large communications centers or companies. The work of dispatchers varies greatly, depending on the industry in which they work.

Police, fire, and ambulance dispatchers, also called public safety dispatchers or 911 operators, monitor the location of emergency services personnel from one or all of the jurisdiction's emergency services departments. These workers dispatch the appropriate type and number of units in response to calls for assistance. Dispatchers, or call takers, often are the first people the public contacts when emergency assistance is required. If certified for emergency medical services, the dispatcher may provide medical instruction to those on the scene of the emergency until the medical staff arrives.

Police, fire, and ambulance dispatchers work in a variety of settings—a police station, a fire station, a hospital, or, increasingly, a centralized communications center. In some areas, one of the major departments serves as the communications center. In these situations, all emergency calls go to that department, where a dispatcher handles their calls and screens the others before transferring them to the appropriate service.

When handling calls, dispatchers question each caller carefully to determine the type, seriousness, and location of the emergency. The information obtained is posted either electronically by computer or, with decreasing frequency, by hand. The dispatcher then quickly decides the priority of the incident, the kind and number of units needed, and the location of the closest and most suitable units available. When appropriate, dispatchers stay in close contact with other service providers—for example, a police dispatcher would monitor the response of the fire department when there is a major fire. In a medical emergency, dispatchers keep in close touch not only with the dispatched units, but also with the caller. They may give extensive first-aid instructions before the emergency personnel arrive, while the caller is waiting for the ambulance. Dispatchers continuously give updates on the patient's condition to the ambulance personnel and often serve as a link between the medical staff in a hospital and the emergency medical technicians in the ambulance. (A separate statement on emergency medical technicians and paramedics appears elsewhere in the *Handbook*.)

Other dispatchers coordinate deliveries, service calls, and related activities for a variety of firms. *Truck dispatchers,* who work for local and long-distance trucking companies, coordinate the movement of trucks and freight between cities. These dispatchers direct the pickup and delivery activities of drivers, receive customers' requests for the pickup and delivery of freight, consolidate freight orders into truckloads for specific destinations, assign drivers and trucks, and draw up routes and pickup and delivery schedules. *Bus dispatchers* make sure that local and long-distance buses stay on schedule. They handle all problems that may disrupt service, and they dispatch other buses or arrange for repairs in order to restore service and schedules. *Train dispatchers* ensure the timely and efficient movement of trains according to orders and schedules. They must be aware of track switch positions, track maintenance areas, and the location of other trains running on the track. *Taxicab dispatchers,* or starters, dispatch taxis in response to requests for service and keep logs on all road service calls. *Tow-truck dispatchers* take calls for emergency road service. They relay the nature of the problem to a nearby service station or a tow-truck service and see to it that the road service is completed. *Gas and water service dispatchers* monitor gaslines and water mains and send out service trucks and crews to take care of emergencies.

Work environment. The work of dispatchers can be very hectic when many calls come in at the same time. The job of public safety dispatchers is particularly stressful because a slow or an improper response to a call can result in serious injury or further harm. Also, callers who are anxious or afraid may become excited and be unable to provide needed information; some may even become abusive. Despite provocations, dispatchers must remain calm, objective, and in control of the situation.

Dispatchers sit for long periods, using telephones, computers, and two-way radios. Much of their time is spent at video display terminals, viewing monitors and observing traffic patterns. As a result of working for long stretches with computers and other electronic equipment, dispatchers can experience significant eyestrain and back discomfort. Generally, dispatchers work a 40-hour week; however, rotating shifts and compressed work schedules are common. Alternative work schedules are necessary to accommodate evening, weekend, and holiday work and 24-hour-per-day, 7-day-per-week operations.

Training, Other Qualifications, and Advancement

Dispatchers generally are entry-level workers who are trained on the job and need no more than a high school diploma. Many States require specific types of training or certification.

Education and training. Workers usually develop the necessary skills on the job. This informal training lasts from several days to a few months, depending on the complexity of the job. While working with an experienced dispatcher, new employees monitor calls and learn how to operate a variety of communications equipment, including telephones, radios, and various wireless devices. As trainees gain confidence, they begin to handle calls themselves. In smaller operations, dispatchers sometimes act as customer service representatives, processing orders. Many public safety dispatchers also participate in structured training programs sponsored by their employer. Increasingly, public safety dispatchers receive training in stress and crisis management as well as in family counseling. This training helps them to provide effective services to others; and, at the same time, it helps them manage the stress involved in their work.

Licensure. Many States require specific types of training or certification from a professional association. Certification often requires several months in a classroom for instruction in computer-assisted dispatching and other emerging technologies as well as radio dispatching and stress management.

Other qualifications. State or local government civil service regulations usually govern police, fire, and emergency medical dispatching jobs. Candidates for these positions may have to pass written, oral, and performance tests. Also, they may be asked to attend training classes in order to qualify for advancement.

Communication skills and the ability to work under pressure are important personal qualities for dispatchers. Residency in the city or county of employment frequently is required for public safety dispatchers. Dispatchers in transportation industries must be able to deal with sudden influxes of shipments and

Projections data from the National Employment Matrix

Occupational Title	SOC Code	Employment, 2006	Projected employment, 2016	Change, 2006-16	
				Number	Percent
Dispatchers..	43-5030	289,000	306,000	16,000	6
Police, fire, and ambulance dispatchers	43-5031	99,000	113,000	13,000	14
Dispatchers, except police, fire, and ambulance	43-5032	190,000	193,000	2,900	2

NOTE: Data in this table are rounded. See the discussion of the employment projections table in the *Handbook* introductory chapter on *Occupational Information Included in the Handbook.*

disruptions of shipping schedules caused by bad weather, road construction, or accidents.

Certification and advancement. Although there are no mandatory licensing requirements, some States require that public safety dispatchers possess a certificate to work on a State network, such as the Police Information Network. Many dispatchers participate in these programs in order to improve their prospects for career advancement.

Dispatchers who work for private firms, which usually are small, will find few opportunities for advancement. In contrast, public safety dispatchers may become a shift or divisional supervisor or chief of communications, or they may move to higher paying administrative jobs. Some become police officers or fire fighters.

Employment

Dispatchers held 289,000 jobs in May of 2006. About 34 percent were police, fire, and ambulance dispatchers, almost all of whom worked for State and local governments—primarily local police and fire departments. About 28 percent of all dispatchers worked in the transportation and warehousing industry, and the rest worked in a wide variety of mainly service-providing industries.

Although dispatching jobs are found throughout the country, most dispatchers work in urban areas, where large communications centers and businesses are located.

Job Outlook

Employment of dispatchers is expected to grow more slowly than average. In addition to those positions resulting from job growth, many openings will arise from the need to replace workers who transfer to other occupations or leave the labor force.

Employment change. Employment of dispatchers is expected to increase 6 percent over the 2006-16 decade, more slowly than the average for all occupations. Population growth and economic expansion are expected to spur employment growth for all types of dispatchers. The growing and aging population will increase demand for emergency services and stimulate employment growth of police, fire, and ambulance dispatchers.

Job prospects. In addition to openings due to growth, job openings will result from the need to replace workers who transfer to other occupations or leave the labor force. Many districts are consolidating their communications centers into a shared area-wide facility. As the equipment becomes more complex, individuals with computer skills and experience will have a greater opportunity for employment as public safety dispatchers.

Employment of some dispatchers is more adversely affected by economic downturns than employment of other dispatchers. For example, when economic activity falls, demand for transportation services declines. As a result, taxicab, train, and truck dispatchers may experience layoffs or a shortened workweek, and jobseekers may have some difficulty finding entry-level jobs. Employment of tow-truck dispatchers, by contrast, is seldom affected by general economic conditions, because of the emergency nature of their business. Likewise, public safety dispatchers are unlikely to be affected by economic downturns.

Earnings

Median annual wage-and-salary earnings of dispatchers, except police, fire, and ambulance in May 2006 were $32,190. The middle 50 percent earned between $24,860 and $42,030. The lowest 10 percent earned less than $19,780, and the highest 10 percent earned more than $53,250.

Median annual wage-and-salary earnings of police, fire, and ambulance dispatchers in 2006 were $31,470. The middle 50 percent earned between $25,200 and $39,040. The lowest 10 percent earned less than $20,010, and the highest 10 percent earned more than $47,190.

Related Occupations

Other occupations that involve directing and controlling the movement of vehicles, freight, and personnel, as well as distributing information and messages, include air traffic controllers, communications equipment operators, customer service representatives, and reservation and transportation ticket agents and travel clerks.

Sources of Additional Information

For further information on training and certification for police, fire, and emergency dispatchers, contact:

➤ Association of Public Safety Communications Officials, International, 351 N. Williamson Blvd., Daytona Beach, FL 32114. Internet: **http://www.apco911.org**

➤ International Municipal Signal Association, P.O. Box 359, 165 E. Union St., Newark, NY 14513.
Internet: **http://www.IMSAsafety.org**

Information on job opportunities for police, fire, and emergency dispatchers is available from personnel offices of State and local governments or police departments. Information about work opportunities for other types of dispatchers is available from local employers and State employment service offices.

Meter Readers, Utilities

(O*NET 43-5041.00)

Significant Points

- Meter reading is one of the fastest-declining occupations, as a result of automated meter reading (AMR) systems that allow meters to be monitored and billed from a central point.

- Most meter readers are employed by electric, gas, or water utilities or by local governments.

- Many workers begin working as meter readers and advance to lineman, power plant operator, or dispatcher jobs.

Nature of the Work

Meter readers read electric, gas, water, or steam consumption meters and record the volume used. They serve both residential and commercial consumers. The basic duty of a meter reader is

Most modern meters are electronic and can be read using a remote device.

to walk or drive along a route and read customers' consumption from a tracking device. Accuracy is the most important part of the job, as companies rely on readers to provide the information they need to bill their customers.

Other duties include inspecting the meters and their connections for any defects or damage, supplying repair and maintenance workers with the necessary information to fix damaged meters. They keep track of customers' average usage and record reasons for any extreme fluctuations in volume. Meter readers are constantly aware of any abnormal behavior or consumption that might indicate an unauthorized connection. They may turn on service for new occupants and turn off service for questionable behavior or nonpayment of charges.

Work environment. Meter readers work outdoors in all types of weather as they travel through communities and neighborhoods taking readings. Those traveling on foot may have to walk several miles a day. Dogs can pose a difficulty for meter readers, although they are generally given precautionary devices to help them avoid encounters. Meter readers generally work 40-hour weeks, although part-time positions are available. The typical workweek is Monday through Friday.

Training, Other Qualifications, and Advancement

Meter readers are entry-level utility employees. Many people start utility careers in this occupation with the goal of advancing to more responsible positions.

Education and training. Most employers prefer to hire workers who have a high school diploma. Until they demonstrate an ability to work alone, inexperienced meter readers usually work with more experienced ones. They learn how to read meters and determine consumption rates on the job and they must also learn the route that they need to travel.

Other qualifications. No experience is required for this position, but employers prefer to hire those familiar with computers and other electronic office and business equipment. Because routes may change, it is important for readers to be able to understand maps. Typing, recordkeeping and other clerical skills are also useful.

Advancement. Meter reading is generally considered an entry-level occupation. Many people start working as meter readers and move up to higher positions in the metering department. Others move on to other positions within the utility, such as dispatcher or distributor. They may also become apprentices to more skilled positions, such as lineman or electrician.

Employment

Meter readers held about 47,000 jobs in 2006. About 42 percent were employed by electric, gas, and water utilities. Most of the rest were employed in local government, reading water meters or meters for other government-owned utilities.

Job Outlook

Despite declining employment, some job openings are expected during the 2006-16 decade.

Employment change. Employment of meter readers is expected to decline by 10 percent through 2016. New AMR systems allow meters to be monitored and billed from a central point, reducing the need for meter readers.

Job prospects. It will be many years before AMR systems can be implemented in all locations, so there still will be some openings for meter readers, mainly to replace workers leaving the occupation. The utilities industry is expecting a large number of retirements from its aging workforce, which should create many job opportunities.

Earnings

Median annual earnings of utility meter readers in May 2006 were $30,330. The middle 50 percent earned between $23,580 and $39,320. The lowest 10 percent earned less than $18,970, and the highest 10 percent earned more than $49,150. Employee benefits vary greatly between companies and may not be offered for part-time workers. If uniforms are required, employers generally provide them or offer an allowance to purchase them.

Projections data from the National Employment Matrix

Occupational Title	SOC Code	Employment, 2006	Projected employment, 2016	Change, 2006-16	
				Number	Percent
Meter readers, utilities	43-5041	47,000	42,000	-4,800	-10

NOTE: Data in this table are rounded. See the discussion of the employment projections table in the *Handbook* introductory chapter on *Occupational Information Included in the Handbook.*

Related Occupations

Other workers responsible for the distribution and control of utilities include line installers and repairers, and power plant operators, distributors, and dispatchers.

Sources of Additional Information

Information about job opportunities may be obtained from local utilities and offices of State employment services, and from:
➤ International Brotherhood of Electrical Workers, 1125 15th St.NW., Washington, DC 20005.
Internet: **http://www.ibew.org**

Postal Service Workers

(O*NET 43-5051.00, 43-5052.00, 43-5053.00)

Significant Points

- Employment of Postal Service workers is expected to experience little or no change overall because of greater efficiencies in the processing and sorting of mail.

- Keen competition is expected as the number of qualified applicants usually exceeds the number of job openings.

- Qualification is based on an examination.

- Applicants customarily wait 1 to 2 years or more after passing the examination before being hired.

Nature of the Work

Each week, the U.S. Postal Service delivers billions of pieces of mail, including letters, bills, advertisements, and packages through heat, snow, or rain. To do this in an efficient and timely manner, the Postal Service employs about 615,000 individuals who process, sort, and deliver mail and packages as well as provide customer services and supplies in post offices. Most Postal Service workers are clerks, mail carriers, or mail sorters, processors, and processing machine operators. Postal clerks wait on customers at post offices, whereas mail sorters, processors, and processing machine operators sort incoming and outgoing mail at post offices and mail processing centers. Mail carriers deliver mail to urban and rural residences and businesses throughout the United States.

Postal Service clerks, also known as window clerks, sell stamps, money orders, postal stationery, and mailing envelopes and boxes in post offices throughout the country. They also weigh packages to determine postage and check that packages are in satisfactory condition for mailing. These clerks register, certify, and insure mail and answer questions about postage rates, post office boxes, mailing restrictions, and other postal matters. Window clerks also help customers file claims for damaged packages.

Postal Service mail sorters, processors, and processing machine operators prepare incoming and outgoing mail for distribution at post offices and at mail processing centers. These workers are commonly referred to as mail handlers, distribution clerks, mail processors, or mail processing clerks. They load and unload postal trucks and move mail around a mail processing center with forklifts, small electric tractors, or hand-pushed carts. They also load and operate mail processing, sorting, and canceling machinery.

Postal Service mail carriers deliver mail, once it has been processed and sorted, to residences and businesses in cities, towns, and rural areas. Although carriers are classified by their type of route—either city or rural—duties of city and rural carriers are similar. Most travel established routes, delivering and collecting mail. Mail carriers start work at the post office early in the morning, when they arrange the mail in delivery sequence. Automated equipment has reduced the time that carriers need to sort the mail, causing them to spend more of their time delivering it.

Mail carriers cover their routes on foot, by vehicle, or a combination of both. On foot, they carry a heavy load of mail in a satchel or push it on a cart. In most urban and rural areas, they use a car or small truck. Although the Postal Service provides vehicles to city carriers, most rural carriers must use their own automobiles for whose use they are reimbursed. Deliveries are made house-to-house, to roadside mailboxes, and to large buildings such as offices or apartments, which generally have all of their tenants' mailboxes in one location.

Besides delivering and collecting mail, carriers collect money for postage-due and COD (cash-on-delivery) fees and obtain signed receipts for registered, certified, and insured mail. If a customer is not home, the carrier leaves a notice that tells where special mail is being held. After completing their routes, carriers return to the post office with mail gathered from homes, businesses, and sometimes street collection boxes, and turn in the mail, receipts, and money collected during the day.

Some city carriers may have specialized duties such as delivering only parcels or picking up mail from mail collection boxes. In contrast to city carriers, rural carriers provide a wider range of postal services, in addition to delivering and picking up mail. For example, rural carriers may sell stamps and money orders and register, certify, and insure parcels and letters. All carriers, however, must be able to answer customers' questions about postal regulations and services and provide change-of-address cards and other postal forms when requested.

Work environment. Window clerks usually work in the public portion of post offices. They have a variety of duties and frequent contact with the public, but they rarely work at night. However, they may have to deal with upset customers, stand for long periods, and be held accountable for an assigned stock of stamps and funds. Depending on the size of the post office in which they work, they also may be required to sort mail.

Despite the use of automated equipment, the work of mail sorters, processors, and processing machine operators can be physically demanding. Workers may have to move heavy sacks of mail around a mail processing center. These workers usually are on their feet, reaching for sacks and trays of mail or placing packages and bundles into sacks and trays. Processing mail can be tiring and tedious. Many sorters, processors, and machine operators work at night or on weekends, because most large post offices process mail around the clock, and the largest volume of mail is sorted during the evening and night shifts.

Postal Service workers examine addresses to ensure that mail gets delivered to the correct location.

Workers can experience stress as they process mail under tight production deadlines and quotas.

Most carriers begin work early in the morning—those with routes in a business district can start as early as 4 a.m. Overtime hours are frequently required for urban carriers. Carriers spend most of their time outdoors, delivering mail in all kinds of weather. Though carriers face many natural hazards, such as extreme temperatures, wet and icy roads and sidewalks, and even dog bites, serious injuries are often due to the nature of the work, which requires repetitive movements, as well as constant lifting and bending. These types of repetitive injuries occur as various kinds of injuries to joints and muscles, as well as carpal tunnel syndrome.

Training, Other Qualifications, and Advancement

All applicants for Postal Service jobs are required to take a postal service examination. After passing the exam, it may take 1 to 2 years or longer before being hired as the number of applicants is generally much greater than the number of jobs that open up.

Education and training. There are no specific education requirements to become a Postal Service worker; however, all applicants must have a good command of the English language. Upon being hired, new Postal Service workers are trained on the job by experienced workers. Many post offices offer classroom instruction on safety and defensive driving. Workers receive additional instruction when new equipment or procedures are introduced. In these cases, workers usually are trained by another postal employee or a training specialist.

Other qualifications. Postal Service workers must be at least 18 years old. They must be U.S. citizens or have been granted permanent resident-alien status in the United States, and males must have registered with the Selective Service upon reaching age 18.

All applicants must pass a written examination that measures speed and accuracy at checking names and numbers and the ability to memorize mail distribution procedures. Jobseekers should contact the post office or mail processing center where they wish to work to determine when an exam will be given. Applicants' names are listed in order of their examination scores. Five points are added to the score of an honorably discharged veteran and 10 points are added to the score of a veteran who was wounded in combat or is disabled. When a vacancy occurs, the appointing officer chooses one of the top three applicants; the rest of the names remain on the list to be considered for future openings until their eligibility expires—usually 2 years after the examination date.

When accepted, applicants must pass a physical examination and drug test, and may be asked to show that they can lift and handle mail sacks weighing 70 pounds. Applicants for mail carrier positions must have a driver's license and a good driving record, and must receive a passing grade on a road test.

Postal clerks and mail carriers should be courteous and tactful when dealing with the public, especially when answering questions or receiving complaints. A good memory and the ability to read rapidly and accurately are important. Good interpersonal skills are important, particularly for mail clerks and mail carriers who deal closely with the public.

Advancement. Postal Service workers often begin on a part-time, flexible basis and become regular or full time in order of seniority, as vacancies occur. Full-time workers may bid for preferred assignments, such as the day shift or a high-level nonsupervisory position. Carriers can look forward to obtaining preferred routes as their seniority increases. Postal Service workers can advance to supervisory positions on a competitive basis.

Employment

The U.S. Postal Service employed 80,000 clerks; 338,000 mail carriers; and 198,000 mail sorters, processors, and processing machine operators in 2006. Most of them worked full time. Most postal clerks provide window service at post office branches. Many mail sorters, processors, and processing machine operators sort mail at major metropolitan post offices; others work at mail processing centers. The majority of mail carriers work in cities and suburbs, while the rest work in rural areas.

Postal Service workers are classified as casual, part-time flexible, part-time regular, or full time. Casuals are hired for 90 days at a time to help process and deliver mail during peak mailing or vacation periods. Part-time flexible workers do not have a regular work schedule or weekly guarantee of hours but are called as

Projections data from the National Employment Matrix

Occupational Title	SOC Code	Employment, 2006	Projected employment, 2016	Change, 2006-16	
				Number	Percent
Postal service workers..	43-5050	615,000	603,000	-12,000	-2
Postal service clerks..	43-5051	80,000	80,000	900	1
Postal service mail carriers	43-5052	338,000	341,000	3,500	1
Postal service mail sorters, processors, and processing machine operators...	43-5053	198,000	181,000	-17,000	-8

NOTE: Data in this table are rounded. See the discussion of the employment projections table in the *Handbook* introductory chapter on *Occupational Information Included in the Handbook.*

the need arises. Part-time regulars have a set work schedule of fewer than 40 hours per week, often replacing regular full-time workers on their scheduled day off. Full-time postal employees work a 40-hour week over a 5-day period.

Job Outlook

Employment of Postal Service workers is expected to experience little or no change through 2016. Still, many jobs will become available for mail clerks and carriers, which are expected to add workers, and because of the need to replace those who retire or leave the occupation.

Employment change. The stable employment overall of Postal Service mail carriers and Postal Service clerks will be offset by declines in Postal Service mail sorters, processors, and processing machine operators, which will cause overall employment of Postal Service workers to decline 2 percent over the 2006-2016 period. An increasing population, the greater use of third class, or bulk, mail by businesses, and more electronic shopping will generate more business for the Postal Service. However, demand will be moderated by the fact that people are sending out fewer pieces of first class mail because of the growing use of electronic communication.

These changes will affect Postal Service occupations in different ways. Efforts by the Postal Service to provide better service and meet the needs of a growing population will increase the demand for Postal Service clerks. However, the declining use of first class mail as the use of electronic communication grows will hold growth in this occupation to a minimum.

Employment of mail sorters, processors, and processing machine operators is expected to decline moderately because of the increasing use of automated materials handling equipment and optical character readers, barcode sorters, and other automated sorting equipment. In addition, companies that mail in bulk have an economic incentive to presort the mail before it arrives at the Post Office to qualify for a reduction in the price.

Employment of mail carriers is expected to grow, but only about 1 percent through 2016. As the population continues to rise, the need for mail carriers will grow. In addition, businesses are using the mail more to deliver advertising, which is making up for the reduced use of first class mail. Also, the Postal Service is moving toward more centralized mail delivery, such as the use of cluster mailboxes, to cut down on the number of door-to-door deliveries. The best employment opportunities for mail carriers are expected to be in less urbanized areas as the number of addresses to which mail must be delivered continues to grow, especially in fast growing rural areas. However, increased use of the "delivery point sequencing" system, which

allows machines to sort mail directly by the order of delivery, should reduce the amount of time that carriers spend sorting their mail, allowing them to spend more time on the streets delivering mail. This will mitigate the demand for more mail carriers.

Job prospects. Those seeking jobs as Postal Service workers can expect to encounter keen competition. The number of applicants usually exceeds the number of job openings because of the occupation's low entry requirements and attractive wages and benefits.

The role of the Postal Service as a government-approved monopoly continues to be a topic of debate. However, in 2003 the Presidential Commission on Postal Services and in 2006 the Congress both rejected the idea of privatizing the United States Postal Service. Employment and schedules in the Postal Service fluctuate with the demand for its services. When mail volume is high, full-time employees work overtime, part-time workers get additional hours, and casual workers may be hired. When mail volume is low, overtime is curtailed, part-timers work fewer hours, and casual workers are discharged.

Earnings

Median annual earnings of Postal Service mail carriers were $44,350 in May 2006. The middle 50 percent earned between $40,290 and $48,400. The lowest 10 percent had earnings of less than $34,810, while the top 10 percent earned more than $50,830. Rural mail carriers are reimbursed for mileage put on their own vehicles while delivering mail.

Median annual earnings of Postal Service clerks were $44,800 in 2006. The middle 50 percent earned between $41,720 and $47,890. The lowest 10 percent had earnings of less than $38,980, while the top 10 percent earned more than $49,750.

Median annual earnings of Postal Service mail sorters, processors, and processing machine operators were $43,900 in 2006. The middle 50 percent earned between $40,350 and $47,440. The lowest 10 percent had earnings of less than $25,770, while the top 10 percent earned more than $49,570.

Postal Service workers enjoy a variety of employer-provided benefits similar to those enjoyed by Federal Government workers. The American Postal Workers Union, the National Association of Letter Carriers, the National Postal Mail Handlers Union, and the National Rural Letter Carriers Association together represent most of these workers.

Related Occupations

Other occupations with duties similar to those of Postal Service clerks include cashiers; counter and rental clerks; file clerks;

and shipping, receiving, and traffic clerks. Others with duties related to those of Postal Service mail carriers include couriers and messengers, and truck drivers and driver/sales workers. Occupations whose duties are related to those of Postal Service mail sorters, processors, and processing machine operators include inspectors, testers, sorters, samplers, and weighers, and material moving occupations.

Sources of Additional Information

Local post offices and State employment service offices can supply details about entrance examinations and specific employment opportunities for Postal Service workers.

Production, Planning, and Expediting Clerks

(O*NET 43-5061.00)

Significant Points

- Production, planning, and expediting clerks work closely with supervisors who must approve production and work schedules.

- Many production, planning, and expediting jobs are at the entry level and do not require more than a high school diploma.

- Manufacturing firms and wholesale and retail trade establishments are the primary employers.

- Slower-than-average employment growth is projected.

Nature of the Work

Production, planning, and expediting clerks coordinate and facilitate the flow of information, work, and materials within or among offices. Most of their work is done according to production, work, or shipment schedules that are developed by supervisors who determine work progress and completion dates. Clerks compile reports on the progress of work and on production problems, and also may set worker schedules, estimate costs, schedule the shipment of parts, keep an inventory of materials, inspect and assemble materials, and write special orders for services and merchandise. In addition, they may route and deliver parts to ensure that production quotas are met and that merchandise is delivered on the date promised.

Production and planning clerks compile records and reports on various aspects of production, such as materials and parts used, products produced, machine and instrument readings, and frequency of defects. These workers prepare work tickets or

other production guides and distribute them to other workers. Production and planning clerks coordinate, schedule, monitor, and chart production and its progress, either manually or electronically. They also gather information from customers' orders or other specifications and use the information to prepare a detailed production sheet that serves as a guide in assembling or manufacturing the product.

Expediting clerks contact vendors and shippers to ensure that merchandise, supplies, and equipment are forwarded on the specified shipping dates. They communicate with transportation companies to prevent delays in transit, and they may arrange for the distribution of materials upon their arrival. They may even visit work areas of vendors and shippers to check the status of orders. Expediting clerks locate materials and distribute them to specified production areas. They may inspect products for quality and quantity to ensure their adherence to specifications. They also keep a chronological list of due dates and may move work that does not meet the production schedule to the top of the list.

Work environment. Although their offices or desks may be near a production plant or warehouse, production, planning, and expediting clerks generally work in clean and environmentally-controlled conditions. They spend most of their day either on the phone or on the computer while working closely with supervisors who must approve production and work schedules. The typical workweek is Monday through Friday.

Training, Other Qualifications, and Advancement

Training requirements for production, planning, and expediting clerks are limited. Usually a high school diploma is sufficient, although computer skills also are essential.

Education and training. Many production, planning, and expediting jobs are at the entry level and do not require more than a high school diploma. However, applicants who have taken business courses or have specific job-related experience may be preferred. Production, planning, and expediting clerks usually learn the job by doing routine tasks under close supervision. They learn how to count and mark stock, and then they start keeping records and taking inventory. Production, planning, and expediting clerks must learn both how their company operates and the company's priorities before they can begin to write production and work schedules efficiently.

Other qualifications. Employers prefer to hire those familiar with computers and other electronic office and business equipment. Because communication with other people is an integral part of some jobs in the occupation, good oral and written communication skills are essential. Typing, filing, recordkeeping, and other clerical skills also are important. Strength, stamina, good eyesight, and an ability to work at repetitive tasks, sometimes under pressure, are other important characteristics that employers look for in prospective workers.

Projections data from the National Employment Matrix

Occupational Title	SOC Code	Employment, 2006	Projected employment, 2016	Change, 2006-16	
				Number	Percent
Production, planning, and expediting clerks...................................	43-5061	293,000	305,000	12,000	4

NOTE: Data in this table are rounded. See the discussion of the employment projections table in the *Handbook* introductory chapter on *Occupational Information Included in the Handbook.*

Production, planning, and expediting clerks monitor reports to ensure a steady flow of materials.

Advancement. Advancement opportunities for production, planning, and expediting clerks vary with the place of employment, but often require additional education.

Employment

Clerks engaged in production, planning, and expediting activities work in almost every sector of the economy, overseeing inventory control and assuring that schedules and deadlines are met. In 2006, production, planning, and expediting clerks held 293,000 jobs. Jobs in manufacturing made up 41 percent. Another 15 percent were in wholesale and retail trade establishments. Others worked in advertising firms and for telecommunications companies, among other places.

Job Outlook

Employment of production, planning, and expediting clerks is expected to increase more slowly than average.

Employment change. The number of production, planning, and expediting clerks is expected to grow by 4 percent from 2016 to 2016, slower than the average for all occupations. As a greater emphasis is placed on the timely delivery of goods and services throughout the economy, there will be increasing need for production, planning, and expediting clerks at all levels of the supply chain. However, the expected employment decline in manufacturing will limit the overall growth of this occupation. The work of production, planning, and expediting clerks is less likely to be automated than the work of many other administrative support occupations.

Job prospects. In addition to openings due to employment growth, job openings will arise from the need to replace production, planning, and expediting clerks who leave the labor force or transfer to other occupations. Opportunities will be better in fields that are experiencing faster growth, such as wholesale trade and warehousing.

Earnings

Median annual earnings of production, planning, and expediting clerks in May 2006 were $38,620. The middle 50 percent earned between $29,560 and $48,900. The lowest 10 percent earned less than $23,470, and the highest 10 percent earned more than $59,080.

These workers usually receive the same benefits as most other workers.

Related Occupations

Other workers who coordinate the flow of information to assist the production process include cargo and freight agents; shipping, receiving, and traffic clerks; stock clerks and order fillers; and weighers, measurers, checkers, and samplers, recordkeeping.

Sources of Additional Information

Information about job opportunities may be obtained from local employers and from local offices of the State employment service.

Shipping, Receiving, and Traffic Clerks

(O*NET 43-5071.00)

Significant Points

- Shipping, receiving, and traffic clerks generally are entry-level workers who need no more than a high school diploma.

- Slower-than-average employment growth is expected as a result of increasing automation; many additional job openings will result from the need to replace workers who leave the occupation.

- Because of increasing automation, employers prefer to hire those familiar with computers and other electronic office and business equipment.

Nature of the Work

Shipping, receiving, and traffic clerks keep records of all goods shipped and received. Their duties depend on the size of the establishment they work for and the level of automation used. Larger companies typically are better able to finance the purchase of computers, scanners, and other equipment to handle some or all of a clerk's responsibilities. In smaller companies, a clerk maintains records, prepares shipments, sorts packages, and accepts deliveries. In both environments, shipping, receiving, and traffic clerks may lift cartons of various sizes.

Shipping clerks keep records of all outgoing shipments. They prepare shipping documents and mailing labels and make sure that orders have been filled correctly. Also, they record items taken from inventory and note when orders were filled. Sometimes they fill the order themselves, taking merchandise from the stockroom, noting when inventories run low, and wrapping or packing the goods in shipping containers. They also address and label packages, look up and compute freight or postal rates, and record the weight and cost of each shipment. In addition, shipping clerks may prepare invoices and furnish information about shipments to other parts of the company, such as the accounting department. Once a shipment is checked and ready to go, shipping clerks may sort and move the goods from the

Shipping, receiving, and traffic clerks maintain records of all goods shipped and received.

warehouse—sometimes by forklift—to the shipping dock or truck terminal and direct their loading.

Receiving clerks perform tasks similar to those of shipping clerks. They determine whether orders have been filled correctly by verifying incoming shipments against the original order and the accompanying bill of lading or invoice. They make a record of the shipment and the condition of its contents. In many firms, receiving clerks either use hand-held scanners to record barcodes on incoming products or manually enter the information into a computer. These data then can be transferred to the appropriate departments. An increasing number of clerks at larger, more automated companies use radio-frequency identification (RFID) scanners, which store and remotely retrieve data using tags or transponders. Clerks then check the shipment for any discrepancies in quantity, price, and discounts. Receiving clerks may route or move shipments to the proper department, warehouse section, or stockroom. They also may arrange for adjustments with shippers if merchandise is lost or damaged. Receiving clerks in small businesses may perform some duties similar to those of stock clerks. In larger establishments, receiving clerks may control all receiving platform operations, such as scheduling of trucks, recording of shipments, and handling of damaged goods.

Traffic clerks maintain records on the destination, weight, and charges on all incoming and outgoing freight. They verify rate charges by comparing the classification of materials with rate charts. In many companies, this work may be automated. Information either is scanned or is entered by hand into a computer for use by the accounting department or other departments within the company. Traffic clerks also keep a file of claims for overcharges and for damage to goods in transit.

Work environment. Most jobs for shipping, receiving, and traffic clerks involve frequent standing, bending, walking, and

stretching. Lifting and carrying smaller items also may be involved, especially at small companies with less automation. Although automated devices have lessened the physical demands of this occupation, their use remains somewhat limited. The work still can be strenuous, even though mechanical material handling equipment, such as computerized conveyor systems, is used to move heavy items at a rapid pace.

The typical workweek is Monday through Friday; however, evening and weekend hours are common in some jobs and may be required when large shipments are involved or during major holiday periods.

Training, Other Qualifications, and Advancement

Shipping, receiving, and traffic clerks generally are entry-level workers who need no more than a high school diploma. Because of increasing automation, however, employers prefer to hire those familiar with computers and other electronic office and business equipment.

Education and training. Shipping, receiving, and traffic clerks usually learn the job by doing routine tasks under close supervision. They first learn how to count and mark stock, and then they start keeping records and taking inventory.

Training in the use of automated equipment usually is done informally, on the job. As these occupations become more automated, however, workers may need longer periods of training to master the use of the equipment and technology. Because of increasing automation, employers prefer to hire those familiar with computers and other electronic office and business equipment.

Other qualifications. Strength, stamina, good eyesight, and an ability to work at repetitive tasks, sometimes under pressure, are important characteristics. Shipping, receiving, and traffic clerks who handle jewelry, liquor, or drugs may need to be bonded.

Advancement. Shipping, receiving, and traffic clerks are commonly promoted to head clerk, and those with a broad understanding of shipping and receiving may sometimes become purchasing agents or enter a related field, such as industrial traffic management. The Warehousing Education and Research Council offers online courses in distribution and logistics, which may enhance a clerk's potential for advancement.

Employment

Shipping, receiving, and traffic clerks held about 769,000 jobs in 2006. About 71 percent were employed in manufacturing or by wholesale and retail establishments. Although jobs for shipping, receiving, and traffic clerks are found throughout the country, most clerks work in urban areas, where shipping depots in factories and wholesale establishments usually are located.

Projections data from the National Employment Matrix

Occupational Title	SOC Code	Employment, 2006	Projected employment, 2016	Change, 2006-16	
				Number	Percent
Shipping, receiving, and traffic clerks	43-5071	769,000	797,000	28,000	4

NOTE: Data in this table are rounded. See the discussion of the employment projections table in the *Handbook* introductory chapter on *Occupational Information Included in the Handbook.*

Job Outlook

Slower-than-average employment growth is expected as a result of increasing automation. However, many additional job openings will result from the need to replace shipping, receiving, and traffic clerks who leave the occupation.

Employment change. Employment of shipping, receiving, and traffic clerks is expected to grow 4 percent between 2006 and 2016, more slowly than the average for all occupations. Job growth will continue to be limited by automation as all but the smallest firms move to reduce labor costs by using computers and high-technology scanners to store and retrieve shipping and receiving records.

Methods of handling materials have changed significantly in recent years. Large warehouses are increasingly becoming automated, with equipment such as automatic sorting systems, robots, computer-directed trucks, and programmed data storage and retrieval systems. This automation, coupled with the growing use of hand-held barcode and RFID scanners in shipping and receiving departments, has increased the productivity of shipping, receiving, and traffic clerks.

Job prospects. In addition to some openings from employment growth, many job openings will occur because of the need to replace shipping, receiving, and traffic clerks who leave the occupation. This is a large entry-level occupation, and many vacancies are created each year as workers leave as part of their normal career progression. Because smaller warehouses, distribution centers, and trucking terminals will continue to rely on sorting and moving goods by hand, job opportunities at those facilities may be better than at larger, more automated centers.

Earnings

Median annual earnings of wage-and-salary shipping, receiving, and traffic clerks in May 2006 were $26,070. The middle 50 percent earned between $20,670 and $32,840. The lowest 10 percent earned less than $16,970, and the highest 10 percent earned more than $40,590.

These workers usually receive the same benefits as most other workers. If uniforms are required, employers generally provide them or offer an allowance to purchase them.

Related Occupations

Shipping, receiving, and traffic clerks record, check, and often store materials that a company receives. They also process and pack goods for shipment. Other workers who perform similar duties are stock clerks and order fillers; production, planning, and expediting clerks; cargo and freight agents; and Postal Service workers.

Sources of Additional Information

For information about career opportunities and online courses in distribution, warehousing, and storage systems, contact:
➤ Warehousing Education and Research Council, 1100 Jorie Blvd., Suite 170, Oak Brook, IL 60523. Internet: **http://www.werc.org**

Additional information about job opportunities may be obtained from local employers and local offices of the State employment service.

Stock Clerks and Order Fillers

(O*NET 43-5081.00, 43-5081.01, 43-5081.02, 43-5081.03, 43-5081.04)

Significant Points

- Stock clerks and order fillers generally are entry-level workers who learn through short-term on-the-job training.

- Despite the projected decline in employment due to the use of automation in factories, warehouses, and stores, numerous job openings are expected due to replacement needs.

- Because of automation, applicants who are familiar with computers and other electronic office and business equipment will have the best job prospects.

Nature of the Work

Stock clerks and order fillers receive, unpack, check, store, track merchandise or materials, and pick up customer orders. They keep records of items entering or leaving the stockroom and inspect damaged or spoiled goods. Stock clerks and order fillers sort, organize, and mark items with identifying codes, such as price, stock, or inventory control codes, so that inventories can be located quickly and easily. They also may be required to lift cartons of various sizes. In larger establishments, where they may be responsible for only one task, they may be called *stock-control clerks, merchandise distributors, or property custodians.* In smaller firms, they also may perform tasks such as packing and mailing items, usually handled by shipping and re-

Numerous job openings for stock clerks and order fillers are expected due to replacement needs.

Projections data from the National Employment Matrix

Occupational Title	SOC Code	Employment, 2006	Projected employment, 2016	Change, 2006-16	
				Number	Percent
Stock clerks and order fillers...	43-5081	1,705,000	1,574,000	-131,000	-8

NOTE: Data in this table are rounded. See the discussion of the employment projections table in the *Handbook* introductory chapter on *Occupational Information Included in the Handbook.*

ceiving clerks. (A separate statement on shipping, receiving, and traffic clerks appears elsewhere in the *Handbook*.)

In many firms, stock clerks and order fillers use hand-held scanners connected to computers to keep inventories up to date. In retail stores, stock clerks bring merchandise to the sales floor and stock shelves and racks. In stockrooms and warehouses, stock clerks store materials in bins, on floors, or on shelves. Instead of putting the merchandise on the sales floor or on shelves, order fillers take customers' orders and either hold the merchandise until the customers can pick it up or send it to them.

Work environment. Working conditions vary considerably by employment setting. Most jobs for stock clerks and order fillers involve frequent standing, bending, walking, and stretching. Some lifting and carrying of smaller items also may be involved. Although automated devices have lessened the physical demands of this occupation, their use remains somewhat limited. Even though mechanical material handling equipment is employed to move heavy items, the work still can be strenuous.

Evening and weekend hours are common and may be required when large shipments are involved or when inventory is taken.

Training, Other Qualifications, and Advancement

Stock clerk and order fillers generally are entry-level workers who do not need more than a high school diploma or GED. Short-term on-the-job training is usually adequate for this occupation.

Education and training. Stock clerks and order fillers usually learn the job by doing routine tasks under close supervision. They learn how to count and mark stock and later to keep records and take inventory. Training in the use of automated equipment usually is done informally, on the job. As this occupation becomes more automated, however, workers may need longer periods of training to master the use of the equipment.

Other qualifications. Strength, stamina, good eyesight, and an ability to work at repetitive tasks, sometimes under pressure, are important characteristics. Stock clerks and order fillers who handle jewelry, liquor, or drugs may be bonded. Employers prefer to hire those familiar with computers and other electronic office and business equipment. Typing, filing, recordkeeping, and other clerical skills also are important in some jobs.

Advancement. Advancement opportunities for stock clerks and order fillers vary with the place of employment. With additional training, some workers advance to jobs as warehouse leads or supervisors, purchasing agents or other jobs within the facility such as inventory control.

Employment

Stock clerks and order fillers held about 1.7 million jobs in 2006. About 78 percent work in wholesale and retail trade. The greatest numbers are found in department stores, followed by grocery stores. Jobs for stock clerks are found in all parts of the country, but most work in large urban areas that have many large suburban shopping centers, warehouses, and factories.

Job Outlook

Employment of stock clerks and order fillers is projected to decline as a result of automation in factories, warehouses, and stores. However, numerous job openings will occur each year due to the need to replace workers who leave the occupation, which is a characteristic of very large occupations with limited training requirements. Because of automation, applicants who are familiar with computers and other electronic office and business equipment will have the best job prospects.

Employment change. Employment of stock clerks and order fillers is expected to decline moderately by 8 percent over the 2006 to 2016 period. The growing use of computers for inventory control and the installation of new, automated equipment are expected to inhibit growth in demand for stock clerks and order fillers, especially in manufacturing and wholesale trade industries, where operations are most easily automated. In addition to using computerized inventory control systems to sort goods more efficiently, firms in these industries are relying more on sophisticated conveyor belts and automatic high stackers to store and retrieve goods. Also, expanded use of battery-powered, driverless, automatically guided vehicles can be expected.

The increasing role of large retail outlets and warehouses, as well as catalog, mail, telephone, and Internet shopping services, however, should bolster employment of stock clerks and order fillers in these sectors of retail trade.

Job prospects. Despite declining employment, numerous job openings will occur each year due to replacement needs. Because of automation, applicants who are familiar with computers and other electronic office and business equipment will have the best job prospects. Since much of the work of stock clerks and order fillers who work in grocery, general merchandise, apparel, accessory, and department stores is done manually and is difficult to automate, workers in these industries should be less affected by automation than workers in manufacturing.

Earnings

In May 2006, median annual wage-and-salary earnings of stock clerks and order fillers in were $20,440. The middle 50 percent earned between $16,670 and $26,440. The lowest 10 percent earned less than $14,490, and the highest 10 percent earned more than $34,200.

These workers usually receive the same benefits as most other workers. If uniforms are required, employers generally provide them or offer an allowance to purchase them.

Related Occupations
Workers who also handle, move, organize, store, and keep records of materials include shipping, receiving, and traffic clerks; production, planning, and expediting clerks; cargo and freight agents; and procurement clerks.

Sources of Additional Information
State employment service offices can provide information about job openings for stock clerks and order fillers.

Weighers, Measurers, Checkers, and Samplers, Recordkeeping

(O*NET 43-5111.00)

Significant Points

- Many jobs are at the entry level and do not require more than a high school diploma.

- Employment of weighers, measurers, checkers, and samplers is expected to decline because of the increased use of automated equipment that performs the function of these workers.

Nature of the Work
Weighers, measurers, checkers, and samplers weigh, measure, and check materials, supplies, and equipment in order to keep accurate records. Most of their duties are clerical. Using either manual or automated data-processing systems, they verify the quantity, quality, and overall value of the items they are responsible for and check the condition of items purchased, sold, or produced against records, bills, invoices, or receipts. They check the items to ensure the accuracy of the recorded data. They prepare reports on warehouse inventory levels and on the use of parts. Weighers, measurers, checkers, and samplers also check for any defects in the items and record the severity of the defects they find.

These workers use weight scales, counting devices, tally sheets, and calculators to get and record information about products. They usually move objects to and from the scales with a handtruck or forklift. They issue receipts for products when needed or requested.

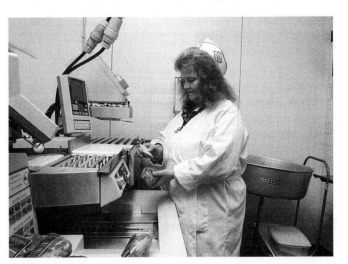

Information obtained by these workers needs to be accurate.

Work environment. Weighers, measurers, checkers, and samplers work in a wide variety of businesses, institutions, and industries. Some work in warehouses, stockrooms, or shipping and receiving rooms that may not be temperature controlled. Others may spend time in cold storage rooms or on loading platforms that are exposed to the weather.

Training, Other Qualifications, and Advancement
Most jobs do not require more than a high school diploma. However preference is given to applicants familiar with computers.

Education and training. Many weigher, measurer, checker, and sampler jobs are entry level and do not require more than a high school diploma or a GED, its equivalent.

Other qualifications. Employers prefer to hire individuals familiar with computers. Applicants who have specific job-related experience may also be preferred. Typing, filing, recordkeeping, and other clerical skills are important.

Advancement. Advancement opportunities vary with the place of employment.

Employment
Weighers, measurers, checkers, and samplers held about 79,000 jobs in 2006. Their employment is spread across many industries. Retail trade accounted for 14 percent of those jobs, manufacturing accounted for about 22 percent, and wholesale trade employed another 18 percent.

Job Outlook
Despite rapid declines in overall employment due primarily to automation, job opportunities should arise from the need to replace workers who leave the labor force or transfer to other occupations.

Projections data from the National Employment Matrix

Occupational Title	SOC Code	Employment, 2006	Projected employment, 2016	Change, 2006-16	
				Number	Percent
Weighers, measurers, checkers, and samplers, recordkeeping..........	43-5111	79,000	70,000	-9,000	-11

NOTE: Data in this table are rounded. See the discussion of the employment projections table in the *Handbook* introductory chapter on *Occupational Information Included in the Handbook*.

Employment change. Employment of weighers, measurers, checkers, and samplers is expected to decline rapidly by 11 percent from 2006 through 2016 because of the increased use of automated equipment that now performs the function of these workers.

Job prospects. Despite employment declines, job opportunities should arise from the need to replace workers who leave the labor force or transfer to other occupations.

Earnings

Median wage-and-salary earnings of weighers, measurers, checkers, and samplers in May 2006 were $12.20. The middle 50 percent earned between $9.66 and $15.83. The lowest 10 percent earned less than $8.03, and the highest 10 percent earned more than $19.78.

These workers usually receive the same benefits as most other workers. If uniforms are required, employers generally provide them or offer an allowance to purchase them.

Related Occupations

Other workers who determine and document characteristics of materials or equipment include cargo and freight agents; production, planning, and expediting clerks; shipping, receiving, and traffic clerks; stock clerks and order fillers; and procurement clerks.

Sources of Additional Information

Information about job opportunities may be obtained from local employers and local offices of the State employment service.

Other Office and Administrative Support Occupations

Communications Equipment Operators

(O*NET 43-2011.00, 43-2021.00, 43-2099.99)

Significant Points

- Switchboard operators hold 7 out of 8 jobs.

- Workers train on the job.

- Employment is expected to decline rapidly, but job prospects should be good.

Nature of the Work

Most communications equipment operators work as *switchboard operators* for a wide variety of businesses, such as hospitals, hotels, telephone call centers, and government agencies. Switchboard operators use private branch exchange (PBX) or voice over Internet protocol (VoIP) systems to relay incoming, outgoing, and interoffice calls. They also may frequently handle other clerical duties, such as supplying information, taking messages, and greeting and announcing visitors.

Technological improvements have automated many of the tasks handled by switchboard operators. New systems automatically connect outside calls to the correct destination or to automated directories, and voice-mail systems take messages without the assistance of an operator. Despite the increasing automation of telephone call routing, however, some callers still require the assistance of an operator. Many callers have general requests, but do not know the person or department with whom they wish to speak. Switchboard operators use their knowledge of the duties and responsibilities of different departments to correctly direct calls.

Telephone operators assist customers in making telephone calls. Some telephone operators are central office operators who help customers to complete local and long-distance calls, usually under special circumstances. Other telephone operators are directory assistance operators who provide customers with information such as telephone numbers or area codes.

When callers dial "0," they usually reach a *central office operator*. Most of these operators work for telephone companies, and many of their responsibilities have been automated. For example, callers can make international, collect, and credit card calls without the assistance of a central office operator. Even so, callers still need a central office operator for a limited number of tasks, including placing person-to-person calls or interrupting busy lines if an emergency warrants the disruption. When natural disasters such as storms or earthquakes occur, central office operators provide callers with emergency phone contacts. They also assist callers who are having difficulty with automated phone systems. For example, an operator monitoring an automated system that aids a caller in placing collect calls may intervene if a caller needs assistance with the system.

When callers dial information, they usually reach a *directory assistance operator* who provides callers with information such as telephone numbers, addresses, and business listings. Most directory assistance operators work for telephone companies; increasingly, they also work for companies that provide business services. Automated systems now handle many of the functions once performed by directory assistance operators. The systems prompt callers for a listing and may even connect the call after providing the telephone number. Directory assistance operators, however, are still needed to monitor many of the calls received by automated systems. The operators listen to recordings of the customer's request and then key information into electronic directories to access the correct telephone numbers. Directory assistance operators also provide personal assistance to customers having difficulty using the automated system.

Other communications equipment operators include workers who operate satellite communications equipment, telegraph equipment, and a wide variety of other communications equipment.

Work environment. Most communications equipment operators work in pleasant, well-lighted surroundings. Because communications equipment operators spend much time seated at keyboards and video monitors, employers often provide workstations designed to decrease glare and other physical discomforts. Such improvements reduce the incidence of eyestrain, back discomfort, and injury due to repetitive motion.

An operator's work may be quite repetitive and the pace hectic during peak calling periods. To maintain operators' efficiency, supervisors at telephone companies often monitor their performance, including the amount of time they spend on each call. The rapid pace of the job—handling up to 1000 calls in a day—and frequent monitoring may cause stress.

Switchboard operators generally work the same hours as other clerical employees at their company. In most organizations, full-time operators work regular business hours over a 5-day workweek. Work schedules are more irregular in hotels, hospitals, and other organizations that require round-the-clock operator services. In these companies, switchboard operators may work in the evenings and on holidays and weekends.

Telephone operators must be accessible to customers 24 hours a day; therefore, they work a variety of shifts. Some operators work split shifts, coming on duty during peak calling periods in the late morning and early evening and going off duty during the intervening hours. Telephone companies normally assign shifts by seniority, allowing the most experienced operators the first choice of schedules. As a result, entry-level operators may have less desirable schedules, including late evening, split-shift, and weekend work. However, companies may allow operators the flexibility to swap shifts with other operators. Telephone company operators may work overtime.

Approximately 1 in 5 communications equipment operators work part time. Because of the irregular nature of telephone operator schedules, many employers seek part-time workers for those shifts that are difficult to fill.

Training, Other Qualifications, and Advancement

Training for communications equipment operators is normally a mix of on-the-job training and classes lasting a few hours to a few weeks.

Switchboard operators direct calls within a business.

Education and training. Communications equipment operators generally receive their training on the job, so a high school diploma is usually sufficient for most operators. Switchboard operators usually receive informal on-the-job training, lasting only a few days or weeks. Because they are often the first contact with the public or client, switchboard operators often receive some training in customer service. Training may vary by place of employment—a switchboard operator in a hospital would learn how to handle different emergencies, for example. Since switchboard operators' duties may include clerical work, training in basic computer and writing skills may also be required.

Entry-level telephone operators at telecommunications companies may receive both classroom and on-the-job instruction that can last a couple of weeks. These operators may be paired with experienced personnel who provide hands-on instruction.

New employees in both specialties are trained in the operation of their equipment and in procedures designed to maximize efficiency. They are familiarized with company policies, and instructors monitor both the time and quality of trainees' responses to customer requests. Supervisors may continue to monitor new employees closely after they complete their initial training session.

Other qualifications. Applicants should have clear speech, good hearing, and strong reading, spelling, and numerical skills. Computer literacy and typing skills also are important, and familiarity with a foreign language is helpful for some positions. Candidates for positions may be required to take an examination covering basic language, computer, data entry, and math skills. Employers emphasize customer service and seek operators who will remain courteous to customers while working quickly and handling difficult customers.

Advancement. After 1 or 2 years on the job, communications equipment operators may advance to other positions within a company. Many switchboard and telephone operators enter clerical occupations, such as customer service representative, dispatcher, and receptionist, in which their operator experience is valuable. (See the *Handbook* sections on these occupations.) Telephone operators interested in more technical work may train for positions in installing and repairing equipment. (See the sections of the *Handbook* on radio and telecommunications equipment installers and repairers, and line installers and repairers.) Promotion to supervisory positions is also possible.

Employment

Communications equipment operators held about 209,000 jobs in 2006. About 7 out of 8 worked as switchboard operators. Employment was distributed as follows:

Switchboard operators, including answering service..........177,000
Telephone operators...27,000
All other communications equipment operators.....................4,300

Switchboard operators work in almost all industries, but they are concentrated in telephone call centers, hospitals, hotels, and the Federal Government. Many work as temporary employees in the employment services industry. Telephone operators are concentrated in the telecommunications industry.

Projections data from the National Employment Matrix

Occupational Title	SOC Code	Employment, 2006	Projected employment, 2016	Change, 2006-16	
				Number	Percent
Communications equipment operators	43-2000	209,000	183,000	-25,000	-12
Switchboard operators, including answering service....................	43-2011	177,000	163,000	-15,000	-8
Telephone operators	43-2021	27,000	16,000	-11,000	-40
Communications equipment operators, all other	43-2099	4,300	4,700	300	7

NOTE: Data in this table are rounded. See the discussion of the employment projections table in the *Handbook* introductory chapter on *Occupational Information Included in the Handbook.*

Job Outlook

Employment of communications equipment operators is projected to decline rapidly. Virtually all job openings will result from the need to replace communications equipment operators who transfer to other occupations or leave the labor force, but job prospects are expected to be good.

Employment change. Employment of communications equipment operators is projected to decline rapidly by 12 percent between 2006 and 2016. Switchboard operators are projected to decline moderately by 8 percent. Telephone operators are expected to decline rapidly by 40 percent. Declining employment will be due largely to new labor-saving communications technologies, the movement of jobs to foreign countries, and consolidation of telephone operator jobs into fewer locations.

Developments in communications technologies—in particular, voice recognition systems—will continue to significantly reduce demand for communications equipment operators. Voice recognition technology allows automated telephone systems to recognize human speech. Callers speak directly to the system, which interprets the speech and then connects the call. Voice recognition systems do not require callers to input data through a telephone keypad so they are easier to use than touch-tone systems. Voice recognition systems are increasingly able to understand sophisticated vocabulary and grammatical structures; however, many companies will continue to employ operators so that those callers who do have problems can access a live employee if they desire.

The proliferation of cell phones has negatively affected employment of both telephone operators and switchboard operators. Cell phones have reduced the demand for directory assistance and collect calls, and have resulted in decreasing use of pay phones that often required operators to assist with the call. The increasing use of cell phones also have reduced demand for switchboard operators in hotels because hotel guests now use in-room phones less frequently.

Internet directory assistance services are reducing the need for directory assistance operators. With Internet access increasingly available on cell phones, the decline in demand for directory assistance services will continue.

As communications technologies have improved and the price of long-distance service has fallen, companies are finding other ways to reduce costs by consolidating operator jobs in low cost locations. Increasingly this has included the movement of telephone operator jobs to other countries with lower prevailing wage rates.

Job prospects. Despite declining employment, job prospects should be good. There are frequent job openings due to turnover. Many communications equipment operator leave the occupation each year, and some must be replaced.

Earnings

Median hourly earnings of wage-and-salary switchboard operators, including answering service, were $10.88 in May 2006. The middle 50 percent earned between $9.14 and $13.29. The lowest 10 percent earned less than $7.71, and the highest 10 percent earned more than $15.93. Median hourly earnings in the industries employing the largest numbers of switchboard operators are:

Offices of physicians..	$11.40
General medical and surgical hospitals...................................	11.07
Automobile dealers	10.04
Business support services	9.60
Telephone call centers..	9.55

Median hourly earnings of wage-and-salary telephone operators in May 2006 were $16.41. The middle 50 percent earned between $10.67 and $20.59. The lowest 10 percent earned less than $8.44, and the highest 10 percent earned more than $22.44.

Some telephone operators working at telephone companies are members of the Communications Workers of America or the International Brotherhood of Electrical Workers. For these operators, union contracts govern wage rates, wage increases, and the time required to advance from one pay step to the next.

Median hourly earnings of all other wage-and-salary communications equipment operators in May 2006 were $15.23. The middle 50 percent earned between $10.04 and $19.91. The lowest 10 percent earned less than $7.91, and the highest 10 percent earned more than $24.58.

Related Occupations

Other workers who provide information to the general public include dispatchers; hotel, motel, and resort desk clerks; customer service representatives; and receptionists and information clerks.

Sources of Additional Information

For more details about employment opportunities, contact companies in the industries that employ communications equipment operators.

Computer Operators

(O*NET 43-9011.00)

Significant Points

- Computer operators are projected to be among the most rapidly declining occupations over the 2006-16 decade because advances in technology are making the duties traditionally performed by computer operators obsolete.

- Computer operators usually receive on-the-job training; the length of training varies with the job and the experience of the worker.

- Opportunities will be best for operators who have formal computer education, are familiar with a variety of operating systems, and keep up with the latest technology.

Nature of the Work

Computer operators oversee the operation of computer hardware systems, ensuring that these machines are used as efficiently and securely as possible. They may work with mainframes, minicomputers, or networks of personal computers. Computer operators must anticipate problems and take preventive action, as well as solve problems that occur during operations.

The duties of computer operators vary with the size of the installation, the type of equipment used, and the policies of the employer. Generally, operators control the console of either a mainframe digital computer or a group of minicomputers. Working from operating instructions prepared by program-

Computer operators monitor computer systems and watch for potential problems.

mers, users, or operations managers, computer operators set controls on the computer and on peripheral devices required to run a particular job.

Computer operators load equipment with tapes, disks, and paper, as needed. While the computer is running—which may be 24 hours a day—computer operators monitor the control console and respond to operating and computer messages. Messages indicate the individual specifications of each job being run. If an error message occurs, operators must locate and solve the problem or terminate the program. Operators also maintain logbooks or operating records that list each job run and events that occur during their shift, such as machine malfunctions. Other computer operators perform and monitor routine tasks, such as tape backup, virus checking, software upgrading, and basic maintenance. In addition, computer operators may help programmers and systems analysts test and debug new programs.

A greater number of computer operators are working on personal computers (PCs) and minicomputers, as the number and complexity of computer networks continues to grow. In many offices, factories, and other work settings, PCs and minicomputers are connected in networks, often referred to as local area networks (LANs) or multi-user systems. While users in the area operate some of these computers, many require the services of full-time operators. The tasks they perform on PCs and minicomputers are very similar to those performed on large computers and include trying to keep the computer networks secure.

As organizations continue to look for opportunities to increase productivity, many tasks formerly performed by computer operators are now being automated. New software enables computers to perform many routine tasks, formerly done by computer operators, without human interaction. Scheduling, loading, and downloading programs, mounting tapes, rerouting messages, and running periodic reports can be done without the intervention of an operator. As technology advances, the responsibilities of many computer operators are shifting to areas such as network operations, user support, and database maintenance.

Work environment. Computer operators generally work in well-lit, ventilated, comfortable rooms. Because many organizations use their computers 24 hours a day, 7 days a week, computer operators may be required to work evening or night shifts and weekends. Shift assignments usually are made based on seniority. However, increasingly automated operations will lessen the need for shift work because many companies can let the computer take over operations during less desirable working hours. In addition, telecommuting technologies, such as faxes, modems, and e-mail, and data center automation, such as automated tape libraries, enable some operators to monitor batch processes, check systems performance, and record problems for the next shift.

Because computer operators generally spend a lot of time in front of a computer monitor and perform repetitive tasks such as loading and unloading printers, they may be susceptible to eyestrain, back discomfort, and hand and wrist problems.

Projections data from the National Employment Matrix

Occupational Title	SOC Code	Employment, 2006	Projected employment, 2016	Change, 2006-16	
				Number	Percent
Computer operators..	43-9011	130,000	98,000	-32,000	-25

NOTE: Data in this table are rounded. See the discussion of the employment projections table in the *Handbook* introductory chapter on *Occupational Information Included in the Handbook.*

Training, Other Qualifications, and Advancement

Computer operators generally require a high school degree and are trained by employers on the job. Most computer operators expect to advance to other positions in the information technology field within a few years.

Education and training. Computer operators usually receive on-the-job training to become acquainted with their employer's equipment and routines. The length of training varies with the job and the experience of the worker. However, previous work experience is key to obtaining an operator job in many large establishments. Employers generally look for specific, hands-on experience with the type of equipment and related operating systems they use. Additionally, formal computer training, perhaps through a community college or technical school, can be useful. Related training also can be obtained through the U.S. Armed Forces and from some computer manufacturers. As computer technology changes and data processing centers become more automated, employers will increasingly require candidates for operator jobs to have formal training and related experience.

Other qualifications. Computer technology changes so rapidly that operators must be adaptable and willing to learn. Operators who work in automated data centers also need analytical and technical expertise to deal with unique or high-level problems that a computer is not programmed to handle. Operators must be able to communicate well and to work effectively with programmers, users, and other operators. Computer operators also must be able to work independently because they may have little or no direct supervision.

Advancement. Some computer operators may advance to supervisory jobs, although most management positions within data processing or computer operations centers require advanced formal education, such as a bachelor's or graduate degree. Computer operators may advance to jobs in areas such as network operations or support through on-the-job experience and additional formal education. As they gain experience in programming, some operators may advance to jobs as programmers or analysts, but a move into these types of jobs is becoming much more difficult because employers increasingly require at least a bachelor's degree for more skilled computer jobs.

Employment

Computer operators held about 130,000 jobs in 2006. Jobs are found in various industries such as government, health care, manufacturing, data processing services and other information industries, and finance and insurance. They are also employed by some firms in computer systems design and related services as more companies contract out their data processing operations.

Job Outlook

Computer operators continue to be one of the occupations with the most rapidly declining employment. Although computers are increasingly prevalent in the workplace, improved software and automation of many systems are quickly reducing the need for this occupation. Some job openings may, nevertheless, be available to replace workers who leave the occupation.

Employment change. Employment of computer operators is projected to decline by 25 percent because advances in technology are making obsolete many of the duties traditionally performed by these workers. Technological advances have reduced both the size and cost of computer equipment while increasing the capacity for data storage and processing automation. Sophisticated computer hardware and software are now used in practically every industry in such areas as factory and office automation, telecommunications, health care, education, and government. The expanding use of software that automates computer operations gives companies the option of making systems more efficient, but greatly reduces the need for operators. Such improvements require operators to monitor a greater number of operations at the same time and solve a broader range of problems that may arise. The result is that fewer operators will be needed to perform more highly skilled work.

Computer operators who are displaced by automation may be reassigned to support staffs that maintain personal computer networks or assist other members of the organization. Operators who keep up with changing technology by updating their skills through additional training should have the best prospects of moving into other areas such as network administration and technical support. Others may be retrained to perform different job duties, such as supervising an operations center, maintaining automation packages, or analyzing computer operations to recommend ways to increase productivity. In the future, operators who wish to take advantage of changing job opportunities in the computer field will need to know more about programming, automation software, graphics interface, client-server environments, and open systems.

Job prospects. Experienced operators are expected to face competition for the few job openings that will arise each year to replace workers who transfer to other occupations or leave the labor force. Opportunities will be best for operators who have formal computer education, familiarity with a variety of operating systems, and knowledge of the latest technology.

Earnings

Median annual earnings of computer operators were $33,560 in May 2006. The middle 50 percent earned between $25,990 and $43,060 per year. The highest 10 percent earned more than $51,970, and the lowest 10 percent earned less than $20,510.

Related Occupations

Other occupations involving work with computers include computer software engineers; computer programmers; computer support specialists and systems administrators; computer systems analysts, and computer scientists and database administrators. Other occupations in which workers operate electronic office equipment include data entry and information processing workers and secretaries and administrative assistants.

Sources of Additional Information

For information about work opportunities in computer operations, contact establishments with large computer centers, such as banks, manufacturing firms, insurance companies, colleges and universities, and data processing service organizations. The local office of the State employment service can supply information about employment and training opportunities.

Data Entry and Information Processing Workers

(O*NET 43-9021.00, 43-9022.00)

Significant Points

- For many people, a job as a data entry and information processing worker is their first job after high school.

- Although overall employment is projected to decline, the need to replace workers who leave this large occupation each year should produce job openings.

- Job prospects should be best for those with expertise in appropriate computer software applications and who meet company requirements for keyboarding speed.

Nature of the Work

Organizations need to process a rapidly growing amount of information. Data entry and information processing workers help ensure the smooth and efficient handling of information. By keying in text, entering data into a computer, operating a variety of office machines, and performing other clerical duties, these workers help organizations keep up with the rapid changes that are characteristic of today's "Information Age." Data entry and information processing workers are known by various other titles, including word processors, typists, and data entry keyers, and less commonly, electronic data processors, keypunch technicians, and transcribers.

Word processors and *typists* usually set up and prepare reports, letters, mailing labels, and other text material. As entry-level workers, word processors may begin by keying headings on form letters, addressing envelopes, or preparing standard forms on computers. As they gain experience, they often are assigned tasks requiring a higher degree of accuracy and independent judgment. Senior word processors may work with highly technical material, plan and key complicated statistical tables, combine and rearrange materials from different sources, or prepare master copies.

Data entry and information processing workers rely on computers to do their work.

Most keyboarding is now done on computers that normally are connected to a monitor, keyboard, and printer and may have "add-on" capabilities, such as optical character recognition readers. Word processors use this equipment to record, edit, store, and revise letters, memos, reports, statistical tables, forms, and other printed materials. Although it is becoming less common, some word processing workers are employed on centralized word processing teams that handle transcription and keying for several departments.

In addition to fulfilling the duties mentioned above, word processors often perform other office tasks, such as answering telephones, filing, and operating copiers or other office machines. Job titles of these workers frequently vary to reflect these duties. For example, administrative clerks combine word processing with filing, sorting mail, answering telephones, and other general office work. Note readers transcribe stenotyped notes of court proceedings into standard formats.

Data entry keyers usually input lists of items, numbers, or other data into computers or complete forms that appear on a computer screen. They also may manipulate existing data, edit current information, or proofread new entries into a database for accuracy. Some examples of data sources include customers' personal information, medical records, and membership lists. Usually, this information is used internally by a company and may be reformatted before other departments or customers use it.

Keyers use various types of equipment to enter data. Many use a machine that converts the information they type to magnetic impulses on tapes or disks for entry into a computer system. Others prepare materials for printing or publication by using data entry composing software. Some keyers operate online terminals or personal computers. Increasingly, data entry keyers work with nonkeyboard forms of data entry, such as scanners and electronically transmitted files. When using the new character recognition systems, data entry keyers often enter only those data which cannot be recognized by machines. In some offices, keyers also operate computer peripheral equipment such as printers and tape readers, act as tape librarians, and perform other clerical duties.

Work environment. Data entry and information processing workers usually work a standard 40-hour week in clean offices. They sit for long periods and sometimes must contend with high noise levels caused by various office machines. These workers are susceptible to repetitive strain injuries such as carpal tunnel syndrome, neck and back injuries, and eyestrain. To help prevent these conditions, many offices have adopted regularly scheduled breaks, ergonomically designed keyboards, and workstations that allow workers to stand or sit as they wish.

Some workers in this occupation telecommute, working from their homes on personal computers linked by telephone lines to those in the main office. This arrangement enables them to key in material at home while still being able to produce printed copy in their offices.

Training, Other Qualifications, and Advancement

Many data entry and information processing workers are hired right out of high school. Most training occurs on the job, and can be learned in a short period of time.

Education and training. Employers generally hire high school graduates who meet their requirements for accuracy and keyboarding speed. Increasingly, employers also expect applicants to have training or experience in word processing or data entry tasks. Spelling, punctuation, and grammar skills are important, as is familiarity with standard office equipment and procedures.

Students acquire skills in keyboarding and in the use of word processing, spreadsheet, and database management computer software in high schools, community colleges, business schools, temporary help agencies, or self-teaching aids such as books, tapes, and Internet tutorials.

Advancement. For many people, a job as a data entry and information processing worker is their first job after high school or after a period of full-time family responsibilities. This work frequently serves as a steppingstone to higher paying jobs with increased responsibilities. Large companies and government agencies usually have training programs to help administrative employees upgrade their skills and advance to higher level positions. It is common for data entry and information processing workers to transfer to other administrative jobs, such as secretary, administrative assistant, or statistical clerk, or to be promoted to a supervisory job in a word processing or data entry center.

Employment

Data entry and information processing workers held about 492,000 jobs in 2006 and were employed in virtually every sector of the economy. Of the data entry and information processing workers, 313,000 were data entry keyers and 179,000 were word processors and typists.

About 1 out of 5 data entry and information processing workers held jobs in firms providing administrative and support services, including temporary help and word processing agencies, and another 15 percent worked for State or local government.

Job Outlook

Although employment of data entry and information processing workers is expected to decline, job prospects will be favorable for those who have good technical skills, familiarity with office equipment, and keyboarding speed and accuracy.

Employment change. Overall employment of data entry and information processing workers is projected to moderately decline by 7 percent through the year 2016. Although data entry and information processing workers are affected by productivity gains stemming from organizational restructuring and the implementation of new technologies, projected employment change differs among these workers. Employment of word processors and typists is expected to decline because of the proliferation of personal computers, which allows other workers to perform duties formerly assigned to word processors and typists. Most professionals and managers, for example, now use desktop personal computers to do their own word processing. However, because technologies affecting data entry keyers tend to be costlier to implement, employment of these workers will decline less than word processors and typists.

Employment growth of data entry keyers will be dampened by productivity gains as various data-capturing technologies, such as barcode scanners, voice recognition technologies, and sophisticated character recognition readers, become more prevalent. These technologies can be applied to a variety of business transactions, such as inventory tracking, invoicing, and placing orders. Moreover, as telecommunications technology improves, many organizations will increasingly take advantage of computer networks that allow data to be transmitted electronically. These networks will permit more data to be entered

Projections data from the National Employment Matrix

Occupational Title	SOC Code	Employment, 2006	Projected employment, 2016	Change, 2006-16	
				Number	Percent
Data entry and information processing workers	43-9020	492,000	457,000	-35,000	-7
Data entry keyers	43-9021	313,000	299,000	-15,000	-5
Word processors and typists..	43-9022	179,000	158,000	-21,000	-12

NOTE: Data in this table are rounded. See the discussion of the employment projections table in the *Handbook* introductory chapter on *Occupational Information Included in the Handbook.*

automatically into computers, reducing the demand for data entry keyers.

In addition to being affected by technology, employment of data entry and information processing workers will be adversely affected by businesses that are increasingly contracting out their work. Many organizations have reduced or even eliminated permanent in-house staff—for example, in favor of temporary employment and staffing services firms. Some large data entry and information processing firms increasingly employ workers in nations with relatively lower wages. As international trade barriers continue to fall and telecommunications technology improves, this transfer of jobs will mean reduced demand for data entry keyers in the United States.

Job prospects. The need to replace workers who transfer to other occupations or leave this large occupation for other reasons will produce numerous job openings each year. Job prospects will be most favorable for those with the best technical skills—in particular, expertise in appropriate computer software applications. Data entry and information processing workers must be willing to upgrade their skills continuously in order to remain marketable.

Earnings

Median annual earnings of word processors and typists in May 2006 were $29,430. The middle 50 percent earned between $24,180 and $35,950. The lowest 10 percent earned less than $20,200, while the highest 10 percent earned more than $43,330. The salaries of these workers vary by industry and by region. In May 2006, median annual earnings in the industries employing the largest numbers of word processors and typists were as follows:

Local government	$31,210
Elementary and secondary schools	29,960
Federal government	29,420
State government	28,520
Employment services	25,220

Median annual earnings of data entry keyers in May 2006 were $24,690. The middle 50 percent earned between $20,460 and $29,700. The lowest 10 percent earned less than $17,050, and the highest 10 percent earned more than $35,970. The following are median annual earnings for May 2006 in the industries employing the largest numbers of data entry keyers:

Management, scientific, and technical consulting services	$25,860
Insurance carriers	25,760
Accounting, tax preparation, bookkeeping, and payroll services	23,600
Data processing, hosting, and related services	22,680
Employment services	22,650

Related Occupations

Data entry and information processing workers must transcribe information quickly. Other workers who deliver information in a timely manner are dispatchers, interpreters and translators, and communications equipment operators. Data entry and in-

formation processing workers also must be comfortable working with office technology, and in this regard they are similar to court reporters, medical records and health information technicians, secretaries and administrative assistants, and computer operators.

Sources of Additional Information

For information about job opportunities for data entry and information processing workers, contact the nearest office of the State employment service.

For information related to administrative occupations, including educational programs and certified designations, contact:

➤ International Association of Administrative Professionals, 10502 NW., Ambassador Dr., P.O. Box 20404, Kansas City, MO 64195-0404. Internet: **http://www.iaap-hq.org**

➤ American Management Association, 1601 Broadway, New York, NY 10019. Internet: **http://www.amanet.org**

Desktop Publishers

(O*NET 43-9031.00)

Significant Points

- About 35 percent work for newspaper, periodical, book, and directory publishers, while almost 25 percent work in the printing industry.

- Overall employment is expected to experience little or no change over the 2006-2016 decade.

- Most employers prefer to hire experienced desktop publishers; among persons without experience, opportunities should be best for those with certificates or degrees in desktop publishing or graphic design.

Nature of the Work

Desktop publishers use computer software to format and combine text, data, photographs, charts, and other graphic art or illustrations into prototypes of pages and other documents that are to be printed. They then may print the document using a high resolution printer or they may send the materials, either in print form or electronically, to a commercial printer. Examples of materials produced by desktop publishers include books, brochures, calendars, magazines, newsletters and newspapers, packaging, and forms.

Desktop publishers typically design and create the graphics that accompany text, convert photographs and illustrations into digital images, and manipulate the text and images to display information in an attractive and readable format. They design page layouts, develop presentations and advertising campaigns, and do color separation of pictures and graphics material. Some desktop publishers may write some of the text or headlines used in newsletters or brochures. They also may translate electronic information onto film or other traditional media if the final product will be sent to an off-set printer. As companies bring the production of marketing, promotional, and other kinds of materials in-house, they increasingly employ desktop publishers to produce such materials in house.

Desktop publishers use a computer and appropriate software to enter and select formatting properties, such as the size and style of type, column width, and spacing. Print formats are stored in the computer and displayed on a computer monitor. Images and text can be rearranged, column widths altered, or material enlarged or reduced. New information, such as charts, pictures, or additional text can be added. Scanners are used to capture photographs, images, or art as digital data that can be either incorporated directly into electronic page layouts or further manipulated with the use of computer software. The desktop publisher can make adjustments or compensate for deficiencies in the original color print or transparency. An entire newspaper, catalog, or book page, complete with artwork and graphics, can be created on the screen exactly as it will appear in print. Digital files are then used to produce printing plates. Like photographers and multimedia artists and animators, desktop publishers also can create special effects or other visual images using film, video, computers, or other electronic media. (Separate statements on photographers and on artists and related workers appear elsewhere in the *Handbook*.)

Desktop publishing encompasses a number of different kinds of jobs. Personal computers enable desktop publishers to more easily perform many of the design and layout tasks that would otherwise require large and complicated equipment and extensive human effort. Advances in computer software and printing technology continue to enhance desktop publishing work, making desktop publishing more economical and efficient than before. For example, desktop publishers get the material as computer files delivered over the Internet or on a portable disk drive instead of receiving simple typed text and instructions from customers. Other innovations in the occupation include digital color page makeup systems, electronic page layout systems, and off-press color proofing systems. In addition, most materials are reproduced on the Internet as well as printed; therefore, desktop publishers may need to know electronic publishing software, such as Hypertext Markup Language (HTML) and may be responsible for converting text and graphics to an Internet-ready format.

Some desktop publishers may write and edit as well as lay out and design pages. For example, in addition to laying out articles for a newsletter, desktop publishers may be responsible for copyediting content or for writing original content themselves. Desktop publisher's writing and editing responsibilities may vary widely from project to project and employer to employer. Smaller firms typically use desktop publishers to perform a wide range of tasks, while desktop publishers at larger firms may specialize in a certain part of the publishing process. (Writers and editors are discussed elsewhere in the *Handbook*.)

Desktop publishers also may be called publications specialists, electronic publishers, DTP operators, desktop publishing editors, electronic prepress technicians, electronic publishing specialists, image designers, typographers, compositors, layout artists, and Web publications designers. The exact name may vary by the specific tasks performed or simply by personal preference.

Work environment. Desktop publishers usually work in clean, air-conditioned office areas with little noise. They generally work a standard workweek; however, some may work night shifts, weekends, or holidays depending upon the production schedule for the project or to meet deadlines.

These workers often are subject to stress and the pressures of short deadlines and tight work schedules. Like other workers who spend long hours working in front of a computer monitor, desktop publishers may be susceptible to eyestrain, back discomfort, and hand and wrist problems.

Training, Other Qualifications, and Advancement
Most desktop publishers learn their skills by taking classes, completing a certificate program offered on line or through an accredited academic program, or through experience on the job. Experience is the best training and many desktop publishers get started just by experimenting with the software and developing a knack for designing and laying out material for publication.

Education and training. There is generally no educational requirement for the job of desktop publisher. Most people learn on the job or by taking classes on line or through local learning centers that teach the latest software. For those who are interested in pursuing a career in desktop publishing, an associate degree or a bachelor's degree in graphic arts, graphic communications, or graphic design is preferred. Graphic arts programs are a good way to learn about the desktop publishing software used to format pages; assign type characteristics; and import text and graphics into electronic page layouts. The programs teach print and graphic design fundamentals and provide an extensive background in imaging, prepress operations, print reproduction, and emerging media. Courses in other aspects of printing also are available at vocational-technical institutes, industry-sponsored update and retraining programs, and private trade and technical schools.

Other qualifications. Although formal training is not always required, those with certificates or degrees will have the best job opportunities. Most employers prefer to hire people who have at least a high school diploma and who possess good communication skills, basic computer skills, and a strong work ethic. Desktop publishers should be able to deal courteously with people, because they have to interact with customers and cli-

Desktop publishers format and design photographs, art, and data with text for electronic page layouts.

Projections data from the National Employment Matrix

Occupational Title	SOC Code	Employment, 2006	Projected employment, 2016	Change, 2006-16	
				Number	Percent
Desktop publishers..	43-9031	32,000	32,000	300	1

NOTE: Data in this table are rounded. See the discussion of the employment projections table in the *Handbook* introductory chapter on *Occupational Information Included in the Handbook.*

ents and be able to express design concepts and layout options with them. They also may have to do simple math calculations and compute ratios to scale graphics and artwork and estimate job costs. A basic understanding and facility with computers, printers, scanners, and other office equipment and technologies also is needed to work as a desktop publisher.

Desktop publishers need good manual dexterity, and they must be able to pay attention to detail and work independently. Good eyesight, including visual acuity, depth perception, a wide field of view, color vision, and the ability to focus quickly also are assets. Artistic ability often is a plus. Employers also seek persons who are even tempered and adaptable—important qualities for workers who often must meet deadlines and learn how to operate new equipment.

Advancement. Workers with limited training and experience assist more experienced staff on projects while they learn the software and gain practical experience. They advance on the basis of their demonstrated mastery of skills. Desktop publishing software continues to evolve and gain in technological sophistication. As a result, desktop publishers need to keep abreast of the latest developments and how to use new software and equipment. As they gain experience, they may advance to positions with greater responsibility. Some may move into supervisory or management positions. Other desktop publishers may start their own companies or work as independent consultants, while those with more artistic talent and further education may find job opportunities in graphic design or commercial art positions.

Employment

Desktop publishers held about 32,000 jobs in 2006. About 35 percent worked for newspaper, periodical, book, and directory publishers, while 24 percent worked in the printing and related support activities industry. Other desktop publishers work for professional, scientific, and technical services firms and in many other industries that produce printed or published materials.

The printing and publishing industries are two of the most geographically dispersed industries in the United States, and desktop publishing jobs are found throughout the country. Although most jobs are in large metropolitan cities, electronic communication networks and the Internet allow some desktop publishers to work from other locations.

Job Outlook

Employment of desktop publishers is expected to experience little or no change over the 2006-2016 decade because more people are learning basic desktop publishing skills as a part of their regular job functions in other occupations and because more organizations are formatting materials for display on the web rather than designing pages for print publication.

Employment change. Employment of desktop publishers is expected to grow 1 percent between 2006 and 2016, which is considered little or no change in employment. Desktop publishing has become a frequently used and common tool for designing and laying out printed matter, such as advertisements, brochures, newsletters, and forms. However, increased computer processing capacity and widespread availability of more elaborate desktop publishing software will make it easier and more affordable to use for people who are not printing professionals. As a result, the need for people who specialize in desktop publishing will slow, as more people are able to do this work.

In addition, organizations are increasingly moving their published material to the Internet to save the cost of printing and distributing materials. This change will slow the growth of desktop publishers, especially in smaller membership and trade organizations, which publish newsletters and small reports. Companies that produce large reports and rely on high quality and high resolution color and graphics within their publications, however, will continue to use desktop publishers to lay out publications for offset printing.

Job prospects. Despite the little to no change in projected employment, job opportunities for desktop publishers are expected to be good because of the need to replace workers who move into managerial positions, transfer to other occupations, or leave the labor force. However, job prospects will be better for those with experience as many employers prefer to hire experienced desktop publishers because of the long time it takes to become good at this work. Among individuals with little or no experience, opportunities should be best for those with computer backgrounds, certification in desktop publishing, or who have completed a postsecondary program in desktop publishing, graphic design, or web design.

Earnings

Earnings for desktop publishers vary according to level of experience, training, geographic location, and company size. Median annual earnings of desktop publishers were $34,130 in May 2006. The middle 50 percent earned between $26,270 and $44,360. The lowest 10 percent earned less than $20,550, and the highest 10 percent earned more than $55,040 a year. Median annual earnings of desktop publishers in May 2006 were $36,460 in printing and related support services and $31,450 in newspaper, periodical, book, and directory publishers.

Related Occupations

Desktop publishers use artistic and editorial skills in their work. These skills also are essential for artists and related workers; commercial and industrial designers; prepress technicians and workers; public relations specialists; and writers and editors.

Sources of Additional Information

Details about training programs may be obtained from local employers such as newspapers and printing shops or from local offices of the State employment service.

For information on careers and training in printing, desktop publishing, and graphic arts, write to:

➤ Graphic Arts Education and Research Foundation, 1899 Preston White Dr., Reston, VA 20191-4367. Internet: **http://www.gaerf.org**

➤ Graphic Arts Information Network, 200 Deer Run Rd., Sewickley, PA 15143. Internet: **http://www.gain.net**

Office and Administrative Support Worker Supervisors and Managers

(O*NET 43-1011.00)

Significant Points

- Most jobs are filled by promoting office or administrative support workers from within the organization.

- Office automation will cause employment in some office and administrative support occupations to grow slowly or even decline, resulting in slower-than-average growth among supervisors and managers.

- Applicants are likely to encounter keen competition because their numbers should greatly exceed the number of job openings.

Nature of the Work

All organizations need timely and effective office and administrative support to operate efficiently. Office and administrative support supervisors and managers coordinate this support. These workers are employed in virtually every sector of the economy, working in positions as varied as teller supervisor, customer services manager, or shipping and receiving supervisor.

Although specific functions of office and administrative support supervisors and managers vary significantly, they share many common duties. For example, supervisors perform administrative tasks to ensure that their staffs can work efficiently. Equipment and machinery used in their departments must be in good working order. If the computer system goes down or a fax machine malfunctions, the supervisors must try to correct the problem or alert repair personnel. They also request new equipment or supplies for their department when necessary.

Planning work and supervising staff are key functions of this job. To do these effectively, the supervisor must know the strengths and weaknesses of each member of the staff, as well as the results required and time allotted to each job. Supervisors must make allowances for unexpected staff absences and other disruptions by adjusting assignments or performing the work themselves if the situation requires it.

After allocating work assignments and issuing deadlines, office and administrative support supervisors and managers oversee the work to ensure that it is proceeding on schedule and meeting established quality standards. This may involve reviewing each person's work on a computer—as in the case of accounting clerks—or listening to how a worker deals with customers—as in the case of customer services representatives. When supervising long-term projects, the supervisor may meet regularly with staff members to discuss their progress.

Office and administrative support supervisors and managers also evaluate each worker's performance. If a worker has done a good job, the supervisor indicates that in the employee's personnel file and may recommend a promotion or other award. Alternatively, if a worker is performing inadequately, the supervisor discusses the problem with the employee to determine the cause and helps the worker to improve his or her performance. This might require sending the employee to a training course or arranging personal counseling. If the situation does not improve, the supervisor may recommend a transfer, demotion, or dismissal.

Office and administrative support supervisors and managers usually interview and evaluate prospective employees. When new workers arrive on the job, supervisors greet them and provide orientation to acquaint them with their organization and its operating routines. Some supervisors may be actively involved in recruiting new workers—for example, by making presentations at high schools and business colleges. They also may

Office and administrative support worker supervisors and managers must ensure that offices operate efficiently.

Projections data from the National Employment Matrix

Occupational Title	SOC Code	Employment, 2006	Projected employment, 2016	Change, 2006-16	
				Number	Percent
First-line supervisors/managers of office and administrative support workers..	43-1011	1,418,000	1,500,000	82,000	6

NOTE: Data in this table are rounded. See the discussion of the employment projections table in the *Handbook* introductory chapter on *Occupational Information Included in the Handbook.*

serve as the primary liaisons between their offices and the general public through direct contact and by preparing promotional information.

Supervisors help train new employees in organization and office procedures. They may teach new employees how to use the telephone system and operate office equipment. Because most administrative support work is computerized, they also must teach new employees to use the organization's computer system. When new office equipment or updated computer software is introduced, supervisors train experienced employees to use it efficiently or, if this is not possible, arrange for their employees to receive special outside training.

Office and administrative support supervisors and managers often act as liaisons between the administrative support staff and the professional, technical, and managerial staff. This may involve implementing new company policies or restructuring the workflow in their departments. They also must keep their superiors informed of their progress and any potential problems. Often, this communication takes the form of research projects and progress reports. Because supervisors and managers have access to information such as their department's performance records, they may compile and present these data for use in planning or designing new policies.

Office and administrative support supervisors and managers also may have to resolve interpersonal conflicts among the staff. In organizations covered by union contracts, supervisors must know the provisions of labor-management agreements and run their departments accordingly. They also may meet with union representatives to discuss work problems or grievances.

Work environment. Office and administrative support supervisors and managers are employed in a wide variety of work settings, but most work in clean and well-lit offices that usually are comfortable.

Most office and administrative support supervisors and managers work a standard 40-hour week. However, some organizations operate around the clock, so some supervisors may have to work nights, weekends, and holidays. Sometimes, supervisors rotate among the three 8-hour shifts in a workday; in other cases, shifts are assigned on the basis of seniority.

Training, Other Qualifications, and Advancement

Most firms fill office and administrative support supervisory and managerial positions by promoting office or administrative support workers from within their organizations. To become eligible for promotion to a supervisory position, administrative support workers must prove they are capable of handling additional responsibilities.

Education and training. Many employers require office and administrative support supervisors and managers to have postsecondary training—and in some cases, an associate or even a bachelor's degree. Good working knowledge of the organization's computer system is also an advantage. In addition, supervisors must pay close attention to detail in order to identify and correct errors made by the staff they oversee.

Most office and administrative support worker supervisors and managers are promoted from within the company. Several years of on-the-job experience are usually the best preparation to become a supervisor or manager. After acquiring some experience, the employee should have a thorough knowledge of other personnel and company operations.

Administrative support workers with potential supervisory abilities may be given occasional supervisory assignments. To prepare for full-time supervisory duties, workers may attend in-house training or take courses in time management, project management, or interpersonal relations.

Other qualifications. When evaluating candidates, supervisors look for strong teamwork, problem-solving, leadership, and communication skills, as well as determination, loyalty, poise, and confidence. They also look for more specific supervisory attributes, such as the ability to organize and coordinate work efficiently, to set priorities, and to motivate others. Increasingly, supervisors need a broad base of office skills coupled with personal flexibility to adapt to changes in organizational structure and move among departments when necessary.

Advancement. For office and administrative supervisors and managers promoted from within, advancement opportunities may be limited without a postsecondary degree, depending on the company. The knowledge required to move into more business and financial related occupations may not necessarily be learned through working in an office or administrative occupation.

In some managerial positions, office and administrative support supervisor positions are filled with people from outside the organization. These positions may serve as entry-level training for potential higher level managers. New college graduates may rotate through departments of an organization at this level to learn the work of the organization before moving on to a higher level position.

Employment

Office and administrative support supervisors and managers held 1.4 million jobs in 2006. Although jobs for office and administrative support supervisors and managers are found in practically every industry, the largest number are found in organizations with a large administrative support workforce, such as banks, wholesalers, government agencies, retail establishments, business service firms, health care facilities, schools, and insurance companies. Because of most organizations' need for continuity of supervision, few office and administrative support supervisors and managers work on a temporary or part-time basis.

Job Outlook

Employment of office and administrative support supervisors and managers is expected to grow more slowly than the average for all occupations through the year 2016. Keen competition is expected for prospective job applicants.

Employment change. Employment is expected to grow by 6 percent during the 2006-16 period, which is more slowly than the average for all occupations. Employment of office and administrative support supervisors and managers is determined largely by the demand for administrative support workers. New technology should increase office and administrative support workers' productivity and allow a wider variety of tasks to be performed by people in professional positions. These trends will cause employment in some administrative support occupations to grow slowly or even decline. As a result, supervisors will direct smaller permanent staffs—supplemented by increased use of temporary administrative support staff—and perform more professional tasks. Office and administrative support managers will coordinate the increasing amount of administrative work and make sure that the technology is applied and running properly. However, organizational restructuring should continue to reduce employment in some managerial positions, distributing more responsibility to office and administrative support supervisors.

Job prospects. Like those seeking other supervisory and managerial occupations, applicants for jobs as office and administrative support worker supervisors and managers are likely to encounter keen competition because the number of applicants should greatly exceed the number of job openings. Besides the job openings arising from growth, a large number of openings will stem from the need to replace workers who transfer to other occupations or leave this large occupation for other reasons.

Earnings

Median annual earnings of office and administrative support supervisors and managers were $43,510 in May 2006; the middle 50 percent earned between $33,730 and $56,130. The lowest paid 10 percent earned less than $26,530, while the highest paid 10 percent earned more than $71,340. In May 2006, median annual earnings in the industries employing the largest numbers of office and administrative support supervisors and managers were:

Management of companies and enterprises	$49,160
Local government	45,520
General medical and surgical hospitals	44,250
Offices of physicians	42,110
Depository credit intermediation	40,900

In addition to typical benefits, some office and administrative support supervisors and managers, particularly in the private sector, may receive additional compensation in the form of bonuses and stock options.

Related Occupations

Office and administrative support supervisors and managers must understand and sometimes perform the work of those whom they oversee, including bookkeeping, accounting, and auditing clerks; secretaries and administrative assistants; communications equipment operators; customer service representatives; data entry and information processing workers; general office clerks; receptionists and information clerks; stock clerks and order fillers; and order clerks. Their supervisory and administrative duties are similar to those of other supervisors and managers, such as education administrators and administrative services managers.

Sources of Additional Information

For information related to a wide variety of management occupations, including educational programs and certified designations, contact:

➤ International Association of Administrative Professionals, 10502 NW. Ambassador Dr., P.O. Box 20404, Kansas City, MO 64195-0404.
Internet: **http://www.iaap-hq.org**
➤ American Management Association, 1601 Broadway, New York, NY 10019.
Internet: **http://www.amanet.org**
➤ Association of Professional Office Managers, 1 Research Court, Suite 450, Rockville, MD 20850.
Internet: **http://www.apomonline.org**

Office Clerks, General

(O*NET 43-9061.00)

Significant Points

- Employment growth and high replacement needs in this large occupation will result in numerous job openings.

- Prospects should be best for those with knowledge of basic computer applications and office machinery as well as good communication skills.

- Part-time and temporary positions are common.

Nature of the Work

Rather than performing a single specialized task, general office clerks have responsibilities that often change daily with the needs of the specific job and the employer. Some clerks spend their days filing or keyboarding. Others enter data at a computer terminal. They also operate photocopiers, fax machines, and other office equipment; prepare mailings; proofread documents; and answer telephones and deliver messages.

The specific duties assigned to a clerk vary significantly, depending on the type of office in which he or she works. An office clerk in a doctor's office, for example, would not perform the same tasks that a clerk in a large financial institution or in the office of an auto parts wholesaler would. Although all clerks may sort checks, keep payroll records, take inventory, and access information, they also perform duties unique to their employer, such as organizing medications in a doctor's office, preparing materials for presentations in a corporate office, or filling orders received by fax machine for a wholesaler.

General office clerks may send faxes and make photocopies as part of their administrative tasks.

Clerks' duties also vary by level of experience. Whereas inexperienced employees make photocopies, stuff envelopes, or record inquiries, experienced clerks usually are given additional responsibilities. For example, they may maintain financial or other records, set up spreadsheets, verify statistical reports for accuracy and completeness, handle and adjust customer complaints, work with vendors, make travel arrangements, take inventory of equipment and supplies, answer questions on departmental services and functions, or help prepare invoices or budgetary requests. Senior office clerks may be expected to monitor and direct the work of lower level clerks.

Work environment. For the most part, general office clerks work in comfortable office settings. Those on full-time schedules usually work a standard 40-hour week; however, some work shifts or overtime during busy periods. About 26 percent of clerks work part time in 2006. Many clerks also work in temporary positions.

Training, Other Qualifications, and Advancement

Office clerks often need to know how to use word processing and other business software and office equipment. Experience working in an office is helpful, but office clerks also learn skills on the job.

Education and training. Although most office clerk jobs are entry-level positions, employers may prefer or require previous office or business experience. Employers usually require a high school diploma or equivalent, and some require basic computer skills, including familiarity with word processing software, as well as other general office skills.

Training for this occupation is available through business education programs offered in high schools, community and junior colleges, and postsecondary vocational schools. Courses in office practices, word processing, and other computer applications are particularly helpful.

Other qualifications. Because general office clerks usually work with other office staff, they should be cooperative and able to work as part of a team. Employers prefer individuals who can perform a variety of tasks and satisfy the needs of the many departments within a company. In addition, applicants should have good communication skills, be detail oriented, and adaptable.

Advancement. General office clerks who exhibit strong communication, interpersonal, and analytical skills may be promoted to supervisory positions. Others may move into different, more senior administrative jobs, such as receptionist, secretary, or administrative assistant. After gaining some work experience or specialized skills, many workers transfer to jobs with higher pay or greater advancement potential. Advancement to professional occupations within an organization normally requires additional formal education, such as a college degree.

Employment

General office clerks held about 3.2 million jobs in 2006. Most are employed in relatively small businesses. Although they work in every sector of the economy, about 43 percent worked in local government, health care and social assistance, administrative and support services, finance and insurance, or professional, scientific, and technical services industries.

Job Outlook

Employment growth and high replacement needs in this large occupation is expected to result in numerous job openings for general office clerks.

Employment change. Employment of general office clerks is expected to grow 13 percent between 2006 and 2016, which is about as fast as the average for all occupations. The employment outlook for these workers will continue to be affected by the increasing use of technology, expanding office automation, and the consolidation of administrative support tasks. These

Projections data from the National Employment Matrix

Occupational Title	SOC Code	Employment, 2006	Projected employment, 2016	Change, 2006-16	
				Number	Percent
Office clerks, general	43-9061	3,200,000	3,604,000	404,000	13

NOTE: Data in this table are rounded. See the discussion of the employment projections table in the *Handbook* introductory chapter on *Occupational Information Included in the Handbook*.

factors have led to a consolidation of administrative support staffs and a diversification of job responsibilities. However, this consolidation will increase the demand for general office clerks because they perform a variety of administrative support tasks, as opposed to clerks with very specific functions. It will become increasingly common within businesses, especially those smaller in size, to find only general office clerks in charge of all administrative support work.

Job prospects. Many job openings for general office clerks are expected to be for full-time jobs; there will also be a demand for part-time and temporary positions. Prospects should be best for those who have good writing and communication skills and knowledge of basic computer applications and office machinery—such as fax machines, telephone systems, and scanners. As general administrative support duties continue to be consolidated, employers will increasingly seek well-rounded individuals with highly developed communication skills and the ability to perform multiple tasks.

Job opportunities may vary from year to year because the strength of the economy affects demand for general office clerks. Companies tend to employ more workers when the economy is strong. Industries least likely to be affected by economic fluctuations tend to be the most stable places for employment.

Earnings

Median annual earnings of general office clerks were $23,710 in May 2006; the middle 50 percent earned between $18,640 and $30,240 annually. The lowest 10 percent earned less than $14,850, and the highest 10 percent earned more than $37,600. Median annual salaries in the industries employing the largest numbers of general office clerks in May 2006 were:

Local government	$26,590
General medical and surgical hospitals	26,050
Elementary and secondary schools	24,230
Colleges, universities, and professional schools	23,980
Employment services	21,890

Related Occupations

The duties of general office clerks can include a combination of bookkeeping, keyboarding, office machine operation, and filing. Other office and administrative support workers who perform similar duties include bookkeeping, accounting, and auditing clerks; communications equipment operators; customer service representatives; data entry and information processing workers; order clerks; receptionists and information clerks; secretaries and administrative assistants; stock clerks and order fillers; and tellers. Nonclerical entry-level workers include cashiers; counter and rental clerks; and food and beverage serving and related workers.

Sources of Additional Information

State employment service offices and agencies can provide information about job openings for general office clerks.

For information related to administrative occupations, including educational programs and certified designations, contact:

➤ International Association of Administrative Professionals, 10502 NW. Ambassador Dr., P.O. Box 20404, Kansas City, MO 64195-0404. Internet: **http://www.iaap-hq.org**

➤ American Management Association, 1601 Broadway, New York, NY 10019. Internet: **http://www.amanet.org**

Secretaries and Administrative Assistants

(O*NET 43-6011.00, 43-6012.00, 43-6013.00, 43-6014.00)

Significant Points

- This occupation is expected to be among those with the largest number of new jobs.

- Opportunities should be best for applicants with extensive knowledge of software applications.

- Secretaries and administrative assistants today perform fewer clerical tasks and are increasingly taking on the roles of information and communication managers.

Nature of the Work

As the reliance on technology continues to expand in offices, the role of the office professional has greatly evolved. Office automation and organizational restructuring have led secretaries and administrative assistants to assume responsibilities once reserved for managerial and professional staff. In spite of these changes, however, the core responsibilities for secretaries and administrative assistants have remained much the same: Performing and coordinating an office's administrative activities and storing, retrieving, and integrating information for dissemination to staff and clients.

Secretaries and administrative assistants perform a variety of administrative and clerical duties necessary to run an organization efficiently. They serve as information and communication managers for an office; plan and schedule meetings and appointments; organize and maintain paper and electronic files; manage projects; conduct research; and disseminate information by using the telephone, mail services, Web sites, and e-mail. They also may handle travel and guest arrangements.

Secretaries and administrative assistants use a variety of office equipment, such as fax machines, photocopiers, scanners, and videoconferencing and telephone systems. In addition, secretaries and administrative assistants often use computers to do tasks previously handled by managers and professionals, such as: create spreadsheets; compose correspondence; manage databases; and create presentations, reports, and documents using desktop publishing software and digital graphics. They also may negotiate with vendors, maintain and examine leased equipment, purchase supplies, manage areas such as stockrooms or corporate libraries, and retrieve data from vari-

Secretaries and administrative assistants use computers to perform clerical and administrative tasks.

ous sources. At the same time, managers and professionals have assumed many tasks traditionally assigned to secretaries and administrative assistants, such as keyboarding and answering the telephone. Because secretaries and administrative assistants do less dictation and word processing, they now have time to support more members of the executive staff. In a number of organizations, secretaries and administrative assistants work in teams to work flexibly and share their expertise.

Many secretaries and administrative assistants now provide training and orientation for new staff, conduct research on the Internet, and operate and troubleshoot new office technologies.

Specific job duties vary with experience and titles. *Executive secretaries and administrative assistants* provide high-level administrative support for an office and for top executives of an organization. Generally, they perform fewer clerical tasks than do secretaries and more information management. In addition to arranging conference calls and supervising other clerical staff, they may handle more complex responsibilities such as reviewing incoming memos, submissions, and reports in order to determine their significance and to plan for their distribution. They also prepare agendas and make arrangements for meetings of committees and executive boards. They also may conduct research and prepare statistical reports.

Some secretaries and administrative assistants, such as legal and medical secretaries, perform highly specialized work requiring knowledge of technical terminology and procedures. For instance, *legal secretaries* prepare correspondence and legal papers such as summonses, complaints, motions, responses, and subpoenas under the supervision of an attorney or a paralegal. They also may review legal journals and assist with legal research—for example, by verifying quotes and citations in legal briefs. Additionally, legal secretaries often teach newly minted lawyers how to prepare documents for submission to the courts. *Medical secretaries* transcribe dictation, prepare correspondence, and assist physicians or medical scientists with reports, speeches, articles, and conference proceedings. They also record simple medical histories, arrange for patients to be hospitalized, and order supplies. Most medical secretaries need to be familiar with insurance rules, billing practices, and hospital or laboratory procedures. Other technical secretaries who assist engineers or scientists may prepare correspondence, maintain their organization's technical library, and gather and edit materials for scientific papers.

Secretaries employed in elementary schools and high schools perform important administrative functions for the school. They are responsible for handling most of the communications between parents, the community, and teachers and administrators who work at the school. As such, they are required to know details about registering students, immunizations, and bus schedules, for example. They schedule appointments, keep track of students' academic records, and make room assignments for classes. Those who work directly for principals screen inquiries from parents and handle those matters not needing a principal's attention. They also may set a principal's calendar to help set her or his priorities for the day.

Work environment. Secretaries and administrative assistants usually work in schools, hospitals, corporate settings, government agencies, or legal and medical offices. Their jobs often involve sitting for long periods. If they spend a lot of time keyboarding, particularly at a computer monitor, they may encounter problems of eyestrain, stress, and repetitive motion ailments such as carpal tunnel syndrome.

Almost one-fifth of secretaries work part time and many others work in temporary positions. A few participate in job-sharing arrangements, in which two people divide responsibility for a single job. The majority of secretaries and administrative assistants, however, are full-time employees who work a standard 40-hour week.

Training, Other Qualifications, and Advancement

Word processing, writing, and communication skills are essential for all secretaries and administrative assistants. However, employers increasingly require extensive knowledge of software applications, such as desktop publishing, project management, spreadsheets, and database management.

Education and training. High school graduates who have basic office skills may qualify for entry-level secretarial positions. They can acquire these skills in various ways. Training ranges from high school vocational education programs that teach office skills and typing to 1- and 2-year programs in office administration offered by business and vocational-technical schools, and community colleges. Many temporary placement agencies also provide formal training in computer and office skills. Most medical and legal secretaries must go through specialized training programs that teach them the language of the industry.

Employers of executive secretaries increasingly are seeking candidates with a college degree, as these secretaries work closely with top executives. A degree related to the business or industry in which a person is seeking employment may provide the job seeker with an advantage in the application process.

Most secretaries and administrative assistants, once hired, tend to acquire more advanced skills through on-the-job instruction by other employees or by equipment and software vendors. Others may attend classes or participate in online education to learn how to operate new office technologies, such as information storage systems, scanners, or new updated software packages. As office automation continues to evolve, retraining and continuing education will remain integral parts of secretarial jobs.

Other qualifications. Secretaries and administrative assistants should be proficient in typing and good at spelling, punctuation, grammar, and oral communication. Employers also look for good customer service and interpersonal skills because secretaries and administrative assistants must be tactful in their dealings with people. Discretion, good judgment, organizational or management ability, initiative, and the ability to work independently are especially important for higher-level administrative positions. Changes in the office environment have increased the demand for secretaries and administrative assistants who are adaptable and versatile.

Certification and advancement. Testing and certification for proficiency in office skills is available through organizations such as the International Association of Administrative Professionals; National Association of Legal Secretaries (NALS), Inc.; and Legal Secretaries International, Inc. As secretaries and administrative assistants gain experience, they can earn several different designations. Prominent designations include the Certified Professional Secretary (CPS) and the Certified Administrative Professional (CAP), which can be earned by meeting certain experience or educational requirements and passing an examination. Similarly, those with 1 year of experience in the legal field, or who have concluded an approved training course and who want to be certified as a legal support professional, can acquire the Accredited Legal Secretary (ALS) designation through a testing process administered by NALS.

NALS offers two additional designations: Professional Legal Secretary (PLS), considered an advanced certification for legal support professionals, and a designation for proficiency as a paralegal. Legal Secretaries International confers the Certified Legal Secretary Specialist (CLSS) designation in areas such as intellectual property, criminal law, civil litigation, probate, and business law to those who have 5 years of legal experience and pass an examination. In some instances, certain requirements may be waived.

Secretaries and administrative assistants generally advance by being promoted to other administrative positions with more responsibilities. Qualified administrative assistants who broaden their knowledge of a company's operations and enhance their skills may be promoted to senior or executive secretary or administrative assistant, clerical supervisor, or office manager. Secretaries with word processing or data entry experience can advance to jobs as word processing or data entry trainers, supervisors, or managers within their own firms or in a secretarial, word processing, or data entry service bureau. Secretarial and administrative support experience also can lead to jobs such as instructor or sales representative with manufacturers of software

or computer equipment. With additional training, many legal secretaries become paralegals.

Employment

Secretaries and administrative assistants held more than 4.2 million jobs in 2006, ranking it among the largest occupations in the U.S. economy. The following tabulation shows the distribution of employment by secretarial specialty:

Secretaries, except legal, medical, and executive 1,940,000
Executive secretaries and administrative assistants 1,618,000
Medical secretaries..408,000
Legal secretaries...275,000

Secretaries and administrative assistants are employed in organizations of every type. Around 9 out of 10 secretaries and administrative assistants are employed in service providing industries, ranging from education and health care to government and retail trade. Most of the rest work for firms engaged in manufacturing or construction.

Job Outlook

Employment of secretaries and administrative assistants is expected to grow about as fast as average for all occupations. Secretaries and administrative assistants will have among the largest numbers of new jobs arise, about 362,000 over the 2006-16 period. Additional opportunities will result from the need to replace workers who transfer to other occupations or leave this occupation.

Employment change. Employment of secretaries and administrative assistants is expected to increase about 9 percent, which is about as fast as average for all occupations, between 2006 and 2016. Projected employment varies by occupational specialty. Above average employment growth in the health care and social assistance industry should lead to faster than average growth for medical secretaries, while moderate growth in legal services is projected to lead to average growth in employment of legal secretaries. Employment of executive secretaries and administrative assistants is projected to grow faster than average for all occupations. Growing industries—such as administrative and support services; health care and social assistance; and professional, scientific, and technical services—will continue to generate the most new jobs. Little or no change in employment is expected for secretaries, except legal, medical, or executive, who account for about 46 percent of all secretaries and administrative assistants.

Increasing office automation and organizational restructuring will continue to make secretaries and administrative assistants

Projections data from the National Employment Matrix

Occupational Title	SOC Code	Employment, 2006	Projected employment, 2016	Change, 2006-16	
				Number	Percent
Secretaries and administrative assistants	43-6000	4,241,000	4,603,000	362,000	9
Executive secretaries and administrative assistants	43-6011	1,618,000	1,857,000	239,000	15
Legal secretaries...	43-6012	275,000	308,000	32,000	12
Medical secretaries..	43-6013	408,000	477,000	68,000	17
Secretaries, except legal, medical, and executive	43-6014	1,940,000	1,962,000	22,000	1

NOTE: Data in this table are rounded. See the discussion of the employment projections table in the *Handbook* introductory chapter on *Occupational Information Included in the Handbook.*

more productive in coming years. Computers, e-mail, scanners, and voice message systems will allow secretaries and administrative assistants to accomplish more in the same amount of time. The use of automated equipment also is changing the distribution of work in many offices. In some cases, traditional secretarial duties as typing, filing, photocopying, and bookkeeping are being done by clerks in other departments or by the professionals themselves. For example, professionals and managers increasingly do their own word processing and data entry, and handle much of their own correspondence. Also, in some law and medical offices, paralegals and medical assistants are assuming some tasks formerly done by secretaries.

Developments in office technology are certain to continue. However, many secretarial and administrative duties are of a personal, interactive nature and, therefore, are not easily automated. Responsibilities such as planning conferences, working with clients, and instructing staff require tact and communication skills. Because technology cannot substitute for these personal skills, secretaries and administrative assistants will continue to play a key role in most organizations.

As paralegals and medical assistants assume more of the duties traditionally assigned to secretaries, there is a trend in many offices for professionals and managers to replace the traditional arrangement of one secretary per manager with secretaries and administrative assistants who support the work of systems, departments, or units. This approach often means that secretaries and administrative assistants assume added responsibilities and are seen as valuable members of a team.

Job prospects. In addition to jobs created from growth, numerous job opportunities will arise from the need to replace secretaries and administrative assistants who transfer to other occupations, especially exceptionally skilled executive secretaries and administrative assistants who often move into professional occupations. Job opportunities should be best for applicants with extensive knowledge of software applications and for experienced secretaries and administrative assistants. Opportunities also should be very good for those with advanced communication and computer skills. Applicants with a bachelor's degree will be in great demand to act more as managerial assistants and to perform more complex tasks.

Earnings

Median annual earnings of secretaries, except legal, medical, and executive, were $27,450 in May 2006. The middle 50 percent earned between $21,830 and $34,250. The lowest 10 percent earned less than $17,560, and the highest 10 percent earned more than $41,550. Median annual earnings in the industries employing the largest numbers of secretaries, except legal, medical, and executive in May 2006 were:

Local government	$30,350
General medical and surgical hospitals	28,810
Colleges, universities, and professional schools	28,700
Elementary and secondary schools	28,120
Employment services	26,810

Median annual earnings of executive secretaries and administrative assistants were $37,240 in May 2006. The middle 50 percent earned between $30,240 and $46,160. The lowest 10

percent earned less than $25,190, and the highest 10 percent earned more than $56,740. Median annual earnings in the industries employing the largest numbers of executive secretaries and administrative assistants in May 2006 were:

Management of companies and enterprises	$41,570
Local government	38,670
Colleges, universities, and professional schools	36,510
State government	35,830
Employment services	31,600

Median annual earnings of legal secretaries were $38,190 in May 2006. The middle 50 percent earned between $29,650 and $48,520. The lowest 10 percent earned less than $23,870, and the highest 10 percent earned more than $58,770. Medical secretaries earned a median annual salary of $28,090 in May 2006. The middle 50 percent earned between $23,250 and $34,210. The lowest 10 percent earned less than $19,750, and the highest 10 percent earned more than $40,870.

Salaries vary a great deal, however, reflecting differences in skill, experience, and level of responsibility. Certification in this field may be rewarded by a higher salary.

Related Occupations

Workers in a number of other occupations also type, record information, and process paperwork. Among them are bookkeeping, accounting, and auditing clerks; receptionists and information clerks; communications equipment operators; court reporters; human resources assistants, except payroll and timekeeping; computer operators; data entry and information processing workers; paralegals and legal assistants; medical assistants; and medical records and health information technicians. A growing number of secretaries and administrative assistants share in managerial and human resource responsibilities. Occupations requiring these skills include office and administrative support supervisors and managers; computer and information systems managers; administrative services managers; and human resources, training, and labor relations managers and specialists.

Sources of Additional Information

State employment offices provide information about job openings for secretaries and administrative assistants.

For information on the latest trends in the profession, career development advice, and the CPS or CAP designations, contact:
➤ International Association of Administrative Professionals, 10502 NW. Ambassador Dr., P.O. Box 20404, Kansas City, MO 64195-0404. Internet: **http://www.iaap-hq.org**
➤ Association of Executive and Administrative Professionals, Suite G-13, 900 South Washington Street, Falls Church, VA 22406-4009. Internet: **http://www.theaeap.com**

Information on the CLSS designation can be obtained from:
➤ Legal Secretaries International Inc., 2302 Fannin Street, Suite 500, Houston, TX 77002-9136.
Internet: **http://www.legalsecretaries.org**

Information on the ALS, PLS, and paralegal certifications are available from:
➤ National Association of Legal Secretaries, Inc., 314 East Third St., Suite 210, Tulsa, OK 74120.
Internet: **http://www.nals.org**

Farming, Fishing, and Forestry Occupations

Agricultural Workers

(O*NET 45-2011.00, 45-2021.00, 45-2041.00, 45-2091.00, 45-2092.00, 45-2092.01, 45-2092.02, 45-2093.00, and 45-2099.99)

Significant Points

- Duties vary widely, from raising plants and livestock to inspecting agricultural products at border crossings.

- Farmworkers learn their jobs through short-term on-the-job training; agricultural inspectors and animal breeders require more work experience or a college degree.

- Most farmworkers receive relatively low pay and do strenuous work in all kinds of weather, but many enjoy the rural lifestyle.

- Job openings are expected to be numerous for some types of work.

Nature of the Work

Agricultural workers play a large role in getting food, plants, and other agricultural products to market. Working mostly on farms or ranches, but also in nurseries, slaughterhouses, and even ports of entry, these workers have numerous and diverse duties. Among their activities are planting and harvesting crops, installing irrigation, delivering animals, and inspecting our food for safety. While most agricultural workers have relatively few technical skills, some have college degrees that train them to breed animals with specific traits or to inspect food, protecting us from harmful bacteria.

More than 80 percent of agricultural workers are farmworkers and laborers. *Crop, nursery, and greenhouse farmworkers* and laborers perform numerous activities related to growing and harvesting grains, fruits, vegetables, nuts, fiber, trees, shrubs, and other crops. They plant and seed, prune, irrigate, harvest, and pack and load crops for shipment. Farmworkers also apply pesticides, herbicides, and fertilizers to crops and repair fences and some farm equipment. Nursery and greenhouse workers prepare land or greenhouse beds for growing horticultural products, such as trees, plants, flowers, and sod. Their duties include planting, watering, pruning, weeding, and spraying the plants. They may cut, roll, and stack sod; stake trees; tie, wrap, and pack plants to fill orders; and dig up or move field-grown and containerized shrubs and trees.

Farm and ranch animal farmworkers care for live farm, ranch, or water animals that may include cattle, sheep, swine, goats, horses, poultry, finfish, shellfish, and bees. The animals are usually raised to supply meat, fur, skins, feathers, eggs, milk, or honey. Duties may include feeding, watering, herding, grazing, castrating, branding, debeaking, weighing, catching, and loading animals. On dairy farms, farmworkers operate milking machines; they also may maintain records on animals, examine animals to detect diseases and injuries, assist in delivering animals at their birth, and administer medications, vaccinations, or insecticides. Many workers clean and maintain animal housing areas every day.

Other agricultural workers known as *agricultural equipment operators* use a variety of farm equipment to plow, sow seeds, and maintain and harvest crops. Equipment may include tractors, fertilizer spreaders, haybines, raking equipment, balers, combines, threshers, and trucks. These workers also operate machines, such as conveyor belts, loading machines, separators, cleaners, and dryers, used in moving and treating crops after their harvest. As part of the job, workers may make adjustments and minor repairs to equipment.

Agricultural inspectors, another type of agricultural worker, are employed by Federal and State governments to ensure compliance with laws and regulations governing the health, safety, and quality of agricultural commodities. Inspectors also make sure that the facilities and equipment used in processing the commodities meet legal standards. Meat safety is a prime responsibility. Inspectors work to ensure that meat is free of harmful ingredients or bacteria. In meat-processing facilities, inspectors may collect samples of meat suspected to be diseased or contaminated and send them to a laboratory for identification and analysis. They also may inspect livestock to help determine the effectiveness of medication and feeding programs. Some inspectors are stationed at export and import sites to weigh and inspect agricultural shipments leaving and entering the country to ensure the quality and quantity of the shipments. A few work at logging sites, making sure that safety regulations are enforced.

Graders and sorters of agricultural products examine agricultural commodities being prepared for market, classifying them according to quality or size: they grade, sort, or classify unprocessed food and other agricultural products by size, weight, color, or condition and discard inferior or defective products. For example, graders sort eggs by color and size and also examine the fat content; others examine the marbling of beef, classifying the meat as "Prime," "Choice," or a lower grade, as appropriate. The grade assigned determines the meat's price.

Animal breeders select and breed animals using their knowledge of genetics and animal science to produce offspring with desired traits and characteristics, such as chickens that lay more eggs, pigs that produce leaner meat, and sheep with more desirable wool. Some animal breeders also breed and raise cats, dogs, and other household pets. Larger and more expensive animals, such as horses and cattle, are usually bred through artificial insemination, which requires the taking of semen from the male and then inseminating the female. This process ensures better results than conventional mating and also enables one prized male to sire many more offspring. To know which animals to breed and when, animal breeders keep detailed records, including the health of the animals, their size and weight, and the amount and quality of the product produced by them. They also keep track of the traits of the offspring. Some animal breeders work as consultants for a number of farmers, but others breed and raise their own animals for sale or future breeding. For those who raise animals, tasks might include fixing and cleaning animal shelters, feeding and watering the animals, and overseeing animals' health. Some breeders supervise others who perform these tasks. Animal breeders also read journals and newsletters to learn the latest information on breeding and veterinary practices.

Work environment. Working conditions for agricultural workers vary widely. Much of the work of farmworkers and laborers on farms and ranches is physically strenuous and takes place outdoors in all kinds of weather. Harvesting fruits and vegetables, for example, may require much bending, stooping, and lifting. Workers may have limited access to sanitation facilities while working in the field and drinking water may also be limited. Nevertheless, some agricultural workers enjoy the variety of their work, the rural setting, the satisfaction of working the land, and raising animals.

Farm work does not lend itself to a regular 40-hour workweek. Work cannot be delayed when crops must be planted or harvested or when animals must be sheltered and fed. Long hours and weekend work is common in these jobs. For example, farmworkers and agricultural equipment operators may work 6- or 7 days a week during planting and harvesting seasons. Some graders and sorters may work evenings or weekends because of the perishable nature of the products they inspect. Agricultural inspectors may also work long and irregular schedules.

Many agricultural worker jobs are seasonal in nature, so some workers also do other jobs during slow seasons. Migrant farmworkers, who move from location to location as crops ripen, live an unsettled lifestyle, which can be stressful. Work also is seasonal for farmworkers in nurseries; spring and summer are the busiest times of the year. Greenhouse workers enjoy relatively comfortable working conditions while tending to plants indoors. However, during the busy seasons, when landscape contractors need plants, work schedules may be more demanding, requiring weekend work. Moreover, the transition from warm weather to cold weather means that nursery workers might have to work overtime with little notice given in order to move plants indoors to protect them from a frost. Farmworkers who work with animals usually have a more regular schedule; their work is steadier and year round, but they sometimes must come to work on short notice to help handle emergencies.

Farmworkers risk exposure to pesticides and other hazardous chemicals sprayed on crops or plants. However, exposure can be minimal if safety procedures are followed. Those who work on mechanized farms must take precautions to avoid injury when working with tools and heavy equipment. Those who work directly with animals risk being bitten or kicked.

Federal meat inspectors may work in highly mechanized plants or with poultry or livestock in confined areas with extremely cold temperatures and slippery floors. Inspectors' jobs often require working with sharp knives, moderate lifting, and walking or standing for long periods. Inspectors may find themselves in adversarial roles when the organization or individual being inspected objects to the inspection or its potential consequences. Some inspectors travel frequently to visit farms and processing facilities. Others work at ports, inspecting cargo on the docks or on boats.

Graders and sorters may work with similar products for an entire shift, or they may be assigned a variety of items. They may be on their feet all day and may have to lift heavy objects, but others may sit during most of their shift and do little strenuous work. Some graders work in clean, air-conditioned environments, suitable for carrying out controlled tests.

Animal breeders spend most of their time outdoors around animals but can also work in offices or laboratories. Breeders who consult may travel from farm to farm. If they need to sell offspring, breeders may travel to attend shows and meet potential buyers. While tending to the animals, breeders may be bitten or kicked.

Training, Other Qualifications, and Advancement

The majority of agricultural workers learn their skills on the job in less than a month. Some occupations, however, require more work experience or formal education.

Education and training. Most farmworkers learn their jobs quickly as they work; many do not have a high school diploma.

Agricultural workers tend to flowers or crops in nurseries and greenhouses.

Projections data from the National Employment Matrix

Occupational Title	SOC Code	Employment, 2006	Projected employment, 2016	Change, 2006-16	
				Number	Percent
Agricultural workers	45-2000	859,000	838,000	-21,000	-2
Agricultural inspectors..	45-2011	16,000	16,000	-200	-1
Animal breeders..	45-2021	11,000	11,000	500	4
Graders and sorters, agricultural products	45-2041	42,000	41,000	-800	-2
Miscellaneous agricultural workers	45-2090	790,000	769,000	-20,000	-3
Agricultural equipment operators	45-2091	59,000	56,000	-3,000	-5
Farmworkers and laborers, crop, nursery, and greenhouse.......	45-2092	603,000	583,000	-20,000	-3
Farmworkers, farm and ranch animals.................................	45-2093	107,000	110,000	2,900	3
Agricultural workers, all other..	45-2099	20,000	20,000	0	0

NOTE: Data in this table are rounded. See the discussion of the employment projections table in the *Handbook* introductory chapter on *Occupational Information Included in the Handbook*.

People without a high school diploma are particularly common in the crop production sector, which is more labor-intensive and employs more migrant farmworkers. Other agricultural workers require a month to a year of training on the job and, maybe, coursework in related subjects. For graders and sorters, training requirements vary on the basis of their responsibilities. For those who perform tests on agricultural products, a high school diploma is preferred and may be required. Simple jobs requiring mostly visual inspection might be filled by those without a high school diploma.

The education and training requirements for animal breeders vary with the type of breeding they do. For those who breed livestock and other large or expensive animals, a bachelor's or graduate degree in animal science is recommended. Courses include genetics, animal breeding, and animal physiology. For those with experience raising animals or who are breeding their own animals, a bachelor's degree often is not needed, but an associate degree or other training in animal breeding is recommended.

Agricultural inspector jobs require relevant work experience or some college coursework in biology, agricultural science, or a related subject. Inspectors also must be trained in the applicable laws and regulations governing inspection before they can start their jobs.

Other qualifications. Experience working on a farm or around animals is helpful but not necessary to qualify for many jobs. For those who operate equipment on the road or drive a truck as part their job, a driver's license or commercial driver's license is required.

Nursery workers who deal directly with customers must be friendly and tactful. Employers also look for responsible, self-motivated individuals because nursery workers sometimes work with little supervision. People who want to become agricultural inspectors should be responsible, able to communicate well, and like detailed work.

Advancement. Farmworkers who work hard and quickly, have good communication skills, and take an interest in the business may advance to crew leader or other supervisory positions. The ability to speak both English and Spanish is quite helpful in supervisory work as well.

Some agricultural workers aspire to become farm, ranch, or other agricultural managers, or own farms or ranches themselves. (Farmers, ranchers, and agricultural managers are dis-

cussed elsewhere in the *Handbook*.) In addition, their knowledge of raising and harvesting produce may provide an excellent background for becoming purchasing agents and buyers of farm products. Knowledge of working a farm as a business can also help agricultural workers become farm and home management advisors. Those who earn a college degree in agricultural science could become agricultural and food scientists.

Federal Government inspectors whose job performance is satisfactory advance through a career ladder to a specified level. Positions above this level are usually supervisory, and advancement to them is competitive and based on agency needs and individual merit. Advancement opportunities in State and local governments and in the private sector often are similar to those in the Federal Government.

Employment

Agricultural workers held about 859,000 jobs in 2006. More than 68 percent of all agricultural workers worked for crop and livestock producers, while about 5 percent worked for agricultural service providers, mostly farm labor contractors. Agricultural inspectors are employed mainly by Federal, State, and local governments.

By far, the State with the largest employment of farmworkers is California, followed by Oregon and Washington. Though these States produce a multitude of agricultural products, they are particularly known for raising grapes, potatoes, tomatoes, lettuce, apples, citrus, and nursery and greenhouse products.

Job Outlook

Job opportunities for agricultural workers occupations should be abundant because large numbers of workers leave these jobs due to their low wages and physical demands. Overall employment of agricultural workers is projected to undergo little or no change over the 2006-16 decade, reflecting in large part the outlook for farmworkers in crops, nurseries, and greenhouses, who make up the large majority of all agricultural workers.

Employment change. Overall employment of agricultural workers is expected to decline about 2 percent, which is considered little or no change. Employment of farmworkers who work in crops, nurseries, or greenhouses and those who work with farm and ranch animals are projected to decline moderately, about 3 percent. Fewer farmworkers will be needed overall because of continued consolidation of farms and technological advancements in farm equipment that make existing farmworkers more efficient. Farmworkers will increasingly work for farm labor contractors rather than being hired directly by a farm. The agriculture industry also is expected to face increased competition from foreign countries and rising imports, particularly from Central America and China because of free trade agreements with those regions. Nursery and greenhouse workers should experience some job growth in this period, reflecting the increasing demand for landscaping plants.

Employment of agricultural inspectors is expected show little or no change. Governments at all levels are not expected to hire significant numbers of new inspectors, and instead to leave more of the routine inspections to businesses. Little or no change in employment is also expected for graders and sorters. Employment of agricultural equipment operators is expected to decline moderately, reflecting the agriculture industry's continuing ability to produce more with fewer workers overall. Consolidation is resulting in fewer small farmers and greater need to hire equipment operators, but on a temporary basis. Animal breeders will grow more slowly than average, around 4 percent over the 2006-16 period, as large commercial farmers continue to try to improve their animals. However, because the occupation is so small, few new jobs are expected.

Job prospects. Job openings should be plentiful because of relatively large numbers of workers who leave these jobs for other occupations. This is especially true for jobs as agricultural inspectors, graders and sorters, agricultural equipment operators, and crop, greenhouse, and nursery farmworkers. Job prospects will not be as good for animal breeders and ranch and animal farmworkers because fewer workers leave these jobs. Those who work with animals tend to have a more settled lifestyle, as the work does not require them to follow crops for harvest.

Earnings

Agricultural workers had the following median hourly earnings in May 2006:

Agricultural inspectors	$18.32
Animal breeders	13.02
Agricultural equipment operators	9.72
Farmworkers, farm and ranch animals	9.17
Graders and sorters, agricultural products	8.27
Farmworkers and laborers, crop, nursery, and greenhouse	7.95

Farmworkers in crop production often are paid piece rates, with earnings based on how much they do instead of how many hours they work. Farmworkers tend to receive fewer benefits than those in many other occupations. Some employers supply seasonal workers with room and board. Agricultural inspectors employed by State and Federal Governments tend to have very good benefits.

Related Occupations

The duties of farmworkers who perform outdoor labor are similar to the duties of grounds maintenance workers; fishers and operators of fishing vessels; and forest, conservation, and logging workers. Farmworkers who work with farm and ranch animals perform tasks similar to those of animal care and service workers. Animal breeders may perform some work similar to those of veterinary technologists or veterinarians.

Sources of Additional Information

Information on agricultural worker jobs is available from:

➤ National FFA Organization, The National FFA Center, Attention: Career Information Requests, P.O. Box 68690, Indianapolis, IN 46268-0960. Internet: **http://www.ffa.org**

Information on obtaining positions as an agricultural inspector with the Federal Government is available from the Office of Personnel Management through USAJOBS, the Federal Government's official employment information system. This resource for locating and applying for job opportunities can be accessed through the Internet at **http://www.usajobs.opm.gov** or through an interactive voice response telephone system at (703) 724-1850 or TDD (978) 461-8404. These numbers are not toll free, and charges may result.

Fishers and Fishing Vessel Operators

(O*NET 45-3011.00)

Significant Points

- This occupation is characterized by strenuous work, long hours, seasonal employment, and some of the most hazardous conditions.

- About two out of three fishers are self-employed, among the highest proportion in the workforce.

- Fishers usually acquire their occupational skills on the job.

- Employment is projected to decline rapidly.

Nature of the Work

Fishers and fishing vessel operators catch and trap various types of marine life for human consumption, animal feed, bait, and other uses. (Aquaculture—the raising and harvesting, under controlled conditions, of fish and other aquatic life in ponds or confined bodies of water—is covered in the *Handbook* statement on farmers, ranchers, and agricultural managers.)

Fishing hundreds of miles from shore with commercial fishing vessels—large boats capable of hauling a catch of tens of thousands of pounds of fish—requires a crew that includes a captain, or skipper, a first mate and sometimes a second mate, a boatswain (called a deckboss on some smaller boats), and deckhands with specialized skills.

The *fishing boat captain* plans and oversees the fishing operation, the fish to be sought, the location of the best fishing grounds, the method of capture, the duration of the trip, and the sale of the catch.

The captain ensures that the fishing vessel is seaworthy; oversees the purchase of supplies, gear, and equipment, such as fuel, netting, and cables; obtains the required fishing permits and licenses; and hires qualified crew members and assigns their duties. The captain plots the vessel's course using com-

Fishers often work near the coast.

passes, charts, and electronic navigational equipment, such as loran systems or GPS navigation systems. Ships also use radar and sonar to avoid obstacles above and below the water and to detect fish. Sophisticated tracking technology allows captains to better locate and analyze schools of fish. The captain directs the fishing operation through the officers' actions and records daily activities in the ship's log. In port, the captain sells the catch to wholesalers, food processors, or through a fish auction and ensures that each crew member receives the prearranged portion of the proceeds. Captains increasingly use the Internet to bypass processors and sell fish directly to consumers, grocery stores, and restaurants often even before they return to port.

The *first mate* is the captain's assistant and assumes control of the vessel when the captain is off duty. Duty shifts, called watches, usually last 6 hours. In this role, the first mate must be familiar with navigation requirements and the operation of all electronic equipment. The mate's regular duty though, with the help of the boatswain and under the captain's oversight, is to direct the fishing operations and sailing responsibilities of the deckhands, including the operation, maintenance, and repair of the vessel and the gathering, preservation, stowing, and unloading of the catch.

The *boatswain*, a highly experienced deckhand with supervisory responsibilities, directs the *deckhands as* they carry out the sailing and fishing operations. Before departure, the deckhands load equipment and supplies. When necessary, boatswains repair fishing gear, equipment, nets, and accessories. They operate the fishing gear, letting out and pulling in nets and lines, and extract the catch, such as cod, flounder, and tuna, from the nets or the lines' hooks. Deckhands use dip nets to prevent the escape of small fish and gaffs to facilitate the landing of large fish. They then wash, salt, ice, and stow away the catch. Deckhands also must ensure that decks are clear and clean at all times and that the vessel's engines and equipment are kept in good working order. Unless "lumpers" (laborers or longshore workers) are hired, the deckhands unload the catch.

Large fishing vessels that operate in deep water generally have technologically advanced equipment, and some may have facilities on board where the fish are processed and prepared for sale. Such vessels are equipped for long stays at sea and can perform the work of several smaller boats.

Some fishers work on small boats in relatively shallow waters, often in sight of land. Navigation and communication needs are vital and constant for almost all types of boats. On these small boats crews usually are small, often only one or two, who work on all aspects of the fishing operation. Their work might include placing gill nets across the mouths of rivers or inlets, entrapment nets in bays and lakes, or pots and traps for fish or shellfish such as lobsters and crabs. Dredges and scrapes are sometimes used to gather shellfish such as oysters and scallops. A very small proportion of commercial fishing is conducted as diving operations. Depending upon the water's depth, divers wearing regulation diving suits with an umbilical (air line) or a scuba outfit and equipment use spears to catch fish and use nets and other equipment to gather shellfish, coral, sea urchins, abalone, and sponges. In very shallow waters, fish are caught from small boats with an outboard motor, from rowboats, or by wading from shore. Fishers use a wide variety of hand-operated equipment, for example, nets, tongs, rakes, hoes, hooks, and shovels, to gather fish and shellfish; catch amphibians and reptiles such as frogs and turtles; and harvest marine vegetation such as Irish moss and kelp.

Although most fishers are involved in commercial fishing, some captains and deckhands use their expertise in fishing for sport or recreational purposes. For this type of fishing, a group of people charter a fishing vessel with a captain, and possibly several deckhands, for periods ranging from several hours to a number of days and embark upon sportfishing, socializing, and relaxation.

Work environment. Fishing operations are conducted under various environmental conditions, depending on the region of the country and the kind of species sought. Storms, fog, and wind may hamper fishing vessels or cause them to suspend fishing operations and return to port. In relatively busy fisheries, boats have to take care to avoid collisions.

Fishers and fishing vessel operators work under some of the most hazardous conditions of any occupation, and transportation to a hospital or doctor is often not readily available when injuries occur. The crew must be on guard against the danger of injury from malfunctioning fishing gear, entanglement in fishing nets and gear, slippery decks, ice formation in the winter, or being swept overboard by a wave. Malfunctioning navigation or communication equipment may lead to collisions or shipwrecks.

Fishers and fishing vessel operators face strenuous outdoor work and long hours. Commercial fishing trips may require a stay of several weeks or even months hundreds of miles away from one's home port. The pace of work may vary, but even during travel between the home port and the fishing grounds, deckhands on smaller boats try to finish their cleaning and maintenance duties so that there are no chores remaining to be done at port. However, lookout watches are a regular responsibility, and crew members must be prepared to stand watch at prearranged times of the day or night. Although fishing gear has improved, and operations have become more mechanized, netting and processing fish are strenuous activities. Newer vessels have improved living quarters and amenities such as television and shower stalls, but crews still experience the aggravations of confined quarters, continuous close personal contact, and the absence of family.

Training, Other Qualifications, and Advancement

Fishers usually acquire their occupational skills on the job. There are no formal academic training requirements.

Education and training. Most fishers begin as deckhands and learn their trade on the job. Deckhands normally start by finding work through family, friends, or simply walking around the docks and asking for employment. Some larger trawlers and processing ships are run by larger companies. New workers can apply through the companies' human resources department. Operators of large commercial fishing vessels are required to complete a Coast Guard-approved training course. Students can expedite their entrance into these occupations by enrolling in 2-year vocational-technical programs offered by secondary schools. In addition, some community colleges and universities offer fishery technology and related programs that include courses in seamanship, vessel operations, marine safety, navigation, vessel repair and maintenance, health emergencies, and fishing gear technology. Courses include hands-on experience. Secondary and postsecondary programs are normally offered in or near coastal areas.

Experienced fishers may find short-term workshops especially useful. These generally are offered through various postsecondary institutions and provide a good working knowledge of electronic equipment used in navigation and communication and offer information on the latest improvements in fishing gear.

Licensure. Captains and mates on large fishing vessels of at least 200 gross tons must be licensed. Captains of sportfishing boats used for charter, regardless of the boats' size, must also be licensed. Crew members on certain fish-processing vessels may need a merchant mariner's document. The U.S. Coast Guard issues these documents and licenses to individuals who meet the stipulated health, physical, and academic requirements. States set licensing requirements for boats operating in State waters, defined as inland waters and waters within 3 miles of the coast.

Fishers need a permit to fish in almost any water. Permits are distributed by States for State waters and by regional fishing councils for Federal waters. The permits specify the season when fishing is allowed, the type of fish that may be caught, and sometimes the type of fishing gear that is permissible. (For information about merchant marine occupations, see the section on water transportation occupations elsewhere in the *Handbook*.)

Other qualifications. Fishers must be in good health and possess physical strength. Good coordination, mechanical aptitude, and the ability to work under difficult or dangerous conditions are necessary to operate, maintain, and repair equipment and fishing gear. Fishers need stamina to work long hours at sea, often under difficult conditions. On large vessels, they must be able to work as members of a team. Fishers must be patient, yet always alert, to overcome the boredom of long watches when they are not engaged in fishing operations. The ability to assume any deckhand's functions on short notice is important. As supervisors, mates must be able to assume all duties, including the captain's, when necessary. The captain must be highly experienced, mature, and decisive and also must possess the business skills needed to run business operations.

Advancement. On fishing vessels, most fishers begin as deckhands. Experienced, reliable deckhands who display supervisory qualities may become boatswains, who, in turn, may become second mates, first mates, and, finally, captains. Deckhands who acquire experience and whose interests are in ship engineering—the maintenance and repair of ship engines and equipment—can eventually become licensed chief engineers on large commercial vessels after meeting the Coast Guard's experience, physical, and academic requirements. Almost all captains become self-employed, and the overwhelming majority eventually own, or have an interest in, one or more fishing ships. Some may choose to run a sport or recreational fishing operation.

Employment

Fishers and fishing vessel operators held an estimated 38,000 jobs in 2006. About two out of three were self-employed. Most fishing takes place off the coasts, particularly off Alaska, the Gulf Coast, Virginia, California, and New England. Alaska ranks the highest in total volume of fish caught, according to the National Marine Fisheries Service. Many fishers are seasonal workers and positions are usually filled by people who work primarily in other occupations, such as teachers, or by students. For example, salmon season causes employment of fishers in Alaska to more than double during the summer. Because fishing is quite seasonal and workers are often self-employed, measuring total employment is quite difficult.

Job Outlook

Employment of fishers and fishing vessel operators is projected to decline rapidly as regulations relating to the replenishment of fish stocks reduce allowable fishing.

Employment change. Employment of fishers and fishing vessel operators is expected to decline rapidly by 16 percent through the year 2016. Fishers and fishing vessel operators depend on the natural ability of fish stocks to replenish themselves through growth and reproduction, as well as on governmental regulation to promote replenishment of fisheries. As the use of sophisticated electronic equipment for navigation, communication, and locating fish has raised the efficiency of finding fish stocks, the need for setting limits to catches has also risen. Ad-

Projections data from the National Employment Matrix

Occupational Title	SOC Code	Employment, 2006	Projected employment, 2016	Change, 2006-16	
				Number	Percent
Fishers and related fishing workers..	45-3011	38,000	32,000	-6,200	-16

NOTE: Data in this table are rounded. See the discussion of the employment projections table in the *Handbook* introductory chapter on *Occupational Information Included in the Handbook*.

ditionally, improvements in fishing gear and the use of highly automated floating processors, where the catch is processed aboard the vessel, have greatly increased fish hauls.

Fisheries councils issue various types of restrictions to prevent over-harvesting and to allow stocks of fish and shellfish to naturally replenish. Fishing councils are shifting to an individual quota system that tends to reduce employment. However, such a system is beneficial for those who remain in the industry because it allows for longer fishing seasons, better investment returns, and steadier employment.

In addition, rising seafood imports and increasing competition from farm-raised fish are adversely affecting fishing income and is also causing some fishers to leave the industry. However, competition from farm-raised and imported seafood tends to be concentrated in specific species and should have more of an impact in some regions than others.

Governmental efforts to replenish stocks are having some positive results, which should increase the stock of fish in the future. Furthermore, efforts by private fishers' associations on the West Coast to increase government monitoring of the fisheries may help to prevent the type of decline in fish stocks found in waters off the East Coast. Nevertheless, fewer fishers and fishing vessel operators are expected to make their living from the Nation's waters in the years ahead.

Job prospects. Many fishers and fishing vessel operators leave the occupation because of the strenuous and hazardous nature of the job and the lack of steady, year-round income. Thus, some job openings will arise from the need to replace workers who leave the occupation or retire. Sportfishing boats will also continue to provide some job opportunities.

Earnings

In May 2006, median annual earnings of wage-and-salary fishers were $27,250. The bottom 10 percent earned less than $15,280, while the top 10 percent earned more than $45,480. Earnings of fishers and fishing vessel operators normally are highest in the summer and fall when demand for their catch and environmental conditions are favorable and lowest during the winter. Many full-time and most part-time workers supplement their income by working in other activities during the off-season.

Earnings of fishers vary widely, depending upon their position, their ownership percentage of the vessel, the size of their ship, and the amount and value of the catch. The costs of the fishing operation such as fuel, repair and maintenance of gear and equipment, and the crew's supplies are deducted from the sale of the catch. Net proceeds are distributed among the crew members in accordance with a prearranged percentage. Generally, the ship's owner, usually its captain, receives half of the net proceeds. From this amount, the owner pays for depreciation, maintenance and repair, and replacement and insurance costs of the ship and its equipment; the money that remains is the owner's profit.

Related Occupations

Other occupations that involve outdoor work with fish and watercraft include water transportation occupations and fish and game wardens. Many ships not only catch the fish but also cut, trim, and preserve it. Seafood processing work done on land is performed by meat, poultry, and fish cutters and trimmers.

Sources of Additional Information

Information on licensing of fishing vessel captains and mates and on requirements for merchant mariner documentation is available from the U.S. Coast Guard Marine Inspection Office or Marine Safety Office in your State. Or contact either of the following agencies:

➤ Office of Compliance, Commandant (G-MOC-3) 2100 Second St.SW., Washington, DC 20593.
Internet:
   http://www.access.gpo.gov/nara/cfr/waisidx_01/46cfr28_01.html

➤ Licensing and Evaluation Branch, National Maritime Center, 4200 Wilson Blvd., Suite 630, Arlington, VA 22203-1804.
Internet: **http://www.uscg.mil/STCW/index.htm**

Forest, Conservation, and Logging Workers

(O*NET 45-4011.00, 45-4021.00, 45-4022.00, 45-4023.00, 45-4029.99)

Significant Points

- Workers spend all their time outdoors, sometimes in poor weather and often in isolated areas.

- Most jobs are physically demanding and can be hazardous.

- Little to no change in overall employment is expected.

Nature of the Work

The Nation's forests are a rich natural resource, providing beauty and tranquility, varied recreational benefits, and wood for commercial use. Managing and harvesting the forests and woodlands require many different kinds of workers. Forest and conservation workers help develop, maintain, and protect the forests by growing and planting new seedlings, fighting insects and diseases that attack trees, and helping to control soil erosion. Timber-cutting and logging workers harvest thousands of acres of forests each year for the timber that provides the raw material for countless consumer and industrial products.

Forest and conservation workers perform a variety of tasks to reforest and conserve timberlands and to maintain forest facilities, such as roads and campsites. Some forest workers, called tree planters, use digging and planting tools called "dibble bars" and "hoedads" to plant seedlings in reforesting timberland areas. Forest workers also remove diseased or undesirable trees with power saws or handsaws, spray trees with insecticides and fungicides to kill insects and to protect against disease, and apply herbicides on undesirable brush to reduce competing vegetation. In private industry, forest workers usually working under the direction of professional foresters, paint boundary lines, assist with controlled burning, aid in marking and measuring trees, and keep tallies of trees examined and counted. Those who work for State and local governments or who are under contract with them also clear away brush and debris from camp trails, roadsides, and camping areas. Some forest workers clean kitchens and rest rooms at recreational facilities and campgrounds.

Other forest and conservation workers work in forest nurseries, sorting out tree seedlings and discarding those not meeting standards of root formation, stem development, and condition of foliage.

Some forest workers are employed on tree farms, where they plant, cultivate, and harvest many different kinds of trees. Their duties vary with the type of farm. Those who work on specialty farms, such as farms growing Christmas or ornamental trees for nurseries, are responsible for shearing treetops and limbs to control the growth of the trees under their care, to increase the density of limbs, and to improve the shapes of the trees. In addition, these workers' duties include planting the seedlings, spraying to control surrounding weed growth and insects, and harvesting the trees.

Other forest workers gather, by hand or with the use of handtools, products from the woodlands, such as decorative greens, tree cones and barks, moss, and other wild plant life. Still others tap trees for sap to make syrup or chemicals.

Logging workers are responsible for cutting and hauling trees in large quantities. The timber-cutting and logging process is carried out by a logging crew. A typical crew might consist of one or two tree fallers or one tree harvesting machine operator to cut down trees, one bucker to cut logs, two logging skidder operators to drag cut trees to the loading deck, and one equipment operator to load the logs onto trucks.

Specifically, *fallers*, commonly known as *tree fallers*, cut down trees with hand-held power chain saws or mobile felling machines. Usually using gas-powered chain saws, buckers trim off the tops and branches and buck (cut) the resulting logs into specified lengths. *Choke setters* fasten chokers (steel cables or chains) around logs to be skidded (dragged) by tractors or forwarded by the cable-yarding system to the landing or deck area, where the logs are separated by species and type of product, such as pulpwood, saw logs, or veneer logs, and loaded onto trucks. *Rigging slingers and chasers* set up and dismantle the cables and guy wires of the yarding system. *Log sorters, markers, movers,* and *chippers* sort, mark, and move logs, based on species, size, and ownership, and tend machines that chip up logs.

Logging equipment operators use tree harvesters to fell the trees, shear the limbs off, and then cut the logs into desired lengths. They drive tractors mounted on crawler tracks and operate self-propelled machines called skidders or forwarders, which drag or transport logs from the felling site in the woods to the log landing area for loading. They also operate grapple loaders, which lift and load logs into trucks. Some logging equipment operators, usually at a sawmill or a pulpmill woodyard, use a tracked or wheeled machine similar to a forklift to unload logs and pulpwood off of trucks or gondola railroad cars. Some newer, more efficient logging equipment has state-of-the-art computer technology, requiring skilled operators with more training.

Log graders and *scalers* inspect logs for defects, measure logs to determine their volume, and estimate the marketable content or value of logs or pulpwood. These workers often use hand-held data collection devices to enter data about individual trees; later, the data can be downloaded or sent from the scaling area to a central computer via modem.

Other timber-cutting and logging workers have a variety of responsibilities. Some hike through forests to assess logging conditions. Some clear areas of brush and other growth to prepare for logging activities or to promote the growth of desirable species of trees.

Most crews work for self-employed logging contractors who have substantial logging experience, the capital to purchase equipment, and the skills needed to run a small business successfully. Many contractors work alongside their crews as supervisors and often operate one of the logging machines, such as the grapple loader or the tree harvester. Some manage more than one crew and function as owner-supervisors.

Although timber-cutting and logging equipment has greatly improved and operations are becoming increasingly mechanized, many logging jobs still are dangerous and very labor intensive. These jobs require various levels of skill, ranging from the unskilled task of manually moving logs, branches, and equipment to skillfully using chain saws to fell trees, and heavy equipment to skid and load logs onto trucks. To keep costs down, many timber-cutting and logging workers maintain and repair the equipment they use. A skillful, experienced logging worker is expected to handle a variety of logging operations.

Work environment. Forestry and logging jobs are physically demanding. Workers spend all their time outdoors, sometimes in poor weather and often in isolated areas. The increased use of enclosed machines has decreased some of the discomforts caused by inclement weather and has generally made tasks much safer. Workers in some sparsely populated western States, as well as northern Maine, commute long distances between their homes and logging sites. A few logging camps in Alaska and Maine house workers in bunkhouses. In the more densely populated eastern and southern States, commuting distances are shorter.

Most logging occupations involve lifting, climbing, and other strenuous activities, although machinery has eliminated some heavy labor. Loggers work under unusually hazardous conditions. Falling branches, vines, and rough terrain are constant

Logging workers use increasingly productive machinery to harvest logs.

hazards, as are the dangers associated with tree-felling and log-handling operations. Special care must be taken during strong winds, which can even halt logging operations. Slippery or muddy ground, hidden roots, or vines not only reduce efficiency, but also present a constant danger, especially in the presence of moving vehicles and machinery. Poisonous plants, brambles, insects, snakes, heat, humidity, and extreme cold are everyday occurrences where loggers work. The use of hearing protection devices is required on logging operations because the high noise level of felling and skidding operations over long periods may impair one's hearing. Workers must be careful and use proper safety measures and equipment such as hardhats, eye and ear protection, safety clothing, and boots to reduce the risk of injury.

The jobs of forest and conservation workers generally are much less hazardous than those of loggers. It may be necessary for some forestry aides or forest workers to walk long distances through densely wooded areas to accomplish their work tasks.

Training, Other Qualifications, and Advancement

Most forest, conservation, and logging workers develop skills through on-the-job training, learning from experienced workers.

Education and training. Generally, a high school diploma is sufficient for most forest, conservation, and logging occupations. Many forest worker jobs offer only seasonal employment during warm-weather months, so many students are hired to perform short-term, labor-intensive tasks, such as planting tree seedlings or conducting precommercial tree thinning.

Through on-the-job training, logging workers become familiar with the character and dangers of the forest environment and the operation of logging machinery and equipment. Safety training is a vital and required part of the instruction of all logging workers. Many State forestry or logging associations provide training sessions for tree fallers, whose job duties require more skill and experience than do other positions on the logging team. Sessions may take place in the field, where trainees, under the supervision of an experienced logger, have the opportunity to practice various felling techniques. Fallers learn how to manually cut down extremely large or expensive trees safely and with minimal damage to the felled or surrounding trees.

Training programs for loggers and foresters are common in many States. These training programs also include sessions on encouraging the health and productivity of the Nation's forests through the forest product industry's Sustainable Forest Initiative program. Logger training programs vary by State but generally include classroom or field training in a number of areas, including best management practices, environmental compliance, wetlands, safety, endangered species, reforestation, and business management. Some programs lead to logger certification.

Logging companies and trade associations, such as the Northeastern Loggers Association, the American Loggers Council, and the Forest Resources Association, Inc. also offer training programs for workers who operate large, expensive machinery and equipment. Often, a representative of the equipment manufacturer spends several days in the field explaining and overseeing the operation of newly purchased machinery.

Some vocational and technical schools and community colleges offer courses leading to a 2-year technical degree in forestry, wildlife management, conservation, and forest harvesting, all of which are helpful in obtaining a job. A curriculum that includes field trips to observe or participate in forestry or logging activities provides a particularly good background. Additionally, a few community colleges offer training for equipment operators.

Other qualifications. Forest, conservation, and logging workers must be in good health and able to work outdoors every day. They also must be able to work as part of a team. Many logging occupations require physical strength and stamina. Maturity and good judgment are important in making quick, intelligent decisions when hazards arise. Mechanical aptitude and coordination are necessary for operators of machinery and equipment, who often are responsible for repair and maintenance. Self-employed loggers need initiative and managerial and business skills to be successful as logging contractors.

Advancement. Logging workers generally advance from tasks requiring a lot of manual labor to those involving the operation of expensive, sometimes complicated logging equipment. Inexperienced entrants usually begin as laborers, carrying tools and equipment, clearing brush, performing equipment maintenance, and loading and unloading logs and brush. For some, familiarization with logging operations may lead to jobs such as log-handling equipment operator. Further experience may lead to jobs involving the operation of more complicated machinery and yarding towers to transport, load, and unload logs. Those who have the motor skills required for the efficient use of power saws and other equipment may become fallers and buckers.

Some experienced logging workers start their own logging contractor businesses, but to do so they also need some basic business skills, which are essential in today's tight business climate.

Employment

Forest, conservation, and logging workers held about 88,000 jobs in 2006 in the following occupations:

Logging equipment operators 40,000
Forest and conservation workers..20,000
Fallers..13,000
Log graders and scalers...7,100
Logging workers, all others 8,000

About 34 percent of all forest and conservation workers work for government, primarily at the State and local level. About 33 percent are employed by companies that operate timber tracts, tree farms, or forest nurseries, or for contractors that supply services to agriculture and forestry industries. Some of those employed in forestry services work on a contract basis for the U.S. Department of Agriculture's Forest Service. Self-employed forest and conservation workers make up nearly 15 percent of the occupation.

Although forest and conservation workers are located in every State, employment is concentrated in the West and Southeast, where many national and private forests and parks are located. Seasonal demand for forest, conservation, and logging workers can vary by region and time of year. For northern States in particular, winter weather can interrupt forestry and logging operations, although some logging can be done in winter.

More than half of all logging workers work for the logging industry. Another 28 percent are self-employed, who mostly work under contract to landowners and the logging industry. About 10 percent work for sawmills and other businesses in the wood product manufacturing industry.

Job Outlook

Overall employment of forest, conservation, and logging workers is expected to experience little or no change through the year 2016. Most job openings will result from replacement needs because some forestry workers are young people who are not committed to the occupation on a long-term basis.

Employment change. Employment of forest, conservation, and logging workers overall is expected to decline slightly by 1 percent over the 2006-16 decade. Forest and conservation workers is the only occupation in this group that is expected to have job growth, increasing 6 percent over the 10 years. Demand for forest and conservation workers will increase as more land is set aside to protect natural resources or wildlife habitats. In addition, more jobs may be created by recent Federal legislation designed to prevent destructive wildfires by thinning the forests and setting controlled burns in dry regions susceptible to forest fires.

Logging workers are expected to decline by 3 percent from 2006 to 2016. New policies allowing some access to Federal timberland may create some logging jobs, and job opportunities also will arise from timber sales of owners of privately owned forests and tree farms. Nevertheless, domestic timber producers continue to face increasing competition from foreign producers, who can harvest the same amount of timber at lower cost. As competition increases, the logging industry is expected to continue to consolidate in order to reduce costs, eliminating some jobs.

Increased mechanization of logging operations and improvements in logging equipment will continue to depress demand for many manual timber-cutting and logging workers. Employment of fallers, buckers, choke setters, and other workers whose jobs are labor intensive should decline as more laborsaving equipment is used. Employment of machinery and equipment operators, such as tree harvesting, skidding, and log-handling equipment operators, will be less adversely affected and should

rise slightly as logging companies switch away from manual tree felling.

Job prospects. Despite the projection for little to no change in overall employment, prospects for forest and conservation workers should be good. Job openings will come from the large numbers of workers who leave these jobs on a seasonal basis and from an increase in retirements expected over the next decade. Also, many logging workers will transfer to other jobs that are less physically demanding, dangerous, and prone to layoffs.

But employment of forest, conservation, and logging workers can sometimes be unsteady. Weather can curtail the work of forest and conservation workers during the muddy spring season and the cold winter months, depending on the geographic region. Changes in the level of construction, particularly residential construction, also cause slowdowns in logging activities in the short term. In addition, logging operations must be relocated when timber in a particular area has been harvested. During prolonged periods of inactivity, some workers may stay on the job to maintain or repair logging machinery and equipment, but others are laid off or forced to find jobs in other occupations.

Earnings

Earnings vary with the particular forestry or logging occupation and with experience. Many beginning or inexperienced workers earn the Federal minimum wage of $5.85 an hour, but many States set minimum wages higher than the Federal minimum. Under Federal law, this wage will increase to $6.55 in the summer of 2008 and to $7.25 in the summer of 2009. Earnings range from the minimum wage in some beginning forestry and conservation positions to over $26.00 an hour for the most experienced fallers.

Median hourly earnings in 2006 for forest, conservation, and logging occupations were as follows:

Logging equipment operators $14.28
Log graders and scalers...14.06
Fallers..13.80
Forest and conservation workers...10.01

Earnings of logging workers vary by size of establishment and by geographic area. Workers in the largest establishments earn more than those in the smallest ones. Workers in Alaska

Projections data from the National Employment Matrix

Occupational Title	SOC Code	Employment, 2006	Projected employment, 2016	Change, 2006-16	
				Number	Percent
Forest, conservation, and logging workers	45-4000	88,000	87,000	-1,200	-1
Forest and conservation workers..	45-4011	20,000	21,000	1,100	6
Logging workers	45-4020	69,000	66,000	-2,300	-3
Fallers..	45-4021	13,000	12,000	-1,000	-7
Logging equipment operators	45-4022	40,000	40,000	-500	-1
Log graders and scalers...	45-4023	7,100	6,700	-400	-5
Logging workers, all other..	45-4029	7,900	7,500	-500	-6

NOTE: Data in this table are rounded. See the discussion of the employment projections table in the *Handbook* introductory chapter on *Occupational Information Included in the Handbook.*

and the Northwest earn more than those in the South, where the cost of living is generally lower.

Forest and conservation workers who work for State and local governments or for large, private firms generally enjoy more generous benefits than do workers in smaller firms. Small logging contractor firms generally offer timber-cutting and logging workers few benefits beyond vacation days. However, some employers offer full-time workers basic benefits, such as medical coverage, and provide safety apparel and equipment.

Related Occupations

Other occupations concerned with the care of trees and their environment include conservation scientists and foresters, forest and conservation technicians, and grounds maintenance workers. Logging equipment operators have skills similar to material-moving occupations and construction equipment operators.

Sources of Additional Information

For information about timber-cutting and logging careers and about secondary and postsecondary programs offering training for logging occupations, contact:

➤ Forest Resources Association, Inc., 600 Jefferson Plaza, Suite 350, Rockville, MD 20852.
Internet: **http://www.forestresources.org**
➤ American Loggers Council. P.O. Box 966, Hemphill, TX 75948. Internet: **http://www.americanloggers.org**

For information on the Sustainable Forestry Initiative training programs, contact:

➤ American Forest & Paper Association, 1111 19th St.NW., Suite 800, Washington, DC 20036.
Internet: **http://www.afandpa.org**

A list of State forestry associations and other forestry-related State associations is available at most public libraries. Schools of Forestry at State land-grant colleges or universities also can be useful sources of information.

Construction Trades and Related Workers

Boilermakers

(O*NET 47-2011.00)

Significant Points

- Boilermakers use potentially dangerous equipment and the work is physically demanding.

- Most boilermakers learn through a formal apprenticeship; people with a welding certification or other welding training get priority in selection to apprenticeship programs.

- Excellent employment opportunities are expected.

Nature of the Work

Boilermakers and *boilermaker mechanics* make, install, and repair boilers, closed vats, and other large vessels or containers that hold liquids and gases. Boilers heat water or other fluids under extreme pressure for use in generating electric power and to provide heat and power in buildings, factories, and ships. Chemicals, oil, beer, and hundreds of other products are processed and stored in the tanks and vats made by the Nation's boilermakers.

In addition to installing and maintaining boilers and other vessels, boilermakers also help erect and repair air pollution equipment, blast furnaces, water treatment plants, storage and process tanks, and smoke stacks. Boilermakers also install refractory brick and other heat-resistant materials in fireboxes or pressure vessels. Some install and maintain the huge pipes used in dams to send water to and from hydroelectric power generation turbines.

Electric power plants harness highly pressurized steam in a boiler to spin the blades of a turbine, which is attached to an electric generator. In most plants, coal burned in a firebox is the dominant fuel used to generate steam in the boiler.

Because boilers last a long time—sometimes 50 years or more—boilermakers regularly maintain them and upgrade components, such as boiler tubes, heating elements, and ductwork, to increase efficiency. They regularly inspect fittings, feed pumps, safety and check valves, water and pressure gauges, boiler controls, and auxiliary machinery. For closed vats and other large vessels, boilermakers clean or supervise cleaning using scrapers, wire brushes, and cleaning solvents. They repair or replace defective parts using hand and power tools, gas torches, and welding equipment, and may operate metalworking machinery to repair or make parts. They also dismantle leaky boilers, patch weak spots with metal stock, replace defective sections, and strengthen joints.

Boilers and other high-pressure vessels used to hold liquids and gases usually are made in sections by casting each piece

Many boilermakers learn their trade through a formal apprenticeship.

out of steel, iron, copper, or stainless steel. Manufacturers are increasingly automating this process to improve the quality of these vessels. Boiler sections are then welded together, often using robotic welding systems or automated orbital welding machines, which make more consistent welds than are possible by hand and eliminates some of the monotony of the task. Small boilers may be assembled in the manufacturing plant; larger boilers usually are prefabricated in numerous pieces and assembled on site, although they may be temporarily assembled in a fabrication shop to ensure a proper fit before final assembly on the permanent site.

Before making or repairing a fabricated metal product, a boilermaker studies design drawings and creates full size patterns or templates, using straightedges, squares, transits, and tape measures. After the various sized shapes and pieces are marked out on metal, boilermakers use hand and power tools or flame cutting torches to make the cuts. The sections of metal are then bent into shape and accurately lined up before they are welded together. If the plate sections are very large, heavy cranes are used to lift the parts into place. Boilermakers align sections using plumb bobs, levels, wedges, and turnbuckles. They use hammers, files, grinders, and cutting torches to remove irregular edges so that metal pieces fit together properly. They then join them by bolting, welding, or riveting. Boilermakers also align and attach water tubes, stacks and liners, safety and check valves, water and pressure gauges, and other parts and test complete vessels for leaks or other defects.

Work environment. Boilermakers often use potentially dangerous equipment, such as acetylene torches and power grinders; handle heavy parts and tools; and work on ladders or on top of large vessels. Dams, boilers, storage tanks, and pressure vessels are usually of substantial size, thus a major portion of boilermaker work is performed at great heights, sometimes hundreds of feet above the ground in the case of dams. The work is physically demanding and may be done in cramped quarters inside boilers, vats, or tanks that are often dark, damp, and poorly ventilated. Field construction work is performed outside so exposure to all types of weather conditions, including extreme heat and cold, is common. To reduce the chance of injuries, boilermakers often wear hardhats, harnesses, protective clothing, ear plugs, safety glasses and shoes, and respirators.

Boilermakers may experience extended periods of overtime when equipment is shut down for maintenance. Overtime work also may be necessary to meet construction or production deadlines. However, since most field construction and repair work is contract work, there may be periods of unemployment when a contract is complete. Many boilermakers must travel to a project and live away from home for long periods of time.

Training, Other Qualifications, and Advancement

Most boilermakers learn this trade through a formal apprenticeship. A few become boilermakers through a combination of trade or technical school training and employer-provided training.

Education and training. Most boilermakers train in both boilermaking and structural fabrication. Apprenticeship programs usually consist of 6,000 hours or 4 years of paid on-the-job training, supplemented by a minimum of 144 hours of classroom instruction each year in subjects such as set-up and assembly rigging, plate and pressure welding, blueprint reading, and layout. Those who finish registered apprenticeships are certified as fully qualified journey-workers.

Most apprentices must be high school graduates or have a GED or its equivalent. Those with welding training or a welding certification will have priority in applying for apprenticeship programs. Experienced boilermakers often attend apprenticeship classes or seminars to learn about new equipment, procedures, and technology. When an apprenticeship becomes available, the local union publicizes the opportunity by notifying local vocational schools and high school vocational programs.

Other qualifications. The work of boilermakers requires a high degree of technical skill, knowledge, and dedication. Because the tools and equipment used by boilermakers are typically heavier and more cumbersome than those in other construction trades, having physical strength and stamina is important. Good manual dexterity is also important. Most apprentices must be at least 18 years old.

Advancement. Some boilermakers advance to supervisory positions. Because of their extensive training, those trained through apprenticeships usually have an advantage in getting promoted over those who have not gone through the full program.

Employment

Boilermakers held about 18,000 jobs in 2006. About 63 percent worked in the construction industry, assembling and erecting boilers and other vessels. Around 18 percent worked in manufacturing, primarily in boiler manufacturing shops, iron and steel plants, petroleum refineries, chemical plants, and shipyards. Some also worked for boiler repair firms or railroads.

Job Outlook

Employment of boilermakers is expected to grow faster than average. Excellent employment opportunities are expected.

Employment change. Overall employment of boilermakers is expected to grow by 14 percent between 2006 and 2016, faster than the average for all occupations. Growth will be driven by the need to maintain and upgrade, rather than replace, the many existing boilers that are getting older, and by the need to meet the growing population's demand for electric power. While boilers historically have lasted over 50 years, the need to replace components, such as boiler tubes, heating elements, and ductwork, is an ongoing process that will continue to spur demand for boilermakers. To meet the requirements of the Clean Air Act, utility companies also will need to upgrade many of their boiler systems in the next few years.

The Energy Policy Act of 2005 is expected to lead to the construction of many new clean-burning coal power plants, spurring demand for boilermakers. The law, designed to promote conservation and use of cleaner technologies in energy production through tax credits and higher efficiency standards, is expected to positively affect the occupation and the energy industry throughout the 2006-16 projection period.

Installation of new boilers and pressure vessels, air pollution equipment, blast furnaces, water treatment plants, storage and process tanks, electric static precipitators, and stacks and liners, will further drive growth of boilermakers, although to a slightly lesser extent than repairs will.

Job prospects. Job prospects should be excellent because of job growth and because the work of a boilermaker remains hazardous and physically demanding, leading some new apprentices to seek other types of work. An even greater number of openings will arise from the numerous boilermakers expected to retire over the projection decade.

People who have welding training or a welding certificate should have the best opportunities for being selected for boilermaker apprenticeship programs.

Most industries that purchase boilers are sensitive to economic conditions. Therefore, during economic downturns, boilermakers in the construction industry may be laid off. However, maintenance and repairs of boilers must continue even during economic downturns so boilermaker mechanics in manufacturing and other industries generally have more stable employment.

Earnings

In May 2006, the median annual earnings of wage and salary boilermakers were about $46,960. The middle 50 percent earned between $37,300 and $59,710. The lowest 10 percent earned

Projections data from the National Employment Matrix

Occupational Title	SOC Code	Employment, 2006	Projected employment, 2016	Change, 2006-16	
				Number	Percent
Boilermakers..	47-2011	18,000	20,000	2,500	14

NOTE: Data in this table are rounded. See the discussion of the employment projections table in the *Handbook* introductory chapter on *Occupational Information Included in the Handbook.*

less than $30,410, and the highest 10 percent earned more than $71,170. Apprentices generally start at about half of journey-level wages, with wages gradually increasing to the journey wage as workers gain skills.

Many boilermakers belong to labor unions, most to the International Brotherhood of Boilermakers. Other boilermakers are members of the International Association of Machinists, the United Automobile Workers, or the United Steelworkers of America.

Related Occupations

Workers in a number of other occupations assemble, install, or repair metal equipment or machines. These occupations include assemblers and fabricators; machinists; industrial machinery mechanics and maintenance workers; millwrights; pipelayers, plumbers, pipefitters, and steamfitters; sheet metal workers; tool and die makers; and welding, soldering, and brazing workers.

Sources of Additional Information

For more information about boilermaking apprenticeships or other training opportunities, contact local offices of the unions previously mentioned, local construction companies and boiler manufacturers, or the local office of your State employment service. You can also find information on the registered apprenticeships together with links to State apprenticeship programs on the U.S. Department of Labor's Web site: **http://www.doleta.gov/atels_bat** Apprenticeship information is also available from the U.S. Department of Labor's toll free helpline: (877) 872-5627.

For information on apprenticeships and the boilermaking occupation, contact:

➤ International Brotherhood of Boilermakers, Iron Ship Builders, Blacksmiths, Forgers, and Helpers, 753 State Ave., Suite 570, Kansas City, KS 66101. Internet: **http://www.boilermakers.org**

For general information on apprenticeships and how to get them, see the *Occupational Outlook Quarterly* article "Apprenticeships: Career training, credentials—and a paycheck in your pocket," online at **http://www.bls.gov/opub/ooq/2002/summer/art01.pdf** and in print at many libraries and career centers.

Brickmasons, Blockmasons, and Stonemasons

(O*NET 47-2021.00, 47-2022.00)

Significant Points

- Job prospects are expected to be very good, especially for workers with restoration skills.
- Most entrants learn informally on the job, but apprenticeship programs provide the most thorough training.
- The work is usually outdoors and involves lifting heavy materials and working on scaffolds.
- About 24 percent were self-employed.

Nature of the Work

Brickmasons, blockmasons, and stonemasons create attractive, durable surfaces and structures. For thousands of years, these workers have built buildings, fences, roads, walkways, and walls using bricks, concrete blocks, and natural stone. The structures that they build will continue to be in demand for years to come.

The work varies in complexity, from laying a simple masonry walkway to installing an ornate exterior on a highrise building. Workers cut or break the materials used to create walls, floors, and other structures. Once their building materials are properly sized, they are laid with or without a binding material. These workers use their own perceptions and a variety of tools to ensure that the structure meets the desired standards. After finishing laying the bricks, blocks, or stone, these workers clean the finished product with a variety of cleaning agents.

Brickmasons and *blockmasons*—who often are called simply *bricklayers*—build and repair walls, floors, partitions, fireplaces, chimneys, and other structures with brick, precast masonry panels, concrete block, and other masonry materials. Some brickmasons specialize in installing firebrick linings in industrial furnaces.

When building a structure, brickmasons use one of two methods, either the corner lead or the corner pole. Using the corner lead method, they begin by constructing a pyramid of bricks at each corner—called a lead. After the corner leads are complete, less experienced brickmasons fill in the wall between the corners using a line from corner to corner to guide each course, or layer, of brick. Due to the precision needed, corner leads are time-consuming to erect and require the skills of experienced bricklayers.

Because of the expense associated with building corner leads, some brickmasons use corner poles, also called masonry guides, which enable them to build an entire wall at the same time. They fasten the corner poles (posts) in a plumb position to define the wall line and stretch a line between them. This line serves as a guide for each course of brick. Brickmasons then spread a bed of mortar (a cement, lime, sand, and water mixture) with a trowel (a flat, bladed metal tool with a handle), place the brick on the mortar bed, and press and tap the brick into place. Depending on blueprint specifications, brickmasons either cut bricks with a hammer and chisel or saw them to fit around windows, doors, and other openings. Mortar joints are then finished with jointing tools for a sealed, neat, uniform appearance. Although brickmasons typically use steel supports, or lintels, at window and door openings, they sometimes build brick arches, which support and enhance the beauty of the brickwork.

Refractory masons are brickmasons who specialize in installing firebrick and refractory tile in high-temperature boilers, furnaces, cupolas, ladles, and soaking pits in industrial establishments. Most of these workers are employed in steel mills, where molten materials flow on refractory beds from furnaces to rolling machines. They also are employed at oil refineries, glass furnaces, incinerators, and other locations requiring high temperatures during the manufacturing process.

After a structure is completed there is still work that often needs to be done. Pointing, cleaning, and caulking workers can be the final workers on a job or the primary workers on a

Brickmasons, blockmasons, and stonemasons usually work outdoors.

restoration project. These workers use chemicals to clean the laid materials to give the structure a finished appearance. Older structures also need to be refurbished as the mortar or binding agents break down. In many cases a grinder or blade is used to carefully remove the old mortar. Special care is taken to not damage the main structural integrity or the bricks, blocks, or stone. New mortar is then inserted. Depending on how much mortar is being replaced and how, it may take several applications to allow the new mortar to cure properly. These same masons replace and repair damaged masonry materials as part of the building's restoration process.

Stonemasons build stone walls, as well as set stone exteriors and floors. They work with two types of stone—natural cut stone, such as marble, granite, and limestone and artificial stone made from concrete, marble chips, or other masonry materials. Stonemasons usually work on nonresidential structures, such as houses of worship, hotels, and office buildings, but they also work on residences.

Stonemasons often work from a set of drawings, in which each stone has been numbered for identification. Helpers may locate and carry these prenumbered stones to the masons. A derrick operator using a hoist may be needed to lift large stone pieces into place.

When building a stone wall, masons set the first course of stones into a shallow bed of mortar. They then align the stones with wedges, plumb lines, and levels, and work them into position with various tools. Masons continue to build the wall by alternating layers of mortar and courses of stone. As the work progresses, masons remove the wedges, fill the joints between stones, and use a pointed metal tool, called a tuck pointer, to smooth the mortar to an attractive finish. To hold large stones in place, stonemasons attach brackets to the stone and weld or bolt these brackets to anchors in the wall. Finally, masons wash the stone with a cleansing solution to remove stains and dry mortar.

When setting stone floors, which often consist of large and heavy pieces of stone, masons first use a trowel to spread a layer of damp mortar over the surface to be covered. Using crowbars and hard rubber mallets for aligning and leveling, they then set the stone in the mortar bed. To finish, workers fill the joints and clean the stone slabs.

Masons use a special hammer and chisel to cut stone. They cut stone along the grain to make various shapes and sizes, and valuable pieces often are cut with a saw that has a diamond blade. Some masons specialize in setting marble which, in many respects, is similar to setting large pieces of stone. Brickmasons and stonemasons also repair imperfections and cracks, and replace broken or missing masonry units in walls and floors.

Most nonresidential buildings now are built with walls made of concrete block, brick veneer, stone, granite, marble, tile, or glass. In the past, masons doing nonresidential interior work mainly built block partition walls and elevator shafts, but because many types of masonry and stone are used in the interiors of today's nonresidential structures, these workers now must be more versatile. For example, some brickmasons and blockmasons now install structural insulated concrete units and wall panels. They also install a variety of masonry anchors and other masonry-associated accessories used in many highrise buildings.

Work environment. Brickmasons, blockmasons, and stonemasons usually work outdoors, but in contrast to the past when work slowed down in the winter months, new processes and materials are allowing these masons to work in a greater variety of weather conditions. Masons stand, kneel, and bend for long periods and often have to lift heavy materials. Common hazards include injuries from tools and falls from scaffolds, but these can often be avoided when proper safety equipment is used and safety practices are followed.

Most workers work a standard 40-hour week. Earnings for workers in these trades can be reduced on occasion because poor weather and slowdowns in construction activity limit the time they can work.

Training, Other Qualifications, and Advancement
Most brickmasons, blockmasons, and stonemasons pick up their skills informally, observing and learning from experienced workers. Many others receive initial training in vocational education schools or from industry-based programs common throughout the country. Others complete an apprenticeship, which generally provides the most thorough training.

Education and training. Individuals who learn the trade on the job usually start as helpers, laborers, or mason tenders. These workers carry materials, move or assemble scaffolds, and mix mortar. When the opportunity arises, they learn from experienced craftworkers how to mix and spread mortar, lay brick and block, or set stone. They also may learn restoration skills such as cleaning, pointing, and repointing. As they gain experience, they learn more difficult tasks and make the transition to full-fledged craftworkers. The learning period on the job may last longer than if trained in an apprenticeship program. Industry-based training programs offered through construction companies usually last between 2 and 4 years.

Apprenticeships for brickmasons, blockmasons, and stonemasons usually are sponsored by local contractors, trade associations, or local union-management committees. Apprenticeship programs usually require 3 years of on-the-job training, in addition to a minimum of 144 hours of classroom instruction each year in blueprint reading, mathematics, layout work, sketching, and other subjects. Applicants for apprenticeships must be at least 17 years old and in good physical condition. A high school education is preferable with courses in mathematics, mechanical drawing, and general shop.

Apprentices often start by working with laborers, carrying materials, mixing mortar, and building scaffolds for about a month. Next, apprentices learn to lay, align, and join brick and block. They may also learn on the job to work with stone and concrete, which enables them to work with more than one masonry material.

Bricklayers who work in nonresidential construction usually work for large contractors and receive well-rounded training—normally through apprenticeship in all phases of brick or stone work. Those who work in residential construction usually work primarily for small contractors and specialize in only one or two aspects of the job.

Some workers learn at technical schools that offer masonry courses. Entrance requirements and fees vary depending on the school and who is funding the program. Some people take courses before being hired, and some take them later as part of the on-the-job training.

Other qualifications. The most desired quality in workers is dependability and a strong work ethic. Knowledge of basic math including measurement, volume, mixing proportions, algebra, plane geometry, and mechanical drawing are important in this trade.

Advancement. With additional training and experience, brickmasons, blockmasons, and stonemasons may become supervisors for masonry contractors. Some eventually become owners of businesses employing many workers and may spend most of their time as managers. Others move into closely related areas such as construction management or building inspection. Many unionized Joint Apprenticeship and Training Committees offer continual "life long learning" through continuing education courses that help those members who want to advance their technical knowledge and their careers.

Employment

Brickmasons, blockmasons, and stonemasons held 182,000 jobs in 2006. The vast majority were brickmasons. Workers in these crafts are employed primarily by building, specialty trade, or general contractors.

About 24 percent of brickmasons, blockmasons, and stonemasons were self-employed. Many of the self-employed are contractors who work on small jobs, such as patios, walkways, and fireplaces.

Job Outlook

Average employment growth is expected. Job prospects should be very good, especially for workers with restoration skills.

Employment change. Jobs for brickmasons, blockmasons, and stonemasons are expected to increase 10 percent over the 2006-16 decade, about as fast as the average for all occupations, as population and business growth create a need for new houses, industrial facilities, schools, hospitals, offices, and other structures. Also stimulating demand for workers will be the need to restore a growing number of old brick buildings. Moreover, the use of brick and stone for decorative work on building fronts, sidewalks, and in lobbies and foyers is increasing. Brick exteriors should remain very popular, reflecting a growing preference for durable exterior materials requiring little maintenance. Increased construction on hillsides also will spur the demand for new masons as designers create attractive areas that need retaining walls to hold soil in place. There is also an increased demand for durable homes that incorporate brick or stone in hurricane-prone areas.

Job prospects. Job opportunities for brickmasons, blockmasons, and stonemasons are expected to be very good through 2016. A large number of masons are expected to retire over the next decade. The large number of aging masonry buildings will increase opportunities for workers with restoration skills. Also, workers able to install new synthetic materials will have improved opportunities. Applicants who take masonry-related courses at technical schools will have better opportunities than those without these courses.

Employment of brickmasons, blockmasons, and stonemasons, like that of many other construction workers, is sensitive to changes in the economy. When the level of construction activity falls, workers in these trades can experience periods of unemployment. On the other hand, shortages of these workers may occur in some areas during peak periods of building activity.

Projections data from the National Employment Matrix

Occupational Title	SOC Code	Employment, 2006	Projected employment, 2016	Change, 2006-16	
				Number	Percent
Brickmasons, blockmasons, and stonemasons..................................	47-2020	182,000	200,000	18,000	10
Brickmasons and blockmasons...	47-2021	158,000	174,000	15,000	10
Stonemasons	47-2022	24,000	26,000	2,400	10

NOTE: Data in this table are rounded. See the discussion of the employment projections table in the *Handbook* introductory chapter on *Occupational Information Included in the Handbook.*

Earnings

Median hourly earnings of wage and salary brickmasons and blockmasons in May 2006 were $20.66. The middle 50 percent earned between $15.96 and $26.26. The lowest 10 percent earned less than $12.24, and the highest 10 percent earned more than $32.43. Median hourly earnings in the two industries employing the largest number of brickmasons in May 2006 were $20.57 in the foundation, structure, and building exterior contractors industry and $20.67 in the masonry contractors industry.

Median hourly earnings of wage and salary stonemasons in May 2006 were $17.29. The middle 50 percent earned between $13.12 and $22.04. The lowest 10 percent earned less than $10.36, and the highest 10 percent earned more than $28.46.

Apprentices or helpers usually start at about 50 percent of the wage rate paid to experienced workers. Pay increases as apprentices gain experience and learn new skills. Employers usually increase apprentices' wages about every 6 months based on specific advancement criteria.

Some brickmasons, blockmasons, and stonemasons are members of the International Union of Bricklayers and Allied Craftsworkers.

Related Occupations

Brickmasons, blockmasons, and stonemasons combine a thorough knowledge of brick, concrete block, stone, and marble with manual skill to erect attractive, yet highly durable, structures. Workers in other occupations with similar skills include carpet, floor, and tile installers and finishers; cement masons, concrete finishers, segmental pavers, and terrazzo workers; and plasterers and stucco masons.

Sources of Additional Information

For details about apprenticeships or other work opportunities in these trades, contact local bricklaying, stonemasonry, or marble-setting contractors; the Associated Builders and Contractors; a local office of the International Union of Bricklayers and Allied Craftsworkers; a local joint union-management apprenticeship committee; or the nearest office of the State employment service or apprenticeship agency. Apprenticeship information is also available from the U.S. Department of Labor's toll free helpline: (877) 872-5627 and online at: **http://www.doleta.gov/atels_bat**

For general information on apprenticeships and how to get them, see the *Occupational Outlook Quarterly* article "Apprenticeships: Career training, credentials—and a paycheck in your pocket," online at **http://www.bls.gov/opub/ooq/2002/summer/art01.pdf** and in print in many libraries and career centers.

For information on training for brickmasons, blockmasons, and stonemasons, contact:

➤ Associated Builders and Contractors, Workforce Development Division, 4250 North Fairfax Dr., 9th Floor, Arlington, VA 22203. Internet: **http://www.trytools.org**

➤ International Union of Bricklayers and Allied Craftworkers, International Masonry Institute National Training Center, 17101 Science Dr., Bowie, MD 20715.
Internet: **http://www.imiweb.org**

➤ Mason Contractors Association of America, 33 South Roselle Rd., Schaumburg, IL 60193.
Internet: **http://www.masoncontractors.org**

➤ National Association of Home Builders, Home Builders Institute, 1201 15th St.NW., Washington, DC 20005.
Internet: **http://www.hbi.org**

➤ National Center for Construction Education and Research, 3600 NW., 43rd St., Bldg. G, Gainesville, FL 32606.
Internet: **http://www.nccer.org**

For general information about the work of bricklayers, contact:

➤ Associated General Contractors of America, Inc., 2300 Wilson Blvd., Suite 400, Arlington, VA 22201.
Internet: **http://www.agc.org**

➤ Brick Industry Association, 11490 Commerce Park Dr., Reston, VA 22091-1525. Internet: **http://www.brickinfo.org**

➤ National Concrete Masonry Association, 13750 Sunrise Valley Dr., Herndon, VA 20171-3499.
Internet: **http://www.ncma.org**

Carpenters

(O*NET 47-2031.00, 47-2031.01, 47-2031.02)

Significant Points

- About 32 percent of all carpenters—the largest construction trade—were self-employed.

- Job opportunities should be best for those with the most training and skills.

- Between 3 and 4 years of both on-the-job training and classroom instruction usually is needed to become a skilled carpenter.

Nature of the Work

Carpenters are involved in many different kinds of construction, from the building of highways and bridges to the installation of kitchen cabinets. Carpenters construct, erect, install, and repair structures and fixtures made from wood and other materials.

Each carpentry task is somewhat different, but most involve the same basic steps. Working from blueprints or instructions from supervisors, carpenters first do the layout—measuring, marking, and arranging materials—in accordance with local building codes. They cut and shape wood, plastic, fiberglass, or drywall using hand and power tools, such as chisels, planes, saws, drills, and sanders. They then join the materials with nails, screws, staples, or adhesives. In the last step, carpenters do a final check of the accuracy of their work with levels, rules, plumb bobs, framing squares, and surveying equipment, and make any necessary adjustments.

When working with prefabricated components, such as stairs or wall panels, the carpenter's task is somewhat simpler because it does not require as much layout work or the cutting and assembly of as many pieces. Prefabricated components

Carpenters cut and shape wood, plastic, fiberglass, or drywall using hand and power tools.

are designed for easy and fast installation and generally can be installed in a single operation.

Some carpenters do many different carpentry tasks, while others specialize in one or two. Carpenters who remodel homes and other structures, for example, need a broad range of carpentry skills. As part of a single job, for example, they might frame walls and partitions, put in doors and windows, build stairs, install cabinets and molding, and complete many other tasks. Because these carpenters are so well-trained, they often can switch from residential building to commercial construction or remodeling work, depending on which offers the best work opportunities.

Carpenters who work for large construction contractors or specialty contractors may perform only a few regular tasks, such as constructing wooden forms for pouring concrete, or erecting scaffolding. Some carpenters build tunnel bracing, or brattices, in underground passageways and mines to control the circulation of air through the passageways and to worksites. Others build concrete forms for tunnel, bridge, or sewer construction projects.

Carpenters employed outside the construction industry perform a variety of installation and maintenance work. They may replace panes of glass, ceiling tiles, and doors, as well as repair desks, cabinets, and other furniture. Depending on the employer, carpenters install partitions, doors, and windows; change locks; and repair broken furniture. In manufacturing firms, carpenters may assist in moving or installing machinery. (For more information on workers who install machinery, see the discussion of millwrights as well as industrial machinery installation, repair, and maintenance workers elsewhere in the *Handbook*.)

Work environment. As is true of other building trades, carpentry work is sometimes strenuous. Prolonged standing, climbing, bending, and kneeling often are necessary. Carpenters risk injury working with sharp or rough materials, using sharp tools and power equipment, and working in situations where they might slip or fall. Although many carpenters work indoors, those that work outdoors are subject to variable weather conditions.

Most carpenters work a standard 40 hour week. Hours may be longer during busy periods.

Training, Other Qualifications, and Advancement

Carpenters learn their trade through formal and informal training programs. Between 3 and 4 years of both on-the-job training and classroom instruction usually is needed to become a skilled carpenter. There are a number of ways to train, but a more formal training program often improves job opportunities.

Education and training. Learning to be a carpenter can start in high school. Classes in English, algebra, geometry, physics, mechanical drawing, blueprint reading, and general shop will prepare students for the further training they will need.

After high school, there are a number of different ways to obtain the necessary training. Some people get a job as a carpenter's helper, assisting more experienced workers. At the same time, the helper might attend a trade or vocational school, or community college to receive further trade-related training and eventually become a carpenter.

Some employers offer employees formal apprenticeships. These programs combine on-the-job training with related classroom instruction. Apprentices usually must be at least 18 years old and meet local requirements. Apprenticeship programs usually last 3 to 4 years, but length varies with the apprentice's skill.

On the job, apprentices learn elementary structural design and become familiar with common carpentry jobs, such as layout, form building, rough framing, and outside and inside finishing. They also learn to use the tools, machines, equipment, and materials of the trade. In the classroom, apprentices learn safety, first aid, blueprint reading, freehand sketching, basic mathematics, and various carpentry techniques. Both in the classroom and on the job, they learn the relationship between carpentry and the other building trades.

The number of apprenticeship programs is limited, however, so only a small proportion of carpenters learn their trade through these programs. Most apprenticeships are offered by commercial and industrial building contractors with union membership.

Some people who are interested in carpentry careers choose to get their classroom training before seeking a job. There are a number of public and private vocational-technical schools and training academies affiliated with unions and contractors that offer training to become a carpenter. Employers often look favorably upon these students and usually start them at a higher level than those without the training.

Other qualifications. Carpenters need manual dexterity, eye-hand coordination, physical fitness, and a good sense of balance. The ability to solve arithmetic problems quickly and accurately also is required. In addition, military service or a good work history is viewed favorably by employers.

Certification and advancement. Carpenters who complete formal apprenticeship programs receive certification as journeypersons. Some carpenters earn other certifications in scaffold building, high torque bolting, or pump work. These certifications prove that carpenters are able to perform these tasks, which can lead to additional responsibilities.

Carpenters usually have more opportunities than most other construction workers to become general construction supervisors because carpenters are exposed to the entire construction process. For those who would like to advance, it is increasingly important to be able to communicate in both English and Spanish in order to relay instructions and safety precautions to workers; Spanish-speaking workers make up a large part of the construction workforce in many areas. Carpenters may advance to carpentry supervisor or general construction supervisor positions. Others may become independent contractors. Supervisors and contractors need good communication skills to deal with clients and subcontractors. They should be able to identify and estimate the quantity of materials needed to complete a job and accurately estimate how long a job will take to complete and what it will cost.

Employment

Carpenters are employed throughout the country in almost every community and make up the largest building trades occupation. They held about 1.5 million jobs in 2006.

About 32 percent worked in construction of buildings and about 23 percent worked for specialty trade contractors. Most of the rest of the wage and salary workers worked for manufacturing firms, government agencies, retail establishments, and a wide variety of other industries. About 32 percent of all carpenters were self-employed. Some carpenters change employers each time they finish a construction job. Others alternate between working for a contractor and working as contractors themselves on small jobs, depending on where the work is available.

Job Outlook

Average job growth, coupled with replacement needs, create a large number of openings each year. Job opportunities should be best for those with the most training and skills.

Employment change. Employment of carpenters is expected to increase by 10 percent during the 2006-16 decade, about as fast as the average for all occupations. The need for carpenters should grow as construction activity increases in response to demand for new housing and office and retail space, and for modernizing and expanding schools and industrial plants. A strong home remodeling market also will create demand for carpenters. Moreover, construction of roads and bridges as well as restaurants, hotels, and other businesses will increase the demand for carpenters in the coming decade.

Some of the demand for carpenters, however, will be offset by expected productivity gains resulting from the increasing use of prefabricated components and improved fasteners and tools. Prefabricated wall panels, roof assemblies, and stairs, as well as prehung doors and windows can be installed very quickly. Instead of having to be built on the worksite, prefabricated walls, partitions, and stairs can be lifted into place in one operation; beams and, in some cases, entire roof assemblies, are lifted into place using a crane. As prefabricated components become more standardized, builders will use them more often. In addition, improved adhesives are reducing the time needed to join materials, and lightweight, cordless, and pneumatic tools—such as nailers and drills—will all continue to make carpenters more productive. New and improved tools, equipment, techniques, and materials also have made carpenters more versatile, allowing them to perform more carpentry tasks.

Job prospects. Job opportunities should be best for those with the most training and skills. Job growth and replacement needs for those who leave the occupation create a large number of openings each year. Many people with limited skills take jobs as carpenters but eventually leave the occupation because they dislike the work or cannot find steady employment.

Carpenters with all-around skills will have better opportunities for steady work than carpenters who can perform only a few relatively simple, routine tasks. Carpenters can experience periods of unemployment because of the short-term nature of many construction projects, winter slowdowns in construction activity in northern areas, and the cyclical nature of the construction industry.

Employment of carpenters, like that of many other construction workers, is sensitive to the fluctuations of the economy. Workers in these trades may experience periods of unemployment when the overall level of construction falls. On the other hand, shortages of these workers may occur in some areas during peak periods of building activity.

Job opportunities for carpenters also vary by geographic area. Construction activity parallels the movement of people and businesses and reflects differences in local economic conditions. The areas with the largest population increases will also provide the best opportunities for jobs as carpenters and for apprenticeships for people seeking to become carpenters.

Earnings

In May 2006, median hourly earnings of wage and salary carpenters were $17.57. The middle 50 percent earned between $13.55 and $23.85. The lowest 10 percent earned less than $10.87, and the highest 10 percent earned more than $30.45. Median hourly earnings in the industries employing the largest numbers of carpenters were as follows:

Projections data from the National Employment Matrix

Occupational Title	SOC Code	Employment, 2006	Projected employment, 2016	Change, 2006-16	
				Number	Percent
Carpenters	47-2031	1,462,000	1,612,000	150,000	10

NOTE: Data in this table are rounded. See the discussion of the employment projections table in the *Handbook* introductory chapter on *Occupational Information Included in the Handbook.*

Residential building construction..$17.39
Foundation, structure, and building exterior contractors 17.03
Nonresidential building construction.....................................15.12
Building finishing contractors..13.76
Employment services...10.88

Earnings can be reduced on occasion, because carpenters lose work time in bad weather and during recessions when jobs are unavailable. Earnings may be increased by overtime during busy periods.

Some carpenters are members of the United Brotherhood of Carpenters and Joiners of America.

Related Occupations

Carpenters are skilled construction workers. Other skilled construction occupations include brickmasons, blockmasons, and stonemasons; cement masons, concrete finishers, segmental pavers, and terrazzo workers; drywall installers, ceiling tile installers, and tapers; electricians; pipelayers, plumbers, pipefitters, and steamfitters; and plasterers and stucco masons.

Sources of Additional Information

For information about carpentry apprenticeships or other work opportunities in this trade, contact local carpentry contractors, locals of the union mentioned above, local joint union-contractor apprenticeship committees, or the nearest office of the State employment service or apprenticeship agency. You can also find information on the registered apprenticeship system with links to State apprenticeship programs on the U.S. Department of Labor's Web site: **http://www.doleta.gov/atels_bat** Apprenticeship information is also available from the U.S. Department of Labor's toll free helpline: (877) 872-5627.

For information on training opportunities and carpentry in general, contact:

➤ Associated Builders and Contractors, 4250 North Fairfax Dr., 9th Floor, Arlington, VA 22203.
Internet: **http://www.trytools.org**
➤ Associated General Contractors of America, Inc., 2300 Wilson Blvd., Suite 400, Arlington, VA 22201.
Internet: **http://www.agc.org**
➤ National Center for Construction Education and Research, 3600 NW., 43rd St., Bldg. G, Gainesville, FL, 32606.
Internet: **http://www.nccer.org**
➤ National Association of Home Builders, Home Builders Institute, 1201 15th St.NW., Washington, DC 20005.
Internet: **http://www.hbi.org**
➤ United Brotherhood of Carpenters and Joiners of America, Carpenters Training Fund, 6801 Placid St., Las Vegas, NV 89119. Internet: **http://www.carpenters.org**

For general information on apprenticeships and how to get them, see the *Occupational Outlook Quarterly* article "Apprenticeships: Career training, credentials—and a paycheck in your pocket," online at **http://www.bls.gov/opub/ooq/2002/summer/art01.pdf** and in print at many libraries and career centers.

Carpet, Floor, and Tile Installers and Finishers

(O*NET 47-2041.00, 47-2042.00, 47-2043.00, 47-2044.00)

Significant Points

- About 42 percent of carpet, floor, and tile installers and finishers are self-employed.

- Most workers learn on the job.

- Projected job growth varies by specialty; for example, tile and marble setters will have faster than average job growth, while little change is expected in the employment of carpet installers.

- Employment is less sensitive to fluctuations in construction activity than other construction trades workers.

Nature of the Work

Carpet, tile, and other types of floor coverings not only serve an important basic function in buildings, but their decorative qualities also contribute to the appeal of the buildings. Carpet, floor, and tile installers and finishers lay floor coverings in homes, offices, hospitals, stores, restaurants, and many other types of buildings. Tile also may be installed on walls and ceilings.

Before installing carpet, *carpet installers* first inspect the surface to be covered to determine its condition and, if necessary, correct any imperfections that could show through the carpet or cause the carpet to wear unevenly. They measure the area to be carpeted and plan the layout, keeping in mind expected traffic patterns and placement of seams for best appearance and maximum wear.

When installing wall-to-wall carpet without tacks, installers first fasten a tackless strip to the floor, next to the wall. They then install the padded cushion or underlay. Next, they roll out, measure, mark, and cut the carpet, allowing for 2 to 3 inches of extra carpet for the final fitting. Using a device called a "knee kicker," they position the carpet, stretching it to fit evenly on the floor and snugly against each wall and door threshold. They then cut off the excess carpet. Finally, using a power stretcher, they stretch the carpet, hooking it to the tackless strip to hold it in place. The installers then finish the edges using a wall trimmer.

Because most carpet comes in 12-foot widths, wall-to-wall installations require installers to join carpet sections together for large rooms. The installers join the sections using heat-taped seams—seams held together by a special plastic tape that is activated by heat.

On special upholstery work, such as stairs, carpet may be held in place with staples. Also, in commercial installations, carpet often is glued directly to the floor or to padding that has been glued to the floor.

Carpet installers use hand tools such as hammers, drills, staple guns, carpet knives, and rubber mallets. They also may use carpetlaying tools, such as carpet shears, knee kickers, wall trimmers, loop pile cutters, heat irons, and power stretchers.

Floor installers and *floor layers* lay floor coverings such as laminate, linoleum, vinyl, cork, and rubber for decorative purposes, or to deaden sounds, absorb shocks, or create air-tight environments. Although they also may install carpet, wood or tile, that is not their main job. Before installing the floor, floor layers inspect the surface to be covered and, if necessary, correct any deficiencies, such as a rotted or unleveled sub-floor, in order to start with a sturdy, smooth, clean foundation. They measure and cut floor covering materials. When installing linoleum or vinyl, they may use an adhesive to cement the material directly to the floor. For laminate floor installation, workers may unroll and install a polyethylene film which acts as a moisture barrier, along with a thicker, padded underlayer which helps reduce noise. Cork and rubber floors often can be installed directly on top of the sub-floor without any underlayer. Finally, floor layers install the floor covering to form a tight fit.

After a carpenter installs a new hardwood floor or when a customer wants to refinish an old wood floor, floor sanders and finishers are called in to smooth any imperfections in the wood and apply finish coats of varnish or polyurethane. To remove imperfections and smooth the surface, they will scrape and sand wooden floors using floor sanding machines. They then inspect the floor and remove excess glue from joints using a knife or wood chisel and may further sand the wood surfaces by hand, using sandpaper. Finally, they apply sealant using brushes or rollers, often applying multiple coats.

Tile installers, tilesetters, and *marble setters* apply hard tile and marble to floors, walls, ceilings, countertops, patios, and roof decks. Tile and marble are durable, impervious to water, and easy to clean, making them a popular building material in bathrooms, kitchens, hospitals, and commercial buildings.

Prior to installation, tilesetters use measuring devices and levels to ensure that the tile is placed in a consistent manner. Tile varies in color, shape, and size, ranging in size from 1 inch to 24 or more inches on a side, so tilesetters sometimes prearrange tiles on a dry floor according to the intended design. This allows them to examine the pattern, check that they have enough of each type of tile, and determine where they will have to cut tiles to fit the design in the available space. To cover all exposed areas, including corners and around pipes, tubs, and wash basins, tilesetters cut tiles to fit with a machine saw or a special cutting tool. To set tile on a flat, solid surface such as drywall, concrete, plaster, or wood, tilesetters first use a tooth-edged trowel to spread a "thin set," or thin layer of cement adhesive or "mastic," a very sticky paste. They then properly position the tile and gently tap the surface with their trowel handle, rubber mallet, or a small block of wood to set the tile evenly and firmly. Spacers are used to maintain exact distance between tiles, and any excess thin set is wiped off the tile immediately after placement.

To apply tile to an area that lacks a solid surface, tilesetters nail a support of metal mesh or tile backer board to the wall or ceiling to be tiled. They use a trowel to apply a cement mortar—called a "scratch coat"—onto the metal screen, and scratch the surface of the soft mortar with a small tool similar to a rake. After the scratch coat has dried, tilesetters apply a brown coat of

Prior to installing tile, tilesetters use measuring devices and levels to ensure that the tile is placed in a consistent manner.

mortar to level the surface, and then apply mortar to the brown coat and place tile onto the surface. Hard backer board also is used in areas where there is excess moisture, such as a shower stall.

When the cement or mastic has set, tilesetters fill the joints with "grout," which is very fine cement and includes sand for joints 1/8th of an inch and larger. They then apply the grout to the surface with a rubber-edged device called a grout float or a grouting trowel to fill the joints and remove excess grout. Before the grout sets, they wipe the tiles and finish the joints with a damp sponge for a uniform appearance.

Marble setters cut and set marble slabs in floors and walls of buildings. They trim and cut marble to specified sizes using a power wet saw, other cutting equipment, or handtools. After setting the marble in place, they polish the marble to high luster using power tools or by hand.

Work environment. Carpet, floor, and tile installers and finishers usually work indoors and have regular daytime hours. However, when floor covering installers need to work in occupied stores or offices, they may work evenings and weekends to avoid disturbing customers or employees. By the time workers install carpets, flooring, or tile in a new structure, most construction has been completed and the work area is relatively clean and uncluttered. Installing these materials is labor intensive; workers spend much of their time bending, kneeling, and reaching—activities that require endurance. The work can be very hard on workers' knees and back. Carpet installers frequently lift heavy rolls of carpet and may move heavy furniture, which requires strength and can be physically exhausting. Safety regulations may require that they wear kneepads or safety goggles when using certain tools. Carpet and floor layers may be exposed to fumes from various kinds of glue and to fibers of certain types of carpet.

Although workers are subject to cuts from tools or materials, falls from ladders, and strained muscles, the occupation is not as hazardous as some other construction occupations.

Training, Other Qualifications, and Advancement
The vast majority of carpet, floor, and tile installers and finishers learn their trade informally on the job. A few, mostly tile setters, learn through formal apprenticeship programs, which include classroom instruction and paid on-the-job training.

Education and training. Informal training for carpet installers often is sponsored by individual contractors. Workers start as helpers, and begin with simple assignments, such as installing stripping and padding, or helping to stretch newly installed carpet. With experience, helpers take on more difficult assignments, such as measuring, cutting, and fitting.

Tile and marble setters also learn their craft mostly through on-the-job training. They start by helping carry materials and learning about the tools of the trade. They then learn to prepare the subsurface for tile or marble. As they progress, they learn to cut the tile and marble to fit the job. They also learn to apply grout and sealants used in finishing the materials to give it its final appearance. Apprenticeship programs and some contractor-sponsored programs provide comprehensive training in all phases of the tilesetting and floor layer trades.

Other floor layers also learn on the job and begin by learning how to use the tools of the trade. They next learn to prepare surfaces to receive flooring. As they progress, they learn to cut and install the various floor coverings.

Other qualifications. Some skills needed to become carpet, floor, and tile installers and finishers include manual dexterity, eye-hand coordination, physical fitness, and a good sense of balance and color. The ability to solve basic arithmetic problems quickly and accurately also is required. In addition, reliability and a good work history are viewed favorably by contractors.

Advancement. Carpet, floor, and tile installers and finishers sometimes advance to become supervisors, salespersons, or estimators. In these positions, they must be able to estimate the time, money, and quantity of materials needed to complete a job.

Some carpet installers may become managers for large installation firms. Many carpet, floor, and tile installers and finishers who begin working for someone else eventually go into business for themselves as independent subcontractors.

For those who would like to advance, it is increasingly important to be able to communicate in both English and Spanish to relay instructions and safety precautions to workers with limited understanding of English; Spanish-speaking workers make up a large part of the construction workforce in many areas. Workers who want to advance to supervisor jobs or become contractors also need good English skills to deal with clients and subcontractors.

Employment
Carpet, floor, and tile installers and finishers held about 196,000 jobs in 2006. About 42 percent of all carpet, floor, and tile installers and finishers were self-employed, compared with 20 percent of all construction trades and related workers. The following tabulation shows 2006 wage-and-salary employment by specialty:

Tile and marble setters 79,000
Carpet installers 73,000
Floor layers, except carpet, wood, and hard tiles.................29,000
Floor sanders and finishers...14,000

Many carpet installers work for flooring contractors or floor covering retailers. Most salaried tilesetters are employed by tilesetting contractors who work mainly on nonresidential construction projects, such as schools, hospitals, and office buildings. Most self-employed tilesetters work on residential projects.

Although carpet, floor, and tile installers and finishers are employed throughout the Nation, they tend to be concentrated in populated areas where there are high levels of construction activity.

Job Outlook
Employment of carpet, floor, and tile installers and finishers is expected to grow more slowly than the average for all occupations. Job growth and opportunities, however, will differ among the individual occupations.

Employment change. Overall employment is expected to grow by 4 percent between 2006 and 2016, more slowly than the average for all occupations. Tile and marble setters, the largest specialty, will experience faster than average job growth because population and business growth will result in more construction of shopping malls, hospitals, schools, restaurants, and other structures in which tile is used extensively. Tiles, including those made of glass, slate, and mosaic, and other less traditional materials, are also becoming more popular, particularly in the growing number of more expensive homes.

Carpet installers, the second largest specialty, will have little or no job growth as residential investors and homeowners increasingly choose hardwood floors because of their durabil-

Projections data from the National Employment Matrix

Occupational Title	SOC Code	Employment, 2006	Projected employment, 2016	Change, 2006-16	
				Number	Percent
Carpet, floor, and tile installers and finishers....................................	47-2040	196,000	203,000	7,500	4
Carpet installers	47-2041	73,000	72,000	-900	-1
Floor layers, except carpet, wood, and hard tiles.........................	47-2042	29,000	25,000	-3,500	-12
Floor sanders and finishers...	47-2043	14,000	14,000	-300	-2
Tile and marble setters	47-2044	79,000	91,000	12,000	15

NOTE: Data in this table are rounded. See the discussion of the employment projections table in the *Handbook* introductory chapter on *Occupational Information Included in the Handbook.*

ity, neutral colors, and low maintenance, and because owners feel these floors will add to the value of their homes. Carpets, on the other hand, stain and wear out faster than wood or tile, which contributes to the decreased demand for carpet installation. Nevertheless, carpet will continue to be used in nonresidential structures such as schools, offices, and hospitals. Also, many multifamily structures will require or recommend carpet because it provides sound dampening.

Workers who install other types of flooring, including laminate, cork, rubber, and vinyl, should experience rapidly declining employment because these materials are used less often and are often laid by other types of construction workers. Employment of floor sanders and finishers—a small specialty—is projected to have little or no job growth due to the increasing use of prefinished hardwood flooring and because their work is heavily concentrated in the relatively small niche market of residential remodeling. There should be some employment growth, however, resulting from restoration of damaged hardwood floors, which is typically more cost effective than installing new floors.

Job prospects. In addition to employment growth, job openings are expected for carpet, floor, and tile installers and finishers because of the need to replace workers who leave the occupation. The strenuous nature of the work leads to high replacement needs because many of these workers do not stay in the occupation long.

Few openings will arise for vinyl and linoleum floor installers because the number of these jobs is comparatively small and because homeowners can increasingly take advantage of easy application products, such as self-adhesive vinyl tiles.

Employment of carpet, floor, and tile installers and finishers is slightly less sensitive to changes in construction activity than most other construction occupations because much of the work involves replacing worn carpet and other flooring in existing buildings. However, workers in these trades may still experience periods of unemployment when the overall level of construction falls. On the other hand, shortages of these workers may occur in some areas during peak periods of building activity.

Earnings

In May 2006, the median hourly earnings of wage and salary carpet installers were $16.62. The middle 50 percent earned between $12.06 and $23.26. The lowest 10 percent earned less than $9.46, and the top 10 percent earned more than $31.11. The median hourly earnings of carpet installers working for building finishing contractors were $17.17, and $15.69 for those working in home furnishings stores. Carpet installers are paid either on an hourly basis or by the number of yards of carpet installed.

Median hourly earnings of wage and salary floor layers except carpet, wood, and hard tiles were $16.44 in May 2006. The middle 50 percent earned between $12.71 and $23.78. The lowest 10 percent earned less than $9.77, and the top 10 percent earned more than $32.32.

Median hourly earnings of wage and salary floor sanders and finishers were $13.89 in May 2006. The middle 50 percent earned between $10.84 and $18.47. The lowest 10 percent

earned less than $9.08, and the top 10 percent earned more than $24.21.

Median hourly earnings of wage and salary tile and marble setters were $17.59 in May 2006. The middle 50 percent earned between $13.16 and $23.50. The lowest 10 percent earned less than $10.26, and the top 10 percent earned more than $29.95.

Earnings of carpet, floor, and tile installers and finishers vary greatly by geographic location and by union membership status. Some carpet, floor, and tile installers and finishers belong to the United Brotherhood of Carpenters and Joiners of America. Some tilesetters belong to the International Union of Bricklayers and Allied Craftsmen, and some carpet installers belong to the International Brotherhood of Painters and Allied Trades.

Apprentices and other trainees usually start out earning about half of what an experienced worker earn; their wage rates increase as they advance through the training program.

Related Occupations

Carpet, floor, and tile installers and finishers measure, cut, and fit materials to cover a space. Workers in other occupations involving similar skills, but using different materials, include brickmasons, blockmasons, and stonemasons; carpenters; cement masons, concrete finishers, segmental pavers, and terrazzo workers; drywall installers, ceiling tile installers, and tapers; painters and paperhangers; roofers; and sheet metal workers.

Sources of Additional Information

For details about apprenticeships or work opportunities, contact local flooring or tilesetting contractors or retailers, locals of the unions previously mentioned, or the nearest office of the State apprenticeship agency or employment service. Apprenticeship information is also available from the U.S. Department of Labor's tollfree helpline: (877) 872-5627.

For general information about the work of carpet installers and floor layers, contact:

➤ Floor Covering Installation Contractors Association, 7439 Milwood Dr., West Bloomfield, MI 48322.
Internet: **http://www.fcica.com/index2.html**

Additional information on training for carpet installers and floor layers is available from:

➤ Finishing Trades Institute, International Union of Painters and Allied Trades, 1750 New York Ave. NW., Washington, DC 20006. Internet: **http://www.finishingtradesinstitute.org**

For general information about the work of tile installers and finishers, contact:

➤ International Union of Bricklayers and Allied Craftworkers, International Masonry Institute, The James Brice House, 42 East St., Annapolis, MD 21401. Internet: **http://www.imiweb.org**
➤ National Association of Home Builders, Home Builders Institute, 1201 15th St. NW., Washington, DC 20005.
Internet: **http://www.hbi.org and http://www.nahb.org**

For more information about tile setting and tile training, contact:

➤ National Tile Contractors Association, P.O. Box 13629, Jackson, MS 39236. Internet: **http://www.tile-assn.com**

For information concerning training of carpet, floor, and tile installers and finishers, contact:

➤ United Brotherhood of Carpenters and Joiners of America, 50 F St.NW., Washington, DC 20001.
Internet: **http://www.carpenters.org**

For general information on apprenticeships and how to get them, see the *Occupational Outlook Quarterly* article "Apprenticeships: Career training, credentials—and a paycheck in your pocket," in print at many libraries and career centers and online at: **http://www.bls.gov/opub/ooq/2002/summer/art01.pdf**

Cement Masons, Concrete Finishers, Segmental Pavers, and Terrazzo Workers

(O*NET 47-2051.00, 47-2053.00, 47-4091.00)

Significant Points

- Job opportunities are expected to be good, especially for those with the most experience and skills.

- Most learn on the job or though a combination of classroom and on-the-job training that can take 3 to 4 years.

- Cement masons often work overtime, with premium pay, because once concrete has been placed, the job must be completed.

Nature of the Work

Cement masons, concrete finishers, and terrazzo workers all work with concrete, one of the most common and durable materials used in construction. Once set, concrete—a mixture of Portland cement, sand, gravel, and water—becomes the foundation for everything from decorative patios and floors to huge dams or miles of roadways.

Cement masons and *concrete finishers* place and finish concrete. They also may color concrete surfaces, expose aggregate (small stones) in walls and sidewalks, or fabricate concrete beams, columns, and panels. In preparing a site to place concrete, cement masons first set the forms for holding the concrete and properly align them. They then direct the casting of the concrete and supervise laborers who use shovels or special tools to spread it. Masons then guide a straightedge back and forth across the top of the forms to "screed," or level, the freshly placed concrete. Immediately after leveling the concrete, masons carefully float it—smooth the concrete surface with a "bull float," a long-handled tool about 8 by 48 inches that covers the coarser materials in the concrete and brings a rich mixture of fine cement paste to the surface.

After the concrete has been leveled and floated, concrete finishers press an edger between the forms and the concrete and guide it along the edge and the surface. This produces slightly rounded edges and helps prevent chipping or cracking. Concrete finishers use a special tool called a "groover" to make joints or grooves at specific intervals that help control cracking. Next, they smooth the surface using either a powered or hand trowel, a small, smooth, rectangular metal tool.

Cement masons first set the forms for holding the concrete and properly align them.

Sometimes, cement masons perform all the steps of laying concrete, including the finishing. As the final step, they retrowel the concrete surface back and forth with powered or hand trowels to create a smooth finish. For a coarse, nonskid finish, masons brush the surface with a broom or stiff-bristled brush. For a pebble finish, they embed small gravel chips into the surface. They then wash any excess cement from the exposed chips with a mild acid solution. For color, they use colored premixed concrete. On concrete surfaces that will remain exposed after the forms are stripped, such as columns, ceilings, and wall panels, cement masons cut away high spots and loose concrete with hammer and chisel, fill any large indentations with a Portland cement paste, and smooth the surface with a carborundum stone. Finally, they coat the exposed area with a rich Portland cement mixture, using either a special tool or a coarse cloth to rub the concrete to a uniform finish.

Throughout the entire process, cement masons must monitor how the wind, heat, or cold affects the curing of the concrete. They must have a thorough knowledge of concrete characteristics so that, by using sight and touch, they can determine what is happening to the concrete and take measures to prevent defects.

Segmental pavers lay out, cut, and install pavers—flat pieces of masonry made from compacted concrete or brick. This masonry is typically installed in patios, sidewalks, plazas, streets, crosswalks, parking lots, and driveways. Installers usually begin their work on a previously prepared base that has been graded to the proper depth, although some projects may include the base preparation. A typical segmental paver installation begins with leveling a layer of sand, followed by placement of the pavers, normally by hand but sometimes by machine. Usually the work includes constructing edges to prevent horizontal movement of the pavers. Sand is then added to fill the joints between the pavers.

Terrazzo workers create attractive walkways, floors, patios, and panels by exposing marble chips and other fine aggregates on the surface of finished concrete. Much of the preliminary work of terrazzo workers is similar to that of cement masons. There are six different types of terrazzo, but the focus of this description is on the most common standard terrazzo: Marble-chip terrazzo, which requires three layers of materials. First, cement masons or terrazzo workers build a solid, level concrete foundation that is 3 to 4 inches deep. Second, after the forms are removed from the foundation, workers add a 1-inch layer of sandy concrete. Terrazzo workers partially embed, or attach with adhesive, metal divider strips in the concrete wherever there is to be a joint or change of color in the terrazzo. For the third and final layer, terrazzo workers blend and place into each of the panels a fine marble chip mixture that may be color-pigmented. While the mixture is still wet, workers add additional marble chips of various colors into each panel and roll a light-weight roller over the entire surface.

When the terrazzo is thoroughly set, helpers grind it with a terrazzo grinder, which is somewhat like a floor polisher, only much heavier. Any depressions left by the grinding are filled with a matching grout material and hand-troweled for a smooth, uniform surface. Terrazzo workers then clean, polish, and seal the dry surface for a lustrous finish.

Work environment. Concrete, segmental paving, or terrazzo work is fast-paced and strenuous, and requires continuous physical effort. Because most finishing is done at floor level, workers must bend and kneel often. Many jobs are outdoors, and work is generally halted during inclement weather. The work, either indoors or outdoors, may be in areas that are muddy, dusty, or dirty. To avoid chemical burns from uncured concrete and sore knees from frequent kneeling, many workers wear kneepads. Workers usually also wear water-repellent boots while working in wet concrete.

Most workers work 40 hours a week, although the number of hours can be increased or decreased by outside factors. Earnings for workers in these trades can be reduced on occasion because poor weather and slowdowns in construction activity limit the time they can work.

Training, Other Qualifications, and Advancement

Most cement masons, concrete finishers, segmental pavers, and terrazzo workers learn their trades through on-the-job training, either as helpers or in apprenticeship programs. Some workers also learn their jobs by attending trade or vocational-technical schools.

Education and training. Many masons and finishers first gain experience as construction laborers. (See the section on construction laborers elsewhere in the *Handbook*.) Most on-the-job training programs consist of informal instruction, in which experienced workers teach helpers to use the tools, equipment, machines, and materials of the trade. Trainees begin with tasks such as edging, jointing, and using a straightedge on freshly placed concrete. As training progresses, assignments become more complex, and trainees can usually do finishing work within a short time.

Other workers train in formal apprenticeship programs usually sponsored by local contractors, trade associations, or local union-management committees. These earn while you learn programs provide on-the-job training and the recommended minimum of 144 hours of classroom instruction each year. In the classroom, apprentices learn applied mathematics, blueprint reading, and safety. Apprentices generally receive special instruction in layout work and cost estimation. Apprenticeships may take 3 to 4 years to complete. Applying for an apprenticeship may require a written test and a physical exam.

Many States have technical schools that offer courses in masonry which improve employment and advancement opportunities. Entrance requirements and fees vary depending on the school and who is funding the program. These schools may offer courses before hiring or after hiring as part of the on-the-job training.

Other qualifications. The most important quality employers look for is dependability and a strong work ethic. When hiring helpers and apprentices, employers prefer high school graduates who are at least 18 years old, possess a driver's license, and are in good physical condition. The ability to get along with others is also important because cement masons frequently work in teams. High school courses in general science, mathematics, and vocational-technical subjects, such as blueprint reading and mechanical drawing provide a helpful background. Cement masons, concrete finishers, segmental pavers, and terrazzo workers should enjoy doing demanding work. They should take pride in craftsmanship and be able to work without close supervision.

Advancement. With additional training, cement masons, concrete finishers, segmental pavers, or terrazzo workers may become supervisors for masonry contractors or move into construction management, building inspection, or contract estimation. Some eventually become owners of businesses, where they may spend most of their time managing rather than practicing their original trade. For those who want to own their own business, taking business classes will help them prepare.

Employment

Cement masons, concrete finishers, segmental pavers, and terrazzo workers held about 229,000 jobs in 2006; segmental pavers and terrazzo workers accounted for only a small portion of the total. Most cement masons and concrete finishers worked

Projections data from the National Employment Matrix

Occupational Title	SOC Code	Employment, 2006	Projected employment, 2016	Change, 2006-16	
				Number	Percent
Cement masons, concrete finishers, segmental pavers, and terrazzo workers..	—	229,000	255,000	26,000	11
Cement masons, concrete finishers, and terrazzo workers.............	47-2050	228,000	254,000	26,000	11
Cement masons and concrete finishers	47-2051	222,000	247,000	25,000	11
Terrazzo workers and finishers	47-2053	6,800	7,500	700	11
Segmental pavers	47-4091	1,000	1,100	100	10

NOTE: Data in this table are rounded. See the discussion of the employment projections table in the *Handbook* introductory chapter on *Occupational Information Included in the Handbook.*

for specialty trade contractors, primarily foundation, structure, and building exterior contractors. They also worked for contractors in residential and nonresidential building construction and in heavy and civil engineering construction on projects such as highways; bridges; shopping malls; or large buildings such as factories, schools, and hospitals. A small number were employed by firms that manufacture concrete products. Most segmental pavers and terrazzo workers worked for specialty trade contractors who install decorative floors and wall panels.

Only about 2 percent of cement masons, concrete finishers, segmental pavers, and terrazzo workers were self-employed, a smaller proportion than in other building trades. Most self-employed masons specialized in small jobs, such as driveways, sidewalks, and patios.

Job Outlook

Average employment growth is expected, and job prospects are expected to be good, especially for those with the most experience and skills.

Employment change. Employment of cement masons, concrete finishers, segmental pavers, and terrazzo workers is expected to grow 11 percent over the 2006-16 decade, about as fast as the average for all occupations. More workers will be needed to build new highways, bridges, factories, and other residential and nonresidential structures to meet the demands of a growing population. Additionally, cement masons will be needed to repair and renovate existing highways and bridges and other aging structures.

The use of concrete for buildings is increasing. For example, residential construction in Florida is using more concrete as building requirements are changed in reaction to the increased frequency and intensity of hurricanes. Concrete use is likely to expand into other hurricane-prone areas as the durability of the Florida homes are demonstrated.

Job prospects. Opportunities for cement masons, concrete finishers, segmental pavers, and terrazzo workers are expected to be good, particularly for those with the most experience and skills. Employers report difficulty in finding workers with the right skills, as many qualified jobseekers often prefer work that is less strenuous and has more comfortable working conditions. There are expected to be a significant number of retirements over the next decade, which will create more job openings. Applicants who take masonry-related courses at technical schools will have better opportunities than those without these courses.

Employment of cement masons, concrete finishers, segmental pavers, and terrazzo workers, like that of many other construction workers, is sensitive to the fluctuations of the economy. Workers in these trades may experience periods of unemployment when the overall level of construction falls. On the other hand, shortages of these workers may occur in some areas during peak periods of building activity.

Earnings

In May 2006, the median hourly earnings of wage and salary cement masons and concrete finishers were $15.70. The middle 50 percent earned between $12.38 and $20.70. The bottom 10 percent earned less than $10.02, and the top 10 percent earned more than $27.07. Median hourly earnings in the industries

employing the largest numbers of cement masons and concrete finishers were as follows:

Masonry contractors..$17.05
Nonresidential building construction......................................16.34
Highway, street, and bridge construction...............................16.20
Other specialty trade contractors 16.15
Poured concrete foundation and structure contractors............15.38

In May 2006, the median hourly earnings of wage and salary terrazzo workers and finishers were $15.21. The middle 50 percent earned between $12.01 and $20.50. The bottom 10 percent earned less than $9.31, and the top 10 percent earned more than $27.22.

In May 2006, the median hourly earnings of wage and salary segmental pavers were $13.80. The middle 50 percent earned between $10.47 and $17.05. The bottom 10 percent earned less than $8.41, and the top 10 percent earned more than $19.11.

Like other construction trades workers, earnings of cement masons, concrete finishers, segmental pavers, and terrazzo workers may be reduced on occasion because poor weather and slowdowns in construction activity limit the amount of time they can work. Nonunion workers generally have lower wage rates than union workers. Apprentices usually start at 50 to 60 percent of the rate paid to experienced workers, and increases are generally achieved by meeting specified advancement requirements every 6 months. Cement masons often work overtime, with premium pay, because once concrete has been placed, the job must be completed.

Some cement masons, concrete finishers, segmental pavers, and terrazzo workers belong to unions, mainly the Operative Plasterers' and Cement Masons' International Association of the United States and Canada, and the International Union of Bricklayers and Allied Craftworkers. A few terrazzo workers belong to the United Brotherhood of Carpenters and Joiners of the United States.

Related Occupations

Cement masons, concrete finishers, segmental pavers, and terrazzo workers combine skill with knowledge of building materials to construct buildings, highways, and other structures. Other occupations involving similar skills and knowledge include brickmasons, blockmasons, and stonemasons; carpet, floor, and tile installers and finishers; drywall installers, ceiling tile installers, and tapers; and plasterers and stucco masons.

Sources of Additional Information

For information about apprenticeships and work opportunities, contact local concrete or terrazzo contractors, locals of unions previously mentioned, a local joint union-management apprenticeship committee, or the nearest office of the State employment service or apprenticeship agency. Apprenticeship information is also available from the U.S. Department of Labor's toll free helpline: (877) 872-5627. You may also check the U.S. Department of Labor's Web site for information on apprenticeships and links to State apprenticeship programs. Internet: **http://www.doleta.gov/atels_bat**

For general information about cement masons, concrete finishers, segmental pavers, and terrazzo workers, contact:

➤ Associated Builders and Contractors, Workforce Development Division, 4250 North Fairfax Dr., 9th Floor, Arlington, VA 22203. Internet: **http://www.trytools.org**

➤ Associated General Contractors of America, Inc., 2300 Wilson Blvd., Suite 400, Arlington, VA 22201.

Internet: **http://www.agc.org**

➤ International Union of Bricklayers and Allied Craftworkers, International Masonry Institute, The James Brice House, 42 East St., Annapolis, MD 21401. Internet: **http://www.imiweb.org**

➤ National Center for Construction Education and Research, 3600 NW., 43rd St., Bldg. G, Gainesville, FL 32606.

Internet: **http://www.nccer.org**

➤ National Concrete Masonry Association, 13750 Sunrise Valley Dr., Herndon, VA 20171-3499.

Internet: **http://www.ncma.org**

➤ National Terrazzo and Mosaic Association, 201 North Maple, Suite 208, Purcellville, VA 20132.

➤ Operative Plasterers' and Cement Masons' International Association of the United States and Canada, 11720 Beltsville Dr., Suite 700, Beltsville, MD 20705.

Internet: **http://www.opcmia.org**

➤ Portland Cement Association, 5420 Old Orchard Rd., Skokie, IL 60077. Internet: **http://www.cement.org**

➤ United Brotherhood of Carpenters and Joiners, 50 F St.NW., Washington, DC 20001. Internet: **http://www.carpenters.org**

For more information about careers and training as a mason, contact:

➤ Mason Contractors Association of America, 33 South Roselle Rd., Schaumburg, IL 60193.

Internet: **http://www.masoncontractors.org**

For general information on apprenticeships and how to get them, see the *Occupational Outlook Quarterly* article "Apprenticeships: Career training, credentials—and a paycheck in your pocket," online at **http://www.bls.gov/opub/ooq/2002/summer/art01.pdf** and in print at many libraries and career centers.

Construction and Building Inspectors

(O*NET 47-4011.00)

Significant Points

- About 41 percent of inspectors worked for local governments, primarily municipal or county building departments.

- Many home inspectors are self-employed.

- Opportunities should be best for experienced construction supervisors and craftworkers who have some college education, engineering or architectural training, or certification as construction inspectors or plan examiners.

Nature of the Work

Construction and building inspectors examine buildings, highways and streets, sewer and water systems, dams, bridges, and other structures. They ensure that their construction, alteration, or repair complies with building codes and ordinances, zoning regulations, and contract specifications. Building codes and standards are the primary means by which building construction is regulated in the United States for the health and safety of the general public. National model building and construction codes are published by the International Code Council (ICC), although many localities have additional ordinances and codes that modify or add to the National model codes. To monitor compliance with regulations, inspectors make an initial inspection during the first phase of construction and follow up with further inspections throughout the construction project. However, no inspection is ever exactly the same. In areas where certain types of severe weather or natural disasters—such as earthquakes or hurricanes—are more common, inspectors monitor compliance with additional safety regulations designed to protect structures and occupants during those events.

There are many types of inspectors. *Building inspectors* inspect the structural quality and general safety of buildings. Some specialize in for example, structural steel or reinforced-concrete structures. Before construction begins, *plan examiners* determine whether the plans for the building or other structure comply with building codes and whether they are suited to the engineering and environmental demands of the building site. To inspect the condition of the soil and the positioning and depth of the footings, inspectors visit the worksite before the foundation is poured. Later, they return to the site to inspect the foundation after it has been completed. The size and type of structure, as well as the rate at which it proceeds toward completion, determine the number of other site visits they must make. Upon completion of the project, they make a final, comprehensive inspection.

In addition to structural characteristics, a primary concern of building inspectors is fire safety. They inspect structures' fire sprinklers, alarms, smoke control systems, and fire exits. Inspectors assess the type of construction, contents of the building, adequacy of fire protection equipment, and risks posed by adjoining buildings.

Electrical inspectors examine the installation of electrical systems and equipment to ensure that they function properly and comply with electrical codes and standards. They visit worksites to inspect new and existing sound and security systems, wiring, lighting, motors, and generating equipment. They also inspect the installation of the electrical wiring for heating and air-conditioning systems, appliances, and other components.

Elevator inspectors examine lifting and conveying devices such as elevators, escalators, moving sidewalks, lifts and hoists, inclined railways, ski lifts, and amusement rides.

For information on *Fire inspectors*, see the *Handbook* statement on *Fire fighting occupations*.

Home inspectors conduct inspections of newly built or previously owned homes, condominiums, town homes, manufactured homes, apartments, and at times commercial buildings. Home inspection has become a standard practice in the home-purchasing process. Home inspectors are most often hired by prospective home buyers to inspect and report on the condition of a home's systems, components, and structure. Although they look for and report violations of building codes, they do not

Construction and building inspectors must check building measurements against construction codes.

have the power to enforce compliance with the codes. Typically, they are hired either immediately prior to a purchase offer on a home or as a contingency to a sales contract. In addition to examining structural quality, home inspectors inspect all home systems and features, including roofing as well as the exterior, attached garage or carport, foundation, interior, plumbing, and electrical, heating, and cooling systems. Some home inspections are done for homeowners who want an evaluation of their home's condition, for example, prior to putting the home on the market or as a way to diagnose problems.

Mechanical inspectors inspect the installation of the mechanical components of commercial kitchen appliances, heating and air-conditioning equipment, gasoline and butane tanks, gas and oil piping, and gas-fired and oil-fired appliances. Some specialize in boilers or ventilating equipment as well.

Plumbing inspectors examine plumbing systems, including private disposal systems, water supply and distribution systems, plumbing fixtures and traps, and drain, waste, and vent lines.

Public works inspectors ensure that Federal, State, and local government construction of water and sewer systems, highways, streets, bridges, and dams conforms to detailed contract specifications. They inspect excavation and fill operations, the placement of forms for concrete, concrete mixing and pouring, asphalt paving, and grading operations. They record the work

and materials used so that contract payments can be calculated. Public works inspectors may specialize in highways, structural steel, reinforced concrete, or ditches. Others specialize in dredging operations required for bridges and dams or for harbors.

The owner of a building or structure under construction employs *specification inspectors* to ensure that work is done according to design specifications. Specification inspectors represent the owner's interests, not those of the general public. Insurance companies and financial institutions also may use their services.

Details concerning construction projects, building and occupancy permits, and other documentation generally are stored on computers so that they can easily be retrieved and updated. For example, inspectors may use laptop computers to record their findings while inspecting a site. Most inspectors use computers to help them monitor the status of construction inspection activities and keep track of permits issued, and some can access all construction and building codes from their computers on the jobsite, decreasing the need for paper binders. However, many inspectors continue to use a paper checklist to detail their findings.

Although inspections are primarily visual, inspectors may use tape measures, survey instruments, metering devices, and equipment such as concrete strength measurers. They keep a log of their work, take photographs, and file reports. Many inspectors also use laptops or other portable electronic devices onsite to facilitate the accuracy of their written reports, as well as e-mail and fax machines to send out the results. If necessary, they act on their findings. For example, government and construction inspectors notify the construction contractor, superintendent, or supervisor when they discover a violation of a code or ordinance or something that does not comply with the contract specifications or approved plans. If the problem is not corrected within a reasonable or otherwise specified period, government inspectors have authority to issue a "stop-work" order.

Many inspectors also investigate construction or alterations being done without proper permits. Inspectors who are employees of municipalities enforce laws pertaining to the proper design, construction, and use of buildings. They direct violators of permit laws to obtain permits and to submit to inspection.

Work environment. Construction and building inspectors usually work alone. However, several may be assigned to large, complex projects, particularly because inspectors tend to specialize in different areas of construction. Although they spend considerable time inspecting construction worksites, inspectors also spend time in a field office reviewing blueprints, answering letters or telephone calls, writing reports, and scheduling inspections.

Many construction sites are dirty and may be cluttered with tools, materials, or debris. Inspectors may have to climb ladders or many flights of stairs or crawl around in tight spaces. Although their work generally is not considered hazardous, inspectors, like other construction workers, wear hardhats and adhere to other safety requirements while at a construction site.

Inspectors normally work regular hours. However, they may work additional hours during periods when a lot of construction is taking place. Also, if an accident occurs at a construction site, inspectors must respond immediately and may work additional hours to complete their report. Non-government inspectors—especially those who are self-employed—may have a varied work schedule, at times working evenings and weekends.

Training, Other Qualifications, and Advancement

Although requirements vary considerably, construction and building inspectors should have a thorough knowledge of construction materials and practices. In some States, construction and building inspectors are required to obtain a special license or certification, so it is important to check with the appropriate State agency.

Education and training. Most employers require at least a high school diploma or the equivalent, even for workers with considerable experience. More often, employers look for persons who have studied engineering or architecture or who have a degree from a community or junior college with courses in building inspection, home inspection, construction technology, drafting, and mathematics. Many community colleges offer certificate or associate degree programs in building inspection technology. Courses in blueprint reading, algebra, geometry, and English also are useful. A growing number of construction and building inspectors are entering the occupation with a college degree, which often can substitute for previous experience. The distribution of all construction and building inspectors by their highest level of educational attainment in 2006 was:

	Percent
High school graduate or less	31
Some college, no degree	28
Associate's degree	12
Bachelor's degree	26
Graduate degree	2

The level of training requirements varies by type of inspector and State. In general, construction and building inspectors receive much of their training on the job, although they must learn building codes and standards on their own. Working with an experienced inspector, they learn about inspection techniques; codes, ordinances, and regulations; contract specifications; and recordkeeping and reporting duties. Supervised onsite inspections also may be a part of the training. Other requirements can include various courses and assigned reading. Some courses and instructional material are available online as well as through formal venues.

Licensure and certification. Many States and local jurisdictions require some type of license or certification for employment as a construction and building inspector. Requirements may vary by State or local municipality. Typical requirements for licensure or certification include previous experience, a minimum educational attainment level, such as a high school diploma, and possibly the passing of a State-approved examination. Some States have individual licensing programs for inspectors, while others may require certification by such associations as the International Code Council, International Association of Plumbing and Mechanical Officials, and National Fire Protection Association.

Similarly, some States require home inspectors to obtain a State issued license or certification. Currently, 33 States have regulations affecting home inspectors. Requirements for a license or certification vary by State, but may include obtaining a minimum level of education, having a set amount of experience with inspections, purchasing liability insurance of a certain amount, and the passing of an examination. Renewal is usually every few years and annual continuing education is almost always required.

Other qualifications. Because inspectors must possess the right mix of technical knowledge, experience, and education, employers prefer applicants who have both formal training and experience. For example, many inspectors previously worked as carpenters, electricians, or plumbers. Home inspectors combine knowledge of multiple specialties, so many of them come into the occupation having a combination of certifications and previous experience in various construction trades.

Construction and building inspectors must be in good physical condition in order to walk and climb about construction and building sites. They also must have a driver's license so that they can get to scheduled appointments.

Advancement. Being a member of a nationally recognized inspection association enhances employment opportunities and may be required by some employers. Even if it is not required, certification can enhance an inspector's opportunities for employment and advancement to more responsible positions. To become certified, inspectors with substantial experience and education must pass examinations on topics including code requirements, construction techniques and materials, standards of practice, and codes of ethics. The International Code Council offers multiple voluntary certifications, as do many other professional associations. Many categories of certification are awarded for inspectors and plan examiners in a variety of specialties, including the Certified Building Official (CBO) certification, for code compliance, and the Residential Building Inspector (RBI) certification, for home inspectors. In a few cases, there are no education or experience prerequisites, and certification consists of passing an examination in a designated field either at a regional location or online. In addition, Federal,

Projections data from the National Employment Matrix

Occupational Title	SOC Code	Employment, 2006	Projected employment, 2016	Change, 2006-16	
				Number	Percent
Construction and building inspectors	47-4011	110,000	130,000	20,000	18

NOTE: Data in this table are rounded. See the discussion of the employment projections table in the *Handbook* introductory chapter on *Occupational Information Included in the Handbook.*

State, and many local governments may require inspectors to pass a civil service exam.

Because they advise builders and the general public on building codes, construction practices, and technical developments, construction and building inspectors must keep abreast of changes in these areas. Continuing education is required by many States and certifying organizations. Numerous employers provide formal training to broaden inspectors' knowledge of construction materials, practices, and techniques. Inspectors who work for small agencies or firms that do not conduct their own training programs can expand their knowledge and upgrade their skills by attending State-sponsored training programs, by taking college or correspondence courses, or by attending seminars and conferences sponsored by various related organizations, including professional organizations. An engineering or architectural degree often is required for advancement to supervisory positions.

Employment

Construction and building inspectors held about 110,000 jobs in 2006. Local governments—primarily municipal or county building departments—employed 41 percent. Employment of local government inspectors is concentrated in cities and in suburban areas undergoing rapid growth. Local governments in larger jurisdictions may employ large inspection staffs, including many plan examiners or inspectors who specialize in structural steel, reinforced concrete, and boiler, electrical, and elevator inspection. In smaller jurisdictions, only one or a few inspectors who specialize in multiple areas may be on staff.

Another 26 percent of construction and building inspectors worked for architectural and engineering services firms, conducting inspections for a fee or on a contract basis. Many of these were home inspectors working on behalf of potential real estate purchasers. Most of the remaining inspectors were employed in other service-providing industries or by State governments. About 1 in 10 construction and building inspectors was self-employed. Since many home inspectors are self-employed, it is likely that most self-employed construction and building inspectors were home inspectors.

Job Outlook

Job opportunities in construction and building inspection should be best for highly experienced supervisors and construction craft workers who have some college education, engineering or architectural training, or certification as inspectors or plan examiners. Inspectors should experience faster than average employment growth.

Employment change. Employment of construction and building inspectors is expected to grow by 18 percent over the 2006-2016 decade, which is faster than the average for all occupations. Concern for public safety and a desire for improvement in the quality of construction should continue to stimulate demand for construction and building inspectors in government as well as in firms specializing in architectural, engineering, and related services. As the result of new technology such as building information modeling (BIM), the availability of a richer set of buildings data in a more timely and transparent manner will make it easier to conduct plan reviews. This will lead to more time and resources spent on inspections. In addition, the

growing focus on natural and manmade disasters is increasing the level of interest in and need for qualified inspectors. Issues such as green and sustainable design are new areas of focus that will also drive the demand for construction and building inspectors.

The routine practice of obtaining home inspections is a relatively recent development, causing employment of home inspectors to increase rapidly. Although employment of home inspectors is expected to continue to increase, the attention given to this specialty, combined with the desire of some construction workers to move into less strenuous and potentially higher paying work, may result in reduced growth of home inspectors in some areas. In addition, increasing State regulations are starting to limit entry into the specialty only to those who have a given level of previous experience and are certified.

Job prospects. Inspectors are involved in all phases of construction, including maintenance and repair work, and are therefore less likely to lose their jobs when new construction slows during recessions. Those who are self-employed, such as home inspectors, are more likely to be affected by economic downturns or fluctuations in the real estate market. However, those with a thorough knowledge of construction practices and skills in areas such as reading and evaluating blueprints and plans will be better off. Inspectors with previous related experience in construction, a postsecondary degree, and engineering or architectural training will have the best prospects. In addition to openings stemming from the expected employment growth, some job openings will arise from the need to replace inspectors who transfer to other occupations or leave the labor force.

Earnings

Median annual earnings of wage and salary construction and building inspectors were $46,570 in May 2006. The middle 50 percent earned between $36,610 and $58,780. The lowest 10 percent earned less than $29,210, and the highest 10 percent earned more than $72,590. Median annual earnings in the industries employing the largest numbers of construction and building inspectors were:

Architectural, engineering, and related services	$46,850
Local government	46,040
State government	43,680

Building inspectors, including plan examiners, generally earn the highest salaries. Salaries in large metropolitan areas are substantially higher than those in small jurisdictions.

Benefits vary by place of employment. Those working for the government and private companies typically receive standard benefits, including health and medical insurance, a retirement plan, and paid annual leave. Those who are self-employed may have to provide their own benefits.

More than a quarter of all construction and building inspectors belonged to a union in 2006.

Related Occupations

Because construction and building inspectors are familiar with construction principles, the most closely related occupations are construction occupations, especially carpenters, plumbers, and electricians. Construction and building inspectors also combine knowledge of construction principles and law with an ability to coordinate data, diagnose problems, and communicate with people. Workers in other occupations using a similar combination of skills include architects, except landscape and naval; appraisers and assessors of real estate; construction managers; civil engineers; cost estimators; engineering technicians; and surveyors, cartographers, photogrammetrists, and surveying technicians.

Sources of Additional Information

Information about building codes, certification, and a career as a construction or building inspector is available from:

➤ International Code Council, 500 New Jersey Avenue, NW., 6th Floor, Washington, DC 20001-2070.
Internet: **http://www.iccsafe.org**

➤ National Fire Protection Association, 1 Batterymarch Park, Quincy, Massachusetts, 02169-7471.
Internet: **http://www.nfpa.org**

For more information about construction inspectors, contact:

➤ Association of Construction Inspectors, 1224 North Nokomis NE., Alexandria, MN 56308.

For more information about electrical inspectors, contact:

➤ International Association of Electrical Inspectors, 901 Waterfall Way, Suite 602, Richardson, TX 75080-7702. Internet: **http://www.iaei.org**

For more information about elevator inspectors, contact:

➤ National Association of Elevator Safety Authorities International, 6957 Littlerock Rd SW., Ste A, Tumwater, WA 98512. Internet: **http://www.naesai.org**

For more information about education and training for mechanical and plumbing inspectors, contact:

➤ International Association for Plumbing and Mechanical Officials, 5001 E. Philadelphia St., Ontario, CA 91761.
Internet: **http://www.iapmo.org/iapmo**

For information about becoming a home inspector, contact any of the following organizations:

➤ American Society of Home Inspectors, 932 Lee St., Suite 101, Des Plaines, IL 60016. Internet: **http://www.ashi.org**

➤ National Association of Home Inspectors, 4248 Park Glen Rd., Minneapolis, MN 55416. Internet: **http://www.nahi.org**

For information about a career as a State or local government construction or building inspector, contact your State or local employment service.

Construction Equipment Operators

(O*NET 47-2071.00, 47-2072.00, 47-2073.00)

Significant Points

- Many construction equipment operators acquire their skills on the job, but formal apprenticeship programs provide more comprehensive training.

- Job opportunities are expected to be very good.

- Hourly pay is relatively high, but operators of some types of equipment cannot work in inclement weather, so total annual earnings may be reduced.

Nature of the Work

Construction equipment operators use machinery to move construction materials, earth, and other heavy materials at construction sites and mines. They operate equipment that clears and grades land to prepare it for construction of roads, buildings, and bridges. They use machines to dig trenches to lay or repair sewer and other pipelines and hoist heavy construction materials. They may even work offshore constructing oil rigs. Construction equipment operators also operate machinery that spreads asphalt and concrete on roads and other structures.

These workers also set up and inspect the equipment, make adjustments, and perform some maintenance and minor repairs. Construction equipment operators control equipment by moving levers, foot pedals, operating switches, or joysticks. Construction equipment is more complicated to use than it was in the past. For example, Global Positioning System (GPS) technology is now being used to help with grading and leveling activities.

Included in the construction equipment operator occupation are paving, surfacing, and tamping equipment operators; piledriver operators; and operating engineers. *Paving and surfacing equipment operators* use levers and other controls to operate machines that spread and level asphalt or spread and smooth concrete for roadways or other structures. *Asphalt paving machine operators* turn valves to regulate the temperature and flow of asphalt onto the roadbed. They must take care that the machine distributes the paving material evenly and without voids, and make sure that there is a constant flow of asphalt going into the hopper. *Concrete paving machine operators* control levers and turn handwheels to move attachments that spread, vibrate, and level wet concrete in forms. They must observe the surface of concrete to identify low spots into which workers must add concrete. They use other attachments to smooth the surface of the concrete, spray on a curing compound, and cut expansion joints. *Tamping equipment operators* operate tamping machines that compact earth and other fill materials for roadbeds or other construction sites. They also may operate machines with interchangeable hammers to cut or break up old pavement and drive guardrail posts into the earth.

Piledriver operators use large machines to hammer piles into the ground.

Piledriver operators use large machines, mounted on skids, barges, or cranes to hammer piles into the ground. Piles are long heavy beams of wood or steel driven into the ground to support retaining walls, bulkheads, bridges, piers, or building foundations. Some piledriver operators work on offshore oil rigs. Piledriver operators move hand and foot levers and turn valves to activate, position, and control the pile-driving equipment.

Operating engineers and other construction equipment operators use one or several types of power construction equipment. They may operate excavation and loading machines equipped with scoops, shovels, or buckets that dig sand, gravel, earth, or similar materials and load it into trucks or onto conveyors. In addition to the familiar bulldozers, they operate trench excavators, road graders, and similar equipment. Sometimes, they may drive and control industrial trucks or tractors equipped with forklifts or booms for lifting materials or with hitches for pulling trailers. They also may operate and maintain air compressors, pumps, and other power equipment at construction sites. Construction equipment operators who are classified as operating engineers are capable of operating several different types of construction equipment.

Work environment. Construction equipment operators work outdoors, in nearly every type of climate and weather condition, although in many areas of the country, some types of construction operations must be suspended in winter. Bulldozers, scrapers, and especially tampers and piledrivers are noisy and shake or jolt the operator. Operating heavy construction equipment can be dangerous. As with most machinery, accidents generally can be avoided by observing proper operating procedures and safety practices. Construction equipment operators are cold in the winter and hot in the summer and often get dirty, greasy, muddy, or dusty. Some operators work in remote locations on large construction projects, such as highways and dams, or in factory or mining operations.

Operators may have irregular hours because work on some construction projects continues around the clock or must be performed late at night or early in the morning.

Training, Other Qualifications, and Advancement

Construction equipment operators usually learn their skills on the job, but formal apprenticeship programs provide more comprehensive training.

Education and training. Employers of construction equipment operators generally prefer to hire high school graduates, although some employers may train non-graduates to operate some types of equipment. High school courses in automobile mechanics are helpful because workers may perform maintenance on their machines. Also useful are courses in science and mechanical drawing.

On the job, workers may start by operating light equipment under the guidance of an experienced operator. Later, they may operate heavier equipment, such as bulldozers and cranes. Technologically advanced construction equipment with computerized controls and improved hydraulics and electronics requires more skill to operate. Operators of such equipment may need more training and some understanding of electronics.

It is generally accepted that formal training provides more comprehensive skills. Some construction equipment operators train in formal operating engineer apprenticeship programs administered by union-management committees of the International Union of Operating Engineers and the Associated General Contractors of America. Because apprentices learn to operate a wider variety of machines than do other beginners, they usually have better job opportunities. Apprenticeship programs consist of at least 3 years, or 6,000 hours, of paid on-the-job training together with and 144 hours of related classroom instruction each year.

Private vocational schools offer instruction in the operation of certain types of construction equipment. Completion of such programs may help a person get a job. However, people considering such training should check the school's reputation among employers in the area and find out if the school offers the opportunity to work on actual machines in realistic situations. A large amount of information can be learned in classrooms. But to become a skilled construction equipment operator, a worker needs to actually perform the various tasks. The best training facilities have equipment on-site so that students can do the tasks that they are learning about.

Licensure. Construction equipment operators often obtain a commercial driver's license so that they can haul their equipment to the various job sites. Commercial driver's licenses are issued by States according to each State's rules and regulations. (See the statement on truck drivers and driver/sales workers elsewhere in the *Handbook* for more information on commercial driver's licenses.)

Certification and other qualifications. Mechanical aptitude and experience operating related mobile equipment, such as farm tractors or heavy equipment, in the Armed Forces or elsewhere is an asset. Operators need to be in good physical condition and have a good sense of balance, the ability to judge distance, and eye-hand-foot coordination. Some operator positions require the ability to work at heights.

Certification or training in the right school will allow a worker to have opportunities across the country. While attending some vocational schools, operators are able to qualify for or attain various certifications. These certifications prove to potential employers that an operator is able to handle specific types of equipment. Certifications last from 3 to 5 years and must be renewed.

Advancement. Construction equipment operators can advance to become supervisors. Some operators choose to teach in training facilities to pass on their knowledge. Other operators start their own contracting businesses although this may be difficult because of high start-up costs.

Employment

Construction equipment operators held about 494,000 jobs in 2006. Jobs were found in every section of the country and were distributed among various types of operators as follows:

Operating engineers and other construction
   equipment operators..424,000
Paving, surfacing, and tamping equipment operators...........64,000
Pile-driver operators...5,600

About 63 percent of construction equipment operators worked in the construction industry. Many equipment operators worked in heavy construction, building highways, bridges, or railroads.

Projections data from the National Employment Matrix

Occupational Title	SOC Code	Employment, 2006	Projected employment, 2016	Change, 2006-16	
				Number	Percent
Construction equipment operators	47-2070	494,000	536,000	42,000	8
Paving, surfacing, and tamping equipment operators	47-2071	64,000	70,000	5,800	9
Pile-driver operators..	47-2072	5,600	6,000	500	8
Operating engineers and other construction equipment operators	47-2073	424,000	460,000	35,000	8

NOTE: Data in this table are rounded. See the discussion of the employment projections table in the *Handbook* introductory chapter on *Occupational Information Included in the Handbook.*

About 17 percent of construction equipment operators worked in State and local government. Others—mostly grader, bulldozer, and scraper operators—worked in mining. Some also worked for manufacturing or utility companies. About 5 percent of construction equipment operators were self-employed.

Job Outlook

Average job growth, reflecting increased demand for their services, and the need to replace workers who leave the occupation should result in very good job opportunities for construction equipment operators.

Employment change. Employment of construction equipment operators is expected to increase 8 percent between 2006 and 2016, about as fast as the average for all occupations. Even though improvements in equipment are expected to continue to raise worker productivity and to moderate the demand for new workers somewhat, employment is expected to increase because population and business growth will create a need for new houses, industrial facilities, schools, hospitals, offices, and other structures.

Specifically, more paving, surfacing, and tamping equipment operators will be needed as a result of expected growth in highway, bridge, and street construction. There has been consistent Congressional support for road projects. Bridge construction is expected to increase most because bridges will need to be repaired or replaced before they become unsafe. In some areas, deteriorating highway conditions also will spur demand for highway maintenance and repair.

More piledriver operators will be needed as construction continues to move into areas that are challenging to build in and require the use of piles as supports. Increases in bridge construction will also create demand for piledriver operators.

Demand for operating engineers and other construction equipment operators will be driven by the demand for new construction. Increases in pipeline construction will also create demand. These operators work in all sectors of construction.

Job prospects. Job opportunities for construction equipment operators are expected to be very good. Some potential workers may choose not to enter training programs because they prefer work that has more comfortable working conditions and is less seasonal in nature. This reluctance makes it easier for willing workers to get operator jobs.

In addition, many job openings will arise from job growth and from the need to replace experienced construction equipment operators who transfer to other occupations, retire, or leave the job for other reasons. Construction equipment operators who can use a large variety of equipment will have the best prospects. Operators with pipeline experience will have especially good opportunities.

Employment of construction equipment operators, like that of many other construction workers, is sensitive to the fluctuations in the economy. Workers in these trades may experience periods of unemployment when the overall level of construction falls. On the other hand, shortages of these workers may occur in some areas during peak periods of building activity.

Earnings

Earnings for construction equipment operators vary. In May 2006, median hourly earnings of wage and salary operating engineers and other construction equipment operators were $17.74. The middle 50 percent earned between $13.89 and $23.98. The lowest 10 percent earned less than $11.54, and the highest 10 percent earned more than $30.83. Median hourly earnings in the industries employing the largest numbers of operating engineers were:

Highway, street, and bridge construction.............................$19.88
Utility system construction 18.62
Other specialty trade contractors 18.00
Other heavy and civil engineering construction.....................17.63
Local government 15.95

Median hourly earnings of wage and salary paving, surfacing, and tamping equipment operators were $15.05 in May 2006. The middle 50 percent earned between $11.98 and $19.71. The lowest 10 percent earned less than $9.97, and the highest 10 percent earned more than $25.30. Median hourly earnings in the industries employing the largest numbers of paving, surfacing, and tamping equipment operators in were as follows:

Other specialty trade contractors $15.26
Highway, street, and bridge construction...............................15.11
Local government 14.86

In May 2006, median hourly earnings of wage and salary piledriver operators were $22.20. The middle 50 percent earned between $16.31 and $31.65. The lowest 10 percent earned less than $12.83, and the highest 10 percent earned more than $37.28. Median hourly earnings in the industries employing the largest numbers of pile driver operators were as follows:

Other heavy and civil engineering construction....................$28.60
Highway, street, and bridge construction...............................22.50
Other specialty trade contractors 20.60
Utility system construction 18.62

Hourly pay is relatively high, particularly in large metropolitan areas. However, annual earnings of some workers may be lower than hourly rates would indicate because work time may be limited by bad weather. About 28 percent of construction equipment operators belong to a union.

Related Occupations

Other workers who operate mechanical equipment include agricultural equipment operators; truck drivers, heavy and tractor trailer; logging equipment operators; and a variety of material moving occupations.

Sources of Additional Information

For further information about apprenticeships or work opportunities for construction equipment operators, contact a local of the International Union of Operating Engineers, a local apprenticeship committee, or the nearest office of the State apprenticeship agency or employment service. You can also find information on the registered apprenticeship system with links to State apprenticeship programs on the U.S. Department of Labor's Web site: **http://www.doleta.gov/atels_bat** Apprenticeship information is also available from the U.S. Department of Labor's toll free helpline: (877) 872-5627.

For general information about the work of construction equipment operators, contact:

➤ Associated General Contractors of America, 2300 Wilson Blvd., Suite 400, Arlington, VA 22201. Internet: **http://www.agc.org**
➤ International Union of Operating Engineers, 1125 17th St.NW., Washington, DC 20036. Internet: **http://www.iuoe.org**
➤ National Center for Construction Education and Research, P.O. Box 141104, Gainesville, FL 32614-1104. Internet: **http://www.nccer.org**
➤ Pile Driving Contractors Association, P.O. Box 66208, Orange Park, FL 32065. Internet: **http://www.piledrivers.org**

For general information on apprenticeships and how to get them, see the *Occupational Outlook Quarterly* article "Apprenticeships: Career training, credentials—and a paycheck in your pocket," online at **http://www.bls.gov/opub/ooq/2002/summer/art01.pdf** and in print at many libraries and career centers.

Construction Laborers

(O*NET 47-2061.00)

Significant Points

- Many construction laborer jobs require a variety of basic skills, but others require specialized training and experience.

- Most construction laborers learn on the job, but formal apprenticeship programs provide the most thorough preparation.

- Job opportunities vary by locality, but in many areas there will be competition, especially for jobs requiring limited skills.

- Laborers who have specialized skills or who can relocate near new construction projects should have the best opportunities.

Nature of the Work

Construction laborers can be found on almost all construction sites performing a wide range of tasks from the very easy to the potentially hazardous. They can be found at building, highway, and heavy construction sites; residential and commercial sites; tunnel and shaft excavations; and demolition sites. Many of the jobs they perform require physical strength, training, and experience. Other jobs require little skill and can be learned in a short amount of time. While most construction laborers specialize in a type of construction, such as highway or tunnel construction, some are generalists who perform many different tasks during all stages of construction. Construction laborers, who work in underground construction, such as in tunnels, or in demolition are more likely to specialize in only those areas.

Construction laborers clean and prepare construction sites. They remove trees and debris, tend pumps, compressors and generators, and build forms for pouring concrete. They erect and disassemble scaffolding and other temporary structures. They load, unload, identify, and distribute building materials to the appropriate location according to project plans and specifications. Laborers also tend machines; for example, they may mix concrete using a portable mixer or tend a machine that pumps concrete, grout, cement, sand, plaster, or stucco through a spray gun for application to ceilings and walls. They often help other craftworkers, including carpenters, plasterers, operating engineers, and masons.

Construction laborers are responsible for oversight of the installation and maintenance of traffic control devices and patterns. At highway construction sites, this work may include clearing and preparing highway work zones and rights of way; installing traffic barricades, cones, and markers; and controlling traffic passing near, in, and around work zones. They also dig trenches, install sewer, water, and storm drain pipes, and place concrete and asphalt on roads. Other highly specialized tasks include operating laser guidance equipment to place pipes; operating air, electric, and pneumatic drills; and transporting and setting explosives for tunnel, shaft, and road construction.

Some construction laborers help with the removal of hazardous materials, such as asbestos, lead, or chemicals. (Workers who specialize in and are certified for the removal of hazardous

Construction laborers remove excess materials after a job is completed.

materials are discussed in the *Handbook* statement on hazardous materials removal workers.)

Construction laborers operate a variety of equipment including pavement breakers; jackhammers; earth tampers; concrete, mortar, and plaster mixers; electric and hydraulic boring machines; torches; small mechanical hoists; laser beam equipment; and surveying and measuring equipment. They may use computers and other high-tech input devices to control robotic pipe cutters and cleaners. To perform their jobs effectively, construction laborers must be familiar with the duties of other craftworkers and with the materials, tools, and machinery they use.

Construction laborers often work as part of a team with other skilled craftworkers, jointly carrying out assigned construction tasks. At other times, construction laborers may work alone, reading and interpreting instructions, plans, and specifications with little or no supervision.

Work environment. Most laborers do physically demanding work. They may lift and carry heavy objects, and stoop, kneel, crouch, or crawl in awkward positions. Some work at great heights, or outdoors in all weather conditions. Some jobs expose workers to harmful materials or chemicals, fumes, odors, loud noise, or dangerous machinery. Some laborers may be exposed to lead-based paint, asbestos, or other hazardous substances during their work especially when working in confined spaces. To avoid injury, workers in these jobs wear safety clothing, such as gloves, hardhats, protective chemical suits, and devices to protect their eyes, respiratory system, or hearing. While working in underground construction, construction laborers must be especially alert to safely follow procedures and must deal with a variety of hazards.

Construction laborers generally work 8-hour shifts, although longer shifts are common. Overnight work may be required when working on highways. In some parts of the country, construction laborers may work only during certain seasons. They may also experience weather-related work stoppages at any time of the year.

Training, Other Qualifications, and Advancement

Many construction laborer jobs require a variety of basic skills, but others require specialized training and experience. Most construction laborers learn on the job, but formal apprenticeship programs provide the most thorough preparation.

Education and training. While some construction laborer jobs have no specific educational qualifications or entry-level training, apprenticeships for laborers require a high school diploma or equivalent. High school classes in English, mathematics, physics, mechanical drawing, blueprint reading, welding, and general shop can be helpful.

Most workers start by getting a job with a contractor who provides on-the-job training. Increasingly, construction laborers find work through temporary help agencies that send laborers to construction sites for short-term work. Entry-level workers generally help more experienced workers. They perform routine tasks, such as cleaning and preparing the worksite and unloading materials. When the opportunity arises, they learn from experienced construction trades workers how to do more difficult tasks, such as operating tools and equipment. Construction laborers may also choose or be required to attend a trade or vocational school or community college to receive further trade-related training.

Some laborers receive more formal training. A number of employers, particularly large nonresidential construction contractors with union membership, offer employees formal apprenticeships, which provide the best preparation. These programs include between 2 and 4 years of classroom and on-the-job training. In the first 200 hours, workers learn basic construction skills such as blueprint reading, the correct use of tools and equipment, and safety and health procedures. The remainder of the curriculum consists of specialized skills training in three of the largest segments of the construction industry: building construction, heavy and highway construction, and environmental remediation, such as lead or asbestos abatement, and mold or hazardous waste remediation.

Workers who use dangerous equipment or handle toxic chemicals usually receive specialized safety training. Laborers who remove hazardous materials are required to take union or employer-sponsored Occupational Safety and Health Administration safety training.

Apprenticeship applicants usually must be at least 18 years old and meet local requirements. Because the number of apprenticeship programs is limited, however, only a small proportion of laborers learn their trade in this way.

Other qualifications. Laborers need manual dexterity, eye-hand coordination, good physical fitness, a good sense of balance, and an ability to work as a member of a team. The ability to solve arithmetic problems quickly and accurately may be required. In addition, military service or a good work history is viewed favorably by contractors.

Certification and advancement. Laborers may earn certifications in welding, scaffold erecting, and concrete finishing. These certifications help workers prove that they have the knowledge to perform more complex tasks.

Through training and experience, laborers can move into other construction occupations. Laborers may also advance to become construction supervisors or general contractors. For those who would like to advance, it is increasingly important to be able to communicate in both English and Spanish in order to relay instructions and safety precautions to workers with limited understanding of English; Spanish-speaking workers make up a large part of the construction workforce in many areas. Supervisors and contractors need good communication skills to deal with clients and subcontractors.

In addition, supervisors and contractors should be able to identify and estimate the quantity of materials needed to complete a job, and accurately estimate how long a job will take to complete

Projections data from the National Employment Matrix

Occupational Title	SOC Code	Employment, 2006	Projected employment, 2016	Change, 2006-16	
				Number	Percent
Construction laborers..	47-2061	1,232,000	1,366,000	134,000	11

NOTE: Data in this table are rounded. See the discussion of the employment projections table in the *Handbook* introductory chapter on *Occupational Information Included in the Handbook.*

and what it will cost. Computer skills also are important for advancement as construction becomes increasingly mechanized and computerized.

Employment

Construction laborers held about 1.2 million jobs in 2006. They worked throughout the country but, like the general population, were concentrated in metropolitan areas. About 67 percent of construction laborers work in the construction industry, including 30 percent who work for specialty trade contractors. About 17 percent were self-employed in 2006.

Job Outlook

Employment is expected to grow about as fast as the average. In many areas, there will be competition for jobs, especially for those requiring limited skills. Laborers who have specialized skills or who can relocate near new construction projects should have the best opportunities.

Employment change. Employment of construction laborers is expected to grow by 11 percent between 2006 and 2016, about as fast as the average for all occupations. The construction industry in general is expected to grow more slowly than it has in recent years. Due to the large variety of tasks that laborers perform, demand for laborers will mirror the level of overall construction activity.

Construction laborer jobs will be adversely affected by automation as some jobs are replaced by new machinery and equipment that improves productivity and quality. Also, laborers will be increasingly employed by staffing agencies that will contract out laborers to employers on a temporary basis, and in many areas employers will continue to rely on day laborers instead of full-time laborers on staff.

Job prospects. In many geographic areas there will be competition, especially for jobs requiring limited skills, due to a plentiful supply of workers who are willing to work as day laborers. In other areas, however, opportunities will be better. Overall opportunities will be best for those with experience and specialized skills and for those who can relocate to areas with new construction projects. Opportunities will also be better for laborers specializing in road construction.

Employment of construction laborers, like that of many other construction workers, is sensitive to the fluctuations of the economy. Workers in these trades may experience periods of unemployment when the overall level of construction falls. On the other hand, shortages of these workers may occur in some areas during peak periods of building activity.

Earnings

Median hourly earnings of wage and salary construction laborers in May 2006 were $12.66. The middle 50 percent earned between $9.95 and $17.31. The lowest 10 percent earned less than $8.16, and the highest 10 percent earned more than $24.19. Median hourly earnings in the industries employing the largest number of construction laborers were as follows:

Nonresidential building construction	$13.62
Other specialty trade contractors	12.93
Residential building construction	12.82
Foundation, structure, and building exterior contractors	12.41
Employment services	9.90

Earnings for construction laborers can be reduced by poor weather or by downturns in construction activity, which sometimes result in layoffs. Apprentices or helpers usually start out earning about 60 percent of the wage rate paid to experienced workers. Pay increases as apprentices gain experience and learn new skills. Some laborers belong to the Laborers' International Union of North America.

Related Occupations

The work of construction laborers is closely related to other construction occupations. Other workers who perform similar physical work include persons in material moving occupations; forest, conservation, and logging workers; and grounds maintenance workers.

Sources of Additional Information

For information about jobs as a construction laborer, contact local building or construction contractors, local joint labor-management apprenticeship committees, apprenticeship agencies, or the local office of your State Employment Service. You can also find information on the registered apprenticeships together with links to State apprenticeship programs on the U.S. Department of Labor's Web site: **http://www.doleta.gov/atels_bat** Apprenticeship information is also available from the U.S. Department of Labor's toll-free helpline: (877) 872-5627. For general information on apprenticeships and how to get them, see the *Occupational Outlook Quarterly* article "Apprenticeships: Career training, credentials—and a paycheck in your pocket," online at **http://www.bls.gov/opub/ooq/2002/summer/art01.pdf** and in print at many libraries and career centers.

For information on education programs for laborers, contact:
➤ Laborers-AGC Education and Training Fund, 37 Deerfield Rd., P.O. Box 37, Pomfret Center, CT 06259.
Internet: **http://www.laborerslearn.org**
➤ National Center for Construction Education and Research, P.O. Box 141104, Gainesville, FL 32614-1104.
Internet: **http://www.nccer.org**

Drywall Installers, Ceiling Tile Installers, and Tapers

(O*NET 47-2081.00, 47-2082.00)

Significant Points

- Most workers learn this trade on the job by starting as helpers to more experienced workers; additional classroom instruction may also be needed.

- Job prospects are expected to be good.

- Inclement weather seldom interrupts work, but workers may be idled when downturns in the economy slow construction activity.

Nature of the Work

Drywall consists of a thin layer of gypsum between two layers of heavy paper. It is used to make walls and ceilings in most buildings today because it is faster and cheaper to install than plaster.

There are two kinds of drywall workers—installers and tapers—although many workers do both types of work. *Installers,* also called *framers* or *hangers,* fasten drywall panels to the inside framework of houses and other buildings. *Tapers* or *finishers*, prepare these panels for painting by taping and finishing joints and imperfections. In addition to drywall workers, ceiling tile installers and lathers also help to build walls and ceilings.

Because drywall panels are manufactured in standard sizes—usually 4 feet by 8 or 12 feet—drywall installers must measure, cut, fit, and fasten them to the inside framework of buildings. Workers cut smaller pieces to go around doors and windows. Installers saw, drill, or cut holes in panels for electrical outlets, air-conditioning units, and plumbing. After making these alterations, installers may glue, nail, or screw the wallboard panels to the wood or metal framework, called studs. Because drywall is heavy and cumbersome, another worker usually helps the installer to position and secure the panel. Installers often use a lift when placing ceiling panels.

After the drywall is installed, tapers fill joints between panels with a joint compound, also called spackle or "mud." Using the wide, flat tip of a special trowel, they spread the compound into and along each side of the joint with brush-like strokes. They immediately use the trowel to press a paper tape—used to reinforce the drywall and to hide imperfections—into the wet compound and to smooth away excess material. Nail and screw depressions also are covered with this compound, as are imperfections caused by the installation of air-conditioning vents and other fixtures. On large projects, finishers may use automatic taping tools that apply the joint compound and tape in one step. Using increasingly wider trowels, tapers apply second and third coats of the compound, sanding the treated areas after each coat to make them as smooth as the rest of the wall surface. This results in a seamless and almost perfect surface. For hard to reach heights and ceilings, sanding poles are commonly used. Some tapers apply textured surfaces to walls and ceilings with trowels, brushes, or spray guns.

Ceiling tile installers, or *acoustical carpenters*, apply or mount acoustical tiles or blocks, strips, or sheets of shock-absorbing materials to ceilings and walls of buildings to reduce reflection of sound or to decorate rooms. First, they measure and mark the surface according to blueprints and drawings. Then, they nail or screw moldings to the wall to support and seal the joint between the ceiling tile and the wall. Finally, they mount the tile, either by applying a cement adhesive to the back of the tile and then pressing the tile into place, or by nailing, screwing, stapling, or wire-tying the lath directly to the structural framework.

Making walls out of plaster requires the work of lathers. *Lathers* apply the support base for plaster coatings, fireproofing, or acoustical materials. This support base, called lath, is put on walls, ceilings, ornamental frameworks, and partitions of buildings before plaster and other coatings are added. Lathers use handtools and portable power tools, to nail, screw, staple, or wire-tie the lath directly to the structural framework of a building. At one time, lath was made of wooden strips, but now, it is usually made of wire, metal mesh, or gypsum, also known as rockboard. Metal lath is used when the plaster on top of it will be exposed to weather or water or when a surface is curved or irregular and not suitable for drywall.

Work environment. As in many other construction trades, this work is sometimes physically strenuous. Drywall installers, ceiling tile installers, lathers, and tapers spend most of the day on their feet, either standing, bending, stretching, or kneeling. Some tapers use stilts to tape and finish ceiling and angle joints. Installers have to lift and maneuver heavy, cumbersome drywall panels. Hazards include falls from ladders and scaffolds and injuries from power tools and from working with sharp tools, such as utility knives. Because sanding a joint compound to a smooth finish creates a great deal of dust, most finishers wear masks and goggles for protection.

A 40-hour week is standard, but the workweeks often fluctuate depending on the workload. Workers who are paid hourly rates receive premium pay for overtime.

Training, Other Qualifications, and Advancement

Drywall installers, ceiling tile installers, and tapers learn their trade through formal and informal training programs. It can take 3 to 4 years of both classroom and paid on-the-job training to become a fully skilled worker, but many skills can be learned within the first year. In general, the more formal the training process, the more skilled the individual becomes, and the more in demand by employers.

Education and training. Training for this profession can begin in a high school, where classes in English, math, mechanical drawing, blueprint reading, and general shop are recommended. The most common way to get a first job is to find an employer who will provide on-the-job training. Entry-level workers generally start as helpers, assisting more experienced workers. Employers may also send new employees to a trade or vocational school or community college to receive classroom training.

Some employers, particularly large nonresidential construction contractors with union membership, offer employees formal apprenticeships. These programs combine on-the-job training with related classroom instruction—at least 144 hours of instruction each year. The length of the apprenticeship program, usually 3 to 4 years, varies with the apprentice's skill. Because the number of apprenticeship programs is limited, however, only a small proportion of drywall installers, ceiling tile installers, and tapers learn their trade this way.

Most beginners learn this trade on the job by helping experienced workers.

Helpers and apprentices start by carrying materials, lifting and holding panels, and cleaning up debris. They also learn to use the tools, machines, equipment, and materials of the trade. Within a few weeks, they learn to measure, cut, and install materials. Eventually, they become fully experienced workers. Tapers learn their job by taping joints and touching up nail holes, scrapes, and other imperfections. They soon learn to install corner guards and to conceal openings around pipes. At the end of their training, drywall installers, ceiling tile installers, and tapers learn to estimate the cost of installing and finishing drywall.

Other jobseekers may choose to obtain their classroom training before seeking a job. There are a number of vocational-technical schools and training academies affiliated with the unions and contractors that offer training in these occupations. Employers often look favorably upon graduates of these training programs and usually start them at a higher level than those without the training.

Other qualifications. Some skills needed to become a drywall installer, ceiling tile installer, and taper include manual dexterity, eye-hand coordination, good physical fitness, and a good sense of balance. The ability to solve basic arithmetic problems quickly and accurately also is required. In addition, a good work history or military service is viewed favorably by contractors.

Supervisors and contractors need good English skills in order to deal with clients and subcontractors. They also should be able to identify and estimate the quantity of materials needed to complete a job, and accurately estimate how long a job will take to complete and at what cost.

Apprentices usually must be at least 18 years old and have a high school diploma or GED. Those who complete apprenticeships registered with the Federal or State Government receive a journey worker certificate, recognized Nationwide.

Advancement. Drywall installers, ceiling tile installers, and tapers may advance to carpentry supervisor or general construction supervisor positions. Others may become independent contractors. For those who would like to advance, it is increasingly important to be able to communicate in both English and Spanish in order to relay instructions and safety precautions to workers with limited understanding of English because Spanish-speaking workers make up a large part of the construction workforce in many areas. Knowing English well also makes it easier to advance.

Employment

Drywall installers, ceiling tile installers, and tapers held about 240,000 jobs in 2006. Most worked for contractors specializing in drywall and ceiling tile installation; others worked for contractors doing many kinds of construction. About 56,000 were self-employed independent contractors.

Most installers and tapers are employed in populous areas. In other areas, where there may not be enough work to keep a drywall or ceiling tile installer employed full time, carpenters and painters usually do the work.

Job Outlook

Employment is expected to increase about as fast as the average for all occupations, largely reflecting overall growth of the construction industry. Good job prospects are expected overall.

Employment change. Employment is expected to grow by 7 percent between 2006 and 2016, about as fast as the average for all occupations. Growth reflects the number of new construction and remodeling projects. New residential construction projects are expected to provide the majority of new jobs during the projection decade, but home improvement and renovation projects are also expected to create jobs because existing residential and nonresidential buildings are getting old and need repair.

Job prospects. Job opportunities for drywall installers, ceiling tile installers, and tapers are expected to be good. Many potential workers are not attracted to this occupation because they prefer work that is less strenuous and has more comfortable working conditions. Experienced workers will have especially favorable opportunities.

Besides those resulting from job growth, many jobs will open up each year because of the need to replace workers who transfer to other occupations or leave the labor force.

Despite the growing use of exterior panels, most drywall installation and finishing is done indoors. Therefore, drywall workers lose less work time because of inclement weather than do some other construction workers. Nevertheless, like many other construction workers, employment is sensitive to the fluctuations of the economy. Workers in these trades may experience periods of unemployment when the overall level of construction falls. On the other hand, shortages of these workers may occur in some areas during peak periods of building activity.

Earnings

In May 2006, the median hourly earnings of wage and salary drywall and ceiling tile installers were $17.38. The middle 50 percent earned between $13.60 and $22.58. The lowest 10 percent earned less than $10.90, and the highest 10 percent earned more than $28.85. The median hourly earnings in the industries employing the largest numbers of drywall and ceiling tile installers were as follows:

Foundation, structure, and building exterior contractors $18.10
Drywall and insulation contractors 17.42
Nonresidential building construction 17.26
Residential building construction...17.26

Projections data from the National Employment Matrix

Occupational Title	SOC Code	Employment, 2006	Projected employment, 2016	Change, 2006-16	
				Number	Percent
Drywall installers, ceiling tile installers, and tapers	47-2080	240,000	258,000	17,000	7
Drywall and ceiling tile installers	47-2081	186,000	199,000	14,000	7
Tapers..	47-2082	54,000	58,000	3,900	7

NOTE: Data in this table are rounded. See the discussion of the employment projections table in the *Handbook* introductory chapter on *Occupational Information Included in the Handbook.*

In May 2006, the median hourly earnings of wage and salary tapers were $19.85. The middle 50 percent earned between $14.65 and $25.70. The lowest 10 percent earned less than $11.59, and the highest 10 percent earned more than $31.23.

Some contractors pay these workers according to the number of panels they install or finish per day; others pay an hourly rate.

Trainees usually start at about half the rate paid to experienced workers and receive wage increases as they became more skilled.

Related Occupations

Drywall installers, ceiling tile installers, and tapers combine strength and dexterity with precision and accuracy to make materials fit according to a plan. Other occupations that require similar abilities include carpenters; carpet, floor, and tile installers and finishers; insulation workers; and plasterers and stucco masons.

Sources of Additional Information

For information about work opportunities in drywall application and finishing and ceiling tile installation, contact local drywall installation and ceiling tile installation contractors, a local joint union-management apprenticeship committee, a State or local chapter of the Associated Builders and Contractors, or the nearest office of the State employment service or apprenticeship agency. You can also find information on the registered apprenticeship system with links to State apprenticeship programs on the U.S. Department of Labor's Web site: **http://www.doleta.gov/atels_bat** Apprenticeship information is also available from the U.S. Department of Labor's toll free helpline: (877) 282-5627.

For details about job qualifications and training programs in drywall application and finishing and ceiling tile installation, contact:

➤ Associated Builders and Contractors, 4250 North Fairfax Dr., 9th Floor, Arlington, VA 22203. Internet: **www.trytools.org**
➤ Finishing Trades Institute, International Union of Painters and Allied Trades, 1750 New York Ave. NW., Washington, DC 20006. Internet: **http://www.finishingtradesinstitute.org**
➤ National Association of Home Builders, Home Builders Institute, 1201 15th St.NW., Washington, DC 20005. Internet: **http://www.hbi.org**
➤ National Center for Construction Education and Research, P.O. Box 141104, Gainesville, FL 32614-1104. Internet: **http://www.nccer.org**
➤ United Brotherhood of Carpenters and Joiners of America, Carpenters Training Fund, 6801 Placid St., Las Vegas, NV 89119. Internet: **http://www.carpenters.org**

For general information on apprenticeships and how to get them, see the *Occupational Outlook Quarterly* article "Apprenticeships: Career training, credentials—and a paycheck in your pocket," online at **http://www.bls.gov/opub/ooq/2002/summer/art01.pdf** and in print at many libraries and career centers.

Electricians

(O*NET 47-2111.00)

Significant Points

- Job opportunities should be very good, especially for those with the broadest range of skills.

- Most electricians acquire their skills by completing an apprenticeship program lasting 4 to 5 years.

- About 4 out of 5 electricians work in the construction industry or are self-employed, but there also will be opportunities for electricians in other industries.

Nature of the Work

Electricians bring electricity into homes, businesses, and factories. They install and maintain the wiring, fuses, and other components through which electricity flows. Many electricians also install and maintain electrical machines in factories.

Electricians usually start their work by reading blueprints. Blueprints are technical diagrams that show the locations of circuits, outlets, load centers, panel boards, and other equipment. To ensure public safety, electricians follow the National Electrical Code, and State and local building codes.

Electricians connect all types of wires to circuit breakers, transformers, outlets, or other components. They join the wires in boxes with various specially designed connectors. When installing wiring, electricians use hand tools such as conduit benders, screwdrivers, pliers, knives, hacksaws, and wire strippers, as well as power tools such as drills and saws. Later, they use ammeters, ohmmeters, voltmeters, oscilloscopes, and other equipment to test connections and ensure the compatibility and safety of components.

Electricians generally focus on either construction or maintenance, although many do both. Electricians specializing in construction primarily install wiring systems into factories, businesses, and new homes. Electricians specializing in maintenance work fix and upgrade existing electrical systems and repair electrical equipment.

When electricians install wiring systems in factories and commercial settings, they first place conduit (pipe or tubing) inside partitions, walls, or other concealed areas as designated by the blueprints. They also fasten small metal or plastic boxes to the walls that will house electrical switches and outlets. They pull insulated wires or cables through the conduit to complete circuits between these boxes. The diameter and number of wires installed depends on how much power will need to run through it. The greater the diameter of the wire, the more electricity it can handle. In residential construction, electricians usually install insulated wire encased in plastic, which does not need to run through conduit.

Some electricians also install low-voltage wiring systems in addition to electrical systems, although line installers and repairers specialize in this work. Low-voltage wiring accommodates voice, data, and video equipment, such as telephones, computers, intercoms, and fire alarm and security systems. Electricians also may install coaxial or fiber optic cable for telecommunications equipment and electronic controls for industrial uses.

Maintenance electricians repair or replace electric and electronic equipment when it breaks. They make needed repairs as quickly as possible in order to minimize inconvenience. They may replace items such as circuit breakers, fuses, switches, electrical and electronic components, or wire. Electricians also periodically inspect all equipment to ensure it is operating properly and to correct problems before breakdowns occur.

Maintenance work varies greatly, depending on where an electrician works. Electricians who focus on residential work perform a wide variety of electrical work for homeowners. They may rewire a home and replace an old fuse box with a new circuit breaker box to accommodate additional appliances, or they may install new lighting and other electric household items, such as ceiling fans. These electricians might also do some construction and installation work.

Electricians in large factories usually do maintenance work that is more complex. They may repair motors, transformers, generators, and electronic controllers on machine tools and industrial robots. Electricians also advise management whether continued operation of equipment could be hazardous. When working with complex electronic devices, they may consult with engineers, engineering technicians, line installers and repairers, or industrial machinery mechanics and maintenance workers. (Statements on these occupations appear elsewhere in the *Handbook*.)

Work environment. Electricians work indoors and out, at construction sites, in homes, and in businesses or factories. Work may be strenuous at times and may include bending conduit, lifting heavy objects, and standing, stooping, and kneeling for long periods. Electricians risk injury from electrical shock, falls, and cuts. They must follow strict safety procedures to avoid injuries. When working outdoors, they may be subject to inclement weather conditions. Some electricians may have to travel long distances to jobsites.

Most electricians work a standard 40-hour week, although overtime may be required. Those who do maintenance work may work nights or weekends and be on call to go to the worksite when needed. Electricians in industrial settings may have

Electricians may rewire a home and replace an old fuse box with a new circuit breaker box to accommodate additional appliances.

periodic extended overtime during scheduled maintenance or retooling periods. Companies that operate 24 hours a day may employ three shifts of electricians.

Training, Other Qualifications, and Advancement
Most electricians learn their trade through apprenticeship programs. These programs combine on-the-job training with related classroom instruction.

Education and training. Most electricians learn their trade through apprenticeship programs. These programs combine paid on-the-job training with related classroom instruction. Joint training committees made up of local unions of the International Brotherhood of Electrical Workers and local chapters of the National Electrical Contractors Association; individual electrical contracting companies; or local chapters of the Associated Builders and Contractors and the Independent Electrical Contractors Association usually sponsor apprenticeship programs.

Because of the comprehensive training received, those who complete apprenticeship programs qualify to do both maintenance and construction work. Apprenticeship programs usually last 4 years. Each year includes at least 144 hours of classroom instruction and 2,000 hours of on-the-job training. In the classroom, apprentices learn electrical theory, blueprint reading, mathematics, electrical code requirements, and safety and first aid practices. They also may receive specialized training in soldering, communications, fire alarm systems, and cranes and elevators.

On the job, apprentices work under the supervision of experienced electricians. At first, they drill holes, set anchors, and attach conduit. Later, they measure, fabricate, and install conduit and install, connect, and test wiring, outlets, and switches. They also learn to set up and draw diagrams for entire electrical systems. Eventually, they practice and master all of an electrician's main tasks.

Some people start their classroom training before seeking an apprenticeship. A number of public and private vocational-technical schools and training academies offer training to become an electrician. Employers often hire students who complete these programs and usually start them at a more advanced level than those without this training. A few people become electricians by first working as helpers—assisting electricians by setting up job sites, gathering materials, and doing other nonelectrical work—before entering an apprenticeship program. All apprentices need a high school diploma or a General Equivalency Diploma (G.E.D.). Electricians may also need classes in mathematics because they solve mathematical problems on the job.

Education can continue throughout an electrician's career. Electricians often complete regular safety programs, manufacturer-specific training, and management training courses. Classes on installing low-voltage voice, data, and video systems have recently become common as these systems become more prevalent. Other courses teach electricians how to become contractors.

Licensure. Most States and localities require electricians to be licensed. Although licensing requirements vary from State to State, electricians usually must pass an examination that tests their knowledge of electrical theory, the National Electrical

Projections data from the National Employment Matrix

Occupational Title	SOC Code	Employment, 2006	Projected employment, 2016	Change, 2006-16	
				Number	Percent
Electricians..	47-2111	705,000	757,000	52,000	7

NOTE: Data in this table are rounded. See the discussion of the employment projections table in the *Handbook* introductory chapter on *Occupational Information Included in the Handbook*.

Code, and local electric and building codes. Experienced electricians periodically take courses offered by their employer or union to learn about changes in the National Electrical Code.

Electrical contractors who do electrical work for the public, as opposed to electricians who work for electrical contractors, often need a special license. In some States, electrical contractors need certification as master electricians. Most States require master electricians to have at least 7 years of experience as an electrician. Some States require a bachelor's degree in electrical engineering or a related field.

Other qualifications. Applicants for apprenticeships usually must be at least 18 years old and have a high school diploma or a G.E.D. They also may have to pass a test and meet other requirements.

Other skills needed to become an electrician include manual dexterity, eye-hand coordination, physical fitness, and a good sense of balance. They also need good color vision because workers frequently must identify electrical wires by color. In addition, apprenticeship committees and employers view a good work history or military service favorably.

Advancement. Experienced electricians can advance to jobs as supervisors. In construction, they also may become project managers or construction superintendents. Those with sufficient capital and management skills can start their own contracting business, although this often requires a special electrical contractor's license. Supervisors and contractors should be able to identify and estimate costs and prices and the time and materials needed to complete a job. Many electricians also become electrical inspectors.

For those who seek to advance, it is increasingly important to be able to communicate in both English and Spanish in order to relay instructions and safety precautions to workers with limited understanding of English; Spanish-speaking workers make up a large part of the construction workforce in many areas. Spanish-speaking workers who want to advance in this occupation need very good English skills to understand electrician classes and installation instructions, which are usually written in English. and are highly technical.

Employment

Electricians held about 705,000 jobs in 2006. About 68 percent of wage-and-salary workers were employed in the construction industry and the remainder worked as maintenance electricians in other industries. In addition, about 11 percent of electricians were self-employed.

Job Outlook

Average employment growth is expected. Job prospects should be very good, particularly for workers with the widest range of skills, including voice, data, and video wiring.

Employment change. Employment of electricians should increase 7 percent between 2006 and 2016, about as fast as the average for all occupations. As the population and economy grow, more electricians will be needed to install and maintain electrical devices and wiring in homes, factories, offices, and other structures. An increase in power plant construction over the next ten years will require many additional electricians. New technologies also are expected to continue to spur demand for these workers. For example, buildings increasingly need wiring to accommodate computers and telecommunications equipment. Robots and other automated manufacturing systems in factories also will require the installation and maintenance of more complex wiring systems. As the economy rehabilitates and retrofits older structures, which usually require electrical improvements to meet modern codes, it will create additional jobs.

Job prospects. In addition to jobs created by the increased demand for electrical work, many openings are expected over the next decade as a large number of electricians retire. This will create very good job opportunities, especially for those with the widest range of skills, including voice, data, and video wiring. Job openings for electricians will vary by location and specialty, however, and will be best in the fastest growing regions of the country, especially those areas where power plants are being constructed.

Employment of electricians, like that of many other construction workers, is sensitive to the fluctuations of the economy. Workers in these trades may experience periods of unemployment when the overall level of construction falls. On the other hand, shortages of these workers may occur in some areas during peak periods of building activity.

Although employment of maintenance electricians is steadier than that of construction electricians, those working in the automotive and other manufacturing industries that are sensitive to cyclical swings in the economy may experience lay offs during recessions. In addition, opportunities for maintenance electricians may be limited in many industries by the increased contracting out for electrical services in an effort to reduce operating costs. However, increased job opportunities for electricians in electrical contracting firms should partially offset job losses in other industries.

Earnings

In May 2006, median hourly earnings of wage and salary electricians were $20.97. The middle 50 percent earned between $16.07 and $27.71. The lowest 10 percent earned less than $12.76, and the highest 10 percent earned more than $34.95. Median hourly earnings in the industries employing the largest numbers of electricians were:

Motor vehicle parts manufacturing $31.90
Electric power generation, transmission,
    and distribution 26.32
Local government 23.80
Nonresidential building construction 20.58
Electrical contractors 20.47
Plumbing, heating, and air-conditioning contractors 19.56
Employment services 17.15

Apprentices usually start at between 40 and 50 percent of the rate paid to fully trained electricians, depending on experience. As apprentices become more skilled, they receive periodic pay increases throughout their training.

Some electricians are members of the International Brotherhood of Electrical Workers. Among unions representing maintenance electricians are the International Brotherhood of Electrical Workers; the International Union of Electronic, Electrical, Salaried, Machine, and Furniture Workers; the International Association of Machinists and Aerospace Workers; the International Union, United Automobile, Aircraft and Agricultural Implement Workers of America; and the United Steelworkers of America.

Related Occupations

To install and maintain electrical systems, electricians combine manual skill and knowledge of electrical materials and concepts. Workers in other occupations involving similar skills include heating, air-conditioning, and refrigeration mechanics and installers; line installers and repairers; electrical and electronics installers and repairers; electronic home entertainment equipment installers and repairers; and elevator installers and repairers.

Sources of Additional Information

For details about apprenticeships or other work opportunities in this trade, contact the offices of the State employment service, the State apprenticeship agency, local electrical contractors or firms that employ maintenance electricians, or local union-management electrician apprenticeship committees. Apprenticeship information is also available from the U.S. Department of Labor's toll free helpline: (877) 872-5627.

Information also may be available from local chapters of the Independent Electrical Contractors, Inc.; the National Electrical Contractors Association; the Home Builders Institute; the Associated Builders and Contractors; and the International Brotherhood of Electrical Workers.

For information about union apprenticeship and training programs, contact:

➤ National Joint Apprenticeship Training Committee, 301 Prince George's Blvd., Upper Marlboro, MD 20774.
Internet: **http://www.njatc.org**
➤ National Electrical Contractors Association, 3 Metro Center, Suite 1100, Bethesda, MD 20814.
Internet: **http://www.necanet.org**
➤ International Brotherhood of Electrical Workers, 1125 15th St.NW., Washington, DC 20005.
Internet: **http://www.ibew.org**

For information about independent apprenticeship programs, contact:

➤ Associated Builders and Contractors, Workforce Development Department, 4250 North Fairfax Dr., 9th Floor, Arlington, VA 22203. Internet: **http://www.trytools.org**
➤ Independent Electrical Contractors, Inc., 4401 Ford Ave., Suite 1100, Alexandria, VA 22302.
Internet: **http://www.ieci.org**
➤ National Association of Home Builders, Home Builders Institute, 1201 15th St.NW., Washington, DC 20005.
Internet: **http://www.hbi.org**
➤ National Center for Construction Education and Research, 3600 NW 43rd St., Bldg. G, Gainesville, FL 32606.
Internet: **http://www.nccer.org**

For general information on apprenticeships and how to get them, see the *Occupational Outlook Quarterly* article "Apprenticeships: Career training, credentials—and a paycheck in your pocket," in print at many libraries and career centers and online at: **http://www.bls.gov/opub/ooq/2002/summer/art01.pdf**

Elevator Installers and Repairers

(O*NET 47-4021.00)

Significant Points

- Most workers belong to a union and enter the occupation through a 4-year apprenticeship program.

- Excellent employment opportunities are expected.

- Elevator installers and repairers are less affected by downturns in the economy and inclement weather than other construction trades workers.

Nature of the Work

Elevator installers and repairers—also called *elevator constructors* or *elevator mechanics*—assemble, install, and replace elevators, escalators, chairlifts, dumbwaiters, moving walkways, and similar equipment in new and old buildings. Once the equipment is in service, they maintain and repair it as well. They also are responsible for modernizing older equipment.

To install, repair, and maintain modern elevators, which are almost all electronically controlled, elevator installers and repairers must have a thorough knowledge of electronics, electricity, and hydraulics. Many elevators are controlled with microprocessors, which are programmed to analyze traffic conditions in order to dispatch elevators in the most efficient manner. With these controls, it is possible to get the greatest amount of service with the fewest number of cars.

Elevator installers and repairers usually specialize in installation, maintenance, or repair work. Maintenance and repair workers generally need greater knowledge of electricity and electronics than do installers because a large part of maintenance and repair work is troubleshooting.

When installing a new elevator, installers and repairers begin by studying blueprints to determine the equipment needed to install rails, machinery, car enclosures, motors, pumps, cylinders, and plunger foundations. Then, they begin equipment installation. Working on scaffolding or platforms, installers bolt or weld steel rails to the walls of the shaft to guide the elevator.

Elevator installers put in electrical wires and controls by running tubing, called conduit, along a shaft's walls from floor to floor. Once the conduit is in place, mechanics pull plastic-covered electrical wires through it. They then install electrical components and related devices required at each floor and at the main control panel in the machine room.

Installers bolt or weld together the steel frame of an elevator car at the bottom of the shaft; install the car's platform, walls, and doors; and attach guide shoes and rollers to minimize the lateral motion of the car as it travels through the shaft. They also install the outer doors and door frames at the elevator entrances on each floor.

For cabled elevators, these workers install geared or gearless machines with a traction drive wheel that guides and moves heavy steel cables connected to the elevator car and counter-weight. (The counterweight moves in the opposite direction from the car and balances most of the weight of the car to reduce the weight that the elevator's motor must lift.) Elevator installers also install elevators in which a car sits on a hydraulic plunger that is driven by a pump. The plunger pushes the elevator car up from underneath, similar to a lift in an auto service station.

Installers and repairers also install escalators. They place the steel framework, the electrically powered stairs, and the tracks and install associated motors and electrical wiring. In addition to elevators and escalators, installers and repairers also may install devices such as dumbwaiters and material lifts—which are similar to elevators in design—as well as moving walkways, stair lifts, and wheelchair lifts.

Once an elevator is operating properly, it must be maintained and serviced regularly to keep it in safe working condition. Elevator installers and repairers generally do preventive maintenance—such as oiling and greasing moving parts, replacing worn parts, testing equipment with meters and gauges, and adjusting equipment for optimal performance. They insure that the equipment and rooms are clean. They also troubleshoot and may be called to do emergency repairs. Unlike most elevator installers, those who specialize in elevator maintenance are on their own most of the day and typically service the same elevators periodically.

A service crew usually handles major repairs—for example, replacing cables, elevator doors, or machine bearings. This may require the use of cutting torches or rigging equipment—tools that an elevator repairer would not normally carry. Service crews also do major modernization and alteration work, such as moving and replacing electrical motors, hydraulic pumps, and control panels.

The most highly skilled elevator installers and repairers, called "adjusters," specialize in fine-tuning all the equipment after installation. Adjusters make sure that an elevator works according to specifications and stops correctly at each floor within a specified time. Adjusters need a thorough knowledge of electricity, electronics, and computers to ensure that newly installed elevators operate properly.

Work environment. Elevator installers lift and carry heavy equipment and parts, and they may work in cramped spaces

or awkward positions. Potential hazards include falls, electrical shock, muscle strains, and other injuries related to handling heavy equipment. Most of their work is performed indoors in existing buildings or buildings under construction.

Most elevator installers and repairers work a 40-hour week. However, overtime is required when essential equipment must be repaired, and some workers are on 24-hour call. Because most of their work is performed indoors in buildings, elevator installers and repairers lose less work time due to inclement weather than do other construction trades workers.

Training, Other Qualifications, and Advancement

Most elevator installers receive their education through an apprenticeship program. High school classes in mathematics, science, and shop may help applicants compete for apprenticeship openings.

Education and training. Most elevators installers and repairers learn their trade in an apprenticeship program administered by local joint educational committees representing the employers and the union—the International Union of Elevator Constructors. In nonunion shops, workers may complete training programs sponsored by independent contractors.

Apprenticeship programs teach a range of skills, usually during a 4-year period. Programs combine paid on-the-job training with classroom instruction in blueprint reading, electrical and electronic theory, mathematics, applications of physics, and safety.

Most apprentices assist experienced elevator installers and repairers. Beginners carry materials and tools, bolt rails to walls, and assemble elevator cars. Eventually, apprentices learn more difficult tasks such as wiring.

Applicants for apprenticeship positions must have a high school diploma or the equivalent. High school courses in electricity, mathematics, and physics provide a useful background. As elevators become increasingly sophisticated, workers may need to get more advanced education—for example, a certificate or associate degree in electronics. Workers with education beyond high school usually advance more quickly than their counterparts without a degree.

Many elevator installers and repairers receive additional training in their particular company's equipment.

Repairers make sure that an elevator operates according to specifications and stops at each floor within a specified time.

Projections data from the National Employment Matrix

Occupational Title	SOC Code	Employment, 2006	Projected employment, 2016	Change, 2006-16	
				Number	Percent
Elevator installers and repairers..	47-4021	22,000	24,000	1,900	9

NOTE: Data in this table are rounded. See the discussion of the employment projections table in the *Handbook* introductory chapter on *Occupational Information Included in the Handbook.*

Licensure. Most cities and States require elevator installers and repairers to pass a licensing examination. Other requirements for licensure vary.

Certification and other qualifications. Workers who also complete an apprenticeship registered by the U.S. Department of Labor or their State board earn a journeyworker certificate recognized Nationwide. Applicants for apprenticeship positions must be at least 18 years old, have a high school diploma or equivalent, and pass a drug test and an aptitude test. Good physical condition and mechanical aptitude also are important.

Jobs with many employers require membership in the union. To be considered fully qualified by the union, workers must complete an apprenticeship and pass a standard exam administered by the National Elevator Industry Educational Program.

The National Association of Elevator Contractors also offers certification as a Certified Elevator Technician or Certified Accessibility and Private Residence Lift Technician.

Advancement. Ongoing training is very important if a worker is to keep up with technological developments in elevator repair. In fact, union elevator installers and repairers typically receive training throughout their careers, through correspondence courses, seminars, or formal classes. This training greatly improves one's chances for promotion and retention.

Some installers may receive further training in specialized areas and advance to the position of mechanic-in-charge, adjuster, supervisor, or elevator inspector. Adjusters, for example, may be picked for their position because they possess particular skills or are electronically inclined. Other workers may move into management, sales, or product design jobs.

Employment

Elevator installers and repairers held about 22,000 jobs in 2006. Most were employed by specialty trades contractors, particularly elevator maintenance and repair contractors. Others were employed by field offices of elevator manufacturers, machinery wholesalers, government agencies, or businesses that do their own elevator maintenance and repair.

Job Outlook

Even with average job growth, excellent job opportunities are expected in this occupation.

Employment change. Employment of elevator installers and repairers is expected to increase 9 percent during the 2006-16 decade, about as fast as the average for all occupations. Demand for additional elevator installers depends greatly on growth in nonresidential construction, such as commercial office buildings and stores that have elevators and escalators. This sector of the construction industry is expected to grow during the decade as the economy expands. In addition, the need to continually update and repair old equipment, provide access to the disabled, and install increasingly sophisticated equipment

and controls should add to the demand for elevator installers and repairers. The demand for elevator installers and repairers will also increase as a growing number of the elderly require easier access to their homes through stair lifts and residential elevators.

Job prospects. Workers should have excellent opportunities when seeking to enter this occupation. Elevator installer and repairer jobs have relatively high earnings and good benefits. However, the dangerous and physically challenging nature of this occupation and the significant training it requires reduces the number of applicants and creates better opportunities for those who apply. Job prospects should be best for those with postsecondary education in electronics or experience in the military.

Elevators, escalators, lifts, moving walkways, and related equipment need to be kept in good working condition year round, so employment of elevator repairers is less affected by economic downturns and seasonality than other construction trades.

Earnings

Earnings of elevator installers and repairers are among the highest of all construction trades. Median hourly earnings of wage and salary elevator installers and repairers were $30.59 in May 2006. The middle 50 percent earned between $23.90 and $35.76. The lowest 10 percent earned less than $17.79, and the top 10 percent earned more than $42.14. Median hourly earnings in the building equipment contractors industry were $30.74.

Earnings for members of the International Union of Elevator Constructors vary based on the local and specialty. Check with a local in your area for exact wages.

About three out of four elevator installers and repairers were members of unions or covered by a union contract, one of the highest proportions of all occupations. The largest numbers were members of the International Union of Elevator Constructors. In addition to free continuing education, elevator installers and repairers receive basic benefits enjoyed by most other workers.

Related Occupations

Elevator installers and repairers combine electrical and mechanical skills with construction skills, such as welding, rigging, measuring, and blueprint reading. Other occupations that require many of these skills are boilermakers; electricians; electrical and electronics installers and repairers; industrial machinery mechanics and maintenance workers; millwrights; sheet metal workers; and structural and reinforcing iron and metal workers.

Sources of Additional Information

For information about apprenticeships or job opportunities as an elevator mechanic, contact local contractors, a local chapter of the International Union of Elevator Constructors, a local joint union-management apprenticeship committee, or the nearest office of your State employment service or apprenticeship agency. You can also find information on the registered apprenticeship system with links to State apprenticeship programs on the U.S. Department of Labor's Web site: **http://www.doleta.gov/atels_bat** Apprenticeship information is also available from the U.S. Department of Labor's toll free helpline: (877) 872-5627.

For further information on opportunities as an elevator installer and repairer, contact:

➤ International Union of Elevator Constructors, 7154 Columbia Gateway Dr., Columbia, MD 21046.
Internet: **http://www.iuec.org**

For additional information about the Certified Elevator Technician (CET) program or the Certified Accessibility and Private Residence Lift Technician (CAT) program, contact:

➤ National Association of Elevator Contractors, 1298 Wellbrook Circle, Suite A, Conyers, GA 30012.
Internet: **http://www.naec.org**

For general information on apprenticeships and how to get them, see the *Occupational Outlook Quarterly* article "Apprenticeships: Career training, credentials—and a paycheck in your pocket," online at **http://www.bls.gov/opub/ooq/2002/summer/art01.pdf** and in print at many libraries and career centers.

Glaziers

(O*NET 47-2121.00)

Significant Points

- Many glaziers learn the trade by helping experienced workers.

- Job opportunities are expected to be good.

Nature of the Work

Glass serves many uses in modern life. Insulated and specially treated glass keeps in warmed or cooled air and provides good condensation and sound control. Tempered and laminated glass makes doors and windows more secure. In large commercial buildings, glass panels give office buildings a distinctive look while reducing the need for artificial lighting. The creative use of large windows, glass doors, skylights, and sunroom additions makes homes bright, airy, and inviting.

Glaziers are responsible for selecting, cutting, installing, replacing, and removing all types of glass. They generally work on one of several types of projects. Residential glazing involves work such as replacing glass in home windows; installing glass mirrors, shower doors, and bathtub enclosures; and fitting glass for tabletops and display cases. On commercial interior projects, glaziers install items such as heavy, often etched, decorative room dividers or security windows. Glazing projects also may involve replacement of storefront windows for establishments such as supermarkets, auto dealerships, or banks. In the construction of large commercial buildings, glaziers build metal framework extrusions and install glass panels or curtain walls. (Workers who replace and repair glass in motor vehicles are not covered in this statement. See the statement on automotive body and related repairers elsewhere in the *Handbook*.)

Besides working with glass, glaziers also may work with plastics, granite, marble, and other similar materials used as glass substitutes and with films or laminates that improve the durability or safety of the glass. They may mount steel and aluminum sashes or frames and attach locks and hinges to glass doors.

For most jobs, the glass is precut and mounted in frames at a factory or a contractor's shop. It arrives at the jobsite ready for glaziers to position and secure it in place. They may use a crane or hoist with suction cups to lift large, heavy pieces of glass. They then gently guide the glass into position by hand.

Once glaziers have the glass in place, they secure it with mastic, putty, or other paste-like cement, or with bolts, rubber gaskets, glazing compound, metal clips, or metal or wood moldings. When they secure glass using a rubber gasket—a thick, molded rubber half-tube with a split running its length—they first secure the gasket around the perimeter within the opening, then set the glass into the split side of the gasket, causing it to clamp to the edges and hold the glass firmly in place.

When they use metal clips and wood moldings, glaziers first secure the molding to the opening, place the glass in the molding, and then force springlike metal clips between the glass and the molding. The clips exert pressure and keep the glass firmly in place.

When a glazing compound is used, glaziers first spread it neatly against and around the edges of the molding on the inside of the opening. Next, they install the glass. Pressing it against the compound on the inside molding, workers screw or nail outside molding that loosely holds the glass in place. To hold it firmly, they pack the space between the molding and the glass with glazing compound and then trim any excess material with a glazing knife.

For some jobs, the glazier must cut the glass manually at the jobsite. To prepare the glass for cutting, glaziers rest it either

Most glaziers learn their trade by helping experienced workers, sometimes with supplemental classroom training.

on edge on a rack, or "A-frame," or flat against a cutting table. They then measure and mark the glass for the cut.

Glaziers cut glass with a special tool that has a small, very hard metal wheel. Using a straightedge as a guide, the glazier presses the cutter's wheel firmly on the glass, guiding and rolling it carefully to make a score just below the surface. To help the cutting tool move smoothly across the glass, workers brush a thin layer of oil along the line of the intended cut or dip the cutting tool in oil. Immediately after cutting, the glazier presses on the shorter end of the glass to break it cleanly along the cut.

In addition to handtools such as glasscutters, suction cups, and glazing knives, glaziers use power tools such as saws, drills, cutters, and grinders. An increasing number of glaziers use computers in the shop or at the jobsite to improve their layout work and reduce the amount of wasted glass.

Work environment. Glaziers often work outdoors, sometimes in inclement weather. Their work can, at times, result in injuries as they work with sharp tools and may need to remove broken glass. They must be prepared to lift heavy glass panels and work on scaffolding, sometimes at great heights. Glaziers do a considerable amount of bending, kneeling, lifting, and standing during the installation process.

Training, Other Qualifications, and Advancement

Most glaziers learn their trade by helping experienced workers, sometimes with supplemental classroom training. A few formal apprenticeship programs are available.

Education and training. Glaziers learn their trade through formal and informal training programs. Usually 3 years of classroom and on-the-job training are required to become a skilled glazier. There are a number of different avenues that one can take to obtain the necessary training. Most glaziers start by obtaining a job with a contractor who then provides on-the-job training. Entry-level workers generally start as helpers, assisting more experienced workers. During this time, employers may send the employee to a trade or vocational school or community college to receive further classroom training.

Some employers offer formal apprenticeships. These programs combine paid on-the-job training with related classroom instruction. Apprenticeship applicants usually must be at least 18 years old and meet local requirements. The length of the program is usually 3 years, but varies with the apprentice's skill. Because the number of apprenticeship programs is limited, however, only a small proportion of glaziers learn their trade through these programs.

On the job, apprentices or helpers often start by carrying glass and cleaning up debris in glass shops. They often practice cutting on discarded glass. Later, they are given an opportunity to cut glass for a job and assist experienced workers on simple installation jobs. By working with experienced glaziers, they eventually acquire the skills of a fully qualified glazier. On the job, they learn to use the tools and equipment of the trade; handle, measure, cut, and install glass and metal framing; cut and fit moldings; and install and balance glass doors. In the classroom, they are taught about glass and installation techniques as well as basic mathematics, blueprint reading and sketching, general construction techniques, safety practices, and first aid.

Licensure. Only the State of Connecticut currently requires glaziers to have a license. In addition to passing a test, workers need education, experience, and an apprenticeship to be licensed. There is a voluntary license in Florida. Other States may require licenses in the future.

Other qualifications. Skills needed to become a glazier include manual dexterity, eye-hand coordination, physical fitness, and a good sense of balance. The ability to solve arithmetic problems quickly and accurately also is required. In addition, a good work history or military service is viewed favorably by employers.

Certification and advancement. Glaziers who learn the trade through a formal registered apprenticeship program become certified journeyworkers. Some associations offer other certifications. The National Glass Association, for example, offers a series of written examinations that certify an individual's competency to perform glazier work at three progressively difficult levels of proficiency: Level I Glazier; Level II Commercial Interior or Residential Glazier, or Storefront or Curtainwall Glazier; and Level III Master Glazier.

Advancement for glaziers generally consists of increases in pay; some advance to glazier supervisors, general construction supervisors, independent contractors, or cost estimators. For those who would like to advance, it is increasingly important to be able to communicate in both English and Spanish in order to relay instructions and safety precautions to workers with limited understanding of English because Spanish-speaking workers make up a large part of the construction workforce in many areas. Supervisors and contractors need good communication skills to deal with clients and subcontractors and should be able to identify and estimate the quantity of materials needed to complete a job and accurately estimate how long a job will take to complete and at what cost.

Employment

Glaziers held 55,000 jobs in 2006. About 68 percent of glaziers worked for glazing contractors engaged in new construction, alteration, and repair. About 16 percent of glaziers worked in retail glass shops that install or replace glass, and for wholesale distributors of products containing glass.

Job Outlook

Average employment growth is projected. Good job opportunities are expected, especially for those with a range of skills.

Projections data from the National Employment Matrix

Occupational Title	SOC Code	Employment, 2006	Projected employment, 2016	Change, 2006-16	
				Number	Percent
Glaziers	47-2121	55,000	62,000	6,600	12

NOTE: Data in this table are rounded. See the discussion of the employment projections table in the *Handbook* introductory chapter on *Occupational Information Included in the Handbook.*

Employment change. Employment is expected to grow 12 percent from 2006 to 2016, about as fast as the average for all occupations. Employment of glaziers is expected to increase as a result of growth in residential and nonresidential construction. Demand for glaziers also will be spurred by the continuing need to modernize and repair existing structures, which often involves installing new windows. Also, more homeowners now prefer rooms with more sunlight and are adding sunrooms and skylights to houses. Demand for specialized safety glass and glass coated with protective laminates is also growing in response to a higher need for security and the need to withstand hurricanes, particularly in many commercial and government buildings. Homes and buildings that have been built recently are less likely to need replacement windows than older structures.

Counteracting these factors, however, is the ability of other workers such as carpenters to install windows, which reduces employment growth for glaziers.

Job prospects. Job opportunities for glaziers are expected to be good. Since employers prefer workers who can do a variety of tasks, glaziers with a range of skills will have the best opportunities.

Like other construction trades workers, glaziers employed in the construction industry should expect to experience periods of unemployment because of the limited duration of construction projects and the cyclical nature of the construction industry. During downturns in the economy, job openings for glaziers are reduced as the level of construction declines. However, construction activity varies from area to area, so job openings fluctuate with local economic conditions. Employment opportunities should be greatest in metropolitan areas, where most glazing contractors and glass shops are located.

Earnings

In May 2006, median hourly earnings of wage and salary glaziers were $16.64. The middle 50 percent earned between $12.85 and $22.18. The lowest 10 percent earned less than $10.19, and the highest 10 percent earned more than $30.52. Median hourly wage-and-salary earnings in the foundation, structure, and building exterior contractors industry were $17.03. Median hourly earnings for glaziers employed by building materials and supply dealers, where most glass shops are found, were $15.51.

Glaziers covered by union contracts generally earn more than their nonunion counterparts. Apprentice wage rates usually start at 40 to 50 percent of the rate paid to experienced glaziers and increase as they gain experience. Because glaziers can lose work time due to weather conditions and fluctuations in construction activity, their overall earnings may be lower than their hourly wages suggest.

Some glaziers employed in construction are members of the International Union of Painters and Allied Trades.

Related Occupations

Glaziers use their knowledge of construction materials and techniques to install glass. Other construction workers whose jobs also involve skilled, custom work are brickmasons, blockmasons, and stonemasons; carpenters; carpet, floor, and tile installers and finishers; cement masons, concrete finishers, seg-

mental pavers, and terrazzo workers; sheet metal workers; and painters and paperhangers. In addition, automotive body and related repairers install broken or damaged glass on the vehicles they repair.

Sources of Additional Information

For more information about glazier apprenticeships or work opportunities, contact local glazing or general contractors, a local of the International Union of Painters and Allied Trades, a local joint union-management apprenticeship agency, or the nearest office of the State employment service or State apprenticeship agency. You can also find information on the registered apprenticeships together with links to State apprenticeship programs on the U.S. Department of Labor's Web site: **http://www.doleta.gov/atels_bat** Apprenticeship information is also available from the U.S. Department of Labor's toll free helpline: (877) 872-5627.

For general information about the work of glaziers, contact:

➤ International Union of Painters and Allied Trades, 1750 New York Ave. NW., Washington, DC 20006.
Internet: **http://www.iupat.org**

For information concerning training for glaziers, contact:

➤ Associated Builders and Contractors, Workforce Development Department, 4250 North Fairfax Dr., 9th Floor, Arlington, VA 22203. Internet: **www.trytools.org**

➤ National Glass Association, Education and Training Department, 8200 Greensboro Dr., Suite 302, McLean, VA 22102. Internet: **http://www.glass.org**

For general information on apprenticeships and how to get them, see the *Occupational Outlook Quarterly* article "Apprenticeships: Career training, credentials—and a paycheck in your pocket," online at **http://www.bls.gov/opub/ooq/2002/summer/art01.pdf** and in print at many libraries and career centers.

Hazardous Materials Removal Workers

(O*NET 47-4041.00)

Significant Points

- Working conditions can be hazardous.

- Formal education beyond high school is not required, but government standards require specific types of on-the-job training.

- Good job opportunities are expected, mainly due to the need to replace workers who leave the occupation.

Nature of the Work

Increased public awareness and Federal and State regulations are resulting in the removal of more hazardous materials from buildings, facilities, and the environment to prevent further contamination of natural resources and to promote public health and safety. Hazardous materials typically possess at least one of four characteristics—ignitability, corrosivity, reactivity, or toxicity. Hazardous materials removal workers identify, remove, package, transport, and dispose of various hazardous materials, including asbestos, radioactive and nuclear materials, arsenic, lead, and mercury. These workers are sometimes called abatement, remediation, or decontamination workers. Removal workers often respond to emergencies where harmful substances are present.

Hazardous materials removal workers use a variety of tools and equipment, depending on the work at hand. Equipment ranges from brooms to personal protective suits that completely isolate workers from the hazardous material. Because of the threat of contamination, workers often wear disposable or reusable coveralls, gloves, hardhats, shoe covers, safety glasses or goggles, chemical-resistant clothing, face shields, and devices to protect one's hearing. Most workers are also required to wear respirators while working, to protect them from airborne particles or noxious gases. The respirators range from simple versions that cover only the mouth and nose to self-contained suits with their own air supply.

Asbestos and lead are two of the most common contaminants that hazardous materials removal workers encounter. Through the 1970s, asbestos was used to fireproof roofing and flooring, for heat insulation, and for a variety of other purposes. It was durable, fire retardant, resisted corrosion, and insulated well, making it ideal for such applications. Embedded in materials, asbestos is fairly harmless; airborne, however, it can cause several lung diseases, including lung cancer and asbestosis. Today, asbestos is rarely used in buildings, but there are still structures that contain the material that must be remediated. Similarly, lead was a common building component found in paint and plumbing fixtures and pipes until the late 1970s. Because lead is easily absorbed into the bloodstream, often from breathing lead dust or from eating chips of paint containing lead, it can cause serious health risks, especially in children. Due to these risks, it has become necessary to remove lead-based products from buildings and structures.

Asbestos abatement workers and *lead abatement workers* remove asbestos, lead, and other materials from buildings scheduled to be renovated or demolished. Using a variety of hand and power tools, such as vacuums and scrapers, these workers remove the asbestos and lead from surfaces. A typical residential lead abatement project involves the use of a chemical to strip the lead-based paint from the walls of the home. Lead abatement workers apply the compound with a putty knife and allow it to dry. Then they scrape the hazardous material into an impregnable container for transport and storage. They also use sandblasters and high-pressure water sprayers to remove lead from large structures. The vacuums utilized by asbestos abatement workers have special, highly efficient filters designed to trap the asbestos, which later is disposed of or stored. During the abatement, special monitors measure the amount of asbestos and lead in the air, to protect the workers; in addition, lead abatement workers wear a personal air monitor that indicates the amount of lead to which a worker has been exposed. Workers also use monitoring devices to identify the asbestos, lead, and other materials that need to be removed from the surfaces of walls and structures.

Transportation of hazardous materials is safer today than it was in the past, but accidents still occur. *Emergency and disaster response workers* clean up hazardous materials after train derailments and trucking accidents. These workers also are needed when an immediate cleanup is required, as would be the case after an attack by biological or chemical weapons.

Some hazardous materials removal workers specialize in radioactive substances. These substances range from low-level contaminated protective clothing, tools, filters, and medical equipment, to highly radioactive nuclear reactor fuels used to produce electricity. *Decontamination technicians* perform duties similar to those of janitors and cleaners, but the items and areas they clean are radioactive. They use brooms, mops, and other tools to clean exposed areas and remove exposed items for decontamination or disposal. Some of these jobs are now being done by robots controlled by people away from the contamination site. Increasingly, many of these remote devices are being used to automatically monitor and survey surfaces, such as floors and walls, for contamination.

With experience, decontamination technicians can advance to *radiation-protection technician* jobs and use radiation survey meters and other remote devices to locate and evaluate materials, operate high-pressure cleaning equipment for decontamination, and package radioactive materials for transportation or disposal.

Decommissioning and decontamination workers remove and treat radioactive materials generated by nuclear facilities and power plants. With a variety of handtools, they break down contaminated items such as "gloveboxes," which are used to process radioactive materials. At decommissioning sites, the workers clean and decontaminate the facility, as well as remove any radioactive or contaminated materials.

Treatment, storage, and disposal workers transport and prepare materials for treatment or disposal. To ensure proper treatment of the materials, laws, typically regulated by the U.S. Environmental Protection Agency (EPA) or Occupational Safety and Health Administration (OSHA), require these workers to be able to verify shipping manifests. At incinerator facilities, treatment, storage, and disposal workers transport materials from the customer or service center to the incinerator. At landfills, they follow a strict procedure for the processing and storage of hazardous materials. They organize and track the location of items in the landfill and may help change the state of a material from liquid to solid in preparation for its storage. These workers typically operate heavy machinery, such as forklifts, earthmoving machinery, and large trucks and rigs.

To help clean up the Nation's hazardous waste sites, a Federal program, called Superfund, was created in 1980. Under the Superfund program, abandoned, accidentally spilled, or illegally dumped hazardous waste that poses a current or future threat to human health or the environment is cleaned up. In doing so, the EPA along with potentially responsible parties, communities, local, State, and Federal authorities, identify hazardous waste sites, test site conditions, formulate cleanup plans, and clean up the sites.

Mold remediation is a new aspect of some hazardous materials removal work. Some types of mold can cause allergic reactions, especially in people who are susceptible to them. Although mold is present in almost all structures and is not usually defined as a hazardous material, some mold—especially the types that cause allergic reactions—can infest a building to such a degree that extensive efforts must be taken to remove it safely. Molds are fungi that typically grow in warm, damp conditions both indoors and outdoors year round. They can be found in heating and air-conditioning ducts, within walls, and in showers, attics, and basements. Although mold remediation is often undertaken by other construction workers, large scale mold removal is usually handled by hazardous materials removal workers, who take special precautions to protect themselves and surrounding areas from being contaminated.

Hazardous materials removal workers also may be required to construct scaffolding or erect containment areas prior to abatement or decontamination. In most cases, government regulation dictates that hazardous materials removal workers be closely supervised on the worksite. The standard usually is 1 supervisor to every 10 workers. The work is highly structured, sometimes planned years in advance, and team oriented. There is a great deal of cooperation among supervisors and workers. Because of the hazard presented by the materials being removed, work areas are restricted to licensed hazardous materials removal workers, thus minimizing exposure to the public.

Work environment. Hazardous materials removal workers function in a highly structured environment to minimize the danger they face. Each phase of an operation is planned in ad-

Most hazardous materials removal workers are required to wear respirators to protect them from airborne particles.

vance, and workers are trained to deal with safety breaches and hazardous situations. Crews and supervisors take every precaution to ensure that the worksite is safe. Whether they work with asbestos, mold, lead abatement, or in radioactive decontamination, hazardous materials removal workers must stand, stoop, and kneel for long periods. Some must wear fully enclosed personal protective suits for several hours at a time; these suits may be hot and uncomfortable and may cause some individuals to experience claustrophobia.

Hazardous materials removal workers face different working conditions, depending on their area of expertise. Although many work a standard 40-hour week, overtime and shift work are common, especially for emergency and disaster response workers. Asbestos and lead abatement workers usually work in structures such as office buildings, schools, or historic buildings under renovation. Because they are under pressure to complete their work within certain deadlines, workers may experience fatigue. Completing projects frequently requires night and weekend work, because hazardous materials removal workers often work around the schedules of others. Treatment, storage, and disposal workers are employed primarily at facilities such as landfills, incinerators, boilers, and industrial furnaces. These facilities often are located in remote areas, due to the kinds of work being done. As a result, workers employed by treatment, storage, or disposal facilities may commute long distances to their jobs.

Decommissioning and decontamination workers, decontamination technicians, and radiation protection technicians work at nuclear facilities and electric power plants. Like treatment, storage, and disposal facilities, these sites often are far from urban areas. Workers, who often perform jobs in cramped conditions, may need to use sharp tools to dismantle contaminated objects. A hazardous materials removal worker must have great self-control and a level head to cope with the daily stress associated with handling hazardous materials.

Hazardous materials removal workers may be required to travel outside their normal working areas in order to respond to emergencies, the cleanup of which sometimes take several days or weeks to complete. During the cleanup, workers may be away from home for the entire time.

Training, Other Qualifications, and Advancement

No formal education beyond a high school diploma is required for a person to become a hazardous materials removal worker. However, Federal, State, and local government standards require specific types of on-the-job training. The regulations vary by specialty and sometimes by State or locality. Employers are responsible for employee training.

Education and training. Hazardous materials removal workers usually need at least 40 hours of formal on-the-job training. For most specialties, this training must meet specific requirements set by the Federal Government or individual States.

Licensure. Workers who treat asbestos and lead, the most common contaminants, must complete a training program through their employer that meets Occupational Safety and Health Administration (OSHA) standards. Employer-sponsored training is usually performed in-house, and the employer

Projections data from the National Employment Matrix

Occupational Title	SOC Code	Employment, 2006	Projected employment, 2016	Change, 2006-16	
				Number	Percent
Hazardous materials removal workers	47-4041	39,000	44,000	4,400	11

NOTE: Data in this table are rounded. See the discussion of the employment projections table in the *Handbook* introductory chapter on *Occupational Information Included in the Handbook*.

is responsible for covering all technical and safety subjects outlined by OSHA.

To become an emergency and disaster response worker and treatment, storage, and disposal worker, candidates must obtain a Federal license as mandated by OSHA. Employers are responsible for ensuring that employees complete a formal 40-hour training program, given either in house or in OSHA-approved training centers. The program covers health hazards, personal protective equipment and clothing, site safety, recognition and identification of hazards, and decontamination.

In some cases, workers may discover one hazardous material while abating another. If they are not licensed to work with the newly discovered material, they cannot continue to work with it. Many experienced workers opt to take courses in additional types of hazardous material removal to avoid this situation. Mold removal is not regulated by OSHA, but is regulated by each State.

For decommissioning and decontamination workers employed at nuclear facilities, training is most extensive. In addition to obtaining licensure through the standard 40-hour training course in hazardous waste removal, workers must take courses dealing with regulations governing nuclear materials and radiation safety as mandated by the Nuclear Regulatory Commission. These courses add up to approximately 3 months of training, although most are not taken consecutively. Many agencies, organizations, and companies throughout the country provide training programs that are approved by the U.S. Environmental Protection Agency, the U.S. Department of Energy, and other regulatory bodies. Workers in all fields are required to take refresher courses every year to maintain their license.

Other qualifications. Workers must be able to perform basic mathematical conversions and calculations when mixing solutions that neutralize contaminants and should have good physical strength and manual dexterity. Because of the nature of the work and the time constraints sometimes involved, employers prefer people who are dependable, prompt, and detail-oriented. Because much of the work is done in buildings, a background in construction is helpful.

Employment

Hazardous materials removal workers held about 39,000 jobs in 2006. About 79 percent were employed in waste management and remediation services. Another 5 percent were employed in construction, primarily in asbestos abatement and lead abatement. A small number worked at nuclear and electric plants as decommissioning and decontamination workers and radiation safety and decontamination technicians.

Job Outlook

Employment of hazardous materials removal workers is expected to grow about as fast as average. Good job opportunities

are expected because of the need to replace the large number of workers who leave the occupation each year.

Employment change. Employment of hazardous materials removal workers is expected to grow 11 percent between 2006 and 2016, about as fast as the average for all occupations. Since the 1970s, asbestos and lead-based paints and plumbing fixtures and pipes have not been used and much of the remediation stemming from those products has taken place. With the continuing decline in the number of structures that contain asbestos and lead, demand for asbestos and lead abatement workers will be somewhat limited. Some growth, however, will result from the need to abate lead and asbestos from Federal and historic buildings. Mold remediation is a small and previously rapidly growing part of the occupation. However, builders have reduced the mold problem by improving the quality of construction to prevent moisture from entering buildings, limiting job growth for this specialty. Also, as more workers in other occupations, such as painters and heating, ventilation, and air-conditioning workers, are able to perform mold, lead, and asbestos removal on small-scale projects, employment growth of hazardous materials removal workers will continue to be negatively impacted.

Employment of decontamination technicians, radiation safety technicians, and decommissioning and decontamination workers, however, is expected to grow in response to increased pressure for safer and cleaner nuclear and electric generation facilities. Renewed interest in nuclear power production could lead to the construction of additional facilities, resulting in the need for many new workers.

Numerous Superfund projects will require cleanup of hazardous materials waste sites, spurring demand for hazardous materials removal workers. However, employment growth will largely be determined by Federal funding, which has been declining in recent years.

Job prospects. In addition to some job openings from employment growth, many openings are expected for hazardous materials removal workers because of the need to replace workers who leave the occupation, leading to good opportunities. The often dangerous aspects of the job lead to high turnover because many workers do not stay in the occupation long. Opportunities for decontamination technicians, radiation safety technicians, and decontamination workers should be particularly good as a number of new workers will be needed to replace those who retire or leave the occupation for other reasons.

Lead and asbestos workers will have some opportunities at specialty remediation companies as restoration of Federal buildings and historic structures continues, although at a slower pace. The best employment opportunities for mold remediation workers will be in Southeast, and parts of the Northeast and Northwest, where mold tends to thrive.

These workers are not greatly affected by economic fluctuations because the facilities in which they work must operate, regardless of the state of the economy.

Earnings

Median hourly earnings of wage and salary hazardous materials removal workers were $17.04 in May 2006. The middle 50 percent earned between $13.31 and $22.75 per hour. The lowest 10 percent earned less than $11.02 per hour, and the highest 10 percent earned more than $28.45 per hour. The median hourly earnings in remediation and other waste management services, the largest industry employing hazardous materials removal workers, were $16.75.

Related Occupations

Asbestos abatement workers and lead abatement workers share skills with other construction trades workers, including painters and paperhangers; insulation workers; and sheet metal workers. Treatment, storage, and disposal workers, decommissioning and decontamination workers, and decontamination and radiation safety technicians work closely with plant and system operators, such as power plant operators, distributors, and dispatchers and water and liquid waste treatment plant and system operators. Police officers and firefighters also respond to emergencies and often are the first ones to respond to incidents where hazardous materials may be present.

Sources of Additional Information

For more information on hazardous materials removal workers in the construction industry, including information on training, contact:

➤ Laborers-AGC Education and Training Fund, 37 Deerfield Rd., P.O. Box 37, Pomfret, CT 06259.
Internet: **http://www.laborerslearn.org**

Insulation Workers

(O*NET 47-2131.00, 47-2132.00)

Significant Points

- Workers must follow strict safety guidelines to protect themselves from insulating irritants.

- Most insulation workers learn their work informally on the job; others complete formal apprenticeship programs.

- Job opportunities are expected to be excellent.

Nature of the Work

Properly insulated buildings reduce energy consumption by keeping heat in during the winter and out in the summer. Vats, tanks, vessels, boilers, steam and hot-water pipes, and refrigerated storage rooms also are insulated to prevent the wasteful loss of heat or cold and to prevent burns. Insulation also helps to reduce the noise that passes through walls and ceilings. Insulation workers install the materials used to insulate buildings and equipment.

Insulation workers cement, staple, wire, tape, or spray insulation. When covering a steam pipe, for example, insulation workers measure and cut sections of insulation to the proper length, stretch it open along a cut that runs the length of the material, and slip it over the pipe. They fasten the insulation with adhesive, staples, tape, or wire bands. Sometimes, they wrap a cover of aluminum, plastic, or canvas over the insulation and cement or band the cover in place. Insulation workers may screw on sheet metal around insulated pipes to protect the insulation from weather conditions or physical abuse.

When covering a wall or other flat surface, workers may use a hose to spray foam insulation onto a wire mesh that provides a rough surface to which the foam can cling and that adds strength to the finished surface. Workers may then install drywall or apply a final coat of plaster for a finished appearance.

In attics or exterior walls, workers may blow in loose-fill insulation. A helper feeds a machine with fiberglass, cellulose, or rock-wool insulation, while another worker blows the insulation with a compressor hose into the space being filled.

In new construction or on major renovations, insulation workers staple fiberglass or rock-wool batts to exterior walls and ceilings before drywall, paneling, or plaster walls are put in place. In making major renovations to old buildings or when putting new insulation around pipes and industrial machinery, insulation workers often must first remove the old insulation. In the past, asbestos—now known to cause cancer in humans—was used extensively in walls and ceilings and to cover pipes, boilers, and various industrial equipment. Because of this danger, U.S. Environmental Protection Agency regulations require that asbestos be removed before a building undergoes major renovations or is demolished. When asbestos is present, specially trained workers must remove it before insulation workers can install the new insulating materials. (See the statement on hazardous materials removal workers elsewhere in the *Handbook*.)

Insulation workers use common handtools, including trowels, brushes, knives, scissors, saws, pliers, and stapling guns. They may use power saws to cut insulating materials, welding machines to join sheet metal or secure clamps, and compressors to blow or spray insulation.

Insulation workers must follow strict safety guidelines to protect themselves.

Projections data from the National Employment Matrix

Occupational Title	SOC Code	Employment, 2006	Projected employment, 2016	Change, 2006-16	
				Number	Percent
Insulation workers...	47-2130	61,000	66,000	5,200	8
Insulation workers, floor, ceiling, and wall..................................	47-2131	32,000	35,000	2,700	8
Insulation workers, mechanical...	47-2132	28,000	31,000	2,500	9

NOTE: Data in this table are rounded. See the discussion of the employment projections table in the *Handbook* introductory chapter on *Occupational Information Included in the Handbook.*

Work environment. Insulation workers generally work indoors in residential and industrial settings. They spend most of the workday on their feet, either standing, bending, or kneeling. They also work from ladders or in confined spaces. Their work usually requires more coordination than strength. In industrial settings, these workers often insulate pipes and vessels at temperatures that may cause burns. Minute particles from insulation materials, especially when blown, can irritate the eyes, skin, and respiratory system. Workers must follow strict safety guidelines to protect themselves. They keep work areas well ventilated; wear protective suits, masks, and respirators; and take decontamination showers when necessary. Most insulation is applied after buildings are enclosed, so weather conditions have less effect on the employment of insulation workers than some other construction workers.

Training, Other Qualifications, and Advancement

Most insulation workers learn their trade informally on the job, although some complete formal apprenticeship programs.

Education and training. Employers prefer to hire high school graduates. High school courses in blueprint reading, shop mathematics, science, sheet metal layout, woodworking, and general construction provide a helpful background.

Most new workers receive instruction and supervision from experienced insulation workers. Trainees begin with simple tasks, such as carrying insulation or holding material while it is fastened in place. On-the-job training can take up to 2 years, depending on the nature of the work, but most training is completed in 3 to 6 months. Learning to install insulation in homes generally requires less training than does learning to apply insulation in commercial and industrial settings. As they gain experience, trainees receive less supervision, more responsibility, and higher pay

Trainees in formal apprenticeship programs receive in-depth instruction in all phases of insulation. Apprenticeships are generally offered by contractors that install and maintain industrial insulation. Apprenticeship programs may be provided by a joint committee of local insulation contractors and the local union of the International Association of Heat and Frost Insulators and Asbestos Workers, to which some insulation workers belong. Programs normally consist of 4 or 5 years of on-the-job training coupled with classroom instruction, and trainees must pass practical and written tests to demonstrate their knowledge of the trade.

Licensure. The Environmental Protection Agency offers mandatory certification for insulation workers who remove and handle asbestos.

Other qualifications. For entry-level jobs, insulation contractors prefer to hire workers who are in good physical condi-

tion and licensed to drive. Applicants seeking apprenticeship positions should have a high school diploma or its equivalent and be at least 18 years old. Supervisors and contractors, especially, need good communication skills to deal with clients and subcontractors.

Certification and advancement. A voluntary certification program has been developed by insulation contractor organizations to help workers prove their skills and knowledge of residential insulation. Certification in insulation of industrial settings is being developed. Workers need at least 6 months of experience before they can complete certification. The North American Insulation Manufacturer's Association also offers a certification for insulation energy appraisal.

Skilled insulation workers may advance to supervisor, shop superintendent, or insulation contract estimator, or they may set up their own insulation business.

For those who would like to advance, it is increasingly important to be able to relay instructions and safety precautions to workers in both English and Spanish because Spanish-speaking workers make up a large part of the construction workforce in many areas.

Employment

Insulation workers held about 61,000 jobs in 2006. The construction industry employed 91 percent of workers; 53 percent work for drywall and insulation contractors. Other insulation workers held jobs in the Federal Government, in wholesale trade, and in shipbuilding and other manufacturing industries that have extensive installations for power, heating, and cooling. In less populated areas, carpenters, heating and air-conditioning installers or drywall installers may do insulation work.

Job Outlook

Insulation workers should have excellent employment opportunities due to about average job growth coupled with the need to replace many workers who leave this occupation.

Employment change. Employment of insulation workers is expected to increase 8 percent during the 2006-16 decade, about as fast as the average for all occupations. Demand for insulation workers will be spurred by the continuing need for energy efficient buildings and power plant construction, both of which will generate work in existing structures and new construction. Growth might be tempered as other workers—such as carpenters, heating and air-conditioning installers, or drywall installers—do some insulation work.

Job prospects. Job opportunities for insulation workers are expected to be excellent. In addition to opportunities created by job growth, there will be a need to replace many workers. The irritating nature of many insulation materials, combined with the often difficult working conditions, causes many insulation workers to leave the occupation each year. Job openings will also arise from the need to replace workers who retire or leave the labor force for other reasons.

Insulation workers in the construction industry may experience periods of unemployment because of the short duration of many construction projects and the cyclical nature of construction activity. Workers employed to perform industrial plant maintenance generally have more stable employment because maintenance and repair must be done continually.

Earnings

In May 2006, median hourly earnings of wage and salary insulation workers, floor, ceiling, and wall were $14.67. The middle 50 percent earned between $11.26 and $20.00. The lowest 10 percent earned less than $9.25, and the highest 10 percent earned more than $27.76. Median hourly earnings of insulation workers, mechanical were $17.74. The middle 50 percent earned between $13.55 and $25.12. The lowest 10 percent earned less than $10.51, and the highest 10 percent earned more than $33.39. Median hourly earnings in the industries employing the largest numbers of insulation workers were:

Insulation workers, mechanical
    Building finishing contractors $18.69
    Building equipment contractors 16.60
Insulation workers, floor, ceiling, and wall
    Building finishing contractors $14.53

Union workers tend to earn more than nonunion workers. Apprentices start at about one-half of the journey worker's wage. Insulation workers doing commercial and industrial work earn substantially more than those working in residential construction, which does not require as much skill.

Related Occupations

Insulation workers combine their knowledge of insulation materials with the skills of cutting, fitting, and installing materials. Workers in occupations involving similar skills include carpenters; carpet, floor, and tile installers and finishers; drywall installers, ceiling tile installers, and tapers; roofers; and sheet metal workers.

Sources of Additional Information

For information about training programs or other work opportunities in this trade, contact a local insulation contractor, the nearest office of the State employment service or apprenticeship agency, or the following organization:

➤ National Insulation Association, 99 Canal Center Plaza, Suite 222, Alexandria, VA 22314.
Internet: **http://www.insulation.org**

For more information about residential insulation, contact:

➤ Insulation Contractors Association of America, 1321 Duke St., Suite 303, Alexandria, VA 22314.
Internet: **http://www.insulate.org**

You can also find information on the registered apprenticeships together with links to State apprenticeship programs on the U.S. Department of Labor's Web site: **http://www.doleta.gov/atels_bat** Apprenticeship information is also available from the U.S. Department of Labor's toll free helpline: (877) 872-5627.

For general information on apprenticeships and how to get them, see the *Occupational Outlook Quarterly* article "Apprenticeships: Career training, credentials—and a paycheck in your pocket," online at **http://www.bls.gov/opub/ooq/2002/summer/art01.pdf** and in print at many libraries and career centers.

Painters and Paperhangers

(O*NET 47-2141.00, 47-2142.00)

Significant Points

- Employment prospects for painters should be excellent due to the large numbers of workers who leave the occupation for other jobs; paperhangers will face very limited opportunities.

- Most workers learn informally on the job as helpers, but some experts recommend completion of an apprenticeship program.

- About 42 percent of painters and paperhangers are self-employed.

Nature of the Work

Paint and wall coverings make surfaces clean, attractive, and bright. In addition, paints and other sealers protect exterior surfaces from wear caused by exposure to the weather.

Painters apply paint, stain, varnish, and other finishes to buildings and other structures. They choose the right paint or finish for the surface to be covered, taking into account durability, ease of handling, method of application, and customers' wishes. Painters first prepare the surfaces to be covered, so that the paint will adhere properly. This may require removing the old coat of paint by stripping, sanding, wire brushing, burning, or water and abrasive blasting. Painters also wash walls and trim to remove dirt and grease, fill nail holes and cracks, sandpaper rough spots, and brush off dust. On new surfaces, they apply a primer or sealer to prepare the surface for the finish coat. Painters also mix paints and match colors, relying on knowledge of paint composition and color harmony. In large paint shops or hardware stores, mixing and matching are automated.

There are several ways to apply paint and similar coverings. Painters must be able to choose the right paint applicator for each job, depending on the surface to be covered, the characteristics of the finish, and other factors. Some jobs need only a good bristle brush with a soft, tapered edge; others require a dip or fountain pressure roller; still others are best done using a paint sprayer. Many jobs need several types of applicators. In fact, painters may use an assortment of brushes, edgers, and rollers for a single job. The right tools speed the painter's work and also produce the most attractive surface.

Some painting artisans specialize in creating unique finishes by using one of many decorative techniques. These techniques often involve "broken color," a process created by applying one or more colors in broken layers over a different base coat to pro-

scaffolds suspended by ropes, or cables attached to roof hooks. When painting steeples and other conical structures, they use a bosun's chair, a swing-like device.

Paperhangers cover walls and ceilings with decorative wall coverings made of paper, vinyl, or fabric. They first prepare the surface to be covered by applying "sizing," which seals the surface and makes the covering adhere better. When redecorating, they may first remove the old covering by soaking, steaming, or applying solvents. When necessary, they patch holes and take care of other imperfections before hanging the new wall covering.

After the surface has been prepared, paperhangers must prepare the paste or other adhesive, unless they are using pretreated paper. They then measure the area to be covered, check the covering for flaws, cut the covering into strips of the proper size, and closely examine the pattern in order to match it when the strips are hung. Much of this process can now be handled by specialized equipment.

The next step is to brush or roll the adhesive onto the back of the covering, if needed, and to then place the strips on the wall or ceiling, making sure the pattern is matched, the strips are straight, and the edges are butted together to make tight, closed seams. Finally, paperhangers smooth the strips to remove bubbles and wrinkles, trim the top and bottom with a razor knife, and wipe off any excess adhesive.

Work environment. Most painters and paperhangers work 40 hours a week or less; about 24 percent have variable schedules or work part time. Painters and paperhangers must stand for long periods, often working from scaffolding and ladders. Their jobs also require a considerable amount of climbing, bending, and stretching. These workers must have stamina because much of the work is done with their arms raised overhead. Painters, especially industrial painters, often work outdoors, almost always in dry, warm weather. Those who paint bridges or building infrastructure may be exposed to extreme heights and uncomfortable positions; some painters work suspended with ropes or cables.

Some painting jobs can leave a worker covered with paint. Drywall dust created by electric sanders prior to painting requires workers to wear protective safety glasses and a dust mask. Painters and paperhangers sometimes work with materials that are hazardous or toxic, such as when they are required to remove lead-based paints. In the most dangerous situations, painters work in a sealed self-contained suit to prevent inhalation of or contact with hazardous materials. Although workers are subject to falls from ladders, the occupation is not as hazardous as some other construction occupations.

Training, Other Qualifications, and Advancement

Painting and paperhanging is learned mostly on the job, but some experts recommend completion of an apprenticeship program.

Education and training. Most painters and paperhangers learn through on-the-job training and by working as a helper to an experienced painter. However, there are a number of formal and informal training programs that provide more thorough instruction and a better career foundation. In general, the more formal the training received, the more likely the individual will

Self-employed, independent painting contractors account for 2 out of 5 painters and paperhangers.

duce a mottled or textured effect. Often these techniques employ glazes or washes applied over a solid colored background. Glazes are made of oil-based paints and give a sleek glow to walls. Washes are made of latex-based paints that have been thinned with water and can add a greater sense of depth and texture. Other decorative painting techniques include sponging, rag-rolling, stippling, sheen striping, dragging, distressing, color blocking, marbling, and faux finishes.

Some painters specialize in painting industrial structures to prevent deterioration. One example is applying a protective coating to steel bridges to fight corrosion. The coating most commonly used is a waterborne acrylic solvent that is easy to apply and environmentally friendly, but other specialized and sometimes difficult-to-apply coatings may be used. Painters may also coat interior and exterior manufacturing facilities and equipment such as storage tanks, plant buildings, lockers, piping, structural steel, and ships.

When painting any industrial structure, workers must take necessary safety precautions depending on their project. Those who specialize in interior applications such as painting the inside of storage tanks, for example, must wear a full-body protective suit. When working on bridges, painters are often suspended by cables and may work at extreme heights. When working on tall buildings, painters erect scaffolding, including "swing stages,"

enter the profession at a higher level. There are limited informal training opportunities for paperhangers because there are fewer paperhangers and helpers are usually not required.

If available, apprenticeships generally provide a mixture of classroom instruction and paid on-the-job training. Apprenticeships for painters and paperhangers consist of 2 to 4 years of on-the-job training, supplemented by a minimum of 144 hours of related classroom instruction each year. A high school education or its equivalent, with courses in mathematics, usually is required to enter an apprenticeship program. Apprentices receive instruction in color harmony, use and care of tools and equipment, surface preparation, application techniques, paint mixing and matching, characteristics of different finishes, blueprint reading, wood finishing, and safety.

Besides apprenticeships, some workers gain skills by attending technical schools that offer training prior to employment. These schools can take about a year to complete. Others receive training through local vocational high schools.

Whether a painter learns the trade through a formal apprenticeship or informally as a helper, on-the-job instruction covers similar skill areas. Under the direction of experienced workers, trainees carry supplies, erect scaffolds, and do simple painting and surface preparation tasks while they learn about paint and painting equipment. As they gain experience, trainees learn to prepare surfaces for painting and paperhanging, to mix paints, and to apply paint and wall coverings efficiently and neatly. Near the end of their training, they may learn decorating concepts, color coordination, and cost-estimating techniques. In addition to learning craft skills, painters must become familiar with safety and health regulations so that their work complies with the law.

Other qualifications. Painters and paperhangers should have good manual dexterity, vision, and color sense. They also need physical stamina and balance to work on ladders and platforms. Apprentices or helpers generally must be at least 18 years old and in good physical condition, in addition to the high school diploma or equivalent that most apprentices need.

Certification and advancement. Some organizations offer training and certification to enhance the skills of their members. People interested in industrial painting, for example, can earn several designations from the National Association of Corrosion Engineers in several areas of specialization, including one for coating applicators, called Protective Coating Specialist. Courses range from 1 day to several weeks depending on the certification program and specialty.

Painters and paperhangers may advance to supervisory or estimating jobs with painting and decorating contractors. Many establish their own painting and decorating businesses. For those who would like to advance, it is increasingly important to be able to communicate in both English and Spanish in order to relay instructions and safety precautions to workers with limited English skills; Spanish-speaking workers make up a large part of the construction workforce in many areas. Painting contractors need good English skills to deal with clients and subcontractors.

Employment

Painters and paperhangers held about 473,000 jobs in 2006; about 98 percent were painters. Around 38 percent of painters and paperhangers work for painting and wall covering contractors engaged in new construction, repair, restoration, or remodeling work. In addition, organizations that own or manage large buildings—such as apartment complexes—may employ painters, as do some schools, hospitals, factories, and government agencies.

Self-employed independent painting contractors accounted for 42 percent of all painters and paperhangers, significantly greater than the 20 percent of all construction trades workers combined.

Job Outlook

Employment of painters and paperhangers is expected to grow about as fast as the average for all occupations, reflecting increases in the stock of buildings and other structures that require maintenance and renovation. Excellent employment opportunities are expected for painters due to the need to replace the large number of workers who leave the occupation; paperhangers will have very limited opportunities.

Employment change. Overall employment is expected to grow by 11 percent between 2006 and 2016, about as fast as the average for all occupations. Driving employment growth will be retiring baby boomers who either purchase second homes or otherwise leave their existing homes that then require interior painting. Investors who sell properties or rent them out will also require the services of painters prior to completing a transaction. The relatively short life of exterior paints in residential homes as well as changing color and application trends will continue to support demand for painters. Painting is labor-intensive and not susceptible to technological changes that might make workers more productive and slow employment growth.

Growth of industrial painting will be driven by the need to prevent corrosion and deterioration of the many industrial structures by painting or coating them. Applying a protective coating to steel bridges, for example, is cost effective and can add years to the life expectancy of a bridge.

Employment of paperhangers should decline rapidly as many homeowners take advantage of easy application materials and resort to cheaper alternatives, such as painting.

Projections data from the National Employment Matrix

Occupational Title	SOC Code	Employment, 2006	Projected employment, 2016	Change, 2006-16	
				Number	Percent
Painters and paperhangers..	47-2140	473,000	526,000	53,000	11
Painters, construction and maintenance......................................	47-2141	463,000	517,000	54,000	12
Paperhangers...	47-2142	9,900	8,700	-1,200	-12

NOTE: Data in this table are rounded. See the discussion of the employment projections table in the *Handbook* introductory chapter on *Occupational Information Included in the Handbook.*

Job prospects. Job prospects for painters should be excellent because of the need to replace workers who leave the occupation for other jobs. There are no strict training requirements for entry into these jobs, so many people with limited skills work as painters or helpers for a relatively short time and then move on to other types of work with higher pay or better working conditions.

Opportunities for industrial painters should be excellent as the positions available should be greater than the pool of qualified individuals to fill them. While industrial structures that require painting are located throughout the Nation, the best employment opportunities should be in the petrochemical industry in the Gulf Coast region, where strong demand and the largest concentration of workers exists.

Very few openings will arise for paperhangers because the number of these jobs is comparatively small and cheaper, more modern decorative finishes such as faux effects and sponging have gained in popularity at the expense of paper, vinyl, or fabric wall coverings.

Jobseekers considering these occupations should expect some periods of unemployment, especially until they gain experience. Many construction projects are of short duration, and construction activity is cyclical in nature. Remodeling, restoration, and maintenance projects, however, should continue as homeowners undertake renovation projects and hire painters even in economic downturns. Nonetheless, workers in these trades may experience periods of unemployment when the overall level of construction falls. On the other hand, shortages of these workers may occur in some areas during peak periods of building activity.

Earnings

In May 2006, median hourly earnings of wage and salary painters, construction and maintenance, were $15.00, not including the earnings of the self-employed. The middle 50 percent earned between $12.19 and $19.51. The lowest 10 percent earned less than $9.97, and the highest 10 percent earned more than $25.62. Median hourly earnings in the industries employing the largest numbers of painters were as follows:

Local government	$20.11
Drywall and insulation contractors	16.18
Nonresidential building construction	15.68
Residential building construction	15.04
Painting and wall covering contractors	14.62

In May 2006, median earnings for wage and salary paperhangers were $16.21. The middle 50 percent earned between $13.12 and $20.62. The lowest 10 percent earned less than $10.34, and the highest 10 percent earned more than $26.77.

Earnings for painters may be reduced on occasion because of bad weather and the short-term nature of many construction jobs. Hourly wage rates for apprentices usually start at 40 to 50 percent of the rate for experienced workers and increase periodically.

Some painters and paperhangers are members of the International Brotherhood of Painters and Allied Trades. Some painters are members of other unions.

Related Occupations

Painters and paperhangers apply various coverings to decorate and protect wood, drywall, metal, and other surfaces. Other construction occupations in which workers do finishing work include carpenters; carpet, floor, and tile installers and finishers; drywall installers, ceiling tile installers, and tapers; painting and coating workers, except construction and maintenance; and plasterers and stucco masons.

Sources of Additional Information

For details about painting and paperhanging apprenticeships or work opportunities, contact local painting and decorating contractors, local trade organizations, a local of the International Union of Painters and Allied Trades, a local joint union-management apprenticeship committee, or an office of the State apprenticeship agency or employment service.

For information about the work of painters and paperhangers and training opportunities, contact:

➤ Associated Builders and Contractors, Workforce Development Department, 4250 North Fairfax Dr., 9th Floor, Arlington, VA 22203. Internet: **http://www.trytools.org**

➤ International Union of Painters and Allied Trades, 1750 New York Ave. NW., Washington, DC 20006.
Internet: **http://www.iupat.org**

➤ National Center for Construction Education and Research, P.O. Box 141104, Gainesville, FL 32614.
Internet: **http://www.nccer.org**

➤ Painting and Decorating Contractors of America, 1801 Park 270 Dr., Suite 220, St.Louis, MO 63146.
Internet: **http://www.pdca.org**

For general information about the work of industrial painters and opportunities for training and certification as a protective coating specialist, contact:

➤ National Association of Corrosion Engineers, 1440 South Creek Dr., Houston, TX 77084.
Internet: **http://www.nace.org**

Pipelayers, Plumbers, Pipefitters, and Steamfitters

(O*NET 47-2151.00, 47-2152.00, 47-2152.01, 47-2152.02)

Significant Points

- Job opportunities should be very good, especially for workers with welding experience.

- Pipelayers, plumbers, pipefitters, and steamfitters comprise one of the largest and highest paid construction occupations.

- Most States and localities require plumbers to be licensed.

- Apprenticeship programs generally provide the most comprehensive training, but many workers train in career or technical schools or community colleges.

Nature of the Work

Most people are familiar with plumbers who come to their home to unclog a drain or install an appliance. In addition to these activities, however, pipelayers, plumbers, pipefitters, and steamfitters install, maintain, and repair many different types of pipe systems. For example, some systems move water to a municipal water treatment plant and then to residential, commercial, and public buildings. Other systems dispose of waste, provide gas to stoves and furnaces, or provide for heating and cooling needs. Pipe systems in powerplants carry the steam that powers huge turbines. Pipes also are used in manufacturing plants to move material through the production process. Specialized piping systems are very important in both pharmaceutical and computer-chip manufacturing.

Although pipelaying, plumbing, pipefitting, and steamfitting sometimes are considered a single trade, workers generally specialize in one of five areas. *Pipelayers* lay clay, concrete, plastic, or cast-iron pipe for drains, sewers, water mains, and oil or gas lines. Before laying the pipe, pipelayers prepare and grade the trenches either manually or with machines. After laying the pipe, they weld, glue, cement, or otherwise join the pieces together. *Plumbers* install and repair the water, waste disposal, drainage, and gas systems in homes and commercial and industrial buildings. Plumbers also install plumbing fixtures—bathtubs, showers, sinks, and toilets—and appliances such as dishwashers and water heaters. *Pipefitters* install and repair both high-pressure and low-pressure pipe systems used in manufacturing, in the generation of electricity, and in the heating and cooling of buildings. They also install automatic controls that are increasingly being used to regulate these systems. Some pipefitters specialize in only one type of system. *Steamfitters* install pipe systems that move liquids or gases under high pressure. *Sprinklerfitters* install automatic fire sprinkler systems in buildings.

Pipelayers, plumbers, pipefitters, and steamfitters use many different materials and construction techniques, depending on the type of project. Residential water systems, for example, incorporate copper, steel, and plastic pipe that can be handled and installed by one or two plumbers. Municipal sewerage systems, on the other hand, are made of large cast-iron pipes; installation normally requires crews of pipefitters. Despite these differences, all pipelayers, plumbers, pipefitters, and steamfitters must be able to follow building plans or blueprints and instructions from supervisors, lay out the job, and work efficiently with the materials and tools of their trade. Computers and specialized software are used to create blueprints and plan layouts.

When construction plumbers install piping in a new house, for example, they work from blueprints or drawings that show the planned location of pipes, plumbing fixtures, and appliances. Recently, plumbers have become more involved in the design process. Their knowledge of codes and the operation of plumbing systems can cut costs. They first lay out the job to fit the piping into the structure of the house with the least waste of material. Then they measure and mark areas in which pipes will be installed and connected. Construction plumbers also check for obstructions such as electrical wiring and, if necessary, plan the pipe installation around the problem.

Pipelayers lay clay, concrete, plastic, or cast-iron pipe for drains, sewers, water mains, and oil or gas lines.

Sometimes, plumbers have to cut holes in walls, ceilings, and floors of a house. For some systems, they may hang steel supports from ceiling joists to hold the pipe in place. To assemble a system, plumbers—using saws, pipe cutters, and pipe-bending machines—cut and bend lengths of pipe. They connect lengths of pipe with fittings, using methods that depend on the type of pipe used. For plastic pipe, plumbers connect the sections and fittings with adhesives. For copper pipe, they slide a fitting over the end of the pipe and solder it in place with a torch.

After the piping is in place in the house, plumbers install the fixtures and appliances and connect the system to the outside water or sewer lines. Finally, using pressure gauges, they check the system to ensure that the plumbing works properly.

Work environment. Pipefitters and steamfitters most often work in industrial and power plants. Plumbers work in commercial and residential settings where water and septic systems need to be installed and maintained. Pipelayers work outdoors, sometime in remote areas, as they build the pipelines that connect sources of oil, gas, and chemicals with the users of these materials. Sprinklerfitters work in all buildings that require the use of fire sprinkler systems.

Because pipelayers, plumbers, pipefitters, and steamfitters frequently must lift heavy pipes, stand for long periods, and sometimes work in uncomfortable or cramped positions, they need physical strength and stamina. They also may have to work outdoors in inclement weather. In addition, they are subject to possible falls from ladders, cuts from sharp tools, and burns from hot pipes or soldering equipment.

Pipelayers, plumbers, pipefitters, and steamfitters engaged in construction generally work a standard 40-hour week; those involved in maintaining pipe systems, including those who provide maintenance services under contract, may have to work evening or weekend shifts and work on call. These maintenance workers may spend a lot of time traveling to and from worksites.

Training, Other Qualifications, and Advancement

Most pipelayers, plumbers, pipefitters, and steamfitters train in career or technical schools or community colleges, and on the job through apprenticeships.

Education and training. Pipelayers, plumbers, pipefitters, and steamfitters enter into the occupation in a variety of ways. Most residential and industrial plumbers get their training in career and technical schools and community colleges and from on-the-job training. Pipelayers, plumbers, pipefitters, and steamfitters who work for nonresidential enterprises are usually trained through formal apprenticeship programs.

Apprenticeship programs generally provide the most comprehensive training available for these jobs. They are administered either by union locals and their affiliated companies or by nonunion contractor organizations. Organizations that sponsor apprenticeships include: the United Association of Journeymen and Apprentices of the Plumbing and Pipefitting Industry of the United States and Canada; local employers of either the Mechanical Contractors Association of America or the National Association of Plumbing-Heating-Cooling Contractors; a union associated with a member of the National Fire Sprinkler Association; the Associated Builders and Contractors; the National Association of Plumbing-Heating-Cooling Contractors; the American Fire Sprinkler Association, or the Home Builders Institute of the National Association of Home Builders.

Apprenticeships—both union and nonunion—consist of 4 or 5 years of paid on-the-job training and at least 144 hours of related classroom instruction per year. Classroom subjects include drafting and blueprint reading, mathematics, applied physics and chemistry, safety, and local plumbing codes and regulations. On the job, apprentices first learn basic skills, such as identifying grades and types of pipe, using the tools of the trade, and safely unloading materials. As apprentices gain experience, they learn how to work with various types of pipe and how to install different piping systems and plumbing fixtures. Apprenticeship gives trainees a thorough knowledge of all aspects of the trade. Although most pipelayers, plumbers, pipefitters, and steamfitters are trained through apprenticeship, some still learn their skills informally on the job.

Licensure. Although there are no uniform national licensing requirements, most States and communities require plumbers to be licensed. Licensing requirements vary, but most localities require workers to have 2 to 5 years of experience and to pass an examination that tests their knowledge of the trade and of local plumbing codes before working independently. Several States require a special license to work on gas lines. A few States require pipe fitters to be licensed. These licenses usually require a test, experience, or both.

Other qualifications. Applicants for union or nonunion apprentice jobs must be at least 18 years old and in good physical condition. A drug test may be required. Apprenticeship committees may require applicants to have a high school diploma or its equivalent. Armed Forces training in pipelaying, plumbing,

and pipefitting is considered very good preparation. In fact, people with this background may be given credit for previous experience when entering a civilian apprenticeship program. High school or postsecondary courses in shop, plumbing, general mathematics, drafting, blueprint reading, computers, and physics also are good preparation.

Advancement. With additional training, some pipelayers, plumbers, pipefitters, and steamfitters become supervisors for mechanical and plumbing contractors. Others, especially plumbers, go into business for themselves, often starting as a self-employed plumber working from home. Some eventually become owners of businesses employing many workers and may spend most of their time as managers rather than as plumbers. Others move into closely related areas such as construction management or building inspection.

For those who would like to advance, it is increasingly important to be able to communicate in both English and Spanish in order to relay instructions and safety precautions to workers with limited understanding of English; Spanish-speaking workers make up a large part of the construction workforce in many areas. Supervisors and contractors need good communication skills to deal with clients and subcontractors.

Employment

Pipelayers, plumbers, pipefitters, and steamfitters constitute one of the largest construction occupations, holding about 569,000 jobs in 2006. About 55 percent worked for plumbing, heating, and air-conditioning contractors engaged in new construction, repair, modernization, or maintenance work. Others did maintenance work for a variety of industrial, commercial, and government employers. For example, pipefitters were employed as maintenance personnel in the petroleum and chemical industries, both of which move liquids and gases through pipes. About 12 percent of pipelayers, plumbers, pipefitters, and steamfitters were self-employed.

Job Outlook

Average employment growth is projected. Job opportunities are expected to be very good, especially for workers with welding experience.

Employment change. Employment of pipelayers, plumbers, pipefitters, and steamfitters is expected to grow 10 percent between 2006 and 2016, about as fast as the average for all occupations. Demand for plumbers will stem from new construction and building renovation. Bath remodeling, in particular, is expected to continue to grow and create more jobs for plumbers. In addition, repair and maintenance of existing residential systems will keep plumbers employed. Demand for pipefitters and steamfitters will be driven by maintenance and construc-

Projections data from the National Employment Matrix

Occupational Title	SOC Code	Employment, 2006	Projected employment, 2016	Change, 2006-16	
				Number	Percent
Pipelayers, plumbers, pipefitters, and steamfitters............................	47-2150	569,000	628,000	59,000	10
Pipelayers..	47-2151	67,000	72,000	5,800	9
Plumbers, pipefitters, and steamfitters	47-2152	502,000	555,000	53,000	11

NOTE: Data in this table are rounded. See the discussion of the employment projections table in the *Handbook* introductory chapter on *Occupational Information Included in the Handbook.*

tion of places such as powerplants, water and wastewater treatment plants, office buildings, and factories, with extensive pipe systems. Growth of pipelayer jobs will stem from the building of new water and sewer lines and pipelines to new oil and gas fields. Demand for sprinklerfitters will increase because of changes to State and local rules for fire protection in homes and businesses.

Job prospects. Job opportunities are expected to be very good, as demand for skilled pipelayers, plumbers, pipefitters, and steamfitters is expected to outpace the supply of workers well trained in this craft in some areas. Some employers report difficulty finding workers with the right qualifications. In addition, many people currently working in these trades are expected to retire over the next 10 years, which will create additional job openings. Workers with welding experience should have especially good opportunities.

Traditionally, many organizations with extensive pipe systems have employed their own plumbers or pipefitters to maintain equipment and keep systems running smoothly. But, to reduce labor costs, many of these firms no longer employ full-time, in-house plumbers or pipefitters. Instead, when they need a plumber, they rely on workers provided under service contracts by plumbing and pipefitting contractors.

Construction projects generally provide only temporary employment. When a project ends, some pipelayers, plumbers, pipefitters, and steamfitters may be unemployed until they can begin work on a new project, although most companies are trying to limit these periods of unemployment to retain workers. In addition, the jobs of pipelayers, plumbers, pipefitters, and steamfitters are generally less sensitive to changes in economic conditions than jobs in other construction trades. Even when construction activity declines, maintenance, rehabilitation, and replacement of existing piping systems, as well as the increasing installation of fire sprinkler systems, provide many jobs for pipelayers, plumbers, pipefitters, and steamfitters.

Earnings

Pipelayers, plumbers, pipefitters, and steamfitters are among the highest paid construction occupations. Median hourly earnings of wage and salary plumbers, pipefitters, and steamfitters were $20.56. The middle 50 percent earned between $15.62 and $27.54. The lowest 10 percent earned less than $12.30, and the highest 10 percent earned more than $34.79. Median hourly earnings in the industries employing the largest numbers of plumbers, pipefitters, and steamfitters were:

Natural gas distribution	$24.91
Nonresidential building construction	21.30
Plumbing, heating, and air-conditioning contractors	20.44
Utility system construction	19.18
Local government	17.86

In May 2006, median hourly earnings of wage and salary pipelayers were $14.58. The middle 50 percent earned between $11.75 and $19.76. The lowest 10 percent earned less than $9.73, and the highest 10 percent earned more than $25.73.

Apprentices usually begin at about 50 percent of the wage rate paid to experienced workers. Wages increase periodically as skills improve. After an initial waiting period, apprentices receive the same benefits as experienced pipelayers, plumbers, pipefitters, and steamfitters.

About 30 percent of pipelayers, plumbers, pipefitters, and steamfitters belonged to a union. Many of these workers are members of the United Association of Journeymen and Apprentices of the Plumbing and Pipefitting Industry of the United States and Canada.

Related Occupations

Other workers who install and repair mechanical systems in buildings include boilermakers; electricians; elevator installers and repairers; heating, air-conditioning, and refrigeration mechanics and installers; industrial machinery mechanics and maintenance workers; millwrights; sheet metal workers; and stationary engineers and boiler operators. Other related occupations include construction managers and construction and building inspectors.

Sources of Additional Information

For information about apprenticeships or work opportunities in pipelaying, plumbing, pipefitting, and steamfitting, contact local plumbing, heating, and air-conditioning contractors; a local or State chapter of the National Association of Plumbing, Heating, and Cooling Contractors; a local chapter of the Mechanical Contractors Association; a local chapter of the United Association of Journeymen and Apprentices of the Plumbing and Pipefitting Industry of the United States and Canada; or the nearest office of your State employment service or apprenticeship agency. Apprenticeship information is also available from the U.S. Department of Labor's toll free helpline: (877) 872-5627.

For information about apprenticeship opportunities for pipelayers, plumbers, pipefitters, and steamfitters, contact:

➤ United Association of Journeymen and Apprentices of the Plumbing and Pipefitting Industry, 901 Massachusetts Ave. NW., Washington, DC 20001. Internet: **http://www.ua.org**

For more information about training programs for pipelayers, plumbers, pipefitters, and steamfitters, contact:

➤ Associated Builders and Contractors, Workforce Development Department, 4250 North Fairfax Dr., 9th Floor, Arlington, VA 22203. Internet: **http://www.trytools.org**

➤ Home Builders Institute, National Association of Home Builders, 1201 15th St.NW., Washington, DC 20005. Internet: **http://www.hbi.org**

For general information about the work of pipelayers, plumbers, and pipefitters, contact:

➤ Mechanical Contractors Association of America, 1385 Piccard Dr., Rockville, MD 20850. Internet: **http://www.mcaa.org**

➤ National Center for Construction Education and Research, 3600 NW 43rd St., Bldg. G, Gainesville, FL 32606. Internet: **http://www.nccer.org**

➤ Plumbing-Heating-Cooling Contractors—National Association, 180 S. Washington St, Falls Church, VA 22040. Internet: **http://www.phccweb.org**

For general information about the work of sprinklerfitters, contact:

➤ American Fire Sprinkler Association, Inc., 12750 Merit Dr., Suite 350 Dallas, TX 75251. Internet:**http://www.firesprinkler.org**

➤ National Fire Sprinkler Association, 40 Jon Barrett Rd., Patterson, NY 12563. Internet: **http://www.nfsa.org**

For general information on apprenticeships and how to get them, see the *Occupational Outlook Quarterly* article "Apprenticeships: Career training, credentials—and a paycheck in your pocket," in print at many libraries and career centers and online at: **http://www.bls.gov/opub/ooq/2002/summer/art01.pdf**

Plasterers and Stucco Masons

(O*NET 47-2161.00)

Significant Points

- Plastering is physically demanding work.

- Becoming a skilled plasterer or stucco mason generally requires 3 or 4 years of training, either informally on the job or through a formal apprenticeship.

- Good employment opportunities are expected.

- The best employment opportunities should continue to be in Florida, California, and the Southwest.

Nature of the Work

Plastering—one of the oldest crafts in the building trades—remains popular due to the durability and relatively low cost of the material. Plasterers apply plaster to interior walls and ceilings to form fire-resistant and relatively soundproof surfaces. They also apply plaster veneer over drywall to create smooth or textured abrasion-resistant finishes. In addition, plasterers install prefabricated exterior insulation systems over existing walls—for good insulation and interesting architectural effects—and cast ornamental designs in plaster. Stucco masons apply durable plasters, such as polymer-based acrylic finishes and stucco, to exterior surfaces. Plasterers and stucco masons should not be confused with drywall installers, ceiling tile installers, and tapers—discussed elsewhere in the *Handbook*—who use drywall instead of plaster to make interior walls and ceilings.

Plasterers can plaster either solid surfaces, such as concrete block, or supportive wire mesh called lath. When plasterers work with hard interior surfaces, such as concrete block and concrete, they first apply a brown coat of gypsum plaster that provides a base, which is followed by a second, or finish coat, also called "white coat," made of a lime-based plaster. When plastering metal-mesh lath foundations, they apply a preparatory, or "scratch coat" with a trowel. They spread this rich plaster mixture into and over the metal lath. Before the plaster sets, plasterers scratch its surface with a rake-like tool to produce ridges, so that the subsequent brown coat will bond tightly. They then apply the brown coat and the finish, white coat.

Applying different types of plaster coating requires different techniques. When applying the brown coat, plasterers spray or trowel the mixture onto the surface, then finish by smoothing it to an even, level surface. Helpers usually prepare this mixture.

For the finish, or white coat, plasterers themselves usually prepare a mixture of lime, plaster of Paris, and water. They quickly apply this using a "hawk," that is a light, metal plate

Most plasterers and stucco masons are employed in Florida, Texas, California, and the Southwest, where exterior stucco with decorative finishes is very popular.

with a handle, along with a trowel, brush, and water. This mixture, which sets very quickly, produces a very smooth, durable finish.

Plasterers also work with a plaster material that can be finished in a single coat. This "thin-coat" or gypsum veneer plaster is made of lime and plaster of Paris and is mixed with water at the jobsite. This plaster provides a smooth, durable, abrasion-resistant finish on interior masonry surfaces, special gypsum baseboard, or drywall prepared with a bonding agent.

Plasterers create decorative interior surfaces as well. One way that they do this is by pressing a brush or trowel firmly against a wet plaster surface and using a circular hand motion to create decorative swirls. Plasterers sometimes do more complex decorative and ornamental work that requires special skill and creativity. For example, they may mold intricate wall and ceiling designs, such as cornice pieces and chair rails. Following an architect's blueprint, plasterers pour or spray a special plaster into a mold and allow it to set. Workers then remove the molded plaster and put it in place, according to the plan.

Stucco masons usually apply stucco—a mixture of Portland cement, lime, and sand—over cement, concrete, masonry or wire lath. Stucco may also be applied directly to a wire lath with a scratch coat, followed by a brown coat, and then a finish coat. Stucco masons may also embed marble or gravel chips into the finish coat to achieve a pebblelike, decorative finish.

When required, plasterers and stucco masons apply insulation to the exteriors of new and old buildings. They cover the outer wall with rigid foam insulation board and reinforcing mesh, and then trowel on a polymer-based or polymer-modified base coat. They may apply an additional coat of this material with a decorative finish.

Work environment. Most plasters work indoors, except for the few who apply decorative exterior finishes. Stucco masons, however, work outside when applying stucco or exterior wall insulation. Plasterers and stucco masons may work on scaffolds high above the ground.

Plastering and stucco work is physically demanding, requiring considerable standing, bending, lifting, and reaching overhead, sometimes causing neck and upper back cramps. The work can also be dusty and dirty. It can irritate the skin, eyes, and lungs unless protective masks and gloves are used.

Training, Other Qualifications, and Advancement

Becoming a skilled plasterer or stucco mason generally requires 3 or 4 years of training, either informally on the job or through a formal apprenticeship.

Education and training. Preparation for a career as a plasterer or stucco mason can begin in high school, with classes in mathematics, mechanical drawing, and shop. After high school, there are many different ways to train.

The most common way is to get a job with a contractor who will provide on-the-job training. Entry-level workers usually start as helpers, assisting more experienced workers. They may start by carrying materials, setting up scaffolds, and mixing plaster. Later, they learn to apply the scratch, brown, and finish coats and may also learn to replicate plaster decorations for restoration work. Some employers enroll helpers in an employer-provided training program or send the employee to a trade or vocational school, or community college to receive further classroom training.

Depending on the region, some employers say a formal apprenticeship is the best way to learn plastering. Apprenticeship programs, sponsored by local joint committees of contractors and unions, usually include 3 or 4 years of paid on-the-job training and 160 hours of classroom instruction each of those years. In class, apprentices learn drafting, blueprint reading, and basic mathematics for layout work. They also learn how to estimate materials and costs and how to cast ornamental plaster designs.

On the job, apprentices learn about lath bases, plaster mixes, methods of plastering and safety practices. They learn how to use various tools, such as hand and powered trowels, floats, brushes, straightedges, power tools, plaster-mixing machines, and piston-type pumps. Some apprenticeship programs also allow individuals to train in related occupations, such as cement masonry and bricklaying.

Applicants for apprentice or helper jobs who have a high school education are preferred. Courses in general mathematics, mechanical drawing, and shop provide a useful background.

Other qualifications. Workers need to be in good physical condition and have good manual dexterity. Artistic creativity is helpful for those who apply decorative finishes. Applicants for apprenticeships usually must be at least 18 years old.

Certification and advancement. Some organizations related to masonry trades offer training and certification intended to enhance the skills of their members. For example, the International Union of Bricklayers and Allied Craftworkers, International Masonry Institute confers designations in several areas of specialization, including one for plastering. Candidates who complete a 12-week certification program can earn a designa-

tion as a "journey level plasterer" by passing a competency based exam. Experienced candidates can become trainers and earn a designation as "Certified Instructor of Journeyworkers and Apprentices in the Trowel Trades."

With additional training and experience, plasterers and stucco masons may advance to jobs as supervisors, superintendents, or estimators for plastering contractors. Many become self-employed contractors. Others become building inspectors.

Employment

Plasterers and stucco masons held about 61,000 jobs in 2006. Many plasterers and stucco masons are employed in Florida, Texas, California, and the Southwest, where exterior stucco with decorative finishes is very popular. Use of exterior stucco on homes in other parts of the country is gaining popularity as well.

Most plasterers and stucco masons work for independent contractors. About 16 percent of plasterers and stucco masons are self-employed.

Job Outlook

Employment of plasterers and stucco masons is expected to grow about as fast as the average for all occupations as a result of increased appreciation for the durability and attractiveness of troweled finishes. Good job prospects are expected.

Employment change. Employment is expected to grow by 8 percent between 2006 and 2016, about as fast as the average for all occupations. In recent years, there has been an increased appreciation for the attractive finishes and durability that plaster provides. Thin-coat plastering—or veneering—in particular, is gaining wide acceptance as more builders recognize its ease of application, durability, quality of finish, and sound-proofing and fire-retarding qualities, although the increased use of fire sprinklers will reduce the demand for fire-resistant plaster work. Prefabricated wall systems and new polymer-based or polymer-modified acrylic exterior insulating finishes also are gaining popularity, particularly in the South and Southwest regions of the country, because of their relatively low cost. In addition, plasterers will be needed to renovate plasterwork in old structures and to create special architectural effects, such as curved surfaces, which are not practical with drywall materials.

Job prospects. Job opportunities for plasterers and stucco masons are expected to be good because many potential candidates prefer work that is less strenuous and more comfortable. Additionally, some prospects may be deterred by the lengthy apprenticeship. This creates more opportunity for people who want these jobs.

Job openings will come from employment growth and from the need to replace plasterers and stucco masons who transfer to other occupations or leave the labor force. Skilled, experienced

Projections data from the National Employment Matrix

Occupational Title	SOC Code	Employment, 2006	Projected employment, 2016	Change, 2006-16	
				Number	Percent
Plasterers and stucco masons...	47-2161	61,000	66,000	5,000	8

NOTE: Data in this table are rounded. See the discussion of the employment projections table in the *Handbook* introductory chapter on *Occupational Information Included in the Handbook.*

plasterers with artistic ability should have excellent opportunities, especially with restoration projects. The best employment opportunities should continue to be in Florida, California, and the Southwest, where the use of stucco is expected to remain popular. But decorative custom finishes, expensive homes, and large-scale restoration projects will continue to drive demand for plastering in the Northeast, particularly in urban areas.

Employment of plasterers and stucco masons, like that of many other construction workers, is sensitive to the fluctuations of the economy. Workers in these trades may experience periods of unemployment when the overall level of construction activity falls. On the other hand, shortages of these workers may occur in some areas during peak periods of building activity.

Bad weather affects plastering less than other construction trades because most work is indoors. On exterior surfacing jobs, however, plasterers and stucco masons may lose time because plastering materials cannot be applied under wet or freezing conditions.

Earnings
In May 2006, median hourly earnings of wage and salary plasterers and stucco masons were $16.68. The middle 50 percent earned between $13.53 and $21.25. The lowest 10 percent earned less than $10.84, and the top 10 percent earned more than $27.31.

The median hourly earnings in the largest industries employing plasterers and stucco masons were $16.92 in drywall and insulation contractors and $15.55 in masonry contractors.

Apprentices begin by earning about half the rate paid to experienced workers. Annual earnings for plasterers and stucco masons can be less than the hourly rate suggests because poor weather and periodic declines in construction activity can limit work hours.

Related Occupations
Other construction workers who use a trowel as their primary tool include brickmasons, blockmasons, and stonemasons; cement masons, concrete finishers, segmental pavers, and terrazzo workers; and drywall installers, ceiling tile installers, and tapers.

Sources of Additional Information
For information about apprenticeships or other work opportunities, you may contact local plastering contractors, locals of the unions mentioned below, local joint union-management apprenticeship committees, or the nearest office of your State apprenticeship agency or employment service. You can also find information on the registered apprenticeship system with links to State apprenticeship programs on the U.S. Department of Labor's Web site: **http://www.doleta.gov/atels_bat** Apprenticeship information is also available from the U.S. Department of Labor's toll free helpline: (877) 282-5627.

For general information about the work of plasterers and stucco masons, contact:

➤ Association of Wall and Ceiling Industries International, 803 West Broad St., Falls Church, VA 22046. Internet: **http://www.awci.org**

For information about plasterers, contact:

➤ Operative Plasterers' and Cement Masons' International Association of the United States and Canada, 11720 Beltsville Dr., Suite 700, Beltsville, MD 20705. Internet: **http://www.opcmia.org**

For information on certification and the training of plasterers and stucco masons, contact:

➤ International Union of Bricklayers and Allied Craftworkers, International Masonry Institute, The James Brice House, 42 East St., Annapolis, MD 21401. Internet: **http://www.imiweb.org**

For general information on apprenticeships and how to get them, see the *Occupational Outlook Quarterly* article "Apprenticeships: Career training, credentials—and a paycheck in your pocket," in print at many libraries and career centers and online at: **http://www.bls.gov/opub/ooq/2002/summer/art01.pdf**.

Roofers

(O*NET 47-2181.00)

Significant Points

- Most roofers learn their skills informally on the job; some roofers train through 3-year apprenticeships.

- Most job openings will arise from the need to replace those who leave the occupation because the work is hot, strenuous, and dirty, causing many people to switch to jobs in other construction trades.

- Demand for roofers is less susceptible to downturns in the economy than demand for other construction trades because most roofing work consists of repair and reroofing.

Nature of the Work
A leaky roof can damage ceilings, walls, and furnishings. Roofers repair and install roofs made of tar or asphalt and gravel; rubber or thermoplastic; metal; or shingles to protect buildings and their contents from water damage. Repair and reroofing—replacing old roofs on existing buildings—makes up the majority of work for roofers.

There are two types of roofs—low-slope and steep-slope. Low-slope roofs rise 4 inches per horizontal foot or less and are installed in layers. Steep-slope roofs rise more than 4 inches per horizontal foot and are usually covered in shingles. Most commercial, industrial, and apartment buildings have low-slope roofs. Most houses have steep-slope roofs. Some roofers work on both types; others specialize.

Most low-slope roofs are covered with several layers of materials. Roofers first put a layer of insulation on the roof deck. Over the insulation, they often spread a coat of molten bitumen, a tarlike substance. Next, they install partially overlapping layers of roofing felt—a fabric saturated in bitumen—over the surface. Roofers use a mop to spread hot bitumen over the felt before adding another layer of felt. This seals the seams and makes the surface watertight. Roofers repeat these steps to build up the desired number of layers, called "plies." The top

Most residential steep-slope roofs are covered with shingles.

layer is glazed to make a smooth finish or has gravel embedded in the hot bitumen to create a rough surface.

An increasing number of low-slope roofs are covered with a single-ply membrane of waterproof rubber or thermoplastic compounds. Roofers roll these sheets over the roof's insulation and seal the seams. Adhesive, mechanical fasteners, or stone ballast hold the sheets in place. Roofers must make sure the building is strong enough to hold the stone ballast.

A small but growing number of buildings now have "green" roofs that incorporate plants. A "green" roof begins with a single or multi-ply waterproof layer. After it is proven to be leak free, roofers put a root barrier over it, and then layers of soil, in which trees and grass are planted. Roofers are usually responsible for making sure the roof is watertight and can withstand the weight and water needs of the plants.

Most residential steep-slope roofs are covered with shingles. To apply shingles, roofers first lay, cut, and tack 3-foot strips of roofing felt over the entire roof. Starting from the bottom edge, the roofer then staples or nails overlapping rows of shingles to the roof. Roofers measure and cut the felt and shingles to fit intersecting roof surfaces and to fit around vent pipes and chimneys. Wherever two roof surfaces intersect, or shingles reach a vent pipe or chimney, roofers cement or nail flashing-strips of metal or shingle over the joints to make them watertight. Finally, roofers cover exposed nailheads with roofing cement or caulking to prevent water leakage. Roofers who use tile, metal shingles, or shakes (rough wooden shingles) follow a similar process.

Roofers also install equipment that requires cutting through roofs, such as ventilation ducts and attic fans. Some roofers are expert in waterproofing; some waterproof and dampproof masonry and concrete walls, floors, and foundations. To prepare surfaces for waterproofing, they hammer and chisel away rough spots or remove them with a rubbing brick, before applying a coat of liquid waterproofing compound. They also may paint or spray surfaces with a waterproofing material or attach waterproofing membrane to surfaces. Roofers usually spray a bitumen-based coating on interior or exterior surfaces when dampproofing.

Work environment. Roofing work is strenuous. It involves heavy lifting, as well as climbing, bending, and kneeling. Roofers work outdoors in all types of weather, particularly when making repairs. However, they rarely work when it rains or in very cold weather as ice can be dangerous. In northern States, roofing work is generally not performed during winter months. During the summer, roofers may work overtime to complete jobs quickly, especially before forecasted rainfall.

Workers risk slips or falls from scaffolds, ladders, or roofs or burns from hot bitumen, but safety precautions, can prevent most accidents. In addition, roofs can become extremely hot during the summer, causing heat-related illnesses. In 2005, the rate of injuries for roofing contractors in construction was almost twice that of workers overall.

Training, Other Qualifications, and Advancement

Most roofers learn their skills informally by working as helpers for experienced roofers and by taking classes, including safety training, offered by their employers; some complete 3-year apprenticeships.

Education and training. A high school education, or its equivalent, is helpful and so are courses in mechanical drawing and basic mathematics. Although most workers learn roofing as helpers for experienced workers, some roofers train through 3-year apprenticeship programs administered by local union-management committees representing roofing contractors and locals of the United Union of Roofers, Waterproofers, and Allied Workers. Apprenticeship programs usually include at least 2,000 hours of paid on-the-job training each year, plus a minimum of 144 hours of classroom instruction a year in tools and their use, arithmetic, safety, and other topics. On-the-job training for apprentices is similar to the training given to helpers, but an apprenticeship program is more structured and comprehensive. Apprentices, for example, learn to dampproof and waterproof walls.

Trainees start by carrying equipment and material and erecting scaffolds and hoists. Within 2 or 3 months, they are taught to measure, cut, and fit roofing materials and, later, to lay asphalt or fiberglass shingles. Because some roofing materials are used infrequently, it can take several years to get experience working on all types of roofing.

Other qualifications. Good physical condition and good balance are essential for roofers. They cannot be afraid of heights. Experience with metal-working is helpful for workers who install metal roofing. Usually, apprentices must be at least 18 years old.

Projections data from the National Employment Matrix

Occupational Title	SOC Code	Employment, 2006	Projected employment, 2016	Change, 2006-16	
				Number	Percent
Roofers..	47-2181	156,000	179,000	22,000	14

NOTE: Data in this table are rounded. See the discussion of the employment projections table in the *Handbook* introductory chapter on *Occupational Information Included in the Handbook.*

Advancement. Roofers may advance to become supervisors or estimators for a roofing contractor or become contractors themselves.

Employment

Roofers held about 156,000 jobs in 2006. Almost all salaried roofers worked for roofing contractors. About 20 percent of roofers were self-employed. Many self-employed roofers specialized in residential work.

Job Outlook

Most job openings will arise from turnover, because the work is hot, strenuous, and dirty, causing many people to switch to jobs in other construction trades. Faster-than-average employment growth is expected.

Employment change. Employment of roofers is expected to grow 14 percent between 2006 and 2016, which is faster than the average for all occupations. Roofs deteriorate faster than most other parts of buildings, and they need to be repaired or replaced more often. So as the number of buildings continues to increase, demand for roofers is expected to grow. In addition to repair work, the need to install roofs on new buildings is also expected to add to the demand for roofers.

Job prospects. Job opportunities for roofers will arise primarily because of the need to replace workers who leave the occupation. The proportion of roofers who leave the occupation each year is higher than in most construction trades—roofing work is hot, strenuous, and dirty, and a significant number of workers treat roofing as a temporary job until they find other work. Some roofers leave the occupation to go into other construction trades. Jobs should be easiest to find during spring and summer.

Employment of roofers who install new roofs, like that of many other construction workers, is sensitive to the fluctuations of the economy. Workers in these trades may experience periods of unemployment when the overall level of construction falls. On the other hand, shortages of these workers may occur in some areas during peak periods of building activity. Nevertheless, roofing is more heavily concentrated on repair and replacement rather than new installation, making demand for roofers less susceptible to the business cycle than it is for some other construction trades.

Earnings

In May 2006, median hourly earnings of wage and salary roofers were $15.51. The middle 50 percent earned between $12.12 and $20.79. The lowest 10 percent earned less than $9.81, and the highest 10 percent earned more than $26.79. The median hourly earnings of roofers in the foundation, structure, and building exterior contractors industry were $15.54. Earnings may be reduced on occasion when poor weather limits the time roofers can work.

Apprentices usually start earning about 40 percent to 50 percent of the rate paid to experienced roofers. They receive periodic raises as they master the skills of the trade.

Some roofers are members of the United Union of Roofers, Waterproofers, and Allied Workers. Hourly wages and fringe benefits are generally higher for union workers.

Related Occupations

Roofers use shingles, bitumen and gravel, single-ply plastic or rubber sheets, or other materials to waterproof building surfaces. Workers in other occupations who cover surfaces with special materials for protection and decoration include carpenters; carpet, floor, and tile installers and finishers; cement masons, concrete finishers, segmental pavers, and terrazzo workers; drywall installers, ceiling tile installers, and tapers; plasterers and stucco masons; and sheet metal workers.

Sources of Additional Information

For information about apprenticeships or job opportunities in roofing, contact local roofing contractors, a local chapter of the roofers union, a local joint union-management apprenticeship committee, or the nearest office of your State employment service or apprenticeship agency. You can also find information on the registered apprenticeship system with links to State apprenticeship programs on the U.S. Department of Labor's Web site: **http://www.doleta.gov/atels_bat** Apprenticeship information is also available from the U.S. Department of Labor's toll free helpline: (877) 872-5627.

For information about the work of roofers, contact:

➤ National Roofing Contractors Association, 10255 W. Higgins Rd., Suite 600, Rosemont, IL 60018-5607.
Internet: **http://www.nrca.net**

➤ United Union of Roofers, Waterproofers, and Allied Workers, 1660 L St.NW., Suite 800, Washington, DC 20036.
Internet: **http://www.unionroofers.org**

For general information on apprenticeships and how to get them, see the *Occupational Outlook Quarterly* article "Apprenticeships: Career training, credentials—and a paycheck in your pocket," online at **http://www.bls.gov/opub/ooq/2002/summer/art01.pdf** and in print at many libraries and career centers.

Sheet Metal Workers

(O*NET 47-2211.00)

Significant Points

- About 66 percent of sheet metal workers are found in the construction industry; around 21 percent are in manufacturing.

- Workers learn through informal on-the-job training or formal apprenticeship programs.

- Job opportunities in construction should be good, particularly for individuals who have apprenticeship training or who are certified welders; applicants for jobs in manufacturing may experience competition.

Nature of the Work

Sheet metal workers make, install, and maintain heating, ventilation, and air-conditioning duct systems; roofs; siding; rain gutters; downspouts; skylights; restaurant equipment; outdoor signs; railroad cars; tailgates; customized precision equipment; and many other products made from metal sheets. They also may work with fiberglass and plastic materials. Although some workers specialize in fabrication, installation, or maintenance, most do all three jobs. Sheet metal workers do both construction-related work and mass production of sheet metal products in manufacturing.

Sheet metal workers first study plans and specifications to determine the kind and quantity of materials they will need. They then measure, cut, bend, shape, and fasten pieces of sheet metal to make ductwork, countertops, and other custom products. In an increasing number of shops, sheet metal workers use computerized metalworking equipment. This enables them to perform their tasks more quickly and to experiment with different layouts to find the one that wastes the least material. They cut, drill, and form parts with computer-controlled saws, lasers, shears, and presses.

In shops without computerized equipment, and for products that cannot be made on such equipment, sheet metal workers make the required calculations and use tapes, rulers, and other measuring devices for layout work. They then cut or stamp the parts on machine tools.

Before assembling pieces, sheet metal workers check each part for accuracy using measuring instruments such as calipers and micrometers and, if necessary, finish pieces using hand, rotary, or squaring shears and hacksaws. After inspecting the pieces, workers fasten seams and joints together with welds, bolts, cement, rivets, solder, specially formed sheet metal drive clips, or other connecting devices. They then take the parts to the construction site, where they further assemble the pieces as they install them. These workers install ducts, pipes, and tubes by joining them end to end and hanging them with metal hangers secured to a ceiling or a wall. They also use shears, hammers, punches, and drills to make parts at the worksite or to alter parts made in the shop.

Some jobs are done completely at the jobsite. When installing a metal roof, for example, sheet metal workers usually measure and cut the roofing panels on site. They secure the first panel in place and interlock and fasten the grooved edge of the next panel into the grooved edge of the first. Then, they nail or weld the free edge of the panel to the structure. This two-step process is repeated for each additional panel. Finally, the workers fasten machine-made molding at joints, along corners, and around windows and doors for a neat, finished effect.

In addition to installation, some sheet metal workers specialize in testing, balancing, adjusting, and servicing existing air-conditioning and ventilation systems to make sure they are functioning properly and to improve their energy efficiency. Properly installed duct systems are a key component to heating, ventilation, and air-conditioning (HVAC) systems; sometimes duct installers are called *HVAC technicians*. A growing activity for sheet metal workers is building commissioning, which is a complete mechanical inspection of a building's HVAC, water, and lighting systems.

Sheet metal workers in manufacturing plants make sheet metal parts for products such as aircraft or industrial equipment. Although some of the fabrication techniques used in large-scale manufacturing are similar to those used in smaller shops, the work may be highly automated and repetitive. Sheet metal workers doing such work may be responsible for repro-

Sheet metal workers often take additional training, provided by the union or by their employer, to improve their skills.

gramming the computer control systems of the equipment they operate.

Work environment. Sheet metal workers usually work a 40-hour week. Those who fabricate sheet metal products work in shops that are well-lighted and well-ventilated. However, they stand for long periods and lift heavy materials and finished pieces. Sheet metal workers must follow safety practices because working around high-speed machines can be dangerous. They also are subject to cuts from sharp metal, burns from soldering and welding, and falls from ladders and scaffolds. They are often required to wear safety glasses and must not wear jewelry or loose-fitting clothing that could easily be caught in a machine. They may work at a variety of different production stations to reduce the repetitiveness of the work.

Those performing installation work do considerable bending, lifting, standing, climbing, and squatting, sometimes in close quarters or awkward positions. Although duct systems and kitchen equipment are installed indoors, the installation of siding, roofs, and gutters involves much outdoor work, exposing sheet metal workers to various kinds of weather.

Training, Other Qualifications, and Advancement

Sheet metal workers learn their trade through both formal apprenticeships and informal on-the-job training programs. Formal apprenticeships are more likely to be found in construction.

Education and training. To become a skilled sheet metal construction worker usually takes between 4 and 5 years of both classroom and on-the-job training. While there are a number of different ways to obtain this training, generally the more formalized the training received by an individual, the more thoroughly skilled they become, and the more likely they are to be in demand by employers. For some, this training begins in a high school, where classes in English, algebra, geometry, physics, mechanical drawing and blueprint reading, and general shop are recommended.

After high school, there are a number of different ways to train. One way is to get a job with a contractor who will provide training on the job. Entry-level workers generally start as helpers, assisting more experienced workers. Most begin by carrying metal and cleaning up debris in a metal shop while they learn about materials and tools and their uses. Later, they learn to operate machines that bend or cut metal. In time, helpers go out on the jobsite to learn installation. Employers may send the employee to courses at a trade or vocational school or community college to receive further formal training. Helpers may be promoted to the journey level if they show the requisite knowledge and skills. Most sheet metal workers in large-scale manufacturing receive on-the-job training, with additional class work or in-house training as necessary. The training needed to become proficient in manufacturing takes less time than the training in construction.

Some employers, particularly large nonresidential construction contractors with union membership, offer formal apprenticeships. These programs combine paid on-the-job training with related classroom instruction. Usually, apprenticeship applicants must be at least 18 years old and meet local requirements. The length of the program, usually 4 to 5 years, varies with the apprentice's skill. Apprenticeship programs provide comprehensive instruction in both sheet metal fabrication and installation. They may be administered by local joint committees composed of the Sheet Metal Workers' International Association and local chapters of the Sheet Metal and Air-Conditioning Contractors National Association.

Sheet metal workers can choose one of many specialties. Workers can specialize in commercial and residential HVAC installation and maintenance, industrial welding and fabrication, exterior or architectural sheet metal installation, sign fabrication, and testing and balancing of building systems.

On the job, apprentices first receive safety training and then training in tasks that allow them to immediately begin work. They learn the basics of pattern layout and how to cut, bend, fabricate, and install sheet metal. They begin by learning to install and maintain basic ductwork and gradually advance to more difficult jobs, such as making more complex ducts, commercial kitchens, and decorative pieces. They also use materials such as fiberglass, plastics, and other nonmetallic materials. Workers often focus on a sheet metal specialty. In the classroom, apprentices learn drafting, plan and specification reading, trigonometry and geometry applicable to layout work, welding, the use of computerized equipment, and the principles of heating, air-conditioning, and ventilation systems. In addition, apprentices learn the relationship between sheet metal work and other construction work.

Other qualifications. Sheet metal workers need to be in good physical condition and have mechanical and mathematical aptitude and good reading skills. Good eye-hand coordination, spatial and form perception, and manual dexterity also are important. Courses in algebra, trigonometry, geometry, mechanical drawing, and shop provide a helpful background for learning the trade, as does related work experience obtained in the U.S. Armed Services.

It is important for experienced sheet metal workers to keep abreast of new technological developments, such as the use of computerized layout and laser-cutting machines. Workers often take additional training, provided by the union or by their employer, to improve existing skills or to acquire new ones.

Certification and advancement. Certifications in one of the specialties can be beneficial to workers. Certifications related to sheet metal specialties are offered by a wide variety of associations, some of which are listed in the sources of more information at the end of this statement. Those that complete registered apprenticeships are certified as journey workers, which can help to prove their skills to employers.

Sheet metal workers in construction may advance to supervisory jobs. Some of these workers take additional training in welding and do more specialized work. Workers who perform building and system testing are able to move into construction and building inspection. Others go into the contracting business for themselves. Because a sheet metal contractor must have a shop with equipment to fabricate products, this type of contracting business is more expensive to start than other types of construction contracting.

Sheet metal workers in manufacturing may advance to positions as supervisors or quality inspectors. Some of these workers may move into other management positions.

Employment

Sheet metal workers held about 189,000 jobs in 2006. About 66 percent of all sheet metal workers were in the construction industry, including 45 percent who worked for plumbing, heating, and air-conditioning contractors; most of the rest in construction worked for roofing and sheet metal contractors. Some worked for other special trade contractors and for general contractors engaged in residential and commercial building.

About 21 percent of all sheet metal workers were in manufacturing industries, such as the fabricated metal products, machinery, and aerospace products and parts industries. Some sheet metal workers work for the Federal Government.

Compared with workers in most construction craft occupations, relatively few sheet metal workers are self-employed.

Job Outlook

Average employment growth is projected. Job opportunities in construction should be good, particularly for individuals who have apprenticeship training or who are certified welders; applicants for jobs in manufacturing may experience competition.

Employment change. Employment of sheet metal workers is expected to increase 7 percent between 2006 and 2016, about as fast as the average for all occupations. This reflects growth in the number of industrial, commercial, and residential structures being built. The need to install energy-efficient air-conditioning, heating, and ventilation systems in older buildings and to

Projections data from the National Employment Matrix

Occupational Title	SOC Code	Employment, 2006	Projected employment, 2016	Change, 2006-16	
				Number	Percent
Sheet metal workers..	47-2211	189,000	201,000	13,000	7

NOTE: Data in this table are rounded. See the discussion of the employment projections table in the *Handbook* introductory chapter on *Occupational Information Included in the Handbook.*

perform other types of renovation and maintenance work also should boost employment. In addition, the popularity of decorative sheet metal products and increased architectural restoration are expected to add to the demand for sheet metal workers.

Job prospects. Job opportunities are expected to be good for sheet metal workers in the construction industry, reflecting both employment growth and openings arising each year as experienced sheet metal workers leave the occupation. Opportunities should be particularly good for individuals who have apprenticeship training or who are certified welders. Applicants for jobs in manufacturing may experience competition because a number of manufacturing plants that employ sheet metal workers are moving to other countries and the plants that remain are becoming more productive.

Sheet metal workers in construction may experience periods of unemployment, particularly when construction projects end and economic conditions dampen construction activity. Nevertheless, employment of sheet metal workers is less sensitive to declines in new construction than is the employment of some other construction workers, such as carpenters. Maintenance of existing equipment—which is less affected by economic fluctuations than is new construction—makes up a large part of the work done by sheet metal workers. Installation of new air-conditioning and heating systems in existing buildings continues during construction slumps, as individuals and businesses adopt more energy-efficient equipment to cut utility bills. In addition, a large proportion of sheet metal installation and maintenance is done indoors, so sheet metal workers usually lose less worktime due to bad weather than other construction workers.

Earnings

In May 2006, median hourly earnings of wage and salary sheet metal workers were $17.96. The middle 50 percent earned between $13.30 and $24.89. The lowest 10 percent of all sheet metal workers earned less than $10.36, and the highest 10 percent earned more than $32.30. The median hourly earnings of the largest industries employing sheet metal workers were:

Building finishing contractors..$18.84
Plumbing, heating, and air-conditioning contractors..............18.60
Roofing contractors..17.27
Architectural and structural metals manufacturing.................16.60

Apprentices normally start at about 40 to 50 percent of the rate paid to experienced workers. As apprentices acquire more skills, they receive periodic pay increases until their pay approaches that of experienced workers. In addition, union workers in some areas receive supplemental wages from the union when they are on layoff or shortened workweeks.

Related Occupations

To fabricate and install sheet metal products, sheet metal workers combine metalworking skills and knowledge of construction materials and techniques. Other occupations in which workers lay out and fabricate metal products include assemblers and fabricators; machinists; machine setters, operators, and tenders—metal and plastic; and tool and die makers. Construction occupations requiring similar skills and knowledge include gla-

ziers and heating, air-conditioning, and refrigeration mechanics and installers.

Sources of Additional Information

For more information about apprenticeships or other work opportunities, contact local sheet metal contractors or heating, refrigeration, and air-conditioning contractors; a local of the Sheet Metal Workers International Association; a local of the Sheet Metal and Air-Conditioning Contractors National Association; a local joint union-management apprenticeship committee; or the nearest office of your State employment service or apprenticeship agency. You can also find information on the registered apprenticeship system with links to State apprenticeship programs on the U.S. Department of Labor's Web site: **http://www.doleta.gov/atels_bat** Apprenticeship information is also available from the U.S. Department of Labor's toll free helpline: 1 (877) 872-5627.

For general and training information about sheet metal workers, contact:

➤ International Training Institute for the Sheet Metal and Air-Conditioning Industry, 601 N. Fairfax St., Suite 240, Alexandria, VA 22314. Internet: **http://www.sheetmetal-iti.org**
➤ National Center for Construction Education and Research, P.O. Box 141104, Gainesville, FL 32614.
Internet: **http://www.nccer.org**
➤ Sheet Metal and Air-Conditioning Contractors' National Association, 4201 Lafayette Center Dr., Chantilly, VA 20151.
Internet: **http://www.smacna.org**
➤ Sheet Metal Workers International Association, 1750 New York Ave. NW., Washington, DC 20006.
Internet: **http://www.smwia.org**

For general information on apprenticeships and how to get them, see the *Occupational Outlook Quarterly* article "Apprenticeships: Career training, credentials—and a paycheck in your pocket," online at **http://www.bls.gov/opub/ooq/2002/summer/art01.pdf** and in print at many libraries and career centers.

Structural and Reinforcing Iron and Metal Workers

(O*NET 47-2171.00, 47-2221.00)

Significant Points

- Workers must be in good physical condition and must not fear heights.

- Most employers recommend completion of a formal 3-year or 4-year apprenticeship, but some workers learn on the job.

- Earnings of structural iron and steel workers are among the highest of all construction trades.

- In most areas, job opportunities should be excellent.

Nature of the Work

Structural and reinforcing iron and metal workers place and install iron or steel girders, columns, and other construction materials to form buildings, bridges, and other structures. They also position and secure steel bars or mesh in concrete forms in order to reinforce the concrete used in highways, buildings, bridges, tunnels, and other structures. In addition, they repair and renovate older buildings and structures. Even though the primary metal involved in this work is steel, these workers often are known as *ironworkers* or *erectors*. Some ironworkers make structural metal in fabricating shops, which are usually located away from the construction site. These workers are covered in the statement on assemblers and fabricators found elsewhere in the *Handbook*.

Before construction can begin, ironworkers must erect steel frames and assemble the cranes and derricks that move structural steel, reinforcing bars, buckets of concrete, lumber, and other materials and equipment around the construction site. Once this job has been completed, workers begin to connect steel columns, beams, and girders according to blueprints and instructions from supervisors and superintendents. Structural steel, reinforcing rods, and ornamental iron generally come to the construction site ready for erection—cut to the proper size, with holes drilled for bolts and numbered for assembly.

Ironworkers at the construction site unload and stack the prefabricated steel so that it can be hoisted easily when needed. To hoist the steel, ironworkers attach cables (slings) to the steel and to the crane or derrick. One worker directs the hoist operator with hand signals while another worker holds a rope (tag line) attached to the steel to prevent it from swinging. The crane or derrick hoists steel into place in the framework, whereupon two ironworkers called connectors position the steel with connecting bars and spud wrenches—a long wrench with a pointed handle. Workers using driftpins or the handle of a spud wrench align the holes in the steel with the holes in the framework. Ironworkers check vertical and horizontal alignment with plumb bobs, laser equipment, transits, or levels; then they bolt or weld the piece permanently in place.

Reinforcing iron and rebar workers, sometimes called rod busters, set reinforcing bars (often called rebar) in the forms that hold concrete, following blueprints showing the location, size, and number of bars. They then fasten the bars together by tying wire around them with pliers. When reinforcing floors, ironworkers place spacers under the rebar to hold the bars off the deck. Although these materials usually arrive ready to use, ironworkers occasionally must cut bars with metal shears or acetylene torches, bend them by hand or machine, or weld them with arc-welding equipment. Some concrete is reinforced with welded wire fabric that ironworkers put into position using hooked rods. Post-tensioning is another technique used to reinforce concrete. In this technique, workers substitute cables for rebar. When the concrete is poured, the ends of the cables are left exposed. After the concrete cures, ironworkers tighten the cables with jacking equipment specially designed for the purpose. Post-tensioning allows designers to create larger open areas in a building, because supports can be placed further apart. This technique is commonly employed in parking garages and arenas.

Ornamental ironworkers install stairs, handrails, curtain walls (the nonstructural walls and window frames of many large buildings), and other miscellaneous metal after the struc-

ture of the building has been completed. As they hoist pieces into position, ornamental ironworkers make sure that the pieces are properly fitted and aligned before bolting or welding them for a secure fit.

Work environment. Structural and reinforcing iron and metal workers usually work outside in all kinds of weather. However, those who work at great heights do not work during wet, icy, or extremely windy conditions. Because the danger of injuries from falls is great, ironworkers use safety devices such as safety harnesses, scaffolding, and nets to reduce risk.

Training, Other Qualifications, and Advancement
Many workers learn to be ironworkers through formal apprenticeships, but others learn on the job less formally. Certifications in welding and rigging can increase a worker's usefulness on the job site.

Education and training. Most employers recommend a 3- or 4-year apprenticeship consisting of paid on-the-job training and evening classroom instruction as the best way to learn this trade. Apprenticeship programs are administered by committees made up of representatives of local unions of the International Association of Bridge, Structural, Ornamental and Reinforcing Iron Workers or the local chapters of contractors' associations.

In the classroom, apprentices study blueprint reading; mathematics, the basics of structural erecting, rigging, reinforcing, welding, assembling, and safety training. Apprentices also study the care and safe use of tools and materials. On the job, apprentices work in all aspects of the trade, such as unloading

Earnings of structural iron and steel workers are among the highest of all construction trades.

Projections data from the National Employment Matrix

Occupational Title	SOC Code	Employment, 2006	Projected employment, 2016	Change, 2006-16	
				Number	Percent
Structural and reinforcing iron and metal workers	—	102,000	110,000	7,800	8
Reinforcing iron and rebar workers	47-2171	30,000	34,000	3,500	12
Structural iron and steel workers	47-2221	72,000	76,000	4,300	6

NOTE: Data in this table are rounded. See the discussion of the employment projections table in the *Handbook* introductory chapter on *Occupational Information Included in the Handbook.*

and storing materials at the job site, rigging materials for movement by crane, connecting structural steel, and welding.

Some ironworkers learn the trade informally on the job, without completing an apprenticeship. These workers generally do not receive classroom training, although some large contractors have extensive training programs. On-the-job trainees usually begin by assisting experienced ironworkers on simple jobs, such as carrying various materials. With experience, trainees perform more difficult tasks, such as cutting and fitting different parts; however, learning through work experience alone may not provide training as complete as an apprenticeship program, and it usually takes longer.

Other qualifications. Ironworkers must be at least 18 years old. A high school diploma is preferred by employers and local apprenticeship committees. High school courses in general mathematics, mechanical drawing, English, and welding are considered helpful. Because materials used in iron working are heavy and bulky, ironworkers must be in good physical condition. They also need good agility, balance, eyesight, and depth perception to work safely at great heights on narrow beams and girders. Ironworkers should not be afraid of heights or suffer from dizziness.

Certification and advancement. Ironworkers who complete apprenticeships are certified as journey workers, which often make them more competitive for jobs and promotions. Those who meet education and experience requirements can become welders certified by the American Welding Society. Apprenticeship programs often provide trainees the opportunity to become certified as part of their coursework because welding skills are useful for many ironworker tasks.

Some experienced workers are promoted to supervisor. Others may go into the contracting business for themselves. The ability to communicate in both English and Spanish will improve opportunities for advancement.

Employment

Ironworkers held about 102,000 jobs in 2006; structural iron and steel workers held about 72,000 jobs; and reinforcing iron and rebar workers held about 30,000 jobs. About 88 percent worked in construction, with 50 percent working for foundation, structure, and building exterior contractors. Most of the remaining ironworkers worked for contractors specializing in the construction of homes; factories; commercial buildings; religious structures; schools; bridges and tunnels; and water, sewer, communications, and power lines.

Structural and reinforcing iron and metal workers are employed in all parts of the country, but most work in metropolitan areas, where the bulk of commercial and industrial construction takes place.

Job Outlook

Average job growth is projected, but in most areas of the country job opportunities should be excellent.

Employment change. Employment of structural and reinforcing iron and metal workers is expected to grow 8 percent between 2006 and 2016, about as fast as the average for all occupations. Nonresidential and heavy construction is expected to increase, creating jobs. The rehabilitation, maintenance, and replacement of a growing number of older buildings, powerplants, highways, and bridges also are expected to create employment opportunities. State and Federal legislatures continue to support and fund the building of roads, which will secure jobs for the near future. However, a lack of qualified applicants may restrain employment growth in some areas.

Job prospects. In addition to new jobs from employment growth, many job openings will result from the need to replace experienced ironworkers who leave the occupation or retire. In most areas, job opportunities should be excellent, although the number of job openings can fluctuate from year to year with economic conditions and the level of construction activity. Many workers prefer to enter other occupations with better working conditions, leading to opportunities for those who wish to become structural and reinforcing iron and metal workers.

Employment of structural and reinforcing iron and metal workers, like that of many other construction workers, is sensitive to the fluctuations of the economy. Workers in these trades may experience periods of unemployment when the overall level of construction falls. On the other hand, shortages of these workers may occur in some areas during peak periods of building activity. Similarly, job opportunities for ironworkers may vary widely by geographic area. Population growth in the South and West should create more job opportunities than elsewhere as bridges, buildings, and roads are constructed. Job openings for ironworkers usually are more abundant during the spring and summer months, when the level of construction activity increases. Workers who are willing to relocate are often able to find work in another area.

Earnings

Earnings of structural iron and steel workers are among the highest of all construction trades. In May 2006, median earnings of wage and salary structural iron and steel workers in all industries were $19.46 an hour. The middle 50 percent earned between $14.11 and $27.08. The lowest 10 percent earned less than $10.94, and the highest 10 percent earned more than $34.78.

Median hourly earnings of wage and salary reinforcing iron and rebar workers in all industries were $18.38. The middle 50 percent earned between $13.15 and $27.03. The lowest 10 percent earned less than $10.25, and the highest 10 percent earned more than $34.15.

Median hourly earnings of wage and salary structural iron and steel workers in foundation, structure, and building exterior contractors were $20.54 and in nonresidential building construction, $16.76. Reinforcing iron and rebar workers earned median hourly earnings of $18.67 in foundation, structure, and building exterior contractors.

About 31 percent of the workers in this trade are union members. According to International Association of Bridge, Structural, Ornamental, and Reinforcing Iron Workers, average hourly earnings, including benefits, for structural and reinforcing metal workers who belonged to a union and worked full time were slightly higher than the hourly earnings of nonunion workers. Structural and reinforcing iron and metal workers in New York, Boston, San Francisco, Chicago, Los Angeles, Philadelphia, and other large cities received the highest wages.

Apprentices generally start at about 50 to 60 percent of the rate paid to experienced journey workers. Throughout the course of the apprenticeship program, as they acquire skills, they receive periodic increases until their pay approaches that of experienced workers.

Earnings for ironworkers may be reduced on occasion because work can be limited by bad weather, the short-term nature of construction jobs, and economic downturns.

Related Occupations

Structural and reinforcing iron and metal workers play an essential role in erecting buildings, bridges, highways, power lines, and other structures. Others who work on these construction jobs include assemblers and fabricators; boilermakers; civil engineers; cement masons, concrete finishers, segmental pavers, and terrazzo workers; construction managers; and welding, soldering, and brazing workers.

Sources of Additional Information

For more information on apprenticeships or other work opportunities, contact local general contractors; a local of the International Association of Bridge, Structural, Ornamental, and Reinforcing Iron Workers Union; a local ironworkers' joint union-management apprenticeship committee; a local or State chapter of the Associated Builders and Contractors or the Associated General Contractors; or the nearest office of your State employment service or apprenticeship agency. You can also find information on the registered apprenticeship system with links to State apprenticeship programs on the U.S. Department of Labor's Web site: **http://www.doleta.gov/atels_bat** Apprenticeship information is also available from the U.S. Department of Labor's toll free helpline: 1 (877) 872-5627.

For apprenticeship information, contact

➤ International Association of Bridge, Structural, Ornamental, and Reinforcing Iron Workers, Apprenticeship Department, 1750 New York Ave. NW., Suite 400, Washington, DC 20006. Internet: **http://www.ironworkers.org**

For general information about ironworkers, contact either of the following sources:

➤ Associated Builders and Contractors, Workforce Development Department, 4250 North Fairfax Dr., 9th Floor, Arlington, VA 22203. Internet: **http://www.trytools.org**

➤ Associated General Contractors of America, Inc., 2300 Wilson Blvd., Suite 400., Arlington, VA 22201. Internet: **http://www.agc.org**

For general information on apprenticeships and how to get them, see the *Occupational Outlook Quarterly* article "Apprenticeships: Career training, credentials—and a paycheck in your pocket," in print at many libraries and career centers and online at: **http://www.bls.gov/opub/ooq/2002/summer/art01.pdf**

Installation, Maintenance, and Repair Occupations

Electrical and Electronic Equipment Mechanics, Installers, and Repairers

Computer, Automated Teller, and Office Machine Repairers

(O*NET 49-2011.00, 49-9091.00)

Significant Points

- Workers qualify for these jobs by receiving training in electronics from associate degree programs, the military, vocational schools, equipment manufacturers, or employers.

- Employment is expected to grow more slowly than the average for all occupations.

- Job prospects will be best for applicants with knowledge of electronics, and who have formal training and repair experience.

Nature of the Work

Computer, automated teller, and office machine repairers install, fix, and maintain many of the machines that are common to businesses and households. Some repairers travel to customers' workplaces or other locations to make the necessary repairs. These workers—known as *field technicians*—often have assigned areas in which they perform preventive maintenance on a regular basis. *Bench technicians* work in repair shops located in stores, factories, or service centers. In small companies, repairers may work both in repair shops and at customer locations.

Computer repairers, also known as *computer service technicians* or *data processing equipment repairers*, service mainframe, server, and personal computers; printers; and auxiliary computer equipment. These workers primarily perform hands-on repair, maintenance, and installation of computers and related equipment. Workers who provide technical assistance, in person or by telephone, to computer system users are known as computer support specialists or computer support technicians. (See the section on computer support specialists and systems administrators elsewhere in the *Handbook*.)

Computer repairers usually replace subsystems instead of repairing them. Replacement is common because subsystems are inexpensive and businesses are reluctant to shut down their computers for time-consuming repairs. Subsystems commonly replaced by computer repairers include video cards, which transmit signals from the computer to the monitor; hard drives, which store data; and network cards, which allow communication over the network. Defective modules may be given to bench technicians, who use software programs to diagnose the problem and who may repair the modules, if possible.

Office machine and cash register servicers work on photocopiers, cash registers, mail-processing equipment, and fax machines. Newer models of office machinery include computerized components that allow them to function more effectively than earlier models.

Office machine repairers usually work on machinery at the customer's workplace. However, if the machines are small enough, customers may bring them to a repair shop for maintenance. Common malfunctions include paper misfeeds caused by worn or dirty parts, and poor-quality copy resulting from problems with lamps, lenses, or mirrors. These malfunctions usually can be resolved simply by cleaning the relevant components. Breakdowns also may result from the failure of commonly used parts. For example, heavy use of a photocopier may wear down the printhead, which applies ink to the final copy. In such cases, the repairer usually replaces the part instead of repairing it.

Automated teller machine servicers install and repair automated teller machines (ATMs). These machines allow customers to carry out bank transactions without the assistance of a teller. ATMs also provide a growing variety of other services, including stamp, phone card, and ticket sales.

When ATMs malfunction, computer networks recognize the problem and alert repairers. Common problems include worn magnetic heads on card readers, which prevent the equipment from recognizing customers' bankcards, and "pick failures," which prevent the equipment from dispensing the correct amount of cash. Field technicians travel to the locations of ATMs and usually repair equipment by removing and replacing defective components. Broken components are taken to a repair shop, where bench technicians make the necessary repairs. Field technicians perform routine maintenance on a regular basis, replacing worn parts and running diagnostic tests to ensure that the equipment functions properly.

To install large equipment, such as mainframe computers and ATMs, repairers connect the equipment to power sources and communication lines that allow the transmission of information over computer networks. For example, when an ATM dispenses cash, it transmits the withdrawal information to the customer's bank. Workers also may install operating software and peripheral equipment, checking that all components are configured to function together correctly.

Computer, automated teller, and office machine repairers use a variety of tools for diagnostic tests and repair. To diagnose malfunctions, they use multimeters to measure voltage, current, resistance, and other electrical properties; signal generators to provide test signals; and oscilloscopes to monitor equipment signals. To diagnose computerized equipment, repairers use software programs. To repair or adjust equipment, workers use handtools, such as pliers, screwdrivers, soldering irons, and wrenches.

Work environment. Repairers usually work in clean, well-lighted surroundings. Because computers and office machines are sensitive to extreme temperatures and humidity, repair shops usually are air-conditioned and well ventilated. Field repairers must travel frequently to various locations to install, maintain, or repair customers' equipment. ATM repairers may have to perform their jobs in small, confined spaces that house the equipment.

Because computers and ATMs are critical for many organizations to function efficiently, data processing equipment repairers and ATM field technicians often work around the clock. Their schedules may include evening, weekend, and holiday shifts, sometimes assigned on the basis of seniority. Office machine and cash register servicers usually work regular business hours because the equipment they repair is not as critical. Most repairers work about 40 hours per week, but about 12 percent work more than 50 hours per week.

Although their jobs are not strenuous, repairers must lift equipment and work in a variety of postures. Repairers of computer monitors need to discharge voltage from the equipment to avoid electrocution. Workers may have to wear protective goggles.

Training, Other Qualifications, and Advancement

Knowledge of electronics is required, and employers prefer workers with formal training. Office machine and ATM repairers usually have an associate degree. Certification is available for entry-level workers, as well as experienced workers seeking advancement.

Education and training. Knowledge of electronics is necessary for employment as a computer, automated teller, or office machine repairer. Employers prefer workers who are certified or who have training in electronics from an associate degree program, the military, a vocational school, or an equipment manufacturer. Employers generally provide some training to new repairers on specific equipment; however, workers are expected to arrive on the job with a basic understanding of equipment repair. Employers may send experienced workers to training sessions to keep up with changes in technology and service procedures.

Most office machine and ATM repairer positions require an associate degree in electronics. A basic understanding of mechanical equipment also is important because many of the parts that fail in office machines and ATMs, such as paper loaders, are mechanical. Entry-level employees at large companies normally receive on-the-job training lasting several months. Such training may include a week of classroom instruction, followed by a period of 2 weeks to several months assisting an experienced repairer.

Certification and other qualifications. Various organizations offer certification. Certification demonstrates a level of competency, and can make an applicant more attractive to employers.

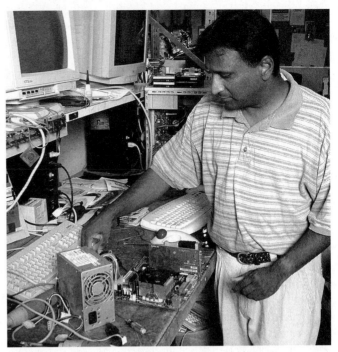

Computer repairers perform hands-on repair, maintenance, and installation of computers and related equipment.

Field technicians work closely with customers and must have good communications skills and a neat appearance. Employers may require that field technicians have a driver's license.

Certification and advancement. Newly hired computer repairers may work on personal computers or peripheral equipment. With experience, they can advance to positions maintaining more sophisticated systems, such as networking equipment and servers. Field repairers of ATMs may advance to bench technician positions responsible for more complex repairs. Experienced workers may become specialists who help other repairers diagnose difficult problems or who work with engineers in designing equipment and developing maintenance procedures. Experienced workers also may move into management positions responsible for supervising other repairers.

Because of their familiarity with equipment, experienced repairers may move into customer service or sales positions. Some experienced workers open their own repair shops or become wholesalers or retailers of electronic equipment.

Certification may also increase one's opportunities for advancement. Certification is available for workers with varying levels of skills and experience. To obtain certification, workers generally must pass an examination corresponding to their skill level.

Employment

Computer, automated teller, and office machine repairers held about 175,000 jobs in 2006. Wholesale trade establishments employed about 31 percent of the workers in this occupation; most of these establishments were wholesalers of professional and commercial equipment and supplies. Many workers also were employed in computer and software stores and office supply stores. Others worked in electronic and precision equipment repair shops and computer systems design firms. About 20 percent of computer, automated teller, and office machine

Projections data from the National Employment Matrix

Occupational Title	SOC Code	Employment, 2006	Projected employment, 2016	Change, 2006-16	
				Number	Percent
Computer, automated teller, and office machine repairers................	49-2011	175,000	180,000	5,200	3

NOTE: Data in this table are rounded. See the discussion of the employment projections table in the *Handbook* introductory chapter on *Occupational Information Included in the Handbook*.

repairers were self-employed, compared to 7 percent for all installation, maintenance, and repair occupations.

Job Outlook

Employment is expected to grow more slowly than the average for all occupations. Opportunities will be best for applicants with knowledge of electronics, formal training, and previous experience.

Employment change. Employment of computer, automated teller, and office machine repairers is expected to grow by 3 percent from 2006 to 2016, which is slower than the average for all occupations. Limited job growth will be driven by the increasing dependence of business and individuals on computers and other sophisticated office machines. The need to maintain this equipment will create new jobs for repairers.

Although computer equipment continues to become less expensive and more reliable, malfunctions still occur and can cause severe problems for users, most of whom lack the knowledge to make repairs. Computers are critical to most businesses today and will become even more so as companies increasingly engage in electronic commerce, and as individuals continue to bank, shop, and pay bills online.

People also are becoming increasingly reliant on ATMs. Besides offering bank and retail transactions, ATMs provide an increasing number of other services, such as employee information processing and distribution of government payments. The relatively slow rate at which new ATMs are installed, however, and the fact that they are becoming easier to repair, will limit demand for ATM repairers.

Conventional office machines, such as calculators, are inexpensive, and often are replaced instead of repaired. However, digital copiers and other, newer office machines are more costly and complex. This equipment often is computerized, designed to work on a network, and capable of performing multiple functions. But because this equipment is becoming more reliable, job growth in office machine repairers will be limited as well.

Job prospects. In addition to new job growth, a number of openings will result from the need to replace workers who retire or leave the occupation. Job prospects will be best for applicants with knowledge of electronics, formal training, and repair experience.

Earnings

Median hourly earnings of wage-and-salary computer, automated teller, and office machine repairers were $17.54 in May 2006. The middle 50 percent earned between $13.56 and $22.44. The lowest 10 percent earned less than $10.65, and the highest 10 percent earned more than $27.36. Median hourly earnings in the industries employing the largest numbers of computer, automated teller, and office machine repairers in May 2006 were:

Computer systems design and related services	$19.41
Professional and commercial equipment and supplies merchant wholesalers	19.09
Office supplies, stationery, and gift stores	16.64
Electronic and precision equipment repair and maintenance	15.82
Computer and software stores	15.20
Electronics and appliance stores	14.71

Related Occupations

Workers in other occupations who repair and maintain electronic equipment include electronic home entertainment equipment installers and repairers; home appliance repairers; broadcast and sound engineering technicians and radio operators; precision instrument and equipment repairers; electrical and electronics installers and repairers; electricians; radio and telecommunications equipment installers and repairers; coin, vending, and amusement machine servicers and repairers; industrial machinery mechanics and maintenance workers; and maintenance and repair workers, general.

Sources of Additional Information

For information on careers and certification, contact:

➤ ACES International, 5241 Princess Anne Rd., Suite 110, Virginia Beach, VA 23462.
Internet: **http://www.acesinternational.org**
➤ Electronics Technicians Association International, 5 Depot St., Greencastle, IN 46135. Internet: **http://eta-i.org**
➤ International Society of Certified Electronics Technicians, 3608 Pershing Ave., Fort Worth, TX 76107-4527.
Internet: **http://www.iscet.org**

Electrical and Electronics Installers and Repairers

(O*NET 49-2092.00, 49-2093.00, 49-2094.00, 49-2095.00, 49-2096.00, 49-9031.00)

Significant Points

- Knowledge of electrical equipment and electronics is necessary for employment; employers often prefer applicants with an associate degree in electronics.

- Employment is projected to grow more slowly than average for all occupations.

- Job opportunities will be best for applicants with an associate degree, certification, and related experience.

Nature of the Work

Businesses and other organizations depend on complex electronic equipment for a variety of functions. Industrial controls automatically monitor and direct production processes on the factory floor. Transmitters and antennae provide communication links for many organizations. Electric power companies use electronic equipment to operate and control generating plants, substations, and monitoring equipment. The Federal Government uses radar and missile control systems to provide for the national defense and to direct commercial air traffic. These complex pieces of electronic equipment are installed, maintained, and repaired by electrical and electronics installers and repairers.

Installers and repairers, known as *field technicians*, often travel to factories or other locations to repair equipment. These workers usually have assigned areas in which they perform preventive maintenance on a regular basis. When equipment breaks down, field technicians go to a customer's site to repair the equipment. Bench technicians work in repair shops located in factories and service centers, fixing components that cannot be repaired on the factory floor.

Electrical and electronic equipment are two distinct types of industrial equipment, although much equipment contains both electrical and electronic components. In general, electrical portions provide the power for the equipment, while electronic components control the device, although many types of equipment still are controlled with electrical devices.

Some industrial electronic equipment is self-monitoring and alerts repairers to malfunctions. When equipment breaks down, repairers will first check for common causes of trouble, such as loose connections or obviously defective components. If routine checks do not locate the trouble, repairers may refer to schematics and manufacturers' specifications that show connections and provide instructions on how to locate problems. Automated electronic control systems are becoming increasingly complex, making diagnosis more challenging. With these systems, repairers use software programs and testing equipment to diagnose malfunctions. Among their diagnostic tools are multimeters, which measure voltage, current, and resistance, and advanced multimeters, which measure capacitance, inductance, and current gain of transistors. Repairers also use signal generators, which provide test signals, and oscilloscopes, which display signals graphically. Finally, repairers use handtools such as pliers, screwdrivers, soldering irons, and wrenches to replace faulty parts and adjust equipment.

Because repairing components is a complex activity and factories cannot allow production equipment to stand idle, repairers on the factory floor usually remove and replace defective units, such as circuit boards, instead of fixing them. Defective units are discarded or returned to the manufacturer or a specialized shop for repair. Bench technicians at these locations have the training, tools, and parts needed to thoroughly diagnose and repair circuit boards or other complex components. These workers also locate and repair circuit defects, such as poorly soldered joints, blown fuses, or malfunctioning transistors.

Electrical and electronics installers often fit older manufacturing equipment with new automated control devices. Older manufacturing machines are frequently in good working order but are limited by inefficient control systems for which replacement parts are no longer available. Installers replace old electronic control units with new programming logic controls (PLCs). Setting up and installing a new PLC involves connecting it to different sensors and electrically powered devices (electric motors, switches, and pumps) and writing a computer program to operate the PLC. Electronics installers coordinate their efforts with those of other workers who are installing and maintaining equipment. (See the section on industrial machinery mechanics and maintenance workers elsewhere in the *Handbook*.)

Electrical and electronics installers and repairers, transportation equipment install, adjust, or maintain mobile electronic communication equipment, including sound, sonar, security, navigation, and surveillance systems on trains, watercraft, or other vehicles. *Electrical and electronics repairers, powerhouse, substation, and relay* inspect, test, maintain, or repair electrical equipment used in generating stations, substations, and in-service relays. These workers may be known as powerhouse electricians, relay technicians, or power transformer repairers. *Electric motor, power tool, and related repairers*—such as armature winders, generator mechanics, and electric golf cart repairers—specialize in installing, maintaining, and repairing electric motors, wiring, or switches.

Electronic equipment installers and repairers, motor vehicles have a significantly different job. They install, diagnose, and repair communication, sound, security, and navigation equipment in motor vehicles. Most installation work involves either new alarm or sound systems. New sound systems vary significantly in cost and complexity of installation. Replacing a head unit (radio) with a new CD player is simple, requiring the removal of a few screws and the connection of a few wires. Installing a new sound system with a subwoofer, amplifier, and fuses is far more complicated. The installer builds a fiberglass or wood box designed to hold the subwoofer and to fit inside the unique dimensions of the automobile. Installing sound-deadening material, which often is necessary with more

Some repairers install, diagnose, and repair equipment in cars and other motor vehicles.

powerful speakers, requires an installer to remove many parts of a car (for example, seats, carpeting, or interiors of doors), add sound-absorbing material in empty spaces, and reinstall the interior parts. The installer also runs new speaker and electrical cables. The new system may require additional fuses, a new electrical line to be run from the battery through a newly drilled hole in the firewall into the interior the vehicle, or an additional or more powerful alternator or battery. Motor vehicle installers and repairers work with an increasingly complex range of electronic equipment, including DVD players, satellite navigation equipment, passive security systems, and active security systems.

Work environment. Many electrical and electronics installers and repairers work on factory floors, where they are subject to noise, dirt, vibration, and heat. Bench technicians primarily work in repair shops, where the surroundings are relatively quiet, comfortable, and well lighted.

Installers and repairers may have to do heavy lifting and work in a variety of positions. They must follow safety guidelines and often wear protective goggles and hardhats. When working on ladders or on elevated equipment, repairers must wear harnesses to avoid falls. Before repairing a piece of machinery, these workers must follow procedures to ensure that others cannot start the equipment during the repair process. They also must take precautions against electric shock by locking off power to the unit under repair.

Motor vehicle electronic equipment installers and repairers normally work indoors in well-ventilated and well-lighted repair shops. Minor cuts and bruises are common, but serious accidents usually are avoided when safety practices are observed.

Training, Other Qualifications, and Advancement

Applicants with an associate degree in electronics are preferred, and professional certification often is required.

Education and training. Knowledge of electrical equipment and electronics is necessary for employment. Employers often prefer applicants with an associate degree from a community college or technical school, although a high school diploma may be sufficient for some jobs. Entry-level repairers may begin by working with experienced technicians who provide technical guidance, and work independently only after developing the necessary skills.

Certification and other qualifications. Many employers require applicants to be certified. Certification is available from various professional and education organizations, and usually requires applicants to pass an exam demonstrating their level of expertise.

Installers and repairers should have good eyesight and color perception to work with the intricate components used in electronic equipment. Field technicians work closely with customers and should have good communication skills and a neat appearance. Employers also may require that field technicians have a driver's license.

Certification and advancement. Certification can also serve as a form of advancement. Workers who become certified in a specialty area may gain additional responsibilities and be awarded higher pay.

Experienced repairers with advanced training may become specialists or troubleshooters who help other repairers diagnose difficult problems. Workers with leadership ability may become supervisors of other repairers. Some experienced workers open their own repair shops.

Employment

Electrical and electronics installers and repairers held about 169,000 jobs in 2006. The following tabulation breaks down their employment by occupational specialty:

Electrical and electronics repairers, commercial
and industrial equipment.......................................80,000
Electric motor, power tool, and related repairers.................25,000
Electrical and electronics repairers, powerhouse,
substation, and relay...22,000
Electrical and electronics installers and repairers,
transportation equipment 21,000
Electronic equipment installers and repairers,
motor vehicles...20,000

Many repairers worked for utilities; building equipment contractors; machinery and equipment repair shops; electrical and electronics wholesalers; electronics and appliance retailers; motor vehicle and parts dealers; manufacturers of electrical, electronic, and transportation equipment; and Federal, State, and local government.

Job Outlook

Employment is expected to increase more slowly than the average through the year 2016. Job prospects should be best for applicants with an associate degree, certification, and related experience.

Employment change. Overall employment of electrical and electronics installers and repairers is expected to grow by 3 percent through the year 2016, which is slower than the average for all occupations. Growth rates will vary by occupational specialty.

Employment of electrical and electronics installers and repairers of commercial and industrial equipment is expected to grow by 7 percent, which is about as fast as the average for all occupations. This equipment will become more sophisticated and will be used more frequently as businesses strive to lower costs by increasing and improving automation. Companies will install electronic controls, robots, sensors, and other equipment to automate processes such as assembly and testing. In addition, as prices decline, this equipment will be used more frequently throughout a number of industries, including services, utilities, and construction, as well as manufacturing. Improved reliability of equipment should not constrain employment growth, however: companies increasingly will rely on repairers because malfunctions that idle commercial and industrial equipment will continue to be costly.

Employment of motor vehicle electronic equipment installers and repairers is expected to grow by 5 percent, which is slower than the average for all occupations. As motor vehicle manufacturers install more and better sound, security, entertainment, and navigation systems in new vehicles, and as newer electronic systems require progressively less maintenance, employment

Projections data from the National Employment Matrix

Occupational Title	SOC Code	Employment, 2006	Projected employment, 2016	Change, 2006-16	
				Number	Percent
Electrical and electronics installers and repairers............................	—	169,000	174,000	5,200	3
Electric motor, power tool, and related repairers.........................	49-2092	25,000	24,000	-1,100	-4
Electrical and electronics installers and repairers, transportation equipment...	49-2093	21,000	22,000	900	4
Electrical and electronics repairers, commercial and industrial equipment...	49-2094	80,000	86,000	5,500	7
Electrical and electronics repairers, powerhouse, substation, and relay...	49-2095	22,000	21,000	-1,000	-5
Electronic equipment installers and repairers, motor vehicles	49-2096	20,000	21,000	900	5

NOTE: Data in this table are rounded. See the discussion of the employment projections table in the *Handbook* introductory chapter on *Occupational Information Included in the Handbook.*

growth for aftermarket electronic equipment installers will be limited.

Employment of electric motor, power tool, and related repairers is expected to decline slowly, decreasing by 4 percent. Improvements in electrical and electronic equipment design, as well as the increased use of disposable tool parts should suppress job growth.

Employment of electrical and electronic installers and repairers of transportation equipment is expected to grow by 4 percent, which is slower than the average for all occupations. Declining employment in the rail transportation industry will dampen growth in this occupational specialty.

Employment of electrical and electronics installers and repairers, powerhouse, substation, and relay is expected to decline slowly, decreasing by 5 percent. Consolidation and privatization in utilities industries should improve productivity, reducing employment. Newer equipment will be more reliable and easier to repair, further limiting employment.

Job prospects. Job opportunities should be best for applicants with an associate degree in electronics, certification, and related experience. In addition to employment growth, the need to replace workers who transfer to other occupations or leave the labor force will result in some openings.

Earnings

Median hourly earnings of wage-and-salary electrical and electronics repairers, commercial and industrial equipment were $21.72 in May 2006. The middle 50 percent earned between $17.18 and $26.59. The lowest 10 percent earned less than $13.43, and the highest 10 percent earned more than $30.90. In May 2006, median hourly earnings were $23.49 in the Federal Government and $19.92 in building equipment contractors, the industries employing the largest numbers of electrical and electronics repairers, commercial and industrial equipment.

Median hourly earnings of wage-and-salary electric motor, power tool, and related repairers were $15.80 in May 2006. The middle 50 percent earned between $12.56 and $20.24. The lowest 10 percent earned less than $9.97, and the highest 10 percent earned more than $25.37. In May 2006, median hourly earnings were $15.32 in commercial and industrial machinery and equipment (except automotive and electronic) repair and maintenance, the industry employing the largest number of electronic motor, power tool, and related repairers.

Median hourly earnings of wage-and-salary electrical and electronics repairers, powerhouse, substation, and relay were $27.60 in May 2006. The middle 50 percent earned between $23.62 and $32.07. The lowest 10 percent earned less than $19.42, and the highest 10 percent earned more than $35.49. In May 2006, median hourly earnings were $28.30 in electric power generation, transmission, and distribution, the industry employing the largest number of these repairers.

Median hourly earnings of wage-and-salary electronics installers and repairers, motor vehicles were $13.57 in May 2006. The middle 50 percent earned between $10.78 and $17.41. The lowest 10 percent earned less than $9.13, and the highest 10 percent earned more than $23.45.

Median hourly earnings of wage-and-salary electrical and electronics repairers, transportation equipment were $20.72 in May 2006. The middle 50 percent earned between $16.79 and $25.10. The lowest 10 percent earned less than $13.24, and the highest 10 percent earned more than $28.78.

Related Occupations

Workers in other occupations who install and repair electronic equipment include broadcast and sound engineering technicians and radio operators; computer, automated teller, and office machine repairers; electronic home entertainment equipment installers and repairers; radio and telecommunications equipment installers and repairers; electricians; elevator installers and repairers; aircraft and avionics equipment mechanics and service technicians; coin, vending, and amusement machine servicers and repairers; and maintenance and repair workers, general. Industrial machinery mechanics and maintenance workers also install, maintain, and repair industrial machinery.

Sources of Additional Information

For information on careers and certification, contact any of the following organizations:

➤ ACES International, 5241 Princess Anne Rd., Suite 110, Virginia Beach, VA 23462.
Internet: **http://www.acesinternational.org**

➤ Electronics Technicians Association International, 5 Depot St., Greencastle, IN 46135. Internet: **http://eta-i.org/**

➤ International Society of Certified Electronics Technicians, 3608 Pershing Ave., Fort Worth, TX 76107-4527.
Internet: **http://www.iscet.org**

Electronic Home Entertainment Equipment Installers and Repairers

(O*NET 49-2097.00)

Significant Points

- Employers prefer applicants who have basic knowledge and skills in electronics; many applicants gain these skills at vocational training programs and community colleges.

- Employment is expected to grow more slowly than the average for all occupations because it often is cheaper to replace equipment than to repair it.

- Job opportunities will be best for applicants with knowledge of electronics, related hands-on experience, and good customer service skills.

Nature of the Work

Electronic home entertainment equipment installers and repairers—also called *service technicians*—repair a variety of equipment. They may specialize in one type of product, or may be trained in many different ones. The most common products include televisions and radios, stereo components, video and audio disc players, and video cameras. They also install and repair home security systems, intercom equipment, satellite television dishes, and home theater systems, which consist of large-screen televisions and sophisticated surround-sound audio components.

Customers usually bring small, portable equipment to repair shops for servicing. Repairers at these locations, known as *bench technicians*, are equipped with a full array of electronic tools and parts. When larger, less mobile equipment breaks down, customers may pay repairers to come to their homes. These repairers, known as field technicians, travel with a limited set of tools and parts, and attempt to complete the repair at the customer's location. If the job is complex, technicians may bring defective components back to the shop for diagnosis and repair.

When equipment breaks down, repairers check for common causes of trouble, such as dirty or defective components. Many repairs consist simply of cleaning and lubricating equipment. If routine checks do not locate the trouble, repairers may refer to schematics and manufacturers' specifications that provide instructions on how to locate problems. Repairers use a variety of test equipment to diagnose and identify malfunctions. Multimeters detect short circuits, failed capacitors, and blown fuses by measuring voltage, current, and resistance. Color-bar and dot generators provide onscreen test patterns, signal generators test signals, and oscilloscopes and digital storage scopes measure complex waveforms produced by electronic equipment. Repairs may involve removing and replacing a failed capacitor, transistor, or fuse. Repairers use hand tools, such as pliers, screwdrivers, soldering irons, and wrenches, to replace faulty parts. They also make adjustments to equipment, such as focus-

ing and converging the picture of a television set or balancing the audio on a surround-sound system.

Improvements in technology have miniaturized and digitized many audio and video recording devices. Miniaturization has made repair work significantly more difficult because both the components and the acceptable tolerances are smaller. Also, components now are mounted on the surface of circuit boards, instead of plugged into slots, requiring more precise soldering when a new part is installed. Improved technologies have lowered the price of electronic home entertainment equipment to the point where customers often replace broken equipment instead of repairing it.

Work environment. Most repairers work in well-lighted electrical repair shops. Field technicians, however, spend much time traveling in service vehicles and working in customers' residences.

Repairers may have to work in a variety of positions and carry heavy equipment. Although the work of repairers is comparatively safe, they must take precautions against minor burns and electric shock. Because television monitors carry high voltage even when they are turned off, repairers need to discharge the voltage before servicing such equipment.

Training, Other Qualifications, and Advancement

Employers prefer applicants who have basic electronics skills, good problem-solving skills, and previous repair experience. Good customer service skills are essential for field technicians, as they spend a majority of their time working in customers' homes.

Education and training. Employers prefer applicants who have basic knowledge and skills in electronics as well as previous repair experience. Many applicants gain these skills at vocational training programs and community colleges. Training programs should include both hands-on experience and theoretical education in digital consumer electronics. Entry-level repairers may work closely with more experienced technicians, who provide technical guidance.

Other qualifications. Field technicians work closely with customers and must have good communication skills and a neat appearance. Repairers also must have good problem solving skills, as their main duty is to diagnose and solve problems. Employers also may require that field technicians have a driver's license.

Most home entertainment equipment installers and repairers work in electronic stores.

Projections data from the National Employment Matrix

Occupational Title	SOC Code	Employment, 2006	Projected employment, 2016	Change, 2006-16	
				Number	Percent
Electronic home entertainment equipment installers and repairers ..	49-2097	40,000	41,000	1,200	3

NOTE: Data in this table are rounded. See the discussion of the employment projections table in the *Handbook* introductory chapter on *Occupational Information Included in the Handbook*.

Certification and advancement. Various organizations offer certification for electronic home entertainment equipment installers and repairers. Repairers may specialize in a variety of skill areas, including consumer electronics. To receive certification, repairers must pass qualifying exams corresponding to their level of training and experience.

Experienced repairers with advanced training may become specialists or troubleshooters, helping other repairers to diagnose difficult problems. Workers with leadership ability may become supervisors of other repairers. Some experienced workers open their own repair shops.

Employment

Electronic home entertainment equipment installers and repairers held about 40,000 jobs in 2006. Many repairers worked in electronics and appliance stores that sell and service electronic home entertainment products or in electronic and precision equipment repair and maintenance shops. About 12 percent of electronic home entertainment equipment installers and repairers were self-employed, compared to 7 percent for all installation, maintenance, and repair occupations.

Job Outlook

Employment is expected to increase more slowly than the average for all occupations. Job prospects will be best for applicants with knowledge of electronics, related experience, and good customer service skills.

Employment change. Employment of electronic home entertainment equipment installers and repairers is expected to grow by 3 percent from 2006 to 2016, which is slower than average for all occupations. Demand will be driven by the rising sales of home entertainment equipment.

The need for repairers is expected to grow slowly, however, because home entertainment equipment is less expensive than in the past. As technological developments have lowered the price and improved the reliability of equipment, the demand for repair services has decreased. When a malfunction does occur, it often is cheaper for consumers to replace equipment than to pay for repairs.

Employment growth will be spurred somewhat by the introduction of sophisticated digital equipment, such as high-definition digital televisions and digital camcorders. So long as the price of such equipment remains high, purchasers will be willing to hire repairers when malfunctions occur. There also will be demand to install sophisticated home entertainment systems, such as home theaters.

Job prospects. Job openings will come about because of employment growth and from the need to replace workers who retire or who leave the occupation. Opportunities will be best for applicants with knowledge of electronics and who have related hands-on experience and good customer service skills.

Earnings

Median hourly earnings of wage-and-salary electronic home entertainment equipment installers and repairers were $14.42 in May 2006. The middle 50 percent earned between $11.52 and $18.24. The lowest 10 percent earned less than $8.96, and the highest 10 percent earned more than $22.42. In May 2006, median hourly earnings of electronic home entertainment equipment installers and repairers were $14.46 in electronics and appliance stores and $13.18 in electronic and precision equipment repair and maintenance.

Related Occupations

Other workers who install, repair, and maintain electronic equipment include computer, automated teller, and office machine repairers; electrical and electronics installers and repairers; radio and telecommunications equipment installers and repairers; precision instrument and equipment repairers; home appliance repairers; coin, vending, and amusement machine servicers and repairers; maintenance and repair workers, general; and electricians.

Sources of Additional Information

For information on careers and certification, contact:
➤ ACES International, 5241 Princess Anne Rd., Suite 110, Virginia Beach, VA 23462.
Internet: **http://www.acesinternational.org**
➤ Electronics Technicians Association International, 5 Depot St., Greencastle, IN 46135. Internet: **http://www.eta-i.org**
➤ International Society of Certified Electronics Technicians, 3608 Pershing Ave., Fort Worth, TX 76107-4527.
Internet: **http://www.iscet.org**

Radio and Telecommunications Equipment Installers and Repairers

(O*NET 49-2021.00, 49-2022.00)

Significant Points

- Little or no change in employment is projected.

- Job opportunities vary by specialty; good opportunities are expected for central office installers and repairers, but station installers and repairers can expect keen competition.

- Applicants with computer skills and postsecondary electronics training should have the best opportunities.

- Repairers may be on-call around the clock in case of emergencies—night, weekend, and holiday hours are common.

Nature of the Work

Telephones, computers, and radios depend on a variety of equipment to transmit communications signals and connect to the Internet. From electronic and optical switches that route telephone calls and packets of data to their destinations to radio transmitters and receivers that relay signals from radios in airplanes, boats, and emergency vehicles, complex equipment is needed to keep us communicating. The workers who set up and maintain this sophisticated equipment are called radio and telecommunications equipment installers and repairers.

Telecommunications equipment installers and repairers have a range of skills and abilities, which vary by the type of work they do and where it is performed. Most work indoors. (Equipment installers who work mainly outdoors are classified as telecommunications line installers and repairers—a separate occupation discussed elsewhere in the *Handbook*.)

Central office installers and repairers—telecommunications equipment installers and repairers who work at switching hubs called central offices—do some of the most complex work. Switching hubs contain the switches and routers that direct packets of information to their destinations. Installers and repairers set up those switches and routers as well as cables and other equipment.

Although most telephone lines connecting houses to central offices and switching stations are still copper, the lines connecting central hubs to each other are fiber optic. Fiber optic lines, along with newer packet switching equipment, have greatly increased the transmission capacity of each line, allowing an ever increasing amount of information to pass through the lines. Switches and routers are used to transmit, process, amplify, and direct a massive amount of information. Installing and maintaining this equipment requires a high level of special technical knowledge.

The increasing reliability of switches and routers has simplified maintenance, however. New self-monitoring telecommunications switches alert central office repairers to malfunctions. Some switches allow repairers to diagnose and correct problems from remote locations. When faced with a malfunction, the repairer may refer to manufacturers' manuals that provide maintenance instructions.

As cable television and telecommunications technology converge, the equipment used in both technologies is becoming more similar. The distribution centers for cable television companies, which are similar to central offices in the telecommunications sector, are called *headends*. Headend technicians perform essentially the same work as central office technicians, but they work in the cable industry.

When problems with telecommunications equipment arise, telecommunications equipment repairers diagnose the source of the problem by testing each part of the equipment. This requires understanding how the software and hardware interact. Repairers often use spectrum analyzers, network analyzers, or both to locate the problem. A network analyzer sends a signal through the equipment to detect any distortion in the signal. The nature of the signal distortion often directs the repairer to the source of the problem. To fix the equipment, repairers may use small hand tools, including pliers and screwdrivers, to remove and replace defective components such as circuit boards or wiring.

Newer equipment is easier to repair because whole boards and parts are designed to be quickly removed and replaced. Repairers also may install updated software or programs that maintain existing software.

Another type of telecommunications installer and repairer, *PBX installers and repairers* set up private branch exchange (PBX) switchboards, which relay incoming, outgoing, and interoffice telephone calls within a single location or organization. To install switches and switchboards, installers first connect the equipment to power lines and communications cables and install frames and supports. They test the connections to ensure that adequate power is available and that the communication links work properly. They also install equipment such as power systems, alarms, and telephone sets. New switches and switchboards are computerized and workers often need to install software or program the equipment to provide specific features. Finally, the installer performs tests to verify that the newly installed equipment functions properly. If a problem arises, PBX repairers determine whether it is located within the PBX system or whether it originates in the telephone lines maintained by the local telephone company. Newer installations use voice-over Internet protocol (VoIP) systems. VoIP systems operate like a PBX system, but they use a company's computer wiring to run Internet access, network applications, and telephone communications.

Station installers and repairers, telephone—commonly known as *home installers and repairers or telecommunications service technicians*—install and repair telecommunications wiring and equipment in customers' home or business premises. They install telephone, VoIP, Internet, and other communications services by installing wiring inside the home or connecting existing wiring to outside service lines. Depending upon the service required, they may setup television capability or connect modems and install software on a customer's computer. To complete the connection to an outside service line, the installer may need to climb telephone poles or ladders and test the line. Later on, if a maintenance problem occurs, station repairers test the customer's lines to determine if the problem is located in the customer's premises or in the outside service lines and attempt to fix the problem if it is inside. If the problem is with the outside service lines, telecommunications line repairers are usually called to fix it.

Radio mechanics install and maintain radio transmitting and receiving equipment, excluding cellular communications systems. This includes stationary equipment mounted on transmission towers or tall buildings and mobile equipment, such as two-way radio communications systems in taxis, airplanes, ships, and emergency vehicles. Aviation and marine radio mechanics also may work on other electronic equipment, in addition to radios. Newer radio equipment is self-monitoring and may alert mechanics to potential malfunctions. When malfunctions occur, these mechanics examine equipment for damaged components and either fix them, replace the part, or make a software modification. They may use electrical measuring instruments to monitor signal strength, transmission capacity, interference, and signal delay, as well as hand tools to replace defective components and parts and to adjust equipment so that it performs within required specifications.

Work environment. Radio and telecommunications equipment installers and repairers generally work in clean, well-lighted, air-conditioned surroundings, such as a telecommunications company's central office, a customer's location, or an electronic repair shop or service center. Traveling to the site of the installation or repair is common among station installers and repairers, PBX and VoIP installers and repairers, and radio mechanics. The installation may require access to rooftops, ladders, and telephone poles to complete the repair. Radio mechanics may need to work on transmissions towers, which may be located on top of tall buildings or mountains, as well as aboard airplanes and ships. These workers are subject to a variety of weather conditions while working outdoors.

The work of most repairers involves lifting, reaching, stooping, crouching, and crawling. Adherence to safety precautions is important in order to guard against work hazards. These hazards include falls, minor burns, electrical shock, and contact with hazardous materials.

Nearly all radio and telecommunications equipment installers and repairers work full time. Many work regular business hours to meet the demand for repair services during the workday. Schedules are more irregular at employers that provide repair services 24 hours a day, such as for police radio communications operations or where installation and maintenance must take place after normal business hours. At these locations, mechanics work a variety of shifts, including weekend and holiday hours. Repairers may be on call around the clock, in case of emergencies, and may have to work overtime.

Training, Other Qualifications, and Advancement

Postsecondary education in electronics and computer technology is increasingly required for radio and telecommunications equipment installers and repairer jobs, and a few employers even prefer people with a bachelor's degree for some of the most complex types of work. About half of all radio and telecommunications equipment installers and repairers have completed some college courses or an associate degree.

Education and training. As telecommunications technology becomes more complex, the education required for radio and telecommunications equipment installers and repairer jobs has increased. Most employers prefer applicants with postsecondary training in electronics and familiarity with computers. The education needed for these jobs may vary from a certification to work on certain equipment to a 2- or 4-year degree in electronics or a related subject. Sources of training include 2- and 4-year college programs in electronics or communications technology, military experience in radios and electronics, trade schools, and programs offered by equipment and software manufacturers. Educational requirements are higher for central office installers and repairers and for those working in nonresidential settings.

Many in the telecommunications industry work their way up into this occupation by gaining experience at less difficult jobs. Experience as a telecommunications line installer or station installer is helpful before moving up to the job of central office installer and other more complex jobs, for example. Military experience with communications equipment is also

Telecommunications equipment installers make adjustments in central offices.

valued by many employers in both telecommunications and radio repair.

Newly hired repairers usually receive some training from their employers. This may include formal classroom training in electronics, communications systems, or software and informal hands-on training assisting an experienced repairer. Large companies may send repairers to outside training sessions to learn about new equipment and service procedures. As networks have become more sophisticated—often including equipment from a variety of companies—the knowledge needed for installation and maintenance also has increased.

Licensure. Aviation and marine radio mechanics are required to have a license from the Federal Communications Commission before they can work on these types of radios. This requires passing several exams on radio law, electronics fundamentals, and maintenance practices.

Other qualifications. Familiarity with computers, being mechanically inclined, and being able to solve problems are traits that are highly regarded by employers. Repairers must also be able to distinguish colors, because wires are color-coded. For positions that require climbing poles and towers, workers must be in good physical shape and not afraid of heights. Repairers who handle assignments alone at a customer's site must be able to work without close supervision. For workers who frequently contact customers, a pleasant personality, neat appearance, and good communications skills also are important.

Certification and advancement. This is an occupation where the technology is changing rapidly. Workers must keep abreast of the latest equipment available and know how to repair it. Telecommunications equipment installers and repairers often need to be certified to perform certain tasks or to work on specific equipment. Certification often requires taking classes. Some of certifications are needed before entering an occupation; others are meant to improve one's current abilities or to advance in the occupation.

The Society of Cable and Telecommunications Engineers and the Telecommunications Industry Association offer voluntary certifications to workers in this field. Telecommunica-

Projections data from the National Employment Matrix

Occupational Title	SOC Code	Employment, 2006	Projected employment, 2016	Change, 2006-16	
				Number	Percent
Radio and telecommunications equipment installers and repairers..	49-2020	205,000	209,000	4,800	2
Radio mechanics	49-2021	6,500	6,300	-300	-4
Telecommunications equipment installers and repairers, except line installers	49-2022	198,000	203,000	5,000	3

NOTE: Data in this table are rounded. See the discussion of the employment projections table in the *Handbook* introductory chapter on *Occupational Information Included in the Handbook.*

tions equipment manufacturers also provide training on specific equipment.

Experienced repairers with advanced training may become specialists or troubleshooters who help other repairers diagnose difficult problems, or may work with engineers in designing equipment and developing maintenance procedures. Home installers may advance to wiring computer networks or working as a central office installer and repairer. Because of their familiarity with equipment, repairers are particularly well qualified to become manufacturers' sales workers. Workers with leadership ability also may become maintenance supervisors or service managers. Some experienced workers open their own repair services or shops, or become wholesalers or retailers of electronic equipment.

Employment

Radio and telecommunications equipment installers and repairers held about 205,000 jobs in 2006. About 198,000 were telecommunications equipment installers and repairers, except line installers. The remaining 6,500 were radio mechanics.

Telecommunications equipment installers and repairers work mostly in the telecommunications industry. Increasingly, however, they can be found in the construction industry working as contractors to the telecommunications industry.

Radio mechanics work in the electronic and precision equipment repair and maintenance industry, the telecommunications industry, electronics and appliance stores, government, and other industries.

Job Outlook

Little or no change in employment of radio and telecommunications equipment installers and repairers is projected. Job opportunities vary by specialty. Job prospects are best for those with computer skills and postsecondary training in electronics.

Employment change. Employment of radio and telecommunications equipment installers and repairers is expected to increase 2 percent, reflecting little or no change, during the 2006-16 period. Over the next decade, telecommunications companies will provide faster Internet connections, provide video-on-demand, add hundreds of television stations, and many services that haven't even been invented yet. Although building the new networks required to provide these services will create jobs, these gains will be offset by a decline in maintenance work. The new equipment requires much less maintenance work because it is newer, more reliable, easier to repair, and more resistant to damage from the elements.

The increased reliability of radio equipment and the use of self-monitoring systems also will continue to lessen the need for radio mechanics. However, technological changes are also creating new wireless applications that create jobs for radio mechanics.

Job prospects. Applicants with computer skills and postsecondary training in electronics should have the best opportunities for radio and telecommunications equipment installer and repairer jobs, but opportunities will vary by specialty. Good opportunities should be available for central office and PBX installers and repairers experienced in current technology, as the growing popularity of VoIP, expanded multimedia offerings such as video on demand, and other telecommunications services continue to place additional demand on telecommunications networks. These new services require high data transfer rates, which can be achieved only by installing new optical switching and routing equipment. Extending high-speed communications from central offices to customers also will require telecommunications equipment installers to put in place more advanced switching and routing equipment, but opportunities for repairers will be limited by the increased reliability and automation of the new switching equipment.

Station installers and repairers can expect keen competition. Prewired buildings and the increasing reliability of telephone equipment will reduce the need for installation and maintenance of customers' telephones, as will the declining number of pay telephones in operation as use of cellular telephones grows. However, some of these losses should be offset by the need to upgrade internal lines in businesses and the wiring of new homes and businesses with fiber optic lines.

Radio mechanics should find good opportunities if they have a strong background in electronics and an ability to work independently. Increasing competition from cellular services is limiting the growth of radio services, but employers report difficulty finding adequate numbers of qualified radio mechanics to perform repair work.

Earnings

In May 2006, median hourly earnings of telecommunications equipment installers and repairers, except line installers were $25.21. The middle 50 percent earned between $20.43 and $28.66. The bottom 10 percent earned less than $14.96, whereas the top 10 percent earned more than $32.84. The median hourly earnings of these workers in the wired telecommunications carriers industry were $26.25 in May 2006.

Median hourly earnings of radio mechanics in May 2006 were $18.12. The middle 50 percent earned between 14.04 and

$23.02. The bottom 10 percent earned less than $10.94, whereas the top 10 percent earned more than $28.54.

About 4 percent of radio and telecommunications equipment installers and repairers were self-employed. About 26 percent of radio and telecommunication equipment installers and repairers are members of unions, such as the Communications Workers of America (CWA) and the International Brotherhood of Electrical Workers (IBEW.)

Telecommunications equipment installers and repairers employed by large telecommunications companies who also belong to unions often have very good benefits, including health, dental, vision, and life insurance. They also usually have good retirement and leave policies. Those working for small independent companies and contractors may get fewer benefits.

Radio mechanics tend to work for small electronics firms or government. Benefits vary widely depending upon the type of work and size of firm. Government jobs usually have good benefits.

Related Occupations

Related occupations that involve work with electronic equipment include broadcast and sound engineering technicians and radio operators; computer, automated teller, and office machine repairers; and electrical and electronics installers and repairers. Line installers and repairers also set up and install telecommunications equipment. Engineering technicians also may repair electronic equipment as part of their duties.

Sources of Additional Information

For information on career and training opportunities, contact:
➤ International Brotherhood of Electrical Workers, Telecommunications Department, 900 7th St.NW., Washington, DC 20001.
➤ Communications Workers of America, 501 3rd St.NW., Washington, DC 20001.
Internet: **http://www.cwa-union.org/jobs**

For information on training and professional certifications for those already employed by cable telecommunications firms, contact:
➤ Society of Cable Telecommunications Engineers, Certification Department, 140 Phillips Rd., Exton, PA 19341-1318. Internet: **http://www.scte.org**

For information on training and licensing for aviation and marine radio mechanics, contact:
➤ The Federal Communications Commission (FCC), 445 12th St.SW., Washington, DC 20554.
Internet: **http://wireless.fcc.gov/commoperators**

For more information on employers, education, and training in marine electronics and radios, contact:
➤ National Marine Electronics Association, 7 Riggs Ave., Severna Park, MD 21164. Internet: **http://www.nmea.org**

Vehicle and Mobile Equipment Mechanics, Installers, and Repairers

---

Aircraft and Avionics Equipment Mechanics and Service Technicians

(O*NET 49-2091.00, 49-3011.00)

Significant Points

- Most workers learn their jobs in 1 of about 170 schools certified by the Federal Aviation Administration (FAA).

- Job opportunities should be favorable for persons who have completed an aircraft mechanic training program, but keen competition is likely for jobs at major airlines, which offer the best pay and benefits.

- Job opportunities are likely to continue to be best at small commuter and regional airlines, at FAA repair stations, and in general aviation.

Nature of the Work

To keep aircraft in peak operating condition, aircraft and avionics equipment mechanics and service technicians perform scheduled maintenance, make repairs, and complete inspections required by the Federal Aviation Administration (FAA).

Many aircraft mechanics, also called airframe mechanics, power plant mechanics, and avionics technicians, specialize in preventive maintenance. They inspect aircraft engines, landing gear, instruments, pressurized sections, accessories—brakes, valves, pumps, and air-conditioning systems, for example—and other parts of the aircraft, and do the necessary maintenance and replacement of parts. They also keep records related to the maintenance performed on the aircraft. Mechanics and technicians conduct inspections following a schedule based on the number of hours the aircraft has flown, calendar days since the last inspection, cycles of operation, or a combination of these factors. In large, sophisticated planes equipped with aircraft monitoring systems, mechanics can gather valuable diagnostic information from electronic boxes and consoles that monitor the aircraft's basic operations. In planes of all sorts, aircraft mechanics examine engines by working through specially designed openings while standing on ladders or scaffolds or by using hoists or lifts to remove the entire engine from the craft. After taking an engine apart, mechanics use precision instruments to measure parts for wear and use x-ray and magnetic inspection equipment to check for invisible cracks. They repair or replace worn or defective parts. Mechanics also may repair sheet metal or composite surfaces; measure the tension of control cables; and check for corrosion, distortion, and cracks in the fuselage, wings, and tail. After completing all repairs, they must test the equipment to ensure that it works properly.

Other mechanics specialize in repair work rather than inspection. They find and fix problems that pilot's describe. For example, during a preflight check, a pilot may discover that the aircraft's fuel gauge does not work. To solve the problem, mechanics may troubleshoot the electrical system, using electrical test equipment to make sure that no wires are broken or shorted out, and replace any defective electrical or electronic components. Mechanics work as fast as safety permits so that the aircraft can be put back into service quickly.

Some mechanics work on one or many different types of aircraft, such as jets, propeller-driven airplanes, and helicopters. Others specialize in one section of a particular type of aircraft, such as the engine, hydraulics, or electrical system. *Airframe mechanics* are authorized to work on any part of the aircraft except the instruments, power plants, and propellers. Powerplant mechanics are authorized to work on engines and do limited work on propellers. *Combination airframe-and-powerplant mechanics*—called A&P mechanics—work on all parts of the plane except the instruments. Most mechanics working on civilian aircraft today are A&P mechanics. In small, independent repair shops, mechanics usually inspect and repair many different types of aircraft.

Avionics systems—components used for aircraft navigation and radio communications, weather radar systems, and other instruments and computers that control flight, engine, and other primary functions—are now an integral part of aircraft design and have vastly increased aircraft capability. *Avionics technicians* repair and maintain these systems. Their duties may require additional licenses, such as a radiotelephone license issued by the U.S. Federal Communications Commission (FCC). Because of the increasing use of technology, more time is spent repairing electronic systems, such as computerized controls. Technicians also may be required to analyze and develop solutions to complex electronic problems.

Work environment. Mechanics usually work in hangars or in other indoor areas. When hangars are full or when repairs must be made quickly, they may work outdoors, sometimes in unpleasant weather. Mechanics often work under time pressure to maintain flight schedules or, in general aviation, to keep from inconveniencing customers. At the same time, mechanics have a tremendous responsibility to maintain safety standards, and this can cause the job to be stressful.

Frequently, mechanics must lift or pull objects weighing more than 70 pounds. They often stand, lie, or kneel in awkward positions and occasionally must work in precarious positions, such as on scaffolds or ladders. Noise and vibration are common when engines are being tested, so ear protection is necessary.

Aircraft mechanics usually work 40 hours a week on 8-hour shifts around the clock. Overtime and weekend work is frequent.

Training, Other Qualifications, and Advancement

Most workers learn their jobs in 1 of about 170 trade schools certified by the FAA. Most mechanics who work on civilian

aircraft are certified by the FAA as an "airframe mechanic" or a "powerplant mechanic."

Education and training. Although a few people become mechanics through on-the-job training, most learn their jobs in 1 of about the 170 schools certified by the FAA. About one-third of these schools award 2-year and 4-year degrees in avionics, aviation technology, or aviation maintenance management.

FAA standards established by law require that certified mechanic schools offer students a minimum of 1,900 class hours. Coursework in schools normally lasts from 18 to 24 months and provides training with the tools and equipment used on the job. Aircraft trade schools are placing more emphasis on technologies such as turbine engines, composite materials—including graphite, fiberglass, and boron—and aviation electronics, which are increasingly being used in the construction of new aircraft.

Courses in mathematics, physics, chemistry, electronics, computer science, and mechanical drawing are helpful because they demonstrate many of the principles involved in the operation of aircraft, and knowledge of these principles is often necessary to make repairs. Recent technological advances in aircraft maintenance require mechanics to have an especially strong background in electronics to get or keep jobs in this field.

Courses that develop writing skills also are important because mechanics are often required to submit reports. Mechanics must be able to read, write, and understand English.

A few mechanics are trained on the job by experienced mechanics. They must be supervised by certified mechanics until they have FAA certificates.

Licensure. The FAA requires at least 18 months of work experience for an airframe or powerplant certificate, although completion of a program at an FAA-certified mechanic school can be substituted for the work experience requirement. Mechanics and technicians also must pass an exam for certification and take at least 16 hours of training every 24 months to keep their certificate current. Many mechanics take train-

Avionics technicians repair and maintain components used for aircraft navigation, radio communications, and weather radar systems, as well as instruments and computers that control flight, engine, and other functions.

Projections data from the National Employment Matrix

Occupational Title	SOC Code	Employment, 2006	Projected employment, 2016	Change, 2006-16	
				Number	Percent
Aircraft and avionics equipment mechanics and service technicians..	—	138,000	152,000	14,000	10
Avionics technicians	49-2091	16,000	17,000	1,300	8
Aircraft mechanics and service technicians............................	49-3011	122,000	135,000	13,000	11

NOTE: Data in this table are rounded. See the discussion of the employment projections table in the *Handbook* introductory chapter on *Occupational Information Included in the Handbook.*

ing courses offered by manufacturers or employers, usually through outside contractors.

The FAA also offers a combined certificate that allows for certification as both an airframe and a powerplant mechanic, the A&P certificate. For a combined A&P certificate, mechanics must acquire at least 30 months of experience working with both engines and airframes, or experience combined with the completion of an FAA-certified mechanic school program. FAA regulations also require current work experience to keep the A&P certificate valid. Applicants must have at least 1,000 hours of work experience in the previous 24 months or take a refresher course. Most airlines require that mechanics have a high school diploma and an A&P certificate. Applicants for all certificates must pass written and oral tests and demonstrate that they can do the work authorized by the certificate.

Avionics technicians need an FAA mechanics' certificate. They also must be trained and qualified and have the proper tools to work on avionics equipment. Many have avionics repair experience from the military or from working for avionics manufacturers.

Other qualifications. Applicants must be at least 18 years of age. Some aircraft mechanics in the Armed Forces acquire enough general experience to satisfy the work experience requirements for the FAA certificate. With additional study, they may pass the certifying exam. In general, however, jobs in the military services are too specialized to provide the broad experience required by the FAA. Most Armed Forces mechanics have to complete the entire FAA training program, although a few receive some credit for the material they learned in the service. In any case, military experience is a great advantage when seeking employment; employers consider applicants with formal training to be the most desirable applicants.

Aircraft mechanics must do careful and thorough work that requires a high degree of mechanical aptitude. Employers seek applicants who are self-motivated, hard working, enthusiastic, and able to diagnose and solve complex mechanical problems. Additionally, employers prefer mechanics who can perform a variety of tasks. Agility is important for the reaching and climbing necessary to do the job. Because they may work on the tops of wings and fuselages on large jet planes, aircraft mechanics must not be afraid of heights.

Advances in computer technology, aircraft systems, and the materials used to manufacture airplanes have made mechanics' jobs more highly technical. Aircraft mechanics must possess the skills necessary to troubleshoot and diagnose complex aircraft systems. They also must continually update their skills with and knowledge of new technology and advances in aircraft technology

Advancement. As aircraft mechanics gain experience, they may advance to lead mechanic (or crew chief), inspector, lead inspector, or shop supervisor positions. Opportunities are best for those who have an aircraft inspector's authorization. To obtain an inspector's authorization, a mechanic must have held an A&P certificate for at least 3 years, with 24 months of hands-on experience.

In the airlines, where promotion often is determined by examination, supervisors sometimes advance to executive positions. Those with broad experience in maintenance and overhaul might become inspectors with the FAA. With additional business and management training, some open their own aircraft maintenance facilities. Mechanics with the necessary pilot licenses and flying experience may take the FAA examination for the position of flight engineer, with opportunities to become pilots.

Mechanics and technicians learn many different skills in their training that can be applied to other jobs, and some transfer to other skilled repairer occupations or electronics technician jobs. For example, some avionics technicians continue their education and become aviation engineers, electrical engineers (specializing in circuit design and testing), or communication engineers. Others become repair consultants, in-house electronics designers, or join research groups that test and develop products.

Employment

Aircraft and avionics equipment mechanics and service technicians held about 138,000 jobs in 2006; about 5 in 6 of these workers was an aircraft mechanic and service technician.

Employment of aircraft and avionics equipment mechanics and service technicians primarily is concentrated in a small number of industries. More than half of aircraft and avionics equipment mechanics and service technicians worked in air transportation and support activities for air transportation. Around 18 percent worked in aerospace product and parts manufacturing and about 16 percent worked for the Federal Government. Most of the rest worked for companies that operate their own planes to transport executives and cargo.

Most airline mechanics and service technicians work at major airports near large cities. Civilian mechanics employed by the U.S. Armed Forces work at military installations. Mechanics who work for aerospace manufacturing firms typically are located in California or in Washington State. Others work for the FAA, many at the facilities in Oklahoma City, Atlantic City, Wichita, or Washington, DC. Mechanics for independent repair shops work at airports in every part of the country.

Job Outlook

Job growth for these mechanics and technicians is expected to be about as fast as the average for all occupations. Job opportunities should be favorable for people who have completed an aircraft mechanic training program, but keen competition is likely for jobs at major airlines.

Employment change. Employment is expected to increase by 10 percent during the 2006-16 period, about as fast as the average for all occupations. Passenger traffic is expected to increase as the result of an expanding economy and a growing population, and the need for aircraft mechanics and service technicians will grow accordingly.

Job prospects. Most job openings for aircraft mechanics through the year 2016 will stem from the need to replace the many mechanics expected to retire over the next decade. In addition, some mechanics will leave to work in related fields, such as automobile repair, as their skills are largely transferable to other maintenance and repair occupations.

Also contributing to favorable future job opportunities for mechanics is the long-term trend toward fewer students entering technical schools to learn skilled maintenance and repair trades. Many of the students who have the ability and aptitude to work on planes are choosing to go to college, work in computer-related fields, or go into other repair and maintenance occupations with better working conditions. If this trend continues, the supply of trained aviation mechanics may not keep up with the needs of the air transportation industry.

Job opportunities will continue to be the best at small commuter and regional airlines, at FAA repair stations, and in general aviation. Commuter and regional airlines is the fastest growing segment of the air transportation industry, but wages in these airlines tend to be lower than those in the major airlines, so they attract fewer job applicants. Also, some jobs will become available as experienced mechanics leave for higher paying jobs with the major airlines or transfer to other occupations. At the same time, general aviation aircraft are becoming increasingly sophisticated, boosting the demand for qualified mechanics. Mechanics will face more competition for jobs with large airlines because the high wages and travel benefits that these jobs offer generally attract more qualified applicants than there are openings. Also, there is an increasing trend for large airlines to outsource aircraft and avionics equipment mechanic jobs overseas; however, most airline companies prefer that aircraft maintenance be performed in the U.S. because overseas contractors may not comply with more stringent U.S. safety regulations.

In spite of these factors, job opportunities with the airlines are expected to be better than they have been in the past. But, in general, prospects will be best for applicants with experience. Mechanics who keep abreast of technological advances in electronics, composite materials, and other areas will be in greatest demand. Also, mechanics who are mobile and willing to relocate to smaller rural areas will have better job opportunities. The number of job openings for aircraft mechanics in the Federal Government should decline as the Government increasingly contracts out service and repair functions to private repair companies.

Avionics technicians who do not have FAA certification, but who are prepared to master the intricacies of the aircraft while working with certified A&P mechanics, should have good opportunities. However, certified technicians who are trained to work with complex aircraft systems, performing some duties normally performed by certified A&P mechanics, should have the best job prospects. Additionally, technicians with licensing that enables them to work on the airplane, either removing or reinstalling equipment, are expected to be in especially high demand.

Earnings

Median hourly earnings of aircraft mechanics and service technicians were about $22.95 in May 2006. The middle 50 percent earned between $18.96 and $28.12. The lowest 10 percent earned less than $14.94, and the highest 10 percent earned more than $34.51. Median hourly earnings in the industries employing the largest numbers of aircraft mechanics and service technicians in May 2006 were:

Scheduled air transportation	$27.46
Nonscheduled air transportation	23.33
Federal Government	23.19
Aerospace product and parts manufacturing	21.58
Support activities for air transportation	19.57

Median hourly earnings of avionics technicians were about $22.57 in May 2006. The middle 50 percent earned between $19.02 and $26.65. The lowest 10 percent earned less than $15.65, and the highest 10 percent earned more than $30.33.

Mechanics who work on jets for the major airlines generally earn more than those working on other aircraft. Those who graduate from an aviation maintenance technician school often earn higher starting salaries than individuals who receive training in the Armed Forces or on the job. Airline mechanics and their immediate families receive reduced-fare transportation on their own and most other airlines.

About 3 in 10 aircraft and avionics equipment mechanics and service technicians are members of unions or covered by union agreements. The principal unions are the International Association of Machinists and Aerospace Workers, and the Transport Workers Union of America. Some mechanics are represented by the International Brotherhood of Teamsters.

Related Occupations

Workers in some other occupations that involve similar mechanical and electrical work are electricians, electrical and electronics installers and repairers, and elevator installers and repairers.

Sources of Additional Information

Information about jobs with a particular airline can be obtained by writing to the personnel manager of the company.

For general information about aircraft and avionics equipment mechanics and service technicians, contact:

➤ Professional Aviation Maintenance Association, 400 Commonwealth Dr., Warrendale, PA 15096. Internet: **http://www.pama.org**

For information on jobs in a particular area, contact employers at local airports or local offices of the State employment service.

Information on obtaining positions as aircraft and avionics equipment mechanics and service technicians with the Federal Government is available from the Office of Personnel Management through USAJOBS, the Federal Government's official employment information system. This resource for locating and applying for job opportunities can be accessed through the Internet at **http://www.usajobs.opm.gov** or through an interactive voice response telephone system at (703) 724-1850 or TDD (978) 461-8404. These numbers are not toll free, and charges may result.

Automotive Body and Related Repairers

(O*NET 49-3021.00, 49-3022.00)

Significant Points

- To become a fully skilled automotive body repairer, formal training followed by on-the-job instruction is recommended because fixing newer automobiles requires advanced skills.

- Excellent job opportunities are projected because of the large number of older workers who are expected to retire in the next 10 to 15 years.

- Repairers need good reading ability and basic mathematics and computer skills to use print and digital technical manuals.

Nature of the Work

Most of the damage resulting from everyday vehicle collisions can be repaired, and vehicles can be refinished to look and drive like new. *Automotive body repairers*, often called collision repair technicians, straighten bent bodies, remove dents, and replace crumpled parts that cannot be fixed. They repair all types of vehicles, and although some work on large trucks, buses, or tractor-trailers, most work on cars and small trucks. They can work alone, with only general direction from supervisors, or as specialists on a repair team. In some shops, helpers or apprentices assist experienced repairers.

Each damaged vehicle presents different challenges for repairers. Using their broad knowledge of automotive construction and repair techniques, automotive body repairers must decide how to handle each job based on what the vehicle is made of and what needs to be fixed. They must first determine the extent of the damage and order any needed parts.

If the car is heavily damaged, an automotive body repairer might start by realigning the frame of the vehicle. Repairers chain or clamp frames and sections to alignment machines that use hydraulic pressure to align damaged components. "Unibody" vehicles—designs built without frames—must be restored to precise factory specifications for the vehicle to operate correctly. For these vehicles, repairers use benchmark systems to accurately measure how much each section is out of alignment, and hydraulic machinery to return the vehicle to its original shape.

Once the frame is aligned, repairers can begin to fix or replace damaged body parts. If the vehicle or part is made of metal, body repairers will use a pneumatic metal-cutting gun or other tools to remove badly damaged sections of body panels and then weld in replacement sections. Less serious dents are pulled out with a hydraulic jack or hand prying bar or knocked out with handtools or pneumatic hammers. Small dents and creases in the metal are smoothed by holding a small anvil against one side of the damaged area while hammering the opposite side. Repairers also remove very small pits and dimples with pick hammers and punches in a process called metal finishing. Body repairers use plastic or solder to fill small dents that cannot be worked out of plastic or metal panels. On metal panels, they file or grind the hardened filler to the original shape and clean the surface with a media blaster—similar to a sand blaster—before repainting the damaged portion of the vehicle.

Body repairers also repair or replace the plastic body parts that are increasingly used on new vehicles. They remove damaged panels and identify the type and properties of the plastic used. With most types of plastic, repairers can apply heat from a hot-air welding gun or immerse the panel in hot water and press the softened section back into shape by hand. Repairers replace plastic parts that are badly damaged or very difficult to fix. A few body repairers specialize in fixing fiberglass car bodies.

Some body repairers specialize in installing and repairing glass in automobiles and other vehicles. *Automotive glass installers and repairers* remove broken, cracked, or pitted windshields and window glass. Glass installers apply a moisture-proofing compound along the edges of the glass, place the glass in the vehicle, and install rubber strips around the sides of the windshield or window to make it secure and weatherproof.

Many large shops make repairs using an assembly-line approach where vehicles are fixed by a team of repairers who each specialize in one type of repair. One worker might straighten frames while another repairs doors and fenders, for example. In most shops, automotive painters do the painting and refinishing, but in small shops, workers often do both body repairing and painting. (Automotive painters are discussed in the section on painting and coating workers, except construction and maintenance elsewhere in the *Handbook*.)

Work environment. Repairers work indoors in body shops that are noisy with the clatter of hammers against metal and the whine of power tools. Most shops are well ventilated to disperse dust and paint fumes. Body repairers often work in awkward or cramped positions, and much of their work is strenuous and dirty. Hazards include cuts from sharp metal edges, burns from torches and heated metal, injuries from power tools, and fumes from paint. However, serious accidents usually are avoided when the shop is kept clean and orderly and safety practices are observed. Automotive repair and maintenance shops averaged 4 cases of work-related injuries and illnesses per 100 full-time workers in 2005, compared to 4.6 per 100 workers in all private industry.

Automotive body repairers remove, repair, and replace car and truck parts that have been damaged.

Most automotive body repairers work a standard 40-hour week. More than 40 hours a week may be required when there is a backlog of repair work to be completed. This may include working on weekends.

Training, Other Qualifications, and Advancement

Automotive technology is rapidly becoming more sophisticated, and most employers prefer applicants who have completed a formal training program in automotive body repair or refinishing. Most new repairers complete at least part of this training on the job. Many repairers, particularly in urban areas, need a national certification to advance past entry-level work.

Education and training. A high school diploma or GED is often all that is required to enter this occupation, but more specific education and training is needed to learn how to repair newer automobiles. Collision repair programs may be offered in high school or in postsecondary vocational schools and community colleges. Courses in electronics, physics, chemistry, English, computers, and mathematics provide a good background for a career as an automotive body repairer. Most training programs combine classroom instruction and hands-on practice.

Trade and technical school programs typically award certificates to graduates after 6 months to a year of collision repair study. Some community colleges offer 2-year programs in collision repair. Many of these schools also offer certificates for individual courses, so that students are able to take classes incrementally or as needed.

New repairers begin by assisting experienced body repairers in tasks such as removing damaged parts, sanding body panels, and installing repaired parts. Novices learn to remove small dents and make other minor repairs. They then progress to more difficult tasks, such as straightening body parts and returning them to their correct alignment. Generally, it takes 3 to 4 years of hands-on training to become skilled in all aspects of body repair, some of which may be completed as part of a formal education program. Basic automotive glass installation and repair can be learned in as little as 6 months, but becoming fully qualified can take several years.

Continuing education and training are needed throughout a career in automotive body repair. Automotive parts, body materials, and electronics continue to change and to become more complex. To keep up with these technological advances, repair-ers must continue to gain new skills by reading technical manuals and furthering their education with classes and seminars. Many companies within the automotive body repair industry send employees to advanced training programs to brush up on skills or to learn new techniques.

Other qualifications. Fully skilled automotive body repairers must have good reading ability and basic mathematics and computer skills. Restoring unibody automobiles to their original form requires repairers to follow instructions and diagrams in technical manuals and to make precise three-dimensional measurements of the position of one body section relative to another. In addition, repairers should enjoy working with their hands and be able to pay attention to detail while they work.

Certification and advancement. Certification by the National Institute for Automotive Service Excellence (ASE), although voluntary, is the pervasive industry credential for non entry-level automotive body repairers. This is especially true in large, urban areas. Repairers may take up to four ASE Master Collision Repair and Refinish Exams. Repairers who pass at least one exam and have 2 years of hands-on work experience earn ASE certification. The completion of a postsecondary program in automotive body repair may be substituted for 1 year of work experience. Those who pass all four exams become ASE Master Collision Repair and Refinish Technicians. Automotive body repairers must retake the examination at least every 5 years to retain their certification. Many vehicle manufacturers and paint manufacturers also have product certification programs that can advance a repairer's career.

As beginners increase their skills, learn new techniques, earn certifications, and complete work more rapidly, their pay increases. An experienced automotive body repairer with managerial ability may advance to shop supervisor, and some workers open their own body repair shops. Other repairers become automobile damage appraisers for insurance companies.

Employment

Automotive body and related repairers held about 206,000 jobs in 2006; about 13 percent specialized in automotive glass installation and repair. Fifty-eight percent of repairers worked for automotive repair and maintenance shops in 2006, while 20 percent worked for automobile dealers. Others worked for organizations, such as trucking companies, that maintain their own motor vehicles. A small number of repairers worked for wholesalers of motor vehicles, parts, and supplies. More than 15 percent of automotive body repairers were self-employed, roughly double the number for all installation, maintenance, and repair occupations.

Job Outlook

Employment of automotive body and related repairers is expected to grow about as fast as average through the year 2016, and job opportunities are projected to be excellent due to a growing number of retirements in this occupation.

Employment change. Employment of automotive body repairers is expected to grow 12 percent over the 2006-16 decade, as compared to 10 percent for all occupations. Demand for qualified body repairers will increase as the number of vehicles on the road continues to grow. With more motor vehicles in use, more vehicles will be damaged in accidents. In addition, new

Projections data from the National Employment Matrix

Occupational Title	SOC Code	Employment, 2006	Projected employment, 2016	Change, 2006-16	
				Number	Percent
Automotive body and related repairers...	—	206,000	232,000	26,000	12
Automotive body and related repairers.......................................	49-3021	183,000	204,000	21,000	12
Automotive glass installers and repairers	49-3022	24,000	28,000	4,400	19

NOTE: Data in this table are rounded. See the discussion of the employment projections table in the *Handbook* introductory chapter on *Occupational Information Included in the Handbook.*

automotive designs of lighter weight are prone to greater collision damage than are older, heavier designs, so more repairs are needed. Employment growth will continue to be concentrated in automotive body, paint, interior, and glass repair shops, with little or no change in automotive dealerships.

Despite the anticipated increase in the number of auto accidents, the increasing demand for automotive body repairers will be tempered by improvements in the quality of vehicles. Also, technological innovations that enhance safety will reduce the likelihood of accidents.

Demand for automotive body repair services will similarly be constrained as more vehicles are declared a total loss after accidents. In many such cases, the vehicles are not repaired because of the high cost of replacing the increasingly complex parts and electronic components and because of the extensive damage that results when airbags deploy. Also, higher insurance premiums and deductibles mean that minor damage is more often going unrepaired. Larger shops are instituting productivity enhancements, such as employing a team approach to repairs, which may limit employment growth by reducing the time it takes to make repairs.

Job prospects. Employment growth will create some opportunities, but the need to replace experienced repairers who transfer to other occupations or who retire or stop working for other reasons will account for the majority of job openings over the next 10 years. Opportunities will be excellent for people with formal training in automotive body repair and refinishing. Those without any training or experience in automotive body refinishing or collision repair—before or after high school—will face competition for these jobs.

Experienced body repairers are rarely laid off during a general slowdown in the economy as the automotive repair business is not very sensitive to changes in economic conditions. Although repair of minor dents and crumpled fenders is often put off when drivers have less money, major body damage must be repaired before a vehicle can be driven safely.

Earnings

Median hourly wage-and-salary earnings of automotive body and related repairers, including incentive pay, were $16.92 in May 2006. The middle 50 percent earned between $13.00 and $22.33 an hour. The lowest 10 percent earned less than $10.10, and the highest 10 percent earned more than $28.71 an hour. Median hourly earnings of automotive body and related repairers were $17.85 in automobile dealers and $16.66 in automotive repair and maintenance.

Median hourly wage-and-salary earnings of automotive glass installers and repairers, including incentive pay, were $14.77. The middle 50 percent earned between $11.44 and $18.42 an

hour. The lowest 10 percent earned less than $9.19, and the highest 10 percent earned more than $22.22 an hour. Median hourly earnings in automotive repair and maintenance shops, the industry employing most automotive glass installers and repairers, were $14.80.

The majority of body repairers employed by independent repair shops and automotive dealers are paid on an incentive basis. Under this system, body repairers are paid a set amount for various tasks, and earnings depend on both the amount of work assigned and how fast it is completed. Employers frequently guarantee workers a minimum weekly salary. Body repairers who work for trucking companies, buslines, and other organizations that maintain their own vehicles usually receive an hourly wage.

Helpers and trainees typically earn between 30 percent and 60 percent of the earnings of skilled workers. They are paid by the hour until they are skilled enough to be paid on an incentive basis.

Employee benefits vary widely from business to business. However, industry sources report that benefits such as paid leave, health insurance, and retirement assistance are increasingly common in the collision repair industry. Automotive dealerships are the most likely to offer such incentives.

Related Occupations

Repairing damaged motor vehicles often involves working on mechanical components, as well as vehicle bodies. Automotive body repairers often work closely with individuals in several related occupations, including automotive service technicians and mechanics, diesel service technicians and mechanics, auto damage appraisers, and painting and coating workers, except construction and maintenance. Automotive glass installers and repairers complete tasks very similar to those of glaziers.

Sources of Additional Information

Additional details about work opportunities may be obtained from automotive body repair shops, automobile dealers, or local offices of your State employment service. State employment service offices also are a source of information about training programs.

For general information about automotive body repairer careers, contact any of the following sources:

➤ Automotive Careers Today, 8400 Westpark Dr., MS#2, McLean, VA 22102. Internet: **http://www.autocareerstoday.org**

➤ Automotive Service Association, P.O. Box 929, Bedford, Texas 76095. Internet: **http://www.asashop.org**

➤ Inter-Industry Conference On Auto Collision Repair Education Foundation (I-CAR), 5125 Trillium Blvd., Hoffman Estates, IL 60192. Internet: **http://www.collisioncareers.org**

➤ National Automobile Dealers Association, 8400 Westpark Dr., McLean, VA 22102. Internet: **http://www.nada.org**

For general information about careers in automotive glass installation and repair, contact:

➤ National Glass Association. 8200 Greensboro Dr., Suite 302, McLean, VA 22102. Internet: **http://www.glass.org**

For information on how to become a certified automotive body repairer, write to:

➤ National Institute for Automotive Service Excellence (ASE), 101 Blue Seal Dr. SE., Suite 101, Leesburg, VA 20175. Internet: **http://www.asecert.org**

For a directory of certified automotive body repairer programs, contact:

➤ National Automotive Technician Education Foundation, 101 Blue Seal Dr., SE., Suite 101, Leesburg, VA 20175. Internet: **http://www.natef.org**

For a directory of accredited private trade and technical schools that offer training programs in automotive body repair, contact:

➤ Accrediting Commission of Career Schools and Colleges of Technology, 2101 Wilson Blvd., Suite 302, Arlington, VA 22201. Internet: **http://www.accsct.org**

Automotive Service Technicians and Mechanics

(O*NET 49-3023.00, 49-3023.01, 49-3023.02)

Significant Points

- Automotive service technicians and mechanics must continually adapt to changing technology and repair techniques as vehicle components and systems become increasingly sophisticated.

- Formal automotive technician training is the best preparation for these challenging technology-based jobs.

- Opportunities should be very good for automotive service technicians and mechanics with diagnostic and problem-solving skills, knowledge of electronics and mathematics, and mechanical aptitude.

Nature of the Work

Automotive service technicians inspect, maintain, and repair automobiles and light trucks that run on gasoline, electricity, or alternative fuels such as ethanol. Automotive service technicians' and mechanics' responsibilities have evolved from simple mechanical repairs to high-level technology-related work. The increasing sophistication of automobiles requires workers who can use computerized shop equipment and work with electronic components while maintaining their skills with traditional handtools. As a result, automotive service workers are now usually called technicians rather than mechanics. (Service technicians who work on diesel-powered trucks, buses, and equipment are discussed in the *Handbook* section on diesel service technicians and mechanics. Motorcycle technicians—who repair and ser-

vice motorcycles, motor scooters, mopeds, and small all-terrain vehicles—are discussed in the *Handbook* section on small engine mechanics.)

Today, integrated electronic systems and complex computers regulate vehicles and their performance while on the road. Technicians must have an increasingly broad knowledge of how vehicles' complex components work and interact. They also must be able to work with electronic diagnostic equipment and digital manuals and reference materials.

When mechanical or electrical troubles occur, technicians first get a description of the problem from the owner or, in a large shop, from the repair service estimator or service advisor who wrote the repair order. To locate the problem, technicians use a diagnostic approach. First, they test to see whether components and systems are secure and working properly. Then, they isolate the components or systems that might be the cause of the problem. For example, if an air-conditioner malfunctions, the technician might check for a simple problem, such as a low coolant level, or a more complex issue, such as a bad drive-train connection that has shorted out the air conditioner. As part of their investigation, technicians may test drive the vehicle or use a variety of testing equipment, including onboard and hand-held diagnostic computers or compression gauges. These tests may indicate whether a component is salvageable or whether a new one is required.

During routine service inspections, technicians test and lubricate engines and other major components. Sometimes technicians repair or replace worn parts before they cause breakdowns or damage the vehicle. Technicians usually follow a checklist to ensure that they examine every critical part. Belts, hoses, plugs, brake and fuel systems, and other potentially troublesome items are watched closely.

Service technicians use a variety of tools in their work. They use power tools, such as pneumatic wrenches to remove bolts quickly; machine tools like lathes and grinding machines to rebuild brakes; welding and flame-cutting equipment to remove and repair exhaust systems, and jacks and hoists to lift cars and engines. They also use common handtools, such as screwdrivers, pliers, and wrenches, to work on small parts and in hard-to-reach places. Technicians usually provide their own handtools, and many experienced workers have thousands of dollars invested in them. Employers furnish expensive power tools, engine analyzers, and other diagnostic equipment.

Computers are also commonplace in modern repair shops. Service technicians compare the readouts from computerized diagnostic testing devices with benchmarked standards given by the manufacturer. Deviations outside of acceptable levels tell the technician to investigate that part of the vehicle more closely. Through the Internet or from software packages, most shops receive automatic updates to technical manuals and access to manufacturers' service information, technical service bulletins, and other databases that allow technicians to keep up with common problems and learn new procedures.

High technology tools are needed to fix the computer equipment that operates everything from the engine to the radio in many cars. In fact, today most automotive systems, such as braking, transmission, and steering systems, are controlled primarily by computers and electronic components. Additionally, luxury vehicles often have integrated global positioning systems, Internet access, and other new features with which technicians will need to become familiar. Also, as more alternate-fuel vehicles are purchased, more automotive service technicians will need to learn the science behind these automobiles and how to repair them.

Automotive service technicians in large shops often specialize in certain types of repairs. For example, *transmission technicians and rebuilders* work on gear trains, couplings, hydraulic pumps, and other parts of transmissions. Extensive knowledge of computer controls, the ability to diagnose electrical and hydraulic problems, and other specialized skills are needed to work on these complex components, which employ some of the most sophisticated technology used in vehicles. *Tuneup technicians* adjust ignition timing and valves and adjust or replace spark plugs and other parts to ensure efficient engine performance. They often use electronic testing equipment to isolate and adjust malfunctions in fuel, ignition, and emissions control systems.

Automotive air-conditioning repairers install and repair air-conditioners and service their components, such as compressors, condensers, and controls. These workers require special training in Federal and State regulations governing the handling and disposal of refrigerants. *Front-end mechanics* align and

Automotive service technicians use several types of diagnostic tools, including pressure gauges and electronic meters.

balance wheels and repair steering mechanisms and suspension systems. They frequently use special alignment equipment and wheel-balancing machines. *Brake repairers* adjust brakes, replace brake linings and pads, and make other repairs on brake systems. Some technicians specialize in both brake and front-end work.

Work environment. While most automotive service technicians worked a standard 40 hour week in 2006, 30 percent worked longer hours. Some may work evenings and weekends to satisfy customer service needs. Generally, service technicians work indoors in well-ventilated and -lighted repair shops. However, some shops are drafty and noisy. Although many problems can be fixed with simple computerized adjustments, technicians frequently work with dirty and greasy parts, and in awkward positions. They often lift heavy parts and tools. Minor cuts, burns, and bruises are common, but technicians can usually avoid serious accidents if safe practices are observed.

Training, Other Qualifications, and Advancement

Automotive technology is rapidly increasing in sophistication, and most training authorities strongly recommend that people seeking work in automotive service complete a formal training program in high school or in a postsecondary vocational school or community college. However, some service technicians still learn the trade solely by assisting and learning from experienced workers. Acquiring National Institute for Automotive Service Excellence (ASE) certification is important for those seeking work in large, urban areas.

Education and training. Most employers regard the successful completion of a vocational training program in automotive service technology as the best preparation for trainee positions. High school programs, while an asset, vary greatly in scope. Graduates of these programs may need further training to become qualified. Some of the more extensive high school programs participate in Automotive Youth Education Service (AYES), a partnership between high school automotive repair programs, automotive manufacturers, and franchised automotive dealers. All AYES high school programs are certified by the National Institute for Automotive Service Excellence. Students who complete these programs are well prepared to enter entry-level technician positions or to advance their technical education. Courses in automotive repair, electronics, physics, chemistry, English, computers, and mathematics provide a good educational background for a career as a service technician.

Postsecondary automotive technician training programs usually provide intensive career preparation through a combination of classroom instruction and hands-on practice. Schools update their curriculums frequently to reflect changing technology and equipment. Some trade and technical school programs provide concentrated training for 6 months to a year, depending on how many hours the student attends each week, and award a certificate. Community college programs usually award a certificate or an associate degree. Some students earn repair certificates in a particular skill and leave to begin their careers. Associate degree programs, however, usually take 2 years to complete and include classes in English, basic mathematics, computers, and other subjects, as well as automotive repair. Recently, some programs have added classes on customer service, stress management, and other employability skills. Some formal training programs have alliances with tool manufacturers that help entry-level technicians accumulate tools during their training period.

Various automobile manufacturers and participating franchised dealers also sponsor 2-year associate degree programs at postsecondary schools across the Nation. Students in these programs typically spend alternate 6- to 12-week periods attending classes full time and working full time in the service departments of sponsoring dealers. At these dealerships, students work with an experienced worker who provides hands-on instruction and timesaving tips.

Those new to automotive service usually start as trainee technicians, technicians' helpers, or lubrication workers, and gradually acquire and practice their skills by working with experienced mechanics and technicians. In many cases, on-the-job training may be a part of a formal education program. With a few months' experience, beginners perform many routine service tasks and make simple repairs. While some graduates of postsecondary automotive training programs are often able to earn promotion to the journey level after only a few months on the job, it typically takes 2 to 5 years of experience to become a fully qualified service technician, who is expected to quickly perform the more difficult types of routine service and repairs. An additional 1 to 2 years of experience familiarizes technicians with all types of repairs. Complex specialties, such as transmission repair, require another year or two of training and experience. In contrast, brake specialists may learn their jobs in considerably less time because they do not need complete knowledge of automotive repair.

Employers increasingly send experienced automotive service technicians to manufacturer training centers to learn to repair new models or to receive special training in the repair of components, such as electronic fuel injection or air-conditioners. Motor vehicle dealers and other automotive service providers may send promising beginners or experienced technicians to manufacturer-sponsored technician training programs to upgrade or maintain employees' skills. Factory representatives also visit many shops to conduct short training sessions.

Other qualifications. The ability to diagnose the source of a problem quickly and accurately requires good reasoning ability and a thorough knowledge of automobiles. Many technicians consider diagnosing hard-to-find troubles one of their most challenging and satisfying duties. For trainee automotive service technician jobs, employers look for people with strong communication and analytical skills. Technicians need good reading, mathematics, and computer skills to study technical manuals. They must also read to keep up with new technology and learn new service and repair procedures and specifications.

Training in electronics is vital because electrical components, or a series of related components, account for nearly all malfunctions in modern vehicles. Trainees must possess mechanical aptitude and knowledge of how automobiles work. Experience working on motor vehicles in the Armed Forces or as a hobby can be very valuable.

Certification and advancement. ASE certification has become a standard credential for automotive service technicians. While not mandatory for work in automotive service, certification is common for all non entry-level technicians in large, urban areas. Certification is available in 1 or more of 8 different areas

of automotive service, such as electrical systems, engine repair, brake systems, suspension and steering, and heating and air-conditioning. For certification in each area, technicians must have at least 2 years of experience and pass the examination. Completion of an automotive training program in high school, vocational or trade school, or community or junior college may be substituted for 1 year of experience. For ASE certification as a Master Automobile Technician, technicians must be certified in all eight areas.

By becoming skilled in multiple auto repair services, technicians can increase their value to their employer and their pay. Experienced technicians who have administrative ability sometimes advance to shop supervisor or service manager. Those with sufficient funds many times open independent automotive repair shops. Technicians who work well with customers may become automotive repair service estimators.

Employment

Automotive service technicians and mechanics held about 773,000 jobs in 2006. Automotive repair and maintenance shops and automotive dealers employed the majority of these workers—29 percent each. In addition, automotive parts, accessories, and tire stores employed 7 percent of automotive service technicians. Others worked in gasoline stations; general merchandise stores; automotive equipment rental and leasing companies; Federal, State, and local governments; and other organizations. Almost 17 percent of service technicians were self-employed, more than twice the proportion for all installation, maintenance, and repair occupations.

Job Outlook

The number of jobs for automotive service technicians and mechanics is projected to grow faster than average for all occupations over the next decade. Employment growth will create many new jobs, but total job openings will be significantly larger because many skilled technicians are expected to retire and will need to be replaced.

Employment change. Employment of automotive service technicians and mechanics is expected to increase 14 percent between 2006 and 2016, compared to 10 percent for all occupations. It will add a large number of new jobs, about 110,000, over the decade. Demand for technicians will grow as the number of vehicles in operation increases, reflecting continued growth in the driving age population and in the number of multi-car families. Growth in demand will be offset somewhat by continuing improvements in the quality and durability of automobiles, which will require less frequent service.

Employment growth will continue to be concentrated in automobile dealerships and independent automotive repair shops. Many new jobs also will be created in small retail operations that offer after-warranty repairs, such as oil changes, brake repair, air-conditioner service, and other minor repairs generally taking less than 4 hours to complete. Employment of automotive service technicians and mechanics in gasoline service stations will continue to decline, as fewer stations offer repair services.

Job prospects. In addition to openings from growth, many job openings will be created by the need to replace a growing number of retiring technicians. Job opportunities in this occupation are expected to be very good for those who complete high school

Projections data from the National Employment Matrix

Occupational Title	SOC Code	Employment, 2006	Projected employment, 2016	Change, 2006-16	
				Number	Percent
Automotive service technicians and mechanics..............................	49-3023	773,000	883,000	110,000	14

NOTE: Data in this table are rounded. See the discussion of the employment projections table in the *Handbook* introductory chapter on *Occupational Information Included in the Handbook*.

or postsecondary automotive training programs and who earn ASE certification. Some employers report difficulty in finding workers with the right skills. People with good diagnostic and problem-solving abilities, and training in basic electronics and computer courses are expected to have the best opportunities. Those without formal automotive training are likely to face competition for entry-level jobs.

Most people who enter the occupation can expect steady work, even during downturns in the economy. Although car owners tend to postpone maintenance and repair on their vehicles when their budgets are strained, employers usually cut back on hiring new workers during economic downturns instead of letting experienced workers go.

Earnings

Median hourly wage-and-salary earnings of automotive service technicians and mechanics, including commission, were $16.24 in May 2006. The middle 50 percent earned between $11.96 and $21.56 per hour. The lowest 10 percent earned less than $9.17, and the highest 10 percent earned more than $27.22 per hour. Median annual earnings in the industries employing the largest numbers of service technicians were as follows:

Local government, excluding schools	$19.07
Automobile dealers	18.85
Automotive repair and maintenance	14.55
Gasoline stations	14.51
Automotive parts, accessories, and tire stores	14.38

Many experienced technicians employed by automobile dealers and independent repair shops receive a commission related to the labor cost charged to the customer. Under this system, weekly earnings depend on the amount of work completed. Employers frequently guarantee commissioned technicians a minimum weekly salary.

Automotive service technicians who are members of labor unions, such as the International Association of Machinists and Aerospace Workers; the International Union, United Automobile, Aerospace, and Agricultural Implement Workers of America; the Sheet Metal Workers' International Association; and the International Brotherhood of Teamsters, may enjoy more benefits than non-union workers do.

Related Occupations

Other workers who repair and service motor vehicles include automotive body and related repairers, diesel service technicians and mechanics, and small engine mechanics.

Sources of Additional Information

For more details about work opportunities, contact local automobile dealers and repair shops or local offices of the State em-

ployment service. The State employment service also may have information about training programs.

For general information about a career as an automotive service technician, contact:

➤ Automotive Careers Today, 8400 Westpark Dr., MS#2, McLean, VA 22102. Internet: **http://www.autocareerstoday.org**

➤ Career Voyages, U.S. Department of Labor, 200 Constitution Ave., NW., Washington, DC 20210.
Internet:

    http://www.careervoyages.gov/automotive-main.cfm

➤ National Automobile Dealers Association, 8400 Westpark Dr., McLean, VA 22102. Internet: **http://www.nada.org**

A list of certified automotive service technician training programs can be obtained from:

➤ National Automotive Technicians Education Foundation, 101 Blue Seal Dr., SE., Suite 101, Leesburg, VA 20175.
Internet: **http://www.natef.org**

For a directory of accredited private trade and technical schools that offer programs in automotive service technician training, contact:

➤ Accrediting Commission of Career Schools and Colleges of Technology, 2101 Wilson Blvd., Suite 302, Arlington, VA 22201. Internet: **http://www.accsct.org**

Information on automobile manufacturer-sponsored programs in automotive service technology can be obtained from:

➤ Automotive Youth Educational Systems (AYES), 100 W. Big Beaver, Suite 300, Troy, MI 48084.
Internet: **http://www.ayes.org**

Information on how to become a certified automotive service technician is available from:

➤ National Institute for Automotive Service Excellence (ASE), 101 Blue Seal Dr. SE., Suite 101, Leesburg, VA 20175.
Internet: **http://www.asecert.org**

Diesel Service Technicians and Mechanics

(O*NET 49-3031.00)

Significant Points

- A career in diesel engine repair can offer relatively high wages and the challenge of skilled repair work.

- Opportunities are expected to be very good for people who complete formal training programs.

- National certification is the recognized standard of achievement for diesel service technicians and mechanics.

Nature of the Work

Diesel-powered engines are more efficient and durable than their gasoline-burning counterparts. These powerful engines are standard in our Nation's trucks, locomotives, and buses and are becoming more prevalent in light vehicles, including passenger vehicles, pickups, and other work trucks.

Diesel service technicians and mechanics, including *bus and truck mechanics and diesel engine specialists*, repair and maintain the diesel engines that power transportation equipment. Some diesel technicians and mechanics also work on other heavy vehicles and mobile equipment, including bulldozers, cranes, road graders, farm tractors, and combines. Other technicians repair diesel-powered passenger automobiles, light trucks, or boats. (For information on technicians and mechanics working primarily on gasoline-powered automobiles, heavy vehicles and mobile equipment, or boat engines, see the *Handbook* sections on automotive service technicians, heavy vehicle and mobile equipment service technicians, and small engine mechanics.)

Increasingly, diesel technicians must be versatile to adapt to customers' needs and new technologies. It is common for technicians to handle all kinds of repairs, working on a vehicle's electrical system one day and doing major engine repairs the next. Diesel maintenance is becoming increasingly complex, as more electronic components are used to control the operation of an engine. For example, microprocessors now regulate and manage fuel timing, increasing the engine's efficiency. Also, new emissions standards require mechanics to retrofit engines with emissions control systems, such as emission filters and catalysts, to comply with pollution regulations. In modern shops, diesel service technicians use hand-held or laptop computers to diagnose problems and adjust engine functions.

Technicians who work for organizations that maintain their own vehicles spend most of their time doing preventive maintenance. During a routine maintenance check, technicians follow a checklist that includes inspecting brake systems, steering mechanisms, wheel bearings, and other important parts. Following inspection, technicians repair or adjust parts that do not work properly or remove and replace parts that cannot be fixed.

Diesel service technicians use a variety of tools in their work, including power tools, such as pneumatic wrenches that remove bolts quickly; machine tools, such as lathes and grinding machines to rebuild brakes; welding and flame-cutting equipment to remove and repair exhaust systems; and jacks and hoists to lift and move large parts. Common handtools—screwdrivers, pliers, and wrenches—are used to work on small parts and get at hard-to-reach places. Diesel service technicians and mechanics also use a variety of computerized testing equipment to pinpoint and analyze malfunctions in electrical systems and engines. Employers typically furnish expensive power tools, computerized engine analyzers, and other diagnostic equipment, but workers usually accumulate their own hand tools over time.

Work environment. Technicians normally work in well-lighted and ventilated areas. However, some shops are drafty and noisy. Many employers provide lockers and shower facilities. Diesel technicians usually work indoors, although they occasionally repair vehicles on the road. Diesel technicians may lift heavy parts and tools, handle greasy and dirty parts, and stand or lie in awkward positions while making repairs. Minor cuts, burns, and bruises are common, although serious accidents can usually be avoided when safety procedures are followed. Technicians may work as a team or be assisted by an apprentice or helper when doing heavy work, such as removing engines and transmissions.

Most service technicians work a standard 40-hour week, although some work longer hours, particularly if they are self-employed. A growing number of shops have expanded their hours to speed repairs and offer more convenience to customers. Technicians employed by truck and bus firms providing service around the clock may work evenings, nights, and weekends.

Training, Other Qualifications, and Advancement

Employers prefer to hire graduates of formal training programs because those workers are able to advance quickly to the journey level of diesel service. Other workers who learn diesel engine repair through on-the-job training need 3 to 4 years of experience before becoming journey-level technicians.

Education and training. High school courses in automotive repair, electronics, English, mathematics, and physics provide a strong educational background for a career as a diesel service technician or mechanic. Many mechanics also have additional training after high school.

A large number of community colleges and trade and vocational schools offer programs in diesel engine repair. These programs usually last from 6 months to 2 years and may lead to a certificate of completion or an associate degree. Some offer about 30 hours per week of hands-on training with equipment; others offer more lab or classroom instruction. Formal training provides a foundation in the latest diesel technology and instruction in the service and repair of the equipment that technicians will encounter on the job. Training programs also teach technicians to interpret technical manuals and to communicate well with coworkers and customers. Increasingly, employers work closely with representatives of educational programs, providing instructors with the latest equipment, techniques, and tools and offering jobs to graduates.

Diesel service technicians repair and maintain diesel engines in tractor trailers, locomotives, and construction equipment.

Projections data from the National Employment Matrix

Occupational Title	SOC Code	Employment, 2006	Projected employment, 2016	Change, 2006-16	
				Number	Percent
Bus and truck mechanics and diesel engine specialists	49-3031	275,000	306,000	32,000	11

NOTE: Data in this table are rounded. See the discussion of the employment projections table in the *Handbook* introductory chapter on *Occupational Information Included in the Handbook*.

Although formal training programs lead to the best prospects, some technicians and mechanics learn through on-the-job training. Unskilled beginners generally are assigned tasks such as cleaning parts, fueling and lubricating vehicles, and driving vehicles into and out of the shop. Beginners are usually promoted to trainee positions as they gain experience and as vacancies become available.

After a few months' experience, most trainees can perform routine service tasks and make minor repairs. These workers advance to increasingly difficult jobs as they prove their ability and competence. After technicians master the repair and service of diesel engines, they learn to work on related components, such as brakes, transmissions, and electrical systems. Generally, technicians with at least 3 to 4 years of on-the-job experience will qualify as journey-level diesel technicians.

Employers often send experienced technicians and mechanics to special training classes conducted by manufacturers and vendors, in which workers learn about the latest technology and repair techniques.

Other qualifications. Employers usually look for applicants who have mechanical aptitude and strong problem-solving skills and who are at least 18 years old and in good physical condition. Technicians need a State commercial driver's license to test-drive trucks or buses on public roads. Many companies also require applicants to pass a drug test. Practical experience in automobile repair at an automotive service station, in the Armed Forces, or as a hobby is valuable as well.

Certification and advancement. Experienced diesel service technicians and mechanics with leadership ability may advance to shop supervisor or service manager, and some open their own repair shops. Technicians and mechanics with sales ability sometimes become sales representatives.

Although national certification is not required for employment, many diesel engine technicians and mechanics find that it increases their ability to advance. Certification by the National Institute for Automotive Service Excellence (ASE) is the recognized industry credential for diesel and other automotive service technicians and mechanics. Diesel service technicians may be certified as master medium/heavy truck technicians, master school bus technicians, or master truck equipment technicians. They may also be certified in specific areas of truck repair, such as drivetrains, brakes, suspension and steering, electrical and electronic systems, or preventive maintenance and inspection. For certification in each area, a technician must pass one or more of the ASE-administered exams and present proof of 2 years of relevant work experience. To remain certified, technicians must be retested every 5 years.

Employment

Diesel service technicians and mechanics held about 275,000 jobs in 2006. These workers were employed in almost every industry, particularly those that use trucks, buses, and equipment to haul, deliver, and transport materials, goods, and people. The largest employer, the truck transportation industry, employed 1 out of 6 diesel service technicians and mechanics. Less than 1 out of 10 were employed by local governments, mainly to repair school buses, waste removal trucks, and road equipment. A similar number were employed by automotive repair and maintenance facilities. The rest were employed throughout the economy, including construction, manufacturing, retail and wholesale trade, and automotive leasing. About 16,000, a relatively small number, were self-employed. Nearly every area of the country employs diesel service technicians and mechanics, although most work is found in towns and cities where trucking companies, bus lines, and other fleet owners have large operations.

Job Outlook

The number of jobs for diesel service technicians and mechanics is projected to grow about as fast as average. Opportunities should be very good for people who complete formal training in diesel mechanics.

Employment change. Employment of diesel service technicians and mechanics is expected to grow 11 percent from 2006 to 2016, about as fast as the average for all occupations. Additional trucks—and truck repairers—will be needed to keep pace with the increasing volume of freight shipped nationwide. Moreover, the greater durability and economy of the diesel engine relative to the gasoline engine is expected to increase the number of buses, trucks, and other vehicles powered by diesel engines.

And because diesel engines are now cleaner burning and more efficient—to comply with emissions and environmental standards—they are expected to be used in more passenger vehicles, which will create jobs for diesel service technicians and mechanics over the long run. In fact, auto industry executives are projecting more sales of diesel passenger vehicles as gasoline prices increase. In the short-run, many older diesel engines in trucks must be retrofitted to comply with the new emissions regulations, creating more jobs for diesel engine mechanics.

Job prospects. People who enter diesel engine repair will find favorable opportunities, especially as the need to replace workers who retire increases over the next decade. Opportunities should be very good for people who complete formal training in diesel mechanics at community colleges or vocational and technical schools. Applicants without formal training will face stiffer competition for jobs.

Most people entering this occupation can expect relatively steady work because changes in economic conditions have less of an effect on the diesel repair business than on other sectors of the economy. During a downturn in the economy, however, employers may be reluctant to hire new workers.

Earnings

Median hourly earnings of bus and truck mechanics and diesel engine specialists, including incentive pay, were $18.11 in May 2006, more than the $17.65 median hourly earnings for all installation, maintenance, and repair occupations. The middle 50 percent earned between $14.48 and $22.07 an hour. The lowest 10 percent earned less than $11.71, and the highest 10 percent earned more than $26.50 an hour. Median hourly earnings in the industries employing the largest numbers of bus and truck mechanics and diesel engine specialists in May 2006 were as follows:

Local government	$21.22
Motor vehicle and motor vehicle parts and supplies merchant wholesalers	18.27
Automotive repair and maintenance	17.53
General freight trucking	17.14
Specialized freight trucking	16.15

Because many experienced technicians employed by truck fleet dealers and independent repair shops receive a commission related to the labor cost charged to the customer, weekly earnings depend on the amount of work completed. Beginners usually earn from 50 to 75 percent of the rate of skilled workers and receive increases as they become more skilled.

About 23 percent of diesel service technicians and mechanics are members of labor unions, including the International Association of Machinists and Aerospace Workers; the Amalgamated Transit Union; the International Union, United Automobile, Aerospace and Agricultural Implement Workers of America; the Transport Workers Union of America; the Sheet Metal Workers' International Association; and the International Brotherhood of Teamsters. Labor unions may provide additional benefits for their members.

Related Occupations

Diesel service technicians and mechanics repair trucks, buses, and other diesel-powered equipment. Related technician and mechanic occupations include aircraft and avionics equipment mechanics and service technicians, automotive service technicians and mechanics, heavy vehicle and mobile equipment service technicians and mechanics, and small engine mechanics.

Sources of Additional Information

More details about work opportunities for diesel service technicians and mechanics may be obtained from local employers such as trucking companies, truck dealers, or buslines; locals of the unions previously mentioned; and local offices of your State employment service. Local State employment service offices also may have information about training programs. State boards of postsecondary career schools have information on licensed schools with training programs for diesel service technicians and mechanics.

For general information about a career as a diesel service technician or mechanic, write:

➤ Association of Diesel Specialists, 10 Laboratory Dr., PO Box 13966, Research Triangle Park, NC 27709. Internet: **http://www.diesel.org**

Information on how to become a certified diesel technician of medium to heavy-duty vehicles or a certified bus technician is available from:

➤ National Institute for Automotive Service Excellence (ASE), 101 Blue Seal Dr. SE., Suite 101, Leesburg, VA 20175.
➤ Internet: **http://www.asecert.org**

For a directory of accredited private trade and technical schools with training programs for diesel service technicians and mechanics, contact:

➤ Accrediting Commission of Career Schools and Colleges of Technology, 2101 Wilson Blvd., Suite 302, Arlington, VA 22201. Internet: **http://www.accsct.org**
➤ National Automotive Technicians Education Foundation, 101 Blue Seal Dr. SE., Suite 101, Leesburg, VA 20175. Internet: **http://www.natef.org**

Heavy Vehicle and Mobile Equipment Service Technicians and Mechanics

(O*NET 49-3041.00, 49-3042.00, 49-3043.00)

Significant Points

- Opportunities should be excellent for people with formal postsecondary training in diesel or heavy equipment mechanics; those without formal training will face keen competition.

- This occupation offers relatively high wages and the challenge of skilled repair work.

- Skill in using computerized diagnostic equipment is important in this occupation.

Nature of the Work

Heavy vehicles and mobile equipment are indispensable to many industrial activities from construction to railroads. Various types of equipment move materials, till land, lift beams, and dig earth to pave the way for development and production. Heavy vehicle and mobile equipment service technicians and mechanics repair and maintain engines and hydraulic, transmission, and electrical systems for this equipment. Farm machinery, cranes, bulldozers, and railcars are all examples of heavy vehicles that require such service. (For information on service technicians specializing in diesel engines, see the section on diesel service technicians and mechanics elsewhere in the *Handbook*.)

Service technicians perform routine maintenance checks on agricultural, industrial, construction, and rail equipment. They service fuel, brake, and transmission systems to ensure peak performance, safety, and longevity of the equipment. Maintenance checks and comments from equipment operators usually alert technicians to problems. After locating the problem, these technicians rely on their training and experience to use the best possible technique to solve the problem.

With many types of modern heavy and mobile equipment, technicians can plug diagnostic computers into onboard computers to diagnose a component needing adjustment or repair. If necessary, they may partially dismantle affected components to examine parts for damage or excessive wear. Then, using hand-held tools, they repair, replace, clean, and lubricate parts as necessary. In some cases, technicians re-calibrate systems by typing codes into the onboard computer. After reassembling the component and testing it for safety, they put it back into the equipment and return the equipment to the field.

Many types of heavy and mobile equipment use hydraulics to raise and lower movable parts. When hydraulic components malfunction, technicians examine them for fluid leaks, ruptured hoses, or worn gaskets on fluid reservoirs. Occasionally, the equipment requires extensive repairs, as when a defective hydraulic pump needs replacing.

Service technicians diagnose electrical problems and adjust or replace defective components. They also disassemble and repair undercarriages and track assemblies. Occasionally, technicians weld broken equipment frames and structural parts, using electric or gas welders.

Technicians use a variety of tools in their work: power tools, such as pneumatic wrenches to remove bolts quickly; machine tools, like lathes and grinding machines, to rebuild brakes; welding and flame-cutting equipment to remove and repair exhaust systems; and jacks and hoists to lift and move large parts. Service technicians also use common hand tools—screwdrivers, pliers, and wrenches—to work on small parts and to get at hard-to-reach places. They may use a variety of computerized testing equipment to pinpoint and analyze malfunctions in electrical systems and other essential systems. Tachometers and dynamometers, for example, serve to locate engine malfunctions. Service technicians also use ohmmeters, ammeters, and voltmeters when working on electrical systems. Employers typically furnish expensive power tools, computerized engine analyzers, and other diagnostic equipment, but hand tools are normally accumulated with experience, and many experienced technicians have thousands of dollars invested in them.

It is common for technicians in large shops to specialize in one or two types of repair. For example, a shop may have individual specialists in major engine repair, transmission work, electrical systems, and suspension or brake systems. Technicians in smaller shops, on the other hand, generally perform multiple functions.

Technicians also specialize in types of equipment. *Mobile heavy equipment mechanics and service technicians*, for example, keep construction and surface mining equipment, such as bulldozers, cranes, graders, and excavators in working order. Typically, these workers are employed by equipment wholesale distribution and leasing firms, large construction and mining companies, local and Federal governments, and other organizations operating and maintaining heavy machinery and equipment fleets. Service technicians employed by the Federal Government may work on tanks and other armored equipment.

Farm equipment mechanics service, maintain, and repair farm equipment, as well as smaller lawn and garden tractors sold to suburban homeowners. What once was a general repairer's job around the farm has evolved into a specialized technical career. Farmers have increasingly turned to farm equipment dealers to service and repair their equipment because the machinery has grown in complexity. Modern equipment uses more computers, electronics, and hydraulics, making it difficult to perform repairs without specialized training and tools.

Heavy vehicle service technicians often make repairs at work sites rather than in repair shops.

Railcar repairers specialize in servicing railroad locomotives and other rolling stock, streetcars and subway cars, or mine cars. Most railcar repairers work for railroads, public and private transit companies, and railcar manufacturers.

Work environment. Heavy vehicle and mobile equipment service technicians usually work indoors. To repair vehicles and equipment, technicians often lift heavy parts and tools, handle greasy and dirty parts, and stand or lie in awkward positions. Minor cuts, burns, and bruises are common, but serious accidents normally are avoided when safety practices are observed. Although some shops are drafty and noisy, technicians usually work in well-lighted and ventilated areas. Many employers provide uniforms, locker rooms, and shower facilities. Mobile heavy equipment mechanics and railcar repairers generally work a standard 40 hour week.

When heavy or mobile equipment breaks down at a construction site, it may be too difficult or expensive to bring into a repair shop, so the shop will send a field service technician to the site to make repairs. Field service technicians work outdoors and spend much of their time away from the shop. Generally, the more experienced service technicians specialize in field service. They drive trucks specially equipped with replacement parts and tools. On occasion, they must travel many miles to reach disabled machinery.

The hours of work for farm equipment mechanics vary according to the season of the year. During the busy planting and harvesting seasons, farm equipment mechanics often work 6 or 7 days a week, 10 to 12 hours daily. In slow winter months, however, mechanics may work fewer than 40 hours a week.

Training, Other Qualifications, and Advancement

Although industry experts recommend that applicants complete a formal diesel or heavy equipment mechanic training program after graduating from high school, many people qualify for service technician jobs by training on the job. Employers seek people with mechanical aptitude who are knowledgeable about diesel engines, transmissions, electrical systems, computers, and hydraulics.

Education and training. High school courses in automobile repair, physics, chemistry, and mathematics provide a strong foundation for a career as a service technician or mechanic. After high school, those interested in heavy vehicle repair can choose

Projections data from the National Employment Matrix

Occupational Title	SOC Code	Employment, 2006	Projected employment, 2016	Change, 2006-16	
				Number	Percent
Heavy vehicle and mobile equipment service technicians and mechanics............................	49-3040	188,000	206,000	18,000	10
Farm equipment mechanics	49-3041	31,000	31,000	400	1
Mobile heavy equipment mechanics, except engines	49-3042	131,000	147,000	16,000	12
Rail car repairers..	49-3043	27,000	28,000	1,300	5

NOTE: Data in this table are rounded. See the discussion of the employment projections table in the *Handbook* introductory chapter on *Occupational Information Included in the Handbook.*

to attend many community colleges and vocational schools that offer programs in diesel technology. Some of these schools tailor programs to heavy equipment mechanics. These programs teach the basics of analytical and diagnostic techniques, electronics, and hydraulics. The increased use of electronics and computers makes training in electronics essential for new heavy and mobile equipment mechanics. Some 1- to 2-year programs lead to a certificate of completion, whereas others lead to an associate degree in diesel or heavy equipment mechanics. Formal training programs enable trainee technicians to advance to the journey, or experienced worker, level sooner than with informal ones.

Entry-level workers with no formal background in heavy vehicle repair begin to perform routine service tasks and make minor repairs after a few months of on-the-job training. As they prove their ability and competence, workers advance to harder jobs. After trainees master the repair and service of diesel engines, they learn to work on related components, such as brakes, transmissions, and electrical systems. Generally, a service technician with at least 3 to 4 years of on-the-job experience is accepted as fully qualified.

Many employers send trainee technicians to training sessions conducted by heavy equipment manufacturers. The sessions, which typically last up to 1 week, provide intensive instruction in the repair of the manufacturer's equipment. Some sessions focus on particular components found in the equipment, such as diesel engines, transmissions, axles, or electrical systems. Other sessions focus on particular types of equipment, such as crawler-loaders and crawler-dozers. When appropriate, experienced technicians attend training sessions to gain familiarity with new technology or equipment.

Other qualifications. Technicians must read and interpret service manuals, so reading ability and communication skills are both important skills to have. The technology used in heavy equipment is becoming more sophisticated, and technicians should feel comfortable with computers and electronics because hand-held diagnostic computers are often used to make engine adjustments and diagnose problems. Experience in the Armed Forces working on diesel engines and heavy equipment provides valuable background for these positions.

Certification and advancement. Industry certification often allows workers to advance faster. Voluntary certification by the National Institute for Automotive Service Excellence is the recognized industry credential for heavy vehicle and mobile equipment service technicians, who may be certified as master medium/heavy truck technicians or in a specific area of heavy-duty equipment repair, such as brakes, electrical systems, or suspension and steering. For certification in each area, technicians must

pass a written examination and have at least 2 years of experience. High school, vocational or trade school, or community or junior college training in gasoline or diesel engine repair may substitute for up to 1 year of experience. To remain certified, technicians must be retested every 5 years.

Experienced technicians may advance to field service jobs, where they have a greater opportunity to tackle problems independently and earn additional pay. Field positions may require a commercial driver's license and a clean driving record. Technicians with administrative ability may become shop supervisors or service managers. Some technicians open their own repair shops or invest in a franchise.

Employment

Heavy vehicle and mobile equipment service technicians and mechanics held about 188,000 jobs in 2006. Approximately 131,000 were mobile heavy equipment mechanics, 31,000 were farm equipment mechanics, and 27,000 were railcar repairers.

About 29 percent were employed by machinery, equipment, and supplies merchant wholesalers. About 14 percent worked in construction, primarily for specialty trade contractors and highway, street, and bridge construction companies; another 13 percent were employed by Federal, State, and local governments. Other service technicians worked in agriculture; mining; rail transportation and support activities; and commercial and industrial machinery and equipment rental, leasing, and repair. A small number repaired equipment for machinery and railroad rolling stock manufacturers or lawn and garden equipment and supplies stores. About 5 percent of service technicians were self-employed.

Nearly every area of the country employs heavy and mobile equipment service technicians and mechanics, although most work in towns and cities where equipment dealers, equipment rental and leasing companies, and construction companies have repair facilities.

Job Outlook

The number of heavy vehicle and mobile equipment service technicians and mechanics is expected to grow about as fast as average. Those who have completed postsecondary training programs should find excellent opportunities, but those without a formal background in diesel engine or heavy vehicle repair will face keen competition.

Employment change. Employment of heavy vehicle and mobile equipment service technicians and mechanics is expected to grow by 10 percent through the year 2016, about as fast as the average for all occupations. Increasing numbers of heavy duty and mobile equipment service technicians will be required to support growth in the construction and mining industries. Additionally, the agriculture and railroad industries are projected to see more demand over the decade, potentially generating new jobs for farm equipment and railcar repairers, although job opportunities for these repairers will not be as numerous. Finally, as this equipment becomes more complex, repairs increasingly must be made by specially trained technicians. In large part, these service jobs will be with wholesale equipment dealers and rental and leasing companies who do much of the repair work associated with heavy vehicles and mobile equipment.

Job prospects. Opportunities for heavy vehicle and mobile equipment service technicians and mechanics should be excellent for those who have completed formal training programs in diesel or heavy equipment mechanics. People without formal training are expected to encounter growing difficulty entering these jobs.

Most job openings for mobile, rail, and farm equipment technicians will arise from the need to replace experienced repairers who retire. Employers report difficulty finding candidates with formal postsecondary training to fill available service technician positions. This is often because young people with mechanic training and experience opt to take jobs as automotive service technicians or diesel service technicians—jobs that offer more openings and a wider variety of locations in which to work.

Construction and mining operations, which use large numbers of heavy vehicles and mobile equipment, are particularly sensitive to changes in the level of economic activity. While the increased use of such equipment increases the need for periodic service and repair, heavy and mobile equipment may be idle during downturns. Thus, opportunities for service technicians that work on construction and mining equipment may fluctuate with the Nation's economic cycle. In addition, opportunities for farm equipment mechanics are seasonal and are best in warmer months.

Earnings

Median hourly earnings of mobile heavy equipment mechanics were $19.44 in May 2006, as compared to $17.65 per hour for all installation, maintenance, and repair occupations. The middle 50 percent earned between $15.65 and $23.45. The lowest 10 percent earned less than $12.64, and the highest 10 percent earned more than $28.18. Median hourly earnings in the industries employing the largest numbers of mobile heavy equipment mechanics were as follows:

Federal Government	$21.96
Local government	20.33
Machinery, equipment, and supplies merchant wholesalers	19.15
Commercial and industrial machinery and equipment rental and leasing	18.73
Other specialty trade contractors	18.63

Median hourly earnings of farm equipment mechanics were $14.16 in May 2006. The middle 50 percent earned between $11.34 and $17.35. The lowest 10 percent earned less than $9.30, and the highest 10 percent earned more than $20.77. In machinery, equipment, and supplies merchant wholesalers, the industry employing the largest number of farm equipment mechanics, median earnings were $14.37.

Median hourly earnings of railcar repairers were $20.82 in May 2006. The middle 50 percent earned between $16.75 and $24.71. The lowest 10 percent earned less than $12.48, and the highest 10 percent earned more than $28.02. Median hourly earnings were $21.63 in rail transportation, the industry employing the largest number of railcar repairers.

Field technicians normally earn a higher wage than their counterparts because they are required to make on-the-spot decisions to serve their customers.

About 23 percent of heavy vehicle and mobile equipment service technicians and mechanics are members of unions, including the International Association of Machinists and Aerospace Workers, the International Union of Operating Engineers, and the International Brotherhood of Teamsters. Members may enjoy job benefits in addition to what employers provide.

Related Occupations

Workers in related repair occupations include aircraft and avionics equipment mechanics and service technicians; automotive service technicians and mechanics; diesel service technicians and mechanics; industrial machinery mechanics and maintenance workers; and small engine mechanics.

Sources of Additional Information

More details about job openings for heavy vehicle and mobile equipment service technicians and mechanics may be obtained from local heavy and mobile equipment dealers and distributors, construction contractors, and government agencies. Local offices of the State employment service also may have information on job openings and training programs.

For general information about a career as a heavy vehicle and mobile equipment service technician or mechanic, contact:
➤ The AED Foundation (Associated Equipment Dealers affiliate), 615 W. 22nd St., Oak Brook, IL 60523.
Internet: **http://www.aedcareers.com**

A list of certified diesel service technician training programs can be obtained from:
➤ National Automotive Technician Education Foundation (NATEF), 101 Blue Seal Dr., Suite 101, Leesburg, VA 20175.
Internet: **http://www.natef.org**

Information on certification as a heavy-duty diesel service technician is available from:
➤ National Institute for Automotive Service Excellence (ASE), 101 Blue Seal Dr. SE , Suite 101, Leesburg, VA 20175.
Internet: **http://www.asecert.org**

Small Engine Mechanics

(O*NET 49-3051.00, 49-3052.00, 49-3053.00)

Significant Points

- Job prospects should be excellent for people who complete formal training programs.

- Most mechanics learn their skills on the job or while working in related occupations.

- Use of motorcycles, motorboats, and outdoor power equipment is seasonal in many areas, so mechanics may service other types of equipment or work reduced hours in the winter.

Nature of the Work

Small engine mechanics repair and service power equipment ranging from jet skis to chainsaws. Mechanics usually specialize in the service and repair of one type of equipment, although they may work on closely-related products.

When a piece of equipment breaks down, mechanics use various techniques to diagnose the source and extent of the problem. The mark of a skilled mechanic is the ability to diagnose mechanical, fuel, and electrical problems and to make repairs quickly. Quick and accurate diagnosis requires problem-solving ability and a thorough knowledge of the equipment's operation.

Some jobs require minor adjustments or the replacement of a single item, whereas a complete engine overhaul requires hours to disassemble the engine and replace worn valves, pistons, bearings, and other internal parts. Some highly skilled mechanics use specialized components and the latest computerized equipment to customize and tune motorcycles and motorboats for racing.

Handtools are the most important work possessions of mechanics. Small engine mechanics use wrenches, pliers, and screwdrivers on a regular basis. Mechanics usually provide their own tools, although employers will furnish expensive power tools, computerized engine analyzers, and other diagnostic equipment. Computerized engine analyzers, compression gauges, ammeters and voltmeters, and other testing devices help mechanics locate faulty parts and tune engines. This equipment provides a systematic performance report of various components to compare against normal ratings. After pinpointing the problem, the mechanic makes the needed adjustments, repairs, or replacements.

Small engines also require periodic service to minimize the chance of breakdowns and to keep them operating at peak performance. During routine maintenance, mechanics follow a checklist that includes the inspection and cleaning of brakes, electrical systems, fuel injection systems, plugs, carburetors, and other parts. Following inspection, mechanics usually repair or adjust parts that do not work properly or replace unfixable parts.

Motorcycle mechanics specialize in the repair and overhaul of motorcycles, motor scooters, mopeds, dirt bikes, and all-terrain

Small engine mechanics may work on motorcycles, motorboats, lawnmowers, or other outdoor power equipment.

vehicles. Besides repairing engines, they may work on transmissions, brakes, and ignition systems and make minor body repairs. Mechanics often service just a few makes and models of motorcycles because most work for dealers that service only the products they sell.

Motorboat mechanics, or *marine equipment mechanics*, repair and adjust the electrical and mechanical equipment of inboard and outboard boat engines. Most small boats have portable outboard engines that are removed and brought into the repair shop. Larger craft, such as cabin cruisers and commercial fishing boats, are powered by diesel or gasoline inboard or inboard-outboard engines, which are removed only for major overhauls. Most of these repairs, therefore, are performed at docks or marinas. Motorboat mechanics also may work on propellers, steering mechanisms, marine plumbing, and other boat equipment.

Outdoor power equipment and other small engine mechanics service and repair outdoor power equipment such as lawnmowers, garden tractors, edge trimmers, and chain saws. They also may occasionally work on portable generators and go-carts. In addition, small engine mechanics in certain parts of the country may work on snowblowers and snowmobiles, but demand for this type of repair is both seasonal and regional.

Work environment. Small engine mechanics usually work in repair shops that are well lighted and ventilated but are sometimes noisy when engines are tested. Motorboat mechanics may work outdoors in poor weather conditions when making repairs aboard boats. They may also work in cramped or awkward positions to reach a boat's engine. Outdoor power equipment mechanics face similar conditions when they need to make on-site repairs.

During the winter months in the northern United States, mechanics may work fewer than 40 hours a week because the amount of repair and service work declines when lawnmowers, motorboats, and motorcycles are not in use. Many mechanics work full-time only during the busy spring and summer seasons. However, they often schedule time-consuming engine overhauls or work on snowmobiles and snowblowers during winter downtime. Mechanics may work considerably more than 40 hours a week when demand is strong.

Projections data from the National Employment Matrix

Occupational Title	SOC Code	Employment, 2006	Projected employment, 2016	Change, 2006-16	
				Number	Percent
Small engine mechanics...	49-3050	78,000	87,000	9,100	12
Motorboat mechanics..	49-3051	24,000	29,000	4,600	19
Motorcycle mechanics	49-3052	21,000	24,000	2,600	12
Outdoor power equipment and other small engine mechanics	49-3053	33,000	35,000	1,800	6

NOTE: Data in this table are rounded. See the discussion of the employment projections table in the *Handbook* introductory chapter on *Occupational Information Included in the Handbook*.

Training, Other Qualifications, and Advancement

Due to the increasing complexity of motorcycles and motorboats, employers prefer to hire mechanics who have graduated from formal training programs. However, because the number of these specialized postsecondary programs is limited, most mechanics still learn their skills on the job or while working in related occupations.

Education and training. Employers prefer to hire high school graduates for trainee mechanic positions, but many will accept applicants with less education if they possess adequate reading, writing, and math skills. Helpful high school courses include small engine repair, automobile mechanics, science, and business math. Many equipment dealers employ high school students part time and during the summer to help assemble new equipment and perform minor repairs.

Once employed, trainees learn routine service tasks under the guidance of experienced mechanics by replacing ignition points and spark plugs or by taking apart, assembling, and testing new equipment. As they gain experience and proficiency, trainees progress to more difficult tasks, such as advanced computerized diagnosis and engine overhauls. Anywhere from 3 to 5 years of on-the-job training may be necessary before a novice worker becomes competent in all aspects of the repair of motorcycle and motorboat engines. Repair of outdoor equipment, because of fewer moving parts, requires less on-the-job training.

A growing number of motorcycle and marine equipment mechanics graduate from formal motorcycle and motorboat postsecondary programs. Employers prefer to hire these workers for their advanced knowledge of small engine repair. These workers also tend to advance quickly to more demanding small engine repair jobs.

Employers often send mechanics and trainees to courses conducted by motorcycle, motorboat, and outdoor power equipment manufacturers or distributors. These courses, which can last up to 2 weeks, upgrade workers' skills and provide information on repairing new models. Manufacturer classes are usually a prerequisite for any mechanic who performs warranty work for manufacturers or insurance companies.

Other qualifications. For trainee jobs, employers hire people with mechanical aptitude who are knowledgeable about the fundamentals of small 2- and 4-stroke engines. Many trainees get their start by working on automobiles, motorcycles, motorboats, or outdoor power equipment as a hobby. Knowledge of basic electronics is essential because many parts of small vehicles and engines are electric.

Advancement. The skills needed for small engine repair can transfer to other occupations, such as automobile, diesel, or heavy vehicle and mobile equipment mechanics. Experienced mechanics with leadership ability may advance to shop supervisor or service manager jobs. Mechanics with sales ability sometimes become sales representatives or open their own repair shops.

Employment

Small engine mechanics held about 78,000 jobs in 2006. Motorcycle mechanics held around 21,000 jobs. Motorboat mechanics held approximately 24,000 and outdoor power equipment and other small engine mechanics about 33,000. Almost half, 47 percent, of small engine mechanics worked for either other motor vehicle dealers—an industry that includes retail dealers of motorcycles, boats, and miscellaneous vehicles—or for retail hardware, lawn, and garden stores. Most of the remainder were employed by independent repair shops, marinas and boatyards, equipment rental companies, wholesale distributors, and landscaping services. About 23 percent were self-employed, compared to about 7 percent of workers in all installation, maintenance, and repair occupations.

Job Outlook

Average employment growth is projected for of small engine mechanics. Job prospects should be excellent for people who complete formal training programs.

Employment change. Employment of small engine mechanics is expected to grow 12 percent between 2006 and 2016, about as fast as the average for all occupations. An increase in the population of retired people is expected to increase the number of people who have leisure time and income to spend on recreational equipment such as motorcycles and motorboats. Moreover, the increase in the population of coastal and lake regions should add to the popularity of motorboats, and continued motorcycle use among 18- to 24-year-olds will contribute to rising motorcycle sales. The need for mechanics to maintain and repair motorcycles and motorboats is expected to increase with sales.

Outdoor equipment mechanics will not experience the same level of growth. Although the construction of new single-family houses will result in an increase in the sale of lawn and garden machinery and the need for mechanics to repair it, growth will be strongly tempered by a trend toward smaller lawns and the contracting out of maintenance to landscaping firms that often repair their own equipment. Small engine mechanics' growth also will be tempered by the tendency of many consumers to replace relatively inexpensive items rather than have them repaired.

Job prospects. Job prospects should be excellent for people who complete formal training programs. Employers prefer mechanics who have knowledge of both 2- and 4-stroke engines and other emissions-reducing technology as the government increases regulation of the emissions produced by small engines. Many of the job openings for small engine mechanics will result from the need to replace the many experienced small engine mechanics who are expected to transfer to other occupations, retire, or stop working for other reasons.

Work tends to be more available in summer months.

Earnings

Median wage-and-salary earnings of motorcycle mechanics were $14.45 an hour in May 2006, as compared to $17.65 for all installation, maintenance, and repair occupations. The middle 50 percent earned between $11.31 and $18.41. The lowest 10 percent earned less than $8.96, and the highest 10 percent earned more than $23.31. Median hourly earnings in other motor vehicle dealers, the industry employing the largest number of motorcycle mechanics, were $14.42.

Median wage-and-salary earnings of motorboat mechanics were $15.96 an hour in May 2006. The middle 50 percent earned between $12.66 and $20.01. The lowest 10 percent earned less than $9.94, and the highest 10 percent earned more than $24.40. Median hourly earnings in other motor vehicle dealers, the industry employing the largest number of motorboat mechanics, were $15.68.

Median wage-and-salary earnings of outdoor power equipment and other small engine mechanics were $12.94 an hour in May 2006. The middle 50 percent earned between $10.36 and $16.05. The lowest 10 percent earned less than $8.31, and the highest 10 percent earned more than $19.31. Median hourly earnings in lawn and garden equipment and supplies stores, the industry employing the largest number of outdoor power equipment and other small engine mechanics, were $12.74.

Small engine mechanics in small shops usually receive few benefits, but those employed in larger shops often receive paid vacations, sick leave, and health insurance. Some employers also pay for work-related training, provide uniforms, and help mechanics purchase new tools.

Related Occupations

Mechanics and repairers who work on durable equipment other than small engines include automotive service technicians and mechanics, diesel service technicians and mechanics, heavy vehicle and mobile equipment service technicians and mechanics, and home appliance repairers.

Sources of Additional Information

To learn about work opportunities, contact local motorcycle, motorboat, and lawn and garden equipment dealers, boatyards, and marinas. Local offices of the State employment service also may have information about employment and training opportunities.

Other Installation, Maintenance, and Repair Occupations

Coin, Vending, and Amusement Machine Servicers and Repairers

(O*NET 49-9091.00)

Significant Points

- Most workers in this occupation learn their skills on the job.

- Opportunities should be especially good for people with some knowledge of electronics.

Nature of the Work

Coin, vending, and amusement machines give out change, test our gaming skills, and dispense refreshments nearly everywhere we turn. Coin, vending, and amusement machine servicers and repairers install, service, and stock such machines and keep them in good working order.

Occupations in this industry are classified by the type of machine they work on and whether they specialize in servicing or repairing the machines. *Vending machine servicers*, often called route drivers, visit machines that dispense soft drinks, candy and snacks, and other items. They collect money from the coin and cash-operated machines, restock merchandise, and change labels to indicate new selections. They also keep the machines clean and appealing.

Vending machine repairers, often called mechanics or technicians, make sure that the machines operate correctly. On the relatively simple gravity-operated machines, repairers check the keypads, motors, and merchandise chutes. When checking complicated electrical and electronic machines, such as beverage dispensers, they check to see that the machines mix drinks properly and that the refrigeration and heating units work correctly. If the machines are not in good working order, the mechanics repair them. When installing machines, vending machine repairers make the necessary water and electrical connections and check them for proper operation.

Amusement machine servicers and repairers work on jukeboxes, video games, pinball machines, and slot machines. They update selections, repair or replace malfunctioning parts, and rebuild existing equipment.

Vending machine servicers and repairers employed by small companies may both fill and fix machines on a regular basis. These combination servicers-repairers stock machines, collect money, fill coin and currency changers, and repair machines when necessary.

If a machine breaks down, vending and amusement machine repairers inspect it for obvious problems, such as loose electrical wires, malfunctions of the coin mechanism or bill validator, and leaks. When servicing electronic machines, repairers test them

Coin, vending, and amusement machine repairers may make repairs onsite or at their workshop.

with hand-held diagnostic computers that determine the extent and location of any problem. Repairers may only have to replace a circuit board or other component to fix the problem. However, if the problem cannot be readily located, these workers refer to technical manuals and wiring diagrams and use testing devices, such as electrical circuit testers, to find defective parts. Repairers decide whether they must replace a part and whether they can fix the malfunction onsite or whether they have to send the machine to the repair shop.

In the repair shop, vending and amusement machine repairers use power tools, such as grinding wheels, saws, and drills, as well as voltmeters, ohmmeters, oscilloscopes, and other testing equipment. They also use ordinary repair tools, such as screwdrivers, pliers, and wrenches.

Preventive maintenance—avoiding trouble before it starts—is a major job of repairers. For example, they periodically clean refrigeration condensers, lubricate mechanical parts, and adjust machines so that they perform properly. Servicers and repairers also do some paperwork, such as filing reports, preparing repair cost estimates, ordering parts, and keeping daily records of merchandise distributed and money collected. However, new machines with computerized inventory controls reduce the paperwork that a servicer must complete.

Work environment. Repairers generally work a total of 40 hours a week. However, vending and amusement machines operate around the clock, so repairers may be on call to work at night and on weekends and holidays.

Some vending and amusement machine repairers work primarily in company repair shops that generally are quiet, well lighted, and have adequate workspace. Others many spend substantial time on the road, visiting machines wherever they have been placed. Repair work is relatively safe, although servicers and repairers must take care to avoid hazards such as electrical shocks and cuts from sharp tools and other metal objects.

Training, Other Qualifications, and Advancement

Most workers learn their skills on the job. Employers normally hire high school graduates, and give preference to those with high school or vocational school courses in electronics, refrigeration, and machine repair.

Education and training. Electronics have become more prevalent in vending and amusement machines. While employers only require workers to have graduated high school, they give preference to those who have completed programs in basic electronics at vocational high schools and junior colleges. Postsecondary programs in electronics can last 1 to 2 years.

Once hired, new workers are trained informally on the job to fill and fix machines by observing, working with, and receiving instruction from experienced repairers. Beginners start training with simple jobs, such as cleaning or stocking machines. They then learn to rebuild machines by removing defective parts and repairing, adjusting, and testing the machines. Next, they accompany an experienced repairer on service calls and, finally, make visits on their own. This learning process takes from 6 months to 2 years, depending on the individual's abilities, previous education, types of machines serviced, and quality of instruction.

To learn about new machines, repairers and servicers sometimes attend training sessions sponsored by manufacturers and distributors. Both trainees and experienced workers sometimes take evening courses in basic electricity, electronics, microwave ovens, refrigeration, and other related subjects to learn about new techniques and equipment.

Other qualifications. Employers usually require applicants to demonstrate mechanical ability, either through related work experience or by scoring well on mechanical-aptitude tests. Because coin, vending, and amusement machine servicers and repairers sometimes handle thousands of dollars in merchandise and cash, employers try to hire persons who are trustworthy and have no criminal record. Also, the ability to deal tactfully with people is important because servicers and repairers play a significant role in relaying customers' requests and concerns. A driver's license and a good driving record are essential for most vending and amusement machine servicer and repairer jobs, and some employers require their servicers to be bonded.

Certification and advancement. The National Automatic Merchandising Association has two self-study technician training programs, one for vending machine repairers and another for machine servicers. Self-study manuals give instruction in subjects such as customer relations, safety, electronics, and reading schematics. Upon completion of the program, repairers must pass a written test to become certified as a technician or journey-

Projections data from the National Employment Matrix

Occupational Title	SOC Code	Employment, 2006	Projected employment, 2016	Change, 2006-16	
				Number	Percent
Coin, vending, and amusement machine servicers and repairers	49-9091	48,000	46,000	-1,400	-3

NOTE: Data in this table are rounded. See the discussion of the employment projections table in the *Handbook* introductory chapter on *Occupational Information Included in the Handbook*.

man. Certified and other skilled servicers and repairers may be promoted to supervisory jobs or go into business for themselves.

Employment

Coin, vending, and amusement machine servicers and repairers held about 48,000 jobs in 2006. Of these workers, 18 percent were self-employed. Twenty-four percent of these workers were employed by vending machine operators that sell food and other items through machines. Others worked for beverage manufacturing or wholesale companies that have their own machines and for amusement, gambling, and recreation establishments that own video games, jukeboxes, slot machines, and similar types of amusement equipment.

Job Outlook

Employment of coin, vending, and amusement machine servicers and repairers is expected to decline moderately through the year 2016. Opportunities for these workers, however, should be good for those with the proper training or related experience.

Employment change. Employment of coin, vending, and amusement machine services and repairers is expected to decrease by 3 percent between 2006. However, the number of vending machines available to the public is expected to increase. Establishments that are likely to install additional vending machines include industrial plants, hospitals, stores, schools and prisons in order to meet the public demand for inexpensive snacks and other food items. Growth of casino slot machines and coin-operated lottery ticket machines will increase the total number of amusement machines as well.

Despite the expected increase in the number of vending and amusement machines in use, improved technology in newer machines will cause a moderate decline in employment because these machines require less maintenance and need restocking less often. Many will contain computers that record sales and inventory data, reducing the amount of time-consuming paperwork that otherwise would have to be filled out. In addition, some new machines use wireless data transmitters to signal the vending machine company when the machine needs restocking or repairing. This allows servicers and repairers to be dispatched only when needed, instead of having to check each machine on a regular schedule.

Job prospects. Job opportunities should be good for those with training in a related electronic repair field, and who are willing to travel and work at times other than regular business hours. Opportunities will be limited for those with just a high school degree and no training in electronics repair. Job openings will also arise from the need to replace experienced repairers who transfer to other occupations or leave the labor force.

Earnings

Median hourly earnings of coin, vending, and amusement machine servicers and repairers were $13.80 in May 2006. The middle 50

percent earned between $10.84 and $17.23 an hour. The lowest 10 percent earned less than $8.77 an hour, and the highest 10 percent earned more than $21.35 an hour. Median hourly earnings were $12.94 in vending machine operators, the industry employing the largest number of coin, vending, and amusement machine servicers and repairers in May 2006.

Typically, workers who service and repair slot machines in States with some form of legalized gaming have the highest wages. Overtime work usually commands a premium on wages, and some union contracts stipulate higher pay for night work and for emergency repair jobs on weekends and holidays than for regular hours. Some of these workers are members of the International Brotherhood of Teamsters: 17 percent of vending machine repairers and servicers belonged to a union in 2006, as compared with 12 percent for all occupations.

Related Occupations

Other workers who repair equipment with electrical and electronic components include electrical and electronics installers and repairers; electronic home entertainment equipment installers and repairers; heating, air-conditioning, and refrigeration mechanics and installers; and home appliance repairers.

Sources of Additional Information

Information on job opportunities in this field can be obtained from local vending machine firms and local offices of your State employment service.

For general information on vending machine servicing and repair, contact:

➤ National Automatic Merchandising Association, 20 N. Wacker Dr., Suite 3500, Chicago, IL 60606.
Internet: **http://www.vending.org**
➤ Vending Times, 1375 Broadway, New York, NY 10018.

Heating, Air-Conditioning, and Refrigeration Mechanics and Installers

(O*NET 49-9021.00, 49-9021.01, 49-9021.02)

Significant Points

- Employment is projected to grow as fast as the average.

- Job prospects are expected to be excellent.

- Employers prefer to hire those who have completed technical school training or a formal apprenticeship.

Nature of the Work

Heating and air-conditioning systems control the temperature, humidity, and the total air quality in residential, commercial, industrial, and other buildings. Refrigeration systems make it possible to store and transport food, medicine, and other perishable items. Heating, air-conditioning, and refrigeration mechanics and installers—also called technicians—install, maintain, and repair such systems. Because heating, ventilation, air-conditioning, and refrigeration systems often are referred to as HVACR systems, these workers also may be called HVACR technicians.

Heating, air-conditioning, and refrigeration systems consist of many mechanical, electrical, and electronic components, such as motors, compressors, pumps, fans, ducts, pipes, thermostats, and switches. In central forced air heating systems, for example, a furnace heats air, which is then distributed via a system of metal or fiberglass ducts. Technicians must be able to maintain, diagnose, and correct problems throughout the entire system. To do this, they adjust system controls to recommended settings and test the performance of the system using special tools and test equipment.

Technicians often specialize in either installation or maintenance and repair, although they are trained to do both. They also may specialize in doing heating work or air-conditioning or refrigeration work. Some specialize in one type of equipment—for example, hydronics (water-based heating systems), solar panels, or commercial refrigeration. Some technicians also sell service contracts to their clients. Service contracts provide for regular maintenance of the heating and cooling systems and they help to reduce the seasonal fluctuations of this type of work.

Technicians follow blueprints or other specifications to install oil, gas, electric, solid-fuel, and multiple-fuel heating systems and air-conditioning systems. After putting the equipment in place, they install fuel and water supply lines, air ducts and vents, pumps, and other components. They may connect electrical wiring and controls and check the unit for proper operation. To ensure the proper functioning of the system, furnace installers often use combustion test equipment, such as carbon dioxide testers, carbon monoxide testers, combustion analyzers, and oxygen testers. These tests ensure that the system will operate safely and at peak efficiency.

After a furnace or air-conditioning unit has been installed, technicians often perform routine maintenance and repair work to keep the systems operating efficiently. They may adjust burners and blowers and check for leaks. If the system is not operating properly, they check the thermostat, burner nozzles, controls or other parts to diagnose and correct the problem.

Technicians also install and maintain heat pumps, which are similar to air conditioners but can be reversed so that they both heat and cool a home. Because of the added complexity and the fact that they run both in summer and winter, these systems often require more maintenance and need to be replaced more frequently than traditional furnaces and air conditioners.

During the summer, when heating systems are not being used, heating equipment technicians do maintenance work, such as replacing filters, ducts, and other parts of the system that may accumulate dust and impurities during the operating season. During the winter, air-conditioning mechanics inspect the systems and do required maintenance, such as overhauling compressors.

Refrigeration mechanics install, service, and repair industrial and commercial refrigerating systems and a variety of refrigeration equipment. They follow blueprints, design specifications, and manufacturers' instructions to install motors, compressors, condensing units, evaporators, piping, and other components. They connect this equipment to the ductwork, refrigerant lines, and electrical power source. After making the connections, they charge the system with refrigerant, check it for proper operation and leaks, and program control systems.

When air-conditioning and refrigeration technicians service equipment, they must use care to conserve, recover, and recycle the refrigerants used in air-conditioning and refrigeration systems. The release of these refrigerants can be harmful to the environment. Technicians conserve the refrigerant by making sure that there are no leaks in the system; they recover it by venting the refrigerant into proper cylinders; they recycle it for reuse with special filter-dryers; or they ensure that the refrigerant is properly disposed of.

Heating, air-conditioning, and refrigeration mechanics and installers are adept at using a variety of tools, including hammers, wrenches, metal snips, electric drills, pipe cutters and

Excellent job prospects are expected for heating, air-conditioning, and refrigeration mechanics and installers.

benders, measurement gauges, and acetylene torches, to work with refrigerant lines and air ducts. They use voltmeters, thermometers, pressure gauges, manometers, and other testing devices to check airflow, refrigerant pressure, electrical circuits, burners, and other components.

Other craft workers sometimes install or repair cooling and heating systems. For example, on a large air-conditioning installation job, especially where workers are covered by union contracts, ductwork might be done by sheet metal workers and duct installers; electrical work by electricians; and installation of piping, condensers, and other components by pipelayers, plumbers, pipefitters, and steamfitters. Home appliance repairers usually service room air-conditioners and household refrigerators. (Additional information about each of these occupations appears elsewhere in the *Handbook*.)

Work environment. Heating, air-conditioning, and refrigeration mechanics and installers work in homes, retail establishments, hospitals, office buildings, and factories—anywhere there is climate-control equipment that needs to be installed, repaired, or serviced. They may be assigned to specific job sites at the beginning of each day or may be dispatched to a variety of locations if they are making service calls.

Technicians may work outside in cold or hot weather or in buildings that are uncomfortable because the air-conditioning or heating equipment is broken. In addition, technicians might work in awkward or cramped positions and sometimes are required to work in high places. Hazards include electrical shock, burns, muscle strains, and other injuries from handling heavy equipment. Appropriate safety equipment is necessary when handling refrigerants because contact can cause skin damage, frostbite, or blindness. Inhalation of refrigerants when working in confined spaces also is a possible hazard.

The majority of mechanics and installers work at least a 40-hour week. During peak seasons, they often work overtime or irregular hours. Maintenance workers, including those who provide maintenance services under contract, often work evening or weekend shifts and are on call. Most employers try to provide a full workweek year-round by scheduling both installation and maintenance work, and many manufacturers and contractors now provide or even require year-round service contracts. In most shops that service both heating and air-conditioning equipment, employment is stable throughout the year.

Training, Other Qualifications, and Advancement
Because of the increasing sophistication of heating, air-conditioning, and refrigeration systems, employers prefer to hire those who have completed technical school training or a formal apprenticeship. Some mechanics and installers, however, still learn the trade informally on the job.

Education and training. Many secondary and postsecondary technical and trade schools, junior and community colleges, and the U.S. Armed Forces offer 6-month to 2-year programs in heating, air-conditioning, and refrigeration. Students study theory of temperature control, equipment design and construction, and electronics. They also learn the basics of installation, maintenance, and repair. Three accrediting agencies have set academic standards for HVACR programs. These accrediting bodies are HVAC Excellence, the National Center for Con-

struction Education and Research, and the Partnership for Air-Conditioning, Heating, and Refrigeration Accreditation. After completing these programs, new technicians generally need between an additional 6 months and 2 years of field experience before they are considered proficient.

Many technicians train through apprenticeships. Apprenticeship programs frequently are run by joint committees representing local chapters of the Air-Conditioning Contractors of America, the Mechanical Contractors Association of America, Plumbing-Heating-Cooling Contractors—National Association, and locals of the Sheet Metal Workers' International Association or the United Association of Journeymen and Apprentices of the Plumbing and Pipefitting Industry of the United States and Canada. Local chapters of the Associated Builders and Contractors and the National Association of Home Builders sponsor other apprenticeship programs. Formal apprenticeship programs normally last 3 to 5 years and combine paid on-the-job training with classroom instruction. Classes include subjects such as the use and care of tools, safety practices, blueprint reading, and the theory and design of heating, ventilation, air-conditioning, and refrigeration systems. In addition to understanding how systems work, technicians must learn about refrigerant products and the legislation and regulations that govern their use.

Applicants for apprenticeships must have a high school diploma or equivalent. Math and reading skills are essential. After completing an apprenticeship program, technicians are considered skilled trades workers and capable of working alone. These programs are also a pathway to certification and, in some cases, college credits.

Those who acquire their skills on the job usually begin by assisting experienced technicians. They may begin by performing simple tasks such as carrying materials, insulating refrigerant lines, or cleaning furnaces. In time, they move on to more difficult tasks, such as cutting and soldering pipes and sheet metal and checking electrical and electronic circuits.

Several organizations have begun to offer basic self-study, classroom, and Internet courses for individuals with limited experience.

Licensure. Heating, air-conditioning, and refrigeration mechanics and installers are required to be licensed by some States and localities. Requirements for licensure vary greatly, but all States or localities that require a license have a test that must be passed. The contents of these tests vary by State or locality, with some requiring extensive knowledge of electrical codes and others focusing more on HVACR-specific knowledge. Completion of an apprenticeship program or 2 to 5 years of experience are also common requirements.

In addition, all technicians who purchase or work with refrigerants must be certified in their proper handling. To become certified to purchase and handle refrigerants, technicians must pass a written examination specific to the type of work in which they specialize. The three possible areas of certification are: Type I—servicing small appliances; Type II—high-pressure refrigerants; and Type III—low-pressure refrigerants. Exams are administered by organizations approved by the U.S. Environmental Protection Agency, such as trade schools, unions, contractor associations, or building groups.

Projections data from the National Employment Matrix

Occupational Title	SOC Code	Employment, 2006	Projected employment, 2016	Change, 2006-16	
				Number	Percent
Heating, air conditioning, and refrigeration mechanics and installers	49-9021	292,000	317,000	25,000	9

NOTE: Data in this table are rounded. See the discussion of the employment projections table in the *Handbook* introductory chapter on *Occupational Information Included in the Handbook*.

Other qualifications. High school courses in shop math, mechanical drawing, applied physics and chemistry, electronics, blueprint reading, and computer applications provide a good background for those interested in entering this occupation. Some knowledge of plumbing or electrical work also is helpful. A basic understanding of electronics is becoming more important because of the increasing use of electronics in equipment controls. Because technicians frequently deal directly with the public, they should be courteous and tactful, especially when dealing with an aggravated customer. They also should be in good physical condition because they sometimes have to lift and move heavy equipment.

Certification and advancement. Throughout the learning process, technicians may have to take a number of tests that measure their skills. For those with relevant coursework and less than 1 year of experience, the industry has developed a series of exams to test basic competency in residential heating and cooling, light commercial heating and cooling, and commercial refrigeration. These are referred to as "Entry-level" certification exams and are commonly conducted at both secondary and postsecondary technical and trade schools. HVACR technicians who have at least 1 year of experience performing installations and 2 years of experience performing maintenance and repair can take a number of different tests to certify their competency in working with specific types of equipment, such as oil-burning furnaces. These tests are offered through the Refrigeration Service Engineers Society, HVAC Excellence, Carbon Monoxide Safety Association, Air-Conditioning and Refrigeration Safety Coalition, and North American Technician Excellence, Inc., among others. Employers increasingly recommend taking and passing these tests and obtaining certification; doing so may increase advancement opportunities.

Advancement usually takes the form of higher wages. Some technicians, however, may advance to positions as supervisor or service manager. Others may move into sales and marketing. Still others may become building superintendents, cost estimators, system test and balance specialists, or, with the necessary certification, teachers. Those with sufficient money and managerial skill can open their own contracting business.

Employment

Heating, air-conditioning, and refrigeration mechanics and installers held about 292,000 jobs in 2006; about 55 percent worked for plumbing, heating, and air-conditioning contractors. The rest were employed in a variety of industries throughout the country, reflecting a widespread dependence on climate-control systems. Some worked for fuel oil dealers, refrigeration and air-conditioning service and repair shops, schools, and stores that sell heating and air-conditioning systems. Local governments, the Federal Government, hospitals, office buildings, and other organizations that operate large air-conditioning, refrigeration, or heating systems also employed these workers. About 13 percent of these workers were self-employed.

Job Outlook

With average job growth and numerous expected retirements, heating, air-conditioning, and refrigeration mechanics and installers should have excellent employment opportunities.

Employment change. Employment of heating, air-conditioning, and refrigeration mechanics and installers is projected to increase 9 percent during the 2006-16 decade, as fast as the average for all occupations. As the population and stock of buildings grows, so does the demand for residential, commercial, and industrial climate-control systems. Residential HVACR systems generally need replacement after 10 to 15 years; the large number of homes built in recent years will enter this replacement timeframe by 2016. The increased complexity of HVACR systems, which increases the possibility that equipment may malfunction, also will create opportunities for service technicians. A growing focus on improving indoor air quality and the increasing use of refrigerated equipment by a growing number of stores and gasoline stations that sell food should also create more jobs for heating, air-conditioning, and refrigeration technicians.

Concern for the environment has prompted the development of new energy-saving heating and air-conditioning systems. An emphasis on better energy management should lead to the replacement of older systems and the installation of newer, more efficient systems in existing homes and buildings. Also, demand for maintenance and service work should increase as businesses and homeowners strive to keep increasingly complex systems operating at peak efficiency. Regulations prohibiting the discharge and production of older types of refrigerants that pollute the atmosphere should continue to result in the need to replace many existing air conditioning systems or to modify them to use new environmentally safe refrigerants. The pace of replacement in the commercial and industrial sectors will quicken if Congress or individual States change tax rules designed to encourage companies to buy new HVACR equipment.

Job prospects. Job prospects for heating, air-conditioning, and refrigeration mechanics and installers are expected to be excellent, particularly for those who have completed training from an accredited technical school or a formal apprenticeship. Job opportunities should be best in the fastest growing areas of the country. A growing number of retirements of highly skilled technicians are expected to generate many job openings. Many contractors have reported problems finding enough workers to meet the demand for service and installation of HVACR systems.

Technicians who specialize in installation work may experience periods of unemployment when the level of new construction activity declines, but maintenance and repair work usually remains relatively stable. People and businesses depend on their climate-control or refrigeration systems and must keep them in good working order, regardless of economic conditions.

Earnings

Median hourly wage-and-salary earnings of heating, air-conditioning, and refrigeration mechanics and installers were $18.11 in May 2006. The middle 50 percent earned between $14.12 and $23.32 an hour. The lowest 10 percent earned less than $11.38, and the top 10 percent earned more than $28.57. Median hourly earnings in the industries employing the largest numbers of heating, air-conditioning, and refrigeration mechanics and installers were:

Hardware, and plumbing and heating equipment
   and supplies merchant wholesalers.....................................$20.53
Commercial and industrial machinery and equipment (except
   automotive and electronic) repair and maintenance..............19.95
Direct selling establishments 19.12
Plumbing, heating, and air-conditioning contractors..............17.46
Electrical contractors 16.74

Apprentices usually begin at about 50 percent of the wage rate paid to experienced workers. As they gain experience and improve their skills, they receive periodic increases until they reach the wage rate of experienced workers.

Heating, air-conditioning, and refrigeration mechanics and installers enjoy a variety of employer-sponsored benefits. In addition to typical benefits such as health insurance and pension plans, some employers pay for work-related training and provide uniforms, company vans, and tools.

About 14 percent of heating, air-conditioning, and refrigeration mechanics and installers are members of a union. The unions to which the greatest numbers of mechanics and installers belong are the Sheet Metal Workers International Association and the United Association of Journeymen and Apprentices of the Plumbing and Pipefitting Industry of the United States and Canada.

Related Occupations

Heating, air-conditioning, and refrigeration mechanics and installers work with sheet metal and piping, and repair machinery, such as electrical motors, compressors, and burners. Other workers who have similar skills include boilermakers; home appliance repairers; electricians; sheet metal workers; and pipelayers, plumbers, pipefitters, and steamfitters.

Sources of Additional Information

For more information about opportunities for training, certification, and employment in this trade, contact local vocational and technical schools; local heating, air-conditioning, and refrigeration contractors; a local of the unions or organizations previously mentioned; a local joint union-management apprenticeship committee; or the nearest office of the State employment service or apprenticeship agency. You can also find information on the registered apprenticeship system with links to State apprenticeship programs on the U.S. Department of Labor's Web site: **http://www.doleta.gov/atels_bat** Apprenticeship infor-

mation is also available from the U.S. Department of Labor's toll free helpline: (877) 872-5627.

For information on career opportunities, training, and technician certification, contact:

➤ Air-Conditioning Contractors of America, 2800 Shirlington Rd., Suite 300, Arlington, VA 22206.
Internet: **http://www.acca.org**
➤ Air-Conditioning and Refrigeration Institute, 4100 North Fairfax Dr., Suite 200, Arlington, VA 22203.
Internet: **http://www.coolcareers.org** and **http://www.ari.org**
➤ Associated Builders and Contractors, Workforce Development Department, 4250 North Fairfax Dr., 9th Floor, Arlington, VA 22203. Internet: **http://www.trytools.org**
➤ Carbon Monoxide Safety Association, P.O. Box 669, Eastlake, CO 80614. Internet: **http://www.cosafety.org**
➤ Home Builders Institute, National Association of Home Builders, 1201 15th St.NW., 6th Floor, Washington, DC 20005.
Internet: **http://www.hbi.org**
➤ HVAC Excellence, P.O. Box 491, Mt. Prospect, IL 60056.
Internet: **http://www.hvacexcellence.org**
➤ Mechanical Contractors Association of America, Mechanical Service Contractors of America, 1385 Piccard Dr., Rockville, MD 20850. Internet: **http://www.mcaa.org** and **http://www.mcaa.org/msca**
➤ National Center for Construction Education and Research, P.O. Box 141104, Gainesville, FL 32601.
Internet: **http://www.nccer.org**
➤ National Occupational Competency Testing Institute.
Internet: **http://www.nocti.org**
➤ North American Technician Excellence, 4100 North Fairfax Dr., Suite 210, Arlington, VA 22203.
Internet: **http://www.natex.org**
➤ Plumbing-Heating-Cooling Contractors, 180 S. Washington, St., P.O. Box 6808, Falls Church, VA 22046.
Internet: **http://www.phccweb.org org**
➤ Refrigeration Service Engineers Society, 1666 Rand Rd., Des Plaines, IL 60016. Internet: **http://www.rses.org**
➤ Sheet Metal and Air-Conditioning Contractors National Association, 4201 Lafayette Center Dr., Chantilly, VA 20151.
Internet: **http://www.smacna.org**
➤ United Association of Journeymen and Apprentices of the Plumbing and Pipefitting Industry, 901 Massachusetts Ave. NW., Washington, DC 20001. Internet: **http://www.ua.org**

Home Appliance Repairers

(O*NET 49-9031.00)

Significant Points

- Little or no change in employment is projected; however, very good job opportunities are expected, particularly for those with formal training in appliance repair and electronics.

- Workers learn on the job; good customer service skills and a driver's license are essential.

Nature of the Work

Home appliance repairers, also known as in-home service professionals, install and repair home appliances. Some repairers work on small appliances such as microwave ovens and vacuum cleaners. Others specialize in major appliances such as refrigerators, dishwashers, washers and dryers, and window air conditioning units. (Workers whose primary responsibility is the installation and repair of heating and central air conditioning units are covered in a separate *Handbook* statement on heating, air conditioning and refrigeration mechanics and installers—although some worker responsibilities may overlap.) Home appliance repairers install household durable goods such as refrigerators, washing machines, and cooking products. They may have to install pipes in a customer's home to connect the appliances to a gas or water line. In these cases, once the lines are in place, they turn on the gas or water and check for leaks. Home appliance repairers also answer customers' questions about the care and use of appliances.

When problems with home appliances occur, home appliance repairers visually inspect the appliance and check for unusual noises, excessive vibration, leakage of fluid, or loose parts to determine the cause of the failure. Repairers disassemble the appliance to examine its internal parts for signs of wear or corrosion. They follow service manuals and use testing devices such as ammeters, voltmeters, and wattmeters to check electrical systems for shorts and faulty connections.

After identifying problems, home appliance repairers replace or repair defective belts, motors, heating elements, switches, gears, or other items. They tighten, align, clean, and lubricate parts as necessary. Repairers use common handtools, including screwdrivers, wrenches, files, and pliers, as well as soldering guns and tools designed for specific appliances. When repairing appliances with electronic parts, they may replace circuit boards or other electronic components.

When repairing refrigerators and window air-conditioners, repairers must take care to conserve, recover, and recycle chlorofluorocarbon (CFC) and hydrochlorofluorocarbon (HCFC) refrigerants used in the cooling systems, as is required by law. Federal regulations also require that home appliance repairers document the capture and disposal of refrigerants.

Repairers write up estimates of the cost of repairs for customers, keep records of parts used and hours worked, prepare bills, and collect payments. If an appliance is still under warranty, self-employed repairers will talk with the original appliance manufacturer to recoup monetary claims for work performed.

Work environment. Home appliance repairers who handle portable appliances usually work in quiet and adequately lighted and ventilated repair shops. Those who repair major appliances may spend several hours a day driving to and from appointments and emergency calls. Repairers sometimes work in cramped and uncomfortable positions when they are replacing parts in hard-to-reach areas of appliances. Repairer jobs generally are not hazardous, but workers must exercise care and follow safety precautions to avoid electrical shocks and gas leaks, and prevent injuries when lifting and moving large appliances.

Home appliance repairers usually work with little or no direct supervision. Many home appliance repairers work a standard 40-hour week, but may work overtime and weekend hours in the summer months, when they are in high demand to fix refrigerators and window mounted air-conditioners. Some repairers work early morning, evening, and weekend shifts and may remain on call in case of an emergency.

Training, Other Qualifications, and Advancement

Most entry-level workers in this profession enter without any specific training or experience and learn on the job, although employers prefer to hire those who have completed programs in electronics or appliance repair. A driver's license and good customer service skills are essential to work on appliances in customer's homes.

Education and training. Most home appliance repairers enter the occupation with a high school diploma or its equivalent and very little training in repairing appliances. Most learn their jobs while working with more experienced workers, which can last from several months to a few years. In businesses that fix portable appliances in a repair shop, trainees work on a single type of appliance, such as a vacuum cleaner, until they master its repair. Then they move on to others, until they can work on all appliances repaired by the shop. In companies that repair major appliances, beginners assist experienced repairers on service visits. Up to 3 years of on-the-job training may be needed for a technician to become skilled in all aspects of repair.

Home appliance repairers often make house calls to diagnose and fix stoves, refrigerators, dishwashers, or other appliances.

Projections data from the National Employment Matrix

Occupational Title	SOC Code	Employment, 2006	Projected employment, 2016	Change, 2006-16	
				Number	Percent
Home appliance repairers	49-9031	57,000	58,000	900	2

NOTE: Data in this table are rounded. See the discussion of the employment projections table in the *Handbook* introductory chapter on *Occupational Information Included in the Handbook*.

While on-the-job training is the most common method of training, employers prefer to hire students of appliance repair or electronics programs offered in high school vocational programs, postsecondary technical schools or community colleges. These programs can last 1 to 2 years and include courses in basic electricity and electronics as most home appliances contain electronic components. These programs can help reduce the amount of on-the-job training required for entry-level workers.

Whether their basic skills are developed through formal training or on the job, trainees usually receive additional training from their employer and from manufacturers. Some appliance manufacturers and department store chains have formal training programs that include home study and shop classes, in which trainees work with demonstration appliances and other training equipment. Many repairers receive supplemental instruction through 2- or 3-week seminars conducted by appliance manufacturers. Repairers authorized for warranty work by manufacturers are required to attend periodic training sessions.

Licensure. The U.S. Environmental Protection Agency (EPA) has mandated that all repairers who buy or work with refrigerants pass a written examination to become certified in their proper handling. Exams are administered by EPA-approved organizations, such as trade schools, unions, and employer associations. There also are EPA-approved take-home certification exams. Although no formal training is required for certification, many of these organizations offer training programs designed to prepare workers for the certification examination.

A driver's license is necessary in order to drive to customer's homes.

Certification and other qualifications. Mechanical and electrical aptitudes are desirable, and those who work in customers' homes must be courteous and tactful. Those who are self-employed need good business and financial skills to maintain a business.

Home appliance repairers may exhibit their competence by passing one of several certification examinations offered by various organizations. Although voluntary, such certifications can be helpful when seeking employment. The National Appliance Service Technician Certification (NASTeC), which is administered by the International Society of Certified Electronics Technicians (ISCET), requires repairers to pass a comprehensive examination that tests their competence in the diagnosis, repair, and maintenance of major home appliances. The Professional Service Association (PSA) administers a similar certification program. Those who pass the PSA examination earn the Certified Appliance Professional (CAP) designation.

Advancement. Repairers in large shops or service centers may be promoted to supervisor, assistant service manager, or service manager. Some repairers advance to managerial positions such as regional service manager or parts manager for appliance or tool manufacturers. Experienced repairers who have sufficient funds and knowledge of small-business management may open their own repair shops.

Employment

Many communities across the country employ home appliance repairers, but a high concentration of jobs can be found in more populated areas. Home appliance repairers held 57,000 jobs in 2006. About 36 percent of salaried repairers worked for retail trade establishments such as department stores and electronics and appliance stores. About 27 percent of repairers were self-employed. Another 21 percent work in household goods repair and maintenance.

Job Outlook

Little or no change in employment of home appliance repairers is projected. However, very good job opportunities are expected, particularly for individuals with formal training in appliance repair and electronics.

Employment change. The number of home appliance repairers will grow 2 percent between 2006 and 2016, reflecting little or no change. The number of home appliances in use is expected to increase with growth in the numbers of households. The decision to repair an appliance, however, often depends on the price to replace the appliance versus the cost to make the repairs. So while higher priced major appliances designed to have a long life are more likely to be repaired, small appliances are apt to be discarded rather than be repaired. With sales of high-end appliances growing, demand for major appliance repairers should be strong into the future.

Job prospects. In addition to new jobs created over the 2006-16 period, openings will arise as home appliance repairers retire or transfer to other occupations. Very good job opportunities are expected, with job openings continuing to outnumber jobseekers. Individuals with formal training in appliance repair and electronics should have the best opportunities.

Jobs are expected to be increasingly concentrated in larger companies as the number of smaller shops and family-owned businesses decline. Employment is relatively steady and workers are rarely laid off because demand for major appliance repair services is fairly constant.

Earnings

Median hourly earnings, including commissions, of home appliance repairers were $16.28 in May 2006. The middle 50 percent earned between $12.37 and $20.79 a year. The lowest 10 percent earned less than $9.37, and the highest 10 percent earned more than $25.84 a year. In May 2006, median hourly earnings of home appliance repairers in the largest employing industries were $15.18 in electronics and appliance stores and

$17.02 in personal and household goods repair and maintenance.

Earnings of home appliance repairers vary with the skill level required to fix equipment, the geographic location, and the type of equipment repaired. Many repairers receive a commission along with their salary, therefore earnings increase with the number of jobs a repairer can complete in a day.

Many larger dealers, manufacturers, and service stores offer typical benefits such as health insurance coverage, sick leave, and retirement and pension programs. Some home appliance repairers belong to the International Brotherhood of Electrical Workers.

Related Occupations

Other workers who repair electrical and electronic equipment include electrical and electronics installers and repairers; electronic home entertainment equipment installers and repairers; small-engine mechanics; coin, vending, and amusement machine servicers and repairers; and heating, air-conditioning, and refrigeration mechanics and installers.

Sources of Additional Information

For general information on home appliance repairers, contact the following organizations:

➤ National Appliance Service Association, P.O. Box 2514, Kokomo, IN 46904.

➤ United Servicers Association, Inc., P.O. Box 31006, Albuquerque, NM 87190.

Internet: **http://www.unitedservicers.com**

For information on the National Appliance Service Technician Certification program, contact:

➤ International Society of Certified Electronics Technicians, 3608 Pershing Ave., Fort Worth, TX 76107.

Internet: **http://www.nastec.org**

For information on the Certified Appliance Professional program, contact:

➤ Professional Service Association, 71 Columbia St., Cohoes, NY 12047. Internet: **http://www.psaworld.com**

Industrial Machinery Mechanics and Maintenance Workers

(O*NET 49-9041.00, 49-9043.00)

Significant Points

- Most of these workers are employed in manufacturing, but a growing number work for industrial equipment dealers and repair shops.

- Machinery maintenance workers learn on the job, while industrial machinery mechanics usually need some education after high school plus experience working on specific machines.

- Applicants with broad skills in machine repair and maintenance should have favorable job prospects.

Nature of the Work

Imagine an automobile assembly line: a large conveyor system moves unfinished automobiles down the line, giant robotic welding arms bond the different body panels together, hydraulic lifts move the motor into the body of the car, and giant presses stamp body parts from flat sheets of steel. All of these machines—the hydraulic lifts, the robotic welders, the conveyor system, and the giant presses—sometimes break down. When the assembly line stops because a machine breaks down, it costs the company money. Industrial machinery mechanics and machinery maintenance workers maintain and repair these very different, and often very expensive, machines.

The most basic tasks are performed by *machinery maintenance workers*. These employees are responsible for cleaning and lubricating machinery, performing basic diagnostic tests, checking performance, and testing damaged machine parts to determine whether major repairs are necessary. In carrying out these tasks, maintenance workers must follow machine specifications and adhere to maintenance schedules. Maintenance workers may perform minor repairs, but major repairs are generally left to machinery mechanics.

Industrial machinery mechanics, also called industrial machinery repairers or maintenance machinists, are highly skilled workers who maintain and repair machinery in a plant or factory. To do this effectively, they must be able to detect minor problems and correct them before they become major. Machinery mechanics use technical manuals, their understanding of the equipment, and careful observation to discover the cause of the problem. For example, after hearing a vibration from a machine, the mechanic must decide whether it is due to worn belts, weak motor bearings, or some other problem. Mechanics need years of training and experience to diagnose problems, but computerized diagnostic systems and vibration analysis techniques provide aid in determining the nature of the problem.

Industrial machinery mechanics and maintenance workers replace worn drive belts.

After diagnosing the problem, the industrial machinery mechanic disassembles the equipment to repair or replace the necessary parts. When repairing electronically controlled machinery, mechanics may work closely with electronic repairers or electricians who maintain the machine's electronic parts. (Electrical and electronic installers and repairers, as well as electricians, appear elsewhere in the *Handbook*.) Increasingly, mechanics are expected to have the electrical, electronics, and computer programming skills to repair sophisticated equipment on their own. Once a repair is made, mechanics perform tests to ensure that the machine is running smoothly.

Primary responsibilities of industrial machinery mechanics also often include preventive maintenance and the installation of new machinery. For example, they adjust and calibrate automated manufacturing equipment, such as industrial robots. Part of setting up equipment is programming the programmable logic control (PLC), a frequently used type of computer used as the control system for automated industrial machines. Situating and installing machinery has traditionally been the job of millwrights, but as plants retool and invest in new equipment, companies increasingly rely on mechanics to do this task for some machinery. (A section on millwrights appears elsewhere in the *Handbook*.)

Industrial machinery mechanics and machinery maintenance workers use a variety of tools to perform repairs and preventive maintenance. They may use handtools to adjust a motor or a chain hoist to lift a heavy printing press off the ground. When replacements for broken or defective parts are not readily available, or when a machine must be quickly returned to production, mechanics may create a new part using lathes, grinders, or drill presses. Mechanics use catalogs to order replacement parts and often follow blueprints, technical manuals, and engineering specifications to maintain and fix equipment. By keeping complete and up-to-date records, mechanics try to anticipate trouble and service equipment before factory production is interrupted.

Work environment. In production facilities, these workers are subject to common shop injuries such as cuts, bruises, and strains. They also may work in awkward positions, including on top of ladders or in cramped conditions under large machinery, which exposes them to additional hazards. They often use protective equipment such as hardhats, safety glasses, steel-tipped shoes, hearing protectors, and belts.

Because factories and other facilities cannot afford to have industrial machinery out of service for long periods, mechanics may be on call or assigned to work nights or on weekends. Overtime is common among full-time industrial machinery mechanics; about 30 percent work over 40 hours a week.

Training, Other Qualifications, and Advancement

Machinery maintenance workers can usually get a job with little more than a high school diploma or its equivalent—most learn on the job. Industrial machinery mechanics, on the other hand, usually need some education after high school plus experience working on specific machines before they can be considered a mechanic.

Education and training. Employers prefer to hire those who have taken courses in mechanical drawing, mathematics, blueprint reading, computer programming, or electronics. Entry-level machinery maintenance worker positions generally require a high school diploma, GED, or its equivalent. However, employers increasingly prefer to hire machinery maintenance workers with some training in industrial technology or an area of it, such as fluid power. Machinery maintenance workers typically receive on-the-job training lasting a few months to a year to perform routine tasks, such as setting up, cleaning, lubricating, and starting machinery. This training may be offered by experienced workers, professional trainers, or representatives of equipment manufacturers.

Industrial machinery mechanics usually need a year or more of formal education and training after high school to learn the growing range of mechanical and technical skills that they need. While mechanics used to specialize in one area, such as hydraulics or electronics, many factories now require every mechanic to have knowledge of electricity, electronics, hydraulics, and computer programming.

Workers can get this training in a number of different ways. Experience in the military repairing equipment, particularly ships, is highly valued by employers. Also, 2-year associate degree programs in industrial maintenance are good preparation. Some employers offer 4-year apprenticeship programs that combine classroom instruction with paid on-the-job-training. Apprenticeship programs usually are sponsored by a local trade union. Other mechanics may start as helpers or in other factory jobs and learn the skills of the trade informally and by taking courses offered through their employer. Classroom instruction focuses on subjects such as shop mathematics, blueprint reading, welding, electronics, and computer training. In addition to classroom training, it is important that mechanics train on the specific machines they will repair. They can get this training on the job, through dealer or manufacturer's representatives or in a classroom.

Other qualifications. Mechanical aptitude and manual dexterity are important for workers in this occupation. Good reading comprehension is also necessary to understand the technical manuals of a wide range of machines. And, good physical conditioning and agility are necessary because re-

Projections data from the National Employment Matrix

Occupational Title	SOC Code	Employment, 2006	Projected employment, 2016	Change, 2006-16	
				Number	Percent
Industrial machinery mechanics and maintenance workers..............	—	345,000	368,000	23,000	7
Industrial machinery mechanics	49-9041	261,000	284,000	24,000	9
Maintenance workers, machinery	49-9043	84,000	83,000	-900	-1

NOTE: Data in this table are rounded. See the discussion of the employment projections table in the *Handbook* introductory chapter on *Occupational Information Included in the Handbook.*

pairers sometimes have to lift heavy objects or climb to reach equipment.

Advancement. Opportunities for advancement vary by specialty. Machinery maintenance workers, if they take classes and gain additional skills, may advance to industrial machinery mechanic or supervisor. Industrial machinery mechanics also advance by working with more complicated equipment and gaining additional repair skills. The most highly skilled repairers can be promoted to supervisor, master mechanic, or millwright.

Employment

Industrial machinery mechanics and maintenance workers held about 345,000 jobs in 2006. Of these, 261,000 were held by the more highly skilled industrial machinery mechanics, while machinery maintenance workers accounted for 84,000 jobs. The majority of both types of workers were employed in the manufacturing sector in industries such as food processing and chemical, fabricated metal product, machinery, and motor vehicle and parts manufacturing. Additionally, about 9 percent work in wholesale trade, mostly for dealers of industrial equipment. Manufacturers often rely on these dealers to make complex repairs to specific machines. About 7 percent of mechanics work for the commercial and industrial machinery and equipment repair and maintenance industry, often making site visits to companies to repair equipment. Local governments employ a number of machinery maintenance workers, but few mechanics.

Job Outlook

Employment of industrial machinery mechanics and maintenance workers is projected to grow about as fast as average, and job prospects should be favorable for those with a variety of repair skills.

Employment change. Employment of industrial machinery mechanics and maintenance workers is expected to grow 7 percent from 2006 to 2016, about as fast as the average for all occupations. As factories become increasingly automated, these workers will be needed to maintain and repair the automated equipment. However, many new machines are more reliable and capable of self-diagnosis, making repairs easier and quicker and somewhat slowing the growth of repairer jobs.

Industrial machinery mechanics and maintenance workers are not as affected by changes in production levels as other manufacturing workers. During slack periods, when some plant workers are laid off, mechanics often are retained to do major overhaul jobs and to keep expensive machinery in working order. In addition, replacing highly skilled and experienced industrial maintenance workers is quite difficult, which discourages lay-offs.

Job prospects. Applicants with broad skills in machine repair and maintenance should have favorable job prospects. Many mechanics are expected to retire in coming years, and employers have reported difficulty in recruiting young workers with the necessary skills to be industrial machinery mechanics. In addition to openings from growth, most job openings will stem from the need to replace workers who transfer to other occupations or who retire or leave the labor force for other reasons.

Earnings

Median hourly wage-and-salary earnings of industrial machinery mechanics were $19.74 in May 2006. The middle 50 percent earned between $15.87 and $24.46. The lowest 10 percent earned less than $12.84, and the highest 10 percent earned more than $29.85.

Machinery maintenance workers earned somewhat less than the higher skilled industrial machinery mechanics. Median hourly wage-and-salary earnings of machinery maintenance workers were $16.61 in May 2006. The middle 50 percent earned between $12.91 and $21.53. The lowest 10 percent earned less than $10.29, and the highest 10 percent earned more than $26.46.

Earnings vary by industry and geographic region. Median hourly wage-and-salary earnings in the industries employing the largest numbers of industrial machinery mechanics are:

Electric power generation, transmission, and distribution	$26.02
Motor vehicle parts manufacturing	24.97
Machinery, equipment, and supplies merchant wholesalers	18.94
Plastics product manufacturing	18.79
Commercial and industrial machinery and equipment (except automotive and electronic) repair and maintenance	17.78

About 18 percent of industrial machinery mechanics and maintenance workers are union members. Labor unions that represent these workers include the United Steelworkers of America; the United Auto Workers; the International Association of Machinists and Aerospace Workers; the United Brotherhood of Carpenters and Joiners of America; and the International Union of Electronic, Electrical, Salaried, Machine, and Furniture Workers-Communications Workers of America.

Related Occupations

Other occupations that involve repairing and maintaining industrial machinery include machinists; maintenance and repair workers, general; millwrights; electrical and electronics installers and repairers; electricians; and pipelayers, plumbers, pipefitters, and steamfitters.

Sources of Additional Information

Information about employment and apprenticeship opportunities may be obtained from local employers and from local offices of the State employment service. For further information on apprenticeship programs, write to the Apprenticeship Council of your State's labor department or local firms that employ machinery mechanics and repairers. You can also find information on registered apprenticeships, together with links to State apprenticeship programs, on the U.S. Department of Labor's Web site: **http://www.doleta.gov/atels_bat** Apprenticeship information is also available from the U.S. Department of Labor's toll free helpline: (877) 872-5627.

Line Installers and Repairers

(O*NET 49-9051.00, 49-9052.00)

Significant Points

- Earnings are higher than in most other occupations that do not require postsecondary education.

- A growing number of retirements should create very good job opportunities, especially for electrical power-line installers and repairers.

- Line installers and repairers often work outdoors, and conditions can be hazardous.

- Most line installers and repairers require several years of long-term on-the-job training.

Nature of the Work

Line installers and repairers work on the vast networks of wires and cables that provide customers with electrical power and voice, video and data communications services. *Electrical power-line installers and repairers*, also called *line erectors*, install and maintain the networks of powerlines that go from generating plants to the customer. *Telecommunications line installers and repairers* install and repair the lines and cable that provide such services as cable television, telephone service, and the Internet to residential and commercial customers.

All line installers construct new lines by erecting utility poles and towers, or digging underground trenches, to carry the wires and cables. They may use a variety of construction equipment, including digger derricks, trenchers, cable plows, and borers. Digger derricks are trucks equipped with augers and cranes. Workers use augers to dig holes in the ground and use cranes to set utility poles in place. Trenchers and cable plows are used to cut openings in the earth for the laying of underground cables. Borers, which tunnel under the earth, are used to install tubes for the wire without opening a trench in the soil.

When construction is complete, line installers string cable along poles and towers or through tunnels and trenches. While working on poles and towers, installers use truck-mounted buckets to elevate themselves to the top of the structure, but sometimes they have to physically climb the pole or tower. Next, they pull up cable from large reels mounted on trucks, set the line in place, and pull up the slack so that it has the correct amount of tension. Finally, line installers attach the cable securely to the structure using hand and hydraulic tools. When working with electrical powerlines, installers bolt or clamp insulators onto the poles before attaching the cable. Underground cable is laid directly in a trench, pulled through a tunnel, or strung through a conduit running through a trench.

Other installation duties include setting up service for customers and installing network equipment. To set up service, line installers string cable between the customers' premises and the nearest lines running on poles or towers or in trench-es. They connect wiring to houses and check the connection for proper voltage readings. Line installers also may install a variety of network equipment. When setting up telephone and cable television lines, they install amplifiers and repeaters that maintain the strength of communications transmissions. When running electrical powerlines, they install and replace transformers, circuitbreakers, switches, fuses, and other equipment to control and direct the electrical current.

In addition to installation, line installers and repairers are responsible for maintenance of electrical, telecommunications, and cable television lines. Workers periodically travel in trucks, helicopters, and airplanes to visually inspect the wires and cables. Sensitive monitoring equipment can automatically detect malfunctions on the network, such as loss of current flow. When line repairers identify a problem, they travel to the location of the malfunction and repair or replace defective cables or equipment.

Bad weather or natural disasters can cause extensive damage to networks of lines. Line installers and repairers must respond quickly to these emergencies to restore critical utility and communications services. This can often involve working outdoors in adverse weather conditions.

Installation and repair work may require splicing, or joining together, separate pieces of cable. Each cable contains numerous individual wires; splicing the cables together requires that each wire in one piece of cable be joined to another wire in the matching piece. Line installers join these wires and the surrounding cables using small hand tools, epoxy (an especially strong glue), or mechanical equipment. At each splice, they place insulation over the conductor and seal the splice with moistureproof covering. At some companies, specialized *cable splicing technicians* perform splices on larger lines.

Telecommunications networks are in the process of replacing older conventional wire or metal cables with new fiber optic cables. Fiber optic cables are made of hair-thin strands of glass, which convey pulses of light. These cables carry much more information at higher speeds than conventional cables. Splicing fiber optic cable requires specialized equipment that carefully slices, matches, and aligns individual

Line installers and repairers wear safety gear to protect themselves from electrical current.

glass fibers. The fibers are joined by either electrical fusion (welding) or a mechanical fixture and gel (glue).

The work performed by electrical power-line installers and telecommunications line installers and is quite similar, but there are some differences. Working with powerlines requires specialized knowledge of transformers, electrical power distribution systems, and substations. In contrast, working with telecommunications lines requires specialized knowledge of fiber optics and telecommunications switches and routers.

Work environment. Line installers and repairers must climb and maintain their balance while working on poles and towers. They lift equipment and work in a variety of positions, such as stooping or kneeling. Their work often requires that they drive utility vehicles, travel long distances, and work outdoors under a variety of weather conditions.

Line installers and repairers encounter serious hazards on their jobs and must follow safety procedures to minimize potential danger. They wear safety equipment when entering utility holes and test for the presence of gas before going underground. Electric powerline workers have the more hazardous jobs. High-voltage powerlines can instantly electrocute a worker who comes in contact with a live cable, so line installers and repairers must use electrically insulated protective devices and tools when working with such cables. Powerlines are typically higher than telephone and cable television lines, increasing the risk of severe injury due to falls. To prevent these injuries, line installers and repairers must use fall-protection equipment when working on poles or towers.

Since line installers and repairers fix damage from storms, they may be asked to work long and irregular hours. They can expect frequently to be on-call and work overtime. When performing normal maintenance and constructing new lines, line installers work more normal hours.

Training, Other Qualifications, and Advancement

Most line installers and repairers require several years of long-term on-the-job training and some classroom work to become proficient. Formal apprenticeships are common.

Education and training. Line installers and repairers usually need at least a high school diploma. Employers look for people with basic knowledge of algebra and trigonometry and good reading and writing skills. Some also prefer to hire people with technical knowledge of electricity or electronics obtained through vocational programs, community colleges, or the Armed Forces.

Programs in telecommunications, electronics, or electricity, many of which are operated with assistance from local employers and unions, are offered by many community or technical colleges. Some programs work with local companies to offer 1-year certificates that emphasize hands-on field work. More advanced 2-year associate degree programs provide students with a broader knowledge of the technology used in telecommunications and electrical utilities. They offer courses in electricity, electronics, fiber optics, and microwave transmission. Employers often prefer to hire graduates of these programs for line installer and repairer jobs.

Line installers and repairers receive most of their training on the job. Electrical line installers and repairers often must complete formal apprenticeships or other employer training programs. These programs, which can last up to 5 years, combine on-the-job training with formal classroom courses and are sometimes administered jointly by the employer and the union representing the workers. Unions include the International Brotherhood of Electrical Workers, the Communications Workers of America, and the Utility Workers Union of America. Government safety regulations strictly define the training and education requirements for apprentice electrical line installers.

Line installers and repairers working for telephone and cable television companies receive several years of on-the-job training. They also may attend training or take online courses provided by equipment manufacturers, schools, unions, or industry training organizations.

Other qualifications. Line installers and repairers must be able to read instructions, write reports, and solve problems. If they deal directly with customers, they also must have good customer service skills. They should also be mechanically inclined and like working with computers and new technology.

Physical fitness is important because they must be able to climb, lift heavy objects (many employers require applicants to be able to lift at least 50 pounds), and do other physical activity that requires stamina, strength, and coordination. Line installers and repairers often must work at a considerable height above the ground so they cannot be afraid of heights. Normal ability to distinguish colors is necessary because wires and cables may be color-coded. In addition, they often need a commercial driver's licenses to operate company-owned vehicles, so a good driving record is important.

Certification and advancement. Entry-level line installers may be hired as ground workers, helpers, or tree trimmers, who clear branches from telephone and powerlines. These workers may advance to positions stringing cable and performing service installations. With experience, they may advance to more sophisticated maintenance and repair positions responsible for increasingly larger portions of the network. Promotion to supervisory or training positions also is possible, but more advanced supervisory positions often require a college degree.

Advancement for telecommunications line installers is also made easier by earning certifications—formal recognition by a respected organization of one's knowledge of current technology. The Society of Cable Television Engineers (SCTE), for example, offers certification programs for line installers and repairers employed in the cable television industry. Candidates for certification can attend training sessions at local SCTE chapters.

Employment

Line installers and repairers held about 275,000 jobs in 2006. Approximately 162,000 were telecommunications line installers and repairers; the remainder were electrical power-line installers and repairers. Nearly all line installers and repairers worked for telecommunications companies,

Projections data from the National Employment Matrix

Occupational Title	SOC Code	Employment, 2006	Projected employment, 2016	Change, 2006-16	
				Number	Percent
Line installers and repairers...	49-9050	275,000	290,000	16,000	6
Electrical power-line installers and repairers...............................	49-9051	112,000	120,000	8,100	7
Telecommunications line installers and repairers.........................	49-9052	162,000	170,000	7,500	5

NOTE: Data in this table are rounded. See the discussion of the employment projections table in the *Handbook* introductory chapter on *Occupational Information Included in the Handbook.*

including both cable television distribution and telecommunications companies; construction contractors; or electric power generation, transmission, and distribution companies.

Approximately 6,100 line installers and repairers were self-employed. Many of these were contractors employed by the telecommunications companies to handle customer service problems and installations.

Job Outlook

Employment of line installers and repairers is projected to grow more slowly than average, but retirements are expected to create very good job opportunities for new workers, particularly for electrical power-line installers.

Employment change. Overall employment of line installers and repairers will grow 6 percent between 2006 and 2016, slower than the average for all occupations. Growth will reflect an increasing demand for electricity and telecommunications services as the population grows. However, productivity gains—particularly in maintaining these networks—will keep employment growth slow.

Employment of telecommunications line installers and repairers will grow more slowly than the average for all occupations. As the population expands, installers will be needed to lay the wiring for new developments and provide new telecommunications and cable television services. Additionally, old copper wiring will need to be replaced with fiber optic cable, also requiring more installers. The fiber optic lines will allow companies to give customers high-speed access to data, video, and graphics. Fiber optic lines allow for greater amounts of data to be transmitted through the cables at a faster rate. Fiber optic lines are expected to be more reliable in the long run, however, so they will require fewer workers.

Growth of wireless communications will also slow job increases for line installers and repairers in the long run. More households are switching to wireless delivery of their communications, video, and data services. Although wireless networks use lines to connect cellular towers to central offices, they do not require as many line installers to maintain and expand their systems. Satellite television providers—another major portion of the wireless communications industry—will also reduce demand for wire-based phone, Internet, and cable TV.

Employment of electrical power-line installers and repairers is expected to grow about as fast as the average for all occupations. Despite consistently rising demand for electricity, power companies will cut costs by shifting more work to outside contractors and hire fewer installers and repairers. Most new jobs for electrical power-line installers and repair-

ers are expected to arise among contracting firms in the construction industry.

Job prospects. Very good job opportunities are expected, especially for electrical power-line installers and repairers. A growing number of retirements will create many job openings.

Earnings

Earnings for line installers and repairers are higher than those in most other occupations that do not require postsecondary education. Median hourly earnings for electrical power-line installers and repairers were $24.41 in May 2006. The middle 50 percent earned between $18.73 and $28.90. The lowest 10 percent earned less than $13.96, and the highest 10 percent earned more than $34.20. Median hourly earnings in the industries employing the largest numbers of electrical power-line installers and repairers in May 2006 are shown below:

Electric power generation, transmission, and distribution...	$25.90
Wired telecommunications carriers	24.82
Local government	23.06
Building equipment contractors	22.04
Utility system construction	19.29

Median hourly earnings for telecommunications line installers and repairers were $22.25 in May 2006. The middle 50 percent earned between $15.56 and $28.40. The lowest 10 percent earned less than $11.88, and the highest 10 percent earned more than $32.80. Median hourly earnings in the industries employing the largest numbers of telecommunications line installers and repairers in May 2006 are shown below:

Wired telecommunications carriers	$27.61
Building equipment contractors	17.89
Cable and other subscription programming......................	17.72
Cable and other program distribution	17.45
Utility system construction	15.41

Many line installers and repairers belong to unions, principally the Communications Workers of America, the International Brotherhood of Electrical Workers, and the Utility Workers Union of America. For these workers, union contracts set wage rates, wage increases, and the time needed to advance from one job level to the next.

Good health, education, and vacation benefits are common in the occupation.

Related Occupations

Other workers who install and repair electrical and electronic equipment include electricians; power plant operators, distributors, and dispatchers; and radio and telecommunications equipment installers and repairers.

Sources of Additional Information

For more details about employment opportunities, contact the telephone, cable television, or electrical power companies in your community. For general information and educational resources on line installer and repairer jobs, contact:

➤ Communications Workers of America, 501 3rd St.NW., Washington, DC 20001.
Internet: **http://www.cwa-union.org/jobs**

➤ National Joint Apprenticeship and Training Center (NJATC), 301 Prince Georges Blvd., Suite D, Upper Marlboro MD 20774.
Internet: **http://www.njatc.org**

For information on training and professional certifications for those already employed by cable telecommunications firms, contact:

➤ Society of Cable Telecommunications Engineers, Certification Department, 140 Phillips Rd., Exton, PA 19341-1318. Internet: **http://www.scte.org**

Maintenance and Repair Workers, General

(O*NET 49-9042.00)

Significant Points

- General maintenance and repair workers are employed in almost every industry.

- Many workers learn their skills informally on the job.

- Job growth and turnover in this large occupation should result in excellent job opportunities, especially for people with experience in maintenance and related fields.

Nature of the Work

Most craft workers specialize in one kind of work, such as plumbing or carpentry. General maintenance and repair workers, however, have skills in many different crafts. They repair and maintain machines, mechanical equipment, and buildings and work on plumbing, electrical, and air-conditioning and heating systems. They build partitions, make plaster or drywall repairs, and fix or paint roofs, windows, doors, floors, woodwork, and other parts of building structures. They also maintain and repair specialized equipment and machinery found in cafeterias, laundries, hospitals, stores, offices, and factories.

Typical duties include troubleshooting and fixing faulty electrical switches, repairing air-conditioning motors, and unclogging drains. New buildings sometimes have computer-controlled systems that allow maintenance workers to make adjustments in building settings and monitor for problems from a central location. For example, they can remotely control light sensors that turn off lights automatically after a set amount of time or identify a broken ventilation fan that needs to be replaced.

General maintenance and repair workers inspect and diagnose problems and determine the best way to correct them, frequently checking blueprints, repair manuals, and parts catalogs. They obtain supplies and repair parts from distributors or storerooms. Using common hand and power tools such as screwdrivers, saws, drills, wrenches, and hammers, as well as specialized equipment and electronic testing devices, these workers replace or fix worn or broken parts, where necessary, or make adjustments to correct malfunctioning equipment and machines.

General maintenance and repair workers also perform routine preventive maintenance and ensure that machines continue to run smoothly, building systems operate efficiently, and the physical condition of buildings does not deteriorate. Following a checklist, they may inspect drives, motors, and belts, check fluid levels, replace filters, and perform other maintenance actions. Maintenance and repair workers keep records of their work.

Employees in small establishments, where they are often the only maintenance worker, make all repairs, except for very large or difficult jobs. In larger establishments, duties may be limited to the maintenance of everything in a workshop or a particular area.

Work environment. General maintenance and repair workers often carry out several different tasks in a single day, at any number of locations. They may work inside a single building or in several different buildings. They may have to stand for long periods, lift heavy objects, and work in uncomfortably hot or cold environments, in awkward and cramped positions, or on ladders. Those employed in small establishments often work with only limited supervision. Those in larger establishments frequently work under the direct supervision of an experienced worker. Some tasks put workers at risk of electrical shock, burns, falls, cuts, and bruises.

General maintenance and repair workers inspect, diagnose problems, and determine the best way to correct them.

Projections data from the National Employment Matrix

Occupational Title	SOC Code	Employment, 2006	Projected employment, 2016	Change, 2006-16	
				Number	Percent
Maintenance and repair workers, general	49-9042	1,391,000	1,531,000	140,000	10

NOTE: Data in this table are rounded. See the discussion of the employment projections table in the *Handbook* introductory chapter on *Occupational Information Included in the Handbook*.

Most general maintenance workers work a 40-hour week. Some work evening, night, or weekend shifts or are on call for emergency repairs.

Training, Other Qualifications, and Advancement

Many general maintenance and repair workers learn their skills informally on the job as helpers to other repairers or to carpenters, electricians, and other construction workers.

Education and training. General maintenance and repair workers often learn their skills informally on the job. They start as helpers, watching and learning from skilled maintenance workers. Helpers begin by doing simple jobs, such as fixing leaky faucets and replacing light bulbs, and progress to more difficult tasks, such as overhauling machinery or building walls. Some learn their skills by working as helpers to other types of repair or construction workers, including machinery repairers, carpenters, or electricians.

Several months of on-the-job training are required to become fully qualified, depending on the skill level required. Some jobs require a year or more to become fully qualified. Because a growing number of new buildings rely on computers to control their systems, general maintenance and repair workers may need basic computer skills, such as how to log onto a central computer system and navigate through a series of menus. Companies that install computer-controlled equipment usually provide onsite training for general maintenance and repair workers.

Many employers prefer to hire high school graduates. High school courses in mechanical drawing, electricity, woodworking, blueprint reading, science, mathematics, and computers are useful. Because of the wide variety of tasks performed by maintenance and repair workers, technical education is an important part of their training. Maintenance and repair workers often need to do work that involves electrical, plumbing, and heating and air- conditioning systems, or painting and roofing tasks. Although these basic tasks may not require a license to do the work, a good working knowledge of many repair and maintenance tasks is required. Many maintenance and repair workers learn some of these skills in high school shop classes and postsecondary trade or vocational schools or community colleges.

Licensure. Licensing requirements vary by State and locality. In some cases, workers may need to be licensed in a particular specialty such as electrical or plumbing work.

Other qualifications. Mechanical aptitude, the ability to use shop mathematics, and manual dexterity are important. Good health is necessary because the job involves much walking, standing, reaching, and heavy lifting. Difficult jobs require problem-solving ability, and many positions require the ability to work without direct supervision.

Advancement. Many general maintenance and repair workers in large organizations advance to maintenance supervisor or become craftworkers such as electricians, heating and air-conditioning mechanics, or plumbers. Within small organizations, promotion opportunities may be limited.

Employment

General maintenance and repair workers held 1.4 million jobs in 2006. They were employed in almost every industry. Around 19 percent worked in manufacturing industries, almost evenly distributed through all sectors, while about 10 percent worked for Federal, State, and local governments. Others worked for wholesale and retail firms and for real estate firms that operate office and apartment buildings.

Job Outlook

Average employment growth is expected. Job growth and the need to replace those who leave this large occupation should result in excellent job opportunities, especially for those with experience in maintenance and related fields.

Employment change. Employment of general maintenance and repair workers is expected to grow 10 percent during the 2006-16 decade, about as fast as the average for all occupations. Employment is related to the number of buildings—for example, office and apartment buildings, stores, schools, hospitals, hotels, and factories—and the amount of equipment needing maintenance and repair. One factor limiting job growth is that computers allow buildings to be monitored more efficiently, partially reducing the need for workers.

Job prospects. Job opportunities should be excellent, especially for those with experience in maintenance or related fields. General maintenance and repair is a large occupation, generating many job openings due to growth and the need to replace those who leave the occupation. Many job openings are expected to result from the retirement of experienced maintenance workers over the next decade.

Earnings

Median hourly earnings of general maintenance and repair workers were $15.34 in May 2006. The middle 50 percent earned between $11.66 and $19.90. The lowest 10 percent earned less than $9.20, and the highest 10 percent earned more than $24.44. Median hourly earnings in the industries employing the largest numbers of general maintenance and repair workers in May 2006 are shown in the following tabulation:

Local government $15.85
Elementary and secondary schools 15.76
Activities related to real estate 13.44
Lessors of real estate 13.06
Traveler accommodation 11.76

Some general maintenance and repair workers are members of unions including the American Federation of State, County, and Municipal Employees and the United Auto Workers.

Related Occupations

Some duties of general maintenance and repair workers are similar to those of carpenters; pipelayers, plumbers, pipefitters, and steamfitters; electricians; and heating, air-conditioning, and refrigeration mechanics. Other duties are similar to those of coin, vending, and amusement machine servicers and repairers; electrical and electronics installers and repairers; electronic home entertainment equipment installers and repairers; and radio and telecommunications equipment installers and repairers.

Sources of Additional Information

Information about job opportunities may be obtained from local employers and local offices of the State.

For information related to maintenance managers contact:
➤ International Maintenance Institute, P.O. Box 751896, Houston, TX 77275-1896.
Internet: **http://www.imionline.org**

Millwrights

(O*NET 49-9044.00)

Significant Points

- Millwrights usually train in 4-year to 5-year apprenticeships; some learn through community college programs coupled with informal paid on-the-job training.

- Despite projected slower-than-average employment growth, well-qualified applicants should have excellent job opportunities.

- About 50 percent of millwrights belong to labor unions, one of the highest rates of membership in the economy.

Nature of the Work

Millwrights install, replace, dismantle, and repair machinery and heavy equipment used in power generation, including wind power, hydroelectric damns, and natural gas turbines, and in manufacturing plants, construction sites, and mining operations. The development of new technologies requires millwrights to work with new industry-specific and highly complex precision machines. Some of these machines have tolerances smaller than the width of a human hair.

The millwright's responsibilities begin before a new piece of machinery arrives at the jobsite. Millwrights consult with production managers, industrial engineers, and others to determine the optimal placement of the machine in the plant. Some equipment, such as a metal forging press, is so heavy that it must be placed on a new foundation. Millwrights either prepare the foundation themselves or supervise its construc-

tion. As a result, they must know how to read blueprints and to work with a variety of building materials.

When the new machine arrives, millwrights unload, inspect, and move the equipment into position. To lift and move light machinery, millwrights use rigging and hoisting devices, such as pulleys and cables. With heavier equipment, they may use hydraulic-lift trucks or cranes. Lifting such heavy equipment requires millwrights to understand the load properties of cables, ropes, hoists, and cranes. Parts of power plant turbines and other machinery can weigh more than 100 tons and must be precisely positioned; even nuts and bolts can weigh a few hundred pounds each and require a crane to move.

Next, millwrights assemble the machinery. They fit bearings, align gears and wheels, attach motors, and connect belts, according to the manufacturer's blueprints and drawings. Precision leveling and alignment are important in the assembly process, so millwrights measure angles, material thickness, and small distances with calipers, squares, micrometers, and other tools. When a high level of precision is required, they use devices such as lasers and ultrasonic measuring and alignment tools. Millwrights also work with hand and power tools, such as cutting torches, welding machines, hydraulic torque wrenches, hydraulic stud tensioners, soldering guns, and with metalworking equipment, including lathes and grinding machines.

In addition to installing and dismantling machinery, many millwrights work with industrial mechanics and maintenance workers to repair and maintain equipment. This includes preventive maintenance, such as lubrication and fixing or replacing worn parts. If a spare part is unavailable, a millwright may use a lathe or other machine tool to cut a new part. (For further information on machinery maintenance, see the section on industrial machinery mechanics and maintenance workers elsewhere in the *Handbook*.)

Increasingly sophisticated automation means more complicated machines for millwrights to install and maintain, requiring millwrights to specialize in certain machines or machine brands. For example, some millwrights specialize in installing and maintaining turbines in power plants that can weigh hundreds of tons and contain thousands of parts. This machinery requires special care and knowledge, so millwrights

Millwrights repair complex industrial machinery.

Projections data from the National Employment Matrix

Occupational Title	SOC Code	Employment, 2006	Projected employment, 2016	Change, 2006-16	
				Number	Percent
Millwrights...	49-9044	55,000	58,000	3,200	6

NOTE: Data in this table are rounded. See the discussion of the employment projections table in the *Handbook* introductory chapter on *Occupational Information Included in the Handbook*.

receive additional training and are required to be certified by the turbine manufacturer.

Work environment. Millwrights in manufacturing often work in a machine shop and use protective equipment, such as safety belts, protective glasses, and hardhats, to avoid injuries from falling objects or machinery. Those employed in construction may work outdoors in difficult weather conditions.

Millwrights at construction sites may travel long distances to worksites. For example, millwrights who specialize in turbine installation travel to wherever new power plants are being built.

Advanced equipment, such as hydraulic wrenches and hydraulic stud tensioners, have made the work safer and eliminated the need for millwrights to use sledge hammers to pound bolts into position. Other equipment has reduced the strenuous tasks that caused injuries in the past.

Millwrights work independently or as part of a team. Because disabled machinery costs time and money, many millwrights work overtime and some work in shifts; about 39 percent of millwrights report working more than 40 hours during a typical week. During power outages or other emergencies, millwrights often work overtime.

Training, Other Qualifications, and Advancement

Millwrights usually train in 4-year to 5-year apprenticeships that combine paid on-the-job training with classroom instruction. Some learn through community college programs coupled with informal paid on-the-job training.

Education and training. Employers prefer applicants who have a high school diploma, GED, or the equivalent and some vocational training or experience. Courses in science, mathematics, mechanical drawing, computers, and machine shop practice are useful. Once hired, millwrights are trained through 4-year to 5-year apprenticeship programs that combine on-the-job training with classroom instruction, or through community college programs coupled with informal on-the-job training.

Apprenticeships include training in dismantling, moving, erecting, and repairing machinery. Trainees also might learn carpentry, welding, use of concrete, sheet-metal work, and other skills related to installation and repair. Millwright apprentices often attend about 1 week of classes every 3 months. Classroom instruction covers mathematics, blueprint reading, hydraulics, vibration analysis, conveyor systems, electricity, computers, electronics, machining, and instruction in specific machinery. Millwrights are expected to keep their skills up-to-date and may need additional training on technological advances, such as laser shaft alignment.

Other qualifications. Because millwrights assemble and disassemble complicated machinery, mechanical aptitude is very important. Strength and agility also are necessary for lifting and climbing. Millwrights need good interpersonal and communication skills to work as part of a team and to effectively give detailed instructions to others.

Advancement. Advancement for millwrights usually takes the form of higher wages. Some advance to the position of supervisor or superintendent; others may become self-employed contractors.

Employment

Millwrights held about 55,000 jobs in 2006. About half work in manufacturing, primarily in industries such as transportation equipment manufacturing and primary metals manufacturing. About 40 percent of millwrights are employed in construction, where most work for contracting firms that assemble and maintain machinery and equipment for the manufacturing and utility industries, among others. Although millwrights work in every State, employment is concentrated in heavily industrialized areas.

Job Outlook

Employment of millwrights is projected to grow more slowly than average. Opportunities for well-qualified applicants should be excellent, however, as many experienced millwrights retire.

Employment change. Employment of millwrights is projected to grow 6 percent during the 2006-16 decade, slower than the average for all occupations. To remain competitive in coming years, firms will continue to need millwrights to dismantle old equipment and install new high-technology machinery. Highly automated systems that are installed and maintained by millwrights often allow manufacturing companies to remain competitive with producers in lower-wage countries. Warehouse and distribution companies also are deploying highly automated conveyor systems, which are assembled and maintained by millwrights. In addition, growth in both power generation, including wind power and turbines for natural gas and coal plants, and oil and gas extraction and refining will help drive employment growth.

Employment growth will be dampened somewhat by foreign competition in manufacturing. In addition, the demand for millwrights will be adversely affected as other workers, such as industrial machinery mechanics and maintenance workers, assume some installation and maintenance duties.

Job prospects. The large number of expected retirements and the difficulty of recruiting new workers will create excellent job opportunities for well-qualified applicants. Job prospects should be especially good for those who have experience in machining, welding, or doing mechanical work.

Employment prospects for millwrights are better than for some other manufacturing workers because they work across a wide range of industries, including power generation, paper mills, mining, and motor vehicle parts manufacturing. When a downturn occurs in one industry, millwrights can more easily switch to another industry. There will always be a need to maintain and repair existing machinery, dismantle old machinery, and install new equipment.

Earnings

Median hourly wage-and-salary earnings of millwrights were $21.94 in May 2006. The middle 50 percent earned between $17.13 and $29.42. The lowest 10 percent earned less than $13.84, and the highest 10 percent earned more than $34.39. Earnings vary by industry and geographic location. Median hourly wage-and-salary earnings in the industries employing the largest numbers of millwrights were:

Pulp, paper, and paperboard mills	$25.43
Iron and steel mills and ferroalloy manufacturing	20.91
Nonresidential building construction	20.34
Building equipment contractors	19.67
Sawmills and wood preservation	17.55

About 50 percent of millwrights belong to labor unions, one of the highest rates of membership in the economy.

Related Occupations

Other workers who install and maintain manufacturing equipment include industrial machinery mechanics and maintenance workers; tool and die makers; aircraft and avionics equipment mechanics and service technicians; structural and reinforcing iron and metal workers; boilermakers; and assemblers and fabricators. Millwrights also machine parts and operate computer-controlled machine tools as do machinists and computer control programmers and operators. Millwrights often use welding and soldering to assemble and repair machines as do welding, soldering, and brazing workers.

Sources of Additional Information

For further information on apprenticeship programs, write to the Apprenticeship Council of your State's labor department, local offices of your State employment service, or local firms that employ millwrights. You can also find information on the registered apprenticeships, together with links to State apprenticeship programs, on the U.S. Department of Labor's Web site: **http://www.doleta.gov/atels_bat** Apprenticeship information is also available from the U.S. Department of Labor's tollfree helpline: (877) 872-5627.

In addition, you may contact:

➤ Associated Builders and Contractors, Workforce Development Dept., 4250 N. Fairfax Dr., 9th Floor, Arlington, VA 22203. Internet: **http://www.trytools.org**

➤ United Brotherhood of Carpenters and Joiners of America, 6801 Placid St., Las Vegas, NV 89119. Internet: **http://www.ubcmillwrights.org**

Precision Instrument and Equipment Repairers

(O*NET 49-9061.00, 49-9062.00, 49-9063.00, 49-9064.00, 49-9069.99)

Significant Points

- Training requirements include a high school diploma and, in most cases, postsecondary education, coupled with significant on-the-job training.

- Overall employment is expected to grow about as fast as average, and good opportunities are expected for most types of jobs.

- About 1 out of 6 are self-employed.

Nature of the Work

Repairing and maintaining watches, cameras, musical instruments, medical equipment, and other precision instruments requires a high level of skill and attention to detail. Some devices contain tiny gears that must be manufactured to within one one-hundredth of a millimeter of design specifications, and other devices contain sophisticated electronic controls. Job descriptions vary greatly, depending on the type of instrument being repaired.

Camera and photographic equipment repairers fix broken cameras and other optical devices. The repairer must first determine whether a repair should be attempted, because many inexpensive cameras cost more to repair than to replace. The most complicated or expensive repairs are usually referred back to the manufacturer or to a large repair center. If the repairer decides to proceed with the job, the problem must be diagnosed, often by disassembling numerous small parts in order to reach the source. The defective parts are then replaced or repaired. Many problems are caused by the electronic circuits used in cameras, and fixing these circuits requires an understanding of electronics. Camera repairers also maintain cameras by removing and replacing broken or worn parts and cleaning and lubricating gears and springs. Because many of the components involved are extremely small, repairers must have a great deal of manual dexterity. Frequently, older camera parts are no longer available, requiring repairers to build replacement parts or to strip junked cameras. When machining new parts, workers often use a small lathe, a grinding wheel, and other metalworking tools.

Repairs on digital cameras are similar to those on conventional cameras, but because digital cameras have no film to wind, they have fewer moving parts. Digital cameras rely on software, so any repair to the lens requires that it be calibrated with the use of software and by connecting the camera to a personal computer. Because digital cameras are generally more expensive and more widely used than film cameras, they are quickly becoming the most important source of business for camera repairers.

Watch and clock repairers work almost exclusively on expensive and antique timepieces, because moderately priced time-

Watch repairers must work with very small, sensitive parts.

pieces are cheaper to replace than to repair. Electrically powered clocks and quartz watches and clocks function with almost no moving parts, limiting necessary maintenance to replacing the battery. Many expensive timepieces still employ old-style mechanical movements and a manual or automatic winding mechanism. This type of timepiece must be regularly adjusted and maintained. Repair and maintenance work on a mechanical timepiece requires using hand tools to disassemble many fine gears and components. Each part is inspected for signs of wear. Some gears or springs may need to be replaced or machined. Exterior portions of the watch may require polishing and buffing. Specialized machines are used to clean all of the parts with ultrasonic waves and a series of baths in cleaning agents. Reassembling a watch often requires lubricating key parts.

As with older cameras, replacement parts are frequently unavailable for antique watches or clocks. In such cases, watch repairers must machine their own parts. They employ small lathes and other machines in creating tiny parts.

Musical instrument repairers and tuners combine their love of music with a highly skilled craft. These artisans, often referred to as technicians, work in four specialties: Band instruments, pianos and organs, orchestral string instruments, and guitars. (Repairers and tuners who work on electronic organs are discussed in the *Handbook* statement on electronic home entertainment equipment installers and repairers.)

Band instrument repairers, brass and wind instrument repairers, and *percussion instrument repairers* focus on woodwind, brass, reed, and percussion instruments damaged through deterioration or by accident. In most cases, the problem with the instrument will be clear, but in some cases the repairers must diagnose the issue. They may unscrew and remove rod pins, keys, worn cork pads, and pistons and remove soldered parts by means of gas torches. Using filling techniques or a mallet, they repair dents in metal and wood. They also use gas torches,

grinding wheels, lathes, shears, mallets, and small hand tools and, are skilled in metalworking and woodworking.

Violin and guitar repairers adjust and repair stringed instruments. Some repairers work on both stringed and band instruments. Initially, repairers play and inspect the instrument to find any defects. They replace or repair cracked or broken sections and damaged parts. They also restring the instruments and repair damage to their finish. Because the specifications of all types of instruments vary greatly, custom parts machining is considered an essential skill.

Piano tuners and repairers use different techniques, skills, and tools. Most workers in this group are tuners; only a few workers in this occupation specialize in refurbishing older pianos. Tuning involves tightening and loosening different strings to achieve the proper tone or pitch. Pitch matching is usually done by ear—an experienced tuner can compare the sound of a pitch with a tuning fork, and then with other pitches on the piano to make sure it is tuned properly. Tuners must make house calls, as piano tuning is sensitive to movement and most pianos cannot be transported easily. Some repairers specialize in restoring older pianos. Restoration is complicated work, often involving replacing many of the parts, which number more than 12,000 in some pianos. With proper maintenance and restoration, pianos often survive more than 100 years.

Pipe organ repairers do work similar to that of piano repairers, but with organ pipes rather than piano strings. Tuning pipe organs is very complicated, as most organs have thousands of pipes, and different pipes are tuned in different ways. Additionally, many repairers assemble new organs or expand organs with new ranks of pipes. Even with repairers working in teams or with assistants, organ maintenance can take several weeks or even months, depending upon the size of the organ.

Medical equipment repairers, also known as *biomedical equipment technicians*, maintain, adjust, calibrate, and repair electronic, electromechanical, and hydraulic equipment used in hospitals and other medical environments. They use various tools, including multimeters, specialized software, and computers designed to communicate with specific pieces of hardware. These repairers use hand tools, soldering irons, and other electronic tools to repair and adjust equipment. Among the tools they use is equipment designed to simulate water or air pressure. Faulty circuit boards and other parts are normally removed and replaced. Medical equipment repairers must maintain careful, detailed logs of all maintenance and repair that they perform on each piece of equipment.

Medical equipment repairers work on medical equipment such as defibrillators, heart monitors, medical imaging equipment (x-rays, CAT scanners, and ultrasound equipment), voice-controlled operating tables, and electric wheelchairs. Because most equipment repairs take place within a hospital, medical equipment repairers must be comfortable working around patients. In some cases, repairs may take place while equipment is being used. When this is the case, the repairer must take great care to make sure that repairs do not disturb the patient.

Other precision instrument and equipment repairers service, repair, and replace a wide range of equipment associated with automated or instrument-controlled manufacturing processes. For most of these repairers, the emphasis is on determining the problem and how to best approach the solution. In many cases, replacement is preferable to repair, since precision parts are often very sensitive and may cost more to repair than replace. Replacement parts are not always available, so repairers sometimes machine or fabricate new parts. Repairers may also be responsible for preventive maintenance and calibration, which involves regular lubrication, cleaning, and adjustment of many measuring devices. Increasingly, it also involves solving computer software problems as more control devices, such as valves, are controlled by software. To adjust a control device, a technician may need to connect a laptop computer to the control device's computer and make adjustments through changes to the software commands.

Work environment. Camera, watch, and musical instrument repairers work under fairly similar solitary, low-stress conditions with minimal supervision. A quiet, well-lit workshop or repair shop is typical. Piano and organ tuners must travel to the instruments being repaired. Often, these workers can adjust their schedules, allowing for second jobs as needed. Musical instrument repairer jobs are attractive to many professional musicians and retirees because the flexible hours common to repair work allow these individuals time for other pursuits.

Medical equipment and other precision instrument and equipment repairers normally work daytime hours, but are often expected to be on call. Still, like other hospital and factory employees, some repairers work irregular hours. Medical equipment repairers must work in a patient environment, which has the potential to expose them to diseases and other health risks, but occupational injuries are relatively uncommon.

Precision instrument repairers work under a wide array of conditions, from hot, dirty, noisy factories, to air-conditioned workshops, to the outdoors on fieldwork. Attention to safety is essential, as the work sometimes involves dangerous machinery, toxic chemicals, or radiation. Due to the individualized nature of the work, supervision is fairly minimal.

Training, Other Qualifications, and Advancement

For most precision equipment repairers, the most significant source of postsecondary education is on-the-job training. Even in positions where an associate or bachelor's degree is required, an internship or apprenticeship is generally required before a technician is fully qualified. In some cases, learning these trades can take as many as seven years.

Education and training. Most employers require at least a high school diploma for beginning precision instrument and equipment repairers. Many employers prefer applicants with some postsecondary education.

The educational background required for camera and photographic equipment repairers varies, but some knowledge of electronics is necessary. Some workers complete postsecondary training, such as an associate degree, in electronics. The job requires the ability to read electronic schematic diagrams and comprehend other technical information, in addition to manual dexterity. New employees are trained on the job in two stages over about a year. First, they learn to repair a single product over a couple of weeks. Then, they learn to repair other products and refine their skills for 6 to 12 months while working under the close supervision of an experienced repairer. Finally,

repairers continually teach themselves through studying manuals and attending manufacturer-sponsored seminars on the specifics of new models.

Training also varies for watch and clock repairers. Several associations, including the American Watchmakers-Clockmakers Institute and the National Association of Watch and Clock Collectors, offer certifications. Some certifications can be completed in a few months; others require simply passing an examination; the most demanding certifications require 3,000 hours, taken over 2 years, of classroom time in technical institutes or colleges. Those who have earned the most demanding certifications are usually the most sought-after by employers. Clock repairers generally require less training than do watch repairers, because watches have smaller components and require greater precision. Some repairers opt to learn through assisting a master watch repairer. Nevertheless, developing proficiency in watch or clock repair requires several years of education and experience.

For musical instrument repairers and tuners, employers prefer individuals with post-high school training in music repair technology. According to a Piano Technicians Guild membership survey, the overwhelming majority of respondents had at least some college education; most had a bachelor's or higher degree, although not always in music repair technology. Almost all repairers have a strong musical background; many are musicians themselves. Also, a basic ability to play the instruments being repaired is normally required. Courses in instrument repair are offered only at a few technical schools and colleges. Correspondence courses are common for piano tuners. Graduates of these programs normally receive additional training on the job, working with an experienced repairer. Many musical instrument repairers and tuners begin learning their trade on the job as assistants or apprentices. Trainees perform a variety of tasks around the shop. Full qualification usually requires 2 to 5 years of training and practice. Musical instrument repair and tuning requires good manual dexterity, a strong sense of pitch, and good hand-eye coordination.

Medical equipment repairers' training includes on-the-job training, manufacturer training classes, and associate degree programs. While an associate degree in electronics or medical technology is normally required, training varies by specialty. For those with a background in electronics, on-the-job training is more common for workers repairing less electronically sophisticated equipment, such as hospital beds or electric wheelchairs. An associate or even a bachelor's degree, often in medical technology or engineering, and a passing grade on a certification exam is likely to be required of persons repairing more complicated equipment, such as CAT scanners and defibrillators. Many repairers are trained in the military. New repairers begin by observing and assisting an experienced worker over a period of 3 to 6 months, learning a single piece of equipment at a time. Gradually, they begin working independently, while still under close supervision. Biomedical equipment repairers are constantly learning new technologies and equipment through seminars, self-study, and certification exams.

Educational requirements for other precision instrument and equipment repair jobs also vary, but include a high school diploma, with a focus on mathematics and science courses. Because

Projections data from the National Employment Matrix

Occupational Title	SOC Code	Employment, 2006	Projected employment, 2016	Change, 2006-16	
				Number	Percent
Precision instrument and equipment repairers.................................	49-9060	68,000	77,000	8,700	13
Camera and photographic equipment repairers	49-9061	4,400	4,300	-100	-2
Medical equipment repairers..	49-9062	38,000	46,000	8,200	22
Musical instrument repairers and tuners.................................	49-9063	6,000	6,200	200	3
Watch repairers	49-9064	3,800	3,600	-200	-5
Precision instrument and equipment repairers, all other..............	49-9069	16,000	17,000	700	4

NOTE: Data in this table are rounded. See the discussion of the employment projections table in the *Handbook* introductory chapter on *Occupational Information Included in the Handbook.*

repairers need to understand blueprints, electrical schematic diagrams, and electrical, hydraulic, and electromechanical systems, most employers require an associate or sometimes a bachelor's degree in instrumentation and control, electronics, or a related engineering field. In addition to formal education, a year or two of on-the-job training is required before a repairer is considered fully qualified. Many instrument and equipment repairers begin by working in a factory in another capacity, such as repairing electrical equipment. As companies seek to improve efficiency, other types of repair workers are trained to repair precision measuring equipment.

Certification and other qualifications. Much training takes place on the job. The ability to read and understand technical manuals is important. Necessary physical qualities include good fine-motor skills and acute vision. Those working with musical instruments must also have good hearing. Also, precision equipment repairers must be able to pay close attention to details, enjoy problem solving, and have the desire to disassemble machines to see how they work. Most precision equipment repairers must be able to work alone with minimal supervision.

Because many precision instrument and equipment repairers are self-employed, they must also have business skills. Although business most often comes from word-of-mouth advertising, repairers must nevertheless work to establish themselves in the industry. Further, they must manage their business operations, which may mean purchasing insurance and managing their own accounting.

Although most of the positions in this field do not require certification, it may be helpful in finding a job or demonstrating competency to prospective clients. There are several certifications possible in this diverse group of repairers. Information on various certifications is available from the sources of additional information at the end of the statement.

Advancement. Advancement opportunities vary greatly among precision instrument and equipment repairers. For self-employed repairers, advancement may mean the ability to charge more for their services. For workers who are employed by firms, supervisory opportunities are available. In both cases, an experienced worker may become a mentor to someone who is new to the field.

Employment

Precision instrument and equipment repairers held 68,000 jobs in 2006. Employment was distributed among the detailed occupations as follows:

Medical equipment repairers	38,000
Musical instrument repairers and tuners	6,000
Camera and photographic equipment repairers	4,400
Watch repairers	3,800
Precision instrument and equipment repairers, all other	16,000

Medical equipment repairers often work for hospitals or wholesale equipment suppliers, while those in the occupation titled "all other precision instrument repairers" frequently work for manufacturing companies and wholesalers of durable goods. About 1 out of 6 precision instrument and equipment repairers was self-employed—most are proprietors of jewelry, camera, medical equipment, or music repair services.

Job Outlook

Good opportunities are expected for most types of precision instrument and equipment repairer jobs. Overall employment growth is projected to be about as fast as the average for all occupations over the 2006-16 period; however, projected growth varies by detailed occupation.

Employment change. Projected employment growth for precision instrument and equipment repairers varies greatly by specialty.

Employment of camera and photographic equipment repairers is projected to decline by about 2 percent between 2006 and 2016, and employment of watch repairers is projected to decline 5 percent over the same period. These occupations are in decline primarily because the products they service are often less expensive to replace than to repair. Most of the workers who remain in this industry will specialize in repair of expensive watches and cameras, as well as antiques.

Over the same time period, the employment of musical instrument repairers and tuners is projected to increase 3 percent, which is slower than average. Band and orchestra programs in high schools continue to provide most of the business for these workers, and they have been declining for several years. With fewer new musicians, there will be a slump in instrument rentals, purchases, and repairs. In the meantime, however, there continues to be a demand for these services, and new opportunities should continue to arise as the population grows.

The medical equipment repairer occupation is projected to increase 22 percent between 2006 and 2016, which is much faster than the average for all occupations, as a result of increased demand for medical services and increasing complexity of the equipment used in hospitals and clinics. Opportunities should be increasingly good for those who have a strong understanding of software and electronics, as many new medical devices are increasingly reliant on computers.

Over the same time period, employment of other precision instrument and equipment repairers is projected to increase 4 percent, more slowly than average, as most of them work in declining manufacturing industries. Nevertheless, these workers can expect to play an increasingly large role in those industries, as automation continues to dominate modern manufacturing.

Job prospects. Despite varying levels of growth in the various occupations, almost all workers in these fields can expect good job prospects over the next decade. As the baby boomer generation nears retirement, many skilled workers in these occupations are expected to leave the workforce. Additionally, many technical schools and other programs offering courses in these occupations have closed, leading to a shortage of qualified workers. Individuals with strong apprenticeships or internships should have the best prospects as instrumentation continues to become more complex and requires ever greater skill to repair.

Earnings

The following tabulation shows median annual earnings for various precision instrument and equipment repairers in May 2006:

Medical equipment repairers...$40,580
Camera and photographic equipment repairers 34,850
Watch repairers 30,900
Musical instrument repairers and tuners...............................29,200
Precision instrument and equipment repairers, all other.......46,250

Earnings ranged from less than $16,230 for the lowest 10 percent of musical instrument repairers and tuners to more than $69,280 for the highest 10 percent in the occupation all other precision instrument and equipment repairers in May 2006.

Earnings within the different occupations vary significantly, depending upon skill levels. For example, a lesser skilled watch and clock repairer may simply change batteries and replace worn wrist straps, while a highly skilled watch and clock repairer with years of training and experience may rebuild and replace worn parts.

Related Occupations

Many precision instrument and equipment repairers work with precision mechanical and electronic equipment. Other workers who repair precision mechanical and electronic equipment include computer, automated teller, and office machine repairers and coin, vending, and amusement machine servicers and repairers. Other workers who make precision items include medical, dental, and ophthalmic laboratory technicians. Some precision instrument and equipment repairers work with a wide array of industrial equipment. Their work environment and responsibilities are similar to those of industrial machinery mechanics and maintenance workers. Much of the work of watch repairers is similar to that of jewelers and precious stone and metal workers. Camera repairers' work is similar to that of electronic home entertainment equipment installers and repairers; both occupations work with consumer electronics that are based around a circuit board, but that also involve numerous moving mechanical parts.

Sources of Additional Information

For information on musical instrument repair, including schools offering training, contact:

➤ National Association of Professional Band Instrument Repair Technicians (NAPBIRT), P.O. Box 51, Normal, IL 61761. Internet: **http://www.napbirt.org**

For additional information on piano tuning and repair work, contact:

➤ Piano Technicians Guild, 4444 Forest Ave., Kansas City, KS 66106. Internet: **http://www.ptg.org**

For information about training, mentoring programs, employers, and schools with programs in precision instrumentation, automation, and control, contact:

➤ ISA-The Instrumentation, Systems, and Automation Society, 67 Alexander Dr, Research Triangle Park, NC 27709. Internet: **http://www.isa.org**

For information about watch and clock repair and a list of schools with related programs of study, contact:

➤ American Watchmakers-Clockmakers Institute (AWI), 701 Enterprise Dr., Harrison, OH 45030-1696. Internet: **http://www.awi-net.org**

➤ National Association of Watch and Clock Collectors, 514 Poplar St., Columbia, PA 17512-2130. Internet: **http://www.nawcc.org**

For information about medical equipment technicians and a list of schools with related programs of study, contact:

➤ Association for the Advancement of Medical Instrumentation (AAMI), 1110 North Glebe Rd., Suite 220, Arlington, VA 22201-4795. Internet: **http://www.aami.org**

Production Occupations

Assemblers and Fabricators

(O*NET 51-2011.00, 51-2021.00, 51-2022.00, 51-2023.00, 51-2031.00, 51-2041.00, 51-2091.00, 51-2092.00, 51-2093.00, 51-2099.99)

Significant Points

- Most assemblers work on teams, making good communication skills and the ability to get along with others important.

- A high school diploma is sufficient for most jobs, but experience and extra training is needed for more advanced assembly work.

- Employment is projected to decline slowly.

- Job opportunities are expected to be good for qualified applicants in the manufacturing sector, particularly in jobs needing more training.

Nature of the Work

Assemblers and fabricators play an important role in the manufacturing process. They assemble both finished products and the pieces that go into them. The products they assemble using tools, machines, and their hands range from entire airplanes to intricate timing devices. They fabricate and assemble household appliances, automobiles and automobile engines and parts, computers, electronic devices, and more.

Changes in technology have transformed the manufacturing and assembly process. Automated manufacturing systems now use robots, computers, programmable motion control devices, and various sensing technologies. These systems change the way in which goods are made and affect the jobs of those who make them. The more advanced assemblers must be able to work with these new technologies and use them to produce goods.

The job of an assembler or fabricator ranges from very easy to very complicated, requiring a range of knowledge and skills. Skilled assemblers putting together complex machines, for example, begin by reading detailed schematics or blueprints that show how to assemble the machine. After determining how parts should connect, they use hand or power tools to trim, shim, cut, and make other adjustments to fit components together and align properly. Once the parts are properly aligned, they connect them with bolts and screws or by welding or soldering pieces together.

Careful quality control is important throughout the assembly process, so assemblers look for faulty components and mistakes in the assembly process. They help to fix problems before more defective products are produced.

Manufacturing techniques are evolving away from traditional assembly line systems toward "lean" manufacturing systems, which are causing the nature of assemblers' work to change.

Lean manufacturing uses teams of workers to produce entire products or components. *Team assemblers* may still work on an assembly line, but they rotate through different tasks, rather than specializing in a single task. The team also may decide how the work is assigned and how different tasks are performed. This worker flexibility helps companies cover for absent workers, improves productivity, and increases companies' ability to respond to changes in demand by shifting labor from one product line to another. For example, if demand for a product drops, companies may reduce the total number of workers producing it, asking the remaining workers to perform more stages of the assembly process. Some aspects of lean production, such as rotating tasks and seeking worker input on improving the assembly process, are common to all assembly and fabrication occupations.

Although more than half of all assemblers and fabricators are classified as "team assemblers," others specialize in producing one type of product or perform the same or similar functions throughout the assembly process. These workers are classified according to the products they assemble or produce. *Electrical and electronic equipment assemblers*, for example, build products such as electric motors, computers, electronic control devices, and sensing equipment. Automated systems have eliminated much of the mass production work in electronic assembly, so a growing amount of the work of electrical and electronic assemblers is manual assembly during the small-scale production of electronic devices used in avionic systems, military systems, and medical equipment.

Electromechanical equipment assemblers assemble and modify electromechanical devices such as household appliances, dynamometers, actuators, or vending machines. *Coil winders, tapers, and finishers* wind wire coil used in resistors, transformers, generators, and electric motors. *Engine and other machine assemblers* construct, assemble, or rebuild engines and turbines, and machines used in agriculture, construction, mining, and almost all manufacturing industries, including rolling mills, textiles, paper, and food processing. *Aircraft structure, surfaces, rigging, and systems assemblers* assemble, fit, fasten, and install parts of airplanes, space vehicles, or missiles, including tails and wings, landing gear, and heating and ventilation systems. *Structural metal fabricators and fitters* cut, align, and fit together structural metal parts prior to welding or riveting. *Fiberglass laminators and fabricators* create products made of fiberglass, mainly boat decks and hulls and automobile body parts. *Timing device assemblers, adjusters, and calibrators* perform precision assembling or adjusting of timing devices within very narrow tolerances.

It has become more common to involve assemblers and fabricators in product development. Designers and engineers consult manufacturing workers during the design stage to improve product reliability and manufacturing efficiency. For example, an assembler may tell a designer that the dash of a new car design will be too difficult to install quickly and consistently. The designer could then redesign the dash to make it easier to install.

Some experienced assemblers work with designers and engineers to build prototypes or test products. These assemblers must be able to read and interpret complex engineering specifications from text, drawings, and computer-aided drafting systems. They also may need to use a variety of tools and precision measuring instruments.

Work environment. The working environment for assemblers and fabricators is improving, but varies by plant and by industry. Many physically difficult tasks have been made much easier through the use of hydraulic and electromechanical equipment, such as manually tightening massive bolts or moving heavy parts into position. Assembly work, however, may still involve long periods of standing or sitting.

Most factories today are generally clean, well-lit, and well-ventilated, and depending on what type of work is being performed, they may also need to be dirt and dust-free. Electronic and electromechanical assemblers particularly must work in environments free of dust that could affect the operation of the products they build. Some assemblers may also come into contact with potentially harmful chemicals or fumes, but ventilation systems and other safety precautions normally minimize any harmful effects. Other assemblers may come in contact with oil and grease, and their working areas may be quite noisy.

Most full-time assemblers work a 40-hour week, although overtime and shift work is common in some industries. Work schedules of assemblers may vary at plants with more than one shift.

Training, Other Qualifications, and Advancement

The education level and qualifications needed to enter these jobs vary depending on the industry and employer. While a high school diploma or GED is sufficient for most jobs, experience and extra training is needed for more advanced assembly work.

Education and training. Most applicants for assembler positions need only a high school diploma or GED. However, some employers may require specialized training or an associate degree for the most skilled assembly jobs. For example, jobs with electrical, electronic, and aircraft and motor vehicle products manufacturers typically require more education and experience. Other positions may require only brief on-the-job training, sometimes including employer-sponsored classroom instruction.

Other qualifications. Assembly workers must be able to follow instructions carefully, which may require some basic reading skills and the ability to follow diagrams and pictures. Manual dexterity and the ability to carry out complex, repetitive tasks quickly and methodically also are important. For some positions, the ability to lift heavy objects may be needed. Team assemblers also need good interpersonal and communication skills to be able to work well with their teammates. Good eyesight is necessary for assemblers and fabricators who work with small parts. Plants that make electrical and electronic products may test applicants for color vision because their products often contain many differently colored wires.

Advancement. As assemblers and fabricators become more experienced, they may progress to jobs that require greater skill and may be given more responsibility. Experienced assemblers

Electrical and electronics assemblers solder electronic parts together.

may become product repairers if they have learned the many assembly operations and understand the construction of a product. These workers fix assembled pieces that operators or inspectors have identified as defective. Assemblers also can advance to quality control jobs or be promoted to supervisor. Experienced assemblers and fabricators also may become members of research and development teams, working with engineers and other project designers to design, develop, and build prototypes, and test new product models. In some companies, assemblers can become trainees for one of the skilled trades, such as machinist. Those with a background in math, science, and computers may advance to become programmers or operators of more highly automated production equipment.

Employment

Assemblers and fabricators held nearly 2.1 million jobs in 2006. They worked in almost every industry, but 3 out of 4 worked in manufacturing. Within the manufacturing sector, assembly of transportation equipment, such as aircraft, autos, trucks, and buses, accounted for 19 percent of all jobs. Assembly of computers and electronic products accounted for another 11 percent of all jobs. Other industries that employ many assemblers and fabricators are machinery manufacturing: heating and air-conditioning equipment; agriculture, construction, and mining machinery; and engine, turbine, and power transmission equipment; electrical equipment, appliance, and component manufacturing: lighting, household appliances, and electrical equipment; and fabricated metal products.

The following tabulation shows the employment of assemblers and fabricators in the manufacturing industries that employed the most workers in 2006:

Motor vehicle parts manufacturing..................................145,000
Motor vehicle manufacturing..106,000
Semiconductor and other electronic component
  manufacturing...88,000
Navigational, measuring, electromedical, and control
  instruments manufacturing...76,000
Architectural and structural metals manufacturing............74,000

Assemblers and fabricators also work in many other non-manufacturing industries. Twelve percent were employed by employment services firms, mostly as temporary workers; most of these temporary workers were likely assigned to manufacturing plants. Wholesale and retail trade firms employed the next highest number of assemblers and fabricators. Many of these assemblers perform the final assembly of goods before the item is delivered to the customer. For example, most imported furniture is shipped in pieces and assemblers for furniture wholesalers and retailers put together the furniture prior to delivery.

Team assemblers, the largest specialty, accounted for 61 percent of assembler and fabricator jobs. The distribution of employment among the various types of assemblers was as follows in 2006:

Team assemblers..1,274,000
Electrical and electronic equipment assemblers 213,000
Structural metal fabricators and fitters............................103,000
Electromechanical equipment assemblers 60,000
Engine and other machine assemblers..............................45,000
Fiberglass laminators and fabricators 33,000
Aircraft structure, surfaces, rigging, and systems
  assemblers 28,000
Coil winders, tapers, and finishers...................................23,000
Timing device assemblers, adjusters, and calibrators 2,500
Assemblers and fabricators, all other...............................292,000

Job Outlook

Employment of assemblers and fabricators is projected to decline slowly, primarily reflecting productivity growth and strong foreign competition in manufacturing. Job opportunities are expected to be good for qualified applicants in the manufacturing sector, particularly in jobs needing more training.

Employment change. Employment of assemblers and fabricators is expected to decline slowly by 4 percent between 2006 and 2016. Within the manufacturing sector, employment of assemblers and fabricators will be determined largely by the growth or decline in the production of certain manufactured goods. In general, despite projected growth in the output of manufactured goods, employment overall is expected to decline as the whole sector becomes more automated and is able to produce more with fewer workers. However, some individual industries are projected to have more jobs than others. The aircraft products and parts industry is projected to gain jobs over the decade as demand for new commercial and military planes grows significantly. Thus, the need for aircraft structure, surfaces, rigging, and systems assemblers is expected to grow. In addition, because much of the assembly in the aerospace industry is done in hard-to-reach locations—inside airplane fuselages or gear boxes, for example—which are unsuited to robots, aircraft assemblers will not be as easily replaced by automated processes.

In most other manufacturing industries, employment of assemblers and fabricators will be negatively affected by increasing automation, improving productivity, and the shift of assembly to countries with lower labor costs. The effects of automation, though, will be felt more among some types of assemblers and fabricators than among others. Automation will replace workers in operations with a large volume of repetitive work. Automation will have less effect on the assembly of parts that are irregular in size or location.

The use of team production techniques has been one factor in the continuing success of the manufacturing sector, boosting productivity and improving the quality of goods. Thus, while the number of assemblers overall is expected to decline in manufacturing, the number of team assemblers will grow or remain stable as more manufacturing plants convert to using team production techniques.

Other manufacturers have sent their assembly functions to countries where labor costs are lower. Decisions by U.S. corporations to move assembly to other nations should limit employment growth for assemblers in some industries, but a free trade environment also may lead to growth in the export of goods assembled in the United States.

The largest increase in the number of assemblers and fabricators is projected to be in the employment services industry, which supplies temporary workers to various industries. Temporary workers are gaining in importance in the manufacturing sector and elsewhere as companies strive for a more flexible workforce to meet the fluctuations in the market. There will also be more jobs for assemblers and fabricators in the wholesale and retail sectors of the economy. As more goods come unassembled from foreign countries to save on shipping costs, wholesalers and retailers are increasingly assembling products before selling them to their customers.

Job prospects. Job opportunities for assemblers are expected to be good for qualified applicants in the manufacturing sector, particularly in jobs needing more training. Some employers report difficulty finding qualified applicants looking for manufacturing employment. The best opportunities should be with smaller manufacturers as large, high-profile companies tend to attract more applicants. In addition to new jobs stemming from growth in this occupation, many job openings will result from the need to replace workers leaving or retiring from this large occupational group. For example, foreign automobile manufacturers who built plants in the 1980s are expecting a large number of retirements in the next decade and a surge in demand for team assemblers.

Projections data from the National Employment Matrix

Occupational Title	SOC Code	Employment, 2006	Projected employment, 2016	Change, 2006-16	
				Number	Percent
Assemblers and fabricators	51-2000	2,075,000	1,982,000	-93,000	-4
Aircraft structure, surfaces, rigging, and systems assemblers	51-2011	28,000	32,000	3,600	13
Electrical, electronics, and electromechanical assemblers	51-2020	297,000	227,000	-70,000	-23
Coil winders, tapers, and finishers	51-2021	23,000	16,000	-7,000	-30
Electrical and electronic equipment assemblers	51-2022	213,000	156,000	-57,000	-27
Electromechanical equipment assemblers	51-2023	60,000	55,000	-5,500	-9
Engine and other machine assemblers	51-2031	45,000	41,000	-3,900	-9
Structural metal fabricators and fitters.....................................	51-2041	103,000	103,000	-200	0
Miscellaneous assemblers and fabricators	51-2090	1,602,000	1,579,000	-23,000	-1
Fiberglass laminators and fabricators	51-2091	33,000	35,000	2,100	6
Team assemblers..	51-2092	1,274,000	1,275,000	700	0
Timing device assemblers, adjusters, and calibrators	51-2093	2,500	2,300	-200	-8
Assemblers and fabricators, all other..	51-2099	292,000	266,000	-25,000	-9

NOTE: Data in this table are rounded. See the discussion of the employment projections table in the *Handbook* introductory chapter on *Occupational Information Included in the Handbook*.

Earnings

Earnings vary by industry, geographic region, skill, educational level, and complexity of the machinery operated. Median hourly wage-and-salary earnings of team assemblers were $11.63 in May 2006. The middle 50 percent earned between $9.22 and $14.93. The lowest 10 percent earned less than $7.69, and the highest 10 percent earned more than $19.14. Median hourly wage-and-salary earnings in the manufacturing industries employing the largest numbers of team assemblers were as follows:

Motor vehicle manufacturing...$21.60
Motor vehicle parts manufacturing.......................................13.06
Other wood products manufacturing.....................................11.11
Plastics products manufacturing 10.64
Employment services..9.20

Median hourly wage-and-salary earnings of electrical and electronic equipment assemblers were $12.29 in May 2006. The middle 50 percent earned between $9.84 and $15.80. The lowest 10 percent earned less than $8.25, and the highest 10 percent earned more than $19.81. Median hourly wage-and-salary earnings in the manufacturing industries employing the largest numbers of electrical and electronic equipment assemblers were as follows:

Navigational, measuring, electromedical, and control
  instruments manufacturing..$13.42
Electrical equipment manufacturing......................................13.05
Computer and peripheral equipment manufacturing 12.80
Communications equipment manufacturing...........................11.96
Semiconductor and other electronic component
  manufacturing 11.45

In May 2006, other assemblers and fabricators had the following median hourly wage-and-salary earnings:

Aircraft structure, surfaces, rigging, and systems
  assemblers...$21.83
Engine and other machine assemblers 15.99
Structural metal fabricators and fitters....................................14.56
Timing device assemblers, adjusters, and calibrators 13.86
Electromechanical equipment assemblers 13.25
Coil winders, tapers, and finishers...12.64
Fiberglass laminators and fabricators 12.49
Assemblers and fabricators, all other.....................................12.85

Many assemblers and fabricators are members of labor unions. These unions include the International Association of Machinists and Aerospace Workers; the United Automobile, Aerospace and Agricultural Implement Workers of America; the International Brotherhood of Electrical Workers; and the United Steelworkers of America.

Related Occupations

Other occupations that involve operating machines and tools and assembling products include welding, soldering, and brazing workers and machine setters, operators, and tenders—metal and plastic. Also, both millwrights and tool and die makers assemble complex manufacturing equipment. Assemblers and fabricators also are responsible for some quality control and product testing, as are inspectors, testers, sorters, samplers, and weighers.

Sources of Additional Information

Information about employment opportunities for assemblers is available from local offices of the State employment service and from locals of the unions mentioned earlier.

Food Processing Occupations

(O*NET ,51-3011.00, 51-3021.00, 51-3022.00, 51-3023.00, 51-3091.00, 51-3092.00, 51-3093.00, 35-1011.00)

Significant Points

- Most workers in manual food processing jobs require little or no training prior to being hired.

- As more jobs involving cutting and processing meat shift from retail stores to food processing plants, job growth will be concentrated among lesser skilled workers, who are employed primarily in manufacturing.

- Highly skilled bakers should be in demand.

Nature of the Work

Food processing occupations include many different types of workers who process raw food products into the finished goods sold by grocers, wholesalers, restaurants, or institutional food services. These workers perform a variety of tasks and are responsible for producing many of the food products found in every household. Some of these workers are bakers, others process meat, and still others operate food processing equipment.

Bakers mix and bake ingredients according to recipes to produce varying quantities of breads, pastries, and other baked goods. Bakers commonly are employed in grocery stores and specialty shops and produce small quantities of breads, pastries, and other baked goods for consumption on premises or for sale as specialty baked goods. While the quantities are often small, the varieties of bread usually are not. Specialty handcrafted—or artisan—bread, comes with seeds, nuts, fruits, olives, and cheese, which can be included in a crusty loaf, round loaf, flat or even focaccia bread. Bakers can also add a variety of flavors, too, such as rosemary, pecan, fig, garlic, red pepper, sesame, and anise.

In manufacturing, bakers produce goods in large quantities, using high-volume mixing machines, ovens, and other equipment. Goods produced in large quantities usually are available for sale through distributors, grocery stores, supermarkets, or manufacturers' outlets.

Other food processing workers convert animal carcasses into manageable pieces of meat, known as boxed meat or case-ready meat, suitable for sale to wholesalers and retailers. The nature of their jobs varies significantly depending on the stage of the process in which they are involved. Butchers and meat cutters, for example, work primarily in groceries and wholesale establishments that provide meat to restaurants and other retailers; whereas, meat, poultry, and fish cutters and trimmers commonly work in animal slaughtering and processing plants.

In animal slaughtering and processing plants, slaughterers and *meat packers* slaughter cattle, hogs, goats, and sheep, and cut the carcasses into large wholesale cuts, such as rounds, loins, ribs, tenders, and chucks, to facilitate the handling, distribution,

marketing, and sale of meat. In most plants, some slaughterers and meat packers further process the large parts into cuts that are ready for retail stores. Retailers and grocers increasingly prefer such prepackaged meat products because a butcher isn't needed to display and sell them. Slaughterers and meat packers also produce hamburger meat and meat trimmings, preparing sausages, luncheon meats, and other fabricated meat products. They usually work on assembly lines, with each individual responsible for only a few of the many cuts needed to process a carcass. Depending on the type of cut, these workers use knives; cleavers; meat saws; bandsaws; or other potentially dangerous equipment.

Poultry cutters and trimmers slaughter and cut up chickens, turkeys, and other types of poultry. Although the poultry processing industry is becoming increasingly automated, many jobs, such as trimming, packing, and deboning, are still done manually. Most poultry cutters and trimmers perform routine cuts on poultry as it moves along production lines.

Meat, poultry, and fish cutters and trimmers also prepare ready-to-heat foods, usually at processing plants. This preparation often entails filleting meat, poultry, or fish; cutting it into bite-sized pieces or tenders; preparing and adding vegetables; and applying sauces and flavorings, marinades, or breading. These case-ready products are gaining in popularity as they offer quick and easy preparation for consumers while, in many cases, also offering a healthier option.

Manufacturing and retail establishments are likely to employ fish cutters and trimmers, also called *fish cleaners*. These workers primarily scale, cut, and dress fish by removing the head, scales, and other inedible portions and cutting the fish into steaks or fillets. In retail markets, these workers may also wait on customers and clean fish to order.

Butchers and meat cutters process meat at later stages of production. Those who work for large grocery stores, wholesale establishments that supply meat to restaurants, or institutional food service facilities separate wholesale cuts of meat into retail cuts or smaller pieces, known as primals. These butchers cut meat into steaks and chops, shape and tie roasts, and grind beef for sale as chopped meat. Boneless cuts are prepared using knives, slicers, or power cutters, while bandsaws and cleavers are required to cut bone-in pieces of meat. Butchers and meat cutters in retail food stores also may weigh, wrap, and label the cuts of meat; arrange them in refrigerated cases for display; and prepare special cuts to fill unique orders by customers.

Others in food processing occupations include *food batchmakers*, who set up and operate equipment that mixes, blends, or cooks ingredients used in the manufacture of food products according to formulas or recipes; *food cooking machine operators and tenders*, who operate or tend cooking equipment, such as steam-cooking vats, deep-fry cookers, pressure cookers, kettles, and boilers to prepare food products, such as meat, sugar, cheese, and grain; and *food and tobacco roasting, baking, and drying machine operators and tenders*, who use equipment to reduce the moisture content of food or tobacco products or to prepare food for canning. The machines they use include hearth ovens, kiln driers, roasters, char kilns, steam ovens, and vacuum drying equipment.

Work environment. Working conditions vary by type and size of establishment. Most traditional bakers work in bakeries, cake shops, hot-bread shops, hotels, restaurants, cafeterias, and in the bakery departments of supermarkets. Bakers may work under hot and noisy conditions. They typically work under strict order deadlines and critical time-sensitive baking requirements, both of which can induce stress.

Although many bakers often work as part of a team, they also may work alone when baking particular items. These workers may supervise assistants and teach apprentices and trainees. Bakers in retail establishments may be required to serve customers. Bakers usually work odd hours in shifts and may work early mornings, evenings, weekends, and holidays.

In animal slaughtering and processing plants and in large retail food establishments, butchers and meat cutters work in large meat cutting rooms equipped with power machines and conveyors. In small retail markets, the butcher or fish cleaner may work in a cramped space behind the meat or fish counter. To prevent viral and bacterial infections, work areas are kept clean and sanitary.

Butchers and meat cutters, poultry and fish cutters and trimmers, and slaughterers and meatpackers often work in cold, damp rooms. Refrigerated work areas prevent meat from spoiling; they are damp because meat cutting generates large amounts of blood, condensation, and fat. Cool, damp floors increase the likelihood of slips and falls. In addition, cool temperatures, long periods of standing, and repetitive physical tasks make the work tiring. As a result, butchers as well as meat, poultry, and fish cutters and trimmers are more susceptible to injury than are most other workers.

Injuries include cuts and occasional amputations, which occur when knives, cleavers, or power tools are used improperly. Also, repetitive slicing and lifting often lead to cumulative trauma injuries, such as carpal tunnel syndrome. To reduce the incidence of cumulative trauma injuries, some employers have reduced employee workloads, added prescribed rest periods, redesigned jobs and tools, and promoted increased awareness of early warning signs as steps to prevent further injury. Nevertheless, workers in the occupation still face the serious threat of disabling injuries.

Workers who operate food processing machinery typically work in production areas that are specially designed for food preservation or processing. Food batchmakers, in particular, work in kitchen-type, assembly-line production facilities. Because this work involves food, work areas must meet governmental sanitary regulations. The ovens, as well as the motors of blenders, mixers, and other equipment, often make work areas very warm and noisy. There are some hazards, such as burns, created by the equipment that these workers use.

Food batchmakers; food and tobacco roasting, baking, and drying machine operators; and food cooking machine operators and tenders spend a great deal of time on their feet and generally work a regular 40-hour week that may include evening and night shifts.

Training, Other Qualifications, and Advancement

Training varies widely among food processing occupations. However, most manual food processing workers require little or no training before being hired.

Education and training. Bakers often start as apprentices or trainees. Apprentice bakers usually start in craft bakeries, while trainees usually begin in store bakeries, such as those in supermarkets. Bakers need to become skilled in baking, icing, and decorating. Knowledge of bakery products and ingredients, as well as mechanical mixing and baking equipment, is also important. Many apprentice bakers participate in correspondence study and may work towards a certificate in baking. Working as a baker's assistant or at other activities that involve handling food is also a useful way to train.

The skills needed to be a baker are often underestimated. Bakers need to know about ingredients and nutrition, government health and sanitation regulations, business concepts, applied chemistry—including how ingredients combine and how they are affected by heat, and production processes, including how to operate and maintain machinery. Computers often operate high-speed automated equipment typically found in modern food plants.

Most butchers as well as poultry and fish cutters and trimmers acquire their skills through on-the-job training programs. The length of training varies significantly. Simple cutting operations require a few days to learn, while more complicated tasks, such as eviscerating slaughtered animals, generally require several months of training. The training period for highly skilled butchers at the retail level may be 1 or 2 years.

Generally, trainees begin by doing less difficult jobs, such as making simple cuts or removing bones. Under the guidance of experienced workers, trainees learn the proper use and care of tools and equipment, while also learning how to prepare various cuts of meat. After demonstrating skill with various meat cutting tools, trainees learn to divide carcasses into wholesale cuts and wholesale cuts into retail and individual portions. Trainees also may learn to roll and tie roasts, prepare sausage, and cure meat. Those employed in retail food establishments often are taught operations, such as inventory control, meat buying, and

In large grocery stores, butchers and meat cutters separate wholesale cuts of meat into retail cuts or individually sized servings.

Projections data from the National Employment Matrix

Occupational Title	SOC Code	Employment, 2006	Projected employment, 2016	Change, 2006-16	
				Number	Percent
Food processing occupations	51-3000	705,000	764,000	59,000	8
Bakers	51-3011	149,000	164,000	15,000	10
Butchers and other meat, poultry, and fish processing workers....	51-3020	398,000	431,000	34,000	8
Butchers and meat cutters	51-3021	131,000	134,000	2,500	2
Meat, poultry, and fish cutters and trimmers...........................	51-3022	144,000	160,000	16,000	11
Slaughterers and meat packers...	51-3023	122,000	138,000	16,000	13
Miscellaneous food processing workers	51-3090	158,000	169,000	10,000	7
Food and tobacco roasting, baking, and drying machine operators and tenders	51-3091	19,000	21,000	2,000	11
Food batchmakers	51-3092	95,000	105,000	10,000	11
Food cooking machine operators and tenders...........................	51-3093	44,000	42,000	-2,100	-5

NOTE: Data in this table are rounded. See the discussion of the employment projections table in the *Handbook* introductory chapter on *Occupational Information Included in the Handbook*.

recordkeeping. In addition, growing concern about food-borne pathogens in meats has led employers to offer numerous safety seminars and extensive training in food safety to employees.

On-the-job training is common among food machine operators and tenders. They learn to run the different types of equipment by watching and helping other workers. Training can last anywhere from a month to a year, depending on the complexity of the tasks and the number of products involved. A degree in an appropriate area—dairy processing for those working in dairy product operations, for example—is helpful for advancement to a lead worker or a supervisory role. Most food batchmakers participate in on-the-job training, usually from about a month to a year. Some food batchmakers learn their trade through an approved apprenticeship program.

Other qualifications. Bakers need to be able to follow instructions, have an eye for detail, and communicate well with others.

Meat, poultry, and fish cutters and trimmers need manual dexterity, good depth perception, color discrimination, and good hand-eye coordination. They also need physical strength to lift and move heavy pieces of meat. Butchers and fish cleaners who wait on customers should have a pleasant personality, a neat appearance, and the ability to communicate clearly. In some States, a health certificate is required for employment.

Certification and advancement. Bakers have the option of obtaining certification through the Retails Bakers of America. While not mandatory, obtaining certification assures the public and prospective employers that the baker has sufficient skills and knowledge to work at a retail baking establishment.

The Retail Bakers of America offer certification for four levels of competence with a focus on several broad areas, including baking sanitation, management, retail sales, and staff training. Those who wish to become certified must satisfy a combination of education and experience requirements prior to taking an examination. The education and experience requirements vary by the level of certification desired. For example, a certified journey baker requires no formal education but a minimum of 1 year of work experience. On the other hand, a certified master baker must have earned the certified baker designation, and must have completed 30 hours of sanitation coursework approved by a culinary school or government agency, 30 hours of professional development courses or workshops, and a minimum of 8 years of commercial or retail baking experience.

Food processing workers in retail or wholesale establishments may progress to supervisory jobs, such as department managers or team leaders in supermarkets. A few of these workers may become buyers for wholesalers or supermarket chains. Some food processing workers go on to open their own markets or bakeries. In processing plants, workers may advance to supervisory positions or become team leaders.

Employment

Food processing workers held 705,000 jobs in 2006. Employment among the various types of food processing occupations was distributed as follows:

Bakers	149,000
Meat, poultry, and fish cutters and trimmers	144,000
Butchers and meat cutters	131,000
Slaughterers and meat packers	122,000
Food batchmakers	95,000
Food cooking machine operators and tenders	44,000
Food and tobacco roasting, baking, and drying machine operators and tenders	19,000

Thirty-four percent of all food processing workers were employed in animal slaughtering and processing plants. Grocery stores employed another 24 percent. Most of the remainder worked in other food manufacturing industries. Butchers, meat cutters, and bakers are employed in almost every city and town in the Nation, while most other food processing jobs are concentrated in communities with food processing plants.

Job Outlook

Job opportunities should be available in all food processing specialties due to the need to replace experienced workers who transfer to other occupations or leave the labor force. Overall employment is expected to increase about as fast as average.

Employment change. Overall employment in the food processing occupations is projected to increase 8 percent during the 2006-16 decade, about as fast as the average for all occupations. Increasingly, cheaper meat imports from abroad will have a negative effect on domestic employment in many food processing occupations. As more jobs involving cutting and processing meat shift from retail stores to food processing plants, job growth will be concentrated among lesser skilled workers, who are employed primarily in manufacturing.

As the Nation's population grows, the demand for meat, poultry, and seafood should continue to increase. Successful marketing by the poultry industry is likely to increase demand for chicken and ready-to-heat products. Similarly, the development of prepared food products that are lower in fat and more nutritious promises to stimulate the consumption of red meat. The trend toward preparing case-ready meat at the processing level also should contribute to demand for animal slaughterers and meat packers, especially as those products become available at lower prices.

Lesser skilled meat, poultry, and fish cutters and trimmers—who work primarily in animal slaughtering and processing plants—should experience 11 percent growth, about as fast as the average for all occupations, and employment of slaughters and meat packers is expected to increase 13 percent, also about as fast as the average. With the growing popularity of labor-intensive, ready-to-heat poultry products, demand for poultry workers should rise steadily. Potentially offsetting growth will be increased automation and plant efficiency, although some technological breakthroughs may be years away. Fish cutters also will be in demand, as the task of preparing ready-to-heat fish goods gradually shifts from retail stores to processing plants. Advances in fish farming, or "aquaculture," should also help meet the growing demand for fish and produce job growth for fish cutters.

Employment of more highly skilled butchers and meat cutters, who work primarily in large supermarkets, is expected to grow 2 percent, which is considered little or no change in employment. The proliferation of case-ready meat products and automation in the animal slaughtering and processing industries are enabling employers to transfer employment from higher paid butchers to lower wage slaughterers and meat packers in meat packing plants. At present, most red meat arrives at grocery stores partially cut up, but a growing share of meat is being delivered prepackaged with additional fat removed to wholesalers and retailers. This trend is resulting in less work and, thus, fewer jobs for retail butchers.

While high-volume production equipment limits the demand for lesser skilled bakers in manufacturing, overall employment of bakers, particularly highly skilled bakers, should increase 10 percent, about as fast as the average for all occupations, due to growing numbers of bakers in stores, specialty shops, and traditional bakeries. In addition to the growing numbers of cookie, muffin, and cinnamon roll bakeries, the numbers of specialty bread and bagel shops have been growing, spurring demand for artisan bread and pastry bakers.

Employment of food batchmakers and food and tobacco cooking and roasting machine operators and tenders, are expected to grow 11 percent each, about as fast as the average for all occupations. However, as more of this work is being done at the manufacturing level rather than at the retail level, potential employment gains may be offset by productivity gains from automated blending and roasting equipment.

Employment of food cooking machine operators and tenders is expected to decline moderately, about 5 percent, as cooking equipment such as steam vats, deep fryers, kettles, and broilers is increasingly automated.

Job prospects. Jobs should be available in all food processing specialties because of the need to replace experienced workers who transfer to other occupations or leave the labor force. Highly skilled bakers should be especially in demand because of growing demand for specialty products and because of the time it takes to learn to make them.

Earnings

Earnings vary by industry, skill, geographic region, and educational level. Median annual earnings of bakers were $22,030 in May 2006. The middle 50 percent earned between $17,720 and $28,190. The highest 10 percent earned more than $35,380, and the lowest 10 percent earned less than $15,180. Median annual earnings in the industries employing the largest numbers of bakers in May 2006 are given in the following tabulation:

Bakeries and tortilla manufacturing	$22,580
Grocery stores	22,170
Specialty food stores	21,900
Full-service restaurants	20,770
Limited-service eating places	19,990

Median annual earnings of butchers and meat cutters were $26,930 in May 2006. The middle 50 percent earned between $20,630 and $35,240. The highest 10 percent earned more than $43,260 annually, while the lowest 10 percent earned less than $16,520. Butchers and meat cutters employed at the retail level typically earn more than those in manufacturing. Median annual earnings in the industries employing the largest numbers of butchers and meat cutters in May 2006 were:

Other general merchandise stores	$34,190
Grocery stores	27,830
Grocery and related product wholesalers	25,690
Specialty food stores	23,180
Animal slaughtering and processing	23,080

Meat, poultry, and fish cutters and trimmers typically earn less than butchers and meat cutters. In May 2006, median annual earnings for these lower skilled workers were $20,370. The middle 50 percent earned between $17,100 and $24,120. The highest 10 percent earned more than $29,070, while the lowest 10 percent earned less than $14,960. The following tabulation shows median annual earnings in the industries employing the largest numbers of meat, poultry, and fish cutters and trimmers in May 2006:

Other general merchandise stores	$25,150
Grocery stores	20,680
Animal slaughtering and processing	20,530
Specialty food stores	19,990
Seafood product preparation and packaging	18,180

Median annual earnings of food batchmakers were $23,100 in May 2006. The middle 50 percent earned between $17,730 and $30,120. The highest 10 percent earned more than $37,930, and the lowest 10 percent earned less than $15,060. The following tabulation presents median annual earnings in the industries employing the largest numbers of food batchmakers in May 2006:

Dairy product manufacturing..$28,570
Fruit and vegetable preserving and specialty food
  manufacturing 25,100
Other food manufacturing..23,550
Sugar and confectionery product manufacturing..................22,370
Bakeries and tortilla manufacturing.......................................21,720

In May 2006, median annual earnings for slaughterers and meat packers were $21,690. The middle 50 percent earned between $18,290 and $25,440. The highest 10 percent earned more than $28,570, and the lowest 10 percent earned less than $15,950. Median annual earnings in animal slaughtering and processing, the industry employing the largest number of slaughterers and meat packers, were $21,730 in May 2006.

Median annual earnings for food cooking machine operators and tenders were $21,280 in May 2006. The middle 50 percent earned between $17,160 and $27,140. The highest 10 percent earned more than $34,350, and the lowest 10 percent earned less than $14,600. Median annual earnings in grocery stores, the industry employing the largest number of food cooking machine operators and tenders, were $19,400 in May 2006.

In May 2006, median annual earnings for food and tobacco roasting, baking, and drying machine operators and tenders were $23,510. The middle 50 percent earned between $18,820 and $31,540. The highest 10 percent earned more than $38,740, and the lowest 10 percent earned less than $15,910.

Food processing workers generally received typical benefits, including pension plans for union members or those employed by grocery stores. However, poultry workers rarely earned substantial benefits. In 2006, 21 percent of all food processing workers were union members or were covered by a union contract. Many food processing workers are members of the United Food and Commercial Workers International Union.

Related Occupations

Food processing workers must be skilled at both hand and machine work and must have some knowledge of processes and techniques that are involved in handling and preparing food. Other occupations that require similar skills and knowledge include chefs, cooks, and food preparation workers.

Sources of Additional Information

For information on various levels of certification as a baker, contact:

➤ Retail Bakers of America, 8201 Greensboro Dr., Suite 300, McLean, VA, 22102

State employment service offices can provide information about job openings for food processing occupations.

Metal Workers and Plastic Workers

Computer Control Programmers and Operators

(O*NET 51-4011.00, 51-4012.00)

Significant Points

- Manufacturing industries employ almost all of these workers.

- Workers learn in apprenticeship programs, informally on the job, and in secondary, vocational, or postsecondary schools; many entrants have previously worked as machinists or machine setters, operators, and tenders.

- Despite the projected slow decline in employment, job opportunities should be excellent, as employers are expected to continue to have difficulty finding qualified workers.

Nature of the Work

Computer control programmers and operators use computer numerically controlled (CNC) machines to cut and shape precision products, such as automobile, aviation, and machine parts. CNC machines operate by reading the code included in a computer-controlled module, which drives the machine tool and performs the functions of forming and shaping a part formerly done by machine operators. CNC machines include machining tools such as lathes, multi-axis spindles, milling machines, laser cutting machines, and wire electrical discharge machines. CNC machines cut away material from a solid block of metal or plastic—known as a workpiece—to form a finished part. Computer control programmers and operators normally produce large quantities of one part, although they may produce small batches or one-of-a-kind items. They use their knowledge of the working properties of metals and their skill with CNC programming to design and carry out the operations needed to make machined products that meet precise specifications.

CNC programmers—also referred to as *numerical tool and process control programmers*—develop the programs that run the machine tools. They review three-dimensional computer aided/automated design (CAD) blueprints of the part and determine the sequence of events that will be needed to make the part. This may involve calculating where to cut or bore into the workpiece, how fast to feed the metal into the machine, and how much metal to remove.

Next, CNC programmers turn the planned machining operations into a set of instructions. These instructions are translated into a computer aided/automated manufacturing (CAM) program containing a set of commands for the machine to follow. These commands normally are a series of numbers (hence, numerical control) that describes where cuts should occur, what type of cut should be used, and the speed of the cut. After the program is developed, CNC programmers and operators check the programs to ensure that the machinery will function properly and that the output will meet specifications. Because a problem with the program could damage costly machinery and cutting tools or simply waste valuable time and materials, computer simulations may be used to check the program before a trial run. If errors are found, the program must be changed and retested until the problem is resolved. In addition, growing connectivity between CAD/CAM software and CNC machine tools is raising productivity by automatically translating designs into instructions for the computer controller on the machine tool. These new CAM technologies enable programs to be easily modified for use on other jobs with similar specifications.

After the programming work is completed, *CNC setup operators*—also referred to as computer-controlled machine tool operators, metal and plastic—set up the machine for the job. They download the program into the machine, load the proper cutting tools into the tool holder, position the workpiece (piece of metal or plastic that is being shaped) on the CNC machine tool—spindle, lathe, milling machine, or other machine—and then start the machine. During the test run of a new program, the setup operator, who may also have some programming skills, or the CNC programmer closely monitors the machine for signs of problems, such as a vibrating work piece, the breakage of cutting tools, or an out-of-specification final product. If a problem is detected, a setup operator or CNC programmer will modify the program using the control module to eliminate the problems or to improve the speed and accuracy of the program.

Once a program is completed, the operation of the CNC machine may move from the more experienced setup operator to a less-skilled machine operator. Operators load workpieces and cutting tools into a machine, press the start button, monitor the machine for problems, and measure the parts produced to check that they match specifications. If they encounter a problem that requires modification to the cutting program, they shut down the machine and wait for a more experienced CNC setup operator to fix the problem. Many CNC operators start at this basic level and gradually perform more setup tasks as they gain experience.

Regardless of skill level, all CNC operators detect some problems by listening for specific sounds—for example, a dull cutting tool that needs changing or excessive vibration. Machine tools rotate at high speeds, which can create problems with harmonic vibrations in the workpiece. Vibrations cause the machine tools to make minor cutting errors, hurting the quality of the product. Operators listen for vibrations and then adjust the cutting speed to compensate. CNC operators also ensure that the workpiece is being properly lubricated and cooled, because the machining of metal products generates a significant amount of heat.

Since CNC machines can operate with limited input from the operator, a single operator may monitor several machines simultaneously. Typically, an operator might monitor two machines cutting relatively simple parts from softer materials, while devoting most of his or her attention to a third machine cutting a much more difficult part from hard metal, such as stainless steel. Operators are often expected to carefully schedule their work so that all of the machines are always operating.

Work environment. Most machine shops are clean, well lit, and ventilated. Most modern CNC machines are partially or totally enclosed, minimizing the exposure of workers to noise, debris, and the lubricants used to cool workpieces during machining. Nevertheless, working around machine tools can be noisy and presents certain dangers, and workers must follow safety precautions. Computer-controlled machine tool operators, metal and plastic, wear protective equipment, such as safety glasses to shield against bits of flying metal and earplugs to dampen machinery noise. They also must exercise caution when handling hazardous coolants and lubricants. The job requires stamina because operators stand most of the day and, at times, may need to lift moderately heavy workpieces.

Numerical tool and process control programmers work on desktop computers in offices that typically are near, but separate from, the shop floor. These work areas usually are clean, well lit, and free of machine noise. Numerical tool and process control programmers occasionally need to enter the shop floor to monitor CNC machining operations. On the shop floor, CNC programmers encounter the same hazards and exercise the same safety precautions as do CNC operators.

Many computer control programmers and operators work a 40-hour week. CNC operators increasingly work evening and weekend shifts as companies justify investments in more expensive machinery by extending hours of operation. Overtime is common during peak production periods.

Training, Other Qualifications, and Advancement

Computer control programmers and operators train in various ways—in apprenticeship programs, informally on the job, and in secondary, vocational, or postsecondary schools. In general, the more skills needed for the job, the more education and training are needed to qualify. Many entrants have previously worked as machinists or machine setters, operators, and tenders.

Education and training. The amount and type of education and training needed depends on the type of job. Entry-level CNC machine operators may need only a couple of weeks of on-the-job training to reach proficiency. Setup operators and programmers, however, may need years of experience or formal training to write or modify programs. Programmers and operators can receive their training in various ways—in ap-

Computer control operators reprogram computer numerically controlled machines.

prenticeship programs, informally on the job, and in secondary, vocational, or postsecondary schools. A growing number of computer control programmers and more skilled operators receive their formal training from community or technical colleges. For some specialized types of programming, such as that needed to produce complex parts for the aerospace or shipbuilding industries, employers may prefer individuals with a degree in engineering.

For those interested in becoming computer control programmers or operators, high school or vocational school courses in mathematics (trigonometry and algebra), blueprint reading, computer programming, metalworking, and drafting are recommended. Apprenticeship programs consist of shop training and related classroom instruction. In shop training, apprentices learn filing, handtapping, and dowel fitting, as well as the operation of various machine tools. Classroom instruction includes math, physics, programming, blueprint reading, CAD software, safety, and shop practices. Skilled computer control programmers and operators need an understanding of the machining process, including the complex physics that occur at the cutting point. Thus, most training programs teach CNC operators and programmers to perform operations on manual machines prior to operating CNC machines.

As new automation is introduced, computer control programmers and operators normally receive additional training to update their skills. This training usually is provided by a representative of the equipment manufacturer or a local technical school. Many employers offer tuition reimbursement for job-related courses.

Certification and other qualifications. Employers prefer to hire workers who have a basic knowledge of computers and electronics and experience with machine tools. In fact, many entrants to these occupations have previously worked as machinists or machine setters, operators, and tenders. Persons interested in becoming computer control programmers or operators should be mechanically inclined and able to work independently and do highly accurate work.

To boost the skill level of all metalworkers and to create a more uniform standard of competency, a number of training facilities and colleges have recently begun implementing curriculums by incorporating national skills standards developed by the National Institute of Metalworking Skills (NIMS). After completing such a curriculum and passing a performance requirement and written exam, trainees are granted an NIMS credential that provides formal recognition of competency in a metalworking field. Completion of a formal certification program provides expanded career opportunities.

Advancement. Computer control programmers and operators can advance in several ways. Experienced CNC operators may become CNC programmers, and some are promoted to supervisory or administrative positions in their firms. A few open their own shops.

Employment

Computer control programmers and operators held about 158,000 jobs in 2006. About 89 percent were computer-controlled machine tool operators, metal and plastic, and about 11 percent were numerical tool and process control programmers. Manufacturing employs almost all of these workers. Employment was concentrated in fabricated metal products manufacturing, machinery manufacturing, plastics products manufacturing, and transportation equipment manufacturing making mostly aerospace and automobile parts. Although computer control programmers and operators work in all parts of the country, jobs are most plentiful in the areas where manufacturing is concentrated.

Job Outlook

Despite the projected slow decline in employment of computer control programmers and operators, job opportunities should be excellent, as employers are expected to continue to have difficulty finding qualified workers.

Employment change. Employment of computer control programmers and operators is expected to decline slowly by 4 percent through 2016. While CNC machine tools will be increasingly used, advances in CNC machine tools and manufacturing technology will further automate the production process, boosting CNC operator productivity and limiting employment. The demand for computer control programmers also will be negatively affected by the increasing use of software (CAD/CAM) that automatically translates part and product designs into CNC machine tool instructions.

Job prospects. Computer control programmers and operators should have excellent job opportunities despite the projected slow decline in employment. Due to the limited number of people entering training programs, employers are expected to continue to have difficulty finding workers with the necessary skills and knowledge.

Earnings

Median hourly earnings of computer-controlled machine tool operators, metal and plastic, were $15.23 in May 2006. The middle 50 percent earned between $12.10 and $18.84. The lowest 10 percent earned less than $9.91, whereas the top 10 percent earned more than $22.45. Median hourly earnings in the manufacturing industries employing the largest numbers of computer-controlled machine tool operators, metal and plastic, in May 2006 were:

Projections data from the National Employment Matrix

Occupational Title	SOC Code	Employment, 2006	Projected employment, 2016	Change, 2006-16	
				Number	Percent
Computer control programmers and operators	51-4010	158,000	153,000	-5,700	-4
Computer-controlled machine tool operators, metal and plastic ..	51-4011	141,000	136,000	-4,200	-3
Numerical tool and process control programmers........................	51-4012	18,000	16,000	-1,500	-8

NOTE: Data in this table are rounded. See the discussion of the employment projections table in the *Handbook* introductory chapter on *Occupational Information Included in the Handbook.*

Metalworking machinery manufacturing $17.45
Other fabricated metal product manufacturing 15.34
Machine shops; turned product; and screw, nut,
  and bolt manufacturing..14.85
Motor vehicle parts manufacturing 14.12
Plastics product manufacturing 12.32

Median hourly earnings of numerical tool and process control programmers were $20.42 in May 2006. The middle 50 percent earned between $16.14 and $25.61. The lowest 10 percent earned less than $13.11, while the top 10 percent earned more than $31.85.

Many employers, especially those with formal apprenticeship programs, offer tuition assistance for training classes.

Related Occupations

Occupations most closely related to computer control programmers and operators are other metal and plastic working occupations, which include machinists; tool and die makers; machine setters, operators, and tenders—metal and plastic; and welding, soldering, and brazing workers. Numerical tool and process control programmers apply their knowledge of machining operations, metals, blueprints, and machine programming to write programs that run machine tools. Computer programmers also write detailed programs to meet precise specifications.

Sources of Additional Information

For general information about computer control programmers and operators, contact:

➤ Precision Machine Products Association, 6700 West Snowville Rd., Brecksville, OH 44141-3292. Internet: **http://www.pmpa.org/industry-careers/**

For a list of training centers and apprenticeship programs, contact:

➤ National Tooling and Metalworking Association, 9300 Livingston Rd., Fort Washington, MD 20744.

For more information on credential standards and apprenticeship, contact:

➤ The National Institute for Metalworking Skills, 10565 Fairfax Blvd., Suite 203, Fairfax, VA 22030. Internet: **http://www.nims-skills.org/home/index.htm**

Machinists

(O*NET 51-4041.00)

Significant Points

- Machinists learn in apprenticeship programs, informally on the job, in vocational high schools, and in community or technical colleges.

- Many entrants previously have worked as machine setters, operators, or tenders.

- Although employment is projected to decline, job opportunities are expected to be good.

Nature of the Work

Machinists use machine tools, such as lathes, milling machines, and machining centers, to produce precision metal parts. Although they may produce large quantities of one part, precision machinists often produce small batches or one-of-a-kind items. They use their knowledge of the working properties of metals and their skill with machine tools to plan and carry out the operations needed to make machined products that meet precise specifications.

Machinists first review electronic or written blueprints or specifications for a job before they machine a part. Next, they calculate where to cut or bore into the workpiece—the piece of steel, aluminum, titanium, plastic, silicon or any other material that is being shaped. They determine how fast to feed the workpiece into the machine and how much material to remove. They then select tools and materials for the job, plan the sequence of cutting and finishing operations, and mark the workpiece to show where cuts should be made.

After this layout work is completed, machinists perform the necessary machining operations. They position the workpiece on the machine tool—drill press, lathe, milling machine, or other type of machine—set the controls, and make the cuts. During the machining process, they must constantly monitor the feed rate and speed of the machine. Machinists also ensure that the workpiece is properly lubricated and cooled because the machining of metal products generates a significant amount of heat. The temperature of the workpiece is a key concern because most metals expand when heated; machinists must adjust the size of their cuts relative to the temperature.

During the cutting process, machinists detect problems by listening for specific sounds—for example, that of a dull cutting tool or excessive vibration. Dull cutting tools are removed and replaced. Cutting speeds are adjusted to compensate for harmonic vibrations, which can decrease the accuracy of cuts, particularly on newer high-speed spindles and lathes. After the work is completed, machinists use both simple and highly sophisticated measuring tools to check the accuracy of their work against blueprints.

Some machinists, often called production machinists, may produce large quantities of one part, especially parts requiring the use of complex operations and great precision. Many modern machine tools are computer numerically controlled (CNC). CNC machines, following a computer program, control the cutting tool speed, change dull tools, and perform all of the necessary cuts to create a part. Frequently, machinists work with computer control programmers to determine how the automated equipment will cut a part. (See the section on computer control programmers and operators elsewhere in the *Handbook*.) The machinist determines the cutting path, speed of the cut and the feed rate, and the programmer converts path, speed, and feed information into a set of instructions for the CNC machine tool.

Because most machinists train in CNC programming, they may write basic programs themselves and often modify programs in response to problems encountered during test runs. Modifications, called offsets, not only fix problems, but they also improve efficiency by reducing manufacturing time and tool wear. After the production process is designed, computer control operators implement it by performing relatively simple and repetitive operations.

Some manufacturing techniques employ automated parts loaders, automatic tool changers, and computer controls, allowing machines to operate without anyone present. One production machinist, working 8 hours a day, might monitor equipment, replace worn cutting tools, check the accuracy of parts being produced, adjust offsets, and perform other tasks on several CNC machines that operate 24 hours a day. In the off-hours, during what is known as "lights-out manufacturing," a factory may need only a few machinists to monitor the entire factory.

Maintenance machinists repair or make new parts for existing machinery. After an industrial machinery mechanic or maintenance worker discovers the broken part of a machine, they give the broken part to the machinist. (See the section on industrial machinery mechanics and maintenance workers elsewhere in the *Handbook*.) To replace broken parts, maintenance machinists refer to blueprints and perform the same machining operations that were needed to create the original part. While production machinists are concentrated in a few industries, maintenance machinists work in many manufacturing industries.

Because the technology of machining is changing rapidly, machinists must learn to operate a wide range of machines. Some newer machines use lasers, water jets, or electrified wires to cut the workpiece. While some of the computer controls are similar to other machine tools, machinists must understand the unique cutting properties of these different machines. As engineers create new types of machine tools and new materials to machine, machinists must constantly learn new machining properties and techniques.

Work environment. Today, most machine shops are relatively clean, well lit, and ventilated. Many computer-controlled machines are partially or totally enclosed, minimizing the exposure of workers to noise, debris, and the lubricants used to cool workpieces during machining. Nevertheless, working around machine tools presents certain dangers, and workers must follow safety precautions. Machinists wear protective equipment, such as safety glasses to shield against bits of flying metal and earplugs to dampen machinery noise. They also must exercise caution when handling hazardous coolants and lubricants, although many common water-based lubricants present little hazard. The job requires stamina because machinists stand most of the day and, at times, may need to lift moderately heavy workpieces. Modern factories use autoloaders and overhead cranes to reduce heavy lifting.

Many machinists work a 40-hour week. Evening and weekend shifts are becoming more common as companies extend hours of operation to make better use of expensive machines. However, this trend is somewhat offset by lights-out manufacturing that uses fewer machinists and the use of machine operators for less desirable shifts. Overtime is common during peak production periods.

Training, Other Qualifications, and Advancement

Machinists train in apprenticeship programs, vocational schools, or community or technical colleges, or informally on the job.

Many entrants previously have worked as machine setters, operators, or tenders.

Education and training. There are many different ways to become a skilled machinist. Many entrants previously have worked as machine setters, operators, or tenders. In high school, students should take math courses, especially trigonometry, and, if available, courses in blueprint reading, metalworking, and drafting. After high school, some machinists learn entirely on the job, but most acquire their skills in a mix of classroom and on-the-job training. Formal apprenticeship programs, typically sponsored by a union or manufacturer, are an excellent way to learn the job of machinist, but are often hard to get into. Apprentices usually must have a high school diploma, GED, or the equivalent, and most have taken algebra and trigonometry classes.

Apprenticeship programs consist of paid shop training and related classroom instruction lasting up to 4 years. In shop training, apprentices work almost full time and are supervised by an experienced machinist while learning to operate various machine tools. Classroom instruction includes math, physics, materials science, blueprint reading, mechanical drawing, and quality and safety practices. In addition, as machine shops have increased their use of computer-controlled equipment, training in the operation and programming of CNC machine tools has become essential. Apprenticeship classes are often taught in cooperation with local community colleges or vocational-technical schools. A growing number of machinists are learning the trade through 2-year associate degree programs at community or technical colleges. Graduates of these programs still need significant on-the-job experience before they are fully qualified.

Certification and other qualifications. People interested in becoming machinists should be mechanically inclined, have good problem-solving abilities, be able to work independently, and be able to do highly accurate work (tolerances may reach 50/1,000,000ths of an inch) that requires concentration and physical effort. Experience working with machine tools is helpful. In fact, many entrants have worked as machine setters, operators, or tenders.

Machinists change worn cutting tools on computer-controlled machines.

Projections data from the National Employment Matrix

Occupational Title	SOC Code	Employment, 2006	Projected employment, 2016	Change, 2006-16	
				Number	Percent
Machinists	51-4041	397,000	384,000	-12,000	-3

NOTE: Data in this table are rounded. See the discussion of the employment projections table in the *Handbook* introductory chapter on *Occupational Information Included in the Handbook.*

To boost the skill level of machinists and to create a more uniform standard of competency, a number of training facilities, State apprenticeship boards, and colleges are implementing curriculums that incorporate national skills standards developed by the National Institute of Metalworking Skills (NIMS). After completing such a curriculum and passing practical and written exams, trainees are granted a NIMS credential. Completing a recognized certification program provides a machinist with better career opportunities and helps employers better judge the abilities of new hires. Journeyworker certification can be obtained from State apprenticeship boards after completing an apprenticeship.

As new automation is introduced, machinists normally receive additional training to update their skills. This training usually is provided by a representative of the equipment manufacturer or a local technical school. Some employers offer tuition reimbursement for job-related courses.

Advancement. Machinists can advance in several ways. Experienced machinists may become CNC programmers, tool and die makers, or mold makers, or be promoted to supervisory or administrative positions in their firms. A few open their own machine shops.

Employment

Machinists held about 397,000 jobs in 2006. About 78 percent of machinists work in manufacturing industries, such as machine shops and machinery, motor vehicle and parts, aerospace products and parts, and other transportation equipment manufacturing. Maintenance machinists work in most industries that use production machinery.

Job Outlook

Although employment of machinists is projected to decline slowly, job prospects are expected to be good.

Employment change. Employment of machinists is projected to decline slowly by 3 percent over the 2006-16 decade because of rising productivity among these workers and strong foreign competition in the manufacture of goods. Machinists will become more efficient as a result of the expanded use of and improvements in technologies such as CNC machine tools, autoloaders, and high-speed machining. This allows fewer machinists to accomplish the same amount of work. Technology is not expected to affect the employment of machinists as significantly as that of some other production workers, however, because machinists monitor and maintain many automated systems. Due to modern production techniques, employers prefer workers, such as machinists, who have a wide range of skills and are capable of performing almost any task in a machine shop.

Job prospects. Despite the projected decline in employment, job opportunities for machinists should continue to be good

as employers value the wide-ranging skills of these workers. Also, many young people with the necessary educational and personal qualifications needed to become machinists prefer to attend college or may not wish to enter production occupations. Therefore, the number of workers learning to be machinists is expected to be less than the number of job openings arising each year from the need to replace experienced machinists who retire or transfer to other occupations.

Employment levels in this occupation are influenced by economic cycles—as the demand for machined goods falls, machinists involved in production may be laid off or forced to work fewer hours. Employment of machinists involved in plant maintenance, however, often is more stable because proper maintenance and repair of costly equipment remains critical to manufacturing operations, even when production levels fall.

Earnings

Median hourly wage-and-salary earnings of machinists were $16.71 in May 2006. The middle 50 percent earned between $13.14 and $20.82. The lowest 10 percent earned less than $10.29, while the top 10 percent earned more than $25.31. Median hourly wage-and-salary earnings in the manufacturing industries employing the largest number of machinists were:

Aerospace product and parts manufacturing	$18.46
Motor vehicle parts manufacturing	18.27
Metalworking machinery manufacturing	17.36
Machine shops; turned product; and screw, nut, and bolt manufacturing	16.24
Employment services	11.98

Apprentices earn much less than experienced machinists, but earnings increase quickly as they improve their skills. Also most employers pay for apprentices' training classes.

Related Occupations

Occupations most closely related to that of machinist are other machining occupations, which include tool and die makers; machine setters, operators, and tenders—metal and plastic; and computer control programmers and operators. Maintenance machinists work closely with industrial machinery mechanics and maintenance workers.

Sources of Additional Information

For general information about a career in machining, contact:
➤ Precision Machine Products Association, 6700 West Snowville Rd., Brecksville, OH 44141. Internet: **http://www.pmpa.org**

For a list of training centers and apprenticeship programs, contact:
➤ National Tooling and Machining Association, 9300 Livingston Rd., Fort Washington, MD 20744.

For more information on credential standards and apprenticeship, contact:

➤ The National Institute for Metalworking Skills, 10565 Fairfax Blvd., Suite 203, Fairfax, VA 22030. Internet: **http://www.nims-skills.org/home/index.htm**

Information on the registered apprenticeship system with links to State apprenticeship programs may also be found on the U.S. Department of Labor's Web site: **http://www.doleta.gov/atels_bat** Apprenticeship information is also available from the U.S. Department of Labor's toll free helpline: (877) 872-5627.

Machine Setters, Operators, and Tenders—Metal and Plastic

(O*NET 51-4021.00, 51-4022.00, 51-4023.00, 51-4031.00, 51-4032.00, 51-4033.00, 51-4034.00, 51-4035.00, 51-4051.00, 51-4052.00, 51-4061.00, 51-4062.00, 51-4071.00, 51-4072.00, 51-4081.00, 51-4191.00, 51-4192.00, 51-4193.00, 51-4194.00, 51-4199.99)

Significant Points

- Manufacturing industries employ more than 90 percent of workers.

- A few weeks of on-the-job training is sufficient for most workers to learn basic machine operations, but a year or more is required to become a highly skilled operator or setter.

- Overall employment of machine setters, operators, and tenders is projected to decline rapidly over the 2006-16 period as a result of productivity improvements and competition for jobs from abroad.

- Those who can operate multiple machines will have the best opportunities for advancement and for gaining jobs with more long-term potential.

Nature of the Work

Consider the parts of a toaster, such as the metal or plastic housing or the lever that lowers the toast. These parts, and many other metal and plastic products, are produced by machine setters, operators, and tenders—metal and plastic. In fact, machine operators in the metalworking and plastics industries play a major role in producing most of the consumer products on which we rely daily.

In general, these workers can be separated into two groups— those who set up machines for operation and those who operate the machines during production. Setup workers prepare the machines *prior* to production, perform initial test runs producing a part, and may adjust and make minor repairs to the machinery *during* its operation. Operators and tenders primarily monitor the machinery during its operation; sometimes they load or unload the machine or make minor adjustments to the controls. Many workers both set up and operate equipment. Because the setup process requires an understanding of the en-

tire production process, setters usually have more training and are more highly skilled than those who simply operate or tend machinery. As new automation simplifies the setup process, however, less skilled workers also are increasingly able to set up machines for operation.

Setters, operators, and tenders usually are identified by the type of machine with which they work. Some examples of specific titles are drilling- and boring-machine toolsetters, milling- and planing-machine tenders, and lathe- and turning-machine tool operators. Job duties usually vary with the size of the firm and the type of machine being operated. Although some workers specialize in one or two types of machinery, many are trained to set up or operate a variety of machines. Increasing automation allows machine setters to operate multiple machines simultaneously. In addition, newer production techniques, such as team-oriented "lean" manufacturing, require machine operators to rotate between different machines. Rotating assignments results in more varied work, but also requires workers to have a wider range of skills.

Machine setters, operators, and tenders—metal set up and tend machines that cut and form all types of metal parts. Setup workers plan and set up the sequence of operations according to blueprints, layouts, or other instructions. Often this involves loading a computer program with instructions into the machine's computer controls. On all machines, including those with computer controls, setup workers respond to problems during operation by adjusting the speed, feed and other variables. They also choose the proper coolants and lubricants and select the instruments or tools for each operation. Using micrometers, gauges, and other precision measuring instruments, setup workers compare the completed work within the required tolerances.

Although there are many different types of metalworking machine tools that require specific knowledge and skills, most operators perform similar tasks. Whether tending grinding machines that remove excess material from the surface of solid piece of metal or presses that extrude molten metal through a die to form wire, operators usually perform simple, repetitive operations that can be learned quickly. Typically, these workers place metal stock in a machine on which the operating specifications have already been set. They watch one or more ma-

Machine setters, operators, and tenders operate a wide range of machine tools.

chines and make adjustments to the machines based on either reading from computers and gauges or measuring the resulting product. Regardless of the type of machine they operate, machine operators usually depend on more skilled and experienced setup workers for major adjustments when the machines are not functioning properly.

Machine setters, operators, and tenders—plastic set up and tend machines that transform plastic compounds—chemical-based products that can be produced in powder, pellet, or syrup form—into a wide variety of consumer goods such as toys, tubing, and auto parts. These products are manufactured by various methods, of which injection molding is the most common. The injection-molding machine heats and liquefies a plastic compound and forces it into a mold. After the part has cooled and hardened, the mold opens and the part is released. Many common kitchen products are produced with this method. To produce long parts, such as pipes or window frames, an extruding machine usually is used. These machines force a plastic compound through a die that contains an opening with the desired shape of the final product. Blow molding is another common plasticsworking technique. Blow-molding machines force hot air into a mold that contains a plastic tube. As the air moves into the mold, the tube is inflated to the shape of the mold, and a plastic container is formed. The familiar 2-liter soft-drink bottles are produced by this method.

Work environment. Most machine setters, operators, and tenders—metal and plastic work in areas that are clean, well lit, and well ventilated. Nevertheless, many operators require stamina, because they are on their feet much of the day and may do moderately heavy lifting. Also, these workers operate powerful, high-speed machines that can be dangerous if strict safety rules are not observed. Most operators wear protective equipment, such as safety glasses and earplugs, to protect against flying particles of metal or plastic and against noise from the machines. However, many modern machines are enclosed, minimizing the exposure of workers to noise, dust, and lubricants used during machining. Other required safety equipment varies by work setting and machine. For example, those in the plastics industry who work near materials that emit dangerous fumes or dust must wear face masks or self-contained breathing apparatus.

Overtime is common during periods of increased production for most machine setters, operators, and tenders—metal and plastic, but they usually work a 40-hour week. Because many metalworking and plastics working shops operate more than one shift daily, some operators work nights and weekends.

Training, Other Qualifications, and Advancement

A few weeks of on-the-job training is sufficient for most workers to learn basic machine operations, but a year or more is required to become a highly skilled operator or setter.

Education and training. Employers generally prefer workers who have a high school diploma or equivalent for jobs as machine setters, operators, and tenders. Being able to read, write, and speak English is important. Those interested in this occupation can improve their employment opportunities by completing high school courses in shop and blueprint reading and by gaining a working knowledge of the properties of met-

als and plastics. A solid math background, including courses in algebra, geometry, trigonometry, and basic statistics, also is useful, along with experience working with computers.

Trainees begin by observing and assisting experienced workers, sometimes in formal training programs or apprenticeships. Under supervision, they may start as tenders, supplying materials, starting and stopping the machine, or removing finished products from it. Then they advance to the more difficult tasks performed by operators, such as adjusting feed speeds, changing cutting tools, or inspecting a finished product for defects. Eventually, they develop the skills and experience to setup machines and assist newer operators.

The complexity of the equipment largely determines the time required to become an operator. Most operators learn the basic machine operations and functions in a few weeks, but a year or more may be needed to become skilled operators or to advance to the more highly skilled job of setter. Although many operators learn on the job, some community colleges and other educational institutions offer courses and certifications in operating metal and plastics machines. In addition to providing on-the-job training, some employers send promising machine tenders to classes. Other employers prefer to hire workers who have completed, or currently are enrolled in, a training program.

Setters or technicians often plan the sequence of work, make the first production run, and determine which adjustments need to be made. As a result, these workers need a thorough knowledge of the machinery and of the products being manufactured. Strong analytical abilities are particularly important for this job. Some companies have formal training programs for operators and setters, which often combine classroom instruction with on-the-job training. For some positions, such as grinders and rolling or pressing setup workers, formal apprenticeships are available. These programs require 300-600 hours of classroom training, and 2000-4000 hours of on-the-job experience. Workers complete these programs in about 2 to 4 years, depending upon the program.

Other qualifications. As the machinery in manufacturing plants becomes more complex and with changes to shop-floor organization that require more teamwork among employees, employers increasingly look for persons with good communication and interpersonal skills. Mechanical aptitude, manual dexterity, and experience working with machinery also are helpful.

Certification and advancement. Job opportunities and advancement can be enhanced by becoming certified in a particular machining skill. The National Institute for Metalworking Skills has developed standards for machine setters, operators, and tenders—metal. After taking an approved course and passing a written exam and performance requirement, the worker is issued a credential that signifies competence in a specific machining operation. The Society of Plastics Industry, the national trade association representing plastics manufacturers, also certifies workers in that industry. Certifications vary greatly depending upon the skill level involved. Both organizations offer multiple levels of operator and setter certifications. Certifications allow operators and setters to switch jobs more easily because they can prove their skills to a potential employer.

Projections data from the National Employment Matrix

Occupational Title	SOC Code	Employment, 2006	Projected employment, 2016	Change, 2006-16	
				Number	Percent
Machine setters, operators, and tenders—metal and plastic	—	1,141,000	975,000	-166,000	-15
Forming machine setters, operators, and tenders, metal and plastic	51-4020	161,000	140,000	-20,000	-13
Extruding and drawing machine setters, operators, and tenders, metal and plastic	51-4021	94,000	87,000	-6,700	-7
Forging machine setters, operators, and tenders, metal and plastic	51-4022	31,000	22,000	-9,400	-30
Rolling machine setters, operators, and tenders, metal and plastic	51-4023	36,000	32,000	-4,200	-12
Machine tool cutting setters, operators, and tenders, metal and plastic	51-4030	513,000	425,000	-88,000	-17
Cutting, punching, and press machine setters, operators, and tenders, metal and plastic	51-4031	272,000	231,000	-40,000	-15
Drilling and boring machine tool setters, operators, and tenders, metal and plastic	51-4032	43,000	33,000	-9,500	-22
Grinding, lapping, polishing, and buffing machine tool setters, operators, and tenders, metal and plastic	51-4033	101,000	85,000	-16,000	-16
Lathe and turning machine tool setters, operators, and tenders, metal and plastic	51-4034	68,000	52,000	-16,000	-23
Milling and planing machine setters, operators, and tenders, metal and plastic	51-4035	29,000	23,000	-6,100	-21
Metal furnace and kiln operators and tenders	51-4050	33,000	27,000	-6,100	-18
Metal-refining furnace operators and tenders	51-4051	18,000	15,000	-3,500	-19
Pourers and casters, metal	51-4052	15,000	12,000	-2,600	-17
Model makers and patternmakers, metal and plastic	51-4060	16,000	15,000	-1,000	-6
Model makers, metal and plastic	51-4061	8,800	8,200	-600	-6
Patternmakers, metal and plastic	51-4062	7,400	7,000	-400	-5
Molders and molding machine setters, operators, and tenders, metal and plastic	51-4070	171,000	148,000	-23,000	-14
Foundry mold and coremakers	51-4071	15,000	11,000	-3,300	-23
Molding, coremaking, and casting machine setters, operators, and tenders, metal and plastic	51-4072	157,000	137,000	-20,000	-13
Multiple machine tool setters, operators, and tenders, metal and plastic	51-4081	97,000	97,000	300	0
Miscellaneous metalworkers and plastic workers	51-4190	150,000	122,000	-28,000	-18
Heat treating equipment setters, operators, and tenders, metal and plastic	51-4191	27,000	23,000	-4,000	-15
Lay-out workers, metal and plastic	51-4192	10,000	8,100	-2,000	-20
Plating and coating machine setters, operators, and tenders, metal and plastic	51-4193	42,000	37,000	-5,100	-12
Tool grinders, filers, and sharpeners	51-4194	22,000	18,000	-4,200	-19
Metal workers and plastic workers, all other	51-4199	49,000	36,000	-12,000	-25

NOTE: Data in this table are rounded. See the discussion of the employment projections table in the *Handbook* introductory chapter on *Occupational Information Included in the Handbook*.

Advancement for operators usually takes the form of higher pay and a wider range of responsibilities, eventually than can advance to be setup workers. With experience and training they can become multiple-machine operators, or trainees for more highly skilled positions, such as, machinists, tool and die makers, or computer-control programmers. (See the statements on machinists, computer control programmers and operators, and tool and die makers elsewhere in the *Handbook*.) Some setup workers may advance to supervisory positions.

Employment

Machine setters, operators, and tenders—metal and plastic held about 1.1 million jobs in 2006. More than 90 percent of jobs were found in manufacturing, primarily in fabricated metal product manufacturing, plastics and rubber products manufacturing, primary metal manufacturing, machinery manufacturing, and motor vehicle parts manufacturing.

Job Outlook

Overall employment in the various machine setter, operator, and tender occupations is expected to decline rapidly during the projection period. Those who can operate multiple machines will have the best opportunities for advancement and for gaining jobs with more long-term potential.

Employment change. Overall employment in the various machine setter, operator, and tender occupations is expected to decline rapidly by 15 percent from 2006 to 2016. In general, employment growth of these workers will be affected by technological advances, changing demand for the goods they produce, foreign competition, and the reorganization of production processes.

One of the most important factors influencing employment change in this occupation is the implementation of labor-saving machinery. Many firms are adopting new technologies, such as computer-controlled machine tools and robots in order to improve quality, lower production costs, and remain competitive. Computer-controlled equipment allows operators to tend a greater number of machines simultaneously and often makes setup easier, thereby reducing the amount of time setup workers spend on each machine. Robots are being used to load and unload parts from machines. The lower-skilled manual machine tool operators and tenders jobs are more likely to be eliminated by these new technologies, because the functions they perform are more easily automated.

The demand for machine setters, operators, and tenders—metal and plastic largely mirrors the demand for the parts they produce. The consumption of plastic products has grown as they have been substituted for metal goods in many products in recent years. The process is likely to continue and should result in stronger demand for machine operators in plastics than in metal.

Both the plastics and metal industries, however, face stiff foreign competition that is limiting the demand for domestically produced parts. One way in which larger U.S. producers have responded to this competition is by moving production operations to other countries where labor costs are lower. These moves are likely to continue and will further reduce employment growth for machine operators, setters, and tenders—metal and plastic in the United States. Another way domestic manufacturers compete with low-wage foreign competition is by increasing their use of automated systems, which can make manufacturing establishments more competitive by improving their productivity. However, increased automation also limits employment growth.

Job prospects. Despite the overall rapid employment decline, a large number of machine setter, operator, and tender jobs will become available because of an expected surge in retirements, primarily baby boomers, by the end of the decade. Workers with a thorough background in machine operations, certifications from industry associations, exposure to a variety of machines, and a good working knowledge of the properties of metals and plastics will be better able to adjust to the changing environment. In addition, new shop-floor arrangements will reward workers with good basic mathematics and reading skills, good communication skills, and the ability and willingness to learn new tasks. As workers adapt to team-oriented production methods, those who can operate multiple machines will have the best opportunities for advancement and for gaining jobs with more long-term potential.

Earnings

Earnings for machine operators can vary by size of the company, union status, industry, and skill level and experience of the operator. Also, temporary employees, who are being hired in greater numbers, usually get paid less than permanently employed work-

ers. The median hourly earnings in May 2006 for a variety of machine setters, operators, and tenders—metal and plastic were:

Model makers, metal and plastic...$20.22
Patternmakers, metal and plastic..17.01
Lay-out workers, metal and plastic...16.15
Metal-refining furnace operators and tenders............................15.69
Lathe and turning machine tool setters, operators,
    and tenders, metal and plastic...15.46
Milling and planing machine setters, operators,
    and tenders, metal and plastic...15.18
Rolling machine setters, operators, and tenders,
    metal and plastic...14.93
Heat treating equipment setters, operators, and tenders,
    metal and plastic...14.83
Tool grinders, filers, and sharpeners...14.73
Multiple machine tool setters, operators, and tenders,
    metal and plastic...14.68
Drilling and boring machine tool setters, operators,
    and tenders, metal and plastic...14.36
Pourers and casters, metal...14.22
Forging machine setters, operators, and tenders,
    metal and plastic...13.94
Foundry mold and coremakers...13.82
Extruding and drawing machine setters,
    operators, and tenders, metal and plastic..............................13.58
Grinding, lapping, polishing, and buffing machine
    tool setters, operators, and tenders, metal and plastic...........13.50
Plating and coating machine setters, operators,
    and tenders, metal and plastic...13.21
Cutting, punching, and press machine setters,
    operators, and tenders, metal and plastic..............................12.66
Molding, coremaking, and casting machine setters,
    operators, and tenders, metal and plastic..............................12.29
Metal workers and plastic workers, all other............................16.69

Related Occupations

Workers in occupations closely related to machine setters, operators, and tenders—metal and plastic include machinists; tool and die makers; assemblers and fabricators; computer control programmers and operators; painting and coating workers, except construction and maintenance; and welding, soldering, and brazing workers. Often, machine operators are responsible for checking the quality of parts being produced, work similar to that of inspectors, testers, sorters, samplers, and weighers.

Sources of Additional Information

For general information about careers and companies employing metal machine setters, operators, and tenders, contact:
➤ National Tooling and Machining Association, 9300 Livingston Rd., Fort Washington, MD 20744.
Internet: **http://www.ntma.org**
➤ Precision Metalforming Association Educational Foundation, 6363 Oak Tree Blvd., Independence, OH 44131.
Internet: **http://www.pmaef.org**
➤ Precision Machine Products Association, 6700 West Snowville Rd., Brecksville, OH 44141-3292.
Internet: **http://www.pmpa.org**

For information on schools and employers with training programs in plastics, contact:

➤ Society of Plastics Industry, 1667 K St.NW., Suite 1000, Washington, DC 20006.

Internet:

http://www.plasticsindustry.org/outreach/careers.htm

Tool and Die Makers

(O*NET 51-4111.00)

Significant Points

- Most tool and die makers need 4 or 5 years of classroom instruction and on-the-job training to become fully qualified.

- Employment is projected to decline because of strong foreign competition and advancements in automation.

- Despite the decline in employment, excellent job opportunities are expected.

Nature of the Work

Tool and die makers are among the most highly skilled workers in manufacturing. These workers produce and repair tools, dies, and special guiding and holding devices that enable machines to manufacture a variety of products we use daily—from clothing and furniture to heavy equipment and parts for aircraft.

Toolmakers craft precision tools and machines that are used to cut, shape, and form metal and other materials. They also produce jigs and fixtures—devices that hold metal while it is bored, stamped, or drilled—and gauges and other measuring devices. Die makers construct metal forms, called dies, that are used to shape metal in stamping and forging operations. They also make metal molds for diecasting and for molding plastics, ceramics, and composite materials. Some tool and die makers craft prototypes of parts, and then, working with engineers and designers, determine how best to manufacture the part. In addition to developing, designing, and producing new tools and dies, these workers also may repair worn or damaged tools, dies, gauges, jigs, and fixtures.

To perform these functions, tool and die makers employ many types of machine tools and precision measuring instruments. They also must be familiar with the machining properties, such as hardness and heat tolerance, of a wide variety of common metals, alloys, plastics, ceramics, and other composite materials. Tool and die makers are knowledgeable in machining operations, mathematics, and blueprint reading. In fact, tool and die makers often are considered highly specialized machinists. The main difference between tool and die makers and machinists is that machinists normally make a single part during the production process, while tool and die makers make many parts and assemble and adjust machines used in the production process. (See the section on machinists elsewhere in the *Handbook*.)

While many tools and dies are designed by engineers or tool designers, tool and die makers are also trained to design tools and often do. They may travel to a customer's plant to observe the operation and suggest ways in which a new tool could improve the manufacturing process.

Once a tool or die is designed, tool and die makers, working from blueprints, plan the sequence of operations necessary to manufacture the tool or die. They measure and mark the pieces of metal that will be cut to form parts of the final product. At this point, tool and die makers cut, drill, or bore the part as required, checking to ensure that the final product meets specifications. Finally, these workers assemble the parts and perform finishing jobs such as filing, grinding, and polishing surfaces. While manual machining has declined, it is still used for unique or low-quantity parts that are often required in building tools and dies.

Tool and die makers use computer-aided design (CAD) to develop products and parts. Specifications entered into computer programs can be used to electronically develop blueprints for the required tools and dies. Numerical tool and process control programmers use computer-aided design or computer-aided manufacturing (CAD/CAM) programs to convert electronic drawings into CAM-based computer programs that contain instructions for a sequence of cutting tool operations. (See the section on computer control programmers and operators elsewhere in the *Handbook*.) Once these programs are developed, computer numerically controlled (CNC) machines follow the set of instructions contained in the program to produce the part. Computer-controlled machine tool operators or machinists normally operate CNC machines, but tool and die makers are trained in both operating CNC machines and writing CNC programs, and they may perform either task. CNC programs are stored electronically for future use, saving time and increasing worker productivity.

After machining the parts, tool and die makers carefully check the accuracy of the parts using many tools, including coordinate measuring machines, which use sensor arms and software to compare the dimensions of the part to electronic blueprints. Next, they assemble the different parts into a functioning machine. They file, grind, shim, and adjust the different parts to properly fit them together. Finally, tool and die makers set up a test run using the tools or dies they have made to make sure that the manufactured parts meet specifications. If problems occur, they compensate by adjusting the tools or dies.

Work environment. Tool and die makers usually work in toolrooms that are normally quieter than typical manufacturing production floors because there are fewer machines running at once. Toolrooms also are generally kept clean and cool to minimize heat-related expansion of metal workpieces. To minimize the exposure of workers to moving parts, machines have guards and shields. Most computer-controlled machines are totally enclosed, minimizing workers' exposure to noise, dust, and the lubricants used to cool workpieces during machining. Tool and die makers also must follow safety rules and wear protective equipment, such as safety glasses to shield against bits of flying metal, earplugs to protect against noise, and gloves and masks to reduce exposure to hazardous lubricants and cleaners. These workers also need stamina because they often spend much of the day on their feet and may do moderately heavy lifting. Companies employing tool and die makers have traditionally

Tool and die makers use manual lathes to make custom parts or small batches of parts.

operated only one shift per day. Overtime and weekend work are common, especially during peak production periods.

Training, Other Qualifications, and Advancement

It usually takes 4 or 5 years of classroom and paid on-the-job training to become a fully trained tool and die maker. Good math, problem-solving, and computer skills are important requirements for these workers.

Education and training. Most tool and die makers learn their trade through 4 or 5 years of education and training in formal apprenticeships or in other postsecondary programs offered at local community colleges or technical schools. These programs often include a mix of classroom instruction and paid hands-on experience. According to most employers, apprenticeship programs are the best way to learn all aspects of tool and die making. Most apprentices must have a high school diploma, GED, or equivalent, and high school mathematics and shop classes make it easier to get into an apprenticeship program.

Traditional apprenticeships usually require that the apprentice complete a specific number of work and classroom hours to complete the program, which typically takes 4 or 5 years. Some companies and State apprenticeship programs, however, are now shifting from time-based programs to competency-based programs. Under competency-based programs, apprentices can move ahead more quickly by passing a series of exams and demonstrating competency in a particular job skill.

While formal apprenticeship programs may be the best way to learn the job, many tool and die makers receive most of their formal classroom training from community and technical colleges while working for a company that often supports the employee's training goals and provides the needed on-the-job training less formally. These trainees often begin as machine operators and gradually take on more difficult assignments. Many machinists become tool and die makers.

During their training, tool and die maker trainees learn to operate milling machines, lathes, grinders, laser and water cutting machines, wire electrical discharge machines, and other machine tools. They also learn to use handtools for fitting and assembling gauges and other mechanical and metal-forming equipment. In addition, they study metalworking processes, such as heat treating and plating. Classroom training usually

consists of tool designing, tool programming, blueprint reading, and, if needed, mathematics courses, including algebra, geometry, trigonometry, and basic statistics. Tool and die makers must have good computer skills to work with CAD/CAM technology, CNC machine tools, and computerized measuring machines.

Even after completing a formal training program, tool and die makers still need years of experience to become highly skilled. Most specialize in making certain types of tools, molds, or dies.

Certification and other qualifications. State apprenticeship boards certify tool and die makers as journey workers after they have completed a licensed program. While a State certification is not necessary to work as a tool and die maker, it gives workers more flexibility in employment and is required by some employers. Apprentices usually must be at least 18 years old, in addition to having a high school education and high school mathematics classes.

Because tools and dies must meet strict specifications—precision to one ten-thousandth of an inch is common—the work of tool and die makers requires skill with precision measuring devices and a high degree of patience and attention to detail. Good eyesight is essential. People entering this occupation also should be mechanically inclined, able to work and solve problems independently, have strong mathematical skills, and be capable of doing work that requires concentration and physical effort. Tool and die makers who visit customers' plants need good interpersonal and sales skills.

Employers generally look for someone with a strong educational background as an indication that the person can more easily adapt to change, which is a constant in this occupation. As automation continues to change the way tools and dies are made, workers regularly need to update their skills to learn how to operate new equipment. Also, as materials such as alloys, ceramics, polymers, and plastics are increasingly used, tool and die makers need to learn new machining techniques to deal with the new materials.

Advancement. There are several ways for skilled workers to advance. Some move into supervisory and administrative positions in their firms or they may start their own shop. Others may take computer courses and become computer-controlled machine tool programmers. With a college degree, a tool and die maker can go into engineering or tool design.

Employment

Tool and die makers held about 101,000 jobs in 2006. Most worked in industries that manufacture metalworking machinery, transportation equipment such as motor vehicle parts, fabricated metal products, and plastics products. Although they are found throughout the country, jobs are most plentiful in the Midwest and the Northeast, where many of metalworking companies are located.

Job Outlook

Employment of tool and die makers is projected to decline rapidly. However, excellent job opportunities are expected as many employers report difficulty finding qualified applicants.

Employment change. Employment of tool and die makers is projected to decline rapidly by 10 percent over the 2006-16

Projections data from the National Employment Matrix

Occupational Title	SOC Code	Employment, 2006	Projected employment, 2016	Change, 2006-16	
				Number	Percent
Tool and die makers	51-4111	101,000	91,000	-9,700	-10

NOTE: Data in this table are rounded. See the discussion of the employment projections table in the *Handbook* introductory chapter on *Occupational Information Included in the Handbook.*

decade because of strong foreign competition in manufacturing and advances in automation, including CNC machine tools and computer-aided design, that should improve worker productivity. On the other hand, tool and die makers play a key role in building and maintaining advanced automated manufacturing equipment, which makes them less susceptible to lay-offs than other less-skilled production workers. As firms invest in new equipment, modify production techniques, and implement product design changes more rapidly, they will continue to rely heavily on skilled tool and die makers for retooling.

Job prospects. Despite declining employment, excellent job opportunities are expected. Employers in certain parts of the country report difficulty attracting skilled workers and apprenticeship candidates with the necessary abilities to replace retiring workers and fill other openings. The number of workers receiving training in this occupation is expected to continue to be fewer than the number of openings created each year by tool and die makers who retire or transfer to other occupations. A major factor limiting the number of people entering the occupation is that many young people who have the educational and personal qualifications necessary to learn tool and die making usually prefer to attend college or do not wish to enter production occupations.

Earnings

Median hourly wage-and-salary earnings of tool and die makers were $21.29 in May 2006. The middle 50 percent earned between $17.29 and $26.77. The lowest 10 percent had earnings of less than $13.85, while the top 10 percent earned more than $32.41. Median hourly wage-and-salary earnings in the manufacturing industries employing the largest numbers of tool and die makers were as follows:

Motor vehicle parts manufacturing $26.45
Plastics product manufacturing 20.79
Forging and stamping 20.24
Metalworking machinery manufacturing 20.08
Machine shops; turned product; and screw, nut,
    and bolt manufacturing 19.41

The pay of apprentices is tied to their skill level. As they gain more skills and reach specific levels of performance and experience, their pay increases.

Related Occupations

The occupations most closely related to the work of tool and die makers are other machining occupations. These include machinists; computer control programmers and operators; and machine setters, operators, and tenders—metal and plastic. Another occupation that requires precision and skill in working with metal is welding, soldering, and brazing workers.

Like tool and die makers, assemblers and fabricators assemble and repair complex machinery. Millwrights and industrial machinery mechanics also repair and assemble manufacturing equipment. When measuring parts, tool and die makers use some of the same tools and equipment that inspectors, testers, sorters, samplers, and weighers use in their jobs.

Sources of Additional Information

For career information and to have inquiries on training and employment referred to member companies, contact:
➤ Precision Machine Products Association, 6700 West Snowville Rd., Brecksville, OH 44141. Internet: **http://www.pmpa.org**

For lists of schools and employers with tool and die apprenticeship and training programs, contact:
➤ National Tooling and Machining Association, 9300 Livingston Rd., Ft. Washington, MD 20744.
Internet: **http://www.ntma.org**

For information on careers, education and training, earnings, and apprenticeship opportunities in metalworking, contact:
➤ Precision Metalforming Association Educational Foundation, 6363 Oak Tree Blvd., Independence, OH 44131.
Internet: **http://www.pmaef.org**
➤ The National Institute for Metalworking Skills, 10565 Fairfax Boulevard, Suite 203, Fairfax, VA 22030.
Internet: **http://www.nims-skills.org**

Information on the registered apprenticeship system with links to State apprenticeship programs can be found on the U.S. Department of Labor's Web site: **http://www.doleta.gov/atels_bat** Apprenticeship information is also available from the U.S. Department of Labor's toll free helpline: (877) 872-5627.

Welding, Soldering, and Brazing Workers

(O*NET 51-4121.00, 51-4121.06, 51-4121.07, 51-4122.00)

Significant Points

- About 2 out of 3 jobs are in manufacturing industries.

- Training ranges from a few weeks of school or on-the-job training to several years of combined school and on-the-job training.

- Employment is projected to grow more slowly than average.

- Job prospects should be excellent as employers report difficulty finding enough qualified people.

Nature of the Work

Welding is the most common way of permanently joining metal parts. In this process, heat is applied to metal pieces, melting and fusing them to form a permanent bond. Because of its strength, welding is used in shipbuilding, automobile manufacturing and repair, aerospace applications, and thousands of other manufacturing activities. Welding also is used to join beams when constructing buildings, bridges, and other structures and to join pipes in pipelines, power plants, and refineries.

There are over 80 different welding processes that a welder can employ. Some are performed manually, and the work is entirely controlled by the welder. Others are semiautomatic, and the welder uses machinery, such as a wire feeder, to perform welding tasks.

One of the most common types of welding is arc welding. Standard arc welding involves two large metal alligator clips that carry a strong electrical current. One clip is attached to any part of the piece being welded. The second clip is connected to a thin welding rod. When the rod touches the piece, a powerful electrical circuit is created. The massive heat created by the electrical current causes both the piece and the steel core of the rod to melt together, cooling quickly to form a solid bond. The speed with which the welder works can affect the strength of the weld.

Two common and advanced types of arc welding are Tungsten Inert Gas (TIG) and Metal Inert Gas (MIG) welding. TIG welding often is used with stainless steel or aluminum. The welder holds the welding rod in one hand and an electric torch in the other hand. The torch is used to simultaneously melt the rod and the piece. MIG uses a spool of continuously fed wire instead of a rod, which allows the welder to join longer stretches of metal without stopping to replace a rod. The welder holds the wire feeder, which functions like the alligator clip in arc welding.

Like arc welders, soldering and brazing workers use molten metal to join two pieces of metal. However, the metal added during the soldering and brazing process has a melting point lower than that of the piece, so only the added metal is melted, not the piece. Soldering uses metals with a melting point below 800 degrees Fahrenheit; brazing uses metals with a higher melting point. Because soldering and brazing do not melt the piece, these processes normally do not create the distortions or weaknesses in the piece that can occur with welding. Soldering commonly is used to join electrical, electronic, and other small metal parts. Brazing produces a stronger joint than does soldering and often is used to join metals other than steel, such as brass. Brazing can also be used to apply coatings to parts to reduce wear and protect against corrosion.

Skilled welding, soldering, and brazing workers generally plan work from drawings or specifications and use their knowledge of welding processes and base metals to determine how best to join the parts. The difficulty of the weld is determined by its position—horizontal, vertical, overhead, or 6G (circular, such as in large pipes)—and by the type of metals to be fused. Highly skilled welders often are trained to work with a wide variety of materials, such as titanium, aluminum, or plastics, in addition to steel. Welders then select and set up welding equipment, execute the planned welds, and examine welds to ensure that they meet standards or specifications.

By observing problems during the welding process, welders can compensate by adjusting the speed, voltage, amperage, or feed of the rod. Some welders have more limited duties, however. They perform routine jobs that already have been planned and laid out and do not require extensive knowledge of welding techniques.

Automated welding is used in an increasing number of production processes. In these instances, a machine or robot performs the welding tasks while being monitored by a welding machine operator. Welding, soldering, and brazing machine setters, operators, and tenders follow specified layouts, work orders, or blueprints. Operators must load parts correctly and constantly monitor the machine to ensure that it produces the desired bond.

The work of arc, plasma, and oxy-gas cutters is closely related to that of welders. However, instead of joining metals, cutters use the heat from an electric arc, a stream of ionized gas called plasma, or burning gases to cut and trim metal objects to specific dimensions. Cutters also dismantle large objects, such as ships, railroad cars, automobiles, buildings, or aircraft. Some operate and monitor cutting machines similar to those used by welding machine operators. Plasma cutting has been increasing in popularity because, unlike other methods, it can cut a wide variety of metals, including stainless steel, aluminum, and titanium.

Work environment. Welding, soldering, and brazing workers often are exposed to a number of hazards, including very hot materials and the intense light created by the arc. They wear safety shoes, goggles, hoods with protective lenses, and other devices designed to prevent burns and eye injuries and to protect them from falling objects. They normally work in well-ventilated areas to limit their exposure to fumes. Automated welding, soldering, and brazing machine operators are not exposed to as many dangers, and a face shield or goggles usually provide adequate protection for these workers.

Welders and cutters may work outdoors, often in inclement weather, or indoors, sometimes in a confined area designed to contain sparks and glare. Outdoors, they may work on a scaffold or platform high off the ground. In addition, they may be required to lift heavy objects and work in a variety of awkward positions, while bending, stooping, or standing to perform work overhead.

Although about 50 percent of welders, solderers, and brazers work a 40-hour week, overtime is common, and nearly 1 out of 5 welders work 50 hours per week or more. Welders also may work in shifts as long as 12 hours. Some welders, solderers, brazers, and machine operators work in factories that operate around the clock, necessitating shift work.

Training, Other Qualifications, and Advancement

Training for welding, soldering, and brazing workers can range from a few weeks of school or on-the-job training for low-skilled positions to several years of combined school and on-the-job training for highly skilled jobs.

Education and training. Formal training is available in high schools and postsecondary institutions, such as vocation-

Welders inspect their work to ensure a strong bond.

al-technical institutes, community colleges, and private welding schools. The U.S. Armed Forces operate welding schools as well. Although some employers provide training, they prefer to hire workers who already have experience or formal training. Courses in blueprint reading, shop mathematics, mechanical drawing, physics, chemistry, and metallurgy are helpful. An understanding of electricity also is very helpful, and knowledge of computers is gaining importance, especially for welding, soldering, and brazing machine operators, who are becoming more responsible for the programming of robots and other computer-controlled machines. Since understanding the welding process and inspecting welds is important for both welders and welding machine operators, companies hiring machine operators prefer workers with a background in welding.

Certification and other qualifications. Some welding positions require general certifications in welding or certifications in specific skills such as inspection or robotic welding. The American Welding Society certification courses are offered at many welding schools. Some employers have developed their own internal certification tests.

Welding, soldering, and brazing workers need good eyesight, hand-eye coordination, and manual dexterity. They should be able to concentrate on detailed work for long periods and be able to bend, stoop, and work in awkward positions. In addi-

tion, welders increasingly must be willing to receive training and perform tasks in other production jobs.

Advancement. Welders can advance to more skilled welding jobs with additional training and experience. For example, they may become welding technicians, supervisors, inspectors, or instructors. Some experienced welders open their own repair shops. Other welders, especially those who obtain a bachelor's degree, become welding engineers.

Employment

Welding, soldering, and brazing workers held about 462,000 jobs in 2006. About 2 of every 3 welding jobs were found in manufacturing. Jobs were concentrated in fabricated metal product manufacturing, transportation equipment manufacturing, machinery manufacturing, architectural and structural metals manufacturing, and construction.

Job Outlook

Employment of welding, soldering, and brazing workers is expected to grow more slowly than average. They will have excellent job opportunities as some welding employers report difficulty finding trained welders.

Employment change. Employment of welding, soldering, and brazing workers is expected to grow about 5 percent over the 2006-16 decade, slower than the average for all occupations. Welding has grown significantly over the long term because of advances that have allowed it to replace other joining technologies in many applications. Thus, demand for welders is increasing in the construction, manufacturing, and utilities industries. Despite overall employment declines in the manufacturing industry, the outlook for welders in manufacturing is far stronger than for other occupations. The basic skills of welding are the same across industries, so welders can easily shift from one industry to another depending on where they are needed most. For example, welders laid off in the auto industry have been able to find work in the booming oil and gas industry, although the shift may require relocating.

Automation is less of a threat to welders and welding machine operators than to other manufacturing occupations. Welding machines must still be operated by someone who is knowledgeable about welding and can inspect the weld and make adjustments. In custom applications, much of the work is difficult or impossible to automate. This includes manufacturing small batches of items, construction work, and making repairs in factories.

Job prospects. Retirements and job growth in the oil and gas and other industries are expected to create excellent opportunities for welders. Welding schools report that graduates have little difficulty finding work, and some welding employers report difficulty finding trained welders.

Earnings

Median wage-and-salary earnings of welders, cutters, solderers, and brazers were $15.10 an hour in May 2006. The middle 50 percent earned between $12.30 and $18.47. The lowest 10 percent had earnings of less than $10.08, and the top 10 percent earned over $22.50. The range of earnings of welders reflects the wide range of skill levels. Median hourly

Projections data from the National Employment Matrix

Occupational Title	SOC Code	Employment, 2006	Projected employment, 2016	Change, 2006-16	
				Number	Percent
Welding, soldering, and brazing workers..	51-4120	462,000	484,000	22,000	5
Welders, cutters, solderers, and brazers	51-4121	409,000	430,000	21,000	5
Welding, soldering, and brazing machine setters, operators, and tenders..	51-4122	53,000	54,000	1,600	3

NOTE: Data in this table are rounded. See the discussion of the employment projections table in the *Handbook* introductory chapter on *Occupational Information Included in the Handbook.*

wage-and-salary earnings of welders, cutters, solderers, and brazers in the industries employing the largest numbers of them were:

Other general purpose machinery manufacturing $15.43
Agriculture, construction, and mining machinery
  manufacturing..14.90
Commercial and industrial machinery and equipment (except
  automotive and electronic) repair and maintenance...........14.59
Architectural and structural metals manufacturing 14.39
Motor vehicle body and trailer manufacturing.....................13.68

Median wage-and-salary earnings of welding, soldering, and brazing machine setters, operators, and tenders were $14.90 an hour in May 2006. The middle 50 percent earned between $12.02 and $18.90. The lowest 10 percent had earnings of less than $9.95, and the top 10 percent earned over $25.44. Their median wage-and-salary earnings in motor vehicle parts manufacturing, the industry employing them in the largest numbers, were $17.75 an hour in May 2006.

Many welders belong to unions. Among these are the International Association of Machinists and Aerospace Workers; the International Brotherhood of Boilermakers, Iron Ship Builders, Blacksmiths, Forgers and Helpers; the International Union, United Automobile, Aerospace and Agricul-tural Implement Workers of America; the United Association of Journeymen and Apprentices of the Plumbing, Pipefitting, Sprinkler Fitting Industry of the United States and Canada; and the United Electrical, Radio, and Machine Workers of America.

Related Occupations

Welding, soldering, and brazing workers are skilled metal workers. Other skilled metal workers include machinists; machine setters, operators, and tenders—metal and plastic; computer control programmers and operators; tool and die makers; sheet metal workers; and boilermakers. Assemblers and fabricators of electrical and electronic equipment often assemble parts using soldering. Pipelayers, plumbers, pipefitters, and steamfitters also need welding skills.

Sources of Additional Information

For information on training opportunities and jobs for welding, soldering, and brazing workers, contact local employers, the local office of the State employment service, or schools providing welding, soldering, or brazing training.

Information on careers, certifications, and educational opportunities in welding is available from:

➤ American Welding Society, 550 N.W. Lejeune Rd., Miami, FL 33126. Internet: **http://www.aws.org**

Printing Occupations

Bookbinders and Bindery Workers

(O*NET 51-5011.00, 51-5012.00)

Significant Points

- Employment is expected to decline rapidly, reflecting the use of more productive machinery and the growth of imports of bound printed material.

- Opportunities for hand bookbinders are limited because only a small number of establishments do this highly specialized work.

- Most bookbinders and bindery workers train on the job.

Nature of the Work

The process of combining printed sheets into finished products such as books, magazines, catalogs, folders, and directories is known as "binding." When a publication or advertising supplement has been printed, it must then be folded, glued, stitched, stapled, or otherwise turned into the finished product that will be seen by the public. *Bindery workers* set up, operate, and maintain the machines that perform these various tasks, while *bookbinders* perform highly skilled hand finishing operations.

Job duties depend on the material being bound. Some types of binding and finishing jobs consist of only one step. Preparing leaflets or newspaper inserts, for example, requires only folding. Binding of books and magazines, on the other hand, requires a number of steps. Bindery workers first assemble the books and magazines from large, flat, printed sheets of paper. They then operate machines that first fold printed sheets into "signatures," which are groups of pages arranged sequentially.

Bookbinders pay careful attention to detail to avoid binding pages incorrectly.

They then assemble the signatures in sequence and join them by means of a saddle-stitch process or perfect binding (where no stitches are used). In firms that do "edition binding", workers bind books produced in large numbers, or "runs."

In libraries where repair work on rare books is needed, bookbinders sew, stitch, or glue the assembled printed sheets, shape the book bodies with presses and trimming machines, and reinforce them with glued fabric strips. Covers are created separately and glued, pasted, or stitched onto the book bodies. The books then undergo a variety of finishing operations, often including wrapping in paper jackets. In establishments that print new books, this work is done mechanically.

A small number of bookbinders work in hand binderies. These highly skilled workers design original or special bindings for limited editions, or restore and rebind rare books. Some binders repair books and provide other specialized binding services to libraries.

Bookbinders and bindery workers in small shops may perform many binding tasks, while those in large shops tend to specialize. Tasks may include performing perfect binding or operating laminating machinery. Others specialize as folder operators or cutter operators, and may perform adjustments and minor repairs to equipment as needed.

Work environment. Binderies often are noisy and jobs can be strenuous, requiring considerable lifting, standing, and carrying. Binding often resembles an assembly line on which workers perform repetitive tasks. The jobs also may require stooping, kneeling, and crouching, but equipment that minimizes such activity is now widely available.

Bookbinders and bindery workers normally work 40 hours per week, although weekend and holiday hours may be necessary if production on a job is behind schedule. Many large printers operate around the clock, so some bindery workers may work on shifts. Part-time workers made up 11 percent of this occupation in 2006.

Training, Other Qualifications, and Advancement
On-the-job training remains the most common form of training for entry level bindery workers, but new technology will require workers to obtain more formal training. Attention to detail and mechanical aptitude are important for these jobs.

Education and training. High school students interested in bindery careers should take shop courses or attend a vocational-technical high school. Occupational skill centers also provide an introduction to bindery work and bookbinding. For entry-level positions, most employers look for high school graduates or those with associate degrees.

Training in graphic communications also can be an asset. Vocational-technical institutes offer postsecondary programs in the graphic arts, as do some skill-updating or retraining programs and community colleges. Other programs are made available by unions to their members. Four-year colleges also offer programs related to printing and publishing, but their emphasis is on preparing people for careers as graphic artists, educators, or managers in the graphic arts field.

While postsecondary education is available, most bookbinders and bindery workers learn the craft through on-the-job training. Inexperienced workers usually are assigned simple tasks such as moving paper from cutting machines to folding machines. They learn basic binding skills, including the characteristics of paper and how to cut large sheets of paper into different sizes with the least amount of waste. Usually, it takes one to three months to learn to operate the simpler machines but it can take up to one year to become completely familiar with more complex equipment, such as computerized binding machines. As workers gain experience, they learn to operate more types of equipment. To keep pace with changing technology, retraining is increasingly important for bindery workers.

Formal apprenticeships are not as common as they used to be, but still are offered by some employers. Apprenticeships allow beginners to acquire skills by working alongside skilled workers while also taking classes. The more structured program provided by an apprenticeship enables workers to acquire the high levels of specialization and skill needed for some bindery and bookbinding jobs.

Other qualifications. Bindery work requires careful attention to detail. Accuracy, patience, neatness, and good eyesight are all important. Mechanical aptitude is necessary to operate the newer, more automated equipment, and workers with computer skills will increasingly be in demand. Manual dexterity is needed in order to count, insert, and fold. In addition, creativity and artistic ability are necessary for hand bookbinding.

Certification and advancement. With experience, binders can expect increased salaries and more responsibility. Completion of a formal certification program can further advancement opportunities. Without additional training, advancement opportunities outside of bindery work are limited. In large binderies, experienced bookbinders or bindery workers may advance to supervisory positions.

Employment
In 2006, bookbinders and bindery workers held about 72,000 jobs, including 7,200 as skilled bookbinders and 65,000 as bindery workers. More than 3 out of 4 bookbinding and bindery jobs are in printing and related support activities. Traditionally, the largest employers of bindery workers were bindery trade shops, which are companies that specialize in providing binding services for printers without binderies or whose printing production exceeds their binding capabilities. However,

Projections data from the National Employment Matrix

Occupational Title	SOC Code	Employment, 2006	Projected employment, 2016	Change, 2006-16	
				Number	Percent
Bookbinders and bindery workers	51-5010	72,000	57,000	-15,000	-21
Bindery workers..	51-5011	65,000	51,000	-14,000	-22
Bookbinders	51-5012	7,200	6,000	-1,200	-17

NOTE: Data in this table are rounded. See the discussion of the employment projections table in the *Handbook* introductory chapter on *Occupational Information Included in the Handbook*.

this type of binding is now being done increasingly in-house, and is now called "in-line finishing."

The publishing industry employed less than 1 in 10 bindery workers. Other bindery workers were found in the employment services industry, which supplies temporary workers to companies that require their services.

Job Outlook
Employment of bookbinders and bindery workers is projected to decline rapidly between 2006 and 2016, but opportunities should be good because many job openings are created by bindery workers who transfer to other occupations.

Employment change. Overall employment of bookbinders and bindery workers is expected to decline rapidly by 21 percent between 2006 and 2016. Over this period, demand for domestic bindery workers will slow as productivity in printing and bindery operations increases. Computers have caused binding to become increasingly automated, and coupled with other technological advances, have reduced labor requirements. Consequently, more printing companies are expected to perform bindery services in-house rather than send the work to specialized binding shops. Also, some bindery jobs will be lost because of outsourcing of work to firms in foreign countries where books and other materials that take a long time to make can be produced more cheaply.

More efficient binding machinery will slow growth in demand for specialized bindery workers who assist skilled bookbinders. The number of establishments that do hand bookbinding is small, also limiting growth.

Job prospects. Bindery workers generally face favorable job opportunities because many workers leave these jobs and there is a recurring need to replace them. However, improvements in binding machinery mean fewer will be replaced than leave. Additionally, many skilled bookbinders are older and will likely retire in the next decade. Experienced workers will continue to have the best opportunities for these skilled jobs. Prospects for all bindery jobs will be best for workers who have completed training or certification programs, internships, or who have experience in a related production occupation.

Earnings
Median hourly earnings of bookbinders were $14.55 in May 2006, compared to $13.16 per hour for all production occupations. The middle 50 percent earned between $10.48 and $19.34 an hour. The lowest 10 percent earned less than $8.30, and the highest 10 percent earned more than $22.69.

Median hourly earnings of bindery workers were $12.29 in May 2006. The middle 50 percent earned between $9.67 and

$16.02 an hour. The lowest 10 percent earned less than $7.93, and the highest 10 percent earned more than $20.14.

Related Occupations
Other workers who set up and operate production machinery include prepress technicians and workers; printing machine operators; machine setters, operators, and tenders—metal and plastic; and various other precision machine operators.

Sources of Additional Information
Information about apprenticeships and other training opportunities may be obtained from local printing industry associations, local bookbinding shops, local offices of the Graphic Communications Conference or local offices of the State employment service. Apprenticeship information is also available from the U.S. Department of Labor's toll-free helpline: (877) 282-5627.

For general information on bindery occupations, write to:
➤ Graphic Communications Conference of the International Brotherhood of Teamsters, 1900 L St.NW., Washington, DC 20036-5007.

For information on careers and training programs in printing and the graphic arts, contact:
➤ Graphic Arts Education and Research Foundation, 1899 Preston White Dr., Reston, VA 20191-5468.
Internet: **http://www.makeyourmark.org**
➤ Printing Industries of America/Graphic Arts Technical Foundation, 200 Deer Run Rd., Sewickley, PA 15143.
➤ NPES The Association for Suppliers of Printing Publishing, and Converting Technologies, 1899 Preston White Dr., Reston, VA 20191-4367.
Internet: **http://www.npes.org/education/index.html**

Prepress Technicians and Workers

(O*NET 51-5021.00, 51-5022.00)

Significant Points

- Most prepress technician jobs now require formal postsecondary graphic communications training in the various types of computer software used in digital imaging.

- Employment is projected to decline rapidly as the increased use of computers in typesetting and page layout requires fewer prepress technicians.

Nature of the Work

The printing process has three stages: prepress, press, and binding or finishing. While workers in small print shops are usually responsible for all three stages, in most printing firms, formatting print jobs and correcting layout errors before the job goes to print is the responsibility of a specialized group of workers. *Prepress technicians and workers* are responsible for this prepress work. They perform a variety of tasks to help transform text and pictures into finished pages and prepare the pages for print.

Prepress technicians receive images from in-house graphic designers or directly from customers and see the job through the process of preparing print-ready pages to create a finished printing plate. Printing plates are thin sheets of metal that carry the final image to be printed. Printing presses use this plate to copy the image to the printed products we see every day. Once a printing plate has been created, prepress technicians collaborate with printing machine operators to check for any potential printing problems. Several plates may be needed if a job requires color, but advanced printing technology does not require plates.

For a long time, prepress workers used a photographic process to make printing plates. This is a complex process involving ultraviolet light and chemical exposure through which the text and images of a print job harden on a metal plate and become water repellent. These hard, water repellent portions of the metal plate are in the form of the text and images that will be printed on paper. More recently, the printing industry has largely moved to technology known as "direct-to-plate", by which the prepress technicians send the data directly to a plating system, by-passing the need for the photographic technique.

The direct-to-plate technique is just one example of digital imaging technology that has largely replaced cold type print technology. Prepress technicians known as "preflight technicians" or production coordinators are using digital imaging technology to complete more and more print jobs. Using this technology, technicians take electronic files received from customers and check them for completeness. They then format the jobs using electronic page layout software in order to fit the pages to dimensions of the paper stock to be used. When color printing is required, the technicians produce an electronic image of the printed pages and then print a copy, or "proof," of the pages as they will appear when printed. The technician then has the proofs delivered or mailed to the customer for a final check. Once the customer approves the proofs, technicians use laser "imagesetters" to expose digital images of the pages directly onto the thin metal printing plates.

Advances in computer software and printing technology continue to change prepress work. Today, customers of print shops often use their own computers to do much of the typesetting and page layout work formerly done by prepress technicians. This process, called "desktop publishing," provides printers with pages of material that look like the desired finished product. This work is usually done by desktop publishers or graphic designers with knowledge of publishing software. (Sections on desktop publishers and graphic designers appear elsewhere in the *Handbook*.) As a result, prepress workers often receive files from customers on a computer disk or via e-mail that contain typeset material already laid out in pages. Other more advanced technologies now allow prepress technicians to send printing files directly to the printer and skip the plate-making process altogether. Despite the shortcuts that technological advancements allow, workers still need to understand the basic processes behind prepress, press, and finishing operations. Some workers, known as *job printers*, perform prepress and print operations. Job printers often are found in small establishments where work combines several job skills.

Work environment. Prepress technicians and workers usually work in clean, air-conditioned areas with little noise. Some workers may develop eyestrain from working in front of a video display terminal or other minor problems, such as backaches. Those platemakers who still work with toxic chemicals face the hazard of skin irritations. Workers are often subject to stress and the pressures of deadlines and tight work schedules.

Prepress employees usually work an 8-hour day. Some workers—particularly those employed by newspapers—work night shifts. Weekend and holiday work may be required, particularly when a print job is behind schedule. Part-time prepress technicians made up 12 percent of this occupation in 2006.

Training, Other Qualifications, and Advancement

Employers prefer workers with formal training in printing or publishing. Familiarity with the printing process, including the technology used, and attention to detail are the qualities that employers will seek most in job applicants.

Education and training. Many employers consider the best candidates for prepress jobs to be individuals with a combination of work experience in the printing industry and formal training in the new digital technology. The experience of these applicants provides them with an understanding of how printing plants operate and demonstrates their interest in advancing within the industry.

Traditionally, prepress technicians and workers started as helpers and were trained on the job. Some of these jobs re-

Prepress technicians and workers increasingly use direct-to-plate technologies that eliminate direct contact with ink and chemicals.

Projections data from the National Employment Matrix

Occupational Title	SOC Code	Employment, 2006	Projected employment, 2016	Change, 2006-16	
				Number	Percent
Prepress technicians and workers	—	119,000	100,000	-19,000	-16
Job printers...	51-5021	48,000	44,000	-4,500	-9
Prepress technicians and workers	51-5022	71,000	56,000	-15,000	-21

NOTE: Data in this table are rounded. See the discussion of the employment projections table in the *Handbook* introductory chapter on *Occupational Information Included in the Handbook.*

quired years of experience performing detailed manual work to become skillful enough to perform the most difficult tasks. Today, however, employers expect workers to have some formal postsecondary graphic communications training in the various types of computer software used in digital imaging and will train workers on the job as needed.

For beginners, 2-year associate degree programs offered by community colleges, junior colleges, and technical schools teach the latest prepress skills and allow students to practice applying them. There are also 4-year bachelor's degree programs in graphic design aimed primarily at students who plan to move into management positions in printing or design. For workers who do not wish to enroll in a degree program, prepress-related courses are offered at many community colleges, junior colleges, 4-year colleges and universities, vocational-technical institutes, and private trade and technical schools. Workers with experience in other printing jobs can take a few college-level graphic communications courses to upgrade their skills and qualify for prepress jobs.

Other qualifications. Employers prefer workers with good communication skills, both oral and written. When prepress problems arise, prepress technicians and workers should be able to deal courteously with customers to resolve them. Also, in small shops, they may take customer orders. Persons interested in working for firms using advanced printing technology need to be comfortable with electronics and computers. At times, prepress personnel may have to perform computations in order to estimate job costs or operate many of the electronics used to run modern equipment.

Prepress technicians and workers need manual dexterity and accurate eyesight. Good color vision helps workers find mistakes and locate potential problems. It is essential for prepress workers to be able to pay attention to detail and work independently. Artistic ability is often a plus. Employers also seek persons who are comfortable with the pressures of meeting deadlines, using new software, and operating new equipment.

Advancement. Employers may send experienced technicians to industry-sponsored update and retraining programs to develop new skills or hone current ones. This kind of prepress training is sometimes offered in-house or through unions in the printing industry.

Employment

Prepress technicians and workers overall held about 119,000 jobs in 2006. Most prepress jobs are found in the printing industry, while newspaper publishing employs the second largest number of prepress technicians and workers.

The printing and publishing industries are two of the most geographically dispersed in the United States. While prepress jobs are found throughout the country, large numbers are concentrated in large printing centers such as Chicago, Los Angeles–Long Beach, New York City, Minneapolis–St. Paul, Philadelphia, Boston, and Washington, DC.

Job Outlook

Employment of prepress technicians and workers is projected to decline rapidly through 2016, because of improvements in printing technology that require fewer of these workers. Despite this, job prospects are good for prepress technicians with good computer and customer service skills.

Employment change. Overall employment of prepress technicians and workers is expected to decline by 16 percent over the 2006-2016 period. Demand for printed material should continue to grow, spurred by rising levels of personal income, increasing school enrollments, higher levels of educational attainment, and expanding markets. But the use of computers and publishing software—often by the clients of the printing company—will result in rising productivity of prepress technicians, and thus halting the creation of new jobs.

Computer software now allows office workers at a desktop computer terminal to specify text typeface and style and to format pages. This development shifts traditional prepress functions away from printing plants into advertising and public relations agencies, graphic design firms, and large corporations. As page layout and graphic design capabilities of computer software have become less expensive and more user-friendly, many companies are turning to in-house desktop publishing. Some firms also are finding it less costly to prepare their own newsletters and other reports. At newspapers, writers and editors also are doing more composition using publishing software. This rapid growth in the use of desktop publishing software has eliminated most prepress typesetting and composition technician jobs associated with the older printing technologies. In addition, new technology is increasing the amount of automation that printing companies can employ, which leaves less work for prepress workers. The duties of prepress workers will likely begin to merge with those of other printing industry workers—such as those of customer service representatives—which will also curb prepress job growth.

Job prospects. Despite a decline in the number of new prepress positions, opportunities will be favorable for workers with strong computer and customer service skills, such as preflight technicians who electronically check materials prepared by clients and adapt them for printing.

In order to compete in the desktop publishing environment, commercial printing companies are adding desktop publishing and electronic prepress work to the list of services they provide. Electronic prepress technicians, digital proofers, platemakers, and graphic designers are using new equipment and ever-improving software to design and lay out publications and complete their printing more quickly. The increasing range of services offered by printing companies using new digital technologies mean that opportunities in prepress work will be best for those with computer backgrounds who have completed postsecondary programs in printing technology or graphic communications. Workers with this background will be better able to adapt to the continuing evolution of publishing and printing technology.

Earnings

While wage rates for prepress technicians and workers depend on basic factors such as employer, education, and location, the median hourly earnings of prepress technicians and workers were $16.01 in May 2006, compared to $13.16 per hour for all production occupations. The middle 50 percent earned between $11.98 and $20.69 an hour. The lowest 10 percent earned less than $9.37, and the highest 10 percent earned more than $25.71 an hour. Median hourly earnings in printing and related support activities, the industry employing the largest number of prepress technicians and workers, were $16.44 in May 2006, while workers in the newspaper, periodical, and book publishing industry earned $15.17 an hour.

For job printers, median hourly earnings were $15.58 in May 2006. The middle 50 percent earned between $12.15 and $19.83 an hour. The lowest 10 percent earned less than $9.56, and the highest 10 percent earned more than $24.70 an hour. Median hourly earnings in the industries employing the largest numbers of job printers May 2006 were $16.19 in the newspaper, periodical, and book publishing industry and $15.76 in printing and related support activities.

Related Occupations

Prepress technicians and workers use artistic skills in their work. These skills also are essential for artists and related workers, graphic designers, and desktop publishers. Moreover, many of the skills used in Web site design also are employed in prepress technology. Prepress technicians' work also is tied in closely with that of printing machine operators.

Sources of Additional Information

Details about training programs may be obtained from local employers such as newspapers and printing shops, or from local offices of the State employment service.

For information on careers and training in printing and the graphic arts, write to:

➤ Graphic Arts Education and Research Foundation, 1899 Preston White Dr., Reston, VA 20191-5468.
Internet: **http://www.makeyourmark.org**
➤ Graphic Communications Conference of the International Brotherhood of Teamsters, 1900 L St.NW., Washington, DC 20036-5007.
➤ Printing Industries of America/Graphic Arts Technical Foundation, 200 Deer Run Rd., Sewickley, PA 15143-2324.

Printing Machine Operators

(O*NET 51-5023.00)

Significant Points

- Most printing machine operators are trained on the job.

- Retirements of older press operators are expected to create openings for skilled workers.

- Rising demand for customized print jobs will mean those skilled in digital printing operations will have the best job opportunities.

Nature of the Work

Printing machine operators, also known as press operators, prepare, operate, and maintain printing presses. Duties of printing machine operators vary according to the type of press they operate. Traditional printing methods, such as offset lithography, gravure, flexography, and letterpress, use a plate or roller that carries the final image that is to be printed and copies the image to paper. In addition to the traditional printing processes, plateless or nonimpact processes are coming into general use. Plateless processes—including digital, electrostatic, and inkjet printing—are used for copying, duplicating, and document and specialty printing. Plateless processes usually are done by quick printing shops and smaller in-house printing shops, but increasingly are being used by commercial printers for short-run or customized printing jobs.

Machine operators' jobs differ from one shop to another because of differences in the types and sizes of presses. Small commercial shops can be operated by one person and tend to have relatively small presses, which print only one or two colors at a time. Large newspaper, magazine, and book printers use giant "in-line web" presses that require a crew of several press operators and press assistants.

After working with prepress technicians (who are covered in the *Handbook* statement on prepress technicians and workers) to identify and resolve any potential problems with a job, printing machine operators prepare machines for printing. To prepare presses, operators install the printing plate with the images to be printed and adjust the pressure at which the machine prints. Then they ink the presses, load paper, and adjust the press to the paper size. Operators ensure that paper and ink meet specifications, and adjust the flow of ink to the inking rollers accordingly. They then feed paper through the press cylinders and adjust feed and tension controls. New digital technology, in contrast, is able to automate much of this work.

While printing presses are running, printing machine operators monitor their operation and keep the paper feeders well stocked. They make adjustments to manage ink distribution, speed, and temperature in the drying chamber, if the press has one. If paper tears or jams and the press stops, which can happen with some offset presses, operators quickly correct the problem to minimize downtime. Similarly, operators working with other high-speed presses constantly look for problems, and when necessary make quick corrections to avoid expensive losses of paper and ink. Throughout the run, operators must regularly pull sheets to check for any printing imperfections. Most printers have, or will soon have, presses with computers and sophisticated instruments to control press operations, making it possible to complete printing jobs in less time. With this equipment, printing machine operators set up, monitor, and adjust the printing process on a control panel or computer monitor, which allows them to control the press electronically.

In most shops, machine operators also perform preventive maintenance. They oil and clean the presses and make minor repairs.

Work environment. Operating a press can be physically and mentally demanding, and sometimes tedious. Printing machine operators are on their feet most of the time. Often, operators work under pressure to meet deadlines. Most printing presses are capable of high printing speeds, and adjustments must be made quickly to avoid waste. Pressrooms are noisy, and workers in certain areas wear ear protection. Working with press machinery can be hazardous, but the threat of accidents has decreased with newer computerized presses that allow operators to make most adjustments from a control panel.

Many printing machine operators, particularly those who work for newspapers, work weekends, nights, and holidays as many presses operate continually. They also may work overtime to meet deadlines. The average operator worked 40 hours per week in 2006.

Training, Other Qualifications, and Advancement

Although employers prefer that beginners complete a formal apprenticeship or a postsecondary program in printing equipment operation, most printing machine operators are trained on the job. Attention to detail and familiarity with electronics and computers are essential for operators.

Education and training. Beginning printing machine operators load, unload, and clean presses. With time and training, they may become fully qualified to operate that type of press. Operators can gain experience on more than one kind of printing press during the course of their career.

Experienced operators will periodically receive retraining and skill updating. For example, printing plants that change

Printing machine operators execute production orders through an increasingly automated process.

from sheet-fed offset presses to digital presses have to retrain the entire press crew because skill requirements for the two types of presses are different.

Apprenticeships for printing machine operators, once the dominant method for preparing for this occupation, are becoming less prevalent. When they are offered by the employer, they include on-the-job instruction and some related classroom training or correspondence school courses.

Formal postsecondary programs in printing equipment operation offered by technical and trade schools, community colleges, and universities are growing in importance. Postsecondary courses in printing provide the theoretical and technical knowledge needed to operate advanced equipment that employers look for in an entry-level worker. Some postsecondary school programs require two years of study and award an associate degree.

Because of technical developments in the printing industry, courses in chemistry, electronics, color theory, and physics are helpful in secondary or postsecondary programs.

Other qualifications. Persons who wish to become printing machine operators need mechanical aptitude to make press adjustments and repairs. Workers need good vision and attention to detail to locate and fix problems with print jobs. Oral and written communication skills also are required. Operators should possess the mathematical skills necessary to compute percentages, weights, and measures, and to calculate the amount of ink and paper needed to do a job. Operators now also need basic computer skills to work with newer printing machines.

Certification and advancement. As printing machine operators gain experience, they may advance in pay and responsibility by working on a more complex printing press. For example, operators who have demonstrated their ability to work with a one-color sheet-fed press may be trained to operate a four-color sheet-fed press. Voluntarily earning a formal certification may also help advance a career in printing. An operator also may advance to pressroom supervisor and become responsible for an entire press crew. In addition, printing machine operators can draw on their knowledge of press operations to become cost estimators, providing estimates of printing jobs to potential customers.

Employment

Printing machine operators held about 198,000 jobs in 2006. Half of all operator jobs were in printing and related support activities. Paper manufacturers and newspaper publishers also were large employers. Additional jobs were in advertising agencies, employment services firms, and colleges and universities that do their own printing.

The printing and newspaper publishing industries are two of the most geographically dispersed in the United States. While printing machine operators can find jobs throughout the country, large numbers of jobs are concentrated in large printing centers such as Chicago, Los Angeles-Long Beach, New York, Minneapolis-St. Paul, Philadelphia, Boston, and Washington, DC.

Job Outlook

Employment of printing machine operators is projected to decline moderately through 2016, as newer printing presses require fewer operators. Despite this, job opportunities are ex-

Projections data from the National Employment Matrix

Occupational Title	SOC Code	Employment, 2006	Projected employment, 2016	Change, 2006-16	
				Number	Percent
Printing machine operators	51-5023	198,000	186,000	-11,000	-6

NOTE: Data in this table are rounded. See the discussion of the employment projections table in the *Handbook* introductory chapter on *Occupational Information Included in the Handbook.*

pected to be favorable because a large number of these workers are expected to retire over the next decade. The best opportunities will be available to skilled operators.

Employment change. Employment of printing machine operators is expected to decline moderately by six percent over the 2006-16 decade even as the output of printed materials is expected to increase. Employment will fall because of increasing automation in the printing industry and because of the outsourcing of some production to foreign countries.

Book and magazine circulation will increase as school enrollments rise and niche publications continue to enjoy success. Additional growth will also come from the increasing ability of the printing industry to profitably print smaller quantities, which should widen the market for printed materials as production costs decline.

Commercial printing will continue to be driven by increased expenditures for print advertising materials. New marketing techniques are leading advertisers to increase spending on messages targeted to specific audiences, and should continue to require the printing of a wide variety of catalogs, direct mail enclosures, newspaper inserts, and other kinds of print advertising.

However, employment will not grow at the same pace as output because increased use of new computerized printing equipment will require fewer operators. This will especially be true with the increasing automation of the large printing presses used in the newspaper industry. In addition, some companies are lowering their printing costs by having their work printed out of the country when it does not need to be completed quickly. New business practices within the publishing industry, such as printing-on-demand and electronic publishing, will reduce the size of print runs, further moderating output.

Job prospects. Opportunities for employment in printing machine operation should be favorable. Retirements of older printing machine operators and the need for workers trained on increasingly computerized printing equipment will create many job openings over the next decade. For example, small printing jobs will increasingly be run on sophisticated high-speed digital printing equipment that requires a complex set of operator skills, such as knowledge of database management software. Those who complete postsecondary training programs in printing and who are comfortable with computers will have the best employment opportunities.

Earnings

Median hourly earnings of printing machine operators were $14.90 in May 2006, as compared to $13.16 per hour for all production occupations. The middle 50 percent earned between $11.11 and $19.49 an hour. The lowest 10 percent earned less than $8.84, and the highest 10 percent earned more than $24.23 an hour. Median hourly earnings in the industries employing the largest numbers of printing machine operators in May 2006 were:

Newspaper, periodical, book, and directory publishers $17.27
Converted paper product manufacturing................................16.37
Printing and related support activities...................................15.55
Plastics product manufacturing...13.81
Advertising and related services 11.95

The basic wage rate for a printing machine operator depends on the geographic area in which the work is located and on the size and complexity of the printing press being operated.

Related Occupations

Other workers who set up and operate production machinery include machine setters, operators, and tenders—metal and plastic; bookbinders and bindery workers; and various precision machine operators.

Sources of Additional Information

Details about apprenticeships and other training opportunities may be obtained from local employers, such as newspapers and printing shops, local offices of the Graphic Communications Conference of the International Brotherhood of Teamsters, local affiliates of Printing Industries of America/Graphic Arts Technical Foundation, or local offices of the State employment service.

For general information about printing machine operators, contact:

➤ Graphic Communications Conference of the International Brotherhood of Teamsters, 1900 L St.NW., Washington, DC 20036-5007.

For information on careers and training in printing and the graphic arts contact:

➤ NPES The Association for Suppliers of Printing Publishing, and Converting Technologies, 1899 Preston White Dr., Reston, VA 20191-4367.
Internet: **http://www.npes.org/education/index.html**

➤ Printing Industry of America/Graphic Arts Technical Foundation, 200 Deer Run Rd., Sewickley, PA 15143.

➤ Graphic Arts Education and Research Foundation, 1899 Preston White Dr., Reston, VA 20191-5468.
Internet: **http://www.makeyourmark.org**

Textile, Apparel, and Furnishings Occupations

(O*NET 51-6011.00, 51-6021.00, 51-6031.00, 51-6041.00, 51-6042.00, 51-6051.00, 51-6052.00, 51-6061.00, 51-6062.00, 51-6063.00, 51-6064.00, 51-6091.00, 51-6092.00, 51-6093.00, 51-6099.99)

Significant Points

- Most workers learn through on-the-job training.

- This group ranks among the rapidly declining occupations because of increases in imports, offshore assembly, productivity gains from automation, and new fabrics that do not need as much processing.

- Earnings of most workers are low.

Nature of the Work

Textile, apparel, and furnishings workers produce fibers, cloth, and upholstery, and fashion them into a wide range of products that we use in our daily lives. Textiles are the basis of towels, bed linens, hosiery and socks, and nearly all clothing, but they also are a key ingredient in products ranging from roofing to tires. Jobs range from those that involve programming computers to those in which the worker operates large industrial machinery and to those that require substantial handwork.

Textile machine setters, operators, and tenders run machines that make textile products from fibers. The first step in manufacturing textiles is preparing the natural or synthetic fibers. *Extruding and forming machine operators, synthetic and glass fibers*, set up and operate machines that extrude or force liquid synthetic material such as rayon, fiberglass, or liquid polymers through small holes and draw out filaments. Other operators put natural fibers such as cotton, wool, flax, or hemp through carding and combing machines that clean and align them into short lengths collectively called "sliver." In making sliver, operators may combine different types of natural fibers and synthetics filaments to give the product a desired texture, durability, or other characteristic. *Textile winding, twisting, and drawing-out machine operators* take the sliver and draw out, twist, and wind it to produce yarn, taking care to repair any breaks.

Textile bleaching and dyeing machine operators control machines that wash, bleach, or dye either yarn or finished fabrics and other products. *Textile knitting and weaving machine operators* put the yarn on machines that weave, knit, loop, or tuft it into a product. Woven fabrics are used to make apparel and other goods, whereas some knitted products (such as hosiery) and tufted products (such as carpeting) emerge in near-finished form. Different types of machines are used for these processes, but operators perform similar tasks, repairing breaks in the yarn and monitoring the yarn supply while tending many machines at once. *Textile cutting machine operators* trim the fabric into various widths and lengths, depending on its intended use.

Apparel workers cut fabric and other materials and sew it into clothing and related products. Workers in a variety of occupations fall under the heading of apparel workers. *Tailors, dressmakers, and sewers* make custom clothing and alter and repair garments for individuals. However, workers in most apparel occupations are found in manufacturing, performing specialized tasks in the production of large numbers of garments that are shipped to retail establishments for sale.

Fabric and apparel patternmakers convert a clothing designer's original model of a garment into a pattern of separate parts that can be laid out on a length of fabric. After discussing the item with the designer, these skilled workers usually use a computer to outline the parts and draw in details to indicate the positions of pleats, buttonholes, and other features. (In the past, patternmakers laid out the parts on paper, using pencils and drafting instruments such as rulers.) Patternmakers then alter the size of the pieces in the pattern to produce garments of various sizes, and they may mark the fabric to show the best layout of pattern pieces to minimize waste of material.

Once an item's pattern has been made and marked, mass production of the garment begins. Cutters and trimmers take the patterns and cut out material, paying close attention to their work because mistakes are costly. Following the outline of the pattern, they place multiple layers of material on the cutting table and use an electric knife or other tools to cut out the various pieces of the garment; delicate materials may be cut by hand. In some companies, computer-controlled machines do the cutting.

Sewing machine operators join the parts of a garment together, reinforce seams, and attach buttons, hooks, zippers, and accessories to produce clothing. After the product is sewn, other workers remove lint and loose threads and inspect and package the garments.

Shoe and leather workers are employed either in manufacturing or in personal services. In shoe manufacturing, *shoe machine operators and tenders* operate a variety of specialized machines that perform cutting, joining, and finishing functions. In personal services, *shoe and leather workers and repairers* perform a variety of repairs and custom leatherwork for the general public. They construct, decorate, or repair shoes, belts, purses, saddles, luggage, and other leather products. They also may repair some products made of canvas or plastic. When making custom shoes or modifying existing footwear for people with foot problems or special needs, shoe and leather workers and repairers cut pieces of leather, shape them over a form shaped like a foot, and sew them together. They then attach soles and heels, using sewing machines or cement and nails. They also dye and polish the items, using a buffing wheel to produce a smooth surface and lustrous shine. When making luggage, they fasten leather to a frame and attach handles and other hardware. They also cut and secure linings inside the frames and sew or stamp designs onto the exterior of the luggage. In addition to performing all of the preceding steps, saddle makers often apply leather dyes and liquid topcoats to produce a glossy finish on a saddle. They also may decorate the surface of the saddle by hand stitching or by stamping the leather with decorative patterns and designs. Shoe and leather workers and repairers who own their own shops keep records and supervise other workers.

Upholsterers make, fix, and restore furniture that is covered with fabric. Using hammers and tack pullers, upholsterers who restore furniture remove old fabric and stuffing to get down to the springs and wooden frame. Then they reglue loose sections of the frame and refinish exposed wood. The springs sit on a cloth mat, called webbing, that is attached to the frame. Upholsterers replace torn webbing, examine the springs, and replace broken or bent ones.

Upholsterers who make new furniture start with a bare wooden frame. First, they install webbing, tacking it to one side of the frame, stretching it tight, and tacking it to the other side. Then, they tie each spring to the webbing and to its neighboring springs. Next, they cover the springs with filler, such as foam, a polyester batt, or similar fibrous batting material, to form a smooth, rounded surface. Then they measure and cut fabric for the arms, backs, seats, sides, and other surfaces, leaving as little waste as possible. Finally, sewing the fabric pieces together and attaching them to the frame with tacks, staples, or glue, they affix any ornaments, such as fringes, buttons, or rivets. Sometimes, upholsterers provide pickup and delivery of the furniture they work on. They also help customers select new coverings by providing samples of fabrics and pictures of finished pieces.

Laundry and drycleaning workers clean cloth garments, linens, draperies, blankets, and other articles. They also may clean leather, suede, furs, and rugs. When necessary, they treat spots and stains on articles before laundering or drycleaning. They tend machines during cleaning and ensure that items are not lost or misplaced with those of another customer. *Pressers, textile, garment, and related materials*, shape and remove wrinkles from items after steam pressing them or ironing them by hand. Workers then assemble each customer's items, box or bag them, and prepare an itemized bill for the customer.

Work environment. Most people in textile, apparel, and furnishings occupations work a standard 5-day, 35- to 40-hour week. Working on evenings and weekends is common for shoe and leather workers, laundry and drycleaning workers, and tailors, dressmakers, and sewers employed in retail stores. Many textile and fiber mills often use rotating schedules of shifts so that employees do not continuously work nights or days. But these rotating shifts sometimes cause workers to have sleep disorders and stress-related problems.

Although much of the work in apparel manufacturing still is based on a piecework system that allows for little interpersonal contact, some apparel firms are placing more emphasis on teamwork and cooperation. Under this new system, individuals work closely with one another, and each team or module often governs itself, increasing the overall responsibility of each operator.

Working conditions vary by establishment and by occupation. In manufacturing, machinery in textile mills is often noisy, as are areas in which sewing and pressing are performed in apparel

Textile machine setters, operators, and tenders tend machines that weave yarn into apparel.

factories; patternmaking and spreading areas tend to be much quieter. Many older factories are cluttered, hot, and poorly lit and ventilated, but more modern facilities usually have more workspace and are well lit and ventilated. Textile machinery operators use protective glasses and masks that cover their noses and mouths to protect against airborne particles. Many machines operate at high speeds, and textile machinery workers must be careful not to wear clothing or jewelry that could get caught in moving parts. In addition, extruding and forming machine operators wear protective shoes and clothing when working with certain chemical compounds.

Work in apparel production can be physically demanding. Some workers sit for long periods, and others spend many hours on their feet, leaning over tables and operating machinery. Operators must be attentive while running sewing machines, pressers, automated cutters, and the like. A few workers wear protective devices such as gloves. In some instances, new machinery and production techniques have decreased the physical demands on workers. For example, newer pressing machines are controlled by foot pedals or by computer and do not require much strength to operate.

Laundries and drycleaning establishments are often hot and noisy. Employees also may be exposed to harsh solvents, but newer environmentally-friendly and less toxic cleaning solvents are improving the work environment in these establishments. Areas in which shoe and leather workers make or repair shoes and other leather items can be noisy, and odors from leather dyes and stains frequently are present. Workers need to pay close attention when working with machines, to avoid punctures, lacerations, and abrasions.

Upholstery work is not dangerous, but upholsterers usually wear protective gloves and clothing when using sharp tools and lifting and handling furniture or springs. During most of the workday, upholsterers stand and may do a lot of bending and heavy lifting. They also may work in awkward positions for short periods.

Training, Other Qualifications, and Advancement

A high school diploma is sufficient for most jobs in textile, apparel, and furnishings occupations. Most people learn their jobs by working alongside more experienced workers.

Education and training. Most workers in these jobs have a high school diploma or less education. However, applicants with postsecondary vocational training or previous work experience may have a better chance of getting a more skilled job and advancing to a supervisory position.

Machine operators usually are trained on the job by more experienced employees or by machinery manufacturers' representatives. Operators begin with simple tasks and are assigned more difficult operations as they gain experience.

Precision shoe and leather workers and repairers generally also learn their skills on the job. Manual dexterity and the mechanical aptitude to work with handtools and machines are important in shoe repair and leatherworking. Shoe and leather workers who produce custom goods should have artistic ability as well. Beginners start as helpers for experienced workers, but, in manufacturing, they may attend more formal in-house training programs. Beginners gradually take on more tasks until they are fully qualified workers, a process that takes about 2 years in an apprenticeship program or as a helper in a shop. Other workers spend 6 months to a year in a vocational training program. Learning to make saddles takes longer. Shoe repairers need to keep their skills up to date to work with the rapidly changing footwear styles and materials. Some attend trade shows or specialized training seminars and workshops in custom shoemaking, shoe repair, and other leatherwork sponsored by associations.

Custom tailors, dressmakers, and sewers often have previous experience in apparel production, design, or alteration. Knowledge of fabrics, design, and construction is very important. Custom tailors sometimes learn these skills through courses in high school or a community college. Some experienced custom tailors open their own tailoring shop. Custom tailoring is a highly competitive field, however, and training in small-business operations can mean the difference between success and failure.

Laundry and dry cleaning workers usually learn on the job also. Although laundries and drycleaners prefer entrants with previous work experience, they routinely hire inexperienced workers.

Most upholsterers learn their skills on the job, but a few do so through apprenticeships. Inexperienced persons also may take training in basic upholstery in vocational schools and some community colleges. The length of training may vary from 6 weeks to 3 years. Upholsterers who work on custom-made pieces may train for 8 to 10 years.

Other qualifications. In manufacturing, textile and apparel workers need good hand-eye coordination, manual dexterity, physical stamina, and the ability to perform repetitive tasks for long periods. As machinery in the industry continues to become more complex, knowledge of the basics of computers and electronics will increasingly be an asset. In addition, the trends toward cross-training of operators and working in teams will increase the time needed to become fully trained on all machines and require interpersonal skills to work effectively with others.

Upholsterers should have manual dexterity, good coordination, and the strength needed to lift heavy furniture. An eye for detail, a flair for color, and the ability to use fabrics creatively also are helpful.

Advancement. Some production workers may become first-line supervisors, but most can advance only to more skilled operator jobs. Some in the shoemaking and leatherworking occupations begin as workers or repairers and advance to salaried supervisory and managerial positions. Some open their own shop. They are more likely to succeed if they understand business practices and management and offer good customer service in addition to their technical skills.

Upholsterers, too, can open their own shops. The upholstery business is highly competitive, however, so operating a shop successfully is difficult. Some experienced or highly skilled upholsterers may become supervisors or sample makers in large shops and factories.

Employment

Textile, apparel, and furnishings workers held 873,000 jobs in 2006. Employment in the detailed occupations that make up this group was distributed as follows:

Laundry and dry-cleaning workers	239,000
Sewing machine operators	233,000
Pressers, textile, garment, and related materials	77,000
Upholsterers	55,000
Tailors, dressmakers, and custom sewers	54,000
Textile winding, twisting, and drawing out machine setters, operators, and tenders	43,000
Textile knitting and weaving machine setters, operators, and tenders	40,000
Sewers, hand	23,000
Textile bleaching and dyeing machine operators and tenders	19,000
Textile cutting machine setters, operators, and tenders	19,000
Extruding and forming machine setters, operators, and tenders, synthetic and glass fibers	18,000
Shoe and leather workers and repairers	16,000
Fabric and apparel patternmakers	9,200
Shoe machine operators and tenders	4,100
All other textile, apparel, and furnishings workers	24,000

Manufacturing jobs are concentrated in California, North Carolina, Georgia, New York, Texas, and South Carolina. Jobs in reupholstery, shoe repair and custom leatherwork, and laundry and drycleaning establishments are found in cities and towns throughout the Nation. Overall, about 12 percent of all workers in textile, apparel, and furnishings occupations were self-employed; however, about half of all tailors, dressmakers, and sewers and about a quarter of all upholsterers were self-employed.

Job Outlook

Overall employment of textile, apparel, and furnishings workers is expected to decline rapidly through 2016, but some openings will be created by the need to replace workers who leave the occupation.

Employment change. Employment in textile, apparel, and furnishing occupations is expected to decline by 11 percent between 2006 and 2016. Apparel workers have been among the most rapidly declining occupational groups in the economy. Increasing imports, the use of offshore assembly, and greater productivity through automation will contribute to additional job losses. Also, many new textiles require less production and processing.

Domestic production of apparel and textiles will continue to move abroad, and imports to the U.S. market are expected to increase. Fierce competition in the market for apparel will keep domestic apparel and textile firms under intense pressure to cut costs and produce more with fewer workers. Although the textile industry already is highly automated, it will continue to seek to increase worker productivity through the introduction of labor-saving machinery and the invention of new fibers and fabrics that reduce production costs. Technological developments, such as computer-aided marking and grading, computer-controlled cutters, semiautomatic sewing and pressing machines, and automated material-handling systems have increased output while reducing the need for some workers in larger firms.

Despite advances in technology, the apparel industry has had difficulty employing automated equipment for many assembly tasks because of the delicate properties of many textiles. Also, the industry produces a wide variety of apparel items that change frequently with changes in style and season. Even so, increasing numbers of sewing machine operator jobs are expected to be lost to low-wage workers abroad.

Outside of the manufacturing sector, tailors, dressmakers, and sewers—the most skilled apparel workers—are expected to experience little to no change in employment. Most of these workers are self-employed or work in clothing stores. The demand for custom home furnishings and tailored clothes is diminishing in general, but remains steady in upscale stores and by certain clients. Designer apparel and other handmade goods also appeal to people looking for one-of-a-kind items.

Employment of shoe and leather workers is expected to decline rapidly through 2016 as a result of growing imports of less expensive shoes and leather goods and of increasing productivity of U.S. manufacturers. Also, buying new shoes often is cheaper than repairing worn or damaged ones. However, declines might be offset somewhat as the population continues to age and more people need custom shoes for health reasons.

Employment of upholsterers is expected to decline moderately through 2016 as new furniture and automotive seats use more durable coverings and as manufacturing firms continue to become more automated and efficient. Demand for the reupholstery of furniture also is expected to decline as the increasing manufacture of new, relatively inexpensive upholstered furniture causes many consumers simply to replace old, worn furniture. However, demand will continue to be steady for upholsterers who restore very valuable furniture. Most reupholstery work is labor intensive and not easily automated.

Job prospects. Even though the overall number of jobs in this occupation is decreasing, job openings do arise each year from the need to replace some of the many workers who transfer to other occupations, retire, or leave the occupation for other reasons.

Earnings

Earnings of textile, apparel, and furnishings workers vary by occupation. Because many production workers in apparel manufacturing are paid according to the number of acceptable pieces they produce, their total earnings depend on skill,

Projections data from the National Employment Matrix

Occupational Title	SOC Code	Employment, 2006	Projected employment, 2016	Change, 2006-16	
				Number	Percent
Textile, apparel, and furnishings occupations...................................	51-6000	873,000	777,000	-97,000	-11
Laundry and dry-cleaning workers..	51-6011	239,000	262,000	23,000	10
Pressers, textile, garment, and related materials..........................	51-6021	77,000	74,000	-3,400	-4
Sewing machine operators...	51-6031	233,000	170,000	-63,000	-27
Shoe and leather workers..	51-6040	20,000	17,000	-3,100	-16
Shoe and leather workers and repairers..................................	51-6041	16,000	14,000	-1,600	-10
Shoe machine operators and tenders......................................	51-6042	4,100	2,600	-1,500	-36
Tailors, dressmakers, and sewers	51-6050	77,000	76,000	-1,800	-2
Sewers, hand...	51-6051	23,000	21,000	-2,900	-12
Tailors, dressmakers, and custom sewers..............................	51-6052	54,000	55,000	1,000	2
Textile machine setters, operators, and tenders.........................	51-6060	122,000	88,000	-34,000	-28
Textile bleaching and dyeing machine operators and tenders...	51-6061	19,000	14,000	-5,900	-30
Textile cutting machine setters, operators, and tenders	51-6062	19,000	14,000	-5,100	-27
Textile knitting and weaving machine setters, operators, and tenders...	51-6063	40,000	28,000	-12,000	-31
Textile winding, twisting, and drawing out machine setters, operators, and tenders	51-6064	43,000	33,000	-11,000	-24
Miscellaneous textile, apparel, and furnishings workers..............	51-6090	106,000	92,000	-14,000	-13
Extruding and forming machine setters, operators, and tenders, synthetic and glass fibers	51-6091	18,000	15,000	-3,100	-18
Fabric and apparel patternmakers..	51-6092	9,200	6,600	-2,600	-29
Upholsterers...	51-6093	55,000	50,000	-4,900	-9
Textile, apparel, and furnishings workers, all other.................	51-6099	24,000	21,000	-3,600	-15

NOTE: Data in this table are rounded. See the discussion of the employment projections table in the *Handbook* introductory chapter on *Occupational Information Included in the Handbook.*

speed, and accuracy. Workers covered by union contracts tend to have higher earnings. Median hourly earnings by occupation in May 2006 were as follows:

Fabric and apparel patternmakers $15.74
Extruding and forming machine setters, operators,
   and tenders, synthetic and glass fibers 13.78
Upholsterers 13.09
Textile knitting and weaving machine setters,
   operators, and tenders 11.68
Textile bleaching and dyeing machine
   operators and tenders 11.20
Textile winding, twisting, and drawing out machine
   setters, operators, and tenders 11.08
All other textile, apparel, and furnishings workers.................11.03
Tailors, dressmakers, and custom sewers................................11.01
Shoe machine operators and tenders.......................................10.54
Textile cutting machine setters, operators, and tenders 10.39
Shoe and leather workers and repairers 9.83
Sewers, hand 9.79
Sewing machine operators 9.04
Laundry and dry-cleaning workers 8.58
Pressers, textile, garment, and related materials.....................8.56

Benefits vary by size of company and work that is done. Large employers typically offer all usual benefits. Apparel workers in retail trade also may receive a discount on their purchases from the company for which they work. In addition, some of the larger manufacturers operate company stores from which employees can purchase apparel products at significant discounts. Some small firms and drycleaning establishments, however, offer only limited benefits. Self-employed workers generally have to purchase their own insurance.

Related Occupations

Textile, apparel, and furnishings workers apply their knowledge of textiles and leathers to fashion products with the use of handtools and machinery. Others who produce products using handtools, machines, and their knowledge of the materials with which they work include assemblers and fabricators; food-processing workers; jewelers and precious stone and metal workers; and woodworkers.

Sources of Additional Information

Information about job opportunities in textile, apparel, and furnishings occupations is available from local employers and local offices of State employment services.

Woodworkers

(O*NET 51-7011.00, 51-7021.00, 51-7031.00, 51-7032.00, 51-7041.00, 51-7042.00, 51-7099.99)

Significant Points

- Most woodworkers are trained on the job; basic machine operations may be learned in a few months, but becoming a skilled woodworker often requires several years of experience.

- Job prospects will be best for highly skilled woodworkers who produce customized work, which is less susceptible to automation and import competition, and for those who can operate computerized numerical control machines.

- Employment is highly sensitive to economic cycles; during economic downturns, workers are subject to layoffs or reductions in hours.

Nature of the Work

Despite the abundance of plastics and other materials, wood products continue to be useful and popular. Woodworkers help to meet the demand for wood products by creating finished products from lumber. Many of these products are mass produced, such as many types of furniture, kitchen cabinets, and musical instruments. Other products are crafted in small shops that make architectural woodwork, handmade furniture, and other specialty items.

Although the term woodworker often evokes images of a craftsman who builds ornate furniture using hand tools, the modern wood industry is highly technical. Some woodworkers still build by hand, but more often, handtools have been replaced by power tools, and much of the work has been automated. Work is usually done on an assembly line, meaning that most individuals learn to perform a single part of a complex process. Different types of woodworkers are employed in every stage of the building process, from sawmill to finished product. Their activities vary greatly.

Many woodworkers use computerized numerical control (CNC) machines to operate factory tools. Using these machines, woodworkers can create complex designs with fewer human steps. This technology has raised worker productivity by allowing one operator to simultaneously tend a greater number of machines. The integration of computers with equipment has improved production speed and capability, simplified setup and maintenance requirements, and increased the demand for workers with computer skills.

Production woodworkers set up, operate, and tend all types of woodworking machines. In sawmills, *sawing machine operators and tenders* set up, operate, or tend wood-sawing machines that cut logs into planks, timbers, or boards. In manufacturing plants, woodworkers first determine the best method of shaping and assembling parts, working from blueprints, supervisors' instructions, or shop drawings that woodworkers themselves produce. Before cutting, they often must measure and mark the materials. They verify dimensions and may trim parts using handtools such as planes, chisels, wood files, or sanders to ensure a tight fit.

Woodworking machine operators and tenders set up, operate, or tend specific woodworking machines, such as drill presses, lathes, shapers, routers, sanders, planers, and wood-nailing machines. New operators may simply press a switch on a woodworking machine and monitor the automatic operation, but more highly skilled operators set up the equipment, cut and shape wooden parts, and verify dimensions using a template, caliper, or rule.

After wood parts are made, woodworkers add fasteners and adhesives and connect the pieces to form a complete unit. The product is then finish-sanded; stained, and, if necessary, coated with a sealer, such as lacquer or varnish. Woodworkers may perform this work in teams or be assisted by helpers.

Precision or custom woodworkers, such as *cabinetmakers and bench carpenters, modelmakers and patternmakers,* and *furniture finishers*, often build one-of-a-kind items. These highly skilled precision woodworkers usually perform a complete cycle of tasks—cutting, shaping, and preparing surfaces and assembling complex wood components into a finished wood product. Precision workers normally need substantial training and an ability to work from detailed instructions and specifications. In addition, they often are required to exercise independent judgment when undertaking an assignment. They may still use heavy machinery and power tools in their everyday work. As CNC machines have become less expensive, many smaller firms have started using them.

Work environment. Working conditions vary by industry and specific job duties. In logging and sawmills, for example, workers handle heavy, bulky material and often encounter excessive noise, dust, and other air pollutants. However, the use of earplugs and respirators may alleviate these problems. Safety precautions and computer-controlled equipment minimize risk of injury from rough wood stock, sharp tools, and power equipment.

In furniture and kitchen cabinet manufacturing, employees who operate machinery also must wear ear and eye protection. They follow operating safety instructions and use safety shields or guards to prevent accidents. Those who work in areas where wood is cut or finishings applied often must wear an appropriate dust or vapor mask or a complete protective safety suit. Prolonged standing, lifting, and fitting of heavy objects are common characteristics of the job.

Training, Other Qualifications, and Advancement

Many woodworkers are highly skilled and require significant on-the-job training. Mathematics skills, especially geometry, are essential and computer skills are increasingly important,

Education and training. Employers seek applicants with a high school diploma or the equivalent because of the growing sophistication of machinery and the constant need for retraining. People seeking woodworking jobs can enhance their employment and advancement prospects by completing high school and receiving training in mathematics, science, and computer applications.

Woodworkers increasingly acquire skills through higher education. For many workers, this means earning a degree from a vocational or trade school. Others may attend colleges or universities that offer training in wood technology, furniture manufacturing, wood engineering, and production management.

Woodworkers use sophisticated equipment to make wood into furniture.

These programs prepare students for positions in production, supervision, engineering, and management and are increasingly important as woodworking technology advances.

Most woodworkers are trained on the job, however, picking up skills informally from experienced workers. They can learn basic machine operations and job tasks in a few months, but becoming a skilled woodworker often requires 2 or more years.

Beginners usually observe and help experienced machine operators. They may supply material to, or remove fabricated products from, machines. Trainees also do simple machine operating jobs while closely supervised by experienced workers. As beginners gain experience, they perform more complex jobs with less supervision. Some may learn to read blueprints, set up machines, and plan the sequence of the work.

Other qualifications. In addition to training, woodworkers need mechanical ability, manual dexterity, and the ability to pay attention to detail and safety. As the industry becomes more sophisticated, skill with computers and computer-controlled machinery is becoming more important.

Advancement. Advancement opportunities are often limited and depend on education and training, seniority, and a worker's skills and initiative. Sometimes experienced woodworkers become inspectors or supervisors responsible for the work of a group of woodworkers. Production workers can advance into these positions by assuming additional responsibilities and attending workshops, seminars, or college programs. Those who are highly skilled may set up their own woodworking shops.

Employment

Woodworkers held about 370,000 jobs in 2006. Self-employed woodworkers, mostly cabinetmakers and furniture finishers, accounted for 12 percent of these jobs.

Three out of 4 woodworkers were employed in manufacturing. About 2 out of 5 worked in establishments manufacturing household and office furniture and fixtures, and 1 in 3 worked in wood product manufacturing, producing a variety of raw, intermediate, and finished woodstock. Wholesale and retail lumber dealers, furniture stores, reupholstery and furniture repair shops, and construction firms also employ woodworkers.

Projections data from the National Employment Matrix

Occupational Title	SOC Code	Employment, 2006	Projected employment, 2016	Change, 2006-16	
				Number	Percent
Woodworkers	51-7000	370,000	380,000	11,000	3
Cabinetmakers and bench carpenters..	51-7011	149,000	153,000	4,100	3
Furniture finishers	51-7021	31,000	30,000	-1,000	-3
Model makers and patternmakers, wood	51-7030	4,200	2,500	-1,700	-40
Model makers, wood..	51-7031	1,900	1,100	-800	-41
Patternmakers, wood..	51-7032	2,300	1,400	-900	-40
Woodworking machine setters, operators, and tenders.................	51-7040	165,000	173,000	8,800	5
Sawing machine setters, operators, and tenders, wood.............	51-7041	65,000	68,000	2,500	4
Woodworking machine setters, operators, and tenders, except sawing	51-7042	100,000	106,000	6,400	6
Woodworkers, all other..	51-7099	20,000	21,000	300	2

NOTE: Data in this table are rounded. See the discussion of the employment projections table in the *Handbook* introductory chapter on *Occupational Information Included in the Handbook.*

Woodworking jobs are found throughout the country. However, lumber and wood products-related production jobs are concentrated in the Southeast, Midwest, and Northwest, close to the supply of wood. Furniture-making jobs are more prevalent in the Southeast. Custom shops can be found everywhere, but generally are concentrated in or near highly populated areas.

Job Outlook

Overall employment of woodworkers is expected to grow slower than average. Opportunities should be good for skilled applicants.

Employment change. Overall employment of woodworkers is expected to grow by 3 percent during the 2006-16 decade, which is slower than the average of all occupations. This slow growth will be a result of increased automation in the wood products manufacturing industry. Technology is becoming increasingly important to this industry, and automation has greatly reduced the number of people required to produce a finished product. Furthermore, international competition—especially from China—has led to a significant decline in domestic employment of these workers.

Employment of sawing and woodworking machine setters, operators, and tenders is expected to grow more slowly than the average through 2016. Import growth will lead to job losses in the U.S. industry. To remain competitive, some domestic firms are expected to move their production processes to foreign countries, further reducing employment. Firms that stay are increasingly using advanced technology, such as robots and CNC machinery. These developments will prevent employment from rising with the demand for wood products, particularly in the mills and manufacturing plants where many processes can be automated.

Employment of furniture finishers is expected to decline slowly. Since furniture is largely mass-produced, it is highly susceptible to import competition; the percentage of imported furniture sold in the United States has steadily increased over the years, a trend that is expected to continue. Labor is significantly less expensive in developing countries, so these forces will likely affect the industry for quite some time.

Employment of bench carpenters and cabinetmakers is expected to grow more slowly than average, while modelmakers and patternmakers are expected to decline rapidly. Other specialized woodworking occupations will experience little or now change in growth. Demand for these workers will stem from increases in population, personal income, and business expenditures and from the continuing need for repair and renovation of residential and commercial properties. Therefore, opportunities should be available for workers who specialize in items such as moldings, cabinets, stairs, and windows. Firms that focus on custom woodwork will be best able to compete against imports without transferring jobs offshore.

Job prospects. Despite slower than average employment growth, prospects should be good for qualified workers. Many experienced woodworkers will soon reach retirement age, and this will create a need for new workers. In general, opportunities for more highly skilled woodworkers will be better than for woodworkers in specialties susceptible to automation and competition from imported wood products. The need for woodworkers with technical skills to operate their increasingly advanced computerized machinery will be especially great. Custom workers and modelmakers and patternmakers who know how to create and execute designs on a computer may have the best opportunities. These jobs require an understanding of wood and a strong understanding of computers—a combination that can be somewhat difficult to find.

The number of new workers entering these occupations has declined greatly in recent years, as training programs become less available or popular. Competition for jobs is expected to be mild, and opportunities should be best for woodworkers who, through vocational education or experience, develop highly specialized woodworking skills or knowledge of CNC machine tool operation.

Employment in all woodworking specialties is highly sensitive to economic cycles. During economic downturns, workers are subject to layoffs or reductions in hours.

Earnings

Median annual wage-and-salary earnings of cabinetmakers and bench carpenters were $27,010 in May 2006. The middle 50 percent earned between $21,350 and $34,290. The lowest 10 percent earned less than $17,660, and the highest 10 percent earned more than $43,060.

Median annual wage-and-salary earnings of sawing machine setters, operators, and tenders, wood were $24,280. The middle 50 percent earned between $19,620 and $29,930. The lowest

10 percent earned less than $16,290, and the highest 10 percent earned more than $36,220.

Median annual wage-and-salary earnings of woodworking machine setters, operators, and tenders, except sawing were $23,940. The middle 50 percent earned between $19,460 and $29,480. The lowest 10 percent earned less than $16,410, and the highest 10 percent earned more than $35,950.

Median annual wage-and-salary earnings were $25,010 for furniture finishers and $22,580 for all other woodworkers.

Related Occupations

Like woodworkers, carpenters also work with wood. In addition, many woodworkers follow blueprints and drawings and use machines to shape and form raw wood into a final product. Workers who perform similar functions working with other materials include sheet metal workers; structural and reinforcing iron and metal workers; computer control programmers and operators; machinists; textile, apparel, and furnishings occupations; and tool and die makers.

Sources of Additional Information

For information about careers and education and training programs in woodworking, contact:

➤ WoodLINKS USA, P.O. Box 1153, Point Roberts, WA 98281.
Internet: **http://www.woodlinks.com/USA/home.html**

Plant and System Operators

Power Plant Operators, Distributors, and Dispatchers

(O*NET 51-8011.00, 51-8012.00, 51-8013.00)

Significant Points

- Job prospects are expected to be good as many workers retire and new plants are built.

- Most entry-level workers start as helpers or laborers, and several years of training and experience are required to become fully qualified.

- Familiarity with computers and a basic understanding of science and math is helpful for those entering the field.

Nature of the Work

Electricity is vital for most everyday activities. From the moment you flip the first switch each morning, you are connecting to a huge network of people, electric lines, and generating equipment. Power plant operators control the machinery that generates electricity. Power plant distributors and dispatchers control the flow of electricity from the power plant, over a network of transmission lines, to industrial plants and substations, and, finally, over distribution lines to residential users.

Power plant operators control and monitor boilers, turbines, generators, and auxiliary equipment in power-generating plants. Operators distribute power demands among generators, combine the current from several generators, and monitor instruments to maintain voltage and regulate electricity flows from the plant. When power requirements change, these workers start or stop generators and connect or disconnect them from circuits. They often use computers to keep records of switching operations and loads on generators, lines, and transformers. Operators also may use computers to prepare reports of unusual incidents, malfunctioning equipment, or maintenance performed during their shift.

Operators in plants with automated control systems work mainly in a central control room and usually are called *control room operators* or *control room operator trainees* or *assistants*. In older plants, the controls for the equipment are not centralized; *switchboard operators* control the flow of electricity from a central point, while *auxiliary equipment operators* work throughout the plant, operating and monitoring valves, switches, and gauges.

In nuclear power plants, most operators start working as *equipment operators* or *auxiliary operators*. They help the more senior workers with equipment maintenance and operation while learning the basics of plant operation. With experience and training they may be licensed by the Nuclear Regulatory Commission as *reactor operators* and authorized to control equipment that affects the power of the reactor in a nuclear power plant. *Senior reactor operators* supervise the operation of all controls in the control room. At least one senior operator must be on duty during each shift to act as the plant supervisor.

Power distributors and dispatchers, also called *load dispatchers* or *systems operators*, control the flow of electricity through transmission lines to industrial plants and substations that supply residential needs for electricity. They monitor and

Power plant operators spent most of their time monitoring systems for problems.

Projections data from the National Employment Matrix

Occupational Title	SOC Code	Employment, 2006	Projected employment, 2016	Change, 2006-16	
				Number	Percent
Power plant operators, distributors, and dispatchers.........................	51-8010	47,000	48,000	900	2
Nuclear power reactor operators..	51-8011	3,800	4,200	400	11
Power distributors and dispatchers...	51-8012	8,600	8,200	-400	-5
Power plant operators..	51-8013	35,000	36,000	900	3

NOTE: Data in this table are rounded. See the discussion of the employment projections table in the *Handbook* introductory chapter on *Occupational Information Included in the Handbook*.

operate current converters, voltage transformers, and circuit breakers. Dispatchers also monitor other distribution equipment and record readings at a pilot board—a map of the transmission grid system showing the status of transmission circuits and connections with substations and industrial plants.

Dispatchers also anticipate power needs, such as those caused by changes in the weather. They call control room operators to start or stop boilers and generators, in order to bring production into balance with needs. Dispatchers handle emergencies such as transformer or transmission line failures and route current around affected areas. In substations, they also operate and monitor equipment that increases or decreases voltage, and they operate switchboard levers to control the flow of electricity in and out of the substations.

Work environment. Operators, distributors, and dispatchers who work in control rooms generally sit or stand at a control station. This work is not physically strenuous, but it does require constant attention. Operators who work outside the control room may be exposed to danger from electric shock, falls, and burns.

Nuclear power plant operators are subject to random drug and alcohol tests, as are most workers at such plants. Additionally, they have to pass a medical examination every two years and may be exposed to small amounts of ionizing radiation as part of their jobs.

Because electricity is provided around the clock, operators, distributors, and dispatchers usually work one of three 8-hour shifts or one of two 12-hour shifts on a rotating basis. Shift assignments may change periodically, so that all operators share less desirable shifts. Work on rotating shifts can be stressful and fatiguing because of the constant change in living and sleeping patterns.

Training, Other Qualifications, and Advancement

Power plant operators, dispatchers, and distributors generally need a combination of education, on-the-job training, and experience. Candidates with strong computer and technical skills are generally preferred.

Education and training. Employers often seek recent high school graduates for entry-level operator, distributor, and dispatcher positions. Workers with college or vocational school degrees will have more advancement opportunities, especially in nuclear power plants. Although it is not a prerequisite, many senior reactor operators have a bachelor's degree in engineering or the physical sciences.

Workers selected for training as power plant operators or distributors undergo extensive on-the-job and classroom instruction. Several years of training and experience are re-

quired for a worker to become a fully qualified control room operator or power plant distributor.

In addition to receiving initial training to become fully qualified as a power plant operator, distributor, or dispatcher, most workers are given periodic refresher training—especially the nuclear power plant operators. Refresher training usually is taken on plant simulators designed specifically to replicate procedures and situations that might be encountered at the trainee's plant.

Licensure. Power plant operators, distributors, and dispatchers may need licenses depending on jurisdiction and specific job function. Requirements vary greatly from place to place and may be administered by State, county, or local governments.

Extensive training and experience are necessary to pass the Nuclear Regulatory Commission (NRC) examinations required for nuclear reactor operators and senior nuclear reactor operators. Before beginning training, a nuclear power plant worker must have 3 years of power plant experience. At least 6 months of this must be on-site at the nuclear power plant where the operator is to be licensed. Training generally takes at least 1 year, after which the worker must take an NRC-administered examination. To maintain their licenses, reactor operators must pass an annual practical plant operation exam and a biennial written exam administered by their employers. Reactor operators can upgrade their licenses to the senior reactor operator level after a year of licensed experience at the plant by taking another examination given by the NRC. Training may include simulator and on-the-job training, classroom instruction, and individual study. Experience in other power plants or with Navy nuclear propulsion plants also is helpful.

Advancement. Most entry-level workers start as helpers or laborers and advance to more responsible positions as they become comfortable in the plant. In many cases, there are mandatory waiting times between starting a position and advancing to the next level due to licensing requirements. With sufficient training and experience, workers can become shift supervisors or, in nuclear power plants, senior reactor operators.

Because power plants have different systems and safety mechanisms, it is often very difficult to advance by changing companies or plants. Most utilities promote from within; most workers advance within a particular plant or by moving to another plant owned by the same utility.

Employment

Power plant operators, distributors, and dispatchers held about 47,000 jobs in 2006, of which 3,800 were nuclear power plant operators, 8,600 were power distributors and dispatchers, and 35,000 were other power plant operators. Jobs were located throughout the country. About 70 percent of jobs were in electric power generation, transmission, and distribution. About 16 percent worked in government, mainly in local government. Others worked for manufacturing establishments that produced electricity for their own use.

Job Outlook

Employment of power plant operators, distributors, and dispatchers is projected to experience little or no employment change, but job opportunities are expected to be very good due to the large number of retiring workers who must be replaced, increased demand for energy, and recent legislation which paves the way for a number of new plants.

Employment change. Between 2006 and 2016, employment of power plant operators, distributors, and dispatchers is projected to experience little or no employment change, growing by about 2 percent. Electric utilities are expected to build new power plants in response to the Energy Policy Act of 2005, which provides a number of subsidies. Growth will be tempered by a continued emphasis on cost reduction and automation. Although new power plants will require fewer workers than their older counterparts, the machinery in the new plants will be more technologically complex and environmental regulations will require much closer attention to emissions, so workers will be required to have higher skill levels.

Job prospects. Job opportunities are expected to be very good for people who are interested in becoming power plant operators, distributors, and dispatchers. During the 1990s, the emphasis on cost cutting among utilities led to hiring freezes and the laying off of younger workers. The result is an aging workforce, half of which is expected to retire within the next 10 years. Utilities have responded by setting up new education programs at community colleges and high schools throughout the country. Prospects should be especially good for people with computer skills and a basic understanding of science and mathematics.

Earnings

Median annual earnings of power plant operators were $55,000 in May 2006. The middle 50 percent earned between $45,110 and $65,460. The lowest 10 percent earned less than $35,590, and the highest 10 percent earned more than $75,240.

Median annual earnings of nuclear power reactor operators were $69,370 in May 2006. The middle 50 percent earned between $61,590 and $78,150. The lowest 10 percent earned less than $54,180, and the highest 10 percent earned more than $92,240.

Median annual earnings of power distributors and dispatchers were $62,590 in May 2006. The middle 50 percent earned between $52,510 and $73,920. The lowest 10 percent earned less than $42,370, and the highest 10 percent earned more than $85,740.

Related Occupations

Other workers who monitor and operate plant and system equipment include chemical plant and system operators; petroleum pump system operators, refinery operators, and gaug-ers; stationary engineers and boiler operators; and water and liquid waste treatment plant and system operators.

Sources of Additional Information

For information about employment opportunities, contact local electric utility companies, local unions, and State employment service offices.

For general information about power plant operators, nuclear power reactor operators, and power plant distributors and dispatchers, contact:

➤ American Public Power Association, 2301 M St.NW., Washington, DC 20037-1484.
Internet: **http://www.appanet.org**
➤ International Brotherhood of Electrical Workers, 1125 15th St.NW., Washington, DC 20005.
Internet: **http://www.ibew.org**
➤ National Association of Power Engineers, Inc., 1 Springfield St., Chicopee, MA 01013.

Information on licensing for nuclear reactor operators and senior reactor operators is available from:
➤ Nuclear Regulatory Commission, Washington, DC 20555-0001. Internet: **http://www.nrc.gov**

Stationary Engineers and Boiler Operators

(O*NET 51-8021.00)

Significant Points

- Workers usually acquire their skills through a formal apprenticeship program or through on-the-job training supplemented by courses at a trade or technical school.

- Most workers need to be licensed, but licensing requirements vary across the Nation.

- Employment is projected to grow slowly, and applicants may face competition for jobs.

- Opportunities will be best for workers with training in computerized controls and instrumentation.

Nature of the Work

Most large office buildings, malls, warehouses, and other commercial facilities have extensive heating, ventilation, and air-conditioning systems that keep them comfortable all year long. Industrial plants often have additional facilities to provide electrical power, steam, or other services. Stationary engineers and boiler operators control and maintain these systems, which include boilers, air-conditioning and refrigeration equipment, diesel engines, turbines, generators, pumps, condensers, and compressors. The equipment that stationary engineers and boiler operators control is similar to equipment operated by locomotive or marine engineers, except that it is used to generate heat or electricity, rather than to move a train or ship.

Stationary engineers and boiler operators start up, regulate, repair, and shut down equipment. They ensure that the equipment operates safely, economically, and within established limits by monitoring meters, gauges, and computerized controls. Stationary engineers and boiler operators control equipment manually in many older buildings and, if necessary, make adjustments. They watch and listen to machinery and routinely check safety devices, identifying and correcting any trouble that develops.

In newer buildings, stationary engineers typically use computers to operate the mechanical, electrical, and fire safety systems. They monitor, adjust, and diagnose these systems from a central location, using a computer linked into the buildings' communications network.

Routine maintenance is a regular part of the work of stationary engineers and boiler operators. Engineers use hand and power tools to perform maintenance and repairs ranging from a complete overhaul to replacing defective valves, gaskets, or bearings. They lubricate moving parts, replace filters, and remove soot and corrosion that can reduce the boiler's operating efficiency. They also test the water in the boiler and add chemicals to prevent corrosion and harmful deposits. In most facilities, stationary engineers are responsible for the maintenance and balancing of air systems, as well as hydronic systems that heat or cool buildings by circulating fluid (such as water or water vapor) in a closed system of pipes. They may check the air quality of the ventilation system and make adjustments to keep the operation of the boiler within mandated guidelines. Servicing, troubleshooting, repairing, and monitoring modern systems all require the use of sophisticated electrical and electronic test equipment. Additionally, many stationary engineers perform other maintenance duties, such as carpentry, plumbing, locksmithing, and electrical repairs.

Stationary engineers and boiler operators keep a record of relevant events and facts concerning the operation and maintenance of the equipment. When working with steam boilers, for example, stationary engineers and boiler operators observe, control, and record steam pressure, temperature, water level, chemistry, power output, fuel consumption, and emissions from the boiler. They also note the date and nature of all maintenance and repairs.

In a large building or industrial plant, a senior stationary engineer may be in charge of all mechanical systems in the building and may supervise a team of assistant stationary engineers, turbine operators, boiler tenders, and air-conditioning and refrigeration operators and mechanics. In a small building or industrial plant, there may be only one stationary engineer.

Work environment. Engine rooms, power plants, boiler rooms, mechanical rooms, and electrical rooms are usually clean and well lighted. Even under the most favorable conditions, however, some stationary engineers and boiler operators are exposed to high temperatures, dust, dirt, and high noise levels from the equipment. Maintenance duties also may require contact with oil, grease, or smoke. Workers spend much of the time on their feet. They also may have to crawl inside boilers and work in crouching or kneeling positions to inspect, clean, or repair equipment.

Stationary engineers and boiler operators work around hazardous machinery, such as low- and high-pressure boilers and electrical equipment. They must follow procedures to guard against burns, electric shock, and noise, danger from moving parts, and exposure to hazardous materials, such as asbestos or toxic chemicals.

Stationary engineers and boiler operators generally have steady, year-round employment. The average workweek is 40 hours. In facilities that operate around the clock, engineers and operators usually work one of three daily 8-hour shifts on a rotating basis. Weekend and holiday work often is required.

Training, Other Qualifications, and Advancement

Many stationary engineers and boiler operators begin their careers in mechanic or helper positions and are trained on-the-job by more experienced engineers. Others begin by entering formal apprenticeships or training programs. After completing the required training, workers can become licensed, which allows them to work on boilers of a certain size without supervision.

Education and training. Most employers prefer to hire persons with at least a high school diploma or the equivalent for stationary engineers and boiler operator jobs. Workers primarily acquire their skills on the job and usually start as boiler tenders or as helpers to more experienced workers. This practical experience may be supplemented by postsecondary vocational training in subjects such as computerized controls and instrumentation. Other workers complete formal apprenticeship programs. Becoming an engineer or operator without completing a formal apprenticeship program usually requires many years of work experience.

The International Union of Operating Engineers sponsors apprenticeship programs and is the principal union for stationary engineers and boiler operators. In selecting apprentices, most local labor-management apprenticeship committees prefer applicants with a basic understanding of mathematics, science,

Stationary engineers monitor boilers and make necessary adjustments and repairs.

computers, mechanical drawing, machine shop practice, and chemistry. An apprenticeship usually lasts 4 years and includes 8,000 hours of on-the-job training. In addition, apprentices receive 600 hours of classroom instruction in subjects such as boiler design and operation, elementary physics, pneumatics, refrigeration, air-conditioning, electricity, and electronics.

Continuing education—such as vocational school or college courses—is becoming increasingly important for stationary engineers and boiler operators, in part because of the growing complexity of the equipment with which engineers and operators now work. In 2006, roughly half of all stationary engineers between the ages of 25 and 44 had at least some college coursework.

Most large and some small employers encourage and pay for skill-improvement training for their employees. These employers often realize major cost savings due to greater efficiency of their workers; improved maintenance, reliability, and effective lifespan of equipment; and a better safety record. Well-trained workers manage energy better, which can also greatly reduce an employer's energy costs. Training is almost always provided when new equipment is introduced or when regulations concerning some aspect of the workers' duties change.

Licensure. Most States and cities have licensing requirements for stationary engineers and boiler operators. Applicants for licensure usually must be at least 18 years of age, reside for a specified period in the State or locality in which they wish to work, meet experience requirements, and pass a written examination. A stationary engineer or boiler operator who moves from one State or city to another may have to pass an examination for a new license due to regional differences in licensing requirements.

There are several classes of stationary engineer licenses. Each class specifies the type and size of equipment the engineer is permitted to operate without supervision. A licensed first-class stationary engineer is qualified to run a large facility, supervise others, and operate equipment of all types and capacities. An applicant for this license may be required to have a high school education, have completed an apprenticeship or lengthy on-the-job training, and have several years of experience working with a lower class license. Licenses below first class limit the types or capacities of equipment the engineer may operate without supervision.

Other qualifications. In addition to training, stationary engineers and boiler operators need mechanical aptitude and manual dexterity. Being in good physical condition is also important.

Advancement. Stationary engineers and boiler operators advance by being placed in charge of larger, more powerful, or more varied equipment. Generally, engineers advance to these jobs as they obtain higher class licenses. Some stationary engineers and boiler operators advance to become boiler inspectors, chief plant engineers, building and plant superintendents, or building managers. A few obtain jobs as examining engineers or technical instructors.

Because most stationary engineering staffs are relatively small, workers may find it difficult to advance, especially within a company. Most high-level positions are held by experienced workers with seniority. Workers wishing to move up to these positions must often change employers or wait for older workers to retire before they can advance.

Employment

Stationary engineers and boiler operators held about 45,000 jobs in 2006. They worked throughout the country, generally in the more heavily populated areas in which large industrial and commercial establishments are located. Jobs were dispersed throughout a variety of industries. The majority of jobs were in State and local government, manufacturing, and hospitals.

Job Outlook

Employment in this occupation is expected to grow more slowly than the average through 2016. Applicants may face competition for jobs. Employment opportunities will be best for those with apprenticeship training and experience using computerized systems.

Employment change. Employment of stationary engineers and boiler operators is expected to grow by 3 percent between 2006 and 2016, which is more slowly than the average for all occupations. Continuing commercial and industrial development will increase the amount of equipment to be operated and maintained. However, automated systems and computerized controls are making newly installed equipment more efficient, thus reducing the number of jobs needed for its operation.

Job prospects. People interested in working as stationary engineers and boiler operators should expect to face competition for these relatively high-paying positions. Slow job growth coupled with the tendency of experienced workers to stay in a job for decades should continue to make openings scarce. While many workers will reach retirement age within the next decade, the number of workers who need to be replaced will be small relative to other occupations.

Earnings

Median annual earnings of stationary engineers and boiler operators were $46,040 in May 2006. The middle 50 percent earned between $36,490 and $57,380. The lowest 10 percent earned less than $28,370, and the highest 10 percent earned more than $68,690.

Related Occupations

Workers who monitor and operate stationary machinery include chemical plant and system operators; gas plant operators; petroleum pump system operators, refinery operators, and gaugers;

Projections data from the National Employment Matrix

Occupational Title	SOC Code	Employment, 2006	Projected employment, 2016	Change, 2006-16	
				Number	Percent
Stationary engineers and boiler operators...	51-8021	45,000	47,000	1,600	3

NOTE: Data in this table are rounded. See the discussion of the employment projections table in the *Handbook* introductory chapter on *Occupational Information Included in the Handbook.*

power plant operators, distributors, and dispatchers; and water and liquid waste treatment plant and system operators. Other workers who maintain the equipment and machinery in a building or plant are industrial machinery mechanics and maintenance workers, and millwrights.

Sources of Additional Information

Information about apprenticeships, vocational training, and work opportunities is available from State employment service offices, locals of the International Union of Operating Engineers, vocational schools, and State and local licensing agencies. Apprenticeship information is also available from the U.S. Department of Labor's toll-free helpline: (877) 282-5627.

Specific questions about this occupation should be addressed to:

➤ International Union of Operating Engineers, 1125 17th St. NW., Washington, DC 20036. Internet: **http://www.iuoe.org**

➤ National Association of Power Engineers, Inc., 1 Springfield St., Chicopee, MA 01013.
Internet: **http://www.powerengineers.com**

➤ Building Owners and Managers Institute International, 1521 Ritchie Hwy., Arnold, MD 21012.
Internet: **http://www.bomi-edu.org**

Water and Liquid Waste Treatment Plant and System Operators

(O*NET 51-8031.00)

Significant Points

- Employment is concentrated in local government and private water, sewage, and other systems utilities.

- Because of a large number of upcoming retirements and the difficulty of filling these positions, job opportunities will be excellent.

- Completion of an associate degree or a 1-year certificate program increases an applicant's chances for employment and promotion.

Nature of the Work

Clean water is essential for everyday life. *Water treatment plant and system operators* treat water so that it is safe to drink. *Liquid waste treatment plant and system operators*, also known as wastewater treatment plant and system operators, remove harmful pollutants from domestic and industrial liquid waste so that it is safe to return to the environment.

Water is pumped from wells, rivers, streams, and reservoirs to water treatment plants, where it is treated and distributed to customers. Wastewater travels through customers' sewer pipes to wastewater treatment plants, where it is treated and either returned to streams, rivers, and oceans or reused for irrigation and landscaping. Operators in both types of plants control equipment and processes that remove or destroy harmful materials, chemicals, and microorganisms from the water. Operators also control pumps, valves, and other equipment that moves the water or wastewater through the various treatment processes, after which they dispose of the removed waste materials.

Operators read, interpret, and adjust meters and gauges to make sure that plant equipment and processes are working properly. Operators control chemical-feeding devices, take samples of the water or wastewater, perform chemical and biological laboratory analyses, and adjust the amounts of chemicals, such as chlorine, in the water. They employ a variety of instruments to sample and measure water quality, and they use common hand and power tools to make repairs to valves, pumps, and other equipment.

Water and wastewater treatment plant and system operators increasingly rely on computers to help monitor equipment, store the results of sampling, make process-control decisions, schedule and record maintenance activities, and produce reports. In some modern plants, operators also use computers to monitor automated systems and determine how to address problems.

Occasionally, operators must work during emergencies. A heavy rainstorm, for example, may cause large amounts of wastewater to flow into sewers, exceeding a plant's treatment capacity. Emergencies also can be caused by conditions inside a plant, such as chlorine gas leaks or oxygen deficiencies. To handle these conditions, operators are trained to make an emergency management response and use special safety equipment and procedures to protect public health and the facility. During these periods, operators may work under extreme pressure to correct problems as quickly as possible. Because working conditions may be dangerous, operators must be extremely cautious.

The specific duties of plant operators depend on the type and size of the plant. In smaller plants, one operator may control all of the machinery, perform tests, keep records, handle complaints, and perform repairs and maintenance. Operators in this type of plant may have to be on-call 24 hours a day in case of an emergency. In medium-sized plants, operators monitor the plant throughout the night by working in shifts. In large plants, operators may be more specialized and monitor only one process. They might work with chemists, engineers, laboratory technicians, mechanics, helpers, supervisors, and a superintendent.

Water quality standards are largely set by two major Federal environmental statutes: the Safe Drinking Water Act, which specifies standards for drinking water, and the Clean Water Act,

Many water and liquid waste treatment plant and system operators work alone, managing small plants.

Projections data from the National Employment Matrix

Occupational Title	SOC Code	Employment, 2006	Projected employment, 2016	Change, 2006-16	
				Number	Percent
Water and liquid waste treatment plant and system operators	51-8031	111,000	126,000	15,000	14

NOTE: Data in this table are rounded. See the discussion of the employment projections table in the *Handbook* introductory chapter on *Occupational Information Included in the Handbook.*

which regulates the discharge of pollutants. Industrial facilities that send their wastes to municipal treatment plants must meet certain minimum standards to ensure that the wastes have been adequately pretreated and will not damage municipal treatment facilities. Municipal water treatment plants also must meet stringent standards for drinking water. The list of contaminants regulated by these statutes has grown over time. As a result, plant operators must be familiar with the guidelines established by Federal regulations and how they affect their plant. In addition, operators must be aware of any guidelines imposed by the State or locality in which the plant operates.

Work environment. Water and wastewater treatment plant and system operators work both indoors and outdoors and may be exposed to noise from machinery and to unpleasant odors. Operators' work is physically demanding and often is performed in unclean locations; they must pay close attention to safety procedures because of the presence of hazardous conditions, such as slippery walkways, dangerous gases, and malfunctioning equipment.

Plants operate 24 hours a day, 7 days a week. In small plants, operators may work during the day and be on-call in the evening, nights and weekends. Medium and large plants that require constant monitoring may employ workers in three 8-hour shifts. Because larger plants require constant monitoring, weekend and holiday work is generally required. Operators may be required to work overtime.

Training, Other Qualifications, and Advancement

Employers usually hire high school graduates who are trained on-the-job, and later become licensed. Education after high school improves job prospects.

Education and training. A high school diploma usually is required for an individual to become a water or wastewater treatment plant operator. The completion of an associate degree or a 1-year certificate program in water quality and wastewater treatment technology increases an applicant's chances for employment and promotion because plants are becoming more complex. The majority of such programs are offered by trade associations, and can be found throughout the country. These programs provide a good general knowledge of water and wastewater treatment processes, as well as basic preparation for becoming an operator. In some cases, a degree or certificate program can be substituted for experience, allowing a worker to become licensed at a higher level more quickly.

Trainees usually start as attendants or operators-in-training and learn their skills on the job under the direction of an experienced operator. They learn by observing and doing routine tasks such as recording meter readings, taking samples of wastewater and sludge, and performing simple maintenance and repair work on pumps, electric motors, valves, and other plant equipment. Larg-

er treatment plants generally combine this on-the-job training with formal classroom or self-paced study programs.

Most State drinking water and water pollution control agencies offer courses to improve operators' skills and knowledge. The courses cover principles of treatment processes and process control, laboratory procedures, maintenance, management skills, collection systems, safety, chlorination, sedimentation, biological treatment, sludge treatment and disposal, and flow measurements. Some operators take correspondence courses on subjects related to water and wastewater treatment, and some employers pay part of the tuition for related college courses in science or engineering.

Licensure. The Safe Drinking Water Act Amendments of 1996, enforced by the U.S. Environmental Protection Agency, specify national minimum standards for certification of public water system operators. Operators must pass an examination certifying that they are capable of overseeing water treatment operations. Mandatory certification is implemented at the State level, and licensing requirements and standards vary widely depending on the State. There are generally three to four different levels of certification, depending on the operator's experience and training. Higher levels qualify the operator to oversee a wider variety of treatment processes. Although relocation may mean having to become certified in a new jurisdiction, many States accept other States' certifications.

Other qualifications. Water and wastewater treatment plant operators need mechanical aptitude and the ability to solve problems intuitively. They should also be competent in basic mathematics, chemistry, and biology. They must have the ability to apply data to formulas that determine treatment requirements, flow levels, and concentration levels. Some basic familiarity with computers also is necessary, as operators generally use them to record data. Some plants also use computer-controlled equipment and instrumentation.

Certification and advancement. In addition to mandatory certifications required by law, operators can earn voluntary certifications that demonstrate their skills and knowledge. The Association of Boards of Certification offers several levels and types of certification to people who pass exams and have sufficient education and experience.

As operators are promoted, they become responsible for more complex treatment processes. Some operators are promoted to plant supervisor or superintendent; others advance by transferring to a larger facility. Postsecondary training in water and wastewater treatment, coupled with increasingly responsible experience as an operator, may be sufficient to qualify a worker to become superintendent of a small plant, where a superintendent also serves as an operator. However, educational requirements are rising as larger, more complex treatment plants are built to meet new drinking water and water pollution control standards. With each promotion, the operator must have greater knowledge of Federal, State, and local regulations. Superintendents of large plants generally need an engineering or science degree.

A few operators get jobs as technicians with State drinking water or water pollution control agencies. In that capacity, they monitor and provide technical assistance to plants throughout the State. Vocational-technical school or community college training generally is preferred for technician jobs. Experienced operators may transfer to related jobs with industrial liquid waste treatment plants, water or liquid waste treatment equipment and chemical companies, engineering consulting firms, or vocational-technical schools.

Employment

Water and wastewater treatment plant and system operators held about 111,000 jobs in 2006. Almost 4 in 5 operators worked for local governments. Others worked primarily for private water, sewage, and other systems utilities and for private waste treatment and disposal and waste management services companies. Private firms are increasingly providing operation and management services to local governments on a contract basis.

Water and wastewater treatment plant and system operators were employed throughout the country, but most jobs were in larger towns and cities. Although nearly all operators worked full time, those in small towns may work only part time at the treatment plant, with the remainder of their time spent handling other municipal duties.

Job Outlook

Water and wastewater treatment plant and system operators jobs are expected to grow faster than the average for all occupations. Job opportunities should be excellent for qualified workers.

Employment change. Employment of water and wastewater treatment plant and system operators is expected to grow by 14 percent between 2006 and 2016, which is faster than the average for all occupations. An increasing population and the growth of the economy are expected to boost demand for water and wastewater treatment services. As new plants are constructed to meet this demand, new water and wastewater treatment plant and system operator new jobs will arise.

Local governments are the largest employers of water and wastewater treatment plant and system operators. Employment in privately owned facilities will grow faster, as Federal certification requirements have increased utilities' reliance on private firms specializing in the operation and management of water and wastewater treatment facilities.

Job prospects. Job opportunities should be excellent because the retirement of the baby boomer generation will require that many operators with years of experience be replaced. Further, the number of applicants for these jobs is normally low, due primarily to the physically demanding and unappealing nature of some of the work. Opportunities should be best for persons with mechanical aptitude and problem solving skills.

Earnings

Median annual earnings of water and wastewater treatment plant and system operators were $36,070 in May 2006. The middle 50 percent earned between $28,120 and $45,190. The lowest 10 percent earned less than $21,860, and the highest 10 percent earned more than $55,120. Median annual earnings of water and liquid waste treatment plant and systems operators in May 2006 were $36,200 in local government and $34,180 in water, sewage, and other systems.

In addition to their annual salaries, water and wastewater treatment plant and system operators usually receive benefits that may include health and life insurance, a retirement plan, and educational reimbursement for job-related courses.

Related Occupations

Other workers whose main activity consists of operating a system of machinery to process or produce materials include chemical plant and system operators; gas plant operators; petroleum pump system operators, refinery operators, and gaugers; power plant operators, distributors, and dispatchers; and stationary engineers and boiler operators.

Sources of Additional Information

For information on employment opportunities, contact State or local water pollution control agencies, State water and liquid waste operator associations, State environmental training centers, or local offices of the State employment service.

For information on certification, contact:

➤ Association of Boards of Certification, 208 Fifth St., Ames, IA 50010-6259. Internet: **http://www.abccert.org**

For educational information related to a career as a water or liquid waste treatment plant and system operator, contact:

➤ American Water Works Association, 6666 West Quincy Ave., Denver, CO 80235. Internet: **http://www.awwa.org**

➤ National Rural Water Association, 2915 S. 13th St., Duncan, OK 73533. Internet: **http://www.nrwa.org**

➤ Water Environment Federation, 601 Wythe St., Alexandria, VA 22314-1994. Internet: **http://www.wef.org**

Other Production Occupations

Inspectors, Testers, Sorters, Samplers, and Weighers

(O*NET 51-9061.00)

Significant Points

- Almost 7 in 10 are employed in manufacturing establishments.

- While a high school diploma is sufficient for basic testing of products, complex precision-inspecting positions are filled by experienced assemblers, machine operators, or mechanics who already have a thorough knowledge of the products and production processes.

- Employment is expected to decline slowly, reflecting the growth of automated inspection and the redistribution of quality-control responsibilities from inspectors to other production workers.

Nature of the Work

Inspectors, testers, sorters, samplers, and weighers ensure that your food will not make you sick, that your car will run properly, and that your pants will not split the first time you wear them. These workers monitor or audit quality standards for virtually all domestically manufactured products, including foods, textiles, clothing, glassware, motor vehicles, electronic components, computers, and structural steel. As product quality becomes increasingly important to the success of many manufacturing firms, daily duties of inspectors have changed. In some cases, the job titles of these workers also have been changed to *quality-control inspector* or a similar name, reflecting the growing importance of quality. (A separate statement on construction and building inspectors appears elsewhere in the *Handbook*.)

Regardless of title, all inspectors, testers, sorters, samplers, and weighers work to guarantee the quality of the goods their firms produce. Specific job duties also vary across the wide range of industries in which these workers are found. For example, materials inspectors may check products by sight, sound, feel, smell, or even taste to locate imperfections such as cuts, scratches, bubbles, missing pieces, misweaves, or crooked seams. These workers also may verify dimensions, color, weight, texture, strength, or other physical characteristics of objects. Mechanical inspectors generally verify that parts fit, move correctly, and are properly lubricated; check the pressure of gases and the level of liquids; test the flow of electricity; and do a test run to check for proper operation. Some jobs involve only a quick visual inspection; others require a longer, detailed one. Sorters may separate goods according to length, size, fabric type, or color, while samplers test or inspect a sample taken from a batch or production run

for malfunctions or defects. Weighers weigh quantities of materials for use in production.

Inspectors, testers, sorters, samplers, and weighers are involved at every stage of the production process. Some inspectors examine materials received from a supplier before sending them to the production line. Others inspect components and assemblies or perform a final check on the finished product. Depending on their skill level, inspectors also may set up and test equipment, calibrate precision instruments, repair defective products, or record data.

Inspectors, testers, sorters, samplers, and weighers rely on a number of tools to perform their jobs. Although some still use hand held measurement devises such as micrometers, calipers, and alignment gauges, it is more common for them to operate electronic inspection equipment, such as coordinate measuring machines (CMMs). These machines use sensitive probes to measure a part's dimensional accuracy and allow the inspector to analyze the results using computer software. Inspectors testing electrical devices may use voltmeters, ammeters, and oscilloscopes to test insulation, current flow, and resistance. All the tools that inspectors use are maintained by calibration technicians, who ensure that they work properly and generate accurate readings.

Inspectors mark, tag, or note problems. They may reject defective items outright, send them for repair or correction, or fix minor problems themselves. If the product is acceptable, inspectors may screw a nameplate onto it, tag it, stamp it with a serial number, or certify it in some other way. Inspectors, testers, sorters, samplers, and weighers record the results of their inspections, compute the percentage of defects and other statistical measures, and prepare inspection and test reports. Some electronic inspection equipment automatically provides test reports containing these inspection results. When defects are found, inspectors notify supervisors and help to analyze and correct the production problems.

The emphasis on finding the root cause of defects is a basic tenet of modern management and production philosophies. Industrial production managers (see the statement on this occupation elsewhere in the *Handbook*) work closely with the inspectors to reduce defects and improve quality. In the past, a certain level of defects was considered acceptable because variations would always occur. Current philosophies emphasize constant quality improvement through analysis and correction of the causes of defects. The nature of inspectors' work has changed from merely checking for defects to determining the cause of those defects.

Increased emphasis on quality control in manufacturing means that inspection is more fully integrated into the production process than in the past. Now, companies have integrated teams of inspection and production workers to jointly review and improve product quality. In addition, many companies now use self-monitoring production machines to ensure that the output is produced within quality standards. Self-monitoring machines can alert inspectors to production problems and automatically repair defects in some cases.

Some firms have completely automated inspection with the help of advanced vision inspection systems, using machinery installed at one or several points in the production process. Inspectors in these firms monitor the equipment, review output, and perform random product checks.

Testers repeatedly test existing products or prototypes under real-world conditions. For example, they may purposely abuse a machine by not changing its oil to see when failure occurs. They may devise automated machines to repeat a basic task thousands of times, such as opening and closing a car door. Through these tests, companies determine how long a product will last, what parts will break down first, and how to improve durability.

Work environment. Working conditions vary by industry and establishment size. As a result, some inspectors examine similar products for an entire shift, whereas others examine a variety of items.

In manufacturing, it is common for most inspectors to remain at one workstation. Inspectors in some industries may be on their feet all day and may have to lift heavy objects, whereas in other industries, they sit during most of their shift and read electronic printouts with massive quantities of data. Workers in heavy manufacturing plants may be exposed to the noise and grime of machinery; in other plants, inspectors work

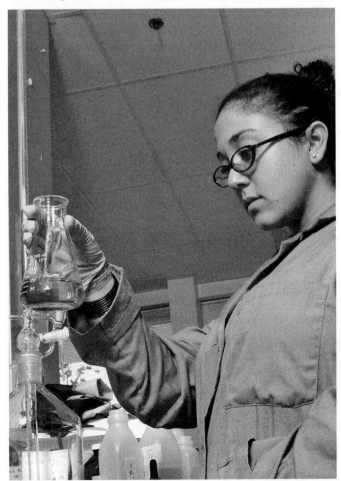

Inspectors, testers, sorters, samplers, and weighers often work in laboratories and may need a background in science.

in clean, air-conditioned environments suitable for carrying out controlled tests. Other inspectors rarely see the products they are inspecting and instead do the majority of their work examining electronic readouts in front of a computer.

Some inspectors work evenings, nights, or weekends. Shift assignments generally are made on the basis of seniority. Overtime may be required to meet production goals.

Training, Other Qualifications, and Advancement
Most inspectors, testers, sorters, samplers, and weighers enter the occupation after spending years at a particular company or in an industry. They usually get their training on the job.

Education and training. Training requirements vary, based on the responsibilities of the inspector, tester, sorter, sampler, or weigher. For workers who perform simple "pass/fail" tests of products, a high school diploma generally is sufficient, together with basic in-house training. Training for new inspectors may cover the use of special meters, gauges, computers and other instruments; quality-control techniques; blueprint reading; safety; and reporting requirements. There are some postsecondary training programs in testing, but many employers prefer to train inspectors on the job.

Chances of finding work in this occupation can be improved by studying industrial trades, including computer-aided design, in high school or in a postsecondary vocational program. Laboratory work in the natural or biological sciences may also improve one's analytical skills and enhance the ability to find work in medical or pharmaceutical labs where many of these workers are employed.

As companies implement more automated inspection techniques that require less manual inspection, workers in this occupation have to learn to operate and program more sophisticated equipment and learn software applications. Since this requires additional skills, the need for higher education may be necessary. To address this need, some colleges are offering associate degrees in fields such as quality control management.

Other qualifications. In general, inspectors, testers, sorters, samplers, and weighers need mechanical aptitude, math and communication skills, and good hand-eye coordination and vision. Another important skill is the ability to analyze and interpret blueprints, data, manuals, and other material to determine specifications, inspection procedures, formulas, and methods for making adjustments.

Certification and advancement. Complex inspection positions are filled by experienced assemblers, machine operators, or mechanics who already have a thorough knowledge of the products and production processes. To advance to these positions, experienced workers may need training in statistical process control, new automation, or the company's quality assurance policies. As automated inspection equipment and electronic recording of results is common, computer skills are also important.

Training has become more formalized with the advent of standards from the International Organization for Standardization. As a result, certification as a quality inspector, offered by the American Society for Quality, is designed to certify that someone is trained in the field and may enable workers to

Projections data from the National Employment Matrix

Occupational Title	SOC Code	Employment, 2006	Projected employment, 2016	Change, 2006-16	
				Number	Percent
Inspectors, testers, sorters, samplers, and weighers.........................	51-9061	491,000	457,000	-35,000	-7

NOTE: Data in this table are rounded. See the discussion of the employment projections table in the *Handbook* introductory chapter on *Occupational Information Included in the Handbook*.

advance within the occupation. To take the exam for certification, two years of on the job experience in mechanical inspection or a related field is required.

Advancement for workers with the necessary skills frequently takes the form of higher pay. They may also advance to inspector of more complex products, supervisor, or related positions such as purchaser of materials and equipment.

Employment

Inspectors, testers, sorters, samplers, and weighers held about 491,000 jobs in 2006. About 7 in 10 worked in manufacturing establishments that produced such products as motor vehicle parts, plastics products, semiconductor and other electronic components, and aerospace products and parts. Inspectors, testers, sorters, samplers, and weighers also were found in employment services, wholesale trade, architectural, engineering, and related services, and government agencies.

Job Outlook

Like that of many other occupations concentrated in manufacturing industries, employment of inspectors, testers, sorters, samplers, and weighers is expected to decline moderately through the year 2016. The decline stems primarily from the growing use of automated inspection and the redistribution of some quality-control responsibilities from inspectors to production workers. Additionally, as manufacturing companies continue to move some production offshore, the need for these workers will lessen.

Employment change. Employment of inspectors, testers, sorters, samplers, and weighers is expected to decline moderately by 7 percent between 2006 and 2016. Because the majority of inspectors, testers, sorters, samplers, and weighers work in the manufacturing sector, their outlook is greatly affected by what happens to manufacturing companies. As this sector becomes more automated and productive and as some production moves offshore, the number of inspectors, testers, sorters, samplers, and weighers is expected to decline. However, the continuing emphasis on producing quality goods and the need for accuracy in the growing medical and biotechnology fields will positively affect this occupation and moderate the decline.

In some industries, however, automation is not a feasible alternative to manual inspection. Where key inspection elements are oriented toward size, such as length, width, or thickness, automation will become more important in the future. But where taste, smell, texture, appearance, fabric complexity, or product performance is important, inspection will continue to be done by workers. Employment of inspectors, testers, sorters, samplers, and weighers is expected to increase faster than average in the employment services industry, as manu-

facturers and industrial firms hire more temporary inspectors to increase the flexibility of their staffing.

The emphasis on improving quality and productivity has led manufacturers to invest in automated inspection equipment and to take a more systematic approach to quality inspection. Continued improvements in technologies, such as spectrophotometers and computer-assisted visual inspection systems, allow firms to effectively automate inspection tasks, increasing workers' productivity and reducing the demand for inspectors. Inspectors will continue to operate these automated machines and monitor the defects they detect. Thus, while the growing emphasis on quality has increased the importance of inspection, the increased automation of inspection has limited the demand for inspectors.

Apart from automation, firms are integrating quality control into the production process. Many inspection duties are being redistributed from specialized inspectors to fabrication and assembly workers who monitor quality at every stage of the production process. In addition, the growing implementation of statistical process control is resulting in "smarter" inspection. Using this system, firms survey the sources and incidence of defects so that they can better focus their efforts on reducing production of defective products.

Job prospects. Although numerous job openings will arise due to the need to replace workers who move out of this large occupation, many of these jobs will be open only to experienced workers with advanced skills.

Earnings

Median hourly earnings of inspectors, testers, sorters, samplers, and weighers were $14.14 in May 2006. The middle 50 percent earned between $10.84 and $18.79 an hour. The lowest 10 percent earned less than $8.65 an hour, and the highest 10 percent earned more than $24.85 an hour. Median hourly earnings in the industries employing the largest numbers of inspectors, testers, sorters, samplers, and weighers in May 2006 were:

Aerospace product and parts manufacturing......................$20.62
Motor vehicle parts manufacturing......................................16.74
Semiconductor and other electronic component
  manufacturing..13.32
Plastics product manufacturing..12.85
Employment services...11.12

Related Occupations

Other workers who conduct inspections include agricultural inspectors, construction and building inspectors, fire inspectors and investigators, occupational health and safety specialists and technicians, and transportation inspectors.

Sources of Additional Information

For general information about inspection, testing, and certification, contact:

➤ American Society for Quality, 600 North Plankinton Ave., Milwaukee, WI 53203. Internet: **http://www.asq.org**

Jewelers and Precious Stone and Metal Workers

(O*NET 51-9071.00, 51-9071.01, 51-9071.06, 51-9071.07)

Significant Points

- About half of all jewelers are self-employed.

- Jewelers usually learn their trade in vocational or technical schools, through distance-learning centers, or on the job.

- Prospects for bench jewelers and other skilled jewelers should be favorable; keen competition is expected for lower-skilled manufacturing jobs, such as assemblers and polishers.

Nature of the Work

Jewelers and precious stone and metal workers use a variety of common and specialized handtools and equipment to design and manufacture new pieces of jewelry; cut, set, and polish gem stones; repair or adjust rings, necklaces, bracelets, earrings, and other jewelry; and appraise jewelry, precious metals, and gems. Jewelers usually specialize in one or more of these areas and may work for large jewelry manufacturing firms, for small retail jewelry shops, or as owners of their own businesses. Regardless of the type of work done or the work setting, jewelers need a high degree of skill, precision, and attention to detail.

Some jewelers design or make their own jewelry. Following their own designs or those created by designers or customers, they begin by shaping the metal or by carving wax to make a model for casting the metal. The individual parts then are soldered together, and the jeweler may mount a diamond or other gem or may engrave a design into the metal. Other jewelers do finishing work, such as setting stones, polishing, or engraving, or make repairs. Typical repair work includes enlarging or reducing ring sizes, resetting stones, and replacing broken clasps and mountings.

Bench jewelers usually work in jewelry retailers. They perform a wide range of tasks, from simple jewelry cleaning and repair to moldmaking and fabricating pieces from scratch. In larger manufacturing businesses, jewelers usually specialize in a single operation. *Mold and model makers* create models or tools for the jewelry that is to be produced. *Assemblers* solder or fuse jewelry and their parts; they also may set stones. *Engravers* etch designs into the metal with specialized tools, and *polishers* bring a finished luster to the final product.

Jewelers typically do the handiwork required to produce a piece of jewelry, while *gemologists* and laboratory graders analyze, describe, and certify the quality and characteristics of gem stones. Gemologists may work in gemological laboratories or

as quality control experts for retailers, importers, or manufacturers. After using microscopes, computerized tools, and other grading instruments to examine gem stones or finished pieces of jewelry, they write reports certifying that the items are of a particular quality. Many jewelers also study gemology to become familiar with the physical properties of the gem stones with which they work.

Jewelry appraisers carefully examine jewelry to determine its value, after which they write appraisal documents. They determine the value of a piece by researching the jewelry market, using reference books, auction catalogs, price lists, and the Internet. They may work for jewelry stores, appraisal firms, auction houses, pawnbrokers, or insurance companies. Many gemologists also become appraisers.

In small retail stores or repair shops, jewelers and appraisers may be involved in all aspects of the work. Those who own or manage stores or shops also hire and train employees; order, market, and sell merchandise; and perform managerial duties.

New technology is helping to produce jewelry of higher quality at a reduced cost and in a shorter amount of time. For example, lasers are often used for cutting and improving the quality of stones, for applying intricate engraving or design work, and for inscribing personal messages or identification on jewelry. Jewelers also use lasers to weld metals together in milliseconds with no seams or blemishes, improving the quality and appearance of jewelry.

Some manufacturing firms use computer-aided design and manufacturing (CAD/CAM) to facilitate product design and automate some steps in the moldmaking and modelmaking process. CAD allows jewelers to create a virtual-reality model of a piece of jewelry. Using CAD, jewelers can modify the design, change the stone, or try a different setting and see the changes on a computer screen before cutting a stone or performing other costly steps. Once they are satisfied with the model, CAM produces it in a waxlike or other material. After the mold of the model is made, it is easier for manufacturing firms to produce numerous copies of a given piece of jewelry, which are then distributed to retail establishments across the country. Similar techniques may be used in the retail setting, allowing customers to review their jewelry designs with the jeweler and make modifications before committing themselves to the expense of a customized piece of jewelry.

Work environment. A jeweler's work involves a great deal of concentration and attention to detail. Trying to satisfy customers' and employers' demands for speed and quality while working on precious stones and metal can cause fatigue or stress. However, the use of more ergonomically correct jewelers' benches has eliminated most of the strain and discomfort caused by spending long periods over a workbench.

Lasers require both careful handling to avoid injury and steady hands to direct precision tasks. In larger manufacturing plants and some smaller repair shops, chemicals, sharp or pointed tools, and jewelers' torches pose safety threats and may cause injury if proper care is not taken. Most dangerous chemicals, however, have been replaced with synthetic, less toxic products to meet safety requirements.

In repair shops, jewelers usually work alone with little supervision. In retail stores, they may talk with customers about repairs, perform custom design work, and even do some selling. Because many of their materials are valuable, jewelers must observe strict security procedures, including working behind locked doors that are opened only by a buzzer, working on the other side of barred windows, making use of burglar alarms, and, in larger jewelry establishments, working in the presence of armed guards.

Training, Other Qualifications, and Advancement

Jewelers usually learn their trade in vocational or technical schools, through distance-learning centers, or on the job. Formal training enhances employment and advancement opportunities.

Education and training. Jewelers usually learn their trade in vocational or technical schools, through distance-learning centers, or on the job. For those interested in working in a jewelry store or repair shop, vocational and technical training or courses offered by public and private colleges are the best sources of training. In these programs, which can vary in length from 6 months to 1 year, students learn the use and care of jewelers' tools and machines and basic jewelrymaking and jewelry-repairing skills, such as designing, casting, and setting and polishing stones.

Jewelers usually learn their trade in vocational or technical schools, through distance-learning centers, or on the job.

Technical school courses also cover topics such as blueprint reading, math, and shop theory. To enter some technical school programs and most college programs, a high school diploma or its equivalent is required. However, some schools specializing in jewelry training do not require graduation from high school.

Colleges and art and design schools offer programs that can lead to the degree of bachelor of fine arts, or master of fine arts, in jewelry design. Various institutes offer courses and programs in gemology. Programs cover a wide range of topics, including the identification and grading of diamonds and gem stones.

Computer-aided design is becoming increasingly common, and students—especially those interested in design and manufacturing—may wish to obtain training in it; however, most employers will provide such training.

Most employers feel that vocational school and technical school graduates need up to a year of additional supervised on-the-job training or an apprenticeship to refine their repair skills and learn more about the operation of the store or shop. In addition, some employers encourage workers to improve their skills by enrolling in short-term technical school courses such as fabricating, jewelry design, jewelry manufacturing, wax carving, and gemology. Employers may pay all or part of the cost of this additional training.

In jewelry manufacturing plants, workers traditionally develop their skills through informal apprenticeships and on-the-job training. The apprenticeship or training period lasts up to 1 year, depending on the difficulty of the specialty. Training usually focuses on casting, setting stones, making models, or engraving. In recent years, a growing number of technical schools have begun to offer training designed for jewelers working in manufacturing. Employers in manufacturing may prefer graduates of these programs because they are familiar with the production process and require less on-the-job training.

Other qualifications. The precise and delicate nature of jewelry work requires finger and hand dexterity, good hand-eye coordination, patience, and concentration. Artistic ability and fashion consciousness are major assets, particularly in jewelry design and jewelry shops, because jewelry must be stylish and attractive. Those who work in jewelry stores have frequent contact with customers and should be neat, personable, and knowledgeable about the merchandise. In addition, employers require workers of good character because jewelers work with valuable materials.

Certification and advancement. Jewelers of America offers four credentials, ranging from Certified Bench Jeweler Technician to Certified Master Bench Jeweler, for bench jewelers who pass a written and practical exam. Certification is not required to work as a bench jeweler, but it may help jewelers to show expertise and to advance.

Advancement opportunities are limited and depend greatly on an individual's skill and initiative. In manufacturing, some jewelers advance to supervisory jobs, such as master jeweler or head jeweler, but for most, advancement means earning higher pay for the same job. Jewelers who work in jewelry stores or repair shops may become managers; some open their own businesses.

Those interested in starting their own business should first establish themselves and build a reputation for their work with-

Projections data from the National Employment Matrix

Occupational Title	SOC Code	Employment, 2006	Projected employment, 2016	Change, 2006-16	
				Number	Percent
Jewelers and precious stone and metal workers.............................	51-9071	52,000	51,000	-1,200	-2

NOTE: Data in this table are rounded. See the discussion of the employment projections table in the *Handbook* introductory chapter on *Occupational Information Included in the Handbook.*

in the jewelry trade. Once they obtain sufficient credit from jewelry suppliers and wholesalers, they can acquire the necessary inventory. Also, because the jewelry business is highly competitive, jewelers who plan to open their own store should have sales experience and knowledge of marketing and business management. Courses in these subjects are often available from technical schools and community colleges.

Employment

Jewelers and precious stone and metal workers held about 52,000 jobs in 2006. About 51 percent of these workers were self-employed; many operated their own store or repair shop, and some specialized in designing and creating custom jewelry.

About 22 percent of wage-and-salary jobs for jewelers and precious stone and metal workers were in retail trade, primarily in jewelry, luggage, and leather goods stores. Another 17 percent of jobs were in jewelry and silverware manufacturing. A small number of jobs were with merchant wholesalers of miscellaneous durable goods and in repair shops providing repair and maintenance of personal and household goods. Although jewelry stores and repair shops were found in every city and in many small towns, most jobs were in larger metropolitan areas. Many jewelers employed in manufacturing worked in Rhode Island, New York, Chicago, Dallas, Florida, or California.

Job Outlook

Employment of jewelers and precious stone and metal workers is expected to experience little or no change. Prospects for bench jewelers and other skilled jewelers should be favorable; keen competition is expected for lower-skilled manufacturing jobs, such as assemblers and polishers.

Employment change. Employment of jewelers and precious stone and metal workers is expected to experience little or no change, declining 2 percent between 2006 and 2016.

The increasing numbers of affluent individuals, working women, double-income households, and fashion-conscious men are expected to keep jewelry sales strong. The population aged 45 and older, which accounts for a major portion of jewelry sales, also is on the rise. However, most jewelry manufacturing has already moved abroad, and this trend is expected to continue.

Nontraditional jewelry marketers, such as discount stores, mail-order and catalogue companies, television shopping networks, and Internet retailers, have expanded the number of buying options and increased their sales volume. However, these establishments require fewer sales staff, limiting employment opportunities for jewelers and precious stone and metal workers who work mainly in sales.

Traditional jewelers may continue to lose some of their market share to nontraditional outlets, but they will maintain a large customer base. Many buyers prefer to see and try on jewelry before purchasing it or enjoy the experience of shopping in a store. Jewelry stores also have the advantage of being able to offer personalized service and build client relationships. Additionally, new jewelry sold by nontraditional retailers will create demand for skilled jewelers for sizing, cleaning, and repair work. There may also be increased demand for bench jewelers as baby boomers seek customization and repair of heirloom jewelry.

Job prospects. Despite little or no change in employment, opportunities should be favorable for bench jewelers and other skilled jewelers. New jewelers will be needed to replace those who retire or who leave the occupation for other reasons. When master jewelers retire, they take with them years of experience that require substantial time and financial resources to replace. Many employers have difficulty finding and retaining jewelers with the right skills and the necessary knowledge. Opportunities in jewelry stores and repair shops will be best for graduates from training programs for jewelers or gemologists.

Keen competition is expected for lower-skilled manufacturing jobs that are amenable to automation, such as assemblers and polishers. Jewelry designers who wish to create their own jewelry lines should expect intense competition. Although demand for customized and boutique jewelry is strong, it is difficult for independent designers to establish themselves.

The jewelry industry can be cyclical. During economic downturns, demand for jewelry products and for jewelers tends to decrease. However, demand for repair workers should remain strong even during economic slowdowns because maintaining and repairing jewelry is an ongoing process. In fact, demand for jewelry repair may increase during recessions, as people repair or restore existing pieces rather than purchase new ones.

Earnings

Median annual wage-and-salary earnings for jewelers and precious stone and metal workers were $29,750 in May 2006. The middle 50 percent earned between $22,390 and $40,160. The lowest 10 percent earned less than $17,760, and the highest 10 percent earned more than $54,940.

Most jewelers start out with a base salary, but once they become more proficient, they may begin charging by the number of pieces completed. Jewelers who work in retail stores may earn a commission for each piece of jewelry sold. Many jewelers also enjoy a variety of benefits, including reimbursement from their employers for work-related courses and discounts on jewelry purchases.

Related Occupations

Jewelers and precious stone and metal workers do precision handwork. Other skilled workers who do similar jobs include precision instrument and equipment repairers; welding, soldering, and brazing workers; and woodworkers. Some jewelers and precious stone and metal workers create their own jewelry designs. Other occupations that require visual arts abilities include artists and related workers, and various designers—commercial and industrial, fashion, floral, graphic, and interior. Finally, some jewelers and precious stone and metal workers are involved in the buying and selling of stones, metals, or finished pieces of jewelry. Similar occupations include retail salespersons and sales representatives in wholesale trade.

Sources of Additional Information

Information on job opportunities and training programs for jewelers and gemologists is available from:

➤ Gemological Institute of America, 5345 Armada Dr., Carlsbad, CA 92008. Internet: **http://www.gia.edu**

For more information about bench jeweler certification and careers in jewelry design and retail, including different career paths, training options, and schools, contact:

➤ Jewelers of America, 52 Vanderbilt Ave., 19th Floor, New York, NY 10017. Internet: **http://www.jewelers.org**

For information on jewelry design and manufacturing, training, and schools offering jewelry-related programs and degrees by State, contact:

➤ Manufacturing Jewelers and Suppliers of America, 45 Royal Little Dr., Providence, RI 02904.
Internet: **http://www.mjsa.org**

To receive a list of accredited technical schools that have programs in gemology, contact:

➤ Accrediting Commission of Career Schools and Colleges of Technology, 2101 Wilson Blvd., Suite 302, Arlington, VA 22201. Internet: **http://www.accsct.org**

Medical, Dental, and Ophthalmic Laboratory Technicians

(O*NET 51-9081.00, 51-9082.00, 51-9083.00)

Significant Points

- Around 55 percent of salaried jobs were in medical equipment and supply manufacturing laboratories, which usually are small, privately owned businesses with fewer than 5 employees.

- Most technicians learn their craft on the job, but many employers prefer to hire those with formal training.

- Slower-than-average employment growth is expected for dental and ophthalmic laboratory technicians, while average employment growth is expected for medical appliance technicians.

- Job opportunities should be favorable because few people seek these positions.

Nature of the Work

When patients require a medical device to help them see clearly, chew and speak well, or walk, their health care providers send requests to medical, dental, and ophthalmic laboratory technicians. These technicians produce a variety of implements to help patients.

Medical appliance technicians construct, fit, maintain, and repair braces, artificial limbs, joints, arch supports, and other surgical and medical appliances. They follow prescriptions or detailed instructions from podiatrists or orthotists, who request braces, supports, corrective shoes, or other devises; prosthetists, who order prostheses—replacement limbs, such as an arm, leg, hand, or foot—for patients who need them due to a birth defect, accident, or amputation; or other health care professionals. Medical appliance technicians who work with these types of devices are called orthotic and prosthetic technicians. Other medical appliance technicians work with appliances that help correct other medical problems, such as hearing aids.

Creating medical devices takes several steps. To make arch supports, for example, technicians first make a wax or plastic impression of the patient's foot. Then they bend and form a material so that it conforms to prescribed contours required to fabricate structural components. If a support is mainly required to correct the balance of a patient with legs of different lengths, a rigid material is used. If the support is primarily intended to protect those with arthritic or diabetic feet, a soft material is used. Supports and braces are polished with grinding and buffing wheels. Technicians may cover arch supports with felt to make them more comfortable.

For prostheses, technicians construct or receive a plaster cast of the patient's limb to use as a pattern. Then, they lay out parts and use precision measuring instruments to measure them. Technicians may use wood, plastic, metal, or other material for the parts of the artificial limb. Next, they carve, cut, or grind the material using hand or power tools. Then, they drill holes for rivets and glue, rivet, or weld the parts together. They are able to do very precise work using common tools. Next, technicians use grinding and buffing wheels to smooth and polish artificial limbs. Lastly, they may cover or pad the limbs with rubber, leather, felt, plastic, or another material. Also, technicians may mix pigments according to formulas to match the patient's skin color and apply the mixture to the artificial limb.

After fabrication, medical appliance technicians test devices for proper alignment, movement, and biomechanical stability using meters and alignment fixtures. They also may fit the appliance on the patient and adjust them as necessary. Over time the appliance will wear down, so technicians must repair and maintain the device. They also may service and repair the machinery used for the fabrication of orthotic and prosthetic devices.

Dental laboratory technicians fill prescriptions from dentists for crowns, bridges, dentures, and other dental prosthetics. First, dentists send a specification of the item to be manufactured, along with an impression or mold of the patient's mouth or teeth. With new technology, a technician may receive a digital impression rather than a physical mold. Then dental laboratory technicians, also called dental technicians, create a model of the patient's mouth by pouring plaster into the impression and allowing it to set. They place the model on an apparatus that mimics the bite and movement of the patient's jaw. The model serves as the basis of the prosthetic device. Technicians examine the model, noting the size and shape of the adjacent teeth, as well as gaps within the gumline. Based upon these observations and the dentist's specifications, technicians build and shape a wax tooth or teeth model, using small hand instruments called wax spatulas and wax carvers. The wax model is used to cast the metal framework for the prosthetic device.

After the wax tooth has been formed, dental technicians pour the cast and form the metal and, using small hand-held tools, prepare the surface to allow the metal and porcelain to bond. They then apply porcelain in layers, to arrive at the precise shape and color of a tooth. Technicians place the tooth in a porcelain furnace to bake the porcelain onto the metal framework, and then adjust the shape and color, with subsequent grinding and addition of porcelain to achieve a sealed finish. The final product is a nearly exact replica of the lost tooth or teeth.

In some laboratories, technicians perform all stages of the work, whereas in other labs, each technician does only a few. Dental laboratory technicians can specialize in 1 of 5 areas: orthodontic appliances, crowns and bridges, complete dentures, partial dentures, or ceramics. Job titles can reflect specialization in these areas. For example, technicians who make porcelain and acrylic restorations are called *dental ceramists.*

Ophthalmic laboratory technicians—also known as manufacturing opticians, optical mechanics, or optical goods workers—make prescription eyeglass or contact lenses. Prescription lenses are curved in such a way that light is correctly focused onto the retina of the patient's eye, improving his or her vision. Some ophthalmic laboratory technicians manufacture lenses for other optical instruments, such as telescopes and binoculars. Ophthalmic laboratory technicians cut, grind, edge, and finish lenses according to specifications provided by dispensing opticians, optometrists, or ophthalmologists and may insert lenses into frames to produce finished glasses. Although some lenses still are produced by hand, technicians are increasingly using automated equipment to make lenses.

Ophthalmic laboratory technicians should not be confused with workers in other vision care occupations. Ophthalmologists and optometrists are "eye doctors" who examine eyes, diagnose and treat vision problems, and prescribe corrective lenses. Ophthalmologists are physicians who also perform eye

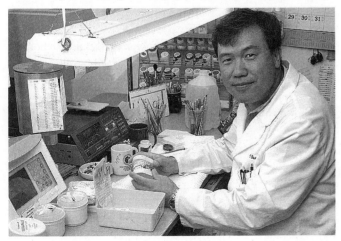

Dental laboratory technicians create models of a patient's mouth, and use those models to create dental prosthetics such as dentures.

surgery. Dispensing opticians, who also may do the work of ophthalmic laboratory technicians, help patients select frames and lenses, and adjust finished eyeglasses. (See the statement on physicians and surgeons, which includes ophthalmologists, as well as the statement on optometrists and opticians, dispensing, elsewhere in the *Handbook.*)

Ophthalmic laboratory technicians read prescription specifications, select standard glass or plastic lens blanks, and then mark them to indicate where the curves specified on the prescription should be ground. They place the lens in the lens grinder, set the dials for the prescribed curvature, and start the machine. After a minute or so, the lens is ready to be "finished" by a machine that rotates it against a fine abrasive, to grind it and smooth out rough edges. The lens is then placed in a polishing machine with an even finer abrasive, to polish it to a smooth, bright finish.

Next, the technician examines the lens through a lensometer, an instrument similar in shape to a microscope, to make sure that the degree and placement of the curve are correct. The technician then cuts the lenses and bevels the edges to fit the frame, dips each lens into dye if the prescription calls for tinted or coated lenses, polishes the edges, and assembles the lenses and frame parts into a finished pair of glasses.

In small laboratories, technicians usually handle every phase of the operation. In large ones, in which virtually every phase of the operation is automated, technicians may be responsible for operating computerized equipment. Technicians also inspect the final product for quality and accuracy.

Work environment. Medical, dental, and ophthalmic laboratory technicians generally work in clean, well-lighted, and well-ventilated laboratories. They have limited contact with the public. Salaried laboratory technicians usually work 40 hours a week, but some work part time. At times, technicians wear goggles to protect their eyes, gloves to handle hot objects, or masks to avoid inhaling dust. They may spend a great deal of time standing.

Dental technicians usually have their own workbenches, which can be equipped with Bunsen burners, grinding and polishing equipment, and hand instruments, such as wax spatulas and wax carvers. Some dental technicians have computer-aided milling equipment to assist them with creating artificial teeth.

Training, Other Qualifications, and Advancement
Most medical, dental, and ophthalmic laboratory technicians learn their craft on the job; however, many employers prefer to hire those with formal training.

Education and training. High school students interested in becoming medical appliance technicians should take mathematics, metal and wood shop, and drafting. Medical appliance technicians usually begin as helpers and gradually learn new skills as they gain experience.

Formal training is also available. In 2006, there were four orthotic and prosthetic technician programs accredited by the National Commission on Orthotic and Prosthetic Education (NCOPE). These programs offer either an associate degree or a 1-year certificate for orthotic or prosthetic technicians. The programs instruct students on human anatomy and physiology, orthotic and prosthetic equipment and materials, and applied biomechanical principles to customize orthotics or prostheses. The programs also include clinical rotations to provide hands-on experience.

Dental laboratory technicians begin by learning simple tasks, such as pouring plaster into an impression, and progress to more complex procedures, such as making porcelain crowns and bridges. Becoming a fully trained technician requires an average of 3 to 4 years, depending upon the individual's aptitude and ambition, but it may take a few years more to become an accomplished technician. High school students interested in becoming dental laboratory technicians should take courses in art, metal and wood shop, drafting, and sciences. Courses in management and business may help those wishing to operate their own laboratories.

Training in dental laboratory technology also is available through community and junior colleges, vocational-technical institutes, and the Armed Forces. Formal training programs vary greatly both in length and in the level of skill they impart. In 2006, 20 programs in dental laboratory technology were accredited by the Commission on Dental Accreditation in conjunction with the American Dental Association. These programs provide classroom instruction in dental materials science, oral anatomy, fabrication procedures, ethics, and related subjects. In addition, each student is given supervised practical experience in a school or an associated dental laboratory. Accredited programs normally take 2 years to complete and lead to an associate degree. A few programs take about 4 years to complete and offer a bachelor's degree in dental technology. Graduates of 2-year training programs need additional hands-on experience to become fully qualified.

Each dental laboratory owner operates in a different way, and classroom instruction does not necessarily expose students to techniques and procedures favored by individual laboratory owners. Students who have taken enough courses to learn the basics of the craft usually are considered good candidates for training, regardless of whether they have completed a formal program. Many employers will train someone without any classroom experience.

Ophthalmic laboratory technicians start on simple tasks if they are training to produce lenses by hand. They may begin with marking or blocking lenses for grinding; then, they progress to grinding, cutting, edging, and beveling lenses; finally, they are trained in assembling the eyeglasses. Depending on individual aptitude, it may take up to 6 months to become proficient in all phases of the work.

Employers filling trainee jobs prefer applicants who are high school graduates. Courses in science, mathematics, and computers are valuable; manual dexterity and the ability to do precision work are essential. Technicians using automated systems will find computer skills valuable.

A few ophthalmic laboratory technicians learn their trade in the Armed Forces or in the few programs in optical technology offered by vocational-technical institutes or trade schools. These programs have classes in optical theory, surfacing and lens finishing, and the reading and applying of prescriptions. Programs vary in length from 6 months to 1 year and award certificates or diplomas.

Other qualifications. A high degree of manual dexterity, good vision, and the ability to recognize very fine color shadings and variations in shape also are necessary for dental technicians. An artistic aptitude for detailed and precise work also is important.

Certification and advancement. Voluntary certification for orthotic and prosthetic technicians is available through the American Board for Certification in Orthotics and Prosthetics (ABC). Applicants are eligible for an exam after completing a program accredited by NCOPE or obtaining 2 years of experience as a technician under the direct supervision of an ABC-certified practitioner. After successfully passing the appropriate exam, technicians receive the Registered Orthotic Technician, Registered Prosthetic Technician, or Registered Prosthetic-Orthotic Technician credential. Certification may help those orthotic and prosthetic technicians seeking to advance.

With additional formal education, medical appliance technicians who make orthotics and prostheses can advance to become orthotists or prosthetists, technicians who work with patients who need braces, artificial limbs, or related devices and help to determine the specifications for those devices.

In large dental laboratories, dental technicians may become supervisors or managers. Experienced technicians may teach or take jobs with dental suppliers in such areas as product development, marketing, and sales. Opening one's own laboratory is another, and more common, way to advance and earn more.

The National Board for Certification, an independent board established by the National Association of Dental Laboratories, offers certification in dental laboratory technology. Certification, which is voluntary except in three states, can be obtained in five specialty areas: crowns and bridges, ceramics, partial dentures, complete dentures, and orthodontic appliances. Certification may increase chances of advancement.

Ophthalmic laboratory technicians can become supervisors and managers. Some become dispensing opticians, although further education or training generally is required in that occupation.

Employment

Medical, dental, and ophthalmic laboratory technicians held about 95,000 jobs in 2006. About 55 percent of salaried jobs were in medical equipment and supply manufacturing laboratories, which usually are small, privately owned businesses with fewer than 5 employees. However, some laboratories are large; a few employ more than 1,000 workers. The following tabulation shows employment by detailed occupation:

Dental laboratory technicians 53,000
Opthalmic laboratory technicians 29,000
Medical appliance technicians 12,000

In addition to manufacturing laboratories, many medical appliance technicians worked in health and personal care stores, while others worked in public and private hospitals, professional and commercial equipment and supplies merchant wholesalers, or consumer goods rental centers. Some were self-employed.

Projections data from the National Employment Matrix

Occupational Title	SOC Code	Employment, 2006	Projected employment, 2016	Change, 2006-16	
				Number	Percent
Medical, dental, and ophthalmic laboratory technicians	51-9080	95,000	100,000	5,000	5
Dental laboratory technicians	51-9081	53,000	55,000	2,000	4
Medical appliance technicians..	51-9082	12,000	13,000	1,200	9
Ophthalmic laboratory technicians...	51-9083	29,000	31,000	1,900	7

NOTE: Data in this table are rounded. See the discussion of the employment projections table in the *Handbook* introductory chapter on *Occupational Information Included in the Handbook.*

In addition to manufacturing laboratories, many dental laboratory technicians worked in offices of dentists. Some dental laboratory technicians open their own offices.

Most ophthalmic laboratory technician jobs were in medical equipment and supplies manufacturing laboratories, about 29 percent. Another 29 percent of jobs were in health and personal care stores, such as optical goods stores that manufacture and sell prescription glasses and contact lenses. Some jobs were in offices of optometrists or ophthalmologists, while others worked at professional and commercial equipment and supplies merchant wholesalers. A few worked in commercial and service industry machine manufacturing firms that produce lenses for other optical instruments, such as telescopes and binoculars.

Job Outlook

Overall, slower-than-average growth is expected for employment of medical, dental, and ophthalmic laboratory technicians. However, job opportunities should be favorable because few people seek these positions.

Employment change. Overall employment for these occupations is expected to grow five percent from 2006 to 2016, slower than the average for all occupations.

Medical appliance technicians will grow at nine percent, about as fast as the average for all occupations, because of the increasing prevalence of the two leading causes of limb loss—diabetes and cardiovascular disease. In addition, advances in technology may spur demand for prostheses that allow for greater movement.

Employment of dental laboratory technicians is expected to grow more slowly than average, at four percent. During the last few years, demand has arisen from an aging public that is growing increasingly interested in cosmetic prostheses. For example, many dental laboratories are filling orders for composite fillings that are the same shade of white as natural teeth to replace older, less attractive fillings. However, job growth for dental laboratory technicians will be limited. The overall dental health of the population has improved because of fluoridation of drinking water and greater emphasis on preventive dental care, which has reduced the incidence of dental cavities. As a result, full dentures will be less common, as most people will need only a bridge or crown.

Ophthalmic laboratory technicians are expected to experience employment growth of seven percent, about as fast as the average for all occupations. Demographic trends make it likely that many more Americans will need vision care in the years ahead. Not only will the population grow, but also the proportion of middle-aged and older adults is projected to increase rapidly. Middle age is a time when many people use corrective lenses for the first time, and elderly persons usually require more vision care than others. However, the increasing use of automated machinery will temper job growth for ophthalmic laboratory technicians.

Job prospects. Job opportunities for medical, dental, and ophthalmic laboratory technicians should be favorable, despite expected slower-than-average growth. Few people seek these jobs, reflecting the relatively limited public awareness and low starting wages. In addition to openings from job growth, many job openings also will arise from the need to replace technicians who transfer to other occupations or who leave the labor force.

Earnings

Median hourly earnings of wage-and-salary medical appliance technicians were $14.99 in May 2006. The middle 50 percent earned between $11.34 and $19.65 an hour. The lowest 10 percent earned less than $8.93, and the highest 10 percent earned more than $27.00 an hour

Median hourly earnings of wage-and-salary dental laboratory technicians were $15.67 in May 2006. The middle 50 percent earned between $11.61 and $20.57 an hour. The lowest 10 percent earned less than $9.16, and the highest 10 percent earned more than $26.13 an hour. In the two industries that employed the most dental laboratory technicians, medical equipment and supplies manufacturing and offices of dentists, median hourly earnings were $15.09 and $17.74, respectively.

Median hourly earnings of wage-and-salary ophthalmic laboratory technicians were $12.24 in May 2006. The middle 50 percent earned between $9.86 and $15.82 an hour. The lowest 10 percent earned less than $8.38, and the highest 10 percent earned more than $19.98 an hour. Median hourly earnings were $11.63 in medical equipment and supplies manufacturing and $11.49 in health and personal care stores, the two industries that employ the most ophthalmic laboratory technicians.

Related Occupations

Medical, dental, and ophthalmic laboratory technicians manufacture and work with the same devices that are used by dispensing opticians and orthotists and prosthetists. Other occupations that work with or manufacture goods using similar tools and skills are precision instrument and equipment repairers and textile, apparel, and furnishings occupations.

Sources of Additional Information

For information on careers in orthotics and prosthetics, contact:

➤ American Academy of Orthotists and Prosthetists, 526 King St., Suite 201, Alexandria, VA 22314. Internet: **http://www.opcareers.org**

For a list of accredited programs for orthotic and prosthetic technicians, contact:

➤ National Commission on Orthotic and Prosthetic Education, 330 John Carlyle St., Suite 200, Alexandria, VA 22314. Internet: **http://www.ncope.org**

For information on requirements for certification of orthotic and prosthetic technicians, contact:

➤ American Board for Certification in Orthotics and Prosthetics, 330 John Carlyle St., Suite 210, Alexandria, VA 22314. Internet: **http://www.abcop.org**

For a list of accredited programs in dental laboratory technology, contact:

➤ Commission on Dental Accreditation, American Dental Association, 211 E. Chicago Ave., Chicago, IL 60611. Internet: **http://www.ada.org**

For information on requirements for certification of dental laboratory technicians, contact:

➤ National Board for Certification in Dental Technology, 325 John Knox Rd., L103, Tallahassee, FL 32303. Internet: **http://www.nbccert.org**

For information on career opportunities in commercial dental laboratories, contact:

➤ National Association of Dental Laboratories, 325 John Knox Rd., L103, Tallahassee, FL 32303. Internet: **http://www.nadl.org**

For information on an accredited program in ophthalmic laboratory technology, contact:

➤ Commission on Opticianry Accreditation, P.O. Box 4342, Chapel Hill, NC 27515.

General information on grants and scholarships is available from individual schools. State employment service offices can provide information about job openings for medical, dental, and ophthalmic laboratory technicians.

Painting and Coating Workers, Except Construction and Maintenance

(O*NET 51-9121.00, 51-9122.00, 51-9123.00)

Significant Points

- About 7 out of 10 jobs are in manufacturing establishments.

- Most workers acquire their skills on the job; training usually lasts from a few days to several months, but becoming skilled in all aspects of painting can require 1 to 2 years of training.

- Overall employment is projected to decline, but employment change will vary by specialty.

- Good job prospects are expected for those with painting experience.

Nature of the Work

Millions of items ranging from cars to candy are covered by paint, plastic, varnish, chocolate, or some other type of coating solution. Painting or coating is used to make a product more attractive or protect it from the elements. The paint finish on an automobile, for example, makes the vehicle more attractive and provides protection from corrosion. Achieving this end result is the work of painting and coating workers.

Before painting and coating workers can begin to apply the paint or other coating, they often need to prepare the surface. A metal, wood, or plastic part may need to be sanded or ground to correct imperfections or rough up a surface so that paint will stick to it. After preparing the surface, the product is carefully cleaned to prevent any dust or dirt from becoming trapped under the paint. Metal parts are often washed or dipped in chemical baths to prepare the surface for painting and protect against corrosion. If the product has more than one color or has unpainted parts, masking is required. Masking normally involves carefully covering portions of the product with tape and paper.

After the product is prepared for painting, coating, or varnishing, a number of techniques may be used to apply the paint. Perhaps the most straightforward technique is simply dipping an item in a large vat of paint or other coating. This is the technique used by *dippers*, who immerse racks or baskets of articles in vats of paint, liquid plastic, or other solutions by means of a power hoist.

Spraying products with a solution of paint or some other coating is also quite common. *Spray machine operators* use spray guns to coat metal, wood, ceramic, fabric, paper, and food products with paint and other coating solutions. Following a formula, operators fill the machine's tanks with a mixture of paints or chemicals, adding prescribed amounts of solution. Then they adjust nozzles on the spray guns to obtain the proper dispersion of the spray, and they hold or position the guns so as to direct the spray onto the article. Operators also check the flow and viscosity of the paint or solution and visually inspect the quality of the coating. When products are drying, these workers often must regulate the temperature and air circulation in drying ovens.

Some factories use automated painting systems that are operated by *coating, painting, and spraying machine setters, operators, and tenders*. When setting up the systems, operators position the automatic spray guns, set the nozzles, and synchronize the action of the guns with the speed of the conveyor carrying articles through the machine and drying ovens. The operator also may add solvents or water to the paint vessel to prepare the paint for application. During the operation of the painting machines, these workers tend the equipment, observe gauges on the control panel, and check articles for evidence of any variation from specifications. The operator uses a manual spray gun to "touch up" flaws.

Powder coating is another common technique for painting manufactured goods. Powder coating machines achieve a smooth finish on metal objects. Workers oversee machines that electrically charge the metal object so that it acts like a magnet. The object enters a powder room filled with powdered paint that is attracted to the magnetic object. After being covered in the powder, the object is baked in an oven where the paint melts into a smooth paint finish.

Individuals who paint, coat, or decorate articles such as furniture, glass, pottery, toys, cakes, and books are known as *painting, coating, and decorating workers.* Some workers coat confectionery, bakery, and other food products with melted chocolate, cheese, oils, sugar, or other substances. Paper is often coated to give it its gloss or finish and silver, tin, and copper solutions are often sprayed on glass to make mirrors.

The best known group of painting and coating workers are those who refinish old or damaged cars, trucks, and buses in automotive body repair and paint shops. *Transportation equipment painters*, also called *automotive painters*, who work in repair shops are among the most highly skilled manual spray operators because they perform intricate, detailed work and mix paints to match the original color, a task that is especially difficult if the color has faded. The preparation work on an old car is similar to painting other metal objects. The paint is normally applied with a manually controlled spray gun.

Transportation equipment painters who work on new cars oversee several automated steps. A modern car is first dipped in an anti-corrosion bath, then painted with the color of the car, and then painted in several coats of clear paint. The clear paint prevents scratches from damaging the colored paint on the car.

Most other transportation equipment painters either paint equipment too large to paint automatically—such as ships or giant construction equipment—or perform touch-up work to repair flaws in the paint caused either by damage during assembly or flaws during the automated painting process.

Whatever object is being painted and in whatever method, the painting process is often repeated several times to achieve a thick, smooth, protective coverage.

Transportation equipment painters work in well-ventilated paint rooms.

Work environment. Painting and coating workers typically work indoors and may be exposed to dangerous fumes from paint and coating solutions, although in general, workers' exposure to hazardous chemicals has decreased because of regulations limiting emissions of volatile organic compounds and other hazardous air pollutants. Painting usually is done in special ventilated booths with workers typically wearing masks or respirators that cover their noses and mouths. More sophisticated paint booths and fresh-air systems are increasingly used to provide a safer work environment.

Operators have to stand for long periods, and when using a spray gun, they may have to bend, stoop, or crouch in uncomfortable positions to reach different parts of the article. Some painters work suspended from ropes to reach high places.

Most painting and coating workers work a normal 40-hour week, but automotive painters in repair shops can work more than 50 hours a week, depending on the number of vehicles that need repainting.

Training, Other Qualifications, and Advancement

Most workers acquire their skills on the job; training usually lasts from a few days to several months, but becoming skilled in all aspects of painting can require 1 to 2 years of training.

Education and training. Training for beginning painting and coating machine setters, operators, and tenders and for painting, coating, and decorating workers, may last from a few days to a couple of months. Coating, painting, and spraying machine setters, operators, and tenders who modify the operation of computer-controlled equipment may require additional training in computer operations and minor programming. Most transportation equipment painters start as helpers and also gain their skills informally on the job.

Becoming skilled in all aspects of painting usually requires 1 to 2 years of on-the-job training and sometimes requires some formal classroom instruction. Beginning helpers usually remove trim, clean, and sand surfaces to be painted; mask surfaces they do not want painted; and polish finished work. As helpers gain experience, they progress to more complicated tasks, such as mixing paint to achieve a good match and using spray guns to apply primer coats or final coats to small areas.

Additional instruction in safety, equipment, and techniques is offered at some community colleges and vocational or technical schools. Some automotive painters are sent to technical schools to learn the intricacies of mixing and applying different types of paint. Such programs can improve employment prospects and speed promotion. Employers also sponsor training programs to help their workers become more productive. Additional training is available from manufacturers of chemicals, paints, or equipment, explaining their products and giving tips about techniques.

Other qualifications. Painting and coating workers in factories need to be able to read and follow detailed plans or blueprints. Some workers also need artistic talent to paint furniture, decorate cakes, or make sure that the paint on a car or other object is the right color. Applicants should be able to breathe comfortably wearing a respirator.

Certification and advancement. Voluntary certification by the National Institute for Automotive Service Excellence

Projections data from the National Employment Matrix

Occupational Title	SOC Code	Employment, 2006	Projected employment, 2016	Change, 2006-16	
				Number	Percent
Painting workers	51-9120	192,000	184,000	-8,000	-4
Coating, painting, and spraying machine setters, operators, and tenders..	51-9121	106,000	93,000	-14,000	-13
Painters, transportation equipment..	51-9122	54,000	59,000	4,600	8
Painting, coating, and decorating workers	51-9123	31,000	32,000	1,100	4

NOTE: Data in this table are rounded. See the discussion of the employment projections table in the *Handbook* introductory chapter on *Occupational Information Included in the Handbook*.

(ASE) is recognized as the standard of achievement for automotive painters. For certification, painters must pass a written examination and have at least 2 years of experience in the field. High school, trade or vocational school, or community or junior college training in automotive refinishing that meets ASE standards may substitute for up to 1 year of experience. To retain the certification, painters must retake the examination at least every 5 years.

Experienced painting and coating workers with leadership ability may become team leaders or supervisors. Many become paint and coating inspectors. Those who get practical experience or formal training may become sales or technical representatives for chemical or paint companies. Some automotive painters eventually open their own shops.

Employment

Painting and coating workers held about 192,000 jobs in 2006. Coating, painting, and spraying machine setters, operators, and tenders accounted for about 106,000 jobs, while transportation equipment painters constituted about 54,000. Another 31,000 jobs were held by painting, coating, and decorating workers.

Approximately 7 out of 10 wage-and-salary workers were employed by manufacturing establishments, particularly those that manufacture fabricated metal products, transportation equipment, industrial machines, household and office furniture, and plastic, wood, and paper products. Outside of manufacturing, workers were employed by independent automotive repair shops and by motor vehicle dealers. Less than 4 percent were self-employed.

Job Outlook

Overall employment of painting and coating workers is expected to decline slowly, but employment change will vary by specialty. Good job prospects are expected for those with painting experience.

Employment change. Overall employment of painting and coating workers is expected to decline slowly by 4 percent from 2006 to 2016. Declining employment is expected because better spraying and coating machines and techniques allow fewer workers to produce the same amount of work. But employment change will vary by specialty.

Employment of coating, painting, and spraying machine setters, operators, and tenders is expected to decline 13 percent as improvements in the automation of paint and coating applications raise worker productivity, allowing fewer workers to accomplish the same work. For example, operators will

be able to coat goods more rapidly as sophisticated industrial machinery moves and aims spray guns more efficiently.

Employment of transportation equipment painters is projected to grow 8 percent. Many transportation equipment painters work in autobody repair and the need for these workers is expected to increase as the number of cars on the road goes up. Growth in the ship building industry is expected to create additional openings for those who paint ships.

Painting, coating, and decorating workers are projected to grow 4 percent. Growth will be driven by growing employment in retail operations. In manufacturing, competition from imports and automation should reduce employment. However, the specialized skills required by these workers should limit job losses from automation.

Job prospects. Like many manufacturing occupations, employers report difficulty finding qualified workers. Opportunities should be good for those with painting experience. Excellent opportunities will exist for experienced painters in the oil and gas industry and the ship building industry over the next decade.

Earnings

Median hourly earnings of wage-and-salary coating, painting, and spraying machine setters, operators, and tenders were $12.90 in May 2006. The middle 50 percent earned between $10.34 and $16.28 an hour. The lowest 10 percent earned less than $8.67, and the highest 10 percent earned more than $19.87 an hour.

Median hourly earnings of wage-and-salary transportation equipment painters were $17.15 in May 2006. The middle 50 percent earned between $13.29 and $23.08 an hour. The lowest 10 percent earned less than $10.82, and the highest 10 percent earned more than $28.10 an hour. Median hourly earnings of transportation equipment painters were $17.15 in automotive repair and maintenance shops and $23.98 in motor vehicle manufacturing.

Median hourly earnings of wage-and-salary painting, coating, and decorating workers were $11.04 in May 2006. The middle 50 percent earned between $9.00 and $14.09 an hour. The lowest 10 percent earned less than $7.55, and the highest 10 percent earned more than $18.23 an hour.

Many automotive painters employed by motor vehicle dealers and independent automotive repair shops receive a commission based on the labor cost charged to the customer. Under this method, earnings depend largely on the amount of work a painter does and how fast it is completed. Employers frequently guarantee commissioned painters a minimum weekly salary. Helpers and trainees usually receive an hourly rate until they become sufficiently skilled to work on commission. Trucking companies, bus lines, and other organizations that repair and refinish their own vehicles usually pay by the hour.

Many painting and coating machine operators belong to unions, including the International Union of Painters and Allied Trades, the Sheet Metal Workers International Association, the United Auto Workers, and the International Brotherhood of Teamsters. Most union operators work for manufacturers and large motor vehicle dealers.

Related Occupations

Other occupations similar to painting and coating workers include painters and paperhangers and machine setters, operators, and tenders—metal and plastic. Painters who work in auto body repair work closely with automotive body and related repairers.

Sources of Additional Information

For more details about work opportunities, contact local manufacturers, automotive body repair shops, motor vehicle dealers, vocational schools, locals of unions representing painting and coating workers, or the local offices of the State employment service. The State employment service also may be a source of information about training programs.

For a directory of certified automotive painting programs, contact:

➤ National Automotive Technician Education Foundation, 101 Blue Seal Dr., SE., Suite 101, Leesburg, VA 20175. Internet: **http://www.natef.org**

Photographic Process Workers and Processing Machine Operators

(O*NET 51-9131.00, 51-9132.00)

Significant Points

- Most workers receive on-the-job training from their companies, manufacturers' representatives, and experienced workers.

- A rapid decline in employment is expected as digital photography becomes commonplace.

- Job opportunities will be best for individuals with experience using computers and digital technology.

Nature of the Work

Both amateur and professional photographers rely heavily on photographic process workers and processing machine operators to develop film, make prints or slides, and do related tasks, such as enlarging or retouching photographs. *Photographic processing machine operators* operate various machines, such as mounting presses and motion picture film printing, photographic printing, and film developing machines. *Photographic process workers* perform more delicate tasks, such as retouching photographic negatives, prints, and images to emphasize or correct specific features.

Processing machine operators who work with digital images first load the raw images onto a computer, either directly from the camera or, more commonly, from a storage device such as a flash card or CD. Most processing of the images is done automatically by software, but images may also be reviewed manually by the operator, who then selects the images the customer wants printed and the quantity. Some digital processors also upload images onto a Web site so that the customer can view them from a home computer and share them with others.

Photographic processing machine operators often have specialized jobs. *Film process technicians* operate machines that develop exposed photographic film or sensitized paper in a series of chemical and water baths to produce negative or positive images. First, technicians mix developing and fixing solutions, following a formula. They then load the film in the machine, which immerses the exposed film in the various solutions to bring out the image. Finally they rinse it in water to remove the chemicals. The technician then dries the film. In some cases, these steps are performed by hand.

Color printer operators control equipment that produces color prints from negatives. These workers read customer instructions to determine processing requirements. They load film into color printing equipment, examine negatives to determine equipment control settings, set controls, and produce a specified number of prints. Finally, they inspect the finished prints for defects, remove any that are found, and insert the processed negatives and prints into an envelope for return to the customer.

Photographic process workers, sometimes known as *digital imaging technicians*, use computer images of conventional negatives and specialized computer software to vary the contrast of images, remove unwanted background, or combine features from different photographs.

Although computers and digital technology are replacing much manual work, some photographic process workers, especially those who work in portrait studios, still perform many specialized tasks by hand directly on the photo or negative. *Airbrush artists* restore damaged and faded photographs, and may color or shade drawings to create photographic likenesses using an airbrush. *Photographic retouchers* alter photographic negatives, prints, or images to accentuate the subject. *Colorists* apply oil colors to portrait photographs to create natural, lifelike appearances. *Photographic spotters* remove imperfections on photographic prints and images.

Work environment. Photographic process workers and processing machine operators generally work in clean, appropriately lighted, well-ventilated, and air-conditioned offices, photofinishing laboratories, or one-hour minilabs. In recent years, more commercial photographic processing has been done on computers than in darkrooms, and this trend is expected to continue.

Some photographic process workers and processing machine operators are exposed to the chemicals and fumes associated with developing and printing. These workers must wear rubber gloves and aprons and take precautions against these hazards. Those who use computers for extended periods may experience back pain, eyestrain, or fatigue.

Photographic processing machine operators must do repetitive work accurately and at a rapid pace. Photographic process workers do detailed tasks, such as airbrushing and spotting, which can contribute to eye fatigue.

Training, Other Qualifications, and Advancement

Most photographic process workers and processing machine operators receive on-the-job training from their companies, manufacturers' representatives, and experienced workers. New employees gradually learn to use the machines and chemicals that develop and print film and the computer techniques to process and print digital images.

Education and training. Employers prefer applicants who are high school graduates or who have some experience in the field. Familiarity with computers is essential for photographic processing machine operators. The ability to perform simple mathematical calculations also is helpful.

Photography courses that include instruction in film processing are valuable preparation. Such courses are available through high schools, vocational-technical institutes, private trade schools, and colleges and universities; some colleges offer degrees in photographic technology.

On-the-job training in photographic processing occupations can range from just a few hours for print machine operators to several months for photographic processing workers such as airbrush artists and colorists. Some workers attend periodic training seminars to maintain a high level of skill. With much of the processing and editing work now being done on computers, employees must continually learn new programs as they become available.

Other qualifications. Manual dexterity, good hand-eye coordination, and good vision, including normal color perception, are important qualifications for photographic process workers.

Advancement. Photographic process machine workers can sometimes advance from jobs as machine operators to supervisory positions in laboratories or to management positions within retail stores.

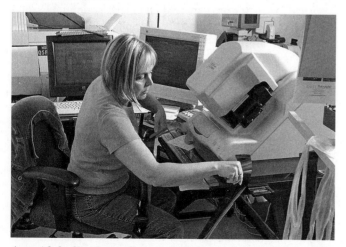

A rapid decline in employment of photographic process workers and processing machining operators is expected as digital photography becomes commonplace.

Employment

Photographic process workers held about 24,000 jobs in 2006. Photographic processing machine operators held about 49,000 jobs in 2006.

About 20 percent of photographic process workers were employed in photographic services. An additional 13 percent were employed by electronic and appliance stores and drug stores, and 14 percent worked in the publishing, internet services, and motion picture industries.

About 70 percent of photographic processing machine operators worked in retail establishments, primarily in general merchandise stores and drug stores Small numbers were employed in the printing industry and in portrait studios and commercial laboratories that process the work of professional photographers.

Job Outlook

A rapid decline in employment is expected for photographic process workers and processing machine operators through the year 2016. Job opportunities will be best for individuals with experience using computers and digital technology.

Employment change. Employment of photographic process workers and processing machine operators is expected to decline rapidly by 45 percent over the 2006-16 decade. Digital cameras, which use electronic memory rather than film to record images, have in recent years become standard among professional photographers. They are rapidly gaining in popularity among amateur photographers as well as the cost of these cameras continues to fall. This will continue to reduce the demand for traditional photographic processing machine operators. However, while many digital camera owners will choose to print their own pictures with their own equipment, a growing number of casual photographers are choosing not to acquire the needed equipment and skills to print the photos themselves. For them, self-service machines and online ordering services will be able to meet most of the demand, but there will still be some demand for professionals to print digital photos and operate the machines, as well as to develop and print photos from those who continue to use film cameras.

Digital photography also will reduce demand for photographic process workers. Using digital cameras and technology, consumers who have a personal computer and the proper software are able to download and view pictures on their computer, as well as to manipulate, correct, and retouch their own photographs. No matter what improvements occur in camera technology, though, some photographic processing tasks will still require skillful manual treatment.

Job prospects. Job opportunities will be best for individuals with experience using computers and digital technology. Employment fluctuates somewhat over the course of the year, typically peaking during school graduation and summer vacation periods.

Earnings

Earnings of photographic process workers vary greatly depending on skill level, experience, and geographic location. Median hourly earnings for photographic process workers were $11.19 in May 2006. The middle 50 percent earned between $8.61 and $15.12. The lowest 10 percent earned less than $7.32, and the

Projections data from the National Employment Matrix

Occupational Title	SOC Code	Employment, 2006	Projected employment, 2016	Change, 2006-16	
				Number	Percent
Photographic process workers and processing machine operators ...	51-9130	73,000	40,000	-33,000	-45
Photographic process workers	51-9131	24,000	15,000	-8,600	-36
Photographic processing machine operators..............................	51-9132	49,000	25,000	-25,000	-50

NOTE: Data in this table are rounded. See the discussion of the employment projections table in the *Handbook* introductory chapter on *Occupational Information Included in the Handbook*.

highest 10 percent earned more than $21.43. Median hourly earnings were $11.65 in photographic services.

Median hourly earning for photographic processing machine operators were $9.38 in May 2006. The middle 50 percent earned between $8.01 and $11.44. The lowest 10 percent earned less than $7.16, and the highest 10 percent earned more than $14.92. Median hourly earnings in the two industries employing the largest numbers of photographic processing machine operators were $9.58 in photographic services and $8.50 in health and personal care stores.

Related Occupations

Photographic process workers and processing machine operators need specialized knowledge of the photo developing process. Other workers who apply specialized technical knowledge include clinical laboratory technologists and technicians, computer operators, jewelers and precious stone and metal workers, prepress technicians and workers, printing machine operators, and science technicians.

Sources of Additional Information

For information about employment opportunities in photographic laboratories and schools that offer degrees in photographic technology, contact:
➤ Photo Marketing Association International, 3000 Picture Place, Jackson, MI 49201. Internet: **http://www.pmai.org**

Semiconductor Processors

(O*NET 51-9141.00)

Significant Points

- Employment is expected to decline over the next 10 years because of increasing automation and the building of many new plants abroad.

- Opportunities will be best for applicants who have an associate degree in a relevant subject.

Nature of the Work

Semiconductors are unique substances, which, under different conditions, can act as either conductors or insulators of electricity. Semiconductor processors turn one of these substances—silicon—into microchips, also known as integrated circuits. These microchips contain millions of tiny electronic components and are used in a wide range of products, from personal computers and cellular telephones to airplanes and missile guidance systems.

To manufacture microchips, *semiconductor processors* start with cylinders of silicon called ingots. First, the ingots are sliced into thin wafers. Using automated equipment, workers or robots polish the wafers, imprint precise microscopic patterns of the circuitry onto them using photolithography, etch out patterns with acids, and replace the patterns with conductors, such as aluminum or copper. The wafers then receive a chemical bath to make them smooth, and the imprint process begins again on a new layer with the next pattern. A complex chip may contain more than 20 layers of circuitry. Once the process is complete, wafers are then cut into individual chips, which are enclosed in a casing and shipped to equipment manufacturers.

The manufacturing and slicing of wafers to create semiconductors takes place in cleanrooms—production areas that are kept free of all airborne matter because the circuitry on a chip is so small that even microscopic particles can make it unusable. All semiconductor processors working in cleanrooms must wear special lightweight outer garments known as "bunny suits". These garments fit over clothing to prevent lint and other particles from contaminating the cleanroom.

There are two types of semiconductor processors: operators and technicians. *Operators* start and monitor the equipment that performs the various production tasks. They spend the majority of their time at computer terminals, monitoring the operation of equipment to ensure that each of the tasks in the production of the wafer is performed correctly. Operators may also transfer wafer carriers from one station to the next, though the lifting of heavy wafer carriers is done by robots in most new fabricating plants.

Technicians are generally more experienced workers who troubleshoot production problems and make equipment adjustments and repairs. They take the lead in assuring quality control and in maintaining equipment. They also test completed chips to make sure they work properly. To keep equipment repairs to a minimum, technicians perform diagnostic analyses and run computations. For example, technicians may determine if a flaw in a chip is due to contamination and peculiar to that wafer, or if the flaw is inherent in the manufacturing process.

Work environment. The work pace in cleanrooms is deliberately slow. Limited movement keeps the air in cleanrooms as free as possible of dust and other particles, which can destroy microchips during their production. Because the machinery sets the operators' rate of work, workers maintain a relaxed pace. Although workers spend some time alone monitoring equipment, operators and technicians spend much of their time working in teams.

Technicians are on their feet most of the day, walking through the cleanroom to oversee production activities. Operators spend a great deal of time sitting or standing at workstations, monitoring computer readouts and indicators.

The temperature in the cleanrooms must be kept within a narrow range and is generally comfortable for workers. Although bunny suits cover virtually the entire body, their lightweight fabric keeps the temperature inside fairly comfortable. Entry and exit of workers from the cleanroom are controlled to minimize contamination, and workers must be reclothed in a clean bunny suit and decontaminated each time they return to the cleanroom.

Several highly toxic chemicals are used at various points in the process of manufacturing microchips. Workers who are exposed to such chemicals can be seriously harmed. However, fabrication plants are designed with safeguards to ensure that these chemicals are handled, used, and disposed of without exposing workers or the surrounding environment. Toxic chemicals are applied to wafers by computer-controlled machine tools in sealed chambers, and there is normally little risk of workers coming into contact with them.

Semiconductor fabricating plants operate around the clock. Night and weekend work is common. In some plants, workers maintain standard 8-hour shifts, 5 days a week. In other plants, employees are on duty for 12-hour shifts to minimize the disruption of cleanroom operations brought about by changes. Managers may also allow workers to alternate schedules, thereby distributing the overnight shift equitably.

Training, Other Qualifications, and Advancement

People interested in becoming semiconductor processors—either operators or technicians—need strong technical skills, an ability to solve problems intuitively, and an ability to work in teams. Mathematics, including statistics, and physical science knowledge are also very useful. Communication skills and an understanding of manufacturing principles are also very important.

Education and training. For semiconductor processor jobs, employers prefer applicants who have completed an associate degree. However, experience plus completion of a 1-year certificate program in semiconductor technology, offered by some community colleges, may also be sufficient. Some semiconductor technology programs at community colleges include internships at semiconductor fabricating plants. Other applicants may qualify by completing a degree in high-tech manufacturing. Hands-on training is an important part of degree and certificate programs.

To ensure that operators and technicians keep their skills current, employers provide regular on-the-job training. Some employers also provide financial assistance to employees who want to earn an associate or bachelor's degree, especially if the employee is working toward becoming a technician.

Advancement. Workers advance as they become more comfortable with the equipment and better understand the manufacturing process. Employees train workers for several months, after which they become entry-level operators or technicians. After a few years, as they become more knowledgeable about the operations of the plant, they generally advance to the intermediate level. This entails greater responsibilities. Over time, usually 7 to 10 years, workers may become senior technicians,

Semiconductor processors wear protective garments called "bunny suits" to avoid contaminating the chips they produce.

who lead teams of technicians and work directly with engineers to develop processes in the plant.

Employment

Semiconductor processors held approximately 42,000 jobs in 2006. Nearly all of them were employed in the computer and electronic product manufacturing industry.

Job Outlook

Employment of semiconductor processors is projected to decline through 2016. Opportunities will be best for those with a 2-year degree and experience working in high-tech manufacturing.

Employment change. Employment of semiconductor processors is projected to decline moderately, decreasing by 13 percent between 2006 and 2016. Although the demand for microchips is growing at a very rapid rate, employment levels in the industry will not increase over the next 10 years because of automation and the opening of fabricating plants in other countries. As the electrical components of chips become smaller, they become more sensitive. This means that chip manufacturers prefer precise robotics to human workers, who could potentially damage the chips. Additionally, there is a trend toward moving production to the areas where demand is most concentrated, thus, reducing the demand for U.S. exports of microchips. While this has not decreased U.S. production, fewer new plants are being constructed here.

Because of increased automation, most of the new positions created will be for technicians. While operator jobs will decline as older plants close and newer plants use more robotics, technician jobs will become more prevalent as the machinery becomes more complex and needs more monitoring. Technicians are responsible for understanding more of the fabrication process, so companies hiring new employees will expect a higher level of competency.

The demand for semiconductor chips remains very high, stemming from the many existing and future applications for semiconductors in computers, appliances, machinery, biotechnology, vehicles, cell phones, and other equipment.

Job prospects. Despite the decline in employment, some jobs will open up due to the need to replace workers who leave the

Projections data from the National Employment Matrix

Occupational Title	SOC Code	Employment, 2006	Projected employment, 2016	Change, 2006-16	
				Number	Percent
Semiconductor processors	51-9141	42,000	37,000	-5,500	-13

NOTE: Data in this table are rounded. See the discussion of the employment projections table in the *Handbook* introductory chapter on *Occupational Information Included in the Handbook.*

occupation. Because specialized training is required to excel in this field, the number of openings is expected to remain in rough balance with the number of qualified job seekers. Prospects will be best for applicants with an associate degree and experience in high-tech manufacturing.

Earnings

Median annual earnings of wage-and-salary semiconductor processors were $32,860 in May 2006. The middle 50 percent earned between $26,680 and $40,620 an hour. The lowest 10 percent earned less than $21,700, and the top 10 percent earned more than $49,470 an hour.

Technicians with an associate degree in electronics or semiconductor technology generally start at higher salaries than those with less education.

Semiconductor processors generally received good benefits packages, including health care, disability plans and life insurance, stock options and retirement.

Related Occupations

Semiconductor processors do production work that resembles the work of precision assemblers and fabricators of other high-tech equipment. Also, many electronic semiconductor processors have academic training in semiconductor technology, which emphasizes scientific and engineering principles. Other occupations that require some college or postsecondary vocational training emphasizing such principles are engineering technicians, electrical engineers, and science technicians.

Sources of Additional Information

For more information on semiconductor processor careers, contact:

➤ Maricopa Advanced Technology Education Center, 2323 West 14th St., Suite 540, Tempe, AZ 85281.
Internet: **http://www.matec.org**
➤ Semiconductor Industry Association, 181 Metro Dr., Suite 450, San Jose., CA 95110. Internet: **http://www.sia-online.org**

Transportation and Material Moving Occupations

Air Transportation Occupations

Aircraft Pilots and Flight Engineers

(O*NET 53-2011.00, 53-2012.00)

Significant Points

- Regional and low-cost airlines offer the best opportunities; pilots attempting to get jobs at the major airlines will face strong competition.

- Pilots usually start with smaller commuter and regional airlines to acquire the experience needed to qualify for higher paying jobs with national or major airlines.

- Many pilots have learned to fly in the military, but growing numbers have college degrees with flight training from civilian flying schools that are certified by the Federal Aviation Administration (FAA).

- Earnings of airline pilots are among the highest in the Nation.

Nature of the Work

Pilots are highly trained professionals who either fly airplanes or helicopters to carry out a wide variety of tasks. Most are *airline pilots, copilots*, and *flight engineers* who transport passengers and cargo. However, 1 out of 5 pilots is a commercial pilot involved in dusting crops, spreading seed for reforestation, testing aircraft, flying passengers and cargo to areas not served by regular airlines, directing firefighting efforts, tracking criminals, monitoring traffic, and rescuing and evacuating injured persons.

Before departure, pilots plan their flights carefully. They thoroughly check their aircraft to make sure that the engines, controls, instruments, and other systems are functioning properly. They also make sure that baggage or cargo has been loaded correctly. They confer with flight dispatchers and aviation weather forecasters to find out about weather conditions en route and at their destination. Based on this information, they choose a route, altitude, and speed that will provide the safest, most economical, and smoothest flight. When flying under instrument flight rules—procedures governing the operation of the aircraft when there is poor visibility—the pilot in command, or the company dispatcher, normally files an instrument flight plan with air traffic control so that the flight can be coordinated with other air traffic.

Takeoff and landing are the most difficult parts of the flight, and require close coordination between the two pilots. For example, as the plane accelerates for takeoff, the pilot who is flying the take off concentrates on the runway while the other pilot scans the instrument panel. To calculate the speed they must attain to become airborne, pilots consider the altitude of the airport, outside temperature, weight of the plane, and speed and direction of the wind. The moment the plane reaches takeoff speed, the nonflying pilot informs the flying pilot, who then pulls back on the controls to raise the nose of the plane. Captains and first officers usually alternate flying each leg from takeoff to landing.

Unless the weather is bad, the flight itself is relatively routine. Airplane pilots, with the assistance of autopilot and the flight management computer, steer the plane along their planned route and are monitored by the air traffic control stations they pass along the way. They regularly scan the instrument panel to check their fuel supply; the condition of their engines; and the air-conditioning, hydraulic, and other systems. Pilots may request a change in altitude or route if circumstances dictate. For example, if the ride is rougher than expected, pilots may ask air traffic control if pilots flying at other altitudes have reported better conditions; if so, they may request an altitude change. This procedure also may be used to find a stronger tailwind or a weaker headwind to save fuel and increase speed. In contrast, because helicopters are used for short trips at relatively low altitude, helicopter pilots must be constantly on the lookout for trees, bridges, power lines, transmission towers, and other dangerous obstacles as well as low-flying general aviation aircraft. Regardless of the type of aircraft, all pilots must monitor warning devices designed to help detect sudden shifts in wind conditions that can cause crashes.

Pilots must rely completely on their instruments when visibility is poor. On the basis of altimeter readings, they know how high above ground they are and whether they can fly safely over mountains and other obstacles. Special navigation radios give pilots precise information that, with the help of special charts, tells them their exact position. Other very sophisticated equipment provides directions to a point just above the end of a runway and enables pilots to land completely without an outside visual reference. Once on the ground, pilots must complete records on their flight and the aircraft maintenance status for their company and the FAA.

The number of nonflying duties that pilots have depends on the employment setting. Airline pilots have the services of large support staffs and, consequently, perform few nonflying duties. However, because of the large numbers of passengers, airline pilots may be called upon to coordinate handling of disgruntled or disruptive passengers. Also, under the Federal Flight Deck

Officer program airline pilots who undergo rigorous training and screening are deputized as Federal law enforcement officers and are issued firearms to protect the cockpit against intruders and hijackers. Pilots employed by other organizations, such as charter operators or businesses, have many other duties. They may load the aircraft, handle all passenger luggage to ensure a balanced load, and supervise refueling; other nonflying responsibilities include keeping records, scheduling flights, arranging for major maintenance, and performing minor aircraft maintenance and repairs.

Except on small aircraft, two pilots usually make up the cockpit crew. Generally, the most experienced pilot, the *captain*, is in command and supervises all other crew members. The pilot and the copilot, often called the first officer, share flying and other duties, such as communicating with air traffic controllers and monitoring the instruments. Some large aircraft have a third crewmember, the flight engineer, who assists the pilots by monitoring and operating many of the instruments and systems, making minor in-flight repairs, and watching for other aircraft. The flight engineer also assists the pilots with the company, air traffic control, and cabin crew communications. New technology can perform many flight tasks, however, and virtually all new aircraft now fly with only two pilots, who rely more heavily on computerized controls.

Some pilots are flight instructors. They teach their students in ground-school classes, in simulators, and in dual-controlled planes and helicopters. A few specially trained pilots are examiners or check pilots. They periodically fly with other pilots or pilot's license applicants to make sure that they are proficient.

Work environment. Most pilots spend a considerable amount of time away from home because the majority of flights involve overnight layovers. When pilots are away from home, the airlines provide hotel accommodations, transportation between the hotel and airport, and an allowance for meals and other expenses.

Airline pilots, especially those on international routes, often experience jet lag—fatigue caused by many hours of flying through different time zones. To guard against pilot fatigue, which could result in unsafe flying conditions, the FAA requires

Pilots have many nonflying duties that include keeping records, scheduling flights, arranging for major maintenance, and performing minor aircraft maintenance and repairs.

airlines to allow pilots at least 8 hours of uninterrupted rest in the 24 hours before finishing their flight duty.

Commercial pilots face other types of job hazards. The work of test pilots, who check the flight performance of new and experimental planes, may be dangerous. Pilots who are crop-dusters may be exposed to toxic chemicals and seldom have the benefit of a regular landing strip. Helicopter pilots involved in rescue and police work may be subject to personal injury.

Although flying does not involve much physical effort, the mental stress of being responsible for a safe flight, regardless of the weather, can be tiring. Pilots must be alert and quick to react if something goes wrong, particularly during takeoff and landing.

FAA regulations limit flying time of airline pilots of large aircraft to a maximum of 100 hours a month or 1,000 hours a year. Most airline pilots fly an average of 65 to 75 hours a month and work at least an additional 65 to 75 hours a month performing nonflying duties. Most pilots have variable work schedules, working several days on, then several days off. Airlines operate flights at all hours of the day and night, so work schedules often are irregular. Flight assignments are based on seniority; the sooner pilots are hired, the stronger their bidding power is for preferred assignments.

Commercial pilots also may have irregular schedules, flying 30 hours one month and 90 hours the next. Because these pilots frequently have many nonflying responsibilities, they have much less free time than do airline pilots. Except for corporate flight department pilots, most commercial pilots do not remain away from home overnight. But, they may work odd hours. However, if the company owns a fleet of planes, pilots may fly a regular schedule.

Flight instructors may have irregular and seasonal work schedules, depending on their students' available time and the weather. Instructors frequently work in the evening or on weekends.

Training, Other Qualifications, and Advancement

All pilots who are paid to transport passengers or cargo must have a commercial pilot's license with an instrument rating issued by the FAA. Helicopter pilots also must hold a commercial pilot's license with a helicopter rating.

Education and training. Although some small airlines hire high school graduates, most airlines require at least 2 years of college and prefer to hire college graduates. In fact, most entrants to this occupation have a college degree. Because the number of college-educated applicants continues to increase, many employers are making a college degree an educational requirement. For example, test pilots often are required to have an engineering degree.

Pilots also need flight experience to qualify for a license. Completing classes at a flight school approved by the FAA can reduce the amount of flight experience required for a pilot's license. In 2006, the FAA certified about 600 civilian flying schools, including some colleges and universities that offer degree credit for pilot training. Initial training for airline pilots typically includes a week of company indoctrination; 3 to 6 weeks of ground school and simulator training; and 25 hours of initial operating experience, including a check-ride with an

Projections data from the National Employment Matrix

Occupational Title	SOC Code	Employment, 2006	Projected employment, 2016	Change, 2006-16	
				Number	Percent
Aircraft pilots and flight engineers	53-2010	107,000	121,000	14,000	13
Airline pilots, copilots, and flight engineers	53-2011	79,000	90,000	10,000	13
Commercial pilots..	53-2012	28,000	31,000	3,600	13

NOTE: Data in this table are rounded. See the discussion of the employment projections table in the *Handbook* introductory chapter on *Occupational Information Included in the Handbook.*

FAA aviation safety inspector. Once trained, pilots are required to attend recurrent training and simulator checks once or twice a year throughout their career.

Licensure. To qualify for FAA licensure, applicants must be at least 18 years old and have at least 250 hours of flight experience.

The U.S. Armed Forces have always been an important source of experienced pilots because of the extensive flying time and experience on jet aircraft and helicopters. Those without Armed Forces training may become pilots by attending flight schools or by taking lessons from FAA-certified flight instructors. Applicants also must pass a strict physical examination to make sure that they are in good health and have 20/20 vision with or without glasses, good hearing, and no physical handicaps that could impair their performance. They must pass a written test that includes questions on the principles of safe flight, navigation techniques, and FAA regulations, and must demonstrate their flying ability to FAA or designated examiners.

To fly during periods of low visibility, pilots must be rated by the FAA to fly by instruments. Pilots may qualify for this rating by having the required hours of flight experience, including 40 hours of experience in flying by instruments; they also must pass a written examination on procedures and FAA regulations covering instrument flying and demonstrate to an examiner their ability to fly by instruments. Requirements for the instrument rating vary depending on the certification level of flight school.

Airline pilots must fulfill additional requirements. Captains must have an airline transport pilot's license. Applicants for this license must be at least 23 years old and have a minimum of 1,500 hours of flying experience, including night and instrument flying, and must pass FAA written and flight examinations. Usually, they also have one or more advanced ratings depending on the requirements of their particular job. Because pilots must be able to make quick decisions and accurate judgments under pressure, many airline companies reject applicants who do not pass required psychological and aptitude tests. All licenses are valid so long as a pilot can pass the periodic physical and eye examinations and tests of flying skills required by the FAA and company regulations.

Other qualifications. Depending on the type of aircraft, new airline pilots start as first officers or flight engineers. Although some airlines favor applicants who already have a flight engineer's license, they may provide flight engineer training for those who have only the commercial license. Many pilots begin with smaller regional or commuter airlines, where they obtain experience flying passengers on scheduled flights into busy airports in all weather conditions. These jobs often lead to higher paying jobs with bigger, national or major airlines.

Companies other than airlines usually require less flying experience. However, a commercial pilot's license is a minimum requirement, and employers prefer applicants who have experience in the type of craft they will be flying. New employees usually start as first officers, or fly less sophisticated equipment.

Advancement. Advancement for pilots usually is limited to other flying jobs. Many pilots start as flight instructors, building up their flying hours while they earn money teaching. As they become more experienced, these pilots occasionally fly charter planes or perhaps get jobs with small air transportation firms, such as air-taxi companies. Some advance to flying corporate planes. A small number get flight engineer jobs with the airlines.

In the airlines, advancement usually depends on seniority provisions of union contracts. After 1 to 5 years, flight engineers advance according to seniority to first officer and, after 5 to 15 years, to captain. Seniority also determines which pilots get the more desirable routes. In a nonairline job, a first officer may advance to captain and, in large companies, to chief pilot or director of aviation in charge of aircraft scheduling, maintenance, and flight procedures.

Employment

Civilian aircraft pilots and flight engineers held about 107,000 jobs in 2006. About 79,000 worked as airline pilots, copilots, and flight engineers. The rest were commercial pilots who worked as flight instructors at local airports or for large businesses that fly company cargo and executives in their own airplanes or helicopters. Some commercial pilots flew small planes for air-taxi companies, usually to or from lightly traveled airports not served by major airlines. Others worked for a variety of businesses, performing tasks such as dusting crops, inspecting pipelines, or conducting sightseeing trips.

Pilots are located across the country, but airline pilots usually are based near major metropolitan airports or airports operating as hubs for the major airlines.

Federal, State, and local governments employed pilots. A few pilots were self-employed.

Job Outlook

Regional airlines and low-cost carriers will present the best opportunities; pilots attempting to get jobs at the major airlines will face strong competition.

Employment change. Employment of aircraft pilots and flight engineers is projected to grow 13 percent from 2006 to 2016, about as fast as the average for all occupations. Population growth and an expanding economy are expected to boost the demand for air travel, contributing to job growth. New jobs will be created as airlines expand their capacity to meet this rising demand by increasing the number of planes in operation. However, employment growth will be limited by productivity improvements as airlines switch to larger planes and adopt the low-cost carrier model that emphasizes faster turnaround times for flights, keeping more pilots in the air rather than waiting on the ground. Also, fewer flight engineers will be needed as new planes requiring only two pilots replace older planes that require flight engineers.

Job prospects. Job opportunities are expected to continue to be better with the regional airlines and low-cost carriers, which are growing faster than the major airlines. Opportunities with air cargo carriers also should arise because of increasing security requirements for shipping freight on passenger airlines, growth in electronic commerce, and increased demand for global freight. Business, corporate, and on-demand air taxi travel also should provide some new jobs for pilots.

Pilots attempting to get jobs at the major airlines will face strong competition, as those firms tend to attract many more applicants than the number of job openings. Applicants also will have to compete with laid-off pilots for any available jobs. Pilots who have logged the greatest number of flying hours using sophisticated equipment typically have the best prospects. For this reason, military pilots often have an advantage over other applicants.

In the long run, demand for air travel is expected to grow along with the population and the economy. In the short run, however, employment opportunities of pilots generally are sensitive to cyclical swings in the economy. During recessions, when a decline in the demand for air travel forces airlines to curtail the number of flights, airlines may temporarily furlough some pilots.

Earnings

Earnings of aircraft pilots and flight engineers vary greatly depending whether they work as airline or commercial pilots. Earnings of airline pilots are among the highest in the Nation, and depend on factors such as the type, size, and maximum speed of the plane and the number of hours and miles flown. For example, pilots who fly jet aircraft usually earn higher salaries than pilots who fly turboprops. Airline pilots and flight engineers may earn extra pay for night and international flights. In May 2006, median annual earnings of airline pilots, copilots, and flight engineers were $141,090.

Median annual earnings of commercial pilots were $57,480 in May 2006. The middle 50 percent earned between $40,780 and $83,760. The lowest 10 percent earned less than $28,450, and the highest 10 percent earned more than $115,220.

Airline pilots usually are eligible for life and health insurance plans. They also receive retirement benefits and, if they fail the FAA physical examination at some point in their careers, they get disability payments. In addition, pilots receive an expense allowance, or "per diem," for every hour they are away from home. Some airlines also provide allowances to pilots for purchasing and cleaning their uniforms. As an additional benefit, pilots and their immediate families usually are entitled to free or reduced-fare transportation on their own and other airlines.

More than half of all aircraft pilots are members of unions. Most of the pilots who fly for the major airlines are members of the Air Line Pilots Association, International, but those employed by one major airline are members of the Allied Pilots Association.

Related Occupations

Although they are not in the cockpit, air traffic controllers and airfield operations specialists also play an important role in making sure flights are safe and on schedule, and participate in many of the decisions that pilots must make.

Sources of Additional Information

For information about job opportunities, salaries, and qualifications, write to the personnel manager of the particular airline.

For information on airline pilots, contact:

➤ Air Line Pilots Association, International, 1625 Massachusetts Ave. NW., Washington, DC 20036.
➤ Air Transport Association of America, Inc., 1301 Pennsylvania Ave. NW., Suite 1100, Washington, DC 20004.
➤ Federal Aviation Administration, 800 Independence Ave. SW., Washington, DC 20591. Internet: **http://www.faa.gov**

For information on helicopter pilots, contact:

➤ Helicopter Association International, 1635 Prince St., Alexandria, VA 22314.

For information about job opportunities in companies other than airlines, consult the classified section of aviation trade magazines and apply to companies that operate aircraft at local airports.

Air Traffic Controllers

(O*NET 53-2021.00)

Significant Points

- Nearly all air traffic controllers are employed by the Federal Aviation Administration (FAA), an agency of the Federal Government.

- Replacement needs will continue to account for most job openings, reflecting the large number of air traffic controllers who will be eligible to retire over the next decade.

- Competition to get into FAA training programs is expected to remain keen; however, graduates of these programs have good job prospects.

- Air traffic controllers earn relatively high pay and have good benefits.

Nature of the Work

The air traffic control system is a vast network of people and equipment that ensures the safe operation of commercial and private aircraft. Air traffic controllers coordinate the movement of air traffic to make certain that planes stay a safe distance apart. Their immediate concern is safety, but controllers also must direct planes efficiently to minimize delays. Some regulate airport traffic through designated airspaces; others regulate airport arrivals and departures.

Although *airport tower controllers* or *terminal controllers* watch over all planes traveling through the airport's airspace, their main responsibility is to organize the flow of aircraft into and out of the airport. Relying on radar and visual observation, they closely monitor each plane to ensure a safe distance between all aircraft and to guide pilots between the hangar or ramp and the end of the airport's airspace. In addition, controllers keep pilots informed about changes in weather conditions such as wind shear, a sudden change in the velocity or direction of the wind that can cause the pilot to lose control of the aircraft.

During arrival or departure, several controllers direct each plane. As a plane approaches an airport, the pilot radios ahead to inform the terminal of the plane's presence. The controller in the radar room, just beneath the control tower, has a copy of the plane's flight plan and already has observed the plane on radar. If the path is clear, the controller directs the pilot to a runway; if the airport is busy, the plane is fitted into a traffic pattern with other aircraft waiting to land. As the plane nears the runway, the pilot is asked to contact the tower. There, another controller, who also is watching the plane on radar, monitors the aircraft the last mile or so to the runway, delaying any departures that would interfere with the plane's landing. Once the plane has landed, a ground controller in the tower directs it along the taxiways to its assigned gate. The ground controller usually works entirely by sight, but may use radar if visibility is very poor.

The procedure is reversed for departures. The ground controller directs the plane to the proper runway. The local controller then informs the pilot about conditions at the airport, such as weather, speed and direction of wind, and visibility. The local controller also issues runway clearance for the pilot to take off. Once in the air, the plane is guided out of the airport's airspace by the departure controller.

After each plane departs, airport tower controllers notify *enroute controllers* who will next take charge. There are 21 air route traffic control centers located around the country, each employing 300 to 700 controllers, with more than 150 on duty during peak hours at the busiest facilities. Airplanes usually fly along designated routes; each center is assigned a certain airspace containing many different routes. Enroute controllers work in teams of up to three members, depending on how heavy traffic is; each team is responsible for a section of the center's airspace. A team, for example, might be responsible for all planes that are between 30 and 100 miles north of an airport and flying at an altitude between 6,000 and 18,000 feet.

To prepare for planes about to enter the team's airspace, the radar associate controller organizes flight plans coming off a printer. If two planes are scheduled to enter the team's airspace at nearly the same time, location, and altitude, this controller may arrange with the preceding control unit for one plane to change its flight path. The previous unit may have been another team at the same or an adjacent center, or a departure controller at a neighboring terminal. As a plane approaches a team's airspace, the radar controller accepts responsibility for the plane from the previous controlling unit. The controller also delegates responsibility for the plane to the next controlling unit when the plane leaves the team's airspace.

The radar controller, who is the senior team member, observes the planes in the team's airspace on radar and communicates with the pilots when necessary. Radar controllers warn pilots about nearby planes, bad weather conditions, and other potential hazards. Two planes on a collision course will be directed around each other. If a pilot wants to change altitude in search of better flying conditions, the controller will check to determine that no other planes will be along the proposed path. The team responsible for the aircraft notifies the next team in charge of the airspace ahead as the flight progresses. Through team coordination, the plane arrives safely at its destination.

Both airport tower and enroute controllers usually control several planes at a time; often, they have to make quick decisions about completely different activities. For example, a controller might direct a plane on its landing approach and at the same time provide pilots entering the airport's airspace with information about conditions at the airport. While instructing these pilots, the controller also might observe other planes in the vicinity, such as those in a holding pattern waiting for permission to land, to ensure that they remain well separated.

The FAA has implemented an automated air traffic control system, called the National Airspace System (NAS) Architecture. The NAS Architecture is a long-term strategic plan that will allow controllers to more efficiently deal with the demands of increased air traffic. It encompasses the replacement of aging equipment and the introduction of new systems, technologies, and procedures to enhance safety and security and support future aviation growth. The NAS Architecture facilitates continuing discussion of modernization between the FAA and the aviation community.

In addition to airport towers and enroute centers, air traffic controllers also work in flight service stations at more than 35 locations, including 17 locations in Alaska. These *flight service specialists* provide pilots with preflight and inflight weather information, suggested routes, and other aeronautical information important to the safety of a flight. Flight service specialists relay air traffic control clearances to pilots not in direct communications with a tower or center, assist pilots in emergency situations, and initiate and coordinate searches for missing or overdue aircraft. At certain locations where there is no airport tower or the tower has closed for the day, flight service specialists provide airport advisory services to landing and departing aircraft. However, they are not involved in actively managing and separating air traffic.

Some air traffic controllers work at the FAA's Air Traffic Control Systems Command Center in Herndon, VA, where they oversee the entire system. They look for situations that will create bottlenecks or other problems in the system and then respond with a management plan for traffic into and out of the troubled sector. The objective is to keep traffic levels in the trouble spots manageable for the controllers working at enroute centers.

Work environment. During busy times, controllers must work rapidly and efficiently. Total concentration is required

Air traffic controllers are primarily concerned with safety, but they also must direct planes efficiently to minimize delays.

to keep track of several planes at the same time and to make certain that all pilots receive correct instructions. The mental stress of being responsible for the safety of several aircraft and their passengers can be exhausting. Unlike tower controllers, radar controllers also have the extra stress of having to work in semi-darkness, never seeing the actual aircraft they control except as a small "bleep" on the radarscope. Controllers who work in flight service stations work in offices close to the communications and computer equipment.

Controllers work a basic 40-hour week; however, they may work additional hours, for which they receive overtime, or premium pay, or equal time off. Because most control towers and centers operate 24 hours a day, 7 days a week, controllers rotate night and weekend shifts. Contract flight service station working conditions may vary somewhat from the FAA.

Training, Other Qualifications, and Advancement

To become an air traffic controller, a person must complete an FAA-approved education program; pass a pre-employment test; receive a school recommendation; meet the basic qualification requirements in accordance with Federal law; and achieve a qualifying score on the FAA-authorized pre-employment test. Candidates also must pass a medical exam, undergo drug screening, and obtain a security clearance before they can be hired.

Education and training. Individuals must enroll in an FAA-approved education program and pass a pre-employment test that measures the applicant's ability to learn the controller's duties. Exceptions are air traffic controllers with prior experience and military veterans. The pre-employment test is currently offered only to students in the FAA Air Traffic Collegiate Training Initiative Program or the Minneapolis Community and Technical College, Air Traffic Control Training Program. The test is administered by computer and takes about 8 hours to complete. To take the test, an applicant must apply under an open

advertisement for air traffic control positions and be chosen to take the examination. When there are many more applicants than available positions, applicants are selected to take the test through random selection. In addition to the pre-employment test, applicants must have 3 years of full-time work experience, have completed a full 4 years of college, or a combination of both. In combining education and experience, 1 year of undergraduate study—30 semester or 45 quarter hours—is equivalent to 9 months of work experience. Certain kinds of aviation experience also may be substituted for these requirements.

Upon successful completion of an FAA-approved program, individuals who receive school recommendation, meet the basic qualification requirements (including being less than 31 years of age) in accordance with Federal law, and achieve a qualifying score on the FAA-authorized pre-employment test become eligible for employment as an air traffic controller.

Upon selection, employees attend the FAA Academy in Oklahoma City, OK, for 12 weeks of training, during which they learn the fundamentals of the airway system, FAA regulations, controller equipment, and aircraft performance characteristics, as well as more specialized tasks.

After graduation from the FAA Academy in Oklahoma City, candidates are assigned to an air traffic control facility and are classified as "developmental controllers" until they complete all requirements to be certified for all of the air traffic control positions within a defined area of a given facility. Generally, it takes new controllers with only initial controller training between 2 and 4 years, depending on the facility and the availability of facility staff or contractors to provide on-the-job training, to complete all the certification requirements to become certified professional controllers. Individuals who have had prior controller experience normally take less time to become fully certified. Controllers who fail to complete either the academy or the on-the-job portions of the training usually are dismissed. Controllers must pass a physical examination each year and a job performance examination twice each year. Failure to become certified in any position at a facility within a specified time also may result in dismissal. Controllers also are subject to drug screening as a condition of continuing employment.

Other qualifications. Air traffic controllers must be articulate to give pilots directions quickly and clearly. Intelligence and a good memory also are important because controllers constantly receive information that they must immediately grasp, interpret, and remember. Decisiveness also is required because controllers often have to make quick decisions. The ability to concentrate is crucial because controllers must make these decisions in the midst of noise and other distractions.

Advancement. At airports, new controllers begin by supplying pilots with basic flight data and airport information. They then advance to the position of ground controller, then local controller, departure controller, and, finally, arrival controller. At an air route traffic control center, new controllers first deliver printed flight plans to teams, gradually advancing to radar associate controller and then to radar controller.

Controllers can transfer to jobs at different locations or advance to supervisory positions, including management or staff jobs—such as air traffic control data systems computer specialist—in air traffic control, and top administrative jobs in

Projections data from the National Employment Matrix

Occupational Title	SOC Code	Employment, 2006	Projected employment, 2016	Change, 2006-16	
				Number	Percent
Air traffic controllers..	53-2021	25,000	28,000	2,600	10

NOTE: Data in this table are rounded. See the discussion of the employment projections table in the *Handbook* introductory chapter on *Occupational Information Included in the Handbook.*

the FAA. However, there are only limited opportunities for a controller to switch from a position in an enroute center to a tower. Contract flight service station working conditions may vary somewhat from the FAA.

Employment

Air traffic controllers held about 25,000 jobs in 2006. The vast majority were employed by the FAA. Air traffic controllers work at airports—in towers and flight service stations—and in air route traffic control centers. Some professional controllers conduct research at the FAA's national experimental center near Atlantic City, NJ. Others serve as instructors at the FAA Academy in Oklahoma City. A small number of civilian controllers work for the U.S. Department of Defense. In addition to controllers employed by the Federal Government, some work for private air traffic control companies providing service to non-FAA towers and contract flight service stations.

Job Outlook

Most employment opportunities are expected to result from the need to replace workers who retire or leave the occupation for other reasons; graduates of an FAA training program have good prospects.

Employment change. Employment of air traffic controllers is projected to grow 10 percent from 2006 to 2016, about as fast as the average for all occupations. Increasing air traffic will require more controllers to handle the additional work. Job growth, however, is not expected to keep pace with the increasing number of aircraft flying. New computerized systems will assist the controller by automatically making many of the routine decisions. This will allow controllers to handle more traffic, thus increasing their productivity. In addition, Federal budget constraints may limit hiring of air traffic controllers.

Job prospects. Most job opportunities are expected as the result of replacement needs from workers leaving the occupation. The majority of today's air traffic controllers will be eligible to retire over the next decade, although not all are expected to do so. Nevertheless, replacement needs will result in job opportunities each year for those graduating from the FAA training programs. Despite the increasing number of jobs coming open, competition to get into the FAA training programs is expected to remain keen, as there generally are many more applicants to get into the schools than there are openings, but those who graduate have good prospects of getting a job as a controller.

Air traffic controllers who continue to meet the proficiency and medical requirements enjoy more job security than do most workers. The demand for air travel and the workloads of air traffic controllers decline during recessions, but controllers seldom are laid off.

Earnings

Air traffic controllers earn relatively high pay and have good benefits. Median annual earnings of air traffic controllers in May 2006 were $117,240. The middle 50 percent earned between $86,860 and $142,210. The lowest 10 percent earned less than $59,410, and the highest 10 percent earned more than $145,600. The average annual salary, excluding overtime earnings, for air traffic controllers in the Federal Government—which employs 90 percent of all controllers—was $122,220 in May 2006.

The Air Traffic Control pay system classifies each air traffic facility into one of eight levels with corresponding pay bands. Under this pay system, controllers' salaries are determined by the rating of the facility. Higher ratings usually mean higher controller salaries and greater demands on the controller's judgment, skill, and decision-making ability.

Depending on length of service, air traffic controllers receive 13 to 26 days of paid vacation and 13 days of paid sick leave each year, in addition to life insurance and health benefits. Controllers also can retire at an earlier age and with fewer years of service than other Federal employees. Air traffic controllers are eligible to retire at age 50 with 20 years of service as an active air traffic controller or after 25 years of active service at any age. There is a mandatory retirement age of 56 for controllers who manage air traffic. However, Federal law provides for exemptions to the mandatory age of 56, up to age 61, for controllers having exceptional skills and experience. Earnings and benefits for controllers working in contract towers or flight service stations may vary.

Related Occupations

Airfield operations specialists also are involved in the direction and control of traffic in air transportation.

Sources of Additional Information

For further information on how to qualify and apply for a job as an air traffic controller, contact the FAA:

➤ Federal Aviation Administration, 800 Independence Ave. SW., Washington, DC 20591. Internet: **http://www.faa.gov**

Motor Vehicle Operators

Bus Drivers

(O*NET 53-3021.00, 53-3022.00)

Significant Points

- Opportunities should be good, particularly for school bus drivers; applicants for higher paying public transit bus driver positions may encounter competition.

- State and Federal governments establish bus driver qualifications and standards, which include a commercial driver's license.

- Work schedules vary considerably among various types of bus drivers.

- Bus drivers must possess strong customer service skills, including communication skills and the ability to manage large groups of people with varying needs.

Nature of the Work

Bus drivers provide transportation for millions of people, from commuters to school children to vacationers. There are two major kinds of bus drivers. *Transit and intercity bus drivers* transport people within or across States, along routes run within a metropolitan area or county, or on chartered excursions and tours. *School bus drivers* take children to and from schools and related events.

Bus drivers pick up and drop off passengers at bus stops, stations, or—in the case of students—at regularly scheduled neighborhood locations, all according to strict time schedules. Drivers must operate vehicles safely, sometimes in heavy traffic. They also cannot let light traffic put them ahead of schedule so that they miss passengers. Bus drivers drive a range of vehicles from 15-passenger buses to 60-foot articulated buses that can carry more than 100 passengers.

Local transit and intercity bus drivers stock up on tickets or transfers and prepare trip reports after reporting to their assigned terminal or garage. In some transportation firms, maintenance departments are responsible for keeping vehicles in good condition; in others, drivers check their vehicle's tires, brakes, windshield wipers, lights, oil, fuel, and water supply before beginning their routes. Drivers usually verify that the bus has safety equipment, such as fire extinguishers, first aid kits, and emergency reflectors.

During their shift, local transit and intercity bus drivers collect fares; answer questions about schedules, routes, and transfer points; and sometimes announce stops. Intercity bus drivers may make only a single one-way trip to a distant city or a round trip each day. They may stop at towns just a few miles apart or only at large cities hundreds of miles apart. Local transit bus drivers may make several trips each day over the same city and suburban streets, stopping as frequently as every few blocks.

Local transit bus drivers submit daily trip reports with a record of trips, significant schedule delays, and mechanical problems. Intercity drivers who drive across State or national boundaries must comply with U.S. Department of Transportation regulations. These include completing vehicle inspection reports and recording distances traveled and the times they spend driving, performing other duties, and off duty.

Some intercity drivers operate motor coaches which transport passengers on chartered trips and sightseeing tours. Drivers routinely interact with customers and tour guides to make the trip as comfortable and informative as possible. They are directly responsible for keeping to strict schedules, adhering to the guidelines of the tour's itinerary, and ensuring the overall success of the trip. These drivers act as customer service representatives, tour guides, program directors, and safety guides. Trips frequently last more than a day. The driver may be away for more than a week if assigned to an extended tour.

School bus drivers usually drive the same routes each day, stopping to pick up pupils in the morning and returning them to their homes in the afternoon. Some school bus drivers also transport students and teachers on field trips or to sporting events. In addition to driving, some school bus drivers work part time in the school system as janitors, mechanics, or classroom assistants when not driving buses.

Bus drivers must be alert to prevent accidents, especially in heavy traffic or in bad weather, and to avoid sudden stops or swerves that jar passengers. School bus drivers must exercise particular caution when children are getting on or off the bus. They must maintain order on their bus and enforce school safety standards by allowing only students to board. In addition, they must know and enforce the school system's rules regarding student conduct. As the number of students with physical or behavioral disabilities increases, school bus drivers must learn how to accommodate their special needs.

Some school bus drivers can take their bus home or park it in a more convenient area rather than reporting to an assigned terminal or garage. School bus drivers do not collect fares. Instead, they prepare weekly reports on the number of students, trips or "runs," work hours, miles, and fuel consumption. Their supervisors set time schedules and routes for the day or week.

Work environment. Driving a bus through heavy traffic while dealing with passengers is more stressful and fatiguing than physically strenuous. Many drivers enjoy the opportunity to work without direct supervision, with full responsibility for their bus and passengers. To improve working conditions and retain drivers, many bus lines provide ergonomically designed seats and controls for drivers. Many bus companies use Global Positioning Systems to help dispatchers manage their bus fleets and help drivers navigate.

Work schedules vary considerably among various types of bus drivers. Intercity bus drivers may work nights, weekends, and holidays and often spend nights away from home, during which they stay in hotels at company expense. Senior drivers with regular routes have regular weekly work schedules, but others do not have regular schedules and must be prepared to report for work on short notice. They report for work only when called for a charter assignment or to drive extra buses on a regular route. Intercity bus travel and charter work tend to be seasonal. From May through August, drivers might work the maximum number of hours per week that regulations allow. During winter, junior drivers might work infrequently, except for busy holiday travel periods, and may be furloughed at times.

School bus drivers work only when schools are in session. Many work 20 hours a week or less, driving one or two routes in the morning and afternoon. Drivers taking field or athletic trips, or who also have midday kindergarten routes, may work more hours a week.

Regular local transit bus drivers usually have a 5-day work-week; Saturdays and Sundays are considered regular workdays. Some drivers work evenings and after midnight. To accommodate commuters, many work "split shifts"—for example, 6 a.m. to 10 a.m. and 3 p.m. to 7 p.m., with time off in between.

Intercity bus drivers operating tour and charter buses may work any day and all hours of the day, including weekends and holidays. Their hours are dictated by the destinations, schedules, and itineraries of chartered tours. Like all commercial drivers, their weekly hours must be consistent with the Department of Transportation's rules and regulations concerning hours of service. For example, drivers may drive for 10 hours and work for up to 15 hours—including driving and non-driving duties—before having 8 hours off duty. Drivers may only drive for 60 hours in 7 days or 70 hours in 8 days. They are required to document their time in a logbook.

Training, Other Qualifications, and Advancement

State and Federal governments establish bus driver qualifications and standards, which include a commercial driver's license (CDL) with the proper endorsements. Many employers provide

Bus drivers are responsible for the safety of passengers.

several weeks of training and help new employees obtain their CDL. Other employers prefer those with truck or other driving experience.

Education and training. Many employers prefer high school graduates and require a written test of ability to follow complex bus schedules. Some intercity and public transit bus companies require several years of experience driving a bus or truck. Most intercity bus companies and local transit systems give driver trainees 2 to 8 weeks of classroom and behind-the-wheel instruction. In the classroom, trainees learn Department of Transportation and company work rules, safety regulations, State and municipal driving regulations, and safe driving practices. They also learn to read schedules, determine fares, keep records, and deal courteously with passengers.

School bus drivers receive between 1 and 4 weeks of driving instruction and classroom training on State and local laws, regulations, and policies; safe driving practices; driver-pupil relations; first aid; emergency evacuation procedures; and the special needs of students who are disabled or emotionally troubled. School bus drivers also must be aware of the school system's rules for discipline and conduct for bus drivers and the students they transport. Many people who become school bus drivers have never driven any vehicle larger than an automobile.

During training, all bus drivers practice driving on set courses. They practice turns and zigzag maneuvers, backing up, and driving in narrow lanes. Then, they drive in light traffic and, eventually, on congested highways and city streets. They also make trial runs without passengers to improve their driving skills and learn the routes. Local transit trainees memorize and drive each of the runs operating out of their assigned garage. New drivers make regularly scheduled trips with passengers, accompanied by an experienced driver who gives helpful tips, answers questions, and evaluates the new driver's performance. Most bus drivers get brief supplemental training periodically to stay informed of safety issues and regulatory changes.

Licensure. Bus driver qualifications and standards are established by State and Federal regulations. All drivers must comply with Federal regulations and with any State regulations that exceed Federal requirements. Federal regulations require drivers who operate commercial motor vehicles in excess of 26,000 pounds gross vehicle weight rating or designed to carry 16 or more people, including the driver, to hold a commercial driver's license with the appropriate endorsements from the State in which they live. As with all commercial drivers, bus drivers who drive across State or national boundaries, as motor coach drivers frequently do, must comply with U.S. Department of Transportation regulations, State regulations, and the regulations of other countries.

To qualify for a commercial driver's license, applicants must pass a knowledge test on rules and regulations and then demonstrate in a skills test that they can operate a bus safely. A national database records all driving violations incurred by people who hold commercial licenses, and a State may not issue a license to a person who has already had a license suspended or revoked in another State. To be issued a commercial license, a driver must surrender all other driver's licenses. All bus drivers must also have a passenger endorsement for their license, which requires passing a knowledge test and demonstrating the necessary skills in a vehicle of the same type as the one they would be driving on the job. Information on how to apply for a commercial driver's license and each type of endorsement can be obtained from State motor vehicle administrations.

Although many States allow those who are 18 years of age and older to drive buses within State borders, the U.S. Department of Transportation establishes minimum qualifications for bus drivers engaged in interstate commerce. Federal Motor Carrier Safety Regulations require drivers to be at least 21 years old and to pass a physical examination once every 2 years. The main physical requirements include good hearing, at least 20/40 vision with or without glasses or corrective lenses, and a 70-degree field of vision in each eye. Drivers cannot be color-blind. They must be able to hear a forced whisper in one ear at not less than 5 feet, with or without a hearing aide. Drivers must have normal blood pressure and normal use of their arms and legs. They may not use any controlled substances, unless prescribed by a licensed physician. People with epilepsy or with diabetes controlled by insulin are not permitted to be interstate bus drivers. Federal regulations also require employers to test their drivers for alcohol and drug use as a condition of employment and require periodic random tests of the drivers while they are on duty. In addition, a driver must not have been convicted of a felony involving the use of a motor vehicle or a crime involving drugs, driving under the influence of drugs or alcohol, refusing to submit to an alcohol test required by a State or its implied consent laws or regulations, leaving the scene of a crime, or causing a fatality through negligent operation of a commercial vehicle.

All drivers also must be able to read and speak English well enough to read road signs, prepare reports, and communicate with law enforcement officers and the public. In addition, drivers must take a written examination on the Motor Carrier Safety Regulations of the U.S. Department of Transportation.

School bus drivers are required to obtain a commercial driver's license with a school bus endorsement from the State in which they live. To receive this endorsement, they must pass a written test and demonstrate necessary skills in a bus of the same type that they would be driving on their route. Both of these tests are specific to school buses and are in addition to the testing required to receive a commercial license and the passenger endorsement.

Other qualifications. Many intercity and public transit bus companies prefer applicants who are at least 24 years old. Because bus drivers deal with passengers, they must be courteous. They need an even temperament and emotional stability because driving in heavy, fast-moving, or stop-and-go traffic and dealing with passengers can be stressful. Drivers must have strong customer service skills, including communication skills and the ability to coordinate and manage large groups of people. In some States, school bus drivers must pass a background investigation to uncover any criminal record or history of mental problems.

Advancement. New intercity and local transit drivers usually are placed on an "extra" list to drive chartered runs, extra buses on regular runs, and special runs, such as those during morning and evening rush hours and to sports events. New drivers also substitute for regular drivers who are ill or on vacation. New drivers remain on the extra list and may work only part time, perhaps for several years, until they have enough seniority to get a regular run.

Senior drivers may bid for the runs that they prefer, such as those with more work hours, lighter traffic, weekends off, or—in the case of intercity bus drivers—higher earnings or fewer workdays per week.

Opportunities for promotion are generally limited. However, experienced drivers may become supervisors or dispatchers—assigning buses to drivers, checking whether drivers are on schedule, rerouting buses to avoid blocked streets or other problems, and dispatching extra vehicles and service crews to scenes of accidents and breakdowns. In transit agencies with rail systems, drivers may become train operators or station attendants. Some bus drivers become either instructors of new bus drivers or master-instructors, who train new instructors. Few drivers become managers. Promotion in publicly owned bus systems is often determined by competitive civil service examination. Some motor coach drivers purchase their own equipment and open their own business.

Employment

Bus drivers held about 653,000 jobs in 2006. About 34 percent worked part time. Around 70 percent of all bus drivers were school bus drivers working primarily for school systems or for companies providing school bus services under contract. Most of the remainder worked for private and local government transit systems; some also worked for intercity and charter bus lines.

Job Outlook

Average job growth and good employment opportunities are expected for bus drivers. Those seeking higher paying public transit bus driver positions may encounter competition. Individuals who have good driving records and who are willing to work a part-time or irregular schedule will probably have the best job prospects.

Employment change. Overall employment of bus drivers is expected to grow 10 percent between 2006 and 2016, about as fast as the average for all occupations. New drivers will be

Projections data from the National Employment Matrix

Occupational Title	SOC Code	Employment, 2006	Projected employment, 2016	Change, 2006-16 Number	Change, 2006-16 Percent
Bus drivers	53-3020	653,000	721,000	67,000	10
Bus drivers, transit and intercity	53-3021	198,000	223,000	25,000	13
Bus drivers, school....................................	53-3022	455,000	497,000	42,000	9

NOTE: Data in this table are rounded. See the discussion of the employment projections table in the *Handbook* introductory chapter on *Occupational Information Included in the Handbook.*

needed primarily to meet the transportation needs of the growing general population and school-aged population.

Employment growth for local transit and intercity bus drivers is projected to be 13 percent over the 2006-16 decade, about as fast as average for all occupations, primarily because of the increasing popularity of mass transit due to congestion and rising fuel prices and the demand for transit services in expanding metropolitan areas. Competition from other modes of transportation—airplane, train, or automobile—will temper job growth among intercity bus drivers. Most growth in intercity bus transportation will occur in group charters to locations not served by other modes of transportation. Like automobiles, buses have a far greater number of possible destinations than airplanes or trains. Since they offer greater cost savings and convenience than automobiles do, buses usually are the most economical option for tour groups traveling to out-of-the-way destinations.

The number of school bus drivers is expected to increase 9 percent over the next 10 years, which is also about as fast as the average for all occupations. This growth is somewhat slower than in the past. School enrollments are projected to increase in 37 States, decrease in 12 States and stay constant in 1 State. However, the net effect will still be a slowdown in the rate of school enrollment and, therefore, in employment growth of school bus drivers. This, as well as the part-time nature of the occupation, will result in most openings for school bus drivers being to replace those who leave the occupation.

Job prospects. People seeking jobs as bus drivers likely will have good opportunities. Employment growth will create jobs, but most job openings are expected because of the need to replace workers who take jobs in other occupations or who retire or leave the occupation for other reasons.

Individuals who have good driving records and who are willing to work a part-time or irregular schedule probably will have the best job prospects. School bus driving jobs, particularly in rapidly growing suburban areas, should be easiest to acquire because most are part-time positions with high turnover and less training required than for other bus-driving jobs. Those seeking higher paying public transit bus driver positions may encounter competition. Opportunities for intercity driving positions should be good, although employment prospects for motor coach drivers will depend on tourism, which fluctuates with the economy.

Full-time bus drivers rarely are laid off during recessions. In local transit and intercity bus systems, if the number of passengers decreases, employers might reduce the hours of part-time bus drivers or consolidate routes since fewer buses would be required. Seasonal layoffs are common. Many intercity bus drivers with little seniority, for example, are furloughed during the winter when regularly scheduled and charter business declines. School bus drivers seldom work during the summer or school holidays.

Earnings

Median hourly wage-and-salary earnings of transit and intercity bus drivers were $15.43 in May 2006. The middle 50 percent earned between $11.56 and $19.86 per hour. The lowest 10 percent earned less than $9.26, and the highest 10 percent earned

more than $24.08 per hour. Median hourly earnings in the industries employing the largest numbers of transit and intercity bus drivers were:

Interurban and rural bus transportation	$17.16
Urban transit systems	14.07
School and employee bus transportation	12.35
Other transit and ground passenger transportation	11.51
Charter bus industry	11.50

Median hourly wage-and-salary earnings of school bus drivers were $11.93 in May 2006. The middle 50 percent earned between $8.99 and $14.82 per hour. The lowest 10 percent earned less than $6.58, and the highest 10 percent earned more than $17.61 per hour. Median hourly earnings in the industries employing the largest numbers of school bus drivers were:

School and employee bus transportation	$12.55
Elementary and secondary schools	11.59
Other transit and ground passenger transportation	11.11
Child day care services	9.50
Individual and family services	9.17

The benefits bus drivers receive from their employers vary greatly. Most intercity and local transit bus drivers receive paid health and life insurance, sick leave, vacation leave, and free bus rides on any of the regular routes of their line or system. School bus drivers receive sick leave, and many are covered by health and life insurance and pension plans. Because they generally do not work when school is not in session, they do not get vacation leave.

About 41 percent of bus drivers were members of or were covered by union contracts in 2006. Many intercity and local transit bus drivers are members of the Amalgamated Transit Union. Some drivers belong to the United Transportation Union or to the International Brotherhood of Teamsters.

Related Occupations

Other workers who drive vehicles on highways and city streets include taxi drivers and chauffeurs, and truck drivers and driver/sales workers. Some local transit bus drivers enter rail transportation occupations by becoming subway or light rail operators.

Sources of Additional Information

For information on employment opportunities, contact local transit systems, intercity bus lines, school systems, or the local offices of the State employment service.

General information on school bus driving is available from:
➤ National Association of State Directors of Pupil Transportation Services, P.O. Box 5446, Steamboat Springs, CO 80477. Internet: **http://www.nasdpts.org**
➤ National School Transportation Association, 113 South West St., 4th Floor, Alexandria, VA 22314.
Internet: **http://www.yellowbuses.org**

General information on motor coach driving is available from:
➤ United Motorcoach Association, 113 South West St., 4th Floor, Alexandria, VA 22314. Internet: **http://www.uma.org**

Taxi Drivers and Chauffeurs

(O*NET 53-3041.00)

Significant Points

- Taxi drivers and chauffeurs may work any schedule, including full-time, part-time, night, evening, weekend, and on a seasonal basis.

- Many taxi drivers like the independent, unsupervised work of driving their automobile.

- Local governments set license standards for driving experience and training; many taxi and limousine companies set higher standards.

- Job opportunities should be plentiful; applicants with good driving records, good customer service instincts, and the ability to work flexible schedules should have the best prospects.

Nature of the Work

Anyone who has been in a large city knows the importance of taxi and limousine services. *Taxi drivers* and *chauffeurs* take passengers to and from their homes, workplaces, and recreational pursuits, such as dining, entertainment, and shopping, and to and from business-related events. These professional drivers also help out-of-town business people and tourists get around in unfamiliar surroundings. Some drivers offer sightseeing services around their city.

Drivers must be alert to conditions on the road, especially in heavy and congested traffic or in bad weather. They must take precautions to prevent accidents and avoid sudden stops, turns, and other driving maneuvers that would jar passengers.

Taxi drivers. At the beginning of their driving shift, taxi drivers usually report to a taxicab service or garage where they are assigned a vehicle, most frequently a large, conventional automobile modified for commercial passenger transport. They record their name, the date, and the cab's identification number on a trip sheet. Drivers check the cab's fuel and oil levels and make sure that the lights, brakes, and windshield wipers are in good working order. Drivers adjust rear and side mirrors and their seat for comfort. Any equipment or part not in good working order is reported to the dispatcher or company mechanic.

Taxi drivers pick up passengers by "cruising" for fares, prearranging pickups, and picking up passengers from taxistands in high-traffic areas. In urban areas, many passengers flag down drivers cruising the streets. Customers also may prearrange a pickup by calling a cab company and giving a location, approximate pickup time, and destination. The cab company dispatcher then relays the information to a driver by two-way radio, cellular telephone, or onboard computer. Outside of urban areas, the majority of trips are dispatched in this manner. Drivers also pick up passengers waiting at cabstands or in taxi lines at airports, train stations, hotels, restaurants, and other places where people frequently seek taxis.

Some taxi commissions force cabs to specialize in either cruising or prearranged pick ups. In other cases, not all drivers are allowed to pick up riders in certain parts of a city (a business district) or at certain landmarks (a convention center or airport). These restrictions aim to make taxis available to people in areas that drivers find less profitable.

Good drivers are familiar with streets in the areas they serve so they can choose the most efficient route to destinations. They know the locations of frequently requested destinations, such as airports, bus and railroad terminals, convention centers, hotels, and other points of interest. In case of emergency, drivers should know the location of fire and police stations as well as hospitals.

Upon reaching the destination, drivers determine the fare and announce it to their riders. Each jurisdiction determines the rate and structure of the fare system covering licensed taxis. In many cabs, a taximeter measures the fare based on the distance covered and the amount of time the trip took. Drivers turn on the meter when passengers enter the cab and turn it off when they reach the final destination. The fare also may include surcharges to help cover fuel costs as well as fees for additional passengers, tolls, handling luggage, and a drop charge—an additional flat fee added for use of the cab. In some cases, fares are determined by a system of zones through which the taxi passes during a trip.

Passengers usually add a tip or gratuity to the fare. The amount of the gratuity depends, in part, on the passengers' satisfaction with the quality and efficiency of the ride and the courtesy of the driver.

Drivers issue receipts upon request by the passenger. They enter onto the trip sheet all information regarding the trip, including the place and time of pickup and drop off and the total fee; these logs help taxi company management check drivers' activity and efficiency. Drivers also must fill out accident reports when necessary.

Some drivers transport individuals with special needs, such as those with disabilities and the elderly. These drivers, known as *paratransit drivers*, operate specially equipped vehicles designed to accommodate a variety of needs in non-emergency situations. Although special certification is not necessary, some additional training on the equipment and passenger needs may be required.

Chauffeurs. Chauffeurs operate limousines, vans, and private cars for limousine companies, private businesses, government agencies, and wealthy individuals. Chauffeur service differs from taxi service in that all trips are prearranged. Many chauffeurs transport customers in large vans between hotels and airports, bus terminals, or train stations. Others drive luxury automobiles, such as limousines, to business events, entertainment venues, and social events. Still others provide full-time personal transportation for wealthy families and private companies.

At the beginning of the workday, chauffeurs prepare their automobiles or vans for use. They inspect the vehicle for cleanliness and, when needed, clean the interior and wash the exterior body, windows, and mirrors. They check fuel and oil levels and make sure the lights, tires, brakes, and windshield wipers work. Chauffeurs may perform routine maintenance and make minor repairs, such as changing tires or adding oil and other fluids. If a vehicle requires a more complicated repair, they take it to a professional mechanic.

Chauffeurs cater to passengers by providing attentive customer service and paying attention to detail. They help riders into the car by holding open doors, holding umbrellas when it is raining, and loading packages and luggage into the trunk of the car. Chauffeurs may perform errands for their employers such as delivering packages or picking up clients arriving at airports. To ensure a pleasurable ride in their limousines, many chauffeurs offer conveniences and luxuries such as newspapers, magazines, music, drinks, televisions, and telephones. Increasingly, chauffeurs work as full-service executive assistants, simultaneously acting as driver, secretary, and itinerary planner.

Work environment. Taxi drivers and chauffeurs occasionally have to load and unload heavy luggage and packages. Driving for long periods can be tiring and uncomfortable, especially in densely populated urban areas. Taxi drivers risk robbery because they work alone and often carry large amounts of cash.

Design improvements in newer cars have reduced the stress and increased the comfort and efficiency of drivers. Many regulatory bodies overseeing taxi and chauffeur services require standard amenities such as air-conditioning and general upkeep of the vehicles. Some modern taxicabs also are equipped with sophisticated tracking devices, fare meters, and dispatching equipment. Satellites and tracking systems link many of these state-of-the-art vehicles with company headquarters. In a matter of seconds, dispatchers can deliver directions, traffic advisories, weather reports, and other important communications to drivers anywhere in the area. The satellite link also allows dispatchers to track vehicle location, fuel consumption, and engine performance. Automated dispatch systems help dispatchers locate the closest driver to a customer in order to minimize individual wait time and increase the quality of service. Drivers easily can communicate with dispatchers to discuss delivery schedules and courses of action if there are mechanical problems. When threatened with crime or violence, drivers may have special "trouble lights" to alert authorities of emergencies.

Work hours of taxi drivers and chauffeurs vary greatly. Some jobs offer full-time or part-time employment with work hours that can change from day to day or remain the same. It is often necessary for drivers to report to work on short notice. Chauffeurs who work for a single employer may be on call much of the time. Evening and weekend work is common for drivers and chauffeurs employed by limousine and taxicab services.

Whereas the needs of the client or employer dictate the work schedule for chauffeurs, the work of taxi drivers is much less structured. Working free of supervision, they may break for a meal or a rest whenever their vehicle is unoccupied. Many taxi drivers like the independent, unsupervised work of driving.

This occupation is attractive to individuals, such as college and postgraduate students, seeking flexible work schedules and to anyone seeking a second source of income. Other service workers, such as ambulance drivers and police officers, sometimes moonlight as taxi drivers or chauffeurs.

Full-time taxi drivers usually work one shift a day, which may last 8 to 12 hours. Part-time drivers may work half a shift each day, or work a full shift once or twice a week. Drivers may work shifts at all times of the day and night because most taxi companies offer services 24 hours a day. Early morning and late night shifts are not uncommon. Drivers work long hours during holidays, weekends, and other special times when demand for their services is heavier. Independent drivers set their own hours and schedules.

Training, Other Qualifications, and Advancement

Local governments set licensing standards and requirements for taxi drivers and chauffeurs, which may include minimum amounts of driving experience and training. Many taxi and limousine companies set higher standards than those required by law. It is common for companies to review an applicant's medical, credit, criminal, and driving record. In addition, many companies require an applicant to be at least 21 years old, which is higher than the age typically required by law. Most companies also prefer that an applicant be a high school graduate.

Education and training. Little formal education is needed for taxi drivers or chauffeurs, but most have at least a high school diploma, GED, or its equivalent. Drivers need to be able to communicate effectively, use basic math, and often need knowledge of basic mechanics. Beyond having these skills, most drivers take a course offered by the government or their employer.

Some taxi and limousine companies give new drivers on-the-job training. This training typically is informal and often lasts only about a week. Companies show drivers how to operate the taximeter and communications equipment and how to complete paperwork. Other topics covered may include driver safety and the best routes to popular sightseeing and entertainment destinations. Many companies have contracts with social service agencies and transportation services to transport elderly and disabled citizens in non-emergency situations. To support these services, new drivers may get special training in how to handle wheelchair lifts and other mechanical devices.

Licensure. People interested in driving a taxicab or a limousine first must have a regular automobile driver's license. Usually, applicants then must get a taxi driver or chauffeur's license, commonly called a "hack" license. Some States require only a passenger endorsement, which allows the driver to carry passengers in the vehicle, on a regular driver's license; some require only that drivers be certified by their employer; but the Federal Government requires a commercial driver's li-

Taxi drivers may work shifts at all times of the day and night.

Projections data from the National Employment Matrix

Occupational Title	SOC Code	Employment, 2006	Projected employment, 2016	Change, 2006-16	
				Number	Percent
Taxi drivers and chauffeurs	53-3041	229,000	258,000	30,000	13

NOTE: Data in this table are rounded. See the discussion of the employment projections table in the *Handbook* introductory chapter on *Occupational Information Included in the Handbook.*

cense with a passenger endorsement for drivers transporting 16 or more passengers.

While States set licensing requirements, local regulatory bodies usually set other terms and conditions. These often include requirements for training, which can vary greatly. Some localities require new drivers to enroll in up to 80 hours of classroom instruction, to take an exam, or both before they are allowed to work, Applicants must know local geography, motor vehicle laws, safe driving practices, and relevant regulations. Often, they must also display some aptitude for customer service. Some localities require an English proficiency test, usually in the form of listening comprehension; applicants who do not pass the English exam must take an English course in addition to any formal driving programs.

Some classroom instruction includes route management, map reading, and service for passengers with disabilities. Many taxicab or limousine companies sponsor applicants, giving them a temporary permit that allows them to drive before they have finished the training program and passed the test. Some jurisdictions, such as New York City, have discontinued this practice and now require driver applicants to complete the licensing process before operating a taxi or limousine.

Other qualifications. Taxi drivers and chauffeurs work almost exclusively with the public, and should be able to get along with many different types of people. They must be patient when waiting for passengers and when dealing with rude customers. It also is helpful for drivers to be tolerant and level-headed when driving in heavy and congested traffic. Drivers should be dependable since passengers expect to be picked up at a prearranged time and taken to the correct destination. To be successful, drivers must be responsible and self-motivated because they work with little supervision. Increasingly, companies encourage drivers to develop their own loyal customer base, so as to improve their business.

Many municipalities and taxicab and chauffeur companies require drivers to have a neat appearance. Many chauffeurs wear formal attire, such as a tuxedo, a coat and tie, a dress, or a uniform and cap.

Advancement. Taxi drivers and chauffeurs have limited advancement opportunities. Experienced drivers may obtain preferred routes or shifts. Some advance to become lead drivers, who help to train new drivers. Others take dispatching and managerial positions. Many managers start their careers as drivers. Some people start their own limousine companies.

In small and medium-size communities, drivers sometimes are able to buy their own taxi, limousine, or other type of automobile and go into business for themselves. These independent owner-drivers require an additional permit allowing them to operate their vehicle as a company. Some big cities limit the number of operating permits. In these cities, drivers become owner-drivers by buying permits from owner-drivers who leave the business, or by purchasing or leasing them from the city. Although many owner-drivers are successful, some fail to cover expenses and eventually lose their permits and automobiles. Individuals starting their own taxi company face many obstacles because of the difficulty in running a small fleet. The lack of dispatch and maintenance facilities often is hard for an owner to overcome. Chauffeurs often have a good deal of success and many companies begin as an individually owned and operated business.

For both taxi and limousine service owners, good business sense and courses in accounting, business, and business arithmetic can help an owner-driver to be successful. Knowledge of mechanics enables owner-drivers to perform their own routine maintenance and minor repairs to cut expenses.

Employment

Taxi drivers and chauffeurs held about 229,000 jobs in 2006. About 30 percent of taxi drivers and chauffeurs were self-employed.

Job Outlook

Employment is expected to grow about as fast as average. Job opportunities should be plentiful because of the need to replace the many people who work in this occupation for short periods and then leave. Applicants with good driving records, good customer service instincts, and the ability to work flexible schedules should have the best prospects.

Employment change. Employment of taxi drivers and chauffeurs is expected to grow 13 percent during the 2006-16 projection period—about as fast as the average for all occupations—as local and suburban travel increases. Job growth also will stem from Federal legislation requiring increased services for people with disabilities. Demand for paratransit drivers will grow in response to the increase in the number of elderly people, who often have difficulty driving and using public transportation.

Job prospects. People seeking jobs as taxi drivers and chauffeurs are expected to have plentiful opportunities because of the need to replace the many people who work in this occupation for short periods and then transfer to other occupations or leave the labor force. Earnings, work hours, and working conditions vary greatly, depending on economic and regulatory conditions. Applicants with good driving records, good customer service instincts, and the ability to work flexible schedules should have the best prospects.

The number of job opportunities can fluctuate with the overall movements of the economy because the demand for taxi and limousine transportation depends on travel and tourism. During economic slowdowns, drivers seldom are laid off, but they may have to increase their work hours, and earnings may decline. When the economy is strong, job prospects are numerous as many drivers transfer to other occupations. Extra drivers may be hired during holiday seasons as well as during peak travel and tourist times.

Rapidly growing metropolitan areas and cities experiencing economic growth should offer the best job opportunities.

Earnings

Earnings of taxi drivers and chauffeurs vary greatly, depending on factors such as the number of hours worked, regulatory conditions, customers' tips, and geographic location. Hybrid vehicles, which have improved gas mileage, offer taxi drivers better earnings because drivers pay for their gas out of pocket. Median hourly earnings of salaried taxi drivers and chauffeurs, including tips, were $9.78 in May 2006. The middle 50 percent earned between $8.00 and $12.19 an hour. The lowest 10 percent earned less than $6.85, and the highest 10 percent earned more than $15.80 an hour. Median hourly earnings in the industries employing the largest numbers of taxi drivers and chauffeurs were:

Taxi and limousine service	$10.62
Other transit and ground passenger transportation	9.32
Traveler accommodation	9.09
Individual and family services	8.94
Automobile dealers	8.86

Many taxi drivers and chauffeurs are *lease drivers*. These drivers pay a daily, weekly, or monthly fee to the company allowing them to lease their vehicles. In the case of limousines, leasing also permits the driver access to the company's dispatch system. The fee also may include charges for vehicle maintenance, insurance, and a deposit on the vehicle. Lease drivers may take their cars home with them when they are not on duty.

Most taxi drivers and chauffeurs do not receive benefits. This is unlikely to change because companies have little incentive to offer them. However, a few cities have made an attempt to provide health insurance for drivers.

Related Occupations

Other workers who have similar jobs include bus drivers and truck drivers and driver/sales workers.

Sources of Additional Information

Information on necessary permits and the registration of taxi drivers and chauffeurs is available from local government agencies that regulate taxicabs. Questions regarding licensing should be directed to your State motor vehicle administration. For information about work opportunities as a taxi driver or chauffeur, contact local taxi or limousine companies or State employment service offices in your area.

For general information about the work of taxi drivers, chauffeurs, and paratransit drivers, contact:

➤ Taxicab, Limousine and Paratransit Association, 3849 Farragut Ave., Kensington, MD 20895.

For general information about the work of limousine drivers, contact:

➤ National Limousine Association, 49 South Maple Ave., Marlton, NJ 08053. Internet: **http://www.limo.org**

Truck Drivers and Driver/ Sales Workers

(O*NET 53-3031.00, 53-3032.00, 53-3033.00)

Significant Points

- Overall job opportunities should be favorable.
- Competition is expected for jobs offering the highest earnings or most favorable work schedules.
- A commercial driver's license is required to operate large trucks.

Nature of the Work

Truck drivers are a constant presence on the Nation's highways and interstates. They deliver everything from automobiles to canned food. Firms of all kinds rely on trucks to pick up and deliver goods because no other form of transportation can deliver goods door-to-door. Even though many goods travel at least part of their journey by ship, train, or airplane, almost everything is carried by trucks at some point.

Before leaving the terminal or warehouse, truck drivers check the fuel level and oil in their trucks. They also inspect the trucks to make sure that the brakes, windshield wipers, and lights are working and that a fire extinguisher, flares, and other safety equipment are aboard and in working order. Drivers make sure their cargo is secure and adjust the mirrors so that both sides of the truck are visible from the driver's seat. Drivers report equipment that is inoperable, missing, or loaded improperly to the dispatcher.

Drivers keep a log of their activities, as required by the U.S. Department of Transportation, to the condition of the truck, and the circumstances of any accidents.

Heavy truck and tractor-trailer drivers operate trucks or vans with a capacity of at least 26,000 pounds Gross Vehicle Weight (GVW). They transport goods including cars, livestock, and other materials in liquid, loose, or packaged form. Many routes are from city to city and cover long distances. Some companies use two drivers on very long runs—one drives while the other sleeps in a berth behind the cab. These "sleeper" runs can last for days, or even weeks. Trucks on sleeper runs typically stop only for fuel, food, loading, and unloading.

Some heavy truck and tractor-trailer drivers who have regular runs transport freight to the same city on a regular basis. Other drivers perform ad hoc runs because shippers request varying service to different cities every day.

Long-distance heavy truck and tractor-trailer drivers spend most of their working time behind the wheel but also may have to load or unload their cargo. This is especially common when drivers haul specialty cargo because they may be the only ones at the destination familiar with procedures or certified to handle the materials. Auto-transport drivers, for example, position cars on the trailers at the manufacturing plant and remove them at the dealerships. When picking up or delivering furniture, drivers of long-distance moving vans hire local workers to help them load or unload.

Light or delivery services truck drivers operate vans and trucks weighing less than 26,000 pounds GVW. They pick up or deliver merchandise and packages within a specific area. This may include short "turnarounds" to deliver a shipment to a nearby city, pick up another loaded truck or van, and drive it back to their home base the same day. These services may require use of electronic delivery tracking systems to track the whereabouts of the merchandise or packages. Light or delivery services truck drivers usually load or unload the merchandise at the customer's place of business. They may have helpers if there are many deliveries to make during the day or if the load requires heavy moving. Typically, before the driver arrives for work, material handlers load the trucks and arrange items for ease of delivery. Customers must sign receipts for goods and pay drivers the balance due on the merchandise if there is a cash-on-delivery arrangement. At the end of the day, drivers turn in receipts, payments, records of deliveries made, and any reports on mechanical problems with their trucks.

A driver's responsibilities and assignments change according to the type of loads transported and their vehicle's size. The duration of runs depends on the types of cargo and the destinations. Local drivers may provide daily service for a specific route or region, while other drivers make longer, intercity and interstate deliveries. Interstate and intercity cargo tends to vary from job to job more than local cargo does.

Some local truck drivers have sales and customer service responsibilities. The primary responsibility of *driver/sales workers*, or *route drivers*, is to deliver and sell their firms' products over established routes or within an established territory. They sell goods such as food products, including restaurant takeout items, or pick up and deliver items such as laundry. Their response to customer complaints and requests can make the difference between a large order and a lost customer. Route drivers may also take orders and collect payments.

The duties of driver/sales workers vary according to their industry, the policies of their employer, and the emphasis placed on their sales responsibility. Most have wholesale routes that deliver to businesses and stores, rather than to homes. For example, wholesale bakery driver/sales workers deliver and arrange bread, cakes, rolls, and other baked goods on display racks in grocery stores. They estimate how many of each item to stock by paying close attention to what is selling. They may recommend changes in a store's order or encourage the manager to stock new bakery products. Laundries that rent linens, towels, work clothes, and other items employ driver/sales workers to visit businesses regularly to replace soiled laundry. Their duties also may include soliciting new customers along their sales route.

After completing their route, driver/sales workers place orders for their next deliveries based on product sales and customer requests.

Satellites and the Global Positioning System link many trucks with their company's headquarters. Troubleshooting information, directions, weather reports, and other important communications can be instantly relayed to the truck. Drivers can easily communicate with the dispatcher to discuss delivery schedules and what to do in the event of mechanical problems. The satellite link also allows the dispatcher to track the truck's location, fuel consumption, and engine performance. Some drivers also

Overall job opportunities for truck drivers should be favorable.

work with computerized inventory tracking equipment. It is important for the producer, warehouse, and customer to know their products' location at all times so they can maintain a high quality of service.

Work environment. Truck driving has become less physically demanding because most trucks now have more comfortable seats, better ventilation, and improved, ergonomically designed cabs. Although these changes make the work environment less taxing, driving for many hours at a stretch, loading and unloading cargo, and making many deliveries can be tiring. Local truck drivers, unlike long-distance drivers, usually return home in the evening. Some self-employed long-distance truck drivers who own and operate their trucks spend most of the year away from home.

The U.S. Department of Transportation governs work hours and other working conditions of truck drivers engaged in interstate commerce. A long-distance driver may drive for 11 hours and work for up to 14 hours—including driving and non-driving duties—after having 10 hours off-duty. A driver may not drive after having worked for 60 hours in the past 7 days or 70 hours in the past 8 days unless they have taken at least 34 consecutive hours off. Most drivers are required to document their time in a logbook. Many drivers, particularly on long runs, work close to the maximum time permitted because they typically are compensated according to the number of miles or hours they drive. Drivers on long runs face boredom, loneliness, and fatigue. Drivers often travel nights, holidays, and weekends to avoid traffic delays.

Local truck drivers frequently work 50 or more hours a week. Drivers who handle food for chain grocery stores, produce markets, or bakeries typically work long hours—starting late at night or early in the morning. Although most drivers have regular routes, some have different routes each day. Many local truck drivers, particularly driver/sales workers, load and unload their own trucks. This requires considerable lifting, carrying, and walking each day.

Training, Other Qualifications, and Advancement

A commercial driver's license (CDL) is required to drive large trucks and a regular driver's license is required to drive all other trucks. Training for the CDL is offered by many private and public vocational-technical schools. Many jobs driving smaller trucks require only brief on-the-job training.

Education and training. Taking driver-training courses is a good way to prepare for truck driving jobs and to obtain a commercial drivers license (CDL). High school courses in driver training and automotive mechanics also may be helpful. Many private and public vocational-technical schools offer tractor-trailer driver training programs. Students learn to maneuver large vehicles on crowded streets and in highway traffic. They also learn to inspect trucks and freight for compliance with regulations. Some States require prospective drivers to complete a training course in basic truck driving before getting their CDL.

Completion of a program does not guarantee a job. Some programs provide only a limited amount of actual driving experience. People interested in attending a driving school should check with local trucking companies to make sure the school's training is acceptable. The Professional Truck Driver Institute (PTDI), a nonprofit organization established by the trucking industry, manufacturers, and others, certifies driver-training courses at truck driver training schools that meet industry standards and Federal Highway Administration guidelines for training tractor-trailer drivers.

Training given to new drivers by employers is usually informal and may consist of only a few hours of instruction from an experienced driver, sometimes on the new employee's own time. New drivers may also ride with and observe experienced drivers before getting their own assignments. Drivers receive additional training to drive special types of trucks or handle hazardous materials. Some companies give 1 to 2 days of classroom instruction covering general duties, the operation and loading of a truck, company policies, and the preparation of delivery forms and company records. Driver/sales workers also receive training on the various types of products their company carries so that they can effectively answer questions about the products and more easily market them to their customers.

New drivers sometimes start on panel trucks or other small straight trucks. As they gain experience and show competent driving skills, new drivers may advance to larger, heavier trucks and finally to tractor-trailers.

Licensure. State and Federal regulations govern the qualifications and standards for truck drivers. All drivers must comply with Federal regulations and any State regulations that are in excess of those Federal requirements. Truck drivers must have a driver's license issued by the State in which they live, and most employers require a clean driving record. Drivers of trucks designed to carry 26,000 pounds or more—including most tractor-trailers, as well as bigger straight trucks—must obtain a commercial driver's license. All truck drivers who operate trucks transporting hazardous materials must obtain a CDL, regardless of truck size. In order to receive the hazardous materials endorsement, a driver must be fingerprinted and submit to a criminal background check

by the Transportation Security Administration. In many States, a regular driver's license is sufficient for driving light trucks and vans.

To qualify for a CDL, an applicant must have a clean driving record, pass a written test on rules and regulations, and demonstrate that they can operate a commercial truck safely. A national database permanently records all driving violations committed by those with a CDL. A State will check these records and deny a CDL to those who already have a license suspended or revoked in another State. Licensed drivers must accompany trainees until they get their own CDL. A person may not hold more than one license at a time and must surrender any other licenses when a CDL is issued. Information on how to apply for a CDL may be obtained from State motor vehicle administrations.

Many States allow those who are as young as 18 years old to drive trucks within their borders. To drive a commercial vehicle between States one must be at least 21 years of age, according to the Federal Motor Carrier Safety Regulations published by the U.S. Department of Transportation (U. S. DOT). Regulations also require drivers to pass a physical examination once every 2 years. Physical qualifications include good hearing, at least 20/40 vision with glasses or corrective lenses, and a 70-degree field of vision in each eye. Drivers may not be colorblind. Drivers must also be able to hear a forced whisper in one ear at not less than 5 feet, with a hearing aid if needed. Drivers must have normal use of arms and legs and normal blood pressure. People with epilepsy or diabetes controlled by insulin are not permitted to be interstate truck drivers.

Federal regulations also require employers to test their drivers for alcohol and drug use as a condition of employment and require periodic random tests of the drivers while they are on duty. Drivers may not use any controlled substances, unless prescribed by a licensed physician. A driver must not have been convicted of a felony involving the use of a motor vehicle or a crime involving drugs, driving under the influence of drugs or alcohol, refusing to submit to an alcohol test required by a State or its implied consent laws or regulations, leaving the scene of a crime, or causing a fatality through negligent operation of a motor vehicle. All drivers must be able to read and speak English well enough to read road signs, prepare reports, and communicate with law enforcement officers and the public.

Other qualifications. Many trucking companies have higher standards than those described here. Many firms require that drivers be at least 22 years old, be able to lift heavy objects, and have driven trucks for 3 to 5 years. Many prefer to hire high school graduates and require annual physical examinations. Companies have an economic incentive to hire less risky drivers, as good drivers use less fuel and cost less to insure.

Drivers must get along well with people because they often deal directly with customers. Employers seek driver/sales workers who speak well and have self-confidence, initiative, tact, and a neat appearance. Employers also look for responsible, self-motivated individuals who are able to work well with little supervision.

Advancement. Although most new truck drivers are assigned to regular driving jobs immediately, some start as extra drivers—substituting for regular drivers who are ill or on vacation. Extra drivers receive a regular assignment when an opening occurs.

Projections data from the National Employment Matrix

Occupational Title	SOC Code	Employment, 2006	Projected employment, 2016	Change, 2006-16	
				Number	Percent
Driver/sales workers and truck drivers...	53-3030	3,356,000	3,614,000	258,000	8
Driver/sales workers...	53-3031	445,000	421,000	-24,000	-5
Truck drivers, heavy and tractor-trailer.......................................	53-3032	1,860,000	2,053,000	193,000	10
Truck drivers, light or delivery services.....................................	53-3033	1,051,000	1,140,000	89,000	8

NOTE: Data in this table are rounded. See the discussion of the employment projections table in the *Handbook* introductory chapter on *Occupational Information Included in the Handbook.*

Truck drivers can advance to driving runs that provide higher earnings, preferred schedules, or better working conditions. Local truck drivers may advance to driving heavy or specialized trucks or transfer to long-distance truck driving. Working for companies that also employ long-distance drivers is the best way to advance to these positions. Few truck drivers become dispatchers or managers.

Many long-distance truck drivers purchase trucks and go into business for themselves. Although some of these owner-operators are successful, others fail to cover expenses and go out of business. Owner-operators should have good business sense as well as truck driving experience. Courses in accounting, business, and business mathematics are helpful. Knowledge of truck mechanics can enable owner-operators to perform their own routine maintenance and minor repairs.

Employment

Truck drivers and driver/sales workers held about 3.4 million jobs in 2006. Of these workers, 445,000 were driver/sales workers and 2.9 million were truck drivers. Most truck drivers find employment in large metropolitan areas or along major interstate roadways where trucking, retail, and wholesale companies tend to have their distribution outlets. Some drivers work in rural areas, providing specialized services such as delivering newspapers to customers.

The truck transportation industry employed 26 percent of all truck drivers and driver/sales workers in the United States. Another 25 percent worked for companies engaged in wholesale or retail trade. The remaining truck drivers and driver/sales workers were distributed across many industries, including construction and manufacturing.

Around 9 percent of all truck drivers and driver/sales workers were self-employed. Of these, a significant number were owner-operators who either served a variety of businesses independently or leased their services and trucks to a trucking company.

Job Outlook

Overall job opportunities should be favorable for truck drivers, although opportunities may vary greatly in terms of earnings, weekly work hours, number of nights spent on the road, and quality of equipment. Competition is expected for jobs offering the highest earnings or most favorable work schedules. Average growth is expected.

Employment change. Overall employment of truck drivers and driver/sales workers is expected to increase by 8 percent over the 2006-16 decade, which is about as fast as the average for all occupations, due to growth in the economy and in the amount of freight carried by truck. Because it is such a large occupation,

truck drivers will have a very large number of new jobs arise, over 258,000 over the 2006-16 period. Competing forms of freight transportation—rail, air, and ship transportation—require trucks to move the goods between ports, depots, airports, warehouses, retailers, and final consumers who are not connected to these other modes of transportation. Demand for long-distance drivers will remain strong because they can transport perishable and time-sensitive goods more effectively than alternate modes of transportation.

Job prospects. Job opportunities should be favorable for truck drivers. In addition to growth in demand for truck drivers, numerous job openings will occur as experienced drivers leave this large occupation to transfer to other fields of work, retire, or leave the labor force for other reasons. Jobs vary greatly in terms of earnings, weekly work hours, the number of nights spent on the road, and quality of equipment. There may be competition for the jobs with the highest earnings and most favorable work schedules. There will be more competition for jobs with local carriers than for those with long-distance carriers because of the more desirable working conditions of local carriers.

Job opportunities may vary from year to year since the output of the economy dictates the amount of freight to be moved. Companies tend to hire more drivers when the economy is strong and their services are in high demand. When the economy slows, employers hire fewer drivers or may lay off some drivers. Independent owner-operators are particularly vulnerable to slowdowns. Industries least likely to be affected by economic fluctuation, such as grocery stores, tend to be the most stable employers of truck drivers and driver/sales workers.

Earnings

Median hourly earnings of heavy truck and tractor-trailer drivers were $16.85 in May 2006. The middle 50 percent earned between $13.33 and $21.04 an hour. The lowest 10 percent earned less than $10.80, and the highest 10 percent earned more than $25.39 an hour. Median hourly earnings in the industries employing the largest numbers of heavy truck and tractor-trailer drivers in May 2006 were:

General freight trucking	$18.38
Grocery and related product wholesalers	18.01
Specialized freight trucking	16.40
Cement and concrete product manufacturing	15.26
Other specialty trade contractors	14.94

Median hourly earnings of light or delivery services truck drivers were $12.17 in May 2006. The middle 50 percent earned between $9.31 and $16.16 an hour. The lowest 10 percent earned less than $7.47, and the highest 10 percent earned more than $21.23 an hour. Median hourly earnings in the industries employing the largest numbers of light or delivery services truck drivers in May 2006 were:

Couriers..$17.80
General freight trucking...15.33
Grocery and related product wholesalers................12.84
Building material and supplies dealers 11.54
Automotive parts, accessories, and tire stores 8.38

Median hourly earnings of driver/sales workers, including commissions, were $9.99 in May 2006. The middle 50 percent earned between $7.12 and $15.00 an hour. The lowest 10 percent earned less than $6.19, and the highest 10 percent earned more than $20.30 an hour. Median hourly earnings in the industries employing the largest numbers of driver/sales workers in May 2006 were:

Drycleaning and laundry services..........................$14.81
Direct selling establishments 13.72
Grocery and related product wholesalers................12.37
Full-service restaurants 7.11
Limited-service eating places 7.02

Local truck drivers tend to be paid by the hour, with extra pay for working overtime. Employers pay long-distance drivers primarily by the mile. The per-mile rate can vary greatly from employer to employer and may even depend on the type of cargo being hauled. Some long-distance drivers are paid a percent of each load's revenue. Typically, earnings increase with mileage driven, seniority, and the size and type of truck driven.

Most driver/sales workers receive commissions based on their sales in addition to their hourly wages.

Most self-employed truck drivers are primarily engaged in long-distance hauling. Many truck drivers are members of the International Brotherhood of Teamsters. Some truck drivers employed by companies outside the trucking industry are members of unions representing the plant workers of the companies for which they work.

Related Occupations

Other driving occupations include ambulance drivers and attendants, except emergency medical technicians; bus drivers; and taxi drivers and chauffeurs. Another occupation involving sales duties is sales representatives, wholesale and manufacturing.

Sources of Additional Information

Information on truck driver employment opportunities is available from local trucking companies and local offices of the State employment service.

Information on career opportunities in truck driving may be obtained from:

➤ American Trucking Associations, Inc., 950 North Glebe Road., Suite 210, Arlington, VA 22203.
Internet: **http://www.trucking.org**

A list of certified tractor-trailer driver training courses may be obtained from:

➤ Professional Truck Driver Institute, 2200 Mill Rd., Alexandria, VA 22314. Internet: **http://www.ptdi.org**

Information on union truck driving can be obtained from:

➤ The International Brotherhood of Teamsters, 25 Louisiana Ave. NW., Washington, DC 20001.

Information on becoming a truck driver may be obtained from: **http://www.gettrucking.com**

Rail Transportation Occupations

(O*NET 53-4011.00, 53-4012.00, 53-4013.00, 53-4021.00, 53-4031.00, 53-4041.00, 53-4099.99)

Significant Points

- Opportunities are expected to be good for qualified applicants since a large number of workers are expected to retire or leave these occupations in the next decade.

- Seventy-four percent of these workers are members of unions, and earnings are relatively high.

Nature of the Work

Rail transportation workers are employed by three different types of railroads: freight, passenger, and urban transit (subway and light-rail). Freight railroads transport billions of tons of goods to destinations within the U.S. and to ports to be shipped abroad. Passenger railroads deliver millions of passengers and long-distance commuters to destinations through-

out the country. Subways and light-rail systems move passengers within metropolitan areas and their surrounding suburbs. All of these modes of rail transportation require employees to operate, oversee, and assist in rail operations. Rail transportation workers not only work on trains, but also can be found working in rail yards where railcars are inspected, repaired, coupled, and uncoupled as necessary.

Locomotive engineers operate large trains carrying cargo or passengers between stations. Most engineers run diesel-electric locomotives, although a few operate locomotives powered by battery or externally supplied electricity. Before each run, engineers check the mechanical condition of their locomotives, making any minor adjustments necessary and documenting issues that require more thorough inspection. While trains are in motion, engineers move controls such as throttles and airbrakes. They also monitor instruments that measure speed, amperage, battery charge, and air pressure, both in the brake lines and in the main reservoir. Engineers must have thorough knowledge of their routes and must be constantly aware of the condition and makeup of their train, because trains react differently to the grade and condition of the rail, the number of cars, the ratio of empty cars to loaded cars, and the amount of slack in the train.

Railroad conductors coordinate all activities of freight or passenger train crews. Conductors assigned to freight trains review schedules, switching orders, waybills, and shipping records to obtain loading and unloading information regarding their cargo. In addition, they are responsible for the distribution of tonnage in the train and the operation of freight cars within rail yards and terminals that use remote control locomotive technology. Conductors assigned to passenger trains also ensure passenger safety and comfort as they go about collecting tickets and fares, making announcements for the benefit of passengers, and coordinating the activities of the crew.

Before trains leave a terminal, the conductor and the engineer discuss any concerns regarding the train's route, timetable, and cargo. During runs and in rail yards, engineers and conductors interface electronically with monitoring equipment, traffic control center personnel, dispatchers, and personnel on other trains to issue or receive information concerning stops, delays, and the locations of trains. While engineers interpret and comply with orders, signals, speed limits, and railroad rules and regulations, conductors use dispatch or electronic monitoring devices to relay information about equipment problems on the train or the rails. Conductors may arrange for the removal of defective cars from the train for repairs at the nearest station or stop, and discuss alternative routes with the engineer and dispatcher if there is a defect in, or obstruction on, the rails.

Railroad brake operators assist with the coupling and uncoupling of cars as well as operate some switches. In an effort to reduce costs, most railroads have phased out brake operators, and many trains use only an engineer and a conductor. *Signal operators* install, maintain, and repair the signals on tracks and in yards.

Yardmasters, where present, coordinate the activities of workers engaged in railroad yard operations. These activities, which are also performed by conductors, include making up or breaking up trains and switching inbound or outbound traffic to a specific section of the line. Some cars are sent to unload their cargo on special tracks, while others are moved to different tracks to await assembly into new trains, based on their destinations. Yardmasters tell yard engineers or other personnel where to move the cars to fit the planned train configuration. Switches—many of them operated remotely by computer—divert trains or railcars to the proper track for coupling and uncoupling.

Also included in rail transportation occupations are several smaller occupations. *Switch operators* control the track switches within a rail yard. In rail yards without remote control technology, *rail yard engineers* operate engines within the rail yard. Similarly, *hostlers* operate engines—without attached cars—within the yard, as well as driving them to and from maintenance shops.

In contrast to other rail transportation workers, subway and streetcar operators generally work for public transit authorities instead of railroads. *Subway operators* control trains that transport passengers through cities and their suburbs. The trains run in underground tunnels, on the surface, or on elevated tracks. Operators must stay alert to observe signals along the track that indicate when they must start, slow, or stop their train. They also make announcements to riders, may open and close the doors of the train, and ensure that passengers get on and off the subway safely. Increasingly, the train's speed and the amount of time spent at each station are controlled by computers and not by the operator. During breakdowns or emergencies, operators contact their dispatcher or supervisor and may have to evacuate cars.

Streetcar operators drive electric-powered streetcars, trolleys, or light-rail vehicles that transport passengers around metropolitan areas. Some tracks may be built directly into street pavement or have grade crossings, so operators must observe traffic signals and cope with car and truck traffic. Operators start, slow, and stop their cars so that passengers may get on and off easily. Operators may collect fares and issue change and transfers. They also interact with passengers who have questions about fares, schedules, and routes.

Work environment. Rail transportation employees work nights, weekends, and holidays to operate trains that run 24 hours a day, 7 days a week. Many work more than a 40-hour workweek, although minimum rest hours are mandated by Federal regulations. Engineers and conductors may be placed on an "extra board" on which workers receive assignments only when a railroad needs substitutes for workers who are absent because of vacation, illness, or other reasons. Seniority usually dictates who receives the more desirable shifts, as do union agreements at large unionized railroads. Working conditions vary by the mode of rail transport.

Freight trains generally are dispatched according to the needs of customers; as a result train crews may have irregular schedules. It is common for workers to place their name on a list and wait for their turn to work. Jobs usually are assigned on short notice and often at odd hours. Working weekends is common in freight train transportation. Those who work on trains operating between points hundreds of miles apart may spend consecutive nights away from home. Because of the distances involved on some routes, many railroad employees work without direct supervision.

Rail transportation workers may spend significant time on the road.

Projections data from the National Employment Matrix

Occupational Title	SOC Code	Employment, 2006	Projected employment, 2016	Change, 2006-16	
				Number	Percent
Rail transportation occupations..	53-4000	125,000	127,000	1,800	1
Locomotive engineers and operators	53-4010	47,000	48,000	1,300	3
Railroad brake, signal, and switch operators	53-4021	25,000	22,000	-2,800	-11
Railroad conductors and yardmasters...........................	53-4031	40,000	44,000	3,600	9
Subway and streetcar operators	53-4041	6,900	7,800	800	12
Rail transportation workers, all other...........................	53-4099	6,800	5,500	-1,300	-19

NOTE: Data in this table are rounded. See the discussion of the employment projections table in the *Handbook* introductory chapter on *Occupational Information Included in the Handbook*.

Workers on passenger trains ordinarily have regular and reliable shifts. Also, the appearance, temperature, and accommodations of passenger trains are more comfortable than those of freight trains.

Rail yard workers spend most of their time outdoors and work regardless of weather conditions. These workers climb up and down equipment, which can be strenuous and dangerous if safety rules are not followed. The work of conductors and engineers on local runs, on which trains frequently stop at stations or local rail yards to pick up and deliver cars, is physically demanding as well.

Training, Other Qualifications, and Advancement

Rail transportation workers start out in a variety of positions as they gain experience needed for more demanding assignments. Rail transportation workers generally start out training to become a conductor before they may be considered for an engineer position. Engineer positions require Federal licensure, and nearly all rail transportation workers complete formal classroom and hands-on training before beginning work. Most applicants must pass a drug screening, background check, and physical examination before being hired.

Education and training. Railroads require that applicants have a minimum of a high school diploma or its equivalent, and most training is done through a company's formal training program and on-the-job training. Entry-level jobs and rail yard jobs usually require the successful completion of a company training program before workers are allowed to begin. For brake and signal operator jobs, railroad firms will train applicants either in a company program or—especially with smaller railroads—at an outside training facility. Typical training programs combine classroom and on-site training lasting from a few weeks to a few months. Entry-level conductors are either trained by their employers or are required to complete a formal conductor training program through a community college.

Most transit systems that operate subways and streetcars also operate buses. In these systems, subway or streetcar operators usually gain experience by first driving buses. New operators then complete training programs that last from a few weeks to 6 months. At the end of the period of classroom and on-the-job training, operators usually must pass qualifying examinations covering the operating system, troubleshooting, and evacuation and emergency procedures.

Licensure. Locomotive engineers are unique within rail transportation occupations in that they must be federally li-

censed to operate freight and passenger trains. Federal regulations require beginning engineers to complete a formal engineer training program, including classroom, simulator, and hands-on instruction in locomotive operation. The instruction usually is administered by the rail company in programs approved by the Federal Railroad Administration. At the end of the training period, candidates must pass a hearing and visual acuity test, a safety conduct background check, a railroad operation knowledge test, and a skills performance test before receiving an engineer's license.

Engineers must periodically pass an operational rules efficiency test to maintain their licensure. The test is an unannounced event requiring engineers to take active or responsive action in certain situations, such as maintaining a particular speed through a curve or yard or complying with a signal.

For yard occupations, a commercial driver's license may be required because these workers often operate trucks and other heavy vehicles.

Other qualifications. Rail transportation workers must have good hearing, eyesight, and color vision, as well as good hand-eye coordination, manual dexterity, and mechanical aptitude. Physical stamina is required for most rail transportation jobs. Applicants for locomotive engineer jobs and some conductor jobs must be at least 21 years old.

All applicants must be in good health, have good communication skills, and be able to make quick, responsible judgments. Employers require railroad transportation job applicants to pass a physical examination, drug and alcohol screening, and a criminal background check. Under Federal regulation, all persons licensed to operate engines are subject to random drug and alcohol testing while on duty, and engineers also undergo periodic physical examinations. In some cases, engineers who fail to meet these physical and conduct standards are restricted to yard service, trained to perform other work, or discharged.

Advancement. Most railroad transportation workers begin as a laborer, brake operator, or conductor after completing training on signals, timetables, operating rules, and related subjects. Although new employees may be hired as conductors, seniority determines whether an employee may hold a conductor position full-time. Employers almost always fill engineer positions with workers who have experience in other railroad-operating occupations. Subway and streetcar operators with sufficient seniority can advance to station manager or another supervisory position.

Employment

Rail transportation workers held 125,000 jobs in 2006, distributed among the detailed occupations as follows:

Locomotive engineers and operators......................................47,000
Railroad conductors and yardmasters...................................40,000
Railroad brake, signal, and switch operators..........................25,000
Subway and streetcar operators..6,900
Rail transportation workers, all other 6,800

Most rail transportation workers were employed in the rail transportation industry or support activities for the industry. Rail transportation and rail transportation support activities made up 109,000 jobs in 2006. The rest worked primarily for local governments as subway and streetcar operators, who held 11,000 jobs, while 1,700 workers were employed in mining and manufacturing establishments that operate their own locomotives to move railcars containing ore, coal, and other bulk materials.

Job Outlook

Although employment in most railroad transportation occupations is expected to change little through the year 2016, opportunities are expected to be good for qualified applicants, in large part due to the number of workers expected to retire or leave these occupations in the next decade.

Employment change. Employment is expected to increase by 1 percent, which is considered little or no change. This will occur despite expected increases in the amount of freight volume, which will be due to railroads' advantages over other modes of shipping.

Demand for railroad freight service will grow as the economy and the intermodal transportation of goods continue to expand. Intermodal transportation involves loading cargo in large containers that can be moved by ship, rail, or truck. Improved delivery times and on time service along with reduced shipping rates will help railroads compete with other modes of transportation, such as trucks, ships, and aircraft. Railroads will also benefit from congested highways and relative savings on rising fuel costs. However, technology will allow railroads to improve productivity and consolidate duties, which will offset the need for new employees in occupations not essential for railroad operations. For example, the need for rail yard engineers who operate trains inside rail yards will see a rapid decline as a result of remote control locomotive technology, while employment of locomotive engineers will grow as fast as the average because of the continued need for train operators on open rail. For similar reasons, railroad brake, signal, and switch operators and other rail transportation occupations will see a decline in employment, whereas railroad conductors will continue to be necessary for train operation for the foreseeable future and are expected to grow about as fast as average through 2016.

Passenger rail service is anticipated to increase volume on pace with the growing population, as are public transit authorities. Employment of subway and streetcar operators will see average growth due to increased demand for light-rail transportation systems around the country.

Job prospects. Opportunities for rail transportation workers will be favorable as a large number of older workers are expected to retire over the next decade. Other workers will leave the occupation for various personal and professional reasons, creating further opportunities. Prospects will be best for those positions that are also expected to see growth, for example locomotive engineers and conductors. There will also be job opportunities for those positions that are expected to decline, for example brake, signal, and switch operators. These openings will be the result of retirements and other separations. Entry-level occupations such as brake operator and conductor should be plentiful for applicants with clean drug and criminal records. Opportunities for long-distance train crews are also expected to be good as many of those working in the yards prefer not to travel long distances.

Earnings

Median hourly earnings of rail transportation occupations in May 2006 are indicated in the tabulation below. These earnings were relatively high, compared to $12.17 per hour for all transportation occupations.

Locomotive engineers...$27.88
Railroad conductors and yardmasters......................................26.70
Subway and streetcar operators...23.55
Railroad brake, signal, and switch operators..........................23.49

Most railroad transportation workers are paid according to miles traveled or hours worked, whichever leads to higher earnings. Factors such as seniority, job assignments, and location impact potential earnings.

Seventy-four percent of railroad transportation workers are members of unions compared to 12 percent for all occupations. Many different railroad unions represent various crafts on the railroads. Among the largest of the railroad employee unions are the United Transportation Union and the Brotherhood of Locomotive Engineers and Trainmen. Many subway operators are members of the Amalgamated Transit Union, while others belong to the Transport Workers Union of North America.

Related Occupations

Other related transportation workers include bus drivers, truck drivers and driver/sales workers, and those working in water transportation occupations. Employees who repair and maintain railroad rolling stock are included in heavy vehicle and mobile equipment service technicians and mechanics. Rail transportation workers sometimes work closely with workers in material moving occupations to load and unload freight.

Sources of Additional Information

To obtain information on employment opportunities, contact either the employment offices of railroads and rail transit systems or State employment service offices.

General information about the rail transportation industry is available from:

➤ Association of American Railroads, 50 F St. N.W., Washington, DC 20001.
Internet: **http://www.aar.org**

General information about career opportunities in passenger transportation is available from:

➤ American Public Transportation Association, 1666 K Street N.W., Washington, DC 20006.
Internet: **http://www.apta.com**
➤ National Railroad Passenger Corporation, 60 Massachusetts Ave. N.E., 4th floor, Washington, DC 20002.
Internet: **http://www.amtrak.com**
  General information on career opportunities as a locomotive engineer is available from:

➤ Brotherhood of Locomotive Engineers and Trainmen, 1370 Ontario St.Mezzanine, Cleveland, OH 44113.
Internet: **http://www.ble.org**
  General information on career opportunities as a conductor, yardmaster, or brake operator is available from:
➤ United Transportation Union, 14600 Detroit Ave., Cleveland, OH 44107.
Internet: **http://www.utu.org**

Water Transportation Occupations

(O*NET 53-5011.00, 53-5021.00, 53-5021.01, 53-5021.02, 53-5021.03, 53-5022.00, 53-5031.00)

Significant Points

- Merchant mariners spend extended periods at sea.

- Entry, training, and educational requirements for many water transportation occupations are established and regulated by the U.S. Coast Guard.

- Faster-than-average growth and good job opportunities are expected.

Nature of the Work

The movement of huge amounts of cargo, as well as passengers, between nations and within our Nation depends on workers in water transportation occupations, also known on commercial ships as merchant mariners. They operate and maintain deep-sea merchant ships, tugboats, towboats, ferries, dredges, offshore supply vessels, excursion vessels, and other waterborne craft on the oceans, the Great Lakes, rivers, canals, and other waterways, as well as in harbors. (Workers who operate watercraft used in commercial fishing are described in the section on fishers and fishing vessel operators elsewhere in the *Handbook*.)

Captains, mates, and pilots of water vessels command or supervise the operations of ships and water vessels, both within domestic waterways and on the deep sea. *Captains* or *masters* are in overall command of the operation of a vessel, and they supervise the work of all other officers and crew. Together with their department heads, captains ensure that proper procedures and safety practices are followed, check to make sure that machinery and equipment are in good working order, and oversee the loading and discharging of cargo or passengers. They also maintain logs and other records tracking the ships' movements, efforts at controlling pollution, and cargo and passengers carried.

Deck officers or *mates* direct the routine operation of the vessel for the captain during the shifts when they are on watch. On smaller vessels, there may be only one mate (called a *pilot* on some inland towing vessels), who alternates watches with the captain. The mate would assume command of the ship if the captain became incapacitated. When more than one mate is necessary aboard a ship, they typically are designated chief mate or first mate, second mate, third mate, etc. Mates also supervise and coordinate activities of the crew aboard the ship. Captains and mates determine the course and speed of the vessel, maneuvering to avoid hazards and continuously monitoring the vessel's position with charts and navigational aides. Captains and mates oversee crew members who steer the vessel, determine its location, operate engines, communicate with other vessels, perform maintenance, handle lines, and operate equipment on the vessel. They inspect the cargo holds during loading to ensure that the load is stowed according to specifications and regulations. Captains and mates also supervise crew members engaged in maintenance and the primary upkeep of the vessel.

Pilots guide ships in and out of harbors, through straits, and on rivers and other confined waterways where a familiarity with local water depths, winds, tides, currents, and hazards such as reefs and shoals are of prime importance. Pilots on river and canal vessels usually are regular crew members, like mates. Harbor pilots are generally independent contractors who accompany vessels while they enter or leave port. Harbor pilots may pilot many ships in a single day.

Ship engineers operate, maintain, and repair propulsion engines, boilers, generators, pumps, and other machinery. Merchant marine vessels usually have four engineering officers: A chief engineer and a first, second, and third assistant engineer. Assistant engineers stand periodic watches, overseeing the safe operation of engines and machinery.

Marine oilers and more experienced *qualified members of the engine department*, or QMEDs, assist the engineers to maintain the vessel in proper running order in the engine spaces below decks. These workers lubricate gears, shafts, bearings, and other moving parts of engines and motors; read pressure and temperature gauges; record data; and sometimes assist with repairs and adjust machinery.

Sailors or *deckhands* operate the vessel and its deck equipment under the direction of the ship's officers and keep the nonengineering areas in good condition. They stand watch, looking out for other vessels and obstructions in the ship's path, as well as for navigational aids such as buoys and lighthouses. They also steer the ship, measure water depth in shallow water, and maintain and operate deck equipment such as lifeboats, anchors, and cargo-handling gear. On vessels handling liquid cargo, mariners designated as *pumpmen* hook up hoses, operate pumps, and clean tanks; on tugboats or tow vessels, they tie barges together into tow units, inspect them periodically, and disconnect them when the destination is reached. When docking or departing, they handle lines. They also perform routine maintenance chores, such as repairing lines, chipping rust, and painting and cleaning decks or other areas. Experienced sailors are designated *able seamen* on oceangoing vessels, but may be called simply deckhands on inland waters; larger vessels usually have a *boatswain*, or *head seaman*.

A typical deep-sea merchant ship has a captain, three deck officers or mates, a chief engineer and three assistant engineers, plus six or more seamen, such as able seamen, oilers, QMEDs, and a cook. The size and service of the ship determine the number of crewmembers for a particular voyage. Small vessels operating in harbors, on rivers, or along the coast may have a crew comprising only a captain and one deckhand. On smaller vessels the cooking responsibilities usually fall under the deckhands' duties.

On larger coastal ships, the crew may include a captain, a mate or pilot, an engineer, and seven or eight seamen. Some ships may have special unlicensed positions for entry level apprentice trainees. Unlicensed positions on a large ship may include a full-time cook, an electrician, and machinery mechanics.

Motorboat operators operate small, motor-driven boats that carry six or fewer passengers on fishing charters. They also take depth soundings in turning basins and serve as liaisons

Captains direct all operations on their vessels.

between ships, between ship and shore, between harbors and beaches, or on area patrol.

Work environment. Water transportation workers' schedules vary based upon the type of ship and length of voyage. While on the water, crews are normally on duty for half of the day, 7 days a week.

Merchant mariners on survey and long distance cargo vessels can spend extended periods at sea. Most deep-sea mariners are hired for one or more voyages that last for several months; there is no job security after that. The length of time between voyages varies depending on job availability and personal preference.

Workers on supply vessels transport workers, supplies (water, drilling mud, fuel, and food), and equipment to oil and gas drilling platforms mostly in the Gulf of Mexico. Their voyages can last a few hours to a couple of weeks. As oil and gas exploration pushes into deeper waters, these trips take more time.

Workers on tugs and barges operate on the rivers, lakes, inland waterways, and along the coast. Most tugs have two crews and operate constantly. The crews will alternate, each working for 2-3 weeks and then taking 2-3 weeks off.

Many of those employed on Great Lakes ships work 60 days and have 30 days off, but do not work in the winter when the lakes are frozen. Others work steadily for a week or a month and then have an extended period off. Those on smaller vessels, such as tugs, supply boats and Great Lakes ships, are normally assigned to one vessel and have steady employment.

Workers on ferries transporting commuters work on weekdays in the morning and evening. Other ferries make frequent trips lasting a few hours. Ferries servicing vacation destinations often operate on seasonal schedules. Workers in harbors generally have year-round work. Work in harbors and on ferries is sought after because workers return home every day.

People holding water transportation jobs work in all kinds of weather, except when frozen waters make travel impossible. Although merchant mariners try to avoid severe storms while at sea, working in damp and cold conditions often is inevitable. While it is uncommon for vessels to suffer disasters such as fire, explosion, or a sinking, workers face the possibility that they may have to abandon their craft on short notice if it collides with other vessels or runs aground. They also risk injury or death from falling overboard and hazards associated with working with machinery, heavy loads, and dangerous cargo. However, modern safety management procedures, advanced emergency communications, and effective international rescue systems have greatly improved mariner safety.

Many companies are working to improve the living conditions on vessels to reduce employee turnover. Most of the Nation's newest vessels are air conditioned, soundproofed to reduce machinery noise, and equipped with comfortable living quarters. Some companies have added improved entertainment systems and hired full-time cooks. These amenities lessen the difficulty of spending long periods away from home. Advances in communications, particularly e-mail, better link mariners to their families. Nevertheless, some mariners dislike the long periods away from home and the confinement aboard ship and consequently leave the occupation.

Training, Other Qualifications, and Advancement

Entry, training, and educational requirements for many water transportation occupations are established and regulated by the U.S. Coast Guard. Most officers and operators of commercially operated vessels must be licensed by the Coast Guard, which offers various kinds of licenses, depending on the position, body of water, and type of vessel. Individuals must be relicensed when they change the type of ship or the body of water they are on.

Education and training. Entry-level workers are classified as ordinary seamen or deckhands. Workers take some basic training, lasting a few days, in areas such as first aid and fire-fighting.

There are two paths of education and training for a deck officer or an engineer: applicants must either accumulate thousands of hours of experience while working as a deckhand, or graduate from the U.S. Merchant Marine Academy or another maritime academy. In both cases, applicants must pass a written examination. It is difficult to pass the examination without substantial formal schooling or independent study. The academies offer a 4-year academic program leading to a bachelor-of-science degree, a license (issued only by the Coast Guard) as a third mate (deck officer) or third assistant engineer (engineering officer), and, if the person chooses, a commission as ensign in the U.S. Naval Reserve, Merchant Marine Reserve, or Coast Guard Reserve. With experience and additional training, third officers may qualify for higher rank. Generally officers on deep water vessels are academy graduates and those in supply boats, inland waterways, and rivers rose to their positions through years of experience.

Harbor pilot training usually consists of an extended apprenticeship with a towing company or a habor pilots' association. Entrants may be able seamen or licensed officers.

Licensure. Coast Guard licensing requirements vary by occupational specialty, type of vessel, and by body of water (river, inland waterway, Great Lakes, and oceans.) The requirements increase as the skill level of the occupational specialty increases and the size of the vessel increases.

Entry level seamen or deckhands on vessels operating in harbors or on rivers or other waterways do not need a license. All others working on larger, ocean-going vessels do need a license. To get the basic entry level license, workers must pass a drug screen, take a medical exam, and be U.S. citizens.

Workers on ocean-going or Great Lakes vessels need specialty licenses to work as engineering officers, or deck officers. On rivers or inland waterways, only the captain or anyone who steers the boat needs a license. For more information on licensing requirements see the Coast Guard's Web site listed in the sources of additional information. Radio operators are licensed by the Federal Communications Commission.

Other qualifications. Most positions require excellent health, good vision, and color perception. Good general physical condition is needed because many jobs require the ability to lift heavy objects, withstand heat and cold, stand or stoop for long periods of time, dexterity to maneuver through tight spaces, and good balance on uneven and wet surfaces and in rough water.

Advancement. Experience and passing exams are required to advance. Deckhands who wish to advance must decide whether they want to work in the wheelhouse or the engine room. They will then assist the engineers or deck officers. With experience, assistant engineers and deck offices can advance to become chief engineers or captains. On smaller boats, such as tugs, a captain may choose to become self-employed by buying a boat and working as an owner-operator.

Employment

Water transportation workers held more than 84,000 jobs in 2006. The total number who worked at some point in the year was significantly larger because many merchant marine officers and seamen worked only part of the year. The following tabulation shows employment in the occupations that make up this group:

Captains, mates, and pilots of water vessels 34,000
Sailors and marine oilers...33,000
Ship engineers 15,000
Motorboat operators..3,000

About 40 percent of all workers were employed in water transportation services. About 17 percent worked in inland water transportation—primarily the Mississippi River system—while the other 23 percent were employed in water transportation on the deep seas, along the coasts, and on the Great Lakes. Another 24 percent worked in establishments related to port and harbor operations, marine cargo handling, or navigational services to shipping. Governments employed 9 percent of all water transportation workers, many of whom worked on supply ships and are civilian mariners of the Navy Department's Military Sealift Command.

Projections data from the National Employment Matrix

Occupational Title	SOC Code	Employment, 2006	Projected employment, 2016	Change, 2006-16	
				Number	Percent
Water transportation occupations...	53-5000	84,000	98,000	14,000	16
Sailors and marine oilers...	53-5011	33,000	38,000	5,200	16
Ship and boat captains and operators...	53-5020	37,000	43,000	6,300	17
Captains, mates, and pilots of water vessels	53-5021	34,000	40,000	6,000	18
Motorboat operators..	53-5022	3,000	3,300	300	11
Ship engineers..	53-5031	15,000	17,000	2,100	14

NOTE: Data in this table are rounded. See the discussion of the employment projections table in the *Handbook* introductory chapter on *Occupational Information Included in the Handbook.*

Job Outlook

Employment in water transportation occupations is projected to grow faster than average. Good job opportunities are expected.

Employment change. Employment in water transportation occupations is projected to grow 16 percent over the 2006-2016 period, faster than the average for all occupations. Job growth will stem from increasing tourism and growth in offshore oil and gas production. Employment will also increase in and around major port cities due to rapidly increasing international trade.

Employment in deep-sea shipping for American mariners is expected to remain stable. A fleet of deep-sea U.S.-flagged ships is considered vital to the Nation's defense, so some receive Federal support through a maritime security subsidy and other provisions in laws that limit certain Federal cargoes to ships that fly the U.S. flag.

Employment growth also is expected in passenger cruise ships within U.S. waters. Vessels that operate between U.S. ports are required by law to be U.S.-flagged vessels. The staffing needs for several new U.S. flagged cruise ships that will travel to the Hawaiian Islands will create new opportunities for employment. In addition, increasing use of ferries to handle commuter traffic around major metropolitan areas should increase employment.

Some growth in water transportation occupations is projected in vessels operating in the Great Lakes and inland waterways. Growth will be driven by increasing demand for bulk products, such as coal, iron ore, petroleum, sand and gravel, grain, and chemicals. Since current pipelines cannot transport ethanol, some growth will come from shipping ethanol. Problems with congestion in the rail transportation system will increase demand for inland water transportation.

Job prospects. Good job opportunities will result from growth and the need to replace those leaving the occupation. Most water transportation occupations require workers to be away from home for extended periods of time, causing some to leave these jobs.

Maritime academy graduates who have not found licensed shipboard jobs in the U.S. merchant marine find jobs in related industries. Many academy graduates are ensigns in the Naval or Coast Guard Reserve; some are selected or apply for active duty in those branches of the Service. Some find jobs as seamen on U.S.-flagged or foreign-flagged vessels, tugboats, and other watercraft or enter civilian jobs with the U.S. Navy or Coast Guard. Some take land-based jobs with shipping companies, marine insurance companies, manufacturers of boilers or related machinery, or other related jobs.

Earnings

Earnings vary widely with the particular water transportation position and the worker's experience. Earnings are higher than most other occupations with similar educational requirements for entry-level positions. While wages are lower for sailors than for mates and engineers, sailors' on-board experience is important for advancing into those higher paying positions. Workers are normally paid by the day. Since companies provide food and housing at sea and it is difficult to spend money while working, sailors are able to save a large portion of their pay.

Median annual wage-and-salary earnings of sailors and marine oilers were $30,630 in May 2006. The middle 50 percent earned between $23,790 and $39,380. The lowest 10 percent had earnings of less than $19,220, while the top 10 percent earned over $49,650.

Median annual wage-and-salary earnings of captains, mates, and pilots of water vessels were $53,430 in May 2006. The middle 50 percent earned between $38,880 and $69,570. The lowest 10 percent had earnings of less than $29,360, while the top 10 percent earned over $89,230. Annual pay for captains of larger vessels, such as container ships, oil tankers, or passenger ships may exceed $100,000, but only after many years of experience. Similarly, earnings of captains of tugboats are dependent on the port and the nature of the cargo.

Median annual wage-and-salary earnings of ship engineers were $54,820 in May 2006. The middle 50 percent earned between $41,190 and $74,360. The lowest 10 percent had earnings of less than $34,140, while the top 10 percent earned over $92,860.

Median annual wage-and-salary earnings of motorboat operators were $32,350 in May 2006. The middle 50 percent earned between $23,340 and $45,850. The lowest 10 percent had earnings of less than $17,270, while the top 10 percent earned over $55,170.

The rate of unionization for these workers is about 16 percent, higher than the average for all occupations. Unionization rates vary by region. In unionized areas, merchant marine officers and seamen, both veterans and beginners, are hired for voyages through union hiring halls or directly by shipping companies. Hiring halls rank the candidates by the length of time the person has been out of work and fill open slots accordingly. Most major seaports have hiring halls.

Related Occupations

Workers in other occupations who make their living on the seas and coastal waters include fishers and fishing vessel operators and members of the Navy and the Coast Guard. Heavy vehicle and mobile equipment service technicians and mechanics perform work similar to shipboard engineers.

Sources of Additional Information

Information on a program called "Careers Afloat", which includes a substantial listing of training and employment information and contacts in the U.S., may be obtained through:

➤ Maritime Administration, U.S. Department of Transportation, 400 7th St.SW., Room 7302, Washington, DC 20590.
Internet: **http://www.marad.dot.gov/acareerafloat**

Information on merchant marine careers, training, and licensing requirements is available from:

➤ U.S. Coast Guard National Maritime Center, 4200 Wilson Blvd., Suite 630, Arlington, VA 22203-1804.
Internet: **http://www.uscg.mil/stcw/index.htm**

Information on careers with the Military Sealift Command can be found at:

➤ Military Sealift Command, CIVMAR Support Center, 6353 Center Drive, Building 8, Suite 202, Norfolk, VA 23502.
Internet: **http://www.sealiftcommand.com**

Material Moving Occupations

(O*NET 53-1021.00, 53-7011.00, 53-7021.00, 53-7031.00, 53-7032.00, 53-7033.00, 53-7041.00, 53-7051.00, 53-7061.00, 53-7062.00, 53-7063.00, 53-7064.00, 53-7071.00, 53-7072.00, 53-7073.00, 53-7081.00, 53-7111.00, 53-7121.00, 53-7199.99)

Significant Points

- Despite little or no change in employment, job openings should be plentiful because these occupations are very large and numerous openings will be created to replace workers who leave them.

- Most jobs require little work experience or training.

- Pay is low, and the seasonal nature of the work may reduce earnings.

Nature of the Work

Material moving workers are categorized into two groups—operators and laborers. Operators use machinery to move construction materials, earth, petroleum products, and other heavy materials. Generally, they move materials over short distances—around construction sites, factories, or warehouses. Some move materials onto or off of trucks and ships. Operators control equipment by moving levers, wheels, and/or foot pedals; operating switches; or turning dials. They also may set up and inspect equipment, make adjustments, and perform minor maintenance or repairs.

Laborers and hand material movers move freight, stock, or other materials by hand; clean vehicles, machinery, and other equipment; feed materials into or remove materials from machines or equipment; and pack or package products and materials.

Material moving occupations are classified by the type of equipment they operate or the goods they handle. Each piece of equipment requires different skills, as do different types of loads. (For information on operating engineers; paving, surfacing, and tamping equipment operators; and pile-driver operators, see the statement on construction equipment operators elsewhere in the *Handbook*.)

Industrial truck and tractor operators drive and control industrial trucks or tractors equipped to move materials around warehouses, storage yards, factories, construction sites, or other worksites. A typical industrial truck, often called a forklift or lift truck, has a hydraulic lifting mechanism and forks for moving heavy and large objects. Industrial truck and tractor operators also may operate tractors that pull trailers loaded with materials, goods, or equipment within factories and warehouses or around outdoor storage areas.

Excavating and loading machine and dragline operators tend or operate machinery equipped with scoops, shovels, or buckets to dig and load sand, gravel, earth, or similar materials into trucks or onto conveyors. Construction and mining industries employ the majority of excavation and loading machine and dragline operators. *Dredge operators* excavate waterways, removing sand, gravel, rock, or other materials from harbors, lakes, rivers, and streams. Dredges are used primarily to maintain navigable channels but also are used to restore wetlands and other aquatic habitats; reclaim land; and create and maintain beaches. *Underground mining loading machine operators* use underground loading machines to load coal, ore, or rock into shuttles and mine cars or onto conveyors. Loading equipment may include power shovels, hoisting engines equipped with cable-drawn scrapers or scoops, and machines equipped with gathering arms and conveyors.

Crane and tower operators work mechanical boom and cable or tower and cable equipment to lift and move materials, machinery, and other heavy objects. Operators extend and retract horizontally mounted booms and lower and raise hooks attached to load lines. Most operators are guided by other workers using hand signals or a radio. Operators position loads from an onboard console or from a remote console at the site. While crane and tower operators are noticeable at office building and other construction sites, the biggest group works in primary metal, metal fabrication, and transportation equipment manufacturing industries that use heavy, bulky materials. Operators also work at major ports, loading and unloading large containers on and off ships. *Hoist and winch operators* control movement of cables, cages, and platforms to move workers and materials for manufacturing, logging, and other industrial operations. They work in positions such as derrick operators and hydraulic boom operators. Many hoist and winch operators are found in manufacturing or construction industries.

Pump operators tend, control, and operate pump and manifold systems that transfer gases, oil, or other materials to vessels or equipment. They maintain the equipment and regulate the flow of materials according to a schedule set up by petroleum engineers or production supervisors. *Gas compressor and gas pumping station operators* operate steam, gas, electric motor, or internal combustion engine-driven compressors. They transmit, compress, or recover gases, such as butane, nitrogen, hydrogen, and natural gas. *Wellhead pumpers* operate pumps and auxiliary equipment to produce flows of oil or gas from extraction sites.

Tank car, truck, and ship loaders operate ship-loading and -unloading equipment, conveyors, hoists, and other specialized material-handling equipment such as railroad tank car-unloading equipment. They may gauge or sample shipping tanks and test them for leaks. *Conveyor operators and tenders* control and tend conveyor systems that move materials to or from stockpiles, processing stations, departments, or vehicles. *Shuttle car operators* run diesel or electric-powered shuttle cars in underground mines, transporting materials from the working face to mine cars or conveyors.

Laborers and hand freight, stock, and material movers manually move materials and perform other unskilled, general labor. These workers move freight, stock, and other materials to and from storage and production areas, loading docks, delivery vehicles, ships, and containers. Their specific duties vary by industry and work setting. In factories, they may move raw materials or finished goods between loading docks, storage areas, and work areas, as well as sort materials and supplies and prepare them according to their work orders. Specialized workers within this group include baggage and cargo handlers—who work in transportation industries—and truck loaders and unloaders.

Hand packers and packagers manually pack, package, or wrap a variety of materials. They may inspect items for defects, label cartons, stamp information on products, keep records of items packed, and stack packages on loading docks. This group also includes order fillers, who pack materials for shipment, as well as grocery store courtesy clerks. In grocery stores, they may bag groceries, carry packages to customers' cars, and return shopping carts to designated areas.

Machine feeders and offbearers feed materials into or remove materials from equipment or machines tended by other workers.

Cleaners of vehicles and equipment clean machinery, vehicles, storage tanks, pipelines, and similar equipment using water and cleaning agents, vacuums, hoses, brushes, cloths, or other cleaning equipment.

Refuse and recyclable material collectors gather refuse and recyclables from homes and businesses into their trucks for transport to a dump, landfill, or recycling center. They lift and empty garbage cans or recycling bins by hand or, using hydraulic lift trucks, pick up and empty dumpsters. They work along scheduled routes.

Work environment. Material moving work tends to be repetitive and physically demanding. Workers may lift and carry heavy objects and stoop, kneel, crouch, or crawl in awkward positions. Some work at great heights and some work outdoors—regardless of weather and climate. Some jobs expose workers to fumes, odors, loud noises, harmful materials and chemicals, or dangerous machinery. To protect their eyes, respiratory systems, and hearing, these workers wear safety clothing, such as gloves, hardhats, and other safety devices such as respirators. These jobs have become much less dangerous as safety equipment—such as overhead guards on lift trucks—has become common. Accidents usually can be avoided by observing proper operating procedures and safety practices.

Material movers generally work 8-hour shifts—though longer shifts are not uncommon. In industries that work around the clock, material movers may work overnight shifts. Some do this because their employers do not want to disturb customers during normal business hours. Refuse and recyclable material collectors often work shifts starting at 5 or 6 a.m. Some material movers work only during certain seasons, such as when the weather permits construction activity.

Training, Other Qualifications, and Advancement

Many material moving occupations require little or no formal training. Most training for these occupations are done on the job. For those jobs requiring physical exertion, employers may require that applicants pass a physical exam. Some employers also require drug testing or background checks.

Education and training. Material movers generally learn skills informally, on the job, from more experienced workers or their supervisors. Some employers prefer applicants with a high school diploma, but most simply require workers to be at least 18 years old and physically able to perform the work.

Workers who handle toxic chemicals or use industrial trucks or other dangerous equipment must receive specialized training in safety awareness and procedures. Many of the training requirements are standardized through the U.S. Occupational Safety and Health Administration. This training is usually provided by the employer. Employers also must certify that each operator has received the training and evaluate each operator at least once every 3 years.

For other operators, such as crane operators and those working with specialized loads, there are some training and apprenticeship programs available, such as that offered by the International Union of Operating Engineers. Apprenticeships combine paid on-the-job training with classroom instruction.

Licensure. Fifteen States and 6 cities have laws requiring crane operators to be licensed. Licensing requirements typically include a written as well as a skills test to demonstrate that the licensee can operate a crane safely.

Certification and other qualifications. Some types of equipment operators can become certified by professional associations, such as the National Commission for the Certification of Crane Operators, and some employers may require operators to be certified.

Material moving equipment operators need a good sense of balance, the ability to judge distances, and eye-hand-foot coordination. For jobs that involve dealing with the public, such as grocery store courtesy clerks, workers should be pleasant and courteous. Most jobs require basic arithmetic skills and the ability to read procedural manuals, to understand orders, and other billing documents. Mechanical aptitude and training in automobile or diesel mechanics can be helpful because some operators may perform basic maintenance on their equipment. Experience operating mobile equipment—such as tractors on farms or heavy equipment in the Armed Forces—is an asset. As material moving equipment becomes more advanced, workers will need to be increasingly comfortable with technology.

Advancement. In many of these occupations, experience may allow workers to qualify or become trainees for jobs such as construction trades workers; assemblers or other production workers; motor vehicle operators; or vehicle and mobile equipment mechanics, installers, and repairers. In many workplaces new employees gain experience in a material moving position before

Many job openings are expected in material moving occupations.

Projections data from the National Employment Matrix

Occupational Title	SOC Code	Employment, 2006	Projected employment, 2016	Change, 2006-16	
				Number	Percent
Material moving occupations..	53-7000	4,825,000	4,800,000	-25,000	-1
Conveyor operators and tenders..............................	53-7011	50,000	46,000	-3,700	-7
Crane and tower operators	53-7021	46,000	48,000	1,300	3
Dredge, excavating, and loading machine operators	53-7030	85,000	92,000	6,900	8
Dredge operators...	53-7031	2,100	2,300	100	7
Excavating and loading machine and dragline operators..........	53-7032	80,000	87,000	6,700	8
Loading machine operators, underground mining....................	53-7033	3,100	3,200	100	4
Hoist and winch operators	53-7041	3,000	3,000	0	-1
Industrial truck and tractor operators........................	53-7051	637,000	624,000	-13,000	-2
Laborers and material movers, hand............................	53-7060	3,766,000	3,741,000	-25,000	-1
Cleaners of vehicles and equipment...........................	53-7061	368,000	420,000	52,000	14
Laborers and freight, stock, and material movers, hand..........	53-7062	2,416,000	2,466,000	50,000	2
Machine feeders and offbearers	53-7063	148,000	125,000	-22,000	-15
Packers and packagers, hand.................................	53-7064	834,000	730,000	-104,000	-12
Pumping station operators.....................................	53-7070	29,000	25,000	-3,800	-13
Gas compressor and gas pumping station operators................	53-7071	4,200	3,400	-700	-17
Pump operators, except wellhead pumpers............................	53-7072	11,000	9,200	-1,300	-13
Wellhead pumpers..	53-7073	14,000	13,000	-1,700	-12
Refuse and recyclable material collectors.....................................	53-7081	136,000	146,000	10,000	7
Shuttle car operators	53-7111	2,900	2,600	-200	-8
Tank car, truck, and ship loaders..........................	53-7121	16,000	18,000	1,500	9
Material moving workers, all other............................	53-7199	54,000	54,000	400	1

NOTE: Data in this table are rounded. See the discussion of the employment projections table in the *Handbook* introductory chapter on *Occupational Information Included in the Handbook*.

being promoted to a better paying and more highly skilled job. Some may eventually advance to become supervisors.

Employment

Material movers held 4.8 million jobs in 2006. They were distributed among the detailed occupations as follows:

Laborers and freight, stock, and material movers, hand.....2,416,000
Packers and packagers, hand................................834,000
Industrial truck and tractor operators 637,000
Cleaners of vehicles and equipment.........................368,000
Machine feeders and offbearers 148,000
Refuse and recyclable material collectors............................136,000
Excavating and loading machine and dragline operators........80,000
Conveyor operators and tenders................................50,000
Crane and tower operators....................................46,000
Tank car, truck, and ship loaders 16,000
Wellhead pumpers 14,000
Pump operators, except wellhead pumpers...........................11,000
Gas compressor and gas pumping station operators.................4,200
Loading machine operators, underground mining....................3,100
Hoist and winch operators.......................................3,000
Shuttle car operators..2,900
Dredge operators 2,100
Material moving workers, all other.............................54,000

About 29 percent of all material movers worked in the wholesale trade or retail trade industries. Another 21 percent worked in manufacturing; 16 percent in transportation and warehousing; 4 percent in construction and mining; and 14 percent in the employment services industry, on a temporary or contract basis. For example, companies that need workers for only a few days, to move materials or to clean up a site, may contract with temporary help agencies specializing in providing suitable workers on a short-term basis. A small proportion of material movers were self-employed.

Material movers work in every part of the country. Some work in remote locations on large construction projects such as highways and dams, while others work in factories, warehouses, or mining operations.

Job Outlook

Job openings should be numerous because these occupations is very large and turnover is relatively high, even though little or no change in employment is expected because of automation.

Employment change. Employment in material moving occupations is projected to decline by 1 percent between 2006 and 2016, which is considered little or no change in employment. Improvements in equipment, such as automated storage and retrieval systems and conveyors, will continue to raise productivity and moderate the demand for material movers.

Job growth for material movers depends on the growth or decline of employing industries and the type of equipment the workers operate or the materials they handle. Employment will grow in the warehousing and storage industry as more firms contract out their warehousing functions to this industry. For example, a frozen food manufacturer may reduce its costs by outsourcing these functions to a refrigerated warehousing firm, which can more efficiently deal with the specialized storage needs of frozen food. Jobs in mining are expected to decline due to continued productivity increases within that industry. Opportunities for material movers will also decline in manufacturing due to productivity improvements and outsourcing of warehousing and other activities that depend on material movers. Job growth generally will be slower in large establishments, which can afford to invest in automated systems for their material moving needs.

Construction is very sensitive to changes in economic conditions, so the number of job openings in this industry will fluctuate. Although increasing automation will eliminate some routine tasks, new jobs will be created by the need to operate and maintain new equipment. Additionally, firms are more likely initially to use workers when expanding their businesses as opposed to using automated systems due to the large fixed costs associated with such systems.

Job prospects. Despite the little or no employment growth expected, job openings should be plentiful due to the fact that these occupations are very large and there will be a relatively high number of openings created by the need replace workers who transfer to other occupations or who retire or leave the labor force for other reasons—characteristic of occupations requiring little prior or formal training.

Earnings

Median hourly earnings of material moving workers in May 2006 were relatively low, as indicated by the following tabulation:

Gas compressor and gas pumping station operators	$21.83
Pump operators, except wellhead pumpers	19.13
Shuttle car operators	18.78
Crane and tower operators	18.77
Loading machine operators, underground mining	17.91
Wellhead pumpers	17.38
Dredge operators	16.26
Hoist and winch operators	16.16
Excavating and loading machine and dragline operators	15.83
Tank car, truck, and ship loaders	15.37
Refuse and recyclable material collectors	13.93
Industrial truck and tractor operators	13.11
Conveyor operators and tenders	13.09
Machine feeders and offbearers	10.88
Laborers and freight, stock, and material movers, hand	10.20
Cleaners of vehicles and equipment	8.68
Packers and packagers, hand	8.48
Material moving workers, all other	14.55

Wages vary according to experience and job responsibilities. Wages usually are higher in metropolitan areas. Seasonal peaks and lulls in workload can affect the number of hours scheduled which affects earnings. Some crane operators, such as those unloading containers from ships at major ports earn substantially more then their counterparts in other industries or establishments. Certified crane operators tend to have a slightly higher hourly rate than those who are not certified.

Related Occupations

Other workers who operate mechanical equipment include construction equipment operators; machine setters, operators, and tenders—metal and plastic; rail transportation workers; and truck drivers and driver/sales workers. Other entry-level workers who perform mostly physical work include agricultural workers; building cleaning workers; construction laborers; forest, conservation, and logging workers; and grounds maintenance workers.

Sources of Additional Information

For information about job opportunities and training programs, contact local State employment service offices, building or construction contractors, manufacturers, and wholesale and retail establishments.

Information on safety and training requirements is available from:

➤ U.S. Department of Labor, Occupational Safety and Health Administration (OSHA), 200 Constitution Ave., NW., Washington, DC 20210. Internet: **http://www.osha.gov**

Information on training and apprenticeships for industrial truck operators is available from:

➤ International Union of Operating Engineers, 1125 17th St. NW., Washington, D.C. 20036. Internet: **http://www.iuoe.org**

Information on crane and derrick certification and licensure is available from:

➤ National Commission for the Certification of Crane Operators, 2750 Prosperity Ave., Suite 505, Fairfax, VA 22031. Internet: **http://www.nccco.org**

Job Opportunities in the Armed Forces

(O*NET 55-1011.00, 55-1012.00, 55-1013.00, 55-1014.00, 55-1015.00, 55-1016.00, 55-1017.00, 55-1019.99, 55-2011.00, 55-2012.00, 55-2013.00, 55-3011.00, 55-3012.00, 55-3013.00, 55-3014.00, 55-3015.00, 55-3016.00, 55-3017.00, 55-3018.00, 55-3019.99)

Significant Points

- Some training and duty assignments are hazardous, even in peacetime; hours and working conditions can be arduous and vary substantially, and personnel must strictly conform to military rules at all times.

- Enlisted personnel need at least a high school diploma or its equivalent while officers need a bachelor's or graduate degree.

- Opportunities should be excellent in all branches of the Armed Forces for applicants who meet designated standards.

- Military personnel are eligible for retirement after 20 years of service.

Nature of the Work

Maintaining a strong national defense requires workers who can do such diverse tasks as run a hospital, command a tank, program a computer system, operate a nuclear reactor, or repair and maintain a helicopter. The military provides training and work experience in these and many other fields for more than 2.6 million people. More than 1.4 million people serve in the active Army, Navy, Marine Corps, and Air Force, and more than 1.2 million serve in their Reserve components and the Air and Army National Guard. The Coast Guard, which is also discussed in this *Handbook* statement, is part of the Department of Homeland Security.

The military distinguishes between enlisted and officer careers. Enlisted personnel, who make up about 84 percent of the Armed Forces, carry out the fundamental operations of the military in combat, administration, construction, engineering, health care, human services, and other areas. Officers, who make up the remaining 16 percent of the Armed Forces, are the leaders of the military, supervising and managing activities in every occupational specialty.

The sections that follow discuss the major occupational groups for enlisted personnel and officers.

Enlisted occupational groups. *Administrative careers* include a wide variety of positions. The military must keep accurate information for planning and managing its operations. Both paper and electronic records are kept on personnel and on equipment, funds, supplies, and all other aspects of the military. Administrative personnel record information, prepare reports, maintain files, and review information to assist military officers.

Personnel may work in a specialized area such as finance, accounting, legal affairs, maintenance, supply, or transportation.

Combat specialty occupations include enlisted specialties such as infantry, artillery, and Special Forces, whose members operate weapons or execute special missions during combat. People in these occupations normally specialize by type of weapon system or combat operation. These personnel maneuver against enemy forces and position and fire artillery, guns, mortars, and missiles to destroy enemy positions. They also may operate tanks and amphibious assault vehicles in combat or scouting missions. When the military has especially difficult or specialized missions to perform, they call upon Special Forces teams. These elite combat forces maintain a constant state of readiness to strike anywhere in the world on a moment's notice. Team members from the Special Forces conduct offensive raids, demolitions, intelligence, search-and-rescue missions, and other operations from aboard aircraft, helicopters, ships, or submarines.

Construction occupations in the military include personnel who build or repair buildings, airfields, bridges, foundations, dams, bunkers, and the electrical and plumbing components of these structures. Personnel in construction occupations operate bulldozers, cranes, graders, and other heavy equipment. Construction specialists also may work with engineers and other building specialists as part of military construction teams. Some personnel specialize in areas such as plumbing or electrical wiring. Plumbers and pipefitters install and repair the plumbing and pipe systems needed in buildings and on aircraft and ships. Building electricians install and repair electrical-wiring systems in offices, airplane hangars, and other buildings on military bases.

Electronic and electrical equipment repair personnel repair and maintain electronic and electrical equipment used in the military. Repairers normally specialize by type of equipment, such as avionics, computer, optical, communications, or weapons systems. For example, electronic instrument repairers install, test, maintain, and repair a wide variety of electronic systems, including navigational controls and biomedical instruments. Weapons maintenance technicians maintain and repair weapons used by combat forces; most of these weapons have electronic components and systems that assist in locating targets and in aiming and firing the weapon.

Engineering, science, and technical personnel in the military require specific knowledge to operate technical equipment, solve complex problems, or provide and interpret information. Personnel normally specialize in one area, such as space operations, information technology, environmental health and safety, or intelligence. Space operations specialists use and repair ground-control command equipment related to spacecraft, including electronic systems that track the location and operation of a craft. Information technology specialists develop software programs and operate computer systems. Environmental health and safety specialists inspect military facilities and food supplies for the presence of disease, germs, or other conditions hazardous to health and the environment. Intelligence specialists gather and study aerial photographs and various types of radar and surveillance systems to discover information needed by the military.

Health care personnel assist medical professionals in treating and providing services for men and women in the military. They may work as part of a patient-service team in close contact with doctors, dentists, nurses, and physical therapists. Some specialize in emergency medical treatment, the operation of diagnostic tools such as x-ray and ultrasound equipment, laboratory testing of tissue and blood samples, maintaining pharmacy supplies or patients' records, constructing and repairing dental equipment or eyeglasses, or some other health care task.

Human resources development specialists recruit and place qualified personnel and provide training programs. Personnel in this career area normally specialize by activity. For example, recruiting specialists provide information about military careers to young people, parents, schools, and local communities and explain the Armed Service's employment and training opportunities, pay and benefits, and service life. Personnel specialists collect and store information about the people in the military, including information on their previous and current training, job assignments, promotions, and health. Training specialists and instructors teach classes, give demonstrations, and teach military personnel how to perform their jobs.

Machine operator and production personnel operate industrial equipment, machinery, and tools to fabricate and repair parts

for a variety of items and structures. They may operate engines, turbines, nuclear reactors, and water pumps. Often, they specialize by type of work performed. Welders and metalworkers, for instance, work with various types of metals to repair or form the structural parts of ships, submarines, buildings, or other equipment. Survival equipment specialists inspect, maintain, and repair survival equipment such as parachutes and aircraft life support equipment.

Media and public affairs personnel assist with the public presentation and interpretation of military information and events. They take and develop photographs; film, record, and edit audio and video programs; present news and music programs; and produce artwork, drawings, and other visual displays. Other public affairs specialists act as interpreters and translators to convert written or spoken foreign languages into English or other languages.

Protective service personnel include those who enforce military laws and regulations and provide emergency response to natural and human-made disasters. For example, military police control traffic, prevent crime, and respond to emergencies. Other law enforcement and security specialists investigate crimes committed on military property and guard inmates in military correctional facilities. Firefighters put out, control, and help prevent fires in buildings, on aircraft, and aboard ships.

Support service personnel provide subsistence services and support the morale and well-being of military personnel and their families. Food service specialists prepare all types of food in dining halls, hospitals, and ships. Counselors help military personnel and their families deal with personal issues. They work as part of a team that may include social workers, psychologists, medical officers, chaplains, personnel specialists, and commanders. Religious program specialists assist chaplains with religious services, religious education programs, and related administrative duties.

Transportation and material handling specialists ensure the safe transport of people and cargo. Most personnel within this occupational group are classified according to mode of transportation, such as aircraft, motor vehicle, or ship. Aircrew members operate equipment on aircraft. Vehicle drivers operate all types of heavy military vehicles, including fuel or water tank trucks, semi-trailers, heavy troop transports, and passenger buses. Quartermasters and boat operators navigate and pilot many types of small watercraft, including tugboats, gunboats, and barges. Cargo specialists load and unload military supplies, using equipment such as forklifts and cranes.

Vehicle and machinery mechanics conduct preventive and corrective maintenance on aircraft, automotive and heavy equipment, heating and cooling systems, marine engines, and powerhouse station equipment. These workers typically specialize by the type of equipment that they maintain. For example, aircraft mechanics inspect, service, and repair helicopters, airplanes, and drones. Automotive and heavy equipment mechanics maintain and repair vehicles such as humvees, trucks, tanks, self-propelled missile launchers, and other combat vehicles. They also repair bulldozers, power shovels, and other construction equipment. Heating and cooling mechanics install and repair air-conditioning, refrigeration, and heating equipment. Marine

Many Marines are in combat specialty occupations.

engine mechanics repair and maintain gasoline and diesel engines on ships, boats, and other watercraft. They also repair shipboard mechanical and electrical equipment. Powerhouse mechanics install, maintain, and repair electrical and mechanical equipment in power-generating stations.

Officer occupational groups. *Combat specialty officers* plan and direct military operations, oversee combat activities, and serve as combat leaders. This category includes officers in charge of tanks and other armored assault vehicles, artillery systems, Special Forces, and infantry. Combat specialty officers normally specialize by the type of unit that they lead. Within the unit, they may specialize by type of weapon system. Artillery and missile system officers, for example, direct personnel as they target, launch, test, and maintain various types of missiles and artillery. Special operations officers lead their units in offensive raids, demolitions, intelligence gathering, and search-and-rescue missions.

Engineering, science, and technical officers have a wide range of responsibilities based on their area of expertise. They lead or perform activities in areas such as space operations, environmental health and safety, and engineering. These officers may direct the operations of communications centers or the development of complex computer systems. Environmental health and safety officers study the air, ground, and water to identify and analyze sources of pollution and its effects. They also direct programs to control safety and health hazards in the workplace. Other personnel work as aerospace engineers to design and direct the development of military aircraft, missiles, and spacecraft.

Executive, administrative, and managerial officers oversee and direct military activities in key functional areas such as finance, accounting, health administration, international relations, and supply. Health services administrators, for instance, are responsible for the overall quality of care provided at the hospitals and clinics they operate. They must ensure that each department works together. As another example, purchasing and contracting managers negotiate and monitor contracts for the purchase of the billions of dollars worth of equipment, supplies, and services that the military buys from private industry each year.

Health care officers provide health services at military facilities, on the basis of their area of specialization. Officers who examine, diagnose, and treat patients with illness, injury, or disease include physicians, registered nurses, and dentists. Other health care officers provide therapy, rehabilitative treatment, and additional services for patients. Physical and occupational therapists plan and administer therapy to help patients adjust to disabilities, regain independence, and return to work. Speech therapists evaluate and treat patients with hearing and speech problems. Dietitians manage food service facilities and plan meals for hospital patients and for outpatients who need special diets. Pharmacists manage the purchase, storage, and dispensing of drugs and medicines. Physicians and surgeons in this occupational group provide the majority of medical services to the military and their families. Dentists treat diseases, disorders, and injuries of the mouth. Optometrists treat vision problems by prescribing eyeglasses or contact lenses. Psychologists pro-

vide mental health care and also conduct research on behavior and emotions.

Human resource development officers manage recruitment, placement, and training strategies and programs in the military. Recruiting managers direct recruiting efforts and provide information about military careers to young people, parents, schools, and local communities. Personnel managers direct military personnel functions such as job assignment, staff promotion, and career counseling. Training and education directors identify training needs and develop and manage educational programs designed to keep military personnel current in the skills they need.

Media and public affairs officers oversee the development, production, and presentation of information or events for the public. These officers may produce and direct motion pictures, videos, and television and radio broadcasts that are used for training, news, and entertainment. Some plan, develop, and direct the activities of military bands. Public information officers respond to inquiries about military activities and prepare news releases and reports to keep the public informed.

Protective service officers are responsible for the safety and protection of individuals and property on military bases and vessels. Emergency management officers plan and prepare for all types of natural and human-made disasters. They develop warning, control, and evacuation plans to be used in the event of a disaster. Law enforcement and security officers enforce all applicable laws on military bases and investigate crimes when the law has been broken.

Support services officers manage food service activities and perform services in support of the morale and well-being of military personnel and their families. Food services managers oversee the preparation and delivery of food services within dining facilities located on military installations and vessels. Social workers focus on improving conditions that cause social problems such as drug and alcohol abuse, racism, and sexism.

A sailor in the Navy updates a status board on a ship.

Chaplains conduct worship services for military personnel and perform other spiritual duties according to the beliefs and practices of all religious faiths.

Transportation officers manage and perform activities related to the safe transport of military personnel and material by air and water. These officers normally specialize by mode of transportation or area of expertise because, in many cases, they must meet licensing and certification requirements. Pilots in the military fly various types of specialized airplanes and helicopters to carry troops and equipment and to execute combat missions. Navigators use radar, radio, and other navigation equipment to determine their position and plan their route of travel. Officers on ships and submarines work as a team to manage the various departments aboard their vessels. Ship engineers direct engineering departments aboard ships and submarines, including engine operations, maintenance, repair, heating, and power generation.

Work environment. Most military personnel live and work on or near military bases and facilities throughout the United States and the world. These bases and facilities usually offer comfortable housing and amenities, such as stores and recreation centers. Service members move regularly to complete their training or to meet the needs of their branch of service. Some are deployed to defend national interests. Military personnel must be physically fit, mentally stable, and ready to participate in or support combat missions that maybe difficult and dangerous and involve time away from family. Some, however, are never deployed near combat areas. Specific work environments and conditions depend on branch of service, occupational specialty, and other factors.

In many circumstances, military personnel work standard hours, but personnel must be prepared to work long hours to fulfill missions, and they must conform to strict military rules at all times. Work hours depend on occupational specialty and mission.

Training, Other Qualifications, and Advancement

To join the military, people must meet age, educational, aptitude, physical, and character requirements. These requirements vary by branch of service and vary between officers, who usually have a college degree, and enlisted personnel, who often do not. People are assigned an occupational specialty based on their aptitude, former training, and the needs of the military. All service members must sign a contract and commit to a minimum term of service. After joining the military, all receive general and occupation-specific training.

People thinking about enlisting in the military should learn as much as they can about military life before making a decision. Doing so is especially important if you are thinking about making the military a career. Speaking to friends and relatives with military experience is a good idea. Find out what the military can offer you and what it will expect in return. Then, talk to a recruiter, who can determine whether you qualify for enlistment, explain the various enlistment options, and tell you which military occupational specialties currently have openings. Bear in mind that the recruiter's job is to recruit promising applicants into his or her branch of military service, so the information that

Some Army personnel are construction specialists.

the recruiter gives you is likely to stress the positive aspects of military life in the branch in which he or she serves.

Ask the recruiter for the branch you have chosen to assess your chances of being accepted for training in the occupation of your choice, or, better still, take the aptitude exam to see how well you score. The military uses this exam as a placement exam, and test scores largely determine an individual's chances of being accepted into a particular training program. Selection for a particular type of training depends on the needs of the service, your general and technical aptitudes, and your personal preference. Because all prospective recruits are required to take the exam, those who do so before committing themselves to enlist have the advantage of knowing in advance whether they stand a good chance of being accepted for training in a particular specialty. The recruiter can schedule you for the Armed Services Vocational Aptitude Battery without any obligation. Many high schools offer the exam as an easy way for students to explore the possibility of a military career, and the test also affords an insight into career areas in which the student has demonstrated aptitudes and interests. The exam is not part of the process of joining the military as an officer.

If you decide to join the military, the next step is to pass the physical examination and sign an enlistment contract. Negotiating the contract involves choosing, qualifying for, and agreeing on a number of enlistment options, such as the length of active-duty time, which may vary according to the option. Most active-duty programs have first-term enlistments of 4 years, although there are some 2-year, 3-year, and 6-year programs. The contract also will state the date of enlistment and other options—for example, bonuses and the types of training to be received. If the service is unable to fulfill any of its obligations under the contract, such as providing a certain kind of training, the contract may become null and void.

All branches of the Armed Services offer a delayed entry program (DEP) by which an individual can delay entry into active

Table 1. Military rank and employment for active duty personnel, January 2007

Grade	Rank and title				
	Army	Navy	Air Force	Marine Corps	Total Employment
Commissioned officers:					
O-10	General	Admiral	General	General	40
O-9	Lieutenant General	Vice Admiral	Lieutenant General	Lieutenant General	136
O-8	Major General	Rear Admiral (U)	Major General	Major General	285
O-7	Brigadier General	Rear Admiral (L)	Brigadier General	Brigadier General	449
O-6	Colonel	Captain	Colonel	Colonel	11,345
O-5	Lieutenant Colonel	Commander	Lieutenant Colonel	Lieutenant Colonel	28,566
O-4	Major	Lieutenant Commander	Major	Major	44,908
O-3	Captain	Lieutenant	Captain	Captain	70,131
O-2	1st Lieutenant	Lieutenant (JG)	1st Lieutenant	1st Lieutenant	26,894
O-1	2nd Lieutenant	Ensign	2nd Lieutenant	2nd Lieutenant	23,331
Warrant officers:					
W-5	Chief Warrant Officer	Chief Warrant Officer	—	Chief Warrant Officer	591
W-4	Chief Warrant Officer	Chief Warrant Officer	—	Chief Warrant Officer	2,661
W-3	Chief Warrant Officer	Chief Warrant Officer	—	Chief Warrant Officer	4,676
W-2	Chief Warrant Officer	Chief Warrant Officer	—	Chief Warrant Officer	5,627
W-1	Warrant Officer	Warrant Officer	—	Warrant Officer	3,084
Enlisted personnel:					
E-9	Sergeant Major	Master Chief Petty Officer	Chief Master Sergeant	Sergeant Major/ Master Gunnery Sergeant	10,596
E-8	1st Sergeant/Master Sergeant	Senior Chief Petty Officer	Senior Master Sergeant	1st Sergeant/Master Sergeant	26,987
E-7	Sergeant First Class	Chief Petty Officer	Master Sergeant	Gunnery Sergeant	98,497
E-6	Staff Sergeant	Petty Officer 1st Class	Technical Sergeant	Staff Sergeant	169,725
E-5	Sergeant	Petty Officer 2nd Class	Staff Sergeant	Sergeant	248,226
E-4	Corporal	Petty Officer 3rd Class	Senior Airman	Corporal	257,974
E-3	Private First Class	Seaman	Airman 1st Class	Lance Corporal	186,830
E-2	Private	Seaman Apprentice	Airman	Private 1st Class	83,987
E-1	Private	Seaman Recruit	Airman Basic	Private	57,644

SOURCE: U.S. Department of Defense, Defense Manpower Data Center

duty for up to 1 year after enlisting. High school students can enlist during their senior year and enter a service after graduation. Others choose this program because the job training they desire is not currently available, but will be within the coming year, or because they need time to arrange their personal affairs.

The process of joining the military as an officer is different. Officers must meet educational, physical, and character requirements, but they do not take an aptitude test, for example. The education and training section that follows includes more information.

Education and training. All branches of the Armed Forces usually require their members to be high school graduates or have equivalent credentials, such as a GED. In 2006, more than 98 percent of recruits were high school graduates. Officers usually need a bachelor's or graduate degree. Training varies for enlisted and officer personnel and varies by occupational specialty.

Enlisted personnel training. Following enlistment, new members of the Armed Forces undergo initial-entry training, better known as "basic training" or "boot camp." Through courses in military skills and protocol recruit training provides a 6- to 13-week introduction to military life. Days and nights are carefully structured and include rigorous physical exercise designed to improve strength and endurance and build each unit's cohesion.

Following basic training, most recruits take additional training at technical schools that prepare them for a particular military occupational specialty. The formal training period generally lasts from 10 to 20 weeks, although training for certain occupations—nuclear power plant operator, for example—may take as long as a year. Recruits not assigned to classroom instruction receive on-the-job training at their first duty assignment.

Many service people get college credit for the technical training they receive on duty, which, combined with off-duty courses, can lead to an associate degree through programs in community colleges such as the Community College of the Air Force. In addition to on-duty training, military personnel may choose from a variety of educational programs. Most military installations have tuition assistance programs for people wishing to take courses during off-duty hours. The courses may be correspondence courses or courses in degree programs offered by local colleges or universities. Tuition assistance pays up to 100 percent of college costs up to a credit-hour and annual limit. Each branch of the service provides opportunities for full-time study to a limited number of exceptional applicants. Military personnel accepted into these highly competitive programs receive full pay, allowances, tuition, and related fees. In return, they must agree to serve an additional amount of time in the service. Other highly selective programs enable enlisted personnel to qualify as commissioned officers through additional military training.

Warrant officer training. Warrant officers are technical and tactical leaders who specialize in a specific technical area; for example, Army aviators make up one group of warrant officers. The Army Warrant Officer Corps constitutes less than 5 percent of the total Army. Although the Corps is small in size, its level of responsibility is high. Its members receive extended career opportunities, worldwide leadership assignments, and increased pay and retirement benefits. Selection to attend the Warrant Officer Candidate School is highly competitive and restricted to those who meet rank and length-of-service requirements. The only exception is the Army aviator warrant officer, which has no prior military service requirements.

Officer training. Officer training in the Armed Forces is provided through the Federal service academies (Military, Naval, Air Force, and Coast Guard); the Reserve Officers Training Corps (ROTC) program offered at many colleges and universities; Officer Candidate School (OCS) or Officer Training School (OTS); the National Guard (State Officer Candidate School programs); the Uniformed Services University of Health Sciences; and other programs. All are highly selective and are good options for those wishing to make the military a career. Some are directly appointed. People interested in obtaining training through the Federal service academies must be unmarried and without dependants to enter and graduate, while those seeking training through OCS, OTS, or ROTC need not be single.

Federal service academies provide a 4-year college program leading to a Bachelor of Science (B.S.) degree. Midshipmen or cadets are provided free room and board, tuition, medical and dental care, and a monthly allowance. Graduates receive regular or reserve commissions and have a 5-year active-duty obligation or more if they are entering flight training.

To become a candidate for appointment as a cadet or midshipman in one of the service academies, applicants are required to obtain a nomination from an authorized source, usually a member of Congress. Candidates do not need to know a member of Congress personally to request a nomination. Nominees must have an academic record of the requisite quality, college apti-

tude test scores above an established minimum, and recommendations from teachers or school officials; they also must pass a medical examination. Appointments are made from the list of eligible nominees. Appointments to the Coast Guard Academy, however, are based strictly on merit and do not require a nomination.

ROTC programs train students in 273 Army, 130 Navy and Marine Corps, and 144 Air Force units at participating colleges and universities. Trainees take 3 to 5 hours of military instruction a week, in addition to regular college courses. After graduation, they may serve as officers on active duty for a stipulated period. Some may serve their obligation in the Reserves or National Guard. In the last 2 years of an ROTC program, students typically receive a monthly allowance while attending school, as well as additional pay for summer training. ROTC scholarships for 2, 3, and 4 years are available on a competitive basis. All scholarships pay for tuition and have allowances for textbooks, supplies, and other costs.

College graduates can earn a commission in the Armed Forces through OCS or OTS programs in the Army, Navy, Air Force, Marine Corps, Coast Guard, and National Guard. These programs consist of several weeks of intensive academic, physical, and leadership training. These officers generally must serve their obligation on active duty.

Those with training in certain health professions may qualify for direct appointment as officers. In the case of people studying for the health professions, financial assistance and internship opportunities are available from the military in return for specified periods of military service. Prospective medical students can apply to the Uniformed Services University of Health Sciences, which offers a salary and free tuition in a program leading to a Doctor of Medicine (M.D.) degree. In return, graduates must serve for 7 years in either the military or the Public Health Service. Direct appointments also are available for those qualified to serve in other specialty areas, such as the judge advocate general (legal) or chaplain corps. Flight training is available to commissioned officers in each branch of the Armed Forces. In addition, the Army has a direct enlistment option to become a warrant officer aviator.

Table 2. Military enlisted personnel by broad occupational category and branch of military service, January 2007

Occupational Group - Enlisted	Army	Air Force	Coast Guard	Marine Corps	Navy	Total, all services
Administrative occupations	8,912	23,366	1,683	9,460	22,512	65,933
Combat specialty occupations	120,297	427	856	47,250	5,508	174,338
Construction occupations	16,848	4,979	—	5,597	5,927	33,351
Electronic and electrical repair occupations	35,932	37,722	4,351	14,656	51,424	144,085
Engineering, science, and technical occupations	36,451	46,304	1,110	22,915	38,853	145,633
Health care occupations	29,242	16,805	821	—	24,950	71,818
Human resource development occupations	16,464	12,741	1	6,113	6,756	42,075
Machine operator and precision work occupations	5,727	7,134	1,583	2,301	7,913	24,658
Media and public affairs occupations	6,541	7,574	136	2,340	4,726	21,317
Protective service occupations	25,455	31,483	3,050	5,872	13,122	78,982
Support services occupations	12,014	1,608	1,268	2,289	9,930	27,109
Transportation and material handling occupations	58,237	32,464	11,479	22,344	43,026	167,550
Vehicle machinery mechanic occupations	49,679	44,025	5,821	19,340	49,166	168,031
Total, by service (1)	421,855	271,009	32,477	160,484	287,118	1,172,913

(1) Occupational employment does not sum to totals because occupational information is not available for all personnel.

SOURCE: U.S. Department of Defense, Defense Manpower Data Center

Table 3. Military officer personnel by broad occupational category and branch of service, January 2007

Occupational Group - Officer	Army	Air Force	Coast Guard	Marine Corps	Navy	Total, all services
Combat specialty occupations	19,421	2,861	81	4,684	1,260	28,307
Engineering, science, and technical occupations	20,189	19,852	1,057	3,639	7,873	52,610
Executive, administrative, and managerial occupations	11,262	9,013	231	2,572	5,437	28,515
Health care occupations	9,953	8,970	5	—	7,737	26,665
Human resource development occupations	2,151	2,275	184	293	643	5,546
Media and public affairs occupations	237	408	19	170	265	1,099
Protective service occupations	2,611	1,229	96	327	275	4,538
Support services occupations	1,596	768	—	38	884	3,286
Transportation occupations	13,112	23,540	1,736	7,188	27,049	72,625
Total, by service (1)	82,884	69,284	7,853	18,998	51,558	230,577

(1) Occupational employment does not sum to totals because occupational information is not available for all personnel.
SOURCE: U.S. Department of Defense, Defense Manpower Data Center

Other qualifications. In order to join the services, enlisted personnel must sign a legal agreement called an enlistment contract, which usually involves a commitment of up to 8 years of service. Depending on the terms of the contract, 2 to 6 years are spent on active duty, and the balance is spent in the National Guard or Reserves. The enlistment contract obligates the service to provide the agreed-upon job, rating, pay, cash bonuses for enlistment in certain occupations, medical and other benefits, occupational training, and continuing education. In return, enlisted personnel must serve satisfactorily for the period specified.

Requirements for each service vary, but certain qualifications for enlistment are common to all branches. In order to enlist, usually one must be at least 17 years old, be a U.S. citizen or an alien holding permanent resident status, not have a felony record, and possess a birth certificate. Applicants who are 17 years old must have the consent of a parent or legal guardian before entering the service. For active service in the Army, the maximum age is 42; for the Navy and Air Force the maximum age is 35. Coast Guard enlisted personnel must enter active duty before their 28th birthday, whereas Marine Corps enlisted personnel must not be over the age of 29 when entering. Applicants must pass a written examination—the Armed Services Vocational Aptitude Battery—and meet certain minimum physical standards, such as height, weight, vision, and overall health. Officers must meet different age and physical standards depending on their branch of service.

Women are eligible to enter most military specialties; for example, they may become mechanics, missile maintenance technicians, heavy equipment operators, and fighter pilots, or they may enter into medical care, administrative support, and intelligence specialties. Generally, only occupations involving direct exposure to combat are excluded.

Advancement. Each service has different criteria for promoting personnel. Generally, the first few promotions for both enlisted and officer personnel come easily; subsequent promotions are much more competitive. Criteria for promotion may include time in service and in grade, job performance, a fitness report (supervisor's recommendation), and passing scores on written examinations. Table 1 shows the officer, warrant officer, and enlisted ranks by service.

People planning to apply the skills gained through military training to a civilian career should first determine how good the prospects are for civilian employment in jobs related to the military specialty that interests them. Second, they should know the prerequisites for the related civilian job. Because many civilian occupations require a license, certification, or minimum level of education, it is important to determine whether military training is sufficient for a person to enter the civilian equivalent occupation or, if not, what additional training will be required. Other *Handbook* statements discuss the job outlook, training requirements, and other aspects of civilian occupations for which military training and experience are helpful. Additional information often can be obtained from school counselors.

Employment

In 2007, more than 2.6 million people served in the Armed Forces. More than 1.4 million were on active duty—about 505,000 in the Army, 339,000 in the Navy, 340,000 in the Air Force, and 179,000 in the Marine Corps. In addition, more than 1.2 million people served in their Reserve components and the Air and Army National Guard, and 40,000 individuals served in the Coast Guard, which is now part of the Department of Homeland Security. Table 2 shows the occupational composition of the active-duty enlisted personnel in January 2007; table 3 presents similar information for active-duty officers, including noncommissioned warrant officers.

The Air Force's fleet of planes need regular maintenance to ensure readiness.

Military personnel are stationed throughout the United States and in many countries around the world. About half of all military jobs in the U.S. are located in California, Texas, North Carolina, Virginia, Florida, and Georgia. Approximately 250,000 service members were deployed in support of Operations Enduring Freedom and Iraqi Freedom as of April 30, 2007. An additional 363,000 individuals were stationed outside the United States, including 168,000 assigned to ships at sea. About 105,000 were stationed in Europe, mainly in Germany, and another 70,000 were assigned to East Asia and the Pacific area, mostly in Japan and the Republic of Korea.

Job Outlook

Opportunities should be excellent for qualified individuals in all branches of the Armed Forces through 2016.

Employment change. The United States spends a significant portion of its overall budget on national defense. Despite reductions in personnel due to the elimination of the threats of the Cold War, the number of active-duty personnel is expected to remain roughly constant through 2016. However, recent conflicts and the resulting strain on the military may lead to an increase in the number of active-duty personnel. The current goal of the Armed Forces is to maintain a force sufficient to fight and win two major regional conflicts at the same time. Political events, however, could lead to a significant restructuring with or without an increase in size.

Job prospects. Opportunities should be excellent for qualified individuals in all branches of the Armed Forces through 2016. Many military personnel retire with a pension after 20 years of service, while they still are young enough to start a new career. About 168,000 personnel must be recruited each year to replace those who complete their commitment or retire. Since the end of the draft in 1973, the military has met its personnel requirements with volunteers. When the economy is good and civilian employment opportunities generally are more favorable, it is more difficult for all the services to meet their recruitment quotas. It is also more difficult to meet these goals during times of war, when recruitment goals typically rise.

Educational requirements will continue to rise as military jobs become more technical and complex. High school graduates and applicants with a college background will be sought to fill the ranks of enlisted personnel, while virtually all officers will need at least a bachelor's degree and, in some cases, a graduate degree as well.

Earnings

The earnings structure for military personnel is shown in table 4. Most enlisted personnel started as recruits at Grade E-1 in 2007; however, those with special skills or above-average education started as high as Grade E-4. Most warrant officers had started at Grade W-1 or W-2, depending upon their occupational and academic qualifications and the branch of service of which they were a member, but warrant officer typically is not an entry-level occupation and, consequently, most of these individuals had previous military service. Most commissioned officers started at Grade O-1; some with advanced education started at Grade O-2, and some highly trained officers—for example, physicians and dentists—started as high as Grade O-3. Pay varies by total years of service as well as rank. Because it usually takes many years to reach the higher ranks, most personnel in

Table 4. Military basic monthly pay by grade for active duty personnel, April 2007

Years of service						
Grade	Less than 2	Over 4	Over 8	Over 12	Over 16	Over 20
O-10	—	—	—	—	—	$13,659.00
O-9	—	—	—	—	—	11,946.60
O-8	$8,453.10	$8,964.90	$9,577.20	$10,030.20	$10,447.80	11,319.00
O-7	7,023.90	7,621.20	8,052.90	8,548.80	9,577.20	10,236.00
O-6	5,206.20	6,094.50	6,380.10	6,414.60	7,423.80	8,180.10
O-5	4,339.80	5,291.10	5,628.60	6,110.10	6,776.40	7,158.00
O-4	3,744.60	4,688.40	5,244.60	5,882.40	6,187.50	6,252.30
O-3	3,292.20	4,392.00	4,833.00	5,228.40	5,355.90	5,355.90
O-2	2,844.30	3,857.40	3,936.60	3,936.60	3,936.60	3,936.60
O-1	2,469.30	3,106.50	3,106.50	3,106.50	3,106.50	3,106.50
W-5	—	—	—	—	—	5,845.80
W-4	3,402.00	3,868.50	4,222.20	4,574.10	5,035.50	5,392.20
W-3	3,106.80	3,412.80	3,711.30	4,129.20	4,515.60	4,751.40
W-2	2,732.70	3,124.50	3,443.70	3,755.10	3,973.80	4,191.00
W-1	2,413.20	2,828.40	3,193.50	3,451.20	3,622.80	3,856.20
E-9	—	—	—	4,203.90	4,459.50	4.821.60
E-8	—	—	3,364.80	3,606.00	3,835.80	4,161.30
E-7	2,339.10	2,780.70	3,055.20	3,250.20	3,511.20	3,644.10
E-6	2,023.20	2,419.80	2,744.10	2,928.30	3,043.50	3,064.50
E-5	1,854.00	2,171.40	2,454.90	2,582.10	2,582.10	2,582.10
E-4	1,699.50	1,978.50	2,062.80	2,062.80	2,062.80	2,062.80
E-3	1,534.20	1,729.20	1,729.20	1,729.20	1,729.20	1,729.20
E-2	1,458.90	1,458.90	1,458.90	1,458.90	1,458.90	1,458.90
E-1 4 months of more	1,301.40	1,301.40	1,301.40	1,301.40	1,301.40	1,301.40
E-1 Less than 4 months	1,203.90	—	—	—	—	—

SOURCE: U.S. Department of Defense—Defense Finance and Accounting Service

higher ranks receive the higher pay rates awarded to those with many years of service.

In addition to receiving their basic pay, military personnel are provided with free room and board (or a tax-free housing and subsistence allowance), free medical and dental care, a military clothing allowance, military supermarket and department store shopping privileges, 30 days of paid vacation a year (referred to as leave), and travel opportunities. In many duty stations, military personnel may receive a housing allowance that can be used for off-base housing. This allowance can be substantial, but varies greatly by rank and duty station. For example, in fiscal year 2007, the average housing allowance for an E-4 with dependents was $1,151.24 per month; for a comparable individual without dependents, it was $910.66. The allowance for an O-4 with dependents was $1,856.97 per month; for a comparable individual without dependents, it was $1,611.69. Other allowances are paid for foreign duty, hazardous duty, submarine and flight duty, and employment as a medical officer. Athletic and other facilities—such as gymnasiums, tennis courts, golf courses, bowling centers, libraries, and movie theaters—are available on many military installations. Military personnel are eligible for retirement benefits after 20 years of service.

The Veterans Administration (VA) provides numerous benefits to those who have served at least 24 months of continuous active duty in the Armed Forces. Veterans are eligible for free care in VA hospitals for all service-related disabilities, regardless of time served; those with other medical problems are eligible for free VA care if they are unable to pay the cost of hospitalization elsewhere. Admission to a VA medical center depends on the availability of beds, however. Veterans also are eligible for certain loans, including loans to purchase a home. Veterans, regardless of health, can convert a military life insurance policy to an individual policy with any participating company upon separation from the military. In addition, job counseling, testing, and placement services are available.

Veterans who participate in the Montgomery GI Bill Program receive education benefits. Under this program, Armed Forces personnel may elect to deduct up to $100 a month from their pay during the first 12 months of active duty, putting the money toward their future education. In fiscal year 2007, veterans who served on active duty for 3 or more years or who spent 2 years in active duty plus 4 years in the Selected Reserve received $1,075 a month in basic benefits for 36 months of full-time institutional training. Those who enlisted and serve less than 3 years received $873 a month for 36 months for the same. In addition, each service provides its own contributions to the enlistee's future education. The sum of the amounts from all these sources becomes the service member's educational fund. Upon separation from active duty, the fund can be used to finance educational costs at any VA-approved institution. Among those institutions which are approved by the VA are many vocational, correspondence, certification, business, technical, and flight training schools; community and junior colleges; and colleges and universities.

The Coast Guard patrols U.S. waterways and helps those in distress.

Sources of Additional Information

Each of the military services publishes handbooks, fact sheets, and pamphlets describing entrance requirements, training and advancement opportunities, and other aspects of military careers. These publications are widely available at all recruiting stations, at most State employment service offices, and in high schools, colleges, and public libraries. Information on educational and other veterans' benefits is available from VA offices located throughout the country.

In addition, the Defense Manpower Data Center, an agency of the Department of Defense, publishes *Military Career Guide Online*, a compendium of military occupational, training, and career information designed for use by students and jobseekers. This information is available on the Internet:

http://www.todaysmilitary.com

The *Occupational Outlook Quarterly* also provides information about military careers and training in its spring 2007 article "Military training for civilian careers (Or: How to gain practical experience while serving your country)," available online at:

http://www.bls.gov/opub/ooq/2007/spring/art02.pdf

Data for Occupations Not Studied in Detail

Employment in the hundreds of occupations covered in detail in the main body of the *Handbook* accounts for more than 133 million or 89 percent of all jobs in the economy. Although occupations covering the full spectrum of work are included, those requiring lengthy education or training generally are given the most attention.

This chapter presents summary data on 128 additional occupations, for which employment projections are prepared, but for which detailed occupational information is not developed. These occupations account for about 7 percent of all jobs. For each occupation, the *Occupational Information Network* (O*NET) code, a brief description of the nature of the work, the number of jobs in 2006, a phrase describing the projected employment change from 2006 to 2016, and the most significant source of postsecondary education or training are presented. For a complete list of O*NET codes cited in the *Handbook*, refer to a later chapter, *Occupational Information Network Coverage*. For guidelines on interpreting the description of projected employment change, refer to a chapter in the front of the *Handbook*, Occupational Information Included in the *Handbook*.

The approximately 4 percent of all jobs not covered either in the detailed occupational descriptions in the main body of the *Handbook* or in the summary data presented in this chapter are mainly residual categories, such as "all other managers," for which little meaningful information could be developed.

Management, business, and financial occupations

Agents and business managers of artists, performers, and athletes

(O*NET 13-1011.00)

Represent and promote artists, performers, and athletes to prospective employers. May handle contract negotiations and other business matters for clients.

> 2006 Employment: 25,000
> Projected 2006-16 employment change: About as fast as average
> Most significant source of postsecondary education or training: Bachelor's or higher degree, plus work experience

Compliance officers, except agriculture, construction, health and safety, and transportation

(O*NET 13-1041.01, 13-1041.02, 13-1041.03, 13-1041.04, 13-1041.06)

Examine, evaluate, and investigate eligibility for or conformity with laws and regulations governing contract compliance of licenses and permits, and other compliance and enforcement inspection activities not classified elsewhere. Exclude tax examiners, collectors, and revenue agents and financial examiners.

> 2006 Employment: 237,000
> Projected 2006-16 employment change: More slowly than average
> Most significant source of postsecondary education or training: Long-term on-the-job training

Credit analysts

(O*NET 13-2041.00)

Analyze current credit data and financial statements of individuals or firms to determine the degree of risk involved in extending credit or lending money. Prepare reports with this credit information for use in decisionmaking.

> 2006 Employment: 67,000
> Projected 2006-16 employment change: Little or no change
> Most significant source of postsecondary education or training: Bachelor's degree

Emergency management specialists

(O*NET 13-1061.00)

Coordinate disaster response or crisis management activities, provide disaster preparedness training, and prepare emergency plans and procedures for natural (e.g. hurricanes, floods, earthquakes), wartime, or technological (e.g., nuclear power plant emergencies, hazardous materials spills) disasters or hostage situations.

> 2006 Employment: 12,000
> Projected 2006-16 employment change: About as fast as average
> Most significant source of postsecondary education or training: Work experience in a related occupation

Financial examiners

(O*NET 13-2061.00)

Enforce or ensure compliance with laws and regulations governing financial and securities institutions and financial and real estate transactions. May examine, verify correctness of, or establish authenticity of records.

> 2006 Employment: 26,000
> Projected 2006-16 employment change: About as fast as average
> Most significant source of postsecondary education or training: Bachelor's degree

Legislators

(O*NET 11-1031.00)

Develop laws and statutes at the Federal, State, or local level. Includes only elected officials.

> 2006 Employment: 65,000
> Projected 2006-16 employment change: Little or no change
> Most significant source of postsecondary education or training: Bachelor's or higher degree, plus work experience

Loan counselors

(O*NET 13-2071.00)

Provide guidance to prospective loan applicants who have problems qualifying for traditional loans. Guidance may include determining the best type of loan and explaining loan requirements or restrictions.

2006 Employment: 33,000
Projected 2006-16 employment change: More slowly than average
Most significant source of postsecondary education or training:
  Bachelor's degree

Logisticians

(O*NET 13-1081.00)

Analyze and coordinate the logistical functions of a firm or organization. Responsible for the entire life cycle of a product, including acquisition, distribution, internal allocation, delivery, and final disposal of resources.

2006 Employment: 83,000
Projected 2006-16 employment change: Faster than average
Most significant source of postsecondary education or training:
  Bachelor's degree

Postmasters and mail superintendents

(O*NET 11-9131.00)

Direct and coordinate operational, administrative, management, and supportive services of a U.S. post office; or coordinate activities of workers engaged in postal and related work in assigned post office.

2006 Employment: 26,000
Projected 2006-16 employment change: Little or no change
Most significant source of postsecondary education or training:
  Work experience in a related occupation

Social and community service managers

(O*NET 11-9151.00)

Plan, organize, or coordinate the activities of a social service program or community outreach organization. Oversee the program or organization's budget and polices regarding participant involvement, program requirement, and benefits. Work may involve directing social workers, counselors, or probation officers.

2006 Employment: 130,000
Projected 2006-16 employment change: Much faster than average
Most significant source of postsecondary education or training:
  Bachelor's degree

Tax preparers

(O*NET 13-2082.00)

Prepare tax returns for individuals or small businesses but do not have the background or responsibilities of an accredited or certified public accountant.

2006 Employment: 100,000
Projected 2006-16 employment change: Decline slowly
Most significant source of postsecondary education or training:
  Moderate-term on-the-job training

Transportation, storage, and distribution managers

(O*NET 11-3071.01, 11-3071.02)

Plan, direct, or coordinate transportation, storage, or distribution activities in accordance with governmental policies and regulations. Includes logistics managers.

2006 Employment: 94,000

Projected 2006-16 employment change: About as fast as average
Most significant source of postsecondary education or training:
  Work experience in a related occupation

Professional and related occupations

Audio-visual collections specialists

(O*NET 25-9011.00)

Prepare, plan, and operate audio-visual teaching aids for use in education. May record, catalogue, and file audio-visual materials.

2006 Employment: 7,300
Projected 2006-16 employment change: Decline rapidly
Most significant source of postsecondary education or training:
  Bachelor's degree

Clergy

(O*NET 21-2011.00)

Conduct religious worship and perform other spiritual functions associated with beliefs and practices of religious faith or denomination.

Provide spiritual and moral guidance and assistance to members.

2006 Employment: 404,000
Projected 2006-16 employment change: Faster than average
Most significant source of postsecondary education or training:
  Master's degree

Dietetic technicians

(O*NET 29-2051.00)

Assist dieticians in the provision of food service and nutritional programs. Under the supervision of dieticians, may plan and produce meals based on established guidelines, teach principles of food and nutrition, or counsel individuals.

2006 Employment: 25,000
Projected 2006-16 employment change: Faster than average
Most significant source of postsecondary education or training:
  Postsecondary vocational award

Directors, religious activities and education

(O*NET 21-2021.00)

Direct and coordinate activities of a denominational group to meet religious needs of students. Plan, direct, or coordinate church school programs designed to promote religious education among church membership. May provide counseling and guidance relative to marital, health, financial, or religious problems.

2006 Employment: 99,000
Projected 2006-16 employment change: Faster than average
Most significant source of postsecondary education or training:
  Bachelor's degree

Farm and home management advisors

(O*NET 25-9021.00)

Advise, instruct, and assist individuals and families engaged in agriculture, agricultural-related processes, or home economics activities. Demonstrate procedures and apply research findings to solve problems; instruct and train in product development, sales, and the utilization of machinery and equipment to promote general welfare. Include county agricultural agents, feed and farm management advisors, home economists, and extension service advisors.

2006 Employment: 15,000
Projected 2006-16 employment change: More slowly than average
Most significant source of postsecondary education or training: Bachelor's degree

Law clerks

(O*NET 23-2092.00)

Assist lawyers or judges by researching or preparing legal documents. May meet with clients or assist lawyers and judges in court. Excludes lawyers, and paralegal and legal assistants.

2006 Employment: 37,000
Projected 2006-16 employment change: Little or no change
Most significant source of postsecondary education or training: Bachelor's degree

Mathematical technicians

(O*NET 15-2091.00)

Apply standardized mathematical formulas, principles, and methodology to technological problems in engineering and physical sciences in relation to specific industrial and research objectives, processes, equipment, and products.

2006 Employment: 1,300
Projected 2006-16 employment change: About as fast as average
Most significant source of postsecondary education or training: Master's degree

Merchandise displayers and window trimmers

(O*NET 27-1026.00)

Plan and erect commercial displays, such as those in windows and interiors of retail stores and at trade exhibitions.

2006 Employment: 87,000
Projected 2006-16 employment change: About as fast as average
Most significant source of postsecondary education or training: Moderate-term on-the-job training

Orthotists and prosthetists

(O*NET 29-2091.00)

Assist patients with disabling conditions of limbs and spine or with partial or total absence of limb by fitting and preparing orthopedic braces and prostheses.

2006 Employment: 5,700
Projected 2006-16 employment change: About as fast as average
Most significant source of postsecondary education or training: Bachelor's degree

Psychiatric technicians

(O*NET 29-2053.00)

Care for mentally impaired or emotionally disturbed individuals, following physician instructions and hospital procedures. Monitor patients' physical and emotional well-being and report to medical staff.

May participate in rehabilitation and treatment programs, help with personal hygiene, and administer oral medications and hypodermic injections.

2006 Employment: 62,000
Projected 2006-16 employment change: Decline slowly
Most significant source of postsecondary education or training: Postsecondary vocational award

Set and exhibit designers

(O*NET 27-1027.00)

Design special exhibits and movie, television, and theater sets. May study scripts, confer with directors, and conduct research to determine appropriate architectural styles.

2006 Employment: 12,000
Projected 2006-16 employment change: Faster than average
Most significant source of postsecondary education or training: Bachelor's degree

Social science research assistants

(O*NET 19-4061.00)

Assist social scientists in laboratory, survey, and other social research. May perform publication activities, laboratory analysis, quality control, or data management. Normally these individuals work under the direct supervision of a social scientist and assist in those activities which are more routine. Excludes graduate teaching assistants, who both teach and do research.

2006 Employment: 18,000
Projected 2006-16 employment change: About as fast as average
Most significant source of postsecondary education or training: Associate degree

Title examiners, abstractors, and searchers

(O*NET 23-2093.00)

Search real estate records, examine titles, or summarize pertinent legal or insurance details for a variety of purposes. May compile lists of mortgages, contracts, and other instruments pertaining to titles by searching public and private records for law firms, real estate agencies, or title insurance companies.

2006 Employment: 69,000
Projected 2006-16 employment change: Little or no change
Most significant source of postsecondary education or training: Moderate-term on-the-job training

Service occupations

Amusement and recreation attendants

(O*NET 39-3091.00)

Perform a variety of attending duties at amusement or recreation facilities. May schedule use of recreations facilities, maintain and provide equipment to participants of sporting events or recreational pursuits, or operate amusement concessions and rides.

2006 Employment: 247,000
Projected 2006-16 employment change: Much faster than average
Most significant source of postsecondary education or training: Short-term on-the-job training

Animal control workers

(O*NET 33-9011.00)

Handle animals for the purpose of investigations of mistreatment, or control of abandoned, dangerous, or unattended animals.

2006 Employment: 15,000
Projected 2006-16 employment change: About as fast as average
Most significant source of postsecondary education or training: Moderate-term on-the-job training

Baggage porters and bellhops

(O*NET 39-6011.00)

Handle baggage for travelers at transportation terminals or for guests at hotels or similar establishments.

2006 Employment: 49,000
Projected 2006-16 employment change: About as fast as average
Most significant source of postsecondary education or training: Short-term on-the-job training

Concierges

(O*NET 39-6012.00)

Assist patrons at hotel, apartment or office building with personal services. May take messages, arrange or give advice on transportation, business services or entertainment, or monitor guest requests for housekeeping and maintenance.

2006 Employment: 20,000
Projected 2006-16 employment change: Faster than average
Most significant source of postsecondary education or training: Moderate-term on-the-job training

Costume attendants

(O*NET 39-3092.00)

Select, fit and take care of costumes for cast members, and aid entertainers.

2006 Employment: 4,300
Projected 2006-16 employment change: Faster than average
Most significant source of postsecondary education or training: Short-term on-the-job training

Crossing guards

(O*NET 33-9091.00)

Guide or control vehicular or pedestrian traffic at such places as streets, schools, railroad crossings, or construction sites.

2006 Employment: 69,000
Projected 2006-16 employment change: Little or no change
Most significant source of postsecondary education or training: Short-term on-the-job training

Embalmers

(O*NET 39-4011.00)

Prepare bodies for interment in conformity with legal requirements.

2006 Employment: 9,000
Projected 2006-16 employment change: Faster than average

Most significant source of postsecondary education or training: Postsecondary vocational award

First-line supervisors/managers of food preparation and serving workers

(O*NET 35-1012.00)

Supervise workers engaged in preparing and serving food.

2006 Employment: 817,000
Projected 2006-16 employment change: About as fast as average
Most significant source of postsecondary education or training: Work experience in a related occupation

First-line supervisors/managers of personal service workers

(O*NET 39-1021.00)

Supervise and coordinate activities of personal service workers, such as supervisors of flight attendants, hairdressers, or caddies.

2006 Employment: 215,000
Projected 2006-16 employment change: Faster than average
Most significant source of postsecondary education or training: Work experience in a related occupation

Funeral attendants

(O*NET 39-4021.00)

Perform a variety of tasks during a funeral, such as placing casket in parlor or chapel prior to service; arranging floral offerings or lights around casket; directing or escorting mourners; closing casket; and issuing and storing funeral equipment.

2006 Employment: 33,000
Projected 2006-16 employment change: Faster than average
Most significant source of postsecondary education or training: Short-term on-the-job training

Lifeguards, ski patrol, and other recreational protective services

(O*NET 33-9092.00)

Monitor recreational areas, such as pools, beaches, or ski slopes to provide assistance and protection to participants.

2006 Employment: 114,000
Projected 2006-16 employment change: Faster than average
Most significant source of postsecondary education or training: Short-term on-the-job-training

Locker room, coatroom and dressing room attendants

(O*NET 39-3093.00)

Provide personal items to patrons or customers in locker rooms, dressing rooms, or coatrooms.

2006 Employment: 19,000
Projected 2006-16 employment change: Much faster than average
Most significant source of postsecondary education or training: Short-term on-the-job training

Medical equipment preparers

(O*NET 31-9093.00)

Prepare, sterilize, install, or clean laboratory or healthcare equipment. May perform routine laboratory tasks and operate or inspect equipment.

2006 Employment: 45,000
Projected 2006-16 employment change: Faster than average
Most significant source of postsecondary education or training: Short-term on-the-job training

Motion picture projectionists

(O*NET 39-3021.00)

Set up and operate motion picture projection and related sound reproduction equipment.

2006 Employment: 11,000
Projected 2006-16 employment change: Decline slowly
Most significant source of postsecondary education or training: Short-term on-the-job training

Parking enforcement workers

(O*NET 33-3041.00)

Patrol assigned area, such as public parking lot or section of city to issue tickets to overtime parking violators and illegally parked vehicles.

2006 Employment: 11,000
Projected 2006-16 employment change: About as fast as average
Most significant source of postsecondary education or training: Short-term on-the-job training

Residential advisors

(O*NET 39-9041.00)

Coordinate activities for residents of boarding schools, college fraternities or sororities, college dormitories, or similar establishments. Order supplies and determine need to maintenance, repairs, and furnishings. May maintain household records and assign rooms. May refer residents to counseling resources if needed.

2006 Employment: 57,000
Projected 2006-16 employment change: Faster than average
Most significant source of postsecondary education or training: Short-term on-the-job training

Tour guides and escorts

(O*NET 39-6021.00)

Escort individuals or groups on sightseeing tours or through places of interest, such as industrial establishments, public buildings, and art galleries.

2006 Employment: 40,000
Projected 2006-16 employment change: Much faster than average
Most significant source of postsecondary education or training: Moderate-term on-the-job training

Transportation attendants, except flight attendants and baggage porters

(O*NET 39-6032.00)

Provide services to ensure the safety and comfort of passengers aboard ships, buses, trains, or within the station or terminal. Perform duties, such as greeting passengers, explaining the use of safety equipment, serving meals or beverages, or answering questions related to travel.

2006 Employment: 21,000
Projected 2006-16 employment change: Faster than average
Most significant source of postsecondary education or training: Short-term on-the-job training

Travel guides

(O*NET 39-6022.00)

Plan, organize, and conduct long distance cruises, tours, and expeditions for individuals or groups.

2006 Employment: 4,700
Projected 2006-16 employment change: About as fast as average
Most significant source of postsecondary education or training: Moderate-term on-the-job training

Ushers, lobby attendants, and ticket takers

(O*NET 39-3031.00)

Assist patrons at entertainment events by performing duties, such as collecting admission tickets and passes from patrons, assisting in finding seats, searching for lost articles, and locating such facilities as rest rooms and telephones.

2006 Employment: 103,000
Projected 2006-16 employment change: Faster than average
Most significant source of postsecondary education or training: Short-term on-the-job training

Veterinary assistants and laboratory animal caretakers

(O*NET 31-9096.00)

Feed, water, and examine pets and other nonfarm animals for signs of illness, disease, or injury in laboratories and animal hospitals and clinics. Clean and disinfect cages and work areas, and sterilize laboratory and surgical equipment. May provide routine postoperative care, administer medication orally or topically, or prepare samples for laboratory examination under the supervision of veterinary or laboratory animal technologists or technicians, veterinarians, or scientists. Excludes nonfarm animal caretakers.

2006 Employment: 75,000
Projected 2006-16 employment change: Faster than average
Most significant source of postsecondary education or training: Short-term on-the-job training

Sales and related occupations

Door-to-door sales workers, news and street vendors, and related workers

(O*NET 41-9091.00)

Sell goods or services door-to-door or on the street.

2006 Employment: 200,000
Projected 2006-16 employment change: More slowly than average
Most significant source of postsecondary education or training:
Short-term on-the-job training

Parts salespersons

(O*NET 41-2022.00)

Sell spare and replacement parts and equipment in repair shop or parts store.

2006 Employment: 238,000
Projected 2006-16 employment change: Little or no change
Most significant source of postsecondary education or training:
Moderate-term on-the-job training

Telemarketers

(O*NET 41-9041.00)

Solicit orders for goods and services over the telephone.

2006 Employment: 395,000
Projected 2006-16 employment change: Decline rapidly
Most significant source of postsecondary education or training:
Short-term on-the-job training

Office and administrative support occupations

Correspondence clerks

(O*NET 43-4021.00)

Compose letters in reply to request for merchandise, damage claims, credit and other information, delinquent accounts, incorrect billings, or unsatisfactory services. Duties may include gathering data to formulate reply and typing correspondence.

2006 Employment: 17,000
Projected 2006-16 employment change: About as fast as average
Most significant source of postsecondary education or training:
Short-term-on-the-job training

Court, municipal, and license clerks

(O*NET 43-4031.01, 43-4031.02, 43-4031.03)

Perform clerical duties in courts of law, municipalities, and governmental licensing agencies and bureaus. May prepare docket of cases to be called; secure information for judges and court; prepare draft agendas or bylaws for town or city council; answer official correspondence; keep fiscal records and accounts; issue licenses or permits; record data, administer tests, or collect fees.

2006 Employment: 115,000
Projected 2006-16 employment change: About as fast as average
Most significant source of postsecondary education or training:
Short-term-on-the-job training

Insurance claims and policy processing clerks

(O*NET 43-9041.01, 43-9041.02)

Process new insurance policies, modifications to existing policies, and claims forms. Obtain information from policyholders to verify the accuracy and completeness of information on claims forms, applications and related documents, and company records. Update existing policies and company records to reflect changes requested by policyholders and insurance company representatives. Excludes claims adjusters, examiners, and investigators.

2006 Employment: 254,000
Projected 2006-16 employment change: Little or no change
Most significant source of postsecondary education or training:
Moderate-term on-the-job training

Mail clerks and mail machine operators, except Postal Service

(O*NET 43-9051.00)

Prepare incoming and outgoing mail for distribution. Use hand or mail handling machines to time, stamp, open, read, sort, and route incoming mail; and address, seal, stamp, fold, stuff, and affix postage to outgoing mail or packages. Duties may also include keeping necessary records and completed forms.

2006 Employment: 152,000
Projected 2006-16 employment change: Decline rapidly
Most significant source of postsecondary education or training:
Short-term on-the-job training

New account clerks

(O*NET 43-4141.00)

Interview persons desiring to open bank accounts. Explain banking services available to prospective customers and assist them in preparing application form.

2006 Employment: 81,000
Projected 2006-16 employment change: Decline rapidly
Most significant source of postsecondary education or training:
Work experience in a related occupation

Office machine operators, except computer

(O*NET 43-9071.01)

Operate one or more of a variety of office machines, such as photocopying, photographic, and duplicating machines, or other office machines. Excludes computer operators; mail clerks and mail machine operators; and billing and posting clerks and machine operators.

2006 Employment: 94,000
Projected 2006-16 employment change: Decline slowly
Most significant source of postsecondary education or training:
Short-term on-the-job training

Proofreaders and copy markers

(O*NET 43-9081.00)

Read transcript or proof type setup to detect and mark for correction any grammatical, typographical, or compositional errors. Excludes workers whose primary duty is editing copy. Includes proofreaders of Braille.

2006 Employment: 18,000
Projected 2006-16 employment change: More slowly than average
Most significant source of postsecondary education or training:
Short-term on-the-job training

Statistical assistants

(O*NET 43-9111.00)

Compile and compute data according to statistical formulas for use in statistical studies. May perform actuarial computations and compile charts and graphs for use by actuaries. Includes actuarial clerks.

2006 Employment: 23,000
Projected 2006-16 employment change: About as fast as average
Most significant source of postsecondary education or training: Moderate-term on-the-job training

Farming, fishing, and forestry occupations

Hunters and trappers

(O*NET 45-3021.00)

Hunt and trap wild animals for human consumption, fur, feed, bait, or other purposes.

2006 Employment: 500
Projected 2006-16 employment change: Decline rapidly
Most significant source of postsecondary education or training: Moderate-term on-the-job training

Supervisors, farming, fishing, and forestry workers

(O*NET 45-1011.01, 45-1011.02, 45-1011.03, 45-1011.04, 45-1011.05, 45-1011.06, 45-1012.00)

This broad occupation includes two detailed occupations—first-line supervisors/managers of farming, fishing, and forestry workers; and farm labor contractors. First-line supervisors/managers of farming, fishing, and forestry workers directly supervise and coordinate the activities of agricultural, forestry, aquacultural, and related workers. Farm labor contractors recruit, hire, furnish, and supervise seasonal or temporary agricultural laborers for a fee. May transport, house, and provide meals for workers. Excludes first-line supervisors/managers of landscaping, lawn service, and groundskeeping workers.

2006 Employment: 53,000
Projected 2006-16 employment change: Little or no change
Most significant source of postsecondary education or training: Work experience in a related occupation

Construction and extraction occupations

Continuous mining machine operators

(O*NET 47-5041.00)

Operate self-propelled mining machines that rip coal, metal and nonmetal ores, rock, stone, or sand form the face and load it onto conveyors or into shuttle cars in a continuous operation.

2006 Employment: 10,000
Projected 2006-16 employment change: More slowly than average
Most significant source of postsecondary education or training: Moderate-term on-the-job training

Derrick operators, oil and gas

(O*NET 47-5011.00)

Rig derrick equipment and operate pumps to circulate mud through drill hole.

2006 Employment: 19,000
Projected 2006-16 employment change: Decline slowly
Most significant source of postsecondary education or training: Moderate-term on-the-job training

Earth drillers, except oil and gas

(O*NET 47-5021.00)

Operate a variety of drills—such as rotary, churn, and pneumatic—to tap subsurface water and salt deposits, to remove core samples during mineral exploration or soil testing, and to facilitate the use of explosives in mining or construction. May use explosives. Includes horizontal and earth boring machine operators.

2006 Employment: 22,000
Projected 2006-16 employment change: About as fast as average
Most significant source of postsecondary education or training: Moderate-term on-the-job training

Explosives workers, ordnance handling experts, and blasters

(O*NET 47-5031.00)

Place and detonate explosives to demolish structures or to loosen, remove, or displace earth, rock, or other materials. May perform specialized handling, storage, and accounting procedures. Includes seismograph shooters. Excludes earth drillers, except oil and gas who may also work with explosives.

2006 Employment: 5,300
Projected 2006-16 employment change: Little or no change
Most significant source of postsecondary education or training: Moderate-term on-the-job training

Fence erectors

(O*NET 47-4031.00)

Erect and repair metal and wooden fences and fence gates around highways, industrial establishments, residences, or farms, using hand and power tools.

2006 Employment: 32,000
Projected 2006-16 employment change: About as fast as average
Most significant source of postsecondary education or training: Moderate-term on-the-job training

First-line supervisors/managers of construction trades and extraction workers

(O*NET 47-1011.00)

Directly supervise and coordinate activities of construction or extraction workers.

2006 Employment: 772,000
Projected 2006-16 employment change: About as fast as average
Most significant source of postsecondary education or training: Work experience in a related occupation

Helpers—brickmasons, blockmasons, stonemasons, and tile and marble setters

(O*NET 47-3011.00)

Help brickmasons, blockmasons, stonemasons, or tile and marble setters by performing duties of lesser skill. Duties include using, supplying, or holding materials or tools, and cleaning work area and equipment. Excludes apprentice workers and report them with the appropriate skilled construction trade occupation. Excludes construction laborers who do not primarily assist brickmasons, blockmasons, and stonemasons or tile and marble setters.

2006 Employment: 65,000
Projected 2006-16 employment change: About as fast as average
Most significant source of postsecondary education or training: Short-term on-the-job training

Helpers—carpenters

(O*NET 47-3012.00)

Help carpenters by performing duties of lesser skill. Duties include using, supplying, or holding materials or tools, and cleaning work area and equipment. Excludes apprentice workers and report them with the appropriate skilled construction trade occupation. Excludes construction laborers who do not primarily assist carpenters.

2006 Employment: 109,000
Projected 2006-16 employment change: About as fast as average
Most significant source of postsecondary education or training: Short-term on-the-job training

Helpers—electricians

(O*NET 47-3013.00)

Help electricians by performing duties of lesser skill. Duties include using, supplying, or holding materials or tools, and cleaning work area and equipment. Excludes apprentice workers and report them with them the appropriate skilled construction trade occupation. Excludes construction laborers who do not primarily assist electricians.

2006 Employment: 105,000
Projected 2006-16 employment change: About as fast as average
Most significant source of postsecondary education or training: Short-term on-the-job training

Helpers—extraction workers

(O*NET 47-5081.00)

Help extraction craft workers, such as earth drillers, blasters and explosives workers, derrick operators, and mining machine operators, by performing duties of lesser skill. Duties include supplying equipment or cleaning work area. Excludes apprentice workers.

2006 Employment: 25,000
Projected 2006-16 employment change: Little or no change
Most significant source of postsecondary education or training: Short-term on-the-job training

Helpers—painters, paperhangers, plasterers, and stucco masons

(O*NET 47-3014.00)

Help painters, paperhangers, plasterers, or stucco masons by performing duties of lesser skill. Duties including using, supplying, or holding materials or tools, and cleaning work area and equipment. Excludes apprentice workers and report them with the appropriate skilled construction trade occupation. Excludes construction laborers who do not primarily assist painters, paperhangers, plasterers, or stucco masons.

2006 Employment: 24,000
Projected 2006-16 employment change: Little or no change
Most significant source of postsecondary education or training: Short-term on-the-job training

Helpers—pipelayers, plumbers, pipefitters, and steamfitters

(O*NET 47-3015.00)

Help pipelayers, plumbers, pipefitters, or steamfitters by performing duties of lesser skill. Duties including using, supplying, or holding materials or tools, and cleaning work area and equipment. Excludes apprentice workers and report them with the appropriate skilled construction trade occupation. Excludes construction laborers who do not primarily assist pipelayers, plumbers, pipefitters or steamfitters.

2006 Employment: 85,000
Projected 2006-16 employment change: About as fast as average
Most significant source of postsecondary education or training: Short-term on-the-job training

Helpers—roofers

(O*NET 47-3016.00)

Help roofers by performing duties of lesser skill. Duties include using, supplying, or holding materials or tools, and cleaning work area and equipment. Excludes apprentice workers and report them with the appropriate skilled construction trade occupation. Excludes construction laborers who do not primarily assist roofers.

2006 Employment: 22,000
Projected 2006-16 employment change: About as fast as average
Most significant source of postsecondary education or training: Short-term on-the-job training

Highway maintenance workers

(O*NET 47-4051.00)

Maintain highways, municipal and rural roads, airport runways, and rights-of-way. Duties include patching broken or eroded pavement, repairing guard rails, highway markers, and snow fences. May also mow or clear brush from along road or plow snow from roadway. Excludes tree trimmers and pruners.

2006 Employment: 145,000
Projected 2006-16 employment change: About as fast as average
Most significant source of postsecondary education or training: Moderate-term on-the-job training

Mine cutting and channeling machine operators

(O*NET 47-5042.00)

Operate machinery—such as longwall shears, plows, and cutting machines—to cut or channel along the face or seams of coal mines, stone quarries, or other mining surfaces to facilitate blasting, separating, or removing minerals or materials from mines or from the earth's surface. Includes shale planers.

2006 Employment: 7,900
Projected 2006-16 employment change: More slowly than average
Most significant source of postsecondary education or training: Moderate-term on-the-job training

Rail-track laying and maintenance equipment operators

(O*NET 47-4061.00)

Lay, repair, and maintain track for standard or narrow-gauge railroad equipment used in regular railroad service or in plant yards, quarries, sand and gravel pits, and mines. Includes ballast cleaning machine operators and railroad bed tamping machine operators.

2006 Employment: 15,000
Projected 2006-16 employment change: More slowly than average
Most significant source of postsecondary education or training: Moderate-term on-the-job training

Rock splitters, quarry

(O*NET 47-5051.00)

Separate blocks of rough dimension stone from quarry mass using jackhammer and wedges.

2006 Employment: 3,900
Projected 2006-16 employment change: Much faster than average
Most significant source of postsecondary education or training: Moderate-term on-the-job training

Roof bolters, mining

(O*NET 47-5061.00)

Operate machinery to install roof support bolts in underground mine.

2006 Employment: 4,300
Projected 2006-16 employment change: Little or no change
Most significant source of postsecondary education or training: Moderate-term on-the-job training

Rotary drill operators, oil and gas

(O*NET 47-5012.00)

Set up or operate a variety of drills to remove petroleum products from the earth and to find and remove core samples for testing during oil and gas exploration.

2006 Employment: 20,000
Projected 2006-16 employment change: Decline slowly
Most significant source of postsecondary education or training: Moderate-term on-the-job training

Roustabouts, oil and gas

(O*NET 47-5071.00)

Assemble or repair oil field equipment using hand and power tools. Perform other tasks as needed.

2006 Employment: 44,000
Projected 2006-16 employment change: Decline slowly
Most significant source of postsecondary education or training: Moderate-term on-the-job training

Septic tank servicers and sewer pipe cleaners

(O*NET 47-4071.00)

Clean and repair septic tanks, sewer lines, or drains. May patch walls and partitions of tank, replace damaged drain tile, or repair breaks in underground piping.

2006 Employment: 24,000
Projected 2006-16 employment change: About as fast as average
Most significant source of postsecondary education or training: Moderate-term on-the-job training

Service unit operators, oil, gas, and mining

(O*NET 47-5013.00)

Operate equipment to increase oil flow from producing wells or to remove stick pipe, casing, tools, or other obstructions from drilling wells. May also perform similar services in mining exploration operations. Includes fishing-tool technicians.

2006 Employment: 28,000
Projected 2006-16 employment change: Decline slowly
Most significant source of postsecondary education or training: Moderate-term on-the-job training

Installation, maintenance, and repair occupations

Bicycle repairers

(O*NET 49-3091.00)

Repair and service bicycles.

2006 Employment: 8,600
Projected 2006-16 employment change: About as fast as average
Most significant source of postsecondary education or training: Moderate-term on-the-job training

Commercial divers

(O*NET 49-9092.00)

Work below surface of water, using scuba gear to inspect, repair, remove, or install equipment and structures. May use a variety of power and hand tools, such as drills, sledgehammers, torches, and welding equipment. May conduct tests or experiments, rig explosives, or photograph structures or marine life. Excludes fishers and related fishing workers, athletes and sports competitors, and police and sheriff's patrol officers.

2006 Employment: 3,100
Projected 2006-16 employment change: Faster than average

Most significant source of postsecondary education or training: Postsecondary vocational award

Control and valve installers and repairers, except mechanical door

(O*NET 49-9012.00)

Install, repair, and maintain mechanical regulating and controlling devices, such as electric meters, gas regulators, thermostats, safety and flow valves, and other mechanical governors.

2006 Employment: 43,000
Projected 2006-16 employment change: Little or no change
Most significant source of postsecondary education or training: Moderate-term on-the-job training

Fabric menders, except garment

(O*NET 49-9093.00)

Repair tears, holes, and other defects in fabrics, such as draperies, linens, parachutes, and tents.

2006 Employment: 1,800
Projected 2006-16 employment change: Little or no change
Most significant source of postsecondary education or training: Moderate-term on-the-job training

First-line supervisors/managers of mechanics, installers, and repairers

(O*NET 49-1011.00)

Supervise and coordinate the activities of mechanics, installers, and repairers. Excludes team or work leaders.

2006 Employment: 465,000
Projected 2006-16 employment change: About as fast as average
Most significant source of postsecondary education or training: Work experience in a related occupation

Helpers—installation, maintenance, and repair workers

(O*NET 49-9098.00)

Help installation, maintenance, and repair workers in maintenance, parts replacement, and repair of vehicles, industrial machinery, and electrical and electronic equipment. Perform duties, such as furnishing tools, materials, and supplies to other workers; cleaning work area, machines, and tools; and holding materials or tools for other workers.

2006 Employment: 163,000
Projected 2006-16 employment change: About as fast as average
Most significant source of postsecondary education or training: Short-term on-the-job training

Locksmiths and safe repairers

(O*NET 49-9094.00)

Repair and open locks; make keys; change locks and safe combinations; and install and repair safes.

2006 Employment: 26,000
Projected 2006-16 employment change: Much faster than average
Most significant source of postsecondary education or training: Moderate-term on-the-job training

Manufactured building and mobile home installers

(O*NET 49-9095.00)

Move or install mobile homes or prefabricated buildings.

2006 Employment: 12,000
Projected 2006-16 employment change: Decline slowly
Most significant source of postsecondary education or training: Moderate-term on-the-job training

Mechanical door repairers

(O*NET 49-9011.00)

Install, service, or repair opening and closing mechanisms of automatic doors and hydraulic door closers. Includes garage door mechanics.

2006 Employment: 15,000
Projected 2006-16 employment change: Faster than average
Most significant source of postsecondary education or training: Moderate-term on-the-job training

Recreational vehicle service technicians

(O*NET 49-3092.00)

Diagnose, inspect, adjust, repair, or overhaul recreational vehicles including travel trailers. May specialize in maintaining gas, electrical, hydraulic, plumbing, or chassis/towing systems as well as repairing generators, appliances, and interior components. Includes workers who perform customized van conversions. Excludes automotive service technicians and mechanics, and bus and truck mechanics and diesel engine specialists who also work on recreation vehicles.

2006 Employment: 14,000
Projected 2006-16 employment change: Faster than average
Most significant source of postsecondary education or training: Long-term on-the-job training

Refractory materials repairers, except brickmasons

(O*NET 49-9045.00)

Build or repair furnaces, kilns, cupolas, boilers, converters, ladles, soaking pits, ovens, etc., using refractory materials.

2006 Employment: 3,500
Projected 2006-16 employment change: Decline rapidly
Most significant source of postsecondary education or training: Moderate-term on-the-job training

Riggers

(O*NET 49-9096.00)

Set up or repair rigging for construction projects, manufacturing plants, logging yards, ships and shipyards, or for the entertainment industry.

2006 Employment: 12,000
Projected 2006-16 employment change: Little or no change
Most significant source of postsecondary education or training: Short-term on-the-job training

Security and fire alarm systems installers

(O*NET 49-2098.00)

Install, program, maintain, and repair security and fire alarm wiring and equipment. Ensure that work is in accordance with relevant codes. Excludes electricians who do a broad range of electrical wiring.

2006 Employment: 57,000
Projected 2006-16 employment change: Faster than average
Most significant source of postsecondary education or training: Postsecondary vocational award

Signal and track switch repairers

(O*NET 49-9097.00)

Install, inspect, test, maintain, or repair electric gate crossings, signals, signal equipment, track switches, section lines, or intercommunications systems within a railroad system.

2006 Employment: 7,200
Projected 2006-16 employment change: Decline slowly
Most significant source of postsecondary education or training: Moderate-term on-the-job training

Tire repairers and changers

(O*NET 49-3093.00)

Repair and replace tires.

2006 Employment: 106,000
Projected 2006-16 employment change: Faster than average
Most significant source of postsecondary education or training: Short-term on-the-job training

Production occupations

Cementing and gluing machine operators and tenders

(O*NET 51-9191.00)

Operate or tend cementing and gluing machines to join items for further processing or to form a completed product. Processes include joining veneer sheets into plywood; gluing paper; joining rubber and rubberized fabric parts, plastic, simulated leather, or other materials. Excludes shoe machine operators and tenders.

2006 Employment: 23,000
Projected 2006-16 employment change: Decline slowly
Most significant source of postsecondary education or training: Moderate-term on-the-job training

Chemical equipment operators and tenders

(O*NET 51-9011.00)

Operate or tend equipment to control chemical changes or reactions in the processing of industrial or consumer products. Equipment used includes devulcanizers, steam-jacketed kettles, and reactor vessels. Excludes chemical plant and system operators.

2006 Employment: 53,000
Projected 2006-16 employment change: Decline slowly
Most significant source of postsecondary education or training: Moderate-term on-the-job training

Chemical plant and system operators

(O*NET 51-8091.00)

Control or operate an entire chemical process or system of machines.

2006 Employment: 53,000
Projected 2006-16 employment change: Decline rapidly
Most significant source of postsecondary education or training: Long-term on-the-job training

Cleaning, washing, and metal pickling equipment operators and tenders

(O*NET 51-9192.00)

Operate or tend machines to wash or clean products, such as barrels or kegs, glass items, tin plate, food, pulp, coal, plastic, or rubber, to remove impurities.

2006 Employment: 16,000
Projected 2006-16 employment change: Decline rapidly
Most significant source of postsecondary education or training: Moderate-term on-the-job training

Cooling and freezing equipment operators and tenders

(O*NET 51-9193.00)

Operate or tend equipment, such as cooling and freezing units, refrigerators, batch freezers, and freezing tunnels, to cool or freeze products, food, blood plasma, and chemicals.

2006 Employment: 11,000
Projected 2006-16 employment change: Decline slowly
Most significant source of postsecondary education or training: Moderate-term on-the-job training

Crushing, grinding, and polishing machine setters, operators, and tenders

(O*NET 51-9021.00)

Set up, operate, or tend machines to crush, grind, or polish materials, such as coal, glass, grain, stone, food, or rubber.

2006 Employment: 42,000
Projected 2006-16 employment change: Decline rapidly
Most significant source of postsecondary education or training: Moderate-term on-the-job training

Cutters and trimmers, hand

(O*NET 51-9031.00)

Use hand tools or hand-held power tools to cut and trim a variety of manufactured items, such as carpet, fabric, stone, glass, or rubber.

2006 Employment: 29,000
Projected 2006-16 employment change: Decline slowly
Most significant source of postsecondary education or training: Short-term on-the-job training

Cutting and slicing machine setters, operators, and tenders

(O*NET 51-9032.00)

Set up, operate, or tend machines that cut or slice materials, such as glass, stone, cork, rubber, tobacco, food, paper, or insulating material. Excludes woodworking machines setters, operators, and tenders; cutting, punching, and press machine setters, operators, and tenders, metal and plastic; and textile cutting machine setters, operators, and tenders.

2006 Employment: 79,000
Projected 2006-16 employment change: Decline slowly
Most significant source of postsecondary education or training: Moderate-term on-the-job training

Etchers and engravers

(O*NET 51-9194.00)

Engrave or etch metal, wood, rubber, or other materials for identification or decorative purposes. Includes such workers as etcher-circuit processors, pantograph engravers, and silk screen etchers. Includes photoengravers with prepress technicians and workers.

2006 Employment: 14,000
Projected 2006-16 employment change: Decline slowly
Most significant source of postsecondary education or training: Long-term on-the-job training

Extruding, forming, pressing, and compacting machine setters, operators, and tenders

(O*NET 51-9041.00)

Set up, operate, or tend machines, such as glass forming machines, plodder machines, and tuber machines, to shape and form products, such as glassware, food, rubber, soap, brick, tile, clay, wax, tobacco, or cosmetics. Excludes paper goods machine setters, operators, and tenders; and shoe machine operators and tenders.

2006 Employment: 81,000
Projected 2006-16 employment change: Decline slowly
Most significant source of postsecondary education or training: Moderate-term on-the-job training

First-line supervisors/managers of production and operating workers

(O*NET 51-1011.00)

Supervise and coordinate the activities of production and operating workers, such as inspectors, precision workers, machine setters, and operators, assemblers, fabricators, and plant and system operators. Excludes team or work leaders.

2006 Employment: 699,000
Projected 2006-16 employment change: Decline slowly
Most significant source of postsecondary education or training: Work experience in a related occupation

Furnace, kiln, oven, drier, and kettle operators and tenders

(O*NET 51-9051.00)

Operate or tend heating equipment other than basic metal, plastic or food processing equipment. Includes activities, such as annealing glass, drying lumber, curing rubber, removing moisture from materials, or boiling soap.

2006 Employment: 32,000
Projected 2006-16 employment change: Decline slowly
Most significant source of postsecondary education or training: Moderate-term on-the-job training

Gas plant operators

(O*NET 51-8092.00)

Distribute or process gas for utility companies and others by controlling compressors to maintain specified pressures on main pipelines.

2006 Employment: 12,000
Projected 2006-16 employment change: Decline rapidly
Most significant source of postsecondary education or training: Long-term on-the-job training

Grinding and polishing workers, hand

(O*NET 51-9022.00)

Grind, sand, or polish, using hand tools or hand-held power tools, a variety of metal, wood, stone, clay, plastic, or glass objects. Includes chippers, buffers, and finishers.

2006 Employment: 45,000
Projected 2006-16 employment change: Decline slowly
Most significant source of postsecondary education or training: Moderate-term on-the-job training

Helpers—production workers

(O*NET 51-9198.00)

Help production workers by performing duties of lesser skill. Duties include supplying or holding materials or tools, and cleaning work area and equipment. Excludes apprentice workers.

2006 Employment: 542,000
Projected 2006-16 employment change: Little or no change
Most significant source of postsecondary education or training: Short-term on-the-job training

Mixing and blending machine setters, operators, and tenders

(O*NET 51-9023.00)

Set up, operate, or tend machines to mix or blend materials, such as chemicals, tobacco, liquids, color pigments, or explosive ingredients. Excludes food batchmakers.

2006 Employment: 143,000
Projected 2006-16 employment change: Decline slowly
Most significant source of postsecondary education or training: Moderate-term on-the-job training

Molders, shapers, and casters, except metal and plastic

(O*NET 51-9195.03, 51-9195.04, 51-9195.05, 51-9195.07)

Mold, shape, form, cast, or carve products such as food products, figurines, tile, pipes, and candles consisting of clay, glass, plaster, concrete, stone, or combinations of materials.

2006 Employment: 56,000
Projected 2006-16 employment change: Little or no change
Most significant source of postsecondary education or training: Moderate-term on-the-job training

Packaging and filling machine operators and tenders

(O*NET 51-9111.00)

Operate or tend machines to prepare industrial or consumer products for storage or shipment. Includes cannery workers who pack food products.

> 2006 Employment: 386,000
> Projected 2006-16 employment change: Decline slowly
> Most significant source of postsecondary education or training: Short-term on-the-job training

Paper goods machine setters, operators, and tenders

(O*NET 51-9196.00)

Set up, operate, or tend paper goods machines that perform a variety of functions, such as converting, sawing, corrugating, banding, wrapping, boxing, stitching, forming, or sealing paper or paperboard sheets into products.

> 2006 Employment: 113,000
> Projected 2006-16 employment change: Decline rapidly
> Most significant source of postsecondary education or training: Moderate-term on-the-job training

Petroleum pump system operators, refinery operators, and gaugers

(O*NET 51-8093.00)

Control the operation of petroleum refining or processing units. May specialize in controlling manifold and pumping systems, gauging or testing oil in storage tanks, or regulating the flow of oil into pipelines.

> 2006 Employment: 42,000
> Projected 2006-16 employment change: Decline rapidly
> Most significant source of postsecondary education or training: Long-term on-the-job training

Separating, filtering, clarifying, precipitating, and still machine setters, operators and tenders

(O*NET 51-9012.00)

Set up, operate, or tend continuous flow or vat-type equipment; filter presses; shaker screens; centrifuges; condenser tubes; precipitating, fermenting, or evaporating tanks; scrubbing towers; or batch stills. These machines extract, sort, or separate liquids, gases, or solids from other materials to recover a refined product. Includes dairy processing equipment operators. Excludes chemical equipment operators and tenders.

> 2006 Employment: 44,000
> Projected 2006-16 employment change: Decline slowly
> Most significant source of postsecondary education or training: Moderate-term on-the-job training

Tire builders

(O*NET 51-9197.00)

Operate machines to build tires from rubber components.

> 2006 Employment: 23,000
> Projected 2006-16 employment change: Decline rapidly
> Most significant source of postsecondary education or training: Moderate-term on-the-job training

Transportation and material moving occupations

Aircraft cargo handling supervisors

(O*NET 53-1011.00)

Direct ground crew in the loading, unloading, securing, and staging of aircraft cargo and baggage. Determine the quantity and orientation of cargo and compute aircraft center of gravity. May accompany aircraft as member of flight crew and monitor and handle cargo in flight, and assist and brief passengers on safety and emergency procedures. Includes loadmasters.

> 2006 Employment: 5,800
> Projected 2006-16 employment change: Much faster than average
> Most significant source of postsecondary education or training: Work experience in a related occupation

Airfield operations specialists

(O*NET 53-2022.00)

Ensure the safe takeoff and landing of commercial and military aircraft. Duties include coordination between air-traffic control and maintenance personnel; dispatching; using airfield landing and navigational aids; implementing airfield safety procedures; monitoring and maintaining flight records; and applying knowledge of weather information.

> 2006 Employment: 4,900
> Projected 2006-16 employment change: About as fast as average
> Most significant source of postsecondary education or training: Long-term on-the-job training

Ambulance drivers and attendants, except emergency medical technicians

(O*NET 53-3011.00)

Drive ambulance or assist ambulance drivers in transporting sick, injured, or convalescent persons. Assist in lifting patients.

> 2006 Employment: 22,000
> Projected 2006-16 employment change: Much faster than average
> Most significant source of postsecondary education or training: Moderate-term on-the-job training

Bridge and lock tenders

(O*NET 53-6011.00)

Operate and tend bridges, canal locks, and lighthouses to permit marine passage on inland waterways, near shores, and at danger points in waterway passages. May supervise such operations. Includes drawbridge operators, lock tenders and operators, and slip bridge operators.

> 2006 Employment: 3,900
> Projected 2006-16 employment change: Decline slowly
> Most significant source of postsecondary education or training: Short-term on-the-job training

First-line supervisors/managers of helpers, laborers, and material movers, hand

(O*NET 53-1021.00)

Supervise and coordinate the activities of helpers, laborers, or material movers.

2006 Employment: 182,000
Projected 2006-16 employment change: About as fast as average
Most significant source of postsecondary education or training:
 Work experience in a related occupation

First-line supervisors/managers of transportation and material moving machine and vehicle operators

(O*NET 53-1031.00)

Directly supervise and coordinate activities of transportation and material-moving machine and vehicle operators and helpers.

2006 Employment: 226,000
Projected 2006-16 employment change: About as fast as average
Most significant source of postsecondary education or training:
 Work experience in a related occupation

Parking lot attendants

(O*NET 53-6021.00)

Park automobiles or issue tickets for customers in parking lot or garage. May collect fee.

2006 Employment: 135,000
Projected 2006-16 employment change: About as fast as average
Most significant source of postsecondary education or training:
 Short-term on-the-job training

Service station attendants

(O*NET 53-6031.00)

Service automobiles, buses, trucks, boats, and other automotive or marine vehicles with fuel, lubricants, and accessories. Collect payment for services and supplies. May lubricate vehicle, change motor oil, install antifreeze, or replace lights or other accessories, such as windshield wiper blades or fan belts. May repair or replace tires.

2006 Employment: 96,000
Projected 2006-16 employment change: About as fast as average
Most significant source of postsecondary education or training:
 Short-term on-the-job training

Traffic technicians

(O*NET 53-6041.00)

Conduct field studies to determine traffic volume, speed, effectiveness of signals, adequacy of lighting, and other factors influencing traffic conditions, under direction of traffic engineer.

2006 Employment: 6,900
Projected 2006-16 employment change: About as fast as average
Most significant source of postsecondary education or training:
 Short-term on-the-job training

Transportation inspectors

(O*NET 53-6051.01, 53-6051.07, 53-6051.08)

Inspect equipment or goods in connection with the safe transport of cargo or people. Includes rail transport inspectors, such as freight inspectors, car inspectors, rail inspectors, and other nonprecision inspectors of other types of transportation vehicles.

2006 Employment: 26,000
Projected 2006-16 employment change: Faster than average
Most significant source of postsecondary education or training:
 Work experience in a related occupation

Assumptions and Methods Used in Preparing Employment Projections

Occupational statements in the *Handbook* use one of seven phrases to describe the projected change in employment between 2006 and 2016. (See page 26.) These phrases are based on numerical projections developed using the Bureau of Labor Statistics (BLS) employment projections model system. Projections of occupational employment are the sixth and final step in the system; the six steps are listed in the discussion of methods below. A discussion of projections methods also is accessible on the Internet at: **http://www.bls.gov/emp/empmth01.htm** The November 2007 *Monthly Labor Review* presents a comprehensive discussion of the 2006-16 projections of the economy, labor force, and industry and occupation employment. The winter 2007-08 *Occupational Outlook Quarterly* presents the projections in a series of charts.

The projections reflect the knowledge and judgment of staff in the BLS Office of Occupational Statistics and Employment Projections and of knowledgeable people from other BLS offices, other government agencies, colleges and universities, industries, unions, professional societies, and trade associations, who furnished data and information, prepared reports, or reviewed the projections. BLS takes full responsibility, however, for the projections.

Assumptions. The information in the *Handbook* is based on an economic projection, which is characterized by slower growth in labor force (0.8 percent annually from 2006 to 2016 compared with 1.2 percent annually over the past 10-year period, 1996-2006), an expected unemployment rate of 5.0 percent in 2016, a slowdown in labor productivity (2.2 percent average annual growth compared with 2.6 percent annually over the 1996-2006 period), and an increasing deficit of foreign trade. The Federal budget deficit is assumed to grow due to growth in expenditures for Federal defense and for Medicare and Social Security. Other assumptions include consumer spending on durable goods that grows faster than consumer spending on services and nondurable goods. The declining share of nondurable goods as a percent of total consumer spending is expected to continue. Within services, consumer spending on medical care is expected to drive growth. Investment spending is expected to grow 3.1 percent annually from 2006 to 2016, slower than the 4.5 percent average annual growth in the previous 10 years. This slowdown will stem largely from a decline in the annual average growth rate of spending on computers and software. Expenditures for construction of residential structures will settle down after the 2005 record high to a 1.7 percent average annual growth rate over the 2006-16 projection period. Spending on nonresidential construction will grow faster than the historical pace—1.5 percent annually over the projection period, compared with 0.3 percent annual growth between 1996 and 2006.

Although BLS considers these assumptions reasonable, the economy may follow a different course, resulting in a different pattern of occupational growth. Real growth also could be different because most occupations are sensitive to a much wider variety of factors than those considered in the various projections models. Unforeseen changes in consumer, business, or government spending patterns and in the ways in which goods and services are produced could greatly alter the growth of individual occupations.

Methods. This section summarizes the steps involved in BLS projections of employment by occupation. BLS uses U.S. Census Bureau projections of the population by age, gender, and race, combined with projections of labor force participation rates—the percent of the specified group of the population working or seeking work—to arrive at estimates of the civilian labor force for the projected year.

BLS projections are developed in a series of six steps, each of which is based on separate projections procedures and models and various related assumptions. These six steps, or system components, deal with:

1. Size and demographic composition of the labor force
2. Growth of the aggregate economy
3. Final demand or gross domestic product (GDP)
4. Interindustry relationships (input-output)
5. Industry output and employment
6. Occupational employment

These components provide the overall analytical framework needed to develop detailed employment projections. Each component is developed in order, with the results of each used as input for successive components and with some results feeding back into earlier steps. Each step is repeated a number of times to ensure internal consistency as assumptions and results are reviewed and revised.

The projections of the labor force and assumptions about other demographic variables, fiscal and monetary policies, foreign economic activity, and energy prices and availability form the input to the macroeconomic model. This model projects GDP (sales to all final consuming sectors in the economy) and the distribution of GDP by its major demand components (consumer expenditures, investment, government consumption and gross investments, and exports and imports). Estimating the intermediate flows of goods and services—for example, the steel incorporated into automobiles—is the next step in the projections process. The resulting estimates of demand for goods and services are used to project industry output of final products as well as total output by industry.

Industry output of goods and services is then converted to industry employment. Studies of trends in productivity and technology are used to estimate future output per worker hour, and regression analysis is used to estimate worker hours. These estimates, along with output projections, are used to develop the final industry employment projections.

An industry-occupation matrix, also known as the national employment matrix, is used to project employment for wage and salary workers. The matrix shows occupational staffing patterns—each occupation as a percent of employment in every industry. The matrix covering the 2006-16 period includes 311 detailed industries and 754 detailed occupations. Data for current staffing patterns in the matrix come from the BLS Occupational Employment Statistics (OES) surveys, which collect data from employers on a 3-year cycle.

The occupational staffing patterns for each industry were projected based on anticipated changes in the ways in which goods and services are produced, and were then applied to projected industry employment. The resulting employment was summed across industries to derive total wage and salary employment by occupation. Using this method, rapid employment growth is projected for health care workers, while employment of footwear manufacturing workers is expected to decline, reflecting the projected changes in the health care and footwear manufacturing industries, respectively.

Employment in an occupation also may grow or decline as a result of many other factors. For example, relatively fast growth is expected among computer support specialists as organiza-

tions continue to adopt increasingly sophisticated technology. On the other hand, automation, the expanding use of computers, and developments in computer software will result in declining employment among procurement clerks, order clerks, and word processors and typists. The projected-year matrix incorporates these expected changes.

Data on self-employed workers in each occupation come from the Current Population Survey (CPS). Numbers of self-employed workers were projected separately.

Replacement needs. In most occupations, replacement needs provide more job openings than growth. Replacement openings occur as people leave occupations. Some individuals transfer to other occupations as a step up the career ladder or to change careers; some stop working temporarily, perhaps to return to school or care for a family; other workers—retirees for example—leave the labor force permanently. A discussion of replacements and the methods used to prepare estimates is presented in *Occupational Projections and Training Data, 2008-09 Edition*, BLS Bulletin 2702.

Occupational Information Network Coverage

The *Occupational Information Network* (O*NET), which replaced the *Dictionary of Occupational Titles*, is used by public employment service offices to classify and place job-seekers. O*NET was developed by job analysts. The information on job duties, knowledge and skills, education and training, and other occupational characteristics comes directly from workers and employers. Information on O*NET is available from O*NET Project, U.S. Department of Labor/ETA, 200 Constitution Ave. NW., Room S-4231, Washington, DC 20210-0001. Telephone (202) 693-3660. Internet: **http://www.doleta.gov/programs/onet/**

The structure of O*NET reflects the 2000 *Standard Occupational Classification* (SOC) system. With 822 detailed occupations, SOC represents the Federal Government's most recent effort to analyze the occupational structure in the United States and to provide a national occupational classification system. Information on the SOC, including its occupational structure, is available on the Internet: **http://www.bls.gov/soc/**

Occupational statements in this 2008-09 edition of the *Handbook* list the O*NET codes that relate to or match the definitions used in the Bureau's Occupational Employment Statistics (OES) survey—the principal source of occupational employment data in the *Handbook*. All numbers listed also appear in the table below. The table is arranged by the O*NET code, followed by the O*NET title and the page on which the corresponding *Handbook* statement begins.

Index

F

G

N

Q

R

T

X

Y

Z